Civil Procedure

EDITORIAL ADVISORS

ASPEN PUBLISHERS

Civil Procedure

Cases and Problems

Fourth Edition

Barbara Allen Babcock
Judge John Crown Professor of Law, Emerita
Stanford Law School

Toni M. Massaro
Dean and Milton O. Riepe Chair in Constitutional Law
University of Arizona College of Law

Norman W. Spaulding
Nelson Bowman Sweitzer and Marie B. Sweitzer Professor of Law and Associate Dean for Curriculum
Stanford Law School

Wolters Kluwer
Law & Business

AUSTIN BOSTON CHICAGO NEW YORK THE NETHERLANDS

Aspen Publishers
Attn: Permissions Department
76 Ninth Avenue, 7th Floor
New York, NY 10011-5201

To contact Customer Care, e-mail customer.care@aspenpublishers.com, call 1-800-234-1660, fax 1-800-901-9075, or mail correspondence to:

Aspen Publishers
Attn: Order Department
PO Box 990
Frederick, MD 21705

Printed in the United States of America.

1 2 3 4 5 6 7 8 9 0

ISBN 978-0-7355-8292-7

Library of Congress Cataloging-in-Publication Data

Babcock, Barbara Allen.
Civil procedure : cases and problems / Barbara Allen Babcock, Toni M. Massaro, Norman W. Spaulding. — 4th ed.
p. cm.
ISBN 978-0-7355-8292-7
1. Civil procedure — United States — Cases. I. Massaro, Toni Marie, 1955- II. Spaulding, Norman W. III. Title.

KF8839.B33 2009
347.73'5 — dc22

This book contains paper from well-managed forests to SFI standards.

About Wolters Kluwer Law & Business

Wolters Kluwer Law & Business is a leading provider of research information and workflow solutions in key specialty areas. The strengths of the individual brands of Aspen Publishers, CCH, Kluwer Law International and Loislaw are aligned within Wolters Kluwer Law & Business to provide comprehensive, in-depth solutions and expert-authored content for the legal, professional and education markets.

CCH was founded in 1913 and has served more than four generations of business professionals and their clients. The CCH products in the Wolters Kluwer Law & Business group are highly regarded electronic and print resources for legal, securities, antitrust and trade regulation, government contracting, banking, pension, payroll, employment and labor, and healthcare reimbursement and compliance professionals.

Aspen Publishers is a leading information provider for attorneys, business professionals and law students. Written by preeminent authorities, Aspen products offer analytical and practical information in a range of specialty practice areas from securities law and intellectual property to mergers and acquisitions and pension/benefits. Aspen's trusted legal education resources provide professors and students with high-quality, up-to-date and effective resources for successful instruction and study in all areas of the law.

Kluwer Law International supplies the global business community with comprehensive English-language international legal information. Legal practitioners, corporate counsel and business executives around the world rely on the Kluwer Law International journals, loose-leafs, books and electronic products for authoritative information in many areas of international legal practice.

Loislaw is a premier provider of digitized legal content to small law firm practitioners of various specializations. Loislaw provides attorneys with the ability to quickly and efficiently find the necessary legal information they need, when and where they need it, by facilitating access to primary law as well as state-specific law, records, forms and treatises.

Wolters Kluwer Law & Business, a unit of Wolters Kluwer, is headquartered in New York and Riverwoods, Illinois. Wolters Kluwer is a leading multinational publisher and information services company.

To Tom, Jerry, and Ticien,
Our better halves.

Summary of Contents

Contents *xi*
Preface *xxvii*
Acknowledgments *xxxi*
Special Notice on Citations *xxxv*

Chapter 1 Due Process of Law **1**
Chapter 2 Constructing a Civil Lawsuit **269**
Chapter 3 Discovery of the Adversary's Case **469**
Chapter 4 Dispositions and Adjudications **601**
Chapter 5 Decision Makers and Decision Models **679**
Chapter 6 More Complex Litigation **865**
Chapter 7 Repose: Ending Disputes **1115**

Appendix *1233*
Table of Cases *1351*
Table of Federal Rules of Civil Procedure *1373*
Table of Judicial Code Citations *1377*
Index *1379*

Contents

Preface *xxvii*
Acknowledgments *xxxi*
Special Notice on Citations *xxxv*

1 *Due Process of Law* *1*

A. Notice and the Opportunity To Be Heard 1
Problem Case: The Due Process Game 1
1. The Process Due: Of Context and Subtext 2
Hamdi v. Rumsfeld 2
Note: Reading Procedure Cases 16
Note: Citizens and Non-Citizens 16
Note: Due Process as Notice and a Chance To Be Heard 21
Note: Private Actors and Due Process 23
Note: The *Mathews* Test 24
2. Notice: The Constitutional Dimension 25
Problem Case: The Elusive Defendant 25
Greene v. Lindsey 26
Notes and Questions 31
Note: Mullane v. Central Hanover Bank and Trust Co. 32
Note: Jones v. Flowers 33
3. Notice: Constitutional Requirements Ritualized: Rule 4 35
National Development Co. v. Triad Holding Corp. & Adnan Khashoggi 38
Note: Serving and Being Served 42
Note: Serving Process Abroad 42
Mid-Continent Wood Products v. Harris 44
Notes and Questions 50
4. Improper Conduct to Effect Service 53
Wyman v. Newhouse 53
Note: Impropriety and Immunity from Service of Process 55
B. What Kind of Hearing Does Due Process Require? 56
Problem Case: The Well-Meaning Legislator 56

Stephan Landsman, Readings on Adversarial Justice: The American Approach to Adjudication 58
Notes and Questions 61
Robert Kagan, Adversarial Legalism: The American Way of Law 61
Notes and Questions 68
Note: The Common Understanding of Due Process 68
Tom R. Tyler, Why People Obey the Law 69
Notes and Questions 70
Note: Global Rules of Civil Procedure 71
Lassiter v. Department of Social Services 72
Note: Adding Lawyers: A Functional Approach 81
Note: Lawyers and Due Process 83

1. Access to Lawyers: The Price of Advice 84
   a. The Contingent Fee 85
   b. Other Methods for Providing Legal Services 86
   c. Access to Justice as a Fundamental Right 92
   Walters v. National Association of Radiation Survivors 93
   Note: The Second Act — Legislation 100
   Note: Further Radiation Survivors Proceedings in the Lower Courts 100
   Note: Tennessee v. Lane 102

C. Due Process and Jurisdiction: The Limits of State Power over Persons and Property 103
   Problem Case: An Unhappy Wanderer 103
1. Introduction: State Boundaries and Jurisdiction 104
2. Pennoyer v. Neff: The Human Drama 105
   Wendy Perdue, Sin, Scandal, and Substantive Due Process: Personal Jurisdiction and *Pennoyer* Reconsidered 105
3. Pennoyer v. Neff: The Legal Story 107
4. Minimum Contacts and Substantial Justice 110
   International Shoe Co. v. Washington 110
   Note: The World After *Shoe* 115
   Note: General and Specific Jurisdiction 117
5. Minimum Contacts and Foreseeability 118
   World-Wide Volkswagen Corp. v. Woodson (Oklahoma Supreme Court) 118
   Notes and Questions 120
   World-Wide Volkswagen Corp. v. Woodson (U.S. Supreme Court) 121
   Notes and Questions 128
   Note: The Robinson Saga 129

6. Directing a "Product" Toward a Forum State: Minimum Contacts and Fair Play in a Post-Modern Age 130
   Problem Case: A Troubled Young Man 130
   Note: Keeton v. Hustler Magazine, Inc. 131
   Asahi Metal Industry Co. v. Superior Court 132
   Note: Criticism of *Asahi* 139
   Note: Why Does the Forum Matter? 141
   Note: Litigating Personal Jurisdiction 143
7. Contacts and Contracts 144
   Burger King Corp. v. Rudzewicz 145
   Notes and Questions 154
8. Persons or Property Within the State 155
   Problem Case: Just Passing Through 155
   Shaffer v. Heitner 158
   Note: Post-*Shaffer* Legislation 165
   Burnham v. Superior Court 165
   Notes and Questions 174
   Note: Choice of Law 176
9. Persons and Property in Cyberspace 177
   Problem Case: The Ubiquitous Defendant 177
   Introduction: Personal Jurisdiction and Cyberspace 178
   Zippo Mfg. Co. v. Zippo Dot Com 178
   Note: Traditional Concepts 187
   Note: Substance and Procedure 189
   Note: Enforceability 189
   Note: Purposeful Availment and Dot-Com Litigation Overseas 190
10. Waiving Due Process Objections by Agreement: Autonomy or Adhesion? 192
   Carnival Cruise Lines v. Shute 193
   Notes and Questions 199
   National Equipment Rental, Ltd. v. Szukhent 202
   Note: Applying the Case Law 205

D. Due Process and the Dual Court System: A First Look at Subject Matter Jurisdiction and Venue 207
   Problem Case: The Due Process Game (Part Two) 207
1. A Dual Court System 207
   a. Legislative Authority — Federal Versus State 207
   b. Federal Judicial Authority 208
2. Federal Diversity Jurisdiction 209
   Problem Case: Down with Diversity! Viva Diversity! 209
   a. Determining Diversity of Citizenship 209
   Problems 211
   Mas v. Perry 211

Note: The Domicile of Married Women 213
Tanzymore v. Bethlehem Steel Corp. 213
Notes and Questions 218
b. Historical Backdrop and Current Controversies 225
c. Joinder and the Amount in Controversy 228
Note: Litigating Subject Matter Jurisdiction 229
3. Federal Question Jurisdiction: Statutory Requirements 230
Problem Case: Making a Federal Case 230
Franchise Tax Board v. Construction Laborers Vacation Trust 232
a. Some Easy Cases 233
b. The Well-Pleaded Complaint Requirement 234
Louisville & Nashville R.R. Co. v. Mottley 234
Note: The Aftermath of *Mottley* 235
c. Hard Cases: *Merrell Dow* and the Private Right of Action Requirement 237
Merrell Dow Pharmaceutical v. Thompson 237
Note: Following *Merrell Dow* 246
Grable & Sons Metal Products, Inc. v. Darue Engineering & Mfg. 247
Note: Reconciling *Grable* and *Merrell Dow* 253
4. Tribal Courts 257
Williams v. Lee 258
William C. Canby Jr., American Indian Law 260
5. Venue 265
Applying the Basic Federal Venue Statutes 266
Review Problem: Choosing Systems in Retrospect 267

2 *Constructing a Civil Lawsuit* **269**

Problem Case: The Due Process Game (Part Three) 269
A. A Brief History of Civil Procedure 270
1. Common Law Procedure 271
a. The Pleading Process 271
b. The Writ System 273
c. Methods of Proof 277
d. Equity 280
2. Code Procedure 282
3. Modern Procedure in Federal Courts 283
B. The Allegations: Pleading and Responding Under the Federal Rules of Civil Procedure 290
1. The Complaint 290
Problem Case: The Aggrieved Nurses 290

a. The Basic Standard: Rule 8 291
Conley v. Gibson 291
Notes and Questions 293
American Nurses' Ass'n. v. Illinois 294
Notes and Questions 301
Note: Pleading and Substantive Law 305
Bell Atlantic Corp. v. Twombly 306
Notes and Questions 330
b. Special Pleading Requirements: Rule-Imposed and Judge-Made Burdens 336
Leatherman v. Tarrant County Narcotics Intelligence and Coordination Unit 336
Note: Telling a Story 338
Note: Pleading and Discovery 339
Schultea v. Wood 340
Note: Special Pleading in Civil Rights Cases 346
Note: Rule 9(b) — The Securities Fraud Litigation Example 347
c. Pleading in the Alternative: How Consistent Must the Plaintiff Be? 355
McCormick v. Kopmann 355
2. Responding to the Complaint 361
Problem Case: A Woman Partner 361
a. The Rules and Forms 361
b. The Pre-Answer Motion 362
c. The Answer 364
Fuentes v. Tucker 364
Zielinski v. Philadelphia Piers, Inc. 366
Notes and Questions 369
d. Affirmative Defenses 370
Problem Case: A Woman Partner (Part Two) 370
Gomez v. Toledo 370
Ingraham v. United States 374
Notes and Questions 377
e. Amending the Pleadings 379
Problem Case: A Woman Partner (Part Three) 379
Note: Liberal Pleading and Liberal Amendments 379
Barcume v. City of Flint 381
Notes and Questions 386
Nelson v. Adams USA, Inc., et al. 389
Note: Adding a Party After Judgment 393
Note: Waiting Too Long to Amend 394
C. Policing the Pleadings: Ethical Constraints, Frivolous Cases, and Creative Advocacy 395
Problem Case: The Worker with the "Bad" Accent 395

Mari J. Matsuda, Voices of America: Accent, Antidiscrimination Law, and a Jurisprudence for the Last Reconstruction 396
The History and Importance of Rule 11 400
1. "An Inquiry Reasonable Under the Circumstances" 406
Kraemer v. Grant County 407
Note: The Effect of Rule 11 on Lawyers' Work 412
Christian v. Mattel, Inc. 413
Note: No-Holds-Barred Advocacy 421
Note: "Later Advocating" Written Submissions 423
Note: The Standard of Review on Appeal 425
2. "Improper Purpose," Frivolous Claims, and Arguments for Legal Change 426
Saltany v. Reagan 426
Saltany v. Bush 428
Note: Lawyers for Causes 430
Note: Post-Pleading Improper Purposes 433
3. "Warranted by Existing Law . . ." 434
Frantz v. U.S. Powerlifting Federation 434
Note: Nonfrivolous Arguments for Extension of the Law 438
4. "Factual Contentions Have Evidentiary Support" 438
Arista Records LLC v. Does 1-27 438
Notes and Questions 447
Young v. City of Providence ex rel. Napolitano 448
Note: Tension Between Zealous and Accurate Advocacy? 454
Note: De-emphasizing Monetary Sanctions — Turning Down the Heat 455
5. The Inherent Power to Sanction 457
Chambers v. NASCO, Inc. 457
Note: The Relationship Between Rule 11 and the Court's Inherent Power to Sanction 466
Note: The Contempt Power 467
Note: Contracting for Sanctions? 468

3 *Discovery of the Adversary's Case* 469

Problem Case: The Elusive Defendant (Part Two) 469
A. An Overview of the Discovery Tools and Their Deployment 469
Lawrence J. Zweifach, Deposition Strategy in the Framework of an Overall Discovery Plan 470
B. Discovery Reform Redux: How the Solution Became the Problem 475

Problem Case: The Secret Memo 478
Chalick v. Cooper Hospital, et al. 479
Notes and Questions 485
C. The Scope of Discovery 489
1. "Relevant to the Subject Matter" 489
Blank v. Sullivan & Cromwell 489
Note: Relevance: Three Takes on Scope Under Rule 26 491
Note: Unduly Burdensome or Expensive 494
2. "Any Matter Not Privileged" 495
Problem Case: A Literary Law Student 495
Note: Privileges in Civil Litigation 496
Hickman v. Taylor 498
Note: The Necessities of Adversary Litigation 505
Note: The Scope of Work Product and Anticipating Litigation 506
Upjohn Co. v. United States 509
Note: The Lifetime of the Privilege: Swidler & Berlin v. United States 515
Note: Waiving the Privilege 517
Note: The Privilege as Applied to Government Attorneys 519
Note: Opinion Work Product 520
Note: Privilege in a Corporate Context 523
Note: The Role of Privileges in Assuring Accurate Outcomes 524
Note: Administering a Claim of Privilege 525
Note: Spoliation and the Duty to Preserve Evidence 528
3. Digital Data and the Problem of Electronic Discovery 530
Qualcomm Inc. v. Broadcom Corp. 531
Note: A Problem of Divided Responsibility? 546
Note: E-Discovery Amendments to Rule 26 549
Note: The Discovery of "Metadata" 550
Note: Privilege Logs and Inadvertent Disclosure in E-Discovery 552
4. The Adversary's Experts 554
Problem Case: XRT and the SafeTeeTot 554
Note: Berkey Photo, Inc. v. Eastman Kodak Co. 554
David Margolik, The Long Road Back for a Disgraced Patrician 556
Note: The Temptations of Expert Witnesses 559
Cordy v. The Sherwin-Williams Co. 559
Coates v. AC & S, Inc. 562
Notes and Questions 564
D. Interrogatories and the Adversarial Advocate 569
Problem Case: Rozier v. Ford Motor Co. 569

Rozier v. Ford Motor Co. 569
Note: Discovery Against Complex Organizations 577
E. Depositions and the Adversarial Advocate 586
Problem Case: The Secret Memo (Part Two) 586
Paramount Communications v. Viacom, Inc. 587
Notes and Questions 593
Note: The Appealability of Discovery Orders 594
F. Discovery in International Litigation 596

4 *Dispositions and Adjudications* ***601***

A. Ending Litigation Without Judgment: Settlements, Pretrial Conferences, and Other Maneuvers 602
Problem Case: Pressured to Settle 602
1. Settlement 602
Marek v. Chesny 603
Note: Evans v. Jeff D. 613
Notes and Questions 616
2. The Pretrial Conference — Helpful Judicial Oversight or Unwelcome Coercion? 622
Robert Zampano, Settlement Strategies for Trial Judges 624
Strandell v. Jackson County, Illinois 626
Note: Special Procedures to Encourage Settlement 629
Note: "Litigotiation" 632
Note: Motions in Limine 633
B. Summary Judgment 633
Problem Case: A Literary Law Student (Part Two) 633
1. The Development of Modern Summary Judgment Doctrine 633
a. Piercing the Pleadings: Historical Perspectives 633
Adickes v. S.H. Kress & Co. 635
b. The Supreme Court Trilogy 640
Celotex Corp. v. Catrett 640
Catrett, Administratrix of the Estate of Louis H. Catrett, Deceased v. Johns-Manville Sales Corp. 648
Note: Burdens of Proof, Pleading, and Production 651
Matsushita Elec. Indus. Co. v. Zenith Radio Corp. 654
Note: Anderson v. Liberty Lobby, Inc. 664
Notes and Questions 666
c. A New Standard for Summary Judgment? 668
2. Summary Judgment Problems 671

Sample Issues 671
Exercise: A Literary Law Student 672
C. An Overview of a Trial 674
Problem Case: Hailing a Cab 674
Note: The Problem of Proof 675
D. The Stages of a Trial 676
1. Opening Arguments 676
2. Presentation of Evidence 676
3. Motions Testing the Sufficiency of the Evidence 677
4. Closing Arguments and Jury Instructions 677
5. Jury Deliberations and Verdicts 678
6. Post-Verdict Motions 678

5 *Decision Makers and Decision Models* ***679***

Introduction 679
A. The Judge 679
Problem Case: Judicial Positioning 679
1. Judicial Selection: Appointment and Election 680
a. Selection of Federal Judges 680
b. Federal Magistrates and Special Masters 680
c. Selection of State Judges 683
Glenn Winters, Selection of Judges — An Historical Introduction 684
2. Judicial Qualifications 686
3. Disqualification of Judges in Individual Cases 689
Problem Case: The Prejudiced Judge 689
Statutes and Precedents 690
Note: Liteky v. United States 693
Problem Case: The Prejudiced Judge, Revisited 695
Note: Duckhunting with the Vice President 695
B. The Judge's Powers 697
1. Injunctions and Contempt 697
Walker v. City of Birmingham 697
New York State National Organization for Women v. Terry 713
Notes and Questions 721
C. The Jury: The Seventh Amendment Right 723
Problem Case: The Harassed Student 723
1. The Jury Trial Advantage 723
2. Incidents of Jury Trial: Size and Unanimity 725
3. Interpreting the Seventh Amendment: The Historical Test 727
Curtis v. Loether 728
Note: Other Applications of the Historical Test 731
Note: Jury Trials and Civil Rights 733

4. Preserving the Right: The Order of Trial 735
Beacon Theaters, Inc. v. Westover 735
5. The Jury's Competence: A Functional Analysis 740
Markman v. Westview Instruments, Inc. 740
Notes and Questions 744
D. Choosing a Jury 747
Problem Case: The Harassed Student (Part 2) 747
1. The Law of Jury Selection 749
Thiel v. Southern Pacific Co. 749
Note: Reversal as the Remedy for Improper Jury Selection 752
Edmonson v. Leesville Concrete Co. 753
Note: The Right of the Individual Potential Juror 757
J.E.B. v. Alabama ex rel. T.B. 758
Note: Equal Protection for Jurors and the Future of the Peremptory Challenge 763
Barbara Allen Babcock, A Place in the Palladium: Women's Rights and Jury Service 764
E. Managing the Jury 767
Problem Case: The Bereaved Widow 767
1. Guiding Jury Deliberations: Instructions and the Form of the Verdict 769
Gallick v. Baltimore & Ohio R.R. Co. 769
Notes and Questions 775
2. Taking the Case Away: Judgment as a Matter of Law 778
Galloway v. United States 778
Notes and Questions 786
Reeves v. Sanderson Plumbing Prods., Inc. 789
Notes and Questions 799
3. Starting Over: The New Trial Motion 801
Sanders-El v. Wencewicz 801
Notes and Questions 804
4. Appellate Review of Jury Verdicts 807
Weisgram v. Marley Co. 807
Notes and Questions 814
5. Excessive Verdicts 816
a. Prejudice, Passion, and Punitive Damages 816
Curtis Publishing Co. v. Butts 816
b. Additur and Remittitur 820
c. The Role of the Appellate Court in Administering Remittitur 821
Donovan v. Penn Shipping Co. 821
d. Excessive Verdicts and Due Process 822
6. Anticipating Jury Verdicts 829
7. Trials in the Courtroom of the Future 831

F. Alternative Decision Makers 833
Problem Case: An Injured Quarterback 833
1. Arbitration 834
Gilmer v. Interstate/Johnson Lane Corp. 834
Note: Arbitration Procedure 842
Note: Post-*Gilmer* Developments 842
Note: Paying for Private Justice 845
Note: Justifying Private Justice 848
Note: The Appealability of Arbitration Awards 850
Note: Court-Annexed ADR 851
Note: The Rise of International Arbitration 853
2. Mediation 854
Problem Case: An Injured Quarterback (Part Two) 854
Woods v. Holy Cross Hospital 855
Notes and Questions 860
3. Other Forms of ADR 861
4. Critical Perspectives on ADR 862

6 *More Complex Litigation* 865

A. Subject Matter Jurisdiction in a Dual Court System: A Second Look 865
1. The Governing Law in a Diversity Case 865
Problem Case: Having It Whose Way? 865
a. From *Erie* to *Hanna* 866
Edward A. Purcell Jr., Litigation and Inequality: Federal Diversity Jurisdiction in Industrial America, 1870-1958 866
Erie R.R. Co. v. Tompkins 871
Note: The Personal and Political Aspects of *Erie* 876
b. Substance and Procedure—Illustrative Cases 877
i. Cohen v. Beneficial Industrial Loan Corp. 877
ii. Ragan v. Merchants Transfer & Warehouse Co. 878
iii. Woods v. Interstate Realty Co. 878
iv. Byrd v. Blue Ridge Rural Electric Coop., Inc. 879
c. The *Hanna* Presumption 880
Hanna v. Plumer 881
Notes and Questions 887
d. Gasperini v. Center for Humanities: Separating Substance from Procedure, Balancing State and Federal Interests, and Other Nagging Questions of *Erie-Hanna* Jurisprudence 890
Gasperini v. Center for Humanities, Inc. 890
Notes and Questions 899
2. Supplemental Jurisdiction of the Federal Courts 901
Problem Case: Suing the HMO 901

a. Background to the Statute (28 U.S.C. § 1367) 902
i. The *Gibbs* Test 902
ii. Post-*Gibbs* Developments 904
b. The Modern Approach 904
c. Solving the Problem Case 906
d. Operation of § 1367 in the Class Action Context 907
Exxon Mobil Corp. v. Allapattah 907
Note: Efficiency and Institutional Competence 922
Note: The Class Action Fairness Act of 2005 922
Note: The Multiparty, Multiforum Trial Jurisdiction Act of 2002 925
e. Declining to Exercise Supplemental Jurisdiction 927
f. Tolling of Statutes of Limitation and Supplemental Jurisdiction 928
Note: Pendent Personal Jurisdiction 928
3. Federal Removal Jurisdiction 929
a. Introduction 929
b. Remand 930
Caterpillar Inc. v. Lewis 930
Notes and Questions 938
4. Venue Transfers Within the Federal Court System 945
5. Sua Sponte Transfer 948
Republic of Bolivia v. Philip Morris Companies, Inc. 948
6. Forum Non Conveniens 950
Piper Aircraft Co. v. Reyno 950
Note: Placing Conditions on Dismissal 955
Note: The Degree of Deference to Plaintiff's Choice 956
Note: Venue Transfers for Reasons Other than Inconvenience 957
Review Problem: Choosing Systems in a More Complex World 958
B. Extending the Lawsuit: More on Joinder 958
1. Joinder of Multiple Parties 958
Problem Case: A Woman Partner (Once Again) 959
a. Real Party in Interest 960
b. Capacity to Sue or Be Sued 960
c. Constitutional Limitations—Standing 961
d. Fictitious Names 961
e. Anonymous Parties 961
2. The Rules of Party Joinder 962
a. Permissive Joinder (Rule 20) 962
Mosley v. General Motors Corp. 962
Note: Fraudulent Joinder 966
b. Compulsory Joinder (Rule 19) 966
Temple v. Synthes Corp. 966
Helzberg's Diamond Shops, Inc. v. Valley West Des Moines Shopping Center, Inc. 968

Notes and Questions 971
c. Impleader (Rule 14) 972
Toberman v. Copas 972
United States v. Joe Grasso & Son, Inc. 975
d. Interpleader (Rule 22) and Statutory Interpleader: The Stakeholder's Remedy 978
State Farm Fire & Casualty Co. v. Tashire 979
Note: Transfer for Consolidation 984
e. Intervention (Rule 24) 985
American Lung Ass'n v. Reilly 985
Notes and Questions 987
C. Advanced Issues in Discovery 992
1. Protective Orders, Public Access, and Joinder Strategies 992
Grove Fresh Distributors, Inc. v. Everfresh Juice Co. 992
Note: Collateral Litigation 998
2. Private Investigation and the Duty of Third Parties to Give Evidence 998
a. Private Investigation 998
International Business Machines Corp. v. Edelstein 998
b. Nonparties' Duty to Give Evidence: The Subpoena Power 1001
Mount Sinai School of Medicine v. American Tobacco Co. 1001
Note: The Tobacco Industry Lawyers — Hired Guns' Smoke 1011
Note: Unduly Burdensome Subpoenas 1014
D. Class Actions — An Introduction (Rule 23) 1019
1. Introduction 1019
In re Wells Fargo Home Mortgage Overtime Pay Litigation 1020
Notes and Questions 1032
Note: The Class Suit in Equity 1044
Note: The Right to Jury Trial 1046
2. Appeal of Class Certification 1046
Blair v. Equifax Check Services, Inc. 1046
Notes and Questions 1053
3. Who Is Bound? — Of Civil Rights and Class Actions 1056
Hansberry v. Lee 1056
Note: *Hansberry* and the Concept of Persons Whose Interests Are Affected by Litigation 1060
Note: Defendant Classes 1061
Martin v. Wilks 1061
Notes and Questions 1067
Civil Rights Act of 1991 1067

4. Notice and the Opportunity to Be Heard 1070
    Eisen v. Carlisle & Jacquelin 1070
    Notes and Questions 1075
5. Choice of Forum and Mode of Trial Issues: Personal Jurisdiction 1080
    Phillips Petroleum Co. v. Shutts 1080
    Note: Venue in Class Actions 1087
    Note: Federal Jurisdiction in Class Actions 1088
6. Settlement 1090
    Amchem Products, Inc. v. Windsor 1090
    Notes and Questions 1102
    Jonathan R. Macey and Geoffrey Miller, The Plaintiffs' Attorney's Role in Class Action and Derivative Litigation: Economic Analysis and Recommendations for Reform 1107
    Example: A Lawyer's Fairy Tale 1109
    Note: Rule 68 and Class Actions 1110
    Note: The Aggregation Alternative 1112

7 *Repose: Ending Disputes* *1115*

A. Direct Attacks on Judgments 1115
    Problem Case: A Time to Reconsider 1115
1. Judgments of Courts Lacking Jurisdiction 1116
    Durfee v. Duke 1116
2. Judgments Obtained by Fraud or Mistake 1120
    Kupferman v. Consolidated Research & Mfg. Co. 1120
    Note: Rozier v. Ford Motor Co. 1123
    Note: Extrinsic Fraud 1123
3. Judgments Contrary to Law 1124
    Pierce v. Cook & Co. 1124
    Notes and Questions 1128
B. Collateral Effects of Judgments—Claim and Issue Preclusion 1130
    Note: Planned Parenthood v. Casey 1132
1. Claim Preclusion 1133
    a. In General 1133
    b. Conditions of Claim Preclusion 1134
    Problem Case: A Woman Partner (Yet Again) 1135
    McConnell v. Travelers Indemnity Co. 1136
    Consumers Union of United States v. Consumer Product Safety Commission 1137
    Note: GTE Sylvania, Inc. v. Consumers Union 1143
    Federated Department Stores v. Moitie 1144
    Note: Pleading and Preclusion 1149

Note: Are Defects in Subject Matter Jurisdiction Ever Res Judicata? 1149
Note: Subject Matter Jurisdiction and Remedies 1150
c. Counterclaims and Cross-Claims 1151
Problem Case: A Woman Partner (One More Time) 1152
Martino v. McDonald's System, Inc. 1153
d. Sources of Preclusion Law 1158
Restatement (Second) of Judgments 1158
Notes and Questions 1163
2. Issue Preclusion 1165
Problem Case: Using a Friendly Decision 1165
a. In General 1165
Examples 1166
Commissioner of Internal Revenue v. Sunnen 1166
Allen v. McCurry 1169
b. Mutuality of Estoppel 1174
Parklane Hosiery Co. v. Shore 1174
Notes and Questions 1182
Montana v. United States 1184
Notes and Questions 1188
3. Preclusion in a Federal System 1189
a. State Court Judgments in Federal Courts 1190
Kremer v. Chemical Corp. 1190
Note: England v. Louisiana State Bd. of Medical Examiners 1198
Note: Matsushita Electrical Indus. Co. v. Epstein 1199
Note: Effect of Res Judicata on Amount in Controversy 1200
Brown v. Felsen 1200
Baker v. General Motors Corporation 1204
Exxon Mobil Corp. v. Saudi Basic Indus. Corp. 1213
b. Federal Court Judgments in State Courts 1220
Watkins v. Resorts International Hotel and Casino, Inc. 1220
Notes and Questions 1229

Appendix *1233*
Table of Cases *1351*
Table of Federal Rules of Civil Procedure *1373*
Table of Judicial Code Citations *1377*
Index *1379*

Preface

When the last edition went to press, the nation was on a war footing, raising profound questions about whether the principles and practices associated with due process of law are an impediment to security or a condition of liberty. Even as a new administration looks to strike a different balance in foreign and domestic policy between security and liberty, the constitutional and practical questions about bringing due process to life for those who turn to the law to vindicate their rights remain as pressing as ever. Thus in the case that opens the book, traditional principles of due process meet arguments of exigency, national security, and executive authority.

As before, we begin with constitutional due process, not only to frame the principal themes of the course, but to lay a proper foundation for the study of jurisdiction. There is no better place to start because the study of due process invites sustained reflection about the enduring values that define procedural law: the belief in the power of rules to constrain government decision makers and fellow citizens; the commitment to equal access to law; the peculiarly American zest for adversarial exchange; and the belief in meaningful participation in decisions affecting one's substantive legal rights. With this grounding in procedural first principles, we turn to old chestnuts and new developments in each stage of the modern litigation process.

We have extended treatment of the pleading process in the new edition, primarily because the Supreme Court has intervened in new and surprising ways to enhance the power of judges to dispose of cases early in litigation, before either side knows much about the facts. Although the effects of this development remain uncertain—indeed, there is new litigation before the Supreme Court to clarify the scope of changes to the pleading process—the development is of a piece with general trends in the law of procedure evincing judicial skepticism about the kinds of litigants and disputes that belong in court. We live in an era in which full adversary litigation is both more important and more uncommon than ever. We have structured the new material to highlight and provoke reflection on this seeming contradiction.

We also have addressed the much-discussed style changes to the Federal Rules of Civil Procedure. The restyled rules took effect on

December 1, 2006, with the Advisory Committee promising that the amendments were stylistic only. For those of us in practice long enough to have developed a practitioner's sensitivity to the nuances of the old language, the changes have in some respects been jarring, and there is of course concern about whether and to what extent they will produce new interpretations of the rules and bring new consequences. For the new student of procedure, however, the changes can be learned as any rule change is learned — using precedent and principle to give meaning to new language. For that reason, rather than anticipate substantive changes the courts have yet to find, we include a comprehensive Appendix to support side-by-side comparison of the new and old rules.

We also have deepened coverage of cases and readings on Rule 11 sanctions, sanctions in discovery practice, and the increasingly difficult and important issues surrounding the preservation, storage, and disclosure of digital data. Discovery now dominates modern law practice, and the development of digital data, metadata, and new means of storage and recovery, among other technological advances, has complicated nearly all the traditional burdens and opportunities of discovery practice. Finally, we have continued to expand the treatment of emerging doctrines governing the burgeoning transnational litigation attendant on the growth of a global economy.

As with the third edition, increases in the discretion of the trial judge over both litigants and the jury have caused us to retain our coverage of some old favorites, including extended treatment of the 1986 trilogy of summary judgment decisions by the Supreme Court, *Walker v. City of Birmingham* on pre-judgment remedies and contempt, and discussion of the inherent powers doctrine. We canvass recent efforts by Congress and the Supreme Court to clarify the scope of federal jurisdiction, and to charge lower federal courts with the task of managing increasingly complex, multiparty litigation. And throughout the text we have sought to place greater emphasis on empirical studies of the practical consequences of procedural change, as well as the relationship between procedural rules and both ethical and social understandings of the lawyering role.

For the new edition, invaluable assistance with research was provided by a cadre of dedicated students at Stanford Law School: Samantha Bateman, Sarah Edwards, Caroline Jackson, Menaka Kalaskar, Rakesh Kilaru, David Owens, and Priyanka Rajagopalan. We are immensely grateful for their diligence, creativity, and passion for procedure. For outstanding administrative support, we once again thank Donna Fung, who now has provided uncommonly generous and expert help with three editions. We are also grateful to the editors at Aspen for supporting a new edition. Special thanks are due to John Devins, our patient development editor; Katy Thompson, our diligent project manager; and to the manuscript editors.

Over the years we have been uncommonly fortunate in the support others have provided to the production of this book at both Stanford and Arizona, including Esther Kim, Melanie Wachtell, Kathryn Johnson, Nancy B. Leong, and Naomi Ruth Tsu. Ms. Leong and Ms. Tsu dedicated especially long hours, thoughtful comments, and close editing to enrich the third edition. The exceptional research support of Robyn Kool and Joanna Grossman was instrumental in the first and second editions. Laura Gomez, Kara Mikulich, Jason Richards, Lisa Sitkin, Joseph Vigil, Matthew Gowdy, Jill Harrison, Katherine Wilson, Mary Jensen, Beth Smith, Melinda Evans, Susan Hightower, Maureen Lewis, Julie Loughran, Melinda Mattingly, and Amy Ruskin also contributed much appreciated research assistance.

As always, we are deeply grateful to our fellow procedure teachers who have offered new ideas and input to improve the book. We are particularly indebted to Professor Mary Twitchell for her extremely insightful substantive suggestions, and to Paul Carrington, whose book decades ago started us on this course. He remains our intellectual mentor, still raising fresh insights even as we preserve much of what he has left behind.

Thanks to all for the inspiration.

Barbara Allen Babcock
Toni M. Massaro
Norman W. Spaulding

April 2009

Acknowledgments

We wish to thank those who have given permission for the use of excerpts from the following articles and books:

Babcock, Barbara A., A Place in the Palladium: Women's Rights and Jury Service, 61 U. Cin. L. Rev. 1139 (1993). Copyright © 1993 by the University of Cincinnati. Reprinted by permission of the author and the Cincinnati Law Review from the Cincinnati Law Review, Vol. 61.

Canby, Hon. William C., Tribal Court, Federal Court, State Court: A Jurisdiction Primer, Arizona Attorney (July 1993). Copyright © 1993 State Bar of Arizona. Reprinted by permission of the author and Arizona Attorney.

Carrington, Paul D. and Barbara A. Babcock, American Civil Procedure (3d ed. 1983). Copyright © 1983 by Paul D. Carrington and Barbara A. Babcock. Reprinted by permission of the authors and Little, Brown and Company.

Cohen, Jerome A., Chinese Mediation on the Eve of Modernization, 54 Cal. L. Rev. 1201 (1966). Reprinted by permission of the author and the California Law Review from California Law Review, Vol. 54, pp.1206-1208.

Dawson, John, Lawyers and Involuntary Clients in Public Interest Litigation, 88 Harv. L. Rev. 849 (1975). Copyright © 1975 by the Harvard Law Review Association. Reprinted by permission of the Harvard Law Review Association from the Harvard Law Review, Vol. 88.

Fowler, W. Gary, A Comparison of Initial Recommendation Procedures: Judicial Selection Under Reagan and Carter, 1 Yale L. & Poly. Rev. 199 (1983). Copyright © 1983 by The Yale Law and Policy Review. Reprinted by permission of the author and The Yale Law and Policy Review from The Yale Law and Policy Review, Vol. 1, pp. 303-304, 307-310, 317-318, 331, 332.

Friedenthal, Jack H., Mary Kay Kane, and Arthur R. Miller, Civil Procedure (4th ed. 2005). Copyright © 2005 by West Publishing Corporation. Reprinted with permission of the authors and West Publishing Corporation from Civil Procedure 4th ed., pp. 575, 620, 690-698.

Hazard, Geoffrey, Panel Discussion on Professional Responsibility and the Model Rules of Professional Conduct. Reprinted from the University of Miami Law Review, 35 U. Miami L. Rev. 639, 659-660, 662 (1981), which holds copyright on this article.

Hensler, Deborah, et al., Class Action Dilemmas, reprinted by permission of the RAND Corporation. Copyright © 2000, pp. 375-401.

Higginbotham, A. Leon, The Case of Missing Black Judges, N.Y. Times, July 29, 1992, Op-Ed. Copyright © 1992 by the New York Times Company. Reprinted by permission.

Hinds, Michael deCourcy, Computer Gives Odds on Jury Awards, N.Y. Times, Jan. 21, 1994. Copyright © 1994 by the New York Times Company. Reprinted by permission.

Kagan, Robert, Adversarial Legalism: The American Way of Law, pp.6-16 (2001)

Landers, Jonathan M., Of Legalized Blackmail and Legalized Theft: Consumer Class Actions and the Substance Procedure Dilemma, 47 S. Cal. L. Rev. 842 (1974). Reprinted by permission of the author and the Southern California Law Review from the Southern California Law Review, Vol. 47, pp. 845-847.

Landsman, Stephan, Readings on Adversarial Justice: The American Approach to Adjudication (1988). Copyright © 1988 by Thomson West. Reprinted with permission of the author and Thomson West from Readings on Adversarial Justice: The American Approach to Adjudication, 1st ed., pp. 2-5.

Levy, Jerome S. and Robert C. Prather, Sr., Texas Practice Guide, ADR Strategies, 3:10. Copyright © 1998 by Thomson West. Reprinted with permission of Thomson West.

Luban, David, Taking Out the Adversary: The Assault on Progressive Public Interest Lawyers, 91 Cal. L. Rev. 209, 211- 13 (2003).

Macey, Jonathan R. and Geoffrey Miller, The Plaintiff's Attorney's Role in Class Action and Derivative Litigation: Economic Analysis and Recommendations for Reform, 58 U. Chi. L. Rev. 1, 22-26 (1991).

Margolick, David, The Long Road Back for a Disgraced Patrician, N.Y. Times, Jan. 19, 1990, as reprinted in the S.F. Chronicle, Jan. 28, 1990. Copyright © 1990 by the New York Times Company. Reprinted by permission.

Massaro, Toni M., Rethinking Sixth Amendment Doctrine, Images, and Procedures, 64 N.C. L. Rev. 501 (1986). Copyright © 1986 by the North Carolina Law Review Association. Reprinted with permission from the North Carolina Law Review, Vol. 64, pp. 517-518.

Matsuda, Mari J., Voices of America: Accent, Antidiscrimination Law and a Jurisprudence for the Last Reconstruction, 100 Yale L.J. 1329 (1991). Reprinted by permission of the author, the Yale Law Journal Company, and William S. Hein Company from the Yale Law Journal, Vol. 100, pp.1329-1407.

McElhaney, James W., Nine Ways to Use Depositions, 19:2 Litigation (1993). Copyright © by James W. McElhaney of Case Western Reserve University School of Law. "Nine Ways to Use Depositions" first appeared in Vol. 19, No. 2, Winter (1993) issue of Litigation journal. Reprinted with permission of the copyright holder and the American Bar Association.

Nelson, William E., Americanization of the Common Law: The Impact of Legal Change on Massachusetts Society, 1760-1830, 69-78, 86-87 (1975).

Perdue, Wendy, Sin, Scandal, and Substantive Due Process: Personal Jurisdiction and Pennoyer Reconsidered, 62 Wash. L. Rev. 479 (1987). Reprinted by permission of the author and the Washington Law Review, from the Washington Law Review, Vol. 62, pp. 480-490.

Posner, Richard, An Economic Analysis of Sex Discrimination Laws, 56 U. Chi. L. Rev. 1311 (1989). Reprinted by permission of the author and University of Chicago Law Review from the University of Chicago Law Review, Vol. 56, p.1334.

Purcell, Edward Jr., Geography as Litigation Weapon: Forum Selection Clauses and the Rehnquist Court. Originally published in 40 UCLA L. Rev. 423, 446-449 (1992). Copyright © 1992 by The Regents of the University of California. All Rights Reserved. Reprinted by permission of the author, UCLA Law Review, and Fred B. Rothman & Company.

Purcell, Edward Jr., Litigation and Inequality: Federal Diversity Jurisdiction in Industrial America, 1870-1958 (1992). Copyright © 1992 by Oxford University Press, Inc. Reprinted by permission of the author and Oxford University Press, Inc.

Rabin, Robert L., A Sociolegal History of the Tobacco Tort Litigation, 44 Stan. L. Rev. 853 (1992). Copyright © 1992 by Robert L. Rabin. Reprinted by permission of the author from Stanford Law Review, Vol. 44, pp. 857-860.

Resnik, Judith, Revising the Canon: Feminist Help in Teaching Procedure, 61 Univ. Cincinnati L. Rev. 1181 (1993). Copyright © 1993 by Judith Resnik and the University of Cincinnati. Reprinted by permission of the author and the Cincinnati Law Review from Cincinnati Law Review, Vol. 61, p.1191.

Restatement Second of Judgments §§ 17-29, 86-87 (ALI 1982). Copyright © 1982 by the American Law Institute. Reprinted with permission.

Rhode, Deborah L., Professional Responsibility: Teaching Ethics by the Pervasive Method (1994). Copyright © 1994 by Deborah L. Rhode. Published by Little, Brown and Company. Reprinted by permission of the author and Little, Brown and Company.

Setterberg, Fred, Service with a Smile: Selecting the Right Process Server, 5 Cal. Lawyer 55 (July 1985). Copyright © 1985 by

California Lawyer. Reprinted by permission of the author and California Lawyer from California Lawyer, Vol. 5, pp. 5-56.

Sherwyn, Estreicher and Heise, Assessing the Case for Employment Arbitration, 57 Stan. L. Rev. 1557, 1578-80 (2005).

Stichman, Barton I., The Veterans' Judicial Act of 1988; Congress Introduces Courts and Attorneys to Veterans' Benefits Proceedings, 23 Clearinghouse Rev. 517 (1989). Copyright © 1989 by the Natural Veterans Legal Services Program. Reprinted by permission of the author and the National Veterans Legal Services Program.

Taylor-Thompson, Kim, Empty Votes in Jury Deliberations, 113 Harv. L. Rev. 1261, 1264 (2000).

Thornberg, Elizabeth, Sanctifying Secrecy: The Mythology of the Corporate Attorney-Client Privilege, 69 Notre Dame L. Rev. 157, 193-197 (1993).

Tyler, Tom, Why People Obey the Law (1990). Published by Yale University Press. Copyright © 1990 by Yale University. Reprinted with permission by the author and Yale University Press.

Welles, Edmund O., They Also Serve, San Jose Mercury News, Dec. 28, 1986, at 4. Copyright © 1986 by the San Jose Mercury News. Reprinted with permission from the San Jose Mercury News.

Wells, Catherine, Clarence Thomas: The Invisible Man, 67 S. Cal. L. Rev. 117 (1993). Reprinted by permission of the author and Southern California Law Review from Southern California Law Review, Vol. 67, pp. 119-120.

Winters, Glenn R., Selection of Judges — An Historical Introduction, 44 Tex. L. Rev. 1081 (1966). Copyright © 1966 by the Texas Law Review Association. Reprinted by permission.

Woods, Winton, Carnival Cruise Lines v. Shute: An Amicus Inquiry into the Future of "Purposeful Availment," 36 Wayne L. Rev. 1393 (1990). Reprinted by permission of the author and Wayne Law Review from Wayne Law Review, Vol. 36, p.1396.

Yeazell, Stephen, The Misunderstood Consequences of Modern Civil Procedure, 1994 Wis. L. Rev. 631. Copyright © 1994 by the Board of Regents of the University of Wisconsin System. Reprinted by permission of the author and Wisconsin Law Review from Wisconsin Law Review, pp. 632-633, 636-639, 648, 651, 661-663.

Zampano, Robert, "From the Bench" Settlement Strategies for Trial Judges, Litigation Magazine, Volume 22, No. 1, Fall 1995. Reprinted with permission of the American Bar Association, pp. 3-6.

Zweifach, Lawrence J., Deposition Strategy in the Framework of an Overall Discovery Plan (PLI 1992). Copyright © by the Practicing Law Institute. Reprinted by permission of the Practicing Law Institute.

Special Notice on Citations

Some citations have been omitted from case excerpts without notation, including parallel citations, string citations, and footnotes. Other omissions are indicated with ellipses or bracketed text. We have preserved the original footnote numbers for those notes that have been retained; editors' footnotes are designated with an asterisk and the notation "EDS." when they occur within an excerpt.

Civil Procedure

1 *Due Process of Law*

A. NOTICE AND THE OPPORTUNITY TO BE HEARD

Problem Case: The Due Process Game

In your second week of law school, you find a letter from the President of the University in your mailbox. On official letterhead, it reads:

> You have been accused of a serious Honor Code violation. Please discontinue class attendance immediately and make arrangements to leave campus.

What further information would you want from the University? What procedures would you expect? What kind of hearing would you seek? Would you want someone else to speak for you? What sort of decision maker would you desire? What rights would you assume? Are your assumptions about rights dependent on whether you are innocent or guilty of the violation? On the severity of the penalty?

Most Americans, especially law students, will construct a fairly elaborate model for deciding whether there was an Honor Code violation and what penalty should apply. A sense of the process due, of how facts should be found, and what results should follow is part of the larger, as well as the legal, culture of our society.

Due process, both as aspiration and method, is at the heart of our study of procedure. Rules, statutes, formal and informal decision making must all meet a due process standard. The United States Supreme Court has spoken on the subject in many settings. Sometimes, the process due is only what the legislature says must be done before the government takes property or liberty.

Even then, however, the government must notify the persons affected and afford them some chance to "tell the other side." How much notice, what kind of hearing—these are the due process questions. Here is a recent Supreme Court case on due process, followed by interpretive and explanatory notes. This first section introduces the core of our study and our method in this book. Each unit starts with a problem case, followed by cases and materials for solving it. In reading these, think about the problem case; how does the doctrine fit with your intuitions about due process?

1. The Process Due: Of Context and Subtext

Hamdi v. Rumsfeld
542 U.S. 507 (2004)

Justice O'Connor announced the judgment of the Court and delivered an opinion, in which Chief Justice Rehnquist, Justice Kennedy, and Justice Breyer join.

At this difficult time in our Nation's history, we are called upon to consider the legality of the Government's detention of a United States citizen on United States soil as an "enemy combatant" and to address the process that is constitutionally owed to one who seeks to challenge his classification as such. The United States Court of Appeals for the Fourth Circuit held that petitioner's detention was legally authorized and that he was entitled to no further opportunity to challenge his enemy-combatant label. We now vacate and remand. We hold that although Congress authorized the detention of combatants in the narrow circumstances alleged here, due process demands that a citizen held in the United States as an enemy combatant be given a meaningful opportunity to contest the factual basis for that detention before a neutral decision maker.

I

On September 11, 2001, the al Qaeda terrorist network used hijacked commercial airliners to attack prominent targets in the United States. Approximately 3,000 people were killed in those attacks. One week later, in response to these "acts of treacherous violence," Congress passed a resolution authorizing the President to "use all necessary and appropriate force against those nations, organizations, or persons he determines planned, authorized, committed, or aided the terrorist attacks" or "harbored such organizations or persons, in order to prevent any future acts of international terrorism against the United States by such nations, organizations or persons." Authorization for Use of Military Force ("the AUMF"), 115 Stat. 224. Soon thereafter, the President ordered United States Armed Forces to Afghanistan, with a mission to subdue al Qaeda and quell the Taliban regime that was known to support it.

This case arises out of the detention of a man whom the Government alleges took up arms with the Taliban during this conflict. His name is Yaser Esam Hamdi. Born an American citizen in Louisiana in 1980, Hamdi moved with his family to Saudi Arabia as a child. By 2001, the parties agree, he resided in Afghanistan. At some point that year, he was seized by members of the Northern Alliance, a coalition of military groups opposed to the Taliban government, and eventually was turned over to the United States military. The Government asserts that it initially detained and interrogated Hamdi in Afghanistan before transferring him to the United States Naval Base in Guantanamo Bay in January 2002. In

April 2002, upon learning that Hamdi is an American citizen, authorities transferred him to a naval brig in Norfolk, Virginia, where he remained until a recent transfer to a brig in Charleston, South Carolina. The Government contends that Hamdi is an "enemy combatant," and that this status justifies holding him in the United States indefinitely—without formal charges or proceedings—unless and until it makes the determination that access to counsel or further process is warranted.

In June 2002, Hamdi's father, Esam Fouad Hamdi, filed the present petition for a writ of habeas corpus under 28 U.S.C. § 2241 in the Eastern District of Virginia. . . . The elder Hamdi alleges in the petition that he has had no contact with his son since the Government took custody of him in 2001, and that the Government has held his son "without access to legal counsel or notice of any charges pending against him." App. 103, 104. The petition contends that Hamdi's detention was not legally authorized. Id., at 105. It argues that, "[a]s an American citizen, . . . Hamdi enjoys the full protections of the Constitution," and that Hamdi's detention in the United States without charges, access to an impartial tribunal, or assistance of counsel "violated and continue[s] to violate the Fifth and Fourteenth Amendments to the United States Constitution." Id., at 107. The habeas petition asks that the court, among other things, (1) appoint counsel for Hamdi; (2) order respondents to cease interrogating him; (3) declare that he is being held in violation of the Fifth and Fourteenth Amendments; (4) "[t]o the extent Respondents contest any material factual allegations in this Petition, schedule an evidentiary hearing, at which Petitioners may adduce proof in support of their allegations"; and (5) order that Hamdi be released from his "unlawful custody." Id., at 108-109. Although his habeas petition provides no details with regard to the factual circumstances surrounding his son's capture and detention, Hamdi's father has asserted in documents found elsewhere in the record that his son went to Afghanistan to do "relief work," and that he had been in that country less than two months before September 11, 2001, and could not have received military training. Id., at 188-189. The 20-year-old was traveling on his own for the first time, his father says, and "[b]ecause of his lack of experience, he was trapped in Afghanistan once that military campaign began." Id., at 188-189. The District Court found that Hamdi's father was a proper next friend, appointed the federal public defender as counsel for the petitioners, and ordered that counsel be given access to Hamdi. Id., at 113-116. . . .

[T]he Government filed a response and a motion to dismiss the petition. It attached to its response a declaration from one Michael Mobbs (hereinafter "Mobbs Declaration"), who identified himself as Special Advisor to the Under Secretary of Defense for Policy. Mobbs indicated that in this position, he has been "substantially involved with matters related to the detention of enemy combatants in the current war against the al Qaeda terrorists and those who support and harbor them (including the Taliban)." Id., at 148. He expressed his "familiar[ity]" with Department of Defense and United States military policies and procedures applicable to the detention, control, and transfer of al Qaeda and Taliban personnel, and declared that "[b]ased upon my review of relevant records and reports, I am also familiar with the facts and circumstances related to the capture of . . . Hamdi and his detention by U.S. military forces." Id.

Mobbs then set forth what remains the sole evidentiary support that the Government has provided to the courts for Hamdi's detention. The declaration states that Hamdi "traveled to Afghanistan" in July or August 2001, and that he thereafter "affiliated with a Taliban military unit and received weapons training." Id. It asserts that Hamdi "remained with his Taliban unit following the attacks of September 11" and that, during the time when Northern Alliance forces were "engaged in battle with the Taliban," "Hamdi's Taliban unit surrendered" to those forces, after which he "surrender[ed] his Kalishnikov assault rifle" to them. Id., at 148-149. The Mobbs Declaration also states that, because al Qaeda and the Taliban "were and are hostile forces engaged in armed conflict with the armed forces of the United States," "individuals associated with" those groups "were and continue to be enemy combatants." Id., at 149. Mobbs states that Hamdi was labeled an enemy combatant "[b]ased upon his interviews and in light of his association with the Taliban." Id. According to the declaration, a series of "U.S. military screening team[s]" determined that Hamdi met "the criteria for enemy combatants," and "a subsequent interview of Hamdi has confirmed that he surrendered and gave his firearm to Northern Alliance forces, which supports his classification as an enemy combatant." Id., at 149-150. . . .

The District Court found that the Mobbs Declaration fell "far short" of supporting Hamdi's detention. Id., at 292. It criticized the generic and hearsay nature of the affidavit, calling it "little more than the government's 'say-so.'" Id., at 298. It ordered the Government to turn over numerous materials for *in camera* review, including copies of all of Hamdi's statements and the notes taken from interviews with him that related to his reasons for going to Afghanistan and his activities therein; a list of all interrogators who had questioned Hamdi and their names and addresses; statements by members of the Northern Alliance regarding Hamdi's surrender and capture; a list of the dates and locations of his capture and subsequent detentions; and the names and titles of the United States Government officials who made the determinations that Hamdi was an enemy combatant and that he should be moved to a naval brig. Id., at 185-186. The court indicated that all of these materials were necessary for "meaningful judicial review" of whether Hamdi's detention was legally authorized and whether Hamdi had received sufficient process to satisfy the Due Process Clause of the Constitution and relevant treaties or military regulations. Id., at 291-292. . . .

The Fourth Circuit reversed . . . stress[ing] that, because it was "undisputed that Hamdi was captured in a zone of active combat in a foreign theater of conflict," no factual inquiry or evidentiary hearing allowing Hamdi to be heard or to rebut the Government's assertions was necessary or proper. 16 F.3d 450, 459. Concluding that the factual averments in the Mobbs Declaration, "if accurate," provided a sufficient basis upon which to conclude that the President had constitutionally detained Hamdi pursuant to the President's war powers, it ordered the habeas petition dismissed. Id., at 473. . . .

On the more global question of whether legal authorization exists for the detention of citizen enemy combatants at all, the Fourth Circuit . . . expressed doubt as to Hamdi's argument that 18 U.S.C. § 4001(a), which provides that "[n]o citizen shall be imprisoned or otherwise detained by the United States except pursuant to an Act of Congress,"* required express congressional authorization of detentions of this sort. But it held that, in any event, such authorization was found in the post-September 11 Authorization for Use of Military Force. Id., at 467. Because "capturing and detaining enemy combatants is an inherent part of warfare," the court held, "the 'necessary and appropriate force' referenced in the congressional resolution necessarily includes the capture and detention of any and all hostile forces arrayed against our troops." Id. . . .

"The privilege of citizenship," the court held, "entitles Hamdi to a limited judicial inquiry into his detention, but only to determine its legality under the war powers of the political branches. . . ." 316 F.3d, at 475.

. . . We now vacate the judgment below and remand.

II

[On the threshold question whether the President has the authority to detain citizens who qualify as "enemy combatants," Justice O'Connor wrote:]

The AUMF authorizes the President to use "all necessary and appropriate force" against "nations, organizations, or persons" associated with the September 11, 2001, terrorist attacks. 115 Stat. 224. There can be no doubt that individuals who fought against the United States in Afghanistan as part of the Taliban, an organization known to have supported the al Qaeda terrorist network responsible for those attacks, are individuals Congress sought to target in passing the AUMF. We conclude that detention of individuals falling into the limited category we are considering, for the duration of the particular conflict in which they were captured, is so fundamental and accepted an incident to war as to be an exercise of the "necessary and appropriate force" Congress has authorized the President to use. . . .

III

[Justice O'Connor then turned to the due process issue:]

Even in cases in which the detention of enemy combatants is legally authorized, there remains the question of what process is constitutionally due to a citizen who disputes his enemy-combatant status. Hamdi argues

* 18 U.S.C. § 4001 is the Non-Detention Act, passed by Congress in response to the illegal detention of nearly 120,000 Americans of Japanese ancestry during World War II. Eds.

that he is owed a meaningful and timely hearing and that "extra-judicial detention [that] begins and ends with the submission of an affidavit based on third-hand hearsay" does not comport with the Fifth and Fourteenth Amendments. Brief for Petitioners 16. The Government counters that any more process than was provided below would be both unworkable and "constitutionally intolerable." Brief for Respondents 46. Our resolution of this dispute requires a careful examination both of the writ of habeas corpus, which Hamdi now seeks to employ as a mechanism of judicial review, and of the Due Process Clause, which informs the procedural contours of that mechanism in this instance.

A

. . . All agree that, absent suspension, the writ of habeas corpus remains available to every individual detained within the United States. U.S. Const., Art. I, § 9, cl. 2 ("The Privilege of the Writ of Habeas Corpus shall not be suspended, unless when in Cases of Rebellion or Invasion the public Safety may require it"). Only in the rarest of circumstances has Congress seen fit to suspend the writ. See, e.g., Act of Mar. 3, 1863, ch. 81, § 1; Act of April 20, 1871, ch. 22, § 4. At all other times, it has remained a critical check on the Executive, ensuring that it does not detain individuals except in accordance with law. See INS v. St. Cyr, 533 U.S. 289, 301 (2001). *All agree suspension of the writ has not occurred here.* [Emphasis added.] Thus, it is undisputed that Hamdi was properly before an Article III court to challenge his detention under 28 U.S.C. § 2241. . .

. . . The Government . . . asks us to hold that, given both the flexibility of the habeas mechanism and the circumstances presented in this case, the presentation of the Mobbs Declaration to the habeas court completed the required factual development. . .

C

The Government . . . [argues] that further factual exploration is unwarranted and inappropriate in light of the extraordinary constitutional interests at stake. Under the Government's most extreme rendition of this argument, "[r]espect for separation of powers and the limited institutional capabilities of courts in matters of military decision-making in connection with an ongoing conflict" ought to eliminate entirely any individual process, restricting the courts to investigating only whether legal authorization exists for the broader detention scheme. Brief for Respondents 26. At most, the Government argues, courts should review its determination that a citizen is an enemy combatant under a very deferential "some evidence" standard. Id., at 34 ("Under the some evidence standard, the focus is exclusively on the factual basis supplied by the Executive to support its own determination" (citing Superintendent, Mass. Correctional Institution at Walpole v. Hill, 472 U.S. 445, 455-457 (1985) (explaining that the some evidence standard "does not require" a "weighing of the evidence," but rather calls for assessing "whether there is any evidence in the record that could support the conclusion")). Under this review, a court would assume the accuracy of the Government's articulated basis for Hamdi's detention, as set forth in the Mobbs Declaration, and assess only whether that articulated basis was a legitimate one. Brief for Respondents 36. . . .

In response, Hamdi emphasizes that this Court consistently has recognized that an individual challenging his detention may not be held at the will of the Executive without recourse to some proceeding before a neutral tribunal to determine whether the Executive's asserted justifications for that detention have basis in fact and warrant in law. See, e.g., Zadvydas v. Davis, 533 U.S. 678, 690 (2001); Addington v. Texas, 441 U.S. 418, 425-427 (1979). . . . The District Court, agreeing with Hamdi, apparently believed that the appropriate process would approach the process that accompanies a criminal trial. It therefore disapproved of the hearsay nature of the Mobbs Declaration and anticipated quite extensive discovery of various military affairs. Anything less, it concluded, would not be "meaningful judicial review." App. 291.

Both of these positions highlight legitimate concerns. And both emphasize the tension that often exists between the autonomy that the Government asserts is necessary in order to pursue effectively a particular goal and the process that a citizen contends he is due before he is deprived of a constitutional right. The ordinary mechanism that we use for balancing such serious competing interests, and for determining the procedures that are necessary to ensure that a citizen is not "deprived of life, liberty, or property, without due process of law," U.S. Const., Amt. 5, is the test that we articulated in Mathews v. Eldridge, 424 U.S. 319 (1976). See, e.g., Heller v. Doe, 509 U.S. 312, 330-331 (1993); Zinermon v. Burch, 494 U.S. 113, 127-128 (1990); United States v. Salerno, 481 U.S. 739, 746 (1987); Schall v. Martin, 467 U.S. 253, 274-275 (1984); Addington v. Texas, supra, at 425. *Mathews* dictates that the process due in any given instance is determined by weighing "the private interest that will be affected by the official action" against the Government's asserted interest, "including the function involved" and the burdens the Government would face in providing greater process. 424 U.S., at 335. The *Mathews* calculus then contemplates a judicious balancing of these concerns, through an analysis of "the risk of an erroneous deprivation" of the private interest if the process were reduced and the "probable value, if any, of additional or substitute safeguards." Id. We take each of these steps in turn.

1

It is beyond question that substantial interests lie on both sides of the scale in this case. Hamdi's "private interest . . . affected by the official action," id., is the most elemental of liberty interests—the interest in being free from physical detention by one's own government. Foucha v. Louisiana, 504 U.S. 71, 80 (1992) ("Freedom from bodily restraint has always been at the core of the liberty protected by the Due Process Clause from arbitrary governmental action"); see also Parham v. J.R., 442 U.S.

584, 600 (1979) (noting the "substantial liberty interest in not being confined unnecessarily"). "In our society liberty is the norm," and detention without trial "is the carefully limited exception." *Salerno,* supra, at 755. "We have always been careful not to 'minimize the importance and fundamental nature' of the individual's right to liberty," *Foucha*, supra, at 80, and we will not do so today.

Nor is the weight on this side of the *Mathews* scale offset by the circumstances of war or the accusation of treasonous behavior, for "[i]t is clear that commitment for *any* purpose constitutes a significant deprivation of liberty that requires due process protection," Jones v. United States, 463 U.S. 354, 361 (1983), and at this stage in the *Mathews* calculus, we consider the interest of the *erroneously* detained individual. Carey v. Piphus, 435 U.S. 247, 259 (1978) ("Procedural due process rules are meant to protect persons not from the deprivation, but from the mistaken or unjustified deprivation of life, liberty, or property"). . . . Moreover, as critical as the Government's interest may be in detaining those who actually pose an immediate threat to the national security of the United States during ongoing international conflict, history and common sense teach us that an unchecked system of detention carries the potential to become a means for oppression and abuse of others who do not present that sort of threat. See Ex parte Milligan, 4 Wall. 2, 125 (1866) ("[The Founders] knew—the history of the world told them—the nation they were founding, be its existence short or long, would be involved in war; how often or how long continued, human foresight could not tell; and that unlimited power, wherever lodged at such a time, was especially hazardous to freemen"). Because we live in a society in which "[m]ere public intolerance or animosity cannot constitutionally justify the deprivation of a person's physical liberty," O'Connor v. Donaldson, 422 U.S. 563, 575 (1975), our starting point for the *Mathews* analysis is unaltered by the allegations surrounding the particular detainee or the organizations with which he is alleged to have associated. We reaffirm today the fundamental nature of a citizen's right to be free from involuntary confinement by his own government without due process of law, and we weigh the opposing governmental interests against the curtailment of liberty that such confinement entails.

2

On the other side of the scale are the weighty and sensitive governmental interests in ensuring that those who have in fact fought with the enemy during a war do not return to battle against the United States. As discussed above, the law of war and the realities of combat may render such detentions both necessary and appropriate, and our due process analysis need not blink at those realities. Without doubt, our Constitution recognizes that core strategic matters of warmaking belong in the hands of those who are best positioned and most politically accountable for making them. Department of Navy v. Egan, 484 U.S. 518, 530 (1988) (noting the reluctance of the courts "to intrude upon the authority of the Executive in military and national security affairs").

The Government also argues at some length that its interests in reducing the process available to alleged enemy combatants are heightened by the practical difficulties that would accompany a system of trial-like process. In its view, military officers who are engaged in the serious work of waging battle would be unnecessarily and dangerously distracted by litigation half a world away, and discovery into military operations would both intrude on the sensitive secrets of national defense and result in a futile search for evidence buried under the rubble of war. . . .

3

Striking the proper constitutional balance here is of great importance to the Nation during this period of ongoing combat. But it is equally vital that our calculus not give short shrift to the values that this country holds dear or to the privilege that is American citizenship. It is during our most challenging and uncertain moments that our Nation's commitment to due process is most severely tested; and it is in those times that we must preserve our commitment at home to the principles for which we fight abroad. . . .

With due recognition of these competing concerns, we believe that neither the process proposed by the Government nor the process apparently envisioned by the District Court below strikes the proper constitutional balance when a United States citizen is detained in the United States as an enemy combatant. That is, "the risk of erroneous deprivation" of a detainee's liberty interest is unacceptably high under the Government's proposed rule, while some of the "additional or substitute procedural safeguards" suggested by the District Court are unwarranted in light of their limited "probable value" and the burdens they may impose on the military in such cases. *Mathews*, 424 U.S., at 335.

We therefore hold that a citizen-detainee seeking to challenge his classification as an enemy combatant must receive notice of the factual basis for his classification, and a fair opportunity to rebut the Government's factual assertions before a neutral decisionmaker. See Cleveland Bd. of Ed. v. Loudermill, 470 U.S. 532, 542 (1985) ("An essential principle of due process is that a deprivation of life, liberty, or property 'be preceded by notice and opportunity for hearing appropriate to the nature of the case'" (quoting Mullane v. Central Hanover Bank & Trust Co., 339 U.S. 306, 313 (1950)); Concrete Pipe & Products of Cal., Inc. v. Construction Laborers Pension Trust for Southern Cal., 508 U.S. 602, 617 (1993) ("due process requires a 'neutral and detached judge in the first instance'"). "For more than a century the central meaning of procedural due process has been clear: 'Parties whose rights are to be affected are entitled to be heard; and in order that they may enjoy that right they must first be notified.' It is equally fundamental that the right to notice and an opportunity to be heard 'must be granted at a meaningful time and in a meaningful manner.'" Fuentes v. Shevin, 407 U.S. 67, 80 (1972). These essential constitutional promises may not be eroded.

At the same time, the exigencies of the circumstances may demand that, aside from these core elements, enemy combatant proceedings may be tailored to alleviate their uncommon potential to burden the Executive at a time of ongoing military conflict. Hearsay, for example, may need to be accepted as the most reliable available evidence from the Government in such a proceeding. Likewise, the Constitution would not be offended by a presumption in favor of the Government's evidence, so long as that presumption remained a rebuttable one and fair opportunity for rebuttal were provided. Thus, once the Government puts forth credible evidence that the habeas petitioner meets the enemy-combatant criteria, the onus could shift to the petitioner to rebut that evidence with more persuasive evidence that he falls outside the criteria. A burden-shifting scheme of this sort would meet the goal of ensuring that the errant tourist, embedded journalist, or local aid worker has a chance to prove military error while giving due regard to the Executive once it has put forth meaningful support for its conclusion that the detainee is in fact an enemy combatant. In the words of *Mathews*, process of this sort would sufficiently address the "risk of erroneous deprivation" of a detainee's liberty interest while eliminating certain procedures that have questionable additional value in light of the burden on the Government. 424 U.S., at 335.

We think it unlikely that this basic process will have the dire impact on the central functions of warmaking that the Government forecasts. . . . While we accord the greatest respect and consideration to the judgments of military authorities in matters relating to the actual prosecution of a war, and recognize that the scope of that discretion necessarily is wide, it does not infringe on the core role of the military for the courts to exercise their own time-honored and constitutionally mandated roles of reviewing and resolving claims like those presented here. . . .

In sum, while the full protections that accompany challenges to detentions in other settings may prove unworkable and inappropriate in the enemy-combatant setting, the threats to military operations posed by a basic system of independent review are not so weighty as to trump a citizen's core rights to challenge meaningfully the Government's case and to be heard by an impartial adjudicator.

D

In so holding, we necessarily reject the Government's assertion that separation of powers principles mandate a heavily circumscribed role for the courts in such circumstances. . . . We have long since made clear that a state of war is not a blank check for the President when it comes to the rights of the Nation's citizens. Youngstown Sheet & Tube, 343 U.S. 579, 587 (1952). Whatever power the United States Constitution envisions for the Executive in its exchanges with other nations or with enemy organizations in times of conflict, it most assuredly envisions a role for all three branches when individual liberties are at stake. Home Building & Loan Assn. v. Blaisdell, 290 U.S. 398, 426 (1934) (The war power "is a power to wage war successfully, and thus it permits the harnessing of the entire energies of the people in a supreme cooperative effort to preserve the nation. But even the war power does not remove constitutional limitations safeguarding essential liberties"). . . .

Because we conclude that due process demands some system for a citizen detainee to refute his classification, the proposed "some evidence" standard is inadequate. Any process in which the Executive's factual assertions go wholly unchallenged or are simply presumed correct without any opportunity for the alleged combatant to demonstrate otherwise falls constitutionally short. . . .

. . . . Aside from unspecified "screening" processes, and military interrogations in which the Government suggests Hamdi could have contested his classification, Hamdi has received no process. An interrogation by one's captor, however effective an intelligence-gathering tool, hardly constitutes a constitutionally adequate factfinding before a neutral decision maker. . . .

IV

Hamdi asks us to hold that the Fourth Circuit also erred by denying him immediate access to counsel upon his detention and by disposing of the case without permitting him to meet with an attorney. Since our grant of certiorari in this case, Hamdi has been appointed counsel, with whom he has met for consultation purposes on several occasions, and with whom he is now being granted unmonitored meetings. He unquestionably has the right to access to counsel in connection with the proceedings on remand. No further consideration of this issue is necessary at this stage of the case.

* * *

The judgment of the United States Court of Appeals for the Fourth Circuit is vacated, and the case is remanded for further proceedings.

It is so ordered.

[The opinion of JUSTICE SOUTER, with whom JUSTICE GINSBURG joins, concurring in part, dissenting in part, and concurring in the judgment, is omitted. Justice Souter's view is that the case should have been resolved without reaching the due process issue. Hamdi's detention is illegal, Justice Souter concludes, because neither the 2001 Authorization for Use of Military Force, nor any other law, overrides the Non-Detention Act.]

JUSTICE SCALIA, with whom JUSTICE STEVENS joins, dissenting.

. . . This case brings into conflict the competing demands of national security and our citizens' constitutional right to personal liberty. Although I share the Court's evident unease as it seeks to reconcile the two, I do not agree with its resolution.

Where the Government accuses a citizen of waging war against it, our constitutional tradition has been to prosecute him in federal court for treason or some other crime. Where the exigencies of war prevent that, the Constitution's Suspension Clause, Art. I, § 9, cl. 2, allows Congress to relax the usual protections temporarily. Absent suspension, however, the Executive's assertion of military exigency has not been thought sufficient to permit detention without charge. No one contends that the congressional Authorization for Use of Military Force, on which the Government relies to justify its actions here, is an implementation of the Suspension Clause. Accordingly, I would reverse the decision below.

I

. . . The gist of the Due Process Clause, as understood at the founding and since, was to force the Government to follow those common-law procedures traditionally deemed necessary before depriving a person of life, liberty, or property. When a citizen was deprived of liberty because of alleged criminal conduct, those procedures typically required committal by a magistrate followed by indictment and trial. . . .

These due process rights have historically been vindicated by the writ of habeas corpus. In England before the founding, the writ developed into a tool for challenging executive confinement. . . .

The writ of habeas corpus was preserved in the Constitution—the only common-law writ to be explicitly mentioned. See Art. I, § 9, cl. 2. Hamilton lauded "the establishment of the writ of *habeas corpus*" in his Federalist defense as a means to protect against "the practice of arbitrary imprisonments . . . in all ages, [one of] the favourite and most formidable instruments of tyranny." The Federalist No. 84, at 444. Indeed, availability of the writ under the new Constitution (along with the requirement of trial by jury in criminal cases, see Art. III, § 2, cl. 3) was his basis for arguing that additional, explicit procedural protections were unnecessary. See The Federalist No. 83, at 433.

II

The allegations here, of course, are no ordinary accusations of criminal activity. Yaser Esam Hamdi has been imprisoned because the Government believes he participated in the waging of war against the United States. The relevant question, then, is whether there is a different, special procedure for imprisonment of a citizen accused of wrongdoing *by aiding the enemy in wartime.*

A

Justice O'Connor, writing for a plurality of this Court, asserts that captured enemy combatants (other than those suspected of war crimes) have traditionally been detained until the cessation of hostilities and then released. That is probably an accurate description of wartime practice with respect to enemy *aliens*. The tradition with respect to American citizens, however, has been quite different. Citizens aiding the enemy have been treated as traitors subject to the criminal process. . . .

B

There are times when military exigency renders resort to the traditional criminal process impracticable. English law accommodated such exigencies by allowing legislative suspension of the writ of habeas corpus for brief periods. . . . Where the Executive has not pursued the usual course of charge, committal, and conviction, it has historically secured the Legislature's explicit approval of a suspension. In England, Parliament on numerous occasions passed temporary suspensions in times of threatened invasion or rebellion. . . .

Our Federal Constitution contains a provision explicitly permitting suspension, but limiting the situations in which it may be invoked: "The privilege of the Writ of Habeas Corpus shall not be suspended, unless when in Cases of Rebellion or Invasion the public Safety may require it." Art. I, § 9, cl. 2. Although this provision does not state that suspension must be effected by, or authorized by, a legislative act, it has been so understood, consistent with English practice and the Clause's placement in Article I. See Ex parte Bollman, 4 Cranch 75, 101 (1807); Ex parte Merryman, 17 F. Cas.144, 151-152 (C.D. Md. 1861) (Taney, C.J., rejecting Lincoln's unauthorized suspension); 3 Story § 1336, at 208-209.

The Suspension Clause was by design a safety valve, the Constitution's only "express provision for exercise of extraordinary authority because of a crisis," Youngstown Sheet & Tube Co. v. Sawyer, 343 U.S. 579, 650 (1952) (Jackson, J., concurring). . . .

III

. . . Writings from the founding generation also suggest that, without exception, the only constitutional alternatives are to charge the crime or suspend the writ. . . .

The proposition that the Executive lacks indefinite wartime detention authority over citizens is consistent with the Founders' general mistrust of military power permanently at the Executive's disposal. In the Founders' view, the "blessings of liberty" were threatened by "those military establishments which must gradually poison its very fountain." The Federalist No. 45, p. 238 (J. Madison). No fewer than 10 issues of the Federalist were devoted in whole or part to allaying fears of oppression from the proposed Constitution's authorization of standing armies in peacetime. . . . A view of the Constitution that gives the Executive authority to use military force rather than the force of law against citizens on

American soil flies in the face of the mistrust that engendered these provisions. . . .

V

. . . Hamdi is entitled to a habeas decree requiring his release unless (1) criminal proceedings are promptly brought, or (2) Congress has suspended the writ of habeas corpus. A suspension of the writ could, of course, lay down conditions for continued detention, similar to those that today's opinion prescribes under the Due Process Clause. Cf. Act of Mar. 3, 1863, 12 Stat. 755. But there is a world of difference between the people's representatives' determining the need for that suspension (and prescribing the conditions for it), and this Court's doing so.

. . . Having found a congressional authorization for detention of citizens where none clearly exists; and having discarded the categorical procedural protection of the Suspension Clause; the plurality then proceeds, under the guise of the Due Process Clause, to prescribe what procedural protections *it* thinks appropriate. It "weigh[s] the private interest . . . against the Government's asserted interest," *ante,* and—just as though writing a new Constitution—comes up with an unheard-of system in which the citizen rather than the Government bears the burden of proof, testimony is by hearsay rather than live witnesses, and the presiding officer may well be a "neutral" military officer rather than judge and jury. See *ante,* at 26-27. It claims authority to engage in this sort of "judicious balancing" from Mathews v. Eldridge, 424 U.S. 319 (1976), a case involving . . . *the withdrawal of disability benefits!* Whatever the merits of this technique when newly recognized property rights are at issue (and even there they are questionable), it has no place where the Constitution and the common law already supply an answer. . . .

There is a certain harmony of approach in the plurality's making up for Congress's failure to invoke the Suspension Clause and its making up for the Executive's failure to apply what it says are needed procedures—an approach that reflects what might be called a Mr. Fix-it Mentality. The plurality seems to view it as its mission to Make Everything Come Out Right, rather than merely to decree the consequences, as far as individual rights are concerned, of the other two branches' actions and omissions. Has the Legislature failed to suspend the writ in the current dire emergency? Well, we will remedy that failure by prescribing the reasonable conditions that a suspension should have included. And has the Executive failed to live up to those reasonable conditions? Well, we will ourselves make that failure good, so that this dangerous fellow (if he is dangerous) need not be set free. The problem with this approach is not only that it steps out of the courts' modest and limited role in a democratic society; but that by repeatedly doing what it thinks the political branches ought to do it encourages their lassitude and saps the vitality of government by the people.

VI

. . . The Founders well understood the difficult tradeoff between safety and freedom. "Safety from external danger," Hamilton declared,

> is the most powerful director of national conduct. Even the ardent love of liberty will, after a time, give way to its dictates. The violent destruction of life and property incident to war; the continual effort and alarm attendant on a state of continual danger, will compel nations the most attached to liberty, to resort for repose and security to institutions which have a tendency to destroy their civil and political rights. To be more safe, they, at length, become willing to run the risk of being less free. The Federalist No. 8, p. 33.

The Founders warned us about the risk, and equipped us with a Constitution designed to deal with it. . . .

JUSTICE THOMAS, dissenting.

I

The plurality agrees that Hamdi's detention is lawful if he is an enemy combatant. But the question whether Hamdi is actually an enemy combatant is "of a kind for which the Judiciary has neither aptitude, facilities nor responsibility and which has long been held to belong in the domain of political power not subject to judicial intrusion or inquiry." Chicago & Southern Air Lines, Inc. v. Waterman S.S. Corp., 333 U.S. 103, 111 (1948). . . .

IV

. . . Although I do not agree with the plurality that the balancing approach of *Mathews* is the appropriate analytical tool with which to analyze this case, I cannot help but explain that the plurality misapplies its chosen framework. . . . The plurality devotes two paragraphs to its discussion of the Government's interest, though much of those two paragraphs explain why the Government's concerns are misplaced. But: "It is 'obvious and unarguable' that no governmental interest is more compelling than the security of the Nation." Haig v. Agee, 453 U.S. 280, 307 (1981). . . .

Additional process, the Government explains, will destroy the intelligence gathering function. It also does seem quite likely that, under the process envisioned by the plurality, various military officials will have to take time to litigate this matter. And though the plurality does not say so, a meaningful ability to challenge the Government's factual allegations will probably require the Government to divulge highly classified information to the purported enemy combatant, who might then upon release return to the fight armed with our most closely held secrets. . . .

Undeniably, Hamdi has been deprived of a serious interest, one actually protected by the Due Process Clause. Against this, however, is the Government's overriding interest in protecting the Nation. . . .

I would affirm the judgment of the Court of Appeals.

Note: Reading Procedure Cases

On its face, *Hamdi* seems like a case right on point for deciding what process is due the student in the problem case. And in many respects, it is. But you should recognize that certain aspects of the case are atypical for a procedural due process case. First, Yaser Asam Hamdi was imprisoned by the military. Although he had not been charged with a crime, that possibility hangs over the case, giving it a quasi-criminal dimension. (Recall Justice Scalia's argument that the only constitutional options for the government are to charge Hamdi with a crime or release him.) Second, his lawsuit is not just a standard civil claim, but a petition for a writ of habeas corpus. As the opinions in the case describe, this is a unique and longstanding procedural tool designed specifically for challenges to detention at the hands of the government. Although many lawsuits, like Hamdi's, are brought against the government to force it to comply with the Constitution or other laws, the habeas petition is a special tool. Third, most civil cases arise from disputes between private parties. Finally, in the background of *Hamdi* is a dire national threat. The procedural due process cases on which Justice O'Connor relies, by contrast, deal with things like procedures for terminating government benefits.

Justices Thomas and Scalia object to the idea that the Court should borrow a balancing test from these other contexts. Are there some contexts in which the governmental interest is so great that no balancing should be done at all?

Notice that only three members of the Court join Justice O'Connor's "plurality" opinion. Justice Souter and Justice Ginsburg write separately, disagreeing with Justice O'Connor's reasoning, but joining in the judgment. You will see other important cases in which a majority of the Court is unable to agree on a compelling rationale for the decision. Especially over the last three decades, sharply divided opinions have become commonplace. Can you see why a plurality opinion is less persuasive as precedent?

Note: Citizens and Non-Citizens

A few months after the case was decided, the government released Hamdi from the naval brig under negotiated terms. By that time, Hamdi had been detained without charges for almost three years. To secure his release, Hamdi agreed to give up his U.S. citizenship, to be deported to

Saudi Arabia, and to abide by travel restrictions prohibiting him from returning to the United States or going to Israel, the West Bank, the Gaza Strip, Syria, Afghanistan, and Pakistan. He also was required to waive any right to sue the United States for the harm caused by his detention.

Hamdi is a United States citizen. Should the Due Process Clause of the Fifth Amendment distinguish between citizens and non-citizens? One of the reasons non-citizens are being detained at Guantanamo Bay is that standard constitutional restraints on the government do not apply to non-citizens detained outside the United States.

Hamdi is not the only United States citizen who has been subjected to detention without charges. Jose Padilla, the so-called "dirty bomber," was first arrested in May of 2002 at an airport terminal in Chicago. After being designated an enemy combatant by the Department of Defense, he was sent to a military brig. Following the hearing procedures set out in *Hamdi*, a federal judge in South Carolina granted Padilla's petition for habeas relief in February 2005, more than two and a half years after his initial arrest. The Fourth Circuit Court of Appeals reversed that decision, finding that the government's designation of Padilla as an enemy combatant was correct. Padilla v. Hanft, 432 F.3d 582 (4th Cir. 2005).

When it became clear that Padilla would seek Supreme Court review of the Fourth Circuit's opinion upholding executive authority to designate and detain enemy combatants, the government radically changed course. It filed emergency motions with the Fourth Circuit requesting that the court (1) withdraw its earlier opinion upholding the government's position and (2) authorize the government to transfer Padilla from the brig in South Carolina to civilian law enforcement officials in Florida. The move to Florida was requested so that Padilla could be criminally prosecuted on different charges pursuant to an indictment that the government issued the same day it filed its motions with the Fourth Circuit. The Florida indictment, tellingly, included no mention of the acts upon which the government purported to base its indefinite detention of Padilla (that he was an enemy combatant who had "taken up arms against United States forces in Afghanistan and had thereafter entered into this country for the purpose of blowing up buildings in American cities"). Instead, it charged Padilla with involvement in a Florida "cell" that provided material support to overseas Islamic terrorists.

In August 2007, after the Supreme Court authorized Padilla's transfer to Florida for indictment, a jury convicted Padilla and his codefendants on three counts: conspiracy to commit murder, conspiracy to provide material support to terrorists, and providing material support to terrorists. Judge Cooke sentenced Padilla to 208 months on the first count, 60 months on the second count, and 180 months on the third count, all sentences to be served concurrently. Padilla has appealed his conviction and sentence to the Eleventh Circuit, and the government has cross-appealed his sentence.

The security/due process debate that underlies *Hamdi* and *Padilla* is likely to remain notwithstanding a change in the administration. Even before the 2008 election, it provoked a heated exchange between the legislative, executive, and judicial branches. As you read what follows, dealing with technicalities of habeas corpus and federal court jurisdiction (the power of the federal courts to hear petitions from detainees), consider the role of procedure and its interaction with the assumed merits of the cases involved. You will see that Congress, the executive branch, and the courts appear as concerned with what we might call rules of decision and who gets to decide as with what gets decided. See Jenny Martinez, Process and Substance in the "War on Terror," 108 Colum. L. Rev. 1013 (2008).

In Rasul v. Bush, 542 U.S. 466, 475-484 (2004), decided on the same day as *Hamdi*, the Court held that federal courts have jurisdiction under 28 U. S.C. § 2241 to consider habeas challenges to the legality of detention at Guantanamo of foreign nationals captured abroad. Congress responded to *Hamdi* and *Rasul* by passing the Detainee Treatment Act of 2005 (DTA), Pub. L. No. 109-148, § 1005(e)(1), 119 Stat. 2680, 2741-2742, which amended § 2241 and eliminated federal court jurisdiction over habeas actions filed by alien enemy combatants held at Guantanamo Bay. In place of standard habeas proceedings, the DTA substituted a "Combatant Status Review Tribunal," or CSRT, conducted pursuant to procedures described by the Secretary of Defense and followed by limited review by the United States Court of Appeals for the District of Columbia Circuit.

The very next Term, the Court decided Hamdan v. Rumsfeld, 126 S. Ct. 2749, 2762-2769 (2006), which held that the DTA did not bar Supreme Court review of a habeas petition by a Yemeni national captured during hostilities in Afghanistan and detained at Guantanamo Bay. Proceeding to the merits of Hamdan's claim, the Court held that the structure and procedures of the military commission convened to try Hamdan violated both the Uniform Code of Military Justice and the Geneva Conventions by failing to provide due process guarantees "recognized as indispensable by civilized peoples." Id. at 2795-2796. However, as Justice Breyer noted in his concurrence, "[n]othing prevents the President from returning to Congress to seek the authority he believes necessary." Id. at 2799. President Bush did just that, and in 2006 Congress passed the Military Commissions Act of 2006 (MCA), Pub. L. No. 109-366, 120 Stat. 2600, which again amended § 2241 to strip federal courts of statutory jurisdiction to hear pending habeas petitions brought by individuals "properly detained" as enemy combatants.

Almost immediately following the Act's passage, federal courts began to impose limits to protect detainees' procedural and substantive rights. See Al-Marri v. Wright, 487 F.3d 160, 164 (4th Cir. 2007) ("in the United States, the military cannot seize and imprison civilians—let alone imprison them indefinitely"; rejecting the government's claim that the 2001 Authorization for Use of Military Force or the president's "inherent powers" justify indefinite detention of civilians), reviewed en banc in Al-Marri v. Pucciarelli, No. 06-7427, 2008 WL 2736787 (4th Cir. July 15, 2008).

The en banc decision came in the wake of the Supreme Court's most recent intervention in the now burgeoning law of indefinite detention,

Boumediene v. Bush, 128 S. Ct. 2229 (2008). In *Boumediene*, the D.C. Circuit concluded that the MCA strips the federal courts of jurisdiction to hear habeas claims by detainees. At oral argument in the Supreme Court, Seth Waxman, counsel for Boumediene and former Solicitor General, emphasized that petitioners had been confined at Guantanamo for six years without "ever [having] meaningful notice of the factual grounds of detention or a fair opportunity to dispute those grounds before a neutral decision-maker"—a clear reminder of the plurality's due process concerns in *Hamdi*. Transcript of Oral Argument at 4, Boumediene v. Bush, 128 S. Ct. 2229 (2008) (No. 06-1195).

In June 2008, the Court took Waxman's view of the case, holding that even if the MCA stripped detainees of statutory rights to habeas corpus, the detainees have a constitutional habeas right to challenge their detention. *Boumediene*, 128 S. Ct. at 2262. The Court determined that the Combatant Status Review Tribunals and limited D.C. Circuit review, designed to meet the requirements laid out in *Hamdi*, are not adequate substitutes for review via petitions for habeas corpus. Id. at 2271-2274. The limits Congress imposed on review in the D.C. Circuit prevent detainees from receiving what is "constitutionally required in this context: an opportunity . . . to present relevant exculpatory evidence that was not made part of the record in the earlier proceedings," and the opportunity for the D.C. Circuit to order their release. Id. at 2272. The CSRT system was deemed flawed as well:

> [A]t the CSRT stage the detainee has limited means to find or present evidence to challenge the Government's case against him. He does not have the assistance of counsel and may not be aware of the most critical allegations that the Government relied upon to order his detention. . . . The detainee can confront witnesses that testify during the CSRT proceedings. But given that there are in effect no limits on the admission of hearsay evidence—the only requirement is that the tribunal deem the evidence "relevant and helpful"—the detainee's opportunity to question witnesses is likely to be more theoretical than real. (Citations omitted.) . . . Although we do not hold that an adequate substitute must duplicate § 2241 in all respects, it suffices that the Government has not established that the detainees' access to the statutory review provisions at issue is an adequate substitute for the writ of habeas corpus.

Id. at 2269-2274.

The Court concluded that the MCA was an unconstitutional suspension of the writ of habeas corpus. The holding stems, in part, from the problematic use of hearsay evidence in the CSRT. That is particularly significant given the Court's earlier suggestion in *Hamdi* that "[h]earsay . . . may need to be accepted as the most reliable available evidence from the Government in such a proceeding." The Court directly addressed its ruling in *Hamdi* later in the opinion:

> Although we make no judgment as to whether the CSRTs, as currently constituted, satisfy due process standards, we agree with petitioners that,

> even when all the parties involved in this process act with diligence and in good faith, there is considerable risk of error in the tribunal's findings of fact. This is a risk inherent in any process that, in the words of the former Chief Judge of the [D.C. Circuit] Court of Appeals, is "closed and accusatorial." And given that the consequence of error may be detention of persons for the duration of hostilities that may last a generation or more, this is a risk too significant to ignore.

Id. at 2269-2270. At the same time, the Court reiterated its position in *Hamdi* that "[t]he law must accord the Executive substantial authority to apprehend and detain those who pose a real danger to our security," and that some accommodations to the government's security and administrative efficiency interests are appropriate:

> Although we hold that the DTA is not an adequate and effective substitute for habeas corpus, it does not follow that a habeas corpus court may disregard the dangers the detention in these cases was intended to prevent. . . . Certain accommodations can be made to reduce the burden habeas corpus proceedings will place on the military without impermissibly diluting the protections of the writ. [For example, i]n the DTA Congress sought to consolidate review of petitioners' claims in the Court of Appeals. Channeling future cases to one district court would no doubt reduce administrative burdens on the Government.

Id. at 2276.

Chief Justice Roberts, joined by Justices Scalia, Thomas, and Alito, dissented. He argued that "[t]he DTA system of military tribunal hearings followed by Article III review looks a lot like the procedure *Hamdi* blessed." *Boumediene*, 128 S. Ct. at 2285. "[T]he *Hamdi* plurality," he added, "concluded that this type of review would be enough to satisfy due process, even for citizens. Congress followed the Court's lead, only to find itself the victim of a constitutional bait and switch." Id. at 2284-2285.

Boumediene does not overrule *Hamdi*; indeed, the foundation of the opinion is the Suspension Clause, not due process. But the majority subtly alludes to the *Mathews* test in discussing the "consequence" and "risk" of error, along with "accommodations" of the government's interests. Thus, the Court may have applied a new balancing analysis in reaching the conclusion that Congress had not met constitutional standards for procedures to adjudicate the rights of detainees. As of this writing, a new administration, and a new Congress, will have to go back to the drawing board. President Obama has ordered the facility at Guantanamo closed, but the status of this and other detention sites (e.g., in Afghanistan) remains to be determined. Having completely removed the detainees from the regular system of criminal justice and due process, it is not entirely clear how those who cannot be released can be brought back within the domain of law.

In the note that follows, we trace the genealogy of the due process analysis that has become so central to the enemy combatant cases.

Note: Due Process as Notice and a Chance To Be Heard

The first step in due process analysis is to determine whether life, liberty, or property is at stake. In *Hamdi*, it is liberty—a citizen's right to be free from confinement at the hands of the government. In *Loudermill*, one of the cases cited in Justice O'Connor's opinion, the Court found a property right in a tenured government job and held that a public employee has a right to "oral or written notice of the charges against him, an explanation of the employer's evidence, and an opportunity to present his side of the story" before being fired. Other classic due process cases have held that various government benefits are a form of property and that the government must give beneficiaries notice and a chance to be heard before these benefits are revoked. Justice O'Connor's opinion relies heavily on these cases to support the claim that Hamdi is entitled to a fair process for determining the legality of his detention. In our problem case, does the student have a property interest in attending college, or is it more of a liberty, or associational interest?

Sniadach v. Family Finance Corp., 395 U.S. 337 (1969), was the case that started the due process revolution in the 1960s. Betty Sniadach allegedly owed a bill for some eyeglasses. Her optometrist hired a collection agency, whose lawyer filed suit demanding the money. The court then issued a preliminary order directing Sniadach's employer to hold in escrow a part of her weekly wage of $63.18, so that there would be a pool of money from which to pay a judgment against her.

Ms. Sniadach never had a chance to contest the order before it was sent to her employer. Represented by the legal arm of the NAACP (the National Association for the Advancement of Colored People), Ms. Sniadach, a white woman, took her case to the Supreme Court, arguing that wage garnishment, as practiced in her state and most others, denied the debtor due process of law.

Think about the factors that make her situation an appealing one for a test case.

In a decision from which only Justice Black dissented, the Court held: "The right to be heard 'has little reality or worth unless one is informed that the matter is pending, and can choose for himself whether to appear or default, acquiesce or contest' [quoting Mullane v. Central Hanover Trust Co., 339 U.S. 306, 314 (1950)]. . . . [A] prejudgment garnishment of the Wisconsin type may as a practical matter drive a wage-earning family to the wall." Sniadach v. Family Finance Corp., 395 U.S. 337, 339-340 (1969).

Though the short opinion in this revolutionary case spoke only to the peculiar hardships of wage garnishment, it opened most other forms of prejudgment seizure of property to attack. After *Sniadach* was decided the legal community, to say nothing of the creditor community, anxiously awaited the next case.

The long legal journey of Margarita Fuentes to the Supreme Court started with her visit to a Legal Services Office in Miami, Florida. See

C. Michael Abbott and Donald C. Peters, Fuentes v. Shevin: A Narrative of Federal Test Litigation in the Legal Services Program, 57 Iowa L. Rev. 955 (1972). Fuentes had purchased a stove and a stereo and fallen behind on her payments. One day the sheriff, waving a writ of replevin, came to her house, unhooked both items, and carted them away. Again the Court wrote broadly and based its decision squarely on the lack of notice before seizure of the property. Fuentes v. Shevin, 407 U.S. 67 (1972) (holding that prejudgment replevin without notice and opportunity to be heard violates due process).

Though the Florida statute was called "replevin," it was like the provisions of virtually all states that allowed pretrial repossession of property in which both creditor and debtor had some interest. In Louisiana the procedure allowing prejudgment attachment of property was entitled "sequestration." Just two years after *Fuentes,* that statute was upheld. Mitchell v. W.T. Grant, 416 U.S. 600 (1974). Lawrence Mitchell allegedly owed $574.17 on a stove, stereo, refrigerator, and washing machine when they were seized from him.

In an unusually bitter dissent, Justice Stewart, writing for three members of the Court, said that *Mitchell* was "constitutionally indistinguishable from *Fuentes.*" 416 U.S. at 600. But the majority found that the statute was saved by provisions for the exercise of real judicial discretion in issuing prejudgment orders, the posting of a bond, and a quick post-seizure hearing.

Essentially *Mitchell* held that it was possible for creditors' remedies to pass constitutional muster. But the final case in the series, North Georgia Finishing, Inc. v. Di-Chem, Inc., 419 U.S. 601 (1975), holding Georgia's prejudgment attachment statute unconstitutional, made plain that due process scrutiny was still alive:

> Here, a bank account, surely a form of property, was impounded and, absent a bond, put totally beyond use during the pendency of the litigation on the alleged debt, all by a writ of garnishment issued by a court clerk without notice or opportunity for an early hearing and without participation by a judicial officer.

Id. at 606.

For almost 20 years, the Supreme Court did not speak again on the subject of prejudgment remedies. The action moved instead to the state legislatures, which scrambled to revise their procedures in order to reach the proper balance between the property interests of both creditors and debtors, plaintiffs, and defendants, as well as commercial actors.

One state's typical efforts to update its prejudgment remedies were in the background of the 1991 Supreme Court opinion in Connecticut v. Doehr, 501 U.S. 1 (1991). In that case, a personal quarrel led to the placing of a lien on Doehr's house in connection with a tort action for assault and battery. Relying on the *Sniadach* line, the Court held that, as applied in this case, the Connecticut statute violated due process.

Though it revived procedural due process in a rather dramatic way, *Doehr* was different because it involved real property. All the prior cases had dealt with some form of personalty and the physical seizure of the property itself, which triggered due process concerns. What other types of attachments might fall within *Doehr*'s scope? See, for instance, Shaumyan v. O'Neill, 987 F.2d 122 (2d Cir. 1993), upholding the application of the same Connecticut statute involved in *Doehr* in a case where homeowners were dissatisfied with painting and repairs on their house and refused to pay. The contractors sued in state court and obtained an attachment of the home without either a prior hearing or the posting of a bond.

Think about the interaction of legislatures and courts that this set of cases illustrates. Does it seem a good way for the legal system to operate, or do you agree with the judge who dissented from the Second Circuit's earlier holding that the *Doehr* statute was unconstitutional? He wrote:

> The Due Process Clause is not a code of civil procedure. . . . An *ex parte* prejudgment attachment of real estate does not deprive the owner of any possessory rights in his property. At most, it impairs the market value of the property during the brief interval between the *ex parte* attachment and expeditious adversary hearing required by state law. . . .

Pinsky v. Duncan, 898 F.2d 852 (2d Cir. 1990) (Newman, J., dissenting).

Note how much the personnel of the Court have changed since the early due process cases were decided. In 1997, Justice Scalia wrote for a unanimous court in Gilbert v. Homar, 520 U.S. 924 (1997), that a university's failure to provide notice and a hearing before suspending a university police officer without pay did not violate the officer's right to due process. The officer had been arrested and formally charged with a felony drug charge, which was dropped a few days later. *Homar* did not overrule but distinguished *Loudermill*. What are the distinctions?

Note: Private Actors and Due Process

In the problem case, we do not specify whether the university is public or private. Only the government is required by the Constitution to render due process in its dealings, so the second part of the due process calculus is determining whether there is state action.

As you will learn in other courses, the line between private and official conduct is sometimes blurred such that it is difficult to decide whether state action is present. In one sense, even the thoroughly "private" decision to ask an obnoxious party guest to leave one's house could be characterized as having "official" force to the extent that state property laws determine who owns certain property, subject to interests of others. Yet the Court clearly would not treat the homeowner's eviction of the guest as an action that triggers due process constraints. Less clear is whether the self-help actions of private creditors should be subject to due process simply because state laws regulate some aspects of these contractual relationships. See Flagg Bros., Inc. v. Brooks, 436 U.S. 149 (1978) (holding there was no state action in the sale of a debtor's goods, as authorized by state law, by a warehouse that had the goods in its possession and that had a lien on the goods for unpaid storage charges).

In general, you may assume that when the challenged actions are those of the "state" itself—such as the admission decisions of a public (but not private) employer—then they satisfy state action and thereby may implicate constitutional rights. This does not mean that private actions are *legal* simply because they are beyond constitutional reach. On the contrary, actions that would be unconstitutional in the public sector likewise may be unlawful in the private based on statutory, contract, tort, or other law.

Note: The Mathews *Test*

The test for when a hearing is necessary before deprivation, and how complete the hearing must be, is set out in Mathews v. Eldridge, 424 U.S. 319 (1976), discussed in *Hamdi* and virtually every other due process case since 1976. That case held that no evidentiary hearing was necessary before the government terminated Social Security disability payments. Usually, the balancing mandated by *Mathews* comes out in favor of the government and restricted rather than elaborate process. Recall, for example, that the process afforded Hamdi was quite limited—Scalia's position, that the government must charge a detainee and provide full-blown criminal trial rights or release him, is far more expansive than the plurality's requirement of a hearing with a presumption favoring the government. Yet Justice Thomas's dissent in *Hamdi* attacked the balancing test. He thought it should not apply to matters of national security, and, even if it is applied, he added, the plurality got the balance wrong by giving undue weight to Hamdi's interests and insufficient weight to the government's. His dissent parallels arguments Justice Rehnquist raised in his dissent from the Court's decision in *Loudermill*. There, Rehnquist attacked the incommensurability and subjectivity of the three factors, from a conservative viewpoint:

> Today the balancing test requires a pretermination opportunity to respond. In *Goldberg* we required a full-fledged trial-type hearing, and in *Mathews* we declined to require any pretermination process other than those required by the statute. *At times this balancing process looks as if it were undertaken with a thumb on the scale, depending on the result the Court desired.* . . . The lack of any principled standards in this area means that these procedural due process cases will recur time and time again. Every different set of facts will present a new issue on what process was due and when.

Loudermill, 470 U.S. at 562, n.* (emphasis added). Note that even Justice Scalia, who supports more process for Hamdi, is equally critical of the

Mathews test, arguing that it invites the Court "to prescribe what procedural protections it thinks appropriate" and adopt a "Mr. Fix-it Mentality" well beyond the competence and authority of the judicial branch.

The more usual assault on the *Mathews* balancing test is from the left. Professor Jerry Mashaw's critique has been particularly influential, as his qualms about the case resonate with so many people. Jerry Mashaw, The Supreme Court's Due Process Calculus—Three Factors in Search of a Theory, 44 U. Chi. L. Rev. 28 (1976). His primary concern is that the Court's account of the values of due process was incomplete. Due process is not only about the risk of error, but also about individual dignity, equality, and tradition. Yet nothing in *Mathews* refers to these important aspects of "fair procedure." Moreover, although the due process calculus set forth in *Mathews* appears scientific, it actually is highly subjective and manipulable. How is the judge to measure the risk of error referred to in the test? As Mashaw says, "the calculus asks unanswerable questions. For example, what is the social value, and the social cost, of continuing disability payments until after an oral hearing for persons initially determined to be ineligible?" Finally, Mashaw argues that the Bill of Rights "is meant to insure individual liberty in the face of contrary collective action." This suggests that the *Mathews* calculus is focusing on constitutionally irrelevant factors by emphasizing state interest rather than individual liberty. Thus, whether or not the result in *Mathews* was defensible, according to Mashaw the due process test it deploys was not well conceived.

Yet this critique may ignore the positive features of *Mathews*, especially its realistic appraisal of the significance of procedural costs to procedural rights, and of how any basic constitutional test must be flexible enough to apply to a vast range of due process scenarios. Particularly in the context of administrative law, which *Mathews* addressed, procedural costs must be taken seriously, given the number of hearings involved. Moreover, one must consider that administrative procedures are intended to be an alternative to civil litigation. If due process is construed to require a full-blown adversary hearing in every instance, then most alternative forms of dispute resolution would violate due process.

2. Notice: The Constitutional Dimension

Problem Case: The Elusive Defendant

You are a lawyer consulted by Paulette Peinture, who has a grievance against Gisele Fourchette, international art dealer and all-around world citizen. Peinture was employed to redecorate Fourchette's fabulous condominium for one million dollars. Some weeks into the work, Fourchette suddenly shouted, "I loathe this faux belle époque junk," and shoved the decorator, causing her to fall and dislocate her shoulder. Fourchette then picked up a vase on loan from a gallery and smashed it against the newly papered wall. In ordering Peinture out of the apartment forever, Fourchette said she didn't intend to pay for the work previously done. Peinture's assistant witnessed these events.

Fourchette has the life-style of a very rich woman, but preliminary investigation shows few liquid assets. On the other hand, she owns three late-model luxury cars and the condominium and undoubtedly has some money in a local checking account. Although a resident of the state, she retains her Swiss citizenship, and has five other residences all over the world. The incident itself suggests a certain instability and Fourchette's frequent travels might make her difficult to bring to court.

Nevertheless, you decide to file suit in federal district court in your state claiming damages for breach of contract and tortious assault. You tell your associate to do everything possible to make sure Fourchette has adequate notice, starting (but not concluding) with meeting the requirements of Fed. R. Civ. P. 4.

Your associate first scanned Rule 4 and mailed a copy of the summons to Fourchette at the condominium address. He then faxed a copy of the summons to her condominium, as well as to three art galleries in town where Fourchette is known to have business dealings. He also sent her an e-mail greeting card with the message, "You are being sued" and the law firm's return number on it.

Not satisfied that he had done everything possible, your associate hired a company called "You Sue, We Deliver" to effect in-hand service. The company took the papers to the condominium address, where they were met at the door by Roxanne DeSilva, Fourchette's elderly housekeeper, one of five assistants at the place. DeSilva would later testify that she took some papers from "a kid, a teen-ager who couldn't be more than 16 years old."

When he learned that Fourchette was in town as a defendant in an unrelated criminal trial, your associate mailed a copy of the summons and complaint to Fourchette's lawyer in that case. Even more ingeniously, he employed an actor to pose as a birthday messenger to deliver the papers to Fourchette on the courthouse steps as she emerged from the criminal trial. Singing "A Summons and Complaint Just for You" to a familiar tune, the actor gave, and Fourchette took, a birthday cake, under which the papers rested.

Fourchette has now moved to dismiss the complaint on the basis that she did not receive proper notice and was therefore denied due process of law. How will you respond to the motion that she has been denied due process in this action?

Greene v. Lindsey

456 U.S. 444 (1982)

JUSTICE BRENNAN delivered the opinion of the Court.

Appellees Linnie Lindsey, Barbara Hodgens, and Pamela Ray are tenants in a Louisville, Ky., housing project. Appellants are the Sheriff of

Jefferson County, Ky., and certain unnamed Deputy Sheriffs charged with responsibility for serving process in forcible entry and detainer actions. In 1975, the Housing Authority of Louisville initiated detainer actions against each of appellees, seeking repossession of their apartments. Service of process was made pursuant to Ky. Rev. Stat. § 454.030 (1975), which states:

> If the officer directed to serve notice on the defendant in forcible entry or detainer proceedings cannot find the defendant on the premises mentioned in the writ, he may explain and leave a copy of the notice with any member of the defendant's family thereon over sixteen (16) years of age, and if no such person is found he may serve the notice by posting a copy thereof in a conspicuous place on the premises. The notice shall state the time and place of meeting of the court.

In each instance, notice took the form of posting a copy of the writ of forcible entry and detainer on the door of the tenant's apartment.[1] Appellees claim never to have seen these posted summonses; they state that they did not learn of the eviction proceedings until they were served with writs of possession, executed after default judgments had been entered against them, and after their opportunity for appeal had lapsed.

Thus without recourse in the state courts, appellees filed this suit as a class action in the United States District Court for the Western District of Kentucky, seeking declaratory and injunctive relief under 42 U.S.C. § 1983.* They claimed that the notice procedure employed as a predicate to these eviction proceedings did not satisfy the minimum standards of constitutionally adequate notice described in Mullane v. Central Hanover Bank & Trust Co., 339 U.S. 306 (1950), and that the Commonwealth of Kentucky had thus failed to afford them the due process of law guaranteed by the Fourteenth Amendment. Named as defendants were the Housing Authority of Louisville, several public officials charged with responsibility

1. "Posting" refers to the practice of placing the writ on the property by use of a thumbtack, adhesive tape, or other means. App. 74, 77 (deposition of process servers). Appellants describe the usual method of effecting service pursuant to § 454.030 in the following terms:

> The officer of the court who is charged with serving notice in a forcible entry and detainer action, usually a Jefferson County Deputy Sheriff, takes the following steps in notifying a tenant. First the officer goes to the apartment in an effort to effectuate personal in-hand service. Second, if the named tenant is absent or will not appear at the door, personal in-hand service is made on any member of the tenant's family over sixteen years of age. Finally, if no one answers the door, a copy of the notice is posted on the premises, usually the door.

Brief for Appellants 3.

* Section 1983 provides in full: "Every person who, under color of any statute, ordinance, regulation, custom, or usage, of any State or Territory, subjects, or causes to be subjected, any citizen of the United States or other person within the jurisdiction thereof to the deprivation of any rights, privileges, or immunities secured by the Constitution and laws, shall be liable to the party injured in an action at law, suit in equity, or other proper proceeding for redress." EDS.

over particular Louisville public housing projects, Joseph Greene, the Jefferson County Sheriff, and certain known and unknown Deputy Sheriffs.

On cross-motions for summary judgment, the District Court granted judgment for appellants. In an unreported opinion, the court noted that some 70 years earlier, in Weber v. Grand Lodge of Kentucky, F. & A.M., 169 F. 522 (1909), the Court of Appeals for the Sixth Circuit had held that constructive notice by posting on the door of a building, pursuant to the predecessor statute to § 454.030, provided an adequate constitutional basis upon which to commence an eviction action, on the ground that it was reasonable for the State to presume that a notice posted on the door of the building in dispute would give the tenant actual notice in time to contest the action. Although the District Court recognized that "conditions have changed since the decision in *Weber* . . . and . . . that there is undisputed testimony in this case that notices posted on the apartment doors of tenants are often removed by other tenants," App. 41-42, the court nevertheless concluded that the procedures employed did not deny due process in light of the fact "that posting only comes into play after the officer directed to serve notice cannot find the defendant on the premises," id. at 42.

The Court of Appeals for the Sixth Circuit reversed the grant of summary judgment in favor of appellants and remanded the case for further proceedings. . . .[2] We noted probable jurisdiction, 454 U.S. 938 (1981), and now affirm.

"The fundamental requisite of due process of law is the opportunity to be heard." Gannis v. Ordean, 234 U.S. 385, 394 (1914). And the "right to be heard has little reality or worth unless one is informed that the matter is pending and can choose for himself whether to appear or default, acquiesce or contest," *Mullane*, supra, at 314. Personal service guarantees actual notice of the pendency of a legal action; it thus presents the ideal circumstance under which to commence legal proceedings against a person, and has traditionally been deemed necessary in actions styled *in personam*. McDonald v. Mabee, 243 U.S. 90, 92 (1917). Nevertheless, certain less rigorous notice procedures have enjoyed substantial acceptance throughout our legal history; in light of this history and the practical obstacles to providing personal service in every instance, we have allowed judicial proceedings to be prosecuted in some situations on the basis of procedures that do not carry with them the same certainty of actual notice that inheres in personal service. But we have also clearly recognized that the Due Process Clause does prescribe a constitutional minimum: "An elementary and fundamental requirement of due process in any

2. The Court of Appeals concluded that "[r]equiring Kentucky to provide notice by mail when personal service proves infeasible will not be overly burdensome. The cost will be minimal, and the state's conceded interest in providing a summary procedure for settlement of landlord-tenant disputes will not be seriously circumscribed." 649 F.2d, at 428. The court then noted with approval the provisions of the New York counterpart of § 454.030, which provides that when notice is served by posting, a copy of the petition must be sent by registered or certified mail within a day of the posting. Ibid., citing Velazquez v. Thompson, 451 F.2d 202, 205 (2d Cir. 1971).

proceeding which is to be accorded finality is *notice reasonably calculated, under all the circumstances, to apprise interested parties of the pendency of the action* and afford them an opportunity to present their objections." *Mullane*, 339 U.S. at 314 (emphasis added). It is against this standard that we evaluate the procedures employed in this case. . . .

It is, of course, reasonable to assume that a property owner will maintain superintendence of his property, and to presume that actions physically disturbing his holding will come to his attention. See *Mullane*, supra, at 316. The frequent restatement of this rule impresses upon the property owner the fact that a failure to maintain watch over his property may have significant legal consequences for him, providing a spur to his attentiveness, and a consequent reinforcement to the empirical foundation of the principle. Upon this understanding, a State may in turn conclude that in most cases, the secure posting of a notice on the property of a person is likely to offer that property owner sufficient warning of the pendency of proceedings possibly affecting his interests.

The empirical basis of the presumption that notice posted upon property is adequate to alert the owner or occupant of property of the pendency of legal proceedings would appear to make the presumption particularly well founded where notice is posted at a residence. With respect to claims affecting the continued possession of that residence, the application of this presumption seems particularly apt: If the tenant has a continuing interest in maintaining possession of the property for his use and occupancy, he might reasonably be expected to frequent the premises; if he no longer occupies the premises, then the injury that might result from his not having received actual notice as a consequence of the posted notice is reduced. Short of providing personal service, then, posting notice on the door of a person's home would, in many or perhaps most instances, constitute not only a constitutionally acceptable means of service, but indeed a singularly appropriate and effective way of ensuring that a person who cannot conveniently be served personally is actually apprised of proceedings against him.

But whatever the efficacy of posting in many cases, it is clear that, in the circumstances of this case, merely posting notice on an apartment door does not satisfy minimum standards of due process. In a significant number of instances, reliance on posting pursuant to the provisions of § 454.030 results in a failure to provide actual notice to the tenant concerned. Indeed, appellees claim to have suffered precisely such a failure of actual notice. As the process servers were well aware, notices posted on apartment doors in the area where these tenants lived were "not infrequently" removed by children or other tenants before they could have their intended effect. Under these conditions, notice by posting on the apartment door cannot be considered a "reliable means of acquainting interested parties of the fact that their rights are before the courts." *Mullane*, 339 U.S. at 315.

Of course, the reasonableness of the notice provided must be tested with reference to the existence of "feasible and customary" alternatives and supplements to the form of notice chosen. Ibid. In this connection, we reject appellants' characterization of the procedure contemplated by § 454.030 as one in which "'posting' is used as a method of service only as a last resort." To be sure, the statute requires the officer serving notice to make a visit to the tenant's home and to attempt to serve the writ personally on the tenant or some member of his family. But if no one is at home at the time of that visit, as is apparently true in a "good percentage" of cases, posting follows forthwith. Neither the statute, nor the practice of the process servers, makes provision for even a second attempt at personal service, perhaps at some time of day when the tenant is more likely to be at home. The failure to effect personal service on the first visit hardly suggests that the tenant has abandoned his interest in the apartment such that mere *pro forma* notice might be held constitutionally adequate. Cf. *Mullane*, 339 U.S., at 317-318.

As noted by the Court of Appeals, and as we noted in *Mullane*, the mails provide an "efficient and inexpensive means of communication," id., at 319, upon which prudent men will ordinarily rely in the conduct of important affairs, id., at 319-320. Notice by mail in the circumstances of this case would surely go a long way toward providing the constitutionally required assurance that the State has not allowed its power to be invoked against a person who has had no opportunity to present a defense despite a continuing interest in the resolution of the controversy. Particularly where the subject matter of the action also happens to be the mailing address of the defendant, and where personal service is ineffectual, notice by mail may reasonably be relied upon to provide interested persons with actual notice of judicial proceedings. We need not go so far as to insist that in order to "dispense with personal service the substitute that is most likely to reach the defendant is the least that ought to be required," McDonald v. Mabee, 243 U.S., 90, 92 (1917), in order to recognize that where an inexpensive and efficient mechanism such as mail service is available to enhance the reliability of an otherwise unreliable notice procedure, the State's continued exclusive reliance on an ineffective means of service is not notice "reasonably calculated to reach those who could easily be informed by other means at hand." *Mullane*, supra, at 319.

We conclude that in failing to afford appellees adequate notice of the proceedings against them before issuing final orders of eviction, the State has deprived them of property without the due process of law required by the Fourteenth Amendment. The judgment of the Court of Appeals is therefore *Affirmed*.

JUSTICE O'CONNOR, with whom THE CHIEF JUSTICE and JUSTICE REHNQUIST join, dissenting.

Today, the Court holds that the Constitution prefers the use of the Postal Service to posted notice. The Court reaches this conclusion despite the total absence of any evidence in the record regarding the speed and reliability of the mails. The sole ground for the Court's result is the scant and conflicting testimony of a handful of process servers in Kentucky. On this flimsy basis, the Court confidently overturns the work of the Kentucky Legislature and, by implication, that of at least 10 other States. I must respectfully dissent. . . .

Kentucky's forcible entry and detainer action is a summary proceeding for quickly determining whether or not a landlord has the right to immediate possession of leased premises and, if so, for enabling the landlord speedily to obtain the property from the person in wrongful possession. Ky. Rev. Stat. §§ 383.200, 383.210 (1972). As this Court has recognized, such circumstances call for special procedures:

> There are unique factual and legal characteristics of the landlord-tenant relationship that justify special statutory treatment inapplicable to other litigants. The tenant is, by definition, in possession of the property of the landlord; unless a judicially supervised mechanism is provided for what would otherwise be swift repossession by the landlord himself, the tenant would be able to deny the landlord the rights of income incident to ownership by refusing to pay rent and by preventing sale or rental to someone else. Many expenses of the landlord continue to accrue whether a tenant pays his rent or not. Speedy adjudication is desirable to prevent subjecting the landlord to undeserved economic loss and the tenant to unmerited harassment and dispossession when his lease or rental agreement gives him the right to peaceful and undisturbed possession of the property. Lindsey v. Normet, 405 U.S. 56, 72-73 (1972).

The means chosen for making service of process, therefore, must be prompt and certain, for otherwise the principal purpose of a forcible entry and detainer action could be thwarted before the judicial proceedings even began.

The Kentucky statute meets this need. . . .

The Court, however, holds that notice via the mails is so far superior to posted notice that the difference is of constitutional dimension. How the Court reaches this judgment remains a mystery, especially since the Court is unable, on the present record, to evaluate the risks that notice mailed to public housing projects might fail due to loss, misdelivery, lengthy delay, or theft. Furthermore, the advantages of the mails over posting, if any, are far from obvious. It is no secret, after all, that unattended mailboxes are subject to plunder by thieves. Moreover, unlike the use of the mails, posting notice at least gives assurance that the notice has gotten as far as the tenant's door.

Notes and Questions

1. Note that the Court in *Greene* did not hold that posting is always unconstitutional; rather, the circumstances were such that posting was an unreliable method of service in light of the available alternatives. What is the basis for this conclusion?

2. Service by posting has a long historical pedigree that may make the result in *Greene* surprising. After all, if due process is informed by one's reasonable expectations about the process due, including the notice due, then the long history of permitting notice by posting suggests that the practice is constitutional. Moreover, as you will see in connection with personal jurisdiction and due process, infra, some members of the current Court believe that traditional practices are extremely important measures of contemporary understandings of due process. How do you imagine these Justices would have ruled in *Greene*? Revisit this question after you have read Burnham v. Superior Court of California, 495 U.S. 604 (1990), infra.

Greene is an example of a case in which obedience to statutory requirements did not satisfy the constitutional requirements. Don't such rulings make it difficult for plaintiffs to rely on statutory methods? What might plaintiffs do to reduce the risk that their chosen method of service will later be ruled unconstitutional? Consider, in light of *Greene*, Miserandino v. Resort Properties, Inc., 691 A.2d 208 (1997), *cert. denied*, 522 U.S. 963 (1997), involving Maryland defendants against whom a default judgment had been entered in Virginia state court. The Maryland defendants claimed that they had not received notice of the Virginia lawsuit and challenged the validity of the default judgment when enforcement was sought in Maryland. The means of notice used by the Virginia plaintiffs—mailing by first class mail, without a return receipt or acknowledgment—would not have been valid under Maryland law, nor would it have been satisfactory under Virginia law if the defendants had been Virginia residents. The Maryland court concluded that service by first class mail did not meet the requirements of due process. As Virginia law required service by mail *with a signed return receipt* for residents, the court reasoned, Maryland residents were due the same courtesy.

Note: Mullane v. Central Hanover Bank and Trust Co.

The practice of serving individuals by publication was rendered constitutionally suspect in Mullane v. Central Hanover Bank & Trust Co., 339 U.S. 306 (1950), which involved a common trust fund administered by the Central Hanover Bank. The New York banking statute permitted smaller trust estates to be pooled into a larger fund, enabling small investors to afford professional money managers. State law required the trustee to petition the New York Surrogate Court to settle or audit its activities as trustee. Pursuant to statute, the trustee gave notice of the petition by publishing it in a local newspaper. And months earlier, when each participating trust fund first invested in the common fund, known beneficiaries of the pooled trust had been mailed notice of the procedure for settling the pooled trust.

The court appointed Mullane as representative of all persons with an interest in the income of the common fund and appointed Vaughan as representative of all persons with an interest in the principal of the fund. Mullane challenged the proceeding on the grounds, inter alia, that process had not been served personally on nonresident beneficiaries of the trust and that service by publication violated due process. The Court held that the statutory notice by publication was adequate only for those beneficiaries whose whereabouts were unknown or whose rights were conjectural when the action began. Known beneficiaries, whose whereabouts were reasonably ascertainable, were entitled to notice by mail. The Court in *Mullane* also set forth the general standard for constitutionally sufficient notice that appears in Greene v. Lindsey.

The Supreme Court has continued to invoke the standard of *Mullane*—notice "reasonably calculated" to apprise interested parties—in a wide range of notice settings. In Dusenbery v. United States, 534 U.S. 161 (2002), the Court held, in a 5-4 decision, that notice by certified mail is sufficient to put a prisoner on notice of the administrative forfeiture of cash seized at the time of his arrest. The prisoner claimed he did not receive the certified letter, and that the Bureau of Prisons could have assured actual delivery of the letter to him while he was incarcerated. The majority disagreed, observing that actual notice is not required by *Mullane* and that the methods used were reasonably certain to inform the prisoner.

Note: Jones v. Flowers

Certified mail was good enough for service on prisoners in *Dusenbery*, but the Court rejected service by certified mail on a taxpayer in Jones v. Flowers, 547 U.S. 220, 126 S. Ct. 1708 (2006). Gary Jones bought a house on North Bryan Street in Little Rock, Arkansas, in 1967. He lived there with his wife until they separated in 1993 and Jones moved into an apartment. He continued to pay the mortgage on the house to a mortgage company that deducted and paid the property taxes each month. Once the house was paid off, however, Jones neglected to pay the property taxes and the property was certified as delinquent. In 2000 the State Lands Commissioner mailed a notice of delinquency to Jones at the North Bryan address via certified mail. No one was home, and no one came to the post office in the next 15 days to retrieve the letter, so it was returned to the Commissioner "unclaimed."

In 2002, a few weeks before the property was to be sold at public auction, the Commissioner published a notice of public sale in the *Arkansas Democrat Gazette*. Jones did not come forward. Although no bids were received at the auction, Linda Flowers made an offer a few months later, and the Commissioner again sent a certified letter to Jones at the North Bryan address stating that the land would be sold to Flowers if he did not pay his back taxes. The letter was returned unclaimed and the property, estimated to be worth $80,000, was sold to Flowers for $21,042.15. Flowers then brought proceedings to evict Jones's daughter from the property.

Jones did not learn of the tax sale until his daughter brought him the notice of unlawful detainer Flowers had served on her. Jones responded by filing an action in state court claiming that the Commissioner's attempts at notice were constitutionally deficient under *Mullane* and thus a taking of private property without due process of law. The state trial and appellate courts agreed with the Commissioner that two certified letters are all state law requires and, citing *Dusenbery,* all the process Jones was due under the Constitution.

Writing for the majority, Chief Justice Roberts observed that while due process "does not require that a property owner receive actual notice before the government may take his property," id. at 1713, when the government learns that its chosen method of notice has failed, *Mullane* requires that the government take additional steps. Following *Greene,* the Court observed that the Commissioner could have resent the letter by regular mail or posted notice at the house. Id. at 1719. As the Court admonished:

> We do not think that a person who actually desired to inform a real property owner of an impending tax sale of a house he owns would do nothing when a certified letter sent to the owner is returned unclaimed. If the Commissioner prepared a stack of letters to mail to delinquent taxpayers, handed them to the postman, and then watched as the departing postman accidentally dropped the letters down a storm drain, one would certainly expect the Commissioner's office to prepare a new stack of letters and send them again. No one "desirous of actually informing" the owners would simply shrug his shoulders as the letters disappeared and say "I tried." Failure to follow up would be unreasonable, despite the fact that the letters were reasonably calculated to reach their intended recipients when delivered to the postman. . . .
>
> In prior cases, we have required the government to consider unique information about an intended recipient regardless of whether a statutory scheme is reasonably calculated to provide notice in the ordinary case. In Robinson v. Hanrahan, we held that notice of forfeiture proceedings sent to a vehicle owner's home address was inadequate when the State knew that the property owner was in prison. 409 U.S. at 40. In Covey v. Town of Somers, 351 U.S. 141 (1956), we held that notice of foreclosure by mailing, posting, and publication was inadequate when town officials knew that the property owner was incompetent and without a guardian's protection. Id. at 146-147.
>
> The Commissioner points out that in these cases, the State was aware of such information *before* it calculated how best to provide notice. But it is difficult to explain why due process would have settled for something less if the government had learned after notice was sent, but before the taking occurred, that the property owner was in prison or was incompetent. Under *Robinson* and *Covey,* the government's knowledge that notice pursuant to the normal procedure was ineffective triggered an obligation on the government's part to take additional steps to effect notice. That knowledge was one of the "practicalities and peculiarities of the case," *Mullane,* supra, at 314-315, that the Court took into account in determining whether

> constitutional requirements were met. It should similarly be taken into account in assessing the adequacy of notice in this case. . . .
>
> It is certainly true, as the Commissioner and Solicitor General contend, that the failure of notice in a specific case does not establish the inadequacy of the attempted notice; in that sense, the constitutionality of a particular procedure for notice is assessed *ex ante*, rather than *post hoc*. But if a feature of the State's chosen procedure is that it promptly provides additional information to the government about the effectiveness of notice, it does not contravene the *ex ante* principle to consider what the government does with that information in assessing the adequacy of the chosen procedure. After all, the State knew *ex ante* that it would promptly learn whether its effort to effect notice through certified mail had succeeded. It would not be inconsistent with the approach the Court has taken in notice cases to ask, with respect to a procedure under which telephone calls were placed to owners, what the State did when no one answered. Asking what the State does when a notice letter is returned unclaimed is not substantively different.

Id. at 1716-1717. The Court rejected the Commissioner's argument that notice was reasonably calculated to reach Jones because he was under a legal obligation to keep his address up to date with the tax assessor. It noted, however, that the Commissioner was under no obligation to check to see if Jones's address had changed after he took reasonable additional steps such as resending and posting notice.

Three Justices dissented, arguing that notice by certified mail to an owner's record address should be all that due process requires and insisting that the sufficiency of a state's method of notice must be assessed *ex ante*, at the time notice in any case is sent, not *ex post*, when considerations that go to whether a particular defendant actually received notice inevitably creep in.

Why would resending or posting have improved notice to Jones if he no longer lived at the property? Perhaps, despite its disclaimer, the majority is in effect requiring actual notice. The Court also may have inadvertently resuscitated posting as an alternative or supplemental way of giving notice. Maybe when the notice pertains to an inhabited dwelling, posting might actually be better than certified mail, though the Court's larger point is surely that those giving notice must attend to context in choosing a method of service and implementing it.

3. Notice: Constitutional Requirements Ritualized: Rule 4

Rule 4 sets out specifically how to give constitutional notice. While a lawyer may want to do more than required, she must not do less. Has the associate in the problem case succeeded in giving notice? In meeting the requirements of the Rule?

In its original version, Rule 4 assumed that in-hand delivery of a summons, often by a federal marshal, would be the usual form of service. Major changes in 1983 and 1993 moved mail delivery, with waiver of further service, to the heart of the process. As one commentator rather wistfully noted: "The awesome impact of the sheriff arriving in armor and on horseback . . . and the authority of the sovereign sealed in the hot, red wax of earlier times has been replaced by a bland manila envelope carrying a postage stamp that may celebrate notions of love or poetry." Kent Sinclair, Service of Process: Rethinking the Theory and Procedure of Serving Process Under Federal Rule 4(c), 73 Va. L. Rev. 1183, 1188-1189 (1987).

It took many years, and repeated expressions of preference for mail by the Supreme Court, like those in *Greene*, before Rule 4 was changed significantly. Yet now that notice short of in-hand delivery is accepted, the next move may come more quickly. In the not-too-distant future, the mails may give way to the even greater impersonality of e-mail and the fax machine. New York led the country in passing a statute that would, with the consent of the parties, permit service by fax, although some predicted that this would only lead to further gamesmanship. "Large firms will refuse service to put smaller firms to the considerable expense of messenger delivery," said one observer. N.Y.L.J., July 21, 1989, at 1.

Rule 5(b)(2)(E), effective December 2001, now allows electronic service on parties who give their written consent. Such service is complete upon transmission. See also Rule 6(d) (providing an additional three days to respond to a paper served via electronic means). And, in the first federal appellate case to address the point, the U.S. Court of Appeals for the Ninth Circuit held that a foreign defendant could be served via e-mail. Rio Properties, Inc. v. Rio Int'l Interlink, 284 F.3d 1007 (9th Cir. 2002). The court noted that Rule 4(f)(3) permits courts to direct service "by other means not prohibited by international agreement," and concluded that e-mail service fell within this rule and satisfied due process. The defendant in question had a Web site and had structured its business such that it could only be contacted via e-mail. See also In re Int'l Telemedia Assocs., Inc., 245 B.R. 713 (Bankr. N.D. Ga. 2000) (holding that e-mail service is authorized under Rule 4(f)(3) where it was the only means of communication between plaintiff and defendant).

The Ninth Circuit is not the only court to permit e-mail service. Snyder v. Alternate Energy, Inc., 857 N.Y.S.2d 442 (Civ. Ct. 2008), allowed e-mail service under New York state law provisions permitting the court to direct the manner of service upon individuals and corporations alike when the other methods outlined in the state rules proved "impracticable." Plaintiffs had unsuccessfully attempted to locate the defendants' physical whereabouts and contact them via telephone, but were in frequent contact with defendants over e-mail and instant messenger software. Noting the "pervasive role the internet plays in today's world," id. at 443, and citing *Rio* and *Telemedia*, id. at 447-478, the court crafted an order requiring that plaintiffs e-mail service on two consecutive dates with "prominent subject line[s] indicating that what was being sent were legal papers in an attachment that was to be opened immediately." Id. at 449. "To better insure the effectiveness of the notice to defendants," the court also required plaintiffs to send paper copies of the e-mailed documents to the defendants' last known physical addresses, and contact them at their last known phone numbers." Id. The court concluded its opinion by stating that the "broad constitutional principle" underlying judicially devised alternative service "unshackles the . . . courts from anachronistic methods of service and permits them entry into the technological renaissance." Id. at 449-450 (quoting *Rio*, 284 F.3d at 1017).

Experiments with electronic filing of pleadings and motions may further encourage electronic service of process. Many state courts and some federal district courts have set up systems for online filing. See, e.g., Special Report, Electronic Filing, 67 U.S.L.W. 2563 (1999). The Advisory Committee on Civil Rules has amended Rule 5(d)(3) to authorize all federal district courts by local rule to require papers to be filed, signed, or verified electronically, as long as the rules permit the courts to define "reasonable exceptions." Electronic case file systems are used in 71 federal district courts, and one-third of all federal district courts now require filings to be sent electronically.

Despite modern innovations, personal service has in the past continued to play a major role in the process, and will likely do so even under the waiver of service revision, which still contemplates hand delivery as the major fallback if service by mail should fail.

In most places these days, personal service is seldom done by the sheriff or marshal. Rather, professionals hired by the litigant seek out both easy-to-find and reclusive defendants. One commentator says that this "curious band of white collar soldiers of fortune" often supplies the "grease that gets the ponderous wheels of justice turning." Here is his description of the business of one such office:

> Batzi's (the 26-year-old owner) business ebbs and flows with the season. This time of year he hears a lot from one client, Western Appliance. People whose budgets were blown on Christmas are falling behind on the freezer payments. He works on a lot of child support cases in August and September. "A lot of ex-wives are taking their husbands back to court to get more money for the kid's clothes for school." July and August are the petty crime months when kids are out of school with too much time on their hands. "People are getting divorced all the time—except December. . . . They try to stick it through till the first of the year for tax reasons." In the fall Batzi serves a lot of roofers—the rainy season has begun, exposing shoddy work done the season before.
>
> To serve papers, a process server can do anything short of impersonating an officer of the law. He can lie about his identity or intent. Batzi always carries a change of clothes in the back of his car for disguise. He delights in making "gag" phone calls to people he is tracking down, verifying their presence by informing them that they have just won a lifetime subscription to *Field and Stream*. . . .

Edward O. Welles, They Also Serve, San Jose Mercury West, Dec. 28, 1986, at 4.

A lawyer's magazine details the consumer's point of view:

> "Early in my practice," says Marc Alan Fong, a partner with Fong & Fong of Oakland, "I had some bad experiences with gutter service. I was looking for the cheapest way to serve, and cheapest isn't always the best."
>
> Indeed, "gutter service"—the unauthorized drop-off or posting of papers—is the bane of the process-serving industry. Incompetent process servers can easily ruin a case by slipping papers through a mail slot, leaving them with an unauthorized substitute or even falsifying proof of service and tossing the actual documents. For an attorney, this unethical practice leads to loss of time, costly re-servicing and default judgments. The process server may also face a suit by the person mis-served.
>
> Problems range from the mundane to the melodramatic. First, there's the task of locating the person to be served. Since process servers are generally regarded as door-to-door salesmen specializing in bad news, it's not surprising that all but the most pedestrian jobs require some degree of ingenuity. Seasoned veterans talk romantically about all-night stakeouts, scaling third-story ledges and devising elaborate ruses to trick a recalcitrant subject into identifying himself.
>
> And there is always the prospect of violence. Some irate recipients of process, particularly in bitter domestic cases, take too literally the classical notion of killing the messenger.
>
> "I've been threatened, chased, and had guns pointed under my nose," says Judith A. Cochran, owner of A and T Legal Process Service in Oakland. "One guy led a German shepherd right up against my jugular." Another time, Cochran served the owners of a circus while elephants trained in a yard next to the house. When Cochran handed over the papers, the housemaid energetically beckoned to the elephants in an indecipherable foreign tongue. "The elephants trumpeted and came running towards me," says Cochran. "I don't know to this day whether they were coming after me, or if they were just frightened by the maid."

Fred Setterberg, Service with a Smile: Selecting the Right Process Server, 5 Cal. Law. 55 (July 1985).

Whatever choices the lawyer makes about the method of service, the technicalities of Rule 4 should be observed precisely, as the following case excerpts show.

National Development Co. v. Triad Holding Corp. & Adnan Khashoggi

930 F.2d 253 (2d Cir. 1991)

McLaughlin, Circuit Judge.

[On facts quite similar to the problem case on page 22, the Second Circuit wrote]:

For more than a half-century, the Federal Rules of Civil Procedure have permitted service upon an individual by leaving a summons and complaint "at the individual's dwelling house or usual place of abode." For a half-century before that, Equity Rule 13 had the same provision.

With approximately 1.16 billion passengers annually engaging in international airline travel, see Washington Times, Jan. 1, 1991, at C1 col. 1, and an estimated five million people with second homes in the United States, see Stern, Steal This House, Forbes, Oct. 1, 1990, at 81, determining a person's "dwelling house or usual place of abode" is no longer as easy as in those early days of yesteryear.

We ponder this problem upon review of an order of the United States District Court for the Southern District of New York (Milton Pollack, District Judge), refusing, under Fed. R. Civ. P. 60(b)(4), to vacate a default judgment entered against defendant-appellant Adnan Khashoggi ("Khashoggi"). In essence, Khashoggi argues that, although he has numerous residences world-wide, his "dwelling house or usual place of abode" is in Saudi Arabia and, absent personal delivery, service of process pursuant to Rule 4(d)(1)* is proper only at his compound there. Therefore, he concludes that a purported service at his apartment at the Olympic Tower in New York was void and conferred no jurisdiction. We disagree and affirm the order of the district court. . . .

It is the service of the summons and complaint on Khashoggi on December 22, 1986 that forms the basis of this appeal. On that day, NDC handed a copy of the summons and complaint to Aurora DaSilva, a housekeeper at Khashoggi's Olympic Tower condominium apartment on Fifth Avenue. . . .

On September 23, 1987, after Khashoggi failed to appear in the district court action, a default judgment was entered compelling him to arbitrate NDC's claim.

On October 25, 1989, Khashoggi filed a motion pursuant to Fed. R. Civ. P. 60(b)(4) to vacate the 1987 default judgment compelling him to arbitrate. . . .

The district court held an evidentiary hearing on the service of process issue, at which Khashoggi and his housekeeper, Ms. DaSilva, testified. Ms. DaSilva confirmed that Khashoggi was in New York and staying at his Olympic Tower apartment from December 15 through December 23, 1986. The parties stipulated that Ms. DaSilva accepted delivery of a copy of the summons and complaint on December 22, 1986. Ms. DaSilva testified that during 1986, Khashoggi stayed at his Olympic Tower apartment for a total of 34 days.

To call it an apartment is perhaps to denigrate it. Valued at approximately $20-25 million, containing more than 23,000 square feet on at least two floors, the Olympic Tower apartment contains a swimming pool, a sauna, an office and four separate furnished "apartments" to accommodate guests and Khashoggi's brother. The complex requires the attention of two full-time and three part-time staff persons.

Khashoggi testified that he is a citizen of Saudi Arabia and resides in a ten-acre, six-villa compound in its capital city, Riyadh. In 1986, Khashoggi stayed in the Riyadh compound for only three months. During the

* The provision of the Rule referred to in the case as Rule 4(d)(1) now appears as Rule 4 (e)(2) of the Rule, as revised in 1993. Eds.

remaining nine months, Khashoggi travelled throughout the world, staying another two months at a "home" in Marabella, Spain. Khashoggi testified that he purchased the Olympic Tower apartment in 1974. Shortly thereafter, Khashoggi transferred ownership to Akorp, N.V., a company that is wholly owned by A.K. Holdings, Ltd., which, in turn, is wholly owned by Khashoggi. Before Khashoggi transferred ownership of the Olympic Tower apartment to Akorp, he personally hired contractors to complete a remodeling project costing over $1 million. The results of the remodeling project were prominently featured in the June 1984 issue of *House and Garden*. . . .

[T]he district court found that the Olympic Tower apartment was not a "dwelling house or usual place of abode" for purposes of either Fed. R. Civ. P. 4(d)(1) or N.Y.C.P.L.R. § 308(2), but that service was nevertheless proper because Khashoggi had actual notice. We reject the notion that "actual notice" suffices to cure a void service, but we affirm the district court because we conclude that the Olympic Tower apartment is properly characterized under Rule 4(d)(1) as Khashoggi's "dwelling house or usual place of abode," and service at that location was therefore valid. . . .

There is no dispute that Ms. DaSilva, with whom the papers were left, is a "person of suitable age and discretion then residing" at the Olympic Tower apartment. We are called upon only to determine whether the Olympic Tower apartment was Khashoggi's "dwelling house or usual place of abode," terms that thus far have eluded "any hard and fast definition." 2 J. Moore, Moore's Federal Practice ¶ 4.11[2] at 4-128 (2d ed. 1990). Indeed, these quaint terms are now archaic and survive only in religious hymns, romantic sonnets and, unhappily, in jurisdictional statutes.

The phrase "dwelling house or usual place of abode" to describe where service can be made has its origin in Equity Rule 13. Yet, "[d]espite the length of time the language . . . has been a part of federal practice, the decisions do not make clear precisely what it means." 4A C. Wright & A. Miller, Federal Practice and Procedure § 1096, at 73 (2d ed. 1987). We do not here intend to reconcile decades of conflicting authority. Instead, we decide this case on the facts presented with a recognition of the realities of life in this the winter of the twentieth century.

As leading commentators observe, "[i]n a highly mobile and affluent society, it is unrealistic to interpret Rule 4(d)(1) so that the person to be served has only one dwelling house or usual place of abode at which process may be left." Id. at 79-80 (footnote omitted). This case presents a perfect example of how ineffectual so wooden a rule would be.

Khashoggi is a wealthy man and a frequent intercontinental traveller. Although he is a citizen of Saudi Arabia and considers the Riyadh compound his domicile, he spent only three months there in 1986. Khashoggi testified that the Olympic Tower apartment was only one of twelve locations around the world where he spends his time, including a "home" which he owns in Marabella, Spain, and "houses" in Rome, Paris, and Monte Carlo. The conclusion that only *one* of these locations is Khashoggi's "usual place of abode," since he does not "usually" stay at any one of them, commends itself to neither common sense nor sound policy.

There is nothing startling in the conclusion that a person can have two or more "dwelling houses or usual places of abode," provided each contains sufficient indicia of permanence. State courts construing state statutes containing similar language have arrived at this result where the defendant maintained one residence for certain days of the week or certain months of the year and another residence for the balance of his time. See, e.g., Mangold v. Neuman, 87 A.D.2d 780, 449 N.Y.S.2d 232 (1st Dept.), *aff'd*, 57 N.Y.2d 627, 454 N.Y.S.2d 58, 439 N.E.2d 867 (1982) (a defendant with a house in Wayne, Pennsylvania, an apartment in Philadelphia, a house in Palm Beach and an apartment in a New York City hotel had a "dwelling place," but not a "residence" in New York). Some courts have expressly required that the defendant sought to be served be actually living at the residence at the time service is effected.

Although federal practice under Rule 4(d)(1) has not produced consistent results, compare Capitol Life Ins. Co. v. Rosen, 69 F.R.D. 83 (E.D. Pa. 1975) (service at defendant's brother's house sufficient where defendant frequently journeyed but kept a room and personal belongings at brother's house and paid rent therefor), and Blackhawk Heating & Plumbing Co. v. Turner, 50 F.R.D. 144 (D. Ariz. 1970) (service at house in Arizona deemed proper where evidence suggested that defendant was living at the time in California but received actual notice), with First Natl. Bank & Trust Co. v. Ingerton, 207 F.2d 793 (10th Cir. 1953) (usual place of abode was hotel in New Mexico notwithstanding defendant's temporary stay in Denver), and Shore v. Cornell-Dubilier Elec. Corp., 33 F.R.D. 5 (D. Mass. 1963) (service on defendant who divided his time between residences in New York and New Jersey improper where made at a house he owned in Massachusetts that was used by him only when conducting business there); we believe that application of the rule to uphold service is appropriate under these facts.

It cannot seriously be disputed that the Olympic Tower apartment has sufficient indicia of permanence. Khashoggi owned and furnished the apartment and spent a considerable amount of money remodelling it to fit his lifestyle. Indeed, in July 1989, Khashoggi listed the Olympic Tower apartment as one of his residences in a bail application submitted in connection with the criminal proceedings. Since Khashoggi was actually living in the Olympic Tower apartment on December 22, 1986, service there on that day was, if not the most likely method of ensuring that he received the summons and complaint, reasonably calculated to provide actual notice of the action. See Mullane v. Central Hanover Bank & Trust Co., 339 U.S. 306, 314 (1950). Surely, with so itinerant a defendant as Khashoggi, plaintiff should not be expected to do more.

We conclude, therefore, that service of process on Khashoggi should be sustained under Rule 4(d)(1) because the Olympic Tower apartment was a "dwelling house or usual place of abode" in which he was actually living at the time service was effected. We express no opinion upon the validity of service had Khashoggi not been actually living at the Olympic Tower apartment when service was effected.

Note: Serving and Being Served

The Rule requires that persons served be of "suitable age and discretion," 4(e)(2)(B). What does it say about the person doing the serving? See 4(c). In Benny v. Pipes, 799 F.2d 489 (9th Cir. 1986), *cert. denied*, 484 U.S. 870 (1987), a suit by prisoners against their guards, a fellow prisoner served process on the defendant guards. The guards threw the summons in the trash and then suffered a default judgment. The Ninth Circuit held that "Rule 4 means precisely what it says; save for those few special situations expressly enumerated in the Rule, *any* person over 18 who is not a party to the suit, may serve the summons and complaint." Id. at 890 (emphasis in original).

If, as in the problem case, there is a contest over the underlying facts of service, where should the court look first to determine them? See Rule 4(l). It is, however, to avoid such disputes that the mail and waiver provisions in 4(d) were added. What are the incentives to waive that are built into the Rule?

Rule 4 also provides for service in special situations—such as upon foreign defendants, incompetents, and the non-monolithic United States government. Rule 4(k)(2) is still fairly new and its reach is uncertain. The idea is that a foreign entity may not have sufficient contacts with any one state to subject it to that court's processes, yet it would be fair to require it to appear in the United States. The First Circuit offered a primer on the new provision in United States v. Swiss American Bank, Ltd., 191 F.3d 30 (1st Cir. 1999); see also Graduate Admission Council v. Raju, 241 F. Supp. 2d 589 (E.D. Va. 2003) (relying upon Rule 4(k)(2) to support jurisdiction over Indian citizen who operated a foreign Internet site selling GMAT study materials that allegedly violated United States trademark and copyright laws). One interesting wrinkle is that often defendants will try to prove that they are amenable to service in a particular state, and therefore that 4(k)(2) does not apply. This is an unusual litigation posture for a defendant to maintain.

How about seizure of the defendant's assets in the jurisdiction as a way to give notice, as well as to assure that a judgment will be paid? Would you consider it in the problem case? Remember the line of cases starting with *Sniadach* in the first part of this chapter. See Rule 4(n).

Note: Serving Process Abroad

If you think it was difficult to serve Khashoggi in the United States, consider the challenges of effecting service abroad. Globalization and the rise of multinational corporations have made suits in federal court against foreign individuals and corporations quite common, but these defendants often do not have a presence in the United States making them amenable to service under Rule 4(e). Rule 4(f) sets out procedures for serving individuals in foreign countries, Rule 4(j) covers service upon foreign governments, and Rule 4(h)(2) directs that service on foreign corporations shall be effected in the same manner as service on foreign individuals. Rule 4(f)(1) refers to an important treaty governing international service of process called the Hague Convention on the Service Abroad of Judicial and Extrajudicial Documents. Ratified in 1965 to standardize and simplify service of process in international civil suits, the Hague Convention requires each member country to establish a "Central Authority" to receive documents from other member countries. Each Central Authority may set certain rules for the form of documents it receives (e.g., that the documents be translated into the language of the receiving country), and as long as the documents comply with those requirements, the Convention requires the Central Authority to effect service of process.

Because the U.S. is a signatory, any attempt to hale a foreign defendant into federal court by service abroad must begin with a method of service recognized by the Convention, or, as Rule 4(f)(1) states, another international agreement. Relying on the Central Authority in the defendant's country is standard, but the Convention explicitly provides that it does not "interfere" with other methods, including "the freedom to send judicial documents, by postal channels, directly to persons abroad," as long as "the State of destination does not object." Hague Convention, Article 10 (a); see also Brockmeyer v. May, 383 F.3d 798 (9th Cir. 2004) (noting split among Circuit Courts over whether the reference to "send[ing] judicial documents" in Article 10(a) includes service of process by mail; joining the Second Circuit in holding that "send" includes "serve"). Tempting as it may be to just drop a summons and complaint in the mail, any alternative method chosen also must be valid under Rule 4, see *Brockmeyer*, 383 F.3d at 804 ("in order for the postal channel to be utilized, it is necessary that it be authorized by the law of the forum state") (internal quotations omitted), and U.S. courts demand strict compliance. Id. at 804-806 (invalidating service on a British defendant by regular mail because Rule 4 (f)(2)(C)(ii) demands "mail requiring a signed receipt . . . dispatched by the clerk of the court"; narrowly construing Rule 4(f)(2)(A) as limited to personal service).

This may seem quite technical, and it is true that plaintiffs still trip up on the minutiae, but it is an improvement over the pre-Convention system.

What about international organizations? Can they be served wherever their headquarters are located? Typically, international organizations enter into a "Headquarters Agreement" with the sovereign states in which they have their headquarters. These agreements commonly prohibit service of process upon the headquarters without the express consent of the organization's leadership. This can make it very difficult to effect service on an international organization.

In Prewitt Enterprises Inc. v. Organization of Petroleum Exporting Countries, 353 F.3d 916 (11th Cir. 2003), the plaintiff, a gas station owner in Birmingham, Texas, filed a complaint in federal district court alleging OPEC had engaged in a price-fixing conspiracy with non-member states to limit the production and export of oil. Plaintiff attempted service on OPEC by having the clerk of the court send a copy of the complaint by registered, return-service mail to OPEC's headquarters in Vienna, Austria. Although OPEC received and signed for the complaint, it failed to appear and the district court entered a default judgment. When OPEC received a copy of the order from the triumphant plaintiff, it immediately filed a motion to set aside the default judgment and for dismissal on grounds of insufficient service of process. The Eleventh Circuit affirmed the dismissal, agreeing with the district court that (1) service upon an international organization is governed by Rule 4(h), which provides that service on a corporation or association (including foreign corporations and associations) "shall be effected . . . in any manner prescribed for individuals by subdivision (f) except personal delivery . . . "; and (2) that OPEC could not legally be served by any means listed in Rule 4(f) without its consent because of its Headquarters Agreement with the Austrian government. Id. at 923-928.

Mid-Continent Wood Products v. Harris

936 F.2d 297 (7th Cir. 1991)

COFFEY, Circuit Judge.

Lawrence A. Harris appeals the district court's order denying his Rule 60(b)(4) motion to vacate and dismiss a default judgment on the grounds of improper service of process. We reverse.

I. Facts and Disposition Below

Harris Plywood, Inc. ("Harris Plywood") purchased lumber from the plaintiff, Mid-Continent Wood Products, Inc. ("Mid-Continent") on three separate occasions between May and August of 1980. When Harris Plywood failed to make any payments on the three shipments, the parties entered into negotiations in October 1980 and Harris agreed that the amount due would bear interest at the rate of fourteen percent per annum and that payments would commence within a few weeks. After Harris Plywood failed to make any payments, Mid-Continent filed suit in April 1981 for breach of contract. The parties entered into negotiations for a second time and after these discussions proved fruitless, Mid-Continent filed a motion for a default judgment. On October 28, 1981, the district court granted Mid-Continent's motion for a default judgment in Mid-Continent Wood Products, Inc. v. Harris Plywood, Inc., in the amount of $28,544.75. Instead of executing on the default judgment, Mid-Continent accepted a promissory note for the judgment amount from the defendant Lawrence Harris, President of Harris Plywood, in December of 1981. When Harris failed to pay the amount due, Mid-Continent filed this action to collect on Harris' promissory note.

Mid-Continent makes clear that (to state it mildly) it had a rather difficult time locating Harris and serving him with the complaint and summons. Initially, Mid-Continent attempted to serve Harris personally through a U.S. Marshal in December 1982. One month later on January 5, 1983, the marshal again attempted service by certified mail at Harris' place of employment, Superb Realty Corporation. Harris denied receipt of this mailing.

Mid-Continent states it next attempted service in May 1983 through a private process server at what was thought to be Harris' residence at 13 Secor Drive, Port Washington, New York. On two separate occasions the server attempted personal service but found no one at the address. On the third attempt, the server left the complaint and summons attached to the door of the residence, and followed this up by mailing another copy addressed to Harris at the same address.

At the request of the district court, Mid-Continent's attorney sent a letter on June 3, 1983, to the residence at 13 Secor Drive in order to notify Harris of an upcoming status hearing. A copy of this letter was also sent to Harris' counsel of record in the previous lawsuit, Samuel Panzer. Neither the letter to Harris nor the copy sent to Harris' attorney included copies of the complaint and summons. Harris' attorney contacted Mid-Continent on June 9, 1983, and proposed a settlement in which Harris would pay the entire amount due on the note in monthly installments. Mid-Continent's attorney rejected the offer and stated that if the full amount was not received, Mid-Continent would seek a judgment order against Harris. Nevertheless, Harris' attorney confirmed in writing Harris' intention of forwarding a check and promissory notes in partial satisfaction of the amount due under Harris' guaranty. As promised by Harris' attorney, a mailing arrived from Superb Realty, Harris' place of business, containing a check for $1,000.00 signed on behalf of Superb Realty and three notes for $1,000.00 each, also signed by agents acting on behalf of Superb Realty. On June 16, 1983, Mid-Continent's attorney again informed Harris' attorney that no settlement for less than the full amount would suffice and that if full payment was not received before the next status hearing on June 28, 1983, Mid-Continent would seek a default judgment against Harris. When no further payments were made, Mid-Continent obtained a default judgment against Harris on July 20, 1983, in the amount of $24,549.92.

After securing the judgment, Mid-Continent alleges that it attempted but was unable to locate Harris' assets for some time for purposes of executing on the judgment. Six years later, in June of 1989, Mid-Continent located certain assets of Harris' in Massachusetts and attempted to execute upon the 1983 judgment. However, on August 31, 1989, Harris filed a motion for relief in the district court pursuant to Rule 60(b)(4) of the Federal Rules of Civil Procedure[3] claiming that because service on him did not properly comply with Rule 4 of the Federal Rules of Civil Procedure, the district court lacked personal jurisdiction over him at the time

3. Rule 60(b)(4) provides relief from a final judgment when the judgment is void.

of the entry of judgment in 1983 and further that he never received a copy of the complaint and summons in this action. In support of his motion, Harris offered exhibits and affidavits stating that he never resided at 13 Secor Drive, Port Washington, New York, but stated that he lived at 15 Secor Drive, Port Washington, New York in 1983. He further stated that no one at 13 Secor Drive ever brought any documents pertaining to the case to his house at 15 Secor Drive. The district court issued an opinion denying Harris' motion to vacate and dismiss the default judgment on the grounds of improper service of process on November 1, 1989. While the district court acknowledged in its opinion that service upon Harris did not strictly comply with Rule 4, it nonetheless determined that strict compliance was unnecessary because of: 1) Harris' "actual knowledge of the lawsuit" based on Harris' former attorney's negotiations with Mid-Continent; 2) Mid-Continent's diligent efforts "to obtain technically proper service upon Harris"; and 3) Harris' evasive conduct in responding to the attempts at service of process.

II. Issue for Review

The issue before us is whether a district court may formulate its own test to determine whether to assert personal jurisdiction over a defendant in the absence of service of complaint and summons in accordance with Rule 4 of the Federal Rules of Civil Procedure.

III. Discussion

. . . The district court found that Mid-Continent's attempted service of process on Harris did not comply with Rule 4. The district court then proceeded to devise a three-part test and fashioned an exception to the usual requirements of strict compliance with Rule 4:

> When the cases are examined, three requirements present themselves as requisite to finding an exception to strict compliance. First, it is imperative to upholding faulty service that the defendant actually know of a lawsuit. . . . Second, the server must show that he duly tried to serve the defendant properly; in other words, show that more than a minimum effort was made and that the service actually made on the defendant came reasonably close to satisfying the requirements. This is often stated in terms of the plaintiff having "substantially complied" with Rule 4's mandate. . . . Third, the equities of the situation must warrant an exception from the usual strict compliance requirement. Specifically, the focus here is on the conduct of the defendant in responding to the situation.

The district court determined that these three factors "point clearly toward an exception from strict compliance in this case."

Rule 4(d)(1) provides that the complaint and summons shall, with respect to an individual defendant who is not an infant or incompetent, be made:

> by delivering a copy of the summons and of the complaint to the individual personally or by leaving copies thereof at the individual's dwelling house or usual place of abode with some person of suitable age and discretion then residing therein or by delivering a copy of the summons and of the complaint to an agent authorized by appointment or by law to receive service of process.

The Supreme Court recently addressed the issue of judicially created rules authorizing the service of process:

> We would consider it unwise for a court to make its own rule authorizing service of summons. It seems likely that Congress has been acting on the assumption that federal courts cannot add to the scope of service of summons Congress has authorized. . . . The strength of this long-standing assumption, and the network of statutory enactments and judicial decisions tied to it, argue strongly against devising common law service of process provisions at this late date for at least two reasons. First, since Congress concededly has the power to limit service of process, circumspection is called for in going beyond what Congress has authorized. Second, as statutes and rules have always provided the measures for service, courts are inappropriate forums for deciding whether to extend them. Omni Capital International v. Rudolf Wolff & Company, Ltd., 484 U.S. 97 (1987).

This court has previously stated that a liberal construction of the rules of service of process "cannot be utilized as a substitute for the plain legal requirement as to the manner in which service of process may be had." United States v. Mollenhauer Laboratories, Inc., 267 F.2d 260, 262 (7th Cir. 1959).

. . . [T]he factors considered by the district court have questionable validity, and as a result, the district court's three-part test must fail. The first factor the district court considered in determining the jurisdictional question concerning Harris was its finding that Harris had "actual knowledge of the lawsuit" based on Harris' former attorney's negotiations with Mid-Continent. The district court quotes Armco, Inc. v. Penrod-Stauffer Building Systems, Inc. for the proposition that "[w]hen there is actual notice, every technical violation of the rule or failure of strict compliance may not invalidate the service of process." 733 F.2d 1087, 1089 (4th Cir. 1984). However, the appellate court in *Armco* found the service of process to be invalid despite the defendant's knowledge of the suit and thus, the trial court was without jurisdiction and the default judgment was void. Id., at 1089.

This court has long recognized that valid service of process is necessary in order to assert personal jurisdiction over a defendant. Rabiolo v. Weinstein, 357 F.2d 167 (7th Cir. 1966). Moreover, it is well recognized that a "defendant's actual notice of the litigation . . . is insufficient to satisfy Rule 4's requirements."

In a case similar to ours, the District Court for the Northern District of Indiana held that a defendant's knowledge of a lawsuit will not serve to "cure the deficiencies in service." Bennett v. Circus U.S.A., 108 F.R.D. 142, 148 (1985). In *Bennett*, the plaintiff was unable to locate the defendant and attempted service of the complaint and summons by sending them certified mail to the law firm which had represented the defendant in a previous matter.

. . . [T]he *Bennett* court initially held that service of the summons and complaint upon the defendant's attorney was insufficient because the attorney had not been specifically appointed as an agent to accept service of process. Next, the court rejected the plaintiff's argument that the court had personal jurisdiction over the defendant because the defendant knew of the lawsuit prior to the entry of the default judgment. . . .

We agree with the *Bennett* court and hold that actual knowledge of the existence of a lawsuit is insufficient to confer personal jurisdiction over a defendant in the absence of valid service of process. Even though Harris may have had knowledge of the lawsuit as a result of Harris' former attorney's negotiations with Mid-Continent, "actual notice alone is insufficient to give the court the jurisdiction necessary to allow it to enter a judgment against a defendant." Id. Thus, the district court's reliance on actual notice in determining that it had personal jurisdiction over Harris is erroneous.

The second part of the district court's three-part test focused on whether "the service actually made on the defendant came reasonably close to satisfying the requirements [of Rule 4]." The district court characterized this factor as whether the plaintiff "substantially complied" with Rule 4's mandate. The district court determined that Mid-Continent "tried diligently to obtain technically proper service upon Harris." The court further noted that these attempts "were sufficient to result in settlement discussions between the parties."

This court is reluctant to find jurisdiction based upon whether Mid-Continent "tried diligently" to serve Harris. Indeed, the extent to which the plaintiff "tried" to serve process should not be a factor as to whether a federal court has personal jurisdiction over a defendant. Rather, the requirements of Rule 4 are satisfied only when the plaintiff is successful in serving the complaint and summons on the defendant.

The district court cites United Food & Commercial Workers Union v. Alpha Beta Company, 736 F.2d 1371 (9th Cir. 1984), for its erroneous conclusion that a plaintiff need only come "reasonably close" to satisfying the requirements of Rule 4. However, *United Food* is applicable only to those cases in which the "substantial compliance" is used to prevent a technical error in the form of the documents under Rule 4 from defeating an otherwise proper and successful delivery of process. . . . Thus, to the extent that the "substantial compliance" doctrine has any validity, it is applicable to only those cases such as *United Food*, where it was involved to prevent a purely technical error in the form of the documents under Rule 4 from invalidating an otherwise proper and successful delivery of process.

Even if we agreed with the district court's interpretation of the "substantial compliance" doctrine (which we do not), the facts lead us to believe that ours is a case of "substantial *non*-compliance." The extent of Mid-Continent's efforts to obtain service on Harris consisted of the following: 1) one certified mailing of the complaint and summons to a business address of Harris (which Harris denies receiving), and neither the envelope containing the complaint and summons nor the return receipt evidencing delivery were ever returned; 2) three attempts at personal service by a private process server over a four-day period at an incorrect address; and 3) a noncertified mailing to the same incorrect address.

The district court also cites the settlement discussions between the parties' attorneys as proof that the above-cited attempts at service were sufficient. However, nowhere in Rule 4 is there an exception for settlement discussions in the absence of the usual requirements of proper service of process, nor does the district court cite any case law in support of this proposition. . . .

The third and final factor of the district court's three-part test is whether the "equities" of the case warrant an exception from the usual strict compliance requirement: "Specifically, the focus here is on the conduct of the defendant in responding to the situation." The court cites evasion of process by the defendant as "the most typical example" of this kind of conduct. . . .

The cases cited by the district court involve clear-cut examples of evasion: both involve defendants who specifically refused to acknowledge service and are thus distinguishable. The facts in the case before us fall short of establishing clear and convincing evidence of evasion on the part of the defendant. Unlike the defendants in *Nikwei* and *Benage*, there is no evidence that Harris either refused to accept his mail or actually received mail service but refused to acknowledge it. The district court infers evasion on the part of Harris because of the repeated, *though faulty*, attempts at service of process by Mid-Continent. As we stated supra, valid service of process is a must in order to assert personal jurisdiction over a defendant. Furthermore, the district court found that Harris had acted inequitably by allowing his attorney to engage in settlement discussions with Mid-Continent's attorney and then challenging the service of process six years after the judgment was entered: "Defendant in this case simply sat on his potential defense until the plaintiff finally found some of his assets and only then attempted to assert it." While we certainly do not condone Harris' or his attorney's conduct, we are of the opinion that the record falls short of supporting a finding of evasion or inequitable conduct by Harris.

IV. Conclusion

The three-part test devised by the district court to uphold the default judgment entered against Harris fails to support an exception to the service of process requirements of Rule 4. Therefore, the district court's order denying Harris' Rule 60(b)(4) motion to vacate and dismiss the default judgment on the grounds of improper service of process is *reversed*.

Notes and Questions

1. Some might consider *Mid-Continent* the worst kind of insistence on legal technicality, while others might view it as the best example of the rule of law. What are the arguments for these two positions? What would happen if judges did *not* insist on the technicalities of Rule 4?

2. Note the differences among proper service of process in the sense of (a) whether proper *methods* for service are deployed, versus (b) whether the contents of the process are sufficient, versus (c) (explored later) whether the court to which the defendant is haled has power over that defendant or the defendant's property. If anything is improper, the defendant in federal court may move to dismiss the action on the grounds of "improper service." (Note, however, that some state procedure codes require that the defendant distinguish among these types of process defects.)

If, as in *Mid-Continent*, a default judgment has already been entered, the defendant will have to move to vacate the judgment under Rule 60(b)(4). The defendant will bear the burden of proving she is entitled to relief even though the plaintiff normally has the burden of establishing the court's power to hear the case and its power to bind the defendant to any judgment. In *Mid-Continent*, the court held that it did not matter that Harris had actual notice of the litigation against him: Rule 4 had to be followed to obtain personal jurisdiction over him.

But actual notice is not totally irrelevant when a default judgment is challenged. It can affect the burden of proof on a motion to vacate. The Second, Seventh, and Ninth Circuits have held that a defendant who had actual notice of the litigation carries a "substantial burden" of proving that service was improper, particularly when the plaintiff presents a signed return of service. SEC v. Internet Solutions for Bus. Inc., 509 F.3d 1161, 1163 (9th Cir. 2007) (following Burda Media, Inc. v. Viertel, 417 F.3d 292, 299 (2d Cir. 2005)); O'Brien v. R.J. O'Brien & Assocs. Inc., 998 F.2d 1394, 1398 (7th Cir. 1993); Bally Exp. Corp. v. Balicar, Ltd., 804 F.2d 398, 400-401 (7th Cir. 1986). In *Internet Solutions*, the SEC presented a signed return of service by a process server with a "long and reputable" history and a sworn declaration from the process server claiming that the defendant verified his identity before accepting the summons and complaint for securities fraud. 509 F.3d at 1166. After moving to vacate the $100,000 default judgment, the defendant conceded he knew about the lawsuit but claimed he was at a meeting in another town the day the process server supposedly effected service. Id. Neither the district court nor the Ninth Circuit was convinced:

> Each time Shaw's story was challenged he came up with new and often contradictory evidence to support his version of the facts. In the face of the process server's sworn affidavits, and given the district court's credibility findings in favor of the process server against Shaw, we find that Shaw did not meet his burden to prove by strong and convincing evidence that he was not served with process.

Id. at 1167 (characterizing e-mail correspondence suggesting defendant might have been out of town as "rank hearsay").

3. Courts are not always as inflexible regarding strict compliance with the Rule 4 mandates as the court was in *Mid-Continent*. Consider the following passage from Ortiz v. County of Westchester, 1994 U.S. Dist. LEXIS 11147 (S.D.N.Y. 1994):

> On March 11, 1994, Plaintiff sent to defendant Jackson, by first class mail, a copy of the Summons and Complaint, Plaintiff's First Discovery Demand, a postage prepaid envelope, and two copies of a form entitled "Notice of Acknowledgement of Receipt of Summons and Complaint" (the "Acknowledgment"). The Acknowledgement asserted that service was being effected pursuant to Fed. R. Civ. P. 4(c)(2)(C)(ii). Although Jackson signed the Acknowledgement and returned it without objection to Plaintiff's counsel, who filed it with the Court, Jackson now asserts that service upon him was ineffective. He contends that at the time Plaintiff attempted to effect such service, the method used was invalid, having been superseded by amendments to the Federal Rules of Civil Procedure which took effect December 1, 1993. On this basis, Defendants seek dismissal of the claims against Jackson pursuant to Rule 12(b)(5). . . .
>
> Because the new waiver procedure comports substantially with the former mail service provision, the return of the Acknowledgment by Jackson to Plaintiff's counsel, together with the subsequent filing of the same with the Court, constitutes a waiver of service of process under Rule 4(d). The new Rule 4(d), like the Former Rule 4(c)(2)(C)(ii), aims to eliminate unnecessary costs of service; it effects little change other than the name of the provision, reflecting that "it is more accurate to describe the communication sent to the defendant [formerly the Acknowledgement] as a request for a waiver of formal service. . . ." Fed. R. Civ. P. 4, 28 U.S.C.A., Advisory Committee Notes to 1993 Amendments at 115 (Supp. 1994). Thus, the former service by mail provision and the current waiver of service provision are functional equivalents and Plaintiff's attempt to effect service of process pursuant to the old rule is valid, having been met with Jackson's compliance in returning the Acknowledgment.

Prior to restyling in 2007, Rule 4(m) provided that a complaint must be served on the defendant within 120 days of its filing. Indeed, failure to meet this deadline resulted in dismissal unless the court permits an extension. As the rule provided, the district court "shall dismiss the action without prejudice . . . or direct that service be effected within a specified time; provided that the plaintiff shows good cause for the failure, the court shall extend the time for service for an appropriate period." Fed. R. Civ. P. 4(m). The language seemed clear enough, but consider what precisely a court should have done when the plaintiff failed to show good cause for her failure to meet the 120-day deadline.

In United States v. McLaughlin, 470 F.3d 698 (7th Cir. 2006), government attorneys filed a tax collection suit against Thomas McLaughlin seeking $3 million in unpaid income taxes just five days before the expiration of the 10-year statute of limitations. The government attorneys mailed McLaughlin a copy of the complaint with a request to waive service under Rule 4(d)(2). McLaughlin refused. Rather than hire a professional process server, the Justice Department sent an IRS officer to serve McLaughlin in person. After failing to find McLaughlin at his home, the IRS officer went to his business and left the complaint with his daughter, wrongly assuming that leaving the complaint with an adult at a defendant's place of business is permitted under Rule 4(e)(2). By the time the Justice Department lawyer handling the case discovered the error, the 120-day deadline had passed, so she filed a motion for a 30-day extension. After the motion was granted, she hired a professional process server, who failed to serve McLaughlin, despite repeated attempts. Ultimately, it took two additional extensions and a second process server to serve McLaughlin 271 days after the complaint had been filed and long after the statute of limitations had expired.

As you now know from *Khashoggi* and *Mid-Continent*, and as every first-year law student learns, Rule 4 requirements are to be strictly observed. Those cases and Rule 4 strongly suggest that the first time the lawyer in *McLaughlin* missed the deadline, there was no good cause for an extension.

The Seventh Circuit agreed that there was no good cause ("the government has not much in the way of excuses for missing the deadline in this case by almost five months," id. at 701), but in an opinion that opens up a split with the Fifth and Sixth Circuits, see Turner v. City of Taylor, 412 F.3d 629, 650 (6th Cir. 2005) (plaintiff must show "excusable neglect" for missing the 120-day deadline, borrowing standard from Rule 6(b)(2)), and McGuire v. Turnbo, 137 F.3d 321, 324 (5th Cir. 1998) (same), Judge Richard Posner nevertheless refused to dismiss the complaint for improper service. According to Judge Posner, the plain language of Rule 4(m) leaves the district court discretion to grant an extension even if the plaintiff has *not* shown good cause: "if good cause for the delay is shown, the court *must* extend the time for service, while if good cause is not shown, the court has a choice between dismissing the suit and giving the plaintiff more time ('direct that service be effected within a specified time')." *McLaughlin*, 470 F.3d at 700. Semicolons, it turns out, really matter. Note the change in the restyled rule.

As for McLaughlin's objections grounded in notice, the court emphasized that McLaughlin had received actual notice even if he hadn't been properly served:

> This case is a good example of the wisdom of Rule 4(m) in allowing a judge to excuse delay in service even if the plaintiff has no excuse at all. Since McLaughlin admits liability, he could not be prejudiced by having to defend a case that might have become harder to defend by passage of time, for example because of the death or fading memory of defense witnesses. Anyway he received a copy of the complaint within the 120-day period—probably two copies; almost certainly his daughter showed him the ominous document that the IRS officer had left with her addressed to him. He knew he'd been sued, and armed with that knowledge he could begin his defensive efforts if he wished to contest liability—which he did not. He could not have been prejudiced to even the slightest extent by the government's service fumbles.
>
> When a delay in service causes zero prejudice to the defendant or third parties (or the court itself), the granting of extensions of time for service, whether before or after the 120-day period has expired, cannot be an abuse of discretion. The icing on the cake is that the suit if dismissed could not be reinstated, the statute of limitations having expired five days after the complaint was filed, and the defendant having admitted liability, dismissal would have presented him with a windfall—and a big one. It would have amounted to fining the government $3 million for doing something that did no harm to anyone and handing over the proceeds of the fine to a wrongdoer.

Id. at 701 (citations omitted).

4. Improper Conduct to Effect Service

Wyman v. Newhouse

93 F.2d 313 (2d Cir. 1937)

MANTON, Circuit Judge.

This appeal is from a judgment entered dismissing the complaint on motion before trial. The action is on a judgment entered by default in a Florida state court, a jury having assessed the damages. The recovery there was for money loaned, money advanced for appellee, and for seduction under promise of marriage.

Appellee's answer pleads facts supporting his claim that he was fraudulently enticed into the Florida jurisdiction, appellant's state of residence, for the sole purpose of service of process. . . .

The affidavits submitted by the appellee deemed to be true for the purpose of testing the alleged error dismissing the complaint established that he was a resident of New York and never lived in Florida. On October 25, 1935, while appellee was in Salt Lake City, Utah, he received a telegram from the appellant, which read: "Account illness home planning leaving. Please come on way back. Must see you." Upon appellee's return to New York he received a letter from appellant stating that her mother was dying in Ireland; that she was leaving the United States for good to go to her mother; that she could not go without seeing the appellee once more; and that she wanted to discuss her affairs with him before she left. Shortly after the receipt of this letter, they spoke to each other on the telephone, whereupon the appellant repeated, in a hysterical and distressed voice, the substance of her letter. Appellee promised to go to Florida in a week or ten days and agreed to notify her when he would arrive. This he did, but before leaving New York by plane he received a letter couched in endearing terms and expressing love and affection for him, as well as her delight at his coming. Before leaving New York, appellee telegraphed appellant, suggesting arrangements for their accommodations together while in Miami, Fla. She telegraphed him at a hotel in Washington, D.C., where he was to stop en route, advising him that the arrangements requested had been made. Appellee arrived at 6 O'clock in the morning at the Miami Airport and saw the appellant standing with her sister some 75 feet distant. He was met by a deputy sheriff who, upon identifying appellee, served him with process in a suit for $500,000. A photographer was present who attempted to take his picture. Thereupon a stranger introduced himself and offered to take appellee to his home, stating that he knew a lawyer who was acquainted with the appellant's attorney. . . . Appellee did not retain the Florida attorney to represent him. He returned to New York by plane that evening and consulted his New York counsel, who advised him to ignore the summons served in Florida. He did so, and judgment was entered by default. . . .

These facts and reasonable deductions therefrom convincingly establish that the appellee was induced to enter the jurisdiction of the state of Florida by a fraud perpetrated upon him by the appellant in falsely representing her mother's illness, her intention to leave the United States, and her love and affection for him, when her sole purpose and apparent thought was to induce him to come within the Florida jurisdiction so as to serve him in an action for damages. Appellant does not deny making these representations. All her statements of great and undying love were disproved entirely by her appearance at the airport and participation in the happenings there. She never went to Ireland to see her mother, if indeed the latter was sick at all.

In asking for judgment based on these Florida proceedings, appellant relies upon article 4, section 1, of the United States Constitution, providing that "Full Faith and Credit shall be given in each State to the public Acts, Records, and Judicial Proceedings of every other State." Congress has provided that judicial proceedings duly authenticated, "shall have such faith and credit given to them in every court within the United States as they have by law or usage in the courts of the State from which they are taken." 28 U.S.C.A. § 687. The first inquiry is what faith and credit would be given to this judgment within the state of Florida. On these facts, the service of process was fraudulent, and under the circumstances we think would have been vacated there. . . .

This judgment is attacked for fraud perpetrated upon the appellee which goes to the jurisdiction of the Florida court over his person. A judgment procured fraudulently, as here, lacks jurisdiction and is null and void. The appellee was not required to proceed against the judgment in Florida. His equitable defense in answer to a suit on the judgment is sufficient. A judgment recovered in a sister state, through the fraud of the party procuring the appearance of another, is not binding on the latter when an attempt is made to enforce such judgment in another state.

Note: Impropriety and Immunity from Service of Process

Wyman is the classic case drawing the line against trickery and undignified behavior when such tactics induce a defendant to enter the jurisdiction. Along the same lines is Ticke v. Barton, 95 S.E.2d 427 (W. Va. 1956), which found that service was fraudulently effected when the plaintiff lured the defendant to town by calls about a football banquet honoring his son. The dissent pointed out that the banquet was actually held and that the defendant knew a suit was pending against him in the country to which he traveled.

Generally, however, courts are sympathetic to the efforts to serve elusive defendants. Typical is another old favorite, Sawyer v. LaFlamme, 185 A.2d 466 (Vt. 1962), where the defendant was not only served, but physically held to answer the complaint after being invited and entreated to come to Vermont to settle the case. In holding that this was not fraudulent behavior, the court relied on the fact that the plaintiff's lawyer made no promises about what would happen if the defendant appeared.

There is a common law immunity-from-process rule of long standing to protect witnesses who come from outside the jurisdiction to testify in cases unrelated to the one in which some plaintiff seeks to serve them. Because the purpose is to encourage people to appear and testify, many courts have refused to apply this common law standard to litigants themselves (who have other incentives for appearing) or to witnesses who appear voluntarily rather than under subpoena. Lamb v. Schmitt, 285 U.S. 222 (1932), is the only Supreme Court case on the subject. There an attorney who had come into a state to set aside a fraudulent conveyance was served in an action to recover funds paid as fees in the main suit. The trial court denied the attorney immunity because the two proceedings were integrally related so that service of process in the second suit would not impede but rather would facilitate the administration of justice in the principal case. The Supreme Court made it clear that the immunity is for the benefit of the trial court's processes and is not "a right of the person against whom service is sought." The Court also indicated that whether to allow such immunity is a matter of considerable trial court discretion.

B. WHAT KIND OF HEARING DOES DUE PROCESS REQUIRE?

Problem Case: The Well-Meaning Legislator

You are the legislative assistant for State Senator Veliz, who has asked for your advice about a proposed piece of legislation, summarized below. Specifically, the Senator (who is a lawyer and well-versed in the applicable law) wants to know if the legislation comports with the procedural due process requirements of the Fourteenth Amendment.

Prepare a memorandum that discusses the *procedural due process* implications of each section of the bill. Be specific in identifying any due process problems and the reasons you think they exist. Also discuss any changes or additions that you think would help to protect the bill from a successful procedural due process challenge.

Conclude your memorandum with some observations on whether the bill is a good idea from a procedural standpoint, e.g., is it fair, does it properly take into account the various interests that enter the due process calculation?

Proposed Legislation:

Preamble: WHEREAS, the state of California seeks to assure the prompt, inexpensive, and nonadversarial resolution of all domestic disputes and disputes that involve juveniles, and WHEREAS adversarial process imposes undue expense and delay, exacerbates domestic disharmony, and ill serves the interests of all affected parties, the state adopts the following procedures for permanent and temporary termination of foster parent placements.

Section A. When the Department of Child Protective Services (CPS) has any reason to believe that a child placed by the state in a foster care home is in peril of physical, mental, or emotional abuse, CPS may intervene immediately and remove the child from the custody of the foster parent(s).

Section B. Within 24 hours of removing the child from the custody of the foster parent(s), CPS shall mail notice to the home address of the foster parent(s), stating that the child is in the protective custody of the state, pending a hearing to determine whether the allegations of peril are well founded.

Section C. A hearing shall be commenced within 5 days of delivery of the notice described in (B). Written notice of the time, date, and place of the hearing must be delivered to the home address of the foster parent(s) at least 24 hours before the scheduled hearing.

Section D. The hearing shall be held before an impartial arbitrator, appointed by the state. At the hearing, the arbitrator shall conduct all questioning of relevant parties. No party shall be represented by counsel at this hearing.

Section E. If the arbitrator finds the evidence of peril is well founded, he or she shall enter an order removing any and all other foster children from the foster care home and barring any future placements of foster children in the home of the censured foster parent(s).

Section F. Appeal of the arbitrator's decision may be had by the foster parent(s) or CPS by filing a complaint in the California Superior (trial) court. No attorney shall be provided at state expense for the foster parents on such appeals.

Look back to the Due Process Game problem case at the beginning of this chapter. Did you want a lawyer, or at least an advocate other than yourself, to present your case? Having a lawyer is the "top of the line" of due process and is also the chief cost of a meaningful hearing. Think about a lawyer's work and about when a lawyer, with his or her set of skills, is needed to make the system fair.

The introduction of a lawyer into the case, at least in the United States, brings with it the adversary approach. Most lawyers would not feel competent or adequate unless they zealously represented their clients to the exclusion, or at least significant downplaying, of all other interests—and under the state malpractice laws and bar rules that govern lawyers, professional sanctions and malpractice liability could be imposed on an advocate who fails to zealously represent her clients. Codes of ethics enforced by state bar associations and many of the rules we will study in the pages that follow take cognizance of the interests of third parties, but fidelity to the client's (lawful) interests is paramount. It is not too soon in your legal education to start asking whether and why such professional responsibility should trump personal morality or natural human response to a situation. Should we endorse a role that, as one philosopher put it, promotes "institutionalized immunity from the requirements of conscience" in the legal profession? David Luban, Lawyers and Justice: An Ethical Study at xxi (1988).

This is a difficult question that not only admits of many answers, but raises other, deeper questions. Is law separate from morality? Will the truth emerge from a clash of zealous advocates who put their clients' interests before societal interests? Can a lawyer give good legal advice without talking about the moral, economic, and political consequences of her client's legal position and/or the likely impact on third parties? Can a lawyer identify and make the best legal arguments for a client if she confuses her own moral, economic, and political views with what the law requires or permits? If lawyers are *not* held to be immune from the requirements of conscience, will unpopular, controversial, or morally suspect clients be represented in the legal system? Who will agree to take their cases?

A lawyer for each side totally devoted to that side's cause is the hallmark of the adversary system. The next two readings discuss this and other essential attributes of the system. As you read, think about what it means to make a lawyer's representation a requisite of due process.

Stephan Landsman, Readings on Adversarial Justice: The American Approach to Adjudication
Pages 2-5 (1988)*

The adversary process should not be viewed as a single technique or collection of techniques; it is a unified concept that works by use of a number of interconnecting procedures, each of real importance to the process as a whole. The central precept of the adversary process is that out of the sharp clash of proofs presented by adversaries in a highly structured forensic setting is most likely to come the information upon which a neutral and passive decision maker can base the resolution of a litigated dispute acceptable to both the parties and society. This formulation is advantageous not only because it expresses the overarching adversarial concept, but also because it identifies the method to be utilized in adjudication (the sharp clash of proofs in a highly structured setting), the actors essential to the process (two adversaries and a decision maker), the nature of their functions (presentation of proofs and adjudication of disputes, respectively), and the goal of the entire endeavor (the resolution of disputes in a manner acceptable to the parties and to society).

Like any brief definition of a complex subject the foregoing description of the adversary system fails to indicate some of the most important principles and practices inherent in adversary methodology. The key elements in the system—utilization of a neutral and passive fact finder, reliance on party presentation of evidence, and use of a highly structured forensic procedure—must be more fully discussed to present an accurate picture. This additional information will also be of particular importance in helping to assess the value and shortcomings of the adversary process.

1. Neutral and Passive Decision Maker

The adversary system relies on a neutral and passive decision maker to adjudicate disputes after they have been aired by the adversaries in a contested proceeding. The decision maker is expected to refrain from making any judgments until the conclusion of the contest and is prohibited from becoming actively involved in the gathering of evidence or the settlement of the case. Adversary theory suggests that if the decision maker strays from the passive role, she runs a serious risk of prematurely committing herself to one or another version of the facts and of failing to appreciate the value of all the evidence.

Adversary theory further suggests that neutrality and passivity are essential not only to ensure an evenhanded consideration of each case, but also to convince society at large that the judicial system is trustworthy. When a decision maker becomes an active questioner or otherwise

* Reprinted from Readings on Adversarial Justice: The American Approach to Adjudication 1st ed., © 1988, with permission of West Publishing Company.

participates in a case, she is likely to be perceived as partisan rather than neutral. Judicial passivity helps to ensure the appearance of fairness.

The judicial process is generally used to satisfy two objectives: first, the search for material truth, and second, the resolution of disputes between contending parties. Although most court systems seek to accomplish both these goals, the procedural mechanisms best suited to the achievement of each are different. Where judges are assigned an active, inquisitorial part in the litigation process, they will be expected to undertake an uninhibited search for truth. Perhaps the best examples of this approach are to be found in the justice systems of the Socialist states of Eastern Europe. Where judges are assigned a neutral and passive function, however, they will, in all likelihood, be expected to devote their energies to resolving the disputes framed by the litigants. One of the most significant implications of the American adoption of the principles of neutrality and passivity is that it tends to commit the adversary system to the objective of resolving disputes rather than searching for material truth.

Another major implication of insistence on the neutrality and passivity of the decision maker is that it favors the use of lay juries rather than professional judges. Judges are deeply involved in the management of lawsuits. They are constantly being called upon to make rulings and otherwise oversee the contest. Their passivity and neutrality are likely to be strained as they perform these functions. Except in cases of unusual notoriety, juries are unlikely to face similar strains or to become embroiled in the contest. Further, the members of the jury are likely to be free of those predispositions judges develop because of their training and daily experience in the handling of legal matters. In addition, because the jury comprises a number of individuals, the prejudices of a single juror are not likely to destroy the capacity of the group to render a fair decision. This is to be contrasted with the situation of the solitary judge whose biases can easily influence the decisions she renders. Finally, potential jurors can be questioned before they are permitted to take a seat on the jury and can be excluded if biased. There is no similar mechanism to ensure judicial neutrality. For all these reasons the jury is more likely than the judge to meet adversarial expectations of neutrality and passivity and is therefore favored in adversarial proceedings.

2. Party Presentation of Evidence

Intimately connected with the requirements of decision maker passivity and neutrality is the procedural principle that the parties are responsible for producing all the evidence upon which the decision will be based. This principle insulates the adjudicator from involvement in the contest. It also encourages the adversaries to find and present their most persuasive evidence. Adherence to this principle affords the decision maker the advantage of seeing what each litigant believes to be his most consequential proof. It also focuses the litigation upon the questions of greatest importance to the parties, making more likely a decision tailored to their needs. The benefits of such an approach may be measured in economic terms. A judge-dominated procedure increases the likelihood that the needs of the litigants will not be fully appreciated or satisfied. When this is the case "impositional costs" (those caused by an unbargained for and poorly tailored solution) are substantially increased. Such costs can, in large measure, be avoided in a system relying on participant direction and control.

Because of the potential complexity of legal questions and the intricacy of the legal mechanism, parties generally cannot manage their own lawsuits. Rather, they, and the adversary system, have come to rely upon a class of skilled professional advocates to assemble and to present the testimony upon which decisions will be based. The advocates are expected to provide the forensic talents necessary to organize the evidence and to formulate the legal issues. If the lawyers fail to carry out their duty, development of the case will be impeded, and the adversary process may be undermined. Additionally, the inadequacy of counsel may draw the judge into the contest either in search of material truth or in an attempt to ensure a balanced presentation. Such intervention may impair judicial neutrality.

3. Highly Structured Forensic Procedure

Elaborate sets of rules to govern the pretrial and posttrial periods (rules of procedure), the trial itself (rules of evidence), and the behavior of counsel (rules of ethics) are all important to the adversary system. Rules of procedure serve at least two functions in the adversary scheme. First, they structure litigation to produce a climactic confrontation between the parties in a single trial session or set of trial sessions. Such a confrontation yields the evidence upon which the decision will be based and diminishes the opportunity for the decision maker to undertake a potentially biasing independent investigation. Second, adversarial rules of procedure help to ensure the fairness of the contest by affording each litigant an equal opportunity to make the best possible case. The primary mechanism for ensuring equality is pretrial discovery, a technique allowing each party to examine his opponent's proof.

The trial or evidence rules protect the integrity of the testimonial segment of adversary proceedings. They prohibit the use of evidence that is likely to be unreliable and thereby insulate the trier from misleading information. The evidence rules also prohibit the use of evidence that poses a serious threat of exciting unfair prejudice against one of the parties. Rather than allow the use of such information the adversary system seeks to preserve the neutrality and passivity of the decision maker by a strictly enforced prohibition. Rules of evidence also enhance the power of the attorney to control the presentation of facts by providing him with a precisely formulated set of principles to measure the admissibility of every piece of evidence. In this way the rules confine the authority of the judge in managing the proceedings. Judges are not free to pick and choose the evidence they think most appropriate; rather, they are bound to obey previously fixed evidentiary prescripts.

Since the rough-and-tumble of adversary procedure exacerbates the natural tendency of advocates to seek to win by any means available, the adversary system employs rules of ethics to control the behavior of counsel. To ensure the integrity of the process certain tactics are forbidden, including those designed to harass or to intimidate an opponent as well as those intended to mislead or to prejudice the trier of fact. In addition to their prohibitory function, the rules of ethics are designed to promote vigorous adversarial contests by requiring that each attorney zealously represent his client's interests at all times. To ensure zeal, attorneys are required to give their undivided loyalty to their clients.

Notes and Questions

1. Landsman identifies the objective of procedure as "the resolution of a litigated dispute acceptable to both the parties and society," not as "truth." Are these necessarily different aims? How could the first goal be accomplished without process that promotes accurate outcomes?

2. What resource assumptions undergird the adversary model? Doesn't it assume two equally able—and thus equally funded—adversaries? Doesn't it assume both will have lawyers? Are these assumptions met in all cases? Most? Does anything in the Constitution guarantee that they are met? (Revisit this question at the end of this chapter.)

3. Why wouldn't an inquisitorial model—one in which the judge asked the questions and otherwise controlled the selection and appearance of the witnesses and evidence—satisfy the objectives of procedure? What about a mediation model, under which the parties appear before a mediator who would facilitate discussion and attempt to lead the parties to agreement, but would not impose any settlement on them? Think about these alternatives as you read the following excerpt comparing the American adversary system to other legal regimes.

Robert Kagan, Adversarial Legalism: The American Way of Law

Pages 6-16 (2001)

American Legal Exceptionalism

Everywhere in the modern world legal control of social, political, and economic life is intensifying (Galanter, 1992; Dewees et al. 1991). Law grows from the relentless pressures of technological change, geographic mobility, global economic competition, and environmental pollution—all of which generate social and economic disruption, new risks to health and security, new forms of injustice, and new cultural challenges to traditional norms. Some citizens, riding the waves of change, demand new rights of inclusion, political access, and economic opportunity. Others, threatened by the change, demand legal protection from harm and loss of control. Democratic governments pass laws and issue judicial rulings responsive to both sets of demands (Schuck, 2000; Kagan, 1995).

In some spheres of activity, such as land use regulation and worker protection, Western European polities typically have more restrictive laws than does the United States. Compared to the United States, Japan has a more detailed and extensive set of legally mandated product standards and premarket testing requirements (Edelman, 1988: 292, Vogel, 1990). . . . An increasing number of nations, as well as the European Union, now have active constitutional courts, supporting Torbjorn Vallinder's (1995: 13) claim of a worldwide trend toward the "judicialization of politics," defined as "(1) the expansion of the province of courts or the judges at the expense of politicians and/or the administrators . . . or . . . (2) the spread of judicial decision making methods outside the judicial province proper."

The United States, however, has a unique legal "style." That is the message of an accumulating body of careful cross-national studies. . . . For one social problem after another, the studies show, the American system for making and implementing public policy and resolving disputes is distinctive. "It generally entails (1) more complex bodies of legal rules; (2) more formal, adversarial procedures for resolving political and scientific disputes; (3) more costly forms of legal contestation; (4) stronger, more punitive legal sanctions; (5) more frequent judicial review of and intervention into administrative decisions and processes; (6) more political controversy about legal rules and institutions; (7) more politically fragmented, less closely coordinated decision making systems; and (8) more legal uncertainty and instability."

Comparative studies are hardly necessary, moreover, to show that in no other democracy is litigation so often employed by contestants in political struggles over the delineation of electoral district boundaries, the management of forests, the breakup of business monopolies, the appropriate funding level for inner-city versus suburban public schools, or the effort to discourage cigarette smoking. In no other countries are the money damages assessed in environmental and tort suits nearly so high, or have major manufacturers been driven into bankruptcy by liability claims. . . . The United States has by far the world's largest cadre of special "cause lawyers" seeking to influence public policy and institutional practices by means of innovative litigation. In no other country are lawyers so entrepreneurial in seeking out new kinds of business, so eager to challenge authority, or so quick to propose new liability-expanding legal theories. Finally, referring merely to the last few years, the United States is remarkable in its propensity to stage highly publicized, knock-down-drag-out legal donnybrooks such as the investigation and impeachment trial of President Bill Clinton, the custody battle over the six-year old Cuban refuge Elian Gonzales, the antitrust cases against Microsoft, and the multicourt battle over Florida's votes in the 2000 presidential election—struggles that inject huge televised doses of politicized legal argument into the nation's everyday experience.

What Is Adversarial Legalism?

All these legal propensities are manifestations of what I call "adversarial legalism"—a method of policymaking and dispute resolution with two salient characteristics. The first is *formal legal contestation*—competing interests and disputants readily invoke legal rights, duties and procedural requirements, backed by recourse to formal law enforcement, strong legal penalties, litigation, and/or judicial review. The second is *litigant activism*—a style of legal contestation in which the assertion of claims, the search for controlling legal arguments, and the gathering and submission of evidence are dominated not by judges or government officials but by disputing parties or interests, acting primarily through lawyers. Organizationally, adversarial legalism typically is associated with and is embedded in decision-making institutions in which *authority is fragmented* and in which *hierarchical control is relatively weak.*

These defining features of adversarial legalism have two characteristic consequences. The first is costliness—litigant-controlled, adversarial decision making tends to be particularly complex, protracted and costly. The second is legal uncertainty—when potent adversarial advocacy is combined with fragmented, relatively nonhierarchical decision-making authority, legal norms are particularly malleable and complex, and legal decisions are particularly variable and unpredictable. It is the combination of costliness and legal uncertainty that makes adversarial legalism especially fearsome and controversial.

Table 2 contrasts adversarial legalism with other modes of policy implementation and dispute resolution. The horizontal dimension refers to legal formality—the extent to which contending parties or interests, as well as government officials, invoke and insist on conformity to written legal procedures and preexisting legal rights and duties. At one end of the informal-formal continuum, policy elaboration and dispute resolution can be labeled *legalistic*, in the sense that they are controlled by formal legal rules and procedures rather than by discretionary judgment, bargaining, and informal processes. . . .

The vertical dimension of Table 2 concerns the extent to which the implementation or decision-making process is hierarchical—dominated by an official decisionmaker, applying authoritative norms or standards—as opposed to participatory—that is, influenced by disputing parties and their lawyers, their normative arguments, and the evidence they deem relevant. Taking each of these dimensions to their extreme form produces four "ideal types."

TABLE 2
Modes of Policy Implementation and Dispute Resolution

Organization of decision making authority	*Decisionmaking style*		
	INFORMAL	↔	FORMAL
HIERARCHICAL	Expert or political judgment		Bureaucratic legalism
↕			
PARTICIPATORY	Negotiation/mediation		Adversarial legalism

Negotiation/Mediation

A process in the lower left quadrant of Table 2 is adversarial in the sense that it is dominated by the contending parties, not by an authoritative governmental decision maker. But it is informal or nonlegalistic, since neither procedures nor normative standards are dictated by formal law. One example would be dispute resolution by negotiation, with or without lawyers.... The quadrant would also include mediation, whereby an "official" third party attempts to induce contending parties to agree on a policy or settlement but refrains from imposing a settlement based on law or official policy.

Expert/Political Judgment

The more an official decision maker or institution (as opposed to the contending interests) controls the process and the standards for decision, and the more authoritative and final the institution's decisions are, the more "hierarchical" the process. As suggested by the upper left quadrant in Table 2, hierarchical processes can be legally informal. For example . . . [in] Japan disputes over fault in motor vehicle accidents typically are resolved by special traffic police who rush to the scene, question the parties, "hammer out a consensual story as to what happened," and file a detailed report on their findings (Tanase, 1990: 651-674).

Bureaucratic Legalism

A policy-implementing or decision-making process characterized by a high degree of hierarchical authority and legal formality (the upper right quadrant of Table 2) resembles the ideal-typical bureaucratic process as analyzed by Max Weber. Governance by means of bureaucratic legalism emphasizes uniform implementation of centrally devised rules, vertical accountability, and official responsibility for fact-finding. The more hierarchical the system, the more restricted the role for legal representation and influence by affected citizens or contending interests. In contemporary democracies the pure case of bureaucratic legalism usually is softened in some respects, but it is an ideal systematically pursued, for example, by tax collection agencies. Also tending toward this ideal are German and French courts, where bureaucratically recruited and embedded judges—not the parties' lawyers and not lay juries—dominate both the evidence-gathering and the decision-making processes (Langbein, 1994). . . .

Adversarial Legalism

The lower right quadrant of Table 2 includes policy-implementing and decision processes that are procedurally formalistic but in which hierarchy is weak and party influence on the process is strong. American methods for compensating victims of highway and medical accidents, for example, prominently include a decentralized and adversarial tort law system driven by claimants and their lawyers, as contrasted with Western European compensation systems, which operate primarily though social insurance or benefit-payment bureaucracies. In American civil and criminal adjudication, the introduction of evidence and invocation of legal rules are dominated not by the judge (as in Europe) but by the contending parties' lawyers. . . . From a comparative perspective, American judges are more political, their decisions less uniform (Levin, 1972: 193-221; Rowland and Carp, 1983: 109-134). . . . Lay jurors, whose decisions are not explained and largely shielded from hierarchical review, still play an important role in the American system, which reduces legal certainty and magnifies the influence of skillful advocacy.

Similarly, compared to European democracies, regulatory decision making in the United States entails many more legal formalities—complex legal rules concerning public notice and comment, restrictions on ex parte and other informal contacts with decisionmakers, legalistically specified evidentiary and scientific standards, mandatory official "findings" and responses to interest group arguments. . . . But hierarchical authority is correspondingly weak. . . . Agency decisions are frequently challenged in court by dissatisfied parties and reversed by judges, who dictate further changes in administrative policymaking routines. Lawyers, scientists, and economists hired by contending industry and advocacy groups play a large role in presenting evidence and arguments. Overall, the clash of adversarial argument has a larger influence on decisions than in other countries' regulatory systems, where policy decisions are characterized by a combination of political and expert judgment and consultation with affected interests (Badaracco, 1985; Brickman et al., 1985).

No modern democratic legal system is characterized entirely by any of the quadrants in Table 2. National legal styles are not monolithic. . . . British libel law is more threatening to the press than American libel law, which has been restricted by judicial interpretations of the First Amendment (Weaver and Bennett, 1993). The German Constitutional Court, interpreting a more recent and more detailed constitution than the U.S. Constitution, has been more activist than the U.S. Supreme Court in some important policy areas, thereby stimulating a good deal of constitutional litigation (Currie, 1990; Landfried, 1995: 113). Adversarial legalism can and does occur in more "cooperation"-oriented nations, such as the Netherlands and Japan (Niemeijer, 1989: 121-152; Upham, 1987). . . .

Conversely, Americans often refrain from and disparage adversarial legalism. Contrary to one popular belief, ordinary people often do not demand tougher laws, prosecutions, and lawsuits for every kind of offense. Research indicates that accident victims, disappointed purchasers, and regulatory inspectors who encounter violations generally do *not* resort to law suits as their first recourse (Hensler et al., 1991; Miller and Sarat, 1981; Bardach and Kagan, 1982). They are often willing to submit to bureaucratic or expert judgment or negotiate solutions to their legal claims. Politicians and legal elites often devise less adversarial, less costly alternatives to adversarial litigation—juvenile courts, family courts, small claims courts, workers' compensation tribunals, commercial arbitration, mandatory mediation, negotiated rulemaking and compliance plans, and so on.

American judges and legislatures periodically issue rulings and enact statutes that are designed to *discourage* lawsuits and appeals; the 1980s and 1990s saw a wave of such efforts to dampen adversarial legalism. . . . In principle and in practice, institutionalizing the methods or structures of adversarial legalism—that is, establishing the kinds of judiciaries, legal rules, and law firms that facilitate adversarial litigation—does not completely determine how often conflicting parties actually *use* those institutions.

Yet viewed in comparative perspective, the United States is distinctive in both dimensions. It is especially inclined to encourage the use of adversarial litigation to implement public policies and resolve disputes. And . . . adversarial legalism as a matter of day-to-day practice is far more common in the United States than in other democracies. . . .

The dual aspect of adversarial legalism—as decision-making structure or method and as day-to-day practice—is crucial to understanding its social consequences. It means that adversarial legalism's importance cannot be measured by litigation or adjudication rates alone, any more than the significance of nuclear weapons rests in the frequency of nuclear war. For example, even if only a small minority of aggrieved persons or organizations actually file lawsuits that result in jury trials, the mere threat of costly and potentially punitive adversarial litigation can deter malpractice by hospitals, business organizations and government bodies. . . . Because its structures always stand ready to be mobilized, adversarial legalism—lawyer-dominated, perennially costly contestation—is a barely latent, easily triggered potentiality in virtually all contemporary American political, economic, and administrative processes. It creates a set of incentives and expectations that have come to loom very large in American governmental, commercial and social life.

The Roots of Adversarial Legalism

. . . Students of comparative politics have long observed that in relation to other economically advanced democracies, the United States "has a strong society but a weak state" (Krasner, 1978: 61). Among the rich democracies, American government is the most easily penetrated by organized interest groups and extracts less tax revenue as a proportion of gross national product (Steinmo, 1993; Wilensky, 1975). In a comparative analysis of political cultures, Seymour Martin Lipset (1996: 21) writes that due to its long-standing emphasis on individualism and mistrust of government, "America began and continues as the most antistatist, legalistic, and rights-oriented nation." American government, accordingly, is designed to fragment and limit power. Both the federal and the state constitutions subject governmental power to crosscutting institutional checks and judicially enforceable individual rights. . . .

A structurally fragmented state is especially open to popular and interest group demands. And in contemporary societies—far richer, better informed, and with higher expectations than any in human history—citizens demand a great deal of their government. . . . But getting . . . things from an institutionally fragmented, tax-averse, "antistatist" political system, as in the United States, presents a problem.

American adversarial legalism, therefore, can be viewed as arising from a fundamental tension between two powerful elements: first, a political culture (or set of popular political attitudes) that expects and demands comprehensive governmental protections from serious harm, injustice, and environmental dangers—and hence a powerful, activist government—and, second, a set of governmental structures that reflect mistrust of concentrated power and hence that limit and fragment political and governmental authority.

Adversarial legalism helps resolve the tension. In a "weak," structurally fragmented state, lawsuits and courts provide "nonpolitical," nonstatist mechanisms through which individuals can demand high standards of justice from government. Lawsuits and courts empower interest groups to prod the government to implement ambitious public policies. It is only a slight oversimplification to say that in the United States, lawyers, legal rights, judges, and lawsuits are the functional equivalent of the large central bureaucracies that dominate governance in high-tax, activist welfare states.

Adversarial legalism gives the United States the most politically and socially responsive court system in the world. Compared to most national judiciaries, America judges are less constrained by legal formalisms; they are more policy-oriented, more attentive to the equities (and inequities) of the particular situation. In the decentralized American legal system, if one judge closes the door on a novel legal argument, claimants can often find a more receptive judge in another court. Adversarial legalism makes the judiciary and lawyers more fully part of the governing process and more full democratic in character. But this kind of "responsive law" . . . is a "high-risk strategy" of governance. With its high costs and penalties, and with its responsiveness to private claims, adversarial litigation enables ideologues or opportunists to use the law as a tool for exploitation. In its eagerness to put aside legal formalism in order to seek good outcomes, responsive law generates high levels of legal unpredictability, at least when it is implemented through adversarial legalism. Thus adversarial legalism is an extremely inefficient and hence often unfair way of meeting the public's demand for justice and protection. The world's most responsive legal system does not necessarily give Americans the world's most reliable legal system or the world's most responsive system of governance.

Notes and Questions

1. Professor Kagan concludes with the observation that the adversary system is costly and an inefficient way to meet modern demands for justice. How relevant is efficiency to justice? There is, of course, the timeworn expression that justice delayed is justice denied. Is this the kind of inefficiency he is describing? We are all also familiar with the expression "rubber-stamping." Are hasty, superficial procedures for decision-making any less pernicious than inefficient ones? Efficiency, you will see, looms large in all efforts to define due process in the American legal system.

2. Recall the skepticism Justices Scalia and Thomas expressed about the institutional competence of the courts in *Hamdi*. Does Professor Kagan share their skepticism, or are his concerns about adversarial legalism of a different kind? Is he suggesting that the United States offers too much due process?

3. Professor Kagan argues that adversarial legalism is used and abused by a wide range of institutions, interest groups, and individuals. Which social groups would fare the worst if access to courts for social change is restricted and people had to bring their grievances to the politically accountable, majoritarian branches of government? Which social groups would fare the best?

Note: The Common Understanding of Due Process

Professor Landsman stated that the goal of the adversarial process is to resolve disputes in a manner acceptable to the parties and to society. This suggests that laypeople's procedural expectations should be a primary factor in determining what process is due in a given setting.

Professor Tom Tyler has tried, in different sociological contexts, to measure the expectations of laypeople. His conclusions below are based on telephone interviews with 1,575 citizens of Chicago, Illinois, identified through a random selection process. The respondents were interviewed about their views of the police and courts in Chicago and about their level of behavioral compliance with the law. Does his study suggest that the adversarial model is an inadequate account of procedural justice? That nonadversarial procedures might be acceptable to the parties and society for at least some disputes?

Tom R. Tyler, Why People Obey the Law

Pages 137-138, 143, 147-148 (1990)

Citizens are not using any simple, unidimensional approach to assessing procedural justice. Instead, they pay attention to seven distinct aspects of procedure: the authorities' motivation, honesty, bias, and ethicality; their opportunities for representation; the quality of the decisions; and the opportunity for correcting errors. Each of these seven aspects of procedure has a significant independent influence on judgments about procedural justice. Both aspects of procedure related to decision making and those unrelated to it are important to judgments of procedural justice. The elements of procedural justice most directly linked to decision making are judgments about the neutrality of the decision-making procedure. People believe that decisions should be made by neutral, unbiased decision makers, and they expect the decision makers to be honest and to make their decisions based on objective information about the issues.

People also feel that procedures are fairer when they believe they have had some control in the decision-making procedure. Such control includes having the opportunity to present one's arguments, being listened to, and having one's view considered. As previously noted, this influence includes elements of control over the decisions made, but also includes interpersonal issues not directly linked to decision making. Procedural fairness is further linked to interpersonal aspects of the decision-making procedure. People place great weight on being treated politely and having respect shown both for their rights and for themselves as people. In addition, assessments of procedural fairness are strongly linked to judgments about whether the authorities being dealt with are trying to be fair. These interpersonal factors were not of minor importance. Inferences about the effort to be fair were the most important criterion of procedural fairness; concerns about politeness and rights (jointly labeled ethicality) were the second-most important. Clearly, there are important noninstrumental elements to the meaning of procedural justice. . . .

. . . [T]he meaning of procedural justice changes in response to the nature of the experience that citizens have with legal authorities. Apparently, individuals do not have a single schema of a fair procedure that they apply on all occasions, but instead are concerned with different issues in different circumstances. As a result, it is likely that there are no universally fair procedures for allocation and the resolution of disputes. . . .

If citizens are allowed to convey to authorities their suggestions for solving problems, they feel that their experience is procedurally fairer, and this judgment in turn leads their experience to have positive effects on their views about legal authorities. Such process control effects are larger than the effects of control over the decisions made by the third party. In addition, process control effects increase in magnitude as the outcomes involved become more important. When people feel that they had an opportunity to present their evidence but that they had no influence over the decisions made by the authorities, they may have several possible reactions. First, they may feel a lack of influence and decision control, and these feelings may lead to a loss of support for the authorities that made decisions without heeding their views. This reaction reflects an instrumental perspective. It is a reaction based on the lack of correspondence between the person's advocated outcomes and the outcomes actually obtained. Alternatively, people may react favorably to the opportunity to present their views, even if their views had no effect on the decision made. This has been called the value-expressive effect (Tyler, Rasinski, and Spodick 1985) because the value of process control is not linked to its impact on outcomes.

That process control without decision control generally enhances judgments of fairness and support for the authorities is a result consistent with the value-expressive perspective on process control. People do not seem sensitive only to whether their opportunity to speak influences decisions made by a third party. The implication for legal authorities is that they can gain public support by setting up decision-making structures that allow opportunities for process control. Irrespective of whether their long-term accountability is based on the quality of the outcomes they produce, authorities can clearly obtain short-term support from their constituents by providing opportunities for process control. For authorities motivated to follow policies that are sound in the long term, this discretionary authority gives them the flexibility to do so (see Tyler, Rasinski, and Griffin 1986).

Unfortunately, value-expressive effects also provide opportunities to authorities less interested in helping people: opportunities to mislead and beguile the public by providing chances to speak not linked to any short- or long-term influence over decisions (Tyler and McGraw 1986). If the focus on having opportunities to speak draws people's attention away from the tangible benefits they might receive from the authorities, it makes "false consciousness" possible. People may be satisfied in situations that should be viewed as unfair if judged on objective grounds. . . .

A recent analysis of the content of the speeches of revolutionary leaders found that the speeches focused heavily on distributive justice as opposed to procedural justice (Martin, Scully, and Levitt 1986). Perhaps revolutionary leaders recognize that successfully undermining the legitimacy of existing authorities involves directing people's attention toward distributive injustices. . . .

Notes and Questions

1. If, as Landsman suggested, supra, the goal of procedure is acceptable outcomes, why aren't more studies like Professor Tyler's undertaken?

2. To what extent should the "common understanding" of due process inform the constitutional standard? Does it matter if these common understandings change over time, or should the Constitution be interpreted solely against the backdrop of the framers' common understandings? If the framers' intentions should govern, do studies like Tyler's suggest that inquiries into these intentions may be quite complicated—even impossible?

3. Look at the significance of participants' control over process and their satisfaction with the outcomes. What are the implications of this finding for the due process game in the Problem Case at the beginning of the chapter? For administrators and others who want to deflect complaints about their decisions?

4. Tyler suggests that process preferences are socialized, not intellectualized. Does this mean our taste for due process is wholly learned, not innate? Can it be unlearned? If so, are there educational implications of this study, as well as legal ones? When do you think you learned your process preferences? From whom?

5. Having read Tyler's account, what do you make of Kagan's claim that adversarial legalism results more from structural than cultural factors?

Note: Global Rules of Civil Procedure

The extent to which procedural expectations become culturally ingrained has a significant, practical effect on projects like the American Law Institute's (ALI) effort to draft Transnational Rules of Civil Procedure which would "harmonize" differences among the procedural laws of national legal systems. Such a project immediately encounters skepticism about the possibility, if not the desirability, of "global" procedural rules. One profound obstacle is the difference between the common-law systems—e.g., in the United States—and civil law systems, e.g., in France. In civil law systems, most law derives from legislatively created codes, whereas in common law systems, judges have authority to craft new rules in response to new circumstances. The adversary system, as we know it, and the ideas of due process explored in this chapter, developed in common law systems. There are understandable objections to any transnational procedure that takes as its baseline characteristic U.S. procedure.

In light of both concerns, ALI reporters Geoffrey C. Hazard, Jr., and Michele Taruffo conclude as follows:

> [A] system of procedure acceptable generally throughout the world could not include jury trial and would require much more limited discovery than is typical in the United States. This in turn leads us to conclude that the scope of the proposed Transnational Civil Rules should exclude personal-injury and wrongful-death actions, because barring jury trial in such cases would be unacceptable in the United States. Hence, the scope is now conceived in terms of "business disputes."

Preface, The American Law Institute, Transnational Rules of Civil Procedure, Preliminary Draft No. 2, March 17, 2000. Despite these limitations, the reporters remain optimistic. The Proposed Final Draft, issued in March 2004 and joined by the International Institute for the Unification of Private Law, emphasizes that "the cost and distress resulting from legal conflict can be mitigated by reducing differences in legal systems, whereby the same or similar 'rules of the game' apply no matter where the participants may find themselves." The American Law Institute, Proposed Final Draft, p. 1, March 9, 2004.

Can you see the tension here between the need to harmonize and standardize procedural rules, in the age of e-commerce and global trade, and the cultural and other adverse consequences of imposing any "dominant" cultural model of procedure on "nondominant," dissenting systems? Yet isn't procedural standardizing inescapable, whether through intergovernmental agreements or through private contractual arrangements between commercial actors?

If so, will civil procedure go the way of European currency, i.e., will a new "American-Europrocess," eventually become a similarly controversial, but still growing norm of intercultural exchange?

Assume that you are a participant in the ongoing debates about Transnational Procedure. What would you insist upon, as procedural minima? Would you be willing to sacrifice trial by jury in civil cases? Party-conducted discovery of the opposing party's evidence?

Lassiter v. Department of Social Services

452 U.S. 18 (1981)

JUSTICE STEWART delivered the opinion of the Court.

In the late Spring of 1975, after hearing evidence that the petitioner, Abby Gail Lassiter, had not provided her infant son William with proper medical care, the District Court of Durham County, N.C., adjudicated him a neglected child and transferred him to the custody of the Durham County Department of Social Services, the respondent here. A year later, Ms. Lassiter was charged with first-degree murder, was convicted of second-degree murder, and began a sentence of 25 to 40 years of imprisonment. In 1978 the Department petitioned the court to terminate Ms. Lassiter's parental rights because, the Department alleged, she "has not had any contact with the child since December of 1975" and

> has willfully left the child in foster care for more than two consecutive years without showing that substantial progress has been made in correcting the conditions which led to the removal of the child, or without showing a positive response to the diligent efforts of the Department of Social Services to strengthen her relationship to the child, or to make and follow through with constructive planning for the future of the child.

Ms. Lassiter was served with the petition and with notice that a hearing on it would be held. Although her mother had retained counsel for her in connection with an effort to invalidate the murder conviction, Ms. Lassiter never mentioned the forthcoming hearing to him (or, for that matter, to any other person except, she said, to "someone" in the prison). At the behest of the Department of Social Services' attorney, she was brought from prison to the hearing, which was held August 31, 1978. The hearing opened, apparently at the judge's insistence, with a discussion of whether Ms. Lassiter should have more time in which to find legal assistance. Since the court concluded that she "has had ample opportunity to seek and obtain counsel prior to the hearing of this matter, and [that] her failure to do so is without just cause," the court did not postpone the proceedings. Ms. Lassiter did not aver that she was indigent, and the court did not appoint counsel for her.

A social worker from the respondent Department was the first witness. She testified that in 1975 the Department "received a complaint from Duke Pediatrics that William had not been followed in the pediatric clinic for medical problems and that they were having difficulty in locating Ms. Lassiter. . . . " She said that in May of 1975 a social worker had taken William to the hospital, where doctors asked that he stay "because of breathing difficulties [and] malnutrition and [because] there was a great deal of scarring that indicated that he had a severe infection that had gone untreated." The witness further testified that except for one "prearranged" visit and a chance meeting on the street, Ms. Lassiter had not seen William after he had come into the State's custody, and that neither Ms. Lassiter nor her mother had "made any contact with the Department of Social Services regarding that child." When asked whether William should be placed in his grandmother's custody, the social worker said he should not, since the grandmother "has indicated to me on a number of occasions that she was not able to take responsibility for the child" and since "I have checked with people in the community and from Ms. Lassiter's church who also feel that this additional responsibility would be more than she can handle." The social worker added that William has not seen his grandmother since the chance meeting in July of '76 and that was the only time.

After the direct examination of the social worker, the judge said:

> I notice we made extensive findings in June of '75 that you were served with papers and called the social services and told them you weren't coming; and the serious lack of medical treatment. And, as I have said in my findings of the 16th day of June '75, the Court finds that the grandmother, Ms. Lucille Lassiter, mother of Abby Gail Lassiter, filed a complaint on the 8th day of May, 1975, alleging that the daughter often left the children, Candina, Felicia and William L. with her for days without providing money or food while she was gone.

Ms. Lassiter conducted a cross-examination of the social worker, who firmly reiterated her earlier testimony. The judge explained several times, with varying degrees of clarity, that Ms. Lassiter should only ask questions at this stage; many of her questions were disallowed because they were not really questions, but arguments.

Ms. Lassiter herself then testified, under the judge's questioning, that she had properly cared for William. Under cross-examination, she said that she had seen William more than five or six times after he had been taken from her custody and that, if William could not be with her, she wanted him to be with her mother since "He knows us. Children know they family.... They know they people, they know they family and that child knows us anywhere.... I got four more other children. Three girls and a boy and they know they little brother when they see him."

Ms. Lassiter's mother was then called as a witness. She denied, under the questioning of the judge, that she had filed the complaint against Ms. Lassiter, and on cross-examination she denied both having failed to visit William when he was in the State's custody and having said that she could not care for him.

The court found that Ms. Lassiter "has not contacted the Department of Social Services about her child since December 1975, has not expressed any concern for his care and welfare, and has made no efforts to plan for his future." Because Ms. Lassiter thus had "willfully failed to maintain concern or responsibility for the welfare of the minor," and because it was "in the best interests of the minor," the court terminated Ms. Lassiter's status as William's parent.

On appeal, Ms. Lassiter argued only that, because she was indigent, the Due Process Clause of the Fourteenth Amendment entitled her to the assistance of counsel, and that the trial court had therefore erred in not requiring the State to provide counsel for her. The North Carolina Court of Appeals decided that "[w]hile this State action does invade a protected area of individual privacy, the invasion is not so serious or unreasonable as to compel us to hold that appointment of counsel for indigent parents is constitutionally mandated." In the Matter of William L. Lassiter, 43 N.C. App. 525, 527, 259 S.E.2d 336, 337. The Supreme Court of North Carolina summarily denied Ms. Lassiter's application for discretionary review, 299 N.C. 120, 262 S.E.2d 6, and we granted certiorari to consider the petitioner's claim under the Due Process Clause of the Fourteenth Amendment, [449] U.S. [819] 1980....

The pre-eminent generalization that emerges from this Court's precedents on an indigent's right to appointed counsel is that such a right has been recognized to exist only where the litigant may lose his physical liberty if he loses the litigation. Thus, when the Court overruled the principle of Betts v. Brady, 316 U.S. 455 [(1942)], that counsel in criminal trials need be appointed only where the circumstances in a given case demand it, the Court did so in the case of a man sentenced to prison for five years. Gideon v. Wainwright, 372 U.S. 335 [(1963).]

And thus Argersinger v. Hamlin, 407 U.S. 25 [(1967)], established that counsel must be provided before any indigent may be sentenced to prison, even where the crime is petty and the prison term brief.

That it is the defendant's interest in personal freedom, and not simply the special Sixth and Fourteenth Amendments right to counsel in criminal cases, which triggers the right to appointed counsel is demonstrated by the Court's announcement in In re Gault, 387 U.S. 1 [(1965)], that "the Due Process Clause of the Fourteenth Amendment requires that in respect of proceedings to determine delinquency *which may result in commitment to an institution in which the juvenile's freedom is curtailed*," the juvenile has a right to appointed counsel even [though] those proceedings may be styled "civil" and not "criminal." Id., at 41 . . . (emphasis added). Similarly, four of the five Justices who reached the merits in Vitek v. Jones, 445 U.S. 480 [(1980)], concluded that an indigent prisoner is entitled to appointed counsel before being involuntarily transferred for treatment to a state mental hospital. The fifth Justice differed from the other four only in declining to exclude the "possibility that the required assistance may be rendered by a competent layman in some cases." Id., at 497 [(1980)] (separate opinion of Powell, J.).

Significantly, as a litigant's interest in personal liberty diminishes, so does his right to appointed counsel. In Gagnon v. Scarpelli, 411 U.S. 778 [(1973)], . . . the Court gauged the due process rights of a previously sentenced probationer at a probation-revocation hearing. In Morrissey v. Brewer, 408 U.S. 471, 480 [(1972),] which involved an analogous hearing to revoke parole, the Court had said: "Revocation deprives an individual, not of the absolute liberty to which every citizen is entitled, but only of the conditional liberty properly dependent on observance of special parole restrictions." Relying on that discussion, the Court in *Scarpelli* declined to hold that indigent probationers have, per se, a right to counsel at revocation hearings, and instead left the decision whether counsel should be appointed to be made on a case-by-case basis. . . .

The case of Mathews v. Eldridge, 424 U.S. 319, 335 [(1976),] propounds three elements to be evaluated in deciding what due process requires, viz., the private interests at stake, the government's interest, and the risk that the procedures used will lead to erroneous decisions. We must balance these elements against each other, and then set their net weight in the scales against the presumption that there is a right to appointed counsel only where the indigent, if he is unsuccessful, may lose his personal freedom.

This Court's decisions have by now made plain beyond the need for multiple citation that a parent's desire for and right to "the companionship, care, custody and management of his or her children" is an important interest that "undeniably warrants deference and, absent a powerful countervailing interest, protection." Stanley v. Illinois, 405 U.S. 645, 651 [(1972)]. Here the State has sought not simply to infringe upon that interest, but to end it. If the State prevails, it will have worked a unique kind of deprivation. Cf. May v. Anderson, 345 U.S. 528, 533 [(1953)]; Armstrong v. Manzo, 380 U.S. 545 [(1965)]. A parent's interest in the accuracy and justice of the decision to terminate his or her parental status is, therefore, a commanding one.

Since the State has an urgent interest in the welfare of the child, it shares the parent's interest in an accurate and just decision. For this reason, the State may share the indigent parent's interest in the availability of appointed counsel. If, as our adversary system presupposes, accurate and just results are most likely to be obtained through the equal contest of opposed interests, the State's interest in the child's welfare may perhaps best be served by a hearing in which both the parent and the State acting for the child are represented by counsel, without whom the contest of interests may become unwholesomely unequal. North Carolina itself acknowledges as much by providing that where a parent files a written answer to a termination petition, the State must supply a lawyer to represent the child. N.C. Gen. Stat. § 7A-289.29 (Supp. 1979).

The State's interests, however, clearly diverge from the parent's insofar as the State wishes the termination decision to be made as economically as possible and thus wants to avoid both the expense of appointed counsel and the cost of the lengthened proceedings his presence may cause. But though the State's pecuniary interest is legitimate, it is hardly significant enough to overcome private interests as important as those here, particularly in light of the concession in the respondent's brief that the "potential costs of appointed counsel in termination proceedings . . . is [sic] admittedly de minimis compared to the costs in all criminal actions."

Finally, consideration must be given to the risk that a parent will be erroneously deprived of his or her child because the parent is not represented by counsel. North Carolina law now seeks to assure accurate decisions by establishing the following procedures: A petition to terminate parental rights may be filed only by a parent seeking the termination of the other parent's rights, by a county department of social services or licensed child-placing agency with custody of the child, or by a person with whom the child has lived continuously for the two years preceding the petition. N.C.G.S. § 7A-289.24. A petition must describe facts sufficient to warrant a finding that one of the grounds for termination exists, N.C.G. S. § 7A-289.25(6), and the parent must be notified of the petition and given 30 days in which to file a written answer to it, N.C.G.S. § 7A-289.27. If that answer denies a material allegation, the court must, as has been noted, appoint a lawyer as the child's guardian ad litem and must conduct a special hearing to resolve the issues raised by the petition and the answer. N.C.G.S. § 7A-289.29. If the parent files no answer, "the court shall issue an order terminating all parental and custodial rights . . . ; provided the court shall order a hearing on the petition and may examine the petitioner or others on the facts alleged in the petition." N.C.G.S. § 7A-289.28. Findings of fact are made by a court sitting without a jury and must "be based on clear," cogent, and "convincing evidence." N.C.G.S. § 7A-289.30. Any party may appeal who gives notice of appeal within 10 days after the hearing. N.C.G.S. § 7A-289.34.

The respondent argues that the subject of a termination hearing—the parent's relationship with her child—far from being abstruse, technical, or unfamiliar, is one as to which the parent must be uniquely well informed and to which the parent must have given prolonged thought. The respondent also contends that a termination hearing is not likely to produce difficult points of evidentiary law, or even of substantive law, since the evidentiary problems peculiar to criminal trials are not present and since the standards for termination are not complicated. In fact, the respondent reports, the North Carolina Departments of Social Services are themselves sometimes represented at termination hearings by social workers instead of by lawyers.

Yet the ultimate issues with which a termination hearing deals are not always simple, however commonplace they may be. Expert medical and psychiatric testimony, which few parents are equipped to understand and fewer still to confute, is sometimes presented. The parents are likely to be people with little education, who have had uncommon difficulty in dealing with life, and who are, at the hearing, thrust into a distressing and disorienting situation. That these factors may combine to overwhelm an uncounselled parent is evident from the findings some courts have made.

. . . Thus, courts have generally held that the State must appoint counsel for indigent parents at termination proceedings. State ex rel. Heller v. Miller, 61 Ohio St. 2d 6, 399 N.E.2d 66 (1980); Dept. of Public Welfare v. J. K.B., 393 N.E.2d 406 (Mass. 1979); Matter of Chad S., 580 P.2d 983 (Okla. Sup. Ct. 1978); In re Myricks, 85 Wash. 2d 252, 533 P.2d 841 (1975); Crist v. Division of Youth and Family Services, 128 N.J. Super. 402, 320 A.2d 203 (N.J. Super. Ct. 1974); Danforth v. Maine Dept. of Health and Welfare, 303 A.2d 794 (Me. Sup. Ct. 1973); In re Freisz, 190 Neb. 347, 208 N.W.2d 259 (1973). The respondent is able to point to no presently authoritative case, except for the North Carolina judgment now before us, holding that an indigent parent has no due process right to appointed counsel in termination proceedings. . . .

If, in a given case, the parent's interests were at their strongest, the State's interests were at their weakest, and the risks of error were at their peak, it could not be said that the *Eldridge* factors did not overcome the presumption against the right to appointed counsel, and that due process did not therefore require the appointment of counsel. But since the *Eldridge* factors will not always be so distributed, and since "due process is not so rigid as to require that the significant interests in informality, flexibility and economy must always be sacrificed," Gagnon v. Scarpelli, supra, 411 U.S. at 788, neither can we say that the Constitution requires the appointment of counsel in every parental termination proceeding. We therefore adopt the standard found appropriate in Gagnon v. Scarpelli, and leave the decision whether due process calls for the appointment of counsel for indigent parents in termination proceedings to be answered in the first instance by the trial court, subject, of course, to appellate review. . . .

Here, as in *Scarpelli*, "[i]t is neither possible nor prudent to attempt to formulate a precise and detailed set of guidelines to be followed in determining when the providing of counsel is necessary to meet the applicable due process requirements," since here, as in that case, "[t]he facts and circumstances . . . are susceptible of almost infinite variation. . . ."

Supra, 411 U.S. at 788. . . . Nevertheless, because child-custody litigation must be concluded as rapidly as is consistent with fairness,[7] we decide today whether the trial judge denied Ms. Lassiter due process of law when he did not appoint counsel for her.

The respondent represents that the petition to terminate Ms. Lassiter's parental rights contained no allegations of neglect or abuse upon which criminal charges could be based, and hence Ms. Lassiter could not well have argued that she required counsel for that reason. The Department of Social Services was represented at the hearing by counsel, but no expert witnesses testified and the case presented no especially troublesome points of law, either procedural or substantive. While hearsay evidence was no doubt admitted, and while Ms. Lassiter no doubt left incomplete her defense that the Department had not adequately assisted her in rekindling her interest in her son, the weight of the evidence that she had few sparks of such interest was sufficiently great that the presence of counsel for Ms. Lassiter could not have made a determinative difference. True, a lawyer might have done more with the argument that William should live with Ms. Lassiter's mother—but that argument was quite explicitly made by both Lassiters, and the evidence that the elder Ms. Lassiter had said she could not handle another child, that the social worker's investigation had led to a similar conclusion, and that the grandmother had displayed scant interest in the child once he had been removed from her daughter's custody was, though controverted, sufficiently substantial that the absence of counsel's guidance on this point did not render the proceedings fundamentally unfair. Finally, a court deciding whether due process requires the appointment of counsel need not ignore a parent's plain demonstration that she is not interested in attending a hearing. Here, the trial court had previously found that Ms. Lassiter had expressly declined to appear at the 1975 child custody hearing, Ms. Lassiter had not even bothered to speak to her retained lawyer after being notified of the termination hearing, and the court specifically found that Ms. Lassiter's failure to make an effort to contest the termination proceeding was without cause. In view of all these circumstances, we hold that the trial court did not err in failing to appoint counsel for Ms. Lassiter. . . .

In its Fourteenth Amendment, our Constitution imposes on the States the standards necessary to ensure that judicial proceedings are fundamentally fair. A wise public policy, however, may require that higher standards be adopted than those minimally tolerable under the Constitution. Informed opinion has clearly come to hold that an indigent parent is entitled to the assistance of appointed counsel not only in parental termination proceedings, but in dependency and neglect proceedings as

7. According to the respondent's brief, William Lassiter is now living "in a preadoptive home with foster parents committed for formal adoption to become his legal parents." He cannot be legally adopted, nor can his status otherwise be finally clarified, until this litigation ends.

well. Most significantly, 33 States and the District of Columbia provide statutorily for the appointment of counsel in termination cases. The Court's opinion today in no way implies that the standards increasingly urged by informed public opinion and now widely followed by the States are other than enlightened and wise.

For the reasons stated in this opinion, the judgment is affirmed.

It is so ordered. . . .

JUSTICE BLACKMUN, with whom JUSTICE BRENNAN and JUSTICE MARSHALL join, dissenting.

The Court today denies an indigent mother the representation of counsel in a judicial proceeding initiated by the State of North Carolina to terminate her parental rights with respect to her youngest child. The Court most appropriately recognizes that the mother's interest is a "commanding one," . . . and it finds no countervailing state interest of even remotely comparable significance. . . . Nonetheless, the Court avoids what seems to me the obvious conclusion that due process requires the presence of counsel for a parent threatened with judicial termination of parental rights, and instead, revives an ad hoc approach thoroughly discredited nearly 20 years ago in Gideon v. Wainwright, 372 U.S. 335 (1963). Because I believe that the unique importance of a parent's interest in the care and custody of his or her child cannot constitutionally be extinguished through formal judicial proceedings without the benefit of counsel, I dissent. . . .

The method chosen by North Carolina to extinguish parental rights resembles in many respects a criminal prosecution. Unlike the probation revocation procedure reviewed in Gagnon v. Scarpelli, on which the Court so heavily relies, the termination procedure is distinctly formal and adversarial. The State initiates the proceedings by filing a petition in district court, N.C. Gen. Stat. §§ 7A-289.23 and 7A-289.25 (Supp. 1979), and serving a summons on the parent, § 7A-289.27(1). A state judge presides over the adjudicatory hearing that follows, and the hearing is conducted pursuant to the formal rules of evidence and procedure. N.C. Gen. Stat. § 1A-1, Rule 1 (Supp. 1979). In general, hearsay is inadmissible and records must be authenticated. See, e.g., § 1A-1, Rules 1, 43, 44, 46.

In addition, the proceeding has an obvious accusatory and punitive focus. In moving to terminate a parent's rights, the State has concluded that it no longer will try to preserve the family unit, but instead will marshal an array of public resources to establish that the parent-child separation must be made permanent. The State has legal representation through the county attorney. This lawyer has access to public records concerning the family and to professional social workers who are empowered to investigate the family situation and to testify against the parent. The State's legal representative may also call upon experts in family relations, psychology, and medicine to bolster the State's case. And, of course, the State's counsel himself is an expert in the legal standards and techniques employed at the termination proceeding, including the methods of cross-examination.

In each of these respects, the procedure devised by the State vastly differs from the informal and rehabilitative probation revocation decision in *Scarpelli*. . . . Indeed, the State here has prescribed virtually all the attributes of a formal trial as befits the severity of the loss at stake in the termination decision—every attribute, that is, except counsel for the defendant parent. The provision of counsel for the parent would not alter the character of the proceeding, which is already adversarial, formal, and quintessentially legal. It, however, would diminish the prospect of an erroneous termination, a prospect that is inherently substantial, given the gross disparity in power and resources between the State and the uncounselled indigent parent.

The prospect of error is enhanced in light of the legal standard against which the defendant parent is judged. As demonstrated here, that standard commonly adds another dimension to the complexity of the termination proceeding. Rather than focusing on the facts of isolated acts or omissions, the State's charges typically address the nature and quality of complicated ongoing relationships among parent, child, other relatives, and even unrelated parties. . . .

The legal issues posed by the State's petition are neither simple nor easily defined. The standard is imprecise and open to the subjective values of the judge. A parent seeking to prevail against the State must be prepared to adduce evidence about his or her personal abilities and lack of fault, as well as proof of progress and foresight as a parent that the State would deem adequate and improved over the situation underlying a previous adverse judgment of child neglect. The parent cannot possibly succeed without being able to identify material issues, develop defenses, gather and present sufficient supporting nonhearsay evidence, and conduct cross-examination of adverse witnesses.

The Court, of course, acknowledges that these tasks "may combine to overwhelm an uncounselled parent." I submit that that is a profound understatement. Faced with a formal accusatory adjudication, with an adversary—the State—that commands great investigative and prosecutorial resources, with standards that involve ill-defined notions of fault and adequate parenting, and with the inevitable tendency of a court to apply subjective values or to defer to the State's "expertise," the defendant parent plainly is outstripped if he or she is without the assistance of "'the guiding hand of counsel.'" In re Gault, 387 U.S. [1, 36 (1967)], quoting Powell v. Alabama, 287 U.S. 45, 69 (1932). When the parent is indigent, lacking in education, and easily intimidated by figures of authority, the imbalance may well become insuperable. . . .

The problem of inadequate representation is painfully apparent in the present case. . . .

At the termination hearing, the State's sole witness was the county worker who had met petitioner on the one occasion at the prison. This worker had been assigned to William's case in August 1977, yet much of her testimony concerned events prior to that date; she represented these events as contained in the agency record. . . . Petitioner failed to uncover this weakness in the worker's testimony. That is hardly surprising, for there is no indication that an agency record was introduced into evidence or was present in court, or that petitioner or the grandmother ever had an opportunity to review any such record. The social worker also testified about her conversations with members of the community. In this hearsay testimony, the witness reported the opinion of others that the grandmother could not handle the additional responsibility of caring for the fifth child. . . . There is no indication that these community members were unavailable to testify, and the country attorney did not justify the admission of the hearsay. Petitioner made no objection to its admission. . . .

. . . An experienced attorney might have translated petitioner's reaction and emotion into several substantive legal arguments. The State charged petitioner with failing to arrange a "constructive plan" for her child's future or to demonstrate a "positive response" to the Department's intervention. A defense would have been that petitioner had arranged for the child to be cared for properly by his grandmother, and evidence might have been adduced to demonstrate the adequacy of the grandmother's care of the other children. The Department's own "diligence" in promoting the family's integrity was never put in issue during the hearing, yet it is surely significant in light of petitioner's incarceration and lack of access to her child. Finally, the asserted willfulness of petitioner's lack of concern could obviously have been attacked since she was physically unable to regain custody or perhaps even to receive meaningful visits during 21 of the 24 months preceding the action.

Petitioner plainly has not led the life of the exemplary citizen or model parent. It may well be that if she were accorded competent legal representation, the ultimate result in this particular case would be the same. But the issue before the Court is not petitioner's character; it is whether she was given a meaningful opportunity to be heard when the State moved to terminate absolutely her parental rights. In light of the unpursued avenues of defense, and of the experience petitioner underwent at the hearing, I find virtually incredible the Court's conclusion today that her termination proceeding was fundamentally fair. To reach that conclusion, the Court simply ignores the defendant's obvious inability to speak effectively for herself, a factor the Court has found to be highly significant in past cases. . . .

I respectfully dissent.

[Dissenting opinion of JUSTICE STEVENS omitted.]

Note: Adding Lawyers: A Functional Approach

You may be wondering how Ms. Lassiter got her case all the way to the United States Supreme Court without a lawyer. At the close of the termination proceeding, the trial judge informed her of the right to appeal, and gave her the name and address of the North Central Legal Assistance

Program, a free legal aid office for indigents. She contacted them immediately after the hearing. The record is silent about why the judge did not inform her of the availability of free counsel before the hearing.

In their brief to the Supreme Court, Lassiter's attorneys emphasized three ways in which a lawyer could have helped her present her case: by effectively cross-examining the social worker, who was the only witness against her; by contesting the accuracy and hearsay nature of the secondhand and carelessly maintained records of the social service agency; and by helping her and her mother tell their side of the story on direct examination. As it was, Ms. Lassiter delivered most of her direct testimony in response to impatient and sometimes hostile questions by the court.

The National Center on Women and Family Law, Inc., framed the ways in which counsel could significantly decrease the risk of an erroneous decision: 1) by presenting defenses that the parent would be unlikely to come up with on her own; 2) by insuring that the state's burden of proof is met and supported by reliable evidence; and 3) by protecting the client against bias and impropriety. Excerpts from the *Lassiter* briefs and transcripts offer concrete examples of these points. See Elizabeth G. Thornburg, The Story of *Lassiter:* The Importance of Counsel in an Adversary Setting, in Kevin M. Clermont, Civil Procedure Stories 489 (2004).

The adversary courtroom setting of *Lassiter* makes the absence of a lawyer very striking. Think about a lawyer's due process role in other kinds of hearings and proceedings. A related case study is Lucie White, Subordination, Rhetorical Survival Skills, and Sunday Shoes: Notes on the Hearing of Mrs. G., 38 Buff. L. Rev. 1 (1990). She tells the story of a poor woman engaged in an administrative hearing at a welfare office, and asks whether there might be a humanist model of due process that would allow more meaningful participation by the clients in the decisions that affect their lives.

Finally, for a view that the occasional introduction of counsel at hearings meant to be informal is not an unmixed blessing, see Richard Lempert & Karl Monsma, Lawyers and Informal Justice: The Case of a Public Housing Eviction Board, 51 Law & Contemp. Probs. 135 (1988).

In M.L.B. v. S.L.J., 519 U.S. 102 (1996), the Court faced another case terminating a mother's parental interests in her children. Under Mississippi procedures, the mother had a judicial hearing and was represented by counsel. An appeal was allowed from this procedure, but only upon payment of the costs of preparing a record. In this case, that would be over two thousand dollars.

M.L.B. argued in the Supreme Court that conditioning her right to appeal on payment of this sum when she was indigent denied her due process of law. Citing *Lassiter* for the proposition that "the interest of parents in their relationship with their children is sufficiently fundamental to come within the finite class of liberty interests protected by the Fourteenth Amendment," 519 U.S. at 108, the Court held that a transcript must be provided to M.L.B. Read together, the two cases would seem to assure a transcript but not a lawyer to use it effectively. How can you reconcile these cases? Is this a case in which the identity of the judge might make a difference in the outcome?

Note: Lawyers and Due Process

In the problem case of *The Well-Meaning Legislator*, would you design a process with lawyers in it? At what point are lawyers necessary to fundamental fairness? One way to think about this is to consider the place of the adversary tradition, which assures each side an appropriate chance to present its case. In our civil procedure, the adversary tradition is linked to a much grander principle, the rule of law—that is, the impersonal application of generally accepted principles to disputes. Both are embraced in the deathless words of due process forbidding the government to deprive any person of "life, liberty or property without due process of law."

Due process links the adversary tradition to the rule of law in several ways. For example, the accurate application of law depends on our knowing the truth about the underlying facts of the particular case. The expression of and competition between the adversaries' ideas is thought by many observers to be the best (or the most culturally compatible) means for learning the truth. Moreover, the effort to apply objective legal principles lends an appearance of equal treatment to the adversary tournament, which can enhance the satisfaction of the contestants.

Yet despite their linkage, the rule of law and the adversary tradition are sometimes rivals. The latter seeks to gratify the individual by glorifying her procedural rights while the former focuses on the whole society or its leadership by seeking to enforce society's substantive commands.

This rivalry has economic and ethical dimensions. In economic terms, the decisional process is a scarce resource. A limited amount of time and treasure can be invested in the resolution of any dispute. Thus, the value of any substantive right must be discounted by the cost of enforcement: If the cost to the individual is too high, the "right" is a deception and the game is unfair and ungratifying. But if the cost to the public is exorbitant, the right is contrary to the general interest. Consequently, if we are to be effective in the enforcement of substantive law, we cannot be too fastidious about costly adversary procedures; and if we are to provide fair opportunity for adversary competition, we cannot be excessively demanding about the absolute accuracy and consistent application of substantive principles.

The ethical aspect of the uneasy relationship between the adversary tradition and the rule of law lies in the ambivalent role of professional advocates. If duty to client is unqualified, the advocate would be bound to subvert the process by purposefully twisting the law. On the other hand, if the lawyer's duty to the law is absolute, the adversary relationship would be undermined by self-defeating advocacy. This particular tension is beyond complete reconciliation, and it is complicated by the fact that legal rules are often ambiguous. Even if the lawyer's duty to the law is absolute, it is not at all obvious what obligations would follow from such absolute fidelity. Alternatively, if the lawyer's duty to the client is absolute, legal indeterminacy can make it difficult to identify the boundaries of a client's entitlements, and thus difficult to say how far it is fair to push for that client. Add to this the fact that we are a culturally and morally pluralistic society and you will begin to grasp the depth of the tensions that define the role of professional advocates. See Norman W. Spaulding, Reinterpreting Professional Identity, 74 U. Colo. L. Rev. 1 (2003).

The advocate's skills apply to both the adversary tradition and the rule of law ideal. As the client's representative, the lawyer should maintain a professional detachment in order to present the case at the level of abstraction needed to apply the law, and, of course, to say "no" to the client when the law so requires. Also, the advocate's learning and verbal skill may influence the selection of the legal principle to be applied by judge and jury. The blend of the adversary tradition and the rule of law that makes due process is thus further intertwined with the development and availability of professional skills, attitudes, and learning.

1. Access to Lawyers: The Price of Advice

If the outcome of *Lassiter* (no lawyer at state expense unless the judge so orders) disturbs you, what do you propose as a solution? Legislative action? An appeal to private attorneys to handle such cases pro bono? Mandatory referral to a legal aid attorney?

Rather than have the loser pay the fees of the prevailing party, the so-called American Rule is that each party in a lawsuit bears its own attorneys' fees. In refusing to award fees where there was deliberate infringement of a valid trademark, the Supreme Court strongly reaffirmed the American Rule: "[S]ince litigation is at best uncertain one should not be penalized for merely defending or prosecuting a lawsuit, and . . . the poor might be unjustly discouraged from instituting actions to vindicate their rights. . . . Also, the time, expense and difficulties of proof inherent in litigating the question of what constitutes reasonable attorney's fees would pose substantial burdens for judicial administration." Fleischman Distilling Co. v. Maier Brewing Co., 366 U.S. 714, 718 (1967).

But the American Rule is riddled with statutory exceptions on both the federal and state level, and it is increasingly common for service and commercial contracts of all kinds to include a clause providing that in the case of litigation, the loser will pay attorneys' fees. Moreover, there have been recent proposals for civil justice reform that include a "loser pays" rule in all cases. The proponents argue that this reform is necessary to prevent plaintiffs from filing insubstantial suits in the hope that defendants will settle to avoid the expense of defending the action. Opponents, which include the ABA section on litigation, argue that the rule would deter many meritorious lawsuits and impose a regressive tax on the right to litigate.

Regardless of how the fees are paid, they must be "reasonable," insofar as the legal profession treats the charging of unreasonable fees as a matter of ethics. The Bar of every state has adopted a code that includes some provision similar to that of the ABA Model Rules of Professional Conduct:

Rule 1.5(a) Fees

(a) A lawyer shall not make an agreement for, charge, or collect and unreasonable fee or an unreasonable amount for expenses. The factors to be considered in determining the reasonableness of a fee include the following:

(1) the time and labor required, the novelty and difficulty of the questions involved, and the skill requisite to perform the legal service properly;

(2) the likelihood, if apparent to the client, that the acceptance of the particular employment will preclude other employment by the lawyer;

(3) the fee customarily charged in the locality for similar legal services;

(4) the amount involved and the results obtained;

(5) the time limitations imposed by the client or by the circumstances;

(6) the nature and length of the professional relationship with the client;

(7) the experience, reputation, and ability of the lawyer or lawyers performing the services; and

(8) whether the fee is fixed or contingent.

a. The Contingent Fee

Contingent fee contracts are common for plaintiffs in the collection of commercial debts, personal injury claims, treble damage antitrust suits, minority shareholder litigation, condemnation proceedings, and will contests. Prospective clients usually welcome the contingent fee not only because it relieves them of the immediate burden of litigation costs, but also because they perceive that lawyers having a stake in their claims will be more aggressive.

Other observers have complained of this aggression, attributing to it certain unethical side effects such as the improper coaching of witnesses. On the other hand, the lawyer on contingent fee is sometimes accused of selling out his client by premature settlement of large claims. And even where there is no early settlement, critics have assailed contingent fee agreements according to which lawyers sometimes take over 40 percent of the plaintiff's damage award.

Although the professional codes of most states and the ABA Model Rules generally approve contingent fee arrangements in all but domestic relations and criminal cases, e.g., Model Rule 1.5, there is widespread unease with the practice.

Dissatisfaction with contingency fees that offer huge windfalls to some lawyers has prompted the Manhattan Institute in Washington to propose an alternative scheme. The proposal—endorsed by over two dozen prominent lawyers across a wide political spectrum—would give defendants in civil suits a chance to make an early settlement offer. If the offer was accepted, compensation to the lawyers would be limited to an hourly fee or modest share of the gross. If the offer was refused, it would set a baseline on which contingency fees would be calculated. Thus, for example, if the defense offers $90,000 but is refused, and the case ultimately settles for $100,000, then the most plaintiff's lawyer could charge would be a reasonable hourly fee for the work done up to the time of the first offer, plus a contingent percentage of $10,000—the difference between the offer and the final settlement figure. See Peter Passell, Contingency Fees in Injury Cases Under Attack by Legal Scholars, N.Y. Times, Feb. 11, 1994, at A-1. Compare Fed. R. Civ. P. 68, discussed in Chapter 4.

b. Other Methods for Providing Legal Services

i. Government-Provided Legal Services

Even if the American Rule means you don't have to pay the other side's fees if you lose, you still have to "pay to play"—whether by contingency fee or some other arrangement, you have to pay a lawyer to represent you. As part of the War on Poverty in the 1960s, the federal government established civil legal services offices for those unable to pay. The Legal Services Corporation Act once was funded at over $100 million dollars a year to provide legal help to the indigent through a network of legal aid agencies spread over the country.

The early years of Legal Aid were turbulent because, for instance, poverty lawyers and their clients sued state institutions in "test" cases and, in the minds of some, stirred up litigation and cost to the taxpayers without regard to the overall needs of the community. Think, for instance, of the *Fuentes* case described earlier in this chapter. Without legal aid lawyers, Ms. Fuentes would never have fought the repossession of her stove and stereo all the way to the U.S. Supreme Court. Similarly, Ms. Lassiter appealed the termination of her parental rights with the help of lawyers paid by the federal government.

As the Legal Aid program has matured, its first conservative critics, concerned about subsidizing law reform and class warfare, have in some instances been replaced by those who charge that the original ideals of the program have not been realized, or even that they have been betrayed. For critical analyses of the Legal Aid program and community lawyering, see Gary Bellow, Turning Solutions into Problems: The Legal Aid Experience, 34 NLADA Briefcase 106 (1977); Gerald P. Lopez, Rebellious Lawyering: One Chicano's Vision of Progressive Law Practice (1992); Ann Southworth, Taking the Lawyer Out of Progressive Lawyering, 46 Stan. L. Rev. 213 (1993). The problems with the legal aid system pointed out by Gary

Bellow are several. First, most cases dealt with in legal services offices are treated perfunctorily, unless the client's case presents an interesting or unique legal problem. Second, clients have very little control over their cases; lawyers present the options they see and effectively make the decisions. Third, many lawyers too narrowly define the client's concerns, focusing only on the "legal" problem presented. Finally, many cases result in settlements that may not be desirable for the client. Lopez presents an alternative vision of community lawyering, advocating more collaboration between clients and attorneys, and focusing on political mobilization rather than litigation. Southworth, in her critique of Lopez's model, makes additional suggestions to help lawyers facilitate clients' assertion of control and best use their lawyering skills to make a difference.

By the turn of the century, federally funded legal services had been greatly weakened over the years by legislation that cut the budgets of the programs and that restricted sharply the kinds of cases to which federally funded legal services could be applied. Congress cut the budget of the Legal Services Corporation by about one third in 1996 and passed restrictions that prohibited legal aid lawyers from participating in certain kinds of law reform. Some of these restrictions have been struck down because they interfere with the attorney-client relationship and First Amendment rights. See Legal Servs. Corp. v. Velasquez, 531 U.S. 533 (2001) (striking down statutory provisions that prohibited legal aid lawyers representing welfare beneficiaries from raising challenges to welfare rules that led to the denial of benefits for their clients). Writing for the majority in *Velasquez*, Justice Kennedy emphasized that

> [r]estricting LSC attorneys in advising their clients and in presenting arguments and analyses to the courts distorts the legal system by altering the attorney's traditional role. . . . [According to the statute] upon determining [that] a question of statutory validity is present in any anticipated or pending case or controversy, the LSC-funded attorney must cease the representation at once. . . . The Constitution does not permit the Government to confine litigants and their attorneys in this manner. We must be vigilant when Congress imposes rules and conditions which in effect insulate its own laws from legitimate judicial challenge.

531 U.S. at 534, 544, 548. Other restrictions, however, such as the ban on representing undocumented aliens, prison inmates, and accused drug dealers, and the ban on filing class action lawsuits, remain.

Overall, as David Luban describes, the effect is that legal aid and other public interest legal organizations do not even begin to meet the legal needs of the poor:

> Law is a $100 billion per year industry. Of that $100 billion, however, less than $1 billion is dedicated to delivering legal services to low-income Americans. Put in terms of people rather than dollars, there is about one lawyer for every 240 nonpoor Americans, but only one lawyer for every 9,000 Americans whose low income would qualify them for legal aid. Forty-five

> million Americans qualify for civil legal aid, and they are served by a mere 4,000 legal-aid lawyers plus an estimated 1,000 to 2,000 additional poor people's lawyers. Although the myth persists that the very rich and the very poor have no trouble getting lawyers (because the rich have money and the poor qualify for legal aid), and that only the middle class is squeezed, these numbers reveal the true scarcity of lawyers and services available to low-income people. In very real effect, low-income Americans are denied access to justice. The reason is simple: one lawyer per 9,000 clients.

David Luban, Taking Out the Adversary: The Assault on Progressive Public-Interest Lawyers, 91 Cal. L. Rev. 209, 211-213 (2003); see also Erwin Chemerinsky, Closing the Courthouse Doors to Civil Rights Litigants, 5 U. Pa. J. Const. L. 537 (2003). On the history of efforts to ensure legal services for the poor, see Houseman and Perle, Securing Equal Justice for All: A Brief History of Civil Legal Assistance in the United States (2003); Ruth Bader Ginsburg, Access to Justice: The Social Responsibility of Lawyers, In Pursuit of the Public Good: Access to Justice in the United States, 7 Wash. U. J.L. & Pol'y 1 (2001).

ii. *Group Legal Services*

The American Bar Association Model Rules of Professional Conduct encourage limited use of group legal service plans, which are plans that, like group health care plans, enable consumers to purchase legal services at substantial savings by participating in a group program that covers certain legal services. There arguably is a contradiction between the two purposes of many contemporary American plans. One purpose is to use risk spreading to protect individuals from disastrous costs associated with infrequent and uncontrollable events. The other is to assure access, a policy that proceeds from the expectation that everyone covered by the insurance scheme will employ services in regard to matters or controversies that they are able to resolve outside the law. If all beneficiaries of the plans were to claim all their benefits, they would each bear the full cost of their own services plus the costs of administering the plan. Reasonable persons appraising the value of such plans might perhaps choose to "self-insure" and pay their own legal costs as they go, rather than to contribute to the financing of legal expenses voluntarily incurred by others. It may be for this reason that prepaid legal services have not yet been firmly established in this country as a useful social institution. Nevertheless, many bar organizations as well as many social and political groups maintain a continuing interest in the promotion of prepaid plans.

iii. *The Prepayment Movement*

In many European systems, the costs of some kinds of litigation are distributed among large numbers of users and potential users of the legal system through various schemes of insurance, often private but sometimes public.

This approach to the access problem first made an appearance in the United States during the 1930s, when automobile clubs began to provide insurance against legal costs associated with the purchase and use of automobiles. Such insurance plans were often successfully resisted by the organized bar, which enforced rules against advertising, rules against the presence of intermediaries between lawyers and clients, and rules against unauthorized practice of law by intermediary associations or corporations.

Such resistance was overcome in NAACP v. Button, 371 U.S. 415 (1963), which held that Virginia could not prohibit the NAACP from paying the legal costs of its members in school desegregation litigation; the Virginia law prohibiting third-party payment of costs was said in this instance to violate the First Amendment rights of the group members. The principle was also applied in Railroad Trainmen v. Virginia Bar, 377 U.S. 1 (1964), to bar Virginia's attempt to prohibit the union from telling its members which law firms had agreed to give effective representation to members in industrial accident litigation at reduced contingent rates. Today prepaid legal services have become an increasingly significant means by which middle-income consumers gain access to legal services.

iv. *Private Agreements*

Just as parties can waive or modify other rights by contract, they also can contract to pay attorneys' fees that they would otherwise not have to pay. In Burger King v. Rudzewicz, 471 U.S. 462 (1985), which we will study in the next section, a franchise agreement provided that "[i]n any litigation to enforce the terms of this Agreement, the prevailing party shall be paid by the other party all costs, including attorney's fees, incurred as a result of the legal action." This sort of arrangement is common in contracts between commercial actors.

v. *Pro Bono Legal Services*

Lawyers are encouraged to provide legal services on a pro bono basis to clients who cannot afford their services and who may not qualify for legal aid. Should this obligation be a mandatory one? Would making it mandatory violate the lawyer's constitutional rights?

In fact, the American Bar Association's requirements for pro bono are nonmandatory—that is, they take the form of rules *not* subject to disciplinary action. The ethical guideline, embodied in Model Rule of Professional Conduct 6.1, is reprinted below:

> Every lawyer has a professional responsibility to provide legal services to those unable to pay. A lawyer should aspire to render at least (50) hours of pro bono publico services per year. In fulfilling this responsibility, the lawyer should:
>
> (a) provide a substantial majority of the (50) hours of legal services without fee or expectation of fee to:
> (1) persons of limited means; or
> (2) charitable, religious, civic, community, governmental and educational organizations in matters which are designed primarily to address the needs of persons of limited means; and
>
> (b) provide any additional services through:
> (1) delivery of legal services at no fee or substantially reduced fee to individuals, groups or organizations seeking to secure or protect civil rights, civil liberties or public rights, or charitable, religious, civic, community, governmental and educational organizations in matters in furtherance of their organizational purposes, where the payment of standard legal fees would significantly deplete the organization's economic resources or would be otherwise inappropriate;
> (2) delivery of legal services at a substantially reduced fee to persons of limited means; or
> (3) participation in activities for improving the law, the legal system or the legal profession.
>
> In addition, a lawyer should voluntarily contribute financial support to organizations that provide legal services to persons of limited means.

The notes following the Model Rule suggest that states "may decide to choose a higher or lower number of annual service . . . depending upon local needs and local conditions. . . . Services can be performed in civil matters or in criminal matters for which there is no government obligation to provide funds for legal representation. . . . The responsibility set forth in this Rule is not intended to be enforced through disciplinary process." The Model Rules also encourage lawyers to take advisory roles in legal services organizations or law reform efforts where doing so does not create conflicts with the lawyer's clients.

In addition to providing pro bono service on a volunteer basis, lawyers are expected to accept appointments by courts to represent indigent litigants or defendants. ABA Model Rule 6.2 provides that a "lawyer shall not seek to avoid appointment by a tribunal to represent a person except for good cause, such as: (a) representing the client is likely to result in violation of the Rules of Professional Conduct or other law; (b) representing the client is likely to result in an unreasonable financial burden on the lawyer; or (c) the client or the cause is so repugnant to the lawyer as to be likely to impair the client-lawyer relationship or the lawyer's ability to represent the client." See also United States v. Dillon, 346 F.2d 633, 635 (9th Cir. 1965) (holding that lawyers implicitly consent to court-compelled representation by appointment in part because it is an established tradition of lawyers as officers of the court).

Rules governing the appointment of lawyers by courts for service appear in other places as well. The statute providing for in forma pauperis proceedings, 28 U.S.C. § 1915, places a similar obligation on lawyers, though the case law illustrates the nonenforceable nature of these rules. See, e.g., Mallard v. United States Dist. Court, 490 U.S. 296 (1989).

In reality, although there are instances of dedication and altruism, state bars and courts have consistently rejected proposals to create mandatory pro bono programs, and, as Deborah Rhode reports, "few lawyers come close to satisfying the American Bar Association's" 50-hour aspiration. "Recent estimates," she adds, "suggest that most attorneys do not perform significant pro bono work, and that only between ten and twenty percent of those who do are assisting low-income clients." Deborah Rhode, Cultures of Commitment: Pro Bono for Lawyers and Law Students, in Ethics in Practice: Lawyers' Roles, Responsibilities and Regulation 264 (2000); see also Norman W. Spaulding, The Prophet and the Bureaucrat: Positional Conflicts of Interest in Service Pro Bono Publico, 50 Stan. L. Rev. 1395 (1998).

vi. *Lay Competition*

One of the classic arguments for pro bono service is that lawyers enjoy a monopoly on the provision of legal advice. It is a crime in most states to engage in the unauthorized practice of law, and bar associations have aggressively protected their turf by lobbying for strict enforcement of unauthorized practice rules against non-lawyers. In exchange for the monopoly rights, so the argument goes, lawyers should ensure that the needs of those who cannot afford a lawyer are met. But in the gap between the bar's pro bono aspirations and the mass of unmet legal needs among the poor, low-income, and middle classes, there is now a burgeoning market for inexpensive information about the law and legal process produced by non-lawyers. This includes publishers of so-called legal form books and software programs that guide users through the creation of legal instruments such as wills, contracts, real estate leases, and trusts. Lay purveyors have responded to prosecutions for unauthorized practice by arguing that the First Amendment protects their business—that they have a right to produce, and citizens have a right to purchase, information about how to protect one's legal interests.

In a recent case, the producers of Quicken Family Lawyer 8.0 were sued by the Texas Unauthorized Practice of Law Committee for violating the state's unauthorized practice of law statute, which prohibits "the preparation of a pleading or other document . . . or the rendering of any service requiring the use of legal skill or knowledge, such as preparing a will, contract, or other instrument, the legal effect of which . . . must be carefully determined." Unauthorized Practice of Law Comm. v. Parsons Tech., Inc., 1999 WL 47235 (N.D. Tex. 1999). Quicken Family Lawyer is a software program offering over 100 legal forms with instructions on how to fill them out and an "Ask Arthur Miller" feature that prompts a video image of Harvard Law Professor Arthur Miller answering predetermined questions in a variety of legal fields.

The court held that while publishing legal forms with instructions is permissible, Quicken Family Lawyer constitutes unauthorized practice because it helps users choose the "right" form and customizes the forms users select by adding or removing clauses depending on information the user provides. The court further held that the unauthorized practice statute imposes an acceptable burden on the free speech rights of the software producer because the state has a substantial interest in protecting consumers from misleading, unprofessional legal advice.

The decision caused a stir and the Texas legislature quickly amended the statute to provide that the practice of law does not include software programs or similar products, as long as they state that they "are not a substitute for the advice of an attorney." Following the legislature's action, the Fifth Circuit vacated the district court's injunction. Unauthorized Practice of Law Comm. v. Parsons Tech., Inc., 179 F.3d 956 (5th Cir. 1999).

c. Access to Justice as a Fundamental Right

Rather obviously, civil cases can address rights that are at least as powerful as many involved in criminal proceedings. *Lassiter,* which involved child custody, is an excellent example. Thus you can appreciate why some commentators have urged the United States Supreme Court to find a constitutional right to counsel as an extension of equal protection. Indeed, Professor Frank Michelman has argued that litigating, like voting, is "preservative of all rights" and thus may deserve comparable constitutional protection. Frank Michelman, The Supreme Court and Litigation Access Fees: The Right to Protect One's Rights—Part 1, 1973 Duke L.J. 1153.

Professor Deborah Rhode summarizes other commentators' resistance to such arguments as follows:

> As a threshold matter, how could such rights to counsel be limited? If money were no object, what would deter parties from pursuing trivial claims and inflicting unwarranted costs, not only on the state but also on innocent opponents? . . .
>
> A more fundamental concern involves the magnitude of assistance necessary to assure truly effective representation in civil matters. While efforts to measure legal needs present substantial methodological problems, existing studies suggest the scope of the problem. In a national sample of households at or below 125 percent of the government poverty line, 43 percent of those surveyed reported civil legal problems in the last year;

for about 80 percent of those problems, no legal assistance was available. Major areas of unmet need involved claims concerning medical treatment (14.6 percent), public benefits (13.4 percent), utilities (12 percent), family issues (12 percent), discrimination (11 percent), consumer disputes (10 percent) and housing (9 percent). Moreover, these studies have obvious limitations. They measure only subjective perception, and if parties lack awareness of potential claims, these would not be reported. Nor do such surveys generally measure group needs or collective problems, such as environmental risks or inequitable educational financing.

Deborah L. Rhode, Professional Responsibility: Ethics by the Pervasive Method 542-543 (1994).

Absent a right to counsel at state expense, litigants who cannot afford legal counsel must rely on the other methods for paying lawyers—for example, the contingency fee, legal aid, and pro bono—described above.

In the next case, the Supreme Court deals in another setting with the question of whether lawyers are necessary to due process. As you read, think how the Court views the work of lawyers and their contributions to efficiency.

Walters v. National Association of Radiation Survivors

473 U.S. 305 (1985)

JUSTICE REHNQUIST delivered the opinion of the Court. . . .

I

Congress has by statute established an administrative system for granting service-connected death or disability benefits to veterans. See 38 U.S.C. §§ 301 et seq. The amount of the benefit award is not based upon need, but upon service connection—that is, whether the disability is causally related to an injury sustained in the service—and the degree of incapacity caused by the disability. A detailed system has been established by statute and Veterans' Administration (VA) regulation for determining a veteran's entitlement, with final authority resting with an administrative body known as the Board of Veterans' Appeals (BVA). Judicial review of VA decisions is precluded by statute. The controversy in this case centers on the opportunity for a benefit applicant or recipient to obtain legal counsel to aid in the presentation of his claim to the VA. Section 3404(c) of Title 38 provides:

> The Administrator shall determine and pay fees to agents or attorneys recognized under this section in allowed claims for monetary benefits under laws administered by the Veterans' Administration. Such fees— . . .
>
> (2) shall not exceed $10 with respect to any one claim. . . .

Section 3405 provides criminal penalties for any person who charges fees in excess of the limitation of § 3404.

Appellees here are two veterans' organizations, three individual veterans, and a veteran's widow. . . .

Appellees contended in the District Court that the fee limitation provision of § 3404 denied them any realistic opportunity to obtain legal representation in presenting their claims to the VA and hence violated their rights under the Due Process Clause of the Fifth Amendment and under the First Amendment. The District Court agreed with the appellees on both of these grounds, and entered a nationwide "preliminary injunction" barring appellants from enforcing the fee limitation. 589 F. Supp. 1302 (1984). To understand fully the posture in which the case reaches us it is necessary to discuss the administrative scheme in some detail.

Congress began providing veterans pensions in early 1789, and after every conflict in which the Nation has been involved Congress has, in the words of Abraham Lincoln, "provided for him who has borne the battle, and his widow and his orphan." The VA was created by Congress in 1930, and since that time has been responsible for administering the congressional program for veterans' benefits. In 1978, the year covered by the report of the Legal Services Corporation to Congress that was introduced into evidence in the District Court, approximately 800,000 claims for service-connected disability or death and pensions were decided by the 58 regional offices of the VA. Slightly more than half of these were claims for service-connected disability or death, and the remainder were pension claims. Of the 800,000 total claims in 1978, more than 400,000 were allowed, and some 379,000 were denied. Sixty-six thousand of these denials were contested at the regional level; about a quarter of these contests were dropped, 15% prevailed on reconsideration at the local level, and the remaining 36,000 were appealed to the BVA. At that level some 4,500, or 12%, prevailed, and another 13% won a remand for further proceedings. Although these figures are from 1978, the statistics in evidence indicate that the figures remain fairly constant from year to year.

As might be expected in a system which processes such a large number of claims each year, the process prescribed by Congress for obtaining disability benefits does not contemplate the adversary mode of dispute resolution utilized by courts in this country. It is commenced by the submission of a claim form to the local veterans agency, which form is provided by the VA either upon request or upon receipt of notice of the death of a veteran. Upon application a claim generally is first reviewed by a three-person "rating board" of the VA regional office—consisting of a medical specialist, a legal specialist, and an "occupational specialist." A claimant is "entitled to a hearing at any time on any issue involved in a claim. . . ." 38 C.F.R. § 3.103 (c) (1984). Proceedings in front of the rating board "are *ex parte* in nature," § 3.103(a); no Government official appears in opposition. The principal issues are the extent of the claimant's disability and whether it is service connected. The board is required by regulation "to assist a claimant in developing the facts pertinent to his claim," § 3.103(a), and to consider any evidence offered by the claimant. In deciding the claim the board generally will request the applicant's Armed Service and medical records, and will order a medical examination by a VA hospital. Moreover, the board is directed by regulation to resolve all reasonable doubts in favor of the claimant.

After reviewing the evidence the board renders a decision either denying the claim or assigning a disability "rating" pursuant to detailed regulations developed for assessing various disabilities. Money benefits are calculated based on the rating. The claimant is notified of the board's decision and its reasons, and the claimant may then initiate an appeal by filing a "notice of disagreement" with the local agency. If the local agency adheres to its original decision it must then provide the claimant with a "statement of the case"—a written description of the facts and applicable law upon which the board based its determination—so that the claimant may adequately present his appeal to the BVA. Hearings in front of the BVA are subject to the same rules as local agency hearings—they are *ex parte,* there is no formal questioning or cross-examination, and no formal rules of evidence apply. The BVA's decision is not subject to judicial review.

The process is designed to function throughout with a high degree of informality and solicitude for the claimant. There is no statute of limitations, and a denial of benefits has no formal res judicata effect; a claimant may resubmit as long as he presents new facts not previously forwarded. Although there are time limits for submitting a notice of disagreement and although a claimant may prejudice his opportunity to challenge factual or legal decisions by failing to challenge them in that notice, the time limit is quite liberal—up to one year—and the VA boards are instructed to read any submission in the light most favorable to the claimant.

Perhaps more importantly for present purposes, however, various veterans' organizations across the country make available trained service agents, free of charge, to assist claimants in developing and presenting their claims. These service representatives are contemplated by the VA statute, and they are recognized as an important part of the administrative scheme....

In support of their claim that the present statutory and administrative scheme violates the Constitution, appellees submitted affidavits and declarations of 16 rejected claimants or recipients and 24 practicing attorneys, depositions of several VA employees, and various exhibits. The District Court held a hearing and then issued a 52-page opinion and order granting the requested "preliminary injunction." . . .

. . . In holding that the process described above was "fundamentally unfair," the court relied on the analysis developed by this Court in Mathews v. Eldridge, supra, in which we stated the factors that must be weighed in determining what process is due an individual subject to a deprivation. . . .

In applying this test the District Court relied heavily on appellees' evidence; it noted that the veterans' interest in receiving benefits was significant in that many recipients are disabled, and totally or primarily dependent on benefits for their support. 589 F. Supp. at 1315. With respect to the likelihood of error under the present system, and the value of the additional safeguard of legal representation, it first noted that some of the appellees had been represented by service agents and had been dissatisfied with their representation, and had sought and failed to obtain legal counsel due solely to the fee limitation. The court found that absent expert legal counsel claimants ran a significant risk of forfeiting their rights, because of the highly complex issues involved in some cases. VA processes, the court reasoned, allow claimants to waive points of disagreement on appeal, or to waive appeal altogether by failing to file the notice of disagreement; in addition, claimants simply are not equipped to engage in the factual or legal development necessary in some cases, or to spot errors made by the administrative boards. . . .

. . . In defining the process necessary to ensure "fundamental fairness" we have recognized that the Clause does not require that "the procedures used to guard against an erroneous deprivation . . . be so comprehensive as to preclude any possibility of error," Mackey v. Montrym, 443 U.S. 1, 13 (1979), and in addition we have emphasized that the marginal gains from affording an additional procedural safeguard often may be outweighed by the societal cost of providing such a safeguard. . . .

The Government interest, which has been articulated in congressional debates since the fee limitation was first enacted in 1862 during the Civil War, has been this: that the system for administering benefits should be managed in a sufficiently informal way that there should be no need for the employment of an attorney to obtain benefits to which a claimant was entitled, so that the claimant would receive the entirety of the award without having to divide it with a lawyer. . . .

There can be little doubt that invalidation of the fee limitation would seriously frustrate the oft-repeated congressional purpose for enacting it. Attorneys would be freely employable by claimants to veterans' benefits, and the claimant would as a result end up paying part of the award, or its equivalent, to an attorney. But this would not be the only consequence of striking down the fee limitation that would be deleterious to the congressional plan.

A necessary concomitant of Congress' desire that a veteran not need a representative to assist him in making his claim was that the system should be as informal and nonadversarial as possible. This is not to say that complicated factual inquiries may be rendered simple by the expedient of informality, but surely Congress desired that the proceedings be as informal and nonadversarial as possible. The regular introduction of lawyers into the proceedings would be quite unlikely to further this goal. . . .

Knowledgeable and thoughtful observers have made the same point in other language:

> To be sure, counsel can often perform useful functions even in welfare cases or other instances of mass justice; they may bring out facts ignored by or

> unknown to the authorities, or help to work out satisfactory compromises. But this is only one side of the coin. Under our adversary system the role of counsel is not to make sure the truth is ascertained but to advance his client's cause by any ethical means. Within the limits of professional propriety, causing delay and sowing confusion not only are his right but may be his duty. The appearance of counsel for the citizen is likely to lead the government to provide one—or at least to cause the government's representative to act like one. The result may be to turn what might have been a short conference leading to an amicable result into a protracted controversy. . . .
>
> These problems concerning counsel and confrontation inevitably bring up the question whether we would not do better to abandon the adversary system in certain areas of mass justice. . . . While such an experiment would be a sharp break with our tradition of adversary process, that tradition, which has come under serious general challenge from a thoughtful and distinguished judge, was not formulated for a situation in which many thousands of hearings must be provided each month.

Friendly, Some Kind of Hearing, 123 U. Pa. L. Rev. 1267, 1287-1290 (1975).

Thus, even apart from the frustration of Congress' principal goal of wanting the veteran to get the entirety of the award, the destruction of the fee limitation would bid fair to complicate a proceeding which Congress wished to keep as simple as possible. It is scarcely open to doubt that if claimants were permitted to retain compensated attorneys the day might come when it could be said that an attorney might indeed be necessary to present a claim properly in a system rendered more adversary and more complex by the very presence of lawyer representation. It is only a small step beyond that to the situation in which the claimant who has a factually simple and obviously deserving claim may nonetheless feel impelled to retain an attorney simply because so many other claimants retain attorneys. And this additional complexity will undoubtedly engender greater administrative costs, with the end result being that less Government money reaches its intended beneficiaries. . . .

. . . Simple factual questions are capable of resolution in a nonadversarial context, and it is less than crystal clear why *lawyers* must be available to identify possible errors in *medical* judgment. . . .

JUSTICE STEVENS, with whom JUSTICE BRENNAN and JUSTICE MARSHALL join, dissenting.

The Court does not appreciate the value of individual liberty. It may well be true that in the vast majority of cases a veteran does not need to employ a lawyer, and that the system of processing veterans benefit claims, by and large, functions fairly and effectively without the participation of retained counsel. Everyone agrees, however, that there are at least some complicated cases in which the services of a lawyer would be useful to the veteran and, indeed, would simplify the work of the agency by helping to organize the relevant facts and to identify the controlling issues. What is the reason for denying the veteran the right to counsel of his choice in such cases? The Court gives us two answers: First, the paternalistic interest in protecting the veteran from the consequences of his own improvidence; and second, the bureaucratic interest in minimizing the cost of administering the benefit program. I agree that both interests are legitimate, but neither provides an adequate justification for the restraint on liberty imposed by the $10-fee limitation. . . .

II

The Court's opinion blends its discussion of the paternalistic interest in protecting veterans from unscrupulous lawyers and the bureaucratic interest in minimizing the cost of administration in a way that implies that each interest reinforces the other. Actually the two interests are quite different and merit separate analysis.

In my opinion, the bureaucratic interest in minimizing the cost of administration is nothing but a red herring. Congress has not prohibited lawyers from participating in the processing of claims for benefits and there is no reason why it should. The complexity of the agency procedures can be regulated by limiting the number of hearings, the time for argument, the length of written submissions, and in other ways, but there is no reason to believe that the *agency's* cost of administration will be increased because a claimant is represented by counsel instead of appearing *pro se*. The informality that the Court emphasizes is desirable because it no doubt enables many veterans, or their lay representatives, to handle their claims without the assistance of counsel. But there is no reason to assume that lawyers would add confusion rather than clarity to the proceedings. As a profession, lawyers are skilled communicators dedicated to the service of their clients. Only if it is assumed that the average lawyer is incompetent or unscrupulous can one rationally conclude that the efficiency of the agency's work would be undermined by allowing counsel to participate whenever a veteran is willing to pay for his services. I categorically reject any such assumption.

The fact that a lawyer's services are unnecessary in most cases, and might even be counterproductive in a few, does not justify a total prohibition on their participation in all pension claim proceedings. . . .

The paternalistic interest in protecting the veteran from his own improvidence would unquestionably justify a rule that simply prevented lawyers from overcharging their clients. Most appropriately, such a rule might require agency approval, or perhaps judicial review, of counsel fees. It might also establish a reasonable ceiling, subject to exceptions for especially complicated cases. In fact, I assume that the $10-fee limitation was justified by this interest when it was first enacted in 1864. But time has brought changes in the value of the dollar, in the character of the legal profession, in agency procedures, and in the ability of the veteran to proceed without the assistance of counsel. . .

. . . [T]he statute is unconstitutional for a reason that is more fundamental than its apparent irrationality. What is at stake is the right of an individual to consult an attorney of his choice in connection with a controversy with the Government. In my opinion that right is firmly protected by the Due Process Clause of the Fifth Amendment and by the First Amendment.

The Court recognizes that the Veterans' Administration's procedures must provide claimants with due process of law, but then concludes that the constitutional requirement is satisfied because the appellees have not proved that the "probability of error under the present system" is unacceptable. In short, if 80 or 90 percent of the cases are correctly decided, why worry about those individuals whose claims have been erroneously rejected and who might have prevailed if they had been represented by counsel?

The fundamental error in the Court's analysis is its assumption that the individual's right to employ counsel of his choice in a contest with his sovereign is a kind of second-class interest that can be assigned a material value and balanced on a utilitarian scale of costs and benefits. It is true that the veteran's right to benefits is a property right and that in fashioning the procedures for administering the benefit program, the Government may appropriately weigh the value of additional procedural safeguards against their pecuniary costs. It may, for example, properly decide not to provide free counsel to claimants. But we are not considering a procedural right that would involve any cost to the Government. We are concerned with the individual's right to spend his own money to obtain the advice and assistance of independent counsel in advancing his claim against the Government.

In all criminal proceedings, that right is expressly protected by the Sixth Amendment. As I have indicated, in civil disputes with the Government I believe that right is also protected by the Due Process Clause of the Fifth Amendment and by the First Amendment. If the Government, in the guise of a paternalistic interest in protecting the citizen from his own improvidence, can deny him access to independent counsel of his choice, it can change the character of our free society. Even though a dispute with the sovereign may only involve property rights, or as in this case a statutory entitlement, the citizen's right of access to the independent, private bar is itself an aspect of liberty that is of critical importance in our democracy. Just as I disagree with the present Court's crabbed view of the concept of "liberty," so do I reject its apparent unawareness of the function of the independent lawyer as a guardian of our freedom.

In my view, regardless of the nature of the dispute between the sovereign and the citizen—whether it be a criminal trial, a proceeding to terminate parental rights, a claim for social security benefits, a dispute over welfare benefits, or a pension claim asserted by the widow of a soldier who was killed on the battlefield—the citizen's right to consult an independent lawyer and to retain that lawyer to speak on his or her behalf is an aspect of liberty that is priceless. It should not be bargained away on the notion that a totalitarian appraisal of the mass of claims processed by the Veterans' Administration does not identify an especially high probability of error. Unfortunately, the reason for the Court's mistake today is all too obvious. It does not appreciate the value of individual liberty.

Note: The Second Act—Legislation

After ten years of debate, in which the *Radiation Survivors* case was an important spur, Congress passed the Veterans Judicial Review Act of 1988, 102 Stat. 4105 (38 U.S.C. § 4063) (popularly known as the JRA). In sum, the JRA established a Court of Veterans' Appeals (CVA) that was empowered to review the previously final decisions of the Board of Veterans' Appeals, and also made the decisions of the CVA subject to review by the U.S. Court of Appeals for the Federal Circuit.

In removing the $10 cap on the cost of representation, Congress responded to hearings replete with stories of injured veterans denied their rights because they could not negotiate the intricacies of hearings without representation and because there was no appeal from unjust adverse decisions. S. Rep. No. 418, 100th Cong., 2d Sess. (1988).

For a full discussion of the intricacies of the law, see Barton F. Stichman, The Veterans' Judicial Review Act of 1988: Congress Introduces Courts and Attorneys to Veterans' Benefit Proceedings, 23 Clearinghouse Rev. 515 (1989). He summarizes the attorneys' fees provisions as follows:

> For services rendered in cases appealed to the CVA, the appellant and his or her representative are free to negotiate any fee agreement they desire . . . [though] the advocate must file a copy of the fee agreement with the CVA which may order a reduction if it finds that the fee agreed upon is "excessive or unreasonable." The CVA need not take affirmative action to approve a fee agreement. CVA review of the reasonableness of particular fee agreements can be initiated by motion of the CVA itself or by one of the parties, including apparently, the VA. A decision by the CVA on the reasonableness of a fee is final and cannot be appealed to any other court.

Note: Further Radiation Survivors *Proceedings in the Lower Courts*

The Supreme Court found that the fee-cap statute was not unconstitutional on its face, leaving open the question of whether it might be unconstitutionally applied. On remand, Federal District Judge Marilyn Hall Patel ruled the fee cap unconstitutional when applied to a particular type of plaintiff, notably those not covered by the Veteran's Review Act of 1988:

> On remand, plaintiffs amended their complaint to challenge the constitutionality of the fee limit as applied to claimants with service-connected disability or death ("SCDD") compensation claims based on exposure to

> ionizing radiation. This court granted plaintiffs' motion for certification of a class consisting of "all past, present and future ionizing radiation [IR] claimants who have, or will have, some form of 'active' claim relating to SCDD benefits before the VA." National Assn. of Radiation Survivors v. Walters, 111 F.R.D. 595, 598 (N.D. Cal. 1986) ("NARS III"). After extensive pretrial proceedings, the matter was tried to the court over a period of nearly two months. The trial included testimony by numerous expert witnesses regarding the medical, scientific and legal complexities characteristic of ionizing radiation claims.
>
> During and after the trial Congress worked to change the manner in which veterans' claims were adjudicated and reviewed. After adoption of the Veterans' Judicial Review Act of 1988, Pub. L. No. 100-687, 102 Stat. 4105 (1988), the parties went to great lengths to settle this action in light of the new legislation. Ultimately, the efforts to settle were unsuccessful and the parties returned to this court for a decision on the merits based upon the trial record and other post-trial submissions. . . .
>
> . . . Applying the *Mathews* test to the evidence in the record regarding IR claims, the court concludes as a matter of law both that the "private interest" at stake in IR claims is great and that the risk of erroneous deprivation of that interest is high. *Mathews*, 424 U.S. at 335.
>
> The court further concludes that those features of the existing adjudication procedure which are intended to safeguard the interests of the IR claimant in fact do not serve that purpose. Specifically, the court concludes that the regulatory presumptions in favor of the client, the supposedly informal and non-adversarial nature of the VA adjudication procedure for IR claims, and the availability of service representatives from volunteer veterans organizations do not contribute in any significant way to ensuring that the legitimate interests of the claimant are protected and that IR claims are properly adjudicated.
>
> In addition, the court concludes, based on the above findings of fact, that allowing IR claimants access to attorneys would be of great value as a procedural safeguard. Attorneys would provide extremely valuable and presently unavailable assistance to claimants in such key areas as factual development, marshalling of expert opinion on scientific and medical issues in dispute and effective utilization of statutorily guaranteed procedural rights. Volunteer service representatives are not effectively providing such assistance to claimants.

Nat'l Ass'n of Radiation Survivors v. Derwinski, 782 F. Supp. 1392, 1394, 1407-1408 (N.D. Cal. 1991).

The final act of the due process drama occurred in the Ninth Circuit when it reversed Judge Patel in a long opinion that considered her specific findings and compared them to the observations of the Supreme Court in *Walters.* Nat'l Ass'n of Radiation Survivors v. Derwinski, 994 F.2d 583 (9th Cir. 1992), *cert. denied sub nom.* Nat'l Ass'n of Radiation Survivors v. Brown, 114 S. Ct. 634 (1993). Typical of the court's opinion is the following passage:

> The Supreme Court in *Walters* stated that it is less than crystal clear why *lawyers* must be available to identify possible errors in *medical* judgment.

Walters, 473 U.S. at 330. The district court found that IR claims present many tasks for which attorneys particularly are well suited. Attorneys could secure government documents with relevant information, help claimants avoid procedural errors, enhance the effective use of medical and scientific experts, conduct detailed factual development, and prepare briefs. *Derwinski*, 782 F. Supp. at 1406. The government concedes that attorneys could assist with a number of tasks but asserts that this does not indicate that lawyers are *necessary* to ensure procedural fairness in the adjudication of IR claims. See *Walters*, 473 U.S. at 331.

In support of its finding, the district court stated that "evidence demonstrates that IR claimants who employ attorneys have had significantly higher success rates than those relying on service representatives." *Derwinski*, 782 F. Supp. at 1407. The evidence referenced in that quote showed that in IR claims handled by lawyers the claims were granted in 5 out of 31 cases (16%) while in IR claims not handled by lawyers the claims were granted in 35 out of 5,456 cases (.6%).

Note: Tennessee v. Lane

So far, we have talked about access to the courts in terms of access to counsel, notice, and the right to be heard. But the right of "access" can be impaired in even more basic ways. Consider the case of George Lane. He is a paraplegic and uses a wheelchair. In August 1998, he was compelled to appear in county court in Tennessee to face two misdemeanor criminal charges. When he arrived at the courthouse, he learned that all the courtrooms were located on the second floor and that the building had no elevator, so he left his wheelchair and dragged himself up two flights of stairs to get to the courtroom. When he arrived for his second appearance in October, he refused to drag himself up again, sending word to the court that he would not crawl to the courtroom and that he did not want to put his safety at risk by being carried up by police officers. The court ordered Lane arrested and held in contempt for "failure to appear." In subsequent proceedings, to avoid another contempt citation, Lane remained at the bottom of the stairs while his attorney shuttled between him and the courtroom.

Lane then filed a separate civil action against the state of Tennessee, contending that the state violated Title II of the Americans with Disabilities Act ("ADA"), which requires that public entities ensure access to disabled persons. The State moved to dismiss the case on the ground that it is immune from suits brought by private individuals to enforce federal law. See U.S. Const. amend. XI. However, the Supreme Court upheld the district court's denial of the motion to dismiss, emphasizing that the right of access to the courts under the Due Process Clause is a fundamental right and that Congress has the power under Section 5 of the Fourteenth Amendment to legislate to ensure that disabled persons are not deprived of this fundamental right. Tennessee v. Lane, 541 U.S. 509 (2004). See also id. at 523 (discussing defendant's Sixth Amendment right of confrontation "to be present at all stages of the trial where his absence might frustrate the fairness of the proceedings"). The Court cited a report before Congress in 1990 when it voted on the ADA showing that "76% of public services and programs housed in state-owned buildings were inaccessible to and unusable by persons with disabilities." Id. at 527. The Court concluded that the ADA's duty to accommodate disabled persons in gaining access to public facilities "is perfectly consistent with the well-established due process principle that, within the limits of practicability, a State must afford to all individuals a meaningful opportunity to be heard in its courts." Id. at 532 (internal quotation marks and citations omitted). "[O]rdinary considerations of cost and convenience alone cannot justify a State's failure to provide individuals with a meaningful right of access to the courts." Id. at 533 (internal quotation marks and citations omitted).

C. DUE PROCESS AND JURISDICTION: THE LIMITS OF STATE POWER OVER PERSONS AND PROPERTY

Problem Case: An Unhappy Wanderer

Luckett, a Californian returning from a visit in Arizona, left the interstate highway to visit a rest stop, the Last Chance Curio Shop. Last Chance is advertised on billboards along the highway. It specializes in the sale of Navajo wares and Navajo replicas made in Hong Kong. Luckett passed up the curios, made use of the plumbing facility, and purchased a soft drink from the vending machine.

Shortly after she left Last Chance and just inside the California border, the bottle exploded, causing her car to leave the road. She was injured and her new car was totally wrecked.

Luckett would like to sue Last Chance and/or the Arizona bottler in a California court. In contemplation of such an action, her counsel has conducted an investigation that reveals that:

1. Last Chance gets its Hong Kong curios from a Long Beach, California, importer. Title probably passes to Last Chance in Hong Kong.
2. The Arizona bottler is actually a franchise of a large nationwide soft drink company that is headquartered in Los Angeles. The beverages sold in Last Chance's vending machine are made and bottled in Arizona, and the Arizona bottler has never visited the franchisor's California offices. Yet the franchise contract provides that California law governs it, and that financial transactions and other paperwork must be forwarded to the Los Angeles headquarters.

Can California constitutionally exercise jurisdiction over this claim against the Arizona bottler? Against Last Chance? If a shipment of Last

Chance's goods can be found in Long Beach? If Luckett can serve process on the bottler's headquarters in Los Angeles?

1. Introduction: State Boundaries and Jurisdiction

The concept that courts must have jurisdiction—the authority to speak—is rooted in the State's power over the people and property within its boundaries. Until well into the sixteenth century, the physical expression of this power occurred when plaintiffs used the writ of *capias ad respondendum,* which directed the sheriff to arrest defendants and bring them before the court. Today service of process substitutes for bodily seizure—but behind that innocent-looking piece of paper titled "Summons" stands the full coercive power of the State.

The State is also sovereign over all tangible property located within its borders. When there is a dispute over title, a writ of attachment symbolically seizes the property and gives the court *in rem* jurisdiction to adjudicate the conflicting claims of ownership. In theory, the court has jurisdiction over only the property, or *res,* and not over the people claiming ownership of it. In practice, of course, seizure of the property effectively forces the claimants to come in and defend their interests or suffer a default judgment extinguishing their claims.

Attachment was also the traditional basis for *quasi in rem* jurisdiction, which allowed seizure of a defendant's property even when the property was not related to the claim before the court. Once the court had control of the defendant's property, it could adjudicate the unrelated claim against him—an action for breach of contract, for example—and then, if the defendant lost, order a judicial sale of the property to satisfy the judgment. As with regular *in rem* jurisdiction, a court exercising *quasi in rem* jurisdiction had power over only the property. If the seized property was worth less than the plaintiff's damages on the contract claim, for example, the court had no power to enter an *in personam* judgment against the defendant for the difference.

All three classes of jurisdiction—*capias ad respondendum, in rem,* and *quasi in rem*—are based on ancient notions of territoriality, that is, the State's (and therefore the court's) power over property and persons within its borders. The first case to turn territorial conceptions of jurisdiction into constitutional requirements, and to define these requirements as due process limits on state power, was Pennoyer v. Neff, 95 U.S. 714 (1877), which was technically overruled in 1977, exactly 100 years after it was decided. Shaffer v. Heitner, 433 U.S. 186 (1977). Yet the case remains important because its central holding is still vital—that due process of law is the measure of personal jurisdiction.

We present the *Pennoyer* case through a legal historian's account rather than that of an appellate judge. Think about the differences between the disciplines of law and history in the way facts are stated and used.

2. Pennoyer v. Neff: The Human Drama

Wendy Perdue, Sin, Scandal, and Substantive Due Process: Personal Jurisdiction and Pennoyer Reconsidered

62 Wash. L. Rev. 479, 481-489 (1987)

Our story begins with a young man, Marcus Neff, heading across the country by covered wagon train, presumably to seek his fortune. Neff left Iowa in early 1848 at the age of 24, joining a wagon train of five companies of wagons. At that time, the question of Oregon statehood was being considered in Congress, and there was much speculation that large tracts of the vast, undeveloped land of Oregon would be made available to homesteaders. The speculation proved to be correct and Marcus Neff was one of the earliest settlers to claim land under the Oregon Donation Act.

To qualify for land under the Donation Act, one had to be a citizen living in Oregon and had to submit a request for land by December 1, 1850. Interestingly, Neff's land request was originally dated December 15, 1850, which would have made it too late, but "December" was crossed out and "September" written in above. This is the first instance of many to suggest that events surrounding Pennoyer v. Neff may have been tainted by fraud and deception.

Not surprisingly, registration of a Donation Act claim required a certain amount of paperwork. In addition to the initial claim, the homesteader was required after four years to submit the affidavits of two disinterested persons affirming that the homesteader had cultivated the land for his own use. Neff secured two affidavits, which were submitted prematurely in 1853 and resubmitted in 1856. The 1856 submission should have entitled Neff to receive a patent to the land, but the government was notoriously slow in processing claims, and ten years passed before Neff received his land patent.

Early in 1862 Neff made the unfortunate decision to consult a local Portland attorney, J. H. Mitchell. Although the nature of the legal services is unclear, Neff may have consulted Mitchell in an attempt to expedite the paperwork concerning his land patent. Neff was illiterate, and at the time he consulted Mitchell the government had still not issued his patent. Mitchell, moreover, specialized in land matters. In mid-1862, several months after Neff first consulted Mitchell, another affidavit was filed on Neff's behalf. Several months thereafter Neff received a document from the government certifying that he had met the criteria for issuance of a patent.

Whatever Neff's reasons for seeking Mitchell's legal services, he certainly could have done better in his choice of lawyers. "J. H. Mitchell" was actually the Oregon alias of one John Hipple. Hipple had been a teacher in Pennsylvania who, after being forced to marry the 15-year-old student whom he had seduced, left teaching and took up law. He practiced with a partner for several years, but apparently concluded that it was time to move on to greener pastures. Thus, in 1860 Hipple headed west taking with him four thousand dollars of client money and his then current paramour, a local school teacher. They made their way to California where Hipple abandoned the teacher, ostensibly because she was sick and her medical expenses had become too burdensome, and moved on to Portland, Oregon. There, using the name John H. Mitchell, he quickly established himself as a successful lawyer, specializing in land litigation and railroad right-of-way cases. He also remarried without bothering to divorce his first wife. As one historian has observed, Mitchell's success as a lawyer cannot be attributed to either intellectual or oratorical skills; rather, his strengths included exceptional political instincts, a generous disposition, and a friendly handshake. What he lacked in ethics and ability, he made up for with persistence and desire for success. In his subsequent political career, he became known as a man whose "political ethics justified any means that would win the battle."[33]

Mitchell's ethical standards as a lawyer were no higher than his ethics as a politician. As the *Oregonian* observed: "His political methods are indeed pitched on a sufficiently low scale, but not below his methods as a lawyer." Given Mitchell's reputation, one might at least question whether Neff in fact owed the money Mitchell claimed was due. Neff paid Mitchell $6.50, but Mitchell claimed he was owed an additional $209. Although Mitchell's services were rendered between early 1862 and mid-1863, Mitchell waited several years to take legal action against Neff, perhaps purposely waiting until Neff left the state.

On November 3, 1865, Mitchell filed suit against Neff in Oregon state court, seeking $253.14 plus costs. Mitchell secured jurisdiction under Oregon statute section 55, which provided that if the defendant, after due diligence, cannot be found within the state, he may be served by publication. Mitchell supplied an affidavit in which he asserted that Neff was living somewhere in California and could not be found. Mitchell provided no details as to what he had done to locate Neff, and given Mitchell's lack of scruples, one might wonder whether Neff's whereabouts were indeed unknown to Mitchell and whether Mitchell made any attempt to locate Neff. Notice of the lawsuit was published for six weeks in the *Pacific Christian Advocate,* a weekly newspaper published under the authority of the Methodist Episcopal Church and devoted primarily to religious news and inspirational articles.

In initiating the litigation, Mitchell made what ultimately proved to be a critical mistake. Mitchell's affidavit asserted that Neff owned property, but he did not attach the property at that time. Mitchell most likely neglected this step because Oregon law did not appear to require attachment as a prerequisite for reliance on section 55.

A default judgment in the amount of $294.98 was entered against Neff on February 19, 1866. Although Mitchell had an immediate right to

33. [J. Gaston, The Centennial History of Oregon 1811-1912, at 665 (1912).] Mitchell had an extremely successful political career. He was first elected to the State Senate in 1862, became president of the State Senate in 1864, was seven times a candidate for the United States Senate, and was elected in four of those contests.

execute on the judgment, he waited until early July 1866 to seek a writ of execution, possibly waiting for the arrival of Neff's land patent. The title, which was sent from Washington, D.C. on March 22, 1866, would have taken several months to arrive in Oregon, and thus probably arrived in Oregon shortly before Mitchell sought the writ of execution. Interestingly, although Mitchell had alleged that Neff could not be found, the Oregon land office apparently had no difficulty delivering the patent to Neff.

Under Oregon law, to secure execution one had to obtain a writ of execution and post and publish notice for four weeks. All of the steps were apparently taken. On August 7, 1866, the property was sold at a sheriff's auction for $341.60. Notably, the buyer was not Sylvester Pennoyer, as the Supreme Court opinion and commentators have implied. The property was purchased by none other than J. H. Mitchell, who three days later assigned the property to Sylvester Pennoyer. Pennoyer had much in common with Mitchell. He, like Mitchell, was a Portland lawyer, involved in politics, and active in real estate speculation. There is no evidence available on whether Pennoyer had actual knowledge of, or connection to, the original action, though it is certainly possible. Moreover, since he took title through Mitchell, it is not clear that he should have been treated as a true innocent third-party purchaser.

It appears that for the next eight years Pennoyer peacefully minded his own business, doing those things one would expect of any property owner—he paid the taxes, cut some timber, and sold a small portion of the land. The peace was broken in 1874 when Neff reappeared on the scene. . . .

The case of Neff v. Pennoyer was filed in federal court on September 10, 1874, and the ensuing battle confirms that vindictive and protracted litigation is not a recent phenomenon. Neff apparently had prospered in California. He had settled in San Joaquin with a wife and family, as well as servants, property, and livestock. He was prepared, however, to leave his home in California and move himself, his wife, and his daughter to Oregon for a year to pursue his various legal actions.

3. Pennoyer v. Neff: The Legal Story

Even putting personalities aside, right and justice were clearly with Marcus Neff and nineteenth-century law supplied adequate doctrine for his protection. The lower court decided in his favor by interpreting Oregon's jurisdictional statutes; it found that Mitchell's affidavit describing his efforts to notify Neff failed to meet statutory requirements. Therefore, the default judgment in Mitchell v. Neff was void because it was entered by a court without jurisdiction.

On Pennoyer's appeal to the U.S. Supreme Court, Justice Field brushed aside the lower court's statutory argument but found another jurisdictional defect instead. Mitchell had failed to attach the property *before filing suit*. Establishing a course that held for 100 years, the Court declared: "The authority of every tribunal is necessarily restricted by the territorial limits of the State in which it is established." Pennoyer v. Neff, 95 U.S. at 720. The Court continued:

> [T]he property here in controversy sold under the judgment rendered was not attached, nor in any way brought under the jurisdiction of the court. Its first connection with the case was caused by a levy of the execution. It was not, therefore, disposed of pursuant to any adjudication, but only in enforcement of a personal judgment, having no relation to the property, rendered against a non-resident without service of process upon him in the action, or his appearance therein.

Id. Then, having decided the case, the Court went on to discuss *in personam* jurisdiction more generally:

> [E]very State possesses exclusive jurisdiction and sovereignty over persons and property within its territory. . . . [N]o State can exercise direct jurisdiction and authority over persons or property without its territory. The several States are of equal dignity and authority, and the independence of one implies the exclusion of power from all others. . . . [T]he laws of one State have no operation outside of its territory, except so far as is allowed by comity: . . . no tribunal established by it can extend its process beyond that territory so as to subject either persons or property to its decisions. "Any extension of authority of this sort beyond this limit," says Story, "is a mere nullity, and incapable of binding such persons or property in any other tribunals." Story, Confl. Laws, sect. 539.

Id. at 722-723.

In short, each state's complete power within its own boundaries completely excluded any exercise of extraterritorial jurisdiction by another state. Thus, the limits of judicial power under *Pennoyer* were defined by the dotted lines on a map of the United States. In this rigidly geographical scheme, the distinction between a writ of attachment obtained before judgment to perfect jurisdiction over property and a writ of execution obtained after the fact to enforce an *in personam* judgment assumed constitutional significance.

But Justice Field did not stop with his observations on territoriality and personal jurisdiction. He went on to strike down the state's original action—the entry of "jurisdictionless" judgment—on the ground that it deprived Neff of his property without due process of law.

Justice Field was not speaking in the due process terms that we have dealt with earlier in this chapter—notice and the opportunity to be heard; these, in an unarticulated sense, had been the bases of the lower court opinion. Rather, he established due process as a regulatory canon for the relations among the sovereign states:

> Since the adoption of the Fourteenth Amendment to the Federal Constitution, the validity of such judgments [those rendered against nonresidents] may be directly questioned, and their enforcement in the State resisted, on

> the ground that proceedings in a court of justice to determine the personal rights and obligations of parties over whom that court has no jurisdiction do not constitute due process of law. . . . [A] tribunal [must be] competent by its constitution—that is, by the law of its creation—to pass upon the subject-matter of the suit; and, if that involves merely a determination of the personal liability of the defendant, he must be brought within its jurisdiction by service of process within the State, or his voluntary appearance.

95 U.S. at 733.

In the background of *Pennoyer* was not only the Fourteenth Amendment (adopted less than a decade before the opinion) but also Article IV of the Constitution itself, which requires that "Full Faith and Credit shall be given in each State to the judicial proceedings of every other state." This means that a *valid* judgment of another state or federal court must be enforced according to its terms, without relitigating the underlying claims or defenses. But a judgment entered without obtaining personal jurisdiction over the defendant is invalid and void.

What *Pennoyer* did in the paragraph quoted above was to "identif[y] the test under the Full Faith and Credit clause with the test under the Due Process Clause, making a judgment which would not be enforceable beyond the borders of the state unenforceable within its boundaries. . . ." Philip Kurland, The Supreme Court, the Due Process Clause and the *In Personam* Jurisdiction of State Courts From *Pennoyer* to *Denckla*: A Review, 25 U. Chi. L. Rev. 569 (1958). In short, *Pennoyer* declared that a judgment entered without jurisdiction was unenforceable even by the state that rendered it and even on property within the state's borders. The legal effects of the great old case have reverberated through the twentieth century. Here is the end of the human drama as related by Professor Perdue:

> The opening salvo between Neff and Pennoyer was fired when Neff sued to evict Pennoyer, but the war did not end there. After Pennoyer lost the eviction suit, and costs were awarded against him, he battled bitterly over the amount of those costs. Neff was again the winner, and adding insult to injury, he proceeded to sue Pennoyer again—this time to recover money damages sustained as a result of Pennoyer cutting down timber on the property. Pennoyer counter-claimed to collect property taxes that he had paid from 1866 to 1875. The counterclaim was dismissed and Pennoyer's defense of the damage action proved to be the closest that he got to a victory: the jury found for Neff but awarded only nominal damages.
>
> When the dust had settled, Pennoyer, whom the Supreme Court assumed was a bona fide purchaser for value, was left holding the bag. Pennoyer had purchased the land for "valuable consideration" and paid taxes on it for a number of years, yet he found himself evicted, with nothing to show for his money and subject to suit for trespass for entering the land he thought he owned. There is no evidence that Pennoyer did or could ever recover the loss from anyone.
>
> Following the litigation, Neff disappeared into obscurity; not so Pennoyer and Mitchell. Pennoyer went on to be Governor of Oregon, but he remained bitter about his defeat in Pennoyer v. Neff. Ten years after the

> Supreme Court decision, in his inaugural address as governor, Pennoyer decried that decision as a usurpation of state power. He remained a vociferous critic of the Supreme Court, urging at one point that the entire Court should be impeached, explaining: "We have during this time been living under a government not based upon the Federal Constitution, but under one created by the plausible sophistries of John Marshall. . . . Our constitutional government has been supplanted by a judicial oligarchy."

Perdue, supra, 62 Wash. L. Rev. at 487-488.

By the early twentieth century, the notion that a state's judicial power stopped abruptly at its territorial boundary was being strained by the increasingly interstate character of American society. The modern business corporation and the automobile were two developments that exacerbated the *Pennoyer* restraints; each could inflict damage in a state without necessarily leaving the sort of jurisdictional footprints that *Pennoyer* required. The states responded by enacting statutes based on a theory of "consent" to jurisdiction, which *Pennoyer* had approved.

A Massachusetts statute, for example, declared that by using the state's highways, an out-of-state motorist was deemed to have appointed the state registrar as agent for service of process in actions arising out of accidents on the highways. Jurisdiction under the statute was sustained in Hess v. Pawloski, 274 U.S. 352 (1927). And most states had statutes requiring foreign corporations to appoint a local agent for service of process as a condition of conducting business within the state. If the corporation failed to do so, it was deemed to have appointed a state official, such as the secretary of state, by virtue of undertaking to transact business in the state. The extent and nature of business activities necessary to support this implication of consent to jurisdiction was the subject of considerable litigation. Smolik v. Philadelphia & Reading Co., 222 F. 148 (S.D.N.Y. 1915), *aff'd sub nom.* Penn. Fire Ins. Co. v. Gold Issue Mining Co., 243 U.S. 93 (1917).

The doctrine of implied consent to jurisdiction was a classic example of a "legal fiction" that served to bridge a period of transition in the development of the law. In International Shoe Co. v. Washington, 326 U.S. 310 (1945), the Supreme Court cast those fictions aside, and made explicit the underlying basis of these decisions: due process does not necessarily *require* the States to adhere to the unbending territorial limits on jurisdiction set forth in *Pennoyer*. Burnham v. Superior Court, 495 U.S. 604 (1990).

4. Minimum Contacts and Substantial Justice

International Shoe Co. v. Washington

326 U.S. 310 (1945)

CHIEF JUSTICE STONE delivered the opinion of the Court.

The questions for decision are (1) whether, within the limitations of the due process clause of the Fourteenth Amendment, appellant, a Delaware corporation, has by its activities in the State of Washington rendered itself amenable to proceedings in the courts of that state to recover unpaid contributions to the state unemployment compensation fund exacted by the state statutes, and (2) whether the state can exact those contributions consistently with the due process clause of the Fourteenth Amendment. . . .

In this case notice of assessment for the years in question was personally served upon a sales solicitor employed by appellant in the State of Washington, and a copy of the notice was mailed by registered mail to appellant at its address in St. Louis, Missouri. Appellant appeared specially before the office of unemployment and moved to set aside the order and notice of assessment on the ground that the service upon appellant's salesman was not proper service upon appellant; that appellant was not a corporation of the State of Washington and was not doing business within the state; that it had no agent within the state upon whom service could be made; and that appellant is not an employer and does not furnish employment within the meaning of the statute. . . .

The facts, as found by the appeal tribunal and accepted by the state Superior Court and Supreme Court, are not in dispute. Appellant is a Delaware corporation, having its principal place of business in St. Louis, Missouri, and is engaged in the manufacture and sale of shoes and other footwear. It maintains places of business in several states, other than Washington, at which its manufacturing is carried on and from which its merchandise is distributed interstate through several sales units or branches located outside the State of Washington.

Appellant has no office in Washington and makes no contracts either for sale or purchase of merchandise there. It maintains no stock of merchandise in that state and makes there no deliveries of goods in intrastate commerce. During the years from 1937 to 1940, now in question, appellant employed eleven to thirteen salesmen under direct supervision and control of sales managers located in St. Louis. These salesmen resided in Washington; their principal activities were confined to that state; and they were compensated by commissions based upon the amount of their sales. The commissions for each year totaled more than $31,000. Appellant supplies its salesmen with a line of samples, each consisting of one shoe of a pair, which they display to prospective purchasers. On occasion they rent permanent sample rooms, for exhibiting samples, in business buildings, or rent rooms in hotels or business buildings temporarily for that purpose. The cost of such rentals is reimbursed by appellant.

The authority of the salesmen is limited to exhibiting their samples and soliciting orders from prospective buyers, at prices and on terms fixed by appellant. The salesmen transmit the orders to appellant's office in St. Louis for acceptance or rejection, and when accepted the merchandise for filling the orders is shipped f.o.b. from points outside Washington to the purchasers within the state. All the merchandise shipped into Washington is invoiced at the place of shipment from which collections are made. No salesman has authority to enter into contracts or make collections.

The Supreme Court of Washington was of opinion that the regular and systematic solicitation of orders in the state by appellant's salesmen, resulting in a continuous flow of appellant's product into the state, was sufficient to constitute doing business in the state so as to make appellant amenable to suit in its courts. But it was also of opinion that there were sufficient additional activities shown to bring the case within the rule frequently stated, that solicitation within a state by the agents of a foreign corporation plus some additional activities there are sufficient to render the corporation amenable to suit brought in the courts of the state to enforce an obligation arising out of its activities there. International Harvester Co. v. Kentucky, 234 U.S. 579, 587 [1914]. The court found such additional activities in the salesmen's display of samples sometimes in permanent display rooms, and the salesmen's residence within the state, continued over a period of years, all resulting in a substantial volume of merchandise regularly shipped by appellant to purchasers within the state. . . .

Historically the jurisdiction of courts to render judgment *in personam* is grounded on their *de facto* power over the defendant's person. Hence his presence within the territorial jurisdiction of court was prerequisite to its rendition of a judgment personally binding him. Pennoyer v. Neff, 95 U.S. 714, 733. But now that the *capias ad respondendum* has given way to personal service of summons or other form of notice, due process requires only that in order to subject a defendant to a judgment *in personam*, if he be not present within the territory of the forum, *he have certain minimum contacts with it* such that the maintenance of the suit does not offend "traditional notions of fair play and substantial justice." Milliken v. Meyer, 311 U.S. 457, 463. . . .

Since the corporate personality is a fiction, although a fiction intended to be acted upon as though it were a fact, Klein v. Board of Supervisors, 282 U.S. 19, 24 [1930], it is clear that unlike an individual its "presence" without, as well as within, the state of its origin can be manifested only by activities carried on in its behalf by those who are authorized to act for it. To say that the corporation is so far "present" there as to satisfy due process requirements, for purposes of taxation or the maintenance of suits against it in the courts of the state, is to beg the question to be decided. For the terms "present" or "presence" are used merely to symbolize those activities of the corporation's agent within the state which courts will deem to be sufficient to satisfy the demands of due process. L. Hand, J., in Hutchinson v. Chase & Gilbert, 45 F.2d 139, 141 [2d Cir. 1930]. Those demands may be met by such contacts of the corporation with the state of the forum as make it reasonable, in the context of our federal system of government, to require the corporation to defend the particular suit which is brought there. An "estimate of the inconveniences" which would result to the corporation from a trial away from its "home" or principal place of business is relevant in this connection. Hutchinson v. Chase & Gilbert, supra, 141.

"Presence" in the state in this sense has never been doubted when the activities of the corporation there have not only been continuous and systematic, but also give rise to the liabilities sued on, even though no consent to be sued or authorization to an agent to accept service of process has been given. . . . Conversely it has been generally recognized that the casual presence of the corporate agent or even his conduct of single or isolated items of activities in a state in the corporation's behalf are not enough to subject it to suit on causes of action unconnected with the activities there. To require the corporation in such circumstances to defend the suit away from its home or other jurisdiction where it carries on more substantial activities has been thought to lay too great and unreasonable a burden on the corporation to comport with due process.

While it has been held in cases on which appellant relies that continuous activity of some sorts within a state is not enough to support the demand that the corporation be amenable to suits unrelated to that activity, there have been instances in which the continuous corporate operations within a state were thought so substantial and of such a nature as to justify suit against it on causes of action arising from dealings entirely distinct from those activities.

Finally, although the commission of some single or occasional acts of the corporate agent in a state sufficient to impose an obligation or liability on the corporation has not been thought to confer upon the state authority to enforce it, other such acts, because of their nature and quality and the circumstances of their commission, may be deemed sufficient to render the corporation liable to suit. Cf. . . . Hess v. Pawloski, 274 U.S. 352 (1927). True, some of the decisions holding the corporation amenable to suit have been supported by resort to the legal fiction that it has given its consent to service and suit, consent being implied from its presence in the state through the acts of its authorized agents. But more realistically it may be said that those authorized acts were of such a nature as to justify the fiction. . . .

It is evident that the criteria by which we mark the boundary line between those activities which justify the subjection of a corporation to suit, and those which do not, cannot be simply mechanical or quantitative. The test is not merely, as has sometimes been suggested, whether the activity, which the corporation has seen fit to procure through its agents in another state, is a little more or a little less. International Harvester Co. v. Kentucky, supra, 587. Whether due process is satisfied must depend rather upon the quality and nature of the activity in relation to the fair and orderly administration of the laws which it was the purpose of the due process clause to insure. That clause does not contemplate that a state may make binding a judgment *in personam* against an individual or corporate defendant with which the state has no contacts, ties, or relations. Cf. Pennoyer v. Neff, supra; Minnesota Commercial Assn. v. Benn, 261 U.S. 140 [1923].

But to the extent that a corporation exercises the privilege of conducting activities within a state, it enjoys the benefits and protection of the laws of that state. The exercise of that privilege may give rise to obligations, and, so far as those obligations arise out of or are connected with the activities within the state, a procedure which requires the corporation to respond to a suit brought to enforce them can, in most instances, hardly be said to be undue. . . .

Applying these standards, the activities carried on in behalf of appellant in the State of Washington were neither irregular nor casual. They were systematic and continuous throughout the years in question. They resulted in a large volume of interstate business, in the course of which appellant received the benefits and protection of the laws of the state, including the right to resort to the courts for the enforcement of its rights. The obligation which is here sued upon arose out of those very activities. It is evident that these operations establish sufficient contacts or ties with the state of the forum to make it reasonable and just, according to our traditional conception of fair play and substantial justice, to permit the state to enforce the obligations which appellant has incurred there. Hence we cannot say that the maintenance of the present suit in the State of Washington involves an unreasonable or undue procedure. . . .

We are likewise unable to conclude that the service of the process within the state upon an agent . . . was not sufficient notice of the suit. . . . Nor can we say that the mailing of the notice of suit to appellant by registered mail at its home office was not reasonably calculated to apprise appellant of the suit. . . .

JUSTICE BLACK, concurring.

[I]t is unthinkable that the vague due process clause was ever intended to prohibit a State from regulating or taxing a business carried on within its boundaries simply because this is done by agents of a corporation organized and having its headquarters elsewhere. To read this into the due process clause would in fact result in depriving a State's citizens of due process by taking from the State the power to protect them in their business dealings within its boundaries with representatives of a foreign corporation. Nothing could be more irrational or more designed to defeat the function of our federative system of government. Certainly a State, at the very least, has power to tax and sue those dealing with its citizens within its boundaries, as we have held before. . . . It is true that this Court did use the terms "fair play" and "substantial justice" in explaining the philosophy underlying the holding that it could not be "due process of law" to render a personal judgment against a defendant without notice to and an opportunity to be heard by him. . . .

[This] did not mean thereby that all legislative enactments which this Court might deem to be contrary to natural justice ought to be held invalid under the due process clause. None of the cases purport to support or could support a holding that a State can tax and sue corporations only if its action comports with this Court's notions of "natural justice." I should have thought the Tenth Amendment settled that.

I believe that the Federal Constitution leaves to each State, without any "ifs" or "buts," a power to tax and to open the doors of its courts for its citizens to sue corporations whose agents do business in those States. Believing that the Constitution gave the States that power, I think it a judicial deprivation to condition its exercise upon this Court's notion of "fair play," however appealing that term may be. Nor can I stretch the meaning of due process so far as to authorize this Court to deprive a State of the right to afford judicial protection to its citizens on the ground that it would be more "convenient" for the corporation to be sued somewhere else.

Note: The World After Shoe

As the second great constitutional case on personal jurisdiction, *International Shoe* reaffirmed the due process basis of *Pennoyer* but cut the analysis loose from the mooring of territoriality and set it upon the uncharted sea of "minimum contacts" and "fair play and substantial justice." The Court does emphasize the corporation's continuous contacts with the state, which would indicate that it was "present" in Washington, but also stresses that the state's claim arises from the very activities that provide the basis for jurisdiction. Much ink in opinions and commentary has flowed over cases that fall in between: where the corporation's activities are "continuous and systematic" but do *not* give rise to the liabilities sued upon; or where there are only "isolated items of activity in a state," but these activities are closely connected with the plaintiff's cause of action.

In McGee v. International Life Ins. Co., 355 U.S. 220 (1957), a resident of California had purchased an insurance policy from a company doing business with Californians by mail only. He received premium notices in California and made remittances. Upon his death, the beneficiary sought double indemnity; she brought suit in California, serving the state insurance commissioner and notifying the defendant by registered mail, in accordance with California insurance laws. The insurer defaulted. The beneficiary sought to enforce the resulting judgment by means of an action in Texas. It was held that Texas was obliged to recognize the validity of the California judgment. "California has a manifest interest in providing effective means of redress for its residents when their insurers refuse to pay claims." Id. at 223.

Another famous case was Gray v. American Radiator & Standard Sanitary Corp., 22 Ill. 2d 432, 176 N.E.2d 761 (1961), in which the Illinois court found that it had jurisdiction over an Ohio manufacturer of valves. The defendant had sold his valves to a Pennsylvania manufacturer of water heaters who in turn had sold a heater to an Illinois resident who was ultimately injured by an explosion, allegedly resulting from a defective valve. See also Buckeye Boiler Co. v. Superior Court of Los Angeles County, 71 Cal. 2d 893, 458 P.2d 57 (1969).

The possibilities suggested by *McGee* and *Gray* invited a wave of so-called long-arm statutes, in which states undertook to define the circumstances under which they would attempt to exercise jurisdiction over nonresident defendants. Some states took an expansive approach. See, e.g., Cal. Civ. Proc. Code § 410.10: "A court of this state may exercise jurisdiction on any basis not inconsistent with the Constitution of this state or of the United States." Other states, however, chose not to open the doors of their courts to the full extent permitted by the Constitution. An early model was Ill. Rev. Stat. 1959, ch. 100, para. 17:

> (1) Any person, whether or not a citizen or resident of this State, who in person or through an agent does any of the acts hereinafter enumerated, thereby submits such person, and, if an individual, his personal representative, to the jurisdiction of the courts of this State as to any cause of action arising from the doing of any of such acts:
> (a) The transaction of any business within this State;
> (b) The commission of a tortious act within this State;
> (c) The ownership, use, or possession of any real estate situated in this State;
> (d) Contracting to insure any person, property or risk located within this State at the time of contracting. . . .

For thirty-five years, states expanded their reach over nonresidents, particularly corporate defendants. In only two cases—once believed to be limited to their factual contexts—did the Court deny a state court's effort to exercise jurisdiction. In the first case, Hanson v. Denckla, 357 U.S. 235 (1958), the Court held that a Florida court did not have jurisdiction over a Delaware trust company that had entered into a trust agreement with Dora Donner. Donner was a resident of Pennsylvania when the trust was formed. She later moved to Florida, where she eventually died. Although the trust company continued to perform tasks in connection with the trust after she moved to Florida, the Court concluded that the trustee's tie to Florida was too slight for minimum contacts:

> The unilateral activity of those who claim some relationship with a nonresident defendant cannot satisfy the requirement of contact with the forum State. The application of that rule will vary with the quality and nature of the defendant's activity, but it is essential in each case that there be some act by which the defendant purposefully avails itself of the privilege of conducting activities within the forum State, thus invoking the benefits and protections of its laws.

Id. at 253.

In the second case denying jurisdiction, Kulko v. Superior Court, 436 U.S. 84 (1978), the Court held unconstitutional California's exercise of jurisdiction over a New York father who was sued for divorce, full child custody, and increased child support payments by his former wife, a California resident. California courts had held that by consenting to his daughter's move to California to live with her mother, he had "purposefully availed" himself of the benefits and protections of California. Id. at 89.

The Supreme Court reversed, reasoning that "[a] father who agrees, in the interests of family harmony and his children's preferences, to allow them to spend more time in California than was required under a separation agreement" does not meet the "purposeful availment" standard. Id. at 94. Additionally, the Kulkos' separation was completed in New York, and "basic considerations of fairness point decisively in favor of [that state as the] proper forum for adjudication of this case. . . . It is appellant who has remained in the State of the marital domicile." Id. at 97. Finally, the Court reiterated that "appellant did no more than acquiesce in the stated preference of one of his children to live with her mother in California. This single act is surely not one that a reasonable parent would expect to result in the substantial financial burden and strain of litigating a child-support suit in a forum 3,000 miles away."

Note: General and Specific Jurisdiction

The Court in *Shoe* acknowledged cases in which "the continuous corporate operations within a state were thought so substantial and of such a nature as to justify suit against it on causes of action arising from dealings entirely distinct from those activities." 326 U.S. at 318. The Court later restated this principle in Helicopteros Nacionales de Columbia v. Hall, 466 U.S. 408 (1984), as follows: "Even when the cause of action doesn't arise out of or relate to the foreign corporation's activities in the forum State, due process is not offended by a State's subjecting the corporation to its *in personam* jurisdiction when there are sufficient contacts between the State and the foreign corporation." Id. at 18.

Where the defendant's activities in the forum are not "continuous" and "substantial" enough to satisfy this test, then the Court's minimum contacts and reasonableness analysis is the standard. In these cases it matters whether the dispute "arises out of" or is "related to" the defendant's forum ties. Courts refer to the first type of "dispute-blind" jurisdiction as *general jurisdiction.* The latter "dispute-specific" type of jurisdiction is called *specific jurisdiction.*

For a corporate defendant, the state of incorporation is thought to satisfy the "continuous and systematic" test for general jurisdiction, even if the corporation has its principal place of business in another state. It likely, though not surely, also would be subject to general jurisdiction in the state where its nerve center or main place of business is located. For an individual defendant, the place where she is domiciled has general jurisdiction over her. As Burnham v. Superior Court, 495 U.S. 604 (1990), shows, however, she may also be subject to general (dispute-blind) jurisdiction in any state in which she is served with a summons while physically present in the forum.

Be aware that the term *general jurisdiction* has multiple meanings. It not only refers to the personal jurisdiction concept described in this section, but also can refer to subject matter jurisdiction of some courts. Likewise, the term *limited jurisdiction* may surface in both contexts. It may avoid confusion later to be aware now that the terms have different meanings in different contexts.

The balance of the cases in this chapter, with the exception of *Burnham*, all deal with specific jurisdiction. Why do you suppose the Court has on more occasions reviewed *specific* jurisdiction cases than *general* jurisdiction ones?

The rest of the Supreme Court cases in this chapter were decided since 1978. As you read them, be especially alert to the distinction between statutory and constitutional limits on jurisdiction. You will note that the statutory question is always considered first, since the constitutional issue does not arise unless the state purports to exercise jurisdiction. Note also the different styles of argument and the various roles that statutory arguments play in shaping the constitutional issues.

5. Minimum Contacts and Foreseeability

World-Wide Volkswagen Corp. v. Woodson

585 P.2d 351 (Okla. 1978)

BARNES, J.

This case concerns an original action brought on behalf of World-Wide Volkswagen Corporation and Seaway Volkswagen, Inc., in which the petitioners ask this Court to assume original jurisdiction and issue a writ of prohibition, prohibiting the respondent trial judge, the Honorable Charles S. Woodson, from exercising personal jurisdiction over the petitioners, through service under the Uniform Interstate and International Procedure Act, as adopted in Oklahoma at 12 O.S. 1971, §§ 1701.01 et seq., commonly referred to as the Oklahoma Long-Arm Statute.

The test for applying Long-Arm jurisdiction in Oklahoma is to determine whether the exercise of jurisdiction is authorized by statute, and, if so, whether such exercise of jurisdiction is consistent with the constitutional requirements of due process.

After examining Oklahoma's Long-Arm Statute and the facts present in this case, we conclude that jurisdiction over the nonresident petitioners is authorized by statute.

The facts before us in this case are as follows: In September of 1977, an Audi automobile, driven by Kay Eloise Robinson, was struck in the rear by an automobile being driven by a party not involved in the case before us. Mrs. Robinson and her two children, Eva May and George Samuel, were seriously injured in that collision when the gasoline tank of their Audi automobile ruptured, causing a fire in the passenger compartment of that car. As a result of that collision, manufacturers products liability actions were brought on behalf of Mrs. Robinson, her husband and her children against (1) the manufacturer of the automobile, Volkswagenwerk Aktiengesellschaft; (2) against the U.S. importer of the automobile, Volkswagen of America, Inc.; (3) against the distributor of the automobile, World-Wide Volkswagen Corporation; and (4) against the retail dealer who sold the Robinsons the car, Seaway Volkswagen, Inc.

It is World-Wide Volkswagen, distributor of Audis in Connecticut, New York and New Jersey, and Seaway Volkswagen, Inc., the dealer who sold the car, that petition this Court seeking a writ of prohibition. . . .

In the case before us, the respondents contend that the courts of Oklahoma have jurisdiction over the petitioners because they caused a tortious injury in this State, giving rise to jurisdiction under the provisions of 12 O.S. 1971, § 1701.03(a)(3) or (4).

Title 12 O.S. 1971, § 1701.03, provides in part:

> (a) A court may exercise personal jurisdiction over a person, who acts directly or by an agent, as to a cause of action or claim for relief arising from the person's: . . .
>
> (3) causing tortious injury in this state *by an act or omission in this state;*
>
> (4) causing tortious injury in this state *by an act or omission outside* this state *if he regularly does or solicits business or engages in any other persistent course of conduct, or derives substantial revenue from goods used or consumed or services rendered, in this state.* . . . (Emphasis added.)

While it is true that the alleged acts or omissions of the petitioners allegedly caused tortious injury in this State, none of the acts or omissions alleged took place in this State. The defects in the product allegedly existed at the time the product left the hands of the petitioners, and at that time the automobile was not, and had not been, in the State of Oklahoma. We therefore conclude that no acts or omissions on the part of the petitioners took place within the State. In attempting to convince us that acts or omissions of the petitioners did take place within the State, the respondents rely on Gray v. American Radiator & Standard Sanitary Corp., 22 Ill. 2d 432, 176 N.E.2d 761 (1961).

We do not find the analysis used in Gray v. American Radiator, supra, persuasive. In that case, the Illinois Supreme Court was interpreting a provision of the Illinois Revised Statutes which provided that a nonresident, who either in person or through an agent *commits a tortious act within Illinois,* submits to the jurisdiction of Illinois, and may be served by means of the State Long-Arm Statute. In determining whether the manufacturer of a defective safety valve, which was allegedly defective at the time of manufacture in Ohio, committed a "tortious act" in the State of Illinois, the Court held that a tort had been committed within the jurisdiction because the injury which resulted from the defect occurred in Illinois. In so ruling, the Court held that the place of a wrong is where the last event necessary to render the actor liable takes place, and that the last act to render the manufacturer liable was the sustaining of an injury in Illinois by the plaintiff.

Our statute is *unlike* the Illinois statute. The Illinois statute merely requires that a tortious act be committed within Illinois. The Illinois court ruling makes a party subject to Illinois jurisdiction if his acts ultimately result in tortious injury within Illinois. Our statute requires more than the occurrence of tortious injury within the State before a party is subject to personal jurisdiction. . . .

. . . Accordingly, we hold that the acts or omissions of the petitioners, which are alleged in the petition, were not acts or omissions in this State, and therefore no power to exercise personal jurisdiction over the petitioners existed by virtue of the provisions of 12 O.S. 1971, § 1701.03(a)(3).

We next consider whether the power to exercise personal jurisdiction over the petitioners existed by virtue of 12 O.S. 1971, § 1701.03(a)(4). . . .

In the case before us, the product being sold and distributed by the petitioners is by its very design and purpose so mobile that petitioners can foresee its possible use in Oklahoma. This is especially true of the distributor, who has the exclusive right to distribute such automobile in New York, New Jersey and Connecticut. The evidence presented below demonstrated that goods sold and distributed by the petitioners were used in the State of Oklahoma, and under the facts we believe it reasonable to infer, given the retail value of the automobile, that the petitioners derive substantial income from automobiles which from time to time are used in the State of Oklahoma. This being the case, we hold that under the facts presented, the trial court was justified in concluding that the petitioners derive substantial revenue from goods used or consumed in this State. . . .

[The court then concluded that this assertion of jurisdiction did not violate due process.]

Notes and Questions

1. The Oklahoma Supreme Court opinion first examines the Oklahoma long-arm statute before turning to the constitutional analysis. This is the order in which the jurisdiction issue commonly is addressed, as courts prefer to avoid constitutional issues when possible. If the state long-arm statute does not permit the assertion of jurisdiction, then the court need not reach the difficult constitutional question of whether the assertion would violate due process under the Fourteenth Amendment. What are the efficiencies of this approach? What other policy issues support it?

2. As you might imagine, states have strong incentives in this area to draft long-arm measures that go to the limits of due process. Why? Is there any reason a state might not extend its reach to the maximum extent possible?

3. Despite the incentives to draft long-arm measures that go to the limits of due process, not all states have amended their rules to take advantage of this power. In practice you may encounter three types of long-arm rules, two of which look identical on the books. The first is the type that California, to take one example, has adopted. This "one-step" measure simply asserts, as shown supra, that the state courts have jurisdiction "to the limits of due process," thereby collapsing the state law test into the constitutional one. Be aware, however, that state courts still may interpret

such a measure to require a higher, or different, level of contacts than the federal due process case law requires.

Other states list the conditions under which a court will have jurisdiction. Yet some state courts have interpreted this language to go to the limits of due process, making the statute operationally identical to the one-step measures described above. These might be described as "quasi two-step" measures, insofar as they appear to require two separate analyses—state law and constitutional—but case law reveals that the analysis is the same. Why would state courts interpret language in this manner? Have they usurped legislative power in doing so?

Still other states, dwindling in numbers, have a true two-step process and do not interpret their long-arm statutes to be coterminous with the Fourteenth Amendment. Distinguishing between this type of true two-step statute and the quasi two-step statute is impossible without research into the case law interpreting the scope of long-arm jurisdiction.

What kind of long-arm statute did Oklahoma have when it decided *World-Wide*?

We now turn to the United States Supreme Court's review of the Oklahoma decision. Note that the Court does not reconsider whether the Oklahoma court properly interpreted its long-arm statute, only whether that interpretation violated due process. Why? Whose word is final on the issue of a state statute's meaning?

World-Wide Volkswagen Corp. v. Woodson

444 U.S. 286 (1980)

JUSTICE WHITE delivered the opinion of the Court.

The issue before us is whether, consistently with the Due Process Clause of the Fourteenth Amendment, an Oklahoma court may exercise *in personam* jurisdiction over a nonresident automobile retailer and its wholesale distributor in a products-liability action, when the defendants' only connection with Oklahoma is the fact that an automobile sold in New York to New York residents became involved in an accident in Oklahoma. . . .

The facts presented to the District Court showed that World-Wide is incorporated and has its business office in New York. It distributes vehicles, parts, and accessories, under contract with Volkswagen, to retail dealers in New York, New Jersey, and Connecticut. Seaway, one of these retail dealers, is incorporated and has its place of business in New York. Insofar as the record reveals, Seaway and World-Wide are fully independent corporations whose relations with each other and with Volkswagen and Audi are contractual only. Respondents adduced no evidence that either World-Wide or Seaway does any business in Oklahoma, ships or sells any products to or in that State, has an agent to receive process there, or purchases advertisements in any media calculated to reach Oklahoma. In fact, as respondents' counsel conceded at oral argument, Tr. of Oral Arg. 32, there was no showing that any automobile sold by

World-Wide or Seaway has ever entered Oklahoma with the single exception of the vehicle involved in the present case. . . .

As has long been settled, and as we reaffirm today, a state court may exercise personal jurisdiction over a nonresident defendant only so long as there exist "minimum contacts" between the defendant and the forum State. International Shoe Co. v. Washington, supra, at 316. The concept of minimum contacts, in turn, can be seen to perform two related, but distinguishable, functions. It protects the defendant against the burdens of litigating in a distant or inconvenient forum. And it acts to ensure that the States, through their courts, do not reach out beyond the limits imposed on them by their status as coequal sovereigns in a federal system.

The protection against inconvenient litigation is typically described in terms of "reasonableness" or "fairness." We have said that the defendant's contacts with the forum State must be such that maintenance of the suit "does not offend 'traditional notions of fair play and substantial justice.'" International Shoe Co. v. Washington, supra, at 316, quoting Milliken v. Meyer, 311 U.S. 457, 463 (1940). The relationship between the defendant and the forum must be such that it is "reasonable . . . to require the corporation to defend the particular suit which is brought there." 326 U.S., at 317. Implicit in this emphasis on reasonableness is the understanding that the burden on the defendant, while always a primary concern, will in an appropriate case be considered in light of other relevant factors, including the forum State's interest in adjudicating the dispute, see McGee v. International Life Ins. Co., 355 U.S. 220, 223 (1957); the plaintiff's interest in obtaining convenient and effective relief, see Kulko v. California Superior Court, [436 U.S. 84, 92 (1978),] at least when that interest is not adequately protected by the plaintiff's power to choose the forum, cf. Shaffer v. Heitner, 433 U.S. 186, 211, n. 37 (1977); the interstate judicial system's interest in obtaining the most efficient resolution of controversies; and the shared interest of the several States in furthering fundamental substantive social policies, see Kulko v. California Superior Court, supra, at 93, 98.

The limits imposed on state jurisdiction by the Due Process Clause, in its role as guarantor against inconvenient litigation, have been substantially relaxed over the years. As we noted in McGee v. International Life Ins. Co., supra, at 222-223, this trend is largely attributable to a fundamental transformation in the American economy:

> Today many commercial transactions touch two or more States and may involve parties separated by the full continent. With this increasing nationalization of commerce has come a great increase in the amount of business conducted by mail across state lines. At the same time modern transportation and communication have made it much less burdensome for a party sued to defend himself in a State where he engages in economic activity.

The historical developments noted in *McGee*, of course, have only accelerated in the generation since that case was decided.

Nevertheless, we have never accepted the proposition that state lines are irrelevant for jurisdictional purposes, nor could we, and remain faithful to the principles of interstate federalism embodied in the Constitution. The economic interdependence of the States was foreseen and desired by the Framers. In the Commerce Clause, they provided that the Nation was to be a common market, a "free trade unit" in which the States are debarred from acting as separable economic entities. H. P. Hood & Sons, Inc. v. Du Mond, 336 U.S. 525, 538 (1949). But the Framers also intended that the States retain many essential attributes of sovereignty, including, in particular, the sovereign power to try causes in their courts. The sovereignty of each State, in turn, implied a limitation on the sovereignty of all of its sister States—a limitation express or implicit in both the original scheme of the Constitution and the Fourteenth Amendment. Even if the defendant would suffer minimal or no inconvenience from being forced to litigate before the tribunals of another State; even if the forum State has a strong interest in applying its law to the controversy; even if the forum State is the most convenient location for litigation, the Due Process Clause, acting as an instrument of interstate federalism, may sometimes act to divest the State of its power to render a valid judgment. Hanson v. Denckla, supra, at 251, 254.

Applying these principles to the case at hand, we find in the record before us a total absence of those affiliating circumstances that are a necessary predicate to any exercise of state-court jurisdiction. Petitioners carry on no activity whatsoever in Oklahoma. They close no sales and perform no services there. They avail themselves of none of the privileges and benefits of Oklahoma law. They solicit no business there either through salespersons or through advertising reasonably calculated to reach the State. Nor does the record show that they regularly sell cars at wholesale or retail to Oklahoma customers or residents or that they indirectly, through others, serve or seek to serve the Oklahoma market. In short, respondents seek to base jurisdiction on one, isolated occurrence and whatever inferences can be drawn therefrom: the fortuitous circumstance that a single Audi automobile, sold in New York to New York residents, happened to suffer an accident while passing through Oklahoma.

It is argued, however, that because an automobile is mobile by its very design and purpose it was "foreseeable" that the Robinsons' Audi would cause injury in Oklahoma. Yet "foreseeability" alone has never been a sufficient benchmark for personal jurisdiction under the Due Process Clause. . . . In Kulko v. California Superior Court, 436 U.S. 84 (1978), it was surely "foreseeable" that a divorced wife would move to California from New York, the domicile of the marriage, and that a minor daughter would live with the mother. Yet we held that California could not exercise jurisdiction in a child-support action over the former husband who had remained in New York.

If foreseeability were the criterion, a local California tire retailer could be forced to defend in Pennsylvania when a blowout occurs there, see Erlanger Mills, Inc. v. Cohoes Fibre Mills, Inc. 239 F.2d 502, 507 (4th Cir.

1956); a Wisconsin seller of a defective automobile jack could be haled before a distant court for damage caused in New Jersey, Reilly v. Phil Tolkan Pontiac, Inc., 372 F. Supp. 1205 (D.N.J. 1974), or a Florida soft drink concessionaire could be summoned to Alaska to account for injuries happening there, see Uppgren v. Executive Aviation Services, Inc., 304 F. Supp. 165, 170-171 (D. Minn. 1969). Every seller of chattels would in effect appoint the chattel his agent for service of process. His amenability to suit would travel with the chattel. . . .[11]

This is not to say, of course, that foreseeability is wholly irrelevant. But the foreseeability that is critical to due process analysis is not the mere likelihood that a product will find its way into the forum State. Rather, it is that the defendant's conduct and connection with the forum State are such that he should reasonably anticipate being haled into court there. See Kulko v. California Superior Court, supra at 97-98; Shaffer v. Heitner, 433 U.S. at 216; and see id. at 217-219 (Stevens, J., concurring in judgment). The Due Process Clause, by ensuring the "orderly administration of the laws," International Shoe Co. v. Washington, 326 U.S. at 319, gives a degree of predictability to the legal system that allows potential defendants to structure their primary conduct with some minimum assurance as to where that conduct will and will not render them liable to suit.

When a corporation "purposefully avails itself of the privilege of conducting activities within the forum State," Hanson v. Denckla, 357 U.S. [235,] 253 [1958], it has clear notice that it is subject to suit there, and can act to alleviate the risk of burdensome litigation by procuring insurance, passing the expected costs on to customers, or, if the risks are too great, severing its connection with the State. Hence if the sale of a product of a manufacturer or distributor such as Audi or Volkswagen is not simply an isolated occurrence, but arises from the efforts of the manufacturer or distributor to serve, directly or indirectly, the market for its product in other States, it is not unreasonable to subject it to suit in one of those States if its allegedly defective merchandise has there been the source of injury to its owner or to others. The forum State does not exceed its powers under the Due Process Clause if it asserts personal jurisdiction over a corporation that delivers its products into the stream of commerce with the expectation that they will be purchased by consumers in the forum State. Cf. Gray v. American Radiator & Standard Sanitary Corp., 22 Ill. 2d 432, 176 N.E.2d 761 (1961).

11. Respondents' counsel, at oral argument . . . sought to limit the reach of the foreseeability standard by suggesting that there is something unique about automobiles. It is true that automobiles are uniquely mobile . . . , that they did play a crucial role in the expansion of personal jurisdiction through the fiction of implied consent, e.g., Hess v. Pawloski, 274 U.S. 352, 47 S. Ct. 632 (1927), and that some of the cases have treated the automobile as a "dangerous instrumentality." But today, under the regime of *International Shoe,* we see no difference for jurisdictional purposes between an automobile and any other chattel. The "dangerous instrumentality" concept apparently was never used to support personal jurisdiction; and to the extent it has relevance today it bears not on jurisdiction but on the possible desirability of imposing substantive principles of tort law such as strict liability.

But there is no such or similar basis for Oklahoma jurisdiction over World-Wide or Seaway in this case. Seaway's sales are made in Massena, [New York]. World-Wide's market, although substantially larger, is limited to dealers in New York, New Jersey, and Connecticut. There is no evidence of record that any automobiles distributed by World-Wide are sold to retail customers outside this tristate area. It is foreseeable that the purchasers of automobiles sold by World-Wide and Seaway may take them to Oklahoma. But the mere "unilateral activity of those who claim some relationship with a nonresident defendant cannot satisfy the requirement of contact with the forum State." Hanson v. Denckla, supra, at 253.

In a variant on the previous argument, it is contended that jurisdiction can be supported by the fact that petitioners earn substantial revenue from goods used in Oklahoma. The Oklahoma Supreme Court so found, 585 P.2d at 354-355, drawing the inference that because one automobile sold by petitioners had been used in Oklahoma, others might have been used there also. While this inference seems less than compelling on the facts of the instant case, we need not question the court's factual findings in order to reject its reasoning.

This argument seems to make the point that the purchase of automobiles in New York, from which the petitioners earn substantial revenue, would not occur *but for* the fact that the automobiles are capable of use in distant States like Oklahoma. Respondents observe that the very purpose of an automobile is to travel, and that travel of automobiles sold by petitioners is facilitated by an extensive chain of Volkswagen service centers throughout the country, including some in Oklahoma. However, financial benefits accruing to the defendant from a collateral relation to the forum State will not support jurisdiction if they do not stem from a constitutionally cognizable contact with that State. See Kulko v. California Superior Court, 436 U.S. at 94-95. In our view, whatever marginal revenues petitioners may receive by virtue of the fact that their products are capable of use in Oklahoma is far too attenuated a contact to justify that State's exercise of *in personam* jurisdiction over them.

Because we find that petitioners have no "contacts, ties, or relations" with the State of Oklahoma, International Shoe Co. v. Washington, supra, at 319, the judgment of the Supreme Court of Oklahoma is

Reversed.

JUSTICE BRENNAN, dissenting. . . .

. . . [T]he interest of the forum State and its connection to the litigation is strong. The automobile accident underlying the litigation occurred in Oklahoma. The plaintiffs were hospitalized in Oklahoma when they brought suit. Essential witnesses and evidence were in Oklahoma. See Shaffer v. Heitner, 433 U.S. at 208. The State has a legitimate interest in enforcing its laws designed to keep its highway system safe, and the trial can proceed at least as efficiently in Oklahoma as anywhere else.

The petitioners are not unconnected with the forum. Although both sell automobiles within limited sales territories, each sold the automobile which in fact was driven to Oklahoma where it was involved in an accident. It may be true, as the Court suggests, that each sincerely intended to limit its commercial impact to the limited territory, and that each intended to accept the benefits and protection of the laws only of those States within the territory. But obviously these were unrealistic hopes that cannot be treated as an automatic constitutional shield.

An automobile simply is not a stationary item or one designed to be used in one place. An automobile is *intended* to be moved around. Someone in the business of selling large numbers of automobiles can hardly plead ignorance of their mobility or pretend that the automobiles stay put after they are sold. It is not merely that a dealer in automobiles foresees that they will move. The dealer actually intends that the purchasers will use the automobiles to travel to distant States where the dealer does not directly "do business." The sale of an automobile does *purposefully* inject the vehicle into the stream of interstate commerce so that it can travel to distant States. See *Kulko*, 436 U.S. at 94; Hanson v. Denckla, 357 U.S. 235, 253 (1958). . . .

The Court accepts that a State may exercise jurisdiction over a distributor which "serves" that State "indirectly" by "deliver[ing] its products into the stream of commerce with the expectation that they will be purchased by consumers in the forum State." It is difficult to see why the Constitution should distinguish between a case involving goods which reach a distant State through a chain of distribution and a case involving goods which reach the same State because a consumer, using them as the dealer knew the customer would, took them there. In each case the seller purposefully injects the goods into the stream of commerce and those goods predictably are used in the forum State.

Furthermore, an automobile seller derives substantial benefits from States other than its own. A large part of the value of automobiles is the extensive, nationwide network of highways. Significant portions of that network have been constructed by and are maintained by the individual States, including Oklahoma. The States, through their highway programs, contribute in a very direct and important way to the value of petitioners' businesses. Additionally, a network of other related dealerships with their service departments operates throughout the country under the protection of the laws of the various States, including Oklahoma, and enhances the value of petitioners' businesses by facilitating their customers' traveling. . . .

Justice Marshall, with whom Justice Blackmun joins, dissenting. . . .

This is a difficult case, and reasonable minds may differ as to whether respondents have alleged a sufficient "relationship among the defendant [s], the forum, and the litigation," Shaffer v. Heitner, 433 U.S. 186, 204 (1977), to satisfy the requirements of *International Shoe*. I am concerned, however, that the majority has reached its result by taking an unnecessarily narrow view of petitioners' forum-related conduct. . . [T]he basis for the assertion of jurisdiction is not the happenstance that an individual over whom petitioners had no control made a unilateral decision to take a chattel with him to a distant State. Rather, jurisdiction is premised on the deliberate and purposeful actions of the defendants themselves in choosing to become part of a nationwide, indeed a global, network for marketing and servicing automobiles.

Petitioners are sellers of a product whose utility derives from its mobility. . . . Petitioners know that their customers buy cars not only to make short trips, but also to travel long distances. In fact, the nationwide service network with which they are affiliated was designed to facilitate and encourage such travel. Seaway would be unlikely to sell many cars if authorized service were available only in Massena, N.Y. Moreover, local dealers normally derive a substantial portion of their revenues from their service operations and thereby obtain a further economic benefit from the opportunity to service cars which were sold in other States. It is apparent that petitioners have not attempted to minimize the chance that their activities will have effects in other States; on the contrary, they have chosen to do business in a way that increases that chance, because it is to their economic advantage to do so.

To be sure, petitioners could not know in advance that this particular automobile would be driven to Oklahoma. They must have anticipated, however, that a substantial portion of the cars they sold would travel out of New York. Seaway, a local dealer in the second most populous State, and World-Wide, one of only seven regional Audi distributors in the entire country, would scarcely have been surprised to learn that a car sold by them had been driven in Oklahoma on Interstate 44, a heavily traveled transcontinental highway. In the case of the distributor, in particular, the probability that some of the cars it sells will be driven in every one of the contiguous States must amount to a virtual certainty. This knowledge should alert a reasonable businessman to the likelihood that a defect in the product might manifest itself in the forum State—not because of some unpredictable, aberrant, unilateral action by a single buyer, but in the normal course of the operation of the vehicles for their intended purpose. . . .

JUSTICE BLACKMUN, dissenting. . . .

For me, a critical factor in the disposition of the litigation is the nature of the instrumentality under consideration. It has been said that we are a nation on wheels. What we are concerned with here is the automobile and its peripatetic character. One need only examine our national network of interstate highways, or make an appearance on one of them, or observe the variety of license plates present not only on those highways but in any metropolitan area, to realize that any automobile is likely to wander far from its place of licensure or from its place of distribution and retail sale. Miles per gallon on the highway (as well as in the city) and mileage per tankful are familiar allegations in manufacturers' advertisements today. To expect that any new automobile will remain in the vicinity of its retail sale—like the 1914 electric car driven by the proverbial "little old lady"—is to blink at reality. The automobile is intended for distance as well as for transportation within a limited area.

It therefore seems to me not unreasonable—and certainly not unconstitutional and beyond the reach of the principles laid down in International Shoe Co. v. Washington, 326 U.S. 310 (1945), and its progeny—to uphold Oklahoma jurisdiction over this New York distributor and this New York dealer when the accident happened in Oklahoma. . . .

Notes and Questions

1. Would it have mattered if the Robinsons had told the retailer that they were headed for Oklahoma? If they had been from a neighboring state and been injured there, rather than a distant one?

2. What do you think of Justice Brennan's "hey, hop on a plane" approach? Isn't the burden of distant litigation easily overstated, given modern procedure and technology? What, exactly, is the burden of distant litigation?

3. If the test for minimum contacts had to do with one's reasonable expectations, then why couldn't the expectations simply be changed by an announcement that all states heretofore will have nationwide service of process? Or that all manufacturers, distributors, and sellers of mobile products can anticipate being sued wherever they cause injury within the United States? If strict liability is justifiable, why isn't "strict amenability"?

4. Justice White states that the sovereignty of each state implies a limitation on the sovereignty of others, and suggests that this interstate sovereignty factor is relevant to the personal jurisdiction puzzle. Yet the defendant has always been able to consent to jurisdiction, even by a state with which he has no minimum contacts. How can an individual waive a state's sovereignty interests?

In Insurance Corp. of Ireland v. Compagnie des Bauxites de Guinee, 456 U.S. 694, 702 n.10 (1982), Justice White revisited this aspect of *World-Wide*, and offered this explanation:

> It is true that we have stated that the requirement of personal jurisdiction, as applied to the state courts, reflects an element of federalism and the character of state sovereignty vis-à-vis other states. . . . The restriction on state sovereign power described in *World-Wide Volkswagen Corp.*, however, must be seen as ultimately a function of the liberty interest preserved by the Due Process Clause. That clause is the only source of the personal jurisdiction requirement and the clause itself makes no mention of federalism concerns. Furthermore, if federalism operated as an independent restriction on the sovereign power of the court, it would not be possible to waive the personal jurisdiction requirement: Individual actions cannot change the powers of sovereignty, although the individual can subject himself to powers from which he may otherwise be protected.

So what, then, is the proper role of the sovereignty factor in the personal jurisdiction calculus?

5. Look at the Court's reference to Gray v. American Radiator. How are the two cases different? How does the Court's apparent approval of *Gray* modify the *World-Wide* test for jurisdiction in product liability cases?

Note: The Robinson Saga

Think of yourself as the lawyer for the Robinsons. Why might you prefer to litigate in Oklahoma rather than New York or Arizona? In many cases involving personal jurisdiction, the most interesting question is why the plaintiff chose the questionable forum since there is almost always some relatively uncontestable place where he could sue instead.

Often the answer turns on the other advantages that plaintiff's lawyer hoped (or defendant's lawyer feared) would come from filing in a particular forum. From some of the statements and pleadings in the subsequent litigation in the Robinson case, outlined below, it appears that the decision to fight for jurisdiction over the retailer and distributor was based on the mistaken assumption that their presence would destroy potential diversity in the case, and thus prevent its removal to federal court. (In fact, diversity might not have been destroyed because the Robinsons arguably were no longer citizens of New York, though whether they had effectively established a new domicile was contested). You will learn about such intricacies of subject matter jurisdiction later in this chapter.

The reason the Robinsons' original trial attorney preferred state over federal courts was that he believed his style would be better appreciated by the more local jury drawn from the state court pool. The county where the Robinsons' gas tank caught fire was, moreover, noted for the size of plaintiffs' verdicts that the local juries returned.

After the Supreme Court opinion releasing the retailer and distributor from the case, the Robinsons' fortunes took further sad and protracted turns. The remaining defendants (the importer and the manufacturer) removed the case to federal court based on diversity of citizenship. A jury found for the defendants, and the Robinsons appealed. In Robinson v. Audi NSU Auto Union Aktiengesellschaft, 739 F.2d 1481 (10th Cir. 1984), the court reversed as to the importer, holding that the trial judge improperly excluded evidence that the importer had prior knowledge that the fuel tank design was dangerous.

Back in the trial court, the judge granted summary judgment for the defendant importer on the basis of an Oklahoma Supreme Court decision, handed down after the Robinsons' appeal, holding that an importer cannot be held responsible for a defect attributable solely to the manufacturing process. This time the Robinsons lost on appeal. Robinson v. Volkswagen of America, 803 F.2d 572 (10th Cir. 1986).

With new counsel, the Robinsons turned to malpractice claims against their original lawyers, as well as fraud claims against some of the defendants and their lawyers. Some of these were lost. See, e.g., Robinson

v. Volkswagenwerk, 940 F.2d 1369 (10th Cir. 1991), *cert. denied sub nom.* Herzfeld & Rubin v. Robinson, 502 U.S. 1091 (1992). See Charles W. Adams, World-Wide Volkswagen v. Woodson—The Rest of the Story, 72 Neb. L. Rev. 1122 (1993).

Looking back over the course of the litigation, we can now see that the Robinsons' physical injuries started with an exploding gas tank, and their legal wounds with the questionable and expensive tactical decision to join the retailer and regional distributor and to fight to keep them in the case, even though there were other "deep-pocket" defendants subject to personal jurisdiction in Oklahoma.

6. Directing a "Product" Toward a Forum State: Minimum Contacts and Fair Play in a Post-Modern Age

Problem Case: A Troubled Young Man

Dr. Anna Froid is a psychiatrist who lives and works in San Francisco. One of her patients is a deeply troubled 19-year-old man named Alvin Baites. She has been treating Baites with medication and psychotherapy since October 1987. During the course of his treatment, Baites has expressed repeatedly his hatred of his family, including his widower father, who lives in Sedona, Arizona, and his two sisters, Ellen Baites Plath of Washington state and Sally Baites of Jefferson City, Missouri.

The holidays are always a time of particular unhappiness and frustration for Baites. During two prior Christmas seasons, Baites became violent and irrational after drinking heavily at employee Christmas parties. Though he did not harm anyone, Baites was institutionalized for several months in 1988, after the second episode. Froid knows all of this, since Baites was under her care at that time.

During the fall of 1990, Baites seemed to be making some progress. New medication was helping, and his level of anger toward others decreased modestly as therapy continued. Shortly before the Christmas holidays, however, Baites seemed to suffer a setback. Froid linked this regression to the impending holidays and Baites's plans to spend Christmas with his father and sisters in Arizona. Froid increased the dosage of his medication, but she did not renew her usual warning about mixing alcohol with the medication, since it was typed on the vial.

Baites flew home to Arizona for the holidays. The visit reintroduced old family tensions, which triggered a violent argument between Baites and his family. Unhinged by a combination of medication, alcohol, and stress, Baites lost control and struck and injured his father and sisters. Baites has again been hospitalized, this time in Arizona. At his request, Dr. Froid flew to Arizona to see him there. She consulted with his doctors and talked to Alvin for 50 minutes. Dr. Froid left Arizona in the evening of the day she arrived there.

Her only other contact with Arizona is a one-quarter interest in a rental property in Scottsdale, Arizona. She has never visited the property or indeed been in Arizona except for her visit to Alvin Baites.

Mr. Baites (Alvin's father) has filed a lawsuit against Dr. Froid in Arizona, alleging that she had a duty to warn foreseeable plaintiffs such as himself of Alvin's violent tendencies.

Assume, *arguendo*, that the Arizona long-arm rules provide, in relevant part:

Section 1.03

(a) A court may exercise personal jurisdiction over a person, who acts directly or by an agent as to a claim arising from the person's . . .

> (3) causing tortious injury by an act or omission in this state; or
>
> (4) causing tortious injury in this state by an act or omission outside this state if he or she regularly does or solicits business, or engages in any other persistent course of conduct, or derives substantial revenue from goods used or consumed or services rendered, in this state; or meets the conditions of (5) of this section.
>
> (5) having an interest in, using, or possessing real property in this state. . . .

Can Arizona constitutionally exercise jurisdiction over Mr. Baites's claim against Dr. Froid? If process was served on her when she visited Alvin in the hospital?

Note: Keeton v. Hustler Magazine, Inc.

In Keeton v. Hustler Magazine, Inc., 465 U.S. 770 (1984), Kathy Keeton, a New York resident, sued *Hustler* magazine, an Ohio corporation headquartered in California, for libel in U.S. District Court in New Hampshire. Keeton had originally filed suit in Ohio, but the court held she was time barred there. She then initiated the same action in New Hampshire, where the statute of limitations for libel claims is longer than in most states. The only connection between the forum state and *Hustler* magazine was the monthly sale of 10,000 to 15,000 copies of the magazine there.

Both the district court and the court of appeals dismissed Keeton's complaint, holding that her lack of contacts rendered the State's interest "too attenuated" for an assertion of personal jurisdiction. The court of appeals also pointed out that it would be "unfair" to the magazine to allow jurisdiction under New Hampshire's exceptionally long statute of limitations, especially since the "single publication rule" relied on in libel cases would mean that the New Hampshire court would have to award a prevailing Keeton damages equivalent to the total harm she had suffered, rather than just that sustained in New Hampshire.

The Supreme Court reversed, holding that *Hustler*'s "regular circulation of magazines in the forum State is sufficient to support an assertion of jurisdiction in a libel action based on the contents of the magazine" since "regular monthly sales of thousands of magazines cannot by any stretch of the imagination be characterized as random, isolated, or fortuitous." The Court reasoned that, despite the fact that Keeton was unknown in New Hampshire, the state still had an interest in "employ[ing] its libel laws to discourage the deception of its citizens." The Court also pointed to New Hampshire's "substantial interest" in abiding by the "single publication rule," which preserves judicial resources nationwide by prohibiting multiple libel actions against the same defendant in different states.

Finally, the Court brushed aside concerns about the unfairness of subjecting *Hustler* to the state's unusual approach to libel suits, finding that "the chance duration of statutes of limitations in non-forum jurisdictions has nothing to do with the contacts among respondent, New Hampshire, and this multistate libel action."

In a companion case, Calder v. Jones, 465 U.S. 783 (1984), the Court again addressed the issue of personal jurisdiction in a libel context. In this case, Shirley Jones, the entertainer, sued the editor of the *National Enquirer* and a writer in California for libel related to a defamatory piece about Jones in the magazine. Jones lives in California, the editor and staff writer in Florida. The Court held that the editor and writer reasonably should have anticipated that litigation might be initiated in the home state of a libel plaintiff. Though a plaintiff's domicile is not always a proper forum, where the plaintiff resides can be relevant to a minimum contacts analysis in some cases. The Court noted that this was an intentional tort that involved a particular target, Shirley Jones, and that the writer and editor would have realized at the time of writing and publishing the piece that the injury would be felt primarily where the plaintiff lives. In such a case, the plaintiff's domicile was a proper forum. Moreover, the Court pointed out, more issues of the *Enquirer* are sold in California—the hub of the entertainment industry—than in any other state.

The Court continues, post-*Calder*, to struggle with the issue of when extraterritorial conduct has a sufficient, directed impact on the forum to justify jurisdiction there. In the following case the Court addresses the matter in an international context, but is unable to agree on how courts ought to approach this issue. Which opinion do you find most persuasive?

Asahi Metal Industry Co. v. Superior Court

480 U.S. 102 (1987)

[JUSTICE O'CONNOR delivered the opinion of a Court that was severely fractured on all but the statement of facts and a few paragraphs of standard due process analysis. We print excerpts from these parts first.]

I

On September 23, 1978, on Interstate Highway 80 in Solano County, California, Gary Zurcher lost control of his Honda motorcycle and collided with a tractor. Zurcher was severely injured, and his passenger and wife, Ruth Ann Moreno, was killed. In September 1979, Zurcher filed a product liability action in the Superior Court of the State of California in and for the County of Solano. Zurcher alleged that the 1978 accident was caused by a sudden loss of air and an explosion in the rear tire of the motorcycle, and alleged that the motorcycle tire, tube, and sealant were defective. Zurcher's complaint named, *inter alia*, Cheng Shin Rubber Industrial Co., Ltd. (Cheng Shin), the Taiwanese manufacturer of the tube. Cheng Shin in turn filed a cross-complaint seeking indemnification from its codefendants and from petitioner, Asahi Metal Industry Co., Ltd. (Asahi), the manufacturer of the tube's valve assembly. Zurcher's claims against Cheng Shin and the other defendants were eventually settled and dismissed, leaving only Cheng Shin's indemnity action against Asahi.

California's long-arm statute authorizes the exercise of jurisdiction "on any basis not inconsistent with the Constitution of this state or of the United States." Cal. Civ. Proc. Code Ann. § 410.10 (West 1973). Asahi moved to quash Cheng Shin's service of summons, arguing the State could not exert jurisdiction over it consistent with the Due Process Clause of the Fourteenth Amendment.

In relation to the motion, the following information was submitted by Asahi and Cheng Shin. Asahi is a Japanese corporation. It manufactures tire valve assemblies in Japan and sells the assemblies to Cheng Shin, and to several other tire manufacturers, for use as components in finished tire tubes. Asahi's sales to Cheng Shin took place in Taiwan. The shipments from Asahi to Cheng Shin were sent from Japan to Taiwan. Cheng Shin bought and incorporated into its tire tubes 150,000 Asahi valve assemblies in 1978; 500,000 in 1979; 500,000 in 1980; 100,000 in 1981; and 100,000 in 1982. Sales to Cheng Shin accounted for 1.24 percent of Asahi's income in 1981 and 0.44 percent in 1982. Cheng Shin alleged that approximately 20 percent of its sales in the United States are in California. Cheng Shin purchases valve assemblies from other suppliers as well, and sells finished tubes throughout the world.

In 1983 an attorney for Cheng Shin conducted an informal examination of the valve stems of the tire tubes sold in one cycle store in Solano County. The attorney declared that of the approximately 115 tire tubes in the store, 97 were purportedly manufactured in Japan or Taiwan, and of those 97, 21 valve stems were marked with the circled letter "A," apparently Asahi's trademark. Of the 21 Asahi valve stems, 12 were incorporated into Cheng Shin tire tubes. The store contained 41 other Cheng Shin tubes that incorporated the valve assemblies of other manufacturers. An affidavit of a manager of Cheng Shin whose duties included the purchasing of component parts stated: "'In discussions with Asahi regarding the purchase of valve stem assemblies the fact that my Company sells tubes throughout the world and specifically the United States has been discussed. I am informed and believe that Asahi was fully aware that valve stem assemblies sold to my Company and to others would end up throughout the United States and in California.'" An affidavit of the president of Asahi, on the other hand, declared that Asahi "'has never contemplated that its limited sales of tire valves to Cheng Shin in Taiwan would subject it to lawsuits in California.'" The record does not include any contract between Cheng Shin and Asahi.

Primarily on the basis of the above information, the Superior Court denied the motion to quash summons, stating: "Asahi obviously does business on an international scale. It is not unreasonable that they defend claims of defect in their product on an international scale." Order Denying Motion to Quash Summons.

The Court of Appeal of the State of California issued a peremptory writ of mandate commanding the Superior Court to quash service of summons. The court concluded that "it would be unreasonable to require Asahi to respond in California solely on the basis of ultimately realized foreseeability that the product into which its component was embodied would be sold all over the world including California."

The Supreme Court of the State of California reversed and discharged the writ issued by the Court of Appeal. The court observed: "Asahi has no offices, property or agents in California. It solicits no business in California and has made no direct sales [in California]." 39 Cal. 3d 35, 705 P.2d 543 (1985). Moreover, "Asahi did not design or control the system of distribution that carried its valve assemblies into California." Id. at 48, 702 P.2d at 549. Nevertheless, the court found the exercise of jurisdiction over Asahi to be consistent with the Due Process Clause. It concluded that Asahi knew that some of the valve assemblies sold to Cheng Shin would be incorporated into tire tubes sold in California, and that Asahi benefited indirectly from the sale in California of products incorporating its components. The court considered Asahi's intentional act of placing its components into the stream of commerce—that is, by delivering the components to Cheng Shin in Taiwan—coupled with Asahi's awareness that some of the components would eventually find their way into California, sufficient to form the basis for state court jurisdiction under the Due Process Clause.

We granted certiorari and now reverse.

[All but JUSTICE SCALIA agreed with the following part of the opinion (labeled in the Opinion as Part II(B)):]

The strictures of the Due Process Clause forbid a state court to exercise personal jurisdiction over Asahi under circumstances that would offend "'traditional notions of fair play and substantial justice.'"

We have previously explained that the determination of the reasonableness of the exercise of jurisdiction in each case will depend on an evaluation of several factors. A court must consider the burden on the defendant, the interests of the forum State, and the plaintiff's interest in obtaining relief. It must also weigh in its determination "the interstate judicial system's interest in obtaining the most efficient resolution of controversies; and the shared interest of the several States in furthering fundamental substantive social policies." Cf. *World Wide Volkswagen*, 444 U.S. at 292 (citations omitted).

A consideration of these factors in the present case clearly reveals the unreasonableness of the assertion of jurisdiction over Asahi, even apart from the question of the placement of goods in the stream of commerce.

Certainly the burden on the defendant in this case is severe. Asahi has been commanded by the Supreme Court of California not only to traverse the distance between Asahi's headquarters in Japan and the Superior Court of California in and for the County of Solano, but also to submit its dispute with Cheng Shin to a foreign nation's judicial system. The unique burdens placed upon one who must defend oneself in a foreign legal system should have significant weight in assessing the reasonableness of stretching the long arm of personal jurisdiction over national borders.

When minimum contacts have been established, often the interests of the plaintiff and the forum in the exercise of jurisdiction will justify even the serious burdens placed on the alien defendant. In the present case, however, the interests of the plaintiff and the forum in California's assertion of jurisdiction over Asahi are slight. All that remains is a claim for indemnification asserted by Cheng Shin, a Taiwanese corporation, against Asahi. The transaction on which the indemnification claim is based took place in Taiwan; Asahi's components were shipped from Japan to Taiwan. Cheng Shin has not demonstrated that it is more convenient for it to litigate its indemnification claim against Asahi in California rather than in Taiwan or Japan.

Because the plaintiff is not a California resident, California's legitimate interests in the dispute have considerably diminished. The Supreme Court of California argued that the State had an interest in "protecting its consumers by ensuring that foreign manufacturers comply with the state's safety standards." The State Supreme Court's definition of California's interest, however, was overly broad. The dispute between Cheng Shin and Asahi is primarily about indemnification rather than safety standards. Moreover, it is not at all clear at this point that California law should govern the question whether a Japanese corporation should indemnify a Taiwanese corporation on the basis of a sale made in Taiwan and a shipment of goods from Japan to Taiwan. The possibility of being haled into a California court as a result of an accident involving Asahi's components undoubtedly creates an additional deterrent to the manufacture of unsafe components; however, similar pressures will be placed on Asahi by the purchasers of its components as long as those who use Asahi components in their final products, and sell those products in California, are subject to the application of California tort law.

World-Wide Volkswagen also admonished courts to take into consideration the interests of the "several States," in addition to the forum State, in the efficient judicial resolution of the dispute and the advancement of substantive policies. In the present case, this advice calls for a court to consider the procedural and substantive policies of other *nations* whose interests are affected by the assertion of jurisdiction by the California court. The procedural and substantive interests of other nations in a state court's assertion of jurisdiction over an alien defendant will differ from case to case. In every case, however, those interests, as well as the Federal Government's interest in its foreign relations policies, will be best served by a careful inquiry into the reasonableness of the assertion of jurisdiction in the particular case, and an unwillingness to find the serious burdens on an alien defendant outweighed by minimal interests on the part of the plaintiff or the forum State. "Great care and reserve should be exercised when extending our notions of personal jurisdiction into the international field." United States v. First National City Bank, 379 U.S. 378, 404 (1965) (Harlan, J., dissenting). See Born, Reflections on Judicial Jurisdiction in International Cases, 17 Ga. J. Int'l & Comp. L. 1 (1987).

Considering the international context, the heavy burden on the alien defendant, and the slight interests of the plaintiff and the forum State, the exercise of personal jurisdiction by a California court over Asahi in this instance would be unreasonable and unfair.

[JUSTICE O'CONNOR, joined by JUSTICES REHNQUIST, POWELL, and SCALIA, put forth the following theory.]

The Due Process Clause of the Fourteenth Amendment limits the power of a state court to exert personal jurisdiction over a nonresident defendant.... Most recently we have reaffirmed... that minimum contacts must have a basis in "some act by which the defendant purposefully avails itself of the privilege of conducting activities within the forum State, thus invoking the benefits and protections of its laws." Burger King [Corp. v. Rudzewicz, 471 U.S. 462, 475 (1985)]. "Jurisdiction is proper... where the contacts proximately result from actions by the defendant *himself* that create a 'substantial connection' with the forum State." Ibid., quoting McGee v. International Life Insurance Co.[, 355 U.S. 220, 223 (1957)] (emphasis in original).

Applying the principle that minimum contacts must be based on an act of the defendant, the Court in World-Wide Volkswagen Corp. v. Woodson, 444 U.S. 286 (1980), rejected the assertion that a *consumer's* unilateral act of bringing the defendant's product into the forum State was a sufficient constitutional basis for personal jurisdiction over the defendant. It had been argued in *World-Wide Volkswagen* that because an automobile retailer and its wholesale distributor sold a product mobile by design and purpose, they could foresee being haled into court in the distant States into which their customers might drive. The Court rejected this concept of foreseeability as an insufficient basis for jurisdiction under the Due Process Clause. Id. at 295-296. The Court disclaimed, however, the idea that "foreseeability is wholly irrelevant" to personal jurisdiction, concluding that "[t]he forum State does not exceed its powers under the Due Process Clause if it asserts personal jurisdiction over a corporation that delivers its products into the stream of commerce with the expectation that they will be purchased by consumers in the forum State." . . .

In *World-Wide Volkswagen* itself, the state court sought to base jurisdiction not on any act of the defendant, but on the foreseeable unilateral actions of the consumer. Since *World-Wide Volkswagen*, lower courts have been confronted with cases in which the defendant acted by placing a product in the stream of commerce, and the stream eventually swept defendant's product into the forum State, but the defendant did nothing else to purposefully avail itself of the market in the forum State. Some courts have understood the Due Process Clause, as interpreted in *World-Wide Volkswagen*, to allow an exercise of personal jurisdiction to be based on no more than the defendant's act of placing the product in the stream of commerce. Other courts have understood the Due Process Clause and the above-quoted language in *World-Wide Volkswagen* to require the action of the defendant to be more purposefully directed at the forum State than the mere act of placing a product in the stream of commerce.

The reasoning of the Supreme Court of California in the present case illustrates the former interpretation of *World-Wide Volkswagen*. The Supreme Court of California held that, because the stream of commerce eventually brought some valves Asahi sold Cheng Shin into California, Asahi's awareness that its valves would be sold in California was sufficient to permit California to exercise jurisdiction over Asahi consistent with the requirements of the Due Process Clause. The Supreme Court of California's position was consistent with those courts that have held that mere foreseeability or awareness was a constitutionally sufficient basis for personal jurisdiction if the defendant's product made its way into the forum State while still in the stream of commerce.

Other courts, however, have understood the Due Process Clause to require something more than that the defendant was aware of its product's entry into the forum State through the stream of commerce in order for the State to exert jurisdiction over the defendant. In the present case, for example, the State Court of Appeal did not read the Due Process Clause, as interpreted by *World-Wide Volkswagen*, to allow "mere foreseeability that the product will enter the forum state [to] be enough by itself to establish jurisdiction over the distributor and retailer." . . .

We now find this latter position to be consonant with the requirements of due process. The "substantial connection" between the defendant and the forum State necessary for a finding of minimum contacts must come about by *an action of the defendant purposefully directed toward the forum State*. The placement of a product into the stream of commerce, without more, is not an act of the defendant purposefully directed toward the forum State. Additional conduct of the defendant may indicate an intent or purpose to serve the market in the forum State, for example, designing the product for the market in the forum State, advertising in the forum State, establishing channels for providing regular advice to customers in the forum State, or marketing the product through a distributor who has agreed to serve as the sales agent in the forum State. But a defendant's awareness that the stream of commerce may or will sweep the product into the forum State does not convert the mere act of placing the product into the stream into an act purposefully directed toward the forum State.

Assuming, *arguendo,* that respondents have established Asahi's awareness that some of the valves sold to Cheng Shin would be incorporated into tire tubes sold in California, respondents have not demonstrated any action by Asahi to purposefully avail itself of the California market.

[JUSTICES BRENNAN, WHITE, MARSHALL, and BLACKMUN wrote separately to disagree with the "stream of commerce theory" propounded by the four plurality Justices.]

. . . This is one of those rare cases in which "minimum requirements inherent in the concept of 'fair play and substantial justice' . . . defeat the reasonableness of jurisdiction even [though] the defendant has purposefully engaged in forum activities." [*Burger King,* 471 U.S. at 477-478.] . . .

. . . The stream of commerce refers not to unpredictable currents or eddies, but to the regular and anticipated flow of products from manufacture to distribution to retail sale. As long as a participant in this process is aware that the final product is being marketed in the forum State, the possibility of a lawsuit there cannot come as a surprise. Nor will the litigation present a burden for which there is no corresponding benefit. A defendant who has placed goods in the stream of commerce benefits economically from the retail sale of the final product in the forum State, and indirectly benefits from the State's laws that regulate and facilitate commercial activity. These benefits accrue regardless of whether that participant directly conducts business in the forum State, or engages in additional conduct directed toward that State. Accordingly, most courts and commentators have found that jurisdiction premised on the placement of a product into the stream of commerce is consistent with the Due Process Clause, and have not required a showing of additional conduct.

[Finally, JUSTICE STEVENS, joined by JUSTICES WHITE and BLACKMUN, wrote:]

. . . [E]ven assuming [the validity of the stream-of-commerce-*plus* theory of the plurality, the opinion] misapplies it to the facts of this case. The plurality seems to assume that an unwavering line can be drawn between "mere awareness" that a component will find its way into the forum State and "purposeful availment" of the forum's market. Over the course of its dealings with Cheng Shin, Asahi has arguably engaged in a higher quantum of conduct than "[t]he placement of a product into the stream of commerce, without more. . . ." Whether or not this conduct rises to the level of purposeful availment requires a constitutional determination that is affected by the volume, the value, and the hazardous character of the components.

Note: Criticism of Asahi

Commentators have been very critical of *Asahi*. The mixed messages of the split Court and the addition of factors that are not analytically distinct from minimum contacts are common grounds of the almost universal condemnation.

Another objection is that the plurality creates confusion in an effort to prevent jurisdictional surprise. The plurality holds that the standard of "minimum contacts" has not been met on this record. But what does that mean? Why should it be necessary, as Justice O'Connor suggests, that a component part manufacturer *do* something directed toward the forum? Why isn't actual or constructive awareness that the products reach the forum state enough?

A significant post-*Asahi* issue is whether the case modifies the stream of commerce analysis set forth in *World-Wide*. One could easily argue that the international features of the case make it inapplicable to suits that involve domestic parties. Assume, however, that courts interpret *Asahi* to have more general application. Specifically, they might ask, if a product exits the chain of distribution in the forum and causes injury there, are all parties "up the chain" amenable to process there? Or is some additional forum-directed conduct required, as Justice O'Connor suggests? The lower courts have split over the matter, making it ripe for eventual Supreme Court treatment. Consider the following proposed analysis of the matter by the Court of Appeals for the Fourth Circuit, in Lesnick v. Hollingsworth & Vose Co., 35 F.3d 939 (4th Cir. 1994):

> Hollingsworth & Vose is a Massachusetts corporation with its principal place of business in Massachusetts. It has demonstrated that it had no presence in Maryland by having any office, agent, or employee there, and it had no customers in Maryland. It was not registered to do business there and directed no marketing effort or other activities toward the state. It acknowledges, however, that less than one percent of its income has derived from Maryland through Lorillard's sale of cigarettes there. Hollingsworth & Vose entered into a filter supply arrangement with Lorillard under which Hollingsworth & Vose shipped filter material to Lorillard's plants in Kentucky and New Jersey. It acknowledges that, to the extent that it sold filter material to Lorillard in Kentucky and New Jersey, it placed the product in commerce, and it did so with knowledge that Kent cigarettes manufactured with its filter material would be sold in Maryland.
>
> Lesnick relies principally upon the language in *World-Wide Volkswagen* that a state does not violate the Due Process Clause if it asserts personal jurisdiction over a corporation "that delivers its products into the stream of commerce with the expectation that they will be purchased in the forum State." 444 U.S. at 298. Hollingsworth & Vose concedes that if this language fully states the jurisdictional test it is subject to personal jurisdiction in Maryland. As we have already concluded, however, *World-Wide Volkswagen*'s holding is not so broad as Lesnick would have us believe, and the long-standing principles of personal jurisdiction that began with

International Shoe have not been overruled. Thus, Lesnick cannot rely simply upon the "stream of commerce" logic to establish jurisdiction.

Lesnick falls back on the contention that because Hollingsworth & Vose had such a close relationship with Lorillard, Hollingsworth & Vose would be subject to jurisdiction derivatively through Lorillard's contacts. In support of her contention, Lesnick relies upon the close cooperation that existed between the two defendants by reason of the contract entered into in 1952. Under that agreement, the two jointly owned the patent to the "Micronite Filter" and agreed to share information about technical advances in the field. The two also shared equally the costs of developing the filter, including the costs of creating manufacturing facilities, and they agreed to share any royalties they might earn from licensing the process. In addition, the price Lorillard paid for the filters was a multiple of Hollingsworth & Vose's cost, with Lorillard given a right to inspect production and financial records. Hollingsworth & Vose agreed to sell filter material for tobacco use only to Lorillard for at least the first five years of their dealings. Finally, Lorillard agreed to indemnify Hollingsworth & Vose for any liabilities arising from the harmful effects of the product. The record shows that the two companies exercised some measure of cooperation during the course of the agreement to ensure that the filter was successful.

Although this arrangement represents "additional conduct" beyond the mere sale to Lorillard of filter material,[2] it does not rise to the level of establishing jurisdiction because none of the conduct is in any way directed *toward the state of Maryland.* All of the listed contacts between Lorillard and Hollingsworth & Vose relate only to Hollingsworth & Vose's agreement to supply filters from its plant in Massachusetts to Lorillard in Kentucky and New Jersey. While the result might be different if Hollingsworth & Vose had changed production to comply with Maryland regulations or if it had set up a customer relations network there, see *Asahi,* 480 U.S. at 112 (O'Connor, J.), on the record in this case, we can discover no affirmative action by Hollingsworth & Vose rising to the level of purposeful availment. Therefore, the Maryland courts may not exercise personal jurisdiction over Hollingsworth & Vose in this case, and the judgment of the district court is affirmed.

Compare the court's application of Justice O'Connor's stream of commerce analysis in *Lesnick* with that of the court in these other cases: Boit v. Gar-Tec Prod., Inc., 967 F.2d 671 (1st Cir. 1992) (an Indiana manufacturer's "awareness that the hot air gun might end up in Maine, without more, does not convert [the manufacturer's] sale of the hot air gun to Brookstone [a catalog company] into an act of purposeful availment," id. at 683); Falkirk Mining Co. v. Japan Steel Works, Ltd., 906 F.2d 369 (8th Cir. 1990) (despite North Dakota's long-arm statute allowing jurisdiction over a nonresident defendant who commits a tort within the state, exercising jurisdiction over defendant company offends due process; the New York

2. Lesnick does not contend that Lorillard and Hollingsworth & Vose engaged in a joint venture as defined by Maryland law. We understand, rather, that her allegation rests on the notion that the closeness of the corporations' activities created a *de-facto* agency for jurisdictional purposes.

company's "placement of a product into the stream of commerce, without more, does not constitute an act of the defendant purposefully directed toward the forum State," id. at 376); Dehmlow v. Austin Fireworks, 963 F.2d 941 (7th Cir. 1992) (Illinois' exercise of jurisdiction over a Kansas fireworks company does not offend due process; "[b]ecause the Supreme Court established the stream of commerce theory, and a majority of the Court has not yet rejected it, we consider that theory to be determinative"; this defendant, however, also satisfies "the more stringent minimum contacts test set forth" by Justice O'Connor, id. at 947); and Irving v. Owens-Corning Fiberglass Corp., 864 F.2d 383 (5th Cir. 1989) (Yugoslavian supplier of asbestos is subject to jurisdiction in Texas; "[b]ecause the Court's splintered view of minimum contacts in *Asahi* provides no clear guidance on this issue, we continue to gauge [the Yugoslavian company's] contacts with Texas by the stream of commerce standard. . . ." Id. at 386).

The debate over the vitality of the stream of commerce analysis thus continues. See IMO Indus. v. Kiekert AG, 155 F.3d 254 (3d Cir. 1998) (noting conflict among the circuits regarding whether it is sufficient that the victim of the tort be located in the forum, or whether the defendant must have targeted its tortious conduct at the forum). See also Pennzoil Prod. Co. v. Colelli Assoc., Inc., 149 F.3d 197 (3d Cir. 1998). The majority of circuits have required "targeting" of the forum, which may indicate that Justice O'Connor's approach ultimately will prevail.

Note: Why Does the Forum Matter?

In the following excerpt, Edward Purcell describes how geography can become a litigation weapon that is especially powerful when deployed against individual parties of modest means:

> The deterrent effects of geography are numerous and weighty. The threshold task of merely retaining counsel in a distant location, which may seem routine to attorneys and judges, is profoundly daunting to ordinary people. The very decision to retain an attorney is so troublesome, in fact, that most claimants are content to accept a settlement without one. The result of that commonplace decision, as numerous studies have repeatedly shown, is that such claimants almost invariably obtain much less from their adversaries than they otherwise would. . . .
>
> If a claimant does eventually retain an attorney, he may likely begin by securing counsel who resides near his home and outside of the contractual forum state. In such a case, his hopes are immediately subject to two related risks that geography creates. First, the claimant's leverage in negotiating a settlement is minimized because he has not yet established his willingness or capacity to bring suit in the contractual forum, or even to hire an attorney in the forum state. Second, his local attorney has a strong incentive to arrange an out-of-court settlement—especially if she is acting, as she most probably is, under a contingent fee agreement—in order to maximize her

return and prevent the great bulk of the fee from eventually going to an attorney in the contractual forum state. Those facts by themselves increase the likelihood that the claimant will wind up with a relatively low and unfavorable out-of-court settlement.

If the claimant does secure representation in the distant contractual forum, he begins to shoulder other and more palpable burdens. He may, for example, wind up with two attorneys, one local and one in the contractual forum, an arrangement that can complicate the representation and drive up his costs. Further, his need to rely on a distant attorney compounds his anxieties and uncertainties. The distant attorney is an unknown quantity. The claimant has fewer reasons to trust her, and the possibility that some subtle conflict of interest may emerge between the client and his distant attorney increases. The claimant can scarcely monitor the distant attorney's performance closely, and any attempt to do so would drive up his costs yet again. For her part, the attorney in the contractual forum is not particularly concerned with her reputation in the relatively remote town where her client lives, and she most likely does not represent or hope to represent other individuals or organizations from her client's distant home town.

Once litigation begins, the process quickly piles on additional burdens. One is the obvious need to travel and communicate over long distances, which makes the suit more costly as well as more inconvenient in terms of both litigation planning and client-attorney consultation. Another is the compounded costs and risks created by the attorney's need to communicate with the client's witnesses and to prepare them for depositions and trial testimony. The party may either have to pay additional travel costs for in-person meetings or risk the creation of potentially discoverable documents that could spur additional and costly motion practice and, if disclosed, weaken the party's position in negotiations and at trial. A third burden is the likely additional delays involved in prosecuting the case, as distance and inconvenience combine to complicate various pretrial events and to remove from the attorney the spur of a human client who can or does present himself in person at his attorney's office. A fourth burden is the added cost of participating in a distant trial, including the costs and risks involved in securing the attendance of witnesses at such a location. All of these burdens will be especially heavy if the plaintiff's claim arises from events in his home state and many or all of his witnesses reside there.

Yet another burden is the fact that, whatever else happens, psychologically the claimant feels more cut off, more vulnerable, and even more anxious than he otherwise would. That burden is magnified by the fact that the attorneys representing his corporate adversary feel relatively comfortable and secure litigating in their home court. Those attorneys are, moreover, fully aware of the extra-legal burdens the plaintiff is facing. Consciously or unconsciously, they will tend to drive a harder bargain, hold off settling for a longer period in the hope of obtaining increasingly more favorable terms, and drag their feet while forcing the out-of-state litigant continually to press for action at each stage of the litigation.

A final burden is the risk that the cumulative effect of some or all of the preceding complications may combine to so hamper the party's trial preparations that he will ultimately feel compelled to "cave" on the courthouse steps or end up putting on a materially weaker case than he otherwise would have. If settlement comes after full pretrial discovery and motion practice, costs will consume a larger proportion of any settlement payment. If trial presentation is weak, the party may win little or nothing. The risks of geography increase the likelihood of such unfavorable outcomes, and that ultimate concern further compounds the pressures that push nonresident claimants toward earlier and less favorable settlements.

Edward A. Purcell Jr., Geography as a Litigation Weapon: Forum-Selection Clauses and the Rehnquist Court, 40 UCLA L. Rev. 423, 446-449 (1992).

Note: Litigating Personal Jurisdiction

Consider the following comments of Professor Winton Woods:

> We need constantly to remind ourselves that personal jurisdiction decisions are usually made in the dimly-lit factual arena of the initial choice of forum. Moreover, they are made by trial lawyers with no admitted expertise in constitutional adjudication, but who claim great skill at common law argumentation concerning fairness and equity. At this preliminary litigation juncture, simplicity and clarity of doctrine are principles with stature equal to that of coherency.

Winton Woods, Carnival Cruise Lines v. Shute: An Amicus Inquiry Into the Future of "Purposeful Availment," 36 Wayne L. Rev. 1393, 1396 (1990).

To what extent are the Court's cases unduly confusing for lawyers who are trying to select a forum that will have jurisdiction over all defendants? Is it easy to determine where a corporation has "minimum contacts" or where it has "purposefully directed" its commercial activities? Would a simple, bright-line test be preferable to the context-sensitive due process analysis we now have?

The complexities of the law of personal jurisdiction prompt many lawyers simply to avoid confronting them whenever possible. The simplest way to do this, of course, is to file the action in a forum that clearly has power over the defendant, and in most cases there is such a forum. Whatever the attractions of a questionable forum, the expenses of waging a jurisdiction battle and the likely prolonging of the litigation often lead lawyers to decline a case or to refer the client instead to a lawyer in the forum where jurisdiction is most likely to be established.

Yet when questions of personal jurisdiction do arise, they are fundamental to fairness and to the ability of our procedural system to deal with the nationalization and globalization of commerce.

How exactly does the defendant's lawyer raise the question of personal jurisdiction? There are two principal methods of attack: collateral and direct. By far the more important of these is the direct attack, outlined briefly here and presented more fully in its tactical dimensions in Chapter 2.

The risky indirect, or collateral, attack on personal jurisdiction is raised by doing nothing in response to the service of the summons and complaint. A default judgment will probably be entered; when the plaintiff seeks to execute on the judgment, the defendant can argue that it is void because it was entered by a court without personal jurisdiction. A void judgment is not enforceable as a matter of due process and of full faith and credit. In addition to personal jurisdiction, the requisites of a valid and enforceable judgment are subject-matter jurisdiction and notice to the defendant.

Collateral attack is not for the faint-hearted or risk-averse, however, because the defendant who loses his jurisdictional argument cannot then argue the merits of his defense. These he has defaulted away. The only objections that can be raised on collateral attack are those that go to the power of the court entering the default judgment.

The much more common method of objecting is to raise the issue in the court where the plaintiff asserts jurisdiction. Note that an objection to personal jurisdiction is waived if it is not made in the first response to the complaint filed in the action, whether that is an answer or a motion prior to answering. See Fed. R. Civ. P. 12.

In the direct attack procedure, the defendant who loses on personal jurisdiction may then go on to defend on the merits. If there is an appeal, she may argue that the lower court erred in its ruling on personal jurisdiction. To put it another way, a defendant does not submit to the jurisdiction of the court by moving on to defend the merits. Typically, in state and appellate courts, those who contest jurisdiction directly must wait for a final judgment in the trial court before appealing its assertion of jurisdiction.

Finally, although procedure on contesting personal jurisdiction varies in its details from state to state, the overall approach is close to that of the federal system, outlined above. A few states still provide for "special" and a few for "limited" appearances to contest jurisdiction. The theory behind these practices is that a court must have jurisdiction to decide whether it has jurisdiction, or that by coming in and contesting jurisdiction, a defendant submits to the court's power. In such states, a special appearance must be made for the purpose of objecting to jurisdiction. Similarly, in some places a defendant in a *quasi in rem* action makes a "limited appearance" to defend his cause without exposing himself to an *in personam* judgment that would be enforceable against all of his assets, wherever they may be located.

7. Contacts and Contracts

The identity of the parties is a constant, though usually subtextual, issue in personal jurisdiction cases. As you look back on the cases, most of them deal with bringing a distant defendant to the plaintiff's home court. Add to the mix that the defendant is a multistate corporation and the plaintiff an injured individual, and you have a potent recipe for extending jurisdiction.

So far, we have dealt with fairness determinations after the fact; now we turn to the possibility of deciding in advance the location of some future lawsuit. Here, principles of contract law, as well as of waiver, enter the jurisdictional calculus. The identity of the parties remains important here as well, coming into play in the decisions about whether a contract was fair or fairly agreed to, or whether execution of its terms violates due process of law.

Burger King Corp. v. Rudzewicz
471 U.S. 462 (1985)

JUSTICE BRENNAN delivered the opinion of the Court.

The State of Florida's long-arm statute extends jurisdiction to "[a]ny person, whether or not a citizen or resident of this state," who, *inter alia*, "[b]reach[es] a contract in this state by failing to perform acts required by the contract to be performed in this state," so long as the cause of action arises from the alleged contractual breach. Fla. Stat. § 48.193(1)(g) (Supp. 1984). The United States District Court for the Southern District of Florida, sitting in diversity, relied on this provision in exercising personal jurisdiction over a Michigan resident who allegedly had breached a franchise agreement with a Florida corporation by failing to make required payments in Florida. The question presented is whether this exercise of long-arm jurisdiction offended "traditional conception[s] of fair play and substantial justice" embodied in the Due Process Clause of the Fourteenth Amendment. International Shoe Co. v. Washington, 326 U.S. 310, 320 (1945).

I

A

Burger King Corporation is a Florida corporation whose principal offices are in Miami. It is one of the world's largest restaurant organizations, with over 3,000 outlets in the 50 States, the Commonwealth of Puerto Rico, and 8 foreign nations. Burger King conducts approximately 80% of its business through a franchise operation that the company styles the "Burger King System"—"a comprehensive restaurant format and operating system for the sale of uniform and quality food products." Burger King licenses its franchisees to use its trademarks and service marks for a period of 20 years and leases standardized restaurant facilities to them for the same term. In addition, franchisees acquire a variety of proprietary information concerning the "standards, specifications, procedures and methods for operating a Burger King Restaurant." They also receive market research and advertising assistance, ongoing training in restaurant management,[2] and accounting, cost-control, and inventory-control guidance. By permitting franchisees to tap into Burger King's established national reputation and to benefit from proven procedures for dispensing standardized fare, this system enables them to go into the restaurant business with significantly lowered barriers to entry.

In exchange for these benefits, franchisees pay Burger King an initial $40,000 franchise fee and commit themselves to payment of monthly royalties, advertising and sales promotion fees, and rent computed in part from monthly gross sales. Franchisees also agree to submit to the national organization's exacting regulation of virtually every conceivable aspect of their operations. Burger King imposes these standards and undertakes its rigid regulation out of conviction that "[u]niformity of service, appearance, and quality of product is essential to the preservation of the Burger King image and the benefits accruing therefrom to both Franchisee and Franchisor."

Burger King oversees its franchise system through a two-tiered administrative structure. The governing contracts provide that the franchise relationship is established in Miami and governed by Florida law, and call for payment of all required fees and forwarding of all relevant notices to the Miami headquarters. The Miami headquarters sets policy and works directly with its franchisees in attempting to resolve major problems. Day-to-day monitoring of franchisees, however, is conducted through a network of 10 district offices which in turn report to the Miami headquarters.

The instant litigation grows out of Burger King's termination of one of its franchisees, and is aptly described by the franchisee as "a divorce proceeding among commercial partners." The appellee John Rudzewicz, a Michigan citizen and resident, is the senior partner in a Detroit accounting firm. In 1978, he was approached by Brian MacShara, the son of a business acquaintance, who suggested that they jointly apply to Burger King for a franchise in the Detroit area. MacShara proposed to serve as the manager of the restaurant if Rudzewicz would put up the investment capital; in exchange, the two would evenly share the profits. Believing that MacShara's idea offered attractive investment and tax-deferral opportunities, Rudzewicz agreed to the venture.

Rudzewicz and MacShara jointly applied for a franchise to Burger King's Birmingham, Michigan, district office in the autumn of 1978. The application was forwarded to Burger King's Miami headquarters, which entered into a preliminary agreement with them in February 1979. During the ensuing four months it was agreed that Rudzewicz and MacShara would assume operation of an existing facility in Drayton Plains, Michigan. MacShara attended the prescribed management courses in Miami during this period, see no. 2, supra, and the franchisees purchased $165,000 worth of restaurant equipment from Burger King's Davmor Industries division in Miami. Even before the final agreements were

2. Mandatory training seminars are conducted at Burger King University in Miami and at Whopper College Regional Training Centers around the country.

signed, however, the parties began to disagree. . . . During these disputes Rudzewicz and MacShara negotiated both with the Birmingham district office and with the Miami headquarters.[7] With some misgivings, Rudzewicz and MacShara finally obtained limited concessions from the Miami headquarters,[8] signed the final agreements, and commenced operations in June 1979. By signing the final agreements, Rudzewicz obligated himself personally to payments exceeding $1 million over the 20-year franchise relationship.

The Drayton Plains facility apparently enjoyed steady business during the summer of 1979, but patronage declined after a recession began later that year. Rudzewicz and MacShara soon fell far behind in their monthly payments to Miami. Headquarters sent notices of default, and an extended period of negotiations began among the franchisees, the Birmingham district office, and the Miami headquarters. After several Burger King officials in Miami had engaged in prolonged but ultimately unsuccessful negotiations with the franchisees by mail and by telephone,[9] headquarters terminated the franchise and ordered Rudzewicz and MacShara to vacate the premises. They refused and continued to occupy and operate the facility as a Burger King restaurant.

B

Burger King commenced the instant action in the United States District Court for the Southern District of Florida in May 1981. . . . Burger King alleged that Rudzewicz and MacShara had breached their franchise obligations "within [the jurisdiction of] this district court" by failing to make the required payments "at plaintiff's place of business in Miami, Dade Country, Florida," and also charged that they were tortiously infringing its trademarks and service marks through their continued, unauthorized operation as a Burger King restaurant. Burger King sought damages, injunctive relief, and costs and attorney's fees. Rudzewicz and MacShara entered special appearances and argued, *inter alia*, that because they were Michigan residents and because Burger King's claim did not "arise" within the Southern District of Florida, the District Court lacked personal jurisdiction over them. The District Court denied their motions after a hearing, holding that, pursuant to Florida's long-arm statute, "a

7. Although Rudzewicz and MacShara dealt with the Birmingham district office on a regular basis, they communicated directly with the Miami headquarters in forming the contracts; moreover, they learned that the district office had "very little" decision-making authority and accordingly turned directly to headquarters in seeking to resolve their disputes.

8. They were able to secure a $10,439 reduction in rent for the third year.

9. Miami's policy was to "deal directly" with franchisees when they began to encounter financial difficulties, and to involve district office personnel only when necessary. In the instant case, for example, the Miami office handled all credit problems, ordered cost-cutting measures, negotiated for a partial refinancing of the franchisees' debts, communicated directly with the franchisees in attempting to resolve the dispute, and was responsible for all termination matters.

non-resident Burger King franchisee is subject to the personal jurisdiction of this Court in actions arising out of its franchise agreements." . . .

After a 3-day bench trial, the court again concluded that it had "jurisdiction over the subject matter and the parties to this cause." Finding that Rudzewicz and MacShara had breached their franchise agreements with Burger King and had infringed Burger King's trademarks and service marks, the court entered judgment against them, jointly and severally, for $228,875 in contract damages. The court also ordered them "to immediately close Burger King Restaurant Number 775 from continued operation or to immediately give the keys and possession of said restaurant to Burger King Corporation," found that they had failed to prove any of the required elements of their counterclaim, and awarded costs and attorney's fees to Burger King.

Rudzewicz appealed to the Court of Appeals for the Eleventh Circuit.[11] A divided panel of that Circuit reversed the judgment, concluding that the District Court could not properly exercise personal jurisdiction over Rudzewicz pursuant to Fla. Stat. § 48.193(1)(g) (Supp. 1984) because "the circumstances of the Drayton Plains franchise and the negotiations which led to it left Rudzewicz bereft of reasonable notice and financially unprepared for the prospect of franchise litigation in Florida." Burger King Corp. v. MacShara, 724 F.2d 1505, 1513 (1984). Accordingly, the panel majority concluded that "[j]urisdiction under these circumstances would offend the fundamental fairness which is the touchstone of due process." Ibid. . . .

II

A

The Due Process Clause protects an individual's liberty interest in not being subject to the binding judgments of a forum with which he has established no meaningful "contacts, ties, or relations." International Shoe Co. v. Washington, 326 U.S., at 319.[13] By requiring that individuals have "fair warning that a particular activity may subject [them] to the jurisdiction of a foreign sovereign," Shaffer v. Heitner, 433 U.S. 186, 218 (1977) (Stevens, J., concurring in judgment), the Due Process Clause "gives a degree of predictability to the legal system that allows potential defendants to structure their primary conduct with some minimum assurance

11. MacShara did not appeal his judgment. See Burger King Corp. v. MacShara, 724 F.2d 1505, 1506, n.1 (11th cir. 1984). In addition, Rudzewicz entered into a compromise with Burger King and waived his right to appeal the District Court's finding of trademark infringement and its entry of injunctive relief. . . .

13. Although this protection operates to restrict state power, it "must be seen as ultimately a function of the individual liberty interest preserved by the Due Process Clause" rather than as a function "of federalism concerns." Insurance Corp. of Ireland v. Compagnie des Bauxites de Guinee, 456 U.S. 694, 702-703, n.10 (1982).

as to where that conduct will and will not render them liable to suit," World-Wide Volkswagen Corp. v. Woodson, 444 U.S. 286, 297 (1980).

Where a forum seeks to assert specific jurisdiction over an out-of-state defendant who has not consented to suit there, this "fair warning" requirement is satisfied if the defendant has "purposefully directed" his activities at residents of the forum, Keeton v. Hustler Magazine, Inc., 465 U.S. 770, 774 (1984).[15] . . . And with respect to interstate contractual obligations, we have emphasized that parties who "reach out beyond one state and create continuing relationships and obligations with citizens of another state" are subject to regulation and sanctions in the other State for the consequences of their activities. . . .

. . . [T]he constitutional touchstone remains whether the defendant purposefully established "minimum contacts" in the forum State. International Shoe Co. v. Washington, supra, at 316. Although it has been argued that foreseeability of causing *injury* in another State should be sufficient to establish such contacts there when policy considerations so require,[16] the Court has consistently held that this kind of foreseeability is not a "sufficient benchmark" for exercising personal jurisdiction. World-Wide Volkswagen Corp. v. Woodson, 444 U.S. at 295. Instead, "the foreseeability that is critical to due process analysis . . . is that the defendant's conduct and connection with the forum State are such that he should reasonably anticipate being haled into court there." Id. at 297. In defining when it is that a potential defendant should "reasonably anticipate" out-of-state litigation, the Court frequently has drawn from the reasoning of Hanson v. Denckla, 357 U.S. 235, 253 (1958):

> [I]t is essential in each case that there be some act by which the defendant purposefully avails itself of the privilege of conducting activities within the forum State, thus invoking the benefits and protections of its laws. . . .

Jurisdiction in these circumstances may not be avoided merely because the defendant did not *physically* enter the forum State. Although territorial presence frequently will enhance a potential defendant's affiliation with a State and reinforce the reasonable foreseeability of suit there, it is an inescapable fact of modern commercial life that a substantial amount of business is transacted solely by mail and wire communications across state lines, thus obviating the need for physical presence within a State in which business is conducted. So long as a commercial actor's efforts are "purposefully directed" toward residents of another State, we have

15. "Specific" jurisdiction contrasts with "general" jurisdiction, pursuant to which "a State exercises personal jurisdiction over a defendant in a suit not arising out of or related to the defendant's contacts with the forum." Helicopteros Nacionales de Colombia, S.A. v. Hall, 466 U.S. at 414, n.9; see also Perkins v. Benguet Consolidated Mining Co., 342 U.S. 437 (1952).

16. See, e.g., World-Wide Volkswagen Corp. v. Woodson, 444 U.S. 286, 299 (1980) (Brennan, J., dissenting); Shaffer v. Heitner, 433 U.S. 186, 219 (1977) (Brennan, J., concurring in part and dissenting in part).

consistently rejected the notion that an absence of physical contacts can defeat personal jurisdiction there. Keeton v. Hustler Magazine, Inc., supra.

Once it has been decided that a defendant purposefully established minimum contacts within the forum State, these contacts may be considered in light of other factors to determine whether the assertion of personal jurisdiction would comport with "fair play and substantial justice." International Shoe Co. v. Washington, 326 U.S. at 320. Thus courts in "appropriate case[s]" may evaluate "the burden on the defendant," "the forum State's interest in adjudicating the dispute," "the plaintiff's interest in obtaining convenient and effective relief," "the interstate judicial system's interest in obtaining the most efficient resolution of controversies," and the "shared interest of the several States in furthering fundamental substantive social policies." World-Wide Volkswagen Corp. v. Woodson, 444 U.S. at 292. . . .

B

(1)

. . . [W]e believe there is substantial record evidence supporting the District Court's conclusion that the assertion of personal jurisdiction over Rudzewicz in Florida for the alleged breach of his franchise agreement did not offend due process. . . .

In this case, no physical ties to Florida can be attributed to Rudzewicz other than MacShara's brief training course in Miami. Rudzewicz did not maintain offices in Florida and, for all that appears from the record, has never even visited there. Yet this franchise dispute grew directly out of "a contact which had a *substantial* connection with that State." McGee v. International Life Insurance Co., 355 U.S. at 223 (emphasis added). Eschewing the option of operating an independent local enterprise, Rudzewicz deliberately "reach[ed] out beyond" Michigan and negotiated with a Florida corporation for the purchase of a long-term franchise and the manifold benefits that would derive from affiliation with a nationwide organization. Upon approval, he entered into a carefully structured 20-year relationship that envisioned continuing and wide-reaching contacts with Burger King in Florida. . . .

The Court of Appeals concluded, however, that in light of the supervision emanating from Burger King's district office in Birmingham, Rudzewicz reasonably believed that "the Michigan office was for all intents and purposes the embodiment of Burger King" and that he therefore had no "reason to anticipate a Burger King suit outside of Michigan." 724 F.2d at 511.

This reasoning overlooks substantial record evidence indicating that Rudzewicz most certainly knew that he was affiliating himself with an enterprise based primarily in Florida. The contract documents themselves emphasize that Burger King's operations are conducted and supervised from the Miami headquarters, that all relevant notices and payments must be sent there, and that the agreements were made in and enforced from

Miami. Moreover, the parties' actual course of dealing repeatedly confirmed that decisionmaking authority was vested in the Miami headquarters and that the district office served largely as an intermediate link between the headquarters and the franchisees. When problems arose over building design, site-development fees, rent computation, and the defaulted payments, Rudzewicz and MacShara learned that the Michigan office was powerless to resolve their disputes and could only channel their communications to Miami. Throughout these disputes, the Miami headquarters and the Michigan franchisees carried on a continuous course of direct communications by mail and by telephone, and it was the Miami headquarters that made the key negotiating decisions out of which the instant litigation arose.

Moreover, we believe the Court of Appeals gave insufficient weight to provisions in the various franchise documents providing that all disputes would be governed by Florida law. The franchise agreement, for example, stated:

> This Agreement shall become valid when executed and accepted by BKC at Miami, Florida; it shall be deemed made and entered into in the State of Florida and shall be governed and construed under and in accordance with the laws of the State of Florida. The choice of law designation does not require that all suits concerning this Agreement be filed in Florida.

The Court of Appeals reasoned that choice-of-law provisions are irrelevant to the question of personal jurisdiction. . . . Nothing in our cases . . . suggests that a choice-of-law *provision* should be ignored in considering whether a defendant has "purposefully invoked the benefits and protections of a State's laws" for jurisdictional purposes. Although such a provision standing alone would be insufficient to confer jurisdiction, we believe that, when combined with the 20-year interdependent relationship Rudzewicz established with Burger King's Miami headquarters, it reinforced his deliberate affiliation with the forum State and the reasonable foreseeability of possible litigation there. As Judge Johnson argued in his dissent below, Rudzewicz "purposefully availed himself of the benefits and protections of Florida's laws" by entering into contracts expressly providing that those laws would govern franchise disputes.[24]

Nor has Rudzewicz pointed to other factors that can be said persuasively to outweigh the considerations discussed above and to establish the *unconstitutionality* of Florida's assertion of jurisdiction. We cannot conclude that Florida had no "legitimate interest in holding [Rudzewicz] answerable on a claim related to" the contacts he had established in that

24. . . . The lease also provided for binding arbitration in Miami of certain condemnation disputes, and Rudzewicz conceded the validity of this provision at oral argument. Although it does not govern the instant dispute, this provision also should have made it apparent to the franchisees that they were dealing directly with the Miami headquarters and that the Birmingham district office was *not* "for all intents and purposes the embodiment of Burger King."

State.[25] Moreover, although Rudzewicz has argued at some length that Michigan's Franchise Investment Law, Mich. Comp. Laws §§ 445.1501 et seq. (1979), governs many aspects of this franchise relationship, he has not demonstrated how Michigan's acknowledged interest might possibly render jurisdiction in Florida *unconstitutional*. Finally, the Court of Appeals' assertion that the Florida litigation "severely impaired [Rudzewicz's] ability to call Michigan witnesses who might be essential to his defense and counterclaim," 724 F.2d at 1511-1512, and n.10, is wholly without support in the record. And even to the extent that it is inconvenient for a party who has minimum contacts with a forum to litigate there, such considerations most frequently can be accommodated through a change of venue. Although the Court has suggested that inconvenience may at some point become so substantial as to achieve *constitutional* magnitude, this is not such a case.

The Court of Appeals also concluded, however, that the parties' dealings involved "a characteristic disparity of bargaining power" and "elements of surprise," and that Rudzewicz "lacked fair notice" of the potential for litigation in Florida because the contractual provisions suggesting to the contrary were merely "boilerplate declarations in a lengthy printed contract." United States v. United States Gypsum Co., 333 U.S. 364, 395 (1948). Rudzewicz presented many of these arguments to the District Court, contending that Burger King was guilty of misrepresentation, fraud, and duress; that it gave insufficient notice in its dealings with him; and that the contract was one of adhesion. After a 3-day bench trial, the District Court found that Burger King had made no misrepresentations, that Rudzewicz and MacShara "were and are experienced and sophisticated businessmen," and that "at no time" did they "ac[t] under economic duress or disadvantage imposed by" Burger King.

Federal Rule of Civil Procedure 52(a) requires that "[f]indings of fact shall not be set aside unless clearly erroneous," and neither Rudzewicz nor the Court of Appeals has pointed to record evidence that would support a "definite and firm conviction" that the District Court's findings are mistaken. To the contrary, Rudzewicz was represented by counsel throughout these complex transactions and, as Judge Johnson observed in dissent below, was himself an experienced accountant "who for five months conducted negotiations with Burger King over the terms of the franchise and lease agreements, and who obligated himself personally to contracts requiring over time payments that exceeded $1 million." 724 F.2d at 1514. Rudzewicz was able to secure a modest reduction in rent and other concessions from Miami headquarters[;] moreover, to the extent

25. Complaining that "when Burger King is the plaintiff, you won't 'have it your way' because it sues all franchisees in Miami," Rudzewicz contends that Florida's interest in providing a convenient forum is negligible given the company's size and ability to conduct litigation anywhere in the country. We disagree. Absent compelling considerations, a defendant who has purposefully derived commercial benefit from his affiliations in a forum may not defeat jurisdiction there simply because of his adversary's greater net wealth.

that Burger King's terms were inflexible, Rudzewicz presumably decided that the advantages of affiliating with a national organization provided sufficient commercial benefits to offset the detriments.

III

Notwithstanding these considerations, the Court of Appeals apparently believed that it was necessary to reject jurisdiction in this case as a prophylactic measure, reasoning that an affirmance of the District Court's judgment would result in the exercise of jurisdiction over "out-of-state consumers to collect payments due on modest personal purchases" and would "sow the seeds of default judgments against franchisees owing smaller debts." Kulko v. Superior Court, 436 U.S. 84, 92 (1978). We share the Court of Appeals' broader concerns and therefore reject any talismanic jurisdictional formulas; "the facts of each case must [always] be weighed" in determining whether personal jurisdiction would comport with "fair play and substantial justice." . . .

. . . The judgment of the Court of Appeals is accordingly reversed, and the case is remanded for further proceedings consistent with this opinion.

It is so ordered.

JUSTICE POWELL took no part in the consideration or decision of this case.

JUSTICE STEVENS, with whom JUSTICE WHITE joins, dissenting.

In my opinion there is a significant element of unfairness in requiring a franchisee to defend a case of this kind in the forum chosen by the franchisor. It is undisputed that appellee maintained no place of business in Florida, that he had no employees in that State, and that he was not licensed to do business there. Appellee did not prepare his French fries, shakes, and hamburgers in Michigan, and then deliver them into the stream of commerce "with the expectation that they [would] be purchased by consumers in" Florida. To the contrary, appellee did business only in Michigan, his business, property, and payroll taxes were payable in that State, and he sold all of his products there.

Throughout the business relationship, appellee's principal contacts with appellant were with its Michigan office. Notwithstanding its disclaimer, the Court seems ultimately to rely on nothing more than standard boiler-plate language contained in various documents to establish that appellee "'purposefully availed himself of the benefits and protections of Florida's laws.'" Such superficial analysis creates a potential for unfairness not only in negotiations between franchisors and their franchisees but, more significantly, in the resolution of the disputes that inevitably arise from time to time in such relationships. . . .

Accordingly, I respectfully dissent.

Notes and Questions

1. *Burger King* followed after the signal in *World-Wide Volkswagen* to retract the long arm, yet it is fairly unrestrained in its explication of Florida's interest. Re-read footnote 13. What is left of the "interstate sovereignty" explanation for limits on personal jurisdiction that the Court gave in *World-Wide*?

2. Although suit was filed in a federal district court, the governing law is the Florida long-arm statute. This occurs by operation of Fed. R. Civ. P. 4.

Read Rule 4 and think about whether the federal courts are entitled to extend their reach beyond that of the state in which they sit. Could there be nationwide service of process by federal courts, without regard to the jurisdictional boundaries of individual states? Note that one congressional act, the interpleader statute, provides that a federal court subpoena may reach any state. 28 U.S.C. § 2361.

Given that federal courts in some cases thus have broader service reach than any state court, should parties' reasonable expectations of being haled into a foreign court extend to this broadest range whenever the matter could be filed in federal court?

In connection with our study of federal question jurisdiction in this chapter and Chapter 6, we will return to these questions, in particular whether there should be some distinction between federal question and diversity cases, and the operation of Rule 4(k), a 1993 amendment to the Federal Rules of Civil Procedure.

3. Observe that *Burger King* sets forth a two-step process for assessing whether a court has jurisdiction over a nonresident defendant. First, it determines whether "minimum contacts" exist; second, it determines whether jurisdiction is "reasonable." How would you describe the factors relevant to each step? Recall that in *Asahi* all Justices agreed that even if minimum contacts were present, jurisdiction nevertheless was unreasonable. Thus the Court really does see these as independent prongs. But how is the "burden on the defendant" factor under the reasonableness prong different from purposeful direction or foreseeability under minimum contacts?

4. *Burger King* offers some guidance for future cases in which a plaintiff seeks to sue a nonresident defendant in a contract dispute. The Court identifies several factors to consider. These factors fall into two groups: those that are contained within the contract itself and those that are external to the contract. As to the first group, what contract terms would improve the chances that a party to the contract would be amenable to process in a particular jurisdiction? Post-*Burger King,* what changes do you imagine occurred in contract negotiations among sophisticated commercial actors?

5. Is there reason to believe that a nonresident seller is more vulnerable to jurisdiction in the state where the buyer lives than a nonresident buyer is in the state where the seller lives? Think about the problem case of

Durand v. Intact Hearing, below, and the effect of *Burger King* on actions brought by a seller of goods against a stay-at-home individual consumer.

In Quill v. North Dakota, 504 U.S. 298 (1992), the United States Supreme Court held that a nonresident mail order firm was amenable to process in a suit to collect a sales-type tax from the firm. Although the firm had no office, plant, or salespeople there, it mailed catalogues and items worth millions of dollars in annual sales to North Dakota customers. What if one of the consumers failed to pay her bill? Would she be amenable to process in the state where the mail order firm is located? Is an L.L. Bean customer at risk of suit in Freeport, Maine?

6. Whether you think *Burger King* was correctly decided depends partly on whether you see Rudzewicz and MacShara as competent commercial actors or two little guys from Detroit. In this regard, consider the remark of a civil procedure student at Stanford in Fall 1993:

> I found the two perspectives of the Burger King restaurant in Michigan interesting. The corporation itself viewed the restaurant as part of a large chain with specific quality control measures, price standards, and a uniform nationwide reputation to preserve. The dissent viewed the restaurant as "a local concern serving, at best, a neighborhood or a community." I relate to the latter since I live in an urban area where you can walk from one Burger King to another. Although you can get the same food at another Burger King, the one in your neighborhood is *your* Burger King.

8. Persons or Property Within the State

Problem Case: Just Passing Through

You are an associate with a law firm in San Jose, California. As part of your firm's pro bono obligation, you take on the defense of a case against a local 70-year-old widow, Dinah Durand. Durand was recently served with a summons while sitting in the Phoenix, Arizona, airport en route to her brother's funeral in Richmond, Virginia. The plaintiff is Intact Hearing, Inc., based in Phoenix.

The complaint correctly alleges that Dinah Durand ordered from Intact an in-ear hearing aid, but paid only one installment: the one that accompanied her order. The cost of the hearing aid was $1,200, payable in 12 monthly installments.

You learn that Durand ordered the hearing aid by mail after seeing it advertised on television as a "revolutionary new break-through." But when it arrived, she was extremely disappointed to find that, in her words, "it was a piece of plastic junk that made things louder but not clearer." Along with the aid, she received a piece of paper labeled Acceptance of Order and 11 payment envelopes. The Acceptance form had a schedule of payments due and in large letters at the top stated "Arizona Courts Have Jurisdiction over Any Disputes Under this Agreement." All payments, like the first, were to be mailed to the company in Phoenix, Arizona.

Durand sent the hearing aid back in one of the envelopes provided for the monthly payments and simply threw away all further correspondence from the company. After nine months of this, a company representative telephoned her and warned that if she did not pay the balance due within seven days, she would be sued. Durand told the representative that she had sent the aid back and that he wouldn't be able to sue her in any event because she was leaving the next morning at 6:05 A.M. for Richmond, Virginia, and wouldn't be back for more than seven days. The company representative happened to know that there was a 6:05 flight from San Jose, California, to Richmond that had a plane change in Phoenix. With a quick call to a travel agent, he confirmed that this was the only 6:05 flight to Richmond originating from an airport in or near San Jose.

The company representative passed this information on to the company lawyers and told them as well that "she claims to have returned the aid, but that's what they all say." Since it was already afternoon, the lawyers decided not to institute a search of the company's mail room or to talk to the mail room personnel, but instead quickly filled in Durand's name and the relevant dates on their form complaint, filed it in the Arizona district court (the state trial court), and hired a process server to deliver the complaint and summons to Dinah Durand during her stop-over in Phoenix. She says she was humiliated when a beefy red-faced man thrust the papers at her and said loudly: "Here's a complaint against you, lady. I guess you can hear that."

Assume that the Arizona long-arm provision reads as stated on page 131 above in the problem case of the "Troubled Young Man."

What would be your advice to Ms. Durand? Do you have legitimate objections to the exercise of personal jurisdiction by Arizona? Would you raise them by motion or by taking a default judgment in Arizona? What policy considerations and other considerations would enter your decision about how and whether to object to personal jurisdiction? How would you raise them?

If you were an appellate judge deciding whether jurisdiction was properly exercised, how would you vote, and why?

International Shoe and all its case and statute progeny explicitly and implicitly rejected the principle that presence of the defendant or his property was *essential* for jurisdiction. Unanswered for many years, and still not definitively decided, was whether the presence of either is *sufficient* for the constitutional exercise of jurisdiction.

Recall that under *Pennoyer,* both types of presence-based jurisdiction were constitutional. Presence of a person in the forum—sometimes called "transient" or "gotcha" jurisdiction—would suffice for any lawsuit against the defendant, even if the defendant had no other ties to the state and the lawsuit arose out of activities elsewhere. Moreover, the jurisdiction over the defendant would be general, which in this context means that the defendant's liability would extend to the full value of her (non-exempt) assets.

Presence of a person's property (not self) in the forum was also sufficient for jurisdiction under *Pennoyer.* But the defendant's liability in a case based on attachment of property—called "attachment jurisdiction"—typically was limited to the value of the property attached (though in some states the moment the defendant appeared to defend against that attachment she was deemed to "consent" to *in personam* and thus general jurisdiction over her). Thus the defendant's financial exposure was more limited than if she were physically present and served during the forum visit.

The following chart outlines the four ways in which a court might attempt to obtain jurisdiction over a nonresident:

In personam (person-based)	*Quasi in rem, in rem (property-based)*
1. Nonresident served outside the forum	3. Attachment of property unrelated to lawsuit
2. Nonresident served within the forum	4. Attachment of property related to lawsuit

We have already addressed in depth the post-*Pennoyer* response to the first category, that is, lawsuits in which a nonresident is served outside the forum. The statutory and case law developments from *Shoe* onward established that jurisdiction over the nonresident will be constitutional if the defendant has minimum contacts with the forum and it is reasonable for the court to assert jurisdiction.

At the same time, most legal actors assumed that minimum contacts provided an alternative to traditional territorial jurisdiction—that *in rem* and *quasi in rem* jurisdiction were essentially unaffected by modern notions of fair play and substantial justice. The great expansions of state court jurisdiction took place on a track that paralleled traditional territorial authority over property.

But in a pattern similar to the pressure put on territoriality by the development of the automobile and the corporation, new forms of highly mobile property whose situs was uncertain finally brought the due process analysis of *Shoe* to bear on the *quasi in rem* hybrid jurisdiction. Shaffer v. Heitner, 433 U.S. 186 (1977), overruled *Pennoyer* in so many words and held that *"all assertions of state-court jurisdiction must be evaluated according to the standards set forth in* International Shoe *and its progeny. . . ."* Id. at 212 (emphasis added). For the first time, minimum contacts provided the basis for limiting, rather than expanding, traditional bases of jurisdiction.

The Court's logic in *Shaffer* suggested that a nonresident who is served within the forum *cannot* be amenable to process there *unless* she has "minimum contacts" with the state. Read on, and see how *Shaffer* forms the historical backdrop for the surprising decision of Burnham v. Superior Court. *Burnham* dealt with category two—*in personam* jurisdiction based on physical presence in the forum. *Shaffer* dealt with category three and, by implication, category four—jurisdiction based on the presence of property related to the lawsuit.

Shaffer v. Heitner
433 U.S. 186 (1977)

JUSTICE MARSHALL delivered the opinion of the Court.

The controversy in this case concerns the constitutionality of a Delaware statute that allows a court of that State to take jurisdiction of a lawsuit by sequestering any property of the defendant that happens to be located in Delaware. Appellants contend that the sequestration statute as applied in this case violates the Due Process Clause of the Fourteenth Amendment both because it permits the state courts to exercise jurisdiction despite the absence of sufficient contacts among the defendants, the litigation, and the State of Delaware and because it authorizes the deprivation of defendants' property without providing adequate procedural safeguards. We find it necessary to consider only the first of these contentions.

Appellee Heitner, a nonresident of Delaware, is the owner of one share of stock in the Greyhound Corp., a business incorporated under the laws of Delaware with its principal place of business in Phoenix, Ariz. On May 22, 1974, he filed a shareholder's derivative suit in the Court of Chancery for New Castle County, Del., in which he named as defendants Greyhound, its wholly owned subsidiary Greyhound Lines, Inc., and 28 present or former officers or directors of one or both of the corporations. In essence, Heitner alleged that the individual defendants had violated their duties to Greyhound by causing it and its subsidiary to engage in actions that resulted in the corporations being held liable for substantial damages in a private antitrust suit and a large fine in a criminal contempt action. The activities which led to these penalties took place in Oregon.

Simultaneously with his complaint, Heitner filed a motion for an order of sequestration of the Delaware property of the individual defendants pursuant to Del. Code Ann., Tit. 10, § 366 (1975). This motion was accompanied by a supporting affidavit of counsel which stated that the individual defendants were nonresidents of Delaware. The affidavit identified the property to be sequestered as

> common stock, 3% Second Cumulative Preferenced Stock and stock unit credits of the Defendant Greyhound Corporation, a Delaware corporation, as well as all options and all warrants to purchase said stock issued to said individual Defendants and all contractural [sic] obligations, all rights, debts or credits due or accrued to or for the benefit of any of the said Defendants under any type of written agreement, contract or other legal instrument of any kind whatever between any of the individual Defendants and said corporation.

The requested sequestration order was signed the day the motion was filed. Pursuant to that order, the sequestrator "seized" approximately 82,000 shares of Greyhound common stock belonging to 19 of the defendants, and options belonging to another 2 defendants. These seizures were accomplished by placing "stop transfer" orders or their equivalents on the books of the Greyhound Corp. So far as the record shows, none of the certificates representing the seized property was physically present in Delaware. The stock was considered to be in Delaware, and so subject to seizure, by virtue of Del. Code Ann., Tit. 8, § 169 (1975), which makes Delaware the situs of ownership of all stock in Delaware corporations.

All 28 defendants were notified of the initiation of the suit by certified mail directed to their last known addresses and by publication in a New Castle County newspaper. The 21 defendants whose property was seized (hereafter referred to as appellants) responded by entering a special appearance for the purpose of moving to quash service of process and to vacate the sequestration order. They contended that the *ex parte* sequestration procedure did not accord them due process of law and that the property seized was not capable of attachment in Delaware. In addition, appellants asserted that under the rule of International Shoe Co. v. Washington, 326 U.S. 310 (1945), they did not have sufficient contacts with Delaware to sustain the jurisdiction of that State's courts.

The Court of Chancery rejected these arguments. . . .

On appeal, the Delaware Supreme Court affirmed the judgment of the Court of Chancery. . . .

We noted probable jurisdiction. We reverse.

The Delaware courts rejected appellants' jurisdictional challenge by noting that this suit was brought as a *quasi in rem* proceeding. Since *quasi in rem* jurisdiction is traditionally based on attachment or seizure of property present in the jurisdiction, not on contacts between the defendant and the State, the courts considered appellants' claimed lack of contacts with Delaware to be unimportant. This categorical analysis assumes the continued soundness of the conceptual structure founded on the century-old case of Pennoyer v. Neff, 95 U.S. 714 (1878).

Pennoyer was an ejectment action brought in federal court under the diversity jurisdiction. Pennoyer, the defendant in that action, held the land under a deed purchased in a sheriff's sale conducted to realize on a judgment for attorney's fees obtained against Neff in a previous action by one Mitchell. At the time of Mitchell's suit in an Oregon State court, Neff was a nonresident of Oregon. An Oregon statute allowed service by publication on nonresidents who had property in the State, and Mitchell had used that procedure to bring Neff before the court. The United States Circuit Court for the District of Oregon, in which Neff brought his ejectment action, refused to recognize the validity of the judgment against Neff in Mitchell's suit, and accordingly awarded the land to Neff. This Court affirmed. . . .

. . . As we have noted, under *Pennoyer* state authority to adjudicate was based on the jurisdiction's power over either persons or property. This fundamental concept is embodied in the very vocabulary which we use to describe judgments. If a court's jurisdiction is based on its authority over the defendant's person, the action and judgment are denominated *"in personam"* and can impose a personal obligation on the defendant in favor of the plaintiff. If jurisdiction is based on the court's power over property within its territory, the action is called "*in rem*" or "*quasi in rem*." The effect of a judgment in such a case is limited to the property that supports jurisdiction and does not impose a personal liability on the property owner, since he is not before the court. In *Pennoyer*'s terms, the owner is affected only "indirectly" by an *in rem* judgment adverse to his interest in the property subject to the court's disposition.

By concluding that "[t]he authority of every tribunal is necessarily restricted by the territorial limits of the State in which it is established," 95 U.S. at 720, *Pennoyer* sharply limited the availability of *in personam* jurisdiction over defendants not resident in the forum State. If a nonresident defendant could not be found in a State, he could not be sued there. On the other hand, since the State in which property was located was considered to have exclusive sovereignty over that property, *in rem* actions could proceed regardless of the owner's location. Indeed, since a State's process could not reach beyond its borders, this Court held after *Pennoyer* that due process did not require any effort to give a property owner personal notice that his property was involved in an *in rem* proceeding.

The *Pennoyer* rules generally favored nonresident defendants by making them harder to sue. This advantage was reduced, however, by the ability of a resident plaintiff to satisfy a claim against a nonresident defendant by bringing into court any property of the defendant located in the plaintiff's State. For example, in the well-known case of Harris v. Balk, 198 U.S. 215 (1905), Epstein, a resident of Maryland, had a claim against Balk, a resident of North Carolina. Harris, another North Carolina resident, owed money to Balk. When Harris happened to visit Maryland, Epstein garnished his debt to Balk. Harris did not contest the debt to Balk and paid it to Epstein's North Carolina attorney. When Balk later sued Harris in North Carolina, this Court held that the Full Faith and Credit Clause, U.S. Const., Art. IV, § 1, required that Harris' payment to Epstein be treated as a discharge of his debt to Balk. This Court reasoned that the debt Harris owed Balk was an intangible form of property belonging to Balk, and that the location of that property traveled with the debtor. By obtaining personal jurisdiction over Harris, Epstein had "arrested" his debt to Balk, and brought it into the Maryland court. Under the structure established by *Pennoyer,* Epstein was then entitled to proceed against that debt to vindicate his claim against Balk, even though Balk himself was not subject to the jurisdiction of a Maryland tribunal.

Pennoyer itself recognized that its rigid categories, even as blurred by the kind of action typified by *Harris,* could not accommodate some necessary litigation. Accordingly, Mr. Justice Field's opinion carefully noted that cases involving the personal status of the plaintiff, such as divorce actions, could be adjudicated in the plaintiff's home State even though the defendant could not be served within that State. Similarly, the opinion approved the practice of considering a foreign corporation doing business in a State to have consented to being sued in that State. This basis for *in personam* jurisdiction over foreign corporations was later supplemented by the doctrine that a corporation doing business in a State could be deemed "present" in the State, and so subject to service of process under the rule of *Pennoyer*. . . . [In *International Shoe*,] the relationship among the defendant, the forum, and the litigation, rather than the mutually exclusive sovereignty of the States on which the rules of *Pennoyer* rest, became the central concern of the inquiry into personal jurisdiction. The immediate effect of this departure from *Pennoyer*'s conceptual apparatus was to increase the ability of the state courts to obtain personal jurisdiction over nonresident defendants.

No equally dramatic change has occurred in the law governing jurisdiction *in rem*. There have, however, been intimations that the collapse of the *in personam* wing of *Pennoyer* has not left that decision unweakened as a foundation for *in rem* jurisdiction. Well-reasoned lower court opinions have questioned the proposition that the presence of property in a State gives that State jurisdiction to adjudicate rights to the property regardless of the relationship of the underlying dispute and the property owner to the forum. The overwhelming majority of commentators have also rejected *Pennoyer*'s premise that a proceeding "against" property is not a proceeding against the owners of that property. . . .

Although this Court has not addressed this argument directly, we have held that property cannot be subjected to a court's judgment unless reasonable and appropriate efforts have been made to give the property owners actual notice of the action. This conclusion recognizes, contrary to *Pennoyer*, that an adverse judgment *in rem* directly affects the property owner by divesting him of his rights in the property before the court. . . .

It is clear, therefore, that the law of state-court jurisdiction no longer stands securely on the foundation established in *Pennoyer*. We think that the time is ripe to consider whether the standard of fairness and substantial justice set forth in *International Shoe* should be held to govern actions *in rem* as well as *in personam*.

The case for applying to jurisdiction *in rem* the same test of "fair play and substantial justice" as governs assertions of jurisdiction *in personam* is simple and straightforward. It is premised on recognition that "[t]he phrase, 'judicial jurisdiction over a thing,' is a customary elliptical way of referring to jurisdiction over the interests of persons in a thing." Restatement (Second) of Conflict of Laws § 56, Introductory Note (1971). . . .

This argument, of course, does not ignore the fact that the presence of property in a State may bear on the existence of jurisdiction by providing contacts among the forum State, the defendant, and the litigation. For example, when claims to the property itself are the source of the underlying controversy between the plaintiff and the defendant, it would be unusual for the State where the property is located not to have jurisdiction. In such cases, the defendant's claim to property located in the State would normally indicate that he expected to benefit from the State's protection of his interest. The State's strong interests in assuring the marketability of property within its borders and in providing a procedure for peaceful resolution of disputes about the possession of that property would also support jurisdiction, as would the likelihood that important records and witnesses will be found in the State. The presence of property may also favor jurisdiction in cases, such as suits for injury suffered on the land of an absentee owner, where the defendant's ownership of the property is conceded but the cause of action is otherwise related to rights and duties growing out of that ownership.

It appears, therefore, that jurisdiction over many types of actions which now are or might be brought *in rem* would not be affected by a holding that any assertion of state-court jurisdiction must satisfy the *International Shoe* standard. For the type of *quasi in rem* action typified by Harris v. Balk and the present case, however, accepting the proposed analysis would result in significant change. These are cases where the property which now serves as the basis for state-court jurisdiction is completely unrelated to the plaintiff's cause of action. Thus, although the presence of the defendant's property in a State might suggest the existence of other ties among the defendant, the State, and the litigation, the presence of property alone would not support the State's jurisdiction. If those other ties did not exist, cases over which the State is now thought to have jurisdiction could not be brought in that forum.

. . . [I]n cases such as *Harris* and this one, the only role played by the property is to provide the basis for bringing the defendant into court. Indeed, the express purpose of the Delaware sequestration procedure is to compel the defendant to enter a personal appearance. In such cases, if a direct assertion of personal jurisdiction over the defendant would violate the Constitution, it would seem that an indirect assertion of that jurisdiction should be equally impermissible.

The primary rationale for treating the presence of property as a sufficient basis for jurisdiction to adjudicate claims over which the State would not have jurisdiction if *International Shoe* applied is that a wrongdoer "should not be able to avoid payment of his obligations by the expedient of removing his assets to a place where he is not subject to an in personam suit." Restatement § 66, Comment a. This justification, however, does not explain why jurisdiction should be recognized without regard to whether the property is present in the State because of an effort to avoid the owner's obligations. Nor does it support jurisdiction to adjudicate the underlying claim. At most, it suggests that a State in which property is located should have jurisdiction to attach that property, by use of proper procedures, as security for a judgment being sought in a forum where the litigation can be maintained consistently with *International Shoe.* Moreover, we know of nothing to justify the assumption that a debtor can avoid paying his obligations by removing his property to a State in which his creditor cannot obtain personal jurisdiction over him. The Full Faith and Credit Clause, after all, makes the valid *in personam* judgment of one State enforceable in all other States.

It might also be suggested that allowing *in rem* jurisdiction avoids the uncertainty inherent in the *International Shoe* standard and assures a plaintiff of a forum. We believe, however, that the fairness standard of

International Shoe can be easily applied in a vast majority of cases. Moreover, when the existence of jurisdiction in a particular forum under *International Shoe* is unclear, the cost of simplifying the litigation by avoiding the jurisdictional question may be the sacrifice of "fair play and substantial justice." That cost is too high.

We are left, then, to consider the significance of the long history of jurisdiction based solely on the presence of property in a State. . . . This history must be considered as supporting the proposition that jurisdiction based solely on the presence of property satisfies the demands of due process, but it is not decisive. "[T]raditional notions of fair play and substantial justice" can be as readily offended by the perpetuation of ancient forms that are no longer justified as by the adoption of new procedures that are inconsistent with the basic values of our constitutional heritage. The fiction that an assertion of jurisdiction over property is anything but an assertion of jurisdiction over the owner of the property supports an ancient form without substantial modern justification. Its continued acceptance would serve only to allow state-court jurisdiction that is fundamentally unfair to the defendant.

We therefore conclude that all assertions of state-court jurisdiction must be evaluated according to the standards set forth in *International Shoe* and its progeny.

The Delaware courts based their assertion of jurisdiction in this case solely on the statutory presence of the appellants' property in Delaware. Yet that property is not the subject matter of this litigation, nor is the underlying cause of action related to the property. Appellants' holdings in Greyhound do not, therefore, provide contacts with Delaware sufficient to support the jurisdiction of that State's courts over appellants. If it exists, that jurisdiction must have some other foundation.

Appellee Heitner did not allege and does not now claim that appellants have ever set foot in Delaware. Nor does he identify any act related to his cause of action as having taken place in Delaware. Nevertheless, he contends that appellants' positions as directors and officers of a corporation chartered in Delaware provide sufficient "contacts, ties, or relations," International Shoe Co. v. Washington, 326 U.S. at 319, with that State to give its courts jurisdiction over appellants in this stockholder's derivative action. This argument is based primarily on what Heitner asserts to be the strong interest of Delaware in supervising the management of a Delaware corporation. That interest is said to derive from the role of Delaware law in establishing the corporation and defining the obligations owed to it by its officers and directors. In order to protect this interest, appellee concludes, Delaware's courts must have jurisdiction over corporate fiduciaries such as appellants.

This argument is undercut by the failure of the Delaware Legislature to assert the state interest appellee finds so compelling. Delaware law bases jurisdiction, not on appellants' status as corporate fiduciaries, but rather on the presence of their property in the State. Although the sequestration procedure used here may be most frequently used in derivative suits against officers and directors, the authorizing statute evinces no specific concern with such actions. Sequestration can be used in any suit against a nonresident, and reaches corporate fiduciaries only if they happen to own interests in a Delaware corporation, or other property in the State. But as Heitner's failure to secure jurisdiction over seven of the defendants named in his complaint demonstrates, there is no necessary relationship between holding a position as a corporate fiduciary and owning stock or other interests in the corporation. If Delaware perceived its interest in securing jurisdiction over corporate fiduciaries to be as great as Heitner suggests, we would expect it to have enacted a statute more clearly designed to protect that interest. . . .

Appellee suggests that by accepting positions as officers or directors of a Delaware corporation, appellants performed the acts required by Hanson v. Denckla. He notes that Delaware law provides substantial benefits to corporate officers and directors, and that these benefits were at least in part the incentive for appellants to assume their positions. It is, he says, "only fair and just" to require appellants, in return for these benefits, to respond in the State of Delaware when they are accused of misusing their power.

But like Heitner's first argument, this line of reasoning establishes only that it is appropriate for Delaware law to govern the obligations of appellants to Greyhound and its stockholders. It does not demonstrate that appellants have "purposefully avail[ed themselves] of the privilege of conducting activities within the forum State," Hanson v. Denckla, 357 U.S. 235, 253 (1958), in a way that would justify bringing them before a Delaware tribunal. Appellants have simply had nothing to do with the State of Delaware. Moreover, appellants had no reason to expect to be haled before a Delaware court. Delaware, unlike some States, has not enacted a statute that treats acceptance of a directorship as consent to jurisdiction in the State. . . .

. . . Delaware's assertion of jurisdiction over appellants in this case is inconsistent with that constitutional limitation on state power. The judgment of the Delaware Supreme Court must, therefore, be reversed.

It is so ordered.

JUSTICE REHNQUIST took no part in the consideration or decision of this case.

JUSTICE POWELL, concurring.

I agree that the principles of International Shoe Co. v. Washington, 326 U.S. 310 (1945), should be extended to govern assertions of *in rem* as well as *in personam* jurisdiction in a state court. I also agree that neither the statutory presence of appellants' stock in Delaware nor their positions as directors and officers of a Delaware corporation can provide sufficient contacts to support the Delaware courts' assertion of jurisdiction in this case.

I would explicitly reserve judgment, however, on whether the ownership of some forms of property whose situs is indisputably and permanently located within a State may, without more, provide the contacts necessary to subject a defendant to jurisdiction within the State to the extent of the value of the property. In the case of real property, in particular, preservation of the common-law concept of *quasi in rem* jurisdiction arguably would avoid the uncertainty of the general *International Shoe* standard without significant cost to "'traditional notions of fair play and substantial justice.'" [*International Shoe*, at 316, quoting Milliken v. Meyer, 311 U.S. 457, 463 (1940).] . . .

[The concurring opinion of JUSTICE STEVENS is omitted.]

JUSTICE BRENNAN, concurring in part and dissenting in part.

. . . I fully agree that the minimum-contacts analysis developed in International Shoe Co. v. Washington, 326 U.S. 310 (1945), represents a far more sensible construct for the exercise of state-court jurisdiction than the patchwork of legal and factual fictions that has been generated from the decision in Pennoyer v. Neff, 95 U.S. 714 (1878). . . .

. . . [O]nce having properly and persuasively decided that the *quasi in rem* statute that Delaware admits to having enacted is invalid, the Court then proceeds to find that a minimum-contacts law that Delaware expressly *denies* having enacted also could not be constitutionally applied in this case.

. . . I certainly would not want to rule out the possibility that Delaware's courts might decide that the legislature's overriding purpose of securing the personal appearance in state courts of defendants would best be served by reinterpreting its statute to permit state jurisdiction on the basis of constitutionally permissible contacts rather than stock ownership. Were the state courts to take this step, it would then become necessary to address the question of whether minimum contacts exist here. But in the present posture of this case, the Court's decision of this important issue is purely an abstract ruling.

---

*Note: Post-*Shaffer *Legislation*

After *Shaffer* was decided, Delaware enacted a new law that afforded its courts jurisdiction over officers and directors of Delaware corporations in cases related to their corporate activities. 10 Del. Code § 3114. Is that statute constitutional? That is, are these contacts always sufficient for the assertion of specific jurisdiction by a Delaware court? See Armstrong v. Pomerance, 423 A.2d 174 (Del. 1980) (holding the statute is constitutional).

Burnham v. Superior Court
495 U.S. 604 (1990)

JUSTICE SCALIA announced the judgment of the Court and delivered an opinion in which CHIEF JUSTICE REHNQUIST and JUSTICE KENNEDY join, and in which JUSTICE WHITE joins with respect to Parts I, II-A, II-B, and II-C.

The question presented is whether the Due Process Clause of the Fourteenth Amendment denies California courts jurisdiction over a nonresident, who was personally served with process while temporarily in that State, in a suit unrelated to his activities in the State.

I

Petitioner Dennis Burnham married Francie Burnham in 1976, in West Virginia. In 1977, the couple moved to New Jersey, where their two children were born. In July 1987, the Burnhams decided to separate. They agreed that Mrs. Burnham, who intended to move to California, would take custody of the children. Shortly before Mrs. Burnham departed for California that same month, she and petitioner agreed that she would file for divorce on grounds of "irreconcilable differences."

In October 1987, petitioner filed for divorce in New Jersey state court on grounds of "desertion." Petitioner did not, however, obtain an issuance of summons against his wife and did not attempt to serve her with process. Mrs. Burnham, after unsuccessfully demanding that petitioner adhere to their prior agreement to submit to an "irreconcilable differences" divorce, brought suit for divorce in California state court in early January 1988.

In late January, petitioner visited southern California on business, after which he went north to visit his children in the San Francisco Bay area, where his wife resided. He took the older child to San Francisco for the weekend. Upon returning the child to Mrs. Burnham's home on January 24, 1988, petitioner was served with a California court summons and a copy of Mrs. Burnham's divorce petition. He then returned to New Jersey.

Later that year, petitioner made a special appearance in the California Superior Court, moving to quash the service of process on the ground that the court lacked personal jurisdiction over him because his only contacts with California were a few short visits to the State for the purposes of conducting business and visiting his children. The Superior Court denied the motion, and the California Court of Appeal denied mandamus relief, rejecting petitioner's contention that the Due Process Clause prohibited California courts from asserting jurisdiction over him because he lacked "minimum contacts" with the State. The court held it to be "a valid jurisdictional predicate for *in personam* jurisdiction" that the "defendant [was] present in the forum state and personally served with process."

II

A

The proposition that the judgment of a court lacking jurisdiction is void traces back to the English Year Books. . . . Traditionally that proposition was embodied in the phrase *coram non judice,* "before a person not a judge"—meaning, in effect, that the proceeding in question was not a *judicial* proceeding because lawful judicial authority was not present, and could therefore not yield a *judgment*. American courts invalidated, or denied recognition to, judgments that violated this common-law principle long before the Fourteenth Amendment was adopted. In Pennoyer v. Neff, 95 U.S. 714, 732 (1878), we announced that the judgment of a court lacking personal jurisdiction violated the Due Process Clause of the Fourteenth Amendment as well.

To determine whether the assertion of personal jurisdiction is consistent with due process, we have long relied on the principles traditionally followed by American courts in marking out the territorial limits of each State's authority. That criterion was first announced in Pennoyer v. Neff, in which we stated that due process "mean[s] a course of legal proceedings according to those rules and principles which have been established in our systems of jurisprudence for the protection and enforcement of private rights," id. at 733, including the "well-established principles of public law respecting the jurisdiction of an independent State over persons and property," id. at 722. In what has become the classic expression of the criterion, we said in International Shoe Co. v. Washington, 326 U.S. 310 (1945), that a state court's assertion of personal jurisdiction satisfies the Due Process Clause if it does not violate "'traditional notions of fair play and substantial justice.'" Id. at 316 (quoting Milliken v. Meyer, 311 U.S. 457, 463 (1940)).

Since *International Shoe,* we have only been called upon to decide whether these "traditional notions" permit States to exercise jurisdiction over absent defendants in a manner that deviates from the rules of jurisdiction applied in the 19th century. We have held such deviations permissible, but only with respect to suits arising out of the absent defendant's contacts with the State. The question we must decide today is whether due process requires a similar connection between the litigation and the defendant's contacts with the State in cases where the defendant is physically present in the State at the time process is served upon him.

B

Among the most firmly established principles of personal jurisdiction in American tradition is that the courts of a State have jurisdiction over nonresidents who are physically present in the State. The view developed early that each State had the power to hale before its courts any individual who could be found within its borders, and that once having acquired jurisdiction over such a person by properly serving him with process, the State could retain jurisdiction to enter judgment against him, no matter how fleeting his visit. . . .

. . . Particularly striking is the fact that, as far as we have been able to determine, *not one* American case from the period (or, for that matter, not one American case until 1978) held, or even suggested, that in-state personal service on an individual was insufficient to confer personal jurisdiction. . . .

This American jurisdictional practice is, moreover, not merely old; it is continuing. It remains the practice of, not only a substantial number of the States, but as far as we are aware *all* the States and the Federal Government—if one disregards (as one must for this purpose) the few opinions since 1978 that have erroneously said, on grounds similar to those that petitioner presses here, that this Court's due process decisions render the practice unconstitutional. We do not know of a single state or federal statute, or a single judicial decision resting upon state law, that has abandoned in-state service as a basis of jurisdiction. Many recent cases reaffirm it.

C

Despite this formidable body of precedent, petitioner contends, in reliance on our decisions applying the *International Shoe* standard, that in the absence of "continuous and systematic" contacts with the forum, a nonresident defendant can be subjected to judgment only as to matters that arise out of or relate to his contacts with the forum. This argument rests on a thorough misunderstanding of our cases. . . . [The Court goes on to discuss the development of due process analysis in state court jurisdiction cases from *Pennoyer* forward.]

. . . Our opinion in *International Shoe* made explicit . . . [that] due process does not necessarily *require* the States to adhere to the unbending territorial limits on jurisdiction set forth in *Pennoyer*. The validity of assertion of jurisdiction over a nonconsenting defendant who is not present in the forum depends upon whether "the quality and nature of [his] activity" in relation to the forum renders such jurisdiction consistent with "'traditional notions of fair play and substantial justice.'" . . .

. . . As *International Shoe* suggests, the defendant's litigation-related "minimum contacts" may take the place of physical presence as the basis for jurisdiction. . . .

Nothing in *International Shoe* or the cases that have followed it, however, offers support for the very different proposition petitioner seeks to establish today: that a defendant's presence in the forum is not only unnecessary to validate novel, nontraditional assertions of jurisdiction, but is itself no longer sufficient to establish jurisdiction. That proposition is unfaithful to both elementary logic and the foundations of our due process jurisprudence. The distinction between what is needed to support novel procedures and what is needed to sustain traditional ones is fundamental, as we observed over a century ago:

> [A] process of law, which is not otherwise forbidden, must be taken to be due process of law, if it can show the sanction of settled usage both in England and in this country; but it by no means follows that nothing else can be due process of law. . . . [That which], in substance, has been immemorially the actual law of the land . . . therefor[e] is due process of law. But to hold that such a characteristic is essential to due process of law, would be

> to deny every quality of the law but its age, and to render it incapable of progress or improvement. It would be to stamp upon our jurisprudence the unchangeableness attributed to the laws of the Medes and Persians. Hurtado v. California, 110 U.S. 516, 528-529 (1884).

The short of the matter is that jurisdiction based on physical presence alone constitutes due process because it is one of the continuing traditions of our legal system that define the due process standard of "traditional notions of fair play and substantial justice." That standard was developed by *analogy* to "physical presence," and it would be perverse to say it could now be turned against that touchstone of jurisdiction.

D

Petitioner's strongest argument, though we ultimately reject it, relies upon our decision in Shaffer v. Heitner, 433 U.S. 186 (1977). . . .

It goes too far to say, as petitioner contends, that *Shaffer* compels the conclusion that a State lacks jurisdiction over an individual unless the litigation arises out of his activities in the State. *Shaffer,* like *International Shoe,* involved jurisdiction over an *absent defendant,* and it stands for nothing more than the proposition that when the "minimum contact" that is a substitute for physical presence consists of property ownership it must, like other minimum contacts, be related to the litigation. . . . *Shaffer* was saying, in other words, not that all bases for the assertion of *in personam* jurisdiction (including, presumably, in-state service) must be treated alike and subjected to the "minimum contacts" analysis of *International Shoe;* but rather that *quasi in rem* jurisdiction, that fictional "ancient form," and *in personam* jurisdiction, are really one and the same and must be treated alike—leading to the conclusion that *quasi in rem* jurisdiction, i.e., that form of *in personam* jurisdiction based upon a "property ownership" contact and by definition unaccompanied by personal, in-state service, must satisfy the litigation-relatedness requirement of *International Shoe.* The logic of *Shaffer*'s holding—which places all suits against absent nonresidents on the same constitutional footing, regardless of whether a separate Latin label is attached to one particular basis of contact—does not compel the conclusion that physically present defendants must be treated identically to absent ones. . . .

It is fair to say, however, that while our holding today does not contradict *Shaffer,* our basic approach to the due process question is different. We have conducted no independent inquiry into the desirability or fairness of the prevailing in-state service rule, leaving that judgment to the legislatures that are free to amend it; for our purposes, its validation is its pedigree, as the phrase "*traditional notions* of fair play and substantial justice" makes clear. *Shaffer* did conduct such an independent inquiry, asserting that "'traditional notions of fair play and substantial justice' can be as readily offended by the perpetuation of ancient forms that are no longer justified as by the adoption of new procedures that are inconsistent with the basic values of our constitutional heritage." 433 U.S., at 212. Perhaps that assertion can be sustained when the "perpetuation of ancient forms" is engaged in by only a very small minority of the States.[4] Where, however, as in the present case, a jurisdictional principle is both firmly approved by tradition and still favored, it is impossible to imagine what standard we could appeal to for the judgment that it is "no longer justified." . . .

III

A few words in response to Justice Brennan's opinion concurring in the judgment: It insists that we apply "contemporary notions of due process" to determine the constitutionality of California's assertion of jurisdiction. But our analysis today comports with that prescription, at least if we give it the only sense allowed by our precedents. The "contemporary notions of due process" applicable to personal jurisdiction are the enduring "*traditional* notions of fair play and substantial justice" established as the test by *International Shoe*. By its very language, that test is satisfied if a state court adheres to jurisdictional rules that are generally applied and have always been applied in the United States.

But the concurrence's proposed standard of "contemporary notions of due process" requires more: It measures state-court jurisdiction not only against traditional doctrines in this country, including current state-court practice, but also against each Justice's subjective assessment of what is fair and just. Authority for that seductive standard is not to be found in any of our personal jurisdiction cases. It is, indeed, an outright break with the test of "traditional notions of fair play and substantial justice," which would have to be reformulated "*our* notions of fair play and substantial justice."

The subjectivity, and hence inadequacy, of this approach becomes apparent when the concurrence tries to explain *why* the assertion of jurisdiction in the present case meets its standard of continuing-American-tradition-*plus*-innate-fairness. Justice Brennan lists the "benefits" Mr. Burnham derived from the State of California—the fact that, during the few days he was there, "[h]is health and safety [were] guaranteed by the State's police, fire, and emergency medical services; he [was] free to travel on the State's roads and waterways; he likely enjoy[ed] the fruits of the State's economy." Three days' worth of these benefits strike us as powerfully inadequate to establish, as an abstract matter, that it is "fair" for California to decree the ownership of all Mr. Burnham's worldly goods acquired during the 10 years of his marriage, and the custody over his children. We daresay a contractual exchange swapping those benefits for

4. *Shaffer* may have involved a unique state procedure in one respect: Justice Stevens noted that Delaware was the only State that treated the place of incorporation as the situs of corporate stock when both owner and custodian were elsewhere. See 433 U.S. at 218 (opinion concurring in judgment).

that power would not survive the "unconscionability" provision of the Uniform Commercial Code. Even less persuasive are the other "fairness" factors alluded to by Justice Brennan. It would create "an asymmetry," we are told, if Burnham were *permitted* (as he is) to appear in California courts as a plaintiff, but were not *compelled* to appear in California courts as defendant; and travel being as easy as it is nowadays, and modern procedural devices being so convenient, it is no great hardship to appear in California courts. The problem with these assertions is that they justify the exercise of jurisdiction over *everyone, whether or not* he ever comes to California. The only "fairness" elements setting Mr. Burnham apart from the rest of the world are the three days' "benefits" referred to above—and even those, do not set him apart from many other people who have enjoyed three days in the Golden State (savoring the fruits of its economy, the availability of its roads and police services) but who were fortunate enough not to be served with process while they were there and thus are not (simply by reason of that savoring) subject to the general jurisdiction of California's courts. See, e.g., Helicopteros Nacionales de Columbia v. Hall, 466 U.S. [408,] 414-416 [(1986)]. In other words, even if one agreed with Justice Brennan's conception of an equitable bargain, the "benefits" we have been discussing would explain why it is "fair" to assert general jurisdiction over Burnham-returned-to-New-Jersey-after-service only at the expense of proving that it is also "fair" to assert general jurisdiction over Burnham-returned-to-New-Jersey-*without*-service—which we *know* does not conform with "contemporary notions of due process." . . .

. . . Nothing we say today prevents individual States from limiting or entirely abandoning the in-state-service basis of jurisdiction. And nothing prevents an overwhelming majority of them from doing so, with the consequence that the "traditional notions of fairness" that this Court applies may change. But the States have overwhelmingly declined to adopt such limitation or abandonment, evidently not considering it to be progress.[5] The question is whether, armed with no authority other than individual Justices' perceptions of fairness that conflict with both past and current practice, this Court can compel the States to make such a change on the ground that "due process" requires it. We hold that it cannot. . . .

5. I find quite unacceptable as a basis for this Court's decisions Justice Brennan's view that "the *raison d'être* of various constitutional doctrines designed to protect out-of-staters, such as the Art. IV Privileges and Immunities Clause and the Commerce Clause," entitles this Court to brand as "unfair," and hence unconstitutional, the refusal of all 50 States "to limit or abandon bases of jurisdiction that have become obsolete." "Due process" (which is the constitutional text at issue here) does not mean that process which shifting majorities of this Court feel to be "due"; but that process which American society—self-interested American society, which expresses its judgments in the laws of self-interested States—has traditionally considered "due." The notion that the Constitution, through some penumbra emanating from the Privileges and Immunities Clause and the Commerce Clause, establishes this Court as a Platonic check upon the society's greedy adherence to its traditions can only be described as imperious.

Because the Due Process Clause does not prohibit the California courts from exercising jurisdiction over petitioner based on the fact of in-state service of process, the judgment is

Affirmed.

JUSTICE WHITE, concurring in part and concurring in the judgment.

I join Parts I, II-A, II-B, and II-C of Justice Scalia's opinion and concur in the judgment of affirmance. The rule allowing jurisdiction to be obtained over a nonresident by personal service in the forum State, without more, has been and is so widely accepted throughout this country that I could not possibly strike it down, either on its face or as applied in this case, on the ground that it denies due process of law guaranteed by the Fourteenth Amendment. Although the Court has the authority under the Amendment to examine even traditionally accepted procedures and declare them invalid, e.g., Shaffer v. Heitner, 433 U.S. 186 (1977), there has been no showing here or elsewhere that as a general proposition the rule is so arbitrary and lacking in common sense in so many instances that it should be held violative of due process in every case. Furthermore, until such a showing is made, which would be difficult indeed, claims in individual cases that the rule would operate unfairly as applied to the particular nonresident involved need not be entertained. At least this would be the case where presence in the forum State is intentional, which would almost always be the fact. Otherwise, there would be endless, fact-specific litigation in the trial and appellate courts, including this one. Here, personal service in California, without more, is enough, and I agree that the judgment should be affirmed.

JUSTICE BRENNAN, with whom JUSTICE MARSHALL, JUSTICE BLACKMUN, and JUSTICE O'CONNOR join, concurring in the judgment.

I agree with Justice Scalia that the Due Process Clause of the Fourteenth Amendment generally permits a state court to exercise jurisdiction over a defendant if he is served with process while voluntarily present in the forum State.[1] I do not perceive the need, however, to decide that a jurisdictional rule that "'has been immemorially the actual law of the land,'" quoting Hurtado v. California, 110 U.S. 516, 528 (1884), automatically comports with due process simply by virtue of its "pedigree." Although I agree that history is an important factor in establishing whether a jurisdictional rule satisfies due process requirements, I cannot agree that it is the *only* factor such that all traditional rules of jurisdiction are, *ipso facto,* forever constitutional. Unlike Justice Scalia, I would undertake an "independent inquiry into the . . . fairness of the prevailing in-state service rule." I therefore concur only in the judgment.

1. I use the term "transient jurisdiction" to refer to jurisdiction premised solely on the fact that a person is served with process while physically present in the forum State.

I

I believe that the approach adopted by Justice Scalia's opinion today—reliance solely on historical pedigree—is foreclosed by our decisions in International Shoe Co. v. Washington, 326 U.S. 310 (1945), and Shaffer v. Heitner, 433 U.S. 186 (1977). . . . The critical insight of *Shaffer* is that all rules of jurisdiction, even ancient ones, must satisfy contemporary notions of due process. . . . We recognized that "'[t]raditional notions of fair play and substantial justice' can be as readily offended by the perpetuation of ancient forms that are no longer justified as by the adoption of new procedures that are inconsistent with the basic values of our constitutional heritage." Id. at 212 (citations omitted). I agree with this approach and continue to believe that "the minimum-contacts analysis developed in *International Shoe* . . . represents a far more sensible construct for the exercise of state-court jurisdiction than the patchwork of legal and factual fictions that has been generated from the decision in Pennoyer v. Neff." Id. at 219 (citation omitted) (Brennan, J., concurring in part and dissenting in part). . . .

II

Tradition, though alone not dispositive, is of course *relevant* to the question whether the rule of transient jurisdiction is consistent with due process.[7] Tradition is salient not in the sense that practices of the past are automatically reasonable today; indeed, under such a standard, the legitimacy of transient jurisdiction would be called into question because the rule's historical "pedigree" is a matter of intense debate. . . .

. . . I find the historical background relevant because, however murky the jurisprudential origins of transient jurisdiction, the fact that American courts have announced the rule for perhaps a century (first in dicta, more recently in holdings) provides a defendant voluntarily present in a particular State *today* "clear notice that [he] is subject to suit" in the forum. World-Wide Volkswagen Corp. v. Woodson, 444 U.S. at 297. . . .

By visiting the forum State, a transient defendant actually "avail[s]" himself, Burger King [v. Rudzewicz, 471 U.S. 462, 476 (1985),] of significant benefits provided by the State. His health and safety are guaranteed by the State's police, fire, and emergency medical services; he is free to

7. I do not propose that the "contemporary notions of due process" to be applied are no more than "each Justice's subjective assessment of what is fair and just." Rather, the inquiry is guided by our decisions beginning with International Shoe Co. v. Washington, 326 U.S. 310 (1945), and the specific factors that we have developed to ascertain whether a jurisdictional rule comports with "traditional notions of fair play and substantial justice." See, e.g., Asahi Metal Industry Co. v. Superior Court of California, Solano County, 480 U.S. 102, 113 (1987) (noting "several factors," including "the burden on the defendant, the interests of the forum State, and the plaintiff's interest in obtaining relief"). This analysis may not be "mechanical or quantitative," *International Shoe*, 326 U.S. at 319, but neither is it "freestanding," or dependent on personal whim. Our experience with this approach demonstrates that it is well within our competence to employ.

travel on the State's roads and waterways; he likely enjoys the fruits of the State's economy as well. . . .

The potential burdens on a transient defendant are slight. "'[M]odern transportation and communications have made it much less burdensome for a party sued to defend himself'" in a State outside his place of residence. *Burger King*, supra, at 474, quoting McGee v. International Life Ins. Co., 355 U.S. 220, 223 (1957). That the defendant has already journeyed at least once before to the forum—as evidenced by the fact that he was served with process there—is an indication that suit in the forum likely would not be prohibitively inconvenient. Finally, any burdens that do arise can be ameliorated by a variety of procedural devices.[13] For these reasons, as a rule the exercise of personal jurisdiction over a defendant based on his voluntary presence in the forum will satisfy the requirements of due process.

In this case, it is undisputed that petitioner was served with process while voluntarily and knowingly in the State of California. I therefore concur in the judgment.

JUSTICE STEVENS, concurring in the judgment.

As I explained in my separate writing, I did not join the Court's opinion in Shaffer v. Heitner, 433 U.S. 186 (1977), because I was concerned by its unnecessarily broad reach. Id. at 217-219 (opinion concurring in judgment). The same concern prevents me from joining either Justice Scalia's or Justice Brennan's opinion in this case. For me, it is sufficient to note that the historical evidence and consensus identified by Justice Scalia, the consideration of fairness identified by Justice Brennan, and the common sense displayed by Justice White, all combine to demonstrate that this is, indeed, a very easy case. Accordingly, I agree that the judgment should be affirmed.

Notes and Questions

1. Is reasonableness irrelevant, post-*Burnham*, whenever a defendant is served in the forum? This case is like *Asahi* in showing a fractured Court and in leaving the reader with no clear sense of direction. Do you agree with Professor Mary Twitchell that "the case leaves us with the

13. For example, in the federal system, a transient defendant can avoid protracted litigation of a spurious suit through a motion to dismiss for failure to state a claim or through a motion for summary judgment. Fed. Rules Civ. Proc. 12(b)(6) and 56. He can use relatively inexpensive methods of discovery, such as oral deposition by telephone (Rule 30 (b)(7)), deposition upon written questions (Rule 31), interrogatories (Rule 33), and requests for admission (Rule 36), while enjoying protection from harassment (Rule 26(c)), and possibly obtaining costs and attorney's fees for some of the work involved (Rules 37(a)(4), (b)-(d)). Moreover, a change of venue may be possible. 28 U.S.C. § 1404. In state court, many of the same procedural protections are available, as is the doctrine of *forum non conveniens*, under which the suit may be dismissed. See generally Abrams, Power, Convenience, and the Elimination of Personal Jurisdiction in the Federal Courts, 58 Ind. L. J. 1, 23-25 (1982).

unpalatable result of a clear rule with two mutually destructive explanations of how the rule fits into our jurisprudence"? *Burnham* and Constitutionally Permissible Levels of Harm, 22 Rutgers L.J. 659 (1991).

What is the impact of a plurality opinion? Is there any reason to give Justice Scalia's four-vote rationale more weight than Justice Brennan's four-vote rationale? Why does Justice Scalia's opinion appear first? What is the unanimous part of the opinion? Do you sympathize with Justice Stevens's "a pox on both your houses" approach?

2. Look again at Justice White's concurrence. Is he placing a burden on the defendant to show that jurisdiction is arbitrary in a particular case, or in so many cases that it is unreasonable in every case? Is the latter showing one that a defendant can ever make? Is it the correct inquiry under due process, which—one might argue—is an individual-centered right that assures due process to *each* defendant rather than to *most* of them over time?

3. None of the opinions in *Burnham* pays much heed to the Court's 1978 decision in *Kulko*. Why not? Although *Burnham* did not overrule *Kulko*, and is superficially easy to distinguish because Ezra Kulko was not served in California, isn't the Court's reasoning in *Kulko* hard to reconcile with either the result or the plurality opinions in *Burnham*?

4. Among the most interesting of the issues raised by *Burnham* is the struggle between Justice Scalia and Justice Brennan over the role of tradition in constitutional interpretation. What is the best case one can make in favor of the static approach proposed by Justice Scalia, which emphasizes tradition-bound interpretation? What is the best case for the dynamic approach to interpretation that Justice Brennan believes is appropriate? Is it "imperious"? Is the excerpt from Tom Tyler on page 61, regarding the common understanding of fair process, relevant to this discussion?

Obviously, quite a bit more is at stake in this debate over original intent, tradition, and Platonic checks than simply the vitality of transient jurisdiction. *Burnham* is but one illustration of a fundamental question that recurs in constitutional law: What are the proper limits of judicial review in this area? Yet *Burnham* is an excellent vehicle for launching that debate in the context of procedure, given its straightforward facts and potentially harsh results.

We encourage you to approach this important issue from the standpoint of one seeking to develop the arguments on both sides as fully as possible, rather than as one committed *ab initio* to a particular result. Remember that the composition of the judiciary can and does change over time. So, too, does society. If you embrace the dynamic approach to interpretation, does it matter to you who is doing the interpreting? Should it? Likewise, if you endorse the static approach, have you thought about how you would determine what "our traditions" are? As of what date would you pinpoint the applicable tradition? Does your experience with jurisdiction issues thus far assure you that legislators "know what they are doing" when they draft a jurisdiction statute? Or are the interpretation and refining of jurisdiction issues best left to the judiciary? Should judges be "imperious"?

Burnham inspired a flurry of scholarly activity, mostly critical. For a sampling of concerns about the decision by commentators with a procedural bent, see The Future of Personal Jurisdiction: A Symposium on Burnham v. Superior Court, 22 Rutgers L.J. 559 (1991). For other commentary on *Burnham,* see Earl M. Maltz, Personal Jurisdiction and Constitutional Theory—A Comment on Burnham v. Superior Court, 22 Rutgers L.J. 689 (1991); Linda A. Silberman, Reflections on Burnham v. Superior Court: Toward Presumptive Rules of Jurisdiction and Implications for Choice of Law, 22 Rutgers L.J. 569 (1991); Russell J. Weintraub, An Objective Basis for Rejecting Transient Jurisdiction, 22 Rutgers L.J. 611 (1991); see also Richard B. Cappalli, Locke as the Key: A Unifying and Coherent Theory of *in Personam* Jurisdiction, 43 Case W. Res. L. Rev. 97 (1992); Robert Taylor-Manning, An Easy Case Makes Bad Law—Burnham v. Superior Court, 66 Wash. L. Rev. 623 (1991).

Note: Choice of Law

Simply because a court has jurisdiction over the defendant does not necessarily mean it has the power to apply its substantive laws to the controversy. It may, however, apply its own procedural rules—though the distinction between procedural and substantive rules is sometimes hazy.

If the applicable substantive law is federal, then the court—federal or state—will apply that federal law to the matter. Where an action is based on state law but has multistate features—such as *World-Wide Volkswagen*—the forum may be obliged to apply the substantive law of another jurisdiction rather than its own. The choice of law decision depends on two sets of constraints.

First, each state has its own statutory rules regarding which law to apply, called "conflicts" laws. Second, the United States Supreme Court has held that due process and full faith and credit limitations prevent a state from applying its own laws to a controversy unless it has "a significant contact or significant aggregation of contacts, creating state interests, such that choice of its law is neither arbitrary nor fundamentally unfair." Allstate Ins. Co. v. Hague, 449 U.S. 302, 312-313 (1981) (plurality opinion). See also Phillips Petroleum Co. v. Shutts, 472 U.S. 797 (1985). In defining fundamental fairness for choice of law purposes the Court has relied on factors that track closely the factors relevant to "minimum contacts." While in theory the inquiries are distinct, they tend to converge such that a court with personal jurisdiction typically will also have constitutional power to apply its state law to the controversy.

Full treatment of the range of choice of law problems in state courts is beyond the scope of this text and most Civil Procedure courses. For discussion of the substantive law applied to a controversy brought in a federal court on the basis of diversity jurisdiction, see Chapter 6.

9. Persons and Property in Cyberspace

Problem Case: The Ubiquitous Defendant

You are a law clerk for a federal district court judge in Washington, D.C., who is considering a motion to dismiss for lack of personal jurisdiction. She has asked you to draft an opinion for her in the case of Marcus Neff, a U.S. congressman from Oregon, who is suing Sylvester Sleeze for the tort of defamation.

Sleeze is the editor of *The Naked Truth*, an electronic gossip magazine focusing on the doings of politicians and people in the entertainment industry. Anyone in the world may access his magazine through his Web site, www.thenakedtruth.com, after registering a free user name and obtaining a free password. The site relies on word-of-mouth to gain readers and does not pay to advertise itself.

A few months ago, the lead story, printed under the headline "Vicious Rumor," was to the effect that Marcus Neff, "the scion of a long line of Oregonians," was guilty of repeated acts of domestic violence against his wife, over a period of many years. The Neff story appeared on the Web site 24 hours a day for three days, during which the Web site received 30,000 hits (visitors to the Web site), significantly more than the usual 3,000-hit total for each new posting. There is no way to tell how many of these hits were from D.C., or how many visitors to the Web site read the Neff story.

If untrue, the publication is clearly an actionable tort under District of Columbia law. Less clear is whether this court has personal jurisdiction over Sleeze, who is a resident of Los Angeles, where he puts out the magazine from his home computer.

During the time period involved in this suit, Sleeze was trying to develop a regular list of subscribers to whom he e-mailed each new edition of *The Naked Truth*. At the time of the Neff story, there were a few thousand subscribers. But since the e-mail address gives no geographical information, Sleeze did not know precisely how many of these were in the District of Columbia. At oral argument, however, counsel for Sleeze said that, in a preliminary effort to locate subscribers geographically, they had traced several hundred to Los Angeles, but only a few dozen to the District of Columbia.

The Naked Truth Web site has hyperlinks that allow visitors to the Web site to connect with other publications, some of which are based in Washington, D.C. At the Web site, and in the e-mailed editions of the report, Sleeze seeks financial contributions to the magazine, but he has received very few so far, and only one or two from the District of Columbia.

Visitors to the Web site may leave comments and gossip of their own on the Web site. Again, since e-mail identities are not generally geographical, it is impossible to say how much of the interaction on the Web site comes from the District of Columbia.

Sleeze has been to Washington, D.C., only once over the last five years, for the christening of his niece. His sister paid his way, and while he was in town he appeared on C-SPAN (a nationwide cable TV service) to talk about putting out an electronic magazine. He did not pay for the airtime, nor was he paid for appearing. Sleeze has not advertised his magazine in any media located in the District of Columbia.

The D.C. long-arm statute provides for personal jurisdiction over anyone who:

(1) causes tortious injury in the District of Columbia by an act or omission in the District of Columbia, or
(2) causes tortious injury by an act or omission outside the District of Columbia if he reasonably expects the act to have consequences in the District of Columbia *and* derives substantial revenue from interstate or international commerce.

Introduction: Personal Jurisdiction and Cyberspace

Almost overnight (especially quick in legal time), the World Wide Web has become a force in the global economy, as well as a part of the daily lives of millions. The Web's new and unstructured interactions stir up all sorts of litigation. People sue over the use and ownership of intellectual property such as domain names. Torts are committed, contracts made and broken in cyberspace. Where is the center of gravity of such lawsuits, and where is the location of the wrongs sued upon? Where can the plaintiff make the defendant appear?

The challenge is fairness to the defendant who is, in one sense, everywhere and, at the same time, potentially nowhere. Should a person who causes harm, as in our problem case, be held to suit wherever the Internet reaches? Technological change has often shaped concepts of due process. Think about how the early Internet cases compare with the impact of the automobile and the corporate form of doing business on jurisdiction.

Appellate courts are beginning to decide important cases dealing with the Internet and jurisdiction; still, much of the law is in the form of trial court opinions. Virtually all of these apply traditional jurisdictional analysis, looking first to the scope of the local long-arm statute, then to due process fairness in the usual sense. Though courts and commentators often mention the Web's potential to revolutionize state court jurisdiction, the cases so far are only beginning to face these implications.

Zippo Mfg. Co. v. Zippo Dot Com

952 F. Supp. 1119 (W.D. Pa. 1997)

McLaughlin, District Judge.

This is an Internet domain name[1] dispute. At this stage of the controversy, we must decide the constitutionally permissible reach of Pennsylvania's

1. Domain names serve as a primary identifier of an Internet user. Panavision Intern., L. P. v. Toeppen, 938 F. Supp. 616 (C.D. Cal. 1996). Businesses using the Internet commonly use their business names as part of the domain name (e.g., IBM.com). Id. The designation ".com" identifies the user as a commercial entity. Id.

Long Arm Statute, 42 Pa. C.S.A. § 5322, through cyberspace. Plaintiff Zippo Manufacturing Corporation ("Manufacturing") has filed a five count complaint against Zippo Dot Com, Inc. ("Dot Com") alleging trademark dilution, infringement, and false designation under the Federal Trademark Act, 15 U.S.C. §§ 1051-1127. In addition, the Complaint alleges causes of action based on state law trademark dilution under 54 Pa. C.S.A. § 1124, and seeks equitable accounting and imposition of a constructive trust. Dot Com has moved to dismiss for lack of personal jurisdiction. . . . For the reasons set forth below, Defendant's motion is denied.

I. Background

The facts relevant to this motion are as follows. Manufacturing is a Pennsylvania corporation with its principal place of business in Bradford, Pennsylvania. Manufacturing makes, among other things, well known "Zippo" tobacco lighters. Dot Com is a California corporation with its principal place of business in Sunnyvale, California. Dot Com operates an Internet Web site and an Internet news service and has obtained the exclusive right to use the domain names "zippo.com", "zippo.net" and "zipponews.com" on the Internet.[3]

Dot Com's Web site contains information about the company, advertisements, and an application for its Internet news service. The news service itself consists of three levels of membership— "public/free," "Original," and "Super." Each successive level offers access to a greater number of Internet newsgroups. A customer who wants to subscribe to either the "Original" or "Super" level of service, fills out an online application that asks for a variety of information including the person's name and address. Payment is made by credit card over the Internet or the telephone. The application is then processed and the subscriber is assigned a password which permits the subscriber to view and/or download Internet newsgroup messages that are stored on the Defendant's server in California.

Dot Com's contacts with Pennsylvania have occurred almost exclusively over the Internet. Dot Com's offices, employees and Internet servers are located in California. Dot Com maintains no offices, employees or agents in Pennsylvania. Dot Com's advertising for its service to Pennsylvania residents involves posting information about its service on its Web page, which is accessible to Pennsylvania residents via the Internet. Defendant has approximately 140,000 paying subscribers worldwide. Approximately two percent (3,000) of those subscribers are Pennsylvania residents. These subscribers have contracted to receive Dot Com's service by visiting its Web site and filling out the application. Additionally,

3. Dot Com has registered these domain names with Network Solutions, Inc. which has contracted with the National Science Foundation to provide registration services for Internet domain names. Once a domain name is registered to one user, it may not be used by another.

Dot Com has entered into agreements with seven Internet access providers in Pennsylvania to permit their subscribers to access Dot Com's news service. Two of these providers are located in the Western District of Pennsylvania.

The basis of the trademark claims is Dot Com's use of the word "Zippo" in the domain names it holds, in numerous locations in its Web site and in the heading of Internet newsgroup messages that have been posted by Dot Com subscribers. When an Internet user views or downloads a newsgroup message posted by a Dot Com subscriber, the word "Zippo" appears in the "Message-Id" and "Organization" sections of the heading. The news message itself, containing text and/or pictures, follows. Manufacturing points out that some of the messages contain adult oriented, sexually explicit subject matter....

III. Discussion

A. *Personal Jurisdiction*

1. *The Traditional Framework*

Our authority to exercise personal jurisdiction in this case is conferred by state law. Fed. R. Civ. P. 4(e); Mellon Bank (East) FSFS, N.A. v. Farino, 960 F.2d 1217, 1221 (3d Cir. 1992). The extent to which we may exercise that authority is governed by the Due Process Clause of the Fourteenth Amendment to the Federal Constitution. Kulko v. Superior Court of California, 436 U.S. 84, 91 (1978).

Pennsylvania's long arm jurisdiction statute is codified at 42 Pa. C.S.A. § 5322(a). The portion of the statute authorizing us to exercise jurisdiction here permits the exercise of jurisdiction over non-resident defendants upon "(2) Contracting to supply services or things in this Commonwealth." 42 Pa. C.S.A. § 5322(a). It is undisputed that Dot Com contracted to supply Internet news services to approximately 3,000 Pennsylvania residents and also entered into agreements with seven Internet access providers in Pennsylvania. Moreover, even if Dot Com's conduct did not satisfy a specific provision of the statute, we would nevertheless be authorized to exercise jurisdiction to the "fullest extent allowed under the Constitution of the United States." 42 Pa. C.S.A. § 5322(b).

The constitutional limitations on the exercise of personal jurisdiction differ depending upon whether a court seeks to exercise general or specific jurisdiction over a non-resident defendant. *Mellon*, 960 F.2d at 1221. General jurisdiction permits a court to exercise personal jurisdiction over a non-resident defendant for non-forum related activities when the defendant has engaged in "systematic and continuous" activities in the forum state. Helicopteros Nacionales de Colombia, S.A. v. Hall, 466 U.S. 408, 414-416 (1984). In the absence of general jurisdiction, specific jurisdiction permits a court to exercise personal jurisdiction over a non-resident defendant for forum-related activities where the "relationship between the defendant and the forum falls within the 'minimum contacts' framework" of International Shoe Co. v. Washington, 326 U.S. 310 (1945), and its progeny. *Mellon*, 960 F.2d at 1221. Manufacturing does not contend that we should exercise general personal jurisdiction over Dot Com. Manufacturing concedes that if personal jurisdiction exists in this case, it must be specific.

A three-pronged test has emerged for determining whether the exercise of specific personal jurisdiction over a non-resident defendant is appropriate: (1) the defendant must have sufficient "minimum contacts" with the forum state, (2) the claim asserted against the defendant must arise out of those contacts, and (3) the exercise of jurisdiction must be reasonable. Id. The "Constitutional touchstone" of the minimum contacts analysis is embodied in the first prong, "whether the defendant purposefully established" contacts with the forum state. Burger King Corp. v. Rudzewicz, 471 U.S. 462, 475 (1985) (citing International Shoe Co. v. Washington, 326 U.S. 310, 319 (1945)). Defendants who "'reach out beyond one state' and create continuing relationships and obligations with the citizens of another state are subject to regulation and sanctions in the other State for consequences of their actions." Id. (citing Travelers Health Assn. v. Virginia, 339 U.S. 643, 647 (1950)). "[T]he foreseeability that is critical to the due process analysis is . . . that the defendant's conduct and connection with the forum State are such that he should reasonably expect to be haled into court there." World-Wide Volkswagen Corp. v. Woodson, 444 U.S. 286, 297 (1980). This protects defendants from being forced to answer for their actions in a foreign jurisdiction based on "random, fortuitous or attenuated" contacts. Keeton v. Hustler Magazine, Inc., 465 U.S. 770, 774 (1984). "Jurisdiction is proper, however, where contacts proximately result from actions by the defendant *himself* that create a 'substantial connection' with the forum State." *Burger King*, 471 U.S. at 475 (citing McGee v. International Life Insurance Co., 355 U.S. 220, 223 (1957)).

The "reasonableness" prong exists to protect defendants against unfairly inconvenient litigation. *World-Wide Volkswagen*, 444 U.S. at 292. Under this prong, the exercise of jurisdiction will be reasonable if it does not offend "traditional notions of fair play and substantial justice." *International Shoe*, 326 U.S. at 316. When determining the reasonableness of a particular forum, the court must consider the burden on the defendant in light of other factors including: "the forum state's interest in adjudicating the dispute; the plaintiff's interest in obtaining convenient and effective relief, at least when that interest is not adequately protected by the plaintiff's right to choose the forum; the interstate judicial system's interest in obtaining the most efficient resolution of controversies; and the shared interest of the several states in furthering fundamental substantive social policies." *World-Wide Volkswagen*, 444 U.S. at 292.

2. *The Internet and Jurisdiction*

In Hanson v. Denckla, the Supreme Court noted that "[a]s technological progress has increased the flow of commerce between States, the need for jurisdiction has undergone a similar increase." Hanson v. Denckla, 357

U.S. 235, 250-251 (1958). Twenty seven years later, the Court observed that jurisdiction could not be avoided "merely because the defendant did not *physically* enter the forum state." *Burger King*, 471 U.S. at 476. The Court observed that:

> [I]t is an inescapable fact of modern commercial life that a substantial amount of commercial business is transacted solely by mail and wire communications across state lines, thus obviating the need for physical presence within a State in which business is conducted.

Id.

Enter the Internet, a global "'super-network' of over 15,000 computer networks used by over 30 million individuals, corporations, organizations, and educational institutions worldwide." Panavision Intern., L.P. v. Toeppen, 938 F. Supp. 616 (C.D. Cal. 1996). "In recent years, businesses have begun to use the Internet to provide information and products to consumers and other businesses." Id. The Internet makes it possible to conduct business throughout the world entirely from a desktop. With this global revolution looming on the horizon, the development of the law concerning the permissible scope of personal jurisdiction based on Internet use is in its infant stages. The cases are scant. Nevertheless, our review of the available cases and materials[5] reveals that the likelihood that personal jurisdiction can be constitutionally exercised is directly proportionate to the nature and quality of commercial activity that an entity conducts over the Internet. This sliding scale is consistent with well developed personal jurisdiction principles. At one end of the spectrum are situations where a defendant clearly does business over the Internet. If the defendant enters into contracts with residents of a foreign jurisdiction that involve the knowing and repeated transmission of computer files over the Internet, personal jurisdiction is proper. *E.g.*, CompuServe, Inc. v. Patterson, 89 F.3d 1257 (6th Cir. 1996). At the opposite end are situations where a defendant has simply posted information on an Internet Web site which is accessible to users in foreign jurisdictions. A passive Web site that does little more than make information available to those who are interested in it is not grounds for the exercise of personal jurisdiction. *E.g.*, Bensusan Restaurant Corp., v. King, 937 F. Supp. 295 (S.D.N.Y. 1996). The middle ground is occupied by interactive Web sites where a user can exchange information with the host computer. In these cases, the exercise of jurisdiction is determined by examining the level of interactivity and commercial nature of the exchange of information that occurs on the Web site. *E.g.*, Maritz, Inc. v. Cybergold, Inc., 947 F. Supp. 1328 (E.D. Mo. 1996).

5. See generally, Robert A. Bourque and Kerry L. Konrad, Avoiding Jurisdiction Based on Internet Web Site, New York Law Journal (Dec. 10, 1996); David Bender, Emerging Personal Jurisdiction Issues on the Internet, 453 PLI/Pat 7 (1996); Comment, Richard S. Zembek, Jurisdiction and the Internet: Fundamental Fairness in the Networked World of Cyberspace, 6 Alb. L.J. Sci. & Tech. 339 (1996).

Traditionally, when an entity intentionally reaches beyond its boundaries to conduct business with foreign residents, the exercise of specific jurisdiction is proper. *Burger King,* 471 U.S. at 475. Different results should not be reached simply because business is conducted over the Internet. In CompuServe, Inc. v. Patterson, 89 F.3d 1257 (6th Cir. 1996), the Sixth Circuit addressed the significance of doing business over the Internet. In that case, Patterson, a Texas resident, entered into a contract to distribute shareware[6] through CompuServe's Internet server located in Ohio. *CompuServe,* 89 F.3d at 1260. From Texas, Patterson electronically uploaded thirty-two master software files to CompuServe's server in Ohio via the Internet. Id. at 1261. One of Patterson's software products was designed to help people navigate the Internet. Id. When CompuServe later began to market a product that Patterson believed to be similar to his own, he threatened to sue. Id. CompuServe brought an action in the Southern District of Ohio, seeking a declaratory judgment. Id. The District Court granted Patterson's motion to dismiss for lack of personal jurisdiction and CompuServe appealed. Id. The Sixth Circuit reversed, reasoning that Patterson had purposefully directed his business activities toward Ohio by knowingly entering into a contract with an Ohio resident and then "deliberately and repeatedly" transmitted files to Ohio. Id. at 1264-1266.

In Maritz, Inc. v. Cybergold, Inc., 947 F. Supp. 1328 (E.D. Mo. 1996), the defendant had put up a Web site as a promotion for its upcoming Internet service. The service consisted of assigning users an electronic mailbox and then forwarding advertisements for products and services that matched the users' interests to those electronic mailboxes. *Maritz,* 947 F. Supp. at 1330. The defendant planned to charge advertisers and provide users with incentives to view the advertisements. Id. Although the service was not yet operational, users were encouraged to add their address to a mailing list to receive updates about the service. Id. The court rejected the defendant's contention that it operated a "passive Web site." Id. at 1333-34. The court reasoned that the defendant's conduct amounted to "active solicitations" and "promotional activities" designed to "develop a mailing list of Internet users" and that the defendant "indiscriminately responded to every user" who accessed the site. Id. at 1333-34.

Inset Systems, Inc. v. Instruction Set, 937 F. Supp. 161 (D. Conn. 1996) represents the outer limits of the exercise of personal jurisdiction based on the Internet. In *Inset Systems,* a Connecticut corporation sued a Massachusetts corporation in the District of Connecticut for trademark infringement based on the use of an Internet domain name. *Inset Systems,* 937 F. Supp. at 162. The defendant's contacts with Connecticut consisted of posting a Web site that was accessible to approximately 10,000 Connecticut residents and maintaining a toll free number. Id. at 165. The court exercised personal jurisdiction, reasoning that advertising on the Internet constituted the purposeful

6. "Shareware" is software which a user is permitted to download and use for a trial period, after which the user is asked to pay a fee to the author for continued use. *CompuServe,* 89 F.3d at 1260.

doing of business in Connecticut because "unlike television and radio advertising, the advertisement is available continuously to any Internet user." Id. at 165.

Bensusan Restaurant Corp., v. King, 937 F. Supp. 295 (S.D.N.Y. 1996) reached a different conclusion based on a similar Web site. In *Bensusan,* the operator of a New York jazz club sued the operator of a Missouri jazz club for trademark infringement. *Bensusan,* 937 F. Supp. at 297. The Internet Web site at issue contained general information about the defendant's club, a calendar of events and ticket information. Id. However, the site was not interactive. Id. If a user wanted to go to the club, she would have to call or visit a ticket outlet and then pick up tickets at the club on the night of the show. Id. The court refused to exercise jurisdiction based on the Web site alone, reasoning that it did not rise to the level of purposeful availment of that jurisdiction's laws. The court distinguished the case from *CompuServe,* supra, where the user had "'reached out' from Texas to Ohio and 'originated and maintained' contacts with Ohio." Id. at 301.

Pres-Kap, Inc. v. System One, Direct Access, Inc., 636 So. 2d 1351 (Fla. App. 1994), *review denied,* 645 So. 2d 455 (Fla. 1994), is not inconsistent with the above cases. In *Pres-Kap,* a majority of a three-judge intermediate state appeals court refused to exercise jurisdiction over a consumer of an online airline ticketing service. *Pres-Kap* involved a suit on a contract dispute in a Florida court by a Delaware corporation against its New York customer. *Pres-Kap,* 636 So. 2d at 1351-1352. The defendant had leased computer equipment which it used to access an airline ticketing computer located in Florida. Id. The contract was solicited, negotiated, executed and serviced in New York. Id. at 1352. The defendant's only contact with Florida consisted of logging onto the computer located in Florida and mailing payments for the leased equipment to Florida. Id. at 1353. *Pres-Kap* is distinguishable from the above cases and the case at bar because it addressed the exercise of jurisdiction over a consumer of online services as opposed to a seller. When a consumer logs onto a server in a foreign jurisdiction he is engaging in a fundamentally different type of contact than an entity that is using the Internet to sell or market products or services to residents of foreign jurisdictions. The *Pres-Kap* court specifically expressed concern over the implications of subjecting users of "online" services with contracts with out-of-state networks to suit in foreign jurisdictions. Id. at 1353.

3. *Application to This Case*

First, we note that this is not an Internet advertising case in the line of *Inset Systems* and *Bensusan,* supra. Dot Com has not just posted information on a Web site that is accessible to Pennsylvania residents who are connected to the Internet. This is not even an interactivity case in the line of *Maritz,* supra. Dot Com has done more than create an interactive Web site through which it exchanges information with Pennsylvania residents in hopes of using that information for commercial gain later. We are not being asked to determine whether Dot Com's Web site alone constitutes the purposeful availment of doing business in Pennsylvania. This is a "doing business over the Internet" case in the line of *CompuServe,* supra. We are being asked to determine whether Dot Com's conducting of electronic commerce with Pennsylvania residents constitutes the purposeful availment of doing business in Pennsylvania. We conclude that it does. Dot Com has contracted with approximately 3,000 individuals and seven Internet access providers in Pennsylvania. The intended object of these transactions has been the downloading of the electronic messages that form the basis of this suit in Pennsylvania.

We find Dot Com's efforts to characterize its conduct as falling short of purposeful availment of doing business in Pennsylvania wholly unpersuasive. At oral argument, Defendant repeatedly characterized its actions as merely "operating a Web site" or "advertising." Dot Com also cites to a number of cases from this Circuit which, it claims, stand for the proposition that merely advertising in a forum, without more, is not a sufficient minimal contact.[7] This argument is misplaced. Dot Com has done more than advertise on the Internet in Pennsylvania. Defendant has sold passwords to approximately 3,000 subscribers in Pennsylvania and entered into seven contracts with Internet access providers to furnish its services to their customers in Pennsylvania.

Dot Com also contends that its contacts with Pennsylvania residents are "fortuitous" within the meaning of *World-Wide Volkswagen,* 444 U.S. 286 (1980). Defendant argues that it has not "actively" solicited business in Pennsylvania and that any business it conducts with Pennsylvania residents has resulted from contacts that were initiated by Pennsylvanians who visited the Defendant's Web site. The fact that Dot Com's services have been consumed in Pennsylvania is not "fortuitous" within the meaning of *World-Wide Volkswagen.* In *World-Wide Volkswagen,* a couple that had purchased a vehicle in New York, while they were New York residents, were injured while driving that vehicle through Oklahoma and brought suit in an Oklahoma state court. *World-Wide Volkswagen,* 444 U.S. at 288. The [defendant] did not sell its vehicles in Oklahoma and had not made an effort to establish business relationships in Oklahoma. Id. at 295. The Supreme Court characterized the [defendant's] ties with Oklahoma as fortuitous because they resulted entirely out the fact that the plaintiffs had driven their car into that state. Id.

Here, Dot Com argues that its contacts with Pennsylvania residents are fortuitous because Pennsylvanians happened to find its Web site or heard about its news service elsewhere and decided to subscribe. This argument misconstrues the concept of fortuitous contacts embodied in *World-Wide*

7. Defendant has cited to: Gehling v. St. George's School of Medicine, Ltd., 773 F.2d 539 (3d Cir. 1985); Fields v. Ramada Inn Inc., 816 F. Supp. 1033 (E.D. Pa. 1993); and Garofalo v. Praiss, 1990 WL 97800 (E.D. Pa. 1990). We note that these cases all involve the issue of whether advertising can rise to the level of "systematic and continuous" contacts for the purpose of general jurisdiction.

Volkswagen. Dot Com's contacts with Pennsylvania would be fortuitous within the meaning of *World-Wide Volkswagen* if it had no Pennsylvania subscribers and an Ohio subscriber forwarded a copy of a file he obtained from Dot Com to a friend in Pennsylvania or an Ohio subscriber brought his computer along on a trip to Pennsylvania and used it to access Dot Com's service. That is not the situation here. Dot Com repeatedly and consciously chose to process Pennsylvania residents' applications and to assign them passwords. Dot Com knew that the result of these contracts would be the transmission of electronic messages into Pennsylvania. The transmission of these files was entirely within its control. Dot Com cannot maintain that these contracts are "fortuitous" or "coincidental" within the meaning of *World-Wide Volkswagen*. When a defendant makes a conscious choice to conduct business with the residents of a forum state, "it has clear notice that it is subject to suit there." *World-Wide Volkswagen*, 444 U.S. at 297. Dot Com was under no obligation to sell its services to Pennsylvania residents. It freely chose to do so, presumably in order to profit from those transactions. If a corporation determines that the risk of being subject to personal jurisdiction in a particular forum is too great, it can choose to sever its connection to the state. Id. If Dot Com had not wanted to be amenable to jurisdiction in Pennsylvania, the solution would have been simple—it could have chosen not to sell its services to Pennsylvania residents.

Next, Dot Com argues that its forum-related activities are not numerous or significant enough to create a "substantial connection" with Pennsylvania. Defendant points to the fact that only two percent of its subscribers are Pennsylvania residents. However, the Supreme Court has made clear that even a single contact can be sufficient. *McGee,* 355 U.S. at 223. The test has always focused on the "nature and quality" of the contacts with the forum and not the quantity of those contacts. *International Shoe,* 326 U.S. at 320. The Sixth Circuit also rejected a similar argument in *CompuServe* when it wrote that the contacts were "deliberate and repeated even if they yielded little revenue." *CompuServe*, 89 F.3d at 1265.

We also conclude that the cause of action arises out of Dot Com's forum-related conduct in this case. The Third Circuit has stated that "a cause of action for trademark infringement occurs where the passing off occurs." Cottman Transmission Systems Inc. v. Martino, 36 F.3d 291, 294 (citing Tefal, S.A. v. Products Int'l Co., 529 F.2d 495, 496 n. 1 (3d Cir. 1976); Indianapolis Colts v. Metro. Baltimore Football, 34 F.3d 410 (7th Cir. 1994). . . .

In *Indianapolis Colts,* also case cited by the Third Circuit in *Cottman,* an Indiana National Football League franchise sued a Maryland Canadian Football League franchise in the Southern District of Indiana, alleging trademark infringement. *Indianapolis Colts,* 34 F.3d at 411. On appeal, the Seventh Circuit held that personal jurisdiction was appropriate in Indiana because trademark infringement is a tort-like injury and a substantial amount of the injury from the alleged infringement was likely to occur in Indiana. Id. at 412.

In the instant case, both a significant amount of the alleged infringement and dilution, and resulting injury have occurred in Pennsylvania. The object of Dot Com's contracts with Pennsylvania residents is the transmission of the messages that Plaintiff claims dilute and infringe upon its trademark. When these messages are transmitted into Pennsylvania and viewed by Pennsylvania residents on their computers, there can be no question that the alleged infringement and dilution occur in Pennsylvania. Moreover, since Manufacturing is a Pennsylvania corporation, a substantial amount of the injury from the alleged wrongdoing is likely to occur in Pennsylvania. Thus, we conclude that the cause of action arises out of Dot Com's forum-related activities under the authority of both *Tefal* and *Indianapolis Colts*, supra.

Finally, Dot Com argues that the exercise of jurisdiction would be unreasonable in this case. We disagree. There can be no question that Pennsylvania has a strong interest in adjudicating disputes involving the alleged infringement of trademarks owned by resident corporations. We must also give due regard to the Plaintiff's choice to seek relief in Pennsylvania. *Kulko*, 436 U.S. at 92. These concerns outweigh the burden created by forcing the Defendant to defend the suit in Pennsylvania, especially when Dot Com consciously chose to conduct business in Pennsylvania, pursuing profits from the actions that are now in question. The Due Process Clause is not a "territorial shield to interstate obligations that have been voluntarily assumed." *Burger King*, 471 U.S. at 474. . . .

IV. Conclusion

We conclude that this Court may appropriately exercise personal jurisdiction over the Defendant. . . .

Note: Traditional Concepts

The contracts between "Dot Com" and its Pennsylvania customers are really driving the outcome, aren't they? Does the existence of the Web add to the analysis or is this just *Burger King* in cyberspace? Compare the jurisdictional facts in *Zippo* with those in the problem case. Are they equally compelling cases for exercising jurisdiction? What do you make of the "reasonableness" analysis in the penultimate paragraph of the opinion? Are Internet vendors open to suit anywhere they have clients? Almost anywhere?

If you were a lawyer representing a Web entrepreneur, like Sleeze in our problem case, how would you advise him to avoid potential worldwide personal jurisdiction? One device for websites selling products is the "clickwrap agreement" that includes a choice of venue clause, which a consumer must agree to before being allowed to buy anything. Stomp Inc. v. NeatO LLC, 61 F. Supp. 2d 1074 (S.D. Cal. 1999).

Zippo's "sliding scale test" is now the rule in a number of circuits. See, e.g., Best Van Lines, Inc. v. Walker, 490 F.3d 239 (2d Cir. 2007) (using the *Zippo* test to frame the inquiry into whether the defendant transacted any business in the jurisdiction); Lakin v. Prudential Sec., Inc., 348 F.3d 704 (8th Cir. 2003) (distinguishing use of test for specific and general jurisdiction); Carefirst of Md., Inc. v. Carefirst Pregnancy Ctrs., Inc., 334 F.3d 390 (4th Cir. 2003); Toys "R" Us, Inc. v. Step Two, S.A., 318 F.3d 446, 452 (3d Cir. 2003) (calling *Zippo* the "seminal authority regarding personal jurisdiction based upon the operation of an Internet web site"); Soma Medical Int'l v. Standard Chartered Bank, 196 F.3d 1292 (10th Cir. 1999); Mink v. AAAA Dev. LLC, 190 F.3d 333, 336 (5th Cir. 1999); Cybersell, Inc. v. Cybersell, Inc., 130 F.3d 414 (9th Cir. 1997); CompuServe, Inc. v. Patterson, 89 F.3d 1257 (6th Cir. 1996).

However, a small minority of lower courts have signaled their willingness to break from the *Zippo* framework. See, e.g., Shamsuddin v. Vitamin Research Prods., 346 F. Supp. 2d 804, 811 (D. Md. 2004) (holding that "website interactivity may have some bearing on the jurisdictional analysis, but it is not determinative"); Hy Cite Corp. v. Badbusinessbureau.com L.L.C., 297 F. Supp. 2d 1154 (W.D. Wis. 2004) (finding interactive Web site, sale of one book, and e-mail exchange between Wisconsin company and West Indies-based Web site insufficient to establish minimum contacts); Howard v. Mo. Bone & Joint Ctr., Inc., 869 N.E.2d 207, 212 (Ill. App. 5th 2007) (calling the *Zippo* sliding-scale approach "arbitrary" and concluding that "the web page's level of interactivity is irrelevant").

Several recent articles have argued that the *Zippo* test should be abandoned. See Eric C. Hawkins, General Jurisdiction and Internet Contacts: What Role, If Any, Should the *Zippo* Sliding Scale Test Play in the Analysis?, 74 Fordham L. Rev. 2371 (2006); Bunmi Awoyemi, *Zippo* Is Dying—Should It Be Dead? The Exercise of Personal Jurisdiction by U.S. Federal Courts over Non-Domiciliary Defendants in Trademark Infringement Lawsuits Arising Out of Cyberspace, 9 Marq. Intell. Prop. L. Rev. 37 (2005).

Two courts have gone further than *Zippo*, holding that Internet companies with interactive, commercially successful Web sites may be subject to *general* jurisdiction in any state where sales and use of the Web site are substantial. See Gator.Com Corp. v. L.L. Bean, Inc., 341 F.3d 1072, 1079-1080 (9th Cir. 2003), *rehearing en banc granted by* 366 F.3d 789 (2004) (finding general jurisdiction arising from L.L. Bean's "highly interactive, as opposed to 'passive,' website," its extensive Internet catalogue sales in California, and its targeted electronic advertising in the state), *dismissed as moot by* 398 F.3d 1125 (9th Cir. 2005) (en banc); Gorman v. Ameritrade Holding Corp., 293 F.3d 506, 512-513 (D.C. Cir. 2002) (finding general jurisdiction where D.C. customers of defendant online brokerage firm used the Web site "to open accounts, transmit funds to those accounts electronically, use the accounts to buy and sell securities, and enter into bidding contracts with the defendant").

Zippo discusses most of the significant cases that preceded it on jurisdiction and the Internet. There also has been a good deal of commentary on the subject. Here is a selective list of some of these early attempts to, as Professor Redish says, "put new wine in old bottles." Michael E. Allen, Analyzing Minimum Contacts Through the Internet, 31 Ind. L. Rev. 385 (1998); Dan L. Burk, Federalism in Cyberspace, 28 Conn. L. Rev. 1095 (1996); Christopher McWhinney, Sean Wooden, Jeremy McKown, John Ryan, & Joseph Green, The "Sliding Scale" of Personal Jurisdiction Via the Internet, 2000 Stan. Tech. L. Rev. 1; Martin H. Redish, Of New Wine and Old Bottles: Personal Jurisdiction, the Internet, and the Nature of Constitutional Evolution, 38 Jurimetrics J. 575 (1998); Howard B. Stravitz, Personal Jurisdiction in Cyberspace: Something More Is Required on the Electronic Stream of Commerce, 49 S.C. L. Rev. 925 (1998); E. Costa, Comment: Minimum Contacts in Cyberspace: A Taxonomy of the Case Law, 35 Hous. L. Rev. 453 (1998); Veronica M. Sanchez, Comment: Taking a Byte Out of Minimum Contacts: A Reasonable Exercise of Personal Jurisdiction in Cyberspace Trademark Disputes, 46 UCLA L. Rev. 1671 (1999).

Note: Substance and Procedure

The nature of the Internet comes up first in connection with personal jurisdiction. In many cases, the issue is also central to the merits. What kinds of facts would Plaintiff Neff want to show about *The Naked Truth* Web site at the trial? Questions about who owns what in cyberspace are often contested in huge, bet-the-store jury trials, replete with many experts and multi-media presentations.

One of the most interesting trials of the twentieth century was the government's case against Microsoft for antitrust violations and unfair competition. Though it was tried by a judge, the intense media and market interest gave it the flavor and community connection of a jury trial. The existential features of the Web and who controls access to it were at issue in the case, and much of the evidence was in electronic form, including crucial e-mails. See, e.g., U.S. v. Microsoft: How a Case Gained Momentum, N.Y. Times, June 9, 2000, at A-1; Laureen Seeger and Beth Rogers, Computer Compliance Issues: U.S. v. Microsoft & E-mail, 1121 PLI/Corp 11 (1999). The case also required the trial judge to master the intricacies of contemporary computer markets and technology, fomenting discussions of the judiciary's institutional competence to deal with emerging technological issues. For further discussion of issues surrounding the *Microsoft* trial, see Steve Bickerstaff, Shackles on the Giant: How the Federal Government Created Microsoft, Personal Computers, and the Internet, 78 Tex. L. Rev. 1 (1999); Symposium, United States v. Microsoft, 31 Conn. L. Rev. 1245 (1999).

Note: Enforceability

One concern for a judge ruling on personal jurisdiction is whether he or she will be able to enter enforceable judgments. Distant defendants with only Web contacts in the forum state may be able simply to ignore court orders. Consider, for instance, the case of the toymaker, Mattel Inc., the manufacturer of the Barbie doll. It owns Cyber Patrol, a popular Internet filtering program intended to help parents block children's access to harmful sites, and also used by libraries and schools.

Two computer enthusiasts, one in Canada and one in Sweden, each independently designed programs to defeat Cyber Patrol, and posted them for free on the Internet. Mattel sued, claiming violation of the Cyber Patrol copyright. Mattel filed its case in Massachusetts, and the two original defendants caved in immediately, stipulating to the entry of a far-ranging injunction against not only the named defendants but "all persons in active concert or participation" with them. All these "un-named parties" were enjoined from "publishing the software source code and binaries known as 'Cphack.exe' or any derivative thereof."

The injunction would presumably cover the hundred or so other people in the United States and elsewhere who had set up mirror sites of the original two, from which Cphack. exe could be downloaded and used. None of these people received notice or had the opportunity to be heard. Few have ever been in Massachusetts. Are they bound by the injunction? Should they be bound? What is the remedy if they continue to display their Web sites? See Microsystems Software, Inc. v. Scandinavia Online AB, 98 F. Supp. 2d 74 (D. Mass. 2000). See also Chapter 5, section B, infra.

Note: Purposeful Availment and Dot-Com Litigation Overseas

How can a Web-based company protect itself against judgments obtained by foreign users in foreign courts? Popular search engines are especially susceptible to foreign litigation because they are used by people all around the world and they must constantly balance the goal of providing open access to wide-ranging Internet content against the risk that content accessed through their search engines will offend users and/or the law where users are logging on. To give but one example, Yahoo! runs chat rooms and an auction Web site. Nazi rhetoric has surfaced in some of its chat rooms and Nazi paraphernalia has appeared for sale on its auction Web site. Two French organizations recently filed suit in French court against Yahoo! alleging violations of the French Criminal Code, which prohibits exhibition of Nazi propaganda for sale and the purchase or possession of such material by French citizens, and other French hate speech laws. The Web site www.fr.yahoo.com, run by the company's subsidiary in France, edits the Web site to exclude all Nazi material, but French users can easily access the unedited American Web site. The French court granted an injunction requiring Yahoo!, among other things, "to destroy all Nazi-related messages, images, and text stored on its server, particularly any Nazi relics, objects, insignia, emblems, and flags on its auction site, and to remove any excerpts from Mein Kampf and Protocole des Sages de Sion, books promoting Nazism." Yahoo!, Inc. v. La

Ligue Contre le Racisme et L'Antisemitisme, 379 F.3d 1120, 1122 (9th Cir. 2004). The injunction authorized sanctions of about $13,300 U.S. *per day* for failure to comply.

Rather than comply with or appeal the decision in France, Yahoo! filed a complaint in the Northern District of California seeking a declaration that the French court's orders were unenforceable in the United States because they abridge the First Amendment. The French organizations responded by moving to dismiss the complaint for want of personal jurisdiction. The district court denied the motion, holding that it could exercise specific jurisdiction because the French organizations had (1) sent a cease and desist letter to Yahoo!'s corporate headquarters in Santa Clara, California, demanding that Yahoo! remove the offending Nazi material, (2) used the United States Marshals Service to effect service on Yahoo! in California, and (3) asked the French court for an injunction ordering Yahoo! to make changes to its Web sites. Id. at 1124. The court decided that these actions met the purposeful availment requirement, because, like the libelous newspaper article in Calder v. Jones, see supra page 126, they were "'expressly aim[ed]'" at Yahoo! in California. Id. at 1124 (quoting *Calder*).

The Ninth Circuit reversed on appeal, noting that *Calder*'s "express aiming" test requires that the conduct aimed at the forum state must be "wrongful," like the intentionally tortious article the journalist and editor in *Calder* were sued for publishing. The French organization's actions, by contrast, were simply efforts to enforce French law—efforts, the court stressed, that a French court had already deemed legitimate. Id. at 1125-1126. A lengthy dissenting opinion argued that wrongful conduct is only one form of express aiming that can meet the purposeful availment requirement. Id. at 1132 ("although an intentional tortious act clearly satisfies the *Calder* 'effects test,' so too can other conduct 'targeted' or 'expressly aimed' at residents of the forum state") (Brunetti, J., dissenting opinion).

In 2006, after rehearing the case en banc, the Ninth Circuit reversed the panel decision, finding the exercise of personal jurisdiction proper. The court pointed out that if conduct had to be wrongful in order to create personal jurisdiction, a court would lose its jurisdiction, and hence its ability to decide a case, the moment it ruled the questionable conduct to be permissible. 433 F.3d 1199, 1208 (2006). In evaluating the French organization's contacts with the forum state, the court agreed with earlier decisions that the cease and desist letter alone was not enough to establish minimum contacts. See Inamed Corp. v. Kuzmak, 249 F.3d 1356 (Fed. Cir. 2001); Bancroft & Masters, Inc. v. Augusta National Inc., 223 F.3d 1082 (9th Cir. 2000); Cascade Corp. v. Hiab-Foco AB, 619 F.2d 36 (9th Cir. 1980). But taken together with the interim orders from the French court, the Ninth Circuit found sufficient contacts for personal jurisdiction.

Additionally, whether or not the French court had infringed Yahoo!'s First Amendment rights, the court noted that enforcement of the fines was highly unlikely because "American courts do not enforce monetary fines or penalties awarded by foreign courts." 433 F.3d at 1211. A plurality of the court further held that the First Amendment question was not ripe, and remanded the case to the district court to be dismissed without prejudice.

10. Waiving Due Process Objections by Agreement: Autonomy or Adhesion?

As we saw in *Burger King*, parties can by private agreement affect what law will be applied to a controversy. Whether and when courts will respect these choice of law clauses depends on several practical and policy considerations, including the extent to which the agreement was freely negotiated.

In the following case, the parties agreed to a particular forum for the litigation. The case demonstrates again that a party *can* waive procedural rights that she otherwise would enjoy. We later will encounter other limits on courts and parties that are not waivable, such as the limits on a federal court's power to hear matters that are not within the court's subject matter jurisdiction.

What principle justifies giving effect to a forum selection clause? Does it matter if the forum is one that would otherwise be proper, in the sense of having jurisdiction over the defendant? How knowing and voluntary must the execution of the clause (versus the entire contract) be to warrant giving that clause effect? Read on to see what the United States Supreme Court has said on the matter.

In Shute v. Carnival Cruise Lines, 783 P.2d 78 (1989), Eulala Shute, a Washington resident, fell while touring the galley of the cruise ship *Tropicale* while it was off the coast of Mexico. She had purchased her ticket in Washington through a travel agent who forwarded the payment to Carnival's headquarters in Miami. The cruise sailed from Los Angeles to Puerto Vallarta, Mexico.

Factors cutting for the exercise of jurisdiction were Carnival's advertisements in local newspapers, its provision of brochures to travel agents within the state, and its periodic seminars for travel agents in order to update them on Carnival's offerings. Carnival also pays a 10 percent commission on proceeds from tickets sold for Carnival cruises. On the other hand, Carnival is a Panamanian corporation with its principal place of business in Miami. It is not registered to do business in Washington, owns no property, and maintains no office or bank account there. None of its ships call at Washington ports.

The suit was filed in federal district court, which held that it had no jurisdiction. Initially, the Ninth Circuit reversed and found that there was jurisdiction. The court then withdrew its opinion and certified to the Supreme Court of Washington the question whether the long-arm statute applied to Carnival Cruise Lines. In deciding that its statute would bring

Carnival Cruise Lines to Washington to defend, the state Supreme Court held that its statute requires that three factors must coincide:

> (1) The nonresident defendant or foreign corporation must purposefully do some act or consummate some transaction in the forum state;
> (2) the cause of action must arise from, or be connected with, such act or transaction; and
> (3) the assumption of jurisdiction by the forum state must not offend traditional notions of fair play and substantial justice, consideration being given to the quality, nature, and extent of the activity in the forum state, the relative convenience of the parties, the benefits and protection of the laws of the forum state afforded the respective parties, and the basic equities of the situation.

783 P.2d at 80. The Washington court concluded:

> We adopt the "but for" test of Shute v. Carnival Cruise Lines, 863 F.2d 1437 (9th Cir. 1988), *withdrawn*, 872 F.2d 930 (1989), and hold that there is sufficient connection between the Shutes' claim and Carnival's Washington contacts to support long-arm jurisdiction under R.C.W. 4.28.185. "But for" Carnival's "transaction of any business within this state," Mrs. Eulala Shute would not have been injured on respondent's cruise ship. Therefore her claim "arises from" Carnival's Washington contacts within the meaning of Washington's long-arm statute.

Id. at 82.

Thus, as it was litigated through the courts below, *Carnival Cruise* was shaping up to be the next major case on personal jurisdiction, dealing with the sending of advertising messages and other intangibles through the commercial stream. The question on which the United States Supreme Court granted certiorari was: "Can a state long-arm statute constitutionally reach a defendant whose activities in the forum state are insubstantial and bear only a tenuous relationship to the cause of action?" But this question was not to be decided.

Carnival Cruise Lines v. Shute
499 U.S. 585 (1991)

JUSTICE BLACKMUN delivered the opinion of the Court.

In this admiralty case we primarily consider whether the United States Court of Appeals for the Ninth Circuit correctly refused to enforce a forum-selection clause contained in tickets issued by petitioner Carnival Cruise Lines, Inc., to respondents Eulala and Russel Shute.

I

The Shutes, through an Arlington, Wash., travel agent, purchased passage for a 7-day cruise on petitioner's ship, the *Tropicale*. Respondents paid the fare to the agent who forwarded the payment to petitioner's headquarters in Miami, Fla. Petitioner then prepared the tickets and sent them to respondents in the State of Washington. The face of each ticket, at its left-hand lower corner, contained this admonition:

SUBJECT TO CONDITIONS OF
CONTRACT ON LAST PAGES
IMPORTANT! PLEASE READ CONTRACT
ON LAST PAGES 1, 2, 3

The following appeared on "contract page 1" of each ticket:

Terms and Conditions of Passage Contract Ticket

> 3. (a) The acceptance of this ticket by the person or persons named hereon as passengers shall be deemed to be an acceptance and agreement by each of them of all of the terms and conditions of this Passage Contract Ticket.
> 8. It is agreed by and between the passenger and the Carrier that all disputes and matters whatsoever arising under, in connection with or incident to this Contract shall be litigated, if at all, in and before a Court located in the State of Florida, U.S. A., to the exclusion of the Courts of any other state or country.

The last quoted paragraph is the forum-selection clause at issue. . . .

Turning to the forum-selection clause, the Court of Appeals acknowledged that a court concerned with the enforceability of such a clause must begin its analysis with The Bremen v. Zapata Off-Shore Co., 407 U.S. 1 (1972), where this Court held that forum-selection clauses, although not "historically . . . favored," are "prima facie valid." Id., at 9-10. See [Shute v. Carnival Cruise Lines,] 897 F.2d at 388 [9th Cir. 1990]. The appellate court concluded that the forum clause should not be enforced because it "was not freely bargained for." Id. at 389. As an "independent justification" for refusing to enforce the clause, the Court of Appeals noted that there was evidence in the record to indicate that "the Shutes are physically and financially incapable of pursuing this litigation in Florida" and that the enforcement of the clause would operate to deprive them of their day in court and thereby contravene this Court's holding in *The Bremen*. 897 F.2d at 389.

We granted certiorari to address the question whether the Court of Appeals was correct in holding that the District Court should hear respondents' tort claim against petitioner. 498 U.S. 807-808 (1990). Because we find the forum-selection clause to be dispositive of this question, we need not consider petitioner's constitutional argument as to personal jurisdiction.

We begin by noting the boundaries of our inquiry. First, this is a case in admiralty, and federal law governs the enforceability of the forum-selection clause we scrutinize. Second, we do not address the question whether respondents had sufficient notice of the forum clause before entering the contract for passage. Respondents essentially have conceded that they had notice of the forum-selection provision. Additionally, the Court of Appeals evaluated the enforceability of the forum clause under the assumption, although "doubtful," that respondents could be deemed to have had knowledge of the clause.

Within this context, respondents urge that the forum clause should not be enforced because, contrary to this Court's teachings in *The Bremen*, the clause was not the product of negotiation, and enforcement effectively would deprive respondents of their day in court. . . .

Both petitioner and respondents argue vigorously that the Court's opinion in *The Bremen* governs this case, and each side purports to find ample support for its position in that opinion's broad-ranging language. This seeming paradox derives in large part from key factual differences between this case and *The Bremen*, differences that preclude an automatic and simple application of *The Bremen*'s general principles to the facts here.

In *The Bremen*, this Court addressed the enforceability of a forum-selection clause in a contract between two business corporations. An American corporation, Zapata, made a contract with Unterweser, a German corporation, for the towage of Zapata's ocean-going drilling rig from Louisiana to a point in the Adriatic Sea off the coast of Italy. The agreement provided that any dispute arising under the contract was to be resolved in the London Court of Justice. After a storm in the Gulf of Mexico seriously damaged the rig, Zapata ordered Unterweser's ship to tow the rig to Tampa, Fla., the nearest point of refuge. Thereafter, Zapata sued Unterweser in admiralty in federal court at Tampa. Citing the forum clause, Unterweser moved to dismiss. The District Court denied Unterweser's motion, and the Court of Appeals for the Fifth Circuit, sitting en banc on rehearing, and by a sharply divided vote, affirmed. 446 F.2d 907 (1971).

This Court vacated and remanded, stating that, in general, "a freely negotiated private international agreement, unaffected by fraud, undue influence, or overweening bargaining power, such as that involved here, should be given full effect." 407 U.S. at 12-13 (footnote omitted). The Court further generalized that "in the light of present-day commercial realities and expanding international trade we conclude that the forum clause should control absent a strong showing that it should be set aside." Id., at 15. The Court did not define precisely the circumstances that would make it unreasonable for a court to enforce a forum clause. Instead, the Court discussed a number of factors that made it reasonable to enforce the clause at issue in *The Bremen* and that, presumably, would be pertinent in any determination whether to enforce a similar clause.

In this respect, the Court noted that there was "strong evidence that the forum clause was a vital part of the agreement, and [that] it would be unrealistic to think that the parties did not conduct their negotiations, including fixing the monetary terms, with the consequences of the forum clause figuring prominently in their calculations." Id., at 14 (footnote omitted). Further, the Court observed that it was not "dealing with an agreement between two Americans to resolve their essentially local disputes in a remote alien forum," and that in such a case, "the serious inconvenience of the contractual forum to one or both of the parties might carry greater weight in determining the reasonableness of the forum clause." Id. at 17. The Court stated that even where the forum clause establishes a remote forum for resolution of conflicts, "the party claiming [unfairness] should bear a heavy burden of proof." Ibid.

In applying *The Bremen,* the Court of Appeals in the present litigation took note of the foregoing "reasonableness" factors and rather automatically decided that the forum-selection clause was unenforceable because, unlike the parties in *The Bremen,* respondents are not business persons and did not negotiate the terms of the clause with petitioner. Alternatively, the Court of Appeals ruled that the clause should not be enforced because enforcement effectively would deprive respondents of an opportunity to litigate their claim against petitioner. *The Bremen* concerned a "far from routine transaction between companies of two different nations contemplating the tow of an extremely costly piece of equipment from Louisiana across the Gulf of Mexico and the Atlantic Ocean, through the Mediterranean Sea to its final destination in the Adriatic Sea." Id. at 13. These facts suggest that, even apart from the evidence of negotiation regarding the forum clause, it was entirely reasonable for the Court in *The Bremen* to have expected Unterweser and Zapata to have negotiated with care in selecting a forum for the resolution of disputes arising from their special towing contract.

In contrast, respondents' passage contract was purely routine and doubtless nearly identical to every commercial passage contract issued by petitioner and most other cruise lines. In this context, it would be entirely unreasonable for us to assume that respondents—or any other cruise passenger—would negotiate with petitioner the terms of a forum-selection clause in an ordinary commercial cruise ticket. Common sense dictates that a ticket of this kind will be a form contract the terms of which are not subject to negotiation, and that an individual purchasing the ticket will not have bargaining parity with the cruise line. But by ignoring the crucial differences in the business contexts in which the respective contracts were executed, the Court of Appeals' analysis seems to us to have distorted somewhat this Court's holding in *The Bremen.*

In evaluating the reasonableness of the forum clause at issue in this case, we must refine the analysis of *The Bremen* to account for the realities of form passage contracts. As an initial matter, we do not adopt the Court of Appeals' determination that a nonnegotiated forum-selection clause in a form ticket contract is never enforceable simply because it is not the subject of bargaining. Including a reasonable forum clause in a form contract of this kind well may be permissible for several reasons: First, a cruise line has a special interest in limiting the fora in which it potentially could be subject to suit. Because a cruise ship typically carries passengers from many locales, it is not unlikely that a mishap on a cruise could subject the cruise line to litigation in several different fora. Additionally, a clause establishing *ex ante* the forum for dispute resolution has the salutary effect of dispelling any confusion about where suits arising from the contract must be brought and defended, sparing litigants the time and expense of pretrial motions to determine the correct forum and conserving judicial resources that otherwise would be devoted to deciding those motions. Finally, it stands to reason that passengers who purchase tickets containing a forum clause like that at issue in this case benefit in the form of reduced fares reflecting the savings that the cruise line enjoys by limiting the fora in which it may be sued.

We also do not accept the Court of Appeals' "independent justification" for its conclusion that *The Bremen* dictates that the clause should not be enforced because "[t]here is evidence in the record to indicate that the Shutes are physically and financially incapable of pursuing this litigation in Florida." 897 F.2d at 389. We do not defer to the Court of Appeals' findings of fact. In dismissing the case for lack of personal jurisdiction over petitioner, the District Court made no finding regarding the physical and financial impediments to the Shutes' pursuing their case in Florida. The Court of Appeals' conclusory reference to the record provides no basis for this Court to validate the finding of inconvenience. . . . In the present case, Florida is not a "remote alien forum," nor—given the fact that Mrs. Shute's accident occurred off the coast of Mexico—is this dispute an essentially local one inherently more suited to resolution in the State of Washington than in Florida. In light of these distinctions, and because respondents do not claim lack of notice of the forum clause, we conclude that they have not satisfied the "heavy burden of proof" required to set aside the clause on grounds of inconvenience.

It bears emphasis that forum-selection clauses contained in form passage contracts are subject to judicial scrutiny for fundamental fairness. In this case, there is no indication that petitioner set Florida as the forum in which disputes were to be resolved as a means of discouraging cruise passengers from pursuing legitimate claims. Any suggestion of such a bad-faith motive is belied by two facts: Petitioner has its principal place of business in Florida, and many of its cruises depart from and return to Florida ports. Similarly, there is no evidence that petitioner obtained respondents' accession to the forum clause by fraud or overreaching. Finally, respondents have conceded that they were given notice of the forum provision and, therefore, presumably retained the option of rejecting the contract with impunity. In the case before us, therefore, we conclude that the Court of Appeals erred in refusing to enforce the forum-selection clause. . . .

The judgment of the Court of Appeals is reversed.

It is so ordered.

JUSTICE STEVENS, with whom JUSTICE MARSHALL joins, dissenting.

The Court prefaces its legal analysis with a factual statement that implies that a purchaser of a Carnival Cruise Lines passenger ticket is fully and fairly notified about the existence of the choice of forum clause in the fine print on the back of the ticket. Even if this implication were accurate, I would disagree with the Court's analysis. But, given the Court's preface, I begin my dissent by noting that only the most meticulous passenger is likely to become aware of the forum-selection provision. I have therefore appended to this opinion a facsimile of the relevant text, using the type size that actually appears in the ticket itself. A careful reader will find the forum-selection clause in the 8th of the 25 numbered paragraphs.

Of course, many passengers, like the respondents in this case, will not have an opportunity to read paragraph 8 until they have actually purchased their tickets. By this point, the passengers will already have accepted the condition set forth in paragraph 16(a), which provides that "[t]he Carrier shall not be liable to make any refund to passengers in respect of . . . tickets wholly or partly not used by a passenger." Not knowing whether or not that provision is legally enforceable, I assume that the average passenger would accept the risk of having to file suit in Florida in the event of an injury, rather than canceling—without a refund—a planned vacation at the last minute. The fact that the cruise line can reduce its litigation costs, and therefore its liability insurance premiums, by forcing this choice on its passengers does not, in my opinion, suffice to render the provision reasonable. . . .

Forum-selection clauses in passenger tickets involve the intersection of two strands of traditional contract law that qualify the general rule that courts will enforce the terms of a contract as written. Pursuant to the first strand, courts traditionally have reviewed with heightened scrutiny the terms of contracts of adhesion, form contracts offered on a take-or-leave basis by a party with stronger bargaining power to a party with weaker power. Some commentators have questioned whether contracts of adhesion can justifiably be enforced at all under traditional contract theory because the adhering party generally enters into them without manifesting knowing and voluntary consent to all their terms.

The common law, recognizing that standardized form contracts account for a significant portion of all commercial agreements, has taken a less extreme position and instead subjects terms in contracts of adhesion to scrutiny for reasonableness. Judge J. Skelly Wright set out the state of the law succinctly in Williams v. Walker-Thomas Furniture Co., 350 F.2d 445, 449-450 (1965) (footnotes omitted):

> Ordinarily, one who signs an agreement without full knowledge of its terms might be held to assume the risk that he has entered a one-sided bargain. But when a party of little bargaining power, and hence little real choice, signs a commercially unreasonable contract with little or no knowledge of its terms, it is hardly likely that his consent, or even an objective manifestation of his consent, was ever given to all of the terms. In such a case the usual rule that the terms of the agreement are not to be questioned should be abandoned and the court should consider whether the terms of the contract are so unfair that enforcement should be withheld.

The second doctrinal principle implicated by forum-selection clauses is the traditional rule that "contractual provisions, which seek to limit the place or court in which an action may . . . be brought, are invalid as contrary to public policy." See Dougherty, Validity of Contractual Provision Limiting Place or Court in Which Action May Be Brought, 31 A.L.R. 4th 404, 409 § 3 (1984). Although adherence to this general rule has declined in recent years, particularly following our decision in The Bremen v. Zapata Off-Shore Co., 407 U.S. 1 (1972), the prevailing rule is still that forum-selection clauses are not enforceable if they were not freely bargained for, create additional expense for one party, or deny one party a remedy. A forum-selection clause in a standardized passenger ticket would clearly have been unenforceable under the common law before our decision in *The Bremen,* and, in my opinion, remains unenforceable under the prevailing rule today. . . .

I respectfully dissent.

Notes and Questions

1. The Court in *Carnival Cruise* suggests that forum selection clauses should be enforced only if they are fundamentally fair. Yet it upheld a small-type forum clause against the Shutes. Is the concept of fundamental fairness related to due process?

2. The Supreme Court's decision in *Carnival Cruise* has been the subject of criticism from many angles. A sampling of the criticism is listed here. For the contracts perspective, see Patrick J. Borchers, Forum Selection Agreements in the Federal Courts after *Carnival Cruise*: A Proposal for Congressional Reform, 78 Wash. L. Rev. 55 (1992); For an economic perspective, see Lee Goldman, My Way and the Highway: The Law and Economics of Choice of Forum Clauses in Consumer Form Contracts, 86 Nw. U. L. Rev. 700 (1992). For the personal jurisdiction perspective, see John McKinley Kirby, Consumer's Right to Sue at Home Jeopardized Through Forum Selection Clause in Carnival Cruise Lines v. Shute, 70 N. C. L. Rev. 888 (1992); Edward A. Purcell Jr., Geography as a Litigation Weapon: Consumer's Forum-Selection Clauses and the Rehnquist Court, 40 UCLA L. Rev. 423 (1992); David H. Taylor, The Forum Selection Clause: A Tale of Two Concepts, 66 Temp. L. Rev. 785 (1993); Linda S. Mullenix, Forum-Shoppers Should Discover a Wider Market, Nat'l L.J., Aug. 19, 1991, at S12.

For an especially thorough examination of the consequences of forum selection clauses, see Walter W. Heiser, Forum Selection Clauses in State Court: Limitations on Enforcement After *Steward* and *Carnival Cruise,* 45 Fla. L. Rev. 361 (1993). And for an important historical study of forum selection clause enforcement, see David Marcus, The Perils of Contract Procedure: A Revised History of Forum Selection Clauses in the Federal Courts, 82 Tulane L. Rev. 973 (2008).

Notwithstanding the criticism, lower courts generally have followed the Court's lead. But see Walker v. Carnival Cruise Lines, 107 F. Supp. 2d 1135 (N.D. Cal. 2000) (refusing to enforce a forum selection clause in a suit alleging that Carnival Cruise violated the Americans with Disabilities Act by failing to provide accessible accommodations on a cruise ship; the court reasoned that, "in combination, plaintiffs' physical disabilities and economic constraints are so severe that . . . they would preclude plaintiffs from having their day in court" if they had to travel to bring suit against Carnival Cruise); id. at 1143 ("This Court is persuaded that enforcing defendants' forum selection clause, under the circumstances presented here, would contravene the strong national policy of eradicating disability discrimination and promoting full and equal access to the legal system for civil rights plaintiffs."). See also O'Brien v. Okemo Mountain, Inc., 17 F. Supp. 2d 98 (D. Conn. 1998) (inadequate notice on lift ticket rendered forum selection clause unenforceable).

Some courts have even extended the enforceability of forum selection clauses to third parties. In Medtronic, Inc. v. Endologix, Inc., 530 F. Supp. 2d 1054 (D. Minn. 2008), a district court held that Medtronic (a heart valve manufacturer with a long-standing corporate presence in Minnesota) could bind not only two former employees who had signed employment contracts that included forum selection clauses requiring litigation in Minnesota state court, but also their new employer. The court reasoned that "[a]lthough Endologix did not sign those agreements, a third party may be bound by a forum-selection clause where it is 'closely related to the dispute such that it becomes foreseeable that it will be bound.'" Id. at 1056 (quoting and following Marano Enters. of Kan. v. Z-Teca Rests., L.P., 254 F.3d 753, 757 (8th Cir. 2001)). The court concluded that Endologix could "reasonably foresee being bound by the forum-selection clause" because the litigation arose from Endologix's decision to hire the two former Medtronic employees, it knew of the agreements the employees had signed with Medtronic, and it shared a common interest with the employees in defending against the Medtronic suit. Id. at 1057. Even if Endologix could not be bound as a third party, the court continued, the forum selection clauses precluded the employees from giving their consent to Endologix's attempt to remove the case from Minnesota state court. Id.

3. In *Carnival Cruise,* the Court treated the issues of personal jurisdiction and forum selection clauses as analytically distinct. Yet by effectively upholding Florida jurisdiction over the case, the Court may have missed the boat. Perhaps the *plaintiffs* have a due process right, akin to that of nonresident defendants, not to be forced to litigate in a foreign forum.

Due process for defendants requires that a court have personal jurisdiction over them before entering judgment. Thus a forum selection clause operates against a defendant as a waiver of personal jurisdiction in the specified forum, limiting venue to that forum. Against a plaintiff, a forum selection clause forces an individual to bring suit in a specified place. Isn't there a parallel due process concern? See John McKinley

Kirby, Consumer's Right to Sue at Home Jeopardized Through Forum Selection Clause in Carnival Cruise Line v. Shute, 70 N.C. L. Rev. 888 (1992).

In the next case we return to the issue of service of process—not to be confused with *amenability* to service of process or personal jurisdiction. This too can be the subject of private agreements whereby the parties waive their right to constitutional *notice*.

Under what circumstances should people be allowed to give up (or waive) their constitutional right to due process? This question arises with respect to all aspects of due process—notice, the right to a hearing, and, as you just saw above, personal jurisdiction. Waiver of due process rights can come in many forms; a somewhat crude example of such a waiver—waiving notice and the opportunity to be heard—is that of a Texas bank which responded to *Fuentes*, page 22 supra, by requiring loan applicants to sign this form:

> IN THE EVENT I/WE DEFAULT IN ANY OF THE OBLIGATIONS IMPOSED BY THIS CONTRACT, I/WE HEREBY WAIVE NOTICE AND HEARING AND AGREE THAT THE COLLATERAL MAY BE REPOSSESSED.

If you were the bank's lawyer, what advice would you give them about whether they can seize the savings account of a defaulting debtor who has signed this form? What considerations would enter into your advice?

A form of this type, known as a "cognovit note," was upheld by the Court against a due process claim in D.H. Overmyer Co. v. Frick Co., 405 U.S. 174 (1972). The Court described a cognovit note as an "ancient legal device by which the debtor consents in advance to the holder's obtaining a judgment without notice or hearing, and possibly even with the appearance, on the debtor's behalf, of an attorney designated by the holder." Id. at 176. But the Court noted specifically that its holding applied in

> the commercial world . . . and is not controlling precedent for other facts of other cases. For example, where the contract is one of adhesion, where there is great disparity in bargaining power, and where the debtor receives nothing for the cognovit provision, other legal consequences may ensue.

Id. at 188.

In the treatment of waiver of any constitutional rights, the Supreme Court has acted with some trepidation. In the process context, the Court has suggested that waiver can be validly executed only in negotiated contracts, see *Burger King*, supra (finding that "where . . . forum-selection provisions have been obtained through 'freely negotiated' agreements and are not 'unreasonable and unjust,' their enforcement does not offend due process," 471 U.S. at 473); or where the contracting parties are both sophisticated, commercial entities, see *The Bremen*. Compare Justice Black's dissent in the following case, where he suggests that form contracts are never sufficient to validly waive due process rights. What do you think should be required to waive due process rights?

National Equipment Rental, Ltd. v. Szukhent

375 U.S. 311 (1964)

JUSTICE STEWART delivered the opinion of the Court.

The Federal Rules of Civil Procedure provide that service of process upon an individual may be made "by delivering a copy of the summons and of the complaint to an agent authorized by appointment . . . to receive service of process." The petitioner is a corporation with its principal place of business in New York. It sued the respondents, residents of Michigan, in a New York federal court, claiming that the respondents had defaulted under a farm equipment lease. The only question now before us is whether the person upon whom the summons and complaint were served was "an agent authorized by appointment" to receive the same, so as to subject the respondents to the jurisdiction of the federal court in New York.

The respondents obtained certain farm equipment from the petitioner under a lease executed in 1961. The lease was on a printed form less than a page and a half in length, and consisted of 18 numbered paragraphs. The last numbered paragraph, appearing just above the respondent's signatures and printed in the same type used in the remainder of the instrument, provided that "the Lessee hereby designates Florence Weinberg, 47-21 Forty-first Street, Long Island City, N.Y., as agent, for the purpose of accepting service of any process within the State of New York." The respondents were not acquainted with Florence Weinberg.

In 1962, the petitioner commenced the present action by filing in the federal court in New York a complaint which alleged that the respondents had failed to make any of the periodic payments specified by the lease. The Marshal delivered two copies of the summons and complaint to Florence Weinberg. That same day she mailed the summons and complaint to the respondents, together with a letter stating that the documents had been served upon her as the respondents' agent for the purpose of accepting service of process in New York, in accordance with the agreement contained in the lease. The petitioner itself also notified the respondents by certified mail of the service of process upon Florence Weinberg.

Upon motion of the respondents, the District Court quashed service of the summons and complaint, holding that, although Florence Weinberg had promptly notified the respondents of the service of process and mailed copies of the summons and complaint to them, the lease agreement itself had not explicitly required her to do so, and there was therefore a "failure of the agency arrangement to achieve intrinsic and continuing reality." 30 F.R.D. 3, 5. The Court of Appeals affirmed, 311 F.2d 79, and we granted certiorari, 372 U.S. 974. For the reasons stated in this opinion, we have concluded that Florence Weinberg was "an agent authorized by appointment . . . to receive service of process," and accordingly we reverse the judgment before us.

We need not and do not in this case reach the situation where no personal notice has been given to the defendant. Since the respondents did in fact receive complete and timely notice of the lawsuit pending against them, no due process claim has been made. The case before us is therefore quite different from cases where there was no actual notice, such as Schroeder v. City of New York, 371 U.S. 208; Walker v. Hutchinson City, 352 U.S. 112; and Mullane v. Central Hanover Tr. Co., 339 U.S. 306. Similarly, as the Court of Appeals recognized, this Court's decision in Wuchter v. Pizzutti, 276 U.S. 13, is inapposite here. In that case a state nonresident motorist statute which failed to provide explicitly for communication of notice was held unconstitutional, despite the fact that notice had been given to the defendant in that particular case. *Wuchter* dealt with the limitations imposed by the Fourteenth Amendment upon a statutory scheme by which a State attempts to subject nonresident individuals to the jurisdiction of its courts. The question presented here, on the other hand, is whether a party to a private contract may appoint an agent to receive service of process within the meaning of Federal Rule of Civil Procedure 4(d)(1),* where the agent is not personally known to the party, and where the agent has not expressly undertaken to transmit notice to the party.

The purpose underlying the contractual provision here at issue seems clear. The clause was inserted by the petitioner and agreed to by the respondents in order to assure that any litigation under the lease should be conducted in the State of New York. The contract specifically provided that "This agreement shall be deemed to have been made in Nassau County, New York, regardless of the order in which the signatures of the parties shall be affixed hereto, and shall be interpreted, and the rights and liabilities of the parties here determined, in accordance with the laws of the State of New York." And it is settled, as the courts below recognized, that parties to a contract may agree in advance to submit to the jurisdiction of a given court, to permit notice to be served by the opposing party, or even to waive notice altogether.

Under well-settled general principles of the law of agency, Florence Weinberg's prompt acceptance and transmittal to the respondents of the summons and complaint pursuant to the authorization was itself sufficient to validate the agency. . . .

It is argued, finally, that the agency sought to be created in this case was invalid because Florence Weinberg may have had a conflict of interest. This argument is based upon the fact that she was not personally known

* In the current rule, this language appears in Rule 4(e)(2). EDS.

to the respondents at the time of her appointment and upon a suggestion in the record that she may be related to an officer of the petitioner corporation. But such a contention ignores the narrowly limited nature of the agency here involved. Florence Weinberg was appointed the respondents' agent for the single purpose of receiving service of process. An agent with authority so limited can in no meaningful sense be deemed to have had an interest antagonistic to the respondents, since both the petitioner and the respondents had an equal interest in assuring that, in the event of litigation, the latter be given that adequate and timely notice which is a prerequisite to a valid judgment....

The judgment of the Court of Appeals is reversed and the case is remanded for further proceedings consistent with this opinion.

It is so ordered.

JUSTICE BLACK, dissenting....

... This Court should reject any construction of Rule 4(d)(1) or formulation of federal standards under it to help powerful litigants to achieve by unbargained take-it-or-leave-it contracts what Congress has consistently refused to permit by legislation.

The end result of today's holding is not difficult to foresee. Clauses like the one used against the Szukhents—clauses which companies have not inserted, I suspect, because they never dreamed a court would uphold them—will soon find their way into the "boilerplate" of everything from an equipment lease to a conditional sales contract. Today's holding gives a green light to every large company in this country to contrive contracts which declare with force of law that when such a company wants to sue someone with whom it does business, that individual must go and try to defend himself in some place, no matter how distant, where big business enterprises are concentrated, like, for example, New York, Connecticut, or Illinois, or else suffer a default judgment. In this very case the Court holds that by this company's carefully prepared contractual clause the Szukhents must, to avoid a judgment rendered without a fair and full hearing, travel hundreds of miles across the continent, probably crippling their defense and certainly depleting what savings they may have, to try to defend themselves in a court sitting in New York City. I simply cannot believe that Congress, when by its silence it let Rule 4(d)(1) go into effect, meant for that rule to be used as a means to achieve such a far-reaching, burdensome, and unjust result. Heretofore judicial good common sense has, on one ground or another, disregarded contractual provisions like this one, not encouraged them. It is a long trip from San Francisco—or from Honolulu or Anchorage—to New York, Boston, or Wilmington. And the trip can be very expensive, often costing more than it would simply to pay what is demanded. The very threat of such a suit can be used to force payment of alleged claims, even though they be wholly without merit. This fact will not be news to companies exerting their economic power to wangle such contracts. No statute and no rule requires this Court to place its imprimatur upon them. I would not....

. . . In effect the Court treats the provision as a waiver of the Szukhents' constitutional right not to be compelled to go to a New York court to defend themselves against the company's claims. This printed form provision buried in a multitude of words is too weak an imitation of genuine agreement to be treated as a waiver of so important a constitutional safeguard as is the right to be sued at home. Waivers of constitutional rights to be effective, this Court has said, must be deliberately and understandingly made and can be established only by clear, unequivocal, and unambiguous language. It strains credulity to suggest that these Michigan farmers ever read this contractual provision about Mrs. Weinberg and about "accepting service of any process within the State of New York." And it exhausts credulity to think that they or any other laymen reading these legalistic words would have known or even suspected that they amounted to an agreement of the Szukhents to let the company sue them in New York should any controversy arise. This Court should not permit valuable constitutional rights to be destroyed by any such sharp contractual practices. The idea that there was a knowing consent of the Szukhents to be sued in the courts of New York is no more than a fiction—not even an amiable one at that.

JUSTICE BRENNAN, with whom THE CHIEF JUSTICE and JUSTICE GOLDBERG join, dissenting. . . .

. . . We must bear in mind what was said in United States v. Rumely, 345 U.S. 41, 44, that we must strive not to be "that 'blind' Court, against which Mr. Chief Justice Taft admonished in a famous passage, . . . that does not see what '[a]ll others can see and understand.'" It offends common sense to treat a printed form which closes an installment sale as embodying terms to all of which the individual knowingly assented. The sales pitch aims solely at getting the signature on the form and wastes no time explaining or even mentioning the print. Before I would find that an individual purchaser has knowingly and intelligently consented to be sued in another State, I would require more proof of that fact than is provided by his mere signature on the form.

Note: Applying the Case Law

Review your understanding of the Court's personal jurisdiction case law by analyzing the following questions:

1. What if a nonresident defendant has substantial, continuous contacts with a forum, but the cause of action arose elsewhere, the state has no interest in the dispute, and no witnesses or other evidence are located in the forum? Should the "unreasonableness" factors that apply in specific jurisdiction cases apply in general jurisdiction cases? See Metropolitan Life Ins. Co. v. Robertson-Ceco Corp., 84 F.3d 560 (2d Cir. 1996) (applying *International Shoe*'s "unreasonableness" factors and declining jurisdiction).

2. Should placement of advertisements in internationally circulated magazines constitute a sufficient tie to a U.S. forum, where the plaintiff in a defamation suit resides in the forum and experienced injuries there, but the defendant, a French advertising agency, had no other ties to the forum and the allegedly defamatory publication was written in French and was aimed at French consumers? See Noonan v. Winston Co., 135 F.3d 85 (1st Cir. 1998) (finding contacts with the forum insufficient to establish jurisdiction).

3. In a breach of contract case, are only the parties' dealings with respect to the disputed contracts relevant, or are all of defendant's contracts with the state relevant, however dissimilar in terms of time, geography, or substance? See R.A.R., Inc. v. Turner Diesel, Ltd., 107 F.3d 1272 (7th Cir. 1997) (concluding that prior sales transactions between a foreign corporation and an Illinois corporation were not sufficiently related to a later contract to establish minimum contacts for purposes of jurisdiction).

4. What if a Hong Kong hotel that solicited a Massachusetts firm's business is sued in Massachusetts in a wrongful death action arising from the death of a firm employee in the hotel swimming pool? See Nowak v. Tak How Investment Ltd., 94 F.3d 708 (1st Cir. 1996), *cert. denied*, 520 U.S. 1155 (1997) (finding personal jurisdiction because the hotel's solicitation of business in Massachusetts brought plaintiffs to the hotel and was therefore related to the drowning that gave rise to the suit).

5. Should California courts have jurisdiction over Washington-based fast food franchisees named as defendants in a cross-complaint filed by a California meat processor? The meat processor was a defendant in an action brought by franchisees whose customers were exposed to E-coli bacteria. The E-coli bacteria were traced to the hamburgers processed at a California plant. The cross-plaintiff claimed that the Washington franchisee failed to cook the hamburgers properly, and sought both damages and indemnification for any liability in the main action. The Washington franchisee had contractual arrangements with the California-based franchiser, including a forum selection clause and choice of law provision pointing toward California and California law, respectively. Were the tort claims listed in the cross-complaint sufficiently related to the franchisee's California contacts to satisfy due process? See Vons, Inc. v. Seabest Foods, Inc., 926 P.2d 1085 (1997) (finding purposeful availment by cross-defendants because of ongoing franchise relationship with California franchiser).

6. Is a Bennington, Vermont, doctor who regularly treats patients from New York amenable to process in New York, in a malpractice suit filed by a New York resident who was seen by the doctor in Vermont? See Ingraham v. Carroll, 687 N.E.2d 1293 (1997) (holding that although the doctor could anticipate that his actions might cause injury in New York, he did not derive substantial revenue from interstate or international commerce; a physician's services are "inherently personal, and local, in nature").

D. DUE PROCESS AND THE DUAL COURT SYSTEM: A FIRST LOOK AT SUBJECT MATTER JURISDICTION AND VENUE

Problem Case: The Due Process Game (Part Two)

Assume that a public university expels an undergraduate without a hearing of any kind. The student decides to sue the University on two grounds: violation of due process under the Fourteenth Amendment and breach of an implied contract based on the terms of the Student Handbook, which sets forth a list of grounds for expulsion. The student's position is that she violated none of the stated grounds for expulsion, and that the school cannot expel her for reasons not listed in the Handbook. Moreover, she contends, she was entitled to notice and a hearing regarding the University's basis for the expulsion and a chance to respond to the accusations.

Could the student file this action in a federal district court? In a state court? In either? Does the University have any control over the choice of forum?

1. A Dual Court System

The federal and state courts have distinct and overlapping jurisdiction, such that some actions may be brought in either system whereas others may be brought in only one of them. In general, state courts are courts of "general jurisdiction" and federal courts are courts of "limited jurisdiction." This means that state courts have broader subject matter jurisdiction than do federal courts. On rare occasions, however, an action may fall within the exclusive jurisdiction of the federal courts, and would thus be heard only by a federal judge.

To understand the division of judicial power and labor between the federal and state courts, one must review the United States Constitution. The Constitution says that the federal government, including the federal judiciary, has only as much power as the Constitution allows. That is, under the Tenth Amendment, all powers not expressly given to the federal government are reserved to the states and to the people.

a. Legislative Authority—Federal Versus State

In general, Congress has power over matters of national concern, which include matters involving interstate commerce, money, naturalization, post offices, roads, and a host of other concerns that require national legislation and control. Article I of the Constitution sets forth these areas of federal concern, and adds that the power to control these issues includes the power to make all laws that are "necessary and proper" for executing that authority. The most significant basis for congressional action is the Commerce Clause, which has been interpreted to justify broad-reaching federal legislation over a wide range of private activities. For example, the United States Congress has passed laws that prevent any business that employs a modest number of employees from discriminating against its employees on the basis of race, gender, ethnicity, or religion. This intervention of federal legislative authority into private, local businesses has been held to be constitutional because the business may affect interstate commerce, which Congress has the right to regulate.

Simply because Congress has the power to legislate in an area, however, does not mean that it must do so. Nor does it mean that states are powerless to draft legislation that addresses the same matter. When a state law and a federal law conflict, however, the federal law trumps the state law, under the Supremacy Clause (Article VI). Moreover, federal law may preempt state law in areas where there is congressional intention to do so or where there is a particularly compelling reason not to allow both federal and state standards to control that subject.

b. Federal Judicial Authority

Just as Congress possesses limited legislative authority, the federal courts have limited judicial authority. Again, the explanation lies in the constitutional allocation of power.

First read Article III of the Constitution. In Section 1, Congress is given the power to establish the "inferior" federal courts. Thus the only court that Congress cannot abolish, or that does not exist subject to congressional discretion, is the United States Supreme Court.

Now read Section 2 of Article III. This sets forth the major areas of subject matter jurisdiction for the federal courts. It cites the types of cases that can be litigated in federal (as opposed to state) courts. The two most significant areas include cases that arise between "citizens of different states" (diversity jurisdiction) and cases "arising under this Constitution, the laws of the United States, and Treaties made" (federal question jurisdiction).

The Court, pursuant to its authority under Marbury v. Madison, 5 U.S. (1 Cranch) 137 (1803), to determine the meaning and scope of the Constitution, has interpreted Article III fairly liberally. For example, the Court has interpreted the phrase "between citizens of different states" to mean merely that at least one of the plaintiffs is from a different state than at least one defendant or adverse party. Complete diversity of all plaintiffs from all defendants is not *constitutionally* required.

The Court has been even more generous in construing the phrase "arising under." It is enough, according to the Court, if federal law is an "ingredient" of the dispute; it need not be central or the gravamen of the matter. Thus, for example, the Court said that the Constitution is satisfied when a federal court hears a case that involves a federally chartered bank, even if the case turns entirely on state law. The federal charter gives the bank its legal existence and thus its capacity to sue or be sued. This federal law is an original ingredient that, though a slender reed, is enough to satisfy Article III. Osborn v. Bank of United States, 22 U.S. (9 Wheat.) 738, 819-823 (1824).

Finally, the Court has interpreted Article III to permit federal courts to hear state law claims, even when they arise between citizens of the same state, provided that the state law claims grow out of the same "common nucleus of operative facts" as a claim that meets Article III requirements. That is, if there is a solid federal subject matter jurisdiction "trunk," then the court can hear state claim "branches" from that trunk. The test is one of factual connectedness. The current name applied to this "branch" jurisdiction is *supplemental* jurisdiction. Older terms for this type of jurisdiction are *pendent* and *ancillary,* or *incidental,* jurisdiction.

The foregoing passages, however, describe only the constitutional possibilities of federal court jurisdiction—the limits to which Congress *could* go in giving the courts subject matter jurisdiction. The power that federal courts actually have been given by Congress is, according to the Supreme Court, much narrower. The statutory power of the federal courts has been construed to be much narrower than the constitutional potential power described above. The key statutes are 28 U.S.C. §§ 1331, 1332, 1367, and 1441. We will concentrate here on the basic statutes, leaving discussion of supplemental jurisdiction to Chapter 6.

2. Federal Diversity Jurisdiction

Problem Case: Down with Diversity! Viva Diversity!

Assume that you are a member of Congress. The Congress is poised to vote on a bill that would—once and for all—abolish federal court diversity jurisdiction. After reviewing the history of diversity jurisdiction and the legal literature debating its current usefulness, you rise and speak out on the matter. What position will you take? What arguments will you raise in support of your position?

a. Determining Diversity of Citizenship

The federal diversity jurisdiction statute, 28 U.S.C. § 1332, permits federal courts to exercise jurisdiction in actions between "citizens of different States" where the amount in controversy exceeds $75,000. The federal courts' diversity jurisdiction is not exclusive. The litigant may choose either state or federal court to hear the claim. If the plaintiff does choose state court, however, the defendant may be entitled to remove the action to federal court, provided that the defendant is not a resident of the state in which the original action was filed and all other requirements of removal are met. 28 U.S.C. §§ 1446-1447.

The basic requirements of the modern diversity statute may be summarized as follows:

- All plaintiffs must be diverse from all defendants, absent a clear statutory or decisional exception. That is, *complete diversity* is required by the statute, though this is not constitutionally compelled. See Strawbridge v. Curtiss, 7 U.S. (3 Cranch) 267 (1806).
- Diversity of citizenship for an individual is determined by examining where she resides and has the intention of remaining indefinitely.
- A corporation is a citizen, for purposes of diversity, both where it is incorporated and where it has its principal place of business. The principal place of business is the corporation's "nerve center," which often (but not always) means the central office where corporate decision makers are located.
- For other types of businesses, such as partnerships, unincorporated associations, or business trusts, different rules apply—partnerships, for instance, are citizens, for purposes of diversity, of every state in which a partner resides. To determine these rules one must consult decisional law.
- In assessing citizenship, the court generally looks to the status of the parties at the time the action is filed. Thus if the parties are diverse at the start of the lawsuit, the court does not lose jurisdiction simply because the parties later become nondiverse. One exception to this occurs when a case is removed from state court to federal court. Diversity generally must exist both when the action is filed in state court and when the petition for removal to federal court is filed.
- Another important exception to the time-of-filing rule is that defects in diversity jurisdiction usually can be cured by dismissing the nondiverse party when the defect in jurisdiction is discovered.
- The amount in controversy may sometimes be satisfied by aggregating claims within the lawsuit. The summary on page 229, infra, reviews how courts have tended to interpret the amount-in-controversy requirement when multiple parties or claims are involved; a complete treatment, and coverage of 28 U.S.C. § 1367, are reserved for Chapter 6.
- If the plaintiff requests an injunction, rather than money damages, the amount-in-controversy requirement may still be satisfied, provided the value of the controversy exceeds $75,000. Courts have taken several approaches to calculating this value, including 1) assessing the value of the injunction to the plaintiff, 2) assessing the cost of complying with the injunction for the defendant, and 3) analyzing both value to plaintiff and cost to defendant and allowing jurisdiction if either one exceeds $75,000.

Problems

Test your understanding of the basic rules by answering the following hypotheticals. Are the diversity jurisdiction requirements satisfied?

1. *A*, a citizen of Nebraska, sues *B*, a citizen of Delaware, and *C*, a citizen of Nebraska, for $100,000 (each) in federal court.
2. *A*, a citizen of Nebraska, sues *B*, a corporation that is incorporated in Maryland and has its principal place of business in Nebraska, for $100,000 in federal court.
3. *A*, a corporation that is incorporated in Delaware and has its principal place of business in Alaska, sues *B*, a corporation that is incorporated in Delaware and has its principal place of business in California, for $100,000 in federal court.
4. *A*, a citizen of Maine, and *B*, a citizen of Maine, sue *C*, a citizen of Arizona, for $100,000 (each) in federal court.

The following cases and materials demonstrate how courts have interpreted statutory diversity jurisdiction requirements.

Mas v. Perry

489 F.2d 1396 (5th Cir. 1974)

AINSWORTH, Circuit Judge.

[Plaintiffs were a married couple who met while graduate students at Louisiana State University. They were married at Mrs. Mas's home in Jackson, Mississippi, after which they returned to LSU for two more years. They then moved to Park Ridge, Illinois. They sued their Louisiana landlord in federal district court in Louisiana for damages resulting from his undetected use of two-way mirrors to watch them in their bedroom during three of the first four months of their marriage before their move out of state. The husband was a French national; the wife was originally from Mississippi. The landlord challenged the federal court filing on the ground that the wife was not diverse from him. At the time of trial, the couple's intention was to return to Baton Rouge while Mr. Mas completed his Ph.D. They were undecided as to where they would go thereafter. The trial court held that the wife retained her Mississippi citizenship.]

It has long been the general rule that complete diversity of parties is required in order that diversity jurisdiction obtain; that is, no party on one side may be a citizen of the same State as any party on the other side. Strawbridge v. Curtiss [7 U.S. (3 Cranch) 267 (1806)]. This determination of one's State citizenship for diversity purposes is controlled by federal law, not by the law of any State. As is the case in other areas of federal jurisdiction, the diverse citizenship among adverse parties must be present at the time the complaint is filed. Jurisdiction is unaffected by subsequent changes in the citizenship of the parties. The burden of pleading the diverse citizenship is upon the party invoking federal jurisdiction and if the diversity jurisdiction is properly challenged, that party also bears the burden of proof.

To be a citizen of a State within the meaning of section 1332, a natural person must be both a citizen of the United States and a domiciliary of that State. For diversity purposes, citizenship means domicile; mere residence in the State is not sufficient.

A person's domicile is the place of "his true, fixed, and permanent home and principal establishment, and to which he has the intention of returning whenever he is absent therefrom. . . ." [Stine v. Moore, 213 F.2d 446, 448 (5th Cir. 1954).] A change of domicile may be effected only by a combination of two elements: (a) taking up residence in a different domicile with (b) the intention to remain there.

It is clear that at the time of her marriage, Mrs. Mas was a domiciliary of the State of Mississippi. While it is generally the case that the domicile of the wife—and, consequently, her State citizenship for purposes of diversity jurisdiction—is deemed to be that of her husband, we find no precedent for extending this concept to the situation here, in which the husband is a citizen of a foreign state but resides in the United States. Indeed, such a fiction would work absurd results on the facts before us. If Mr. Mas were considered a domiciliary of France—as he would be since he had lived in Louisiana as a student-teaching assistant prior to filing this suit—then Mrs. Mas would also be deemed a domiciliary, and thus, fictionally at least, a citizen of France. She would not be a citizen of any State and could not sue in a federal court on that basis; nor could she invoke the alienage jurisdiction to bring her claim in federal court, since she is not an alien. On the other hand, if Mrs. Mas's domicile were Louisiana, she would become a Louisiana citizen for diversity purposes and could not bring suit with her husband against appellant, also a Louisiana citizen, on the basis of diversity jurisdiction. These are curious results under a rule arising from the theoretical identity of person and interest of the married couple.

An American woman is not deemed to have lost her United States citizenship solely by reason of her marriage to an alien. 8 U.S.C. § 1489. Similarly, we conclude that for diversity purposes a woman does not have her domicile or State citizenship changed solely by reason of her marriage to an alien.

Mrs. Mas's Mississippi domicile was disturbed neither by her year in Louisiana prior to her marriage nor as a result of the time she and her husband spent at LSU after their marriage, since for both periods she was a graduate assistant at LSU.

Though she testified that after her marriage she had no intention of returning to her parents' home in Mississippi, Mrs. Mas did not effect a change of domicile since she and Mr. Mas were in Louisiana only as students and lacked the requisite intention to remain there. Until she acquires a new domicile, she remains a domiciliary, and thus a citizen, of Mississippi. . . .

[The court's discussion of the jurisdictional amount is omitted.]

Thus the power of the federal district court to entertain the claims of appellees in this case stands on two separate legs of diversity jurisdiction: a claim by an alien against a State citizen; and an action between citizens of different States. We also note, however, the propriety of having the federal district court entertain a spouse's action against a defendant, where the district court already has jurisdiction over a claim, arising from the same transaction, by the other spouse against the same defendant. In the case before us, such a result is particularly desirable. The claims of Mr. and Mrs. Mas arise from the same operative facts, and there was almost complete interdependence between their claims with respect to the proof required and the issues raised at trial. Thus, since the district court has jurisdiction of Mr. Mas's action, sound judicial administration militates strongly in favor of federal jurisdiction of Mrs. Mas's claim.

Affirmed.

Note: The Domicile of Married Women

Under the common law, a wife automatically assumed her husband's domicile upon marriage, based primarily upon the assumption that the husband was the breadwinner and could therefore determine where the family would live. Over time, exceptions were created if, for instance, the wife was providing the main financial support for the family. See Herma Hill Kay, Sex-Based Discrimination 177-183 (2d ed. 1981). The court in *Mas* created another exception—that of a female U.S. citizen marrying a foreign national. Since *Mas,* the common-law rule has been successfully challenged under the Equal Protection Clause as well as under Louisiana's equal rights amendment. Samuel v. University of Pittsburgh, 375 F. Supp. 1119 (W.D. Pa. 1974), *decision to decertify class vacated,* 538 F.2d 991 (3d Cir. 1976); Craig v. Craig, 365 So. 2d 1268 (La. 1979). Today, although many spouses are of the same domicile, most courts are quick to accept evidence to the contrary and consider each individual's domicile separately.

Tanzymore v. Bethlehem Steel Corp.

457 F.2d 1320 (3d Cir. 1972)

GIBBONS, Circuit Judge.

Appellant Tanzymore filed a complaint in the District Court for the Eastern District of Pennsylvania seeking damages from Bethlehem Steel Corporation for personal injuries. The complaint alleges that Mr. Tanzymore is "a domiciliary of 7418 Lenwood Street, Apartment 3, City of Cleveland, State of Ohio," and that Bethlehem is a Delaware corporation with its principal place of business in the Eastern District of Pennsylvania. Bethlehem filed an answer, and took Mr. Tanzymore's deposition. When the deposition was filed Bethlehem moved to dismiss the action on the ground that the district court lacked jurisdiction because the controversy is not wholly between citizens of different states. No affidavits were filed by Mr. Tanzymore in opposition to the motion. The court considered the briefs filed by the parties, heard argument on the motion, and without holding an evidentiary hearing, on the basis of Mr. Tanzymore's deposition concluded that there was no diversity of citizenship between the parties and dismissed the complaint. In its opinion, 325 F. Supp. 891, the court stated:

> Both the deposition[s] taken of the plaintiff, and his work record [as disclosed therein], indicate[s] that he is at best a resident of Pennsylvania, and may, in fact, be a citizen of no state. . . . This Court is unable to find that plaintiff is a citizen of the state of Ohio.

This appeal followed.[1] On appeal Mr. Tanzymore concedes, as he must, that determination of the underlying jurisdictional facts may be made by the court. Wetmore v. Rymer, 169 U.S. 115 (1898). Nor does he dispute that where a jurisdictional fact is traversed the burden of showing that the federal court has jurisdiction rests upon the plaintiff. Gibbs v. Buck, 307 U.S. 66, 72 (1939). He contends only that in a case in which the pleadings and depositions show a dispute as to the jurisdictional facts that dispute may not be resolved by the court without an evidentiary hearing. Mr. Tanzymore's deposition does contain the naked assertion that he intended at all times to remain an Ohio domiciliary, but virtually nothing else in the deposition is consistent with the conclusive assertion.[2] Nevertheless, he

1. We are advised that a timely suit has been filed in a Pennsylvania court.

2. In his deposition Tanzymore testified as follows:

Examination by Mr. Holland [Bethlehem's Attorney]

Q. Assuming that it was in May or along about May of 1966 or '65 that you first went to work for Young & Posen, I would like you to tell me where you went to work for them.
A. Philadelphia, Pennsylvania, at the Gulf Oil Company.
Q. All right. Now, before you went to work for Young & Posen at the Gulf Oil plant in Philadelphia, where did you work?
A. I worked for Lachat Construction Company in Baltimore, Maryland—Lachat Steel Construction Company, Baltimore, Maryland. . . .
Q. What is your permanent home address now?
A. 307 East Fourth Street, Bethlehem, Pennsylvania.
Q. And what is 307 East Fourth Street: Is it an apartment or a house or a—
A. This is a lady got a house, and she rent me a room and helps me about, because I can't —I am unable to help myself.
Q. And your accommodations there, then, are a room?
A. Right.
Q. Do you take your meals with this landlady?
A. Up until she unable to cook for me. Now I have to eat in lunchrooms.
Q. How long have you lived at 307 East Fourth Street?
A. Umm, six months. . . .

contends, it was improper to resolve the disputed domicile issue against him without giving him the opportunity to testify in an evidentiary hearing.

A. 543 North New Street.
Q. That's in Bethlehem?
Q. Were you living at the American Hotel—
A. When I got hurt, correct.
Q. —when you were working at the Bethlehem Steel?
Q. Were all of these jobs that you did at Bethlehem Steel right after each other, or did you have assignments somewhere else in between?
A. We had assignment elsewhere. I went down into West Virginia, and then I had an assignment of staying at home until the other job got ready to be done.
A. Oh, I lived in Cleveland, Ohio, off and on, ever since '65. Off and on. . . .
Q. [Y]ou are not registered to vote?
A. No. . . .
A. Well, hell, my license expired in—it must be, for my automobile, what the hell—'63.
Q. And at the time this accident occurred, you didn't own one?
Q. Would I be correct in assuming that you haven't owned one since 1963?
Q. Now, Mr. Tanzymore, at the place where you presently live on 307 East Fourth Street, do you own furnishings in that house?
A. Yeah. I bought my bed, tables, chairs. I have to sleep in a hospital bed, due to my discs in my back resting on the nerves of my spine.
Q. Do you get mail at that address?
A. Yes, I do.
Q. The postmen [sic] delivers the mail to 307—
A. No, he deliver to the front house. I live in the back house.
Q. Well, what was that address?
A. 543—
Q. —North New. Did you own any of the furnishings at that residence?
A. No, I didn't own any. I had the same furniture I have now. I was buying the same stuff that I am buying now.
Q. And did you get your mail at that address also?
A. I did so.
Q. Do you have any furnishings—beds, chairs, sofas, television set, or anything like that —
A. I got a television set, I got a hospital bed. I got a stand, I got a table and five chairs, I got three sheets, I got one blanket, I got two pillows, I got a water glass that I put water aside of the bed on. I got a flower and a pot, about yea long and yea high (demonstrating). I have three suits of clothes, I got a dozen pocket handkerchiefs, a dozen pair of underwears, I got six pair of socks, and I have three neckties. . . .
Q. Do you own any things like these—clothing or furniture—that you keep anywhere else? . . .
A. No, I don't. Not now I don't.
Q. When was the last time that you did?
A. 1967.
Q. Mr. Tanzymore, do you own any real estate?
A. No, I don't.
Q. Any land?
A. No.
Q. Lots?
Q. You don't maintain any bank accounts in any other cities?
A. No.
Q. You don't have a safe deposit box in any bank anywhere?
A. No, I don't.
Q. Do you maintain any memberships in any clubs any places other than Bethlehem?
A. No. I don't.

Appellant's argument confuses the court's role in deciding a motion for summary judgment under Fed. R. Civ. P. 56 with its role in making a jurisdictional determination pursuant to 28 U.S.C. § 1359[3] and Fed. R. Civ. P. 12(h)(3).[4] Since 1875, when the predecessor to 28 U.S.C. § 1359 was first enacted, when a question of federal jurisdiction is raised either by a party as here, or by the court on its own motion, the court may inquire, by affidavits or otherwise, into the facts as they exist. Wetmore v. Rymer, 169 U.S. [115,] 120-121 [1898]. McNutt v. General Motors Acceptance Corp., 298 U.S. 178, 184-190 (1936); KVOS, Inc. v. Associated Press, 299 U.S. 269, 278 (1936); Gibbs v. Buck, 307 U.S. [66,] 71, 72 [1939]; Land v. Dollar, 330 U.S. 731, 735 (1947). In Wetmore v. Rymer, the Court wrote:

> But the questions might arise in such a shape that the court might consider and determine them without the intervention of a jury. And it would appear to have been the intention of congress to leave the mode of raising and trying such issues to the discretion of the trial judge.

Examination by Mr. Baratta [Mr. Tanzymore's attorney]

Q. Now, the address that you gave us in Cleveland, was that a house?
A. Yes. Apartment house.
Q. Did you own that house?
A. No. Rent. I rented a room there, with another lady and her—you know, her family.
Q. Did you own any furniture that was in that particular apartment?
A. No. All that was furnished. That house was a furnished house.
Q. A furnished apartment?
A. Yes.
Q. Did you have a lease?
A. No. Just rent weekly—monthly.
A. My operator license. They expired in 1963.
Q. All right. What state issued that license?
A. Seattle, Washington.
Q. At the time of your accident did you have any bank accounts in Cleveland, Ohio?
A. No. At the time of my accident, no.
Q. At the time of your accident or immediately before the accident, and immediately after the accident did you receive any mail at the Cleveland address that you gave us?
A. No. No.
A. I haven't been back to Cleveland, Ohio, since I left.

Examination by Mr. Holland

Q. But you have since made Bethlehem your home?
A. I made Bethlehem my home on the—under my doctor, I made Pennsylvania my home, under my doctors throughout Pennsylvania. When I say "throughout Pennsylvania" I mean I may be under this doctor if I felt like I wasn't going to get well, like I did before. I'd go somewhere where I can. Due to that, due to all the business of my accident—the same as this meeting here, I can't be in Cleveland and attend your meeting here. All of this stuff comes under the heading of my accident, that I have to stay here until somebody do something about me, other than God himself.

3. § 1359. Parties Collusively Joined or Made: "A district court shall not have jurisdiction of a civil action in which any party, by assignment or otherwise, has been improperly or collusively made or joined to invoke the jurisdiction of such court."

4. Fed. R. Civ. P. 12(h) Waiver or Preservation of Certain Defenses: "(3) Whenever it appears by suggestion of the parties or otherwise that the court lacks jurisdiction of the subject matter, the court shall dismiss the action."

169 U.S. at 121. More recently in Gibbs v. Buck, the Court wrote:

> As there is no statutory direction for procedure upon an issue of jurisdiction, the mode of its determination is left to the trial court.

307 U.S. at 71-72. Shortly after our decision in McSparran v. Weist, 402 F.2d 867 (3d Cir. 1968), *cert. denied sub nom.* Fritzinger v. Weist, 395 U.S. 903 (1969), in which we directed that the district courts make inquiry into diversity manufactured by the appointment of out of state guardians, we had occasion to suggest a standard for the exercise of discretion in the method of determining the jurisdictional issue. In Groh v. Brooks, 421 F.2d 589, 594 (3d Cir. 1970) Judge Stahl wrote:

> If a plaintiff whose assertion of federal jurisdiction is challenged by a motion to dismiss fails to bring forth any factual material to support his claim to jurisdiction, then dismissal may properly be granted against him. However, it should clearly appear from the record that plaintiff has had an opportunity to present facts, either by way of affidavit or in an evidentiary hearing, in support of his position that diversity was not manufactured. (footnotes omitted)

Here the attorney for Tanzymore had an opportunity to cross examine him at the deposition. He did so. There was an opportunity, unavailed of, to file affidavits in opposition to the motion to dismiss. The district court, having discretion as to the procedure to be followed in making its jurisdictional determination, exercised that discretion reasonably in deciding the motion on the basis of the deposition. Had parts of the deposition tended to support Mr. Tanzymore's conclusory statement of domicile and had he then requested an evidentiary hearing to resolve the conflict a different procedure might have been appropriate.

Compare Seideman v. Hamilton, 275 F.2d 224 (3d Cir. 1960), in which we approved the procedure of the court's hearing evidence on the issue of diversity and Shahmoon Industries Inc. v. Imperato, 338 F.2d 449 (3d Cir. 1964), in which this court *sua sponte* returned the case to the district court to enlarge the record on a diversity issue by taking additional evidence. While these cases teach that an evidentiary hearing may be appropriate they do not hold that such a hearing is always required so long as the court has afforded the plaintiff notice and a fair opportunity to be heard. We will not set aside its reasonable exercise of discretion as to the mode of determination of the jurisdictional facts. A different rule applies, of course, where a summary disposition reaches the merits of the claim rather than the jurisdiction of the court. Compare Fed. R. Civ. P. 56(c), 65(a).

Mr. Tanzymore also contends that the district court decision is a holding which accepts the doctrine of cases such as Pannill v. Roanoke Times Co., 252 F. 910 (W.D. Va. 1918), which hold that a person may be "stateless" and that such a stateless person cannot create diversity of citizenship for purposes of 28 U.S.C. § 1332. See also Clapp v. Stearns &

Co., 229 F. Supp. 305 (S.D.N.Y. 1964); Factor v. Pennington Press, Inc., 238 F. Supp. 630 (N.D. Ill. 1964). He urges that we reject this doctrine.

The district court did speculate that Mr. Tanzymore may be a stateless person, but this is not its holding. The plaintiff had the burden of alleging a basis for federal jurisdiction. Fed. R. Civ. P. 8(a)(1). When the jurisdictional allegations were traversed he had the burden of supporting those allegations. McNutt v. General Motors Acceptance Corp., 298 U.S. at 182-189; KVOS v. Associated Press, 299 U.S. at 276-277; Nelson v. Keefer, 451 F.2d 289 (3d Cir. 1971). The holding was only that Mr. Tanzymore failed to meet the burden of establishing that he was, as he alleged, a citizen of Ohio.[5] Since he had the burden of establishing the basis of federal jurisdiction which he alleged, and failed to carry that burden, we need inquire no further for it was his obligation, not that of the court, to establish his citizenship.

The judgment of the district court dismissing the complaint for want of jurisdiction will be affirmed.

Notes and Questions

1. There are two exceptions to the diversity statute: probate and domestic relations claims. Such claims cannot be brought in federal court, regardless of the diversity of the parties. The root of these exceptions lies in the historical division of labor among courts. While probate and domestic relations claims once were heard by the ecclesiastical courts, only actions "of a civil nature in law or equity" were covered by the diversity statute. The historical treatment has persisted because of a modern sense that states have greater expertise in these matters of "local" concern, though this characterization is certainly debatable.

Teasing out matters that fall within the states' exclusive probate jurisdiction from overlapping matters that do not can be difficult. Although it is clear that the federal courts will not probate a will or assume control of property that is in the custody of a state court, this does not mean they cannot hear actions against administrators, executors, and other claimants that are related to such property.

Similarly subtle distinctions can arise in connection with the domestic relations exception. In Ankenbrandt v. Richards, 504 U.S. 689 (1992), the

5. The complaint actually alleges only that Mr. Tanzymore is a "domiciliary" of Ohio:

> A naked averment that one is a "domiciliary" or a "resident" of a state is insufficient. The statute requires that the averment be that one is a "citizen" of a state. "The whole record, however, may be looked to, for the purpose of curing a defective averment of citizenship, . . . and if the requisite citizenship is anywhere expressly averred in the record, or facts are therein stated which in legal intendment constitute such allegation, that is sufficient."

Sun Printing & Pub. Assn. v. Edwards, 194 U.S. 377, 382 (1904).

Court held that despite the exception the federal court could hear an action in which plaintiff sued her ex-husband for abuse of the children while they were visiting their father. Federal courts may not issue divorce, child custody, or alimony decrees, but they can hear tort actions that arise within domestic relations. Anna Nicole Smith's widely reported, and ultimately successful, efforts to establish her right to the multi-million dollar estate of her deceased husband offer a case in point. Smith, whose real name was Vickie Lynn Marshall, married Texas millionaire J. Howard Marshall in 1994 after a three-year courtship. J. Howard died a year later without having provided for Vickie in his will. Although he had apparently promised to provide for her security via a "catch-all" trust, his will at the time of his death left his estate to one of his sons, E. Pierce Marshall.

In 1997, while J. Howard's estate was in probate proceedings in Texas state court, Vickie filed for bankruptcy in the United States Bankruptcy Court for the Central District of California. Federal bankruptcy courts have exclusive jurisdiction over bankruptcy petitions.

Hostilities between Vickie and Pierce broke out almost immediately, with Vickie making public charges that Pierce had engaged in forgery, fraud, and overreaching to win control of his father's estate. Pierce responded by jumping into the bankruptcy proceedings. He filed a "proof of claim" with the bankruptcy court, seeking a declaration that his separate cause of action against Vickie for defamation was not a dischargeable debt. Since Pierce had submitted himself to the jurisdiction of the bankruptcy court by filing his objections, Vickie then filed a counterclaim against Pierce asserting that he had tortiously interfered with the estate gift J. Howard intended to give her.

The bankruptcy court entered judgment for Vickie on her counterclaim, finding that J. Howard had in fact directed his lawyers to prepare a trust for Vickie consisting of half the appreciation of his assets from the date of their marriage, but that Pierce had conspired to suppress or destroy the trust instrument and to strip his father of his assets by backdating, altering, and otherwise falsifying documents, arranging for surveillance of his father and Vickie, and presenting documents to his father under false pretenses. The court awarded Vickie $449 million, less any recovery she made in the Texas probate proceeding, and, on "overwhelming evidence" of Pierce's maliciousness and fraud, $25 million in punitive damages. At the same time, in the Texas proceeding, Pierce succeeded in convincing the probate court that his father's existing will was valid, making Pierce the heir to the entire estate.

The case reached the Supreme Court on Pierce's claim that the federal bankruptcy court judgment was void for want of subject matter jurisdiction due to the probate exception. Marshall v. Marshall, 547 U.S. 293 (2006). Resolving a division in the Circuit Courts over what sorts of actions by a bankruptcy court "interfere with the probate proceedings," 126 S. Ct. at 1748 (quoting Markham v. Allen, 326 U.S. 490, 494 (1946)), the Court held that a bankruptcy court impermissibly "interferes" with probate proceedings only when it "'disturb[s] or affect[s] the possession of property in the custody of a state court.'" Id. (quoting *Markham*, 326 U.S. at 494). As the Court reasoned:

> [T]he probate exception reserves to state probate courts the probate or annulment of a will and the administration of a decedent's estate; it also precludes federal courts from endeavoring to dispose of property that is in the custody of a state probate court. But it does not bar federal courts from adjudicating matters outside those confines and otherwise within federal jurisdiction.

Id. at 311-312. Vickie's tort claim seeking an *in personam* judgment against Pierce was therefore within the jurisdiction of the bankruptcy court. She did not "seek to reach a *res* in the custody of a state court," her claim did not "involve the administration of an estate, the probate of a will, or any other purely probate matter," and it raised common tort issues as to which state probate courts possess "no special proficiency . . . in handling." Id. at 312. The Court also rejected the Texas Probate Court's attempt to claim exclusive jurisdiction: "'[A] State cannot create a transitory cause of action and at the same time destroy the right to sue on that transitory cause of action in any court having jurisdiction.'" Id. at 313 (quoting Tennessee Coal, Iron, & R.R. Co. v. George, 233 U.S. 354, 360 (1914)).

2. Note that the party invoking diversity jurisdiction has the burden of proving it. Discuss the steps you might take to establish this on behalf of an individual client. What questions would you need to ask the client? What other evidence would you seek? Where would you obtain that evidence? In what form would you present it to the court?

Now consider the same questions as they relate to a corporate client. Even though the party invoking diversity jurisdiction has the burden of proving it, opponents who would prefer to be in state court have ample incentive to investigate the issue for themselves. Failure to do so can be costly. See Belleville Catering Co. v. Champaign Market Place, L.L.C., 350 F.3d 691 (7th Cir. 2003).

In *Belleville Catering*, the case went all the way to trial, ending in a $220,000 verdict for defendants on a counterclaim against plaintiffs. On appeal, the court raised *sua sponte* the question whether all the members of Champaign Market Place were indeed diverse (the parties had incorrectly assumed that limited liability companies are treated like corporations for diversity of citizenship analysis). Several members of Champaign Market Place, as it happened, were nondiverse, prompting the Seventh Circuit to dismiss the case for lack of subject matter jurisdiction and to order counsel "to perform, without additional fees, any further services that are necessary to bring this suit to a conclusion in state court, or via settlement. That way the clients will pay just once for the litigation." Id. at 694. The court admonished: "The costs of a doomed foray into federal court should fall on the lawyers who failed to do their homework, not on the hapless clients. . . . Lawyers for defendants, as well as plaintiffs, must investigate rather than assume jurisdiction." Id. at 693-694.

Belleville Catering is a case in which neither party caught a defect in diversity jurisdiction that was present from the very start of the case. What do you think should happen if the citizenship status of a non-diverse party changes during litigation? Under the standard "time-of-filing" rule, post-filing changes in citizenship are not relevant, so the result should be the same—dismissal for lack of subject matter jurisdiction. But this has not stopped parties and sympathetic lower courts from trying to forge exceptions to avoid the harsh consequences of the time-of-filing rule. In Grupo Dataflux v. Atlas Global Group, L.P., 541 U.S. 567 (2004), the Supreme Court rejected the Fifth Circuit's attempt to create an exception to the time of filing rule where the composition of a partnership changes. When the complaint for state law breach of contract was filed, Atlas, a Texas partnership, had two partners who were Mexican citizens. Grupo Dataflux was a Mexican corporation, so there were aliens on both sides, see 28 U.S.C. § 1332(a)(2), but the case went all the way through a jury trial resulting in a $750,000 award for Atlas before Grupo Dataflux caught the jurisdictional defect and filed a motion to dismiss. The Fifth Circuit reversed the lower court's dismissal because the Mexican partners left Atlas a month before the trial began (thus altering its citizenship) and because Grupo Dataflux failed to raise the defect until after court time and resources had been expended on a jury trial. In a sharply divided decision, the Supreme Court reversed, holding that the traditional time-of-filing rule should apply even though the citizenship of Atlas changed, and even though the case had proceeded to a jury verdict before Grupo Dataflux raised the defect. As the majority opinion emphasized,

> [t]o our knowledge, the Court has never approved a deviation from the rule articulated by Chief Justice Marshall in 1829 that "[w]here there is no change of party, a jurisdiction depending on the condition of the party is governed by that condition, as it was at the commencement of the suit."

541 U.S. at 574. Does this holding embrace a venerable but inefficient rule? Why not punish Grupo Dataflux for its lack of diligence in raising the jurisdictional defect? What interests does the time-of-filing rule serve? Atlas and the dissenting opinion raised these questions and received the following response in the majority opinion:

> The time-of-filing rule is what it is precisely because the facts determining jurisdiction are subject to change, and because constant litigation in response to that change would be wasteful. . . . Atlas and Dataflux have thus far litigated this case for more than 6½ years, including 3½ years over a conceded jurisdictional defect. Compared with the one month it took the Magistrate Judge to apply the time-of-filing rule . . . when the jurisdictional problem was brought to her attention, this waste counsels strongly against any course that would impair the certainty of our jurisdictional rules and thereby encourage similar jurisdictional litigation.

Id. at 580-582. Are you persuaded?

3. Recall the controversy in *World-Wide Volkswagen* regarding whether the Robinsons were diverse from all of the defendants in the action. Their lawyer sought to prevent removal of the action from state court to federal court by adding defendants who were not diverse from the Robinsons and those who were. This is permissible, provided that the parties are not nominal parties, in which case their citizenship may be disregarded for diversity purposes. See, e.g., Rose v. Giamatti, 721 F. Supp. 906 (S.D. Ohio 1989) (holding that the Cincinnati Reds and Major League Baseball were nominal parties in the action by Pete Rose against A. Bartlett Giamatti, then Commissioner of Baseball).

Likewise, the court will disregard the citizenship of fictitious parties, also known as Doe allegations. See 28 U.S.C. § 1441(a) (providing that, for purposes of removal, "the citizenship of defendants sued under fictitious names shall be disregarded").

4. What about citizens of foreign countries who are joined to a suit between citizens of different states? 28 U.S.C. § 1332(a)(3) provides for federal jurisdiction in suits between "citizens of different States and in which citizens or subjects of a foreign state are additional parties." In this context, courts have held that "the presence of foreigners on both sides of a diversity case does not destroy diversity" so long as there are properly diverse United States citizens on both sides of the case. Tango Music, LLC v. DeadQuick Music, Inc., 348 F.3d 244, 245 (7th Cir. 2003). The plain language of the statute suggests the same result should follow even if foreigners from the same country are on both sides of the litigation. Id. at 245-246. How would you distinguish *Groupo Dataflux*?

5. Unlike most banks and ordinary businesses, national banks are not incorporated in any of the states in which they operate; they are incorporated by the U.S. Treasury. Don't be deceived by the label, however. Although Congress has rather ambiguously provided that national banks are citizens for purposes of diversity jurisdiction "of the States in which they are respectively located," 28 U.S.C. § 1348, the Supreme Court has held that "located" in this context refers to the state of a national bank's main office, not every state in which the bank has established a branch. Wachovia Bank v. Schmidt, 546 U.S. 303 (2006).

6. The circuits are split, however, on how to treat trusts. The Supreme Court has held that in a suit by individual trustees authorized to manage trust assets and sue on behalf of the trust, the citizenship of the trustees and not the beneficiaries of the trust is assessed for diversity purposes. Navarro Savings Assoc. v. Lee, 446 U.S. 458, 465-466 (1980). The Court did not address how to assess citizenship when the trust itself is a party to a suit. Some circuit courts have extended *Navarro* and held that the citizenship of the trust is always that of the trustee or trustees. See Hicklin Eng'g, L.C. v. Bartell, 439 F.3d 346, 348 (7th Cir. 2006); Johnson v. Columbia Props. Anchorage, LP, 437 F.3d 894, 899 (9th Cir. 2006). The Eleventh Circuit has held that the beneficiaries of a trust are the only relevant group for diversity purposes. See Riley v. Merrill Lynch, 292 F.3d 1334, 1338 (11th Cir. 2002). After canvassing the prior law, the Third

Circuit recently held that the proper approach is to look to the citizenship of *both* the trustees and beneficiaries. Emerald Investors Trust v. Gaunt Parsippany Partners, 492 F.3d 192, 203-205 (3d Cir. 2007). The court placed special emphasis on the Supreme Court's holding in Carden v. Arkoma Assoc., 494 U.S. 185 (1990), that the citizenship of all members of an artificial entity must be assessed for diversity purposes. *Emerald Investors*, 492 F.3d at 200. It also stressed that a broad citizenship rule serves federalism principles by keeping state law cases out of federal court unless diversity is truly complete. Id. at 204. The court remanded for a full evidentiary hearing to determine the citizenship of all beneficiaries and trustees of the plaintiff trust as well as the citizenship of all partners of defendant limited partnership.

What about the relationship between parent and subsidiary corporations? Specifically, what should a court do when a nondiverse parent company assigns its legal claims to a diverse subsidiary? What should a court do when a nondiverse subsidiary assigns legal claims to a diverse parent? These are complex issues involving corporations doctrine, but a few basic principles are clear. First, some courts apply a presumption of collusion—that is, a presumption that diversity jurisdiction has been improperly manufactured under 28 U.S.C. § 1359—when a nondiverse parent company assigns its claims to a diverse subsidiary "engaged in no business other than the prosecution of that claim." Prudential Oil Corp. v. Phillips Petroleum Co., 546 F.2d 469, 476 (2d Cir. 1976) (extended beyond parent-subsidiary relationships in Airlines Reporting Corp. v. S&N Travel, Inc., 58 F.3d 857 (2d Cir. 1995)). The reason is fairly straightforward: a subsidiary whose only business is to create diversity jurisdiction for bringing legal claims on behalf of a parent company is nothing short of a forum selection scam. If it were legal to do this, companies could simply create subsidiaries anytime they wanted to avoid the normal limits on diversity jurisdiction.

Different concerns are implicated when a nondiverse *subsidiary* assigns claims to a diverse *parent*. Here, the parent already may be on the hook for liabilities of the subsidiary or otherwise involved in the events leading to litigation. Still, the circuits are split. The Ninth Circuit has applied a presumption of collusion. See Nike, Inc. v. Comercial Iberica de Exclusivas Deportivas, S.A., 20 F.3d 987, 991-992 (9th Cir. 1994). The Eleventh Circuit, by contrast, applies no presumption. See Ambrosia Coal & Constr. Co. v. Pages Morales, 482 F.3d 1309, 1314-1315 (11th Cir. 2007) (following Seventh Circuit decision, Herzog Contracting Corp. v. McGowen Corp., 976 F.2d 1062, 1067 (7th Cir. 1992) (holding that "no inference of collusive invocation of jurisdiction can be drawn from the simple fact that assignor and assignee are under common ownership")). The Eleventh Circuit emphasized that a number of factors are relevant to determining whether an assignment of claims is collusive: whether the assignor has retained an interest in the assigned claim, whether consideration was exchanged, and whether the assignee has any previous connection to the matter. *Ambrosia Coal*, 482 F.2d at 1315. In the case before it, the court determined that the subsidiary had not collusively assigned its claim to its parent because there was evidence that the parent had funded the real estate purchase at issue and had actively participated in the suit. Id. at 1316.

7. In *Mas* the court held that Mrs. Mas remained a Mississippi domiciliary even though she had no intention of returning there because she had not acquired a new domicile; she was living in Louisiana as a student but "lacked the requisite intention to remain there." This is the so-called presumption of continuing domicile. See Padilla-Mangual v. Pavia Hosp., 516 F.3d 29, 31-32 (1st Cir. 2008). The presumption is overcome by evidence of presence or residence in another state and evidence of intent to remain there. Although things like registering to vote; paying taxes; owning or leasing real or personal property; working; and holding bank accounts, licenses, and church or club memberships are all traditional indicia of intent to remain, notice that most of these activities would be most applicable to a person of means. The First Circuit has emphasized that none of these "typical indicia of domicile are required in order to change one's domicile"; they are only examples. Id. at 33.

In *Padilla*, the district court of Puerto Rico dismissed plaintiff's suit for damages from allegedly negligent medical treatment for lack of diversity, concluding that he had not altered his presumed domicile of Puerto Rico by moving to Florida. The court

> focused on Padilla's apparent failure to cultivate the sort of ties traditionally viewed as manifesting an expression of domicile: "Padilla does not work nor has he indicated that he is looking for work in Florida. He does not go to school. He does not belong to any clubs, nor does he attend a church. He does not have any bank accounts. He has not registered or exercised the right to vote. Other than his driver's license and a stated desire to stay there, Padilla doesn't seem to have established any real presence in Florida."

Id. The district court also rejected Padilla's claim that his physical condition prevented him from working or going to school.

The First Circuit reversed, pointing to record evidence including: two declarations, one by Padilla, and another by his mother, that he is a resident of Florida with no intention to return to Puerto Rico and plans to stay in Florida; copies of payments and charges from four places in Florida where Padilla claimed he had lived; and a copy of a Florida driver's license. Id. at 32. The court noted that "[a]ny number of explanations are possible" for the absence of traditional indicia of domicile—among them "physical or mental incapacity, religious objections, to name a few." Id. at 34.

> The point is that where a party has declared his intent to change and remain in his new domicile, and the opposing written submissions do not demonstrate the falsity of the declaration with reasonable certainty, the absence of typical indicia of domicile is not determinative. More is required of the district court before it concludes that a plaintiff has not met his burden and overcome the presumption. We agree with our sister circuits that in these circumstances an evidentiary hearing is appropriate.

Id. The court remanded for such a hearing.

8. There is an indication at the end of *Tanzymore* that the district court thought Mr. Tanzymore might be "stateless." That would mean he is not a citizen of a state entitled to invoke the diversity jurisdiction of any federal court. See Newman-Green, Inc. v. Alfonzo-Larrain, 490 U.S. 826, 828 (1989). The Third Circuit did not take up the question, deciding instead that Mr. Tanzymore simply failed to meet his burden of establishing that he was in fact a citizen of Ohio. Other courts have, however, dismissed a case for want of complete diversity when it appears one of the parties is indeed "stateless." See Thompson v. Deloitte & Touche LLP, 503 F. Supp. 2d 1118, 1123-1125 (S.D. Iowa 2007) (granting motion to dismiss for want of diversity jurisdiction on ground that U.S. limited liability partnership with one stateless partner, a U.S. citizen living in Asia with no domicile in the United States, who was not registered to vote in the United States, with no U.S. residence for state income tax purposes, and who planned to continue living and working in Asia "indefinitely," renders entire firm stateless); Nat'l City Bank v. Aronson, 474 F. Supp. 2d 925 (S.D. Ohio 2007) (remanding case and awarding attorneys' fees to plaintiff for defendants' improper removal upon finding that a defendant beneficiary of trust living and planning to remain in New Zealand was stateless despite owning a residence in Colorado, holding a Colorado bank account to pay U.S. bills, possessing a Colorado driver's license, owning two cars registered in the state, retaining two state academic certifications, actively serving on a board for a religious organization in the state, and residing in the home for nearly six months in 2005).

b. Historical Backdrop and Current Controversies

The history of diversity jurisdiction is long and conflict-ridden. Unlike federal question jurisdiction, which was not granted fully to the federal courts until after the Civil War, diversity jurisdiction was granted in the first Judiciary Act of 1789. The founders felt strongly that federal courts must be given power to hear conflicts between citizens of different states, lest nonresidents be subject to biased judgments by plaintiffs' home courts.

Whether the diversity option actually was essential to protecting nonresident parties from state court bias, however, was and is contested. In a detailed study of federal diversity jurisdiction from 1870 to 1958, Edward Purcell concludes that the diversity option often worked to the strategic advantage of astute corporate defendants of the late 1800s and early 1900s in ways that had little or nothing to do with local bias. Edward A. Purcell Jr., Litigation and Inequality: Federal Diversity Jurisdiction in Industrial America, 1870-1958 (1992). Corporate lawyers would petition for removal to federal courts, which often sat in cities far from the plaintiffs' homes. Id. at 45-50. The distance factor, coupled with the more pro-business law then available in federal courts, id. at 59-60, made federal court a highly attractive option for corporations. To block the removal, plaintiffs either would discount their claims at the pleading stage and allege less than the jurisdictional amount that then applied to diversity cases ($500), or settle. As Purcell reports, the corporations had significant leverage in these settlement negotiations because of the diversity option. Id. at 63. Those most affected by the combination of procedural and substantive advantages afforded corporations by federal diversity were plaintiffs whose injuries were the most serious. For these plaintiffs to avoid removal, they had to discount their claims far more steeply than parties with less serious injuries. Id. at 100. None of these machinations was inspired by the "fear of state court bias" so often invoked as the primary reason for federal court diversity jurisdiction.

Subsequent changes in the substantive and procedural features of diversity jurisdiction, as well as technological advances that made geographical distance less significant to parties, removed some of the problems outlined by Purcell. Despite the changes, some observers continued to view diversity jurisdiction with skepticism. In particular they questioned whether state lines continued to be significant enough to warrant the expense of diversity jurisdiction. Federal court resources, they argued, might be better applied to federal question cases.

The arguments for and against retaining federal diversity jurisdiction continue to be advanced. Proponents say that out-of-state citizens cannot always count on a fair trial in a state court, that diversity cases keep federal judges up-to-date on state statutory and common law, and that funneling diversity cases into federal courts relieves the caseloads of state courts. Opponents argue that there is no empirical evidence that the state courts are any less fair than federal courts, that state courts lose the opportunity to upgrade and reform state law, that state boundaries are meaningless in today's global community, and that keeping diversity cases at the state level would ease the burden on federal courts. See The Judicial Conference of the United States, Long Range Plan for the Federal Courts 29-31, recommendation 7 (1995) (calling for limits on diversity jurisdiction).

A collateral source of controversy is the fact that while state judges are often elected officials, federal judges are appointed for life. State judges are regarded by some as tainted by this political aspect, whereas others see their accountability to a constituency as making them more responsible. Some practicing lawyers suggest that federal judges are better trained and more objective; others argue that defendants have a better chance in federal than in state courts. Out-of-state lawyers also may prefer trying cases in federal court because the rules of court and procedure are the same throughout the country, while local court rules vary substantially from state to state, even county to county. Backlog is also a factor: Parties may try to have the lawsuit removed to federal court if there is a greater backlog (and resulting delay) in the state court. See Neal Miller, An Empirical Study of Forum Choices in Removal Cases Under Diversity and Federal Question Jurisdiction, 41 Am. U. L. Rev. 369, 400-423 (1992) (discussing studies that compare attorney preferences in choosing between state and federal courts).

The 95th Congress, in 1978, came close to abolishing diversity jurisdiction —the bill passed the House but died in the Senate. See Thomas D. Rowe, Abolishing Diversity Jurisdiction: The Silver Lining, A.B.A. J., Feb. 1980, at 177; see also Thomas D. Rowe, Abolishing Diversity Jurisdiction: Positive Side Effects and Potential for Further Reforms, 92 Harv. L. Rev. 963 (1979). Commenting on the bill, Professor Rowe argued that abolishing the random benefits and manipulable aspects of diversity jurisdiction might not be such a bad thing, after all. He says that abolishing diversity jurisdiction would: result in a "sheer reduction in the incidence of difficult jurisdictional and procedural issues," particularly complete diversity; facilitate judicial reform of federal pendent and ancillary jurisdiction and procedures for removal of actions from state court to federal court; and pave the way for further reforms in federal practice. Id. at 178. To arguments that not all state courts are equipped to handle foreign service of process, multistate discovery, and interstate enforcement of judgments, Rowe responded that the abolition of diversity jurisdiction might give them just the incentive they need to develop their capacities. Id. at 180.

Other legal scholars disagree. For example, Professors Moore and Weckstein have suggested that "[t]he large number of diversity cases brought to the federal courts and their apparently satisfactory disposition is itself evidence of the value of diversity jurisdiction." James William Moore & Donald T. Weckstein, Diversity Jurisdiction: Past, Present, and Future, 43 Tex. L. Rev. 1, 19 n.116 (1964). They even argue that diversity jurisdiction be expanded at the federal level, to help build federal common law and expound national rules of conflict of laws. Id. at 20. They credit the federal courts with having brought most state courts up to standard, but warn that some states "have not come as far as others, and only in federal courts is an out-of-state litigant always afforded the best available pleading practices and pre-trial and trial procedures, a judge free of the pressures of re-election or reappointment, and a jury without parochial attachment to a single county or municipality."

Daniel J. Meador has taken a third approach, suggesting that rather than abolishing diversity jurisdiction altogether or restricting it with periodic adjustments to the amount in controversy, a more effective controlling device would be to eliminate diversity cases based on subject matter, particularly personal injury. Daniel Meador, A New Approach to Limiting Diversity Jurisdiction, 46 A.B.A. J. 383 (1960). Not only do personal injury cases congest the federal court docket—they constitute about 60 percent of all diversity cases and 80 percent of those that go through completed jury trials—but tort actions for personal injury tend to be "local" in nature, in that they are based on a single local occurrence, relevant evidence is available locally, and interstate aspects tend to revolve more around the defendant's business, not the occurrence itself. Id. at 384. Insurance and contract law, on the other hand, are considered more appropriate issues for the federal forum.

The strongest arguments currently being made in the area of diversity jurisdiction involve the creation of a multiparty, multiforum federal court jurisdiction. As one proponent has stated, "[t]he problem is the unavailability of any single forum in which to consolidate scattered, related litigation—a difficulty that is becoming more and more common given the increasing number of complex tort actions, such as those growing out of mass accidents and product liability claims." Rowe, supra, at 8.

Although bills to abolish diversity jurisdiction have been perennially introduced, none has succeeded thus far. Thus, diversity cases continue to be an important part of the federal court dockets. Diversity cases accounted for 51,992, or 20 percent, of total federal civil cases in 1974, and 49,793, or 19 percent, of total federal civil cases filed in 1988. Compare this with the early days, when the 368 cases heard by the federal courts between 1790 and 1815 constituted over 57 percent of the total cases heard. The 1996 amendment to 28 U.S.C. § 1332, which raised the amount in controversy to $75,000, does not appear to have lowered the number of filings. In 2008, 88,457 diversity cases were filed, 34 percent of all federal cases.

Arguments against diversity jurisdiction have prevailed to the limited extent that the diversity statute has been amended to increase the amount in controversy necessary to qualify for federal court jurisdiction, but without reducing filings. Congress and the courts also have been unwilling to expand the scope of diversity jurisdiction by allowing nondiverse parties to tack themselves on to a suit between diverse parties, even though the nondiverse parties have claims that are factually connected to the pending diversity suit. Thus, while the diversity option remains, it is controversial.

c. Joinder and the Amount in Controversy

In addition to establishing complete diversity of citizenship, the party invoking federal diversity jurisdiction must demonstrate that the amount in controversy is greater than $75,000.

The jurisdictional amount stated in 28 U.S.C. § 1332 can be difficult to calculate. Questions immediately arise that cannot be resolved on the face of the statute, such as whether two plaintiffs can aggregate their claims against one defendant to meet the jurisdictional amount. Most of these questions have been answered by case law that construes the statute. Some of them also require an understanding of 28 U.S.C. § 1367, which addresses supplemental jurisdiction. In each example below, we assume the action is based *solely* on diversity. We summarize the case law under 28 U.S.C. § 1332 and the basic rules that it establishes. We leave a more thorough examination of § 1367 and supplemental jurisdiction to Chapter 6.

1. Two or more claims of *one* plaintiff against a defendant *can* be aggregated to reach the amount-in-controversy requirement, even if the claims are factually unrelated.

P v. D

P claim(1) $45,000	+	P claim(2) $31,000	=	Amount in controversy $76,000 *meets requirement*

2. The claims of *more than one* plaintiff, each of which fails to meet the amount in controversy requirement standing alone, *cannot* be aggregated to reach the jurisdictional amount if the plaintiffs' claims are *separate and distinct* (that is, not asserting one right). But if at least one plaintiff's claims, standing alone, meets the amount-in-controversy requirement, the related claims of additional plaintiffs joined under Rule 20 may be joined even if those claims are below the amount-in-controversy requirement.*
3. There is no aggregation of a plaintiff's claims against multiple defendants. Thus where P's claim against D(1) does not meet the amount in controversy requirement, it does not matter that P's claim against D(2), when added to P's claim against D(1), would meet that amount.
4. A defendant's compulsory counterclaim* against the plaintiff falls within the supplemental jurisdiction of the court and thus *can* be heard even if it does not meet the amount-in-controversy requirement.
5. If, on the other hand, D's counterclaim falls below the amount in controversy and is unrelated to plaintiff's claim, then it is *not* within the court's supplemental jurisdiction and must be dismissed.
6. As in situation 1 above, separate counterclaims of a single defendant against a single plaintiff *can* be aggregated to reach the amount-in-controversy requirement. This is true regardless of whether the counterclaims are compulsory or permissive.

Note: Litigating Subject Matter Jurisdiction

Review the mechanics of litigating personal jurisdiction, discussed in section C of this chapter. Now read Fed. R. Civ. P. 12(b)(1). Assume that a claim filed in a federal district court is arguably, but not certainly, outside the court's subject matter jurisdiction, and that dismissal for

* For more on the subtleties of this rule for complex litigation, see the section on supplemental jurisdiction in Chapter 6.

** A "compulsory" counterclaim is one that arises out of the transaction or occurrence that is the subject matter of the opposing party's claims. See Fed. R. Civ. P. 13(a).

lack of personal jurisdiction over the defendant is clearly warranted. May the court address only the dispositive personal jurisdiction issue and thereby avoid the thorny subject matter jurisdiction dispute? Or must the subject matter jurisdiction be faced first, given that it is foundational? In Ruhrgas AG v. Marathon Oil Co., 526 U.S. 574 (1999), the Court held that:

> [In] cases removed from state court to federal court, as in cases originating in federal court, there is no unyielding jurisdictional hierarchy. Customarily, a federal court first resolves doubts about its jurisdiction over the subject matter, but there are circumstances in which a district court appropriately accords priority to a personal jurisdiction inquiry.

Id. at 578. The Court concluded that the case before it was one in which treatment of personal jurisdiction issues first was appropriate, because the challenge to personal jurisdiction involved no complex state law questions and was easier to resolve than the "difficult and novel" subject matter jurisdiction issue. Id. at 579.

3. Federal Question Jurisdiction: Statutory Requirements

Problem Case: Making a Federal Case

Can this case properly be brought in federal court?

Heidi Gesund	)	
	)	
v.	)	COMPLAINT
	)	
The Vita-Men,	)	
Inc.	)	

JURISDICTION

1. Jurisdiction is based on 28 U.S.C. § 1331; this is a case arising under the laws of the United States.

PARTIES

2. Plaintiff Heidi Gesund is a citizen of Albuquerque, New Mexico. She is a professional bodybuilder who has over the past decade won state, national, and world titles in the women's division of the sport.

3. Defendant, trading under the name The Vita-Men, is a company incorporated under the laws of New Mexico and doing business in that state with its principal place of business in Albuquerque.

CAUSE OF ACTION

4. Defendants have advertised on radio, television, and in the print media that their product, Mineral Magic, contains an all-natural vitamin formula guaranteed to enhance muscle tone.

5. On or about June 25, 2000, Plaintiff Heidi Gesund purchased 100 doses of Mineral Magic, and between that date and July 10, 2000, she consumed a total of 40 doses of the product in preparation for a national bodybuilding competition to be held in Albuquerque on July 12, 2000.

6. On the eve of the competition, Plaintiff awoke with a disturbing medical condition characterized by severe swelling of the muscular tissue and the appearance of unsightly, thick black hairs, which now cover her entire body; plaintiff is a natural blond.

7. On information and belief, Mineral Magic contains synthetic testosterone, as well as other animal and human hormones, that have not been adequately tested or approved by the federal Food and Drug Administration.

8. On information and belief, Mineral Magic is sold and distributed in violation of FDA rules and regulations, and is unsafe for human consumption.

WHEREFORE, plaintiff demands judgment against The Vita-Men in the sum of one million dollars and costs.

The Court has interpreted federal question statutory jurisdiction to mean that the federal courts may hear a case under 28 U.S.C. § 1331 provided that federal law has a *substantial* and *direct* bearing on the case. (Recall that the constitutional possibilities may be much broader; the federal law need only be an "ingredient" of the dispute.) In the easiest examples, this statutory test is met because the claim is based directly on an alleged violation of a federal statute. Thus, for example, § 1331 is clearly satisfied if a plaintiff alleges that the defendant violated Title VII of the Civil Rights Act of 1964, a federal statute that protects workers against discrimination. The court inevitably must construe the federal law in order to resolve the dispute, and Title VII explicitly creates a cause of action. The plaintiff therefore has a right to litigate this matter in federal court, if she wishes.

Note, however, that she instead may choose to litigate in state court, because the state courts have *concurrent* power over all but a handful of matters that fall within the *exclusive* judicial authority of the federal courts. That is, simply because a federal statute is involved does not mean that she *must* litigate in federal court, but that she *can* do so, if she wishes.

A more difficult question arises when an action not based directly on a federal statute requires the court to construe a federal law in order to dispose of the case. For example, parties might agree under a contract that *A* will deliver to *B* goods that meet certain federal standards. If *A* sues *B* for breach of contract, alleging that the goods fail to meet these federal standards, then a case based on the state law of contract necessarily will entail federal law as well. The courts have said, in essence, that whether the presence of federal law in the case is enough to "federalize" it under § 1331 is a matter of degree, rather like proximate cause.

In this section, we want to enable you to recognize the nature of federal claims in our dual court system, while at the same time assuring you that complete understanding must await a course in federal jurisdiction. We begin with an exercise on identifying federal claims. We then turn to one of the earliest cases limiting federal court jurisdiction, Louisville & Nashville R.R. Co. v. Mottley, 211 U.S. 149 (1908). Finally, we discuss Merrell Dow Pharmaceutical v. Thompson, 478 U.S. 804 (1986), and Grable & Sons Metal Products, Inc. v. Darue Engineering & Mfg., 545 U.S. 1158 (2005), the two most significant modern cases dealing with limits on federal question jurisdiction.

The following case excerpt summarizes the current test for determining whether a case "arises under" federal law and thus poses a federal question justifying the jurisdiction of the federal courts. Which of the cases that follow the excerpt seem to satisfy the test?

Franchise Tax Board v. Construction Laborers Vacation Trust

463 U.S. 1 (1983)

JUSTICE BRENNAN delivered the opinion of the Court.

Since the first version of § 1331 was enacted, Act of Mar. 3, 1875, ch. 137, § 1, 18 Stat. 470, the statutory phrase "arising under the Constitution, laws, or treaties of the United States" has resisted all attempts to frame a single, precise definition for determining which cases fall within, and which cases fall outside, the original jurisdiction of the district courts. . . .

The most familiar definition of the statutory "arising under" limitation is Justice Holmes' statement, "A suit arises under the law that creates the cause of action." American Well Works Co. v. Layne & Bowler Co., 241 U.S. 257, 260 (1916). However, it is well settled that Justice Holmes' test is more useful for describing the vast majority of cases that come within the district courts' original jurisdiction than it is for describing which cases are beyond district court jurisdiction. We have often held that a case "arose under" federal law where the vindication of a right under state law necessarily turned on some construction of federal law, see, e.g., Smith v. Kansas City Title & Trust Co., 255 U.S. 180 (1921); Hopkins v. Walker, 244 U.S. 486 (1917), and even the most ardent proponent of the Holmes test has admitted that it has been rejected as an exclusionary principle, see Flournoy v. Wiener, 321 U.S. 253, 270-272 (1944) (Frankfurter, J., dissenting). See also T. B. Harms Co. v. Eliscu, 339 F.2d 823, 827 (2d Cir. 1964) (Friendly, J.). Leading commentators have suggested that for purposes of § 1331 an action "arises under" federal law "if in order for the plaintiff to secure the relief sought he will be obliged to establish both the correctness and the applicability to his case of a proposition of federal law." P. Bator, P. Mishkin, D. Shapiro, & H. Wechsler, Hart and Wechsler's The Federal Courts and the Federal System 889 (2d ed. 1973); cf. T. B. Harms Co., supra, at 827 ("a case may 'arise under' a law of the United States if the complaint discloses a need for determining the meaning or application of such a law"). . . .

. . . "[A] right or immunity created by the Constitution or laws of the United States must be an element, and an essential one, of the plaintiff's cause of action." Gully v. First National Bank in Meridian, 299 U.S. 109, 112 (1936). . . . Even though state law creates appellant's causes of action, its case might still "arise under" the laws of the United States if a well-pleaded complaint established that its right to relief under state law requires resolution of a substantial question of federal law in dispute between the parties. . . .

. . . Under our interpretations, Congress has given the lower federal courts jurisdiction to hear, originally or by removal from a state court, only those cases in which a well-pleaded complaint establishes either that federal law creates the cause of action or that the plaintiff's right to relief necessarily depends on resolution of a substantial question of federal law. . . .

---

a. Some Easy Cases

Below are short summaries of claims filed in federal court under the federal question statute. Can you see why they might satisfy the statute?

Bender v. City of St. Ann, 816 F. Supp. 1372 (E.D. Mo. 1993). Deli owner brought § 1983 action alleging constitutional violations stemming from enforcement of ordinance restricting the number of commercial signs his establishment could display.

Hudson v. National Acad. of Sciences, Inst. of Medicine, 816 F. Supp. 774 (D. D.C. 1993). Title VII race discrimination case was filed by former employee of nonprofit corporation alleging discrimination in failure to promote, retaliation in nonselection for promotion, harassment, and demotion based on race, and discriminatory termination.

Ware v. Howard Univ., 816 F. Supp. 737 (D.D.C. 1993). University employee brought action against university alleging violations of Age Discrimination in Employment Act (ADEA).

Adler v. Berg Harmon Assocs., 816 F. Supp. 919 (S.D.N.Y. 1993). Investors in limited partnership interests in real estate tax shelters brought suit against joint venture which syndicated and promoted sale of interests, its parent corporations, and corporate officer. Investors asserted violations of the Securities and Exchange Act, the Racketeer Influenced and Corrupt Organizations Act (RICO), common-law fraud, negligence, and breach of fiduciary duty.

b. The Well-Pleaded Complaint Requirement

The above cases should reinforce for you the first requirement of federal question jurisdiction, that federal courts may hear a case if federal law has a substantial and direct bearing on the case. A second requirement is that the federal question must appear on the face of the "well-pleaded" complaint. Simply put, the plaintiff's claim—not the defendant's response—must include the federal question. Below is the famous case that established this limitation on federal court power. To understand *Mottley*, you need to appreciate that "well-pleaded" does not mean *actually* pleaded in the complaint filed with the court. Rather, "well-pleaded" here means the least the plaintiff needed to include in the complaint to state fully her complaint against the defendant, without anticipating defendant's likely response to that claim. Read on to find out what happened to the Mottley crew.

Louisville & Nashville R.R. Co. v. Mottley

211 U.S. 149 (1908)

Statement by Justice Moody.

The appellees (husband and wife), being residents and citizens of Kentucky, brought this suit in equity in the circuit court of the United States for the western district of Kentucky against the appellant, a railroad company and a citizen of the same state. The object of the suit was to compel the specific performance of the following contract:

> Louisville, KY., Oct. 2d, 1871. The Louisville & Nashville Railroad Company, in consideration that E. L. Mottley and wife, Annie E. Mottley, have this day released company from all damages or claims for damages for injuries received by them on the 7th of September, 1871, in consequence of a collision of trains on the railroad of said company at Randolph's Station, Jefferson County, Kentucky, hereby agrees to issue free passes on said railroad and branches now existing or to exist, to said E. L. & Annie E. Mottley for the remainder of the present year, and thereafter to renew said passes annually during the lives of said Mottley and wife or either of them.

The bill alleged that in September, 1871, plaintiffs, while passengers upon the defendant railroad, were injured by the defendant's negligence, and released their respective claims for damages in consideration of the agreement for transportation during their lives, expressed in the contract. It is alleged that the contract was performed by the defendant up to January 1, 1907, when the defendant declined to renew the passes. The bill then alleges that the refusal to comply with the contract was based solely upon that part of the act of Congress of June 29, 1906 (34 Stat. at L. 584, chap. 3591), which forbids the giving of free passes or free transportation. The bill further alleges: First, that the act of Congress referred to does not prohibit the giving of passes under the circumstances of this case; and, second, that, if the law is to be construed as prohibiting such passes, it is in conflict with the 5th Amendment of the Constitution, because it deprives the plaintiffs of their property without due process of law. The defendant demurred to the bill. The judge of the circuit court overruled the demurrer, entered a decree for the relief prayed for, and the defendant appealed directly to this court. . . .

JUSTICE MOODY, after making the foregoing statement, delivered the opinion of the court:

Two questions of law were raised by the demurrer to the bill, were brought here by appeal, and have been argued before us. They are, first, whether that part of the act of Congress of June 29, 1906 (34 Stat. at L. 584, chap. 3591), which forbids the giving of free passes or the collection of any different compensation for transportation of passengers than that specified in the tariff filed, makes it unlawful to perform a contract for transportation of persons who, in good faith, before the passage of the act, had accepted such contract in satisfaction of a valid cause of action against the railroad; and, second, whether the statute, if it should be construed to render such a contract unlawful, is in violation of the 5th Amendment of the Constitution of the United States. We do not deem it necessary, however, to consider either of these questions, because, in our opinion, the court below was without jurisdiction of the cause. Neither party has questioned that jurisdiction, but it is the duty of this court to see to it that the jurisdiction of the circuit court, which is defined and limited by statute, is not exceeded. This duty we have frequently performed of our own motion.

There was no diversity of citizenship, and it is not and cannot be suggested that there was any ground of jurisdiction, except that the case was a "suit . . . arising under the Constitution or laws of the United States." 25 Stat. at L. 434, chap. 866. It is the settled interpretation of these words, as used in this statute, conferring jurisdiction, that a suit arises under the Constitution and laws of the United States only when the plaintiff's statement of his own cause of action shows that it is based upon those laws or that Constitution. It is not enough that the plaintiff alleges some anticipated defense to his cause of action, and asserts that the defense is invalidated by some provision of the Constitution of the United States. Although such allegations show that very likely, in the course of the litigation, a question under the Constitution would arise, they do not show that the suit, that is, the plaintiff's original cause of action, arises under the Constitution. . . .

It is ordered that the judgment be reversed and the case remitted to the circuit court with instructions to dismiss the suit for want of jurisdiction.

Note: The Aftermath of Mottley

Assume that you are the lawyer for the Mottleys and must turn to redrafting the complaint. Try your hand at rewriting the complaint so that it does not anticipate the defendant's response.

Your efforts at doing this are likely to reflect real life in which the lawyer for the Mottleys could not draft a federal question complaint, and so turned to state court. Naturally, the railroad responded by raising the authority of the federal statute for its actions. Again the case made its way to the United States Supreme Court, which construed the statute to uphold the railroad's action in rescinding the passes. Louisville & Nashville R.R. Co. v. Mottley, 219 U.S. 467 (1911). Thus, two long and expensive journeys led to a dead end for the Mottleys.

The Court recently reaffirmed the well-pleaded complaint rule in Rivet v. Regions Bank of Louisiana, 522 U.S. 470 (1998). See further discussion of *Rivet* in Chapters 6 and 7. See also Holmes Group, Inc. v. Vornado Air Circulation Syst., Inc., 535 U.S. 826 (2002) (holding that a federal patent infringement claim asserted as a counterclaim did not create federal subject matter jurisdiction because the well-pleaded complaint, not the counterclaim, determines whether a civil action "arises under" federal patent law).

At first glance, the Declaratory Judgment Act, 28 U.S.C. § 2201, which allows potential defendants like the railroad to become plaintiffs instead and test whether they are excused from renewing passes like those granted the Mottleys, would seem an avenue for a more fair and speedy resolution of questions like that about the statute in *Mottley*. In Skelly Oil Co. v. Phillips Petroleum Co., 339 U.S. 667 (1950), however, the Supreme Court held that the Declaratory Judgment Act did not alter the jurisdiction of the federal courts, so that if plaintiffs like the Mottleys could not plead "well" in the federal courts, neither could defendants like the railroad who did not want to wait to be sued before determining the constitutionality and viability of their potential defenses.

For a recent discussion of federal question jurisdiction in the Declaratory Judgment and Labor Management Relations Act § 301(a) context, which discusses (and distinguishes) *Skelly Oil Co.*, see Textron Lycoming Reciprocating Engine Division Arvo Corp. v. United Automobile Aerospace and Agricultural Implement Workers of America, Intl. Union and Its Local 787, 523 U.S. 653 (1998). The Court noted that "[n]o decision of this Court has squarely confronted and explicitly upheld federal-question jurisdiction on the basis of the anticipatory claim against which the declaratory-judgment plaintiff presents a nonfederal defense." 523 U.S. at 659, 660. Although it acknowledged that the Declaratory Judgment Act might be read to allow such anticipation, past cases have not presented that issue, and have had language to suggest "that the declaratory-judgment plaintiff must himself have a federal claim." Id. at 660. See also Household Bank v. JFS Group, 320 F.3d 1249, 1251 (11th Cir. 2003) (joining seven other circuits in holding that "federal-question jurisdiction exists in a declaratory judgment action if the plaintiff has alleged facts in a well-pleaded complaint which demonstrate that the defendant could file a coercive action arising under federal law").

c. Hard Cases: *Merrell Dow* and the Private Right of Action Requirement

In our next case, Merrell Dow Pharmaceutical v. Thompson, 478 U.S. 804 (1986), the U.S. Supreme Court addressed the question whether a federal statute must provide an express or implied private right of action when a plaintiff seeks to rely on that statute as the basis for federal jurisdiction over state law claims. A private right of action is created when a statute gives to private persons, not merely public authorities, the right to enforce the statute through litigation. This happens in one of two ways. Either the statute expressly provides for this private right of action, or a court may conclude that such a right is implied by the statute, despite the absence of explicit congressional language granting such a right.

Cort v. Ash, 422 U.S. 66 (1975), sets forth four factors relevant to a finding of an implied private right of action: 1) whether the statute was enacted for the benefit of a special class of which the plaintiff is a member; 2) whether the legislative history evinces an intent to create a private right of action; 3) whether finding a private right of action would frustrate the purpose of the legislative scheme; and 4) whether implying a private right of action is inappropriate because the subject matter involves an area basically of concern to the states. The Court's growing unease with the subjectivity of this four-factor test has led it to ignore it in recent cases.

To understand *Merrell Dow,* you thus need to focus on two facts: not all statutes that impose particular legal obligations can be enforced by private citizens, even though the statutes likely were drafted to protect those citizens; and the Court is increasingly wary of finding an "implied" private right of action. If, for example, Congress were to pass a law regulating the disposal of chemical waste by certain industries, this law may be enforceable only by the government rather than by private individuals. That is, there may be no express or implied private right of action for such an act. *Merrell Dow* discusses the subject matter jurisdiction consequences of such an act.

Merrell Dow Pharmaceutical v. Thompson

478 U.S 804 (1986)

JUSTICE STEVENS delivered the opinion of the Court.

The question presented is whether the incorporation of a federal standard in a state-law private action, when Congress has intended that there not be a federal private action for violations of that federal standard, makes the action one "arising under the Constitution, laws, or treaties of the United States," 28 U.S.C. § 1331.

The Thompson respondents are residents of Canada and the MacTavishes reside in Scotland. They filed virtually identical complaints against petitioner, a corporation, that manufactures and distributes the drug Bendectin. The complaints were filed in the Court of Common Pleas in

Hamilton County, Ohio. Each complaint alleged that a child was born with multiple deformities as a result of the mother's ingestion of Bendectin during pregnancy. In five of the six counts, the recovery of substantial damages was requested on common-law theories of negligence, breach of warranty, strict liability, fraud, and gross negligence. In Count IV, respondents alleged that the drug Bendectin was "misbranded" in violation of the Federal Food, Drug, and Cosmetic Act (FDCA), 52 Stat. 1040, as amended, 21 U.S.C. §§ 301 et seq. (1982 ed. and Supp. III), because its labeling did not provide adequate warning that its use was potentially dangerous. Paragraph 26 alleged that the violation of the FDCA "in the promotion" of Bendectin "constitutes a rebuttable presumption of negligence." Paragraph 27 alleged that the "violation of said federal statutes directly and proximately caused the injuries suffered" by the two infants.

Petitioner filed a timely petition for removal from the state court to the Federal District Court alleging that the action was "founded, in part, on an alleged claim arising under the laws of the United States." After removal, the two cases were consolidated. Respondents filed a motion to remand to the state forum on the ground that the federal court lacked subject-matter jurisdiction. Relying on our decision in Smith v. Kansas City Title & Trust Co., 255 U.S. 180 (1921), the District Court held that Count IV of the complaint alleged a cause of action arising under federal law and denied the motion to remand.

The Court of Appeals for the Sixth Circuit reversed. . . .

We granted certiorari, and we now affirm.

Article III of the Constitution gives the federal courts power to hear cases "arising under" federal statutes. That grant of power, however, is not self-executing, and it was not until the Judiciary Act of 1875 that Congress gave the federal courts general federal-question jurisdiction. Although the constitutional meaning of "arising under" may extend to all cases in which a federal question is "an ingredient" of the action, Osborn v. Bank of the United States, 9 Wheat. 738, 823 (1824), we have long construed the statutory grant of federal-question jurisdiction as conferring a more limited power.

Under our longstanding interpretation of the current statutory scheme, the question whether a claim "arises under" federal law must be determined by reference to the "well-pleaded complaint." A defense that raises a federal question is inadequate to confer federal jurisdiction. Louisville & Nashville R.R. Co. v. Mottley, 211 U.S. 149 (1908). Since a defendant may remove a case only if the claim could have been brought in federal court, 28 U.S.C. § 1441(b), moreover, the question for removal jurisdiction must also be determined by reference to the "well-pleaded complaint."

. . . [T]he propriety of the removal in this case thus turns on whether the case falls within the original "federal question" jurisdiction of the federal courts. There is no "single, precise definition" of that concept; rather, "the phrase 'arising under' masks a welter of issues regarding the interrelation of federal and state authority and the proper management of the federal judicial system."

This much, however, is clear. The "vast majority" of cases that come within this grant of jurisdiction are covered by Justice Holmes' statement that a "'suit arises under the law that creates the cause of action.'" Thus, the vast majority of cases brought under the general federal-question jurisdiction of the federal courts are those in which federal law creates the cause of action. . . .[5]

This case does not pose a federal question of the first kind; respondents do not allege that federal law creates any of the causes of action that they have asserted. This case thus poses what Justice Frankfurter called the "litigation-provoking problem," Textile Workers v. Lincoln Mills, 353 U.S. 448, 470 (1957) (dissenting opinion)—the presence of a federal issue in a state-created cause of action.

In undertaking this inquiry into whether jurisdiction may lie for the presence of a federal issue in a nonfederal cause of action, it is, of course, appropriate to begin by referring to our understanding of the statute conferring federal-question jurisdiction. We have consistently emphasized that, in exploring the outer reaches of § 1331, determinations about federal jurisdiction require sensitive judgments about congressional intent, judicial power, and the federal system. "If the history of the interpretation of judiciary legislation teaches us anything, it teaches the duty to reject treating such statutes as a wooden set of self-sufficient words. . . . The Act of 1875 is broadly phrased, but is has been continuously construed and limited in the light of the history that produced it, the demands of reason and coherence, and the dictates of sound judicial policy which have emerged from the Act's function as a provision in the mosaic of federal judiciary legislation." Romero v. International Terminal Operating Co., 358 U.S. 354, 379 (1959). . . .

In this case, both parties agree with the Court of Appeals' conclusion that there is no federal cause of action for FDCA violations. For purposes of our decision, we assume that this is a correct interpretation of the FDCA. Thus, as the case comes to us, it is appropriate to assume that, under the settled framework for evaluating whether a federal cause of action lies, some combination of the following factors is present: (1) the plaintiffs are not part of the class for whose special benefit the statute was passed; (2) the indicia of legislative intent reveal no congressional purpose to provide a private cause of action; (3) a federal cause of action would not further the underlying purposes of the legislative scheme; and (4) the respondents' cause of action is a subject traditionally relegated to state law. In short, Congress did not intend a private federal remedy for violations of the statute that it enacted.

5. "The general rule is that where it appears from the bill or statement of the plaintiff that the right to relief depends upon the construction or application of the Constitution or laws of the United States, and that such federal claim is not merely colorable, and rests upon a reasonable foundation, the District Court has jurisdiction under this provision." Smith v. Kansas City Title & Trust Co., 255 U.S. 180, 199 (1921). The effect of this view, expressed over Justice Holmes' vigorous dissent, . . . has been often noted.

This is the first case in which we have reviewed this type of jurisdictional claim in light of these factors. That this is so is not surprising. The development of our framework for determining whether a private cause of action exists has proceeded only in the 11 years, and its inception represented a significant change in our approach to congressional silence on the provision of federal remedies.

The recent character of that development does not, however, diminish its importance. Indeed, the very reasons for the development of the modern implied remedy doctrine—the "increased complexity of federal legislation and the increased volume of federal litigation," as well as "the desirability of a more careful scrutiny of legislative intent," Merrill Lynch, Pierce, Fenner & Smith, Inc. v. Curran, 456 U.S. 353, 377 (1982)—are precisely the kind of considerations that should inform the concern for "practicality and necessity" for the construction of § 1331 when jurisdiction is asserted because of the presence of a federal issue in a state cause of action.

The significance of the necessary assumption that there is no federal private cause of action thus cannot be overstated. For the ultimate import of such a conclusion, as we have repeatedly emphasized, is that it would flout congressional intent to provide a private federal remedy for the violation of the federal statute. We think it would similarly flout, or at least undermine, congressional intent to conclude that the federal courts might nevertheless exercise federal-question jurisdiction and provide remedies for violations of that federal statute solely because the violation of the federal statute is said to be a "rebuttable presumption" or a "proximate cause" under state law, rather than a federal action under federal law.

Petitioner advances three arguments to support its position that, even in the face of this congressional preclusion of a federal cause of action for a violation of the federal statute, federal-question jurisdiction may lie for the violation of the federal statute as an element of a state cause of action.

First, petitioner contends that the case represents a straightforward application of the statement that federal-question jurisdiction is appropriate when "it appears that some substantial, disputed question of federal law is a necessary element of one of the well-pleaded state claims." 463 U.S. at 13. [But] the mere presence of a federal issue in a state cause of action does not automatically confer federal-question jurisdiction. Indeed, in determining that federal-question jurisdiction was not appropriate in the case before us, we stressed Justice Cardozo's emphasis on principled, pragmatic distinctions: "'What is needed is something of that common-sense accommodation of judgment to kaleidoscopic situations which characterizes the law in its treatment of causation . . . a selective process which picks the substantial causes out of the web and lays the other ones aside.'" Gully v. First National Bank, 299 U.S. 109, 117-118 (1936).

. . . Given the significance of the assumed congressional determination to preclude federal private remedies, the presence of the federal issue as an element of the state tort is not the kind of adjudication for which jurisdiction would serve congressional purposes and the federal system.

We simply conclude that the congressional determination that there should be no federal remedy for the violation of this federal statute is tantamount to a congressional conclusion that the presence of a claimed violation of the statute as an element of a state cause of action is insufficiently "substantial" to confer federal-question jurisdiction.

Second, petitioner contends that there is a powerful federal interest in seeing that the federal statute is given uniform interpretations, and that federal review is the best way of insuring such uniformity. In addition to the significance of the congressional decision to preclude a federal remedy, we do not agree with petitioner's characterization of the federal interest and its implications for federal-question jurisdiction. To the extent that petitioner is arguing that state use and interpretation of the FDCA pose a threat to the order and stability of the FDCA regime, petitioner should be arguing, not that federal courts should be able to review and enforce state FDCA-based causes of action as an aspect of federal-question jurisdiction, but that the FDCA pre-empts state-court jurisdiction over the issue in dispute. Petitioner's concern about the uniformity of interpretation, moreover, is considerably mitigated by the fact that, even if there is no original district court jurisdiction for these kinds of action, this Court retains power to review the decision of a federal issue in a state cause of action.

Finally, petitioner argues that, whatever the general rule, there are special circumstances that justify federal-question jurisdiction in this case. Petitioner emphasizes that it is unclear whether the FDCA applies to sales in Canada and Scotland; there is, therefore, a special reason for having a federal court answer the novel federal question relating to the extraterritorial meaning of the Act. We reject this argument. We do not believe the question whether a particular claim arises under federal law depends on the novelty of the federal issue. Although it is true that federal jurisdiction cannot be based on a frivolous or insubstantial federal question, "the interrelation of federal and state authority and the proper management of the federal judicial system," Franchise Tax Board v. Construction Laborers Vacation Trust, 463 U.S. 1, 8 (1983), would be ill served by a rule that made the existence of federal-question jurisdiction depend on the district court's case-by-case appraisal of the novelty of the federal question asserted as an element of the state tort. The novelty of an FDCA issue is not sufficient to give it status as a federal cause of action; nor should it be sufficient to give a state-based FDCA claim status as a jurisdiction-triggering federal question.

We conclude that a complaint alleging a violation of a federal statute as an element of a state cause of action, when Congress has determined that there should be no private, federal cause of action for the violation, does not state a claim "arising under the Constitution, laws, or treaties of the United States." 28 U.S.C. § 1331.

The judgment of the Court of Appeals is affirmed.

It is so ordered.

JUSTICE BRENNAN, with whom JUSTICE WHITE, JUSTICE MARSHALL, and JUSTICE BLACKMUN join, dissenting. . . .

I believe that the limitation on federal jurisdiction recognized by the Court today is inconsistent with the purposes of § 1331. Therefore, I respectfully dissent.

While the majority of cases covered by § 1331 may well be described by Justice Holmes' adage that "[a] suit arises under the law that creates the cause of action," American Well Works Co. v. Layne & Bowler Co., 241 U. S. 257, 260 (1916), it is firmly settled that there may be federal-question jurisdiction even though both the right asserted and the remedy sought by the plaintiff are state created. The rule as to such cases was stated in what Judge Friendly described as "[t]he path-breaking opinion" in Smith v. Kansas City Title & Trust Co., 255 U.S. 180 (1921). In *Smith*, a shareholder of the defendant corporation brought suit in the federal court to enjoin the defendant from investing corporate funds in bonds issued under the authority of the Federal Farm Loan Act. The plaintiff alleged that Missouri law imposed a fiduciary duty on the corporation to invest only in bonds that were authorized by a valid law and argued that, because the Farm Loan Act was unconstitutional, the defendant could not purchase bonds issued under its authority. Although the cause of action was wholly state created, the Court held that there was original federal jurisdiction over the case:

> The general rule is that where it appears from the bill or statement of the plaintiff that the right to relief depends upon the construction or application of the Constitution or laws of the United States, and that such federal claim is not merely colorable, and rests upon a reasonable foundation, the District Court has jurisdiction under [the statute granting federal question jurisdiction].

Id. at 199.

The continuing vitality of *Smith* is beyond challenge. We have cited it approvingly on numerous occasions, and reaffirmed its holding several times. . . .

There is, to my mind, no question that there is federal jurisdiction over the respondents' fourth cause of action under the rule set forth in *Smith*. Respondents pleaded that petitioner's labeling of the drug Bendectin constituted "misbranding" in violation of §§ 201 and 502(f)(2) and (j) of the Federal Food, Drug, and Cosmetic Act (FDCA), 52 Stat. 1040, as amended, 21 U.S.C. §§ 301 et seq. (1982 ed. and Supp. III), and that this violation "directly and proximately caused" their injuries. Respondents asserted in the complaint that this violation established petitioner's negligence *per se* and entitled them to recover damages without more. No other basis for finding petitioner negligent was asserted in connection with this claim. As pleaded, then, respondents' "right to relief depend[ed] upon the construction or application of the Constitution or laws of the United States." *Smith*, 255 U.S. at 199. Furthermore, although petitioner disputes its liability under the FDCA, it concedes that respondents' claim that petitioner violated the FDCA is "colorable, and rests upon a reasonable foundation." . . . As stated in the complaint, a drug is "misbranded" under the FDCA if "the labeling or advertising fails to reveal facts material . . . with respect to consequences which may result from the use of the article to which the labeling or advertising relates. . . ." 21 U.S.C. § 321(n). Obviously, the possibility that a mother's ingestion of Bendectin during pregnancy could produce malformed children is material. Petitioner's principal defense is that the Act does not govern the branding of drugs that are sold in foreign countries. It is certainly not immediately obvious whether this argument is correct. Thus, the statutory question is one which "discloses a need for determining the meaning or application of [the FDCA]"and the claim raised by the fourth cause of action is one "arising under" federal law within the meaning of § 1331.

The Court apparently does not disagree with any of this—except, of course, for the conclusion. According to the Court, if we assume that Congress did not intend that there be a private federal cause of action under a particular federal law (and, presumably, *a fortiori* if Congress' decision not to create a private remedy is express), we must also assume that Congress did not intend that there be federal jurisdiction over a state cause of action that is determined by that federal law. Therefore, assuming—only because the parties have made a similar assumption—that there is no private cause of action under the FDCA, the Court holds that there is no federal jurisdiction over the plaintiffs' claim. . . .

The Court nowhere explains the basis for this conclusion. Yet it is hardly self-evident. Why should the fact that Congress chose not to create a private federal *remedy* mean that Congress would not want there to be federal *jurisdiction* to adjudicate a state claim that imposes liability for violating the federal law? Clearly, the decision not to provide a private federal remedy should not affect federal jurisdiction unless the reasons Congress withholds a federal remedy are also reasons for withholding federal jurisdiction. Thus, it is necessary to examine the reasons for Congress' decisions to grant or withhold both federal jurisdiction and private remedies, something the Court has not done.

In the early days of our Republic, Congress was content to leave the task of interpreting and applying federal laws in the first instance to the state courts; with one short-lived exception, Congress did not grant the inferior federal courts original jurisdiction over cases arising under federal law until 1875. Judiciary Act of 1875, ch. 137, § 1, 18 Stat. 470. The reasons Congress found it necessary to add this jurisdiction to the district courts are well known. First, Congress recognized "the importance, and even necessity of *uniformity* of decisions throughout the whole United States, upon all subjects within the purview of the constitution." Martin v. Hunter's Lessee, [14 U.S. (1 Wheat.) 304, 347-348 (1816)]. Concededly, because federal jurisdiction is not always exclusive and because federal courts may disagree with one another, absolute uniformity has not been obtained even under § 1331. However, while perfect uniformity may not have been achieved, experience indicates that the availability of a federal forum in federal-question cases has done much to advance that goal. This, in fact, was the conclusion of the American Law Institute's Study of the Division of Jurisdiction Between State and Federal Courts. A.L.I. 164-168.

In addition, § 1331 has provided for adjudication in a forum that specializes in federal law and that is therefore more likely to apply that law correctly. Because federal-question cases constitute the basic grist for federal tribunals, "[t]he federal courts have acquired a considerable expertness in the interpretation and application of federal law." [American Law Institute Study of the Division of Jurisdiction Between State and Federal Courts, A.L.I. at 164-165.] By contrast, "it is apparent that federal question cases must form a very small part of the business of [state] courts." Id. at 165. As a result, the federal courts are comparatively more skilled at interpreting and applying federal law, and are much more likely correctly to divine Congress' intent in enacting legislation.

These reasons for having original federal-question jurisdiction explain why cases like this one and *Smith*—i.e., cases where the cause of action is a creature of state law, but an essential element of the claim is federal—"arise under" federal law within the meaning of § 1331. Congress passes laws in order to shape behavior; a federal law expresses Congress' determination that there is a federal interest in having individuals or other entities conform their actions to a particular norm established by that law. Because all laws are imprecise to some degree, disputes inevitably arise over what specifically Congress intended to require or permit. It is the duty of courts to interpret these laws and apply them in such a way that the congressional purpose is realized. As noted above, Congress granted the district courts power to hear cases "arising under" federal law in order to enhance the likelihood that federal laws would be interpreted more correctly and applied more uniformly. In other words, Congress determined that the availability of a federal forum to adjudicate cases involving federal questions would make it more likely that federal laws would shape behavior in the way that Congress intended.

By making federal law an essential element of a state-law claim, the State places the federal law into a context where it will operate to shape behavior: the threat of liability will force individuals to conform their conduct to interpretations of the federal law made by courts adjudicating the state-law claim. It will not matter to an individual found liable whether the officer who arrives at his door to execute judgment is wearing a state or a federal uniform; all he cares about is the fact that a sanction is being imposed—and may be imposed again in the future—because he failed to comply with the federal law. Consequently, the possibility that the federal law will be incorrectly interpreted in the context of adjudicating the state-law claim implicates the concerns that led Congress to grant the district courts power to adjudicate cases involving federal questions in precisely the same way as if it was federal law that "created" the cause of action. It therefore follows that there is federal jurisdiction under § 1331.

The only remaining question is whether the assumption that Congress decided not to create a private cause of action alters this analysis in a way that makes it inappropriate to exercise original federal jurisdiction. According to the Court, "the very reasons for the development of the modern implied remedy doctrine" support the conclusion that, where the legislative history of a particular law shows (whether expressly or by inference) that Congress intended that there be no private federal remedy, it must also mean that Congress would not want federal courts to exercise jurisdiction over a state-law claim making violations of that federal law actionable. These reasons are "'the increased complexity of federal legislation,'" "'the increased volume of federal litigation,'" and "'the desirability of a more careful scrutiny of legislative intent.'"

These reasons simply do not justify the Court's holding. Given the relative expertise of the federal courts in interpreting federal law, the increased complexity of federal legislation argues rather strongly in *favor* of recognizing federal jurisdiction. And, while the increased volume of litigation may appropriately be considered in connection with reasoned arguments that justify limiting the reach of § 1331, I do not believe that the day has yet arrived when this Court may trim a statute solely because it thinks that Congress made it too broad.

This leaves only the third reason: "'the desirability of a more careful scrutiny of legislative intent.'" I certainly subscribe to the proposition that the Court should consider legislative intent in determining whether or not there is jurisdiction under § 1331. But the Court has not examined the purposes underlying either the FDCA or § 1331 in reaching its conclusion that Congress' presumed decision not to provide a private federal remedy under the FDCA must be taken to withdraw federal jurisdiction over a private state remedy that imposes liability for violating the FDCA. Moreover, such an examination demonstrates not only that it is consistent with legislative intent to find that there is federal jurisdiction over such a claim, but, indeed, that it is the Court's contrary conclusion that is inconsistent with congressional intent.

The enforcement scheme established by the FDCA is typical of other, similarly broad regulatory schemes. Primary responsibility for overseeing implementation of the Act has been conferred upon a specialized administrative agency, here the Food and Drug Administration (FDA). Congress has provided the FDA with a wide-ranging arsenal of weapons to combat violations of the FDCA, including authority to obtain an *ex parte* court order for the seizure of goods subject to the Act, authority to initiate proceedings in a federal district court to enjoin continuing violations of the FDCA, and authority to request a United States Attorney to bring criminal proceedings against violators. Significantly, the FDA has no independent enforcement authority; final enforcement must come from the federal courts, which have exclusive jurisdiction over actions under the FDCA. . . .

Given that Congress structured the FDCA so that all express remedies are provided by the federal courts, it seems rather strange to conclude that it either "flout[s]" or "undermine[s]" congressional intent for the federal courts to adjudicate a private state-law remedy that is based upon violating the FDCA. . . .

Note: Following Merrell Dow

1. Re-read Justice Holmes's test for federal question jurisdiction quoted in *Franchise Tax Board* and *Merrell Dow*. The core of his dissenting opinion in *American Well Works* is that there is no federal question jurisdiction unless federal law creates the cause of action on which the plaintiff sues—it is a simple, bright line definition of "arising under." Is the result in *Merrell Dow* any different from what would follow under Holmes's test? The plaintiffs' state tort claims in *Merrell Dow* could not be heard in federal court because the federal statute they invoked did not provide a private cause of action.

2. What does it signal when Congress creates a private right of action to enforce federal rights? Think about the array of federal legislation that *does not* create a private right of action but could become a necessary component of state law claims. In the wake of the New Deal and the rise of the administrative state there are countless federal statutes regulating everything from emission standards for automobiles to the labeling of nutrition facts in food—most of these statutes do not establish private rights of action even though they are intended to protect the public at large. Should the federal courts be open to all cases in which a federal statute must be applied or construed in order to decide a state law claim? Well before *Merrell Dow*, the Court said "no," federal issues must not only be necessary to the resolution of a state law claim, but *substantial*, and not all federal issues raised in state law cases are substantial. See the majority opinion's discussion of Gully v. First National Bank, page 240, supra.

3. *Merrell Dow* tells us we can be certain that federal issues are "substantial" when Congress creates a private right of action. But does the decision limit federal question jurisdiction to cases in which the plaintiff has a private right of action? In other words, after *Merrell Dow*, can a plaintiff establish federal question jurisdiction by invoking a federal statute even if the statute does not create, either expressly or by implication, a private right of action?

Lower courts were sharply divided on this question until the following case cleared the air. *Grable* began as a suit to "quiet title" to land in Michigan seized and resold by the IRS to pay for back taxes. Like the tort law claims in *Merrell Dow*, a suit to resolve a dispute regarding title to land is typically a matter of state common law property doctrine. Plaintiff, the original owner, brought suit in state court against the company that bought the land at an IRS sale. As the case describes in Section II below, there is a specific statutory vehicle for accomplishing this called "removal." See 28 U.S.C. § 1441. Removal jurisdiction is discussed in some detail in Chapter 6. For now you need only know that for a defendant to remove a case to federal court, the case must meet the same test for federal question jurisdiction under § 1331 we have been examining here. As you read, pay close attention to how the Court treats *Merrell Dow*.

Grable & Sons Metal Products, Inc. v. Darue Engineering & Mfg.

545 U.S. 308 (2005)

JUSTICE SOUTER delivered the opinion of the Court.

The question is whether want of a federal cause of action to try claims of title to land obtained at a federal tax sale precludes removal to federal court of a state action with nondiverse parties raising a disputed issue of federal title law. We answer no, and hold that the national interest in providing a federal forum for federal tax litigation is sufficiently substantial to support the exercise of federal question jurisdiction over the disputed issue on removal, which would not distort any division of labor between the state and federal courts, provided or assumed by Congress.

I

In 1994, the Internal Revenue Service seized Michigan real property belonging to petitioner Grable & Sons Metal Products, Inc., to satisfy Grable's federal tax delinquency. Title 26 U.S.C. § 6335 required the IRS to give notice of the seizure, and there is no dispute that Grable received actual notice by certified mail before the IRS sold the property to respondent Darue Engineering & Manufacturing. Although Grable also received notice of the sale itself, it did not exercise its statutory right to redeem the property within 180 days of the sale, § 6337(b)(1), and after that period had passed, the Government gave Darue a quitclaim deed. § 6339.

Five years later, Grable brought a quiet title action in state court, claiming that Darue's record title was invalid because the IRS had failed to notify Grable of its seizure of the property in the exact manner required by § 6335(a), which provides that written notice must be "given by the Secretary to the owner of the property [or] left at his usual place of abode or business." Grable said that the statute required personal service, not service by certified mail.

Darue removed the case to Federal District Court as presenting a federal question, because the claim of title depended on the interpretation of the notice statute in the federal tax law. The District Court declined to remand the case at Grable's behest after finding that the "claim does pose a significant question of federal law," Tr. 17 (Apr. 2, 2001), and ruling that Grable's lack of a federal right of action to enforce its claim against Darue did not bar the exercise of federal jurisdiction. . . .

The Court of Appeals for the Sixth Circuit affirmed. 377 F.3d 592 (2004). On the jurisdictional question, the panel thought it sufficed that the title claim raised an issue of federal law that had to be resolved, and implicated a substantial federal interest (in construing federal tax law). The court went on to affirm the District Court's judgment on the merits. We granted certiorari on the jurisdictional question alone, to resolve a split within the Courts of Appeals on whether Merrell Dow Pharmaceuticals Inc. v. Thompson, 478 U.S. 804 (1986), always requires a federal cause of action as a condition for exercising federal-question jurisdiction.[2] We now affirm.

II

Darue was entitled to remove the quiet title action if Grable could have brought it in federal district court originally, 28 U.S.C. § 1441(a), as a civil action "arising under the Constitution, laws, or treaties of the United States," § 1331. This provision for federal-question jurisdiction is invoked by and large by plaintiffs pleading a cause of action created by federal law (e.g., claims under 42 U.S.C. § 1983). There is, however, another long-standing, if less frequently encountered, variety of federal "arising under" jurisdiction, this Court having recognized for nearly 100 years that in certain cases federal question jurisdiction will lie over state-law claims that implicate significant federal issues. E.g., Hopkins v. Walker, 244 U.S. 486, 490-491 (1917). The doctrine captures the commonsense notion that a federal court ought to be able to hear claims recognized under state law that nonetheless turn on substantial questions of federal law, and thus justify resort to the experience, solicitude, and hope of uniformity that a federal forum offers on federal issues, see ALI, Study of the Division of Jurisdiction Between State and Federal Courts 164-166 (1968).

The classic example is Smith v. Kansas City Title & Trust Co., 255 U.S. 180 (1921), a suit by a shareholder claiming that the defendant corporation could not lawfully buy certain bonds of the National Government because their issuance was unconstitutional. Although Missouri law provided the cause of action, the Court recognized federal-question jurisdiction because the principal issue in the case was the federal constitutionality of the bond issue. *Smith* thus held, in a somewhat generous statement of the scope of the doctrine, that a state-law claim could give rise to federal-question jurisdiction so long as it "appears from the [complaint] that the right to relief depends upon the construction or application of [federal law]." Id. at 199.

2. Compare Seinfeld v. Austen, 39 F.3d 761, 764 (7th Cir. 1994) (finding that federal-question jurisdiction over a state-law claim requires a parallel federal private right of action), with Ormet Corp. v. Ohio Power Co., 98 F.3d 799, 806 (4th Cir. 1996) (finding that a federal private action is not required).

The *Smith* statement has been subject to some trimming to fit earlier and later cases recognizing the vitality of the basic doctrine, but shying away from the expansive view that mere need to apply federal law in a state-law claim will suffice to open the "arising under" door. As early as 1912, this Court had confined federal-question jurisdiction over state-law claims to those that "really and substantially involv[e] a dispute or controversy respecting the validity, construction or effect of [federal] law." Shulthis v. McDougal, 225 U.S. 561, 569 (1912). This limitation was the ancestor of Justice Cardozo's later explanation that a request to exercise federal-question jurisdiction over a state action calls for a "common-sense accommodation of judgment to [the] kaleidoscopic situations" that present a federal issue, in "a selective process which picks the substantial causes out of the web and lays the other ones aside." Gully v. First Nat. Bank in Meridian, 299 U.S. 109, 117-118 (1936). It has in fact become a constant refrain in such cases that federal jurisdiction demands not only a contested federal issue, but a substantial one, indicating a serious federal interest in claiming the advantages thought to be inherent in a federal forum. E.g., Chicago v. International College of Surgeons, 522 U.S. 156, 164 (1997); *Merrell Dow*, supra, at 814, and n. 12; Franchise Tax Bd. of Cal. v. Construction Laborers Vacation Trust for Southern Cal., 463 U.S. 1, 28 (1983).

But even when the state action discloses a contested and substantial federal question, the exercise of federal jurisdiction is subject to a possible veto. For the federal issue will ultimately qualify for a federal forum only if federal jurisdiction is consistent with congressional judgment about the sound division of labor between state and federal courts governing the application of § 1331. Thus, *Franchise Tax Bd.* explained that the appropriateness of a federal forum to hear an embedded issue could be evaluated only after considering the "welter of issues regarding the interrelation of federal and state authority and the proper management of the federal judicial system." Id. at 8. Because arising-under jurisdiction to hear a state-law claim always raises the possibility of upsetting the state-federal line drawn (or at least assumed) by Congress, the presence of a disputed federal issue and the ostensible importance of a federal forum are never necessarily dispositive; there must always be an assessment of any disruptive portent in exercising federal jurisdiction. See also *Merrell Dow*, supra, at 810.

These considerations have kept us from stating a "single, precise, all-embracing" test for jurisdiction over federal issues embedded in state-law claims between nondiverse parties. Christianson v. Colt Industries Operating Corp., 486 U.S. 800, 821 (1988) (Stevens, J., concurring). We have not kept them out simply because they appeared in state raiment, as Justice Holmes would have done, see *Smith*, supra, at 214 (dissenting opinion), but neither have we treated "federal issue" as a password opening federal courts to any state action embracing a point of federal law. Instead, the question is, does a state-law claim necessarily raise a stated federal issue, actually disputed and substantial, which a federal forum may entertain without disturbing any congressionally approved balance of federal and state judicial responsibilities.

III

A

This case warrants federal jurisdiction. Grable's state complaint must specify "the facts establishing the superiority of [its] claim," Mich. Ct. Rule 3.411(B)(2)(c) (West 2005), and Grable has premised its superior title claim on a failure by the IRS to give it adequate notice, as defined by federal law. Whether Grable was given notice within the meaning of the federal statute is thus an essential element of its quiet title claim, and the meaning of the federal statute is actually in dispute; it appears to be the only legal or factual issue contested in the case. The meaning of the federal tax provision is an important issue of federal law that sensibly belongs in a federal court. The Government has a strong interest in the "prompt and certain collection of delinquent taxes," United States v. Rodgers, 461 U.S. 677, 709 (1983), and the ability of the IRS to satisfy its claims from the property of delinquents requires clear terms of notice to allow buyers like Darue to satisfy themselves that the Service has touched the bases necessary for good title. The Government thus has a direct interest in the availability of a federal forum to vindicate its own administrative action, and buyers (as well as tax delinquents) may find it valuable to come before judges used to federal tax matters. Finally, because it will be the rare state title case that raises a contested matter of federal law, federal jurisdiction to resolve genuine disagreement over federal tax title provisions will portend only a microscopic effect on the federal-state division of labor. See n. 3, infra.

This conclusion puts us in venerable company, quiet title actions having been the subject of some of the earliest exercises of federal-question jurisdiction over state-law claims. . . .[3]

B

Merrell Dow Pharmaceuticals Inc. v. Thompson, 478 U.S. 804 (1986), on which Grable rests its position, is not to the contrary. *Merrell Dow*

3. The quiet title cases also show the limiting effect of the requirement that the federal issue in a state-law claim must actually be in dispute to justify federal-question jurisdiction. In Shulthis v. McDougal, 225 U.S. 561 (1912), this Court found that there was no federal question jurisdiction to hear a plaintiff's quiet title claim in part because the federal statutes on which title depended were not subject to "any controversy respecting their validity, construction, or effect." Id. at 570. As the Court put it, the requirement of an actual dispute about federal law was "especially" important in "suit[s] involving rights to land acquired under a law of the United States," because otherwise "every suit to establish title to land in the central and western states would so arise [under federal law], as all titles in those States are traceable back to those laws." Id. at 569-570.

considered a state tort claim resting in part on the allegation that the defendant drug company had violated a federal misbranding prohibition, and was thus presumptively negligent under Ohio law. Id. at 806. The Court assumed that federal law would have to be applied to resolve the claim, but after closely examining the strength of the federal interest at stake and the implications of opening the federal forum, held federal jurisdiction unavailable. Congress had not provided a private federal cause of action for violation of the federal branding requirement, and the Court found "it would . . . flout, or at least undermine, congressional intent to conclude that federal courts might nevertheless exercise federal-question jurisdiction and provide remedies for violations of that federal statute solely because the violation . . . is said to be a . . . 'proximate cause' under state law." Id. at 812.

Because federal law provides for no quiet title action that could be brought against Darue, Grable argues that there can be no federal jurisdiction here, stressing some broad language in *Merrell Dow* (including the passage just quoted) that on its face supports Grable's position, see Note, Mr. *Smith* Goes to Federal Court: Federal Question Jurisdiction over State Law Claims Post-*Merrell Dow*, 115 Harv. L. Rev. 2272, 2280-2282 (2002) (discussing split in Circuit Courts over private right of action requirement after *Merrell Dow*). But an opinion is to be read as a whole, and *Merrell Dow* cannot be read whole as overturning decades of precedent, as it would have done by effectively adopting the Holmes dissent in *Smith*, see supra, at 5, and converting a federal cause of action from a sufficient condition for federal-question jurisdiction into a necessary one.

In the first place, *Merrell Dow* disclaimed the adoption of any bright-line rule, as when the Court reiterated that "in exploring the outer reaches of § 1331, determinations about federal jurisdiction require sensitive judgments about congressional intent, judicial power, and the federal system." 478 U.S. at 810. The opinion included a lengthy footnote explaining that questions of jurisdiction over state-law claims require "careful judgments," id. at 814, about the "nature of the federal interest at stake," id., at 814, n. 12 (emphasis deleted). And as a final indication that it did not mean to make a federal right of action mandatory, it expressly approved the exercise of jurisdiction sustained in *Smith*, despite the want of any federal cause of action available to *Smith*'s shareholder plaintiff. 478 U.S. at 814, n. 12. *Merrell Dow* then, did not toss out, but specifically retained the contextual enquiry that had been *Smith*'s hallmark for over 60 years. At the end of *Merrell Dow*, Justice Holmes was still dissenting.

Accordingly, *Merrell Dow* should be read in its entirety as treating the absence of a federal private right of action as evidence relevant to, but not dispositive of, the "sensitive judgments about congressional intent" that § 1331 requires. The absence of any federal cause of action affected *Merrell Dow*'s result two ways. The Court saw the fact as worth some consideration in the assessment of substantiality. But its primary importance emerged when the Court treated the combination of no federal cause of action and no preemption of state remedies for misbranding as an important clue to Congress's conception of the scope of jurisdiction to be exercised under § 1331. The Court saw the missing cause of action not as a missing federal door key, always required, but as a missing welcome mat, required in the circumstances, when exercising federal jurisdiction over a state misbranding action would have attracted a horde of original filings and removal cases raising other state claims with embedded federal issues. For if the federal labeling standard without a federal cause of action could get a state claim into federal court, so could any other federal standard without a federal cause of action. And that would have meant a tremendous number of cases.

One only needed to consider the treatment of federal violations generally in garden variety state tort law. "The violation of federal statutes and regulations is commonly given negligence per se effect in state tort proceedings." Restatement (Third) of Torts (proposed final draft) § 14, Comment *a*. See also W. Keeton, D. Dobbs, R. Keeton, & D. Owen, Prosser and Keeton on Torts, § 36, p. 221, n. 9 (5th ed. 1984) ("[T]he breach of a federal statute may support a negligence per se claim as a matter of state law" (collecting authority)). A general rule of exercising federal jurisdiction over state claims resting on federal mislabeling and other statutory violations would thus have heralded a potentially enormous shift of traditionally state cases into federal courts. Expressing concern over the "increased volume of federal litigation," and noting the importance of adhering to "legislative intent," *Merrell Dow* thought it improbable that the Congress, having made no provision for a federal cause of action, would have meant to welcome any state-law tort case implicating federal law "solely because the violation of the federal statute is said to [create] a rebuttable presumption [of negligence] . . . under state law." 478 U.S. at 811-812 (internal quotation marks omitted). In this situation, no welcome mat meant keep out. *Merrell Dow*'s analysis thus fits within the framework of examining the importance of having a federal forum for the issue, and the consistency of such a forum with Congress's intended division of labor between state and federal courts.

As already indicated, however, a comparable analysis yields a different jurisdictional conclusion in this case. Although Congress also indicated ambivalence in this case by providing no private right of action to Grable, it is the rare state quiet title action that involves contested issues of federal law, see n. 3, supra. Consequently, jurisdiction over actions like Grable's would not materially affect, or threaten to affect, the normal currents of litigation. Given the absence of threatening structural consequences and the clear interest the Government, its buyers, and its delinquents have in the availability of a federal forum, there is no good reason to shirk from federal jurisdiction over the dispositive and contested federal issue at the heart of the state-law title claim.

IV

The judgment of the Court of Appeals, upholding federal jurisdiction over Grable's quiet title action, is affirmed.

It is so ordered.

[The concurring opinion of JUSTICE THOMAS is omitted]

Note: Reconciling Grable *and* Merrell Dow

1. *Grable* holds that while the presence of a private cause of action is sufficient to establish federal question jurisdiction, it is not necessary. Instead, the Court endorses the long-standing "contextual enquiry" focusing on whether allowing cases into federal court will upset "the sound division of labor between state and federal courts," or, more precisely, the "congressionally approved balance of federal and state judicial responsibilities." Allowing jurisdiction in *Grable* presented no threat to the federal/state balance, at least in part, the Court reasoned, because state title cases involving disputed issues of federal law are rare (unlike state tort cases involving violations of federal standards like *Merrell Dow*, which are quite common and would therefore overwhelm the federal courts). Does that mean there is a presumption against federal question jurisdiction whenever a federal issue involved in state law claims arises frequently? Shouldn't cases that frequently present important, contested issues of federal law be heard in federal court?

2. Because *Grable* doesn't overrule *Merrell Dow*, it is still important to ask whether an express or implied private cause of action is provided in the federal law invoked as part of a state law claim. When the federal statute expressly creates a cause of action, this is easy work—the statute says private individuals can sue to enforce the rights it protects. But how do we know when Congress has created a private right of action by implication?

In Cannon v. University of Chicago, 441 U.S. 677 (1979) (finding a private right of action under Title IX where plaintiff claimed sex-based exclusion from the university's medical education program), the Court offered the following answer:

> As our recent cases—particularly Cort v. Ash, 422 U.S. 66 (1975)—demonstrate, the fact that a federal statute has been violated and some person harmed does not automatically give rise to a private cause of action in favor of that person. Instead, before concluding that Congress intended to make a remedy available to a special class of litigants, a court must carefully analyze the four factors that *Cort* identifies as indicative of such an intent. Our review of those factors persuades us, however, that the Court of Appeals reached the wrong conclusion and that petitioner does have a statutory right to pursue

her claim that respondents rejected her application on the basis of her sex. After commenting on each of the four factors, we shall explain why they are not overcome by respondents' countervailing arguments.

First, the threshold question under *Cort* is whether the statute was enacted for the benefit of a special class of which the plaintiff is a member. That question is answered by looking to the language of the statute itself.... There would be far less reason to infer a private remedy in favor of individual persons if Congress, instead of drafting Title IX with an unmistakable focus on the benefited class, had written it simply as a ban on discriminatory conduct by recipients of federal funds or as a prohibition against the disbursement of public funds to educational institutions engaged in discriminatory practices.

Unquestionably, therefore, the first of the four factors identified in *Cort* favors the implication of a private cause of action. Title IX explicitly confers a benefit on persons discriminated against on the basis of sex, and petitioner is clearly a member of that class for whose special benefit the statute was enacted.

Second, the *Cort* analysis requires consideration of legislative history. We must recognize, however, that the legislative history of a statute that does not expressly create or deny a private remedy will typically be equally silent or ambiguous on the question. Therefore, in situations such as the present one in which it is clear that federal law has granted a class of persons certain rights, it is not necessary to show an intention to *create* a private cause of action, although an explicit purpose to *deny* such cause of action would be controlling. *Cort,* 422 U.S. at 82 (emphasis in original). But this is not the typical case. Far from evidencing any purpose to *deny* a private cause of action, the history of Title IX rather plainly indicates that Congress intended to create such a remedy.

Title IX was patterned after Title VI of the Civil Rights Act of 1964. Except for the substitution of the word "sex" in Title IX to replace the words "race, color, or national origin" in Title VI, the two statutes use identical language to describe the benefited class. Both statutes provide the same administrative mechanism for terminating federal financial support for institutions engaged in prohibited discrimination. Neither statute expressly mentions a private remedy for the person excluded from participation in a federally funded program. The drafters of Title IX explicitly assumed that it would be interpreted and applied as Title VI had been during the preceding eight years.

In 1972 when Title IX was enacted, the critical language in Title VI had already been construed as creating a private remedy. Most particularly, in 1967, a distinguished panel of the Court of Appeals for the Fifth Circuit squarely decided this issue in an opinion that was repeatedly cited with approval and never questioned during the ensuing five years....

Third, under *Cort,* a private remedy should not be implied if it would frustrate the underlying purpose of the legislative scheme. On the other hand, when that remedy is necessary or at least helpful to the accomplishment of the statutory purpose, the Court is decidedly receptive to its implication under the statute.

Title IX, like its model Title VI, sought to accomplish two related, but nevertheless somewhat different, objectives. First, Congress wanted to avoid the use of federal resources to support discriminatory practices; second, it wanted to provide individual citizens effective protection against those practices. Both of these purposes were repeatedly identified in the debates on the two statutes.

The first purpose is generally served by the statutory procedure for the termination of federal financial support for institutions engaged in discriminatory practices. That remedy is, however, severe and often may not provide an appropriate means of accomplishing the second purpose if merely an isolated violation has occurred. In that situation, the violation might be remedied more efficiently by an order requiring an institution to accept an applicant who had been improperly excluded. Moreover, in that kind of situation it makes little sense to impose on an individual, whose only interest is in obtaining a benefit for herself, or on HEW [Health, Education, and Welfare], the burden of demonstrating that an institution's practices are so pervasively discriminatory that a complete cut-off of federal funding is appropriate. The award of individual relief to a private litigant who has prosecuted her own suit is not only sensible but is also fully consistent with—and in some cases even necessary to—the orderly enforcement of the statute.

The Department of Health, Education, and Welfare, which is charged with the responsibility for administering Title IX, perceives no inconsistency between the private remedy and the public remedy. On the contrary, the agency takes the unequivocal position that the individual remedy will provide effective assistance to achieving the statutory purposes. The agency's position is unquestionably correct.

Fourth, the final inquiry suggested by *Cort* is whether implying a federal remedy is inappropriate because the subject matter involves an area basically of concern to the States. No such problem is raised by a prohibition against invidious discrimination of any sort, including that on the basis of sex. Since the Civil War, the Federal Government and the federal courts have been the "'*primary* and powerful reliances'" in protecting citizens against such discrimination. Steffel v. Thompson, 415 U.S. 452, 464 (1974) (emphasis in original), quoting F. Frankfurter & J. Landis, The Business of the Supreme Court 65 (1928). Moreover, it is the expenditure of federal funds that provides the justification for this particular statutory prohibition. There can be no question but that this aspect of the *Cort* analysis supports the implication of a private federal remedy.

In sum, there is no need in this case to weigh the four *Cort* factors; all of them support the same result. Not only the words and history of Title IX, but also its subject matter and underlying purposes, counsel implication of a cause of action in favor of private victims of discrimination. . . .

3. Since *Grable,* the Court has continued to take a dim view of assertions of federal question jurisdiction where Congress has not explicitly "set out the welcome mat." In Empire Healthchoice Assurance, Inc. v. McVeigh, 547 U.S. 677 (2006), a 5-4 majority of the Court rejected federal question jurisdiction over an action to recover health care payments made to an injured federal employee after the employee prevailed in a tort action against the individuals responsible for his injuries. Although the plaintiff was a private insurer and the cause of action for reimbursement a standard state law

claim, the company provided health benefits to federal employees under a federally regulated contract, the action for reimbursement against the federal employee was authorized by that contract, and the contract required that any reimbursements obtained be returned to the Federal Employees Health Benefits Fund, against which private insurance carriers draw to pay for benefits of enrolled federal employees.

While conceding that "distinctly federal interests are involved," id. at 696, the majority placed great weight on the fact that "Congress has not expressly created a federal right of action enabling insurance carriers like Empire to sue health-care beneficiaries in federal court to enforce reimbursement rights. . . ." Id. at 693. Indeed, the Court drew a further inference against federal question jurisdiction for reimbursement actions from the fact that the statute creating the program expressly recognized a right for beneficiaries to sue in federal court if carriers denied benefits. "Had Congress found it necessary or proper to extend federal jurisdiction further, in particular, to encompass contract-derived reimbursement claims between carriers and insured workers, it would have been easy enough for Congress to say so." Id. at 696. Even the statute's broad federal preemption provision (which states that the contract provisions the government negotiates with private carriers "shall supercede and preempt any State or local law" on questions relating to "the nature or extent of coverage or benefits," id. at 685) was insufficient to convince the Court that Congress intended reimbursement claims to be adjudicated in federal court. Id. at 698. The Court found the case "poles apart from *Grable*," because plaintiff's reimbursement claim was fact-bound, would not aid the resolution of future cases, and "was triggered, not by the action of any federal department, agency, or service, but by the settlement of a personal-injury action launched in state court. . . ." Id. at 700.

Justice Breyer, in dissent, emphasized the incongruity of denying federal question jurisdiction where

> the statute is federal, the program it creates is federal, the program's beneficiaries are federal employees working throughout the country, the Federal Government pays all relevant costs, and the Federal Government receives all relevant payments. The private carrier's only role in this scheme is to administer the health benefits plan for the federal agency in exchange for a fixed service charge.

Id. at 704.

But the majority flatly rejected the view that a case arises under federal law simply because the dispute concerns the application of terms in a federal contract. "[U]niform federal law need not be applied to all questions in federal government litigation, even in cases involving government contracts. The prudent course, we have recognized, is often to adopt the readymade body of state law as the federal rule of decision until Congress strikes a different accommodation." Id. at 691-692. Absent evidence of a "significant conflict . . . between an identifiable federal policy or interest and the operation of state law . . . there is no cause to displace state law, much less to lodge this case in federal court." Id. at 693.

As in *Merrell Dow*, the central inquiry for the majority is whether Congress has expressly created a federal right of action. Does the majority give adequate weight to the interest in uniformity in the law that governs the health benefits of federal employees? Why should it make a difference, in distinguishing *Grable*, that this case involves adjudication of facts, whereas *Grable* presented a fairly pure question of law?

4. What if the four factors in *Cannon* had not all pointed in the same direction? Is there any meaningful way to balance them? Again, the Court's growing unease with the unpredictability of the four-factor test, derived from *Cort*, has led to the decline of the use of the test. Although *Cannon* has not been overruled, the current Supreme Court has been markedly reluctant to construe a federal statute that does not *expressly* authorize a private right of action to implicitly authorize such an action. See, e.g., Stoneridge Inv. Partners v. Scientific-Atlanta, 128 S. Ct. 761 (2008) (concluding that the implied right of action found in the Securities Exchange Act does not extend to customers or suppliers of the investment company); Gonzaga Univ. v. Doe, 536 U.S. 273 (2002) (holding that federal law that requires schools and colleges to protect the privacy of student educational records does not establish a private right of action for improper disclosures); Alexander v. Sandoval, 532 U.S. 275 (2001) (holding that Title VI implies no private right of action to enforce disparate impact regulations); cf. Blessing v. Freestone, 520 U.S. 329 (1997) (setting forth a three-part test for determining whether a federal statute creates an individual right to sue the state). The current Court's reluctance is part of a larger pattern of exalting "plain meaning" over purposive interpretation of statutes and of favoring less aggressive judicial review. What are the strengths of this philosophy? The limitations? If Congress is free to insert an express private right of action if it wants one, should a failure to do so be dispositive under the rule of statutory construction that the mention of one thing excludes another? Does anything in *Grable* alter your views on these questions?

4. Tribal Courts

Often overlooked in studies of jurisdiction is that within the geographical boundaries of the United States is Native American territory, within which tribes have judicial authority along with, in certain circumstances, the states and the federal government. Below, we present a Supreme Court case dealing with the issue of tribal jurisdiction in civil cases. We then turn to an analysis by Judge William C. Canby Jr., outlining the main features of civil tribal court authority. As you read these materials, consider the radically different historical trajectory of tribal jurisdiction relative to our study of civil jurisdiction in state and federal court. Notice, however, that concepts of sovereignty, territoriality, the status of the litigants, and the relationship between the dispute and the forum, though considerably more complex in this context, are still present. For a fuller account of federal Indian law see David H. Getches, Charles F. Wilkinson, & Robert A. Williams Jr., Federal Indian Law: Cases and Materials (5th ed. 2004). For a discussion of the interrelationship of tribal, federal, and state courts, see Judith Resnick, Dependent Sovereigns: Indian Tribes, States and the Federal Courts, 56 U. Chi. L. Rev. 671 (1989).

Williams v. Lee

358 U.S. 217 (1959)

Mr. JUSTICE BLACK delivered the opinion of the Court.

Respondent, who is not an Indian, operates a general store in Arizona on the Navajo Indian Reservation under a license required by federal statute. He brought this action in the Superior Court of Arizona against petitioners, a Navajo Indian and his wife who live on the Reservation, to collect for goods sold them there on credit. Over petitioners' motion to dismiss on the ground that jurisdiction lay in the tribal court rather than in the state court, judgment was entered in favor of respondent. The Supreme Court of Arizona affirmed, holding that since no Act of Congress expressly forbids their doing so Arizona courts are free to exercise jurisdiction over civil suits by non-Indians against Indians though the action arises on an Indian reservation. 83 Ariz. 241. Because this was a doubtful determination of the important question of state power over Indian affairs, we granted certiorari.

Originally the Indian tribes were separate nations within what is now the United States. Through conquest and treaties they were induced to give up complete independence and the right to go to war in exchange for federal protection, aid, and grants of land. When the lands granted lay within States these governments sometimes sought to impose their laws and courts on the Indians. Around 1830 the Georgia Legislature extended its laws to the Cherokee Reservation despite federal treaties with the Indians which set aside this land for them. The Georgia statutes forbade the Cherokees from enacting laws or holding courts and prohibited outsiders from being on the Reservation except with permission of the State Governor. The constitutionality of these laws was tested in Worcester v. State of Georgia, 6 Pet. 515, when the State sought to punish a white man, licensed by the Federal Government to practice as a missionary among the Cherokees, for his refusal to leave the Reservation. Rendering one of his most courageous and eloquent opinions, Chief Justice Marshall held that Georgia's assertion of power was invalid.

> The Cherokee nation . . . is a distinct community, occupying its own territory . . . in which the laws of Georgia can have no force, and which the citizens of Georgia have no right to enter, but with the assent of the Cherokees themselves, or in conformity with treaties, and with the acts of Congress. The whole intercourse between the United States and this nation, is, by our

constitution and laws, vested in the government of the United States. 6 Pet. at page 561.

Despite bitter criticism and the defiance of Georgia which refused to obey this Court's mandate in *Worcester* the broad principles of that decision came to be accepted as law. Over the years this Court has modified these principles in cases where essential tribal relations were not involved and where the rights of Indians would not be jeopardized, but the basic policy of *Worcester* has remained. Thus, suits by Indians against outsiders in state courts have been sanctioned. And state courts have been allowed to try non-Indians who committed crimes against each other on a reservation. But if the crime was by or against an Indian, tribal jurisdiction or that expressly conferred on other courts by Congress has remained exclusive.[5] Essentially, absent governing Acts of Congress, the question has always been whether the state action infringed on the right of reservation Indians to make their own laws and be ruled by them.

Congress has also acted consistently upon the assumption that the States have no power to regulate the affairs of Indians on a reservation. To assure adequate government of the Indian tribes it enacted comprehensive statutes in 1834 regulating trade with Indians and organizing a Department of Indian Affairs. 4 Stat. 729, 735. Not satisfied solely with centralized government of Indians, it encouraged tribal governments and courts to become stronger and more highly organized. See, e.g., the Wheeler-Howard Act, §§ 16, 17, 48 Stat. 987, 988, 25 U.S.C. §§ 476, 477, 25 U.S.C.A. §§ 476, 477. Congress has followed a policy calculated eventually to make all Indians full-fledged participants in American society. This policy contemplates criminal and civil jurisdiction over Indians by any State ready to assume the burdens that go with it as soon as the educational and economic status of the Indians permits the change without disadvantage to them. See H.R. Rep. No. 848, 83d Cong., 1st Sess. 3, 6, 7 (1953). Significantly, when Congress has wished the States to exercise this power it has expressly granted them the jurisdiction which Worcester v. State of Georgia had denied.

No departure from the policies which have been applied to other Indians is apparent in the relationship between the United States and the Navajos. On June 1, 1868, a treaty was signed between General William T. Sherman, for the United States, and numerous chiefs and headmen of the "Navajo nation or tribe of Indians."[7] At the time this document was signed the Navajos were an exiled people, forced by the United States to

5. For example, Congress has granted to the federal courts exclusive jurisdiction upon Indian reservations over 11 major crimes. And non-Indians committing crimes against Indians are now generally tried in federal courts. See 18 U.S.C. §§ 437-439, 1151-1163, 18 U. S.C.A. §§ 437-439, 1151-1163.

7. 15 Stat. 667. In 16 Stat. 566 (1871), Congress declared that no Indian tribe or nation within the United States should thereafter be recognized as an independent power with whom the United States could execute a treaty but provided that this should not impair the obligations of any treaty previously ratified. Thus the 1868 treaty with the Navajos survived this Act.

live crowded together on a small piece of land on the Pecos River in eastern New Mexico, some 300 miles east of the area they had occupied before the coming of the white man. In return for their promises to keep peace, this treaty "set apart" for "their permanent home" a portion of what had been their native country, and provided that no one, except United States Government personnel, was to enter the reserved area. Implicit in these treaty terms, as it was in the treaties with the Cherokees involved in Worcester v. State of Georgia, was the understanding that the internal affairs of the Indians remained exclusively within the jurisdiction of whatever tribal government existed. Since then, Congress and the Bureau of Indian Affairs have assisted in strengthening the Navajo tribal government and its courts. See the Navajo-Hopi Rehabilitation Act of 1950, § 6, 64 Stat. 46, 25 U.S.C. § 636, 25 U.S.C.A. § 636; 25 CFR §§ 11.1 through 11.87NH. The Tribe itself has in recent years greatly improved its legal system through increased expenditures and better-trained personnel. Today the Navajo Courts of Indian Offenses exercise broad criminal and civil jurisdiction which covers suits by outsiders against Indian defendants. No Federal Act has given state courts jurisdiction over such controversies. In a general statute Congress did express its willingness to have any State assume jurisdiction over reservation Indians if the State Legislature or the people vote affirmatively to accept such responsibility. To date, Arizona has not accepted jurisdiction, possibly because the people of the State anticipate that the burdens accompanying such power might be considerable.

There can be no doubt that to allow the exercise of state jurisdiction here would undermine the authority of the tribal courts over Reservation affairs and hence would infringe on the right of the Indians to govern themselves. It is immaterial that respondent is not an Indian. He was on the Reservation and the transaction with an Indian took place there. The cases in this Court have consistently guarded the authority of Indian governments over their reservations. Congress recognized this authority in the Navajos in the Treaty of 1868, and has done so ever since. If this power is to be taken away from them, it is for Congress to do it.

Reversed.

William C. Canby Jr., American Indian Law

124-128, 131-133, 138-141, 199-208 *(2004)*

Chapter VII

A. *Introduction*

The most complex problems in the field of Indian Law arise in jurisdictional disputes among the federal government, the tribes and the states.

To resolve those problems it is essential to know the basic limits of jurisdiction of each of the three contending powers. . . .

B. Indian Country

After many years of change and development, the concept of Indian country was given its present definition by Congress in 1948. 18 U.S.C. § 1151 provides:

> [T]he term "Indian country," as used in this chapter, means (a) all land within the limits of any Indian reservation under the jurisdiction of the United States government, notwithstanding the issuance of any patent, and including rights-of-way running through the reservation, (b) all dependent Indian communities within the borders of the United States whether within the original or subsequently acquired territory thereof, and whether within or without the limits of a state, and (c) all Indian allotments, the Indian titles to which have not been extinguished, including rights-of-way running through the same.

Although this definition is for purposes of the criminal code, it is also used for civil jurisdiction. . . .

Subsection (a) includes all of the territory within an Indian reservation. It is most important to note that even land owned by non-Indians in fee simple . . . is still "Indian country" if it is within the exterior boundaries of an Indian reservation. There exist within many reservations large tracts of land long since settled by non-Indians, and even entire towns incorporated by non-Indians under state law, but all of those tracts and towns are Indian country for purposes of jurisdiction. . . .

Although the mere opening up of a reservation for non-Indian settlement does not remove the newly settled lands from Indian country, a congressional decision to abandon the reservation status of those lands does. In cases where Congress has opened reservations to heavy settlement, there is often a difficult question of fact whether the intent was to permit non-Indians to live and own land on a reservation or whether it was to extinguish a portion of the reservation (to "diminish" the reservation) and open it for settlement as public, non-Indian land. . . .

In Solem v. Bartlett, 465 U.S. 463 (1984), the Court . . . stated that . . . "[e]xplicit reference to cession or other language evidencing the present and total surrender of all tribal interests" was strongly indicative of intent to diminish, and created an almost insurmountable presumption when combined with a commitment to compensate the tribe for the opened land. 465 U.S. at 470-71. Even without language of cession, a diminishment could be found from other factors, although it would not lightly be implied. The other factors were the manner in which the transaction was arranged or considered at the time; subsequent treatment of the area by the concerned governments; and later demographic consequences of the opening. . . .

Subsection (b) of 18 U.S.C. § 1151 . . . is a codification of the Supreme Court's holding in United States v. Sandoval, 231 U.S. 28 (1913). That case involved the New Mexico Pueblos, which held their land in fee simple under Spanish grants and which were not formally designated as reservations. The Court held that the Pueblo lands were Indian country nevertheless, since the Pueblos were wards dependent upon the federal government's guardianship. . . .

Subsection (c) of § 1151 is self-explanatory; it includes within Indian country any allotment that is either still in trust . . . or is owned in fee by an Indian with a restriction on alienation in favor of the United States. . . . Such allotments are Indian country whether or not they are located within a reservation.

C. *Historical Background of Jurisdiction in Indian Country*

In colonial days, the Indian territory was entirely the province of the tribes, and they had jurisdiction in fact and theory over all persons and subjects present there. Shortly after the Revolution, federal jurisdiction was extended to non-Indians committing crimes against Indians in Indian territory, as part of the overall federal policy of providing a buffer between the non-Indian and Indian populations. Federal jurisdiction was further extended in 1817 to cover crimes by both Indians and non-Indians in Indian country with the notable exception of crimes by Indians against Indians; the latter were left entirely to be dealt with by tribal law or custom. . . .

One of the basic premises underlying the constitutional allocation of Indian affairs to the federal government was that the states could not be relied upon to deal fairly with the Indians. Severe limitations upon the exercise of state power in Indian territory therefore seemed implicit in the nation's early Indian policy, but the extent of these limitations was not dealt with authoritatively until John Marshall's decision in the second of the famous Cherokee cases, Worcester v. Georgia, 31 U.S. 515 (1832). At the heart of the case lay Georgia's attempt to exercise total jurisdiction within Cherokee territory—to divide that territory among several Georgia counties, to apply Georgia law to all persons within the area, and to prohibit the Cherokees from exercising any governmental powers of their own. Chief Justice Marshall's opinion for the Court totally rejected Georgia's attempt, and characterized Cherokee territory as one "in which the laws of Georgia can have no force. . . . " 31 U.S. at 561. . . .

For fifty years, Marshall's view that state law and power could not intrude into Indian country held sway. Then a major change occurred in United States v. McBratney, 104 U.S. 621 (1881). In that case a non-Indian had been convicted in federal circuit court of murdering another non-Indian on the Ute reservation in Colorado. The Supreme Court, in a highly doubtful construction of the applicable federal statutes, first held that the federal court could exercise criminal jurisdiction only over places within the exclusive jurisdiction of the federal government. If the state had any jurisdiction over this crime, then the federal court necessarily had none. The state of Colorado must have jurisdiction, the Court ruled, because Congress had admitted it to the union "upon an equal footing with the original States" and no exception was made for jurisdiction over the Ute reservation. The laws of Colorado therefore extend throughout the state, including the Ute reservation, insofar as they relate to crimes by non-Indians against non-Indians. The federal conviction was reversed, and the lower court was directed to deliver the defendant to state authorities. . . .

In both theoretical and practical terms . . . the decision[] had an enormous and complicating impact on the law of jurisdiction in Indian country, for they made it impossible ever after to deal with questions of state jurisdiction on a purely geographical basis. Marshall's rule in *Worcester* that state laws can have no force in Indian country had several virtues, but perhaps the greatest was simplicity. When tribal and state powers were viewed in purely territorial terms, it was necessary only to discover the location of a transaction or occurrence in order to determine which of two competing systems of law and courts had control over it. McBratney [and its progeny], on the other hand, require not only a determination of location, but also an inquiry into the nature of the subject matter and the identity of the parties involved in the case. They open the door to judicial balancing of state and tribal interests whenever arguable questions of jurisdiction arise. . . .

F. *Present Division of Civil Jurisdiction in Indian Country*

2.1 Tribal Civil Jurisdiction

a. General Civil Litigation

The civil jurisdiction of tribal courts, unlike their criminal jurisdiction, is subject to no statutory limit on the relief courts may grant. . .

With regard to subject matter, tribal courts have exclusive jurisdiction over a suit by any person against an Indian for a claim arising in Indian country. Williams v. Lee, 358 U.S. 217 (1959). Necessarily, then, the tribe has exclusive jurisdiction over disputes between tribal members arising on the reservation. It also has exclusive jurisdiction over wholly internal tribal subject matter, such as membership disputes. The exclusive jurisdiction recognized by Williams v. Lee had always been assumed to extend to suits against Indians from recognized tribes other than the one upon whose reservation the claim arose, but the Supreme Court in recent years has rendered this assumption unsafe. . . . In Washington v. Confederated Tribes of the Colville Indian Reservation, 447 U.S. 134 (1980), the Court permitted a state to impose a sales tax on Indians making purchases on a reservation other than their own. The Court stated that, "[f]or most practical purposes those Indians stand on the same footing as non-Indians resident on the reservation." 447 U.S. at 161. Then, in Strate v. A-1 Contractors, 520 U.S. 438 (1997), the Court held that a tribal court had no jurisdiction over a dispute between "nonmembers" arising out of a vehicle accident on a state right-of-way within the reservation. In *Strate*, the nonmembers were non-Indians, but the Court talked only of nonmembers and tribal members in drawing a line of adjudicatory jurisdiction. . . .

In addition to their exclusive jurisdiction over reservation-based claims against tribal members, tribal courts also probably have the power to adjudicate claims against tribal members domiciled or present within their territory even though those claims arose outside of Indian country. Many tribes, however, have chosen not to exercise such jurisdiction.

Much recent litigation has been concerned with the power of tribal courts to entertain claims against non-Indian (or nonmember) defendants that arise in Indian country. For years the tribes made no attempt to exercise that power by compulsion; some tribal codes still provide for such jurisdiction only when the non-Indian defendant stipulates to it. Recently, however, numbers of tribes have revised their codes to permit their tribal courts generally to exercise jurisdiction over non-Indians for reservation-based claims. A non-Indian defendant contested such jurisdiction in National Farmers Union Ins. Cos. v. Crow Tribe, 471 U.S. 845 (1985). The Supreme Court did not resolve the question, but deferred to the tribal court so that it could determine its jurisdiction in the first instance. . . .

[The Crow Tribe decision, along with language in Iowa Mutual Ins. Co. v. LaPlante, 480 U.S. 9 (1987),] encouraged many tribes, and numbers of lower courts, to assume that tribal courts could exercise general civil jurisdiction over all reservation-based litigation, particularly if one of the parties was the tribe or a tribal member. The seeds of a narrower view had already been planted, however, in Montana v. United States, 450 U.S. 544 (1981). *Montana* held that an Indian tribe had no authority to regulate hunting and fishing by non-Indians on non-Indian-owned fee land within the reservation. The Court stated that the tribe's domestic dependent sovereignty extended only to self-government and the control of internal relations. Hunting and fishing by non-Indians on non-Indian fee lands was neither. *Montana* at one point went considerably farther, however, and announced a general proposition that "the inherent sovereign powers of an Indian tribe do not extend to the activities of nonmembers of the tribe." The only exceptions were (1) that a tribe could regulate "activities of nonmembers who enter consensual relationships with the tribe or its members," as through commercial dealings, and (2) that a tribe could exercise "civil authority over the conduct of non-Indians on fee lands within its reservation when that conduct threatens or has some direct effect on the political integrity, the economic security, or the health or welfare of the tribe." *Montana*, 450 U.S. at 565-66.

The Supreme Court carried *Montana* a step farther in 1997, when it held that a tribal court had no jurisdiction over litigation between nonmembers arising out of a vehicle accident on a state highway within a reservation. Strate v. A-1 Contractors, 520 U.S. 438 (1997). The Court narrowed the statement in *LaPlante* that civil jurisdiction over non-Indian activities within a reservation "presumptively lies in the tribal courts"; that statement, according to *Strate,* meant nothing more than that the tribal court presumptively had jurisdiction over those non-Indian activities that the tribe could regulate under *Montana*. . . . The Court also stated that the second *Montana* exception should be read narrowly, in light of *Montana*'s description of tribal authority as the power to punish tribal offenders, to determine membership, and to regulate the domestic relations and inheritance for members.

Strate was the forerunner of further restrictions on tribal jurisdiction over nonmembers. . . .

Atkinson Trading Co. v. Shirley, 532 U.S. 645 (2001), held that the tribe had no power to tax hotel occupancy by non-Indians on fee land within the Navajo reservation. The Court clearly regarded *Montana* not as an exception to presumed power of a tribe over its reservation but as a "general rule that Indian tribes lack civil authority over nonmembers on non-Indian fee land." Id. at 654. *Montana*'s exceptions were narrowly construed lest they "swallow the rule." Id. at 655. Then, in Nevada v. Hicks, 533 U.S. 353 (2001), the Court for the first time applied to trust land *Montana*'s presumption against tribal authority over nonmembers. The Court held that the tribe had no power to regulate a search by state officers investigating off-reservation crime even though the search was of an Indian-owned residence on tribal trust land. . . . [T]he tribal court could not entertain a suit against [the state officers] brought by the offended tribal member.

With the *Montana* "rule" broadly applicable throughout reservations, the extent of tribal regulation and tribal court jurisdiction over nonmembers is subject to great limitation. . . .

Hicks also held that tribal courts did not qualify as courts of general jurisdiction, which would permit them to entertain general federal civil claims such as those arising under 42 U.S.C. § 1983. . . .

Frequently, when a nonmember (usually a non-Indian) is sued in tribal court, he or she will bring an action in federal court either to challenge the tribal court's jurisdiction or to attempt to litigate the underlying dispute in federal court. In such cases, federal courts have regularly abstained or stayed their proceedings . . . to permit the tribal court to determine in the first instance whether it has jurisdiction. Thus a party seeking in federal court to challenge a tribal court's jurisdiction must first exhaust tribal remedies.

---

5. Venue

Selecting the proper forum for a dispute also involves the rules of venue. Unlike personal jurisdiction or subject matter jurisdiction restrictions on the plaintiff's choice of forum, venue restrictions are purely statutory and not constitutionally mandated. The rules of venue attempt to allocate court business in a reasonable and efficient manner, mindful of the interests of the litigants and the judicial system.

The primary sources of venue requirements in the federal courts are 28 U.S.C. §§ 1391 and 1392. There also are specialty venue statutes for particular types of actions, such as shareholder's derivative suits. See, e.g., 28 U.S.C. § 1401. Note that § 1391 was amended in 1990, so that cases decided before that date may be inapplicable.

At this point we deal with venue in its simplest form: choosing a court within a state's boundaries. More complicated issues, and more aggressive gaming, occur with the possibility of venue transfers among federal courts in a multistate system. We deal with these statutes—28 U.S.C. §§ 1404 and 1406—in Chapter 6. See also Hart & Wechsler, The Federal Courts and the Federal System 1515 (5th ed. 2003).

Applying the Basic Federal Venue Statutes

Read 28 U.S.C. §§ 1391 and 1392 and Fed. R. Civ. P. 12(b)(3) and (h)(1) carefully, and then attempt to answer the following questions:

1. Who can object to improper venue? Can the court raise this issue *sua sponte*, or is this solely a defendant-centered concern?

2. How does a party raise an objection to improper venue? See Fed. R. Civ. P. 12(b)(3) and (h)(1). What happens if the defendant fails to make the objection in the answer or pre-answer motion? What happens if the defendant makes a timely motion and it is granted? Return to this last question after you have studied the venue transfer statutes, 28 U.S.C. §§ 1404 and 1406.

3. Note that where a person or a corporation "resides" for purposes of the venue statute may differ from "domicile" for purposes of determining diversity jurisdiction. For an individual, residence and domicile typically are the same. But for a corporation, they are not.

A defendant corporation "resides" in any judicial district in which it is subject to personal jurisdiction. If the state has more than one district, then each district is treated like a separate state for determining this.

A plaintiff or defendant corporation is "domiciled" in the state(s) where it is incorporated *and* where it has its principal place of business ("dual citizenship").

4. Where would venue be proper in the following cases? If you would need additional information to determine this, what would it be?

a. *P*, a resident of California, sues *D*(1), a resident of the northern district of Illinois, and *D*(2), a resident of the southern district of Illinois, in federal court. The sole basis for federal court jurisdiction is diversity. The action concerns a car accident that occurred in southern Illinois.

b. *P*, a resident of California, sues *D*(1), who lives in Arkansas, and *D*(2), who lives in Tennessee, in federal court. The action is based on federal question jurisdiction and concerns a contract that was entered into and executed in California.

c. *P* is a corporation that is incorporated in Delaware and does business throughout the northeast. *D* is a corporation that is incorporated in Maine and that has its principal place of business in Maine. It does business solely in Maine, Vermont, and New Hampshire. *P* sues *D* in federal court, based solely on diversity, regarding the sale by *D* to *P* of a defective machine. The machine was shipped from Maine to *P*'s plant in Vermont.

Review Problem: Choosing Systems in Retrospect

Now that you have mastered the territorial restrictions on forum selection (personal jurisdiction and venue) as well as the power restrictions imposed by the subject matter jurisdiction rules, you should test your skills by answering the following questions based on the hypothetical of the "Troubled Young Man."

> A patient of a San Francisco-based psychiatrist injures his father, an Arizona resident, in Arizona. The father wishes to sue the California psychiatrist on the theory that she had a duty to warn the Arizonan of her patient's foreseeable violent acts toward his father. All therapy took place in California. The psychiatrist knew that her patient was going to visit his father in Arizona and increased his medication to ease the inevitable stress of family encounters.

1. Would a state court have subject matter jurisdiction?
2. Would a federal district court have subject matter jurisdiction, assuming there is an adequate amount in controversy?
3. Where would personal jurisdiction over Dr. Froid be found?
4. Assuming that a federal court would have jurisdiction to hear the dispute, where within the federal system would venue be proper?
5. What law would govern Dr. Froid's liability—federal or state?

2 *Constructing a Civil Lawsuit*

Problem Case: The Due Process Game (Part Three)

Recall the due process game, which we encountered in Chapter 1. Assume that the student was expelled without the requisite notice and opportunity to be heard, and now wishes to file an action in federal court complaining that the expulsion was unlawful. What do you imagine that the complaint would contain? Which of the following do you think should be included in the complaint?

1) All facts concerning the expulsion. (What should be included in "all facts"?)
2) The specific law that is violated by the expulsion.
3) The basis for federal court power to hear the matter.
4) The specific relief requested, e.g., money damages or injunctive relief.

What are the costs of demanding that a plaintiff include this information? Of allowing the plaintiff to plead less information?

Do you think that the plaintiff should also be allowed to include information about another, unrelated matter that involves one or all of the same defendants? What if, for example, the administrator had hit the student's car in the school parking lot? Could this tort action be included in the due process lawsuit against the same administrator?

Assume that the student alleges only the due process violation. Assume also that the defendant believes that the facts are not as the student alleges, that the student has no legal right to recover even if the facts as alleged are true, and that since the time for complaining about the matter has passed, the lawsuit is too late. Should the defendant be able to make all three objections, or must he choose one and stick to it?

What if, after the complaint and defendant's response have been filed, additional facts come to light that change the facts alleged in the complaint? Should the plaintiff be allowed to amend the complaint? Required to do so?

In the following sections, we will consider all of these questions from a historical and a contemporary perspective. As the materials will explain, attitudes about pleadings and the amount of work pleadings should do to narrow and resolve the claims have changed dramatically over time. At one point, pleadings, which dominated the procedural world, were expected to produce one and only one issue for trial. In 1938, however, the law of federal pleading rejected this view of the paper conversation and liberalized the rules. Plaintiffs were allowed merely to state the basic facts of the dispute, in order to put the defendant on notice of the nature of the case. Gone were the days of artful pleaders and the triumph of arcane pleading form over litigation substance.

The changes produced their own forms of abuse, however, including a perceived rise in insubstantial claims that cost defendants time and money, as defendants no longer could rely on the burdens of pleading to weed out the frivolous pleaders. As of this writing, proceduralists remain divided about the proper role of pleading in establishing the contours of a lawsuit. Indeed, the divisions may be sharper than ever, and Congress and the courts have begun to revise the balance struck in 1938. Plaintiffs, of course, prefer less strict rules in order to move the case forward without the burden of elaborate and expensive prediscovery fact-finding. Defendants prefer rules that require plaintiffs to uncover facts that support their claims before discovery and before the defendant must answer these claims. No rule, as we shall see, is costless or uncontroversial among the lawyers who know best the litigation implications of pleading obligations.

We begin with the history of pleading, which remains relevant to modern-day pleading in three ways: first, some modern terminology and practices reflect the older locutions; second, the right to trial by jury in civil cases depends in part on whether the right in question would have been heard on the "law" or "equity" side of the old courts of England; and third, knowing the history of modern pleading gives the modern lawyer a richer sense of the problems the new rules hoped to cure. This history also may be an important corrective to some contemporary reformers' claims about the benefits of tailoring pleading rules to particular substantive rights.

A. A BRIEF HISTORY OF CIVIL PROCEDURE

In modern usage, pleadings are the documents that initially frame a lawsuit: the plaintiff's complaint, the defendant's answer, and possibly the plaintiff's reply to new matters raised in the answer. There has long been considerable controversy about the function of pleadings—whether they serve merely to notify the court and the parties that a legal dispute is beginning, to screen frivolous cases out of the system, or to define and limit the issues for trial. Some background on the ancestry of today's pretrial procedure aids the understanding of the cycles of reform and reaction that characterize the practice of pleading.

1. Common Law Procedure

a. The Pleading Process

The first pleadings were oral exchanges in court between the parties. The exchanges quickly came to adhere to established patterns; thus, in debt, the plaintiff would orally swear: "In the name of the living God, as I money demand, so have I lack of that which [defendant's name] promised me when I mine to him sold." To this the defendant would make an appropriate, equally formulaic response.

The first lawyers entered the picture as assistants to the parties in their oral pleas to the court. Early in the Norman period, it became the custom to make a record of oral altercations by entering them on the plea roll, which was maintained by a clerk. In 1256, Bracton's Note Book was published. This study of the plea rolls increased attention to the written words. Plucknett explains the natural result of this new focus:

> [C]ounsel no longer directed their attention solely to the oral words; on the contrary, it is plain that their great concern was to get some things on the record, and to keep other things off. Pleading was therefore the art of saying things in court in such a way as to produce a particular result on the roll. . . .
>
> . . . It demanded great learning and still greater skill from the serjeants [lawyers] for they were in effect settling the pleadings in the heat of battle, and in the presence of the adversary. On the other hand, there was the substantial advantage that the court joined in the discussion, which thus sometimes became a round-table conference of judges and counsel who joined in trying to find a way of pleading a cause which would bring out the real points. . . .
>
> Then [in the fifteenth century] a change took place: instead of leaving it to the clerks to enroll a case in accordance with their own ideas of the way it was pleaded, the legal profession provided the clerks with drafts of the entries they desired to have. . . . By this means the lawyers secured absolute control of what was written on the rolls. . . .

Theodore Plucknett, A Concise History of the Common Law 405-407 (5th ed. 1956).

Over the centuries two basic rules that were originally sensible and straightforward were elaborated until common law pleading became arcane and accessible only to the most skilled. The first rule was that the plea must abide the writ. The writs were a kind of order, or form of action, that the King's courts issued to begin a suit. Even if a plaintiff alleged a good case under, for instance, the writ of trespass, his suit would be thrown out of court if he pleaded some aspect of moral fault; this could be included only in a pleading under the writ of trespass on the case. The rigidity of the writ system meant that legal fictions arose as parties sought to bring the facts of their cases within established writs. At the same time that such fictions abounded, new forms of action were devised to meet society's increasing complexity.

The second rule was that the pleading exchange must proceed until a single issue emerged. Roy McDonald, Alternative Pleading, 48 Mich. L. Rev. 311, 314-317 (1950), explains:

> As is well known, the unique object of classical common law pleading was to reduce litigation to a single issue of law or fact. The dominant precept which had been developed to effectuate this objective was that the "facts" be alleged with certainty. Three subordinate rules—that pleadings not be duplicitous, or repugnant, or in the alternative—tended to the "chief object . . . that the parties be brought to issue, and that the issue be material, single and certain in its quality."[10] Apologists had supported the requirement with argument as to economy and expedience: the decision of one material issue would dispose of the controversy, so it was unnecessary to consider more. This, of course, was true, provided one did not inquire too closely into the justice of the decision. . . .
>
> . . . The classical common law rule was that so long as new matter responsive to the immediately preceding pleading of the opponent could be introduced without departure, the exchange continued, each pleading limited to its single issue, until the parties ultimately clashed head-on at a single point.
>
> Such rules were by their very nature incompatible with alternative pleadings. Accordingly, alternatives were prohibited upon the theory that the party must take a stand and notify his opponent with precision as to his contention. Neither party could assert in a single count or defense two theories, either of which independently would sustain his claim or defense, and each of which would require a separate response. . . .

By the early eighteenth century, several methods emerged to avoid the hazards of single-issue pleading. Most notable among these were the "common counts," which were pattern pleadings used for simple contract actions, known as assumpsit. For instance, under the "indebitatus" count, the plaintiff could simply state that at the defendant's request he had furnished him with goods and services at an agreed price, that the plaintiff had demanded the price, and defendant had not paid. Similarly, in the "in quantum valebant" count the plaintiff alleged that he had delivered goods for which no price was agreed upon; the "in quantum meruit" count was used for services performed where no price was agreed.

But ease in pleading was the exception, and by the nineteenth century, legal technicalities had earned their still-surviving bad name. In an ironic twist, the first reform efforts made matters worse by insisting on even greater precision in pleadings. The Hilary Rules of 1834 had the effect of increasing the number of dispositions based on shortcomings in the pleadings, rather than permanently settling pleading rules promptly with a minimal number of cases being decided on the basis of pleading technicalities, as proponents of the reform claimed would happen.

10. Stephen, Pleading, 5th Am. Ed., p. 135 (1845).

b. The Writ System

No overview of the history of pleading would be complete without a glance at the type of actions covered by the common law writs and their relationship to modern substantive law. The principal writs were those of debt, covenant, account, assumpsit (special and general), trespass, trespass on the case, ejectment, trover, detinue, and replevin.

Each writ had its own procedure, as we have seen, and each covered its own distinct form of legal wrong. The distinctions between some of them—such as trespass and trespass on the case—were rather fine, however, making writ selection a sometimes complex decision that would doom the pleading if made incorrectly. These precursors to your modern common law subjects—contracts, property, and torts—included actions to recover property, breach of contracts (express and implied in law or fact), assault and battery, theft of personal property, trespass onto real property, negligence, injuries to reputation, nuisances, actions to try title to land, actions to recover damages for conversion of or injury to personal property, and actions to recover property wrongfully taken or detained.

In the mighty writ of trespass and its offshoot—trespass on the case—lie the history of much of modern tort and property law. The writ of assumpsit gave rise to much of modern contract law. Students may want to examine their casebooks in all of these courses to see whether they contain early English cases involving trespass, case, or assumpsit. The historical distinction between trespass and trespass on the case, to take one important example, is the root of the modern distinction between intentional torts and negligence.

Perhaps the most interesting, even amusing, bit of writ history is that of ejectment. It underwent a series of modifications that transformed ejectment from a literal matter of physical ejectment of a hostile person on the owner's land, to a staged performance (with live "actors"—so-called John Does and Richard Roes engaged to act out for the landowner the steps necessary to bring the matter of trying his title to the land before the court), to fictitious allegations of entry onto the land, lease, and ouster without an actual entry or ouster.

As the following excerpt from Professor William E. Nelson's study of procedural reform in post-Revolutionary Massachusetts describes, the writ system made for an exceedingly complex pleading regime. And the complexities generated resentment, especially among farmers and other working class people who believed that the legal system should be accessible to the common citizen. Byzantine pleading procedures, in their view, rendered justice illusory. Many decisions turned on technicalities rather than the merits, leaving litigants without redress for wrongs while enhancing not only the power and purse of lawyers but the undemocratic authority of judge-made law inherited from England:

> Although the [state] Constitution of 1780 had enjoined that "every subject . . . ought to obtain right and justice freely," the costs of litigation were

such that many agrarian debtors felt that right and justice were unobtainable. To them "judicial proceeding[s]" appeared so "intricate" that their usual outcome was only "to throw an honest man out of three quarters of his property" if he put his case to law. Agrarian leaders were determined "to vindicate the rights of the poor against the aggressions of power and violence."

The reform movement was in part directed against the legal profession. The less thoughtful reformers argued that the legal system's expense resulted from a conspiracy among lawyers "to perplex and embarrass every judicial proceeding . . . [and] to delay every process. . . ." Their remedy was to abolish lawyers and have every litigant plead his own cause. Some concessions were made to this antiprofessionalism during the 1780s: litigants were granted permission by statute to plead their own cause, they were forbidden to employ more than two attorneys simultaneously in any one case, and they were permitted to employ as attorneys persons not admitted to the bar. But then the bar regrouped and fought vigorously and successfully to resist any further concessions and to erode those already granted. . . . The antiprofessional movement of the 1780s, in short, was simply overwhelmed by a professional countermovement. . . .

[Another] way the reformers sought to make justice freely and equally accessible was by simplifying the rules of procedure. They contended that "the state of pleading in this Commonwealth [had become such] that an honest man . . . [could] not obtain" right and justice "without being obliged to employ a lawyer, at a great expense. . . . " "Artful men in England," they explained, "ha[d] so entangled the mode of managing a cause with the nice distinction of special pleas (and . . . [the courts in Massachusetts had] unfortunately adopted the pernicious practice) that in short justice . . . [could] scarcely be obtained unless it [was] dearly purchased." "[I]nstead of obtaining justice 'freely,' 'completly,' and 'promptly,'" many litigants saw their "causes . . . carried through every tedious labyrinth" and juries "hindered from coming to a speedy decision of a cause, by the labouring pleadings" of the common law.

The reformers sought to abandon technical and outmoded pleading forms and to have judgments rendered "according to the merits of the case. . . . " "[P]leas," it was urged, should "be simple, and the clerk [should be] authorized to write them in short form for each of the parties." There was no "occasion or need . . . of all the parade of written pleas, replications, rejoinders, etc., etc. in common trials at law," since all that a court needed to know was "the fact, the law, and the equity of the case"; then the issue of causes would not "depend upon adroitness of advocates . . . [but] upon their intrinsic justice." . . .

Although the system of common law pleading was not the principal cause of the high cost of litigation, it was a factor. . . .

Under the common law system a plaintiff was required to name the form of action under which he was bringing his suit. If he did "not name . . . his plea," "give any name to this his Action," or "declare . . . in an action of Debt or Trespass on the Case, or in any other Action or Plea known in the Register or in the Law," his writ would be abated. Writs were also abated when a plaintiff brought the wrong cause of action—trespass, for example, instead of a case for obstructing the flow of water to a milldam; case instead of debt on a bond; debt instead of trespass for a statutory penalty for cutting the plaintiff's trees; debet and detinet, a variety of debt, instead of detinet only on an administrator's bond.

Each form of action, moreover, had its own form of general denial, so called because it imported an absolute and complete denial by a defendant of each and every allegation in a plaintiff's declaration. . . . If the defendant pleaded the wrong general issue, as not guilty to a plea of assumpsit, or owes nothing to a plea of trespass . . . , that he was a Son of Liberty and therefore ought not to be sued, or, as John Adams colorfully pleaded in two cases, "Law is perfect reason without passion" and "the Law of nature is common to brutes & men," then judgment would be given on demurrer for the plaintiff.

If a defendant did not wish to plead the general issue, he could plead specially. . . . Special pleas could be of a great variety, depending upon the circumstances of a defendant's case. . . .

The response to a special plea by a defendant was a replication by the plaintiff, traversing or confessing and avoiding the special plea. That could be followed by a rejoinder by the defendant, followed in turn by a surrejoinder, a rebutter, and a surrebutter. A number of technical rules made special pleading a supremely refined and difficult art. First, a plea was required to be single—that is, it could contain only one factual allegation; moreover, a party could set forth only one plea, unless he obtained the court's permission to plead double. Second, a party's plea had to answer his opponent's allegations in every material point. A plea also had to be direct, positive, and nonargumentative, certain as to time, place, and persons, capable of trial and properly averred in the common form—"and this he is ready to verify." A final rule was that the defendant could not put in a special plea that amounted merely to a denial of all or part of the plaintiff's charge but had to advance some new fact not mentioned in the declaration. . . .

After the plaintiff had selected the correct writ, he was required to have it served on the defendant . . . [and the] plaintiff also had to be certain that all the parties who ought to be joined in the litigation were joined and that the parties who ought not to be joined were not. Rules on this subject were quite technical. Joint obligors and joint promissors, for example, both had to be joined in a suit on their promise. . . . Tenants in common were also required to join in land pleas and in personal actions such as trespass, assumpsit, and nuisance. Joint bailors, on the other hand, did not have to sue their bailee together, and agents were not required to be joined in suits against their principals. . . .

The most technical of all the pleading rules was one requiring parties to litigation to be precisely identified. Pursuant to this requirement, civil and criminal actions were dismissed when there was no person by the exact name and description given the named defendant. Civil and criminal actions were similarly dismissed for failing to state the full name of a party to the writ or for misspelling or otherwise misstating a party's name—either his Christian name or his surname. There was an even greater need for certainty in naming parties in suits involving corporate litigants, and here too writs were abated for misnomers.

In addition to making a plaintiff give all parties their proper names, the law required him to state correctly without any misspelling the town and county in which all parties resided. . . . [T]he plaintiff also had to state correctly the addition, that is the occupation or social rank, of both plaintiff and defendant. Failure to do so was ground for abatement of a writ. . . . More suits were abated or dismissed for improper additions than on any other ground, and much elaborate learning proliferated on the subject of additions: one finds the bench and bar of the Superior Court debating, for instance, whether the description of a blacksmith should include a nailer, and whether a militia captain was a gentleman by way of commission, reputation, or courtesy. . . .

Even before Shay's Rebellion, in which high litigation costs, high taxes, and lack of currency were the chief complaints, the courts and the legal profession had begun to take hesitant steps toward reform. . . . Reform occurred piecemeal, as individual lawyers, either lacking precise knowledge of common law pleading rules or seeking some strategic advantage in litigation at hand, entered pleas that were not in proper form. . . . The courts, sensing the validity of reformers' complaints about the undue expense of technical pleading rules and seeing that reduced adherence to form threatened no tangible interest of the law or of the legal profession, often decided to permit counsel either to ignore or to amend the informality. As various decisions of this sort cumulated over time, the ancient system of common law pleading was destroyed, and new rules of pleading emerged in its place. . . .

By the early nineteenth century, then, the emerging concern in pleading was with substance, not with form. This concern was of great significance, for it compelled the bench and the bar to think about law in substantive categories, such as "tort" and "contract," rather than in the old procedural categories of trespass, assumpsit, and the like.

William E. Nelson, Americanization of the Common Law: The Impact of Legal Change on Massachusetts Society, 1760-1830, at 69-78 (1975).

Nelson emphasizes that the transition away from the writ system was not without "consequences that were unforeseen and that required compensatory modification of other rules of law." Id. at 86. These problems are worth enumerating here, as you will see that they resurface in our study of the modern pleading rules that emerged from the nineteenth-century rejection of the writ system.

One advantage of common law pleading is that in addition to giving parties notice of the essence of each others' claims it narrows the issues that can arise upon trial by requiring the parties to select before trial, at least in part, the legal theory they plan to pursue. Particularly if the parties have engaged in special pleading, the issues on which litigation will turn are precisely identified before trial begins. With the abolition of common law pleading, issues were no longer formulated and defined before trial but during the very course of trial, as the parties offered evidence and made legal contentions on the basis of that evidence. . . . [P]reparation for trial [thus] became more difficult and hazardous; as one defendant argued, the complaint to which he had to respond was "so general, that it . . . [was] impossible [that] any man . . . [could] prepare to defend himself in the same. . . ."

> Whereas litigants at common law had often had to prepare evidence only on a small number of precisely defined issues, a litigant under the new pleading system had to prepare to meet many potential issues, only some of which would arise. Moreover, he faced the danger that issues he had never anticipated might be brought up and that he might "be surprised by a piece of evidence which at another time he could have explained or answered."

Id. at 86-87.

Can you imagine any procedural tools that would address these problems? Is it more efficient to force parties to plead to and try a single issue, or to have more liberal pleading and grant new trials if a litigant is unfairly surprised by unanticipated or undiscovered evidence? Nelson reports that, after the reforms in Massachusetts,

> [n]ewly discovered evidence became . . . the most common cause for granting new trials. As a general matter, new trials were granted whenever a party had not had adequate opportunity to present his claim. . . . Although common law pleading was antiquated, unduly technical, and expensive, and hence in need of reform, it nonetheless provided a working system for the trial of cases.

Id. at 87.

Following is a diagram of the primary writs—what Nelson calls "the old procedural categories." Again, recall that each had its own procedure, which included its own method of proof. In the next section we take up the matter of methods of proof, with special emphasis on the evolution of the trial by jury and the decline of wager of law, trial by battle, and—most students' personal favorite—trial by ordeal.

c. Methods of Proof

Before the emergence of the jury as a method of proof, the common law system employed wager of law, trial by battle, and the ordeal as mechanisms for determining the victor in litigation. The jury system eventually replaced these older methods, for reasons that should become obvious as you learn more about each.

Wager of law, abolished in 1833, referred to a litigant's use of oaths to "make his law." For example, in a debt action (see the chart), the defendant would solemnly swear that he owed the plaintiff nothing. He then would bring in *compurgators*, or "oath helpers," who would swear that the defendant's oath was clean. The defendant might say the following: "By the Lord, I am guiltless both in deed and counsel of the charge of which N. accuses me." To which the compurgators would swear, "By the Lord, the oath is clear and unperjured which M. has sworn."

The purpose of these oaths was not to convince the court, or to submit the defendant to cross-examination; it was to bring upon the swearers the wrath of God if they lied. Yet the wrath of God was not all these oath

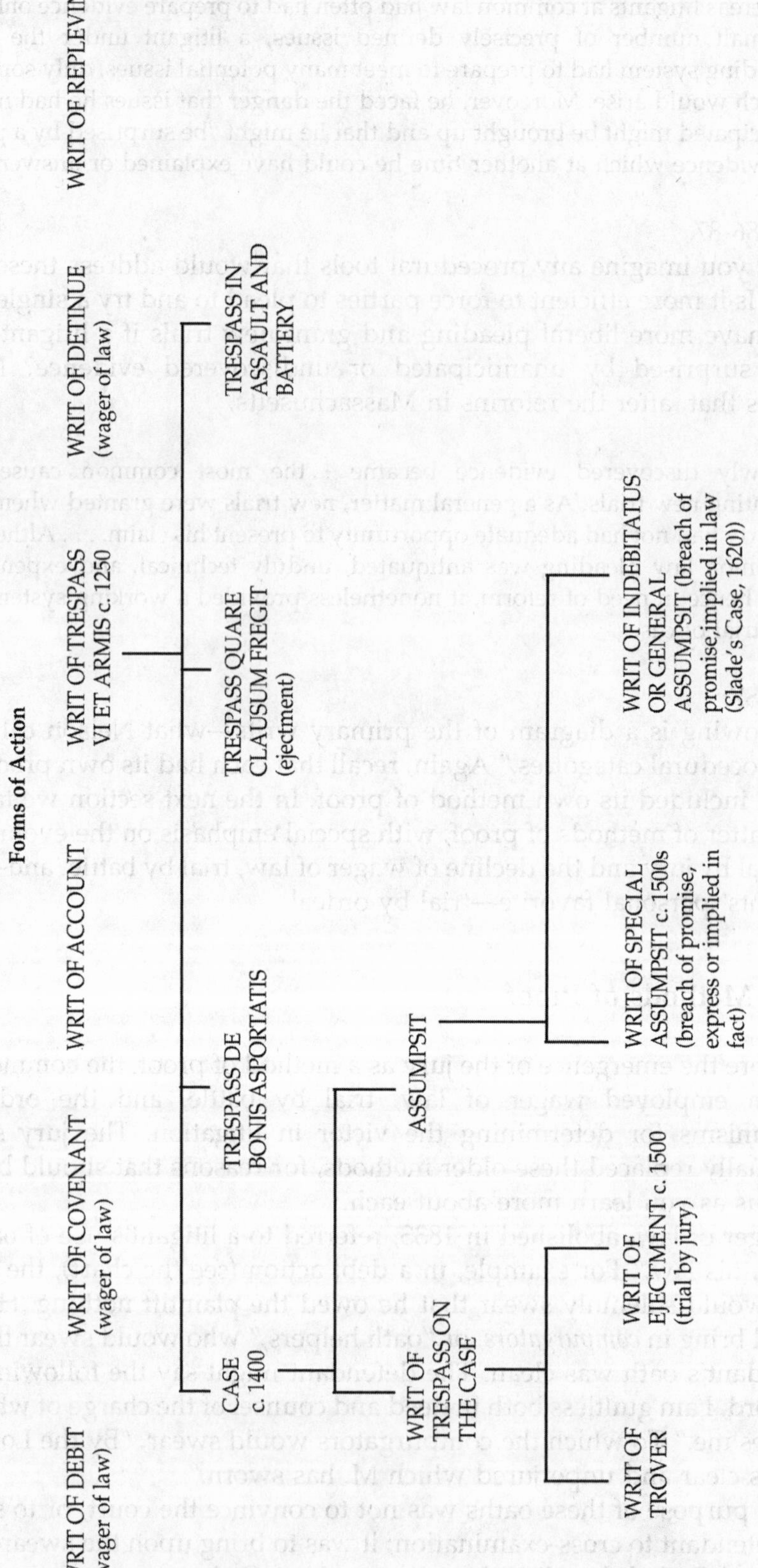
Forms of Action
WRIT OF DEBT (wager of law)
WRIT OF COVENANT (wager of law)
WRIT OF ACCOUNT
WRIT OF TRESPASS VI ET ARMIS c.1220
WRIT OF DETINUE (wager of law)
WRIT OF REPLEVIN
CASE c. 1400
TRESPASS DE BONIS ASPORTATIS
TRESPASS QUARE CLAUSUM FREGIT (ejectment)
TRESPASS IN ASSAULT AND BATTERY
WRIT OF TRESPASS ON THE CASE
ASSUMPSIT
WRIT OF TROVER
WRIT OF EJECTMENT c. 1500 (trial by jury)
WRIT OF SPECIAL ASSUMPSIT c.1500s (breach of promise, express or implied in fact)
WRIT OF INDEBITATUS OR GENERAL ASSUMPSIT (breach of promise, implied in law (Slade's Case, 1620))

helpers had to fear. By swearing for the defendant, they put their worth as well as their souls on the line, for the price of swearing falsely was to lose one's *wergeld* (the value, set in monetary terms, of each person, which varied with one's status—each person quite literally had his "price"), as well as community respect and confidence. People who lived in small agrarian communities depended heavily on their neighbors and needed a good reputation.

How many compurgators one needed depended on the defendant's rank. A person of low rank or bad character might be required to produce three times the usual number of compurgators, or be required to undergo the ordeal. In many respects, the wager of law was less about truth than about community support for the defendant.

Trial by battle, abolished in 1819, is self-explanatory; less obvious was the provision for hiring a champion, thus transforming the battle into one of economic, rather than physical strength. (Some would say that this method of proof resembles most closely modern methods of proof, though parties now hire the best legal rather than physical competitors.)

And, of course, there was the ordeal, abolished in 1215 by the Lateran Council, but still used well into the fifteenth century. The ordeal is traced by some historians to a certain Bishop Poppo, who preached to the Jutlanders (Danes) with no success. Frustrated by his failures, Bishop Poppo asked the Jutlanders whether they might believe his message was divine if he could touch a hot iron and suffer no harm. Receiving an affirmative response, Bishop Poppo allegedly heated an iron glove until red hot, put his hand inside, and withdrew it uninjured. The Danes apparently were impressed.

The theory behind the ordeal, perhaps based on Numbers 5:12-13, was that God would spare the innocent. One ordeal required the party to carry a one pound red hot iron a distance of nine feet. The party's hands would then be bound for three days. If his hands healed, he was innocent; if not, he was deemed guilty. Similarly, a party might be ordered to put his hand in a boiling cauldron and pull out a stone. A third ordeal was to bind a party with rope and throw him into the river. If he sank, he was innocent, because the water would reject the guilty. (Being proved innocent seems small comfort, though, if it meant being tied up at the bottom of the river.) Such methods were bound to produce some bad results, as the community witnessed some innocent (in the modern sense) people deemed guilty in the eyes of God. The Church effectively ended the practice in 1215 by withdrawing its support.

The most enduringly important common-law method of proof was the trial by jury, though its early form bore little resemblance to its modern counterpart. The early jury was a group of neighbors who were sworn to tell the truth about something they had observed, usually in an effort to preserve the King's rights. They were summoned by a royal officer to give impartial testimony about their knowledge. As such, the early jurors were more like modern-day witnesses than jurors. Moreover, the right to trial by jury was a matter of royal prerogative, not a common right. Benefit of that right was one that the King could give or sell to people in his grace. This gave rise to the expression "One could not wage law against the King." This meant that when the King was the plaintiff, one had to submit to trial by jury, which then included certain incentives for jurors to find for the crown. The right to a trial of one's peers is traced to the Magna Carta, but the notion then was that the Barons at Runnymede should be entitled to trial by *their* "peers"—noblemen, not lower echelon citizens.

Over time, of course, the right to trial by jury became available to all citizens who filed writs that carried with them this method of proof. Moreover, jurors no longer were selected on the basis of their knowledge of a controversy; on the contrary, actual knowledge would disqualify a person from serving as a juror in the case.

Today, under the Seventh Amendment, the right to trial by jury in civil cases hinges primarily on whether the right in question was one that would have fallen on the common law (versus equity) side of Anglo-American jurisdiction. This means that modern actions sounding in tort and contract, as well as many in property, could involve jury trials should one of the parties request it in a timely manner. You will learn more about how this analysis goes in Chapter 5's section on the right to jury trial.

As the discussion below on equity jurisdiction will explain, another guide to whether one is entitled to a trial by jury is the relief requested. If it is money damages, this often—though not always—means that the action is one at law and jury triable.

d. Equity

Adding to the confusion of the common law system was the existence of a separate court system, Chancery, which administered a body of "equitable" doctrine applying to allegations of fraud, mistake, and breach of fiduciary duty. The Court of Chancery differed from the common law courts in important ways. First, Chancery developed the concept of formal pretrial proceedings through which parties could learn facts beyond the pleadings—"discovery" in modern parlance. But this ameliorative alternative to the burden of pleading was soon itself weighted with Byzantine complexity and protracted delays, made infamous by Dickens in *Bleak House*. Second, the Chancery trial had no jury; the judge decided questions of fact. Finally, Chancery had remedies unavailable at common law, where the only favorable plaintiff's outcome was an award of monetary damages. The Chancellor typically issued affirmative orders requiring that the rightful situation be effected—orders that were the ancestors of the modern injunction.

Resort to Chancery was proper only when an action at law was inadequate, either because the court of law was unfair or unwilling to do justice, or because the available common law writs and their remedies were inadequate. The system was not meant to act contrary to the principles of the law courts, but as an essential supplement to them.

Unlike actions at law, which were considered actions against property (*in rem*), equity acted against the person (*in personam*). The order of the Chancellor was a personal order against the affected party, and was enforceable by contempt power and imprisonment, if necessary. A judgment at law would operate against the party's property, such that the court (through the sheriff) would enforce the judgment by attaching the property in an execution on the judgment, selling it, and satisfying the plaintiff's judgment through the proceeds of the sale. Any balance, minus costs, was returned to the defendant.

Chancery was a highly discretionary and flexible system, prompting the remark by Selden that equitable relief depended on the "size of the Chancellor's foot." The reason for this discretion, again, makes sense in light of the origins of equity. In its earliest forms, equity was not a formal system of judicial relief, but the Chancellor's response to an individual's appeal. The Chancellor did not see this as a judicial act, but as an administrative and political response to a dispute. Thus it never occurred to the Chancellor to employ the common-law methods of proof, such as a jury or wager of law.

By the fifteenth century, however, the Chancellor was clearly acting as a judge, and was recognized as such. In ruling on the petitions, the Chancellor invoked moral grounds that continue to influence one's right to secure an equitable remedy. For example, "clean hands" were necessary before one could receive equitable relief. Likewise, delay ("laches") might defeat one's right to recover, even if no formal statute of limitations barred recovery. Conduct that misled an opponent or otherwise caused him to rely on a state of affairs might "estop" one from disrupting his expectations.

The remedies available in equity included injunctions, specific performance, restitution, constructive trusts, equitable liens, and remedies for fiduciary misconduct, among others. Recall that in Chapter 1, we dealt with the flexible equitable doctrines in considering whether injunctions, wage garnishment, and attachment of property without an *ex ante* adversary hearing may violate due process.

The subjects commonly heard in equity rather than in law included matters involving the enforcement of uses or trusts, those involving mortgage foreclosures, family matters, and equitable conversion. The need for a system like equity to relieve the unforgiving nature of law, and the interplay between the two, is well illustrated by a mortgage foreclosure example. The mortgage itself is a contract between the mortgagor and mortgagee that typically provides that failure to make timely payments constitutes a material breach. Legal title, as readers with mortgages will know, is held by the lender, and does not pass to the borrower unless he makes timely payments, as prescribed by the mortgage agreement. The term *legal* title is important here, and refers to title acknowledged on the law side of the common law courts.

The harshness of mortgage law, enforced by the law side of common law courts, was that a borrower who paid a significant number of payments, but who later defaulted on the mortgage, was deemed to have breached the contract and thereby lost the value of any payments he already made. Moreover, he had no chance to redeem the mortgage.

Over time, equity recognized the severity of this result and came to respect the borrower's right to recovery of the money already paid—called *equity* today, and now you know why.

In the early seventeenth century, equity courts acted to soften further the hard edges of the law of mortgage by providing a right of redemption to the borrower even in the absence of fraud or mistake in the making of the mortgage. It tempered the redemption opportunity, though, by giving the lender the right to foreclose. This meant that the lender went to the equity court and asked that the right of redemption be foreclosed, such that if the borrower did not redeem (pay up) within a reasonable period of time, then the mortgage would be foreclosed.

Needless to say, the existence of Chancery as a separate, supplemental system of justice complicated procedure. Some actions had both legal and equitable characteristics, which might not become apparent until well into the pleading process. Should the action be bifurcated at this late date? Dismissed and refiled? Also, questions inevitably arose about the relative powers of law and equity courts, with periods of quite bitter turf conflicts.

The complicating aspects of the formal division between equity and law persisted for centuries. In the American federal courts, some of the problems ultimately were resolved when, in 1938, law and equity finally were merged so that one judge had power to award both equitable and legal remedies. But this is getting ahead of the story. Before turning to 1938 and its cataclysmic procedural changes, we first need to review the interim stage of pleading history—Code procedure.

2. Code Procedure

Colonial legislatures in the United States sought, largely unsuccessfully, to mitigate the rigors of common law pleading and to simplify equity procedures. Judicial reforms, such as those discussed by Nelson above, were also fairly limited. Not until the mid-nineteenth century, when complaints about litigation cost, delay, and complexity became a part of Jacksonian Democratic reform agitation, was there a significant departure from the basic structure of English procedure. By that time, frustration among Democratic lawyers and laymen with the subtleties of the writ system had sharpened considerably. William Sampson, a New York lawyer and early advocate of procedural reform, derisively referred to

> those odious volumes of special pleading . . . where the suitor's story is told in twenty different ways, and answered in as many, and must be hunted for with fear and trembling in printed books . . . and made conformable to precedents composed before the party was in being, and which, in no single instance, conform to the truth: insomuch, that he who dares to tell his case according to the simple and honest truth, will for that very reason . . fail in his suit.

William Sampson, An Anniversary Discourse, Delivered Before the Historical Society of New York, Dec. 6, 1823, in Perry Miller, The Legal Mind in America from Independence to the Civil War 132 (1962). A strong egalitarian element ran through the reform proposals—a concern, as in post-Revolutionary Massachusetts, that the writ system was inconsistent with democratic principles and biased in favor of the rich. As Henry Dwight Sedgwick, another New York lawyer, wrote:

> Americans will not long believe . . . that there is any necessity that the forms of conducting a legal controversy should be so multiplied and expensive, that the mere costs of suit . . . should be so great, that none but the rich can indulge the luxury of the law.

Henry Dwight Sedgwick, Review of Sampson's Anniversary Discourse, in Perry Miller, The Legal Mind in America from Independence to the Civil War 145-146 (1962).

The signal reform was the New York Act of 1848, drafted by David Dudley Field. The "Field Code," as it came to be known, provided "one form of action," thus abolishing the writ system and embracing all claims previously known at law and in equity. The Code also abandoned the goal of reducing the dispute to a single issue, which might require years of pleading. Instead, the pleadings were limited to the Complaint, the Answer, and possibly a Reply. But this streamlining did not mean that the pleadings were unimportant. To the contrary, they were the primary vehicle for controlling and defining the dispute. As such they served two distinct but related functions. First, the parties were supposed to learn each other's factual contentions from the pleadings, so that they could be fully prepared and not surprised by developments at trial. Full disclosure through the pleadings was also intended to promote the early resolution of issues not actually in dispute.

The hopes for the Code were expressed in the First Report of the Commissioners on Practice and Pleadings, 141-142 (1848):

> We propose that the plaintiff shall state his case according to the facts, and as for relief as he supposed himself entitled to; that the defendant shall by his answer point out his defense distinctly. This form of allegation and counter allegation will make the parties disclose the cause of action and defense, so that they may come to the trial prepared with the necessary proofs.

In his published notes to the new Code, Field emphasized:

> The object of every suit, so far as modes of proceeding are concerned, is to place the parties, whose rights are involved in it, in a proper and convenient manner, before the tribunal by which they are to be adjudicated; to present their conflicting allegations plainly and intelligibly to each other and to the Court; to secure by adequate means a trial or hearing of the contested points; to obtain a judgment or determination adapted to the justice of the

> case; and to effect the enforcement of that judgment by vigorous and efficient means.... Let our Courts be hereafter confined in their adjudications to questions of substantial right, and not to the nice balancing of the question whether the party has conformed himself to the arbitrary and absurd nomenclature imposed upon him by rules, the reason of which, if they ever possessed that quality, has long since ceased to exist, and the continuance of which is a reproach to the age in which we live.

First Report, Extracts from the Notes to Title I, Part II, in 1 A.P. Sprague, Speeches, Arguments, and Misc. Papers of David Dudley Field, 266-267 (1884). California adopted a version of the Field Code in 1849, and it was carried eastward from California and westward from New York until by the turn of the century more than half of the states had switched from common law to Code pleading and merged law and equity.

With the hope that facts would be disclosed in the pleadings, the codifiers made sparing use of the costly discovery devices developed in equity. Depositions were permitted only in rare circumstances and documents were discoverable only if they were found necessary to an issue on which the moving party had the burden of producing evidence.

The plan for adversaries to disclose their cases fully in their pleadings, and thus reduce the area of dispute, proved visionary. Before the dust had settled, the liberalization of pleading created as many pitfalls for the unwary as the common law system it had revamped. A typical Code section required a statement of the facts constituting the cause of action, written in ordinary and concise language. To be avoided were "conclusions" and "evidence." But the distinction between facts and evidence, or even facts and conclusions, soon proved impossible to make. The attempt produced some grand legal writing:

> The distinction between propositions of fact and conclusions of law is this: Propositions of fact are descriptive; conclusions of law are dispositive. Propositions of fact state history; conclusions of law assign legal significance to that history. But since useful propositions of fact must be relevant, and the relevancy of statements of ultimate fact depends on legal considerations, this distinction is not as easy as it seems. While statements of ultimate fact only describe, and do not decide cases, yet they must describe legally relevant aspects of the events to which they refer. A description of a totally irrelevant aspect cannot be a fact-of-the-case.

Clarence Morris, Law and Fact, 55 Harv. L. Rev. 1303, 1329 (1942). Walter Wheeler Cook was especially influential on the distinction between facts and conclusions, finding that it is one of degree only, and that no rational argument can settle the question of whether a particular allegation is too abstract. Only precedent or officially approved form books can guide the pleader. Walter Wheeler Cook, "Facts" and "Statements of Fact," 4 U. Chi. L. Rev. 233 (1937); Walter Wheeler Cook, Statements of Fact in Pleading Under the Codes, 21 Colum. L. Rev. 416 (1921).

In practice, courts developed exceptions to the Code pleading requirements by, for instance, allowing or even requiring the pleading of evidence when it was needed to give full notice to the opponent. Or, on the other hand, courts endorsed the pleading of conclusions:

> In cases of negligence, the sufferer may only know the general, the immediate, cause of the injury, and may be entirely ignorant as to the specific acts or omissions which lead up to it. The term "negligence," for the purpose of pleading, is a fact to be pleaded, an ultimate fact, which qualifies an act otherwise not wrongful. Negligence is not the act itself, but the fact which defines the character of the act, and makes it a legal wrong.

Rannard v. Lockheed Aircraft Corp., 157 P.2d 1, 5 (1945). Contra Kramer v. Kansas City Power & Light Co., 279 S.W. 43 (1925).

Such language by the California Supreme Court hardly comports with the ideal of Code pleading that "the allegations must be of dry, naked actual facts, while the rules of law applicable thereto, and the legal rights and duties arising therefrom, must be left entirely to the courts." John Norton Pomeroy, Code Remedies 640 (5th ed. 1929).

The entrenched habits of mind of judges and pleaders made them resist Code pleading. As Justice Grier opined: "The distinction between the different forms of action for different wrongs, requiring different remedies, lies in the nature of things; it is absolutely inseparable from the correct administration of justice in common-law courts." McFaul v. Ramsey, 61 U.S. 523, 525 (1857). Maitland summed up all the difficulties with pleading reform when he wrote: "the forms of action we have buried, but they still rule us from their graves." Frederick William Maitland, Equity and the Forms of Action at Common Law 296 (1909).

Despite Maitland's famous bon mot, Code pleading was not a dark failure in the history of pleading reform. California and New York, as well as several other states, retain their Codes, with a decisional gloss stretching over more than a hundred years. And the rulemakers who drafted the Federal Rules of Civil Procedure in 1938 were richly informed by the experience under the Codes.

3. Modern Procedure in Federal Courts

The limitations of older forms of pleading that plagued the state courts likewise plagued the federal courts, as the federal courts for many years conformed their procedure in actions arising on the law side of their jurisdiction (rather than the equity side) to that of local state courts. For actions arising in equity the federal courts had their own nationally uniform rules of procedure. Thus a federal district court in Maryland would in nonequity cases conform its civil procedure to that of Maryland state courts, though even in these cases exceptions existed to the general rule of borrowing state procedural law.

The problems with this often confusing system of borrowing state procedure, and with the anachronistic state procedures it borrowed, prompted a protracted fight for revised, uniform rules of federal procedure. The reform effort was spearheaded by Thomas Shelton, who instigated a resolution by the American Bar Association in 1911 favoring court-made rules of civil procedure for the federal courts. These efforts, however, did not bear fruit for over 20 years. It was not until 1934 that Congress finally adopted a bill that authorized the United States Supreme Court to promulgate rules of "pleading and practice" that would be uniform among all of the federal district courts of the United States. See Rules Enabling Act of 1934, 28 U.S.C. §§ 2071-2077.

The Rules Enabling Act of 1934 contains the caveat that no rule shall "abridge, enlarge, or modify any substantive rights." 28 U.S.C. § 2072(b); see generally Stephen B. Burbank, The Rules Enabling Act of 1934, 130 U. Pa. L. Rev. 1015 (1982) (describing the history that gave rise to the 1934 Act); Stephen N. Subrin, How Equity Conquered Common Law: The Federal Rules of Civil Procedure in Historical Perspective, 130 U. Pa. L. Rev. 909 (1982) (describing how the rules of equity, rather than common law procedure, became the model for the federal rules). The Court appointed an Advisory Committee, composed of law professors, practicing lawyers, and former judges, that was charged with responsibility for drafting uniform rules of procedure for the district courts. Charles E. Clark, Dean of Yale Law School, was named the Reporter of the Advisory Committee and became the principal draftsperson of the rules it eventually proposed. Dean Clark had for years before his appointment devoted considerable scholarly energy to denouncing the way in which procedural technicalities often stood in the way of substantive merits of disputes, and to proposals for minimizing the role of procedure in determining legal outcomes. See Subrin, supra, at 961-962.

In 1938, the first uniform rules adopted pursuant to the 1934 Act took effect. The changes affected by the rules were sweeping and massively influential, as the new streamlined rules became models for reform of state procedure in many jurisdictions. Significant among the changes were the abolition of the forms of action in favor of one form of action for all types of lawsuits, expanded discovery, greatly simplified pleading requirements, and the merger of law and equity. The overriding goal, stated with elegant simplicity in Rule 1, was "to secure the just, speedy, and inexpensive determination of every action." See Brooke Coleman, Recovering Access: Rethinking the Structure of Federal Civil Rulemaking (forthcoming 2009) (describing commitment of original Advisory Committee to opening access to the courts).

The centerpiece of the new rules was Rule 8, which required only a "short and plain statement of the claim showing that the pleader is entitled to relief." Almost immediately, the shibboleth became "notice pleading": The pleader was required only to state enough of anything— facts, conclusions, law—to give the court and the opponent notice of the nature of his claim. Supplementing the limited pleadings were elaborate provisions for pretrial discovery and Rule 16, which provided for a pretrial conference to shape the issues for trial.

The new Rules were greeted with high hopes but have failed to conclude the eternal debate about the function of pleadings. In the early 1950s, one critic observed as follows:

> The conversion of Rule 8 to notice pleadings is part of a broader tendency of deferring the inevitable necessity of thinking through one's case. . . . [T]he necessary job of coming to grips with the issues is deferred with the consoling assurance to counsel that the issues can be found and framed by discovery procedures and the pretrial conference.
>
> . . . [But d]iscovery does not define the issues. It simply throws into the hopper the whole undigested mass of facts. Anything goes.
>
> . . . Discovery . . . ought not to be required until some preliminary definition of issues has occurred.

Harold Lasky, Memorandum for the Committee on Rule 8, 13 F.R.D. 275 (1952).

The tone of the debate grew increasingly sharp, and there were many ready on the fiftieth birthday of the Rules to declare them another failed procedural reform. In addition to the dissatisfaction with notice pleading, the Rules were criticized for encouraging overly adversarial behavior, unfairly advantaging rich litigants, vesting too much discretion in judges, and being subject to unpredictable application. In the normal course, such concerns might have resulted in some fairly sweeping Rule changes. But in the 1980s the profession's expressed unhappiness with the operation of the Rules joined with the public's outrage at the social, political, and economic costs of "excessive" litigation to create an unusual political constituency for immediate procedural reform.

Congress passed The Civil Justice Reform Act of 1990, Pub. L. No. 101-650, 104 Stat. 5089 (1990). Among the main reforms suggested by the Act were: (1) the "tracking" of cases, that is, allowing more time and attention for complex cases and expediting less complex ones, and (2) the encouragement of the use of alternative dispute resolution. But the Act's major innovation was the creation of a rulemaking group in each of the 94 federal districts that would devise means "from the bottom up" for reducing delay and expense.

Local rulemaking was encouraged, as was local experimentation with various new procedures (like voluntary disclosure under the discovery rules; see more in Chapter 3). One of the Act's chief critics, Professor Linda Mullinex, complained that it "mandates local, grassroots rulemaking by civilian advisory groups, a novel process that essentially circumvents the usual judicial advisory committee system for civil procedure rule reform that has been in place since 1938. In this respect alone, the Act is revolutionary." Linda S. Mullinex, The Counter-Reformation in Procedural Justice, 77 Minn. L. Rev. 375, 377-379 (1992).

Before the ink was dry, the Act stirred up more criticism than the ills it was meant to reform, including the fundamental attack that it was unnecessary. There was no excessive litigation, according to many commentators, only an overworked federal judiciary with unfilled vacancies making the situation worse. For an excellent compilation of early commentary on the working of the Act and its various reform proposals, see Symposium: Civil Justice Reform, 46 Stan. L. Rev. 1285-1634 (1994).

Despite all the furor of its creation, the Act went out with hardly a whimper. It presumably expired Dec. 1, 1997, although Congress did not specifically mandate its conclusion. See Carl Tobias, Fin-de-Siécle Federal Civil Procedure, 51 Fla. L. Rev. 641 (1999). In the final analysis, it was something of a wash. After a five-year study mandated by the Act itself, the RAND Corporation's Institute for Civil Justice found that the Act as a whole had no impact at all on the problems of unnecessary cost and delay. Even positive effects had unintended consequences; thus while strict deadlines for completing discovery reduced delay, they also increased costs. See Stephanie B. Goldberg, Rand-ly Criticized: Congressional Court Fix Had Little Effect on Cost and Delay, 83 APR A.B.A. J. 14 (1997).

Professor Edward Cavanagh considered the Act's failure in a thoughtful commentary on the whole unhappy experience. He noted the "confusion and uncertainty" created by the Act, because "it often added yet another layer of local and sometimes conflicting procedures to the existing patchwork quilt of local rules, standing orders and individual judges' rules, further balkanizing an already fragmented federal system." Another unintended consequence was the billable hours lawyers now spent on figuring out what rules and procedures to follow. Finally, Congress lost interest, and the funding became "shockingly minimal." Professor Cavanagh's article concludes that the CJRA

> should be buried but not forgotten, for though the Act failed to achieve its principal goals, it has taught us some valuable lessons. First, the CJRA experience has demonstrated that the federal civil justice system, far from being on the brink of imminent collapse, is functioning well. Second, the experience has underscored the fact that true procedural reform proceeds at a glacial pace and cannot be attained overnight. Third, attempts to reform a national court system through local initiatives are costly, confusing and, on balance, these drawbacks outweigh the benefits that might be derived from local experimentation. If nothing else, the CJRA has taught us that we needed fewer—not more—local rules. Fourth, a reform program, to be truly effective, must first identify the underlying problems afflicting the system as well as their causes and then tailor the reforms to address these causes.

Edward D. Cavanagh, The Civil Justice Reform Act of 1990: Requiescat in Pace, 173 F.R.D. 565, 568-570 (1997).

In the spirit of simplicity and accessibility that animated Dean Clark and other early drafters, the Civil Rules Advisory Committee began restyling the Federal Rules of Civil Procedure in 2003. In what became the most comprehensive overhaul since the Rules were first adopted, the Committee restyled every one, from Rule 1 to Rule 86, and redesigned the practice forms. The proposed amendments to the Rules were approved by the Supreme Court in April 2007 and took effect on December 1, 2007.

There were two kinds of amendments to the Rules in the style project. The first were "style only" amendments, intended to simplify every Rule by updating the language to reflect contemporary usage and improve readability. These "stylistic" changes included minor alterations to the body of the Rules, along with the addition of new labels and internal subparts. The second was a set of "style-substance" changes to Rules 4(a), 9(h), 11(a), 14(b), 16(c), 26(g), 30(b), 31(c), 40, 71.1(d), and 78(a); these changes were also intended to improve the Rules but arguably involve changes to their substantive meaning. The "style-substance" alterations were approved separately from the stylistic changes and also took effect on December 1, 2007. For an overview of all of the 2007 revisions, see Memorandum from the Comm. on Rules of Practice and Procedure of the Judicial Conference of the U.S. to C.J. John Roberts, Summary of Proposed Amendments to the Federal Rules (Nov. 1, 2006), available at http://www.uscourts.gov/rules/supct1106/summary_proposed_amend.pdf.

A looming question is whether the style changes, even those intended to be purely stylistic, will have substantive effects in the interpretation of the rules. The Advisory Committee Note to each rule now contains the explicit disclaimer "The language of Rule ____ has been amended as a part of the general restyling of the Civil Rules to make them more easily understood. . . . These changes are intended to be stylistic only." The Supreme Court has indicated its agreement with the Advisory Committee's view, "advis[ing that] the changes were stylistic only." Republic of Philippines v. Pimentel, 128 S. Ct. 2180, 2184 (2008) (interpreting the new Rule 19).

But, of course, any alteration to language in the field of law has the potential to reshape meaning, even if it is for "style only." Critics of the new Rules argue that "clarity without change" is impossible, and they worry that the new Rules will create, rather than eliminate, confusion. See, e.g., Edward H. Cooper, Restyling the Civil Rules: Clarity Without Change, 79 Notre Dame L. Rev. 1761 (2004); Edward A. Hartnett, Against (Mere) Restyling, 82 Notre Dame L. Rev. 155 (2006); Memorandum from Stephen B. Burbank & Gregory P. Joseph to the Fed. Comm. on Rules of Practice and Procedure, Restyled Federal Rules of Civil Procedure (Oct. 24, 2005), available at http://www.uscourts.gov/rules/CV%20Comments%202005/05-CV-022.pdf. Practicing lawyers must now consider whether the judicial gloss given to the prior language in each Rule over the last 70 years is still relevant and binding. To aid your analysis of the cases that follow we urge you to consult Appendix A, which provides a side-by-side comparison of the pre-restyled text and the new text of every rule appearing in the casebook. some of the most significant revisions in the cases that follow.

As you read the materials in this chapter about pleading, keep in mind the cycles of reform and reaction that are the background of the governing rules. Remember that the dream of the rulemakers was to simplify pretrial procedure. Is this an impossible dream? Do the style changes simplify the rules?

B. THE ALLEGATIONS: PLEADING AND RESPONDING UNDER THE FEDERAL RULES OF CIVIL PROCEDURE

1. The Complaint

Problem Case: The Aggrieved Nurses

IN THE UNITED STATES DISTRICT COURT
FOR THE NORTHERN DISTRICT OF ILLINOIS

American Nurses Association,	)	
Plaintiff	)	
v.	)	Civil Action
	)	File No. xx-xxx
State of Illinois,	)	
Defendant	)	

This court has jurisdiction under 28 U.S.C.S. § 1331 [Federal Question Jurisdiction]. This case arises under Title VII of the Civil Rights Act of 1964, 42 U.S.C. § 2000e.

COMPLAINT

1. Plaintiffs are two associations of nurses plus 21 individuals, mostly women, who work for the state in jobs like nursing that are mainly filled by women. They represent a class of all current women employees of the state.
2. Defendants are the State of Illinois, its departments and other Agencies subject to the State Personnel Code, and State Officials.
3. Defendants have intentionally discriminated and continue to intentionally discriminate against female state employees in the terms and conditions of their employment because of their sex and because of their employment in historically female-dominated sex-segregated job classifications.

Wherefore plaintiffs demand judgment against defendant, and the entry of such relief in damages, backpay, and such other relief as the court deems proper and the evidence supports.

Signed: ____________
Attorney for the Plaintiff
45 La Salle St.
Chicago, Illinois

Does this complaint meet the requirements of Rule 8? Can it survive a motion to dismiss under Rule 12(b)(6)? Passing the issue of whether it meets a minimum standard, is this a good complaint? Are you impressed by the justice of the cause?

a. The Basic Standard: Rule 8

Conley v. Gibson

355 U.S. 42 (1957)

JUSTICE BLACK delivered the opinion of the Court. This class suit was brought in a Federal District Court in Texas by certain Negro members of the Brotherhood of Railway and Steamship Clerks, petitioners here, on behalf of themselves and other Negro employees similarly situated against the Brotherhood, its Local Union No. 28 and certain officers of both. In summary, the complaint made the following allegations relevant to our decision: Petitioners were employees of the Texas and New Orleans Railroad at its Houston Freight House. Local 28 of the Brotherhood was the designated bargaining agent under the Railway Labor Act for the bargaining unit to which petitioners belonged. A contract existed between the Union and the Railroad which gave the employees in the bargaining unit certain protection from discharge and loss of seniority. In May 1954, the Railroad purported to abolish 45 jobs held by petitioners or other Negroes all of whom were either discharged or demoted. In truth the 45 jobs were not abolished at all but instead filled by whites as the Negroes were ousted, except for a few instances where Negroes were rehired to fill their old jobs but with loss of seniority. Despite repeated pleas by petitioners, the Union, acting according to plan, did nothing to protect them against these discriminatory discharges and refused to give them protection comparable to that given white employees. The complaint then went on to allege that the Union had failed in general to represent Negro employees equally and in good faith. It charged that such discrimination constituted a violation of petitioners' rights under the Railway Labor Act to fair representation from their bargaining agent. And it concluded by asking for relief in the nature of declaratory judgment, injunction and damages.

The respondents appeared and moved to dismiss the complaint on several grounds[, including that] the complaint failed to state a claim upon which relief could be given. . . . [The District Court granted the motion to dismiss and the Fifth Circuit affirmed. 229 F.2d 436. The part of the opinion dealing with other grounds for dismissal is omitted.]

. . . In appraising the sufficiency of the complaint we follow, of course, the accepted rule that a complaint should not be dismissed for failure to state a claim unless it appears beyond doubt that the plaintiff can prove no set of facts in support of his claim which would entitle him to relief.[5] Here, the complaint alleged, in part, that petitioners were discharged wrongfully by the Railroad and that the Union, acting according to plan, refused to protect their jobs as it did those of white employees or to help them with their grievances all because they were Negroes. If these

5. See, e.g., Leimer v. State Mutual Life Assur. Co., 108 F.2d 302 [8th Cir. 1940]; Dioguardi v. Durning, 139 F.2d 774 [2d Cir. 1944]; Continental Collieries v. Shober, 130 F.2d 631 [3d Cir. 1942].

allegations are proven there has been a manifest breach of the Union's statutory duty to represent fairly and without hostile discrimination all of the employees in the bargaining unit. This Court squarely held in *Steele* and subsequent cases that discrimination in representation because of race is prohibited by the Railway Labor Act. The bargaining representative's duty not to draw "irrelevant and invidious"[6] distinctions among those it represents does not come to an abrupt end, as the respondents seem to contend, with the making of an agreement between union and employer. Collective bargaining is a continuing process. Among other things, it involves day-to-day adjustments in the contract and other working rules, resolution of new problems not covered by existing agreements, and the protection of employee rights already secured by contract. The bargaining representative can no more unfairly discriminate in carrying out these functions than it can in negotiating a collective agreement. A contract may be fair and impartial on its face yet administered in such a way, with the active or tacit consent of the union, as to be flagrantly discriminatory against some members of the bargaining unit.

The respondents also argue that the complaint failed to set forth specific facts to support its general allegations of discrimination and that its dismissal is therefore proper. The decisive answer to this is that the Federal Rules of Civil Procedure do not require a claimant to set out in detail the facts upon which he bases his claim. To the contrary, all the Rules require is "a short and plain statement of the claim"[8] that will give the defendant fair notice of what the plaintiff's claim is and the grounds upon which it rests. The illustrative forms appended to the Rules plainly demonstrate this. Such simplified "notice pleading" is made possible by the liberal opportunity for discovery and the other pretrial procedures established by the Rules to disclose more precisely the basis of both claim and defense and to define more narrowly the disputed facts and issues.[9] Following the simple guide of Rule 8(f) that "all pleadings shall be so construed as to do substantial justice," we have no doubt that petitioners' complaint adequately set forth a claim and gave the respondents fair notice of its basis. The Federal Rules reject the approach that pleading is a game of skill in which one misstep by counsel may be decisive to the outcome and accept the principle that the purpose of pleading is to facilitate a proper decision on the merits.

The judgment is reversed and the cause is remanded to the District Court for further proceedings not inconsistent with this opinion.

It is so ordered.

---

6. Steele v. Louisville & Nashville R. Co., 323 U.S. 192, 203 [1944].

8. Rule 8(a)(2).

9. See, e.g., Rule 12(e) (motion for a more definite statement); Rule 12(f) (motion to strike portions of the pleading); Rule 12(c) (motion for judgment on the pleadings); Rule 16 (pre-trial procedure and formulation of issues); Rules 26-37 (depositions and discovery); Rule 56 (motion for summary judgment); Rule 15 (right to amend).

Notes and Questions

1. *The Ideals of Notice Pleading. Conley*'s requirement that a complaint should not be dismissed "unless it appears beyond doubt that the plaintiff can prove no set of facts in support of the claim that entitle him to relief" sets an almost impossible standard, doesn't it?

One reason for this wide interpretation of Rule 8's requirements was that the plaintiffs appeared particularly deserving. Look at the date of the case, well before Title VII of the Civil Rights Act of 1964 would have allowed a suit against the employer, the natural defendant, as well as providing a sure statutory basis for a suit against the union.

Moreover, the plaintiffs, black workers in the South, may have feared that they could not get a fair hearing on breach of contract claims against the employers in their state courts. They needed a federal forum, and it would certainly have been against the spirit of the rules to throw them out on a pleading technicality.

Another reason that *Conley* sets such a high standard for dismissing a complaint is that details and evidence regarding the actions charged, a conspiracy between the union and the employer to deprive African-Americans of their jobs, were peculiarly within the knowledge of the defendants. Access to information is often a consideration when courts are considering who should bear the burden of pleading or failing to plead more fully.

2. *Pleading and Subject Matter Jurisdiction.* Recall that Rule 8 not only requires a short and plain statement of the claim, but also "a short and plain statement of the grounds for the court's jurisdiction." Rule 8(a)(1). This refers to the federal court's subject matter jurisdiction, the basic rules of which you encountered in Chapter 1, supra.

Quickly review those jurisdictional principles, and consider their pleading implications before responding to the following questions:

a. In an action based solely on diversity, brought by two plaintiffs against one defendant, what would the jurisdictional allegations need to include? See Fed. R. Civ. P. Form 7 and the materials at Chapter 1, section D(2), supra.
b. In an action based solely on a federal statute, what must the jurisdictional allegation include? See Fed. R. Civ. P. Form 7 and the materials at Chapter 1, section D(3), supra.
c. In an action based on a federal question that also asserts a related state law claim, what must the jurisdictional allegation include? See Fed. R. Civ. P. Form 7 and the materials at Chapter 6, section A(2), infra.

3. *Factual Versus Substantive Sufficiency.* Note that there are two ways in which a complaint may fail to state a claim. The first occurs when the complaint is insufficiently detailed to allege the violation of an existing, valid law. The second occurs when the complaint satisfies the "notice

pleading" baseline of *Conley* but nevertheless fails to state a claim because no law exists, at the moment, to support plaintiff's claim. In the former situation, plaintiff can attempt to amend the complaint to provide the missing details. In the latter, plaintiff cannot amend to cure the defect; her only recourse may be to appeal, should the trial judge refuse to extend existing law to fit her situation. As we will see in section C, infra, however, there are ethical and other limits on lawyers' license to file lawsuits to forge new legal paths, as opposed to following familiar ones.

4. *Pleading Too Much.* All that *Conley* requires is that the complaint set forth a claim and give fair notice of its basis. You would think from reading Justice Black's opinion that the complaint here was very short and unspecific. Actually, the opposite was true. The complaint was a rambling affair, with dark allegations of secret meetings and conspiratorial cover-ups. All the facts alleged did not add up to a coherent, much less a concise story, however. Justice Black artfully redrew their complaint to make it a short and plain statement, and declared that the standard for the future.

In the next case, very like *Conley* in many ways, the plaintiffs also were thrown out of the trial court for pleading too much rather than for giving inadequate notice of their case and its basis.

American Nurses' Ass'n. v. Illinois

783 F.2d 716 (7th Cir. 1986)

POSNER, Circuit Judge.

This class action charges the State of Illinois with sex discrimination in employment, in violation of Title VII of the Civil Rights Act of 1964, 42 U.S.C. § 2000e, and the equal protection clause of the Fourteenth Amendment. The named plaintiffs are two associations of nurses plus 21 individuals, mostly but not entirely female, who work for the state in jobs such as nursing and typing that are filled primarily by women. The suit is on behalf of all state employees in these job classifications. The precise allegations of the complaint will require our careful attention later, but for now it is enough to note that they include as an essential element the charge that the state pays workers in predominantly male job classifications a higher wage not justified by any difference in the relative worth of the predominantly male and the predominantly female jobs in the state's roster.

The complaint was filed in May 1984, and before the state answered, an amended complaint was filed early in July. Less than a month later the state moved to dismiss the complaint or, in the alternative, for summary judgment. In November the plaintiffs filed a memorandum in opposition to the state's motion, to which they attached exhibits not obtained in the course of pretrial discovery—for there had been no discovery. In April 1985, the district judge dismissed the complaint under Fed. R. Civ. P. 12(b)(6) but without ruling on the state's alternative request for summary judgment, 606 F. Supp. 1313. The ground for dismissal was that the complaint pleaded a comparable worth case and that a failure to pay employees in accordance with comparable worth does not violate federal antidiscrimination law. The plaintiffs appeal. They argue that their case is not (or perhaps not just) a comparable worth case and that in characterizing the complaint as he did the district judge terminated the lawsuit by a semantic manipulation. . . . [A]s we understand the plaintiffs' position it is not that a mere failure to rectify traditional wage disparities between predominantly male and predominantly female jobs violates federal law. The circuits that have considered this contention have rejected it, see Spaulding v. University of Washington, 740 F.2d 686, 706-707 (9th Cir. 1984). . . . The relevance of a comparable worth study in proving sex discrimination is that it may provide the occasion on which the employer is forced to declare his intentions toward his female employees. . .

. . . Knowledge of a disparity is not the same thing as an intent to cause or maintain it; if for example the state's intention was to pay market wages, its knowledge that the consequence would be that men got higher wages on average than women and that the difference might exceed any premium attributable to a difference in relative worth would not make it guilty of intentionally discriminating against women. Similarly, even if the failure to act on the comparable worth study could be regarded as "reaffirming" the state's commitment to pay market wages, this would not be enough to demonstrate discriminatory purpose. To demonstrate such a purpose the failure to act would have to be motivated at least in part by a desire to benefit men at the expense of women. . . .

Another point is that the Bennett Amendment to Title VII (the last sentence in 42 U.S.C. § 2000e-2(h)) authorizes employers to pay different wages to men and women provided that the difference would be lawful under the Equal Pay Act, which allows unequal pay for equal work if the inequality results from "any . . . factor other than sex," 29 U.S.C. § 206(d)(1)(iv). The Supreme Court in [County of Washington v.] Gunther[, 452 U.S. 161 (1981),] assumed without quite deciding that the Bennett Amendment allows an employer charged (necessarily under Title VII rather than the Equal Pay Act) with paying unequal wages for unequal work to defend by showing that the inequality is based on something other than sex, even if the result is a disparate impact. See 452 U.S. at 171. This reading would confine the scope of Title VII in a case such as the present to intentional discrimination.

So if all that the plaintiffs in this case are complaining about is the State of Illinois' failure to implement a comparable worth study, they have no case and it was properly dismissed. We must therefore consider what precisely they are complaining about. Our task would be easier if the complaint had been drafted with the brevity that the Federal Rules of Civil Procedure envisage though do not require. Before the era of modern pleading ushered in the promulgation of the rules in 1938, a plaintiff to survive a motion to dismiss the complaint had to plead facts which if true showed that his legal rights had been invaded. The problem was that without pretrial discovery, which ordinarily could not be conducted before the complaint was filed, the plaintiff might not know enough facts to be able to make the required showing. For fact pleading the federal rules substituted notice pleading. The complaint would have to indicate the nature of the plaintiff's claim with only enough specificity to enable the parties to determine the preclusive effect of a judgment disposing of the claim ("a short and plain statement of the claim showing that the pleader is entitled to relief," Rule 8 (a)(2)). The Appendix of Forms to the federal rules illustrates with a complaint for negligence that, so far as the invasion of the plaintiff's legal rights are concerned, says only: "On June 1, 1936, in a public highway called Boylston Street in Boston, Massachusetts, defendant negligently drove a motor vehicle against plaintiff who was then crossing said highway." Form 9, ¶2*; and see Rule 84 ("the forms contained in the Appendix of Forms are sufficient under the rules and are intended to indicate the simplicity and brevity of statement which the rules contemplate"). The plaintiff was expected to use pretrial discovery to gather the facts showing the defendant's negligence and the defendant could serve contention interrogatories on the plaintiff to learn the theory behind the claim. See Rule 33(b), and Note of Advisory Committee to the 1970 amendment thereto. When discovery was complete, a pretrial order would be issued formulating the issues for trial; this order would perform many of the functions of the complaint in a system of fact pleading. See Rule 16; see generally Wright, The Law of Federal Courts § 68 (4th ed. 1983).

The idea of "a plain and short statement of the claim" has not caught on. Few complaints follow the models in the Appendix of Forms. Plaintiffs' lawyers, knowing that some judges read a complaint as soon as it is filed in order to get a sense of the suit, hope by pleading facts to "educate" (that is to say, influence) the judge with regard to the nature and probable merits of the case, and also hope to set the stage for an advantageous settlement by showing the defendant what a powerful case they intend to prove. The pleading of facts is well illustrated by the present case. The complaint is twenty pages long and has a hundred page appendix (the comparable worth study).

A plaintiff who files a long and detailed complaint may plead himself out of court by including factual allegations which if true show that his legal rights were not invaded. Kaiser Aluminum & Chemical Sales, Inc. v. Avondale Shipyards, Inc., 677 F.2d 1045, 1050 (5th Cir. 1982); Associated Builders, Inc. v. Alabama Power Co., 505 F.2d 97, 100 (5th Cir. 1974); Orthmann v. Apple River Campground, Inc., 757 F.2d 909, 915 (7th Cir. 1985) (dictum); 5 Wright & Miller, Federal Practice and Procedure § 1357, at p. 604 (1969). The district judge thought the plaintiffs had done that here. Let us see.

The key paragraph of the complaint is paragraph 9, which reads as follows:

> Defendants State of Illinois, its Departments and other Agencies subject to the State Personnel Code, and State Officials, have intentionally discriminated

* Form 9 now appears as Form 11 in the restyled Federal Rules. Eds.

> and continue to intentionally discriminate against female state employees in the terms and conditions of their employment because of their sex and because of their employment in historically female-dominated sex-segregated job classifications. Defendants have intentionally discriminated and continue to discriminate against male state employees because of their employment in historically female-dominated sex-segregated job classifications. The acts, practices and policies of discrimination for which defendants are responsible include, but are not limited to, the following:
>
> (a) Use of a sex-biased system of pay and classification which results in and perpetuates discrimination in compensation against women employed in historically female-dominated sex-segregated job classifications;
>
> (b) Use of a sex-biased system of pay and classification which, because it results in and perpetuates discrimination in compensation against women employed in historically female-dominated sex-segregated job classifications, adversely affects males employed in such historically female-dominated sex-segregated job classifications;
>
> (c) Compensation at lower rates of pay of female employees in historically female-dominated sex-segregated job classifications which are or have been evaluated as being of comparable, equal, or greater worth than historically male-dominated sex-segregated job classifications which receive higher rates of pay;
>
> (d) Compensation at lower rates of pay of male employees in historically female-dominated sex-segregated job classifications which are or have been evaluated as being of comparable, equal, or greater worth than historically male sex-segregated job classifications which receive higher rates of pay;
>
> (e) Compensation at lower rates of pay of female employees than male employees performing work of equal skill, effort and responsibility under similar working conditions;
>
> (f) More favorable treatment in compensation of male state employees than of similarly situated female employees;
>
> (g) Discrimination in classification.

If this were the entire charging part of the complaint, there would be no question of dismissing it for failure to state a claim. The paragraph initially charges the state with intentional discrimination against its female employees, because of their sex; and this, standing alone, would be quite enough to state a claim under Title VII. It continues, "and because of their employment in historically female-dominated sex-segregated job classifications," and then adds a claim on behalf of male employees in those classifications. The continuation could be interpreted as an allegation that the state's failure to adopt a wage scale based on the principle of comparable worth violates Title VII, and if so fails to state a claim. But the mention of "sex-segregated" blurs the picture. If the state has deliberately segregated jobs by sex, it has violated Title VII. Anyway a complaint cannot be dismissed merely because it includes invalid claims along with a valid one....

Subparagraphs (a) through (g) present a list of particular discriminatory practices; and since they are merely illustrative ("not limited to"), the complaint would not fail even if none of them were actionable. Some are, some aren't. If (a), the "use of a sex-biased system for pay and classification which results in and perpetuates discrimination in compensation against women employed in historically female-dominated sex-segregated job classifications," just means that the state is paying wages determined by the market rather than by the principle of comparable worth, it states no claim. But if it means to allege that the state has departed from the market measure on grounds of sex—not only paying higher than market wages in predominantly male job classifications and only market wages in predominantly female classifications, but keeping women from entering the predominantly male jobs ("sex-segregated")—it states a claim. Subparagraph (b) adds nothing. If the state is discriminating against women by maintaining unwarranted wage differentials between predominantly male and predominantly female jobs, any men who happen to find themselves in predominantly female jobs will be, as it were, dragged down with the women—will be incidental victims of a discrimination targeted against others.

Subparagraph (c) is an effort to fit the case to the mold of *Gunther*.... But as we said earlier, the failure to accept the recommendations in a comparable worth study is not actionable. Paragraph 9(c) thus fails to state a claim—as does (d), which is the same as (c) except that it, like subparagraph (b), complains on behalf of male occupants of predominantly female jobs.

Subparagraphs (e) and (f) are inscrutable. If they complained about payment of unequal pay for the same work they would state a claim under the Equal Pay Act. But that Act is not cited in the complaint, perhaps deliberately, and the substitution of "work of equal skill" etc. for "equal work . . . of equal skill" etc. may also be deliberate. The intention may be to claim that different pay for different *but comparable* work violates Title VII—and if so this is a comparable worth claim by a different name, and fails. However, when a defendant is unclear about the meaning of a particular allegation in the complaint, the proper course is not to move to dismiss but to move for a more definite statement. See Fed. R. Civ. P. 12(e); United States v. Employing Plasterers Assn., 347 U.S. 186, 189 (1954).

That leaves subparagraph (g)—"Discrimination in classification." This could be a reprise of the comparable worth allegations or it could mean that in classifying jobs for pay purposes the responsible state officials had used the fraction of men in each job as a factor in deciding how high a wage to pay—which would be intentional discrimination.

Maybe the allegations in paragraph 9 are illuminated by subsequent paragraphs of the complaint. Paragraph 10, after summarizing the comparable worth study, says, "Defendants knew or should have known of the historical and continuing existence of patterns and practices of discrimination in compensation and classification, as documented at least in part by the State of Illinois Study." All that the study "documents," however, is that 28 percent of the employees subject to the state's personnel code are employed in 24 job classifications, in each of which at least 80 percent of the employees are of the same sex, and that based on the principles of comparable worth the 12 predominantly female job classifications are underpaid by between 29 and 56 percent. For example, an electrician whose job is rated in the study at only 274 points in skill, responsibility, etc. has an average monthly salary of $2,826, compared to $2,104 for a nurse whose job is rated at 480 points. These disparities are consistent, however, with the state's paying market wages, and of course the fact that the state knew that market wages do not always comport with the principles of comparable worth would not make a refusal to abandon the market actionable under Title VII. But at the very end of paragraph 10 we read, "Moreover, defendants have knowingly and *willfully* failed to take any action to correct such discrimination" (emphasis added), and in the word "willfully" can perhaps be seen the glimmerings of another theory of violation that could survive a motion to dismiss. Suppose the state has declined to act on the results of the comparable worth study not because it prefers to pay (perhaps is forced by labor-market or fiscal constraints to pay) market wages but because it thinks men deserve to be paid more than women. Cf. Crawford v. Board of Education, 458 U.S. 527, 539 n. 21 (1982). This would be the kind of deliberate sex discrimination that Title VII forbids, once the statute is understood to allow wage disparities between dissimilar jobs to be challenged (*Gunther*).

"Willfully" is, however, a classic legal weasel word. Sometimes it means with wrongful intent but often it just means with knowledge of something or other. Willful evasion of taxes means not paying when you know you owe tax. After reading the comparable worth study the responsible state officials knew that the state's compensation system might not be consistent with the principles of comparable worth ("might" because there has been no determination that the comparable worth study is valid even on its own terms—maybe it's a lousy comparable worth study). But it would not follow that their failure to implement the study was willful in a sense relevant to liability under Title VII. They may have decided not to implement it because implementation would cost too much or lead to excess demand for some jobs and insufficient demand for others. The only thing that would make the failure a form of intentional and therefore actionable sex discrimination would be if the motivation for not implementing the study was the sex of the employees—if for example the officials thought that men ought to be paid more than women even if there is no difference in skill or effort or in the conditions of work. . . .

We have said that a plaintiff can plead himself right out of court. But the court is not to pounce on the plaintiff and by a crabbed and literal reading of the complaint strain to find that he has pleaded facts which show that his claim is not actionable, and then dismiss the complaint on the merits so that the plaintiff cannot replead. (The dismissal would preclude another suit based on any theory that the plaintiff could have advanced on the basis of the facts giving rise to the first suit. Alexander v.

Chicago Park District, 773 F.2d 850, 854 (7th Cir. 1985); Bunker Ramo Corp. v. United Business Forms, Inc., 713 F.2d 1272, 1277 (7th Cir. 1983).) The district judge did not quite do that here, because this complaint can easily be read to allege a departure from the principles of comparable worth, and no more. But that reading is not inevitable, and the fact that it is logical and unstrained is not enough to warrant dismissal. In the system created by the Federal Rules of Civil Procedure a complaint "should not be dismissed for failure to state a claim unless it appears beyond doubt that the plaintiff can prove no set of facts in support of his claim which would entitle him to relief." Conley v. Gibson, 355 U.S. 41, 45-46 (1957). This language, repeated though it has been in countless later cases (see, e. g., Hishon v. King & Spaulding, 467 U.S. 69 (1984)), should not be taken literally; for taken literally it would permit dismissal only in frivolous cases. As we said earlier, if the plaintiff, though not required to do so, pleads facts, and the facts show that he is entitled to no relief, the complaint should be dismissed. There would be no point in allowing such a lawsuit to go any further; its doom is foretold. But this is not such a case....

Furthermore, a complaint is not required to allege all, or any, of the facts logically entailed by the claim. If Illinois is overpaying men relative to women, this must mean—unless the market model is entirely inapplicable to labor markets—that it is paying women at least their market wage (and therefore men more), for women wouldn't work for less than they could get in the market; and if so the state must also be refusing to hire women in the men's jobs, for above-market wages in those jobs would be a magnet drawing the women from their lower-paying jobs. Maybe the references in the complaint to the segregation of jobs by sex are meant to allege such refusals but if not this pleading omission would not be critical. A plaintiff does not have to plead evidence. If these plaintiffs admitted or the defendants proved that there was no steering or other method of segregating jobs by sex, the plaintiff's theory of discrimination might be incoherent, and fail. But a complaint does not fail to state a claim merely because it does not set forth a complete and convincing picture of the alleged wrongdoing. So the plaintiffs do not have to allege steering even if it is in some sense implicit in their claim.... It is premature to conclude that there is *no* worthwhile remedy for the intentional discrimination that consists of overpaying workers in predominantly male jobs because most of those workers are male. We emphasize, however, that proof of this causality is essential and is not to be inferred merely from the results of a comparable worth study and from the refusal of the employer to implement the study's recommendations.... But the plaintiffs are entitled to make additional efforts to prove a case of intentional discrimination within the boundaries sketched in this opinion.

Reversed and Remanded.

Notes and Questions

1. Several years after Judge Posner decided *American Nurses*, he wrote about his view of sex discrimination claims, concluding:

> What has been the net effect of the cascade of laws and lawsuits aimed at eliminating sex discrimination in employment? This is maddeningly difficult to say, but it is possible that women as a whole have not benefited and have in fact suffered. Because of the heterogeneity of women as an economic class and their interdependence with men, laws aimed at combating sex discrimination are more likely to benefit particular groups of women at the expense of other groups rather than women as a whole. And to the extent that the overall effect of the law is to reduce aggregate social welfare because of the allocative and administrative costs of the law, women as a group are hurt along with men. Sex discrimination has long been on the decline, for reasons unrelated to law, and this makes it all the more likely that the principal effect of public intervention may have been to make women as a group worse off by reducing the efficiency of the economy. The case for ambitious extensions of sex discrimination law—for example in the direction of comparable worth—is therefore weak.
>
> These suggestions should not be surprising, in light of the extensive, and largely negative, economic literature on regulation. There is a tendency to suppose that laws forbidding discrimination are somehow exempt from the critique of regulation. This position is difficult to sustain.
>
> It is possible that the economic costs of sex discrimination law are offset by gains not measured in an economic analysis—gains in self-esteem, for example. But it is not clear that, if the canvas is broadened in this fashion, the picture brightens. For example, if by reducing the wages of men sex discrimination law propels more wives into the job market, with the result that (since they still bear the principal burden of household production) they work harder, have fewer children, and have less stable marriages, it is not clear that they are better off on balance than they were when their husbands had higher wages and they stayed home. The social, like the economic, consequences of sex discrimination law are murky, and not necessarily positive. In any event it is important to know what the sex discrimination laws cost; the price tag for an increase in women's self-esteem, if known, might be thought too high by society.

An Economic Analysis of Sex Discrimination Laws, 56 U. Chi. L. Rev. 1311, 1334 (1989). Do these views shed further light on *American Nurses*?

2. As we saw in Chapter 1, defects in subject matter jurisdiction, unlike objections to personal jurisdiction and failure to state a claim, are generally non-waivable and may be raised at any time by either party or the court. (Recall *Belleville Catering*, supra page 220, in which the Seventh Circuit discovered a lack of complete diversity in a case that had gone all the way to trial below. The court dismissed the case *sua sponte*.).

But how do we know when a defect is "jurisdictional" such that the court lacks subject matter jurisdiction? You learned in Chapter 1 how to evaluate citizenship and the amount in controversy in diversity cases, and, in federal question cases, how to apply the well-pleaded complaint rule. These are the core doctrines. But how should a court treat a motion to dismiss arguing that the plaintiff has not met a specific statutory requirement that is a predicate to determining liability? Consider, for example, in an employment discrimination case, a requirement that limits Title VII liability to "employers," which the statute defines as businesses with more than 15 employees.

If the defendant has fewer than 15 employees, and Title VII's prohibitions therefore do not apply, can she raise this at any time as a defect in the court's subject matter jurisdiction, or is it properly considered a substantive challenge for failure to state a claim? And what about statutes providing strict time limits for certain rights and remedies to apply—does a party's failure to meet these deadlines leave the court without subject matter jurisdiction, or does it merely present a ground for dismissal under Rule 12(b)(6) in the same way that statutes of limitation do?

You can see the temptation, both for defendants and docket-burdened courts, to characterize a defect as "jurisdictional" if it would get rid of the case. The defect can be raised whenever it is discovered and it immediately strips the court of its power to hear the case. The court, moreover, can reassure itself that it has deferred to the federalism interests that limit federal court jurisdiction. However, the indiscriminate extension of limits on subject matter jurisdiction is not without its costs, not the least of which is the confusion created by blurring the distinction between jurisdictional defects and substantive or other procedural deficiencies in a case. There is, too, the rather serious risk that cases will be thrown out of federal court late in the game, perhaps after the expenses of adjudicating the merits have already been incurred.

The Supreme Court has tried to curtail the trend toward expanding the category of so-called jurisdictional defects, simultaneously decrying the proliferation of "drive-by jurisdictional rulings" and conceding that the Court itself, "no less than other courts, has sometimes been profligate in its use of the term [jurisdiction]." Arbaugh v. Y&H Corp., 546 U.S. 500, 510 (2006). *Arbaugh* resolved a circuit split in the Title VII setting over whether the size of defendant's business is a jurisdictional issue. The plaintiff, a bartender and waitress in defendant's Moonlight Café, sued for sexual harassment. Two weeks after the trial court entered judgment for the plaintiff following a bench trial, defendant filed a Rule 12(h)(3) motion to dismiss for lack of subject matter jurisdiction, arguing for the very first time that it was not an "employer" within the meaning of Title VII. Reversing the trial court and the Fifth Circuit, the Court held that the statutory definition of an "employer" as a business with 15 or more employees is not a requirement going to the subject matter jurisdiction of federal courts.

To begin with, the Court reasoned, the definition of an employer is not included in the jurisdictional provisions of the statute authorizing a federal cause of action. It "appears in a separate provision that does not speak in jurisdictional terms or refer in any way to the jurisdiction of the district courts." Id. at 515 (internal quotation marks omitted). Just as important,

> [g]iven the unfair[ness] and waste of judicial resources entailed in tying the employee-numerosity requirement to subject-matter jurisdiction, we think it the sounder course to refrain from constricting § 1331 or Title VII's jurisdictional provision, 42 U.S.C. § 2000e-5(f)(3), and to leave the ball in Congress' court. If the Legislature clearly states that a threshold limitation on a statute's scope shall count as jurisdictional, then courts and litigants will be duly instructed and will not be left to wrestle with the issue. But when Congress does not rank a statutory limitation on coverage as jurisdictional, courts should treat the restriction as nonjurisdictional in character.

Id. at 515-516 (internal quotation marks, citations, and footnote omitted). The Court reached a similar conclusion in the context of mandatory time limits, holding in Scarborough v. Principi that time prescriptions, however emphatic, "are not properly typed 'jurisdictional.'" 541 U.S. 401, 414 (2004). See also Eberhart v. United States, 546 U.S. 12 (2005) (rule setting forth time limit for a motion for new trial is not "jurisdictional"); Kontrick v. Ryan, 540 U.S. 443, 453 (2004) (time limits for objections to bankruptcy discharge are not "jurisdictional"); Faranza K. v. Indiana Dep't of Educ., 473 F.3d 703, 705 (7th Cir. 2007) (filing deadline and verification requirements are not jurisdictional defects). Cf. Kircher v. Putnam Funds Trust, 547 U.S. 633, 642-44 (decision about whether removal was proper under Securities Litigation Uniform Standards Act of 1998 is "jurisdictional").

3. Notice that Judge Posner assesses the sufficiency of each claim separately because so long as any one of the plaintiffs' theories of discrimination states a claim, the case may go forward. Whatever you make of his resolution of each claim, he is surely aided in that endeavor by the fact that plaintiffs have set out each claim in their complaint. But does notice pleading *require* the plaintiff to do so, or can she just describe what happened and leave it to the defendant and the court to sort out how many legitimate claims those facts raise? Some courts have come to refer to jumbled claims rather derisively as "shotgun pleading."

For a case demonstrating judicial frustration, bordering on hostility, with so-called shotgun pleadings in civil rights cases, see Davis v. Coca-Cola Bottling Co., 516 F.3d 955, 980 (11th Cir. 2008). In reviewing this Title VII case, the exasperated appellate judge wrote:

> If the framers of the Federal Rules of Civil Procedure could read the record in this case—beginning with the plaintiffs' complaint and [defendant's] answer and continuing to the district court's final order granting [defendant] summary judgment—they would roll over in their graves. In fashioning the Rules, they assumed that complaints would be drafted as clearly and definitively as possible, so that the defendant could understand the cause(s) of action the plaintiff was asserting and frame a responsive pleading, and the district court, having a clear and definitive response

before it, could recognize the parties' claims and defenses, identify the issues of fact to be litigated, and proceed to a just result. The framers also assumed that the lawyers appearing before the district court would adhere to the standards of professional responsibility and conduct, and that, as officers of the court, would be aware that the federal courts constitute a scarce resource for resolving disputes and that their failure to adhere to these standards would likely yield countless untoward, and totally unacceptable, consequences.

This case confounds these assumptions. The complaint is a model of "shotgun" pleading of the sort this court has been roundly, repeatedly, and consistently condemning for years, long before this lawsuit was filed. And the defendant's answer is no better. . . .

Plaintiffs' complaint, first amended complaint, and second amended complaint are nearly identical, each containing three counts. . . . [In the 121 paragraphs of Count I] plaintiffs were contending . . . race discrimination in "pay, raises, benefits, ability to advance, and right to be free of racial discrimination, harassment and intimidation, and other terms and conditions of employment," all in violation of Title VII. This all-encompassing discrimination gave the eight named plaintiffs (and the unnamed members of their class) untold causes of action, all bunched together in one count contrary to the requirements of Federal Rule of Civil Procedure 10(b). With one exception . . . Count I failed explicitly to link a particular plaintiff to a particular cause of action. . . .

No competent lawyer . . . could compose an answer to these sweeping and multifaceted acts of discrimination that would be in keeping with what the framers of the Rules intended. Yet [defendant's] lawyers framed one. They used the same shotgun strategy plaintiffs had employed. Their answer contained fourteen defenses. . . . The second through the fourteenth defense were affirmative defenses, and except for the seventh defense, consisted of one sentence. These affirmative defenses did not respond to specific causes of action, because the drafter of the answer could not identify the specific causes of action each named plaintiff was purporting to allege. . . .

It took several rounds of pleadings . . . for the court even to begin the process of narrowing the issues. In the end, as our preceding analysis of plaintiffs' arguments discloses, the court missed some claims altogether. . . .

The unvarnished truth is that this court puts no credence in briefs written against a backdrop of a case disposed of on shotgun pleadings. . . . Had we not approached the appeal in this manner, there is no telling how many mistakes we might have made in identifying plaintiffs' claims, the district court's treatment of those claims, and the issues plaintiffs reserved for appeal.

Davis, 516 F.3d at 979-983. The court noted that a simple motion for more definite statement by defendants under Rule 12(e) would have saved countless hours of attorney and court time. Id. at 983-984. Remarkably, after its five-page diatribe, and after concluding that plaintiffs' case was almost entirely without merit, the court declined to sanction either side or award the prevailing party attorneys' fees. Id. at 984.

Is the problem here just lazy pleading and bad lawyering, or is it relevant that courts have gradually required parties to plead more facts than would be required by simple notice pleading? Perhaps modern cases have grown too complex to fit the notice pleading framework of Rule 8. Gone in any case is the attitude of generosity reflected in Justice Black's reframing of the complaint in *Conley*.

Note: Pleading and Substantive Law

A law-trained person reading the complaint must be able to infer from it that at least one legal theory arguably would justify the request for a remedy, if the facts are as alleged. Knowing what facts to plead therefore requires some substantive knowledge. Given this interdependence of substance and procedure, many law students find this first encounter with pleading fairly abstract; after all, you are just learning the elements of torts, contracts, and other legal wrongs.

Nevertheless, some general principles about pleading should be obvious even at this early stage in your legal career. For example, you likely already have studied (or can intuit) the basic elements of the tort of negligence. Now examine Form 11, which you will find in the Appendix to the Federal Rules of Civil Procedure (located after the Rules in your Rule book), which gives specific content to Rule 8 in a concrete tort setting. Form 11 suggests that a plaintiff in a negligence case should allege—at least—facts that show a duty, breach of that duty, and injuries that were proximately caused by that breach. Put another way, the complaint should tell the judge who did what to whom, where, and how, then ask for relief. Many attorneys will do more than Form 11, of course, in describing the event and its consequences. Also, many districts require lawyers to fill out a civil cover sheet when they file a complaint, on which they must indicate what kind of case it is by checking the appropriate box, for example, negligence or contract. This means the lawyer is expected to have a theory of the case when she files a lawsuit, even if it is only a general idea and may change as discovery dictates. Our inquiry at this point, however, is not whether more can or should be included in a complaint filed in federal court, but what—at the least—*must* be.

Notwithstanding the simplicity of the Forms in the Appendix to the Rules, this turns out to be a rather difficult question to answer. Take a look once again at the final two paragraphs of Judge Posner's opinion in *American Nurses*. Taking up the most frequently cited part of *Conley*, he writes that

> [i]n the system created by the Federal Rules of Civil Procedure a complaint "should not be dismissed for failure to state a claim unless it appears beyond doubt that the plaintiff can prove no set of facts in support of his claim which would entitle him to relief." Conley v. Gibson, 355 U.S. 41, 45-46 (1957). This language, repeated though it has been in countless other cases, *should not be taken literally; for taken literally it would permit dismissal only in frivolous cases.*

783 F.2d at 727 (emphasis added) (citation omitted). How, then, *should* we take this language? Consider the torts example from Form 11. Can a plaintiff simply plead that the defendant "negligently struck plaintiff" without describing any specific details of the incident other than the location and the date on which it occurred? Must the plaintiff include facts that, if true, reveal the manner in which defendant was negligent (e.g., driving while talking on his cell phone, reaching into the back seat to assist a passenger, driving under the influence of medications that reduce reaction time)?

Whatever his reservations about the "any set of facts" language from *Conley*, Judge Posner rightly observes at the start of the last paragraph that, under Rule 8, "a complaint is not required to allege all, or any, of the facts logically entailed by the claim. . . . [Nor does a plaintiff] have to plead evidence. . . . [A] complaint does not fail to state a claim merely because it does not set forth a complete and convincing picture of the alleged wrongdoing." Id. So it would appear that our tort victim may allege negligence generally.

Still, Judge Posner appears to be ill at ease with the plaintiffs' claim in *American Nurses* and, in the same paragraph, he goes on to question the plausibility of their case, emphasizing that they cannot prevail without showing intentional steering or sex segregation between traditionally male and female jobs. As he puts it, "proof of this causality is essential and is not to be inferred merely from the results of a comparable worth study and from the refusal of the employer to implement the study's recommendations." Id. at 730. The complaint survives, but plaintiffs will have to meet a high threshold of proof to prevail on the merits (so high, indeed, that they dropped their case after Posner's ruling).

Notice too that Judge Posner seems on the verge of concluding that plaintiffs' claim was too economically implausible to survive the motion to dismiss. Only proof of intentional steering or sex segregation would convince him of the existence of the pay discrimination scheme plaintiffs have alleged. The case reveals not only the risks of notice pleading for plaintiffs, but the perennial temptation on the part of judges with crowded dockets to use Rule 12(b)(6) motions to screen out cases that, while not frivolous, seem unlikely to succeed.

American Nurses proved prescient. In 2007 the Supreme Court revisited *Conley* and answered the question whether the oft-cited "any set of facts" language should be taken literally.

Bell Atlantic Corp. v. Twombly

550 U.S. 544 (2007)

Justice Souter delivered the opinion of the Court.

Liability under § 1 of the Sherman Act, 15 U.S.C. § 1, requires a "contract, combination . . . , or conspiracy, in restraint of trade or commerce." The question in this putative class action is whether a § 1 complaint can survive a motion to dismiss when it alleges that major telecommunications providers engaged in certain parallel conduct unfavorable to competition, absent some factual context suggesting agreement, as distinct from identical, independent action. We hold that such a complaint should be dismissed.

I

The upshot of the 1984 divestiture of the American Telephone & Telegraph Company's (AT&T) local telephone business was a system of regional service monopolies (variously called "Regional Bell Operating Companies," "Baby Bells," or "Incumbent Local Exchange Carriers" (ILECs)), and a separate, competitive market for long-distance service from which the ILECs were excluded. More than a decade later, Congress withdrew approval of the ILECs' monopolies by enacting the Telecommunications Act of 1996 (1996 Act), 110 Stat. 56, which "fundamentally restructure[d] local telephone markets" and "subject[ed] [ILECs] to a host of duties intended to facilitate market entry." AT&T Corp. v. Iowa Utilities Bd., 525 U.S. 366, 371 (1999). In recompense, the 1996 Act set conditions for authorizing ILECs to enter the long-distance market. See 47 U.S.C. § 271.

"Central to the [new] scheme [was each ILEC's] obligation . . . to share its network with competitors," Verizon Communications Inc. v. Law Offices of Curtis V. Trinko, LLP, 540 U.S. 398, 402 (2004), which came to be known as "competitive local exchange carriers" (CLECs). A CLEC could make use of an ILEC's network in any of three ways: by (1) "purchas[ing] local telephone services at wholesale rates for resale to end users," (2) "leas[ing] elements of the [ILEC's] network 'on an unbundled basis,'" or (3) "interconnect[ing] its own facilities with the [ILEC's] network." *Iowa Utilities Bd.*, supra, at 371 (quoting 47 U.S.C. § 251(c)). . . .

Respondents William Twombly and Lawrence Marcus (hereinafter plaintiffs) represent a putative class consisting of all "subscribers of local telephone and/or high speed internet services . . . from February 8, 1996 to present." Amended Complaint ¶ 53. In this action against petitioners, a group of ILECs,[1] plaintiffs seek treble damages and declaratory and injunctive relief for claimed violations of § 1 of the Sherman Act, 15 U.S.C. § 1, which prohibits "[e]very contract, combination in the form of trust or otherwise, or conspiracy, in restraint of trade or commerce among the several States, or with foreign nations."

1. The 1984 divestiture of AT&T's local telephone service created seven Regional Bell Operating Companies. Through a series of mergers and acquisitions, those seven companies were consolidated into the four ILECs named in this suit: BellSouth Corporation, Qwest Communications International, Inc., SBC Communications, Inc., and Verizon Communications, Inc. (successor-in-interest to Bell Atlantic Corporation). Complaint ¶ 21. Together, these ILECs allegedly control 90 percent or more of the market for local telephone service in the 48 contiguous States. Id., ¶ 48.

The complaint alleges that the ILECs conspired to restrain trade in two ways, each supposedly inflating charges for local telephone and high-speed Internet services. Plaintiffs say, first, that the ILECs "engaged in parallel conduct" in their respective service areas to inhibit the growth of upstart CLECs. Their actions allegedly included making unfair agreements with the CLECs for access to ILEC networks, providing inferior connections to the networks, overcharging, and billing in ways designed to sabotage the CLECs' relations with their own customers. . . .

Second, the complaint charges agreements by the ILECs to refrain from competing against one another. These are to be inferred from the ILECs' common failure "meaningfully [to] pursu[e]" "attractive business opportunit[ies]" in contiguous markets where they possessed "substantial competitive advantages," and from a statement of Richard Notebaert, chief executive officer (CEO) of the ILEC Qwest, that competing in the territory of another ILEC "'might be a good way to turn a quick dollar but that doesn't make it right.'"

The complaint couches its ultimate allegations this way:

> In the absence of any meaningful competition between the [ILECs] in one another's markets, and in light of the parallel course of conduct that each engaged in to prevent competition from CLECs within their respective local telephone and/or high speed internet services markets and the other facts and market circumstances alleged above, Plaintiffs allege upon information and belief that [the ILECs] have entered into a contract, combination or conspiracy to prevent competitive entry in their respective local telephone and/or high speed internet services markets and have agreed not to compete with one another and otherwise allocated customers and markets to one another.

The United States District Court for the Southern District of New York dismissed the complaint for failure to state a claim upon which relief can be granted. The District Court acknowledged that "plaintiffs may allege a conspiracy by citing instances of parallel business behavior that suggest an agreement," but emphasized that "while '[c]ircumstantial evidence of consciously parallel behavior may have made heavy inroads into the traditional judicial attitude toward conspiracy[, . . .] "conscious parallelism" has not yet read conspiracy out of the Sherman Act entirely.'" 313 F. Supp. 2d 174, 179 (2003) (quoting Theatre Enterprises, Inc. v. Paramount Film Distributing Corp., 346 U.S. 537, 541 (1954)). Thus, the District Court understood that allegations of parallel business conduct, taken alone, do not state a claim under § 1; plaintiffs must allege additional facts that "ten [d] to exclude independent self-interested conduct as an explanation for defendants' parallel behavior." 313 F. Supp. 2d at 179. . . . As to the ILECs' supposed agreement against competing with each other, the District Court found that the complaint does not "alleg[e] facts . . . suggesting that refraining from competing in other territories as CLECs was contrary to [the ILECs'] apparent economic interests, and consequently [does] not rais[e] an inference that [the ILECs'] actions were the result of a conspiracy." Id. at 188.

The Court of Appeals for the Second Circuit reversed, holding that the District Court tested the complaint by the wrong standard.... Although the Court of Appeals took the view that plaintiffs must plead facts that "include conspiracy among the realm of 'plausible' possibilities in order to survive a motion to dismiss," it then said that "to rule that allegations of parallel anticompetitive conduct fail to support a plausible conspiracy claim, a court would have to conclude that there is no set of facts that would permit a plaintiff to demonstrate that the particular parallelism asserted was the product of collusion rather than coincidence." Id.

We granted certiorari to address the proper standard for pleading an antitrust conspiracy through allegations of parallel conduct and now reverse.

II

A

Because § 1 of the Sherman Act "does not prohibit [all] unreasonable restraints of trade... but only restraints effected by a contract, combination, or conspiracy," Copperweld Corp. v. Independence Tube Corp., 467 U.S. 752, 775 (1984), "[t]he crucial question" is whether the challenged anticompetitive conduct "stem[s] from independent decision or from an agreement, tacit or express," *Theatre Enterprises*, 346 U.S. at 540. While a showing of parallel "business behavior is admissible circumstantial evidence from which the fact finder may infer agreement," it falls short of "conclusively establish[ing] agreement or... itself constitut[ing] a Sherman Act offense." Id. at 540-541. Even "conscious parallelism," a common reaction of "firms in a concentrated market [that] recogniz[e] their shared economic interests and their interdependence with respect to price and output decisions" is "not in itself unlawful." Brooke Group Ltd. v. Brown & Williamson Tobacco Corp., 509 U.S. 209, 227 (1993); see 6 P. Areeda & H. Hovenkamp, Antitrust Law ¶ 1433a, p. 236 (2d ed. 2003) (hereinafter Areeda & Hovenkamp) ("The courts are nearly unanimous in saying that mere interdependent parallelism does not establish the contract, combination, or conspiracy required by Sherman Act § 1")....

The inadequacy of showing parallel conduct or interdependence, without more, mirrors the ambiguity of the behavior: consistent with conspiracy, but just as much in line with a wide swath of rational and competitive business strategy unilaterally prompted by common perceptions of the market. See, e.g., AEI-Brookings Joint Center for Regulatory Studies, Epstein, Motions to Dismiss Antitrust Cases: Separating Fact from Fantasy, Related Publication 06-08, pp. 3-4 (2006) (discussing problem of "false positives" in § 1 suits). Accordingly, we have previously hedged against false inferences from identical behavior at a number of points in the trial sequence. An antitrust conspiracy plaintiff with evidence showing nothing beyond parallel conduct is not entitled to a directed verdict; proof of a § 1 conspiracy must include evidence tending to exclude the possibility of independent action; and at the summary judgment stage a § 1 plaintiff's offer of conspiracy evidence must tend to rule out the possibility that the defendants were acting independently, see Matsushita Elec. Industrial Co. v. Zenith Radio Corp., 475 U.S. 574 (1986).

B

This case presents the antecedent question of what a plaintiff must plead in order to state a claim under § 1 of the Sherman Act. Federal Rule of Civil Procedure 8(a)(2) requires only "a short and plain statement of the claim showing that the pleader is entitled to relief," in order to "give the defendant fair notice of what the . . . claim is and the grounds upon which it rests," Conley v. Gibson, 355 U.S. 41, 47 (1957). While a complaint attacked by a Rule 12(b)(6) motion to dismiss does not need detailed factual allegations, id., a plaintiff's obligation to provide the "grounds" of his "entitle [ment] to relief" requires more than labels and conclusions, and a formulaic recitation of the elements of a cause of action will not do. Factual allegations must be enough to raise a right to relief above the speculative level, see 5 C. Wright & A. Miller, Federal Practice and Procedure § 1216, pp. 235-236 (3d ed. 2004) ("[T]he pleading must contain something more . . . than . . . a statement of facts that merely creates a suspicion [of] a legally cognizable right of action"),[3] on the assumption that all the allegations in the complaint are true (even if doubtful in fact), see, e.g., Swierkiewicz v. Sorema N.A., 534 U.S. 506, 508, n.1 (2002); Neitzke v. Williams, 490 U.S. 319, 327 (1989) ("Rule 12(b)(6) does not countenance . . . dismissals based on a judge's disbelief of a complaint's factual allegations"); Scheuer v. Rhodes, 416 U.S. 232, 236 (1974) (a well-pleaded complaint may proceed even if it appears "that a recovery is very remote and unlikely").

In applying these general standards to a § 1 claim, we hold that stating such a claim requires a complaint with enough factual matter (taken as true) to suggest that an agreement was made. Asking for plausible grounds to infer an agreement does not impose a probability requirement

3. The dissent greatly oversimplifies matters by suggesting that the Federal Rules somehow dispensed with the pleading of facts altogether. See post, at 10 (opinion of Stevens, J.) (pleading standard of Federal Rules "does not require, or even invite, the pleading of facts"). While, for most types of cases, the Federal Rules eliminated the cumbersome requirement that a claimant "set out *in detail* the facts upon which he bases his claim," Conley v. Gibson, 355 U.S. 41, 47 (1957) (emphasis added), Rule 8(a)(2) still requires a "showing," rather than a blanket assertion, of entitlement to relief. Without some factual allegation in the complaint, it is hard to see how a claimant could satisfy the requirement of providing not only "fair notice" of the nature of the claim, but also "grounds" on which the claim rests. See 5 Wright & Miller § 1202, at 94, 95 (Rule 8(a) "contemplate[s] the statement of circumstances, occurrences, and events in support of the claim presented" and does not authorize a pleader's "bare averment that he wants relief and is entitled to it").

at the pleading stage; it simply calls for enough fact to raise a reasonable expectation that discovery will reveal evidence of illegal agreement. And, of course, a well-pleaded complaint may proceed even if it strikes a savvy judge that actual proof of those facts is improbable, and "that a recovery is very remote and unlikely." Id. In identifying facts that are suggestive enough to render a § 1 conspiracy plausible, we have the benefit of the prior rulings and considered views of leading commentators, already quoted, that lawful parallel conduct fails to bespeak unlawful agreement. It makes sense to say, therefore, that an allegation of parallel conduct and a bare assertion of conspiracy will not suffice. Without more, parallel conduct does not suggest conspiracy, and a conclusory allegation of agreement at some unidentified point does not supply facts adequate to show illegality. Hence, when allegations of parallel conduct are set out in order to make a § 1 claim, they must be placed in a context that raises a suggestion of a preceding agreement, not merely parallel conduct that could just as well be independent action.

The need at the pleading stage for allegations plausibly suggesting (not merely consistent with) agreement reflects the threshold requirement of Rule 8(a)(2) that the "plain statement" possess enough heft to "sho[w] that the pleader is entitled to relief." A statement of parallel conduct, even conduct consciously undertaken, needs some setting suggesting the agreement necessary to make out a § 1 claim; without that further circumstance pointing toward a meeting of the minds, an account of a defendant's commercial efforts stays in neutral territory. An allegation of parallel conduct is thus much like a naked assertion of conspiracy in a § 1 complaint: it gets the complaint close to stating a claim, but without some further factual enhancement it stops short of the line between possibility and plausibility of "entitle[ment] to relief."

We alluded to the practical significance of the Rule 8 entitlement requirement in Dura Pharmaceuticals, Inc. v. Broudo, 544 U.S. 336 (2005), when we explained that something beyond the mere possibility of loss causation must be alleged, lest a plaintiff with "'a largely groundless claim'" be allowed to "'take up the time of a number of other people, with the right to do so representing an *in terrorem* increment of the settlement value.'" Id. at 347 (quoting Blue Chip Stamps v. Manor Drug Stores, 421 U.S. 723, 741 (1975)). So, when the allegations in a complaint, however true, could not raise a claim of entitlement to relief, "'this basic deficiency should . . . be exposed at the point of minimum expenditure of time and money by the parties and the court.'" 5 Wright & Miller § 1216, at 233-234 (quoting Daves v. Hawaiian Dredging Co., 114 F. Supp. 643, 645 (D. Haw. 1953)); see also *Dura*, supra, at 346; Asahi Glass Co. v. Pentech Pharmaceuticals, Inc., 289 F. Supp. 2d 986, 995 (N.D. Ill. 2003) (Posner, J., sitting by designation) ("[S]ome threshold of plausibility must be crossed at the outset before a patent antitrust case should be permitted to go into its inevitably costly and protracted discovery phase").

Thus, it is one thing to be cautious before dismissing an antitrust complaint in advance of discovery, but quite another to forget that proceeding to antitrust discovery can be expensive. As we indicated over 20 years ago in Associated Gen. Contractors of Cal., Inc. v. Carpenters, 459 U.S. 519, 528, n.17 (1983), "a district court must retain the power to insist upon some specificity in pleading before allowing a potentially massive factual controversy to proceed." See also Car Carriers, Inc. v. Ford Motor Co., 745 F.2d 1101, 1106 (7th Cir. 1984) ("[T]he costs of modern federal antitrust litigation and the increasing caseload of the federal courts counsel against sending the parties into discovery when there is no reasonable likelihood that the plaintiffs can construct a claim from the events related in the complaint"); . . . Memorandum from Paul V. Niemeyer, Chair, Advisory Committee on Civil Rules, to Hon. Anthony J. Scirica, Chair, Committee on Rules of Practice and Procedure (May 11, 1999), 192 F.R.D. 354, 357 (2000) (reporting that discovery accounts for as much as 90 percent of litigation costs when discovery is actively employed). That potential expense is obvious enough in the present case: Plaintiffs represent a putative class of at least 90 percent of all subscribers to local telephone or high-speed Internet service in the continental United States, in an action against America's largest telecommunications firms (with many thousands of employees generating reams and gigabytes of business records) for unspecified (if any) instances of antitrust violations that allegedly occurred over a period of seven years.

It is no answer to say that a claim just shy of a plausible entitlement to relief can, if groundless, be weeded out early in the discovery process through "careful case management," post, given the common lament that the success of judicial supervision in checking discovery abuse has been on the modest side. See, e.g., Easterbrook, Discovery as Abuse, 69 B.U. L. Rev. 635, 638 (1989) ("Judges can do little about impositional discovery when parties control the legal claims to be presented and conduct the discovery themselves"). And it is self-evident that the problem of discovery abuse cannot be solved by "careful scrutiny of evidence at the summary judgment stage," much less "lucid instructions to juries," post; the threat of discovery expense will push cost-conscious defendants to settle even anemic cases before reaching those proceedings. Probably, then, it is only by taking care to require allegations that reach the level suggesting conspiracy that we can hope to avoid the potentially enormous expense of discovery in cases with no "'reasonably founded hope that the [discovery] process will reveal relevant evidence'" to support a § 1 claim. *Dura*, 544 U.S., at 347 (quoting *Blue Chip Stamps*, supra, at 741; alteration in *Dura*).[6]

6. The dissent takes heart in the reassurances of plaintiffs' counsel that discovery would be "phased" and "limited to the existence of the alleged conspiracy and class certification." Post. But determining whether some illegal agreement may have taken place between unspecified persons at different ILECs (each a multibillion dollar corporation with legions of management level employees) at some point over seven years is a sprawling, costly, and hugely time-consuming undertaking not easily susceptible to the kind of line drawing and case management that the dissent envisions. Perhaps the best answer to the dissent's optimism that antitrust discovery is open to effective judicial control is a more extensive quotation of the authority just cited, a judge with a background in antitrust law. Given the system that we have, the hope of effective judicial supervision is slim: "The timing is all

Plaintiffs do not, of course, dispute the requirement of plausibility and the need for something more than merely parallel behavior explained in *Theatre Enterprises*, *Monsanto*, and *Matsushita*, and their main argument against the plausibility standard at the pleading stage is its ostensible conflict with an early statement of ours construing Rule 8. Justice Black's opinion for the Court in Conley v. Gibson spoke not only of the need for fair notice of the grounds for entitlement to relief but of "the accepted rule that a complaint should not be dismissed for failure to state a claim unless it appears beyond doubt that the plaintiff can prove no set of facts in support of his claim which would entitle him to relief." 355 U.S. at 45-46. This "no set of facts" language can be read in isolation as saying that any statement revealing the theory of the claim will suffice unless its factual impossibility may be shown from the face of the pleadings; and the Court of Appeals appears to have read *Conley* in some such way when formulating its understanding of the proper pleading standard.

On such a focused and literal reading of *Conley*'s "no set of facts," a wholly conclusory statement of claim would survive a motion to dismiss whenever the pleadings left open the possibility that a plaintiff might later establish some "set of [undisclosed] facts" to support recovery. So here, the Court of Appeals specifically found the prospect of unearthing direct evidence of conspiracy sufficient to preclude dismissal, even though the complaint does not set forth a single fact in a context that suggests an agreement. It seems fair to say that this approach to pleading would dispense with any showing of a "'reasonably founded hope'" that a plaintiff would be able to make a case, see *Dura*, 544 U.S. at 347 (quoting *Blue Chip Stamps*, 421 U.S. at 741); Mr. Micawber's optimism would be enough.*

Seeing this, a good many judges and commentators have balked at taking the literal terms of the *Conley* passage as a pleading standard. See, e.g., *Car Carriers*, 745 F.2d at 1106 ("*Conley* has never been interpreted literally" and, "[i]n practice, a complaint . . . must contain either direct or inferential allegations respecting all the material elements necessary to

---

wrong. The plaintiff files a sketchy complaint (the Rules of Civil Procedure discourage fulsome documents), and discovery is launched. A judicial officer does not know the details of the case the parties will present and in theory *cannot* know the details. Discovery is used to find the details. The judicial officer always knows less than the parties, and the parties themselves may not know very well where they are going or what they expect to find. A magistrate supervising discovery does not—cannot—know the expected productivity of a given request, because the nature of the requester's claim and the contents of the files (or head) of the adverse party are unknown. Judicial officers cannot measure the costs and benefits to the requester and so cannot isolate impositional requests. Requesters have no reason to disclose their own estimates because they gain from imposing costs on rivals (and may lose from an improvement in accuracy). The portions of the Rules of Civil Procedure calling on judges to trim back excessive demands, therefore, have been, and are doomed to be, hollow. We cannot prevent what we cannot detect; we cannot detect what we cannot define; we cannot define 'abusive' discovery except in theory, because in practice we lack essential information." Easterbrook, Discovery as Abuse, 69 B.U. L. Rev. 635, 638-639 (1989).

* [A reference to a character in Charles Dickens's *David Copperfield*. EDS.]

sustain recovery under *some* viable legal theory" (internal quotation marks omitted; emphasis and omission in original)); Ascon Properties, Inc. v. Mobil Oil Co., 866 F.2d 1149, 1155 (9th Cir. 1989) (tension between *Conley*'s "no set of facts" language and its acknowledgment that a plaintiff must provide the "grounds" on which his claim rests); O'Brien v. DiGrazia, 544 F.2d 543, 546, n.3 (1st Cir. 1976) ("[W]hen a plaintiff . . . supplies facts to support his claim, we do not think that *Conley* imposes a duty on the courts to conjure up unpleaded facts that might turn a frivolous claim of unconstitutional . . . action into a substantial one"); Hazard, From Whom No Secrets Are Hid, 76 Tex. L. Rev. 1665, 1685 (1998) (describing *Conley* as having "turned Rule 8 on its head"); Marcus, The Revival of Fact Pleading Under the Federal Rules of Civil Procedure, 86 Colum. L. Rev. 433, 463-465 (1986) (noting tension between *Conley* and subsequent understandings of Rule 8).

We could go on, but there is no need to pile up further citations to show that *Conley*'s "no set of facts" language has been questioned, criticized, and explained away long enough. To be fair to the *Conley* Court, the passage should be understood in light of the opinion's preceding summary of the complaint's concrete allegations, which the Court quite reasonably understood as amply stating a claim for relief. But the passage so often quoted fails to mention this understanding on the part of the Court, and after puzzling the profession for 50 years, this famous observation has earned its retirement. The phrase is best forgotten as an incomplete, negative gloss on an accepted pleading standard: once a claim has been stated adequately, it may be supported by showing any set of facts consistent with the allegations in the complaint. See *Sanjuan*, 40 F.3d at 251 (once a claim for relief has been stated, a plaintiff "receives the benefit of imagination, so long as the hypotheses are consistent with the complaint"); accord, *Swierkiewicz*, 534 U.S. at 514. *Conley*, then, described the breadth of opportunity to prove what an adequate complaint claims, not the minimum standard of adequate pleading to govern a complaint's survival.[8]

III

When we look for plausibility in this complaint, we agree with the District Court that plaintiffs' claim of conspiracy in restraint of trade comes up short. To begin with, the complaint leaves no doubt that

8. . . . The dissent finds relevance in Court of Appeals precedents from the 1940s, which allegedly gave rise to *Conley*'s "no set of facts" language. See post. Even indulging this line of analysis, these cases do not challenge the understanding that, before proceeding to discovery, a complaint must allege facts suggestive of illegal conduct. . . . Rather, these cases stand for the unobjectionable proposition that, when a complaint adequately states a claim, it may not be dismissed based on a district court's assessment that the plaintiff will fail to find evidentiary support for his allegations or prove his claim to the satisfaction of the factfinder. Cf. Scheuer v. Rhodes, 416 U.S. 232, 236 (1974) (a district court weighing a motion to dismiss asks "not whether a plaintiff will ultimately prevail but whether the claimant is entitled to offer evidence to support the claims").

plaintiffs rest their § 1 claim on descriptions of parallel conduct and not on any independent allegation of actual agreement among the ILECs. Supra. Although in form a few stray statements speak directly of agreement, on fair reading these are merely legal conclusions resting on the prior allegations. Thus, the complaint first takes account of the alleged "absence of any meaningful competition between [the ILECs] in one another's markets," "the parallel course of conduct that each [ILEC] engaged in to prevent competition from CLECs," "and the other facts and market circumstances alleged [earlier]"; "in light of" these, the complaint concludes "that [the ILECs] have entered into a contract, combination or conspiracy to prevent competitive entry into their . . . markets and have agreed not to compete with one another." Complaint ¶51.[10] The nub of the complaint, then, is the ILECs' parallel behavior, consisting of steps to keep the CLECs out and manifest disinterest in becoming CLECs themselves, and its sufficiency turns on the suggestions raised by this conduct when viewed in light of common economic experience.

We think that nothing contained in the complaint invests either the action or inaction alleged with a plausible suggestion of conspiracy. As to the ILECs' supposed agreement to disobey the 1996 Act and thwart the CLECs' attempts to compete, we agree with the District Court that nothing in the complaint intimates that the resistance to the upstarts was anything more than the natural, unilateral reaction of each ILEC intent on keeping its regional dominance. The 1996 Act did more than just subject the ILECs to competition; it obliged them to subsidize their competitors with their own equipment at wholesale rates. The economic incentive to resist was powerful, but resisting competition is routine market conduct, and even if the ILECs flouted the 1996 Act in all the ways the plaintiffs allege, there is no reason to infer that the companies had agreed among themselves to do what was only natural anyway; so natural, in fact, that if alleging parallel decisions to resist competition were enough to imply an antitrust conspiracy, pleading a § 1 violation against almost any group of competing businesses would be a sure thing.

The complaint makes its closest pass at a predicate for conspiracy with the claim that collusion was necessary because success by even one CLEC

10. If the complaint had not explained that the claim of agreement rested on the parallel conduct described, we doubt that the complaint's references to an agreement among the ILECs would have given the notice required by Rule 8. Apart from identifying a seven-year span in which the § 1 violations were supposed to have occurred (i.e., "[b]eginning at least as early as February 6, 1996, and continuing to the present," id. ¶64), the pleadings mentioned no specific time, place, or person involved in the alleged conspiracies. This lack of notice contrasts sharply with the model form for pleading negligence, Form 9, which the dissent says exemplifies the kind of "bare allegation" that survives a motion to dismiss. Post. Whereas the model form alleges that the defendant struck the plaintiff with his car while plaintiff was crossing a particular highway at a specified date and time, the complaint here furnishes no clue as to which of the four ILECs (much less which of their employees) supposedly agreed, or when and where the illicit agreement took place. A defendant wishing to prepare an answer in the simple fact pattern laid out in Form 9 would know what to answer; a defendant seeking to respond to plaintiffs' conclusory allegations in the § 1 context would have little idea where to begin.

in an ILEC's territory "would have revealed the degree to which competitive entry by CLECs would have been successful in the other territories." Id. ¶50. But, its logic aside, this general premise still fails to answer the point that there was just no need for joint encouragement to resist the 1996 Act; as the District Court said, "each ILEC has reason to want to avoid dealing with CLECs" and "each ILEC would attempt to keep CLECs out, regardless of the actions of the other ILECs." 313 F. Supp. 2d at 184.[12]

Plaintiffs' second conspiracy theory rests on the competitive reticence among the ILECs themselves in the wake of the 1996 Act, which was supposedly passed in the "'hop[e] that the large incumbent local monopoly companies . . . might attack their neighbors' service areas, as they are the best situated to do so.'" Complaint ¶38 (quoting Consumer Federation of America, Lessons from 1996 Telecommunications Act: Deregulation Before Meaningful Competition Spells Consumer Disaster, p. 12 (Feb. 2000)). Contrary to hope, the ILECs declined "'to enter each other's service territories in any significant way,'" Complaint ¶38, and the local telephone and high speed Internet market remains highly compartmentalized geographically, with minimal competition. Based on this state of affairs, and perceiving the ILECs to be blessed with "especially attractive business opportunities" in surrounding markets dominated by other ILECs, the plaintiffs assert that the ILECs' parallel conduct was "strongly suggestive of conspiracy." Id. ¶40.

But it was not suggestive of conspiracy, not if history teaches anything. In a traditionally unregulated industry with low barriers to entry, sparse competition among large firms dominating separate geographical segments of the market could very well signify illegal agreement, but here we have an obvious alternative explanation. In the decade preceding the 1996 Act and well before that, monopoly was the norm in telecommunications, not the exception. The ILECs were born in that world, doubtless liked the world the way it was, and surely knew the adage about him who lives by the sword. Hence, a natural explanation for the noncompetition alleged is that the former Government-sanctioned monopolists were sitting tight, expecting their neighbors to do the same thing.[13]

12. From the allegation that the ILECs belong to various trade associations, see Complaint ¶46, the dissent playfully suggests that they conspired to restrain trade, an inference said to be "buttressed by the common sense of Adam Smith." Post. If Adam Smith is peering down today, he may be surprised to learn that his tongue-in-cheek remark would be authority to force his famous pinmaker to devote financial and human capital to hire lawyers, prepare for depositions, and otherwise fend off allegations of conspiracy; all this just because he belonged to the same trade guild as one of his competitors when their pins carried the same price tag.

13. The complaint quoted a reported statement of Qwest's CEO, Richard Notebaert, to suggest that the ILECs declined to compete against each other despite recognizing that it "'might be a good way to turn a quick dollar.'" ¶42 (quoting Chicago Tribune, Oct. 31, 2002, Business Section, p. 1). This was only part of what he reportedly said, however, and the District Court was entitled to take notice of the full contents of the published articles referenced in the complaint, from which the truncated quotations were drawn. See Fed. Rule Evid. 201. Notebaert was also quoted as saying that entering new markets as a CLEC

. . . We agree with the District Court's assessment that antitrust conspiracy was not suggested by the facts adduced under either theory of the complaint, which thus fails to state a valid § 1 claim.[14]

Plaintiffs say that our analysis runs counter to Swierkiewicz v. Sorema N.A., 534 U.S. 506, 508 (2002), which held that "a complaint in an employment discrimination lawsuit [need] not contain specific facts establishing a prima facie case of discrimination under the framework set forth in *McDonnell Douglas Corp. v. Green*, 411 U.S. 792 (1973)." They argue that just as the prima facie case is a "flexible evidentiary standard" that "should not be transposed into a rigid pleading standard for discrimination cases," *Swierkiewicz*, supra, at 512, "transpos[ing] 'plus factor' summary judgment analysis woodenly into a rigid Rule 12(b)(6) pleading standard . . . would be unwise," Brief for Respondents 39. As the District Court correctly understood, however, "*Swierkiewicz* did not change the law of pleading, but simply re-emphasized . . . that the Second Circuit's use of a heightened pleading standard for Title VII cases was contrary to the Federal Rules' structure of liberal pleading requirements." 313 F. Supp. 2d at 181 (citation and footnote omitted). Even though *Swierkiewicz*'s pleadings "detailed the events leading to his termination, provided relevant dates, and included the ages and nationalities of at least some of the relevant persons involved with his termination," the Court of Appeals dismissed his complaint for failing to allege certain additional facts that Swierkiewicz would need at the trial stage to support his claim in the absence of direct evidence of discrimination. *Swierkiewicz*, 534 U.S. at 514. We reversed on the ground that the Court of Appeals had impermissibly applied what amounted to a heightened pleading requirement by insisting that Swierkiewicz allege "specific facts" beyond those necessary to state his claim and the grounds showing entitlement to relief. Id. at 508.

Here, in contrast, we do not require heightened fact pleading of specifics, but only enough facts to state a claim to relief that is plausible on its face. Because the plaintiffs here have not nudged their claims across the line from conceivable to plausible, their complaint must be dismissed.

---

would not be "a sustainable economic model" because the CLEC pricing model is "just . . . nuts." Chicago Tribune, Oct. 31, 2002, Business Section, p. 1 (cited at Complaint ¶42). Another source cited in the complaint quotes Notebaert as saying he thought it "unwise" to "base a business plan" on the privileges accorded to CLECs under the 1996 Act because the regulatory environment was too unstable. Chicago Tribune, Dec. 19, 2002, Business Section, p. 2 (cited at Complaint ¶45).

14. In reaching this conclusion, we do not apply any "heightened" pleading standard, nor do we seek to broaden the scope of Federal Rule of Civil Procedure 9, which can only be accomplished "'by the process of amending the Federal Rules, and not by judicial interpretation.'" Swierkiewicz v. Sorema N.A., 534 U.S. 506, 515 (2002) (quoting Leatherman v. Tarrant County Narcotics Intelligence and Coordination Unit, 507 U.S. 163, 168 (1993)). On certain subjects understood to raise a high risk of abusive litigation, a plaintiff must state factual allegations with greater particularity than Rule 8 requires. Fed. Rules Civ. Proc. 9(b)-(c). Here, our concern is not that the allegations in the complaint were insufficiently "particular[ized]", id.; rather, the complaint warranted dismissal because it failed *in toto* to render plaintiffs' entitlement to relief plausible.

The judgment of the Court of Appeals for the Second Circuit is reversed, and the cause is remanded for further proceedings consistent with this opinion.

It is so ordered.

JUSTICE STEVENS, with whom JUSTICE GINSBURG joins except as to Part IV, dissenting.

. . . [T]his is a case in which there is no dispute about the substantive law. If the defendants acted independently, their conduct was perfectly lawful. If, however, that conduct is the product of a horizontal agreement among potential competitors, it was unlawful. Plaintiffs have alleged such an agreement and, because the complaint was dismissed in advance of answer, the allegation has not even been denied. Why, then, does the case not proceed? Does a judicial opinion that the charge is not "plausible" provide a legally acceptable reason for dismissing the complaint? I think not.

Respondents' amended complaint describes a variety of circumstantial evidence and makes the straightforward allegation that petitioners

> "entered into a contract, combination or conspiracy to prevent competitive entry in their respective local telephone and/or high speed internet services markets and have agreed not to compete with one another and otherwise allocated customers and markets to one another." Complaint ¶ 51.

The complaint explains that, contrary to Congress' expectation when it enacted the 1996 Telecommunications Act, and consistent with their own economic self-interests, petitioner Incumbent Local Exchange Carriers (ILECs) have assiduously avoided infringing upon each other's markets and have refused to permit nonincumbent competitors to access their networks. The complaint quotes Richard Notebaert, the former CEO of one such ILEC, as saying that competing in a neighboring ILEC's territory "might be a good way to turn a quick dollar but that doesn't make it right." Id. ¶ 42. Moreover, respondents allege that petitioners "communicate amongst themselves" through numerous industry associations. Id. ¶ 46. In sum, respondents allege that petitioners entered into an agreement that has long been recognized as a classic *per se* violation of the Sherman Act. See Report of the Attorney General's National Committee to Study the Antitrust Laws 26 (1955).

Under rules of procedure that have been well settled since well before our decision in *Theatre Enterprises*, a judge ruling on a defendant's motion to dismiss a complaint, "must accept as true all of the factual allegations contained in the complaint." Swierkiewicz v. Sorema N.A., 534 U.S. 506, n.1 (2002). But instead of requiring knowledgeable executives such as Notebaert to respond to these allegations by way of sworn depositions or other limited discovery—and indeed without so much as requiring petitioners to file an answer denying that they entered into any agreement—the majority permits immediate dismissal based on the assurances of company lawyers that nothing untoward was afoot. The Court embraces the argument of those lawyers that "there is no reason to infer that the companies had agreed among themselves to do what was only natural anyway," ante; that "there was just no need for joint encouragement to resist the 1996 Act," ante; and that the "natural explanation for the noncompetition alleged is that the former Government-sanctioned monopolists were sitting tight, expecting their neighbors to do the same thing," ante.

The Court and petitioners' legal team are no doubt correct that the parallel conduct alleged is consistent with the absence of any contract, combination, or conspiracy. But that conduct is also entirely consistent with the *presence* of the illegal agreement alleged in the complaint. And the charge that petitioners "agreed not to compete with one another" is not just one of "a few stray statements," ante; it is an allegation describing unlawful conduct. As such, the Federal Rules of Civil Procedure, our longstanding precedent, and sound practice mandate that the District Court at least require some sort of response from petitioners before dismissing the case.

Two practical concerns presumably explain the Court's dramatic departure from settled procedural law. Private antitrust litigation can be enormously expensive, and there is a risk that jurors may mistakenly conclude that evidence of parallel conduct has proved that the parties acted pursuant to an agreement when they in fact merely made similar independent decisions. Those concerns merit careful case management, including strict control of discovery, careful scrutiny of evidence at the summary judgment stage, and lucid instructions to juries; they do not, however, justify the dismissal of an adequately pleaded complaint without even requiring the defendants to file answers denying a charge that they in fact engaged in collective decisionmaking. More importantly, they do not justify an interpretation of Federal Rule of Civil Procedure 12(b)(6) that seems to be driven by the majority's appraisal of the plausibility of the ultimate factual allegation rather than its legal sufficiency.

I

Rule 8(a)(2) of the Federal Rules requires that a complaint contain "a short and plain statement of the claim showing that the pleader is entitled to relief." The rule did not come about by happenstance and its language is not inadvertent. The English experience with Byzantine special pleading rules—illustrated by the hypertechnical Hilary rules of 1834—made obvious the appeal of a pleading standard that was easy for the common litigant to understand and sufficed to put the defendant on notice as to the nature of the claim against him and the relief sought. Stateside, David Dudley Field developed the highly influential New York Code of 1848, which required "[a] statement of the facts constituting the cause of action, in ordinary and concise language, without repetition, and in such a manner as to enable a person of common understanding to know what is intended." An Act to Simplify and Abridge the Practice, Pleadings and Proceedings of the Courts of this State, ch. 379, § 120(2), 1848 N.Y. Laws pp. 497, 521. Substantially similar language appeared in the Federal Equity Rules adopted in 1912. See Fed. Equity Rule 25 (requiring "a short and simple statement of the ultimate facts upon which the plaintiff asks relief, omitting any mere statement of evidence").

A difficulty arose, however, in that the Field Code and its progeny required a plaintiff to plead "facts" rather than "conclusions," a distinction that proved far easier to say than to apply. As commentators have noted,

> "it is virtually impossible logically to distinguish among 'ultimate facts,' 'evidence,' and 'conclusions.' Essentially any allegation in a pleading must be an assertion that certain occurrences took place. The pleading spectrum, passing from evidence through ultimate facts to conclusions, is largely a continuum varying only in the degree of particularity with which the occurrences are described." Weinstein & Distler, Comments on Procedural Reform: Drafting Pleading Rules, 57 Colum. L. Rev. 518, 520-521 (1957).

See also Cook, Statements of Fact in Pleading Under the Codes, 21 Colum. L. Rev. 416, 417 (1921) (hereinafter Cook) ("[T]here is no logical distinction between statements which are grouped by the courts under the phrases 'statements of fact' and 'conclusions of law'"). Rule 8 was directly responsive to this difficulty. Its drafters intentionally avoided any reference to "facts" or "evidence" or "conclusions." . . .

Under the relaxed pleading standards of the Federal Rules, the idea was not to keep litigants out of court but rather to keep them in. The merits of a claim would be sorted out during a flexible pretrial process and, as appropriate, through the crucible of trial. See *Swierkiewicz*, 534 U.S. at 514 ("The liberal notice pleading of Rule 8(a) is the starting point of a simplified pleading system, which was adopted to focus litigation on the merits of a claim"). Charles E. Clark, the "principal draftsman" of the Federal Rules, put it thus:

> "Experience has shown . . . that we cannot expect the proof of the case to be made through the pleadings, and that such proof is really not their function. We can expect a general statement distinguishing the case from all others, so that the manner and form of trial and remedy expected are clear, and so that a permanent judgment will result." The New Federal Rules of Civil Procedure: The Last Phase—Underlying Philosophy Embodied in Some of the Basic Provisions of the New Procedure, 23 A.B.A. J. 976, 977 (1937) (hereinafter Clark, New Federal Rules).

The pleading paradigm under the new Federal Rules was well illustrated by the inclusion in the appendix of Form 9, a complaint for negligence. As relevant, the Form 9 complaint states only: "On June 1, 1936, in a public highway called Boylston Street in Boston, Massachusetts, defendant negligently drove a motor vehicle against plaintiff who was then crossing said highway." Form 9, Complaint for Negligence, Forms App., Fed. Rules Civ. Proc., 28 U.S.C. App., p. 829 (hereinafter Form 9). The complaint then describes the plaintiff's injuries and demands judgment. The asserted ground for relief—namely, the defendant's negligent driving —would have been called a "'conclusion of law'" under the code pleading of old. See, e.g., Cook 419. But that bare allegation suffices under a system that "restrict[s] the pleadings to the task of general notice-giving and invest[s] the deposition-discovery process with a vital role in the preparation for trial." Hickman v. Taylor, 329 U.S. 495, 501 (1947); see also *Swierkiewicz*, 534 U.S. at 513, n.4 (citing Form 9 as an example of "'the simplicity and brevity of statement which the rules contemplate'"); Thomson v. Washington, 362 F.3d 969, 970 (7th Cir. 2004) (Posner, J.) ("The federal rules replaced fact pleading with notice pleading").

II

. . . Consistent with the design of the Federal Rules, *Conley*'s "no set of facts" formulation permits outright dismissal only when proceeding to discovery or beyond would be futile. Once it is clear that a plaintiff has stated a claim that, if true, would entitle him to relief, matters of proof are appropriately relegated to other stages of the trial process. Today, however, in its explanation of a decision to dismiss a complaint that it regards as a fishing expedition, the Court scraps *Conley*'s "no set of facts" language. . . .

If *Conley*'s "no set of facts" language is to be interred, let it not be without a eulogy. That exact language, which the majority says has "puzzl[ed] the profession for 50 years," ibid., has been cited as authority in a dozen opinions of this Court and four separate writings. In not one of those 16 opinions was the language "questioned," "criticized," or "explained away." Indeed, today's opinion is the first by any Member of this Court to express *any* doubt as to the adequacy of the *Conley* formulation. Taking their cues from the federal courts, 26 States and the District of Columbia utilize as their standard for dismissal of a complaint the very language the majority repudiates: whether it appears "beyond doubt" that "no set of facts" in support of the claim would entitle the plaintiff to relief.[5]

5. See, e.g., EB Invs., LLC v. Atlantis Development, Inc., 930 So. 2d 502, 507 (Ala. 2005); Department of Health & Social Servs. v. Native Village of Curyung, 151 P.3d 388, 396 (Alaska 2006); Newman v. Maricopa Cty., 167 Ariz. 501, 503, 808 P.2d 1253, 1255 (App. 1991); Public Serv. Co. of Colo. v. Van Wyk, 27 P.3d 377, 385-386 (Colo. 2001) (en banc); Clawson v. St. Louis Post-Dispatch, LLC, 906 A.2d 308, 312 (D.C. 2006); Hillman Constr. Corp. v. Wainer, 636 So. 2d 576, 578 (Fla. App. 1994); Kaplan v. Kaplan, 266 Ga. 612, 613, 469 S.E.2d 198, 199 (1996); Wright v. Home Depot U.S.A., 111 Haw. 401, 406, 142 P.3d 265, 270 (2006); Taylor v. Maile, 142 Idaho 253, 257, 127 P.3d 156, 160 (2005); Fink v. Bryant, 2001-CC-0987, p. 4 (La. 11/28/01), 801 So. 2d 346, 349; Gagne v. Cianbro Corp., 431 A.2d 1313, 1318-1319 (Me. 1981); Gasior v. Massachusetts Gen. Hospital, 446 Mass. 645, 647, 846 N.E.2d 1133, 1135 (2006); Ralph Walker, Inc. v. Gallagher, 926 So. 2d 890, 893 (Miss. 2006); Jones v. Montana Univ. System, 337 Mont. 1, 7, 155 P.3d 1247, 1254 (2007); Johnston v. Nebraska Dept. of Correctional Servs., 270 Neb. 987, 989, 709 N.W.2d 321, 324 (2006); Blackjack Bonding v. Las Vegas Munic. Ct., 116 Nev. 1213, 1217, 14 P.3d 1275, 1278 (2000);

. . . I would not rewrite the Nation's civil procedure textbooks and call into doubt the pleading rules of most of its States without far more informed deliberation as to the costs of doing so. Congress has established a process—a rulemaking process—for revisions of that order. See 28 U.S.C. §§ 2072-2074.

Today's majority calls *Conley*'s "'no set of facts'" language "an incomplete, negative gloss on an accepted pleading standard: once a claim has been stated adequately, it may be supported by showing any set of facts consistent with the allegations in the complaint." Ante. This is not and cannot be what the *Conley* Court meant. First, as I have explained, and as the *Conley* Court well knew, the pleading standard the Federal Rules meant to codify does not require, or even invite, the pleading of facts.[6] . . . Second, it is pellucidly clear that the *Conley* Court was interested in what a

---

Shepard v. Ocwen Fed. Bank, 361 N.C. 137, 139, 638 S.E.2d 197, 199 (2006); Rose v. United Equitable Ins. Co., 2001 ND 154, ¶10, 632 N.W.2d 429, 434; State ex rel. Turner v. Houk, 112 Ohio St. 3d 561, 562, 2007-Ohio-814, ¶5, 862 N.E.2d 104, 105 (per curiam); Moneypenney v. Dawson, 2006 OK 53, ¶2, 141 P.3d 549, 551; Gagnon v. State, 570 A.2d 656, 659 (R.I. 1990); Osloond v. Farrier, 2003 SD 28, ¶4, 659 N.W.2d 20, 22 (per curiam); Smith v. Lincoln Brass Works, Inc., 712 S.W.2d 470, 471 (Tenn. 1986); Association of Haystack Property Owners v. Sprague, 145 Vt. 443, 446, 494 A.2d 122, 124 (1985); In re Coday, 156 Wash. 2d 485, 497, 130 P.3d 809, 815 (2006) (en banc); Haines v. Hampshire Cty. Comm'n, 216 W. Va. 499, 502, 607 S.E.2d 828, 831 (2004); Warren v. Hart, 747 P.2d 511, 512 (Wyo. 1987); see also Malpiede v. Townson, 780 A.2d 1075, 1082-1083 (Del. 2001) (permitting dismissal only "where the court determines with reasonable certainty that the plaintiff could prevail on no set of facts that may be inferred from the well-pleaded allegations in the complaint" (internal quotation marks omitted)); Canel v. Topinka, 212 Ill. 2d 311, 318, 818 N.E.2d 311, 317 (2004) (replacing "appears beyond doubt" in the *Conley* formulation with "is clearly apparent"); In re Young, 522 N.E.2d 386, 388 (Ind. 1988) (per curiam) (replacing "appears beyond doubt" with "appears to a certainty"); Barkema v. Williams Pipeline Co., 666 N.W.2d 612, 614 (Iowa 2003) (holding that a motion to dismiss should be sustained "only when there exists no conceivable set of facts entitling the non-moving party to relief"); Pioneer Village v. Bullitt Cty., 104 S.W.3d 757, 759 (Ky. 2003) (holding that judgment on the pleadings should be granted "if it appears beyond doubt that the nonmoving party cannot prove any set of facts that would entitle him/her to relief"); Corley v. Detroit Bd. of Ed., 470 Mich. 274, 277, 681 N.W.2d 342, 345 (2004) (per curiam) (holding that a motion for judgment on the pleadings should be granted only "'if no factual development could possibly justify recovery'"); Oberkramer v. Ellisville, 706 S.W.2d 440, 441 (Mo. 1986) (en banc) (omitting the words "beyond doubt" from the *Conley* formulation); Colman v. Utah State Land Bd., 795 P.2d 622, 624 (Utah 1990) (holding that a motion to dismiss is appropriate "only if it clearly appears that [the plaintiff] can prove no set of facts in support of his claim"); NRC Management Servs. Corp. v. First Va. Bank-Southwest, 63 Va. Cir. 68, 70 (2003) ("The Virginia standard is identical [to the *Conley* formulation], though the Supreme Court of Virginia may not have used the same words to describe it").

6. The majority is correct to say that what the Federal Rules require is a "'showing'" of entitlement to relief. Ante, at 8, n.3. Whether and to what extent that "showing" requires allegations of fact will depend on the particulars of the claim. For example, had the amended complaint in this case alleged *only* parallel conduct, it would not have made the required "showing." See supra. Similarly, had the pleadings contained only an allegation of agreement, without specifying the nature or object of that agreement, they would have been susceptible to the charge that they did not provide sufficient notice that the defendants may answer intelligently. Omissions of that sort instance the type of "bareness" with which the Federal Rules are concerned. A plaintiff's inability to persuade a district court that the allegations actually included in her complaint are "plausible" is an altogether different kind of failing, and one that should not be fatal at the pleading stage.

complaint *must* contain, not what it *may* contain. In fact, the Court said without qualification that it was "appraising the *sufficiency* of the complaint." 355 U.S. at 45 (emphasis added). It was, to paraphrase today's majority, describing "the minimum standard of adequate pleading to govern a complaint's survival," ante.

We can be triply sure as to *Conley*'s meaning by examining the three Court of Appeals cases the *Conley* Court cited as support for the "accepted rule." . . . 355 U.S. at 45-46. In the first case, Leimer v. State Mut. Life Assur. Co. of Worcester, Mass., 108 F.2d 302 (8th Cir. 1940), the plaintiff alleged that she was the beneficiary of a life insurance plan and that the insurance company was wrongfully withholding proceeds from her. In reversing the District Court's grant of the defendant's motion to dismiss, the Eighth Circuit noted that court's own longstanding rule that, to warrant dismissal, "'it should appear from the allegations that a cause of action does not exist, rather than that a cause of action has been defectively stated.'" Id. at 305 (quoting Winget v. Rockwood, 69 F.2d 326, 329 (8th Cir. 1934).

The *Leimer* court viewed the Federal Rules—specifically Rules 8(a)(2), 12 (b)(6), 12(e) (motion for a more definite statement), and 56 (motion for summary judgment)—as reinforcing the notion that "there is no justification for dismissing a complaint for insufficiency of statement, except where it appears to a certainty that the plaintiff would be entitled to no relief under any state of facts which could be proved in support of the claim." 108 F.2d at 306. The court refuted in the strongest terms any suggestion that the unlikelihood of recovery should determine the fate of a complaint: "No matter how improbable it may be that she can prove her claim, she is entitled to an opportunity to make the attempt, and is not required to accept as final a determination of her rights based upon inferences drawn in favor of the defendant from her amended complaint." Ibid.

The Third Circuit relied on *Leimer*'s admonition in Continental Collieries, Inc. v. Shober, 130 F.2d 631 (1942), which the *Conley* Court also cited in support of its "no set of facts" formulation. In a diversity action the plaintiff alleged breach of contract, but the District Court dismissed the complaint on the ground that the contract appeared to be unenforceable under state law. The Court of Appeals reversed, concluding that there were facts in dispute that went to the enforceability of the contract, and that the rule at the pleading stage was as in *Leimer*: "No matter how likely it may seem that the pleader will be unable to prove his case, he is entitled, upon averring a claim, to an opportunity to try to prove it." 130 F.2d at 635.

The third case the *Conley* Court cited approvingly was written by Judge Clark himself. In Dioguardi v. Durning, 139 F.2d 774 (2d Cir. 1944), the *pro se* plaintiff, an importer of "tonics," charged the customs inspector with auctioning off the plaintiff's former merchandise for less than was bid for it . . . and complained that two cases of tonics went missing three weeks before the sale. The inference, hinted at by the averments but never stated in so many words, was that the defendant fraudulently denied the plaintiff his rightful claim to the tonics, which, if true, would have violated federal law. Writing six years after the adoption of the Federal Rules he held the lead rein in drafting, Judge Clark said that the defendant

> "could have disclosed the facts from his point of view, in advance of a trial if he chose, by asking for a pre-trial hearing or by moving for a summary judgment with supporting affidavits. But, as it stands, we do not see how the plaintiff may properly be deprived of his day in court to show what he obviously so firmly believes and what for present purposes defendant must be taken as admitting." Id. at 775.

. . . Judge Clark's opinion disquieted the defense bar and gave rise to a movement to revise Rule 8 to require a plaintiff to plead a "'cause of action.'" See 5 Wright & Miller § 1201, at 86-87. The movement failed; *Dioguardi* was explicitly approved in *Conley*; and "[i]n retrospect the case itself seems to be a routine application of principles that are universally accepted," 5 Wright & Miller § 1220, at 284-285.

In light of *Leimer*, *Continental Collieries*, and *Dioguardi*, *Conley*'s statement that a complaint is not to be dismissed unless "no set of facts" in support thereof would entitle the plaintiff to relief is hardly "puzzling." It reflects a philosophy that, unlike in the days of code pleading, separating the wheat from the chaff is a task assigned to the pretrial and trial process. *Conley*'s language, in short, captures the policy choice embodied in the Federal Rules and binding on the federal courts.

We have consistently reaffirmed that basic understanding of the Federal Rules in the half century since *Conley*. For example, in *Scheuer v. Rhodes*, 416 U.S. 232 (1974), we reversed the Court of Appeals' dismissal on the pleadings when the respondents, the Governor and other officials of the State of Ohio, argued that petitioners' claims were barred by sovereign immunity. In a unanimous opinion by then-Justice Rehnquist, we emphasized that

> "[w]hen a federal court reviews the sufficiency of a complaint, before the reception of any evidence either by affidavit or admissions, its task is necessarily a limited one. The issue is not whether a plaintiff will ultimately prevail but whether the claimant is entitled to offer evidence to support the claims. *Indeed it may appear on the face of the pleadings that a recovery is very remote and unlikely but that is not the test.*" Id. at 236 (emphasis added).

The *Rhodes* plaintiffs had "alleged generally and in conclusory terms" that the defendants, by calling out the National Guard to suppress the Kent State University student protests, "were guilty of wanton, willful and negligent conduct." Krause v. Rhodes, 471 F.2d 430, 433 (6th Cir. 1972). . . .

We again spoke with one voice against efforts to expand pleading requirements beyond their appointed limits in Leatherman v. Tarrant County Narcotics Intelligence and Coordination Unit, 507 U.S. 163 (1993). Writing for the unanimous Court, Chief Justice Rehnquist rebuffed the Fifth Circuit's effort to craft a standard for pleading municipal liability that accounted for "the enormous expense involved today in litigation," Leatherman v. Tarrant Cty. Narcotics Intelligence and Coordination Unit, 954 F.2d 1054, 1057 (1992) (internal quotation marks omitted), by requiring a plaintiff to "state with factual detail and particularity the basis for the claim which necessarily includes why the defendant-official cannot successfully maintain the defense of immunity." *Leatherman*, 507 U.S. at 167 (internal quotation marks omitted). We found this language inconsistent with Rules 8(a)(2) and 9(b) and emphasized that motions to dismiss were not the place to combat discovery abuse: "In the absence of [an amendment to Rule 9(b)], federal courts and litigants must rely on summary judgment and control of discovery to weed out unmeritorious claims sooner rather than later." Id. at 168-169.

Most recently, in *Swierkiewicz*, 534 U.S. 506, we were faced with a case more similar to the present one than the majority will allow. In discrimination cases, our precedents require a plaintiff at the summary judgment stage to produce either direct evidence of discrimination or, if the claim is based primarily on circumstantial evidence, to meet the shifting evidentiary burdens imposed under the framework articulated in *McDonnell Douglas Corp. v. Green*, 411 U.S. 792 (1973). Swierkiewicz alleged that he had been terminated on account of national origin in violation of Title VII of the Civil Rights Act of 1964. The Second Circuit dismissed the suit on the pleadings because he had not pleaded a prima facie case of discrimination under the *McDonnell Douglas* standard.

We reversed in another unanimous opinion, holding that "under a notice pleading system, it is not appropriate to require a plaintiff to plead facts establishing a prima facie case because the *McDonnell Douglas* framework does not apply in every employment discrimination case." *Swierkiewicz*, 534 U.S. at 511. We also observed that Rule 8(a)(2) does not contemplate a court's passing on the merits of a litigant's claim at the pleading stage. Rather, the "simplified notice pleading standard" of the Federal Rules "relies on liberal discovery rules and summary judgment motions to define disputed facts and issues and to dispose of unmeritorious claims." Id. at 512. . . .

As in the discrimination context, we have developed an evidentiary framework for evaluating claims under § 1 of the Sherman Act when those claims rest on entirely circumstantial evidence of conspiracy. See Matsushita Elec. Industrial Co. v. Zenith Radio Corp., 475 U.S. 574 (1986). Under *Matsushita*, a plaintiff's allegations of an illegal conspiracy may not, at the summary judgment stage, rest solely on the inferences that may be drawn from the parallel conduct of the defendants. In order to survive a Rule 56 motion, a § 1 plaintiff "must present evidence 'that tends to exclude the possibility' that the alleged conspirators acted independently.'" Id. at 588 (quoting Monsanto Co. v. Spray-Rite Service Corp., 465 U.S. 752, 764 (1984)). That is, the plaintiff "must show that the inference of conspiracy is reasonable in light of the competing inferences of independent action or collusive action." 475 U.S. at 588.

Everything today's majority says would therefore make perfect sense if it were ruling on a Rule 56 motion for summary judgment and the evidence included nothing more than the Court has described. But it should go without saying in the wake of *Swierkiewicz* that a heightened production burden at the summary judgment stage does not translate into a heightened pleading burden at the complaint stage. The majority rejects the complaint in this case because—in light of the fact that the parallel conduct alleged is consistent with ordinary market behavior—the claimed conspiracy is "conceivable" but not "plausible." I have my doubts about the majority's assessment of the plausibility of this alleged conspiracy. But even if the majority's speculation is correct, its "plausibility" standard is irreconcilable with Rule 8 and with our governing precedents. . . .

This case is a poor vehicle for the Court's new pleading rule, for we have observed that "in antitrust cases, where 'the proof is largely in the hands of the alleged conspirators,' . . . dismissals prior to giving the plaintiff ample opportunity for discovery should be granted very sparingly." Hospital Building Co. v. Trustees of Rex Hospital, 425 U.S. 738, 746 (1976) (quoting Poller v. Columbia Broadcasting System, Inc., 368 U.S. 464, 473 (1962)). . . . Moreover, the fact that the Sherman Act authorizes the recovery of treble damages and attorney's fees for successful plaintiffs indicates that Congress intended to encourage, rather than discourage, private enforcement of the law. It is therefore more, not less, important in antitrust cases to resist the urge to engage in armchair economics at the pleading stage.

The same year we decided *Conley*, Judge Clark wrote, presciently,

> "I fear that every age must learn its lesson that special pleading cannot be made to do the service of trial and that live issues between active litigants are not to be disposed of or evaded on the paper pleadings, i.e., the formalistic claims of the parties. Experience has found no quick and easy short cut for trials in cases generally *and antitrust cases in particular.*" Special Pleading in the "Big Case"? in Procedure—The Handmaid of Justice 147, 148 (C. Wright & H. Reasoner eds., 1965) (hereinafter Clark, Special Pleading in the Big Case) (emphasis added).

In this "Big Case," the Court succumbs to the temptation that previous Courts have steadfastly resisted. While the majority assures us that it is not applying any "'heightened'" pleading standard, see ante, n.14, I shall now explain why I have a difficult time understanding its opinion any other way.

III

The Court does not suggest that an agreement to do what the plaintiffs allege would be permissible under the antitrust laws. Nor does the Court hold that these plaintiffs have failed to allege an injury entitling them to sue for damages under those laws. Rather, the theory on which the Court permits dismissal is that, so far as the Federal Rules are concerned, no agreement has been alleged at all. This is a mind-boggling conclusion.

As the Court explains, prior to the enactment of the Telecommunications Act of 1996 the law prohibited the defendants from competing with each other. The new statute was enacted to replace a monopolistic market with a competitive one. The Act did not merely require the regional monopolists to take affirmative steps to facilitate entry to new competitors; it also permitted the existing firms to compete with each other and to expand their operations into previously forbidden territory. See 47 U.S.C. § 271. Each of the defendants decided not to take the latter step. That was obviously an extremely important business decision, and I am willing to presume that each company acted entirely independently in reaching that decision. I am even willing to entertain the majority's belief that any agreement among the companies was unlikely. But the plaintiffs allege in three places in their complaint, ¶¶ 4, 51, 64, that the ILECs did in fact agree both to prevent competitors from entering into their local markets and to forgo competition with each other. And as the Court recognizes, at the motion to dismiss stage, a judge assumes "that all the allegations in the complaint are true (even if doubtful in fact)."

The majority circumvents this obvious obstacle to dismissal by pretending that it does not exist. The Court admits that "in form a few stray statements in the complaint speak directly of agreement," but disregards those allegations by saying that "on fair reading these are merely legal conclusions resting on the prior allegations" of parallel conduct. The Court's dichotomy between factual allegations and "legal conclusions" is the stuff of a bygone era. That distinction was a defining feature of code pleading, see generally Clark, The Complaint in Code Pleading, 35 Yale L.J. 259 (1925-1926), but was conspicuously abolished when the Federal Rules were enacted in 1938. . . .[9]

Even if I were inclined to accept the Court's anachronistic dichotomy and ignore the complaint's actual allegations, I would dispute the Court's suggestion that any inference of agreement from petitioners' parallel conduct is "implausible." Many years ago a truly great economist perceptively observed that "[p]eople of the same trade seldom meet together, even for merriment and diversion, but the conversation ends in a conspiracy against the public, or in some contrivance to raise prices." A. Smith, An Inquiry into the Nature and Causes of the Wealth of Nations, in 39 Great Books of the Western World 55 (R. Hutchins & M. Adler eds.,

9. The Court suggests that the allegation of an agreement, even if credited, might not give the notice required by Rule 8 because it lacks specificity. The remedy for an allegation lacking sufficient specificity to provide adequate notice is, of course, a Rule 12(e) motion for a more definite statement. See Swierkiewicz v. Sorema N.A., 534 U.S. 506, 514 (2002). Petitioners made no such motion and indeed have conceded that "[o]ur problem with the current complaint is not a lack of specificity, it's quite specific." Tr. of Oral Arg. 14. Thus, the fact that "the pleadings mentioned no specific time, place, or persons involved in the alleged conspiracies," ante, at 18, n.10, is, for our purposes, academic.

1952). I am not so cynical as to accept that sentiment at face value, but I need not do so here. Respondents' complaint points not only to petitioners' numerous opportunities to meet with each other, Complaint ¶46, but also to Notebaert's curious statement that encroaching on a fellow incumbent's territory "might be a good way to turn a quick dollar but that doesn't make it right," id. ¶ 42. What did he mean by that? One possible (indeed plausible) inference is that he meant that while it would be in his company's economic self-interest to compete with its brethren, he had agreed with his competitors not to do so. According to the complaint, that is how the Illinois Coalition for Competitive Telecom construed Notebaert's statement, id. ¶ 44, and that is how Members of Congress construed his company's behavior, id. ¶ 45.

Perhaps Notebaert meant instead that competition would be sensible in the short term but not in the long run. That's what his lawyers tell us anyway. But I would think that no one would know better what Notebaert meant than Notebaert himself. Instead of permitting respondents to ask Notebaert, however, the Court looks to other quotes from that and other articles and decides that what he meant was that entering new markets as a CLEC would not be a "'sustainable economic model.'" . . . But . . . the District Court was required at this stage of the proceedings to construe Notebaert's ambiguous statement in the plaintiffs' favor. The inference the statement supports—that simultaneous decisions by ILECs not even to attempt to poach customers from one another once the law authorized them to do so were the product of an agreement—sits comfortably within the realm of possibility. That is all the Rules require. . . .

Respondents in this case proposed a plan of "'phased discovery'" limited to the existence of the alleged conspiracy and class certification. . . . Given the charge in the complaint—buttressed by the common sense of Adam Smith—I cannot say that the possibility that joint discussions and perhaps some agreements played a role in petitioners' decisionmaking process is so implausible that dismissing the complaint before any defendant has denied the charge is preferable to granting respondents even a minimal opportunity to prove their claims. See Clark, New Federal Rules 977 ("[T]hrough the weapons of discovery and summary judgment we have developed new devices, with more appropriate penalties to aid in matters of *proof*, and do not need to force the pleadings to their less appropriate function").[13]

13. The potential for "sprawling, costly, and hugely time-consuming" discovery, ante, at 13, n.6, is no reason to throw the baby out with the bathwater. The Court vastly underestimates a district court's case-management arsenal. Before discovery even begins, the court may grant a defendant's Rule 12(e) motion; Rule 7(a) permits a trial court to order a plaintiff to reply to a defendant's answer; and Rule 23 requires "rigorous analysis" to ensure that class certification is appropriate, General Telephone Co. of Southwest v. Falcon, 457 U.S. 147, 160 (1982). Rule 16 invests a trial judge with the power, backed by sanctions, to regulate pretrial proceedings via conferences and scheduling orders, at which the parties may discuss, *inter alia*, "the elimination of frivolous claims or defenses," Rule 16 (c)(1); "the necessity or desirability of amendments to the pleadings," Rule 16(c)(2); "the control and scheduling of discovery," Rule 16(c)(6); and "the need for adopting special

I fear that the unfortunate result of the majority's new pleading rule will be to invite lawyers' debates over economic theory to conclusively resolve antitrust suits in the absence of any evidence. It is no surprise that the antitrust defense bar—among whom "lament" as to inadequate judicial supervision of discovery is most "common," see ante—should lobby for this state of affairs. But "we must recall that their primary responsibility is to win cases for their clients, not to improve law administration for the public." Clark, Special Pleading in the Big Case 152. As we did in our prior decisions, we should have instructed them that their remedy was to seek to amend the Federal Rules—not our interpretation of them. See *Swierkiewicz*, 534 U.S. at 515.

IV

Just a few weeks ago some of my colleagues explained that a strict interpretation of the literal text of statutory language is essential to avoid judicial decisions that are not faithful to the intent of Congress. Zuni Public School Dist. No. 89 v. Department of Education, 127 S. Ct. 1534 (2007) (Scalia, J., dissenting). I happen to believe that there are cases in which other tools of construction are more reliable than text, but I agree of course that congressional intent should guide us in matters of statutory interpretation. Id. at 1534 (Stevens, J., concurring). This is a case in which the intentions of the drafters of three important sources of law—the Sherman Act, the Telecommunications Act of 1996, and the Federal Rules of Civil Procedure—all point unmistakably in the same direction, yet the Court marches resolutely the other way. . . .

The transparent policy concern that drives the decision is the interest in protecting antitrust defendants—who in this case are some of the

---

procedures for managing potentially difficult or protracted actions that may involve complex issues, multiple parties, difficult legal questions, or unusual proof problems," Rule 16(c)(12). Subsequently, Rule 26 confers broad discretion to control the combination of interrogatories, requests for admissions, production requests, and depositions permitted in a given case; the sequence in which such discovery devices may be deployed; and the limitations imposed upon them. Indeed, Rule 26(c) specifically permits a court to take actions "to protect a party or person from annoyance, embarrassment, oppression, or undue burden or expense" by, for example, disallowing a particular discovery request, setting appropriate terms and conditions, or limiting its scope. In short, the Federal Rules contemplate that pretrial matters will be settled through a flexible process of give and take, of proffers, stipulations, and stonewalls, not by having trial judges screen allegations for their plausibility *vel non* without requiring an answer from the defendant. And should it become apparent over the course of litigation that a plaintiff's filings bespeak an *in terrorem suit*, the district court has at its call its own *in terrorem* device, in the form of a wide array of Rule 11 sanctions. See Rules 11(b), (c) (authorizing sanctions if a suit is presented "for any improper purpose, such as to harass or to cause unnecessary delay or needless increase in the cost of litigation"); see Business Guides, Inc. v. Chromatic Communications Enterprises, Inc., 498 U.S. 533 (1991) (holding that Rule 11 applies to a represented party who signs a pleading, motion, or other papers, as well as to attorneys); Atkins v. Fischer, 232 F.R.D. 116, 126 (D.D.C. 2005) ("As possible sanctions pursuant to Rule 11, the court has an arsenal of options at its disposal").

wealthiest corporations in our economy—from the burdens of pretrial discovery. Even if it were not apparent that the legal fees petitioners have incurred in arguing the merits of their Rule 12(b) motion have far exceeded the cost of limited discovery, or that those discovery costs would burden respondents as well as petitioners, that concern would not provide an adequate justification for this law-changing decision. For in the final analysis it is only a lack of confidence in the ability of trial judges to control discovery, buttressed by appellate judges' independent appraisal of the plausibility of profoundly serious factual allegations, that could account for this stark break from precedent. . . .

Accordingly, I respectfully dissent.

Notes and Questions

1. Does *Twombly* reverse *Conley*? Many civil procedure and constitutional law scholars think the Court overruled *Conley*, at least in effect. The Court said it was merely clarifying the meaning of a sentence—though the sentence it "clarifies" is the centerpiece of the Rule 8 pleading regime *Conley* endorsed. In June 2007, when *Twombly* was decided, *Conley* had been cited 78,133 times by courts and commentators. Much of that huge body of law and precedent was surely unsettled by *Twombly*, and as the dissent notes, the civil procedure texts must now all be rewritten. The Court gave short shrift to the history of *Conley* and to the fact that it settled for 50 years an intense debate in American procedure about what due process requires of pleading. You can be sure that there will now be a great outpouring on subjects long dormant and assumed to be well settled. For an article predicting the erosion of the *Conley* standard, see Richard L. Marcus, The Revival of Fact Pleading Under the Federal Rules of Civil Procedure, 86 Colum. L. Rev. 433 (1986). For the argument that *Twombly* represents a sea change in the application and interpretation of Rule 8(a), see A. Benjamin Spencer, Plausibility Pleading, 49 B.C. L. Rev. 431 (2008); see also David Marcus, Charles Clark, Legal Realism, and the Jurisprudential Basis of the Federal Rules of Civil Procedure 85-87 (draft on file with casebook authors) (arguing that *Twombly*'s interpretation of Rule 8 departs from the intent of the Rule's framers).

Most of the circuit courts grappling with the ramifications of the decision have concluded that it imposes some form of "plausibility" requirement according to which the plaintiff must now allege enough facts to render her claim plausible, not merely possible. See, e.g., ACA Fin. Guar. Corp. v. Advest, Inc., 512 F.3d 46, 58 (1st Cir. 2008) (concluding that *Twombly* gave 12(b)(6) "more heft"); Ridge at Red Hawk, L.L.C. v. Schneider, 493 F.3d 1174, 1177 (10th Cir. 2007) (holding that after *Twombly*, the mere possibility that some plaintiff could prove some set of facts in support of the claim is insufficient; instead, the complaint "must give the court reason to believe that *this* plaintiff has a reasonable likelihood of mustering factual support for *these* claims"); Iqbal v. Hasty 490 F.3d 143, 157-158 (2d Cir. 2007) (holding that *Twombly* does not impose a "universal standard of heightened fact pleading" but does require a pleader "to amplify a claim with some factual allegations in those contexts where such amplification is needed to render the claim *plausible*").

A few courts, however, have continued to apply *Conley*-style notice pleading even in the wake of *Twombly*. See, e.g., Aktieselskabet AF 21. November 2001 v. Fame Jeans, Inc., 525 F.3d 8, 15 (D.C. Cir. 2008) ("*Twombly* leaves the long-standing fundamentals of notice pleading intact."); Skaff v. Meridien N. Amer. Beverly Hills, L.L.C., 506 F.3d 832, 842 (9th Cir. 2007) (citing *Twombly* for the proposition that courts should not "impose . . . heightened [pleading] standards in the absence of an explicit requirement in a statute or federal rule"); McZeal v. Sprint Nextel Corp., 501 F.3d 1354, 1357 n.4 (Fed. Cir. 2007) (holding that *Twombly* did not materially change the pleading requirement "as articulated in *Conley*"); Airborne Beepers & Video, Inc. v. AT&T Mobility, L.L.C., 499 F.3d 663, 667 (7th Cir. 2007) ("*Twombly* did not signal a switch to fact-pleading.").

Just 18 days after issuing its opinion in *Twombly*, the Supreme Court itself seemed to backtrack in a brief per curiam opinion in Erickson v. Pardus, 127 S. Ct. 2197 (2007). Erickson, a Colorado prisoner, filed a lawsuit against prison officials alleging wrongful termination of medical treatment for hepatitis C. Id. at 2197-2198. The district court dismissed his complaint, and the Tenth Circuit affirmed, holding that Erickson's complaint was merely "conclusory." Id. The Supreme Court reversed, stating that the Tenth Circuit's holding "departs in [a] stark . . . manner from the pleading standard mandated by the Federal Rules of Civil Procedure." Id. at 2198. The Court cited *Twombly* only once, for the proposition that a complaint need only "give the defendant fair notice of what the . . . claim is and the grounds upon which it rests." Id. at 2200. *Twombly*'s "plausibility" language was entirely absent.

Does the result in *Erickson* affect your view of *Twombly*? On the one hand, *Erickson* appears to follow a more liberal pleading standard reminiscent of *Conley*—the plaintiff's complaint stated only that prison officials had wrongly terminated his hepatitis treatment for at least 18 months based on an erroneous belief that plaintiff was using drugs. On the other hand, *Erickson* might be limited to its facts. Consider the Court's observation that the Tenth Circuit's "departure from the liberal pleading standards set forth by Rule 8(a)(2) is even more pronounced in this particular case because petitioner has been proceeding, from the litigation's outset, without counsel." Id. at 2200.

2. What do you make of the *Twombly* majority's sweeping declaration that *Conley*'s "no set of facts" formulation "is best forgotten as an incomplete, negative gloss on an accepted pleading standard"?

One of the main questions the case leaves open is whether it applies across the board or only to antitrust cases. The Court's language suggests broad application, but one could reasonably believe that the Court only wants to see more detailed pleadings in antitrust cases of the *Twombly* type, and perhaps other "big cases." For the argument that the *Twombly* holding should be construed narrowly, see Keith Bradley, Pleading Standards Should Not Change After Bell Atlantic v. Twombly, 102 Nw. U. L. Rev. Colloquy 117 (2007), http://www.law.northwestern.edu/lawreview/Colloquy/2007/31, and Scott Dodson, Pleading Standards After Bell Atlantic Corp. v. Twombly, 93 Va. L. Rev. In Brief (July 9, 2007), http://www.virginialawreview.org/inbrief.php?sinbrief&p2007/07/09/dodson. As you will see when we come to summary judgment in Chapter 4, there are unique reasons to worry about antitrust suits when the effect of defendant companies' conduct—whether conspiratorial or not—is to lower prices for the consumer. See Matsushita Elec. Indus. Co. v. Zenith Radio Corp., 475 U.S. 574 (1986). Does it look like this is the effect of defendants' conduct in *Twombly*?

Nevertheless, courts have already applied the new *Twombly* standard in a number of cases outside of its original antitrust context, including RICO cases, see Limestone Dev. Corp. v. Vill. of Lemont, 520 F.3d 797 (7th Cir. 2008); constitutional civil rights cases, see *Iqbal*, 490 F.3d 143; wrongful discharge cases, see Hicks v. Ass'n of Am. Med. Colls., 503 F. Supp. 2d 48 (D.D.C. 2007); and intellectual property cases, see U2 Home Entm't, Inc. v. Kylin TV, Inc., No. 06-CV-02770, 2007 WL 2028108 (E.D.N.Y. July 11, 2007).

Empirical analyses suggest that *Twombly*'s effects are likely to be felt most acutely in Section 1983 and other civil rights cases of the sort that we will see in *Leatherman*, our next case. A study comparing post-*Twombly* cases to a control group of cases using the old *Conley* standard found that the new "plausibility" requirement had little impact on the rate of 12(b)(6) dismissals in most areas of law. However, in civil rights cases that cited *Twombly*, the plaintiffs' claims were dismissed at a statistically higher rate than under the old *Conley* framework. See Kendall W. Hannon, Note, Much Ado About *Twombly*: A Study on the Impact of *Bell Atlantic Corp. v. Twombly* on 12(b)(6) Motions, 83 Notre Dame L. Rev. 1811 (2008), available at http://papers.ssrn.com/sol3/papers.cfm?abstract_id1091246.

One such case, currently pending in the Supreme Court, may end up confirming Hannon's observation. In Iqbal v. Hasty, 490 F.3d 143 (2d Cir. 2007), the Second Circuit concluded that *Twombly* did not bar a civil rights action against former Attorney General John Ashcroft and FBI Director Robert Mueller. Iqbal, a Pakistani national detained in Brooklyn after 9/11, filed a lawsuit alleging that the conditions of his detention were unconstitutional. Id. at 147-149. Among Iqbal's many allegations were claims that Ashcroft and Mueller had helped set up discriminatory detention policies and were aware of Iqbal's mistreatment in the Brooklyn detention facility. Id. After an extensive discussion of *Twombly*, the Second Circuit concluded that the case presented no bar to all but one of Iqbal's claims, and permitted him access to "carefully limited and tightly controlled" discovery. Id. at 177-178. The Supreme Court recently heard oral argument in *Iqbal*, and at the time of this publication had not yet rendered its decision. But *Twombly* came up early and often at oral argument, with the government arguing that *Twombly*'s "disavow[al]" of *Conley* required dismissal of Iqbal's complaint. See Transcript of Oral Argument at 17, 22-23, Ashcroft v. Iqbal, No. 07-1075 (S. Ct. Feb. 6, 2008). The government also argued that officials like Ashcroft and Mueller should get the same "protections" as civil antitrust defendants given that both have "extraordinarily busy schedules." Id.

If the Court has begun to carve out special rules for certain types of cases, this is a real departure from the trans-substantive nature of the Federal Rules, thought by the original rulemakers to be one of their greatest accomplishments, and a vindication of core due process values. At the limit, *Twombly* may mark a return to a version of writ system pleading, in which different pleading procedures are required for different substantive claims. As the dissent suggests, and as we'll shortly see in *Leatherman* and its progeny, such a departure from trans-substantivity would also implicate Rule 9(b).

3. Consider the tension between the due process values of efficiency and access to justice in the case. The Court decries the way in which costly discovery can yield "*in terrorem*" increases in settlement values, and *Twombly* seeks to prevent the injustice that results when defendants are forced to spend significant time and money responding to claims that later turn out to be baseless. On the other hand, in antitrust and other cases, the "smoking gun" evidence often rests exclusively in the hands of defendants. It is not at all clear how plaintiffs in such cases could prevail without reaching discovery to develop the necessary proof.

The *Twombly* decision may not even be efficient on its own terms. Many lower courts have professed confusion over exactly what it requires. See, e.g., *Iqbal*, 490 F.3d at 157 ("These conflicting signals create some uncertainty as to the intended scope of the Court's decision."). The Third Circuit predicts that "[t]he issues raised by *Twombly* are not easily resolved, and likely will be a source of controversy for years to come." Phillips v. County of Allegheny, 515 F.3d 224, 234 (3d Cir. 2008). This suggests that the litigation seeking to interpret *Twombly*'s tea leaves could prove as "sprawling, costly, and hugely time-consuming" as the Court worries that discovery has become.

4. How must our tort victim now plead her case? Can she still simply follow Form 11 and state that the defendant drove "negligently," or is that a mere conclusion unsupported by any facts? And what about the plaintiffs in *American Nurses*—would their case survive a Rule 12(b)(6) motion under the interpretation of *Conley* given in *Twombly*? The issue Judge Posner spent so much time wrestling with—whether failure to respond to a comparable worth study revealing significant, gender-based pay disparities supports an inference of discrimination—seems very similar to the *Twombly* plaintiffs' attempt to support a claim of conspiracy by evidence of "parallel action."

In both complaints, what we might think of as the "ultimate fact" (intentional discrimination on the one hand, and agreement in restraint of trade on the other), is alleged generally and then supported by more specific allegations about behavior, the legality of which depends entirely on the inferences one draws. In both cases, the courts believed the general allegations of illegality were economically "implausible" because innocent explanations could be inferred. What exactly must the *Twombly* plaintiffs now plead for their suit to continue? As in *American Nurses*, plaintiffs threw in the towel after the 12(b)(6) ruling; what would they have had to plead to go forward?

5. Consider whether some or all of the following recently decided cases would come out differently after *Twombly*:

- Simpson v. Nickel, 450 F.3d 303, 305 (7th Cir. 2006) (reversing dismissal of § 1983 civil rights claim by prisoner claiming retaliation for exercise of First Amendment rights where district court found that prisoner's complaint failed to show that the speech triggering retaliation by prison officials was truthful, holding that the complaint need only contain "'claims' (which is to say, grievances) rather than legal theories and factual specifics").
- Kolupa v. Roselle Park Dist., 438 F.3d 713, 714-715 (7th Cir. 2006) (reversing dismissal of Title VII suit on ground that complaint survives if it "recite[s] that the employer has caused some concrete injury by holding the worker's religion against him"; "[a]ny decision declaring 'this complaint is deficient because it does not allege X' is a candidate for summary reversal, unless X is on the list in Fed. R. Civ. P. 9(b)").*
- Doe v. Smith, 429 F.3d 706, 708 (7th Cir. 2005) (reversing dismissal of suit claiming ex-boyfriend illegally disseminated video of the couple having sex because complaint did not allege "interception," an element required for liability under federal wiretapping statute, and holding that "pleadings in federal court need not allege facts corresponding to each 'element' of a statute. . . . Usually they need do no more than narrate a grievance simply and directly, so that the defendant knows what he has been accused of").**

6. Perhaps Swierkiewicz v. Sorema helps us determine what the post-*Twombly* results would be in these cases. Recall that the majority in *Twombly* took pains to distinguish *Swierkiewicz* at the very end of its opinion. *Swierkiewicz* is a 2002 age and national origin discrimination case that (at the time anyway) was assumed to have conclusively settled the status of liberal notice pleading. The plaintiff, a 53-year-old Hungarian native and chief underwriting officer for an insurance company, filed suit after being demoted and seeing his underwriting responsibilities transferred to a 32-year-old with only 1 year of experience. When Swierkiewicz

* The Seventh Circuit has held that *Kolupa* is abrogated by *Twombly*, see EEOC v. Concentra Health Servs., Inc., 496 F.3d 773, 777 (7th Cir. 2007).

** We thank Cathie Struve, Univ. of Penn., for calling these Seventh Circuit cases to our attention.

brought his concerns to his supervisor, he was asked to resign without severance and was then fired.

The trial court dismissed his complaint on the ground that Swierkiewicz failed to allege facts sufficient to constitute a prima facie case of discrimination. A prima facie case requires (i) membership in a protected group, (ii) qualification for the job, (iii) an adverse employment action, and (iv) circumstances that support an inference of discrimination. Swierkiewicz, the court reasoned, would have to show all four elements to shift the burden of proof at trial, but his complaint lacked any evidence to support an inference of discrimination. The Second Circuit affirmed.

Writing for a unanimous Court, Justice Thomas emphasized that "[t]his Court has never indicated that the requirements for establishing a prima facie case . . . also apply to the pleading standard that plaintiff must satisfy in order to survive a motion to dismiss. . . . Consequently, the ordinary rules for assessing the sufficiency of a complaint apply. See e.g. Scheuer v. Rhodes, 416 U.S. 232, 236 (1974) ("When a federal court reviews the sufficiency of a complaint, before the reception of any evidence either by affidavit or admissions, its task is necessarily a limited one. The issue is not whether a plaintiff will ultimately prevail, but whether the claimant is entitled to offer evidence in support of its claims.")." *Swierkiewicz*, 534 U.S. at 511. Justice Thomas found the trial court's approach equally inconsistent with Rule 8:

> Furthermore, imposing the [lower courts'] heightened pleading standard in employment discrimination cases conflicts with Federal Rule of Civil Procedure 8(a)(2), which provides that a complaint must include only "a short and plain statement of the claim showing that the pleader is entitled to relief." Such a statement must simply "give the defendant fair notice of what the plaintiff's claim is and the ground upon which it rests." Conley v. Gibson, 355 U.S. 41, 47 (1957). This simplified notice pleading standard relies on liberal discovery rules and summary judgment motions to define disputed facts and issues and to dispose of unmeritorious claims. . . . Rule 8's simplified pleading standard applies to all civil actions, with limited exceptions.

Id. at 512-513. Under this standard, Swierkiewicz's complaint should have survived the motion to dismiss because it alleged termination on account of his age and national origin and identified the events leading up to his termination, including "the ages and nationalities of at least some of the relevant persons involved with his termination." Id. at 514. The Court was untroubled by what the defendant and lower courts called the complaint's "conclusory allegations of discrimination"—the ultimate fact in the case—or the prospect that liberal notice pleading would "burden the courts and encourage disgruntled employees to bring unsubstantiated suits." Id. Are you convinced by the attempt to distinguish *Swierkiewicz* in *Twombly*? General allegations of discrimination, supported only by allegations regarding the plaintiff's status and evidence of adverse employment actions, seem analogous to general allegations of antitrust conspiracy, supported only by parallel conduct.

7. Finally, *Twombly* may exert influence on future revisions of the Federal Rules of Civil Procedure. The Supreme Court appears to have fired a shot across the bow of the Advisory Committee, signaling that it will intervene and reinterpret the rules if the Advisory Committee does not do more to address what the Court takes to be serious defects in litigation practice and procedure.

b. Special Pleading Requirements: Rule-Imposed and Judge-Made Burdens

Well before *Twombly,* Congress and the lower courts had begun to develop rules to increase the screening function of pleadings, particularly for causes of action they took to be crowding their dockets or "disfavored" for other reasons. As you read the cases below and the materials on pleading standards in securities cases, note the different premises about the proper role of pleading in the old *Conley* standard, *Twombly*'s plausibility standard, and Rule 9(b).

Leatherman v. Tarrant County Narcotics Intelligence and Coordination Unit

507 U.S. 163 (1993)

CHIEF JUSTICE REHNQUIST delivered the opinion of the Court.

We granted certiorari to decide whether a federal court may apply a "heightened pleading standard"—more stringent than the usual pleading requirements of Rule 8(a) of the Federal Rules of Civil Procedure—in civil rights cases alleging municipal liability under Rev. Stat. § 1979, 42 U.S.C. § 1983. We hold it may not.

We review here a decision granting a motion to dismiss, and therefore must accept as true all the factual allegations in the complaint. This action arose out of two separate incidents involving the execution of search warrants by local law enforcement officers. Each involved the forcible entry into a home based on the detection of odors associated with the manufacture of narcotics. One home-owner claimed that he was assaulted by the officers after they had entered; another claimed that the police had entered her home in her absence and killed her two dogs. Plaintiffs sued several local officials in their official capacity and the county and two municipal corporations that employed the police officers involved in the incidents, asserting that the police conduct had violated the Fourth Amendment to the United States Constitution. The stated basis for municipal liability under Monell v. New York City Dept. of Social Services, 436 U.S. 658 (1978), was the failure of these bodies adequately to train the police officers involved. See Canton v. Harris, 489 U.S. 378 (1989).

The United States District Court for the Northern District of Texas ordered the complaints dismissed, because they failed to meet the "heightened pleading standard" required by the decisional law of the Court of Appeals for the Fifth Circuit. 755 F. Supp. 726 (1991). The Fifth Circuit, in turn, affirmed the judgment of dismissal, 954 F.2d 1054 (1992), and we granted certiorari, 112 S. Ct. 2989 (1992), to resolve a conflict among the Courts of Appeals concerning the applicability of a heightened pleading standard to § 1983 actions alleging municipal liability. Cf., e.g., Karim-Panahi v. Los Angeles Police Dept., 839 F.2d 621, 624 (9th Cir 1988) ("a claim of municipal liability under section 1983 is sufficient to withstand a motion to dismiss even if the claim is based on nothing more than a bare allegation that the individual officers' conduct conformed to official policy, custom, or practice") (internal quotation marks omitted). We now reverse.

Respondents seek to defend the Fifth Circuit's application of a more rigorous pleading standard on two grounds. First, respondents claim that municipalities' freedom from *respondeat superior* liability, see *Monell*, supra, necessarily includes immunity from suit. In this sense, respondents assert, municipalities are no different from state or local officials sued in their individual capacity. Respondents reason that a more relaxed pleading requirement would subject municipalities to expensive and time consuming discovery in every § 1983 case, eviscerating their immunity from suit and disrupting municipal functions.

This argument wrongly equates freedom from liability with immunity from suit. To be sure, we reaffirmed in *Monell* that "a municipality cannot be held liable under § 1983 on a *respondeat superior* theory." 436 U.S., at 691. But, contrary to respondents' assertions, this protection against liability does not encompass immunity from suit. . . .

Second, respondents contend that the Fifth Circuit's heightened pleading standard is not really that at all. . . . According to respondents, the degree of factual specificity required of a complaint by the Federal Rules of Civil Procedure varies according to the complexity of the underlying substantive law. To establish municipal liability under § 1983, respondents argue, a plaintiff must do more than plead a single instance of misconduct. This requirement, respondents insist, is consistent with a plaintiff's Rule 11 obligation to make a reasonable pre-filing inquiry into the facts.

But examination of the Fifth Circuit's decision in this case makes it quite evident that the "heightened pleading standard" is just what it purports to be: a more demanding rule for pleading a complaint under § 1983 than for pleading other kinds of claims for relief. See 954 F.2d at 1057-1058. This rule was adopted by the Fifth Circuit in Elliott v. Perez, 751 F.2d 1472 (1985), and described in this language:

> In cases against government officials involving the likely defense of immunity we require of trial judges that they demand that the plaintiff's complaints state with factual detail and particularity the basis for the claim which necessarily includes why the defendant-official cannot successfully maintain the defense of immunity.

Id. at 1473.

In later cases, the Fifth Circuit extended this rule to complaints against municipal corporations asserting liability under § 1983. See, e.g., Palmer v. San Antonio, 810 F.2d 514 ([5th Cir.] 1987).

We think that it is impossible to square the "heightened pleading standard" applied by the Fifth Circuit in this case with the liberal system of "notice pleading" set up by the Federal Rules. Rule 8(a)(2) requires that a complaint include only "a short and plain statement of the claim showing that the pleader is entitled to relief." In Conley v. Gibson, 355 U.S. 41 (1957), we said in effect that the Rule meant what it said:

> [T]he Federal Rules of Civil Procedure do not require a claimant to set out in detail the facts upon which he bases his claim. To the contrary, all the Rules require is "a short and plain statement of the claim" that will give the defendant fair notice of what the plaintiff's claim is and the grounds upon which it rests.

Id. at 47 (footnote omitted).

Rule 9(b) does impose a particularity requirement in two specific instances. It provides that "[i]n all averments of fraud or mistake, the circumstances constituting fraud or mistake shall be stated with particularity." Thus, the Federal Rules do address in Rule 9(b) the question of the need for greater particularity in pleading certain actions, but do not include among the enumerated actions any reference to complaints alleging municipal liability under § 1983. *Expressio unius est exclusio alterius.*

The phenomenon of litigation against municipal corporations based on claimed constitutional violations by their employees dates from our decision in *Monell*, supra, where we for the first time construed § 1983 to allow such municipal liability. Perhaps if Rules 8 and 9 were rewritten today, claims against municipalities under § 1983 might be subjected to the added specificity requirement of Rule 9(b). But that is a result which must be obtained by the process of amending the Federal Rules, and not by judicial interpretation. In the absence of such an amendment, federal courts and litigants must rely on summary judgment and control of discovery to weed out unmeritorious claims sooner rather than later.

The judgment of the Court of Appeals is reversed, and the case remanded for further proceedings consistent with this opinion.

It is so ordered.

Note: Telling a Story

Recall that *Leatherman* is cited and distinguished in *Twombly*: the *Twombly* Court denied that it was creating a heightened pleading standard. The details of the police misconduct in *Leatherman* get very little attention, however, even in Justice Rehnquist's majority opinion. Consider the following excerpt from the Fifth Circuit opinion:

> This civil rights case arose out of two separate incidents involving the execution of search warrants by law enforcement officers with the Tarrant County Narcotics Intelligence and Coordination Unit. One incident involved Charlene Leatherman, her son Travis, and her two dogs, Shakespeare and Ninja. Ms. Leatherman and Travis were driving in Fort Worth when they were suddenly stopped by police cars. Police officers surrounded the two of them, shouting instructions and threatening to shoot them. The officers informed Ms. Leatherman that other law enforcement officers were in the process of searching her residence. The officers also informed her that the search team had shot and killed their two dogs. Ms. Leatherman and Travis returned to their home to find Shakespeare lying dead some twenty-five feet from the front door. He had been shot three times, once in the stomach, once in the leg, and once in the head. Ninja was lying in a pool of blood on the bed in the master bedroom. He had been shot in the head at close range, evidently with a shotgun, and brain matter was splattered across the bed, against the wall, and on the floor around the bed. The officers found nothing in the home relevant to their investigation. Rather than departing with dispatch, they proceeded to lounge on the front lawn of the Leatherman home for over an hour, drinking, smoking, talking, and laughing, apparently celebrating their seemingly unbridled power.
>
> The other incident alleged in plaintiffs' amended complaint involved a police raid of the home of Gerald Andert pursuant to a search warrant. The warrant was issued on the basis that police officers had smelled odors associated with the manufacture of amphetamines emanating from the Andert home. At the time of the raid, Andert, a sixty-four year old grandfather, was at home with his family mourning the death of his wife; she had died after a three year battle with cancer. Without knocking or identifying themselves, the officers burst into the home and, without provocation, began beating Andert. First, an unidentified officer knocked him backwards. When Andert turned, he was greeted by two swift blows to the head inflicted by a club, presumably of the billy-style. His head wound would require eleven stitches. Other officers, in the meantime, shouted obscenities at the family members, who were still unaware of the intruders' identities. At gunpoint, the officer forced the family members to lie face down on the floor. The officers did not relent: they continued to insult the residents and threatened to harm them. After searching the residence for one and one-half hours and finding nothing in the residence related to narcotics activity, the officers finally left.

Leatherman v. Tarrant County Narcotics Intelligence and Coordination Unit, 954 F.2d 1054, 1055-1056 (5th Cir. 1992). Should these details have been part of plaintiff's complaint? Or are they more properly matters to be developed in discovery? Why might plaintiff's counsel want to include such detail in a complaint, even if not required to by the Federal Rules of Civil Procedure? What must be included after *Twombly*?

Note: Pleading and Discovery

Keep in mind the intimate relation of pleading and discovery. Part of the original purpose of the Rules was to allow easy access to court through simplified pleading, and then fill in the allegations through discovery. Thus, as we will see in Chapter 3, the original scope of discovery in Rule 26 was very broad; parties might seek from each other any information "relevant to the subject matter involved in the action."

The most recent amendment to Rule 26 restricts initial mandatory disclosures among the parties to discovery of information that is *relevant to the claims or defenses* of the disclosing party, and restricts later discovery to information relevant to claims and defenses of any party. Only for good cause may the court permit more liberal discovery. Doesn't this new discovery rule have to affect pleading behavior? It offers a huge incentive to plead claims and defenses with more specificity than Rule 8 would warrant, in order to justify broader discovery.

Another link between pleading and discovery arises in complaints of misconduct against government officials, like *Leatherman*. Trial and appellate courts have often been reluctant to impose full discovery obligations on public servants without some more indication than Rule 8 requires that the suit is meritorious. For an example of what might be taken as the opposite conclusion about the impingement of a lawsuit and discovery on a public official's time, see Clinton v. Jones, 520 U.S. 681 (1997).

Despite the language in *Leatherman* rejecting a heightened pleading requirement in cases not covered by Rule 9, some lower courts construed it to allow such a requirement in civil rights suits against individual government officials (as opposed to municipalities). See Branch v. Tunnell, 14 F.3d 449 (9th Cir. 1994); Kimberlin v. Quinlan, 6 F.3d 789 (D.C. Cir. 1993). The courts relied on language in *Leatherman* specifically reserving judgment on whether heightened pleading was required in suits against individual government officials under the Supreme Court's qualified immunity doctrine. In his review of post-*Leatherman* case law, Professor Richard Marcus argued that "*Leatherman* has been a nudge, not a hammerstroke, against high pleading requirements," and that the case has not effected a "dramatic shift" in pleading practice. Richard L. Marcus, The Puzzling Persistence of Pleading Practice, 76 Tex. L. Rev. 1749, 1764-1765, 1767 (1998).

The following case shows how the Fifth Circuit struggled with the lingering desire, post-*Leatherman,* to require more specific pleading of certain claims.

Schultea v. Wood

47 F.3d 1427 (5th Cir. 1995) (en banc)

HIGGINBOTHAM, Circuit Judge.

I

A former chief of police for Tomball, Texas, alleges that three city councilmen and the city manager conspired to demote him after he reported to state authorities that one of the councilmen might be involved in illegal activity.

As chief of police, Joseph M. Schultea began investigating allegations in March 1992, that David R. Wood, a councilman, was involved in criminal activity. On April 8, 1992, Schultea told Warren K. Driver, the city manager of this home rule city, about his investigation. The next day, Schultea and Driver discussed the investigation with Mario Del Osso, the city's attorney. The three decided that Schultea would forward his investigative report to the Texas Department of Public Safety.

The next day, Wood demanded that Driver add to the upcoming council agenda possible action against Schultea. Driver, however, persuaded Wood not to pursue the matter.

With the next report about Wood to the TDPS, events took a different turn. After consulting with Driver, Schultea sent additional information about Wood to the TDPS on May 27, 1992. Later that same day, Schultea learned that Wood and the two other councilmen, Homer Ford and W. F. "Slim" Plagens, had instructed Driver to add to the agenda of the June 1, 1992, city council meeting, discussion of adverse action against Schultea. Schultea alleges that Driver told him that "he had no option but to place me on the agenda because Councilmen Wood, Ford and Plagens have all told him that either I go or he goes." Schultea requested that the city council consider the agenda item in public, but the city council made its decision in a closed executive session. The next day, Driver told Schultea that he had been demoted from police chief to assistant police chief.

Schultea immediately requested an administrative appeal or grievance hearing to challenge his demotion and to stop city councilmen Wood, Ford, and Plagens from making "libelous and slanderous comments" about him. On June 9, 1992, Driver told Schultea that the city did not have a grievance or administrative appeal procedure for his case. Schultea nevertheless again asked the city council for a hearing. Driver responded with a memorandum that, Schultea alleges, led people to believe that he deserved his demotion. Driver eventually put Schultea on the June 15, 1992, city council agenda at which Schultea could again request a hearing to contest his demotion and to clear his name. The record is not clear but the city council appears to have tacitly denied his request for a hearing at the June 15 meeting.

Schultea then filed this suit. He alleges that by demoting him, the council members deprived him of his property and liberty interests without due process and violated his First Amendment rights by retaliating against him for reporting Wood's allegedly criminal activities to the state. Schultea also claims several violations of Texas state law.

The councilmen moved to dismiss. The district court denied the motion, stating simply that "the complaint . . . states a claim against the defendants." The four individual defendants brought this interlocutory appeal challenging the denial of their qualified immunity from suit.

A panel of this court affirmed in part, reversed in part, and remanded for further proceedings. It agreed with the district court that Schultea's First Amendment claim should have survived the motion to dismiss, because "[n]o reasonable public official in 1992 [i.e., the year the alleged retaliation occurred] could have assumed that he could retaliate against an employee because the employee disclosed instances of misconduct by a public official."

The panel disagreed with the district court's conclusion that Schultea's procedural due process claims, at least in their present form, should go forward. The first of Schultea's two procedural due process claims alleges a constitutionally protected property interest in his employment. In Texas, employment is terminable at will absent a contract to the contrary; Schultea had to allege such a contract. The panel found that neither the city charter nor the representations of the official who hired Schultea created such a contract.

Schultea's second procedural due process claim alleges that his demotion, combined with the city councilmen's stigmatizing slander, deprived him of his liberty interest. The panel held that to establish a deprivation of this liberty interest, Schultea had to show more than demotion. Schultea retained city employment without a reduction in salary or fringe benefits. The panel concluded that this negated his liberty interest claim.

The panel reversed the order denying the motion to dismiss these due process claims, but remanded to permit Schultea to amend and restate them. The court noted that the complaint did not state Schultea's "best case." Schultea had filed his complaint himself, and had only later retained counsel.

The panel gave guidance for the remand . . . [holding] that this circuit's pleading standard survives the recent Supreme Court decision in Leatherman v. Tarrant County Narcotics Intelligence & Coordination Unit, 507 U.S. 163 (1993). The panel reasoned that the *Leatherman* court did not "'consider whether [its] qualified immunity jurisprudence would require a heightened pleading in cases involving individual government officials.'" (quoting Leatherman, 113 S. Ct. at 1162). The panel observed and we agree that nothing in *Leatherman* disturbed our holding in Elliott v. Perez, 751 F.2d 1472 (5th Cir. 1985), that complaints in such cases be pled with "factual detail and particularity."

Our task today is to explain the measure by which to judge the adequacy of any amended complaint Schultea may file on remand. It is the occasion for our revisit of *Elliott*. As we will explain, we stand by our insistence that complaints plead more than conclusions, and that a plaintiff can, at the pleading stage, be required to engage the affirmative defense of qualified immunity when invoked. However, we will no longer insist that plaintiff fully anticipate the defense in his complaint at the risk of dismissal under Rule 12.

It is important to follow the shifts in application of *Elliott* as qualified immunity has evolved. Our statement of the measure, "heightened pleading," has not changed, but in application it has moved, linked as it is to the substantive principle. This is the age-old dance of procedure and substance, here with the music of qualified immunity.

We are persuaded that we can balance plaintiffs' rights to challenge lawless government action against public officials' rights to be free of the difficulties of the discovery process without judicial additions to Rule 9(b) and with no change in the day-to-day procedure in these cases, except one. We will draw to center stage a judicial tool explicitly preserved by the Civil Rules, the reply. See Fed. R. Civ. P. 7(a).

II

In *Elliott,* we held that in suits filed under 42 U.S.C. § 1983 against public officials in their private capacity, a claim must be stated with particularity. Judge Brown, writing for the panel majority, forthrightly insisted on this greater detail to accommodate the substantive right of officials sued for money damages to be free both of individual liability and the discovery process—at least where a defendant's actions, although illegal at the time of suit, were not certainly so when the complained of actions were taken. The panel saw qualified immunity as a substantive right overriding liberal pleading rules, often termed notice pleading, the conventional but misleading description of the Civil Rules. A concurring opinion doubted judicial authority to impose a pleading rule. (Higginbotham, J., concurring specially). It urged that insistence on greater pleading detail ought to rest on the reality that what is short and plain is inseparable from the legal and factual complexity of the case at issue. It reasoned that federal trial judges could insist that to state a claim, short and plain, against a public official, a plaintiff must at least chart a factual path to the defeat of the defendant's immunity, free of conclusion.

The majority in *Elliott* and the cases that followed treated pleading questions as a choice between polar opposites—notice pleading and pleading with particularity. In many if not most cases, however, our insistence on pleading with particularity translated to no more than an insistence that the complaint not plead conclusions. To be sure, we have invoked "heightened pleading" and "pleading with particularity" as a pleading requirement in kinship with Rule 9(b)—but again our "particularity" seldom bit harder in application than an insistence that a plaintiff plead more than conclusions. Had we simply insisted that plaintiffs plead more than conclusions in their complaints, our holdings in these post-*Elliott* cases would not have changed.

The pleading hurdle erected was, in actual fact, somewhere between the poles of this perceived bipolar set. Significantly, the requirement of making a short and plain statement demands more than a statement of conclusions even without the support of Rule 9(b). This is because the Federal Rules of Civil Procedure have, since their inception in 1938, insisted on more than conclusions, and in this sense, have never been a system of notice pleading.

Because the Supreme Court has further defined the contours of qualified immunity since *Elliott*, we first consider that doctrine. We must define the demands qualified immunity now makes upon the Civil Rules and, in particular, the Rules' preference for discovery over pleading, before we return to pleading standards. We will then describe the array of procedural tools available to a trial judge.

III

In 1993, the Court in *Leatherman* concluded that the heightened pleading requirement of *Elliott* could not be applied in a § 1983 suit against a municipality, reserving the question of whether it might survive in cases against public officials. We need not answer that question today because henceforth we do not rely upon Rule 9's particularity requirements for the simple reason that it is unnecessary to do so. A practical working marriage of pleading and qualified immunity is achievable without looking to Rule 9. We look instead to Rule 7.

IV

Qualified immunity's limits upon access to the discovery process create a new and large role for the Rule 7(a) reply, a vestige of pre-1938 common law and code pleading expressly preserved in the Civil Rules. At the heart of the 1938 transition to the Civil Rules was the over-arching policy judgment that pleadings would henceforth play a far less important role in the winnowing process. This reduced role for pleadings in general came with the implicit direction to use the discovery processes to put flesh on claims and defenses.

In the 1938 transition, the reply was preserved but put on the shelf, seldom to be used. Both common law and code pleading required a response to any new matter in an initial responsive pleading at the pain of admitting the assertion. Under Rule 7(a), it is not necessary to reply to such new matter, and under Rule 8(d), allegations in a pleading for which no response is required are deemed denied.

Thus the Civil Rules anticipate a reduced, but not eradicated, role for the Rule 7 reply. Professors Wright and Miller observe that "[i]n certain instances, an additional pleading by the plaintiff may be helpful to the defendant in laying the groundwork for a motion to test the sufficiency of the claim." Charles A. Wright & Arthur R. Miller, Federal Practice and Procedure § 1185, at 23. We believe that ordering a reply to the affirmative defense of qualified immunity is one of those certain instances.

When a public official pleads the affirmative defense of qualified immunity in his answer, the district court may, on the official's motion or on its own, require the plaintiff to reply to that defense in detail. By definition, the reply must be tailored to the assertion of qualified immunity and fairly engage its allegations. A defendant has an incentive to plead his defense with some particularity because it has the practical effect of requiring particularity in the reply.

The Federal Rules of Civil Procedure permit the use of Rule 7 in this manner. The only Civil Rule that governs the content of Rule 7 replies is Rule 8(e)(1), which demands that "[e]ach averment of a pleading shall be simple, concise, and direct." We do not read Rule 8(e)(1) as a relevant limitation upon the content of a Rule 7 reply. Indeed, a party pleading fraud or mistake with particularity under Rule 9(b) is also required to do so in a simple, concise and direct manner. Nor is Rule 8(a)(2)'s "short and plain" standard a limitation on the content of a Rule 7 reply. Rule 8 applies only to the subset of pleadings that "set forth a claim for relief, whether an original claim, counterclaim, cross-claim, or third-party claim." Rule 8(a) does not encompass pleadings that it does not list, including Rule 7 replies. Employing the maxim that the Supreme Court used in Leatherman—*expressio unius est exclusio alterius*—we hold that because Rule 8(a) does not list Rule 7 replies, Rule 8(a)'s "short and plain" standard does not govern Rule 7 replies.

There is a powerful argument that the substantive right of qualified immunity supplants the Federal Rules's scheme of pleading by short and plain statement. Yet, the issue is complex and difficult. The contention that a federal procedural rule conflicts with a substantive right is problematic. "[A]ll federal rules of court enjoy presumptive validity. Indeed, to date the Supreme Court 'has never squarely held a provision of the civil rules to be invalid on its face or as applied.'" Exxon Corp. v. Burglin, 42 F.3d 948 (5th Cir. 1995). In any event, finding a civil rule inapplicable does not solve the problem. We would have to supply a new rule in its place. Nor will it do to insist that avoiding qualified immunity is an element of a claim. . . .

V

Our answer to *Leatherman* is that the district court has an array of procedures that will carry the load as far as pleadings can. First, the district court must insist that a plaintiff suing a public official under § 1983 file a short and plain statement of his complaint, a statement that rests on more than conclusions alone. Second, the court may, in its discretion, insist that a plaintiff file a reply tailored to an answer pleading the defense of qualified immunity. Vindicating the immunity doctrine will ordinarily require such a reply, and a district court's discretion not to do so is narrow indeed when greater detail might assist. The district court may ban discovery at this threshold pleading stage and may limit any necessary discovery to the defense of qualified immunity. The district court need not allow any discovery unless it finds that plaintiff has supported his claim with sufficient precision and factual specificity to raise a genuine issue as to the illegality of defendant's conduct at the time of the alleged acts. Even if such limited discovery is allowed, at its end, the court can again determine whether the case can proceed and consider any motions for summary judgment under Rule 56.

None of this draws upon the authority of Rule 9(b). The ultimate outcome of a confrontation between Rule 9(b) and qualified immunity, we no longer need to decide and we do not. We do not abandon the insistence in Elliott v. Perez that a complaint must do more than allege conclusions. Rather, we embrace it, retaining the practical core of the writing of both Judge Brown and the concurring opinion.

Our answer to the question of whether *Elliott* survived *Leatherman* is this: Since our first efforts in *Elliott* nine years ago, the law of qualified immunity has developed, and our perception of its practical demands upon the Civil Rules has moved in tandem. The confrontation we saw in 1984 is not the confrontation today, and we can insist upon all the particularity of practical use, with no draw upon Rule 9(b)....

We affirm the district court's denial of the motion to dismiss Schultea's first amendment claim, *but reverse its denial of the motion to dismiss* Schultea's claims of denied procedural due process. These claims are remanded to allow plaintiff to amend and for further proceedings consistent with this opinion.

Affirmed in part and reversed in part.

Note: Special Pleading in Civil Rights Cases

In Crawford-El v. Britton, 523 U.S. 574 (1998), the Supreme Court gave an implicit nod to the use of Rule 7(a) as an end run around *Leatherman*. In a 5-4 decision (from which *Leatherman*'s author, Chief Justice Rehnquist, dissented), the Court rejected the imposition of a clear and convincing standard of proof as applied to constitutional claims that require proof of improper intent. More generally, the Court emphasized its limited role in resolving rulemaking issues that overlap with congressional legislative power, stressing that "questions regarding pleading, discovery, and summary judgment are most frequently and effectively resolved either by the rulemaking process or the legislative process." Id. at 595. It also noted that trial courts have other means at their disposal besides heightened pleading standards for preventing unnecessary and burdensome discovery against government defendants, including Rule 7(a) power to order a reply to an answer, and Rule 12(e) power to grant a defendant's motion for a more definite statement.

Following *Crawford-El*, most circuits abandoned heightened pleading standards in cases other than those governed by Rule 9(b). See, e.g.,

Galbraith v. County of Santa Clara, 307 F.3d 1119, 1125 (9th Cir. 2002) (citing cases and overruling Branch v. Turnell, 14 F.3d 449 (9th Cir. 1994); Goad v. Mitchell, 297 F.3d 497, 502-503 (6th Cir. 2002). There was some lingering resistance, but especially after the Supreme Court reaffirmed *Conley*'s notice pleading rule in *Swierkiewicz*, supra at page 333, lower courts for the most part came into alignment. As the First Circuit put it, "*Swierkiewicz* has sounded the death knell for the imposition of a heightened pleading standard except in cases in which either a federal statute or specific Civil Rule requires that result." Puertorriquenos en Accion v. Hernandez, 367 F.3d 61, 66 (1st Cir. 2004).

It is unclear how *Twombly* affects this line of cases. As the notes following *Twombly* reveal, supra at page 329, the preliminary signs are not encouraging. Indeed, *Schultea* remains good law in the Fifth Circuit, with many courts citing it right alongside *Twombly*. For example, Foreman v. Texas A&M Univ. Sys. Health Science Ctr., uses the *Twombly* 12(b)(6) standard throughout but cites *Schultea* for the proposition that "in cases involving claims of qualified immunity, it is often appropriate to require a plaintiff to file a detailed reply . . . when the complaint itself does not meet the required standard—'that plaintiff has supported his claim with sufficient precision and factual specificity to raise a genuine issue as to the illegality of defendant's conduct at the time of the alleged acts.'" No. 3:08-CV-1469-L, 2008 WL 4949267 at *3 (N.D. Tex. Nov. 12, 2008). See also Nicholas W. v. Nw. Indep. Sch. Dist., No. 4:07-CV-14, 2008 WL 5101547 (E.D. Tex. Nov. 26, 2008); Greenwood v. City of Yoakum, No. V-07-78, 2008 WL 4615779 (S.D. Tex. Oct. 17, 2008).

In any case, the Rule 7(a) strategy you saw at work in *Schultea*, as well as resistance to the farthest reach of *Leatherman*, reveal that *Leatherman* was not immediately transformative. The breadth and depth of appellate litigation on pleading standards over the last two decades indicate a strong desire on the part of the lower courts, and among repeat-player defendants, to establish stricter standards. The resistance to *Leatherman* may also indicate a reluctance to adhere to the opinion's textualist interpretation of the pleading rules and the principle of transubstantivity they embody. Having seen both the rules and the resistance to them, do you think uniform rules make sense in all cases? Should certain claims be disfavored? Is pleading the right stage in which to filter disfavored actions?

Note: Rule 9(b)—The Securities Fraud Litigation Example

A very important area in which heightened pleading requirements *do* apply is securities fraud litigation. The federal securities laws—Securities and Exchange Act of 1934 § 10(b) and Rule 10b-5—prohibit corporate officers and directors from misleading the investing public with statements and omissions that contain material misrepresentations. Given that Fed. R. Civ. P. 9(b) lists "fraud" as one of the allegations that must be pleaded with particularity, and given that § 10(b) and Rule 10b-5 are directed at fraudulent acts, the courts have had little trouble concluding that the "plain meaning" of Fed. R. Civ. P. 9(b) dictates that heightened pleading standards govern these cases. See In re Glenfed, Inc. Sec. Litig., 42 F.3d 1541 (9th Cir. 1994). But see William M. Richman, Donald E. Lively, and Patricia Mell, The Pleading of Fraud: Rhymes Without Reason, 60 S. Cal. L. Rev. 959 (1987); Note, Pleading Securities Fraud Claims with Particularity Under Rule 9(b), 97 Harv. L. Rev. 1432 (1984). Yet, as the Second Circuit has explained, Rule 9(b) produces an irresolvable tension:

> On the one hand, there is the interest in deterring fraud in the securities markets and remedying it when it occurs. That interest is served by recognizing that the victims of fraud often are unable to detail their allegations until they have had some opportunity to conduct discovery of those reasonably suspected of having perpetrated a fraud. . . .
>
> On the other hand, there is the interest in deterring the use of the litigation process as a device for extracting undeserved settlements as the price of avoiding the extensive discovery costs that frequently ensue once a complaint survives dismissal, even though no recovery would occur if the suit were litigated to completion. It has never been clear how these competing interests are to be accommodated, and the adjudication process is not well suited to the formulation of a universal resolution of the tensions between them. In the absence of a more refined statutory standard than the vague contours of section 10(b) or a more detailed attempt at rulemaking than the SEC has managed in Rule 10b-5, despite 50 years of unavailed opportunity, courts must adjudicate the precise cases before them, striking the balance as best they can. . . .

In re Time Warner, Inc. Sec. Litig., 9 F.3d 259, 263-264 (2d Cir. 1993).

The tension between these two interests, along with the internal conundrum of Fed. R. Civ. P. 9(b)—which demands that fraud be pleaded "with particularity" but that intent may be "averred generally"—has led to conflicting results. Some courts read the rule to require fairly specific allegations for pleadings in securities cases. For example, in Ross v. A.H. Robins Co. (2d Cir. 1976), the Second Circuit held that the plaintiffs had failed to plead with the requisite degree of specificity in an action alleging that defendants had manipulated and artificially inflated the market price of Robins's common stock by disseminating false and misleading information about the effectiveness and safety of the Dalkon Shield, an intrauterine birth control device that Robins manufactured. Reviewing prior case law on pleading in securities actions, the court concluded as follows:

> These decisions taken together establish that a plaintiff alleging fraud in connection with a securities transaction must specifically allege the acts or omissions upon which his claim rests. It will not do merely to track the language of Rule 10b-5 and rely on such meaningless phrases as "scheme and conspiracy" or "plan and scheme and course of conduct to deceive." A defendant is entitled to a reasonable opportunity to answer the complaint and must be given adequate information to frame a response.

> There is no question that the plaintiffs in this instance adequately identified the alleged "misrepresentations." However, we believe that the pleading is deficient in other important respects.
>
> The complaint alleges only in a most sketchy fashion circumstances which would give rise to an inference of fraud. The complaint sets forth numerous facts which, it is alleged, indicate that "there were serious questions as to the safety and efficiency of the Dalkon Shield. . . . " (Complaint ¶ 18.) . . .
>
> As indicated above, although Rule 9(b) requires that "circumstances constituting fraud . . . shall be stated with particularity" it provides that "[m]alice, intent, *knowledge*, and other condition of mind of a person may be averred generally." (Emphasis added.) Of course, defendants' awareness of the facts alleged by the plaintiffs in paragraph 18 indicating that there were serious questions about the safety and efficacy of the Dalkon Shield is central to plaintiffs' Rule 10b-5 claim. However, at this stage of the litigation, we cannot realistically expect plaintiffs to be able to plead defendants' actual knowledge. On the other hand, plaintiffs can be required to supply a factual basis for their conclusory allegations regarding that knowledge. It is reasonable to require that the plaintiffs specifically plead those events which they assert give rise to a strong inference that the defendants had knowledge of the facts contained in paragraph 18 of the complaint or recklessly disregarded their existence. And, of course, plaintiffs must fix the time when these particular events occurred.
>
> Finally, the complaint is deficient in that it fails to specify the time period during which Robins' stock allegedly fell from $19 a share to $13 a share. (Complaint ¶ 45.) Absent such a statement, including a claim that the stock has not, since it was acquired, risen above $19 a share, it is impossible to determine whether the named plaintiffs or any members of the proposed class have any viable claim that they sustained a loss due to defendants' alleged misconduct.
>
> However, notwithstanding the deficiencies which exist in the pleading, we believe, as we indicated at the outset, that plaintiffs should be given a final chance to replead.

Id. at 557-559. Is the holding in *Ross* consistent with the general rule that "Rule 9(b) pleading standards may be relaxed . . . 'when the opposing party is the only practical source for discovering the specific facts supporting a pleader's conclusion'"? U.S. ex rel. Karvelas v. Melrose-Wakefield Hosp., 360 F.3d 220, 229 (1st Cir. 2004) (stating but declining to apply this rule in a qui tam suit) (quoting Boston Maritime Corp. v. Hampton, 987 F.2d 855, 866 (1st Cir. 1993)). Under this relaxed standard, when facts are particularly within the defendant's control, a court will allow limited discovery before requiring the plaintiff to plead with particularity.

Contrast the approach of the Second Circuit in *Ross* with that of the Ninth Circuit in In re Glenfed, Inc., 42 F.3d 1541 (9th Cir. 1994) (en banc), in which the court concluded that plaintiffs in securities fraud cases need *not* plead facts giving rise to a strong inference of fraudulent intent. As the court noted,

> The Second Circuit's test may or may not have the effect of deterring or weeding out "strike suits," which various courts have seen as imposing undesirable social and economic costs. Blue Chip Stamps v. Manor Drug Stores. 421 U.S. 723, 741 [1975]; Denny v. Barbar, 576 F.2d 465, 470 (2d Cir. 1978); see also Semegen, 780 F.2d [727,] 731 [9th Cir. 1985]. Whether the test has such an effect is beside the point. We are not permitted to add new requirements to Rule 9(b) simply because we like the effects of doing so. This is a job for Congress, or for the various legislative, judicial, and advisory bodies involved in the process of amending the Federal Rules. Leatherman v. Tarrant County Narcotics Intelligence & Coordination Unit, 113 S. Ct. 1160, 1163 [1993] (courts may not impose a heightened pleading standard for civil rights claims against municipalities, which are nowhere mentioned in Rule 9(b); such a result "must be obtained by the process of amending the Federal Rules, and not by judicial interpretation").

Id. at 1546.

Yet while intent ("scienter") could be averred generally, the court recognized that under Fed. R. Civ. P. 9(b), fraud could not. The court explained the pleading requirements for fraud as follows:

> To allege fraud with particularity, a plaintiff must set forth *more* than the neutral facts necessary to identify the transaction. The plaintiff must set forth what is false or misleading about a statement, and why it is false. In other words, the plaintiff must set forth an explanation as to why the statement or omission complained of was false or misleading. A plaintiff might do less and still identify the statement complained of; indeed, the plaintiff might do less and still set forth some of the circumstances of the fraud. But the plaintiff cannot do anything less and still comply with Rule 9 (b)'s mandate to set forth with particularity those circumstances which *constitute* the fraud.
>
> In certain cases, to be sure, the requisite particularity might be supplied with great simplicity. At argument, counsel for plaintiffs hypothesized that a plaintiff might allege that he bought a house from defendant, that defendant assured him that it was in perfect shape, and that in fact the house turned out to be built on landfill, or in a highly irradiated area; plaintiff could simply set forth these facts (presumably along with time and place), allege scienter in conclusory fashion, and be in compliance with Rule 9(b). We agree that such a pleading would satisfy the rule. Since "in perfect shape" and "built on landfill" are at least arguably inconsistent, plaintiff would have set forth the most central "circumstance constituting fraud"—namely, that what defendant said was false. Notably, the statement would have been just as false when defendant uttered it as when plaintiff discovered the truth. The house was *always* defective because it was *always* built on landfill.
>
> What makes many securities fraud cases more complicated is that often there is no reason to assume that what is true at the moment plaintiff discovers it was also true at the moment of the alleged misrepresentation, and that therefore simply because the alleged misrepresentation conflicts with the current state of facts, the charged statement must have been false. Securities fraud cases often involve some more or less catastrophic event

> occurring between the time the complained-of statement was made and the time a more sobering truth is revealed (precipitating a drop in stock price). Such events might include, for example, a general decline in the stock market, a decline in other markets affecting the company's product, a shift in consumer demand, the appearance of a new competitor, or a major lawsuit. When such an event has occurred, it is clearly insufficient for plaintiffs to say that the later, sobering revelations make the earlier, cheerier statement a falsehood. In the face of such intervening events, a plaintiff must set forth, as part of the circumstances constituting fraud, an explanation as to why the disputed statement was untrue or misleading *when made.* This can be done most directly by pointing to inconsistent contemporaneous statements or information (such as internal reports) which were made by or available to the defendants. The contemporaneous existence of such statements may support an inference of scienter, but that is *not required* under Rule 9(b).

The conflict over these two approaches, and the invitation by the Ninth Circuit to legislative intervention—this is "a job for Congress"—led to congressional hearings in 1995 that resulted in the controversial Private Securities Litigation Reform Act of 1995. Passed over the veto of President Clinton, the Act makes several significant changes in securities litigation, including a modification of the pleading requirements. A plaintiff now must "state with particularity facts giving rise to a strong inference that the defendant acted with the required state of mind," essentially adopting the Second Circuit position. See Elliott J. Weiss, The New Securities Fraud Pleading Requirements: Speed Bump or Road Block?, 38 Ariz. L. Rev. 675 (1996).

The ambiguity of the new, more stringent pleading standard has led to a great deal of litigation in the past decade over precisely what plaintiffs must plead to survive a motion to dismiss, which has resulted in a wide variety of court interpretations. Compare the Sixth Circuit's formulation: "[W]e hold that plaintiffs may meet PSLRA pleading requirements by alleging facts that give rise to a strong inference of reckless behavior but not by alleging facts that illustrate nothing more than a defendant's motive and opportunity to commit fraud." In re Comshare, Inc. Sec. Litig., 183 F.3d 542, 551 (6th Cir. 1999), with that of the Ninth Circuit: "We hold that a private securities plaintiff proceeding under the PSLRA must plead, in great detail, facts that constitute strong circumstantial evidence of deliberately reckless or conscious misconduct." In re Silicon Graphics, Inc., Sec. Litig, 183 F.3d 970, 974 (9th Cir. 1999). See also Southland Sec. Corp. v. INSpire Ins. Solutions, Inc., 365 F.3d 353 (5th Cir. 2004) (holding that the "group pleading" doctrine, which treats unattributed company statements in public documents as the "collective work of those individuals with direct involvement in the everyday business of the company," does not survive the PSLRA; instead plaintiffs must allege facts demonstrating each individual defendant's participation in company communications alleged to be fraudulent).

The emerging consensus seems to be that while allegations of a generalized desire to raise capital or increase compensation, for example, will not meet the new standard, showing material departures from generally accepted accounting principles generally will. See Steven B. Rosenfeld, Pleading Scienter Under the Private Securities Litigation Reform Act of 1995, 1085 PLI/Corp. 791 (1998). Courts

> require that a securities fraud complaint plead specific facts from which a strong inference can be drawn that each defendant sued was really up to no good. No matter which side of the analytical debate a particular court lines up on, generalized allegations of wrongdoing will not suffice; nor will allegations of mercenary motive that could be leveled against almost any corporate executive. Thus, plaintiffs alleging securities fraud under the PSLRA will have to come up with specific facts painting their particular defendants as more than run-of-the-mill greedy tycoons, and defendants will and should continue to move for dismissal of those complaints that do not do that.

Id. at 803.

It seems equally clear that the PSLRA increases the front end costs for plaintiffs, since more extensive prefiling investigation is a predicate to more detailed pleading. This suggests that new suits are especially likely to be filed where the government or third parties have already investigated and publicly revealed corporate fraud. Cases requiring plaintiffs' lawyers to invest time and money in extensive prefiling investigations of their own, on the other hand, may not be pursued. Is this a salutary consequence? At least one feature of the recent corporate accounting and mortgage lending scandals is that companies became extremely adept at concealing their true financial condition from regulators and investors. Moreover, as the collapse of Enron and Anderson Consulting shows, when legally questionable means of concealment failed, some troubled corporations turned to blatantly criminal methods such as document destruction to thwart investigators. See Nancy B. Rapoport and Bala G. Dharan, Enron: Corporate Fiascos and Their Implications (2004).

Whether the PSLRA was even necessary to deter meritless securities fraud filings also is debatable. Compare Janet Cooper Alexander, Do the Merits Matter? A Study of Settlements in Securities Class Actions, 43 Stan. L. Rev. 497 (1991), with Elliott J. Weiss and John S. Beckman, Let the Money Do the Monitoring: How Institutional Investors Can Eliminate Agency Costs in Securities Class Actions, 104 Yale L.J. 2053 (1995). The significance of the 1995 Act to pleading reform generally, and to the issue of congressional versus judicial control over procedural reform, is addressed by Stephen Burbank in an essay in which he states that "[i]f . . . the Civil Justice Reform Act was a wake-up call, the Private Securities Litigation Act of 1995 was a fire alarm." Procedure and Power, 46 J. Legal Educ. 513, 516 (1996).

One reason the courts (and many defendants) have been so concerned about pleading burdens in securities fraud cases is the fear of "strike suits"—baseless suits or suits plaintiffs otherwise doubt they could win but nevertheless file in the hope that defendants will settle to avoid litigation costs. Surviving a motion to dismiss is often the primary—perhaps sole—objective of plaintiff's counsel, as no further steps often are necessary. What are the consequences of permitting such an important, ultimately dispositive ruling to take place so early in the litigation?

Consider also the following observations by Joel Seligman regarding the effectiveness of motions to dismiss and Rule 11 sanctions to deal with baseless securities fraud complaints:

> The proponents of new restrictions [on securities fraud actions] . . . urge that none of the judiciary's devices to discourage frivolous litigation . . . successfully winnows out nonmeritorious lawsuits.
>
> Data available to the Senate Securities Subcommittee suggest that the facts are quite different. Senator Domenici, for example, summarized the litigation experience of a leading—if not *the* leading—plaintiff's litigation firm, which in 1990 and 1991 filed 111 cases, and found that 38% were dismissed on a motion, with the balance subsequently settled. . . .
>
> In addition, the Securities Industry Association reported that in 1992, forty-six motions to dismiss for failure to meet the requirements of Rule 9(b) were filed, and twenty-nine lawsuits were dismissed. . . . One may reasonably infer from such data that the courts have at least some success in winnowing out nonmeritorious lawsuits.

Joel Seligman, The Merits Do Matter, 108 Harv. L. Rev. 438, 445-446 (1994). For a response to Professor Seligman, see Joseph A. Grundfest, Why Disimply?, 108 Harv. L. Rev. 727 (1995), and an earlier work by the same author that triggered the Seligman article, Disimplying Private Rights of Action Under the Federal Securities Laws: The Commission's Authority, 107 Harv. L. Rev. 961 (1994).

One thing is clear: special pleading rules now apply to federal private securities litigation quite independent of Fed. R. Civ. P. 9(b). Will this development, along with *Twombly*'s broad plausibility standard, lead to a proliferation of special pleading rules in other areas? If so, is this a potential revival of the writs?

The special federal pleading rules for securities cases do not apply to state courts. In an effort to prevent investors from eluding the 1995 Act by filing in state court, Congress passed S. 1260, the Securities Litigation Uniform Standards Act of 1998. The Act requires that securities class actions against nationally traded companies be brought in federal, rather than state court. Private surveys, however, suggest that securities class actions have not migrated to state courts to evade the 1995 Private Securities Litigation Reform Act requirements. Moreover, according to SEC research findings, federal securities class action suit filings did not decline after adoption of the 1995 Private Securities Reform Act. Rather, they increased. See 66 U.S.L.W. 2524 (March 3, 1998). The Act likewise apparently has not resulted in a substantial increase in the number of institutional investors serving as lead plaintiffs. 66 U.S.L.W. 2587 (March 31, 1998). See Elliott J. Weiss and Janet Moser, Enter *Yossarian*: How to

Resolve the Procedural Catch-22 that the Private Securities Litigation Reform Act Creates, 76 Wash. U. L.Q. 457 (1998); see generally Symposium, The Implications of the Private Securities Litigation Reform Act, 76 Wash. U. L.Q. 447 (1998) (articles by Richard H. Walker, Elliott J. Weiss, Janet E. Moser, Douglas M. Branson, Hillary A. Sale, William S. Lerach, and Richard A. Rosen).

Does the securities litigation experience suggest caution before modifying pleading rules in other scenarios? If it does, should recent congressional legislation that customizes civil procedure rules in prisoners' suits, see Prison Litigation Reform Act, Pub. L. No. 104-134, 110 Stat. 1321 (codified as amended in scattered titles and sections of the U.S.C.), and in cases under the Biomaterials Access Assurance Act of 1998, 21 U.S.C. §§ 1601-1606 (2000) be reconsidered?

Keep in mind that not every aspect of a securities fraud claim is subject to heightened pleading under Rule 9(b) and the PSLRA. Proximate causation and economic loss, both essential elements in a securities fraud claim, need only meet the notice pleading standard. But plaintiffs still have to be careful not to plead too little. In Dura Pharmaceuticals, Inc. v. Broudo, 544 U.S. 336 (2005), for example, the Supreme Court upheld the dismissal of a securities fraud complaint alleging that plaintiffs suffered damages by paying "artificially inflated prices for Dura securities." Id. at 340. Plaintiffs bought stock in the company because of assurances that its drugs, including a new asthmatic spray device, would be approved by the Food and Drug Administration and become profitable products. When neither assurance proved true, the company's stock fell.

Although the complaint was quite detailed in other respects, the Supreme Court held that alleging an inflated stock price on the date of purchase does not meet the notice requirements for causation and economic loss. "For one thing, as a matter of pure logic, at the moment the transaction takes place, the plaintiff has suffered no loss; the inflated purchase payment is offset by ownership of a share that *at that instant* possesses equivalent value." 544 U.S. at 342. And even if the shares are later resold at a lower price, the lower price may or may not be the effect of the market correcting for company misrepresentations. The "lower price may reflect, not the earlier misrepresentation, but changed economic circumstances, changed investor expectations, new industry-specific or firm-specific facts, conditions, or other events, which taken separately or together account for some or all of that lower price. . . . Other things being equal, the longer the time between purchase and sale . . . the more likely that other factors caused the loss." Id. at 343. So alleging an inflated purchase price does not establish a loss without further allegations regarding the price when the stocks are later resold *and* the reasons for the lower price at that time. Liberal notice pleading, the Court concluded, would not save the complaint from dismissal:

> We concede that the Federal Rules of Civil Procedure require only a "short and plain statement of the claim showing that the pleader is entitled to

> relief." Fed. R. Civ. Proc. 8(a)(2). . . . But, even so, the "short and plain statement" must provide the defendant with "fair notice of what the plaintiff's claim is and the grounds upon which it rests." Conley v. Gibson, 355 U.S. 41, 47 (1957). The complaint before us fails this simple test. . . . [O]rdinary pleading rules are not meant to impose a great burden upon a plaintiff. Swierkiewicz v. Sorema N. A., 534 U.S. 506, 513-515 (2002). But it should not prove burdensome for a plaintiff who has suffered an economic loss to provide a defendant with some indication of the loss and the causal connection that the plaintiff has in mind. At the same time, allowing a plaintiff to forgo giving any indication of the economic loss and proximate cause that the plaintiff has in mind would bring about harm of the very sort the [securities laws and the PSLRA] seek to avoid. . . . It would permit a plaintiff "with a largely groundless claim to take up the time of a number of other people, with the right to do so representing an *in terrorem* increment of the settlement value, rather than a reasonably founded hope that the [discovery] process will reveal relevant evidence." Blue Chip Stamps, 421 U.S. at 741.

Id. at 1634. Is this really liberal notice pleading? Did the Court fairly apply *Conley* (the standard at the time), or did it smuggle a heightened pleading requirement into Rule 8(a)? If the complaint alleges an inflated price on a certain date when stocks are purchased, reliance on false company assurances, and a later drop in prices, aren't defendants put on notice that the plaintiffs believe their losses arise from the drop in stock price and that the losses are tied to false company assurances?

The Court found the complaint inadequate because other factors could account for the post-purchase decline in stock price. Even if, under *Conley,* we would have assumed the company's misrepresentations were the proximate cause, it is far from clear this assumption would be warranted under *Twombly.* Did *Dura* open the door for *Twombly*?

c. Pleading in the Alternative: How Consistent Must the Plaintiff Be?

Recall that the complaint is filed before formal discovery has begun. Sometimes the plaintiff does not know precisely what happened, yet has an adequate basis for filing a lawsuit. How should the plaintiff handle these ambiguities and fact gaps in the pleading? Should pleading alternative legal theories or alternative statements of the facts be permitted? Subject to what limits? See Fed. R. Civ. P. 8(e).

McCormick v. Kopmann

161 N.E.2d 720 (1959)

On the evening of November 21, 1956, Lewis McCormick was killed on Main Street in Gifford, Illinois, when a truck being operated by defendant

Lorence Kopmann collided with the automobile which McCormick was driving.

This action was brought by McCormick's widow in the Circuit Court of Champaign County against Kopmann and Anna, John and Mary Huls. The complaint contains four counts; the issues raised on this appeal concern only the first and fourth counts.

Count I is brought by plaintiff as Administratrix of McCormick's Estate, against Kopmann, under the Illinois Wrongful Death Act. Plaintiff sues for the benefit of herself and her eight children, to recover for the pecuniary injury suffered by them as a result of McCormick's death. It is charged that Kopmann negligently drove his truck across the center line of Main Street and collided with McCormick's automobile. In paragraph 3 of Count I, plaintiff alleges:

> That at the time of the occurrence herein described, and for a reasonable period of time preceding it, the said decedent was in the exercise of ordinary care for his own safety and that of his property.

Count IV is brought by plaintiff as Administratrix of McCormick's Estate, against the Huls, under the Illinois Dram Shop Act. Plaintiff avers that County IV is brought "in the alternative to Count I." She sues for the benefit of herself and her four minor children, to recover for the injury to their means of support suffered as a result of McCormick's death. It is alleged that Anna Huls operated a dramshop in Penfield, Illinois; that John and Mary Huls operated a dramshop in Gifford; that on November 21, 1956 the Huls sold alcoholic beverages to McCormick which he consumed and which rendered him intoxicated; and that "as a result of such intoxication" McCormick drove his automobile "in such a manner as to cause a collision with a truck" being driven by Kopmann on Main Street in Gifford.

Kopmann, defendant under Count I, moved to dismiss the complaint on the theory that the allegations of that Count I and Count IV were fatally repugnant and could not stand together, because McCormick could not be free from contributory negligence as alleged in Count I, if his intoxication caused the accident as alleged in Count IV. Kopmann also urged that the allegation in Count IV that McCormick's intoxication was the proximate cause of his death, is a binding judicial admission which precludes an action under the Wrongful Death Act. Kopmann's motion was denied. He raised the same defenses in his answer.

The Huls, defendants under Count IV, answered. They did not file a motion directed against Count IV.

Neither defendant sought a severance (see Civil Practice Act, Sections 44(2) and 51), and both counts came on for trial at the same time.

Plaintiff introduced proof that at the time of the collision, McCormick was proceeding North in the northbound traffic lane, and that Kopmann's truck, travelling South, crossed the center line and struck McCormick's car. Plaintiff also introduced testimony that prior to the accident McCormick drank a bottle of beer in Anna Huls' tavern in Penfield and one or two bottles of beer in John and Mary Huls' tavern in Gifford. Plaintiff's witness Roy Lowe, who was with McCormick during the afternoon and evening of November 21, and who was seated in the front seat of McCormick's car when the collision occurred, testified on cross examination that in his opinion McCormick was sober at the time of the accident.

At the close of plaintiff's evidence, all defendants moved for directed verdicts. The motions were denied.

Kopmann, the defendant under the Wrongful Death count, introduced testimony that at the time of the collision, his truck was in the proper lane; that McCormick's automobile was backed across the center line of Main Street, thus encroaching on the southbound lane, and blocking it; that the parking lights on McCormick's automobile were turned on, but not the headlights; that Kopmann tried to swerve to avoid hitting McCormick's car; and that there was an odor of alcohol on McCormick's breath immediately after the accident. Over plaintiff's objection, the trial court permitted Kopmann's counsel to read to the jury the allegations of Count IV relating to McCormick's intoxication, as an admission.

The Huls, defendants under the Dram Shop count, introduced opinion testimony of a number of witnesses that McCormick was not intoxicated at the time of the accident. Anna Huls testified that McCormick drank one bottle of beer in her tavern. Several witnesses testified that McCormick had no alcoholic beverages in John and Mary Huls' tavern.

All defendants moved for directed verdicts at the close of all the proof. The motions were denied. The jury was instructed that Count IV was an alternative to Count I; that Illinois law permits a party who is uncertain as to which state of facts is true to plead in the alternative, and that it is for the jury to determine the facts. At Kopmann's request, the court instructed the jury on the law of contributory negligence, and further:

> [I]f you find from all of the evidence in the case that (McCormick) was operating his automobile while intoxicated and that such intoxication, if any, contributed proximately to cause the collision in question, then in that case . . . you should find the defendant, Lorence Kopmann, not guilty.

The jury returned a verdict against Kopmann for $15,500 under Count I. The jury found the Huls not guilty under Count IV. Kopmann's motions for judgment notwithstanding the verdict, and in the alternative for a new trial, were denied.

Kopmann has appealed. His first contention is that the trial court erred in denying his pretrial motion to dismiss the complaint. Kopmann is correct in asserting that the complaint contains inconsistent allegations. The allegation of Count I that McCormick was free from contributory negligence, cannot be reconciled with the allegation of Count IV that McCormick's intoxication was the proximate cause of his death. Freedom from contributory negligence is a prerequisite to recovery under the

Wrongful Death Act. Russell v. Richardson, 31 N.E.2d 427, at p. 434. If the jury had found that McCormick was intoxicated and that his intoxication caused the accident, it could not at the same time have found that McCormick was not contributorily negligent. The Illinois Supreme Court has held that "voluntary intoxication will not excuse a person from exercising such care as may reasonably be expected from one who is sober." Keeshan v. Elgin A. & S. Traction Co., 82 N.E. 360, 362. . . .

Counts I and IV, therefore, are mutually exclusive; plaintiff may not recover upon both counts. It does not follow, however, that these counts may not be pleaded together. Section 24(1) of the Illinois Civil Practice Act (Ill. Rev. Stat. Ch. 110, Sec. 24) authorizes joinder of defendants against whom a liability is asserted in the alternative arising out of the same transaction. Section 24(3) of the Act provides:

> If the plaintiff is in doubt as to the person from whom he is entitled to redress, he may join two or more defendants, and state his claim against them in the alternative in the same count or plead separate counts in the alternative against different defendants, to the intent that the question which, if any, of the defendants is liable, and to what extent, may be determined as between the parties.

Section 34 of the Act states in part that "Relief, whether based on one or more counts, may be asked in the alternative." Section 43(2) of the Act provides:

> When a party is in doubt as to which of two or more statements of fact is true, he may, regardless of consistency, state them in the alternative or hypothetically in the same or different counts or defenses, whether legal or equitable. A bad alternative does not affect a good one.

Thus, the Civil Practice Act expressly permits a plaintiff to plead inconsistent counts in the alternative, where he is genuinely in doubt as to what the facts are and what the evidence will show. The legal sufficiency of each count presents a separate question. It is not ground for dismissal that allegations in one count contradict those in an alternative count. . . .

The 1955 revision of Section 43(2) of the Civil Practice Act was designed to make it clear that inconsistent facts or theories could be pleaded alternatively, whether in the same or different counts. In their note respecting the revised section, the drafters of the 1955 Act, having explained why clarifying language was needed, concluded: "Under the revision the inconsistency may exist either in the statement of the facts, or in the legal theories adopted." S.H.A. ch. 110, sec. 43, p. 514. This provision was modelled after Rule 8(e)(2) of the Federal Rules of Civil Procedure, 28 U.S.C.A. Federal courts have held that where the plaintiff in personal injury cases is uncertain as to who is liable, he may assert his claims against the several defendants alternatively. . . .

Sound policy weighs in favor of alternative pleading, so that controversies may be settled and complete justice accomplished in a single action. Illinois Civil Practice Act, Section 4; City of Nokomis v. Sullivan, 153 N.E.2d 48; Fleshner v. Copeland, 147 N.E.2d 329. If the right is abused, as where the pleader has knowledge of the true facts (viz., he knows that the facts belie the alternative) pleading in the alternative is not justified. Thus in Church v. Adler, 113 N.E.2d 327 at page 332, we said:

> [A]lternative pleading is not permitted when in the nature of things the pleader must know which of the inconsistent averments is true and which is false. Plaintiff must know whether she will be sick, sore, lame and disordered for the rest of her life or whether on the contrary she has regained her health, as alleged in Count II. She must make up her mind which is the fact, and strike the inconsistent allegation from her pleading on remand.

There is nothing in the record before us to indicate that plaintiff knew in advance of the trial, that the averments of Count I, and not Count IV, were true. In fact, at the trial, Kopmann attempted to establish the truth of the allegations of Count IV that McCormick was intoxicated at the time of the collision and that his intoxication caused his death. He can hardly be heard now to say that before the trial, plaintiff should have known that these were not the facts. Where, as in the *Church* case, the injured party is still living and able to recollect the events surrounding the accident, pleading in the alternative may not be justified, but where, as in the case at bar, the key witness is deceased, pleading alternative sets of facts is often the only feasible way to proceed. . . .

We hold that, in the absence of a severance, plaintiff had the right to go to trial on both Counts I and IV, and to adduce all the proof she had under both Count I and Count IV. . . . Plaintiff pleaded alternative counts because she was uncertain as to what the true facts were. Even assuming she introduced proof to support all essential allegations of both Count I and Count IV, she was entitled to have all the evidence submitted to the trier of fact, and to have the jury decide where the truth lay. She was not foreclosed *ipso facto* from going to the jury under Count I, merely because she submitted proof, under Count IV, tending to prove that McCormick's intoxication proximately caused his death. If this were the rule, one who in good faith tried his case on alternative theories, pursuant to the authorization, if not the encouragement of Section 43, would run the risk of having his entire case dismissed. The provisions of the Civil Practice Act authorizing alternative pleading, necessarily contemplate that the pleader adduce proof in support of both sets of allegations or legal theories, leaving to the jury the determination of the facts. . . .

What we have said is not to say that a plaintiff assumes no risks in adducing proof to support inconsistent counts. The proof in support of one inconsistent count necessarily tends to negate the proof under the other count and to have its effect upon the jury. While the fact alone of inconsistent evidence will not bar submission of the case to the jury, it may very well affect the matter of the weight of the evidence and warrant the granting of a new trial, even though, as we have held, it does not warrant *ipso facto* a directed verdict or judgment notwithstanding the verdict.

Kopmann argues that plaintiff should have been required to elect between her alternative counts before going to the jury. The doctrine known as "election of remedies" has no application to the case at bar. Here, either of two defendants may be liable to plaintiff, depending upon what the jury finds the facts to be. It has been aptly said that "truth cannot be stated until known, and, for purposes of judicial administration, cannot be known until the trier of facts decides the fact issues." McCaskill, Illinois Civil Practice Act Annotated (1933), p. 103. Plaintiff need not choose between the alternative counts. Such a requirement would, to a large extent, nullify the salutary purposes of alternative pleading. Since she could bring actions against the defendants seriatim, or at the same time in separate suits, she is entitled to join them in a single action, introduce all her proof, and submit the entire case to the jury under appropriate instructions. . . .

Kopmann contends he was prejudiced because Counts I and IV were submitted together to the jury, in that the jury was confused by plaintiff's inconsistent positions as to liability. We believe this argument is no longer open to Kopmann, since he failed to seek a separate trial pursuant to Section 51 of the Illinois Civil Practice Act. Russell v. Chicago Trust & Savings Bank, 29 N.E. 37; cf. People v. Skaggs, 76 N.E.2d 455. We also note that Kopmann's counsel repeatedly sought to establish McCormick's intoxication, indicating that this issue would have been injected into the case whether or not Count IV was presented concurrently with Count I. And, in any event, the jury was carefully instructed as to the law and the position of each party. The verdict itself shows that the instructions were understood and followed.

Kopmann argues that the practical effect of the trial court's instructions was to direct the jury to determine whether he or the Huls were liable to plaintiff, depending upon whether or not McCormick was intoxicated. The instructions given belie this contention. At Kopmann's request, the jury was repeatedly admonished that Kopmann was not liable to plaintiff if the jury found McCormick was guilty of contributory negligence, as well as if the jury found McCormick was intoxicated and his intoxication contributed proximately to cause the accident. No error was committed in this regard. . . .

Plaintiff has perfected a cross appeal, contending that the verdict is inadequate as a matter of law. We believe the jury could reasonably fix plaintiff's damages under Count I at $15,500. . . .

We conclude that the verdict and judgment below are correct and the judgment is affirmed.

---

2. Responding to the Complaint

Problem Case: A Woman Partner

Attorney Shayes sued her former law firm partners at McKenzie, Brachman et al. for violation of Title VII of the Civil Rights Act, alleging that she was "forced out" of the partnership because of conduct and attitudes that discriminated against her on the basis of sex. She also claimed that she was fired from the partnership because she had refused to go along with the cover-up of malpractice toward an unknowing client.

McKenzie filed a timely motion to dismiss for failure to state a claim upon which relief can be granted, based on his argument that Title VII does not cover professional legal partnerships. Relying on Hishon v. King and Spalding, 467 U.S. 69 (1984), the district court rejected the motion.

Can McKenzie now:

a) move to dismiss for improper venue?
b) move to dismiss for lack of subject matter jurisdiction?
c) make a motion for a more definite statement?
d) include in its answer the defense of lack of jurisdiction over the person?

a. The Rules and Forms

We now consider the options available to the defendant in responding to the complaint. The alternatives may be clustered, in general, as the following types of objections, in terms coined by the late Professor Delmar Karlen:

1) "'Tain't so." The defendant may deny the factual allegations of the complaint. The means for denying allegations is the answer. See Fed. R. Civ. P. 8(b) and Fed. R. Civ. P. Form 30, ¶ 3 (forms follow the text of the Rules).
2) "Yes, but." This is an affirmative defense, once called a "confession and avoidance." Here, the defendant may concede that the plaintiff's facts are true, and even that the law would entitle the plaintiff to relief under those facts, but asserts that other facts or law provide the defendant with a legal "out." For example, the plaintiff may properly allege the existence of a contract and that the contract was breached, but the defendant may have an affirmative defense because the contract was not in writing and is one for which a writing is required under the statute of frauds. See Fed. R. Civ. P. 8(c). An affirmative defense is raised in the answer, if any is filed. See Fed. R. Civ. P. Form 30, ¶ 6.
3) "So what!" The defense is the motion to dismiss for failure to state a claim in which the movant admits the facts as stated (for purposes of

the motion only), but insists that the law does not support the claim. For example, the complaint may allege, in some detail, how the defendant's lawn decorations offend plaintiff's tastes, but no law may protect plaintiff from a neighbor defendant's bad taste. The defendant may raise this defense in a pre-answer motion *or* in the answer. See Fed. R. Civ. P. 12(b)(6) and Fed. R. Civ. P. Form 30, ¶4.

4) "Not here." The plaintiff may have chosen the wrong court system or the wrong court within the system—jurisdiction and venue problems. Defendant can object to these either by pre-answer motion or in the answer, but with venue and personal jurisdiction the defendant must be careful to include the objection in whichever document is filed first. These are *waivable* defenses. Subject matter jurisdiction objections are more resilient and can be raised at any time during the proceedings, even on appeal. See Fed. R. Civ. P. 12 (b)(1)-(3) and Fed. R. Civ. P. Form 40.
5) "Right back at ya." This is a counterclaim. The defendant may have an independent claim for relief against the plaintiff. If so, defendant can raise this counterclaim in the answer. See Fed. R. Civ. P. 8(c)(2), 13 and Form 30, ¶7 Counterclaim.
6) Other defenses—bad notice, service of process, or other defects in the complaint—may be raised either in the answer or in a pretrial motion. Again, however, beware: some must be raised in the first document filed or else are waived. See Fed. R. Civ. P. 12(g) and (h).

In working with the materials that follow, be aware that a full explanation of some of the defenses—such as lack of subject matter jurisdiction, venue, or personal jurisdiction—appears elsewhere in the book. We focus here on the means by which these objections are made and where they fit in the defendant's arsenal of responses to the complaint.

b. The Pre-Answer Motion

The first option available to the attorney is to file a pre-answer motion. How does a motion differ from a pleading? Fed. R. Civ. P. 7 defines the *pleadings* as the *complaint*, the *answer*, and the *reply*, if any. A *motion* is a request that the court enter an order of some kind. See, e.g., Fed. R. Civ. P. Forms 40-42.

A motion has four parts: a notice of the motion, the motion, a certificate of service, and a memorandum in support of the motion. The first part tells your opponent when the motion will be heard. The second part is the specific request that the judge enter an order. For example, you may file a motion that requests that the judge dismiss the complaint for failure to state a claim. The third part is simply your averment to the court that you served the motion on your opponent, and how. The final part is a legal brief explaining to the court why you believe the motion should be granted under the applicable facts and law. If the motion cannot be granted on the basis of the pleadings, and rests on facts that lie outside the pleadings, then you may need to add a fifth document—an affidavit that sets forth the facts on which the motion depends.

Why might an attorney elect to file a motion, rather than an answer, when the answer can include all of the pre-answer objections (except the little-used 12(e)) plus the responses that can be made only in an answer? Isn't the lawyer risking the expense of filing two sets of papers instead of one, should the pre-answer motion fail?

One answer is that there are motions that will serve to defeat a case at a very early stage, and thus save the defendant from costly investigation and discovery. Challenging subject matter or personal jurisdiction, for instance, may quickly dispose of a case.

Defendants who think the case against them is hopeless often move to dismiss under Rule 12(b)(6). Used properly, this motion asks the court to dismiss the complaint because, as written, it cannot be construed to state a claim upon which legal relief may be granted.

The modern 12(b)(6) motion is an outgrowth of the common law demurrer, a term still used in many courts. These older forms carried with them many technicalities no longer observed. For example, the distinction between a general demurrer—which went to the merits of a case—and a special demurrer—which went to defects of form—has disappeared.

As we saw in *Twombly*, to survive the modern 12(b)(6) motion, the complaint must state facts that, if true, would give rise to a legally enforceable right. The judge must not decide the facts at this stage; rather, the facts alleged in the complaint are assumed to be true. Note that the plaintiff is not required to state her legal theory in the complaint, only facts sufficient to put defendant on notice of the matter about which plaintiff is suing.

Given the bare pleading requirement of Rule 8, as interpreted in *Conley* and *Twombly*, how often do you think the 12(b)(6) motion should be granted? Also consider the possibility that your motion will educate your opponent about defects in her case. In some situations, therefore, some lawyers may elect to file a motion for summary judgment or even take a case to trial rather than use 12(b)(6) prematurely. See, e.g., Jean Maclean Snyder, Tripping at the Threshold, 17 Litig. 17, 21 (1990).

Sufficiency of a complaint refers not only to the allegations in the pleading, but also to the available legal theories. A complaint may be very detailed, yet still lose on a motion to dismiss for failure to state a claim because no law supports plaintiff's alleged right to recover. Isn't this the heart of the *American Nurses* case?

Other means by which a party may attack a claim or counterclaim that is "hopeless" are through a motion for judgment on the pleadings, Fed. R. Civ. P. 12(c), and the motion for summary judgment, Fed. R. Civ. P. 56. The difference between the 12(c) and 12(b)(6) motions is timing; 12(c) is the proper designation for a motion to dismiss an action for failure to state a claim that is filed *after* the pleadings are closed—that is, after the complaint and answer (and reply, if any) have been filed. The difference between the motion for summary judgment and both the 12(c) and

12(b)(6) motions is that a summary judgment motion looks outside the pleadings to discover that plaintiff's claim is hopeless. Formerly called a "speaking demurrer," the summary judgment motion presents information, usually in the form of an affidavit that demonstrates that a trial would be pointless because no material issue of fact exists. The judge therefore may rule in advance of any fact-finding, as a matter of law. You will work more closely with summary judgment in Chapter 4, infra.

c. The Answer

Fuentes v. Tucker

187 P.2d 752 (1947)

GIBSON, Chief Justice.

The minor sons of the respective plaintiffs were killed by an automobile operated by defendant. The two actions were consolidated for trial, and in each case the verdict of the jury awarded the plaintiffs $7,500. Defendant appealed from the judgments claiming the trial court erred in permitting plaintiffs to present evidence of facts outside the issues framed by the pleadings.

On the day of the trial defendant filed an amended answer in each case which admitted "that he was and is liable for the death of the deceased . . . and the damages directly and proximately caused thereby." Plaintiffs were nevertheless permitted to prove the circumstances of the accident, including the facts that defendant was intoxicated and that the children were thrown eighty feet by the force of the impact.

It is defendant's position that the introduction of evidence as to the circumstances of the accident was error because it was not relevant or material to the amount of the damages, which was the only issue to be determined by the jury. Plaintiffs contend that defendant could not, by acknowledging legal responsibility for the deaths of the children, deprive them of the right to show the circumstances surrounding the accident, and that therefore it was not error to admit evidence of such facts. They do not claim, however, that the evidence was material to any of the facts in dispute under the pleadings as they stood at the commencement of the trial.

It is a doctrine too long established to be open to dispute that the proof must be confined to the issues in the case and that the time of the court should not be wasted, and the jury should not be confused, by the introduction of evidence which is not relevant or material to the matters to be adjudicated. This is merely one aspect of the larger problem of delay in the conduct of litigation. Every court has a responsibility to the public to see that justice is administered efficiently and expeditiously and that the facilities of the court are made available at the first possible moment to those whose cases are awaiting trial. It would be an unwarranted waste of public funds, and a manifest injustice to the many litigants seeking an early trial date, to allow counsel in a particular case to occupy substantial periods of time in the useless presentation of evidence on matters not in controversy; and we know of no well considered opinion which asserts such a right.

One of the functions of pleadings is to limit the issues and narrow the proofs. If facts alleged in the complaint are not controverted by the answer, they are not in issue, and no evidence need be offered to prove their existence. Travelers Ins. Co. v. Byers, 11 P.2d 444 [1932]; Code Civ. Proc., §§ 462, 588, 1868, 1870, subds. (1), (15); see I Wigmore on Evidence, 3d Ed. 1940, p. 9, § 2. Evidence which is not pertinent to the issues raised by the pleadings is immaterial, and it is error to allow the introduction of such evidence.

It follows, therefore, if an issue has been removed from a case by an admission in the answer, that it is error to receive evidence which is material solely to the excluded matter. This, of course, does not mean that an admission of liability precludes a plaintiff from showing how an accident happened if such evidence is material to the issue of damages. In an action for personal injuries, where liability is admitted and the only issue to be tried is the amount of damage, the force of the impact and the surrounding circumstances may be relevant and material to indicate the extent of plaintiff's injuries. Johnson v. McRee, 152 P.2d 526 [1944]; Martin v. Miqueu, 98 P.2d 816 [1940]. Such evidence is admissible because it is relevant and material to an issue remaining in the case.

The defendant here by an unqualified statement in his answer admitted liability for the deaths of the children, and the sole remaining question in issue was the amount of damages suffered by the parents. In an action for wrongful death of a minor child the damages consist of the pecuniary loss to the parents in being deprived of the services, earnings, society, comfort and protection of the child. Bond v. United Railroads, 113 P. 366 [1911]. The manner in which the accident occurred, the force of the impact, or defendant's intoxication could have no bearing on these elements of damage. The evidence, therefore, was not material to any issue before the jury, and its admission was error. . . .

The introduction of evidence of admitted facts is permissible in cases where the admission is ambiguous in form or limited in scope or where, during the trial of a case, a party seeks to deprive his opponents of the legitimate force and effect of material evidence by the bald admission of a probative fact. . . .

. . . The boys involved in this accident were approximately twelve years old when they were killed. Certainly the sum of $7,500, which was awarded by the jury in each case, cannot be said to be an unreasonable amount to allow for the wrongful death of a child of that age, and the verdicts are not so large as to indicate that the jury was unduly influenced by the admission of the immaterial testimony in question. It does not appear, therefore, that the error resulted in a miscarriage of justice. . . .

The judgments are affirmed.

CARTER, Justice (concurring). . . .

The effect of the majority holding in this case is to deny to an injured person the benefit of presenting to the trier of fact the entire factual situation surrounding the accident out of which the injury arose. It cannot be denied that either a jury or a trial judge is more disposed to award a substantial amount of damages in a case where the defendant is shown to have been guilty of gross negligence and his conduct was such as to indicate a reckless disregard for the safety of others, than where the negligence amounted to only an error in judgment. The present holding will make it possible for a defendant who has been guilty of the most heinous kind of reckless and wanton conduct, including intoxication, to conceal from the trier of fact the extent of his culpability, and thereby gain any advantage which might flow from the absence of such disclosure. Theoretically and technically, and judged by academic standards, this practice may be justified, but when gauged by actual experience in the administration of justice it favors the worst offenders by permitting them to escape from a larger award of damages which the trier of fact might feel justified in awarding if the entire picture were presented. . . .

Zielinski v. Philadelphia Piers, Inc.

139 F. Supp. 408 (E.D. Pa. 1956)

VAN DUSEN, District Judge.

Plaintiff requests a ruling that, for the purposes of this case, the motor-driven fork lift operated by Sandy Johnson on February 9, 1953, was owned by defendant and that Sandy Johnson was its agent acting in the course of his employment on that date. The following facts are established by the pleadings, interrogatories, depositions and uncontradicted portions of affidavits:

1. Plaintiff filed his complaint on April 28, 1953, for personal injuries received on February 9, 1953, while working on Pier 96, Philadelphia, for J. A. McCarthy, as a result of a collision of two motor-driven fork lifts.

2. Paragraph 5 of this complaint stated that "a motor-driven vehicle known as a fork lift or chisel, owned, operated and controlled by the defendant, its agents, servants and employees, was so negligently and carelessly managed . . . that the same . . . did come into contact with the plaintiff causing him to sustain the injuries more fully hereinafter set forth."

3. The "First Defense" of the Answer stated "Defendant . . . (c) denies the averments of paragraph 5. . . ."

4. The motor-driven vehicle known as a fork lift or chisel, which collided with the McCarthy fork lift on which plaintiff was riding, had on it the initials "P.P.I."

5. On February 10, 1953, Carload Contractors, Inc. made a report of this accident to its insurance company, whose policy No. CL 3964 insured Carload Contractors, Inc. against potential liability for the negligence of its employees contributing to a collision of the type described in paragraph 2 above.

6. By letter of April 29, 1953, the complaint served on defendant was forwarded to the above-mentioned insurance company. This letter read as follows:

> Gentlemen:
>
> As per telephone conversation today with your office, we attach hereto "Complaint in Trespass" as brought against Philadelphia Piers, Inc. by one Frank Zielinski for supposed injuries sustained by him on February 9, 1953.
>
> We find that a fork lift truck operated by an employee of Carload Contractors, Inc. also insured by yourselves was involved in an accident with another chisel truck, which, was alleged, did cause injury to Frank Zielinski, and same was reported to you by Carload Contractors, Inc. at the time, and you assigned Claim Number OL 0153-94 to this claim.
>
> Should not this Complaint in Trespass be issued against Carload Contractors, Inc. and not Philadelphia Piers, Inc.?
>
> We forward for your handling.

7. Interrogatories 1 to 5 and the answers thereto, which were sworn to by defendant's General Manager on June 12, 1953, and filed on June 22, 1953, read as follows:

> 1. State whether you have received any information of an injury sustained by the plaintiff on February 9, 1953, South Wharves. If so, state when and from whom you first received notice of such injury. A. We were first notified of this accident on or about February 9, 1953 by Thomas Wilson.
>
> 2. State whether you caused an investigation to be made of the circumstances of said injury and if so, state who made such investigation and when it was made. A. We made a very brief investigation on February 9, 1953 and turned the matter over to (our insurance company) for further investigation. . . .

8. At a deposition taken August 18, 1953, Sandy Johnson testified that he was the employee of defendant on February 9, 1953, and had been their employee for approximately fifteen years.

9. At a pretrial conference held on September 27, 1955, plaintiff first learned that over a year before February 9, 1953, the business of moving freight on piers in Philadelphia, formerly conducted by defendant, had been sold by it to Carload Contractors, Inc. and Sandy Johnson had been transferred to the payroll of this corporation without apparently realizing it, since the nature or location of his work had not changed. . . .

11. Defendant now admits that on February 9, 1953, it owned the fork lift in the custody of Sandy Johnson and that this fork lift was leased to Carload Contractors, Inc. It is also admitted that the pier on which the accident occurred was leased by defendant.

12. There is no indication of action by either party in bad faith and there is no proof of inaccurate statements being made with intent to deceive. Because defendant made a prompt investigation of the accident, its insurance company has been representing the defendant since suit was

brought, and this company insures Carload Contractors, Inc. also, requiring defendant to defend this suit will not prejudice it.

Under these circumstances, and for the purposes of this action, it is ordered that the following shall be stated to the jury at the trial:

> It is admitted that, on February 9, 1953, the towmotor or fork lift bearing the initials "P.P.I." was owned by defendant and that Sandy Johnson was a servant in the employ of defendant and doing its work on that date.

This ruling is based on the following principles:

1. Under the circumstances of this case, the answer contains an ineffective denial of that part of paragraph 5 of the complaint which alleges that "a motor-driven vehicle known as a fork lift or chisel (was) owned, operated and controlled by the defendant, its agents, servants and employees."

Fed. R. Civ. P. 8(b) provides:

> A party shall state in short and plain terms his defenses to each claim asserted and shall admit or deny the averments upon which the adverse party relies. . . . Denials shall fairly meet the substance of the averments denied. When a pleader intends in good faith to deny only a part or a qualification of an averment, he shall specify so much of it as is true and material and shall deny only the remainder.

For example, it is quite clear that defendant does not deny the averment in paragraph 5 that the fork lift came into contact with plaintiff, since it admits, in the answers to interrogatories, that an investigation of an occurrence of the accident had been made and that a report dated February 10, 1953, was sent to its insurance company stating "While Frank Zielinski was riding on bumper of chisel and holding rope to secure cargo, the chisel truck collided with another chisel truck operated by Sandy Johnson causing injuries to Frank Zielinski's legs and hurt head of Sandy Johnson." Compliance with the above-mentioned rule required that defendant file a more specific answer than a general denial. A specific denial of parts of this paragraph and specific admission of other parts would have warned plaintiff that he had sued the wrong defendant.

Paragraph 8.23 of Moore's Federal Practice (2nd Edition) Vol. II, p. 1680, says: "In such a case, the defendant should make clear just what he is denying and what he is admitting." This answer to paragraph 5 does not make clear to plaintiff the defenses he must be prepared to meet.

Under circumstances where an improper and ineffective answer has been filed, the Pennsylvania courts have consistently held that an allegation of agency in the complaint requires a statement to the jury that agency is admitted where an attempt to amend the answer is made after the expiration of the period of limitation. See Burns v. Joseph Flaherty Co., 1924, 278 Pa. 579, 582-583; Boles v. Federal Electric Co., 1926, 89 Pa. Super. 160, 163-164. Although the undersigned has been able to find no federal court decisions on this point, he believes the principle of these Pennsylvania appellate court decisions may be considered in view of all the facts of this case, where jurisdiction is based on diversity of citizenship, the accident occurred in Pennsylvania, and the federal district court is sitting in Pennsylvania. . . .

2. Under the circumstances of this case, principles of equity require that defendant be estopped from denying agency because, otherwise, its inaccurate statements and statements in the record, which it knew (or had the means of knowing within its control) were inaccurate, will have deprived plaintiff of his right of action.

If Interrogatory 2 had been answered accurately by saying that employees of Carload Contractors, Inc. had turned the matter over to the insurance company, it seems clear that plaintiff would have realized his mistake. The fact that if Sandy Johnson had testified accurately, the plaintiff could have brought its action against the proper party defendant within the statutory period of limitations is also a factor to be considered, since defendant was represented at the deposition and received knowledge of the inaccurate testimony.

At least one appellate court has stated that the doctrine of equitable estoppel will be applied to prevent a party from taking advantage of the statute of limitations where the plaintiff has been misled by conduct of such party. See Peters v. Public Service Corporation, 29 A.2d 189, 195 (1942). . . .

> Of course, defendants were under no duty to advise complainants' attorney of his error, other than by appropriate pleadings, but neither did defendants have a right, knowing of the mistake, to foster it by its acts of omission.

This doctrine has been held to estop a party from taking advantage of a document of record where the misleading conduct occurred after the recording, so that application of this doctrine would not necessarily be precluded in a case such as this where the misleading answers to interrogatories and depositions were subsequent to the filing of the answer, even if the denial in the answer had been sufficient. . . .

Since this is a pre-trial order, it may be modified at the trial if the trial judge determines from the facts which then appear that justice so requires.

Notes and Questions

1. *Strategy in Pleading.* Remember that in our problem case, Shayes pleaded inconsistently about the reasons for her being fired. Why might she want to plead both theories, even though she would not proceed to trial on both at once? Defendants also plead strategically—as illustrated by *Fuentes*. Note the tactical advantages of admitting certain facts, even if untrue or possible to contest.

2. *Insufficient Denials Treated as Admissions.* Note that Rule 8(b) was thoroughly "restyled" in 2007. Harsh applications of the strictures of Fed. R. Civ. P. 8(b) on the pleading of denials have generally been avoided and the sanction of Fed. R. Civ. P. 8(b)(6) has been applied sparingly. On the other hand, gross departures from the requirements of the Rule, such as those that could mislead the adversary, may be treated as admissions. For example, a denial of sufficient knowledge under Fed. R. Civ. P. 8(b) may be deemed an admission if the party denying the knowledge clearly has it, see e.g., Mesirow v. Duggan, 240 F.2d 751 (8th Cir. 1957).

3. *The Relation Between Fed. R. Civ. P. 8(b)(6) and Fed. R. Civ. P. 9(c).* Fed. R. Civ. P. 8(b)(6) may also be read with Fed. R. Civ. P. 9(c). In Lumbermen's Mutual Insurance Co. v. Bowman, 313 F.2d 381 (10th Cir. 1963), it was held that a general denial was not sufficient to put in issue noncompliance with conditions precedent to liability.

4. *Failing to Respond.* What if the defendant simply fails to respond at all? See Fed. R. Civ. P. 55; see also Honda Power Equip. Mfr., Inc. v. Woodhouse, 219 F.R.D. 2, 4-5 (D.D.C. 2003) (entering default judgment against British defendants in patent litigation who, nine months after the complaint was filed and six months after seeking an extension of time to answer, "had neither filed responsive pleadings nor entered an appearance in this case"; defendants sought a stay of the motion for default judgment pending the outcome of parallel litigation in the United Kingdom between the parties as well as leave to file an answer and counterclaim, but then dropped out of contact with their lawyers in the United States).

d. Affirmative Defenses

Problem Case: A Woman Partner (Part Two)

In the lawsuit by Shayes against her former partners, McKenzie intends to raise as a defense that Shayes was paid a substantial severance bonus upon leaving the partnership, and that there was an oral agreement that she would not sue the firm. Must McKenzie include this defense in his answer, or may he simply deny the allegations of her complaint? Read Rule 8(c) and consider the following cases.

Gomez v. Toledo

446 U.S. 635 (1980)

Justice Marshall delivered the opinion of the Court.

The question presented is whether, in an action brought under 42 U.S.C. § 1983 against a public official whose position might entitle him to qualified immunity, a plaintiff must allege that the official has acted in bad faith in order to state a claim for relief or, alternatively, whether the defendant must plead good faith as an affirmative defense.

I

Petitioner Carlos Rivera Gomez brought this action against respondent, the Superintendent of the Police of the Commonwealth of Puerto Rico, contending that respondent had violated his right to procedural due process by discharging him from employment with the Police Department's Bureau of Criminal Investigation.[1] Basing jurisdiction on 28 U.S.C. § 1343(3),[2] petitioner alleged the following facts in his complaint.[3] Petitioner had been employed as an agent with the Puerto Rican police since 1968. In April 1975, he submitted a sworn statement to his supervisor in which he asserted that two other agents had offered false evidence for use in a criminal case under their investigation. As a result of this statement, petitioner was immediately transferred from the Criminal Investigation Corps for the Southern Area to Police Headquarters in San Juan, and a few weeks later to the Police Academy in Gurabo, where he was given no investigative authority. In the meantime respondent ordered an investigation of petitioner's claims, and the Legal Division of the Police Department concluded that all of petitioner's factual allegations were true.

In April 1976, while still stationed at the Police Academy, petitioner was subpoenaed to give testimony in a criminal case arising out of the evidence that petitioner had alleged to be false. At the trial petitioner, appearing as a defense witness, testified that the evidence was in fact false. As a result of this testimony, criminal charges, filed on the basis of information furnished by respondent, were brought against petitioner for the allegedly unlawful wiretapping of the agents' telephones. Respondent suspended petitioner in May 1976 and discharged him without a hearing in July. In October, the District Court of Puerto Rico found no probable cause to believe that petitioner was guilty of the allegedly unlawful wiretapping and, upon appeal by the prosecution, the Superior Court affirmed. Petitioner in turn sought review of his discharge before the Investigation, Prosecution, and Appeals Commission of Puerto Rico, which, after a hearing, revoked the discharge order rendered by respondent and ordered that petitioner be reinstated with backpay.

Based on the foregoing factual allegations, petitioner brought this suit for damages, contending that his discharge violated his right to procedural due process, and that it had caused him anxiety, embarrassment, and injury to his reputation in the community. In his answer, respondent denied a number of petitioner's allegations of fact and asserted several affirmative defenses. Respondent then moved to dismiss the complaint

1. The complaint originally named the Commonwealth of Puerto Rico and the police of the Commonwealth of Puerto Rico as additional defendants, but petitioner consented to their dismissal from the action.

2. That section grants the federal district courts jurisdiction "[t]o redress the deprivation, under color of any State law, statute, ordinance, regulation, custom or usage, of any right, privilege or immunity secured by the Constitution of the United States or by any Act of Congress providing for equal rights of citizens or of all persons within the jurisdiction of the United States."

3. At this state of proceedings, of course, all allegations of the complaint must be accepted as true.

for failure to state a cause of action, see Fed. Rule Civ. Proc. 12(b)(6), and the District Court granted the motion. Observing that respondent was entitled to qualified immunity for acts done in good faith within the scope of his official duties, it concluded that petitioner was required to plead as part of his claim for relief that, in committing the actions alleged, respondent was motivated by bad faith. The absence of any such allegation, it held, required dismissal of the complaint. The United States Court of Appeals for the First Circuit affirmed. 602 F.2d 1018 (1979).

We granted certiorari to resolve a conflict among the Courts of Appeals. We now reverse.

Good faith is aff def.

II

Section 1983 provides a cause of action for "the deprivation of any rights, privileges, or immunities secured by the Constitution and laws" by any person acting "under color of any statute, ordinance, regulation, custom, or usage, of any State or Territory." 42 U.S.C. § 1983.[6] This statute, enacted to aid in "'the preservation of human liberty and human rights,'" Owen v. City of Independence, 445 U.S. 622, 636 (1980), quoting Cong. Globe, 42d Cong., 1st Sess., App. 68 (1871) (Rep. Shellabarger), reflects a congressional judgment that a "damages remedy against the offending party is a vital component of any scheme for vindicating cherished constitutional guarantees," 445 U.S. at 651. As remedial legislation, § 1983 is to be construed generously to further its primary purpose. See 445 U.S. at 636.

In certain limited circumstances, we have held that public officers are entitled to a qualified immunity from damages liability under § 1983. This conclusion has been based on an unwillingness to infer from legislative silence a congressional intention to abrogate immunities that were both "well established at common law" and "compatible with the purposes of the Civil Rights Act." 445 U.S. at 638. Findings of immunity have thus been "predicated upon a considered inquiry into the immunity historically accorded the relevant official at common law and the interests behind it." Imbler v. Pachtman, 424 U.S. 409, 421 (1976). In Pierson v. Ray, 386 U.S. 547, 555 (1967), for example, we concluded that a police officer would be "excus[ed] from liability for acting under a statute that he reasonably believed to be valid but that was later held unconstitutional, on its face or as applied." And in other contexts we have held, on the basis of "[c]ommon law tradition . . . and strong public-policy reasons," Wood v. Strickland, 420 U.S. 308, 318 (1975), that certain categories of executive officers should be allowed qualified immunity from liability for acts done on the basis of an objectively reasonable belief that those acts were lawful.

6. Section 1983 provides in full: "Every person who, under color of any statute, ordinance, regulation, custom, or usage, of any State or Territory, subjects, or causes to be subjected, any citizen of the United States or other person within the jurisdiction thereof to the deprivation of any rights, privileges, or immunities secured by the Constitution and laws, shall be liable to the party injured in an action at law, suit in equity, or other proper proceeding for redress."

Nothing in the language or legislative history of § 1983, however, suggests that in an action brought against a public official whose position might entitle him to immunity if he acted in good faith, a plaintiff must allege bad faith in order to state a claim for relief. By the plain terms of § 1983, two—and only two—allegations are required in order to state a cause of action under that statute. First, the plaintiff must allege that some person has deprived him of a federal right. Second, he must allege that the person who has deprived him of that right acted under color of state or territorial law. See Monroe v. Pape, 365 U.S. 167, 171 (1961). Petitioner has made both of the required allegations. He alleged that his discharge by respondent violated his right to procedural due process, see Board of Regents v. Roth, 408 U.S. 564 (1972), and that respondent acted under color of Puerto Rican law.

Moreover, this Court has never indicated that qualified immunity is relevant to the existence of the plaintiff's cause of action; instead we have described it as a defense available to the official in question. See Procunier v. Navarette, [434 U.S. 555,] 562 [1978]; Pierson v. Ray, supra, at 556, 557; Butz v. Economou, 438 U.S. 478, 508 (1978). Since qualified immunity is a defense, the burden of pleading it rests with the defendant. See Fed. Rule Civ. Proc. 8(c) (defendant must plead any "matter constituting an avoidance or affirmative defense"); 5 C. Wright & A. Miller, Federal Practice and Procedure § 1271 (1969). It is for the official to claim that his conduct was justified by an objectively reasonable belief that it was lawful. We see no basis for imposing on the plaintiff an obligation to anticipate such a defense by stating in his complaint that the defendant acted in bad faith.

Our conclusion as to the allocation of the burden of pleading is supported by the nature of the qualified immunity defense. As our decisions make clear, whether such immunity has been established depends on facts peculiarly within the knowledge and control of the defendant. Thus we have stated that "[i]t is the existence of reasonable grounds for the belief formed at the time and in light of all the circumstances, coupled with good-faith belief, that affords a basis for qualified immunity of executive officers for acts performed in the course of official conduct." Scheuer v. Rhodes, [416 U.S. 232,] at 247-248 [1974]. The applicable test focuses not only on whether the official has an objectively reasonable basis for that belief, but also on whether "[t]he official himself [is] acting sincerely and with a belief that he is doing right," Wood v. Strickland, supra, at 321. There may be no way for a plaintiff to know in advance whether the official has such a belief or, indeed, whether he will even claim that he does. The existence of a subjective belief will frequently turn on factors which a plaintiff cannot reasonably be expected to know. For example, the official's belief may be based on state or local law, advice of counsel, administrative practice, or some other factor of which the official alone is aware. To impose the pleading burden on the plaintiff would ignore this elementary fact and be contrary to the established practice in analogous areas of the law.[8]

8. As then-Dean Charles Clark stated over 40 years ago: "It seems to be considered only fair that certain types of things which in common law pleading were matters in confession and avoidance—i.e., matters which seemed more or less to admit the general complaint and

The decision of the Court of Appeals is reversed, and the case is remanded to that court for further proceedings consistent with this opinion.

It is so ordered.

JUSTICE REHNQUIST joins the opinion of the Court, reading it as he does to leave open the issue of the burden of persuasion, as opposed to the burden of pleading, with respect to a defense of qualified immunity.

Ingraham v. United States

808 F.2d 1075 (5th Cir. 1987)

POLITZ, Circuit Judge.

The appellees in these consolidated cases sued the United States, under the Federal Tort Claims Act, for severe injuries caused by the negligence of government physicians. In each case, after entry of adverse judgment the government moved for relief from the judgment to the extent that the damages exceeded the limit imposed on medical malpractice awards by the Medical Liability and Insurance Improvement Act of Texas, Tex. Rev. Civ. Stat. Ann. art. 4590i. The respective district courts denied these posttrial motions. Concluding that the government did not raise the issue timely before the trial courts, that the issues were not preserved for appeal, and, in the Bonds case, that the challenged awards were not otherwise excessive, we affirm both judgments.

Background

In 1977, in response to what was perceived to be a medical malpractice crisis, the Legislature of Texas, like several other state legislatures, adopted certain limitations on damages to be awarded in actions against health care providers, for injuries caused by negligence in the rendering of medical care and treatment. Of particular significance to these appeals is the $500,000 cap placed on the *ex delicto* recovery,[1] not applicable to past and future medical expenses.[2]

---

yet to suggest some other reason why there was no right—must be specifically pleaded in the answer, and that has been a general rule." ABA, Proceedings Institute at Washington and Symposium at New York City on the Federal Rules of Civil Procedure 49 (1939).

1. Tex. Rev. Civ. Stat. Ann. art. 4590i, § 11.02(a), provides:

> In an action on a health care liability claim where final judgment is rendered against a physician or health care provider, the limit of civil liability for damages of the physician or health care provider shall be limited to an amount not to exceed $500,000.

2. Tex. Rev. Civ. Stat. Ann. art. 4590i, § 11.02(b), provides:

> Subsection (a) of this section does not apply to the amount of damages awarded on a health care liability claim for the expenses of necessary medical, hospital, and custodial care received before judgment or required in the future for treatment of the injury.

On February 12, 1979, Dwight L. Ingraham was operated on by an Air Force surgeon. During the back surgery a drill was negligently used and Ingraham's spinal cord was damaged, causing severe and permanent injuries. The court awarded Ingraham judgment for $1,264,000. This total included $364,000 for lost wages and $900,000 for pain, suffering, and disability. There is no reference to the Medical Liability and Insurance Improvement Act of Texas in the pleadings, nor was any reference made to the Act during the trial. After entry of judgment the United States filed a notice of appeal. Thereafter, urging the Act's limitations, the government sought relief from judgment under Fed. R. Civ. P. 60(b). The district court denied that motion. No appeal was taken from that ruling.

Similarly, in March of 1979, Jocelyn and David Bonds, and their infant daughter Stephanie, were victims of the negligent performance by an Air Force physician. Because of the mismanagement of the 43rd week of Jocelyn Bonds's first pregnancy, and the failure to perform timely a caesarian section delivery, Stephanie suffered asphyxiation *in utero*. The loss of oxygen caused extensive brain damage, resulting in spastic quadriparesis, cortical blindness, seizures, and mental retardation. In their FTCA action the court awarded Stephanie $1,814,959.70 for medical expenses and $1,675,595.90 for the other losses. Jocelyn Bonds was awarded $750,000 for her losses, including loss of the society of her daughter. As in the Ingraham case, the government did not invoke the Texas malpractice limitation in pleading or at trial. Postjudgment the government filed a motion to amend the judgment under Fed. R. Civ. P. 59, but, again, there was no mention of the limitations Act. Subsequently, three months after entry of the judgment, the government filed a pleading entitled "Motion for Reconsideration," in which it advanced the malpractice Act. That motion was denied. The government appealed the judgment and motion to amend, but did not appeal the denial of the "motion for reconsideration."

These appeals do not challenge the courts' findings of liability, but object only to quantum, contending that damages are limited by the Medical Liability and Insurance Improvement Act and, in the case of Stephanie and Jocelyn Bonds, are otherwise excessive.

Analysis

Appellees maintain that we should not consider the statutory limitation of liability invoked on appeal because it is an affirmative defense under Rule 8(c) of the Federal Rules of Civil Procedure, and the failure to raise it timely constitutes a waiver. We find this argument persuasive.

Rule 8(c) first lists 19 specific affirmative defenses, and concludes with the residuary clause "any other matter constituting an avoidance or affirmative defense." In the years since adoption of the rule, the residuary clause has provided the authority for a substantial number of additional defenses which must be timely and affirmatively pleaded. These include:

exclusions from a policy of liability insurance; breach of warranty; concealment of an alleged prior undissolved marriage; voidable preference in bankruptcy; noncooperation of an insured; statutory limitation on liability; the claim that a written contract was incomplete; judgment against a defendant's joint tortfeasor; circuity of action; discharge of a contract obligation through novation or extension; recission or mutual abandonment of a contract; failure to mitigate damages; adhesion contract; statutory exemption; failure to exhaust state remedies; immunity from suit; good faith belief in lawfulness of action; the claim that a lender's sale of collateral was not commercially reasonable; a settlement agreement or release barring an action; and custom of trade or business. See 5 C. Wright & A. Miller, Federal Practice and Procedure: Civil, § 1271 (1969 & supp.), and 27 Fed. Proc., L. Ed. § 62. 63 (1984 & supp.), for discussion and citations.

Determining whether a given defense is "affirmative" within the ambit of Rule 8(c) is not without some difficulty. We find the salient comments of Judge Charles E. Clark, Dean of the Yale Law School, later Chief Judge of the United States Second Circuit Court of Appeals, and the principal author of the Federal Rules, to be instructive:

> [J]ust as certain disfavored allegations made by the plaintiff . . . must be set forth with the greatest particularity, so like disfavored defenses must be particularly alleged by the defendant. These may include such matters as fraud, statute of frauds . . . , statute of limitations, truth in slander and libel . . . and so on. In other cases the mere question of convenience may seem prominent, as in the case of payment, where the defendant can more easily show the affirmative payment at a certain time than the plaintiff can the negative of nonpayment over a period of time. Again it may be an issue which may be generally used for dilatory tactics, such as the question of the plaintiff's right to sue . . . a vital question, but one usually raised by the defendant on technical grounds. These have been thought of as issues "likely to take the opposite party by surprise," which perhaps conveys the general idea of fairness or the lack thereof, though there is little real surprise where the case is well prepared in advance.

Clark, Code Pleading, 2d ed. 1947, § 96 at 609-610, quoted in 5 C. Wright & A. Miller, Federal Practice and Procedure: Civil, § 1271, p. 313 (1969).

Also pertinent to the analysis is the logical relationship between the defense and the cause of action asserted by the plaintiff. This inquiry requires a determination (1) whether the matter at issue fairly may be said to constitute a necessary or extrinsic element in the plaintiff's cause of action; (2) which party, if either, has better access to relevant evidence; and (3) policy considerations: should the matter be indulged or disfavored? See 27 Fed. Proc., L. Ed. § 62.63.

Central to requiring the pleading of affirmative defenses is the prevention of unfair surprise. A defendant should not be permitted to "lie behind a log" and ambush a plaintiff with an unexpected defense. The instant cases illustrate this consideration. Plaintiffs submit that, had they known the statute would be applied, they would have made greater efforts to prove medical damages which were not subject to the statutory limit. In addition, plaintiffs maintain that they would have had an opportunity and the incentive to introduce evidence to support their constitutional attacks on the statute.

This distinction separates the present cases from our recent decision in Lucas v. United States, 807 F.2d 414 (5th Cir. 1986). In *Lucas*, although the limitation of recovery issue was not pleaded, it was raised at trial. We held that the trial court was within its discretion to permit the defendant to effectively amend its pleadings and advance the defense. The treatment we accorded this issue in *Lucas* is consistent with long-standing precedent of this and other circuits that "'where [an affirmative defense] is raised in the trial court in a manner that does not result in unfair surprise, . . . technical failure to comply with Rule 8(c) is not fatal.'" Bull's Corner Restaurant v. Director, Federal Emergency Management Agency, 759 F.2d 500, 502 (5th Cir. 1985), quoting Allied Chemical Corp. v. Mackay, 695 F.2d 854, 855 (5th Cir. 1983).

We view the limitation on damages as an "avoidance" within the intendment of the residuary clause of 8(c). Black's Law Dictionary, 5th ed. 1979, defines an avoidance in pleadings as "the allegation or statement of new matter, in opposition to a former pleading, which, admitting the facts alleged in such former pleading, shows cause why they should not have their ordinary legal effect." Applied to the present discussion, a plaintiff pleads the traditional tort theory of malpractice and seeks full damages. The defendant responds that assuming recovery is in order under the ordinary tort principles, because of the new statutory limitation, the traditional precedents "should not have their ordinary legal effect."

Considering these factors, against the backdrop and with the illumination provided by other applications of Rule 8(c), we conclude that the Texas statutory limit on medical malpractice damages is an affirmative defense which must be pleaded timely and that in the cases at bar the defense has been waived.

Notes and Questions

1. *Identifying an Affirmative Defense.* The line between an affirmative defense and a denial is not always easily discerned or drawn. For substantial assistance in identifying defenses that the federal courts deem "affirmative," see Fed. R. Civ. P. 8(c). Note that the list is not exhaustive. In the problem case, does the alleged settlement between Shayes and her old law firm fall within any of the named affirmative defenses? Who should logically plead it, and thus probably have to prove it?

In Gomez v. Toledo, qualified immunity is not on the 8(c) list but there are many prudential reasons for making it an affirmative defense; the same reasons may explain the extraordinary position taken by the Fifth

Circuit in *Schultea* and the pre-*Leatherman* cases that the defense of qualified immunity can affect the pleading burden of the *plaintiff*. Which issues are for the plaintiff to plead and which for the defendant continues to be a difficult question in many cases. For a typical instance where the court found that a defense need not be specially pleaded, see Sanden v. Mayo Clinic, 495 F.2d 221 (8th Cir. 1974), holding that the fraudulent pretense of injury in a malpractice action is not an affirmative defense.

2. *Unpleaded Defenses*. Fed. R. Civ. P. 8 does not explicitly state that affirmative defenses not pleaded are waived. Fed. R. Civ. P. 12(h) is explicit in regard to a few defenses that may be the subject of motions to dismiss. Nevertheless, a number of cases have applied Fed. R. Civ. P. 8(c) to preclude untimely consideration of unpleaded defenses. Thus, in Radio Corp. of Am. v. Radio Station KYFM, Inc., 424 F.2d 14 (10th Cir. 1970), a defendant tried unsuccessfully to raise on a posttrial motion the defenses of the statute of frauds, illegality of contract, and lack of authority. An amazingly harsh case is Crawford v. Zeitler, 326 F.2d 119 (6th Cir. 1964), which imposed a waiver on a defendant who had pleaded the wrong statute of limitations. Certainly the better view is that the defendant need not identify the particular statute in his answer because the court can take notice of the correct law, e.g., Wade v. Lynn, 181 F. Supp. 361 (N.D. Ohio 1960). See also Harris v. Secretary, Dep't of Veterans Affairs, 126 F.3d 339 (D.C. Cir. 1997), which held that where no statute of limitations defense was raised in the responsive pleading, the defense cannot be raised in a motion to dismiss or motion for summary judgment, even if no prejudice to the opponent has been shown; rather, the party must file an amended pleading under Rule 15(a) to preserve the structure of notice pleading. Leave to amend should be freely granted if no prejudice would occur, but the technical requirements of 8(c) cannot be elided.

3. *Affirmative Defenses Apparent on the Face of the Complaint*. Some defenses may be raised on a pre-answer motion to dismiss as well as by the answer, if the factual basis for the defense is disclosed in the complaint. See, e.g., Larter & Sons, Inc. v. Dinkler Hotels Co., 199 F.2d 854 (5th Cir. 1952). The statute of limitations is the most frequent example, but the limitations period may be extended by facts not revealed in the complaint. Perhaps the plaintiff who alleges an apparently stale claim should anticipate the defense of limitations and make the appropriate allegations that might negate it; this is suggested in Kincheloe v. Farmer, 214 F.2d 604 (7th Cir. 1954). On the other hand, if a defendant files a general motion to dismiss for failure to state a claim that is not specifically based on the statute of limitations, the court may not view this motion as sufficient to preserve the issue of statute of limitations. Wagner v. Fawcett Publ'n, 307 F.2d 409 (7th Cir. 1962). To be safe, therefore, a defendant who uses the pre-answer motion to attack a stale complaint should follow up with an answer that asserts "statute of limitations" as an affirmative defense, lest the defense be deemed waived.

4. *Other Causes of Waivers*. The pleading of an affirmative defense is not a guarantee against waiver. In Demsey & Assocs. v. S.S. Sea Star, 461 F.2d

1009 (2d Cir. 1972), *abrogated on other grounds by* Seguros Illimani S.A. v. M/V popi, 929 F.2d 89 (2d Cir. 1991), a defendant pleaded an arbitration clause as a defense, but proceeded to litigate other defenses without moving for a stay. It was held that the failure to move for a stay was an effective waiver of the arbitration clause.

e. Amending the Pleadings

Problem Case: A Woman Partner (Part Three)

After McKenzie, Brachman had answered the complaint, Shayes learned that one of the reasons things turned sour for her at the firm was that a fellow partner, Arnie Becker, was having an affair with a woman associate he wanted to advance in her place. Becker and the woman associate have since left the firm.

How should Shayes go about amending the complaint to include this information and these parties? What if she learned this information after the statute of limitations had passed for filing a suit based on this information?

Note: Liberal Pleading and Liberal Amendments

Free leave to amend pleadings as the case develops is part of the Rules' original design. Read Rule 15 carefully. Note that it progresses chronologically from the point before the defendant has answered through post-judgment amendment. Of course, the requirements vary at each stage that amendment is sought, and the judge's discretion about allowing the amendment is extremely broad. A further complication is the increasing use of the pretrial order in Rule 16 which frames the issues for trial, and has a high standard for amendment. First, read Rule 15, with special emphasis on 15(a) and (b). What do these sections suggest about the following questions:

1) Can you amend a complaint without court permission or agreement by your opponent? Under what circumstances?
2) Can you amend an answer without court permission or agreement by your opponent? Under what circumstances?
3) If the time for amending as of course (without permission) has elapsed, what must you do to amend a pleading?
4) If a party files an amended pleading to which a response must be filed, how much time does the opponent get to respond?
5) If a matter proceeds to trial and evidence is introduced that departs from the pleadings, what happens to the pleadings? Does it depend on whether an objection to the evidence is made?
6) Now read Rule 16. Does the answer to 5) change when there is a pretrial order that frames the issues for trial?

The real difficulty occurs when a party seeks to amend a pleading after the statute of limitations has run. The general rule is that the amendment will relate back to the time the original pleading was filed, provided the amended claim arises from the same transaction or occurrence as that described in the original pleading. The idea here is that the opponent had adequate notice within the applicable statute of limitations of the amended claim because it is factually related to the claim first described. Also, if the law of the jurisdiction that supplies the applicable statute of limitations would allow the amendment, it will be allowed in federal court even if the amended claim is *not* factually related to the original claim.

The most difficult amendment situation is one in which the amendment seeks to change parties, not just claims, after the statute of limitations has elapsed. This usually is impermissible *unless* the narrow requirements of Rule 15(c) are met. Essentially, this means that the case must be one of mistaken identity, and the real party must have been aware within the period described in Rule 15(c) that, but for an error, the original pleading would have named him as the defendant.

Before proceeding to questions that test your comprehension of Rule 15(c), you need to appreciate the distinction between filing a pleading and serving it on your opponent. *Filing* means carrying the papers to the courthouse and handing them to the clerk. Filing gives the court notice of your request, but not other parties to the lawsuit. *Service* means delivering the pleading to all parties of record, whether by hand-carrying it, mailing it, or other means. Only service assures that your opponents are on notice of the pleadings. To be safe, a lawyer should assure whenever possible that *both* filing *and* service occur before the statute of limitations elapses. Some states require that *both* occur within the statute of limitations. In other states, however, and in federal court actions for which federal law governs the statute of limitations, only filing must occur before the statute of limitations runs out. This *tolls* the statute of limitations. Thereafter, in federal court a lawyer has 120 days within which to serve the complaint or risk dismissal, which would mean the lawyer would have to refile the matter, thus losing any interim "tolling" time.

Now, how would you analyze the following problems?

a) The applicable statute of limitations is two years, and requires that both filing and service occur within this period. On June 1, 2004, *A* and Company *B* are involved in an accident. On May 31, 2006, *A* files suit against *B* in federal court. Service of the complaint follows on June 15, 2006. May *B* move to dismiss on the ground that the complaint is untimely?

b) Assume instead that filing and service occur within the statute of limitations period. May *A* now move to amend the complaint to add a claim for damages in a contract matter that arose in 2003?

c) Same as b) except that *A* moves in July 2006 to amend to add a claim for physical injuries that occurred in the June 1 accident. Permissible?

d) Same as a), and *A* moves to amend the complaint in July 2006. The amendment seeks to change the name of the party against whom the complaint is filed, because the plaintiff since has learned Company *C* actually owns the vehicle involved in the June 1 collision, though the name on the vehicle read "Co. *B*." The president of Co. *B* is also the president of Co. *C*, and she read the original complaint when it was served on June 15, 2006. What result?

Barcume v. City of Flint

819 F. Supp. 631 (E.D. Mich. 1993)

NEWBLATT, District Judge.

Before the Court is defendant City of Flint's ("City") motion for summary judgment, plaintiffs' response, and defendant City's reply. For the reasons that follow, defendant's motion is GRANTED IN PART and DENIED IN PART.

This civil rights action arises out of the alleged discriminatory hiring and promotion practices of the City of Flint and alleged discriminatory employment practices and sexually hostile working environment within the Flint Police Department ("FPD"). The thirteen plaintiffs are all female law enforcement officers employed by, or previously employed by, the FPD. This case is not a class action lawsuit, but rather consists of thirteen separate plaintiffs alleging personal discrimination and harassment at the hands of fellow male police officers, supervisory personnel, the FPD and its command staff, and the City of Flint through its alleged policy and practice of discrimination and tacit approval of the harassment that allegedly exists within the FPD.

Plaintiffs filed their original complaint on January 30, 1984. In that complaint, plaintiffs made various claims against both the City of Flint and the Flint Police Officers Association ("FPOA"). The original complaint consisted of five counts: (I) a claim of discrimination in hiring and promotion practices in violation of 42 U.S.C. § 1983 against defendant City; (II) a claim for violation of the duty of fair representation against defendant FPOA; (III) a claim of conspiracy to deprive plaintiffs of their civil rights in violation of 42 U.S.C. § 1985(3) against both defendants; (IV) a claim of discrimination in hiring and promotion practices and in terms, conditions and privileges of employment in violation of the Elliott-Larsen Civil Rights Act against defendant City; and (V) a claim against defendant FPOA for violation of the Elliott-Larsen Civil Rights Act.

On December 4, 1985, after extensive discovery had already taken place, plaintiffs moved the Court for leave to file a Second Amended Complaint. A hearing on this motion was held on June 23, 1986. At that hearing, the Court granted plaintiffs' motion to file an amended complaint, provided that the amended pleading separated plaintiffs' claims regarding the constitutionality of defendant City's Affirmative Action Plan ("AAP") from those alleging "traditional" or "garden variety" discrimination on the basis of sex. Id. at 26. The Court indicated that the AAP's exclusion of women may be evidence relevant to a classic discrimination claim, but that the determination regarding the constitutionality of the AAP is a separate claim to be filed as a separate count. Id. As noted in the Court's Memorandum Opinion and Order of January 26, 1987, leave for plaintiffs to amend their complaint had been granted at the June 23, 1986 hearing. Nevertheless, it was not until February 26, 1987 that plaintiffs filed their Second Amended Complaint and Jury Demand. The Second Amended Complaint contains six counts, two of which still remain to be adjudicated as to defendant City; count II, a claim pursuant to 42 U.S.C. § 1983 that defendant City violated plaintiffs' rights to equal protection in the terms and conditions of employment; and count VI, a claim that defendant City violated plaintiffs' rights secured by the Elliott-Larsen Civil Rights Act in the terms and conditions of employment.[1] Through their motion, defendant City seeks summary judgment to dismiss or limit plaintiffs' claims under counts II and VI.

I. Factual Background

The specific facts alleged by plaintiffs shall be addressed as necessary in context of discussion regarding defendant City's motion. Defendant City's arguments shall be addressed seriatim.

II. Statute of Limitations

Defendant's first argument is that plaintiffs' claims of alleged discriminatory conduct occurring before February 26, 1984 are barred by the statute of limitations. Plaintiffs do not dispute that the statute of limitations for both 42 U.S.C. § 1983 and the Elliott-Larsen Civil Rights Act ("Elliott-Larsen"), M.C.L. §§ 37. 2101 et seq., is three years. Conlin v. Blanchard 890 F.2d 811 (6th Cir. 1989); Browning v. Pendleton, 869 F.2d 989 (6th Cir. 1989). Thus, argues defendant City, to the extent that plaintiffs' claims are based upon conduct and events occurring more than three years before the filing of the Second Amended Complaint, these claims are time-barred. Of course, defendant City's position presumes that plaintiffs' Second Amended Complaint neither relates back to plaintiffs' original complaint, filed January 30, 1984, nor alleges a continuing violation that would allow plaintiffs to recover damages for the entire period of the continuing illegal conduct.

1. Count I was a § 1983 claim challenging the constitutionality of the AAP for its failure to include women in its remedial provisions. The Court granted summary judgment to defendants on count I, upholding the constitutionality of the AAP. Count IV of the Second Amended Complaint was a claim against defendants City and FPOA alleging conspiracy to deprive plaintiffs of their civil rights through implementation of the AAP to the exclusion of women. Because this Court has upheld the constitutionality of the AAP, plaintiffs concede that count IV is also effectively dismissed. Thus, the Court will not address defendant City's motion as it relates to count IV.

A. Relation Back

Federal Rule of Civil Procedure 15(c) provides in relevant part that:

> An amendment of a pleading relates back to the date of the original pleading when . . . the claim . . . asserted in the amended pleading arose out of the conduct, transaction, or occurrence set forth or attempted to be set forth in the original pleading. . . .

Fed. R. Civ. P. 15(c)(2) [Now 15(c)(1)(B)] . The effect of this rule is that

> once litigation involving particular conduct or a given transaction or occurrence has been instituted, the parties are not entitled to the protection of the statute of limitations against the later assertion by amendment of defenses or claims that arise out of the same conduct, transaction, or occurrence as set forth in the original pleading.

Wright, Miller & Kane, Federal Practice and Procedure: Civil 2d § 1496 (1990) at 64. The rationale behind Rule 15(c) is to allow an amendment to relate back to the filing of the original complaint where the defendant has been put on notice, through the pleadings or from other sources, of the entire scope of the transaction or occurrence out of which the amended claims arise. See id. at § 1497. Thus,

> amendments that merely correct technical deficiencies or expand or modify the facts alleged in the earlier pleading meet the Rule 15(c) test and will relate back. . . . [A]mendments that do no more than restate the original claim with greater particularity or amplify the details of the transaction alleged in the preceding pleading fall within Rule 15(c). But, if the alteration of the original statement is so substantial that it cannot be said that defendant [sic] was given adequate notice of the conduct, transaction, or occurrence that forms the basis of the claim or defense, then the amendment will not relate back and will be time barred if the limitations period has expired.

Id. at § 1497 pp. 74-79; see also Tiller v. Atlantic Coast Line R.R. Co., 323 U.S. 574, 581 (1995); Boddy v. Dean, 821 F.2d 346, 351 (6th Cir. 1987) (amendment that alleges added events leading up to same injury may relate back). Furthermore, that the amendment changes the legal theory upon which the action initially was brought will not automatically bar relation back. Id. at § 1497 p. 94. Thus,

> [t]the fact that an amendment changes the legal theory on which the action initially was brought is of no consequence if the factual situation upon which the action depends remains the same and has been brought to defendant's [sic] attention by the original pleading.

Id. at § 1497 pp. 94-95; see also Hageman v. Signal L.P. Gas, Inc., 486 F.2d 479, 484 (6th Cir. 1973) (added theory of liability for same occurrence may relate back). An amendment will not relate back, however, if it asserts a new claim for relief based on different facts than set forth in the original complaint. Koon v. Lakeshore Contractors, 128 F.R.D. 650, 653 (W.D. Mich. 1988).

In their response brief, plaintiffs argue that defendant City was not surprised by plaintiffs' allegations made in the Second Amended Complaint. Plaintiffs' response brief at 23. Plaintiffs argue that the original complaint gave defendant City ample notice that plaintiffs were suffering from continuing sexual discrimination in a variety of forms by the FPD and its agents. Id. At the very least, argue plaintiffs, the allegations of the Second Amended Complaint were an "attempt" to raise claims of sex discrimination which merely were particularized from the more broad allegations of the original complaint. Id. Plaintiffs further argue that, apart from the notice provided by the original complaint, defendant City became aware through its deposition of plaintiffs in 1984 and 1985 "that plaintiffs' exclusion from the AAP was but one act in a long line of discriminatory events." Id. Because defendant City, through discovery, knew of the sexually discriminatory and hostile work environment at the FPD, plaintiffs assert that their sexual discrimination and sexual harassment claims relate back to the filing of the original complaint. Id. at 24.

Defendant City argues in its motion that the Second Amended Complaint does not relate back to the original complaint. Defendant City argues that the original complaint only presented a challenge to the validity of the AAP, adopted and implemented in 1984, which excluded women from its definition of minorities to receive the benefits of affirmative action. Defendant City asserts that any mention of sexually discriminatory practices was limited to creating an historical perspective upon which to justify the necessity for the inclusion of women in the AAP. No specific persons were identified in the complaint as perpetrators of sexual discrimination. Rather, plaintiffs discussed generally the historical hiring practices of the FPD and the concomitant effect this had on promotional opportunities for women. Conversely, argues defendant City, the Second Amended Complaint alleges different causes of action based upon vastly different facts not pleaded in the original complaint. Defendant City asserts that the Second Amended Complaint implicates an entirely new set of actors who allegedly engaged in inappropriate conduct independent of that alleged in the original complaint. Finally, defendant City argues that the original complaint did not provide notice of the subsequently filed claims of sexual discrimination and sexual harassment; in fact, plaintiffs will need to introduce entirely different evidence to establish their claims set forth in the Second Amended Complaint as opposed to that required to support their claims in the original complaint.

In support of their position, plaintiffs cite several cases as authority that claims based upon new legal theories may relate back to the original pleading where the facts upon which they are derived were included in the original complaint, or are similar and related to the facts set forth originally. See Maty v. Grasselli Co., 303 U.S. 197 (1938); Boddy v. Dean, 821 F.2d 346 (6th Cir. 1987); Carter v. Delta Air Lines, Inc., 441 F. Supp. 808

(S.D.N.Y. 1977); Baruan v. Young, 536 F. Supp. 356 (D. Md.1982). Thus, the question before the Court regarding this issue is whether the claims raised in plaintiffs' Second Amended Complaint constitute different legal theories, and whether these claims arise out of the same or related occurrences or transactions as those pleaded in the original complaint.

A review of the original complaint, filed on January 30, 1984, reveals absolutely no claims of sexual harassment. Moreover, the entire complaint, consisting of eighty-four paragraphs, is devoid of any reference to conduct that could be interpreted as sexual harassment by the most reasonably prudent defense attorney. The original complaint also fails to allege a single incident of harassment or any other discrimination attributable to any individual person acting as an agent of the City of Flint. The original complaint does, however, make claims of discrimination in hiring and promotion of women in violation of their civil rights secured by 42 U.S.C. § 1983 (count I) and the Elliott-Larsen Civil Rights Act (count IV).

Plaintiffs' Second Amended Complaint, filed February 26, 1987, states much broader claims under § 1983 and Elliott-Larsen. Not only do counts II and VI allege discrimination in hiring and promotional practices of defendant City, they further allege claims of disparate treatment and harassment that were not included in the original pleading. Most notably, both counts II and VI allege that defendant City condones and ratifies sexual harassment toward women in the workplace, and that defendant City has done so with knowledge or notice of the sexually hostile environment. These claims with regard to sexual harassment and hostile work environment are new to the Second Amended Complaint. There was not an inkling of factual support for such claims in the original complaint. Therefore, defendant City did not have notice that plaintiffs were pursuing that particular type of discrimination claim in this law-suit.

Plaintiffs' original complaint alleges a violation of 42 U.S.C. § 1983 by defendant City for traditional and historical discrimination against women in hiring police officers. This historical discrimination, it is alleged, has adversely impacted women in the promotion to sergeant. The AAP's failure to include women allegedly acts to perpetuate the past discrimination against women in the FPD.

To the extent that count II of the Second Amended Complaint alleges discrimination in hiring and promotion practices, and disparate impact upon present opportunities for promotion of women to the rank of sergeant, plaintiffs' claims relate back to the original complaint for statute of limitations purposes. To the extent, however, that plaintiffs' claims under count II allege disparate treatment based upon sex, sexual harassment, and the existence of a hostile work environment within the FPD, plaintiffs' claims do not relate back to the original complaint.

The same is true with regard to count VI of the Second Amended Complaint. Although count IV of the original complaint stated a claim of discrimination against plaintiffs in the terms and conditions of employment, there was no notice to defendant City that this claim was for any violation other than discrimination in hiring and promotion practices, and in the exclusion of women from the relief prescribed by the AAP. No facts were alleged that would support, or that would indicate an attempt to support, a sexual harassment claim. Plaintiffs' view that defendant City was on notice from defendants' depositions of plaintiffs in 1984 and 1985 is rejected. Plaintiffs had ample opportunity to amend the complaint to state the expanded scope of their Elliott-Larsen and § 1983 claims—to include sexual harassment—or to notify defendant City directly that such claims were being pursued. As a result of the filing of plaintiffs' Second Amended Complaint, defendant City was required to engage extensively in further discovery, including redeposition of the thirteen plaintiffs. This would not have been the case had defendant City been made aware of the sexual harassment claim. Therefore, the Court finds that defendant City did not have notice of the added claims.

Plaintiffs' position that the Second Amended Complaint merely particularized allegations made or attempted to be raised in the original pleadings also is rejected. As stated previously, there is no indication from the original complaint that plaintiff was making a claim of sexual harassment. Therefore, to the extent that count VI alleges that defendant City discriminated against plaintiffs in hiring and promotional practices, plaintiffs' claim relates back to the original pleading. Plaintiffs' claims of sexual harassment and disparate treatment in terms and conditions of employment, other than in hiring or promotional decisions, do not relate back and, unless they constitute a continuing violation as discussed below, they are barred by the statute of limitations for those incidents occurring more than three years prior to the filing of the Second Amended Complaint.

Notes and Questions

1. *Amending the Legal Theory.* To what extent does the ability to file an amended complaint hinge on how generally the plaintiff words the original complaint? Should a plaintiff always be allowed to amend a complaint to add a new theory of recovery based on the same facts? If so, was *Barcume* wrongly decided? Wouldn't the plaintiff in some cases be able to ascertain the proper theory (or theories) only after some discovery? Yet in *Barcume,* shouldn't the plaintiffs have known at the time they filed the complaint whether the workplace was hostile?

2. *Adding Related Claims.* As the cases indicate, the test for determining whether an added claim is sufficiently related to the original claim is hardly wooden. Context matters much here, as it does in determining relatedness under Rule 13(a) (compulsory counterclaims) and under 28 U.S.C. § 1367 (supplemental jurisdiction).

3. *Some Examples.* What do you think about the following proposed amendments that were offered after the statute of limitations period had elapsed?

a. In an action against a surgeon for lack of informed consent, may the plaintiff amend the complaint to add a claim that the surgeon was negligent during and after the surgery? See Moore v. Baker, 989 F.2d 1129 (11th Cir. 1993) (concluding amendment did not relate back).

b. In an action against a union for refusal to file a grievance on behalf of an employee, may the plaintiff-employee amend the complaint to add a claim that the union refused on a second occasion to file a grievance on the employee's behalf? See Gomes v. Avco Corp., 964 F.2d 1330 (2d Cir. 1992) (concluding amendment did not relate back).

c. In a securities fraud action, may the plaintiff amend the complaint to add a claim against a defendant when the plaintiff knew the identity of the defendant but was not fully aware of the defendant's responsibility for the alleged harm? See Powers v. Graff, 148 F.3d 1223 (11th Cir. 1998) (concluding amendment did not relate back).

d. In a habeas petition challenging a criminal conviction on the ground that evidence from a witness for the prosecution was admitted in violation of the Confrontation Clause of the Sixth Amendment, may the petitioner amend the complaint to add a claim that coercive tactics were used to obtain damaging statements from him and introduced at trial in violation of his Fifth Amendment right against self-incrimination? See Mayle v. Felix, 545 U.S. 644 (2005) (concluding amendment did not relate back; the relevant underlying "conduct, transaction, or occurrence" was not petitioner's trial and conviction in state court, in which both pieces of evidence were introduced, but the circumstances surrounding the extraction of evidence from the prosecution witness before trial).

4. *Amending the Pleadings After 12(b)(6) Dismissal.* Given the constricted use of the dismissal for failure to state a claim, we might be less free with the right to amend following the ruling on the motion: If it is impossible to imagine a winning case based on the initial pleading, there is less risk that the pleader would be unjustly defeated by a denial of leave to amend. There is, indeed, a manifest tendency of federal courts to be less tolerant of multiple repleadings. See, e.g., Kamsler v. H.A. Seinscheimer Co., 347 F.2d 740 (7th Cir. 1965). But there may still be a right to amend without leave of court, at least once. Note the first sentence of Fed. R. Civ. P. 15(a). It has been held that a motion under Fed. R. Civ. P. 12(b)(6) is not a "responsive pleading," Breier v. N. Cal. Bowling Proprietors' Assn., 316 F.2d 787 (9th Cir. 1963). Where the plaintiff has repleaded after his first complaint had been successfully attacked, and then gone to trial on an amended complaint, the first complaint may be regarded as withdrawn; if so, the ruling on it is no longer open to appellate review. Blazer v. Black, 196 F.2d 139 (10th Cir. 1965). If dismissals for failure to state a claim increase under *Twombly,* should courts be even more generous in granting leave to amend?

Note that the judge has no explicit power to dismiss a complaint *sua sponte,* and Fed. R. Civ. P. 12(i) cannot be disregarded. Armstrong v. Rushing, 352 F.2d 836 (9th Cir. 1965), *superseded on other grounds by statute,* 28 U.S.C. § 1915(e), *as recognized in* Lopez v. Smith, 160 F.3d 567, 570 (9th Cir. 1988).

The Fourth Circuit and the Ninth Circuit have split on whether a plaintiff may amend a complaint as a matter of right under 15(a) even after 12(b)(6) dismissal. Compare Zachair Ltd. v. Driggs, 141 F.3d 1162 (4th Cir. 1998) (no) (unpublished opinion), with Doe v. United States, 58 F.3d 494 (9th Cir. 1995) (yes).

5. *Adding Nondiverse Parties.* Rule 15(c) makes it seem fairly easy to add a party if a litigant discovers she has made a mistake in naming her opponent. More generally, Rule 15(a) suggests parties have the right to amend once as of right before an answer or other responsive pleading is filed. But using either rule to add a party is always risky where subject matter jurisdiction rests on diversity. In Am. Fiber & Finishing, Inc. v. Tyco Healthcare Group, LP, 362 F.3d 136 (1st Cir. 2004), a suit to recover the costs of cleaning up an industrial site, the plaintiff used Rule 15(a) to switch defendants when it learned that Tyco was the corporate successor to the original polluter. Three years later, after Tyco prevailed in the trial court, American Fiber moved to vacate the judgment on appeal claiming that the addition of Tyco destroyed the requisite diversity. Although the Supreme Court has held that "if jurisdiction exists at the time an action is commenced, such jurisdiction may not be divested by subsequent events," Freeport-McMoRan, Inc. v. K N Energy, Inc., 498 U.S. 426, 428 (1991), the First Circuit reasoned that plaintiff's discovery that it named the wrong defendant is not a "subsequent event" within the meaning of *Freeport-McMoRan.* The court admitted that there "is something unsettling about a party bringing a case in a federal court, taking the case to final judgment, losing, and then invoking a jurisdictional defect that it created—with the result that it escapes from the judgment and returns, albeit in a different venue, to relitigate the merits." *American Fiber*, 362 F.3d at 142. But "the shoe could have been on the other foot," the court noted, since American Fiber might have won "only to have its victory snatched away by the belated discovery of the jurisdictional snafu." Id. at 143. The court at least charged plaintiff for the costs of the appeal.

6. *Amending Other Documents.* Take another look at the text of Rule 15(c). Does the doctrine of relation back apply exclusively to "pleadings"? In Scarborough v. Principi, 541 U.S. 401 (2004), plaintiff prevailed before the Court of Appeals for Veterans Claims in an action seeking disability benefits. His lawyer then filed a timely application for attorney fees under the Equal Access to Justice Act, which provides that the prevailing party in an action against the federal government may recover attorney's fees. The government opposed the application and sought to have it dismissed on the ground that it failed to include an allegation, required under the EAJA, that the government's position in the underlying case for disability benefits "was not substantially justified." Scarborough's lawyer responded right away by filing an amended application including the necessary language, but the 30-day fee application period had already expired and the court dismissed his application for that reason. The Supreme Court reversed, holding that the lawyer's amended application "related back" to his initial timely application even though an application for attorney's

fees is not a "pleading" within the meaning of Rule 15(c). As the Court reasoned, the doctrine of relation back was applied "well before 1938, the year the Federal Rules became effective," and had "'roots in the former federal equity practice and a number of state codes.'" 541 U.S. at 1867. See also Edleman v. Lynchburg Coll., 535 U.S. 106 (2002) (failure to verify by oath a Title VII discrimination charge timely filed with the EEOC); Becker v. Montgomery, 532 U.S. 757 (2001) (failure to sign a timely notice of appeal).

Nelson v. Adams USA, Inc., et al.

529 U.S. 460 (2000)

JUSTICE GINSBURG delivered the opinion of the Court.

This litigation began when Ohio Cellular Products Corporation (OCP) sued respondent Adams USA, Inc. (Adams), claiming patent infringement. The District Court eventually dismissed OCP's claim and ordered OCP to pay Adams' costs and attorney fees. Adams feared that OCP might be unable to pay the fee award and therefore sought a means to recover from petitioner Nelson, president and sole shareholder of OCP, in his individual capacity. In pursuit of that objective, Adams moved under Rule 15 of the Federal Rules of Civil Procedure to amend its pleading to add Nelson as a party; Adams also asked the court, under Rule 59(e), to amend the fee award. The District Court granted the motion in full, simultaneously making Nelson a party and subjecting him to judgment. The Court of Appeals affirmed. We hold that the District Court erred in amending the judgment immediately upon permitting amendment of the pleading. Due process, as reflected in Rule 15 as well as Rule 12, required that Nelson be given an opportunity to respond and contest his personal liability for the award after he was made a party and before the entry of judgment against him.

OCP and its successor corporation held two patents relating to the method of manufacturing a foamed padding used in athletic equipment. In 1994, OCP sued Adams for infringement. Adams maintained that the patents had been anticipated by prior art and were therefore invalid under 35 U.S.C. § 102(b). The District Court ruled in Adams' favor and dismissed the infringement complaint.

Adams then moved for attorney fees and costs. The District Court granted the motion on the ground that Nelson, who was at all relevant times president and sole shareholder of OCP, had deceitfully withheld the prior art from the United States Patent and Trademark Office. This behavior, the District Court concluded, constituted inequitable conduct chargeable to OCP. On January 20, 1998, the District Court awarded Adams costs and fees in the amount of $178,888.51 against OCP.

Adams feared, however, that it would be unable to collect the award. This was an altogether understandable concern; it stemmed from a letter OCP's counsel had sent Adams warning that OCP would be liquidated if exposed to a judgment for fees more than nominal in amount. Adams therefore moved to amend its pleading to add Nelson, personally, as a party from whom fees could be collected. In this post judgment endeavor, Adams reasoned that Nelson was the flesh-and-blood party behind OCP, the person whose conduct in withholding prior art precipitated the fee award, and a person with funds sufficient to satisfy that award. The District Court granted the motion.

The Court of Appeals for the Federal Circuit affirmed the amended judgment against Nelson. Ohio Cellular Prods., Inc. v. Adams USA, Inc., 175 F.3d 1343 (1999). It was "uncommon," the appeals court acknowledged, to add a party after the entry of judgment. Id. at 1348. The court concluded, however, that Nelson had not been prejudiced by the post judgment joinder. The Federal Circuit based that conclusion on Nelson's failure to show that "anything different or additional would have been done" to stave off the judgment had Nelson been a party, in his individual capacity, from the outset of the litigation. . . .

The Federal Rules of Civil Procedure are designed to further the due process of law that the Constitution guarantees. Cf. Fed. Rule Civ. Proc. 1 (Rules "shall be construed and administered to secure the just, speedy, and inexpensive determination of every action."). Rule 15 sets out the requirements for amended and supplemental pleadings. On that score, the Court of Appeals observed that as long as no undue prejudice is shown, "due process requirements are met if the requirements of Rule 15 are met." 175 F.3d at 1349, n.5. But in the instant case, the requirements of Rule 15 were not met. As Judge Newman recognized in her dissent below, due process does not countenance such swift passage from pleading to judgment in the pleader's favor. See id. at 1352.

The propriety of allowing a pleading alteration depends not only on the state of affairs prior to amendment but also on what happens afterwards. Accordingly, Rule 15 both conveys the circumstances under which leave to amend shall be granted and directs how the litigation will move forward following an amendment. When a court grants leave to amend to add an adverse party after the time for responding to the original pleading has lapsed, the party so added is given "10 days after service of the amended pleading" to plead in response. Fed. Rule Civ. Proc. 15(a). This opportunity to respond, fundamental to due process, is the echo of the opportunity to respond to original pleadings secured by Rule 12. See Fed. Rule Civ. Proc. 12(a)(1). Thus, Rule 15 assumes an amended pleading will be filed and anticipates service of that pleading on the adverse party.

Nelson was never served with an amended pleading. Indeed, no such pleading was ever actually composed and filed in court. Nor, after the amendment naming him as a party, was Nelson accorded 10 days to state his defenses against personal liability for costs and fees. Instead, judgment was entered against him the moment permission to amend the pleading was granted. Appeal after judgment, in the circumstances this case presents, did not provide an adequate opportunity to defend against the imposition of liability. Cf. American Surety Co. v. Baldwin, 287 U.S. 156

(1932). Adams points to nothing in the record indicating that Nelson affirmatively relinquished his right to respond on the merits of the case belatedly stated against him in his individual capacity. Accordingly, the proceedings did not comply with Rule 15, and neither did they comport with due process [citations omitted].

It is true that Nelson knew as soon as Adams moved to amend the pleading and alter the judgment that he might ultimately be subjected to personal liability. One could ask, therefore, whether Nelson in fact had a fair chance, before alteration of the judgment, to respond and be heard. Rule 15 and the due process for which it provides, however, demand a more reliable and orderly course. First, as the Rule indicates, pleading in response to an amended complaint is a prerogative of parties, see Fed. Rule Civ. Proc. 15(a), and Nelson was not a party prior to the District Court's ruling on Adams' motion to amend. Second, as Rule 15 further prescribes, the clock on an added party's time to respond does not start running until the new pleading naming that party is served, see ibid., just as the clock on an original party's time to respond does not start running until the original pleading is served, see Fed. Rule Civ. Proc. 12(a)(1)(A). This is not to say that Rule 15 is itself a constitutional requirement. Beyond doubt, however, a prospective party cannot fairly be required to answer an amended pleading not yet permitted, framed, and served.

To summarize, Nelson was never afforded a proper opportunity to respond to the claim against him. Instead, he was adjudged liable the very first moment his personal liability was legally at issue. Procedure of this style has been questioned even in systems, real and imaginary, less concerned than ours with the right to due process.[1]

Adams strongly urges, however, that Nelson waived his objections to the swift process of the District Court. Adams first maintains that Nelson waived arguments based on personal jurisdiction and the absence of service of process by failing to raise them promptly after being added as a party. Nelson's winning argument, however, is based neither on personal jurisdiction nor on service of process. It rests on his right to have time and opportunity to respond to the claim once Adams gained leave to sue Nelson in his individual capacity, and thereby to reach beyond OCP's corporate till into Nelson's personal pocket. Waiver of arguments

1. A well-known work offers this example:

"'Herald, read the accusation!' said the King.

On this the White Rabbit blew three blasts on the trumpet, and then unrolled the parchment scroll, and read as follows:

'The Queen of Hearts, she made some tarts,
All on a summer day:
The Knave of Hearts, he stole those tarts,
And took them quite away!'

'Consider your verdict,' the King said to the jury.

'Not yet, not yet!' the Rabbit interrupted. 'There's a great deal to come before that!'"

L. Carroll, Alice in Wonderland and Through the Looking Glass 108 (Messner, 1982).

based on personal jurisdiction and service of process is therefore beside the point.

In a similar vein, and this time coming closer to the dispositive issue, Adams submits that the Federal Circuit "did not address the 'due process' issues now sought to be presented, . . . because these issues were never raised by Petitioner" before that court. Id. at 47 (emphasis deleted). It is indeed the general rule that issues must be raised in lower courts in order to be preserved as potential grounds of decision in higher courts. But this principle does not demand the incantation of particular words; rather, it requires that the lower court be fairly put on notice as to the substance of the issue. See, e.g., Beech Aircraft Corp. v. Rainey, 488 U.S. 153, 174-175 (1988). And the general rule does not prevent us from declaring what due process requires in this case, for that matter was fairly before the Court of Appeals.

In response to questioning from the appellate bench, Nelson's counsel explained that the core of his client's argument was the fundamental unfairness of imposing judgment without going through the process of litigation our rules of civil procedure prescribe.[4] Both the majority and the dissent in the Federal Circuit understood that an issue before them concerned the process due after Adams' postjudgment motion. See 175 F.3d at 1349, n.5 (majority opinion); 175 F.3d at 1352 (Newman, J., dissenting). Our resolution of the case as a matter of due process therefore rests on a ground considered and passed upon by the court below.

Beneath Adams' technical and ultimately unavailing arguments about waiver, its essential position in the litigation is reflected in the Federal Circuit's decision: There was sufficient identity between Nelson and OCP to bind Nelson, without further ado, to a judgment already entered against OCP. Nelson was president and sole shareholder of OCP. See 175 F.3d at 1346. It was Nelson who withheld prior art from the Patent Office. See id. at 1349. He had actual notice that Adams was seeking to collect a fee award from OCP, because he was the "effective controller" of the litigation for OCP and personally participated as a witness at the hearing on whether OCP had engaged in inequitable conduct. . . .

"No basis has been advanced," the panel majority concluded, "to believe anything different or additional would have been done to defend against the allegation of inequitable conduct had Nelson individually already been added as a party or had he been a party from the outset." 175 F.3d at 1351. We neither dispute nor endorse the substance of this speculation. We say instead that judicial predictions about the outcome of hypothesized litigation cannot substitute for the actual opportunity to defend that due process affords every party against whom a claim is

4. Nelson's counsel stated his position as follows: "It's legally wrong to subject the individual, nonserved, nonsued, nonlitigated-against person to liability for that judgment. Because there are rules. The rules say if you want a judgment against somebody, you sue them, you litigate against them, you get a judgment against them." Tape of Oral Arg. in No. 98-1448 (Fed. Cir. Feb. 3, 1999).

stated. As Judge Newman wrote in dissent: "The law, at its most fundamental, does not render judgment simply because a person might have been found liable had he been charged." 175 F.3d at 1354.

Our decision surely does not insulate Nelson from liability. As counsel twice represented at oral argument, Nelson seeks only the right to contest on the merits his personal liability for fees originally sought and awarded solely against OCP. That right, we hold, is just what due process affords him. . . .

For the reasons stated, the judgment of the Court of Appeals is reversed, and the case is remanded for further proceedings consistent with this opinion.

It is so ordered.

Note: Adding a Party After Judgment

What is a simple little case like this doing in the Supreme Court, you might ask? So trifling are the issues that no one bothers to dissent. It is unusual for a case that deals with pleading issues to reach the appellate stage, much less the Supreme Court. Why is this true, and what propelled Nelson v. Adams so far? Though it reads like an easy case, the decision is potentially very important. Rendering a corporation judgment-proof by bankruptcy or other maneuvers is a common (though ethically dubious) tactic, especially in intellectual property litigation; this case provides an important tool for fighting such tactics.

The Court clearly indicates that it is possible to amend the pleadings to add a party after the case has gone to judgment. All one must do is observe Rule 15's niceties. This is not only an endorsement of Rule 15's expansive tendencies, but also reveals the Court's continued acceptance of liberal pleading rules. For post-*Nelson* lower court decisions, see Insituform Technologies, Inc. v. Cat Contracting, Inc., 385 F.3d 1360 (Fed. Cir. 2004) (allowing amendment adding executive officer of defendant corporation post-judgment; distinguishing *Nelson* on the grounds that the officer had notice of the suit and was liable as an individual tortfeasor); Johns v. Harborage I, Ltd., 664 N.W.2d 291 (Minn. 2003) (plaintiff allowed to amend pleadings after judgment in sexual harassment suit).

What exactly does the Court say Adams should have done? What would Nelson have said if he had an opportunity to be heard? Is he urging that he had important evidence to produce at a hearing? What prevented him from seeking a hearing, or a reconsideration when he was personally made a party for purposes of judgment enforcement? The District Court and the Federal Circuit (which handles patent appeals) seemed hostile to Nelson on the merits. Can you see why?

Note: Waiting Too Long to Amend

Rule 15(a) provides that a court "should be freely give leave when justice so requires," and Rule 16 permits modification of scheduling orders "only for good cause and with the judge's consent." Are these standards identical? The language in both seems to reflect the liberal spirit of notice pleading—that parties should be able to adjust their claims and defenses as they learn the details of the dispute, and that cases should be decided on their merits rather than technicalities. Note that the pre-2007 Rule 1 said leave "*shall* be freely given." Is the verb change merely stylistic?

As with any discretionary standard, pleaders are at the mercy of the court deciding just what "justice requires" and just what constitutes "good cause." And, however important liberal pleading is, at a certain point amendments jeopardize efficiency and fair notice to opponents. We saw the potential problems with notice in *Nelson,* where amendment followed the entry of judgment—an extreme example. More commonly, courts are asked to consider amendments as a case approaches trial and discovery deepens or as some claims are dismissed and plaintiffs struggle to keep their case alive. Eleventh hour amendments can affect pretrial scheduling orders, the pace and scope of discovery, and preparations for trial. See Southland Sec. Corp. v. INSpire Ins. Solutions, Inc., 365 F.3d 353, 384 (5th Cir. 2005) (affirming denial of third request for leave to amend in securities case where district court had repeatedly warned plaintiffs of deficiencies in their pleadings and offered "'one more opportunity to amend their pleadings in accordance with the requirements of Rule 9(b) and the PSLRA'"); Leary v. Daeschner, 349 F.3d 888 (6th Cir. 2003) (affirming denial of second request for leave to amend filed almost two years after the deadline set by the lower court's scheduling order for the close of discovery and dispositive motions). See also Brzozowski v. Corr. Physician Servs., Inc., 360 F.3d 173 (3d Cir. 2004) (even where there is no statute of limitations, late attempts to amend are subject to the equitable doctrine of laches; remanding to consider reasonableness of delay and prejudice to added party where plaintiff sought to add successor entity in gender discrimination suit after learning that her employer was going bankrupt and had already sold its major assets to the successor entity).

As the advisory committee notes to Rule 16 emphasize, the Rule "is designed to ensure that at some point both the parties and the pleadings will be fixed." Permitting late amendments in disregard of pretrial scheduling orders may simply "reward the indolent and the cavalier." Johnson v. Mammoth Recreations, Inc., 975 F.2d 604, 611 (9th Cir. 1992). Courts are even less tolerant of attempts to modify claims mid-course by parties who do not formally request leave to amend under Rule 15. See Gilmour v. Gates, McDonald & Co., 382 F.3d 1312, 1315 (11th Cir. 2004) (holding that a plaintiff cannot add a claim by raising it in a brief filed in opposition to defendant's motion for summary judgment: "Liberal pleading does not require that, at the summary judgment stage, defendants must infer all possible claims that could arise out of facts set forth in the complaint. The proper procedure for Gilmour to assert a new contract claim was to seek to amend her complaint.").

What general principles should guide lower courts in deciding whether to grant leave to amend? "Freely give" is capacious language—what else besides delay might weigh against granting leave to amend? The Supreme Court has held that several factors are relevant:

> In the absence of any apparent or declared reason—such as undue delay, bad faith, or dilatory motive on the part of the movant, repeated failure to cure deficiencies by amendments previously allowed, undue prejudice to the opposing party by virtue of allowance of the amendment, futility of the amendment, etc.—the leave sought should, as the rules require, be "freely given."

Foman v. Davis, 371 U.S. 178, 182 (1962). Thus, if the party seeking to amend has been diligent, and the other side can adjust to the added claims, leave should generally be granted. But where leave to amend is requested after the deadline set in a Rule 16 scheduling order, the standard is more exacting. See Parker v. Columbia Pictures Indus., 204 F.3d 326, 340 (2d Cir. 2000) ("[D]espite the lenient standard of Rule 15(a), a district court does not abuse its discretion in denying leave to amend the pleadings after the deadline set in the scheduling order where the moving party has failed to establish good cause" under Rule 16).

C. POLICING THE PLEADINGS: ETHICAL CONSTRAINTS, FRIVOLOUS CASES, AND CREATIVE ADVOCACY

Problem Case: The Worker with the "Bad" Accent

Manuel Perfume sued the State of Hawaii in federal court for national origin discrimination in violation of Title VII of the Civil Rights Act. He claimed as well that the state's hiring procedures denied him due process of law. His suit asked for $1 million in damages.

In a lengthy complaint he made the following allegations: 1) He had immigrated from the Philippines, become a naturalized citizen, and sought work as a clerk at the Department of Motor Vehicles. 2) He had placed first among 500 people who took the Civil Service Examination, which tests, among other skills, the ability to read, write, and understand English. 3) After being interviewed for the job he was turned down because of his Filipino accent. 4) This reason was a proxy for national origin discrimination, as evidenced partly by the fact that the DMV has never hired any clerks of Filipino origin. 5) The State of Hawaii did not follow its own procedures in denying him a job, in that the ability to speak "unaccented English" was not listed as a job qualification, nor was there a rating on the official interview form for such a qualification. 6) Finally, Perfume claimed that he speaks perfectly clearly, though with an identifiable Filipino accent.

Accent discrimination is a novel claim under antidiscrimination laws. Attached as an exhibit to Perfume's original complaint was a 100-page study commissioned by the Hawaii Civil Rights Commission showing that Filipinos are heavily discriminated against in Hawaii. One example of prejudicial attitudes was that many people simply fail to listen to people of Philippine ancestry.

On the day the suit was filed there was a press conference in the offices of Perfume's lawyers, at which copies of the complaint were provided to the media and where Perfume discussed his background and decision to litigate. "Million-Dollar Discriminators" was the headline the next day in the major Honolulu newspaper.

The State moved for sanctions under Fed. R. Civ. P. 11, alleging the following as to the original complaint: 1) The job description had included the ability to deal with the public among the qualifications. 2) Clear communication with a great number of contentious and disgruntled people was a bona fide occupational qualification of the DMV clerk job (and thus a statutory exception to Title VII). 3) Perfume's accent was extremely strong, making him unintelligible to many people. 4) At the time of Perfume's application 4 out of 40 clerks at the DMV were Filipino.

The State also claims that the suit was filed in bad faith. The press conference and the "preposterous" damages are alleged as evidence of improper purpose: to force an unwarranted settlement. Moreover, the State claims that the plaintiff is continuing to generate adverse publicity, and that this excuses them from observing the 21-day waiting period, see Rule 11(c)(2), before filing the sanctions motion with the court.

If you were the district court judge, how would you rule on the State's motion for sanctions? What would you say about the failure to observe the waiting period? Suppose you feel that there are too many employment discrimination cases on your docket—can this legitimately enter your decision?

Professor Mari Matsuda has written about the actual case on which our problem is built:

Mari J. Matsuda, Voices of America: Accent, Antidiscrimination Law, and a Jurisprudence for the Last Reconstruction

100 Yale L.J. 1329, 1333-1340 (1991)

I come from a place that is farther away from any place than any place. The islands of Hawaii, geographically isolated and peopled from all corners of the world, are a linguist's dream. The linguistic and ethnic heritage of the islands is more diverse than that of any other state in the United States. In the voices of the islands one hears traces of Hawaiian, Portuguese, New England English, Japanese, Chinese, Filipino, and Spanish. It is thus no accident that two significant Title VII cases falling in the middle of the doctrinal puzzle of accent discrimination come from Hawaii.

Perhaps in explaining the puzzle, it is best to begin where all cases begin, with a person and the story they bring to court.

A. Manuel Fragante's Story

. . . In 1981 Manuel Fragante took a civil service examination along with over 700 other applicants. He is an intelligent and educated man, and he was not surprised when he received the highest score of all applicants who took the test. Fragante was ranked first on the list of eligibles, but, after a brief interview, he was turned down for the job of clerk in the Division of Motor Vehicles. When he asked why, he learned that he was rejected because of his Filipino accent. Manuel Fragante, combat veteran of two wars and true believer in the rhetoric of equality, promptly contacted a Filipino American state legislator, who in turn recommended that Fragante visit the run-down office of a neighborhood public interest law firm.

The lawyers advised Mr. Fragante that Title VII litigation is costly and difficult, that money damages in a case such as his are often nominal, and that although he was treated unfairly, discrimination is difficult to prove. Mr. Fragante listened carefully and replied that his case was a strong one, and that discrimination is not allowed under American law. He was prepared for a fight, even a long and bitter one, in order to show the truth about his case.

The lawyers were impressed. Here was an articulate and passionate plaintiff, unquestionably qualified in every respect for the job, turned down because of his accent. The issues were clean. The client was committed. The lawyers realized they would never get another plaintiff as good as Mr. Fragante to test the application of Title VII to accent cases. They agreed to fight the case to the end. And so they did, losing at every level before the federal courts.

Manuel Fragante was born and raised in the Philippines, during a time of heavy American influence there. He is an educated man, with a university degree in law. The Philippines is a land of many languages, including Ilocano, Ilongo, Visayan, Cebuano Visayan, Tagalog, and English—the last four of which Mr. Fragante speaks. In part because of this diversity, and in part because of the influence of the United States, English is the language used in many Filipino schools, universities, businesses, and media. All of Manuel Fragante's schooling was in English, and his command of the English language—given the strict, no-nonsense, prewar style of his early teachers—exceeds that of many Americans.

Manuel Fragante loves two countries: the Philippines, his birth home, and the United States, his adopted home. When Japan occupied the Philippine Islands, Fragante was one of thousands of young men who took to the hills to join the resistance. As a guerilla fighter, he swore to outlast the occupation, predicting the eventual liberation of his homeland. He fought for three years, surviving several bouts of malaria. After the war, like veterans of many nations of that time, Fragante started a family, furthered his education, and made modest economic gains as he continued to work in the military and in civilian enterprises. He believed in self-reliance, hard work, and respect for authority—the kind of ideas questioned and ridiculed by the generation that followed his. Fragante's loyalty to the United States, liberator of the Philippines, was solid. He volunteered from Manila to serve on the American side for a twenty-three-month tour of duty in the Vietnam War, and he continued military training in places like Fort Harrison, Indiana, and Fort Leavenworth, Kansas. He is particularly proud of his performance in U.S. military schools, where his intellectual skills frequently put him ahead of American officers in test scores. . . .

The Division of Motor Vehicles (DMV) of the City and County of Honolulu is much like similar departments all over the United States. . . .

It is in the nature of such places that people are not always at their best. Some customers become impatient and demanding. The job of motor vehicle clerk is the lowest paying job in the city employment hierarchy. It has the highest turnover. Employees rarely last over a year, and the city is constantly looking for new clerks.

Because the DMV creates constant demand for new employees, the personnel department sent a specialist to study the job and devise a screening test to help identify a large pool of prospective clerks. This is a well-established procedure used by large employers. The specialist observed clerks on the job. The key skills she identified included alphabetizing, reproducing numbers and letters with accuracy, making change, exhibiting courtesy, and other routine clerical skills. A test was devised to measure these skills.

In these days of skepticism toward standardized tests, this particular type of test is still highly regarded by employment specialists. Clerical skills are measurable with considerable accuracy, and performance in tasks such as accurately addressing large numbers of envelopes is largely predictable from test results. If such a test is devised with actual job functions in mind, it tends to predict fairly, and is less susceptible to racial or cultural bias than other tests. . . .

This was the premise Manuel Fragante relied on when he took the civil service examination and out-tested his 700 competitors. He was proud of his score and felt assured of the job. While others thought the job was beneath him given his age and experience, he was looking forward to the simplicity of its tasks, to the official feel of working for the government in an air-conditioned building, and to the chance to earn some spending money instead of wasting his time in boring idleness. He found warnings that the job was stressful mildly amusing. Having lived through invasion, war, and economic uncertainty, Manuel Fragante figured he could handle an irate taxpayer complaining about a long wait in line. He thus walked in for his interview with a calm and assured dignity. He knew the job was his.

The interviewers were other employees of the DMV: a supervisor and a secretary. The interview surprised Mr. Fragante. It was less of an interview than a brief conversation, lasting ten to fifteen minutes. The interviewers had no list of standard questions. They did have a rating sheet devised by one of the interviewers. After Mr. Fragante left, the interviewers conferred and entered scores on the rating sheet. . . . The interviewers made these comments:

"Difficult manner of pronunciation."

"Pronounced" and "Heavy Filipino" accent.

Manuel Fragante was passed over for the job. The administrator in charge of hiring recommendations stated, "because of his accent, I would not recommend him for this position." The interviewers heard what any listener would hear in a brief conversation with Mr. Fragante: he speaks with a heavy Filipino accent, one that he is unlikely to lose at his age.

At the trial in the *Fragante* case, a linguist who studies Filipino and non-Filipino interactions stated that Mr. Fragante speaks grammatically correct, standard English, with the characteristic accent of someone raised in the Philippines. There is a history, in Hawaii and elsewhere, of prejudice against this accent, the linguist explained, that will cause some listeners to "turn off" and not comprehend it. The degree of phonological—or sound—deviation in Fragante's speech was not, however, so far afield from other accents of English-speakers in Hawaii that he would not be understood. Any non-prejudiced speaker of English would have no trouble understanding Mr. Fragante, the linguist concluded. . . .

The linguist sat through the trial and noted the proceedings with interest. Attorneys for both sides suffered lapses in grammar and sentence structure, as did the judge. Mr. Fragante's English, a review of the transcript confirmed, was more nearly perfect in standard grammar and syntax than any other speaker in the courtroom. Mr. Fragante testified for two days, under the stress of both direct and cross-examination. The judge and the examiners spoke to Fragante in English and understood his answers. A court reporter understood and took down his words verbatim. In the functional context of the trial, everyone understood Manuel Fragante's speech. Yet the defendant's interviewers continued to claim Fragante could not be understood well enough to serve as a DMV clerk. . . .

The judge was on assignment from Arizona. He listened to four days of testimony and concluded that Manuel Fragante was denied the job *not* because of national origin, but because of legitimate difficulties with his accent.[34] . . .

Manuel Fragante was upset by the opinion. Soon after losing out on the DMV job, he was hired by the State of Hawaii as a statistician. Much of his

34. Fragante v. City and County of Honolulu, 699 F. Supp. 1429, 1432 (D. Haw. 1987).

work involved telephone interviews. Fragante felt his employment with the State proved his claim that the city misjudged his accent. He told his attorneys he wanted to press forward with his case.

Fragante lost on appeal before the Ninth Circuit although he did gain the symbolic victory of the court's sympathetic recognition that accent discrimination could violate Title VII.* The U.S. Supreme Court denied certiorari.[40]

Manuel Fragante met his pledge to take his case as far as he could. His case has brought him a notoriety he is proud of, and he continues to argue against accent discrimination to community groups. Manuel Fragante, denied a job because of the way he speaks, has been interviewed on radio and television. He has spoken at fundraisers in California and Hawaii. He has campaigned actively, speaking in his own voice, against accent discrimination.

The History and Importance of Rule 11

Many of you, at least on first reading, might think it ridiculous that a man with a difficult accent would sue for a position that required dealing with an irascible public. Did Professor Matsuda's article modify your initial reaction? As a lawyer would you have accepted Perfume's case? As a judge, would you find it professionally fulfilling to have it on your docket?

The original design of the Rules to increase access and simplify procedure also made it easier for people to file unmerited, even frivolous, cases. Rule 11, framed in terms of the lawyer's duty to the court, was intended, from the first, to deal with this problem. It provided for striking pleadings filed for "delay" or without good ground to support them. One of the shortest and least used Rules, it lay dormant for many years. In 1976, one commentator wrote that there were only eleven reported cases. Michael Risinger, Honesty in Pleading and Its Enforcement: Some "Striking" Problems with Federal Rule of Procedure 11, 61 Minn. L. Rev. 1, 36 (1976).

This all changed in 1983 when Rule 11 was amended to require that attorneys certify that they had made "a reasonable inquiry" before filing a complaint. But most significantly, the new rule made a monetary sanction, attorneys' fees, available for the amount incurred because of the filing of the "bad" pleading. By this provision, the rulemakers assured that Rule 11 would arise from its desuetude, because for defendants especially, practically everything that happened in the litigation up to and including the

* Fragante v. City and County of Honolulu, 888 F.2d 591, 594-595 (9th Cir. 1989). Eds.

40. Fragante v. City and County of Honolulu, 110 S. Ct. 1811 (1990).

filing of the Rule 11 motion could be ascribed to the original "bad" pleading. Here is the relevant language from the 1983 rule:

Rule 11. Signature of Pleadings, Motions and Other Papers; Sanctions

> Every pleading, motion, and other paper of a party represented by an attorney shall be signed by at least one attorney of record in the attorney's individual name, whose address shall be stated. A party who is not represented by an attorney shall sign the party's pleading, motion, or other paper and state the party's address. Except when otherwise specifically provided by rule or statute, pleadings need not be verified or accompanied by affidavit. The rule in equity that averments of an answer under oath must be overcome by the testimony of two witnesses or of one witness sustained by corroborating circumstances is abolished. The signature of an attorney or party constitutes a certificate by the signer that the signer has read the pleading, motion, or other paper; that to the best of the signer's knowledge, information, and belief formed after reasonable inquiry it is well grounded in fact and is warranted by existing law or a good faith argument for the extension, modification, or reversal of existing law, and that it is not interposed for any improper purpose, such as to harass or to cause unnecessary delay or needless increase in the cost of litigation. If a pleading, motion, or other paper is not signed, it shall be stricken unless it is signed promptly after the omission is called to the attention of the pleader or movant. If a pleading, motion, or other paper is signed in violation of this rule, the court, upon motion or upon its own initiative, shall impose upon the person who signed it, a represented party, or both, an appropriate sanction, which may include an order to pay to the other party or parties the amount of the reasonable expenses incurred because of the filing of the pleading, motion, or other paper, including a reasonable attorney's fee.

Note that, once a court finds that the rule has been violated, it *must* impose sanctions. The prospect of automatic sanctions under the amended Rule generated "collateral disputes of unprecedented—and perhaps unanticipated—magnitude" and over 3,000 published opinions. George Cochran, Rule 11: The Road to Amendment, 2 Att'y Sanctions Newsl. 141 (1991); John Frank, Bench-Bar Proposal to Revise Civil Procedure Rule 11, 137 F.R.D. 159 (1991) (noting that courts were *"drowning in satellite litigation"* under the 1983 rule) (emphasis added). Virtually every circuit produced lengthy, often *en banc* (i.e., all judges sitting), decisions about various aspects of the Rule, dealing with such questions as the standard of review, the content and timing of a hearing on Rule 11 motions, standing to make the motion, and many other issues.

The United States Supreme Court decided four cases under the 1983 version of Rule 11, the first coming six years into the new regime. Though these cases shared a "get tough" tone, they offered no structure or vision for the burgeoning Rule 11 case law. Two of them have been superseded by the 1993 amendments to the Rule. In Pavelic & LeFlore v. Marvel Entm't Group, 493 U.S. 120 (1989) (superseded), the Court held that only the individual attorney who signed a pleading, and not the law firm with which she was associated, could be sanctioned. The majority opinion scanted any discussion of which method might better serve the Rule's purposes or the intent of the rulemakers.

With the same "plain meaning" approach, the Court found that a represented party could be sanctioned directly for actions her lawyer took at her behest. Bus. Guides, Inc. v. Chromatic Commc'ns Enters., 498 U.S. 533 (1991). Again, the Court showed little concern about the impact of its decision on the administration of the Rule, that is, that making the client a target for sanctions would have the effect of turning up the heat in practice. Cooter and Gell v. Hartmarx, 496 U.S. 384 (1990) (superseded), held that a Rule 11 sanction motion survived the voluntary dismissal of an action by the plaintiff under Rule 41(a)(1)(i). In other words, a plaintiff might not "cure" a violation by giving up his court action. Many commentators criticized this opinion for its tendency to keep litigation alive instead of streamlining it. Similarly, in Willy v. Coastal Corp., 504 U.S. 935 (1992), the Court held that sanctions imposed against a plaintiff would be upheld even though the court imposing them lacked subject matter jurisdiction over the dispute at the time of the sanctionable conduct.

In considering all of the ink spilled over the 1983 Amendments to Rule 11, remember that the published decisions may be the tip of the iceberg in terms of the impact of an active sanctions practice on lawyer's work. In an impressively designed empirical study of the Rule's operation, the authors found that 82 percent of the federal litigators in three circuits reported having been affected by the Rule. Lawrence C. Marshall, Herbert M. Kritzer, and Frances Kahn Zemans, The Use and Impact of Rule 11, 86 Nw. U. L. Rev. 943 (1992). Positive effects ranged from declining a case to withholding a claim or defense. On the negative side, a substantial number of lawyers reported that they failed to assert a claim or defenses that had merit because of sanction fears. Id. at 959-962.

The following passage became a rallying cry for those who would reform the Rule:

> Sometimes there are reasons to sue even when one cannot win. Bad court decisions must be challenged if they are to be overruled, but the early challenges are certainly hopeless. The first attorney to challenge Plessy v. Ferguson was certainly bringing a frivolous action, but his efforts and the efforts of others eventually led to Brown v. Board of Education.

Eastway Constr. Corp. v. City of New York, 637 F. Supp. 558, 575 (E.D.N.Y. 1986).

The reformers won, and a new version of Rule 11 went into effect in December 1993. It was meant to moderate the heat of the adversary practice under the previous Rule. What place the huge jurisprudence generated by the prior Rule will play in interpreting the new Rule, as well as the meaning of the Rule itself, are subjects that will continue to stir and confound proceduralists well into the twenty-first century.

Read the current Rule 11 and the Advisory Committee Notes. The major changes in the 1993 Rule were to increase the discretion of the trial judge on whether to impose sanctions and to de-emphasize monetary sanctions in administering the Rule. A 21-day "safe harbor" provision was also added in part (c). The 1993 version of Rule 11 retains the duty of investigation, and the same basic categories of disapproved pleadings: improper purpose; inadequate legal basis; inadequate factual basis.

The 1993 amendments had the desired effect of cutting down substantially the cases and commentary under Rule 11. Several studies and articles indicate general satisfaction with the functioning of the new Rule, particularly with the safe harbor provision. See, e.g., Theodore Hirt, A Second Look at Amended Rule 11, 48 Am. U. L. Rev. 1007, 1027-1028 (1999); Laura Duncan, Sanctions Litigation Declining, A.B.A. J., Mar. 1995 (concluding on the basis of interviews with judges, lawyers, and law professors that there has been a marked decline in Rule 11 litigation). A 2005 Federal Judicial Center survey found that "the percentage of judges supporting the safe harbor has increased from 70% to 86% since 1995; the percentage of judges showing strong support has increased from 32% to 60%. The percentage of judges opposing the safe harbor has decreased from 16% to 10%." Federal Judicial Center, Report of a Survey of United States District Judges' Experiences and Views Concerning Rule 11, at 5 (2005). Likewise, "[a]pproximately 85% of the district judges view groundless litigation in [cases where the plaintiff is represented by counsel] as no more than a small problem and another 12% see such litigation as a moderate problem." Id. at 3. Remarkably, beyond occasionally noting the availability of sanctions, the Supreme Court has remained largely silent on the interpretation of Rule 11 after the 1993 amendments. For a comprehensive survey on the ten-year anniversary of the 1993 amendments, see Symposium: Happy (?) Birthday Rule 11, 37 Loyola L.A. L. Rev. 515 (2004).

Still, skeptics remain. On the one hand, some have suggested that the safe harbor provision has not eliminated the chilling effect of sanctions targeted at civil rights plaintiffs. See Danielle Kie Hart, Symposium: Happy Birthday (?) Rule 11: And the Chill Goes On, 37 Loy. L.A. L. Rev. 645, 662 (2004) (arguing that courts have shifted to other sanctions tools such as the inherent power doctrine and 28 U.S.C. § 1927); Georgene Vairo, Rule 11 and the Profession, 67 Fordham L. Rev. 589, 643 (1998) (same). On the other hand, concerns about "litigation abuse" have prompted calls to do away with the safe harbor and return to the mandatory sanctions provision of the 1983 amendments. These critics worry that the safe harbor provision "actually can increase the number of frivolous actions because attorneys can file those suits with impunity, knowing that, if challenged, they can simply withdraw or amend their complaints within the twenty-one day period." Friedenthal, Kane, and Miller, Civil Procedure 269 (1999) (citing scholars who advocate eliminating the safe harbor).

As in 1983 and 1993, Rule 11 has become a focal point in the larger debate about "litigation abuse." H.R. 420, the Lawsuit Abuse Reduction

Act of 2005, which would have restored 1983-style mandatory sanctions, was reported out of the House Judiciary Committee on May 25, 2005, and a similar bill was passed by the House of Representatives in 2004, though it failed in the Senate. Concerns about litigation abuse, particularly in the area of medical malpractice, also were prominent in the 2004 presidential campaign. Reviewing the broader arguments on litigation abuse and arguments for Rule 11 reform, Aaron Hiller contends that circumstances have changed since the 1990s:

> From 1992 to 2001, the overall number of civil lawsuits filed in America dropped by 47%. The number of tort suits fell by 31.8% and the number of medical malpractice claims—an area of litigation often cited by tort reformers and insurance companies for increasing abuse—declined by 14.2%.
>
> As the amount of litigation on the docket has declined, so have the jury awards so often decried as outrageous and skyrocketing by tort reformers. The median jury award in 2001 was $37,000, representing a 43.1% decrease over the previous decade. Limiting that analysis only to tort cases, the median jury award stood at $28,000, a 56% drop since 1992. Moreover, juries rarely award punitive damages at all—less than 3% of all plaintiff winners in tort trials were awarded punitive damages; the median award was $38,000.

Aaron Hiller, Rule 11 and Tort Reform: Myth, Reality, and Legislation, 18 Geo. J. Legal Ethics 809, 818 (2005).

If these are the facts on the ground, what is driving public and political debate on litigation abuse? First, there is certainly some distortion in the cases covered by the media. As Deborah Rhode puts it, "[t]he public gets anecdotal glimpses of atypical cases without a sense of their overall significance." Deborah L. Rhode, In the Interests of Justice: Reforming the Legal Profession 121 (2000). Second, politicians seeking stricter rules often offer "polemics that take considerable poetic license." Id. (quoting former California Governor Pete Wilson's comment that the "'lawyer's briefcase has become a weapon of terror,'" and then Governor George W. Bush's denunciation of "'junk lawsuits that clog our courts'"). Third, and perhaps most important, in a pluralistic society we are bound to disagree on what amounts to "abuse" of the litigation system. As Professor Rhode elaborates:

> [W]hat qualifies as a frivolous claim depends on the eye of the beholder. While a few commonly cited examples meet almost anyone's definition, the line between vindictiveness and vindication is often difficult to draw. Sexual harassment claims were once routinely dismissed as matters beneath judicial notice. In some quarters, the situation has not significantly improved. Press commentators have a field day with harassment "witch trials" and "corporate McCarthyism," which assertedly allow radical feminists to "sue anybody about anything." To some (usually male) judges, it is a mistake to allow antidiscrimination law to redress the "petty slights of the hypersensitive." Yet only through these ostensibly petty claims have Americans finally begun to recognize the real costs of harassment. Women

> pay the highest price in terms of direct economic and psychological injuries, but all of us pay more indirectly. Harassment costs the average Fortune 500 company an estimated $6 million annually in turnover, worker absences, and lost productivity.

"Many of the media's favorite examples of trivial claims and outrageous verdicts," she continues,

> rely on highly selective factual excerpts. A textbook illustration involves a recent multimillion dollar punitive damages award against McDonald's for serving coffee at scalding temperatures. To most journalists, this case served as an all-purpose indictment of the legal profession and legal process; an avaricious lawyer paraded a petty incident before an out-of-control jury and extracted an absurd recovery. Newspaper editorials, radio talk shows, and magazine commentaries replayed endless variations on the theme summarized by the national Chamber of Commerce: "Is it fair to get a couple of million dollars from a restaurant just because you spilled hot coffee on yourself?"
>
> On closer examination, the question no longer looks rhetorical. The plaintiff, a seventy-nine-year-old woman, suffered acutely painful third degree burns from 180 degree coffee. She spent eight days in the hospital and returned again for skin grafts. Only after McDonald's refused to reimburse her medical expenses did she bring suit. At trial, jurors learned of seven hundred other burn cases involving McDonald's coffee during the preceding decade. Although medical experts had warned that such high temperatures were causing serious injuries, the corporation's safety consultant had viewed the number of complaints as "trivial." The jury's verdict of $2.3 million was not an arbitrary choice. Its punitive damages award represented two days of coffee sales revenues, and the judge reduced the judgment to $640,000. To avoid an appeal, the plaintiff then settled the case for a smaller, undisclosed amount. McDonald's put up warning signs, and other fast-food chains adopted similar measures. While evaluations of this final result may vary, it was not the patently "ridiculous" travesty that media critics described. . . .
>
> All too often, anecdotes substitute for analysis and masquerade as reflective of broader trends. . . . Commentators point to dramatic growth in certain kinds of cases, such as bankruptcy and product liability suits in federal courts. But federal filings account for only 2 percent of American litigation. And in state courts, product liability suits have been declining. While business leaders raise the most complaints about legal hypochondria, disputes between businesses are the largest and fastest growing category of civil litigation. . . . Higher per capita caseloads occurred in previous centuries in some American communities [and] United States court filings are now in the same range, when adjusted for population, as those in Canada, Australia, New Zealand, England, and Denmark.

Id. at 121-123.

Media and political distortion surely play a role in framing the debate on litigation abuse along with lack of consensus on what interests we expect the legal system to serve. Are there other elements at work?

Consider the following cases in thinking about the "Bad Accent" problem case, the debate on litigation abuse, and the efficacy of Rule 11 in general.

1. "An Inquiry Reasonable Under the Circumstances"

Although their holdings did not deal directly with the point, two of the cases to reach the United States Supreme Court on the 1983 version of Rule 11 were cases of inadequate investigation. In Cooter & Gell v. Hart-Marx, 496 U.S. 384 (1990), the lawyers apparently filed a major antitrust case on the basis of a few phone calls to men's clothing stores in four cities, from which they determined that only one store in each place sold Hart, Schaffner & Marx suits.

The other case, Business Guides, Inc. v. Chromatic Commc'ns Enters., 498 U.S. 533 (1991), held that Rule 11 imposes an objective standard of reasonable inquiry on parties who sign pleadings, motions, or other papers. The plaintiffs in *Business Guides* filed an application for a temporary restraining order against a competitor, claiming that Chromatic was copying from Business Guides' trade directory. Id. at 535-536. To support its TRO application, Business Guides filed signed affidavits identifying ten false directory listings (called "seeds") that Chromatic had allegedly copied along with other accurate listings. The company did not, however, specify the false information it had planted in the seeds. Id. at 536. When lawyers for Business Guides were asked to specify the false data in the seeds by the law clerk for the district court judge, they contacted their clients and then promptly withdrew their claims as to three of the ten listings. This was apparently the first time the lawyers had asked anyone at Business Guides about the accuracy of the seeds. Having become suspicous, the district judge's law clerk made an independent investigation and discovered that *nine* of the ten seeds contained no inaccuracies. Id.

Unaware, the lawyers for Business Guides prepared a supplemental affidavit for a company employee identifying "false" information in the seven remaining listings. On the day of the hearing, the employee realized that at least one seed in the affdavit was accurate and crossed it out by hand. Armed with the law clerk's more comprehensive findings, the district court denied the TRO application and referred the matter to a magistrate judge to determine whether sanctions should be imposed. The magistrate recommended sanctions against the client for failing to conduct a proper prefiling inquiry, and against the client and law firm for failing to inquire into the accuracy of the listings after learning that four contained no misinformation. Id. at 537-538.

Affirming the lower courts' decision to apply a standard of objective reasonableness to both the client's and attorney's conduct, the Supreme Court observed that

> the essence of Rule 11 is that *signing is no longer a meaningless act; it denotes merit*. A signature sends a message to the district court that this document is

> to be taken seriously. This case is illustrative. Business Guides sought a TRO on the strength of an initial application accompanied by five signed statements to the effect that Chromatic was pirating its directory. Because these documents were filed under seal, the District Court had to determine the credibility of the allegations without the benefit of hearing the other side's view. The court might plausibly have attached some incremental significance to the fact that Business Guides itself risked being sanctioned if the factual allegations contained in these signed statements proved to be baseless. Business Guides asks that we construe Rule 11 in a way that would render the signatures on these statements risk free. Because this construction is at odds with the Rule's general admonition that signing denotes merit, we are loath to do so.

Id. at 546 (emphasis added).

Business Guides and *Cooter & Gell* make clear that it is risky business to file a complaint simply because you believe your client's story. In the case that follows, consider whether you think the lawyer did enough before filing.

Kraemer v. Grant County

892 F.2d 686 (7th Cir. 1990)

PER CURIAM.

Attorney Mark D. Lawton appeals from the district court's order requiring him to pay $3,000 to William and Betty Baker, defendants below and appellees here, as a sanction under Fed. R. Civ. P. 11 for having filed a lawsuit on behalf of his client without first having made reasonable investigation into the facts of the case. We hold that under the circumstances presented here the imposition of sanctions was erroneous and we reverse.

Lawton was contacted in the late summer of 1986 by Laura Kraemer. Kraemer told him that Herbert Hottenstein, the sheriff of Grant County, Wisconsin, had conspired with the Bakers to evict her from her home and steal her belongings. Lawton asked Kraemer to write a detailed letter explaining what had happened. In her letter, Kraemer gave this account of events relevant to this appeal: She and her fiance Steven Baker had been living together for about three years. In late April 1986, they discovered that Kirk and Cindy Novinski had a house for rent in rural Grant County, and they chose to take it. The Novinskis demanded a $150 security deposit and $150 per month in rent, and Steven Baker agreed to pay it. A couple of days later Kraemer gave the Novinskis $100 and the Novinskis gave her the key. The rest of the rent was never paid because Steven Baker was killed in a work-related accident on May 8. The funeral took place on May 10. At the funeral, Steven Baker's parents, Bill and Betty Baker, asked Kraemer if they could come over to the house to pick up Steven Baker's belongings the next day. Kraemer reluctantly gave her permission. Before going home, Kraemer stopped at a friend's house. When she finally returned home she found that almost everything had been taken from the house, and she found a note from Betty Baker stating that they had taken the things they wanted. Kraemer immediately notified the sheriff's department.

The sheriff's officer on duty called the Bakers and told them to return what they had taken by 10:30 the next morning, May 11. At that time, however, Sheriff Hottenstein himself came out to Kraemer's house and said that the Bakers were within their rights. While Kraemer and the sheriff were talking, the Bakers arrived. Sheriff Hottenstein ordered Kraemer to turn her car keys and ownership papers over to the Bakers, telling her that the car was both unregistered and unsafe, and that the Bakers would make sure the car was not driven in that condition.

Kraemer went to visit her mother in another city for a few days. When she returned, she found a note on the front door, signed by a sheriff's deputy, which read: "To whom it may concern—Nothing is to be removed from the premises until you contact Grant County Sheriff's Department." The electricity had been cut off on orders of the Bakers. Kraemer went to the utility company and ordered service restored. When she got back to the house, on June 4, she met the landlord, Kirk Novinski. She tried to give him the money owing on May's rent, but Novinski refused to take it, telling her to hold off until she could straighten things out with the Bakers. At the time, someone from the utility company arrived to hook up the electricity, but Novinski objected. Kraemer convinced the man to leave the power on at least for the night. That evening, Sheriff Hottenstein returned and told Kraemer that she had to leave the house right then. The next day, the sheriff and the Bakers watched as Kraemer moved her belongings out of the house.

On July 29, when Kraemer was five months pregnant, she had another brush with the law. She was arrested by a Wisconsin State Patrol officer for driving with a defective brakelight. She was unable to produce a valid driver's license (the trooper knew the license was on file with the Wisconsin Department of Transportation), or the $33 bond required for that offense, and she was jailed for several hours until someone posted bond for her.

On the strength of this letter, Lawton made an administrative claim against the county on Kraemer's behalf for damages. When the claim was denied, Lawton hired (at his own expense) a private investigator to look into the allegations Kraemer had made. The investigator's report is not in the record, but Lawton conceded that he was unable to confirm or to discredit any part of Kraemer's story except that he had been given a statement by one of the Bakers' relatives saying that she had been with the Bakers when they took property out of Kraemer's house, and that she felt that action was "wrong." The investigator reported that the potential defendants had been "hostile."

This is all the information Lawton had been able to gather when he filed this suit against the Bakers and Hottenstein (and others not involved in this appeal) on January 29, 1987, alleging violations of Kraemer's constitutional rights and seeking damages under 42 U.S.C. § 1983 and 28 U.S.C. § 1343. Both of these statutes require the plaintiff to show state action before recovery can be had. Many of the allegations of the complaint are undisputed. The complaint stated a claim sufficient to withstand a motion for dismissal under Fed. R. Civ. P. 12(b)(6). Through discovery it was learned, among other things, that at the time of the events charged in the complaint there had been lengthy and frequent telephone conversations between the Bakers and the sheriff's office. Lawton was not able, however, to produce through discovery sufficient facts with respect to state action to defeat the defendants' motion for summary judgment. This court affirmed the grant of summary judgment in an unpublished order, Kraemer v. Grant County, 870 F.2d 659 (7th Cir. 1989), with one judge concurring specially to state that he considered the issue of state action to be a close one on summary judgment. It appeared that the sheriff played an active role in the dispute between the parties, although not necessarily an improper role.

Along with their motion for summary judgment, the Bakers requested that the court require Kraemer or Lawton to pay their legal fees in defending a frivolous or vexatious action under 42 U.S.C. § 1988. See Christiansburg Garment Co. v. EEOC, 434 U.S. 412 (1978). The district court held a hearing on the request on October 28, 1988, and found that an award of attorneys' fees was not proper in this case under § 1988 due to Kraemer's poverty, but also found that an award against Lawton personally was appropriate under Fed. R. Civ. P. 11. On November 10, 1989 the court ordered Lawton to pay $3,000 of the Bakers' total legal bill of about $8,000. The court ruled that Lawton should have known that there was no factual or legal basis for the allegation of state action at the time the complaint was filed. The award was less than the actual damages caused by his actions because Lawton is a fairly recent law school graduate, and had done some investigation before filing Kraemer's complaint. Lawton filed a motion to amend findings under Fed. R. Civ. P. 52(b), which was denied on December 14, 1988. Lawton filed a timely notice of appeal and we reverse.

Under our decision en banc in Mars Steel Corp. v. Continental Bank N.A., 880 F.2d 928 (7th Cir. 1989), our review of an order imposing Rule 11 sanctions (or refusing to impose them, see Tabrizi v. Village of Glen Ellyn, 883 F.2d 587 (7th Cir. 1989)) is deferential—we review only for abuse of discretion. But deferential review is different from no review at all, even when there is no controlling legal issue in the case. *Mars Steel*, 880 F.2d at 936. "Concerns for the effect on both an attorney's reputation and for the vigor and creativity of advocacy by other members of the bar necessarily require that we exercise less than total deference to the district court in its decision to impose Rule 11 sanctions." In re Ronco, Inc., 838 F.2d 212, 217 (7th Cir. 1988) (quoted with approval in *Mars Steel*). See also *Mars Steel*, 880 F.2d at 940-941 (Flaum, J., concurring) (no single abuse of discretion standard exists). In reviewing the imposition of sanctions under Rule 11, then, we will give deference to the decision of the district court, but with careful reference to the standards governing the exercise of the court's discretion and to the purposes Rule 11 is meant to serve.

In this case, our focus is on the reasonableness of Lawton's prefiling research into the facts of the case. Although the district court referred to Lawton's failure to establish a basis for the complaint in fact and in law, the legal problems drop out if his version of the facts was correct. If Sheriff Hottenstein was in fact conspiring with the Bakers to deprive Kraemer of her property, then there would be a remedy under 42 U.S.C. § 1983 for violation of Kraemer's civil rights. See Dennis v. Sparks, 449 U.S. 24, 27-28 (1980). Absent the sheriff's involvement, of course, there is no state action and no legal basis for a federal claim. But Kraemer's claim ultimately failed because she could not establish the necessary facts, not because the law did not provide a federal remedy for the wrongs she alleged in her complaint. Indeed, the complaint survived a Fed. R. Civ. P. 12(b)(6) motion for dismissal for failure to state a claim upon which relief could be granted. Therefore we need only determine whether the district court properly found that Lawton had not performed reasonable research into the facts of the case before filing the complaint.

It is not necessary that an investigation into the facts be carried to the point of absolute certainty. Nemmers v. United States, 795 F.2d 628, 632 (7th Cir. 1986). The investigation need merely be reasonable under the circumstances. S.A. Auto Lube, Inc. v. Jiffy Lube Intl., Inc., 842 F.2d 946, 948 (7th Cir. 1988). Relevant factors for the court to consider include:

> Whether the signer of the documents had sufficient time for investigation; the extent to which the attorney had to rely on his or her client for the factual foundation underlying the pleading, motion, or other paper; whether the case was accepted from another attorney; the complexity of the facts and the attorney's ability to do a sufficient pre-filing investigation; and whether discovery would have been beneficial to the development of the underlying facts.

Brown v. Federation of State Medical Bds., 830 F.2d 1429, 1435 (7th Cir. 1987). An analysis of these factors shows that it was error to conclude that Lawton's conduct in filing the complaint was sanctionable.

The key fact that Lawton and Kraemer had to establish was the sheriff's involvement in a conspiracy with the Bakers. "Because conspiracies are carried out in secret, direct proof of agreement is rare." United States v. Koenig, 856 F.2d 843, 854 (7th Cir. 1988). We cannot require an attorney to procure a confession of participation in a conspiracy from one of the prospective defendants before filing suit—if there were such a confession, no lawsuit would be necessary. Lawton did all he reasonably could have done to investigate his client's account of events before the complaint was filed. He hired a private investigator to interview the prospective defendants and to determine what had actually happened. The defendants refused to cooperate with the investigator. We cannot insist that a lawyer abandon his client's cause simply because the investigator was unable to obtain the cooperation of the prospective defendants.

When the defendants refused to cooperate voluntarily, Lawton had only two options: he could advise his client to give up, or he could file a complaint on her behalf and try to develop the necessary facts through discovery. Absent some official coercion, the defendants had proved unwilling to provide any evidence whatever relating to Kraemer's case, and their unwillingness was reflected in their hostile reactions to Lawton's investigator. No one else could be expected to have knowledge of the conspiracy. Until some other source of information became available, then, Lawton had to rely on his client for the factual foundation of the claim. There was simply no other source to which he could turn.

Once Lawton was armed with the coercive power of the federal courts to enforce the rules of discovery, he was able to get telephone records showing frequent and lengthy telephone conversations between the sheriff and the Bakers during May and June 1986, including a 22-minute conversation in the early morning of May 11, after Kraemer had reported to the sheriff's office that her house had been broken into, and just before Sheriff Hottenstein came out to the house to tell Kraemer that the Bakers had acted within their rights. Lawton was even able to get tapes of some later conversations between the sheriff and the Bakers, including one in which William Baker told the sheriff that "if we all stick together and find out she's lying then they'll call it [the lawsuit] off quick."[2] The particular facts that Lawton unearthed during discovery are irrelevant to the reasonableness of his filing the complaint, *Mars Steel*, 880 F.2d at 932 (focus of Rule 11 is on what should have been done before filing rather than on results), but the fact that he had to use discovery to learn them is relevant. If discovery is necessary to establish a claim, then it is not unreasonable to file a complaint so as to obtain the right to conduct that discovery. "Rule 11 must not bar the courthouse door to people who have some support for a complaint but need discovery to prove their case." Frantz v. United States Powerlifting Federation, 836 F.2d 1063 (7th Cir. 1987).

Rule 11 cannot be allowed to thoroughly undermine zealous advocacy. "The rule is not intended to chill an attorney's enthusiasm or creativity in pursuing factual or legal theories." Advisory Committee Notes to 1983 Amendment to Fed. R. Civ. P. 11. This is especially so in civil rights cases involving unpopular clients. Lawton's client is a young woman who appears to be exceedingly unpopular with the authorities in Grant County, as indicated by the fact that she was jailed for a minor traffic offense. It may on occasion take the power of the federal courts to keep state officials from harassing unpopular and powerless citizens. If that is the case, a federal forum must be available to them. We cannot allow such officials to avoid their constitutional duties simply by stonewalling an investigator.

Lawton took all the steps he reasonably could have taken before filing suit to determine the truth of Kraemer's allegations. He should not have

2. Apparently this tape was not available at the time summary judgment was entered, and it was not considered by the district court or by this court in affirming on the merits.

been sanctioned for turning to the judiciary, whose function is to find truth, when his own resources failed.

Reversed.

Note: The Effect of Rule 11 on Lawyers' Work

Rule 11 cases open incomparable insights into the practice of law. In these two cases, we see a large law firm and a solo practitioner fined for essentially the same conduct: filing a complaint founded on little more than what the clients told them. Why is this more justified in *Kraemer*?

The bulk of the opinion in *Business Guides* was directed to whether the client should be sanctioned, along with the law firm (for signing an affidavit supporting the TRO). Can you see why the law firm was eager to "take the rap" for the client in this case? Though *Business Guides* was decided under the 1983 version of the rule, parties may still be sanctioned under current practice, though not for mistakes about the law. See Rule 11(c)(5)(A).

Think about the sanctioned lawyer in *Kraemer.* One Stanford student called him in 1993 and found him still embittered. From his standpoint, he had worked hard on the case, perhaps devoting more effort than it required because it was early in his career and he was sympathetic to the client. In reaction to the sanctions, he claimed that he "would never, ever, file a civil rights suit in federal court again."

The present version of the Rule is meant to reduce the adversariness and anger that has resulted from the effort in the previous decade to put teeth into the requirements of nonfrivolous pleading. One major way the Rule seeks to accomplish this is to eliminate the emphasis courts gave monetary sanctions under the previous Rule. Professors Marshall, Kritzer, and Zemans in their excellent empirical study of sanctions in three federal circuits found that monetary sanctions were the norm under the 1983 rule. Yet the amount was not "as large as many media accounts of sensational cases may lead some to imagine." About 90 percent of the cases involved sanctions of $25,000 or less. The median sanction was $2,500. The authors concluded that "much of the bar's resistance to Rule 11 has its source in the stigma attached to being labelled a Rule 11 violator," rather than the amount of money paid. They acknowledged, however, a possible *in terrorem* effect of newspaper accounts of huge monetary awards. The Use and Impact of Rule 11, 86 Nw. U. L. Rev. 943, 956-957 (1992).

What are some possible nonmonetary sanctions? One that could have considerable bite is reference to the bar disciplinary committee. If the bar decides to discipline the attorney, it must first conduct its own investigation of the alleged misconduct, and otherwise follow its own rules regarding lawyer discipline. In a case of severe misconduct, the lawyer may face suspension of his license to practice law or even disbarment. But public bar sanctions are exceedingly rare. Not only do most state bar associations lack sufficient resources to investigate and prosecute complaints of misconduct, they, like other self-regulating bodies, often lack the will to aggressively pursue misconduct by their members. This means that judges bear a heavy burden in choosing sanctions that will adequately compensate for and deter misconduct.

In the case that follows, we see a trial judge eager to bear that burden. As you read, consider the factors that provoked the judge to enter such a high sanctions award.

Christian v. Mattel, Inc.

286 F.3d 1118 (9th Cir. 2002)

McKEOWN, Circuit Judge.

It is difficult to imagine that the Barbie doll, so perfect in her sculpture and presentation, and so comfortable in every setting, from "California girl" to "Chief Executive Officer Barbie," could spawn such acrimonious litigation and such egregious conduct on the part of her challenger. In her wildest dreams, Barbie could not have imagined herself in the middle of Rule 11 proceedings. But the intersection of copyrights on Barbie sculptures and the scope of Rule 11 is precisely what defines this case.

James Hicks appeals from a district court order requiring him, pursuant to Federal Rule of Civil Procedure 11, to pay Mattel, Inc. $501,565 in attorneys' fees that it incurred in defending against what the district court determined to be a frivolous action. Hicks brought suit on behalf of [his client] Harry Christian, claiming that Mattel's Barbie dolls infringed Christian's Claudene doll sculpture copyright. . . .

We hold that the district court did not abuse its discretion in determining that the complaint filed by Hicks was frivolous under Rule 11. In parsing the language of the district court's sanctions orders, however, we cannot determine with any degree of certainty whether the district court grounded its Rule 11 decision on Hicks' misconduct that occurred outside the pleadings, such as in oral argument, at a meeting of counsel, and at a key deposition. . . . Consequently, we vacate the district court's orders and remand for further proceedings consistent with this opinion. . . .

Background

As context for examinimg the district court's determination that the underlying action was frivolous, we begin by discussing the long history of litigation between Matel and Hicks' past and correct clients: Harry Christian; Christian's daughter, Claudene; and the Collegiate Doll Company ("COC"), Claudene's proprietorships.

I. Prior Litigation Between Mattel and CDC

Mattel is a toy company that is perhaps best recognized as the manufacturer of the world-famous Barbie doll. Since Barbie's creation in 1959, Mattel has outfitted her in fashions and accessories that have evolved over time. In perhaps the most classic embodiment, Barbie is depicted as a slender-figured doll with long blonde hair and blue eyes. Mattel has sought to protect its intellectual property by registering various Barbie-related copyrights, including copyrights protecting the doll's head sculpture. Mattel has vigorously litigated against putative infringers.

In 1990, Claudene Christian, then an undergraduate student at the University of Southern California ("USC"), decided to create and market a collegiate cheerleader doll. The doll, which the parties refer to throughout their papers as "Claudene," had blonde hair and blue eyes and was outfitted to resemble a USC cheerleader.

Mattel soon learned about the Claudene doll. After concluding that it infringed certain Barbie copyrights, Mattel brought an administrative action before the United States Customs Service in 1996 in which it alleged that the Claudene doll, manufactured abroad, had pirated the head sculpture of the "Teen Talk" and "SuperStar" Barbies. The Customs Service ruled in CDC's favor and subsequently released a shipment of Claudene dolls. Undaunted, Mattel commenced a federal court action in 1997 in which it once again alleged that CDC infringed various of Mattel's copyrights. At the time, Claudene Christian was president of CDC and Harry Christian was listed as co-founder of the company and chief financial officer. CDC retained Hicks as its counsel. After the court dismissed CDC's multiple counterclaims, the case . . . settled. . . .

II. The Present Action

Seizing on a loophole in the parties' settlement agreement, within weeks of the agreement, Harry Christian, who was not a signatory to the agreement, retained Hicks as his counsel and filed a federal court action against Mattel. In the complaint . . . Christian alleged that Mattel obtained a copy of the copyrighted Claudene doll in 1996, the year of its creation, and then infringed its overall appearance, including its face paint, by developing a new Barbie line called "Cool Blue" that was substantially similar to Claudene. Christian sought damages in the amount of $2.4 billion and various forms of injunctive relief. . . . [In a letter to Mattel's counsel, Hicks claimed] that an additional doll called "Virginia Tech University Barbie" also infringed the Claudene doll copyright. Hicks, however, never amended the complaint to plead allegations about Virginia Tech Barbie.

Two months after the complaint was filed, Mattel moved for summary judgment. In support of its motion, Mattel proffered evidence that the Cool Blue Barbie doll contained a 1991 copyright notice on the back of its head, indicating that it predated Claudene's head sculpture copyright by approximately six years. Mattel . . . argued that Cool Blue Barbie could not as a matter of law infringe Claudene's head sculpture copyright. Mattel similarly contended that the copyright on the Virginia Tech Barbie's head sculpture also significantly predated the purported copyright on the Claudene head sculpture. Virginia Tech Barbie and other Barbie dolls contained a head sculpture that was copyrighted in 1976 and originally appeared on SuperStar Barbie.

At a follow-up counsel meeting required by a local rule, Mattel's counsel attempted to convince Hicks that his complaint was frivolous. During the videotaped meeting, they presented Hicks with copies of various Barbie dolls that not only had been created prior to 1996 (the date of Claudene's creation), but also had copyright designations on their heads that pre-dated Claudene's creation. Additionally, Mattel's counsel noted that the face paint on some of the earlier-created Barbie dolls was virtually identical to that used on Claudene. Hicks declined Mattel's invitation to inspect the dolls and, later during the meeting, hurled them in disgust from a conference table.

Having been unsuccessful in convincing Hicks to dismiss Christian's action voluntarily, Mattel served Hicks with a motion for Rule 11 sanctions.... Hicks declined to withdraw the complaint during the 21-day safe harbor period provided by Rule 11, and Mattel filed its motion.

Seemingly unfazed by Mattel's Rule 11 motion, Hicks proceeded with the litigation and filed a motion pursuant to Federal Rule of Civil Procedure 56(f) to obtain additional discovery.... Hicks then began filing additional papers that were characterized by frequency and volume. Following official completion of the summary judgment briefing schedule, Hicks filed what was styled as a "supplemental opposition." In those papers, Christian asserted for the first time that the head sculpture of Mattel's CEO Barbie (which was created in 1998) infringed Christian's copyright in the Claudene doll. He did not, however, move for leave to amend the complaint.

Hicks later filed additional papers alleging that several additional Barbie dolls infringed the Claudene sculpture. As with CEO Barbie, no motion for leave to amend the complaint was filed....

III. The District Court Orders

The district court granted Mattel's motions for summary judgment and Rule 11 sanctions. The court ruled that Mattel did not infringe the 1997 Claudene copyright because it could not possibly have accessed the Claudene doll at the time it created the head sculptures of the Cool Blue (copyrighted in 1991) and Virginia Tech (copyrighted in 1976) Barbies. The court also rejected Christian's theory that the Mattel dolls had infringed the totality of Claudene's appearance, including its face paint, because the copyright is "limited in scope and extends only to 3-dimensional sculptures and not 2-dimensional artwork...." Alternatively, the court found that Mattel had been using lighter-colored face paint "on dolls produced before the Claudene doll was created in 1996, such as Colonial Barbie (1994) and Pioneer Barbie (1995)," and therefore could not have infringed the later-created Claudene doll even if the Claudene copyright protected two-dimensional artwork. Finally, the court found that Mattel, as owner of various Barbie head sculpture copyrights, had "the exclusive right to prepare derivative works of its own copyrighted works. See 17 U.S.C. § 106(2). Thus, Mattel has the right to paint and repaint its own copyrighted sculptures."...

As for Mattel's Rule 11 motion, the district court found that Hicks had "filed a meritless claim against defendant Mattel. A reasonable investigation by Mr. Hicks would have revealed that there was no factual foundation for [Christian's] copyright claim." Indeed, the district court noted that Hicks needed to do little more than examine "the back of the heads of the Barbie dolls he claims were infringing," because such a perfunctory inquiry would have revealed "the pre-1996 copyright notices on the Cool Blue and [Virginia Tech] Barbie doll heads." . . .

The district court awarded Mattel $501,565 in attorneys' fees. At the outset of its order, the court summarized the findings in its earlier order, namely that it had "predicated its [Rule 11] decision" on Hicks' filing a frivolous complaint and "further found" that he had "'behaved boorishly, misrepresented the facts and misstated the law.'" In discussing Rule 11's purpose of deterring such conduct, the district court made further findings about Hicks' behavior during prior proceedings—some of which were completely unrelated to this case.

The district court next considered various arguments that Hicks had advanced in opposition to Mattel's fee application. Hicks first contended, without much elaboration, that a fee award would have a "ruinous" effect on his finances and ability to practice law.[4] The district court held, however, that "repeated reprimands and sanctions" imposed in prior litigations "clearly have not had the desired deterrent effect on his behavior," and it concluded that Hicks would not be punished sufficiently if the court were to impose mere "non-monetary sanctions." Hicks also argued (somewhat ironically) that Mattel's fees request was excessive in light of how simplistic it should have been to defend against Christian's action. The district court disagreed, reasoning [as] in Brandt v. Schal Assocs., Inc., 960 F.2d 640, 648 (7th Cir. 1992), [that] the judiciary has "'little sympathy for the litigant who fires a big gun, and when the adversary returns fire, complains because he was firing blanks.'"

Discussion

I. Standard of Review

We review the district court's decision to impose Rule 11 sanctions—and, if they are warranted, the reasonableness of the actual amount

4. Hicks argues that the district court erred in failing to consider his ability to pay such considerable sanctions. Although we note language in In re Yagman, 796 F.2d 1165 (9th Cir. 1986) that appears to require the district court to make such a determination, see id. at 1185, the Yagman case predated the 1993 amendments to Rule 11. The Advisory Committee's notes concerning the amendments indicate that an attorney's financial wherewithal is only one of several factors that a district court may consider in deciding the amount of sanctions. See Fed. R. Civ. P. 11, advisory committee notes, 1993 Amendments, Subdivisions (b) and (c). Here, Hicks had an opportunity to present specific financial information to the district court, but merely argued conclusorily that the sanctions would be "ruinous." The district court acknowledged this argument. Nothing in Rule 11 mandates a specific weighing of this factor, however.

imposed—for abuse of discretion. Cooter & Gell v. Hartmarx Corp., 496 U.S. 384, 401, 405 (1990). . . .

II. Imposition of Rule 11 Sanctions

. . . .

A. General Rule 11 Principles

Filing a complaint in federal court is no trifling undertaking. An attorney's signature on a complaint is tantamount to a warranty that the complaint is well grounded in fact and "existing law" (or proposes a good faith extension of the existing law) and that it is not filed for an improper purpose. . . .

The attorney has a duty prior to filing a complaint not only to conduct a reasonable factual investigation, but also to perform adequate legal research that confirms whether the theoretical underpinnings of the complaint are "warranted by existing law or a good faith argument for an extension, modification or reversal of existing law." Golden Eagle Distrib. Corp. v. Burroughs Corp., 801 F.2d 1531, 1537 (9th Cir. 1986). One of the fundamental purposes of Rule 11 is to "reduce frivolous claims, defenses or motions and to deter costly meritless maneuvers, . . . [thereby] avoid[ing] delay and unnecessary expense in litigation." Id. at 1536. Nonetheless, a finding of significant delay or expense is not required under Rule 11. Where, as here, the complaint is the primary focus of Rule 11 proceedings, a district court must conduct a two-prong inquiry to determine (1) whether the complaint is legally or factually "baseless" from an objective perspective, and (2) if the attorney has conducted "a reasonable and competent inquiry" before signing and filing it. Buster v. Greisen, 104 F.3d 1186, 1190 (9th Cir. 1997).

B. The District Court's Findings Regarding the Meritless Claim

1. Did Hicks Have an Adequate Legal or Factual Basis for Filing the Complaint? Hicks filed a single claim of copyright infringement against Mattel. The complaint charges that the Cool Blue Barbie infringed the copyright in the Claudene doll head. In addition, in a subsequent letter to Mattel's counsel, he claimed that Virginia Tech Barbie also infringed Claudene. Hicks cannot seriously dispute the district court's conclusions that, assuming the applicability of the doctrine of prior creation, Christian's complaint was legally and factually frivolous. Indeed, as a matter of copyright law, it is well established that a prior-created work cannot infringe a later-created one. See Grubb v. KMS Patriots, L.P., 88 F.3d 1, 5 (1st Cir. 1996) (noting that "prior creation renders any conclusion of access or inference of copying illogical").

Copyright infringement requires proof that a plaintiff owns a valid copyright in the work and that the defendant copied the work. Feist Publ'n, Inc. v. Rural Tel. Serv. Co., Inc., 499 U.S. 340, 361 (1991). Proof of copying often revolves around whether the defendant had sufficient access to copy the work. Access is only a theoretical issue in this case, however. By simple logic, it is impossible to copy something that does not exist. Thus, if Mattel created its doll sculptures before CDC created Claudene in 1994, it is factually and legally impossible for Mattel to be an infringer.

The record of creation is telling and conclusive. The Cool Blue Barbie doll uses the Neptune's Daughter doll head which was created in 1991, some six years before the Claudene doll. The Virginia Tech Barbie doll uses the SuperStar sculpture which Mattel created in 1976. The SuperStar doll was the subject of the just-completed federal court litigation, and Hicks should have been well aware of the prior creation, not to mention that the copyright notice (including date of creation) appears prominently on the back of the dolls' heads.

Recognizing the futility of attacking prior creation, Hicks argues that the paint on the Claudene doll's face features a light makeup that is distinctive and that the two Barbie dolls thus infringe Claudene's overall appearance and presentation. This argument fails because, among other things, Mattel used the light face paint on the Pioneer Barbie, which was created two years before the Claudene doll, thus defeating once again any claim of copying.[7] It also bears noting that Mattel has been repainting various doll heads for decades. Under Hicks' theory, CDC's use of an infringing doll head coupled with "new" face paint would result in liability for Mattel's repainting of its prior-created Barbie doll sculptures. Neither common sense nor copyright law countenances such a result, even if the Claudene doll were deemed a derivative work. See Entm't Research Group, Inc. v. Genesis Creative Group, Inc., 122 F.3d 1211, 1220 (9th Cir. 1997) (holding that owners of copyrighted works have broad latitude to copyright derivatives thereof if they have "adequate originality").

In the face of facts and law clearly against his client, Hicks sought to resurrect the copyright claim by deluging the district court with supplemental filings, including entirely new claims regarding a different assortment of Barbie dolls and non-Barbie dolls. The dolls included, for example, the CEO doll, which used the 1991 Neptune's Daughter head with a modified mouth.

The district court did not consider any of Hicks' supplemental filings, noting that Hicks failed to comply with local rules regarding page limitations and typefaces. Given the chameleon nature of the claims and Hicks' flip-flop from the sculpture-plus-painting theory back to the sculpture-only theory, the district court was justified in putting an end to Hicks' serial filings. The district court has considerable latitude in managing the parties' motion practice and enforcing local rules that place parameters on briefing. We cannot say that the court abused its discretion by declining to consider Hicks' multitudinous efforts to circumvent the

7. When shown a Pioneer Barbie doll at his deposition, Christian claimed that it infringed the Claudene doll. This fatal admission, which was made just before Hicks whisked him from the deposition room, underscores the frivolousness of Christian's claim.

court's local rules and to expand the scope of an already frivolous suit. At some point, enough is enough. . . .

2. *Did Hicks Conduct an Adequate Factual Investigation?* The district court concluded that Hicks "filed a case without factual foundation." Hicks, having argued unsuccessfully that his failure to perform even minimal due diligence was irrelevant as a matter of copyright law, does not contest that he would have been able to discover the copyright information simply by examining the doll heads. Instead he argues that the district court did not understand certain "complex" issues. Simply saying so does not make it so. The district court well understood the legal and factual background of the case. It was Hicks' absence of investigation, not the district court's absence of analysis, that brought about his downfall.

The district court did not abuse its discretion in concluding that Hicks' failure to investigate fell below the requisite standard established by Rule 11.

III. The District Court's Additional Findings Regarding Misconduct

Hicks argues that even if the district court were justified in sanctioning him under Rule 11 based on Christian's complaint and the follow-on motions, its conclusion was tainted because it impermissibly considered other misconduct that cannot be sanctioned under Rule 11, such as discovery abuses, misstatements made during oral argument, and conduct in other litigation.

[This] argument has merit. While Rule 11 permits the district court to sanction an attorney for conduct regarding "pleading[s], written motion[s], and other paper[s]" that have been signed and filed in a given case, Fed. R. Civ. P. 11(a), it does not authorize sanctions for, among other things, discovery abuses or misstatements made to the court during an oral presentation. See Bus. Guides, Inc. v. Chromatic Communications Enter., 892 F.2d 802, 813 (9th Cir. 1989) (holding that misstatements made during oral argument cannot constitute sanctionable offenses under Rule 11); In re Yagman, 796 F.2d at 1187 (holding that discovery abuses cannot be sanctioned under Rule 11); see also Fed. R. Civ. P. 11, advisory committee notes, 1993 Amendments, Subdivisions (b) and (c) ("The rule applies only to assertions contained in papers filed with or submitted to the court. It does not cover matters arising for the first time during oral presentations to the court, when counsel may make statements that would not be made if there had been more time for study and reflection.").

In its January 5, 2000, order, the district court cited multiple bases for its Rule 11 findings:

> Mr. Hicks has filed a case without factual foundation. Moreover, while this court cannot evaluate Mr. Hicks' conduct in the litigation before Judge Matz, his conduct in this case and the related one pending before this court has fallen below the standards expected of attorneys practicing in the Central District of California. In the related case, this court has already

> ordered Mr. Hicks to personally pay plaintiff's attorney's fees incurred as a result of his culpable conduct. Order of July 13, 1999 in CV99-4667. In connection with the instant motion and the discovery preceding it, he has behaved boorishly, misrepresented the facts, and misstated the law. Accordingly, the court grants defendant's motion for Rule 11 sanctions against Mr. Hicks.

In connection with the conclusion on boorish behavior, the court cited Hicks' conduct ("tossing Barbie dolls off a table") at a meeting of counsel and his interruption of a deposition following a damaging admission by his client. The charge of misrepresentation of facts was based on a statement made at oral argument that he had never seen a particular catalogue while a videotape of exhibit inspections showed him "leisurely thumbing through the catalogue." Hicks' conflicting representations in pleadings as to the identity of allegedly infringing Barbie dolls was an additional example of misrepresentation noted by the court. Finally, the court determined that Hicks made misrepresentations in his briefs concerning the law of joint authorship in the copyright context. . . .

The orders clearly demonstrate that the district court decided, at least in part, to sanction Hicks because he signed and filed a factually and legally meritless complaint and for misrepresentations in subsequent briefing. But the orders, coupled with the supporting examples, also strongly suggest that the court considered extra-pleadings conduct as a basis for Rule 11 sanctions. . . .

The laundry list of Hicks' outlandish conduct is a long one and raises serious questions as to his respect for the judicial process. Nonetheless, Rule 11 sanctions are limited to "paper[s]" signed in violation of the rule. Conduct in depositions, discovery meetings of counsel, oral representations at hearings, and behavior in prior proceedings do not fall within the ambit of Rule 11. Because we do not know for certain whether the district court granted Mattel's Rule 11 motion as a result of an impermissible intertwining of its conclusion about the complaint's frivolity and Hicks' extrinsic misconduct, we must vacate the district court's Rule 11 orders.

We decline Mattel's suggestion that the district court's sanctions orders could be supported in their entirety under the court's inherent authority. To impose sanctions under its inherent authority, the district court must "make an explicit finding [which it did not do here] that counsel's conduct constituted or was tantamount to bad faith." Primus Auto. Fin. Serv., Inc. v. Batarse, 115 F.3d 644, 648 (9th Cir. 1997) (internal quotation marks omitted). We acknowledge that the district court has a broad array of sanctions options at its disposal: Rule 11, 28 U.S.C. § 1927,[11] and the court's inherent authority. Each of these sanctions alternatives has its own particular requirements, and it is important that the grounds be separately articulated to assure that the conduct at issue falls within the scope of the sanctions

11. Section 1927 provides for imposition of "excess costs, expenses, and attorneys' fees" on counsel who "multiplies the proceedings in any case unreasonably and vexatiously."

remedy. See, e.g., B.K.B. v. Maui Police Dep't, 276 F.3d 1091, 1107 (9th Cir. 2002) (holding that misconduct committed "in an unreasonable and vexatious manner" that "multiplies the proceedings" violates § 1927); Fink v. Gomez, 239 F.3d 989, 991-992 (9th Cir. 2001) (holding that sanctions may be imposed under the court's inherent authority for "bad faith" actions by counsel, "which includes a broad range of willful improper conduct"). On remand, the district court will have an opportunity to delineate the factual and legal basis for its sanctions orders.

IV. The District Court's Decision to Award Attorney's Fees

... Because we are vacating the district court's Rule 11 orders on other legal grounds, we express no opinion at this stage about the particular reasonableness of any of the fees the district court elected to award Mattel. We do, however, encourage the district court on remand to ensure that the time spent by Mattel's attorneys was reasonably and appropriately spent in relation to both the patent frivolousness of Christian's complaint and the services directly caused by the sanctionable conduct.[12] See Fed. R. Civ. P. 11, advisory committee notes, 1993 Amendments, Subdivisions (b) and (c) (noting that attorneys' fees may only be awarded under Rule 11 for those "services directly and unavoidably caused" by the sanctionable conduct).

Conclusion

We vacate the district court's Rule 11 orders and remand for further proceedings consistent with this opinion.

Vacated and Remanded.

Note: No-Holds-Barred Advocacy

Counsel for Business Guides could plausibly claim to have been under time pressure to file. Counsel for Kraemer could plausibly claim to have made as diligent a prefiling inquiry as limited resources and the recalcitrance of the defendant would permit. Is there any excuse for Hicks's

12. For example, because the action was frivolous on its face, why would Mattel's attorneys need to spend 700 hours ($173,151.50 in fees) for the summary judgment motion and response? Although Hicks clearly complicated the proceedings through multiple filings, Mattel's theory and approach was stunningly simple and required little explication: (1) Mattel's Barbie dolls and face paint were prior copyright creations that could not infringe the after-created Claudene doll and (2) Christian was neither a contributor to nor owner of the copyright. This is not to say that Hicks' defense of the motion necessarily called for a timid response, but neither does it compel a bazooka approach.

conduct in *Christian*, or does he seem to you like the kind of lawyer for whom Rule 11 sanctions are obviously appropriate? Should it matter that the amount of the sanctions might end his practice (see footnote 4 supra)? Is the evidence of Hicks's misconduct in other cases relevant to the question whether he should be sanctioned in this case?

Even if Hicks made a woefully inadequate prefiling inquiry, what would a reasonable lawyer have done? Would it have been enough to check the copyright stamps on the back of Barbie's head when Mattel's counsel made the dolls available for inspection? In *Kraemer*, the Seventh Circuit places a lot of weight on the fact that Lawton hired a private investigator who was stonewalled. That leaves open the question how far a lawyer should go when there is no stonewalling, when time and money permit open inquiry into the facts. Consider Intamin Ltd. v. Magnetar Tech. Corp., 483 F.3d 1328 (Fed. Cir. 2007), in which the Federal Circuit upheld a district court's decision not to impose sanctions in a patent infringement case involving competing brake systems for roller coasters. The defendant, Magnetar, argued that Intamin's prefiling inquiry was inadequate

> because it did not obtain and physically cut open the metal casing on the magnets in Magnetar's brake system. The record shows that Magnetar's system encased the magnets in metal tubes. Accordingly, a visual inspection would not disclose the orientation of the magnets within the tubes. In Judin v. United States, 110 F.3d 780, 784 (Fed. Cir. 1997), this court held that the district court abused its discretion in not granting Rule 11 sanctions against a patentee who failed to obtain a sample of the product as part of its pre-filing investigation. However, *Judin* did not create a blanket rule that a patentee must obtain and thoroughly deconstruct a sample of a defendant's product to avoid violating Rule 11. Rather, in *Judin*, the patentee could have easily obtained a sample of the accused device (a bar code scanner) for a nominal price from the post office. In this case, the technology presented the patentee with unreasonable obstacles to any effort to obtain a sample of Magnetar's amusement ride brake system, let alone the difficulty of opening the casing.
>
> In lieu of cutting open the casing, Intamin might have tested a Magnetar device for magnetic polarities. In *Q-Pharma*, however, this court did not impose on a patentee a Rule 11 obligation to perform a simple chemical test on a sample to determine its composition. 360 F.3d at 1302. Instead, this court found that the patentee satisfied its Rule 11 obligations with other reasonable pre-filing inquiries. Id. Here, the district court determined: "In light of the other information [Intamin] had at the time of filing . . . [its] pre-filing inquiry was reasonable." Reconsideration Decision, slip op. at 7. In particular, the district court noted that Intamin "evaluated the patent portfolio, analyzed the patent's validity, determined the scope of the patent's claims, and performed an infringement analysis." Id. The district court further determined that Intamin "reviewed publicly available documents on [Magnetar's] brakes, inspected [Magnetar's] brakes as installed on a roller coaster, took photos of the brakes, and reviewed the brakes with experts." Id. Thus the district court determined that Intamin's pre-filing inquiry was reasonable under the circumstances. Id. This court discerns no abuse of discretion in the district court's determination.

483 F.3d at 1338. Cf. United Stars Ind. v. Plastech Engineered Prods., Inc., 525 F.3d 605 (7th Cir. 2008) (defendant sanctioned for filing counterclaim in commercial contract dispute with no evidentiary support); Garr v. U.S. Healthcare Inc., 22 F.3d 1274 (3d Cir. 1994) (inadequate investigation by attorney who relied on *Wall Street Journal* story and copied another attorney's complaint before filing securities fraud suit); Ideal Instruments, Inc. v. Rivard Instruments, Inc., 243 F.R.D. 322 (N.D. Iowa 2007) (awarding sanctions for reliance on bogus expert report in motion for preliminary injunction without proper prefiling investigation), 245 F.R.D. 381 (N.D. Iowa 2007) (adjusting attorney fee award downward to comport with Rule 11 focus on deterrence and to punish attorneys seeking sanctions for block billing); Guidry v. Clare, 442 F. Supp. 2d 282 (E.D. Va. 2006) (inadequate investigation in frivolous unfair debt collection practices suit arising from attempts by defendant to collect $62 bounced check for daughter's cheerleading lessons).

Note: "Later Advocating" Written Submissions

The Ninth Circuit remanded *Christian* for a reassessment of the sanctions award in part because it worried the trial court had punished Hicks for "boorishness" and for misrepresentations made during oral argument. The opinion emphasizes that Rule 11 sanctions are "limited to '*paper*[s]' signed in violation of the rule." The 1993 Amendments, however, make sanctions available for "presenting to the court a pleading, written motion, or other paper," and "presenting" explicitly includes "signing, filing, submitting, or *later advocating*" a written submission. See Fed. R. Proc. 11, 1993 Advisory Committee Notes. Has the Ninth Circuit ignored the "later advocating" language of the rule?

Compare the reasoning in *Christian* with the analysis of the Second Circuit in O'Brien v. Alexander:

> Our review of the sanctions imposed is a more difficult and delicate task [than the review of the sufficiency of the complaint]. A lawyer fighting for his client's rights in a courtroom is expected to be as wily and resourceful as Daniel Webster was in his defense of Jabez Stone in the foreclosure action brought against him by the Devil, to whom Stone had sold his soul. Stephen Vincent Benét, The Devil and Daniel Webster, reprinted in Law in Action: An Anthology of the Law in Literature 139 (Crown Publishers 1947). Counsel must be able to think and argue on his or her feet in a courtroom, a forum where conditions change rapidly. Yet zealous oral advocacy must be conducted according to the rules and counsel may not "knowingly make a false statement of law or fact," Model Code of Professional Responsibility DR 7-102(A.5). To violate this professional standard may result in sanctions under Rule 11. Such sanctions were imposed for two oral statements made by counsel. In our view, one violated Rule 11, the other did not. . . .
>
> [T]he 1993 amendment expanded the scope of litigating lawyers' obligations in a manner directly relevant to the present case. It permits sanctions

based upon the "presenting" of a paper—rather than limiting sanctions to those papers that bear an attorney's signature—and defining "presenting" broadly as "signing, filing, submitting, or later advocating." Fed. R. Civ. P. 11 (b). The Advisory Committee explained the new provision as follows:

> The rule applies only to assertions contained in papers filed with or submitted to the court. It does not cover matters arising for the first time during oral presentations to the court, when counsel may make statements that would not have been made if there had been more time for study and reflection. However, a litigant's obligations with respect to the contents of these papers are not measured solely as of the time they are filed with or submitted to the court, but include reaffirming to the court and advocating positions contained in those pleadings and motions after learning that they cease to have any merit. For example, an attorney who during a pretrial conference insists on a claim or defense should be viewed as "presenting to the court" that contention and would be subject to the obligations of subdivision (b) measured as of that time.

The new language and the Advisory Committee's comments make evident that although sanctions may now be based on litigants' oral representations, not all oral statements are sanctionable under Rule 11, even when they advance baseless allegations or objectively frivolous arguments. Moreover, to avoid imposing sanctions for oral statements regarding matters that do not flow directly from the signed paper—even when such new matters arise in the course of a presentation relating generally to the paper—the amended Rule 11 requires a close nexus between the oral statement and the underlying written paper. As the Advisory Committee stated, the rule applies only to "assertions" contained in the underlying paper, not to that paper generally or in the abstract.

Consequently, we are unable to accept the district court's view that Rule 11 applies to oral advocacy whenever an attorney advocates a signed paper. *O'Brien*, 898 F. Supp. at 176. Such a broad rule is completely contrary to the Advisory Committee's recognition that oral advocacy often requires lawyers to address new matters without much opportunity for study and reflection. In fact, because oral advocacy almost always relates in some way to a prior signed paper, adopting the district court's proposition would entail a significant and unintended expansion of Rule 11's scope.

That an oral statement is made in the course of advocating a pleading or motion is not enough; to be sanctionable the oral statement must relate directly to a particular representation contained in the document that the lawyer is then advocating. Thus, to be sanctionable an oral representation must meet two requirements: (1) it must violate the certification requirement of Rule 11(b), e.g., by advocating baseless allegations, and (2) it must relate directly to a matter addressed in the underlying paper and be in furtherance of that matter to constitute advocating within the meaning of subsection (b).

101 F.3d 1479 (2d Cir. 1996) (upholding sanctions for misrepresentations linked directly to frivolous complaint made by plaintiff's counsel during oral argument).

Note: The Standard of Review on Appeal

Recall that the Seventh Circuit in *Kraemer* reviewed the lower court's decision on what it called an "abuse of discretion" standard. At least in theory, this means that the lower court's decision should be treated with great deference. The Supreme Court endorsed this deferential standard of review for Rule 11 sanctions in Cooter & Gell v. Hartmarx Corp.:

> The considerations involved in the Rule 11 context are similar to those involved in determining negligence, which is generally reviewed deferentially. . . . Familiar with the issues and litigants, the district court is better situated than the court of appeals to marshall the pertinent facts and apply the fact-dependent legal standard mandated by Rule 11. Of course, this standard would not preclude the appellate court's correction of a district court's legal errors, e.g., . . . relying on a materially incorrect view of the relevant law in determining that a pleading was not "warranted by existing law or a good faith argument" for changing the law. An appellate court would be justified in concluding that, in making such errors, the district court abused its discretion. . . . Pierce v. Underwood, 487 U.S. 552 (1988), strongly supports applying a unitary abuse of discretion standard to all aspects of a Rule 11 proceeding. In *Pierce,* the Court held a District Court's determination under the Equal Access to Justice Act (EAJA), 28 U.S.C. § 2412(d) (1982 ed.), that "the position of the United States was substantially justified" should be reviewed for an abuse-of-discretion. As a position is "substantially justified" if it "has a reasonable basis in law and fact," 487 U.S. at 566, n.2, EAJA requires an inquiry similar to the Rule 11 inquiry as to whether a pleading is "well grounded in fact" and legally tenable. . . .
>
> Two factors the Court found significant in *Pierce* are equally pertinent here. First, the Court indicated that "as a matter of the sound administration of justice," deference was owed to the "judicial actor . . . better positioned than another to decide the issue in question." 487 U.S. at 559-560. Because a determination whether a legal position is "substantially justified" depends greatly on factual determinations, the Court reasoned that the district court was "better positioned" to make such factual determinations. See 487 U.S. at 560. A district court's ruling that a litigant's position is factually well grounded and legally tenable for Rule 11 purposes is similarly fact specific. . . .
>
> Second, *Pierce* noted that only deferential review gave the district court the necessary flexibility to resolve questions involving "multifarious, fleeting, special, narrow facts that utterly resist generalization." Id. at 561-562. . . . The issues involved in determining whether an attorney has violated Rule 11 likewise involve "fact-intensive, close calls." Shaffer & Sandler 15. . . . The district court is best acquainted with the local bar's litigation practices and thus best situated to determine when a sanction is warranted to serve Rule 11's goal of specific and general deterrence. Deference to the determination of courts on the front lines of litigation will enhance these courts' ability to control the litigants before them. Such deference will streamline the litigation process by freeing appellate courts from the duty of reweighing evidence and reconsidering facts already weighed and considered by the district court; it will also discourage litigants from pursuing marginal appeals, thus reducing the amount of satellite litigation.

496 U.S. 384, 402-404 (1990).

Was the Seventh Circuit appropriately deferential to the district court's decision in *Kraemer*? Isn't the district court in a better position to know the facts and circumstances supporting sanctions in the case? As you read the cases that follow, notice how the standard of review affects the way the appellate courts treat the decision to grant or deny sanctions made by the courts below.

2. "Improper Purpose," Frivolous Claims, and Arguments for Legal Change

Saltany v. Reagan

886 F.2d 438 (D.C. Cir. 1989)

BUCKLEY, D.H. GINSBURG, and SENTELLE, Circuit Judges.
PER CURIAM.

On April 13, 1988, fifty-five Libyan citizens and residents filed suit in the district court seeking damages for injuries, death, and property loss sustained in the 1986 United States air strike on Libya. Substantial damages were sought from the United States, President Reagan, senior civilian and military officials, and from the United Kingdom and Prime Minister Thatcher as well. Plaintiffs sought to hold the British defendants liable on the basis that the Prime Minister gave the United States permission to use British air bases in the air strike. Plaintiffs asserted claims under the Federal Tort Claims Act, 28 U.S.C. § 2671, et seq., the Foreign Claims Act, 10 U.S.C. § 2734, the Alien Tort Claims Act, 28 U.S.C. § 1350, the Racketeer Influenced and Corrupt Organizations Act, 18 U.S.C. § 1961, et seq., and various constitutional and common law theories, including the "tort law of Libya."

Upon motions, the district court dismissed plaintiffs' claims as to all defendants. See Saltany v. Reagan, 702 F. Supp. 319 (D.D.C. 1988). Plaintiffs appealed and defendants have moved this court for summary affirmance: By separate order this date, we affirm the decision dismissing plaintiffs' case.

Both the United States and the British defendants also moved the district court for sanctions pursuant to Federal Rule of Civil Procedure 11, on the grounds that plaintiffs abused the judicial process and needlessly imposed upon defendants the cost of defending against an action not supported by existing law or by any good faith argument for the extension, modification, or reversal of existing law. The district court found that plaintiffs' counsel "surely knew" that the case "offered no hope whatsoever of success," but it declined to impose sanctions in the interest of keeping the courthouse door open as a forum for suits "brought as a public statement of protest of Presidential action with which counsel (and, to be sure, their clients) were in profound disagreement."

The United Kingdom has cross-appealed from, and seeks summary reversal of, the decision denying sanctions. Additionally, the United Kingdom seeks attorneys' fees and costs, pursuant to both Federal Rule of Appellate Procedure 38 and 28 U.S.C. § 1927, for the costs of defending against a frivolous appeal. For the reasons stated below, we reverse and remand the district court decision with regard to the Rule 11 sanction, and grant the United Kingdom's motion for attorneys' fees and costs on appeal pursuant to Rule 38.

I. Federal Rule of Civil Procedure 11

The United Kingdom asserts that the district court erred in denying its Rule 11 motion for attorneys' fees and costs, relying upon the well established principle that the court must impose a sanction "once it has found a violation of the rule." Weil v. Markowitz, 829 F.2d 166, 171 (D.C. Cir. 1987) (footnote omitted); Westmoreland v. CBS, 770 F.2d 1168, 1174-1175 (D.C. Cir. 1985). Thus, the question is whether the district court found, or should have found, that plaintiffs violated Rule 11. If so, then a sanction must be imposed.

Here, the district court observed that plaintiffs, citizens or residents of Libya, could not be "presumed to be familiar with the rules of law of the United States." *Saltany*, 702 F. Supp. at 322. The court noted, however, that "[i]t is otherwise . . . with their counsel. The case offered no hope whatsoever of success, and plaintiffs' attorneys surely knew it." Id.

The court thus found, in substance if not in terms, that plaintiffs' counsel had violated Rule 11; yet the court did not impose a sanction. Instead, the court went on to observe that because the "injuries for which the suit is brought are not insubstantial," the case is not "frivolous so much as it is audacious." Id. The seriousness of the injury, however, has no bearing upon whether a complaint is properly grounded in law and fact. We may agree with the district court that the suit is audacious—that is not sanctionable in itself—but, we do not see how filing a complaint that "plaintiffs' attorneys surely knew" had "no hope whatsoever of success" can be anything but a violation of Rule 11.

Nonetheless, surmising that the suit was brought as a public statement of protest, the district court opined that courts can "serve in some respects as a forum for making such statements, and should continue to do so." Id. (citing Talamini v. Allstate Insurance Co., 470 U.S. 1067, 1070-71 (1985) (Stevens, J., concurring in dismissal of appeal)). We do not conceive it a proper function of a federal court to serve as a forum for "protests," to the detriment of parties with serious disputes waiting to be heard. In any event, reliance upon *Talamini* was inappropriate. That opinion, representing the views of Justice Stevens and three other justices, argued in opposition to awarding sanctions against an attorney who had pursued an unmeritorious application for review in an otherwise unremarkable unfair trade practices action. It in no way speaks to the use of the courts as any sort of political or protest forum. Whether punitive sanctions should be imposed for invoking the judicial process is properly fit into the equation when considering whether a Rule 11 violation has occurred. Here, the district court had already determined in effect that a violation had occurred. Therefore, we grant the United Kingdom's motion for summary reversal and remand the matter to the district court for imposition of an appropriate sanction.

II. Federal Rule of Appellate Procedure 38

The United Kingdom (with the support of the United States) seeks to recover the attorneys' fees and costs it incurred by reason of plaintiffs' pursuit of a frivolous appeal. We grant attorneys' fees and costs under Rule 38, and thus do not consider the alternate claim under 28 U.S.C. § 1927.

The basis for the United Kingdom's request is that the Supreme Court's decision in Argentine Republic v. Amerada Hess Corp., 109 S. Ct. 683 (1989), which was issued about a month after the decision of the district court, utterly foreclosed plaintiff's argument that the United Kingdom is subject to the jurisdiction of the courts of the United States.

In *Amerada Hess*, the Court ruled unanimously and unequivocally that the Foreign Sovereign Immunities Act ("FSIA") provides the "sole basis for obtaining jurisdiction over a foreign state in our courts." *Amerada Hess*, 109 S. Ct. at 688. Furthermore, the Court held that a foreign state's use of military force allegedly in violation of international law fell outside any of the exceptions to sovereign immunity provided by the FSIA. . . .

. . . [W]e find that *Amerada Hess* clearly bars plaintiffs' claim against the United Kingdom, and that so much was apparent to counsel for plaintiffs before they imposed upon the United Kingdom the burden of this appeal. Accordingly, we grant the United Kingdom's motion for attorneys' fees and costs to be assessed against counsel. . . .

So ordered.

---

*Saltany v. Bush**

960 F.2d 1060 (D.C. Cir. 1992)

WALD, EDWARDS and D.H. GINSBURG, Circuit Judges.

PER CURIAM.

. . . Counsel challenge the award of Rule 11 and Rule 38 sanctions against them, as directed by a previous panel. The law of the case doctrine bars this challenge. See, e.g., Melong v. Micronesian Claims Commn., 643

* President Bush is substituted for former President Reagan, insofar as the latter is sued in his official capacity. See Fed. R. App. P. 43(c).

F.2d 10, 17 (D.C. Cir. 1980). We see no clear error combined with manifest injustice, nor does Cooter & Gell v. Hartmarx Corp., 496 U.S. 384 (1990), constitute intervening law on the Rule 11 issue. The prior panel determined that the District Court had found a Rule 11 violation, see Saltany v. Reagan, and there is no basis under *Cooter* or any other precedent for us to reconsider this determination. Moreover, *Cooter* makes clear that sanctions must be imposed once a violation is found. See 100 S. Ct. at 2454, 2460.

Counsel also argue for a nonmonetary Rule 11 sanction, but the District Court considered this possibility and reasonably exercised its discretion to impose a fine instead. . . .

WALD, Circuit Judge, dissenting.

I regretfully dissent from the majority's affirmance of the district court's imposition of Rule 11 sanctions against plaintiffs' counsel. The district court had originally denied appellees' motion for Rule 11 sanctions, concluding that "[i]t cannot . . . be said that the case is frivolous so much as it is audacious." Saltany v. Reagan, 702 F. Supp. 319, 322 (D.D.C. 1988).

On the first appeal, this court nonetheless concluded that, when the district judge commented in his opinion that "[t]he case offered no hope whatsoever of success, and plaintiffs' attorneys surely knew it," id., he "found, in substance if not in terms, that plaintiffs' counsel had violated Rule 11; yet the court did not impose a sanction." The prior panel remanded to the district court for the "imposition of an appropriate sanction." Id. On remand, the district judge not unreasonably interpreted the remand order "as an unequivocal direction to it" to impose Rule 11 sanctions, and he ordered plaintiffs' counsel to pay $10,000 each to the British appellees.

Under the "law of the case" doctrine, a decision on an issue of law made at one stage of a case ordinarily becomes a binding precedent to be followed in successive stages of the same case. However, this doctrine "is not an inexorable command that rigidly binds a court to its former decisions but rather is an expression of good sense and wise judicial practice." Carpa, Inc. v. Ward Foods, Inc., 567 F.2d 1316, 1320 (5th Cir. 1978). As this court has stated on several occasions, "[t]o warrant divergence from the law of the case, a court must not only be convinced that its earlier decision was erroneous; it must also be satisfied that adherence to the law of the case will work a grave injustice." Melong v. Micronesian Claims Commn., 643 F.2d 10, 17 (D.C. Cir 1980); Laffey v. Northwest Airlines, Inc., 642 F.2d 578, 585 (D.C. Cir. 1980); see also Browning v. Navarro, 887 F.2d 553, 556 (5th Cir. 1989) ("We have the discretion to ignore a previous decision if substantially different evidence has been presented, there has been an intervening change in the law, or the prior decision was clearly erroneous and it would work a manifest injustice.").

Despite the extremely high threshold that any departure from past holdings in the same case must meet, I feel one is justified here. Cooter & Gell v. Hartmarx Corp., 496 U.S. 384 (1990), decided after the first appeal in this case, does represent an "intervening change in the law" to the extent that it establishes a "clearly erroneous" standard rather than a *de novo* review standard for a review of a decision to impose (or not to impose) Rule 11 sanctions. Although the prior panel opinion did not expressly identify its standard in reviewing the district judge's denial of Rule 11 sanctions, in my view, it did not treat his express decision not to impose sanctions with the required deference by finding that he had ruled on the factual predicates of Rule 11 but had erred in not properly applying the law to those findings.

In order to find a violation of Rule 11, the district judge must conclude that, to the best of counsel's knowledge, information, and belief formed after reasonable inquiry, the pleading was neither "well grounded in fact" nor "warranted by existing law or a good faith argument for the extension, modification, or reversal of existing law," or that the pleading was "interposed for an[] improper purpose, such as to harass or to cause unnecessary delay or needless increase in the cost of litigation." Fed. R. Civ. P. 11. The district judge here explicitly declined to make any such finding. His remark that the case "offered no hope whatsoever of success, and plaintiffs' attorneys surely knew it" is not an appropriate substitute for the conclusions required by Rule 11. Even if the district judge's conclusion that appellants' counsel knew that they had no hope of prevailing was correct—a "fact" put in some doubt both by the enormous time and energy expended by counsel in preparation of their case and the expert opinions they were able to assemble on behalf of the legitimacy of their clients' cause of action—that conclusion is still not equivalent to a finding that counsel did not have a "good faith argument for the extension, modification, or reversal of existing law." Surely the propriety of Rule 11 sanctions should not depend on the degree of optimism with which counsel approach litigation. The prior panel's conclusion that the district judge had found "in substance" that appellants' counsel had violated Rule 11 was itself, in my view, "clearly erroneous," and the sanctions imposed on the basis of that substituted finding have created a "manifest injustice."

The effect of reaching beyond a district judge's clear exercise of his discretion not to impose Rule 11 sanctions and not to make the specific fact findings required by Rule 11 by reconstructing that decision out of side comments about the likelihood of plaintiffs' prevailing (and counsels' knowledge thereof) cannot but chill well-founded future suits, whose time in the law may not yet have come, but whose value in exposing abuses and educating courts and the public is substantial. Cognizant that the district judge had no realistic choice but to impose sanctions on remand, I dissent from the result which our prior decision required of him.

Note: Lawyers for Causes

One of the lawyers sanctioned in this case was Ramsey Clark, a former Attorney General of the United States. Here is his professional biography, reprinted from Martindale-Hubbell Law Directory, a selective directory of practicing lawyers:

> *RAMSEY CLARK,* born Dallas, Texas, December 18, 1927; admitted to bar, 1951, Texas; 1956, U.S. Supreme Court; 1969, District of Columbia; 1970, New York. *Education:* University of Texas (B.A., 1949); University of Chicago (M.A., 1950; J.D., 1950). Assistant Attorney General, 1961-1964, Deputy Attorney General, 1965-1966 and Attorney General of the United States, 19670-1969.
>
> *General Civil and Criminal Practice. Constitutional Trials and Appeals.*

Why would a man with this impeccable resume bring a case like *Saltany,* which had so little chance of success? Do you think that if the 1993 version of the Rule applied, and defendants had warned Mr. Clark of their intention to seek sanctions, he would have used the so-called safe harbor and withdrawn the complaint?

Your political view of whether bombing is a "proper" response to state-sponsored terrorism influences whether you think the case was properly filed, doesn't it? Brian L. Davis, in Quaddafi, Terrorism and the Origins of the U.S. Attack on Libya (1990), argues strongly that bombing with a high risk of hitting civilian populations is misguided policy and wrong morally. Should a lawyer deciding whether to take a case read up on its moral and political implications?

Generally speaking, when you think of yourself as a lawyer deciding whether to take a case that reaches beyond disputes between individuals, what factors enter your decision? Would the fact that the clients have an arguable claim and are able to pay handsomely for representation be enough to induce you to take the case?

There is a long-standing professional norm of providing legal services without attempting to prejudge the moral, political, or ideological merits of a case. Scholars refer to this as the neutrality norm, the service norm, or, more precisely, "thin professional identity." Norman W. Spaulding, Reinterpreting Professional Identity, 74 U. Colo. L. Rev. 1 (2003). It reflects both a professional ideal of diligently serving all who require legal services (or at least all who require services for the purpose of bringing *nonfrivolous* claims) and two practical considerations: First, because human judgment is fallible, lawyers are likely to misjudge a case or client, particularly at the outset when they know little about the specific facts. Second, if lawyers prejudge cases, popular, or at least well-paying and uncontroversial, clients will likely enjoy meaningful access to the law, but others will not—both the quantity of clients served and the quality of client service provided would vary according to the preferences of individual lawyers. The rules of professional conduct generally endorse the service norm, see ABA Model Rule 1.2(b), but they do not require it. A lawyer is *encouraged* to be open to take all clients she can competently serve, especially clients who cannot afford to pay, and clients whose claims are controversial and who may therefore have trouble finding another lawyer. But, excepting court-ordered appointment, a lawyer generally cannot be *sanctioned* for refusing a case. In practice, this means lawyers are free to pick and choose.

Another tradition endorses "cause lawyering"—not only allowing, but encouraging, lawyers to seek out (or refuse) cases based on moral, political, and ideological criteria or personal identification with a client and/or her cause. It too reflects the professional ideal of expanding access to legal services. Many cause lawyers have dedicated themselves to serving clients others will not, either because the clients cannot pay, or because they are members of marginalized social groups, or, as is all too often the case, both. See Austin Sarat and Stuart Scheingold, Cause Lawyering: Political Commitments and Professional Responsibilities (1998).

Anthony D'Amato argues, in The Imposition of Sanctions for Claims Arising from the U.S. Air Raid on Libya, 84 Am. J. Int'l L. 705 (1990), that the underlying claims in *Saltany* were strong ones, and that it was wrong in the face of international law precedent to dismiss the case summarily. As to the sanctions against the plaintiffs' lawyers, he notes:

> It may very well be true that there was no hope of success in a case brought before these particular judges. The three-judge panel on appeal consisted of judges who had all been appointed by President Reagan. The complaint accused President Reagan of being a war criminal. It is not unreasonable to suppose that such judges would view the complaint with abhorrence and disgust.

Id. at 707. Are hopeless claims the same as frivolous ones? Are lawsuits in federal courts one way to express political opinion and dissent? Or is this an improper purpose?

Indeed, you might wonder why an "improper purpose" should matter if the underlying claim is nonfrivolous. Is this language in Rule 11 superfluous? Or does it only seem so as it applies to complaints, versus other pleadings governed by Rule 11? Compare Sussman v. Bank of Israel (Appeal of Lewin), 56 F.3d 450 (2d Cir. 1995) (holding that a party should not be sanctioned for filing a nonfrivolous complaint simply because one of his multiple motives in filing it may have been improper), with F.D.I.C. v. Maxxam, Inc, 523 F.3d 566 (5th Cir. 2008) (plaintiff "would violate Rule 11 if it filed a case that it reasonably thought had merit, but pursued it in a manner calculated to increase the costs of defense," rejecting view that "the filing of a paper for an improper purpose is immunized from Rule 11 sanctions simply because it is well grounded in fact and law"), and Szabo Food Serv., Inc. v. Canteen Corp., 823 F.2d 1073, 1083 (7th Cir. 1987) (stating that "filing a colorable suit for the purpose of imposing expense on the defendant rather than for the purpose of winning" is sanctionable under Rule 11). But see Townsend v. Holman Consulting Corp., 929 F.2d 1358, 1362 (9th Cir. 1990) (holding that "a determination of improper purpose must be supported by a determination of frivolousness when a complaint is at issue").

Note: Post-Pleading Improper Purposes

The *Saltany* cases involve attempts to get in the courthouse door. But the obligations of Rule 11 do not end with the pleadings. The Rule covers not just pleadings, but every "written motion, and other paper" presented to the court, and sanctions can be imposed for "later advocating" any prior filing. See Rule 11(b). Consider Whitehead v. Food Max of Mississippi, Inc., 332 F.3d 796 (5th Cir. 2003) (en banc). After winning a $3.4 million jury verdict against Kmart for negligently failing to provide adequate parking lot security (the plaintiff and her daughter were abducted from a Kmart parking lot in Jackson, Mississippi), plaintiff's lawyer used a handwritten request to obtain a writ of execution from the clerk of the court before Kmart had a chance to appeal. He then notified the media and proceeded to the nearest Kmart with two federal Marshalls in order to seize money from the cash registers and store vault. Although interrupted by a stay order from the court once it learned of the lawyer's conduct, the lawyer proceeded to give statements to the media about Kmart's "outrageous" and "arrogant" actions and claimed that Kmart had refused to pay the judgment. Id. at 800. The district court fined the lawyer $8,000 (Kmart's attorney's fees for opposing the writ of execution) and the Fifth Circuit affirmed, reasoning that shameless self-promotion and deliberately seeking to embarrass Kmart were improper purposes within the meaning of Rule 11(b)(1). In his defense, the lawyer claimed that "almost everything an attorney in litigation does . . . is designed to embarrass an opponent in one way or another" and "establishing a reputation for success in the representation of clients is the most professional way for a lawyer to build a practice," id. at 807. The court categorically rejected this argument:

> The execution did not require Minor to accompany the two United States Marshalls to the Kmart (especially where, as here, the involved property was well-known, open, and obvious). See Fed. R. Civ. P. 69. And, the execution certainly did not require the media's presence at the Kmart or the improper comments Minor made there to the media.

Id. at 806-807. Notice that the improper purpose here is not linked to the content of the lawyer's written application for a writ of execution, but rather to conduct following the issuance of the writ. Cf. *Christian*, supra.

Would your view of the case change if it turned out that plaintiff was not even legally entitled to a writ of execution when her lawyer applied for it? See id. at 800, 803-804 (Kmart claimed, and the district court agreed, that Kmart was entitled to an automatic 10-day stay of execution; the Fifth Circuit held that improper purpose was sufficient ground for sanction and declined to consider, as an additional ground, whether the application for the writ was based on a reasonable inquiry into the law).

A postscript: In a separate opinion, the Fifth Circuit reversed the jury verdict and remanded for a new trial because it found that the jury was unduly influenced by the "passion and prejudice" of the plaintiff's lawyer's closing argument. See Whitehead v. Food Max of Miss., Inc., 163 F.3d 265, 276-281 (5th Cir. 1998).

3. "Warranted by Existing Law..."

Frantz v. U.S. Powerlifting Federation

836 F.2d 1063 (7th Cir. 1987)

EASTERBROOK, Circuit Judge.

The complaint charged the International Powerlifting Federation (IPF), its American affiliate the United States Powerlifting Federation (USPF), and Conrad Cotter, the president of the USPF, with conspiring to monopolize the sport of weight lifting. The plaintiffs include two weight lifters who were disqualified from participating in events sponsored by the IPF because they participated in events sponsored by the American Powerlifting Federation (APF), a rival to the USPF....

The IPF did not file an appearance, and a default judgment was entered against it. The district court dismissed the complaint against the USPF and Cotter under Fed. R. Civ. P. 12(b)(6) for failure to state a claim on which relief may be granted, after plaintiffs' counsel conceded that the complaint was insufficient. The plaintiffs then filed an amended complaint against USPF, dropping Cotter as a defendant. The district court dismissed this complaint under Rule 12(b)(6), finding it dependent on a theory of conspiracy between the USPF and the IPF that could not be sustained. The court also held that Cotter is entitled to attorneys' fees as a sanction under Fed. R. Civ. P. 11 for the initial complaint against him, because the plaintiffs did not have a plausible argument about how the USPF could conspire with its officers. The court denied the USPF's request for sanctions, however, because it concluded that the plaintiffs' amended complaint had a colorable, though unsuccessful, theory.

Cotter's request for fees came to $44,700: $4,300 to obtain dismissal of the initial complaint, and $40,400 to pursue the request for fees (and ask the district court to ensure that the amended complaint did not apply to him). The size of the request surprised—shocked—the district judge. The court vacated its award under Rule 11, writing:

> Sanctions were awarded because it was extremely clear to the court that there was no legal or factual basis for naming Cotter as a defendant. Cotter's attorneys, however, contend that they have spent at least 39.535 hours drafting that portion of the motion to dismiss, memorandum in support of the motion and summary of the motion which pertained to Cotter. They

> have requested $4,289.48 in fees as to this activity (they also request an additional $40,401.40 in legal fees). Apparently, the issues regarding Cotter's legal and factual involvement in the case were vastly more complicated than this court had determined. . . . Therefore, the court is sua sponte reconsidering the award . . . and is hereby denying the award of attorneys' fees in toto.

Cotter appeals from the vacation of the award in his favor, and the USPF appeals the denial of its request for sanctions.

I

The suit against Cotter was frivolous, given Copperweld Corp. v. Independence Tube Corp., 467 U.S. 752 (1984), decided a year before this suit began. Rule 11 requires counsel to do legal research before filing, and to be aware of legal rules established by the Supreme Court. A party may not strike out blindly and rely on its opponent to do the research to make the case or expose its fallacies. . . .

The court vacated the sanction because the request for fees showed that counsel spent about 40 hours preparing and filing the motion to dismiss. This showed, according to the court, that the case was "vastly more complicated" than the court had believed. Perhaps this is a droll way to say that Cotter's total bill was out of line. We consider this possibility later. If the court meant the remark seriously, it is insufficient. Whether the complaint violated Rule 11 depends on what the plaintiffs and their lawyer did—whether they performed the legal and factual work necessary to avoid filing an unwarranted paper—not on what the defendants did with the complaint. That the defendants may have taken too long to find *Copperweld* does not absolve plaintiffs; the violation of Rule 11 exists at the moment the paper is filed. If Cotter's lawyers were inefficient, then Cotter must pay them (or counsel must swallow the costs, as counsel who waste time recognize when exercising billing judgment). The defendants' inefficiency does not show that the case was "vastly more complex" than the district court first thought. *Copperweld* holds that corporate officers cannot conspire with their corporations for purposes of the antitrust laws. The complaint was based on a conspiracy between officer and corporation; this was doomed after *Copperweld*, and sanctions were in order.

For what it is worth, we doubt that 40 hours is preposterous for preparing a response to this complaint. Cotter's lawyers had to find *Copperweld* and then consider the possibility that plaintiffs were trying to create an exception to that case. This might entail researching the treatment of *Copperweld* in later cases and interviewing Cotter, a resident of Florida, to discover whether there were facts (and therefore a theory) lurking behind the outline provided by the complaint. Antitrust suits are easy to file yet notoriously costly to defend, and achieving the dismissal of an antitrust case in under 40 hours is unusual.

What is even more unusual is that counsel took about 400 hours to pursue the compensation for 40 hours, a ratio of billing time to productive time that would be fatal when collecting from one's own clients. The request for sanctions was an adversarial proceeding, which eats up time that need not be spent when collecting from friendlier clients, but a ratio of ten to one still is extreme. The district court was entitled to be skeptical of this bill. . . .

The complaint in this case was frivolous, which calls at a minimum for censure of Victor D. Quilici, the plaintiffs' lawyer. Whether it calls for amercement—and, if so, whether Cotter or the Treasury is the appropriate beneficiary—is something the district court should consider as an initial matter. . . .

There is no single "right" sanction, any more than there is one "right" penalty for bank robbery. Much must be left to the good judgment of the courts of first instance. . . . Because this case involved a request for a tidy sum, the court should explain why it chose to equate the two sanctions (if that remains its disposition after reconsideration). . . . [A]n explanation need not be complex, and a judge need not pretend that there is a single right answer that can be reached by deductive logic or defended with precision. The absence of ineluctable answers does not imply the privilege to indulge an unexamined gestalt. This case must be remanded so that the district court may put its reasoning on record—a process that, by inducing critical scrutiny of one's initial reactions, often improves the quality of decisions.

II

The district court rejected outright the USPF's request for attorneys' fees under Rule 11[, saying] only this about the USPF's request for sanctions under Rule 11:

> The allegations of seven types of anticompetitive conduct by the USPF and the IPF are largely conclusory. However, there are at least a few facts in the complaint which describe the anti-competitive conduct. Although it is difficult to determine the exact nature of the alleged anti-competitive conduct in the absence of greater specificity, the allegations on the whole appear to be based on plausible legal theories.

The court appears to be making two points. One is that if a complaint contains any formally correct statement of a legal theory, then the pleader's obligation under Rule 11 has been satisfied. This is incorrect. A claim may be sufficient in form but sanctionable because, for example, counsel failed to conduct a reasonable investigation before filing. And the inclusion of one sufficient (and adequately investigated) claim does not permit counsel to file a stream of unsubstantiated claims as riders.

Each claim takes up the time of the legal system and the opposing side. A single claim in an antitrust case may occasion the expenditure of hundreds or thousands of hours, as opposing counsel try to verify or refute the allegations and theories. Rule 18(a) permits the liberal joinder of claims, but each joined claim, potentially the basis of separate litigation, must have a foundation—the same foundation it would have needed if the claims had been pursued separately. Just as evidence that Perkins is a thief does not justify an accusation that he is a murderer, so a colorable legal theory about boycotts of weight lifters does not excuse a baseless allegation about price fixing in the television business. Rule 11 applies to all statements in papers it covers. Each claim must have sufficient support; each must be investigated and researched before filing.

The court's other point is that the complaint contains sufficient facts from which the judge may discern the legal claims. The USPF takes issue with this, arguing that the complaint was shy the necessary facts. The USPF's reply brief asserts: "This court has made clear that even if Mr. Quilici possessed sufficient information in his files to support plaintiffs' claims, his failure to include it in the complaint violated Rule 11." The USPF does not cite the cases where we "made clear" this proposition. There aren't any such cases. The USPF has confused Rule 8 with Rule 11. Rule 8 determines how much information has to be in the complaint—not much, as both the language of Rule 8 and the forms attached to the Rules show. The complaint should contain a "short and plain statement of the claim showing that the pleader is entitled to relief," Rule 8(a)(2). It is not only unnecessary but also undesirable to plead facts beyond limning the nature of the claim (with exceptions, see Rule 9, that do not concern us). Bloated, argumentative pleadings are a bane of modern practice. American Nurses' Assn. v. Illinois, 783 F.2d 716 (7th Cir. 1986). Rule 11 requires not that counsel *plead* facts but that counsel *know* facts after conducting a reasonable investigation—and then only enough to make it reasonable to press litigation to the point of seeking discovery. Rule 11 neither modifies the "notice pleading" approach of the federal rules nor requires counsel to prove the case in advance of discovery. See also Szabo [Food Servs. v. Canteen Corp., 823 F.2d 1073 (7th Cir. 1987)] (Rule 11 requires only an "outline of a case" before filing the complaint, though it does require enough investigation to discover that outline).

This is a fine line. Rule 11 must not bar the courthouse door to people who have some support for a complaint but need discovery to prove their case, yet the need for discovery does not excuse the filing of a vacuous complaint. No matter how such inquiries come out, however, courts must ask the right question: whether the side filing the pleading knew enough at the time, not whether it spread all on the record. Rule 11 states that the signature verifies that the paper is "well grounded in fact," not that all the facts are contained in the paper.

The case is remanded for further inquiry, under the standards of [our previous cases,] into the support for each of the theories contained in the complaint.

Reversed and Remanded.

Note: Nonfrivolous Arguments for Extension of the Law

Read Rule 11(b)(2) about the duty of the lawyer (and parties representing themselves) to get the law right. The pleader who wants to change or extend the law must make a "nonfrivolous" argument for doing so. Previously, the Rule tracked most professional ethics by requiring that lawyers seeking extension, modification, or reversal of existing law do so in "good faith." The Advisory Committee notes that the new wording sets a more objective standard. Do you agree?

In addition to the duty to file only meritorious claims, most codes of professional responsibility also include an injunction to reveal controlling adverse authority to the tribunal. See, e.g., Model Rule 3.3: "A lawyer shall not knowingly: . . . (2) fail to disclose to the tribunal legal authority in the controlling jurisdiction known to the lawyer to be directly adverse to the position of the client and not disclosed by opposing counsel."

For an article about the profession's standards of internal regulation and Rule 11, see Georgene Vairo, Rule 11 and the Profession, 67 Fordham L. Rev. 589 (1998) (finding that Rule 11 replaced bar discipline in many respects and that practice under the 1983 version often decreased civility and professionalism).

Frantz was decided under the previous version of the Rule, making the imposition of sanctions mandatory once a Rule 11 violation was found. Would the result have been different under the current version? One difference that flows from changing the mandatory nature of sanctions is the standard of review by the appellate court. When the trial judge has discretion, the appellate court usually reviews for abuse of discretion, rather than for the correctness of the decision. Are there good reasons for putting the main responsibility for administering Rule 11 in the trial judge's hands?

Judge Easterbrook is not the only judge to express surprise at a fee bill submitted by attorneys prevailing on a Rule 11 motion. See Kathrein v. Monar, 218 F. App'x 530 (7th Cir. 2007) (upholding sanctions against plaintiff found to have filed suit against his ex-wife's new husband for the improper purpose of harassing and "runn[ing] up Monar's legal fees," but reversing the $56,858.15 fee award reflecting 200 hours of attorney time as unreasonable for a case dismissed on the pleadings).

4. "Factual Contentions Have Evidentiary Support"

Arista Records LLC v. Does 1-27

584 F. Supp. 2d 240 (D. Me. 2008)

JOHN A. WOODCOCK, JR., District Judge.

A consortium of copyright owners and licensees claim that unknown University of Maine students have infringed their rights in copyrighted songs in violation of federal copyright laws. The Defendants, who remain anonymous, filed dispositive, discovery, and sanctions motions. The Court denies each motion.

I. Motions to Dismiss

A. *Procedural History*

The Plaintiffs filed two symmetrical cases against Doe Defendants, alleging copyright infringement.[3] . . . Seven Defendants filed the first motion to dismiss on November 14, 2007. Two other defendants later joined that motion. The Court referred the motions to dismiss to the United States Magistrate Judge, who filed her Recommended Decision on January 25, 2008. Defendants filed a joint objection to the Recommended Decision on February 11, 2008, and Plaintiffs filed their response on February 28, 2008. . . . The Court has reviewed and considered the magistrate judge's Recommended Decision, together with the entire record, and has made a de novo determination of all matters adjudicated by the magistrate judge's Recommended Decision.

B. The Court Can Consider the Purpose of the Complaint When Applying the Newly-Refined Pleading Standards of Twombly

The Defendants first pin their hopes on *Twombly*. Acknowledging that under pre-*Twombly* standards, there "would have been no question but that the conclusory complaint filed by plaintiffs here satisfied the 'short and plain statement' requirement of [Rule 8]," they nevertheless contend that *Twombly* mandates a "new and significant construction" of Rule 8, which justifies dismissal. Defendants argue that *Twombly* not only directs courts to consider the purpose and context of the litigation when deciding motions to dismiss pursuant to Rule 12(b)(6), but also changes significantly the notice pleading standards of Rule 8(a). In her Recommended Decision, the magistrate judge wrote that she was "not persuaded that *Twombly* ushered in a new era for Rule 12(b)(6) contests in which federal courts are expected to adjust the pleading standard depending on an assessment of the social value of a particular litigation." The Court agrees.

. . . [In Part 1 of Section B, the Court discussed the *Twombly* pleading standard. EDS.]

2. *Twombly* and the Context of the Litigation

. . . Seizing on dicta, Defendants claim *Twombly* invites a cost/benefit analysis at this stage of a litigation: the higher the cost of proceeding to judgment, the more beneficial to hold the pleadings to a higher standard

3. Aside from differences in the parties, the complaints in the cases are identical. Each contains an attachment setting forth the Internet Protocol (IP) addresses for each Doe Defendant. Though necessarily different, the attachments are formally identical; neither alleges more legally relevant facts about any Defendant Doe.

under Rules 8(a) and 12(b)(6). There is some language in *Twombly* that supports this view. Responding to the dissent's contention that discovery would be phased and limited, *Twombly* noted that "determining whether some illegal agreement may have taken place between unspecified persons at different [Incumbent Local Exchange Carriers] (each a multibillion dollar corporation with legions of management level employees) at some point over seven years is a sprawling, costly, and hugely time-consuming undertaking not easily susceptible to the kind of line drawing and case management that the dissent envisions." *Twombly*, 127 S. Ct. at 1967 n.6. *Twombly* also observed that care at summary judgment and well-crafted jury instructions will do nothing to cure the problem of discovery abuse, given that "the threat of discovery expense will push cost-conscious defendants to settle even anemic cases before reaching those proceedings." Id. at 1967. The heightened *Twombly* standard thus responded to factors which, though not unique to antitrust litigation, apply with special force to large-scale litigation based on an inherently ambiguous cause of action. What remains unclear is how the court should take *Twombly* concerns into account in simpler litigation.[7] . . .

The First Circuit has answered the threshold question of whether *Twombly* announces a new standard. It does. Since *Twombly*, the First Circuit has reiterated that the standard for assessing a motion to dismiss is whether "the complaint states facts sufficient to establish a 'claim to relief that is plausible on its face.'" Trans-Spec Truck Serv., Inc. v. Caterpillar Inc., 524 F.3d 315, 320 (1st Cir. 2008) (quoting *Twombly*, 127 S. Ct. at 1974); Rodriguez-Ortiz v. Margo Caribe, Inc., 490 F.3d 92, 95-96 (1st Cir. 2007). In ACA Fin, Guar. Corp. v. Advest, Inc., the First Circuit summed up *Twombly* by saying that it gave Rule 12(b)(6) "more heft." 512 F.3d 46, 58 (1st Cir. 2008).

. . . [Nevertheless,] *Twombly* is not to be construed to create a sliding scale of heightened review, depending on the complexity and potential expense of the underlying litigation.[8] If this analysis is correct, the

7. Interpreting and applying *Twombly*, courts have puzzled over the difficulties associated with disentangling the holding and the dicta. See, e.g., United States ex rel. Snapp, Inc. v. Ford Motor Co., 532 F.3d 496, 502 n.6 (6th Cir. 2008); Aktieselskabet AF 21 November 2001 v. Fame Jeans Inc., 525 F.3d 8, 15 (D.C. Cir. 2008) (concluding that *Twombly* "leaves the long-standing fundamentals of notice pleading intact"); Limestone Dev. Corp. v. Vill. of Lemont, 520 F.3d 797, 803-04 (7th Cir. 2008) (cautioning that *Twombly* "must not be overread"); Robbins v. Okla. ex rel. Dep't of Human Servs., 519 F.3d 1242, 1247 (10th Cir. 2008) (describing the new formulation as "less than pellucid"); Phillips v. County of Allegheny, 515 F.3d 224, 233-35 (3d Cir. 2008) (describing *Twombly* as "confusing"); Anderson v. Sara Lee Corp., 508 F.3d 181, 188 n.7 (4th Cir. 2007); Iqbal v. Hasty, 490 F.3d 143, 155-58 (2d Cir. 2007) (referring to "conflicting signals" in *Twombly*).

8. Extrapolating from a recent case in which the Third Circuit stated that "[c]ontext matters in notice pleading," *Phillips*, 515 F.3d at 233; see *Robbins*, 519 F.3d at 1248 (agreeing with *Phillips* that "context matters"), Defendants contend that the Plaintiffs' "nationwide, systematic and coordinated campaign," alleged strong-arm settlement tactics, and the possible asymmetry between actual and statutory damages provide the relevant context here. See Defs.' Obj. at 3-5. Even under *Phillips*, the only material context under Rule 8(a) is "the type of case" being litigated. *Phillips*, 515 F.3d at 233. In other words, the elements of the claim and the historical facts alleged in the complaint provide the relevant

Defendants' contentions about how the recording industry Plaintiffs have addressed similar lawsuits are not properly considerations for a Rule 12 (b)(6) dismissal.

Assuming, for the sake of argument, that *Twombly* requires an assessment of context in addition to an analysis of pleadings, the Defendants here can hardly be said to be in the same position as the defendants there. The only discovery Plaintiffs have sought is from Defendants' Internet Service Provider (ISP), third party University of Maine. Perhaps recognizing that *Twombly*'s discovery-related concerns do not apply to them, Defendants instead base their argument for a higher pleading standard on the type of information likely to be discovered and the extent of their possible liability for statutory damages. In the context of this case, the Family Educational and Privacy Rights Act (FERPA), 20 U.S.C. § 1232g, affords comparatively weak protections, which do not transform Plaintiffs' Complaint into one that improperly seeks nothing more than confidential information. Furthermore, the Court does not share Defendants' view that their potential liability for statutory damages in excess of Plaintiffs' actual damages somehow requires that they remain anonymous. Although the Court has not found in any party's motion papers reference to the Online Copyright Infringement Liability Limitation provisions of the Digital Millennium Copyright Act (DMCA), 17 U.S.C. § 512, that statute specifically provides for copyright owners' discovery of the very information Plaintiffs seek here. See 17 U.S.C. § 512(h) ("A copyright owner . . . may request the clerk of any United States district court to issue a subpoena to a service provider for identification of an alleged infringer. . . ."). Accordingly, the DMCA specifically sanctions the disclosure of anonymous internet users' identities. Even if the Court agreed that *Twombly* granted the discretion to hold a complaint to a higher standard where discovery could be expensive, or result in lost anonymity and liability for statutory damages, the Court is not persuaded that present circumstances warrant exercise of such discretion.[12]

3. Applying the Newly Refined Pleading Standards of *Twombly*

After *Twombly*, the task under Rule 12(b)(6) remains essentially the same with a slightly enhanced degree of scrutiny. First, a court "continues to take all factual allegations as true and to draw all *reasonable* inferences in favor of the plaintiff." Rodriguez-Ortiz, 490 F.3d at 96 (emphasis in original). Second, a court "need not credit a complaint's bald assertions or legal conclusions." Glassman v. Computervision Corp., 90 F.3d 617, 628 (1st Cir. 1996) (citation and internal quotation omitted). Third, a court

---

Rule 12(b)(6) context. Extraneous suggestions of the Plaintiffs' conduct in other, similar cases, including possible, even probable, voluntary dismissal by Plaintiffs following limited discovery, are irrelevant. *Twombly* cannot fairly be read to instruct otherwise.

12. The Defendants contradict themselves. They first claim that the Plaintiffs use this type of lawsuit for discovery and settlement purposes only, pressuring the revealed defendants to quick settlement in the face of exorbitant statutory damages. In the next breath, they liken these law suits to expensive and complex antitrust litigation.

must determine whether the complaint's factual allegations "'possess enough heft' to set forth 'a plausible entitlement to relief.'" Gagliardi v. Sullivan, 513 F.3d 301, 305 (1st Cir. 2008) (quoting *Twombly*, 127 S. Ct. at 1966-67). . . .

Defendants object to the Recommended Decision on the grounds that it does not, under the proper standard, satisfactorily analyze the fit between the Complaint's factual allegations and the elements of copyright infringement. Defendants protest that Plaintiffs' Complaint contains only "bald assertions" and "problematic suppositions" that fall short of alleging "'a plausible entitlement to relief.'" Id. (quoting *Twombly*, 127 S. Ct. at 1967). . . .

The Complaint, considered with the two Exhibits A, survives Defendants' motion to dismiss. Plaintiffs' Complaint alleges facts that set forth "a plausible entitlement to relief," Rodriguez-Ortiz, 490 F.3d at 95 (1st Cir. 2007), under the Copyright Act, 17 U.S.C. § 101 et seq. There are only two elements to a claim of copyright infringement: (1) copyright ownership and (2) violation of "any of the exclusive rights of the copyright owner," which include reproduction and distribution rights. 17 U.S.C. §§ 106, 501. Plaintiffs have alleged ownership, and pleaded facts in support of those allegations. Plaintiffs have also alleged that "each Defendant, without the permission or consent of Plaintiffs, has continuously used, and continues to use, an online media distribution system to download and/or distribute to the public" the same copyrighted recordings. Compl. ¶24.

Here, the Complaint does not merely allege distribution and reproduction; it contains factual allegations specific to each Defendant. Each Defendant is identified by his or her IP address. Associated with each IP address is a detailed list of songs that were allegedly distributed to or downloaded from others on the file sharing network. The Complaint, as drafted, gives the Defendants "fair notice of what the . . . claim is and the grounds upon which it rests." *Twombly*, 127 S. Ct. at 1964 (alteration in original) (internal quotation omitted).

Furthermore, each IP address is alleged to have actively participated in either "Gnutella" or "AresWarez," networks that allow users to share electronic files anonymously over the internet. "Gnutella technology," no stranger to copyright litigation, was used in certain "Morpheus" software that, as the Supreme Court recently observed, allows users to "download desired files directly from peers' computers." Metro-Goldwyn-Mayer Studios Inc. v. Grokster, Ltd., 545 U.S. 913, 922 (2005). In *Grokster*, the Court held StreamCast, the distributor of the Morpheus software, liable for the copyright infringing acts of its users. Id. at 919. Although it is true that StreamCast and Grokster conceded their users' copyright infringement in that case, id. at 923, *Grokster* demonstrates that it is plausible under *Twombly* to infer that Defendants in fact both downloaded copyrighted songs and shared them with other users. After all, the *Grokster* Court distinguished "item[s] with substantial lawful as well as unlawful uses" from those "good for nothing else but infringement," and found that Morpheus and the Gnutella technology belong in the latter category. *Grokster*, 545 U.S. at 932. Because it is reasonable to infer that the

Defendants downloaded and shared files, the Court draws those inferences in Plaintiffs' favor, as it should. *Rodriguez-Ortiz*, 490 F.3d at 96. Unlike the allegations of parallel conduct in *Twombly*, which were consistent with both independent action and conspiracy, allegations of file sharing and membership in a peer-to-peer network are most consistent with downloading and distribution in violation of Plaintiffs' exclusive rights.

Defendants nonetheless argue that although ownership of copyrighted music files and membership in a file sharing network may allow for an inference that they made copyrighted songs available to others, a claim for infringement requires more. In their original motion to dismiss, Defendants make passing reference to one authority on this critical question. Defendants claim "[i]t is highly unlikely that merely offering to sell or give away a copy (as opposed to selling it or giving it away) is an infringing act." . . . It is regrettable that the parties did not more fully develop this point, because there is considerable authority for the proposition that storage of copyrighted recordings and making them available on a network does not amount to copyright infringement. See, e.g., Atl. Recording Corp. v. Howell, 554 F. Supp. 2d 976, 981-82, 987 (D. Ariz. 2008) (denying summary judgment to recording company and holding that "[m]erely making a copy available does not constitute distribution").

There is also authority for the [contrary] proposition that infringement of exclusive distribution rights under 17 U.S.C. § 106(3) includes "making available" liability based on the fact that an infringer has taken all but the ultimate step of actual "distribution." See, e.g., Hotaling v. Church of Jesus Christ of Latter-Day Saints, 118 F.3d 199, 203 (4th Cir. 1997) (finding libraries infringed exclusive distribution rights by maintaining unauthorized copies of microfiche in collection, listing them in their catalogs, and making them available to the borrowing or browsing public). . . .

The most recent First Circuit opinion on the issue . . . stated that posting songs on a website "might be infringing." Whether it is likely infringing or "highly unlikely," as Defendants claim, the Court need not resolve at this early stage.

Twombly did not "impose a probability requirement at the pleading stage." 127 S. Ct. at 1965. All that is required are "enough fact[s] to raise a reasonable expectation that discovery will reveal evidence," id., of either distribution or downloading. By alleging facts regarding (1) Plaintiffs' ownership of copyrighted songs, (2) Defendants' membership in a file-sharing network, and (3) Defendants' holding out those songs in such a way that final distribution for downloading depends only on the proper functioning of file-sharing software installed on Defendants' computers, Plaintiffs' Complaint survives Defendants' motions to dismiss.

C. The Plaintiffs Violated the Rules of Joinder

In her Recommended Decision, the magistrate judge suggested that the Court enter an order to show cause why Plaintiffs should not be sanctioned pursuant to Rule 11. The magistrate judge recommended that the order direct the Plaintiffs to demonstrate that they have adequate evidentiary support for their factual contentions regarding joinder of Plaintiffs and Defendants in this action. Id.; see Fed. R. Civ. P. 11(b)(3). The Court did not act on the recommendation, and did not issue the show cause order. Presumably encouraged by the magistrate judge's recommendation, the Defendants moved for sanctions pursuant to Rule 11 based in large part on the joinder issue. The merits of Defendants' sanctions motion are discussed infra Part III.

Rule 20(a)(2) permits joinder of a number of defendants in one cause of action if:

> (A) any right to relief is asserted against them jointly, severally, or in the alternative with respect to or arising out of the same transaction, occurrence, or series of transactions or occurrences; and (B) any question of law or fact common to all defendants will arise in the action.

Fed. R. Civ. P. 20(a)(2). Rule 20 is permissive. Compare Fed. R. Civ. P. 20 (a)(2) (stating that "[p]ersons . . . *may* be joined in one action as defendants"), with Fed. R. Civ. P. 19 (addressing required joinder of parties). The purpose of the rule is "to promote trial convenience and expedite the final determination of disputes, thereby preventing multiple lawsuits." 7 Charles Alan Wright, Arthur R. Miller & Mary Kay Kane, Federal Practice and Procedure § 1652, at 395 (3d ed. 2001). The Court's discretion, however, is not unlimited. To be joined, the right to relief must relate to or arise out of the same transaction or occurrence. Id. § 1653.

The Plaintiffs point out that the Complaint alleges the Doe Defendants (1) engaged in copyright infringement on the internet; (2) uploaded and downloaded copyrighted sound recordings using peer-to-peer networks; and (3) accessed the peer-to-peer network though a common ISP—the same University. The Plaintiffs further assert that twenty-five of the twenty-seven Doe Defendants used the same peer-to-peer network and many infringed the same copyrighted sound recording or different copyrighted sound recordings from the same artist. Finally, they allege that the Doe Defendants have been "active participants in what can only be described as an on-line music swap meet, unlawfully copying copyrighted works from other users and distributing such works to other users."

Based on these allegations, the Court is not as troubled as the magistrate judge by joinder of these Doe Defendants in one lawsuit. In fact, the Plaintiffs attached a list of over three hundred court orders which they claim have approved joinder in similar cases. At the very least, it seems premature to make a final determination that joinder is not permissible under Rule 20. Finally, as Rule 21 makes clear, "[m]isjoinder of parties is not a ground for dismissing an action." Fed. R. Civ. P. 21. Absent dismissal, the Court could sua sponte "on just terms, add or drop a party." Id. The remedy, then, would be to break up this one lawsuit into individual causes of action, an alternative that does not exactly resonate with practicality.

Regarding the magistrate judge's concern about the possibility of abuse of the litigation process by the Plaintiffs, the Court is again more sanguine. It is true, as the magistrate judge observes, that the Plaintiffs have not identified and served the Doe Defendants and that they seek their names through this lawsuit. It is also possible that once identified and served, the Doe Defendants will determine that it is in their best interests to resolve the case. But, the Court begins with the premise that the Plaintiffs have a statutorily protected interest in their copyrighted material and that the Doe Defendants, at least by allegation, have deliberately infringed that interest without consent or payment. Under the law, the Plaintiffs are entitled to protect their copyrighted material and it is difficult to discern how else in this unique circumstance the Plaintiffs could act. Not to act would be to allow those who would take what is not theirs to remain hidden behind their ISPs and to diminish and even destroy the intrinsic value of the Plaintiffs' legal interests.

. . . [The court's discussion of discovery requests and plaintiff's allegedly unlawful investigative techniques is omitted. EDS.]

III. Rule 11 Motion for Sanctions

Defendants argue that Plaintiffs violated Rule 11 by filing a complaint "solely for the improper purpose of obtaining discovery of confidential educational records," in violation of Rule 11(b)(1), and by joining all Plaintiffs and all Defendants in one action without "good faith evidentiary support" for such joinder under Rule 20 in violation of Rule 11(b)(3).

The Court is perplexed by the Defendants' first claim. They start with the proposition that "[i]f a complaint is not filed to vindicate a plaintiff's rights in court, its purpose is improper per se," and it therefore does exactly what Rule 11(b)(1) proscribes. The Defendants further reason that because Plaintiffs do not know the identities of the Defendants, the Plaintiffs cannot possibly hope to vindicate their rights until these identities are discovered. The Defendants conclude that the Plaintiffs' only possible purpose in filing this suit must be to discover identifying information, not to vindicate their rights, all in violation of Rule 11(b)(1). However, simply because the Plaintiffs' first step in this lawsuit was to move for expedited discovery does not make their purpose for commencing it either improper or unrelated to vindicating their rights under the Copyright Act. After all, it is undisputed that without such discovery, the Plaintiffs have no hope of vindicating their rights.

The only way the Defendants' argument has any force is to assume that the Plaintiffs' access to the identifying information itself is somehow "improper" in the Rule 11(b)(1) sense. The Court is unwilling to make this assumption; indeed, the Court has decided it is proper for Plaintiffs to discover this information. On two occasions, the Defendants' own arguments belie this supposition: "Plaintiffs' sole purpose . . . is to . . . seek immediate discovery that would otherwise be protected by [FERPA],"; Plaintiffs' use of a Complaint "to gain access to otherwise shielded information . . . supports a finding of improper purpose." The Court does not share the Defendants' view that a litigant's animating purpose becomes improper under Rule 11(b)(1) by merely engaging the judicial machinery in pursuit of a necessary and proper remedy, otherwise out of reach, whether by expedited discovery order or other preliminary relief.

The Defendants' second claim, that Plaintiffs have no "good faith evidentiary support" for joining Plaintiffs and Defendants in this case, relies on a misreading of Rule 11(b)(3) that they borrowed, it appears, from the magistrate judge's recommendation for a show cause order.[26] For the Defendants to gain any traction, they must point the Court to factual contentions for which Plaintiffs lack evidentiary support. The Defendants, like the magistrate judge, suggest that allegations of conformity with the permissive joinder requirement are factual allegations that require evidentiary support, which Plaintiffs do not have.[27] At the same time, however, the Defendants do not believe that Plaintiffs' factual contentions—that Defendants belonged to the same file sharing network and engaged in copyright infringement by similar means—"create the common nexus of facts required to meet the transaction test set forth in Rule 20." The Defendants cannot have it both ways: the Rule 20(a) requirements are either factual matters or legal tests.

The Court is not alone in finding that the "transaction test" is what Defendants think it is, a legal test: "The transaction and common-question requirements prescribed by Rule 20(a) are not rigid tests. They are flexible concepts used by the courts to implement the purpose of Rule 20 and therefore are to be read as broadly as possible whenever doing so is likely to promote judicial economy." Wright, Miller & Kane § 1653, at 415; cf. Abdullah v. Acands, Inc., 30 F.3d 264, 269 n.5 (1st Cir. 1994) (approving of another court's application of the "same transaction or occurrence test" to

26. The magistrate judge took Plaintiffs to task for appearing to run afoul of Rule 11(b)(3), which she quoted as requiring "that a representation in a pleading have evidentiary support." Rec. Dec. at 11 n.5; but see Fed. R. Civ. P. 11(b)(2)-(3) (distinguishing between "factual contentions" and "legal contentions," and requiring "evidentiary support" only of the former, and allowing "legal contentions [to pass it] warranted by existing law or by a nonfrivolous argument for extending, modifying, or reversing existing law or for establishing new law"). In the magistrate judge's view, Plaintiffs' allegation that their claims "arise[] out of the same series of transactions or occurrences," Compl. ¶20, are factual contentions that require evidentiary support. The Court disagrees.

27. In their Complaint, Plaintiffs allege that

> each Defendant [has] . . . committed violations of the same law (e.g., copyright law), by committing the same acts (e.g., the downloading and distribution of copyrighted sound recordings owned by Plaintiffs), and by using the same means (e.g., a file-sharing network) that each Defendant accessed via the same ISP. Accordingly, Plaintiffs' right to relief arises out of the same series of transactions or occurrences, and there are questions of law or fact common to all Defendants such that joinder is warranted and appropriate here.

Compl. ¶20.

a set of facts similar to those before the Acands court). Accordingly, while Plaintiffs' factual allegations may or may not support the legal contention that the transaction test is satisfied, the Court will not sanction Plaintiffs for making legal contentions in their Complaint and denies Defendants' motion for sanctions.

IV. Conclusion

The Court concurs with the recommendation of the United States Magistrate Judge for the reasons set forth in her Recommended Decision and for the reasons set forth in Part I supra that the motions to dismiss should be denied. . . .

In accordance with Part III supra, the Court denies Defendant Does #16 and #18's Motion for Sanctions Pursuant to Rule 11.

So Ordered.

Notes and Questions

1. We have not yet reached the rules for joinder in our study, but, much like the test for the doctrine of relation back, which we covered in our analysis of Rule 15, the basic test for permissive joinder focuses on whether parties are joined for claims arising from the same "transaction or occurrence." Are you satisfied by the court's holding that this test is not "factual" within the meaning of Rule 11(b)(3)? Even if the test is purely a question of law, Rule 11(b)(2) would apply, wouldn't it? Defendants seem to be arguing that plaintiffs could not possibly have known, at the time the complaint was filed, whether the defendants had coordinated their copyright infringement. Common use of the university's ISP seems a slender reed for joining them, but the recording industry has regularly invoked this procedural tool to thwart file sharing. Can you see the reasons why (apart from the *in terrorem* effect it creates on campus when lots of students are served with process)? One possible reason is that the scope of discovery, as we will see in Chapter 3, is affected by the scope of the pleadings. Alleging widespread infringement at a school opens up the prospect of broader discovery than litigation against individual students.

2. In *Frantz*, Judge Easterbrook rightly observes that mere failure to state a claim is not the same as filing a frivolous suit—the Rule 11 and Rule 12 (b)(6) standards are indeed different. In *Arista Records*, however, we have the opposite issue: whether a complaint that survives a motion to dismiss (now assessed under the more strict *Twombly* standard) could nevertheless give rise to Rule 11 sanctions. The court in *Arista Records* focuses on improper purpose and the grounds for joinder in the Rule 11 section, but one has the feeling that the court may have been influenced in its Rule 11 inquiry by its earlier determination that the case states a claim under

Twombly. Whether each defendant is properly joined is not entirely independent of whether one sees file sharing as a form of copyright infringement.

Young v. City of Providence ex rel. Napolitano

404 F.3d 33 (1st Cir. 2005)

BOUDIN, Chief Judge.

In the course of a civil rights action, the district court determined that three attorneys for the plaintiff had violated Rule 11 of the Federal Rules of Civil Procedure. The court revoked the pro hac vice status of the two attorneys who were not members of the court's bar and formally censured one of the two. Young v. City of Providence, 301 F. Supp. 2d 187 (D.R.I. 2004). In this decision, we address appeals by all three attorneys; the merits of the civil rights action are the subject of the plaintiff's separate appeal resolved in our companion decision issued today sub nom.

The civil rights action grew out of a tragedy that occurred in January 2000 in Providence, Rhode Island. Two police officers (Michael Solitro and Carlos Saraiva), responding to the scene of a nighttime disturbance at a restaurant, shot and killed an off-duty officer—Cornel Young, Jr., who, with his weapon drawn, was attempting to assist them. In June 2001, Young's mother, acting on her own behalf and as executor of Young's estate, brought a civil rights action in district court asserting claims under section 1983, 42 U.S.C. § 1983 (2000), and under state law, against the city, various officials and the two officers.

The case, assigned to Judge Mary Lisi, was a complex one. This was due in part to the difficulty in reconstructing exactly what had happened in the nighttime encounter, in part to the different tiers of liability asserted against various defendants (direct, supervisory and municipal) and in part to plaintiff's aim to show a pattern or policy of incompetent hiring and inadequate training. Both Barry Scheck and Nicholas Brustin of the New York firm of Cochran, Neufeld & Scheck LLP were admitted pro hac vice to represent the plaintiff; Robert Mann of the Providence firm of Mann & Mitchell acted as local counsel. Scheck was admitted, to replace his partner Johnnie Cochran, Jr., only in September 2003—shortly before a "phase I" trial was to begin focusing on the conduct of Solitro and Saraiva.

The litigation was the subject of extensive publicity; among other facets, the officers who fired the shots were white while Cornel Young was black (and the son of a senior Providence police officer). Scheck, who acted as lead counsel after his admission, was at odds with the district judge over various matters, including the division of the trial into two phases. Yet the incident that gave rise to the Rule 11 findings, censure and revocation of pro hac vice status was narrowly focused and arose against the following background.

By September 2003, extensive discovery had been conducted. One of the issues in the discovery, and in the ensuing trial, concerned the precise movements of Cornel Young and of Solitro. The former had been inside the restaurant; Solitro and Saraiva had approached the building through the parking lot to find a man (later identified as Aldrin Diaz, who had caused an earlier disturbance) pointing a gun out of the window of a Chevrolet Camaro parked in the lot in front of the restaurant. Solitro broke cover and started toward the car. Young, moving to assist, emerged from the restaurant with his own weapon drawn and was shot by Solitro and Saraiva. Just where Young and Solitro had stood and moved had a bearing on who was at fault in the episode.

During discovery, Solitro had drawn a line indicating his own movement in relation to other physical landmarks including the Camaro; the line was drawn on a clear overlay laid atop a made-to-scale diagram prepared by the state attorney general in his own investigation. Scheck planned to rely importantly on the diagram in his opening to explain to the jury the defense version of what had happened. However, in September 2003, out-takes filmed by a local TV station on the night of the shooting became available and, from defense counsel's viewpoint, raised questions about the accuracy of the diagram—at least as to the location of the Camaro. Until then it had apparently been expected that both sides would agree to the admission of the diagram.

At the final pre-trial conference on September 19, 2003, the district court was told briefly that there was a dispute about the diagram. . . . Defense counsel then told the district judge that the defense objected to the diagram as inconsistent with photographs made from the out-takes, and the judge responded that the parties should confer to see whether they could stipulate as to the matter. The judge told plaintiff's counsel: "If you can't agree to a stipulation on that, then I'm going to have to tell you to stay away from it because you're going to need testimony to explain it to the jury."

Scheck then offered as a compromise to stipulate that the diagram conflicted with photographs made from the film out-takes, but the next morning defense counsel declined the offer. Scheck again sought unsuccessfully to persuade the judge that he ought to be allowed to refer to the diagram in the opening. Then, with the opening statements about to begin, Scheck signed a stipulation drafted by defense counsel that the diagram was inaccurate as to the location of the Camaro and that the actual alignment of the car was as described in the stipulation. On this basis, Scheck was allowed to use the diagram in the opening, but he was not allowed thereafter to elicit testimony contradicting the stipulation.

Over the next several days of trial, further examination of the photographs persuaded Scheck and his colleagues that the out-takes did not contradict the diagram. A young associate at Scheck's firm was told to draft a memorandum to support a motion seeking relief from the stipulation on grounds of mistake. The memorandum was filed with the court on October 16, 2003 in mid-trial, after being reviewed and then signed by all three counsel—Scheck, Brustin and Mann. That same morning the judge directed counsel to re-read the memorandum, saying that she was disturbed by representations made in the memorandum, "particularly as they relate to the actions of the court."

The memorandum, set forth in full at 301 F. Supp. 2d at 199-204, started with an introductory paragraph that conflated the earlier events by saying that counsel had believed prior to trial that the diagram could be used at trial and then continued:

> It was only on the eve of opening statements, once plaintiff had prepared her entire opening based on that stipulation, that defendants first said they would not stipulate to Exhibit 18, based on two new photographs they had found, Exhibits X and Y. Plaintiff, moments before her opening, was informed by the Court she had to agree to defendants' stipulation. Plaintiff was genuinely confused about the import of photographs X and Y. Plaintiff's opening relied critically on using that exhibit to explain events to the jury. In this state of confusion and uncertainty, plaintiff felt little choice but to accept any stipulation defendant provided.

Id. at 200.

Thereafter, the memorandum provided a much more detailed recitation of events, together with legal arguments to justify relief from the stipulation entered into in such circumstances. Later, the memorandum blamed defense counsel for rejecting Scheck's October 7 compromise stipulation, adding that "[u]nder the circumstances, plaintiff had no choice but to sign a stipulation without any chance to review the photographs at issue." Id. at 208. It there quoted a well known treatise that "'courts will look at the facts carefully to see that one litigant has not been coerced into the stipulation.'" Id. at 208 n.5 (quoting 22 Wright & Graham, Federal Practice and Procedure § 5194 (1978)).

After filing the motion and then hearing the judge's statement that she was disturbed by its representations, plaintiff's counsel returned to their office after the trial ended for the day and, assertedly unable to determine what had so troubled the judge, prepared a letter of general apology, which was immediately delivered to court. It apologized for any misstatement and said that "we do not seek to shift responsibility to the Court [for the stipulation], and if we have created a contrary impression, we are sorry." It did not withdraw any specific statement; plaintiff's counsel's position is that at that time they did not fully appreciate what had so concerned the district judge.

The following morning, during argument on the motion for relief from the stipulation, the judge made clear her view that "the reference [in the memorandum] to the Court instructing you that you had to stipulate is, again, a misrepresentation." Scheck now sought to explain that he had been misunderstood, but the judge denied the motion for relief from the stipulation. Later that day the court called counsel before it and ruled that, based on the memorandum's misrepresentation, the pro hac vice admissions of Scheck and Brustin were revoked. Mann was directed to proceed to represent plaintiff at the trial. The trial proceeded to its completion and to a final judgment on February 12, 2004. [One of the two officers was found to have used excessive force.]

After the trial but before final judgment was entered, the district court on November 7, 2003, issued a show cause order to the three plaintiff's counsel. The order said that all three counsel had violated Rule 11(b)(3) and directed the parties to show cause why sanctions should not be imposed. Counsel filed a memorandum and affidavits arguing that they had had no deceptive intent and that, read as a whole and in context, their memorandum asking to withdraw the stipulation had not misrepresented any facts. The Rhode Island Bar Association filed an amicus brief in support of the lawyers; the ACLU also sought unsuccessfully to do so. . . .

[T]he Rule 11 findings focused solely upon two specific "misrepresentations" in the memorandum: one was the above block-quoted language including the key statement that "[p]laintiff, moments before her opening, was informed by the Court she had to agree to defendants' stipulation." 301 F. Supp. 2d at 200. The other was the statement that defense counsel "had no choice" but to sign the stipulation without any chance to review the photographs. Id. at 208. Both statements, said the court, falsely indicated that the court had ordered the stipulation to be signed; and, the court noted, the memorandum's references to injustice and coercion gave the impression that the court was responsible for such wrongs.

The court accepted that the memorandum had been drafted by a young associate and that plaintiff's counsel had denied instructing the younger lawyer to say that the court had directed the stipulation. However, the court said that plaintiff's counsel were responsible under Rule 11 for statements made in a memorandum that they had reviewed and signed. Assessing relative responsibility, the court sanctioned Scheck by imposing "a public censure," 301 F. Supp. 2d at 198; Brustin, an associate whom the court said took direction from Scheck, was merely "admonished" to be more careful, id.; and as to Mann, whose role was ascribed to "inattention," id. at 199, the court said that his reputation in Rhode Island for integrity was well established and a sanction was unnecessary to deter repetition.

All three of plaintiff's counsel have appealed from the order determining that they committed Rule 11 violations, and Scheck and Brustin have asked that their censure and admonition be overturned and their pro hac vice status restored. . . .

Rule 11(b) is not a strict liability provision. It prohibits filings made with "any improper purpose," the offering of "frivolous" arguments, and the assertion of factual allegations without "evidentiary support" or the "likely" prospect of such support. A lawyer who makes an inaccurate factual representation must, at the very least, be culpably careless to commit a violation. See Fed. R. Civ. P. 11(b) (requiring that factual contentions have evidentiary support only "to the best of the person's knowledge, information, and belief, formed after an inquiry reasonable under the circumstances"). The question presented by plaintiff's counsel's first argument is whether something more than falsity and serious carelessness is required; counsel contend that where the court itself initiates the Rule 11 inquiry, the conduct must involve "situations that are akin to a contempt of court." The phrase is taken from an Advisory Committee's Note, to which we will return.

This distinction urged by plaintiff's counsel is at odds with the plain language of Rule 11. Rule 11(b), creating duties, sets out the substantive obligations of counsel (e.g., that factual claims must have evidentiary support or a likely prospect of it) without in any way suggesting that the substantive obligations differ depending on whether a later claim of violation is raised by opposing counsel or the court. Nor is it obvious why anyone would wish such duties governing "primary conduct" to depend on who might thereafter raise objections in a remedial proceeding. . . .

The only hint of such a distinction as to the substantive standard appears in the Advisory Committee's Note, which explains the absence of a safe harbor for court-initiated inquiries as follows: "Since show cause orders will ordinarily be issued only in situations that are akin to a contempt of court, the rule does not provide a [comparable] 'safe harbor' [to withdraw the objected-to statement]." This language has, indeed, been taken by several circuits as suggesting that only egregious conduct can be reached where the court begins the inquiry,[4] but we think mistaken any inference that this language requires malign subjective intent.

It is true that courts ought not invoke Rule 11 for slight cause; the wheels of justice would grind to a halt if lawyers everywhere were sanctioned every time they made unfounded objections, weak arguments, and dubious factual claims. However, this is an argument for requiring serious misconduct, whoever initiated the inquiry into a violation—not for distinguishing between the judge and opposing counsel. The "akin to contempt" language used by the Advisory Committee's Note may well have meant only that no safe harbor was needed because judges would act only in the face of serious misconduct.

A specific purpose of the 1993 revision of Rule 11 was to reject such a bad faith requirement. See Advisory Committee's Note saying that the amendments were "intended to eliminate any 'empty-head pure-heart' justification for patently frivolous arguments." Since then only one circuit court has read the present rule to require bad faith, In re Pennie & Edmonds LLP, 323 F.3d 86, 90-93 (2d Cir. 2003), and it did so in the teeth of a strong dissent, id. at 93-102. True, judges must be especially careful where they are both prosecutor and judge; but careful appellate review is the answer to this concern, whether the charge is negligence or deliberate dishonesty and whether it is contempt or a Rule 11 violation. If anything, opposing counsel has far greater incentive than the trial judge to invoke Rule 11 for slight cause.

We come, then, to the question whether the two objected-to statements in the memorandum were false and, if so, sufficiently careless to warrant

4. See Kaplan v. DaimlerChrysler, A.G., 331 F.3d 1251, 1255-56 (11th Cir. 2003); In re Pennie & Edmonds LLP, 323 F.3d 86, 90-93 (2d Cir. 2003); Hunter v. Earthgrains Co. Bakery, 281 F.3d 144, 151, 153 (4th Cir. 2002); United Nat'l Ins. Co. v. R & D Latex Corp., 242 F.3d 1102, 1115, 1118 (9th Cir. 2001).

sanction. The trial judge read both statements to suggest that the court had forced plaintiff's counsel to sign the stipulation. In our view, read as a whole, the memorandum makes it clear that the judge did not require that the stipulation be signed but only said that a stipulation was a condition to use of the diagram in Scheck's opening statement—which is entirely accurate. There is some warrant for criticism of the memorandum but the central charge of falsity on which the Rule 11 findings rest cannot be sustained, so the issue of carelessness disappears.

The first paragraph of the memorandum (block-quoted above) did say that plaintiff was informed at the opening that "she had to agree to defendants' stipulation," omitting to add the phrase "in order to use the diagram in the opening argument." But the memorandum soon makes it explicitly clear that the judge required the stipulation only in the sense that it was a condition of using the diagram in the opening. Describing the events of October 8 after defense counsel rejected Scheck's stipulation, the memorandum states: "The Court instructed plaintiff again that the exhibit could be only used under stipulation."

As for the second quotation objected to by the judge—the statement that "plaintiff had no choice but to sign a stipulation"—the memorandum did not assert that the judge had directed Scheck to sign; indeed, the statement followed immediately after the memorandum's statement that defendants had rejected the Scheck stipulation "minutes before the opening" (in which, as the memorandum had already explained, the diagram was crucial to Scheck's planned presentation). "Forced" refers to these circumstances and not to any directive from the judge that Scheck sign the stipulation.

The main problem in this memorandum is that in the introductory summary the drafter took as an unexplained premise what the lawyers and the judge full well knew: that the judge had made clear, before the fatal stipulation was signed, that a disputed document could not be used in the opening argument absent a stipulation. Yet, as we have just seen, even this premise is made explicit later in the memorandum. The general rule is that statements must be taken in context, United States v. Moran, 393 F.3d 1, 16 (1st Cir. 2004), and that related parts of a document must be taken together, Nadherny v. Roseland Property Co., 390 F.3d 44, 49 (1st Cir. 2004). That a hasty reader might take the first paragraph out of context is not in the present circumstances enough to brand the memorandum as false.

We are not suggesting that a deliberate lie would be immune to sanction merely because corrective language can be found buried somewhere else in the document. But here the trial judge did not find, and in these circumstances could not have found, that plaintiff's counsel had intended to deceive. The memorandum was drafted under pressure, by a younger lawyer not admitted as counsel in the case; and it was reviewed and signed by Mann, whose established reputation and integrity the opinion praises, and by Brustin, whose trial conduct is also approved of by the judge in her decision. Nor, of course, can anyone suppose that the judge would have been misled as to what she herself had earlier directed.

As it happens, the memorandum may otherwise have been misleading or inaccurate in certain of its detail. If one accepts the account of defense counsel at the show cause hearing, the memorandum left out both the fact of prior warnings from defense counsel that they were concerned about the diagram and the fact that the photographs themselves were furnished to Brustin on September 25 or 26. By omitting such detail, the memorandum enhances the "surprise" element tincturing the memorandum's gloss on the events of October 7 and 8 ("for the first time," "last minute choice"). Further, assuming that the photographs were provided on September 25 or 26, the memorandum's statement that the stipulation was signed "without any chance to review the photographs at issue" is doubtful; perhaps Scheck meant only that he had not focused on the issue but it would have been better to say that.

However, the district court made no definitive findings as to what warnings were given and when. The basis for the Rule 11 charges was the suggestion that the judge had required the stipulation. We also do not know how far defense counsel had gone, prior to receiving the out-takes, in leading plaintiff's counsel to believe that the diagram was common ground. Nor can we tell how far Scheck was involved in trial preparations before his last-minute pro hac vice appearance. The final period before a large trial, like the trial itself, involves late nights, multiplying tasks and resulting confusions that are hard to imagine for one who has not experienced them. The burden upon the trial judge is scarcely less.

The district judge is well known for both patience and care. It is easy to imagine why, in the course of a tense and contentious trial, she was greatly displeased at a document, emblazoned with references to injustice, that could be publicly read as blaming the trial judge for what had patently been plaintiff's counsel's own miscalculation. But on a close reading and a consideration of all the circumstances, the memorandum taken as a whole did no more than say, albeit inartfully, that the trial judge had required the stipulation to be signed as a condition of using the diagram in the opening.

Accordingly, the findings that plaintiff's counsel violated Rule 11 cannot stand; and, as those findings are the only grounds for the censure, admonition and revocation of pro hac vice status, they too must be undone. The findings of Rule 11 violations are set aside, the sanction and admonition are vacated, and the pro hac vice status of Scheck and Brustin is restored. No costs.

It is so ordered.

Note: Tension Between Zealous and Accurate Advocacy?

At first glance *Young* seems to be about factual assertions that took on exaggerated significance—first in the eyes of the plaintiff, then in the eyes of the trial judge. The judge appears to have become quite upset about the implication that she forced the hand of plaintiff's counsel with respect to evidence central to his case. The appellate court, from a distance, seems to have recognized that the trial was heated, that things might have gotten overblown, and that innocent mistakes (mistakes that do not bespeak *over-zealous advocacy*) can happen under the pressure of trial.

Rule 11(b)(3) cases typically concern misrepresentations about facts in the world material to the merits of the case, not misrepresentations of prior statements made by the trial judge. There is, however, a hint that what was really at stake in *Young* was concern about misrepresentations about facts in the world—indeed, the fact most material to this case, the precise location of the threat that caused the white officers to shoot their plainclothes colleague. The appellate court seems to have recognized that the ultimate difference of opinion had more to do with the accuracy of the diagram that was the subject of the contested eve-of-trial stipulation than with anything the judge said. But without specific findings on what prior representations the lawyers made to the court and to each other regarding the accuracy of the diagram, the appellate court could not get to the bottom of the matter. Hence the reversal.

It is clear that if either side knew the diagram was false, introducing it at trial would be sanctionable misconduct. But the real issue here seems to have been that defendants either knew the diagram to be accurate, as the testimony at trial tended to confirm, or they knew the diagram would be inculpating (whether accurate or not). Does their resistance to the stipulation that plaintiff's counsel initially sought trouble you? What about factual contentions about the video out-take photographs in support of that resistance?

Note: De-emphasizing Monetary Sanctions—Turning Down the Heat

The current Rule 11 not only makes sanctions discretionary, even when the judge finds a violation, but also downgrades the award of monetary sanctions. Do you see how the rulemakers do this? See, for example, (c)(4) and think about deterrence as a rationale. Isn't it likely to produce fewer monetary awards than goals of punishment or compensation? What other provisions might make lawyers less likely to file Rule 11 motions?

What sorts of nonmonetary sanctions might a court impose? The advisory committee suggests some possibilities: "striking the offending paper; issuing an admonition, reprimand, or censure; requiring participation in seminars or other educational programs; ordering a fine payable to the court; referring the matter to disciplinary authorities. . . ." Again, trial courts have wide authority in fashioning sanctions. Consider for instance this shaming technique:

> Counsel is admonished about her reliance on [inapplicable case law] and is warned that her advocacy will receive strict scrutiny in future cases. . . .

> Counsel is hereby reprimanded for what was at the least a careless reading of the caselaw. She is ordered to show a copy of this Order and Reasons to her supervisor and to certify to this Court that she has done so.

Traina v. United States, 911 F.2d 1155, 1158 (5th Cir. 1990) (holding that this was a severe sanction even under the 1983 version of the Rule).

Note that Rule 11(c)(3) allows the court to impose sanctions on its own initiative (*sua sponte*). What kinds of sanctions may the court impose when it is acting without a motion? Courts that have considered the issue have concluded that the "plain meaning" of the pre-style change Rule 11(c)(2) is that a sanction of attorneys' fees is not permitted. A payment of sanctions may be directed to the court only. See Nuwesra v. Merrill Lynch, Fenner & Smith, Inc., 174 F.3d 87 (2d Cir. 1999); Johnson v. Wadell & Reed, Inc., 74 F.3d 147 (7th Cir. 1995). There is, however, another way for a court to award attorneys' fees in this situation. See Clark v. United Parcel Serv., Inc., 460 F.3d 1004, 1011 (8th Cir. 2006) (upholding award of attorneys' fees under 28 U.S.C. § 1927, in addition to *sua sponte* Rule 11 sanctions, where counsel's conduct was found to be vexatious by the trial court). Plaintiff's counsel in *Clark* filed a 480-page opposition brief replete with misrepresentations and misstatements in response to defendants' summary judgment motion. The Eighth Circuit agreed with the district court that counsel's filing was a deplorable form of "litigation by attrition, wherein *the practitioner's intent* was to force the opposition either to yield to its position or be crushed under a great weight of misstated factual assertions and drowned in a sea of bombast." Id. at 1010-1011.

Should a court be allowed to impose sanctions *sua sponte* when the lawyer has no opportunity to withdraw or correct her sanctionable conduct? Remember that one of the most significant changes in the 1993 Amendments is Rule 11(c)(2), providing a 21-day safe harbor in which attorneys can remedy potentially offending conduct and avoid sanctions. Parties, to be sure, cannot file for sanctions without offering the requisite safe harbor, and this means that any motion for sanctions must be filed at least 21 days before a case ends. See Brickwood Contractors Inc. v. Datanet Engineering Inc., 369 F.3d 385, 389 (4th Cir. 2004) ("Because the rule requires that the party submitting the challenged pleading be given an opportunity to withdraw the pleading, sanctions cannot be sought after summary judgment has been granted."); Barber v. Miller, 146 F.3d 707 (9th Cir. 1998) (disallowing sanctions where Rule 11 motion was filed after complaint dismissed); Ridder v. City of Springfield, 109 F.3d 288 (6th Cir. 1997) (same result where motion was filed after summary judgment granted). See also Rule 11 Advisory Committee Notes 1993 ("Given the 'safe harbor' provisions . . . a party cannot delay serving its Rule 11 motion until conclusion of the case (or judicial rejection of the offending contention)."). What if the party who receives the sanctions motion does not object when it is deprived of the safe harbor? See *Brickwood Contractors*, 369 F.3d at 395 (noting that "the issue of whether a party has complied with the [safe harbor] rule is subject to forfeiture if not timely raised").

Should the result be different where a court imposes sanctions on its own motion? Recall the First Circuit's discussion of this in *Young*. But see In re Pennie & Edmonds LLP, 323 F.3d 86 (2d Cir. 2003) (court may impose sanctions *sua sponte* even if lawyers had no opportunity to correct their offending submission, but sanctions appropriate only where, as in findings of contempt, lawyers acted in bad faith); *Brickwood Contractors*, 369 F.3d at 389 n.2; *Clark*, 460 F.3d at 1010 (noting that whenever a court acts *sua sponte* to impose Rule 11 sanctions, the new rule should be applied with "particular strictness," but declining to expressly adopt standard set out by the Second Circuit in *In re Pennie & Edmonds LLP*).

5. The Inherent Power to Sanction

As the following case illustrates, Rule 11 is neither the exclusive, nor the most powerful, means for regulating the conduct of lawyers and litigants appearing before a court.

Chambers v. NASCO, Inc.

501 U.S. 32 (1991)

JUSTICE WHITE delivered the opinion of the Court.

This case requires us to explore the scope of the inherent power of a federal court to sanction a litigant for bad-faith conduct. Specifically, we are asked to determine whether the District Court, sitting in diversity, properly invoked its inherent power in assessing as a sanction for a party's bad-faith conduct attorney's fees and related expenses paid by the party's opponent to its attorneys. We hold that the District Court acted within its discretion, and we therefore affirm the judgment of the Court of Appeals.

I

This case began as a simple action for specific performance of a contract, but it did not remain so. Petitioner G. Russell Chambers was the sole shareholder and director of Calcasieu Television and Radio, Inc. (CTR), which operated television station KPLC-TV in Lake Charles, Louisiana. On August 9, 1983, Chambers, acting both in his individual capacity and on behalf of CTR, entered into a purchase agreement to sell the station's facilities and broadcast license to respondent NASCO, Inc., for a purchase price of $18 million. The agreement was not recorded in the parishes in which the two properties housing the station's facilities were located. Consummation of the agreement was subject to the approval of the

Federal Communications Commission (FCC); both parties were obligated to file the necessary documents with the FCC no later than September 23, 1983. By late August, however, Chambers had changed his mind and tried to talk NASCO out of consummating the sale. NASCO refused. On September 23, Chambers, through counsel, informed NASCO that he would not file the necessary papers with the FCC.

NASCO decided to take legal action. On Friday, October 14, 1983, NASCO's counsel informed counsel for Chambers and CTR that NASCO would file suit the following Monday in the United States District Court for the Western District of Louisiana, seeking specific performance of the agreement, as well as a temporary restraining order (TRO) to prevent the alienation or encumbrance of the properties at issue. NASCO provided this notice in accordance with Federal Rule of Civil Procedure 65 and Rule 11 of the District Court's Local Rules (now Rule 10), both of which are designed to give a defendant in a TRO application notice of the hearing and an opportunity to be heard.

The reaction of Chambers and his attorney, A. J. Gray III, was later described by the District Court as having "emasculated and frustrated the purposes of these rules and the powers of [the District] Court by utilizing this notice to prevent NASCO's access to the remedy of specific performance." NASCO, Inc. v. Calcasieu Television & Radio, Inc., 623 F. Supp. 1372, 1383 (W.D. La. 1985). On Sunday, October 16, 1983, the pair acted to place the properties at issue beyond the reach of the District Court by means of the Louisiana Public Records Doctrine. Because the purchase agreement had never been recorded, they determined that if the properties were sold to a third party, and if the deeds were recorded before the issuance of a TRO, the District Court would lack jurisdiction over the properties.

To this end, Chambers and Gray created a trust, with Chambers' sister as trustee and Chambers' three adult children as beneficiaries. The pair then directed the president of CTR, who later became Chambers' wife, to execute warranty deeds conveying the two tracts at issue to the trust for a recited consideration of $1.4 million. Early Monday morning, the deeds were recorded. The trustee, as purchaser, had not signed the deeds; none of the consideration had been paid; and CTR remained in possession of the properties. Later that morning, NASCO's counsel appeared in the District Court to file the complaint and seek the TRO. With NASCO's counsel present, the District Judge telephoned Gray. Despite the judge's queries concerning the possibility that CTR was negotiating to sell the properties to a third person, Gray made no mention of the recordation of the deeds earlier that morning. NASCO, Inc. v. Calcasieu Television & Radio, Inc., 124 F.R.D. 120, 126, n.8 (W.D. La. 1989). That afternoon, Chambers met with his sister and had her sign the trust documents and a $1.4 million note to CTR. The next morning, Gray informed the District Court by letter of the recordation of the deeds the day before, and admitted that he had intentionally withheld the information from the court.

Within the next few days, Chambers' attorneys prepared a leaseback agreement from the trustee to CTR, so that CTR could remain in possession of the properties and continue to operate the station. The following week, the District Court granted a preliminary injunction against Chambers and CTR and entered a second TRO to prevent the trustee from alienating or encumbering the properties. At that hearing, the District Judge warned that Gray's and Chambers' conduct had been unethical.

Despite this early warning, Chambers, often acting through his attorneys, continued to abuse the judicial process. In November 1983, in defiance of the preliminary injunction, he refused to allow NASCO to inspect CTR's corporate records. The ensuing civil contempt proceedings resulted in the assessment of a $25,000 fine against Chambers personally. NASCO, Inc. v. Calcasieu Television & Radio, Inc., 583 F. Supp. 115 (W.D. La. 1984). Two subsequent appeals from the contempt order were dismissed for lack of a final judgment. See NASCO, Inc. v. Calcasieu Television & Radio, Inc., No. 84-9037 (5th Cir May 29, 1984); NASCO, Inc. v. Calcasieu Television & Radio, Inc., 752 F.2d 157 (5th Cir 1985).

Undeterred, Chambers proceeded with "a series of meritless motions and pleadings and delaying actions." 124 F.R.D., at 127. These actions triggered further warnings from the court. At one point, acting sua sponte, the District Judge called a status conference to find out why bankers were being deposed. When informed by Chambers' counsel that the purpose was to learn whether NASCO could afford to pay for the station, the court canceled the depositions consistent with its authority under Federal Rule of Civil Procedure 26(g).

At the status conference nine days before the April 1985 trial date, the District Judge again warned counsel that further misconduct would not be tolerated. Finally, on the eve of trial, Chambers and CTR stipulated that the purchase agreement was enforceable and that Chambers had breached the agreement on September 23, 1983, by failing to file the necessary papers with the FCC. At trial, the only defense presented by Chambers was the Public Records Doctrine.

In the interlude between the trial and the entry of judgment during which the District Court prepared its opinion, Chambers sought to render the purchase agreement meaningless by seeking permission from the FCC to build a new transmission tower for the station and to relocate the transmission facilities to that site, which was not covered by the agreement. Only after NASCO sought contempt sanctions did Chambers withdraw the application.

The District Court entered judgment on the merits in NASCO's favor, finding that the transfer of the properties to the trust was a simulated sale and that the deeds purporting to convey the property were "null, void, and of no effect." 623 F. Supp. at 1385. Chambers' motions, filed in the District Court, the Court of Appeals, and this Court, to stay the judgment pending appeal were denied. Undeterred, Chambers convinced CTR officials to file formal oppositions to NASCO's pending application for FCC approval of the transfer of the station's license, in contravention of both the District Court's injunctive orders and its judgment on the merits. NASCO then sought contempt sanctions for a third time, and the oppositions were withdrawn.

When Chambers refused to prepare to close the sale, NASCO again sought the court's help. A hearing was set for July 16, 1986, to determine whether certain equipment was to be included in the sale. At the beginning of the hearing, the court informed Chambers' new attorney, Edwin A. McCabe, that further sanctionable conduct would not be tolerated. When the hearing was recessed for several days, Chambers, without notice to the court or NASCO, removed from service at the station all of the equipment at issue, forcing the District Court to order that the equipment be returned to service.

Immediately following oral argument on Chambers' appeal from the District Court's judgment on the merits, the Court of Appeals, ruling from the bench, found the appeal frivolous. The court imposed appellate sanctions in the form of attorney's fees and double costs, pursuant to Federal Rule of Appellate Procedure 38, and remanded the case to the District Court with orders to fix the amount of appellate sanctions and to determine whether further sanctions should be imposed for the manner in which the litigation had been conducted. NASCO, Inc., v. Calcasieu Television & Radio, Inc., 797 F.2d 975 (5th Cir. 1986) (per curiam) (unpublished order).

On remand, NASCO moved for sanctions, invoking the District Court's inherent power, Fed. Rule Civ. Proc. 11, and 28 U.S.C. § 1927. After full briefing and a hearing, see 124 F.R.D. at 141, n.11, the District Court determined that sanctions were appropriate "for the manner in which this proceeding was conducted in the district court from October 14, 1983, the time that plaintiff gave notice of its intention to file suit to this date." Id., at 123. At the end of an extensive opinion recounting what it deemed to have been sanctionable conduct during this period, the court imposed sanctions against Chambers in the form of attorney's fees and expenses totaling $996,644.65, which represented the entire amount of NASCO's litigation costs paid to its attorneys.[5] In so doing, the court rejected Chambers' argument that he had merely followed the advice of counsel, labeling him "the strategist." . . .

5. In calculating the award, the District Court deducted the amounts previously awarded as compensatory damages for contempt, as well as the amount awarded as appellate sanctions. 124 F.R.D. at 133-134.

The court also sanctioned other individuals, who are not parties to the action in this Court. Chambers' sister, the trustee, was sanctioned by a reprimand; attorney Gray was disbarred and prohibited from seeking readmission for three years; attorney Richard A. Curry, who represented the trustee, was suspended from practice before the court for six months; and attorney McCabe was suspended for five years. Id. at 144-146. Although these sanctions did not affect the bank accounts of these individuals, they were nevertheless substantial sanctions and were as proportionate to the conduct at issue as was the monetary sanction imposed on Chambers. Indeed, in the case of the disbarment of attorney Gray, the court recognized that the penalty was among the harshest possible sanctions and one which derived from its authority to supervise those admitted to practice before it. See id. at 140-141.

In imposing the sanctions, the District Court first considered Federal Rule of Civil Procedure 11. It noted that the alleged sanctionable conduct was that Chambers and the other defendants had "(1) attempted to deprive this Court of jurisdiction by acts of fraud, nearly all of which were performed outside the confines of this Court, (2) filed false and frivolous pleadings, and (3) attempted, by other tactics of delay, oppression, harassment and massive expense to reduce plaintiff to exhausted compliance." Id. at 138. The court recognized that the conduct in the first and third categories could not be reached by Rule 11, which governs only papers filed with a court. As for the second category, the court explained that the falsity of the pleadings at issue did not become apparent until after the trial on the merits, so that it would have been impossible to assess sanctions at the time the papers were filed. Id. at 138-139. Consequently, the District Court deemed Rule 11 "insufficient" for its purposes. Id. at 139. The court likewise declined to impose sanctions under § 1927, both because the statute applies only to attorneys, and therefore would not reach Chambers, and because the statute was not broad enough to reach "acts which degrade the judicial system," including "attempts to deprive the Court of jurisdiction, fraud, misleading and lying to the Court." Ibid. The court therefore relied on its inherent power in imposing sanctions, stressing that "[t]he wielding of that inherent power is particularly appropriate when the offending parties have practiced a fraud upon the court."

The Court of Appeals affirmed. NASCO, Inc. v. Calcasieu Television & Radio, Inc., 894 F.2d 696 (5th Cir. 1990). The court rejected Chambers' argument that a federal court sitting in diversity must look to state law, not the court's inherent power, to assess attorney's fees as a sanction for bad-faith conduct in litigation. The court further found that neither 28 U.S.C. § 1927 nor Federal Rule of Civil Procedure 11 limits a court's inherent authority to sanction bad-faith conduct "when the party's conduct is not within the reach of the rule or the statute." 894 F.2d at 702-703. Although observing that the inherent power "is not a broad reservoir of power, ready at an imperial hand, but a limited source; an implied power squeezed from the need to make the court function," id. at 702, the court also concluded that the District Court did not abuse its discretion in awarding to NASCO the fees and litigation costs paid to its attorneys. Because of the importance of these issues, we granted certiorari, 498 U.S. 807 (1990).

II

Chambers maintains that 28 U.S.C. § 1927 and the various sanctioning provisions in the Federal Rules of Civil Procedure[8] reflect a legislative

8. A number of the rules provide for the imposition of attorney's fees as a sanction. See Fed. Rule Civ. Proc. 11 (certification requirement for papers), 16(f) (pretrial conferences), 26(g) (certification requirement for discovery requests), 30(g) (oral depositions), 37 (sanctions for failure to cooperate with discovery), 56(g) (affidavits accompanying

intent to displace the inherent power. At least, he argues that they obviate or foreclose resort to the inherent power in this case. We agree with the Court of Appeals that neither proposition is persuasive.

A

It has long been understood that "[c]ertain implied powers must necessarily result to our Courts of justice from the nature of their institution," powers "which cannot be dispensed with in a Court, because they are necessary to the exercise of all others." United States v. Hudson, 7 Cranch 32, 34 (1812); see also Roadway Express, Inc. v. Piper, 447 U.S. 752, 764 (1980) (citing *Hudson*). For this reason, "Courts of justice are universally acknowledged to be vested, by their very creation, with power to impose silence, respect, and decorum, in their presence, and submission to their lawful mandates." Anderson v. Dunn, 6 Wheat. 204, 227 (1821); see also Ex parte Robinson, 19 Wall. 505, 510 (1874). These powers are "governed not by rule or statute but by the control necessarily vested in courts to manage their own affairs so as to achieve the orderly and expeditious disposition of cases." Link v. Wabash R. Co., 370 U.S. 626, 630-631 (1962).

Prior cases have outlined the scope of the inherent power of the federal courts. For example, the Court has held that a federal court has the power to control admission to its bar and to discipline attorneys who appear before it. See Ex parte Burr, 9 Wheat. 529, 531 (1824). While this power "ought to be exercised with great caution," it is nevertheless "incidental to all Courts." Ibid.

In addition, it is firmly established that "[t]he power to punish for contempts is inherent in all courts." *Robinson,* supra, at 510. This power reaches both conduct before the court and that beyond the court's confines, for "[t]he underlying concern that gave rise to the contempt power was not . . . merely the disruption of court proceedings. Rather, it was disobedience to the orders of the Judiciary, regardless of whether such disobedience interfered with the conduct of trial." Young v. United States ex rel. Vuitton et Fils S.A., 481 U.S. 787, 798 (1987) (citations omitted).

Of particular relevance here, the inherent power also allows a federal court to vacate its own judgment upon proof that a fraud has been perpetrated upon the court. See Hazel-Atlas Glass Co. v. Hartford-Empire Co., 322 U.S. 238 (1944); Universal Oil Products Co. v. Root Refining Co., 328 U.S. 575 (1946). This "historic power of equity to set aside fraudulently begotten judgments," *Hazel-Atlas,* 322 U.S. at 245, is necessary to the

---

summary judgment motions). In some instances, the assessment of fees is one of a range of possible sanctions, see, e.g., Fed. Rule Civ. Proc. 11, while in others, the court must award fees, see, e.g., Fed. Rule Civ. Proc. 16(f). In each case, the fees that may be assessed are limited to those incurred as a result of the rule violation. In the case of Rule 11, however, a violation could conceivably warrant an imposition of fees covering the entire litigation, if, for example, a complaint or answer was filed in violation of the rule. The court generally may act sua sponte in imposing sanctions under the rules.

integrity of the courts, for "tampering with the administration of justice in [this] manner . . . involves far more than an injury to a single litigant. It is a wrong against the institutions set up to protect and safeguard the public." Id. at 246. Moreover, a court has the power to conduct an independent investigation in order to determine whether it has been the victim of fraud. *University Oil*, supra, 328 U.S., at 580.

There are other facets to a federal court's inherent power. The court may bar from the courtroom a criminal defendant who disrupts a trial. Illinois v. Allen, 397 U.S. 337 (1970). It may dismiss an action on grounds of forum non conveniens, Gulf Oil Corp. v. Gilbert, 330 U.S. 501, 507-508 (1947); and it may act sua sponte to dismiss a suit for failure to prosecute, *Link*, supra, 370 U.S. at 630, 631.

Because of their very potency, inherent powers must be exercised with restraint and discretion. See *Roadway Express*, supra, 447 U.S. at 764. A primary aspect of that discretion is the ability to fashion an appropriate sanction for conduct which abuses the judicial process. As we recognized in *Roadway Express*, outright dismissal of a lawsuit, which we had upheld in *Link*, is a particularly severe sanction, yet is within the court's discretion. 447 U.S. at 765. Consequently, the "less severe sanction" of an assessment of attorney's fees is undoubtedly within a court's inherent power as well. Ibid. See also Hutto v. Finney, 437 U.S. 678, 689, n.14 (1978).

Indeed, "[t]here are ample grounds for recognizing . . . that in narrowly defined circumstances federal courts have inherent power to assess attorney's fees against counsel," *Roadway Express*, supra, 447 U.S. at 765, even though the so-called American Rule prohibits fee-shifting in most cases. See Alyeska Pipeline Service Co. v. Wilderness Society, 421 U.S. 240, 259 (1975). As we explained in *Alyeska*, these exceptions fall into three categories. The first, known as the "common fund exception," derives not from a court's power to control litigants, but from its historic equity jurisdiction, see Sprague v. Ticonic National Bank, 307 U.S. 161 (1939), and allows a court to award attorney's fees to a party whose litigation efforts directly benefit others. *Alyeska*, 421 U.S. at 257-258. Second, a court may assess attorney's fees as a sanction for the "'willful disobedience of a court order.'" Id. at 258 (quoting Fleischmann Distilling Corp. v. Maier Brewing Co., 386 U.S. 714, 718 (1967)). Thus, a court's discretion to determine "[t]he degree of punishment for contempt" permits the court to impose as part of the fine attorney's fees representing the entire cost of the litigation. Toledo Scale Co. v. Computing Scale Co., 261 U.S. 399, 428 (1923).

Third, and most relevant here, a court may assess attorney's fees when a party has "'acted in bad faith, vexatiously, wantonly, or for oppressive reasons.'" *Alyeska*, supra, 421 U.S. at 258-259 (quoting F.D. Rich Co. v. United States ex rel. Industrial Lumber Co., 417 U.S. 116 (1974)). In this regard, if a court finds "that fraud has been practiced upon it, or that the very temple of justice has been defiled," it may assess attorney's fees against the responsible party, *Universal Oil*, supra, 328 U.S. at 580, as it may when a party "shows bad faith by delaying or disrupting the litigation or by hampering enforcement of a court order,"[10] *Hutto*, 437 U.S. at 689, n.14. The imposition of sanctions in this instance transcends a court's equitable power concerning relations between the parties and reaches a court's inherent power to police itself, thus serving the dual purpose of "vindicat[ing] judicial authority without resort to the more drastic sanctions available for contempt of court and mak[ing] the prevailing party whole for expenses caused by his opponent's obstinacy." Id.

B

We discern no basis for holding that the sanctioning scheme of the statute and the rules displaces the inherent power to impose sanctions for the bad-faith conduct described above. These other mechanisms, taken alone or together, are not substitutes for the inherent power, for that power is both broader and narrower than other means of imposing sanctions. First, whereas each of the other mechanisms reaches only certain individuals or conduct, the inherent power extends to a full range of litigation abuses. At the very least, the inherent power must continue to exist to fill in the interstices. Even the dissent so concedes. . . . Second, while the narrow exceptions to the American Rule effectively limit a court's inherent power to impose attorney's fees as a sanction to cases in which a litigant has engaged in bad-faith conduct or willful disobedience of a court's orders, many of the other mechanisms permit a court to impose attorney's fees as a sanction for conduct which merely fails to meet a reasonableness standard. Rule 11, for example, imposes an objective standard of reasonable inquiry which does not mandate a finding of bad faith.[11]

It is true that the exercise of the inherent power of lower federal courts can be limited by statute and rule, for "[t]hese courts were created by act of Congress." *Robinson*, 19 Wall. at 511. Nevertheless, "we do not lightly assume that Congress has intended to depart from established principles" such as the scope of a court's inherent power. Weinberger v. Romero-Barcelo, 456 U.S. 305, 313 (1982); see also *Link*, 370 U.S. at 631-632. . . .

The Court's prior cases have indicated that the inherent power of a court can be invoked even if procedural rules exist which sanction the same conduct. In *Link*, it was recognized that a federal district court has

10. In this regard, the bad-faith exception resembles the third prong of Rule 11's certification requirement, which mandates that a signer of a paper filed with the court warrant that the paper "is not interposed for any improper purpose, such as to harass or to cause unnecessary delay or needless increase in the cost of litigation."

11. Indeed, Rule 11 was amended in 1983 precisely because the subjective bad-faith standard was difficult to establish and courts were therefore reluctant to invoke it as a means of imposing sanctions. See Advisory Committee Notes on the 1983 Amendment to Rule 11, 28 U.S.C. App., pp. 575-576. Consequently, there is little risk that courts will invoke their inherent power "to chill the advocacy of litigants attempting to vindicate all other important federal rights." See [dissent]. To the extent that such a risk does exist, it is no less present when a court invokes Rule 11. See Cooter & Gell v. Hartmarx Corp., 496 U.S. 384 (1990).

the inherent power to dismiss a case sua sponte for failure to prosecute, even though the language of Federal Rule of Civil Procedure 41(b) appeared to require a motion from a party. . . . A court must, of course, exercise caution in invoking its inherent power, and it must comply with the mandates of due process, both in determining that the requisite bad faith exists and in assessing fees. Furthermore, when there is bad-faith conduct in the course of litigation that could be adequately sanctioned under the rules, the court ordinarily should rely on the rules rather than the inherent power. But if in the informed discretion of the court, neither the statute nor the rules are up to the task, the court may safely rely on its inherent power.

Like the Court of Appeals, we find no abuse of discretion in resorting to the inherent power in the circumstances of this case. It is true that the District Court could have employed Rule 11 to sanction Chambers for filing "false and frivolous pleadings," 124 F.R.D. at 138, and that some of the other conduct might have been reached through other rules. Much of the bad-faith conduct by Chambers, however, was beyond the reach of the rules, his entire course of conduct throughout the lawsuit evidenced bad faith and an attempt to perpetrate a fraud on the court, and the conduct sanctionable under the rules was intertwined within conduct that only the inherent power could address. In circumstances such as these in which all of a litigant's conduct is deemed sanctionable, requiring a court first to apply rules and statutes containing sanctioning provisions to discrete occurrences before invoking inherent power to address remaining instances of sanctionable conduct would serve only to foster extensive and needless satellite litigation, which is contrary to the aim of the rules themselves. See, e.g., Advisory Committee Notes on the 1983 Amendment to Rule 11, 28 U.S.C. App., pp. 575-576. . . .

For the foregoing reasons, the judgment of the Court of Appeals for the Fifth Circuit is

Affirmed.

JUSTICE SCALIA, dissenting.

[Justice Scalia generally agreed with the majority's view of the law, but agreed with Justice Kennedy that the District Court here had no power to impose any sanctions for petitioner's flagrant, bad-faith breach of contract; and he agreed with Justice Kennedy that it appears to have done so.]

JUSTICE KENNEDY, with whom The Chief Justice and Justice Souter join, dissenting.

Today's decision affects a vast expansion of the power of federal courts, unauthorized by rule or statute. I have no doubt petitioner engaged in sanctionable conduct that warrants severe corrective measures. But our outrage at his conduct should not obscure the boundaries of settled legal categories. . . .

Upon a finding of bad faith, courts may now ignore any and all textual limitations on sanctioning power. By inviting district courts to rely on inherent authority as a substitute for attention to the careful distinctions contained in the rules and statutes, today's decision will render these sources of authority superfluous in many instances. A number of pernicious practical effects will follow.

The Federal Rules establish explicit standards for, and explicit checks against, the exercise of judicial authority. Rule 11 provides a useful illustration. . . .

By contrast, courts apply inherent powers without specific definitional or procedural limits. True, if a district court wishes to shift attorney's fees as a sanction, it must make a finding of bad faith to circumvent the American Rule. But today's decision demonstrates how little guidance or limitation the undefined bad-faith predicate provides. The Court states without elaboration that courts must "comply with the mandates of due process . . . in determining that the requisite bad faith exists," ante, . . . but the Court's bad-faith standard, at least without adequate definition, thwarts the first requirement of due process, namely, that "[a]ll are entitled to be informed as to what the State commands or forbids." Lanzetta v. New Jersey, 306 U.S. 451, 453 (1939). This standardless exercise of judicial power may appear innocuous in this litigation between commercial actors. But the same unchecked power also can be applied to chill the advocacy of litigants attempting to vindicate all other important federal rights.

Note: The Relationship Between Rule 11 and the Court's Inherent Power to Sanction

After *Chambers* courts are free to sanction attorneys for "bad faith" conduct. As a lower court has emphasized, "[i]t is axiomatic that courts have the authority to impose sanctions *sua sponte* under the various sources of the sanctioning power—i.e. federal statutes, the Federal Rules of Civil Procedure, and the inherent power of the courts." Wolters Kluwer Fin. Servs. Inc. v. Scivantage, 525 F. Supp. 2d 448, 452 n.8 (S.D.N.Y. 2007). This "axiomatic" power, however, has raised concerns. First, exercising "inherent" power in an area where Congress has already legislated procedural rules is at least potentially controversial. See John Papachristos, Comment, Inherent Power Found, Rule 11 Lost: Taking a Shortcut to Impose Sanctions in Chambers v. NASCO, 59 Brook. L. Rev. 1225, 1265 (1993); see also Danielle Kie Hart, And the Chill Goes On—Federal Civil Rights Plaintiffs Beware: Rule 11 Vis-a-Vis 28 U.S.C. § 1927 and the Court's Inherent Power, 38 Loy. L.A. L. Rev. 645 (2004); Danielle Kie Hart, Still Chilling After All These Years: Rule 11 of the Federal Rules of Civil Procedure and Its Impact on Federal Civil Rights Plaintiffs After the 1993 Amendments, 37 Val. U. L. Rev. 1 (2002).

Finally, note that while Rule 11 is evaluated for objective reasonableness, a finding of subjective bad faith is required when a court imposes sanctions under its inherent power. How might this difference play out in practice? See Charles Yablon, Hindsight, Regret and Safe Harbors In Rule 11 Litigation, 37 Loy. L.A. L. Rev. 599, (2004) (arguing that amended Rule 11's safe harbor reduces the potential for hindsight bias); see also Gillette Foods Inc. v. Bayerwald-Fruchteverwertung, 977 F.2d 809, 813 (3d Cir. 1992) (holding that courts have the inherent power to sanction conduct that does not violate Rule 11 since such inherent power is necessary to "fill in the interstices" between the range of potential bad faith conduct and the scope of Rule 11 (quoting *Chambers*, 111 S. Ct. at 2134)).

Note: The Contempt Power

One form of the court's inherent power discussed in *Chambers*, and in more detail in Chapter 5, is the contempt sanction. The history of the contempt power of the judge lies in English equity procedure. If the Chancellor found an addressee of an injunction or other court order to be in contempt, he might impose the sanctions of *civil* or *criminal* contempt. The latter was strictly punitive in purpose and would take the form of a fine or a term of imprisonment. The former was intended to be coercive and remedial. Usually, it would take the form of an imprisonment until such time as the addressee complied with the court's order. It was said, somewhat glibly, that the defendant carries his own jail keys in his pocket. It also was said that the power exercised by the Chancellor was the minimum necessary to secure compliance. Nevertheless, there were numerous instances in which defiant litigants remained imprisoned for many years.

In some instances, it was possible that a contempt proceeding would be conducted summarily. This would occur if the contempt could be classified as direct, meaning presumably that the chancellor had direct knowledge of the defiance. This kind of proceeding had also been known to the law courts, where criminal contempt sanctions had long been applied to those who disturbed proceedings or offended the dignity of the court, but the instances of the exercise of this power were always few. A notable example of a summary contempt proceeding occurred in a law court in the eighteenth century when a subject flung an ax at the judge. Although he missed, he was executed on the spot in the courtroom.

The basic provision of modern federal law on contempt, 18 U.S.C. § 401, is representative of much similar state legislation:

> A court of the United States shall have power to punish by fine or imprisonment, at its discretion, such contempt of its authority, and none other, as:
>
> (1) Misbehavior of any person in its presence or so near thereto as to obstruct the administration of justice;
> (2) Misbehavior of any of its officers in their official transactions;
> (3) Disobedience or resistance to its lawful writ, process, order, rule, decree, or command.

Note that the basic statute does not distinguish between civil and criminal contempt. In a series of cases on contempt, culminating in United Mine Workers of America v. Bagwell, 512 U.S. 821 (1994), the Supreme Court has clarified the distinction. What follows on whether a contempt is labeled criminal or civil?

Note: Contracting for Sanctions?

In addition to Rule 11 and the courts' inherent power to sanction, a party may be sanctioned if she has agreed to it as a penalty for disobedience. In Baella-Silva v. Hulsey, 454 F.3d 5 (1st Cir. 2006), an attorney sued co-counsel to recover fees allegedly owed according to a fee-sharing agreement. The parties entered a settlement agreement, which the court incorporated into its judgment disposing of the case. The settlement agreement contained a confidentiality clause, as almost all settlement agreements do, but this particular confidentiality clause provided liquidated damages in the amount of $50,000 for breach. When Baella-Silva filed a motion for disbursement of funds using the court's new-fangled e-filing system, he neglected to file it under seal, so it was posted live on the court's online docket.

Although Baella-Silva realized his mistake within an hour and promptly withdrew the motion, defendant Hulsey immediately filed a motion to suspend disbursement of Baella-Silva's fee and to collect the $50,000 specified in the contract as a sanction for his breach of the confidentiality clause. The First Circuit upheld the sanction, as well as an additional $20,320 sanction imposed by the district court under its inherent powers when Baella-Silva violated a separate provision of the settlement contract prohibiting contact between the parties. Baella-Silva violated the latter provision when he filed two new suits against defendants. The district court chose $20,320 because it equaled the damages sought in Baella-Silva's new suits. The First Circuit agreed that the amount was not excessive, observing that "[s]o long as a sanction is reasonably proportionate to the offending conduct, the trial court's quantification of it ought not to be disturbed." Id. at 13 (internal quotation marks omitted).

3 *Discovery of the Adversary's Case*

Problem Case: The Elusive Defendant (Part Two)

Return to your client, the disappointed decorator, in Chapter 1. Assume that you have managed to serve the complaint and have received in return a form answer that denies all the factual allegations of the complaint. What happens next in the case?

Read Rules 26(a) and (f).

What would you turn over voluntarily to the other side? What would you expect to get from them?

What formal discovery will you undertake? Sketch out a discovery plan.

A. AN OVERVIEW OF THE DISCOVERY TOOLS AND THEIR DEPLOYMENT

Discovery is the process by which parties learn the evidence relevant to a case. More Rules are devoted to discovery than to any other subject, yet the interpretive case law is not large. Can you see why this is? Part of the answer lies in the fact-specific nature of discovery fights, making it less likely that any case will serve as a far-ranging precedent. Part of the answer is that judges dislike getting caught up in discovery disputes and find ways to avoid spending too much time and energy on them. Rather than dealing with all the Rule permutations through cases, therefore, we offer instead a practicing lawyer's advice about investigating a case and planning discovery. We then turn to a more general consideration of the ambitions for and frustrations with the modern discovery regime revealed in decisional law.

Lawrence J. Zweifach, Deposition Strategy in the Framework of an Overall Discovery Plan

Pages 9-20 (1999)

I. Preliminary Considerations for the Development of a Discovery Plan

A. The attorney and the client should work together closely as a team in the development of a discovery plan.

B. Define major objectives in the litigation.

C. Evaluate alternative courses of action.

D. Formulate a "theory of the case."

1. The initial theory of the case is a working hypothesis that undoubtedly will change during the course of discovery and other pretrial proceedings.
2. At the outset of the litigation, draft a tentative outline setting forth the major points that would be made in summation after the trial of the case. This outline, which should be revised on a regular basis throughout the litigation, will be a valuable tool for ensuring that you are "litigating with a purpose."

E. The client should develop a litigation budget based on a careful analysis of the potential gains and losses involved in the litigation, as well as the client's resources.

1. The budget should be broken down to include expenses as well as pretrial, trial and post-trial activities.
2. The budget should also reflect the possibility that the litigation will give rise to activities beyond the initial claims; for example, counterclaims and third-party claims.
3. Ideally, the attorney should be directly involved in the budgeting process. At the very least, the attorney must be fully apprised of all budgetary constraints.

F. Define short-range and medium-range goals.

1. Temporary restraining order and/or preliminary injunction.
2. Motion for summary judgment.
3. Settlement goals.

G. Formulate strategies to achieve objectives.

1. The discovery plan should be based on the client's overall litigation objectives and strategies for achieving those objectives.
2. Objectives must be clearly defined. For example, if your principal goal is to set the stage for an early settlement, your strategy might be to pursue selected discovery on a fast track. Or, if your goal is to make an early summary judgment motion, you might want to focus your preliminary discovery on only those issues that will be the subject of that motion. On the other hand, if your ultimate goal is to be prepared fully to take the case to trial, your discovery plan will be directed towards maximizing your ability to prevail at trial.

3. In preparing a plan, consider the cost and potential benefits of all available discovery tools.
4. Carefully analyze alternative approaches to discovery, paying particular attention to all available discovery devices, and the timing and sequence of discovery. . . .

II. The Primary Discovery Tools

A. Informal discovery
   1. In some situations, informal witness interviews can be more advantageous than formal deposition testimony.
   2. An interview of a potential non-party witness can help you decide whether or not you should subpoena the witness for a deposition.
   3. Witnesses can be "locked in" to positions on the facts by having them sign written statements or by having them swear to affidavits.
   4. Before attempting to contact a potential witness, make sure that you understand the ethical proscriptions that govern whom you may contact directly. For example, you generally will not be permitted to contact (without the permission of your adversary) the opposing party or its employees. See Model Code of Professional Responsibility DR7-104(A)(1) (1980). . . .
   5. In some cases, private investigators can be valuable sources of information.
   6. It is critical to remember that the attorney-client privilege will not protect your statements to a witness during an informal interview. Moreover, the work-product doctrine, to the extent that it is applicable, will rarely afford lasting protection. Finally, you never know what a witness will ultimately claim that you said to him during an interview. In sum, be discreet and avoid conducting any one-on-one interviews.

B. Formal discovery.
   1. Interrogatories.
   2. Depositions.
   3. Notice of subpoena to produce documents and things.
   4. Requests for admissions.
   5. Physical and mental examinations.

C. In deciding which discovery devices to use, pay careful attention to all applicable procedural rules, local rules, individual judge's rules and standing orders. . . .

D. Uses and advantages of interrogatories.
   1. Determine the existence and location of documents.
   2. Learn the identity of persons with knowledge relevant to the litigation.
   3. Learn the specific contentions of the opposing party.
   4. Interrogatories are less expensive and time-consuming than depositions.

E. Uses and advantages of requests for admissions.

1. Narrow issues.
2. Can obviate need for complicated proof regarding foundations for admissibility of documents.
3. Can help to avoid unnecessary areas of discovery and trial preparation.

III. Uses and Advantages of Depositions

A. Secure admissions and impeachment evidence from an adverse party.

B. Learn what adverse party and non-party witnesses know about the issues in the case and what their testimony will be at trial.
   1. "Lock" adverse party and non-party witnesses into facts and positions so that there will be no surprises at trial.

C. Depositions, unlike interrogatories, allow the examiner to receive spontaneous answers from the witness and to ask follow-up questions.

D. The examiner has an opportunity to observe the demeanor of a potential trial witness.

E. Depositions can narrow and clarify issues for trial.

F. Determine the location, nature, and availability of documents and other physical evidence.

G. Learn the identity of other potential witnesses.

H. Preserve for trial the testimony of individuals who might be beyond subpoena power at the time of trial or who might otherwise be unavailable.

I. To obtain the production of documents and other physical evidence and to lay the foundation for their admission into evidence at trial.

IV. The Timing and Sequence of Discovery

A. The timing and sequence of discovery will sometimes be dictated by an individual judge's rules or by a pre-trial order issued after a pre-trial conference.

B. One traditional approach to discovery is to issue general discovery requests first, and to have subsequent discovery requests build on the previous general requests, so that the information obtained becomes increasingly detailed. This approach is particularly useful when the attorney does not have substantial knowledge about the claims and the underlying facts at the outset of the litigation. Here, the adverse party would be deposed only after all relevant documents and answers to the principal interrogatories have been received. This approach enables the attorney to maximize her ability to take a thorough deposition of the adverse party and to avoid duplicative discovery. Under this approach, the following sequence of discovery might be employed:
   1. First, issue interrogatories of a general nature to identify potential witnesses and the existence of documents. At the same time, issue an

initial request for the production of documents. Also, if appropriate, issue a preliminary request to admit in order to narrow the issues.
2. Depose secondary witnesses.
3. Issue follow-up document requests and interrogatories.
4. Depose key witnesses.
5. Depose the adverse party.
6. Issue follow-up requests to admit.
7. Depose expert witnesses.
8. Issue contention interrogatories.
9. Issue final, "clean up" discovery requests.

C. In some circumstances, it is desirable to take the deposition of a plaintiff shortly after the pleadings have been filed and prior to the taking of other discovery.
   1. This approach enables defense counsel to obtain admissions before the plaintiff has had a full opportunity to learn about the defendant's theory of the case, and prior to the time that the issues have become refined . . .

D. The sequence of discovery must be tailored to the particular circumstances of each case. In most cases, it will be extremely difficult to take a useful deposition without first having had an opportunity to examine relevant documents. However, under certain circumstances, the taking of depositions to "lock in" the testimony of witnesses at the outset of discovery can be invaluable.

V. Deciding Whether to Depose a Witness

A. As a general rule, always depose the adverse party.
B. Depositions are expensive and time-consuming.
C. Many of the purposes of a deposition can be accomplished with an informal interview.
D. Depositions can influence settlement valuation. . . .
E. The deposition of the "favorable" nonparty witness.
   1. The consequences of taking the deposition:
      a. You eliminate the opportunity of having a tactical advantage at trial—i.e., calling a witness to testify who has not been deposed.
      b. Your adversary gets two big bites at the apple. That is, assuming that the witness will be available for trial, your adversary can "experiment" impeachment techniques at the deposition, knowing that she will have a full opportunity to cross-examine the witness at trial. This opportunity to take risks at the deposition (that one otherwise wouldn't take during their first confrontation with the witness at trial) is extremely advantageous.
      c. On the other hand, a strong performance by a key, non-party witness can facilitate the settlement of a case and save the cost of additional litigation.
   2. The consequences of not taking the deposition:

a. You might lose the benefit of the witness's potentially favorable testimony because the witness might become unavailable to testify at trial.

b. Even worse, today's seemingly "friendly" witness could be a hostile witness at trial. By the time of trial, the witness could have a change of heart (if not a change of recollection) and testify for your adversary. . .

F. The deposition of the adverse non-party witness

1. The consequences of taking the deposition:

a. You might direct your adversary to a witness that they did not know about.

b. You might preserve for trial the unfavorable testimony of a witness who otherwise would be unavailable to testify at trial.

2. The consequences of not taking the deposition:

a. You might be called upon to cross-examine the witness at trial without having any prior knowledge of the nature of the witness's testimony.

b. If you do not learn about the damaging nature of the witness's testimony during the discovery stage of the case, you might miss the opportunity to reach a reasonable settlement.

VI. Determining the Sequence of Depositions

A. One popular school of thought is to take the depositions of secondary witnesses before the deposition of key witnesses and the adverse party.

1. This approach enables the attorney to gather as much information as possible before attempting to depose the critical witnesses and the adverse party. By starting at the bottom of the pyramid, the examiner will be able to take more thorough depositions at the end of discovery.

2. The downside is that you enable the adverse party and principal witnesses to become better-educated by the time they are deposed.

B. Taking the depositions of principal witnesses and the adverse party before the depositions of secondary witnesses

1. If the attorney has an understanding of the basic facts and contentions underlying the litigation, this approach might be attractive.

2. Here, admissions can be obtained from the adverse party before he has an opportunity to learn all of the facts, issues and available defense in the case.

3. This approach contemplates a rapid pace of discovery. It can foster an early settlement and lay the groundwork for a relatively early motion for summary judgment.

B. DISCOVERY REFORM REDUX:* HOW THE SOLUTION BECAME THE PROBLEM

The greatest single innovation of the Federal Rules was their provision for open-handed, self-executing discovery. In one of its first major cases dealing with the Rules, the Supreme Court expressed the goal of the new order: "Mutual knowledge of all the relevant facts gathered by both parties is essential to proper litigation." Hickman v. Taylor, 329 U.S. 495, 507 (1947). The idea was that full disclosure not only would promote reasonable settlements and allow cases to be shaped for summary judgment, but also would prevent trials from becoming sporting events where each side tried to surprise the other with evidence for which it was unprepared.

As originally promulgated, and for more than four decades, Rule 26 invited all-out inquiry in terms of its scope and methods, providing for good measure that unless the court ordered otherwise, "the frequency of use" of the various discovery methods was not to be limited. The parties were expected to work together to share information without, at least in the first instance, relying on the power of the court to compel disclosure.

But in the seventies, liberal discovery came under increasing attack. One of the underlying arguments against the original conception of the discovery rules was that, in combination with liberal pleading, it created a potent and unfair shift of advantage to plaintiffs in litigation. Clearing the pleading hurdle means that the plaintiff can use the discovery process to obtain evidence in support of her claims from the defendant, essentially at the defendant's expense. Indeed, some analysts assert that the 1938 Federal Rules represented an effort, "under the guise of procedural reform,... to gain an advantage for New Deal constituencies, particularly plaintiffs, in pursuing litigation." Jay S. Goodman, On the Fiftieth Anniversary of the Federal Rules of Civil Procedure: What Did the Drafters Intend?, 21 Suffolk U. L. Rev. 351, 352 (1987) (citing Stephen N. Subrin, The New Era in American Civil Procedure, 67 A.B.A. J. 1648, 1651 (1981)). Chief among these "New Deal constituencies" were individual consumers and shareholders who were thought to be at a disadvantage in litigation against corporate defendants. See, e.g., Harry Kalven Jr. and Maurice Rosenfield, The Contemporary Function of the Class Suit, 8 U. Chi. L. Rev. 684 (1941). In effect, the Rules transferred power, in the form of access to information, from corporate defendants to individual plaintiffs.

A second attack, applicable to both parties but perhaps more common to corporate litigants, is the use of wide-ranging discovery not to find facts but to impose transaction costs on the other side, forcing settlement to avoid the even higher costs of litigating. Judges also voiced frustration with the extent of collateral litigation over compliance with discovery

* This title is taken from an article by Carl Tobias of the same name in 31 Conn. L. Rev. 1433 (1999).

obligations by parties who were "stonewalling" or engaged in so-called fishing expeditions.

The widespread sense that there was discovery abuse led to the 1983 Amendments to the Rules, which provided more court intervention to limit and sanction bad and excessive practice. In terms of the overall approach to formal discovery, however, the Rules were unchanged: each party remained responsible for formulating its own requests, which could be resisted if not correct or if they invaded some zone of privacy or privilege belonging to the other party.

In 1993, Rule 26 was further amended to require parties to provide certain information to their opponents *without* awaiting a discovery request. Such mandatory disclosure was already required in some states, and had by most accounts been working well. Under the Civil Justice Reform Act of 1991, moreover, a number of federal courts were in the midst of experimenting with mandatory disclosure rules.

Nevertheless, the mandatory disclosure option triggered a massive outpouring of commentary, pro and con. On one side of the debate were those like Judge Schwarzer and Magistrate Judge Brazil, who have argued for years that mandatory disclosure of the type called for in the amended Rule is simply what an ethical lawyer would disclose at any rate, especially in response to skilled queries from the other side. See William W. Schwarzer, The Federal Rules, the Adversary Process, and Discovery Reform, 50 U. Pitt. L. Rev. 703 (1989); Wayne D. Brazil, The Adversary Character of Civil Discovery: A Critique and Proposals for Change, 31 Vand. L. Rev. 1295 (1978).

On the other side of the debate were many observers who felt that the mandatory disclosure provisions were a radical, dangerous incursion into the lawyer's ethical obligations of respect for a client's confidences and of zealous representation. Justice Scalia dissented from the amendments to Rule 26 in the same opinion in which he had excoriated the new Rule 11 (see Chapter 2): "[T]he new Rule would place intolerable strain upon lawyers' ethical duty to represent their clients and not to assist the opposing side. Requiring a lawyer to make a judgment as to what information is 'relevant to disputed facts' plainly requires him to use his professional skills in the service of the adversary." Justice Scalia, Dissenting Statement to Amendments to the Federal Rules of Civil Procedure, 146 F.R.D. 507, 511 (1993). Justice Scalia was joined by many a practitioner at local and national bar meetings who insisted that faithfulness to one's client, a sense of working out one's case in private, and the very nature of the adversary system were at stake. Still other critics of discovery reform argued that the claim of widespread abuse was ungrounded. See, e.g., Linda S. Mullinex, Discovery in Disarray: The Pervasive Myth of Pervasive Discovery Abuse and the Consequences for Unfounded Rulemaking, 46 Stan. L. Rev. 1393 (1994).

To appease the contingent that argued that the adversary system was at stake, the 1993 Amendments allowed any district to opt out of the mandatory disclosure provisions. Although opinion was divided, and nearly half the federal districts chose not to implement the rule, there was substantial evidence that the new Rule 26(a)(1) was achieving its intended goals of cutting litigation costs and speeding case disposition. Surveys of lawyers and judges in Minnesota—among the federal districts that chose to implement Rule 26(a)(1)—indicated that the rule worked well. See Robert E. Oliphant, Four Years of Experience with Rule 26(a)(1): The Rule Is Alive and Well, 24 Wm. Mitchell L. Rev. 323 (1998). In one national survey of litigators, more than half of the attorneys who took part in discovery either gave or received initial disclosures, even though many of them were litigating in districts that had opted out of Rule 26(a)(1). See Thomas E. Willing et al., An Empirical Study of Discovery and Disclosure Practice Under the 1993 Federal Rule Amendments, 39 B.C. L. Rev. 525, 534 (1998).

This encouraging empirical evidence, together with a growing sense of unease about undercutting the uniformity of practice in federal courts, brought about a broader shift in Rule 26 in 2000. Under the newly amended rule, pretrial exchange is mandatory unless a case qualifies for one of several exceptions, such as habeas corpus petitions, actions by the United States to collect on student loans, and enforcement of arbitration awards. See Rule 26(a)(1)(B).

Other significant changes were made in the disclosure provisions that may undermine the flow of party-initiated disclosure. Originally, the scope of discovery as set out in Rule 26 was very broad indeed, applying to any information "relevant to the subject matter." The 1993 rule limited mandatory disclosure to "disputed facts pleaded with particularity." The 2000 amendments, however, eliminated this formulation and provided instead that the scope of mandatory discovery is limited to material that the disclosing party may use to support its claims or defense." Information "relevant to the subject matter" may be obtained only upon court order upon a showing of good cause under Rule 26(b)(1). Can you see how these changes may affect notice pleading?

Another new part of the mandatory disclosure rule exempts the disclosure of material to be used "solely for impeachment." Parties can, of course, move the court for further discovery, but even here things may have changed. A new sentence added to Rule 26(b)(1) reminds the court that "all discovery is subject to the limitations imposed by Rule 26(b)(2)(c)." These provisions require that the court apply a cost-benefit analysis to discovery. The Advisory Committee explains this unusual approach to drafting as follows: "The Committee has been told repeatedly that courts have not implemented these limitations with the vigor that was contemplated.... This otherwise redundant cross-reference has been added to emphasize the need for active judicial use of subdivision (b)(2) to control excessive discovery."

Finally, lawyers' "duties in discovery [are] evolv[ing] rapidly" as a result of the proliferation of means for data storage and communication by means that leave a digital trail (so-called e-discovery). Christopher D. Wall, Ethics in the Era of Electronic Evidence, 41 Trial, Oct. 2005, at 56.

Today, as much as "90 percent of potentially discoverable information is generated and stored electronically." Id. To begin to meet this huge shift in discovery practice, the Advisory Committee drafted amendments that took effect in 2006. See, e.g., Rule 26(b)(2)(B) (setting out specific limitations on discovery of electronically stored information).

The recent amendments are not likely to be the last in the great ongoing re-examination of discovery and its place in procedure. Our goal in this chapter is to help you understand and participate in this debate rather than master all the discovery rules and their considerable technicalities. We focus, therefore, on the topics of scope, privilege, the use of experts, and the regulation of discovery practice by the appellate courts. In the study of discovery, we see the full flowering of the adversary system, for better and for worse.

Problem Case: The Secret Memo

You represent DiChem, a small San Diego corporation whose business is assessing air and water quality for private industries to determine compliance with environmental and occupational safety regulations. In the fall of 2006, DiChem advertised nationally to fill the position of Director of Advertising, and interviewed several applicants. Charles Morris from New Mexico won the job, sold his house, and came on board in December. Shortly thereafter, the company went through hard financial times and laid him off.

Morris has sued DiChem and its president Eve Barrie, alleging that the company should have disclosed the precarious fiscal state to him and had failed to do so. Eve Barrie tells you that neither she nor anyone else said anything at all about DiChem's financial situation at the interviews. She adds, "any management-level employee knows that the job depends on the company's continued financial viability."

When you ask for Eve Barrie's complete file on the hiring of the Director of Advertising, she gives you a meaningful look, and says, "Shall I go through it first?" You smile back and say: "I need to know everything. Anything detrimental to our position will be covered by a privilege, I'm sure."

Back at your office, you go through the file and make notes on each item in it, using special firm letterhead on which is preprinted in large capital letters, "Attorney Work Product." You attach a separate sheet of this special letterhead, with your notes on it, to each item in Barrie's file.

Your heart misses a beat when you come to an undated scrawled note in what you have come to recognize as Eve Barrie's handwriting. It says, "If we ever get into a court fight, must decide how much to tell re black hole—company collapse????" You make the following note: "Item 5—looks like a possible damning admission that company knew they were in danger of collapse. Was it bad enough to verge over into fraud? Did they misrepresent? Get associate to research this if it becomes relevant. Barrie is a smart cookie, but it may be better not to ask her too many more questions until and unless we have to prepare her for deposition."

Must you turn the note over under Rule 26(a)(1)(A)? How will you respond if your opponent moves the court under Rule 26(b) for the complete file on the hiring of the new director? Suppose the court orders disclosure of everything in the file; does that include your memorandum attached to the Eve Barrie note? How will you protect your work?

In order to fully answer these questions, you will need to read through the end of this chapter. For now, you should begin to consider the urgency of these basic discovery questions: what must you disclose to an opponent, in what form, and under what circumstances?

Chalick v. Cooper Hospital, et al.

192 F.R.D. 145 (D.N.J. 2000)

KUGLER, United States Magistrate Judge.

This matter comes before the Court upon Plaintiff Conrad Chalick's Motion to Amend the Complaint. Plaintiff seeks to replace a fictitiously-named John Doe defendant with Richard Burns, M.D., pursuant to Fed. R. Civ. P. 15(c). It is uncontested that the original complaint was filed within the limitations period, but the request to add Dr. Burns as a defendant was made after the limitations period expired, and that, therefore, the question before this Court is whether the addition of Dr. Burns relates back to the filing of the original complaint under Fed. R. Civ. P. 15(c). Because, as discussed below, the court finds that defendants' violations of Fed. R. Civ. P. 26(a) preclude them from claiming that Dr. Burns did not receive notice and was unaware that he was a proper defendant, plaintiff's motion shall be granted.

I. Background

Plaintiff initiated this medical malpractice action by filing a complaint in this court on or about March 9, 1999, claiming diversity jurisdiction under 28 U.S.C. § 1332. Plaintiff named Cooper Hospital-University Medical Center and University Radiology Services, P.A., as defendants, along with four individual physicians: Raja Salem, M.D., Chin-Wei Huang, M.D., Edward G. Moss, M.D., and Robert M. White, M.D. Plaintiff also named as defendants John Does 1-50 and Jane Does 1-50, whom plaintiff identified as [other hospital personnel whose names were presently unknown who had participated in caring for the plaintiff's son].

Plaintiff alleged that defendants were responsible for the death of plaintiff's decedent, Michael Ellis Chalick, who was admitted to Cooper Hospital-University Medical Center on May 30, 1997, following a parachuting accident. . . . There is no dispute that the named defendants were timely served. Defendants University Radiology and Drs. White and Moss [hereinafter referred to as the "University Radiology defendants"] filed their answer to the amended complaint on or about May 5, 1999. Defendants Cooper Hospital and Drs. Salem and Huang [hereinafter referred to as the "Cooper Hospital defendants"] filed their answer to the amended complaint on or about May 19, 1999.

A. Rule 26(a) Disclosures

On or about June 2, 1999, the Cooper Hospital defendants served plaintiff with their Rule 26(a) disclosures. With respect to persons with relevant knowledge, defendants identified the four individual physician defendants, along with five other physicians or nurses, including Dr. Richard Burns. Defendants provided nothing other than Dr. Burns' name; they did not provide Dr. Burns' address or the basis of his knowledge, as is required under Fed. R. Civ. P. 26(a)(1)(A).

On or about June 14, 1999, the University Radiology defendants served plaintiff's counsel with their Rule 26(a) disclosures, also identifying Dr. Richard Burns as an individual with relevant knowledge. These defendants also failed to provide the information required by Rule 26(a)(1)(A), other than Dr. Burns' name.

B. Interrogatories and Depositions

Plaintiff's counsel then served interrogatories and deposition notices. On or about July 14, 1999, Defendant Dr. Huang responded to plaintiff's interrogatories. Form C(3) Interrogatory No. 15 stated in relevant part:

> 15. State the names and addresses of all consultants or other physicians who saw, examined and treated plaintiff at your request for the condition forming the basis of the complaint. . . .

Defendant Huang responded: "No consultations per se, however, thoracic and lumbar spine x-rays were ordered and trauma attending Dr. Burns was notified of the change in patient's condition." In addition, in response to Supplemental Interrogatory No. 2, which asked for the identities of all persons known to fit the description of the John Doe defendants, [Any and all other individuals named in the Cooper Hospital records who may have discoverable information about the care and treatment of the decedent and history of the decedent's injury], Defendant Huang objected to the interrogatory, but referred plaintiff to his response to Form C Interrogatory No. 4, which identified Dr. Richard Burns, among others, as persons with relevant knowledge.[3]

3. There is no indication that the response did anything to explain the nature of Dr. Burns' knowledge, other than to merely identify him by name as a person with relevant knowledge.

On or about August 18, 1999, defendant Dr. Salem served plaintiff with responses to interrogatories. In response to Form C Interrogatory No. 4, Dr. Salem also identified Dr. Richard Burns as a person with relevant knowledge. He did not, however, identify Dr. Burns in response to Form C(3) Interrogatory No. 15.

Plaintiff's counsel initially scheduled depositions of the individual doctor defendants for August 24, 1999. Those depositions were then rescheduled to October, 1999, then to November, 1999, and again to December, 1999. It was not until the deposition of Defendant Dr. Salem on December 10, 1999, that plaintiff claims he first became aware that he had a claim against Dr. Burns.

It was from Dr. Salem's testimony that plaintiff learned that Dr. Burns was a trauma surgeon at Cooper Hospital-University Medical Center who filled in as attending physician in the trauma unit for Dr. Salem during the early morning hours of May 31, 1997, while Dr. Salem was in the operating room. Salem testified that he asked Dr. Burns to check on Michael Chalick in response to his complaints of pain, tingling, and numbness, that Dr. Burns did check on Michael Chalick, made a notation of Mr. Chalick's complaints on his chart, and reviewed Mr. Chalick's x-rays with Dr. Salem. Dr. Salem further testified that Dr. Burns discussed Michael Chalick's condition with Dr. Salem on the morning of May 31, 1997. As a result of this testimony, on or about December 27, 1999, plaintiff filed this motion to amend the amended complaint to add Richard Burns, M.D., as a defendant, conceding that the statute of limitations ran on plaintiff's claim against Dr. Burns, but claiming that the amendment relates back to the filing of the original Complaint under Fed. R. Civ. P. 15(c). In the proposed Second Amended Complaint, plaintiff identifies Dr. Burns as "an individual licensed to practice medicine in the State of New Jersey, who at all times relevant herein maintained a practice of medicine at Three Cooper Plaza, Suite 411, Camden, New Jersey." Plaintiff further alleges in the First Count that "at all relevant times defendants Salem, Huang, Moss, Burns, and White were duly authorized agents, servants, workmen or employees of defendant Cooper Hospital-University Medical Center, acting within the course and scope of their employment."

All other allegations in the proposed Second Amended Complaint remain the same.

The Cooper Hospital defendants filed a brief in opposition to plaintiff's motion. In their opposition, the Cooper Hospital defendants argue that Dr. Burns did not receive actual or constructive notice of this lawsuit, and did not have reason to know that plaintiff intended to sue him until he received plaintiff's motion to amend.

II. Relation Back of Amendments

[Most of the Rule 15 discussion is omitted. Suffice it to say that the Magistrate started from this proposition: "The Third Circuit has shown a strong liberality in allowing amendments under Rule 15 in order to ensure that claims will be decided on the merits rather than on technicalities." It then reached the following conclusion:

> These relation back conditions are subject to equitable considerations. In Bechtel v. Robinson, 886 F.2d 644 (3d Cir. 1989), the Third Circuit held that a defendant, by virtue of misleading the plaintiff as to the proper party to sue, was equitably estopped from asserting he did not receive notice under Rule 15(c). The court examined the principles of equitable estoppel under Delaware law and found that they prevented the defendant from relying upon the statute of limitations defense.
>
> While we recognize that "the statute of limitations is important to a defendant to protect it from the unfair surprise of a stale claim," in this case any surprise to [the defendant] is not "unfair." It was through [the defendant's] own conduct, by misleading the appellants as to the proper party to sue, that appellants were forced to bring a stale claim against him.

EDS.]

III. Disclosure Requirements

In medical malpractice wrongful death cases such as this, it is the defendants who possess the indisputably relevant information about who the decedent's treating physicians were during the decedent's stay in the hospital. The only information that plaintiffs often have at the time of filing a lawsuit are medical records and charts that contain undecipherable handwriting and signatures.[6] It is the obligation of defendants to provide plaintiff with the identities and roles of the decedent's treating physicians so that the case can be decided on the merits. Simply put, defendants must tell a plaintiff who did what, and when, with regard to plaintiff's care and treatment. Just as important, however, is defendants' obligation to provide this information early in the action pursuant to Rule 26(a).

Rule 26(a) obligations are clear and established in this District. . . . While some courts chose to opt-out of certain provisions of the 1993 amendments to Rule 26, this court adopted the new Rule 26(a) in its entirety. . . .

The voluntary disclosure provision of Rule 26(a) that was amended in response to the Civil Justice Reform Act of 1990 was a dramatic and unprecedented shift in federal discovery practice — a shift that was necessitated by the progressively increasing undue time and expense spent on obtaining undisputedly relevant discovery, which was a waste of the litigants' time, as well as that of the court in enforcing the federal discovery rules against recalcitrant parties. This District does not take Rule 26(a) lightly. See Local Civil Rule 26.1, comment. The purpose of voluntary

6. Dr. Richard Burns' notes and signature appear in Michael Chalick's medical records — specifically, a progress notation made at 4:30 A.M. on May 31, 1997, on Michael Chalick's chart — but plaintiff argues, and the court agrees, that the signature was illegible.

disclosures is to streamline discovery and thereby avoid the practice of serving multiple, boilerplate interrogatories and document requests, which themselves bring into play a concomitant set of delays and costs. The requirement of the identification of persons with relevant knowledge in Rule 26(a)(1)(A), along with the subject matter of their knowledge, serves the important purpose of assisting the parties in deciding whom to depose.

Particularly in medical negligence cases, Rule 26(a) disclosure requirements should eliminate what has degenerated into a ritualistic jousting over who should be a defendant. Strict enforcement of the rule leads to early identity of the proper parties so that the litigants can focus on the real issue — who, if anyone, was negligent. This aids defendants as well as plaintiffs, for consistent with the obligations under Rule 11, plaintiff's counsel will be expected to dismiss those defendants who had no role in the care and treatment of the plaintiff.

Litigants are warned not to "indulge in gamesmanship with respect to the disclosure obligations." Advisory Committee Notes, Rule 26(a). To curb such "gamesmanship," Rule 37(c)(1) provides the court with broad latitude in fashioning an appropriate sanction for failure to provide the information required under Rule 26(a). This provision is self-executing; there is no need for a litigant to make a motion to compel. Nor does the imposition of a sanction under this provision require a violation of a court order as a prerequisite.

The automatic enforcement power of Rule 37(c)(1) has been well documented since its revision in 1993. See, e.g., Newman v. GHS Osteopathic, Inc., 60 F.3d 153, 156 (3d Cir. 1995) ("Rule 37 is written in mandatory terms and 'is designed to provide a strong inducement for disclosure of Rule 26(a) material.'" (citation omitted)); Vance v. United States of America, 1999 U.S. App. LEXIS 14943, *8[-*9] (6th Cir. 1999) ("It is well-established that Fed. R. Civ. P. 37(c)(1), enacted in 1993, mandates that a trial court punish a party for discovery violations in connection with Rule 26 unless the violation was harmless or is substantially justified."); Salgado v. General Motors Corp., 150 F.3d 735, 742 and n.6 (7th Cir. 1998) (holding that Rule 37(c)(1) provides enforcement mechanism for violations of Rule 26(a) and that "the district court is not required to fire a warning shot"); Klonoski v. Mahlab, 156 F.3d 255, 269 (1st Cir. 1998) ("The new rule [37(c)(1)] clearly contemplates stricter adherence to discovery requirements, and harsher sanctions for breaches of this rule, and the required sanction in the ordinary case is mandatory preclusion."). The sanctions available to this court under Rule 37(c)(1) are those set forth in subparagraphs (A), (B) and (C) of subdivision (b)(2). . . .

With these rules in mind, the court makes the following findings. Defendants failed to comply with their disclosure obligations under Rule 26(a)(1)(A), because they provided no information about Dr. Burns other than his name. They did not provide the basis of his knowledge, as required by the rule. Had they complied with their Rule 26(a)(1)(A) obligations, plaintiff would have been duly informed by June 2, 1999, that

Dr. Burns was one of the physicians responsible for the care of Michael Chalick on the day that he died.

Defendants have not provided "substantial justification" for their failure to explain the role of Dr. Burns, nor was this failure harmless. The prejudice resulting to plaintiff is obvious. If he had received that information on June 2, 1999, plaintiff would reasonably have had the time and information necessary to add Dr. Burns as a defendant and provide notice to him before July 29, 1999. That not only would have allowed Dr. Burns to participate in the litigation from the outset, but it also would have prevented defendants from arguing now that Dr. Burns did not receive notice within the Rule 15(c) period. That prejudice also extends to the court, for defendants' refusal to provide plaintiff with the information necessary to determine who the physicians were who were responsible for the care of Michael Chalick has hindered the efficient management of the pretrial process with which the court is charged under Rule 16 and has delayed a resolution of this action on its merits. Defendants' failure to comply with Rule 26(a), along with the resulting prejudice, warrants a sanction.

The court further finds that an appropriate sanction is to refuse to allow defendants to rely on their claim that Dr. Burns, within the Rule 15(c) period, did not receive notice of the action and did not have reason to believe that he would be a named defendant.[8] See Fed. R. Civ. P. 37(b)(2)(B); Bechtel v. Robinson, 886 F.2d at 652 (applying equitable estoppel to bar defendant from claiming that he did not receive notice within the limitations period). Dr. Burns cannot claim to have suffered prejudice from his late addition to this lawsuit when the defendants, with whom Dr. Burns apparently shares an identity of interest, had reason to know as early as June, 1999, by virtue of the John Doe paragraph in the complaint, that plaintiff intended to name all of the physicians who treated Michael Chalick on the day before and morning of his death, and that Dr. Burns was one of those physicians.[9]

8. The fact that plaintiff had knowledge on July 14, 1999, of Dr. Huang's interrogatory response in which he stated that "trauma attending Dr. Burns was notified of the change in patient's condition" does not undo the prejudice that defendants caused by their earlier Rule 26(a) violation, nor does plaintiff's delay in deposing any of the defendant doctors change the sanction which this court finds is an appropriate remedy for defendants' discovery violations. See Lundy v. Adamar of New Jersey, Inc., 34 F.3d 1173, 1197 (Becker, J., concurring in part, dissenting in part) ("This Court has repeatedly stated outright that unexcused delay unaccompanied by real detriment to the defendant or to the judiciary does not constitute undue delay.").

9. Even if the Cooper Hospital defendants were allowed to rely on their claim that Dr. Burns suffered prejudice, the court finds that defendants' burden of showing actual prejudice has not been met. See Urrutia v. Harrisburg County Police Dept., 91 F.3d 451, 461 ("The prejudice must be actual, not hypothetical."); Bechtel v. Robinson, 886 F.2d 644, 652 (defendant must show that it was unfairly denied opportunity to present facts or evidence which it would have presented had amendment been timely). Any lost opportunity of Dr. Burns to present facts or evidence was not unfair, given the Cooper Hospital defendants' knowledge of his role in Michael Chalick's care and the common interest of Dr. Burns and the Cooper Hospital defendants, who presumably have been engaged in the preparation of a defense that will not differ significantly from that which Dr. Burns will

Accordingly, the court finds that a sanction under Rule 37(c)(1) is warranted by defendants' violation of their disclosure obligations under Rule 26(a).

Notes and Questions

1. *The Rhythm of Discovery. Chalick* shows both the usual progression of discovery and how delays occur. First in line is mandatory discovery. How soon must that be made? How can it be resisted? Next in the usual course are some interrogatories. Who answered the interrogatories that are mentioned in the case? How do you think it happened that there were discrepancies among the defendants in the answers to the interrogatories?

Notice that the interrogatories were followed by depositions of the treating doctors. Some of the delay in the case was the five months in which the depositions were continued again and again. Why does the magistrate not count these against the plaintiff in making his equitable assessment?

If you were the lawyer for Dr. Burns, what arguments would you make about the unfairness of adding him as a defendant after the limitations period? One of the strongest arguments is that the plaintiffs had notice very early on that there was a Dr. Burns in the case; why wasn't it up to them to find out who he was?

2. *The Advantages of Mandatory Disclosure.* What are the strategic consequences of making early disclosures? Might the advantages of disclosure ever be great enough to trigger the exchange of information even without the mandatory disclosure rule? See Robert D. Cooter and Daniel L. Rubinfeld, An Economic Model of Legal Discovery, 23 J. Legal Stud. 435, 436 (1994) (noting that "[r]evealing information to correct the other side's false optimism creates an advantage in settlement bargaining for the disclosing party . . . [that] provides a strong incentive voluntarily to disclose facts correcting the other side's false optimism before trial").

Apparently, many practicing lawyers see the advantage of some mandatory disclosure. Studies done of the operation of Rule 26(a) in the places where it was first tried, found substantial satisfaction with its effect on the cost of discovery and the promotion of settlement. Most significantly, the Rule did not produce the satellite litigation that many opponents predicted. See Thomas E. Willging et al., An Empirical Study of Discovery and Disclosure Practice Under the 1993 Federal Rule Amendments, 39 B. C. L. Rev. 525 (1998).

Still, the risk of abuse, or "gamesmanship," as the court put it in *Chalick*, is ever present. In *Chalick* the problem was failure to fully disclose under

---

present. In any event, there has been no claim of loss of witness testimony or other evidence as a result of the delay in naming Dr. Burns, and the court will permit the parties adequate time to exchange discovery regarding Dr. Burns.

Rule 26(a). Is it possible to defeat the purpose of the rule by disclosing too much? Consider United States ex rel. Bradford Hunt v. Merck-Medco Managed Care, LLC, 223 F.R.D. 330, 333 (E.D. Pa. 2004), a consumer fraud action against a pharmaceutical company in which defendants objected to the plaintiffs' initial disclosures on the grounds of the sheer volume of the names provided (3,900!) and that this hefty disclosure thwarted "the purpose and intent of Rule 26(a) to provide an efficient start to relevant discovery." Defendants sought an order requiring plaintiffs, among other things, to "(1) make a qualitative judgment on the importance or relevance of each individual listed, (2) identify the twenty most significant individuals for Plaintiffs' case in each category [including patients, physicians, as well as former and current employees of the defendant pharmaceutical company], and (3) identify the subject of discoverable information for each individual listed. . . ." Id. at 332.

Are these demands legitimate under Rule 26(a)? Have plaintiffs abused Rule 26(a) by dumping a massive amount of information (a version of the needle-in-the-haystack approach to discovery), or are defendants abusing Rule 26(a) by forcing plaintiffs to reveal more than the rule requires?

The district court sided with the plaintiffs, holding that the sheer volume of a party's initial disclosure statements "cannot, by itself constitute a violation of Rule 26(a) because the self-executing disclosures are merely a starting point for the discovery process," and initial disclosures will vary in each case according to the sophistication of the claims raised in the pleadings. Id. at 333. "Logically," the court reasoned, "the more complex the case in terms of the number of parties and the scope of allegations, the larger the disclosure statements should be." Id. Looking at the facts of this case, the court continued:

> Medco Defendants are alleged to have defrauded patients, clients, and the United States by canceling and destroying prescriptions, by failing to perform needed pharmaceutical services, by switching patient's subscriptions without their knowledge and consent, by . . . billing patients for drugs never ordered, by creating false records, by soliciting and receiving inducements from [other drug companies] to favor their products, and by making false and misleading statements to the government about its conduct. These allegations encompass . . . potentially numerous Merck-Medco facilities across the country, numerous current and former Merck-Medco employees, numerous physicians and patients. Given the broad language of Rule 26(a) — parties must provide information concerning "each individual likely to have discoverable information" — one would expect the self-executing initial disclosures in this case to be voluminous.

Id. Finally, the court chastised defendants' counsel for trying to force plaintiffs to reveal their subjective impressions of the quality of evidence in the disclosures:

> [I]t is apparent that the Medco Defendants seek to use the self-executing disclosure statements of Rule 26(a)(1) not only as a tool for starting relevant

> discovery, but also as a tool to learn details of Plaintiffs' investigation and trial strategy. For example, the Medco Defendants ask this court to require Plaintiffs to make a qualitative determination of the most important witnesses in each category as part of their Amended Initial Disclosure Statement. This request clearly seeks information and analysis that goes well beyond the purpose and intent of Rule 26(a)(1).

Id. at 335.

3. *The Ethics of Nondisclosure.* In the problem case, would Eve Barrie's memorandum be subject to Rule 26(a) required disclosure? To answer this completely, you need to know some evidence law. Is the memorandum something that the company might use to support its defense? Not likely—since it seems to undercut the defense. But who can tell what might happen at trial that might make the memorandum relevant to the defense? In the same vein, can you say with certainty that the memorandum need not be disclosed because it would be used "solely for impeachment" of Eve Barrie? That word "solely" is quite a limitation, isn't it?

The opponents of redefining the scope of discovery argued that this relation to evidence law would lead to wrangles unrelated to the purposes of discovery. They also argued that the change in scope would burden and distort the pleading stage. Can you understand the argument that parties will plead at greater length to limit the discovery that they must give? The previous Rule 26(a) on mandatory discovery related it to matters pleaded with particularity. Many thought that phraseology invited overly elaborate pleading. The new formulation hardly seems better on this score. See *Twombly* and note in Chapter 2 at page 339.

The Secret Memo hypothetical also has obvious ethical implications. What does professional ethics dictate in this situation, apart from *any* rules of procedure? Consider the following discussion of this dilemma from Deborah Rhode's Professional Responsibility: Ethics by the Pervasive Method 442-444 (2d ed. 1998):

> In a well-known passage from his autobiography, Samuel Williston described an incident from practice involving a financial dispute. As counsel for the defendant, Williston had carefully reviewed his client's correspondence with the plaintiff. Opposing counsel had made no inquiries concerning certain letters relevant to the controversy, and no one mentioned them at trial. The court ruled in favor of the defendant and gave an oral explanation of its reasoning that Williston describes as follows:
>
>> In the course of his remarks the Chief Justice stated as one reason for his decision a supposed fact which I knew to be unfounded. I had in front of me a letter that showed his error. Though I have no doubt of the propriety of my behavior in keeping silent, I was somewhat uncomfortable at the time. . . . The lawyer must decide when he takes a case whether it is a suitable one for him to undertake and after this decision is made, he is not justified in turning against his client by exposing injurious evidence entrusted to him. If that evidence was unknown to him when he took the case, he may sometimes withdraw

from it, but while he is engaged as counsel he is not only not obligated to disclose unfavorable evidence, but it is a violation of his duty to his client if he does so.

In another often-discussed case from around the same period, the New York County Bar Ethics Committee was asked for an opinion about disclosures in tort litigation. The plaintiff was a three-year-old child, who was injured by falling off a porch, allegedly because of the defendant owner's negligence. The defendant's attorney successfully moved to dismiss the case for lack of evidence without disclosing that he had an eyewitness to the accident present in court. Neither the judge nor the plaintiff's attorney was aware that any witness existed. The Committee's entire assessment of the case was as follows: "In the opinion of the Committee the conduct of the defendant's attorney is not professionally improper. The fact of infancy does not call for a different reply."

Such dead ends in the search for truth are not uncommon. . . . Nor are the costs insubstantial: consider the nondisclosure of an opponent's life-threatening disease. . . . The rationale for withholding information in such cases rests on two considerations. One involves the need to protect confidential information in order to ensure trust and candor in lawyer-client relationships. The other consideration involves the need to provide incentives in a competitive adversarial structure. If parties begin to assume that they can rely on an opponent's disclosure of material information, they may cease to do adequate preparation themselves. The result would be inequity and inefficiency. One party could end up subsidizing both sides of a lawsuit. And the more that individuals attempted to freeload on their adversaries, the greater the risk that neither side would prepare adequately.

Are these considerations sufficient to justify the bar's current ethical rules concerning disclosure of facts? Disciplinary Rule 7-102(A) provides that a lawyer "shall not conceal or knowingly fail to disclose that which he is required by law to reveal" and "shall not knowingly make a false statement of law or fact." Model Rule 3.3(a) similarly prohibits lawyers from making a "false statement of material fact or law to a tribunal," and from failing "to disclose a material fact to a tribunal when disclosure is necessary to avoid assisting a criminal or fraudulent act by the client." In ex parte proceedings, a lawyer must "inform the tribunal of all material facts known to the lawyer which will enable the tribunal to make an informed decision, whether or not the facts are adverse."

Should the rule governing ex parte proceedings apply to all litigation? . . . A similar obligation applies to prosecutors, who must reveal exculpatory facts under Brady v. Maryland, (373 U.S. 83 (1963)), Model Rule 3.8, and DR 7-103(B). Defenders of a broader duty of disclosure in civil cases point out that these analogous provisions have worked reasonably well in criminal cases without undermining incentive structures or trusting relationships in contexts such as criminal prosecutions or securities regulation. Advocates also argue that additional disclosure requirements would not chill client confidences. . . . From this perspective:

- clients often have no realistic alternative to confiding in counsel;
- lawyers acquire much adverse information through means other than direct client communication;

- clients already are unaware of the scope of confidentiality protections; and
- the bar in many countries and in this nation historically has managed to provide adequate representation without sweeping confidentiality protections.

What is your view? Would you support an initial proposal by the Model Rules Commission that (1) would have required disclosure of adverse facts if they would "probably have a substantial effect on the determination of a material issue" and (2) would have permitted disclosure of evidence favorable to opposing parties?

C. THE SCOPE OF DISCOVERY

1. "Relevant to the Subject Matter"

Blank v. Sullivan & Cromwell
16 Fair Empl. Prac. Cas. (BNA) 87 (S.D.N.Y. 1976)

MOTLEY, District Judge.

[Plaintiffs were women lawyers who had unsuccessfully applied for positions as associates around 1970; they sued, alleging sexual discrimination in hiring.]

Plaintiffs have moved for a rehearing and modification of so much of this court's order of May 24, 1976 as denied plaintiffs the discovery sought in Interrogatories 60(f) and (g), 61, 62, and 63 of their First Interrogatories[1] (filed in court on April 18, 1976). That order adopted the report of Magistrate Harold J. Raby, to whom plaintiffs' Rule 37 motion had previously been referred, but modified the report insofar as it had recommended

1.
60. Identify each and every female permanent associate at Sullivan & Cromwell prior to August 30, 1970 and indicate as to each . . .

(f). whether each was offered an opportunity to become a partner; and
(g). whether each became a partner.

61. State the average length of service at the firm as an associate, of all associates who were offered partnerships in the firm between 1961 and the present date.

62. If any person listed in answer to Question 60 was not offered an opportunity to become a partner within the average length of service period noted in answer to Question 61, state the reason why she was not extended such an offer.

63. State the name of each male attorney hired by the firm after the earliest date listed in answer to Question 60(b) who was offered an opportunity to become a partner at the firm, and indicate:

(a) the date when each person started work at the firm;
(b) the date on which each person was offered the opportunity to become a partner; and
(c) the area of specialization of each person.

compliance with the Interrogatories here in question. Specifically, with respect to these Interrogatories (and certain others not in issue on the motion for rehearing), the court held that "the defendant need not respond in any form to such Interrogatories since the information sought therein relates to defendant's partners and employees who became partners, and is not relevant to the subject matter of the suit before this court." However, upon reconsideration and upon careful examination of the arguments submitted by plaintiffs, defendant, and amicus Equal Employment Opportunity Commission, the court has decided to order defendants to respond to the Interrogatories here in issue. . . .

In reversing its prior ruling, this court also is mindful of the fact that a plaintiff may not sue for injuries that he or she has not suffered, and he or she may not sue on behalf of a class of which he or she is not a member. Plaintiff, therefore, cannot represent in this action those who may be aggrieved by defendant's partner selection criteria. However, defendant is incorrect in suggesting that because the individual plaintiff here has not alleged that she was denied partnership due to her sex, she is not entitled to the requested discovery.

Under Rule 26, Fed. R. Civ. P., a party is entitled to discovery, not only of material which is relevant and admissible at trial, but also of information which "appears reasonably calculated to lead to the discovery of admissible evidence." More specifically, in Title VII cases, in which a plaintiff alleges discriminatory employment practices, both the Supreme Court, in McDonnell Douglas Corp. v. Green, 411 U.S. 792, 804-805 (1973), and the Second Circuit in Kohn v. Royall, Koegel & Wells 496 F.2d 1094 (2d Cir. 1974), have ruled that general information on defendant's labor hierarchy may be reflective of restrictive or exclusionary hiring practices within the contemplation of the statute.

Thus, the narrow inquiry is whether the information requested is so unrelated to plaintiffs' claim that women are discriminated against by defendant on account of sex that it cannot be said to be "relevant" within the expansive meaning of that term in Rule 26. In the court's view, this connection is not nearly so tenuous as defendant suggests.

By order dated June 13, 1975, this court ruled that "the class represented by plaintiff is defined to include all women qualified to hold legal positions at the law firm of Sullivan and Cromwell who have been or would be denied employment because of their sex." Judge Lasker of this Court dealt with a plaintiff class similarly constituted in a suit against the law firm of Royall, Koegel & Wells. By order dated January 7, 1975, he granted plaintiffs in that suit similar discovery with respect to advancement to partnership, endorsing the recommendation of Magistrate, now Judge Goettel, who had commented as follows: "It is difficult to conceive of anything more telling with respect to whether or not these associates [females] are being subject to employment discrimination than whether they proceed on to partnerships in the firm in the same manner as male attorneys with similar capabilities."

The court is, of course, aware that the numerous factors which bear upon the admission to partnership make it impossible to equate that decision with the decision to hire an associate. However, it does not follow from that recognition that a firm's practices in advancing, or failing to advance, associates to partnership have no probative bearing upon allegations of improper discrimination in hiring associates. Even assuming arguendo, that Title VII does not proscribe the use of sex as a criterion for admission to partnership, that legal conclusion does not necessarily indicate that evidence of sexually oriented discrimination at that level might not be probative of a similar pattern in the selection of associates, where it would be illegal.

Accordingly, defendant is directed to answer the Interrogatories referred to above.

Note: Relevance: Three Takes on Scope Under Rule 26

One of the most hotly debated changes in the year 2000 round of Rule revision was the definition of scope in Rule 26. The old standard, "relevance to the subject matter" of the lawsuit, which *Blank* applied, is now applicable *only* on court order for good cause shown. The general standard for discovery under the formal rules is "relevan[ce] to any party's claim or defense." See Rule 26(b)(1). Yet a third standard applies for the Rule 26(a) disclosures: The disclosing party must turn over materials that support his *own* claim or defense.

The intent of the rule-makers is clear, isn't it? They are hoping to limit discovery and to cut down on its excesses. For an early empirical analysis of the 2000 Amendments, see Ann K. Hadrava, The Amendment to Federal Rule of Civil Procedure 26(B)(1) Scope of Discovery: An Empirical Analysis of Its Potential "Relevancy" to Employment Discrimination Actions, 26 Okla. City U. L. Rev. 1111 (2001). For a critique of the amendments, see John S. Beckerman, Confronting Civil Discovery's Fatal Flaws, 84 Minn. L. Rev. 505, 538-543 (2000) (arguing that civil discovery is ill-suited to a party-centric, adversarial court system and that the changes to 26(b)(1) will exacerbate existing problems).

Would the partnership information in *Blank* be discoverable by interrogatory under the new Rule 26(b)(1)? What could Blank's lawyer argue was good cause? Are the cases like *Blank*, ordering discovery under the previous standard (relevance to the subject matter), precedent for determining "good cause" under the new rule?

Authority is divided on whether and how much the new standard limits the scope of discovery. On the one hand, some courts take it for granted that the Advisory Committee intended to restrict discovery. As the Ninth Circuit observed in limiting discovery in a Title VII sexual harassment suit against a church:

> "[T]he ability of the district court to control discovery" will guard against "a wide-ranging intrusion into sensitive religious matters." [Bollard v. California

> Province of the Soc. of Jesus, 196 F.3d 940, 950 (9th Cir. 1999).] Significantly, the district court's control over discovery has been enhanced since our 1999 *Bollard* decision. In 2000, the Federal Rules of Civil Procedure were amended "to involve the court more actively in regulating the breadth of sweeping or contentious discovery." Fed. R. Civ. P. 26 Advisory Committee Notes. In particular, the new rules limit the breadth of discovery that can occur absent court approval. Under Rule 26(b)(1), for example, discovery must now relate more directly to a "claim or defense" than it did previously, and "if there is an objection that discovery goes beyond material relevant to the parties' claims or defenses, the court would become involved." Id.

Elvig v. Calvin Presbyterian Church, 375 F.3d 951, 967-968 (9th Cir. 2004). See also Sanyo Laser Prods. Inc. v. Arista Records, Inc., 214 F.R.D. 496, 500 (S.D. Ind. 2003) ("[T]he scope of discovery has narrowed somewhat under the revised rule. The change, while meaningful, is not dramatic, and broad discovery remains the norm."); Surles v. Air France, 2001 WL 1142231, at *1 n.3 (S.D.N.Y. Sept. 27, 2001) ("[I]t is intended that the scope of discovery be narrower than it was, in some meaningful way." (internal quotation marks and citation omitted)). Other courts have concluded that although there is no fundamental difference between the current and previous versions of Rule 26(b)(1), the difference can be ascertained by applying the principles in Rule 26(b)(2). See, e.g., Thompson v. Dept. of Hous. and Urban Dev., 199 F.R.D. 168, 172 (D. Md. 2001) ("[T]he practical solution to implementing the new Rule changes may be to focus more on whether the requested discovery makes sense in light of the Rule 26(b)(2) factors, than to attempt to divine some bright line difference between the old and new rule."); In re Sealed Case (Medical Records), 381 F.3d 1205, 1215 (D.C. Cir. 2004).

On the other hand, many courts have simply blinked at the idea that the new language requires stricter limits. Consider, for instance, the following opinion in an age and disability discrimination suit brought against Coca-Cola by an employee who was demoted to a lesser-paying job after the company denied him a medical waiver it had granted him for the preceding 20 years for a disability he had from birth.

> Defendant objects to several of plaintiff's interrogatories and production requests on the grounds of relevance. "Parties may obtain discovery regarding any matter, not privileged, that is relevant to the claim or defense of any party." Fed. R. Civ. P. 26(b)(1). Relevance is not defined in the Federal Rules of Civil Procedure. However, the Federal Rules of Evidence defines "relevant evidence" as "evidence having any tendency to make the existence of any fact that is of consequence to the determination of the action more probable or less probable than it would be without the evidence." Fed. R. Evid. 401. By necessary implication, the definition of relevance in the universe of discovery is broader than that in evidence. Under the evidence regime, evidence is admissible only if it is relevant. Fed. R. Evid. 402. However, discovery has no such constraint. "Relevant information need not be admissible at the trial if the discovery appears reasonably calculated to

lead to the discovery of admissible evidence." Fed. R. Civ. P. 26(b)(1). With this in mind, courts have taken the position that relevance, in the realm of discovery, ought to be broadly and liberally construed. See Herbert v. Lando, 441 U.S. 153 (1979).

The definition of relevance continues to be liberally interpreted even after changes to Rule 26 in 2000. Relevance, as it stands after the 2000 amendments, "requires the courts and the parties to focus on the actual claims and defenses involved in the action." 6 Moore's Federal Practice § 26.43 (Matthew Bender 3d ed.) (citing Fed. R. Civ. P. 26(b)(1) advisory committee's note (2000)). Prior to 2000, Rule 26 merely required that discovery be relevant to the "subject matter involved in the pending action." However, *there is no indication that the change in focus from relevance in relation to the subject matter, to relevance in relation to claims and defenses," marks a substantial departure from the traditional liberal construction of the term, which is designed to assure access to the information necessary for the achievement of justice and fair trials."* Id. § 26.41[3][c]. Relevancy continues to be "broadly construed, and a request for discovery should be considered relevant if there is any possibility that the information sought may be relevant to the claim or defense of any party." Favale v. Roman Catholic Diocese of Bridgeport, 233 F.R.D. 243 (D. Conn. 2005) (quoting Merrill v. Waffle House, Inc., 227 F.R.D. 467, 470 (N.D. Tex. 2005)) (emphasis added).

For the foregoing reasons the court finds that interrogatories and production requests objected to on the grounds of relevance are, in fact, relevant or will reasonably lead to the discovery of relevant information.

Interrogatory 8(e) asks defendant to "[i]dentify each year the company refused to hire any individuals possessing state-granted Medical waivers for Commercial Drivers." Defendants admit that the adverse employment decision made in this case was prompted by a company policy. This policy presumably requires both that current employees not be granted medical waivers and that new drivers requiring such waivers not be hired. What interrogatory 8(e) seeks is proof, or lack thereof, of this policy at work before plaintiff's demotion. Defendant voluntarily asserted its policy as a defense to the alleged discrimination. As such, it cannot now claim that historical examples of that policy in action are not relevant. . . .

Interrogatory 19 asks the defendant to articulate its policies and procedures used to record and preserve employee health records. Plaintiff argues that insurance costs are a potential reason to discriminate against disabled employees. The argument continues that if the defendant knew about disabled employees it would place those employees in less hazardous positions in order to minimize insurance costs, even if a disabled employee was qualified to perform a more hazardous task with reasonable accommodation. This argument is plausible in that it sets forth a possible motive defendant might have to maintain a policy of discrimination. Defendant's policy is alleged as discriminatory by plaintiff and asserted as a defense by defendant. As such, the information requested in interrogatory 19 is relevant to a claim or defense in this case.

Production Request 16 asks for information regarding the evaluation of defendant's managers and supervisors. The evaluations may include reports or reprimands for discriminatory activity by defendant's managers or supervisors. As such, evaluations could provide information establishing

> a pattern or practice of discrimination. Therefore, the information is relevant and should be produced.
>
> Production Request 31 asks for "[a]ny and all memos, letters, notes, correspondence, e-mails or other documents written or electronic which describe hiring procedures of the Defendant." Defendant admits that a company policy required the adverse employment decision alleged in this case. It is unclear whether this policy affects only current employees or extends to prospective employees as well. If it is the latter, then plaintiff's request is obviously relevant. Further, the defendant did not address this production request in its response to plaintiff's Motion to Compel. Having no additional information on which to base a contrary decision, the court finds that Production Request 31 seeks relevant information.

Breon v. Coca-Cola Bottling Co. of New England, 232 F.R.D. 49, 52 (D. Conn. 2005) (emphasis added). See also EEOC v. Caesars Entertainment, Inc., 237 F.R.D. 428 (D. Nev. 2006) ("There seems to be a general consensus that the Amendments to Rule 26(b) 'do not dramatically alter the scope of discovery.'") (quoting World Wrestling Fed'n Entm't, Inc., v. William Morris Agency, Inc., 204 F.R.D. 263, 265 n.1 (S.D.N.Y. 2001)).

Note: Unduly Burdensome or Expensive

Responding to discovery can be very burdensome. Written interrogatories, for example, can be cheap to produce and costly to answer; lengthy or numerous depositions can seriously disrupt normal business and the activities of life. Balancing the legitimate need for information against the burden and expense of producing it has proved a nearly intractable problem both for the rule-makers and for the courts.

The original tool for dealing with excessive discovery requests was a motion for a protective order from the court under Rule 26(c). Because the original scope of discovery was so broad, such orders were seldom granted. In the first round of attack on discovery abuse, the 1983 revision called for a court to place limits on the frequency of discovery if it was found "unreasonably cumulative, more readily obtainable from another source, redundant of discovery already taken, unduly burdensome or expensive taking into account the needs of the case, the amount in controversy, limitations on the parties' resources, and the importance of the issues at stake in the litigation."

The 2000 revisions go even further in providing for the court to shift the cost of discovery, and to raise the matter of limits on its own, without waiting for an aggrieved party to complain or seek a protective order. Of particular concern to those who think discovery reform has gone too far is the balancing required in Rule 26(b)(2)(C)(iii) between the benefits and the burdens of proposed discovery.

These provisions signal that parties no longer have an unquestioned right to pursue discovery until "no stone is left unturned" or their adversary collapses from exhaustion (whichever comes first). But they have been criticized on the ground that they call for an impossibly subjective inquiry and authorize the courts to make inappropriate judgments about the relative "importance" of cases.

2. "Any Matter Not Privileged"

Problem Case: A Literary Law Student

Donna Doolittle is a second-year student at Stamford Law School in Stamford, Connecticut. In 2008, she began publishing a book, in weekly installments, in the National Legal Gossip Journal. Entitled *Stamford Law,* the book recounts the trials and tribulations of a first-year law student.

In 2009, Evan Monson, the author of *First Year* (a best-selling book about a first-year student's experience in law school, published in the early 1990s), sued Doolittle and the National Legal Gossip Corporation for copyright infringement, claiming that her book impermissibly copied Monson's book.

Doolittle has retained you as her attorney. You have filed an answer denying that she copied any part of *First Year.* Your answer was based in part on the following:

Donna has never read *First Year*. However, a friend of hers, who read a draft of *Stamford Law,* remarked on the striking similarities between her book and Monson's. As a result, Donna retained Charlie Counsel to advise her about copyright law before she published the first installment. Charlie sent Donna a memorandum, which begins: "Based on your friend's comment that *Stamford Law* bears a 'striking resemblance' to *First Year,* I have done some legal research. . ." The memo goes on to say that one does not infringe a copyrighted work unless one actually copied the work, and it concludes that Donna should not read *First Year.* (You check and determine that this is an accurate account of copyright law.) Donna doesn't have a copy of the memo in her possession; she recalled that she had lent it to a fellow student to assist him in preparing for a copyright exam. Rather than try to track down the student, who has since graduated, you obtained a copy of the memo directly from Charlie Counsel.

Donna says that all of the stories recounted in *Stamford Law* were based on her own experiences or those of law school classmates. There are four sets of documents relating to these experiences:

1) A diary, written during her first year at law school, that, in addition to recounting events at the school, contains much personal material, which she says would be terribly embarrassing to reveal to anyone. She has adamantly refused to let you see the diary, saying that her personal thoughts and revelations are so intertwined with descriptions of events at the school that they can't be separated.
2) Some very rough notes, in an orange notebook, of her conversations with classmates, upon which she drew to write the book.

3) After completing the book, but before the first installment was published, Donna started systematically re-interviewing her classmates to hear their stories again. Rough notes of the re-interviews are in a blue notebook. When you asked her why she did the re-interviews, Donna said that she had the impression that it was important to check out the stories "in case someone claimed they were untrue."
4) Donna was still conducting the re-interviews as the installments were being published, but she stopped when Monson filed suit. You asked her to continue re-interviewing the remainder of her classmates to get their stories. She has completed the project and given you a yellow notebook with these interview notes.

You are Donna's lawyer. Which, if any, of the four sets of documents are you required to disclose under Rule 26(a)(1)? Suppose that Monson's counsel notices Donna's deposition and asks that she bring "all correspondence, notes, interviews, drafts, and other documents relating to the writing and publication of *Stamford Law.*" What will you tell her to produce?

Do you think this is an appropriate case in which to move for a protective order under Rule 26(c)? What would your argument be?

Note: Privileges in Civil Litigation

One principle of discovery has withstood all rule revision and rethinking: privileged information is not discoverable. Some privileges are defined by the law of evidence, though analysis of them occurs in light of long-established common law privileges. A witness who successfully asserts a privilege may avoid giving relevant evidence in a case. The Fifth Amendment privilege against self-incrimination is a familiar example; it applies in civil litigation only if the witness faces a serious threat of *criminal* prosecution. Privileges designed to protect certain professional or confidential relationships—the doctor-patient, priest-penitent, and marital privileges, for example—are also established in most jurisdictions. A less established example, recognized in most but not all jurisdictions, is the journalist's privilege to protect confidential news sources, recognized by a few courts and some statutory law. See, e.g., Baker v. F&F Investment, 470 F.2d 778 (2d Cir. 1972). See also Omokehinede v. Detroit Bd. Of Educ., 251 F.R.D. 261, 264 (E.D. Mich. 2007) (noting that most jurisdictions have adopted some qualified privilege for journalists despite the Sixth Circuit's refusal).

Still another privilege is the so-called self-critical analysis privilege, recognized by some jurisdictions. This privilege protects material that satisfies the following criteria:

> "[F]irst, the information must result from a critical self-analysis undertaken by the party seeking protection; second, the public must have a strong interest in preserving the free flow of the type of information sought; finally,

> the information must be the type whose flow would be curtailed if discovery were allowed." Note, The Privilege of Self-Critical Analysis, 96 Harv. L. Rev. 1083, 1086 (1983). To these requirements should be added the general proviso that no document will be accorded a privilege unless it was prepared with the expectation that it would be kept confidential, and has in fact been kept confidential. See James F. Flanagan, Rejecting a General Privilege for Self-Critical Analyses, 51 Geo. Wash. L. Rev. 551, 574-76 (1983) (citing 8 J. Wigmore, Wigmore on Evidence § 2285, at 527 (1961)); see also Peterson v. Chesapeake & Ohio Rv., 112 F.R.D. 360, 363 (W.D. Mich. 1986) (refusing to apply the privilege to investigative report because report was not "performed with the expectation that the analysis [would] remain confidential" and in fact had not been kept confidential); Westmoreland v. CBS, Inc., 97 F.R.D. 703, 706 (S.D.N.Y. 1983) (same).

Dowling v. American Hawaii Cruises, Inc., 971 F.2d 423, 426 (9th Cir. 1992). See also id. ("Even if such a privilege exists, the justifications for it do not support its application to voluntary routine safety reviews."); Joiner v. Hercules, Inc., 169 F.R.D. 695, 699 (S.D. Ga. 1996). Cf. Cloud v. Superior Court [Little Industries, Inc.], 50 Cal. App. 4th 1552 (1996) (refusing to adopt the "self-critical analysis" privilege).

In all of these areas, a given is that recognizing the privilege will necessarily impede the search for truth, because it will deprive the parties and the court of relevant, often highly probative evidence. The privilege represents a judgment that other social values outweigh the needs and interests of the civil litigation system. Given the strong interest in disclosure of relevant facts, all privileges generally are construed narrowly, and care must be taken not to waive the privilege inadvertently. Thus, for example, submitting an insurance form to recover medical expenses may constitute a waiver of any psychiatrist-patient privilege. (See infra at page 517 on waiving the attorney-client privilege.) Likewise, the privilege may be only as good as the professional in whom one confides. In a New Jersey criminal case that received national attention, the court held that no privilege barred a jailhouse minister from testifying that the defendant confessed to him. Although the minister could not be compelled to testify, he could do so voluntarily. See Wade Lambert, Courts Say Penitent's Secrets May Not Be Secret, Wall St. J., Jan. 13, 1994, at B1.

The privileges most common in civil litigation are the attorney-client privilege and its offshoot, the work-product privilege. Unlike all other privileges, these two are said to promote, or at least be consistent with, the underlying values of the adversary system. Thus, they are more robust and easier to maintain than other privileges. This is true even though they operate, like the others, to deprive the fact-finder of relevant information. In the following cases, you will see the profound conviction expressed by the Supreme Court over many decades that protection of the lawyer's private work is essential to the sound operation of the system as a whole.

The attorney-client privilege is mostly a creature of common law, with local variations. Nowhere does it mean, as lay people tend to think, that telling something to a lawyer turns it into a protected secret. The hornbook elements of attorney-client privilege are (1) a communication (2) from the client to the lawyer (3) without the presence of others (4) for the purpose of seeking legal advice.

In the famous case of Hickman v. Taylor, the privilege argued was attorney-client. The Court found that it did not apply but fashioned a new privilege instead: work-product protection. As you read the following materials, think about the view they give of lawyers' work and of the adversary system.

Hickman v. Taylor

329 U.S. 495 (1947)

JUSTICE MURPHY delivered the opinion of the Court.

This case presents an important problem under the Federal Rules of Civil Procedure as to the extent to which a party may inquire into oral and written statements of witnesses, or other information, secured by an adverse party's counsel in the course of preparation for possible litigation after a claim has arisen. . . .

On February 7, 1943, the tug *J. M. Taylor* sank while engaged in helping to tow a car float of the Baltimore & Ohio Railroad across the Delaware River at Philadelphia. The accident was apparently unusual in nature, the cause of it still being unknown. Five of the nine crew members were drowned. Three days later the tug owners and the underwriters employed a law firm, of which respondent Fortenbaugh is a member, to defend them against potential suits by representatives of the deceased crew members and to sue the railroad for damages to the tug.

A public hearing was held on March 4, 1943, before the United States Steamboat Inspectors, at which the four survivors were examined. This testimony was recorded and made available to all interested parties. Shortly thereafter, Fortenbaugh privately interviewed the survivors and took statements from them with an eye toward the anticipated litigation; the survivors signed these statements on March 29. Fortenbaugh also interviewed other persons believed to have some information relating to the accident and in some cases he made memoranda of what they told him. At the time when Fortenbaugh secured the statements of the survivors, representatives of two of the deceased crew members had been in communication with him. Ultimately claims were presented by representatives of all five of the deceased; four of the claims, however, were settled without litigation. The fifth claimant, petitioner herein, brought suit in a federal court under the Jones Act on November 26, 1943, naming as defendants the two tug owners, individually and as partners, and the railroad.

One year later, petitioner filed 39 interrogatories directed to the tug owners. The 38th interrogatory read:

> State whether any statements of the members of the crews of the Tugs *J.M. Taylor* and *Philadelphia* or of any other vessel were taken in connection with

the towing of the car float and the sinking of the Tug *J.M. Taylor*. Attach hereto exact copies of all such statements if in writing, and if oral, set forth in detail the exact provisions of any such oral statements or reports.

Supplemental interrogatories asked whether any oral or written statements, records, reports, or other memoranda had been made concerning any matter relative to the towing operation, the sinking of the tug, the salvaging and repair of the tug, and the death of the deceased. If the answer was in the affirmative, the tug owners were then requested to set forth the nature of all such records, reports, statements or other memoranda.

The tug owners, through Fortenbaugh, answered all of the interrogatories except No. 38 and the supplemental ones just described. While admitting that statements of the survivors had been taken, they declined to summarize or set forth the contents. They did so, on the ground that such requests called "for privileged matter obtained in preparation for litigation" and constituted "an attempt to obtain indirectly counsel's private files." It was claimed that answering these requests "would involve practically turning over not only the complete files, but also the telephone records and, almost, the thoughts of counsel."

In connection with the hearing on these objections, Fortenbaugh made a written statement and gave an informal oral deposition explaining the circumstances under which he had taken the statements. But he was not expressly asked in the deposition to produce the statements. The District Court for the Eastern District of Pennsylvania, sitting en banc, held that the requested matters were not privileged. 4 F.R.D.479. The court then decreed that the tug owners and Fortenbaugh, as counsel and agent for the tug owners, forthwith

> [A]nswer Plaintiff's 38th interrogatory and supplementary interrogatories; produce all written statements of witnesses obtained by Mr. Fortenbaugh, as counsel and agent for Defendants; state in substance any fact concerning this case which Defendants learned through oral statements made by witnesses to Mr. Fortenbaugh whether or not included in his private memoranda and produce Mr. Fortenbaugh's memoranda containing statements of fact by witnesses or to submit these memoranda to the Court for determination of those portions which should be revealed to Plaintiff.

Upon their refusal, the court adjudged them in contempt and ordered them imprisoned until they complied.

The Third Circuit Court of Appeals, also sitting en banc, reversed the judgment of the District Court. 153 F.2d 212. It held that the information here sought was part of the "work product of the lawyer" and hence privileged from discovery under the Federal Rules of Civil Procedure. The importance of the problem, which has engendered a great divergence of views among district courts, led us to grant certiorari. 328 U.S. 876.

The pretrial deposition-discovery mechanism established by Rules 26 to 37 is one of the most significant innovations of the Federal Rules of Civil Procedure. Under the prior federal practice, the pretrial functions of notice giving, issue formulation and fact revelation were performed primarily and inadequately by the pleadings. Inquiry into the issues and the facts before trial was narrowly confined and was often cumbersome in method. The new rules, however, restrict the pleadings to the task of general notice giving and invest the deposition-discovery process with a vital role in the preparation for trial. The various instruments of discovery now serve (1) as a device, along with the pretrial hearing under Rule 16, to narrow and clarify the basic issues between the parties, and (2) as a device for ascertaining the facts, or information as to the existence or whereabouts of facts relative to those issues. Thus civil trials in the federal courts no longer need be carried on in the dark. The way is now clear, consistent with recognized privileges, for the parties to obtain the fullest possible knowledge of the issues and facts before trial. . . .

In urging that he has a right to inquire into the materials secured and prepared by Fortenbaugh, petitioner emphasizes that the deposition-discovery portions of the Federal Rules of Civil Procedure are designed to enable the parties to discover the true facts and to compel their disclosure wherever they may be found. It is said that inquiry may be made under these rules, epitomized by Rule 26, as to any relevant matter which is not privileged; and since the discovery provisions are to be applied as broadly and liberally as possible, the privilege limitation must be restricted to its narrowest bounds. On the premise that the attorney-client privilege is the one involved in this case, petitioner argues that it must be strictly confined to confidential communications made by a client to his attorney. And since the materials here in issue were secured by Fortenbaugh from third persons rather than from his clients, the tug owners, the conclusion is reached that these materials are proper subjects for discovery under Rule 26.

As additional support for this result, petitioner claims that to prohibit discovery under these circumstances would give a corporate defendant a tremendous advantage in a suit by an individual plaintiff. Thus in a suit by an injured employee against a railroad or in a suit by an insured person against an insurance company the corporate defendant could pull a dark veil of secrecy over all the pertinent facts it can collect after the claim arises merely on the assertion that such facts were gathered by its large staff of attorneys and claim agents. At the same time, the individual plaintiff, who often has direct knowledge of the matter in issue and has no counsel until some time after his claim arises could be compelled to disclose all the intimate details of his case. By endowing with immunity from disclosure all that a lawyer discovers in the course of his duties, it is said, the rights of individual litigants in such cases are drained of vitality and the lawsuit becomes more of a battle of deception than a search for truth.

But framing the problem in terms of assisting individual plaintiffs in their suits against corporate defendants is unsatisfactory. Discovery concededly may work to the disadvantage as well as to the advantage of individual plaintiffs. Discovery, in other words, is not a one-way proposition. It is available in all types of cases at the behest of any party, individual or corporate, plaintiff or defendant. The problem thus far transcends the situation confronting this petitioner. And we must view that problem in light of the limitless situations where the particular kind of discovery sought by petitioner might be used.

We agree, of course, that the deposition-discovery rules are to be accorded a broad and liberal treatment. No longer can the time-honored cry of "fishing expedition" serve to preclude a party from inquiry into the facts underlying his opponent's case. Mutual knowledge of all the relevant facts gathered by both parties is essential to proper litigation. To that end, either party may compel the other to disgorge whatever facts he has in his possession. The deposition-discovery procedure simply advances the stage at which the disclosure can be compelled from the time of trial to the period preceding it, thus reducing the possibility of surprise. But discovery, like all matters of procedure, has ultimate and necessary boundaries. As indicated by [Rule 26(c)] . . . limitations inevitably arise when it can be shown that the examination is being conducted in bad faith or in such a manner as to annoy, embarrass, or oppress the person subject to the inquiry. And as Rule 26(b) provides, further limitations come into existence when the inquiry touches upon the irrelevant or encroaches upon the recognized domains of privilege.

We also agree that the memoranda, statements, and mental impressions in issue in this case fall outside the scope of the attorney-client privilege and hence are not protected from discovery on that basis. It is unnecessary here to delineate the content and scope of that privilege as recognized in the federal courts. For present purposes, it suffices to note that the protective cloak of this privilege does not extend to information which an attorney secures from a witness while acting for his client in anticipation of litigation. Nor does this privilege concern the memoranda, briefs, communications and other writings prepared by counsel for his own use in prosecuting his client's case; and it is equally unrelated to writings which reflect an attorney's mental impressions, conclusions, opinions or legal theories.

But the impropriety of invoking that privilege does not provide an answer to the problem before us. Petitioner has made more than an ordinary request for relevant, nonprivileged facts in the possession of his adversaries or their counsel. He has sought discovery as of right of oral and written statements of witnesses whose identity is well known and whose availability to petitioner appears unimpaired. He has sought production of these matters after making the most searching inquires of his opponents as to the circumstances surrounding the fatal accident, which inquiries were sworn to have been answered to the best of their information and belief. Interrogatories were directed toward all the events prior to, during and subsequent to the sinking of the tug. Full and honest answers to such broad inquiries would necessarily have included all pertinent information gleaned by Fortenbaugh through his interviews with the witnesses. Petitioner makes no suggestion, and we cannot assume, that the tug owners or Fortenbaugh were incomplete or dishonest in the framing of their answers. In addition, petitioner was free to examine the public testimony of the witnesses taken before the United States Steamboat Inspectors. We are thus dealing with an attempt to secure the production of written statements and mental impressions contained in the files and the mind of the attorney Fortenbaugh without any showing of necessity or any indication or claim that denial of such production would unduly prejudice the preparation of petitioner's case or cause him any hardship or injustice. For aught that appears, the essence of what petitioner seeks either has been revealed to him already through the interrogatories or is readily available to him direct from the witnesses for the asking.

The District Court, after hearing objections to petitioner's request, commanded Fortenbaugh to produce all written statements of witnesses and to state in substance any facts learned through oral statements of witnesses to him. Fortenbaugh was to submit any memoranda he had made of the oral statements so that the court might determine what portions should be revealed to petitioner. All of this was ordered without any showing by petitioner, or any requirement that he make a proper showing, of the necessity for the production of any of this material or any demonstration that denial of production would cause hardship or injustice. The court simply ordered production on the theory that the facts sought were material and were not privileged as constituting attorney-client communications.

In our opinion, neither Rule 26 nor any other rule dealing with discovery contemplates production under such circumstances. That is not because the subject matter is privileged or irrelevant, as those concepts are used in these rules. Here is simply an attempt, without purported necessity or justification, to secure written statements, private memoranda and personal recollections prepared or formed by an adverse party's counsel in the course of his legal duties. As such, it falls outside the arena of discovery and contravenes the public policy underlying the orderly prosecution and defense of legal claims. Not even the most liberal of discovery theories can justify unwarranted inquiries into the files and the mental impressions of an attorney.

Historically, a lawyer is an officer of the court and is bound to work for the advancement of justice while faithfully protecting the rightful interests of his clients. In performing his various duties, however, it is essential that a lawyer work with a certain degree of privacy, free from unnecessary intrusion by opposing parties and their counsel. Proper preparation of a client's case demands that he assemble information, sift what he considers to be the relevant from the irrelevant facts, prepare his legal theories and plan his strategy without undue and needless interference. That is the historical and the necessary way in which lawyers act within the framework of our system of jurisprudence to promote justice and to protect their clients' interests. This work is reflected, of course, in interviews, statements, memoranda, correspondence, briefs, mental impressions, personal beliefs, and countless other tangible and intangible ways—aptly though roughly termed by the Circuit Court of Appeals in this case as the "work product of the lawyer." Were such materials open to opposing counsel on mere demand, much of what is now put down in writing would remain unwritten.

An attorney's thoughts, heretofore inviolate, would not be his own. Inefficiency, unfairness, and sharp practices would inevitably develop in the giving of legal advice and in the preparation of cases for trial. The effect on the legal profession would be demoralizing. And the interests of the clients and the cause of justice would be poorly served.

We do not mean to say that all written materials obtained or prepared by an adversary's counsel with an eye toward litigation are necessarily free from discovery in all cases. Where relevant and nonprivileged facts remain hidden in an attorney's file and where production of those facts is essential to the preparation of one's case, discovery may properly be had. Such written statements and documents might, under certain circumstances, be admissible in evidence or give clues as to the existence or location of relevant facts. Or they might be useful for purposes of impeachment or corroboration. And production might be justified where the witnesses are no longer available or can be reached only with difficulty. Were production of written statements and documents to be precluded under such circumstances, the liberal ideals of the deposition-discovery portions of the Federal Rules of Civil Procedure would be stripped of much of their meaning. But the general policy against invading the privacy of an attorney's course of preparation is so well recognized and so essential to an orderly working of our system of legal procedure that a burden rests on the one who would invade that privacy to establish adequate reasons to justify production through a subpoena or court order. That burden, we believe, is necessarily implicit in the rules as now constituted.

Rule [26(c)], as presently written, gives the trial judge the requisite discretion to make a judgment as to whether discovery should be allowed as to written statements secured from witnesses. But in the instant case there was no room for that discretion to operate in favor of the petitioner. No attempt was made to establish any reason why Fortenbaugh should be forced to produce the written statements. There was only a naked, general demand for these materials as of right and a finding by the District Court that no recognizable privilege was involved. That was insufficient to justify discovery under these circumstances and the court should have sustained the refusal of the tug owners and Fortenbaugh to produce.

But as to oral statements made by witnesses to Fortenbaugh, whether presently in the form of his mental impressions or memoranda, we do not believe that any showing of necessity can be made under the circumstances of this case so as to justify production. Under ordinary conditions, forcing an attorney to repeat or write out all that witnesses have told him and to deliver the account to his adversary gives rise to grave dangers of inaccuracy and untrustworthiness. No legitimate purpose is served by such production. The practice forces the attorney to testify as to what he remembers or what he saw fit to write down regarding witnesses' remarks . . . [and] would make the attorney much less an officer of the court and much more an ordinary witness. The standards of the profession would thereby suffer. Denial of production of this nature does not mean that any material, nonprivileged facts can be hidden from the petitioner in this case. He need not be unduly hindered in the preparation of his case, in the discovery of facts or in his anticipation of his opponents' position. Searching interrogatories directed to Fortenbaugh and the tug owners, production of written documents and statements upon a proper showing and direct interviews with the witnesses themselves all serve to reveal the facts in Fortenbaugh's possession to the fullest possible extent consistent with public policy. Petitioner's counsel frankly admits that he wants the oral statements only to help prepare himself to examine witnesses and to make sure that he has overlooked nothing. That is insufficient under the circumstances to permit him an exception to the policy underlying the privacy of Fortenbaugh's professional activities. If there should be a rare situation justifying production of these matters, petitioner's case is not of that type.

We fully appreciate the wide-spread controversy among the members of the legal profession over the problem raised by this case. It is a problem that rests on what has been one of the most hazy frontiers of the discovery process. But until some rule or statute definitely prescribes otherwise, we are not justified in permitting discovery in a situation of this nature as a matter of unqualified right. When Rule 26 and the other discovery rules were adopted, this Court and the members of the bar in general certainly did not believe or contemplate that all the files and mental processes of lawyers were thereby opened to the free scrutiny of their adversaries. And we refuse to interpret the rules at this time so as to reach so harsh and unwarranted a result.

We therefore affirm the judgment of the Circuit Court of Appeals.

Affirmed.

JUSTICE JACKSON, concurring. . . .

The primary effect of the practice advocated here would be on the legal profession itself. But it too often is overlooked that the lawyer and the law office are indispensable parts of our administration of justice. Law-abiding people can go nowhere else to learn the ever changing and constantly multiplying rules by which they must behave and to obtain redress for their wrongs. The welfare and tone of the legal profession is therefore of prime consequence to society, which would feel the consequences of such a practice as petitioner urges secondarily but certainly. . . .

Counsel for the petitioner candidly said on argument that he wanted this information to help prepare himself to examine witnesses, to make sure he overlooked nothing. He bases his claim to it in his brief on the view that the Rules were to do away with the old situation where a law suit developed into "a battle of wits between counsel." But a common law trial is and always should be an adversary proceeding. Discovery was hardly intended to enable a learned profession to perform its functions either without wits or on wits borrowed from the adversary.

The real purpose and the probable effect of the practice ordered by the district court would be to put trials on a level even lower than a "battle of wits." I can conceive of no practice more demoralizing to the Bar than to require a lawyer to write out and deliver to his adversary an account of what witnesses have told him. Even if his recollection were perfect, the statement would be his language, permeated with his inferences. Everyone who has tried it knows that it is almost impossible so fairly to record the expressions and emphasis of a witness that when he testifies in the environment of the court and under the influence of the leading question there will not be departures in some respects. Whenever the testimony of the witness would differ from the "exact" statement the lawyer had delivered, the lawyer's statement would be whipped out to impeach the witness. Counsel producing his adversary's "inexact" statement could lose nothing by saying, "Here is a contradiction, gentlemen of the jury. I do not know whether it is my adversary or his witness who is not telling the truth, but one is not." Of course, if this practice were adopted, that scene would be repeated over and over again. The lawyer who delivers such statements often would find himself branded a deceiver afraid to take the stand to support his own version of the witness's conversation with him, or else he will have to go on the stand to defend his own credibility—perhaps against that of his chief witness, or possibly even his client....

And what is the lawyer to do who has interviewed one whom he believes to be a biased, lying or hostile witness to get his unfavorable statements and know what to meet? He must record and deliver such statements even though he would not vouch for the credibility of the witness by calling him. Perhaps the other side would not want to call him either, but the attorney is open to the charge of suppressing evidence at the trial if he fails to call such a hostile witness even though he never regarded him as reliable or truthful.

Having been supplied the names of the witnesses, petitioner's lawyer gives no reason why he cannot interview them himself. If an employee-witness refuses to tell his story, he, too, may be examined under the Rules. He may be compelled on discovery, as fully as on the trial, to disclose his version of the facts. But that is his own disclosure—it can be used to impeach him if he contradicts it and such a deposition is not useful to promote an unseemly disagreement between the witness and the counsel in the case....

Note: The Necessities of Adversary Litigation

Work-product protection, as recognized by the Supreme Court in Hickman v. Taylor, has been incorporated into and extended by Rule 26(b)(3). Can you see why Rule 26(b)(3) is broader than the rule established in *Hickman*?

In 1947, *Hickman* was among the first cases to reach the Supreme Court after the Federal Rules of Civil Procedure became effective in 1938. Running through the case is the concern that the discovery rules are incompatible with the adversary system, the traditional mode of uncovering truth. Easily discernible as a subtext is the Court's fear that the harder-working, more skilled, and ingenious counsel may not win his just reward under a system of open-handed discovery. See Richard L. Marcus, The Story of *Hickman*: Preserving Adversarial Incentives While Embracing Broad Discovery, in Civil Procedure Stories 323 (Kevin M. Clermont ed., 2d ed. 2008).

In view of the Court's concerns about adversariness in *Hickman*, which, as you will see momentarily, are just as strong in a more recent case, Upjohn Co. v. United States, it seems strange indeed that in some places the practice of taking formal discovery, often depositions under oath, from opposing counsel has emerged. Can you see arguments that this is inoffensive, that it is the easiest way to obtain the information, and that it does not necessarily trench on the lawyer-client relationship?

Would the mandatory disclosure provisions of Rule 26(a) obviate any argument for taking opposing counsel's deposition? Is this an argument in their favor? For a summary of cases and a good exposition on both sides of the issue of whether lawyers may, or should, be allowed to take opposing counsel's deposition, see Timothy Flynn Jr., Note, "On Borrowed Wits": A Proposed Rule for Attorney Depositions, 93 Colum. L. Rev. 1956 (1993). For contrasting views on deposing counsel, compare Shelton v. American Motors Corp., 805 F.2d 1323 (8th Cir. 1986) (adopting a strict rule), with In re Subpoena Issued to Dennis Friedman, 350 F.3d 65 (2d Cir. 2003) (adopting a more flexible standard).

For a case in which opposing counsel were ordered to submit to deposition, due to their waiver of the attorney-client privilege by failing to object and to maintain confidentiality, see Nguyen v. Excel Corp., 197 F.3d 200 (5th Cir. 1999). For a discussion of the ethical and practical considerations an attorney may face when subpoenaed for deposition, see Daniel J. Pope and Suzanne Lee, Discovery on Wits "Borrowed from the Adversary": Deposition of the Trial Attorney, 65 Def. Couns. J. 285, 285 (1998) ("As unusual as it may seem, the practice of deposing opposing trial counsel is not an uncommon method of discovery."). In United States v. Nobles, 422 U.S. 225 (1975), a criminal case, the written report made by a defense investigator was ordered turned over to the prosecutor when the investigator was called to testify at trial. One claim was that the investigator's report was work product and thus shielded from production. The Court held that in the circumstances of this case the privilege had been waived and noted: "At its core, the work-product doctrine shelters the mental processes of the attorney, providing a privileged area within which he can analyze and prepare his client's case. But the doctrine is an intensely practical one, grounded in the realities of litigation in our adversary system." *Nobles*, 422 U.S. at 238.

Note: The Scope of Work Product and Anticipating Litigation

Work product is one of the most frequently litigated privileges, and the phrase "in anticipation of litigation" is often the focus of dispute. See Rule 26(b)(3). To some, almost every business decision in today's world anticipates litigation. Others interpret the words to mean that a specific claim must have been filed, or at least threatened, before the work-product privilege kicks in to protect documents from disclosure.

The Second Circuit has weighed in with the broad view, holding that work-product protection extends to documents created for the primary purpose of informing a business decision where the business decision is influenced by anticipated litigation. See United States v. Adlman, 134 F.3d 1194 (2d Cir. 1998). The case involved an IRS summons to obtain a memorandum prepared by the corporate taxpayer's outside accountants at the request of the company's tax counsel. The aim was to assess the tax consequences of a proposed corporate reorganization on anticipated litigation with the IRS. The court stated that "[n]owhere does Rule 26(b)(3) state that a document must have been prepared *to aid* in the conduct of litigation in order to constitute work product, much less *primarily or exclusively* to aid in litigation; rather, the rule is best read to extend protection to documents prepared *because of* litigation." Id. at 1198 (emphasis in original).

Adlman's "because of" standard is now the majority rule. See In re Grand Jury Subpoena (Mark Torf), 350 F.3d 1010 (9th Cir. 2003), *as amended by* 357 F.3d 900 (9th Cir. 2004); PepsiCo, Inc. v. Baird, Kurtz & Dobson LLP, 305 F.3d 813 (8th Cir. 2002); State of Maine v. U.S. Dept. of Interior, 298 F.3d 60 (1st Cir. 2002); Montgomery County v. MicroVote Corp., 175 F.3d 296 (3d Cir. 1999); Logan v. Commercial Union Ins. Co., 96 F.3d 971 (7th Cir. 1996). As the Ninth Circuit summarized the rule, "a document should be deemed prepared 'in anticipation of litigation' . . . if 'in light of the nature of the document and the factual situation in the particular case, the document can be fairly said to have been prepared or obtained because of the prospect of litigation.'" *Grand Jury Subpoena*, 350 F.3d at 1016 (quoting Wright and Miller, 8 Federal Practice and Procedure § 2020 (2d ed. 1994)).

The District of Columbia Circuit has followed an even broader, *motive-based* test, holding that documents need not have been prepared in connection with a specific claim to be shielded by attorney work-product privilege. The sole criterion is whether they were prepared based on an actual subjective and objectively reasonable belief that litigation was "an even real possibility." See In re Sealed Case, 146 F.3d 881 (D.C. Cir. 1998). Judge Tatel explains that, "[w]ithout a strong work-product privilege, lawyers would keep their thoughts to themselves, avoid communicating with other lawyers, and hesitate to take notes." Id. at 884.

> [A] contrary ruling would undermine lawyer effectiveness at a particularly critical stage of a legal representation. It is often prior to the emergence of specific claims that lawyers are best equipped either to help clients avoid litigation or to strengthen available defenses should litigation occur. For instance, lawyers routinely meet with potential grand jury targets to discuss possible charges, consider whether business decisions might result in antitrust or securities lawsuits, analyze copyright and patent implications of

> new technologies or works of art, and assess the possibility that new products might give rise to tort actions. If lawyers had to wait for specific claims to arise before their writings could enjoy work-product protection, they would not likely risk taking notes about such matters or communicating in writing with colleagues, thus severely limiting their ability to advise clients effectively. A lawyer advising a potential grand jury target, for example, might be reluctant to write something like "the critical facts which could harm my client are . . ." even though it would help the lawyer organize complex thoughts, because in the government's hands, such a note could become a powerful weapon against the client. Likewise, asked by a client to evaluate the antitrust implications of a proposed merger and advised that no specific claim had yet surfaced, a lawyer knowing that work product is unprotected would not likely risk preparing an internal legal memorandum assessing the merger's weaknesses, jotting down on a yellow legal pad possible areas of vulnerability, or sending a note to a partner—"After reviewing the proposed merger, I think it's O.K., although I'm a little worried about. . . . What are your views?" Nor would the partner respond in writing, "I disagree. This merger is vulnerable because. . . ." Discouraging lawyers from engaging in the writing, note-taking, and communications so critical to effective legal thinking would, in Hickman's words, "demoraliz[e]" the legal profession, and "the interests of the clients and the cause of justice would be poorly served."

Id. at 886-887. See also Equal Employment Opportunity Comm'n v. Lutheran Soc. Servs. 186 F.3d 959, 969 (D.C. Cir. 1999), in which the appellate court applied its test in a similar case where "evidence suggest[ed] that litigation lay just over the horizon" and found a report protected by the work-product privilege. Other appellate courts favor a narrower construction of the work-product privilege, one where the disputed document is tailored to particular litigation. See, e.g., United States v. Davis, 636 F.2d 1028 (5th Cir. 1981), *cert. denied*, 454 U.S. 862 (1981); United States v. El Paso Co., 682 F.2d 530 (5th Cir. 1982), *cert. denied*, 466 U.S. 944 (1984).

What about so-called dual purpose documents—documents created both in anticipation of litigation and for independent purposes? As the Second Circuit said in *Adlman*, "the 'because of' formulation . . . withholds protection from documents that are prepared in the ordinary course of business or that would have been created in essentially similar form irrespective of the litigation." 134 F.3d at 1202. The accountant's tax memorandum was prepared in anticipation of litigation in *Adlman*, but also to help the company assess the business consequences of the proposed merger, so the Second Circuit remanded the case for more fact-finding. Under the Second Circuit's approach, then, close attention to the circumstances surrounding a document's preparation is often necessary to draw the line. See *Grand Jury Subpoena*, 350 F.3d at 1017-1018 (work-product protection applies to documents prepared by environmental consultant in anticipation of litigation and in efforts to comply with an EPA civil investigation and supervised cleanup where a criminal investigation later develops: "Having chosen to pursue a criminal investigation, the government now seeks to capitalize on [the paint manufacturer's] earlier cooperation and obtain all of [the consultant's] documents pertaining to the disposal of [the manufacturer's] waste material. . . . The documents are entitled to work product protection because, taking into account the facts surrounding their creation, their litigation purpose so permeates any non-litigation purpose that the two purposes cannot be separated. . . .").

A final issue on the scope of work-product protection: how do you think a court should treat the claim that an attorney's selection among documents produced by an adversary should qualify as protected work product? Say the adversary produces thousands of documents in response to a request for production of documents or to prepare a client's deposition. Won't it reveal mental impressions if the lawyer has to disclose which documents she has selected from the heap?

In the most commonly cited case, the Third Circuit held that an attorney's choice of documents from among those produced qualifies as protected work product "[b]ecause identification of the documents as a group will reveal defense counsel's selection process, and thus his mental impressions. . . ." Sporck v. Peil, 759 F.2d 312, 315 (3d Cir. 1985). The Third Circuit relied on a district court opinion from Delaware in which the court emphasized that "'[i]n selecting and ordering a few documents out of thousands counsel could not help but reveal important aspects of his understanding of the case,'" and especially in cases "'involving extensive document discovery, the process of selection and distillation is often more critical than pure legal research.'" Id. at 316 (quoting James Julian, Inc. v. Raytheon Co., 93 F.R.D. 138, 144 (D. Del. 1982)). Cf. Miller v. Holzmann, 238 F.R.D. 30, 32-33 (D.D.C. 2006) (distinguishing *Sporck* on the ground that the number of documents plaintiffs scanned from defendant's production, around 20,000, was "so large that it would be difficult to conceive of [defendant] gleaning plaintiffs' trial strategy solely by virtue of plaintiffs' disclosing the identity of the documents," concluding that the information was merely fact work product, not opinion work product, and denying plaintiffs' motion for a protective order because defendant's interest in accelerating the progress of litigation qualified as a "substantial need" under Rule 26(b)(3)).

Upjohn Co. v. United States

449 U.S. 383 (1981)

JUSTICE REHNQUIST delivered the opinion of the Court. . . .

Petitioner Upjohn manufactures and sells pharmaceuticals here and abroad. In January 1976 independent accountants conducting an audit of one of petitioner's foreign subsidiaries discovered that the subsidiary made payments to or for the benefit of foreign government officials in order to secure government business. The accountants so informed Mr. Gerard Thomas, petitioner's Vice-President, Secretary, and General Counsel. Thomas is a member of the Michigan and New York bars, and has been petitioner's General Counsel for 20 years. He consulted with outside counsel and R. T. Parfet, Jr., petitioner's Chairman of the Board. It was decided that the company would conduct an internal investigation of what were termed "questionable payments." As part of this investigation the attorneys prepared a letter containing a questionnaire which was sent to "all foreign general and area managers" over the Chairman's signature. The letter began by noting recent disclosures that several American companies made "possibly illegal" payments to foreign government officials and emphasized that the management needed full information concerning any such payments made by Upjohn. The letter indicated that the Chairman had asked Thomas, identified as "the company's General Counsel," "to conduct an investigation for the purpose of determining the nature and magnitude of any payments made by the Upjohn Company or any of its subsidiaries to any employee or official of a foreign government." The questionnaire sought detailed information concerning such payments. Managers were instructed to treat the investigation as "highly confidential" and not to discuss it with anyone other than Upjohn employees who might be helpful in providing the requested information. Responses were to be sent directly to Thomas. Thomas and outside counsel also interviewed the recipients of the questionnaire and some 33 other Upjohn officers or employees as part of the investigation.

On March 26, 1976, the company voluntarily submitted a preliminary report to the Securities and Exchange Commission on Form 8-K disclosing certain questionable payments. A copy of the report was simultaneously submitted to the Internal Revenue Service, which immediately began an investigation to determine the tax consequences of the payments. Special agents conducting the investigation were given lists by Upjohn of all those interviewed and all who had responded to the questionnaire. On November 23, 1976, the Service issued a summons pursuant to 26 U.S.C. § 7602 demanding production of:

> All files relative to the investigation conducted under the supervision of Gerard Thomas to identify payments to employees of foreign governments and any political contributions made by the Upjohn Company or any of its affiliates since January 1, 1971 and to determine whether any funds of the Upjohn Company had been improperly accounted for on the corporate books during the same period.
>
> The records should include but not be limited to written questionnaires sent to managers of the Upjohn Company's foreign affiliates, and memorandums or notes of the interviews conducted in the United States and abroad with officers and employees of the Upjohn Company and its subsidiaries. . . .

The company declined to produce the documents specified in the second paragraph on the grounds that they were protected from disclosure by the attorney-client privilege and constituted the work product of attorneys prepared in anticipation of litigation. On August 31, 1977, the United States filed a petition seeking enforcement of the summons under

26 U.S.C. §§ 7402(b) and 7604(a) in the United States District Court for the Western District of Michigan. That court adopted the recommendation of a Magistrate who concluded that the summons should be enforced. Petitioner appealed to the Court of Appeals for the Sixth Circuit[, which upheld the order requiring production.] . . .

Federal Rule of Evidence 501 provides that "the privilege of a witness . . . shall be governed by the principles of the common law as they may be interpreted by the courts of the United States in light of reason and experience." The attorney-client privilege is the oldest of the privileges for confidential communications known to the common law. . . . Its purpose is to encourage full and frank communication between attorneys and their clients and thereby promote broader public interests in the observance of law and administration of justice. The privilege recognizes that sound legal advice or advocacy serves public ends and that such advice or advocacy depends upon the lawyer being fully informed by the client. . . .

Admittedly complications in the application of the privilege arise when the client is a corporation, which in theory is an artificial creature of the law, and not an individual; but this Court has assumed that the privilege applies when the client is a corporation. United States v. Louisville & Nashville R. Co., 236 U.S. 318, 336 (1915), and the Government does not contest the general proposition. . . . The Court of Appeals, however, considered the application of the privilege in the corporate context to present a "different problem," since the client was an inanimate entity and "only the senior management, guiding and integrating the several operations, . . . can be said to possess an identity analogous to the corporation as a whole." 600 F.2d at 1226. The first case to articulate the so-called "control group test" adopted by the court below, City of Philadelphia v. Westinghouse Electric Corp., 210 F. Supp. 483, 485 (E.D. Pa. 1963), reflected a similar conceptual approach:

> Keeping in mind that the question is, Is it the corporation which is seeking the lawyer's advice when the asserted privileged communication is made?, the most satisfactory solution, I think, is that if the employee making the communication, of whatever rank he may be, is in a position to control or even to take a substantial part in a decision about any action which the corporation may take upon the advice of the attorney, . . . then, in effect, *he is (or personifies) the corporation* when he makes his disclosure to the lawyer and the privilege would apply. (Emphasis supplied.)

Such a view, we think, overlooks the fact that the privilege exists to protect not only the giving of professional advice to those who can act on it but also the giving of information to the lawyer to enable him to give sound and informed advice. . . . See also Hickman v. Taylor, 329 U.S. 495, 511 (1947).

In the case of the individual client the provider of information and the person who acts on the lawyer's advice are one and the same. In the corporate context, however, it will frequently be employees beyond the control group as defined by the court below — "officers and agents . . . responsible for directing [the company's] actions in response to legal advice" — who will possess the information needed by the corporation's lawyers. Middle-level — and indeed lower-level — employees can, by actions within the scope of their employment, embroil the corporation in serious legal difficulties, and it is only natural that these employees would have the relevant information needed by corporate counsel if he is adequately to advise the client with respect to such actual or potential difficulties. . . .

The narrow scope given the attorney-client privilege by the court below not only makes it difficult for corporate attorneys to formulate sound advice when their client is faced with a specific legal problem but also threatens to limit the valuable efforts of corporate counsel to ensure their client's compliance with the law. In light of the vast and complicated array of regulatory legislation confronting the modern corporation, corporations, unlike most individuals, "constantly go to lawyers to find out how to obey the law," Burnham, The Attorney-Client Privilege in the Corporate Arena, 24 Bus. Law. 901, 913 (1969), particularly since compliance with the law in this area is hardly an instinctive matter. . . . The test adopted by the court below is difficult to apply in practice, though no abstractly formulated and unvarying "test" will necessarily enable courts to decide questions such as this with mathematical precision. But if the purpose of the attorney-client privilege is to be served, the attorney and client must be able to predict with some degree of certainty whether particular discussions will be protected. An uncertain privilege, or one which purports to be certain but results in widely varying applications by the courts, is little better than no privilege at all. . . .

The communications at issue were made by Upjohn employees to counsel for Upjohn acting as such, at the direction of corporate superiors in order to secure legal advice from counsel. As the magistrate found, "Mr. Thomas consulted with the Chairman of the Board and outside counsel and thereafter conducted a factual investigation to determine the nature and extent of the questionable payments *and to be in a position to give legal advice to the company with respect to the payments.*" (Emphasis supplied.) . . . Information, not available from upper-echelon management, was needed to supply a basis for legal advice concerning compliance with securities and tax laws, foreign laws, currency regulations, duties to shareholders, and potential litigation in each of these areas. The communications concerned matters within the scope of the employees' corporate duties, and the employees themselves were sufficiently aware that they were being questioned in order that the corporation could obtain legal advice. . . .

The Court of Appeals declined to extend the attorney-client privilege beyond the limits of the control group test for fear that doing so would entail severe burdens on discovery and create a broad "zone of silence" over corporate affairs. Application of the attorney-client privilege to communications such as those involved here, however, puts the adversary in no worse position than if the communications had never taken place. The privilege only protects disclosure of communications; it does not protect disclosure of the underlying facts by those who communicated with the attorney:

> The protection of the privilege extends only to communications and not to facts. A fact is one thing and a communication concerning that fact is an entirely different thing. The client cannot be compelled to answer the question, "What did you say or write to the attorney?" but may not refuse to disclose any relevant fact within his knowledge merely because he incorporated a statement of such fact into his communication to his attorney. [City of Philadelphia v. Westinghouse Electric Corp., 205 F. Supp. 830, 831 (E.D. Pa. 1962).]

See also Diversified Industries[, Inc. v. Meredith,] 572 F.2d [596,] 611 [8th Cir. 1977]; State v. Circuit Court, 34 Wis. 2d 559, 580, 150 N.W.2d 387, 399 (1967) ("the courts have noted that a party cannot conceal a fact merely by revealing it to his lawyer"). Here the Government was free to question the employees who communicated with Thomas and outside counsel.

Our decision that the communications by Upjohn employees to counsel are covered by the attorney-client privilege disposes of the case so far as the responses to the questionnaires and any notes reflecting responses to interview questions are concerned. The summons reaches further, however, and Thomas has testified that his notes and memoranda of interviews go beyond recording responses to his questions. To the extent that the material subject to the summons is not protected by the attorney-client privilege as disclosing communications between an employee and counsel, we must reach the ruling by the Court of Appeals that the work-product doctrine does not apply to summonses issued under 26 U.S.C. sect. 7602. . . .

While conceding the applicability of the work-product doctrine, the Government asserts that it has made a sufficient showing of necessity to overcome its protections. The magistrate apparently so found. The Government relies on the following language in *Hickman*:

> We do not mean to say that all written materials obtained or prepared by an adversary's counsel with an eye toward litigation are necessarily free from discovery in all cases. Where relevant and non-privileged facts remain hidden in an attorney's file and where production of those facts is essential to the preparation of one's case, discovery may properly be had. . . . And production might be justified where the witnesses are no longer available or may be reached only with difficulty. [Hickman v. Taylor, 329 U.S. 495, 511 (1947).]

The Government stresses that interviews are scattered across the globe and that Upjohn has forbidden its employees to answer questions it considers irrelevant. The above-quoted language from *Hickman,* however, did not apply to "oral statements made by witnesses . . . whether presently in the form of [the attorney's] mental impressions or memoranda." Id. at 512. . . . As to such material the Court did "not believe that any showing of necessity can be made under the circumstances of this case so as to justify production.... If there should be a rare situation justifying production of these matters petitioner's case is not of that type." Id. at 512-513.... Forcing an attorney to disclose notes and memoranda of witnesses' oral statements is particularly disfavored because it tends to reveal the attorney's mental processes, [id.] at 513 ... ("what he saw fit to write down regarding witnesses' remarks"); id. at 516-517,... ("the statement would be his [the attorney's] language, permeated with his inferences") (Jackson, J., concurring).[8]

Rule 26 accords special protection to work product revealing the attorney's mental processes. The Rule permits disclosure of documents and tangible things constituting attorney work product upon a showing of substantial need and inability to obtain the equivalent without undue hardship. This was the standard applied by the magistrate.... Rule 26 goes on, however, to state that "[i]n ordering discovery of such materials when the required showing has been made, the court shall protect against disclosure of the mental impressions, conclusions, opinions or legal theories of an attorney or other representative of a party concerning the litigation." Although this language does not specifically refer to memoranda based on oral statements of witnesses, the *Hickman* court stressed the danger that compelled disclosure of such memoranda would reveal the attorney's mental processes. It is clear that this is the sort of material the draftsmen of the Rule had in mind as deserving special protection. Based on the foregoing, some courts have concluded that *no* showing of necessity can overcome protection of work product which is based on oral statements from witnesses. See, e.g., In re Grand Jury Proceedings, 473 F.2d 840, 848 (8th Cir. 1973) (personal recollections, notes and memoranda pertaining to conversation with witnesses).... Those courts declining to adopt an absolute rule have nonetheless recognized that such material is entitled to special protection.

We do not decide the issue at this time. It is clear that the magistrate applied the wrong standard when he concluded that the Government had made a sufficient showing of necessity to overcome the protections of the work-product doctrine. The magistrate applied the "substantial need" and "without undue hardship" standard articulated in the first part of Rule 26(b)(3). The notes and memoranda sought by the Government here, however, are work product based on oral statements. If they reveal communications, they are, in this case, protected by the attorney-client privilege. To the extent they do not reveal communications, they reveal the attorneys' mental processes in evaluating the communications. As Rule 26 and *Hickman* make clear, such work product cannot be disclosed

8. Thomas described his notes of the interviews as containing "what I consider to be the important questions, the substance of the responses to them, my beliefs as to the importance of these, my beliefs as to how they related to the inquiry, my thoughts as to how they related to other questions. In some instances they might even suggest other questions that I would have to ask or things that I needed to find elsewhere."

simply on a showing of substantial need and inability to obtain the equivalent without undue hardship.

While we are not prepared at this juncture to say that such material is always protected by the work-product rule, we think a far stronger showing of necessity and unavailability by other means than was made by the Government or applied by the magistrate in this case would be necessary to compel disclosure. Since the Court of Appeals thought that the work-product protection was never applicable in an enforcement proceeding such as this, and since the magistrate whose recommendations the District Court adopted applied too lenient a standard of protection, we think the best procedure with respect to this aspect of the case would be to reverse the judgment of the Court of Appeals for the Sixth Circuit and remand the case to it for such further proceedings in connection with the work-product claim as are consistent with this opinion.

Accordingly, the judgment of the Court of Appeals is reversed, and the case is remanded for further proceeding

It is so ordered.

Note: The Lifetime of the Privilege: Swidler & Berlin v. United States

In *Upjohn,* both the attorney-client and the work-product privileges were invoked. This is often true, because parties would always prefer the broader, unqualified privilege to the more limited work-product exception. *Upjohn* is often cited for the importance of the attorney-client privilege, which "promotes trust in the representational relationship, thereby facilitating the provision of legal services and ultimately the administration of justice." See, e.g., Swidler & Berlin v. United States, 524 U.S. 399, 412 (1998) (Justice O'Connor, dissenting).

Swidler & Berlin was one of the cases growing out of the investigation of President Clinton. The Supreme Court again strongly endorsed the importance of the privilege, holding that in most circumstances, it extends even beyond the grave.

Here are the facts, as stated by Chief Justice Rehnquist for the majority:

> This dispute arises out of an investigation conducted by the Office of the Independent Counsel into whether various individuals made false statements, obstructed justice, or committed other crimes during investigations of the 1993 dismissal of employees from the White House Travel Office. Vincent W. Foster, Jr., was Deputy White House Counsel when the firing occurred. In July, 1993, Foster met with petitioner James Hamilton, an attorney at petitioner Swidler & Berlin, to seek legal representation concerning possible congressional or other investigations of the firings. During a 2-hour meeting, Hamilton took three pages of handwritten notes. One of the first entries in the notes is the word "Privileged." Nine days later, Foster committed suicide.

> In December 1995, a federal grand jury, at the request of the Independent Counsel, issued subpoenas to petitioners Hamilton and Swidler & Berlin for, inter alia, Hamilton's handwritten notes of his meeting with Foster. Petitioners filed a motion to quash, arguing that the notes were protected by the attorney client privilege and by the work product privilege. The District Court, after examining the notes *in camera*, concluded they were protected from disclosure by both doctrines and denied enforcement of the subpoenas.

Id. at 401-402.

The Court of Appeals for the District of Columbia Circuit reversed, but the Supreme Court found that "the great body of case law," and most commentators supported the survival of the privilege. In addition, the Court discerned

> weighty reasons that counsel in favor of posthumous application. Knowing that communications will remain confidential even after death encourages the client to communicate fully and frankly with counsel. While the fear of disclosure, and the consequent withholding of information from counsel, may be reduced if disclosure is limited to posthumous disclosure in a criminal context, it seems unreasonable to assume that it vanishes altogether. Clients may be concerned about reputation, civil liability or possible harm to friends or family. Posthumous disclosure of such communications may be as feared as disclosure during the client's lifetime. . . .
>
> The Independent Counsel assumes, incorrectly we believe, that the privilege is analogous to the Fifth Amendment's protection against self-incrimination. But as suggested above, the privilege serves much broader purposes. Clients consult attorneys for a wide variety of reasons, only one of which involves possible criminal liability. Many attorneys act as counselors on personal and family matters, where, in the course of obtaining the desired advice, confidences about family members or financial problems must be revealed in order to assure sound legal advice. The same is true of owners of small businesses who may regularly consult their attorneys about a variety of problems arising in the course of the business. These confidences may not come close to any sort of admission of criminal wrongdoing, but nonetheless be matters which the client would not wish divulged.
>
> This is true of disclosure before and after the client's death. Without assurance of the privilege's posthumous application, the client may very well not have made disclosures to his attorney at all, so the loss of evidence is more apparent than real. In the case at hand, it seems quite plausible that Foster, perhaps already contemplating suicide, may not have sought legal advice from Hamilton if he had not been assured the conversation was privileged.

Id. at 407-408

Three Justices (O'Connor, Scalia, and Thomas) dissented even though they agreed that ordinarily the privilege extends beyond the death of the client. They argued that there might be compelling reasons for disclosure in some instances, and that the case should be remanded for the district court to consider whether these existed.

Swidler & Berlin is the most significant of several high-profile cases concerning the scope of evidentiary privileges that grew out of the administration of President Clinton and the activities of Independent Counsel Kenneth Starr. See, e.g., In re Lindsey, 158 F.3d 1263 (D.C. Cir. 1998), *cert. denied*, 525 U.S. 996 (1998) (concerning executive privilege, government privilege, and the president's personal attorney-client privilege); see also Forrest Shea Browning, Swidler & Berlin v. United States: A Grave Decision—When Does Attorney-Client Privilege Have a Life of Its Own?, 22 Am. J. Trial Advoc. 671, 671 n.2 (citing cases); Note, Maintaining Confidence in Confidentiality: The Application of the Attorney-Client Privilege to Government Counsel, 112 Harv. L. Rev. 1995 (1999).

Note: Waiving the Privilege

The privilege extends beyond the grave, but while lawyer and client are alive, it is generally quite easy to waive. The rationale is simple—the privilege is an obstacle to the search for truth in the adversary process and waivers give meaning to the principle that the privilege should be narrowly construed. See United States v. Nixon, 418 U.S. 683 (1974). Most prominently, courts have carved out an exception to the privilege where legal advice is used in furtherance of crime or fraud. As Justice Cardozo wrote: "The privilege takes flight if the relation is abused. A client who consults an attorney for advice that will serve him in the commission of a fraud will have no help from the law." Clark v. United States, 289 U.S. 1, 15 (1933).

In an important opinion for the Ninth Circuit arising from the rise and fall of Napster, Judge William Fletcher offered the following summary of the standard for determining whether the crime-fraud exception applies:

> A party seeking to vitiate the attorney-client privilege under the crime-fraud exception must satisfy a two-part test. First, the party must show that "the client was engaged in or planning a criminal or fraudulent scheme when it sought the advice of counsel to further the scheme." In re Grand Jury Proceedings, 87 F.3d [377, 381 (9th Cir. 1996)]. Second, it must demonstrate that the attorney-client communications for which production is sought are "sufficiently related to" and were made "*in furtherance of* [the] intended, or present, continuing illegality. Id. at 382-83 (internal quotation marks omitted) (emphasis added). . . .
>
> The attorney need not have been aware that the client harbored an improper purpose. Because both the legal advice and the privilege are for the benefit of the client, it is the client's knowledge and intent that are relevant. . . . The planned crime or fraud need not have succeeded for the exception to apply. The client's abuse of the attorney-client relationship, not his or her successful criminal or fraudulent act, vitiates the privilege. . . .
>
> [I]n a civil case the burden of proof that must be carried by a party seeking outright disclosure of attorney-client communications under the crime-fraud exception should be preponderance of the evidence.

In re Napster, Inc., 479 F.3d 1078, 1090-1095 (9th Cir. 2007) (holding that $85 million loan by German conglomerate to Napster, part of which was used by Napster to pay for litigation expenses against American copyright holders, was not an attempted fraud on the court sufficient to pierce attorney-client privilege between German conglomerate and its counsel).

Should the attorney-client privilege cover conversations planning or otherwise encouraging implementation of a document destruction policy to eliminate evidence in anticipation of litigation? See Rambus, Inc. v. Infineon Technologies AG, 220 F.R.D. 264 (E.D. Va. 2004) (holding privilege gives way where software company and its lawyers, anticipating patent litigation with a competitor, drafted and implemented a document destruction policy including "Shred Day," which "culminated in a 5:00 pm beer, pizza, and champagne 'celebration' . . . [for] morale boosting after a day of heavy sack lifting and laborious document review").

The privilege also is destroyed if confidential communications are disclosed to adversaries or other third parties—the privilege needn't protect secrets the client is careless about keeping. See In re Keeper of the Records, 348 F.3d 16 (1st Cir. 2003) (company lost privilege as to any confidential information it shared in a conference call with its co-venturer); Clady v. County of Los Angeles, 770 F.2d 1421 (9th Cir. 1985). Traditionally, even *inadvertent* disclosure of privileged material results in waiver. Compare In re Sealed Case, 877 F.2d 976 (D.C. Cir. 1989) (inadvertence no grounds for relief from waiver), with KL Group v. Case, Kay & Lynch, 829 F.2d 909 (9th Cir. 1987) (lower court has discretion to order return of inadvertently disclosed material), and Rule 26(b)(5)(B).

Lawyers and clients must be equally cautious about making *voluntary* disclosures. Disclosing significant portions of privileged material can waive the privilege as to the remainder on the ground that the privilege should not operate both as a sword and a shield for the privilege holder—allowing her to disclose helpful information while refusing to release countervailing facts. See In re Keeper, 348 F.3d at 23-24 ("fairness concerns" justify extending the waiver "beyond the matter actually revealed"). And courts have deemed the privilege waived for failure to comply with the requirement in Rule 26(b)(5)(A) that claims of privilege be explicit and "describe the nature of the documents, communications or tangible things not disclosed . . . in a manner that . . . will enable other parties to assess the claim." See Clarke v. American Commerce National Bank, 974 F.2d 127, 129 (9th Cir. 1992) ("blanket assertions of the privilege are extremely disfavored") (internal quotations omitted), and United States v. Construction Products Research, Inc., infra, page 525. Finally, because it puts attorney-client communications directly in issue in the litigation, the privilege can be waived if the client asserts as part of a claim or defense that she relied on the advice of counsel. See United States v. Bilzerian, 926 F.2d 1285 (2d Cir. 1991), *overruled on other grounds by* United States v. Mandanici, 205 F.3d (2d Cir. 2000).

Note: The Privilege as Applied to Government Attorneys

Should government employees enjoy the benefits of the attorney-client privilege in their communications with government counsel? On the one hand, we certainly want public servants to engage in full and frank communication with lawyers about how to comply with law. On the other hand, government lawyers and the government officials they represent ultimately work for the public, and we deeply value transparency in government affairs. A government shrouded in secrecy is not a democracy, and an informed electorate and accountability to the public cannot be achieved without transparency.

In the non-governmental setting, once a court determines that the elements of the privilege have been met, the privilege applies even if it means other societal values are undermined. Indeed, we knowingly diminish the truth-finding function of the adversary process to protect the privilege because, as the Court argued in *Upjohn*, full and frank communication promotes compliance with law. When the communication occurs between government lawyer and government client, however, the Seventh, Eighth, and D.C. Circuit Courts of Appeals have endorsed a balancing test, holding that the privilege should give way to further a criminal investigation because the true client of the government lawyer is a public entity and the public interest is served by transparency in government affairs. See In re: A Witness Before the Special Grand Jury 2000-2, 288 F.3d 289 (7th Cir. 2002); In re Lindsey, 158 F.3d 1263 (D.C. Cir. 1998); In re Grand Jury Subpoena Duces Tecum, 112 F.3d 910 (8th Cir. 1997).

The Second Circuit, by contrast, rejected the balancing test in a case in which federal prosecutors sought to compel the testimony of the former chief legal counsel to the Office of the Governor of Connecticut. In re Grand Jury Investigation, 399 F.3d 527 (2d Cir. 2005). The governor was under investigation for receiving gifts in exchange for public favors, including lucrative state contracts. On several occasions the chief legal counsel discussed the receipt of gifts and related state ethics law with the governor and his staff. She also discussed the governor's practice of personally approving state contracts.

The district court entered an order compelling her to testify on the ground that, unlike the private attorney-client relationship, a government lawyer owes loyalty not only to the government official she serves, but to the public. As the district court put it, "any governmental attorney-client privilege must yield because the interests served by the grand jury's fact-finding process clearly outweigh the interests served by the privilege." 399 F.3d at 530. The Second Circuit reversed, holding that weighing the public interest against the interest in confidentiality is inappropriate even for government attorneys. "If anything," the court stated,

> the traditional rationale for the privilege applies with special force in the government context. It is crucial that government officials, who are expected to uphold and execute the law and who may face criminal prosecution

> for failing to do so, be encouraged to seek out and receive fully informed legal advice. Upholding the privilege furthers a culture in which consultation with government lawyers is accepted as a normal, desirable, and even indispensable part of conducting public business. Abrogating the privilege undermines that culture and thereby impairs the public interest.

Id. at 534. Which rule best serves the public interest?

A government official's conversations with a private attorney she retains for her own protection are privileged under the traditional rule. Why provide another privilege for conversations with government lawyers as well? For one thing, the government lawyer has an interest in getting a full picture of the facts so she can discharge her duties. (Recall that *Upjohn* spoke not only of the client's need for advice, but the lawyer's need for a full understanding of the facts to which advice will be tailored.)

Another answer is that there are two entities involved — the office and the office-holder. When the public official seeks legal advice from a government lawyer, she speaks in her capacity as an office-holder. That would imply that the privilege for communications between office-holders and government lawyers "belongs" to the office. If that is right, shouldn't a future occupant of the office be allowed to waive the privilege as to the conversations of earlier office-holders? And if future office-holders can waive the privilege, doesn't that diminish the concern about excessive secrecy in recognizing a governmental attorney-client privilege? For discussion of this issue, see id. at 534-535.

Note: Opinion Work Product

Note that Rule 26(b)(3) distinguishes between ordinary work product and "opinion work product." See Rule 26(b)(3)(B). Distinctions between the two are not easily made, and this has prompted court struggles and decisions that Professor Waits describes as "almost as big a mess as [the case law on] ordinary work product." See Kathleen Waits, Opinion Work Product: A Critical Analysis of Current Law and a New Analytical Framework, 73 Or. L. Rev. 385, 386 (1994).

Consider Holmgren v. State Farm Mutual Automobile Insurance Co., 976 F.2d 573, 576-578 (9th Cir. 1992). Plaintiff sought and obtained production of a memorandum prepared during a personal injury suit by the insurer's adjuster, in which the adjuster set forth a range of potential liability for plaintiff's claims. The insurer argued that the memo was "opinion work product" under Rule 26(b)(3) and thus entitled to absolute protection. The court held that no absolute privilege exists for opinion work product:

> State Farm contends that the district court erred in compelling it to produce and admitting as evidence plaintiff's exhibits 92 and 93. These items are handwritten memoranda drafted during the litigation of the Cannon suit by a State Farm adjuster. They contain a range of values for Holmgren's

claims, including aggravation, medical expenses, lost earnings, pain and suffering, loss of course of life and loss of home, fixing the range of potential liability as from $78,000 to $145,000. State Farm argues that these items are opinion work product and protected under Fed. R. Civ. P. 26(b)(3).

Holmgren contends that State Farm failed to object to the admission of the exhibits. We reject the argument. Counsel objected by affidavit to the production of both items as "opinion work product." The primary purpose of the work product rule is to "prevent exploitation of a party's efforts in preparing for litigation." Admiral Ins. Co. v. United States District Court, 881 F.2d 1486, 1494 (9th Cir. 1989). Like the discovery process that it limits, the work product doctrine encourages efficient development of facts and issues.

Exhibits 92 and 93 meet the threshold requirements for qualification as work product: both are (a) documents sought by Holmgren that were (b) prepared for trial (c) by a representative of State Farm. They reflect the opinion of a State Farm adjuster on the range of potential liability. See Reavis v. Metropolitan Property & Liability Ins. Co., 117 F.R.D. 160, 164 (S.D. Cal. 1987) (recognizing opinion work product of adjusters handling claim).

We need not decide whether Rule 26(b)(3) provides any protection for material prepared for litigation that has terminated. For even if it does, the rule permits discovery when mental impressions are the pivotal issue in the current litigation and the need for the material is compelling.

A party seeking opinion work product must make a showing beyond the substantial need/undue hardship test required under Rule 26(b)(3) for non-opinion work product. Upjohn Co. v. United States, 449 U.S. 383, 401-02 (1981). The Supreme Court, however, has so far declined to decide whether opinion work product is absolutely protected from discovery. Id. at 401.

The leading case denying all discovery of opinion work product is Duplan Corp. v. Moulinage et Retorderie de Chavanoz, 509 F.2d 730, 734 (4th Cir. 1974) (*Duplan II*). The *Duplan II* court reasoned, "[i]n our view, no showing of relevance, substantial need or undue hardship should justify compelled disclosure of an attorney's mental impressions, conclusions, opinions or legal theories. This is made clear by the Rule's use of the term 'shall' as opposed to 'may'". Id. at 734. This argument ignores the Advisory Committee notes to the 1970 amendment to Rule 26(b)(3) which state that the Rule "conform[s] to the holdings of the cases, when viewed in light of their facts." In Hickman [v. Taylor, 329 U.S. 495 (1947)], the Court stated that "[i]f there should be a rare situation justifying production of [work product], petitioner's case is not of that type." 329 U.S. at 513.

The Supreme Court, in 1946, rejected a proposed amendment to Rule 30(b) that would have given opinion work product absolute protection. See Report of Proposed Amendments to Rules of Civil Procedure, 5 F.R.D. 433, 456-57 (1946); Order dated December 27, 1946, 329 U.S. 843 (1946) (omitting reference to Rule 30(b) amendment in enumeration of amendments to rules adopted). That rejection, followed closely by the *Hickman* decision, which ordained a case-by-case approach to work product questions, suggests that the Court did not view the mandatory language of Rule 26(b)(3) as demanding absolute protection of opinion work product.

We agree with the several courts and commentators that have concluded that opinion work product may be discovered and admitted when mental impressions are *at issue* in a case and the need for the material is compelling.

Both elements are met here. In a bad faith insurance claim settlement case, the "strategy, mental impressions and opinion of [the insurer's] agents concerning the handling of the claim are directly at issue." *Reavis,* 117 F.R.D. at 164. Further, Holmgren's need for the exhibits was compelling. Montana permits insureds and third party claimants to proceed under § 33-18-201 against an insurer for bad faith in the settlement process. See Mont. Code Ann. § 33-18-242 (1979) (applicable to claims arising after July 1, 1987); Klaudt v. Flink, 658 P.2d 1065, 1067 (1983), *overruled on other grounds [sub nom.]* Fode v. Farmers Ins. Exch., 719 P.2d 414 (1986). Unless the information is available elsewhere, a plaintiff may be able to establish a compelling need for evidence in the insurer's claim file regarding the insurer's opinion of the viability and value of the claim. We review the question on a case-by-case basis.

If a party has demonstrated the requisite level of need and hardship, the other party must produce the material.

In *Handgards,* "the lawyers who managed and supervised the former litigation for the defendants [were] being called as witnesses to express their opinions as to the merits of the prior suits." Handgards[, Inc. v. Johnson & Johnson,] 413 F. Supp [926,] 931 [N.D. Cal. 1976]. This comment, and others like it in "at issue" cases, is a practical acknowledgment of the fact that, in bad faith settlement cases, insurers may call their adjusters to testify to their opinions as to the lack of viability of the underlying claim. When an insurer chooses to remain mute on the subject, the plaintiff is not foreclosed from developing the same evidence.

Holmgren v. State Farm Mutual Automobile Insurance Co., 976 F.2d 573, 576-578 (9th Cir. 1992).

The court was distinguishing Duplan Corp. v. Moulinage et Retorderie de Chavonoz, 509 F.2d 730, 734-736 (4th Cir. 1974), *cert. denied,* 420 U.S. 997 (1975), in which plaintiff sought discovery of lawyer opinion material prepared for use in an earlier lawsuit against the same defendant. The material sought included the opinions of the defendant's attorneys about dealings with the patent office, which were the subject matter of the pending litigation. The court held that the material was not properly discoverable:

[The trial court] . . . reasoned that what was a mental impression, opinion, conclusion, or legal theory, although absolutely protected during the pendency of a lawsuit, may change to an "operative fact" in a subsequent case once the earlier lawsuit is terminated. And should this happen, upon a proper showing of substantial need and undue hardship, the district court held that it might in its discretion order the production of opinions and conclusions where the denial of such production would frustrate the demands of justice and result in suffocation of the truth. . . .

In our view, this construction fails to comport with the policies underlying Hickman v. Taylor and Rule 26(b)(3).

> It seems clear from the whole tenor of the *Hickman* opinion that the court was concerned with protecting the thought processes of lawyers and thus the very adversary system. . . . And in our view, the fears articulated by the *Hickman* court should apply here with equal force. . . .
>
> In every instance in which an attorney is consulted (even confining our remarks to the words of the Rule) "in anticipation of litigation" he must be free to give his candid, dispassionate opinion, and equally free to record it and his mental impressions and conclusions. No other rule is compatible with the interests of justice. The client seeking the opinion must be similarly uninhibited. . . .
>
> It is true that litigation is no longer a game of hide and seek, and also true that justice is to a large extent equated with truth. But if attorneys may not freely and privately express and record mental impressions, opinions, conclusions, and legal theories, in writing, and clients may not freely seek them, then there is justice for no one, and truth, instead of being more readily ascertainable, will become lost in the murky recesses of the memory in the minds of men, who, after all, are human and subject to the human frailty of rationalization. Cf. *Hickman*, 329 U.S. p. 511.

Id. at 734-736.

Note: Privilege in a Corporate Context

Upjohn takes the attorney-client privilege, which is ordinarily conceived of in terms of an attorney advising an individual client, and applies it to a collective entity—the corporation. In what ways do individual and corporate clients differ that alter the assumptions that tend to drive the privilege? Are the costs inevitably entailed in allowing a privilege to shield information from an opponent compounded in the corporate context?

Upjohn tells us that communication between counsel to a corporation and lower level employees can be protected by the privilege. What about communication with independent professionals like accountants and tax experts who are not employees, but who regularly provide advice that can have important legal consequences? If a company has engaged in Enron-like fast and loose financial accounting, will conversations about the issue with outside accountants be covered by the privilege just because a lawyer working for the company is also in the room? On the facts of *Upjohn*, what if Gerard Thomas brought in accounting consultants and auditors to help the company determine the extent of bribery and the likely implications for tax liability? Would the accountants' conversations with lower level employees be covered? Remember that the privilege disappears upon any voluntary disclosure of confidential information to a third party.

The general rule is that where the services of an agent are used in order to assist the lawyer in giving legal advice to the client, communications between the agent, the client, and the lawyer are covered by the privilege as long as they relate to issues on which legal advice is sought. However, the privilege is waived when privileged information is shared with an agent for purposes unrelated to seeking legal advice. In First Federal Savings Bank v. United States, 55 Fed. Cl. 263 (Fed. Cl. 2003), for instance, First Federal shared confidential minutes of its board meetings with its accounting firm KPMG on two occasions: first, to conduct a fraud audit as part of an internal investigation run by First Federal's lawyers, and second, to prepare annual audits of First Federal's financial statements. The court concluded that while the privilege covered the first disclosure of the board minutes, see id. at 268 ("Lawyers frequently experience difficulty when interpreting and applying accounting principles. . . . Given the complexity of the accounting issues [in this case], the court is persuaded that [the fraud audit] procedures were related to the rendition of legal advice."), disclosures to KPMG so it could prepare annual audits were purely for business purposes and therefore waived the privilege. Id. at 269 ("Just as documents transmitted to an agent for the preparation of a tax return are not privileged, documents transmitted to an agent for the preparation of an audited financial statement likewise are not privileged.").

The same rule regarding agents applies for individual clients, but in the corporate context covering communications with agents raises all the concerns we saw in *Upjohn* about extending the privilege beyond the control group. See notes infra, at 567-69. In light of recent corporate scandals, does the shield of the corporate attorney-client privilege extend too far? Was excessive confidentiality the underlying problem? For an analysis of the role of lawyers and confidentiality rules in the Enron scandal, see Roger C. Cramton, Enron and the Corporate Lawyer: A Primer on Legal and Ethical Issues, 58 Bus. Law. 143 (2002).

Note: The Role of Privileges in Assuring Accurate Outcomes

Assume, arguendo, that the primary and sole aim of civil litigation is accurate outcomes (as opposed to party satisfaction or other potential values of civil process we explored in Chapter 1). Can you nevertheless defend the attorney-client privilege? Work-product privilege? Does it matter whether you allow for sharing of the costs of generating the information that work-product and attorney-client privilege protect?

Consider the following scenarios and their "accurate-outcome" implications, described by Professor Elizabeth Thornberg in Sanctifying Secrecy: The Mythology of the Corporate Attorney-Client Privilege, 69 Notre Dame L. Rev. 157, 193-197 (1993):

> [XYZ Corporation, a manufacturer of consumer widgets, is sued by a consumer who was injured by the widget and alleges that it was defective. The corporation has an employee named Smith whose job is to test new products.] Assume that Jones, the president of XYZ, instructs Green, the vice-president,

to call the corporate attorney and tell him that Smith has admitted that the widget was known to be defective before it was marketed. If the plaintiff deposes Green and asks what the president said to Green or what Green said to the attorney, both Green and Jones would be held to be "representatives of the client," and the privilege would allow Green to refuse to answer the question. This direct method of learning about Smith's warning is thus closed to the plaintiff.

If the plaintiff instead deposes Jones, the president, and asks him what Smith said, the president should be required to testify about what Smith told him, because this communication went straight from employee to employee for business purposes. Unfortunately, the claims and the case law are not so clear. Many corporations would still claim a privilege, based on the attorney's need to gather information. . . .

Assume that a plaintiff-consumer has sent an interrogatory asking whether XYZ adequately tested the widget. Assume further that there are five engineers in XYZ's research and development department, including Smith. Smith has told the corporate attorney that inadequate testing was done, that some of the documentation making it appear that tests were done is actually false, and that the engineers structured the tests so as to avoid exposing a known problem in the widget's design. The other four engineers told the lawyer that the testing was fine. All of these conversations are privileged. XYZ answers the plaintiff's question merely by saying that it adequately tested the widget. If requested it will provide the documentation on the tests. XYZ further identifies the other four engineers as persons with knowledge of the testing procedures. XYZ does not mention Smith's opinion.

Is this response a lie? Not exactly. But it is an incomplete picture of the information available to XYZ and clearly misleading to the plaintiff. The privilege contributes to the scenario by letting the lawyer and corporate entity decide which of the employees' conflicting stories to put forward as the only available information. While presenting its favorite version of the facts, the corporation simultaneously claims privilege as to any document reflecting Smith's concerns (if these documents haven't hit the shredder long ago) and as to any conversation between Smith and the lawyer. If documents do exist and the lawyer acts ethically, the corporation will acknowledge that documents exist, but claim privilege. Less responsible lawyers may make a "silent assertion" of the privilege. Thus the corporation makes and rules on its own privilege objection, and the plaintiff may never know that the information exists in order to pursue it in unprotected form.

Note: Administering a Claim of Privilege

In the previous note, the privilege claim itself, combined with the testing, reveals the likelihood that the results were unfavorable. How can a party make a claim of privilege without risking the revelation of the very information he is seeking to shield? How much does a court need to know in order to assess the validity of a claim of privilege? In United States v. Construction Products Research, Inc., 73 F.3d 464 (2d Cir. 1996), as in *Upjohn*, the court was asked to enforce the subpoena of an administrative agency. The NRC (Nuclear Regulatory Commission) was investigating whether a government contractor had wrongfully discharged a whistle-blower. Here is the description of the subpoena and the privilege claim:

> [T]he NRC issued the subpoena involved here, requiring Respondents to produce: (1) all documents related to Holub's termination; (2) Holub's personnel file; (3) all of Respondents' policies, procedures, and requirements regarding involuntary terminations; (4) and "position descriptions of jobs" held by Holub and two other employees. Respondents refused to comply with it.
>
> The United States, on behalf of the NRC, filed a petition to enforce the subpoena in the United States District Court for the District of Connecticut. The district court referred the petition to a magistrate judge, who recommended that the petition be granted and that Respondents' claim of privilege be rejected as a general defense to enforcement of the subpoena. The district court adopted the magistrate judge's recommended ruling *in toto*, and issued an order of enforcement. This ruling appears not to have considered the applicability of the privilege to any particular document, though it is arguable that the district court's denial of Respondents' motion to reconsider constituted a rejection of the privilege as to all documents for which privilege had been claimed. Respondents appealed, but turned over to the NRC those documents which they conceded were not privileged, while refusing to produce allegedly privileged documents.
>
> The party asserting the privilege must establish the essential elements of the privilege. United States v. Adlman, 68 F.3d 1495, 1499 (2d Cir. 1995); von Bulow by Auersperg v. von Bulow, 811 F.2d 136, 144 (2d Cir.), *cert. denied*, 481 U.S. 1015 (1987). To invoke the attorney-client privilege, a party must demonstrate that there was: (1) a communication between client and counsel, which (2) was intended to be and was in fact kept confidential, and (3) made for the purpose of obtaining or providing legal advice. Fisher v. United States, 425 U.S. 391, 403 (1976); Adlman, 68 F.3d at 1499; United States v. Abrahams, 905 F.2d 1276, 1283 (9th Cir. 1990).
>
> Respondents also assert a work-product privilege. To invoke this privilege, a party generally must show that the documents were prepared principally or exclusively to assist in anticipated or ongoing litigation. . . .
>
> To facilitate its determination of privilege, a court may require "an adequately detailed privilege log in conjunction with evidentiary submissions to fill in any factual gaps." Bowne, 150 F.R.D. at 474; see also In re Grand Jury Investigation, 974 F.2d 1068, 1071 (9th Cir. 1992). The privilege log should identify each document and the individuals who were parties to the communications, providing sufficient detail to permit a judgment as to whether the document is at least potentially protected from disclosure. Other required information, such as the relationship between . . . individuals not normally within the privileged relationship, is then typically supplied by affidavit or deposition testimony. Even under this approach, however, if the party invoking the privilege does not provide sufficient detail to demonstrate fulfillment of all the legal requirements for application of the privilege, his claim will be rejected.
>
> We have reviewed Respondents' privilege log, and find it deficient. The log contains a cursory description of each document, the date, author,

recipient, and "comments." Further, under a heading entitled "Basis of Claim," each of the documents listed is alleged to be an "Attorney-Client Communication."

These general allegations of privilege, however, are not supported by the information provided. For example, descriptions and comments for some of the documents listed are as follows: (a) "Fax Re: DOL Findings" with comment "cover sheet"; (b) "Fax: Whistleblower article" with comment "Self-explanatory"; (c) "Letter Re: Customer Orders" with comment "Re: Five Star Products"; (d) "Summary of Enclosures" with comment "Self-explanatory"; etc. The descriptions and comments simply do not provide enough information to support the privilege claim, particularly in the glaring absence of any supporting affidavits or other documentation. See Bowne, 150 F.R.D. at 475; Allendate Mut. Ins. Co. v. Bull Data Sys., Inc., 145 F.R.D. 84, 88 (N.D. Ill. 1992) (privilege log should provide "a specific explanation of why the document is privileged").

Id. at 468-474.

Once a privilege log is filed, attorneys for the adversary must review it and decide whether to file a motion to compel. If they believe the asserted privilege has been abused in furtherance of crime or fraud (not just that the log is inadequate), there are special procedures to determine whether the privilege should be waived. Typically, in a civil case (there are different procedures when prosecutors seek to put privileged material before a grand jury), the motion to compel will include waiver as a ground for compelling production. The difficulty, of course, is that the party seeking disclosure usually does not have access to the very documents that would most clearly establish whether the attorney-client relationship has been abused. So how can a lawyer prove the crime/fraud exception applies?

Sometimes the underlying criminal or fraudulent behavior has already come to light. This makes it a lot easier to argue for waiver of the privilege, particularly in contexts such as the recent financial accounting and mortgage scandals, where it is obvious that counsel would have been involved in the decision making. But without a proven (or at least publicly exposed) crime or fraud, and in any context where the role of counsel is unknown, establishing the elements of waiver can be exceedingly difficult. Just as thorny is the question of how to decide whether the exception applies without revealing the very information covered by the privilege — public revelation, as you have read above, is itself a form of waiver.

In United States v. Zolin, 491 U.S. 554, 572 (1989), the Supreme Court held that when the party seeking waiver makes a prima facie showing, the trial court has discretion to review the privileged documents *"in camera"* to determine whether the crime/fraud exception indeed applies. This seems reasonable because it preserves the privilege while allowing the issue of waiver to be decided, but it is subject to abuse in practice. To begin with, in order to secure *in camera* review, a party does not have to prove by a preponderance of the evidence that the attorney-client relationship was in fact abused by the other side. As the Court held in *Zolin*, the party seeking waiver need only present "a factual basis adequate to support a good faith belief by a reasonable person . . . that *in camera* review of the material may reveal evidence to establish the claim that the crime-fraud exception applies." 491 U.S. at 572. Perhaps more troublingly, seeking waiver offers a chance to have the judge who will adjudicate the merits of the case see evidence of criminal or fraudulent conduct by an opponent, and her lawyer. Even if the material the judge reviews is not bad enough to result in waiver, it may nonetheless color the judge's view of the case. All of which is just to say that abuse of waiver, not just abuse of the privilege, is possible.

This is not the only approach, though. A party may bypass *in camera* review and move for outright disclosure. But if she does, the Third, Seventh, Eighth, and Ninth Circuits have held that the court must allow the party seeking to preserve the attorney-client privilege an opportunity to present countervailing evidence in support of its claim of privilege. See In re Napster, 479 F.3d 1078, 1093 (9th Cir. 2007); In re Gen. Motors Corp., 153 F.3d 714, 716 (8th Cir. 1998); Haines v. Liggett Group Inc., 975 F.2d 81, 96-97 (3d Cir. 1992); In re Feldberg, 862 F.2d 622, 625-626 (7th Cir. 1988).

Note: Spoliation and the Duty to Preserve Evidence

Both work-product protection and the attorney-client privilege insulate facts from disclosure in litigation. However, lawyers and their clients have an affirmative obligation to preserve documents and other things that may be relevant to pending and anticipated litigation. Nothing can be turned over in discovery if it has not been preserved. Willful destruction of evidence is called "spoliation," and in addition to potential criminal liability for obstruction of justice, courts have inherent power to impose sanctions against parties who commit spoliation. Sanctions can range from shifting the costs of discovery to the party who has destroyed evidence to instructing the jury that it can draw an adverse inference against the offending party that the evidence destroyed was harmful to that party and favorable to the adversary.

Consider Zubulake v. UBS Warburg LLC, 220 F.R.D. 212 (S.D.N.Y. 2003). Laura Zubulake, an equities trader for UBS earning $650,000 a year, sued the company for gender discrimination. Although lawyers for UBS instructed it to preserve all relevant documents once Zubulake filed an administrative charge with the EEOC, UBS employees (possibly fearful for their own jobs if Zubulake's charges proved true) lost or failed to retain backup records of e-mail correspondence between Zubulake, human resources, and others in her working group. Claiming that evidence essential to proving her case was in the lost e-mails, Zubulake filed a motion for sanctions.

The court reasoned that UBS had a duty to preserve relevant evidence once it reasonably anticipated that Zubulake might sue:

> Documents create a paper reality we call proof. The absence of such documentary proof may stymie the search for the truth. Electronic evidence

> only complicates matters. . . . [I]t has become easier to delete or tamper with evidence (both intentionally and inadvertently) and more difficult for litigants to craft policies that ensure all relevant documents are preserved.

Id. at 214. Once a party recognizes that litigation is possible, the court continued, "it must suspend its routine document retention/destruction policy and put in place a 'litigation hold' to ensure the preservation of relevant documents." Id. at 218. Although UBS failed to take these steps, the court concluded that the "in terrorem effect" of an adverse inference sanction would be too harsh and instead shifted the costs of additional discovery to UBS: "In practice, an adverse inference instruction often ends litigation — it is too difficult a hurdle for the spoliator to overcome." Id. at 219-220.

When UBS employees involved in the document destruction were re-deposed two years into the litigation, plaintiff learned that additional e-mails harmful to UBS's defense had been deleted and that other potentially detrimental e-mail correspondence on active UBS servers had never been disclosed in response to valid requests. Plaintiff again moved for sanctions and this time around the court agreed that UBS's conduct was willful, warranting an adverse inference instruction to the jury:

> [A] major consideration in choosing an appropriate sanction — along with punishing UBS and deterring future misconduct — is to restore Zubulake to the position that she would have been in had UBS faithfully discharged its discovery obligations. . . . [T]he jury empanelled to hear this case will be given an adverse inference instruction with respect to e-mails deleted after August 2001, and in particular, with respect to e-mails that were irretrievably lost when UBS's backup tapes were recycled. No one can ever know precisely what was on those tapes, but the content of e-mails recovered from other sources — along with the fact that UBS employees willfully deleted e-mails — is sufficiently favorable to Zubulake that I am convinced that the contents of the lost tapes would have been similarly, if not more, favorable.

Zubulake v. UBS Warburg LLC, 229 F.R.D. 422, 437 (S.D.N.Y. 2004) (also forcing UBS to pay the costs incurred by plaintiff as a result of UBS's tardy compliance with discovery requests, including the costs of moving for sanctions). See also Coleman (Parent) Holdings, Inc. v. Morgan, Stanley & Co., Inc., 2005 WL 679071, at *7 (Fla. Cir. Ct. 2005) (shifting burden of proof at trial and reading description of discovery misconduct to jury).

At trial, the jury found UBS liable and awarded $29.3 million dollars in damages. A court's power to choose among different sanctions for spoliation thus carries with it the power to determine the outcome of the case. See also United States v. Philip Morris USA, Inc., 327 F. Supp. 2d 21 (D.D.C. 2004) (declining to impose adverse inference as sanction where at least 11 high-level corporate officers at Philip Morris deleted numerous e-mails in violation of the company's document retention policy and the court's Case Management Order requiring "preservation of all documents and other records containing information which could be . . . relevant to the subject matter of this litigation"); see also id. at 26 (approving exclusion of testimony by any employees who engaged in document destruction and imposing a $2,750,000 penalty as sanctions for the defendants' "reckless disregard and gross indifference . . . toward their discovery and document preservation obligations").

While laying most of the blame on UBS and its employees, the *Zubulake* court also emphasized that lawyers are bound, ethically and by Rule 26(e), to help ensure that their clients appropriately supplement their initial disclosures and avoid spoliation:

> First, counsel must issue a "litigation hold" at the outset of litigation or whenever litigation is reasonably anticipated. The litigation hold should be periodically reissued so that new employees are aware of it, and so that it is fresh in the minds of all employees.
>
> Second, counsel should communicate directly with the "key players" in the litigation, i.e., the parties identified in a party's initial disclosure and any subsequent supplementation thereto. . . . As with the litigation hold, the key players should be periodically reminded that the preservation duty is still in place.
>
> Finally, counsel should instruct all employees to produce electronic copies of their relevant active files. Counsel must also make sure that all backup media which the party is required to retain is identified and stored in a safe place. . . . One of the primary reasons that electronic data is lost is ineffective communication with information technology personnel.

Id. at 433-434. In this case, the court found that "counsel failed to properly oversee UBS in a number of important ways, both in terms of its duty to locate relevant information and its duty to preserve and timely produce that information." Id. at 435. See also United States v. Philip Morris USA, Inc., 327 F. Supp. 2d 21 (D.D.C. 2004) (fining Philip Morris $2.75 million for failing to follow court's evidence preservation order and destroying e-mails over two-year period, and barring company from presenting any fact witness who participated in spoliation). Cf. Cedars-Sinai Med. Ctr. v. Sup. Ct., 18 Cal. 4th 1 (1998) (rejecting tort liability for intentional spoliation discovered before trial); Temple Community Hosp. v. Sup. Ct., 20 Cal. 4th 464 (1999) (rejecting tort liability for intentional spoliation by third party).

3. Digital Data and the Problem of Electronic Discovery

As *Zubulake* demonstrates, modern discovery disputes increasingly involve digital data. This new form of data is both a blessing and a curse. Unlike work that used to be done orally, or communication that takes place exclusively by phone or in live meetings, digital communication leaves a record. And we are becoming increasingly reliant on digital methods of work and communication. The amount of raw information generated and stored on computers and other electronic media is huge, and growing fast. A recent study found that in 2002 alone, nearly five "exabytes" of new data were created. Five exabytes of data are equivalent to the contents of 37,000 libraries, each with a book collection the size of the Library of Congress. Ninety-two percent of that data is stored on magnetic media such as hard disks, 7 percent on film, just 0.01 percent on paper, and 0.002 on optical media. See www.sims.berkeley.edu/research/projects/how-much-info-2003/execsum.htm#summary. More than two-thirds of electronically stored data is never printed. Tricia Bishop, Electronic Records Open Up Fertile Legal Research Field, L.A. Times, Dec. 27, 2004, at C3.

In addition, digital data can now be stored in tiny, high-volume memory devices. A 1.44-megabyte floppy disk can hold the equivalent of 720 pages of text, a CD-ROM up to 325,000 pages, and storage devices with a terabyte of memory can store the equivalent of 500 billion pages of text. In a 2000 ABA Litigation Section survey, "40% of participating attorneys believed their clients had significant electronic records collections, yet 83% said their clients did not have established protocols to answer requests for electronic documents, and 75% said their clients were not aware electronic records were discoverable." 9 Feb. HIBJ 4. Although "[a] handful of law firms have created units specifically to mine for electronic information and help clients manage it[,] [e]xperts say many lawyers aren't yet comfortable with hunting for electronic data and may be setting themselves up for claims of malpractice because of it." Bishop, supra. For this very reason, private companies have sprung up to fill the gap. "Today, about 160 companies concentrate on electronic discovery, whose total revenues grew to $430 million in 2003 from $40 million in 1999." Id.

Apart from the relative ease of digital file destruction, can you see some of the unique problems this new format for data storage creates for discovery in civil litigation? As you read the case below, consider whether any of the issues that give rise to sanctions are distinctive because of the type of information Qualcomm tried to conceal, or whether the case reflects problems all too familiar in traditional discovery practice.

Qualcomm Inc. v. Broadcom Corp.

2008 WL 66932 (S.D. Cal. Jan. 7, 2008)

BARBARA L. MAHOR, United States Magistrate Judge.

Background

A. The Patent Infringement Case

Qualcomm initiated this patent infringement action on October 14, 2005, alleging Broadcom's infringement of Qualcomm patent numbers 5,452,104 (the "'104 patent") and 5,576,767 (the "'767 patent") based on its manufacture, sale, and offers to sell H.264-compliant products. Qualcomm sought injunctive relief, compensatory damages, attorneys' fees and costs.

On December 8, 2006, Broadcom filed a First Amended Answer and Counterclaims in which it alleged (1) a counterclaim that the '104 patent is unenforceable due to inequitable conduct, and (2) an affirmative defense that both patents are unenforceable due to waiver. Broadcom's waiver defense was predicated on Qualcomm's participation in the Joint Video Team ("JVT") in 2002 and early 2003. The JVT is the [international] standards-setting body that created the H.264 standard, which was released in May 2003 and governs video coding.*

B. *Evidence of Qualcomm's Participation in the JVT*

Over the course of discovery, Broadcom sought information concerning Qualcomm's participation in and communications with the JVT through a variety of discovery devices. For example, as early as January 23, 2006, Broadcom served its First Set of Requests for the Production of Documents and Things (Nos. 1-88), in which it requested:

> [a]ll documents given to or received from a standards setting body or group that concern any standard relating to the processing of digital video signals that pertains in any way to any Qualcomm Patent, including without limitation communications, proposals, presentations, agreements, commitments, or contracts to or from such bodies. . . . [and]
>
> [a]ll documents concerning any Qualcomm membership, participation, interaction, and/or involvement in setting any standard relating to the processing of digital video signals that pertains in any way to any Qualcomm Patent. This request also covers all proposed or potential standards, whether or not actually adopted. . . .
>
> [a]ll documents referring to or evidencing any participation by Qualcomm in the proceedings of the JVT, the ISO, the IEC, and/or the ITU-T; and
>
> [a]ll documents constituting, referring to, or evidencing any disclosure by any party to the JVT, the ISO, the IEC, and/or the ITU-T of any Qualcomm Patent and/or any Related Qualcomm Patent.

Id. Broadcom also requested similar information via interrogatories and multiple Rule 30(b)(6) deposition notices.

On their face, Qualcomm's written discovery responses did not appear unusual. In response to Broadcom's request for JVT documents, Qualcomm, in a discovery response signed by attorney Kevin Leung, stated,

* [The patents at issue cover methods for compressing video image data. H.264/MPEG-AVC creates a global, uniform standard specification that enables High Definition (HD) images to be efficiently stored and delivered over satellite, broadcast, and cable television, as well as Blu-ray disc, mobile phones, and Internet-based television. Since 2001, through the JVT, prominent video technology companies, including Microsoft and Sony, collaborated with others in the development of the H.264 standard for their mutual benefit. The goal was a standard that would allow efficient product creation centered around a single coding mechanism. H.264 has been a substantial breakthrough in HD development—even winning a Primetime Emmy Engineering Award from the U.S. Academy of Television Arts & Science. For more information on H.264 see http://www.apple.com/quicktime/technologies/h264/faq.html. EDS.]

"Qualcomm will produce non-privileged relevant and responsive documents describing Qualcomm's participation in the JVT, if any, which can be located after a reasonable search." Similarly, Qualcomm committed to producing "responsive non-privileged documents that were given to or received from standards-setting body responsible for the [H.264] standard, and which concern any Qualcomm participation in setting the [H.264] standard." When asked for "the facts and circumstances of any and all communications between Qualcomm and any standards setting body relating to video technology, including . . . the JVT . . . ," Qualcomm responded that it first attended a JVT meeting in December 2003 and that it first submitted a JVT proposal in January 2006. . . . Qualcomm stated that it submitted four proposals to the JVT in 2006 but had no earlier involvement. . . . Kevin Leung signed both of these interrogatory responses.

Qualcomm's responses to Broadcom's Rule 30(b)(6) deposition notices were more troubling. Initially, Qualcomm designated Christine Irvine as the corporation's most knowledgeable person on the issue of Qualcomm's involvement in the JVT. Although attorney Leung prepared Irvine for her deposition, Qualcomm did not search her computer for any relevant documents or emails or provide her with any information to review. Irvine testified falsely that Qualcomm had never been involved in the JVT. Broadcom impeached Irvine with documents showing that Qualcomm had participated in the JVT in late 2003. Qualcomm ultimately agreed to provide another Rule 30(b)(6) witness.

Qualcomm designated Scott Ludwin as the new representative to testify about Qualcomm's knowledge of and involvement in the JVT. Leung prepared and defended Ludwin at his deposition. Qualcomm did not search Ludwin's computer for any relevant documents nor take any other action to prepare him. Ludwin testified falsely that Qualcomm only began participating in the JVT in late 2003, after the H.264 standard had been published. In an effort to impeach him (and extract the truth), Broadcom showed Ludwin a December 2002 email reflector list from the Advanced Video Coding ("AVC") Ad Hoc Group that listed the email address viji@qualcomm.com.[2] Although Ludwin did not recognize the document, Broadcom utilized the document throughout the litigation to argue that Qualcomm had participated in the JVT during the development of the H.264 standard.

As the case progressed, Qualcomm became increasingly aggressive in its argument that it did not participate in the JVT during the time the JVT

2. The document is an "Input Document to JVT" entitled "Ad Hoc Report on AVC Verification Test." The Report discusses a meeting to take place among JVT members. The Annex A to the document is entitled a "list of Ad Hoc Members." It includes Raveendran's email address, viji@qualcomm.com, and identifies her as a member of list avc_ce. Id. While the document is not an email sent to or from Raveendran, it indicates that a Qualcomm employee was receiving JVT/AVC reports in 2002. This document became critical to Broadcom as it was the only evidence in Broadcom's possession indicating the truth — that Qualcomm had been actively involved in the JVT and the development of the H.264 standard in 2002.

was creating the H.264 standard.[3] This argument was vital to Qualcomm's success in this litigation because if Qualcomm had participated in the creation of the H.264 standard, it would have been required to identify its patents that reasonably may be essential to the practice of the H.264 standard, including the '104 and '767 patents, and to license them royalty-free or under non-discriminatory, reasonable terms. Thus, participation in the JVT in 2002 or early 2003 during the creation of the H.264 standard would have prohibited Qualcomm from suing companies, including Broadcom, that utilized the H.264 standard. . . .

C. Trial and Decision Not to Produce avc_ce Emails

Trial commenced on January 9, 2007, and throughout trial, Qualcomm argued that it had not participated in the JVT in 2002 and early 2003 when the H.264 standard was being created. In his opening statement, Qualcomm's lead attorney, James Batchelder, stated:

> Later, in May of '03, the standard is approved and published. And then Qualcomm, in the fall of 2003, it begins to participate not in JVT because it's done. H.264 is approved and published. Qualcomm begins to participate in what are called professional extensions, things that sit on top of the standard, additional improvements.

While preparing Qualcomm witness Viji Raveendran to testify at trial, attorney Adam Bier discovered an August 6, 2002 email to viji@qualcomm.com welcoming her to the avc_ce mailing list. Several days later, on January 14, 2007, Bier and Raveendran searched her laptop computer using the search term "avc_ce" and discovered 21 separate emails, none of which Qualcomm had produced in discovery. The email chains bore several dates in November 2002 and the authors discussed various issues relating to the H.264 standard. While Raveendran was not a named author or recipient, the emails were sent to all members of two JVT email groups (jvt-experts and avc_ce) and Raveendran maintained them on her computer for more than four years. The Qualcomm trial team decided not to produce these newly discovered emails to Broadcom, claiming they were not responsive to Broadcom's discovery requests. The attorneys ignored the fact that the presence of the emails on Raveendran's computer undercut Qualcomm's premier argument that it had not participated in the JVT in 2002. The Qualcomm trial team failed to conduct any investigation to determine whether there were more emails that also had not been produced.

3. For example, on September 1, 2006, Qualcomm submitted an expert declaration confirming the absence of any corporate records indicating Qualcomm's participation in the JVT. The declaration was prepared by the Heller Ehrman lawyers and reviewed by numerous Day Casebeer and Qualcomm in-house attorneys. . . . Numerous in-house and outside counsel also [prepared and reviewed other motions, including a motion for summary judgment and motions in limine denying any involvement by Qualcomm with the JVT while the H.264 standard was being created].

Four days later, during a sidebar discussion, Stanley Young argued against the admission of the December 2002 avc_ce email reflector list, declaring: "Actually, there are no emails—there are no emails . . . there's no evidence that any email was actually sent to this list. This is just a list of email . . . addresses. There's no evidence of anything being sent." None of the Qualcomm attorneys who were present during the sidebar mentioned the 21 avc_ce emails found on Raveendran's computer a few days earlier.

During Raveendran's direct testimony on January 24th, attorney Lee Patch pointedly did not ask her any questions that would reveal the fact that she had received the 21 emails from the avc_ce mailing list; instead, he asked whether she had "any knowledge of having read" any emails from the avc_ce mailing list. But on cross-examination, Broadcom asked the right question and Raveendran was forced to admit that she had received emails from the avc_ce mailing list. Immediately following this admission, in response to Broadcom's request for the emails, and despite the fact that he had participated in the decision three days earlier not to produce them, Patch told the Court at sidebar:

> [I]t's not clear to me [the emails are] responsive to anything. So that's something that needs to be determined before they would be produced. . . . I'm talking about whether they were actually requested in discovery. . . . I'm simply representing that I haven't seen [the emails], and [whether Broadcom requested them] hasn't been determined.

Over the lunch recess that same day, Qualcomm's counsel produced the 21 emails they previously had retrieved from Raveendran's email archive.

On January 26, 2007, the jury returned unanimous verdicts in favor of Broadcom regarding the non-infringement of the '104 and '767 patents, and in favor of Qualcomm regarding the validity and non-obviousness of the same. The jury also returned a unanimous advisory verdict in favor of Broadcom that the '104 patent is unenforceable due to inequitable conduct and the '104 and '767 patents are unenforceable due to waiver.

On March 21, 2007, Judge Brewster found (1) in favor of Qualcomm on Broadcom's inequitable conduct counterclaim regarding the '104 patent, and (2) in favor of Broadcom on Broadcom's waiver defense regarding the '104 and '767 patents. Judge Brewster issued a comprehensive order detailing the appropriate remedy for Qualcomm's waiver. After a thorough overview of the JVT, the JVT's policies and guidelines, and Qualcomm's knowledge of the JVT and evidence of Qualcomm's involvement therein, Judge Brewster found:

> by clear and convincing evidence that Qualcomm, its employees, and its witnesses actively organized and/or participated in a plan to profit heavily by (1) wrongfully concealing the patents-in-suit while participating in the JVT and then (2) actively hiding this concealment from the Court, the jury, and opposing counsel during the present litigation.

Id. at 22. Judge Brewster further found that Qualcomm's "counsel participated in an organized program of litigation misconduct and concealment throughout discovery, trial, and post-trial before new counsel took over lead role in the case on April 27, 2007." Based on "the totality of the evidence produced both before and after the jury verdict," and in light of these findings, Judge Brewster concluded that "Qualcomm has waived its rights to enforce the '104 and '767 patents and their continuations, continuations-in-part, divisions, reissues, or any other derivatives of either patent."

Also on August 6, 2007, Judge Brewster granted Broadcom's Motion for an Award of Attorneys' Fees pursuant to 35 U.S.C. § 285. Judge Brewster found clear and convincing evidence that Qualcomm's litigation misconduct, as set forth in his Waiver Order, justified Qualcomm's payment of all "attorneys' fees, court costs, expert witness fees, travel expenses, and any other litigation costs reasonably incurred by Broadcom" in the defense of this case. On December 11, 2007, Judge Brewster adopted this court's recommendation and ordered Qualcomm to pay Broadcom $9,259,985.09 in attorneys' fees and related costs, as well as post-judgment interest on the final fee award of $8,568,633.24 at 4.91 percent accruing from August 6, 2007.

D. *Qualcomm's Post-Trial Misconduct*

Following trial, Qualcomm continued to dispute the relevancy and responsiveness of the 21 Raveendran emails. Qualcomm also resisted Broadcom's efforts to determine the scope of Qualcomm's discovery violation. . . .

But, on April 9, 2007, James Batchelder and Louis Lupin, Qualcomm's General Counsel, submitted correspondence to Judge Brewster in which they admitted Qualcomm had thousands of relevant unproduced documents and that their review of these documents "revealed facts that appear to be inconsistent with certain arguments that [outside counsel] made on Qualcomm's behalf at trial and in the equitable hearing following trial." Batchelder further apologized "for not having discovered these documents sooner and for asserting positions that [they] would not have taken had [they] known of the existence of these documents."

As of June 29, 2007, Qualcomm had searched the email archives of twenty-one employees and located more than forty-six thousand documents (totaling more than three hundred thousand pages), which had been requested but not produced in discovery. Qualcomm continued to produce additional responsive documents throughout the summer.

Discussion

As summarized above, and as found by Judge Brewster, there is clear and convincing evidence that Qualcomm intentionally engaged in conduct designed to prevent Broadcom from learning that Qualcomm had participated in the JVT during the time period when the H.264 standard was being developed. To this end, Qualcomm withheld tens of thousands of emails showing that it actively participated in the JVT in 2002 and 2003 and then utilized Broadcom's lack of access to the suppressed evidence to repeatedly and falsely aver that there was "no evidence" that it had participated in the JVT prior to September 2003. Qualcomm's misconduct in hiding the emails and electronic documents prevented Broadcom from correcting the false statements and countering the misleading arguments.

A. *Legal Standard*

The Federal Civil Rules authorize federal courts to impose sanctions on parties and their attorneys who fail to comply with discovery obligations and court orders. Rule 37 authorizes a party to file a motion to compel an opponent to comply with a discovery request or obligation when the opponent fails to do so initially. Fed. R. Civ. P. 37(a). If such a motion is filed, the rule requires the court to award reasonable attorney's fees to the prevailing party unless the court finds the losing party's position was "substantially justified" or other circumstances make such an award unjust. . . . There is no requirement under this rule that the failure be willful or reckless; "sanctions may be imposed even for negligent failures to provide discovery." Fjelstad v. Am. Honda Motor Co., Inc., 762 F.2d 1334, 1343 (9th Cir. 1985).

The Federal Rules also provide for sanctions against individual attorneys who are remiss in complying with their discovery obligations. . . . See Fed. R. Civ. P. 26(g)(2). "[W]hat is reasonable is a matter for the court to decide on the totality of the circumstances." Fed. R. Civ. P. 26 Advisory Committee Notes (1983 Amendment). The Committee explained that:

> Rule 26(g) imposes an affirmative duty to engage in pretrial discovery in a responsible manner that is consistent with the spirit and purposes of Rules 26 through 37. In addition, Rule 26(g) is designed to curb discovery abuse by explicitly encouraging the imposition of sanctions. This subdivision provides a deterrent to both excessive discovery and evasion by imposing a certification requirement that obliges each attorney to stop and think about the legitimacy of a discovery request, a response thereto, or an objection. . . . If primary responsibility for conducting discovery is to continue to rest with the litigants, they must be obliged to act responsibly and avoid abuse. . . .

In addition to this rule-based authority, federal courts have the inherent power to sanction litigants to prevent abuse of the judicial process. See Chambers v. Nasco, Inc., 501 U.S. 32, 44-46 (1991). . . .

B. *Broadcom Did Not File a Motion to Compel Discovery*

As summarized above, Broadcom served interrogatories and requested documents relating to Qualcomm's participation in the JVT. Qualcomm responded that "Qualcomm will produce non-privileged relevant and responsive documents describing QUALCOMM's participation in the JVT, if any, which can be located after a reasonable search." Qualcomm also committed to producing "responsive non-privileged documents that were given to or received from the standards-setting body responsible for the [H.264] standard, and which concern any Qualcomm participation in setting the [H.264] standard."

Despite these responses, Qualcomm did not produce over 46,000 responsive documents, many of which directly contradict the non-participation argument that Qualcomm repeatedly made to the court and jury. Because Qualcomm agreed to produce the documents and answered the interrogatories (even though falsely), Broadcom had no reason to file a motion to compel. . . .

This dilemma highlights another problem with Qualcomm's conduct in this case. The Federal Rules of Civil Procedure require parties to respond to discovery in good faith; the rules do not require or anticipate judicial involvement unless or until an actual dispute is discovered. As the Advisory Committee explained, "[i]f primary responsibility for conducting discovery is to continue to rest with the litigants, they must be obliged to act responsibly and avoid abuse." Fed. R. Civ. P. 26(g) Advisory Committee Notes (1983 Amendment). The Committee's concerns are heightened in this age of electronic discovery when attorneys may not physically touch and read every document within the client's custody and control. For the current "good faith" discovery system to function in the electronic age, attorneys and clients must work together to ensure that both understand how and where electronic documents, records and emails are maintained and to determine how best to locate, review, and produce responsive documents. Attorneys must take responsibility for ensuring that their clients conduct a comprehensive and appropriate document search. Producing 1.2 million pages of marginally relevant documents while hiding 46,000 critically important ones does not constitute good faith and does not satisfy either the client's or attorney's discovery obligations. Similarly, agreeing to produce certain categories of documents and then not producing all of the documents that fit within such a category is unacceptable. Qualcomm's conduct warrants sanctions.

C. Sanctions

. . .

1. Misconduct by Qualcomm

Qualcomm violated its discovery obligations by failing to produce more than 46,000 emails and documents that were requested in discovery and that Qualcomm agreed to produce. . . .

Qualcomm has not established "substantial justification" for its failure to produce the documents. In fact, Qualcomm has not presented any evidence attempting to explain or justify its failure to produce the documents. Despite the fact that it maintains detailed records showing whose computers were searched and which search terms were used, Qualcomm has not presented any evidence establishing that it searched for pre-September 2003 JVT, avc_ce, or H.264 records or emails on its computer system or email databases. Qualcomm also has not established that it searched the computers or email databases of the individuals who testified on Qualcomm's behalf at trial or in depositions as Qualcomm's most knowledgeable corporate witnesses; in fact, it indicates that it did not conduct any such search. The fact that Qualcomm did not perform these basic searches at any time before the completion of trial indicates that Qualcomm intentionally withheld the documents. This conclusion is bolstered by the fact that when Qualcomm "discovered" the 21 Raveendran emails, it did not produce them and did not engage in any type of review to determine whether there were additional relevant, responsive, and unproduced documents. The conclusion is further supported by the fact that after trial Qualcomm did not conduct an internal investigation to determine if there were additional unproduced documents, but, rather, spent its time opposing Broadcom's efforts to force such a search and insisting, without any factual basis, that Qualcomm's search was reasonable.

Qualcomm's claim that it inadvertently failed to find and produce these documents also is negated by the massive volume and direct relevance of the hidden documents. As Judge Brewster noted, it is inexplicable that Qualcomm was able to locate the post-September 2003 JVT documents that either supported, or did not harm, Qualcomm's arguments but were unable to locate the pre-September 2003 JVT documents that hurt its arguments. Similarly, the inadvertence argument is undercut by Qualcomm's ability to easily locate the suppressed documents using fundamental JVT and avc_ce search terms when forced to do so by Broadcom's threat to return to court. Finally, the inadvertence argument also is belied by the number of Qualcomm employees and consultants who received the emails, attended the JVT meetings, and otherwise knew about the information set forth in the undisclosed emails. It is inconceivable that Qualcomm was unaware of its involvement in the JVT and of the existence of these documents.

Assuming, arguendo, that Qualcomm did not know about the suppressed emails, Qualcomm failed to heed several warning signs that should have alerted it to the fact that its document search and production were inadequate. The first significant concern should have been raised in connection with the Rule 30(b)(6) depositions of Christine Irvine and Scott Ludwin. Both individuals testified as the Qualcomm employee most knowledgeable about Qualcomm's involvement in the JVT. But Qualcomm did not search either person's computer for JVT documents, did not provide either person with relevant JVT documents to review, and did not make any other efforts to ensure each person was in fact knowledgeable about Qualcomm's JVT involvement. These omissions are especially incriminating because many of the suppressed emails were to or from Irvine. If a witness is testifying as an organization's most knowledgeable person on a specific subject, the organization has an obligation to conduct a reasonable investigation and review to ensure that the witness does possess the organization's knowledge.[6] Fed. R. Civ. P. 30(b)(6); In re JDS Uniphase Corp. Sec. Litig., 2007 WL 219857, *1 (N.D. Cal. 2007) (the corporation "must prepare the designee to the extent matters are reasonably available, whether from documents, past employees, or other sources"). An adequate investigation should include an analysis of the sufficiency of the document search and, when electronic documents are involved, an analysis of the sufficiency of the search terms and locations. In the instant case, a reasonable inquiry should have included using the JVT, avc_ce, and H.264 search terms and searching the computers of Raveendran, Irvine, Ludwin (and other Qualcomm employees identified in the emails discovered on the computers of these witnesses). This minimal inquiry would have revealed the existence of the suppressed documents. . . .

Another ignored warning flag was the December 2002 avc_ce email reflector containing Raveendran's email address. Broadcom utilized this document in several ways to argue that Qualcomm was involved in the JVT prior to September 2003. Even though this document indicated that in December 2002, a Qualcomm employee was a member of the avc_ce email group, which related to the JVT and the development of the H.264 standard, there is no evidence that its presence triggered a search by Qualcomm for "avc_ce," "JVT," or any other relevant term on Raveendran's computer or any other Qualcomm database. Again, if Qualcomm had performed this search, it would have located the suppressed emails. The fact that Qualcomm chose not to investigate this document supports the conclusion that Qualcomm intentionally withheld the 46,000 emails. This conclusion is reinforced by the fact that, without any investigation, Qualcomm repeatedly tried to discredit the document and Broadcom's reliance on it.

Qualcomm had the ability to identify its employees and consultants who were involved in the JVT, to access and review their computers, databases and emails, to talk with the involved employees and to refresh their recollections if necessary. . . . Qualcomm chose not to do so and therefore must be sanctioned.

2. Attorneys' Misconduct

The next question is what, if any, role did Qualcomm's retained lawyers play in withholding the documents? The Court envisions four scenarios. First, Qualcomm intentionally hid the documents from its retained lawyers and did so so effectively that the lawyers did not know or suspect that the suppressed documents existed. Second, the retained lawyers

6. Qualcomm also has not presented any evidence that outside counsel knew enough about Qualcomm's organization and operation to identify all of the individuals whose computers should be searched and determine the most knowledgeable witness. And, more importantly, Qualcomm is a large corporation with an extensive legal staff; it clearly had the ability to identify the correct witnesses and determine the correct computers to search and search terms to use. Qualcomm just lacked the desire to do so.

failed to discover the intentionally hidden documents or suspect their existence due to their complete ineptitude and disorganization. Third, Qualcomm shared the damaging documents with its retained lawyers (or at least some of them) and the knowledgeable lawyers worked with Qualcomm to hide the documents and all evidence of Qualcomm's early involvement in the JVT. Or, fourth, while Qualcomm did not tell the retained lawyers about the damaging documents and evidence, the lawyers suspected there was additional evidence or information but chose to ignore the evidence and warning signs and accept Qualcomm's incredible assertions regarding the adequacy of the document search and witness investigation.

Given the impressive education and extensive experience of Qualcomm's retained lawyers, the Court rejects the first and second possibilities. It is inconceivable that these talented, well-educated, and experienced lawyers failed to discover through their interactions with Qualcomm any facts or issues that caused (or should have caused) them to question the sufficiency of Qualcomm's document search and production. Qualcomm did not fail to produce a document or two; it withheld over 46,000 critical documents that extinguished Qualcomm's primary argument of non-participation in the JVT. In addition, the suppressed documents did not belong to one employee, or a couple of employees who had since left the company; they belonged to (or were shared with) numerous, current Qualcomm employees, several of whom testified (falsely) at trial and in depositions. . . .

The Court finds no direct evidence establishing option three. Neither party nor the attorneys have presented evidence that Qualcomm told one or more of its retained attorneys about the damaging emails or that an attorney learned about the emails and that the knowledgeable attorney(s) then helped Qualcomm hide the emails. While knowledge may be inferred from the attorneys' conduct, evidence on this issue is limited due to Qualcomm's assertion of the attorney-client privilege.[8]

Thus, the Court finds it likely that some variation of option four occurred; that is, one or more of the retained lawyers chose not to look in the correct locations for the correct documents, to accept the unsubstantiated assurances of an important client that its search was sufficient, to ignore the warning signs that the document search and production

8. Qualcomm asserted the attorney-client privilege and decreed that its retained attorneys could not reveal any communications protected by the privilege. Several attorneys complained that the assertion of the privilege prevented them from providing additional information regarding their conduct. This concern was heightened when Qualcomm submitted its self-serving declarations describing the failings of its retained lawyers. Recognizing that a client has a right to maintain this privilege and that no adverse inference should be made based upon the assertion, the Court accepted Qualcomm's assertion of the privilege and has not drawn any adverse inferences from it. However, the fact remains that the Court does not have access to all of the information necessary to reach an informed decision regarding the actual knowledge of the attorneys. As a result, the Court concludes for purposes of this Order that there is insufficient evidence establishing option three.

were inadequate, not to press Qualcomm employees for the truth, and/or to encourage employees to provide the information (or lack of information) that Qualcomm needed to assert its non-participation argument and to succeed in this lawsuit. These choices enabled Qualcomm to withhold hundreds of thousands of pages of relevant discovery and to assert numerous false and misleading arguments to the court and jury. This conduct warrants the imposition of sanctions.

a. Identity of Sanctioned Attorneys

The Court finds that each of the following attorneys contributed to Qualcomm's monumental discovery violation and is personally responsible: James Batchelder, Adam Bier, Kevin Leung, Christopher Mammen, Lee Patch, and Stanley Young ("Sanctioned Attorneys").

[Day Casebeer a]ttorneys Leung, Mammen and Batchelder are responsible for the initial discovery failure because they handled or supervised Qualcomm's discovery responses and production of documents. . . . Had Leung, Mammen, Batchelder, or any of the other attorneys insisted on reviewing Qualcomm's records regarding the locations searched and terms utilized, they would have discovered the inadequacy of the search and the suppressed documents.[10] Similarly, Leung's difficulties with the Rule 30(b)(6) witnesses, Irvine and Ludwin, should have alerted him (and the supervising or senior attorneys) to the inadequacy of Qualcomm's document production and to the fact that they needed to review whose computers and databases had been searched and for what. . . .

[Day Casebeer a]ttorneys Bier, Mammen and Patch are responsible for the discovery violation because they also did not perform a reasonable inquiry to determine whether Qualcomm had complied with its discovery obligations. When Bier reviewed the August 6, 2002 email welcoming Raveendran to the avc_ce email group, he knew or should have known that it contradicted Qualcomm's trial arguments and he had an obligation

10. Leung's attorney represented during the OSC hearing that Leung requested a more thorough document search but that Qualcomm refused to do so. If Leung was unable to get Qualcomm to conduct the type of search he deemed necessary to verify the adequacy of the document search and production, then he should have obtained the assistance of supervising or senior attorneys. If Mammen and Batchelder were unable to get Qualcomm to conduct a competent and thorough document search, they should have withdrawn from the case or taken other action to ensure production of the evidence. See The State Bar of California, Rules of Professional Conduct, Rule 5-220 (a lawyer shall not suppress evidence that the lawyer or the lawyer's client has a legal obligation to reveal); Rule 3-700 (a lawyer shall withdraw from employment if the lawyer knows or should know that continued employment will result in a violation of these rules or the client insists that the lawyer pursue a course of conduct prohibited under these rules). Attorneys' ethical obligations do not permit them to participate in an inadequate document search and then provide misleading and incomplete information to their opponents and false arguments to the court. Id.; Rule 5-200 (a lawyer shall not seek to mislead the judge or jury by a false statement of fact or law); see also In re Marriage of Gong and Kwong, 157 Cal. App. 4th 939, 951 (1st Dist. 2007) ("[a]n attorney in a civil case is not a hired gun required to carry out every direction given by the client"; he must act like the professional he is).

to verify that it had been produced in discovery or to immediately produce it. If Bier, as a junior lawyer, lacked the experience to recognize the significance of the document, then a more senior or knowledgeable attorney should have assisted him. To the extent that Patch was supervising Bier in this endeavor, Patch certainly knew or should have recognized the importance of the document from his involvement in Qualcomm's motion practice and trial strategy sessions.

Similarly, when Bier found the 21 emails on Raveendran's computer that had not been produced in discovery, he took the appropriate action and informed his supervisors, Mammen and Patch. Patch discussed the discovery and production issue with Young and Batchelder. While all of these attorneys assert that there was a plausible argument that Broadcom did not request these documents, only Bier and Mammen actually read the emails. Moreover, all of the attorneys missed the critical inquiry: was Qualcomm's document search adequate? If these 21 emails were not discovered during Qualcomm's document search, how many more might exist? The answer, obviously, was tens of thousands. . . . And, these experienced attorneys should have realized that the presence on Raveendran's computer of 21 JVT/avc_ce emails from 2002 contradicted Qualcomm's numerous arguments that it had not participated in the JVT during that same time period. This fact, alone, should have prompted the attorneys to immediately produce the emails and to conduct a comprehensive document search.

Finally, [Heller Ehrman attorney] Young, [and Day Casebeer attorneys] Patch and Batchelder bear responsibility for the discovery failure because they did not conduct a reasonable inquiry into Qualcomm's discovery production before making specific factual and legal arguments to the court. Young decided that Qualcomm should file a motion for summary adjudication premised on the fact that Qualcomm had not participated in the JVT until after the H.264 standard was adopted in May 2003. Given that non-participation was vital to the motion, Young had a duty to conduct a reasonable inquiry into whether that fact was true. And, again, had Young conducted such a search, he would have discovered the inadequacy of Qualcomm's document search and production and learned that his argument was false. Similarly, Young had a duty to conduct a reasonable inquiry into the accuracy of his statement before affirmatively telling the court that no emails were sent to Raveendran from the avc_ce email group. Young also did not conduct a reasonable (or any) inquiry during the following days before he approved the factually incorrect JMOL.[12] A reasonable investigation would have prevented the false filing.

12. While the Court recognizes that the Day Casebeer attorneys were primarily responsible for discovery in this case, the Heller Ehrman attorneys took on the task of preparing witnesses and briefing regarding the JVT and, thus, were in a position to evaluate during this process whether the underlying discovery upon which they relied was adequate. Young, unlike [other, unsanctioned Heller Ehrman attorneys] Venkatesan and Robertson, was the primary liaison with Day Casebeer and also was privy to the evolving theories of the case. As such, he was made aware of some of the red flags such as

Patch was an integral part of the trial team — familiar with Qualcomm's arguments, theories and strategies. He knew on January 14th that 21 avc_ce emails had been discovered on Raveendran's computer. Without reading or reviewing the emails, Patch participated in the decision not to produce them. Several days later, Patch carefully tailored his questions to ensure that Raveendran did not testify about the unproduced emails. And, after Broadcom stumbled into the email testimony, Patch affirmatively misled the Court by claiming that he did not know whether the emails were responsive to Broadcom's discovery requests. This conduct is unacceptable and, considering the totality of the circumstances, it is unrealistic to think that Patch did not know or believe that Qualcomm's document search was inadequate and that Qualcomm possessed numerous, similar and unproduced documents.

Batchelder also is responsible because he was the lead trial attorney and, as such, he was most familiar with Qualcomm's important arguments and witnesses. Batchelder stated in his opening statement that Qualcomm had not participated in the JVT before late 2003. Despite this statement and his complete knowledge of Qualcomm's legal theories, Batchelder did not take any action when he was informed that JVT documents that Qualcomm had not produced in discovery were found on Raveendran's computer. He did not read the emails, ask about their substance, nor inquire as to why they were not located during discovery. And, he stood mute when four days later, Young falsely stated that no emails had been sent to Raveendran from the avc_ce email group. Finally, all of the pleadings containing the lie that Qualcomm had not participated in the JVT in 2002 or early 2003 were sent to Batchelder for review and he approved or ignored all of them. The totality of the circumstances, including all of the previously-discussed warning signs, demanded that Batchelder conduct an investigation to verify the adequacy of Qualcomm's document search and production. His failure to do so enabled Qualcomm to withhold the documents. . . .

3. Imposed Sanctions

The remaining issue, then, is what are the appropriate sanctions.

a. Monetary Sanctions Against Qualcomm

. . .

Because Broadcom prevailed at trial and in the post-trial hearings despite the suppressed evidence, it is reasonable to infer that had Qualcomm intended to produce the 46,000 incriminating emails (and thereby acknowledge its early involvement in the JVT and its accompanying need to

---

the discovery of the JVT emails on Raveendran's computer and was in the best position both to understand their significance and to communicate any concerns to the Day Casebeer attorneys or Qualcomm in-house counsel.

disclose its intellectual property), the instant case may never have been filed. Even if Qualcomm did file this case, the hidden evidence would have dramatically undermined Qualcomm's arguments and likely resulted in an adverse pretrial adjudication, much as it caused the adverse post-trial rulings. Accordingly, Qualcomm's failure to produce the massive number of critical documents at issue in this case significantly increased the scope, complexity and length of the litigation and justifies a significant monetary award.

The Court therefore awards Broadcom all of its attorneys' fees and costs incurred in the instant litigation. Because Judge Brewster already has awarded these costs and fees to Broadcom [under fee shifting provisions of the patent statute] and a double recovery would be improper, this Court directs that Qualcomm receive credit toward this penalty. . . . Accordingly, for its monumental and intentional discovery violation, Qualcomm is ordered to pay $8,568,633.24 to Broadcom; this figure will be reduced by the amount actually paid by Qualcomm to Broadcom to satisfy the exceptional case award.[17]

b. Referral to the California State Bar

As set forth above, the Sanctioned Attorneys assisted Qualcomm in committing this incredible discovery violation by intentionally hiding or recklessly ignoring relevant documents, ignoring or rejecting numerous warning signs that Qualcomm's document search was inadequate, and blindly accepting Qualcomm's unsupported assurances that its document search was adequate. The Sanctioned Attorneys then used the lack of evidence to repeatedly and forcefully make false statements and arguments to the court and jury. As such, the Sanctioned Attorneys violated their discovery obligations and also may have violated their ethical duties. See e.g., The State Bar of California, Rules of Professional Conduct, Rule 5-200 (a lawyer shall not seek to mislead the judge or jury by a false statement of fact or law), Rule 5-220 (a lawyer shall not suppress evidence that the lawyer or the lawyer's client has a legal obligation to reveal or to produce). To address the potential ethical violations, the Court refers the Sanctioned Attorneys to The State Bar of California for an appropriate investigation and possible imposition of sanctions. Within ten days of the date of this Order, each of the Sanctioned Attorneys must forward a copy of this Order and Judge Brewster's Waiver Order to the Intake Unit, The State Bar of California, 1149 South Hill Street, Los Angeles, California 90015 for appropriate investigation.

17. Because the attorneys' fees sanction is so large, the Court declines to fine Qualcomm. If the imposition of an $8.5 million dollar sanction does not change Qualcomm's conduct, the Court doubts that an additional fine would do so.

c. Case Review and Enforcement of Discovery Obligations

The Court also orders Qualcomm and the Sanctioned Attorneys to participate in a comprehensive Case Review and Enforcement of Discovery Obligations ("CREDO") program. . . .

At a minimum, the CREDO protocol must include a detailed analysis (1) identifying the factors that contributed to the discovery violation . . . (2) creating and evaluating proposals, procedures, and processes that will correct the deficiencies identified in subsection (1), (3) developing and finalizing a comprehensive protocol that will prevent future discovery violations (e.g., determining the depth and breadth of case management and discovery plans that should be adopted; identifying by experience or authority the attorney from the retained counsel's office who should interface with the corporate counsel and on which issues; describing the frequency the attorneys should meet and whether other individuals should participate in the communications; identifying who should participate in the development of the case management and discovery plans; describing and evaluating various methods of resolving conflicts and disputes between the client and retained counsel, especially relating to the adequacy of discovery searches; describing the type, nature, frequency, and participants in case management and discovery meetings; and, suggesting required ethical and discovery training; etc.), (4) applying the protocol that was developed in subsection (3) to other factual situations, such as when the client does not have corporate counsel, when the client has a single in-house lawyer, when the client has a large legal staff, and when there are two law firms representing one client, (5) identifying and evaluating data tracking systems, software, or procedures that corporations could implement to better enable inside and outside counsel to identify potential sources of discoverable documents (e.g., the correct databases, archives, etc.), and (6) any other information or suggestions that will help prevent discovery violations.

It is so ordered.

Note: A Problem of Divided Responsibility?

Qualcomm sent shockwaves through the legal community and remains, in many ways, a wake-up call for attorneys regarding the potential uses and abuses of e-discovery. Electronically stored information vastly multiplies the number of potentially relevant documents and, concomitantly, the responsibilities of lawyers to manage them before and during litigation. For an analysis of some of these issues see Hon. Paul W. Grimm, Ethical Issues Associated with Preserving, Accessing, Discovering, and Using Electronically Stored Information, SP003 ALI-ABA 693 (2008) (discussing Rule of Professional Responsibility 3.4 (Fairness to Opposing Party and Counsel) and using *Qualcomm* as a case in point for its ethical discussion); see id. at 718-719 ("There are many lessons to be learned from *Qualcomm*, but chief among them is that lawyers can expect that courts will require them to live up to their obligations under Rule 26(g), and that blind reliance on a client's representations that it adequately searched for and produced all responsive ESI will not insulate a lawyer from sanctions or charges of ethical misconduct when the lawyer knows or should suspect the client's response is inadequate."); Kristine L. Roberts, ABA Section of Litigation, Qualcomm Fined for "Monumental" E-Discovery Violations—Possible Sanctions Against Counsel Remain Pending (May 2008) (discussing steps attorneys should take to "avoid Qualcomm's fate" by making e-discovery checklists), http://www.abanet.org/litigation/litigationnews/2008/may/0508_article_qualcomm.html.

Although the sanction imposed against outside counsel for Qualcomm is still the subject of litigation as of this writing (the attorneys have asked the district court judge to reverse the magistrate judge's order), the trial court's separate attorney fees award against Qualcomm has been upheld. See Qualcomm, Inc. v. Broadcom, Inc., 548 F.3d 1004, 1004 (Fed. Cir. 2008) (upholding attorney fee award under the federal patent statute's fee shifting provision for inequitable conduct). For the posttrial order that got the sanctions ball rolling, see Qualcomm, Inc. v. Broadcom, Inc., 539 F. Supp. 2d 1214 (S.D. Cal. 2007).

Can you discern from the opinion what the division of labor was among the lawyers representing Qualcomm? There were two outside law firms, Heller Ehrman and Day Casebeer, and Qualcomm is a large enough company that it has a substantial in-house counsel's office. The company is also regularly involved in litigation with high-tech industry competitors. In part to save costs, it appears to have divided up its litigation work among outside firms and in-house counsel not only between cases, but *within* cases. In this case, Day Casebeer appears to have been in charge of pleading and discovery, but lawyers from Heller Ehrman were brought in for trial. Doesn't this division of labor inherently increase the risk that lawyers accountable under procedural and ethical rules for the accuracy of their representations may not know or be in a position to verify the truth of what they tell the judge, jury, and opposing counsel? See David Luban, The Ethics of Wrongful Obedience, in Luban, Legal Ethics and Human Dignity 237 (2007) (discussing the problem of divided responsibility in large organizations, especially large law firms); Luban, Contrived Ignorance, 87 Geo. L.J. 957 (1999) (arguing that lawyers often face incentives to remain deliberately ignorant of client misdeeds even when directly confronted with evidence of such wrongdoing).

If Qualcomm's in-house lawyers assured outside counsel that they would take care of providing relevant company documents and witnesses themselves in response to Broadcom's discovery requests, are the outside attorneys and firms within their rights to rely on that assurance? The court says no, at least not when contradictions appear in the record and a reasonable attorney would inquire. What if outside counsel did inquire but was rebuffed? What if outside counsel's retainer agreement specifically limited their duties to dealing with the court and opposing counsel? These are some of the issues that remain open regarding the sanctions imposed on outside counsel. In subsequent briefing the attorneys argued, as they did before the magistrate judge, that they cannot possibly defend their conduct in the case as long as they are bound by the attorney-client privilege.

Should the trial judge waive the attorney-client privilege? As of this writing, the trial judge had vacated the sanctions award against outside counsel and granted a "self-defense exception" to the attorney-client privilege to allow the attorneys to conduct discovery (against their own client) in an effort to prove that in-house counsel and corporate officers were responsible for the deception. Qualcomm, Inc. v. Broadcom, Inc., 2008 WL 638108 *3 (S.D. Cal. 2008) ("The attorneys have a due process right to defend themselves under the totality of circumstances presented in this sanctions hearing where their alleged conduct regarding discovery is in conflict with that alleged by Qualcomm concerning performance of discovery responsibilities.").

What about the lawyers for defendants? Are you troubled that they had the August 6, 2002, e-mail to Viji Raveendran from the JVT avc_ce mailing list in their possession but did not use it as the basis for a motion to compel or for pressing Qualcomm's lawyers for more information about why an employee had such an e-mail if the company was not involved with JVT before late 2003? Could more effective use of discovery tools by the defendant have avoided the debacle of a last-minute revelation on cross-examination at trial, or do you think filing proper requests in the first place was enough? Discovery is supposed to avoid surprise, but that only happens if both sides act both ethically *and* diligently.

Qualcomm is not the only case involving professional misconduct in e-discovery. In Doe v. Norwalk Cmty. Coll., 248 F.R.D. 372 (D. Conn. 2007), for instance, the district court had to decide on an appropriate sanction against defendants who scrubbed their hard drive of the names of key witnesses in a sexual harassment case. The court ultimately decided to issue an adverse inference based on the spoliation of evidence. See also Krumwiede v. Brighton Assocs., 2006 WL 1308629, at *9 (N.D. Ill. May 8, 2006) (unreported) (imposing the "harsh sanction" of a default judgment against a party that altered, modified, and deleted documents on a laptop computer before surrendering it during discovery). For a general survey of case law touching on e-discovery ethics issues, see Dale M. Cendali et al., Potential Ethical Pitfalls in Electronic Discovery, in Ethics in Context 2007, at 105 (PLI/NY Practice Skills, Course Handbook Series No. 10960, 2007), available at 171 PLI/NY 105 (Westlaw). See also Joseph Gallagher, Note, E-Ethics: The Ethical Dimension of the Electronic Discovery Amendments to the Federal Rules of Civil Procedure, 20 Geo. J. Legal Ethics 613, 626 (2007) (concluding that the e-discovery rules represent a "general movement away from boilerplate discovery mechanisms and towards the private resolution of conflicts," making it all the more important for lawyers to act ethically).

Note: E-Discovery Amendments to Rule 26

Concerns about the differences between digital data and traditional materials subject to discovery led the Advisory Committee to propose amendments to the discovery rules in 2004. The amendments, which took effect January 1, 2006, address the need to meet and confer about discovery of electronic data early in the litigation, Fed. R. Civ. P. 26(f)(3)(C); the form in which electronic data should be produced, Rules 33, 34, 45(d)(1); how to deal with privileged information (whether digital or not) that is inadvertently disclosed, Rules 26(b)(5)(B), 26(f)(3)(C); how to manage discovery of data that are not stored in readily accessible formats, Rule 26(b)(2)(B); and protection against sanctions for failing to produce information where a party can make a good faith showing that the data have been destroyed or made inaccessible as a result of the routine operation of an electronic information management system, Rule 37(f). "Electronically stored information" is also now formally recognized as a separate category of discovery along with the traditional categories of "documents" and "things." For an overview of some of the early case law applying these amendments, see Kenneth J. Withers, Federal Court Decisions Involving Electronic Discovery December 1, 2006–June 15, 2007, ALI-ABA Course of Study: Civil Practice and Litigation Techniques in Federal and State Courts 1725, available at SN009 ALI-ABA 1725 (Westlaw). See also Bar v. Lowe's Home Ctrs., Inc., 2007 WL 1299180 (W.D.N.C. May 2, 2007) (model discovery plan to facilitate discovery of electronically stored information under new F.R.C.P. 26(f)).

For commentary on the amendments, see George L. Paul and Bruce H. Naron, The Discovery Revolution: E-Discovery Amendments to the Federal Rules of Civil Procedure (2006); Shira A. Scheindlin, E-Discovery: The Newly Amended Federal Rules of Civil Procedure (2006). See also David K. Isom, Electronic Discovery Primer for Judges, 2005 Fed. Cts. L. Rev. 1 (2005); Ken Withers, Two Tiers and a Safe Harbor: Federal Rulemakers Grapple with Electronic Discovery, Fed. Litigator (Sept. 2004); Hon. Ron Hedges, A View From the Bench and Trenches: A Critical Appraisal of Some Proposed Amendments to the Federal Rules of Civil Procedure, 227 F.R.D. 123 (2005).

As a result of the 2006 amendments e-mail, blogs, and even instant messaging are discoverable. See generally Monique C.M. Leahy, Proof of Instant Message, Blog, or Chat as Evidence, 100 Am. Jurisprudence Proof of Facts 3d 89, § 20 (2008). In Steinbuch v. Cutler, for example, a staff assistant to then U.S. Senator Mike DeWine created a blog, "Washingtonienne," which detailed her social and sexual activities with various men and was later linked to the more popular site "Wonkette." 463 F. Supp. 2d 4 (D.D.C. 2006). In a claim against the staffer for invasion of privacy and intentional infliction of emotional distress that followed, discovery of the blog was challenged and the plaintiff was required to respond to the truth or falsity of *each post*. See id. at 9-10. For a critique of the amendments on the ground that they over-expand the domain of discoverable information, see Douglas L. Rodgers, A Search for Balance in Discovery of ESI Since Dec. 1, 2006, 14 Rich J.L. & Tech 8, 8 (2006) (arguing that discovery of electronically stored information "threatens to clog the federal court system and make judicial determination of the substantive merits of disputes an endangered species").

Note: The Discovery of "Metadata"

The most controversial aspects of the amendments, however, appear to be those dealing with privileges, so-called metadata, and requests for data stored in formats that are not readily accessible. With respect to privileges, the main concern is waiver, loss of the ability to prevent confidential information from being introduced in court once it has been inadvertently disclosed to the other side. That concern applies to both traditional documents and digital data; see the Note on waiver, supra page 517.

"Metadata" refers to electronically stored information that is created any time a digital file is made, used, or altered. A simple example is the "track changes" function in a word processing program. Courts and commentators have been divided over whether metadata must be produced whenever electronically stored information is requested in discovery. Debate has centered on the questions of whether metadata is in fact part of the "document" subject to discovery and whether electronically stored information can be "scrubbed" of its metadata before production. In an employment dispute, for instance, a trail of tracked changes may be the only information revealing workforce changes that were planned or imposed by the employer. Can an employer scrub such metadata from its spreadsheets prior to disclosure? See *Williams v. Sprint/United Mgmt. Co., 230 F.R.D. 640 (D. Kan. 1995)* (holding metadata in employment spreadsheets was relevant and should not have been scrubbed; withholding sanctions but imposing a waiver of privileges and work-product protection as to metadata).

Amended Rule 34 now makes clear that metadata are discoverable, "subject to the relevance limit under Rule 26(b)(1) and the proportionality limits under Rule 26(b)(2)(C) that apply to all discovery." Hon. Lee H. Rosenthal, A Few Thoughts on Electronic Discovery After December 1, 2006, 116 Yale L.J. Pocket Part 167, 185-189 (2006) (discussing *Williams*); see also W. Lawrence Wescott II, The Increasing Importance of Metadata in Electronic Discovery, 14 Rich. J.L. & Tech. 10, 10 (2008) (surveying trends in recent case law and concluding that practitioners should make a "regular practice" of preserving metadata). However, not all scholars agree that the current discovery rules establish an ideal system for metadata discovery. See, e.g., Mike Breen, Nothing to Hide: Why Metadata Should Be Presumed Relevant, 56 U. Kan. L. Rev. 439 (2007) (proposing a rule presuming metadata relevant and requiring the disclosing party to rebut that presumption); Lucia Cucu, Note, The Requirement for Metadata Production Under *Williams v. Sprint/United Management Co.*: An

Unnecessary Burden for Litigants Engaged in Electronic Discovery, 93 Cornell L. Rev. 221 (2007) (articulating another alternative to the *Williams* rule, namely requiring production only of metadata that the opposing party requests).

Finally, the accessibility of the format in which electronically stored information is kept may seem a trivial issue, but it is not. Typically, a business keeps records it regularly uses in digital files that are readily accessible. Computer memory of this sort is costly, though, so as data become less useful, businesses will often either destroy them as part of a document management program or arrange for storage in compressed files that can retain massive amounts of data. Compressed data, however, are functionally inaccessible without payment for their retrieval; the data cannot be searched electronically in compressed format, and restoring them to a searchable format is both time-consuming and very expensive. Amended Rule 26(b)(2)(B) provides that, absent a showing of good cause, "[a] party need not provide discovery of electronically stored information from sources that the party identifies as not reasonably accessible because of undue burden or cost."

Does this Rule create an incentive for parties to move information that may be relevant to litigation into compressed data files? Normally, the producing party pays the costs of production, see Oppenheimer Fund, Inc. v. Sanders, 437 U.S. 340, 358 (1978), though trial courts have authority under Rule 26(c) to condition discovery on payment of costs by the requesting party if the request would otherwise impose "undue burden or expense." Should a defendant have to bear all the costs of restoring compressed data even when the plaintiff has submitted overbroad discovery requests?

In a sex discrimination suit, Quinby v. WestLB AG, 245 F.R.D. 94 (S.D.N.Y. 2006), the court adopted a seven-factor test first articulated in Zubulake v. UBS Warburg, LLC, 217 F.R.D. 309, 322 (S.D.N.Y. 2003), for determining whether the plaintiff was obliged to share production costs for data stored in inaccessible formats. In shifting 30 percent of the $181,013.28 retrieval tab to the plaintiff, the *Quinby* court placed heavy emphasis on the fact that the plaintiff had initially requested "to search nineteen current and former WestLB employees' e-mails for over 170 search terms for approximately a five year period" in order to find references to plaintiff, terms that were "potentially sexist," information "relating to discrimination against other women at WestLB," and "e-mails showing that men were more highly compensated than women." *Quinby*, 245 F.R.D. at 98-99. After reviewing a sample of the data produced and finding little relevant information, the court agreed with defendant that plaintiff's request was overbroad.

Still, the court refused to order cost sharing as to information that defendant improperly converted into an inaccessible format after it knew, or should have known, plaintiff would likely file suit. Id. at 104 ("[I]f a party creates its own burden or expense by converting into an inaccessible format data that it should have reasonably foreseen would be discoverable material at a time when it should have anticipated litigation, then it should not be entitled to shift the costs of restoring and searching the data."). The court grounded this portion of its order on defendant's duty to avoid spoliation, noting that "the downgrading of data to a less accessible form—which systematically hinders future discovery by making the recovery of the information more costly and burdensome—is a violation of the preservation obligation." Id. at 103 n.12 (internal quotation marks omitted).

Similarly, consider PSEG Power N.Y. Inc. v. Alberici Constructors, Inc., 2007 WL 2687670 (N.D.N.Y. 2007) (unreported), where the court adopted a variant of the seven-factor *Zubulake* test to determine whether plaintiffs should exclusively bear the costs of reproducing data already transmitted to defendants in an unusable form. Because of a technical glitch, plaintiff's production of some 3,000 e-mails divorced messages from attachments in a manner that made it impossible to tether them back. Since the controversy would not exist "but for PSEG's vendor creating [the] email attachment fiasco," the court concluded that PSEG should bear the entire costs of production: "Whether created by a software incompatibility or malfunction, such deficiency does not provide a sufficient excuse from presenting an important aspect of discovery in a convoluted fashion.... Alberici should not be resigned to accept a flawed discovery process." Id. at *12. See also In re Bristol-Myers Squibb Securities Litigation, 205 F.R.D. 437 (D.N.J. 2002) (plaintiffs agreed to pay the cost of copying documents requested before learning the data were available in electronic form; plaintiffs obtained production in electronic form but were forced to pay just over $300,000 for the paper copying already completed); Zubulake v. UBS Warburg LLC, 217 F.R.D. 309 (S.D.N.Y. 2003) (dispute over obligation to produce documents from difficult-to-access backup tapes and who should bear costs of such production); Zubulake v. UBS Warburg LLC, 216 F.R.D. 280 (S.D.N.Y. 2003) (same).

Are these results consistent with amended Rule 26(b)(2)(B)?

Note: Privilege Logs and Inadvertent Disclosure in E-Discovery

Privilege logs have long been a burdensome and time-consuming affair, often consuming thousands of hours in complex cases. Many a junior associate can recount memories of long hours spent in windowless rooms surrounded by boxes of documents to be sorted for relevance and privileges. The practice (and the temptation to take shortcuts) has become even more burdensome with electronically stored information. In a recent case, the court threatened waiver as a sanction where attorneys for AT&T improperly listed an entire e-mail strand, consisting of 29 separate e-mails, as privileged in its log when only one e-mail in the strand was privileged. In re Universal Service Fund Telephone Billing Practices Litigation, 232 F.R.D. 669 (D. Kan. 2005). AT&T contended that an e-mail strand is analogous to minutes of a meeting, or a transcript of a conversation, such that individual e-mails should not be separated for purposes of a privilege claim. Id. at 672. The court disagreed, emphasizing the risk of "stealth claims of privilege" and that e-mail strands, unlike meetings and conversations, often span several days and involve different sending and receiving individuals for separate parts of the strand. Id. at 673.

AT&T averted the sanction of waiver only by agreeing to produce the unprivileged portions of the strands it had withheld. The judge observed that

> [t]he undersigned . . . is only five years removed from private practice. He is acutely sensitive to the fact that, as a practical matter, requiring each e-mail within a strand to be listed separately on a privilege log is a laborious, time-intensive task for counsel. And, of course, that task adds considerable expense for the clients involved; even for very well-financed corporate defendants such as those in the case at a bar. . . . But the court finds that adherence to such a procedure is essential to ensuring that privilege is asserted only where necessary to achieve its purpose. . . .

Id. at 674.

The risk of inadvertent disclosure is also far greater with electronically stored information. In Marrero Hernandez v. Esso Standard Oil., 2006 WL 1967364 (D.P.R. 2006), for example, the defendant inadvertently produced information it claimed was privileged after someone accidentally merged two electronic files (one privileged, the other not) through "an errant mouse click." Id. at *1 The court held that disclosure to an adversary, whether privileged or not, waives privilege even though the claim might be valid. Id. at *4-*5.

Notice that because privileges are common law doctrines developed by the courts, nothing about Rule 26(f), which encourages the parties to come to an agreement prior to discovery about how they will handle things like inadvertent disclosure of privileged information, nor Rule 26(b)(5)(B), which requires a party to return inadvertently disclosed information subject to a claim of privilege, resolves the issue of waiver. As one trial judge has explained:

> The Civil Rules cannot . . . change substantive privilege law, including the law of privilege waiver, without an affirmative act of Congress. Under current law, depending on the jurisdiction, even if the parties agree to various protocols under which disclosure will not waive a privilege or protection, and the court includes their agreement in an order, neither the agreement nor order assures that the agreement will bind *third parties*. And although amended Rule 26(b)(5) provides a procedure for asserting claims of privilege or protection after production when the parties have not reached an agreement through the meet-and-confer process, the new rule does not resolve the substantive issue of whether the production has waived a belatedly asserted privilege or work-product protection claim. The risk of waiver and of disclosure will lead some parties, particularly those who are frequently sued, to continue to insist on extensive, time-consuming, and costly preproduction privilege reviews, even with a nonwaiver agreement in place between the parties.

Hon. Lee H. Rosenthal, A Few Thoughts on Electronic Discovery After December 1, 2006, 116 Yale L.J. Pocket Part 167, 183 (2006) (emphasis added).

4. The Adversary's Experts

Problem Case: XRT and the SafeTeeTot

The XRT Corporation, which manufacturers the SafeTeeTot infant car seat, has been sued in federal court by a consumer who claims that the seat design is defective. XRT's in-house counsel, Lucy Lee, hired two engineers, Tony McGee, a university professor, and Mickey Wayne, a private consultant, to render their expert opinions about the design. Pursuant to Lee's instructions each expert made an oral report of his finding to XRT's managing officers, which Lee then reduced to writing.

McGee concluded, based on experiments conducted in his university laboratory, that the SafeTeeTot is "the safest infant seat on the market due to XRT's use of what are known in the trade as 'extra-secure' buckles, which are buckles commonly used in commercial airplanes." Wayne's conclusion, on the other hand, is highly critical of XRT's design, particularly XRT's improper use of "extra-secure" buckles. Wayne bases his conclusion on industry-generated safety reports.

Lee paid Wayne for the preliminary consultation and told him no further work would be required. She then informed McGee that XRT intended to call him as an expert witness at trial, and requested a formal written report, which he duly produced.

In response to properly framed requests by the plaintiff, must XRT:

1) disclose Wayne's and McGee's names?
2) produce Lee's memorandum summarizing Wayne's and McGee's oral reports?
3) disclose the substance of Wayne's and McGee's opinions?
4) produce a copy of McGee's written report?
5) May the plaintiff in the case now retain Wayne? If the plaintiff tried to retain Wayne, what would you do procedurally to try to stop her from using him as an expert? What arguments would you make?

Note: Berkey Photo, Inc. v. Eastman Kodak Co., 603 F.2d 263 (2d Cir. 1979)

In "one of the largest and most significant private antitrust suits in history," Kodak relied upon a single expert witness, Professor Peck of Yale, to explain its view of the relevant markets and the reason for

Kodak's persistently high market shares in the film processing industry. Several weeks before trial this expert was deposed; in connection with this deposition, a number of documents were supplied to Berkey by Perkins, a lawyer for Kodak. Perkins represented that these documents included all those supplied to Peck by Kodak and all reports made by Peck to Kodak. In the course of the deposition, Peck stated that he had sent his own notes and work papers to Perkins because they were confidential and because he lacked storage. Perkins stated that all of these work papers had been destroyed; Peck said that he did not remember when he learned that Perkins was destroying the material, but that he had continued to send material to Perkins after learning that the destruction was happening.

Peck was the last witness at the trial. He testified that Kodak had done well because it was innovative, not because it was predatory. On the 110th day of trial, Berkey counsel, Stein, was allowed to cross-examine Peck on the nature of the materials sent to Perkins that were destroyed. He started by asking whether his memorandum of April 21, 1975, the earliest supplied by Perkins at the time of the deposition, was, indeed, the earliest report prepared by Peck for Kodak. Peck acknowledged that it was not. Kodak then produced a letter of November 25, 1974, in which Peck acknowledged to Kodak that he had no persuasive answers as yet to two troublesome economic questions. Kodak had not supplied the document earlier because they thought it was a "letter," not a "report." Stein was then permitted to question Peck as to why at the time of the deposition he had failed to remember and discuss his letter of November 1974. The judge also asked Kodak to search its files again for any other relevant documents. At the beginning of the next week, the trial counsel for Kodak, Doar, acknowledged that all of the documents previously said to have been destroyed were still in Kodak's possession. Moreover, Peck, who had claimed to have no files, had discovered his copy of the letter of November 1974.

Perhaps as a result of these revelations, the jury found in favor of Berkey on every disputed issue. Judgment was accordingly entered in its favor in an amount exceeding $87 million. Among the contentions made on appeal by Kodak was that the trial judge, Marvin Frankel, had allowed Stein to make too much of the revelations of the missing documents, thus destroying the force of Peck's testimony. The court of appeals complimented the judge on his restraint:

> We are also of the view that the cross-examination of Peck remained within permissible channels, particularly in light of the extraordinary revelations that preceded it. Peck conceded at his deposition that he continued to forward research materials to Kodak's lawyers after learning they were destroyed upon receipt, thereby providing more than a sufficient threshold showing of relevance to permit further inquiry on cross-examination. Suspicion could only have been increased by the sudden appearance of PX 666, a letter of great importance to Berkey's efforts to impeach Peck, which the writer claimed to have forgotten existed. And when Peck revealed on Monday that his files had contained a copy of this letter from the outset, deeper inquiry was certainly justified. As each new fact came to light, Judge

Frankel carefully reassessed its relevance to Peck's credibility and gradually enlarged the scope of permissible inquiry into the witness's actions.

Mr. Stein's questions, therefore, far from consisting of the mere compendium of inflammatory rhetoric that Kodak describes, were legitimate challenges to Peck's credibility and to the independence of his judgment. Indeed, Judge Frankel, who throughout the unusual disclosures described here maintained an attitude of cautious restraint, noted in a colloquy with the attorneys that Peck's credibility had, in his judgment, been destroyed on the witness stand. To be sure, the jury need not have believed Berkey's argument that Peck had deliberately collaborated with Perkins in an effort to destroy or conceal documents unfavorable to Kodak's cause. But there was certainly more than an adequate basis to permit Berkey to contend that this inference was justified, and that, at best, Peck was a willing tool of Kodak.

We are not unmindful that the incidents described, as presented to the jury, led to the unfortunate consequence of casting Kodak's attorneys, and the defendant itself, in a highly unfavorable light. It is no less true, however, that the cross-examination elicited information that was highly relevant to an assessment of the independence of judgment and probity of one of Kodak's principal witnesses. Where the trial judge has taken great care to balance the probative value of the evidence against the prejudice that may accrue from its introduction, we think it inappropriate to substitute our judgment for his.

603 F.2d at 308.

David Margolik, The Long Road Back for a Disgraced Patrician

N.Y. Times, Jan. 19, 1990, at B6 (as reprinted in the San Francisco Chronicle, Jan. 28, 1990, at 8)

At the center [*sic*] for Constitutional Rights, Mahlon F. Perkins Jr. is something of an oddball. Among its young, polyglot legal staff, he is a 71-year-old patrician, who looks and speaks like Robert Frost.

His colleagues wear beards or blue jeans; he favors bow ties. They like rock music; he watches birds. They come to work by subway; he takes the train from Greenwich, Conn.

But incongruity is not his chief distinction. Ten years ago, in a scandal that rocked the Wall Street bar, Perkins, then counsel for Kodak, admitted lying in a major antitrust case brought against his client by Berkey Photo.

After almost 30 years at Donovan, Leisure, Newton & Irvine, one of New York's most prominent law firms, he left in disgrace. Then he was sentenced to a month in prison, an extraordinary punishment for a lawyer of his stature and reputation.

In sentencing Perkins, federal District Judge Robert Ward — a Harvard Law School classmate of his — mourned a career ended and a reputation destroyed.

That assessment, it turns out, was quite premature. In an ending that is not only happy but also quite unforeseeable, Perkins has come back, reincarnated as a civil liberties lawyer.

Three days each week, Perkins volunteers his services at the center, which handles primarily civil rights, First Amendment and criminal justice cases.

In his former life, he represented institutions like the American Association of Advertising Agencies and Hughes Tool Co., and earned $200,000 a year doing it. Now, his clients include Corazon Aquino, president of the Philippines; the White Earth Band of Chippewa Indians, and Harvard alumni seeking South African divestiture — and he serves them without pay, living off past earnings.

Where once he occupied a stately office on the 34th floor of 30 Rockefeller Plaza, with a panoramic view of Central Park, Perkins now works out of a tiny seventh-floor rectangle overlooking the discount houses of lower Broadway.

All of the perquisites of corporate law practice — the secretaries, the tea cart, the lunch clubs — are gone, but so, too, are the time sheets, the pressures and the Brooks Brothers suits, a change that especially pleases him. "I've hated jackets and ties for years," he said. "I thought they were ridiculous."

Perkins' stop at the center is only the most recent leg of an extraordinary journey that has taken him from Shanghai, where he was born the son of a diplomat and lived until he was 13, to Phillips Exeter, to Harvard to the Office of Strategic Services to corporate law to the Metropolitan Correctional Facility, a place he had previously seen only on his way to court. This last transition was not easy.

After prison, he fought off disbarment with the support of friends. Then Perkins found himself, a onetime editor of the Harvard Law Review, unable to sell or even give away his services.

Skeptics at the center wondered whether they were getting damaged goods, or if a strait-laced type could ever passionately represent clients who were black or Hispanic or poor, let alone move from the hierarchy of Wall Street to the anarchy of public interest work.

Their fears have long since been allayed. In more than five years at the center, Perkins has earned a reputation for productivity, effectiveness, dedication, and modesty. He has also become a treasured colleague.

"For a Protestant WASP type coming in from the corporate world, particularly with my history, it was really something for them to let me come here in the first place," said Perkins.

In some ways, he said, his ordeal was a blessing in disguise, forcing him into a career change he had considered but might never have had the courage to make.

"Intellectually, the work here is every bit as satisfying as what I did before," he said. "And politically, I derive a lot more satisfaction than I did at Donovan, Leisure."

"I'm helping in causes I believe in very deeply. This wasn't a very good way to have gotten out, but at this point, I'm very happy not to be there, and very happy to be here."

Perkins was on the legal team defending Kodak against antitrust charges brought by Berkey in 1973. At one point, he informed opposing counsel that some documents it sought had been destroyed. In fact, they were in a suitcase back in his office, and he knew it.

He came forward in January 1978 and acknowledged his misstatement to the court. Quickly, he was suspended from the firm. By March, he had resigned.

For Perkins, a man with a heretofore unblemished record, it was a crushing blow. Dozens of times during the next few months, he was asked—and asked himself—why he had lied.

None of the withheld documents was crucial; virtually all had been duplicated and were produced to the other side anyway. "It was sort of an impromptu kind of thing, and then I sort of got stuck with it," he once said.

Eventually, he pleaded guilty to contempt of court, an offense somewhere in the never-never land between misdemeanors and felonies. . . .

Perkins, who had always been interested in prison reform—he had contributed to the Fortune Society, which helps find jobs for former convicts—soon tasted the humiliations of jail firsthand: the lockups, the strip searches before and after every visitation.

But there were compensations. "I met a lot of very interesting, wonderful people," he said.

"I began to feel that many of the inmates were better than a lot of the guards." . . .

Upon his release, he resolved to go into public-interest law, and he began looking for work the following spring, after a court-appointed referee ruled that he be censured rather than disbarred.

"I had a lot of interviews—at the NAACP, the New York Civil Liberties Union, the New York Legal Aid Society—but I got no offers," he recalled. "They didn't think I was their type. At the Civil Liberties Union, they told me they were looking for women and blacks. I interviewed with Ramsey Clark for an hour, then never heard any more from him."

In the meantime, Perkins worked part time for a small Manhattan law firm and plunged himself into volunteer activities in Greenwich, Conn., for the symphony orchestra, the library, the United Way, the National Association for the Advancement of Colored People, the Audubon Society.

But although his community rallied around him, his old law firm did not. It was his rude introduction to the harsh new realities of large-firm practice.

Few of his former partners visited him in prison. Younger, career-conscious lawyers, many of whom he had hired, were told to keep their distance. He was gently told he was no longer welcome to visit his old offices or even to enter its reception area.

"The only place that I felt shunned was my old law firm, and I resented that," he said. "But to be fair to Donovan, Leisure, this was a very traumatic thing for them. One of my regrets is that what I had done, really unwittingly, had done great harm to the people there."

Note: The Temptations of Expert Witnesses

How did it happen that lawyers as skilled and as concerned with their reputations as Kodak's counsel could have concealed the documents in the *Berkey-Kodak* case? In thinking about that question, never really answered in the decision, consider the organization of many firms into different branches. It may be that the corporate lawyer who was in charge of working with the expert to develop his opinion thought that the litigation branch had lower standards than the rest of the firm ("it's a jungle out there" mentality).

Another explanation could be that the expert and his lawyers had a sense of having a right to work in private and to express doubts and questions, without these being turned over to the other side. Note also, though, that in the hands of a skilled lawyer, the facts that Professor Peck had initial doubts and then changed his mind and that he had thought of all the possibilities could add to his credibility. Good tactics and good ethics are often entwined.

Finally, the importance of expert testimony may posit an irresistible temptation to some lawyers. In most civil cases these days, experts are hired by each side, even in cases where their utility is not immediately apparent, as it is, for instance, in medical or legal malpractice cases. Two aviation lawyers probably spoke for many of their colleagues when they wrote:

> We all have horror stories involving expert witnesses. Cases where too many experts have been used, where experts have been harassed by opposing counsel, and where experts have been qualified on the most mundane or off-the-wall issues, to name a few of the gripes.

William G. Burd and Madelyn Simon Lozano, Experts: Is the End Near for Their Use?, 59 J. Air L. & Com. 77, 77 (1993).

Cordy v. The Sherwin-Williams Co.

156 F.R.D. 575 (D.N.J. 1994)

KUGLER, United States Magistrate Judge.

In this day of divided and shifting loyalties, when it is not unknown for lawyers to change firms in the middle of litigation, we are faced with the phenomenon of an expert essentially doing the same thing by changing sides in the litigation. The question for the Court is whether he should get away with it.

The underlying lawsuit involves a claim by plaintiff Sterling Cordy for damages for massive injuries he suffered while riding his bicycle over a railroad track crossing in Lindenwold, New Jersey, on August 30, 1991. Plaintiff alleges that defendant Sherwin-Williams Company owns the crossing and is liable to him for damages.

Before the Court are cross-motions. Defendant first moved for an Order compelling Plaintiff's counsel to produce the bicycle for examination and testing by their expert, James Marley Green. Plaintiff moved for an Order barring Defendant from using Green as their expert, and further to disqualify the law firm of Marshall, Dennehey, Warner, Coleman & Goggin, from further representing Sherwin-Williams Company in this case. Plaintiff contends that he had first retained Green to work on his behalf, and that Green changed sides in the middle of this litigation. . . .

Any analysis properly begins with a recognition of the Court's inherent power to disqualify experts. . . .

Some jurisdictions have established a two-step inquiry to determine whether to disqualify an expert who had prior relationship with a party. First, was it objectively reasonable for the first party who retained the expert to believe that a confidential relationship existed? Second, did that party disclose any confidential information to the expert? . . .

In addition to the above analysis, the Court should balance the competing policy objectives in determining expert disqualification. The policy objectives favoring disqualification include preventing conflicts of interest and maintaining the integrity of the judicial process. The main policy objectives militating against disqualification are ensuring access to expert witnesses who possess specialized knowledge and allowing experts to pursue their professional calling. Courts have also expressed concern that if experts are too easily subjected to disqualification, unscrupulous attorneys and clients may attempt to create an inexpensive relationship with potentially harmful experts solely to keep them from the opposing party.

Under Federal Rule of Civil Procedure 26, the opposition is entitled to obtain information upon which a testifying expert intends to rely in formulating his or her opinions. Generally, when an expert obtains information from Plaintiff's attorneys, who in turn have obtained that information from the client, the attorney-client privilege applies, subject to a variety of qualifications. . . .

Defendant contends that one reason the Court should not disqualify Green is because Brown & Connery never "retained" him. This argument is based in part on Green's conduct in returning the original retainer payment after he resigned in July, 1993.

Nonsense. Green accepted a retainer from Plaintiff, and later returned it. The fact that he returned it cannot erase his acceptance of it, the significance of it, or the implications arising from it when he later accepted a retainer from Defendant.

Defendant also contends that Green only had "minimal contacts" with Brown & Connery. However, there is no question that Green performed services for Brown & Connery. He entered into a written contract. He was paid. He learned their litigation strategy and reviewed their investigation. He billed for 28 hours of work. He rendered some kind of oral opinion. There was extensive contact between Green and Brown & Connery. Their relationship was clearly not a preliminary interview or consultation in order to determine whether an attorney desired to enter into a relationship with an expert. . . .

Clearly Brown & Connery retained Green. . . .

Defendant contends that Brown & Connery never shared any confidential information with Green. Counsel points to the lack of any "Confidentiality Agreement" or commitment that Green would not work for any other party involved in the lawsuit, relying on Wang Laboratories, Inc. v. Toshiba Corporation, 762 F. Supp. 1246, 1250 (E.D. Va. 1991) (suggesting the steps that an attorney should take to make sure the expert knows that confidentiality is expected) and English Feedlot[, Inc. v. Norden Lab,] 833 F. Supp. [1498,] 1505 [D. Colo. 1993] (". . . a lawyer seeking to retain an expert and establish a confidential relationship should make this intention unmistakably clear and should confirm it in writing").

But there is no "right" way for an attorney to retain an expert for purposes of litigation. No case in New Jersey has held that an attorney must go through the formalistic rituals suggested in *Wang Laboratories*, and this Court declines the invitation to be the first.

The real question is whether Brown & Connery acted reasonably in assuming that a confidential or fiduciary relationship existed with Green. The answer is yes.

Some of the contents of P-10 (the three-ring binder sent by Brown & Connery to Green) are clearly confidential and not subject to disclosure. The selection process used to assemble P-10, and the grouping of the photographs and documents represent the mental impressions of Plaintiff's counsel and are protected work product. Green acknowledges that Plaintiff's firm informed him of their theory of the case and their targeted defendants. This also was protected work product. . . . Plaintiff's counsel had every reason to assume that it had entered into a confidential relationship with Green. Plaintiff's counsel passed confidential information to Green. It is simply not possible for Green to ignore what he learned from Brown & Connery. At the very least, his engagement with Brown & Connery has to "subliminally affect his testimony and assessment of facts." . . .

Defendant, however, raises additional issues. First, counsel seems to imply that Plaintiff's counsel engaged Green simply to disqualify him from serving as an expert for the other side. That kind of odious practice is roundly condemned. However, there is no evidence this was Plaintiff's purpose, and the Court will not impute such motives to one of its own officers. . . .

Moreover, there is no evidence that either side is unable to secure another expert. Although counsel may feel Green is a "world respected expert on the subject of bicycle accident reconstruction and railroad grade crossing accident[s]," Db-19, there is no evidence of anything unique about his services. See *Wang Laboratories*, 762 F. Supp. at 1249 n.6 ("a different result might be warranted if the consultant involved were unique in some relevant sense"). The business of being an expert has become a cottage industry. . . .

This Court need not impute any evil motive to either Green or Defendant's law firm. This analysis does not seek out intentional wrongdoing but addresses an issue of fairness. Any party to a law-suit who retains an expert should not have to worry that the expert will change sides in the middle of the proceeding. To hold otherwise would adversely affect the confidence parties place in this system of justice. As noted in American Protection Insurance Co. v. MGM Grand Hotel-Las Vegas, Inc., CV-LV 82-26 (HDM), 1986 WL 57464 (D. Nev.):

> Were the most important witness' assistance in the litigation to be sold to the highest bidder, the court's integrity would be discredited. In addition, the public estimation of the judicial system would be diminished.

Accordingly, plaintiff's Motion to Disqualify James Marley Green from serving as an expert for defendant Sherwin-Williams shall be granted. The Order shall also provide that any work done to date so far by Green shall not inure to the benefit of defendant Sherwin-Williams.

Coates v. AC & S, Inc.

133 F.R.D. 109 (E.D. La. 1990)

CHARLES SCHWARTZ, JR., District Judge.

This matter is before the Court on the motion of plaintiff to compel discovery of experts consulted by defendants. . . . Plaintiff in this matter, Charles Coates, recently died, allegedly of peritoneal mesothelioma. After his death, tissue samples were taken and sent to both plaintiff's and defendant's experts. Defendants have sent the samples to certain experts whom they have designated pursuant to Rule 26(b)(4)(B) as experts who have been retained in anticipation of litigation but who will not testify at trial. Plaintiff now seeks to depose these experts or to obtain copies of any written reports including the results of all tests made and all conclusions of these experts. . . . The Court finds that the exceptional circumstances contemplated by Rule 26(b)(4)(B) are present in this situation. Moreover, the Court finds that a pathologist's or other expert's examination of tissue samples taken from the body of a person who is now deceased is sufficiently analogous to an examination under Rule 35(b) so that all parties have a right to the type of information set forth in that rule.

The Court issued its original ruling on August 8, 1990, in an effort to curtail the "shopping" of tissue samples by requiring all parties to file into the record the names and addresses of all persons or entities to whom such tissue samples were sent. In that order, the Court stated that it "was of the opinion that without this Order, there is the possibility of 'shopping' of tissue samples and this creates an 'exceptional circumstance.'" The Court is still of the opinion that "shopping" continues to take place and that such "shopping" is sufficient to fall within the Rule's exceptional circumstances exception.

Defendants oppose the instant motion and make much of their "right" to determine their trial strategy, arguing that allowing plaintiffs to depose or to obtain the written reports of experts who will not be called at trial will significantly undermine this "right." Defendants have apparently forgotten, however, that the goal of litigation is not for the side with the best strategy to win; rather the goal should be to seek the ultimate truth at issue in the matter. Hickman v. Taylor, 329 U.S. 495 (1947).

Defendants contend that the fact that they may send tissue samples to more than one doctor does not necessarily mean shopping for a favorable opinion, but only demonstrates the difficulty of making a definitive diagnosis of mesothelioma. If not for this order, both sides may continue to seek for an expert who can render a definitive diagnosis favorable to their position in the case, and at trial, then, it would appear to the jury that the experts in support of each side's position are divided evenly. Those experienced in litigation know that for the most part experts, if they can in good conscience, tend to testify favorably for those who employ them. In my experience I have never known a party to call an expert it knows would testify contrary to its interests. The reality of the situation is that if a number of other experts have been consulted herein, but who could not make a definitive diagnosis, and these experts are not called as witnesses, then the jury could be mislead [*sic*] regarding the truth of plaintiff's condition. Considering the difficulty in diagnosing mesothelioma, the fact finder is entitled to know the extent of any disagreement of those whom a plaintiff or defendant employed, unless we adopt the theory that in a civil case, as part of its trial tactics, a party has the right to suppress the truth. Absent this Order, it is impracticable for either side to obtain this information by other means, and it thus falls within the exceptional circumstances contemplated by Rule 26(b)(4)(B).[1]

Rule 35(b), while not directly on point, is sufficiently analogous to provide support for the Court's decision to permit the discovery sought. In In re Certain Asbestos Cases, 112 F.R.D. 427 (N.D. Tex. 1986), the defendants sought an order permitting an autopsy "for the purpose of determining the exact cause of death." Id. at 429. The defendants also requested that the court regulate the taking and preserving of tissue samples. In that case, the court held that Rule 35(a) permitted the autopsy upon a showing that the physical condition of the party was at issue and there was good cause shown for the examination. The court also noted that "[i]t would be incongruous to terminate at death the search for the true state of a person's physical condition when the precise controversy is his condition at death." Id. at 433. In the instant matter, the tissue samples have already been taken, the only question is how many doctors or other

1. The Court has considered appointing an additional expert pursuant to Rule 706 of the Federal Rules of Evidence and charging his expenses and costs, but feels that the approach herein obviates the necessity of such an appointment.

experts will examine them and whether they must disclose their findings. It is clear that if an autopsy had been performed in this matter pursuant to Rule 35(a), then under Rule 35(b), each doctor so participating would be required to disclose his conclusions. The Court finds no logical distinction between that result and the one plaintiffs seek. The fact that discovery in this matter is conducted by the sending of tissue samples rather than by autopsy should not dictate whether the findings of the doctors participating should be revealed. Accordingly,

IT IS ORDERED that when any party sends a tissue sample to any expert for review, then any other party may discover the result of that review, including obtaining any written report, diagnosis, or test result, or may take the deposition of such expert upon payment of his time and expenses when deposed and if he is not to be called as a witness at trial, also upon payment of his fee and expenses in connection with the preparation of his report.

Notes and Questions

1. *Testing the Limits.* As a powerful example of the expert making the case, consider Haley v. Pan American World Airways, 746 F.2d 311 (5th Cir. 1984), in which the parents of an adult passenger recovered damages for their son's pre-impact fear in a crash that killed everyone. They proved his fear through a psychiatrist who had treated survivors of aircraft accidents, and who testified to the five levels of stress, culminating in panic, that most, if not all, people experience in crisis. Does this seem to you to be an "extreme" reliance on experts? Would your opinion change once you knew that the jury, while finding for the plaintiff, awarded only $15,000 in damages?

2. *Disclosing the Strength of the Experts.* Whether an expert will be allowed to testify, based on how she will look on the stand and how she will stand up under cross-examination, is central to the decision of each side about whether to settle in advance of trial and for how much. In fact, many a settlement has followed from the deposition performance of the expert for one side or the other. The 1993 version of the Rules reflects what had long been the practice in many places, which was to depose the adversary's experts on the eve of trial. Note that in Rule 26(a)(2)(B) there is a special provision for turning over in advance of trial the expert's report and other matters relating to his testimony. Read this provision carefully. Can you see the reasons why the rules provide that one side give the other so much in the way of background information on the experts who will testify?

3. *The History of Rule 26(a)(2).* In light of the importance of experts in today's practice, it may seem surprising that the original Federal Rules had no provision for their discovery by the adversary. For an excellent history of the present Rule that posits that it still may not adequately reflect the

actual practice where the care, feeding, and discovery of experts is a huge part of the litigation, see Note, Discovery of the Nontestifying Expert Witness's Identity Under the Federal Rules of Civil Procedure: You Can't Tell the Players Without a Program, 37 Hastings L.J. 201 (1985).

4. *Nontestifying Experts*. Notice the distinction drawn between two kinds of experts in Rule 26, experts who are likely to testify at trial and those "retained or specially employed in anticipation of litigation" but who are *not* likely to be called as witnesses. The reasons for the different treatment are obvious, but as *Cordy* and *Coates* demonstrate, there may be costs associated with prohibiting routine discovery of experts who are specially retained but won't be called as a witness at trial. Does the "exceptional circumstances" escape hatch in Rule 26(b)(4)(B) respond fully to this concern? Does the "exceptional circumstances only" requirement apply not only to the opinions of nontestifying experts, but also to their *identities*? Courts have divided on this last issue. For a thorough discussion of the conflict in an opinion written by Magistrate Judge Wayne D. Brazil — who is widely respected for his knowledge of procedure — see In re Pizza Time Theatre Securities Litigation, 113 F.R.D. 94, 96-98 (N.D. Cal. 1986) (concluding that the discovery of the identities of nontestifying experts should be subject to the "exceptional circumstances" standard).

Lawyers may, of course, change their minds about whether a designated expert should testify; that decision is often influenced by the quality of the report the expert produces. But redesignating an expert as nontestifying to avoid disclosure of the report and deposition by an opponent can be sticky — the redesignation itself can send a signal that the case is weak. In Plymovent Corp. v. Air Tech Solutions, Inc., 243 F.R.D. 139 (D.N.J. 2007), plaintiffs moved for a preliminary injunction in their false advertising claim relying predominantly on a retained expert's videotape and report purporting to show that Air Tech's product for removing exhaust fumes from closed garages did not work as advertised.

At the hearing, however, before Plymovent called its expert, the following colloquy occurred between the judge and counsel for Plymovent:

THE COURT: [A]re you going to rely on that tape and the report that's based on that tape, or are you going to ignore it and proceed without it — . . . You think that helps your case?

MR. O'NEILL: Absolutely, your Honor. For the purposes of today, it provides —

THE COURT: You don't want to reconsider that position[?]

MR. O'NEILL: Your Honor, what it does —

THE COURT: I will give you a chance.

MR. O'NEILL: What it does, your Honor, is it provides the court with a visual representation. —

THE COURT: It's a travesty of the scientific method, it's a travesty. It's the only word I can think of. I'm not saying that if it's done right you might not reach the same results, but who knows. It's a travesty. . . . I don't have to be much of a scientist to know that that report has about 35 different variables in there, none of which are harmonized. I mean it's a travesty. So, I just want to know if you want to rely on it, or you think you have a good case without it.

MR. O'NEILL: I have a very good case without it.

THE COURT: All right.

Id. at 141-142. The court denied preliminary injunctive relief and the case proceeded to discovery. Plymovent produced the report and videotape, but (probably due to the judge's admonition) it did not designate its expert as a witness for trial. Defendant nonetheless filed a *subpoena duces tecum* seeking all documents "referring or relating to" the expert report and videotape. Against Plymovent's motion to quash the subpoena, defendant argued that Plymovent's expert could not be redesignated as nontestifying under Rule 26(b)(4)(B) because Plymovent attempted to rely on the expert at the preliminary injunction hearing. That attempt, defendant contended, along with disclosure of the report and videotape, waived the protections of Rule 26(b)(4)(B) for any remaining documents related to the expert's work on the case.

The court rejected the argument and granted the motion to quash, emphasizing that Rule 26(b)(4)(B) "creates a safe harbor whereby facts and opinions of non-testifying, consulting experts are shielded from discovery except upon a showing of exceptional circumstances." Id. at 143. The court found "a common theme . . . apparent throughout the cases reviewed from various jurisdictions — the conversion of an expert designated for trial purposes under Rule 26(b)(4)(A), to a consulting expert, under Rule 26(b)(4)(B), is allowed and results in insulating that expert from discovery. . . ." Id. at 144. Here, the court found that Plymovent had never formally designated its expert as a trial witness, no relief had been granted on the basis of the expert's submitted materials, and Plymovent had functionally withdrawn its expert at the preliminary injunction hearing. Id. at 145-146 (following Intervet, Inc. v. Merial Ltd., 2007 WL 1797643 (D. Neb. 2007)).

Other courts have held that relying on or disclosing a nontestifying expert's report does waive the protection of Rule 26(b)(4)(B). See Atari Corp. v. Sega of America, 161 F.R.D. 417, 418-420 (N.D. Cal. 1994); U.S. v. Hooker Chemicals & Plastics Corp., 112 F.R.D. 333, 339 (W.D.N.Y. 1986).

5. *Applying Rule 26(b)(4).* Assume that a research scientist who works for a corporation happens to witness an industrial accident while walking to the corporation cafeteria for lunch. The injured employee sues the company and seeks to depose the scientist. Do any of the restrictions in Rule 26(b)(4) regarding deposing an expert apply? Must the employee pay the expert a reasonable fee for time spent in responding to this discovery?

Assume instead that a consumer of the company's product seeks to depose the research scientist to determine whether the company's research department had knowledge of the alleged defect. Do any of the restrictions in Rule 26(b)(4) regarding deposing an expert apply in this situation? See In re Shell Oil Refinery, 132 F.R.D. 437 (E.D. La. 1990); Ager v. Jane C.

Stormont Hospital & Training School for Nurses, 622 F.2d 496 (10th Cir. 1980). See also David S. Day, Discovery Standards for the Testimonial Expert Under Federal Rule of Civil Procedure 26(b)(4): A Twentieth Anniversary Assessment, 133 F.R.D. 209 (1990); Note, Compelling Experts to Testify: A Proposal, 44 U. Chi. L. Rev. 851 (1977). In analyzing these questions of proper rule interpretation, consider the following excerpt from In re Shell Oil Refinery, 132 F.R.D. at 441-442:

> The court finds that the persuasive authority favors application of Rule 26(b)(4)(B) to non-testifying in-house experts. To rule otherwise would encourage economic waste by requiring an employer to hire independent experts to obtain the protection of Rule 26(b)(4). Protection of an in-house expert's opinion's [sic] supports improved public safety and other social benefits of self-analysis. That the work of an in-house expert is used not only to defend a lawsuit but also to improve a company's operations or product design does not remove him from the parameters of Rule 26(b)(4)(B). See Hermsdorfer v. American Motors Corp., 96 F.R.D. 13, 15 (W.D.N.Y. 1982).
>
> Not all in-house experts fall within the parameters of the retained or specially employed language of Rule 26(b)(4)(B). The Advisory Committee Notes exclude from the scope of Rule 26(b)(4)(B) "an expert who is simply a general employee of the party not specially employed on the case." Those in-house experts who are not retained or specially employed should be treated as ordinary witnesses under Rule 26(b)(1), and if their work was in anticipation of litigation or preparation of trial, then discovery must be analyzed under the work product doctrine, Rule 26(b)(3).
>
> Neither the Rule nor the Notes explain when a general employee may become retained or specially employed. Some courts have found that the terms retained or specially employed mean "something more than simply the assignment of a current employee to a particular problem raised by current litigation." See Kansas-Nebraska Natural Gas Co. [v. Marathon Oil Co.,] 109 F.R.D. [12,] 16 [D. Neb. 1985]. To the contrary, other authority suggests that "a regular employee may become specially employed when he is designated and assigned by a party to apply his expertise to a particular matter in anticipation of litigation or for trial." See Pielemeier, Discovery of Non-Testifying In-House Experts, 58 Ind. L.J. at 602 (citing Graham, Discovery of Experts Under Rule 26(b)(4), 1976 U. Ill. L.F. note 3, at 942).
>
> Whether an in-house expert is retained or specially employed must be decided case-by-case.

6. *Experts and the Attorney-Client Privilege.* Lawyers have to be very careful about what information they share with expert witnesses and whether they are confident they want an expert to testify. Giving privileged information to an expert designated to testify under Rule 26(b)(4)(A) may work a waiver of the privilege that cannot be undone by redesignating the expert as a nontestifying witness. See CP Kelco U.S., Inc. v. Pharmacia Corp., 213 F.R.D. 176 (D. Del. 2003) (privilege waived as to documents reviewed by testifying defense expert but not produced to plaintiff; holding unchanged by redesignation of expert as nontestifying after his deposition).

7. *Litigation Consultants*. Experts on depositions, trials, juries, and the tactics of testimony are increasingly hired to help lawyers and litigants "frame" their evidence in the most persuasive way to the jury. Some worry that these consultants do more than merely "frame" testimony. Should conversations between lawyers, clients, and litigation consultants be covered by the work product doctrine?

In litigation over securities fraud liability between Cedant Corp. and its outside accounting firm, Ernst & Young, Cedant sought discovery of communications between Ernst & Young and its trial consultant about the case, and, more specifically, about how to handle the deposition of Ernst & Young's audit team manager. The Third Circuit held that communications with the litigation consultant should be covered as opinion work product. It rejected Cedant's argument that "a non-attorney's advice regarding witness testimony" should not be covered because "the jury is entitled to know the consultant's communications with the witness . . . in the same way it is entitled to know and assess all other factors that may have informed the witness's testimony and may affect credibility." In re Cedant Corp. Securities Litigation, 343 F.3d 658, 666 (3d Cir. 2003). The court observed that Rule 26 expressly covers work by an attorney's agents in anticipation of litigation and that the communications with the trial consultant "focused on issues that counsel [and the consultant] perceived to be central to the case," including "counsel's view of the important facts of the case, the contentions of the parties, and Ernst & Young's trial themes, theories and strategies." Id. at 667.

The court went out of its way to note that Cedant "conceded that it was not accusing Ernst & Young of fabricating false testimony in the meetings [with the consultant]," and that "[t]he protection afforded opinion or core work product may be breached when there is a charge of false testimony." Id. at 666-667 n.8. Still, if communications with a trial consultant are covered as opinion work product in the first instance, how can anyone know if advice from a consultant crosses the line from friendly assistance and "spin" to suborning perjury?

8. *Court-Appointed Experts.* Note that Rule 706 of the Federal Rules of Evidence authorizes judges to appoint an expert witness on its motion, even without the parties' agreement to the appointment. Fed. R. Evid. 706(a). The rule states that an expert witness so appointed "shall advise the parties of the witness's findings, if any; the witness's deposition may be taken by any party; and the witness may be called to testify by the court on any party." Id. Consider the following description of judges' use of 706:

> The typical expert appointed under Rule 706 is called for opinion testimony on a difficult scientific or technical issue . . . most often for their medical, engineering, or accounting expertise. The medical experts tended to be appointed in personal injury cases where the party experts offered diametrically opposed views on either the proper standard of care and treatment or the causation of the injury. Engineering experts (a category that included those with knowledge of computer technology) were appointed

most often for bench trials that involved technical patent or trade secret issues when the judge felt the need for assistance in understanding the technology. Accountants were typically appointed to offer an opinion on the value of complex financial claims in contract disputes or commercial failures. In addition to these areas of expertise that are most in demand, a wide variety of expert witnesses have been appointed by the trial courts to render opinions. They have testified on issues ranging from whether dwellings the Army Corps of Engineers sought to remove from navigable waters were "houseboats" or "floating homes" to the authenticity of a signature designating a beneficiary under a pension plan.

Ellen E. Deason, Managing the Managerial Expert, 1998 U. Ill. L. Rev. 341, 347-348 (1998) (footnotes omitted). Does this power adequately respond to concerns about partisan experts?

D. INTERROGATORIES AND THE ADVERSARIAL ADVOCATE

Problem Case: Rozier v. Ford Motor Co.

You represent defendant Ford Motor Company in a wrongful death action alleging that the defective design and placement of the fuel tank on a 1980 Ford Galaxie 500 caused a fatal explosion and fire when the car was struck from behind by another car. You have received a set of interrogatories and document requests from plaintiff's counsel that includes the following:

> Interrogatory No. 19: Over the last ten years, has Ford Motor Company prepared any written reports or analyses of the comparative advantages or disadvantages of alternate locations (e.g., on top of the rear axle or in front of the rear axle) for fuel tanks in full-sized sedans and hardtops, including the 1980 Galaxie 500?
>
> Document request No. 19: If your answer to Interrogatory 19 is in the affirmative, produce all such written reports or analyses.

How would you respond to these requests? What would you have to do before deciding how to respond? Where, within a structure that resembles that of the chart on the next page, would you expect to find responsive information?

Rozier v. Ford Motor Co.

573 F.2d 1332 (5th Cir. 1978)

SIMPSON, Circuit Judge.

[The plaintiff, Martha Rozier, was the widow of William Rozier, who died when his 1969 Ford Galaxie 500 was struck from behind and the fuel

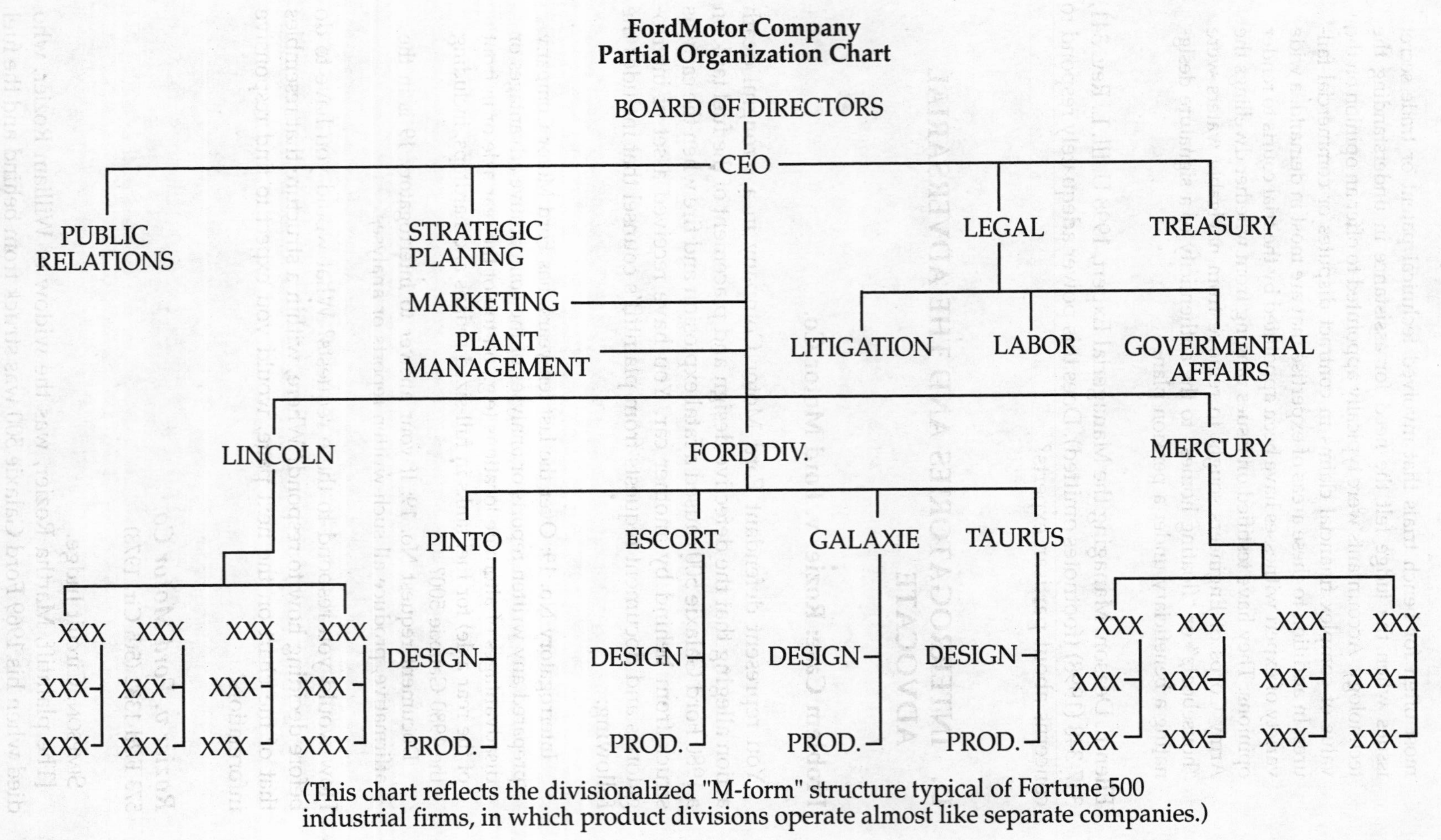

(This chart reflects the divisionalized "M-form" structure typical of Fortune 500 industrial firms, in which product divisions operate almost like separate companies.)

tank exploded. After a one-week trial, the jury returned a verdict for Ford. Approximately ten months thereafter, Mrs. Rozier moved for a new trial on the ground that Ford had failed to disclose a document covered by plaintiffs' interrogatories and that the failure to disclose constituted fraud that entitled Mrs. Rozier to relief under Rule 60(b)(3). The trial judge denied the motion and the plaintiff appealed. On appeal, the court ruled for Mrs. Rozier, concluding that her motion was timely, that the interrogatories did cover the undisclosed document, and that Ford's failure to disclose the document prevented her from fully and fairly presenting her case.]

The facts relevant to Mrs. Rozier's 60(b)(3) motion are as follows.

On August 25, 1975, counsel for Mrs. Rozier served her fourth set of interrogatories upon counsel for defendant Ford. Interrogatories 8, 10, 12, and 16 asked whether Ford had conducted "any cost/benefit analyses" with respect to four possible design modifications of fuel tanks for passenger cars, including full-sized sedans and hard-tops. Interrogatory 19 requested similar information not limited to "cost/benefit analyses":

> 19. In conducting "its own in-house research and development work on . . . alternate fuel tank locations" over the last ten years (Stenning Deposition Vol. II, p. 32), has Ford Motor Company prepared any written reports or analyses of the comparative advantages or disadvantages of alternate locations, (e. g. on top of the rear axle or in front of the rear axle) for fuel tanks in full-sized sedans and hard-tops, including the 1969 Galaxie 500?

The interrogatories also asked whether, in the event such documents exist, Ford would make them available for inspection and copying without the necessity of a request for production.

In response, Ford objected to these and other interrogatories on the grounds that "the information sought therein does not relate to vehicles of the same size, chassis and fuel system as the 1969 Ford Galaxie 500." On December 11, 1975, counsel for Mrs. Rozier moved in writing to compel Ford to answer the fourth set of interrogatories. On January 6, 1976, the district court entered an order directing in part, as follows:

> Defendant shall file with the Court and serve upon Plaintiff's counsel, no later than January 21, 1976, answers to questions numbered 4, 5, 6, 7, 8, 9, 10, 11, 12, 13, 14, 15, 16, 17, 19, and 20 of Plaintiff's Fourth Interrogatories; *provided, however*, that the aforesaid questions are limited to such written requirements, cost/benefit analyses, and written reports or analyses which are applicable to the 1969 Ford Galaxie 500. The fact that a written requirement, cost/benefit analysis or written report may also be applicable to vehicles *other than* the 1969 Ford Galaxie 500 does *not* render it beyond the scope of the aforesaid interrogatory and must be disclosed in response to the aforesaid interrogatories. (Emphasis in original.)

Finally, on January 22, 1976, in purported compliance with this order, Ford filed amended responses to the fourth set of interrogatories. In answering interrogatories 8, 10, 12 and 16 concerning cost/benefit analyses of alternate fuel tank designs, Ford stated: "There would be no formal cost-benefit analysis with regard to this information." In response to interrogatory 19, concerning "written reports of analyses of the comparative advantages and disadvantages of alternate locations . . . for fuel tanks," Ford stated: "Defendant cannot find such written analysis covering the inquiry."

Approximately one year after Ford filed these amended responses—and ten months after the jury returned a verdict favorable to Ford—plaintiff's counsel learned of the document from Ford's files at issue in this appeal. Dated "2/9/71," this "Confidential Cost Engineering Report" states as its subject:

> Trend Cost Estimate—Fuel Tank Proposals (30 MPH Safety Std.)—Prop[osal] I—Tank Over Rear Axle Surrounded by Body Sheet Metal Barrier & Prop[osal] II—Tank in Tank Filled With Polyurethane Vs. 1971 Ford Design—1975 Ford/Mercury.

So far as we can determine from the face of the document and on the basis of remarks by counsel for Ford during oral argument, this "Trend Cost Estimate" was prepared in anticipation of a revised National Highway Traffic Safety Administration safety standard of 30 m.p.h. for rear end collisions. It compares the costs of parts and labor associated with two proposed alternate fuel tank designs based on the design of a 1971 full-sized Ford. Without dispute the 1969 Galaxie 500 model was a full-sized Ford car. Apparently, Ford planned to begin using a new fuel tank design sufficient to satisfy the 30 m.p.h. standard in its 1975 full-sized models.

In her motion for a new trial pursuant to Rule 60(b)(3), Mrs. Rozier contended that the 1971 Trend Cost Estimate should have been produced in response to the district court's January 6, 1976, order because it was "applicable to the 1969 Ford Galaxie 500." In support of her motion, Mrs. Rozier filed affidavits by Frederick E. Arndt, a safety engineering consultant, and Byron Bloch, a product safety consultant, both of whom had testified on her behalf at the trial. Each affidavit stated:

> [T]he 1969 Ford Galaxie 500 is so similar in size, design, and fuel tank location to the 1971 Ford that the subject "Confidential Cost Engineering Report" is as applicable and valid for the 1969 Ford Galaxie 500 as it is for the 1971 Ford.

In response to Mrs. Rozier's motion to vacate, Ford produced an affidavit by Thomas G. Grubba, an attorney on the house legal staff of Ford Motor Company, who "was involved in" the case. Mr. Grubba swore that he was unaware of the Trend Cost Estimate when the answers to plaintiff's interrogatories were prepared, but that he became aware of the document on February 25, 1976. We note that although Ford's answers were filed on January 22, 1976, the trial did not begin until March 1, 1976, a week after Mr. Grubba discovered the document.

By any fair reading, the district court's January 6, 1976, discovery order called for production of this Trend Cost Estimate. Ford, in response to the motion to vacate and in this appeal, has urged that, as a term of art, a "trend cost estimate" is not a "cost/benefit analysis." Whether the document in question technically is or is not a cost/benefit analysis—to our non-expert eyes, the terms are synonymous, as alike as "Tweedledum and Tweedledee"—is largely irrelevant in this case because plaintiff's interrogatories were not limited to "cost/benefit analyses." Interrogatory 19 asked whether Ford had "prepared *any* written reports or analyses of the comparative advantages or disadvantages of alternate locations . . . for fuel tanks" (emphasis added); the court's January 6 order compelled production of all such "written reports or analyses which are applicable to the 1969 Ford Galaxie 500," specifically noting that written reports also applicable to vehicles other than the 1969 Ford Galaxie 500 were not beyond the scope of the discovery order "and must be disclosed in response to the aforesaid interrogatories." Undeniably, the Trend Cost Estimate is a report "of the comparative advantages or disadvantages" of alternate fuel tank locations, since the alternative which could satisfy the safety standard for the least cost would, in terms of Ford's interests, be the most advantageous. Also, in light of the unchallenged assertions made in the Arndt and Bloch affidavits, this estimate based on the design of a 1971 full-sized Ford is applicable to a 1969 full-sized Ford. We recognize that the Trend Cost Estimate does not purport to estimate the cost of installing new fuel tanks on automobiles already manufactured, such as a 1969 Galaxie 500; however, neither the interrogatory nor the court order limited discovery to reports of that description.

We conclude that Mrs. Rozier has proved by clear and convincing evidence that Ford engaged in misrepresentation and other misconduct. Plaintiff's interrogatory 19, as limited by the district court's order, called for production of the Trend Cost Estimate. In its written response, Ford stated that it could find no such report. A month later, an in-house attorney for Ford involved in this case discovered the Trend Cost Estimate but failed to disclose it or to amend the inaccurate response to interrogatory 19.[10] If Ford

10. Ford's duty to amend its inaccurate response is based on Rule 26(e)(2), Fed. R. Civ. P.:

> A party is under a duty seasonably to amend a prior response if he obtains information upon the basis of which (A) he knows that the response was incorrect when made, or (B) he knows that the response though correct when made is no longer true and the circumstances are such that a failure to amend the response is in substance a knowing concealment.

See Havenfied Corp. v. H & R Block, Inc., 509 F.2d 1263 (8th Cir. 1975), *cert. denied,* 421 U.S. 999 [1975].

Although we are unaware of the precise nature of Mr. Grubba's involvement in this case, he did not participate in the trial itself or in the appeal. The attorneys retained by Ford to represent the company at trial and in the appeal have assured this Court that they were personally unaware of the Trend Cost Estimate until Mrs. Rozier filed her motion to vacate almost a year after the trial. We accept their statements.

in good faith believed that the district court's order was not intended to compel production of this document, the appropriate remedy was to seek a ruling by the district court at that point and not a year after the trial and then only when, by chance, the plaintiff learned of it.

The more vexing question is whether nondisclosure of the Trend Cost Estimate prevented Mrs. Rozier from fully and fairly presenting her case. At trial, Mrs. Rozier contended that Ford was negligent in designing a fuel tank that could not withstand an impact such as that involved in the accident which took her husband's life. Prior to trial, she expressed an intention to rely on 14 theories to explain how Ford deviated from the appropriate standard of care. Inevitably, information developed in the discovery stages of the case influenced the decision as to which theories would be emphasized at trial. We are left with the firm conviction that disclosure of the Trend Cost Estimate would "have made a difference in the way plaintiff's counsel approached the case or prepared for trial," Rock Island Bank & Trust Co. v. Ford Motor Co., 54 Mich. App. 278, 220 N.W.2d 799 (1974), and that Mrs. Rozier was prejudiced by Ford's nondisclosure. See Seaboldt v. Pennsylvania R.R. Co., 290 F.2d 296, 299-300 (3d Cir. 1961).

Although Ford does not specifically dispute this conclusion, it has argued, in a related context, that the Trend Cost Estimate, if admissible in trial, would merely have been cumulative because plaintiff's experts testified at length as to the feasibility of alternative fuel tank designs. Additionally, Ford contends that the document would have been inadmissible by virtue of Rule 407, Fed. R. Evid. We think that these arguments misconstrue the significance of the withheld document.

The admissibility of evidence is irrelevant in the discovery process so long as "the information sought appears reasonably calculated to lead to the discovery of admissible evidence." Fed. R. Civ. P. 26(b)(1). The Trend Cost Estimate clearly satisfies this test. It was not an isolated document, but rather one in a series; some of the other documents, also not produced by Ford during discovery, are referred to in the estimate itself: "Request from J. M. Chiara," "Layouts LA-901277 and 901278," "our report dated February 4, 1971," "A proposal for a fuel tank installation over the rear axle is illustrated in the attached drawing." At a minimum, production of the Trend Cost Estimate could have led to discovery of these other documents. . . .

We cannot know what use, if any, plaintiff's counsel would have made of the Trend Cost Estimate had it been produced by Ford prior to trial. However, consideration of one likely use reveals the prejudice that Mrs. Rozier may have suffered as a consequence of Ford's misconduct.

The negligence alleged by Mrs. Rozier may have taken place in one or both of two time frames: (1) up to and including the production of the 1969 Ford Galaxie 500, and (2) between the time of production in 1969 and the time of the fatal collision in 1973. Under the facts of this case, the task of proving negligence in the pre-production period was the most difficult. Given the industry practices and standards in 1969, the jury was less likely to find that Ford's conduct fell below that to be expected from an ordinarily prudent manufacturer in designing the fuel system for a full-sized sedan. In the post-production period, however, Ford may have had a duty to warn consumers of a latent danger such as a defectively designed fuel tank. Here the plaintiff need not have been hamstrung by the less sophisticated state of the art in 1969, and may have been able to make a convincing case based on the Trend Cost Estimate.

Georgia courts[12] recognize a cause of action against automobile manufacturers for negligence in failing to warn of latent dangers arising from defective design. Friend v. General Motors Corp., 18 Ga. App. 763, 165 S. E.2d. 734, 737 (1968). And, as the Eighth Circuit has explained in discussing this duty to warn:

> The failure to use reasonable care in design *or knowledge* of a defective design gives rise to the reasonable duty on the manufacturer to warn of this condition. Larsen v. General Motors Corp., 391 F.2d 495, 505 (8th Cir. 1968) (emphasis added).

Here, arguably, the Trend Cost Estimate furnishes evidence that Ford, in 1971, had knowledge that the fuel tanks on those models with designs comparable to the 1969 Galaxie 500 could not withstand rear-end collisions at 30 m.p.h. or greater and that a design to correct this condition was both economically and structurally feasible. If a jury were persuaded that the fuel tank of the 1969 Galaxie was latently but not negligently defective *at the time of production*, it might still have found that once Ford acquired the knowledge evidenced by the Trend Cost Estimate it negligently failed to warn Galaxie users of the defect.

By a peculiar turn of events, the jury in this case was foreclosed at the last minute from considering Ford's failure to warn as a possible negligent omission. At least as early as December 10, 1975, when the parties filed a "Consolidated Proposed Pre-Trial Order," Mrs. Rozier indicated that one "act of negligence" upon which she intended to rely was "[f]ailure to warn owners and users of the vehicle of the risk of injury or death due to fire in the event of a collision." The trial judge so instructed the jury, noting that although several acts of negligence were alleged, the plaintiff "is merely required to prove one such act. . . ." Counsel for Ford objected to the warning instruction because it did not specify that the duty to warn extended only to unreasonable risks of injury. The exchange which followed this objection suggests that plaintiff's counsel, in the light of the information then available to him, viewed the duty to warn as an inconsequential part of the case:

THE COURT: What do you say about the last exception?

12. In this diversity case, we are of course "*Erie*-bound" to apply the law of Georgia, both the forum state and the state where Mr. Rozier's fatal injury occurred. Erie R.R. Co. v. Tompkins, 304 U.S. 64 (1938).

MR. DEVINE (For Plaintiff): Your Honor, I think it might do well to clarify that. The Jury has to find that there is a danger before the Defendant has a duty to warn of that danger. I believe that there is plenty of evidence to support that there is a danger.
THE COURT: Nevertheless, what do you say . . .
MR. DEVINE: I think it should be clear.
THE COURT: . . . You concede that I should withdraw then that charge from the Jury's consideration?
MR. DEVINE: I have no objection, Your Honor.

The Court thereupon further charged the Jury as follows:

THE COURT: Members of the Jury, I had charged you that the Plaintiff claimed that the Defendant was negligent in failing to warn owners and passengers of the 1969 Ford Galaxie 500 of the risk of burn injury attendant to occupying that vehicle. I now withdraw that charge, and you will not give that charge any weight whatsoever in your deliberations.

The following colloquy ensued out of the presence of the jury:

THE COURT: Any exceptions to that?
MR. WEINBERG: No, sir.
MR. DEVINE: No, sir.

It is apparent, then, that the Trend Cost Estimate, far from being a cumulative tidbit of evidence already subsumed in the case presented to the jury, might have been the catalyst for an entirely different approach to the case on a theory that the plaintiff, lacking the document, let die before it reached the jury. Under these circumstances, we hold that Ford's wrongful withholding of information prevented Mrs. Rozier from fully and fairly presenting her case.

2. Policy Considerations

Our system of civil litigation cannot function if parties, in violation of court orders, suppress information called for upon discovery. "Mutual knowledge of all the relevant facts gathered by both parties is essential to proper litigation. To that end, either party may compel the other to disgorge whatever facts he has in his possession." Hickman v. Taylor, 329 U.S. 495, 507 (1947). The Federal Rules of Civil Procedure substitute the discovery process for the earlier—and inadequate—reliance on pleadings for notice-giving, issue-formulation, and fact-revelation. As the Supreme Court stated in Hickman v. Taylor, supra, "civil trials in the federal courts no longer need be carried on in the dark. The way is now clear, consistent with recognized privileges, for the parties to obtain the fullest possible knowledge of the issues and facts before trial." 329 U.S. at 501. The aim of these liberal discovery rules is to "make a trial less a game of blind man's bluff and more a fair contest with the basic issues and facts disclosed to the fullest practicable extent." United States v. Procter & Gamble Co., 356 U.S. 677 (1958). It is axiomatic that "[d]iscovery by interrogatory requires candor in responding." Dollar v. Long Mfg., N.C., Inc., 561 F.2d 613, 616 (5th Cir. 1977).

Through its misconduct in this case, Ford completely sabotaged the federal trial machinery, precluding the "fair contest" which the Federal Rules of Civil Procedure are intended to assure. Instead of serving as a vehicle for ascertainment of the truth, the trial in this case accomplished little more than the adjudication of a hypothetical fact situation imposed by Ford's selective disclosure of information. The policy protecting the finality of judgments is not so broad as to require protection of judgments obtained in this manner. . . .

We hold that the district court abused its discretion in denying plaintiff's Rule 60(b)(3) motion and that a new trial is required.

Note: Discovery Against Complex Organizations

The court in *Rozier* implicitly assumes that Ford's lawyers at some point made a conscious decision not to disclose the Trend Cost Estimate. In fact, however, the document was never picked up in the search for information responsive to the plaintiff's discovery requests. It was part of a patent application that a lawyer on Ford's legal staff, who had some involvement with the case, became "aware" of about a week before trial, but only in connection with an entirely unrelated matter. Neither he nor anyone else involved in the *Rozier* case ever made an adversarial determination to withhold the document, because it never found its way into the *Rozier* information loop. In order to understand how this might have happened, consider the number of decisions and judgments, each presenting an opportunity for miscue, that go into the design, execution, and management of a responsive search effort.

The obvious place to begin the search is in the department responsible for designing the Galaxie itself, presumably a research and development or design unit within the Ford product division. But the order clearly extends to the R&D and design departments responsible for other "similar" sedans as well, which may well include Lincoln or Mercury products. Since the product divisions in an M-form structure typically compete with each other for the firm's resources, however, they stand in an almost adversarial relationship that may impede the search effort. And since R & D and design departments are often organized in an informal or "organic" rather than "mechanistic" structure, their information structures are especially difficult for an outsider to penetrate.

Certain nonproduction departments might also have responsive information. The Trend Cost Estimate was part of a patent application, which might have been found in the files of the legal department. And it had apparently been prepared "in anticipation of a revised National Highway Traffic Safety Administration safety standard of 30 M.P.H. for rear end collisions," which suggests that the unit responsible for regulatory matters, probably Intergovernmental Affairs, might also be an unexpected source. Finally, consider the effect of changes in the organization over time: people who passed through Ford R&D during the relevant period but have since moved on to other jobs within the company, taking their personal files with them; and subunits reorganized out of existence long ago, whose files are languishing in some forgotten warehouse. When discovery spans a period of 10 or 20 years, as is not uncommon in product liability cases, there are few employees with long enough institutional memories to be of assistance, and document "retention" (i.e., destruction) schedules wreak havoc on the paper record.

In short, designing a search structure requires an understanding of the formal and informal structure of the organization, a form of "local knowledge" that exists only within the organization itself, if indeed it exists at all. The decentralization and mobility of personnel typical of large American corporations often mean that there is literally no single person who has all the necessary information.

Moreover, good design alone does not guarantee a thorough search. Executing the search is equally important, and equally problematic, for several reasons.

Responding to discovery entails real work: work that is outside the normal responsibilities of the employees who must do it, contrary to their institutional interests, and not rewarded within the company's regular compensation and incentive structure. Ford Motor Company builds cars, not lawsuits, and hours devoted to litigation rather than car production will not be rewarded in performance evaluations. When you ask busy people to do something as boring, time consuming, and literally unrewarding as producing documents for litigation, the initial reaction is not likely to be enthusiastic.

One of Ford's responses in *Rozier* hints at the problem: "There *would be* no formal cost benefit analysis with respect to such information" (emphasis added). The peculiar subjunctive evokes a kind of phone conversation that is all too familiar to litigators trying to track down information: "We just don't do that sort of thing—believe me, there's no point in looking any further, I've been here for 25 years, and there's never been a cost-benefit analysis done." Motivating employees to go beyond the easy and the obvious in responding to discovery requests requires both a policy leadership and tangible assurances that the effort is not a wasted one. Litigators often worry about motivational problems when a case actually goes to trial, and they want their star witnesses to put in the work necessary for adequate preparation. A word of praise from a supervisor or a letter of commendation in the personnel file can help matters considerably, but it is probably the unusual litigator or client who exerts that sort of effort in responding to the opponent's discovery.

Even if the corporation does support the discovery effort in both word and deed, however, that still does not guarantee that individual employees will find it in their interests to comply. Since the people with the most information about the case are also the ones whose actions are being attacked in the litigation, self-protection provides a strong motivation for concealment even, and perhaps especially, when the organization is committed to ferreting out the truth.

And even if both management and employees are willing participants in the discovery process, there is an enormous problem of communication. Left to their own devices, employees will respond to a discovery request as laypeople, making their own judgments about the meaning of the request and the nature of the search they are supposed to do. Terms like "cost-benefit analysis," which was at issue in *Rozier,* might have a technical meaning to a design engineer that is far narrower than what the requesting, or even responding, lawyer would assume.

Another common reaction among clients is to think only in terms of formal files or official documents. Ford's response is again suggestive: "There would be no *formal* cost benefit analysis" (emphasis added), implying that the search might have been limited to central files. Trying to convince client employees that a request for "documents" includes their personal, informal notes, even (especially!) those labeled "confidential," is often a major exercise in reeducation. Ensuring that all copies of a responsive document are produced poses a related problem. It is entirely natural for an employee to assume that one final copy of a report or memorandum will be sufficient, as it is for most substantive purposes; but for purposes of discovery each draft and copy, complete with unexpurgated marginal notes, is a distinct document.

Characterizing Ford's failure to produce the Trend Cost Estimate as a failure of the search process, rather than a conscious decision to withhold the document, does not exonerate its behavior. To the contrary, the respondent's first obligation in discovery is to conduct a search reasonably designed to produce all responsive information, and to monitor results so as to ensure compliance by all participants. Ford's failure to demonstrate, or even argue, that it had conducted a reasonable search that reasonably failed to pick up the Trend Cost Estimate is a more persuasive reason for the result in *Rozier* than the court's glib assertion that the Trend Cost Estimate was "clearly" called for.

The importance of systematic compliance with discovery requests was underscored in National Association of Radiation Survivors v. Turnage, 115 F.R.D. 543 (N.D. Cal. 1987). Following the Supreme Court's decision in Walters v. National Association of Radiation Survivors, 473 U.S. 305 (1985) (Chapter 1, supra), that a $10 limit on attorneys' fees in a Veterans Administration hearing was not unconstitutional per se, the plaintiffs commenced discovery to develop evidence that the fee limit was unconstitutional in actual practice. After some four years of acrimonious discovery disputes, plaintiffs' counsel received a letter from an anonymous informant—promptly dubbed "Deep Throat" by the press—alleging that the VA was destroying relevant documents. The investigation sparked by this dramatic development produced evidence that discoverable evidence had been withheld and destroyed, and that VA employees who urged compliance with discovery were being persistently harassed. District Judge Marilyn Hall Patel's opinion awarding sanctions, however, emphasized this more subtle and fundamental point: that the VA's "failure to establish any systematic process to comply with plaintiffs' discovery requests" established its "culpable intent" entirely independent of the "affirmative efforts to stifle full compliance." 115 F.R.D. at 551. Based on this finding Judge Patel not only awarded stiff monetary sanctions,* but also ordered defendant's counsel to present a plan to "insure the proper and orderly circulation of and compliance with future discovery requests, the maintenance of a record of discovery and documents provided, and the establishment of a system to supervise the response of employees who are asked to obtain or compile discovery." Id. at 559.

Thus far we have considered the difficulties inherent in organizational discovery only from the respondent's point of view. For the requesting party, however, the problems are compounded by the constraints of the adversary system. The adversary system forces the requesting lawyer to rely on her opponent to do the real work of ferreting information out of the organization, a task that entails the exercise of subjective judgment on matters of interpretation, emphasis, and effort at every turn. The responding lawyer therefore enjoys a huge area of essentially unmonitored discretion that, according to the traditional rules of the game, will be exercised to promote her own client's interests, rather than her opponent's.

Moreover, the assumption that the requesting lawyer can protect her client's interests through follow-up and enforcement is rendered implausible by the complexity and expense of the tasks. In the language of institutional economics, the problem can be expressed in terms of "information impactedness": the organizational party has far more complete knowledge about the discovery transaction than the requester can obtain at reasonable expense through arms-length adversarial interaction. More often than not, the follow-up effort is abandoned well short of fruition.

In *Rozier*, for example, after four sets of interrogatories, a series of depositions, and a motion and order compelling production, plaintiff had not received a shred of information on the cost of alternative fuel tank designs. In theory, it was up to plaintiff's lawyer to keep on pushing if he was not satisfied. And all the weasel words in Ford's responses—that "there would be no formal cost-benefit analysis" and that it could "not find" information responsive to the request—strongly suggested

* The VA was ordered to pay $105,000 to the plaintiffs and an additional $15,000 to the clerk of the court for costs incurred as a result of its discovery breaches. EDS.

the possibility of organizational failure; that is, they hadn't found any documents because they hadn't looked very far. But with only a month remaining before trial, there was probably not enough time for the laborious ritual of deposing everyone involved in the search effort. And even if there were time on the calendar, it would be difficult to justify the considerable expense in order to chase down a phantom. The most persistent reality of organizational discovery is that time, money, and inertia are on the side of the organization.

A striking example of just how hard the requesting lawyer may have to push to prevail over a savvy, recalcitrant defendant is provided in Network Computing Systems v. Cisco Systems, Inc., 223 F.R.D. 392 (D.S.C. 2004). NCS, a computer network and systems integrator, entered into a contract with Cisco to sell Cisco networking hardware and software. The relationship broke down within 18 months and NCS filed suit against Cisco claiming breach of contract and fraud, among other things. Cisco counterclaimed for failure to pay for goods provided. After being sanctioned once for improper delay by a Magistrate Judge assigned to resolve the parties' burgeoning discovery disputes, NCS's CEO filed an affidavit denying that certain requested documents existed and asserting that the company's customer list and e-mails had already been produced. Cisco, which had already filed a motion to compel and a motion to strike the complaint in order to force disclosures from NCS, didn't buy the CEO's denials. Both the CEO and his lawyer had previously assured the court that there simply was no customer list. Now they were claiming that it already had been produced. A second motion to compel resulted in an order from the Magistrate Judge requiring NCS either to produce the requested documents or indicate the location of those documents in materials it had already produced.

Ten days later, seven months after the court granted Cisco's first motion to compel, and fully a year after they were due in response to Cisco's discovery requests, NCS sent Cisco the customer list and nine pages of never before seen e-mails. Significantly, NCS could not prove to the satisfaction of the judge that any of the disputed documents already had been produced to Cisco. Moreover, the documents bore "Bates stamps" (a numbering system used to keep track of discovery documents when they are delivered to an opponent) that did not match the style of NCS's earlier disclosures. The Magistrate Judge recommended that the district court impose a monetary sanction reflecting the fees and costs Cisco incurred in its extended effort to reveal NCS's deceptive discovery conduct.

The district court's review of the report and recommendation of the Magistrate Judge contains an extended lament about abusive discovery tactics. The judge is in a good position to opine on the subject—unlike most district court judges, he prefers to rule on discovery disputes himself rather than refer them to Magistrate Judges. (The NCS case was exceptional because, initially, it had been assigned to a different judge in the same district.) As you read the following excerpt, consider whether you agree with the court's assessment of the failings of self-executing discovery, and consider whether matters would improve if more district court judges handled discovery disputes personally.

Before addressing the question of whether sanctionable conduct has occurred and, if so, what sanction is appropriate, the court will briefly recount its experience with discovery disputes in recent years. Unlike a majority of District Judges who routinely relegate discovery disputes to Magistrate Judges, this court has always heard and decided its own discovery matters. After seventeen years on the bench, the undersigned has concluded that, despite the best efforts of Congress, the Advisory Committee on Civil Rules and other similar bodies, litigation expenses continue to rise, often due to ever-increasing discovery demands and ensuing discovery disputes.[2] As Judge Patrick Higginbotham has observed, "The discovery beast has yet to be tamed."[3]

Additionally, refereeing contentious discovery disputes is, in my view, perhaps the most unwelcome aspect of a trial judge's work. For example, United States District Judge Wayne Alley once vented his displeasure with discovery battles in the following order:

> Defendant's Motion to Dismiss or in the Alternative to Continue Trial is denied. If the recitals in the briefs from both sides are accepted at face value, neither side has conducted discovery according to the letter and spirit of the Oklahoma County Bar Association Lawyer's Creed. This is an aspirational creed not subject to enforcement by this Court, but violative conduct does call for judicial disapprobation at least. If there is a hell to which disputatious, uncivil, vituperative lawyers go, let it be one in which the damned are eternally locked in discovery disputes with other lawyers of equally repugnant attributes.

Krueger v. Pelican Prod. Corp., C/A No. 87-2385-A (W.D. Okla. Feb. 24, 1989).

Resolving contentious discovery disputes is especially difficult in those cases (and there are many) where both sides have behaved badly. Judges often find themselves in a position similar to NFL referees, who have to peel the players off of each other in an effort to find the player in the middle who started the melee. The answer is not always clear and the decision of what sanction, if any, to impose is especially difficult where there is a degree of fault on both sides.

Also, numerical inflation appears to be setting in. In past years, discovery battles typically involved "thousands of documents." Recently, however, one attorney suggested to me at a discovery hearing that, including the request for electronic mail communications, a production request was "likely to exceed one million pages." Crane v. Int'l Paper Co., C/A No. 3:02-3352 (D.S.C. Apr. 25, 2003) (Defendant's Motion for Protective Order, at 2). Further, the

2. See, e.g., James S. Kakalik, et al., Just Speedy and Inexpensive? An Evaluation of Judicial Case Management Under the Civil Justice Reform Act, Rand Inst. 1 (1996) (concluding that Congress's landmark legislation the 1991 Civil Justice Reform Act "had little effect on time to disposition, litigation costs, and attorneys' satisfaction and views on the fairness of case management").

3. Patrick E. Higginbotham, So Why Do We Call Them Trial Courts?, 55 SMU L. Rev. 1405, 1417 (2002).

parties often overreach in their discovery requests[5] and stonewall interrogatories from their opponents.[6] Hardball discovery, which is still a problem in some cases, is costly to our system and consumes an inordinate amount of judicial resources.

In addition, this court's own firsthand observation of discovery expenditures in civil litigation yields the inescapable conclusion that litigants expend enormous amounts of money on discovery in cases that do not even make it to trial. A recent case on this court's docket is illustrative. Twin City Fire Ins. Co. v. Ben Arnold-Sunbelt Beverage Co., 336 F. Supp. 610, 2004 WL 2165971 (D.S.C. 2004), involved two female employees who had sued their corporation for sexual harassment in state court. The claimed harassment involved one corporate officer who allegedly groped and inappropriately touched the two employees in the privacy of his office, with no third party witnesses. The claims asserted in the cases were all state law claims for assault and battery, intentional infliction of emotional distress, and the like. There were no complicated Title VII claims or other unique issues in either of the cases — the cases presented a pure swearing contest involving no more than three potential eyewitnesses (the two victims and the defendant). The cases eventually settled prior to trial. The controversy made its way to this court's docket in a declaratory judgment action brought by the insurance companies who refused to provide a defense. In that case, which only involved state law claims, the defense team spent a staggering $1.5 million to engage in discovery prior to settling the cases. Id. at 614, 2004 WL 2165971.

In light of the preceding, this court has reluctantly concluded that changes to the rules of civil procedure and other well-intentioned reforms will have only a marginal impact in those cases where abusive and hardball discovery practices occur. It is the undersigned's sincere belief that contentious and expensive discovery battles will continue to present challenges to the judicial system, and that these challenges should be answered by trial judges, who occupy the best vantage point from which to resolve these controversies. . . .

This court's experience has been that monetary sanctions are usually seen by the offending litigant as a cost of doing business. Here, the damages claimed by NCS (the offending litigant) exceed $33 million. A sanction of $3,407.33 (the amount levied by the Magistrate Judge for the first violation) will do little to deter a litigant who has so much at stake. Conversely, dismissal is a sanction so severe that few District Judges are willing to risk the possibility of reversal for imposing such a draconian measure, even when it appears to be appropriate under the circumstances.

This court determines that it has authority to inform the jury of the misconduct under the Federal Rules of Civil Procedure. A recent amendment

5. As one court colorfully observed: Even if one is entitled to embark on a fishing expedition, one must at least use "rod and reel, or even a reasonably sized net[; not] drain the pond and collect the fish from the bottom." In re IBM Peripheral EDP Devices Antitrust Litigation, 77 F.R.D. 39, 42 (N.D. Cal. 1977).

6. I have presided over one discovery dispute where the defendant's attorney objected to an interrogatory, which essentially sought the names of witnesses, on the grounds that it was burdensome and oppressive, while at the same time propounding an identically-worded question in his own interrogatories.

to the Rules, adopted in connection with the mandatory disclosure of core information required by new federal Rule 26, authorizes the court to inform the jury about the failure to make disclosures required by Rule 26. Fed. R. Civ. P. 37(c)(1). ("[S]anctions . . . may include informing the jury of the failure to make the disclosure [required by Rule 26].") Rule 37(d), the Rule that facially applies to the situation presented here, does not contain an explicit reference to informing the jury as a sanction, but does authorize the court to:

> . . . make such orders in regard to the failure [to provide discovery] as are just, and among others it may take any action authorized under subparagraphs (A), (B), and (C) of subdivision (b)(2) of [Rule 37].

Subsection (C) of subdivision (b)(2) of Rule 37 authorizes the court to strike pleadings, dismiss an action with prejudice, or render a default judgment against the disobedient party. Thus, although Rule 37(d) does not contain an explicit authorization to inform the jury of the misconduct by the litigant (as is the case with the failure to make Rule 26 disclosures), the Rule clearly gives this court broad discretion to "make such orders . . . as are just" including the extreme sanctions of dismissal and default judgment. If the court has the express authority to impose such harsh remedies, it certainly has the implied authority to impose a less severe sanction, especially when that sanction is one authorized by a corresponding rule regarding failure to make Rule 26 disclosure responses.

As the Fifth Circuit Court of Appeals has noted, the sanctions enumerated by Rule 37 are not exclusive, but flexible, and "may be applied in as many or varied forms as the court desires by exercising discretion in light of the facts of each case." Guidry v. Continental Oil Co., 640 F.2d 523, 533 (5th Cir. 1981). A leading treatise notes that "Rule 37 is flexible. . . . The court . . . is not limited . . . to a stereotyped response. The sanctions . . . are not exclusive and arbitrary but flexible, selective, and plural." 8A Charles Alan Wright, Arthur R. Miller & Richard L. Marcus, Federal Practice and Procedure § 2284 (2d ed. 1994).

Moreover, at oral argument on the objections to the Report and Recommendation, counsel for both the plaintiff and the defendant acknowledged that this court has the authority to inform the jury of the misconduct as a sanction under the Rules.

A moderate approach of informing the jury about the misconduct is especially appropriate in those rare cases where there has been clear and sanctionable conduct by one of the parties. This case is one of those rare cases. Here, an experienced litigant[10] told a United States Magistrate Judge, vested by one of this court's district judges with the authority to hear and decide all disputes relating to this case, that customer lists did not exist. It is unconvincing and inconceivable, given current technology, that a company in the business of computer software failed to keep a list of its customers or could not readily assemble such a list when requested. In this case, after telling the Magistrate Judge that customer lists did not exist, NCS informed

10. William Charping, a counterclaim defendant who is [NCS's CEO], has been involved in forty separate lawsuits. *See* Plaintiff's Motion in Limine to Exclude Evidence of Other Litigation, dated Jun. 29, 2004.

the Magistrate Judge that they did, in fact, exist, and that they had been produced in an earlier discovery response.

The circumstances of that earlier response are, to say the least, quite suspicious. At the January 21, 2004 hearing, counsel for Cisco produced copies of the lists that were purportedly produced earlier. Yet careful examination of the font styles on the Bates numbers of the customer lists appeared different from the font styles on the earlier discovery responses. Cisco thus established a strong circumstantial case that the documents had been manipulated to appear as though they had been produced with earlier discovery. According to Cisco, this fabrication could have been achieved by using a gap in the Bates number sequencing to place new numbers on documents not previously furnished in an effort to represent to the court that documents had been furnished, when they had not. When the font style controversy arose at oral argument, the court afforded counsel an opportunity to examine the issue thoroughly and to present an affidavit from someone knowledgeable about computer systems and scanners to explain why the font style might have been different. Shortly thereafter, NCS's local counsel sought, and received, permission to withdraw as counsel of record in this case. The explanation for the variant font style has been received and reviewed by this court, though it yields inconclusive results. Therefore, the court resolves the dispute in favor of NCS since the evidence is inconclusive as to whether any "back dating" of discovery responses occurred.

The fact remains, however, that NCS first represented to the Magistrate Judge that certain garden variety documents did not exist. This representation was made on several occasions. It now turns out that the documents did, in fact, exist. NCS asserts that no prejudice has accrued to Cisco because the documents were eventually produced. This conclusion ignores the fact that they were produced only after several contentious discovery battles before the Magistrate Judge. On this record, the court concludes that a monetary sanction is not appropriate and would not deter future violations. The Magistrate Judge has already imposed a monetary sanction on NCS for earlier discovery problems to no avail. The most extreme sanction sought by Cisco, that of a dismissal with prejudice, does not appear to be appropriate in this case given the very high burden a litigant must meet to have its opponent's case dismissed on this ground.

The moderate approach of telling the jury about the misconduct appears to be tailor-made for this case. Accordingly, if this case is reversed and sent back for trial, it is the court's intention to give the jury the following instruction as a sanction for the misconduct set out in this Order:

> "Ladies and gentlemen, in this case as in every civil case in the federal court system, as part of the trial preparation process the parties are entitled to request information from each other in a process that is known as discovery. Occasionally, disputes arise as to exactly what information has to be produced and whether any such information is in existence.
>
> In this case, Cisco Systems, Inc. asked its opponent, Network Computing Services Corporation, for a list of its customers, a request that this court determined to be an appropriate request for information. Network indicated, on more than one occasion to this court that such a list did not exist. It was later learned, however, that such a

> customer list did exist, and that list has now been produced to Cisco. You may consider this conduct by Network, along with all the other evidence that you hear during the trial, in deciding the issues presented for your determination in this case."

In adopting what it perceives to be a middle course, the court has rejected the extreme sanction of dismissal, as requested by Cisco, and has also rejected what it views as an inadequate sanction—a monetary penalty as recommended by the Magistrate Judge. The monetary penalty, already imposed by the Magistrate Judge, yielded no deterrent effect. The extreme sanction of dismissal is also inappropriate under the facts of this case. Moreover, the court has cautiously declined to inform the jury that NCS perpetrated an even greater fraud upon the court by attempting to backdate discovery responses. After carefully and calmly reviewing the totality of the circumstances presented here, this court is of the opinion that the sanction chosen by the court is best for this case and will serve to deter the offending litigant from similar conduct in this and future cases.

It is so ordered.

Id. at 394-401.

E. DEPOSITIONS AND THE ADVERSARIAL ADVOCATE

Problem Case: The Secret Memo (Part Two)

Return to the problem case in which you are representing the president of the company, Eve Barrie. You have decided to turn over the "the smoking gun" memorandum according to the voluntary disclosure provisions of Rule 26.

Your adversaries have now moved to depose Eve Barrie. How do you prepare her, in general and particularly, to answer questions about the memorandum? What would be the most helpful thing she might say about the meaning of the memorandum? What are the ethical and other restraints on putting these words into her mouth?

Assume that at the deposition, the lawyer for the other side presses her very hard in what seems to you an obvious attempt to make her lose her temper and perhaps the benefits of her careful preparation. What is your recourse when this happens? How can you protect your witness?

Remember that interrogatories and, of course, requests to admit may be addressed only to parties. But the deposition of anyone with information about the case may be taken under Rules 30 and 31. Look back also to the material on deposition strategy at the beginning of this chapter.

Usually such depositions are taken in a lawyer's office, with a court reporter who swears the witnesses. There is no judicial officer on hand to rule on objections, and particularly when the client is present, or is being deposed, lawyers sometimes become overly zealous, to put the problem mildly. To give you some idea of the possibilities for abuse, we print the following case. How would you defend the conduct of the famous lawyer in this case, were you called upon to do so before a Bar Disciplinary Committee? The press? A court considering his disbarment?

The Northern California Chapter of the Association of Business Trial Lawyers adopted a guide to legal etiquette that includes admonitions such as: "Only take depositions when they are needed and behave as if a judge were present," and "Do not be offensive even when your client so desires." It might seem that such suggestions would be obvious, yet codes of civility in addition to codes of professional responsibility are becoming increasingly common.

Paramount Communications v. Viacom, Inc.

637 A.2d 34 (Del. 1994)

Addendum

The record in this case is extensive. The appendix filed in this Court comprises 15 volumes, totaling some 7,251 pages. It includes substantial deposition testimony which forms part of the factual record before the Court of Chancery and before this Court. . . . As noted, the Court has commended the parties for their professionalism in conducting expedited discovery, assembling and organizing the record, and preparing and presenting very helpful briefs, a joint appendix, and oral argument.

The Court is constrained, however, to add this Addendum. Although this Addendum has no bearing on the outcome of the case, it relates to a serious issue of professionalism involving deposition practice in proceedings in Delaware trial courts.[23]

The issue of discovery abuse, including lack of civility and professional misconduct during depositions, is a matter of considerable concern to Delaware courts and courts around the nation.[24] One particular instance

23. We raise this matter *sua sponte* as part of our exclusive supervisory responsibility to regulate and enforce appropriate conduct of lawyers appearing in Delaware proceedings. . . .

24. Justice Sandra Day O'Connor recently highlighted the national concern about the deterioration in civility in a speech delivered on December 14, 1993, to an American Bar Association Group on "Civil Justice Improvements":

> I believe that the justice system cannot function effectively when the professionals charged with administering it cannot even be polite to one another. Stress and frustration drive down productivity and make the process more time-consuming and expensive. Many of the best people get driven away from the field. The profession and the system itself lose esteem in the public's eyes.
>
> . . . In my view, incivility disserves the client because it wastes time and energy—time that is billed to the client at hundreds of dollars an hour, and energy that is better spent working on the case than working over the opponent.

of misconduct during a deposition in this case demonstrates such an astonishing lack of professionalism and civility that it is worthy of special note here as a lesson for the future—a lesson of conduct not to be tolerated or repeated.

On November 10, 1993, an expedited deposition of Paramount, through one of its directors, J. Hugh Liedtke, was taken in the state of Texas. The deposition was taken by Delaware counsel for QVC. Mr. Liedtke was individually represented at this deposition by Joseph D. Jamail, Esquire, of the Texas Bar. Peter C. Thomas, Esquire, of the New York Bar appeared and defended on behalf of the Paramount defendants....

Mr. Jamail did not otherwise appear in this Delaware proceeding representing any party, and he was not admitted *pro hac vice.* Under the rules of the Court of Chancery and this Court, lawyers who are admitted *pro hac vice* to represent a party in Delaware proceedings are subject to Delaware Disciplinary Rules, and are required to review the Delaware State Bar Association Statement of Principles of Lawyer Conduct (the "Statement of Principles").[29] During the Liedtke deposition, Mr. Jamail abused the privilege of representing a witness in a Delaware proceeding, in that he: (a) improperly directed the witness not to answer certain questions; (b) was extraordinarily rude, uncivil, and vulgar; and (c) obstructed the ability of the questioner to elicit testimony to assist the Court in this matter.

To illustrate, a few excerpts from the latter stages of the Liedtke deposition follow:

A. [Mr. Liedtke] I vaguely recall [Mr. Oresman's letter].... I think I did read it, probably....

The Honorable Sandra Day O'Connor, "Civil Justice System Improvements," ABA at 5 (Dec. 14, 1993) (footnotes omitted).

29. The following are a few pertinent excerpts from the Statement of Principles:

> The Delaware State Bar Association, for the Guidance of Delaware lawyers, *and those lawyers from other jurisdictions who may be associated with them,* adopted the following Statement of Principles of Lawyer Conduct on [November 15, 1991].... The purpose of adopting these Principles is to promote and foster the ideals of *professional courtesy, conduct and cooperation....* A lawyer should develop and maintain the qualities of integrity, compassion, learning, civility, diligence and public service that mark the most admired members of our profession.... [A] lawyer ... *should treat* all persons, including *adverse lawyers* and parties, *fairly and equitably.... Professional civility is conduct that shows respect not only for the courts and colleagues, but also for all people encountered in practice....* Respect for the court requires ... emotional self-control; [and] the absence of scorn and superiority in words of [sic] demeanor.... A lawyer should use pre-trial procedures, including discovery, solely to develop a case for settlement or trial. *No pre-trial procedure should be used to harass an opponent or delay a case.... Questions and objections at deposition should be restricted to conduct appropriate in the presence of a judge....* Before moving the admission of a lawyer from another jurisdiction, a Delaware lawyer should make such investigation as is required to form an informed conviction that the lawyer to be admitted is ethical and competent, and should furnish the candidate for admission with a copy of this Statement.

(Emphasis supplied.)

Q. (By Mr. Johnston [Delaware counsel for QVC]) Okay. Do you have any idea why Mr. Oresman was calling that material to your attention?
MR. JAMAIL: Don't answer that. How would he know what was going on in Mr. Oresman's mind? Don't answer it. Go on to your next question.
MR. JOHNSTON: No, Joe—.
MR. JAMAIL: He's not going to answer that. Certify it. I'm going to shut it down if you don't go to your next question.
MR. JOHNSTON: No. Joe, Joe—.
MR. JAMAIL: Don't "Joe" me, asshole. You can ask some questions, but get off of that. I'm tired of you. You could gag a maggot off a meat wagon. Now, we've helped you every way we can.
MR. JOHNSTON: Let's just take it easy.
MR. JAMAIL: No, we're not going to take it easy. Get done with this.
MR. JOHNSTON: We will go on to the next question.
MR. JAMAIL: Do it now.
MR. JOHNSTON: We will go on to the next question. We're not trying to excite anyone.
MR. JAMAIL: Come on. Quit talking. Ask the question. Nobody wants to socialize with you.
MR. JOHNSTON: I'm not trying to socialize. We'll go on to another question. We're continuing the deposition.
MR. JAMAIL: Well, go on and shut up.
MR. JOHNSTON: Are you finished?
MR. JAMAIL: Yeah, you—
MR. JOHNSTON: Are you finished?
MR. JAMAIL: I may be and you may be. Now, you want to sit here and talk to me, fine. This deposition is going to be over with. You don't know what you're doing. Obviously someone wrote out a long outline of stuff for you to ask. You have no concept of what you're doing. Now, I've tolerated you for three hours. If you've got another question, get on with it. This is going to stop one hour from now, period. Go.
MR. JOHNSTON: Are you finished?
MR. THOMAS: Come on, Mr. Johnston, move it.
MR. JOHNSTON: I don't need this kind of abuse.
MR. THOMAS: Then just ask the next question.
Q. (By Mr. Johnston) All right. To try to move forward, Mr. Liedtke, . . . I'll show you what's been marked as Liedtke 14 and it is a covering letter dated October 29 from Steven Cohen of Wachtell, Lipton, Rosen & Katz including QVC's Amendment Number 1 to its Schedule 14D-1, and my question—
A. No.
Q. —to you, sir, is whether you've seen that?
A. No. Look, I don't know what your intent in asking all these questions is, but, my God, I am not going to play boy lawyer.
Q. Mr. Liedtke—
A. Okay. Go ahead and ask your question.
Q. —I'm trying to move forward in this deposition that we are entitled to take. I'm trying to streamline it.

MR. JAMAIL: Come on with your next question. Don't even talk with this witness.

MR. JOHNSTON: I'm trying to move forward with it.

MR. JAMAIL: You understand me? Don't talk to this witness except by question. Did you hear me?

MR. JOHNSTON: I heard you fine.

MR. JAMAIL: You fee makers think you can come here and sit in somebody's office, get your meter running, get your full day's fee by asking stupid questions. Let's go with it.

(JA 6002-06).[30]

Staunch advocacy on behalf of a client is proper and fully consistent with the finest effectuation of skill and professionalism. Indeed, it is a mark of professionalism, not weakness, for a lawyer zealously and firmly to protect and pursue a client's legitimate interests by a professional, courteous, and civil attitude toward all persons involved in the litigation process. A lawyer who engages in the type of behavior exemplified by Mr. Jamail on the record of the Liedtke deposition is not properly representing his client, and the client's cause is not advanced by a lawyer who engages in unprofessional conduct of this nature. It happens that in this case there was no application to the Court, and the parties and the witness do not appear to have been prejudiced by this misconduct.[31]

Nevertheless, the Court finds this unprofessional behavior to be outrageous and unacceptable. If a Delaware lawyer had engaged in the kind of misconduct committed by Mr. Jamail on this record, that lawyer would have been subject to censure or more serious sanctions.[32] While the specter of disciplinary proceedings should not be used by the parties as a litigation tactic, conduct such as that involved here goes to the heart of the trial court proceedings themselves. As such, it cries out for relief under

30. Joint Appendix of the parties on appeal.

31. We recognize the practicalities of litigation practice in our trial courts, particularly in expedited proceedings such as this preliminary injunction motion, where simultaneous depositions are often taken in far-flung locations, and counsel have only a few hours to question each witness. Understandably, counsel may be reluctant to take the time to stop a deposition and call the trial judge for relief. Trial courts are extremely busy and overburdened. Avoidance of this kind of misconduct is essential. If such misconduct should occur, the aggrieved party should recess the deposition and engage in a dialogue with the offending lawyer to obviate the need to call the trial judge. If all else fails and it is necessary to call the trial judge, sanctions may be appropriate against the offending lawyer or party, or against the complaining lawyer or party if the request for court relief is unjustified. See Ch. Ct. R. 37. It should also be noted that discovery abuse sometimes is the fault of the questioner, not the lawyer defending the deposition. These admonitions should be read as applying to both sides.

32. See In re Ramunno, Del. Supr., 625 A.2d 248, 250 (1993) (Delaware lawyer held to have violated Rule 3.5 of the Rules of Professional Conduct, and therefore subject to public reprimand and warning for use of profanity similar to that involved here and "insulting conduct toward opposing counsel [found] . . . unacceptable by any standard").

the trial court's rules, including Ch. Ct. R. 37. Under some circumstances, the use of the trial court's inherent summary contempt powers may be appropriate. See In re Butler, Del. Supr., 609 A.2d 1080, 1082 (1992).

Although busy and overburdened, Delaware trial courts are "but a phone call away" and would be responsive to the plight of a party and its counsel bearing the brunt of such misconduct.[34] It is not appropriate for this Court to prescribe in the abstract any particular remedy or to provide an exclusive list of remedies under such circumstances. We assume that the trial courts of this State would consider protective orders and the sanctions permitted by the discovery rules. Sanctions could include exclusion of obstreperous counsel from attending the deposition (whether or not he or she has been admitted *pro hac vice*), ordering the deposition recessed and reconvened promptly in Delaware, or the appointment of a master to preside at the deposition. Costs and counsel fees should follow.

As noted, this was a deposition of Paramount through one of its directors. Mr. Liedtke was a Paramount witness in every respect. He was not there either as an individual defendant or as a third party witness. Pursuant to Ch. Ct. R. 170(d), the Paramount defendants should have been represented at the deposition by a Delaware lawyer or a lawyer admitted *pro hac vice*. A Delaware lawyer who moves the admission *pro hac vice* of an out-of-state lawyer is not relieved of responsibility, is required to appear at all court proceedings (except depositions when a lawyer admitted *pro hac vice* is present), shall certify that the lawyer appearing *pro hac vice* is reputable and competent, and that the Delaware lawyer is in a position to recommend the out-of-state lawyer. Thus, one of the principal purposes of the *pro hac vice* rules is to assure that, if a Delaware lawyer is not to be present at a deposition, the lawyer admitted *pro hac vice* will be there. As such, he is an officer of the Delaware Court, subject to control of the Court to ensure the integrity of the proceeding. Counsel attending the Liedtke deposition on behalf of the Paramount defendants had an obligation to ensure the integrity of that proceeding. The record of the deposition as a whole (JA 5916-6054) demonstrates that, not only Mr. Jamail, but also Mr. Thomas (representing the Paramount defendants), continually interrupted the questioning, engaged in colloquies and objections which sometimes suggested answers to questions,[36]

34. See Hall v. Clifton Precision, E.D. Pa., 150 F.R.D. 525 (1993) (ruling on "coaching," conferences between deposed witnesses and their lawyers, and obstructive tactics):

> Depositions are the factual battleground where the vast majority of litigation actually takes place. . . . Thus, it is particularly important that this discovery device not be abused. Counsel should never forget that even though the deposition may be taking place far from a real courtroom, with no black-robed overseer peering down upon them, as long as the deposition is conducted under the caption of this court and proceeding under the authority of the rules of this court, counsel are operating as officers of this court. They should comport themselves accordingly; should they be tempted to stray, they should remember that this judge is but a phone call away.

150 F.R.D. at 531.

36. Rule 30(d)(1) of the revised Federal Rules of Civil Procedure, which became effective on December 1, 1993, requires objections during depositions to be "stated

and constantly pressed the questioner for time throughout the deposition.[37] As to Mr. Jamail's tactic quoted above, Mr. Thomas passively let matters proceed as they did, and at times even added his own voice to support the behavior of Mr. Jamail. A Delaware lawyer or a lawyer admitted *pro hac vice* would have been expected to put an end to the misconduct in the Liedtke deposition.

This kind of misconduct is not to be tolerated in any Delaware court proceeding, including depositions taken in other states in which witnesses appear represented by their own counsel other than counsel for a party in the proceeding. Yet, there is no clear mechanism for this Court to deal with this matter in terms of sanctions or disciplinary remedies at this time in the context of this case. Nevertheless, consideration will be given to the following issues for the future: (a) whether or not it is appropriate and fair to take into account the behavior of Mr. Jamail in this case in the event application is made by him in the future to appear *pro hac vice* in any Delaware proceeding;[38] and (b) what rules or standards should be adopted to deal effectively with misconduct by out-of-state lawyers in depositions in proceedings pending in Delaware courts.

As to (a), this Court will welcome a voluntary appearance by Mr. Jamail if a request is received from him by the Clerk of this Court within thirty days of the date of this Opinion and Addendum. The purpose of such voluntary appearance will be to explain the questioned conduct and to show cause why such conduct should not be considered as a bar to any future appearance by Mr. Jamail in a Delaware proceeding. As to (b), this Court and the trial courts of this State will undertake to strengthen the existing mechanisms for dealing with the type of misconduct referred to in this Addendum and the practices relating to admissions *pro hac vice.*

---

concisely and in a non-argumentative and non-suggestive manner." The Delaware trial courts and this Court are evaluating the desirability of adopting certain of the new Federal Rules, or modifications thereof, and other possible rule changes.

37. While we do not necessarily endorse everything set forth in the *Hall* case, we share Judge Gawthrop's view not only of the impropriety of coaching witnesses on and off the record of the deposition (see supra note 34), but also the impropriety of objections and colloquy which "tend to disrupt the question-and-answer rhythm of a deposition and obstruct the witness's testimony." See 150 F.R.D. at 530. To be sure, there are also occasions when the questioner is abusive or otherwise acts improperly and should be sanctioned. See supra note 31. Although the questioning in the *Liedtke* deposition could have proceeded more crisply, this was not a case where it was the questioner who abused the process.

38. The Court does not condone the conduct of Mr. Thomas in this deposition. Although the Court does not view his conduct with the gravity and revulsion with which it views Mr. Jamail's conduct, in the future the Court expects that counsel in Mr. Thomas's position will have been admitted *pro hac vice* before participating in a deposition. As an officer of the Delaware Court, counsel admitted *pro hac vice* are now clearly on notice that they are expected to put an end to conduct such as that perpetrated by Mr. Jamail on this record.

Notes and Questions

1. *Deposition Details: Attendance, Location, Limitations.* How do you compel attendance at a deposition if the deponent is

a) a nonparty? See Rules 30(a) and 45(c), (e).
b) a party who is sued or suing in their individual capacity? See Rule 37(d).
c) a corporate entity? See Rules 30(b)(6), 37(d).

Where may a deposition be taken

a) of a party? Any limits on this? See Rule 26(c).
b) of a nonparty? See Rules 45(b)(2), 45(c).

2. *Recourse for Deposition Misconduct.* What is the function of the lawyer who "defends" a deposition? Can she object to a question on the ground that it calls for inadmissible hearsay? That it calls for revelation of privileged information? That it is irrelevant to the issues raised by the pleadings? That it already has been asked and answered twice? Eight times? See Rules 26, 30(d), 32(b). Can the defending lawyer ask the deponent questions? (Who pays for this time on the record?) Why might the lawyer insist on asking follow-up questions to clarify the deponent's testimony? See Rule 32. If the defending lawyer becomes overly protective of the deponent and orders her not to answer questions that are *not* beyond the scope of permissible inquiry, what may the deposing lawyer do? Review the Guide to the Enforcement Scheme at the beginning of this chapter for assistance. The Guide also outlines other misconduct at depositions — such as failing to show — and its consequences. See also A Report on the Conduct of Depositions, Federal Bar Council, Committee on Second Circuit Courts, 131 F.R.D. 613 (1990) (discussing various obstructionist deposition practices, including instructing a witness not to answer, and their consequences).

3. *Video Depositions.* Rule 30(b)(3) allows for video depositions, portions of which may be introduced at trial subject to the same conditions that apply to all depositions. What are the potential benefits of video depositions? The pitfalls? Consider the following advice about use of video depositions:

> Do not think that video depositions are necessarily better than readings or reenactments. A one-camera deposition can be deadly — particularly if it lasts more than an hour. Few things are more boring than watching a video screen that shows a talking head answering questions from a disembodied voice that comes from off screen.
>
> So if you are going to use a video deposition, there are some important things to do:
>
> a. Use two cameras — one for the lawyers and one for the witness. It does not take great technical expertise, fancy equipment, or extra people. The

operator just switches back and forth from one camera to the other, depending on who is talking. That way you won't be stuck with just a talking head.

b. Keep the deposition under an hour—under a half hour is better, if you can. Short and simple is almost always better than long and pedantic.

c. Use a different piece of real or demonstrative evidence every 10 or 15 minutes. Have charts, maps, pictures, or medical illustrations blown up and mounted on an easel so the witness can point out important details that will show up on the video screen. Then when you replay the deposition for the jury, have those same exhibits on the same easel—right next to the video screen. It provides an alternate point of interest for the jury as well as giving a link of reality between the trial and the deposition.

James W. McElhaney, Nine Ways to Use Depositions, 19:2 Litig. 45, 48 (1993). See also Mark A. Neubauer, Videotaping Depositions, 19:4 Litig. 60 (1993); Michael J. Henke, The Taking and Use of Videotaped Depositions, 16 Am. J. Trial Advoc. 151 (1992). Reprinted with permission of the American Bar Association.

4. *Preparing Clients for Deposition.* As much may hinge on the testimony generated at a deposition, lawyers typically prepare their clients for the experience. Most lawyers likely would agree with the following description of basic client preparation for a deposition:

Q. What five basic rules should a lawyer give a witness?

A.
1. Witnesses are under oath and are obliged to tell the truth.
2. Witnesses are not required to answer questions that have not been asked, should not respond to a questioner's tone and should not argue with a questioner.
3. Witnesses should not volunteer information, guess, speculate or assume.
4. Witnesses should make certain that they understand the question that has been asked.
5. A question that calls for a narrative response (*Q*: What happened then?) may be difficult to answer in full. The witness should be advised to preface the answer with "As I recall" or "My current recollection is" so that if something else comes to mind later, the witness will be able to testify to the additional facts without embarrassment.

Steven A. Meyerowitz, Preparing Your Clients for Depositions, 15 Pa. Law. 20 (July 1993). Are there other rules you would add to this list?

Note: The Appealability of Discovery Orders

In this chapter, you have read a number of appellate cases, including cases from the United States Supreme Court, that turned on discovery issues. Yet as a general matter, discovery rulings are not "final district court orders," within the meaning of 28 U.S.C. § 1291, which sets the jurisdiction of the courts of appeal. Nor in most cases do discovery orders fit within the requirements of 28 U.S.C. § 1292, which provides for an interlocutory appeal of some nonfinal orders.

Yet many discovery orders are, at least in the minds of the parties, dispositive of the issues in a case. Parties may settle or suffer dismissal rather than disclose under what they view as a wrong but ruinous discovery order.

One rather extreme method for getting an appeal is the one pioneered in Hickman v. Taylor. In that case, the lawyer, Samuel B. Fortenbaugh, who refused to turn over the interview notes, underwent a contempt citation, presumably criminal, which is appealable, to bring the issue to a higher court. In an interview years after the case, Fortenbaugh termed the contempt order "a deal" between the judge, opposing counsel, and himself. "We were a pretty clubby group here in Philadelphia, the Admiralty bar," Fortenbaugh remarked. Paul Coady, Dredging the Depths of Hickman v. Taylor, Harv. L. Rev, May 6, 1977, at 6. The opposing lawyer, Abraham Freedman, told an interviewer that in retrospect it was a mistake to agree to the contempt citation because that "created" some sympathy in some quarters for Fortenbaugh. Id.

Sometimes the failure to produce some important piece of evidence becomes an issue on appeal after final judgment, as was true in Rozier v. Ford Motor Co. And at other times, the sanction for discovery violations may be dismissal of the lawsuit, which is most certainly a final order. See National Hockey League v. Metropolitan Hockey Club, 427 U.S. 639, 641 (1975) (upholding dismissal of the action for failure to answer interrogatories, "not merely to penalize those whose conduct may be deemed to warrant such a sanction, but to deter those who might be tempted to such conduct in the absence of such a deterrent").

Upjohn, and the note case on administering the privilege, both were appeals from judgments about the enforcement of administrative subpoenas. Neither was technically a final order. Here is what the Second Circuit said about appealability in United States v. Construction Products Research, Inc., 73 F.3d 464, 468-469 (2d Cir. 1996):

> The general rule is that orders enforcing subpoenas issued in connection with civil and criminal actions, or grand jury proceedings, are *not* final, and therefore *not* appealable. United States v. Ryan, 402 U.S. 530, 532-33; Cobbledick v. United States, 309 U.S. 323, 328, (1940); Reich v. National Eng'g & Contracting Co., 13 F.3d 93, 95 (4th Cir. 1993); Kemp v. Gay, 947 F.2d 1493, 1495 (D.C. Cir. 1991). To obtain appellate review, the subpoenaed party must defy the district court's enforcement order, be held in contempt, and then appeal the contempt order, which is regarded as final under § 1291. *Ryan*, 402 U.S. at 532; *Cobbledick*, 309 U.S. at 328; *National Eng'g*, 13 F.3d at 95; *Kemp*, 947 F.2d at 1495. "The purpose of this rule is to discourage parties from pursuing appeals from orders enforcing these subpoenas, which would temporarily halt the district court's litigation process or the grand jury process." *National Eng'g*, 13 F.3d at 95.

> There is a different rule, however, in administrative proceedings. A district court order enforcing a subpoena issued by a government agency in connection with an administrative investigation may be appealed immediately without first performing the ritual of obtaining a contempt order. [citations omitted]. The rationale is that, at least from the district court's perspective, the court's enforcement of an agency subpoena arises out of a proceeding that "may be deemed self-contained, so far as the judiciary is concerned. . . . There is not, as in the case of a grand jury or trial, any further judicial inquiry which would be halted were the offending [subpoenaed party] permitted to appeal." *Cobbledick,* 309 U.S. at 330.

Finally, consider the opinion in *Cordy.* It was rendered by a magistrate judge originally. In many district courts, these subjudicial officers take on major litigation matters, like the pretrial motion to disqualify both the other side's experts, as well as their law firm.

In *Cordy,* supra, Magistrate Kugler disqualified not only the expert, but also the lawyers who had worked with him and their law firm as well. Though he found no wrongdoing or bad faith, his concern was with a certain carelessness on the part of the lawyers in dealing with the expert, as well as the appearance of impropriety.

A magistrate judge's opinion is appealable to the district court under whose direction the magistrate is working. But thenceforth, a motion to disqualify a law firm, like all other discovery matters, may not be appealed before there is a final judgment in the case. In a matter of disqualification of counsel, however, or even of an expert (given his centrality to the case), it is difficult to conceive how the point that the judge made an error might be preserved for appeal. Must the counsel or experts actually involved do a bad job, or worse job than the prior firm or expert would have done to preserve the point? Should they make a record at every major juncture of how much better the previous firm would have handled the matter?

Only extraordinary paths are available to gain review of discovery orders, and it is rare for discovery issues to survive beyond a final order in the case. Can you see why this is? Most civil cases settle without an appealable order of any kind, and among these is a subset of those that settle because of an adverse discovery ruling. For an interesting account of the experience in Texas of allowing parties seriously aggrieved by a discovery order to appeal through an extraordinary writ, see Elizabeth G. Thornburg, Interlocutory Review of Discovery Orders: An Idea Whose Time Has Come, 44 Sw. L.J. 1045 (1990).

F. DISCOVERY IN INTERNATIONAL LITIGATION

The Restatement of Foreign Relations asserts that "[n]o aspect of the extension of the American legal system beyond the territorial frontier of the United States has given rise to so much friction as the requests for documents in investigation and litigation in the United States." Restatement 3d of Foreign Relations § 442, Reporter's Note 1 (1987). In an increasingly global economy, litigation in the United States increasingly involves parties and conduct that stretch well beyond the borders of the United States, and foreign litigation increasingly implicates parties and evidence in the United States. As one court recently put it, "transactions involving participants from many lands have become common fare. This world economic interdependence has highlighted the importance of comity, as international commerce depends to a large extent on the ability of merchants to predict the likely consequences of their conduct in overseas markets. This predictability, in turn, depends on cooperation, reciprocity, and respect among nations." Quaak v. KPMG-Belgium, 361 F.3d 11, 19 (1st Cir. 2004).

Rule 26 and the other federal rules we have covered in this chapter regulate discovery in federal courts but they say nothing about how discovery should proceed in international litigation. How, for instance, should discovery proceed in litigation before foreign tribunals when parties or witnesses with relevant evidence reside in the United States? For nearly 150 years, federal courts have provided assistance to foreign tribunals in gathering evidence in the United States. The traditional mechanism was called a "letter rogatory" — a request from one court to another, delivered through diplomatic channels, to take evidence from a witness within the jurisdiction of the receiving court. But letters rogatory were of strictly limited use. Until Congress passed amendments to the underlying statute in 1948, courts could only meet a request for evidence in a letter rogatory where the government of a foreign country was a party to, or had some interest in, the foreign litigation. And until 1964, the evidence sought had to be testimonial (documentary and other tangible evidence was excluded), the foreign proceeding had to be "judicial," thereby excluding adjudications by administrative and quasi-judicial bodies, and the litigation had to be pending before the courts of a foreign country, making it unclear whether proceedings before international tribunals were covered. On the history of letters rogatory, see Harry Leroy Jones, International Judicial Assistance: Procedural Chaos and a Program for Reform, 62 Yale L.J. 515 (1953); Hans Smit, International Litigation Under the United States Code, 65 Colum. L. Rev. 1015, 1027 (1965). See also 28 U.S.C. § 1781.

The statute as it now stands is quite broad, see 28 U.S.C. § 1782, and the Supreme Court has upheld its application to proceedings before multinational administrative commissions such as the Directorate General for Competition of the European Commission — the division of the executive body of the European Union responsible for regulating competition. See Intel Corp. v. Advanced Micro Devices, Inc., 542 U.S. 241 (2004). In *Intel*, AMD, a global competitor in the microprocessor industry, filed a complaint alleging antitrust violations with the Directorate General and then petitioned the District Court for the Northern District of California for an order directing Intel to hand over documents relevant to its complaint before the European Commission. Intel opposed the request in part on the theory, endorsed by the First and Eleventh Circuits, that § 1782 only permits discovery of information that would be discoverable by the Directorate General under EU law if the documents had been located in the European Union. The Supreme Court rejected this "foreign-discoverability requirement," holding that AMD qualifies as an "interested person" within the meaning of § 1782, that the Commission of the European Communities is properly considered a "foreign or international tribunal" even though it acts in many respects as a public prosecutor, and that while § 1782 protects privileged material from disclosure, "nothing in the text of § 1782 limits a district court's production-order authority to materials that could be discovered in the foreign jurisdiction if the materials were located there." *Intel,* 542 U.S. at 253-254, 260.

This does not mean production under § 1782 is automatic. As the Court emphasized, a district court has discretion in whether to grant a § 1782 request. Factors relevant to the exercise of that discretion include (1) whether the applicant seeks information from individuals who are not party to the foreign proceeding and thus not subject to the discovery powers of the foreign tribunal, (2) whether the requests are "unduly intrusive or burdensome," (3) "the nature of the foreign tribunal," (4) "the character of the proceedings underway abroad," (5) "the receptivity of the foreign government or the court or agency abroad to U.S. federal-court judicial assistance," and (6) "whether the § 1782 request conceals an attempt to circumvent foreign proof-gathering restrictions or other policies of a foreign country or the United States." Id. at 264.

Notice that, apart from the limitation covering privileged material, there is no requirement that district courts consider whether "United States law would allow discovery in domestic litigation analogous to the foreign proceeding." Id. at 263. That means Intel can be forced to disclose information to the European Commission, with the aid of the federal courts, which a federal court could not order disclosed in domestic litigation. Doesn't that invite abuse of § 1782 for "fishing expeditions"?

Would it affect your view to know that the information AMD sought was covered by a protective order issued by the District Court for the Northern District of Alabama in a separate, domestic antitrust suit against Intel? See id. at 251. Is it significant that the Directorate General did not want the information enough to seek assistance from U.S. courts on its own under § 1782, or that the European Commission filed an amicus brief with the Supreme Court emphasizing that it did not want or need the help of the district court in this matter? See id. at 265-266.

What is the risk in allowing a party to obtain discovery beyond the limits of the discovery laws of both the foreign and domestic jurisdictions in an antitrust case like this? If Intel is not engaged in anti-competitive behavior in the EU market, why should it fear open discovery?

And what about problems obtaining discovery overseas to aid in litigation in the United States? Consider Quaak v. KPMG-Belgium, 361 F.3d 11 (1st Cir. 2004). *Quaak* is a consolidation of several class actions and numerous other suits against the Belgian accounting firm KPMG-B alleging securities fraud in the firm's role as the auditor for a publicly traded company that collapsed under financial mismanagement. The cases were consolidated in Massachusetts federal district court. When the case reached pretrial discovery, plaintiffs moved to compel production of relevant auditing records and other work papers located in Belgium. KPMG-B refused to produce, arguing that Article 458 of the Belgian Criminal Code prohibits auditors from disclosing confidential client information. When the district court nevertheless granted plaintiffs' motion to compel, KPMG-B filed an ex parte action with a Belgian court in Brussels "seeking to enjoin the plaintiffs from taking any step' to proceed with the requested discovery. To ensure compliance, they asked the Belgian court to impose a fine of one million Euros for each violation of the proposed injunction." Id. at 15. The Belgian court declined to proceed ex parte, directed notice to the U.S. plaintiffs and scheduled a hearing on the injunction. Plaintiffs responded by immediately seeking an injunction from the Massachusetts district court against KPMG-B to prevent it from proceeding with its suit in Belgium. The court granted the "anti-suit injunction," ordering KPMG-B "to withdraw forthwith its writ in the Court of First Instance in Brussels and . . . not to proceed with the hearing . . . [and to] file proof of compliance with this order." Id. The court also refused to stay its order compelling production of the requested documents.

KPMG-B appealed to the First Circuit, arguing that the international anti-suit injunction was inconsistent with principles of comity and the presumption in favor of concurrent jurisdiction. In a carefully reasoned opinion the First Circuit followed the Second, Third, Sixth, and D.C. Circuits in endorsing a "conservative approach for gauging the propriety of international anti-suit injunctions." Id. at 17 (citing cases). According to this approach, "considerations of international comity must be given substantial weight — and those considerations ordinarily establish a rebuttable presumption against the issuance of an order that has the effect of halting foreign judicial proceedings." Id. at 18.

The Fifth, Seventh, and Ninth Circuits have adopted a more permissive approach toward granting international anti-suit injunctions whenever, as the *Quaak* court put it, parallel international proceedings "would frustrate the speedy and efficient determination of the [local] case." Id. at 17 (citing Kaepa, Inc. v. Achilles Corp. 76 F.3d 624, 626 (5th Cir. 1996); Philips Med. Sys. Int'l B.V. v. Bruetman, 8 F.3d 600, 605 (7th Cir. 1993); and Seattle Totems Hockey Club, Inc. v. Nat'l Hockey League, 652 F.2d 852, 855-856 (9th Cir. 1981)).

Even applying its conservative approach, however, the court upheld the international anti-suit injunction against KPMG-B. Characterizing KPMG-B's Belgian action as an "attempt to chill legitimate discovery by in terrorem tactics [and to] quash the practical power of the United States courts," the court reasoned that "[w]here, as here, a party institutes a foreign action in a blatant attempt to evade the rightful authority of the forum court, the need for an antisuit injunction crests." Id. at 20 (internal quotations and citation omitted).

Assuming Article 458 of the Belgian Criminal Code is valid, and that none of the exceptions to the confidentiality rule it creates apply to this case, is it right to say that KPMG-B is trying to quash or evade the authority of the federal court in Massachusetts? Isn't it just trying to assure that the federal court does not negate its rights and duties under Belgian law? What other options did KPMG-B have facing the court's order compelling production of the documents? The First Circuit admonishes that KPMG-B could have "exhaust[ed] its position in the federal judicial system before attempting to sidetrack that system." Id. at 21. It also might have "sought clarification from the Belgian courts without raising the stakes to a level that necessarily precipitated a direct conflict with the pending securities fraud action." Id. Would either course have been effective? Wouldn't both have favored the U.S. plaintiffs proceeding against KPMG-B in U.S. courts?

4 *Dispositions and Adjudications*

Approximately 98 percent of cases filed in federal court drop out of the system before trial — most often by settlement, but sometimes by rulings on motions to dismiss or to enter summary judgment. Leonidas Ralph Mecham, Judicial Business of the Federal Courts: 2001 Annual Report of the Director 154 (2001); Stephen C. Yeazell, The Misunderstood Consequences of Modern Civil Process, 1994 Wis. L. Rev. 631, 633 & n.6 (reporting a settlement rate of 95 percent). As Professor Yeazell has observed, "[w]e have moved from a trial-based procedure to one centered on the events that occur instead of trial and which typically head off trial." Id. at 639. He explains:

> Specific procedural changes achieved this reallocation of judicial resources. In 1938, the Federal Rules reoriented the trial process of the federal courts. They did not eliminate trial. But they interposed a number of new steps between the commencement of litigation and trial, each of which could yield a judicial ruling and thus require judicial time. As a consequence, trial, once the center of judicial attention, became one among many tasks. Even more significant, these other tasks often produced enough information or sufficiently exhausted resources that the parties settled. Courts now devote the bulk of their civil work to such pretrial tasks — ruling on discovery disputes, deciding joinder issues, conducting pretrial and settlement conferences, and, sadly, punishing lawyers for misbehavior during this phase of proceedings. This work is important, required, and often practically dispositive. But it does not, by itself, produce a judgment that finally disposes of the case in the way that a trial, successful summary judgment motion, or a dismissal on the pleadings does. Instead, these judicial decisions provide a framework within which the parties decide how to evaluate settlement or abandonment of the underlying lawsuits. These developments suggest a quiet revolution in the process of civil litigation in the United States.

Id. The same quiet revolution has occurred in state courts. A 2003 study of 21 states conducted by the National Center for State Courts reports that only 8 percent of civil cases ended in a jury or bench trial. Examining the Work of State Courts 22 (2003). The remaining 92 percent of the caseload was disposed of either by settlement, voluntary dismissal, involuntary dismissal, or summary judgment. Id.

In section A we discuss some of the technically nondispositive judicial activities and procedures that have a great impact on the outcome in the immediate case, as well as succeeding ones. Keep in mind what you know about discovery and motions on the pleadings—other pretrial activities that may result in a final disposition of the case. Settled cases are never reviewed by an appellate court, even though the impetus for settlement may have been an incorrect ruling. One of the results of the new emphasis on the pretrial period is a tremendous increase in the trial judge's power, and in private ordering by the parties also.

In section B we deal with pretrial dispositions that include judgment—in particular, summary judgment—and in sections C and D we briefly introduce the procedural mechanics involved when a case goes to trial. The burgeoning universe of *alternatives* to traditional adversarial litigation, broadly referred to as "alternative dispute resolution" procedures, is covered in Chapter 5.

A. ENDING LITIGATION WITHOUT JUDGMENT: SETTLEMENTS, PRETRIAL CONFERENCES, AND OTHER MANEUVERS

Problem Case: Pressured to Settle

You are a lawyer member of the Advisory Committee considering the following Rule changes designed to promote settlement:

Rule 16: Change to make at least one pretrial conference mandatory, at which the possibility of settlement and the use of extrajudicial procedures to resolve the dispute must be discussed.

Rule 68: Change to provide for an offer of settlement from either party, and for sanctions, including attorneys' fees, to be imposed for the rejection of any reasonable offer, regardless of which party prevails.

What would be your position on making settlement discussion mandatory and its rejection costly? Would you feel differently about it if you were a judge?

1. Settlement

Settlement—often actively encouraged by trial judges—deflects many cases from the trial stage and insulates resolutions from searching appellate review. Professor Yeazell describes this process as follows:

> Judges have long asked parties informally whether they wish to settle. Under the original version of the Rules, judges who were so inclined used

> the pretrial conference, authorized but not required by Rule 16, as an occasion for doing so. In 1983, and again in 1993, Rule 16 was revised to make explicit the propriety of such efforts. Congress has further encouraged judges to direct more attention to this area. One can therefore expect to see more judges encouraging settlement. Some have applauded, while others have criticized this tendency. But the debate has focused on the inherent desirability of such a rule for judges, rather than on the redistribution of power the rule entails.
>
> For the litigants, the summary jury trial and settlement discussions provide another stage of the pretrial process on which time and professional effort must be focused. This stage differs from discovery and joinder motions because it is controlled by the judge rather than the parties; parties can suggest that settlement would be useful, but the judge has almost unbounded discretion to conduct such proceedings whether or not the parties think it useful. Moreover, the amount of such effort lies within the judge's discretion: an enthusiastic judge may order a summary jury trial, a minitrial, arbitration, *and* a settlement conference. The aim of such process is, of course, to avoid a trial. If the judge succeeds, he incidentally removes his prior rulings from appellate scrutiny.

Yeazell, supra, 1994 Wis. L. Rev. at 657.

Of course, settlement may also serve other purposes. The most commonly cited advantages are that it avoids the expense of protracted proceedings and may increase party satisfaction (and thus compliance) with the outcome. The preference for settlement over trial is so strong that it prompted at least one judge to quip that "a bad settlement is almost always better than a good trial." In re Warner Commc'ns Sec. Litig., 618 F. Supp. 735, 740 (S.D.N.Y. 1985), *aff'd*, 798 F.2d 35 (2d Cir. 1986).

The following case addresses Fed. R. Civ. P. 68, which promotes settlement (and its efficiencies) by making it potentially costly to decline a settlement offer. Is the rule unduly coercive, or is it a reasonable inducement to take all serious settlement offers seriously?

Marek v. Chesny

473 U.S. 1 (1985)

CHIEF JUSTICE BURGER delivered the opinion of the Court.

We granted certiorari to decide whether attorney's fees incurred by a plaintiff subsequent to an offer of settlement under Federal Rule of Civil Procedure 68 must be paid by the defendant under 42 U.S.C. § 1988, when the plaintiff recovers a judgment less than the offer.

Petitioners, three police officers, in answering a call on a domestic disturbance, shot and killed respondent's adult son. Respondent, in his own behalf and as administrator of his son's estate, filed suit against the officers in the United States District Court under 42 U.S.C. § 1983 and state tort law.

Prior to trial, petitioners made a timely offer of settlement "for a sum, including costs now accrued and attorney's fees, of one hundred thousand ($100,000) dollars." Respondent did not accept the offer. The case went to trial and respondent was awarded $5,000 on the state-law "wrongful death" claim, $52,000 for the § 1983 violation, and $3,000 in punitive damages.

Respondent filed a request for $171,692.47 in costs, including attorney's fees. This amount included costs incurred after the settlement offer. Petitioners opposed the claim for postoffer costs, relying on Federal Rule of Civil Procedure 68, which shifts to the plaintiff all "costs" incurred subsequent to an offer of judgment not exceeded by the ultimate recovery at trial. Petitioners argued that attorney's fees are part of the "costs" covered by Rule 68. The District Court agreed with petitioners and declined to award respondent "costs, including attorney's fees, incurred after the offer of judgment." 547 F. Supp. 542, 547 (N.D. Ill. 1982). The parties subsequently agreed that $32,000 fairly represented the allowable costs, including attorney's fees, accrued prior to petitioners' offer of settlement. Respondent appealed the denial of postoffer costs.

The Court of Appeals reversed. . . . The plain purpose of Rule 68 is to encourage settlement and avoid litigation. Advisory Committee Note on Rules of Civil Procedure, Report of Proposed Amendments, 5 F.R.D. 433, 483 n.1 (1946), 28 U.S.C. App., p. 637; Delta Air Lines, Inc. v. August, 450 U.S. 346, 352 (1981). The Rule prompts both parties to a suit to evaluate the risks and costs of litigation, and to balance them against the likelihood of success upon trial on the merits. This case requires us to decide whether the offer in this case was a proper one under Rule 68, and whether the term "costs" as used in Rule 68 includes attorney's fees awardable under 42 U.S.C. § 1988.

The first question we address is whether petitioners' offer was valid under Rule 68. Respondent contends that the offer was invalid because it lumped petitioners' proposal for damages with their proposal for costs. Respondent argues that Rule 68 requires that an offer must separately recite the amount that the defendant is offering in settlement of the substantive claim and the amount he is offering to cover accrued costs. Only if the offer is bifurcated, he contends, so that it is clear how much the defendant is offering for the substantive claim, can a plaintiff possibly assess whether it would be wise to accept the offer. He apparently bases this argument on the language of the Rule providing that the defendant "may serve upon the adverse party an offer to allow judgment to be taken against him for the money or property or to the effect specified in his offer, *with costs then accrued*" (emphasis added).

The Court of Appeals rejected respondent's claim, holding that "an offer of the money or property or to the specified effect is, by force of the rule itself, 'with' — that is, plus 'costs then accrued,' whatever the amount of those costs is." 720 F.2d at 476. We, too, reject respondent's argument. We do not read Rule 68 to require that a defendant's offer itemize the respective amounts being tendered for settlement of the underlying substantive claim and for costs.

The critical feature of this portion of the Rule is that the offer be one that allows *judgment to be taken against the defendant for both the damages caused by the challenged conduct and the costs then accrued*. In other words, the drafters' concern was not so much with the particular components of offers, but with the *judgments* to be allowed against defendants. If an offer recites that costs are included or specifies an amount for costs, and the plaintiff accepts the offer, the judgment will necessarily include costs; if the offer does not state that costs are included and an amount for costs is not specified, the court will be obliged by the terms of the Rule to include in its judgment an additional amount which in its discretion, see Delta Air Lines, Inc. v. August, supra, at 362, 365 (Powell, J., concurring), it determines to be sufficient to cover the costs. In either case, however, the offer has *allowed* judgment to be entered against the defendant both for damages caused by the challenged conduct and for costs. Accordingly, it is immaterial whether the offer recites that costs are included, whether it specifies the amount the defendant is allowing for costs, or, for that matter, whether it refers to costs at all. As long as the offer does not implicitly or explicitly provide that the judgment not include costs, a timely offer will be valid.

This construction of the Rule best furthers the objective of the Rule, which is to encourage settlements. If defendants are not allowed to make lump-sum offers that would, if accepted, represent their total liability, they would understandably be reluctant to make settlement offers. As the Court of Appeals observed, "many a defendant would be unwilling to make a binding settlement offer on terms that left it exposed to liability for attorney's fees in whatever amount the court might fix on motion of the plaintiff." 720 F.2d at 477.

Contrary to respondent's suggestion, reading the Rule in this way does not frustrate plaintiffs' efforts to determine whether defendants' offers are adequate. At the time an offer is made, the plaintiff knows the amount in damages caused by the challenged conduct. The plaintiff also knows, or can ascertain, the costs then accrued. A reasonable determination whether to accept the offer can be made by simply adding these two figures and comparing the sum to the amount offered. Respondent is troubled that a plaintiff will not know whether the offer on the substantive claim would be exceeded at trial, but this is so whenever an offer of settlement is made. In any event, requiring itemization of damages separate from costs would not in any way help plaintiffs know in advance whether the judgment at trial will exceed a defendant's offer.

Curiously, respondent also maintains that petitioners' settlement offer did not exceed the judgment obtained by respondent. In this regard, respondent notes that the $100,000 offer is not as great as the sum of the $60,000 in damages, $32,000 in preoffer costs, and $139,692.47 in claimed postoffer costs. This argument assumes, however, that postoffer costs should be included in the comparison. The Court of Appeals correctly recognized that postoffer costs merely offset part of the expense of continuing the litigation to trial, and should not be included in the calculus. Id., at 476.

The second question we address is whether the term "costs" in Rule 68 includes attorney's fees awardable under 42 U.S.C. § 1988. By the time the Federal Rules of Civil Procedure were adopted in 1938, federal statutes had authorized and defined awards of costs to prevailing parties for more than 85 years. See Act of Feb. 26, 1853, 10 Stat. 161; see generally Alyeska Pipeline Service Co. v. Wilderness Society, 421 U.S. 240 (1975). Unlike in England, such "costs" generally had not included attorney's fees; under the "American Rule," each party had been required to bear its own attorney's fees. The "American Rule" as applied in federal courts, however, had become subject to certain exceptions by the late 1930's. Some of these exceptions had evolved as a product of the "inherent power in the courts to allow attorney's fees in particular situations." *Alyeska,* supra, at 259. But most of the exceptions were found in federal statutes that directed courts to award attorney's fees as part of costs in particular cases. 421 U.S. at 260-262.

Section 407 of the Communications Act of 1934, for example, provided in relevant part that, "[i]f the petitioner shall finally prevail, he shall be allowed a reasonable attorney's fee, to be taxed and collected as a part of the costs of the suit." 47 U.S.C. § 407. There was identical language in § 3 (p) of the Railway Labor Act, 45 U.S.C. § 153(p) (1934 ed.). Section 40 of the Copyright Act of 1909, 17 U.S.C. § 40 (1934 ed.), allowed a court to "award to the prevailing party a reasonable attorney's fee as part of the costs." And other statutes contained similar provisions that included attorney's fees as part of awardable "costs." See, e.g., the Clayton Act, 15 U.S.C. § 15 (1934 ed.); the Securities Act of 1933, 15 U.S.C. § 77k(e) (1934 ed.); the Securities Exchange Act of 1934, 15 U.S.C. §§ 78i(e), 78r(a) (1934 ed.).

The authors of Federal Rule of Civil Procedure 68 were fully aware of these exceptions to the American Rule. The Advisory Committee's Note to Rule 54(d), 28 U.S.C. App., p.621, contains an extensive list of the federal statutes which allowed for costs in particular cases; of the 35 "statutes as to costs" set forth in the final paragraph of the Note, no fewer than 11 allowed for attorney's fees as part of costs. Against this background of varying definitions of "costs," the drafters of Rule 68 did not define the term; nor is there any explanation whatever as to its intended meaning in the history of the Rule.

In this setting, given the importance of "costs" to the Rule, it is very unlikely that this omission was mere oversight; on the contrary, the most reasonable inference is that the term "costs" in Rule 68 was intended to refer to all costs properly awardable under the relevant substantive statute or other authority. In other words, all costs properly awardable in an action are to be considered within the scope of Rule 68 "costs." Thus, absent congressional expressions to the contrary, where the underlying statute defines "costs" to include attorney's fees, we are satisfied such fees are to be included as costs for purposes of Rule 68.

Here, respondent sued under 42 U.S.C. § 1983. Pursuant to the Civil Rights Attorney's Fees Awards Act of 1976, 90 Stat. 2641, as amended, 42 U.S.C. § 1988, a prevailing party in a § 1983 action may be awarded attorney's fees "as part of the costs." Since Congress expressly included attorney's fees as "costs" available to a plaintiff in a § 1983 suit, such fees are subject to the cost-shifting provision of Rule 68. This "plain meaning" interpretation of the interplay between Rule 68 and § 1988 is the only construction that gives meaning to each word in both Rule 68 and § 1988.

Unlike the Court of Appeals, we do not believe that this "plain meaning" construction of the statute and the Rule will frustrate Congress' objective in § 1988 of ensuring that civil rights plaintiffs obtain "'effective access to the judicial process.'" Hensley v. Eckerhart, 461 U.S. 424, 429 (1983), quoting H.R. Rep. No. 94-1558, p. 1 (1976). Merely subjecting civil rights plaintiffs to the settlement provision of Rule 68 does not curtail their access to the courts, or significantly deter them from bringing suit. Application of Rule 68 will serve as a disincentive for the plaintiff's attorney to continue litigation after the defendant makes a settlement offer. There is no evidence, however, that Congress, in considering § 1988, had any thought that civil rights claims were to be on any different footing from other civil claims insofar as settlement is concerned. Indeed, Congress made clear its concern that civil rights plaintiffs not be penalized for "helping to lessen docket congestion" by settling their cases out of court. See H.R. Rep. No. 94-1558, supra, at 7.

Moreover, Rule 68's policy of encouraging settlements is neutral, favoring neither plaintiffs nor defendants; it expresses a clear policy of favoring settlement of all lawsuits. Civil rights plaintiffs—along with other plaintiffs—who reject an offer more favorable than what is thereafter recovered at trial will not recover attorney's fees for services performed after the offer is rejected. But, since the Rule is neutral, many civil rights plaintiffs will benefit from the offers of settlement encouraged by Rule 68. Some plaintiffs will receive compensation in settlement where, on trial, they might not have recovered, or would have recovered less than what was offered. And, even for those who would prevail at trial, settlement will provide them with compensation at an earlier date without the burdens, stress, and time of litigation. In short, settlements rather than litigation will serve the interests of plaintiffs as well as defendants.

To be sure, application of Rule 68 will require plaintiffs to "think very hard" about whether continued litigation is worthwhile; that is precisely what Rule 68 contemplates. This effect of Rule 68, however, is in no sense inconsistent with the congressional policies underlying § 1983 and § 1988. Section 1988 authorizes courts to award only "reasonable" attorney's fees to prevailing parties. In Hensley v. Eckerhart, supra, we held that "the most critical factor" in determining a reasonable fee "is the degree of success obtained." Id. at 436. We specifically noted that prevailing at trial "may say little about whether the expenditure of counsel's time was reasonable in relation to the success achieved." Ibid. In a case where a rejected settlement offer exceeds the ultimate recovery, the plaintiff—although technically the prevailing party—has not received any monetary benefits from the postoffer services of his attorney. This case presents a good example: the $139,692 in postoffer legal services resulted in a recovery $8,000 less than petitioners' settlement offer. Given Congress' focus on the success achieved, we are not persuaded that shifting the postoffer costs to respondent in these circumstances would in any sense thwart its intent under § 1988.

Rather than "cutting against the grain" of § 1988, as the Court of Appeals held, we are convinced that applying Rule 68 in the context of a § 1983 action is consistent with the policies and objectives of § 1988. Section 1988 encourages plaintiffs to bring meritorious civil rights suits; Rule 68 simply encourages settlements. There is nothing incompatible in these two objectives.

Congress, of course, was well aware of Rule 68 when it enacted § 1988, and included attorney's fees as part of recoverable costs. The plain language of Rule 68 and § 1988 subjects such fees to the cost-shifting provision of Rule 68. Nothing revealed in our review of the policies underlying § 1988 constitutes "the necessary clear expression of congressional intent" required "to exempt . . . [the] statute from the operation of" Rule 68. Califano v. Yamasaki, 442 U.S. 682, 700 (1979). We hold that petitioners are not liable for costs of $139,692 incurred by respondent after petitioners' offer of settlement.

The judgment of the Court of Appeals is *Reversed*.

JUSTICE POWELL, concurring.

In Delta Airlines, Inc. v. August, 450 U.S. 346 (1981), the offer under Rule 68 stated that it was *"in the amount of $450, which shall include attorney's fees,* together with costs accrued to date." Id. at 365. In a brief concurring opinion, I expressed the view that this offer did not comport with the Rule's requirements. It seemed to me that an offer of judgment should consist of two identified components: (i) the substantive relief proposed, and (ii) costs, including a reasonable attorney's fee. The amount of the fee ultimately should be within the discretion of the court if the offer is accepted. In questioning the form of the offer in *Delta,* I was influenced in part by the fact that it was a Title VII case. I concluded that the "'costs' component of a Rule 68 offer of judgment in a Title VII case must include reasonable attorney's fees accrued to the date of the offer." Id. at 363. My view, however, as to the specificity of the "substantive relief" component of the offer did not depend solely on the fact that *Delta* was a Title VII case.

No other Justice joined my *Delta* concurrence. The Court's decision was upon a different ground. Although I think it the better practice for the offer of judgment expressly to identify the components, it is important to have a Court for a clear interpretation of Rule 68. I noted in *Delta* that "parties to litigation and the public as a whole have an interest—often an overriding one—in settlement rather than exhaustion of protracted court proceedings." Ibid. The purpose of Rule 68 is to "facilitat[e] the early resolution of marginal suits in which the defendant perceives the claim to be without merit, and the plaintiff recognizes its speculative nature." Ibid. See also id. at 363, n.1. We have now agreed as to what specifically is required by Rule 68.

Accordingly, I join the opinion of the Court.

JUSTICE REHNQUIST, concurring.

In Delta Airlines, Inc. v. August, 450 U.S. 346 (1981), I expressed in dissent the view that the term "costs" in Rule 68 did not include attorney's fees. Further examination of the question has convinced me that this view was wrong, and I therefore join the opinion of the Chief Justice. Cf. McGrath v. Kristensen, 340 U.S. 162, 176 (1950) (Jackson, J. concurring).

JUSTICE BRENNAN, with whom JUSTICE MARSHALL and JUSTICE BLACKMUN join, dissenting.

The Court's reasoning is wholly inconsistent with the history and structure of the Federal Rules, and its application to the over 100 attorney's fees statutes enacted by Congress will produce absurd variations in Rule 68's operation based on nothing more than picayune differences in statutory phraseology. Neither Congress nor the drafters of the Rules could possibly have intended such inexplicable variations in settlement incentives. Moreover, the Court's interpretation will "seriously undermine the purposes behind the attorney's fees provisions" of the civil rights laws, Delta Air Lines, Inc. v. August, 450 U.S. 346, 378 (1981) (Rehnquist, J., dissenting)—provisions imposed by Congress pursuant to § 5 of the Fourteenth Amendment. Today's decision therefore violates the most basic limitations on our rulemaking authority as set forth in the Rules Enabling Act, 28 U.S.C. § 2072, and as summarized in Alyeska Pipeline Co. v. Wilderness Society, 421 U.S. 240 (1975). Finally, both Congress and the Judicial Conference of the United States have been engaged for years in considering possible amendments to Rule 68 that would bring attorney's fees within the operation of the Rule. That process strongly suggests that Rule 68 has not previously been viewed as governing fee awards, and it illustrates the wisdom of deferring to other avenues of amending Rule 68 rather than ourselves engaging in "standardless judicial lawmaking." Delta Air Lines, Inc. v. August, supra, at 378 (Rehnquist, J., dissenting)....

For a number of reasons, "costs" as that term is used in the Federal Rules should be interpreted uniformly in accordance with the definition of costs set forth in § 1920:

First. The limited history of the costs provisions in the Federal Rules suggests that the drafters intended "costs" to mean only taxable costs traditionally allowed under the common law or pursuant to the statutory predecessor of § 1920....

Second. The rules provide that "costs" may automatically be taxed by the clerk of the court on one day's notice, Fed. Rule Civ. Proc. 54(d)—

strongly suggesting that "costs" were intended to refer only to those routine, readily determinable charges that could appropriately be left to a clerk, and as to which a single day's notice of settlement would be appropriate. Attorney's fees, which are awardable only by the *court* and which frequently entail lengthy disputes and hearings, obviously do not fall within that category.

Third. When particular provisions of the Federal Rules are *intended* to encompass attorney's fees, they do so *explicitly.* Eleven different provisions of the Rules authorize a court to award attorney's fees as "expenses" in particular circumstances, demonstrating that the drafters knew the difference, and intended a difference, between "costs," "expenses," and "attorney's fees."

Fourth. With the exception of one recent Court of Appeals opinion and two recent District Court opinions, the Court can point to no authority suggesting that courts or attorneys have ever viewed the cost-shifting provisions of Rule 68 as including attorney's fees. . . .

Fifth. We previously have held that words and phrases in the Federal Rules must be given a consistent usage and be read *in pari materia,* reasoning that to do otherwise would "attribute a schizophrenic intent to the drafters." Id. at 353. Applying the Court's "plain language" approach consistently throughout the Rules, however, would produce absurd results that would turn statutes like § 1988 on their heads and plainly violate the restraints imposed on judicial rulemaking by the Rules Enabling Act. . . .

Sixth. As with all of the Federal Rules, the drafters intended Rule 68 to have a uniform, consistent application in *all* proceedings in federal court. In accordance with this intent, Rule 68 should be interpreted to provide uniform, consistent incentives "to encourage the settlement of litigation." Delta Air Lines, Inc. v. August, supra, at 352. Yet today's decision will lead to dramatically different settlement incentives depending on minor variations in the phraseology of the underlying fees-award statutes—distinctions that would appear to be nothing short of irrational and for which the Court has no plausible explanation.

Congress has enacted well over 100 attorney's fees statutes, many of which would appear to be affected by today's decision. As the Appendix to this dissent illustrates, Congress has employed a variety of slightly different wordings in these statutes. It sometimes has referred to the awarding of "attorney's fees *as part of* the costs," to "costs *including* attorney's fees," and to "attorney's fees and *other* litigation costs." Under the "plain language" approach of today's decision, Rule 68 will operate to *include* the potential loss of otherwise recoverable attorney's fees as an incentive to settlement in litigation under these statutes. But Congress frequently has referred in other statutes to the awarding of "costs *and* a reasonable attorney's fee," of "costs *together* with a reasonable attorney's fee," or simply of "attorney's fees" without reference to costs. Under the Court's "plain language" analysis, Rule 68 obviously will *not* include the potential loss of otherwise recoverable attorney's fees as a settlement incentive in litigation under these statutes because they do not refer to fees "as" costs.

The result is to sanction a senseless patchwork of fee shifting that flies in the face of the fundamental purpose of the Federal Rules—the provision of uniform and consistent procedure in federal courts. . . . [M]any statutes contain several fees-award provisions governing actions arising under different subsections, and the phraseology of these provisions sometimes differs slightly from section to section. It is simply preposterous to think that Congress or the drafters of the Rules intended to sanction differing applications of Rule 68 depending on which particular subsection of, *inter alia*, the Privacy Act of 1974, the Home Owners' Loan Act of 1933, the Outer Continental Shelf Lands Act Amendments of 1978, or the Interstate Commerce Act the plaintiff happened to invoke. . . .

Rule 68 . . . is not "sensitive" at all to the merits of an action and to antidiscrimination policy. It is a mechanical *per se* provision automatically shifting "costs" incurred after an offer is rejected, and it deprives a district court of *all* discretion with respect to the matter by using "the strongest verb of its type known to the English language—'must.'" Delta Air Lines, Inc. v. August, supra, at 369. The potential for conflict between § 1988 and Rule 68 could not be more apparent.

Of course, a civil rights plaintiff who *unreasonably* fails to accept a settlement offer, and who thereafter recovers less than the proffered amount in settlement, is barred under § 1988 itself from recovering fees for unproductive work performed in the wake of the rejection. This is because "the extent of a plaintiff's success is *a* crucial factor in determining the proper amount of an award of attorney's fees," 461 U.S. at 440 (emphasis added). . . .

But the results under § 1988 and Rule 68 will *not* always be congruent, because § 1988 mandates the careful consideration of a broad range of other factors and accords appropriate leeway to the district court's informed discretion. . . .

The Court argues, however, that its interpretation of Rule 68 "is neutral, favoring neither plaintiffs nor defendants." This contention is also plainly wrong. As the Judicial Conference Advisory Committee on the Federal Rules of Civil Procedure has noted twice in recent years, Rule 68 "is a 'one-way street,' available only to those defending against claims and not to claimants." Interpreting Rule 68 in its current version to include attorney's fees will lead to a number of skewed settlement incentives that squarely conflict with Congress' intent. To discuss but one example, Rule 68 allows an offer to be made any time after the complaint is filed and gives the plaintiff only 10 days to accept or reject. The Court's decision inevitably will encourage defendants who know they have violated the law to make "low-ball" offers immediately after suit is filed and before plaintiffs have been able to obtain the information they are entitled to by way of discovery to assess the strength of their claims and the reasonableness of the offers. The result will put severe pressure on plaintiffs to settle on the basis of inadequate information in order to avoid the risk of bearing all of their fees even if reasonable discovery might reveal that the defendants were subject to far greater liability. Indeed, because Rule 68 offers may be made recurrently without limitation, defendants will be well advised to make ever-slightly larger offers throughout the discovery process and before plaintiffs have conducted all reasonably necessary discovery.

This sort of so-called "incentive" is fundamentally incompatible with Congress' goals. Congress intended for "private citizens . . . to be able to assert their civil rights" and for "those who violate the Nation's fundamental laws" not to be able "to proceed with impunity." Accordingly, civil rights plaintiffs "'appear before the court cloaked in a mantle of public interest'"; to promote the "*vigorous* enforcement of modern civil rights legislation," Congress has directed that such "private attorneys general" shall not "be deterred from bringing good faith actions to vindicate the fundamental rights here involved." Yet requiring plaintiffs to make wholly uninformed decisions on settlement offers, at the risk of *automatically* losing all of their postoffer fees no matter what the circumstances and notwithstanding the "excellent" results they might achieve after the full picture emerges, will work just such a deterrent effect.

Other difficulties will follow from the Court's decision. For example, if a plaintiff recovers less money than was offered before trial but obtains potentially far-reaching injunctive or declaratory relief, it is altogether unclear how the Court intends judges to go about quantifying the "value" of the plaintiff's success. . . .

Indeed, the judgment of the Court of Appeals below turned on its determination that an interpretation of Rule 68 to include attorney's fees is beyond the pale of the judiciary's rulemaking authority. Congress has delegated its authority to this Court "to prescribe by general rules . . . the practice and procedure of the district courts and courts of appeals of the United States in civil actions." 28 U.S.C. § 2072. This grant is limited, however, by the condition that "[s]uch rules shall not abridge, enlarge or modify any substantive right." Ibid. The right to attorney's fees is "substantive" under any reasonable definition of that term. Section 1988 was enacted pursuant to § 5 of the Fourteenth Amendment, and the House and Senate Reports recurrently emphasized that "fee awards are an integral part of the *remedies* necessary to obtain . . . compliance" with the civil rights laws and to redress violations. Statutory attorney's fees remedies such as that set forth in § 1988 "are far more like new causes of action tied to specific rights than like background procedural rules governing any and all litigation." Hensley v. Eckerhart, 461 U.S. at 443, n.2 (Brennan, J., concurring in part and dissenting in part). See also 720 F.2d at 479 (§ 1988 "does not make the litigation process more accurate and efficient for both parties; even more clearly than the statute of limitations [at issue in Ragan v. Merchants Transfer & Warehouse Co., 337 U.S. 530 (1949)], it is designed instead to achieve a substantive objective—compliance with the civil rights laws").

As construed by the Court today, Rule 68 surely will operate to "abridge" and to "modify" this statutory right to reasonable attorney's fees. "The test must be whether a rule really regulates *procedure*—the judicial process for enforcing rights and duties recognized by substantive law and for justly administering remedy and redress for disregard or infraction of them," or instead operates to abridge a substantive right "in the guise of regulating procedure." Sibbach v. Wilson & Co., 312 U.S. 1, 10, 14 (1941) (emphasis added); see also Hanna v. Plumer, 380 U.S. 460, 464-465 (1965). Unlike those provisions of the Federal Rules that explicitly authorize an award of attorney's fees, Rule 68 is not addressed to bad-faith or unreasonable litigation conduct. The courts always have had inherent authority to assess fees against parties who act "in bad faith, vexatiously, wantonly, or for oppressive reasons," Alyeska Pipeline Service Co. v. Wilderness Society, 421 U.S. at 258-259, and the assessment of fees against parties whose *unreasonable* conduct has violated the rules of litigation falls comfortably into the courts' authority to administer "remedy and redress for disregard or infraction" of those rules, Sibbach v. Wilson & Co., supra, at 14. Rule 68, on the other hand, contains no reasonableness component. As interpreted by the Court, it will operate to divest a prevailing plaintiff of fees to which he otherwise might be entitled under the reasonableness standard simply because he guessed wrong, or because he did not have all information reasonably necessary to evaluate the offer, or because of unforeseen changes in the law or evidence after the offer. The Court's interpretation of Rule 68 therefore clearly collides with the congressionally prescribed substantive standards of § 1988, and the Rules Enabling Act requires that the Court's interpretation give way.

Note: Evans v. Jeff D., 475 U.S. 717 (1986)

A Legal Services lawyer filed a class action against Idaho officials responsible for the education and treatment of children who suffer emotional and mental handicaps, alleging deficiencies in both the educational and health facilities for these children. The complaint sought injunctive relief and costs and attorney's fees.

One week before trial, the defendants offered a settlement giving the plaintiffs "virtually all" the injunctive relief they sought. The offer was conditioned on a waiver of any claim for fees and costs. Holding that approval of a settlement with this condition was within the trial court's discretion, the Supreme Court relied specifically on Marek v. Chesny:

> [We] believe that a general proscription against negotiated waiver of attorney's fees in exchange for a settlement on the merits would itself impede vindication of civil rights, at least in some cases, by reducing the attractiveness of settlement. Of particular relevance in this regard is our recent decision in Marek v. Chesny, 473 U.S. 1 (1985). . . . To promote both settlement and civil rights, we implicitly acknowledged in Marek v. Chesny the possibility of a tradeoff between merits relief and attorney's fees when

we upheld the defendant's lump-sum offer to settle the entire civil rights action, including any liability for fees and costs.

In approving the package offer in Marek v. Chesny we recognized that a rule prohibiting the comprehensive negotiation of all outstanding issues in a pending case might well preclude the settlement of a substantial number of cases:

> If defendants are not allowed to make lump-sum offers that would, if accepted, represent their total liability, they would understandably be reluctant to make settlement offers. As the Court of Appeals observed, "many a defendant would be unwilling to make a binding settlement offer on terms that left it exposed to liability for attorney's fees in whatever amount the court might fix on motion of the plaintiff." 720 F.2d, at 477. [Id. at 6-7.]

. . . Most defendants are unlikely to settle unless the cost of the predicted judgment, discounted by its probability, plus the transaction costs of further litigation, are greater than the cost of the settlement package. If fee waivers cannot be negotiated, the settlement package must either contain an attorney's fee component of potentially large and typically uncertain magnitude, or else the parties must agree to have the fee fixed by the court. Although either of these alternatives may well be acceptable in many cases, there surely is a significant number in which neither alternative will be as satisfactory as a decision to try the entire case.[23]

The adverse impact of removing attorney's fees and costs from bargaining might be tolerable if the uncertainty introduced into settlement negotiations were small. But it is not. The defendants' potential liability for fees in this kind of litigation can be as significant as, and sometimes even more significant than, their potential liability on the merits. This proposition is most dramatically illustrated by the fee awards of district courts in actions seeking only monetary relief.[24] Although it is more difficult to compare fee awards with the cost of injunctive relief, in part because the cost of such relief is seldom reported in written opinions, here too attorney's fees

23. It is unrealistic to assume that the defendant's offer on the merits would be unchanged by redaction of the provision waiving fees. If it were, the defendant's incentive to settle would be diminished because of the risk that attorney's fees, when added to the original merits offer, will exceed the discounted value of the expected judgment plus litigation costs. If, as is more likely, the defendant lowered the value of its offer on the merits to provide a cushion against the possibility of a large fee award, the defendant's offer on the merits will in many cases be less than the amount to which the plaintiff feels himself entitled, thereby inclining him to reject the settlement. Of course, to the extent that the merits offer is somewhere between these two extremes the incentive of both sides to settle is dampened, albeit to a lesser degree with respect to each party.

24. See, e.g., Rivera v. Riverside, 763 F.2d 1580, 1581-1583 (9th Cir. 1985) (city ordered to pay victorious civil rights plaintiffs $245,456.25 following a trial in which they recovered a total of $33,350 in damages), *cert. granted*, 474 U.S. 917 (1985); Cunningham v. City of McKeesport, 753 F.2d 262, 269 (3d Cir. 1985) (city ordered to pay some $35,000 in attorney's fees in a case in which judgment for the plaintiff was entered in the amount of $17,000) [vacated by 478 U.S. 1015 (1986)]; Copeland v. Marshall, 641 F.2d 880, 891 (1980) (en banc) ($160,000 attorney's fees awarded for obtaining $33,000 judgment); Skoda v. Fontani, 646 F.2d 1193, 1194 (7th Cir.), *remanded to* 519 F. Supp. 309, 310 (N.D. Ill. 1981) ($6,086.12 attorney's fees awarded to obtain $1 recovery). Cf. Marek v. Chesny, 473 U.S., at 7 ($171,692.47 in claimed attorney's fees and costs to obtain $60,000 damages judgment).

awarded by district courts have "frequently outrun the economic benefits ultimately obtained by successful litigants." 122 Cong. Rec. 31472 (1976) (remarks of Sen. Kennedy).[25] Indeed, in this very case "[c]ounsel for defendants view[ed] the risk of an attorney's fees award as the most significant liability in the case." Brief for Defendants in Support of Approval of Compromise in Jeff D. v. Evans, No. 80-4091 (D. Idaho), p.5. Undoubtedly there are many other civil rights actions in which potential liability for attorney's fees may overshadow the potential cost of relief on the merits and darken prospects for settlement if fees cannot be negotiated.

475 U.S. at 732-735.

In dissent, Justices Brennan, Marshall, and Blackmun argued:

> . . . As summed up by the Legal Ethics Committee of the District of Columbia Bar:
>
> > Defense counsel . . . are in a uniquely favorable position when they condition settlement on the waiver of the statutory fee: They make a demand for a benefit that the plaintiff's lawyer cannot resist as a matter of ethics and one in which the plaintiff has no interest and therefore will not resist. [Op. No. 147, reprinted in 113 Daily Washington Reporter, at 394.]
>
> . . . And, of course, once fee waivers are permitted, defendants will seek them as a matter of course, since this is a logical way to minimize liability. Indeed, defense counsel would be remiss *not* to demand that the plaintiff waive statutory attorney's fees. A lawyer who proposes to have his client pay more than is necessary to end litigation has failed to fulfill his fundamental duty zealously to represent the best interests of his client. Because waiver of fees does not affect the plaintiff, a settlement offer is not made less attractive to the plaintiff if it includes a demand that statutory fees be waived. Thus, in the future, we must expect settlement offers routinely to contain demands for waivers of statutory fees.
>
> The cumulative effect this practice will have on the civil rights bar is evident. It does not denigrate the high ideals that motivate many civil rights practitioners to recognize that lawyers are in the business of practicing law, and that, like other business people, they are and must be concerned with earning a living.[13] The conclusion that permitting fee waivers will seriously impair the ability of civil rights plaintiffs to obtain legal assistance is embarrassingly obvious.

25. See, e.g., Grendel's Den, Inc. v. Larkin, 749 F.2d 945, 960 (1st Cir. 1984) (awarding $113,640.85 in fees and expenses for successful challenge to law zoning liquor establishments in Larkin v. Grendel's Den, 459 U.S. 116 (1982)).

13. See Earl Johnson, Jr., Lawyers' Choice: A Theoretical Appraisal of Litigation Investment Decisions, 15 Law & Soc. Rev. 567 (1980-1981) (concluding that "fee for service" lawyers will withdraw resources from a given case when total expected costs exceed total expected benefits); Kraus, 29 Vill. L. Rev., at 637 ("No matter how sophisticated the analysis of attorney responses becomes, the conclusion remains that the more we decrease the reasonable expectation of Fees Act awards, the less likely it is that Fees Act cases will be initiated.").

Notes and Questions

1. *The Catalyst Theory of Prevailing Parties.* In *Evans*, the settlement offer was conditioned on the waiver of any claim to attorneys' fees. Can a party obtain attorneys' fees when a civil rights case settles and the settlement agreement does not include a fee waiver clause? In Roberson v. Giuliani, 346 F.3d 75 (2d Cir. 2003), plaintiffs challenged the legality of various policies for the handling of applications for food stamps, Medicaid, and public assistance in New York City. The City agreed to a settlement implementing a variety of improvements in its procedures and the order dismissing the case provided that the court would "retain jurisdiction over the settlement agreement for enforcement purposes." Id. at 78. Plaintiffs subsequently moved for over $140,000 in attorneys' fees and costs as "prevailing parties" under 42 U.S.C. § 1988, on the theory that their lawsuit was the "catalyst" in forcing the City to change its procedures.

This was a bold move coming in the wake of the Supreme Court's decision in Buckhannon Bd. & Care Home, Inc. v. W. Va. Dep't of Health & Human Res., 532 U.S. 598 (2001) (rejecting "catalyst theory" of defining prevailing parties under § 1988 and holding that to "prevail" requires a "judicially sanctioned change in the legal relationship of the parties . . . [a] *judicial imprimatur*"). Citing *Buckhannon*, the district court rejected the request for attorneys' fees. However, the Second Circuit reversed, holding that retaining jurisdiction to enforce a settlement agreement is a sufficient judicial imprimatur to confer prevailing party status on the plaintiffs. *Roberson*, 346 F.3d at 82-83. The court joined five other circuits "in concluding that judicial action other than a judgment on the merits or a consent decree can support an award of attorneys' fees, so long as such action carries with it sufficient judicial imprimatur." Id. at 81 (citing cases). Cf. Torres v. Walker, 356 F.3d 238, 244-245 (2d Cir. 2004) (stipulated dismissal containing no provision reserving jurisdiction for court to monitor compliance with settlement lacked "sufficient judicial imprimatur" to warrant application of Prison Litigation Reform Act's fee cap for prevailing parties).

Still, public interest lawyers had reason to worry following the Court's rejection of the "catalyst theory" in *Buckhannon*. As an amicus brief filed in the case observed:

> The abolition of the catalyst rule would be particularly severe since the attorneys may lose their fees and expenses by action of the defendant at any time during the litigation. The case can be litigated for years. If the defendant then moots the case by granting relief, even when the case is on appeal or in this Court, the abolition of the catalyst rule would mean all the fees and expenses would be lost. Few attorneys would be willing or able to take such a risk.
>
> Many of the cases brought under fee-shifting statutes, such as environmental cases, involve major, complex litigation requiring substantial resources. The clients in this type of litigation rarely can pay any significant

portion of the fees or costs. Hundreds or thousands of hours and tens or hundreds of thousands of dollars may need to be expended.

The *Laidlaw* case is a good example. [Friends of the Earth v. Laidlaw Envtl. Servs. (TOC), Inc., 528 U.S. 167 (2000).] *Laidlaw*, a Clean Water Act case against a private polluter, was brought in June 1992. Since the beginning of this case, over eight years ago, plaintiffs' attorneys' have expended approximately 9,000 hours and $230,000 in expenses on this case. While the case was in this Court, the defendant claimed that the case had become moot because the incinerator had been dismantled. This Court remanded the issue of mootness to the lower courts for resolution. If the case is found moot, and the catalyst rule is abolished, plaintiffs' counsel would be denied fees over eight years after the case was brought.

2000 WL 1701809. See also *Buckhannon*, 532 U.S. at 623 (Ginsburg, J., dissenting) ("[T]he Court's constricted definition of 'prevailing party,' and consequent rejection of the 'catalyst theory,' [will] impede access to court for the less well heeled, and shrink the incentive Congress created for the enforcement of federal law by private attorneys general.").

In 2007, Congress passed the OPEN Government Act. According to this new law, at least with respect to actions to force disclosure of government records under the Freedom of Information Act, the catalyst theory has been revived. The statute provides:

> (i) The court may assess against the United States reasonable attorney fees and other litigation costs reasonably incurred in any case under this section in which the complainant has substantially prevailed. (ii) For purposes of this subparagraph, a complainant has substantially prevailed if the complainant has obtained relief through either—
>
> (I) a judicial order, or an enforceable written agreement or consent decree; or
>
> (II) a voluntary or unilateral change in position by the agency, if the complainant's claim is not insubstantial.

5 U.S.C. § 552(a)(4)(E). See also Wildlands CPR v. U.S. Forest Serv., 558 F. Supp. 2d 1096, 1097-1098 (D. Mont. 2008) (analyzing the new statute).

2. *The Defendant/Offeror's Attorneys' Fees.* In *Marek*, the Court was not presented with the question of whether Rule 68 requires a plaintiff to pay *defendant's* attorneys' fees, in addition to paying defendant's costs and losing the right to recover his own attorney's fees under 42 U.S.C. § 1988. The question has resurfaced in cases similar to *Marek*, where prevailing party fee-shifting statutes define attorneys' fees "as costs." The majority position is that Rule 68 does not require a plaintiff to pay the defendant's attorneys' fees. As the Ninth Circuit has recently held:

> *Marek* holds that "the term 'costs' in Rule 68 was intended to refer to all costs *'properly awardable'* under the relevant substantive statute or other authority." *Marek*, 473 U.S. at 9 (emphasis added). Where the substantive statute permits a "prevailing party" to recover attorneys' fees as costs, a

> defendant who has not "prevailed" may not recover attorneys' fees pursuant to Rule 68. Such costs are not "properly awardable" under the relevant statute.

Champion Produce, Inc. v. Ruby Robinson Co., 342 F.3d 1016, 1029 (9th Cir. 2003). See also Harbor Motor Co. v. Arnell Chevrolet-Geo, Inc., 265 F.3d 638 (7th Cir. 2001) (same); Crossman v. Marcoccio, 806 F.2d 329 (1st Cir. 1986) (same); O'Brien v. City of Greers Ferry, 873 F.2d 1115 (8th Cir. 1989). But see Jordan v. Time, Inc., 111 F.3d 102, 105 (11th Cir. 1997) (because plaintiff "did not obtain a judgment more favorable than the ones contained in Time's offers of judgment, Jordan must pay Time's fees and costs" where the underlying statute allowed prevailing party fees "as part of the costs").

3. *A Lawyer's Competence: Negotiation and Litigation*. The Rule-driven encouragement of settlement surely reflects some ambivalence toward the adversary system and elaborate due process. Does the prevalence of settlement as an alternative to trial modify your image of the lawyer who chooses litigation as a career? To what degree are the skills of a negotiator different from those of a trial advocate? Consider these words of advice in a practice manual, directed toward mediation, but generally applicable to settlement negotiations:

> Practice Tip: For settlement to occur at a mediation conference, litigators have to abandon their well-developed confrontational mode of courtroom behavior and speech. Instead, it is essential that counsel open lines of effective communication with the opposing party. . . . Negotiation entails a totally different focus than the historical objective of "winning."
>
> Adroit negotiators know, or have learned to use non-blaming language when speaking to the opposing counsel or principal. To the contrary, a wise negotiator knows to discuss the mutual dependencies and common interests of the ostensibly hostile interests that are present at the bargaining table.

Jerome S. Levy and Robert C. Prather, Sr., Texas Practice Guide, ADR Strategies 3:13 (1998).

On the other hand, another practice tip in the same section advises coming to the negotiation with a carefully prepared game plan, a "thorough understanding of the undisputed facts," and "an appreciation of where the parties are in terms of their perceptions on the disputed facts and law." Id. This sounds a lot like what litigators do.

4. *Controversy Over Rule 68*. As explained in Gudenkauf v. Stauffer Comm. Inc., 158 F.3d 1074, 1083-1084 (10th Cir. 1998), *Marek* has been at least partially superseded by law. As the Tenth Circuit explained in a Title VII case:

> [T]he Supreme Court held in Marek v. Chesny, 473 U.S. 1, 105 S. Ct. 3012, 87 L. Ed. 2d 1 (1985), that under Rule 68, a successful civil rights plaintiff could be denied attorney's fees otherwise available under subsection (k). The

> legislative history of the [Civil Rights Act of 1991] specifically disapproved of the *Marek* decision and proposed to amend subsection (k) to avoid its application. "*Marek* is particularly problematic in the context of Title VII, because it may impede private actions, which Congress has relied upon for enforcement of the statute's guarantees and advancement of the public's interest." H.R. Rep. No. 102-40(I) at 82. Although subsection (k) ultimately remained unchanged in this regard, the proposed amendment was adopted in the language of subsection (g)(2)(B). Congress therefore clearly did not intend a district court to reduce a mixed motives plaintiff's fee award on the basis of a rejected pretrial settlement.

For an argument that current Rule 68 actually is an ineffective inducement to settle, and that it may increase the likelihood of trial or have an ambiguous result, see David A. Anderson, Improving Settlement Devices: Rule 68 and Beyond, 23 J. Legal Stud. 225 (1994).

One potential harshness of Rule 68 lies in its mandatory nature. For example, in Webb v. James, 147 F.3d 617 (7th Cir. 1998), the court held that a Rule 68 offer is not an ordinary contract and that the contract doctrine of recission is inappropriate with respect to Rule 68 offers. The Rule requires that once an offer is accepted and properly filed, the clerk "shall enter judgment," thereby foreclosing any exercise of discretion to allow recission. The sole remedy available would be to pursue relief from judgment under Rule 60(b). Given this strict construction of Rule 68, it may not be surprising that the same court also held that a defendant could not take advantage of Rule 68's cost-shifting requirement where the defendant's $10,000 settlement offer, "to be divided among all three plaintiffs," was not apportioned on an individualized basis. Gavoni v. Dobbs House, Inc., 164 F.3d 1071 (7th Cir. 1999). The jury had awarded a total of $6,500 to the plaintiffs, apportioning $2,000, $2,000, and $2,500 among them. Plaintiffs had requested $825,000 ($230,000; $320,000; $275,000). Id. at 1073. For an interesting discussion of the duty to specifically apportion Rule 68 offers in multi-defendant, multi-claim actions, see Le v. Univ. of Pa., 321 F.3d 403 (3d Cir. 2003) (holding apportionment not always necessary in suit for national origin discrimination and retaliation).

In *Webb*, the parties disagreed about the meaning of the settlement. What if the defendant's Rule 68 settlement offer contains an error—can the offer be revoked before plaintiff accepts? Courts remain divided on this question. Compare Perkins v. U.S. West Commc'ns, 138 F.3d 336 (8th Cir. 1998) (offer is irrevocable during ten-day acceptance period provided by Rule 68 even if trial court grants summary judgment), and Richardson v. Nat'l R.R. Passenger Corp., 49 F.3d 760 (D.C. Cir. 1995) (Rule 68 offer is irrevocable during ten-day acceptance period, but if the offer is induced by misconduct on the part of plaintiff, judgment may be modified or withdrawn under Rule 60(b)), with Colonial Penn Ins. Co. v. Coil, 887 F.2d 1236 (4th Cir. 1989) (permitting revocation of offer induced by fraud), and Cesar v. Rubie's Costume Co., 219 F.R.D. 257 (E.D.N.Y. 2004) (permitting revocation where defendant's offer contained a clerical error affecting the amount and scope of the settlement) (citing and following Fisher v. Stolaruk Corp., 110 F.R.D. 74 (E.D. Mich. 1986) (articulating test for revocation where mistake in offer is substantial, material to acceptance, not the result of negligent conduct by defendant, and where revocation will still leave plaintiff in the same position prior to the mistake).

What about vague offers—especially offers that fail to quantify damages? Are they valid if plaintiff accepts? The Fifth Circuit has recently upheld a district court's refusal to enter judgment on an offer specifying that the attorneys would confer and agree "upon reasonable compensation for Plaintiff's claimed 'actual damages,' and that said amount is added to this Offer of Judgment." Basha v. Mitsubishi Motor Credit of Am., Inc., 336 F.3d 451, 454 (5th Cir. 2003) (mutual assent is absent and "such a vague offer of judgment did not provide Basha with a clear baseline to evaluate the risks of continued litigation").

5. *Settlement in Complex Litigation.* Settlement may be a more complicated prospect when there are multiple parties with interlocking interests. For an interesting analysis of the impact of joint and several liability on settlement—especially of rules giving a right of contribution to a settling defendant—in cases involving multiple defendants, see Lewis A. Kornhauser and Richard L. Revesz, Settlements Under Joint and Several Liability, 68 N.Y.U. L. Rev. 427 (1993). For a fuller discussion of the issue of settlement in the class action context, see Chapter 6, especially Amchem v. Windsor Products.

6. *Enforcement of Settlement Agreements and Federal Court Jurisdiction.* To understand the enforcement of a settlement agreement, one must consider that the agreement is a private contract between the parties, enforceable under the applicable law of contract. As such, a federal court lacks subject matter jurisdiction over any dispute that may arise over the enforcement of the settlement agreement, unless the conditions of diversity jurisdiction are met. See Kokkonen v. Guardian Life Ins. Co. of America, 511 U.S. 375 (1994). If the settlement produces a dismissal of the action under Rule 41(a)(2), however, the court may make the parties' compliance with the settlement agreement part of its order, and thereby retain jurisdiction over the enforcement. If dismissal occurs pursuant to Rule 41(a)(1)(ii), the court can, with consent of the parties, incorporate the settlement agreement in the order, and thereby retain jurisdiction over the enforcement. Otherwise, the parties must go to state court to enforce the settlement agreement, even if the settlement is of a suit pending in federal court.

7. *Conflicts of Interest in Settlement Negotiations.* An obvious potential problem is that settlement may in some cases prove more attractive to plaintiffs' lawyers than to their clients. Particularly in class action suits, or in other cases in which the lawyers are compensated under a contingency fee arrangement, the temptation to settle early rather than pursue the litigation may be overwhelming. Can you see why? If the lawyer gives in to the temptation, however, the settlement may be vulnerable to subsequent attack, as the disappointed plaintiffs challenge the fairness of the settle-

ment and the adequacy of representation. In egregious cases, it also may expose the lawyers who negotiated the settlement to malpractice suits.

8. *Settlement and Sentiment.* Most discussions of settlement incentives tend to assume that the parties' settlement decisions are based primarily on rational assessments of the expected value of trial, of the likely litigation costs, and of the likely outcome of trial. Might parties also weigh other factors not captured by this economic model? See Russell Korobkin and Chris Guthrie, Psychological Barriers to Litigation Settlement: An Experimental Approach, 93 Mich. L. Rev. 107 (1994) (concluding that individuals do not always behave in the rational way that economic models assume, insofar as psychological processes affect how they perceive, understand, and respond to settlement offers).

The Texas Practice Guide makes the following recommendations:

> PRACTICE TIP: Most litigators have experienced an instance in which a client never advised the attorney of a hidden agenda, such as wanting a portion of the defendant's stock or wishing to "punish" the miscreant. The easiest (and most obvious) manner of clarifying such matters is to ask the following two pointed questions:
>
> 1. "Is the amount of money the only issue in this case?"
> 2. "Is there anything other than financial recovery that you want to achieve as a result of this lawsuit?"
>
> If the answer to either of these questions is vague or ambivalent, it is incumbent upon counsel to cross-examine one's own client. The wise lawyer knows to use counseling and interviewing techniques to draw out the client's real objective in the case.
>
> "I understand how important this matter is to you, but at the same time . . . "
>
> . . . "If we are not talking only about money, what would be the best way of settling this case from your point of view?"
>
> "I recognize that you feel strongly about this particular point, but let me ask you if you would feel differently if the other side was willing to compensate you fairly for giving up this point?"
>
> In short, the client should be encouraged not to take a hard and fast bargaining position on points that may come up during the negotiations. . . . This enables counsel to explore possible alternatives. Be creative.
>
> . . . As stated previously, it is incumbent on counsel to be sure that the client understands the critical distinction between "wants" and "needs." Emotion is the driving force at the "wants" level of discussion. Reality is injected into the equation at the "needs" level. It is a perilous undertaking for an attorney to fail to be sure that the client has a realistic understanding of what is to be reasonably expected as an outcome. . . .
>
> PRACTICE TIP: The client's level of expectation plays a major part in the process. If the client's non-negotiable goal is a result at the "want" level, the attorney at some future date may be faced with a State Bar grievance complaint filed by this same client, due to the disparity between the client's expectation and the attorney's expectation of the most likely result at trial. If the attorney cannot convince the client as to the trial value of the case, it may

> be in the lawyer's best interest to promptly withdraw from this particular representation.
>
> To state the obvious, plaintiffs routinely believe that they were the losers in some tragic situation. A corollary to that belief is the misperception that no one else in the history of civilization has ever suffered that type of loss or injury. A threshold consideration is whether a given situation is a tragedy or merely an inconvenience.

Jerome S. Levy and Robert C. Prather Sr., Texas Practice Guide, ADR Strategies 3:10 (1998).

2. The Pretrial Conference — Helpful Judicial Oversight or Unwelcome Coercion?

The pretrial conference is perhaps the only major feature of the federal rules that is an American invention, although even this innovation had an English ancestor in the early oral pleadings, in which the judge joined in the formulation of the issues. Apparently an idea of Judge Edson Sunderland, the pretrial conference was first used in 1929 in the Wayne County Circuit Court in Detroit. When the Federal Rules were drafted in 1938, the pretrial conference under Rule 16 was seen as the culmination of the revised pretrial process. With pleadings assuming the minor role of giving notice of the dispute, and discovery assuming major importance in exploring and developing factual issues, the pretrial conference was the point at which issues were finally to be defined and limited for trial.

The pretrial conference has not been uniformly popular with lawyers, partly because of resistance to possible settlement pressure from the judge and partly because of the additional work it entails. But the Supreme Court upheld the power of a district judge to render a default judgment against a plaintiff for failure of his counsel to attend a pretrial conference. Link v. Wabash R.R. Co., 370 U.S. 626 (1962).

From the first promulgation of the Rules, the practice under Rule 16 has varied enormously from district to district and even among judges in the same courthouse. In 1983, amid concern about abusive discovery, overworked courts, and the role of the passive, impartial judge, the rule-makers overhauled Rule 16 to make it a tool for streamlining the process. Most significantly, the new Rule included the discussion of settlement in the matters to be covered at a pretrial conference (Rule 16(c)).

The 1993 Amendments to Rule 16 went even further in designating the pretrial conference as a major step in the process and as an important settlement moment. Note, for instance, the suggestion in part (c) that "the court may require that a party or its representative be present or reasonably available by telephone in order to consider possible settlement." As the lawyer for a client, when would you want your client to come to a pretrial conference?

In a classic article, Professor Judith Resnik made a case against the increased activity of judges in shaping the case and promoting settlement:

> I believe that the role of judges before adjudication is undergoing a change as substantial as has been recognized in the posttrial phase of public law cases. Today, federal district judges are assigned a case at the time of its filing and assume responsibility for shepherding the case to completion. Judges have described their new tasks as "case management" — hence my term "managerial judges." As managers, judges learn more about cases much earlier than they did in the past. They negotiate with parties about the course, timing, and scope of both pretrial and posttrial litigation. These managerial responsibilities give judges greater power. Yet the restraints that formerly circumscribed judicial authority are conspicuously absent. Managerial judges frequently work beyond the public view, off the record, with no obligation to provide written, reasoned opinions, and out of reach of appellate review.
>
> This new managerial role has emerged for several reasons. One is the creation of pretrial discovery rights. The 1938 Federal Rules of Civil Procedure embodied contradictory mandates: a discovery system ("give your opponent all information relevant to the litigation") was grafted onto American adversarial norms ("protect your client zealously" and therefore "withhold what you can"). In some cases, parties argued about their obligations under the discovery rules; such disputes generated a need for someone to decide pretrial conflicts. Trial judges accepted the assignment and have become mediators, negotiators, and planners — as well as adjudicators. Moreover, once involved in pretrial discovery, many judges became convinced that their presence at other points in a lawsuit's development would be beneficial; supervision of discovery became a conduit for judicial control over all phases of litigation and thus infused lawsuits with the continual presence of the judge-overseer.
>
> Partly because of their new oversight role and partly because of increasing case loads, many judges have become concerned with the volume of their work. To reduce the pressure, judges have turned to efficiency experts who promise "calendar control." Under the experts' guidance, judges have begun to experiment with schemes for speeding the resolution of cases and for persuading litigants to settle rather than try cases whenever possible. During the past decade, enthusiasm for the "managerial movement" has become widespread; what began as an experiment is likely soon to become obligatory. . . .
>
> In the rush to conquer the mountain of work, no one — neither judges, court administrators, nor legal commentators — has assessed whether relying on trial judges for informal dispute resolution and for case management, either before or after trial, is good, bad, or neutral. Little empirical evidence supports the claim that judicial management "works" either to settle cases or to provide cheaper, quicker, or fairer dispositions. Proponents of judicial management have also failed to consider the systemic effects of the shift in judicial role. Management is a new form of "judicial activism," a behavior that usually attracts substantial criticism. Moreover, judicial management may be teaching judges to value their statistics, such as the number of case dispositions, more than they value the quality of their

> dispositions. Finally, because managerial judging is less visible and usually unreviewable, it gives trial courts more authority and at the same time provides litigants with fewer procedural safeguards to protect them from abuse of that authority. In short, managerial judging may be redefining *sub silentio* our standards of what constitutes rational, fair, and impartial adjudication.

Judith Resnik, Managerial Judges, 96 Harv. L. Rev. 374, 378-380 (1982). But see Steven Flanders, Blind Umpires — A Response to Professor Resnik, 35 Hastings L.J. 505 (1984), for a strident disagreement with her cautions about the pretrial conference.

Judge Robert Zampano, after 30 years on the federal bench, described his approach to settlement in an ABA magazine for practitioners. He agreed with Professor Resnik that trial judges should not be case managers, but he thought they should instead become more actively involved in settling cases ("or" support court-annexed ADR). Most of the article is devoted to the subject of its title: Settlement Strategies for Trial Judges. As you read his suggestions, think about the qualities of personality and intellect that the judge is reflecting. Are these the same qualities that make a good trial judge?

Robert Zampano, Settlement Strategies for Trial Judges

Litigation 3 (Fall 1995). Reprinted with permission of the American Bar Association.

Despite the fact that settlement terminates over 90 percent of civil litigation, many trial judges do not conduct meaningful settlement conferences, but instead rely on superficial formulas or simplistic compromises. I am astonished when judges say to me: "If the lawyers refuse to settle the case between themselves, why should I bother?" I am further horrified when I hear that some judges schedule 10 or 15 settlement conferences in a day with the following stereotypical approach to the settlement of most cases: "Ms. Plaintiff's Counsel, what is your demand?" After receiving the answer, the judge turns to opposing counsel and inquires: "Mr. Defense Attorney, what is your offer?" Then with an amazing display of wisdom and mathematical dexterity, the judge announces his decision that a certain figure, usually exactly in the middle, is the proper settlement. This approach, or one similarly inflexible and passive, does not foster effective and efficient settlement conferences.

The trial judge should play an active, dynamic, and creative role in the settlement process. This may mean injecting herself personally and directly into the settlement negotiations, or it may involve a referral, with specific and well-defined guidelines set by the judge, to a special master or a panel of experts who possess a particular expertise in the subject matter of the lawsuit. . . .

The settlement judge must have the patience, open-mindedness, and skill to fashion a settlement that is fair and reasonable under all circumstances. Sometimes, a method of settlement that neither party has considered opens the door to a satisfactory resolution of the lawsuit. Thus, no particular formula for settlements is available. In effect, each case must be tailored for settlement according to its own characteristics.

Nevertheless, every case on the court docket has a potential for settlement: negligence, contract, trade secret, civil rights, anti-trust, shareholders' derivative actions, patent infringement, and so forth. Almost all cases should be assigned for settlement conferences.

This is not to say that all cases can be, or should be, settled. Public policy may require that a case be litigated rather than settled. Novel legal questions may call for definitive precedential rulings by a court. For example, certain products-liability cases, where public disclosure will benefit hundreds or even thousands of potential claimants, may not be suited for private, undisclosed settlements. . . .

Lawyers, on their own, do manage to settle a fair percentage of civil cases. However, for several reasons, we cannot depend on lawyers to resolve their clients' differences in many of the cases on the trial docket without judicial intervention.

First, law schools have seriously neglected to train students in the art of settlement techniques. "Black letter" law is taught, not the practicalities of lawyering as a business in which people resolve their disputes by negotiation and mediation.

Second, the trial attorney is a professional advocate and not a professional negotiator or decision-maker. His primary role is to advance the client's cause with skill, determination, and diligence. The lawyer earns a fee to win a case, not to compromise it.

Third, lawyers usually settle a case on their own only after following an expensive, cumbersome, awkward route in an adversarial atmosphere. Most lawyers fear that if they initiate settlement discussions, it indicates a sign of weakness to their opponents and portrays a lack of confidence to their clients. . . .

The clients' personal participation in settlement conferences is crucial to success. I can count on the fingers of one hand the cases in which I conducted a settlement conference without the individual parties or the chief executive officer of a corporation being present. If an insurance company was involved, the adjuster was required to attend and the claims manager was asked to be readily available to speak to me by phone. In-house counsel of corporations were also urged to take part in settlement discussions. I conducted no settlement conference unless counsel and their clients expressly consented beforehand to the ground rules.

Although my practices varied depending on the nature of the case, I first met with all counsel and their clients; then I usually saw and spoke with plaintiff and plaintiff's counsel privately. As a general rule, I chatted with the plaintiff about his background and prior experience with litigation. Sooner or later, I asked the person just to sit back and "tell me about your case." Many times we engaged in lively, interesting, and engaging colloquy with respect to the merits of the case. Sometimes I played the devil's advocate; other times I did not.

The most important feature of the discussion was to give the plaintiff a full opportunity to be heard, in his own way. I tried to put myself in the shoes of the party to understand exactly the source of the grievance and what type of settlement he believed would be just and fair. Generally, there was an open and frank discussion of attorneys' fees; the availability of witnesses and documents to support the case; the inconvenience of a trial; and the rock-bottom settlement terms, beyond which the individual would not give in even one degree.

Judge Zampano's view of active judicial intervention is extremely benign. A different picture emerges from cases where the lawyers did not want the judge's help. G. Heileman Brewing Co. v. Joseph Oat Corp., 871 F.2d 648 (7th Cir. 1989) (en banc), is a striking example. In that case, a federal district court ordered the Oat Corporation to send "a corporate representative with authority to settle" to a pretrial conference. The majority, on a fractured court, held that the order was valid under the inherent authority of the trial court. The case was decided before the 1993 amendments to Rule 16(c), which now specifically provides that where appropriate, the court may order parties to appear, or be available by phone. The Advisory Committee notes that the explicit authorization in the Rule "is not intended to limit the reasonable exercise of the court's inherent powers," citing *G. Heileman Brewing.*

Once the judge has everyone before him, what can he make them do? The 1993 Amendments to Rule 16 also provide in (c)(9) that a judge may take appropriate action as to "the use of special procedures to assist in resolving the dispute when authorized by statute or rule." According, again, to the Advisory Committee notes, one of these "special procedures" is the summary jury trial.

Strandell v. Jackson County, Illinois

838 F.2d 884 (7th Cir. 1987)

RIPPLE, Circuit Judge.

In this appeal, we must decide whether a federal district court can require litigants to participate in a nonbinding summary jury trial. In a nonbinding summary jury trial, attorneys summarize their case before a jury, which then renders a nonbinding verdict. The purpose of this device is to motivate litigants towards settlement by allowing them to estimate how an actual jury may respond to their evidence. Thomas Tobin, Esquire, appeals from a judgment of criminal contempt for refusing to participate in such a procedure. We vacated the judgment by an order dated September 10, 1987; we now issue a full opinion.

Mr. Tobin represents the parents of Michael Strandell in a civil rights action against Jackson County, Illinois. The case involves the arrest, strip search, imprisonment, and suicidal death of Michael Strandell. In anticipation of a pretrial conference on September 3, 1986, the plaintiffs filed a written report concerning settlement prospects. The plaintiffs reported that they were requesting $500,000, but that the defendants refused to discuss the issue. At the pretrial conference, the district court suggested that the parties consent to a summary jury trial. A summary jury trial generally lasts one day, and consists of the selection of six jurors to hear approximations by counsel of the expected evidence. After receiving an abbreviated charge, the jury retires with directions to render a consensus verdict. After a verdict is reached, the jury is informed that its verdict is advisory in nature and nonbinding. The objective of this procedure is to induce the parties to negotiate a settlement. Mr. Tobin informed the district court that the plaintiffs would not consent to a summary jury trial, and filed a motion to advance the case for trial. The district court ordered that discovery be closed on January 15, 1987, and set the case for trial.

During discovery, the plaintiffs had obtained statements from 21 witnesses. The plaintiffs learned the identity of many of these witnesses from information provided by the defendants. After discovery closed, the defendants filed a motion to compel production of the witnesses' statements. The plaintiffs responded that these statements constituted privileged work-product; they argued that the defendants could have obtained the information contained in them through ordinary discovery. The district court denied the motion to compel production; it concluded that the defendants had failed to establish "substantial need" and "undue hardship," as required by Rule 26(b)(3) of the Federal Rules of Civil Procedure.

On March 23, 1987, the district court again discussed settlement prospects with counsel. The court expressed its view that a trial could not be accommodated easily on its crowded docket and again suggested that the parties consent to a summary jury trial. On March 26, 1987, Mr. Tobin advised the district court that he would not be willing to submit his client's case to a summary jury trial, but that he was ready to proceed to trial immediately. He claimed that a summary jury trial would require disclosure of the privileged statements. The district court rejected this argument, and ordered the parties to participate in a summary jury trial.

On March 31, 1987, the parties and counsel appeared, as ordered, for selection of a jury for the summary jury trial. Mr. Tobin again objected to the district court's order compelling the summary jury trial. The district court denied this motion. Mr. Tobin then respectfully declined to proceed with the selection of the jury. The district court informed Mr. Tobin that it did not have time available to try this case, nor would it have time for a trial "in the foreseeable months ahead." The court then held Mr. Tobin in criminal contempt for refusing to proceed with the summary jury trial.

The district court postponed disposition of the criminal contempt judgment until April 6, 1987. On that date, the district court asked Mr. Tobin to reconsider his position on proceeding with the summary jury trial. Mr. Tobin reiterated his view that the court lacked the power to compel a summary jury trial, and maintained that such a proceeding would violate his client's rights. The district court entered a criminal contempt judgment of $500 against Mr. Tobin. Mr. Tobin filed a notice of appeal that same day.

The district court filed a memorandum opinion setting forth its reasons for ordering a summary jury trial. The district court noted that trial in this case was expected to last five to six weeks, and that the parties were "poles apart in terms of settlement." It further noted that summary jury trials had been used with great success in such situations.

. . . In turning to the narrow question before us — the legality of compelled participation in a summary jury trial — we must also acknowledge, at the very onset, that a district court no doubt has substantial inherent power to control and to manage its docket. Link v. Wabash R.R., 370 U.S. 626, 629-30 (1962) . . . [t]hat power must, of course, be exercised in a manner that is in harmony with the Federal Rules of Civil Procedure. Those rules are the product of a careful process of study and reflection designed to take "due cognizance both of the need for expedition of cases and the protection of individual rights." That process, set forth in the Rules Enabling Act, 28 U.S.C. § 2072, also reflects the joint responsibility of the legislative and judicial branches of government in striking the delicate balance between these competing concerns. See generally Hanna v.
Plumer, 380 U.S. 460, 471 (1965). Therefore, in those areas of trial practice where the Supreme Court and the Congress, acting together, have addressed the appropriate balance between the needs for judicial efficiency and the rights of the individual litigant, innovation by the individual judicial officer must conform to that balance.

In this case, the district court quite properly acknowledged, at least as a theoretical matter, this limitation on its power to devise a new method to encourage settlement. Consequently, the court turned to Rule 16 of the Federal Rules of Civil Procedure in search of authority for the use of a mandatory summary jury trial. In the district court's view, two subsections of Rule 16(c)[(7) and (11)] authorized such a procedure. . . .*

Here, we must respectfully disagree with the district court. We do not believe that these provisions can be read as authorizing a mandatory summary jury trial. In our view, while the pretrial conference of Rule 16 was intended to foster settlement through the use of extrajudicial procedures, it was not intended to require that an unwilling litigant be sidetracked from the normal course of litigation. The drafters of Rule 16 certainly intended to provide, in the pretrial conference, "a neutral forum" for discussing the matter of settlement. Fed. R. Civ. P. 16 advisory committee's note. However, it is also clear that they did not foresee that the

* These provisions are now subsumed in 16(c)(9). EDS.

conference would be used "to impose settlement negotiations on unwilling litigants. . . ." While the drafters intended that the trial judge "explor[e] the use of procedures other than litigation to resolve the dispute"—including "urging the litigants to employ adjudicatory techniques outside the courthouse," they clearly did not intend to require the parties to take part in such activities. As the Second Circuit, commenting on the 1983 version of Rule 16, wrote: "Rule 16 . . . was not designed as a means for clubbing the parties—or one of them—into an involuntary compromise." Kothe v. Smith, 771 F.2d 667, 669 (2d Cir. 1985).

. . . The use of a mandatory summary jury trial as a pretrial settlement device would also affect seriously the well-established rules concerning discovery and work-product privilege. See Fed. R. Civ. P. 26(b)(3); see also Hickman v. Taylor, 329 U.S. 495 (1947). These rules reflect a carefully-crafted balance between the needs for pretrial disclosure and party confidentiality. Yet, a compelled summary jury trial could easily upset that balance by requiring disclosure of information obtainable, if at all, through the mandated discovery process. We do not believe it is reasonable to assume that the Supreme Court and the Congress would undertake, in such an oblique fashion, such a radical alteration of the considered judgments contained in Rule 26 and in the case law. If such radical surgery is to be performed, we can expect that the national rule-making process outlined in the Rules Enabling Act will undertake it in quite an explicit fashion.

The district court, in explaining its decision to compel the use of the summary jury trial, noted that the Southern District of Illinois faces crushing caseloads. The court suggested that handling that caseload, including compliance with the Speedy Trial Act, required resort to such devices as compulsory summary jury trials. We certainly cannot take issue with the district court's conclusion that its caseload places great stress on its capacity to fulfill its responsibilities. However, a crowded docket does not permit the court to avoid the adjudication of cases properly within its congressionally-mandated jurisdiction. See Thermtron Prods. v. Hermansdorfer, 423 U.S. 336, 344 (1976). As this court said in Taylor v. Oxford, 575 F.2d 152 (5th Cir. 1978): "Innovative experiments may be admirable, and considering the heavy case loads in the district courts, understandable, but experiments must stay within the limitations of the statute."

Because we conclude that the parameters of Rule 16 do not permit courts to compel parties to participate in summary jury trials, the contempt judgment of the district court is vacated.

Note: Special Procedures to Encourage Settlement

Some courts, especially trial courts, have not found *Strandell* persuasive and have continued ordering parties to participate in summary jury trials.

See, e.g., Fed. Reserve Bd. of Minneapolis v. Carrey-Canada, Inc., 123 F.R.D. 603 (D. Minn. 1988), in which the district court found that it had the power under Rules 1 and 16 to order participation in a summary jury trial. The court reasoned that "even if it does not lead to settlement," the summary trial "will be of substantial benefit . . . by clarifying issues for trial, both for the parties and for the court." Id. at 607. See also In re Atl. Pipe Corp., 304 F.3d 135 (1st Cir. 2002); Arabian Am. Oil Co. v. Scarfone, 119 F.R.D. 448 (M.D. Fla. 1988). But see In re NLO, Inc., 5 F.3d 154 (6th Cir. 1993).

Whether the summary jury trial should be open to the public, as a regular (or real) trial would be, has also been contested. See, e.g., Day v. NLO, Inc., 147 F.R.D. 148 (S.D. Ohio 1993) (refusal to close a summary jury trial to the public; rejection of claim that it might taint the actual jury pool), *rev'd*, 5 F.3d 154, 158 (6th Cir. 1993) ("If summary jury trials aid parties in realistically assessing their potential liability or award and facilitate settlement talks, then litigants will voluntarily participate in order to avoid the expenses associated with lengthy trials. . . . Compelling an unwilling litigant to undergo this process improperly interposes the tribunal into the normal adversarial course of litigation. It is error."). Does the rise of these low-visibility alternatives to trial compromise our collective interest in observing civil process? What is that collective interest? Can it be described as a right, or simply a procedure preference?

Summary jury trials are only one of the special procedures to which a court might resort; arbitration and mediation are others (see Chapter 5). Consider Judge Zampano's description of one of his settlement-promotion strategies, and think about where he gets the authority to do this.

> When a case had difficult technical aspects, I at times requested the parties to agree upon the selection of a neutral advisor or panel of experts to sit in on the settlement talks; to listen to the contentions of the parties; and to assist in formulating a settlement plan. Many times, outside experts point out overlooked features in a case, proffer impartial analyses, and advance creative and attractive terms for a reasonable settlement.
>
> The key ingredient to the successful use of special masters or a panel of experts is that all the parties and counsel must agree upon the individuals selected. Several methods for the appointment of neutral advisors have proven acceptable in practice. The usual procedure is for the court to submit to each party a list of 15 or 20 specialists in the field. Peremptory challenges are exercised privately by each party. When the lists are returned, the court appoints a special master or panel from those names acceptable to both sides. Another method is to have the parties provide the court with names. It is surprisingly common for the parties to submit one or more of the same names. On occasion, I have merely called in the parties, their counsel, and trial experts and openly discussed the appointment of a renowned individual from the faculty of a local university or from the staff of a business or utility company in the state, and so forth.
>
> I have followed a few other ground rules: (1) The advisors were permitted to confer with the parties privately and separately, or together; they could

make on-site inspections; they could ask questions of the parties, counsel, or the retained experts who were scheduled to testify at trial; and they could confer with me privately. (2) The predetermined charges for the experts were divided equally between the parties. (3) The recommendations of the advisors for settlement were not binding; however, if the case did not settle, any party could call the experts as witnesses, identify them as "court-appointed experts," and submit their "findings" and "opinions" to the jury within the scope permissible under the Federal Rules of Evidence.

I once employed a panel of experts to help resolve a class action civil rights case brought by a group of women to challenge the validity of the physical agility tests being given to applicants for positions on a municipality's police department. These tests had been developed years ago and had been uniformly adopted by most cities and towns in Connecticut. At the time of the settlement conference, each side had retained the services of experts, extensive discovery was scheduled, and the parties predicted the case would take several weeks to try. The issues attracted wide-scale media attention.

With the agreement of the parties, a three-person panel of experts was selected to meet and hear the parties and their experts; to view the administration of the tests; and to report their findings and recommendations to the court. The panel consisted of a Yale law professor, who was a recognized civil rights scholar; the director of women's athletic activities at Yale University; and a medical doctor, who had considerable experience in treating sports-related injuries and who had written several articles on physical agility training for male and female athletes.

Two full days were set aside for the panel to complete their assignment. They unanimously determined that, in some respects, the municipality's tests were not job-related. They designed a new series of tests that they believed would be fair and reasonable to determine the physical qualifications of the applicants, both female and male.

I reviewed the report of the panel, carefully considered its contents, and made a few minor changes to conform to several valid suggestions by the parties. I then met with the parties who agreed to the conditions of the settlement I proposed. Because it was a class action, I scheduled a formal hearing on the matter, with due notice to the class, and eventually entered judgment. I am now informed that almost every city and town in Connecticut has revised its physical entrance examinations for police and fire departments to conform to the decree entered in this case.

Robert Zampano, Settlement Strategies for Trial Judges, Litigation (Fall 1995), at 6.

Under the Alternative Dispute Resolution Act of 1998, 28 U.S.C. § 651(b), each federal district court is obliged to adopt local rules implementing its own ADR program with formal mechanisms for promoting settlement. A 2005 study reveals that 62 courts authorize mediation, 32 authorize settlement conferences, 21 authorize arbitration, 18 authorize "early neutral evaluation," and 9 simply authorize the use of ADR in general. Summary of Selected Features on Court ADR Research (Nov. 17, 2005). See also John Lande, How Much Justice Can We Afford?, 2006 J. Disp. Resol. 213.

Note: "Litigotiation"

Marc Galanter and Mia Cahill describe modern civil litigation as "a single process of pursuing remedies in the presence of courts. For mnemonic purposes, we attach to it the fanciful neologism 'litigotiation.'" "Most Cases Settle": Judicial Promotion and Regulation of Settlements, 46 Stan. L. Rev. 1339, 1341-1342 (1994). The authors question whether this growing enthusiasm for judicial promotion of settlement is a good thing by carefully analyzing many arguments that have been advanced in support of settlement in general and of judicial encouragement of settlement in particular. They express their conclusions as follows:

> What do we know of the effects of judicial intervention on the number or quality of settlements? As to number, the available studies provide no basis for thinking judicial promotion leads to a number of settlements that is sufficiently higher than would otherwise occur to compensate for the opportunity costs of the judicial attention diverted from litigation. . . . As to the effects of judicial promotion on the quality of settlements, we simply do not know. . . . Are settlements arranged by judges less variable, more principled, more reflective of the merits? No one knows.

Id. at 1388-1389. See also Carrie Menkel-Meadow, For and Against Settlement: Uses and Abuses of the Mandatory Settlement Conference, 33 UCLA L. Rev. 485 (1985).

What do you imagine are the problems that researchers encounter when attempting to answer the questions raised by Galanter and Cahill? If the questions are unanswerable, then why do so many reformers seem sold on expanding (and formalizing through Rules amendments) judicial power to encourage settlements? What is the empirical basis for this movement?

Professor Janet Cooper Alexander offers the following summary of the potential advantages of settlement over trial. What do they imply about the foregoing materials on judicial promotion of settlement?

> Settlement has many positive aspects, to be sure. For example, it may cost the parties less than trial; it avoids all-or-nothing results and allows parties to assure themselves an "average" outcome based on the expected value of the case; it permits consideration of interests that cannot be taken into account in adjudication; it allows innovative "pie-enlarging" solutions that are not possible through remedies available from adjudication; and it produces consensual, rather than coerced, outcomes. Adjudication, however, also serves important public and private interests. . . . [A]djudication produces precedents, which are a public good. Adjudication serves other public interests as well, such as enforcing the substantive law, providing a yardstick for evaluating settlements, assuring public access to information about disputes affecting the public interest, preserving public confidence in the administration of justice, and affording citizen participation in democratic government through jury service. And adjudication advances private

interests such as individual dignity and the interest in securing private rights.

Janet Cooper Alexander, Judges' Self-Interest and Procedural Rules: Comment on Macey, 23 J. Legal Stud. 647, 650 (1994).

Note: Motions in Limine

A number of the subjects for discussion at pretrial conferences deal with matters of evidence. See, e.g., Fed. R. Civ. P. 16 (c)(2). It is not uncommon for the court and the parties to resolve difficult points of evidence before the case starts: The usual tool for doing this is the motion in limine (at the threshold). Although these motions may seem more glamorous in criminal suits, in that many such motions deal with the constitutionality of confessions, unlawful searches and seizures, and the like, they are likewise important in civil suits. If, for example, a case seems to hinge on the admissibility of certain documentary evidence, then a pretrial ruling on its admissibility could be practically dispositive, either by inducing settlement or paving the way to a successful motion for summary judgment. Pretrial rulings on the admissibility of evidence therefore serve an important role in resolving at least some suits at an early stage. Fuller comprehension of the rules that govern such motions will come from your courses in evidence, constitutional criminal procedure, and trial practice.

B. SUMMARY JUDGMENT

Problem Case: A Literary Law Student (Part Two)

Return to the problem case in Chapter 3C.2 (page 495) and assume that you are still Donna's lawyer. She has suggested that you file a motion for summary judgment, appending her affidavit stating that she has never read or heard anyone recount any part of *First Year.* Assuming that the plaintiff has no direct evidence to the contrary, what are your chances of prevailing, and why?

1. The Development of Modern Summary Judgment Doctrine

a. Piercing the Pleadings: Historical Perspectives

The historic antecedents of Rule 56 lie in the nineteenth-century British demurrer's inadequacy in weeding out the spurious defenses raised by obligors on bills of exchange. On the surface the pleadings of these particular debtors looked good enough to escape demurrer but the whole world knew that they were interposed only for delay. Accordingly, in 1855, Parliament enacted legislation to enable the courts to "pierce the pleadings" in such cases in order to render prompt decisions.

In the same period, American codes were enacted to provide for the striking of "sham" pleadings. Rule 56 was originally conceived in reaction to both the English and American experience. Its intention is to allow judges to dismiss cases where there is not enough evidence to justify the time and expense of trial. At the same time, it does not incorporate the condemnation of the pleading as a "sham."

Rule 56 has never been significantly amended. Practice under it has been described in these terms by a judge sitting in the Northern District of California:

> [It] is plagued by confusion and uncertainty. It suffers from misuse by those lawyers who insist on making a motion in the face of obvious fact issues; from neglect by others who, fearful of judicial hostility to the procedure, refrain from moving even where summary judgment would be appropriate; and from the failure of trial and appellate courts to define clearly what is a genuine issue of material fact.

William Schwarzer, Summary Judgment under the Federal Rules: Defining Genuine Issues of Material Fact, 99 F.R.D. 465 (1984).

In 1986, the Supreme Court decided three summary judgment cases in a single term, with the apparent purpose of clarifying the practice and encouraging its use. This, in turn, produced an avalanche of commentary about summary judgment. Here is a sampling of some of the best articles: Daniel P. Collins, Summary Judgment and Circumstantial Evidence, 40 Stan. L. Rev. 491 (1988); D. Michael Risinger, Another Step in the Counter Revolution: A Summary Judgment on the Supreme Court's New Approach to Summary Judgment, 54 Brook. L. Rev. 35 (1988); Melissa L. Nelken, One Step Forward, Two Steps Back: Summary Judgment after *Celotex*, 40 Hastings L.J. 53 (1988); Linda Mullinex, Summary Judgment: Taming the Beast of Burdens, 10 Am. J. Trial Advoc. 433 (1987); Note, Federal Summary Judgment: The "New" Workhorse for an Overburdened Federal Court System, 20 U.C. Davis L. Rev. 955 (1987); David P. Currie, Thoughts on Directed Verdicts and Summary Judgments, 45 U. Chi. L. Rev. 72 (1977); Martin B. Louis, Federal Summary Judgment Doctrine: A Critical Analysis, 83 Yale L.J. 745 (1974).

The proponents of summary judgment tend to be the same people who urge that the pleading stage be more meaningful generally. Summary judgment is, however, a more drastic event than dismissal of a pleading, at least in the usual case; it raises, as well, the specter of denying the right to a jury trial. Excerpts from the major precedent in the path of expanding summary judgment and from the Supreme Court trilogy appear below.

Adickes v. S.H. Kress & Co.

398 U.S. 144 (1970)

JUSTICE HARLAN delivered the opinion of the Court.

Petitioner, Sandra Adickes, a white school teacher from New York, brought this suit in the United States District Court for the Southern District of New York against respondent S.H. Kress & Co. ("Kress") to recover damages under 42 U.S.C. § 1983[1] for an alleged violation of her constitutional rights under the Equal Protection Clause of the Fourteenth Amendment. The suit arises out of Kress' refusal to serve lunch to Miss Adickes at its restaurant facilities in its Hattiesburg, Mississippi, store on August 14, 1964, and Miss Adickes' subsequent arrest upon her departure from the store by the Hattiesburg police on a charge of vagrancy. At the time of both the refusal to serve and the arrest, Miss Adickes was with six young people, all Negroes, who were her students in a Mississippi "Freedom School" where she was teaching that summer. Unlike Miss Adickes, the students were offered service, and were not arrested.

Petitioner's complaint had two counts, each bottomed on § 1983, and each alleging that Kress had deprived her of the right under the Equal Protection Clause of the Fourteenth Amendment not to be discriminated against on the basis of race. The first count charged that Miss Adickes had been refused service by Kress because she was a "Caucasian in the company of Negroes." Petitioner sought, *inter alia,* to prove that the refusal to serve her was pursuant to a "custom of the community to segregate the races in public eating places." However, in a pretrial decision, 252 F. Supp. 140 ([S.D.N.Y.] 1966), the District Court ruled that to recover under this count, Miss Adickes would have to prove that at the time she was refused service, there was a specific "custom . . . of refusing service to whites in the company of Negroes" and that this custom was "enforced by the State" under Mississippi's criminal trespass statute. Because petitioner was unable to prove at the trial that there were other instances in Hattiesburg of a white person having been refused service while in the company of Negroes, the District Court directed a verdict in favor of respondent. A divided panel of the Court of Appeals affirmed on this ground, also holding that § 1983 "requires that the discriminatory custom or usage be proved to exist in the locale where the discrimination took place, and in the State generally," and that petitioner's "proof on both points was deficient," 499 F.2d 121, 124 ([2d Cir.] 1968).

1. Rev. Stat. § 1979, 42 U.S.C. § 1983 provides:

> Every person who, under color of any statute, ordinance, regulation, custom, or usage, of any State or Territory, subjects, or causes to be subjected, any citizen of the United States or other person within the jurisdiction thereof to the deprivation of any rights, privileges, or immunities secured by the Constitution and laws, shall be liable to the party injured in an action at law, suit in equity, or other proper proceeding for redress.

The second count of her complaint, alleging that both the refusal of service and her subsequent arrest were the product of a conspiracy between Kress and the Hattiesburg police, was dismissed before trial on a motion for summary judgment. The District Court ruled that petitioner had "failed to allege any facts from which a conspiracy might be inferred." 252 F. Supp. at 144. This determination was unanimously affirmed by the Court of Appeals, 409 F.2d at 126-127.

Miss Adickes, in seeking review here, claims that the District Court erred both in directing a verdict on the substantive count, and in granting summary judgment on the conspiracy count. Last Term we granted certiorari, 394 U.S. 1011 (1969), and we now reverse and remand for further proceedings on each of the two counts....

We now proceed to consider whether the District Court erred in granting summary judgment on the conspiracy count. In granting respondent's motion, the District Court simply stated that there was "no evidence in the complaint or in the affidavits and other papers from which a 'reasonably-minded person' might draw an inference of conspiracy," 252 F. Supp. at 144, *aff'd*, 409 F.2d, at 126-127. Our own scrutiny of the factual allegations of petitioner's complaint, as well as the material found in the affidavits and depositions presented by Kress to the District Court, however, convinces us that summary judgment was improper here, for we think respondent failed to carry its burden of showing the absence of any genuine issue of fact. Before explaining why this is so, it is useful to state the factual arguments, made by the parties concerning summary judgment, and the reasoning of the courts below.

In moving for summary judgment, Kress argued that "uncontested facts" established that no conspiracy existed between any Kress employee and the police. To support this assertion, Kress pointed first to the statements in the deposition of the store manager (Mr. Powell) that (a) he had not communicated with the police,[8] and that (b) he had, by a prearranged tacit signal,[9] ordered the food counter supervisor to see that Miss Adickes was refused service only because he was fearful of a riot in

8. In his deposition, Powell admitted knowing Hugh Herring, chief of police of Hattiesburg, and said that he had seen and talked to him on two occasions in 1964 prior to the incident with Miss Adickes. When asked how often the arresting officer, Ralph Hillman, came into the store, Powell stated that he didn't know precisely but "Maybe every day." However, Powell said that on August 14 he didn't recall seeing any policemen either inside or outside the store, and he denied (1) that he had called the police, (2) that he had agreed with any public official to deny Miss Adickes the use of the library, (3) that he had agreed with any public official to refuse Miss Adickes service in the Kress store on the day in question, or (4) that he had asked any public official to have Miss Adickes arrested.

9. The signal, according to Powell, was a nod of his head. Powell claimed that at a meeting about a month earlier with Miss Baggett, the food counter supervisor, he "told her not to serve the white person in the group if I... shook my head no. But, if I didn't give her any sign, to go ahead and serve anybody."

Powell stated that he had prearranged this tacit signal with Miss Baggett because "there was quite a lot of violence... in Hattiesburg" directed towards whites "with colored people, in what you call a mixed group."

the store by customers angered at seeing a "mixed group" of whites and blacks eating together.[10] Kress also relied on affidavits from the Hattiesburg chief of police,[11] and the two arresting officers,[12] to the effect that store manager Powell had not requested that petitioner be arrested. Finally, Kress pointed to the statements in petitioner's own deposition that

10. Powell described the circumstances of his refusal as follows:

> On this particular day, just shortly after 12 o'clock, I estimate there was 75 to 100 people in the store, and the lunch counter was pretty—was pretty well to capacity there, full, and I was going up towards the front of the store in one of the aisles, and looking towards the front of the store, and there was a group of colored girls, and a white woman who came into the north door, which was next to the lunch counter.
>
> And the one thing that really stopped me and called my attention to this group, was the fact that they were dressed alike. They all had on, what looked like a light blue denim skirt. And the best I can remember is that they were—they were almost identical, all of them. And they came into the door, and people coming in stopped to look, and they went on to the booths. And there happened to be two empty there. And one group of them and the white woman sat down in one, and the rest of them sat in the second group.
>
> And, almost immediately there—I mean this, it didn't take just a few seconds from the time they came into the door to sit down, but, already the people began to mill around the store and started coming over towards the lunch counter. And, by that time I was up close to the candy counter, and I had a wide open view there. And the people had real sour looks on their faces, nobody was joking, or being corny, or carrying on. They looked like a frightened mob. They really did. I have seen mobs before. I was in Korea during the riots in 1954 and 1955. And I know what they are. And this actually got me.
>
> I looked out towards the front, and we have what they call see-through windows. There is no backs to them. You can look out of the store right into the street. And the north window, it looks right into the lunch counter, 25 or 30 people were standing there looking in, and across the street even, in a jewelry store, people were standing there, and it looked really bad to me. It looked like one person could have yelled "Let's get them," which has happened before, and cause this group to turn into a mob. And, so, quickly I just made up my mind to avoid the riot, and protect the people that were in the store, and my employees, as far as the people in the mob who were going to get hurt themselves. I just knew that something was going to break loose there.

11. The affidavit of the chief of police, who it appears was not present at the arrest, states in relevant part:

> Mr. Powell had made no request of me to arrest Miss Sandra Adickes or any other person, in fact, I did not know Mr. Powell personally until the day of this statement. [But cf. Powell's statement at his deposition, n.8, supra.] Mr.Powell and I had not discussed the arrest of this person until the day of this statement and we had never previously discussed her in any way.

12. The affidavits of Sergeant Boone and Officer Hillman each state, in identical language:

> I was contacted on this date by Mr. John H. Williams, Jr., a representative of Genesco, owners of S.H. Kress and Company, who requested that I make a statement concerning alleged conspiracy in connection with the aforesaid arrest.
>
> This arrest was made on the public streets of Hattiesburg, Mississippi, and was an officers discretion arrest. I had not consulted with Mr. G.T. Powell, Manager of S.H. Kress and Company in Hattiesburg, and did not know his name until this date. No one at the Kress store asked that the arrest be made and I did not consult with anyone prior to the arrest.

she had no knowledge of any communication between any Kress employee and any member of the Hattiesburg police, and was relying on circumstantial evidence to support her contention that there was an arrangement between Kress and the police.

Petitioner, in opposing summary judgment, pointed out that respondent had failed in its moving papers to dispute the allegation in petitioner's complaint, a statement at her deposition,[13] and an unsworn statement by a Kress employee,[14] all to the effect that there was a policeman in the store at the time of the refusal to serve her, and that this was the policeman who subsequently arrested her. Petitioner argued that although she had no knowledge of an agreement between Kress and the police, the sequence of events created a substantial enough possibility of a conspiracy to allow her to proceed to trial, especially given the fact that the noncircumstantial evidence of the conspiracy could only come from adverse witnesses. Further, she submitted an affidavit specifically disputing the manager's assertion that the situation in the store at the time of the refusal was "explosive," thus creating an issue of fact as to what his motives might have been in ordering the refusal of service.

We think that on the basis of this record, it was error to grant summary judgment. As the moving party, respondent had the burden of showing the absence of a genuine issue as to any material fact, and for these purposes the material it lodged must be viewed in the light most favorable to the opposing party. Respondent here did not carry its burden because of its failure to foreclose the possibility that there was a policeman in the Kress store while petitioner was awaiting service, and that this policeman reached an understanding with some Kress employee that petitioner not be served.... If a policeman were present, we think it

13. When asked whether she saw any policeman in the store up to the time of the refusal of service, Miss Adickes answered: "My back was to the door, but one of my students saw a policeman come in." She went on to identify the student as "Carolyn." At the trial, Carolyn Moncure, one of the students who was with petitioner, testified that "about five minutes" after the group had sat down and while they were still waiting for service, she saw a policeman come in the store. She stated: "[H]e came in the store, my face was facing the front of the store, and he came in the store and he passed, and he stopped right at the end of our booth, and he stood up and he looked around and he smiled, and he went to the back of the store, he came right back and he left out." This testimony was corroborated by that of Dianne Moncure, Carolyn's sister, who was also part of the group. She testified that while the group was waiting for service, a policeman entered the store, stood "for a while" looking at the group, and then "walked to the back of the store."

14. During discovery, respondent gave to petitioner an unsworn statement by Miss Irene Sullivan, a check-out girl. In this statement Miss Sullivan said that she had seen Patrolman Hillman come into the store "[s]hortly after 12:00 noon," while petitioner's group was in the store. She said that he had traded a "hello greeting" with her, and then walked past her check-out counter toward the back of the store "out of [her] line of vision." She went on: "A few minutes later Patrolman Hillman left our store by the northerly front door just slightly ahead of a group composed of several Negroes accompanied by a white woman. As Hillman stepped onto the sidewalk outside our store the police car pulled across the street and into an alley that is alongside our store. The police car stopped and Patrolman Hillman escorted the white woman away from the Negroes and into the police car."

would be open to a jury, in light of the sequence that followed, to infer from the circumstances that the policeman and a Kress employee had a "meeting of the minds" and thus reached an understanding that petitioner should be refused service. Because "[o]n summary judgment the inferences to be drawn from the underlying facts contained in [the moving party's] materials must be viewed in the light most favorable to the party opposing the motion," United States v. Diebold, Inc., 369 U.S. 654, 655 (1962), we think respondent's failure to show there was no policeman in the store requires reversal.

Pointing to Rule 56(e), as amended in 1963, respondent argues that it was incumbent on petitioner to come forward with an affidavit properly asserting the presence of the policeman in the store, if she were to rely on that fact to avoid summary judgment. Respondent notes in this regard that none of the materials upon which petitioner relied met the requirements of Rule 56(e).[19]

This argument does not withstand scrutiny, however, for both the commentary on and background of the 1963 amendment conclusively show that it was not intended to modify the burden of the moving party under Rule 56(c) to show initially the absence of a genuine issue concerning any material fact. The Advisory Committee note on the amendment states that the changes were not designed to "affect the ordinary standards applicable to the summary judgment." And, in a comment directed specifically to a contention like respondent's, the Committee stated that "[w]here the evidentiary matter in support of the motion does not establish the absence of a genuine issue, summary judgment must be denied *even if no opposing evidentiary matter is presented.*" Because respondent did not meet its initial burden of establishing the absence of a policeman in the store, petitioner here was not required to come forward with suitable opposing affidavits.

If respondent had met its initial burden by, for example, submitting affidavits from the policemen denying their presence in the store at the time in question, Rule 56(e) would then have required petitioner to have done more than simply rely on the contrary allegation in her complaint. To have avoided conceding this fact for purposes of summary judgment, petitioner would have had to come forward with either (1) the affidavit of someone who saw the policeman in the store or (2) an affidavit under Rule 56(f) explaining why at that time it was impractical to do so. Even though not essential here to defeat respondent's motion, the submission of such an affidavit would have been the preferable course for petitioner's counsel to have followed. As one commentator has said:

> It has always been perilous for the opposing party neither to proffer any countering evidentiary materials nor file a 56(f) affidavit. And the peril rightly continues [after the amendment to Rule 56(e)]. Yet the party moving

19. Petitioner's statement at her deposition, see n.13, supra, was, of course, hearsay; and the statement of Miss Sullivan, see n.14, supra, was unsworn. And, the rule specifies that reliance on allegations in the complaint is not sufficient. See Fed. Rule Civ. Proc. 26(e).

> for summary judgment has the burden to show that he is entitled to judgment under established principles; and if he does not discharge that burden then he is not entitled to judgment. No defense to an insufficient showing is required.

J. Moore, Federal Practice ¶56.22[2], pp.2824-2825 (2d ed. 1966)....

Adickes bears indicia of its proximity to the height of the civil rights movement—the Court seems reluctant to give an interpretation of Rule 56 that would sanction judicial indifference to the powerful social forces at play in the restaurant that day. The decision also reflects traditional skepticism toward summary judgment and toward the enhanced role for trial judges Rule 56 implies. It is perhaps not surprising then that *Adickes* was read broadly in the lower courts for the principle that the movant bears a heavy burden to establish the absence of genuine issues for trial. Critics complained that this unduly limited the role of summary judgment as a tool for weeding out cases unworthy of a full blown trial.

In 1986, the Supreme Court intervened, reframing the standard governing summary judgment decisions in three separate cases. As you read these cases, consider what assumptions about summary judgment and pretrial litigation lie behind the Court's analysis, and consider whether and to what extent the standard articulated in *Adickes* is altered by the trilogy.

b. The Supreme Court Trilogy

Celotex Corp. v. Catrett

477 U.S. 317 (1986)

JUSTICE REHNQUIST delivered the opinion of the Court.

Respondent commenced this lawsuit in September 1980, alleging that the death in 1979 of her husband, Louis H. Catrett, resulted from his exposure to products containing asbestos manufactured or distributed by 15 named corporations. Respondent's complaint sounded in negligence, breach of warranty, and strict liability.... [Thirteen defendants], including petitioner, filed motions for summary judgment. Petitioner's motion... argued that summary judgment was proper because respondent had "failed to produce evidence that any [Celotex] product... was the proximate cause of the injuries alleged...."... In response to petitioner's summary judgment motion, respondent then produced three documents which she claimed "demonstrate that there is a genuine material factual dispute" as to whether the decedent had ever been exposed to petitioner's asbestos products. The three documents included a transcript of a deposition of the decedent, a letter from an official of one of the decedent's former employers whom petitioner planned to call as a trial witness, and a letter from an insurance company to respondent's attorney, all tending to establish that the decedent had been exposed to petitioner's asbestos products in Chicago during 1970-1971. Petitioner, in turn, argued that the three documents were inadmissible hearsay and thus could not be considered in opposition to the summary judgment motion.

... [T]he District Court granted all of the motions filed by the various defendants. The court explained that it was granting petitioner's summary judgment motion because "there [was] no showing that the plaintiff was exposed to the defendant Celotex's product...." Respondent appealed only the grant of summary judgment in favor of petitioner, and a divided panel of the District of Columbia Circuit reversed. The majority of the Court of Appeals held that petitioner's summary judgment motion was rendered "fatally defective" by the fact that petitioner "made no effort to adduce *any* evidence, in the form of affidavits or otherwise, to support its motion." According to the majority, Rule 56(e) of the Federal Rules of Civil Procedure, and this Court's decision in Adickes v. S.H. Kress & Co., 398 U.S. 144, 159 (1970), establish that "the party opposing the motion for summary judgment bears the burden of responding *only after* the moving party has met its burden of coming forward with proof of the absence of any genuine issues of material fact."

We think that the position taken by the majority of the Court of Appeals is inconsistent with the standard for summary judgment set forth in Rule 56(c) of the Federal Rules of Civil Procedure. Under Rule 56(c), summary judgment is proper "if the pleadings, depositions, answers to interrogatories, and admissions on file, together with the affidavits, if any, show that there is no genuine issue as to any material fact and that the moving party is entitled to a judgment as a matter of law." In our view, the plain language of Rule 56(c) mandates the entry of summary judgment, after adequate time for discovery and upon motion, against a party who fails to make a showing sufficient to establish the existence of an element essential to that party's case, and on which that party will bear the burden of proof at trial. In such a situation, there can be "no genuine issue as to any material fact," since a complete failure of proof concerning an essential element of the nonmoving party's case necessarily renders all other facts immaterial. The moving party is "entitled to a judgment as a matter of law" because the nonmoving party has failed to make a sufficient showing on an essential element of her case with respect to which she has the burden of proof. "[The] standard [for granting summary judgment] mirrors the standard for a directed verdict under Federal Rule of Civil Procedure 50(a)...." Anderson v. Liberty Lobby, Inc., [477 U.S. 242, 250 (1986)].

Of course, a party seeking summary judgment always bears the initial responsibility of informing the district court of the basis for its motion, and identifying those portions of "the pleadings, depositions, answers to interrogatories, and admissions on file, together with the affidavits, if any," which it believes demonstrate the absence of a genuine issue of material fact. But unlike the Court of Appeals, we find no express or implied requirement in Rule 56 that the moving party support its motion with affidavits or other similar materials *negating* the opponent's claim. On the contrary, Rule 56(c), which refers to "the affidavits, *if any*" (emphasis added), suggests the absence of such a requirement. And if there were any doubt about the meaning of Rule 56(c) in this regard, such doubt is clearly removed by Rules 56(a) and (b), which provide that claimants and defendants, respectively, may move for summary judgment *"with or without supporting affidavits"* (emphasis added). The import of these subsections is that, regardless of whether the moving party accompanies its summary judgment motion with affidavits, the motion may, and should, be granted so long as whatever is before the district court demonstrates that the standard for the entry of summary judgment, as set forth in Rule 56(c), is satisfied. One of the principal purposes of the summary judgment rule is to isolate and dispose of factually unsupported claims or defenses, and we think it should be interpreted in a way that allows it to accomplish this purpose.[5]

Respondent argues, however, that Rule 56(e), by its terms, places on the nonmoving party the burden of coming forward with rebuttal affidavits, or other specified kinds of materials, only in response to a motion for summary judgment "made and supported as provided in this rule." According to respondent's argument, since petitioner did not "support" its motion with affidavits, summary judgment was improper in this case. But as we have already explained, a motion for summary judgment may be made pursuant to Rule 56 "with or without supporting affidavits." In cases like the instant one, where the nonmoving party will bear the burden of proof at trial on a dispositive issue, a summary judgment motion may properly be made in reliance solely on the "pleadings, depositions, answers to interrogatories, and admissions on file." Such a motion, whether or not accompanied by affidavits, will be "made and supported as provided in this rule," and Rule 56(e) therefore requires the nonmoving party to go beyond the pleadings and by her own affidavits, or by the "depositions, answers to interrogatories, and admissions on file," designate "specific facts showing that there is a genuine issue for trial."

. . . Obviously, Rule 56 does not require the nonmoving party to depose her own witnesses. Rule 56(e) permits a proper summary judgment motion to be opposed by any of the kinds of evidentiary materials listed in Rule 56(c), except the mere pleadings themselves, and it is from this list that one would normally expect the nonmoving party to make the showing to which we have referred.

The Court of Appeals in this case felt itself constrained, however, by language in our decision in Adickes v. S.H. Kress & Co., 398 U.S. 144 (1970). There we held that summary judgment had been improperly entered in favor of the defendant restaurant in an action brought under 42

5. See Louis, Federal Summary Judgment Doctrine: A Critical Analysis, 83 Yale L.J. 745, 752 (1974); Currie, Thoughts on Directed Verdicts and Summary Judgments, 45 U. Chi. L. Rev. 72, 79 (1977).

U.S.C. § 1983. In the course of its opinion, the *Adickes* Court said that "both the commentary on and the background of the 1963 amendment conclusively show that it was not intended to modify the burden of the moving party . . . to show initially the absence of a genuine issue concerning any material fact." Id. at 159. We think that this statement is accurate in a literal sense, since we fully agree with the *Adickes* Court that the 1963 amendment to Rule 56(e) was not designed to modify the burden of making the showing generally required by Rule 56(c). It also appears to us that, on the basis of the showing before the Court in *Adickes,* the motion for summary judgment in that case should have been denied. But we do not think the *Adickes* language quoted above should be construed to mean that the burden is on the party moving for summary judgment to produce evidence showing the absence of a genuine issue of material fact, even with respect to an issue on which the nonmoving party bears the burden of proof. Instead, as we have explained, the burden on the moving party may be discharged by "showing"—that is, pointing out to the district court—that there is an absence of evidence to support the nonmoving party's case.

The last two sentences of Rule 56(e) were added, as this Court indicated in *Adickes,* to disapprove a line of cases allowing a party opposing summary judgment to resist a properly made motion by reference only to its pleadings. While the *Adickes* Court was undoubtedly correct in concluding that these two sentences were not intended to *reduce* the burden of the moving party, it is also obvious that they were not adopted to *add to* that burden. Yet that is exactly the result which the reasoning of the Court of Appeals would produce. . . .

Respondent commenced this action in September 1980, and petitioner's motion was filed in September 1981. The parties had conducted discovery, and no serious claim can be made that respondent was in any sense "railroaded" by a premature motion for summary judgment. Any potential problem with such premature motions can be adequately dealt with under Rule 56(f), which allows a summary judgment motion to be denied, or the hearing on the motion to be continued, if the nonmoving party has not had an opportunity to make full discovery.

In this Court, respondent's brief and oral argument have been devoted as much to the proposition that an adequate showing of exposure to petitioner's asbestos products was made as to the proposition that no such showing should have been required. But the Court of Appeals declined to address either the adequacy of the showing made by respondent in opposition to petitioner's motion for summary judgment, or the question whether such a showing, if reduced to admissible evidence, would be sufficient to carry respondent's burden of proof at trial. We think the Court of Appeals with its superior knowledge of local law is better suited than we are to make these determinations in the first instance.

The Federal Rules of Civil Procedure have for almost 50 years authorized motions for summary judgment upon proper showings of the lack of a genuine, triable issue of material fact. Summary judgment procedure is properly regarded not as a disfavored procedural shortcut, but rather as an integral part of the Federal Rules as a whole, which are designed "to secure the just, speedy and inexpensive determination of every action." Fed. R. Civ. Proc. 1; see Schwarzer, Summary Judgment Under the Federal Rules: Defining Genuine Issues of Material Fact, 99 F.R.D. 465, 467 (1984). Before the shift to "notice pleading" accomplished by the Federal Rules, motions to dismiss a complaint or to strike a defense were the principal tools by which factually insufficient claims or defenses could be isolated and prevented from going to trial with the attendant unwarranted consumption of public and private resources. But with the advent of "notice pleading," the motion to dismiss seldom fulfills this function any more, and its place has been taken by the motion for summary judgment. Rule 56 must be construed with due regard not only for the rights of persons asserting claims and defenses that are adequately based in fact to have those claims and defenses tried to a jury, but also for the rights of persons opposing such claims and defenses to demonstrate in the manner provided by the Rule, prior to trial, that the claims and defenses have no factual basis.

The judgment of the Court of Appeals is accordingly reversed, and the case is remanded for further proceedings consistent with this opinion.

It is so ordered.

JUSTICE WHITE, concurring.

I agree that the Court of Appeals was wrong in holding that the moving defendant must always support his motion with evidence or affidavits showing the absence of a genuine dispute about a material fact. . . . But the movant must discharge the burden the Rules place upon him: It is not enough to move for summary judgment without supporting the motion in any way or with a conclusory assertion that the plaintiff has no evidence to prove his case.

A plaintiff need not initiate any discovery or reveal his witnesses or evidence unless required to do so under the discovery Rules or by court order. Of course, he must respond if required to do so; but he need not also depose his witnesses or obtain their affidavits to defeat a summary judgment motion asserting only that he has failed to produce any support for his case. It is the defendant's task to negate, if he can, the claimed basis for the suit. . . .

JUSTICE BRENNAN, with whom THE CHIEF JUSTICE and JUSTICE BLACKMUN join, dissenting.

. . . [T]he Court has not clearly explained what is required of a moving party seeking summary judgment on the ground that the nonmoving party cannot prove its case. This lack of clarity is unfortunate: district courts must routinely decide summary judgment motions, and the Court's opinion will very likely create confusion. For this reason, even if I agreed with the Court's result, I would have written separately to explain more clearly the law in this area. However, because I believe that Celotex did not meet its burden of production under Federal Rule of Civil Procedure 56, I respectfully dissent from the Court's judgment.

I

. . . The burden of establishing the nonexistence of a "genuine issue" is on the party moving for summary judgment. This burden has two distinct components: an initial burden of production, which shifts to the nonmoving party if satisfied by the moving party; and an ultimate burden of persuasion, which always remains on the moving party. The court need not decide whether the moving party has satisfied its ultimate burden of persuasion[2] unless and until the court finds that the moving party has discharged its initial burden of production. Adickes v. S.H. Kress & Co., 398 U.S. 144, 157-161 (1970); 1963 Advisory Committee's Notes on Fed. Rule Civ. Proc. 56(e).

The burden of production imposed by Rule 56 requires the moving party to make a prima facie showing that it is entitled to summary judgment. The manner in which this showing can be made depends upon which party will bear the burden of persuasion on the challenged claim at trial. If the *moving* party will bear the burden of persuasion at trial, that party must support its motion with credible evidence—using any of the materials specified in Rule 56(c)—that would entitle it to a directed verdict if not controverted at trial. Such an affirmative showing shifts the burden of production to the party opposing the motion and requires that party either to produce evidentiary materials that demonstrate the existence of a "genuine issue" for trial or to submit an affidavit requesting additional time for discovery. Id.; Fed. Rules Civ. Proc. 56(e), (f).

If the burden of persuasion at trial would be on the *nonmoving* party, the party moving for summary judgment may satisfy Rule 56's burden of production in either of two ways. First, the moving party may submit affirmative evidence that negates an essential element of the nonmoving party's claim. Second, the moving party may demonstrate to the court that the nonmoving party's evidence is insufficient to establish an essential element of the nonmoving party's claim. If the nonmoving party cannot muster sufficient evidence to make out its claim, a trial would be useless and the moving party is entitled to summary judgment as a matter of law.

Where the moving party adopts this second option and seeks summary judgment on the ground that the nonmoving party—who will bear the burden of persuasion at trial—has no evidence, the mechanics of discharging Rule 56's burden of production are somewhat trickier. Plainly, a conclusory assertion that the nonmoving party has no evidence is

2. The burden of persuasion imposed on a moving party by Rule 56 is a stringent one. Summary judgment should not be granted unless it is clear that a trial is unnecessary, and any doubt as to the existence of a genuine issue for trial should be resolved against the moving party, *Adickes*, 398 U.S. at 158-159. . . .

insufficient. See *ante,* (White, J., concurring). Such a "burden" of production is no burden at all and would simply permit summary judgment procedure to be converted into a tool for harassment. Rather, as the Court confirms, a party who moves for summary judgment on the ground that the nonmoving party has no evidence must affirmatively show the absence of evidence in the record. This may require the moving party to depose the nonmoving party's witnesses or to establish the inadequacy of documentary evidence. If there is literally no evidence in the record, the moving party may demonstrate this by reviewing for the court the admissions, interrogatories, and other exchanges between the parties that are in the record. Either way, however, the moving party must affirmatively demonstrate that there is no evidence in the record to support a judgment for the nonmoving party.

If the moving party has not fully discharged this initial burden of production, its motion for summary judgment must be denied, and the court need not consider whether the moving party has met its ultimate burden of persuasion. Accordingly, the nonmoving party may defeat a motion for summary judgment that asserts that the nonmoving party has no evidence by calling the court's attention to supporting evidence already in the record that was overlooked or ignored by the moving party. In that event, the moving party must respond by making an attempt to demonstrate the inadequacy of this evidence, for it is only by attacking all the record evidence allegedly supporting the nonmoving party that a party seeking summary judgment satisfies Rule 56's burden of production.[3] . . .

The result in *Adickes,* is fully consistent with these principles. In that case, petitioner was refused service in respondent's lunchroom and then was arrested for vagrancy by a local policeman as she left. Petitioner brought an action under 42 U.S.C. § 1983 claiming that the refusal of service and subsequent arrest were the product of a conspiracy between respondent and the police; as proof of this conspiracy, petitioner's complaint alleged that the arresting officer was in respondent's store at the time service was refused. Respondent subsequently moved for summary judgment on the ground that there was no actual evidence in the record from which a jury could draw an inference of conspiracy. In response, petitioner pointed to a statement from her own deposition and an unsworn statement by a Kress employee, both already in the record and both ignored by respondent, that the policeman who arrested petitioner was in

3. Once the moving party has attacked whatever record evidence—if any—the nonmoving party purports to rely upon, the burden of production shifts to the nonmoving party, who must either (1) rehabilitate the evidence attacked in the moving party's papers, (2) produce additional evidence showing the existence of a genuine issue for trial as provided in Rule 56(e), or (3) submit an affidavit explaining why further discovery is necessary as provided in Rule 56(f). See 10A C. Wright, A. Miller & M. Kane, Federal Practice and Procedure § 2727, pp. 138-143 (2nd ed. 1983). Summary judgment should be granted if the nonmoving party fails to respond in one or more of these ways, or if, after the nonmoving party responds, the court determines that the moving party has met its ultimate burden of persuading the court that there is no genuine issue of material fact for trial. See, e.g., First National Bank of Arizona v. Cities Service Co., 391 U.S. 253, 289 (1968).

the store at the time she was refused service. We agreed that "[if] a policeman were present, . . . it would be open to a jury, in light of the sequence that followed, to infer from the circumstances that the policeman and Kress employee had a 'meeting of the minds' and thus reached an understanding that petitioner should be refused service." 398 U.S., at 158. Consequently, we held that it was error to grant summary judgment "on the basis of this record" because respondent had "failed to fulfill its initial burden" of demonstrating that there was no evidence that there was a policeman in the store. Id. at 157-158.

The opinion in *Adickes* has sometimes been read to hold that summary judgment was inappropriate because the respondent had not submitted affirmative evidence to negate the possibility that there was a policeman in the store. The Court of Appeals apparently read *Adickes* this way and therefore required Celotex to submit evidence establishing that plaintiff's decedent had not been exposed to Celotex asbestos. I agree with the Court that this reading of *Adickes* was erroneous and that Celotex could seek summary judgment on the ground that plaintiff could not prove exposure to Celotex asbestos at trial. However, Celotex was still required to satisfy its initial burden of production.

II

I do not read the Court's opinion to say anything inconsistent with or different than the preceding discussion. My disagreement with the Court concerns the application of these principles to the facts of this case.

Defendant Celotex sought summary judgment on the ground that plaintiff had "failed to produce" any evidence that her decedent had ever been exposed to Celotex asbestos. Celotex supported this motion with a two-page "Statement of Material Facts as to Which There is No Genuine Issue" and a three-page "Memorandum of Points and Authorities" which asserted that the plaintiff had failed to identify any evidence in responding to two sets of interrogatories propounded by Celotex and that therefore the record was "totally devoid" of evidence to support plaintiff's claim.

Approximately three months earlier, Celotex had filed an essentially identical motion. Plaintiff responded to this earlier motion by producing three pieces of evidence which she claimed "[at] the very least . . . demonstrate that there is a genuine factual dispute for trial": (1) a letter from an insurance representative of another defendant describing asbestos products to which plaintiff's decedent had been exposed; (2) a letter from T.R. Hoff, a former supervisor of decedent, describing asbestos products to which decedent had been exposed; and (3) a copy of decedent's deposition from earlier workmen's compensation proceedings. Plaintiff also apparently indicated at that time that she intended to call Mr. Hoff as a witness at trial.

Celotex subsequently withdrew its first motion for summary judgment. However, as a result of this motion, when Celotex filed its second summary judgment motion, the record *did* contain evidence—including at least one witness—supporting plaintiff's claim....

On these facts, there is simply no question that Celotex failed to discharge its initial burden of production. Having chosen to base its motion on the argument that there was no evidence in the record to support plaintiff's claim, Celotex was not free to ignore supporting evidence that the record clearly contained. Rather, Celotex was required, as an initial matter, to attack the adequacy of this evidence. Celotex'[s] failure to fulfill this simple requirement constituted a failure to discharge its initial burden of production under Rule 56, and thereby rendered summary judgment improper.

This case is indistinguishable from *Adickes*. Here, as there, the defendant moved for summary judgment on the ground that the record contained no evidence to support an essential element of the plaintiff's claim. Here, as there, the plaintiff responded by drawing the court's attention to evidence that was already in the record and that had been ignored by the moving party. Consequently, here, as there, summary judgment should be denied on the ground that the moving party failed to satisfy its initial burden of production.

[The dissenting opinion of JUSTICE STEVENS is omitted.]

On remand, the D.C. Circuit still refused to grant Celotex's motion. As you read the decision, consider why each appellate court to rule on *Celotex* was so sharply divided. Does it have to do with the specific facts of this case, or the implications for summary judgment in future decisions?

Catrett, Administratrix of the Estate of Louis H. Catrett, Deceased v. Johns-Manville Sales Corp.

826 F.2d 33 (D.C. Cir. 1987)

STARR, Circuit Judge, joined by WALD, Chief Judge.

This case is before us on remand from the Supreme Court. The sole question is whether the District Court properly granted summary judgment in favor of an asbestos manufacturer in a suit brought by the survivor of a victim of asbestosis....

The Supreme Court... instructed... [this court] to address questions we had previously found unnecessary to consider, namely

> the adequacy of the showing made by [Mrs. Catrett] in opposition to [Celotex's] motion for summary judgment, or... whether such a showing, if reduced to admissible evidence, would be sufficient to carry [Mrs. Catrett's] burden of proof at trial.

We thus are called upon to determine whether Mrs. Catrett's showing was sufficient to avoid summary judgment under Federal Rule of Civil Procedure 56(e). . . .

II

Upon review, we discern several items pointing to the existence of a genuine issue concerning Mr. Catrett's alleged exposure to Celotex products. First, Mrs. Catrett (twice) submitted the letter from Mr. Hoff, the Anning-Johnson executive. This letter chronicles Mr. Catrett's work for Anning-Johnson, reporting that he worked for the company for "one calendar year ending, 12/22/71." According to the Hoff letter, Mr. Catrett's "duties were to supervise and train crews in the application of Firebar Fireproofing." Thus, on its face, the letter reflects knowledge by a specific Anning-Johnson official of the deceased employee's exposure to Firebar fireproofing. The letter further relates an "understanding" that the manufacturer of Firebar was now owned by Celotex.

Confronted with this potentially damning piece of evidence, Celotex argues that the Hoff letter should be ignored by virtue of its asserted inadmissibility at trial. *See* 10A C. Wright, A. Miller & M. Kane, Federal Practice and Procedure § 2721 (2d ed. 1983) (In passing on a summary judgment motion, a court may consider materials specified in Federal Rule of Civil Procedure 56(c) as well as "any material *that would be admissible or usable at trial*." (emphasis added)).

In the circumstances of this case, we believe that the Hoff letter should be considered. . . . Mrs. Catrett argues that the letter is admissible, asserting that the Hoff letter is admissible as falling within the business records exception to the hearsay rule. See Fed. R. Evid. 803(6). *More importantly, Celotex never objected to the District Court's consideration of the Hoff letter*. . . .

In this situation, it could scarcely be clearer that the letter was before the District Court. . . . [I]t is well established that "inadmissible documents may be considered by the court if not challenged," 10A C. Wright, § 2722, at 60. . . .

The second item also relates to Mr. Hoff. In her supplemental interrogatory responses, Mrs. Catrett listed Hoff as a witness. There can, of course, be no doubt that this response is properly considered in ruling on a summary judgment motion. See Fed. R. Civ. P. 56(c) (specifically listing "answers to interrogatories" as items that may be considered). Taking this response together with the Hoff letter, the record, dispassionately viewed, reflects the existence of a witness who can testify with respect to Mr. Catrett's exposure to Firebar. Thus, even if the Hoff letter itself would not be admissible at trial, Mrs. Catrett has gone on to indicate that the substance of the letter is reducible to admissible evidence in the form of trial testimony.

Third . . . the record contains several documents, *submitted by Celotex*, recording the sale of Firebar to Anning-Johnson during the period when Mr. Catrett worked there. These [purchase orders] operate to put Firebar and Mr. Catrett in the same place at the same time. Since Mrs. Catrett's interrogatory responses make it abundantly clear that Mr. Catrett's particular vocation was the application of fireproofing, these documents go a long way toward creating a genuine issue with respect to Mr. Catrett's exposure to Firebar.

Fourth, the record reflects a direct link among the three corporate entities or divisions of relevance, namely Carey-Canadian Asbestos, Panacon Corporation, and Celotex. Carey-Canadian is identified in the sales records furnished by Celotex as the entity selling Firebar to Anning-Johnson, Mr. Catrett's employer. Those sales records describe Carey-Canadian as "A Division of Panacon Corporation." Celotex's interrogatory responses, in turn, relate that Panacon was merged into Celotex in 1972 (thus corroborating the more general statements as to corporate ownership found in the Hoff letter). The responses stated, in addition, that "this merger was . . . statutory, and The Celotex Corporation assumed the assets and ordinary liabilities of Panacon Corporation." Thus . . . the record before the District Court evinces a clear link between Carey-Canadian and Celotex, and thus between Celotex and Firebar.

III

. . . Considering the record before the District Court when it granted summary judgment — in particular, the four items discussed above — we believe that the issue of exposure was not so one-sided that Celotex was entitled to judgment as a matter of law. The record contains sufficient evidence to create a genuine issue of material fact with respect to Mr. Catrett's exposure to the asbestos product Firebar while working for Anning-Johnson. While the four items taken individually provide less than overpowering support for Mrs. Catrett's position, their cumulative effect is, we believe, sufficient to defeat the summary judgment motion. . . .

On this record, therefore, an unbroken chain links Mr. Catrett to Firebar, and Firebar to Celotex. . . . Accordingly, the District Court's grant of summary judgment was, on the basis of the record then before it, in error. We therefore reverse the judgment and remand the case for further proceedings not inconsistent with this opinion.

It is so ordered.

BORK, Circuit Judge, dissenting.

The central issue here on motion for summary judgment is causation. Defendant alleges that plaintiff has made no showing that anyone can offer personal knowledge that any exposure to asbestos occurred in this case. I agree that plaintiff has not identified "specific facts" that would indicate such exposure occurred, and I certainly think that plaintiff has not made the kind of showing necessary to defeat a directed verdict motion. I would therefore grant defendant's motion for summary judgment.

Plaintiff has identified two items that may bear on whether anyone has personal knowledge of exposure to asbestos in this case. . . .

It would seem apparent that the mere listing of a potential witness, without more, does not constitute setting forth specific facts. Here plaintiff has never claimed that Mr. Hoff has any personal knowledge that her husband was exposed to asbestos during his year of work at this company, and indeed did not specify the grounds of his possible testimony at all, except to say that he would be able to testify about "facts relevant to the subject matter of this lawsuit."

The majority concludes, however, that we should interpret plaintiff's listing of Mr. Hoff as a witness in light of his letter to the insurance company, thereby finding enough evidence to stave off the equivalent of a motion for directed verdict on causation. . . . [But], the sum total of all this "evidence" falls far short of showing, or even suggesting, that anyone has been identified who can testify from personal knowledge about any asbestos exposure. That lack alone requires that defendant's motion for summary judgment be granted. . . .

For these reasons, I think plaintiff has not carried her burden in resisting summary judgment. . . . [D]espite more than two years for discovery, she has been unable to present the district court with any "specific facts" beyond the vague listing of a potential witness not claimed to have any personal knowledge about exposure. My concern is that the majority's view may make decisions on summary judgment both more difficult and more uncertain because the majority's rationale suggests that trial judges must consider various permutations of vague and inadmissible evidence in reaching those decisions. . . . This approach represents a departure from the Supreme Court's admonition [in *Celotex*] that "summary judgment procedure is properly regarded not as a disfavored procedural shortcut, but rather as an integral part of the Federal Rules as a whole, which are designed 'to secure the just, speedy, and inexpensive determination of every action.'" I respectfully dissent.

Note: Burdens of Proof, Pleading, and Production

Reread Justice Brennan's dissent in *Celotex*, in which he describes the burdens of production and proof (persuasion) by a party moving for summary judgment and the interplay between these burdens and the more general burden of persuasion in the case. To understand the opinion, you need to distinguish among three concepts: burdens of proof and persuasion, burdens of pleading, and burdens of production. For good measure, we also add *presumptions* to this list, as they can modify the burdens.

The *burden of proof* is the burden of persuading the fact finder—jury or judge—of a material issue. In a civil case, if the evidence on an issue is in equipoise at the end of the case, then the party with the burden of proof on the issue *loses*, because the burden in most civil cases is the "preponderance of the evidence" standard. A motion for summary judgment is, in effect, an early argument by one party that because her opponent lacks sufficient evidence on an essential element of her case, she could not prevail at trial. Indeed, the party moving for summary judgment (the "movant") must establish that no reasonable fact finder could—were a trial to occur—rule for her opponent, such that the trial judge would be obliged to enter a judgment in favor of the movant as a matter of law. Thus, to evaluate whether a party is entitled to summary judgment one must consider the burden of proof that will govern the matter at trial, as well as all of the available evidence that has been, or might be, uncovered. The burden of prevailing on the *motion*, in other words, hinges in part on the burden of proof at *trial*, which may or may not rest with the party moving for summary judgment.

In allocating burdens of proof, judges are guided by precedent and, on occasion, by statutes. As Professor Morgan has observed, several factors tend to influence decisions about who has the burden:

> In reaching its determination to put this burden upon plaintiff or defendant, it is influenced by substantially the same considerations as those which obtain in the determination of any question of substantive law. . . . These respectively make it fall upon (1) the party having the affirmative of the issues, (2) the party to whose case the fact in question is essential, (3) the party having peculiar means of knowing the fact, and (4) the party who has the burden of pleading it.

Edmund M. Morgan, Some Observations Concerning Presumptions, 44 Harv. L. Rev. 906, 910-911 (1931).

As factor four of Morgan's list suggests, the party with the *burden of pleading* an issue usually—but not always—has the burden of *proving* that issue. Thus the burden of pleading is not necessarily the same as the burden of proof, and one must take care to distinguish between these two concepts, just as one must distinguish between the burden of production and the burden of proof.

Finally, there is the *burden of production*. This is the threshold burden of presenting at least *some* evidence to fulfill the obligation of taking an issue to the jury or judge so they can decide if the burden of proof is satisfied. If the issue is debatable, then the burden of production is met and the fact finder can then weigh the evidence to determine whether the party with the burden of proof should win or lose. If a party fails to meet her burden of production at trial, then her opponent is entitled to judgment as a matter of law. Again, the summary judgment motion is an early, pretrial allegation that the movant's opponent will be unable to satisfy the burden of production at trial. Hence, no trial is necessary and summary judgment is proper.

Put another way, when the plantiff has the burden of proof, the division of labor is as follows:

Pretrial

1) Plaintiff moves for summary judgment. Plaintiff must persuade judge that *defendant* will be unable to produce sufficient evidence at trial to survive plaintiff's motion for judgment as a matter of law. Essentially, this means plaintiff has such weighty or uncontradicted evidence to support each element of her prima facie case that no reasonable fact finder could find for defendant—a difficult standard to meet. (This is the pretrial motion that parallels the trial motion in paragraph 3 below.)

2) Defendant moves for summary judgment. Defendant must show that *plaintiff* will be unable to produce sufficient evidence at trial to satisfy her burden of production, such that defendant would succeed on a motion for judgment as a matter of law. (This is the *Celotex*-type pretrial motion that parallels the trial motion in paragraph 1 below.)

Trial

1) Plaintiff presents her case. If, at the close of plaintiff's evidence, there is insufficient evidence of an essential element of the prima facie case to make it debatable, then plaintiff has *not* met the burden of production. Defendant can now move for judgment as a matter of law. (This is the trial motion that parallels the defendant's summary judgment motion in paragraph 2 above.)

2) Assuming plaintiff meets her burden of production, the case proceeds.

3) Defendant presents her case. If, at the close of defendant's evidence, there is insufficient evidence to *rebut* an essential element of plaintiff's case to make it debatable, then defendant has *not* met the burden of production. Plaintiff can now move for judgment as a matter of law. (This is the trial motion that parallels the plaintiff's summary judgment motion in pretrial paragraph 1 above.)

4) Close of evidence. Assuming the burdens of production are met, the case goes to the fact finder, who weighs the evidence and decides whether the party with the burden of proof—usually the plaintiff—has satisfied the applicable standard.

One final evidentiary concept must be added to this collection. In some areas of law, rebuttable *presumptions* operate to ease a party's burden of proof. For example, a court may presume that a child born to a married woman is the offspring of the woman's legal husband. This presumption, which is based on public policy, must be taken as true once the basic facts are shown (birth of a child, valid marriage) in the absence of adequate rebuttal of either the basic facts or the presumed fact (paternity by the legal husband).

One of the major lingering questions after *Celotex* has been just how little a movant can put in the record to support a motion for summary judgment when the nonmovant has the burden of proof on the issue at trial. In a personal injury case, for instance, may the defendant simply "point out" that the plaintiff's proof of causation is weak? Is that sufficient to shift the burden of production, or must the defendant do more? Do you think the showing in *Celotex* was sufficient? For an excellent study of how *Celotex*'s change in the moving party's initial burden on summary judgment has affected practice, see Brooke D. Coleman, The *Celotex* Initial Burden Standard and an Opportunity to "Revivify" Rule 56, 32 S. Ill. U. L.J. 295 (2008) (surveying district court opinions and finding that a majority of summary judgment decisions come on cross-motions, not an early motion by defendant; that defendants tend to file extensive motions, not the one-page motions theoretically possible under *Celotex;* and that most motions come after significant discovery, not when plaintiff has not had a chance to gather evidence).

In the second summary judgment case decided in the 1986 term, the Supreme Court reversed the Third Circuit's finding that summary judgment was improper in a complex antitrust suit between Japanese and American television manufacturers. Like the other two cases in the 1986 trilogy, this one provoked a heated dissent. In the past, the Supreme Court has indicated that "summary judgment should be used sparingly in complex antitrust litigation where motive and intent play leading roles, the proof is largely in the hands of the alleged conspirators, and hostile witnesses thicken the plot." Poller v. Columbia Broad. Sys., Inc., 368 U.S. 464, 473 (1962).

In *Matsushita*, the majority apparently adhered to the idea that antitrust cases require special analysis on summary judgment, but it found that this analysis cut against the American television manufacturers, who opposed the motion.

Matsushita Elec. Indus. Co. v. Zenith Radio Corp.

475 U.S. 574 (1986)

JUSTICE POWELL delivered the opinion of the Court.

This case requires that we again consider the standard district courts must apply when deciding whether to grant summary judgment in an antitrust conspiracy case.

I

Stating the facts of this case is a daunting task. The opinion of the Court of Appeals for the Third Circuit runs to 69 pages; the primary opinion of the District Court is more than three times as long. Two respected District

Judges each have authored a number of opinions in this case; the published ones alone would fill an entire volume of the Federal Supplement. In addition, the parties have filed a 40-volume appendix in this court that is said to contain the essence of the evidence on which the [lower courts] based their respective decisions. . . . What follows is a summary of this case's long history.

A

Petitioners, defendants below, are 21 corporations that manufacture or sell "consumer electronic products" (CEPs)—for the most part, television sets. Petitioners include both Japanese manufacturers of CEPs and American firms, controlled by Japanese parents, that sell the Japanese-manufactured products. Respondents, plaintiffs below, are Zenith Radio Corporation (Zenith) and National Union Electric Corporation (NUE). Zenith is an American firm that manufactures and sells television sets. NUE is the corporate successor to Emerson Radio Company, an American firm that manufactured and sold television sets until 1970, when it withdrew from the market after sustaining substantial losses. Zenith and NUE began this lawsuit in 1974, claiming that petitioners had illegally conspired to drive American firms from the American CEP market. According to respondents, the gist of this conspiracy was a scheme to raise, fix and maintain artificially *high* prices for television receivers sold by [petitioners] in Japan and, at the same time, to fix and maintain *low* prices for television receivers exported to and sold in the United States. These "low prices" were allegedly at levels that produced substantial losses for petitioners. The conspiracy allegedly began as early as 1953, and according to respondents was in full operation by sometime in the late 1960's. Respondents claimed that various portions of this scheme violated §§ 1 and 2 of the Sherman Act, § 2(a) of the Robinson-Patman Act, § 73 of the Wilson Tariff Act, and the Antidumping Act of 1916. . . .

B

. . . [The district court granted petitioners' motion for summary judgment. The Court of Appeals reversed on the ground] that a factfinder reasonably could draw the following conclusions:

1. The Japanese market for CEPs was characterized by oligopolistic behavior, with a small number of producers meeting regularly and exchanging information on price and other matters. This created the opportunity for a stable combination to raise both prices and profits in Japan. American firms could not attack such a combination because the Japanese Government imposed significant barriers to entry.
2. Petitioners had relatively higher fixed costs than their American counterparts, and therefore needed to operate at something approaching full capacity in order to make a profit.

3. Petitioners' plant capacity exceeded the needs of the Japanese market.
4. By formal agreements arranged in cooperation with Japan's Ministry of International Trade and Industry (MITI), petitioners fixed minimum prices for CEPs exported to the American market. The parties refer to these prices as the "check prices," and to the agreements that require them as the "check price agreements."
5. Petitioners agreed to distribute their products in the United States according to a "five company rule": each Japanese producer was permitted to sell only to five American distributors.
6. Petitioners undercut their own check prices by a variety of rebate schemes. Petitioners sought to conceal these rebate schemes both from the United States Customs Service and from MITI, the former to avoid various customs regulations as well as action under the antidumping laws, and the latter to cover up petitioners' violations of the check-price agreements.

Based on inferences from the foregoing conclusions,[5] the Court of Appeals concluded that a reasonable factfinder could find a conspiracy to depress prices in the American market in order to drive out American competitors, which conspiracy was funded by excess profits obtained in the Japanese market. The court apparently did not consider whether it was as plausible to conclude that petitioners' price-cutting behavior was independent and not conspiratorial. . . .

II

We begin by emphasizing what respondents' claim is *not*. Respondents cannot recover antitrust damages based solely on an alleged cartelization of the Japanese market, because American antitrust laws do not regulate the competitive conditions of other nations' economies. Nor can respondents recover damages for any conspiracy by petitioners to charge higher than competitive prices in the American market. Such conduct would indeed violate the Sherman Act, but it could not injure respondents: as petitioners' competitors, respondents stand to gain from any conspiracy to raise the market price in CEPs. Finally, for the same reason, respondents cannot recover for a conspiracy to impose nonprice restraints that have the effect of either raising market price or limiting output. Such restrictions, though harmful to competition, actually *benefit* competitors by making supracompetitive pricing more attractive. Thus, neither

5. In addition to these inferences, the court noted that there was expert opinion evidence that petitioners' export sales "generally were at prices which produced losses, often as high as twenty-five percent on sales." The court did not identify any direct evidence of below-cost pricing; nor did it place particularly heavy reliance on this aspect of the expert evidence.

petitioners' alleged supracompetitive pricing in Japan, nor the five company rule that limited distribution in this country, nor the check prices insofar as they established minimum prices in this country, can by themselves give respondents a cognizable claim against petitioners for antitrust damages. The Court of Appeals therefore erred to the extent that it found evidence of these alleged conspiracies to be "direct evidence" of a conspiracy that injured respondents.

Respondents nevertheless argue that these supposed conspiracies, if not themselves grounds for recovery of antitrust damages, are circumstantial evidence of another conspiracy that *is* cognizable: a conspiracy to monopolize the American market by means of pricing below the market level.

The thrust of respondents' argument is that petitioners used their monopoly profits from the Japanese market to fund a concerted campaign to price predatorily and thereby drive respondents and other American manufacturers of CEPs out of business. Once successful, according to respondents, petitioners would cartelize the American CEP market, restricting output and raising prices above the level that fair competition would produce. The resulting monopoly profits, respondents contend, would more than compensate petitioners for the losses they incurred through years of pricing below market level.

The Court of Appeals found that respondents' allegation of a horizontal conspiracy to engage in predatory pricing,[8] if proved, would be a *per se* violation of § 1 of the Sherman Act. Petitioners did not appeal from that conclusion. The issue in this case thus becomes whether respondents adduced sufficient evidence in support of their theory to survive summary judgment.

III

To survive petitioners' motion for summary judgment, respondents must establish that there is a genuine issue of material fact as to whether petitioners entered into an illegal conspiracy that caused respondents to suffer a cognizable injury. Fed. Rule Civ. Proc. 56(e); First National Bank of Arizona v. Cities Service Co., 391 U.S. 253, 288-289 (1968). This showing has two components. First, respondents must show more than a conspiracy in violation of the antitrust laws; they must show an injury to them resulting from the illegal conduct. Respondents charge petitioners with a whole host of conspiracies in restraint of trade. . . . [However],

8. Throughout this opinion, we refer to the asserted conspiracy as one to price "predatorily." This term has been used chiefly in cases in which a single firm, having a dominant share of the relevant market, cuts its prices in order to force competitors out of the market, or perhaps to deter potential entrants from coming in. In such cases, "predatory pricing" means pricing below some appropriate measure of cost. . . .

unless, in context, evidence of these "other" conspiracies raises a genuine issue concerning the existence of a predatory pricing conspiracy, that evidence cannot defeat petitioners' summary judgment motion.

Second, the issue of fact must be "genuine." Fed. Rules Civ. Proc. 56(c), (e). When the moving party has carried its burden under Rule 56(c), its opponent must do more than simply show that there is some metaphysical doubt as to the material facts. Clark, Special Problems in Drafting and Interpreting Procedural Codes and Rules, 3 Vand. L. Rev. 493, 504-505 (1950). In the language of the Rule, the nonmoving party must come forward with "specific facts showing that there is a *genuine issue for trial*." Fed. Rule Civ. Proc. 56(e) (emphasis added). See also Advisory Committee Note to 1963 Amendment of Fed. Rule Civ. Proc. 56(e), 28 U.S.C. App., p.626 (purpose of summary judgment is to "pierce the pleadings and to assess the proof in order to see whether there is a genuine need for trial"). Where the record taken as a whole could not lead a rational trier of fact to find for the nonmoving party, there is no "genuine issue for trial." *Cities Service*, 391 U.S. at 289.

It follows from these settled principles that if the factual context renders respondents' claim implausible—if the claim is one that simply makes no economic sense—respondents must come forward with more persuasive evidence to support their claim than would otherwise be necessary. . . .

Respondents correctly note that "[on] summary judgment the inferences to be drawn from the underlying facts . . . must be viewed in the light most favorable to the party opposing the motion." United States v. Diebold, Inc., 369 U.S. 654, 655 (1962). But antitrust law limits the range of permissible inferences from ambiguous evidence in a § 1 case. Thus, in Monsanto Co. v. Spray-Rite Service Corp., 465 U.S. 752 (1984), we held that conduct as consistent with permissible competition as with illegal conspiracy does not, standing alone, support an inference of antitrust conspiracy. Id. at 764. See also *Cities Service*, 391 U.S., at 280. To survive a motion for summary judgment or for a directed verdict, a plaintiff seeking damages for a violation of § 1 must present evidence "that tends to exclude the possibility" that the alleged conspirators acted independently. *Monsanto*, 465 U.S. at 764. Respondents in this case, in other words, must show that the inference of conspiracy is reasonable in light of the competing inferences of independent action or collusive action that could not have harmed respondents. See *Cities Service*, 391 U.S. at 280.

Petitioners argue that these principles apply fully to this case. According to petitioners, the alleged conspiracy is one that is economically irrational and practically infeasible. Consequently, petitioners contend, they had no motive to engage in the alleged predatory pricing conspiracy; indeed, they had a strong motive *not* to conspire in the manner respondents allege. . . . This argument requires us to consider the nature of the alleged conspiracy and the practical obstacles to its implementation.

IV

A

A predatory pricing conspiracy is by nature speculative. Any agreement to price below the competitive level requires the conspirators to forgo profits that free competition would offer them. The forgone profits may be considered an investment in the future. For the investment to be rational, the conspirators must have a reasonable expectation of recovering, in the form of later monopoly profits, more than the losses suffered. As then-Professor Bork, discussing predatory pricing by a single firm, explained:

> Any realistic theory of predation recognizes that the predator as well as his victims will incur losses during the fighting, but such a theory supposes it may be a rational calculation for the predator to view the losses as an investment in future monopoly profits (where rivals are to be killed) or in future undisturbed profits (where rivals are to be disciplined). The future flow of profits, appropriately discounted, must then exceed the present size of the losses. R. Bork, The Antitrust Paradox 145 (1978).

See also McGee, Predatory Pricing Revisited, 23 J. Law & Econ. 289, 295-297 (1980). As this explanation shows, the success of such schemes is inherently uncertain: the short-run loss is definite, but the long-run gain depends on successfully neutralizing the competition. Moreover, it is not enough simply to achieve monopoly power, as monopoly pricing may breed quick entry by new competitors eager to share in the excess profits. The success of any predatory scheme depends on *maintaining* monopoly power for long enough both to recoup the predator's losses and to harvest some additional gain. Absent some assurance that the hoped-for monopoly will materialize, *and* that it can be sustained for a significant period of time, "[t]he predator must make a substantial investment with no assurance that it will pay off." Easterbrook, Predatory Strategies and Counterstrategies, 48 U. Chi. L. Rev. 263, 268 (1981). For this reason, there is a consensus among commentators that predatory pricing schemes are rarely tried, and even more rarely successful.

These observations apply even to predatory pricing by a *single firm* seeking monopoly power. In this case, respondents allege that a large number of firms have conspired over a period of many years to charge below-market prices in order to stifle competition. Such a conspiracy is incalculably more difficult to execute than an analogous plan undertaken by a single predator. The conspirators must allocate the losses to be sustained during the conspiracy's operation, and must also allocate any gains to be realized from its success. Precisely because success is speculative and depends on a willingness to endure losses for an indefinite period, each conspirator has a strong incentive to cheat, letting its partners suffer the losses necessary to destroy the competition while sharing in any gains if the conspiracy succeeds. The necessary allocation is therefore difficult to accomplish. . . .

Finally, if predatory pricing conspiracies are generally unlikely to occur, they are especially so where, as here, the prospects of attaining monopoly power seem slight. In order to recoup their losses, petitioners must obtain enough market power to set higher than competitive prices, and then must sustain those prices long enough to earn in excess profits what they earlier gave up in below-cost prices. Two decades after their conspiracy is alleged to have commenced, petitioners appear to be far from achieving this goal: the two largest shares of the retail market in television sets are held by RCA and respondent Zenith, not by any of petitioners. Moreover, those shares, which together approximate 40% of sales, did not decline appreciably during the 1970's. Petitioners' collective share rose rapidly during this period, from one-fifth or less of the relevant markets to close to 50%. Neither the District Court nor the Court of Appeals found, however, that petitioners' share presently allows them to charge monopoly prices; to the contrary, respondents contend that the conspiracy is ongoing — that petitioners are still artificially *depressing* the market price in order to drive Zenith out of the market. The data in the record strongly suggest that that goal is yet far distant.

The alleged conspiracy's failure to achieve its ends in the two decades of its asserted operation is strong evidence that the conspiracy does not in fact exist. Since the losses in such a conspiracy accrue before the gains, they must be "repaid" with interest. . . . If the losses have been substantial — as would likely be necessary in order to drive out the competition — petitioners would most likely have to sustain their cartel for years simply to break even.

Nor does the possibility that petitioners have obtained supracompetitive profits in the Japanese market change this calculation. Whether or not petitioners have the *means* to sustain substantial losses in this country over a long period of time, they have no *motive* to sustain such losses absent some strong likelihood that the alleged conspiracy in this country will eventually pay off. The courts below found no evidence of any such success, and — as indicated above — the facts actually are to the contrary: RCA and Zenith, not any of the petitioners, continue to hold the largest share of the American retail market in color television sets. . . .

B

In *Monsanto*, we emphasized that courts should not permit factfinders to infer conspiracies when such inferences are implausible, because the effect of such practices is often to deter procompetitive conduct. *Monsanto*, 465 U.S. at 762-764. Respondents, petitioners' competitors, seek to hold petitioners liable for damages caused by the alleged conspiracy to cut prices. Moreover, they seek to establish this conspiracy indirectly, through evidence of other combinations (such as the check-price agreements and the five company rule) whose natural tendency is to raise prices, and through evidence of rebates and other price-cutting activities that respondents argue tend to prove a combination to suppress prices. But cutting prices in order to increase business often is the very essence of competition. Thus, mistaken inferences in cases such as this one are especially costly, because they chill the very conduct the antitrust laws are designed to protect. See id. at 763-764. "[We] must be concerned lest a rule or precedent that authorizes a search for a particular type of undesirable pricing behavior end up by discouraging legitimate price competition." Barry Wright Corp. v. ITT Grinnell Corp., 724 F.2d 227, 234 (1st Cir. 1983).

In most cases, this concern must be balanced against the desire that illegal conspiracies be identified and punished. That balance is, however, unusually one-sided in cases such as this one. As we earlier explained, predatory pricing schemes require conspirators to suffer losses in order eventually to realize their illegal gains; moreover, the gains depend on a host of uncertainties, making such schemes more likely to fail than to succeed. These economic realities tend to make predatory pricing conspiracies self-deterring: unlike most other conduct that violates the antitrust laws, failed predatory pricing schemes are costly to the conspirators. See Easterbrook, The Limits of Antitrust, 63 Texas L. Rev. 1, 26 (1984). Finally, unlike predatory pricing by a single firm, *successful* predatory pricing conspiracies involving a large number of firms can be identified and punished once they succeed, since some form of minimum price-fixing agreement would be necessary in order to reap the benefits of predation. Thus, there is little reason to be concerned that by granting summary judgment in cases where the evidence of conspiracy is speculative or ambiguous, courts will encourage such conspiracies.

V

[P]etitioners had no motive to enter into the alleged conspiracy. To the contrary, as presumably rational businesses, petitioners had every incentive *not* to engage in the conduct with which they are charged, for its likely effect would be to generate losses for petitioners with no corresponding gains. The Court of Appeals did not take account of the absence of a plausible motive to enter into the alleged predatory pricing conspiracy. . . .

The "direct evidence" on which the court relied was evidence of *other* combinations, not of a predatory pricing conspiracy. Evidence that petitioners conspired to raise prices in Japan provides little, if any, support for respondents' claims: a conspiracy to increase profits in one market does not tend to show a conspiracy to sustain losses in another. Evidence that petitioners agreed to fix *minimum* prices (through the check-price agreements) for the American market actually works in petitioners' favor, because it suggests that petitioners were seeking to place a floor under prices rather than to lower them. The same is true of evidence that petitioners agreed to limit the number of distributors of their products in the

American market—the so-called five company rule. That practice may have facilitated a horizontal territorial allocation, but its natural effect would be to raise market prices rather than reduce them. Evidence that tends to support any of these collateral conspiracies thus says little, if anything, about the existence of a conspiracy to charge below-market prices in the American market over a period of two decades.

That being the case, the absence of any plausible motive to engage in the conduct charged is highly relevant to whether a "genuine issue for trial" exists within the meaning of Rule 56(e). Lack of motive bears on the range of permissible conclusions that might be drawn from ambiguous evidence: if petitioners had no rational economic motive to conspire, and if their conduct is consistent with other, equally plausible explanations, the conduct does not give rise to an inference of conspiracy. . . .

The decision of the Court of Appeals is reversed, and the case is remanded for further proceedings consistent with this opinion.

It is so ordered.

JUSTICE WHITE, with whom JUSTICE BRENNAN, JUSTICE BLACKMUN, and JUSTICE STEVENS join, dissenting.

. . . In defining what respondents must show in order to recover, the Court makes assumptions that invade the factfinder's province. The Court states with very little discussion that respondents can recover under § 1 of the Sherman Act only if they prove that "petitioners conspired to drive respondents out of the relevant markets by (i) pricing below the level necessary to sell their products, or (ii) pricing below some appropriate measure of cost." This statement is premised on the assumption that "[an] agreement without these features would either leave respondents in the same position as would market forces or would actually benefit respondents by raising market prices." In making this assumption, the Court ignores the contrary conclusions of respondents' expert DePodwin, whose report in very relevant part was erroneously excluded by the District Court.

The DePodwin Report, on which the Court of Appeals relied along with other material, indicates that respondents were harmed in two ways that are independent of whether petitioners priced their products below "the level necessary to sell their products or . . . some appropriate measure of cost." First, the Report explains that the price-raising scheme in Japan resulted in lower consumption of petitioners' goods in that country and the exporting of more of petitioners' goods to this country than would have occurred had prices in Japan been at the competitive level. Increasing exports to this country resulted in depressed prices here, which harmed respondents.[2] Second, the DePodwin Report indicates that

2. Dr. DePodwin summarizes his view of the harm caused by Japanese cartelization as follows:

> When we consider the injuries inflicted on United States producers, we must again look at the Japanese television manufacturers' export agreement as part of a generally collusive scheme embracing the Japanese domestic market as well. This

petitioners exchanged confidential proprietary information and entered into agreements such as the five company rule with the goal of avoiding intragroup competition in the United States market. The Report explains that petitioners' restrictions on intragroup competition caused respondents to lose business that they would not have lost had petitioners competed with one another.[3]

The DePodwin Report alone creates a genuine factual issue regarding the harm to respondents caused by Japanese cartelization and by agreements restricting competition among petitioners in this country. No doubt the Court prefers its own economic theorizing to Dr. DePodwin's,

---

scheme increased the supply of television receivers to the United States market while restricting supply in the Japanese market. If Japanese manufacturers had competed in both domestic and export markets, they would have sold more in the domestic market and less in the United States. A greater proportion of Japanese production capacity would have been devoted to domestic sales. Domestic prices would have been lower and export prices would have been higher. The size of the price differential between domestic and export markets would have diminished practically to the vanishing point. Consequently, competition among Japanese producers in both markets would have resulted in reducing exports to the United States and United States prices would have risen. In addition, investment by the United States industry would have increased. As it was, however, the influx of sets at depressed prices cut the rates of return on television receiver production facilities in the United States to so low a level as to make such investment uneconomic.

We can therefore conclude that the American manufacturers of television receivers would have made larger sales at higher prices in the absence of the Japanese cartel agreements. Thus, the collusive behavior of Japanese television manufacturers resulted in a very severe injury to those American television manufacturers, particularly to National Union Electric Corporation, which produced a preponderance of television sets with screen sizes of nineteen inches and lower, especially those in the lower range of prices.

3. The DePodwin Report has this, among other things, to say in summarizing the harm to respondents caused by the five company rule, exchange of production data, price coordination, and other allegedly anti-competitive practices of petitioners:

The impact of Japanese anti-competitive practices on United States manufacturers is evident when one considers the nature of competition. When a market is fully competitive, firms pit their resources against one another in an attempt to secure the business of individual customers. However, when firms collude, they violate a basic tenet of competitive behavior, i.e., that they act independently. United States firms were confronted with Japanese competitors who collusively were seeking to destroy their established customer relationships. Each Japanese company had targeted customers which it could service with reasonable assurance that its fellow Japanese cartel members would not become involved. But just as importantly, each Japanese firm would be assured that what was already a low price level for Japanese television receivers in the United States market would not be further depressed by the actions of its Japanese associates.

The result was a phenomenal growth in exports, particularly to the United States. Concurrently, Japanese manufacturers, and the defendants in particular, made large investments in new plant and equipment and expanded production capacity. It is obvious, therefore, that the effect of the Japanese cartel's concerted actions was to generate a larger volume of investment in the Japanese television industry than would otherwise have been the case. This added capacity both enabled and encouraged the Japanese to penetrate the United States market more deeply than they would have had they competed lawfully.

but that is not a reason to deny the factfinder an opportunity to consider Dr. DePodwin's views on how petitioners' alleged collusion harmed respondents.

The Court, in discussing the unlikelihood of a predatory conspiracy, also consistently assumes that petitioners valued profit-maximization over growth. In light of the evidence that petitioners sold their goods in this country at substantial losses over a long period of time, I believe that this is an assumption that should be argued to the factfinder, not decided by the Court.

The majority relies on a lot of scholarly commentary about the economics of anti-competitive behavior. Is relying on this commentary still viewing the evidence in the light most favorable to the nonmovant? What value does the evidence of additional conspiracies have for the material issue of whether a predatory pricing conspiracy existed in the United States market? Is the Court's analysis limited to antitrust cases, or does it have broader implications for summary judgment in all cases?

Note: Anderson v. Liberty Lobby, Inc., 477 U.S. 242 (1986)

In *Anderson*, the final case in the 1986 trilogy, the Court made summary judgment more readily available in libel cases. The Court, in an opinion by Justice White, explained its view of the relationship between a motion for summary judgment under Fed. R. Civ. P. 56 and one for a directed verdict under Fed. R. Civ. P. 50(a) as follows:

> [T]he "genuine issue" summary judgment standard is "very close" to the "reasonable jury" directed verdict standard: "The primary difference between the two motions is procedural; summary judgment motions are usually made before trial and decided on documentary evidence, while directed verdict motions are made at trial and decided on the evidence that has been admitted." Bill Johnson's Restaurants, Inc. v. NLRB, 461 U.S. 731, 745, n.11 (1983). In essence, though, the inquiry under each is the same: whether the evidence presents a sufficient disagreement to require submission to a jury or whether it is so one-sided that one party must prevail as a matter of law.
>
> Progressing to the specific issue in this case, we are convinced that the inquiry involved in a ruling on a motion for summary judgment or for a directed verdict necessarily implicates the substantive evidentiary standard of proof that would apply at the trial on the merits. If the defendant in a run-of-the-mill civil case moves for summary judgment or for a directed verdict based on the lack of proof of a material fact, the judge must ask himself not whether he thinks the evidence unmistakably favors one side or the other but whether a fair-minded jury could return a verdict for the plaintiff on the

evidence presented. The mere existence of a scintilla of evidence in support of the plaintiff's position will be insufficient; there must be evidence on which the jury could reasonably find for the plaintiff. The judge's inquiry, therefore, unavoidably asks whether reasonable jurors could find by a preponderance of the evidence that the plaintiff is entitled to a verdict—"whether there is [evidence] upon which a jury can properly proceed to find a verdict for the party producing it, upon whom the *onus* of proof is imposed." [Improvement Co. v. Munson, 81 U.S. (14 Wall.) 442, 448 (1872).]

In terms of the nature of the inquiry, this is no different from the consideration of a motion for acquittal in a criminal case, where the beyond-a-reasonable-doubt standard applies and where the trial judge asks whether a reasonable jury could find guilt beyond a reasonable doubt. See Jackson v. Virginia, 443 U.S. 307, 318-319 (1979). Similarly, where the First Amendment mandates a "clear and convincing" standard, the trial judge in disposing of a directed verdict motion should consider whether a reasonable factfinder could conclude, for example, that the plaintiff had shown actual malice with convincing clarity. . . .

In sum, we conclude that the determination of whether a given factual dispute requires submission to a jury must be guided by the substantive evidentiary standards that apply to the case. This is true at both the directed verdict and summary judgment stages. Consequently, where the *New York Times* [376 U.S. 254, 285 (1964)] "clear and convincing" evidence requirement applies, the trial judge's summary judgment inquiry as to whether a genuine issue exists will be whether the evidence presented is such that a jury applying that evidentiary standard could reasonably find for either the plaintiff or the defendant. Thus, where the factual dispute concerns actual malice, clearly a material issue in a *New York Times* case, the appropriate summary judgment question will be whether the evidence in the record could support a reasonable jury finding either that the plaintiff has shown actual malice by clear and convincing evidence or that the plaintiff has not. . . . Because the Court of Appeals did not apply the correct standard in reviewing the District Court's grant of summary judgment, we vacate its decision and remand the case for further proceedings consistent with this opinion.

477 U.S. at 251-255.

Justice Brennan dissented on the following grounds:

I simply cannot square the direction that the judge "is not himself to weigh the evidence" with the direction that the judge also bear in mind the "quantum" of proof required and consider whether the evidence is of sufficient "caliber or quantity" to meet that "quantum." I would have thought that a determination of the "caliber and quantity," i.e., the importance and value, of the evidence in light of the "quantum," i.e., amount "required," could *only* be performed by weighing the evidence.

If in fact, this is what the Court would, under today's decision, require of district courts, then I am fearful that this new rule—for this surely would be a brand new procedure—will transform what is meant to provide an expedited "summary" procedure into a full-blown paper trial on the merits. It is hard for me to imagine that a responsible counsel, aware that the judge

> will be assessing the "quantum" of the evidence he is presenting, will risk either moving for or responding to a summary judgment motion without coming forth with *all* of the evidence he can muster in support of his client's case. Moreover, if the judge on motion for summary judgment really is to weigh the evidence, then in my view grave concerns are raised concerning the constitutional right of civil litigants to a jury trial. . . .
>
> In my view, if a plaintiff presents evidence which either directly or by permissible inference (and these inferences are a product of the substantive law of the underlying claim) supports all of the elements he needs to prove in order to prevail on his legal claim, the plaintiff has made out a prima facie case and a defendant's motion for summary judgment must fail regardless of the burden of proof that the plaintiff must meet. In other words, whether evidence is "clear and convincing," or proves a point by a mere preponderance, is for the factfinder to determine. As I read the case law, this is how it has been, and because of my concern that today's decision may erode the constitutionally enshrined role of the jury, and also undermine the usefulness of summary judgment procedure, this is how I believe it should remain.

477 U.S. at 266-268.

Justice Rehnquist, joined by Chief Justice Burger, also dissented.

A study by the Libel Defense Resource Center reports that media defendants' ultimate success rate on summary judgment motions reached 82.3 percent during 1995-1996. This marks an increase in success rate that is likely attributable to Anderson v. Liberty Lobby, 477 U.S. 242 (1986). See Mass Media — Defamation: Study Finds Media Success in Summary Judgments at Peak, 66 U.S.L.W. 2186 (Sept. 30, 1997).

Notes and Questions

1. *Appeal*. When a district court grants summary judgment on all claims in a case, this creates a final judgment which can be appealed. But what if summary judgment is denied, the case goes to trial, and the movant loses before the jury as well? Can the movant raise the denial of summary judgment on appeal? Generally, appellate courts will not review the denial of summary judgment after a trial on the merits. Can you see why? Think about the standard set out in the Supreme Court trilogy. Can you imagine grounds for an exception to this general rule? What if the summary judgment motion involves only questions of law?

As one court describes the general rule:

> [A] denial of summary judgment is a prediction that the evidence will be sufficient to support a verdict in favor of the nonmovant. Once the trial has taken place, our focus is on the evidence actually admitted and not on the earlier summary judgment record. After the trial, the merits should be judged in relation to the fully-developed record emerging from trial. . . . We will not at that point step back in time to determine whether a different judgment may have been warranted on the record at summary judgment.

Chemetall GMBH v. ZR Energy, Inc., 320 F.3d 714, 718-719 (7th Cir. 2003) (internal citations and quotation marks omitted). Nevertheless, the court recognized an exception on the facts before it because the summary judgment motion denied by the lower court involved only questions of law—specifically, the validity of a confidentiality agreement and covenant not to compete signed by the plaintiff employee: "But when, as in this case, the court's denial of summary judgment is not based on the adequacy of the evidence, the justification we just described does not apply." Id. at 719. Reviewing the denial of summary judgment on a question of law after the jury trial would not put the court in the position of re-judging the case on incomplete proof. In so holding, the Seventh Circuit joined six other circuits, see id. at 719 (listing other decisions), and widened the split with the Fourth Circuit, which held in Chesapeake Paper Prods. Co. v. Stone & Webster Eng'g Corp., 51 F.3d 1229, 1236 (4th Cir. 1995), that summary judgment denials are unreviewable because it is often difficult to separate legal and factual grounds and because any legal issue can be preserved for appeal by making a motion for judgment as a matter of law under Rule 50 at the close of evidence at trial. In *Chemetall*, the appealability of a denial of summary judgment was presented precisely because counsel for plaintiff failed to make a proper Rule 50 motion challenging once again the validity of the confidentiality agreement. See 320 F.3d at 719-720.

2. *Partial Summary Judgment*. Read Rules 56(b) and 54(d). Particularly in complex cases with multiple parties and claims, these rules permit the judge to dispose of portions of the case as to which no factual dispute exists. The result is a better-defined, simpler lawsuit at trial than would be possible without partial summary judgment.

3. *Sua Sponte Summary Judgment*. As *Celotex* noted, a motion by a party is not necessary for a judge to award summary judgment *sua sponte*, but due process requires notice and an opportunity to be heard when a judge acts on her own to dispose of a claim or the entire case. See also DL Res., Inc. v. FirstEnergy Solutions Corp., 506 F.3d 209, 223 (3d Cir. 2007) ("District courts may grant summary judgment *sua sponte* in appropriate circumstances. However, a district court may not generally grant summary judgment *sua sponte* unless it gives prior notice and an opportunity to oppose summary judgment."). That means a judge cannot isolate weak claims and throw them out just because the parties have filed for summary judgment on other aspects of the case. See *DL Res.*, 506 F.3d at 223. The parties must be informed that the court is considering granting summary judgment *sua sponte* on that claim and given a chance to respond.

A recognized exception to the notice requirement is where "(1) the point at issue is purely legal; (2) the record was fully developed[;] and (3) the failure to give notice does not prejudice the party." Gibson v. Mayor & Council of Wilmington, 355 F.3d 215, 219-224 (3d Cir. 2004).

c. A New Standard for Summary Judgment?

Plainly, the Supreme Court hoped its reframing of the Rule 56 standard in the 1986 trilogy would enhance the role of summary judgment. In an early commentary, Professor Jack Friedenthal suggested that the ultimate effect of the cases was actually "uncertain and could prove to be limited, in part because a number of the Justices dissented in each of these cases, and in part because the Court has somewhat of a history of deciding one summary judgment case one way, only to return later with an opinion leaning the other way." Cases on Summary Judgment: Has There Been a Material Change in Standards?, 63 Notre Dame L. Rev. 770 (1988). Other commentators took a less sanguine view; see, for instance, Jeffrey W. Stempel, A Distorted Mirror: The Supreme Court's Shimmering View of Summary Judgment, Directed Verdict, and the Adjudication Process, 49 Ohio St. L.J. 95, 161 (1988) (warning against the unfairness to plaintiffs of a regime in which summary judgment is freely granted).

Some, however, have hailed the three cases as harbingers of a new day when the "summary judgment motion is a viable and welcome alternative to needless and extended litigation in federal courts." Judge Lawrence Pierce, Summary Judgment: A Favored Means of Summarily Resolving Disputes, 53 Brook. L. Rev. 279, 286 (1987). One study found a "widespread and dramatic recasting of summary judgment doctrine by the lower courts" since the 1986 trilogy, with many such motions freely granted at the district court level. Samuel Issacharoff and George Loewenstein, Second Thoughts About Summary Judgment, 100 Yale L.J. 73, 88 (1990).

Judge Patricia M. Wald, one of the circuit judges in *Celotex*, who insisted on remand from the Supreme Court that summary judgment could not stand, Catrett v. Johns-Manville Sales Corp., 826 F.2d 33 (D.C. Cir. 1987), *cert. denied*, 484 U.S. 1066 (1988), has written of the course of summary judgment practice since the trilogy:

> [W]e are now at a stage where the focus should be on ensuring that summary judgment stays within its proper boundaries, rather than on encouraging its unimpeded growth. Its expansion across subject matter boundaries and its frequent conversion from a careful calculus of factual disputes (or the lack thereof) to something more like a gestalt verdict based on an early snapshot of the case have turned it into a potential juggernaut which, if not carefully monitored, could threaten the relatively small residue of civil trials that remain.

Patricia M. Wald, Summary Judgment at Sixty, 76 Tex. L. Rev. 1897, 1917 (1998).

More recent studies indicate that summary judgment is both more frequently sought, and more frequently granted, but the data also show these trends beginning well before the 1986 trilogy. See, e.g., Joe S. Cecil et al., Trends in Summary Judgment Practice: A Preliminary Analysis 1-3

(Federal Judicial Center 2001); see also Stephen B. Burbank, Vanishing Trials and Summary Judgment in Federal Civil Cases: Drifting Towards Bethlehem or Gomorrah?, 1 J. Empirical Legal Stud. 591 (2004); Stephen B. Burbank, Keeping Our Ambition Under Control: The Limits of Data and Inference in Searching for the Causes and Consequences of Vanishing Trials in Federal Court, 1 J. Empirical Legal Stud. 571 (2004). For arguments that the trilogy has indeed made an impact, see Martin H. Redish, Summary Judgment and the Vanishing Trial: Implications of the Litigation Matrix, 57 Stan. L. Rev. 1329 (2005) (arguing that liberalized summary judgment is one of the main reasons why a lower percentage of cases go to trial today); Marc Galanter, The Vanishing Trial: An Examination of Trials and Related Matters in Federal and State Courts, 1 J. Empirical Legal Stud. 459 (2004); Arthur R. Miller, The Pretrial Rush to Judgment: Are the "Litigation Explosion," "Liability Crisis," and Efficiency Clichés Eroding Our Day in Court and Jury Trial Commitments?, 78 N.Y.U. L. Rev. 982 (2003). No one disputes that fewer cases are going to trial, but the underlying reasons are difficult to isolate and measure. See Marc Galanter, The Hundred-Year Decline of Trials and the Thirty Years War, 57 Stan. L. Rev. 1255, 1257-1260 (2005) (reporting that federal civil trials fell "from a high of 12,570 in 1985 to 4,206 in 2003" and a gradual decline in state trials, but also pointing to evidence of a "steady downward trend . . . in progress for more than a century, marking a long historic movement away from trial as a mode of disposing of civil cases").

Professor Suja Thomas has recently argued that modern summary judgment procedure is unconstitutional because it denies civil litigants their Seventh Amendment right to a jury trial. See Suja A. Thomas, Why Summary Judgment Is Unconstitutional, 93 Va. L. Rev. 139 (2007). The Seventh Amendment guarantees litigants the right to a jury trial in all legal actions that would have been tried to a jury at English common law. Professor Thomas contends that "no procedure similar to summary judgment existed under the English common law" and that summary judgment in fact "violates the core principles or 'substance' of the English common law," id. at 139-140. She adds that

> the substance of the common law is surprisingly clear. First, under the common law, the jury or the parties determined the facts. . . . A court itself never decided the case without such a determination by the jury or the parties, however improbable the evidence might be. Second, only after the parties presented evidence at trial and only after a jury rendered a verdict, would a court ever determine whether the evidence was sufficient to support a jury verdict. If the court decided that the evidence was insufficient to support the verdict, it would order a new trial. Another jury would determine the facts and decide which party won. In other words, if the court itself believed the evidence was insufficient, it would never determine who should win. Third, a jury would decide every case in which there was any evidence, however improbable the evidence was, unless the moving party admitted the facts and conclusions of the nonmoving party, including the improbable facts and conclusions.

> These core principles of the common law reveal that summary judgment is unconstitutional. Under summary judgment, a court decides whether a "genuine issue as to any material fact" exists or, in other words, whether "a reasonable jury could return a verdict for the nonmoving party." Under this standard, in contrast to under the common law, the court decides whether factual inferences from the evidence are reasonable, applies the law to any "reasonable" factual inferences, and as a result makes the determination as to whether a claim could exist. In other words, the court decides whether the case should be dismissed before a jury hears the case. Under the common law, a court would never engage in this determination. Cases that would have been decided by a jury under the common law are now dismissed by a judge under summary judgment.

Id. at 143. See also John Bronsteen, Against Summary Judgment, 75 Geo. Wash. L. Rev. 522 (2007) (noting strong evidence that summary judgment violates the Seventh Amendment and arguing that the civil justice system would be both fairer and more efficient without it).

Professor Thomas's article provoked a stir both on the bench and in legal journals. Several federal court judges cited the article and commented on its conclusions in their opinions. See In re Zyprexa Prods. Liab. Litig., 489 F. Supp. 2d 230, 263 (E.D.N.Y. 2007) (noting that the increasing use of early dismissal procedures like summary judgment "poses a threat to the continued viability of the Seventh Amendment jury trial"); In re One Star Class Sloop Sailboat Built in 1930 with Hull No. 721, Named "Flash II," 517 F. Supp. 2d 546, 555 (D. Mass. 2007) ("[F]ederal courts overuse summary judgment as a case management tool."). See also Cook v. McPherson, No. 07-5552, 2008 WL 904736, at *3 (6th Cir. Apr. 2, 2008) (noting that the "historical examination [in the article] . . . is interesting," but ultimately rejecting the plaintiff's argument that summary judgment is unconstitutional).

Other scholars have defended the use of Rule 56 as a constitutional and necessary expedient to resolve modern cases. See William E. Nelson, Summary Judgment and the Progressive Constitution, 93 Iowa L. Rev. 1653 (2008) (largely agreeing with Thomas's historical findings, but arguing that the Constitution should not be tied to anachronistic, centuries-old law and instead should be capable of evolution in response to changing societal needs); Edward Brunet, Summary Judgment Is Constitutional, 93 Iowa L. Rev. 1625 (2008) (arguing that modern summary judgment is consistent with the Seventh Amendment and that two historical antecedents used by common law courts, trial by inspection and demurrer to the evidence, justify its use). But see Suja Thomas, Why Summary Judgment Is Still Unconstitutional: A Reply to Professors Brunet and Nelson, 93 Iowa L. Rev. 1667 (2008) (rejecting the analogies to trial by inspection and demurrer to the evidence and arguing that the substance of common law jury trials should continue to control the question of summary judgment's constitutionality); Suja Thomas, Why the Motion to Dismiss Is Now Unconstitutional, 92 Minn. L. Rev. 1851 (2008) (extending her analysis to 12(b)(6) motions).

The Supreme Court's only full-dress opinion on the standard for summary judgment since the trilogy is Cleveland v. Policy Management System Corp., 526 U.S. 795 (1999). Cleveland swore that she was totally disabled in her application for Social Security benefits after a stroke. Later she went back to work, but was fired. She brought suit under the Americans with Disabilities Act (ADA), alleging that the employer had failed to make a reasonable accommodation to her disability, which would have enabled her to "perform the essential functions of her job." The lower courts found that she was judicially estopped from bringing a claim under the ADA because of her prior sworn statement, and granted summary judgment. The Supreme Court reversed, holding that the prior statement raised only a rebuttable presumption against her:

> Summary judgment for a defendant is appropriate when the plaintiff "fails to make a showing sufficient to establish the existence of an element essential to [her] case, and on which [she] will bear the burden of proof at trial." *Celotex*, 477 U.S. at 322. An ADA plaintiff bears the burden of proving that she is a "qualified individual with a disability"—that is, a person "who, with or without reasonable accommodation, can perform the essential functions" of her job.... And a plaintiff's sworn assertion in an application for disability benefits that she is, for example, "unable to work" will appear to negate an essential element of her ADA case—at least if she does not offer a sufficient explanation. For that reason, we hold that an ADA plaintiff cannot simply ignore the apparent contradiction that arises out of the earlier SSDI total disability claim. Rather, she must proffer a sufficient explanation.... To defeat summary judgment that explanation must be sufficient to warrant a reasonable juror's concluding that, assuming the truth of, or the plaintiff's good faith belief in, the earlier statement, the plaintiff could nonetheless "perform the essential functions" of her job, with or without "reasonable accommodation."

What might the plaintiff be able to show, by way of explanation, to overcome her sworn statement in her application for Social Security benefits?

2. Summary Judgment Problems

Sample Issues

Based on the foregoing materials on summary judgment, how would you answer the following questions?

a. Assume that a corporation is sued for employment discrimination in hiring. One person, a supervisor, was solely responsible for hiring for the open position. He denies intent to discriminate. Can the plaintiff survive a motion for summary judgment on the ground that the fact finder might disbelieve the supervisor?

b. Assume instead that a plaintiff sues the city for negligence in failure to repair a large pothole, which she claims caused her to swerve into a parked car on the side of the road. There is only one witness, who says plaintiff's car did not swerve; rather, plaintiff drove straight into the back of the parked car while plaintiff seemed to be distracted. Evidence at the scene indicates that plaintiff had a cup of hot coffee in the car, which she had just purchased at a drive-through restaurant, and that an opened but half-full container of cream was on the front seat next to her. Should the city's motion for summary judgment be granted?

c. Assume that 90 percent of all taxicabs in Dodge City are owned by defendant Orange Cab Co. Plaintiff was injured in a hit-and-run accident in the early morning hours. Plaintiff sues Orange Cab Co. She states at her deposition that the vehicle that hit her was a taxicab, but she can recall nothing more specific. The only other taxicab company in town is the Yellow Cab Co., whose cabs look very similar to Orange Cab Co.'s though they are a slightly lighter color. Their records indicate that only one of their drivers was out that morning, and he claims that he was in a different part of town that morning. Plaintiff and defendant Orange Cab Co. file cross-motions for summary judgment. Should either one be granted?

d. Plaintiff, a lawyer, sues defendant, her law partner, for defamation, claiming that defendant had made false statements that plaintiff was padding clients' bills for personal profit. Defendant denies making the statements. Defendant deposes the three people to whom the defamatory statements allegedly were made, all of whom deny that defendant made the statements. Defendant then moves for summary judgment. Should it be granted? See Dyer v. MacDougall, 201 F.2d 265 (2d Cir. 1952).

Consider in this regard the following language from Colosi v. Electri-Flex Co., 965 F.2d 500, 503 (7th Cir. 1992), in an opinion by Judge Posner:

> If a party presents multiple affidavits on summary judgment, covering the same ground, and some are shown to be unworthy of belief but others are not, do those others entitle the party to summary judgment or can the falsity of some support a negative inference about the others? We should think the latter, at least in extreme cases. If (to choose a number at random) a party presents nine affidavits each saying the same thing, and eight are shown to be perjurious, we would doubt that the party was entitled to summary judgment merely because the last stood uncontradicted.

Exercise: A Literary Law Student

Prepare a motion for summary judgment on behalf of Doolittle in the matter of Doolittle v. Turow, in the form that you would use to file it in a federal district court. Assume that the action is pending in the United

States District Court for the Northern District of California and has been assigned Case No. 97-909. You can see from Form 19 that a motion for summary judgment consists of several basic parts: 1) notice of the motion; 2) the motion itself; 3) any attachments to the motion, for example, affidavits; 4) a brief entitled "Memorandum in Support of Motion for Summary Judgment," explaining why the movant is entitled to prevail; and 5) a certificate of service. The judge's name is Wisdom. Below is a sample certificate of service:

Certificate of Service

The undersigned certifies that a true and exact copy of the foregoing Motion for Summary Judgment Pursuant to Rule 56 of the Federal Rules of Civil Procedure, and Memorandum in Support of Motion for Summary Judgment was, this 10th day of August, 2000, served upon the following party of record:

Dorothy B. Spornak
Venable and Gold, P.C.
115 South Main Street
San Francisco, California 90013

/s/
____
William A. Loomis, Attorney for Defendant

The form for Doolittle's affidavit would be along these lines:

Doolittle)
)
v.
)
)
Monson)

AFFIDAVIT

I, Donna Doolittle, being first duly sworn on oath, depose and state as follows:

1. I am [fill in the appropriate description].

2. (and 3. or more) [List the allegation(s) Doolittle would swear to in order to make her case for summary judgment.]

FURTHER AFFIANT SAYETH NOT

____

Subscribed and Sworn to before me this

________ day of ___________ 200____.

/s/

____

Notary Public

C. AN OVERVIEW OF A TRIAL

Some cases, about 2 to 5 percent of those filed in federal court, survive the blandishments of settlement and the hurdles of early adverse rulings, and actually go to trial — sometimes even trial by jury. As rare as it is, the trial drama nevertheless defines American procedure, and everything happens in its looming shadow. Here is an outline of the basic features of the civil trial, though, like all dramas, it needs enactment for full understanding.

Problem Case: Hailing a Cab

P was walking his dog late one summer night in Whittier, a small community in Montana, when a cab jumped the curb and injured him. *P*, who is from Idaho, was visiting a cousin in Montana. *P* sued Checker Cab Co., one of only two cab companies in Whittier, in federal court based on diversity of citizenship. Is *P* entitled to trial by jury in this matter?

Assume *P* is entitled to trial by jury. *P* has little recollection of the moments before the incident other than his vivid memory that it was a taxicab that hit him. As he says, "The last thing I saw was a flash of black and white and a meter sign bearing down on me!" At trial, *P* produces no other evidence of the identity of the cab that hit him. Checker Cabs are all black and white. The only other cab company in Whittier is the Domino Cab Co., whose cabs also are black and white. After *P* rests, Checker introduces documentary and other evidence that none of its cabs were on *P*'s street at the time and date in question. The jury returns a verdict for *P*. Checker then moves (for the first time) for judgment as a matter of law.

What result? What other evidence of identity of the cab could *P* have introduced? How might *P* have obtained that evidence?

Note: The Problem of Proof

Now that you have mastered pleading and several important pretrial motions, you might consider how, exactly, a lawyer "proves" her case or otherwise demonstrates that there is a factual dispute worth trying. While the pleading should put defendant on notice of a legal claim raised by the alleged facts, the pleading is not proof, only allegations.

Proof is, of course, the testimony of any witnesses to the alleged event, which can be supplied on the stand, in a deposition, or both. Likewise, there may be physical evidence that supports the claim, such as tire tracks or a bloody glove. Documentary evidence, such as business records or memoranda, may be introduced through a witness who can lay the proper foundation for the evidence.

There also may be expert witnesses who can offer opinions about the allegations that shore up or negate a party's claim. Experts must be qualified as such, and, their testimony is subject to special rules in discovery and at trial. As we saw in Chapter 3, expert testimony is expensive and may be subject to abuse. For these and other reasons, the use of experts in litigation has been the subject of substantial critical commentary. See, e.g., J. Alexander Tanford, The Ethics of Evidence, 25 Am. J. Trial Advoc. 487, 547-549 (2002); L. Timothy Perin, Expert Witness Testimony, 29 U. Rich. L. Rev. 389 (1995); Peter Huber, Galileo's Revenge: Junk Science in the Courtroom (1991); John William Strong, Language and Logic in Expert Testimony: Limiting Expert Testimony by Restrictions of Function, Reliability and Form, 71 Or. L. Rev. 349 (1992); cf. Gross and Mnookin, Expert Evidence and Expert Information: A Preliminary Taxonomy, 34 Seton Hall L. Rev. 139 (2003). But the most common complaints are not new. See, e.g., Learned Hand, Historical and Practical Considerations Regarding Expert Testimony, 15 Harv. L. Rev. 40 (1901).

Facts can also, on occasion, be established without formal proof through the doctrine of "judicial notice." Essentially, judicial notice is allowed when the facts in question lie within common knowledge or can otherwise be determined from an irrefutable source, such that it makes little sense to force the parties to prove them through affirmative evidence. For example, a court might take judicial notice that "where cypress grows, pine doesn't grow." See Fox v. City of W. Palm Beach, 383 F.2d 189, 195 n.2 (5th Cir. 1967). The doctrine has also been referred to as a means by which things that "any damn fool knows" need not be established, but can instead be judicially noticed.

And finally, the parties can simply stipulate to certain facts and thereby avoid the time and expense of generating the evidence to prove them.

With respect to all of these means of establishing facts, except stipulations, the lawyers must consider the applicable law of evidence. If the only evidence on a crucial point is inadmissible hearsay, then it is of no help to the party invoking it. The opponent can object to the introduction of that evidence, and the judge must grant the objection.

Careful litigators often outline the essential elements of their claims and make a list of witnesses or other available admissible evidence that supports these elements. As a trial progresses, the lawyer may make a notation on the outline when evidence of each element is introduced and actually admitted into the record. This assures that *all* elements are supported by evidence both presented and *admitted* into the record before the lawyer rests, a step much easier to overlook than you might imagine, especially in a complex case.

D. THE STAGES OF A TRIAL

1. Opening Arguments

The trial begins with opening statements by plaintiff, in which the plaintiff's lawyer outlines for the decision maker — judge or jury — what the case is about, what arguments she will make, and how she intends to prove them. The defendant may follow with her opening statements, or may reserve the right to do this later, after the plaintiff has presented her case.

2. Presentation of Evidence

The plaintiff then presents her case by calling witnesses to the stand and asking them questions on direct examination. After the plaintiff completes her examination of a witness, the defendant is entitled to cross-examine the witness. The plaintiff then may respond with redirect examination, and the defendant may follow with recross-examination, and so on until the witness is excused.

Formal rules of evidence govern the permissible nature and content of the lawyers' questioning. Under the rules the lawyers have the primary responsibility for raising evidentiary objections and doing so in a timely fashion; if the lawyers make no objection to otherwise inadmissible evidence, it usually will be admitted. For example, a witness may repeat the statement of another person in her testimony, to which the opposing lawyer may object on the ground of "hearsay." The judge then must rule on whether the statement violates the federal rules regarding hearsay evidence — there are numerous exceptions to the ban on hearsay — after hearing the lawyers' arguments about the statement's admissibility. If the opposing lawyer does not raise the hearsay objection, however, then the statement will be admitted. The judge's role is—primarily—to umpire, not advocate, though judges have some authority to call and interrogate witnesses, and they vary widely in their willingness to actively supervise the trial.

"Evidence" can take multiple forms, such as expert testimony, documents, pictures, physical evidence, and lay testimony. The verdict must be based solely on the evidence that is accepted by the court. Thus the lawyers must be careful to assure that some credible evidence has been admitted to support every element of their case before they rest.

When the plaintiff has presented all of her witnesses and evidence, she will rest. If, after the plaintiff rests, the defendant believes that the plaintiff has failed to establish a prima facie case, then the defendant will move for a judgment as a matter of law (also known as directed verdict) on the ground that no reasonable fact finder could rule in the plaintiff's favor. The judge usually will deny or reserve a ruling on this motion, and the defendant typically will proceed to present her case. At the close of the defendant's case, the plaintiff may present any additional evidence as necessary to meet any new matters raised by the defendant's witnesses; the defendant, in turn, may follow with such evidence as may be necessary to respond to plaintiff's evidence.

3. Motions Testing the Sufficiency of the Evidence

After both sides have rested, either or both may move for judgment as a matter of law. If the motions are denied, the case goes to the jury or—in a bench trial—to the judge.

4. Closing Arguments and Jury Instructions

If the case is tried to a jury, the judge issues instructions to guide the jury's deliberation, with input from the lawyers. Each lawyer offers proposed instructions, which the trial judge considers in crafting the final instructions. Typically, the lawyers prepare these instructions before trial, as this helps them to focus on what must be established to prevail and to prepare their cases accordingly.

The lawyers' closing statements may precede the jury instructions (jurisdictions vary on this), though the instruction conference between the judge and lawyers occurs before the closing statements. In closing arguments, the lawyers review the evidence actually introduced and explain how it supports their party's theory. Although the judge, not the lawyer, instructs the jury on the law, effective closing arguments explain in detail why that law supports the party's position. Lawyers also often parallel the opening statements so that they offer the fact finder a logical conclusion to a coherently and logically presented case.

5. Jury Deliberations and Verdicts

In a jury case, the jury will retire to deliberate after the closing arguments and delivery of instructions. The judge may request that the jurors deliver one of three types of verdicts: general, general with interrogatories, or special. Which type of verdict to request is usually left to the discretion of the trial judge.

The general verdict, which is the most common type, asks only that the jury decide who wins and the amount of damages. A general verdict with interrogatories asks for the same information as a general verdict, plus answers to several specific questions. If the jury's general verdict is inconsistent with its specific answers, the specific answers control. Finally, the special verdict asks the jury to answer specific factual questions only; the judge then applies the law to their responses and decides who wins.

In a case tried to a judge, the case merely concludes after closing arguments and the judge later delivers her ruling. In some cases, the judge may ask the lawyers to submit proposed findings of fact and conclusions of law, which the judge may incorporate into her final opinion.

6. Post-Verdict Motions

In a case tried to a jury, after the jury returns its verdict the judgment will be entered on the verdict. The losing party may then move for a judgment notwithstanding the verdict ("jnov")—now called a renewed motion for judgment as a matter of law—or may move for a new trial. The grounds for a renewed motion are the same as those for judgment as a matter of law. A new trial motion, in contrast, addresses a broader range of defects of a trial, such as admission of improper evidence, jury misconduct, improper jury instructions, or other grounds.

In the case of a bench trial, the losing party typically responds to an unfavorable ruling by appealing, rather than seeking further relief from the trial judge.

For an excellent, practical introduction to the basic elements of trial practice, see Thomas A. Mauet, Trials (2d ed. 2009); Thomas A. Mauet and Warren D. Wolfson, Trial Evidence (4th ed. 2009); Thomas A. Mauet, Trial Techniques (7th ed. 2007).

5 *Decision Makers and Decision Models*

INTRODUCTION

It matters who decides. Lawyers invest much skill and energy in efforts to reach the "right" decision maker. The legal system invests at least as much effort and expense in trying to prevent the identity of the decision maker from assuming significance. The effort to reach the same result, no matter who decides, is the essence of the rule of law.

Although our ideal is that all litigants are treated the same, regardless of their own, or the decision maker's, identity, we know that ideals are never fully attained, so that lawyers will continue to worry about the procedures for determining who decides. In an adversary system, moreover, one side's choice of decision maker is constantly subject to the charge of bias, incompetence, or inconvenience by the other side. You have already seen in our study of jurisdiction how the issue of who decides is a question that can itself stir great litigation battles.

This chapter will examine some of the bimodal choices that confront lawyers in their quest for an understanding tribunal in a particular case: judge or jury; litigation or an alternative. We look first at how judges are chosen and at the great powers they wield. Then we consider the jury, how it is chosen, and its powers (which we study through the efforts of the trial judge and the appellate courts to manage the jury). Finally, we introduce you to some of the leading methods of alternative dispute resolution.

A. THE JUDGE

Problem Case: Judicial Positioning

Many lawyers regard a judicial appointment, especially to the federal bench, as the crown of a successful legal career. If you were to begin now in shaping your professional life so as to be in the best position for a judgeship sometime in the future, what steps would you take? What law school or other activities would you pursue? What jobs, post-law school? What professional and personal contacts would you cultivate?

Why would a person want to become a judge? Why might someone *not* want such a job? To what sorts of people is such a position likely to be most appealing? Are they likely to be the best ones for the job?

1. Judicial Selection: Appointment and Election

a. Selection of Federal Judges

Article II of the Constitution provides that the President shall nominate and appoint federal judges, with the "Advice and Consent" of the Senate. For Supreme Court Justices, the President has often nominated candidates without significant senatorial consultation. Although most Supreme Court nominations have been approved by the Senate, on occasion this practice has resulted in heated confirmation fights within the Senate, and some nominations have been rejected or withdrawn in the face of likely rejection.

By contrast, the traditional practice for nominating federal district court judges has been for the nomination to originate with the senior senator of the President's political party from the nominee's state.

Federal court of appeals judges have traditionally been selected through a joint effort of the executive and legislative branches. The President has more power with regard to these appointments because the circuits include multiple states; a President having difficulty with a senator on a court of appeals appointment has the option of appointing a judge from a different state.

The procedures to be observed by the President in selecting judicial candidates and the Senate in considering nominees are not specified in any constitutional or statutory provisions. As objectives have shifted over the years, the process has taken on a variety of forms. See Judith Resnik, Judicial Selection and Democratic Theory: Demand, Supply, and Life Tenure, 26 Cardozo L. Rev. 579 (2005); Symposium: Federal Judicial Selection, 39 U. Rich. L. Rev. 793 (2004).

As the chart on the following page depicts, regardless of selection procedures, presidential priorities can dramatically shape the profile of federal judicial nominees.

b. Federal Magistrates and Special Masters

In 1968, Congress created the office of United States Magistrate to replace a former system of U.S. Commissioners. Unlike the commissioner, the magistrate was to be paid a fixed salary, to be an attorney if at all possible, to serve a fixed term of eight years, and to be subject to removal from office only for cause. 28 U.S.C. § 636; Fed. R. Civ. P. 72-76. Section 636 provided that any district court "may establish rules pursuant to which any full-time United States magistrate . . . may be assigned such

Percentage of Female and Minority Appointees by George W. Bush Compared to Prior Presidents

President/Term	*Total appointments*	*Male*	*Female*	*White*	*African American*	*Latino*	*Asian American*	*Native American*	*Arab American*
George W. Bush 2001-2008	311	242 (77.8%)	69 (22.2%)	258 (83%)	21 (6.8%)	28 (9%)	4 (1.3%)	0	N/A
Clinton 1993-2000	378	267 (70.6%)	111 (29.4%)	285 (75.4%)	62 (16.4%)	24 (6.3%)	5 (1.3%)	1 (0.26%)	1 (0.26%)
Bush 1989-1992	192	156 (81.2%)	36 (18.8%)	172 (89.6%)	11 (5.7%)	8 (4.2%)	1 (0. 5%)	0	0
Reagan 1981-1988	378	347 (91.8%)	31 (8.2%)	356 (94.2%)	7 (1.9%)	13 (3.4%)	2 (0.5%)	0	0
Carter 1977-1980	258	217 (84.1%)	41 (15.9%)	202 (78.3%)	37 (14.3%)	16 (6.2%)	2 (0.8%)	1 (0.4%)	0
Ford 1974-1976	65	64 (98.5%)	1 (1.5%)	59 (90.8%)	3 (4.6%)	1 (1.5%)	2 (3.1%)	0	0
Nixon 1969-1974	227	226 (99.6%)	1 (0.4%)	218 (96.0%)	6 (2.6%)	2 (0.9%)	1 (0.4%)	0	0

* Of the twenty one, one was Roger Gregory, President Clinton's recess appointment to the Fourth Circuit.

Source: Judicial Selection During the Bush Administration (2008); Alliance for Justice Judicial Selection Project 2001-02 Biennial Report.

additional duties as are not inconsistent with the Constitution and laws of the United States." Magistrates are appointed by the district courts that they serve, and these courts determine their duties.

Congressional concern about the increased burdens on federal trial judges motivated the creation of the magistrate position. The legislation's goal of diverting to magistrates many matters that would otherwise consume judicial time has been realized. Since the statute was passed in 1968, there has been a steady increase in both the number and complexity of matters referred to magistrates.

Magistrates are not appointed by the President in the manner prescribed by Article III of the Constitution, but are appointed by the judges to whom they are subordinate. They also do not enjoy life tenure. This arrangement has led many to argue—so far unsuccessfully—that delegating federal judicial authority to magistrates violates Article III. In a criminal case, United States v. Raddatz, 447 U.S. 667, 681 (1980), the Supreme Court rejected the argument that Article III was violated when an evidentiary ruling was referred to a magistrate:

> Congress made clear that the district court has plenary discretion whether to authorize a magistrate to hold an evidentiary hearing and that the magistrate acts subsidiary to and only in aid of the district court. Thereafter, the entire process takes place under the district court's total control and jurisdiction.
>
> We need not decide whether . . . Congress could constitutionally have delegated the task of rendering a final decision on a suppression motion to a non-Article III officer . . . Congress has not sought to make any such delegation.

Pressures to increase the authority of magistrate judges remain strong. Citing the "mounting queue of civil cases" in the district courts and a desire to "improve access to the courts for all groups," Congress substantially expanded the power of magistrate judges to conduct jury trials, decide dispositive motions, and enter final judgment in the Federal Magistrate Act of 1979. S. Rep. No. 96-74, at 4 (1979). Under the statute, magistrates can now handle "any or all proceedings in a jury or nonjury civil matter and order the entry of judgment in the case" if the parties consent to disposition by the magistrate and if the judge has been "specially designated" by the district court. 28 U.S.C. § 636(c)(1). Significantly, § 636(c)(1) proceedings conducted by magistrate judges occur without any supervision or review by district courts and a judgment entered by the magistrate judge pursuant to section 636(c)(1) is treated as a final judgment of the district court.

The parties' consent is the only effective way to prevent busy or biased district courts from coercing certain litigants into trials before magistrate judges. Nonetheless, Congress amended the Act in 1990 to permit district courts to "again advise the parties of the availability of the magistrate" even after they have declined referral. Judicial Improvements Act, 28 U.S.C. § 636(c)(2). And more recently, the Supreme Court has held that consent to case-dispositive authority for a magistrate judge need not be express if the circumstances indicate that the parties "clearly implied their consent." Roell v. Withrow, 538 U.S. 580, 586 (2003) (finding implied consent where defendants appeared before the magistrate judge and did not express any reservation after being notified of their right to refuse the judge's exercise of case-dispositive authority). Defendants prevailed before the magistrate judge and the plaintiff attempted to use their failure expressly to consent as grounds for vacating the judgment. The Court observed that its implied consent rule would "check[] the risk of gamesmanship by depriving parties of the luxury of waiting for the outcome before denying the magistrate judge's authority. Judicial efficiency is served; the Article III right is substantially honored." Id. at 590. Four Justices dissented, emphasizing that express consent "ensures that the parties knowingly and voluntarily waive their right to an Article III judge." Id. at 595.

Under Rule 53, district court judges also have the power to appoint special masters in exceptional, complex cases. The powers and compensation of the master are subject to the judge's discretion. The master is to assist the judge or jury, as directed, but the master's factual findings are accepted unless clearly erroneous in nonjury cases, and may be admissible as evidence in jury cases. Fed. R. Civ. P. 53(e).

As a practical matter, the sub-judiciary has become indispensable. Federal judges likely could not manage their caseloads effectively without delegating some tasks to magistrates and special masters. The question, therefore, is not whether to deploy these assistants, but how, and according to what system of appointment, compensation, and judicial review. See Mark A. Fellows & Roger S. Haydock, Federal Court Special Masters: A Vital Resource in the Era of Complex Litigation, 31 Wm. Mitchell L. Rev. 1269 (2005); 2004 Special Masters Conference: Transcript of Proceedings, 31 Wm. Mitchell L. Rev. 1193 (2005).

Amendments to Rule 53 in 2003 confirm the indispensability of and increasingly extensive reliance on special masters. Gone is the language of section (b) that "[a] reference to a master shall be the exception and not the rule." Fed. R. Civ. P. 53(b) (1993). The new Rule also explicitly permits special masters to "address pretrial and post-trial matters that cannot be addressed effectively and timely by an available district judge or magistrate judge of the district." Rule 53(a)(1)(C). Before the amendments, the Rule only discussed "trial" masters, implying that special masters should not be assigned to handle pre- and posttrial issues. The amendment recognizes facts on the ground since special masters have long been assigned non-trial matters.

c. Selection of State Judges

The judges who serve in the judicial systems of the states are selected by diverse methods. The history and extent of this variety are summarized in the following article.

Glenn Winters, Selection of Judges—An Historical Introduction

44 Tex. L. Rev. 1081, 1082-1086 (1966)

The early years of our national existence probably stand without parallel in the intensity of popular interest in government. The hardships of emigration from the comfortable, settled life of the old country and the struggle for survival in the new world placed a premium on self-reliance and independence which found expression in all aspects of life, including government. The new nation as a whole was a grand experiment in popular self-government, and the spirit of experimentation did not cease with the adoption of the federal and state constitutions. There had never been an elected judiciary, but with the new concept of sovereignty in the populace as a whole, it was inevitable that someone would propose popular election of judges, since governors and legislators were already being elected. This was not particularly designed for improving justice but was simply another manifestation of the populism movement. However, there is some indication that it was inspired in part by a feeling that judges were being appointed too frequently from the ranks of the wealthy and privileged. Apparently the first elected judges were lower court judges in Georgia, elected as early as 1812. Mississippi, in 1832, was the first state to adopt a completely elective judiciary. New York, however, by action of its constitutional convention in 1846, led the switch from legislative and gubernatorial appointment to election. All states entering the Union from then until the entrance of Alaska in 1958 came in with an elected judiciary, and even the colonial states of Georgia, Maryland, Virginia, and Pennsylvania joined in the switch from appointment to election. New Hampshire, Massachusetts, Connecticut, Rhode Island, New Jersey, Delaware, and South Carolina resisted and to this day have never had elected judges.

Dissatisfaction began to develop almost immediately after election of the judiciary came into vogue in the mid-1800's. In the 1860's, the Tammany Hall organization in New York City seized control of the elected judiciary and aroused public indignation by ousting able judges and putting in incompetent ones. As a result, the question of a return to the appointment method was submitted to the people by referendum in 1873 but was defeated. Tammany control of the judiciary continued, and similar conditions in other states led to a revulsion against the elective system soon after it was established. Virginia went back to legislative selection after fourteen years of judicial elections. Vermont elected minor court judges for twenty years but abandoned this method in 1870. Even Mississippi went back to appointment in 1868 and retained it until 1910. Furthermore, states which retained the elective system became increasingly concerned about the adverse effects of political selection on the quality of judicial personnel and developed the nonpartisan ballot as a means of "taking the judges out of politics."

The nonpartisan-ballot system gained its greatest acceptance around the turn of the century in the states of the Northwest, from Ohio and

Michigan to the Pacific coast, but it was also adopted in others such as Arizona and Tennessee. It soon became clear, however, that this was not the answer. As early as 1913, William Howard Taft, then ex-President of the United States and destined to be Chief Justice of the United States Supreme Court, told the American Bar Association that the nonpartisan ballot was a failure. He asserted that the system would only further lower the quality of judicial personnel by making it possible for unqualified persons who could not even get political support to run entirely on their own and to get elected by means of aggressive campaigning.

The early years of the twentieth century were times of activity, interest, and progress in judicial administration. In 1906, Roscoe Pound, a youthful professor at the University of Nebraska, delivered his historic address before the American Bar Association on "Causes of Popular Dissatisfaction with the Administration of Justice," in which he declared that popular election of judges had almost destroyed the traditional respect for the bench. In 1913, the same year that Taft addressed the American Bar Association, the American Judicature Society was founded by Pound, John H. Wigmore, Herbert Harley, and others as an instrumentality through which persons interested in the administration of justice might work together for its improvement.

Albert M. Kales, a member of Wigmore's faculty at Northwestern University and also one of the founders of the American Judicature Society, was director of research for the new organization. A brilliant lawyer and student of judicial administration, Kales set out to devise a method of judicial selection that would combine the benefits and avoid the weaknesses of both election and appointment. He saw the strength of the appointive system in its pinpointing of responsibility for the selections and in the opportunity it offered for intelligent appraisal of the candidate's qualifications, in contrast to the usual unfamiliarity of the voter with the requirements of the office and the extent to which the candidates met them. Kales viewed the latter as the chief weakness of the elective system, along with the preeminence election naturally gave to political rather than judicial qualifications, a fault to be found also, however, under a political appointive system. He felt that there was some merit in the desire of the people to keep in their own hands as much control over their government as possible, and he saw a positive benefit in the reminder to the elected judge that he is the people's servant and not their master.

The system which Kales devised and which the American Judicature Society took up and promoted consisted of appointment and election with the addition of a third element—a nonpolitical nominating commission. Under this plan, judicial vacancies would be filled through appointment by a high elected official from a list of names submitted by the commission, which would have an affirmative responsibility to seek out the best available judicial talent. The judges nominated and appointed would thereafter go before the voters, without competing candidates, on the sole question of their retention in office. In the event of a rejection, the resulting vacancy would be filled as before by nomination and appointment.

In 1937, nearly twenty-five years after its formulation, this plan was given the endorsement of the American Bar Association. Three years later it was voted into the constitution of Missouri and has since been commonly known as the Missouri Plan. Its application in Missouri was limited to the supreme court, the court of appeals, the circuit and probate courts of St. Louis and Jackson County (Kansas City), and the St. Louis Court of Criminal Correction. . . .

California almost preceded Missouri's action by six years, having adopted a combination appointive-elective plan for its appellate courts in 1934. A last-minute legislative compromise, however, removed the vital nominating commission and substituted a confirming commission instead.

During the twenty-five years since adoption of the Missouri Plan in 1940, some or all of its features have been adopted for use in selecting some or all of the judges of a dozen states. . . .

The nominating-commission plan has also been used on a voluntary basis, without a constitutional or statutory mandate, in several other states.

In recent years, campaign battles over judgeships have grown intense and costly, sometimes inducing opponents to spend millions of dollars. Hot button political issues including abortion, tort reform, same-sex marriage, and school financing and reform have made the races more contentious, increasingly high profile, and often more dependent on the support of political parties. Those who favor the election of judges argue that campaigning forces judges to be accountable to those who live under the law and requires them to be responsive to and represent a wider array of views. Critics allege that leaving judicial selection to political whims forces judges and their opponents to shape their views according to public opinion rather than their interpretation of the law and to abdicate the impartiality that justice requires. Currently, 42 states choose at least some of their judges through political elections. Over 80 percent of state appeals court judges retain their power through the electoral process. William Glaberson, Fierce Campaigns Signal a New Era for State Courts, N.Y. Times, June 5, 2000, at A1.

2. Judicial Qualifications

In America there is no formal, extended training program for judges beyond those required for certification as a lawyer. This is not true of all systems. In many European countries, for example, it is usual to establish a separate career track for judges who undergo longer educational programs and meet somewhat more rigorous academic standards than other members of the legal profession. One possible consequence is reduced social mobility, since those who are willing and able to undergo the longer and more rigorous program will tend to be from a more privileged socioeconomic class. This may mean, in turn, that the degree to which the judicial establishment reflects the politics and values of minorities and the disadvantaged is lessened. If these consequences are real, are there offsetting advantages? It may depend on the extent to which the attributes required for judicial work can be inculcated by formal training. In the absence of convincing data, is it intuitively reasonable to suppose that those who have undergone more rigorous academic training will be more courageous, decisive, fair, patient, or sane? Or is it reasonable to suppose that those who invested more in their judicial careers will be more likely to manifest the desired traits?

As an alternative to the separate track approach, the idea that judges should continue their education after attaining judicial office has gained credence in recent decades. While a substantial effort to move in this direction has been made by various public agencies and private institutions, the appropriate subjects of on-the-job training for judges have not yet been settled.

What about the candidate's philosophy regarding judicial authority? To what extent should the candidate's belief in *stare decisis*, statutory language, or the "plain meaning" of constitutional provisions as restraints on judicial discretion be relevant?

Catherine Pierce Wells has described two basic strands of judicial philosophy — formalism and realism — as follows:

> In analyzing the judicial task, legal theorists have generally divided into two camps. On the one hand, there are formalists who argue that legal decision making is a matter of applying preexisting rules or theories to the facts of a given case. On the other hand, there are realists who reject this idea and argue that substantive legal theories do not decide concrete cases. Not surprisingly, these two camps possess different attitudes towards judicial selection. The formalist places the emphasis on substantive law and normative theory, beginning the process with assumptions about the correctness of certain legal views and proceeding to make an evaluation by examining the candidate's grasp of and commitment to these views. The realist, by contrast, focuses on character and background, asking whether the prospective judge has the kind of character and background that would produce sound intuitions for resolving legal controversies. . . .

Catherine Pierce Wells, Clarence Thomas: The Invisible Man, 67 S. Cal. L. Rev. 117, 119-120 (1993). See also Gregory C. Sisk and Michael Heise, Judges and Ideology: Public and Academic Debates About Statistical Measures, 99 Nw. U. L. Rev. 743 (2005).

Controversy over the issue of judicial philosophy and over the extent to which inquiries into the candidate's position on particular legal disputes are fair game was fever-pitched during the failed confirmation hearings of Judge Robert Bork. These hearings, during which the nominee underwent intense and specific questioning on a range of legal issues, gave rise to a new verb: "Borking" a nominee. The disappointed candidate thereafter penned a work in which he angrily denounced the process that led to his defeat and the legal philosophy of his detractors. Robert H. Bork, The Tempting of America: The Political Seduction of the Law (1990).

What about race, ethnicity, or gender? Some commentators have argued that a judge should decide a case "from the bottom up," which means, among other things, that the judge should be "sensitive to a diverse range of interests." See Wells, supra, at 128-131. Does this imply the further step of assuring that the bench as a whole be diverse, in order to improve its overall ability to hear a wide range of voices? If it does, what kind of diversity will further this end? Of particular, sometimes divisive, concern is whether a candidate's race, ethnicity, or gender should be relevant factors in judicial appointments. Here again, Supreme Court nominations have been the most visible example of how these factors can bear on judicial selections.

In a letter published in the New York Times, Judge A. Leon Higginbotham made the following argument in favor of treating racial diversity as a relevant factor in making judicial appointments:

> Since Justice Thomas moved from the Court of Appeals to the Supreme Court, *no* African-Americans appointed by President Bush remain on the Courts of Appeals. As Judge Reinhardt has said: "In President Bush's view, Clarence Thomas is apparently all there is out there. Clarence Thomas *is* black America to our President."
>
> By 1993, six of the 10 African-Americans sitting on the Courts of Appeals will be eligible for retirement. As the African-American judges appointed by President Carter have retired, Presidents Reagan and Bush have replaced them largely with white judges in their 30's and early 40's. Why is it important for the Federal bench to be pluralistic? Pluralism, more often than not, creates a milieu in which the judiciary, the litigants — indeed, our democratic system — benefit from the experience of those whose backgrounds reflect the breadth of the American experience.
>
> I do not want to be misunderstood. Pluralism does not mean that only a judge of the same race as a litigant will be able to adjudicate the case fairly. Rather, by creating a pluralistic court, we make sure judges will reflect a broad perspective. For example, speaking of Justice Thurgood Marshall, Justice Sandra Day O'Connor said: "At oral arguments and conference meetings, in opinions and dissents, Justice Marshall imparted not only his legal acumen but also his life experiences, pushing and prodding us to respond not only to the persuasiveness of legal argument but also to the power of moral truth."
>
> Judicial pluralism is important for another reason. It is difficult to have a court that in the long run has the respect of most segments of the population if the court has no or minuscule pluralistic strands. Of course, pluralism does not absolutely and forever guarantee an effective and fair judiciary. Nothing really does. However, pluralism is a sine qua non in building a court that is both substantively excellent *and* respected by the general population. In other words, judicial pluralism breeds judicial legitimacy. Judicial homogeneity, by contrast, is more often than not a deterrent to, rather than a promoter of, equal justice for all.

A. Leon Higginbotham, The Case of the Missing Black Judges, N.Y. Times, July 29, 1992, at A-21.

Others have argued that gender diversity should likewise be relevant to judicial appointments decisions. Like people of color, women of all races have been underrepresented on the judiciary. See, e.g., Judith Resnik, Revising the Canon: Feminist Help in Teaching Procedure, 61 U. Cin. L. Rev. 1181, 1191 (1993).

Both Judge Higginbotham and Professor Resnik regard the absence of members of certain groups within the judiciary as troublesome. But in what ways, exactly, is that absence potentially problematic? Is the matter similar to the problem produced by a jury that is not cross-representative of the community? If so, what *is* that problem? Does it go to the appearance of justice, its content, or both?

The extent to which one regards racial, gender, and ethnic pluralism on the bench as important also may depend on the extent to which one regards law as open-ended and judges as properly filling in the interstices. As such, the realist versus formalist discussion also may have a bearing on the diversity issue.

3. Disqualification of Judges in Individual Cases

Problem Case: The Prejudiced Judge

Graham Buchanan, the lawyer for the plaintiff in a personal injury case that is in federal court because the parties are diverse, believes that the federal district judge, Rosemary McArthur, is biased against him to such a degree that she cannot fairly try any case in which he appears. His evidence of bias is as follows:

1) That, while in law school in 1985-1988, he and McArthur were academic rivals and that McArthur is biased against Buchanan because he was chosen as editor-in-chief of the law review rather than McArthur; McArthur at that time stated to the law school newspaper that the sole reason he was chosen instead of her was that he was male, which Buchanan told the newspaper was "feminist fantasy."
2) That McArthur is biased against Buchanan for political reasons. He was the head of the law student chapter of the Federalist Society, a politically conservative organization, and she headed the student chapter of the National Lawyers' Guild, a politically liberal organization. During an argument between them over welfare, in spring of 1988, McArthur called Buchanan's position "fascist fantasy."
3) That, before McArthur became a federal judge in 1999, she and Buchanan served together on a state bar committee charged with investigating allegations of ethical violations. During their joint tenure,

Buchanan brought a complaint against McArthur, accusing her of refusing to pursue claims brought against women or minorities. McArthur denied the charge and warned Buchanan that such accusations were slanderous, but filed no action against him. The complaint against her was dismissed for lack of evidence.

4) That, in 1998, Buchanan and McArthur were opposing counsel in a personal injury suit, and McArthur told Buchanan that she would "mop the courtroom floor with him." Her client prevailed in the suit. No other, similar courtroom incidents between them occurred after 1998. They opposed each other in four subsequent lawsuits without problems.
5) That, shortly after McArthur was appointed to the federal bench in 1999, Buchanan saw McArthur at a bar function and said to her, in a joking tone, "Well, now we're even, Rose. You think I got editor-in-chief because I'm a male, and I think you got a federal judgeship because you're a female." McArthur made no response to Buchanan's quip.

Buchanan since has appeared before Judge McArthur in three matters. In the first, his client prevailed when the opponent defaulted. The second is currently in discovery. The third matter is the one at hand.

Statutes and Precedents

Two statutes, 28 U.S.C. Sections 144 and 455, govern the disqualification of judges in federal cases. Section 144 permits a party to file a "timely and sufficient affidavit" alleging that the judge is either biased against that party or in favor of an opponent. Such a challenge may be made only once in each case, with the judge retaining the power to deny the motion and remain on the case. Section 455 mandates that a judge "shall disqualify himself in any proceeding in which his impartiality might reasonably be questioned," and further may not continue to preside over a case if any of a series of specific circumstances obtain.

Virtually every state code has some process by which lawyers may challenge the impartiality of the judge assigned to hear a case. Many state codes, unlike the federal statutes, give each side one free strike — similar to a peremptory challenge to a juror — which may be exercised to excuse a judge without offering a reason. Section 144, by contrast, requires the challenging party to state reasons for alleging bias and leaves it in the judge's discretion to remain on the case despite the challenge.

The following scenarios, drawn from actual federal cases, involve judges accused of being "too partial" to hear the particular disputes before them. As you read them, consider whether you think the judges exhibited bias and whether you believe the challenges were well-founded.

United States v. Hatahley

In this case, the district court judge was deemed too partial to hear an action filed by Native Americans in southeastern Utah for losses of horses and burros that were seized and destroyed by the United States government in pursuance of its range clearance program. Evidence of the judge's bias was thought to lie in his statements describing the range clearance program, with its instances of brutal handling and slaughter of the Native Americans' livestock, as "'horrible,' 'monstrous,' 'atrocious,' 'cruel,' 'coldblooded depredation,' and 'without a sense of decency.'" United States v. Hatahley, 257 F.2d 920 (10th Cir. 1958). The district judge also suggested that Congress or the president should conduct investigations to determine the tribe's aboriginal rights, and threatened to conduct one himself. A public appeal on behalf of the plaintiffs was made for funds and supplies to be cleared through the judge's chambers.

Haines v. Liggett Group, Inc.

In the second case, the district judge was held to have compromised the appearance of impartiality by making the following statements — which were widely publicized in the media — in a case brought against the tobacco industry:

> In the light of the current controversy surrounding breast implants, one wonders when all industries will recognize their obligation to voluntarily disclose risks from the use of their products. All too often in the choice between the physical health of consumers and the financial well-being of business, concealment is chosen over disclosure, sales over safety, and money over morality. Who are these persons who knowingly and secretly decide to put the buying public at risk solely for the purpose of making profits and who believe that illness and death of consumers is an appropriate cost of their own prosperity!
>
> . . . [D]espite some rising pretenders, the tobacco industry may be the king of concealment and disinformation.

Haines v. Liggett Group, Inc., 975 F.2d 81 (3d Cir. 1992).

Pennsylvania v. Local Union 542, International Union of Operating Engineers

The third case involved a petition for disqualification of Judge Higginbotham, on the ground that his involvement in racial justice issues made him too partial to hear a race discrimination case. He said that the evidence of his alleged personal bias included the following:

> 1) That the instant case is a class action, brought under the Civil Rights Act of 1964 and other civil rights statutes, charging that defendants have

discriminated against the twelve black plaintiffs and the class they represent on the basis of race, and seeking extensive equitable and legal remedies for the alleged discrimination;

2) That I will try the instant case without a jury, and that I am black;

3) That on Friday, October 25, 1974, I addressed a luncheon meeting of the Association for the Study of Afro-American Life and History, during the 59th Annual Meeting of that organization, "a group composed of black historians";

4) That in the course of that speech I criticized two recent Supreme Court decisions which involved alleged racial discrimination, and said, *inter alia,* that:

(a) "I do not see the [Supreme] Court of the 1970's or envision the Court of the 1980's as the major instrument for significant change and improvement in the quality of race relations in America";

(b) "The message of these recent decisions is that if we are to deal with the concept of integration, we must probably make our major efforts in another forum";

(c) "As I see it, we must make major efforts in other forums without exclusive reliance on the federal legal process."

5) That I used the pronoun "we" several times in the course of the speech, and that my use of this pronoun evidences my "intimate tie with and emotional attachment to the advancement of black civil rights";

6) That by my agreement to deliver the speech I presented myself as "a leader in the future course of the black civil rights movement";

7) That my speech took place in "an extra-judicial and community context," and not in the course of this litigation;

8) That the following day, Saturday, October 26, 1974, *The Philadelphia Inquirer* published "an article appearing under a predominant headline on the first page of the metropolitan news section, . . . describing the October 25th meeting and publishing the aforementioned quotes";

9) That approximately 450,000 copies of *The Philadelphia Inquirer* containing this account were distributed publicly on or about October 26, 1974;

10) That this account made "the community at large" aware of my "significant role as a spokesman, scholar and active supporter of the advancement of the causes of integration";

11) That I believe "that there has been social injustice to blacks in the United States"; "that these injustices must be corrected and remedied"; and "that they must be remedied by extra-judicial efforts by blacks, including [myself]";

12) That "the very invitation to speak," "the content of [my] remarks" and my "posing for photographs" after the address identify me as "a leader for and among blacks," and "one of the country's leading civil rights proponents";

13) That I am a "celebrity" within the black community;

14) That "I [have] identified, and [do] identify, [myself] with causes of blacks, including the cause of correction of social injustices which [I believe] have been caused to blacks"; that I have made myself "a participant in those causes, including the cause of correction of social injustices which [I believe] have been caused to blacks";

15) That "in view of the applicable federal law," and by reason of my "personal and emotional commitments to civil rights causes of the black community, the black community expectation as to [my] leadership and spokesmanship therein, and the basic tenet of our legal system requiring both actual and apparent impartiality in the federal courts," my "continuation . . . as trier of fact, molder of remedy and arbiter of all issues constitutes judicial impropriety."

Pennsylvania v. Local Union 542, International Union of Operating Engineers, 388 F. Supp. 155 (E.D. Pa. 1974).

Blank v. Sullivan & Cromwell

The fourth case involved a petition requesting Judge Constance Motley to disqualify herself in an action brought by a female plaintiff against a prominent New York law firm alleging that the law firm discriminated in the employment of lawyers on the basis of sex. The basis of the petition was that Judge Motley, who is African-American, "strongly identified with those who suffered discrimination in employment because of sex or race." Blank v. Sullivan & Cromwell, 418 F. Supp. 1 (S.D.N.Y. 1975). Support for this claim was thought to lie in a quote, attributed to the judge, on the crippling effects of discrimination.

Responding to the accusation of bias, Judge Motley had this to say:

> It is beyond dispute that for much of my legal career I worked on behalf of blacks who suffered race discrimination. I am a woman, and before being elevated to the bench, was a woman lawyer. These obvious facts, however, clearly do not, *ipso facto*, indicate or even suggest the personal bias or prejudice required by [28 U.S.C.] § 144. The assertion, without more, that a judge who engaged in civil rights litigation and who happens to be of the same sex as a plaintiff in a suit alleging sex discrimination on the part of a law firm, is, therefore, so biased that he or she could not hear the case, comes nowhere near the standards required for recusal. Indeed, if background or sex or race of each judge were, by definition, sufficient grounds for removal, no judge on this court could hear this case, or many others, by virtue of the fact that all of them were attorneys, of a sex, often with distinguished law firm or public service backgrounds.
>
> Nowhere in their affidavits do defense counsel or defendant indicate that I have any relationship or personal association or interest in this litigation. They merely point to my general background and the obvious facts of my race and sex as evidence of extrajudicial prejudice.

Note: Liteky v. United States, 510 U.S. 540 (1994)

The United States Supreme Court had occasion to consider the nature of judicial bias and the circumstances under which it renders a judge unable to be impartial. Before and during the defendants' 1991 trial on federal criminal charges, the district judge denied defense motions that he recuse himself pursuant to 28 U.S.C. § 455(a) (the companion statute to that involved in the Higginbotham case, supra), which requires a federal judge to "disqualify himself in any proceeding in which his impartiality might reasonably be questioned." These motions were based first on rulings and statements this same judge made, which allegedly displayed impatience, disregard, and animosity toward the defense, and second on the judge's admonishment of the defendants' counsel and codefendants in front of the jury at the 1991 trial. The court of appeals confirmed the defendants' convictions, concluding that matters arising from judicial proceedings are not a proper basis for recusal, and the Supreme Court agreed.

In the opinion for the Court, Justice Scalia wrote:

> [T]he pejorative connotation of the terms "bias" and "prejudice" demands that they be applied only to judicial predispositions that go beyond what is normal and acceptable. We think there is an equivalent pejorative connotation, with equivalent consequences, to the term "partiality." See American Heritage Dictionary 1319 (3d ed. 1992) ("partiality" defined as "[f]avorable prejudice or bias"). A prospective juror in an insurance-claim case may be stricken as partial if he always votes for insurance companies; but not if he always votes for the party whom the terms of the contract support. "Partiality" does not refer to all favoritism, but only to such as is, for some reason, wrongful or inappropriate. Impartiality is not gullibility. . . .
>
> . . . First, judicial rulings alone almost never constitute valid basis for a bias or partiality motion. See United States v. Grinnell Corp., 384 U.S. 563, 583 (1966). In and of themselves (i.e., apart from surrounding comments or accompanying opinion), they cannot possibly show reliance upon an extrajudicial source; and can only in the rarest circumstances evidence the degree of favoritism or antagonism required (as discussed below) when no extrajudicial source is involved. Almost invariably, they are proper grounds for appeal, not for recusal. Second, opinions formed by the judge on the basis of facts introduced or events occurring in the course of the current proceedings, or of prior proceedings, do not constitute a basis for a bias or partiality motion unless they display a deep-seated favoritism or antagonism that would make fair judgment impossible. Thus, judicial remarks during the course of a trial that are critical or disapproving of, or even hostile to, counsel, the parties, or their cases, ordinarily do not support a bias or partiality challenge. They *may* do so if they reveal an opinion that derives from an extrajudicial source; and they *will* do so if they reveal such a high degree of favoritism or antagonism as to make fair judgment impossible. An example of the latter (and perhaps of the former as well) is the statement that was alleged to have been made by the District Judge in Berger v. United States, 255 U.S. 22 (1921), a World War I espionage case against German-American defendants: "One must have a very judicial mind, indeed, not [to be] prejudiced against the German Americans" because their "hearts are reeking with disloyalty." Id., at 28. *Not* establishing bias or partiality, however, are expressions of impatience, dissatisfaction, annoyance, and even anger, that are within the bounds of what imperfect

> men and women, even after having been confirmed as federal judges, sometimes display. A judge's ordinary efforts at courtroom administration — even a stern and short-tempered judge's ordinary efforts at courtroom administration — remain immune.

510 U.S. at 552-556.

Problem Case: The Prejudiced Judge, Revisited

Revisit the problem case at the beginning of this section. Answer the following questions:

1. In your opinion, is Judge McArthur biased against Graham Buchanan within the meaning of Sections 144 and 455? Can she be fair in any matter involving Buchanan?
2. How should Buchanan raise his bias claim? How should McArthur respond?
3. What legal, practical, and policy issues are at stake? Think about the qualities of an ideal judge, the role the judge plays in fair procedure, and the extent to which McArthur may or may not match that ideal.
4. Would Buchanan have a stronger motion if he sought to disqualify McArthur in a sex discrimination case where he represented the male employer?
5. If past experience is relevant to a judge's qualifications, at what point does it imperil her ability to be impartial? When does perspective become bias?

Note: Duckhunting with the Vice President

Matters arising from judicial proceedings are not, as Justice Scalia emphasized in *Liteky*, usually grounds for recusal. What about personal relationships with parties or government officers central to a case? In Cheney v. United States District Court for the District of Columbia, 541 U.S. 913 (2004), Justice Scalia denied a motion to recuse himself from a lawsuit seeking to obtain records of Vice President Richard Cheney's "Energy Task Force" (formally known as the National Energy Policy Development Group) in order to show that the task force was stacked with energy industry representatives.

The Sierra Club, a plaintiff in the underlying case, moved for Justice Scalia's recusal after newspapers reported that, while the case was on appeal before the Supreme Court, Justice Scalia flew with the Vice President from D.C. to Louisiana in a government plane and joined several others for fishing and duck hunting at a hunting camp owned by an oil industry executive and friend of Justice Scalia.

In denying the motion Justice Scalia argued that he was never alone with the Vice President and that he never discussed the case with him. Absent any interaction alone with the Vice President, Scalia continued, the motion amounted to a claim that a Justice's "impartiality might reasonably be questioned," 28 U.S.C. § 455(a), whenever he hears cases in which friends are involved: "But while friendship is a ground for recusal of a Justice where the personal fortune or the personal freedom of the friend is at issue, it has traditionally *not* been a ground for recusal where *official action* is at issue, no matter how important the official action was to the ambitions or the reputation of the Government officer." Id. at 916. Justice Scalia then discussed a number of examples of friendship and social interaction between members of the Court and officers of the executive branch. He emphasized two instances in which no recusal, indeed, no recusal *motion*, followed: (1) Justice Byron White, "close friends with Attorney General Robert Kennedy[,] . . . went on a skiing vacation in Colorado with . . . Kennedy and his family [while] . . . there were pending before the Court at least two cases in which Robert Kennedy, in his official capacity as Attorney General, was a party," id. at 925; and (2) in 1942, Justice Robert Jackson rode to and attended a general's house party in Virginia with President Franklin D. Roosevelt while Wickard v. Filburn was pending before the Court—a case in which Justice Jackson wrote the opinion for the Court. Id. at 925-926.

Do you agree with Justice Scalia that the motion for recusal attacks the fact of his friendship with the Vice President and nothing more? Is his assurance that the case was not discussed on the duck hunting trip enough to allay concerns about his ability to be impartial in the case? Does the presence and hospitality of an oil industry executive distinguish Justice Scalia's case from the examples he gives? Isn't Justice Scalia right that Justices would have to recuse themselves in the vast majority of cases they hear if friendship or acquaintance with a government official were proper grounds for recusal? Assuming Justice Scalia's arguments for denying the motion are persuasive, hasn't the Sierra Club still won? After all, the motion itself brings public attention to Justice Scalia's relationship with the Vice President and the goal of the underlying suit was to bring attention to the impact of the administration's political connections on its policies.

What about the free flight to Louisiana in the Vice President's government jet? Because there was empty space on the flight, Justice Scalia insists it "cost the Government nothing." Id. at 920. Is cost the only issue? Justice Scalia concedes that flying with the Vice President saved some "inconvenience" in getting everyone to the hunt, but insists that this was simply a "social courtes[y]," entirely proper to accept from a government official before the Court solely in his official capacity. Id. at 921.

B. THE JUDGE'S POWERS

1. Injunctions and Contempt

A recurrent theme in our study is the huge power of the trial judge. She is guided by rules that leave much to discretion, she possesses certain inherent powers, and she issues orders that are often dispositive without being appealable. We have seen, moreover, that judges may take an activist (and unsupervised) role in the settlement of cases without trial. In addition to this kind of daily exercise of power, there are two related situations in which the trial judge's authority is at its peak. One is the issuance of preliminary injunctive relief, and the second is the power to hold in contempt one who disobeys a court order. Both of these extraordinary powers, exercised in the most heated circumstances, can be observed in the following cases.

Walker v. City of Birmingham

388 U.S. 307 (1967)

JUSTICE STEWART delivered the opinion of the Court.

On Wednesday, April 10, 1963, officials of Birmingham, Alabama, filed a bill of complaint in a state circuit court asking for injunctive relief against 139 individuals and two organizations. The bill and accompanying affidavits stated that during the preceding seven days:

> [R]espondents had sponsored and/or participated in and/or conspired to commit and/or to encourage and/or to participate in certain movements, plans or projects commonly called "sit-in" demonstrations, "kneel-in" demonstrations, mass street parades, trespasses on private property after being warned to leave the premises by the owners of said property, congregating in mobs upon the public streets and other public places, unlawfully picketing private places of business in the City of Birmingham, Alabama; violation of numerous ordinances and statutes of the City of Birmingham and State of Alabama. . . .

It was alleged that this conduct was "calculated to provoke breaches of the peace," "threaten(ed) the safety, peace and tranquility of the City," and placed "an undue burden and strain upon the manpower of the Police Department."

The bill stated that these infractions of the law were expected to continue and would "lead to further imminent danger to the lives, safety, peace, tranquility and general welfare of the people of the City of Birmingham," and that the "remedy by law (was) inadequate." The circuit judge granted a temporary injunction as prayed in the bill, enjoining the petitioners from, among other things, participating in or encouraging mass street parades or mass processions without a permit as required by a Birmingham ordinance.[1]

Five of the eight petitioners were served with copies of the writ early the next morning. Several hours later four of them held a press conference. There a statement was distributed, declaring their intention to disobey the injunction because it was "raw tyranny under the guise of maintaining law and order."[2] At this press conference one of the petitioners stated: "That they had respect for the Federal Courts, or Federal Injunctions, but in the past the State Courts had favored local law enforcement, and if the police couldn't handle it, the mob would."

That night a meeting took place at which one of the petitioners announced that "[i]njunction or no injunction we are going to march tomorrow." The next afternoon, Good Friday, a large crowd gathered in the vicinity of Sixteenth Street and Sixth Avenue North in Birmingham. A group of about 50 or 60 proceeded to parade along the sidewalk while a crowd of 1,000 to 1,500 onlookers stood by, "clapping, and hollering, and [w]hooping." Some of the crowd followed the marchers and spilled out into the street. At least three of the petitioners participated in this march.

Meetings sponsored by some of the petitioners were held that night and the following night, where calls for volunteers to "walk" and go to jail were made. On Easter Sunday, April 14, a crowd of between 1,500 and 2,000 people congregated in the midafternoon in the vicinity of Seventh Avenue and Eleventh Street North in Birmingham. One of the petitioners was seen organizing members of the crowd in formation. A group of about 50, headed by three other petitioners, started down the sidewalk two abreast. At least one other petitioner was among the marchers. Some 300 or 400 people from among the onlookers followed in a crowd that occupied the entire width of the street and overflowed onto the sidewalks. Violence occurred. Members of the crowd threw rocks that injured a newspaperman and damaged a police motorcycle.

1. The text of the injunction is reproduced as Appendix A to this opinion. The Birmingham parade ordinance, § 1159 of the Birmingham City Code, provides that:

> It shall be unlawful to organize or hold, or to assist in organizing or holding, or to take part or participate in, any parade or procession or other public demonstration on the streets or other public ways of the city, unless a permit therefor has been secured from the commission.
>
> To secure such permit, written application shall be made to the commission, setting forth the probable number of persons, vehicles and animals which will be engaged in such parade, procession or other public demonstration, the purpose for which it is to be held or had, and the streets or other public ways over, along or in which it is desired to have or hold such parade, procession or other public demonstration. The commission shall grant a written permit for such parade, procession or other public demonstration, prescribing the streets or other public ways which may be used therefor, unless in its judgment the public welfare, peace, safety, health, decency, good order, morals or convenience require that it be refused. It shall be unlawful to use for such purposes any other streets or public ways than those set out in said permit.
>
> The two preceding paragraphs, however, shall not apply to funeral processions.

2. The full statement is reproduced as Appendix B to this opinion.

The next day the city officials who had requested the injunction applied to the state circuit court for an order to show cause why the petitioners should not be held in contempt for violating it. At the ensuing hearing the petitioners sought to attack the constitutionality of the injunction on the ground that it was vague and overbroad, and restrained free speech. They also sought to attack the Birmingham parade ordinance upon similar grounds, and upon the further ground that the ordinance had previously been administered in an arbitrary and discriminatory manner.

The circuit judge refused to consider any of these contentions, pointing out that there had been neither a motion to dissolve the injunction, nor an effort to comply with it by applying for a permit from the city commission before engaging in the Good Friday and Easter Sunday parades. Consequently, the court held that the only issues before it were whether it had jurisdiction to issue the temporary injunction, and whether thereafter the petitioners had knowingly violated it. Upon these issues the court found against the petitioners, and imposed upon each of them a sentence of five days in jail and a $50 fine, in accord with an Alabama statute.[3]

The Supreme Court of Alabama affirmed.[4] That court, too, declined to consider the petitioners' constitutional attacks upon the injunction and the underlying Birmingham parade ordinance:

> It is to be remembered that petitioners are charged with violating a temporary injunction. We are not reviewing a denial of a motion to dissolve or discharge a temporary injunction. Petitioners did not file any motion to vacate the temporary injunction until after the Friday and Sunday parades. Instead, petitioners deliberately defied the order of the court and did engage in and incite others to engage in mass street parades without a permit.
>
> We hold that the circuit court had the duty and authority, in the first instance, to determine the validity of the ordinance, and, until the decision of the circuit court is reversed for error by orderly review, either by the circuit court or a higher court, the orders of the circuit court based on its decision are to be respected and disobedience of them is contempt of its lawful authority, to be punished. Howat v. State of Kansas, 258 U.S. 181.

Howat v. State of Kansas, 258 U.S. 181 [1922], was decided by this Court almost 50 years ago. That was a case in which people had been punished by a Kansas trial court for refusing to obey an antistrike injunction issued under the state industrial relations act. They had claimed a right to disobey the court's order upon the ground that the state statute and the injunction based upon it were invalid under the Federal Constitution. The Supreme Court of Kansas had affirmed the judgment, holding that

3. "The circuit court, or judges thereof when exercising equity jurisdiction and powers may punish for contempt by fine not exceeding fifty dollars, and by imprisonment, not exceeding five days, one or both." Ala. Code, Tit. 13, § 143. See also id., §§ 4-5, 126.

4. The Alabama Supreme Court quashed the conviction of one defendant because of insufficient proof that he knew of the injunction before violating it, and the convictions of two others because there was no showing that they had disobeyed the order. 279 Ala. 53, 64 (1965).

the trial court "had general power to issue injunctions in equity, and that even if its exercise of the power was erroneous, the injunction was not void, and the defendants were precluded from attacking it in this collateral proceeding . . . that, if the injunction was erroneous, jurisdiction was not thereby forfeited, that the error was subject to correction only by the ordinary method of appeal, and disobedience to the order constituted contempt." 258 U.S. at 189.

This Court, in dismissing the writ of error, not only unanimously accepted but fully approved the validity of the rule of state law upon which the judgment of the Kansas court was grounded:

> An injunction duly issuing out of a court of general jurisdiction with equity powers, upon pleadings properly invoking its action, and served upon persons made parties therein and within the jurisdiction, must be obeyed by them, however erroneous the action of the court may be, even if the error be in the assumption of the validity of a seeming, but void law going to the merits of the case. It is for the court of first instance to determine the question of the validity of the law, and until its decision is reversed for error by orderly review, either by itself or by a higher court, its orders based on its decision are to be respected, and disobedience of them is contempt of its lawful authority, to be punished. 258 U.S. at 189-190.

The rule of state law accepted and approved in Howat v. State of Kansas is consistent with the rule of law followed by the federal courts.

In the present case, however, we are asked to hold that this rule of law, upon which the Alabama courts relied, was constitutionally impermissible. We are asked to say that the Constitution compelled Alabama to allow the petitioners to violate this injunction, to organize and engage in these mass street parades and demonstrations, without any previous effort on their part to have the injunction dissolved or modified, or any attempt to secure a parade permit in accordance with its terms. Whatever the limits of Howat v. State of Kansas,[6] we cannot accept the petitioners' contentions in the circumstances of this case.

Without question the state court that issued the injunction had, as a court of equity, jurisdiction over the petitioners and over the subject matter of the controversy. And this is not a case where the injunction was transparently invalid or had only a frivolous pretense to validity. We have consistently recognized the strong interest of state and local governments in regulating the use of their streets and other public places. When protest

6. In In re Green, 369 U.S. 689 [1962], the petitioner was convicted of criminal contempt for violating a labor injunction issued by an Ohio court. Relying on the pre-emptive command of the federal labor law, the Court held that the state courts were required to hear Green's claim that the state court was without jurisdiction to issue the injunction. The petitioner in *Green,* unlike the petitioners here, had attempted to challenge the validity of the injunction before violating it by promptly applying to the issuing court for an order vacating the injunction. The petitioner in *Green* had further offered to prove that the court issuing the injunction had agreed to its violation as an appropriate means of testing its validity.

takes the form of mass demonstrations, parades, or picketing on public streets and sidewalks, the free passage of traffic and the prevention of public disorder and violence become important objects of legitimate state concern. As the Court stated, in Cox v. State of Louisiana, "We emphatically reject the notion . . . that the First and Fourteenth Amendments afford the same kind of freedom to those who would communicate ideas by conduct such as patrolling, marching, and picketing on streets and highways, as these amendments afford to those who communicate ideas by pure speech." 379 U.S. 536, 555 [1965]. And as a unanimous Court stated in Cox v. State of New Hampshire:

> Civil liberties, as guaranteed by the Constitution, imply the existence of an organized society maintaining public order without which liberty itself would be lost in the excesses of unrestrained abuses. The authority of a municipality to impose regulations in order to assure the safety and convenience of the people in the use of public highways has never been regarded as inconsistent with civil liberties but rather as one of the means of safeguarding the good order upon which they ultimately depend. 312 U.S. 569, 574 [1941].

The generality of the language contained in the Birmingham parade ordinance upon which the injunction was based would unquestionably raise substantial constitutional issues concerning some of its provisions. The petitioners, however, did not even attempt to apply to the Alabama courts for an authoritative construction of the ordinance. Had they done so, those courts might have given the licensing authority granted in the ordinance a narrow and precise scope, as did the New Hampshire courts in Cox v. State of New Hampshire and Poulos v. State of New Hampshire, both supra. Cf. Shuttlesworth v. City of Birmingham, 382 U.S. 87, 91 [1965]; City of Darlington v. Stanley, 239 S.C. 139 [1961]. Here, just as in *Cox* and *Poulos*, it could not be assumed that this ordinance was void on its face.

The breadth and vagueness of the injunction itself would also unquestionably be subject to substantial constitutional question. But the way to raise that question was to apply to the Alabama courts to have the injunction modified or dissolved. The injunction in all events clearly prohibited mass parading without a permit, and the evidence shows that the petitioners fully understood that prohibition when they violated it.

The petitioners also claim that they were free to disobey the injunction because the parade ordinance on which it was based had been administered in the past in an arbitrary and discriminatory fashion. In support of this claim they sought to introduce evidence that, a few days before the injunction issued, requests for permits to picket had been made to a member of the city commission. One request had been rudely rebuffed,[9]

9. Mrs. Lola Hendricks, not a petitioner in this case, testified that on April 3:

"I went to Mr. Connor's office, the Commissioner's office at the City Hall Building. We went up and Commissioner Connor met us at the door. He asked, and this same official had later made clear that he was without power to grant the permit alone, since the issuance of such permits was the responsibility of the entire city commission.[10] Assuming the truth of this proffered evidence, it does not follow that the parade ordinance was void on its face. The petitioners, moreover, did not apply for a permit either to the commission itself or to any commissioner after the injunction issued. Had they done so, and had the permit been refused, it is clear that their claim of arbitrary or discriminatory administration of the ordinance would have been considered by the state circuit court upon a motion to dissolve the injunction.

This case would arise in quite a different constitutional posture if the petitioners, before disobeying the injunction, had challenged it in the Alabama courts, and had been met with delay or frustration of their constitutional claims. But there is no showing that such would have been the fate of a timely motion to modify or dissolve the injunction. There was an interim of two days between the issuance of the injunction and the Good Friday march. The petitioners give absolutely no explanation of why they did not make some application to the state court during that period. The injunction had issued *ex parte*; if the court had been presented with the petitioners' contentions, it might well have dissolved or at least modified its order in some respects. If it had not done so, Alabama procedure would have provided for an expedited process of appellate review. It cannot be presumed that the Alabama courts would have ignored the petitioners' constitutional claims. Indeed, these contentions were accepted in another case by an Alabama appellate court that struck down on direct review the conviction under this very ordinance of one of these same petitioners.[13]

The rule of law upon which the Alabama courts relied in this case was one firmly established by previous precedents. We do not deal here, therefore, with a situation where a state court has followed a regular past practice of entertaining claims in a given procedural mode, and without notice has abandoned that practice to the detriment of a litigant who finds his claim foreclosed by a novel procedural bar. Barr v. City of Columbia, 378 U.S. 1466 [1964]. This is not a case where a procedural requirement

'May I help you?' I told him, 'Yes, sir, we came up to apply or see about getting a permit for picketing, parading, demonstrating.'" . . .

"I asked Commissioner Connor for the permit, and asked if he could issue the permit, or other persons who would refer me to, persons who would issue a permit. He said, 'No, you will not get a permit in Birmingham, Alabama, to picket. I will picket you over to the City Jail,' and he repeated that twice."

10. Commissioner Connor sent the following telegram to one of the petitioners on April 5:

"Under the provisions of the city code of the City of Birmingham, a permit to picket as requested by you cannot be granted by me individually but is the responsibility (sic) of the entire commission. I insist that you and your people do not start any picketing on the streets in Birmingham, Alabama."

Eugene "Bull" Connor, Commissioner of Public Safety.

13. Shuttlesworth v. City of Birmingham, 43 Ala. App. 68 [1965]. The case is presently pending on certiorari review in the Alabama Supreme Court.

has been sprung upon an unwary litigant when prior practice did not give him fair notice of its existence. Wright v. State of Georgia, 373 U.S. 284, 291 [1963].

The Alabama Supreme Court has apparently never in any criminal contempt case entertained a claim of nonjurisdictional error. In Fields v. City of Fairfield, 273 Ala. 588 [1962], decided just three years before the present case, the defendants, members of a "White Supremacy" organization who had disobeyed an injunction, sought to challenge the constitutional validity of a permit ordinance upon which the injunction was based. The Supreme Court of Alabama, finding that the trial court had jurisdiction, applied the same rule of law which was followed here:

> As a general rule, an unconstitutional statute is an absolute nullity and may not form the basis of any legal right or legal proceedings, yet until its unconstitutionality has been judicially declared in appropriate proceedings, no person charged with its observance under an order or decree may disregard or violate the order or the decree with immunity from a charge of contempt of court; and he may not raise the question of its unconstitutionality in collateral proceedings on appeal from a judgment of conviction for contempt of the order or decree. . . . 273 Ala. at 590.

These precedents clearly put the petitioners on notice that they could not by-pass orderly judicial review of the injunction before disobeying it. Any claim that they were entrapped or misled is wholly unfounded, a conclusion confirmed by evidence in the record showing that when the petitioners deliberately violated the injunction they expected to go to jail.

The rule of law that Alabama followed in this case reflects a belief that in the fair administration of justice no man can be judge in his own case, however exalted his station, however righteous his motives, and irrespective of his race, color, politics, or religion.[16] This Court cannot hold that the petitioners were constitutionally free to ignore all the procedures of the law and carry their battle to the streets. One may sympathize with the petitioners' impatient commitment to their cause. But respect for judicial process is a small price to pay for the civilizing hand of law, which alone can give abiding meaning to constitutional freedom.

Affirmed.

16. The same rule of law was followed in Kasper v. Brittain, 245 F.2d 92 [6th Cir. 1957]. There, a federal court had ordered the public high school in Clinton, Tennessee, to desegregate. Kasper "arrived from somewhere in the East," and organized a campaign "to run the Negroes out of the school." The federal court issued an ex parte restraining order enjoining Kasper from interfering with desegregation. Relying upon the First Amendment, Kasper harangued a crowd "to the effect that although he had been served with the restraining order, it did not mean anything. . . ." His conviction for criminal contempt was affirmed by the Court of Appeals for the Sixth Circuit. That court concluded that "an injunctional order issued by a court must be obeyed," whatever its seeming invalidity, citing Howat v. State of Kansas, 258 U.S. 181. This Court denied certiorari, 355 U.S. 834.

Appendix A to the Opinion of the Court.
Temporary Injunction—April 10, 1963.

A verified Bill of Complaint in the above styled cause having been presented to me on this the 10th of April 1963 at 9:00 o'clock P.M. in the City of Birmingham, Alabama.

Upon consideration of said verified Bill of Complaint and the affidavits of Captain G. V. Evans and Captain George Wall, and the public welfare, peace and safety requiring it, it is hereby considered, ordered, adjudged and decreed that a peremptory or a temporary writ of injunction be and the same is hereby issued in accordance with the prayer of said petition.

It is therefore ordered, adjudged and decreed by the Court that upon the complainant entering into a good and sufficient bond conditioned as provided by law, in the sum of Twenty five Hundred Dollars ($2500.00), same to be approved by the Register of this Court that the Register issue a peremptory or temporary writ of injunction that the respondents and the others identified in said Bill of Complaint, their agents, members, employees, servants, followers, attorneys, successors and all other persons in active concert or participation with the respondents and all persons having notice of said order from continuing any act hereinabove designated particularly: engaging in, sponsoring, inciting or encouraging mass street parades or mass processions or like demonstrations without a permit, trespass on private property after being warned to leave the premises by the owner or person in possession of said private property, congregating on the street or public places into mobs, and unlawfully picketing business establishments or public buildings in the City of Birmingham, Jefferson County, State of Alabama or performing acts calculated to cause breaches of the peace in the City of Birmingham, Jefferson County, in the State of Alabama or from conspiring to engage in unlawful street parades, unlawful processions, unlawful demonstrations, unlawful boycotts, unlawful trespasses, and unlawful picketing or other like unlawful conduct or from violating the ordinances of the City of Birmingham and the Statutes of the State of Alabama or from doing any acts designed to consummate conspiracies to engage in said unlawful acts of parading, demonstrating, boycotting, trespassing and picketing or other unlawful acts, or from engaging in acts and conduct customarily known as "kneel-ins" in churches in violation of the wishes and desires of said churches.

W. A. Jenkins, Jr., As Circuit Judge of the Tenth Judicial Circuit of Alabama, In Equity Sitting.

Appendix B to the Opinion of the Court

In our struggle for freedom we have anchored our faith and hope in the rightness of the Constitution and the moral laws of the universe.

Again and again the Federal judiciary has made it clear that the privileges (sic) guaranteed under the First and the Fourteenth Amendments are to (sic) sacred to be trampled upon by the machinery of state government and police power. In the past we have abided by Federal injunctions out of respect for the forthright and consistent leadership that the Federal judiciary has given in establishing the principle of integration as the law of the land.

However we are now confronted with recalcitrant forces in the Deep South that will use the courts to perpetuate the unjust and illegal system of racial separation.

Alabama has made clear its determination to defy the law of the land. Most of its public officials, its legislative body and many of its law enforcement agents have openly defied the desegregation decision of the Supreme Court. We would feel morally and legal (sic) responsible to obey the injunction if the courts of Alabama applied equal justice to all of its citizens. This would be sameness made legal. However the issuance (sic) of this injunction is a blatant of difference made legal.

Southern law enforcement agencies have demonstrated now and again that they will utilize the force of law to misuse the judicial process.

This is raw tyranny under the guise of maintaining law and order. We cannot in all good conscience obey such an injunction which is an unjust, undemocratic and unconstitutional misuse of the legal process.

We do this not out of any desrespect (sic) for the law but out of the highest respect for the law. This is not an attempt to evade or defy the law or engage in chaotic anarchy. Just as in all good conscience we cannot obey unjust laws, neither can we respect the unjust use of the courts.

We believe in a system of law based on justice and morality. Out of our great love for the Constitution of the U.S. and our desire to purify the judicial system of the state of Alabama, we risk this critical move with an awareness of the possible consequences involved.

CHIEF JUSTICE WARREN, whom JUSTICE BRENNAN and JUSTICE FORTAS join, dissenting.

Petitioners in this case contend that they were convicted under an ordinance that is unconstitutional on its face because it submits their First and Fourteenth Amendment rights to free speech and peaceful assembly to the unfettered discretion of local officials. They further contend that the ordinance was unconstitutionally applied to them because the local officials used their discretion to prohibit peaceful demonstrations by a group whose political viewpoint the officials opposed. The Court does not dispute these contentions, but holds that petitioners may nonetheless be convicted and sent to jail because the patently unconstitutional ordinance was copied into an injunction — issued *ex parte* without prior notice or hearing on the request of the Commissioner of Public Safety — forbidding all persons having notice of the injunction to violate the ordinance without any limitation of time. I dissent because I do not believe that the fundamental protections of the Constitution were meant to be so easily evaded, or that "the civilizing hand of law" would be hampered in the slightest by enforcing the First Amendment in this case.

The salient facts can be stated very briefly. Petitioners are Negro ministers who sought to express their concern about racial discrimination in Birmingham, Alabama, by holding peaceful protest demonstrations in that city on Good Friday and Easter Sunday 1963. For obvious reasons, it was important for the significance of the demonstrations that they be held on those particular dates. A representative of petitioners' organization went to the City Hall and asked "to see the person or persons in charge to issue permits, permits for parading, picketing, and demonstrating." She was directed to Public Safety Commissioner Connor, who denied her request for a permit in terms that left no doubt that petitioners were not going to be issued a permit under any circumstances. "He said, 'No you will not get a permit in Birmingham, Alabama to picket. I will picket you over to the City Jail,' and he repeated that twice." A second, telegraphic request was also summarily denied, in a telegram signed by "Eugene 'Bull' Connor," with the added information that permits could be issued only by the full City Commission, a three-man body consisting of Commissioner Connor and two others.[1] According to petitioners' offer of proof, the truth of which is assumed for purposes of this case, parade permits had uniformly been issued for all other groups by the city clerk on the request of the traffic bureau of the police department, which was under Commissioner Connor's direction. The requirement that the approval of the full Commission be obtained was applied only to this one group.

Understandably convinced that the City of Birmingham was not going to authorize their demonstrations under any circumstances, petitioners proceeded with their plans despite Commissioner Connor's orders. On Wednesday, April 10, at 9 in the evening, the city filed in a state circuit court a bill of complaint seeking an *ex parte* injunction. The complaint recited that petitioners were engaging in a series of demonstrations as "part of a massive effort . . . to forcibly integrate all business establishments,

1. The uncontradicted testimony relating to the rebuffs of petitioners' attempts to obtain a permit is set out in footnotes 9 and 10 of the majority opinion. Petitioners were prevented by a ruling of the trial court from introducing further proof of the intransigence of Commissioner Connor and the other city officials toward any effort by Negroes to protest segregation and racial injustice. The attitude of the city administration in general and of its Public Safety Commissioner in particular are a matter of public record, of course, and are familiar to this Court from previous litigation. See Shuttlesworth v. City of Birmingham, 382 U.S. 87 (1965); Shuttlesworth v. City of Birmingham, 376 U.S. 339 (1964); Shuttlesworth v. City of Birmingham, 373 U.S. 262 (1963); Gober v. City of Birmingham, 373 U.S. 374 (1963); In re Shuttlesworth, 369 U.S. 35 (1962). The United States Commission on Civil Rights found continuing abuse of civil rights protesters by the Birmingham police, including use of dogs, clubs, and firehoses. 1963 Report of the United States Commission on Civil Rights 114 (Government Printing Office, 1963). Commissioner Eugene "Bull" Connor, a self-proclaimed white supremacist (see Congress and the Nation 1945-1964: A Review of Government and Politics in the Postwar Years 1604 (Congressional Quarterly Service, 1965)) made no secret of his personal attitude toward the rights of Negroes and the decisions of this Court. He vowed that racial integration would never come to Birmingham, and wore a button inscribed "Never" to advertise that vow. Yet the Court indulges in speculation that these civil rights protesters might have obtained a permit from this city and this man had they made enough repeated applications.

churches, and other institutions" in the city, with the result that the police department was strained in its resources and the safety, peace, and tranquility were threatened. It was alleged as particularly menacing that petitioners were planning to conduct "kneel-in" demonstrations at churches where their presence was not wanted. The city's police dogs were said to be in danger of their lives. Faced with these recitals, the Circuit Court issued the injunction in the form requested, and in effect ordered petitioners and all other persons having notice of the order to refrain for an unlimited time from carrying on any demonstrations without a permit. A permit, of course, was clearly unobtainable; the city would not have sought this injunction if it had any intention of issuing one.

Petitioners were served with copies of the injunction at various times on Thursday and on Good Friday. Unable to believe that such a blatant and broadly drawn prior restraint on their First Amendment rights could be valid, they announced their intention to defy it and went ahead with the planned peaceful demonstrations on Easter weekend. On the following Monday, when they promptly filed a motion to dissolve the injunction, the court found them in contempt, holding that they had waived all their First Amendment rights by disobeying the court order.

These facts lend no support to the court's charges that petitioners were presuming to act as judges in their own case, or that they had a disregard for the judicial process. They did not flee the jurisdiction or refuse to appear in the Alabama courts. Having violated the injunction, they promptly submitted themselves to the courts to test the constitutionality of the injunction and the ordinance it parroted. They were in essentially the same position as persons who challenge the constitutionality of a statute by violating it, and then defend the ensuing criminal prosecution on constitutional grounds. It has never been thought that violation of a statute indicated such a disrespect for the legislature that the violator always must be punished even if the statute was unconstitutional. On the contrary, some cases have required that persons seeking to challenge the constitutionality of a statute first violate it to establish their standing to sue. Indeed, it shows no disrespect for law to violate a statute on the ground that it is unconstitutional and then to submit one's case to the courts with the willingness to accept the penalty if the statute is held to be valid.

The Court concedes that "(t)he generality of the language contained in the Birmingham parade ordinance upon which the injunction was based would unquestionably raise substantial constitutional issues concerning some of its provisions." That concession is well-founded but minimal. I believe it is patently unconstitutional on its face. Our decisions have consistently held that picketing and parading are means of expression protected by the First Amendment, and that the right to picket or parade may not be subjected to the unfettered discretion of local officials. Although a city may regulate the manner of use of its streets and sidewalks in the interest of keeping them open for the movement of traffic, it may not allow local officials unbridled discretion to decide who shall be allowed to parade or picket and who shall not. "Wherever the title of streets and parks may rest, they have immemorially been held in trust for the use of the public and, time out of mind, have been used for purposes of assembly, communicating thoughts between citizens, and discussing public questions. Such use of the streets and public places has, from ancient times, been a part of the privileges, immunities, rights, and liberties of citizens. The privilege of a citizen of the United States to use the street and parks for communication of views on national questions may be regulated in the interest of all; it is not absolute, but relative, and must be exercised in subordination to the general comfort and convenience, and in consonance with peace and good order; but it must not, in the guise of regulation, be abridged or denied." Hague v. C.I.O., 307 U.S. 496, 515-516 (1939) (opinion of Mr. Justice Roberts). When local officials are given totally unfettered discretion to decide whether a proposed demonstration is consistent with "public welfare, peace, safety, health, decency, good order, morals or convenience," as they were in this case, they are invited to act as censors over the views that may be presented to the public. The unconstitutionality of the ordinance is compounded, of course, when there is convincing evidence that the officials have in fact used their power to deny permits to organizations whose views they dislike. The record in this case hardly suggests that Commissioner Connor and the other city officials were motivated in prohibiting civil rights picketing only by their overwhelming concern for particular traffic problems. Petitioners were given to understand that under no circumstances would they be permitted to demonstrate in Birmingham, not that a demonstration would be approved if a time and place were selected that would minimize the traffic difficulties. The only circumstance that the court can find to justify anything other than a per curiam reversal is that Commissioner Connor had the foresight to have the unconstitutional ordinance included in an ex parte injunction issued without notice or hearing or any showing that it was impossible to have notice or a hearing, forbidding the world at large (insofar as it knew of the order) to conduct demonstrations in Birmingham without the consent of the city officials. This injunction was such potent magic that it transformed the command of an unconstitutional statute into an impregnable barrier, challengeable only in what likely would have been protracted legal proceedings and entirely superior in the meantime even to the United States Constitution.

I do not believe that giving this Court's seal of approval to such a gross misuse of the judicial process is likely to lead to greater respect for the law any more than it is likely to lead to greater protection for First Amendment freedoms. The *ex parte* temporary injunction has a long and odious history in this country, and its susceptibility to misuse is all too apparent from the facts of the case. As a weapon against strikes, it proved so effective in the hands of judges friendly to employers that Congress was forced to take the drastic step of removing from federal district courts the jurisdiction to issue injunctions in labor disputes.[6] The labor injunction fell

6. The Norris-LaGuardia Act, 1932, 47 Stat. 70, 29 U.S.C. §§ 101-115.

into disrepute largely because it was abused in precisely the same way that the injunctive power was abused in this case. Judges who were not sympathetic to the union cause commonly issued, without notice or hearing, broad restraining orders addressed to large numbers of persons of forbidding them to engage in acts that were either legally permissible or, if illegal, that could better have been left to the regular course of criminal prosecution. The injunctions might later be dissolved, but in the meantime strikes would be crippled because the occasion on which concerted activity might have been effective had passed.[7] Such injunctions so long discredited as weapons against concerted labor activities, have now been given new life by this Court as weapons against the exercise of First Amendment freedoms. Respect for the courts and for judicial process was not increased by the history of the labor injunction.[8]

Nothing in our prior decisions, or in the doctrine that a party subject to a temporary injunction issued by a court of competent jurisdiction with power to decide a dispute properly before it must normally challenge the injunction in the courts rather than by violating it, requires that we affirm the convictions in this case. The majority opinion in this case rests essentially on a single precedent, and that a case the authority of which has clearly been undermined by subsequent decisions. Howat v. State of Kansas, 258 U.S. 181 (1922), was decided in the days when the labor injunction was in fashion. Kansas had adopted an Industrial Relations Act, the purpose of which in effect was to provide for compulsory arbitration of labor disputes by a neutral administrative tribunal, the "Court of Industrial Relations." Pursuant to its jurisdiction to investigate and perhaps improve labor conditions in the coal mining industry, the "Court" subpoenaed union leaders to appear and testify. In addition, the State obtained an injunction to prevent a strike while the matter was before the "Court." The union leaders disobeyed both the subpoena and the injunction, and sought to challenge the constitutionality of the Industrial Relations Act in the ensuing contempt proceeding. The Kansas Supreme Court held that the constitutionality of the Act could not be challenged in a contempt proceeding, and this Court upheld that determination.

Insofar as Howat v. State of Kansas might be interpreted to approve an absolute rule that any violation of a void court order is punishable as

7. Frankfurter & Greene, The Labor Injunction 47-48 (1930); Cox & Bok, Cases and Materials on Labor Law 101-107 (1962).

8. "The history of the labor injunction in action puts some matters beyond question. In large part, dissatisfaction and resentment are caused, first, by the refusal of courts to recognize that breaches of the peace may be redressed through criminal prosecution and civil action for damages, and, second, by the expansion of a simple, judicial device to an enveloping code of prohibited conduct, absorbing, en masse, executive and police functions and affecting the livelihood, and even lives, of multitudes. Especially those zealous for the unimpaired prestige of our courts have observed how the administration of law by decrees which through vast and vague phrases surmount law, undermines the esteem of courts upon which our reign of law depends. Not government, but 'government by injunction,' characterized by the consequences of a criminal prosecution without its safeguards, has been challenged." Frankfurter & Greene, supra, at 200.

contempt, it has been greatly modified by later decisions. In In re Green, 369 U.S. 689 (1962), we reversed a conviction for contempt of a state injunction forbidding labor picketing because the petitioner was not allowed to present evidence that the labor dispute was arguably subject to the jurisdiction of the National Labor Relations Board and hence not subject to state regulation. If an injunction can be challenged on the ground that it deals with a matter arguably subject to the jurisdiction of the National Labor Relations Board, then *a fortiori* it can be challenged on First Amendment grounds.[9]

It is not necessary to question the continuing validity of the holding in Howat v. State of Kansas, however, to demonstrate that neither it nor the *Mine Workers*[10] case supports the holding of the majority in this case. In Howat the subpoena and injunction were issued to enable the Kansas Court of Industrial Relations to determine an underlying labor dispute. In the *Mine Workers* case, the District Court issued a temporary anti-strike injunction to preserve existing conditions during the time it took to decide whether it had authority to grant the Government relief in a complex and difficult action of enormous importance to the national economy. In both cases the orders were of questionable legality, but in both cases they were reasonably necessary to enable the court or administrative tribunal to decide an underlying controversy of considerable importance before it at the time. This case involves an entirely different situation. The Alabama Circuit Court did not issue this temporary injunction to preserve existing conditions while it proceeded to decide some underlying dispute. There was no underlying dispute before it, and the court in practical effect merely added a judicial signature to a preexisting criminal ordinance. Just as the court had no need to issue the injunction to preserve its ability to decide some underlying dispute, the city had no need of an injunction to impose a criminal penalty for demonstrating on the streets without a permit. The ordinance already accomplished that. In point of fact, there is only one apparent reason why the city sought this injunction and why the court issued it: to make it possible to punish petitioners for contempt rather than for violating the ordinance, and thus to immunize the unconstitutional statute and its unconstitutional application from any attack. I regret that this strategy has been so successful.

9. The attempt in footnote 6 of the majority opinion to distinguish In re Green is nothing but an attempt to alter the holding of that case. The opinion of the Court states flatly that "a state court is without power to hold one in contempt for violating an injunction that the state court had no power to enter by reason of federal pre-emption." 369 U.S. at 692 (footnote omitted). The alleged circumstance that the court issuing the injunction had agreed to its violation as an appropriate means of testing its validity was considered only a concurring opinion. Although the petitioner in *Green* had attempted to challenge the order in court before violating it, we did not rely on that fact in holding that the order was void. Nor is it clear to me why the Court regards this fact as important, unless it means to imply that the petitioners in this case would have been free to violate the court order if they had first made a motion to dissolve in the trial court.

10. United States v. United Mine Workers, 330 U.S. 258 (1947).

It is not necessary in this case to decide precisely what limits should be set to the *Mine Workers* doctrine in cases involving violations of the First Amendment. Whatever the scope of that doctrine, it plainly was not intended to give a State the power to nullify the United States Constitution by the simple process of incorporating its unconstitutional criminal statutes into judicial decrees. I respectfully dissent.

JUSTICE DOUGLAS, with whom THE CHIEF JUSTICE, JUSTICE BRENNAN, and JUSTICE FORTAS join, dissenting.

We sit as a court of law functioning primarily as a referee in the federal system. Our function in cases coming to us from state courts is to make sure that state tribunals and agencies work within the limits of the Constitution. Since the Alabama courts have flouted the First Amendment, I would reverse the judgment.

Picketing and parading are methods of expression protected by the First Amendment against both state and federal abridgment. Edwards v. South Carolina, 372 U.S. 229, 235-236 [1963]; Cox v. State of Louisiana, 379 U.S. 536, 546-548 [1965]. Since they involve more than speech itself and implicate street traffic, the accommodation of the public and the like, they may be regulated as to the times and places of the demonstrations. But a State cannot deny the right to use streets or parks or other public grounds for the purpose of petitioning for the redress of grievances. See Hague v. C. I. O., 307 U.S. 496, 515-516 [1939].

The rich can buy advertisements in newspapers, purchase radio or television time, and rent billboard space. Those less affluent are restricted to the use of handbills, Murdock v. Commonwealth of Pennsylvania, 319 U.S. 105, 108 [1943], or petitions, or parades, or mass meetings. This "right of the people peaceably to assemble, and to petition the Government for a redress of grievance," guaranteed by the First Amendment, applicable to the States by reason of the Fourteenth, Edwards v. South Carolina, supra, 372 U.S. at 235, was flouted here.

The evidence shows that a permit was applied for. Mrs. Lola Hendricks, a member of the Alabama Christian Movement for Human Rights, authorized by its president, Reverend Shuttlesworth, on April 3, went to the police department and asked to see the person in charge of issuing permits. She then went to the office of Commissioner Eugene "Bull" Connor and told him that "we came up to apply or see about getting a permit for picketing, parading, demonstrating." She asked Connor for the permit, "asked if he could issue the permit, or other persons who would refer me to, persons who would issue a permit." Commissioner Connor replied, "No, you will not get a permit in Birmingham, Alabama to picket. I will picket you over to the City Jail." On April 5, petitioner Shuttlesworth sent a telegram to Commissioner Connor requesting a permit to picket on designated sidewalks on April 5 and 6. The message stated that "the normal rules of picketing" would be observed. The same day, Connor wired back a reply stating that he could not individually grant a permit, that it was the responsibility of the entire Commission and that he "insist[ed] that you and your people do not start any picketing on the streets in Birmingham, Alabama." Petitioners' efforts to show that the City Commission did not grant permits, but that they were granted by the city clerk at the request of the traffic division were cut off.

The record shows that petitioners did not deliberately attempt to circumvent the permit requirement. Rather they diligently attempted to obtain a permit and were rudely rebuffed and then reasonably concluded that any further attempts would be fruitless.

The right to defy an unconstitutional statute is basic in our scheme. Even when an ordinance requires a permit to make a speech, to deliver a sermon, to picket, to parade, or to assemble, it need not be honored when it is invalid on its face. Lovell v. City of Griffin, 303 U.S. 444, 452-453 [1938].

By like reason, where a permit has been arbitrarily denied one need not pursue the long and expensive route to this Court to obtain a remedy. The reason is the same in both cases. For if a person must pursue his judicial remedy before he may speak, parade, or assemble, the occasion when protest is desired or needed will have become history and any later speech, parade, or assembly will be futile or pointless.

Howat v. State of Kansas, states the general rule that court injunctions are to be obeyed until error is found by normal and orderly review procedures. See United States v. United Mine Workers, 330 U.S. 258, 293-294 [1947]. But there is an exception where "the question of jurisdiction" is "frivolous and not substantial." Id. at 293. Moreover, a state court injunction is not per se sacred where federal constitutional questions are involved. In re Green, 369 U.S. 689 [1962], held that contempt could not be imposed without a hearing where the state decree bordered the federal domain in labor relations and only a hearing could determine whether there was federal pre-emption. In the present case the collision between this state court decree and the First Amendment is so obvious that no hearing is needed to determine the issue.

As already related, petitioners made two applications to Commissioner "Bull" Connor for a permit and were turned down. At the trial, counsel for petitioners offered to prove through the city clerk that the Commission never has granted a permit, the issuing authority being the city clerk who acts at the request of the traffic division. But he was not allowed to answer the question. And when asked to describe the practice for granting permits an objection was raised and sustained.

It is clear that there are no published rules or regulations governing the manner of applying for permits, and it is clear from the record that some permits are issued. One who reads this record will have, I think, the abiding conviction that these people were denied a permit solely because their skin was not of the right color and their cause was not popular.

A court does not have *jurisdiction* to do what a city or other agency of a State lacks *jurisdiction* to do. The command of the Fourteenth Amendment, through which the First Amendment is made applicable to the States, is that no "State" shall deprive any person of "liberty" without due process of law. The decree of a state court is "state" action in the constitutional sense, Shelley v. Kraemer, 334 U.S. 1, 14-18 [1948], as much as the action of the state police, the state prosecutor, the state legislature, or the Governor himself. An ordinance — unconstitutional on its face or patently unconstitutional as applied — is not made sacred by an unconstitutional injunction that enforces it. It can and should be flouted in the manner of the ordinance itself. Courts as well as citizens are not free "to ignore all the procedures of the law," to use the Court's language. The "constitutional freedom" of which the Court speaks can be won only if judges honor the Constitution.

[The dissenting opinion of JUSTICE BRENNAN is omitted].

New York State National Organization for Women v. Terry

159 F.3d 86 (2d Cir. 1998)

LEVAL, Circuit Judge:

Plaintiffs are a group of women's organizations, health care clinics, and abortion providers who brought a civil rights action against an anti-abortion organization, its leader, and anti-abortion protestors. The district court, which had earlier enjoined defendants from engaging in various actions in violation of plaintiffs' rights and had found the defendants in contempt for violation of the injunction, granted plaintiffs' motion to reinstate the earlier finding of contempt, and imposed coercive fines. The fines were subject to an opportunity for defendants to purge themselves of contempt and be relieved of the obligation to pay the fines by obeying the injunction and publicly declaring their intention to comply with the injunction. The court also granted plaintiffs' motion to reinstate its award of attorney's fees to plaintiffs for prevailing on their contempt motions and civil rights claim.

On appeal from the finding of contempt with coercive fines and the award of attorney's fees, defendants argue that (1) the contempt sanctions should be vacated for mootness because defendants have not violated the injunctions in over seven years or because of the enactment of the Freedom of Access to Clinic Entrances Act of 1994, 18 U.S.C. § 248 (the "FACE Act"); (2) the fines, notwithstanding the opportunity to purge, are a criminal penalty that may not lawfully be imposed because defendants were not afforded procedural protections required by the Constitution for criminal proceedings; (3) attorney's fees awarded to plaintiffs for prosecuting contempt motions were improperly reinstated; (4) attorney's fees awarded to plaintiffs under 42 U.S.C. § 1988 were improperly reinstated; and (5) the motion for reinstatement of sanctions was time-barred.

We affirm.

Background

Plaintiffs brought this action in the Supreme Court of New York on April 25, 1988, seeking declaratory and injunctive relief to restrain defendants[1] from blocking access to medical facilities that provided abortions during a series of protests planned for April 30 through May 7, 1988. The complaint alleged eight separate causes of action: violations of New York Civil Rights Law § 40-c and New York Executive Law § 296; public nuisance; interference with the business of medical facilities; trespass; infliction of emotional harm on patients and employees of medical facilities; tortious harassment of patients and employees of medical facilities; false imprisonment of patients and employees of medical facilities; and conspiracy to deny women seeking abortion or family planning services the equal protection of the laws and equal privileges and immunities, in violation of 42 U.S.C § 1985(3).

On April 28, 1988, Justice Cahn of the Supreme Court issued a temporary restraining order that did not expressly enjoin defendants from blocking access to abortion clinics.

On May 2, 1988, following a demonstration outside a Manhattan abortion clinic, Justice Cahn issued a second temporary restraining order that enjoined defendants from "trespassing on, blocking, obstructing ingress into or egress from any facility at which abortions are performed in the City of New York, Nassau, Suffolk, or Westchester Counties from May 2, 1988 to May 7, 1988." The following day, May 3, defendant Terry and other protestors violated the order during a demonstration outside a Queens abortion clinic. At a hearing that afternoon before Justice Cahn, defendants removed to federal district court.

On May 4, 1988, the district court adopted a modified version of Justice Cahn's second temporary restraining order. The new temporary restraining order (the "TRO") included coercive sanctions of $25,000 for each day defendants violated the order and required defendants to notify the City of New York in advance of the location of any demonstrations. After defendants violated this TRO on May 5-6, 1988, plaintiffs sought contempt sanctions in accordance with the TRO. The district court adjudged Operation Rescue and Terry in civil contempt of the May 4 Order and held them jointly and severally liable for a $50,000 fine. See New York State Nat'l Org. for Women v. Terry, 697 F. Supp. 1324, 1338 (S.D.N.Y. 1988), *aff'd as modified*, 886 F.2d 1339 (2d Cir. 1989) (*"Terry I"*), *cert. denied*, 495 U.S. 947 (1990).

In response to defendants' publicized plan to carry out more protests on October 28, 29, and 31, 1988, plaintiffs moved to modify the TRO to cover those dates. The district court granted plaintiffs' motion and converted the TRO into a preliminary injunction. In spite of the injunction, on

1. Unless otherwise indicated, "defendants" refers to defendants-appellants, nonparty respondents-appellants, and defendants who did not appeal.

October 29, 1988, hundreds of Operation Rescue protestors blocked access to clinics at two covered locations.

When defendants threatened to block access again on January 12-14, 1989, plaintiffs moved for summary judgment on their claims under 42 U.S.C. § 1985(3) and New York law, and for a Permanent Injunction. The district court granted summary judgment for plaintiffs on their § 1985(3) claim. New York State Nat'l Org. for Women v. Terry, 704 F. Supp. 1247, 1258-1260 (S.D.N.Y. 1989), *aff'd as modified*, 886 F.2d 1339 (2d Cir. 1989) ("*Terry I*"), *cert. denied*, 495 U.S. 947 (1990). The judgment permanently enjoined defendants from

> trespassing on, blocking, or obstructing ingress into or egress from any facility at which abortions are performed in the City of New York, Nassau, Suffolk, or Westchester counties [and] physically abusing or tortiously harassing persons entering, leaving, working at, or using any services at any facility at which abortions are performed in the City of New York, Nassau, Suffolk, or Westchester counties.

Terry I, 886 F.2d at 1345 n. 1, *aff'g* 704 F. Supp. at 1263. The Permanent Injunction also established a schedule of prospective coercive civil sanctions for future violations, providing that

> the failure to comply with this Order by any Operation Rescue participant with actual notice of the provisions of this Order shall subject him or her to civil damages of $25,000 per day for the first violation . . . each successive violation of this Order shall subject the contemnor to a civil contempt fine double that of the previous fine . . . each contemnor shall be jointly and severally liable for all attorneys' fees and related costs incurred by plaintiffs in relation to enforcement of this Order.

Id. We affirmed summary judgment for plaintiffs and the Permanent Injunction. *Terry I*, 886 F.2d at 1357-1364.

In subsequent civil contempt proceedings, the district court found that defendants had violated the TRO, preliminary injunction, and Permanent Injunction ("the district court's orders") on four separate dates: May 6, 1988, October 29, 1988, and January 13-14, 1989. See New York State Nat'l Org. for Women v. Terry, 732 F. Supp. 388, 398 (S.D.N.Y. 1990). The court fined defendant Terry and Operation Rescue, jointly and severally, $100,000 and fined defendant Thomas Herlihy $25,000. Several nonparty respondents who acted in concert with defendants[2] were also fined, including B.O.R.N. ($25,000), Jesse Lee ($100,000), Joseph Foreman ($25,000), Michael McMonagle ($25,000), Jeff White ($25,000), Michael La Penna ($25,000), Florence Talluto ($50,000), Adelle Nathanson ($25,000), and Robert Pearson ($25,000). See 732 F. Supp. at 413-414.

2. Under Fed. R. Civ. P. 65(d), civil contempt sanctions may be assessed against nonparties with actual notice of the order who acted in concert with defendants in violating an order.

The district court also awarded plaintiffs attorney's fees for prevailing on their contempt motions and their civil rights claim. See New York State Nat'l Org. for Women v. Terry, 737 F. Supp. 1350, 1363, 1367 (S.D.N.Y. 1990). We affirmed the contempt judgments and attorney's fees against all defendants and all but two[3] nonparty respondents. See New York State Nat'l Org. for Women v. Terry, 961 F.2d 390, 401 (2d Cir. 1992) ("*Terry II*").

Defendants then petitioned for a writ of certiorari based on the Supreme Court's grant of certiorari in Bray v. Alexandria Women's Health Clinic, 498 U.S. 1119 (1991), a case involving similar facts. Following its decision in Bray v. Alexandria Women's Health Clinic, 506 U.S. 263 (1993), the Supreme Court granted certiorari, vacated the contempt fines and attorney's fees in a memorandum decision, and remanded the case to the Second Circuit for further consideration. See Pearson v. Planned Parenthood Margaret Sanger Clinic (Manhattan), 507 U.S. 901 (1993). On remand, we reinstated the contempt fines and attorney's fees, stating that applications for relief in light of Bray should be addressed in the first instance to the district court. See New York State Nat'l Org. for Women v. Terry, 996 F.2d 1351, 1352 (2d Cir. 1993) ("*Terry III*").

Defendants again sought a writ of certiorari on the ground that the contempt fines were criminal in nature (and could be imposed only with criminal procedural protections) and presented the same issue as was before the Supreme Court in International Union, United Mine Workers of America v. Bagwell, 512 U.S. 821 (1994) ("*Bagwell*"). Certiorari was granted, and the decision of the Court of Appeals was vacated and remanded for further consideration in light of *Bagwell*. See Pearson v. Planned Parenthood Margaret Sanger Clinic (Manhattan), 512 U.S. 1249 (1994).

On remand, we vacated the contempt fines and remanded the case for further proceedings in light of *Bagwell*. See New York State Nat'l Org. for Women v. Terry, 41 F.3d 794, 796, 797 (2d Cir. 1994) ("*Terry IV*"). We also vacated plaintiffs' award of attorney's fees for the contempt motions, and instructed the district court to reconsider in light of Bray v. Alexandria Women's Health, 506 U.S. 263 (1993), its award of attorney's fees under 42 U.S.C. § 1988. See *Terry IV*, 41 F.3d at 797. Plaintiffs then moved the district court for orders that would reinstate the contempt findings and the coercive fines, subject to an opportunity for defendants to purge themselves. Plaintiffs also sought attorney's fees. The district court rejected defendants' contention that the case had been rendered moot by the absence of violations of the Permanent Injunction during the previous seven years or by the enactment of the FACE Act, 18 U.S.C. § 248. See New York State Nat'l Org. for Women v. Terry, 952 F. Supp. 1033, 1039 (S.D.N.Y. 1997). The court reinstated the fines. It ordered "coercive civil penalties" payable to the United States, subject to a "purge provision" under which

3. Contempt judgments against nonparty respondents Florence Talluto and Michael LaPenna were reversed for lack of personal jurisdiction. See *Terry II*, 961 F.2d at 400.

defendants could avoid both the contempt holding and the penalties if they obeyed the injunction and, within sixty days, published an Affirmation of intent to abide by its terms. See id. at 1046; Order Amending and Reinstating Judgments, March 21, 1997, New York State Nat'l Org. for Women v. Terry, 952 F. Supp. 1033 (S.D.N.Y. 1997), at 2-3. The court also reinstated its award of attorney's fees to plaintiffs for prosecuting contempt motions and for prevailing on their civil rights claim. See 952 F. Supp. at 1044, 1046. Defendants appeal.

[Parts I and III are omitted. EDS.]

II. Motion for Reinstatement of Contempt Fines

In *Terry IV* we vacated, in light of International Union, United Mine Workers of America v. Bagwell, 512 U.S. 821 (1994) ("*Bagwell*"), the district court's contempt fines, which were imposed without constitutional criminal procedural protections, and which did not include an opportunity for defendants to purge their contempts. In response to our remand instructions, the district court reinstated the fines, subject to an opportunity to purge. We now must determine if the reinstated fines are consistent with *Bagwell*, which held that defendants were entitled to a criminal jury trial where defendants had "no opportunity to purge [the fines] once imposed," and the circumstances led the Court to conclude that the purpose of the fines was criminal punishment. Defendants argue that the fines, even though subject to a purge provision, are nonetheless a punishment.

Bagwell involved fines levied against a labor union for violations of an injunction, which prohibited the union from, among other things,

> obstructing ingress and egress to company facilities, throwing objects at and physically threatening company employees, placing tire-damaging "jackrocks" on roads used by company vehicles, and picketing with more than a specified number of people at designated sites.

[512 U.S. at 823.] The injunction also required the union to "take all steps necessary to ensure compliance with the injunction, to place supervisors at picket sites, and to report all violations to the court." After a series of non-jury contempt proceedings, at which violations were proven beyond reasonable doubt, the trial court levied approximately $12 million in compensatory fines[4] payable to the aggrieved parties and $52 million in noncompensatory fines payable to the Commonwealth of Virginia and the two counties most seriously affected by the unlawful activity.

Whether a contempt is criminal or civil turns on the character and purpose of the sanction. Civil contempt fines seek one of two objectives.

4. Compensatory fines paid to the aggrieved party for losses sustained are civil. See *Bagwell*, 512 U.S. at 829.

One is coercion—to force the contemnor to conform his conduct to the court's order. The second is compensation. Where the contumacious conduct has caused injury to the beneficiary of the court's order, a civil fine may be imposed on the contemnor to compensate the victim for the loss or harm caused by the unlawful conduct. Criminal fines, by contrast, are intended primarily to punish the contemnor and vindicate the authority of the court. See Gompers v. Bucks Stove & Range Co., 221 U.S. 418, 441-442 (1911), cited in *Bagwell,* 512 U.S. at 827-828; see also Penfield Co. v. Securities & Exchange Comm'n, 330 U.S. 585, 590 (1947).

Several factors contributed to the Court's conclusion that the non-compensatory fines in *Bagwell* were criminal in purpose and could be imposed only through a criminal jury trial. First, the trial court's order imposing the fines included no purge provision enabling defendants to avoid fines by compliance with the court's order. See *Bagwell,* 512 U.S. at 837; Mackler Productions, Inc. v. Cohen, 146 F.3d 126, 129 (2d Cir. 1998). In reaching this conclusion, the Court drew on a line of cases in which it had found sanctions to be civil where "the contemnor is able to purge the contempt and obtain his release by committing an affirmative act, and thus 'carries the keys of his prison in his own pocket.'" *Bagwell,* 512 U.S. at 828, quoting *Gompers,* 221 U.S. at 442; see also United States v. United Mine Workers, 330 U.S. 258, 305 (1947) (stating that a fine would be coercive, rather than punitive, where it was "condition[ed] on the defendant's failure to purge itself within a reasonable time"); Hicks v. Feiock, 485 U.S. 624, 632 (1988) ("a fine that would be payable to the court is . . . remedial when the defendant can avoid paying the fine simply by performing the affirmative act required by the court's order"); Shillitani v. United States, 384 U.S. 364, 370-371 (1966) (noting that when a court confines until compliance a witness refusing to testify at judicial proceedings, the "conditional nature of the imprisonment—based entirely upon the contemnor's continued defiance—justifies holding civil contempt proceedings absent the safeguards of indictment and jury"). The absence of a purge provision was significant because it suggested the trial court's objective was not to coerce but to punish. A purge provision permits the contemnor to escape a fine by conforming his conduct to the court's order or by declaring an intention to do so. The absence of a purge provision means that the fine will be imposed regardless of reform and commitment to obey. A fine without a purge provision therefore suggests an intention to punish past misconduct rather than to insure future lawfulness.

Other factors that helped persuade the *Bagwell* Court that the $52 million in fines in that case were of a punitive, criminal character were that (1) they were not "calibrate[d]" to damages caused by the contumacious activities, 512 U.S. at 834, (2) that they were payable to the Commonwealth and the counties, 512 U.S. at 824-825, rather than to the injured party, and (3) that they were extremely large, amounting to $52 million, 512 U.S. at 837-838 & n.5. See *Mackler,* 146 F.3d at 129. The failure to calibrate the fines to the injuries inflicted on the victims of the contumacious conduct rebutted the inference that the fines were designed to compensate the victims. Similarly, the fact that the $52 million in fines in *Bagwell* were payable to the Commonwealth of Virginia and the counties, rather than to the victims, made unmistakably clear that their purpose was not to compensate. The enormous size of *Bagwell* fines, especially where all other factors pointed to a punitive, rather than a coercive or compensatory purpose, emphasized the need for the protection of the defendant in the adjudication process, reinforcing the conclusion that criminal procedures were required.

The consideration of these factors in the context of this case leads to the conclusion that these fines are civil in nature, because their purpose is coercion. The district court's modified contempt order includes a purge provision that excuses defendants from paying contempt fines if, within 60 days from the date of the court's order, they file and publish an affirmation of their intent to abide by the Permanent Injunction. See Order Amending and Reinstating Judgments, New York State Nat'l Organization for Women v. Terry, 952 F. Supp. 1033 (S.D.N.Y. 1997), at 2-3. Thus, the district court's modified order gives defendants an "opportunity to purge [the fines] once imposed." *Bagwell*, 512 U.S. at 837; see also People v. Operation Rescue National, 80 F.3d 64, 68 n.7 (2d Cir.), *cert. denied*, 117 S. Ct. 85 (1996) ("Under *Bagwell*, a noncompensatory fine is civil, and thus may ordinarily be imposed in the absence of a criminal trial 'only if the contemnor is afforded an opportunity to purge.'").

This purge provision is similar to the provision in United States v. United Mine Workers, 330 U.S. 258 (1947) ("*United Mine Workers*"), that the Supreme Court treated as a model civil fine in *Bagwell*. See *Bagwell*, 512 U.S. at 830 & n.4 (noting, in reference to purge provision in *United Mine Workers*, that "the conduct required of the union to purge the suspended fine was relatively discrete"); id. at 829 ("[*United*] *Mine Workers* . . . held that fixed fines also may be considered purgable and civil when imposed and suspended pending future compliance"); see generally id. at 829-830. In *United Mine Workers*, a union was found guilty beyond reasonable doubt of both criminal and civil contempt and was fined $3.5 million for violating a temporary order that restrained it from terminating the 1946 Krug-Lewis labor agreement,[5] encouraging miners to interfere with the operation of the mines, and interfering with the jurisdiction of the court. *United Mine Workers*, 330 U.S. at 266-267, 269. The Court converted $2.8 million of the fine into a coercive civil fine with a purge provision. See id. at 305; see also *Bagwell*, 512 U.S. at 830 (characterizing this portion of the fine as "civil"). The union could avoid the fine if, within five days of the issuance of the mandate, it showed that it had fully complied with the district court's temporary restraining order and preliminary injunction by (1) withdrawing unconditionally its notice of termination of the Krug-Lewis agreement

5. The agreement addressed relations between the United States government, which was operating a major portion of the country's bituminous coal mines, and the United Mine Workers of America. United Mine Workers, 330 U.S. at 262-263.

and any other notice implying the agreement was not in full force, and (2) notifying its members of the withdrawal of these notices. *United Mine Workers*, 330 U.S. at 305. Similarly, the purge provision in the instant case enables contemnors to avoid their fines if they formally affirm their intention to abide by the Permanent Injunction and publish that intention. The presence of the purge provision tends strongly to support the conclusion that the fines are coercive rather than punitive, and thus civil rather than criminal. The inclusion of the purge provision means that, if the defendants conform their conduct, they escape all obligation to pay the fines. It is therefore clear that punishment for past wrongdoing is not the objective of the fines, but rather coercion of the defendants to conform their conduct to the court's order.

To be sure, that the fines are not calibrated to the harm caused by the defendants' conduct, and are payable to the United States, argues against a conclusion that the fines are intended as compensatory; but this is irrelevant in this case because there is no contention that the fines are intended as compensatory. Those facts are no more indicative of a punitive intent than of an intent to coerce compliance. They are equally compatible with either. By its inclusion of the purge provision, the district court clearly indicated its intent that the fines serve a coercive, rather than a punitive, purpose.

And as for the size of the fines, while they are large enough to warrant concern with the adjudication process, they are nonetheless fully consistent with the court's coercive objective. The size of these fines does not compel the conclusion that the fines are punitive and criminal in the face of the strong indications that the fines are designed to coerce compliance with the court's order, and may be escaped by defendants if they conform their conduct. We conclude they were not imposed as a punishment.

We reject defendants' argument that this imposition of fines represents a finding of criminal contempt as opposed to civil contempt for the purpose of coercion.

Defendants argue that we should follow the result of National Org. for Women v. Operation Rescue, 37 F.3d 646 (D.C. Cir. 1994) ("*Operation Rescue*"), in which the D.C. Circuit, applying *Bagwell*, held that noncompensatory contempt fines were criminal, and that defendants were entitled to the protections of criminal procedure, where the contempts involved out-of-court disobedience to a complex injunction. 37 F.3d at 660-661. There is a crucial difference, however. The order imposing contempt fines in Operation Rescue did not afford contemnors "an opportunity to purge," *Bagwell*, 512 U.S. at 829. See 37 F.3d at 649-650, 661-663.

Defendants also argue that the purge provision is punitive and therefore criminal in nature because it forces defendants to humiliate themselves by publicly confessing wrongdoing. Defendants cite an Eleventh Circuit case in which a purge provision that allowed contemnors to avoid fixed fines by "taking out ads in several newspapers confessing wrongdoing" was held to be "punitive in nature." In re E. I. DuPont De Nemours &

Company-Benlate Litigation, 99 F.3d 363, 369 n.6 (11th Cir. 1996), *cert. denied*, 118 S. Ct. 263 (1997). This order does not require a confession of wrongdoing. The publication of the Affirmation and Explanatory Letter requires statement of an indisputable fact—that "the contemnor has been held in contempt for violating [district court orders]," coupled with statement that "the contemnor has agreed to comply with the Permanent Injunction in the future." See Order Amending and Reinstating Judgments, at 2. The holding of *DuPont* is not pertinent.

Notes and Questions

1. *The Temporary Restraining Order*. *Terry* and *Walker* are cases where the litigants on both sides are implacable and their world views irreconcilable. Each side is also well represented by lawyers who share their clients' goals. Pyrotechnical procedure usually accompanies such a clash, and that is certainly true here. Make a chart of the procedural steps the court describes in each case, and be aware that there were likely many other formal and informal clashes between these adversaries.

The first move in *Terry* was to seek a temporary restraining order against the projected demonstration. The plaintiffs chose to go to state court, where the first order was issued under New York's analog to Fed. R. Civ. P. 65. Later, the defendants removed the case to the federal court. Why do you think the defendants preferred a federal forum?

The federal court essentially continued the injunctive relief in the same form entered by the New York court. Although there was probably a hearing in both state and federal court before the issuance of the TRO here, note that Rule 65 contemplates the possibility that a TRO may issue ex parte, as well as in advance of any adjudication of the merits. This is truly the outer limits of due process—a powerful remedy *before* a proven wrong. Why is this kind of remedy sometimes necessary? Can you identify the provisions of Rule 65 that serve to protect due process values in this unusual context?

Issuance of such a pre-merits order evolved from equity practice in the fourteenth century, and there were never hard and fast rules about when such an order is appropriate. Rule 65, you will note, includes no standards for the issuance of preliminary relief. Instead there is a large body of common law that dictates that a court must find a substantial likelihood of success on the merits, irreparable injury, and that the balance of hardships tips in favor of the party seeking relief, before entering a TRO or a preliminary injunction. See Dan B. Dobbs, 1 Law of Remedies § 2.11, at 21 (2d ed. 1993).

In *Walker*, Dr. King and the others decided to violate the state trial court's order and march on the appointed days because they felt that the momentum of their weeks of demonstrations and months of planning would otherwise be lost. See David Benjamin Oppenheimer, Martin

Luther King, Walker v. City of Birmingham, and the Letter from the Birmingham Jail, 26 U.C. Davis L. Rev. 791 (1993), for a stirring account of the background of the case. In the Supreme Court, a majority of five found that the civil rights leaders were wrong to disobey the order without making some effort to gain its reconsideration, or to appeal it. Was it the protestors who showed disrespect for the law and the courts, or was it the city officials?

Despite *Walker,* the question of whether to obey a court order that almost certainly violates due process (and sometimes other constitutional rights as well) is far from settled.

2. *Another Heated Case: A & M Records et al. v. Napster.* The sweeping equity powers of a single judge were vividly displayed when Judge Marilyn Hall Patel commanded Napster, an Internet company, to remove all links to the plaintiffs' copyrighted material from its online directory by midnight July 28, 2000. The plaintiff companies and the Recording Industry of America sought a preliminary injunction as part of their copyright-infringement suit against Napster. In defense, Napster claimed that it was not storing songs on its own computer servers, but merely facilitating peer swapping of music. It argued, moreover, that the record industry was not harmed by but actually profited from Napster's online activities because peer swapping increased record sales.

Unimpressed by Napster's defenses, Judge Patel ruled from the bench that "to prevail on a preliminary injunction, plaintiffs must demonstrate a combination of probable success on the merits—and the possibility of irreparable harm and a balance of hardships tipping in plaintiff's favor." She went on to hold that plaintiffs had shown a strong likelihood of ultimate success on the merits, and that in a copyright case, this showing actually melded with the showing of irreparable injury. Urging that the preliminary injunction would destroy their business overnight without a full hearing on novel issues raised by new technology, Napster went to the Ninth Circuit and obtained a stay of the preliminary injunction, pending an expedited appeal. A & M Records Inc., et al. v. Napster, Inc. et al., No. C 99-5183 MHP, 2000 WL 1009483 (N.D. Cal.); A & M Records Inc., et al. v Napster, Inc., 114 F. Supp. 2d. 896 (N.D. Cal. 2000), *aff'd in part*, 239 F.3d 1004 (9th Cir. 2001) (remanding with instructions to narrow scope of injunction regarding Napster's contributory liability), *reaffirmed*, 284 F.3d 1091 (9th Cir. 2002).

For an interesting case involving the use of injunctions in the increasingly controversial laws governing elections, see Purcell v. Gonzalez, 549 U.S. 1 (2006) (per curiam) (vacating an injunction issued a month before statewide elections that barred Arizona from enforcing a ballot initiative requiring voters to present proof of citizenship when they register to vote and identification when they vote).

C. THE JURY: THE SEVENTH AMENDMENT RIGHT

Problem Case: The Harassed Student*

Christine Faulkner sued the Mitchell County Public Schools alleging that over a four-year period while she was a student in high school, Thomas Wolfe, a sports coach and teacher, continually sexually harassed her. Among other allegations, Faulkner avers that Wolfe engaged her in sexually oriented conversations in which he asked her about her sexual practices with her boyfriend and about whether she would consider sex with an older man; that he forcibly kissed her on the mouth in the parking lot; and that on three occasions he interrupted a class, requested that the teacher excuse Faulkner, and took her to a private office where he subjected her to coercive intercourse.

She further alleges that though school officials knew that Wolfe was harassing Faulkner and others, and opened an investigation, they took no action to halt it and, in fact, discouraged her from pressing criminal charges. Ultimately, Wolfe resigned on condition that all matters pending against him be dropped, and the school closed its investigation.

Faulkner seeks money damages for the cost of therapy, the loss of educational advantage, and emotional distress. She also wants to enjoin the school from operating in an ad hoc and secret fashion when investigating future sexual harassment claims.

As Faulkner's lawyer, would you file a jury demand under Rule 38? What would you tell your client about the advantages and disadvantages of a jury trial?

As the district judge assigned this case, how would you decide whether it is jury-triable?

1. The Jury Trial Advantage

The right to a jury trial is "preserved" in federal courts by the Seventh Amendment, as reflected in Rule 38. Note that for a fundamental right, jury trial is rather easily waived. See, e.g., Lutz v. Glendale Union High School, 403 F.3d 1061, 1065 (9th Cir. 2005) (holding that because complaint requested, albeit vaguely, jury trial on some issues, plaintiff waived right

* The facts of the problem case are based on Franklin v. Gwinnett Public Schools, 503 U.S. 60 (1992), and have not been significantly altered. Originally, the district court dismissed the complaint on the ground that Title IX of the Education Amendments of 1972, 20 U.S.C. §§ 1681-1688, did not provide a damages remedy. Franklin took her case to the United States Supreme Court, which reversed, holding that there was a right of action for money damages implied in the statute.

to jury trial on others, including the question of liability). Why might Faulkner prefer a jury trial?

What about the school board? Do they want a jury trial? In civil cases, the defendant as well as the plaintiff has a jury trial right. (This contrasts with the criminal system in which the constitutional right to jury trial is guaranteed to the defendant.) Often, if one party strongly prefers a judge, the other side will want a jury for mirror image reasons. Think about the problem case in light of the following, from Professor Steven A. Saltzburg, Improving the Quality of Jury Decision Making, in Verdict: Assessing the Civil Jury System 343-345 (Robert E. Litan ed., 1993):

The trial system in the United States essentially affords two choices, trial by judge or trial by jury. The advantages of trial by judge are many:

- the judge is presumed to know the law, which may eliminate some of the need for trial attorneys to devote part of their opening statements and closing arguments to legal matters and to submit proposed jury instructions;
- the judge is a single decision maker who can indicate more readily than a jury whether he or she is confused and can ask questions with knowledge as to what questioning is permissible and impermissible and what evidence is admissible;
- the judge can deliberate alone, eliminating the possibility of a hung jury;
- the judge often has experience in sifting through evidence, which may help resolving disputed issues of fact; and
- the judge is likely to be more consistent in deciding cases than a group of juries.

The advantages of a jury are perhaps more numerous:

- jurors, who come to each case without the baggage of having heard similar cases, are more likely than a judge to keep open minds and not prejudge a case simply because it bears some resemblance to earlier cases;
- the jury has the benefit of input from a number of people, all of whom have heard the same evidence and analyzed it from their different perspectives, while the judge deliberates alone;
- the jury hears only the evidence the judge has ruled admissible, whereas a judge in a bench trial often hears inadmissible evidence and must perform the difficult task of ignoring that evidence;
- jurors do not speak directly to lawyers, and thus any hostility that might develop in a case between lawyers and the judge will not prejudice the jury's fact-finding;
- a jury selected from a cross-section of the community is likely to have members whose biases or prejudices cancel or neutralize each other, but nothing cancels or neutralizes those of a judge;

- a representative jury offers the possibility that at least some of its members will be from a social class which a litigant can view as a peer group, while a judge may not be perceived as a peer; and
- a jury is by definition drawn from all parts of a community and therefore is in touch with community standards, but a judge may have experience with only a small part of the community.

There is a final aspect of trial by jury that makes the jury preferable to a judge in many cases. Federal judges are appointed for life and are, therefore, totally independent. Such independence is essential if they are to make difficult judgments on important questions, particularly those involving sensitive constitutional issues. But it does create a unique problem: independent judges may take on a regal air that makes litigants feel that judges do not think about things the way "ordinary people" do. Moreover, this independence means that, even if lawyers and litigants have little confidence in the decision making ability of a presiding judge, they have no remedy other than appeal from questionable decisions. Appeals are costly, and the deference appellate courts show to trial court decisions means that truly questionable decisions may be affirmed.

Few state court judges have life tenure. Some are appointed; others are elected. Those who are elected may face opposition in future elections, or they may run on their records. Thus, the danger exists that they may be inclined to make decisions which may help them continue in office.

2. Incidents of Jury Trial: Size and Unanimity

What does the jury look like in a civil case such as that of the harassed student? See Fed. R. Civ. P. 47, 48. By local rule in many federal courts, six-, eight-, or ten-person juries are customary. The Supreme Court upheld this practice in Colgrove v. Battin, 413 U.S. 149 (1973).

Although a prior ruling upholding a six-person jury in a criminal case, Williams v. Florida, 399 U.S. 78 (1970), made the outcome in *Colgrove* inevitable, Justice Marshall was vehement in his dissent:

> [M]y brethren mount a frontal assault on the very nature of the civil jury as that concept has been understood for some seven hundred years. No one need be fooled by reference to the six-man trier of fact utilized in the District Court for the District of Montana as a "jury." This six-man mutation is no more a "jury" than the panel of three judges condemned in Baldwin v. New York, 399 U.S. 66 (1970), or the 12 laymen instructed by a justice of the peace outlawed in Capital Traction Co. v. Hof, [174 U.S. 1 (1899)]. We deal there not with some minor tinkering with the role of the civil jury, but with its wholesale abolition and replacement with a different institution which functions differently, produces different results, and was wholly unknown to the Framers of the Seventh Amendment.

> In my judgment, if such a radical restructuring of the judicial process is deemed wise or necessary, it should be accomplished by constitutional amendment. See, e.g., Tamm, The Five-Man Civil Jury: A Proposed Constitutional Amendment, 51 Geo. L.J. 120 (1962). It appears, however, that the common law jury is destined to expire not with a bang, but a whimper. The proponents of the six-man jury have not secured the approval of two-thirds of both Houses of Congress and three-fourths of the state legislatures for their proposal. Indeed, they have not even secured the passage of simple legislation to accomplish their goal. Instead, they have relied upon the interstitial rulemaking power of the majority of the district court judges sitting in a particular district to rewrite the ancient definition of a civil jury. . . .

Id. at 166-168.

Finally, in Ballew v. Georgia, 435 U.S. 223 (1978), it was held to be a denial of due process of law for the state to convict on the basis of a verdict rendered by only five jurors. The Court justified this result on the basis of scholarship published in the aftermath of *Williams* and *Colgrove* that suggests that progressively smaller juries are less likely to foster effective group deliberation, which "[a]t some point . . . leads to inaccurate fact finding and inaccurate application of the common sense of the community to the facts. Generally, a positive correlation exists between group size and both the quality of group performance and group productivity." Id. at 232-233.

Should Colgrove v. Battin be overruled? Much contemporary social-science research, of the type the Court credited (but, critics claim, misinterpreted) in *Ballew,* suggests that juries of 6 and 12 people do not function in the same ways. Among the advantages ascribed to larger juries are more consistent and reliable verdicts due to more vigorous debate, greater capacity to remember evidence presented during a trial, and the improved ability of jurors with minority views to resist peer pressure when they have allies. A survey of this scholarship can be found in Robert H. Miller, Six of One Is Not a Dozen of the Other: A Reexamination of *Williams v. Florida* and the Size of State Criminal Juries, 146 U. Pa. L. Rev. 621 (1998). Miller concludes: "The consistent findings delivered by these studies probing the differences in the 'essential features' of the jury as cited in *Williams* now clearly establish the functional superiority of the twelve-person jury." Id. at 662.

Shortly after validating smaller juries, the Court ruled in Apodaca v. Oregon, 406 U.S. 404 (1972), that unanimity is not a constitutional requirement, finding a nine-to-three conviction sufficient for state criminal trials. For a mathematical analysis supporting this conclusion, see Robert Timothy Reagan, Supreme Court Decisions and Probability Theory: Getting the Analysis Right, 76 U. Det. Mercy L. Rev. 991, 1019 (1999).

While it may comport with probability theory, elimination of the unanimity requirement might take away the voting power of jurors with minority viewpoints. See Kim Taylor-Thompson, Empty Votes in Jury Deliberations, 113 Harv. L. Rev. 1261 (2000). These silenced voices are likely to belong to women and people of color, who only recently won meaningful access to jury service. According to Professor Taylor-Thompson, non-unanimous voting tends to inhibit inclusion, truncating or even eliminating jury deliberations:

> By discouraging meaningful examination of opposing viewpoints, majority rule decision making impoverishes deliberations. . . . Given that people of color tend to form the numerical minority on juries, the majority could ignore minority views by simply outvoting dissenters. Equally troubling is the fact that studies examining the participation rates of women in a group setting, coupled with jury research on the impact of non-unanimous voting, suggest that a majority of jurors could reach a verdict without ever hearing from women on the jury. Thus, despite the simplistic appeal of making the jury system more "democratic," non-unanimity threatens to eliminate the voices of those who have only recently secured the right to participate in the democratic process.

Id. at 1264.

If you are the counsel for Faulkner in her suit against Mitchell County Public Schools, what would you consider the optimal size of a jury in your case? Would you be concerned about the elimination of the unanimity requirement for the reasons Taylor-Thompson suggests?

3. Interpreting the Seventh Amendment: The Historical Test

Because the Seventh Amendment speaks in terms of "preserving" the jury trial, the Court has tended to rely on history in deciding when the right applies. Simply stated, the test is whether the claim being asserted is one that was tried on the law, versus equity, side of the English courts of law. But the rule is much easier to state than to apply, especially to modern claims that bear little relation to anything known to either law or equity.

The Seventh Amendment does not apply to state courts. Unlike many of the other protections in the first ten amendments, the civil jury trial right has not been incorporated into due process and guaranteed against state encroachment by the Fourteenth Amendment, as illustrated by the historic case of Walker v. Sauvinet, 92 U.S. 90 (1875). Sauvinet charged that a Louisiana statute deprived him of a jury trial in his action against Walker, a licensed keeper of a coffee-house in New Orleans, for refusing him refreshments when called for, on the ground that he was a man of color. The United States Supreme Court held:

> A State cannot deprive a person of his property without due process of law; but this does not necessarily imply that all trials in the State courts affecting the property of persons must be by jury. This requirement of the Constitution is met if the trial is had according to the settled course of judicial proceedings.

92 U.S. at 92-93. Despite the fact that the Seventh Amendment does not apply, most state courts have faced issues of interpretation about the reach of the jury trial right under state constitutions or statutes.

The following case and notes will help you understand the interpretive moves involved in the historical test.

Curtis v. Loether

415 U.S. 189 (1974)

JUSTICE MARSHALL delivered the opinion of the Court.

Section 812 of the Civil Rights Act of 1968, 82 Stat. 88, 42 U.S.C. § 3612, authorizes private plaintiffs to bring civil actions to redress violations of Title VIII, the fair housing provisions of the Act, and provides that "[t]he court may grant as relief, as it deems appropriate, any permanent or temporary injunction, temporary restraining order, or other order, and may award to the plaintiff actual damages and not more than $1,000 punitive damages, together with court costs and reasonable attorney fees. . . ." The question presented in this case is whether the Civil Rights Act or the Seventh Amendment requires a jury trial upon demand by one of the parties in an action for damages and injunctive relief under this section.

Petitioner, a Negro woman, brought this action under § 812, claiming that respondents, who are white, had refused to rent an apartment to her because of her race, in violation of § 804(a) of the Act, 42 U.S.C. § 3604(a). In her complaint she sought only injunctive relief and punitive damages; a claim for compensatory damages was later added. After an evidentiary hearing, the District Court granted preliminary injunctive relief, enjoining the respondents from renting the apartment in question to anyone else pending the trial on the merits. This injunction was dissolved some five months later with the petitioner's consent, after she had finally obtained other housing, and the case went to trial on the issues of actual and punitive damages.

Respondents made a timely demand for jury trial in their answer. The District Court, however, held that jury trial was neither authorized by Title VIII nor required by the Seventh Amendment, and denied the jury request. . . . After trial on the merits, the District Judge found that respondents had in fact discriminated against petitioner on account of her race. Although he found no actual damages, he awarded $250 in punitive damages, denying petitioner's request for attorney's fees and court costs.

The Court of Appeals reversed on the jury trial issue. Rogers v. Loether, 467 F.2d 1110 (7th Cir. 1972). After an extended analysis, the court concluded essentially that the Seventh Amendment gave respondents the right to a jury trial in this action, and therefore interpreted the statute to authorize jury trials so as to eliminate any question of its constitutionality. In view of the importance of the jury trial issue in the administration and enforcement of Title VIII and the diversity of views in the lower courts on the question, we granted certiorari, 412 U.S. 937 (1973). We affirm.

The legislative history on the jury trial question is sparse, and what little is available is ambiguous. There seems to be some indication that supporters of Title VIII were concerned that the possibility of racial prejudice on juries might reduce the effectiveness of civil rights damages actions. On the other hand, one bit of testimony during committee hearings indicates an awareness that jury trials would have to be afforded in damages actions under Title VIII. Both petitioner and respondents have presented plausible arguments from the wording and construction of § 812. We see no point to giving extended consideration to these arguments, however, for we think it is clear that the Seventh Amendment entitles either party to demand a jury trial in an action for damages in the federal courts under § 812.

The Seventh Amendment provides that "[i]n suits at common law, where the value in controversy shall exceed twenty dollars, the right of trial by jury shall be preserved." Although the thrust of the Amendment was to preserve the right to jury trial as it existed in 1791, it has long been settled that the right extends beyond the common-law forms of action recognized at that time. Mr. Justice Story established the basic principle in 1830:

> The phrase "common law," found in this clause, is used in contradistinction to equity, and admiralty, and maritime jurisprudence. . . . By *common law*, [the Framers of the Amendment] meant . . . not merely suits, which the *common* law recognized among its old and settled proceedings, but suits in which *legal* rights were to be ascertained and determined, in contradistinction to those where equitable rights alone were recognized, and equitable remedies were administered. . . . In a just sense, the amendment then may well be construed to embrace all suits which are not of equity and admiralty jurisdiction, whatever might be the peculiar form which they may assume to settle legal rights.

Parsons v. Bedford, 3 Pet. 433, 446-447 (1830) (emphasis in original).

Petitioner nevertheless argues that the Amendment is inapplicable to new causes of action created by congressional enactment. As the Court of Appeals observed, however, we have considered the applicability of the constitutional right to jury trial in actions enforcing statutory rights "as a matter too obvious to be doubted." 467 F.2d at 1114. Although the Court has apparently never discussed the issue at any length, we have often found the Seventh Amendment applicable to causes of action based on statutes. See, e.g., Dairy Queen, Inc. v. Wood, 369 U.S. 469, 477 (1962) (trademark laws); Hepner v. United States, 213 U.S. 103, 115 (1909) (immigration laws); cf. Fleitmann v. Welsbach Street Lighting Co., 240 U.S. 27 (1916) (antitrust laws), and the discussion of *Fleitmann* in Ross v. Bernhard, 396 U.S. 531, 535-536 (1970). Whatever doubt may have existed should now be dispelled. The Seventh Amendment does apply to actions enforcing statutory rights, and requires a jury trial upon demand, if the statute creates legal rights and remedies, enforceable in an action for damages in the ordinary courts of law.

NLRB v. Jones & Laughlin Steel Corp., 301 U.S. 1 (1937), relied on by petitioner, lends no support to her statutory-rights argument. The Court there upheld the award of backpay without jury trial in an NLRB unfair labor practice proceeding, rejecting a Seventh Amendment claim on the ground that the case involved a "statutory proceeding" and "not a suit at common law or in the nature of such a suit." Id. at 48. *Jones & Laughlin* merely stands for the proposition that the Seventh Amendment is generally inapplicable in administrative proceedings, where jury trials would be incompatible with the whole concept of administrative adjudication and would substantially interfere with the NLRB's role in the statutory scheme. Katchen v. Landy, 382 U.S. 323 (1966), also relied upon by petitioner, is to like effect. There the Court upheld, over a Seventh Amendment challenge, the Bankruptcy Act's grant of summary jurisdiction to the bankruptcy court over the trustee's action to compel a claimant to surrender a voidable preference; the Court recognized that a bankruptcy court has been traditionally viewed as a court of equity, and that jury trials would "dismember" the statutory scheme of the Bankruptcy Act. Id. at 339. See also Guthrie National Bank v. Guthrie, 173 U.S. 528 (1899). These cases uphold congressional power to entrust enforcement of statutory rights to an administrative process or specialized court of equity free from the strictures of the Seventh Amendment. But when Congress provides for enforcement of statutory rights in an ordinary civil action in the district courts, where there is obviously no functional justification for denying the jury trial right, a jury trial must be available if the action involves rights and remedies of the sort typically enforced in an action at law.

We think it is clear that a damages action under § 812 is an action to enforce "legal rights" within the meaning of our Seventh Amendment decisions. A damages action under the statute sounds basically in tort — the statute merely defines a new legal duty, and authorizes the courts to compensate a plaintiff for the injury caused by the defendant's wrongful breach. As the Court of Appeals noted, this cause of action is analogous to a number of tort actions recognized at common law.[10] More important, the relief sought here — actual and punitive damages — is the traditional form of relief offered in the courts of law.

We need not, and do not, go so far as to say that any award of monetary relief must necessarily be "legal" relief. A comparison of Title VIII with Title VII of the Civil Rights Act of 1964, where the courts of appeals have

10. For example, the Court of Appeals recognized that Title VIII could be viewed as an extension of the common-law duty of innkeepers not to refuse temporary lodging to a traveler without justification, a duty enforceable in a damages action triable to a jury, to those who rent apartments on a long-term basis. An action to redress racial discrimination may also be likened to an action for defamation or intentional infliction of mental distress. Indeed, the contours of the latter tort are still developing, and it has been suggested that "under the logic of the common-law development of a law of insult and indignity, racial discrimination might be treated as a dignitary tort." C. Gregory & H. Kalven, Cases and Materials on Torts 961 (2d ed. 1969).

held that jury trial is not required in an action for reinstatement and backpay, is instructive, although we of course express no view on the jury trial issue in that context. In Title VII cases the courts of appeals have characterized backpay as an integral part of an equitable remedy, a form of restitution. But the statutory language on which this characterization is based—"[T]he court may enjoin the respondent from engaging in such unlawful employment practice, and order such affirmative action as may be appropriate, which may include, but is not limited to, reinstatement or hiring of employees, with or without back pay . . . , or any other equitable relief as the court deems appropriate," 42 U.S.C. § 2000e-5(g) (1970 ed., Supp. II)—contrasts sharply with § 812's simple authorization of an action for actual and punitive damages. In Title VII cases, also, the courts have relied on the fact that the decision whether to award backpay is committed to the discretion of the trial judge. There is no comparable discretion here: if a plaintiff proves unlawful discrimination and actual damages, he is entitled to judgment for that amount. Nor is there any sense in which the award here can be viewed as requiring the defendant to disgorge funds wrongfully withheld from the plaintiff. Whatever may be the merit of the "equitable" characterization in Title VII cases, there is surely no basis for characterizing the award of compensatory and punitive damages here as equitable relief.

We are not oblivious to the force of petitioner's policy arguments. Jury trials may delay to some extent the disposition of Title VIII damages actions. But Title VIII actions seeking only equitable relief will be unaffected, and preliminary injunctive relief remains available without a jury trial even in damages actions. Dairy Queen, Inc. v. Wood, 369 U.S., at 479 n.20. Moreover, the statutory requirement of expedition of § 812 actions, 42 U.S.C. § 3614, applies equally to jury and non-jury trials. We recognize, too, the possibility that jury prejudice may deprive a victim of discrimination of the verdict to which he or she is entitled. Of course, the trial judge's power to direct a verdict, to grant judgment notwithstanding the verdict, or to grant a new trial provides substantial protection against this risk, and respondents' suggestion that jury trials will expose a broader segment of the populace to the example of the federal civil rights laws in operation has some force. More fundamentally, however, these considerations are insufficient to overcome the clear command of the Seventh Amendment. The decision of the Court of Appeals must be affirmed.

Affirmed.

Note: Other Applications of the Historical Test

Generally, the Supreme Court in modern times has liberally construed the Seventh Amendment, often, as in *Curtis*, finding the right in new statutes. Tull v. United States, 481 U.S. 412 (1987), is another example of the historical test in action. The United States government charged Tull with dumping fill in wetlands in violation of the Clean Water Act, which authorizes both an injunction and a civil penalty of up to $10,000 per day while the violation is occurring. Tull demanded a jury trial, which was refused. After a 15-day bench trial, the judge found violations of the Act and fined Tull $75,000, with further fines to follow unless Tull undertook extremely expensive restoration efforts.

The Court held that Tull had a right to jury trial on the question of liability—whether he had violated the Act—but that the amount of the civil penalties was up to the judge. Recall that one of the historical differences between law and equity is trial by jury in legal actions. Here is how Justice Brennan characterized the historical arguments in *Tull:*

> The petitioner analogizes this Government suit . . . to an action in debt within the jurisdiction of English courts of law. Prior to the enactment of the Seventh Amendment, English courts had held that a civil penalty suit was a particular species of an action in debt that was within the jurisdiction of the courts of law. . . .
>
> The Government argues, however, that—rather than an action in debt—the closer historical analog is an action to abate a public nuisance. . . .
>
> Whether, as the Government argues, a public nuisance action is a better analogy than an action in debt is debatable. But we need not decide the question. As Pernell v. Southall Realty [, 416 U.S. 363 (1974),] cautioned, the fact that the subject matter of a modern statutory action and an 18th century English action are close equivalents "is irrelevant for Seventh Amendment purposes," because "that Amendment requires trial by jury in actions unheard of at common law." It suffices that we conclude that both the public nuisance action and the action in debt are appropriate analogies to the instant statutory action. . . .
>
> A civil penalty was a type of remedy at common law that could only be enforced in courts of law. Remedies intended to punish culpable individuals, as opposed to those intended simply to extract compensation or restore the status quo, were issued by courts of law, not courts of equity. [This] action . . . is of this character. [The Act] does not direct that the "civil penalty" imposed be calculated solely on the basis of equitable determinations, such as the profits gained from violations of the statute, but simply imposes a maximum penalty of $10,000 per day of violation. . . . [The Act's] authorization of punishment to further retribution and deterrence clearly evidences that this subsection reflects more than a concern to provide equitable relief. . . . Because the nature of the relief authorized by [the Act] was traditionally available only in a court of law, the petitioner in this present action is entitled to jury trial on demand.
>
> The punitive nature of the relief sought in the present case is made apparent by a comparison with the relief sought in an action to abate a public nuisance. A public nuisance action was a classic example of the kind of suit that relied on the injunctive relief provided by courts of equity. . . .

Id. at 418-423. The Court went on, however, to hold that there was no right to jury determination of the amount of civil penalties.

In another case applying the historical test, Chauffeurs Local No. 391 v. Terry, 494 U.S. 558 (1990), the Court addressed the question of whether a duty of fair representation suit was jury-triable. The plaintiffs in the case were employees of a trucking company who were represented by the chauffeurs' union. When the union declined to refer to a grievance committee the plaintiffs' charges concerning the company's layoff and recall policies, the employees sought injunctive relief and money damages for the alleged breach of the union's duty of fair representation under Section 301 of the Labor Management Relations Act of 1947. The damage sought was compensation for lost wages and health benefits; all claims for injunctive relief were dismissed when the company filed for bankruptcy. The employees demanded a jury trial.

The Court's opinion applied the *Curtis* two-part test to determine whether the suit would resolve legal—rather than equitable—rights, thereby making the plaintiffs entitled to a jury trial. First, the Court compared the breach of fair representation claim to eighteenth-century causes of action brought in courts of England before the merger of courts of law and equity to determine whether at common law the claim would have been legal or equitable. Because the plaintiff's claim in *Terry* was comparable both to an action by a trust beneficiary for breach of fiduciary duty—an equitable action—and to a breach of contract claim—a legal issue—the Court found that this prong left the jury trial question "in equipoise." Second, the Court analyzed the type of remedy sought in nature. Because plaintiffs sought compensatory damages, which is essentially legal relief, the Court held that they were entitled to a jury trial on all issues. In reaching this conclusion, the Court distinguished the damages sought in this case from those under other statutes where Congress has specifically characterized the damages as equitable relief. Moreover, the Court found the money damages were central to the claim, rather than being simply incidental to a demand for injunctive relief.

The Court held in Feltner v. Columbia Pictures Television, Inc., 523 U.S. 340 (1998), that there is no *statutory* right to a jury trial when a copyright owner elects to recover statutory damages under Section 504(c) of the Copyright Act, in lieu of actual damages. There nevertheless is a *Seventh Amendment* right to jury trial on all issues pertinent to the award of damages under Section 504(c), given close eighteenth-century analogues that were tried before juries. See also City of Monterey v. Del Monte Dunes at Monterey, Ltd., 526 U.S. 687 (1999) (discussing issues properly submitted to jury in a regulatory takings cases brought under 42 U.S.C. § 1983).

Note: Jury Trials and Civil Rights

Curtis was one of the first of a series of late twentieth-century cases dealing with the right to a jury trial, many of which, like *Curtis,* were brought under civil rights statutes. Even those brought under other laws—*Terry,* for instance—often have civil rights undertones.

Title VII of the Civil Rights Act of 1964, which forbids discrimination in employment on the basis of race, sex, religion, and national origin, did not originally address the jury trial issue, with dicta in *Curtis* and *Terry* indicating that such a right would not be available. In its section on remedies, Title VII provides that a "court may enjoin the respondent" and "order such affirmative action as may be appropriate, which may include, but is not limited to, reinstatement for hiring of employees, with or without back pay . . . , or any other *equitable* relief as the court deems appropriate" (emphasis added).

The 1991 Civil Rights Act, 42 U.S.C. § 1981a(a), however, which amends the 1964 Act, adds that a Title VII plaintiff might seek "compensatory and punitive damages," and that if a "complaining party seeks compensatory or punitive damages . . . any party may demand a trial by jury. . . ." Section 102(c). Damages are a classic legal remedy, so this addendum clearly made some cases of employment discrimination, just like housing discrimination, jury-triable.

Determining jury-triability under Title VII can be complicated, however, because the statute provides for several different methods of proving discrimination—mixed motive, intentional, or disparate impact. In disparate impact cases, plaintiffs are not entitled to monetary damages. Thus, those plaintiffs are presumptively not entitled to a jury trial. The opposite is true of mixed motive and intentional discrimination cases, which allow monetary damages as a remedy and thus permit a jury trial.

Allison v. Citgo Petroleum Corp., 151 F.3d 402 (5th Cir. 1998), illustrates the complexity of the jury-triability question. Plaintiffs in the case, the first at the appellate level to examine the effects of the 1991 statute on class certification in Title VII cases, alleged race discrimination against African-American employees and job applicants. The Fifth Circuit found that the new jury trial right precluded class certification. On interlocutory appeal, the circuit court upheld the district court's denial of class certification, finding that the new jury trial right (along with the plaintiffs' claims for money damages) made the case unsuitable for certification: "By injecting jury trials into the Title VII mix, the 1991 Act introduced, in the context of class actions, potential manageability problems with both practical and legal, indeed constitutional, implications." Id. at 410. But see Robinson v. Metro-North Commuter R.R. Co., 267 F.3d 147 (2d Cir. 2001) (disagreeing with Fifth Circuit's analysis in *Allison*).

In a recent civil rights case that was tried to a jury, an appellate court took the unusual step of reversing as a matter of law the jury's $95,000 verdict. Gupta v. Florida Board of Regents, 212 F.3d 571 (11th Cir. 2000), was a Title VII sexual harassment and retaliation case. The plaintiff, an assistant professor at Florida Atlantic University, claimed that a superior had once touched her thigh; lifted the hem of her dress on another occasion; complimented her appearance; frequently called her at home late in the evening; looked at her in ways that made her uncomfortable; and invited her to eat at a Hooter's restaurant while in town for her job interview.

The Eleventh Circuit concluded:

> We have no doubt that Gupta subjectively perceived the alleged harassment to be severe and pervasive. However, the evidence presented at trial does not support a finding that from an objective viewpoint the alleged sexual harassment was so frequent, severe, or pervasive to constitute actionable sexual harassment under Title VII. . . . [A] finding that Gupta's complaints constitute sexual harassment would lower the bar of Title VII to punish mere bothersome and uncomfortable conduct, and would "trivialize true instances of sexual harassment."

Id. at 7, 10 (citation omitted).

What, if any, implications do these decisions involving jury trials and civil rights suits have for our case of the harassed student?

4. Preserving the Right: The Order of Trial

In the problem case, as often happens, the plaintiff is seeking more than one form of relief: money damages, the hallmark of a legal action; and an injunction, the chancellor's tool. Also, remember the extremely loose approach of the Rules to joinder, and to the allowance of counter- and cross-claims. This can result in a case where legal and equitable issues are mixed together. The following case shows how a court may sort out the issues for trial.

Beacon Theaters, Inc. v. Westover

359 U.S. 500 (1959)

JUSTICE BLACK delivered the opinion of the Court.

[Petitioner Beacon Theatres claimed that it had been wrongfully deprived of a jury trial in a suit brought against it by Fox West Coast Theatres, Inc. The theater companies were disputing the issue of "clearances," or contracts giving a theater exclusive rights to show "first run" movies in its geographical area. After building a drive-in theater near San Bernardino, California, Beacon notified Fox—which operated a "first run" movie theater there—that it believed clearances violated antitrust laws. In response, Fox claimed that Beacon's threats deprived Fox of a valuable property right: the right to negotiate for exclusive first-run contracts. Fox filed a "Complaint for Declaratory Relief," asking for a declaration that clearances did not violate the antitrust laws and for an injunction preventing Beacon from bringing any antitrust action until the controversy was resolved. Beacon filed a counterclaim, seeking treble damages under the Sherman Antitrust Act, and demanded a jury trial under Rule 38(b). . . .]

Beacon demanded a jury trial of the factual issues in the case as provided by Federal Rules of Civil Procedure 38(b). The District Court, however, viewed the issues raised by the "Complaint for Declaratory

Relief," including the question of competition between the two theatres, as essentially equitable. Acting under the purported authority of Rules 42(b) and 57, it directed that these issues be tried to the court before jury determination of the validity of the charges of antitrust violations made in the counterclaim and cross-claim. A common issue of the "Complaint for Declaratory Relief," the counterclaim, and the cross-claim was the reasonableness of the clearances granted to Fox, which depended, in part, on the existence of competition between the two theatres. Thus the effect of the action of the District Court could be, as the Court of Appeals believed, "to limit the petitioner's opportunity fully to try to a jury every issue which has a bearing upon its treble damage suit," for determination of the issue of clearances by the judge might "operate either by way of res judicata or collateral estoppel so as to conclude both parties with respect thereto at the subsequent trial of the treble damage claim." 252 F.2d at 874.

The District Court's finding that the Complaint for Declaratory Relief presented basically equitable issues draws no support from the Declaratory Judgment Act, 28 U.S.C. §§ 2201, 2202; Fed. R. Civ. Proc. 57. See also 48 Stat. 955, 28 U.S.C. (1940 ed.) § 400. That statute, while allowing prospective defendants to sue to establish their non-liability, specifically preserves the right to jury trial for both parties. It follows that if Beacon would have been entitled to a jury trial in a treble damage suit against Fox it cannot be deprived of that right merely because Fox took advantage of the availability of declaratory relief to sue Beacon first. Since the right to trial by jury applies to treble damage suits under the antitrust laws, and is, in fact, an essential part of the congressional plan for making competition rather than monopoly the rule of trade, see Fleitmann v. Welsbach Street Lighting Co., 240 U.S. 27, 29 [1916], the Sherman and Clayton Act issues on which Fox sought a declaration were essentially jury questions.

Nevertheless the Court of Appeals [for the Ninth Circuit] refused to upset the order of the district judge. It held that the question of whether a right to jury trial existed was to be judged by Fox's complaint read as a whole. In addition to seeking a declaratory judgment, the court said, Fox's complaint can be read as making out a valid plea for injunctive relief, thus stating a claim traditionally cognizable in equity. . . .

Beacon takes issue with the holding of the Court of Appeals that the complaint stated a claim upon which equitable relief could be granted. . . . Assuming that . . . the complaint can be read as alleging the kind of harassment by a multiplicity of lawsuits which would *traditionally* have justified equity to take jurisdiction and settle the case in one suit we are nevertheless of the opinion that, under the Declaratory Judgment Act and the Federal Rules of Civil Procedure, neither claim can justify denying Beacon a trial by jury of all the issues in the antitrust controversy.

The basis of injunctive relief in the federal courts has always been irreparable harm and inadequacy of legal remedies. At least as much is required to justify a trial court in using its discretion under the Federal Rules to allow claims of equitable origins to be tried ahead of legal ones, since this has the same effect as an equitable injunction of the legal claims . . .

Viewed in this manner, the use of discretion by the trial court under Rule 42(b) to deprive Beacon of a full jury trial on its counterclaim and cross-claim, as well as on Fox's plea for declaratory relief, cannot be justified. Under the Federal Rules the same court may try both legal and equitable causes in the same action. Fed. R. Civ. P. 1, 2, 18. Thus any defenses, equitable or legal, Fox may have to charges of antitrust violations can be raised either in its suit for declaratory relief or in answer to Beacon's counterclaim. On proper showing, harassment by threats of other suits, or other suits actually brought, involving the issues being tried in this case, could be temporarily enjoined pending the outcome of this litigation. Whatever permanent injunctive relief Fox might be entitled to on the basis of the decision in this case could, of course, be given by the court after the jury renders its verdict. In this way the issues between these parties could be settled in one suit giving Beacon a full jury trial of every antitrust issue. Cf. Ring v. Spina, 166 F.2d 546 [2d Cir. 1948]. By contrast, the holding of the court below while granting Fox no additional protection unless the avoidance of jury trial be considered as such, would compel Beacon to split his antitrust case, trying part to a judge and part to a jury. Such a result, which involves the postponement and subordination of Fox's own legal claim for declaratory relief as well as of the counterclaim which Beacon was compelled by the Federal Rules to bring is not permissible.

Our decision is consistent with the plan of the Federal Rules and the Declaratory Judgment Act to effect substantial procedural reform while retaining a distinction between jury and nonjury issues and leaving substantive rights unchanged. Since in the federal courts equity has always acted only when legal remedies were inadequate, the expansion of adequate legal remedies provided by the Declaratory Judgment Act and the Federal Rules necessarily affects the scope of equity. Thus, the justification for equity's deciding legal issues once it obtains jurisdiction, and refusing to dismiss a case, merely because subsequently a legal remedy becomes available, must be reevaluated in the light of the liberal joinder provisions of the Federal Rules which allow legal and equitable causes to be brought and resolved in one civil action. Similarly the need for, and therefore, the availability of such equitable remedies as Bills of Peace, Quia Timet and Injunction must be reconsidered in view of the existence of the Declaratory Judgment Act as well as the liberal joinder provision of the Rules. This is not only in accord with the spirit of the Rules and the Act but is required by the provision in the Rules that "[t]he right to trial by jury as declared by the Seventh Amendment to the Constitution or as given by a statute of the United States shall be preserved . . . inviolate."

If there should be cases where the availability of declaratory judgment or joinder in one suit of legal and equitable causes would not in all respects protect the plaintiff seeking equitable relief from irreparable harm while affording a jury trial in the legal cause, the trial court will necessarily have to use its discretion in deciding whether the legal or equitable cause should be tried first. Since the right to jury trial is a constitutional one, however, while no similar requirement protects trials by the court, that discretion is very narrowly limited and must, wherever possible, be exercised to preserve jury trial. . . .

Respondent claims mandamus is not available under the All Writs Act, 28 U.S.C. § 1651. Whatever differences of opinion there may be in other types of cases, we think the right to grant mandamus to require jury trial where it has been improperly denied is settled.

The judgment of the Court of Appeals is

Reversed.

JUSTICE STEWART, with whom JUSTICE HARLAN and JUSTICE WHITTAKER concur, dissenting.

There can be no doubt that a litigant is entitled to a writ of mandamus to protect a clear constitutional or statutory right to a jury trial. But there was no denial of such a right here. The district judge simply exercised his inherent discretion, now explicitly confirmed by the Federal Rules of Civil Procedure, to schedule the trial of an equitable claim in advance of an action at law. Even an abuse of such discretion could not, I think, be attacked by the extraordinary writ of mandamus. In any event no abuse of discretion is apparent in this case.

The complaint filed by Fox stated a claim traditionally cognizable in equity. That claim, in brief, was that Beacon had wrongfully interfered with the right of Fox to compete freely with Beacon and other distributors for the licensing of films for first-run exhibition in the San Bernardino area. The complaint alleged that the plaintiff was without an adequate remedy at law and would be irreparably harmed unless the defendant were restrained from continuing to interfere — by coercion and threats of litigation — with the plaintiff's lawful business relationships.

The Court of Appeals found that the complaint, although inartistically drawn, contained allegations entitling the petitioner to equitable relief. That finding is accepted in the prevailing opinion today. If the complaint had been answered simply by a general denial, therefore, the issues would under traditional principles have been triable as a proceeding in equity. Instead of just putting in issue the allegations of the complaint, however, Beacon filed pleadings which affirmatively alleged the existence of a broad conspiracy among the plaintiff and other theatre owners to monopolize the first-run exhibition of films in the San Bernardino area, to refrain from competing among themselves, and to discriminate against Beacon in granting film licenses. Based upon these allegations, Beacon asked damages in the amount of $300,000. Clearly these conspiracy allegations stated a cause of action triable as of right by a jury. What was demanded by Beacon, however, was a jury trial not only of this cause of action, but also of the issues presented by the original complaint.

Upon motion of Fox the trial judge ordered the original action for declaratory and equitable relief to be tried separately to the court and in advance of the trial of the defendant's counterclaim and cross-claim for damages. The court's order, which carefully preserved the right to trial by jury upon the conspiracy and damage issues raised by the counterclaim and cross-claim, was in conformity with the specific provisions of the Federal Rules of Civil Procedure. Yet it is decided today that the Court of Appeals must compel the district judge to rescind it.

Assuming the existence of a factual issue common both to the plaintiff's original action and the defendant's counterclaim for damages, I cannot agree that the District Court must be compelled to try the counterclaim first. It is, of course, a matter of no great moment in what order the issues between the parties in the present litigation are tried. What is disturbing is the process by which the Court arrives at its decision — a process which appears to disregard the historic relationship between equity and law.

The Court suggests that "the expansion of adequate legal remedies provided by the Declaratory Judgment Act . . . necessarily affects the scope of equity." Does the Court mean to say that the mere availability of an action for a declaratory judgment operates to furnish "an adequate remedy at law" so as to deprive a court of equity of the power to act? That novel line of reasoning is at least implied in the Court's opinion. But the Declaratory Judgment Act did not "expand" the substantive law. That Act merely provided a new statutory remedy, neither legal nor equitable, but available in the areas of both equity and law. . . .

The availability of a declaratory judgment did not, therefore, operate to confer upon Beacon the right to trial by jury with respect to the issues raised by the complaint.

The Court's opinion does not, of course, hold or even suggest that a court of equity may never determine "legal rights." For indeed it is precisely such rights which the Chancellor, when his jurisdiction has been properly invoked, has often been called upon to decide. Issues of fact are rarely either "legal" or "equitable." All depends upon the context in which they arise. . . .

The Court today sweeps away these basic principles as "precedents decided under discarded procedures." It suggests that the Federal Rules of Civil Procedure have somehow worked an "expansion of adequate legal remedies" so as to oust the District Courts of equitable jurisdiction, as well as to deprive them of their traditional power to control their own dockets. But obviously the Federal Rules could not and did not "expand" the substantive law one whit.

Like the Declaratory Judgment Act, the Federal Rules preserve inviolate the right to trial by jury in actions historically cognizable at common law, as under the Constitution they must. They do not create a right of trial by jury where that right "does not exist under the Constitution or statutes of the United States." Rule 39(a). Since Beacon's counterclaim was compulsory under the Rules, see Rule 13(a), it is apparent that by filing it Beacon could not be held to have waived its jury rights. Compare American Mills Co. v. American Surety Co., 260 U.S. 360 [1922]. But neither can the counterclaim be held to have transformed Fox's original complaint into an action at law. See Bendix Aviation Corp. v. Glass, (D.C. Pa.) 81 F. Supp. 645 [1922].

The Rules make possible the trial of legal and equitable claims in the same proceeding, but they expressly affirm the power of a trial judge to determine the order in which claims shall be heard. Rule 42(b). Certainly the Federal Rules were not intended to undermine the basic structure of equity jurisprudence, developed over the centuries and explicitly recognized in the United States Constitution.

For these reasons I think the petition for a writ of mandamus should have been dismissed.

---

5. The Jury's Competence: A Functional Analysis

Think about the issues in the problem case. What if Wolfe denies that the sexual incidents happened at all, or happened in the way the plaintiff alleges? We think a jury is especially capable of resolving credibility conflicts. Does it have other special competencies?

Generally, in the division of trial labor between the judge and the jury, we say that the judge decides the law, and the jury the facts. Sometimes, however, facts and law merge together, and sometimes the facts are very complicated for a group of lay people to understand. Consider the following case in thinking about the modern role of the civil jury.

Markman v. Westview Instruments, Inc.

517 U.S. 370 (1996)

JUSTICE SOUTER delivered the opinion of the Court.

The question here is whether the interpretation of a so-called patent claim, the portion of the patent document that defines the scope of the patentee's rights, is a matter of law reserved entirely for the court, or subject to a Seventh Amendment guarantee that a jury will determine the meaning of any disputed term of art about which expert testimony is offered. We hold that the construction of a patent, including terms of art within its claim, is exclusively within the province of the court. . . .

The Seventh Amendment provides that "[i]n Suits at common law, where the value in controversy shall exceed twenty dollars, the right of trial by jury shall be preserved . . . ." U.S. Const., Amdt. 7. Since Justice Story's day, United States v. Wonson, 28 F. Cas. 745, 750 (No. 16,750) (CC Mass. 1812), we have understood that "[t]he right of trial by jury thus preserved is the right which existed under the English common law when the Amendment was adopted." Baltimore & Carolina Line, Inc. v. Redman, 295 U.S. 654, 657 (1935). In keeping with our long-standing adherence to this "historical test," Wolfram, The Constitutional History of the Seventh Amendment, 57 Minn. L. Rev. 639, 640-643 (1973), we ask, first, whether we are dealing with a cause of action that either was tried at law at the time of the Founding or is at least analogous to one that was, see, e.g., Tull v. United States, 481 U.S. 412, 417 (1987). If the action in question belongs in the law category, we then ask whether the particular trial decision must fall to the jury in order to preserve the substance of the common-law right as it existed in 1791.[3]

A

As to the first issue, going to the character of the cause of action, "[t]he form of our analysis is familiar. 'First we compare the statutory action to 18th century actions brought in the courts of England prior to the merger of the courts of law and equity.'" Granfinanciera, S.A. v. Nordberg, 492 U.S. 33, 42 (1989) (citation omitted). Equally familiar is the descent of today's patent infringement action from the infringement actions tried at law in the 18th century, and there is no dispute that infringement cases today must be tried to a jury, as their predecessors were more than two centuries ago.

B

This conclusion raises the second question, whether a particular issue occurring within a jury trial (here the construction of a patent claim) is itself necessarily a jury issue, the guarantee being essential to preserve the right to a jury's resolution of the ultimate dispute. In some instances the answer to this second question may be easy because of clear historical evidence that the very subsidiary question was so regarded under the English practice of leaving the issue for a jury. But when, as here, the old practice provides no clear answer, we are forced to make a judgment about the scope of the Seventh Amendment guarantee without the benefit of any fool-proof test.

The Court has repeatedly said that the answer to the second question "must depend on whether the jury must shoulder this responsibility as *necessary to preserve the 'substance of the common-law right of trial by jury.'*" Tull v. United States, supra, at 426, (emphasis added) (quoting Colgrove v. Battin, 413 U.S. 149, 156 (1973)). . . .

The "substance of the common-law right" is, however, a pretty blunt instrument for drawing distinctions. We have tried to sharpen it, to be sure, by reference to the distinction between substance and procedure. We have also spoken of the line as one between issues of fact and law.

But the sounder course, when available, is to classify a mongrel practice (like construing a term of art following receipt of evidence) by using the

3. Our formulations of the historical test do not deal with the possibility of conflict between actual English common-law practice and American assumptions about what that practice was, or between English and American practices at the relevant time. No such complications arise in this case.

historical method, much as we do in characterizing the suits and actions within which they arise. Where there is no exact antecedent, the best hope lies in comparing the modern practice to earlier ones whose allocation to court or jury we do know, seeking the best analogy we can draw between an old and the new.

C

"Prior to 1790 nothing in the nature of a claim had appeared either in British patent practice or in that of the American states," Lutz, Evolution of the Claims of U.S. Patents, 20 J. Pat. Off. Soc. 134 (1938), and we have accordingly found no direct antecedent of modern claim construction in the historical sources. . . .

III

Since evidence of common-law practice at the time of the Framing does not entail application of the Seventh Amendment's jury guarantee to the construction of the claim document, we must look elsewhere to characterize this determination of meaning in order to allocate it as between court or jury. We accordingly consult existing precedent and consider both the relative interpretive skills of judges and juries and the statutory policies that ought to be furthered by the allocation. . . .

B

Where history and precedent provide no clear answers, functional considerations also play their part in the choice between judge and jury to define terms of art. We said in Miller v. Fenton, 474 U.S. 104, 114 (1985), that when an issue "falls somewhere between a pristine legal standard and a simple historical fact, the fact/law distinction at times has turned on a determination that, as a matter of the sound administration of justice, one judicial actor is better positioned than another to decide the issue in question." So it turns out here, for judges, not juries, are the better suited to find the acquired meaning of patent terms.

The construction of written instruments is one of those things that judges often do and are likely to do better than jurors unburdened by training in exegesis. Patent construction in particular "is a special occupation, requiring, like all others, special training and practice. The judge, from his training and discipline, is more likely to give a proper interpretation to such instruments than a jury; and he is, therefore, more likely to be right, in performing such a duty, than a jury can be expected to be." Parker v. Hulme, 18 F. Cas. at 1140. Such was the understanding nearly a century and a half ago, and there is no reason to weigh the respective strengths of judge and jury differently in relation to the modern claim; quite the contrary, for "the claims of patents have become highly technical in many respects as the result of special doctrines relating to the proper form and scope of claims that have been developed by the courts and the Patent Office." Woodward, Definiteness and Particularity in Patent Claims, 46 Mich. L. Rev. 755, 765 (1948).

Markman would trump these considerations with his argument that a jury should decide a question of meaning peculiar to a trade or profession simply because the question is a subject of testimony requiring credibility determinations, which are the jury's forte. It is, of course, true that credibility judgments have to be made about the experts who testify in patent cases, and in theory there could be a case in which a simple credibility judgment would suffice to choose between experts whose testimony was equally consistent with a patent's internal logic. But our own experience with document construction leaves us doubtful that trial courts will run into many cases like that. In the main, we expect, any credibility determinations will be subsumed within the necessarily sophisticated analysis of the whole document, required by the standard construction rule that a term can be defined only in a way that comports with the instrument as a whole. Thus, in these cases a jury's capabilities to evaluate demeanor, to sense the "mainsprings of human conduct," Commissioner of Internal Revenue v. Duberstein, 363 U.S. 278, 289 (1960), or to reflect community standards, United States v. McConney, 728 F.2d 1195, 1204 (9th Cir. 1984) (en banc), are much less significant than a trained ability to evaluate the testimony in relation to the overall structure of the patent. The decisionmaker vested with the task of construing the patent is in the better position to ascertain whether an expert's proposed definition fully comports with the specification and claims and so will preserve the patent's internal coherence. We accordingly think there is sufficient reason to treat construction of terms of art like many other responsibilities that we cede to a judge in the normal course of trial, notwithstanding its evidentiary underpinnings.

C

. . . Finally, we see the importance of uniformity in the treatment of a given patent as an independent reason to allocate all issue of construction to the court. As we noted in General Elec. Co. v. Wabash Appliance Corp., 304 U.S. 364, 369 (1938), "[t]he limits of a patent must be known for the protection of the patentee, the encouragement of the inventive genius of others and the assurance that the subject of the patent will be dedicated ultimately to the public." Otherwise, a "zone of uncertainty which enterprise and experimentation may enter only at the risk of infringement claims would discourage invention only a little less than unequivocal foreclosure of the field," United Carbon Co. v. Binney & Smith Co., 317 U.S. 228, 236 (1942), and "[t]he public [would] be deprived of rights supposed to belong to it, without being clearly told what it is that limits these rights." Merrill v. Yeomans, 94 U.S. 568, 573 (1876). It was just for the sake of such desirable uniformity that Congress created the Court of Appeals for the Federal Circuit as an exclusive appellate court for patent cases, H.R. Rep. No. 97-312, pp. 20-23 (1981), observing that increased uniformity would "strengthen the United States patent system in such a way as to foster technological growth and industrial innovation." Id. at 20.

Uniformity would, however, be ill served by submitting issues of document construction to juries. Making them jury issues would not, to be sure, necessarily leave evidentiary questions of meaning wide open in every new court in which a patent might be litigated, for principles of issue preclusion would ordinarily foster uniformity. . . .

Accordingly, we hold that the interpretation of the word "inventory" in this case is an issue for the judge, not the jury, and affirm the decision of the Court of Appeals for the Federal Circuit.

Notes and Questions

1. *Fairness and Complexity*. Does *Markman* endorse a complexity exception to the Seventh Amendment? At least one commentator thinks so. See Dana C. Butzer, Markman v. Westview: Juries and Patent Infringement Suits (Or Why Is that Jury in the Courtroom Anyway?), 58 Ohio St. L.J. 271 (1997). What is the Court saying about jury competence in patent infringement cases? Does it apply to other highly technical lawsuits, such as antitrust cases, which may turn on sophisticated economic analysis? To mass tort cases, in which difficult scientific evidence is often central?

Markman does not directly address a complexity exception to the jury trial right, though the Court's functional approach was presaged in Ross v. Bernhard, 396 U.S. 531 (1970). In *Ross*, the Court upheld the jury trial right in a stockholder derivative suit, but noted: "As our cases indicate, the 'legal' nature of an issue is determined by considering, first, the premerger custom with reference to such questions; second, the remedy sought; and, third, the practical abilities and limitations of juries." Id. at 538 n.10. The Court arguably built on the third prong — "the practical abilities and limitations of juries" — in its ruling in Markman v. Westview Instruments, Inc., in which the Court stated that "functional considerations" play a part in choosing whether a judge or a jury define terms of art.

The circuits disagree on whether there should be a complexity exception to the jury trial right. The Third Circuit upheld such an exception in an important case, In re Japanese Electronic Products Antitrust Litigation, 631 F.2d 1069 (3d Cir. 1980). The court first noted that the purpose of due process in fact finding was to "minimize the risk of erroneous decisions," and then declared:

> A jury that cannot understand the evidence and the legal rules to be applied provides no reliable safeguard against erroneous decisions. Moreover, in the context of a completely adversarial proceeding like a civil trial, due process requires that "the decision maker's conclusion rest solely on the legal rules and evidence adduced at the hearing." Goldberg v. Kelly, 397 U.

> S. 254, 271 (1970). Unless the jury can understand the legal rules and evidence, we cannot realistically expect that the jury will rest its decision on them.

Id. at 1084.

In dissent, one judge noted values other than accuracy in decision making that are served by the civil jury:

> Part of my difficulty with the majority's position probably results from a perception of the nature of the judicial process and the role of juries in that process. It is often said that the judicial process involves the search for objective truth. We have no real assurance, however, of objective truth whether the trial is to the court or to a jury. The judicial process can do no more than legitimize the imposition of sanctions by requiring that some minimum standards of fair play, which we call due process, are adhered to. In this legitimizing process, the seventh amendment is not a useless appendage to the Bill of Rights, but an important resource in maintaining the authority of the rule of law. In the process of gaining public acceptance for the imposition of sanctions, the role of the jury is highly significant. The jury is a sort of ad hoc parliament convened from the citizenry at large to lend respectability and authority to the process. Judges are often prone to believe that they, alone, can bear the full weight of this legitimizing function. I doubt that they can. Any erosion of citizen participation in the sanctioning system is in the long run likely, in my view, to result in a reduction in the moral authority that supports the process.

Id. at 1093 (Gibbons, J., dissenting).

Both the Ninth Circuit and the Federal Circuit have rejected these due process arguments. The Ninth Circuit did so in In re U.S. Financial Securities Litigation, 609 F.2d 411 (9th Cir. 1979), *cert. denied sub nom.* Gant v. Union Bank, 446 U.S. 929 (1980). Notably, the Federal Circuit, which hears appeals from district court cases involving patents, rejected a "complexity exception" to the jury trial right in patent infringement cases in SRI International v. Matsushita Electric Corp. of America, 775 F.2d 1107 (Fed. Cir. 1985). The court found that "[t]here is no peculiar cachet which removes 'technical' subject matter from the competency of a jury when competent counsel have carefully marshaled and presented the evidence of that subject matter and a competent judge has supplied carefully prepared instructions." Id. at 1130. The Federal Circuit wrote that the argument that a jury "incapable" of understanding evidence could return an "erroneous" result "confuses the route with the destination, for 'due process' is just that, a process. It is an important and constitutionally required process. It is not a result." Id. at 1128. The court added in a footnote: "The requirement is that trials be fair, not perfect. . . . [N]umerous safeguards exist against a clearly 'erroneous result' following a jury trial." Id. at n.6.

Commentators have weighed in on all sides of the debate over whether jurors are competent to decide cases believed to reflect the increasing complexity of our society. See, e.g., Joseph A. Miron Jr., Note, The Constitutionality of a Complexity Exception to the Seventh Amendment, 73 Chi.-Kent L. Rev. 865 (1998) (arguing that a complexity exception is constitutional under the Seventh Amendment because it is consistent with English common law); The Jury's Capacity to Decide Complex Civil Cases, 110 Harv. L. Rev. 1489 (1997) (urging that juries should be empowered to make better decisions in some complex cases, not discarded).

2. *Effects of* Markman *on the Trial and Appellate Processes*. In Markman v. Westview and the Sophistry of Judicial Claim Construction: An Economic Approach [paper on file with the editors], David Berl argues that the *Markman* decision has had the disturbing short-term impact of reducing settlements in patent litigation while increasing costs. Berl writes that the decision has increased uncertainty in the patent litigation process—the opposite of the result the Federal Circuit intended when it made claim construction the province of the judge rather than the jury. "Judicial claim construction has engendered confusion and uncertainty, thus diminishing the incentive for settlement." In part, this is because *Markman* instituted de novo appellate review of judicial claim construction, and the reversal rate has hovered around 40 percent. The *Markman* claim construction procedure also has increased the costs of patent litigation because it generally involves an expensive pretrial hearing, followed by an expensive jury trial. No pretrial appeal of the claim construction is allowed, leading to more waste. Post-*Markman*, "[a]s a result of the uncertainty, the patent litigation process is characterized by less settlement and enormous expenditures—two signs," he concludes, "of the current system's sub-optimality."

3. *Reforms to Improve Jury Performance*. As public perception of problems with juror performance has risen, particularly in the wake of the O.J. Simpson and Rodney King trials of the 1990s, a number of states have studied and experimented with a variety of reforms intended to improve jury performance. Perhaps the most ambitious has been Arizona, which instituted a number of changes in its jury system in 1995. Many of these reforms are aimed at making jurors more active. They include simplifying jury instructions into "plain English"; allowing counsel to make "mini-opening statements" to the entire venire before juror selection; telling jurors that they may take notes; permitting jurors to submit questions to the judge during the trial; providing each juror with copies of the jury instructions and notebooks of trial materials; and, most controversial, permitting jurors to discuss the evidence during trial. See Jacqueline A. Connor, Jury Reform: Notes on the Arizona Seminar, 1 J. Legal Advoc. & Prac. 25, 26 (1999).

Lawyers, judges, social scientists, and jurors participating in a recent symposium on jury reform also agreed that the most urgent need is increased juror involvement:

> [M]any of the proposed reforms are designed to transform jurors from passive sponges to active participants: allowing them to take notes and to ask questions, and providing them with the information they need, when they need it, to make the right decision. The goals are to increase attention

and a sense of continuous engagement, and to reduce confusion. They range from relatively uncontroversial suggestions, such as providing jurors with written copies of the instructions, to more radical reforms, such as allowing jurors to question witnesses or to discuss the case among themselves before the trial is over.

Phoebe C. Ellsworth, Introduction: Jury Reform at the End of the Century: Real Agreement, Real Changes, 32 U. Mich. J.L. Reform 213, 224 (1999). For other discussions and innovations in jury reform, see generally Symposium: The American Civil Jury, 48 DePaul L. Rev. 197 (1998); J. Clark Kelso, Final Report of the Blue Ribbon Commission on Jury System Improvement, 47 Hastings L.J. 1433 (1996); Council for Court Excellence, for the Year 2000 and Beyond: Proposals to Improve the Jury System in Washington, D.C. (setting forth 32 Recommendations for Changes in jury service).

D. CHOOSING A JURY

Problem Case: The Harassed Student (Part 2)

You represent Christine Faulkner, who has sued the school board on the facts recounted at page 723. She seeks money damages for the cost of therapy, the loss of educational advantage, and emotional distress. You have demanded a jury trial, and the day of trial has come.

Your task now is to pick a jury. Those available for selection in your case, called the venire, are pictured below. The larger pool from which this venire was drawn was chosen from the voter registration lists, which in this district are 60 percent male and 10 percent minority. Census data reveal that men and women are about evenly divided and that minorities compose about 20 percent of the population.

In order to reduce the amount of information you would have to assimilate to participate in the task, we will select only a three-person jury from a venire of nine. Each side has one peremptory to supplement the unlimited challenges for cause.

1) Think first about the ideal juror for the plaintiff. What qualities and background should that person have? Who is the ideal juror for the defense? Does anyone in the venire meet your ideal requirements?
2) What else would you like to know about these potential jurors? What nonroutine voir dire questions would each side want to ask?
3) In many places, the practice of designing a questionnaire tailored to the facts of the case and submitting it to the jury beforehand has emerged. What are the advantages and disadvantages of this procedure? Would you want to seek its use in this case?

The Venire for Faulkner v. Mitchell County

(1)

Mikhail Pavlovski
Age 39
Unmarried
1 child
Risk arbitrageur
M.B.A.

(2)

Aisha Jackson
Age 33
Married
1 child
School teacher
B.A.

(3)

Adam Michaels
Age 33
Married
2 children
Contractor
12th grade

(4)

Helen Hardy
Age 58
Unmarried
No children
University professor
Ph.D.

(5)

Jennifer Carmichael
Age 29
Unmarried
No children
Secretary
High school equivalent

(6)

Tony Silver
Age 53
Divorced
Three children
Labor organizer
1 year college

(7)

Randall Li
Age 21
Unmarried
No children
College student
2 years college

(8)

Rose Ibarra
Age 27
Married
1 child
Real estate broker
12th grade

(9)

Jack Prentiss
Age 66
Married
5 children
Retired psychiatrist
M.D.

Start with the first row, and think about whether any of these jurors should be struck for cause. What arguments would you make that one or more of these jurors should be eliminated?

As you look at the total of nine, is there anyone else who might be eliminated for cause? Against whom would you exercise your peremptory challenge for the plaintiff? Against whom for the defense?

As you engage in this exercise, think about the stereotypes you are using and the assumptions you are making. Students are sometimes discomfited by how natural this kind of thinking proves to be. Might it be better to do away with the peremptory challenge altogether, and simply put the first 6 to 12 people in the jury box?

1. The Law of Jury Selection

The jurors who ultimately stand and swear to "do justice in this cause" between Faulkner and the school board will have survived four possible elimination points. Originally summoned from lists that typically do not include, for example, the convicted felon, the unregistered voter, and the homeless (see the Federal Jury Selection Act of 1968, 28 U.S.C. §§ 1861-1878.), each potential juror then had a chance to offer a personal excuse (a sick child, busy time at work). Some of those who remained were later called to the courtroom for trial and questioned by the judge or by counsel about their fitness to serve in the Faulkner case.

After this "voir dire" examination, the judge might have removed some potential jurors for cause — friendship with one of the litigants, or the lawyers, for instance. Finally, lawyers for each side struck others without giving a reason — peremptorily.

The first case deals with the summoning of jurors for the pool, before the selection for an individual case. As you read this venerable precedent, think about its historical context, its doctrinal base, and the remedy the court imposes.

Thiel v. Southern Pacific Co.
328 U.S. 217 (1946)

JUSTICE MURPHY delivered the opinion of the Court.

Petitioner, a passenger, jumped out of the window of a moving train operated by the respondent, the Southern Pacific Company. He filed a complaint in a California state court to recover damages, alleging that the respondent's agents knew that he was "out of his normal mind" and should not be accepted as a passenger or else should be guarded and that, having accepted him as a passenger, they left him unguarded and failed to stop the train before he finally fell to the ground. At respondent's request the case was removed to the federal district court at San Francisco on the ground of diversity of citizenship, respondent being a Kentucky corporation....

After demanding a jury trial, petitioner moved to strike out the entire jury panel, alleging inter alia that

> mostly business executives or those having the employer's viewpoint are purposely selected on said panel, thus giving a majority representation to one class or occupation and discriminating against other occupations and classes, particularly the employees and those in the poorer classes who constitute, by far, the great majority of citizens eligible for jury service.

Following a hearing at which testimony was taken, the motion was denied. Petitioner then attempted to withdraw his demand for a jury trial but the respondent refused to consent. A jury of 12 was chosen. Petitioner thereupon challenged these jurors upon the same grounds previously urged in relation to the entire jury panel and upon the further ground that 6 of the 12 jurors were closely affiliated and connected with the respondent. The court denied this challenge. The trial proceeded and the jury returned a verdict for the respondent.

Petitioner renewed his objections in his motion to set aside the verdict or, in the alternative, to grant a new trial. In denying this motion the court orally found that 5 of the 12 jurors "belong more closely and intimately with the working man and employee class than they do with any other class" and that they might be expected to be "sympathetic with the experiences in life, the affairs of life, and with the economic views, of people who belong to the working or employee class." The Ninth Circuit Court of Appeals affirmed the judgment in its entirety, 149 F.2d 783, and we brought the case here on certiorari "limited to the question whether petitioner's motion to strike the jury panel was properly denied."

The American tradition of trial by jury, considered in connection with either criminal or civil proceedings, necessarily contemplates an impartial jury drawn from a cross-section of the community. Smith v. Texas, 311 U.S. 128, 130 [1940]; Glasser v. United States, 315 U.S. 60, 85 [1942]. This does not mean, of course, that every jury must contain representatives of all the economic, social, religious, racial, political and geographical groups of the community; frequently such complete representation would be impossible. But it does mean that prospective jurors shall be selected by court officials without systematic and intentional exclusion of any of these groups. Recognition must be given to the fact that those eligible for jury service are to be found in every stratum of society. Jury competence is an individual rather than a group or class matter. That fact lies at the very heart of the jury system. To disregard it is to open the door to class distinctions and discriminations which are abhorrent to the democratic ideals of trial by jury.

The undisputed evidence in this case demonstrates a failure to abide by the proper rules and principles of jury selection. Both the clerk of the court and the jury commissioner testified that they deliberately and intentionally excluded from the jury lists all persons who work for a daily wage. They generally used the city directory as the source of names of prospective jurors. In the words of the clerk,

> If I see in the directory the name of John Jones and it says he is a longshoreman, I do not put his name in, because I have found by experience that that man will not serve as a juror, and I will not get people who will qualify. . . . Where I thought the designation indicated that they were day laborers, I mean they were people who were compensated solely when they were working by the day, I leave them out.

The evidence indicated, however, that laborers who were paid weekly or monthly wages were placed on the jury lists, as well as the wives of daily wage earners.

It was further admitted that business men and their wives constituted at least 50 percent of the jury lists, although both the clerk and the commissioner denied that they consciously chose according to wealth or occupation. Thus the admitted discrimination was limited to those who worked for a daily wage, many of whom might suffer financial loss by serving on juries at the rate of $4 a day and would be excused for that reason.

This exclusion of all those who earn a daily wage cannot be justified by federal or state law. Certainly nothing in the federal statutes warrants such an exclusion. And the California statutes are equally devoid of justification for the practice.

Moreover, the general principles underlying proper jury selection clearly outlaw the exclusion practice in this instance. Jury competence is not limited to those who earn their livelihood on other than a daily basis. Wage earners, including those who are paid by the day, constitute a very substantial portion of the community, a portion that cannot be intentionally and systematically excluded in whole or in part without doing violence to the democratic nature of the jury system. Were we to sanction an exclusion of this nature we would encourage whatever desires those responsible for the selection of jury panels may have to discriminate against persons of low economic and social status. We would breathe life into any latent tendencies to establish the jury as the instrument of the economically and socially privileged. That we refuse to do.

It is clear that a federal judge would be justified in excusing a daily wage earner for whom jury service would entail an undue financial hardship. But that fact cannot support the complete exclusion of all daily wage earners regardless of whether there is actual hardship involved. Here there was no effort, no intention, to determine in advance which individual members of the daily wage earning class would suffer an undue hardship by serving on a jury at the rate of $4 a day. All were systematically and automatically excluded. In this connection it should be noted that the mere fact that a person earns more than $4 a day would not serve as an excuse. Jury service is a duty as well as a privilege of citizenship; it is a duty that cannot be shirked on a plea of inconvenience or decreased earning power. Only when the financial embarrassment is such as to impose a real burden and hardship does a valid excuse of this nature appear.

It follows that we cannot sanction the method by which the jury panel was formed in this case. The trial court should have granted petitioner's motion to strike the panel. That conclusion requires us to reverse the judgment below in the exercise of our power of supervision over the administration of justice in the federal courts. See McNabb v. United States, 318 U.S. 332, 340 [1943]. On that basis it becomes unnecessary to determine whether the petitioner was in any way prejudiced by the wrongful exclusion or whether he was one of the excluded class. It is likewise immaterial that the jury which actually decided the factual issue in the case was found to contain at least five members of the laboring class. The evil lies in the admitted wholesale exclusion of a large class of wage earners in disregard of the high standards of jury selection. To reassert those standards, to guard against the subtle undermining of the jury system, requires a new trial by a jury drawn from a panel properly and fairly chosen.

Reversed.

JUSTICE FRANKFURTER, joined by JUSTICE REED, dissents. . . .

Note: Reversal as the Remedy for Improper Jury Selection

Thiel argued on appeal that there should have been more daily wage earners in the pool (that is, among all those summoned to serve), though he did not urge that members of this class were more likely to respond to his claim. Indeed, there had been five apparently unsympathetic daily wage earners actually among the jurors who decided against him.

Yet the Court reversed the judgment in the exercise of its supervisory power in order to "reassert . . . high standards of jury selection." 328 U.S. at 225. Decided the year after World War II ended, *Thiel* rings with affirmations of the jury as fundamental to a democratic society. Selection procedures should draw "every stratum of society into jury service" and treat "jury competence" as "individual rather than a group or class matter." Id. It finds essential to the jury's (somewhat mysterious) functioning that it be inclusive of all elements of the community. When some identifiable group has been excluded, reversal, according to *Thiel,* is the only remedy that will "guard against the subtle undermining of the jury system." Id. at 227. (The quote is from Justice Frankfurter's dissent, who, though he agreed about the importance of maintaining the "broad representative character of the jury . . . as assurance of a diffuse impartiality," thought the remedy of reversal too extreme.)

The fact that reversal is the only remedy for a "mistake" in jury selection puts tremendous pressure on the system for choosing jurors.

In *Thiel*, the challenge was to the entire system of summoning jurors — to the methods used to assemble the pool. The following cases deal with another point of selection: when the individual accepted for the pool is rejected from participating in a specific trial. At the end of the twentieth century, the Supreme Court issued an extraordinary series of cases dealing with the peremptory challenge. Keep in mind the extremity of the remedy — reversed verdicts — as you read the following cases. Think also of what these cases reveal about our conception of juries, and their place in modern adjudication.

What other remedies might there be? What could the trial judge do at the time if he thought jurors were being wrongly excluded?

Edmonson v. Leesville Concrete Co.

500 U.S. 614 (1991)

JUSTICE KENNEDY delivered the opinion of the Court.

We must decide in the case before us whether a private litigant in a civil case may use peremptory challenges to exclude jurors on account of their race. Recognizing the impropriety of racial bias in the courtroom, we hold the race-based exclusion violates the equal protection rights of the challenged jurors. This civil case originated in a United States District Court, and we apply the equal protection component of the Fifth Amendment's Due Process Clause. See Bolling v. Sharpe, 347 U.S. 497 (1954).

I

Thaddeus Donald Edmonson, a construction worker, was injured in a jobsite accident at Fort Polk, Louisiana, a federal enclave. Edmonson sued Leesville Concrete Company for negligence in the United States District Court for the Western District of Louisiana, claiming that a Leesville employee permitted one of the company's trucks to roll backward and pin him against some construction equipment. Edmonson invoked his Seventh Amendment right to a trial by jury.

During voir dire, Leesville used two of its three peremptory challenges authorized by statute to remove black persons from the prospective jury. Citing our decision in Batson v. Kentucky, 476 U.S. 79 (1986), Edmonson, who is himself black, requested that the District Court require Leesville to articulate a race-neutral explanation for striking the two jurors. The District Court denied the request on the ground that *Batson* does not apply in civil proceedings. As empaneled, the jury included 11 white persons and 1 black person. The jury rendered a verdict for Edmonson, assessing his total damages at $90,000. It also attributed 80% of the fault to Edmonson's contributory negligence, however, and awarded him the sum of $18,000.

Edmonson appealed, and a divided panel of the Court of Appeals for the Fifth Circuit reversed, holding that our opinion in *Batson* applies to a private attorney representing a private litigant and that peremptory challenges may not be used in a civil trial for the purpose of excluding jurors on the basis of race. 860 F.2d 1308 (1989). The Court of Appeals panel held that private parties become state actors when they exercise peremptory challenges and that to limit *Batson* to criminal cases "would betray *Batson*'s fundamental principle [that] the state's use, toleration, and approval of peremptory challenges based on race violates the equal protection clause." Id. at 1314. The panel remanded to the trial court to consider whether Edmonson had established a prima facie case of racial discrimination under *Batson*.

The full court then ordered rehearing en banc. A divided en banc panel affirmed the judgment of the District Court, holding that a private litigant in a civil case can exercise peremptory challenges without accountability for alleged racial classifications. 895 F.2d 218 (5th Cir. 1990). The court concluded that the use of peremptories by private litigants does not constitute state action and, as a result, does not implicate constitutional guarantees. The dissent reiterated the arguments of the vacated panel opinion. The Courts of Appeals have divided on the issue. We granted certiorari, 498 U.S. 809 (1990), and now reverse the Court of Appeals.

II

A

In Powers v. Ohio, 499 U.S. 400 (1991), we held that a criminal defendant, regardless of his or her race, may object to a prosecutor's race-based exclusion of persons from the petit jury. Our conclusion rested on a two-part analysis. First, following our opinions in *Batson* and in Carter v. Jury Commission of Greene County, 396 U.S. 320 (1970), we made clear that a prosecutor's race-based peremptory challenge violates the equal protection rights of those excluded from jury service. 499 U.S. at 407-409. Second, we relied on well-established rules of third-party standing to hold that a defendant may raise the excluded jurors' equal protection rights. Id., at 410-415.

Powers relied upon over a century of jurisprudence dedicated to the elimination of race prejudice within the jury selection process. While these decisions were for the most part directed at discrimination by a prosecutor or other government officials in the context of criminal proceedings, we have not intimated that race discrimination is permissible in civil proceedings. See Thiel v. Southern Pacific Co., 328 U.S. 217, 220-221 (1946). Indeed, discrimination on the basis of race in selecting a jury in a civil proceeding harms the excluded juror no less than discrimination in a criminal trial. See id. at 220. In either case, race is the sole reason for denying the excluded venireperson the honor and privilege of participating in our system of justice.

That an act violates the Constitution when committed by a government official, however, does not answer the question whether the same act offends constitutional guarantees if committed by a private litigant or his attorney. The Constitution's protections of individual liberty and equal protection apply in general only to action by the government. National Collegiate Athletic Assn. v. Tarkanian, 488 U.S. 179, 191 (1988). Racial discrimination, though invidious in all contexts, violates the Constitution only when it may be attributed to state action. Moose Lodge No. 107 v. Irvis, 407 U.S. 163, 172 (1972). Thus, the legality of the exclusion at issue here turns on the extent to which a litigant in a civil case may be subject to the Constitution's restrictions. . . .

The trial judge exercises substantial control over *voir dire* in the federal system. See Fed. Rule Civ. Proc. 47. The judge determines the range of information that may be discovered about a prospective juror, and so affects the exercise of both challenges for cause and peremptory challenges. In some cases, judges may even conduct the entire *voir dire* by themselves, a common practice in the District Court where the instant case was tried. See Louisiana Rules of Court, Local Rule 13.02 (W.D. La. 1990). The judge oversees the exclusion of jurors for cause, in this way determining which jurors remain eligible for the exercise of peremptory strikes. In cases involving multiple parties, the trial judge decides how peremptory challenges shall be allocated among them. 28 U.S.C. § 1870. When a lawyer exercises a peremptory challenge, the judge advises the juror he or she has been excused. . . .

The principle that the selection of state officials, other than through election by all qualified voters, may constitute state action applies with even greater force in the context of jury selection through the use of peremptory challenges. Though the motive of a peremptory challenge may be to protect a private interest, the objective of jury selection proceedings is to determine representation on a governmental body. Were it not for peremptory challenges, there would be no question that the entire process of determining who will serve on the jury constitutes state action. The fact that the government delegates some portion of this power to private litigants does not change the governmental character of the power exercised. . . . Here, as in most civil cases, the initial decision whether to sue at all, the selection of counsel, and any number of ensuing tactical choices in the course of discovery and trial may be without the requisite governmental character to be deemed state action. That cannot be said of the exercise of peremptory challenges, however; when private litigants participate in the selection of jurors, they serve an important function within the government and act with its substantial assistance. If peremptory challenges based on race were permitted, persons could be required by summons to be put at risk of open and public discrimination as a condition of their participation in the justice system. The injury to excluded jurors would be the direct result of governmental delegation and participation.

Finally, we note that the injury caused by the discrimination is made more severe because the government permits it to occur within the courthouse itself. Few places are a more real expression of the constitutional authority of the government than a courtroom, where the law itself unfolds. Within the courtroom, the government invokes its laws to determine the rights of those who stand before it. In full view of the public, litigants press their cases, witnesses give testimony, juries render verdicts, and judges act with the utmost care to ensure that justice is done.

Race discrimination within the courtroom raises serious questions as to the fairness of the proceedings conducted there. Racial bias mars the integrity of the judicial system and prevents the idea of democratic government from becoming a reality. Rose v. Mitchell, 443 U.S. 545, 556 (1979); Smith v. Texas, 311 U.S. 128, 130 (1940). In the many times we have addressed the problem of racial bias in our system of justice, we have not "questioned the premise that racial discrimination in the qualification or selection of jurors offends the dignity of persons and the integrity of the courts." *Powers,* 499 U.S. at 402. To permit racial exclusion in this official forum compounds the racial insult inherent in judging a citizen by the color of his or her skin. . . .

We believe the only issue that warrants further consideration in this case is whether a civil litigant can demonstrate a sufficient interest in challenging the exclusion of jurors on account of race. In *Powers,* we held:

> The discriminatory use of peremptory challenges by the prosecution causes a criminal defendant cognizable injury, and the defendant has a concrete interest in challenging the practice. See Allen v. Hardy, 478 U.S. [255,] 259 [(1986)] (recognizing a defendant's interest in "neutral jury selection procedures"). This is not because the individual jurors dismissed by the prosecution may have been predisposed to favor the defendant; if that were true, the jurors might have been excused for cause. Rather, it is because racial discrimination in the selection of jurors "casts doubt on the integrity of the judicial process," Rose v. Mitchell, [supra, at 556], and places the fairness of a criminal proceeding in doubt.

Id. at 411.

The harms we recognized in *Powers* are not limited to the criminal sphere. A civil proceeding often implicates significant rights and interests. Civil juries, no less than their criminal counterparts, must follow the law and act as impartial factfinders. And, as we have observed, their verdicts, no less than those of their criminal counterparts, become binding judgments of the court. Racial discrimination has no place in the courtroom, whether the proceeding is civil or criminal. See Thiel v. Southern Pacific Co., 328 U.S., at 220. Congress has so mandated by prohibiting various discriminatory acts in the context of both civil and criminal trials. See 18 U.S.C. § 243; 28 U.S.C. §§ 1861, 1862. The Constitution demands nothing less. We conclude that courts must entertain a challenge to a private litigant's racially discriminatory use of peremptory challenges in a civil trial.

It may be true that the role of litigants in determining the jury's composition provides one reason for wide acceptance of the jury system and of its verdicts. But if race stereotypes are the price for acceptance of a jury panel as fair, the price is too high to meet the standard of the Constitution. Other means exist for litigants to satisfy themselves of a jury's impartiality without using skin color as a test. If our society is to continue to progress as a multiracial democracy, it must recognize that the automatic invocation of race stereotypes retards that progress and causes continued hurt and injury. By the dispassionate analysis which is its special distinction, the law dispels fears and preconceptions respecting racial attitudes. The quiet rationality of the courtroom makes it an appropriate place to confront race-based fears or hostility by means other than the use of offensive stereotypes. Whether the race generality employed by litigants to challenge a potential juror derives from open hostility or from some hidden and unarticulated fear, neither motive entitles the litigant to cause injury to the excused juror. And if a litigant believes that the prospective juror harbors the same biases or instincts, the issue can be explored in a rational way that consists with respect for the dignity of persons, without the use of classifications based on ancestry or skin color.

[JUSTICE O'CONNOR, joined by CHIEF JUSTICE REHNQUIST and JUSTICE SCALIA, wrote a dissenting opinion. JUSTICE SCALIA also wrote a separate dissent.]

Note: The Right of the Individual Potential Juror

Edmonson began the shift to a focus on the right of the individual juror, rather than on the other interests served by a diverse jury. What are some of these other interests? Consider the following suggestions by Professor Massaro regarding how jury composition in criminal cases may affect interests other than those of individual jurors:

> Because a jury's fairness is determined not only by its verdict but also by its visual appearance, jury selection procedures must produce juries that correspond to people's images of a fair jury. Otherwise, people will distrust jury verdicts regardless of the "correctness" of those results on the merits, and the jury will lose the respect essential to effective decision making.
>
> The visual image of a fair jury can be described as a triptych. A triptych is a picture that has three panels, side by side. The center panel image is fixed, while the flanking panel images overlap the center panel image. In a triptych of the criminal jury, the left panel represents the defendant's image of a fair jury—a group of citizens who will listen to the defendant's version of the facts and who, ideally, will identify in some way with the defendant's life or be empathetic to the defendant's plight. The jury represents the defendant's hope of a hearing by others of common experience.
>
> The right panel represents the government's image of a fair jury—a group of citizens who will listen to the government's version of the facts and who will perform a role in the enforcement of the penal code by convicting

defendants whose guilt is established beyond a reasonable doubt. The government desires a jury that will identify with the victims of crime and that will be not be afraid to punish those who violate the law and injure others.

The center panel of the triptych represents the community's image of the jury—a group of citizens who will sift through the defendant's and the government's evidence and extract the truth. The community may identify with both the defendant and the government, because its members may one day be victims of crime or of government oppression. Fearing both, though perhaps not equally, the community desires a jury system that is reasonably fair to the defendant, yet willing to protect the people from criminals. It probably desires a jury composed of some—but not all—defendant empathizers and some—but not all—victim empathizers.

If this rough concept of the jury is accurate, then a jury selection procedure that allows both sides to challenge prospective jurors for cause and to challenge a limited number of others for no reason through peremptories seems acceptable. What should emerge from this procedure is a jury composed of some defendant-empathizers and some victim-empathizers, with the extremes of either side offset. The defendant might need to be allotted extra peremptories to counterbalance the government's natural advantage in a criminal case. . . .

The problem with the system is that not all defendants have enough empathizers in the community so that at least one of them is sure to get into the jury box after the prosecution has exercised its peremptories. This result is particularly likely when the prosecution intentionally exercises those peremptories to eliminate the defendant's peers. When the jury contains none of the defendant's peers, the defendant's hope of an empathetic hearing vanishes. The left panel image of the jury as citizens who will hear the defendant is distorted or even eliminated, and the center panel image of the jury becomes right-panel skewed.

Toni M. Massaro, Peremptories or Peers?—Rethinking Sixth Amendment Doctrine, Images, and Procedures, 64 N.C. L. Rev. 501, 517-518 (1986).

Are there other interests not canvassed by this image of the jury? Are any of these interests undermined by the uninhibited use of the peremptory challenge?

J.E.B. v. Alabama ex rel. T.B.

511 U.S. 127 (1994)

Justice Blackmun delivered the opinion of the Court.

I

On behalf of relator T.B., the mother of a minor child, respondent State of Alabama filed a complaint for paternity and child support against petitioner J.E.B. in the District Court of Jackson County, Alabama. On October 21, 1991, the matter was called for trial and jury selection began.

The trial court assembled a panel of 36 potential jurors, 12 males and 24 females. After the court excused three jurors for cause, only 10 of the remaining 33 jurors were male. The State then used 9 of its 10 peremptory strikes to remove male jurors; petitioner used all but one of his strikes to remove female jurors. As a result, all the selected jurors were female.

Before the jury was empaneled, petitioner objected to the State's peremptory challenges on the ground that they were exercised against male jurors solely on the basis of gender, in violation of the Equal Protection Clause of the Fourteenth Amendment. Petitioner argued that the logic and reasoning of Batson v. Kentucky [, 476 U.S. 79 (1986)], which prohibits peremptory strikes solely on the basis of race, similarly forbids intentional discrimination on the basis of gender. The court rejected petitioner's claim and empaneled the all-female jury. The jury found petitioner to be the father of the child and the court entered an order directing him to pay child support. . . .

We granted certiorari to resolve a question that has created a conflict of authority — whether the Equal Protection Clause forbids peremptory challenges on the basis of gender as well as on the basis of race. Today we reaffirm what, by now, should be axiomatic: Intentional discrimination on the basis of gender by state actors violates the Equal Protection Clause, particularly where, as here, the discrimination serves to ratify and perpetuate invidious, archaic, and overbroad stereotypes about the relative abilities of men and women.

II

Discrimination on the basis of gender in the exercise of peremptory challenges is a relatively recent phenomenon. Gender-based peremptory strikes were hardly practicable for most of our country's existence, since, until the 19th century, women were completely excluded from jury service. So well-entrenched was this exclusion of women that in 1880 this Court, while finding that the exclusion of African-American men from juries violated the Fourteenth Amendment, expressed no doubt that a State "may confine the selection [of jurors] to males." Strauder v. West Virginia, 100 U.S. 303, 310 [1880]; see also Fay v. New York, 332 U.S. 261, 289-290 (1947).

Many States continued to exclude women from jury service well into the present century, despite the fact that women attained suffrage upon ratification of the Nineteenth Amendment in 1920. States that did permit women to serve on juries often erected other barriers, such as registration requirements and automatic exemptions, designed to deter women from exercising their right to jury service. . . . Under our [modern] equal protection jurisprudence, gender-based classifications require "an exceedingly persuasive justification" in order to survive constitutional scrutiny. Thus, the only question is whether discrimination on the basis of gender in jury selection substantially furthers the State's legitimate interest in achieving a fair and impartial trial. . . .

Far from proffering an exceptionally persuasive justification for its gender-based peremptory challenges, respondent maintains that its decision to strike virtually all the males from the jury in this case "may reasonably have been based upon the perception, supported by history, that men otherwise totally qualified to serve upon a jury might be more sympathetic and receptive to the arguments of a man alleged in a paternity action to be the father of an out-of-wedlock child, while women equally qualified to serve upon a jury might be more sympathetic and receptive to the arguments of the complaining witness who bore the child."

We shall not accept as a defense to gender-based peremptory challenges "the very stereotype the law condemns." Powers v. Ohio, 499 U.S. 400, 410 (1991). Respondent's rationale, not unlike those regularly expressed for gender-based strikes, is reminiscent of the arguments advanced to justify the total exclusion of women from juries. Respondent offers virtually no support for the conclusion that gender alone is an accurate predictor of juror's attitudes; yet it urges this Court to condone the same stereotypes that justified the wholesale exclusion of women from juries and the ballot box. Respondent seems to assume that gross generalizations that would be deemed impermissible if made on the basis of race are somehow permissible when made on the basis of gender.

Discrimination in jury selection, whether based on race or on gender, causes harm to the litigants, the community, and the individual jurors who are wrongfully excluded from participation in the judicial process. . . .

When state actors exercise peremptory challenges in reliance on gender stereotypes, they ratify and reinforce prejudicial views of the relative abilities of men and women. Because these stereotypes have wreaked injustice in so many other spheres of our country's public life, active discrimination by litigants on the basis of gender during jury selection "invites cynicism respecting the jury's neutrality and its obligation to adhere to the law." Powers v. Ohio, 499 U.S. at 412. The potential for cynicism is particularly acute in cases where gender-related issues are prominent, such as cases involving rape, sexual harassment, or paternity. Discriminatory use of peremptory challenges may create the impression that the judicial system has acquiesced in suppressing full participation by one gender or that the "deck has been stacked" in favor of one side. See id. at 413 ("The verdict will not be accepted or understood [as fair] if the jury is chosen by unlawful means at the outset").

In recent cases we have emphasized that individual jurors themselves have a right to nondiscriminatory jury selection procedures. . . . All persons, when granted the opportunity to serve on a jury, have the right not to be excluded summarily because of discriminatory and stereotypical presumptions that reflect and reinforce patterns of historical discrimination. . . . It denigrates the dignity of the excluded juror, and, for a woman, reinvokes a history of exclusion from political participation.[14] The message it sends to all those in the courtroom, and all those who may later learn of the discriminatory act, is that certain individuals, for no reason other than gender, are presumed unqualified by state actors to decide important questions upon which reasonable persons could disagree. . . .

Failing to provide jurors the same protection against gender discrimination as race discrimination could frustrate the purpose of *Batson* itself. Because gender and race are overlapping categories, gender can be used as a pretext for racial discrimination. Allowing parties to remove racial minorities from the jury not because of their race, but because of their gender, contravenes well-established equal protection principles and could insulate effectively racial discrimination from judicial scrutiny.

The judgment of the Court of Civil Appeals of Alabama is reversed and the case is remanded to that court for further proceedings not inconsistent with this opinion.

It is so ordered.

JUSTICE O'CONNOR, concurring.

[T]oday's important blow against gender discrimination is not costless. I write separately to discuss some of these costs, and to express my belief that today's holding should be limited to the *government's* use of gender-based peremptory strikes. . . . In further constitutionalizing jury selection procedures, the Court increases the number of cases in which jury selection — once a sideshow — will become part of the main event.

For this same reason, today's decision further erodes the role of the peremptory challenge. The peremptory challenge is "a practice of ancient origin" and is "part of our common law heritage." Edmonson v. Leesville Concrete Co., 500 U.S. 614, 639 (1991) (O'Connor, J., dissenting). The principal value of the peremptory is that it helps produce fair and impartial juries. Swain v. Alabama, 380 U.S. 202, 218-219 (1965); Babcock, Voir Dire: Preserving "Its Wonderful Power," 27 Stan. L. Rev. 545, 549-558 (1975). "Peremptory challenges, by enabling each side to exclude those jurors it believes will be most partial toward the other side, are a means of eliminat[ing] extremes of partiality on both sides, thereby assuring the selection of a qualified and unbiased jury." Holland v. Illinois, 493 U.S. 474, 484 (1990) (internal quotation marks and citations omitted). The peremptory's importance is confirmed by its persistence: it was well established at the time of Blackstone and continues to endure in all the States. Id. at 481.

14. The popular refrain is that *all* peremptory challenges are based on stereotypes of some kind, expressing various intuitive and frequently erroneous biases. But where peremptory challenges are made on the basis of group characteristics other than race or gender (like occupation, for example), they do not reinforce the same stereotypes about the group's competence or predispositions that have been used to prevent them from voting, participating on juries, pursuing their chosen professions, or otherwise contributing to civic life. See B. Babcock, A Place in the Palladium, Women's Rights and Jury Service, 61 U. Cin. L. Rev. 1139, 1173 (1993).

Moreover, "[t]he essential nature of the peremptory challenge is that it is one exercised without a reason stated, without inquiry and without being subject to the court's control." *Swain*, 380 U.S. at 220. Indeed, often a reason for it cannot be stated, for a trial lawyer's judgments about a juror's sympathies are sometimes based on experienced hunches and educated guesses, derived from a juror's responses at voir dire or a juror's "'bare looks and gestures.'" Ibid. That a trial lawyer's instinctive assessment of a juror's predisposition cannot meet the high standards of a challenge for cause does not mean that the lawyer's instinct is erroneous. Cf. V. Starr & M. McCormick, Jury Selection 522 (1993) (nonverbal cues can be better than verbal responses at revealing a juror's disposition). Our belief that experienced lawyers will often correctly intuit which jurors are likely to be the least sympathetic, and our understanding that the lawyer will often be unable to explain the intuition, are the very reason we cherish the peremptory challenge. But, as we add, layer by layer, additional constitutional restraints on the use of the peremptory, we force lawyers to articulate what we know is often inarticulable. . . .

Nor is the value of the peremptory challenge to the litigant diminished when the peremptory is exercised in a gender-based manner. We know that like race, gender matters. A plethora of studies make clear that in rape cases, for example, female jurors are somewhat more likely to vote to convict than male jurors. See R. Hastie, S. Penrod, & N. Pennington, Inside the Jury 140-141 (1983) (collecting and summarizing empirical studies). Moreover, though there have been no similarly definitive studies regarding, for example, sexual harassment, child custody, or spousal or child abuse, one need not be a sexist to share the intuition that in certain cases a person's gender and resulting life experience will be relevant to his or her view of the case. "'Jurors are not expected to come into the jury box and leave behind all that their human experience has taught them.'" Beck v. Alabama, 447 U.S. 625, 642 (1980). Individuals are not expected to ignore as jurors what they know as men—or women.

[A separate concurrence by JUSTICE KENNEDY and a separate dissenting opinion of CHIEF JUSTICE REHNQUIST have been omitted.]

JUSTICE SCALIA, with whom THE CHIEF JUSTICE and JUSTICE THOMAS join, dissenting.

Today's opinion is an inspiring demonstration of how thoroughly up-to-date and right-thinking we Justices are in matters pertaining to the sexes (or as the Court would have it, the genders), and how sternly we disapprove the male chauvinist attitudes of our predecessors. The price to be paid for this display—a modest price, surely—is that most of the opinion is quite irrelevant to the case at hand. The hasty reader will be surprised to learn, for example, that this lawsuit involves a complaint about the use of peremptory challenges to exclude *men* from a petit jury. To be sure, petitioner, a man, used all but one of *his* peremptory strikes to remove *women* from the jury (he used his last challenge to strike the sole remaining male from the pool), but the validity of *his* strikes is not before us. Nonetheless, the Court treats itself to an extended discussion of the historic exclusion of women not only from jury service, but also from service at the bar (which is rather like jury service, in that it involves going to the courthouse a lot)....[1]

Even if the line of our later cases guaranteed by today's decision limits the theoretically boundless *Batson* principle to race, sex, and perhaps other classifications subject to heightened scrutiny (which presumably would include religious belief), much damage has been done. It has been done, first and foremost, to the peremptory challenge system, which loses its whole character when (in order to defend against "impermissible stereotyping" claims) "reasons" for strikes must be given.... And make no mistake about it: there really is no substitute for the peremptory. Voir dire (though it can be expected to expand as a consequence of today's decision) cannot fill the gap. The biases that go along with group characteristics tend to be biases that the juror himself does not perceive, so that it is no use asking about them. It is fruitless to inquire of a male juror whether he harbors any subliminal prejudice in favor of unwed fathers....

In order, it seems to me, not to eliminate any real denial of equal protection, but simply to pay conspicuous obeisance to the equality of the sexes, the Court imperils a practice that has been considered an essential part of fair jury trial since the dawn of the common law. The Constitution of the United States neither requires nor permits this vandalizing of our people's traditions.

For these reasons, I dissent.

Note: Equal Protection for Jurors and the Future of the Peremptory Challenge

The decision in *J.E.B.* was doctrinally compelled once the right of the prospective juror became the Court's central focus. But *J.E.B.* is important because it finally established that women have a constitutional right to serve on juries, which the Court had never before formally declared, despite the long struggle by women's rights advocates.

For a discussion of this disparate treatment and related issues, see Joanna L. Grossman, Women's Jury Rights: Right of Citizenship or Privilege of Difference?, 46 Stan. L. Rev. 601 (1994). In the article cited by the majority, Professor Babcock argued that *Batson* must be extended to

1. Throughout this opinion, I shall refer to the issue as sex discrimination rather than (as the Court does) gender discrimination. The word "gender" has acquired the new and useful connotation of cultural or attitudinal characteristics (as opposed to physical characteristics) distinctive to the sexes. That is to say, gender is to sex as feminine is to female and masculine to male. The present case does not involve peremptory strikes exercised on the basis of femininity or masculinity (as far as it appears, effeminate men did not survive the prosecution's peremptories). The case involves, therefore, sex discrimination plain and simple.

women in order to prevent gender from becoming an improper proxy for race. Barbara Allen Babcock, A Place in the Palladium: Women's Rights and Jury Service, 61 U. Cin. L. Rev. 1139, 1160-1165 (1993).

What is left of the peremptory challenge now? Has the Court in effect created a third level of challenge, a qualified peremptory for which a reason must be given other than race or gender? What other protected categories will also require an explanation if a potential juror is struck? Religion and national origin are two likely candidates. So may be political affiliation and economic status. Does this leave any room for the operation of a true peremptory challenge, made on the basis of hunch or instinct?

The move to eliminate peremptory challenges altogether might meet constitutional objections, though they have yet to be held constitutionally essential to trial by jury. Consider the following suggestions for preserving the peremptory challenge while generally improving the jury selection process.

Barbara Allen Babcock, A Place in the Palladium: Women's Rights and Jury Service

61 U. Cin. L. Rev. 1139, 1175-1180 (1993)

. . . Aside from the difficulty of accomplishing it, total elimination of the peremptory challenge is ill-advised as it would focus jury selection entirely on the challenge for cause. The judge alone — in a series of highly discretionary, practically unreviewable decisions — would then be permitted to shape the jury in every case. But under the Constitution, the jury trial is guaranteed precisely because our tradition is not to trust the unilateral actions of judges. In particular, the jury is meant to offset the class bias and elitism that characterizes the judiciary, yet we can hardly expect judges to find "cause" — i.e., incipient bias — in jurors who reflect their own image in background or outlook.

Not only would the increased importance of the cause challenge heighten the judge's power, but abolition of the peremptory would make it more difficult for the litigant to lay the groundwork for a cause challenge, as vigorous questioning may antagonize and hence prejudice a potential juror. The peremptory challenge is the insurance that makes genuine inquiry into juror bias possible.

Most important, the peremptory endows the litigant with a role in the process, thus promoting in Blackstone's words "a good opinion of the jury the want of which might totally disconcert him." Although the Supreme Court disallows race as a reason for striking jurors, and should forbid female gender as an explanation also, it does not follow that litigants must relinquish all sense of choice over their shared juries.

The peremptory is important enough that instead of urging our legislatures to abolish it, we should seize the occasion of the Supreme Court's intervention in jury selection to enact modern statutes that will aid our "progress toward a multiracial democracy."[122] This essay concludes by outlining some of the elements such a statute might include, though many of the suggestions could easily be implemented by trial judges or by appellate courts through their respective supervisory powers.

A comprehensive statute would begin by broadening the juror pool beyond voter registration lists to include licensed drivers, utility users, and residents listed in the city directory. Jurors to be summoned should each receive (on the back of the summons), as they now often do, a questionnaire covering items relevant to their basic fitness to serve. . . .

The voir dire process can also be changed to facilitate the exercise of peremptory challenges on a basis other than race or gender. Juror questionnaires can be supplemented by questions, tailored to individual cases designed to probe the attitudes of potential jurors toward sensitive issues that are likely to arise.

Such tailored questionnaires can help the parties base their arguments for cause challenges and their exercise of peremptories on actual suspicion of race prejudice rather than simply on the color of the potential juror's skin. And though they cannot substitute for some public procedures — to see and to hear is, after all, the point of voir dire — the questionnaires can provide grounds for open inquiry that neither humiliates the potential juror nor rouses the ire of the others in the venire.

In order to explore prejudiced attitudes more effectively and efficiently, the parties might give their opening statements to the whole venire and then make inquiries afterward for both cause and peremptory challenges. Potential jurors would then understand how and where their answers fit into the theory of the case and the evidence that will be presented. Once procedures are in place allowing parties to act on intimations of actual bias, rather than on the crude proxy of race or gender, then the requirement for making a prima facie case by letting one or two strikes pass before objecting would no longer be necessary.

Expanding the information available from voir dire responds to the concerns of those who fear that modifying the peremptory challenge will destroy the mystique — or science — of jury selection. Automatic strikes of white women and people of color are not only unnecessary to the art, but they detract from it. When the legendary jury lawyer Clarence Darrow spoke in a much-cited passage of "the knowledge of life, human nature, psychology and the reactions of the human emotions," that a lawyer must bring to jury selection, he was looking at juries that contained no racial minorities and few women.[130] Rather, in shaping the jury he examined "nationality, business, religion, politics, social standing, family ties, friends, habits of life and thought; the books and newspapers he likes and reads and many more matters that combine to make a man."[131] These

122. Edmonson v. Leesville Concrete Co., 111 S. Ct. 2077, 2088 (1991).

130. Clarence Darrow, Attorney for the Defense, Esquire, May 1936, at 35.

131. Id. Darrow did not use the male pronoun generically, since he advised striking any women who might be called.

During the trial, the District Court twice denied oral motions by respondent for judgment as a matter of law under Rule 50 of the Federal Rules of Civil Procedure, and the case went to the jury. The court instructed the jury that "if the plaintiff fails to prove age was a determinative or motivating factor in the decision to terminate him, then your verdict shall be for the defendant." So charged, the jury returned a verdict in favor of petitioner, awarding him $35,000 in compensatory damages, and found that respondent's age discrimination had been "willful." The District Court accordingly entered judgment for petitioner in the amount of $70,000, which included $35,000 in liquidated damages based on the jury's finding of willfulness. Respondent then renewed its motion for judgment as a matter of law and alternatively moved for a new trial, while petitioner moved for front pay. The District Court denied respondent's motions and granted petitioner's, awarding him $28,490.80 in front pay for two years' lost income.

The Court of Appeals for the Fifth Circuit reversed, holding that petitioner had not introduced sufficient evidence to sustain the jury's finding of unlawful discrimination. After noting respondent's proffered justification for petitioner's discharge, the court acknowledged that petitioner "very well may" have offered sufficient evidence for "a reasonable jury [to] have found that [respondent's] explanation for its employment decision was pretextual." The court explained, however, that this was "not dispositive" of the ultimate issue — namely, "whether Reeves presented sufficient evidence that his age motivated [respondent's] employment decision." Addressing this question, the court weighed petitioner's additional evidence of discrimination against other circumstances surrounding his discharge. Specifically, the court noted that Chesnut's age-based comments "were not made in the direct context of Reeves's termination"; there was no allegation that the two other individuals who had recommended that petitioner be fired (Jester and Whitaker) were motivated by age; two of [the decision makers involved in petitioner's discharge (Jester and Sanderson) were over the age of 50; all three of the Hinge Room supervisors were accused of inaccurate recordkeeping; and several of respondent's management positions were filled by persons over age 50 when petitioner was fired. On this basis, the court concluded that petitioner had not introduced sufficient evidence for a rational jury to conclude that he had been discharged because of his age.

We granted certiorari to resolve a conflict among the Courts of Appeals as to whether a plaintiff's prima facie case of discrimination (as defined in McDonnell Douglas Corp. v. Green, 411 U.S. 792 (1973)), combined with sufficient evidence for a reasonable factfinder to reject the employer's nondiscriminatory explanation for its decision, is adequate to sustain a finding of liability for intentional discrimination. . . .

II

Under the ADEA, it is "unlawful for an employer . . . to fail or refuse to hire or to discharge any individual or otherwise discriminate against any individual with respect to his compensation, terms, conditions, or privileges of employment, because of such individual's age." 29 U.S.C. § 623(a)(1). When a plaintiff alleges disparate treatment, "liability depends on whether the protected trait (under the ADEA, age) actually motivated the employer's decision." Hazen Paper Co. v. Biggins, 507 U.S. 604, 610 (1993). That is, the plaintiff's age must have "actually played a role in [the employer's decision making] process and had a determinative influence on the outcome." Id. Recognizing that "the question facing triers of fact in discrimination cases is both sensitive and difficult," and that "there will seldom be 'eyewitness' testimony as to the employer's mental processes," Postal Service Bd. of Governors v. Aikens, 460 U.S. 711, 716 (1983), the Courts of Appeals, including the Fifth Circuit in this case, have employed some variant of the framework articulated in *McDonnell Douglas* to analyze ADEA claims that are based principally on circumstantial evidence. . . . This Court has not squarely addressed whether the *McDonnell Douglas* framework, developed to assess claims brought under § 703(a)(1) of Title VII of the Civil Rights Act of 1964, 78 Stat. 255, 42 U.S.C. § 2000e-2(a)(1), also applies to ADEA actions. Because the parties do not dispute the issue, we shall assume, arguendo, that the *McDonnell Douglas* framework is fully applicable here.

McDonnell Douglas and subsequent decisions have "established an allocation of the burden of production and an order for the presentation of proof in . . . discriminatory-treatment cases." St. Mary's Honor Center v. Hicks, 509 U.S. 502, 506 (1993). First, the plaintiff must establish a prima facie case of discrimination. It is undisputed that petitioner satisfied this burden here: (i) at the time he was fired, he was a member of the class protected by the ADEA ("individuals who are at least 40 years of age," 29 U.S.C. § 631(a)), (ii) he was otherwise qualified for the position of Hinge Room supervisor, (iii) he was discharged by respondent, and (iv) respondent successively hired three persons in their thirties to fill petitioner's position. The burden therefore shifted to respondent to "produce evidence that the plaintiff was rejected, or someone else was preferred, for a legitimate, nondiscriminatory reason." *Burdine,* supra, at 254. This burden is one of production, not persuasion; it "can involve no credibility assessment." *St. Mary's Honor Center,* supra, at 509. Respondent met this burden by offering admissible evidence sufficient for the trier of fact to conclude that petitioner was fired because of his failure to maintain accurate attendance records. Accordingly, "the *McDonnell Douglas* framework—with its presumptions and burdens"—disappeared, *St. Mary's Honor Center,* supra, at 510, and the sole remaining issue was "discrimination vel non," *Aikens,* supra, at 714.

Although intermediate evidentiary burdens shift back and forth under this framework, "the ultimate burden of persuading the trier of fact that the defendant intentionally discriminated against the plaintiff remains at all times with the plaintiff." *Burdine*, 450 U.S. at 253. And in attempting to satisfy this burden, the plaintiff—once the employer produces sufficient evidence to support a nondiscriminatory explanation for its decision—must be afforded the "opportunity to prove by a preponderance of the evidence that the legitimate reasons offered by the defendant were not its true reasons, but were a pretext for discrimination." Id. That is, the plaintiff may attempt to establish that he was the victim of intentional discrimination "by showing that the employer's proffered explanation is unworthy of credence." *Burdine*, supra, at 256. Moreover, although the presumption of discrimination "drops out of the picture" once the defendant meets its burden of production, *St. Mary's Honor Center*, supra at 511, the trier of fact may still consider the evidence establishing the plaintiff's prima facie case "and inferences properly drawn therefrom . . . on the issue of whether the defendant's explanation is pretextual," *Burdine*, supra, at 255 n.10.

In this case, the evidence supporting respondent's explanation for petitioner's discharge consisted primarily of testimony by Chesnut and Sanderson and documentation of petitioner's alleged "shoddy record keeping." Chesnut testified that a 1993 audit of Hinge Room operations revealed "a very lax assembly line" where employees were not adhering to general work rules. As a result of that audit, petitioner was placed on 90 days' probation for unsatisfactory performance. In 1995, Chesnut ordered another investigation of the Hinge Room, which, according to his testimony, revealed that petitioner was not correctly recording the absences and hours of employees. Respondent introduced summaries of that investigation documenting several attendance violations by 12 employees under petitioner's supervision, and noting that each should have been disciplined in some manner. Chesnut testified that this failure to discipline absent and late employees is "extremely important when you are dealing with a union" because uneven enforcement across departments would keep the company "in grievance and arbitration cases, which are costly, all the time." He and Sanderson also stated that petitioner's errors, by failing to adjust for hours not worked, cost the company overpaid wages. Sanderson testified that she accepted the recommendation to discharge petitioner because he had "intentionally falsified company pay records."

Petitioner, however, made a substantial showing that respondent's explanation was false. First, petitioner offered evidence that he had properly maintained the attendance records. Most of the timekeeping errors cited by respondent involved employees who were not marked late but who were recorded as having arrived at the plant at 7 A.M. for the 7 A.M. shift. Respondent contended that employees arriving at 7 A.M. could not have been at their workstations by 7 A.M., and therefore must have been late. But both petitioner and Oswalt testified that the company's automated timeclock often failed to scan employees' timecards, so that the timesheets would not record any time of arrival. On these occasions, petitioner and Oswalt would visually check the workstations and record whether the employees were present at the start of the shift. They stated that if an employee arrived promptly but the timesheet contained no time of arrival, they would reconcile the two by marking "7 A.M." as the employee's arrival time, even if the employee actually arrived at the plant earlier. On cross-examination, Chesnut acknowledged that the timeclock sometimes malfunctioned, and that if "people were there at their workstations" at the start of the shift, the supervisor "would write in seven o'clock." Petitioner also testified that when employees arrived before or stayed after their shifts, he would assign them additional work so they would not be overpaid.

Petitioner similarly cast doubt on whether he was responsible for any failure to discipline late and absent employees. Petitioner testified that his job only included reviewing the daily and weekly attendance reports, and that disciplinary writeups were based on the monthly reports, which were reviewed by Caldwell. Sanderson admitted that Caldwell, and not petitioner, was responsible for citing employees for violations of the company's attendance policy. Further, Chesnut conceded that there had never been a union grievance or employee complaint arising from petitioner's record-keeping, and that the company had never calculated the amount of overpayments allegedly attributable to petitioner's errors. Petitioner also testified that, on the day he was fired, Chesnut said that his discharge was due to his failure to report as absent one employee, Gina Mae Coley, on two days in September 1995. But petitioner explained that he had spent those days in the hospital, and that Caldwell was therefore responsible for any overpayment of Coley. Finally, petitioner stated that on previous occasions that employees were paid for hours they had not worked, the company had simply adjusted those employees' next paychecks to correct the errors.

Based on this evidence, the Court of Appeals concluded that petitioner "very well may be correct" that "a reasonable jury could have found that [respondent's] explanation for its employment decision was pretextual." Nonetheless, the court held that this showing, standing alone, was insufficient to sustain the jury's finding of liability: "We must, as an essential final step, determine whether Reeves presented sufficient evidence that his age motivated [respondent's] employment decision." And in making this determination, the Court of Appeals ignored the evidence supporting petitioner's prima facie case and challenging respondent's explanation for its decision. The court confined its review of evidence favoring petitioner to that evidence showing that Chesnut had directed derogatory, age-based comments at petitioner, and that Chesnut had singled out petitioner for harsher treatment than younger employees. It is therefore apparent that the court believed that only this additional evidence of discrimination was relevant to whether the jury's verdict should stand. That is, the Court of Appeals proceeded from the assumption that a prima facie case of discrimination, combined with sufficient evidence for the trier of fact to disbelieve the defendant's legitimate, nondiscriminatory reason for its decision, is insufficient as a matter of law to sustain a jury's finding of intentional discrimination.

In so reasoning, the Court of Appeals misconceived the evidentiary burden borne by plaintiffs who attempt to prove intentional discrimination through indirect evidence. This much is evident from our decision in *St. Mary's Honor Center.* There we held that the factfinder's rejection of the employer's legitimate, nondiscriminatory reason for its action does not *compel* judgment for the plaintiff. 509 U.S. at 511. The ultimate question is whether the employer intentionally discriminated, and proof that "the employer's proffered reason is unpersuasive, or even obviously contrived, does not necessarily establish that the plaintiff's proffered reason . . . is correct." Id. at 524. In other words, it is not enough . . . to *dis*believe the employer; the factfinder must *believe* the plaintiff's explanation of intentional discrimination. Id. at 519.

In reaching this conclusion, however, we reasoned that it is *permissible* for the trier of fact to infer the ultimate fact of discrimination from the falsity of the employer's explanation. Specifically, we stated:

> The factfinder's disbelief of the reasons put forward by the defendant (particularly if disbelief is accompanied by a suspicion of mendacity) may, together with the elements of the prima facie case, suffice to show intentional discrimination. Thus, rejection of the defendant's proffered reasons will *permit* the trier of fact to infer the ultimate fact of intentional discrimination.

Id. at 511.

Proof that the defendant's explanation is unworthy of credence is simply one form of circumstantial evidence that is probative of intentional discrimination, and it may be quite persuasive. . . . In appropriate circumstances, the trier of fact can reasonably infer from the falsity of the explanation that the employer is dissembling to cover up a discriminatory purpose. Such an inference is consistent with the general principle of evidence law that the factfinder is entitled to consider a party's dishonesty about a material fact as "affirmative evidence of guilt." . . . Moreover, once the employer's justification has been eliminated, discrimination may well be the most likely alternative explanation, especially since the employer is in the best position to put forth the actual reason for its decision. . . . Thus, a plaintiff's prima facie case, combined with sufficient evidence to find that the employer's asserted justification is false, may permit the trier of fact to conclude that the employer unlawfully discriminated.

This is not to say that such a showing by the plaintiff will *always* be adequate to sustain a jury's finding of liability. Certainly there will be instances where, although the plaintiff has established a prima facie case and set forth sufficient evidence to reject the defendant's explanation, no rational factfinder could conclude that the action was discriminatory. For instance, an employer would be entitled to judgment as a matter of law if the record conclusively revealed some other, nondiscriminatory reason for the employer's decision, or if the plaintiff created only a weak issue of fact as to whether the employer's reason was untrue and there was abundant and uncontroverted independent evidence that no discrimination had occurred. To hold otherwise would be effectively to insulate an entire category of employment discrimination cases from review under Rule 50, and we have reiterated that trial courts should not "'treat discrimination differently from other ultimate questions of fact.'" *St. Mary's Honor Center,* 509 U.S. at 524 (quoting *Aikens,* 460 U.S. at 716).

Whether judgment as a matter of law is appropriate in any particular case will depend on a number of factors. Those include the strength of the plaintiff's prima facie case, the probative value of the proof that the employer's explanation is false, and any other evidence that supports the employer's case and that properly may be considered on a motion for judgment as a matter of law. For purposes of this case, we need not—and could not—resolve all of the circumstances in which such factors would entitle an employer to judgment as a matter of law. It suffices to say that, because a prima facie case and sufficient evidence to reject the employer's explanation may permit a finding of liability, the Court of Appeals erred in proceeding from the premise that a plaintiff must always introduce additional, independent evidence of discrimination.

III

A

The remaining question is whether, despite the Court of Appeals' misconception of petitioner's evidentiary burden, respondent was nonetheless entitled to judgment as a matter of law. Under Rule 50, a court should render judgment as a matter of law when "a party has been fully heard on an issue and there is no legally sufficient evidentiary basis for a reasonable jury to find for that party on that issue." Fed. Rule Civ. Proc. 50(a); see also Weisgram v. Marley Co., 528 U.S. 440, 447-48 (2000). The Courts of Appeals have articulated differing formulations as to what evidence a court is to consider in ruling on a Rule 50 motion. Some decisions have stated that review is limited to that evidence favorable to the nonmoving party . . . while most have held that review extends to the entire record, drawing all reasonable inferences in favor of the nonmovant.

On closer examination, this conflict seems more semantic than real. Those decisions holding that review under Rule 50 should be limited to evidence favorable to the nonmovant appear to have their genesis in Wilkerson v. McCarthy, 336 U.S. 53 (1949). In *Wilkerson,* we stated that "in passing upon whether there is sufficient evidence to submit an issue to the jury we need look only to the evidence and reasonable inferences which tend to support the case of" the nonmoving party. 336 U.S. at 57. But subsequent decisions have clarified that this passage was referring to the evidence to which the trial court should *give credence,* not the evidence that the court should *review.* In the analogous context of summary judgment under Rule 56, we have stated that the court must review the record "taken as a whole." Matsushita Elec. Industrial Co. v. Zenith Radio Corp., 475 U.S. 574 (1986). And the standard for granting summary judgment "mirrors" the standard for judgment as a matter of law, such that "the inquiry under each is the same." Anderson v. Liberty Lobby, Inc., 477 U.S. 242, 250-251 (1986); see also Celotex Corp. v. Catrett, 477 U.S. 317, 323 (1986). It therefore follows that, in entertaining a motion for judgment as a matter of law, the court should review all of the evidence in the record.

In doing so, however, the court must draw all reasonable inferences in favor of the nonmoving party, and it may not make credibility determinations or weigh the evidence. "Credibility determinations, the weighing of the evidence, and the drawing of legitimate inferences from the facts are jury functions, not those of a judge." *Liberty Lobby,* supra, at 255. Thus, although the court should review the record as a whole, it must disregard all evidence favorable to the moving party that the jury is not required to believe. That is, the court should give credence to the evidence favoring the nonmovant as well as that "evidence supporting the moving party that is uncontradicted and unimpeached, at least to the extent that that evidence comes from disinterested witnesses." [9A C. Wright & A. Miller, Federal Practice and Procedure § 2529, p. 300 (2d ed. 1995).]

B

Applying this standard here, it is apparent that respondent was not entitled to judgment as a matter of law. In this case, in addition to establishing a prima facie case of discrimination and creating a jury issue as to the falsity of the employer's explanation, petitioner introduced additional evidence that Chesnut was motivated by age-based animus and was principally responsible for petitioner's firing. Petitioner testified that Chesnut had told him that he "was so old [he] must have come over on the Mayflower" and, on one occasion when petitioner was having difficulty starting a machine, that he "was too damn old to do [his] job." According to petitioner, Chesnut would regularly "cuss at me and shake his finger in my face." Oswalt, roughly 24 years younger than petitioner, corroborated that there was an "obvious difference" in how Chesnut treated them. He stated that, although he and Chesnut "had [their] differences," "it was nothing compared to the way [Chesnut] treated Roger." Oswalt explained that Chesnut "tolerated quite a bit" from him even though he "defied" Chesnut "quite often," but that Chesnut treated petitioner "in a manner, as you would . . . treat . . . a child when . . . you're angry with [him]." Petitioner also demonstrated that, according to company records, he and Oswalt had nearly identical rates of productivity in 1993. Yet respondent conducted an efficiency study of only the regular line, supervised by petitioner, and placed only petitioner on probation. Chesnut conducted that efficiency study and, after having testified to the contrary on direct examination, acknowledged on cross-examination that he had recommended that petitioner be placed on probation following the study.

Further, petitioner introduced evidence that Chesnut was the actual decision maker behind his firing. Chesnut was married to Sanderson, who made the formal decision to discharge petitioner. Although Sanderson testified that she fired petitioner because he had "intentionally falsified company pay records," respondent only introduced evidence concerning the inaccuracy of the records, not their falsification. A 1994 letter authored by Chesnut indicated that he berated other company directors, who were supposedly his co-equals, about how to do their jobs. Moreover, Oswalt testified that all of respondent's employees feared Chesnut, and that Chesnut had exercised "absolute power" within the company for "as long as [he] can remember."

In holding that the record contained insufficient evidence to sustain the jury's verdict, the Court of Appeals misapplied the standard of review dictated by Rule 50. Again, the court disregarded critical evidence favorable to petitioner—namely, the evidence supporting petitioner's prima facie case and undermining respondent's nondiscriminatory explanation. The court also failed to draw all reasonable inferences in favor of petitioner. For instance, while acknowledging "the potentially damning nature" of Chesnut's age-related comments, the court discounted them on the ground that they "were not made in the direct context of Reeves's termination." And the court discredited petitioner's evidence that Chesnut was the actual decision maker by giving weight to the fact that there was "no evidence to suggest that any of the other decision makers were motivated by age." Moreover, the other evidence on which the court relied—that Caldwell and Oswalt were also cited for poor recordkeeping, and that respondent employed many managers over age 50—although relevant, is certainly not dispositive. In concluding that these circumstances so overwhelmed the evidence favoring petitioner that no rational trier of fact could have found that petitioner was fired because of his age, the Court of Appeals impermissibly substituted its judgment concerning the weight of the evidence for the jury's.

The ultimate question in every employment discrimination case involving a claim of disparate treatment is whether the plaintiff was the victim of intentional discrimination. Given the evidence in the record supporting petitioner, we see no reason to subject the parties to an additional round of litigation before the Court of Appeals rather than to resolve the matter here. The District Court plainly informed the jury that petitioner was required to show "by a preponderance of the evidence that his age was a determining and motivating factor in the decision of [respondent] to terminate him." The court instructed the jury that, to show that respondent's explanation was a pretext for discrimination, petitioner had to demonstrate "1, that the stated reasons were not the real reasons for [petitioner's] discharge; *and* 2, that age discrimination was the real reason for [petitioner's] discharge" (emphasis added). Given that petitioner established a prima facie case of discrimination, introduced enough evidence for the jury to reject respondent's explanation, and produced additional evidence of age-based animus, there was sufficient evidence for the jury to find that respondent had intentionally discriminated. The District Court was therefore correct to submit the case to the jury, and the Court of Appeals erred in overturning its verdict.

For these reasons, the judgment of the Court of Appeals is reversed.

Notes and Questions

1. *Credibility Again. Galloway* is the classic decision on taking a case from the jury, and *Reeves* deals with the same issue in a very modern context. Do they take different views on resolving inferences from gaps in the testimony? Justice Ginsburg's concurrence in *Reeves* focused especially on this issue:

> The Court today holds that an employment discrimination plaintiff *may* survive judgment as a matter of law by submitting two categories of evidence: first, evidence establishing a "prima facie case," as that term is used in McDonnell Douglas Corp. v. Green, 411 U.S. 792, 802 (1973); and second, evidence from which a rational factfinder could conclude that the employer's proffered explanation for its actions was false. Because the Court of Appeals in this case plainly, and erroneously, required the plaintiff to offer some evidence beyond those two categories, no broader holding is necessary to support reversal.
>
> I write separately to note that it may be incumbent on the Court, in an appropriate case, to define more precisely the circumstances in which plaintiffs will be required to submit evidence beyond these two categories in order to survive a motion for judgment as a matter of law. I anticipate that such circumstances will be uncommon. As the Court notes, it is a principle of evidence law that the jury is entitled to treat a party's dishonesty about a material fact as evidence of culpability. Under this commonsense principle, evidence suggesting that a defendant accused of illegal discrimination has chosen to give a false explanation for its actions gives rise to a rational inference that the defendant could be masking its actual, illegal motivation. Whether the defendant was in fact motivated by discrimination is of course for the finder of fact to decide; that is the lesson of St. Mary's Honor Center v. Hicks, 509 U.S. 502 (1993). But the inference remains—unless it is conclusively demonstrated, by evidence the district court is required to credit on a motion for judgment as a matter of law, that discrimination could not have been the defendant's true motivation. If such conclusive demonstrations are (as I suspect) atypical, it follows that the ultimate question of liability ordinarily should not be taken from the jury once the plaintiff has introduced the two categories of evidence described above. Because the Court's opinion leaves room for such further elaboration in an appropriate case, I join it in full.

Note that virtually every case cited by the Court deals with employment discrimination. Is the Court making special rules about sufficiency of the evidence in this kind of case?

2. *The Procedure for Moving for JMOL.* In the problem case and in *Reeves,* the defendant moved early and often for judgment as a matter of law. This is the common practice, and indeed the legal point is often made on a motion for summary judgment before the trial even begins.

It was held in Slocum v. New York Life Insurance Co., 228 U.S. 364 (1913), that the Seventh Amendment forbade the entry of a judgment contrary to a jury verdict. But in Baltimore & Carolina Line v. Redman, 295 U.S. 654 (1935), it was held that a ruling on a motion for a directed verdict could be postponed until after the jury had delivered its verdict. The language of Fed. R. Civ. P. 50(b) is written to use *Redman* for the purpose of overruling *Slocum.* It remains true, however, that a motion for a judgment as a matter of law made prior to the jury's deliberation is an indispensable prerequisite to the making of a successful renewed motion for judgment as a matter of law. See Starling v. Gulf Life Ins. Co., 382 F.2d 701 (5th Cir. 1967).

The points at which one may make a motion for judgment as a matter of law are outlined in the following chart:

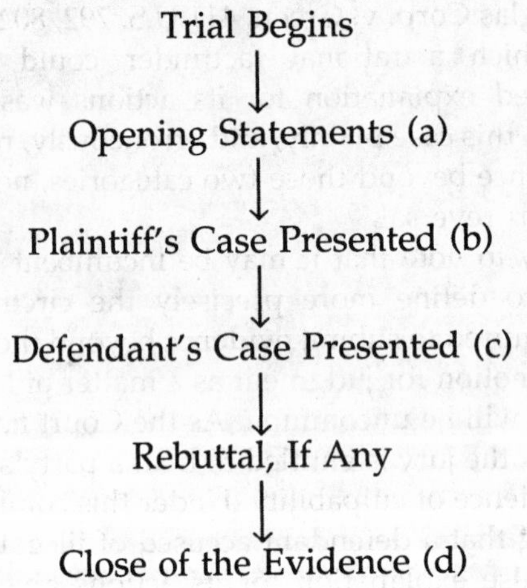

(a) Rare, but parties can move after opening statements.
(b) Defendant may move at close of plaintiff's case. Plaintiff may also, but rarely does so, and even more rarely is such a motion granted.
(c) Either or both parties may move after the close of defendant's case.
(d) After presentation of all of the evidence, either or both parties may move or renew motions made earlier in the trial.

Indeed, the rule in many jurisdictions is that the parties *must renew* the motion at the close of the evidence, or they cannot make the renewed motion for judgment as a matter of law later, and cannot attack the sufficiency of the evidence on appeal.

Note that the judge can reserve ruling on the motion until after the jury has returned with its verdict. The judge almost always will do so, for efficiency reasons. If the jury returns a verdict that the judge considers against the great weight of the evidence, and the judge overturns the verdict by granting the JMOL, then there is a jury verdict to reinstate, should an appellate court disagree with the trial judge's ruling. If the jury never deliberates because the judge has granted a motion for judgment as a matter of law, then there is no verdict to reinstate, and a new trial will be necessary to correct for the trial judge's mistake—an avoidable expense.

The procedure for making a renewed motion for judgment as a matter of law (JNOV) in federal court is quite simple. First, the movant must have made or renewed a motion for judgment as a matter of law at the close of the evidence. Second, the renewed motion must be made within ten days after entry of the judgment. The judge who agrees that the evidence is insufficient to support the verdict has three options, however, when ruling on a renewed motion. She can: 1) direct entry of judgment in favor of the movant; 2) order a new trial; or 3) order a dismissal without prejudice under Fed. R. Civ. P. 41.

A party should always renew the motion for judgment as a matter of law if she wishes to appeal the denial of an earlier motion for judgment as a matter of law or the award of an opponent's motion. See Cone v. West Virginia Pulp & Paper, 330 U.S. 212 (1947).

3. Starting Over: The New Trial Motion

Sanders-El v. Wencewicz

987 F.2d 483 (8th Cir. 1993)

HEANEY, Senior Circuit Judge.

In the morning of 19 May 1989 City of St. Louis police officers stopped the car driven by 22-year-old Sorkis Sanders-El pursuant to a warrant for his arrest. The officers arrested Sanders-El, handcuffed him, and put him in the back seat of a police vehicle. As one of the officers was closing the door of the vehicle, Sanders-El kicked it open and fled. The officers gave chase. When the officers reapprehended Sanders-El—who was still handcuffed—a struggle ensued during which Sanders-El sustained injuries to his eye, face, and head.

Sanders-El filed this action against the officers pursuant to 42 U.S.C. § 1983, alleging the officers used excessive force, depriving him of constitutional rights. A jury first heard the dispute in August 1991, but the magistrate judge declared a mistrial when the jury could not agree on a verdict. A second trial in December 1991 ended with a verdict in favor of the defendant police officers. Sanders-El appeals from the judgment entered on that verdict. We reverse and remand for a new trial.

Sanders-El argues there were numerous prejudicial errors in the trial below, including faulty evidentiary rulings, incomplete instructions to the jury, and racially biased peremptory challenges to members of the venire. What most troubles us, however, was the intentionally prejudicial conduct of defense counsel—particularly an incident in which defense counsel, when cross-examining the plaintiff about prior criminal convictions, dramatically dropped a lengthy computer printout in front of the jury.

The manifest intent of the conduct was to arouse the prejudices of the jury by leading it to believe Sanders-El had the conviction record of a veteran vocational criminal. Counsel conducted this piece of theatrics despite pretrial discussions in which the court indicated its intention not to admit such evidence. After objections by both the plaintiff and his counsel, the court excused the jury and admonished defense counsel against a repetition of the display:

> [T]he record should reflect that defense counsel . . . beginning to question the witness about his prior record dramatically dropped in front of the jury a computer printout of some approximately—what looks like about 10 feet of paper[—]then beginning to question the witness from it. That I think is uncalled for. It's not been shown to me that he has convictions which would warrant that kind of a display in front of the jury and I will caution you not to engage in such displays again in this lawsuit.

Vol. I Noce Trial Transcript at 142 (No. 89-1710-C(2)). Plaintiff also moved the court for sanctions and a mistrial, and the court denied the motion.

The standard of review applicable to a trial court's denial of a motion for mistrial is abuse of discretion. United States v. Muza, 788 F.2d 1309, 1312 (8th Cir. 1986). In appraising the trial court's exercise of its discretion, we bear in mind that "[i]mproper questioning by counsel 'generally entitles the aggrieved party to a new trial' if such questioning 'conveys improper information to the jury and [. . .] prejudices the opposing litigant.'" Williams v. Mensey, 785 F.2d 631, 637 (8th Cir. 1986) (quoting Harris v. Zurich Ins. Co., 527 F.2d 528, 531 (8th Cir. 1975)). . . .

Defendants cite 88 C.J.S. *Trial* § 199 (1955) for the proposition that improper conduct by counsel ordinarily is cured by rebuke or reprimand of counsel if the conduct is not repeated. The same authority, however, states in black letter that "[i]t is highly improper for counsel, acting in bad faith, to make statements or ask questions or engage in other conduct as to witnesses merely to prejudice his opponent's case before the jury." Id. § 162(b). Further, "[t]he misconduct of counsel may be such that its effect cannot be overcome by an admonition to the jury . . . [or] by rebuke or admonition of counsel . . . and in such case the court should grant a discontinuance, mistrial, withdrawal of a juror, discharge of the jury, or a new trial." Id. § 202.

It is not only the conscious impropriety of counsel here that we find troubling, but also the nature of the information counsel improperly intended to convey to the jury. Before the second trial commenced, the judge indicated that Sanders-El's prior felony convictions were admissible for impeachment purposes, but that it was his intention not to allow evidence of prior arrests or probation violations. This sound evidentiary ruling conforms to "[t]he long-standing rule in this circuit . . . that the credibility of a witness may not be impeached by showing that he has been accused of, charged with, or arrested for a crime which has not culminated in a conviction." United States v. Kirk, 496 F.2d 947, 949 (8th Cir. 1974). "This rule is based upon a clear recognition of the fact that the probative value of such evidence is so overwhelmingly outweighed by its inevitable tendency to inflame or prejudice the jury. . . ." United States v. Ling, 581 F.2d 1118, 1121 (4th Cir. 1978). Counsel nonetheless attempted to present the arrest record to the jury first by asking Sanders-El on cross-examination *which* arrest he had been referring to in Sanders-El's response to a prior question. After a sustained objection terminated this line of questioning, counsel continued his cross-examination until it culminated in the computer printout fiasco.

Whether errors had a significant prejudicial influence on the jury in a particular case admittedly is a fine question of judgment in which precedents give little guidance, for what may be harmless in a case where the evidence strongly favors one party may be fatally prejudicial in a close case. Fortunato v. Ford Motor Co., 464 F.2d 962, 976 (2d Cir.) (Mansfield, J., concurring and dissenting), *cert. denied,* 409 U.S. 1038 (1972). In appraising prejudicial remarks and conduct such as involved here, the court must consider "the climate of the contest in which it occurred." Westchester Fire Ins. Co. v. Hanley, 284 F.2d 409, 416 (6th Cir. 1960), *cert. denied,* 365 U.S. 869 (1961).

Even out of context we are dismayed at defense counsel's impertinence, and agree with the trial judge that the conduct was "uncalled for." If this were an isolated incident in a case in which the disputes were not as close, we might have difficulty finding prejudice. In this case, however, we encounter no such difficulty. First, the case was exceedingly close — so close that once already a jury could not agree. Second, the incident was neither isolated nor accidental. Counsel, knowing that such evidence was irrelevant and prejudicial, once already had alluded to the plaintiff's arrest record in front of the jury. After the court sustained the objection to that tactic, counsel resorted to the less candid but equally prejudicial theatrical display at issue. Third, the record does not reveal that the jury received any curative instruction. Left with the distinct impression that the plaintiff was a hardened criminal with a long history of arrests, the jury retired to consider its verdict without an instruction from the court to disregard such evidence in its deliberations. Fourth, as the case law instructs, the nature of this irrelevant evidence is especially prejudicial. Fifth, considering the climate of the contest, we note that this claim by a black plaintiff against white police officers rests largely on the word of Sanders-El against that of the police. Such a case, of necessity, brings the credibility of the witnesses sharply into focus — thus highlighting the significance of the resulting prejudice. See United States v. Pennix, 313 F.2d 524, 531 (4th Cir. 1963).

Considering all the circumstances of the case, we find prejudicial error in defense counsel's courtroom misconduct, and abuse of discretion in the trial court's denial of plaintiff's motion for a mistrial. The other alleged errors we do not reach. Accordingly, based on the foregoing, we reverse and remand for a new trial.

BOWMAN, Circuit Judge, dissenting.

The ruling of a trial court on a motion for mistrial is subject to a deferential standard of review. United States v. Huff, 959 F.2d 731, 735 (8th Cir.), *cert. denied,* 113 S. Ct. 162 (1992). Such rulings are within the broad discretion of the trial court, and we will reverse the trial court only where an abuse of that discretion is shown. United States v. Culver, 929 F.2d 389, 391 (8th Cir. 1991).

Here, the trial court rebuked counsel for dropping the computer printout in front of the jury, and the offending conduct was not repeated. The jury was entitled to weigh plaintiff's prior convictions in assessing his credibility, and aside from anything improperly communicated to the jury about plaintiff's prior arrests, the jury knew by his own admission that he had not led a saintly life. The trial court was in a far better position than we are to make a well-informed judgment as to whether misconduct by the defendants' counsel had unfairly prejudiced the jury's attitude toward the plaintiff. The finding that it had not comes to us from an experienced and respected trial judge, and I see no compelling reason for this Court to disturb that finding.

It is all too easy for this Court, working from a cold record and applying broad principles of trial practice, to assign to events occurring during the course of trial a significance they did not actually have. That is precisely why a reviewing court should give broad deference to the ruling made by the trial court in matters of this sort. As I am unable to conclude that the trial court abused its discretion in denying plaintiff's motion for a mistrial, I would affirm the judgment entered on the jury verdict.

Notes and Questions

1. *Problems Warranting Retrial.* Parties may move for a new trial for a range of reasons, including attorney or juror misconduct, prejudicial errors in evidentiary rulings or jury instructions, or even that the verdict was contrary to the weight of the evidence (more on this below). The trial judge has great discretion in ruling on the motion and may even order a new trial sua sponte.

Sanders-El illustrates one of the grounds—attorney misconduct or mistakes—that may cause a judge to grant a new trial. Should attorneys be subject to personal discipline for these errors, regardless of the ruling on the new trial motion? Below, Professor Deborah Rhode summarizes several ethical norms that govern attorneys' trial behavior. Did defense counsel in *Sanders-El* violate any of these? What about the lawyer in the bereaved widow problem case?

Formal prohibitions include a ban on:

- engaging in conduct intended to disrupt a tribunal or to influence a juror by means prohibited by law (Model Rule [of Professional Responsibility] 3.5);
- engaging in undignified or discourteous conduct which is degrading to a tribunal (DR [Disciplinary Rule] 7-106(C)(6));
- communicating with a juror concerning a case at trial except in official proceedings (DR 7-108(A));
- alluding to any matter that the lawyer does not reasonably believe is relevant or that will not be supported by admissible evidence, asserting personal knowledge of facts in issue except when testifying as a witness, or stating a personal opinion as to the justness of a case, the credibility of a witness, the culpability of a civil litigant or the guilt or innocence of an accused (Model Rule 3.4(e) and DR 7-106(C));
- engaging in conduct involving dishonesty, fraud, deceit, misrepresentation, or conduct prejudicial to the administration of justice (DR 1-102).

In addition, other standards not codified as disciplinary rules provide that a lawyer:

- should not ask a witness a question "solely for the purpose of harassing or embarrassing him . . . and should not by subterfuge put before a jury matters which it cannot properly consider" (EC [Ethical Consideration] 7-25);
- should refrain from argument "calculated to inflame the passions or prejudices of the jury" or "divert the jury from its duty to decide the case on the evidence, by injecting issues broader than the guilt or innocence of the accused under the controlling law, or by making predictions of the consequences of the jury's verdict" (ABA Standards Relating to the Administration of Criminal Justice, The Prosecution Function, Standard 3-5.8).

Deborah L. Rhode, Professional Responsibility: Ethics by the Pervasive Method 710 (1994).

2. *Judges Versus Juries.* The judge may grant a new trial if she believes that the verdict was against the weight of the evidence. It seems fairly clear, moreover, that a new trial may be granted on this basis, even though the evidence would withstand the JMOL motion. In other words, the judge could hold that a reasonable jury could find as it did, but that nonetheless, the verdict is against the weight of the evidence.

This gets tricky when a party argues that the reason the evidence is insufficient is that it is not worthy of belief. We have seen the deference the judge must give to the jury's credibility assessment on the motion for a JMOL. What about a new trial motion on the ground that because the evidence is unbelievable, it is insufficient to support the verdict? Most courts hold that the trial judge may disbelieve the evidence and grant a new trial in the interest of justice. See, e.g., White v. Pence, 961 F.2d 776 (8th Cir. 1991) (reversing a trial judge who doubted his power to order a new trial even though he was dissatisfied with the defendant's evidence).

On the other hand, the Second Circuit upheld a trial judge who refused a new trial even though he felt the defendant's evidence was "overwhelming," but the jury sided with the plaintiff. See Compton v. Luckenbach Overseas Corp., 425 F.2d 1130 (2d Cir. 1970) (upholding the trial judge's denial of the motion for a new trial).

3. *Deadlocked Juries.* Recall our discussion of the importance of the unanimity requirement. See supra at page 725. Juries sometimes stumble on the way to a verdict — clashing viewpoints and personalities can lead to stalemates in jury deliberation. Sometimes juries reach out to the judge for help, often by sending out a note indicating that they are deadlocked, unable to reach a verdict. A judge must be very careful in handling these situations — she cannot cross the line between reminding the jury of its charge and encouraging it to continue deliberating, on the one hand, and coercing jurors to agree on a verdict it would not otherwise have reached. Especially in criminal cases, courts are divided about using "modified *Allen* charges" — supplemental instructions read to deadlocked jurors to urge them to continue deliberations — because of concerns about judicial coercion of jurors. See Allen v. United States, 164 U.S. 492 (1896); see also United States v. Fioravanti, 412 F.2d 407, 419 (3d Cir. 1969) (describing use of *Allen* charge in criminal cases as a "supplemental or 'dynamite charge' to blast a hung jury into a verdict"; use of charge can be reversible error), *followed in* United States v. Eastern Medical Billing, Inc., 230 F.3d 600 (3d. Cir. 2000). Controversy is considerably less sharp in civil trials. See Cary v. Allegheny Technologies Inc., 267 F. Supp. 2d 442, 447 (W.D. Pa. 2003) (denying motion for new trial in gender discrimination suit where judge read modified *Allen* instructions to break deadlocked jury; noting that plaintiff would be "disproportionately burdened by having to bear the expense of a retrial," and, unlike criminal defendants, "[a] civil defendant does not face the loss of his liberty and is not entitled to the presumption of innocence").

4. *Appellate Review of the Grant of a New Trial.* If the trial judge grants a new trial, does the party opposing the motion have to go through the whole thing again before appealing? Yes, said the Court in Allied Chemical Corp. v. Daiflon, Inc., 449 U.S. 33 (1980). Note also that the motion for new trial, like the motion for judgment as a matter of law, can be a use-it-or-lose-it motion. The Fifth Circuit has construed Rule 50(c) to require that a party who wins on a motion for judgment as a matter of law but who does not press for a contemporaneous ruling on its alternative motion for a new trial waives any right to seek a new trial after any appellate reversal on the merits. The rationale is that requiring the party to seek a ruling on both motions assures that the appellate court can review both rulings in one appeal, thereby avoiding piecemeal litigation. See Arenson v. Southern University Law Center, 43 F.3d 194 (5th Cir. 1995).

Traditionally the granting of a new trial is a chance for the trial judge to correct his own errors, or those of the lawyers or the jury, while they are fresh in his mind, and without involving the appellate court. The denial of a new trial is, on the other hand, often grounds for appeal. If the appellate court finds the evidence insufficient, can it order a new trial, or must the appellate court remand for the trial judge to reconsider the Rule 50 motion? The next case answers that question, at least as to the appellate court's power to rule.

4. Appellate Review of Jury Verdicts

Weisgram v. Marley Co.

528 U.S. 440 (2000)

JUSTICE GINSBURG delivered the opinion for a unanimous Court.

This case concerns the respective authority of federal trial and appellate courts to decide whether, as a matter of law, judgment should be entered in favor of a verdict loser. The pattern we confront is this. Plaintiff in a product liability action gains a jury verdict. Defendant urges, unsuccessfully before the federal district court but successfully on appeal, that expert testimony plaintiff introduced was unreliable, and therefore inadmissible, under the analysis required by Daubert v. Merrell Dow Pharmaceuticals, Inc., 509 U.S. 579 (1993). Shorn of the erroneously admitted expert testimony, the record evidence is insufficient to justify a plaintiff's verdict. May the court of appeals then instruct the entry of judgment as a matter of law for defendant, or must that tribunal remand the case, leaving to the district court's discretion the choice between final judgment for defendant or a new trial of plaintiff's case?

Our decision is guided by Federal Rule of Civil Procedure 50, which governs the entry of judgment as a matter of law, and by the Court's pathmarking opinion in Neely v. Martin K. Eby Construction Co., 386 U.S. 317 (1967). As *Neely* teaches, courts of appeals should "be constantly alert" to "the trial judge's first-hand knowledge of witnesses, testimony, and issues"; in other words, appellate courts should give due consideration to the first-instance decision maker's "'feel' for the overall case." Id. at 325. But the court of appeals has authority to render the final decision. If, in the particular case, the appellate tribunal determines that the district court is better positioned to decide whether a new trial, rather than judgment for defendant, should be ordered, the court of appeals should return the case to the trial court for such an assessment. But if, as in the instant case, the court of appeals concludes that further proceedings are unwarranted because the loser on appeal has had a full and fair opportunity to present the case, including arguments for a new trial, the appellate court may appropriately instruct the district court to enter judgment against the jury-verdict winner. Appellate authority to make this determination is no less when the evidence is rendered insufficient by the removal of erroneously admitted testimony than it is when the evidence, without any deletion, is insufficient.

I

Firefighters arrived at the home of Bonnie Weisgram on December 30, 1993, to discover flames around the front entrance. Upon entering the home, they found Weisgram in an upstairs bathroom, dead of carbon monoxide poisoning. Her son, petitioner Chad Weisgram, individually and on behalf of Bonnie Weisgram's heirs, brought a diversity action in the United States District Court for the District of North Dakota seeking wrongful death damages. He alleged that a defect in an electric baseboard heater, manufactured by defendant (now respondent) Marley Company and located inside the door to Bonnie Weisgram's home, caused both the fire and his mother's death.[1]

At trial, Weisgram introduced the testimony of three witnesses, proffered as experts, in an endeavor to prove the alleged defect in the heater and its causal connection to the fire. The District Court overruled defendant Marley's objections, lodged both before and during the trial, that this testimony was unreliable and therefore inadmissible under Federal Rule of Evidence 702 as elucidated by *Daubert*. At the close of Weisgram's evidence, and again at the close of all the evidence, Marley unsuccessfully moved under Federal Rule of Civil Procedure 50(a) for judgment as a matter of law on the ground that plaintiffs had failed to meet their burden of proof on the issues of defect and causation. The jury returned a verdict for Weisgram. Marley again requested judgment as a matter of law, and additionally requested, in the alternative, a new trial, pursuant to Rules 50 and 59; among arguments in support of its post-trial motions, Marley reasserted that the expert testimony essential to prove Weisgram's case was unreliable and therefore inadmissible. The District Court denied the motions and entered judgment for Weisgram. Marley appealed.

The Court of Appeals for the Eighth Circuit held that Marley's motion for judgment as a matter of law should have been granted. Writing for the panel majority, Chief Judge Bowman first examined the testimony of Weisgram's expert witnesses, the sole evidence supporting plaintiffs' product defect charge. Concluding that the testimony was speculative and not shown to be scientifically sound, the majority held the expert evidence incompetent to prove Weisgram's case. The court then considered the remaining evidence in the light most favorable to Weisgram, found it insufficient to support the jury verdict, and directed judgment as a matter of law for Marley. In a footnote, the majority "reject[ed] any contention that [it was] required to remand for a new trial." It recognized its discretion to do so under Rule 50(d), but stated: "[W]e can discern no reason to give the plaintiffs a second chance to make out a case of strict liability. . . . This is not

1. At trial and on appeal, the suit of the Weisgram heirs was consolidated with an action brought against Marley Company by State Farm Fire and Casualty Company, insurer of the Weisgram home, to recover benefits State Farm paid for the damage to the Weisgram townhouse and an adjoining townhouse. State Farm was dismissed from the appeal after certiorari was granted. For purposes of this opinion, we generally refer to the plaintiffs below, and to the petitioners before us, simply as "Weisgram."

a close case. The plaintiffs had a fair opportunity to prove their claim and they failed to do so" (internal citations omitted). The dissenting judge disagreed on both points, concluding that the expert evidence was properly admitted and that the appropriate remedy for improper admission of expert testimony is the award of a new trial, not judgment as a matter of law (citing Midcontinent Broadcasting Co. v. North Central Airlines, Inc., 471 F.2d 357 (8th Cir. 1973)).

Courts of appeals have divided on the question whether Federal Rule of Civil Procedure 50 permits an appellate court to direct the entry of judgment as a matter of law when it determines that evidence was erroneously admitted at trial and that the remaining, properly admitted evidence is insufficient to constitute a submissible case.[2] We granted certiorari to resolve the conflict, 527 U.S. 1069 (1999),[3] and we now affirm the Eighth Circuit's judgment.

II

Federal Rule of Civil Procedure 50 governs motions for judgment as a matter of law in jury trials. It allows the trial court to remove cases or issues from the jury's consideration "when the facts are sufficiently clear that the law requires a particular result." 9A C. Wright & A. Miller, Federal Practice and Procedure § 2521, p. 240 (2d ed. 1995) (hereinafter Wright & Miller). Subdivision (d) [now at Rule 50(e)] controls when, as here, the verdict loser appeals from the trial court's denial of a motion for judgment as a matter of law:

> [T]he party who prevailed on that motion may, as appellee, assert grounds entitling the party to a new trial in the event the appellate court concludes that the trial court erred in denying the motion for judgment. If the appellate court reverses the judgment, nothing in this rule precludes it from determining that the appellee is entitled to a new trial, or from directing the trial court to determine whether a new trial shall be granted.

2. The Tenth Circuit has held it inappropriate for an appellate court to direct the entry of judgment as a matter of law based on the trial court's erroneous admission of evidence, because to do so would be unfair to a party who relied on the trial court's evidentiary rulings. See Kinser v. Gehl Co., 184 F.3d 1259, 1267, 1269 (10th Cir. 1999). The Fourth, Sixth, and Eighth Circuits recently have issued decisions, in accord with the position earlier advanced by the Third Circuit, directing the entry of judgment as a matter of law based on proof rendered insufficient by the deletion of improperly admitted evidence. See Redman v. John D. Brush & Co., 111 F.3d 1174, 1178-1179 (4th Cir. 1997); Smelser v. Norfolk Southern R. Co., 105 F.3d 299, 301, 306 (6th Cir. 1997); Wright v. Willamette Industries, Inc., 91 F.3d 1105, 1108 (8th Cir. 1996); *accord*, Aloe Coal Co. v. Clark Equipment Co., 816 F.2d 110, 115-116 (3d Cir. 1987).

3. We agreed to decide only the issue of the authority of a court of appeals to direct the entry of judgment as a matter of law, and accordingly accept as final the decision of the Eighth Circuit holding the testimony of Weisgram's experts unreliable, and therefore inadmissible under Federal Rule of Evidence 702, as explicated in Daubert v. Merrell Dow Pharmaceuticals, Inc., 509 U.S. 579 (1993). We also accept as final the Eighth Circuit's determination that the remaining, properly admitted, evidence was insufficient to make a submissible case under state law.

Under this Rule, Weisgram urges, when a court of appeals determines that a jury verdict cannot be sustained due to an error in the admission of evidence, the appellate court may not order the entry of judgment for the verdict loser, but must instead remand the case to the trial court for a new trial determination. Nothing in Rule 50 expressly addresses this question.[5]

In a series of pre-1967 decisions, this Court refrained from deciding the question, while emphasizing the importance of giving the party deprived of a verdict the opportunity to invoke the discretion of the trial judge to grant a new trial. See Cone v. West Virginia Pulp & Paper Co., 330 U.S. 212, 216-218 (1947); Globe Liquor Co. v. San Roman, 332 U.S. 571, 573-574 (1948); Johnson v. New York, N.H. & H.R. Co., 344 U.S. 48, 54 n.3 (1952); see also 9A Wright & Miller, § 2540, at 370. Then, in *Neely*, the Court reviewed its prior jurisprudence and ruled definitively that if a motion for judgment as a matter of law is erroneously denied by the district court, the appellate court does have the power to order the entry of judgment for the moving party. 386 U.S. at 326; see also Louis, Post-Verdict Rulings on the Sufficiency of the Evidence: Neely v. Martin K. Eby Construction Co. Revisited, 1975 Wis. L. Rev. 503 (surveying chronologically Court's decisions bearing on appellate direction of judgment as a matter of law).

Neely first addressed the compatibility of appellate direction of judgment as a matter of law (then styled "judgment n.o.v.") with the Seventh Amendment's jury trial guarantee. It was settled, the Court pointed out, that a trial court, pursuant to Rule 50(b), could enter judgment for the verdict loser without offense to the Seventh Amendment. 386 U.S. at 321 (citing Montgomery Ward & Co. v. Duncan, 311 U.S. 243 (1940)). "As far as the Seventh Amendment's right to jury trial is concerned," the Court reasoned, "there is no greater restriction on the province of the jury when an appellate court enters judgment n. o. v. than when a trial court does"; accordingly, the Court concluded, "there is no constitutional bar to an appellate court granting judgment n.o.v." 386 U.S. at 322 (citing Baltimore & Carolina Line v. Redman, 295 U.S. 654 (1935)). The Court next turned to "the statutory grant of appellate jurisdiction to the courts of appeals [in 28 U.S.C. § 2106],"[6] which it found "certainly broad enough to include the power to direct entry of judgment n.o.v. on appeal." 386 U.S. 322. The remainder of the

5. According to the Advisory Committee Notes to the 1963 Rule 50 amendments, this "omission" was not inadvertent:

> Subdivision (d) does not attempt a regulation of all aspects of the procedure where the motion for judgment n.o.v. and any accompanying motion for a new trial are denied, since the problems have not been fully canvassed in the decisions and the procedure is in some respects still in a formative stage. It is, however, designed to give guidance on certain important features of the practice.

Advisory Committee's Notes on Fed. Rule Civ. Proc. 50(d), 28 U.S.C. App., p. 769.

6. Section 2106 reads:

> The Supreme Court or any other court of appellate jurisdiction may affirm, modify, vacate, set aside or reverse any judgment, decree, or order of a court lawfully

Neely opinion effectively complements Rules 50(c) and 50(d), providing guidance on the appropriate exercise of the appellate court's discretion when it reverses the trial court's denial of a defendant's Rule 50(b) motion for judgment as a matter of law. Id. at 322-330; cf. supra, note 5 (1963 observation of Advisory Committee that, as of that year, "problems [concerning motions for judgment coupled with new trial motions] ha[d] not been fully canvassed").

Neely represents no volte-face in the Court's understanding of the respective competences of trial and appellate forums. Immediately after declaring that appellate courts have the power to order the entry of judgment for a verdict loser, the Court cautioned:

> "Part of the Court's concern has been to protect the rights of the party whose jury verdict has been set aside on appeal and who may have valid grounds for a new trial, some or all of which should be passed upon by the district court, rather than the court of appeals, because of the trial judge's first-hand knowledge of witnesses, testimony, and issues—because of his 'feel' for the overall case. These are very valid concerns to which the court of appeals should be constantly alert." 386 U.S. at 325.[7]

Nevertheless, the Court in *Neely* continued, due consideration of the rights of the verdict winner and the closeness of the trial court to the case "do[es] not justify an ironclad rule that the court of appeals should never order dismissal or judgment for the defendant when the plaintiff's verdict has been set aside on appeal." Id. at 326. "Such a rule," the Court concluded, "would not serve the purpose of Rule 50 to speed litigation and to avoid unnecessary retrials." Ibid. *Neely* ultimately clarified that if a court of appeals determines that the district court erroneously denied a motion for judgment as a matter of law, the appellate court may (1) order a new trial at the verdict winner's request or on its own motion, (2) remand the case for the trial court to decide whether a new trial or entry of judgment for the defendant is warranted, or (3) direct the entry of judgment as a matter of law for the defendant. Id. at 327-330; see also 9A Wright & Miller § 2540, at 371-372.

---

brought before it for review, and may remand the cause and direct the entry of such appropriate judgment, decree, or order, or require such further proceedings to be had as may be just under the circumstances.

7. Iacurci v. Lummus Co., 387 U.S. 86 (1967) (per curiam), decided shortly after *Neely*, is illustrative. There, the Court reversed the appellate court's direction of the entry of judgment as a matter of law for the defendant and instructed the appeals court to remand the case to the trial court for a new trial determination; the Court pointed to the jury's failure to respond to four out of five special interrogatories, which left issues of negligence unresolved, and concluded that in the particular circumstances, the trial judge "was in the best position to pass upon the question of a new trial in light of the evidence, his charge to the jury, and the jury's verdict and interrogatory answers." Id. at 88.

III

The parties before us—and court of appeals opinions—diverge regarding *Neely*'s scope. Weisgram, in line with some appellate decisions, posits a distinction between cases in which judgment as a matter of law is requested based on plaintiff's failure to produce enough evidence to warrant a jury verdict, as in *Neely*, and cases in which the proof introduced becomes insufficient because the court of appeals determines that certain evidence should not have been admitted, as in the instant case. Insufficiency caused by deletion of evidence, Weisgram contends, requires an "automatic remand" to the district court for consideration whether a new trial is warranted.

Weisgram relies on cases holding that, in fairness to a verdict winner who may have relied on erroneously admitted evidence, courts confronting questions of judgment as a matter of law should rule on the record as it went to the jury, without excising evidence inadmissible under Federal Rule of Evidence 702. See, e.g., Kinser v. Gehl Co., 184 F.3d 1259, 1267, 1269 (10th Cir. 1999); Schudel v. General Electric Co., 120 F.3d 991, 995-996 (9th Cir. 1997); Jackson v. Pleasant Grove Health Care Center, 980 F.2d 692, 695-696 (11th Cir. 1993); Midcontinent Broadcasting, 471 F.2d, at 358. But see Lightning Lube, Inc. v. Witco Corp., 4 F.3d 1153, 1198-1200 (3d Cir. 1993). These decisions are of questionable consistency with Rule 50(a)(1), which states that in ruling on a motion for judgment as a matter of law, the court is to inquire whether there is any "legally sufficient evidentiary basis for a reasonable jury to find for [the opponent of the motion]." Inadmissible evidence contributes nothing to a "legally sufficient evidentiary basis." See Brooke Group Ltd. v. Brown & Williamson Tobacco Corp., 509 U.S. 209, 242 (1993) ("When an expert opinion is not supported by sufficient facts to validate it in the eyes of the law, or when indisputable record facts contradict or otherwise render the opinion unreasonable, it cannot support a jury's verdict.").[10]

As *Neely* recognized, appellate rulings on post-trial pleas for judgment as a matter of law call for the exercise of "informed discretion," 386 U.S. at 329, and fairness to the parties is surely key to the exercise of that discretion. But fairness concerns should loom as large when the verdict winner, in the appellate court's judgment, failed to present sufficient evidence as when the appellate court declares inadmissible record evidence essential to the verdict winner's case. In both situations, the party whose verdict is set aside on appeal will have had notice, before the close

10. Weisgram additionally urges that the Seventh Amendment prohibits a court of appeals from directing judgment as a matter of law on a record different from the one considered by the jury. *Neely* made clear that a court of appeals may order entry of judgment as a matter of law on sufficiency-of-the-evidence grounds without violating the Seventh Amendment. 386 U.S. at 321-322. Entering judgment for the verdict loser when all of the evidence was properly before the jury is scarcely less destructive of the jury's verdict than is entry of such a judgment based on a record made insufficient by the removal of evidence the jury should not have had before it.

of evidence, of the alleged evidentiary deficiency. See Fed. Rule Civ. Proc. 50(a)(2) (motion for judgment as a matter of law "shall specify . . . the law and facts on which the moving party is entitled to the judgment"). On appeal, both will have the opportunity to argue in support of the jury's verdict or, alternatively, for a new trial. And if judgment is instructed for the verdict loser, both will have a further chance to urge a new trial in a rehearing petition.

Since *Daubert*, moreover, parties relying on expert evidence have had notice of the exacting standards of reliability such evidence must meet. 509 U.S. 579; see also Kumho Tire Co. v. Carmichael, 526 U.S. 137 (1999) (rendered shortly after the Eighth Circuit's decision in Weisgram's case); General Electric Co. v. Joiner, 522 U.S. 136 (1997). It is implausible to suggest, post-*Daubert*, that parties will initially present less than their best expert evidence in the expectation of a second chance should their first try fail. We therefore find unconvincing Weisgram's fears that allowing courts of appeals to direct the entry of judgment for defendants will punish plaintiffs who could have shored up their cases by other means had they known their expert testimony would be found inadmissible. In this case, for example, although Weisgram was on notice every step of the way that Marley was challenging his experts, he made no attempt to add or substitute other evidence. See Lujan v. National Wildlife Federation, 497 U.S. 871, 897 (1990) ("[A] litigant's failure to buttress its position because of confidence in the strength of that position is always indulged in at the litigant's own risk.").

After holding Weisgram's expert testimony inadmissible, the Court of Appeals evaluated the evidence presented at trial, viewing it in the light most favorable to Weisgram, and found the properly admitted evidence insufficient to support the verdict. 169 F.3d at 516-517. Weisgram offered no specific grounds for a new trial to the Eighth Circuit.[13] Even in the petition for rehearing, Weisgram argued only that the appellate court had misapplied state law, did not have the authority to direct judgment, and had failed to give adequate deference to the trial court's evidentiary rulings. The Eighth Circuit concluded that this was "not a close case." 169 F.3d at 517 n.2. In these circumstances, the Eighth Circuit did not abuse its discretion by directing entry of judgment for Marley, instead of returning the case to the District Court for further proceedings. . . .

Neely recognized that there are myriad situations in which the determination whether a new trial is in order is best made by the trial judge. 386 U.S. at 325-326. *Neely* held, however, that there are also cases in which a court of appeals may appropriately instruct the district court to enter judgment as a matter of law against the jury-verdict winner. Id. at 326. We

13. Cf. Neely v. Martin K. Eby Constr. Co., 386 U.S. 317, 327 (1967) (observing that it would not be clear that litigation should be terminated for evidentiary insufficiency when, for example, the trial court excluded evidence that would have strengthened the verdict winner's case or "itself caused the insufficiency . . . by erroneously [imposing] too high a burden of proof").

adhere to *Neely*'s holding and rationale, and today hold that the authority of courts of appeals to direct the entry of judgment as a matter of law extends to cases in which, on excision of testimony erroneously admitted, there remains insufficient evidence to support the jury's verdict.

For the reasons stated, the judgment of the Court of Appeals for the Eighth Circuit is affirmed.

Notes and Questions

1. Weisgram *versus* Neely: *The Path to Greater Control of Juries?* The Court in *Weisgram* relied on its holding in Neely v. Eby Construction Co., 386 U.S. 317 (1967). But there are significant differences between the two cases. *Neely* affirmatively answered the question of whether, faced with insufficient evidence to support a jury verdict, an appellate court could enter judgment as a matter of law without remanding the case to the district court. In *Weisgram,* the Court went a step further. Here, the Court held that an appellate court can enter judgment as a matter of law when expert testimony was admitted into evidence but was later judged unreliable and therefore inadmissible, and the plaintiff had no other evidence to support a verdict. Thus, the plaintiff loses the chance to present her case differently, as she presumably would have had she known at trial that her preferred expert evidence was inadmissible.

Does *Weisgram* lead to more control of juries, if the trial judge's evaluation of expert evidence can now be taken over by the appellate court? What could the bereaved widow have done in the problem case had an appellate court rejected the expert testimony admitted by the trial judge and ordered that she take nothing?

2. *The Special Role of Experts.* As we have seen, judges have a special duty to assess the credibility of scientific testimony before allowing the witness to testify as an expert. Daubert v. Merrell Dow Pharmaceuticals, Inc., 509 U.S. 579 (1993). Is the holding in *Weisgram* limited to such scientific experts? Even if it is so limited, it would still affect a lot of cases because the use of experts is so widespread. What latitude should the trial judge be given to second-guess the jury's view of expert witness credibility in granting a motion for a new trial? This question is complicated by the fact that the trial judge is, in a sense, second-guessing his earlier ruling that the witness was qualified under *Daubert*.

The Supreme Court rejected de novo review of the trial court's application of *Daubert* in General Electric Co. v. Joiner, 522 U.S. 136 (1997), reaffirming the general rule that "abuse of discretion" applies to decisions to admit or exclude expert scientific evidence. For a discussion of *Joiner* and *Daubert*, see Michael H. Gottesman, From *Barefoot* to *Daubert* to *Joiner*: Triple Play or Double Error?, 40 Ariz. L. Rev. 753 (1998). Note that *Daubert* raises a difficult definitional problem: whether the evidence in question is "scientific" versus "nonscientific." The applicability of *Daubert* to the latter category of expert testimony was addressed by the Court in Kumho Tire Co. v. Carmichael, 526 U.S. 137 (1999). The Court concluded that where a mechanical engineer's expert testimony was grounded in personal experience working for a tire manufacturer, the *Daubert* factors — the disputed theory's testability, publication, rate of error, and general acceptance among experts in the relevant field — did apply. But see Marron v. Stromstad, 123 P.3d 992 (Alaska 2005); Logerquist v. McVey, 1 P.3d 113 (Ariz. 2000); CSX Transp., Inc. v. Miller, 858 A.2d 1025 (2004); Watson v. INCO Alloys Int'l, Inc., 545 S.E.2d 294 (2001); West Virginia Div. of Highways v. Butler, 516 S.E.2d 769 (1999).

The ambiguities created by *Daubert* have prompted changes to Federal Rule of Evidence 702, "Testimony by Experts." The amended rule provides as follows:

> If scientific, technical, or other specialized knowledge will assist the trier of fact to understand the evidence or to determine a fact in issue, a witness qualified as an expert by knowledge, skill, experience or training, or education, may testify thereto in the form of an opinion or otherwise if *(1) the testimony is based upon sufficient facts or data, (2) the testimony is the product of reliable principles and methods, and (3) the witness has applied the principles and methods reliably to the facts of the case.*

(New language in italics.)

The Advisory Committee Notes to the amendment indicate that the amendment is designed to resolve the issue presented in *Kumho Tire Co.* as follows:

> [t]he amendment does not distinguish between scientific and other forms of expert testimony. The trial court's gatekeeping function applies to testimony by any expert. . . . While the relevant factors for determining reliability will vary from expertise to expertise, the amendment rejects the premise that an expert's testimony should be treated more permissively simply because it is outside the realm of science. An opinion from an expert who is not a scientist should receive the same degree of scrutiny for reliability as an opinion from an expert who purports to be a scientist.

3. *Limits on Appellate Power to Second-Guess Juries (Reeves v. Sanderson Revisited).* Remember the holding in *Reeves,* supra, that an appellate court impermissibly substituted its judgment for the jury's in an age-discrimination case. Will this ruling remove an important check on runaway jury verdicts? To answer this, think about the effect of the opposite ruling. Plaintiffs in *Reeves,* backed by amici like the Association of Trial Lawyers of America, argued strongly that a contrary decision would undercut the right to jury trial by allowing appellate judges to assess witness credibility.

> Entry of judgment as a matter of law by appellate courts was approved by this Court relatively recently [citing *Weisgram* — EDS.]. However, appellate courts have adopted for themselves the standard of sufficiency of the

> evidence employed by many trial courts, reviewing the sufficiency of evidence de novo, based on review of all the evidence of both parties and applying the "reasonable jury" test. The result has been a dramatic increase in the number of jury verdicts overturned by courts of appeals with entry of judgment as a matter of law, rather than new trial. Such aggressive review of jury verdicts for sufficiency of evidence threatens the essential function of the jury protected by the Seventh Amendment. It is also inconsistent with Federal Rule of Civil Procedure 50, which provides for an informed discretionary decision whether to enter judgment as a matter of law or order a new trial where the evidence has been found insufficient to support the verdict.

Amicus Curiae Brief of the Association of Trial Lawyers of America in Support of the Petitioner at 2-3, Reeves v. Sanderson Plumbing Prods., Inc., 530 U.S. 133 (2000).

Practical considerations, as well as Seventh Amendment rights, compelled more deferential appellate review of the jury's credibility assessment in this case, Reeves argued in his Supreme Court brief:

> The type of tedious, workplace issues involved in this case are those for which appeals court judges have no expertise and little experience. Realities of discipline in a factory workplace are far more familiar to ordinary working people who sit on juries than to appellate judges. . . . Jurors who observe the demeanor of witnesses are in a superior position to judge whether or not Mr. Reeves was truthful when he testified Chesnut dominated the company.

Brief for Petitioner at 45, Reeves v. Sanderson Plumbing Prods., Inc., 530 U.S. 133 (2000).

What could be the potential impact of the *Reeves* decision on our problem case, the bereaved widow? Are there aspects of witness credibility that should be left to the jury, or is a wrongful death case amenable to de novo review of all the evidence on appeal? How would you feel about the implications of the *Reeves* decision if you were the counsel for the bereaved widow? For the manufacturer?

5. Excessive Verdicts

a. Prejudice, Passion, and Punitive Damages

Curtis Publishing Co. v. Butts

351 F.2d 702 (5th Cir. 1965)

SPEARS, Circuit Judge.

This is a libel suit. Curtis Publishing Company published an article in the March 23, 1963 issue of the Saturday Evening Post entitled "The Story of a College Football Fix," characterized by the Post in the subtitle as

"A Shocking Report of How Wally Butts and 'Bear' Bryant Rigged a Game Last Fall."

On March 25, 1963, Wally Butts, former Athletic Director of the University of Georgia, instituted this action against Curtis. In August, 1963, the case was heard before a jury, which returned a verdict against Curtis for $60,000 general and $3,000,000 punitive damages. Conditioned upon the failure of Butts to remit that portion of the award for punitive damages in excess of $400,000, the trial court granted Curtis' motion for new trial. At the same time, Curtis' motion for judgment notwithstanding the verdict was denied. On January 22, 1964, after Butts had filed a remittitur, Curtis' motion for new trial was denied, and judgment for Butts in the amount of $460,000 was entered. Thereafter, Curtis filed motions for new trial under Rule 60(b), F. R. Civ. P., which were denied on April 7, 1964. This appeal is taken from the judgment of January 22, 1964, and from the trial court's denial of Curtis' motions for judgment notwithstanding the verdict and for new trial. We affirm.

Curtis publishes various magazines including the Post. Prior to the publication of the story in question, the editor-in-chief, undoubtedly hoping to attract more readers, had decided to "change the image" of the magazine by making it an "exposé" type, and embarking upon a policy of "sophisticated muckraking," in order "to provoke people" and "make them mad."

The article involved was based upon a claim by one George Burnett that on September 13, 1962 he had accidentally overheard, and made notes of, a long-distance telephone conversation between Butts and "Bear" Bryant, football coach at the University of Alabama, in which Butts divulged certain information about football plays the University of Georgia would use in its opening game against Alabama. Georgia was subsequently defeated 35-0.

About four months after the alleged telephone conversation Burnett contacted various people, including Georgia football coach Johnny Griffith, and then decided to tell his story to the Post. A writer, Frank Graham, Jr., was assigned by the Post to investigate and write the story, and an Atlanta sports editor was retained to advise him. Graham never saw Burnett's notes, as they were at the time in the possession of Georgia school officials; he did not interview a witness known by him to have allegedly discussed the notes with Burnett on the same day the telephone conversation purportedly took place; he never viewed the game films; and neither he nor anyone else on behalf of the Post ever contacted Butts or Bryant. He agreed that both he and Curtis knew publication of the article "would ruin Coach Butts' career."

On March 11, 1963, eleven days before the article was published, Curtis was informed by telegram and letter, both sent by Butts' counsel, of the "absolute falsity of the charges" contained in the proposed story. The record does not disclose that any additional investigation was initiated, and the telegram and letter went unanswered. In addition, a long-distance telephone appeal that the article not be published, made by Butts' daughter prior to publication, was rejected. After the article was published, Curtis refused a demand that it publish a retraction.

The Post took the position from the beginning that the statements made in the article concerning Butts were true, and that because of their nature it had exercised great care by thoroughly checking every significant source of information as to their truthfulness and accuracy, in advance of publication.

Curtis chose not to use as a witness either the author of the article or any of its editors who had made contributions to the article after it had been submitted. Nor did it use the Atlanta sports editor who had assisted in the preparation of the story. As one of its principal witnesses it called upon George Burnett, who was known by Curtis to have been convicted of writing bad checks, and to be on probation at the time he claimed to have listened in on the conversation.

Both Butts and Bryant testified. Each emphatically denied the charges contained in the article and stated that there was never any conversation between them having as its purpose the fixing or rigging of any football game. Several football players, past and present, expressed their opinions to the effect that the outcome of a football game cannot be rigged or fixed without participation by the players themselves, and that there is no way in which two coaches can rig or fix the outcome of a football game without the players' knowledge. Other "experts" stated their opinion that the information contained in the "so-called" Burnett notes would not be of any assistance at all to the University of Alabama in preparing for its game with the University of Georgia. In several instances Butts' witnesses denied direct quotations attributed to them in the article. . . .

Curtis submits twenty-eight specifications of error. . . . The issues involved are: . . . (3) Did the arguments of Butts' counsel, not objected to at the trial, require a new trial? . . .

The trial judge gave his reasons for requiring the remittitur of all punitive damages in excess of $400,000. There is not the slightest suggestion that he thought, or even intimated, that the larger award was based on passion or prejudice. On the contrary, fully aware of the distinction between a verdict excessive in amount which may be reduced by remittitur, and one resulting from improper influences such as passion and prejudice which may not be corrected in this way, the judge necessarily rejected the idea that this verdict had been infected by such destructive elements. . . .

The trial judge had the duty of determining whether as a matter of law (a) any allowance for punitive damages could be made, and (b) what the maximum would be. As to (a), the trial court not only expressed the opinion that the article was extremely defamatory, and that the jury had no choice other than to find Curtis liable, but he also thought that there was "ample evidence from which a jury could have concluded that there was reckless disregard by defendant of whether the article was false or not." Upon determining (b) he had then to decide whether to grant a new trial or require a remittitur as to the excess. The latter is a permissible course and does not infringe upon the Seventh Amendment's guaranty of a jury trial. In making his determination as to (b), he pursued the correct standard of keeping the verdict "within reasonable bounds considering the purpose to be achieved as well as the corporate defendant's wanton or reckless indifference to the plaintiff's rights." Obviously, in deciding the matter the judge had to pick a dollar figure beyond which the law would not go. He selected the sum of $400,000 as the maximum which the law would accept to deter Curtis from repeating the trespass or to compensate the wounded feelings of Butts. Although the reduction required, and the sum remaining, were each substantial, there was ample basis for the trial court's judgment.

To have granted a new trial might appear to have been an easier way out. But that is really no solution. On a retrial, the judge could not instruct the next jury as to the dollar maximum of any such verdict. So that jury would be pretty much on its own, under the unavoidably vague, elastic standards prescribed in the Code, as measured by the enlightened conscience of an impartial jury. The trial judge, on the second trial, would then be forced to repeat the process of testing for (a) and (b). If, as urged by Curtis, the determination by the judge that the amount is too much, necessarily means a new trial, it is quite possible that the case would never end. Georgia has prescribed the "punishment" for aggravated willful torts. The law ought not to frustrate the vindication of that policy by an unrealistic procedure. The jury verdict, as reviewed and reduced by the trial judge, is the tortfeasor's assurance that such damages will not exceed that which the law would tolerate to achieve the Georgia objective of deterring repetition or compensating wounded feelings.

This is no ordinary libel case. The publication of the article by the Post, in the face of several specific appeals that it refrain from doing so, was part and parcel of a general policy of callousness, which recognized from the start that Butts' career would be ruined. The trial judge's appraisal of the evidence, with which we are in complete accord, was that it was sufficiently strong to justify the jury in concluding that what the Post did was done with reckless disregard of whether the article was false or not.

The case was fully developed during extensive pretrials, and in a jury trial lasting two weeks. The record itself comprises 1613 pages. We have given full consideration to the entire record, as well as to the more than 650 pages of briefs submitted by both parties, the numerous authorities cited therein, and the oral arguments of counsel. We think that Curtis has had its day in court. It apparently thought so too until the jury verdict was returned. This is attested by the fact that practically all of its present complaints were not even raised until after the trial.

Believing and so finding that the trial was fair, and that the judgment of the trial court was correct and proper in all respects, it is

Affirmed.

RIVES, Circuit Judge (dissenting). . . .

The punitive damages, either as found by the jury or as fixed by the court, are many times greater in amount than the general damages. Under the court's instructions to the jury, the general damages included compensation "for the mental anguish, pain, mortification, and humiliation he has experienced as a result of the publication." . . . The punitive damages included no element to which the plaintiff was entitled by way of compensation, but, according to the court's instruction to the jury, "the purpose of punitive damages is to deter the defendant from a repetition of the offense and is a warning to others not to commit a like offense. It is intended to protect the community and has an expression of ethical indignation, although the plaintiff receives the award." . . .

For yet another reason the award of $3,000,000 by the jury, or of $400,000 by the court, as punitive damages is unconstitutional and void. There was no semblance of definite standard or controlling guide to govern the award. Can any standard be more vague or arbitrary than "an expression of ethical indignation" first on the part of the jury and then on the part of the trial judge? It must be remembered that stricter standards of permissible vagueness are applicable to a rule having a potentially inhibiting effect on freedom of the press than are applicable to rules relating to less important subjects.

Still further, I submit that the remittitur violates the defendant's rights under the Seventh Amendment. The trial judge concluded "that the award for punitive damages in this case was grossly excessive. It is the court's considered opinion that the maximum sum for punitive damages that should have been awarded against Curtis Publishing Company should be $400,000.00." . . . In another part of his opinion on motion for new trial, the district judge commented: "The award for punitive damages in the case under consideration is more than seventeen times larger than the highest award for punitive damages ever sustained." The district judge's opinion is silent as to the underlying reason for such a grossly excessive verdict. The majority opinion says that " . . . the judge necessarily rejected the idea that the verdict had been infected by such destructive elements [as passion or prejudice]." With deference, I submit that that conclusion is not based on the record or on anything said by the trial judge. . . .

. . . [I]t seems to me that "[t]he public interest requires that the court of its own motion, as is its power and duty, protect suitors in their right to a verdict, uninfluenced by the appeals of counsel to passion or prejudice." New York Central R.R. Co. v. Johnson, 1929, 279 U.S. 310, 318. That would be true even if the prejudicial argument had not been followed by a grossly excessive verdict. I submit that the $3,000,000 punitive damage verdict was so clearly the result of passion and prejudice that it could not be cured by remittitur. . . .

---

b. Additur and Remittitur

Both the problem case and *Curtis Publishing* are examples of remittitur, in which a judge trims a jury verdict that is grossly excessive as a matter of law. The judge may condition the denial of a new trial motion on the plaintiff remitting a portion of the award. The flip side of remittitur is additur, in which the court increases an inadequate verdict.

In Dimick v. Schiedt, 293 U.S. 474 (1934), it was held that the practice of sustaining inadequate verdicts if the defendant should agree to pay a somewhat larger sum was violative of the Seventh Amendment. Is there a plausible distinction between additur and remittitur in the degree to which they offend the right to jury trial? A difference may be said to exist that results from the unanimity requirement; inadequate damages may reflect a compromise. The Court in the *Dimick* case also conceded that remittitur practice was too well established to be repudiated at so late a time. Nevertheless, additurs have been employed in a few exceptional federal cases, e.g., Rocky Mountain Tool & Machine Co. v. Tecon Corp., 371 F.2d 589 (10th Cir. 1966). Many state courts regularly employ additurs as well as remittiturs. Indeed, the Wisconsin practice once condoned new trial orders that were doubly conditional. If the defendant did not exercise the option of paying a sum deemed by the trial judge to be a reasonable maximum, then the plaintiff was given the option of accepting a reasonable minimum; if both refused the court's proposals, a new trial resulted. This practice was abandoned in Powers v. Allstate Insurance Co., 102 N.W. 393 (1960).

c. The Role of the Appellate Court in Administering Remittitur

Donovan v. Penn Shipping Co.
429 U.S. 648 (1977)

PER CURIAM.

The petitioner, while employed by the respondents as a seaman on the SS *Penn Sailor,* slipped on wet paint, injuring his right wrist and elbow. He sued the respondents under the Jones Act, 46 U.S.C. § 688, and obtained a $90,000 verdict at his jury trial. The respondents moved to set aside the verdict as excessive. Fed. Rules Civ. Proc. 50, 59. The District Court granted the motion, and ordered a new trial on damages unless the petitioner agreed to remit $25,000 of the $90,000 award.

After some time the petitioner submitted to the District Court a proposed order stating that he accepted "under protest" the reduced verdict of $65,000, but reserving nonetheless "his right to appeal therefrom." This language was adopted by the District Court in entering a judgment for the petitioner in the amount of $65,000.

The petitioner sought appellate review of the District Court's decision to order a conditional new trial. In so doing he asked the Court of Appeals for the Second Circuit to discard the settled rule that a plaintiff who has accepted a remittitur may not appeal to seek reinstatement of the original verdict. The Court of Appeals refused the petitioner's invitation, and dismissed the appeal. 536 F.2d 536.

The Court of Appeals properly followed our precedents in holding that a plaintiff cannot "protest" a remittitur he has accepted in an attempt to open it to challenge on appeal. A line of decisions stretching back to 1889 has firmly established that a plaintiff cannot appeal the propriety of a remittitur order to which he has agreed.

There are decisions in the Federal Courts of Appeals that depart from these unbroken precedents. Those decisions held or intimated that a plaintiff who accepts a remittitur "under protest" may challenge on appeal the correctness of the remittitur order. Other decisions have suggested that when entertaining cases pursuant to its diversity jurisdiction, a federal court should look to state practice to determine whether such an appeal is permitted.

The proper role of the trial and appellate courts in the federal system in reviewing the size of jury verdicts is, however, a matter of federal law, see Hanna v. Plumer, 380 U.S. 460, 466-469 (1965); Byrd v. Blue Ridge Rural Electric Coop., 356 U.S. 525 (1958), and that law has always prohibited appeals in the situation at bar. The Court of Appeals for the Second Circuit correctly adhered to the consistent rule established by this Court's decisions. In order to clarify whatever uncertainty might exist, we now reaffirm the longstanding rule that a plaintiff in federal court, whether prosecuting a state or federal cause of action, may not appeal from a remittitur order he has accepted.

The petition for a writ of certiorari is granted, and the judgment is *affirmed.*

THE CHIEF JUSTICE and JUSTICE BLACKMUN would grant the petition for certiorari but would have the case argued and given plenary consideration rather than disposed of summarily.

---

d. Excessive Verdicts and Due Process

An issue that has been at the forefront of proposed civil litigation reforms is that of allegedly excessive jury verdicts. Thus far, proposed federal legislation that would cap punitive damages awards has not been adopted. The legislative murmurings, though, are an important backdrop to a trilogy of U.S. Supreme Court cases that address the due process limits on punitive damages awards, and that display sharp divisions among the Justices about federal constitutional limits on these awards.

In the first of these cases, Pacific Mutual Life Insurance Co. v. Haslip, 499 U.S. 1 (1991), the Court concluded that the common-law method for assessing punitive damages did not in itself violate due process, but that this was "not the end of the matter." Id. at 18. The instructions to the jury must make clear the purpose of punitive damages, which is not to compensate the plaintiff but to punish the defendant and deter the defendant and others from engaging in similar misconduct. While juries have discretion in making these awards, their discretion must be exercised within reasonable constraints. Posttrial and appellate review of such awards helps to assure that the awards do not exceed the bounds of reason. Indeed, the Court noted, the Alabama Supreme Court had weighed several factors in determining whether the punitive damage award in *Haslip* was excessive, to wit:

> (a) whether there is a reasonable relationship between the punitive damages award and the harm likely to result from the defendant's conduct as well as the harm that actually has occurred; (b) the degree of reprehensibility of the defendant's conduct, the duration of that conduct, the defendant's awareness, any concealment, and the existence and frequency of similar past conduct; (c) the profitability to the defendant of the wrongful conduct and the desirability of removing that profit and of having the defendant also sustain a loss; (d) the "financial position" of the defendant; (e) all the costs of litigation; (f) the imposition of criminal sanctions on the defendant for its conduct, these to be taken in mitigation; and (g) the existence of other civil awards against the defendant for the same conduct, these also to be taken in mitigation.
>
> The application of these standards, we conclude, imposes a sufficiently definite and meaningful constraint on the discretion of Alabama fact finders in awarding punitive damages. The Alabama Supreme Court's post-verdict review ensures that punitive damages awards are not grossly out of proportion to the severity of the offense and have some understandable relationship to compensatory damages. . . .

Id. at 21-22.

The Court returned to the constitutionality of punitive damages in TXO Production Corp. v. Alliance Resources Corp., 509 U.S. 443 (1993). *TXO* involved a deal between TXO and Alliance Resources over a potentially lucrative tract of land in West Virginia, which TXO hoped to mine for gas and oil. Shortly after concluding the deal, TXO discovered that a previous owner of the site had severed and sold the right to mine coal there. There was no claim made by any of the owners of the coal rights that their interest extended to gas or oil. TXO nevertheless took a quitclaim deed from one of them. It then challenged Alliance's title, finally bringing an action in a West Virginia court for a declaratory judgment against Alliance. Alliance counterclaimed for slander of title.

The court decided the claim adversely to TXO, holding that the Alliance title to the oil and gas was clear. It submitted the counterclaim to trial by jury. Finding that it had cost Alliance $19,000 to defend the declaratory judgment action, it awarded compensatory damages in that amount. It also awarded Alliance punitive damages in the amount of $10,000,000. Judgment entered on that amount was affirmed by the West Virginia Supreme Court of Errors.

Certiorari was granted and the judgment was affirmed. The Court was too divided on the merits to produce an opinion of the Court. Justices Stevens, Blackmun, and Rehnquist held that the amount of the verdict was not so gross as to offend standards of due process, given the evidence that TXO was striving to renegotiate a mineral lease that had been very generous, and could have profited substantially had its tactic worked. They also concluded that it was not constitutionally objectionable for the jury to be allowed to consider the wealth of the defendant in setting the proper amount of the punishment to be imposed. And they held that the following instruction was not unconstitutionally vague:

> In addition to actual or compensatory damages, the law permits the jury, under certain circumstances, to make an award of punitive damages, in order to punish the wrongdoer for his misconduct, to serve as an example or warning to others not to engage in such conduct and to provide additional compensation for the conduct to which the injured parties have been subjected.
>
> If you find from a preponderance of the evidence that TXO Production Corp. is guilty of wanton, wilful, malicious or reckless conduct which shows an indifference to the right of others, then you may make an award of punitive damages in this case.
>
> In assessing punitive damages, if any, you should take into consideration all of the circumstances surrounding the particular occurrence, including the nature of the wrongdoing, the extent of the harm inflicted, the intent of the party committing the act, the wealth of the perpetrator, as well as any mitigating circumstances which may operate to reduce the amount of the damages. The object of such punishment is to deter TXO Production Corp. and others from committing like offenses in the future. Therefore the law recognizes that to in fact deter such conduct may require a larger fine upon one of large means than it would upon one of ordinary means under the same or similar circumstances.

Id. at 464 n.29.

Justice Kennedy concurred in the result:

> To ask whether a particular award of punitive damages is grossly excessive begs the question: excessive in relation to what? The answer excessive in relation to the conduct of the tortfeasor may be correct, but it is unhelpful, for we are still bereft of any standard by which to compare the punishment to the malefaction that gave rise to it. A reviewing court employing this formulation comes close to relying upon nothing more than its own subjective reaction to a particular punitive damages award in deciding whether the award violates the Constitution. This type of review, far from imposing meaningful, law-like restraints on jury excess, could become as fickle as the process it is designed to superintend. Furthermore, it might give the illusion of judicial certainty where none in fact exists, and, in so doing, discourage legislative intervention that might prevent unjust punitive awards.

Id. at 466-467.

Justices Scalia and Thomas concurred in the judgment, holding that the Fourteenth Amendment cannot be read to limit punitive damages. It is not "the secret repository of all sorts of other, unenumerated, substantive rights." Id. at 470.

Justices White and Souter joined in Justice O'Connor's dissent:

> In my view, due process at least requires judges to engage in searching review where the verdict discloses such great disproportions as to suggest the possibility of bias, caprice, or passion....
>
> A comparison of this award and prior ones in West Virginia confirms its unusual nature: It is 20 times larger than the highest punitive damages award *ever* upheld in West Virginia history for any misconduct.... Although TXO's conduct was clearly wrongful, calculated, and improper, the award in this case cannot be upheld as a reasoned retributive response. Not only is it greatly in excess of the actual harm caused, but it is 10 times greater than the largest punitive damages award for the same tort in any jurisdiction....

Id. at 481-482.

Finally, the Court in 1996 decided BMW of North America, Inc. v. Gore, 517 U.S. 559 (1996), a case involving a national car distributor's failure to disclose that certain automobiles had been repainted. Dr. Ira Gore purchased a black BMW sports sedan for $40,750.88 from an authorized BMW dealer. He later learned that the car had been repainted, and sued the American distributor of BMW automobiles for $500,000 in compensatory and punitive damages, and costs.

Dr. Gore's actual damage estimate was $4,000. He argued at trial that a punitive award of $4 million would be an appropriate penalty given that the distributor allegedly sold approximately 1,000 cars without disclosing that they had been repainted.

The jury agreed, and assessed BMW $4,000 in compensatory damages and $4 million in punitive damages, on the ground that the nondisclosure policy of BMW constituted fraud under Alabama law. The trial judge denied BMW's posttrial motion to set aside the punitive damages award as excessive. The Alabama Supreme Court upheld that determination, though it reduced the award to $2 million on the ground that the jury improperly computed the punitive damages.

The United States Supreme Court reversed, holding that the $2 million award was grossly excessive and therefore violated due process. Justice Stevens, writing for the majority, concluded as follows:

> Elementary notions of fairness enshrined in our constitutional jurisprudence dictate that a person receive fair notice not only of the conduct that will subject him to punishment but also of the severity of the penalty that a State may impose. Three guideposts, each of which indicates that BMW did not receive adequate notice of the magnitude of the sanction that Alabama might impose for adhering to the nondisclosure policy adopted in 1983, lead us to the conclusion that the $2 million award against BMW is grossly excessive: the degree of reprehensibility of the nondisclosure; the disparity between the harm or potential harm suffered by Dr. Gore and his punitive damages award; and the difference between this remedy and the civil penalties authorized or imposed in comparable cases....

> The $2 million in punitive damages awarded to Dr. Gore by the Alabama Supreme Court is 500 times the amount of his actual harm as determined by the jury. Moreover, there is no suggestion that Dr. Gore or any other BMW purchaser was threatened with any additional potential harm by BMW's nondisclosure policy. The disparity in this case is thus dramatically greater than those considered in *Haslip* and *TXO*.
>
> Of course, we have consistently rejected the notion that the constitutional line is marked by a simple mathematical formula, even one that compares actual *and potential* damages to the punitive award. *TXO*, 509 U.S., at 458. Indeed, low awards of compensatory damages may properly support a higher ratio than high compensatory awards, if, for example, a particularly egregious act has resulted in only a small amount of economic damages. A higher ratio may also be justified in cases in which the injury is hard to detect or the monetary value of noneconomic harm might have been difficult to determine. It is appropriate, therefore, to reiterate our rejection of a categorical approach. Once again, "we return to what we said . . . in *Haslip*: 'We need not, and indeed we cannot, draw a mathematical bright line between the constitutionally acceptable and the constitutionally unacceptable that would fit every case. We can say, however, that [a] general concer[n] of reasonableness . . . properly enter[s] into the constitutional calculus.'" *TXO*, 509 U.S., at 458 (quoting *Haslip*, 499 U.S., at 18). In most cases, the ratio will be within a constitutionally acceptable range, and remittitur will not be justified on this basis. When the ratio is a breathtaking 500 to 1, however, the award must surely "raise a suspicious judicial eyebrow." *TXO*, 509 U.S., at 482 (O'Connor, J., dissenting).

Id. at 574-575, 582-583.

In a concurring opinion joined by Justices O'Connor and Souter, Justice Breyer observed that the due process protection against excessive verdicts not only provides citizens notice of what actions might subject them to punishment; "it also helps to assure the uniform, general treatment of similarly situated persons that is the essence of the law itself." He continued:

> Legal standards need not be precise in order to satisfy this constitutional concern. But they must offer some kind of constraint upon a jury or court's discretion, and thus protection against purely arbitrary behavior. The standards the Alabama courts applied here are vague and open-ended to the point where they risk arbitrary results. In my view, although the vagueness of those standards does not, by itself, violate due process, it does invite the kind of scrutiny the Court has given the particular verdict before us. This is because the standards, as the Alabama Supreme Court authoritatively interpreted them here, provided no significant constraints or protection against arbitrary results.

Id. at 587-588 (Breyer, J., concurring).

Justice Scalia, joined by Justice Thomas, dissented on the ground that concern about punitive damages run wild was not of constitutional moment, and that "the Court's activities in this area are an unjustified incursion into the province of state governments." Id. at 598 (Scalia, J., dissenting). Even if it were the Court's concern, however, Justice Scalia would have objected to the imposition of a standard as vague and manipulative as the "three guideposts" standard offered by the majority.

Justice Ginsburg likewise dissented, in a separate opinion joined by Chief Justice Rehnquist. She agreed with Justice Scalia that the majority had "venture[d] into territory traditionally within the States' domain, and . . . in the face of reform measures recently adopted or currently under consideration in legislative arenas." Id. at 607 (Ginsburg, J., dissenting). In her view, the Alabama Supreme Court had faithfully applied *Haslip* and *TXO*; the United States Supreme Court thus should have let its judgment stand, in deference to "the Court's longstanding reluctance to countenance review, even by courts of appeals, of the size of verdicts returned by juries in federal district court proceedings." Id. at 613.

On remand, after considering awards in comparable cases involving fraud in the sale of an automobile, the Alabama Supreme Court recalculated the punitive damages at $50,000. The court held that a new trial was warranted unless the plaintiff filed a remittitur of the remainder of the damages. Dr. Gore accepted the remittitur in September 1997. See BMW of N.A. Inc. v. Gore, 701 So. 2d 507 (Ala. 1997); see also State Farm Mutual Auto. Ins. Co. v. Campbell, 538 U.S. 408 (2003) (applying the three-part test of *Gore* to strike down a punitive damages award of $145 million against an insurer for bad faith refusal to settle, fraud, and intentional infliction of emotional distress). The United States Supreme Court returned to the issue of appellate review of punitive damages awards in Cooper Industries, Inc. v. Leatherman Tool Group, Inc., 532 U.S. 424 (2001). It held that the United States Constitution requires de novo appellate review of the "three guideposts" of *Gore*. This is in contrast to the usual appellate deference to lower court findings of fact.

More recently, the Supreme Court invalidated a $79.5 million state court punitive damage verdict in a case brought by a smoker against the cigarette manufacturer Philip Morris, alleging fraud and deceit. Philip Morris USA v. Williams, 549 U.S. 346 (2007) (although juries may consider harm to third parties in deciding how "reprehensible" defendant's conduct was, a punitive damage award is unconstitutional to the extent that it is based on the jury's desire to punish defendant for harm to persons other than the plaintiff). The Court also reduced the $4.5 billion in punitive damages awarded for the Exxon Valdez oil spill to an amount equal to the $507.5 million compensatory damage award. Exxon Shipping Co. v. Baker, 128 S. Ct. 2605 (2008) (purporting to follow maritime common law in adopting a 1:1 ratio of punitive to compensatory damages). Justice Breyer wrote separately to emphasize his disagreement with the way the Court applied its new standard:

> In my view, a limited exception to the Court's 1:1 ratio is warranted here. As the facts set forth in Part I of the Court's opinion make clear, this was no

> mine-run case of reckless behavior. The jury could reasonably have believed that Exxon knowingly allowed a relapsed alcoholic repeatedly to pilot a vessel filled with millions of gallons of oil through waters that provided the livelihood for the many plaintiffs in this case. Given that conduct, it was only a matter of time before a crash and spill like this occurred. And as Justice Ginsburg points out, the damage easily could have been much worse.

See *Baker*, 128 S. Ct. at 2640.

How would you describe the competing interests in these due process cases? Has the Court offered an intelligible standard for due process review of punitive damage awards? Is it any less vague than the other due process standards that you encountered in Chapter 1?

For empirical analysis of jury awards and the difference between awards in judge-tried and jury-tried cases, see Theodore Eisenberg et al., Juries, Judges, and Punitive Damages: An Empirical Study, 87 Cornell L. Rev. 743 (2002) (showing no substantial difference in the rate at which judges and juries award punitive damages or in the relation between sizes of punitive and compensatory awards); Seth A. Seabury et al., Forty Years of Jury Verdicts, 1 J. Empirical Legal Stud. 1, 22-23 (2004) (finding rate of increase in average jury awards since 1960 is less than the growth in real GDP over the same period: "Our results suggest little evidence to support the hypothesis that juries are awarding substantially higher awards on average. . . . On the surface, it seems difficult to reconcile this statement with the kind of headline-grabbing awards that have occurred over the past decade. One explanation for this is that, away from the headlines, the awards in some cases have declined and offset the growth in the larger and more highly publicized awards."); see also Aaron Hiller, Rule 11 and Tort Reform: Myth, Reality, and Legislation, 18 Geo. J. Legal Ethics 809, 818 (2005) ("As the amount of litigation on the docket has declined, so have the jury awards so often decried as outrageous and skyrocketing by tort reformers. The median jury award in 2001 was $37,000, representing a 43.1% decrease over the previous decade. Limiting that analysis only to tort cases, the median jury award stood at $28,000, a 56.3% drop since 1992. Moreover, juries rarely award punitive damages at all—less than 3% of all plaintiff winners in tort trials were awarded punitive damages; the median award was $38,000.").

If the findings of these studies are correct, why have courts constitutionalized their worries over these excessive verdicts? On the other hand, if judge-tried cases result in similar awards, why do plaintiffs' lawyers so often balk at bench trials?

In the recent *Baker* case, Justice Souter offered the following survey of the empirics on punitive damages:

> American punitive damages have been the target of audible criticism in recent decades, see, e.g., Note, Developments, The Paths of Civil Litigation, 113 Harv. L. Rev. 1783, 1784-1788 (2000) (surveying criticism), but the most recent studies tend to undercut much of it. A survey of the literature reveals

> that discretion to award punitive damages has not mass-produced runaway awards, and although some studies show the dollar amounts of punitive-damages awards growing over time, even in real terms, by most accounts the median ratio of punitive to compensatory awards has remained less than 1:1. Nor do the data substantiate a marked increase in the percentage of cases with punitive awards over the past several decades. The figures thus show an overall restraint and suggest that in many instances a high ratio of punitive to compensatory damages is substantially greater than necessary to punish or deter.
>
> The real problem, it seems, is the stark unpredictability of punitive awards. Courts of law are concerned with fairness as consistency, and evidence that the median ratio of punitive to compensatory awards falls within a reasonable zone, or that punitive awards are infrequent, fails to tell us whether the spread between high and low individual awards is acceptable. The available data suggest it is not. A recent comprehensive study of punitive damages awarded by juries in state civil trials found a median ratio of punitive to compensatory awards of just 0.62:1, but a mean ratio of 2.90:1 and a standard deviation of 13.81. Juries, Judges, and Punitive Damages 269. Even to those of us unsophisticated in statistics, the thrust of these figures is clear: the spread is great, and the outlier cases subject defendants to punitive damages that dwarf the corresponding compensatories. The distribution of awards is narrower, but still remarkable, among punitive damages assessed by judges: the median ratio is 0.66:1, the mean ratio is 1.60:1, and the standard deviation is 4.54. Ibid. Other studies of some of the same data show that fully 14% of punitive awards in 2001 were greater than four times the compensatory damages, see Cohen 5, with 18% of punitives in the 1990s more than trebling the compensatory damages, see Ostrom, Rottman, & Goerdt, A Step Above Anecdote: A Profile of the Civil Jury in the 1990s, 79 Judicature 233, 240 (1996). And a study of "financial injury" cases using a different data set found that 34% of the punitive awards were greater than three times the corresponding compensatory damages. Financial Injury Jury Verdicts 333.

128 S. Ct. at 2624-2625. Assuming Justice Souter has properly described "the real problem," are you convinced that the Constitution requires the Court to intervene and correct jury verdicts? Does the risk of an unpredictably high punitive damage award have its own deterrent effect on defendants accustomed to pricing harm so as to internalize it as part of the cost of doing business?

6. Anticipating Jury Verdicts

Given the large dollar values at stake in much civil litigation, it is not surprising that parties and lawyers invest time and money to determine the likely action of a jury in an individual case. Jury research firms compile statistical data on the quantifiable factors involved in jury trials, notably the verdict and the likely monetary award. Well-heeled individual litigants such as large corporations may also choose to conduct mock trials with mock juries in order to predict how a jury might receive certain facts or styles of presentation. A plethora of research has also been conducted on the selection of jurors, in an attempt to predict the verdict likely to be reached by juries of different racial, ethnic, and sexual compositions. This information, in turn, is used by parties to negotiate settlements with insurance companies and other defendants, to plan the presentation of a trial, or to choose between a bench or jury trial.

In the problem case, the bereaved widow, the corporate defendant would be more likely to have the resources to consult jury research firms and possibly conduct a mock trial. What kind of jurors might Ford have sought in hopes of a take-nothing verdict, or at least one lower than $800,000? Could a mock trial have helped Ford choose what evidence to present? Might Christian, the defense counsel, have chosen to alter her style of questioning if mock jurors reacted as unfavorably to her as did Juror 7?

Jury Verdict Research, a legal publishing company, has compiled a database analyzing 90,000 jury verdicts in personal injury cases nationwide, with which, they claim, the statistical likelihood of a plaintiff's winning, as well as the amount of money a jury will award, can be predicted. A snapshot of the results, reported in the New York Times, follows.

Gauging the Chances of Winning

Factors that determine the outcome of typical cases.

- *The size of a jury award varies by location.*

CASE 1: A 35-year-old man falls on the ice in a department store parking lot in Berks Country, Pa. He fractures his ankle and hurts his wrist. His medical expenses are $5,000.
PROBABILITY OF WINNING: 67 percent
LIKELY AWARD: $51,404

CASE 2: The same individual has the same type of accident and the same medical expenses, but the accident occurs in Manhattan.
PROBABILITY OF WINNING: 67 percent
LIKELY AWARD: $56,120

- *The probability of winning a personal injury suit varies with the type of accident and ranges from a little over 30 percent to a little over 90 percent. Medical malpractice suits are the hardest to win, but the awards are more generous.*

CASE 1: A man, 35, fractures his forearm in a boating accident. His medical costs are $5,000. He sues the Berks County, Pa., retail store that sold him the boat.

PROBABILITY OF WINNING: 92 percent
LIKELY AWARD: $51,884

CASE 2: Same circumstances, but the 35-year-old man sues his doctor for not properly setting the fracture.
PROBABILITY OF WINNING: 33 percent
LIKELY AWARD: $59,500

- *In wrongful death suits (and in cases involving severely disabling injuries) juries place a higher cash value on female victims than they do on male victims.*

CASE 1: A married woman, 30, with no children, is killed when a construction company ladder falls on her in Berks County. Her yearly salary was $25,000.
PROBABILITY OF WINNING: 35 percent
LIKELY AWARD: $1,198,208

CASE 2: Same circumstances, but the victim is a man.
PROBABILITY OF WINNING: 35 percent
LIKELY AWARD: $678,700

- *Young adults and middle-aged people tend to receive much larger awards than elderly people, primarily because the younger ones suffer greater loss of wages and, in some cases, because they have to live longer with the pain and suffering from an accident.*

CASE 1: An 18-year-old man becomes a quadriplegic by diving into partly filled swimming pool.
PROBABILITY OF WINNING: 55 percent
LIKELY AWARD: $3,369,251

CASE 2: A 60-year-old becomes a quadriplegic in the same kind of swimming pool accident.
PROBABILITY OF WINNING: 55 percent
LIKELY AWARD: $2,817,885

Compiling Data, and Giving Odds, on Jury Awards, N.Y. Times, Jan. 21, 1994, at B12.

7. Trials in the Courtroom of the Future

Discussions of the trial process evoke images of a judge and jury presiding over a trial presented by live lawyers, with live witnesses and immediate cross-examination. Technological advances are already changing that picture. Electronic images—the "virtual courtroom"—are complementing, and may even supplant, the traditional courtroom scene. Parties already are submitting some claims to "virtual juries" for adjudication online and taking part in online settlement initiatives. See, e.g., Michael Liedtke, New Online Niche: Settling Complaints, Patriot Ledger (Quincy, Mass.), May 1, 2000, at 27; Carolyn Said, Net Services Referee Disputes Between Online Sellers, Buyers, S.F. Chron., June 12, 2000, at C1.

Even in brick-and-mortar courthouses, witnesses can now testify from a distance, thus reducing expensive scheduling conflicts. Documents can be displayed in ways that may enhance their effectiveness, and courtroom computers help trial attorneys organize and present evidence. Rather than reading back testimony, the increasingly popular use of videotaped depositions allows an attorney to impeach a witness with his own image at the touch of a button. Litigators in high-stakes patent cases commission extremely expensive graphics, such as animations intended to demonstrate mechanical processes to judges and jurors.

For explorations of the impact of computer technology on litigation, including the speculation that "[a] trial will normally be a movie presentation," see Paul D. Carrington, Virtual Civil Litigation: A Visit to John Bunyan's Celestial City, 98 Colum. L. Rev. 1516, 1525 (1998). Consider, in this respect, a recently granted motion to conduct an entire trial via video conferencing. See Edwards v. Logan, 38 F. Supp. 2d 463 (W.D. Va. 1999), discussed at 67 U.S.L.W. 1489 (Feb. 12, 1999). In this case, Michael S. Edwards filed a Section 1983 excessive force civil rights lawsuit against officials of a Virginia prison where he was an inmate, claiming he had been forced to take part in a fistfight against a guard. Meanwhile, Edwards was transferred from Virginia to New Mexico to serve out the rest of his sentence. The court decided to conduct the trial by video conference for security reasons and to save the estimated $8,652 it would cost to bring Edwards to Virginia for trial.

The trial court is not the only province where technology is working dramatic change. Court documents are increasingly available online, cutting research and document retrieval time from days to minutes. Courts also are grappling with the issues of electronic filing of documents, and even serving subpoenas via e-mail. Cf. Federal Electronic Case File Project: Changing Way Lawyers Do Business, 67 U.S.L.W. 2547 (Mar. 23, 1999) (discussing federal project involving electronic filing and case management practices); Special Report: State Courts Go Separate Ways in Implementing E-Filing Initiatives, 67 U.S.L.W. 2563 (Mar. 30, 1999) (discussing state court practices regarding electronic filing); Ted Bridis, Judge Allows Delivery by E-Mail, Associated Press Online, March 24, 2000.

Substantive law, as well as procedure, must struggle to keep up with technology. As we have discussed, courts continue to grapple with questions of Internet jurisdiction and other technology-related issues, such as those that arose in the Microsoft antitrust case. Furthermore, rapid advances may present even greater challenges to appellate courts trying to make law that will last, such as when the Supreme Court assessed the validity of Internet decency regulations in Reno v. ACLU, 521 U.S. 844 (1997). See, e.g., Stuart

Minor Benjamin, Stepping into the Same River Twice: Rapidly Changing Facts and the Appellate Process, 78 Tex. L. Rev. 269 (1999).

How might technology have aided the parties in our problem case about the bereaved widow? How high-tech can the trial process get without interfering with the deliberative process that is the jury?

F. ALTERNATIVE DECISION MAKERS

Problem Case: An Injured Quarterback

You are consulted by Sam Wyoming, a professional football quarterback and member of a health maintenance organization(HMO), who has suffered the loss of use of his throwing arm, perhaps as the result of a negligent diagnosis by one of the group doctors. Although nearing the end of his playing life, Sam might well have had several more good seasons. At the time Sam joined the health care group he signed a standard form contract that contained the following clause:

> **Arbitration of Claims**
>
> Any claim arising from the violation of a legal duty incident to this Agreement shall be submitted to binding arbitration if said claim is made on account of death or bodily injury arising out of the rendition or failure to render services under this Agreement, irrespective of the legal theory on which the claim is asserted.
>
> In the event of arbitration, the Member will designate one arbitrator, the Group will designate another, and the two arbitrators thus named will select a third who shall be the chair of the board of arbitration. If the two arbitrators named by the parties are unable to agree on a third arbitrator, the office will be filled by appointment by the American Arbitration Association.

Sam, who is a popular figure in the area, would much prefer a jury trial. Although he had the services of a "sports lawyer" at the time he joined the HMO, he did not ask her to read the contract, nor was he aware of the presence of the clause.

Would you advise him to proceed with the arbitration or to go ahead and file suit? What considerations would enter into your decision?

Thus far, we have been dealing with the resolution of disputes in traditional public settings, where the government pays the judge, or the judge and jury, to make individual decisions in furtherance of the public's broad interest in the administration of justice. But this process is breaking down in many areas, particularly because of its costs of delay, of emotional trauma to the litigants, and of justice no longer recognizable because it has been so long delayed.

The late 1980s and early 1990s saw an unprecedented rise of alternative dispute resolution (ADR) in public and private spheres at both the state and federal levels. The arbitration caseload of the American Arbitration Association, the largest provider of arbitration services in the United States, grew from 92,000 in 1988 to 136,000 in 1999. The caseload of another major ADR provider grew 2,300 percent from 1987 to 1993, averaging 1,200 cases a month in 1993 alone. See Cameron L. Sabin, The Adjudicatory Boat Without a Keel: Private Arbitration and the Need for Public Oversight of Arbitrators, 87 Iowa L. Rev. 1337, 1339-1340 (2002). This movement toward more informal methods of dispute resolution is one of the most significant modern civil justice developments. While there are many permutations of ADR, a few basic questions focus our study: What kind of process is being called for? Is participation mandatory or voluntary? Is the decision to use alternative processes purely private, or is it mandated by a court ("court-annexed")?

Given the expansion of private systems for resolving disputes, it is important to understand ADR's contours and to think critically about its consequences. In what kinds of cases would it be preferable to resolve a dispute through more traditional litigation? By what standards should a trade-off in values be measured in a given case? Does a given ADR procedure implicate constitutional rights to due process, equal protection, the right to a jury trial, or other constitutional guarantees? Does the emphasis on developing alternative processes inhibit the development of the traditional public system?

Although we will deal in this chapter only with the two most widely used alternative dispute resolution systems—arbitration and mediation—there are many other formats for deciding disputes without judges or juries. The concluding portion of this section deals with these other methods, and also offers a critique of ADR.

After you have completed these materials, you should return to the opening problem of the book ("The Due Process Game"). Would ADR satisfy your procedural desires in this scenario? If so, what form of ADR would you prefer and why?

1. Arbitration

Gilmer v. Interstate/Johnson Lane Corp.

500 U.S. 20 (1991)

Justice White delivered the opinion of the Court.

The question presented in this case is whether a claim under the Age Discrimination in Employment Act of 1967 (ADEA), 81 Stat. 602, as amended, 29 U.S.C. § 621 et seq., can be subjected to compulsory arbitration pursuant to an arbitration agreement in a securities registration application. The Court of Appeals held that it could, 895 F.2d 195 (C.A.4 1990), and we affirm.

I

Respondent Interstate/Johnson Lane Corporation (Interstate) hired petitioner Robert Gilmer as a Manager of Financial Services in May 1981. As required by his employment, Gilmer registered as a securities representative with several stock exchanges, including the New York Stock Exchange (NYSE). His registration application, entitled "Uniform Application for Securities Industry Registration or Transfer," provided, among other things, that Gilmer "agree[d] to arbitrate any dispute, claim or controversy" arising between him and Interstate "that is required to be arbitrated under the rules, constitutions or by-laws of the organizations with which I register." Of relevance to this case, NYSE Rule 347 provides for arbitration of "[a]ny controversy between a registered representative and any member or member organization arising out of the employment or termination of employment of such registered representative."

Interstate terminated Gilmer's employment in 1987, at which time Gilmer was 62 years of age. After first filing an age discrimination charge with the Equal Employment Opportunity Commission (EEOC), Gilmer subsequently brought suit in the United States District Court for the Western District of North Carolina.

In response to Gilmer's complaint, Interstate filed in the District Court a motion to compel arbitration of the ADEA claim.

The District Court denied Interstate's motion, based on this Court's decision in Alexander v. Gardner-Denver Co., 415 U.S. 36 (1974), and because it concluded that "Congress intended to protect ADEA claimants from the waiver of a judicial forum." The United States Court of Appeals for the Fourth Circuit reversed, finding "nothing in the text, legislative history, or underlying purposes of the ADEA indicating a congressional intent to preclude enforcement of arbitration agreements." 895 F.2d at 197. We granted certiorari, 498 U.S. 809 (1990), to resolve a conflict among the Courts of Appeals regarding the arbitrability of ADEA claims.[1]

II

The FAA [Federal Arbitration Act] was originally enacted in 1925, 43 Stat. 883, and then reenacted and codified in 1947 as Title 9 of the United States Code. Its purpose was to reverse the longstanding judicial hostility to arbitration agreements that had existed at English common law and had been adopted by American courts, and to place arbitration

1. Compare the decision below with Nicholson v. CPC Int'l Inc., 877 F.2d 221 (C.A.3 1989).

agreements upon the same footing as other contracts. Dean Witter Reynolds Inc. v. Byrd, 470 U.S. 213, 219-220, and n.6 (1985); Scherk v. Alberto-Culver Co., 417 U.S. 506, 510, n.4 (1974). Its primary substantive provision states that "[a] written provision in any maritime transaction or a contract evidencing a transaction involving commerce to settle by arbitration a controversy thereafter arising out of such contract or transaction . . . shall be valid, irrevocable, and enforceable, save upon such grounds as exist at law or in equity for the revocation of any contract." 9 U.S.C. § 2. The FAA also provides for stays of proceedings in federal district courts when an issue in the proceeding is referable to arbitration, § 3, and for orders compelling arbitration when one party has failed, neglected, or refused to comply with an arbitration agreement, § 4. These provisions manifest a "liberal federal policy favoring arbitration agreements." Moses H. Cone Memorial Hospital v. Mercury Construction Corp., 460 U.S. 1, 24 (1983).

It is by now clear that statutory claims may be the subject of an arbitration agreement, enforceable pursuant to the FAA. Indeed, in recent years we have held enforceable arbitration agreements relating to claims arising under the Sherman Act, 15 U.S.C. §§ 1-7; § 10(b) of the Securities Exchange Act of 1934, 15 U.S.C. § 78j(b); the civil provisions of the Racketeer Influenced and Corrupt Organizations Act (RICO), 18 U.S.C. §§ 1961 et seq.; and § 12(2) of the Securities Act of 1933, 15 U.S.C. § 771(2). See Mitsubishi Motors Corp. v. Soler Chrysler-Plymouth, Inc., 473 U.S. 614 (1985); Shearson/American Express Inc. v. McMahon, 482 U.S. 220 (1987); Rodriguez de Quijas v. Shearson/American Express, Inc., 490 U.S. 477 (1989). In these cases we recognized that "[b]y agreeing to arbitrate a statutory claim, a party does not forgo the substantive rights afforded by the statute; it only submits to their resolution in an arbitral, rather than a judicial, forum." *Mitsubishi,* 473 U.S. at 628.

Although all statutory claims may not be appropriate for arbitration, "[h]aving made the bargain to arbitrate, the party should be held to it unless Congress itself has evinced an intention to preclude a waiver of judicial remedies for the statutory rights at issue." Ibid. In this regard, we note that the burden is on Gilmer to show that Congress intended to preclude a waiver of a judicial forum for ADEA claims. See *McMahon,* 482 U.S. at 227. If such an intention exists, it will be discoverable in the text of the ADEA, its legislative history, or an "inherent conflict" between arbitration and the ADEA's underlying purposes. See ibid. Throughout such an inquiry, it should be kept in mind that "questions of arbitrability must be addressed with a healthy regard for the federal policy favoring arbitration." *Moses H. Cone,* 460 U.S. at 24.

III

Gilmer concedes that nothing in the text of the ADEA or its legislative history explicitly precludes arbitration. He argues, however, that compulsory arbitration of ADEA claims pursuant to arbitration agreements would be inconsistent with the statutory framework and purposes of the ADEA. Like the Court of Appeals, we disagree.

A

Congress enacted the ADEA in 1967 "to promote employment of older persons based on their ability rather than age; to prohibit arbitrary age discrimination in employment; [and] to help employers and workers find ways of meeting problems arising from the impact of age on employment." 29 U.S.C. § 621(b). To achieve those goals, the ADEA, among other things, makes it unlawful for an employer "to fail or refuse to hire or to discharge any individual or otherwise discriminate against any individual with respect to his compensation, terms, conditions, or privileges of employment, because of such individual's age." § 623(a)(1). This proscription is enforced both by private suits and by the EEOC. In order for an aggrieved individual to bring suit under the ADEA, he or she must first file a charge with the EEOC and then wait at least 60 days. § 626(d). An individual's right to sue is extinguished, however, if the EEOC institutes an action against the employer. § 626(c)(1). Before the EEOC can bring such an action, though, it must "attempt to eliminate the discriminatory practice or practices alleged, and to effect voluntary compliance with the requirements of this chapter through informal methods of conciliation, conference, and persuasion." § 626(b); see also 29 C.F.R. § 1626.15 (1990).

As Gilmer contends, the ADEA is designed not only to address individual grievances, but also to further important social policies. See, e.g., EEOC v. Wyoming, 460 U.S. 226, 231 (1983). We do not perceive any inherent inconsistency between those policies, however, and enforcing agreements to arbitrate age discrimination claims. It is true that arbitration focuses on specific disputes between the parties involved. The same can be said, however, of judicial resolution of claims. Both of these dispute resolution mechanisms nevertheless also can further broader social purposes. The Sherman Act, the Securities Exchange Act of 1934, RICO, and the Securities Act of 1933 all are designed to advance important public policies, but, as noted above, claims under those statutes are appropriate for arbitration. "[S]o long as the prospective litigant effectively may vindicate [his or her] statutory cause of action in the arbitral forum, the statute will continue to serve both its remedial and deterrent function." *Mitsubishi*, supra, at 637.

We also are unpersuaded by the argument that arbitration will undermine the role of the EEOC in enforcing the ADEA. An individual ADEA claimant subject to an arbitration agreement will still be free to file a charge with the EEOC, even though the claimant is not able to institute a private judicial action. Indeed, Gilmer filed a charge with the EEOC in this case. In any event, the EEOC's role in combating age discrimination is not dependent on the filing of a charge; the agency may receive information concerning alleged violations of the ADEA "from any source," and it has independent authority to investigate age discrimination. . . .

Gilmer also argues that compulsory arbitration is improper because it deprives claimants of the judicial forum provided for by the ADEA. Congress, however, did not explicitly preclude arbitration or other non-judicial resolution of claims, even in its recent amendments to the ADEA. "[I]f Congress intended the substantive protection afforded [by the ADEA] to include protection against waiver of the right to a judicial forum, that intention will be deducible from text or legislative history." *Mitsubishi,* 473 U.S. at 628. Moreover, Gilmer's argument ignores the ADEA's flexible approach to resolution of claims. The EEOC, for example, is directed to pursue "informal methods of conciliation, conference, and persuasion," 29 U.S.C. § 626(b), which suggests that out-of-court dispute resolution, such as arbitration, is consistent with the statutory scheme established by Congress. . .

B

In arguing that arbitration is inconsistent with the ADEA, Gilmer also raises a host of challenges to the adequacy of arbitration procedures. Initially, we note that in our recent arbitration cases we have already rejected most of these arguments as insufficient to preclude arbitration of statutory claims. . . .

Gilmer first speculates that arbitration panels will be biased. However, "[w]e decline to indulge the presumption that the parties and arbitral body conducting a proceeding will be unable or unwilling to retain competent, conscientious and impartial arbitrators." *Mitsubishi,* supra, at 634. In any event, we note that the NYSE arbitration rules, which are applicable to the dispute in this case, provide protections against biased panels. The rules require, for example, that the parties be informed of the employment histories of the arbitrators, and that they be allowed to make further inquiries into the arbitrators' backgrounds. In addition, each party is allowed one peremptory challenge and unlimited challenges for cause. Moreover, the arbitrators are required to disclose "any circumstances which might preclude [them] from rendering an objective and impartial determination." . .

Gilmer also complains that the discovery allowed in arbitration is more limited than in the federal courts, which he contends will make it difficult to prove discrimination. It is unlikely, however, that age discrimination claims require more extensive discovery than other claims that we have found to be arbitrable, such as RICO and antitrust claims. Moreover, there has been no showing in this case that the NYSE discovery provisions, which allow for document production, information requests, depositions, and subpoenas, will prove insufficient to allow ADEA claimants such as Gilmer a fair opportunity to present their claims. Although those procedures might not be as extensive as in the federal courts, by agreeing to arbitrate, a party "trades the procedures and opportunity for review of the courtroom for the simplicity, informality, and expedition of arbitration." *Mitsubishi,* supra, at 628. Indeed, an important counterweight to the reduced discovery in NYSE arbitration is that arbitrators are not bound by the rules of evidence.

A further alleged deficiency of arbitration is that arbitrators often will not issue written opinions, resulting, Gilmer contends, in a lack of public knowledge of employers' discriminatory policies, an inability to obtain effective appellate review, and a stifling of the development of the law. The NYSE rules, however, do require that all arbitration awards be in writing, and that the awards contain the names of the parties, a summary of the issues in controversy, and a description of the award issued. In addition, the award decisions are made available to the public. Furthermore, judicial decisions addressing ADEA claims will continue to be issued because it is unlikely that all or even most ADEA claimants will be subject to arbitration agreements. Finally, Gilmer's concerns apply equally to settlements of ADEA claims, which, as noted above, are clearly allowed.

It is also argued that arbitration procedures cannot adequately further the purposes of the ADEA because they do not provide for broad equitable relief and class actions. As the court below noted, however, arbitrators do have the power to fashion equitable relief. 895 F.2d, at 199-200. Indeed, the NYSE rules applicable here do not restrict the types of relief an arbitrator may award, but merely refer to "damages and/or other relief." The NYSE rules also provide for collective proceedings. But "even if the arbitration could not go forward as a class action or class relief could not be granted by the arbitrator, the fact that the [ADEA] provides for the possibility of bringing a collective action does not mean that individual attempts at conciliation were intended to be barred." Nicholson v. CPC Intl. Inc., 877 F.2d 221, 241 (3d. Cir. 1989) (Becker, J., dissenting). Finally, it should be remembered that arbitration agreements will not preclude the EEOC from bringing actions seeking class-wide and equitable relief.

C

An additional reason advanced by Gilmer for refusing to enforce arbitration agreements relating to ADEA claims is his contention that there often will be unequal bargaining power between employers and employees. Mere inequality in bargaining power, however, is not a sufficient reason to hold that arbitration agreements are never enforceable in the employment context. Relationships between securities dealers and investors, for example, may involve unequal bargaining power, but we nevertheless held in *Rodriguez de Quijas* and *McMahon* that agreements to arbitrate in that context are enforceable. See 490 U.S. at 484; 482 U.S. at 230. As discussed above, the FAA's purpose was to place arbitration agreements on the same footing as other contracts. Thus, arbitration agreements are enforceable "save upon such grounds as exist at law or in equity for the revocation of any contract." 9 U.S.C. § 2. "Of course, courts should remain attuned to well-supported claims that the agreement to arbitrate resulted from the sort of fraud or overwhelming economic power that would provide grounds 'for the revocation of any contract.'" *Mitsubishi,* 473 U.S. at 627. There is no indication in this case, however, that Gilmer, an experienced businessman, was coerced or defrauded into agreeing to the arbitration clause in his registration application. As with the claimed procedural inadequacies discussed above, this claim of unequal bargaining power is best left for resolution in specific cases. . . .

V

We conclude that Gilmer has not met his burden of showing that Congress, in enacting the ADEA, intended to preclude arbitration of claims under that Act. Accordingly, the judgment of the Court of Appeals is

Affirmed.

JUSTICE STEVENS, with whom JUSTICE MARSHALL joins, dissenting.

Section 1 of the Federal Arbitration Act (FAA) states:

> [N]othing herein contained shall apply to contracts of employment of seamen, railroad employees, or any other class of workers engaged in foreign or interstate commerce.

9 U.S.C. § 1. The Court today, in holding that the FAA compels enforcement of arbitration clauses even when claims of age discrimination are at issue, skirts the antecedent question whether the coverage of the Act even extends to arbitration clauses contained in employment contracts, regardless of the subject matter of the claim at issue. In my opinion, arbitration clauses contained in employment agreements are specifically exempt from coverage of the FAA, and for that reason respondent Interstate/Johnson Lane Corporation cannot, pursuant to the FAA, compel petitioner to submit his claims arising under the Age Discrimination in Employment Act to binding arbitration. . . .

There is little dispute that the primary concern animating the FAA was the perceived need by the business community to overturn the common-law rule that denied specific enforcement of agreements to arbitrate in contracts between business entities. The Act was drafted by a committee of the American Bar Association (ABA), acting upon instructions from the ABA to consider and report upon "the further extension of the principle of commercial arbitration." Report of the Forty-third Annual Meeting of the ABA, 45 A.B.A. Rep. 75 (1920). At the Senate Judiciary Subcommittee hearings on the proposed bill, the chairman of the ABA committee responsible for drafting the bill assured the Senators that the bill "is not intended [to] be an act referring to labor disputes, at all. It is purely an act to give the merchants the right or the privilege of sitting down and agreeing with each other as to what their damages are, if they want to do it. Now that is all there is in this." Hearing on S. 4213 and S. 4214 before a

Subcommittee of the Senate Committee on the Judiciary, 67th Cong., 4th Sess., 9 (1923). At the same hearing, Senator Walsh stated:

> The trouble about the matter is that a great many of these contracts that are entered into are really not [voluntary] things at all. Take an insurance policy; there is a blank in it. You can take that or you can leave it. The agent has no power at all to decide it. Either you can make that contract or you can not make any contract. It is the same with a good many contracts of employment. A man says, "These are our terms. All right, take it or leave it." Well, there is nothing for the man to do except to sign it; and then he surrenders his right to have his case tried by the court, and has to have it tried before a tribunal in which he has no confidence at all.

Ibid. . . .

Not only would I find that the FAA does not apply to employment-related disputes between employers and employees in general, but also I would hold that compulsory arbitration conflicts with the congressional purpose animating the ADEA, in particular. As this Court previously has noted, authorizing the courts to issue broad injunctive relief is the cornerstone to eliminating discrimination in society. Albemarle Paper Co. v. Moody, 422 U.S. 405, 415 (1975). The ADEA, like Title VII of the Civil Rights Act of 1964, authorizes courts to award broad, class-based injunctive relief to achieve the purposes of the Act. 29 U.S.C. § 626(b). Because commercial arbitration is typically limited to a specific dispute between the particular parties and because the available remedies in arbitral forums generally do not provide for class-wide injunctive relief, see Shell, ERISA and Other Federal Employment Statutes: When Is Commercial Arbitration an "Adequate Substitute" for the Courts?, 68 Texas L. Rev. 509, 568 (1990), I would conclude that an essential purpose of the ADEA is frustrated by compulsory arbitration of employment discrimination claims. Moreover, as Chief Justice Burger explained:

> Plainly, it would not comport with the congressional objectives behind a statute seeking to enforce civil rights protected by Title VII to allow the very forces that had practiced discrimination to contract away the right to enforce civil rights in the courts. For federal courts to defer to arbitral decisions reached by the same combination of forces that had long perpetuated invidious discrimination would have made the foxes guardians of the chickens.

Barrentine v. Arkansas-Best Freight System, Inc., 450 U.S. 728, 750 (1981) (dissenting opinion). In my opinion the same concerns expressed by Chief Justice Burger with regard to compulsory arbitration of Title VII claims may be said of claims arising under the ADEA. The Court's holding today clearly eviscerates the important role played by an independent judiciary in eradicating employment discrimination.

Note: Arbitration Procedure

Although there are many different types of arbitration, they have in common informal procedures that are less adversarial than the usual civil trial. Parties may choose not to be represented by counsel, and though both sides have an opportunity to present witnesses, physical evidence, and documents, and to challenge the other side's presentation, the rules of evidence and of civil procedure (particularly elaborate discovery) are largely abandoned. As a result, the arbitrator's decision, called an "award," may be rendered quickly on the basis of the arbitrator's general sense of fairness under the circumstances rather than on legal norms.

Choosing arbitration is generally up to the parties at the time of contracting. However, many contracts, like our problem case, provide for procedures in accordance with the American Arbitration Association rules. Compare, for example, the tone of the following excerpt from the Association's Commercial Arbitration Rules to the general tone of the Federal Rules of Civil Procedure:

> It cannot be denied that a large part of what goes on in hearings is people getting things off their chests, and this, of course, bears on your attitude toward evidentiary problems as they arise. The arbitrator's basic problem is to find out as much as possible about what really happened.

Am. Arbitration Assn. R. 29.

Many arbitration clauses specify the venue for the event, for example, where the plaintiff lives or where the claim arose, while others may set venue in the location of the defendant's home office. What are the practical reasons for settling the place of arbitration in advance?

*Note: Post-*Gilmer *Developments*

The United States Supreme Court has held that a union cannot bind nonmember, nonunion employees to arbitration over a union's agency fees if the employees have not agreed to arbitration. Arbitration is inappropriate where one party has not agreed to that remedy. See Air Line Pilots Assn. v. Miller, 523 U.S. 866 (1998). And in suits to compel arbitration under the Federal Arbitration Act, "[t]he question whether the parties have submitted a particular dispute to arbitration, i.e., the *'question of arbitrability,'* is an issue for judicial determination unless the parties clearly and unmistakably provide otherwise." Howsam v. Dean Witter Reynolds, Inc., 537 U.S. 79, 83 (2002). Compare Spahr v. Secco, 330 F.3d 1266 (10th Cir. 2003) (court, not arbitrator, has power to rule on mental capacity challenge to arbitration clause in contract between customer and stockbroker where stockbroker and her firm seek to compel arbitration under FAA), with Primerica Life Ins. Co. v. Brown, 304 F.3d 469 (5th Cir. 2002) (mental capacity defense is for arbitrator to decide), *distinguished in*

Will-Drill Resources Inc. v. Samson Resources Co., 352 F.3d 211, 218 (5th Cir. 2003) ("Where the very existence of any agreement is disputed, it is for the courts to decide at the outset whether an agreement was reached, applying state-law principles of contract.").

The Court also decided Wright v. Universal Maritime Service Corp., 525 U.S. 70 (1998). The Court in *Wright* was asked to consider whether arbitration is mandatory where the union negotiated for arbitration, but an individual seeks to pursue a judicial remedy of an Americans With Disabilities Act (ADA) claim. Wright had argued that because the collective bargaining agreement did not specifically address ADA claims, the Fourth Circuit precedent that treats collective bargaining agreements to arbitrate employment disputes as binding upon individual employees was inapplicable. The Fourth Circuit disagreed, on the grounds that the arbitration clause was particularly broad (covering "all matters affecting wages, hours, and other terms and conditions of employment") and that " [a]n employer need not provide a laundry list of potential disputes in order for them to be covered by an arbitration clause." 121 F.3d 702 (4th Cir. 1997) (unpublished opinion).

The United States Supreme Court reversed the Fourth Circuit in a unanimous opinion written by Justice Scalia. 525 U.S. 70 (1998). The Court concluded that it was unnecessary to resolve a union-negotiated waiver of employees' statutory right to a federal forum, because no such waiver had occurred in this case. The collective bargaining agreement in question had not clearly and unmistakably waived the employees' right to litigate claims under the ADA. Id. at 79-82.

The Court in *Wright* did not resolve a difficult problem that lower courts faced, post-*Gilmer* and post-*Gardner-Denver,* i.e., how to determine the implications and limits of the Court's holding that federal statutory claims may in certain circumstances be submitted to arbitration where a party so contracts, and where the *Gilmer* conditions are met. For example, in Pryner v. Tractor Supply Co., 109 F.3d 354 (7th Cir.), *cert. denied,* 572 U.S. 912 (1997), the Seventh Circuit held in an opinion by Judge Posner that a collective bargaining agreement cannot compel arbitration of a federal anti-discrimination claim by an individual employee. Posner noted that the worker has not necessarily agreed to arbitration in this situation simply because the union has. Cf. EEOC v. Luce, 345 F.3d 742 (9th Cir. 2003); Austin v. Owens-Brockway Glass Container, Inc., 78 F.3d 875 (4th Cir. 1996), *cert. denied,* 519 U.S. 980 (1996) (holding that employees can be compelled to submit Title VII and ADA claims to binding arbitration pursuant to a collective bargaining agreement); see also Bercovitch v. Baldwin School, Inc., 133 F.3d 141 (1st Cir. 1998) (holding that plaintiffs may be compelled to arbitrate ADA claims pursuant to voluntary, pre-dispute agreements); Miller v. Public Storage Mgmt., Inc., 121 F.3d 215 (5th Cir. 1997) (same); Nelson v. Cyprus Bagdad Copper Corp., 119 F.3d 756 (9th Cir. 1997), *cert. denied,* 523 U.S. 1072 (1998) (holding that by signing a form acknowledging that he had read the employee handbook that contained an arbitration provision employee did not waive right to sue under the ADA).

Along with the foregoing conflict over whether unions may bargain away employees' rights to litigate federal statutory claims is a debate over the scope of the Federal Arbitration Act. In Circuit City Stores, Inc. v. Adams, 532 U.S. 105 (2001), the Court held that the Act applies to most employment contracts, and exempts only contracts involving interstate transportation workers. A key aspect of the decision was the Court's conclusion that an arbitration agreement can cover both an employee's federal and state employment law claims. In the wake of *Circuit City*, employees have sought, with mixed success, to avoid arbitration by arguing either that no contract was formed, compare Campbell v. Gen. Dynamics Govt. Sys. Corp., 407 F.3d 546 (1st Cir. 2005) (mass e-mail regarding arbitration policy not enforceable contract), with Gold v. Deutsche AG, 365 F.3d 144 (2d Cir. 2004) (arbitration agreement enforceable where employee signed but did not read form); or by arguing that the arbitration agreement is unconscionable. See, e.g., Alexander v. Anthony Int'l, L.P., 341 F.3d 256 (3d Cir. 2003) (invalidating agreement that imposed a 30-day limitations period on employee but not employer claims, and shifted fees to the loser); Circuit City Stores Inc. v. Adams, 279 F.3d 889 (9th Cir. 2002) (invalidating adhesion contract that required employee, but not employer, to arbitrate disputes, shifted fees, and severely limited remedies); Gannon v. Circuit City Stores Inc., 262 F.3d 677 (8th Cir. 2001) (remanding after severing clause limiting punitive damages to $5,000).

The Court also has held that employee-employer agreements to arbitrate employment-related disputes do not bar the federal Equal Employment Opportunity Commission from pursuing judicial relief, including damages, against an employer who violates federal employment laws. See EEOC v. Waffle House, Inc., 534 U.S. 279 (2002).

Finally, the Court held in a unanimous opinion that the proper course was to compel arbitration of a claim where an arbitration agreement imposed remedial limits on such a claim, but the limits were ambiguous. The arbitrator should have been given an opportunity to construe the ambiguous terms of the agreement. PacifiCare Health Sys., Inc. v. Book, 538 U.S. 401 (2003).

As *Gilmer* and these other cases show, the United States Supreme Court has entered a period of favoring arbitration. Southland Corp. v. Keating, 465 U.S. 1 (1984), was the first extremely broad-based Supreme Court case supporting arbitration. See also Allied-Bruce Terminix Companies, Inc. v. Dobson, 513 U.S. 265 (1995). In recent years, the Court has held that the Federal Arbitration Act compels enforcement of private agreements to arbitrate statutory claims arising under antitrust, securities, and racketeering laws. Mitsubishi Motors Corp. v. Soler Chrysler-Plymouth, Inc., 473 U.S. 614 (1985); Shearson Am. Express, Inc. v. McNulty, 482 U.S. 220 (1987); see also Tenaska Washington Partners II v. United States, 34 Fed. Cl. 434 (1995) (holding that there is no constitutional impediment to allowing federal agencies to enter into agreements to submit to binding arbitration, provided a given agency has the statutory authority to do so).

Note: Paying for Private Justice

Still another issue raised by mandatory arbitration is: who pays for it? The Court of Appeals for the District of Columbia has concluded that where arbitration occurs solely because it is mandated by an employer as a condition of employment, the employer must bear the expense of the arbitrator's fees, given that the employee otherwise could have pursued his or her claims in court without having to pay for the judge's services. Cole v. Burns Int'l Sec. Servs., 105 F.3d 1465 (D.C. Cir. 1997); see also Shankle v. B-G Maint. Mgmt. of Colo., Inc., 163 F.3d 1230, 1235 (10th Cir. 1999) (arbitration agreement requiring litigant to pay half of arbitration costs "failed to provide an accessible forum in which [litigant] could resolve his statutory rights"); Paladino v. Avnet Computer Tech., Inc., 134 F.3d 1054, 1062 (11th Cir. 1999); Armendariz v. Found. Health Psychcare Servs., 6 P.3d 669 (Cal. 2000). But see Rosenberg v. Merrill Lynch, Pierce, Fenner & Smith, Inc., 170 F.3d 1 (1st Cir. 1999) (upholding arbitration requirement that charged plaintiffs forum fees).

The Supreme Court reached a similar issue in a non-employment context, suggesting, without deciding, that large arbitration costs foisted on a consumer by virtue of her contract with a mobile home dealer could invalidate the arbitration clause:

> It may well be that the existence of large arbitration costs could preclude a litigant such as Randolph from effectively vindicating her rights in the arbitral forum.

Green Tree Fin. Corp. v. Randolph, 531 U.S. 79, 90 (2000). The Court remanded the case because the plaintiff had not offered any proof on the likely costs of arbitration that she would face.

After *Green Tree*, circuit courts have agreed that fee-splitting clauses, which require employees to share the costs of arbitration, "can render an arbitration agreement unenforceable where the arbitration fees and costs are so prohibitive as to effectively deny the employee access to the arbitral forum," but there is division between the few courts that struck down such provisions per se, as in *Cole*, and the majority that now read *Green Tree* to require case-by-case review of the burdens imposed by such provisions. Bradford v. Rockwell Semiconductor Sys., Inc., 238 F.3d 549, 554 (4th Cir. 2001) (rejecting *Cole*'s per se rule against fee splitting and adopting a case-by-case approach). In *Bradford*, for example, the Fourth Circuit upheld the arbitration agreement at issue, reasoning that the employee failed to prove that he was unable to pay the $4,470 in arbitration costs he was billed:

> Indeed, this case presents a paradigmatic example of why fee-splitting should not be deemed to automatically render an arbitration agreement unenforceable because Bradford was in no way deterred from attempting to vindicate his rights by means of a full and fair arbitration proceeding.

> Invalidating the arbitration provision now, after the arbitrator has ruled upon his claim, would simply give Bradford a second bite at the apple under circumstances in which there is no evidence that allowing him to pursue his litigation in court would cost him any less than the amount of money that he has already spent in arbitration.

238 F.3d at 558 (suggesting that individuals who object to fee splitting raise their objection prior to the beginning of arbitration); see also LaPrade v. Kidder, Peabody & Co. Inc., 246 F.3d 702, 708 (D.C. Cir. 2001) (upholding arbitration award where plaintiff was required to pay $8,376 in forum fees).

As you might expect, results have varied among courts following the case-by-case approach. In contrast to *Bradford*, the Sixth Circuit, sitting en banc, adopted a broader test for assessing the burdens imposed on litigants, holding that "[a] cost-splitting provision should be held unenforceable whenever it would have the 'chilling effect' of deterring a substantial number of potential litigants from seeking to vindicate their statutory rights." Morrison v. Circuit City Stores, Inc., 317 F.3d 646, 661 (6th Cir. 2003). Although Morrison would have had to pay, at most, only $1,622, the court pointed to studies showing that:

> [A] plaintiff forced to arbitrate a typical $60,000 employment discrimination claim will incur costs . . . that range from three to nearly *fifty* times the basic costs of litigating in a judicial, rather than an arbitral, forum . . . [, that] the average arbitrator fee was $700 per day and that an average employment case incurred a total of $3,750 to $14,000 in arbitration expenses.

Id. at 669. The court rejected the cost-splitting provision on those grounds. As the court reasoned:

> We believe that the following propositions of law can be derived from *Green Tree.* First, in some cases, the potential of incurring large arbitration costs and fees will deter potential litigants from seeking to vindicate their rights in the arbitral forum. Under *Gilmer,* the arbitral forum must provide litigants with an effective substitute for the judicial forum; if the fees and costs of the arbitral forum deter potential litigants, then that forum is clearly not an effective, or even adequate, substitute for the judicial forum. Second, where that prospect deters potential litigants, the arbitration agreement, or at minimum, the cost-splitting provision contained within it, is unenforceable under *Gilmer.* Third, the burden of demonstrating that incurring such costs is likely under a given set of circumstances rests, at least initially, with the party opposing arbitration. . . .
>
> In analyzing this issue, reviewing courts should consider the costs of litigation as the alternative to arbitration, as in *Bradford*, but they must weigh the potential costs of litigation in a realistic manner. In many, if not most, cases, employees (and former employees) bringing discrimination claims will be represented by attorneys on a contingency-fee basis. Thus, many litigants will face minimal costs in the judicial forum, as the attorney will cover most of the fees of litigation and advance the expenses incurred

> in discovery.... In the arbitral forum, the litigant faces an additional expense—the arbitrator's fees and costs—which are never incurred in the judicial forum. Reviewing courts must consider whether the litigant will incur this additional expense and whether that expense, taken together with the other costs and expenses of the differing fora, would deter potential litigants from bringing their statutory claims in the arbitral forum....
>
> In the abstract [the costs of the arbitral forum] may not appear prohibitive, but it must be considered from the vantage point of the potential litigant in a case such as this. Recently terminated, the potential litigant must continue to pay for housing, utilities, transportation, food, and the other necessities of life in contemporary society despite losing her primary, and most likely only, source of income. Unless she is exceedingly fortunate, the potential litigant will experience at least a brief period of unemployment. Turning to the arbitration agreement with her employer, the potential litigant finds that, as the default rule, she will be obligated to pay half the costs of any arbitration which she initiates.
>
> Minimal research will reveal that the potential costs of arbitrating the dispute easily reach thousands, if not tens of thousands, of dollars, far exceeding the costs that a plaintiff would incur in court. Courts charge plaintiffs initial filing fees, but they do not charge extra for in-person hearings, discovery requests, routine motions, or written decisions, costs that are all common in the world of private arbitrators.

Id. at 659-660, 664, 669. The court rejected fee splitting notwithstanding the fact that the arbitration agreement included a provision limiting the employee's exposure to arbitration costs to the greater of $500 or 3 percent of her annual compensation. Such a clause, the court reasoned, "really boils down to risking one's scarce resources in the hopes of an uncertain benefit—it appears to us that a substantial number of similarly situated persons would be deterred from seeking to vindicate their statutory rights under these circumstances." Id. at 670. See also Ingle v. Circuit City Stores, Inc., 328 F.3d 1165, 1177-1178 (9th Cir. 2003) (finding fee-splitting agreement unconscionable on grounds that it gave discretion to arbitrator to require employee to pay total costs of arbitration if employer prevailed while employer would only have to pay half if employee prevailed).

Although the holdings vary, you can see from these cases that employers and retailers have continued to insist on arbitration clauses, and, where possible, fee splitting. The growing trend toward pre-dispute, compelled arbitration and its potential abuses made front-page news in March of 1997. See Barry Meier, In Fine Print, Customers Lose Ability to Sue, N.Y. Times, Mar. 10, 1997, at A1 (noting that "[o]n many occasions, companies have unilaterally wiped out customers' rights to sue by sending out notices of new arbitration requirements in the form of envelope stuffers"). Courts likewise have concluded that arbitration agreements can contain unfairly one-sided terms. See Hooters of Am., Inc. v. Phillips, 173 F.3d 933 (4th Cir. 1999) (holding terms were egregiously unfair to employees).

Note: Justifying Private Justice

For a critique of the trend toward arbitration, see Jean R. Sternlight, Panacea or Corporate Tool?: Debunking the Supreme Court's Preference for Binding Arbitration, 74 Wash. U. L.Q. 637 (1996); Jean R. Sternlight and Elizabeth J. Jensen, Using Arbitration to Eliminate Consumer Class Actions: Efficient Business Practice or Unconscionable Abuse?, 67 Law & Contemp. Probs. 75 (2004).

The data on the impact of arbitration are mixed. In a recent empirical examination of employment arbitration supporting the process, Sherwyn, Estreicher, and Heise summarized the findings of prior studies as follows:

> First, there is no evidence that plaintiffs fare significantly better in litigation. In fact, the opposite may be true. Second, arbitration is faster. Because employment dispute resolution can be both heart wrenching and financially crippling, a quicker resolution is a positive. Third, the question of damages is too difficult to determine based on the available data. While the strongest consensus exists with respect to disposition time, further research is warranted on all three factors, especially on the questions of win/loss records and damages. Of course . . . data will not answer the critical nonempirical questions that greatly influence the debate.

Assessing The Case for Employment Arbitration, 57 Stan. L. Rev. 1557, 1578 (2005); see also id. at 1573-1577 (discussing studies showing *lower* awards generated by arbitration relative to litigation).

The authors further contend that mandatory arbitration is particularly attractive to employers "with a high volume of low-value claims" because (1) quick, efficient resolution minimizes costs, and (2) employers "are tired of what we call 'de facto severance' and wish to limit the value and incidence of nuisance settlements":

> Because it costs employers (1) between $4000 and $10,000 to defend an EEOC charge, (2) at least $75,000 to take a case to summary judgment, and (3) at least $125,000 and possibly over $500,000 to defend a case at trial, it almost always makes good business sense to settle a case for $4000. In other words, it makes economic sense to pay an employee with a salary of $48,000 per year . . . what amounts to one month's severance pay if the employee simply files an EEOC charge. . . . Mandatory arbitration arguably ends de facto severance because arbitration lowers the costs of defense, including potentially adverse publicity. Instead, employers can defend those claims that they believe are baseless.
>
> At the same time that arbitration reduces employers' incentive to settle baseless claims, arbitration programs reduce employers' ability to defeat meritorious claims by delaying or "big firming" the employee into a withdrawal or substandard settlement.

Id. at 1579-1580.

Other, more skeptical scholarship on arbitration includes the following: Paul D. Carrington and Paul H. Haagen, Contract and Jurisdiction, 1996 Sup. Ct. Rev. 331 (commenting on adverse effects of compulsory arbitration in commercial contexts); Developments in the Law, Employment Discrimination, Mandatory Arbitration of Statutory Employment Disputes, 109 Harv. L. Rev. 1568, 1670, 1692 (1996); Samuel Estreicher, Predispute Agreements to Arbitrate Statutory Employment Claims, 72 N.Y.U. L. Rev. 1344 (1997); Stephan Landsman, ADR and the Costs of Compulsion, 57 Stan. L. Rev. 1593 (2005); Carrie Menkel-Meadow, What Will We Do When Adjudication Ends?, 44 UCLA L. Rev. 1613 (1997); Frank E. Sander, H. William Allen, and Debra Hensler, Judicial (Mis)use of ADR: A Debate, 27 U. Tol. L. Rev. 885 (1996); David S. Schwartz, Enforcing Small Print to Protect Big Business: Employee and Consumer Rights in an Age of Compelled Arbitration, 1997 Wis. L. Rev. 33; Jean R. Sternlight, Compelling Arbitration of Claims Under the Civil Rights Act of 1866: What Congress Could Not Have Intended, 47 U. Kan. L. Rev. 273 (1999); Jean R. Sternlight, Creeping Mandatory Arbitration: Is it Just?, 57 Stan. L. Rev. 1631 (2005); Jean R. Sternlight, Rethinking the Constitutionality of the Supreme Court's Preference for Binding Arbitration: A Fresh Assessment of Jury Trial, Separation of Powers, and Due Process Concerns, 72 Tul. L. Rev. 1 (1997).

In a recent work, Deborah Hensler insists that "there are . . . important political values that derive from widespread access to, and use of, the public justice system" that are missing in ADR systems:

> The public spectacle of civil litigation gives life to the "rule of law." To demonstrate that the law's authority can be mobilized by the least powerful as well as the most powerful in society, we need to observe employees and consumers successfully suing large corporations and government agencies, minority group members successfully suing majority group members, and persons engaged in unpopular activities establishing their legal rights to continue those activities. Dispute resolution behind closed doors precludes such observation. In a democracy where many people are shut out of legislative power either because they are too few in number, or too dispersed to elect representatives, or because they do not have the financial resources to influence legislators, collective litigation in class or other mass form provides an alternative strategy for group action. Private individualized dispute resolution extinguishes the possibility of such collective litigation. Conciliation has much to recommend it. But the visible presence of institutionalized and legitimized conflict, channeled productively, teaches citizens that it is not always better to compromise and accept the status quo because, sometimes, great gains are to be had by peaceful contest.

Deborah R. Hensler, Our Courts, Ourselves: How the Alternative Dispute Resolution Movement Is Re-Shaping Our Legal System, 108 Penn St. L. Rev. 165, 196-197 (2003). ADR, she adds, often does not significantly reduce the average time or average transaction costs of dispute resolution, id. at 179-180, 188. See also Kenneth S. Abraham and J.W. Montgomery III, The Lawlessness of Arbitration, 9 Conn. Ins. L.J. 355 (2003); Thomas E.

Carbonneau, Arbitral Justice: The Demise of Due Process in American Law, 70 Tul. L. Rev. 1945 (1996); Bryant G. Garth, Tilting the Justice System: From ADR as Idealistic Movement to a Segmented Market in Dispute Resolution, 18 Ga. St. U. L. Rev. 927, 950-951 (2002) (arguing that by emphasizing ADR, "[w]e have created a segmented and hierarchical system skewed dramatically toward business litigants and a few other players — notably a few sectors of the personal injury bar"); Michael Z. Green, Tackling Employment Discrimination with ADR: Does Mediation Offer a Shield for the Haves or Real Opportunity for the Have-Nots?, 26 Berkeley J. Emp. & Lab. L. 321 (2005); Rex R. Perschbacher and Debra Lyn Bassett, The End of Law, 84 B.U. L. Rev. 1 (2004); Jean R. Sternlight, Is Alternative Dispute Resolution Consistent with the Rule of Law? Lessons from Abroad, 56 DePaul L. Rev. 569, 570-572 (2007) (summarizing scholarship critical of ADR).

Quite apart from arbitration is the growth of so-called claims resolution facilities, described by Deborah Hensler as "privately designed, financed, and administered organizations for giving away money, established as a result of the settlement of mass litigation in trial or bankruptcy courts." Deborah Hensler, Alternative Courts? Litigation-Induced Claims Resolution Facilities, 57 Stan. L. Rev. 1429 (2005). She notes that, in the class action, mass tort context, the "increasing resort to private claims resolution facilities to determine the eligibility for and amount of compensation for civil plaintiffs raises efficiency, equity, and due process questions that deserve broad public policy attention," but the information necessary to support broad public debate is "generally unavailable," in part because the outcomes of claims resolution facilities are "often protected from public scrutiny." Id. at 1429-1430, 1431 (listing as examples the Dalkon Shield Claimants' Trust, the asbestos-related Manville Personal Injury Trust, and the Dow Corning Silicone Gel Implant Trust).

Note: The Appealability of Arbitration Awards

One of the most common features of arbitration clauses in contracts is the nonappealability of the awards. Arbitration awards do show up in the public court system, where they may be entered as a judgment of the court to bolster their enforceability. Most arbitrations are subject to a limited right of review in the form of a motion to modify or set aside the award, but only on the grounds of the arbitrator's bias, fraud, misconduct, or abuse of discretion. In a particularly striking case, the California Supreme Court upheld an award that showed on its face an error in the law. Moncharsh v. Heily & Blase, 3 Cal. 4th 1 (1992); see also E. Assoc. Coal Corp. v. United Mine Workers of Am., Dist. 17, 531 U.S. 57, 62 (2000) ("'as long as [an honest] arbitrator is even arguably construing or applying the contract and acting within the scope of his authority,' the fact that 'a court is convinced he committed serious error does not suffice to overturn his decision'"; refusing to vacate arbitrator's award where employer challenged order reinstating employee on ground that reinstatement violated public policy against operation of dangerous machinery by workers who test positive for drugs).

Either party to an arbitration agreement may claim in court that the issue before the court is not subject to arbitration under the terms of the agreement. Under the Federal Arbitration Act, the other side may request an order compelling arbitration and dismissing the underlying litigation. When a court grants or denies such an order, the Supreme Court has held that the decision is immediately appealable. Thus, the aggrieved party need not await the outcome of arbitration before appealing the order compelling arbitration. See Green Tree Financial Corp. v. Randolph, 531 U.S. 79, 86-87 (2000).

Actions to vacate an unfavorable arbitration award are not, however, to be filed lightly. In the Seventh Circuit, for instance, a long line of cases "[has] discouraged parties from challenging arbitration awards and has upheld Rule 11 sanctions in cases where the challenge to the award was substantially without merit." CUNA Mut. Ins. Soc. v. Office & Prof'l Employees Int'l Union, Local 39, 443 F.3d 556, 561 (7th Cir. 2006). In upholding sanctions against the employer who appealed an arbitration award favoring the union, the court emphasized the following policy grounds against such appeals:

> A company dissatisfied with the decisions of labor arbitrators need not include an arbitration clause in its collective bargaining contracts, but having agreed to include such a clause it will not be permitted to nullify the advantages to the union by spinning out the arbitral process unconscionably through the filing of meritless suits and appeals. For such conduct the law authorizes sanctions that this court will not hesitate to impose. . . . Lawyers practicing in the Seventh Circuit, take heed!

Id. (quoting Dreis & Krump Mfg. Co. v. Int'l Ass'n of Machinists, Dist. No. 8, 802 F.2d 247, 255-256 (7th Cir. 1986)).

"Unconscionable" and "meritless" motions to vacate resonate with the language of Rule 11, but is an appeal that is "substantially without merit" the same as a frivolous motion under Rule 11? It may be easier to get sanctioned for appealing an arbitration award in the Seventh Circuit than for other conduct that might fall under Rule 11.

Note: Court-Annexed ADR

Thus far we have looked at private decisions to arbitrate disputes. The 1980s saw significant growth in state and federal experimentation with court-mandated, also known as "court-annexed," arbitration, often as a condition of trial. As of 1999, 33 states and 22 federal district courts provided for court-annexed arbitration by statute or local rule. See Developments: The Paths of Civil Litigation — VI. ADR, the Judiciary, and

Justice: Coming to Terms with the Alternatives, 113 Harv. L. Rev. 1851 (2000). See generally Susan Keilitz, Court-Annexed Arbitration, National Symposium on Court-Connected Dispute Resolution Research, National Center for State Courts 35 (1994); Deborah R. Hensler, What We Know and What We Don't Know About Court Administered Arbitration, 60 Judicature 270 (1986).

While the goals of court-annexed arbitration are similar to those of private arbitration, court-annexed arbitration is unique in that it operates under the authority of a public court and results in an enforceable decision by that court. State statutes or court rules that provide for court-annexed arbitration generally require certain types of cases (defined primarily by subject matter or the amount in controversy) to be arbitrated before they may be tried in court. California, for example, requires pretrial arbitration of all civil disputes involving claims valued at less than $50,000, while Hawaii requires pretrial arbitration for only personal injury claims valued at less than $150,000. Cal. Civ. P. Code § 1141.11; Haw. Rev. Stat. § 20.

Constitutional challenges to such procedures generally have been rejected, see Kimbrough v. Holiday Inn, 478 F. Supp. 566 (E.D. Pa. 1979); Davis v. Gaona, 260 Ga. 450 (1990); Firelock, Inc. v. Dist. Court of the 20th Judicial Dist., 776 P.2d 1090 (Colo. 1989), and the popularity of ADR has resulted in federal legislation encouraging its use. The Alternative Dispute Resolution Act of 1998, 28 U.S.C. § 652, requires each federal district court to develop procedures for using alternative dispute resolution in all civil actions including, but not limited to, those involving federal contracts. The Act does not mandate a uniform set of procedures, but leaves it to each district court to develop its own local ADR rules. An exception to the mandate is that judges cannot order arbitration in actions based on alleged violations of constitutional law, or where more than $150,000 in damages is requested.

Each court is required to:

- designate a knowledgeable employee to implement the ADR program;
- require that litigants in all civil cases consider the use of an ADR process;
- offer litigants a choice of ADR processes, including mediation, early neutral evaluation, minitrial, and arbitration;
- maintain a panel of neutrals available for each category of process offered; and
- provide for the confidentiality of ADR processes.

Although the bill, as introduced, would have provided for fee shifting if a party demanded a trial de novo after arbitration and then failed to obtain a "substantially more favorable" result, this language was deleted when the bill was approved by the House Judiciary Committee. See 66 U.S.L.W. 2584. Another provision deleted by the committee would have required the use of arbitration in certain cases. As passed, the bill merely provides that if a court elects to require the use of ADR, it may only require the use of mediation or early neutral evaluation. For further discussion of the federal Alternative Dispute Resolution Act and its practical implications, see Eileen Barkas Hoffman, The Impact of the ADR Act of 1998, 6/1/99 Trial-Mag 35.

Do the efficiency benefits to the justice system outweigh the burdens to individual litigants of another layer of procedure? The costs of these processes, including the neutral parties' time, are generally borne by the individual litigants. Do such mandatory procedures discourage low-income litigants from pursuing just claims? Consider, too, that ADR is a process that has both public and private decision makers. Are their motivations the same? Should judges be permitted to work in both the public and private spheres? See Kirk Johnson, Public Judges as Private Contractors: A Legal Frontier, N.Y. Times, Dec. 10, 1994, at B11.

A related development in both state and federal courts is the delegation of decision making power over all or part of a case, such as discovery or calculation of damages, to a collateral authority. In the federal courts, those authorities are known as "special masters" and are authorized by Fed. R. Civ. P. 53. See Wayne Brazil, Special Masters in Complex Cases: Extending the Judiciary or Reshaping Adjudication?, 53 U. Chi. L. Rev. 394 (1986). California has been aggressive in using what it terms "references" to aid courts in the management of cases, frequently permitting, for example, courts to assign discovery to a private judge who will be paid by the parties. While this may help in case management, what are the implications for the parties?

Similarly, federal courts have been encouraged to experiment with different ADR devices. One source of authority is Fed. R. Civ. P. 16, which includes "the possibility of . . . the use of extrajudicial procedures to resolve the dispute" as a proper topic for pretrial conferences. Another source was the Civil Justice Reform Act of 1990, which gave federal courts "authorization to refer appropriate cases to alternative dispute resolution programs that . . . have been designated for use in a district court; or . . . [that] the court may make available, including mediation, mini-trial, and summary jury trial." 28 U.S.C. § 473(a)(6) (Supp. IV 1992).

Note: The Rise of International Arbitration

Globalization has brought many businesses, not just multinational corporations, into contact with foreign partners and competitors. For a variety of reasons, some having to do with the costs of litigation and others with the complexities of jurisdiction and forum selection, arbitration has become a prominent feature of international economic dispute resolution. For a survey of the procedural aspects of international arbitration, see Alan Scott Rau and Edward F. Sherman, Tradition and Innovation in International Arbitration Procedure, 30 Tex. Int'l L.J. 89 (1995). On the enforcement of international arbitration awards in United States courts, see William W. Park and Alexander A. Yanos, Treaty Obligations and National Law: Emerging Conflicts in International Arbitration, 58 Hastings L.J. 251 (2006); Stephen R. Swanson, Antisuit Injunctions in Support of International Arbitration, 81 Tul. L. Rev. 395 (2006).

2. Mediation

Problem Case: An Injured Quarterback (Part Two)

Return to the problem case at the outset of this section (page 833), and suppose that Sam Wyoming did not belong to an HMO (he couldn't stand the long waits for a doctor's care). But when he is injured, arguably by malpractice, he finds that rather than filing his suit, he must first, by state statute, submit to court-annexed mediation.

He feels that mediation is not only a pothole on the road to justice, but that this sort of procedure is a further invasion of his privacy and that it will be personally distasteful to deal with the doctor "who ruined my career" under these circumstances.

Do you advise him to proceed with the mediation? If so, how do you prepare him to participate in it?

Arbitration should be distinguished from mediation. A mediator has no power to decide; he must secure mutual assent to the resolution of the dispute. Mediation is widely used in the family law context. For example, a number of states provide for "conciliation courts" in which the parties must meet with a mediator before formal divorce and custody proceedings can be started or concluded. See, e.g., Cal. FAMILY Code §§ 1800-1842. The purposes of mediation go beyond (or, some would argue, rise above) the determination of rights or the effecting of a compromise. Professor Fuller has written that the central quality of mediation is "its capacity to reorient the parties toward each other, not by imposing rules on them, but by helping them to achieve a new and shared perception of their relationship." Lon Fuller, Mediation — Its Forms and Functions, 44 S. Cal. L. Rev. 305, 327 (1971). Professor Fuller argues that mediation is most appropriate and successful in dyadic relationships such as marriage and employer-employee. The doctor-patient relation can in some instances be dyadic and amenable to mediation.

A strong preference for mediation is embedded in certain cultures. The Confucian approach is described in Jerome Alan Cohen, Chinese Mediation on the Eve of Modernization, 54 Cal. L. Rev. 1201, 1206-1208 (1966):

> According to Confucianists, the legal process was not one of the highest achievements of Chinese civilization but was, rather, a regrettable necessity. Indeed, it was usually considered disreputable to become involved in the

law courts, even as a party with a legitimate grievance. A lawsuit symbolized disruption of the natural harmony that was thought to exist in human affairs. Law was backed by coercion, and therefore tainted in the eyes of Confucianists. Their view was that the optimum resolution of most disputes was to be achieved not by the exercise of sovereign force but by moral persuasion. Moreover, litigation led to litigiousness and to shameless concern for one's own interest to the detriment of the interests of society.

Confucian values emphasized not the rights of the individual but the functioning of the social order, the maintenance of the group. "[I]deas of order, responsibility, hierarchy and harmony" were enshrined in the prevailing social norms, the *li,* which were approved patterns of behavior prescribed in accordance with one's status and the particular social context. Harmony was preeminent among these ideas. Once it had been disturbed it could best be restored through compromise. If one felt he had been wronged, the Confucian ethic taught that it was better to "suffer a little" and smooth the matter over rather than make a fuss over it and create further dissension. If one was recognized as being clearly in the right in a dispute, it was better to be merciful to the offending party and set an example of the kind of cooperation that fostered group solidarity rather than exact one's pound of flesh and further alienate the offender from the group. As Jean Escarra has written: "To take advantage of one's position, to invoke one's 'rights,' has always been looked at askance in China. The great art is to give way (*jang*) on certain points, and thus accumulate an invisible fund of merit whereby one can later obtain advantages in other directions."

This attitude toward dispute settlement reflected the spirit of self-criticism that Confucian ideology sought to inculcate. When the model Confucian gentleman was treated by another in an unreasonable manner, he was supposed to attribute the difficulty to his own personal failings and to examine his own behavior to find the source of the problem. It was expected that by improving his own conduct he would evoke a positive response from the other party and thereby put an end to the matter. Moral men did not insist on their "rights" or on the exclusive correctness of their own position, but settled a dispute through mutual concessions that permitted each to save "face." A lawsuit caused one to lose "face" since it implied either some falling from virtue on one's own part through obstinacy or lack of moderation or, what was also embarrassing, the failure to elicit an appropriate concession from another as a matter of respect for one's own "face." Thus, Confucianism highly prized the art of compromise and, with it, the role of the persuasive intermediary.

Woods v. Holy Cross Hospital

591 F.2d 1164 (5th Cir. 1979)

TJOFLAT, Circuit Judge.

In this case we are called upon to examine portions of Florida's Medical Malpractice Law and determine whether its mandate that a medical malpractice claimant participate in a mediation process prior to bringing an action in court must be enforced by a federal district court in a diversity case. For the reasons set forth below, we find that this requirement meets federal constitutional standards and must be applied in such an action.

I

On July 21, 1975, Nellie Woods, a citizen of Ohio and the administratrix of the estate of her late husband, John N. Woods, filed an action in federal district court in which she claimed damages pursuant to Florida's Wrongful Death Act for Mr. Woods's death. The alleged cause of death was medical malpractice committed by two physicians and a hospital, all named as defendants. Their malpractice insurers were later added as parties-defendant. Jurisdiction was based upon diversity of citizenship, 28 U.S.C. § 1332 (1976). The defendants separately moved to dismiss Mrs. Woods's complaint, alleging that her failure to abide by the mediation panel requirement of Florida Statutes section 768.44 precluded her action. The district court granted the motions to dismiss on the ground that Mrs. Woods had failed to perform a condition precedent to her suit by not proceeding before a Florida malpractice mediation panel. This appeal was taken by Mrs. Woods from the final judgment dismissing her complaint. . . .

[The genesis of the mediation requirement were in these 1975 findings of the Florida Legislature:]

> WHEREAS, the cost of purchasing medical professional liability insurance for doctors and other health care providers has skyrocketed in the past few months; and
>
> WHEREAS, it is not uncommon to find physicians in high-risk categories paying premiums in excess of $20,000 annually; and
>
> WHEREAS, the consumer ultimately must bear the financial burdens created by the high cost of insurance; and
>
> WHEREAS, without some legislative relief, doctors will be forced to curtail their practices, retire, or practice defensive medicine at increased cost to the citizens of Florida; and
>
> WHEREAS, the problem has reached crisis proportion in Florida. . . .

Florida Statutes section 768.44 creates a system under which prior to bringing an action against a medical or osteopathic physician, podiatrist, hospital or health maintenance organization in any court of the state[,] a medical malpractice claimant must submit his claim to a medical liability mediation panel by filing the claim on special forms with the clerk of a state circuit court. If he fails so to file he is precluded from bringing any action based on medical malpractice in "any court of [the state of Florida]."

After a claim is properly filed all defendants must answer within twenty days or else a claimant may proceed in court. If answers are timely filed a claim is heard by a mediation panel consisting of a state circuit judge, an attorney, and a licensed physician. The circuit judge is chosen in a "blind" system; the attorney and physician are chosen from lists compiled by the chief judge of each judicial circuit in Florida. The attorney and physician panel members are each paid one hundred dollars for each day they spend on the panel; both parties to a claim are assessed equally for the payment of these fees. A hearing must be held within ten months of the filing of a claim with the circuit court clerk or else the mediation panel's jurisdiction terminates and a normal lawsuit may be filed; any applicable statute of limitations is tolled from the filing of a claim until at least sixty days after a mediation panel either mails its decision to the parties or has its jurisdiction otherwise terminated. Discovery rules of the Florida Rules of Civil Procedure are applied at panel hearings, and procedural and evidentiary rules are less formal than in ordinary civil litigation. Parties may subpoena and cross-examine witnesses at hearings; counsel for the parties may make opening and closing statements. The judge presiding over a hearing is precluded from presiding over any subsequent judicial proceedings arising out of the claim at issue, and other panel members may act as neither counsel nor witnesses at any subsequent trial of the claim.

Within thirty days of the completion of any hearing a panel files a written decision in which, using specified language, it finds the defendant was or was not negligent and accordingly is or is not liable to the plaintiff. A panel member may concur or dissent to the decision in writing. If liability is found and the parties so agree the panel may proceed to help the parties reach a settlement. In this regard, the panel may recommend a reasonable range of damages, but may not recommend punitive damages. Any damage recommendation is not admissible into evidence at any subsequent trial.

Section 768.47 provides that if any party rejects the decision of a mediation panel he may institute litigation based on his claim in an appropriate court. The panel findings are admissible into evidence in any subsequent litigation, but specific findings of fact are inadmissible. Parties may comment upon panel findings in opening statement or closing argument just as on any other evidence introduced at trial. If there was a dissenting opinion to the panel's decision the numerical vote of the panel is also admissible into evidence. If a defendant fails to participate in the mediation panel process the plaintiff may disclose this fact in any subsequent civil action. Carter v. Sparkman, 335 So. 2d 802, 805 (Fla. 1976). Panel members may not be called to testify as witnesses concerning the merits of a case. The jury is instructed that a panel's finding is not binding upon it but should be accorded such weight as the jury chooses to ascribe to it.

Sections 768.44 and .47 are important parts of Florida's Medical Malpractice Law. They successfully weathered both state and federal constitutional challenges in Carter v. Sparkman. We now turn to Mrs. Woods's various attacks on these provisions in the case before us.

Mrs. Woods's most troublesome argument is that sections 768.44 and .47 are procedural rather than substantive and thus should be inapplicable in a district court diversity case. As a general rule, in a federal diversity case the district court applies the substantive law of the forum state. Erie Railroad v. Tompkins[, 304 U.S. 64 (1938).] . . . Under any of the relevant tests we are convinced that Florida Statutes sections 768.44 and .47 must be applied in federal court. Our opinion on this matter is heightened by the fact that we are guided by "the policies underlying the Erie rule." See Hanna v. Plumer, 380 U.S. [460,] 467-468 [1965].

Section 768.44 provides that a plaintiff whose claim is based on an injury or death allegedly caused by medical malpractice must submit his claim to a medical liability mediation panel before he files an action in court; section 768.47 requires the admission into evidence of the panel's findings at any subsequent trial of such a claim. If federal courts sitting in diversity cases refuse to apply sections 768.44 and .47, Florida's medical malpractice statutory scheme will be inequitably administered. Non-resident plaintiffs will have a substantial advantage over resident ones, as non-resident suitors may avoid the mediation panel provision simply by bringing their actions in federal court; consequently, the worst form of forum-shopping will be encouraged. As we have observed, the Florida Legislature acted in 1975 to avert what it viewed as an impending crisis in the health care field. An integral part of its action was to require malpractice claimants to submit their claims to mediation, "thereby reducing the cost of medical malpractice insurance and ultimately medical expenses." Carter v. Sparkman, 335 So. 2d at 806. We would do grave damage to the legislative response evidenced by Florida's Medical Malpractice Law if we refused to apply the mediation requirement in diversity cases. We decline to take such a step. . . .

[A] constitutional challenge Mrs. Woods raises against sections 768.44 and .47 is a claimed denial of due process. . . . Her contention that these provisions violate due process by requiring arbitration of malpractice claims reflects a confusion between *arbitration* and *mediation*. While arbitration generally implies that parties are bound by an arbitrator's decision, Florida merely requires a mediation, or screening, process after which a party is free to proceed to court and file his claim. State required non-consensual arbitration of medical malpractice claims might present constitutional problems, but no such problems are evident when only mediation is required. As we discuss more fully below, the admissibility of mediation panel findings at a subsequent trial does not unduly affect the fairness of that trial and therefore does not constitute a due process violation. Finally, Mrs. Woods's contention that the method for the selection of mediation panel members violates due process puzzles us. Section 768.44(2)(g) provides that the parties to a malpractice dispute may agree upon a physician and attorney to serve upon the mediation panel, and if they do not so agree they are sent the names of five attorneys and physicians. These names are randomly selected from a list prepared by the chief judge of a Florida judicial circuit. The parties have ten days in which they may challenge the named attorneys and physicians for cause, and if a challenge for cause succeeds the challenged name is stricken and a new name is added to those already under consideration. The actual panel members are chosen when the parties alternately strike names from those provided them until the names of only one attorney and one physician remain. After the panel is chosen the parties may question the physician and attorney to determine if either of them has a state of mind regarding the subject matter at issue, the case at hand, or any parties directly or indirectly involved in said case, that will prevent him from acting with impartiality. Upon a determination by the judicial referee that either panelist cannot act with complete impartiality, the judicial referee shall remove said panelist. We find that this selection process fully comports with due process standards.

Mrs. Woods's final attack against sections 768.44 and .47 is her contention that they combine unconstitutionally to restrict her seventh amendment right to a jury trial. Two seventh amendment questions are presented: (1) does making screening a condition precedent to a jury trial unduly burden the right to such a trial; and (2) does the admission into evidence of a mediation panel's finding on liability usurp the function of a jury.

Mrs. Woods argues that the delay incident to the mediation prerequisite unconstitutionally infringes upon her seventh amendment right. This contention is without merit. The seventh amendment "does not prescribe at what stage of an action a trial by jury must, if demanded, be had, or what conditions may be imposed upon the demand of such a trial, consistently with preserving the right to it." Capital Traction Co. v. Hof, 174 U.S. 1, 23 (1899). Nothing in the seventh amendment requires that a jury make its findings at the earliest possible moment in the course of civil litigation; the requirement is only that the jury *ultimately* determine the issues of fact if they cannot be settled by the parties or determined as a matter of law. As stated by the Florida Supreme Court in Carter v. Sparkman, [335 So. 2d 802, 805 (Fla. 1976), *cert. denied,* 429 U.S. 1041 (1977),]

> [a]lthough courts are generally opposed to any burden being placed on the rights of aggrieved persons to enter the courts . . . there may be reasonable restrictions prescribed by law. Typical examples are the fixing of a time within which suit must be brought, payment of reasonable cost deposits, pursuit of certain administrative relief such as zoning matters or workmen's compensation claims, or the requirement that newspapers be given the right of retraction before an action for libel may be filed.

If a federal court may constitutionally refer a complicated matter to an auditor or special master, it may certainly utilize a medical liability mediation panel without violating the dictates of the seventh amendment. Once the panel has considered the evidence and rendered its decision either party to the claim is free to proceed to a jury trial; the jury will remain the ultimate arbiter of the case. So long as Mrs. Woods's right to have her claim fully and finally determined by a jury is preserved, she cannot be heard to complain that her right to a jury trial has been unconstitutionally restricted.

Mrs. Woods maintains that the presentation of panel findings on liability at a subsequent jury trial will so influence the jury that it will be unable independently to examine the question of liability, particularly since section 768.47 precludes the calling of panel members to testify regarding the merits of the case. We are unable to accept this contention. Section 768.47(2) specifically provides that "[t]he jury shall be instructed that the conclusion of the hearing panel shall not be binding, but shall be accorded such weight as they choose to ascribe to it." The panel finding is a particularly relevant, but not conclusive, form of evidence. The parties to a malpractice dispute are free to present the same witnesses and exhibits before the trial jury that they presented to the mediation panel, and the jury may draw its own conclusions from their testimony, even if in so doing it rejects the panel's finding.

Notes and Questions

1. What are the mediator's obligations — simply encouraging the parties to talk and maintaining order, or carrying messages between the parties and persuading them to accept a particular solution? Is true neutrality possible? Is the mediator legally or morally responsible for the parties' agreement? Compare Lawrence Susskind, Environmental Mediation and the Accountability Problem, 6 Vt. L. Rev. 1 (1981), with Joseph B. Stulberg, The Theory and Practice of Mediation: A Reply to Professor Susskind, 6 Vt. L. Rev. 85 (1981). See also Robert A. Baruch Bush, Efficiency and Protection, or Empowerment and Recognition?: The Mediator's Role and Ethical Standards in Mediation, 41 U. Fla. L. Rev. 253 (1989).

2. What is the role of law and of lawyers in mediation? Does the lawyer-mediator have an obligation to disclose relevant law or to take other steps that would level the parties' power imbalances? A spectrum of views has emerged, ranging from prohibitions on tendering such advice or information to full disclosure. See generally Craig A. McEwen, Nancy H. Rogers, and Richard J. Maiman, Bring in the Lawyers: Challenging the Dominant Approaches to Ensuring Fairness in Divorce Mediation, 79 Minn. L. Rev. 1317 (1995); Leonard Riskin, Toward New Standards for the Neutral Lawyer in Mediation, 26 Ariz. L. Rev. 329 (1984). Many national, state, and local bar associations have developed formal opinions on the subject. See Model Rules of Professional Conduct, Rule 2.2.; Model Code of Professional Responsibility, Ethical Consideration 5-20. See also Robert Mnookin and Lewis Kornhauser, Bargaining in the Shadow of the Law: The Case of Divorce, 88 Yale L.J. 950 (1979).

3. Does the mediation option put the lawyer at odds with her client? By what standards should an attorney measure the legitimacy of a client's mediated settlement? Sandra E. Purnell, Comment, The Attorney as Mediator: Inherent Conflict of Interest?, 32 UCLA L. Rev. 986 (1985).

One consequence of the rise of mediation has been a fast-growing industry of mediators who compete with the judiciary for the "business" of dispute settlement. Some judges in Connecticut are getting a piece of that action by working as private, paid mediators settling lawsuits for a nonprofit mediation service. See Kirk Johnson, Public Judges as Private Contractors: A Legal Frontier, N.Y. Times, Dec. 10, 1994, at B11. An architect of the program, which is called "Sta-Fed," explained that one of its premises is to avoid the drain on the judiciary created by large, private mediation firms that have wooed top judges off the bench with the promise of salaries far higher than those in the public sector. Senior judges who work for Sta-Fed may do so only if they agree not to leave the bench. Is there cause for alarm in the idea of civil justice going private?

3. Other Forms of ADR

Here is a brief description of other forms of dispute resolution. Some of these types build on concepts previously discussed in the sections on arbitration and mediation; others have developed independently.

a. Negotiation. This is probably the most common form of dispute resolution, in which two or more disputing parties try to work out their differences without intervention. While it is easy to overlook negotiation as means of dispute resolution, recent scholarship has more fully developed its principles and applications, and has emphasized its usefulness for fundamental problem-solving that can avoid many of the other dispute resolution techniques. See, e.g., Roger Fisher and William Ury, Getting to Yes (1991).

b. Med-Arb. This form of private dispute resolution combines mediation and arbitration into a single process. The dispute is first mediated, and if that proves unsuccessful, the dispute moves into arbitration. This form of dispute resolution is found in labor-management agreements and, increasingly, in consumer banking. See generally Thomas J. Brewer and Lawrence R. Mills, Combining Mediation & Arbitration, 54 Disp. Resol. J. 32 (1999); Stephen B. Goldberg, The Mediation of Grievances Under a Collective Bargaining Contract: An Alternative to Arbitration, 77 Nw. U. L. Rev. 270 (1982). Should the same neutral party who handled the mediation be allowed to handle the arbitration?

c. Mini-trials. This form of private dispute resolution is best thought of as an aid to settlement. Although forms vary, the concept is that the parties each present their cases in truncated form to a neutral third party who renders an opinion. The opinion generally is not binding, but provides the basis for settlement discussions between the parties, which may or may not include the neutral party. See generally Texas Young Lawyers' Association Committees on ADR, State Bar of Texas, Mini-trials: Opportunities for Compromise, 51 Tex. B.J. 34 (1988).

d. Summary Jury Trials. Pioneered by U.S. District Judge Thomas Lambros, the summary jury trial (SJT) is a form of court-ordered mini-trial in which the neutral party rendering an opinion is a jury drawn from the same population as would be used in a real trial. Again, the SJT should be seen as an aid to settlement. See generally Thomas Lambros, The Summary Jury Trial, 103 F.R.D. 461 (1984); Richard Posner, The Summary Jury Trial and Other Alternative Methods of Dispute Resolution: Some Cautionary Observations, 53 U. Chi. L. Rev. 366 (1986).

e. Early Neutral Evaluation. The Northern District Court of California is among the courts that have experimented with a dispute resolution mechanism known as early neutral evaluation (ENE), under which an evaluator — not the trial judge — is assigned by the judge to meet with the parties to eyeball the case, discuss disputed issues, explore settlement possibilities, and evaluate the parties' relative chances of prevailing. See Joshua D. Rosenberg and H. Jay Folberg, Alternative Dispute Resolution: An Empirical Analysis, 46 Stan. L. Rev. 1487, 1487-1491 (1994).

f. Multidisciplinary Practice. Following on the heels of their European counterparts, American lawyers in growing numbers are weighing the virtues of multidisciplinary practice, in which attorneys partner with nonlawyers to provide a range of corporate services, eschewing the traditional role of lawyers as "firemen," called only in times of trouble. See, e.g., Michael Jonathan Grinfeld, What's Law Got to Do with It?, Cal. Lawyer, June 2000, at 34. The American Bar Association has been wrestling with the ethical and competitive issues raised by such previously prohibited arrangements. An ABA committee has recommended that lawyers "be permitted to share fees and join with nonlawyer professionals in a practice that delivers both legal and nonlegal professional services . . . provided that the lawyers have the control and authority necessary to assure lawyer independence in the rendering of legal services." ABA Commission on Multidisciplinary Practice, Report to the House of Delegates, http://www.abanet.org/cpr/mdp/mdpfinalrep2000.html (last visited Feb. 20, 2009).

4. Critical Perspectives on ADR

Not everyone has been enthusiastic about alternatives to adversarial procedures. One concern, raised by Paul Carrington, is that by tailoring procedure to particular types of disputes we risk reproducing the arcane system of code pleading that the modern rules were intended to eliminate. The advantage of the modern system, some think, is that lawyers need not master the intricacies of multiple procedural devices; rather there is only one form of action that applies to all civil cases. See Paul Carrington, Civil Procedure and Alternative Dispute Resolution, 34 J. Legal Educ. 298 (1984).

Another potential drawback of some forms of ADR is that they may favor informal, discretionary decision making over more formal and bounded methods. This can lead to more impressionistic, idiosyncratic, or standardless decision making, which may result in bias against some litigants or arbitrary outcomes. See, e.g., John Conley and William O'Barr, Fundamentals of Jurisprudence: An Ethnography of Judicial Decision Making in Informal Courts, 66 N.C. L. Rev. 467 (1988); Richard Delgado et al., Fairness and Formality, Minimizing the Risk of Prejudice in Alternative Dispute Resolution, 1985 Wis. L. Rev. 1359; William O'Barr and John Conley, Litigant Satisfaction Versus Legal Adequacy in Small Claims Court Narratives, 19 Law & Soc'y Rev. 661 (1985). See generally 1-2 The Politics of Informal Justice (Richard L. Abel ed., 1982).

In the specific context of domestic disputes, some observers worry that mediation or other nonadversarial techniques may tend to favor the economically or emotionally stronger party or the one who can least tolerate conflict or who most values a harmonious resolution. See, e.g., Martha Fineman, Dominant Discourse, Professional Language, and Legal Change in Child Custody Decision Making, 101 Harv. L. Rev. 727, 765 (1988); Carol Lefcourt, Women, Mediation and Family Law, 18 Clearinghouse Rev. 266, 269 (1984); Lisa Lerman, Mediation of Wife Abuse Cases: The Adverse Impact of Informal Dispute Resolution on Women, 7 Harv. Women's L.J. 57 (1984). This may inspire some parties to settle for far less than they might obtain before a judge in a traditional adversarial proceeding. As one writer has put it, "compromise only is an equitable solution between equals; between unequals, it 'inevitably reproduces inequality.'" Jerold S. Auerbach, Justice Without Law? 136 (1983); see also Owen M. Fiss, Against Settlement, 93 Yale L.J. 1073 (1984).

Other critics of the informalization of procedure insist that it may "neutralize conflict that could threaten state or capital." Richard L. Abel, The Contradictions of Informal Justice, in 1 The Politics of Informal Justice, supra, at 267, 280. As Abel argues, "[i]nformal institutions neutralize conflict by denying its existence, by simulating a society in which conflict is less frequent and less threatening, and by choosing to recognize and handle only those forms of conflict that do not challenge the basic structures. Informal processes moderate the antagonistic adversarial posture of the parties. This is a difficult task because people involved in conflict usually want to win; they seek vindication." Id. at 283.

For a skeptical look at unbounded claims of a litigation explosion in the United States, see Aaron Hiller, Rule 11 and Tort Reform: Myth, Reality, and Legislation, 18 Geo. J. Legal Ethics, 809 (2005); Deborah Rhode, In the Interests of Justice (2000); Marc Galanter, Reading the Landscape of Disputes: What We Know and Don't Know (and Think We Know) About Our Allegedly Contentious and Litigious Society, 31 UCLA L. Rev. 4 (1983). To the extent that ADR is inspired by the sense that the number of claims litigated under traditional methods has sky-rocketed and the attendant costs have become too expensive, Galanter's research obviously is highly relevant to the ADR movement. Indeed, many of the arguments for ADR have been met with rebuttals and surrebuttals, as the debate about ADR measures continues. See, e.g., Owen M. Fiss, Out of Eden, 94 Yale L.J. 1669 (1985); Andrew McThenia and Thomas Shaffer, For Reconciliation, 94 Yale L.J. 1660 (1985).

A very thoughtful analysis of the arguments for and against making civil justice more informal is found in William Simon, Legal Informality and Redistributive Politics, 19 Clearinghouse Rev. 384 (1985). Simon concludes that the matter is more complex than some arguments against informality admit. For example, he argues that informal procedures in welfare hearing systems, while far from perfect,

> facilitate a far more meaningful degree of participation by unrepresented claimants than any other formal system I can think of, and sympathetic and competent official performances are not uncommon. The most serious problems with welfare administration concern, not the hearing procedures, but the frontline bureaucracy and most problems arise from the tendency of increasing *formality* in administration to encumber claimant access to the system.

Id. at 386 (emphasis in original).

To what extent do the alternatives to adversarial procedure sound attractive? Workable? Efficient? On what do your responses to these questions depend?

Obviously, at this early stage in your legal career you may feel unable to judge some of the arguments about the current system's shortcomings and strengths because you have not yet worked within it. But surely you are able—some might say more able than a career-worn veteran lawyer—to judge how the various alternatives might suit the needs of laypeople who must use the civil justice system. In this respect, perhaps the most important of the foregoing materials are those that describe what process "feels fair" to people in various cultures and subcultural contexts. One of the most significant findings of this literature seems to be that people regard procedure as fair when they feel they have some control over it, in the specific sense that they are allowed to participate and *feel* as though they have been heard. Given that the vast majority of legal disputes are handled without a full-blown trial, all lawyers would do well to heed this psychological insight. For even in the nonadversarial, extrajudicial context of the lawyer's office, clients often may need to be heard, and their lawyers often will be the only audience for their grievances. As such, the emerging evidence about what kinds of hearings seem to satisfy laypeoples' sense of just treatment may be as relevant to client counseling as it is to proposals for changes in formal judicial procedures.

6 *More Complex Litigation*

We turn now to some of the elaborations of the basic procedural framework. In the area of federal subject matter jurisdiction, we study first the law to be applied in diversity cases: the jurisprudence of Erie R.R. Co. v. Tompkins, 304 U.S. 64 (1938). Then we turn to issues of when federal courts may hear state claims, as well as take cases from state courts, and allocate business among themselves. On the pleading side, we move beyond the bimodal lawsuit, to joinder, aggregation, and class actions.

The complexities of litigation strain the trans-substantive nature of the rules, and the capacities of judges and juries. Nowhere is this more apparent than in the class action device as applied in mass tort situations. We conclude the chapter with recent cases on subject matter jurisdiction and settlement in class action litigation.

A. SUBJECT MATTER JURISDICTION IN A DUAL COURT SYSTEM: A SECOND LOOK

1. The Governing Law in a Diversity Case

Problem Case: Having It Whose Way?

Recall the facts of *Burger King* in Chapter 1, section C, which involved the franchise agreement dispute between the Miami-based Burger King Corporation and the two businessmen from Michigan. The plaintiff filed the action in a federal district court in Florida.

Yet the plaintiff corporation invoked state law only — trademark infringement and breach of contract — so that jurisdiction was based solely on diversity. (Note that there is also federal law that governs trademark, but it does not preempt all state law in this area.) How is it that a federal court comes to review matters of state substantive law? Which state's law would govern the contract and trademark infringement action — Michigan's or Florida's? Remember that there was a choice of law provision in the franchise agreement. Does that affect your answer?

a. From *Erie* to *Hanna*

Assume that an action is filed in federal district court based solely on diversity; that is, no federal question appears on the face of the well-pleaded complaint. What law should govern this dispute?

The Rules of Decision Act, today found at 28 U.S.C. § 1652, reads as follows:

> The laws of the several states, except where the Constitution or treaties of the United States or Acts of Congress otherwise require or provide, shall be regarded as rules of decision in civil actions in the courts of the United States in cases where they apply.

The key interpretive issue in this clause is: What are "the laws of the several states"? Do they include both substantive and procedural rules? Both statutory and decisional law?

The modern answer, which dates from the famous case of Erie R.R. Co. v. Tompkins, 304 U.S. 64 (1938), is that the Federal Rules govern procedural matters while state law (statutory and decisional) covers substantive issues. You might quickly see that this is necessarily so in a diversity case because, by definition, the case does not involve federal law. But of course, the point is more complicated.

Before *Erie,* decided in the same year that the Federal Rules of Civil Procedure took effect, the situation was just the opposite. So-called federal common law governed the substance of diversity cases whenever no state statute (versus state decisional law) on point existed, and the federal courts (lacking general procedural rules of their own) used the procedure of the state in which the district court was located, except in matters arising in equity. (The equity side versus the law side of federal court jurisdiction is discussed in Chapter 2, supra.)

This pre-*Erie* approach to choice of law in diversity suits was called the *Swift* doctrine, named after the 1842 decision Swift v. Tyson, 41 U.S. (16 Pet.) 1 (1842). Under *Swift,* the "laws of the several states" that federal courts were bound to follow included only state constitutions, statutes, and state judicial opinions interpreting statutes. Federal courts were not bound by other state common law or precedent, but were instead left to develop a body of substantive federal common law to address matters of "general" — as opposed to local — concern.

Edward A. Purcell Jr., Litigation and Inequality: Federal Diversity Jurisdiction in Industrial America, 1870-1958

Pages 226-230 (1992)

Erie was an unusually dramatic case, and its New Deal context and the fact that Brandeis wrote for the majority highlighted its political and intellectual origins. Since the late nineteenth century legal writers had criticized *Swift* on the various grounds that the Court discussed, and the dissents of Field and Holmes had convinced many that *Swift* was unsound in theory as well as in practice. Southerners and westerners, and political progressives generally, had charged for more than half a century that the federal common law favored business interests, encouraged corporate forum shopping, and denigrated the authority of the states. The context of the Court's decision in *Erie,* however, blending easily into the context of both earlier criticisms and the New Deal revolution, tended to obscure the extent to which the challenges of escalating litigation tactics helped move the Court toward abolishing the federal common law by forcing the Justices to recognize its anomalous and discordant nature.

Litigation between individuals and corporations had become increasingly arbitrary and unstable after 1910. The growing arbitrariness—the fact that the value of a case could be determined largely by the tactical possibilities open to the parties, not by its merits—was apparent across the board. The arbitrariness no longer related merely to the basic questions of whether plaintiff lived in a town that was distant from the nearest federal court, or in an area where the federal court had a particularly heavy backlog, or in a state where the local and federal common law conflicted. Instead, litigation tactics had generated new and multiple levels on which arbitrary differences wholly unrelated to the merits of a suit could prove significant or even dispositive. . . .

The use of specialized procedural tactics and countertactics made litigation increasingly volatile and unpredictable. As parties and their attorneys grew more sophisticated, they created an ever-growing number of tactics to squeeze out an advantage. As the methods of transportation and communications improved, they yielded ready access to courts across the nation. As social subgroups organized and gained in experience and as the bar grew more specialized, they opened up for larger numbers of litigants the tactical possibilities that their predecessors had discovered. "For every weapon there is a counter weapon," an attorney for the Brotherhood of Railroad Trainmen explained. "For every form of attack a defense is developed." Tactical inventiveness and organizational development combined to intensify the pressures that pushed against the limits of both doctrine and court structure.

Equally important, the arbitrariness and volatility were becoming more visible to the formal law. Until World War I the problem of distance had been irrelevant as a legal factor, and the problem of delay merely one of administration. The doctrines of the formal law ignored both. The new characteristics of the system, however, were different. The formal law could not ignore the persistence and frequency of certain types of jurisdictional disputes, the widening scope of interstate forum shopping, the pressures for expanded equitable remedies in state and federal courts, and the need to answer increasingly complex questions about personal jurisdiction, choice of law, the full faith and credit clause, the role of *forum non conveniens,* the availability and conditions of declaratory relief, and the scope of the constitutional right to trial by jury. . .

Indeed, diversity litigation in the system and actions under the FELA [Federal Employers' Liability Act] were not the only areas where tactical escalation was developing or threatened. Diversity jurisdiction could offer advantages in other types of litigation as well. Given their greater resources and the much larger amounts at stake, corporations and wealthy individuals were likely to prove even more inventive in disputes involving real estate or commercial transactions. Intracorporate conflicts and shareholder derivative suits could also spur the most determined and byzantine of litigations.

When Congress passed the Rules Enabling Act in 1934, it symbolized and accelerated the changes that the twentieth century was bringing to litigation practice. The act conferred on the Supreme Court the authority to prepare and promulgate, subject to congressional approval, rules of procedure for the federal courts, and it provided for the repeal of the Conformity Act. The new Federal Rules of Civil Procedure were promulgated and went into effect in 1938. The enabling act and the new rules gave further institutional support to the idea that the federal courts constituted a national system of courts, and they in effect recognized that large corporations and a national economy were making twentieth-century corporate legal practice into an interstate enterprise. Separating federal from state practice, the new Federal Rules at once freed the national courts from state procedural rules, confirmed implicitly the higher professional status of federal practice, and facilitated the development by large urban law firms of a national practice in support of the nationwide operations of their corporate clients.

Those nationwide operations were visible in the 1930s when a number of corporations mounted elaborate legal campaigns to stall the New Deal. Companies shopped across the country for the judges and circuits that were most willing to block government agencies, and they cleverly employed shareholder derivative suits to obtain injunctions prohibiting company compliance with the laws. The latter tactic allowed suspiciously "friendly" suits with minimal opposition or agreed-upon facts, and it often prevented the government from even participating in the defense of the challenged laws or administrative actions. Justice Jackson, who had fought many of the New Deal's legal battles when he was Assistant Attorney General, noted the clever uses that the New Deal's opponents made of shareholder derivative suits. The "apparent adversaries were not in real controversy," he explained. "They framed the issues to suit themselves." Small wonder, then, that in his concurrence in Miles [v. Illinois Central R.R. Co., 315 U.S. 698 (1942),] Jackson readily appreciated the "realistic" significance of venue choice under the FELA. "There is nothing which requires a plaintiff to whom such a choice is given," Jackson had remarked, "to exercise it in a self-denying or large-hearted manner."

It was, in short, up to Congress and the Court to regulate federal litigation, and since the 1920s the Court had made sporadic efforts to control many of the new litigation tactics. With few exceptions, the complexity of the issues and conflicts within the Court had blocked any major advance.

Commerce clause venue and the full faith and credit clause seemed of limited use at best, and the tensions between the legal and equitable jurisdiction of the federal courts remained unresolved. In a legal world where sophisticated and complex litigation tactics were growing common, simplicity and order seemed highly desirable. And with a large scholarly and administrative contingent in the legal profession focused on judicial efficiency and concerned with the federal courts as an integrated system, inconsistencies and conflicts stood out ever more sharply. In that context the federal common law appeared increasingly discordant, a wild card that — whatever its merits might otherwise have been — consistently exacerbated the problems of arbitrariness, instability, and tactical escalation that characterized twentieth-century litigation.

As the Court tried to grapple with interstate forum shopping, the tactical escalation in insurance litigation, and similar developments in other areas, so it began gradually to moderate the federal common law in the 1930s. To the extent that differences between the common law of the states and the federal courts could be effectively minimized, the incentives for forum shopping and other tactical maneuvers could be lessened. In 1933 the Court limited the *Swift* doctrine in insurance cases by introducing the principle that the federal courts should accept state common law if the issue was "balanced with doubt." In the mid-1930s it applied the same principle to other common law areas and seemed to defer more often to state courts for the determination of local policies and laws. The fact that the Court itself continued on occasion to apply *Swift* only highlighted the apparent unpredictability of the doctrine. . . .

If the old Supreme Court struggled with the federal common law and the challenges of tactical escalation, however, it still refused to abolish *Swift*. That drastic step required a new Court. When *Erie* came down, six Justices voted to overturn *Swift*: Brandeis and Justice Harlan F. Stone, members of the Court's so-called progressive wing who had joined Holmes's dissent in the *Taxicab* case [Black & White Taxicab & Transfer Co. v. Brown & Yellow Taxicab & Transfer Co., 276 U.S. 518 (1928)]; Chief Justice Charles Evans Hughes and Justice Owen J. Roberts, the two Justices who had apparently switched their positions in 1936-1937; and Justices Hugo L. Black and Stanley Reed, the first two Roosevelt appointees who had recently joined the Court. The remaining Justices, members of the Court's anti-New Deal wing who had been with the majority in the *Taxicab* case, dissented.

Although *Erie* eliminated the wild card of the federal common law, it arguably had some potential to increase incentives for interstate forum shopping. By abolishing the relative interstate uniformity of the federal common law, *Erie* raised the possibility that parties, knowing that the common law applied in the federal courts would no longer be uniform, might be encouraged to seek more favorable substantive law in distant states. The Roosevelt Court discounted that possibility for two reasons. First, it was more hypothetical than real. Choice-of-law rules and the full faith and credit clause restricted forum shopping for more favorable substantive state law. Indeed, interstate forum shopping was inspired in relatively few cases by differences in the states' substantive laws. Rather, it arose for the most part from the advantages offered by different procedural rules and judicial practices or by such extralegal factors as the specialized abilities of local importers, the lure of de facto larger verdicts, and the leverage gained by imposing practical burdens on adversaries. Second, and more important, the Roosevelt Court knowingly made a fundamental value choice. *Erie* protected the 95 percent of individual plaintiffs who sued, usually out of necessity, in their home states. For those plaintiffs intrastate uniformity between state and federal court was infinitely more important than whatever degree of uniformity *Swift* engendered in the common law applied nationally in the federal courts. Whatever instabilities and arbitrariness existed in the legal system, *Erie* would minimize them for the vast majority of individuals.

Although *Erie* was a product of the early Roosevelt Court, the later Roosevelt Court enforced it broadly. The New Deal Justices who subsequently joined the Court shared *Erie*'s hostility to forum shopping but doubted its constitutional language. Although the constitutional basis of the decision was not clear, many of them assumed that it rested on the Tenth Amendment. As good New Dealers, they were suspicious of the Tenth Amendment which, under the old Court, had served as a substantive limitation on the powers of Congress. Accordingly, they simply ignored *Erie*'s constitutional language, embraced it as establishing a broad anti-forum shopping policy, and transformed that policy into a major principle of federal law.

In a series of cases handed down during the 1940s, the Court enforced *Erie* to minimize the legal incentives for intrastate forum shopping. In 1940 it held that the federal courts were bound not just by the decisions of a state's "highest court" but, in the absence of such decisions, also by the rulings of intermediate state appellate courts and even by the rulings of state trial courts. The following year in Klaxon v. Stentor-Electric Manufacturing Co.[, 313 U.S. 487 (1941),] it held that *Erie*'s "prohibition" against "independent determinations" of state laws by federal courts "extends to the field of conflict of laws," even though the field was traditionally classified as an area of "procedural" law. In diversity cases involving state law issues, *Klaxon* held, federal courts were bound to apply the choice-of-law rules of the state in which they sat. In 1945 in Guaranty Trust Co. v. York[, 326 U.S. 99 (1945),] the Roosevelt Court handed down its most far-reaching elaboration of *Erie*, holding that it required federal courts to apply state "procedural" rules if they would "significantly affect the result of a litigation." The "nub of the policy that underlies *Erie*," *York* declared, was that the "accident" of diverse citizenship should not lead to a different result in a federal court than would occur in a state court.

Together *Klaxon*, *York*, and the Court's other decisions in the 1940s implemented *Erie* broadly and reduced to a minimum the differences in the formal law that state and federal courts in the same state would apply. By the end of the decade the federal courts applied not only the common law rules of the state in which they sat but also some of the "procedural" rules that the local state courts followed. Though differences in procedure and institutional structure between state and federal courts remained, the divergent general federal common law had been thoroughly rooted out and the law applied in state and federal courts sitting in the same state brought closely into line.

A workable definition of a "substantive" rule is one that characteristically and reasonably affects people's conduct at the stage of primary activity outside the context of litigation. It is a rule with a purpose other than that of assuring the fairness or efficiency of litigation. Rules of liability are a clear example of substantive rules, because they influence conduct (e.g., reasonable care, safety precautions) outside the courtroom.

A "procedural" rule, generally speaking, is one that is designed to make the process of dispute resolution a fair and efficient mechanism for resolving legal controversies. Rules regarding the filing of a complaint are a clear example.

With these definitions and this simple statement of the *Erie* rule in mind, we now turn to the case itself. When reading it, ask yourself how it was that the federal courts had for nearly 150 years managed to "misread" their rulemaking power. If *Erie* is constitutionally required, what do you make of the Court's failure to recognize its error for so many years? Is there another explanation for the Court's 1938 dramatic reversal?

Erie R.R. Co. v. Tompkins

304 U.S. 64 (1938)

JUDGE BRANDEIS delivered the opinion of the Court.

The question for decision is whether the oft-challenged doctrine of Swift v. Tyson shall now be disapproved.

Tompkins, a citizen of Pennsylvania, was injured on a dark night by a passing freight train of the Erie Railroad Company while walking along its right of way at Hughestown in that State. He claimed that the accident occurred through negligence in the operation, or maintenance, of the train; that he was rightfully on the premises as licensee because on a commonly used beaten footpath which ran for a short distance alongside the tracks; and that he was struck by something which looked like a door projecting from one of the moving cars. To enforce that claim he brought an action in the federal court for southern New York, which had jurisdiction because the company is a corporation of that State. It denied liability; and the case was tried by a jury.

The Erie insisted that its duty to Tompkins was no greater than that owed to a trespasser. It contended, among other things, that its duty to Tompkins, and hence its liability, should be determined in accordance with the Pennsylvania law; that under the law of Pennsylvania, as declared by its highest court, persons who use pathways along the railroad right of way—that is a longitudinal pathway as distinguished from a crossing—are to be deemed trespassers; and that the railroad is not liable for injuries to undiscovered trespassers resulting from its negligence, unless it be wanton or willful. Tompkins denied that any such rule had been established by the decisions of the Pennsylvania courts; and contended that, since there was no statute of the State on the subject, the railroad's duty and liability is to be determined in federal courts as a matter of general law.

The trial judge refused to rule that the applicable law precluded recovery. The jury brought in a verdict of $30,000; and the judgment entered thereon was affirmed by the Circuit Court of Appeals, which held, 90 F.2d 603, 604, that it was unnecessary to consider whether the law of Pennsylvania was as contended, because the question was one not of local, but of general, law and that

> upon questions of general law the federal courts are free, in absence of a local statute, to exercise their independent judgment as to what the law is; and it is well settled that the question of the responsibility of a railroad for injuries caused by its servants is one of general law. . . . Where the public has made open and notorious use of a railroad right of way for a long period of time and without objection, the company owes to persons on such permissive pathway a duty of care in the operation of its trains. . . . It is likewise generally recognized law that a jury may find that negligence exists toward a pedestrian using a permissive path on the railroad right of way if he is hit by some object projecting from the side of the train.

The Erie had contended that application of the Pennsylvania rule was required, among other things, by § 34 of the Federal Judiciary Act of September 24, 1789, chap. 20, 28 U.S.C.A. § 725, which provides: "The laws of the several States, except where the Constitution, treaties, or statutes of the United States otherwise require or provide, shall be regarded as rules of decision in trials at common law, in the courts of the United States, in cases where they apply."

Because of the importance of the question whether the federal court was free to disregard the alleged rule of the Pennsylvania common law, we granted certiorari.

First. Swift v. Tyson, 16 Pet. 1, 18 (1842), held that federal courts exercising jurisdiction on the ground of diversity of citizenship need not, in matters of general jurisprudence, apply the unwritten law of the State as declared by its highest court; that they are free to exercise an independent judgment as to what the common law of the State is—or should be; and that, as there stated by Mr. Justice Story:

> The true interpretation of the thirty-fourth section limited its application to State laws strictly local, that is to say, to the positive statutes of the state, and the construction thereof adopted by the local tribunals, and to rights and titles to things having a permanent locality, such as the rights and titles to

real estate, and other matters immovable and intraterritorial in their nature and character. It never has been supposed by us, that the section did apply, or was designed to apply, to questions of more general nature, not at all dependent upon local statutes or local usages of a fixed and permanent operation, as, for example, to the construction of ordinary contracts or other written instruments, and especially to questions of general commercial law, where the State tribunals are called upon to perform the like functions as ourselves, that is, to ascertain upon general reasoning and legal analogies, what is the true exposition of the contract or instrument, or what is the just rule furnished by the principles of commercial law to govern the case.

The Court in applying the rule of § 34 to equity cases, in Mason v. United States, 260 U.S. 545, 559, said: "The statute, however, is merely declarative of the rule which would exist in the absence of the statute." The federal courts assumed, in the broad field of "general law," the power to declare rules of decision which Congress was confessedly without power to enact as statutes. Doubt was repeatedly expressed as to the correctness of the construction given § 34, and as to the soundness of the rule which it introduced. But it was the more recent research of a competent scholar, who examined the original document, which established that the construction given to it by the Court was erroneous; and that the purpose of the section was merely to make certain that, in all matters except those in which some federal law is controlling, the federal courts exercising jurisdiction in diversity of citizenship cases would apply as their rules of decision the law of the State, unwritten as well as written.[5]

Criticism of the doctrine became widespread after the decision of Black & W. Taxicab & Transfer Co. v. Brown & Y. Taxicab & Transfer Co., 276 U.S. 518. There, Brown and Yellow, a Kentucky corporation owned by Kentuckians, and the Louisville and Nashville Railroad, also a Kentucky corporation, wished that the former should have the exclusive privilege of soliciting passenger and baggage transportation at the Bowling Green, Kentucky, railroad station; and that the Black and White, a competing Kentucky corporation, should be prevented from interfering with that privilege. Knowing that such a contract would be void under the common law of Kentucky, it was arranged that the Brown and Yellow reincorporate under the law of Tennessee, and that the contract with the railroad should be executed there. The suit was then brought by the Tennessee corporation in the federal court for western Kentucky to enjoin competition by the Black and White; an injunction issued by the district court was sustained by the Court of Appeals; and this court, citing many decisions in which the doctrine of Swift v. Tyson had been applied, affirmed the decree.

Second. Experience in applying the doctrine of Swift v. Tyson had revealed its defects, political and social; and the benefits expected to flow

5. Charles Warren, New Light on the History of the Federal Judiciary Act of 1789 (1923), 37 Harv. L. Rev. 49, 51-52, 81-88, 108.

from the rule did not accrue. Persistence of state courts in their own opinions on questions of common law prevented uniformity; and the impossibility of discovering a satisfactory line of demarcation between the province of general law and that of local law developed a new well of uncertainties.

On the other hand, the mischievous results of the doctrine had become apparent. Diversity of citizenship jurisdiction was conferred in order to prevent apprehended discrimination in state courts against those not citizens of the State. Swift v. Tyson introduced grave discrimination by noncitizens against citizens. It made rights enjoyed under the unwritten "general law" vary according to whether enforcement was sought in the state or in the federal court; and the privilege of selecting the court in which the right should be determined was conferred upon the noncitizen. Thus, the doctrine rendered impossible equal protection of the law. In attempting to promote uniformity of law throughout the United States, the doctrine had prevented uniformity in the administration of the law of the State.

The discrimination resulting became in practice far-reaching. This resulted in part from the broad province accorded to the so-called "general law" as to which federal courts exercised an independent judgment. In addition to questions of purely commercial law, "general law" was held to include the obligations under contracts entered into and to be performed within the State, the extent to which a carrier operating within a State may stipulate for exemption from liability for his own negligence or that of his employee; the liability for torts committed within the State upon persons resident or property located there, even where the question of liability depended upon the scope of a property right conferred by the State; and the right to exemplary or punitive damages. Furthermore, state decisions construing local deeds, mineral conveyances, and even devises of real estate were disregarded.

In part the discrimination resulted from the wide range of persons held entitled to avail themselves of the federal rule by resort to the diversity of citizenship jurisdiction. Through this jurisdiction, individual citizens willing to remove from their own State and become citizens of another might avail themselves of the federal rule. And, without even change of residence, a corporate citizen of the State could avail itself of the federal rule by reincorporating under the laws of another state, as was done in the *Taxicab* case.

The injustice and confusion incident to the doctrine of Swift v. Tyson have been repeatedly urged as reasons for abolishing or limiting diversity of citizenship jurisdiction. Other legislative relief has been proposed. If only a question of statutory construction were involved, we should not be prepared to abandon a doctrine so widely applied throughout nearly a century. But the unconstitutionality of the course pursued has now been made clear and compels us to do so.

Third. Except in matters governed by the Federal Constitution or by Acts of Congress, the law to be applied in any case is the law of the State.

And whether the law of the State shall be declared by its Legislature in a statute or by its highest court in a decision is not a matter of federal concern. There is no federal general common law. Congress has no power to declare substantive rules of common law applicable in a State whether they be local in their nature or "general," be they commercial law or a part of the law of torts. And no clause in the Constitution purports to confer such a power upon the federal courts. . . .

The fallacy underlying the rule declared in Swift v. Tyson is made clear by Mr. Justice Holmes. The doctrine rests upon the assumption that there is "a transcendental body of law outside of any particular State but obligatory within it unless and until changed by statute," that federal courts have the power to use their judgment as to what the rules of common law are; and that in the federal courts "the parties are entitled to an independent judgment on matters of general law":

> but law in the sense in which courts speak of it today does not exist without some definite authority behind it. The common law so far as it is enforced in a State, whether called common law or not, is not the common law generally but the law of that State existing by the authority of that State without regard to what it may have been in England or anywhere else. . . . The authority and only authority is the state, and if that be so, the voice adopted by the State as its own [whether it be of its Legislature or of its Supreme Court] should utter the last word.

Thus the doctrine of Swift v. Tyson is, as Mr. Justice Holmes said, "an unconstitutional assumption of power by courts of the United States which no lapse of time or respectable array of opinion should make us hesitate to correct." In disapproving that doctrine we do not hold unconstitutional § 34 of the Federal Judiciary Act of 1789, or any other Act of Congress. We merely declare that in applying the doctrine this Court and the lower courts have invaded rights which in our opinion are reserved by the Constitution to the several States. . . .

Reversed.

JUSTICE CARDOZO took no part in the consideration or decision of this case.

In *Erie,* the Court held that there was no general federal common law upon which federal courts could draw for substantive decisions and mandated that state law apply in diversity suits.

The puzzle is whether this result was constitutionally required, as Justice Brandeis suggested, or if this was merely a statutory requirement. After all, the Constitution gives Congress the power to establish federal courts and to afford these courts power to hear actions arising between citizens of different states. Why, some scholars have asked, does the congressional power to establish these courts not include the power to create courts that may determine both the procedure and the substance of diversity actions?

Regardless of whether the Constitution requires it, however, the Court has interpreted the applicable congressional acts to mean that federal courts sitting in diversity must apply state substantive law. The relevant statutes are the Rules of Decision Act, 28 U.S.C. § 1652, and the Rules Enabling Act, 28 U.S.C. §§ 2072-2077.

The Rules Enabling Act, the current version of which is found at 28 U.S.C. § 2072, provides that the "Supreme Court shall have the power to prescribe general rules of practice and procedure and rules of evidence for cases in the United States district courts" and that "these rules shall not abridge, enlarge, or modify any substantive right." Taken together and grossly simplified, the two acts mean that federal courts apply their own procedure and state substantive law in diversity suits. But see Wilfred J. Ritz, Rewriting the History of the Judiciary Act of 1789, at 134 (Wythe Holt and Lewis LaRue eds., 1990) (arguing that the Judiciary Act of 1789, currently codified at 28 U.S.C. § 1652, directed the federal courts to apply U.S. law rather than English law, and was not intended to compel the application of state law in diversity proceedings); see also Patrick J. Borchers, The Origins of Diversity Jurisdiction, the Rise of Legal Positivism, and a Brave New World for *Erie* and *Klaxon*, 72 Tex. L. Rev. 79 (1993) (arguing that the weight of historical evidence does not support the conclusion that state substantive law must apply in diversity suits); Julius Goebel Jr., History of the Supreme Court of the United States: Antecedents and Beginnings to 1801, at 457-508 (Paul Freund ed., 1971) (recounting the history of the Judiciary Act).

Note: The Personal and Political Aspects of Erie

Professor Purcell, supra, at 790, writes about Justice Brandeis's role in shaping the great case:

> Justice Louis D. Brandeis wrote the Court's opinion. Seizing on an otherwise wholly unremarkable common law tort suit, he persuaded a somewhat hesitant majority to use it as the vehicle to overrule *Swift*. His opinion for the Court, in turn, brought together most of the major themes of his judicial career. In broad constitutional terms, *Erie* expanded the power of the states to control their own common law and at the same time restricted the nonconstitutional lawmaking power of the federal judiciary to those areas over which Congress held the ultimate constitutional authority to legislate. With respect to limiting the scope of federal jurisdiction, *Erie* indirectly restricted both diversity and removal by eliminating one of the major incentives for their use. In terms of rationalizing the nation's judicial system, it sought to eliminate the arbitrariness inherent in a rule that made the applicable substantive law vary depending on the forum that heard an action and — as had Brandeis's opinion in Davis [v. Farmer's Coop. Equity Co., 262 U.S. 312 (1923),] initiating the commerce clause venue doctrine — to discourage jurisdictional manipulation and bring greater order and predictability to litigation practice. In political and

social terms, *Erie* deprived corporations of the favorable rules of the federal common law and remedied one of the major disadvantages that plaintiffs faced in the system of corporate diversity litigation. Finally, in quite personal terms, *Erie* allowed Brandeis to pay public homage to Holmes, his departed friend and colleague, who for more than a quarter-century had been recognized as the major intellectual and constitutional antagonist of *Swift* and the federal common law.

b. Substance and Procedure — Illustrative Cases

After 1938, federal courts sitting in diversity were to follow their own procedure and the substantive laws of the states in which they sat. Perhaps you can imagine the cases that arose next and the existential questions they raised about what is (or is not) a procedural rule. Less than a decade after *Erie,* the Court decided Guaranty Trust Co. v. York, 326 U.S. 99 (1945), which offered this famous guide to interpretation:

> Erie R.R. Co. v. Tompkins was not an endeavor to formulate scientific legal terminology. It expressed a policy that touches vitally the proper distribution of judicial power between State and federal courts. In essence, the intent of that decision was to insure that, in all cases where a federal court is exercising jurisdiction solely because of the diversity of citizenship of the parties, the outcome of the litigation in the federal court should be substantially the same, so far as legal rules determine the outcome of a litigation, as it would be if tried in a State court. The nub of the policy that underlies Erie R.R. Co. v. Tompkins is that for the same transaction the accident of a suit by a non-resident litigant in a federal court instead of in a State court a block away should not lead to a substantially different result.

Id. at 109.

Inevitably, the holding in *Guaranty Trust* was reduced to the following, ultimately unworkable bromide: If a rule is "outcome determinative," it is substantive and state law must govern. The obvious problem with the standard is that even the most relentlessly procedural rules, such as the size and color of the paper used for a complaint, may become "outcome determinative" if a court refuses to accept a complaint that does not comply with the rules.

The following cases highlight the Court's struggle with *Guaranty Trust* and with the distinction between substance and procedure. They remain more important for their results than for their reasoning, and are useful guidelines for the kinds of rules the Court has found to be "substantive."

i. Cohen v. Beneficial Industrial Loan Corp., 337 U.S. 541 (1949)

This case held that a federal court in New Jersey was bound by a statute of that state that imposes on the plaintiff in a derivative shareholder's suit liability for the cost of the defense if he is unsuccessful, and requires security for the payment of this cost to be given by plaintiff as a condition of maintaining the suit. The Court said that the statute could not be disregarded "as a mere procedural device." Id. at 556.

Justice Rutledge, in dissent, said:

> [I]n many situations procedure and substance are so interwoven that rational separation becomes well-nigh impossible. But, even so, this fact cannot dispense with the necessity of making a distinction. For as the matter stands, it is Congress which has power to govern the procedure of the federal courts in diversity cases, and the states which have that power over matters clearly substantive in nature.

Id. at 554.

ii. Ragan v. Merchants Transfer & Warehouse Co., 337 U.S. 530 (1949)

The Court held that the Kansas statute of limitations was not tolled by a filing of a complaint in federal court despite the language of Rule 3, because the federal court was bound to apply the Kansas law that the statute was not tolled until the complaint was served on the defendant. The Court, commenting on Guaranty Trust Co. v. York, said:

> We can draw no distinction in this case because local law brought the cause of action to an end after, rather than before, suit was started in the federal court. In both cases local law created the right which the federal court was asked to enforce. In both cases local law undertook to determine the life of the cause of action. We cannot give it longer life in the federal court than it would have had in the state court without adding something to the cause of action.

Id. at 553.

iii. Woods v. Interstate Realty Co., 337 U.S. 535 (1949)

The Court held that the federal court in Mississippi must dismiss an action brought by a Tennessee corporation that had violated the Mississippi law by doing business without properly qualifying and that was therefore barred from maintaining a suit in the courts of Mississippi. The Court explained at 538:

> The *York* case was premised on the theory that a right which local law creates but which it does not supply with a remedy is no right at all for purposes of enforcement in a federal court in a diversity case; that where in

> such cases one is barred from recovery in the state court, he should likewise be barred in the federal court. The contrary result would create discriminations against citizens of the state in favor of those authorized to invoke the diversity jurisdiction of the federal court. It was that element of discrimination that Erie R. Co. v. Tompkins was designed to eliminate.

Justice Jackson, who had written the opinion in *Cohen*, decided the same day, dissented vigorously at 539-540:

> The state statute as now interpreted by this Court is a harsh, capricious and vindictive measure. It either refuses to entertain a cause of action, not impaired by state law, or it holds it invalid with unknown effects on amounts already collected. In either case the amount of this punishment bears no relation to the amount of the wrong done the State in failure to qualify and pay its taxes. The penalty thus suffered does not go to the State, which sustained the injury, but results in unjust enrichment of the debtor, who has suffered no injury from the creditor's default in qualification. If the state court had held its statute to have this effect, I should agree that federal courts should so apply it; but the whole basis of our decision is contrary to that of the state courts.

iv. Byrd v. Blue Ridge Rural Electric Coop., Inc., 356 U.S. 525 (1958)

Courts quickly realized that strict application of the *York* outcome-determinative test was untenable. Taken to its logical extreme, nearly any rule might conceivably alter the outcome of litigation. In light of the practical difficulties courts encountered with the *York* test, the Supreme Court again took up the *Erie* doctrine in Byrd v. Blue Ridge Rural Electric Coop., Inc., 356 U.S. 525 (1958). *Byrd* involved a negligence action by a North Carolina worker on a construction job being performed in South Carolina for the defendant, a South Carolina utility. The defendant pleaded as a defense that the plaintiff was covered by the local worker's compensation act. It was the practice of South Carolina courts to decide the issue raised by this defense by means of judicial findings, there being no right to trial by jury of the issue of coverage. The Supreme Court nevertheless held that the issue was triable by jury in a federal court:

> We find nothing to suggest that this rule was announced as an integral part of the special relationship created by the statute. Thus the requirement appears to be merely a form and mode of enforcing the immunity, Guaranty Trust Co. v. York, 326 U.S. 99, 108 [1945], and not a rule intended to be bound up with the definition of the rights and obligations of the parties. . . .
>
> But cases following *Erie* have evinced a broader policy to the effect that the federal courts should conform as near as may be — in the absence of other considerations — to state rules even of form and mode where the state

rules may bear substantially on the question whether the litigation would come out one way in the federal court and another way in the state court if the federal court failed to apply a particular local rule. E.g., Guaranty Trust Co. v. York, supra; Bernhardt v. Polygraphic Co., 350 U.S. 198 (1956). Concededly the nature of the tribunal which tries issues may be important in the enforcement of the parcel of rights making up a cause of action or defense, and bear significantly upon achievement of uniform enforcement of the right. It may well be that in the instant personal injury case the outcome would be substantially affected by whether the issue of immunity is decided by a judge or a jury. Therefore, were "outcome" the only consideration, a strong case might appear for saying that the federal court should follow the state practice.

But there are affirmative countervailing considerations at work here. The federal system is an independent system for administering justice to litigants who properly invoke its jurisdiction. An essential characteristic of that system is the manner in which, in civil common-law actions, it distributes trial functions between judge and jury and, under the influence—if not the command—of the Seventh Amendment, assigns the decisions of disputed questions of fact to the jury. Jacob v. New York, 315 U.S. 752 (1942). The policy of uniform enforcement of state created rights and obligations, see, e.g., Guaranty Trust Co. v. York, supra, cannot in every case exact compliance with a state rule—not bound up with rights and obligations—which disrupts the federal system of allocating functions between judge and jury. Herron v. Southern Pacific Co., 283 U.S. 91 (1931). Thus the inquiry here is whether the federal policy favoring jury decisions of disputed fact questions should yield to the state rule in the interest of furthering the objective that the litigation should not come out one way in the federal court and another way in the state court.

We think that in the circumstances of this case the federal court should not follow the state rule. It cannot be gainsaid that there is a strong federal policy against allowing state rules to disrupt the judge-jury relationship in the federal courts. . . .

Id. at 536-538.

The Court in *Byrd* thus rejected a rigid application of *York*'s outcome-determinative test, instead calling on courts to balance competing state and federal policies, particularly where, as in *Byrd*, any difference in outcome was purely speculative. Applying its balancing test, the *Byrd* court concluded that South Carolina's weak interest in judicial determination of *Byrd*'s employment status was outweighed by the strong federal preference for jury trials, as embodied in the Seventh Amendment.

c. The *Hanna* Presumption

The Court further refined *York*'s outcome-determinative test and clarified the *Erie* doctrine in Hanna v. Plumer, which established a powerful presumption in favor of the federal courts' power to use the Federal Rules of Civil Procedure in diversity actions. *Hanna* established that the Federal

Rules are presumed to fall within the Supreme Court's statutory power under the Rules Enabling Act (28 U.S.C. § 2072) to prescribe rules of procedure that do not "abridge, enlarge or modify any substantive right."

Hanna v. Plumer

380 U.S. 460 (1965)

CHIEF JUSTICE WARREN delivered the opinion of the Court.

The question to be decided is whether, in a civil action where the jurisdiction of the United States district court is based upon diversity of citizenship between the parties, service of process shall be made in the manner prescribed by state law or that set forth in Rule 4(d)(1) of the Federal Rules of Civil Procedure.

On February 6, 1963, petitioner, a citizen of Ohio, filed her complaint in the District Court for the District of Massachusetts, claiming damages in excess of $10,000 for personal injuries resulting from an automobile accident in South Carolina, allegedly caused by the negligence of one Louise Plumer Osgood, a Massachusetts citizen deceased at the time of the filing of the complaint. Respondent, Mrs. Osgood's executor and also a Massachusetts citizen, was named as defendant. On February 8, service was made by leaving copies of the summons and the complaint with respondent's wife at his residence, concededly in compliance with Rule 4(d)(1).... Respondent filed his answer on February 26, alleging, *inter alia*, that the action could not be maintained because it had been brought "contrary to and in violation of the provisions of Massachusetts General Laws (Ter. Ed.) Chapter 197, Section 9." That section provides:

> Except as provided in this chapter, an executor or administrator shall not be held to answer to an action by a creditor of the deceased which is not commenced within one year from the time of his giving bond for the performance of his trust, or to such an action which is commenced within said year unless before the expiration thereof the writ in such action has been served by delivery in hand upon such executor or administrator....

On October 17, 1963, the District Court granted respondent's motion for summary judgment, citing Ragan v. Merchants Transfer Co., 337 U.S. 530 (1949), and Guaranty Trust Co. v. York, 326 U.S. 99 (1945), in support of its conclusion that the adequacy of the service was to be measured by § 9, with which, the court held, petitioner had not complied. On appeal, petitioner admitted noncompliance with § 9, but argued that Rule 4(d)(1) defines the method by which service of process is to be effected in diversity actions. The Court of Appeals for the First Circuit, finding that "[r]elatively recent amendments [to § 9] evince a clear legislative purpose to require personal notification within the year," concluded that the conflict of state and federal rules was over "a substantive rather than a procedural matter," and unanimously affirmed. 331 F.2d 157. Because of the threat to the goal of uniformity of federal procedure posed by the decision below, we granted certiorari, 379 U.S. 813.

We conclude that the adoption of Rule 4(d)(1), designed to control service of process in diversity actions, neither exceeded the congressional mandate embodied in the Rules Enabling Act nor transgressed constitutional bounds, and that the Rule is therefore the standard against which the District Court should have measured the adequacy of the service. Accordingly, we reverse the decision of the Court of Appeals.... [The Rules Enabling Act] provides, in pertinent part:

> The Supreme Court shall have the power to prescribe, by general rules, forms of process, writs, pleadings, and motions, and the practice and procedure of the district courts of the United States in civil actions.
>
> Such rules shall not abridge, enlarge or modify any substantive right and shall preserve the right of trial by jury....

Under the cases construing the scope of the Enabling Act, Rule (4)(d)(1) clearly passes muster. Prescribing the manner in which a defendant is to be notified that a suit has been instituted against him, it relates to the "practice and procedure of the district courts." "The test must be whether a rule really regulates procedure—the judicial process for enforcing rights and duties recognized by substantive law and for justly administering remedy and redress for disregard or infraction of them." Sibbach v. Wilson & Co, 312 U.S. 1 [1991]...

Thus were there no conflicting state procedures, Rule 4(d)(1) would clearly control. National Rental v. Szukhent, 375 U.S. 311, 316 [1964]. However, respondent, focusing on the contrary Massachusetts rule, calls to the Court's attention another line of cases, a line which—like the Federal Rules—had its birth in 1938. Erie R.R. Co. v. Tompkins, 304 U.S. 64 [1938], overruling Swift v. Tyson, 16 Pet. 1 [1842], held that federal courts sitting in diversity cases, when deciding questions of "substantive" law, are bound by state court decisions as well as state statutes. The broad command of *Erie* was therefore identical to that of the Enabling Act: federal courts are to apply state substantive law and federal procedural law. However, as subsequent cases sharpened the distinction between substance and procedure, the line of cases following *Erie* diverged markedly from the line construing the Enabling Act. Guaranty Trust Co. v. York, 326 U.S. 99, made it clear the *Erie*-type problems were not to be solved by reference to any traditional or common-sense substance-procedure distinction:

> And so the question is not whether a statute of limitations is deemed a matter of "procedure" in some sense. The question is . . . does it significantly affect the result of a litigation for a federal court to disregard a law of a State that would be controlling in an action upon the same claim by the same parties in a State court?

326 U.S., at 109. Respondent, by placing primary reliance on *York* and *Ragan*, suggests that the *Erie* doctrine acts as a check on the Federal Rules of Civil Procedure, that despite the clear command of Rule 4(d)(1), *Erie*

and its progeny demand the application of the Massachusetts rule. Reduced to essentials, the argument is: (1) *Erie,* as refined in *York,* demands that federal courts apply state law whenever application of federal law in its stead will alter the outcome of the case. (2) In this case, a determination that the Massachusetts service requirements obtain will result in immediate victory for respondent. If, on the other hand, it should be held that Rule 4(d)(1) is applicable, the litigation will continue, with possible victory for petitioner. (3) Therefore, *Erie* demands application of the Massachusetts rule. The syllogism possesses an appealing simplicity, but is for several reasons invalid.

In the first place, it is doubtful that, even if there were no Federal Rule making it clear that in-hand service is not required in diversity actions, the *Erie* rule would have obligated the District Court to follow the Massachusetts procedure. "Outcome-determination" analysis was never intended to serve as a talisman. Byrd v. Blue Ridge Cooperative, 356 U.S. 525, 537 (1958). Indeed, the message of *York* itself is that choices between state and federal law are to be made not by application of any automatic, "litmus paper" criterion, but rather by reference to the policies underlying the *Erie* rule. Guaranty Trust Co. v. York, supra, at 108-112.

The *Erie* rule is rooted in part in a realization that it would be unfair for the character or result of a litigation materially to differ because the suit had been brought in a federal court.

> Diversity of citizenship jurisdiction was conferred in order to prevent apprehended discrimination in state courts against those not citizens of the State. Swift v. Tyson introduced grave discrimination by non-citizens against citizens. It made rights enjoyed under the unwritten "general law" vary according to whether enforcement was sought in the state or in the federal court; and the privilege of selecting the court in which the right should be determined was conferred upon the non-citizen. Thus, the doctrine rendered impossible equal protection of the law.

Erie R.R. Co. v. Tompkins, supra, at 74-75. The decision was also in part a reaction to the practice of "forum-shopping," which had grown up in response to the rule of Swift v. Tyson, 304 U.S. at 73-74. That the *York* test was an attempt to effectuate these policies is demonstrated by the fact that the opinion framed the inquiry in terms of "substantial" variations between state and federal litigation. 326 U.S. at 109. Not only are nonsubstantial, or trivial, variations not likely to raise the sort of equal protection problems which troubled the Court in *Erie;* they are also unlikely to influence the choice of a forum. The "outcome-determination" test therefore cannot be read without reference to the twin aims of the *Erie* rule: discouragement of forum-shopping and avoidance of inequitable administration of the laws.

The difference between the conclusion that the Massachusetts rule is applicable, and the conclusion that it is not, is of course at this point "outcome-determinative" in the sense that if we hold the state rule to apply, respondent prevails, whereas if we hold that Rule 4(d)(1) governs, the litigation will continue. But in this sense *every* procedural variation is "outcome-determinative." For example, having brought suit in a federal court, a plaintiff cannot then insist on the right to file subsequent pleadings in accord with the time limits applicable in the state courts, even though enforcement of the federal timetable will, if he continues to insist that he must meet only the state time limit, result in determination of the controversy against him. So it is here. Though choice of the federal or state rule will at this point have a marked effect upon the outcome of the litigation, the difference between the two rules would be of scant, if any, relevance to the choice of a forum. Petitioner, in choosing her forum, was not presented with a situation where application of the state rule would wholly bar recovery; rather, adherence to the state rule would have resulted only in altering the way in which process was served. Moreover, it is difficult to argue that permitting service of defendant's wife to take the place of in-hand service of defendant himself alters the mode of enforcement of state-created rights in a fashion sufficiently "substantial" to raise the sort of equal protection problems to which the *Erie* opinion alluded.

There is, however, a more fundamental flaw in respondent's syllogism: the incorrect assumption that the rule of Erie R.R. Co. v. Tompkins constitutes the appropriate test of the validity and therefore the applicability of a Federal Rule of Civil Procedure. The *Erie* rule has never been invoked to void a Federal Rule. It is true that there have been cases where this Court has held applicable a state rule in the face of an argument that the situation was governed by one of the Federal Rules. But the holding of each such case was not that *Erie* commanded displacement of a Federal Rule by an inconsistent state rule, but rather that the scope of the Federal Rule was not as broad as the losing party urged, and therefore, there being no Federal Rule which covered the point in dispute, *Erie* commanded the enforcement of state law.

We are reminded by the *Erie* opinion that neither Congress nor the federal courts can, under the guise of formulating rules of decision for federal courts, fashion rules which are not supported by a grant of federal authority contained in Article I or some other section of the Constitution; in such areas state law must govern because there can be no other law. But the opinion in *Erie*, which involved no Federal Rule and dealt with a question which was "substantive" in every traditional sense (whether the railroad owed a duty of care to Tompkins as a trespasser or a licensee), surely neither said nor implied that measures like Rule 4(d)(1) are unconstitutional. For the constitutional provision for a federal court system (augmented by the Necessary and Proper Clause) carries with it congressional power to make rules governing the practice and pleading in those courts, which in turn includes a power to regulate matters which, though falling within the uncertain area between substance and procedure, are rationally capable of classification as either. Cf. McCulloch v. State of Maryland, 4 Wheat. 316, 421, 4 L. Ed. 579 [1819]. Neither *York* nor the cases following it ever suggested that the rule there laid down for coping with situations where no Federal Rule applies is coextensive with the limitation on Congress to which *Erie* had adverted. Although this Court has never before been confronted with a case where the applicable Federal Rule is in direct collision with the law of the relevant State, courts of appeals faced with such clashes have rightly discerned the implications of our decisions.

> One of the shaping purposes of the Federal Rules is to bring about uniformity in the federal courts by getting away from local rules. This is especially true of matters which relate to the administration of legal proceedings, an area in which federal courts have traditionally exerted strong inherent power, completely aside from the powers Congress expressly conferred in the Rules. The purpose of the *Erie* doctrine, even as extended in *York* and *Ragan*, was never to bottle-up federal courts with "outcome-determinative" and "integral-relations" stoppers—when there are "affirmative countervailing (federal) considerations" and when there is a Congressional mandate (the Rules) supported by constitutional authority. Lumbermen's Mut. Cas. Co. v. Wright, 322 F.2d 759, 764 (5th Cir. 1963).

Erie and its offspring cast no doubt on the long-recognized power of Congress to prescribe housekeeping rules for federal courts even though some of those rules will inevitably differ from comparable state rules. Cf. Herron v. Southern Pacific Co., 283 U.S. 91 (1931). "When, because the plaintiff happens to be a non-resident, such a right is enforceable in a federal as well as in a State court, the forms and mode of enforcing the right may at times, naturally enough, vary because the two judicial systems are not identical." Guaranty Trust Co. v. York, supra, at 108; Cohen v. Beneficial Loan Corp., 337 U.S. 541, 555 (1949). Thus, though a court, in measuring a Federal Rule against the standards contained in the Enabling Act and the Constitution, need not wholly blind itself to the degree to which the Rule makes the character and result of the federal litigation stray from the course it would follow in state courts, Sibbach v. Wilson & Co., 312 U.S. 1, 13-14 (1941), it cannot be forgotten that the Erie rule, and the guidelines suggested in *York*, were created to serve another purpose altogether. To hold that a Federal Rule of Civil Procedure must cease to function whenever it alters the mode of enforcing state-created rights would be to disembowel either the Constitution's grant of power over federal procedure or Congress' attempt to exercise that power in the Enabling Act. Rule 4(d)(1) is valid and controls the instant case.

Reversed.

JUSTICE HARLAN, concurring.

It is unquestionably true that up to now *Erie* and the cases following it have not succeeded in articulating a workable doctrine governing choice of law in diversity actions. I respect the Court's effort to clarify the situation in today's opinion. However, in doing so I think it has misconceived the constitutional premises of *Erie* and has failed to deal adequately with those past decisions upon which the courts below relied.

Erie was something more than an opinion which worried about "forum-shopping and avoidance of inequitable administration of the laws," although to be sure these were important elements of the decision. I have always regarded that decision as one of the modern cornerstones of our federalism, expressing policies that profoundly touch the allocation of judicial power between the state and federal systems. *Erie* recognized that there should not be two conflicting systems of law controlling the primary activity of citizens, for such alternative governing authority must necessarily give rise to a debilitating uncertainty in the planning of everyday affairs. And it recognized that the scheme of our Constitution envisions an allocation of law-making functions between state and federal legislative processes which is undercut if the federal judiciary can make substantive law affecting state affairs beyond the bounds of congressional legislative powers in this regard. Thus, in diversity cases *Erie* commands that it be the state law governing primary private activity which prevails.

The shorthand formulations which have appeared in some past decisions are prone to carry untoward results that frequently arise from oversimplification. The Court is quite right in stating that the "outcome-determinative" test of Guaranty Trust Co. v. York, 326 U.S. 99, if taken literally, proves too much, for any rule, no matter how clearly "procedural," can affect the outcome of litigation if it is not obeyed. In turning from the "outcome" test of *York* back to the unadorned forum-shopping rationale of *Erie,* however, the Court falls prey to like oversimplification, for a simple forum-shopping rule also proves too much; litigants often choose a federal forum merely to obtain what they consider the advantages of the Federal Rules of Civil Procedure or to try their cases before a supposedly more favorable judge. To my mind the proper line of approach in determining whether to apply a state or a federal rule, whether "substantive" or "procedural," is to stay close to basic principles by inquiring if the choice of rule would substantially affect those primary decisions respecting human conduct which our constitutional system leaves to state regulation. If so, *Erie* and the Constitution require that the state rule prevail, even in the face of a conflicting federal rule.

The Court weakens, if indeed it does not submerge, this basic principle by finding, in effect, a grant of substantive legislative power in the constitutional provision for a federal court system (compare Swift v. Tyson, 16 Pet. 1), and through it, setting up the Federal Rules as a body of law inviolate.

> [T]he constitutional provision for a federal court system . . . carries with it congressional power . . . to regulate matters which, though falling within the uncertain area between substance and procedure, *are rationally capable of classification as either.*

(Emphasis supplied.) So long as a reasonable man could characterize any duly adopted federal rule as "procedural," the Court, unless I misapprehend what is said, would have it apply no matter how seriously it frustrated a State's substantive regulation of the primary conduct and affairs of its citizens. Since the members of the Advisory Committee, the Judicial Conference, and this Court who formulated the Federal Rules are presumably reasonable men, it follows that the integrity of the Federal Rules is absolute. Whereas the unadulterated outcome and forum-shopping tests may err too far toward honoring state rules, I submit that the Court's "arguably procedural, *ergo* constitutional" test moves too fast and far in the other direction. . . .

Notes and Questions

1. *Arguing State Versus Federal Law.* Post-*Hanna,* when is a debatable *Erie* question likely to arise? *Hanna* makes it very difficult to argue against application of a Federal Rule of Civil Procedure that has been adopted pursuant to the Supreme Court's rulemaking procedure. But federal courts follow many other, non-Fed. R. Civ. P. rules that are arguably "procedural." When these rules conflict with relevant state rules on point, the court must confront the classic *Erie* dilemma: should federal or state rules apply? To argue for application of federal over state law, the lawyer must emphasize the procedural characteristics of the rule, characterize the rule as affecting the fairness and efficiency of litigation (rather than primary human behavior beyond the courtroom), stress the federal court system's interest in applying its own rule, and minimize concerns about outcome determinativeness and forum shopping. Her opponent, of course, will attempt to counter each of these arguments as part of a more general effort to color the rule in question "substantive."

Part of both lawyers' strategies is likely to be analogical reasoning. The lawyers will argue that the rule in question is "just like" a rule that the Court already has deemed "substantive" or "procedural." The following chart is a handy guide for making such arguments.

Rule	*Choice of law*	*Authority*
Standard of care	State law	Erie R.R. Co. v. Tompkins, 304 U.S. 64 (1938)
Conflict of laws	State law	Klaxon Co. v. Stentor Elec., 313 U.S. 487 (1941)
Statute of limitations	State law	Guaranty Trust Co. v. York, 326 U.S. 99 (1945)
Burden of proof	State law	Cities Service Oil v. Dunlap, 308 U.S. 208 (1939)
Burden of pleading	Federal	Palmer v. Hoffman, 318 U.S. 109 (1943)
Discovery — Physical Examinations	Federal	Sibbach v. Wilson & Co., 312 U.S. 1 (1941)
Venue transfers and effect of forum selection clause	Federal	Stewart Org. v. Ricoh Corp., 487 U.S. 22 (1988)
Agreement to arbitrate	State law	Bernhardt v. Polygraphic Co., 350 U.S. 198 (1956)

2. *Determining State Law.* To say that state law applies to an issue leads to another sometimes complex question: What is the controlling state law? State law on point may be sparse, conflicting, or very old. In general, the federal court's job is to forecast what the applicable state's supreme court would say on the matter. In making this forecast, the court will rely on the supreme court's opinions, unless it is fairly confident that the court would not apply its own precedent. In the absence of controlling supreme court decisions, the federal court may consider opinions of state intermediate appellate courts, scholarly articles, the Restatement of Law, and treatises. See generally Bernhardt v. Polygraphic Co. of Am., 350 U.S. 198 (1956); Comm'r v. Estate of Bosch, 387 U.S. 456 (1967).

3. *Applying* Erie *and* Hanna. How would *Erie* and *Hanna* play out in the following cases? (Before learning what the Court actually did in them, see if you can generate the best arguments for each side.)

a. Rule 3 of the Federal Rules of Civil Procedure provides that "[a] civil action is commenced by filing a complaint with the court." Plaintiff files a diversity suit in federal court one day before the applicable statute of limitations elapses. Two weeks later, plaintiff serves defendant with the complaint. Federal law grants plaintiff 120 days after filing a complaint to complete service. State law in this case requires that both filing and service must occur within the applicable statute of limitations. Defendant moves for summary judgment on the ground that the action is barred by the statute of limitations. What result?

See Ragan v. Merchants Transfer & Warehouse Co., 337 U.S. 530 (1949); Walker v. Armco Steel Corp., 446 U.S. 740 (1980).

b. Plaintiff secures a jury verdict against defendant in a federal diversity suit. After the verdict is affirmed on appeal without modification, the appellate court assesses a penalty of 10 percent of the damages, as prescribed by state law, for an unsuccessful appeal of a money judgment. Rule 38 of the Federal Rules of Appellate Procedure holds that "[i]f a court of appeals shall determine that an appeal is frivolous, it may award just damages and single or double costs to the appellee." Defendant objects to the penalty on the ground that Rule 38 governs, and permits penalties to be imposed only when an appeal is frivolous. What result?

See Burlington Northern R.R. Co. v. Woods, 480 U.S. 1 (1987).

c. Plaintiff files a diversity suit against defendant in federal court. State law permits admission into evidence of out-of-court settlements. Federal Rule of Evidence 408 provides as follows:

> Evidence of (1) furnishing or offering or promising to furnish, or (2) accepting or offering or promising to accept, a valuable consideration in compromising or attempting to compromise a claim which was disputed as to either validity or amount, is not admissible to prove liability for or invalidity of the claim or its amount.

Plaintiff offers into evidence (to prove liability) out-of-court settlements between defendant and third parties. Defendant objects, invoking Rule 408. What result?

For a similar issue regarding the application of evidentiary rules, see Carota v. Johns Manville Corp., 893 F.2d 448 (1st Cir. 1990).

In any of these cases, would application of the federal rule (versus the state rule) affect primary behavior outside the courtroom? Produce forum shopping? Promote the integrity and efficiency of the federal courts? Are the federal and state rules in any of them compatible, such that no real conflict exists?

4. *Court-Imposed Sanctions and* Erie. Consider the following excerpt from Chambers v. Nasco, Inc., 501 U.S. 32, 52-53 (1991), previously encountered in Chapter 2, in which the Court held that a federal district judge in a diversity case has "inherent power" to sanction a party for bad faith conduct:

> Only when there is a conflict between state and federal substantive law are the concerns of Erie R.R. Co. v. Tompkins, 304 U.S. 64 (1938), at issue. As we explained in Hanna v. Plumer, 380 U.S. 460, 468 (1965), the "outcome determinative" test of *Erie* and Guaranty Trust Co. v. York, 326 U.S. 99 (1945), "cannot be read without reference to the twin aims of the *Erie* rule: discouragement of forum-shopping and avoidance of inequitable administration of the laws," . . . [N]either of these twin aims is implicated by the assessment of attorney's fees as a sanction for bad-faith conduct before the court which involved disobedience of the court's orders and the attempt to defraud the court itself. . . . [T]he imposition of sanctions under the bad-faith exception depends not on which party wins the lawsuit, but on how the parties conduct themselves during the litigation. Consequently, there is no risk that the exception will lead to forum shopping. Nor is it inequitable to apply the exception to citizens and noncitizens alike, when the party, by controlling his or her conduct in litigation, has the power to determine whether sanctions will be assessed.

5. *Forum Selection Clauses and* Erie. Is a federal court sitting in diversity obliged to respect state law on the enforceability of forum selection clauses in contracts between the parties, or may it follow its own policy?

In Stewart Org., Inc. v. Ricoh, 487 U.S. 22 (1988), the Court held that a federal court could enforce a forum selection clause even when the state whose substantive law applies to the matter would not. When *Ricoh* is read together with Carnival Cruise Lines, Inc. v. Shute, 499 U.S. 585 (1991) (Chapter 1, supra), which upheld the enforcement of a forum selection clause in a form ticket contract, doesn't this give the drafting party considerable control over the location of the lawsuit? For a critical analysis of *Ricoh*, see Richard D. Freer, *Erie*'s Mid-Life Crisis, 63 Tul. L. Rev. 1087, 1113-1131 (1989). Still undecided is the issue of whether state or federal law governs the interpretation of a forum selection clause with respect to personal jurisdiction. In Preferred Capital, Inc. v. Sarasota Kennel Club, Inc., 489 F.3d 303 (6th Cir. 2007), the Sixth Circuit held that state law controls this decision since it is a "substantive" one under *Hanna*. The Seventh and Eleventh Circuits have suggested the same, see IFC Credit Corp. v. Aliano Bros. General Contractors, 437 F.3d 606 (7th Cir. 2006); Alexander Proudfoot Co. World Headquarters v. Thayer, 877 F.2d 912 (11th Cir. 1989), but the Supreme Court has not yet offered a definitive answer.

d. Gasperini v. Center for Humanities: Separating Substance from Procedure, Balancing State and Federal Interests, and Other Nagging Questions of *Erie-Hanna* Jurisprudence

In 1996 the Supreme Court had occasion to revisit the *Erie* doctrine once again in light of *Hanna*. The Court considered two issues: (1) whether New York or federal law should determine the standard of review under which a trial court may alter a jury's damage award; and (2) whether federal appeals courts should adopt New York standards of appellate review that were arguably substantive under *Erie* but implicated strong federal interests.

Gasperini v. Center for Humanities, Inc.
518 U.S. 415 (1996)

JUSTICE GINSBURG delivered the opinion of the Court.

Petitioner William Gasperini, a journalist for CBS News and the Christian Science Monitor, began reporting on events in Central America in 1984. He earned his living primarily in radio and print media and only occasionally sold his photographic work. During the course of his seven year stint in Central America, Gasperini took over 5,000 slide transparencies, depicting active war zones, political leaders, and scenes from daily life. In 1990, Gasperini agreed to supply his original color transparencies to The Center for Humanities, Inc. (Center) for use in an educational videotape, Conflict in Central America. Gasperini selected 300 of his slides for the Center; its videotape included 110 of them. The Center agreed to return the original transparencies, but upon the completion of the project, it could not find them.

Gasperini commenced suit in the United States District Court for the Southern District of New York, invoking the court's diversity jurisdiction pursuant to 28 U.S.C. § 1332. He alleged several state law claims for relief, including breach of contract, conversion, and negligence. The Center conceded liability for the lost transparencies and the issue of damages was tried before a jury.

At trial, Gasperini's expert witness testified that the "industry standard" within the photographic publishing community valued a lost transparency at $1,500. This industry standard, the expert explained, represented the average license fee a commercial photograph could earn over the full course of the photographer's copyright, i.e., in Gasperini's case, his lifetime plus 50 years. . . .

After a three day trial, the jury awarded Gasperini $450,000 in compensatory damages. This sum, the jury foreperson announced, "is [$]1500 each, for 300 slides." Moving for a new trial under Federal Rule of Civil Procedure 59, the Center attacked the verdict on various grounds, including excessiveness. Without comment, the District Court denied the motion.

The Court of Appeals for the Second Circuit vacated the judgment entered on the jury's verdict. 66 F.3d 427 (1995). Mindful that New York law governed the controversy, the Court of Appeals endeavored to apply CPLR § 5501(c), which instructs that, when a jury returns an itemized verdict, as the jury did in this case, the New York Appellate Division "shall determine that an award is excessive or inadequate if it deviates materially from what would be reasonable compensation." . . . Surveying Appellate Division decisions that reviewed damage awards for lost transparencies, the Second Circuit concluded that testimony on industry standard alone was insufficient to justify a verdict. . . .

Guided by Appellate Division rulings, the Second Circuit held that the $450,000 verdict "materially deviates from what is reasonable compensation." 66 F.3d at 431. . . . Remittiturs "presen[t] difficult problems for appellate courts," the Second Circuit acknowledged, for court of appeals judges review the evidence from "a cold paper record." Nevertheless, the Second Circuit set aside the $450,000 verdict and ordered a new trial, unless Gasperini agreed to an award of $100,000.

This case presents an important question regarding the standard a federal court uses to measure the alleged excessiveness of a jury's verdict in an action for damages based on state law. We therefore granted certiorari.

Before 1986, state and federal courts in New York generally invoked the same judge-made formulation in responding to excessiveness attacks on jury verdicts: courts would not disturb an award unless the amount was so exorbitant that it "shocked the conscience of the court." . . .

In 1986, as part of a series of tort reform measures, New York codified a standard for judicial review of the size of jury awards. Placed in CPLR § 5501(c), the prescription reads:

> In reviewing a money judgment . . . in which it is contended that the award is excessive or inadequate and that a new trial should have been granted unless a stipulation is entered to a different award, the appellate division shall determine that an award is excessive or inadequate if it deviates materially from what would be reasonable compensation.

As stated in Legislative Findings and Declarations accompanying New York's adoption of the "deviates materially" formulation, the lawmakers found the "shock the conscience" test an insufficient check on damage awards; the legislature therefore installed a standard "invit[ing] more careful appellate scrutiny." . . .

Although phrased as a direction to New York's intermediate appellate courts, § 5501(c)'s "deviates materially" standard, as construed by New York's courts, instructs state trial judges as well. . . . Application of § 5501(c) at the trial level is key to this case. . . .

As the parties' arguments suggest, CPLR § 5501(c), appraised under Erie R.R. Co. v. Tompkins, 304 U.S. 64 (1938), and decisions in *Erie*'s path, is both "substantive" and "procedural": "substantive" in that § 5501(c)'s "deviates materially" standard controls how much a plaintiff can be awarded; "procedural" in that § 5501(c) assigns decision making authority to New York's Appellate Division. Parallel application of § 5501(c) at the federal appellate level would be out of sync with the federal system's division of trial and appellate court functions, an allocation weighted by the Seventh Amendment. The dispositive question, therefore, is whether federal courts can give effect to the substantive thrust of § 5501(c) without untoward alteration of the federal scheme for the trial and decision of civil cases. . . .

Classification of a law as "substantive" or "procedural" for *Erie* purposes is sometimes a challenging endeavor. Guaranty Trust Co. v. York, 326 U.S. 99 (1945), an early interpretation of *Erie*, propounded an "outcome-determination" test: "[D]oes it significantly affect the result of a litigation for a federal court to disregard a law of a State that would be controlling in an action upon the same claim by the same parties in a State court?" 326 U.S. at 109. Ordering application of a state statute of limitations to an equity proceeding in federal court, the Court said in *Guaranty Trust:* "[W]here a federal court is exercising jurisdiction solely because of the diversity of citizenship of the parties, the outcome of the litigation in the federal court should be substantially the same, so far as legal rules determine the outcome of a litigation, as it would be if tried in a State court." . . . A later pathmarking case, qualifying *Guaranty Trust*, explained that the "outcome determination" test must not be applied mechanically to sweep in all manner of variations; instead, its application must be guided by "the twin aims of the *Erie* rule: discouragement of forum shopping and avoidance of inequitable administration of the laws." Hanna v. Plumer, 380 U.S. 460, 468 (1965). . . .

Informed by these decisions, we address the question whether New York's "deviates materially" standard, codified in CPLR § 5501(c), is outcome affective in this sense: Would "application of the [standard] . . . have so important an effect upon the fortunes of one or both of the litigants that failure to [apply] it would [unfairly discriminate against citizens of the forum State, or] be likely to cause a plaintiff to choose the federal court"? Id., at 468, n.9.

We start from a point the parties do not debate. Gasperini acknowledges that a statutory cap on damages would supply substantive law for *Erie* purposes. . . . New York's Legislature codified in § 5501(c) a new standard, one that requires closer court review than the common law "shock the conscience" test. . . . [Section] 5501(c) contains a procedural instruction, but the State's objective is manifestly substantive.

It thus appears that if federal courts ignore the change in the New York standard and persist in applying the "shock the conscience" test to damage awards on claims governed by New York law, "'substantial' variations between state and federal [money judgments]" may be expected. See *Hanna,* 380 U.S. at 467-468 [n.11]. We therefore agree with the Second Circuit that New York's check on excessive damages implicates what we have called *Erie*'s "twin aims." Just as the *Erie* principle precludes a federal court from giving a state-created claim "longer life . . . than [the claim] would have had in the state court" (citation omitted), so *Erie* precludes a recovery in federal court significantly larger than the recovery that would have been tolerated in state court.

CPLR § 5501(c), as earlier noted, is phrased as a direction to the New York Appellate Division. . . . Concentrating on the authority § 5501(c) gives to the Appellate Division, Gasperini urges that the provision shifts fact-finding responsibility from the jury and the trial judge to the appellate court. Assigning such responsibility to an appellate court, he maintains, is incompatible with the Seventh Amendment's Re-examination Clause, and therefore, Gasperini concludes, § 5501(c) cannot be given effect in federal court. Although we reach a different conclusion than Gasperini, we agree that the Second Circuit did not attend to "[a]n essential characteristic of [the federal court] system," Byrd v. Blue Ridge Rural Elec. Cooperative, Inc., 356 U.S. 525, 537 (1958), when it used § 5501(c) as "the standard for [federal] appellate review," *Consorti,* 72 F.3d at 1013; see also 66 F.3d at 430.

That "essential characteristic" was described in *Byrd,* a diversity suit for negligence in which a pivotal issue of fact would have been tried by a judge were the case in state court. The *Byrd* Court held that, despite the state practice, the plaintiff was entitled to a jury trial in federal court. In so ruling, the Court said that the *Guaranty Trust* "outcome-determination" test was an insufficient guide in cases presenting countervailing federal interests. See *Byrd,* 356 U.S. at 537. The Court described the countervailing federal interests present in *Byrd* this way:

> The federal system is an independent system for administering justice to litigants who properly invoke its jurisdiction. An essential characteristic of that system is the manner in which, in civil common law actions, it distributes trial functions between judge and jury and, under the influence—if not the command—of the Seventh Amendment, assigns the decisions of disputed questions of fact to the jury. Id. (footnote omitted).

The Seventh Amendment, which governs proceedings in federal court, but not in state court, bears not only on the allocation of trial functions between judge and jury, the issue in *Byrd;* it also controls the allocation of authority to review verdicts, the issue of concern here. . . .

In *Byrd,* the Court faced a one-or-the-other choice: trial by judge as in state court, or trial by jury according to the federal practice.[21] In the case

21. The two-trial rule posited by Justice Scalia, post, surely would be incompatible with the existence of "[t]he federal system [as] an independent system for administering justice," Byrd v. Blue Ridge Rural Elec. Cooperative, Inc., 356 U.S. 525, 537 (1958). We

before us, a choice of that order is not required, for the principal state and federal interests can be accommodated. The Second Circuit correctly recognized that when New York substantive law governs a claim for relief, New York law and decisions guide the allowable damages. See 66 F.3d at 430; see also *Consorti,* 72 F.3d at 1011. But that court did not take into account the characteristic of the federal court system that caused us to reaffirm: "The proper role of the trial and appellate courts in the federal system in reviewing the size of jury verdicts is . . . a matter of federal law."

New York's dominant interest can be respected, without disrupting the federal system, once it is recognized that the federal district court is capable of performing the checking function, i.e., that court can apply the State's "deviates materially" standard in line with New York case law evolving under CPLR § 5501(c).[22] We recall, in this regard, that the "deviates materially" standard serves as the guide to be applied in trial as well as appellate courts in New York.

Within the federal system, practical reasons combine with Seventh Amendment constraints to lodge in the district court, not the court of appeals, primary responsibility for application of § 5501(c)'s "deviates materially" check. Trial judges have the "unique opportunity to consider the evidence in the living courtroom context," Taylor v. Washington Terminal Co., 409 F.2d 145, 148 (D.C. Cir. 1969), while appellate judges see only the "cold paper record," 66 F.3d at 431.

District court applications of the "deviates materially" standard would be subject to appellate review under the standard the Circuits now employ when inadequacy or excessiveness is asserted on appeal: abuse of discretion. . . .

It does not appear that the District Court checked the jury's verdict against the relevant New York decisions demanding more than "industry standard" testimony to support an award of the size the jury returned in this case. . . . Accordingly, we vacate the judgment of the Court of Appeals

---

discern no disagreement on such examples among the many federal judges who have considered this case.

22. Justice Scalia finds in Federal Rule of Civil Procedure 59 a "federal standard" for new trial motions in "'direct collision'" with, and "'leaving no room for the operation of,'" a state law like CPLR § 5501(c). . . . The relevant prescription, Rule 59(a), has remained unchanged since the adoption of the Federal Rules by this Court in 1937. 302 U.S. 783. Rule 59(a) is as encompassing as it is uncontroversial. It is indeed "Hornbook" law that a most usual ground for a Rule 59 motion is that "the damages are excessive." See C. Wright, Law of Federal Courts 676-677 (5th ed. 1994). Whether damages are excessive for the claim-in-suit must be governed by laws. And there is no candidate for that governance other than the law that gives rise to the claim for relief — here, the law of New York. See 28 U.S.C. § 2072(a) and (b) ("Supreme Court shall have the power to prescribe general rules of . . . procedure"; "[s]uch rules shall not abridge, enlarge or modify any substantive right"); Browning-Ferris Ind. of Utah, Inc. v. Kelco Disposal, Inc., 492 U.S. 257, 279 (1989) ("standard of excessiveness" is a "matte[r] of state, and not federal, common law"); see also R. Fallon, D. Meltzer, & D. Shapiro, Hart and Wechsler's The Federal Courts and the Federal System 729-730 (4th ed. 1996) (observing that Court "has continued since [Hanna v. Plumer, 380 U.S. 460 (1965),] to interpret the federal rules to avoid conflict with important state regulatory policies," citing Walker v. Armco Steel Corp., 446 U.S. 740 (1980)).

and instruct that court to remand the case to the District Court so that the trial judge, revisiting his ruling on the new trial motion, may test the jury's verdict against CPLR § 5501(c)'s "deviates materially" standard.

It is so ordered.

JUSTICE STEVENS, dissenting [omitted]. . . .

JUSTICE SCALIA, dissenting.

. . . Because the Court and I disagree as to the character of the review that is before us, I recount briefly the nature of the New York practice rule at issue. Section 5501(c) of the N.Y. Civ. Prac. Law and Rules (CPLR) (McKinney 1995) directs New York intermediate appellate courts faced with a claim "that the award is excessive or inadequate and that a new trial should have been granted" to determine whether the jury's award "deviates materially from what would be reasonable compensation." In granting respondent a new trial under this standard, the Court of Appeals necessarily engaged in a two step process. As it has explained the application of § 5501(c), that provision "requires the reviewing court to determine the range it regards as reasonable, and to determine whether the particular jury award deviates materially from that range." Consorti v. Armstrong World Industries, Inc., 72 F.3d 1003, 1013 (1995) (amended). The first of these two steps—the determination as to "reasonable" damages—plainly requires the reviewing court to reexamine a factual matter tried by the jury: the appropriate measure of damages, on the evidence presented, under New York law. The second step—the determination as to the degree of difference between "reasonable" damages and the damages found by the jury (whether the latter "deviates materially" from the former)—establishes the degree of judicial tolerance for awards found not to be reasonable, whether at the trial level or by the appellate court. No part of this exercise is appropriate for a federal court of appeals, whether or not it is sitting in a diversity case.

Granting appellate courts authority to decide whether an award is "excessive or inadequate" in the manner of CPLR § 5501(c) may reflect a sound understanding of the capacities of modern juries and trial judges. That is to say, the people of the State of New York may well be correct that such a rule contributes to a more just legal system. But the practice of federal appellate reexamination of facts found by a jury is precisely what the People of the several States considered not to be good legal policy in 1791. Indeed, so fearful were they of such a practice that they constitutionally prohibited it by means of the Seventh Amendment. . . .

I am persuaded that our prior cases were correct that, at common law, "reexamination" of the facts found by a jury could be undertaken only by the trial court, and that appellate review was restricted to writ of error which could challenge the judgment only upon matters of law. Even if there were some doubt on the point, we should be hesitant to advance our view of the common law over that of our forbears, who were far better acquainted with the subject than we are. . . .

The Court, as is its wont of late, all but ignores the relevant history. It acknowledges that federal appellate review of district court refusals to set aside jury awards as against the weight of the evidence was "once deemed inconsonant with the Seventh Amendment's Re-examination clause," but gives no indication of why ever we held that view; and its citation of only one of our cases subscribing to that proposition fails to convey how long and how clearly it was a fixture of federal practice. . . . That our earlier cases are so poorly recounted is not surprising, however, given the scant analysis devoted to the conclusion that "appellate review for abuse of discretion is reconcilable with the Seventh Amendment." . . .

No precedent of this Court affirmatively supports that proposition. The cases upon which the Court relies neither affirmed nor rejected the practice of appellate weight-of-the-evidence review that has been adopted by the courts of appeals — a development that, in light of our past cases, amounts to studied waywardness by the intermediate appellate bench. . . .

In any event, it is not this Court's statements that the Court puts forward as the basis for dispensing with our prior cases. Rather, it is the Circuit Courts of Appeals' unanimous "agree[ment]" that they may review trial court refusals to set aside jury awards claimed to be against the weight of the evidence. This current unanimity is deemed controlling, notwithstanding the "relatively late" origin of the practice, and without any inquiry into the reasoning set forth in those Court of Appeals decisions. . . .

The Court's holding that federal courts of appeals may review district court denials of motions for new trials for error of fact is not the only novel aspect of today's decision. The Court also directs that the case be remanded to the District Court, so that it may "test the jury's verdict against CPLR § 5501(c)'s 'deviates materially' standard." This disposition contradicts the principle that "[t]he proper role of the trial and appellate courts in the federal system in reviewing the size of jury verdicts is . . . a matter of federal law." Donovan v. Penn Shipping Co., 429 U.S. 648, 649 (1977) (per curiam).

The Court acknowledges that state procedural rules cannot, as a general matter, be permitted to interfere with the allocation of functions in the federal court system. Indeed, it is at least partly for this reason that the Court rejects direct application of § 5501(c) at the appellate level as inconsistent with an "'essential characteristic'" of the federal court system — by which the Court presumably means abuse of discretion review of denials of motions for new trials. But the scope of the Court's concern is oddly circumscribed. The "essential characteristic" of the federal jury, and, more specifically, the role of the federal trial court in reviewing jury judgments, apparently counts for little. The Court approves the "accommodat[ion]" achieved by having district courts review jury verdicts under the "deviates materially" standard, because it regards that as a means of giving effect to the State's purposes "without disrupting the federal system." But changing the standard by which trial judges review jury verdicts does disrupt the federal system, and is plainly inconsistent with "the strong federal policy against allowing state rules to disrupt the judge-jury relationship in federal court." Byrd v. Blue Ridge Rural Elec. Cooperative, Inc., 356 U.S. 525, 538 [n.9] (1958). The Court's opinion does not even acknowledge, let alone address, this dislocation.

We discussed precisely the point at issue here in Browning Ferris Industries of Vt., Inc. v. Kelco Disposal, Inc., 492 U.S. 257 (1989), and gave an answer altogether contrary to the one provided today. *Browning Ferris* rejected a request to fashion a federal common law rule limiting the size of punitive damages awards in federal courts, reaffirming the principle of Erie R.R. Co. v. Tompkins, 304 U.S. 64 (1938), that "[i]n a diversity action, or in any other lawsuit where state law provides the basis of decision, the propriety of an award of punitive damages . . . , and the factors the jury may consider in determining their amount, are questions of state law." 492 U.S. at 278. But the opinion expressly stated that "[f]ederal law . . . will control on those issues involving the proper review of the jury award by a federal district court and court of appeals." Id. at 278-279. "In reviewing an award of punitive damages," it said, "the role of the district court is to determine whether the jury's verdict is within the confines of state law, and to determine, by reference to federal standards developed under Rule 59, whether a new trial or remittitur should be ordered." Id. at 279. The same distinction necessarily applies where the judgment under review is for compensatory damages: State substantive law controls what injuries are compensable and in what amount; but federal standards determine whether the award exceeds what is lawful to such degree that it may be set aside by order for new trial or remittitur.

The Court does not disavow those statements in *Browning Ferris* (indeed, it does not even discuss them), but it presumably overrules them, at least where the state rule that governs "whether a new trial or remittitur should be ordered" is characterized as "substantive" in nature. . . .

A tighter standard for reviewing jury determinations can no more plausibly be called a "substantive" disposition than can a tighter appellate standard for reviewing trial court determinations. The one, like the other, provides additional assurance that the law has been complied with; but the other, like the one, leaves the law unchanged.

The Court commits the classic *Erie* mistake of regarding whatever changes the outcome as substantive. . . . Outcome determination "was never intended to serve as a talisman," Hanna v. Plumer, 380 U.S. 460, 466-467 (1965), and does not have the power to convert the most classic elements of the process of assuring that the law is observed into the substantive law itself. . . .

In any event, the Court exaggerates the difference that the state standard will make. It concludes that different outcomes are likely to ensue depending on whether the law being applied is the state "deviates materially" standard of § 5501(c) or the "shocks the conscience" standard. Of course it is not the federal appellate standard but the federal district court standard for granting new trials that must be compared with the New York standard to determine whether substantially different results will obtain — and it is far from clear that the district court standard ought to be "shocks the conscience."...

In sum, it is at least highly questionable whether the consistent outcome differential claimed by the Court even exists. What seems to me far more likely to produce forum shopping is the consistent difference between the state and federal appellate standards, which the Court leaves untouched. Under the Court's disposition, the Second Circuit reviews only for abuse of discretion, whereas New York's appellate courts engage in a de novo review for material deviation, giving the defendant a double shot at getting the damages award set aside. The only result that would produce the conformity the Court erroneously believes *Erie* requires is the one adopted by the Second Circuit and rejected by the Court: de novo federal appellate review under the § 5501(c) standard....

The foregoing describes why I think the Court's *Erie* analysis is flawed. But in my view, one does not even reach the *Erie* question in this case. The standard to be applied by a district court in ruling on a motion for a new trial is set forth in Rule 59 of the Federal Rules of Civil Procedure, which provides that "[a] new trial may be granted . . . for any of the reasons for which new trials have heretofore been granted in actions at law in the courts of the United States." That is undeniably a federal standard. Federal district courts in the Second Circuit have interpreted that standard to permit the granting of new trials where "'it is quite clear that the jury has reached a seriously erroneous result'" and letting the verdict stand would result in a "'miscarriage of justice.'" Koerner v. Club Mediterranee, S.A., 833 F. Supp. 327 (S.D.N.Y. 1993) (quoting Bevevino v. Saydjari, 574 F.2d 676, 684 (2d Cir. 1978)). Assuming (as we have no reason to question) that this is a correct interpretation of what Rule 59 requires, it is undeniable that the federal rule is "'sufficiently broad' to cause a 'direct collision' with the state law or, implicitly, to 'control the issue' before the court, thereby leaving no room for the operation of that law." Burlington Northern R.R. Co. v. Woods, 480 U.S. 1, 4-5 (1987). It is simply not possible to give controlling effect both to the federal standard and the state standard in reviewing the jury's award. That being so, the court has no choice but to apply the Federal Rule, which is an exercise of what we have called Congress's "power to regulate matters which, though falling within the uncertain area between substance and procedure, are rationally capable of classification as either," *Hanna*, 380 U.S. at 472.

There is no small irony in the Court's declaration today that appellate review of refusals to grant new trials for error of fact is "a control necessary and proper to the fair administration of justice." It is objection to precisely that sort of "control" by federal appellate judges that gave birth to the Reexamination Clause of the Seventh Amendment. Alas, those who drew the Amendment, and the citizens who approved it, did not envision an age in which the Constitution means whatever this Court thinks it ought to mean — or indeed, whatever the courts of appeals have recently thought it ought to mean.

When there is added to the revision of the Seventh Amendment the Court's precedent setting disregard of Congress's instructions in Rule 59, one must conclude that this is a bad day for the Constitution's distinctive Article III courts in general, and for the role of the jury in those courts in particular. I respectfully dissent.

Notes and Questions

1. *An Excessive Verdict?* Think about the resources that have gone into resolving the dispute between the journalist and the Center. We start with the 5-4 decision of the Supreme Court, with a full-dress majority, concurrence, and dissent. This was preceded by briefing, argument, and opinion by the Second Circuit, and a motion for a new trial in the District Court. Thus, a total of 13 judges have passed on the question of whether the jury went too far in its damage award.

The jury trial under review consumed three days of court time and was undoubtedly preceded by copious discovery, the depositions of experts on both sides, and efforts to settle the case. What would be your guess about why the parties failed to settle? What do you think went into the jury's appraisal of the collection? Note that if Gasperini's oeuvre of 5,000 slides were valued at the rate the jury awarded, the collection would be worth over seven million dollars. That seems excessive — or does it? On remand from the Supreme Court, the District Court, applying the New York standard, entered a much smaller remittitur, reducing the jury's verdict to $375,000 instead of $1,000,000, the award granted by the Second Circuit. 972 F. Supp. 765 (S.D.N.Y. 1997).

As to the Second Circuit's decision, the District Court noted that the appellate court's reckoning was entitled to little weight because it had not had the exhibits before it. In addition, the basis for calculating the worth of each slide had not been thoroughly briefed or argued by the attorneys. "The jury," said the District Court, "had the right to consider the superior quality of Mr. Gasperini's work, and the uniqueness of the lost slides as well as the fact that most of them were irreplaceable."

On appeal, the Second Circuit acknowledged that its earlier decision had been based on a "cold-paper record," and noted that the Supreme Court had emphasized that appellate review was limited to determining whether the district court judge had committed an abuse of discretion. Gasperini v. Center for Humanities, Inc. 149 F.3d 137 (2d Cir. 1998).

2. *Rule 59 and the* Hanna *Analysis.* If this were a case in which Rule 59 conflicted with a New York procedural rule governing the grant of a new trial, the federal rule would trump, in an uncomplicated application of *Hanna*. But the majority finds that no federal rule is *involved* in this case. Why not? What is the argument that Rule 59 includes, or at least, implicates, the "shocks the conscience" test?

Instead of the easy case of two procedural rules in opposition, the majority holds that the New York statute is substantive, and that the federal standard is a judge-made procedural rule. Nevertheless, the Court engages in a *Hanna*-type analysis when it asks which standard, state or federal, would best serve the "twin aims of *Erie*." The Court holds that application of the federal standard would encourage forum shopping because there would be both a perceived and a real difference in the size of recoveries on jury verdicts. Moreover, New York citizens would be subjected to unchecked damages in the federal courts when they would be protected in their own courts, and this would be inequitable administration of the laws.

Many commentators and practitioners thought that *Hanna* had created an understanding, even a presumption, that when a Federal Rule was implicated, it would trump other possible rules or standards. At the least, *Gasperini* destabilized that understanding, which may account for some of the hostility with which it has been received. See, e.g., C. Douglas Floyd, *Erie* Awry: A Comment on Gasperini v. Center for Humanities, Inc., 1997 BYU L. Rev. 267; Richard Freer, Some Thoughts on the State of *Erie* After *Gasperini*, 76 Texas L. Rev. 1637 (1998).

The case also has its defenders. Professor Thomas Rowe argues that *Gasperini* does not essentially change the basic framework established by *Hanna*. It merely calls for sensitivity to state interests in construing Federal Rules, and calls for "the clear preservation of the *Byrd* interest analysis in a subset of cases involving judge-made federal procedural rules." Not Bad for Government Work: Does Anyone Else Think the Supreme Court Is Doing a Halfway Decent Job in Its *Erie-Hanna* Jurisprudence?, 73 Notre Dame L. Rev. 963, 1014 (1998).

3. *The Influence of the Seventh Amendment*. Keep in mind that if the New York statute provides for the re-examination of any fact found by a jury, it would violate the Seventh Amendment. (Recall also that the Seventh Amendment does not apply to state courts.) The majority holds that the trial court's review for excessiveness under the New York statute did not constitute such a re-examination.

But the de novo review by the appellate court, which the New York statute also provides, does implicate the Seventh Amendment, according to the Court. This is the point at which the Court reverts to the *Byrd* balancing test. What is in the balance here? How does the majority accommodate the state and federal interests? How is *Gasperini* an extension of *Byrd*?

4. *Semtek Int'l, Inc. v. Lockheed Martin Corp., 531 U.S. 497 (2001).* The Court has continued to interpret potential federal-state procedural conflicts in a manner that accommodates state procedural practices. In *Semtek*, the Court held that the claim-preclusive effect of a federal judgment dismissing a diversity action on statute-of-limitations grounds is determined by the law of the state in which the federal court sits.

The Court relied in part upon an 1875 case, Dupasseur v. Rochereau, 21 Wall. 130 (1875), which held that the res judicata effect of a federal diversity judgment "is such as would belong to judgments of state courts rendered under similar circumstances." The respondent argued that *Dupasseur* was not controlling because it was decided in an era in which federal courts were required by the Conformity Act of 1872 to apply the *procedural* law of the forum state in *nonequity* cases. Moreover, respondent maintained that Rule 41(b) was controlling, because the order of dismissal did not "otherwise specify[]" that the dismissal would "operate[] as an adjudication upon the merits."

The Court disagreed, and concluded that Rule 41(b)'s phrase "on the merits" did not necessarily mean "entitled to claim preclusive effect." Indeed, such an operation of the rule might violate the Rules Enabling Act, insofar as it might "abridge, enlarge or modify [a] substantive right." 28 U.S.C. § 2072(b). "[T]he traditional rule is that expiration of the applicable statute of limitations merely bars the remedy and does not extinguish the substantive right, so that dismissal on that ground does not have claim-preclusive effect in other jurisdictions with longer, unexpired limitations periods." *Semtek*, 531 U.S. at 504. As Justice Scalia noted, if federal court dismissals on statute-of-limitations grounds would bar suit everywhere, this could lead to forum shopping: "[o]ut-of-state defendants sued on stale claims . . . in . . . States adhering to this traditional rule would systematically remove state-law suits brought against them to federal court. . . ." Id.

Given that Rule 41(b) did not determine the outcome, and given these competing federalism principles, the Court concluded that federal common law should incorporate state law regarding the claim-preclusive effect of dismissals, *except* "in situations in which the state law is incompatible with federal interests." Id. Finding no such incompatibility in *Semtek*, the Court held that the state law of preclusion should control. See also Styskal v. Weld County Bd. Of County Comm'rs, 365 F.3d 855 (10th Cir. 2004).

2. Supplemental Jurisdiction of the Federal Courts

Problem Case: Suing the HMO

Plaintiffs Narensky, Chin, and O'Brien sue their health maintenance organization under both federal RICO and ERISA claims and state law claims arising out of the HMO's refusal to provide them treatment. All claims arise out of the same set of facts.

1. A federal district court would have jurisdiction over the RICO and ERISA claims, but what about the state law issues? Must plaintiffs pursue their state law claims in a separate proceeding in state court, assuming federal diversity jurisdiction does not exist?
2. Assume instead that there are no federal claims and federal jurisdiction over all of the original state law claims is based on diversity under 28 U.S.C. § 1332. The HMO impleads the doctors who treated the plaintiffs under Rule 14, thereby making the doctors parties to

the litigation. (Impleader under Rule 14 is discussed more thoroughly later in this chapter.) Plaintiffs seek to make additional state law claims against the doctors, who are not diverse from plaintiffs. May the federal court adjudicate these additional claims, or must plaintiffs sue the doctors separately in state court?

3. The doctors, now third-party defendants, counterclaim against the plaintiffs, alleging slander under state law. May the federal court hear these claims?
4. Instead of suing as individuals, assume the plaintiffs are the named plaintiffs in a class action. Jurisdiction is still based on diversity, which is proper because each of the named plaintiffs alleges over $75,000 in damages. Other class members' claims, however, do not meet the amount in controversy requirements of § 1332. May the federal court take jurisdiction over the class claims of the unnamed parties nonetheless?

a. Background to the Statute (28 U.S.C. § 1367)

Complexities such as those in Narensky et al. v. HMO are common in federal litigation. Multiple claims frequently arise out of the same nucleus of facts and involve at least some of the same parties. How should a federal court proceed when it does not have subject matter jurisdiction over some of the claims? On one hand are fairness and efficiency concerns for the parties, and avoidance of inconsistent outcomes in the federal and state courts. On the other hand, state courts are better at adjudicating state claims, and in many places the federal docket is overloaded (in recent times with criminal cases).

Not unlike the "clean up" doctrine in equity, common law developed over the years allowing state law claims in federal courts under certain conditions. In 1990, Congress passed a statute, intended to codify the best of the common law and to give the federal courts supplemental jurisdiction over some state law claims. 28 U.S.C. § 1367. One advantage of the statute is that it abandons the judge-made distinction between pendent and ancillary jurisdiction — calling all these exercises simply "supplemental jurisdiction." In order, however, to understand the aims of the statute as well as the older case law that still influences its interpretation, you must learn something of the history of supplemental jurisdiction.

i. The Gibbs *Test*

The most important case under the common law regime was United Mine Workers v. Gibbs, 383 U.S. 715 (1966). The Supreme Court stated the basic test for tacking on claims as well as explaining the power to do so:

> Pendent jurisdiction, in the sense of judicial power, exists whenever there is a claim "arising under [the] Constitution, the Laws of the United States,

and Treaties made or which shall be made, under their Authority . . . ," U.S. Const., Art. III, § 2, and the relationship between that claim and the state claim permits the conclusion that the entire action before the court comprises but one constitutional "case." The federal claim must have substance sufficient to confer subject matter jurisdiction on the court. The state and federal claims must derive from a common nucleus of operative fact. But if, considered without regard to their federal or state character, a plaintiff's claims are such that he would ordinarily be expected to try them all in one judicial proceeding, then, assuming substantiality of the federal issues, there is power in federal courts to hear the whole.

That power need not be exercised in every case in which it is found to exist. It has consistently been recognized that pendent jurisdiction is a doctrine of discretion, not of plaintiff's right. Its jurisdiction lies in considerations of judicial economy, convenience and fairness to litigants; if these are not present a federal court should hesitate to exercise jurisdiction over state claims, even though bound to apply state law to them.

Id. at 725-726.

In operation, the *Gibbs* test resulted in the following principles for joining state law "branch" claims to a federal "trunk." First, if the plaintiff asserted a claim based on federal law against the defendant, then she could add as a pendent claim any additional state law claims that arose from the same nucleus of operative facts as the trunk federal law claim. This is the formulation:

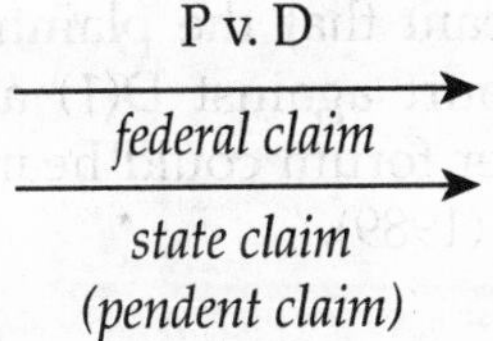

The test was one of factual relatedness, and took into account (1) whether the jury would be unduly confused; and (2) other factors that might weigh against hearing the state claim in federal court, such as whether the federal claim is insubstantial, and whether the claims would ordinarily be tried together.

Second, if the defendant (or unwilling party to a claim) wished to assert a counterclaim against the plaintiff that arose from the same transaction or occurrence as the plaintiff's claim against her, this fell within the ancillary jurisdiction of the court. Thus, compulsory counterclaims could be heard in federal court even if they did not satisfy 28 U.S.C. § 1331 or 1332.

P v. D

→ *federal claim*

← *state counterclaim (ancillary jurisdiction)*

Again, the question was one of factual relatedness — matters that logically should be tried together could be tried together.

ii. *Post-*Gibbs *Developments*

The doctrine of ancillary jurisdiction was extended to allow a party to implead a third-party defendant (see Fed. R. Civ. P. 14) and to assert a factually related cross-claim (see Fed. R. Civ. P. 13) against a codefendant without concern for the statutory jurisdiction demands of § 1331 or § 1332. In all of these cases, the party seeking to add the claim was in a defensive posture, and the claim grew out of the original dispute against her.

In later cases, however, the Supreme Court refused to extend ancillary or pendent jurisdiction principles to other claims that, while factually related to a root federal claim, involved the addition of a new *pendent party*. Thus, for example, supplemental jurisdiction was held not to apply over a plaintiff's claim against a third-party defendant, even though the claim was factually related to the underlying cause of action against the original defendant. See Owen Equip. Co. v. Kroger, 437 U.S. 365 (1978). The Court also upheld a district court's rejection of pendent jurisdiction over state law claims against a nondiverse defendant, even though they were factually related to the underlying federal claims against the original defendants. See Aldinger v. Howard, 427 U.S. 1 (1976), superseded by 28 U.S.C. § 1367.

Most remarkable was a case in which the Court held that a federal court lacked power to hear the factually related state claim against D(2) even when the federal claim against D(1) fell within the *exclusive* jurisdiction of the federal courts. This meant that the plaintiff would have to file two lawsuits, one in federal court against D(1) and another in state court against D(2), because neither forum could hear both claims. See Finley v. United States, 490 U.S. 545 (1989).

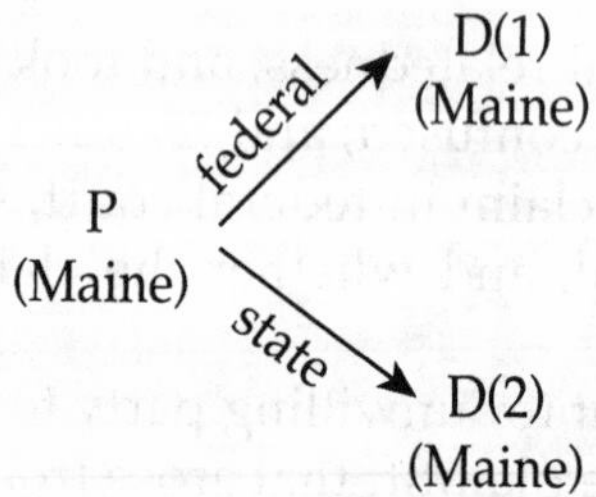

b. The Modern Approach

Shortly after *Finley* was decided, Congress drafted the federal supplemental jurisdiction statute, which codified much of the decisional law regarding ancillary and pendent jurisdiction and changed the hard-hearted approach to pendent party jurisdiction followed by the Court in *Finley*. Read 28 U.S.C. § 1367, and keep it before you as we work through some of the statute's complexities.

The residual ambiguities of the supplemental jurisdiction statute have prompted several decisions. For example, in City of Chicago v.

International College of Surgeons, 522 U.S. 156 (1997), the Supreme Court held that the federal district court properly exercised supplemental jurisdiction over state law claims, including claims for on-the-record review of a municipal agency's denial of a permit to demolish certain facades of designated landmarks in Chicago. Although judicial review was on the agency's record—not de novo—the court ruled that supplemental jurisdiction was appropriate, notwithstanding objections that permitting jurisdiction in such cases could render the federal courts the superintendents of local agencies.

Justice Ginsburg, in an opinion joined by Justice Stevens, dissented, relying on Chicago, R.I. & P.R. Co. v. Stude, 346 U.S. 574 (1954), and Rooker v. Fid. Trust Co., 263 U.S. 413 (1923), which in her view preclude federal courts of first instance from exercising authority under §§ 1331 and 1332 to displace state courts as forums for on-the-record review of state and local agency actions.

The broad grant of supplemental jurisdiction authority contained in § 1367(a) and then limited with respect to diversity cases in § 1367(b) has also proved ambiguous. Section 1367(b) instructs courts not to exercise supplemental jurisdiction in diversity cases over claims by plaintiffs against persons made parties under Rule 14 (impleader), 19 (compulsory joinder), 20 (permissive joinder), or 24 (intervention), or over claims by persons proposed to be joined as plaintiffs under Rule 19, or seeking to intervene as plaintiffs under Rule 24, where exercising such jurisdiction would be inconsistent with the jurisdictional requirements of § 1332 (e.g., complete diversity). (The interplay between joinder, impleader, and intervention and supplemental jurisdiction in diversity cases can give rise to very complex procedural situations that will be somewhat clearer after you study more advanced joinder later in this chapter).

The complexities and likely unintentional consequences of supplemental jurisdiction under § 1367 are underscored by cases like Shanaghan v. Cahill, 58 F.3d 106 (4th Cir. 1995), which noted as follows:

> Section 1367(a) is broadly phrased to provide for supplemental jurisdiction over claims appended to "any civil action" over which the court has "original jurisdiction." . . . Section 1367(b) imposes specific limits on the use of supplemental jurisdiction in diversity cases in order to prevent the addition of parties that would destroy complete diversity as required by § 1332, but otherwise plainly contemplates the use of supplemental jurisdiction in that context. . . . The only possible interpretation of this language is that state law claims between diverse parties that do not, however, satisfy the jurisdictional amount requirements appended to diversity actions are cognizable under supplemental jurisdiction.

Id. at 109.

c. Solving the Problem Case

Armed with § 1367, return to the problem case. Though we supply answers below, keep in mind the fact-charged nature of the inquiry, and the discretionary aspects of the exercise of supplemental jurisdiction.

1. May the federal court exercise supplemental jurisdiction over the state law claims where it has original jurisdiction over federal claims under 28 U.S.C. § 1331, or must plaintiffs sue separately in state court?
   Answer: Because federal jurisdiction is based on claims arising under federal laws, § 1367(a) governs. Assuming that none of the issues discussed in § 1367(c) is present, the court may exercise supplemental jurisdiction over the state law claims because they "are so related to claims in the action within [the court's] original jurisdiction that they form part of the same case or controversy." See 28 U.S.C. § 1367(a).*
2. Where original jurisdiction was based on diversity under § 1332 and the doctors are impleaded under Rule 14, may the court hear plaintiffs' claims against the third-party defendant doctors?
   Answer: Where original jurisdiction is based solely on diversity, federal courts may not exercise supplemental jurisdiction over claims that do not satisfy federal subject matter jurisdiction requirements if the claim is one so specified in § 1367(b). Here, the doctors were made parties to the case by means of impleader under Rule 14. Under § 1367(b), courts may not exercise supplemental jurisdiction over claims made by plaintiffs against persons made parties to a suit under Rule 14. Thus the court may not hear plaintiffs' state law claims against the doctors because federal subject matter jurisdiction is lacking and § 1367 prohibits supplemental jurisdiction over the claims.
3. May the federal court hear the claims alleged by the third-party defendant doctors against plaintiffs?
   Answer: Section 1367(b) carves out exceptions to § 1367(a)'s broad grant of supplemental jurisdiction authority only for claims made by

* If the federal claims are dismissed, a court has discretion under § 1367(c)(3) either to continue exercising supplemental jurisdiction over the remaining state law claims, or dismiss the case altogether. What if the plaintiff *amends* her complaint and drops the federal claims? Should the plaintiff's choice affect the discretion of the court regarding the exercise of supplemental jurisdiction? The Eleventh Circuit has held that it should. In Pintando v. Miami-Dade Hous. Agency, the court held that because an amended pleading supersedes the former pleading, "once the amended complaint [dropping plaintiff's federal Title VII claims] was accepted by the district court . . . there was no longer a federal claim on which the district court could exercise supplemental jurisdiction for the remaining state law claims." 501 F.3d 1241, 1243 (11th Cir. 2007). The court relied upon the Supreme Court's decision in Rockwell Int'l Corp. v. United States, which held that "'when a plaintiff voluntarily amends the complaint, courts look to the amended complaint to determine jurisdiction.'" See Id. (quoting and following *Rockwell*, 127 S. Ct. at 1409 (2007), Wellness Cmty. Nat'l v. Wellness House, 70 F.3d 46, 48-49 (7th Cir. 1995), and Boelens v. Redman Homes, Inc., 759 F.3d 504, 506-508 (5th Cir. 1985)).

plaintiffs against persons added as parties through various rules. Section 1367(b) does not cover claims made by added parties, such as the third-party defendant doctors, against plaintiffs. Thus, the court may exercise supplemental jurisdiction over the doctors' claims against the plaintiffs under § 1367(a).

4. In the class action context where federal jurisdiction is based on diversity, may the federal court adjudicate the claims of unnamed class members whose individual claims would not satisfy the amount in controversy requirement of § 1332?

   Answer: This issue has engendered considerable debate since § 1367 was enacted. One answer is that since Rule 23 class actions are not listed among the exclusions in § 1367(b), then § 1367(a) applies and supplemental jurisdiction is proper. Read on.

d. Operation of § 1367 in the Class Action Context

Interpreting and applying § 1367 has proven particularly problematic in the class action context. Courts and commentators have differed considerably over whether § 1367(b), by omitting class actions under Rule 23 from the list of exceptions to § 1367(a)'s broad grant of supplemental jurisdiction, was meant to overrule Zahn v. International Paper Co., 414 U.S. 291 (1973). *Zahn* prohibited the exercise of supplemental jurisdiction in diversity cases over claims of unnamed class members for less than the jurisdictional amount. (In 1998, the American Law Institute recommended amending § 1367 to make clear that supplemental jurisdiction would be appropriate over such class claims; the amendments have not been adopted.)

Prompted by a sharp split in the circuit courts, the Supreme Court finally addressed the issue in the following decision. Unfortunately, as you will see, the Court itself is badly divided (5-4), so we cannot be certain that its reading of § 1367 will endure. Notice too that the case consolidates two appeals from the circuit courts, one a class action in which the claims of some class members did not meet the amount in controversy requirement, another a standard multi-plaintiff personal injury case in which only one plaintiff met the amount in controversy requirement.

Exxon Mobil Corp. v. Allapattah

545 U.S. 546 (2005)

JUSTICE KENNEDY delivered the opinion of the Court.

These consolidated cases present the question whether a federal court in a diversity action may exercise supplemental jurisdiction over additional plaintiffs whose claims do not satisfy the minimum amount-in-controversy requirement, provided the claims are part of the same case or controversy as the claims of plaintiffs who do allege a sufficient amount in controversy. Our decision turns on the correct interpretation of

28 U.S.C. § 1367. The question has divided the Courts of Appeals, and we granted certiorari to resolve the conflict.

We hold that, where the other elements of jurisdiction are present and at least one named plaintiff in the action satisfies the amount-in-controversy requirement, § 1367 does authorize supplemental jurisdiction over the claims of other plaintiffs in the same Article III case or controversy, even if those claims are for less than the jurisdictional amount specified in the statute setting forth the requirements for diversity jurisdiction. We affirm the judgment of the Court of Appeals for the Eleventh Circuit in *Allapattah,* and we reverse the judgment of the Court of Appeals for the First Circuit in *Star-Kist.*

I

In 1991, about 10,000 Exxon dealers filed a class-action suit against the Exxon Corporation in the United States District Court for the Northern District of Florida. The dealers alleged an intentional and systematic scheme by Exxon under which they were overcharged for fuel purchased from Exxon. The plaintiffs invoked the District Court's § 1332(a) diversity jurisdiction. After a unanimous jury verdict in favor of the plaintiffs, the District Court certified the case for interlocutory review, asking whether it had properly exercised § 1367 supplemental jurisdiction over the claims of class members who did not meet the jurisdictional minimum amount in controversy.

The Court of Appeals for the Eleventh Circuit upheld the District Court's extension of supplemental jurisdiction to these class members. Allapattah Services, Inc. v. Exxon Corp., 333 F.3d 1248 (2003). . . . This decision accords with the views of the Courts of Appeals for the Fourth, Sixth, and Seventh Circuits. See Rosmer v. Pfizer, Inc., 263 F.3d 110 (4th Cir. 2001); Olden v. LaFarge Corp., 383 F.3d 495 (6th Cir. 2004); Stromberg Metal Works, Inc. v. Press Mechanical, Inc., 77 F.3d 928 (7th Cir. 1996); In re Brand Name Prescription Drugs Antitrust Litigation, 123 F.3d 599 (7th Cir. 1997). The Courts of Appeals for the Fifth and Ninth Circuits, adopting a similar analysis of the statute, have held that in a diversity class action the unnamed class members need not meet the amount-in-controversy requirement, provided the named class members do. These decisions, however, are unclear on whether all the named plaintiffs must satisfy this requirement. In re Abbott Labs., 51 F.3d 524 (5th Cir. 1995); Gibson v. Chrysler Corp., 261 F.3d 927 (9th Cir. 2001).

In the other case now before us the Court of Appeals for the First Circuit took a different position on the meaning of § 1367(a). 370 F.3d 124 (2004). In that case, a 9-year-old girl sued Star-Kist in a diversity action in the United States District Court for the District of Puerto Rico, seeking damages for unusually severe injuries she received when she sliced her finger on a tuna can. Her family joined in the suit, seeking damages for emotional distress and certain medical expenses. The District Court granted summary judgment to Star-Kist, finding that none of the plaintiffs met the minimum amount-in-controversy requirement. The Court of Appeals for the First Circuit, however, ruled that the injured girl, but not her family members, had made allegations of damages in the requisite amount.

The Court of Appeals then addressed whether, in light of the fact that one plaintiff met the requirements for original jurisdiction, supplemental jurisdiction over the remaining plaintiffs' claims was proper under § 1367. The court held that § 1367 authorizes supplemental jurisdiction only when the district court has original jurisdiction over the action, and that in a diversity case original jurisdiction is lacking if one plaintiff fails to satisfy the amount-in-controversy requirement. Although the Court of Appeals claimed to "express no view" on whether the result would be the same in a class action, id., at 143 n.19, its analysis is inconsistent with that of the Court of Appeals for the Eleventh Circuit. The Court of Appeals for the First Circuit's view of § 1367 is, however, shared by the Courts of Appeal for the Third, Eighth, and Tenth Circuits, and the latter two Courts of Appeals have expressly applied this rule to class actions. See Meritcare, Inc. v. St. Paul Mercury Ins. Co., 166 F.3d 214 (3d Cir. 1999); Trimble v. Asarco, Inc., 232 F.3d 946 (8th Cir. 2000); Leonhardt v. Western Sugar Co., 160 F.3d 631 (10th Cir. 1998).

II

A

The district courts of the United States, as we have said many times, are "courts of limited jurisdiction. They possess only that power authorized by Constitution and statute." Kokkonen v. Guardian Life Ins. Co. of America, 511 U.S. 375, 377 (1994). In order to provide a federal forum for plaintiffs who seek to vindicate federal rights, Congress has conferred on the district courts original jurisdiction in federal-question cases — civil actions that arise under the Constitution, laws, or treaties of the United States. 28 U.S.C. § 1331. In order to provide a neutral forum for what have come to be known as diversity cases, Congress also has granted district courts original jurisdiction in civil actions between citizens of different States, between U.S. citizens and foreign citizens, or by foreign states against U.S. citizens. § 1332. To ensure that diversity jurisdiction does not flood the federal courts with minor disputes, § 1332(a) requires that the matter in controversy in a diversity case exceed a specified amount, currently $75,000. § 1332(a).

Although the district courts may not exercise jurisdiction absent a statutory basis, it is well established — in certain classes of cases — that, once a court has original jurisdiction over some claims in the action, it may exercise supplemental jurisdiction over additional claims that are part of the same case or controversy. The leading modern case for this principle is Mine Workers v. Gibbs, 383 U.S. 715 (1966). In *Gibbs*, the plaintiff alleged the defendant's conduct violated both federal and state law. The District Court, *Gibbs* held, had original jurisdiction over the action based on the federal claims. *Gibbs* confirmed that the District Court had the additional power (though not the obligation) to exercise supplemental jurisdiction over related state claims that arose from the same Article III case or controversy. Id. at 725 ("The federal claim must have substance sufficient to confer subject matter jurisdiction on the court. . . . [A]ssuming substantiality of the federal issues, there is *power* in federal courts to hear the whole.").

As we later noted, the decision allowing jurisdiction over pendent state claims in *Gibbs* did not mention, let alone come to grips with, the text of the jurisdictional statutes and the bedrock principle that federal courts have no jurisdiction without statutory authorization. Finley v. United States, 490 U.S. 545, 548 (1989). In *Finley*, we nonetheless reaffirmed and rationalized *Gibbs* and its progeny by inferring from it the interpretive principle that, in cases involving supplemental jurisdiction over additional claims between parties properly in federal court, the jurisdictional statutes should be read broadly, on the assumption that in this context Congress intended to authorize courts to exercise their full Article III power to dispose of an "'entire action before the court [which] comprises but one constitutional case.'" 490 U.S. at 549 (quoting *Gibbs*, supra, at 725).

We have not, however, applied *Gibbs'* expansive interpretive approach to other aspects of the jurisdictional statutes. For instance, we have consistently interpreted § 1332 as requiring complete diversity: In a case with multiple plaintiffs and multiple defendants, the presence in the action of a single plaintiff from the same State as a single defendant deprives the district court of original diversity jurisdiction over the entire action. Strawbridge v. Curtiss, 3 Cranch 267 (1806); Owen Equipment & Erection Co. v. Kroger, 437 U.S. 365, 375 (1978). The complete diversity requirement is not mandated by the Constitution, State Farm Fire & Casualty Co. v. Tashire, 386 U.S. 523, 530-531 (1967), or by the plain text of § 1332(a). The Court, nonetheless, has adhered to the complete diversity rule in light of the purpose of the diversity requirement, which is to provide a federal forum for important disputes where state courts might favor, or be perceived as favoring, home-state litigants. The presence of parties from the same State on both sides of a case dispels this concern, eliminating a principal reason for conferring § 1332 jurisdiction over any of the claims in the action. See Wisconsin Dept. of Corrections v. Schacht, 524 U.S. 381, 389 (1998); Newman-Green, Inc. v. Alfonzo-Larrain, 490 U.S. 826, 829 (1989). The specific purpose of the complete diversity rule explains both why we have not adopted *Gibbs'* expansive interpretive approach to this aspect of the jurisdictional statute and why *Gibbs* does not undermine the complete diversity rule. In order for a federal court to invoke supplemental jurisdiction under *Gibbs*, it must first have original jurisdiction over at least one claim in the action. Incomplete diversity destroys original jurisdiction with respect to all claims, so there is nothing to which supplemental jurisdiction can adhere.

In contrast to the diversity requirement, most of the other statutory prerequisites for federal jurisdiction, including the federal-question and amount-in-controversy requirements, can be analyzed claim by claim. True, it does not follow by necessity from this that a district court has authority to exercise supplemental jurisdiction over all claims provided there is original jurisdiction over just one. Before the enactment of § 1367, the Court declined in contexts other than the pendent-claim instance to follow *Gibbs'* expansive approach to interpretation of the jurisdictional statutes. The Court took a more restrictive view of the proper interpretation of these statutes in so-called pendent-party cases involving supplemental jurisdiction over claims involving additional parties — plaintiffs or defendants — where the district courts would lack original jurisdiction over claims by each of the parties standing alone.

Thus, with respect to plaintiff-specific jurisdictional requirements, the Court held in Clark v. Paul Gray, Inc., 306 U.S. 583 (1939), that every plaintiff must separately satisfy the amount-in-controversy requirement. Though *Clark* was a federal-question case, at that time federal-question jurisdiction had an amount-in-controversy requirement analogous to the amount-in-controversy requirement for diversity cases. "Proper practice," *Clark* held, "requires that where each of several plaintiffs is bound to establish the jurisdictional amount with respect to his own claim, the suit should be dismissed as to those who fail to show that the requisite amount is involved." Id. at 590. The Court reaffirmed this rule, in the context of a class action brought invoking § 1332(a) diversity jurisdiction, in Zahn v. International Paper Co., 414 U.S. 291 (1973). It follows "inescapably" from *Clark*, the Court held in *Zahn*, that "any plaintiff without the jurisdictional amount must be dismissed from the case, even though others allege jurisdictionally sufficient claims." 414 U.S. at 300.

The Court took a similar approach with respect to supplemental jurisdiction over claims against additional defendants that fall outside the district courts' original jurisdiction. In Aldinger v. Howard, 427 U.S. 1 (1976), the plaintiff brought a 42 U.S.C. § 1983 action against county officials in district court pursuant to the statutory grant of jurisdiction in 28 U.S.C. § 1343(3) (1976 ed.). The plaintiff further alleged the court had supplemental jurisdiction over her related state-law claims against the county, even though the county was not suable under § 1983 and so was not subject to § 1343(3)'s original jurisdiction. The Court held that supplemental jurisdiction could not be exercised because Congress, in enacting § 1343(3), had declined (albeit implicitly) to extend federal jurisdiction over any party who could not be sued under the federal civil rights statutes. 427 U.S. at 16-19. "Before it can be concluded that [supplemental] jurisdiction [over additional parties] exists," *Aldinger* held, "a federal court must satisfy itself not only that Art[icle] III permits it, but that Congress in the statutes conferring jurisdiction has not expressly or by implication negated its existence." Id. at 18.

In Finley v. United States, 490 U.S. 545 (1989), we confronted a similar issue in a different statutory context. The plaintiff in *Finley* brought a

Federal Tort Claims Act negligence suit against the Federal Aviation Administration in District Court, which had original jurisdiction under § 1346(b). The plaintiff tried to add related claims against other defendants, invoking the District Court's supplemental jurisdiction over so-called pendent parties. We held that the District Court lacked a sufficient statutory basis for exercising supplemental jurisdiction over these claims. Relying primarily on *Zahn, Aldinger,* and *Kroger,* we held in *Finley* that "a grant of jurisdiction over claims involving particular parties does not itself confer jurisdiction over additional claims by or against different parties." 490 U.S. at 556. While *Finley* did not "limit or impair" *Gibbs'* liberal approach to interpreting the jurisdictional statutes in the context of supplemental jurisdiction over additional claims involving the same parties, 490 U.S. at 556, *Finley* nevertheless declined to extend that interpretive assumption to claims involving additional parties. *Finley* held that in the context of parties, in contrast to claims, "we will not assume that the full constitutional power has been congressionally authorized, and will not read jurisdictional statutes broadly." Id. at 549.

As the jurisdictional statutes existed in 1989, then, here is how matters stood: First, the diversity requirement in § 1332(a) required complete diversity; absent complete diversity, the district court lacked original jurisdiction over all of the claims in the action. *Strawbridge,* 3 Cranch, at 267-268; *Kroger,* 437 U.S. at 373-374. Second, if the district court had original jurisdiction over at least one claim, the jurisdictional statutes implicitly authorized supplemental jurisdiction over all other claims between the same parties arising out of the same Article III case or controversy. *Gibbs,* 383 U.S. at 725. Third, even when the district court had original jurisdiction over one or more claims between particular parties, the jurisdictional statutes did not authorize supplemental jurisdiction over additional claims involving other parties. *Clark,* supra, at 590; *Zahn,* supra, at 300-301; *Finley,* supra, at 556.

B

In *Finley* we emphasized that "[w]hatever we say regarding the scope of jurisdiction conferred by a particular statute can of course be changed by Congress." 490 U.S. at 556. In 1990, Congress accepted the invitation. It passed the Judicial Improvements Act, 104 Stat. 5089, which enacted § 1367, the provision which controls these cases.

Section 1367 provides, in relevant part:

> (a) Except as provided in subsections (b) and (c) or as expressly provided otherwise by Federal statute, in any civil action of which the district courts have original jurisdiction, the district courts shall have supplemental jurisdiction over all other claims that are so related to claims in the action within such original jurisdiction that they form part of the same case or controversy under Article III of the United States Constitution. Such supplemental jurisdiction shall include claims that involve the joinder or intervention of additional parties.

> (b) In any civil action of which the district courts have original jurisdiction founded solely on section 1332 of this title, the district courts shall not have supplemental jurisdiction under subsection (a) over claims by plaintiffs against persons made parties under Rule 14, 19, 20, or 24 of the Federal Rules of Civil Procedure, or over claims by persons proposed to be joined as plaintiffs under Rule 19 of such rules, or seeking to intervene as plaintiffs under Rule 24 of such rules, when exercising supplemental jurisdiction over such claims would be inconsistent with the jurisdictional requirements of section 1332.

All parties to this litigation and all courts to consider the question agree that § 1367 overturned the result in *Finley*. There is no warrant, however, for assuming that § 1367 did no more than to overrule *Finley* and otherwise to codify the existing state of the law of supplemental jurisdiction. We must not give jurisdictional statutes a more expansive interpretation than their text warrants, 490 U.S. at 549, 556; but it is just as important not to adopt an artificial construction that is narrower than what the text provides. No sound canon of interpretation requires Congress to speak with extraordinary clarity in order to modify the rules of federal jurisdiction within appropriate constitutional bounds. Ordinary principles of statutory construction apply. In order to determine the scope of supplemental jurisdiction authorized by § 1367, then, we must examine the statute's text in light of context, structure, and related statutory provisions.

Section 1367(a) is a broad grant of supplemental jurisdiction over other claims within the same case or controversy, as long as the action is one in which the district courts would have original jurisdiction. The last sentence of § 1367(a) makes it clear that the grant of supplemental jurisdiction extends to claims involving joinder or intervention of additional parties. The single question before us, therefore, is whether a diversity case in which the claims of some plaintiffs satisfy the amount-in-controversy requirement, but the claims of others plaintiffs do not, presents a "civil action of which the district courts have original jurisdiction." . . .

We now conclude the answer must be yes. When the well-pleaded complaint contains at least one claim that satisfies the amount-in-controversy requirement, and there are no other relevant jurisdictional defects, the district court, beyond all question, has original jurisdiction over that claim. The presence of other claims in the complaint, over which the district court may lack original jurisdiction, is of no moment. If the court has original jurisdiction over a single claim in the complaint, it has original jurisdiction over a "civil action" within the meaning of § 1367(a), even if the civil action over which it has jurisdiction comprises fewer claims than were included in the complaint. Once the court determines it has original jurisdiction over the civil action, it can turn to the question whether it has a constitutional and statutory basis for exercising supplemental jurisdiction over the other claims in the action.

Section 1367(a) commences with the direction that §§ 1367(b) and (c), or other relevant statutes, may provide specific exceptions, but otherwise

§ 1367(a) is a broad jurisdictional grant, with no distinction drawn between pendent-claim and pendent-party cases. In fact, the last sentence of § 1367(a) makes clear that the provision grants supplemental jurisdiction over claims involving joinder or intervention of additional parties. The terms of § 1367 do not acknowledge any distinction between pendent jurisdiction and the doctrine of so-called ancillary jurisdiction. Though the doctrines of pendent and ancillary jurisdiction developed separately as a historical matter, the Court has recognized that the doctrines are "two species of the same generic problem," *Kroger*, 437 U.S., at 370. Nothing in § 1367 indicates a congressional intent to recognize, preserve, or create some meaningful, substantive distinction between the jurisdictional categories we have historically labeled pendent and ancillary.

If § 1367(a) were the sum total of the relevant statutory language, our holding would rest on that language alone. The statute, of course, instructs us to examine § 1367(b) to determine if any of its exceptions apply, so we proceed to that section. While § 1367(b) qualifies the broad rule of § 1367(a), it does not withdraw supplemental jurisdiction over the claims of the additional parties at issue here. The specific exceptions to § 1367(a) contained in § 1367(b), moreover, provide additional support for our conclusion that § 1367(a) confers supplemental jurisdiction over these claims. Section 1367(b), which applies only to diversity cases, withholds supplemental jurisdiction over the claims of plaintiffs proposed to be joined as indispensable parties under Federal Rule of Civil Procedure 19, or who seek to intervene pursuant to Rule 24. Nothing in the text of § 1367(b), however, withholds supplemental jurisdiction over the claims of plaintiffs permissively joined under Rule 20 (like the additional plaintiffs in *Star-Kist*) or certified as class-action members pursuant to Rule 23 (like the additional plaintiffs in *Allapattah*). The natural, indeed the necessary, inference is that § 1367 confers supplemental jurisdiction over claims by Rule 20 and Rule 23 plaintiffs. This inference, at least with respect to Rule 20 plaintiffs, is strengthened by the fact that § 1367(b) explicitly excludes supplemental jurisdiction over claims against defendants joined under Rule 20.

We cannot accept the view, urged by some of the parties, commentators, and Courts of Appeals, that a district court lacks original jurisdiction over a civil action unless the court has original jurisdiction over every claim in the complaint. As we understand this position, it requires assuming either that all claims in the complaint must stand or fall as a single, indivisible "civil action" as a matter of definitional necessity—what we will refer to as the "indivisibility theory"—or else that the inclusion of a claim or party falling outside the district court's original jurisdiction somehow contaminates every other claim in the complaint, depriving the court of original jurisdiction over any of these claims—what we will refer to as the "contamination theory."

The indivisibility theory is easily dismissed, as it is inconsistent with the whole notion of supplemental jurisdiction. If a district court must have original jurisdiction over every claim in the complaint in order to have "original jurisdiction" over a "civil action," then in *Gibbs* there was no civil action of which the district court could assume original jurisdiction under § 1331, and so no basis for exercising supplemental jurisdiction over any of the claims. The indivisibility theory is further belied by our practice—in both federal-question and diversity cases—of allowing federal courts to cure jurisdictional defects by dismissing the offending parties rather than dismissing the entire action. . . .

The contamination theory, as we have noted, can make some sense in the special context of the complete diversity requirement because the presence of nondiverse parties on both sides of a lawsuit eliminates the justification for providing a federal forum. The theory, however, makes little sense with respect to the amount-in-controversy requirement, which is meant to ensure that a dispute is sufficiently important to warrant federal-court attention. The presence of a single nondiverse party may eliminate the fear of bias with respect to all claims, but the presence of a claim that falls short of the minimum amount in controversy does nothing to reduce the importance of the claims that do meet this requirement.

It is fallacious to suppose, simply from the proposition that § 1332 imposes both the diversity requirement and the amount-in-controversy requirement, that the contamination theory germane to the former is also relevant to the latter. There is no inherent logical connection between the amount-in-controversy requirement and § 1332 diversity jurisdiction. After all, federal-question jurisdiction once had an amount-in-controversy requirement as well. If such a requirement were revived under § 1331, it is clear beyond peradventure that § 1367(a) provides supplemental jurisdiction over federal-question cases where some, but not all, of the federal-law claims involve a sufficient amount in controversy. In other words, § 1367(a) unambiguously overrules the holding and the result in *Clark*. If that is so, however, it would be quite extraordinary to say that § 1367 did not also overrule *Zahn*, a case that was premised in substantial part on the holding in *Clark*.

In addition to the theoretical difficulties with the argument that a district court has original jurisdiction over a civil action only if it has original jurisdiction over each individual claim in the complaint, we have already considered and rejected a virtually identical argument in the closely analogous context of removal jurisdiction. In Chicago v. International College of Surgeons, 522 U.S. 156 (1997), the plaintiff brought federal- and state-law claims in state court. The defendant removed to federal court. The plaintiff objected to removal, citing the text of the removal statute, § 1441(a). That statutory provision, which bears a striking similarity to the relevant portion of § 1367, authorizes removal of "any civil action . . . of which the district courts of the United States have original jurisdiction. . . ." The *College of Surgeons* plaintiff urged that, because its state-law claims were not within the District Court's original jurisdiction, § 1441(a) did not authorize removal. We disagreed. The federal law claims, we held, "suffice to make the actions 'civil actions' within the 'original jurisdiction' of the district courts. . . . Nothing in the jurisdictional statutes suggests that the presence of related state law claims somehow alters the fact that [the plaintiff's] complaints, by virtue of their federal claims, were 'civil actions' within the federal courts' 'original jurisdiction.'" Id. at 166. Once the case was removed, the District Court had original jurisdiction over the federal law claims and supplemental jurisdiction under § 1367(a) over the state-law claims. Id. at 165. . . .

More importantly for present purposes, *College of Surgeons* stressed that a district court has original jurisdiction of a civil action for purposes of § 1441(a) as long as it has original jurisdiction over a subset of the claims constituting the action. Even the *College of Surgeons* dissent, which took issue with the Court's interpretation of § 1367, did not appear to contest this view of § 1441(a).

Although *College of Surgeons* involved additional claims between the same parties, its interpretation of § 1441(a) applies equally to cases involving additional parties whose claims fall short of the jurisdictional amount. If we were to adopt the contrary view that the presence of additional parties means there is no "civil action . . . of which the district courts . . . have original jurisdiction," those cases simply would not be removable. To our knowledge, no court has issued a reasoned opinion adopting this view of the removal statute. It is settled, of course, that absent complete diversity a case is not removable because the district court would lack original jurisdiction. Caterpillar Inc. v. Lewis, 519 U.S. 61, 73 (1996). This, however, is altogether consistent with our view of § 1441(a). A failure of complete diversity, unlike the failure of some claims to meet the requisite amount in controversy, contaminates every claim in the action.

We also reject the argument, similar to the attempted distinction of *College of Surgeons* discussed above, that while the presence of additional claims over which the district court lacks jurisdiction does not mean the civil action is outside the purview of § 1367(a), the presence of additional parties does. The basis for this distinction is not altogether clear, and it is in considerable tension with statutory text. Section 1367(a) applies by its terms to any civil action of which the district courts have original jurisdiction, and the last sentence of § 1367(a) expressly contemplates that the court may have supplemental jurisdiction over additional parties. So it cannot be the case that the presence of those parties destroys the court's original jurisdiction, within the meaning of § 1367(a), over a civil action otherwise properly before it. Also, § 1367(b) expressly withholds supplemental jurisdiction in diversity cases over claims by plaintiffs joined as indispensable parties under Rule 19. If joinder of such parties were sufficient to deprive the district court of original jurisdiction over the civil action within the meaning of § 1367(a), this specific limitation on supplemental jurisdiction in § 1367(b) would be superfluous. . . .

Finally, it is suggested that our interpretation of § 1367(a) creates an anomaly regarding the exceptions listed in § 1367(b): It is not immediately obvious why Congress would withhold supplemental jurisdiction over plaintiffs joined as parties "needed for just adjudication" under Rule 19 but would allow supplemental jurisdiction over plaintiffs permissively joined under Rule 20. The omission of Rule 20 plaintiffs from the list of exceptions in § 1367(b) may have been an "unintentional drafting gap," *Meritcare*, 166 F.3d at 221 and n.6. If that is the case, it is up to Congress rather than the courts to fix it. The omission may seem odd, but it is not absurd. An alternative explanation for the different treatment of Rule 19 and Rule 20 is that Congress was concerned that extending supplemental jurisdiction to Rule 19 plaintiffs would allow circumvention of the complete diversity rule: A nondiverse plaintiff might be omitted intentionally from the original action, but joined later under Rule 19 as a necessary party. See *Stromberg Metal Works*, 77 F.3d at 932. The contamination theory described above, if applicable, means this ruse would fail, but Congress may have wanted to make assurance double sure. More generally, Congress may have concluded that federal jurisdiction is only appropriate if the district court would have original jurisdiction over the claims of all those plaintiffs who are so essential to the action that they could be joined under Rule 19. . . .

And so we circle back to the original question. When the well-pleaded complaint in district court includes multiple claims, all part of the same case or controversy, and some, but not all, of the claims are within the court's original jurisdiction, does the court have before it "any civil action of which the district courts have original jurisdiction"? It does. Under § 1367, the court has original jurisdiction over the civil action comprising the claims for which there is no jurisdictional defect. No other reading of § 1367 is plausible in light of the text and structure of the jurisdictional statute. Though the special nature and purpose of the diversity requirement mean that a single nondiverse party can contaminate every other claim in the lawsuit, the contamination does not occur with respect to jurisdictional defects that go only to the substantive importance of individual claims.

It follows from this conclusion that the threshold requirement of § 1367(a) is satisfied in cases, like those now before us, where some, but not all, of the plaintiffs in a diversity action allege a sufficient amount in controversy. We hold that § 1367 by its plain text overruled *Clark* and *Zahn* and authorized supplemental jurisdiction over all claims by diverse parties arising out of the same Article III case or controversy, subject only to enumerated exceptions not applicable in the cases now before us.

C

The proponents of the alternative view of § 1367 insist that the statute is at least ambiguous and that we should look to other interpretive tools, including the legislative history of § 1367, which supposedly demonstrate Congress did not intend § 1367 to overrule *Zahn*. . . .

Those who urge that the legislative history refutes our interpretation rely primarily on the House Judiciary Committee Report on the Judicial Improvements Act. H.R. Rep. No. 101-734 (1990) (House Report or Report). This Report explained that § 1367 would authorize jurisdiction in a case like *Finley*, as well as essentially restore the pre-*Finley* understandings of the authorization for and limits on other forms of supplemental jurisdiction. House Report, at 28. . . . The Report then remarked that § 1367(b) "is not intended to affect the jurisdictional requirements of [§ 1332] in diversity-only class actions, as those requirements were interpreted prior to *Finley*," citing, without further elaboration, *Zahn* and Supreme Tribe of Ben-Hur v. Cauble, 255 U.S. 356 (1921). House Report, at 29, and n.17. . .

As we have repeatedly held, the authoritative statement is the statutory text, not the legislative history or any other extrinsic material. . . . Judicial investigation of legislative history has a tendency to become, to borrow Judge Leventhal's memorable phrase, an exercise in "'looking over a crowd and picking out your friends.'" See Wald, Some Observations on the Use of Legislative History in the 1981 Supreme Court Term, 68 Iowa L. Rev. 195, 214 (1983). Second, judicial reliance on legislative materials like committee reports, which are not themselves subject to the requirements of Article I, may give unrepresentative committee members — or, worse yet, unelected staffers and lobbyists — both the power and the incentive to attempt strategic manipulations of legislative history to secure results they were unable to achieve through the statutory text. . . .

[E]ven if we believed resort to legislative history were appropriate in these cases — a point we do not concede — we would not give significant weight to the House Report. The distinguished jurists who drafted the Subcommittee Working Paper, along with three of the participants in the drafting of § 1367, agree that this provision, on its face, overrules *Zahn*. This accords with the best reading of the statute's text, and nothing in the legislative history indicates directly and explicitly that Congress understood the phrase "civil action of which the district courts have original jurisdiction" to exclude cases in which some but not all of the diversity plaintiffs meet the amount in controversy requirement. . . .

D

Finally, we note that the Class Action Fairness Act (CAFA), Pub. L. 109-2, 119 Stat. 4, enacted this year, has no bearing on our analysis of these cases. Subject to certain limitations, the CAFA confers federal diversity jurisdiction over class actions where the aggregate amount in controversy exceeds $5 million. It abrogates the rule against aggregating claims, a rule this Court recognized in *Ben-Hur* and reaffirmed in *Zahn*. The CAFA, however, is not retroactive, and the views of the 2005 Congress are not relevant to our interpretation of a text enacted by Congress in 1990. The CAFA, moreover, does not moot the significance of our interpretation of § 1367, as many proposed exercises of supplemental jurisdiction, even in the class-action context, might not fall within the CAFA's ambit. The CAFA, then, has no impact, one way or the other, on our interpretation of § 1367.

The judgment of the Court of Appeals for the Eleventh Circuit is affirmed. The judgment of the Court of Appeals for the First Circuit is reversed, and the case is remanded for proceedings consistent with this opinion.

It is so ordered.

JUSTICE GINSBURG, with whom JUSTICE STEVENS, JUSTICE O'CONNOR, and JUSTICE BREYER join, dissenting.

. . . Section 1367, all agree, was designed to overturn this Court's decision in Finley v. United States, 490 U.S. 545 (1989). *Finley* concerned not diversity-of-citizenship jurisdiction (28 U.S.C. § 1332), but original federal-court jurisdiction in cases arising under federal law (28 U.S.C. § 1331). . . . What more § 1367 wrought is an issue on which courts of appeals have sharply divided. . . .

The Court adopts a plausibly broad reading of § 1367, a measure that is hardly a model of the careful drafter's art. There is another plausible reading, however, one less disruptive of our jurisprudence regarding supplemental jurisdiction. If one reads § 1367(a) to instruct, as the statute's text suggests, that the district court must first have "original jurisdiction" over a "civil action" before supplemental jurisdiction can attach, then *Clark* and *Zahn* are preserved, and supplemental jurisdiction does not open the way for joinder of plaintiffs, or inclusion of class members, who do not independently meet the amount-in-controversy requirement. For the reasons that follow, I conclude that this narrower construction is the better reading of § 1367.

II

A

. . . This Court has long held that, in determining whether the amount-in-controversy requirement has been satisfied, a single plaintiff may aggregate two or more claims against a single defendant, even if the claims are unrelated. See, e.g., Edwards v. Bates County, 163 U.S. 269, 273 (1896). But in multiparty cases, including class actions, we have unyieldingly adhered to the nonaggregation rule stated in *Troy Bank*. See *Clark*, 306 U.S., at 589 (reaffirming the "familiar rule that when several plaintiffs assert separate and distinct demands in a single suit, the amount involved in each separate controversy must be of the requisite amount to be within the jurisdiction of the district court, and that those amounts cannot be added together to satisfy jurisdictional requirements"); Snyder v. Harris, 394 U.S. 332, 339-340 (1969) (abandonment of the nonaggregation rule in class actions would undercut the congressional "purpose . . . to check, to some degree, the rising caseload of the federal courts").

B

. . . As explained by the First Circuit in *Ortega*, and applied to class actions by the Tenth Circuit in *Leonhardt*, see supra, § 1367(a) addresses "civil action[s] of which the district courts have original jurisdiction," a formulation that, in diversity cases, is sensibly read to incorporate the rules on joinder and aggregation tightly tied to § 1332 at the time of § 1367's enactment. On this reading, a complaint must first meet that "original jurisdiction" measurement. If it does not, no supplemental jurisdiction is authorized. If it does, § 1367(a) authorizes "supplemental jurisdiction" over related claims. In other words, § 1367(a) would preserve undiminished, as part and parcel of § 1332 "original jurisdiction" determinations, both the "complete diversity" rule and the decisions restricting aggregation to arrive at the amount in controversy. Section 1367(b)'s office, then, would be "to prevent the erosion of the complete diversity [and amount-in-controversy] requirement[s] that might otherwise result from an expansive application of what was once termed the doctrine of ancillary jurisdiction." See Pfander, Supplemental Jurisdiction and Section 1367: The Case for a Sympathetic Textualism, 148 U. Pa. L. Rev. 109, 114 (1999); infra, at 17-18. In contrast to the Court's construction of § 1367, which draws a sharp line between the diversity and amount-in-controversy components of § 1332, see ante, the interpretation presented here does not sever the two jurisdictional requirements.

The more restrained reading of § 1367 just outlined would yield affirmance of the First Circuit's judgment in *Ortega*, and reversal of the Eleventh Circuit's judgment in *Exxon*. It would not discard entirely, as the Court does, the judicially developed doctrines of pendent and ancillary jurisdiction as they existed when *Finley* was decided. Instead, it would recognize § 1367 essentially as a codification of those doctrines, placing them under a single heading, but largely retaining their substance, with overriding *Finley* the only basic change: Supplemental jurisdiction, once the district court has original jurisdiction, would now include "claims that involve the joinder or intervention of additional parties." § 1367(a). . . .

Not only would the reading I find persuasive "alig[n] statutory supplemental jurisdiction with the judicially developed doctrines of pendent and ancillary jurisdiction," id., it would also synchronize § 1367 with the removal statute, 28 U.S.C. § 1441. As the First Circuit carefully explained:

> Section 1441, like § 1367, applies only if the "civil action" in question is one "of which the district courts . . . have original jurisdiction." § 1441(a). Relying on that language, the Supreme Court has interpreted § 1441 to prohibit removal unless the entire action, as it stands at the time of removal, could have been filed in federal court in the first instance. See, e.g., Syngenta Crop Protection, Inc. v. Henson, 537 U.S. 28, 33 (2002); Okla. Tax Comm'n v. Graham, 489 U.S. 838, 840 (1989) (per curiam). Section 1441 has thus been held to incorporate the well-pleaded complaint rule, see City of Chicago [v. Int'l College of Surgeons, 522 U.S. 156, 163 (1997)]; the complete diversity rule, see Caterpillar, Inc. v. Lewis, 519 U.S. 61, 73 (1996); and rules for calculating the amount in controversy, see St. Paul Mercury Indem. Co. v. Red Cab Co., 303 U.S. 283, 291-292 (1938). *Ortega*, 370 F.3d at 138 (citations omitted).

The less disruptive view I take of § 1367 also accounts for the omission of Rule 20 plaintiffs and Rule 23 class actions in § 1367(b)'s text. If one reads § 1367(a) as a plenary grant of supplemental jurisdiction to federal courts sitting in diversity, one would indeed look for exceptions in § 1367(b). Finding none for permissive joinder of parties or class actions, one would conclude that Congress effectively, even if unintentionally, overruled *Clark* and *Zahn*. But if one recognizes that the nonaggregation rule delineated in *Clark* and *Zahn* forms part of the determination whether "original jurisdiction" exists in a diversity case, then plaintiffs who do not meet the amount-in-controversy requirement would fail at the § 1367(a) threshold. Congress would have no reason to resort to a § 1367(b) exception to turn such plaintiffs away from federal court, given that their claims, from the start, would fall outside the court's § 1332 jurisdiction. See Pfander, 148 U. Pa. L. Rev., at 148. . . .

What is the utility of § 1367(b) under my reading of § 1367(a)? Section 1367(a) allows parties other than the plaintiff to assert *reactive* claims once entertained under the heading ancillary jurisdiction. See supra (listing claims, including compulsory counterclaims and impleader claims, over which federal courts routinely exercised ancillary jurisdiction). As earlier observed, see supra, at 14, § 1367(b) stops plaintiffs from circumventing § 1332's jurisdictional requirements by using another's claim as a hook to add a claim that the plaintiff could not have brought in the first instance. *Kroger* is the paradigm case. There, the Court held that ancillary jurisdiction did not extend to a plaintiff's claim against a nondiverse party who had been impleaded by the defendant under Rule 14. Section 1367(b), then, is corroborative of § 1367(a)'s coverage of claims formerly called ancillary, but provides exceptions to assure that accommodation of added claims would not fundamentally alter "the jurisdictional requirements of section 1332." See Pfander, supra, at 135-137.

While § 1367's enigmatic text defies flawless interpretation the precedent-preservative reading, I am persuaded, better accords with the historical and legal context of Congress' enactment of the supplemental jurisdiction statute, and the established limits on pendent and ancillary jurisdiction. It does not attribute to Congress a jurisdictional enlargement broader than the one to which the legislators adverted, cf. *Finley*, 490 U.S., at 549, and it follows the sound counsel that "close questions of [statutory] construction should be resolved in favor of continuity and against change." Shapiro, Continuity and Change in Statutory Interpretation, 67 N.Y.U. L. Rev. 921, 925 (1992).

For the reasons stated, I would hold that § 1367 does not overrule *Clark* and *Zahn*. I would therefore affirm the judgment of the Court of Appeals for the First Circuit and reverse the judgment of the Court of Appeals for the Eleventh Circuit.

[A separate dissenting opinion of JUSTICE STEVENS, joined by JUSTICE BREYER, is omitted.]

Note: Efficiency and Institutional Competence

Put to one side, for a moment, the minutiae of statutory interpretation and the rather Byzantine set of terms and rules for supplemental jurisdiction created by the Court (pendent-claim, pendent-party, and ancillary jurisdiction). Congress and the Court have wrestled with supplemental jurisdiction and created these seemingly over-subtle distinctions for two principal reasons: on the one hand, it is typically most efficient to have one court decide an entire case or controversy; on the other hand, federal courts are courts of limited jurisdiction best suited to hear claims grounded in federal law. As litigation has become more complex (not just because there are multiple parties and multiple claims, but because injuries increasingly cross state and national boundaries), it has become more difficult to define what constitutes a whole case, or, as § 1367 puts it, a "civil action" and "all other claims that are so related . . . that they form part of the same case or controversy." It is also harder to say whether any specific court, state or federal, possesses superior competence to handle the vast array of mixed federal and state law claims these cases present. Assuming the *Allapattah* majority has the correct reading of what Congress intended to accomplish in § 1367, do you think it strikes the right balance between promoting efficiency, respecting federalism, and ensuring institutional competence?

Note: The Class Action Fairness Act of 2005

The majority opinion ends by emphasizing that the Class Action Fairness Act of 2005 had "no bearing" on its decision. Nonetheless, the new statute substantially expands the subject matter jurisdiction of the federal courts. If at least one plaintiff class member is diverse from any defendant, and the amount in controversy exceeds $5 million, the case may be brought in or removed to federal court. See 28 U.S.C. §§ 1332(d) and 1453. This abrogates the complete diversity requirement for class actions meeting the $5 million amount in controversy requirement. The statute also allows aggregation of plaintiffs' claims: "the claims of the individual class members shall be aggregated to determine whether the matter in controversy exceeds the sum or value of $5,000,000, exclusive of interest and costs." See 28 U.S.C. § 1332(d)(6).

The most important exception to the new grant of jurisdiction is for class actions in which there is a substantial connection to a single state. For instance, if more than two thirds of the class members are all citizens of the state in which the action is originally filed, a key defendant is a citizen of that state, and the principal injuries underlying the claim occurred there, federal courts cannot exercise jurisdiction. See 28 U.S.C. § 1332(d)(4). Moreover, district courts have discretion to decline jurisdiction over class actions in which the primary defendants and between one-third and two-thirds of the plaintiff class members are citizens of the same state.

See 28 U.S.C. § 1332(d)(3). The net effect is to place large-stakes, national class actions within the original jurisdiction of the federal courts. The statute passed with a groundswell of support from legislators generally hostile to class actions and concerned about abuse of the procedure, but its effect on the number and outcome of class action cases remains to be seen. (Class actions are discussed in further detail in section D of this chapter.)

For some early scholarly assessments of the Act, see Stephen B. Burbank, The Class Action Fairness Act of 2005 in Historical Context: A Preliminary View, 56 U. Pa. L. Rev. 1439, 1542 (2008) (arguing that while it was not unreasonable for Congress to assert a federal interest in regulating multistate class actions, CAFA may ultimately sweep too far and threaten to interfere with states' regulation of harmful activity within their borders; concluding that "CAFA's exceptions should be amended now to restore the balance of power between plaintiffs and defendants in class actions where a state's interest in regulation through litigation is intense and where the argument for federal jurisdiction relies on the fictions of corporate citizenship and the gathering powers of federal courts"); Lonny Sheinkopf Hoffman, In Retrospect: A First Year Review of the Class Action Fairness Act of 2005, 39 Loy. L.A. L. Rev. 1135 (2006); Samuel Issacharoff, Settled Expectations in a World of Unsettled Law: Choice of Law After the Class Action Fairness Act, 106 Colum. L. Rev. 1839 (2006); David Marcus, *Erie*, the Class Action Fairness Act, and Some Federalism Implications of Diversity Jurisdiction, 45 Wm. & Mary L. Rev. 1247 (2007) (discussing the expansion of diversity jurisdiction and striking parallels between the debate about CAFA and debates over *Erie*); Edward A. Purcell Jr., The Class Action Fairness Act in Perspective: The Old and the New in Federal Jurisdictional Reform, 156 U. Pa. L. Rev. 1823, 1927 (2008) (arguing that CAFA "marks another step in a relatively recent but broad-fronted effort to constrict meaningful remedies against corporate wrongdoing" by centralizing adjudication); Edward Sherman, Class Actions After the Class Action Fairness Act of 2005, 80 Tul. L. Rev. 1593 (2006); Laurens Walker, The Consumer Class Action Bill of Rights: A Policy and Political Mistake, 58 Hastings L.J. 849 (2007) (arguing that the invitation to public participation in class action settlements, including the requirement that defendants notify state attorneys general of proposed settlements, will lead to high transaction costs and to potential political corruption as state attorneys general actively involve themselves in class action cases as a tool for political advancement).

A recent study by the Federal Judicial Center found that CAFA's enactment has led to an increase in the number of class actions filed in or removed to the federal courts based on diversity jurisdiction. Emery G. Lee and Thomas E. Willging, Federal Judicial Center, The Impact of the Class Action Fairness Act of 2005 on the Federal Courts (2008), available at pubcit.typepad.com/clpblog/files/cafa_preliminary_reportiiifinal.pdf. The observed increase was primarily associated with consumer class actions. The study also found that much of the increase in diversity class actions has been driven by an increase in original filings in federal courts, suggesting (contrary to the expectations of many) that plaintiffs' attorneys are choosing the federal forum, rather than leaving it to defense counsel to remove cases to federal court. See also Emery G. Lee III and Thomas Willging, The Impact of the Class Action Fairness Act on the Federal Courts: An Empirical Analysis of Filings and Removals, 156 U. Pa. L. Rev. 1723 (2008) (summarizing some of the same findings, and noting that the monthly average number of diversity class actions filed in or removed to federal courts approximately doubled after CAFA's passage).

One issue worth tracking closely is how the removal provisions of the statute are operating, since removal is the lynchpin. The circuit courts have almost uniformly followed the traditional rule that the party seeking to remove a case to federal court bears the burden of proving that the case belongs there. See Blockbuster, Inc. v. Galeno, 472 F.3d 53 (2d Cir. 2006); Morgan v. Gay, 471 F.3d 469 (3d Cir. 2006), *cert. denied*, 128 S. Ct. 66 (2007); Abrego Abrego v. Dow Chem. Co., 443 F.3d 676 (9th Cir. 2006); Evans v. Walter Industries, Inc., 449 F.3d 1159 (11th Cir. 2006); Brill v. Countrywide Home Loans, Inc., 427 F.3d 446 (7th Cir. 2005). However, H. Hunter Twiford, Anthony Rollo, and John T. Rouse contend that the legislative history of CAFA supports a presumption in favor of federal jurisdiction, with the burden of proof on the party *opposing* federal removal. CAFA's New "Minimal Diversity" Standard For Interstate Class Actions Creates a Presumption That Jurisdiction Exists, with the Burden of Proof Assigned to the Party Opposing Jurisdiction, 25 Miss. C. L. Rev. 7 (2005) (arguing that various district court opinions shifting the burden to the party opposing removal are more faithful to CAFA); see also Twiford, Rollo, and Rouse's CAFA Law Blog (http://www.cafalawblog.com).

Some courts have agreed. See, e.g., Natale v. Pfizer, Inc., 379 F. Supp. 2d 161 (D. Mass. 2005); Lussier v. Dollar Tree Stores, Inc., No. CV05-768-BR, 2005 WL 2211094 (D. Or. Sept. 8, 2005); Waitt v. Merck & Co., No. C05-0759L, 2005 WL 1799740 (W.D. Wash. July 27, 2005); In re Textainer P'ship Sec. Litig., No. C05-0969-MMC, 2005 WL 1791559 (N.D. Cal. July 27, 2005). But see Stephen J. Shapiro, Applying the Jurisdictional Provisions of the Class Action Fairness Act of 2005: In Search of a Sensible Judicial Approach, 59 Baylor L. Rev. 77, 88 (2007) (analyzing the split in the courts and arguing that the removing party bears the burden of proof).

The Fifth Circuit has held that once the party seeking removal makes a prima facie showing of federal jurisdiction, the burden of proof shifts to the party seeking to invoke one of CAFA's exceptions to federal jurisdiction. See Frazier v. Pioneer Americas, 455 F.3d 542 (5th Cir. 2006). In Burdens of Jurisdictional Proof, 59 Ala. L. Rev. 409 (2008), Lonny Shienkopf Hoffman argues that the Fifth Circuit's position is based on flawed assumptions, and that the removing party should carry the burden of proving that these jurisdictional "exceptions" should not apply.

More broadly, the American Law Institute has released a helpful précis of CAFA, designed for practitioners. See Tammy Webb and Kevin Underhill, The Class Action Fairness Act: A Review and Status Report, 2008 ALI-ABA Course of Study: Environmental and Toxic Tort Litigation

177, available at SN082 ALI-ABA 177 (Westlaw). The ALI has also compiled a statistical study outlining the initial impact of CAFA. See Thomas E. Willging and Emery G. Lee III, The Impact of the Class Action Fairness Act of 2005 on the Federal Courts, 2008 ALI-ABA Course of Study: Opinion and Expert Testimony in Federal and State Courts, Sponsored with the Cooperation of the Federal Judicial Center 137, available at SN058 ALI-ABA 137 (Westlaw). Allan Kanner and M. Ryan Casey, Consumer Class Actions After CAFA, 56 Drake L. Rev. 303 (2008), reviews some of the initial cases applying CAFA and discusses emerging trends in CAFA litigation. See also Jay Tidmarsh, Finding Room for State Class Actions in a Post-CAFA World: The Case of the Counterclaim Class Action, 35 W. St. U. L. Rev. 193 (2007) (arguing that counterclaim class actions are one area where state courts can still impact class action practice in the aftermath of CAFA).

Note: The Multiparty, Multiforum Trial Jurisdiction Act of 2002

In another context, Congress has intervened to expand the subject matter jurisdiction of the lower federal courts to deal with complex litigation. The Multiparty, Multiforum Trial Jurisdiction Act (MMTJA) was passed in the wake of the terrorist attacks on September 11, 2001, as a means of centralizing litigation arising from large-scale accidents and disasters involving significant loss of life. See 28 U.S.C. § 1369. The statute grants federal district courts original and removal jurisdiction over "any civil action involving minimal diversity between adverse parties that arises from a single accident, where at least 75 natural persons have died in the accident at a discrete location," and where more than one state is involved because the accident took place in multiple locations, or because of the defendants' place of residence. § 1369(a). Abstention is required if the claims are primarily local, i.e., where the "substantial majority" of the plaintiffs are citizens of a single state "of which the primary defendants are also citizens," and where "the claims asserted will be primarily governed by the laws of that State." § 1369(b).

The first occasion to apply the statute arose out of a tragic fire at a Rhode Island nightclub called "The Station" in 2003. See Passa v. Derderian, 308 F. Supp. 2d 43 (D.R.I. 2004). A rock band well known for using pyrotechnics to enhance its musical performance took the stage at The Station while the band's manager ignited a series of pyrotechnic devices. The fireworks caused an explosion behind the stage area, and within three minutes the entire nightclub was ablaze. Of the 412 people inside the building, 100 died and more than 200 were injured.

A spate of lawsuits were filed in state and federal courts throughout southern New England by fire victims, their estates, and surviving family members, alleging various state law tort claims against a group of defendants including the band members, their agent, their record company and management company, as well as the nightclub owners, the companies that manufactured the insulation in the nightclub, the manufacturer of the fireworks, the corporate event sponsors, and a host of state and local government entities responsible for fire protection. In five such cases before the federal district court of Rhode Island, certain defendants filed motions to dismiss or remand the cases to state court on the theory that the federal court lacked jurisdiction. A "steering committee" of lawyers representing over 180 potential plaintiffs who had not yet sued anyone filed an amicus brief supporting the defendants seeking remand.

The parties seeking dismissal/remand argued that § 1369(b) requires abstention because a substantial majority of the plaintiffs and the defendants were citizens of Rhode Island. The court rejected this claim and retained jurisdiction over the cases. The court first held that § 1369(b) is a mandatory abstention provision, not a limit on the court's subject matter jurisdiction, even though the section heading reads "Limitation of jurisdiction of district courts." The distinction matters because a court is obliged to dismiss a case at any stage if there is a defect in subject matter jurisdiction, but "once a court has determined that abstention is not required, this question is not typically revisited during later stages of the litigation." 308 F. Supp. 2d at 56. On the merits, the court concluded that abstention was not necessary because a substantial majority of the plaintiffs were not from Rhode Island.

The court reached this conclusion by including the citizenship of approximately 335 "potential plaintiffs" who had not yet filed suit. Id. at 59-60. As the court reasoned, "[s]uch an interpretation is consistent with Congress's desire to consolidate all cases arising from one major disaster in one federal court, as it conditions abstention on the citizenship of all potential claimants rather than considering only those who are first to file." Id. at 60.

There is no question that Congress wanted to streamline multidistrict disaster litigation. As the House Conference Report stated:

> It is common after a serious accident to have many lawsuits filed in several states, in both state and federal courts, with many different sets of plaintiffs' lawyers and several different defendants. Despite this multiplicity of suits, the principal issue that must be resolved first in each suit is virtually identical: Is one or more of the defendants liable? . . . The waste of judicial resources—and the costs to both plaintiffs and defendants—of litigating the same liability question several times over in separate lawsuits can be extreme.

Id. at 53. But the MMTJA unambiguously refers to "plaintiffs," in § 1369(b), not to "plaintiffs and potential plaintiffs." Has the court strayed from plain meaning? What if most of the potential plaintiffs, and especially plaintiffs from outside Rhode Island, settle without filing suit or decide not to sue?

The Class Action Fairness Act and the MMTJA hardly bespeak a trend toward the constitutional limit of federal subject matter jurisdiction, but the statutes do suggest that Congress sees the value of letting federal courts shoulder more of the litigation load in certain complex cases. Is efficiency the only concern, or are there reasons to think state courts are inferior forums for these cases?

e. Declining to Exercise Supplemental Jurisdiction

Where supplemental jurisdiction is permissible, a court may nonetheless decline to exercise it. Section 1367(c) describes the grounds upon which courts may refuse to exercise supplemental jurisdiction. The United States Supreme Court construed § 1367(c)'s relationship to United Mine Workers of America v. Gibbs, 383 U.S. 715 (1966), and to abstention doctrine, in City of Chicago v. Int'l College of Surgeons, 522 U.S 156 (1997). The Court described these relationships as follows:

> [T]o say that the terms of § 1367(a) authorize the district courts to exercise supplemental jurisdiction over state law claims . . . does not mean that the jurisdiction *must* be exercised in all cases. Our decisions have established that pendent jurisdiction is a doctrine of discretion, not of plaintiff's right, *Gibbs*, 383 U.S. at 726, and that district courts can decline to exercise jurisdiction over pendent claims for a number of valid reasons, id. at 726-727. Accordingly, we have indicated that district courts [should] deal with cases involving pendent claims in the manner that best serves the principles of economy, convenience, fairness, and comity which underlie the pendent jurisdiction doctrine, Carnegie-Mellon Univ. v. Cohill, 484 U.S. 343, 357 (1988).
>
> The supplemental jurisdiction statute codifies these principles. After establishing that supplemental jurisdiction encompasses other claims, in the same case or controversy as a claim within the district court original jurisdiction, § 1367(a), the statute confirms the discretionary nature of supplemental jurisdiction by enumerating the circumstances in which district courts can refuse its exercise:
>
> > (c) The district courts may decline to exercise supplemental jurisdiction over a claim under subsection (a) if
> >
> > (1) the claim raises a novel or complex issue of State law,
> >
> > (2) the claim substantially predominates over the claim or claims over which the district court has original jurisdiction
> >
> > (3) the district court has dismissed all claims over which it has original jurisdiction, or
> >
> > (4) in exceptional circumstances, there are other compelling reasons for declining jurisdiction, 28 U.S.C. § 1367(c).
>
> Depending on a host of factors, including the circumstances of the particular case, the nature of the state law claims, the character of the governing state law, and the relationship between the state and federal claims, district courts may decline to exercise jurisdiction over supplemental state law claims. The statute thereby reflects the understanding that, when deciding whether to exercise supplemental jurisdiction, a federal court should consider and weigh in each case, and at every stage of the litigation, the values of judicial economy, convenience, fairness, and comity, *Cohill*, supra, at 350.

> In this case, the District Court decided that those interests would be best served by exercising jurisdiction over ICS state law claims. In addition to their discretion under § 1367(c), district courts may be obligated not to decide state law claims (or to stay their adjudication) where one of the abstention doctrines articulated by this Court applies. Those doctrines embody the general notion that federal courts may decline to exercise their jurisdiction, in otherwise exceptional circumstances, where denying a federal forum would clearly serve an important countervailing interest, for example where abstention is warranted by considerations of proper constitutional adjudication, regard for federal-state relations, or wise judicial administration. Quackenbush v. Allstate Ins. Co., 517 U.S. 706, 716 (1996) (citations and internal quotation marks omitted).

522 U.S. at 172-174.

f. Tolling of Statutes of Limitation and Supplemental Jurisdiction

In a case involving 28 U.S.C. § 1367(d) and principles of federalism, the United States Supreme Court upheld the tolling provision of the federal jurisdiction statute. This provision suspends the running of the statute of limitations on state claims while they are pending in federal court. A unanimous court concluded that the tolling process was within Congress's power under the "necessary and proper" clause of the United States Constitution. U.S. Const. Art. 1, section 8, cl. 18. The Court did not regard the provision as an undue intrusion into state sovereignty. Jinks v. Richland County, 538 U.S. 456 (2003).

Assume, however, that a plaintiff brings an action in federal court against a state defendant that alleges both a federal claim and a related state law claim, but the federal action is dismissed on the ground that the state's Eleventh Amendment immunity bars the federal statutory claim. The plaintiff then refiles the state law claim in state court, after the applicable statute of limitations has elapsed. The plaintiff argues that the statute of limitations on the state law claim was tolled by the filing of the original suit in federal court, and that 28 U.S.C. § 1367(d) rescues this state law claim. What result? In Raygor v. Regents of the University of Minnesota, 534 U.S. 533 (2002), the United States Supreme Court held that the statute of limitations is *not* tolled under these circumstances. The dismissals covered by § 1367(d) do not include dismissals based upon the Eleventh Amendment. Rather, a court in such cases should compute the statute of limitations as if the first action had not been filed at all.

Note: Pendent Personal Jurisdiction

In addition to curing problems of subject matter jurisdiction over supplemental claims, some courts have concluded that personal jurisdiction deficiencies may also be cured by "pendent personal jurisdiction."

Assume, for example, that a plaintiff asserts two claims against a defendant in an action filed in federal court. The first claim is based on federal law, and is one for which federal law provides for nationwide service of process. The second claim is based on state law and is factually tied to the first, but involves matters that would not justify assertion of jurisdiction over the defendant on that claim in the forum chosen by the plaintiff. Does the court have personal jurisdiction over the defendant as to both claims?

Some courts that have addressed such circumstances have concluded that there is pendent personal jurisdiction. As stated by the court in IUE AFL-CIO Pension Fund v. Herrmann, 9 F.3d 1049, 1056 (2d Cir. 1993):

> [U]nder the doctrine of pendent personal jurisdiction, where a federal statute authorized nationwide service of process, and the federal and state claims "derive from a common nucleus of operative fact," see United Mine Workers v. Gibbs, 383 U.S. 715, 725 (1996), the district court may assert personal jurisdiction over the parties to the related state law claims even if personal jurisdiction is not otherwise available.

A contrary rule would produce obvious inefficiencies that the supplemental jurisdiction statute as well as the case law it codifies were designed to avoid. Yet is the casual assumption that pendent personal jurisdiction exists persuasive as a matter of due process? Does the factual relatedness required for supplemental subject matter jurisdiction necessarily provide the minimum contact required for due process? See ESAB Group, Inc. v. Centricut, LLC., 126 F.3d 617 (4th Cir. 1997), *cert. denied*, 523 U.S. 1048 (1998).

3. Federal Removal Jurisdiction

a. Introduction

When an action that is filed in state court could have been brought in federal court, the defendant may be entitled to remove the action from state court to federal court, provided the requirements of the federal removal statute (28 U.S.C. § 1441) are met. The federal court to which the defendant may remove is the federal court that embraces the jurisdiction of the state court in which the original action is filed. Thus, for example, if an action is filed in a state court located in Tucson, Arizona, removal would be to the nearest federal district court, which sits in Tucson.

The most important of the removal statute requirements are as follows:

a) The action could originally have been brought in federal court. Removal jurisdiction is no greater than original jurisdiction.
b) All defendants must join in the petition for removal, unless the narrow requirements of § 1441(c) are satisfied.
c) The defendant cannot remove if the basis for federal court jurisdiction is diversity and the defendant is a citizen of the state in

which the original action was filed. This rule is based on the notion that a resident defendant has no reason to fear bias by her own home courts. The rule applies only to diversity-based removal. See Lincoln Property Co. v. Roche, 546 U.S. 81 (2005) (holding that a removing defendant is not obliged to inform federal court of local affiliates who are potential defendants and whose presence, if joined, would defeat removal).

d) The defendant must remove before taking substantial steps to defend the action in the state court. A nontimely petition will be denied.

b. Remand

Once a case has been removed to federal court, the federal judge may remand the case only under the conditions set forth in the removal statutes. Construing these statutes, the U.S. Supreme Court held in Thermtron Products, Inc. v. Hermansdorfer, that a judge could not remand a case merely because of a crowded federal court docket. Since the removal statutes do not list "overcrowded docket" as a basis for remanding a case, the court lacked power to remand on this basis. 423 U.S. 336 (1976), *abrogated on other grounds by* Quackenbush v. Allstate Ins. Co., 517 U.S. 706 (1996).

Despite *Thermtron,* the Court in Carnegie-Mellon University v. Cohill, 484 U.S. 343 (1988), held that a federal court could remand a case when, after removal, the federal claims in the case were dismissed and only the pendent state law claims remained. Three Justices dissented on the ground that because the removal statutes did not expressly provide for remand in such circumstances, they should be construed to disallow remand of residual pendent state law claims. The majority position seems correct, however, especially in light of the federal judiciary's longstanding practice, now codified in the supplemental jurisdiction statute, of declining jurisdiction over pendent state law claims once the anchoring federal claims have been dismissed. 28 U.S.C. § 1367(c)(3).

Motions to remove and to remand are subject to elaborate gaming in which the merits of the case are sometimes buried beneath its procedure. In the following case, which shows you the workings of the removal practice, the U.S. Supreme Court unanimously put considerations of finality and efficiency ahead of technicalities.

Caterpillar Inc. v. Lewis

519 U.S. 61 (1996)

JUSTICE GINSBURG delivered the opinion of the Court.

This case, commenced in a state court, involves personal jury claims arising under state law. The case was removed to a federal court at a time when, the Court of Appeals concluded, complete diversity of citizenship did not exist among the parties. Promptly after the removal, the plaintiff moved to remand the case to the state court, but the District Court denied that motion. Before trial of the case, however, all claims involving the nondiverse defendant were settled, and that defendant was dismissed as a party to the action. Complete diversity thereafter existed. The case proceeded to trial, jury verdict, and judgment for the removing defendant. The Court of Appeals vacated the judgment, concluding that, absent complete diversity at the time of removal, the District Court lacked subject-matter jurisdiction.

The question presented is whether the absence of complete diversity at the time of removal is fatal to federal-court adjudication. We hold that a district court's error in failing to remand a case improperly removed is not fatal to the ensuing adjudication if federal jurisdictional requirements are met at the time judgment is entered.

I

Respondent James David Lewis, a resident of Kentucky, filed this lawsuit in Kentucky state court on June 22, 1989, after sustaining injuries while operating a bulldozer. Asserting state-law claims based on defective manufacture, negligent maintenance, failure to warn, and breach of warranty, Lewis named as defendants both the manufacturer of the bulldozer — petitioner Caterpillar Inc., a Delaware corporation with its principal place of business in Illinois — and the company that serviced the bulldozer — Whayne Supply Company, a Kentucky corporation with its principal place of business in Kentucky.

Several months later, Liberty Mutual Insurance Group, the insurance carrier for Lewis' employer, intervened in the lawsuit as a plaintiff. A Massachusetts corporation with its principal place of business in that State, Liberty Mutual asserted subrogation claims against both Caterpillar and Whayne Supply for workers' compensation benefits Liberty Mutual had paid to Lewis on behalf of his employer.

Lewis entered into a settlement agreement with defendant Whayne Supply less than a year after filing his complaint. Shortly after learning of this agreement, Caterpillar filed a notice of removal, on June 21, 1990, in the United States District Court for the Eastern District of Kentucky. Grounding federal jurisdiction on diversity of citizenship, see 28 U.S.C. § 1332, Caterpillar satisfied with only a day to spare the statutory requirement that a diversity-based removal take place within one year of a lawsuit's commencement, see 28 U.S.C. § 1446(b). Caterpillar's notice of removal explained that the case was nonremovable at the lawsuit's start: Complete diversity was absent then because plaintiff Lewis and defendant Whayne Supply shared Kentucky citizenship. Proceeding on the understanding that the settlement agreement between these two Kentucky parties would result in the dismissal of Whayne Supply from the lawsuit, Caterpillar stated that the settlement rendered the case removable.

Lewis objected to the removal and moved to remand the case to state court. Lewis acknowledged that he had settled his own claims against Whayne Supply. But Liberty Mutual had not yet settled its subrogation claim against Whayne Supply, Lewis asserted. Whayne Supply's presence as a defendant in the lawsuit, Lewis urged, defeated diversity of citizenship. Without addressing this argument, the District Court denied Lewis' motion to remand on September 24, 1990, treating as dispositive Lewis' admission that he had settled his own claims against Whayne Supply.

Discovery, begun in state court, continued in the now federal lawsuit, and the parties filed pretrial conference papers beginning in July 1991. In June 1993, plaintiff Liberty Mutual and defendant Whayne Supply entered into a settlement of Liberty Mutual's subrogation claim, and the District Court dismissed Whayne Supply from the lawsuit. With Caterpillar as the sole defendant adverse to Lewis, the case proceeded to a six-day jury trial in November 1993, ending in a unanimous verdict for Caterpillar. The District Court entered judgment for Caterpillar on November 23, 1993, and denied Lewis' motion for a new trial on February 1, 1994.

On appeal, the Court of Appeals for the Sixth Circuit accepted Lewis' argument that, at the time of removal, Whayne Supply remained a defendant in the case due to Liberty Mutual's subrogation claim against it. Because the party lineup, on removal, included Kentucky plaintiff Lewis and Kentucky defendant Whayne Supply, the Court of Appeals observed that diversity was not complete when Caterpillar took the case from state court to federal court. Consequently, the Court of Appeals concluded, the District Court "erred in denying [Lewis'] motion to remand this case to the state court for lack of subject matter jurisdiction." That error, according to the Court of Appeals, made it necessary to vacate the District Court's judgment.

Caterpillar petitioned for this Court's review. Caterpillar stressed that the nondiverse defendant, Whayne Supply, had been dismissed from the lawsuit prior to trial. It was therefore improper, Caterpillar urged, for the Court of Appeals to vacate the District Court's judgment—entered after several years of litigation and a six-day trial—on account of a jurisdictional defect cured, all agreed, by the time of trial and judgment. We granted certiorari, 517 U.S. 1133 (1996), and now reverse.

II

The Constitution provides, in Article III, § 2, that "[t]he judicial Power [of the United States] shall extend . . . to Controversies . . . between Citizens of different States. "Commencing with the Judiciary Act of 1789, ch. 20, § 11, 1 Stat. 78, Congress has constantly authorized the federal courts to exercise jurisdiction based on the diverse citizenship of parties. In Strawbridge v. Curtiss, 3 Cranch 267 (1806), this Court construed the original Judiciary Act's diversity provision to require complete diversity of citizenship. Id., at 267. We have adhered to that statutory interpretation ever since. See Carden v. Arkoma Associates, 494 U.S. 185, 187 (1990). The current general-diversity statute, permitting federal district court jurisdiction over suits for more than $50,000 "between . . . citizens of different States," 28 U.S.C. § 1332(a), thus applies only to cases in which the citizenship of each plaintiff is diverse from the citizenship of each defendant.

When a plaintiff files in state court a civil action over which the federal district courts would have original jurisdiction based on diversity of citizenship, the defendant or defendants may remove the action to federal court, 28 U.S.C. § 1441(a), provided that no defendant "is a citizen of the State in which such action is brought," § 1441(b). In a case not originally removable, a defendant who receives a pleading or other paper indicating the post-commencement satisfaction of federal jurisdictional requirements—for example, by reason of the dismissal of a nondiverse party—may remove the case to federal court within 30 days of receiving such information.] § 1446(b). No case, however, may be removed from state to federal court based on diversity of citizenship "more than 1 year after commencement of the action."

Once a defendant has filed a notice of removal in the federal district court, a plaintiff objecting to removal "on the basis of any defect in removal procedure" may, within 30 days, file a motion asking the district court to remand the case to state court. § 1447(c). This 30-day limit does not apply, however, to jurisdictional defects: "If at any time before final judgment it appears that the district court lacks subject matter jurisdiction, the case shall be remanded."

III

We note, initially, two "givens" in this case as we have accepted it for review. First, the District Court, in its decision denying Lewis' timely motion to remand, incorrectly treated Whayne Supply, the nondiverse defendant, as effectively dropped from the case prior to removal. Second, the Sixth Circuit correctly determined that the complete diversity requirement was not satisfied at the time of removal. We accordingly home in on this question: Does the District Court's initial misjudgment still burden and run with the case, or is it overcome by the eventual dismissal of the nondiverse defendant?

Petitioner Caterpillar relies heavily on our decisions in American Fire & Casualty Co. v. Finn, 341 U.S. 6 (1951), and Grubbs v. General Elec. Credit Corp., 405 U.S. 699 (1972), urging that these decisions "long ago settled the proposition that remand to the state court is unnecessary even if jurisdiction did not exist at the time of removal, so long as the district court had subject matter jurisdiction at the time of judgment." Caterpillar is right that *Finn* and *Grubbs* are key cases in point and tend in Caterpillar's favor. Each suggests that the existence of subject-matter jurisdiction at time of judgment may shield a judgment against later jurisdictional attack. But neither decision resolves dispositively a controversy of the kind we face, for neither involved a plaintiff who moved promptly, but unsuccessfully, to remand a case improperly removed from state court to federal court, and then challenged on appeal a judgment entered by the federal court.

In *Finn,* two defendants removed a case to federal court on the basis of diversity of citizenship. 341 U.S. at 7-8. Eventually, final judgment was entered for the plaintiff against one of the removing defendants. Id., at 8. The losing defendant urged on appeal, and before this Court, that the judgment could not stand because the requisite diversity jurisdiction, it turned out, existed neither at the time of removal nor at the time of judgment. Agreeing with the defendant, we held that the absence of federal jurisdiction at the time of judgment required the Court of Appeals to vacate the District Court's judgment. Id. at 17-18.[8]

Finn's holding does not speak to the situation here, where the requirement of complete diversity was satisfied at the time of judgment. But Caterpillar points to well-known dicta in *Finn* more helpful to its cause. "There are cases," the Court observed, "which uphold judgments in the district courts even though there was no right to removal." Id., at 16.[9] "In those cases," the *Finn* Court explained, "the federal trial court would have had original jurisdiction of the controversy had it been brought in the federal court in the posture it had at the time of the actual trial of the cause or of the entry of the judgment." Ibid.

The discussion in *Finn* concentrated on cases in which courts held *removing defendants* estopped from challenging final judgments on the basis of removal errors. See id. at 17. The *Finn* Court did not address the situation of a plaintiff such as Lewis, who chose a state court as the forum for his lawsuit, timely objected to removal before the District Court, and then challenged the removal on appeal from an adverse judgment.

In *Grubbs,* a civil action filed in state court was removed to federal court on the petition of the United States, which had been named as a party defendant in a "cross-action" filed by the original defendant. 405 U.S. at 700-701; see 28 U.S.C. § 1444 (authorizing removal of actions brought against the United States, pursuant to 28 U.S.C. § 2410, with respect to property on which the United States has or claims a lien). No party objected to the removal before trial or judgment. See *Grubbs,* 405 U.S. at

8. The Court left open in *Finn* the question whether, on remand to the District Court, "a new judgment [could] be entered on the old verdict without a new trial" if the nondiverse defendant were dismissed from the case. 341 U.S. at 18, n. 18. In the litigation's second round, the District Court allowed the plaintiff to dismiss all claims against the nondiverse defendant. See Finn v. American Fire & Casualty Co., 207 F.2d 113, 114 (C.A.5 1953), *cert. denied,* 347 U.S. 912 (1954). Thereafter, the District Court granted a new trial, on the assumption that the original judgment could not stand for lack of jurisdiction. See 207 F.2d, at 114. Ultimately, the Court of Appeals for the Fifth Circuit set aside the judgment entered after the second trial and ordered the original judgment reinstated. Id., at 117.

9. The Court cited Baggs v. Martin, 179 U.S. 206 (1900), and three lower federal-court cases. *Finn,* 341 U.S. at 16, n. 14.

701. The Court of Appeals nonetheless held, on its own motion, that the "interpleader" of the United States was spurious, and that removal had therefore been improper under 28 U.S.C. § 1444. See *Grubbs*, 405 U.S. at 702. On this basis, the Court of Appeals concluded that the District Court's judgment should be vacated and the case remanded to state court. See ibid.

This Court reversed. Id. at 700. We explained:

> "Longstanding decisions of this Court make clear . . . that where after removal a case is tried on the merits without objection and the federal court enters judgment, the issue in subsequent proceedings on appeal is not whether the case was properly removed, but whether the federal district court would have had original jurisdiction of the case had it been filed in that court." Id. at 702.

We concluded that, "whether or not the case was properly removed, the District Court did have jurisdiction of the parties at the time it entered judgment." Id. at 700. "Under such circumstances," we held, "the validity of the removal procedure followed *may not be raised for the first time on appeal*." Id. (emphasis added). *Grubbs* instructs that an erroneous removal need not cause the destruction of a final judgment, if the requirements of federal subject-matter jurisdiction are met at the time the judgment is entered. *Grubbs*, however, dealt with a case removed without objection. The decision is not dispositive of the question whether a plaintiff, who timely objects to removal, may later successfully challenge an adverse judgment on the ground that the removal did not comply with statutory prescriptions.

Beyond question, as Lewis acknowledges, there was in this case complete diversity, and therefore federal subject-matter jurisdiction, at the time of trial and judgment. . . . The case had by then become, essentially, a two-party law-suit: Lewis, a citizen of Kentucky, was the sole plaintiff; Caterpillar, incorporated in Delaware with its principal place of business in Illinois, was the sole defendant Lewis confronted. Caterpillar maintains that this change cured the threshold *statutory* misstep, i.e., the removal of a case when diversity was incomplete.

Caterpillar moves too quickly over the terrain we must cover. The *jurisdictional* defect was cured, i.e., complete diversity was established before the trial commenced. Therefore, the Sixth Circuit erred in resting its decision on the absence of subject-matter jurisdiction. But a statutory flaw—Caterpillar's failure to meet the § 1441(a) requirement that the case be fit for federal adjudication at the time the removal petition is filed—remained in the unerasable history of the case.

And Lewis, by timely moving for remand, did all that was required to preserve his objection to removal. An order denying a motion to remand, "standing alone," is "[o]bviously . . . not final and [immediately] appealable" as of right. Chicago, R.I. & P.R. Co. v. Stude, 346 U.S. 574, 578 (1954). Nor is a plaintiff required to seek permission to take an interlocutory appeal pursuant to 28 U.S.C. § 1292(b)[10] in order to avoid waiving whatever ultimate appeal right he may have.[11] Indeed, if a party had to invoke § 1292(b) in order to preserve an objection to an interlocutory ruling, litigants would be obliged to seek § 1292(b) certifications constantly. Routine resort to § 1292(b) requests would hardly comport with Congress' design to reserve interlocutory review for "'exceptional'" cases while generally retaining for the federal courts a firm final judgment rule. Coopers & Lybrand v. Livesay, 437 U.S. 463, 475 (1978) (quoting Fisons, Ltd. v. United States, 458 F.2d 1241, 1248 (7th Cir.), *cert. denied,* 405 U.S. 1041 (1972)).

Having preserved his objection to an improper removal, Lewis urges that an "all's well that ends well" approach is inappropriate here. He maintains that ultimate satisfaction of the subject-matter jurisdiction requirement ought not swallow up antecedent statutory violations. The course Caterpillar advocates, Lewis observes, would disfavor diligent plaintiffs who timely, but unsuccessfully, move to check improper removals in district court. Further, that course would allow improperly removing defendants to profit from their disregard of Congress' instructions, and their ability to lead district judges into error.

Concretely, in this very case, Lewis emphasizes, adherence to the rules Congress prescribed for removal would have kept the case in state court. Only by removing prematurely was Caterpillar able to get to federal court inside the one-year limitation set in § 1446(b).[12] Had Caterpillar waited until the case was ripe for removal, i.e., until Whayne Supply was dismissed as a defendant, the one-year limitation would have barred the way, and plaintiff's choice of forum would have been preserved.[14]

These arguments are hardly meritless, but they run up against an overriding consideration. Once a diversity case has been tried in federal court, with rules of decision supplied by state law under the regime of Erie R.R. Co. v. Tompkins, 304 U.S. 64 (1938), considerations of finality, efficiency, and economy become overwhelming.

Our decision in Newman-Green, Inc. v. Alfonzo-Larrain, 490 U.S. 826 (1989), is instructive in this regard. *Newman-Green* did not involve removal, but it did involve the federal courts' diversity jurisdiction and a party defendant whose presence, like Whayne Supply's in this case,

10. Section 1292(b) provides for interlocutory appeals from otherwise not immediately appealable orders, if conditions specified in the section are met, the district court so certifies, and the court of appeals exercises its discretion to take up the request for review.

11. On brief, Caterpillar argued that "Lewis effectively waived his objection to removal by failing to seek an immediate appeal of the district court's refusal to remand." We reject this waiver argument, though we recognize that it has attracted some support in Court of Appeals opinions. See, e.g., Able v. Upjohn Co., 829 F.2d 1330, 1333-1334 (4th Cir. 1987), *cert. denied,* 485 U.S. 963 (1988).

12. Congress amended § 1446(b) in 1988 to include the one-year limitation in order to "reduc[e] the opportunity for removal after substantial progress has been made in state court." H.R. Rep. No. 100-889, p. 72 (1988).

14. Lewis preferred state court to federal court based on differences he perceived in, *inter alia,* the state and federal jury systems and rules of evidence.

blocked complete diversity. *Newman-Green* proceeded to summary judgment with the jurisdictional flaw—the absence of complete diversity—undetected. See Id. at 828-829. The Court of Appeals noticed the flaw, invited the parties to address it, and, en banc, returned the case to the District Court "to determine whether it would be prudent to drop [the jurisdiction spoiler] from the litigation." Id. at 830. We held that the Court of Appeals itself had authority "to dismiss a dispensable nondiverse party," although we recognized that, ordinarily, district courts are better positioned to make such judgments. Id. at 837-838. "[R]equiring dismissal after years of litigation," the Court stressed in *Newman-Green*, "would impose unnecessary and wasteful burdens on the parties, judges, and other litigants waiting for judicial attention." Id. at 836. The same may be said of the remand to state court Lewis seeks here. Cf. Knop v. McMahan, 872 F.2d 1132, 1139, n.16 (3d Cir. 1989) ("To permit a case in which there is complete diversity throughout trial to proceed to judgment and then cancel the effect of that judgment and relegate the parties to a new trial in a state court because of a brief lack of complete diversity at the beginning of the case would be a waste of judicial resources.").

Our view is in harmony with a main theme of the removal scheme Congress devised. Congress ordered a procedure calling for expeditious superintendence by district courts. The lawmakers specified a short time, 30 days, for motions to remand for defects in removal procedure, 28 U.S.C. § 1447(c), and district court orders remanding cases to state courts generally are "not reviewable on appeal or otherwise," § 1447(d). Congress did not similarly exclude appellate review of refusals to remand. But an evident concern that may explain the lack of symmetry relates to the federal courts' subject-matter jurisdiction. Despite a federal trial court's threshold denial of a motion to remand, if, at the end of the day and case, a *jurisdictional* defect remains uncured, the judgment must be vacated. See Fed. Rule Civ. Proc. 12(h)(3) ("Whenever it appears by suggestion of the parties or otherwise that the court lacks jurisdiction of the subject matter, the court shall dismiss the action."); *Finn*, 341 U.S. at 18. In this case, however, no jurisdictional defect lingered through judgment in the District Court. To wipe out the adjudication postjudgment, and return to state court a case now satisfying all federal jurisdictional requirements, would impose an exorbitant cost on our dual court system, a cost incompatible with the fair and unprotracted administration of justice.

Lewis ultimately argues that, if the final judgment against him is allowed to stand, "all of the various procedural requirements for removal will become unenforceable"; therefore, "defendants will have an enormous incentive to attempt wrongful removals." In particular, Lewis suggests that defendants will remove prematurely "in the hope that some subsequent developments, such as the eventual dismissal of nondiverse defendants, will permit th[e] case to be kept in federal court." We do not anticipate the dire consequences Lewis forecasts.

The procedural requirements for removal remain enforceable by the federal trial court judges to whom those requirements are directly addressed. Lewis' prediction that rejection of his petition will "encourag[e] state court defendants to remove cases improperly," rests on an assumption we do not indulge — that district courts generally will not comprehend, or will balk at applying, the rules on removal Congress has prescribed. The prediction furthermore assumes defendants' readiness to gamble that any jurisdictional defect, for example, the absence of complete diversity, will first escape detection, then disappear prior to judgment. The well-advised defendant, we are satisfied, will foresee the likely outcome of an unwarranted removal — a swift and nonreviewable remand order, see 28 U.S.C. §§ 1447(c), (d), attended by the displeasure of a district court whose authority has been improperly invoked. The odds against any gain from a wrongful removal, in sum, render improbable Lewis' projection of increased resort to the maneuver. . . .

For the reasons stated, the judgment of the Court of Appeals is reversed, and the case is remanded for proceedings consistent with this opinion.

It is so ordered.

Notes and Questions

1. *Why Removal?* Why did Caterpillar want to be in federal court? Those reasons are driving this case, yet they could not be gathered or even guessed from the Supreme Court opinion. Nor do we know from the opinion anything about the injuries Mr. Lewis sustained or what caused them. Is it possible that Lewis made Whayne Supply Company a defendant only for purposes of defeating diversity and preventing removal? If so, it was a big tactical error to settle with the nondiverse defendant before the year limitation period ran on removal, wasn't it? Conversely, Caterpillar's lawyers were on the ball to file so quickly for removal, once it was possible. Perhaps they had their petition ready for just such an eventuality.

2. *Appealability.* The Supreme Court assumes that the district court made a mistake on Lewis's motion to remand: that the presence of Liberty Mutual's claim against Whayne did destroy diversity. What were Lewis's options at the point that the federal court denied his motion to remand? It was not appealable as such, since a decision about jurisdiction is a "first" rather than a "final" order. 28 U.S.C. § 1291 (only final orders are appealable).

He also might have tried to get the federal district court to certify this case for an interlocutory appeal under 28 U.S.C. § 1292. The Supreme Court, however, refuses to make an effort to appeal a condition of raising improper removal at the conclusion of the case. Yet the message for practice of this case is that parties had better contest removal in every way possible. Gone are the days when the absence of subject matter jurisdiction (at least as to diversity) was an automatic winner "whenever" it was raised. Cf. Rule 12(h)(3).

Another route for correcting a clearly erroneous district court decision about removal or remand might be an extraordinary writ of mandamus. This was the route taken when the case was tossed back to the state court in *Thermtron Products*, 484 U.S. 343 (1988) (discussed in the introductory note above). Generally speaking, however, there is no effective appeal from an order granting a remand to state court, no matter how clearly wrong the decision may be. See, e.g., Cook v. Wikler, 320 F.3d 431 (3d Cir. 2003) (refusing to review remand order under 28 U.S.C. § 1447(d); district court remanded case on ground that removal by third party defendant is improper). There are a few exceptions to the blanket rule against appeals, such as certain civil rights cases, and exercises of discretion under the supplemental jurisdiction statute, 28 U.S.C. § 1367(c), as well as certain class action lawsuits falling under the recently enacted Class Action Fairness Act. See 28 U.S.C. § 1453(c)(1). See also Weber v. Mobil Oil Corp., 506 F.3d 1311 (5th Cir. 2007) (§ 1453(c)(1) does not allow review of remand order where class action was filed before CAFA; post-CAFA intervention of new parties does not alter date upon which action commenced; distinguishing Prime Care, LLC v. Humana Ins. Co., 447 F.3d 1284 (10th Cir. 2006) (post-CAFA amendment adding new defendants renders remand order appealable as long as the amendment does not relate back to the pre-CAFA pleading); Amalgamated Transit Union Local 1309 v. Laidlaw Transit Servs., Inc., 435 F.3d 1140 (9th Cir. 2006) (discussing and applying § 1453(c)(1)). The Supreme Court's recent interpretations of § 1447(d) have not produced greater clarity on when a remand can be appealed. On the one hand, the Court decisively rejected the claim that either the Private Securities Litigation Reform Act of 1995 (PSLRA) or the Securities Litigation Uniform Standards Act of 1998 creates an exception to the § 1447(d) ban on appealing remands for lack of subject matter jurisdiction. See Kircher v. Putnam Funds Trust, 547 U.S. 633 (2006). Congress passed the second act when it became clear that securities fraud plaintiffs were simply pursuing litigation in state court rather than meet the heightened requirements of federal litigation under the PSLRA. The 1998 Act precludes certain kinds of class actions altogether and it authorizes removal of such suits to federal court so that the preclusion provision can be applied.

Arguing that eight state law class actions were precluded by the 1998 Act, defendants removed the cases to federal district court, but the district court remanded once it found that plaintiffs' cases were not in fact covered by the preclusion provision. Defendants appealed and the Court held that neither it nor the circuit court had authority to entertain the appeal due to § 1447(d). Defendants sought to escape the effect of § 1447(d) by arguing that a decision on coverage by the preclusion provision is not "jurisdictional," and therefore the district court's remand was not for lack of subject matter jurisdiction. The Court flatly rejected this argument, holding that coverage by the preclusion provision is a condition of removal jurisdiction, and emphasizing that

> [t]he policy of Congress opposes "interruption of the litigation of the merits of a removed cause by prolonged litigation of questions of jurisdiction of the

> district court to which the cause is removed," United States v. Rice, 327 U.S. 742, 751 (1946), and nearly three years of jurisdictional advocacy in the cases before us confirm the congressional wisdom. For over a century now, statutes have accordingly limited the power of federal appellate courts to review orders remanding cases removed by defendants from state to federal court. . . . [W]e have relentlessly repeated that "any remand order issued on the grounds specified in § 1447(c) [is immunized from all forms of appellate review], whether or not that order might be deemed erroneous by an appellate court." *Thermtron*, 423 U.S. at 351.

Id. at 640 (citation omitted).

Although eight Justices signed the majority opinion (Justice Scalia concurred separately), *Kircher* may be less decisive than it seems. Six months later, the Court recognized an exception to the § 1447(d) ban on appeals where a federal employee is sued for wrongful or negligent conduct and the Attorney General substitutes the United States as the defendant by certifying that the employee was acting within the scope of his official duties. Osborn v. Haley, 549 U.S. 225 (2007). The Court held that § 1447(d) is trumped by the Federal Employees Liability Reform and Tort Compensation Act of 1988, which provides that the Attorney General's certification is "conclusiv[e] . . . for purposes of removal." 28 U.S.C. § 2679(d)(2). That provision both prevents the district court from reassessing the grounds for certification (whether the employee in fact acted within the scope of her duties when the injury occurred) and gives the government the right to appeal when the district court refuses to recognize the Attorney General's certification. 549 U.S. at 244. The Court so held notwithstanding the fact that the government contended that the incident causing plaintiff's injuries never even took place. Id. at 245-246.

Justice Scalia, exasperated by the majority's disregard for the plain meaning of § 1447(d), decried the Court's gradual, continued erosion of § 1447(d)'s mandate. Id. at 262-263. "How," he asked,

> can a statute explicitly eliminating appellate jurisdiction to review a remand order not "contro[l]" whether an appellate court has jurisdiction to review a remand order? The Court says the answer to this riddle lies in 28 U.S.C. § 2679(d)(2). But that section says only that the Attorney General's certification is "conclusiv[e] . . . for purposes of *removal*" (emphasis added); it says absolutely nothing about the reviewability of remand orders. Thus, the most § 2679(d)(2) can prove is that the District Court should not have remanded the case; that its remand order was erroneous. . . . Just last Term we acknowledged that "a remand premised on an erroneous conclusion of no jurisdiction is unappealable." *Kircher*, 126 S. Ct. at 2155. Today's opinion repudiates that principle. . . . This utterly novel proposition, that a remand order can be set aside when it is contrary to law, leaves nothing remaining of § 1447(d).

Id. at 264-265 (citation omitted). On the scope of the federal officer removal statute, see Watson v. Philip Morris Cos., Inc., 551 U.S. 142 (2007) (regulated industry is not, by virtue of its compliance activities, an agent or officer of the federal government within the meaning of 28 U.S.C. § 1442(a)(1)).

The Court returned to the issue, this time with Justice Scalia writing for a 7-2 majority, in Powerex Corp. v. Reliant Energy Servs., 127 S. Ct. 2411 (2007). *Powerex* was a suit brought by the State of California against a range of companies accused of fixing prices in the California energy market. The suit was filed in California state court and promptly removed by certain defendants under the Foreign Sovereign Immunities Act of 1976, which permits removal by a foreign state. See 28 U.S.C. § 1603(b)(2); see also 28 U.S.C. §§ 1441(d), 1442(a). Plaintiff moved to remand, arguing that Powerex was not a foreign state. The district court agreed and granted remand after concluding that other defendants were entitled to sovereign immunity. Powerex appealed and plaintiff invoked the § 1447(d) bar, but the Ninth Circuit decided it was not precluded from reviewing the appeal. The Supreme Court reversed, holding that "when a district court remands a properly removed case because it nonetheless lacks subject matter jurisdiction, the remand is covered by § 1447(c) and thus shielded from review by § 1447(d)." Id. at 2417. Because the district court here remanded on the express ground that it had no subject matter jurisdiction under the FSIA removal provisions when the defendant is not a foreign state, the decision was unreviewable. Id.

Although acknowledging the division of authority, Justice Scalia reasoned that:

> [t]here is only one plausible explanation of what legal ground the District Court actually relied upon for its remand in the present case. . . . [I]t was the court's lack of *power* to adjudicate the claims against petitioner once it concluded both that petitioner was not a foreign state capable of independently removing and that the claims against other removing cross-defendants were barred by sovereign immunity.

Id. at 2417-2418.

Even though the Court itself has never decided the issue of whether there is subject matter jurisdiction to entertain claims when sovereign immunity bars the claims against the only parties capable of removing the case, Justice Scalia emphasized that § 1447(d) serves important purposes: It "reflects Congress's longstanding policy of not permitting interruption of the litigation of the merits of a removed case by prolonging litigation of questions of jurisdiction of the district court to which the cause is removed. Appellate courts must take that jurisdictional prescription seriously, however pressing the merits of the appeal might seem." Id. at 2421.

The language about the purposes of § 1447(d) seems to have been written with the dissent in mind. Justice Breyer, joined by Justice Stevens, analogized Powerex's appeal to the exception recognized in *Osborn*. If, as in *Osborn*, a district court should not be permitted to trump the Attorney General's statutorily authorized determination of "action within the scope of federal employment," a fortiori a district court should not, by an erroneous remand, be allowed to trump the guarantee in the FSIA that foreign state defendants will enjoy immunity from suit.

> [L]ike *Osborn*, the removing party will have lost considerably more than a choice of forum. The removing party will have lost that which a *different* portion of the special statute sought to provide, namely, the immunity from suit that the FSIA sought to secure. . . . [A] state court [receiving the case on remand] will likely feel bound by the federal court's prior judgment on the lack of immunity (under the state law-of-the-case doctrine) and this Court's review (of an adverse state-court judgment) will come too late.

Id. at 2422-2423. This utterly defeats the purpose of sovereign immunity, "which is to avoid subjecting a foreign sovereign to the rigors and inconvenience of suit." Id. at 2422 (internal quotations omitted).

Can you square *Kircher*, *Osborn*, and *Powerex*? Perhaps at least *Osborn* is explained by the distinctive federal interests involved, or by the explicit congressional directive that district courts are not to mess with the certification decisions that render this type of case removable.

The circuit courts often seem equally intent on finding ways around § 1447(d)'s ban on appellate review of remand orders. See, e.g., Wallace v. La. Citizens Prop. Ins. Co. 444 F.3d 697, 700-701 (5th Cir. 2006) (reviewing district court's remand of case removed under the Multiparty, Multiforum Trial Jurisdiction Act (MMTJA) where Hurricane Katrina victims had filed a class action in state court against their insurers; holding that a district court's decision that it was obliged to abstain under 28 U.S.C. § 1369(b) of the MMTJA is not covered by § 1447(d)).

Once the Fifth Circuit established an exception to § 1447(d) in *Wallace*, it held that the mandatory abstention provision of the MMTJA, 28 U.S.C. § 1369(b), did not in fact require remand to the state court even though the terms of § 1369(b) were met (most of the plaintiffs were from Louisiana, as were defendants, and Louisiana law applied to the case). The court reasoned, rather counter-intuitively, that § 1369(b) abstention does not apply to the MMTJA's removal provision, 28 U.S.C. § 1441(e)(1)(B), notwithstanding the Act's explicit directive that "[a]n action removed under this subsection shall be deemed to be an action under section 1369 and an action in which jurisdiction is based on section 1369. . . ." 28 U.S.C. § 1441(e)(5). The Fifth Circuit simply brushed § 1441(e)(5) aside. See *Wallace*, 444 F.3d at 702.

Perhaps *Powerex* will be a strong enough signal to bring the circuit courts into line. See HIF Bio, Inc. v. Yung Shin Pharm. Ind., 508 F.3d 659 (Fed. Cir. 2007) (appellate court cannot review remand under 28 U.S.C. § 1367(c) where district court concluded it lacked supplemental jurisdiction because of a preponderance of state claims; citing and following *Powerex*); Alvarez v. Uniroyal Tire Co., 508 F.3d 639, 640-641 (11th Cir. 2007) (appellate court cannot review remand for lack of subject matter jurisdiction where remand occurred after plaintiff added a nondiverse party by amendment; citing and following *Powerex*).

What lies behind the desire to review and reverse remands? Is it distrust of state courts? Is it the same kind of distrust that provoked Congress to expand removal jurisdiction during the Reconstruction? See William M. Wiecek, The Reconstruction of Federal Judicial Power, 1863-1875, 13 Am. J. Legal Hist. 333 (1969). The risk that state courts will disregard federal rights can't be a concern in *Wallace*—after all, the case is grounded in Louisiana law.

3. *Removal and Federal Question Jurisdiction.* Litigation over removal and remand of cases under federal question jurisdiction can also raise considerable complications. We meet, for instance, our old friend from Chapter 1, the well-pleaded complaint rule. In Rivet v. Regions Bank of Louisiana, 522 U.S. 470 (1998), the Court summarized the relationship of removal to this rule:

> A state court action may be removed to federal court if it qualifies as a "civil action . . . of which the district courts of the United States have original jurisdiction," unless Congress expressly provides otherwise. 28 U.S.C. § 1441(a). In this case, respondents invoked, in support of removal, the district court's original federal-question jurisdiction over "[a]ny civil action . . . founded on a claim or right arising under the Constitution, treaties or laws of the United States." 28 U.S.C. § 1441(b); see also 28 U.S.C. § 1331.
>
> We have long held that "[t]he presence or absence of federal-question jurisdiction is governed by the 'well-pleaded complaint rule,' which provides that federal jurisdiction exists only when a federal question is presented on the face of the plaintiff's properly pleaded complaint." Caterpillar Inc. v. Williams, 482 U.S. 386, 392 (1987); see also Louisville & Nashville R. Co. v. Mottley, 211 U.S. 149, 152 (1908). A defense is not part of a plaintiff's properly pleaded statement of his or her claim. See Metropolitan Life Ins. Co. v. Taylor, 481 U.S. 58, 63 (1987); Gully v. First Nat. Bank in Meridian, 299 U.S. 109, 112 (1936) ("To bring a case within the [federal-question removal] statute, a right or immunity created by the Constitution or laws of the United States must be an element, and an essential one, of the plaintiff's cause of action"). Thus, "a case may not be removed to federal court on the basis of a federal defense, . . . even if the defense is anticipated in the plaintiff's complaint, and even if both parties admit that the defense is the only question truly at issue in the case." Franchise Tax Bd. of California v. Construction Laborers Vacation Trust for Southern Cal., 463 U.S. 1, 14 (1983).
>
> Allied as an "independent corollary" to the well-pleaded complaint rule is the further principle that "a plaintiff may not defeat removal by omitting to plead necessary federal questions." Id. at 22. If a court concludes that a plaintiff has "artfully pleaded" claims in this fashion, it may uphold removal even though no federal question appears on the face of the plaintiff's complaint. The artful pleading doctrine allows removal where federal law completely preempts a plaintiff's state-law claim. Although federal preemption is ordinarily a defense, "[o]nce an area of state law has been completely pre-empted, any claim purportedly based on that pre-empted state-law claim is considered, from its inception, a federal claim, and therefore arises under federal law." Caterpillar, 482 U.S. at 393.

The United States Supreme Court also decided Wisconsin Dep't of Corrections v. Schacht, 524 U.S. 381 (1998), in which the issue was whether a federal district court to which 42 U.S.C. § 1983 claims were removed, without objection by plaintiff, should have remanded the case to state court, instead of dismissing claims that were barred by sovereign immunity and then granting summary judgment to the defendants on the remaining claims. The Seventh Circuit had held that the presence of an Eleventh Amendment-barred issue deprived the federal court of jurisdiction over the entire case and required remand of the whole case to state court. Schacht v. Wisconsin Dep't of Corrections, 116 F.3d 1151 (7th Cir. 1997). See also McKay v. Boyd Constr. Co., 769 F.2d 1084 (5th Cir. 1985) (accord). Other circuits had held that the federal court should remand only the Eleventh Amendment-barred claims. See Kruse v. Hawaii, 68 F.3d 331 (9th Cir. 1995); Henry v. Metro. Sewer Dist., 922 F.2d 332 (6th Cir. 1990). The Court took the latter view and vacated and remanded the Seventh Circuit case. The Court relied in part on the facts that the state can waive the Eleventh Amendment defense, and that a court may ignore the defect unless raised by the state. The Court further noted that § 1447(c) did not require remand of the entire case, because it refers only to cases in which the federal court lacks subject matter jurisdiction over a "case," not over one claim within the case.

Another subtle issue of removal jurisdiction's requirement of "original" federal court jurisdiction arose in Syngenta Crop Protection, Inc. v. Henson, 537 U.S. 28 (2002). The Court held that 28 U.S.C. § 1441(a) does not authorize removal when federal jurisdiction is based on the "All Writs Act," § 1651 and 28 U.S.C. § 1367. The "All Writs Act" authorizes writs in aid of a court's jurisdiction; it provides no federal subject matter jurisdiction in its own right.

4. *Removal and Forum Shopping*. Section 1446(b) provides a one-year limit for motions to remove "on the basis of jurisdiction conferred by section 1332 of this title," measured from the date the complaint is filed. Can a plaintiff seeking to avoid removal join a nondiverse defendant for 366 days in order to defeat removal based on diversity jurisdiction?

In a case of first impression, the Fifth Circuit held that the one-year limit is subject to equitable exceptions where a plaintiff engages in manipulative conduct designed to defeat removal and preserve the state forum of her choice. See Tedford v. Warner-Lambert Co., 327 F.3d 423 (5th Cir. 2003). Jeretta Kay Tedford filed suit in Texas state court alleging that Warner-Lambert's diabetes drug caused her liver to fail. The only nondiverse defendant in the original complaint was a doctor who treated a co-plaintiff. When the trial court severed the two cases, Warner-Lambert informed Tedford of its intent to remove. "A mere three hours later, Tedford amended her petition to name her treating physician . . . [a Texas resident] as a defendant." Id. at 425. Exactly one year after the complaint was filed, Tedford signed a Notice of Nonsuit voluntarily dismissing her doctor from the case. Ten days later, as soon as it learned of the nonsuit, Warner-Lambert removed the case to federal court.

In affirming the district court's denial of remand, the Fifth Circuit noted that "[t]ime requirements in lawsuits between private litigants are customarily subject to equitable tolling," and concluded that "Tedford's forum manipulation justifies application of an equitable exception in the form of estoppel." Id. at 426-427 (quoting Irwin v. Dep't of Veterans Affairs, 498 U.S. 89, 95 (1990)). The court acknowledged that the one-year limit was designed to protect state proceedings from disruption once substantial progress has been reached, but it reasoned that "[s]trict application of the one year limit would encourage plaintiffs to join nondiverse defendants for 366 days simply to avoid federal court, thereby undermining the very purpose of diversity jurisdiction." Id. at 427.

Is this holding consistent with Congress's intent to limit diversity jurisdiction? See Burns v. Windsor Ins. Co., 31 F.3d 1092, 1097 n.12 (11th Cir. 1994) ("Congress knew when it passed the one year bar on removal that some plaintiffs would attempt to defeat diversity jurisdiction by fraudulently (and temporarily) joining a non-diverse party. . . . *Congress has recognized and accepted that, in some circumstances, plaintiff can and will intentionally avoid federal jurisdiction.*") (emphasis added). And compare the Fifth Circuit's generous treatment of the one-year limit on *removal* with the Third Circuit's strict approach toward an untimely motion for *remand.* See Ariel Land Owners, Inc. v. Dring, 351 F.3d 611, 615 (3d Cir. 2003) (reversing district court's grant of plaintiff's motion for remand filed more than 30 days after the notice of removal; "delay and disruption [caused by removal] is only compounded by permitting federal proceedings to carry on at length (nearly two years in the instant case), only to have the case interrupted again and sent back to the state court"). Interestingly, the motion for remand in Ariel Land Owners was based on defendant's untimely removal.

5. *Exceptions to Removal Jurisdiction.* The United States Supreme Court has held that state court suits under the Fair Labor Standards Act may be removed to federal court, even though the statute gives plaintiffs the right to sue in state *or* federal court. Breuer v. Jim's Concrete of Brevard, Inc., 538 U.S. 691 (2003). Language in the FLSA that a lawsuit "may be maintained . . . in any Federal or State court of competent jurisdiction," did not constitute the unequivocal language needed to overcome the right to removal under 28 U.S.C. § 1441.

4. Venue Transfers Within the Federal Court System

If an action is filed in a federal district court that is the improper venue or that is a substantially less convenient venue than another federal court, the action may be transferred to another district. See 28 U.S.C. §§ 1404 and 1406.

The transferee court must be one in which the defendants would have been subject to personal jurisdiction and where venue would have been proper had the action been filed there originally.

When a party requests a transfer based on inconvenience, rather than because the venue is improper, the court will apply § 1404(a) and will give considerable weight to the plaintiff's choice of forum, among other factors. That means that as between venues equally inconvenient to each party, the plaintiff's choice should prevail. As the Seventh Circuit recently stated: "When plaintiff and defendant are in different states there is no choice of forum that will avoid imposing inconvenience; and when the inconvenience of the alternative venues is comparable there is no basis for a change of venue; the tie is awarded to the plaintiff. . . ." In re National Presto Indus., Inc., 347 F.3d 662, 665 (7th Cir. 2003) (denying defendant's motion for change of venue to home state despite inconvenience of defending action brought by SEC in state where the district court lacked subpoena power over key witnesses).

Section 1406 applies when the reason for the transfer is that the transferor court is the improper forum, rather than merely an inconvenient forum.

Although the venue transfer statutes appear to apply only to transfers based on improper or inconvenient venues, courts have permitted transfers based on personal jurisdiction defects. Thus, if an action is filed in a federal district court that lacks personal jurisdiction over the defendant, the court may use the transfer statutes to send the action to a federal district court where personal jurisdiction and venue requirements are met. The courts disagree, however, about whether the proper statute to cite in this situation is § 1404, § 1406, or a "gloss" on both.

Of great significance to litigants is the effect of a transfer on the law applied to the controversy. If the action is based on a federal statute, then the transfer makes little difference because federal law applies in either forum, though complex questions arise when the federal circuits are in conflict over a question of federal law. See Robert A. Ragazzo, Transfer and Choice of Federal Law: The Appellate Model, 93 Mich. L. Rev. 703 (1995). In a diversity case, however, the transfer may have a bearing on which state's law the federal court will apply to the case. As you learned in the materials on the *Erie* doctrine, federal courts sitting in diversity must apply the substantive law of the applicable state, not federal law, to the controversy. In general, this means that the federal court will apply whatever law a state court would apply. The relevant state court, for diversity purposes, is the state court for the state in which the federal court sits. Thus, a federal court in the northern district of Arizona would apply whatever state law that the Arizona court would apply to a similar action.

Each state has a set of laws, called conflicts laws, that determines which state's laws apply to a particular type of controversy. If all of the relevant events took place within the state, then the state's own laws will apply. But if the lawsuit has multistate features, the conflicts laws typically direct the state court to apply the law of the state that is the "center of gravity" of the controversy. Thus, if an Arizona resident files an action in Arizona regarding a car accident that occurred in California, then the Arizona court may apply California law to the controversy, depending on Arizona's conflicts laws.

These rules of diversity jurisdiction, conflicts, and transfers may enable cagey counsel to forum shop through complex strategic moves. A plaintiff could — in theory — file an action in a federal district court in Arizona that counsel knows is inconvenient, though proper. Then, counsel could move (or wait until opposing counsel moves) for a transfer to the more convenient forum. If the law of forum 1 is more favorable to the plaintiff than the law of forum 2, then counsel might get the advantage of forum 1's law plus the advantage of forum 2's convenience, but only if the law of forum 1 follows the action to forum 2. The following chart shows how courts have responded, regarding the effect of transfer on the law applied to a diversity case, when confronted with precisely these tactics:

Situation	*Transfer?*	*By whom?*	*Law applied*
1) Forum 1 venue proper, but inconvenient. Personal jurisdiction satisfied.	Yes — § 1404	Defendant, plaintiff, or court	Conflicts law of Forum 1
2) Forum 1 venue improper. Personal jurisdiction satisfied.	Yes — § 1406	Defendant, plaintiff, or court	Probably conflicts law of Forum 2
3) Forum 1 venue improper. No personal jurisdiction.	Yes — § 1406	Defendant, plaintiff, or court	Conflicts law of Forum 2
4) Forum 1 venue proper. No personal jurisdiction.	Yes — § 1404, § 1406, or gloss on both	Defendant, plaintiff, or court	Conflicts law of Forum 2

Note: For the third and fourth examples, the defendant must be served with process in Forum 2. Also note that 28 U.S.C. § 1406 is primarily a *defense* tool, so that neither the court nor plaintiff is likely to invoke it, *if defendant does not* (plaintiff, after all, chose the forum, and defendant can waive both venue and personal jurisdiction objections). However, if defendant does object successfully to venue or personal jurisdiction *without* invoking 28 U.S.C. § 1406, i.e., through a 12(b) motion to dismiss, then plaintiff or the court conceivably could resort to § 1406 as authority to transfer, rather than dismiss, the action.

For an empirical analysis of the effect of transfer on plaintiffs' "win rates," see Kevin M. Clermont and Theodore Eisenberg, Exorcising the Evil of Forum-Shopping, 80 Cornell L. Rev. 1507 (1995), and the following exchange: David E. Steinberg, Simplifying The Choice of Forum, 75 Wash. U. L.Q. 1479 (1997); Kevin M. Clermont and Theodore Eisenberg, Simplifying the Choice of Forum: A Reply, 75 Wash. U. L.Q. 1551 (1997). See also Robert A. Ragazzo, Transfer and Choice of Federal Law: The Appellate Model, 93 Mich. L. Rev. 703 (1995).

5. Sua Sponte Transfer

Republic of Bolivia v. Philip Morris Companies, Inc.

39 F. Supp. 2d 1008 (S.D. Tex. 1999)

ORDER OF TRANSFER PURSUANT TO 28 U.S.C. § 1404(a)

KENT, District Judge.

Plaintiff, the Republic of Bolivia, brings this action to recover from numerous tobacco companies various health care costs it allegedly incurred in treating illnesses its residents suffered as a result of tobacco use. This action was originally filed in the District Court of Brazoria County, Texas, 239th Judicial District, and removed to this Court on February 19, 1999, by certain Defendants alleging jurisdiction under 28 U.S.C. § 1331 and 28 U.S.C. § 1332. For the following reasons, the Court exercises its authority and discretion pursuant to 28 U.S.C. § 1404(a) to sua sponte TRANSFER this case to the United States District Court for the District of Columbia.

This is one of at least six similar actions brought by foreign governments in various courts throughout the United States. The governments of Guatemala, Panama, Nicaragua, Thailand, Venezuela, and Bolivia have filed suit in the geographically diverse locales of Washington, D.C., Puerto Rico, Texas, Louisiana, and Florida, in both state and federal courts. Why none of these countries seems to have a court system their own governments have confidence in is a mystery to this Court. Moreover, given the tremendous number of United States jurisdictions encompassing fascinating and exotic places, the Court can hardly imagine why the Republic of Bolivia elected to file suit in the veritable hinterlands of Brazoria County, Texas. The Court seriously doubts whether Brazoria County has ever seen a live Bolivian . . . even on the Discovery Channel. Though only here by removal, this humble Court by the sea is certainly flattered by what must be the worldwide renown of rural Texas courts for dispensing justice with unparalleled fairness and alacrity, apparently in common discussion even on the mountain peaks of Bolivia! Still, the Court would be remiss in accepting an obligation for which it truly does not have the necessary resources. Only one judge presides in the Galveston Division — which currently has before it over seven hundred cases and annual civil filings exceeding such number — and that judge is presently burdened with a significant personal situation which diminishes its ability to always give the attention it would like to all of its daunting docket obligations, despite genuinely heroic efforts to do so. And, while Galveston is indeed an international seaport, the capacity of this Court to address the complex and sophisticated issues of international law and foreign relations presented by this case is dwarfed by that of its esteemed colleagues in the District of Columbia who deftly address such awesome tasks as a matter of course. Indeed, this Court, while doing its very best to address the more prosaic matters routinely before it, cannot think of a Bench better versed and more capable of handling precisely this type of case, which requires a high level of expertise in international matters. In fact, proceedings brought by the Republic of Guatemala are currently well underway in that Court in a related action, and there is a request now before the Judicial Panel on Multidistrict Litigation to transfer to the United States District Court for the District of Columbia all six tobacco actions brought by foreign governments, ostensibly for consolidated treatment. Such a Bench, well-populated with genuinely renowned intellects, can certainly better bear and share the burden of multidistrict litigation than this single judge division, where the judge moves his lips when he reads. . . .

Regardless of, and having nothing to do with, the outcome of Defendants' request for transfer and consolidation, it is the Court's opinion that the District of Columbia, located in this Nation's capital, is a much more logical venue for the parties and witnesses in this action because, among other things, Plaintiff has an embassy in Washington, D.C., and thus a physical presence and governmental representatives there, whereas there isn't even a Bolivian restaurant anywhere near here! Although the jurisdiction of this Court boasts no similar foreign offices, a somewhat dated globe is within its possession. While the Court does not therefrom profess to understand all of the political subtleties of the geographical transmogrifications ongoing in Eastern Europe, the Court is virtually certain that Bolivia is not within the four counties over which this Court presides, even though the words Bolivia and Brazoria are a lot alike and caused some real, initial confusion until the Court conferred with its law clerks. Thus, it is readily apparent, even from an outdated globe such as that possessed by this Court, that Bolivia, a hemisphere away, ain't in south-central Texas, and that, at the very least, the District of Columbia is a more appropriate venue (though Bolivia isn't located there either). Furthermore, as this Judicial District bears no significant relationship to any of the matters at issue, and the judge of this Court simply loves cigars, the Plaintiff can be expected to suffer neither harm nor prejudice by a transfer to Washington, D.C., a Bench better able to rise to the smoky challenges presented by this case, despite the alleged and historic presence there of countless "smoke-filled" rooms. Consequently, pursuant to 28 U.S.C. § 1404(a), for the convenience of parties and witnesses, and in the interest of justice, this case is hereby TRANSFERRED to the United States District Court for the District of Columbia.

It is so ordered.

---

6. Forum Non Conveniens

When the forum chosen by the plaintiff is substantially inconvenient, and the correct forum is that of a different jurisdiction, the doctrine of forum non conveniens may require the court to dismiss the action. No transfer is possible, because the correct court is not within the same judicial system as the inconvenient court. Thus, if an action is filed in state court X, and if the substantially more convenient court is in state court Y, then the action must be dismissed by state X and refiled in state Y. Likewise, if the convenient court is in a foreign country, then the domestic state or federal court must dismiss the lawsuit, and it must be refiled in the foreign jurisdiction.

The following case deals with the doctrine of forum non conveniens and the factors that are relevant to the decision to dismiss an action on this basis.

Piper Aircraft Co. v. Reyno

454 U.S. 235 (1981)

JUSTICE MARSHALL delivered the opinion of the Court.

These cases arise out of an air crash that took place in Scotland. Respondent, acting as representative of the estates of several Scottish citizens killed in the accident, brought wrongful death actions against petitioners in the United States District Court for the Middle District of Pennsylvania. Petitioners moved to dismiss on the ground of *forum non conveniens*. After noting that an alternative forum existed in Scotland, the District Court granted their motions. The United States Court of Appeals for the Third Circuit reversed. . . . [B]ecause we conclude that the District Court did not . . . abuse its discretion, we reverse.

In July 1976, a small commercial aircraft crashed in the Scottish highlands during the course of a charter flight from Blackpool to Perth. The pilot and five passengers were killed instantly. The decedents were all Scottish subjects and residents, as are their heirs and next of kin. There were no eyewitnesses to the accident. At the time of the crash the plane was subject to Scottish air traffic control.

The aircraft, a twin engine Piper Aztec, was manufactured in Pennsylvania by petitioner Piper Aircraft Company ("Piper"). The propellers were manufactured in Ohio by petitioner Hartzell Propeller, Inc. ("Hartzell"). At the time of the crash the aircraft was registered in Great Britain and was owned and maintained by Air Navigation and Trading Co., Ltd. ("Air Navigation"). It was operated by McDonald Aviation, Ltd. ("McDonald"), a Scottish air taxi service. Both Air Navigation and McDonald were organized in the United Kingdom. The wreckage of the plane is now in a hangar in Farnsborough, England.

The British Department of Trade investigated the accident several months after it occurred. A preliminary report found that the plane crashed after developing a spin, and suggested that mechanical failure in the plane or the propeller was responsible. At Hartzell's request, this report was reviewed by a three-member Review Board, which held a nine-day adversary hearing attended by all interested parties. The Review Board found no evidence of defective equipment and indicated that pilot error may have contributed to the accident. The pilot, who had obtained his commercial pilot's license only three months earlier, was flying over high ground at an altitude considerably lower than the minimum height required by his company's operations manual.

In July 1977, a California probate court appointed respondent Gaynell Reyno administratrix of the estates of the five passengers. Reyno is not related to and does not know any of the decedents or their survivors; she was a legal secretary to the attorney who filed this lawsuit. Several days after her appointment, Reyno commenced separate wrongful death actions against Piper and Hartzell in the Superior Court of California, claiming negligence and strict liability. Air Navigation, McDonald, and the estate of the pilot are not parties to this litigation. The survivors of the five passengers whose estates are represented by Reyno filed a separate action in the United Kingdom against Air Navigation, McDonald, and the pilot's estate.[2] Reyno candidly admits that the action against Piper and Hartzell was filed in the United States because its laws regarding liability, capacity to sue, and damages are more favorable to her position than are those of Scotland. Scottish law does not recognize strict liability in tort. Moreover, it permits wrongful death actions only when brought by a decedent's relatives. The relatives may sue only for "loss of support and society."

On petitioner's motion, the suit was removed to the United States District Court for the Central District of California. Piper then moved for transfer to the United States District Court for the Middle District of Pennsylvania, pursuant to 28 U.S.C. § 1404(a). . . . [T]he District Court . . . transferred the case to the Middle District of Pennsylvania. . . .

In May 1978, after the suit had been transferred, both Hartzell and Piper moved to dismiss the action on the ground of *forum non conveniens*. The District Court granted these motions in October 1979. It relied on the balancing test set forth by this Court in Gulf Oil Corporation v. Gilbert, 330 U.S. 501 (1947) and its companion case, Koster v. Lumbermen's Mut. Cas. Co., 330 U.S. 518 (1947). In those decisions, the Court stated that a plaintiff's choice of forum should rarely be disturbed. However, when an alternative forum has jurisdiction to hear the case, and when trial in the chosen forum would "establish . . . oppressiveness and vexation to a defendant out of all proportion to plaintiff's convenience," or when the "chosen forum [is] inappropriate because of considerations affecting the court's own administrative and legal problems," the court may, in the exercise of its sound discretion, dismiss the case. To guide trial court

2. The pilot's estate has also filed suit in the United Kingdom against Air Navigation, McDonald, Piper, and Hartzell.

discretion, the Court provided a list of "private interest factors" affecting the convenience of the litigants, and a list of "public interest factors" affecting the convenience of the forum.[6] . . .

In opposing the motions to dismiss, respondent contended that dismissal would be unfair because Scottish law was less favorable. The District Court explicitly rejected this claim. It reasoned that the possibility that dismissal might lead to an unfavorable change in the law did not deserve significant weight; any deficiency in the foreign law was a "matter to be dealt with in the foreign forum." . . .

The Court of Appeals erred in holding that plaintiffs may defeat a motion to dismiss on the ground of *forum non conveniens* merely by showing that the substantive law that would be applied in the alternative forum is less favorable to the plaintiffs than that of the present forum. The possibility of a change in substantive law should ordinarily not be given conclusive or even substantial weight in the *forum non conveniens* inquiry. . . .

The Court of Appeals' decision is inconsistent with this Court's earlier *forum non conveniens* decisions. . . . Those decisions have repeatedly emphasized the need to retain flexibility. In *Gilbert,* the Court refused to identify specific circumstances "which will justify or require either grant or denial of remedy." . . . Similarly, in *Koster,* the Court rejected the contention that where a trial would involve inquiry into the internal affairs of a foreign corporation, dismissal was always appropriate. "That is one, but only one, factor which may show convenience." . . . [I]n Williams v. Green Bay & Western R., 326 U.S. 549, 557 (1946), we stated that we would "not lay down a rigid rule to govern discretion," and that "each case turns on its facts." If central emphasis were placed on any one factor, the *forum non conveniens* doctrine would lose much of the very flexibility that makes it so valuable.

In fact, if conclusive or substantial weight were given to the possibility of a change in law, the *forum non conveniens* doctrine would become virtually useless. Jurisdiction and venue requirements are often easily satisfied. As a result, many plaintiffs are able to choose from among several forums. Ordinarily, these plaintiffs will select that forum whose choice of law rules are most advantageous. Thus, if the possibility of an unfavorable change in substantive law is given substantial weight in the *forum non conveniens* inquiry, dismissal would rarely be proper. . . . The Court of Appeals' approach is not only inconsistent with the purpose of the *forum non conveniens* doctrine, but also poses substantial practical problems. If the possibility of a change in law were given substantial weight, deciding

6. The factors pertaining to the private interests of the litigants included the "relative ease of access to sources of proof; availability of compulsory process for attendance of unwilling, and the cost of obtaining attendance of willing witnesses; possibility of view of premises, if view would be appropriate to the action; and all other practical problems that make trial of a case easy, expeditious and inexpensive." The public factors bearing on the question included the administrative difficulties flowing from court congestion; the "local interest in having localized controversies decided at home"; the interest in having the trial of a diversity case in a forum that is at home with the law that must govern the action; the avoidance of unnecessary problems in conflict of laws, or in the application of foreign law; and the unfairness of burdening citizens in an unrelated forum with jury duty.

motions to dismiss on the ground of *forum non conveniens* would become quite difficult. Choice-of-law analysis would become extremely important, and the courts would frequently be required to interpret the law of foreign jurisdictions. First, the trial court would have to determine what law would apply if the case were tried in the chosen forum, and what law would apply if the case were tried in the alternative forum. It would then have to compare the rights, remedies, and procedures available under the law that would be applied in each forum. Dismissal would be appropriate only if the court concluded that the law applied by the alternative forum is as favorable to the plaintiff as that of the chosen forum. The doctrine of *forum non conveniens,* however, is designed in part to help courts avoid conducting complex exercises in comparative law. As we stated in *Gilbert,* the public interest factors point towards dismissal where the court would be required to "untangle problems in conflict of laws, and in law foreign to itself." *Gilbert,* supra, 330 U.S. at 509.

Upholding the decision of the Court of Appeals would result in other practical problems. At least where the foreign plaintiff named an American manufacturer as defendant,[17] a court could not dismiss the case on grounds of *forum non conveniens* where dismissal might lead to an unfavorable change in law. The American courts, which are already extremely attractive to foreign plaintiffs,[18] would become even more attractive. The flow of litigation into the United States would increase and further congest already crowded courts.[19]

17. In fact, the defendant might not even have to be American. A foreign plaintiff seeking damages for an accident that occurred abroad might be able to obtain service of process on a foreign defendant who does business in the United States. Under the Court of Appeals' holding, dismissal would be barred if the law in the alternative forum were less favorable to the plaintiff—even though none of the parties are American, and even though there is absolutely no nexus between the subject matter of the litigation and the United States.

18. First, all but 6 of the 50 American States—Delaware, Massachusetts, Michigan, North Carolina, Virginia, and Wyoming—offer strict liability. 1 CCH Prod. Liability Rep. § 4016. Rules roughly equivalent to American strict liability are effective in France, Belgium, and Luxembourg. West Germany and Japan have a strict liability statute for pharmaceuticals. However, strict liability remains primarily an American innovation. Second, the tort plaintiff may choose, at least potentially, from among 50 jurisdictions if he decides to file suit in the United States. Each of these jurisdictions applies its own set of malleable choice-of-law rules. Third, jury trials are almost always available in the United States, while they are never provided in civil law jurisdictions. G. Gloss, Comparative Law 12 (1979); J. Merryman, The Civil Law Tradition 121 (1969). Even in the United Kingdom, most civil actions are not tried before a jury. 1 G. Keeton, The United Kingdom: The Development of its Laws and Constitutions 309 (1955). Fourth, unlike most foreign jurisdictions, American courts allow contingent attorney's fees, and do not tax losing parties with their opponents' attorney's fees. R. Schlesinger, Comparative Law: Cases, Text, Materials 275-277 (3d ed. 1970). Fifth, discovery is more extensive in American than in foreign courts. R. Schlesinger, supra, at 307, 310, and n. 33.

19. In holding that the possibility of a change in law unfavorable to the plaintiff should not be given substantial weight, we also necessarily hold that the possibility of a change in law favorable to defendant should not be considered. Respondent suggests that Piper and Hartzell filed the motion to dismiss, not simply because trial in the United States would be inconvenient, but also because they believe the laws of Scotland are more favorable. She argues that this should be taken into account in the analysis of the private interests. We

The Court of Appeals based its decision, at least in part, on an analogy between dismissals on grounds of *forum non conveniens* and transfers between federal courts pursuant to § 1404(a). In Van Dusen v. Barrack, 376 U.S. 612 (1964), this Court ruled that a § 1404(a) transfer should not result in a change in the applicable law. Quoting dictum in an earlier Third Circuit opinion interpreting *Van Dusen,* the court below stated that "this principle is no less applicable to a dismissal on *forum non conveniens* grounds." However, § 1404(a) transfers are different than dismissals on the ground of *forum non conveniens.*

Congress enacted § 1404(a) to permit change of venue between federal courts. Although the statute was drafted in accordance with the doctrine of *forum non conveniens,* it was intended to be a revision rather than a codification of the common law. District courts were given more discretion to transfer under § 1404(a) than they had to dismiss on grounds of *forum non conveniens.*

The reasoning employed in Van Dusen v. Barrack is simply inapplicable to dismissals on grounds of *forum non conveniens.* That case did not discuss the common-law doctrine. Rather, it focused on "the construction and application" of § 1404(a). Emphasizing the remedial purpose of the statute, *Barrack* concluded that Congress could not have intended a transfer to be accompanied by a change in law. The statute was designed as a "federal housekeeping measure," allowing easy change of venue within a unified federal system. The Court feared that if a change in venue were accompanied by a change in law, forum-shopping parties would take unfair advantage of the relaxed standards for transfer. The rule was necessary to ensure the just and efficient operation of the statute.

We do not hold that the possibility of an unfavorable change in law should *never* be a relevant consideration in a *forum non conveniens* inquiry. Of course, if the remedy provided by the alternative forum is so clearly inadequate or unsatisfactory that it is no remedy at all, the unfavorable change in law may be given substantial weight; the district court may conclude that dismissal would not be in the interests of justice. In this case, however, the remedies that would be provided by the Scottish courts do not fall within this category. Although the relatives of the decedents may not be able to rely on a strict liability theory, and although their potential damage award may be smaller, there is no danger that they will be deprived of any remedy or treated unfairly. . . .

The *forum non conveniens* determination is committed to the sound discretion of the trial court. It may be reversed only when there has been a clear abuse of discretion; where the court has considered all relevant public and private interest factors, and where its balancing of these factors is reasonable, its decision deserves substantial deference. . . .

---

recognize, of course, that Piper and Hartzell may be engaged in reverse forum-shopping. However, this possibility ordinarily should not enter into a trial court's analysis of the private interests. If the defendant is able to overcome the presumption in favor of plaintiff by showing that trial in the chosen forum would be unnecessarily burdensome, dismissal is appropriate—regardless of the fact that defendant may also be motivated by a desire to obtain a more favorable forum.

In analyzing the private interest factors, the District Court stated that the connections with Scotland are "overwhelming." This characterization may be somewhat exaggerated. Particularly with respect to the question of relative ease of access to sources of proof, the private interests point in both directions. As respondent emphasizes, records concerning the design, manufacture, and testing of the propeller and plane are located in the United States. She would have greater access to sources of proof relevant to her strict liability and negligence theories if trial were held here.[25] However, the District Court did not act unreasonably in concluding that fewer evidentiary problems would be posed if the trial were held in Scotland. A large proportion of the relevant evidence is located in Great Britain.

The Court of Appeals found that the problems of proof could not be given any weight because Piper and Hartzell failed to describe with specificity the evidence they would not be able to obtain if trial were held in the United States. It suggested that defendants seeking *forum non conveniens* dismissal must submit affidavits identifying the witnesses they would call and the testimony these witnesses would provide if the trial were held in the alternative forum. Such detail is not necessary. Piper and Hartzell have moved for dismissal precisely because many crucial witnesses are located beyond the reach of compulsory process, and thus are difficult to identify or interview. Requiring extensive investigation would defeat the purpose of their motion. . .

. . . As we stated in *Gilbert*, there is "a local interest in having localized controversies decided at home." [Gulf Oil Co. v. Gilbert, 330 U.S. 501, 509 (1947).] Respondent argues that American citizens have an interest in ensuring that American manufacturers are deterred from producing defective products, and that additional deterrence might be obtained if Piper and Hartzell were tried in the United States, where they could be sued on the basis of both negligence and strict liability. However, the incremental deterrence that would be gained if this trial were held in an American court is likely to be insignificant. The American interest in this accident is simply not sufficient to justify the enormous commitment of judicial time and resources that would inevitably be required if the case were to be tried here.

[JUSTICE WHITE, concurring in part and dissenting in part, wrote a separate opinion. JUSTICE STEVENS, joined by JUSTICE BRENNAN, wrote in dissent.]

Note: Placing Conditions on Dismissal

The defendants in *Piper* agreed that if the case were dismissed for forum non conveniens they would submit to the jurisdiction of the Scottish

25. In the future, where similar problems are presented, district courts might dismiss subject to the condition that defendant corporations agree to provide the records relevant to the plaintiff's claims.

courts and would waive any statute of limitations defense that might be available. Conditioning a forum non conveniens dismissal on steps to recompense in some measure the plaintiff's loss of her chosen forum is not unusual. The same judicial tactic for making the litigation more fair is used under § 1404.

The Supreme Court found in *Piper* that the defendants had described with sufficient detail the problems of proof that would confront them in Pennsylvania. In contrast, under § 1404 some courts have required detailed affidavits about the proof to be presented. See, e.g., Marbury-Patillo Construction Co., Inc. v. Bayside Warehouse Co., 490 F.2d 155 (5th Cir. 1974). In McDonnell Douglas Corp. v. Polin, 429 F.2d 30 (3d Cir. 1970), the court ordered the trial judge, Judge Higginbotham, to limit discovery and rule on a transfer motion under § 1404 without further factual inquiry into the merits. This presented what the judge described as a difficult paradox:

> How can I ascertain whether the many purported "key" witnesses are really the *actual* "key" witnesses for the defense unless I accept either defendants' assertion that ninety "key" witnesses will be needed and called at trial . . . or plaintiff's assertion that the defendant has not sufficiently delineated the issues on which each witness will testify so as to enable me to ascertain whether or not any of the ninety witnesses is in reality a "key" witness[?] . . . Until there is some probe of the merits and of the defenses, how can I determine with reasonable precision whether merely hundreds or many thousands of documents will be required? How can I ascertain whether merely a few man hours or many thousands of man hours of testimony by key personnel would be required at trial?

Polin v. Conductron Corp., 340 F. Supp. 602, 607 (E.D. Pa. 1972). Cf. Sinochem Intern. Co. Ltd. v. Malaysia Intern. Shipping Corp., 549 U.S. 422 (2007) (district court is not obliged to first establish its own jurisdiction before dismissing on grounds of forum non conveniens).

Note: The Degree of Deference to Plaintiff's Choice

Piper correctly states the rule that "a plaintiff's choice of forum should rarely be disturbed." Supra at 871. Should the degree of deference depend on whether there is evidence to suggest that plaintiff engaged in forum shopping? The Second Circuit has held that "circumstances may alter the degree of deference given the plaintiff's forum choice." Pollux Holding Ltd. v. The Chase Manhattan Bank, 329 F.3d 64, 71 (2d Cir. 2003). "Great deference" is accorded a plaintiff suing in her home forum "because it is presumed to be convenient." Id. However, less deference is accorded a foreign plaintiff suing in a United States forum because "it is more likely that forum-shopping for a higher damage award or for some other litigation advantage was the motivation for plaintiff's selection." Id. Do you agree?

In *Pollux*, Greek nationals used Liberian corporations as personal investment vehicles. When investments managed by Chase through its London office collapsed, plaintiffs filed suit in the Southern District of New York, defendant's home forum. The district court granted defendant's motion to dismiss on forum non conveniens grounds and the Second Circuit affirmed, reasoning that England provided an adequate alternate forum:

> Bearing in mind that litigants rarely are concerned with promoting their adversary's convenience at their own expense, a plaintiff's choice of the defendant's home forum over other fora where defendant is amenable to suit and to which the plaintiff and the circumstances or the case are much more closely connected suggests the possibility that plaintiff's choice was made for reasons of trial strategy.

Id. at 74. See also Gross v. British Broad. Corp., 386 F.3d 224 (2d Cir. 2004) (discussing relevance of public and private interests as factors in forum non conveniens analysis); Carey v. Bayerische Hypo-Und Vereinsbank AG, 370 F.3d 234 (2d Cir. 2004) (observing that individual's choice of forum may receive more deference than choice of a large business because hardship on individual forced to litigate abroad is greater).

Note: Venue Transfers for Reasons Other than Inconvenience

Goldlawr, Inc. v. Heiman, 369 U.S. 463 (1962) was an antitrust suit filed originally in the Eastern District of Pennsylvania. Several defendants moved to dismiss for improper venue and for lack of personal jurisdiction. The court, passing only on the venue contention, agreed that venue did not lie. But since the statute of limitations had run, the court did not dismiss the case, but instead transferred it to the Southern District of New York under § 1406. The transferee court then dismissed because the Pennsylvania court had lacked personal jurisdiction.

The Supreme Court reversed, holding that the transfer enabled the plaintiff to cure defects in jurisdiction as well as venue. In dealing with the fact that one effect of transfers under § 1406 is to save claims from statutes of limitations and that it is arguably unfair to effect this saving by filing in a jurisdiction that has no power over the defendant, the Court wrote:

> The language of § 1406(a) is amply broad enough to authorize the transfer of cases, however wrong the plaintiff may have been in filing his case as to venue, whether the court in which it was filed had personal jurisdiction over the defendants or not. This section is thus in accord with the general purpose which has prompted many of the procedural changes of the past few years — that of removing whatever obstacles may impede an expeditious and orderly adjudication of cases and controversies on their merits. When a lawsuit is filed, that filing shows a desire on the part of the plaintiff to begin his case and thereby toll whatever statute of limitations would otherwise apply. The filing itself shows the proper diligence on the part of the plaintiff which such statutes of limitations were intended to insure.

369 U.S. at 466-467. In dissent, Justices Harlan and Stewart wrote:

> The notion that a District Court may deal with an in personam action in such a way as possibly to affect a defendant's substantive rights without first acquiring jurisdiction over him is not a familiar one in federal jurisprudence.

369 U.S. at 467-468.

Review Problem: Choosing Systems in a More Complex World

Return to our Baites v. Froid hypothetical in Chapter 1, Section C(6), and recall the review problem based on it. Now test your skills by answering the following further questions.

A patient of a San Francisco-based psychiatrist injures his father, an Arizona resident, in Arizona. The father wishes to sue the California psychiatrist on the theory that she had a duty to warn the Arizonan of her patient's foreseeable violent acts toward his father. All therapy took place in California. The psychiatrist knew that her patient was going to visit his father in Arizona and increased his medication to ease the inevitable stress of family encounters.

1. Assuming that a federal court would have jurisdiction to hear the dispute, where within the federal system would venue be proper?
2. What law would govern Dr. Froid's liability—federal or state?
3. If the action is filed in federal court, what law will govern whether the plaintiff has the right to a trial by jury—federal or state? Statute of limitations? Burden of proof? Time within which defendant must answer the complaint?
4. Assuming that the action might be filed in either state or federal court, which one would you choose? Why?
5. If you chose to file the action in a state court in California, could Dr. Froid remove the action to federal court? Assume instead that you chose a state court in Arizona. Now can Dr. Froid remove the action to a federal court in Arizona?
6. If you file the action in a federal court in Arizona, could Dr. Froid move to transfer the action to a federal court in California? Would the court be inclined to grant the motion?

B. EXTENDING THE LAWSUIT: MORE ON JOINDER

1. Joinder of Multiple Parties

In the next few pages, we will deal briefly with standing and capacity to sue, issues that assume greater significance as the lawsuit expands. This is not in any sense a full treatment of these complex topics, which are often a matter of substantive law. Rather, this will serve as background to our study of joinder of parties and the many rules that determine when others may, or must, be added to a lawsuit.

Problem Case: A Woman Partner (Once Again)

Recall that Attorney Rosalind Shayes has sued her former partners in an action alleging sex discrimination under Title VII and (after timely amendment of the complaint) libel. The firm partners then counterclaimed for libel, alleging that Shayes had made fairly nasty comments about them that they claim are untrue and that caused damage to their professional reputations.

The counterclaim also alleges that Shayes's significant other, Graham Howard (who is also a prominent attorney), repeated Shayes's defamatory remarks to members of his firm. *Must* Howard be added as a party to the lawsuit? *Can* he be added, provided the partners seek some relief against him?

Assume further that the law firm has an insurance policy that arguably requires the insurance company to indemnify the partners for any recovery that Shayes wins against them. The insurance company, however, denies that the policy extends to the acts of discrimination alleged by Rosalind Shayes. May the partners join the insurance company in the lawsuit and litigate its potential liability on the policy?

Assume instead that Shayes questions several other women lawyers in the firm—past and present—and concludes that many of them also have been discriminated against in terms of promotion and pay. This prompts her to interview the female secretaries and legal assistants. She determines that many of them have been sexually harassed by male lawyers. Shayes now believes that the firm has a pattern or practice of discriminating against its women employees.

Can she expand her lawsuit into a class action suit against the firm, naming herself as the class representative for the 50 to 60 women she thinks were or are subject to unlawful discrimination? If not, could some of these women intervene in Shayes's lawsuit? Could they otherwise become involved in the litigation as parties?

Who can sue or be sued involves interesting questions about legal identity, responsibility, and injury. All litigation, of course, begins with a perceived injury. As modern society has become increasingly interdependent and interconnected, these perceived injuries often have a collective nature. Mass production of goods, for instance, may lead to multiple victims. It also often means that a product is made by a chain of entities—the parts manufacturer, the assembly plant, the packager, the distributor, and the retailer—such that there are many possible defendants when a product is defective.

Determining the proper parties to a lawsuit is even more complex when the immediate entities involved in a dispute are not human beings. Assume, for example, that a client has been severely injured by a dish that melted in her hand. Who, exactly, made the product? Which party (or parties) at the manufacturer was responsible for any alleged defect? As you have seen, an incorrect decision about who to sue cannot always be fixed by amendment, especially after the statute of limitations has elapsed. Is a corporate parent responsible (and thus suable) for the negligence of a subsidiary? Should corporate officers and directors be named as defendants? Who is the proper defendant when the negligent party is "the state"? The state official who committed the negligence, the state itself, or both?

Likewise, determining whether a person or entity has capacity or standing to sue (or be sued) can become complicated. For example, if a public school teacher is negligent in supervising students on a field trip, should she be sued in her individual or official capacity? Does it matter to the outcome?

What about a party who wants to sue anonymously? Should this ever be permissible? If it is a juvenile suing an adult for damages due to sexual abuse?

a. Real Party in Interest

To satisfy the requirement under Rule 17(a) that "[a]n action must be prosecuted in the name of the real party in interest," the party must be one who, under the applicable substantive law, possesses the right sought to be enforced. See generally Jack H. Friedenthal, Mary Kay Kane, and Arthur R. Miller, Civil Procedure 327-337 (3d ed. 1999). Simply because one stands to gain from the litigation, however, does not necessarily mean that he is the real party in interest under the procedural code. Rather, "[t]he court first must ascertain the nature of the substantive right being asserted and then must determine whether the party asserting that right is recognized as the real party in interest under the forum's procedural code." Id. at 320. There is some debate about the need for the real party in interest rule, in that some observers argue that the rules of substantive liability alone should determine who is the real party in interest. In some jurisdictions, parallel real party in interest procedural rules have been abolished.

b. Capacity to Sue or Be Sued

A party must also have capacity to sue or be sued, which refers to an individual's ability to represent her interests in a lawsuit without the assistance of another. Rule 17(b) provides that in federal court actions, capacity "... determined by the law of the individual's domicile." Where the party in question is a corporation, capacity "is determined . . . by the law under which [the corporation] was incorporated." See Friedenthal, Kane, and Miller, supra, at 332-334.

c. Constitutional Limitations — Standing

In your constitutional law studies you will take up the issue of *standing*, which determines whether a party seeking to invoke federal court jurisdiction can satisfy the "case or controversy" requirement of Article III of the Constitution. Simply put, the party must demonstrate three things to have standing: 1) "injury in fact" — an invasion of a legally protected interest that is concrete, particularized, actual, and imminent, not conjectural or hypothetical; 2) a causal relationship between the injury and the challenged conduct, which means that the injury can fairly be traceable to the challenged action of the defendant and is not the result of the independent action of a third party not before the court; and 3) a likelihood that the injury will be redressed by a favorable decision, such that the prospect of relief is not too speculative. See Lujan v. Defenders of Wildlife, 504 U.S. 555 (1992); Allen v. Wright, 468 U.S. 737 (1984); Valley Forge Christian Coll. v. Ams. United for Separation of Church and State, Inc., 454 U.S. 464 (1982); Warth v. Seldin, 422 U.S. 490 (1975).

d. Fictitious Names

Sometimes, a plaintiff may not know the names of the proper defendants, through no fault of his own. Some states allow the plaintiff to file an action against "John Doe" or "XYZ Corporation" defendants, in which he describes but does not name the parties. Once the plaintiff learns the names of the real defendants, he is allowed to amend the pleading. The principal benefit of such statutes is that the statute of limitations typically is deemed to be tolled by the filing of the original complaint, and the amendment relates back to this date.

e. Anonymous Parties

On rare occasions the court may allow a plaintiff to proceed anonymously. These cases involve matters of special sensitivity, described by one court as "personal information of the utmost intimacy." See Southern Methodist Univ. Assoc. v. Wynne & Jaffe, 599 F.2d 707 (5th Cir. 1979). See also Doe v. Blue Cross & Blue Shield of R.I., 794 F. Supp. 72 (D.R.I. 1992) (approving transsexual's use of pseudonym in complaint against insurer). What policy reasons militate against allowing plaintiff anonymity? See generally Joan Steinman, Public Trial, Pseudonymous Parties: When Should Litigants Be Permitted to Keep Their Identities Confidential?, 37 Hastings L.J. 1 (1985).

2. The Rules of Party Joinder

a. Permissive Joinder (Rule 20)

Mosley v. General Motors Corp.
497 F.2d 1330 (8th Cir. 1974)

ROSS, Circuit Judge.

Nathaniel Mosley and nine other persons joined in bringing this action individually and as class representatives alleging that their rights guaranteed under 42 U.S.C. § 2000e et seq. and 42 U.S.C. § 1981 were denied by General Motors and Local 25, United Automobile, Aerospace and Agriculture Implement Workers of America [Union] by reason of their color and race. Each of the ten named plaintiffs had, prior to the filing of the complaint, filed a charge with the Equal Employment Opportunity Commission [EEOC] asserting the facts underlying these claims. Pursuant thereto, the EEOC made a reasonable cause finding that General Motors, Fisher Body Division and Chevrolet Division, and the Union had engaged in unlawful employment practices in violation of Title VII of the Civil Rights Act of 1964. Accordingly, the charging parties were notified by EEOC of their right to institute a civil action in the appropriate federal district court, pursuant to § 706(e) of Title VII, 42 U.S.C. § 2000e-5(e).

In each of the first eight counts of the twelve-count complaint, eight of the ten plaintiffs alleged that General Motors, Chevrolet Division, had engaged in unlawful employment practices by: "discriminating against Negroes as regards promotions, terms and conditions of employment"; "retaliating against Negro employees who protested actions made unlawful by Title VII of the Act and by discharging some because they protested said unlawful acts"; "failing to hire Negro employees as a class on the basis of race"; "failing to hire females as a class on the basis of sex"; "discharging Negro employees on the basis of race"; and "discriminating against Negroes and females in the granting of relief time." Each additionally charged that the defendant Union had engaged in unlawful employment practices "with respect to the granting of relief time to Negro and female employees" and "by failing to pursue 6a grievances." The remaining two plaintiffs made similar allegations against General Motors, Fisher Body Division. All of the individual plaintiffs requested injunctive relief, back pay, attorney's fees, and costs. Counts XI and XII of the complaint were class action counts against the two individual divisions of General Motors. They also sought declaratory and injunctive relief, back pay, attorney's fees and costs.

General Motors moved to strike portions of each count of the twelve-count complaint, to dismiss Counts XI and XII, to make portions of Counts I through XII more definite, to determine the propriety of Counts XI and XII as class actions, to limit the scope of the class purportedly represented, and to determine under which section of Rule 23 Counts XI and XII were maintainable as class actions. The district court ordered that "insofar as the first ten counts are concerned, those ten counts shall be severed into ten separate causes of action," and each plaintiff was directed to bring a separate action based upon his complaint, duly and separately filed. The court also ordered that the class action would not be dismissed, but rather would be left open "to each of the plaintiffs herein, individually or collectively . . . to allege a separate cause of action on behalf of any class of persons which such plaintiff or plaintiffs may separately or individually represent."

In reaching this conclusion on joinder, the district court followed the reasoning of Smith v. North American Rockwell Corp., 50 F.R.D. 515 (N.D. Okla. 1970), which, in a somewhat analogous situation, found there was no right to relief arising out of the same transaction, occurrence or series of transactions or occurrences, and that there was no question of law or fact common to all plaintiffs sufficient to sustain joinder under Federal Rule of Civil Procedure 20(a). Similarly, the district court here felt that the plaintiffs' joint actions against General Motors and the Union presented a variety of issues having little relationship to one another; that they had only one common problem, i.e., the defendant; and that as pleaded the joint actions were completely unmanageable. Upon entering the order, and upon application of the plaintiffs, the district court found that its decision involved a controlling question of law as to which there is a substantial ground for difference of opinion and that any of the parties might make application for appeal under 28 U.S.C. § 1292(b). We granted the application to permit this interlocutory appeal and for the following reasons we affirm in part and reverse in part.

Rule 20(a) of the Federal Rules of Civil Procedure provides:

> All persons may join in one action as plaintiffs if they assert any right to relief jointly, severally, or in the alternative in respect of or arising out of the same transaction, occurrence, or series of transactions or occurrences and if any questions of law or fact common to all these persons will arise in the action. . . .

Additionally, Rule 20(b) and Rule 42(b) vest in the district court the discretion to order separate trials or make such other orders as will prevent delay or prejudice. In this manner, the scope of the civil action is made a matter for the discretion of the district court, and a determination on the question of joinder of parties will be reversed on appeal only upon a showing of abuse of that discretion. Chicago, R.I. & P.R.R. v. Williams, 245 F.2d 397, 404 (8th Cir.), *cert. denied,* 355 U.S. 855 (1957). To determine whether the district court's order was proper herein, we must look to the policy and law that have developed around the operation of Rule 20.

The purpose of the rule is to promote trial convenience and expedite the final determination of disputes, thereby preventing multiple lawsuits. 7 C. Wright, Federal Practice and Procedure § 1652 at 265 (1972). Single trials generally tend to lessen the delay, expense and inconvenience to all concerned. Reflecting this policy, the Supreme Court has said:

> Under the Rules, the impulse is toward entertaining the broadest possible scope of action consistent with fairness to the parties; joinder of claims, parties and remedies is strongly encouraged.

United Mine Workers of America v. Gibbs, 383 U.S. 715, 724 (1966).

Permissive joinder is not, however, applicable in all cases. The rule imposes two specific requisites to the joinder of parties: (1) a right to relief must be asserted by, or against, each plaintiff or defendant relating to or arising out of the same *transaction or occurrence, or series of transactions or occurrences;* and (2) some *question of law or fact common* to all the parties must arise in the action.

In ascertaining whether a particular factual situation constitutes a single transaction or occurrence for purposes of Rule 20, a case by case approach is generally pursued. 7 C. Wright, Federal Practice and Procedure § 1653 at 270 (1972). No hard and fast rules have been established under the rule. However, construction of the terms "transaction or occurrence" as used in the context of Rule 13(a) counterclaims offers some guide to the application of this test. For the purposes of the latter rule,

> "Transaction" is a word of flexible meaning. It may comprehend a series of many occurrences, depending not so much upon the immediateness of their connection as upon their logical relationship.

Moore v. New York Cotton Exchange, 270 U.S. 593, 610 (1926). Accordingly, all "logically related" events entitling a person to institute a legal action against another generally are regarded as comprising a transaction or occurrence. 7 C. Wright, Federal Practice and Procedure § 1653 at 270 (1972). The analogous interpretation of the terms as used in Rule 20 would permit all reasonably related claims for relief by or against different parties to be tried in a single proceeding. Absolute identity of all events is unnecessary.

This construction accords with the result reached in United States v. Mississippi, 380 U.S. 128 (1965), a suit brought by the United States against the State of Mississippi, the election commissioners, and six voting registrars of the State, charging them with engaging in acts and practices hampering and destroying the right of black citizens of Mississippi to vote. The district court concluded that the complaint improperly attempted to hold the six country registrars jointly liable for what amounted to nothing more than individual torts committed by them separately against separate applicants. In reversing, the Supreme Court said:

> But the complaint charged that the registrars had acted and were continuing to act as part of a state-wide system designed to enforce the registration laws in a way that would inevitably deprive colored people of the right to vote solely because of their color. On such an allegation the joinder of all the registrars as defendants in a single suit is authorized by Rule 20(a) of the Federal Rules of Civil Procedure. . . . These registrars were alleged to be carrying on activities which were part of a series of transactions or occurrences the validity of which depended to a large extent upon "questions[s] of law or fact common to all of them."

Id. at 142-143.

Here too, then, the plaintiffs have asserted a right to relief arising out of the same transactions or occurrences. Each of the ten plaintiffs alleged that he had been injured by the same general policy of discrimination on the part of General Motors and the Union. Since a "state-wide system designed to enforce the registration laws in a way that would inevitably deprive colored people of the right to vote" was determined to arise out of the same series of transactions or occurrences, we conclude that a company-wide policy purportedly designed to discriminate against blacks in employment similarly arises out of the same series of transactions or occurrences. Thus the plaintiffs meet the first requisite for joinder under Rule 20(a).

The second requisite necessary to sustain a permissive joinder under the rule is that a question of law or fact common to all the parties will arise in the action. The rule does not require that *all* questions of law and fact raised by the dispute be common. Yet, neither does it establish any qualitative or quantitative test of commonality. For this reason, cases construing the parallel requirement under Federal Rule of Civil Procedure 23(a) provide a helpful framework for construction of the commonality required by Rule 20. In general, those cases that have focused on Rule 23(a)(2) have given it a permissive application so that common questions have been found to exist in a wide range of contexts. 7 C. Wright, Federal Practice and Procedure § 1763 at 604 (1972). Specifically, with respect to employment discrimination cases under Title VII, courts have found that the discriminatory character of a defendant's conduct is basic to the class, and the fact that the individual class members may have suffered different effects from the alleged discrimination is immaterial for the purposes of the prerequisite.

In this vein, one court has said:

> [A]though the actual effects of a discriminatory policy may thus vary throughout the class, the existence of the discriminatory policy threatens the entire class. And whether the Damoclean threat of a racially discriminatory policy hangs over the racial class is a question of fact common to all the members of the class.

Hall v. Werthan Bag Corp., 251 F. Supp. 184, 186 (M.D. Tenn. 1966).

The right to relief here depends on the ability to demonstrate that each of the plaintiffs was wronged by racially discriminatory policies on the part of the defendants General Motors and the Union. The discriminatory character of the defendants' conduct is thus basic to each plaintiff's recovery. The fact that each plaintiff may have suffered different effects from the alleged discrimination is immaterial for the purposes of determining the common question of law or fact. Thus, we conclude that the second requisite for joinder under Rule 20(a) is also met by the complaint.

For the reasons set forth above, we conclude that the district court abused its discretion in severing the joined actions. The difficulties in ultimately adjudicating damages to the various plaintiffs are not so overwhelming as to require such severance. If appropriate, separate trials may be granted as to any particular issue after the determination of common questions.

The judgment of the district court disallowing joinder of the plaintiff's individual actions is reversed and remanded with directions to permit the plaintiffs to proceed jointly. That portion of the district court's judgment that withholds determination of the propriety of the purported class until further discovery is affirmed. We consider the application of the appellants for attorney's fees on this appeal to be premature, and they will be denied without prejudice to their right to reassert that claim upon final disposition of the case.

Note: Fraudulent Joinder

Mosley arose under federal law. Joinder can serve additional purposes in suits based on diversity of citizenship. Consider whether a plaintiff should be permitted to join in-state defendants to defeat a motion to remove a case from state to federal court where removal is predicated on diversity jurisdiction. Generally in-state defendants can be joined (and the case will be remanded) as long as there is a reasonable possibility that state law will impose liability on the facts of the case. Absent such a showing, joinder is fraudulent and will not defeat removal to federal court. See Travis v. Irby, 326 F.3d 644, 647 (5th Cir. 2003); cf. Sweeney v. Sherwin Williams Co., 304 F. Supp. 2d 868 (S.D. Miss. 2004). See supra at 944, Note 4.

b. Compulsory Joinder (Rule 19)

Temple v. Synthes Corp.
498 U.S. 5 (1990)

PER CURIAM.

Petitioner Temple, a Mississippi resident, underwent surgery in October 1986 in which a "plate and screw device" was implanted in his lower spine. The device was manufactured by respondent Synthes, Ltd. (U.S.A.) (Synthes), a Pennsylvania corporation. Dr. S. Henry LaRocca performed the surgery at St. Charles General Hospital in New Orleans, Louisiana. Following surgery, the device's screws broke off inside Temple's back.

Temple filed suit against Synthes in the United States District Court for the Eastern District of Louisiana. The suit, which rested on diversity jurisdiction, alleged defective design and manufacture of the device. At the same time, Temple filed a state administrative proceeding against Dr. LaRocca and the hospital for malpractice and negligence. At the conclusion of the administrative proceeding, Temple filed suit against the doctor and the hospital in Louisiana state court.

Synthes did not attempt to bring the doctor and the hospital into the federal action by means of a third-party complaint, as provided in Federal Rule of Civil Procedure 14(a). Instead, Synthes filed a motion to dismiss Temple's federal suit for failure to join necessary parties pursuant to Federal Rule of Civil Procedure 19. Following a hearing, the District Court ordered Temple to join the doctor and the hospital as defendants within 20 days or risk dismissal of the lawsuit. According to the court, the most significant reason for requiring joinder was the interest of judicial economy. The court relied on this Court's decision in Provident Tradesmen's Bank & Trust Co. v. Patterson, 390 U.S. 102 (1968), wherein we recognized that one focus of Rule 19 is "the interest of the courts and the public in complete, consistent, and efficient settlement of controversies." Id. at 111. When Temple failed to join the doctor and the hospital, the court dismissed the suit with prejudice.

Temple appealed, and the United States Court of Appeals for the Fifth Circuit affirmed. 898 F.2d 152 (1990). The court deemed it "obviously prejudicial to the defendants to have the separate litigations being carried on," because Synthes' defense might be that the plate was not defective but that the doctor and the hospital were negligent, while the doctor and the hospital, on the other hand, might claim that they were not negligent but that the plate was defective. The Court of Appeals found that the claims overlapped and that the District Court therefore had not abused its discretion in ordering joinder under Rule 19. A petition for rehearing was denied.

In his petition for certiorari to this Court, Temple contends that it was error to label joint tortfeasors as indispensable parties under Rule 19(b) and to dismiss the lawsuit with prejudice for failure to join those parties. We agree. Synthes does not deny that it, the doctor, and the hospital are potential joint tortfeasors. It has long been the rule that it is not necessary for all joint tortfeasors to be named as defendants in a single lawsuit. See Lawlor v. National Screen Service Corp., 349 U.S. 322, 329-330 (1955); Bigelow v. Old Dominion Copper Mining & Smelting Co., 225 U.S. 111, 132 (1912). See also Nottingham v. General American Communications Corp., 811 F.2d 873, 880 (5th Cir.) (*per curiam*), *cert. denied*, 484 U.S. 854 (1987). Nothing in the 1966 revision of Rule 19 changed that principle. See Provident Bank, supra, at 116-117, n.12. The Advisory Committee Notes to Rule 19(a) explicitly state that "a tortfeasor with the usual 'joint-and-several' liability is merely a permissive party to an action against another with like liability." 28 U.S.C. App., p.595. There is nothing in Louisiana tort law to the contrary. See Mullin v. Skains, 252 La. 1009, 1014; La. Civ. Code Ann., Arts. 1794, 1795 (West 1987).

The opinion in *Provident Bank*, supra, does speak of the public interest in limiting multiple litigation, but that case is not controlling here. There, the estate of a tort victim brought a declaratory judgment action against an insurance company. We assumed that the policyholder was a person "who, under § (a), should be 'joined if feasible,'" 390 U.S. at 108, and went on to discuss the appropriate analysis under Rule 19(b), because the policyholder could not be joined without destroying diversity. Id., at 109-116. After examining the factors set forth in Rule 19(b), we determined that the action could proceed without the policyholder; he therefore was not an indispensable party whose absence required dismissal of the suit. Id. at 116, 119.

Here, no inquiry under Rule 19(b) is necessary, because the threshold requirements of Rule 19(a) have not been satisfied. As potential joint tortfeasors with Synthes, Dr. LaRocca and the hospital were merely permissive parties. The Court of Appeals erred by failing to hold that the District Court abused its discretion in ordering them joined as defendants and in dismissing the action when Temple failed to comply with the court's order. For these reasons, we grant the petition for certiorari, reverse the judgment of the Court of Appeals for the Fifth Circuit, and remand for further proceedings consistent with this opinion.

It is so ordered.

Helzberg's Diamond Shops, Inc. v. Valley West Des Moines Shopping Center, Inc.

564 F.2d 816 (8th Cir. 1977)

ALSOP, District Judge.

On February 3, 1975, Helzberg's Diamond Shops, Inc. (Helzberg), a Missouri corporation, and Valley West Des Moines Shopping Center, Inc. (Valley West), an Iowa corporation, executed a written Lease Agreement. The Lease Agreement granted Helzberg the right to operate a full line jewelry store at space 254 in the Valley West Mall in West Des Moines, Iowa. Section 6 of Article V of the Lease Agreement provides:

> [Valley West] agrees it will not lease premises in the shopping center for use as a catalog jewelry store nor lease premises for more than two full line jewelry stores in the shopping center in addition to the leased premises. The clause shall not prohibit other stores such as department stores from selling jewelry from catalogs or in any way restrict the shopping center department stores.

Subsequently, Helzberg commenced operation of a full line jewelry store in the Valley West Mall.

Between February 3, 1975 and November 2, 1976, Valley West and two other corporations entered into leases for spaces in the Valley West Mall for use as full line jewelry stores. Pursuant to those leases the two corporations also initiated actual operation of full line jewelry stores.

On November 2, 1976, Valley West and Kirk's Incorporated, Jewelers, an Iowa corporation, doing business as Lord's Jewelers (Lord's), entered into a written Lease Agreement. The Lease Agreement granted Lord's the right to occupy space 261 in the Valley West Mall. Section 1 of Article V of the Lease Agreement provides that Lord's will use space 261

> only as a retail specialty jewelry store (and not as a catalogue or full line jewelry store) featuring watches, jewelry (and the repair of same) and incidental better gift items.

However, Lord's intended to open and operate what constituted a full line jewelry store at space 261. . . . Valley West's motion to dismiss enters into and becomes a part of the District Court's order granting preliminary injunctive relief and because the granting of preliminary injunctive relief is itself appealable, we can and will review the order denying Valley West's motion to dismiss. See United States v. Fort Sill Apache Tribe, 507 F.2d 861 (Ct. Cl. 1974).

Rule 19, Fed. R. Civ. P. provides in pertinent part:

> (a) A person who is subject to service of process and whose joinder will not deprive the court of jurisdiction over the subject matter of the action shall be joined as a party in the action if (1) in his absence complete relief cannot be accorded among those already parties, or (2) he claims an interest relating to the subject of the action and is so situated that the disposition of the action in his absence may (i) as a practical matter impair or impede his ability to protect that interest or (ii) leave any of the persons already parties subject to a substantial risk of incurring double, multiple, or otherwise inconsistent obligations by reason of his claimed interest. . . .
>
> (b) If a person as described in subdivision (a)(1)-(2) hereof cannot be made a party, the court shall determine whether in equity and good conscience the action should proceed among the parties before it, or should be dismissed, the absent person being thus regarded as indispensable. The factors to be considered by the court include: first, to what extent a judgment rendered in the person's absence might be prejudicial to him or those already parties; second, the extent to which, by protective provisions in the judgment, by the shaping of relief, or other measures, the prejudice can be lessened or avoided; third, whether a judgment rendered in the person's absence will be adequate; fourth, whether the plaintiff will have an adequate remedy if the action is dismissed for nonjoinder.

Because Helzberg was seeking and the District Court ordered injunctive relief which may prevent Lord's from operating its jewelry store in the Valley West Mall in the manner in which Lord's originally intended, the District Court correctly concluded that Lord's was a party to be joined if feasible. *See* Rule 19(a)(2)(i), Fed. R. Civ. P. Therefore, because Lord's was not and is not subject to personal jurisdiction in the Western District of Missouri, the District Court was required to determine whether or not Lord's should be regarded as indispensable. After considering the factors which Rule 19(b) mandates be considered, the District Court concluded that Lord's was not to be regarded as indispensable. We agree.

The determination of whether or not a person is an indispensable party is one which must be made on a case-by-case basis and is dependent upon the facts and circumstances of each case. Provident Tradesmens Bank & Trust Co. v. Patterson, 390 U.S. 102 (1968); 7 C. Wright & A. Miller, Federal Practice & Procedure § 1607 (1972); 3A J. Moore, Federal Practice ¶19.07-2[0] (1976). An analysis of the facts and circumstances of the case before us leads us to conclude that Lord's was not an indispensable party and that, therefore, the District Court did not err in denying Valley West's motion to dismiss.

Rule 19(b) requires the court to look first to the extent to which a judgment rendered in Lord's absence might be prejudicial to Lord's or to Valley West. Valley West argues that the District Court's order granting preliminary injunctive relief does prejudice Lord's and may prejudice Valley West. We do not agree.

. . . Even if, as a result of the District Court's granting of the preliminary injunction, Valley West should attempt to terminate Lord's leasehold interest in space 261 in the Valley West Mall, Lord's will retain all of its rights under its Lease Agreement with Valley West. None of its rights or obligations will have been adjudicated as a result of the present proceedings, proceedings to which it is not a party. Therefore, we conclude that Lord's will not be prejudiced in a way contemplated by Rule 19(b) as a result of this action.

Likewise, we think that Lord's absence will not prejudice Valley West in a way contemplated by Rule 19(b). Valley West contends that it may be subjected to inconsistent obligations as a result of a determination in this action and a determination in another forum that Valley West should proceed in a fashion contrary to what has been ordered in these proceedings.

It is true that the obligations of Valley West to Helzberg, as determined in these proceedings, may be inconsistent with Valley West's obligations to Lord's. However, we are of the opinion that any inconsistency in those obligations will result from Valley West's voluntary execution of two Lease Agreements which impose inconsistent obligations rather than from Lord's absence from the present proceedings.

Helzberg seeks only to restrain Valley West's breach of the Lease Agreement to which Helzberg and Valley West were the sole parties. Certainly, all of the rights and obligations arising under a lease can be adjudicated where all of the parties to the lease are before the court. . . . Thus, in the context of these proceedings the District Court can determine all of the rights and obligations of both Helzberg and Valley West based upon the Lease Agreement between them, even though Lord's is not a party to the proceedings.

Valley West's contention that it may be subjected to inconsistent judgments if Lord's should choose to file suit elsewhere and be awarded judgment is speculative at best. In the first place, Lord's has not filed such a suit. Secondly, there is no showing that another court is likely to interpret the language of the two Lease Agreements differently from the way in which the District Court would. Therefore, we also conclude that

Valley West will suffer no prejudice as a result of the District Court's proceeding in Lord's absence. Any prejudice which Valley West may suffer by way of inconsistent judgments would be the result of Valley West's execution of Lease Agreements which impose inconsistent obligations and not the result of the proceedings in the District Court.

Rule 19(b) also requires the court to consider ways in which prejudice to the absent party can be lessened or avoided. The District Court afforded Lord's an opportunity to intervene in order to protect any interest it might have in the outcome of this litigation. Lord's chose not to do so. In light of Lord's decision not to intervene we conclude that the District Court acted in such a way as to sufficiently protect Lord's interests. . . .

Similarly, we also conclude that the District Court's determinations that a judgment rendered in Lord's absence would be adequate and that there is no controlling significance to the fact that Helzberg would have an adequate remedy in the Iowa courts were not erroneous. It follows that the District Court's conclusion that in equity and good conscience the action should be allowed to proceed was a correct one.

In sum, it is generally recognized that a person does not become indispensable to an action to determine rights under a contract simply because that person's rights or obligations under an entirely separate contract will be affected by the result of the action. . . . This principle applies to an action against a lessor who has entered into other leases which also may be affected by the result in the action in which the other lessees are argued to be indispensable parties. . . . We conclude that the District Court properly denied the motion to dismiss for failure to join an indispensable party. . . .

Affirmed.

Notes and Questions

1. *Joinder and Strategy.* Why did the plaintiff in *Temple* choose to sue the defendants separately? And why was plaintiff willing to take a dismissal rather than comply with the court's demand, and then determined to press the point all the way to the Supreme Court?

2. *Compulsory Joinder and the Merits.* Isn't *Helzberg* a puzzling case? The court seems to discount the potential harm to Valley West should two lawsuits with inconsistent results occur. Has the court, in effect, peeked at the merits in deciding the joinder issue, such that it has prejudged Valley West's responsibility for the competing uses of space in the mall?

3. *Compulsory Joinder and Substantive Law.* Determinations about whether a party should be joined in a lawsuit are strongly influenced by substantive law that you may not yet have mastered. Consequently, the issue may have an especially abstract feel to it. But you do know something about tort law, joint and several liability, and contract law. What does this knowledge

suggest about the result in *Temple*? In *Helzberg*? What about a class action suit brought by African-American firefighters who seek a determination that they were denied promotions on the basis of race? Are white firefighters who might be affected by any decree ordering promotion of the African-American firefighters necessary parties in the class action suit? See Martin v. Wilks, 490 U.S. 755 (1989), discussed later in this chapter.

4. *Compulsory Joinder and Complete Relief*. Can a plaintiff join a party under Rule 19 even if the relevant substantive law does not give the plaintiff a cause of action against that party? The Ninth Circuit, relying on International Brotherhood of Teamsters v. United States, 431 U.S. 324 (1977), has said yes, where complete injunctive relief would otherwise be impossible. See EEOC v. Peabody Western Coal Co., 400 F.3d 774 (9th Cir. 2005) (Rule 19 joinder of Navajo Nation appropriate where EEOC complaint for injunctive relief against mining company claims that maintaining a Navajo hiring preference at mines the company leases from the Navajo Nation discriminates against non-Navajo Native Americans; irrelevant that the EEOC cannot assert a cause of action against the Navajo Nation). But see Davenport v. Int'l Bhd. of Teamsters, AFL-CIO, 166 F.3d 356, 366 (D.C. Cir. 1999) (denying injunctive relief where flight attendant union members sued union for unfair representation and sought to join employer Northwest Airlines: "[W]hile Rule 19 provides for joinder of necessary parties, it does not create a cause of action against them. . . . It is not enough that plaintiffs 'need' an injunction against Northwest to obtain full relief. They must also have a right to such an injunction. . . ."), and Vieux Carre Prop. Owners, Residents & Assoc., Inc. v. Brown, 875 F.2d 453, 457 (5th Cir. 1989) (there must be a cause of action for or against party to be joined under Rule 19).

c. Impleader (Rule 14)

Toberman v. Copas

800 F. Supp. 1239 (M.D. Pa. 1992)

RAMBO, District Judge.

Before the court is the motion of Third Party Defendants to dismiss, or in the alternative, for a more definite statement. The motion has been briefed and is ripe for disposition.

Background

On May 6, 1992, Plaintiffs Jon and Carol Toberman filed a complaint against the captioned defendants. The complaint detailed counts of negligence and loss of consortium against each defendant, arising out of a motor vehicle accident which occurred on May 26, 1990 on the Pennsylvania Turnpike in Bedford County, Pennsylvania. Plaintiffs' complaint cited various injuries resulting from the accident, and provided some detail regarding the order of the events involved in the accident, the part played by each of the defendants, and specific conduct that was alleged to be negligent.

One of those defendants was Richard Menendez. On May 26, 1992, Menendez filed a Third Party Complaint against Timothy Swarthout and St. Johnsbury Trucking Company. It is this third party complaint that is the subject of the current motion.

Discussion

The relevant portion of the Third Party complaint, for purposes of this motion, is paragraph four, which reads:

> If the Plaintiffs are entitled to recover for damages alleged and Defendant/Third Party Plaintiff Menendez is held liable, which liability is expressly denied, then and in that event, and in the alternative, Defendant/Third Party Plaintiff Menendez believes and avers that all accidents, injuries, and/or damages involved in this action were caused by and were the direct and proximate result of the negligence of the Third Party Defendants, Timothy Swarthout and St. Johnsbury Trucking Co., in this action, and that each of the Third Party Defendants in this action is solely liable to the Plaintiffs, or in the alternative, each Third Party Defendant is jointly and severally liable and Defendant/Third Party Plaintiff Menendez is entitled to contribution and/or indemnification from the Third Party Defendants.

Third party complaint at ¶4.

Third Party Defendants' motion to dismiss relies on Federal Rule of Civil Procedure 12(b)(1) and (b)(6). Specifically, Third Party Defendants argue that the third party complaint, as worded, does not fall within the court's ancillary jurisdiction and does not comport with the pleading requirements of Federal Rule of Civil Procedure 8.

I. Is the Third Party Complaint a Proper Application of Rule 14?

Third Party Defendants argue that this court lacks jurisdiction over the third party claims that they are solely liable or jointly and severally liable to the Plaintiffs. After examining the issue, this court tends to agree, though not on exactly the same rationale presented by Third Party Defendants.

Third Party Defendants have been impleaded by defendant Menendez under Federal Rule of Civil Procedure 14. Rule 14 allows third-party complaints to be served by a defendant/third party plaintiff upon "a person not a party to the action who is or may be liable to the third-party plaintiff for all or part of the plaintiff's claim against the third-party plaintiff." Fed. R. Civ. P. 14(a).

The underlying purpose of Rule 14 is to promote economy by avoiding the situation where a defendant has been adjudicated liable and then must bring a totally new action against a third party who may be liable to him for all or part of the original plaintiff's claim against him. Charles A. Wright, Arthur Miller & Mary Kane, 6 Federal Practice and Procedure ("Wright & Miller"), § 1441 at 289-290 (1990). True Rule 14 claims fall within "ancillary" or "supplemental" jurisdiction; the latter is a judicially developed concept under which a district court exercises jurisdiction over incidental matters raised by a case over which the court otherwise properly has jurisdiction. See id. § 1444 at 316. Rule 14 neither creates any legal causes of action, nor authorizes the use of impleader practice to violate the limits of federal jurisdiction. Id. § 1442 at 293-294.

Rule 14 was amended in 1946, with the amended version becoming effective in 1948; prior to that time, a defendant could also implead persons directly liable to the plaintiff. Id. § 1441 at 287-288. The 1948 amendment removed a serious jurisdictional issue that had arisen under Rule 14: if a defendant's impleader of a third party who was liable to the plaintiff under ancillary jurisdiction were allowed, this might sanction circumvention of federal jurisdictional requirements, like diversity of citizenship, by encouraging collusion between the original plaintiff and the original defendant.[1] Id. § 1444 at 320. The 1948 amendment was designed to totally eliminate the possibility of this occurring. Id. at 321.[2]

Courts have stringently followed the rule that a third party complaint may not set forth a claim of the third party defendant's liability to the plaintiff. It must set forth a claim of *secondary* liability such that, if the third party plaintiff is found liable, the third party defendant will be liable to him/her under a theory of indemnification, contribution, or some other theory of derivative liability recognized by the relevant substantive law. Jack Friedenthal, Mary Kane and Arthur Miller, Civil Procedure ("Friedenthal, Kane & Miller"), § 6.9 at 362. Any third party complaint which does not facially meet this test is not proper under Rule 14 and thus falls outside of this court's ancillary jurisdiction. A theory that another party is the correct defendant is not appropriate for a third party complaint.

> A defendant sued for negligence, for example, cannot implead a third party whose negligence was totally responsible for plaintiff's injury. When a third party's conduct furnishes a complete defense against the defendant's liability, the defendant may raise that conduct defensively in his answer but may not use it as a foundation for impleader.

Friedenthal, Kane & Miller, § 6.9 at 363.[3] See, e.g., Barab, 98 F.R.D. [455,] 456 [E.D. Pa. 1983] (even if third party defendant's contentions would

1. Hence, before 1948, in cases like the captioned one, a defendant might have impleaded a third party who was allegedly directly liable to the plaintiff, but was not diverse in citizenship; the plaintiff could not have sued the third party in federal court, and to allow the third party's impleader would promote collusion to avoid the requirements of diversity jurisdiction.

2. See Fed. R. Civ. P. 14, Notes of Advisory Committee on Rules, 1946 Amendment.

3. The court would refer counsel to one particular text, Joseph W. Glannon's Civil Procedure, Examples & Explanations (Little, Brown, 1987). Glannon gives several

constitute total defense, they were not proper basis to implead additional party under Rule 14); Donaldson v. United States Steel Corp., 53 F.R.D. 228, 230 (W.D. Pa. 1971) (proposed third party defendant's total responsibility for plaintiff's injuries was a defense, not grounds for third-party complaint).

In the captioned action, Third Party Defendants challenge the language in the third party complaint regarding their sole and direct liability to Plaintiffs. Given the foregoing discussion, this claim of sole and direct liability to Plaintiffs does not comprise a proper third party claim under Rule 14. Again, the third party complaint can only assert a theory of derivative liability to Third Party Plaintiff (recognized by Pennsylvania law) if he is found liable.

Third Party Defendants have raised no challenge to the remainder of the paragraph quoted above, regarding indemnity or contribution. However, there is no indication that the Third Party Plaintiff's theory of recovery is any different with regard to that remaining language. There is no allegation in the third party complaint that Third Party Defendants stand in a joint tortfeasor relationship to Third Party Plaintiff, or that there is any relationship of contribution or indemnity, which would trigger secondary liability under Pennsylvania law. The complaint merely says that Third Party Defendants are liable for indemnity or contribution to Third Party Plaintiff because they are wholly responsible for Plaintiff's injuries. As stated earlier, this is not an acceptable theory for third party liability under Rule 14.

Third Party Plaintiff will be given a chance to amend his third party complaint, if possible, to comport with the requirements of Rule 14. If he does not do so, the motion to dismiss will be granted. Of course, once an amended complaint is submitted, Third Party Defendants will be free to raise any appropriate challenges permitted by the Federal Rules.

United States v. Joe Grasso & Son, Inc.

380 F.2d 749 (5th Cir. 1967)

HUTCHESON, Circuit Judge.

This is an interlocutory appeal growing out of a suit brought for the refund of federal employment taxes.

Joe Grasso & Son, Inc. owns seven shrimp boats used for commercial shrimp fishing in the Gulf of Mexico. Each of the boats is operated by a captain and usually two crewmen. The employment taxes were assessed

instructive hypothetical examples regarding Rule 14, including one concerning "Dillinger," an apprehended robber, who sues "Officer Hayes" for assault in the process of arrest. "Officer Hayes" attempts to implead "Officer Kelly," claiming misidentification, that "Officer Kelly" was the actual arresting officer. However, he cannot do so. Either one officer or the other will be solely liable to the plaintiff; a defendant cannot use impleader merely to suggest new targets for the plaintiff. See Glannon at 150-151.

against Grasso on the ground that it was the employer of these fishermen from the first quarter of 1959 through September 30, 1962. In its answer to Grasso's complaint for refund, the United States brought a third party complaint against the captains, alleging that if Grasso were able to put in issue facts proving that it was not the employer of the fishermen, then the same facts would demonstrate the liability of the captains for the taxes by showing an employer-employee relationship between the captains and the crewmen. The district court dismissed the third party complaint, made the appropriate certification for this appeal under 28 U.S.C. Sec. 1292(b), and placed the case on inactive status pending appeal. We affirm the order of the district court.

Whether the captains may be impleaded is controlled by the language of Fed. R. Civ. P. 14(a) which provides that a defendant may implead a person not a party to the action "who is or may be liable to him for all or part of the plaintiff's claim against him." Thus, in the instant case the government may implead the captains if it is found that the captains may be liable to the government for all or part of Grasso's claim against the government.

After carefully reviewing the nature and purpose of impleader under Rule 14, the district court concluded that it has been "strictly limited to situations where the very existence of potential liability in the third party defendant is dependent upon the outcome of the main claim." While the court agreed that both Grasso and the captains cannot be liable for the employment taxes, it rejected the government's contention that the captains' liability would automatically follow from proof of Grasso's non-liability since the court felt that a third finding is possible, i.e., that the crewmen are not employees of anyone. The court declared that the liability of the captains would not depend upon whether or not Grasso was an employer but only upon whether the government could establish facts bringing the captain-crew relationship within the applicable tax statutes. Of the view that the third party action therefore did not depend upon the outcome of the main claim, the court concluded that the complaint against the captains constituted a separate and independent claim. Accordingly, impleader was denied.

The main thrust of the government's attack is that the district court applied an unduly restrictive definition of the key word in Rule 14, *claim*. Arguing that *claim* refers to the "aggregate of operative facts which give rise to a right enforceable in the courts," the government insists that the operative facts constituting Grasso's claim will establish, if proved, that the captains are employers and self-employed persons who are liable to the government for all Grasso's claim, namely, the employment taxes due on the sums paid to the fishermen. For this to be so, it must be assumed that the crewmen are employed either by Grasso or by the captains.

We can agree with the general principle, as did the court below, that use of the word "claim" in Rule 14 avoids the narrow concepts of "cause of action" and employs instead the idea of the claim as a group of operative facts giving occasion for judicial action. See Dery v. Wyer, 265 F.2d 804,

807 (2d Cir. 1959). Cf. American Fid. & Cas. Co. v. Greyhound Corp., 232 F.2d 89, 92 (5th Cir. 1956). And it is true that when the defendant's right against the third party is merely an outgrowth of the same core of facts which determines the plaintiff's claim, impleader is properly used "to reduce litigation by having one lawsuit do the work of two." Falls Indus., Inc. v. Consolidated Chem. Indus., Inc., 258 F.2d 277, 283 (5th Cir. 1959). But we are also cognizant of the obverse rule, which the government seemingly ignores, that an entirely separate and independent claim cannot be maintained against a third party under Rule 14, even though it does arise out of the same general set of facts as the main claim. . . .

The question whether a defendant's demand presents an appropriate occasion for the use of impleader or else constitutes a separate claim has been resolved consistently by permitting impleader only in cases where the third party's liability was in some way derivative of the outcome of the main claim. In most such cases it has been held that for impleader to be available the third party defendant must be "liable *secondarily* to the original defendant in the event that the latter is held liable to the plaintiff" (emphasis added). Holtzoff, Entry of the Additional Parties in a Civil Action, 31 F.R.D. 101, 106 (1962). . . . Stating the same principle in different words, other authorities declare that the third party must necessarily be *liable over* to the defendant for all or part of the plaintiff's recovery, . . . or that the defendant must attempt to *pass on* to the third party all or part of the liability asserted against the defendant. . . . Whichever expression is preferred, it is clear that impleader under Rule 14 requires that the liability of the third party be dependent upon the outcome of the main claim.

Of course, the government does not contend that the case before us presents the usual situation where impleader is used, i.e., where the third party will be secondarily liable for the judgment against the original defendant. It tells us, however, that the liability of Grasso and the captains is so closely related that one of them will "in all likelihood" be liable for the employment taxes. The government is motivated to implead the captains by the fear that it will be whipsawed in separate trials in which both Grasso and the captains will escape liability by successfully arguing that the other is the employer.

We think that in order for the government to be able to implead the captains as third party defendants in this tax refund suit, it must appear that the liability of the two taxpayers is an either/or proposition as a result of the law or the facts. Such a requirement is consistent in principle with the rationale which underlies impleader as authorized by Rule 14. Although the government has been heard to contend that either Grasso or the captains must be found to be the employer of the crewmen, it has reluctantly conceded the distinct possibility that the crewmen are not employees of anyone but rather operate as independent contractors. Indeed, the government itself on a previous occasion has sought and obtained a finding that other shrimp fishermen were "independent businessmen engaged in business on their own account." Gulf Coast Shrimpers & Oysterman's Assn. v. United States, 236 F.2d 658, 662 n.7 (5th

Cir. [1956]). And in Local 36, International Fishermen & Allied Workers of America v. United States, 177 F.2d 320 (9th Cir. 1949), it was found that the captains and the crewmen were joint venturers. Other decisions have found that the fishermen were not employees of the owners of the vessels but have not considered whether the crewmen were employees of the captains. See United States v. Crawford Packing Co., 330 F.2d 194 (5th Cir. 1964); Williams Packing & Nav. Co. v. Enochs, 176 F. Supp. 168 (S.D. Miss. 1959), *aff'd,* 291 F.2d 402 (5th Cir. 1961), *rev'd, on jurisdictional grounds,* 370 U.S. (1962). Compare Cape Shore Fish Co., Inc. v. United States, 330 F.2d 961 (1964). These decisions illustrate that the determination of whether the crewmen are employees or not will turn on the facts of each case.

While we recognize that allowing impleader of the captains would expedite administratively the entire controversy, the government still has failed to show that the tax liability necessarily will fall upon either Grasso or the captains. The third party complaint against the captains is a separate claim for taxes, and as such must be denied. . . .

The order of the district court is affirmed.

---

d. Interpleader (Rule 22) and Statutory Interpleader: The Stakeholder's Remedy

Interpleader is a method of joining parties in cases where a stakeholder faces two potentially conflicting claims to the same stake. For example, an insurance company may recognize its obligation to pay insurance proceeds to "the wife of *A*" but may find that two women claim to be that person. Interpleader allows the insurance company — the stakeholder — to interplead both putative spouses and thereby protect itself from conflicting claims to the same stake that might result if the women brought two separate actions.

Rule 22 (called Rule interpleader) is one means by which such interpleader can be effected. A far more useful device, however, is the Federal Interpleader Act, codified at 28 U.S.C. §§ 1335, 1397, and 2361. The latter (called statutory interpleader) is more useful than Rule interpleader because the Federal Interpleader Act permits minimal diversity (at least one claimant must be diverse from another claimant), requires only $500 in controversy, permits nationwide service of process, and has liberal venue requirements (venue is proper where one or more of the claimants reside). Likely the only context in which a stakeholder might use the Rule rather than statutory interpleader would be when all of the claimants are from the same state but are diverse from the stakeholder. In this case, statutory interpleader would be unavailable, as it requires diversity between at least two of the claimants.

Useful as the interpleader device may be, it is not an all-purpose "bill of peace," as the following case explains.

State Farm Fire & Casualty Co. v. Tashire

386 U.S. 523 (1967)

JUSTICE FORTAS delivered the opinion of the Court.

Early one September morning in 1964, a Greyhound bus proceeding northward through Shasta Country, California, collided with a southbound pickup truck. Two of the passengers aboard the bus were killed. Thirty-three others were injured, as were the bus driver, the driver of the truck and its lone passenger. One of the dead and 10 of the injured passengers were Canadians; the rest of the individuals involved were citizens of five American States. The ensuing litigation led to the present case, which raises important questions concerning administration of the interpleader remedy in the federal courts.

The litigation began when four of the injured passengers filed suit in California state courts, seeking damages in excess of $1,000,000. Named as defendants were Greyhound Lines, Inc., a California corporation; Theron Nauta, the bus driver; Ellis Clark, who drove the truck; and Kenneth Glasgow, the passenger in the truck who was apparently its owner as well. Each of the individual defendants was a citizen and resident of Oregon. Before these cases could come to trial and before other suits were filed in California or elsewhere, petitioner State Farm Fire & Casualty Company, an Illinois corporation, brought this action in the nature of interpleader in the United States District Court for the District of Oregon.

In its complaint State Farm asserted that at the time of the Shasta County collision it had in force an insurance policy with respect to Ellis Clark, driver of the truck, providing for bodily injury liability up to $10,000 per person and $20,000 per occurrence and for legal representation of Clark in actions covered by the policy. It asserted that actions already filed in California and others which it anticipated would be filed far exceeded in aggregate damages sought, the amount of its maximum liability under the policy. Accordingly, it paid into court the sum of $20,000 and asked the court (1) to require all claimants to establish their claims against Clark and his insurer in this single proceeding and in no other, and (2) to discharge State Farm from all further obligations under its policy—including its duty to defend Clark in lawsuits arising from the accident. Alternatively, State Farm expressed its conviction that the policy issued to Clark excluded from coverage accidents resulting from his operation of a truck which belonged to another and was being used in the business of another. The complaint, therefore, requested that the court decree that the insurer owed no duty to Clark and was not liable on the policy, and it asked the court to refund the $20,000 deposit.

Joined as defendants were Clark, Glasgow, Nauta, Greyhound Lines, and each of the prospective claimants. Jurisdiction was predicated upon 28 U.S.C. § 1335, the federal interpleader statute and upon general diversity of citizenship, there being diversity between two or more of the claimants to the fund and between State Farm and all of the named defendants.

An order issued, requiring the defendants to show cause why they should not be restrained from filing or prosecuting "any proceeding in any state or United States Court affecting the property or obligation involved in this interpleader action, and specifically against the plaintiff and the defendant Ellis D. Clark." Personal service was effected on each of the American defendants, and registered mail was employed to reach the 11 Canadian claimants. Defendants Nauta, Greyhound, and several of the injured passengers responded, contending that the policy did cover this accident and advancing various arguments for the position that interpleader was either impermissible or inappropriate in the present circumstances. Greyhound, however, soon switched sides and moved that the court broaden any injunction to include Nauta and Greyhound among those who could not be sued except within the confines of the interpleader proceeding.

When a temporary injunction along the lines sought by State Farm was issued by the United States District Court for the District of Oregon, the present respondents moved to dismiss the action and, in the alternative, for a change of venue — to the Northern District of California, in which district the collision had occurred. After a hearing, the court declined to dissolve the temporary injunction, but continued the motion for a change of venue. The injunction was later broadened to include the protection sought by Greyhound, but modified to permit the filing — although not the prosecution — of suits. The injunction, therefore, provided that all suits against Clark, State Farm, Greyhound, and Nauta be prosecuted in the interpleader proceeding.

On interlocutory appeal, the Court of Appeals for the Ninth Circuit reversed. 363 F.2d 7. The court found it unnecessary to reach respondents' contentions relating to service of process and the scope of the injunction, for it concluded that interpleader was not available in the circumstances of this case. It held that in States like Oregon which do not permit "direct action" suits against insurance companies until judgments are obtained against the insured, the insurance companies may not invoke federal interpleader until the claims against the insured, the alleged tortfeasor, have been reduced to judgment. Until that is done, said the court, claimants with unliquidated tort claims are not "claimants" within the meaning of § 1335, nor are they "persons having claims against the plaintiff" within the meaning of Rule 22 of the Federal Rules of Civil Procedure.[3] Id., at 10. In accord with that view, it directed dissolution of the temporary

3. We need not pass upon the Court of Appeals' conclusions with respect to the interpretation of interpleader under Rule 22, which provides that "(1) Persons having claims against the plaintiff may be joined as defendants and required to interplead when their claims are such that the plaintiff is or may be exposed to double or multiple liability. . . ." First, as we indicate today, this action was properly brought under § 1335. Second, State Farm did not purport to invoke Rule 22. Third, State Farm could not have invoked it in light of venue and service of process limitations. Whereas statutory interpleader may be brought in the district where any claimant resides (28 U.S.C. § 1397), Rule interpleader based upon diversity of citizenship may be brought only in the district where all plaintiffs or all defendants reside (28 U.S.C. § 1391(a)). And whereas statutory interpleader enables a plaintiff to employ nationwide service of process (28 U.S.C. § 2361),

injunction and dismissal of the action. Because the Court of Appeals' decision on this point conflicts with those of other federal courts, and concerns a matter of significance to the administration of federal interpleader, we granted certiorari. 385 U.S. 811 (1966). Although we reverse the decision of the Court of Appeals upon the jurisdictional question, we direct a substantial modification of the District Court's injunction for reasons which will appear. . . .

We do not agree with the Court of Appeals that, in the absence of a state law or contractual provision for "direct action" suits against the insurance company, the company must wait until persons asserting claims against its insured have reduced those claims to judgments before seeking to invoke the benefits of federal interpleader. That may have been a tenable position under the 1926 and 1936 interpleader statutes. These statutes did not carry forward the language in the 1917 Act authorizing interpleader where adverse claimants "may claim" benefits as well as where they "are claiming" them. In 1948, however, in the revision of the Judicial Code, the "may claim" language was restored. Until the decision below, every court confronted by the question has concluded that the 1948 revision removed whatever requirement there might previously have been that the insurance company wait until at least two claimants reduced their claims to judgments. The commentators are in accord.

Considerations of judicial administration demonstrate the soundness of this view which, in any event, seems compelled by the language of the present statute, which is remedial and to be liberally construed. Were an insurance company required to await reduction of claims to judgment, the first claimant to obtain such a judgment or to negotiate a settlement might appropriate all or a disproportionate slice of the fund before his fellow claimants were able to establish their claims. The difficulties such a race to judgment pose for the insurer, and the unfairness which may result to some claimants, were among the principal evils the interpleader device was intended to remedy.

The fact that State Farm had properly invoked the interpleader jurisdiction under § 1335 did not, however, entitle it to an order both enjoining prosecution of suits against it outside the confines of the interpleader proceeding and also extending such protection to its insured, the alleged tortfeasor. Still less was Greyhound Lines entitled to have that order expanded so as to protect itself and its driver, also alleged to be tortfeasors, from suits brought by its passengers in various state or federal courts. Here, the scope of the litigation, in terms of parties and claims, was vastly more extensive than the confines of the "fund," the deposited proceeds of the insurance policy. In these circumstances, the mere existence of such a fund cannot, by use of interpleader, be employed to accomplish purposes that exceed the needs of orderly contest with respect to the fund.

---

service of process under Rule 22 is confined to that provided in Rule 4. See generally 3 Moore, Federal Practice ¶22. 04. . . .

There are situations, of a type not present here, where the effect of interpleader is to confine the total litigation to a single forum and proceeding. One such case is where a stakeholder, faced with rival claims to the fund itself, acknowledges — or denies — his liability to one or the other of the claimants. In this situation, the fund itself is the target of the claimants. It marks the outer limits of the controversy. It is, therefore, reasonable and sensible that interpleader, in discharge of its office to protect the fund, should also protect the stakeholder from vexatious and multiple litigation. In this context, the suits sought to be enjoined are squarely within the language of 28 U.S.C. § 2361. . . .

But the present case is another matter. Here, an accident has happened. Thirty-five passengers or their representatives have claims which they wish to press against a variety of defendants: the bus company, its driver, the owner of the truck, and the truck driver. The circumstance that one of the prospective defendants happens to have an insurance policy is a fortuitous event which should not of itself shape the nature of the ensuing litigation. For example, a resident of California, injured in California aboard a bus owned by a California corporation should not be forced to sue that corporation anywhere but in California simply because another prospective defendant carried an insurance policy. And an insurance company whose maximum interest in the case cannot exceed $20,000 and who in fact asserts that it has no interest at all, should not be allowed to determine that dozens of tort plaintiffs must be compelled to press their claims — even those claims which are not against the insured and which in no event could be satisfied out of the meager insurance fund — in a single forum of the insurance company's choosing. There is nothing in the statutory scheme, and very little in the judicial and academic commentary upon that scheme, which requires that the tail be allowed to wag the dog in this fashion.

State Farm's interest in this case, which is the fulcrum of the interpleader procedure, is confined to its $20,000 fund. That interest receives full vindication when the court restrains claimants from seeking to enforce against the insurance company any judgment obtained against its insured, except in the interpleader proceeding itself. To the extent that the District Court sought to control claimants' lawsuits against the insured and other alleged tortfeasors, it exceeded the powers granted to it by the statutory scheme.

We recognize, of course, that our view of interpleader means that it cannot be used to solve all the vexing problems of multiparty litigation arising out of a mass tort. But interpleader was never intended to perform such a function, to be an all-purpose "bill of peace." Had it been so intended, careful provision would necessarily have been made to insure that a party with little or no interest in the outcome of a complex controversy should not strip truly interested parties of substantial rights — such as the right to choose the forum in which to establish their claims, subject to generally applicable rules of jurisdiction, venue, service of process, removal, and change of venue. None of the legislative and academic sponsors of a modern federal interpleader device viewed their accomplishment as a "bill of peace," capable of sweeping dozens of lawsuits out of the various state and federal courts in which they were brought and into a single interpleader proceeding. . . .

In light of the evidence that federal interpleader was not intended to serve the function of a "bill of peace" in the context of multiparty litigation arising out of a mass tort, of the anomalous power which such a construction of the statute would give the stakeholder, and of the thrust of the statute and the purpose it was intended to serve, we hold that the interpleader statute did not authorize the injunction entered in the present case. Upon remand, the injunction is to be modified consistently with this opinion.[18]

The judgment of the Court of Appeals is reversed, and the case is remanded to the United States District Court for proceedings consistent with this opinion.

It is so ordered.

JUSTICE DOUGLAS, dissenting in part.

. . . I feel that the use which we today allow to be made of the federal interpleader statute, 28 U.S.C. § 1335, is, with all deference, unwarranted. How these litigants are "claimants" to this fund in the statutory sense is indeed a mystery. . . .

This insurance company's policy provides that it will "pay on behalf of the insured all sums which the insured shall become legally obligated to pay." To date the insured has not become "legally obligated" to pay any sum to any litigant. Since nothing is owed under the policy, I fail to see how any litigant can be a "claimant" as against the insurance company. . . .

. . . Understandably, the insurance company wants the best of two worlds. It does not want an action against it until judgment against its insured. But, at the same time, it wants the benefits of an interpleader statute. Congress could of course confer such a benefit. But it is not for this

18. We find it unnecessary to pass upon respondents' contention, raised in the courts below but not passed upon by the Court of Appeals, that interpleader should have been dismissed on the ground that the 11 Canadian claimants are "indispensable parties" who have not been properly served. The argument is that 28 U.S.C. § 2361 provides the exclusive mode of effecting service of process in statutory interpleader, and that § 2361 — which authorizes a district court to "issue its process for all claimants" but subsequently refers to service of "such process" by marshals "for the respective districts where the claimants reside or may be found" — does not permit service of process beyond the Nation's borders. Since our decision will require basic reconsideration of the litigation by the parties as well as the lower courts, there appears neither need nor necessity to determine this question at this time. We intimate no view as to the exclusivity of § 2361, whether it authorizes service of process in foreign lands, whether in light of the limitations we have imposed on the interpleader court's injunctive powers the Canadian claimants are in fact "indispensable parties" to the interpleader proceeding itself, or whether they render themselves amenable to service of process under § 2361 when they come into an American jurisdiction to establish their rights with respect either to the alleged tortfeasors or to the insurance fund. . . .

Court to grant dispensations from the effects of the statutory scheme which Congress has erected. . . .

Note: Transfer for Consolidation

Read 28 U.S.C. § 1407.

Passed in 1968, this legislation has resulted in thousands of cases being consolidated. Most typical are common disaster cases such as airplane crashes. In re Air Crash Disaster Near Dayton, Ohio, 310 F. Supp. 798 (J.P.M.L. 1970), is a good example. In that case, 13 actions had been filed in three federal district courts. The Judicial Panel on Multidistrict Litigation issued an order to show cause why the actions should not be transferred to a single district for coordinated and consolidated pretrial proceedings. Several plaintiffs and the Tann Corporation opposed transfer. Trans World Airlines and the United States supported it. As is typical in transfer disputes, the arguments made on the motion to transfer were highly practical.

The opponents of the motion argued that informal coordination of the pretrial proceedings was satisfactory, had already led to substantial discovery, and resulted in many settlements. In other words, they didn't need § 1407. Those supporting transfer countered that much discovery was still needed on the question of liability, and that it should be coordinated under the direction of one court.

In ordering a transfer, the Panel must make three findings: that there are one or more common questions of fact; that transfer will promote the just and efficient conduct of the individual suits; and that transfer will be for the convenience of the parties and witnesses. Usually, the transferee court is the one nearest the site of the disaster, or where the most cases are pending, or where there is a judge with unusual experience in mass litigation.

Although § 1407 speaks only to consolidation for pretrial purposes, a note writer in The Judicial Panel and the Conduct of Multidistrict Litigation, 87 Harv. L. Rev. 1001 (1974), found that "[i]n practice . . . the great majority of cases transferred by the Panel under § 1407 have been disposed of by transferee courts and not remanded to their original districts." Id. at 1001-1002. This happens through the grant of partial or complete summary judgment as part of the pretrial proceedings, settlement, trial by agreement among the parties in the transferee forum, and the operation of collateral estoppel. The last of these has occurred most notably in multidistrict litigation in the patent field after Blonder-Tongue Laboratories, Inc. v. University Foundation, 402 U.S. 313 (1971). The Harvard note describes one such case:

> The history of the *Butterfield Patent* litigation, in which a patentee brought numerous infringement actions for relatively small amounts throughout the United States, illustrates both the strengths and weakness[es] of handling

> multidistrict patent litigation by a separate trial on validity followed by collateral estoppel. The Panel granted section 1407 transfer despite arguments by many of the 148 defendants that it would force on them a financial burden disproportionate to the small recoveries sought [In re Butterfield Patent Infringement, 328 F. Supp. 513 (J.P.M.L. 1970).] Despite these fears about expense, the litigation was terminated in the amount of time about normal for one patent infringement case. Thirty-eight defendants agreed to a consolidated trial in the transferee court on the issue of validity. The court's finding of invalidity was then extended by collateral estoppel to 40 other defendants. However, before this scheme for the economical handling of the validity issue was worked out by the transferee court, 70 defendants had settled.

Note, supra, 87 Harv. L. Rev. at 1035-1036.

See Note: The Aggregation Alternative on page 1112 for more about the uses of § 1407.

For a mixed case involving 17 price-fixing suits filed around the country by more than 400 retail drug stores against drug manufacturer and wholesalers, see In re Brand-Name Prescription Drugs Antitrust Litigation, 264 F. Supp. 2d 1372 (M.D.L. Panel 2003) (the MDL panel upheld transferee court's decision to remand remaining individual suits after concluding common expert and fact discovery was complete and after granting summary judgment on the Sherman Act class action claims).

e. Intervention (Rule 24)

American Lung Ass'n v. Reilly

962 F.2d 258 (2d Cir. 1992)

PRATT, Circuit Judge.

Sixty-seven electric utilities and three electric utility industry associations (collectively, "utilities") appeal from an order of the United States District Court for the Eastern District of New York, John R. Bartels, Judge, which denied their motion to intervene as of right as defendants in a citizen suit brought under the Clean Air Act, 42 U.S.C. §§ 7401 et seq., to compel the Environmental Protection Agency (EPA) to review and revise the national ambient air quality standards (NAAQSs) for ozone, 141 F.R.D. 19 (E.D.N.Y. 1992). We conclude that Judge Bartels acted within his discretion in denying the utilities' motion to intervene. We also determine that the district court had subject-matter jurisdiction of the action. Accordingly, we affirm.

I

Under the Clean Air Act, EPA was required to make a final decision (either to revise the NAAQSs or retain the old ones) no later than December 31, 1990. Since EPA had not (and still has not) done so, plaintiffs filed this suit in the Eastern District of New York, alleging that it had breached its non-discretionary, statutory duty of reviewing (and if necessary revising), at five-year intervals, the NAAQSs for ozone, see 42 U.S.C. § 7409(d) (1977). Plaintiffs sought to compel EPA to perform its statutory duties. Specifically, the plaintiffs sought to compel EPA to (a) publish, within 180 days of the district court's order, either proposed revisions to the NAAQSs or a proposed decision formally declining to revise the NAAQSs, (b) provide the public with opportunity for notice and comment, and (c) promulgate final regulations thereafter.

The utilities moved to intervene as parties' defendant. Their proposed answer asserted two defenses: (1) that "[t]he complaint fails to state a claim against Defendants upon which relief can be granted," and (2) that the district court "lacks subject matter jurisdiction over the Plaintiff's complaint." Judge Bartels denied the motion to intervene, and the utilities filed a notice of appeal on February 27, 1992.

The next day, February 28, 1992, Judge Bartels signed a consent order and final judgment which, *inter alia*, ordered EPA, by August 1, 1992, to publish a proposed decision, made pursuant to notice and comment rulemaking procedures, to revise (or not) the existing NAAQSs for ozone. Judge Bartels also ordered EPA to allow a public comment period of at least 60 days, and then to publish a final decision by March 1, 1993.

II

A denial of intervention as of right under Fed. R. Civ. P. 24(a)(2) is reviewed under an abuse of discretion standard, as only the district judge has the "feel of the case" necessary to "weigh the advantages to be derived from appellants' participation as intervenors." United States v. Hooker Chemicals & Plastics Corp., 749 F.2d 968, 991 (2d Cir. 1984) (Friendly, J.). To merit consideration for intervention under rule 24(a)(2), a movant must (1) file a timely application, (2) claiming an interest relating to the property or transaction which is the subject of the action, (3) with the movant so situated that the disposition of the action may as a practical matter impair or impede the movant's ability to protect its interest, (4) unless the movant's interest is adequately represented by existing parties.

Judge Bartels concluded that the motion was timely, but that the utilities fell short on the other three requirements of rule 24(a)(2). With respect to the second requirement, he saw the utilities' interest in the subject matter of the action as based on a "double contingency" of events: "first, the plaintiffs must prevail in this lawsuit and second, the defendants must then downwardly revise the NAAQS[s]." Thus, he concluded, the utilities' interests were too "remote from the subject matter of the proceeding" and too "contingent upon the occurrence of a series of events" (citing Washington Elec. [Coop., Inc. v. Mass. Mun. Wholesale Elec. Co.,] 922 F.2d [92,] 96 [2d Cir. 1990]). With respect to the third requirement, he concluded that since the utilities could participate in any NAAQS rulemaking ordered by the court, a judgment in favor of the plaintiffs could not as a practical matter impair the utilities' ability to challenge any defect of any subsequent rulemaking. As to the fourth requirement, Judge Bartels concluded that the utilities could not demonstrate an interest in the rulemaking schedule that would not be adequately represented by EPA.

On appeal the utilities claim primarily that their interest is not so much in the ultimate rule promulgated by the EPA, as Judge Bartels understood it to be, but in having an opportunity to help shape the schedule for this judicially-compelled rulemaking. The utilities argue that they might have insufficient time to prepare a response to any proposal or to submit comments during the judicially-established comment period. They further point out that absent intervention, they would have no standing to obtain an extension of the deadlines imposed by the district court. To this end, they inform us of numerous cases, mostly from district courts, that have allowed intervention in similar cases.

The utilities' arguments are inadequate to overcome the district court's discretionary denial of intervention. First, as the plaintiffs have correctly pointed out, the cases cited by the utilities that have allowed intervention are primarily cases involving the promulgation of rules for particular industries. In such cases, an industry applying for intervention would have a much less "remote" or "contingent" interest. See, e.g., ManaSota-88, Inc. v. Tidwell, 896 F.2d 1318, 1322 (11th Cir. 1990). Second, the utilities "have asked for little that is new or even particularly different" from the defenses asserted by EPA. Hooker Chemicals, 749 F.2d at 991. Third, even had EPA obeyed the schedule commanded by the statute, there would have been no guarantee that even the seven months prescribed by the district court's order would have been available for "meaningful and effective" comment. See 42 U.S.C. § 7409(d). Finally, the statute requires EPA to base its decisions on the latest scientific knowledge that bears upon a given NAAQS. 42 U.S.C. § 7409(b)(1). There is no reason to believe that EPA will shirk its statutory duty to solicit and consider such information, or that the utilities and their experts will not have adequate opportunity to present their views.

Judge Bartels acted within his discretion. "The circumstances that serve as a basis for decision [on motions to intervene] are so varied and random that the court would virtually need to create a new rule to describe each case." Gene R. Shreve, Questioning Intervention as of Right—Toward a New Methodology of Decisionmaking, 74 Nw. U. L. Rev. 894, 922-923 (1980) (footnotes omitted) (quoted in Hooker Chemicals, 749 F.2d at 991 n.20). . . .

The order of the district court is affirmed.

Notes and Questions

1. *Intervention and Subject Matter Jurisdiction*. As the Sixth Circuit has noted, "[i]ntervention cannot, as a general rule, create jurisdiction where

none exists. Intervention 'presuppose[s] an action duly brought'; it cannot 'cure [the] vice in the original suit' and must 'abide the fate of that suit.' . . . In the absence of jurisdiction over the existing suit, a district court simply has no power to decide a motion to intervene; its only option is to dismiss." Vill. of Oakwood v. State Bank & Trust Co., 481 F.3d 364, 367 (quoting U.S. *ex rel.* Tex. Portland Cement Co. v. McCord, 233 U.S. 157, 163-164 (1914)). In *Village of Oakwood*, depositors sued a bank in state court for improprieties while the bank was held in receivership by the Federal Deposit Insurance Corporation. The FDIC, which the complaint charged with breach of fiduciary duty but failed to name as a party, moved to intervene and then removed the case to federal court before the state court could resolve the motion to intervene. The depositors moved to remand for lack of diversity, but the trial court held onto the case by granting the FDIC's motion to intervene, reasoning that the case was now covered by the Financial Institutions Reform, Recovery, and Enforcement Act of 1989, 12 U.S.C. § 1819(b)(2), which "deems suits to which the FDIC is a party to arise under federal law." *Vill. of Oakwood*, 481 F.3d at 368.

The Sixth Circuit reversed. The court concluded that although there would be subject matter jurisdiction under § 1819(b)(2) and 28 U.S.C. § 1367(a) if the FDIC had substituted itself for the defendant bank under Rule 25(c), or even if the FDIC had been impleaded by the bank, intervention does not produce the same result because of the long-standing rule that "intervention cannot create jurisdiction where none existed." Id. at 368-369. But see Heaton v. Monogram Credit Card Bank, 297 F.3d 416, 426 (5th Cir. 2002) ("[T]he FDIC's attempt to intervene conferred on it sufficient 'party' status to bring this case within the federal court's jurisdiction under § 1819(b)(2)(A).").

2. *Making Decisions About Joinder.* Now that you have reviewed the basic party joinder rules in isolation, reconsider them as an array of devices available to the parties at the pleading stage. What factors, besides the technical aspects of the Rules themselves, are most likely to affect parties' decisions about joinder? A search for assets? Avoiding multiple liability? Convincing a jury to award a substantial verdict? Preventing same? Attracting media interest in the dispute?

If you believe, correctly, that all of these factors (and others not mentioned) may be relevant in at least some cases, then you can appreciate why the Rules are but a small part of the joinder story. Like many aspects of procedure, lawyers make joinder decisions based on a complex array of considerations that range from highly practical, concrete, and case-specific issues to very abstract, systemic issues of fundamental fairness and intelligent allocation of scarce public resources. Thus your ability to make competent joinder decisions will require practical experience as well as the technical proficiency you can gain from this text.

3. *Restraints on Joinder*. It bears repeating (and we have repeated this) that the Federal Rules of Civil Procedure joinder rules are *not* the only constraints on party joinder in federal court. Subject matter jurisdiction, venue,

and personal jurisdiction requirements must also be satisfied. For example, in an action based solely on diversity, a defendant can implead a party under Rule 14 only if the jurisdiction statutes—including the supplemental jurisdiction statute—permit it, and only if the court also has personal jurisdiction over the impleaded party. Likewise, the distinction between necessary and indispensable parties under Rule 19 cannot be made without knowing which persons can (or cannot) be made a party.

4. *Some Examples.* Test your comprehension of the joinder rules we have discussed thus far and federal subject matter jurisdiction requirements by asking whether each claim below could be heard in federal court. Analyze both the Federal Rules of Civil Procedure and subject matter jurisdiction aspects of each claim and—in general—the information you would need to determine each.

Example 1

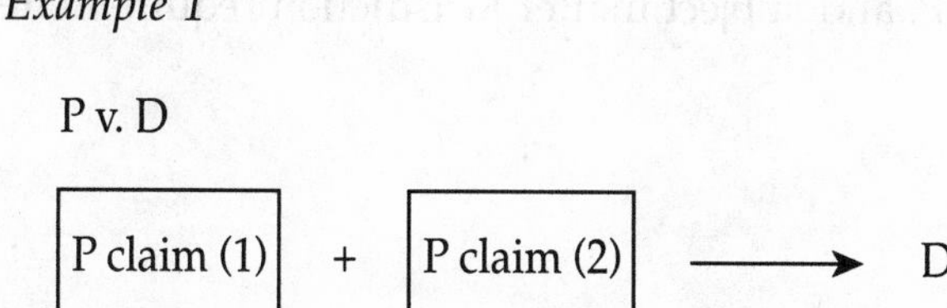

Under what conditions may two or more claims of one plaintiff be asserted against one defendant? Consider both the joinder of claims requirements of the Fed. R. Civ. P. and subject matter jurisdiction requirements.

Example 2

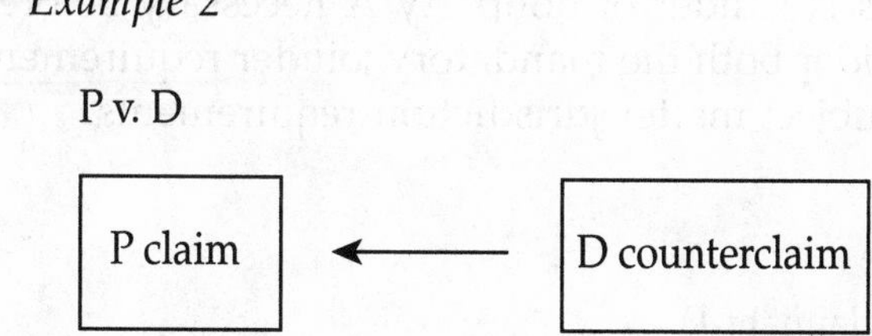

Under what conditions may the defendant assert one or more counterclaims against the plaintiff? Consider both the counterclaim and joinder of claims requirements of the Fed. R. Civ. P. and subject matter jurisdiction requirements.

Example 3

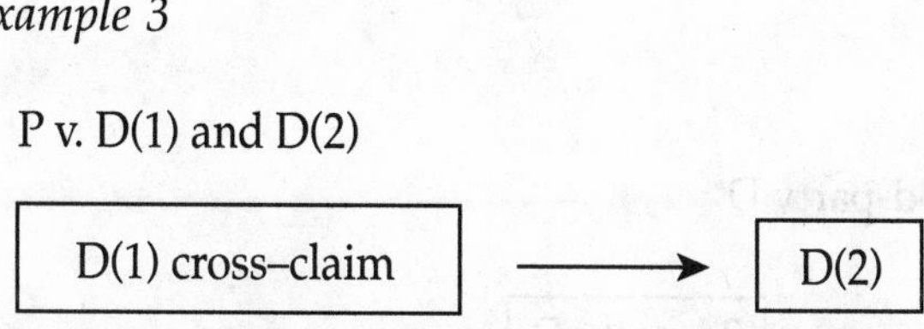

Under what conditions may one defendant assert one or more cross-claims against a codefendant? Consider both the cross-claim and joinder of claims requirements of the Fed. R. Civ. P. and subject matter jurisdiction requirements.

Example 4

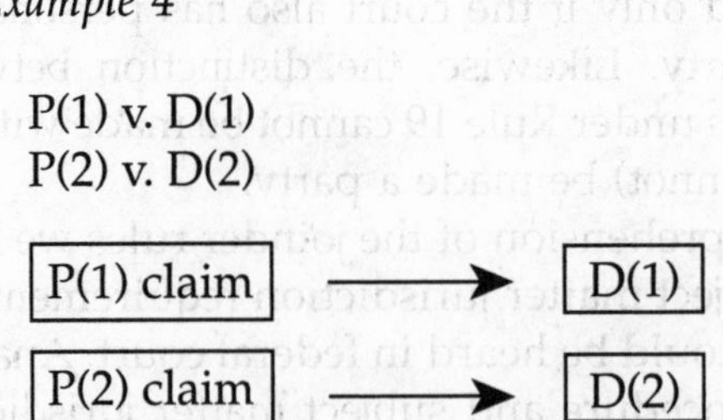

Under what conditions may two plaintiffs join together in asserting claims against two defendants? Consider both the joinder of parties requirements of the Fed. R. Civ. P. and subject matter jurisdiction requirements.

Example 5

P v. D

A (absentee)

a) Under what conditions may a nonparty A intervene in a suit? Consider both the intervention rules of the Fed. R. Civ. P. and subject matter jurisdiction requirements.

b) Under what conditions is joinder of nonparty A necessary before a lawsuit may proceed? Consider both the mandatory joinder requirements of the Fed. R. Civ. P. and subject matter jurisdiction requirements.

Example 6

P (stakeholder) v. D(1) (claimant 1)
and
D(2) (claimant 2)

Under what conditions may a stakeholder interplead claimants to a common fund or a "stake"? Consider both the statutory and Fed. R. Civ. P. interpleader requirements and subject matter jurisdiction requirements.

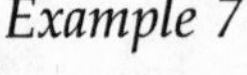

Example 7

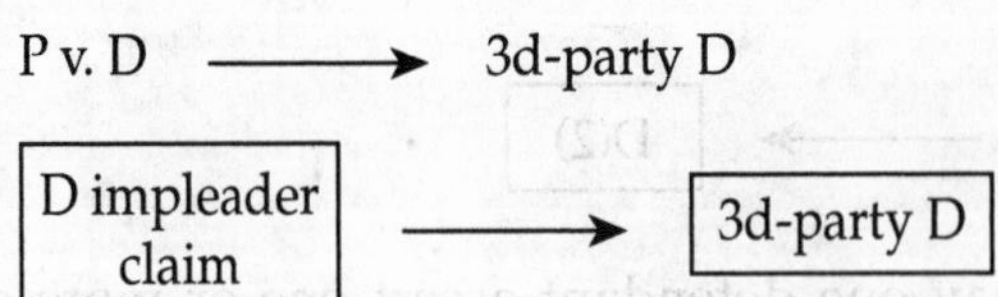

Under what conditions may a defendant implead a third-party defendant and assert one or more claims against the impleaded defendant?

Consider the impleader and joinder of claims requirements of the Fed. R. Civ. P. and subject matter jurisdiction requirements.

5. *Who Are Persons "Affected"?* The joinder devices — especially mandatory joinder and intervention — force courts to consider the fundamental question of who is a person "affected" by the results of civil litigation, both directly and indirectly. In public law cases in particular, such as a school desegregation case, the court often must craft remedies that "involve the adjustment of many competing institutional and human interests, [such that] the decree in a public law case often looks like a discretionary regime addressing a problem governed by multiple and polycentric criteria." Melvin Aron Eisenberg, Participation, Responsiveness, and the Consultative Process: An Essay for Lon Fuller, 92 Harv. L. Rev. 410, 428 (1978). As such, the persons who may be "affected" by the litigation may include the whole community. What are the joinder implications of this feature of public law litigation? Does it point toward greater flexibility in adding parties or permitting absentees to intervene? See also Stephen C. Yeazell, Intervention and the Idea of Litigation: A Commentary on the Los Angeles School Case, 25 UCLA L. Rev. 244 (1977).

For example, must an intervenor have "standing" (that is, meet the applicable Article III requirements of concrete individualized injury), or may this be excused? Compare Ruiz v. Estelle, 161 F.3d 814 (5th Cir. 1998) (holding intervenors need not have Article III standing), with Mausolf v. Babbitt, 85 F.3d 1295, 1300 (8th Cir. 1996) (holding intervenors must have Article III standing). See also Daggett v. Comm'n on Gov't Ethics & Election Practices, 172 F.3d 104 (1st Cir. 1999) (noting split). The United States Supreme Court has reserved judgment on this point. See Diamond v. Charles, 476 U.S. 54, 68-69 & n.21 (1986).

6. *Persons "Affected" and the "Limited Trough."* Persons who may be "affected" by litigation also include those who may be too late to recover assets from a corporation that is forced into bankruptcy by mass tort litigation. These "limited trough" cases present distributional justice issues that are particularly complex, as Thomas A. Smith explains in A Capital Markets Approach to Mass Tort Bankruptcy, 104 Yale L.J. 367 (1994).

The problem captured national attention when asbestos litigation in many forms and forums triggered a rush to the limited assets of the product manufacturers. Mass tort litigation in general raises the distributional justice issues most strikingly. Priorities of claims and the interests of future claimants are the most pressing of these.

Professor Smith proposes a novel capital markets approach to overcoming the distributional justice problems. Under his approach, the bankruptcy court would place the entire value of the defendant company in trust for the tort claimants, and the trust would use these assets to compensate present and future tort creditors under the following scheme: The trust would issue to the tort claimant a security that was designed to be traded on the capital market. The value of the security would be determined by the market, not the trust. Do you see any problems with this proposal? What are its strengths?

C. ADVANCED ISSUES IN DISCOVERY

1. Protective Orders, Public Access, and Joinder Strategies

A controversy that has engaged all three branches of government, and that has tremendous trial strategy implications, is the practice of sealing court records as a condition of settlement or payment of a verdict in civil cases. Closely related to these privately negotiated protective measures are judicially enforced protective orders authorized under Rule 26(c), under which discovery materials may be sealed from nonparty scrutiny. The tension, of course, is between the public interest in access to these materials and the interest in facilitating settlements through agreements not to disclose sensitive material.

At the congressional level, in the 1990s Senator Herb Kohl of Wisconsin proposed the Sunshine in Litigation Act, which would restrict federal courts from issuing protective orders sealing documents without first determining whether public safety or health would be harmed. He cited cases involving silicone breast implants, medical malpractice, and defective heart valves as illustrations of suits in which information on dangerous products uncovered in litigation was sealed from public view. See Henry J. Reske, Secrecy Orders at Issue, A.B.A. J. 32 (Aug. 1994).

Consider the following case and its implications for strategies regarding joinder of parties absent legislation limiting protective orders.

Grove Fresh Distributors, Inc. v. Everfresh Juice Co.
24 F.3d 893 (7th Cir. 1994)

BAUER, Circuit Judge.

This appeal requires us to determine the rights of third parties who wish to intervene in pending litigation for the limited purpose of obtaining access to documents which have been shielded from public scrutiny either by seal or by a protective order. At the heart of this dispute are a pair of lawsuits filed by Grove Fresh Distributors, Inc. against various of its competing orange juice manufacturers. The lawsuits are based on allegations that the defendants engaged in a conspiracy to unlawfully adulterate and misbrand orange juice in violation of federal unfair competition laws, Food and Drug Administration regulations, and the federal Racketeer Influenced and Corrupt Organizations statute (RICO). 18 U.S.C. §§ 1961 et seq. In the first of these cases, filed in 1989 (the "'89 case"), the district court issued a protective order limiting Grove Fresh's ability to disclose information obtained from the defendants by virtue of the discovery process which the defendants classified as confidential. In a subsequent lawsuit involving similar claims, filed in 1990 (the "'90 case"), the district court sealed the entire court file.

Two different sets of intervenors requested leave to intervene in the cases for the purposes of modifying the protective order in the '89 case and vacating the seal in the '90 case. The first group of intervenors are plaintiffs in a separate group of class action cases. Also citing unlawful adulteration and labelling practices, these intervenors ("Consumers") are suing many of the same orange juice manufacturers for consumer fraud and breach of warranty. The Consumers wish to spare the time and expense of a separate pretrial discovery process by obtaining access to the discovery produced in the Grove Fresh cases. They believe that due to the factual similarity between their case and the Grove Fresh cases, much of the relevant material will be the same. The trial court rejected the Consumers' motion to intervene because the court believed that they lacked standing and that they would not suffer any prejudice from the denial.

The second group of intervenors, The Ad Hoc Coalition of In-depth Journalists ("Coalition") represent a group of professional journalists. Their attempt to vacate the seal in the '90 case and modify the protective order in the '89 case was denied by the district court on November 20, 1992. In its opinion, the court recognized that the Coalition had a right to any court decisions in the case and any documents upon which the court relied in making its decisions. Despite this acknowledged right, for reasons of expedience, the court refused to grant access to the Coalition until the proceeding was completed. The district court also denied the Coalition's motion to modify the protective order in the '89 case because in its view the Coalition had no standing nor any rights on the merits to have access to materials which were part of the discovery process.

The '89 case was dismissed pursuant to the defendants' successful motion for summary judgment on February 21, 1992. In late April of 1993, the '90 case was dismissed pursuant to a settlement among the litigants. The Coalition renewed its request to vacate the seal on June 1, 1993. The district court denied the request.

The differences between the two types of intervenors require us to analyze their claims separately. We begin with the Consumers.

I

We address, as a preliminary matter, our appellate jurisdiction here because in their briefs, the defendants in the Grove Fresh case, The Everfresh Juice Company and John Labatt Limited, suggest that the order denying the Consumers' motion was not an appealable order. At oral argument, counsel for the defendants acknowledged that the proceedings in the two cases are now complete and it is not clear whether they adhere to their original position on jurisdiction. Nevertheless even if proceedings below were not complete, our decisions make it evident that an order granting or refusing to grant access in favor of an intervening party is appealable under the collateral order doctrine. Wilk v. American Medical Assn., 635 F.2d 1295 (7th Cir. 1980) (refusing to modify a protective order); American Tel. & Tel. Co. v. Grady, 594 F.2d 594 (7th Cir. 1978) (modifying a protective order), *cert. denied*, 440 U.S. 971 (1979). Thus, even though the order did not end the litigation on its merits, the order was immediately appealable. Everfresh and John Labatt also suggest without elaboration that the Consumers lacked standing to intervene in this case. It is apparent, however, that intervention is the procedurally appropriate course for third-party challenges to protective orders. Hence, Everfresh and John Labatt's jurisdictional challenges are unavailing.

Everfresh and John Labatt also argue that because the Consumers failed to serve them with its motion to intervene, the motion was properly denied. This claim ignores the facts of the case. As originally filed, the motion to intervene was directed only to the '90 case. Due to the seal, which included within its terms the docket sheet, the identities of the defendants and their counsel of record were unknown, and they, therefore, could not be served. The Consumers then amended their motion to include the '89 case, but the court denied the motion before the Consumers had a chance to serve the defendants. Because the failure to serve the defendants in this case was justifiable, Everfresh and John Labatt's procedural challenge is also without merit.

As for the merits of the district court's decision, we find our decision in *Wilk* to be dispositive. In *Wilk*, five chiropractors sued various medical organizations, alleging a conspiracy to violate federal antitrust laws. The State of New York then filed a federal antitrust suit against many of the same organizations. Though the causes of action in the two suits were not identical, both were directed at similar wrongdoings. At the time of the second suit, discovery in the first action was nearly concluded but the court had entered a protective order prohibiting the plaintiffs from revealing the contents of any materials which the defendant had labeled as confidential. The State of New York requested that the protective order in the first case be modified so as to allow it access to discovery materials. The district court denied the motion for intervention.

Reversing the district court, we held that where a third party wishes to modify a protective order so as to avoid duplicative discovery in collateral litigation, policy considerations favoring the efficient resolution of disputes justify modification unless such an order would tangibly prejudice substantial rights of the party opposing modification. *Wilk*, 635 F.2d at 1299. Even if such prejudice is demonstrated, the court has broad discretion in determining whether the injury outweighs the benefits of modification. Id.

Applying this test to the facts in *Wilk*, we recognized that as a bona fide litigant, New York had a legitimate basis for its request, and that because the allegations in the two matters were virtually identical, much of the material produced in the first action would be relevant and eventually discoverable. Thus, we concluded that New York was presumptively entitled to access to the *Wilk* discovery on the same terms as the *Wilk* plaintiffs. On remand, the burden was placed on the parties opposing modification to establish that the intervenors would not be entitled to certain materials. Id. at 1301.

The reasoning of *Wilk* applies with equal force here and we therefore remand the case to the district court with directions to reconsider, in light of *Wilk*, the Consumers' motion to intervene. Our holding in no way diminishes the defendants' rights to limit the Consumers' access so as to retain protection for items which would ordinarily not be discoverable due to privileges or irrelevance. Moreover, if the district court finds that there are legitimate secrecy concerns, the seal and protective order need only be modified to include the Consumers within their parameters.

II

The Coalition argues in its appeal that the district court's order of November 20, 1992 presents three issues for review. First, there is the question of whether the district court's decision to postpone access to the '90 court file after the court had acknowledged the Coalition's rights was proper. Secondly, the Coalition challenges the district court's decision finding that the journalists lacked standing to modify the protective order. Lastly, there is the issue of whether the court should have issued a decision on the record justifying the seal.

The public's right of access to court proceedings and documents is well-established. Press-Enterprise Co. v. Superior Court, 464 U.S. 501 (1984); Nixon v. Warner Communications, 435 U.S. 589 (1978). Public scrutiny over the court system serves to (1) promote community respect for the rule of law, (2) provide a check on the activities of judges and litigants, and (3) foster more accurate fact finding. Richmond Newspapers, Inc. v. Virginia, 448 U.S. 555 (1980). Though its original inception was in the realm of criminal proceedings, the right of access has since been extended to civil proceedings because the contribution of publicity is just as important there. Smith v. United States Dist. Court, 956 F.2d 647, 650 (7th Cir. 1992). In fact, mistakes in civil proceedings may be more likely to inflict costs upon third parties, therefore meriting even more scrutiny. *Richmond Newspapers*, 448 U.S. at 596 (Brennan, J., concurring).

Justified originally by common-law traditions predating the enactment of our Constitution, the right of access belonging to the press and the general public also has a First Amendment basis. Globe Newspaper Co. v. Superior Court, 457 U.S. 596, 603 (1982). Neither the common-law nor the constitutional right is absolute. More general in its contours, the common-law right of access establishes that court files and documents should be open to the public unless the court finds that its records are being used for improper purposes. United States v. Corbitt, 879 F.2d 224, 228 (7th Cir.

1989). The First Amendment presumes that there is a right of access to proceedings and documents which have "historically been open to the public" and where the disclosure of which would serve a significant role in the functioning of the process in question. Id. This presumption is rebuttable upon demonstration that suppression "is essential to preserve higher values and is narrowly tailored to serve that interest." *Press-Enterprise,* 464 U.S. at 510. The difficulties inherent in quantifying the First Amendment interests at issue require that we be firmly convinced that disclosure is inappropriate before arriving at a decision limiting access. Any doubts must be resolved in favor of disclosure. In re Continental Illinois Securities Litigation, 732 F.2d 1302, 1313 (7th Cir. 1984). Though it is not clear whether the district court based its decision on constitutional or common-law grounds, it did find that the Coalition had a right to certain documents in the file. We must decide only whether its decision to postpone access was proper.

In light of the values which the presumption of access endeavors to promote, a necessary corollary to the presumption is that once found to be appropriate, access should be immediate and contemporaneous. Nebraska Press Assn. v. Stuart, 427 U.S. 539 (1976); Continental Illinois Securities Litigation, 732 F.2d at 1310. The newsworthiness of a particular story is often fleeting. To delay or postpone disclosure undermines the benefit of public scrutiny and may have the same result as complete suppression. Chicago Council of Lawyers v. Bauer, 522 F.2d 242, 250 (7th Cir. 1975), *cert. denied,* 427 U.S. 912 (1976). "[E]ach passing day may constitute a separate and cognizable infringement of the First Amendment." Nebraska Press Assn. v. Stuart, 423 U.S. 1327, 1329 (Blackmun, Circuit Justice 1975).

In this case, vacating the seal presented the district court with a peculiar set of problems. In reliance on the seal, the parties had filed documents which otherwise would not be part of the public record. As the district court correctly noted, until admitted into the record, material uncovered during pretrial discovery is ordinarily not within the scope of press access. Seattle Times Co. v. Rhinehart, 467 U.S. 20, 33 (1984). Thus, underlying the district judge's decision to postpone access to the '90 case file was a concern that the effort involved in going through the court file to ascertain which documents were in fact part of the public record was not worth the court's time. We are sensitive to the court's concerns. The time and effort expended in examining the court file to ascertain whether particular documents have been made part of the public record either because the court has relied on them or because the litigants have offered them as evidentiary support is a burden which the district courts should not have to bear. Nevertheless, as we have stated, the right of the press to obtain timely access to judicial decisions and the documents which comprise the bases of those decisions is essential. We conclude, therefore, that once the press has adequately demonstrated that its access has been unjustifiably limited, but where there are legitimate concerns of confidentiality, the burden should shift to the litigants to itemize for the court's approval which documents have been introduced into the public domain. We believe that such an approach provides a legitimate means of reconciling the press's rights with the time constraints facing the trial courts.

With respect to the protective order entered in the '89 case, the district court determined that because the Coalition was not entitled to discovery materials, the Coalition did not have standing to challenge the protective order. The Coalition does not contest the fact that discovery materials are not within the scope of their right of access. Rather, the Coalition believes the defendants are abusing the protective order to prevent the disclosure of harmful information which would otherwise be disseminated. More specifically, the Coalition contends that the defendants are classifying documents as confidential purely because they contain information which if released could harm their own business reputation. The Coalition argues that this is an insufficient justification for protection and constitutes a violation of the term of the protective order and Rule 26(c) of the Federal Rules of Civil Procedure.

Although the media's right of access does not extend to information gathered through discovery that is not part of the public record, the press does have standing to challenge a protective order for abuse or impropriety. Thus to the extent the Coalition's motion was denied for a lack of standing, we reverse the decision of the district court and remand it with instructions to consider the Coalition's allegations concerning abuse of the protective order.

Finally, we are asked to pass on the propriety of the court's failure to issue along with its decision to seal the '90 case file an explanation detailing the court's findings and reasoning. The Supreme Court has stated that when a court finds that the presumption of access has been rebutted by some countervailing interest, that "interest is to be articulated along with findings specific enough that a reviewing court can determine whether the closure order was properly entered." Press Enterprise Co. v. Superior Court, 464 U.S. 501, 510 (1985). Appellate courts have on several occasions emphasized that upon entering orders which inhibit the flow of information between the courts and the public, district courts should articulate on the record their reasons for doing so. In re Continental Illinois Securities Litigation, 732 F.2d 1302, 1313 n.17 (7th Cir. 1984); United States v. Edwards, 672 F.2d 1289, 1294 (7th Cir. 1982); In re State-Record Co., 917 F.2d 124 (4th Cir. 1990) ("[W]ithout specific findings of fact we cannot adequately review closure orders."). In this circuit, we have yet to hold that where such a description is lacking, reversal is *per se* appropriate. See Continental Illinois Securities Litigation, 732 F.2d at 1313 (holding that order granting access did not merit reversal despite insufficiently specific findings but noting that findings on the record are more crucial for orders denying access). In light of our disposition of this case, we need not adopt such a rule here. We ask only that in reaching its decision in this matter on remand that the district court specify the basis for its conclusions.

III

We sympathize with the burdens placed on trial judges today. Nevertheless, where the rights of the litigants come into conflict with the rights of the media and public at large, the trial judge's responsibilities are heightened. In such instances, the litigants' purported interest in confidentiality must be scrutinized heavily. Accordingly, we remand case 93-2438 to the district court for proceedings consistent with this court's decision in *Wilk.* Case 92-4038 is also remanded for proceedings consistent with this opinion.

Note: Collateral Litigation

It is not just the general public that has an interest in learning about dangerous products and consumer fraud. When collateral litigation has been brought against a company for similar misconduct, sealing records in the first case can prevent private litigants in other cases from learning anything about the case and cause repetitive discovery. See Foltz v. State Farm Mut. Auto. Ins. Co., 331 F.3d 1122, 1135 (9th Cir. 2003) (affirming the Circuit's "strong presumption in favor of access to court records" and holding that, absent compelling reasons to maintain a protective order, private intervenors involved in collateral litigation against defendant for fraudulently denying personal injury coverage to insureds are entitled to records filed under seal as part of a dispositive motion filed before a settlement was reached).

2. Private Investigation and the Duty of Third Parties to Give Evidence

a. Private Investigation

International Business Machines Corp. v. Edelstein
526 F.2d 37 (2d Cir. 1975)

PER CURIAM.

International Business Machines ("IBM") petitions this Court for extraordinary relief in the form of a writ of mandamus, pursuant to 28 U.S.C. § 1651 and Fed. R. App. P. 21. The petition focuses on certain rulings and practices adopted by Chief Judge Edelstein of the Southern District of New York in the conduct of a lawsuit currently being tried before him, United States v. International Business Machines Corp., 69 Civ. 200, Civ. No. 72-344.

More specifically, IBM seeks relief from the acts of the trial judge in (1) precluding IBM from privately interviewing adverse witnesses. . . .

This is not an ordinary case, and this will not be an ordinary trial. The complaint was filed on January 17, 1969. In substance, it charged IBM with violations of Section 2 of the Sherman Act (15 U.S.C. § 2). The trial commenced on May 19, 1975 and the Government estimates that it will "last well over a year." It expects to call "more than one hundred witnesses," and to "offer several thousand exhibits." IBM will undoubtedly have a comparable number of witnesses and exhibits. So much for the magnitude of the trial which, having commenced in May 1975 and recessed for the summer, has now resumed. . . .

About a week before the commencement of the trial, at a pretrial conference on May 12, 1975, the trial judge told counsel "that if any one of you seeks to interview a witness in the absence of opposite counsel, that you do it with a stenographer present and *so that it can be available to the Court, for the Court to see it,* and I think that is the kind of condition that I would ask you to live up to." (Emphasis supplied.) This direction was restated, in substance, during the trial.

The Court's ruling grew out of IBM's efforts to interview some of the individuals appearing on the Government's lengthy list of witnesses. We are told (and the Government has submitted no proof in contradiction) that upon learning of these interviews the Government ordered witnesses — two in particular, a Mr. Kraft and Lt. General Phillips — not to proceed with the interviews. Accordingly, both those prospective witnesses cancelled their interview appointments.

As was to be expected, the Court's order proved to be quite unworkable. IBM found it difficult to arrange interviews with witnesses, usually corporate executives with offices outside New York City, at times and places which were convenient to both the witnesses and opposing counsel. Moreover, interviews in the presence of opposing counsel did not lend themselves to the free and open discussion which IBM sought. Interviews transcribed by court reporters were a most unattractive alternative.

The trial judge apparently looked upon an interview as the taking of a deposition. In fact, there is little relation between them. A lawyer talks to a witness to ascertain what, if any, information the witness may have relevant to his theory of the case, and to explore the witness' knowledge, memory and opinion — frequently in light of information counsel may have developed from other sources. This is part of an attorney's so-called work product. It is the common experience of counsel at the trial bar that a potential witness, upon reflection, will often change, modify or expand upon his original statement and that a second or third interview will be productive of greater accuracy. Little wonder then that a witness being interviewed, as in two cases mentioned by IBM, would not wish to have his initial thoughts taken down by a court reporter as if it were sworn testimony in court.

We find disturbing the stated purpose of the order "so that it can be available to the Court, for the Court to see it." This condition is tantamount to an insistence that the trial judge be present at every interview and thus become cognizant of each proposed witness' statements even though such witness may never be called upon to testify. Again, it is common experience that, in presenting his case, counsel will offer the important (in his opinion) testimony which supports his theory of the case and discard the unimportant, his opponent having the same privilege.

We believe that the restrictions on interviewing set by the trial judge exceeded his authority. They not only impair the constitutional right to effective assistance of counsel but are contrary to time-honored and decision-honored principles, namely, that counsel for all parties have a right to interview an adverse party's witnesses (the witness willing) in private, without the presence or consent of opposing counsel and without a transcript being made. And, since the role of the trial judge is to pass upon the admissibility of proof, when and as offered, and to render his decision upon admitted proof, it follows that witness statements, if taken, should not be made available to the court in advance.

There is no question but that the trial judge did not intend adverse results to flow from his rulings. On the contrary, the record indicates that he felt the establishment of formalized interview procedures would aid the Court in its ultimate determination on the merits and would also insure the integrity of the trial by guarding against the exercise of undue influence upon prospective witnesses by interviewing attorneys.

Both of these purposes are indicative of the high standards which Judge Edelstein has set for the conduct of this extraordinarily complex and massive lawsuit, and we agree that it is vital for the Court to make decisions which are as informed as possible, based upon testimony which represents the true opinion and conclusions of the witness who offers it. However, we are in disagreement as to the method best suited to achieve this end. In particular, we are concerned that the means chosen by Judge Edelstein have unduly infringed upon counsels' ability to prepare their case for trial, and have, in addition, lessened the effectiveness of that trial by placing before the Court, not the case as finally prepared and refined by counsel, but rather a hodgepodge of information accumulated in the early stages of counsel's preparation. We believe that it does a disservice both to the parties and to the Court to subject to the Court's scrutiny the process by which counsel researches, develops and integrates the case which he ultimately presents. Counsel cannot be expected to have formulated a finished presentation at the outset of his preparation and endeavors. To require that his initial investigatory efforts be of a quality which counsel would willingly include as part of his client's final case is to set up an impossible standard; to ask him to submit his initial probings, notwithstanding their lack of effectiveness in his client's behalf, is in effect to ask counsel to deny his client the effective representation to which he is entitled. See Code of Professional Responsibility, Canon 7. . . .

The petition for writ of mandamus is granted in accordance with the views expressed in this opinion.

---

b. Nonparties' Duty to Give Evidence: The Subpoena Power

Mount Sinai School of Medicine v. American Tobacco Co.

880 F.2d 1520 (2d Cir. 1989)

KEARSE, Circuit Judge.

Mount Sinai School of Medicine ("Mount Sinai") and The American Cancer Society ("ACS") appeal from a final order of the United States District Court for the Southern District of New York, Kevin Thomas Duffy, Judge, holding them in civil contempt for failing to comply with orders of the court requiring them to respond to subpoenas served by appellees The American Tobacco Company ("American"), R.J. Reynolds Tobacco Company ("Reynolds"), and Philip Morris, Inc. ("Philip Morris") (collectively the "tobacco companies"), requesting research data for use in lawsuits to which Mount Sinai and ACS are not parties. On appeal, Mount Sinai and ACS challenge interlocutory orders that (1) denied their motion to quash the subpoenas on grounds of res judicata, collateral estoppel, and privilege, and (2) denied in part their motion for a protective order permitting redaction of the subpoenaed materials to prevent identification of persons who were subjects of the research. For the reasons below, we uphold the orders of the district court.

Each of the tobacco companies is a defendant in one or more product liability suits pending in state or federal courts around the country (the "underlying suits"), in which the plaintiffs allege that their decedents died of lung cancer caused by a combination of cigarette smoking and exposure to asbestos. Mount Sinai and ACS are not parties to those suits, and neither they nor members of their medical staffs are expected to be called as witnesses. The tobacco companies expect, however, that the plaintiffs will rely on expert testimony that in turn will rely on seminal studies made by certain members of the medical staffs of Mount Sinai and ACS. The tobacco companies seek to subpoena the data underlying these studies.

Dr. Irving J. Selikoff, a professor of medicine at Mount Sinai, is the principal author of, *inter alia,* two articles whose medical conclusions support the plaintiffs' claims in the underlying suits. See Hammond, Selikoff & Seidman, Asbestos Exposure, Cigarette Smoking and Death Rates, 330 Annals N.Y. Acad. Sci. 473 (1979); Selikoff, Seidman & Hammond, Mortality Effects of Cigarette Smoking Among Amosite Asbestos Factory Workers, 65 J. Natl. Cancer Inst. 507 (1980). Earlier studies had shown that cigarette smoking may cause cancer and that exposure to asbestos may also cause cancer. The Selikoff articles suggested that when cigarette smoking was combined with occupational exposure to asbestos, the risks of developing cancer increased geometrically rather than arithmetically. The authors concluded that these data suggested a synergistic relationship between the hazards of smoking and of exposure to asbestos.

For the 1979 article, the period of study ran from 1967 through 1976; for the 1980 article, the period of study ran from 1961 through 1977. Some

11,000 asbestos workers were subjects of the research reported in these two articles. Using a wide range of sources, Dr. Selikoff accumulated a variety of personal data on his subjects. Some information was received through the personal examination of approximately 500 subjects who were treated by Dr. Selikoff in connection with research for the two articles. Along with basic identifying details such as names, places of residence, and union affiliations, the assembled information included such items as dates of birth, dates and causes of death, periods of exposure to asbestos, smoking habits, evidence of cancer, and other relevant medical history. Dr. Selikoff assured his research subjects that the information they provided would remain confidential.

Much of the raw data was eventually recorded on computer tapes to facilitate statistical analysis and convenient storage. The Selikoff research continued after the publication of the 1979 and 1980 articles, and the computer tapes were updated frequently with new information.

In 1986, Reynolds served Mount Sinai and ACS with subpoenas issued by a state court in New York in connection with an action pending in state court in California, see Page v. Lincoln Electric Co., No. 257046 (Cal. Super. Ct.) (the "Page subpoenas"). The Page subpoenas sought all the data underlying the 1979 and 1980 Selikoff articles, as well as data underlying a 1968 article. Each subpoena provided, in pertinent part, as follows:

Documents to Be Produced

1. This subpoena covers documentation, data collections, or data bases (the "raw data") that formed the basis for the [1968, 1979, and 1980 articles];
2. Documents which describe, constitute, comment upon, criticize, review or concern the research design, methodology, sampling protocol, and/or conduct of any of the studies;
3. Copies of the questionnaires, answers to questionnaires, interview forms, responses to interviews, death certificates, autopsy reports, and other cause of death data . . . ;
4. Data sheets, computer tapes and/or copies of computer discs containing all coded data . . . ;

6. *This request is intended to cover all available data used, in as "raw" a form as possible*. . . .

(Emphasis added.)

Mount Sinai and ACS moved to quash the Page subpoenas in New York state court. That court, after discussing both the interests of scholars with respect to their research and the burdens of producing the data called for by the Page subpoenas, granted the motions to quash. In re R.J. Reynolds Tobacco Co., 518 N.Y.S.2d 729 (Sup. Ct. 1987) ("*Reynolds*"). The court stated, in pertinent part, as follows:

> Reynolds' subpoenae . . . are not selective. Rather, they are sweeping and indiscriminate.

A subpoena may be challenged on the grounds that it is overbroad, burdensome or oppressive.... A subpoena may be vacated for reasons of privilege, whether statutory or constitutional, or having its genesis under common law....

CPLR 3101 provides that "[t]here shall be a full disclosure of all evidence ...," which means all relevant information calculated to lead to relevant evidence.... The data requested must be material and necessary although it need not be indispensable.... The rules of evidence may be considered when determining necessity of the requested material. But inadmissibility by itself may not be a reason for denying access to the information, since such information may lead to evidence. In addition, its use in cross-examination can be a consideration.

... [T]he fact that the information is available from other sources or even that Reynolds has or could have obtained the material needed at trial is not reason alone for denying the production of the data. Material subpoenaed may be used for corroborative purposes.

However, when compliance with subpoenae would be so oppressive as to hinder the normal functioning of a Department of the medical school and/or of the American Cancer Society for a prolonged period of time, the Court on motion or on its own initiative may provide appropriate relief.

This is especially so because Mt. Sinai and the American Cancer Society are complete strangers to the underlying litigation. Neither Dr. Selikoff nor his co-authors will be witnesses at the Page trial. They are not consultants in that matter, nor was decedent Page a subject of their medical investigation....

Policy in New York, unlike most other jurisdictions, has accorded privilege to experts.... The United States Supreme Court held in the notable case of Branzburg v. Hayes, 408 U.S. 665, 688 (1972), "that 'the public ... has a right to every man's evidence,' except for those persons protected by a constitutional, common law or statutory privilege." ...

If the production of the material would become oppressive and unreasonably burdensome, the court, in balancing the hardships, should consider whether there are other sources for obtaining the material needed to disprove the conclusions reached by the three studies. In addition, the probative value of the material, if produced, should be considered....

Dr. Selikoff determined by a sample test that it would take thousands of hours to redact all the material which is of a confidential nature. The time required would be the same whether the information is in raw data form or on computer tape.

Reynolds has offered to reimburse Mt. Sinai and the American Cancer Society for the reasonable expenses incurred in their complying with the subpoenae. However, it appears that Dr. Selikoff and his colleagues would still have to spend over a thousand hours of time removing the data identifying the individuals who participated in the study. The loss of the scientists' time in complying with the subpoenae would be an unreasonable burden and would unduly interrupt their ongoing medical investigations.

It is also clear that the medical material requested is not of an archival nature but rather is in constant use as part of ongoing medical research....

Mount Sinai and the American Cancer Society protest, on behalf of their medical scientists, the interference with their ongoing scientific research in this area. While these medical investigations are still in progress, they

> should not be subjected to examination and criticism by people whose interests are arguably antithetical to the medical scientists. It would have the effect of denying to these doctors the opportunity of first publication of their studies. It could also have a chilling effect and discourage future scientific endeavors.
>
> Mount Sinai, the American Cancer Society, the Dean at the Yale University School of Medicine, and other eminent medical scholars claim that forced compliance with the subpoenae would result in an interference with their academic freedom. It was stated in Dow Chemical Co. v. Allen, 7th Cir., 672 F.2d 1262, 1275 [1982] that "whatever constitutional protection is afforded by the First Amendment extends as readily to the scholar in the laboratory as to the teacher in the classroom." Of course, like all other constitutional rights, academic freedom is not absolute and must be balanced against competing interests. . . . For present purposes, respondent's interest in academic freedom may properly figure into the legal calculation of whether forced disclosure would be reasonable.
>
> For the reasons stated above, the court finds that compliance with the subpoenae would place an unreasonable burden upon the medical and scientific institutions involved and would unduly disrupt the ongoing research at both Mount Sinai and the American Cancer Society.
>
> Accordingly, the motion to quash the subpoenae is granted.

Id. at 731-734. The tobacco companies did not appeal.

Shortly after the decision in *Reynolds*, the tobacco companies served on Mount Sinai and ACS the subpoenas at issue here, in connection with actions pending in federal court in Louisiana and Pennsylvania. See Lejeune v. Armstrong World Indus., No. 86-0421 (W.D. La.); Shires v. The Celotex Corp., No. 85-7141 (E.D. Pa.). In these new subpoenas, the tobacco companies seek fewer items than were sought in the Page subpoenas, concentrating primarily on the computer tapes storing the relevant raw data. To the extent relevant here, these subpoenas provide as follows:

> **Documents to Be Produced**
>
> (1) The computer tape(s) for the 1979 study containing all information gathered, or that relates to matters occurring, prior to January 1, 1977.
>
> (2) The computer tape(s) for the 1980 study containing all information gathered, or that relates to matters occurring, prior to January 1, 1978.
>
> (3) The supporting documentation for the 1979 and 1980 studies.

The subpoenas define "supporting documentation" as comprising

> computer code books for the 1979 and 1980 studies; related documentation that would assist in identifying what information is on the computer tapes for the 1979 and 1980 studies and where it is located on the tapes; a blank copy of the coding forms used in transferring information onto the computer tapes for the 1979 and 1980 studies; a blank copy of each type of questionnaire used to gather information for the 1979 and 1980 studies; a copy of the protocol documents for the 1979 and 1980 studies and any addenda thereto; and documents showing the calculations and the

analytical methods and assumptions used in developing the information with respect to the 1979 and 1980 studies. . . .

The subpoenas also make the following provision for confidentiality:

> Where necessary to protect the anonymity of the study participants, identifying information (such as names and street addresses) may be redacted. . . .

Mount Sinai and ACS moved in the district court to quash the subpoenas on the grounds that (1) in light of *Reynolds*, the subpoenas were barred by res judicata and collateral estoppel; (2) under New York law, the data sought by the tobacco companies was subject to the absolute privilege afforded experts; and (3) even if they had no absolute privilege, the researchers enjoyed a qualified privilege and the tobacco companies had not shown that their interests outweighed the interests of researchers. In the alternative, Mount Sinai and ACS moved for a protective order allowing (a) redaction of all identifying information on the computer tapes, (b) a summary by decade of all specific dates, e.g., dates of birth, death, and employment, and (c) restrictions on access by third parties to the subpoenaed materials. They argued that such a protective order was necessary to protect the participants' anonymity and physician-patient privilege.

The district court denied the motion to quash but fashioned a protective order designed to preserve confidentiality. The court rejected the res judicata and collateral estoppel arguments on the ground that "New York State discovery rules and rules [in federal court] are different." It rejected the privilege argument on the ground that no state court precedent definitively established such a privilege; the district court viewed the *Reynolds* court's decision as quashing the Page subpoenas on the ground of burdensomeness and viewed the state court's discussion of privilege as dictum. Finally, though Mount Sinai and ACS argued that even the process of redacting the materials would be burdensome, the court stated that it would not be necessary for Dr. Selikoff himself to perform all the redaction and that a scholar such as he should anticipate that others would wish to scrutinize the bases for his published work. It concluded that "the burdensomeness is not something which is unduly burdensome. . . ." Persuaded nonetheless that the study participants were entitled to some degree of privacy protection, the court entered a protective order granting the Mount Sinai-ACS motion in part. In relevant part, the protective order provides as follows:

> 1. The motion of Mount Sinai and the ACS for a protective order . . . is hereby GRANTED to the extent that Mount Sinai and the ACS may redact the names of the subjects of the two studies . . . , and their street addresses, town or village of residence, names of employers, social security numbers and union registration numbers, provided, however, that Mount Sinai and the ACS shall provide the county of residence of the subjects. The motion is DENIED in all other respects. . . .

> 3. All persons, parties or other entities who are permitted access to the subpoenaed documents . . . shall be . . . prohibited from using any of the information contained therein to identify or attempt to identify the names of any of the subjects of the two studies, and each such person, party or other entity shall execute an Acknowledgment, in the form annexed hereto. . . .
>
> 4. In the event that American, Reynolds or Philip Morris, or any other party, is served with a subpoena . . . or other discovery request . . . seeking production of the subpoenaed documents, such party shall request the person seeking the documents to execute an Acknowledgment as described in paragraph 3. If the person . . . refuses to execute an Acknowledgment and moves or applies to compel production, the party from whom such discovery is sought shall notify counsel for Mount Sinai and the ACS of such motion or application. . . .

The Acknowledgment would require any person seeking access to the data to "agree to be bound by the terms and conditions contained [in the protective order], and . . . consent to the jurisdiction of the Court for the enforcement thereof." The court rejected the Mount Sinai-ACS contention that considerations of physician-patient privilege required further redaction.

Eventually, following an aborted appeal to this Court, see In re American Tobacco Co., 866 F.2d 552, 556 (2d Cir. 1989) ("orders requiring production and denying a further protective order are not final in the absence of a contempt adjudication"), the district court held Mount Sinai and ACS in contempt when they refused to comply with the orders requiring them to respond to the subpoenas. The court imposed on them a sanction of $500 for each day that they remained in contempt, but stayed enforcement of that order pending appeal.

This appeal followed.

II. Discussion

On appeal, Mount Sinai and ACS contend principally that the district court erred in failing to give *Reynolds* the proper preclusive effect and in failing to recognize the state-law privileges afforded to experts and research scholars. In the alternative, they contend that the district court's protective order fails to protect adequately against disclosure of confidential information. We have considered all of their contentions and find no basis for reversal.

A. The Claimed Preclusive Effect of Reynolds

Mount Sinai and ACS contend that the present subpoenas arise out of the same operative facts and give rise to the same issues that were before the state court in *Reynolds* and that therefore principles of res judicata or collateral estoppel bar their enforcement. We disagree.

In order to determine the preclusive effect of the decision in *Reynolds*, we look to the law of New York. See Marrese v. American Academy of Orthopaedic Surgeons, 470 U.S. 373, 380 (1985) (federal court is to "refer to the preclusion law of the State in which judgment was rendered"). Under the transactional approach to res judicata adopted by New York, "once a claim is brought to a final conclusion, all other claims arising out of the same transaction . . . are barred, even if based upon different theories or if seeking a different remedy. . . ." O'Brien v. City of Syracuse, 429 N.E.2d 1158, 1159 (1981). Principles of collateral estoppel will bar relitigation of an issue that is identical to an issue which has necessarily been decided in the prior action. Ryan v. New York Telephone Co., 467 N.E.2d 487, 490 (1984). Issues are considered identical if a different decision in the second suit would necessarily "'destroy or impair rights or interests established by the first.'" Id., 467 N.E.2d at 490 (quoting Schuylkill Fuel Corp. v. B & C Nieberg Realty Corp., 165 N.E. 456 (1929) (Cardozo, J.)).

These principles have been applied in federal court to bar an attack on a subpoena, where a New York state court had previously denied a motion to quash an identical subpoena. Sreter v. Hynes, 419 F. Supp. 546, 548 (E.D.N.Y. 1976) (Pratt, J.); see also Westwood Chemical Co. v. Kulick, 656 F.2d 1224, 1227 (6th Cir. 1981) (res judicata barred party from deposing corporate officers where prior decision quashed subpoenas for depositions of other officers of the same corporation). Where, however, the first subpoena has been quashed as overly broad and a second subpoena is served which is clearly narrower or more specific, New York law does not give preclusive effect to the decision quashing the earlier subpoena. See, e.g., Cunningham and Kaming, P.C. v. Nadjari, 384 N.Y.S.2d 383 (1st Dept. 1976) (mem.). Rather, "any possible future subpoena[] . . . is to be examined on its own merits." Id. at 384.

. . . [T]he subpoenas at issue in the present case are plainly narrower than the subpoenas quashed in *Reynolds*. For example, whereas the Page subpoenas requested the raw data in its original form (e.g., interview notes, completed questionnaires, x-rays), the present subpoenas seek only the computer tapes plus such information as is necessary to interpret those tapes. Further, the present subpoenas, unlike the Page subpoenas, do not seek information that pertains to events occurring subsequent to the periods covered by the published articles.

Since the two sets of subpoenas are significantly different, the district court properly rejected the contention that enforcement of the present subpoenas was precluded by the decision in *Reynolds* quashing the broader subpoenas.

Mount Sinai and ACS also contend that they should not have been ordered to produce the subpoenaed materials in light of the state-law privileges accorded to experts and research scholars. Though in a diversity case the existence of a privilege is to be determined by reference to state law, Dixon v. 80 Pine Street Corp., 516 F.2d 1278, 1280 (2d Cir. 1975); see Fed. R. Evid. 501, an existing privilege should be interpreted no more broadly than necessary. Since privileges shielding information from the reach of the court "contravene the fundamental principle that 'the public . . . has a right to every man's evidence,'" such privileges "must be strictly construed." Trammel v. United States, 445 U.S. 40, 50 (1980) (quoting United States v. Bryan, 339 U.S. 323, 331 (1950)); see Gray v. Board of Higher Education, 692 F.2d 901, 904 (2d Cir. 1982). In light of these principles, we are unpersuaded that the orders of the district court should be overturned.

The claim to protection under the state-law privilege accorded to experts need not detain us long. In New York, experts who have no personal connection to a case enjoy an absolute privilege not to be compelled to give their opinions. Gilly v. City of New York, 508 N.E.2d 901, 901-902 (1987) (per curiam). This privilege has been extended to cover requests, pursuant to a subpoena, for preparation by an expert of a written medical report. See Plummer v. R.H. Macy & Co., 414 N.Y.S.2d 921 (1st Dept. 1979) (mem.).

In the present case, no expert is being asked to testify or to prepare a report. Mount Sinai and ACS have referred us to no New York decision extending the privilege to all existing documentary evidence in the possession of an expert, and our own research has revealed none. Accordingly, we conclude that this privilege is not applicable here.

In support of their claim to protection by a privilege accorded to research scholars, Mount Sinai and ACS are forced to rely on *Reynolds*, for no other New York case can be said to have recognized a scholar's privilege impeding production of research data. The Seventh Circuit has recognized such a qualified privilege, principally to protect scholars from the premature disclosure of their research, see, e.g., Deitchman v. E.R. Squibb & Sons, Inc., 740 F.2d 556, 560-561 (7th Cir. 1984); see also Dow Chemical Co. v. Allen, 672 F.2d 1262, 1274-1276 (7th Cir. 1982), and the *Reynolds* court, citing *Dow Chemical*, explored the possibility that there might be such a privilege. The *Reynolds* court discussed the interests of scholars in their research data, as it did concepts of academic freedom, and it concluded that such concepts were permissible considerations in determining whether to quash the broad subpoenas before it. The court focused primarily on the need to protect the scholar against threats of interference with his ongoing research and against the release of his research findings prior to having had his own opportunity to publish them. 518 N.Y.S.2d at 734.

It is not clear to us, however, that the decision in *Reynolds* establishes the existence of a scholar's privilege as a matter of New York law. The court's discussion was discursive, and its conclusion that the subpoenas should be quashed did not state that the ruling was based on the existence of a privilege. Its concern for burden was plain, as it noted that the Page subpoenas were "not selective" but rather were "sweeping and indiscriminate," and it repeatedly referred to the principles that control where subpoenas are "over-broad, burdensome or oppressive," or "so oppressive as to hinder the normal functioning" of the recipient, or where "the production of the material would become oppressive and unreasonably burdensome," or the burdens would be "unreasonable." Id. at 731-733. The court concluded its discussion by stating that a scholar's "interest in academic freedom may properly figure into the legal calculation of whether forced disclosure would be reasonable," and that for all the reasons discussed, compliance with the Page subpoenas would "place an unreasonable burden upon the medical and scientific institutions involved and would unduly disrupt the ongoing research at both Mount Sinai and the American Cancer Society." Id. at 734. In the absence of a more explicit ruling, it is possible that the court regarded the scholar's interest in his research data as merely a factor to be taken into account in weighing the burdens of production, and that it did not intend to rule that the scholar has a privilege protecting him from having to disclose that data.

Further, if the *Reynolds* court did mean to rule that there is such a privilege, it plainly did not mean to suggest that such a privilege was absolute, for the discussion reveals at least two limiting concerns. First, as discussed above, the court considered at some length whether production would be burdensome, a concern that would have no relevance in the context of an absolute privilege. Second, the court indicated that its concern for research scientists focused in part on their interest in being the first to publish the results of their studies. Thus, the court stated that "*[w]hile these medical investigations are still in progress,* they should not be subjected to examination and criticism by people whose interests are arguably antithetical to the medical scientists," for a premature disclosure "would have the effect of denying to these doctors the opportunity of *first publication* of their studies." Id. at 733-734 (emphasis added). . . . Even were we . . . to conclude that a qualified privilege does exist here, we cannot conclude that reversal is required. Where a qualified privilege is found to exist, a "court 'must apply a balancing test to determine whether the need of the party seeking disclosure outweighs the adverse effect such disclosure would have on the policies underlying the [claimed] privilege.'" Deitchman v. E.R. Squibb & Sons, Inc., 740 F.2d [556,] 559 [7th Cir. 1984] (quoting EEOC v. University of Notre Dame du Lac, 715 F.2d 331, 338 (7th Cir. 1983)) (brackets in *Deitchman*). On appeal, we will not disturb the district court's application of such a balancing test absent an abuse of discretion. . . .

The principal legitimate chilling effect on scientific research, adverted to by the *Reynolds* court, is the possibility that research results discovered prior to their publication would be vulnerable to preemptive or predatory publication by others. But this possibility does not appear to be a factor here since the tobacco companies have narrowed their subpoenas to request only data that was relied upon by Dr. Selikoff in preparing articles that were published some years ago.

Further, if the mere fact that production will require time and effort were dispositive, only rarely would any discovery attempt be successful since most gainfully employed discovery targets could contend that compliance would take time away from their regular work. And though it seems clear that Mount Sinai, ACS, and Dr. Selikoff will be burdened somewhat in complying with the subpoenas, much of the detailed redaction work required in the interests of confidentiality may undoubtedly be performed, given proper instructions, by someone other than Dr. Selikoff or his fellow researchers. The tobacco companies have offered to reimburse Mount Sinai and ACS for the reasonable expenses of compliance.

Finally, though it may be that the tobacco companies could conduct their own studies in an effort to controvert the findings of Dr. Selikoff, it seems that an inordinate length of time would be required in order to duplicate the Selikoff study, and it is clear that scrutiny of the Selikoff data would provide a logically permissible manner in which to attack the findings. Since Dr. Selikoff is acknowledged to be the preeminent authority in the area and it is anticipatable that the expert witnesses to be called by the plaintiffs in the underlying suits will rely on his findings, the district court was not required to relegate the tobacco companies to undertaking independent studies rather than pursuing the most direct method of attack on the Selikoff findings.

We are unpersuaded that a contrary result is required by the fact that the medical researchers have no direct interest in the underlying lawsuits. The publication of their findings and conclusions invites use by persons whom the findings favor and invites reliance by the finders of fact. The public has an interest in resolving disputes on the basis of accurate information. Though under New York law this interest does not warrant requiring scientists to testify or prepare reports in actions with which they have no personal connection, we doubt that New York law would recognize a privilege to withhold the data on which already published findings are based and thereby preclude direct scrutiny of the findings' validity. Thus, even assuming that there is a qualified privilege for research scientists under New York law, we conclude that the scientists may be required to produce data underlying their published findings.

This obligation should not, of course, be without reasonable limitations. We are concerned by the information, given us by counsel for Mount Sinai and ACS at oral argument of this appeal, that there are some 40 extant subpoenas in various lawsuits seeking the data underlying the Selikoff findings. Though we uphold the decision of the district court in the present case requiring compliance with the present subpoenas under the protective order fashioned by the court, we do not foreclose the possibility that repeated requests for production of such data could become unduly burdensome. It may be that any excessive burden could be averted by the creation of a central repository of such data to which current and future suitors could have access, with the proper provisions for confidentiality, or by resort to some other mechanism such as centralized discovery through multidistrict litigation, see 28 U.S.C. § 1407 (1982); see generally In re Asbestos and Asbestos Insulation Material Products Liability Litigation, 431 F. Supp. 906, 910 (J.P.M.L. 1977) (per curiam) (declining to transfer to one district 103 pending actions involving asbestos exposure "under the[] circumstances," where all parties opposed transfer and some actions were far more advanced than others).

We are persuaded, however, that the proper balancing of interests does not warrant a bar against disclosure but only protection against needlessly repetitive disclosures. Hence, in the present case, we conclude that even if

New York law recognizes a qualified privilege for research scholars, the decisions of the district court did not abrogate that privilege.

The protective order entered by the district court allows Mount Sinai and ACS to redact the names of the participants in the studies, their street addresses, towns or villages, social security numbers, employers, and union registration numbers. Mount Sinai and ACS contend that they should also be allowed to redact counties of residence and union local data and to summarize birth and death dates by decade. They assert that without these modifications, the tobacco companies and others could identify the subjects of the studies. We decline to modify the court's protective order.

District court decisions fashioning discovery protective orders are to be reversed only if there has been an abuse of discretion. See Galella v. Onassis, 487 F.2d 986, 997 (2d Cir. 1973). While it might be possible for the tobacco companies to determine the identities of some of the research participants from the information remaining on the computer tapes after the redactions ordered by the district court, the court has enjoined them from doing so. Thus, the protective order provides that "[a]ll persons . . . permitted access to the subpoenaed documents . . . shall be . . . prohibited from . . . identify[ing] or attempt[ing] to identify . . . the subjects of the two studies." Further, any person seeking access to the subpoenaed materials must first execute the Acknowledgment attached to the protective order, which subjects that person to the terms and conditions of the court's order. Presumably the court would impose suitable sanctions against any person who, in violation of these provisions, did attempt to identify a subject of the study. We cannot say that the court was required to grant further redactions as requested by Mount Sinai and ACS.

We also reject the contention that further redaction was required in order to preserve the physician-patient privilege. That privilege can be adequately protected by a court order that prohibits disclosure of the patient's identity. . . .

In sum, the protective order fashioned by the district court was not an abuse of discretion.

The orders of the district court are *affirmed.*

Note: The Tobacco Industry Lawyers—Hired Guns' Smoke

Mount Sinai is a small piece of the tobacco litigation of the 1990s that we will deal with at greater length in the next section, on class actions. You have seen little pieces of the tobacco litigation throughout the text, e.g., *Republic of Bolivia* in the venue section of this chapter. With stakes this high, lawyers for the industry are determined to be as protective of their clients' interests as possible. *Mount Sinai* betrays this tendency by the industry lawyers. Was their protective stance good lawyering or excessively adversarial? Consider the following excerpt from Professor

Rabin's article discussing the tobacco industry lawyers' conduct in these cases:

> . . . From the beginning, the cigarette companies decided that they would defend every claim, no matter what the cost, through trial and any possible appeals. Concomitantly, the companies decided that they would, as a first line of defense, spare no cost in exhausting their adversaries' resources short of the courthouse door.
>
> This no-compromise strategy . . . is unique in the annals of tort litigation. As a general proposition, personal injury lawyers estimate that more than 90 percent of accident claims result in settlement. More specifically, in mass tort litigation — that is, litigation involving a huge number of claims arising out of a single hazardous course of conduct or event, such as the asbestos, Dalkon Shield, and DES cases — there has always come a point when the beleaguered defense has decided that at least some of the persistently arising claims are worth settling. By contrast, over a period exceeding thirty-five years, the tobacco industry never offered to settle a single case.
>
> The cigarette companies' intransigence is simply explained by the size of the projected financial stakes as the initial cases arose in the mid-1950s. The industry was well aware of published figures indicating that in 1954 there were some 25,000 deaths reported from lung cancer, with the annual mortality rising steadily. Studies indicated that more than 60 percent of these deaths among males were attributable to cigarette smoking. It took no great mathematical sophistication to project the number of claims that might be brought against the industry each year if stricken smokers and personal injury lawyers came to believe that tort suits had a good chance of settling for a decent sum of money. The industry saw its very existence threatened and responded in an uncompromising fashion.
>
> The litigation process was, in fact, made to order for a stonewall defense in cigarette cases — as the industry and its attorneys well understood. Personal injury lawyers were, for the most part, lone wolves. They practiced alone or in very small firms, relying on the quick disposition of a high turnover caseload to survive — in some instances, to flourish — in a contingency fee system. Heavy front-end costs, which cannot realistically be recouped in a losing case from an impecunious client, are a major disincentive to involvement in high-risk cases. So, too, are lengthy pretrial delays without prospect of settlement; cash-flow concerns are endemic to contingency fee representation.
>
> The cigarette cases provided ample opportunity to exploit these defense advantages. To begin with, there was the necessity of relying on expert witnesses. From the outset, the industry hotly contested the causal linkage between smoking and lung cancer. Typically, the treating surgeon and various pathologists would be required to testify as to when the claimant contracted the disease, whether the claimant had the type of disease normally associated with smoking, and when the scientific literature first clearly indicated the risks of smoking. While some scientists were willing to volunteer their services on the plaintiff's behalf in the early smoking cases, expert testimony is nonetheless costly; apart from witness fees, there are the travel and time-related costs associated with pretrial depositions of experts on both sides of the case. Moreover, marketing and advertising experts —

and, in the second wave, addiction specialists as well — were essential witnesses if a comprehensive case was to be presented.

More generally, pretrial deposing offered massive leverage to the defense. Relevant litigation issues, such as how much the plaintiff knew about the risks of smoking and whether the plaintiff was generally indifferent to personal risk — issues that have remained salient through both waves of tobacco litigation — created an opening for, in effect, examining every dimension of the claimant's earlier conduct. The tobacco defense was quick to seize on this opportunity by engaging in seemingly endless pretrial interrogation.

But there were also more subtle aspects to the apparent juggernaut that the personal injury lawyer confronted in these cases, extending beyond a continuing onslaught of pretrial motions, procedural challenges, and deposition-taking. Beginning with the earliest cases, the tobacco companies retained counsel from the most prestigious law firms in the country. Those firms, in turn, closely coordinated their litigation efforts. Indeed, in some cases, where the plaintiff had switched brands, the companies were jointly sued and regularly retained local counsel to handle some aspects of the case (with an eye to the courthouse benefits of local counsel if it became necessary to try the case before a local jury). As a consequence, from the earliest pretrial stages, the plaintiff's lawyer, and perhaps an associate, might find ten or fifteen defense attorneys on the other side during the proceedings. . . .

[T]he plaintiffs without exception failed to realize a successful outcome. One reason is that they continued to be overmatched throughout the litigation process. This underlying reality of the litigation is perhaps most revealingly illustrated in an unpublished opinion, Thayer v. Liggett & Myers Tobacco Co., [No. 5314 (W.D. Mich. Feb. 20, 1970),] where the trial judge, stung by defense allegations of personal bias, catalogued in great detail the manner in which the tobacco company lawyers simply wore down the opposition through reliance on protective orders (isolating the plaintiffs from opportunities to collaborate or realize economies of work-product), mass deposing, multiple lawyering, intransigence, and delay. The case was ultimately dropped, at the point when the court was about to grant a new trial (after a defense verdict), due to, in the plaintiff's words, "prohibitive costs." Among the other . . . cases that managed to survive to trial, at least four of the ten were abandoned at some point during the litigation process.

Nor were the plaintiffs' attorneys overmatched only in resources. The cases reveal many instances of dubious lawyering. In Albright v. R.J. Reynolds Tobacco Co., [350 F. Supp. 341 (W.D. Pa. 1972), *aff'd*, 485 F.2d 678 (3d Cir. 1973), *cert. denied*, 416 U.S. 951 (1974),] the court dismissed the plaintiff's suit for failure to reserve the claim when settling a related action for damages against the city of Pittsburgh (plaintiff had argued that his lung cancer was exacerbated by an auto accident caused by the city's negligence). In Cooper v. R.J. Reynolds Tobacco Co., [234 F.2d 170 (1st Cir. 1956),] the claimant's allegation of deceptive advertising was based on a purported ad that, in response to interrogatories, the plaintiff could not produce. In Pritchard v. Liggett & Myers Tobacco Co., [350 F.2d 479, 486 (3d Cir. 1965), *cert. denied*, 382 U.S. 987 (1966),] and Padovani v. Liggett & Myers Tobacco Co., [27 F.R.D. 37, 37-38 (E.D.N.Y. 1961),] both of which were subsequently

> dropped, the court went on record to comment on the incompetence of plaintiffs' attorneys in handling various procedural aspects of the claims. A fairly clear picture emerges of a claimant group both outmanned and outgunned.

Robert Rabin, A Sociological History of the Tobacco Tort Litigation, 44 Stan. L. Rev. 853, 857-860 (1992).

Note: Unduly Burdensome Subpoenas

Recall that the court in *Mount Sinai* expressed concern that multiple requests for production of the scientific studies may become "unduly burdensome." Much of the opinion deals with the preclusion arguments. (On the latter, see Rule 45(c)(3)(A)(iii).) But "undue burden" is an independent ground for quashing a subpoena under Rule 45(c)(3)(A)(iv). As several circuit courts have recognized, this provision requires that a subpoena be quashed if "the burden of compliance with it would exceed the benefit of production of the material sought by it." Nw. Mem'l Hosp. v. Ashcroft, 362 F.3d 923, 927 (7th Cir. 2004) (citing Roberts v. Shawnee Mission Ford, Inc., 352 F.3d 358, 361-362 (8th Cir. 2003)); Misc. Docket Matter #1 v. Misc. Docket Matter #2, 197 F.3d 922, 926-927 (8th Cir. 1999); In re Sealed Case, 162 F.3d 670, 673-674 (D.C. Cir. 1998); Deitchman v. E.R. Squibb & Sons, Inc., 740 F. 2d 556, 563 (7th Cir. 1984)).

Northwestern Memorial is another controversial case involving hospitals. This time the federal government subpoenaed the medical records of women who received late-term abortions as part of an effort to defend the Partial-Birth Abortion Act Ban Act in litigation by certain doctors and pro-choice groups challenging the statute's constitutionality. The subpoena commanded the hospital to produce the records of a doctor for the hospital who performed the abortions, also a plaintiff and expert witness in the underlying case. As the following excerpt indicates, the court was deeply skeptical of the government's motive for seeking the private records of patients treated by the doctor:

> [The district court] pointed out that the "government seeks these records on the *possibility* that it may find something therein which would affect the testimony of Dr. Hammond adversely, that is, for its potential value in impeaching his credibility as a witness. What the government ignores in its argument is how little, if any, probative value lies within these patient records." He contrasted the dearth of probative value "with the potential loss of privacy that would ensue were these medical records used in a case in which the patient was not a party" and concluded that "the balance of harms resulting from disclosure severely out-weighs the loss to the government through non-disclosure."
>
> These findings were solidly based. The hospital had urged both the lack of probative value of the records and the loss of privacy by the patients. The government had responded in generalities, arguing that redaction would

eliminate any privacy concern and that since Dr. Hammond had "made assertions of fact about his experience and his patients that plaintiffs are using to support their claim that, without a health exception, the Act is unconstitutional," the government should be permitted to test those assertions; but the government had not indicated what assertions these were or how the records might bear on them. Although on appeal the hospital repeated at length its reasons for believing that the records sought by the government would have little or no probative value, the government's response in both its opening brief and its reply brief remained vague to the point of being evasive.

At the oral argument we pressed the government's lawyer repeatedly and hard for indications of what he hoped to learn from the hospital records, and drew a blank. (Contrary to our usual practice, we did not limit the length of the oral argument.) The lawyer did suggest that if Hammond testified that patients with leukemia are better off with the D & X procedure than with the conventional D & E procedure but the medical records indicate that not all abortion patients with leukemia undergo D & X abortions, this would both impeach Hammond and suggest that D & X is not the only medically safe abortion procedure available to pregnant women afflicted with leukemia. But such information would be unlikely to be found in Hammond's records, given his strongly expressed preference for using the D & X method in the case of patients in fragile health. The information would be much more likely to be found in the records of physicians who perform D & E rather than D & X abortions on such women. Those records, however, the government didn't seek.

We learned at argument for the first time that Dr. Hammond has been deposed in the New York litigation. The questions and answers in his deposition might illuminate the relevance of the medical records for impeachment of his testimony at the trial. But the government has made no effort to make the deposition a part of the record. . . .

Like the district judge, we think the balance weighs in favor of quashing the subpoena. The government does not deny that the hospital is an appropriate representative of the privacy interests of its patients. Parkson v. Central DuPage Hospital, 435 N.E.2d 140, 142 (Ill. App. 3d 1982). But it argues that since it is seeking only a limited number of records and they would be produced to it minus the information that would enable the identity of the patient to be determined, there is no hardship to either the hospital or the patients of compliance. The argument is unrealistic and incomplete. What is true is that the *administrative* hardship from compliance would be modest. But it is not the only or the main hardship. The natural sensitivity that people feel about the disclosure of their medical records—the sensitivity that lies behind HIPAA—is amplified when the records are of a procedure that Congress has now declared to be a crime. Even if all the women whose records the government seeks know what "redacted" means, they are bound to be skeptical that redaction will conceal their identity from the world. This is hardly a typical case in which medical records get drawn into a lawsuit. Reflecting the fierce emotions that the long-running controversy over the morality and legality of abortion has made combustible, the Partial-Birth Abortion Ban Act and the litigation challenging its constitutionality—and even more so the rash of suits around the country in which the Department of Justice has been seeking the hospital records of abortion patients — have generated enormous publicity. These women must know that, and doubtless they are also aware that hostility to abortion has at times erupted into violence, including criminal obstruction of entry into abortion clinics, the firebombing of clinics, and the assassination of physicians who perform abortions.

Some of these women will be afraid that when their redacted records are made a part of the trial record in New York, persons of their acquaintance, or skillful "Googlers," sifting the information contained in the medical records concerning each patient's medical and sex history, will put two and two together, "out" the 45 women, and thereby expose them to threats, humiliation, and obloquy. As the court pointed out in Parkson v. Central DuPage Hospital, 61 Ill. Dec. 651, 435 N.E.2d at 144, "whether the patients' identities would remain confidential by the exclusion of their names and identifying numbers is questionable at best. The patients' admit and discharge summaries arguably contain histories of the patients' prior and present medical conditions, information that in the cumulative can make the possibility of recognition very high." In its opening brief, as throughout the district court proceeding, the government expressly reserved the right, at a later date, to seek the identity of the patients whose records are produced. Pressed at argument, the government's lawyer abandoned the reservation; but we do not know what would prevent reconsideration should the government, the subpoena having been enforced, discover that particular medical records that it had obtained were incomplete, opaque, or ambiguous.

Even if there were no possibility that a patient's identity might be learned from a redacted medical record, there would be an invasion of privacy. Imagine if nude pictures of a woman, uploaded to the Internet without her consent though without identifying her by name, were downloaded in a foreign country by people who will never meet her. She would still feel that her privacy had been invaded. The revelation of the intimate details contained in the record of a late-term abortion may inflict a similar wound.

If Northwestern Memorial Hospital cannot shield the medical records of its abortion patients from disclosure in judicial proceedings, moreover, the hospital will lose the confidence of its patients, and persons with sensitive medical conditions may be inclined to turn elsewhere for medical treatment. It is not as if the government was seeking medical records from every hospital and clinic that performs late-term abortions, in which event women wanting assurance against the disclosure of their records would have nowhere to turn. It is Dr. Hammond's presence in the New York suit as plaintiff and expert that has resulted in the government's subpoenaing Northwestern Memorial Hospital.

The concerns that the hospital has articulated do not necessarily justify withholding probative evidence from the government; nor can the possibility that medical records of abortion patients would yield evidence germane to the constitutionality of the Partial-Birth Abortion Ban Act be gainsaid. A nearly identical state predecessor of the Act was invalidated by the Supreme Court in Stenberg v. Carhart, 530 U.S. 914 (2000), because it did not permit the D & X procedure in cases in which it is required to protect the health of the pregnant woman. Id. at 930-38. In response, the preamble to the Act contains a finding that the procedure is *never* required for health reasons. 117 Stat. 1201, § 2. The government concedes as it must that this finding, although entitled to respectful consideration, does not bind the courts. . . . The issue of medical necessity remains for determination at the trial in New York, where Dr. Hammond will testify that he believes there are situations in which the D & X procedure is medically indicated. The essential difference between that procedure and the conventional D & E procedure is that in the latter procedure the fetus is destroyed while it is still entirely within the womb, while in the former procedure it is destroyed after the lower extremities, and sometimes the torso, have emerged from the womb and only the head remains inside. It is because part of the fetus is outside the womb when the fetus is destroyed that the supporters of the Act describe the D & X procedure as "partial birth" abortion. Dr. Hammond and other D & X practitioners argue that because less of the fetus is in the womb there is less danger of cutting the woman's tissues with the sharp knives used to dismember the fetus's body in the conventional D & E procedure and causing hemorrhaging, and that if the woman is in fragile health avoiding that danger is medically indicated.

The merits of the dispute are for determination at trial. The only issue for us is whether, given that there is a potential psychological cost to the hospital's patients, and a potential cost in lost goodwill to the hospital itself, from the involuntary production of the medical records even as redacted, the cost is offset by the probative value of the records. The district judge presiding at the trial has said that the records are "relevant," and no doubt they are — in the attenuated sense in which non-privileged materials may be sought in discovery. "Relevant information need not be admissible at the trial if the discovery appears reasonably calculated to lead to the discovery of admissible evidence." Fed. R. Civ. P. 26(b)(1); see Oppenheimer Fund, Inc. v. Sanders, 437 U.S. 340, 350-52 (1978); CSC Holdings, Inc. v. Redisi, 309 F.3d 988, 995-96 (7th Cir. 2002). The trial judge has not opined on the *probative* value of the records, which appears to be meager.

The government has had repeated opportunities to articulate a use for the records that it seeks, and it has failed to do so. What it would like to prove at the trial in New York, to refute Dr. Hammond, is that D & E is always an adequate alternative, from the standpoint of a pregnant woman's health, to the D & X procedure. But the government has failed to explain how the record of a D & X abortion would show this. And it is not as if Hammond had relied on the medical records of his patients in preparing his expert testimony. (Had he done so, they would have had to be disclosed to the government under Fed. R. Civ. P. 26(a)(2).) He doesn't have the records, is not basing his testimony on them, and so far as appears doesn't even remember them.

None of the records is going to state that Dr. Hammond said that he performed a D & X although he believed that a D & E would be just as good. . . . We're still at a loss to understand what it hopes to gain from such discovery. (We begged the government's lawyer to be concrete.) Of course, not having seen the records, the government labors under a disadvantage, although it has surely seen other medical records. And of course, pretrial discovery is a fishing expedition and one can't know what one has caught until one fishes. But Fed. R. Civ. P. 45(c) allows the fish to object, and when they do so the fisherman has to come up with more than the government has been able to do in this case despite the excellence of its lawyers.

The Partial-Birth Abortion Ban Act was passed, as we said, in response to the Supreme Court's decision in the *Stenberg* case. *Stenberg* was one of a number of "first generation" partial-birth cases. . . . In one of the cases decided by this court, Hope Clinic v. Ryan, Dr. Hammond was both a plaintiff and an expert witness. Hope Clinic v. Ryan, 995 F. Supp. 847, 849-50 (N.D. Ill. 1998). Yet in *none* of these many cases, so far as either we or the government is aware, was it so much as suggested that patient records might contain information that would help answer the question, crucial then as now, whether the D & X procedure is ever medically necessary.

Although Hammond is a plaintiff in the New York case, presumably because he actually performs D & X abortions and wants to be allowed to continue doing so, he will be testifying as an expert medical witness. Of all experts who testify in court, physicians are probably the most common. Yet the government has cited to us no case before this one in which medical experts' patient records were used to impeach the expert (Langley v. Coughlin, 1989 WL 436675 (S.D.N.Y. June 19, 1989), rejected the attempt, in a helpful discussion), though in malpractice cases it is not uncommon to use redacted medical records bearing on the defendant's alleged negligence for impeachment. . . .

Were the government sincerely interested in whether D & X abortions are ever medically indicated, one would have expected it to seek from Northwestern Memorial Hospital statistics summarizing the hospital's experience with late-term abortions. Suppose the patients who undergo D & X abortions are identical in all material respects (age, health, number of weeks pregnant, and so on) to those who undergo procedures not forbidden by the Partial-Birth Abortion Ban Act. That would be potent evidence that the D & X procedure does not have a compelling health rationale. No such evidence has been sought, in contrast to Planned Parenthood Federation of America, Inc. v. Ashcroft, at Transcript 26 (Mar. 5, 2004). A variant of the suggested approach would be to obtain a random sample of late-term abortion records from various sources and then determine, through good statistical analysis, whether the patient characteristics that lead Dr. Hammond to perform a D & X lead other physicians to perform a conventional D & E instead, and whether there are differences in the health consequences for these two groups of women. If there are no differences, the government might have a good defense of the Act. Gathering records from Hammond's patients alone will not be useful; but if the government has *other* records (say, from VA hospitals) already in its files, then records of Hammond's procedures might enable a useful comparison. The government hasn't suggested doing anything like that either. Its motives in seeking individuals' medical records remain thoroughly obscure. . . .

The fact that quashing the subpoena comports with Illinois' medical-records privilege is a final factor in favor of the district order's action. As we held in Memorial Hospital for McHenry County v. Shadur, 664 F.2d 1058, 1061 (7th Cir. 1981), comity "impels federal courts to recognize state privileges where this can be accomplished at no substantial cost to federal substantive and procedural policy." See also United States v. One Parcel of Property Located at 31-33 York Street, 930 F.2d 139, 141 (2d Cir. 1991) (per curiam). Patients, physicians, and hospitals in Illinois rely on Illinois' strong policy of privacy of medical records. They cannot rely completely, for they are not entitled to count on the state privilege's being applied in federal court. But in a case such as this in which, so far as we can determine, applying the privilege would not interfere significantly with federal

> proceedings, comity has required us not to apply the Illinois privilege, but to consider with special care the arguments for quashing the subpoena on the basis of relative hardship under Fed. R. Civ. P. 45(c).

We asked whether the position taken by lawyers for the tobacco industry in *Mount Sinai* was good lawyering or excessively adversarial. What do you make of the government's position here? Why seek private medical records of abortion patients if, as the government all but conceded, their probative value is limited? How serious is the privacy concern in light of the government's claim that redaction will prevent the disclosure of any identifying information?

D. CLASS ACTIONS — AN INTRODUCTION (RULE 23)

1. Introduction

In the last decades of the twentieth century, Rule 23 stirred more controversy, reaped larger financial rewards (often for lawyers), and pressed the federal justice system harder than any other rule in the history of procedural law. Whole legal practices and entire law school courses are devoted to this joinder device, which allows representatives to sue on behalf of large numbers of unnamed others, who will be bound by the judgment. Originally, Rule 23 reflected an ancient equitable practice for resolving multiple claims arising out of communal harms. It provided for three kinds of class actions: "true, spurious and hybrid," with the designation turning on whether absent parties were bound by the judgment.

The Rule was little noted or used until 1966, when the present version was enacted in essentially the same form. In Class Action Dilemmas: Pursuing Public Goals for Private Gain (2000), Professor Deborah Hensler writes about the impulses for changing Rule 23 in the 1960s. She quotes John Frank, an influential member of the Advisory Committee, as saying that "the race relations echo of that decade was always in the committee room." Id. at 12. This version of the story of the modern class action finds its genesis in the need for more legal tools to fight discrimination. Others who were also there at the inception deny the grand purposes and say the major impulses behind the changes were to simplify the Rule and make it generally more usable. Id.

The classic argument for Rule 23 is that it enables claims that would otherwise be too small for individuals to mount. Thus, class actions breathe life into rights that would otherwise go unvindicated. Detractors point out that the device in effect may create rights and liabilities that would not otherwise exist. Moreover, the same reasons that made it economically infeasible for the individuals to sue also make it impossible for them to monitor the litigation, supervise the attorney, make decisions about whether to settle or continue — in short, to be a client. In the last section of our class action study, you will see how practice under Rule 23 arguably has created an alternative procedural universe where the focus of litigation is on the lawyer as entrepreneur. But we will start with the basics of the practice; instead of a problem case, we give you a district court judge parsing the Rule as he decides whether to certify a class.

In re Wells Fargo Home Mortgage Overtime Pay Litigation

527 F. Supp. 2d 1053 (N.D. Cal. 2007)

MARILYN HALL PATEL, District Judge.

Background

Plaintiffs in this MDL proceeding are current and former Home Mortgage Consultants (HMCs) employed by Wells Fargo from February 2001 to the present. The nationwide plaintiffs seek certification of two classes. First, plaintiffs seek to certify a class of HMCs who worked nationwide, but not in California,* pursuant to Federal Rule of Civil Procedure 23 to pursue claims for restitution under California's Unfair Competition Law, Cal. Bus. & Prof. Code sections 17200 et seq. ("UCL"). Second, plaintiffs seek to certify a nationwide collective action of non-California HMCs who affirmatively opt in to this case to pursue claims for damages under the Fair Labor Standards Act, 29 U.S.C. section 216(b) ("FLSA").** The UCL provides a vehicle for recovery of restitution predicated on an alleged violation of the FLSA [provisions for overtime pay].

Wells Fargo is a world-wide financial services company, with its headquarters in San Francisco, California. Wells Fargo is subject to the requirements of the FLSA. The exemption status of each position within Wells Fargo is determined by the Corporate Compensation department and the in-house legal department based on the duties and responsibilities of the position.

"Home Mortgage Consultant" is the title given to Wells Fargo employees who sell mortgages. Wells Fargo employs approximately 10,000 HMCs nationwide, and may have employed as many as 25,000 total over the past five years. Approximately 20% of HMCs are employed in California. HMCs are classified according to specialty. Approximately 90-95% of HMCs are designated as "prime" or "sub-prime," while the remaining HMCs are classified as "reverse," "emerging markets,"

* A putative class of California plaintiffs is being represented by a separate lead plaintiff and counsel, and has moved separately for class certification. The putative class in the instant motion consists of plaintiffs from all states other than California, and will be referred to as "the nationwide plaintiffs."

** [We omit discussion of the FLSA procedure for collective action. EDS.]

"renovation" and "builder." Plaintiffs claim that regardless of any variations among HMC classifications, all Wells Fargo HMCs have the same basic job duties and share virtually identical job descriptions.

The primary duty of all HMCs is to sell mortgage loan products. Plaintiffs claim that HMCs spend virtually all of their time in a Wells Fargo office while performing their sales duties, primarily through the use of office telephones and computers. Additionally, plaintiffs claim that HMCs spend considerable time engaged in clerical tasks associated with loan processing. The court notes that . . . plaintiffs' seventeen declarations are substantially identical in format and wording.

All HMCs are paid pursuant to the same basic compensation policy, whereby they receive commissions on the mortgage loans they sell. On January 1, 2005, Wells Fargo began paying HMCs a minimum "draw" of at least $2,000 per month. Prior to that time, there was no guaranteed minimum compensation for HMCs. Wells Fargo classifies all HMCs as "exempt" from the overtime requirements of the FLSA, and no records are kept of the amount of hours HMCs work. Plaintiffs claim that HMCs commonly work more than forty hours per week without additional overtime compensation.

In response to plaintiffs' seventeen HMC declarations, defendant has submitted sixty-seven declarations from other HMCs purporting to show a wide variety in employment experiences. Among defendant's declarants, the time spent working outside a Wells Fargo office ranges from 5-10% to nearly 100% of total time worked, depending upon a variety of factors related to each individual HMC. A similar range appears regarding the frequency with which HMCs are able to meet with their clients in person, and the amount of time spent meeting with clients. Additionally, defendant disputes plaintiffs' claim that HMCs spend a considerable amount of time on clerical tasks, asserting that HMCs who handle a high volume of loans have clerical assistants and that any office tasks performed by HMCs are performed directly in connection with loan originations. In terms of total hours worked, defendant's declarations show a range of thirty to sixty-five hours per week, in contrast to plaintiffs' assertion that HMCs commonly work more than forty hours per week. As with the California HMCs, defendant asserts that these variations in job experiences arise from the varying product specializations among nationwide HMCs. Additional factors affecting work experience include geographic location, work style preferences, compensation objectives, experience, target market and market forces.

Defendant also attacks the reliability of plaintiffs' declarations on a number of grounds. First, defendant cites the similarities and uniformity in the language among the seventeen declarations, suggesting that they are "cookie-cutter" declarations that do not reveal the true experiences of the purported declarants. Second, defendant asserts that nearly all of the declarations come from two offices in the Midwest, and therefore do not represent the 1,600 nationwide offices. Defendant additionally asserts that the declarants lack foundation to opine on the job duties of loan originators other than themselves. Finally, defendant notes that six of the seventeen declarants worked most or all of their time in a refinance center in Des Moines that was established to take advantage of a temporary refinance market, and therefore plaintiffs' declarations are not representative of Midwest HMCs either.

Defendant further claims that current HMCs prefer their current commission-based compensation system, regardless of specialization, and therefore would not benefit from a class action. In response to this, plaintiffs assert that the aim of this litigation is not to do away with Wells Fargo's current commission system, but only to bring the commission system in line with the requirements of the FLSA by establishing record-keeping practices and overtime compensation.

Additionally, plaintiffs attack the reliability of defendant's declarations, claiming that declarations from current employees of a defendant are inherently unreliable and possibly coerced. In a previous order in this litigation, this court noted the "heightened potential for coercion because where the absent class member and the defendant are involved in an ongoing business relationship, such as employer-employee, any communications are more likely to be coercive."

Reviewing the declarations as a whole, there are glaring reliability concerns on both sides. Plaintiffs' declarations represent a very small portion of the full range of HMCs and Wells Fargo locations, and are nearly identical in terms of language and substance. Defendant's declarations, though drawn from a wider sample of Wells Fargo employees and offices, are likewise selectively presented and carry within them possible pressure arising from ongoing employment relationships. It is unremarkable to conclude that both sets of declarations are litigation-driven, and drafted and selected to advance a preferred characterization of the facts. All declarations have therefore been carefully scrutinized.

Even taking these credibility concerns into consideration, however, certain key undisputed and undeniable facts arise. First, it is clear that, from Wells Fargo's perspective, all HMCs are treated exactly the same way in terms of exemption status and compensation. Additionally, the basic function and job description of each HMC is substantively identical—each HMC is charged with selling home mortgages to consumers, with certain differences arising based on the target customer base. Thus, from the perspective of Wells Fargo, there are substantial similarities in the manner in which HMCs are treated, and the manner in which their duties are designated.

From the perspective of individual HMCs, however, there are differences in day-to-day activities and overall employment experiences that cannot be ignored. Within the basic HMC framework, HMCs are given a great deal of flexibility and autonomy in terms of work style and the amount of time they spend working. Though selectively chosen, defendants' declarations indicate a certain degree of variability from one HMC to the next that the court must take into account when determining whether class certification or collective action certification is appropriate.

Legal Standard

I. Motion for Class Certification

A party seeking to certify a class must satisfy the four prerequisites enumerated in Rule 23(a), as well as at least one of the requirements of Rule 23(b). Under Rule 23(a), the party seeking class certification must establish: (1) that the class is so large that joinder of all members is impracticable (i.e., numerosity); (2) that there are one or more questions of law or fact common to the class (i.e., commonality); (3) that the named parties' claims are typical of the class (i.e., typicality); and (4) that the class representatives will fairly and adequately protect the interests of other members of the class (i.e., adequacy of representation). Fed. R. Civ. P. 23(a). In addition to satisfying these prerequisites, parties seeking class certification must show that the action is maintainable under Rule 23(b)(1), (2) or (3). See Rule 23(b). . . .

The party seeking class certification bears the burden of establishing that the requirements of Rules 23(a) and 23(b) have been met. See Zinser v. Accufix Research Inst., Inc., 253 F.3d 1180, 1188 (9th Cir. 2001), amended by 273 F.3d 1266 (9th Cir. 2001); Hanon v. Dataproducts Corp., 976 F.2d 497, 508 (9th Cir. 1992). However, in adjudicating a motion for class certification, the court accepts the allegations in the complaint as true so long as those allegations are sufficiently specific to permit an informed assessment as to whether the requirements of Rule 23 have been satisfied. See Blackie v. Barrack, 524 F.2d 891, 901 n. 17 (9th Cir. 1975). The merits of the class members' substantive claims are generally irrelevant to this inquiry. Eisen v. Carlisle & Jacquelin, 417 U.S. 156, 177-78 (1974); Moore v. Hughes Helicopters, Inc., 708 F.2d 475, 480 (9th Cir. 1983). However, courts are "at liberty to consider evidence which goes to the requirements of Rule 23 even though the evidence may also relate to the underlying merits of the case," and a court may only certify a class after a "rigorous analysis" as to whether the requirements have been satisfied. *Hanon*, 976 F.2d at 509. . . .

Discussion

I. Rule 23 Class Certification

Plaintiffs seek to certify the following class: "all persons who worked as Home Mortgage Consultants outside the state of California for Wells Fargo Bank, N.A. at any time between July 1, 2001 and the present." . . .

A. Rule 23(a) Requirements

1. Numerosity

Pursuant to Rule 23, the class must be "so numerous that joinder of all members is impracticable." Fed. R. Civ. P. 23(a)(1). Defendant acknowledges that the purported class includes approximately 15,000 persons. Accordingly, plaintiffs have satisfied the numerosity requirement.

2. *Commonality*

To fulfill the commonality prerequisite of Rule 23(a)(2), plaintiff must establish that there are questions of law or fact common to the class as a whole. Rule 23(a)(2) does not mandate that each member of the class be identically situated, but only that there be substantial questions of law or fact common to all. See Harris v. Palm Springs Alpine Estates, Inc., 329 F.2d 909, 914 (9th Cir. 1964). Individual variation among plaintiffs' questions of law and fact does not defeat underlying legal commonality, because "the existence of shared legal issues with divergent factual predicates is sufficient" to satisfy Rule 23. Hanlon v. Chrysler Corp., 150 F.3d 1011, 1019 (9th Cir. 1998).

Plaintiffs identify at least four common questions: (1) whether HMCs were properly classified as "exempt" from federal overtime and time-recording statutes; (2) whether Wells Fargo's conduct emanated from California, and thus whether the UCL may be appropriately applied to the class of nationwide plaintiffs; (3) whether Wells Fargo willfully failed to comply with the FLSA; and (4) whether Wells Fargo acted in good faith in classifying HMCs as exempt. Plaintiffs additionally claim that the affirmative defenses raised by defendant—exemption pursuant to the "outside sales" exemption and exemption pursuant to the administrative exemption—involve the common factual question of the HMCs' primary duty. The administrative exemption defense further raises the common question of whether HMCs are paid a salary pursuant to 29 C.F.R. section 541.200(a)(1). The outside sales exemption likewise raises the common factual issue of how certain kinds of work are classified, for example, whether interacting with real estate agents and title company employees outside the office constitutes sales activity. . . .

3. *Typicality*

Under Rule 23(a)(3), the claims of the representative plaintiff must be typical of the claims of the class. To be considered typical for purposes of class certification, the named plaintiff need not have suffered an identical wrong. See *Hanlon*, 150 F.3d at 1020. Rather, the claims of the putative class must be "fairly encompassed by the named plaintiff's claims." General Tel. Co. of the Southwest v. Falcon, 457 U.S. 147, 156 (1982).

Regarding typicality, named plaintiffs Perez and Perry both purportedly had the same job, same job duties, and were subject to the same company practices, policies and decisions that affected their ability to earn overtime wages. Defendants argue that plaintiffs have presented insufficient facts to establish that they adequately represent the 15,000 HMCs from the 1,600 Wells Fargo locations at issue in the nationwide class. Paul v. WinCo Foods, Inc., 2007 WL 1381794, at *4 (D. Idaho Feb. 16, 2007) (finding no typicality where the named plaintiffs "represented only one of the eight Idaho stores and only two the eighteen California locations" and had made only conclusory factual arguments in favor of typicality).

Although "[t]he hurdle imposed by the typicality requirement is not great," named plaintiffs must show more than common issues among themselves and the absent class members. Palmer v. Stassinos, 233 F.R.D. 546, 550 (N.D. Cal. 2006).

Defendants additionally cite testimony from the named plaintiffs indicating their lack of knowledge about the practices of other HMCs. Perez testified that he did not observe the comings and goings of the prime HMCs in his office, and never visited any other Wells Fargo office. Perry testified that he did not know what the other HMCs in his office were doing based on the independent nature of each HMC's business practice.

In sum, the named plaintiffs are typical of the absent class members to the extent that they are subject to the uniform compensation and employment policies that Wells Fargo applies to all HMCs. However, they have not shown that they are typical to the extent that such typicality depends on substantial similarities in day-to-day activities. In light of the fact that plaintiffs are challenging a company-wide policy, however, the fact that the named plaintiffs and the absent class members shared the same job title and were subject to the same policies at issue satisfies the typicality requirement.

4. *Adequacy*

Rule 23(a)(4) dictates that the representative plaintiff must fairly and adequately protect the interests of the class. To satisfy constitutional due process concerns, unnamed class members must be afforded adequate representation before entry of a judgment which binds them. See *Hanlon*, 150 F.3d at 1020 (citing Hansberry v. Lee, 311 U.S. 32, 42-43 (1940)). "Adequate representation depends on the qualifications of counsel for the representatives, an absence of antagonism, a sharing of interests between representatives and absentees, and the unlikelihood that the suit is collusive." Crawford v. Honig, 37 F.3d 485, 487 (9th Cir. 1994).

Plaintiffs assert that the named plaintiffs have no known conflicts with members of the class of HMCs and will fairly and adequately protect the interests of the class. Plaintiffs further claim that their counsel is sufficiently experienced in class and collective actions nationwide regarding wage and hour disputes to provide adequate legal representation to the class.

In response, defendant claims that the nationwide plaintiffs are inadequate representatives because, as former employees, their interests are antagonistic to those of current HMCs. Defendant has cited declarations from several non-California HMCs stating that they prefer the commission-based system due to increased flexibility, control over individual work responsibilities, and the direct correlation between amount of work and compensation level. As noted above, plaintiffs strenuously deny that the end result of a successful class action lawsuit will be to eliminate Wells Fargo's commission-based compensation structure, and therefore assert that these objections are irrelevant.

While courts have held that a former employee may not represent the best interests of current employees where the relief sought may strain the employment relationship between current employees and a defendant employer, defendant has identified no authority stating that former employees are inadequate *per se*. Although the named plaintiffs in this action are primarily concerned with a maximum financial recovery, a determination that current and former employees are entitled to overtime compensation would likely lead to changes within Wells Fargo that would benefit current employees going forward. In other words, defendants have not shown that current employees would be harmed by a successful class action. Accordingly, the named plaintiffs satisfy the adequacy requirement of Rule 23(a).

B. Rule 23(b)(3) Requirements

Class certification pursuant to Rule 23(b)(3) requires the plaintiff to establish that "the questions of law or fact common to the members of the class predominate over any questions affecting only individual members, and that a class action is superior to other available methods for the fair and efficient adjudication of the controversy." The court will address each of these two requirements separately.

1. Predominance

The predominance inquiry "focuses on the relationship between the common and individual issues." Local Joint Executive Bd. of Culinary/Bartender Trust Fund v. Las Vegas Sands, Inc., 244 F.3d 1152, 1162 (9th Cir. 2001). Consequently, the presence of common issues of fact or law sufficient to satisfy the requirements of Rule 23(a)(2) is not by itself sufficient to show that those common issues predominate. *Hanlon*, 150 F.3d at 1022. Nonetheless, "[w]hen common questions present a significant aspect of the case and they can be resolved for all members of the class in a single adjudication, there is clear justification for handling the dispute on a representative rather than on an individual basis." Id. To establish predominance of common issues, a party seeking class certification is not required to show that the legal and factual issues raised by the claims of each class member are identical. Rather, the predominance inquiry focuses on whether the proposed class is "sufficiently cohesive to warrant adjudication by representation." *Culinary/Bartender Trust Fund*, 244 F.3d at 1162. Among the considerations that are central to this inquiry is "the notion that the adjudication of common issues will help achieve judicial economy." *Zinser*, 253 F.3d at 1189.

Plaintiffs assert that the two main questions in this litigation are common to the class. It is clear that the question of whether Wells Fargo's conduct regarding exemption classifications emanated from California is a common question, focusing only on the practices of a handful of individuals within the company. However, plaintiffs further claim that the question of whether HMCs are properly classified as exempt is common as well. Plaintiffs' main point in support of this contention is the fact that Wells Fargo uniformly treats all HMCs as exempt, regardless of any purported variations in duties or work activities. Defendant does not deny that its HMC compensation policy is uniform for all HMCs, and has confirmed that it does not maintain records of hours worked by HMCs.

In the context of overtime pay litigation, courts have often found that common issues predominate where an employer treats the putative class members uniformly with respect to compensation, even where the party opposing class certification presents evidence of individualized variations. For example, in Wang v. Chinese Daily News, 231 F.R.D. 602, 613 (C.D. Cal. 2005), the court held that the defendant "cannot, on the one hand, argue that all [putative class members] are exempt from overtime wages and, on the other hand, argue that the Court must inquire into the job duties of each [putative class member] in order to determine whether that individual is 'exempt.'" . . .

It is undisputed that Wells Fargo's compensation and exemption policy is uniform among all HMCs. Plaintiffs have submitted evidence of other uniform polices regarding HMCs, such as training, recruiting and job descriptions. Accordingly, plaintiffs have made a strong showing that, as a general matter, common questions related to HMC experiences predominate over individual variations. However, courts have recognized that the application of certain specific statutory exemptions requires a highly individualized inquiry, and have resisted class certification on that basis. See, e.g., Perry v. U.S. Bank, No. 2001 WL 34920473 (N.D. Cal. Oct. 16, 2001). In *Perry*, the court denied certification of a class of personal bankers seeking overtime compensation, based on the individual nature of the exemptions. Accordingly, the court will consider the specific exemptions identified by defendant in order to determine whether these exemptions raise predominant individual factual and legal issues.

2. *Exemptions*

Defendant identifies four federal exemptions in its opposition brief: (1) the outside sales exemption, (2) the commissioned sales exemption, (3) the administrative exemption, and (4) the highly paid exemption. The court will consider each exemption in turn.

a. Outside Sales Exemption. Under federal law, employees classified as "outside salespersons" are exempt from overtime requirements. 29 U.S.C. § 213(a)(1). An "outside salesman" is defined as an employee whose primary duty is "(i) making sales . . . , or (ii) obtaining orders or contracts for services or for the use of facilities for which a consideration will be paid by the client or customer; and (2) who is customarily and regularly engaged away from the employer's place or places of business in performing such primary duty." 29 C.F.R. § 541.500(a). Additionally, "work performed incidental to and in conjunction with the employee's own outside sales or solicitations . . . shall be regarded as exempt outside sales work." 29 C.F.R. § 541.500(b). The United States Department of Labor has stated that the outside sales exemption may apply to "employees of finance companies who obtain and solicit mortgages."

Courts have acknowledged that "where liability to each plaintiff will depend on whether that plaintiff was correctly classified as an 'outside salesman,' the Court will be required to make a fact-intensive inquiry into each potential plaintiff's employment situation" and that class certification may therefore be inappropriate. Clausman v. Nortel Networks, Inc., 2003 WL 21314065, at *4 (S.D. Ind. May 1, 2003). Defendant's declarations suggest a wide variation among HMCs in terms of the amount of time spent on outside sales activities, depending on personal preference, experience, efficiency and reliance on support staff.

b. Commissioned Sales Exemption. Federal law provides an exemption for any employee of a "retail or service establishment" where the employee's regular pay rate exceeds one and one half times the minimum wage and "more than half his compensation for a representative period (not less than one month) represents commissions on goods or services." 29 U.S.C. § 207(I). It is unclear whether Wells Fargo would qualify as a "retail or service establishment" for the purposes of this exemption. See Barnett v. Wash. Mut. Bank, FA, 2004 WL 1753400, at *6 (N.D. Cal. Aug. 5, 2004) (holding that credit companies are not "retail or service establishments"); Gatto, 442 F. Supp. 2d at 541-42 (holding that a mortgage broker fit within the definition); see also Martin v. Refrigeration School, Inc., 968 F.2d 3, 5 (9th Cir. 1992) ("The meaning of the term 'retail establishment' is not obvious without further definition, and the statutory definition is of little assistance."). In any case, the question of whether Wells Fargo is a "retail or service establishment" is common to the entire class and does not defeat class certification.

As with the outside sales exemption, a determination of liability pursuant to the commissioned sales exemption will require an individualized inquiry as to the amount and breakdown of each class member's compensation, as well as the amount of time worked by each HMC.

c. Administrative Exemption. The FLSA additionally exempts employees employed in an administrative capacity from overtime requirements. 29 U.S.C. § 213(a). . . . The Department of Labor has stated that employees who service their employer's financial services business by marketing, servicing and promoting financial products, advising customers and recommending products may fall within this exemption. "However, an employee whose *primary* duty is selling financial products does not qualify for the administrative exemption." 29 C.F.R. § 541.203 (emphasis added). In light of this authority, plaintiff has made a strong showing that the administrative exemption may be categorically inapplicable and therefore resolved on a class-wide basis. This favors class certification.

d. Highly Paid Exemption. As a final exemption, Wells Fargo claims that the HMCs are exempt under the federal statute exempting highly compensated employees from overtime laws. Under federal law, "An employee with total annual compensation of at least $100,000 is deemed exempt under section 13(a)(1) of the Act if the employee customarily and regularly performs any one or more of the exempt duties or responsibilities of an executive, administrative or professional employee identified in subparts B, C or D of this part." 29 C.F.R. § 541.601. This, again, will involve an individualized analysis not only of job duties but of the dollar amount of each HMC's compensation.

3. *Conclusion as to Predominance*

Taken together, defendants' declarations have raised serious issues regarding individual variations among HMC job duties and experiences. However, the common factual and legal issues nonetheless predominate. Wells Fargo's uniform policies regarding HMCs weigh heavily in favor of class certification. As numerous courts have recognized, it is manifestly disingenuous for a company to treat a class of employees as a homogenous group for the purposes of internal policies and compensation, and then assert that the same group is too diverse for class treatment in overtime litigation. This is particularly true in a situation such as this, where the difficulty of proving hours worked and compensation received is exacerbated by defendant's complete failure to maintain pertinent records. Accordingly, plaintiffs have satisfied their burden and demonstrated that common issues predominate.

4. *Superiority*

The final prerequisite for certification of a class under Rule 23(b)(3) requires the plaintiff to show that a class action is superior to other methods available for the adjudication of the parties' dispute. "Where classwide litigation of common issues will reduce litigation costs and promote greater efficiency, a class action may be superior to other methods of litigation." *Valentino*, 97 F.3d at 1234. In considering whether a class action is superior, the court must focus on whether the interests of "efficiency and economy" would be advanced by class treatment. *Zinser*, 253 F.3d at 1189. Relevant factors include:

> (A) the interest of members of the class in individually controlling the prosecution or defense of separate actions; (B) the extent and nature of any litigation concerning the controversy already commenced by or against members of the class; (C) the desirability or undesirability of concentrating the litigation of the claims in the particular forum; (D) the difficulties likely to be encountered in the management of a class action.

Fed. R. Civ. P. 23(b)(3).

a. Case Management. Plaintiffs contend that a class action would be superior to individual actions because representative litigation is particularly useful in suits by employees against an employer, and because the various actions that have been previously filed against Wells Fargo regarding HMC overtime compensation have already been consolidated as an MDL action. Defendant claims that the myriad factual issues pertaining to each of the HMCs at each of the numerous Wells Fargo locations throughout the country would make class action case management impracticable and therefore inferior. Defendant further claims that it would be denied due process if the court made determinations regarding a small number of HMCs and then extrapolated those results to the thousands of class members, in light of the individualized analysis required before liability may be determined. Additionally, defendant asserts that the "level of discord" among the putative class members militates against certification. Plaintiffs were also given the names and contact information of 500 putative class members, and have submitted only seventeen declarations in support of their motion. Furthermore, at least one plaintiff is pursuing an FLSA claim individually. Finally, at least some HMCs are content with the present arrangement and would not support a lawsuit geared at altering Wells Fargo's HMC compensation system. However, plaintiffs insist that the current compensation arrangement would not be unduly disturbed by a successful outcome for the plaintiffs, and this purported "discord" is therefore overstated.

As discussed above, many of the issues in this litigation focus on Wells Fargo's policies and practices, including whether any improper classifications were made willfully. Because individual class members have little bearing on these issues, efficiency would be better served by trying these issues on a class-wide basis. Furthermore, although many of the purported exemptions involve individual factual inquiries, plaintiffs have raised categorical challenges to the application of these exemptions which may be resolved on a class-wide basis. In light of the predominance of these common issues over any individualized factual issues, considerations of case management favor class treatment.

b. Alternative Remedies. . . . Defendant claims that pendent state law claims, to the extent they are present in this action, can be litigated as a separate FLSA opt-in action, and therefore class certification of the UCL claim is unnecessary. Defendant further claims that the individual potential recoveries are sufficiently large that HMCs would pursue individual claims if desired.

While the existence of alternative remedies is a factor weighing against class certification, the substantial predominance of common issues coupled with case management techniques tip the balance in favor of class treatment. Plaintiffs have therefore shown that a class action is a superior means of resolving this dispute.

C. Alternative Rule 23 Arguments

In the alternative to a Rule 23(b)(3) action, plaintiffs seek certification pursuant to Rule 23(b)(2) or Rule 23(c)(4)(A).

1. Rule 23(b)(2)

A party seeking certification of a class under Rule 23(b)(2) also bears the burden of establishing that "the party opposing the class has acted or refused to act on grounds generally applicable to the class, thereby making" injunctive relief appropriate. Fed. R. Civ. P. 23(b)(2). Class actions certified under Rule 23(b)(2) are "not limited to actions requesting only injunctive or declaratory relief, but may include cases that also seek monetary damages" where the claim for injunctive relief is the primary claim. Probe v. State Teachers' Ret. Sys., 780 F.2d 776, 780 (9th Cir. 1986). Rule 23(b)(2) certification of a class seeking both injunctive relief and damages is proper only where the claim for injunctive relief is the predominant form of relief sought by the class. See Arnold v. United Artists Theatre Circuit, Inc., 158 F.R.D. 439, 450-51 (N.D. Cal. 1994).

Plaintiff asserts that this action is suitable for Rule 23(b)(2) certification because a ruling that defendants have improperly classified HMCs as exempt would amount to an injunction forcing Wells Fargo to change its policies and practices, and that Wells Fargo could not continue to classify its HMCs as exempt after such a contrary ruling.

In the employment context, courts routinely deny class certification under Rule 23(b)(2) where the named plaintiffs are former employees and therefore will not benefit from any injunctive relief. See, e.g., Jimenez v. Domino's Pizza, Inc., 238 F.R.D. 241, 250 (C.D. Cal. 2006) (holding that claims for monetary relief predominated where plaintiffs were "former employees and thus an injunction as to Domino's behavior to current employees cannot be Plaintiffs' primary concern"). . . . Here, plaintiff is a former employee, and the proposed class definition explicitly envisions a certain proportion of former employees. Accordingly, the predominant claims in this action are monetary, and certification under Rule 23(b)(2) is not available.

2. Rule 23(c)(4)(A)

Rule 23(c) (4)(A) provides that, where appropriate, "an action may be brought or maintained as a class action with respect to particular issues." . . . Because the court has found that common issues predominate over individual issues for the purposes of Rule 23(b)(3), certification under Rule 23(c)(4)(A) is inappropriate. . . .

Conclusion

For the foregoing reasons, plaintiffs' motion for class certification is Granted in part and Denied in Part. Plaintiffs' motion to certify pursuant to Rule 23(b)(2) and Rule 23(c)(A)(4) is Denied. Plaintiffs' motion to certify pursuant to Rule 23(b)(3) is Granted. . . .

Within thirty (30) days of the date of this order the parties shall submit a form or forms of class notice and other appropriate papers to facilitate this order. The Clerk of Court shall set a further Case Management Conference within forty-five (45) days of this order.

Is so ordered.

Notes and Questions

1. *Adequacy of Representation.* Perhaps the most crucial requirement under Rule 23 is that the class representative be "adequate." You can quickly see why this is so, given your extended review of procedural due process in Chapter 1. A class action permits a representative to litigate on behalf of people who are not parties in the usual sense anticipated by the adversary model. The rights of all class members who are properly represented nevertheless are resolved by the lawsuit, without their *own* day in court. Moreover, the rules do not allow represented parties to opt out of the class action in every instance. See Comment 2, infra. Finally, the notice of the suit may not be actually received by all class members, to the extent that their whereabouts may be unknown or they may not receive or comprehend the notice given. See section (ii), infra. Do you see the potential due process issues? The broader implications for the functions of adjudication, as commonly understood? Does a class action satisfy the individual's interest in autonomy and participation as fully as does a single-plaintiff or single-defendant lawsuit? Are deterrence, compensation, and distributional justice ends met adequately by the class action device? Is the expressive nature of a class action suit comparable to that of any individual suit? See Clement v. Am. Honda Fin. Corp., 176 F.R.D. 15 (D. Conn. 1997) (rejecting proposed settlement on ground that it short-changed class members in favor of defendant car leasing company and the attorneys who negotiated the settlement); Epstein v. MCA, Inc., 126 F.3d 1235 (9th Cir. 1997) (concluding that settlement of class action claims violated plaintiffs' rights to adequate representation where it relinquished the right to pursue unasserted federal and state claims).

For a discussion of the problem of intra-group political dissension and its implications for competing procedural and ethical models of class action representations, see William B. Rubenstein, Divided We Litigate: Addressing Disputes Among Group Members and Lawyers in Civil Rights Campaigns, 106 Yale L.J. 1623 (1997). Cf. Marcel Kahan and Linda Silberman, The Inadequate Search for "Adequacy" in Class Actions: A Critique of Epstein v. MCA, Inc., 73 N.Y.U. L. Rev. 765 (1998) (arguing that offering absent class members a broad right to collaterally attack the adequacy of representation is potentially wasteful and may invite forum shopping). See also Richard L. Marcus, Reexamining the Bendectin Litigation Story, 83 Iowa L. Rev. 231, 239 (1977) (reviewing Michael D. Green, Bendectin and Birth Defects: The Challenges of Mass Toxic Substances

Litigation (1996), and noting that "critics of settlement classes can find considerable evidence for their fears in the Bendectin litigation story").

2. *Opting Out: Constitutionally Required?* Look carefully at Rule 23 to determine when a class member can "opt out" of a class action. You will see that not all class members receive this option. How can this be squared with due process? Does it all depend on the adequacy of representation?

The issue continues to divide courts and commentators. In Ticor Title Ins. Co. v. Brown, 114 S. Ct. 1359 (1994), the Court dismissed as "improvidently granted" a writ of certiorari granted to review a decision that due process bars giving preclusive effect to a judgment in a class action suit involving money damages against a plaintiff who had not been given an opportunity to opt out. The Court's refusal to hear the case leaves unresolved whether the non-opt-out provisions of Rules 23(b)(1) and 23(b)(2) are constitutional. See Note, Class Actions in the Asbestos Context: Balancing the Due Process Considerations Implicated by the Right to Opt Out, 70 Tex. L. Rev. 211 (1991).

3. *Predominance of Class Questions.* The requirement that common questions of law or fact should not merely exist, but predominate, has proved nettlesome. It has been especially troublesome in cases that attempt to apply to large classes substantive law drafted with individual claims in mind. In particular, securities and antitrust class actions have absorbed much judicial energy as courts decide whether the elements of these causes of action can be applied to thousands of litigants in one suit without that suit splintering hopelessly into individual trials. Some courts have developed the bifurcated trial, in which elements of the action deemed sufficiently common are heard in one trial and other elements receive individual trial, e.g., Green v. Wolf, 406 F.2d 291, 301 (2d Cir. 1968), *cert. denied*, 395 U.S. 977 (1968). Other courts have simply dismissed the suit as unmanageable as a class action, e.g., Windham v. Am. Brands, Inc., 565 F.2d 59 (4th Cir. 1977). Still other courts have subtly modified the substantive law to accommodate mass claims, loosening or even omitting elements of the action that otherwise would have to be proven for each class member.

Take, for example, Rule 10b-5 of the securities law, which provides a federal remedy for fraud in securities transactions. Two elements of an action under Rule 10b-5 are materiality of the misrepresentation and the plaintiff's reliance on information that he believed to be improperly disclosed — in other words, he thought he was a "tippee," and therefore should not be allowed to recover damages lost, in part, through his own dishonesty. Each of these issues can turn on very particular aspects of individual transactions. Yet there has been an impulse to treat these claims in class actions substituting generalized proof regarding the whole class for the individualized proof originally required. In short, the substantive law has been changed. The need for generalized rather than individual issues has caused the courts to alter or abandon elements of the law that required a certain state of mind on the part of plaintiffs; the class action has thus created a new emphasis in securities laws on the inquiries that are important in strict liability situations, which are amenable to class treatment.

Similar issues have arisen in antitrust cases. For instance, in a price-fixing action under § 1 of the Sherman Antitrust Act, the plaintiff must establish 1) conspiracy to violate the law, 2) the fact that the violation injured the plaintiff, and 3) the extent of the plaintiff's damages. Courts in general have held that the extent of damages will simply have to be heard individually and that the conspiracy will be a common question, e.g., In re Sugar Antitrust Litigation, 559 F.2d 481 (9th Cir. 1977). But the fact of injury, or the causal connection between the defendant's behavior and plaintiff's loss, has proven more problematic. In cases involving only one price-fixed product and uniform market conditions, the fact of injury can easily be proven for all plaintiffs at once.

But as fact situations become more complex, it becomes impossible to prove the fact of injury for the whole class without separate trials. For instance, in Windham v. American Brands, Inc., 565 F.2d 59 (4th Cir. 1977), the plaintiff class alleged a price-fixing conspiracy in the sale of tobacco. The tobacco was classified into 161 grades, and price varied according to the grade and market at which the tobacco was sold. In order to prove the fact of injury, the plaintiffs would have had to show that the conspiracy affected the price of each grade and at each warehouse where class members bought tobacco. The plaintiffs urged the court to accept generalized proof of injury, but the court refused, finding the proposal an invitation to alter the substantive rights of the parties, in contravention of the command of the Rules Enabling Act. If the existence and extent of the injury could not be proven with any accuracy, the court would not award damages; the class certification was reversed. Accord Alabama v. Blue Bird Body Co., 573 F.2d 309 (5th Cir. 1979).

In contrast, other courts that are less concerned with precision have allowed injury to be inferred from the existence of a conspiracy and the purchase of the product in question. The Second Circuit in In re Master Key Antitrust Litigation, 70 F.R.D. 23, 26 n.5 (D. Conn. 1975), *appeal dismissed,* 528 F.2d 5 (2d Cir. 1975), stated: "If the plaintiffs introduce proof . . . that they bought master key systems and that the defendants engaged in a pervasive nationwide course of action that had the effect of stabilizing prices at supra-competitive levels, the jury may conclude that the defendants' conduct caused injury to each plaintiff." Other courts have gone even further to *presume* injury in such a situation, rather than merely allowing an inference of injury, e.g., In re Folding Carton Antitrust Litig., 75 F.R.D. 727, 734 (N.D. Ill. 1977). Thus, the burden of proof on one element of the claim has been shifted from plaintiff to defendant to accommodate the class action procedure.

Yet if the class action is not always a substantively neutral influence, neither does it always have to work against the defendant. The authors of Note, Developments in the Law—Class Action, 89 Harv. L. Rev. 1318 (1976), argue that by bringing the large number of interested parties in a controversy before the court all at once, there is the important substantive influence of forcing the court to see the situation in its entirety, rather than simply adjudicating between two of the many possible litigants. This aspect the authors call "the heuristic function" of class action.

Predominance concerns arise in other contexts as well, perhaps none more controversial than class action suits alleging discrimination under Title VII. The costs of providing notice in Rule 23(b)(3) class actions, and the problem of proving that common questions of law or fact "predominate," create a strong incentive for discrimination plaintiffs to frame their suit under Rule 23(b)(1) or 23(b)(2). Indeed, discrimination is precisely the sort of group-based conduct the Advisory Committee had in mind when it amended Rule 23(b)(2) in 1966. But plaintiffs often run into another "predominance" hurdle.

Consider how a court should treat an attempt to certify a discrimination class action under Rule 23(b)(2) when plaintiffs, in addition to requesting injunctive relief, request compensatory damages for individual class members. What inference should be drawn from the fact that the Advisory Committee Notes say Rule 23(b)(2) is not intended to cover situations where the requested relief "relates exclusively or *predominantly* to money damages" (emphasis added)?

The circuit courts are divided. See Allison v. Citgo Petroleum Corp, 151 F.3d 402, 415 (5th Cir. 1998) (holding that while monetary relief is not totally inconsistent with proceeding under Rule 23(b)(2), a class action shall not proceed under Rule 23(b)(2) unless monetary relief "is incidental to requested injunctive or declaratory relief"), followed in Reeb v. Ohio Dep't of Rehab. & Corr., 435 F.3d 639, 641, 651 (6th Cir. 2006) ("[B]ecause of the individualized nature of damages calculations for Title VII plaintiffs and the ability of those plaintiffs to bring individual actions, the claims for individual compensatory damages of members of a Title VII class necessarily predominate over requested declaratory or injunctive relief, and individual compensatory damages are not recoverable by a Rule 23(b)(2) class"; reversing the district court for failing to conduct a "rigorous analysis" of the Rule 23(a) certification requirements), Murray v. Auslander, 244 F.3d 807 (11th Cir. 2001), and Lemon v. Int'l Union of Operating Eng'rs, Local No. 139, 216 F.3d 577, 581 (7th Cir. 2000). But see Molski v. Gleich, 318 F.3d 937, 950 (9th Cir. 2003) (rejecting *Allison* approach because it "would nullify the discretion vested in the district courts through Rule 23" and would have "troubling implications for the viability of future civil rights actions" since compensatory damages were authorized in the Civil Rights Act of 1991); Robinson v. Metro-North Commuter R.R. Co., 267 F.3d 147, 164 (2d Cir. 2001) (adopting a more flexible balancing test focusing on whether injunctive or declaratory relief would be sought even in the absence of monetary remedies).

4. *Consumer-Type Class Actions. Wells Fargo* is an example of a case where the "little person" who is hurt might not choose to litigate because the potential gain (some overtime pay) is not obviously worth the cost of

litigation. The same is even more true of individuals overcharged for their phone service, or a pair of jeans, or a prescription pill. Though admirers of the class action device think it was made for exactly these kinds of aggregate small injuries, there is not universal agreement even on this apparent purpose for Rule 23.

In a classic article, Professor Jonathan Landers attacked the use of class actions as a means of vindicating small claims:

> To consumerists, the consumer class action is an inviting procedural device to cope with frauds causing small damages to large groups. The slight loss to the individual, when aggregated in the coffers of the wrongdoers, results in gains which are both handsome and tempting. The alternatives to the class action—private suits or governmental actions—have been so often found wanting in controlling consumer frauds that not even the ardent critics of class actions seriously contend that they are truly effective. The consumer class action, when brought by those who have no other avenue of legal redress, provides restitution to the injured, and deterrence of the wrongdoer. Since both of these objectives are, at least partially, goals of the legal system itself, the class action device cannot be all bad.
>
> There is, however, another side of the coin. One can perceive the legal system as set up from a functional point of view to deter the bringing of small claims. Just as consumers have no effective redress within the legal system for small injuries in the absence of the class action device, business concerns are similarly afflicted. The business confronted with unpaid accounts or minor damage claims of a few dollars or even a few hundred dollars is no more able to sue than is the consumer. Many businesses regularly "write off" such small claims, and others turn such claims over to collection agencies which may retain 50 percent of an account in fees. Even those states which have small claims courts frequently prevent business use of the courts either by absolute prohibition, or by such methods as limiting the maximum number of suits which can be filed within a year. Hence, one might argue that in an increasingly complex, impersonal, and interdependent society, there will be an ever increasing number of small grievances and minor disputes, and that such matters are better handled by allowing the loss to lie where it falls than by trying to reallocate the loss though the legal system. In the case of widespread or recurrent situations, a combination of governmental action, criminal penalties, and remedial legislation could be employed.
>
> The consumer class action, as already noted, is seen as the savior for remedying instances of small injuries to large numbers of persons, and it has unquestionably been used in this role numerous times under Rule 23. It is not very clear, however, that the rule was ever intended to serve such a purpose. The Advisory Committee has stated that subsection 23(b)(3) "encompasses those cases in which a class action would achieve economies of time, effort, and expense, and promote uniformity of decision as to persons similarly situated." Such a statement, standing alone, tends to suggest that the draftsmen conceived of the rule as an advanced joinder device to include in a single action all persons of a definable group in a situation where absent the class action at least a portion of the group both could and would sue as individuals. . . . Significantly, this literal reading of

> the Committee's class action comments would support the preclusion of class actions for large groups suing for small amounts. The dominant characteristic of such suits is that they do not involve combinations of persons who would sue anyway, but rather are actions on behalf of persons who, absent the class remedy, would not sue at all. In effect, then, the class action has not simply made an old remedy more efficient; in a realistic sense it has created a new remedy where none existed.

Jonathan M. Landers, Of Legalized Blackmail and Legalized Theft: Consumer Class Actions and the Substance-Procedure Dilemma, 47 S. Cal. L. Rev. 842, 845-847 (1974).

5. *Tobacco-Related Class Actions and Their Progeny*. Though consumer-type class actions have their detractors, the use of Rule 23 in mass tort cases is even more hotly debated. This is particularly true when the tort involves product liability rather than, for instance, some common disaster such as a plane crash. An early example was the Dalkon Shield litigation. Most of the several thousand cases against the defective birth control device were tort actions filed by women who used the device and suffered infertility or other injuries. In a bold and controversial move, a district court in California certified a nationwide class action in the Dalkon Shield mass tort cases, despite the protests of the defendants and many plaintiffs who preferred to litigate independently. The appellate court reversed the district court's certification. In re Northern District of California, Dalkon Shield IUD Products Liability Litigation, 693 F.2d 847 (9th Cir. 1982), *cert. denied*, 459 U.S. 1171 (1983), *abrogation recognized by* Baxter Healthcare Corp. v. U.S. Dist. Court for Cent. Dist. of Cal., 121 F.3d 714 (9th Cir. 1997). Was this the sort of dispute Rule 23 was designed to cover? Isn't typicality a problem when the women each suffered distinctive injuries? Aren't mass torts presumptively inappropriate cases for class action treatment? How would you describe the competing interests at stake?

In addition to the Dalkon Shield cases, courts have been inundated with asbestos injury cases (more later on these), DES cases, Agent Orange cases, and — more recently — cases filed against the tobacco industry. The tobacco industry cases have produced the most dramatic and far-reaching class actions to date. They have also produced some efforts to settle claims outside the court system, never before seen in quite this form.

6. *Legislative Attempts to Manage Class Actions*. Discussions about responding to cases filed against the tobacco industry with federal legislation developed in 1993, when a Mississippi trial lawyer contacted the state attorney general, Michael Moore, and suggested that the state sue the tobacco companies in order to recover Medicaid expenses that were related to smoking. N.Y. Rev., June 25, 1998, at 33. Then, in 1996, one of the lawyers heavily involved in the current discussions, Dick Scruggs, approached Trent Lott, the Senate Majority Leader, and suggested a national settlement. The first proposed deal, $150 billion over 25 years, grew into a proposal of $368.5 billion over 25 years, with several requirements

of the tobacco companies, including restrictions on advertising and marketing, a cigarette price increase, increased warning sign size on packs of cigarettes, FDA regulation of the nicotine levels (with intent to eliminate nicotine by 2009), and penalties for the industry if set reductions in the numbers of teenage smokers were not reached. In return, the tobacco industry was to be given lawsuit immunity from the states, and individuals could not sue for punitive damages for past acts. The limit of liability, per year, was set at $5 billion. See A Worrisome Tobacco Deal, N. Y. Times, June 21, 1997, at A20; John M. Broder, Political Costs Are Clouding Tobacco Talks, N.Y. Times, June 20, 1997, at A1; John M. Broder, Tobacco Critics Begin Heavy Attack on Settlement, Calling It Soft on Cigarette Makers, N.Y. Times, June 24, 1997, at A9; Excerpts from Agreement Between States and Tobacco Industry, N.Y. Times, June 25, 1997, at A16. Barry Meier, Cigarette Makers in a $368 Billion Accord to Curb Lawsuits and Curtail Marketing, N.Y. Times, June 21, 1997, at A1.

Critics of the proposed bill emerged immediately. The two main issues were the FDA's regulation of nicotine and the industry's demand for protection from future lawsuits. See John M. Broder, Political Costs Are Clouding Tobacco Talks, N.Y. Times, June 20, 1997, at A1; Barry Meier, Parties in Tobacco Talks Say Accord May Be Near, N.Y. Times, June 19, 1997, at A10; Sheryl Gay Stolberg, Some Fear that Fine Print Will Limit FDA Authority, N.Y. Times, June 21, 1997, at A9. Opponents of the bill also contended that there were too many concessions to the tobacco industry, including the limit on the penalty that the industry would have to pay if the number of teenage smokers did not decline to the specific limit, see John M. Broder, Tobacco Critics Begin Heavy Attack on Settlement, Calling It Soft on Cigarette Makers, N.Y. Times, June 24, 1997; Holes in the Tobacco Settlement, N.Y. Times, June 27, 1997, at A20; Neil A. Lewis, Panel of Health Experts Rejects Proposed Tobacco Deal, N.Y. Times, June 26, 1997, at A14. Further arguments were that the deal of $368 billion was too low, especially considering that the payments were to be tax deductible for the tobacco industry as an ordinary business expense. John M. Broder, Tobacco Critics Begin Heavy Attack on Settlement, Calling It Soft on Cigarette Makers, N.Y. Times, June 24, 1997, at A9. The restrictions on advertising also had First Amendment implications, because the restrictions could be implemented only if the industry agreed to them. David Rosenbaum, Senators Jockey on Tobacco Agreement, N.Y. Times, Feb. 11, 1998, at A20. Michael Moore, the lead in the negotiations, nevertheless contended that although the bill was not perfect, it was a good start for a compromise. Neil A. Lewis, Panel of Health Experts Rejects Proposed Tobacco Deal, N.Y. Times, June 26, 1997, at A14. The proponents advised others to look at the proposal as a package, taking into account what the tobacco industry was offering. Id.

Discussion of the proposed bill continued throughout 1997, and in March of 1998, Senator John McCain developed a new, tougher bill. His proposal increased the industry's payments to $516 billion, raised the annual cap on liability to $6.5 billion, raised taxes on cigarettes to $1.10, set goals for reduced numbers in teen smoking, and refused to grant tobacco companies any legal immunity. See Susan Headden et al., Marlboro Man to Congress: Drop Dead, U.S. News & World Report, April 20, 1998, at 29; David E. Rosenbaum, Senate Is Offered Sweeping Measure to Fight Smoking, N.Y. Times, March 31, 1998, at A1; Sen. McCain's Comprehensive Tobacco Bill Approved by Senate Commerce Committee, U.S. Law Week, April 7, 1998, at 2604. Passage of the McCain bill was from the start highly uncertain, because too many issues remained unresolved.

One of the main unresolved issues was that of attorneys' fees. A concern with the earlier plan, after the settlement of the lawsuits in Florida, Texas, Mississippi, and Minnesota, was that the attorneys there expected to make billions. In Texas, Governor Bush challenged the attorneys' claims for $2.3 billion in fees while Morales, the state attorney general, argued that a deal is a deal, and the lawyers should be paid based on the original agreement. Florida also faced a claim from lawyers of 25 percent of the $11.3 billion settlement. Sam Howe Verhovek, Fat Fees in Tobacco Deals Signal New Foes for States: The Lawyers, N.Y. Times, Feb. 9, 1998, at A1. Under the $368 billion plan, lawyers for all 37 states involved had been expected to receive the biggest fees in history, over $100 billion. Barry Meier, Record Legal Fees Emerge as Issue in Tobacco Deal, N.Y. Times, June 23, 1997, at A11. The issue divided legislators along political lines, with Republicans pushing for a limit on the fees, and Democrats, traditionally the recipients of donations from trial lawyers, opposing the move. See Barry Meier and Jill Abramson, Tobacco War's New Front: Lawyers Fight for Big Fees, N.Y. Times, June 9, 1998, at A1; David E. Rosenbaum, Senate Again Opposes Limits on Fees in Tobacco Suits, N.Y. Times, June 12, 1998, at A17.

On June 17, 1998, the Senate agreed to limit attorneys' fees on a sliding scale, depending on when the lawyer entered the controversy. For those attorneys who risked the most, entering at the beginning, fees would be up to $4,000 an hour. Those who entered after this date could only be awarded up to $500 an hour. David E. Rosenbaum, Senate Approves Limiting Fees Lawyers Get in Tobacco Cases, N.Y. Times, June 17, 1998, at A1. The matter of attorneys' fees for plaintiffs' lawyers in the Florida, Mississippi, and Texas cases was referred to a fee arbitration panel. A majority of that panel concluded that the lawyers were entitled to fees totaling $8.2 billion.

Some observers expressed concern that these plaintiff attorney beneficiaries of the tobacco litigation would have the financial wherewithal to pursue other tort litigation in ways that may have a difficult-to-predict impact on substantive law, especially tort reform, as well as on the political power of the American Trial Lawyers Association — the national organization of plaintiff lawyers. See Charles W. Wolfram, What Will the Tobacco Fees Set in Motion?, Nat'l L.J., Dec. 28, 1998, at A25. See also Patrick E. Tyler, Tobacco-Busting Lawyers on New Gold-Dusted Trails, N.Y. Times, March 10, 1999, at A1.

On June 17, 1998, however, any chance at enacting tobacco legislation in 1998 failed when the bill was set aside after failing to garner enough votes to move it along. Among the reasons noted for the failure were opposition to the McCain bill by the industry, which claimed it would rather fight the lawsuits, Barry Meier, Tobacco Death Likely to Prompt Litigation Landslide, N.Y. Times, June 19, 1998, at A19; and the industry's ad campaign against the bill, describing it as a tax increase rather than an antismoking measure. See Major Garret and Kenneth T. Walsh, Congress Snuffs Out the Tobacco Bill, U.S. News & World Rep., June 29, 1998, at 30, 32. David Rosenbaum, Senate Drops Tobacco Bill with '98 Revival Unlikely, N.Y. Times, June 18, 1998, at A1; This ad campaign proved to be a winning tactic by the tobacco industry.

When the bill was introduced to the public as an antismoking measure, public support was enthusiastic, especially after the release of internal documents from the industry that acknowledged an awareness of the dangers of nicotine and smoking for many years, and the suppression of evidence related to this awareness. These papers were revealed during the Minnesota lawsuit and published on the Internet. Associated Press, Minnesota Says Tobacco Papers Prove Deception by the Industry, N.Y. Times, January 1998, at A8. However, when the industry started its advertising campaign against the bill, including a toll-free number to contact senators, the public responded, attacking the bill as a tax increase. Major Garret and Kenneth T. Walsh, Congress Snuffs Out the Tobacco Bill, U.S. News & World Rep., June 29, 1998, at 30; David Rosenbaum, Senate Drops Tobacco Bill With '98 Revival Unlikely, N.Y. Times, June 18, 1998, at A25. The bill may also have been a victim of its own size. Amendments were constantly being added in order to make the bill tougher, and many opponents signed on to these amendments on the expectation that each additional amendment would make the bill less likely to pass.

Once the chance of a bill passing in 1998 was gone, the industry faced over 800 pending lawsuits. Barry Meier, Cigarette Producers Face a Fresh Threat in Individuals' Suits, N.Y. Times, Feb. 12, 1999, at A1; Barry Meier, Jury Awards $81 Million to Oregon Smoker's Family: Amount Is Largest in Smoking Related Suit, N.Y. Times, March 31, 1999, at A14; Barry Meier, Tobacco Bill's Death Likely To Prompt Litigation Landslide, N.Y. Times, June 19, 1998, at A19. The chances of the industry's losing these suits were getting stronger, especially after a $1 million verdict handed down by a jury in Florida in early June, and a $51 million verdict (subsequently halved by the judge, though he otherwise upheld the jury verdict) handed down in San Francisco in February of 1999. The industry nevertheless seemed determined to fight the cases, despite settlements with several states. Of special concern to the industry was the chance of a nationwide or statewide class action suit succeeding. The first such case went to trial in July 1998. The class of plaintiffs included 100,000 to 200,000 people seeking $100 billion in compensatory and punitive damages. R.J. Reynolds Tobacco Co. v. Engle, 672 So. 2d 39 (1996), *rev. denied*, 682 So. 2d 1100 (1996) (approving certification of statewide class of tobacco smokers). More on this case appears infra.

The industry reopened talks with state attorneys general in the summer of 1998, and many of the nation's attorneys general stated that they would continue to fight the tobacco industry, both individually and as a group, while also pressuring Congress to regulate the industry. See State Attorneys Will Pursue Tobacco Fight, N.Y. Times, July 15, 1998, at A15. These talks ensued, and in November of 1998 the states announced a proposed settlement of state lawsuits against cigarette makers over the costs of treating smoking-related illnesses. Barry Meier, States Unveil Settlement on Tobacco, N.Y. Times, Nov. 17, 1998, at A18. The $206 billion proposal, to be paid over the next 25 years, is a greatly scaled-back version of the states' earlier, failed proposal. The plan covers 46 states that have sued or have yet to file a suit with the industry. The four excluded states — Florida, Minnesota, Mississippi, and Texas — have already settled suits in deals worth over $40 billion over 25 years. The list of claimants seeking to participate in the settlement includes the federal government, which argues that its portion of health care expenses paid by federal health insurance programs should be compensated under the fund. See Barry Meier, U.S. Takes Step Toward Tobacco Suit, N.Y. Times, April 7, 1999, at A15 (reporting that the Justice Department may consider legal action of its own against the tobacco industry). More on this appears infra.

7. *Revival of Class Actions.* Following Castano v. American Tobacco Co., 84 F.3d 734 (5th Cir. 1996), plaintiffs' groups in individual states sought certification of statewide tobacco classes. States have been reluctant to certify these classes. According to a 1999 law review article, "all federal and most state courts have found tobacco class actions inconsistent with Rule 23 or its state counterparts." Only Louisiana and Florida have entertained the possibility. Susan E. Kearns, Decertification of Statewide Tobacco Class Actions, 74 N.Y.U. L. Rev. 1336 (1999).

As mentioned above, in 1996 the Florida District Court was the first to certify a class of Florida citizens alleging physical injury caused by nicotine addiction. R.J. Reynolds Tobacco Co. v. Engle, 672 So. 2d 39 (Fla. Dist. Ct. App. 1996), *rev. denied*, 682 So. 2d 1100 (Fla. 1996). Following this certification, in July 1999, a Florida jury found against the tobacco industry, holding that it "conspired to hide the danger and addictiveness of cigarettes." Barry Meier, Tobacco Industry Loses First Phase of Broad Lawsuit, N.Y. Times, July 8, 1999, at A1. In July of 2000, a six-person Miami jury returned a stunning verdict of $144.8 billion in punitive damages in the case. The tobacco industry vowed immediately to appeal. See also Scott v. American Tobacco Co., 725 So. 2d 10 (La. Ct. App. 1998), *writ denied*, 731 So. 2d 198 (La. 1999).

A Maryland lower court certified classes of residents suffering injury from smoking and of nicotine-dependent residents seeking medical monitoring. Richardson v. Philip Morris, Inc., No. 9615050/CE212596 (Md. Cir. Ct. Jan. 28, 1998). This certification was reversed on a petition for mandamus. Philip Morris, Inc. v. Angletti, 752 A.2d 200, 222 (Md. 2000) (noting the nationwide trend of refusing to certify or uphold certification of class actions for mass tobacco litigation).

Although most federal and state courts have rejected smoker class actions, plaintiffs continue to pursue the class action option. In 1997, defendant cigarette manufacturers reached a $300 million settlement with a nationwide class of nonsmoking flight attendants who claimed that their illnesses were the result of occupational exposure to second-hand smoke. Broin v. Philip Morris Cos., Fla. Cir. Ct. No. 91-49738CA(22), settlement agreement entered Oct. 10, 1997. The agreement allowed attendants to bring individual actions for compensatory damages, with the defendant companies agreeing to assume the burden of proof on whether second-hand smoke was the cause of any number of medical conditions.

A group of flight attendants who were not satisfied with the settlement filed a subsequent class action, claiming that the settlement gave away too many of the ill plaintiffs' legal rights without sufficient individual compensation. The Florida Third District Court of Appeal upheld the settlement and described it as a "boon to the plaintiffs." Reuters, Tobacco Settlement Is Upheld in Florida, N.Y. Times, March 25, 1999, at A20. Some 300 of the members of the original class have brought individual suits against the cigarette manufacturers. Although lawyers for the cigarette manufacturers assert that the lawsuits have nothing in common, other than the fact that each plaintiff is a flight attendant, others have observed that the presumption of causation in the original settlement will make it easier for the plaintiffs to prevail. Attorneys for Airline Attendants File 300 Individual Suits Against Tobacco Industry, BNA Legal News, Feb. 1, 2000, at 2444.

Union health fund trustees and lung cancer victims who smoked at least "20 pack-years, the equivalent of a pack a day for 20 years," have recently filed suits in the U.S. District Court in Brooklyn, New York. These suits are structured differently in the hope of receiving rulings from a district court judge who has ruled favorably in cases that probably would have been dismissed in other courts. Bob Van Voris, A Carton of New Tobacco Trials: Going Against the Grain, Brooklyn Judge Sets One a Month, Nat'l L.J., April 24, 2000, at A1.

Although courts have tended to side with the defendants on class certification issues, juries have awarded substantial damages to individual plaintiffs. A San Francisco jury awarded both compensatory and punitive damages to a former smoker with lung cancer. The trial judge halved the punitive damage amount, saying that the reduced amount ($26.5 million instead of $51 million) was sufficient to punish the defendant, Philip Morris Companies, for "misleading the public about the dangers of smoking and for marketing cigarettes to teenagers." Associated Press, Award Halved in Suit Against Cigarette Maker, N.Y. Times, March 7, 1999, at A17.

A subsequent San Francisco jury awarded $1.7 million in compensatory damages to a former smoker dying of lung cancer, finding that the "cigarette companies negligently designed cigarettes and knew about the hazards of smoking, then committed fraud by misleading people about how much cigarettes could harm a smoker's health." Associated Press,

Companies Found Liable for Ex-Smoker's Cancer, N.Y. Times, March 22, 2000 at A22. The same jury then awarded the plaintiff $20 million in punitive damages, even though the plaintiff had started smoking after the federal government's 1965 requirement forced cigarette manufacturers to place warning labels on cigarette packages. Previously, the United States Supreme Court had held that the labeling requirements preempted state juries from granting awards to plaintiffs who claimed that they had not received adequate warning about the potential hazards of smoking. Barry Meier, Punitive Damages Added in Smoking Case Verdict, N.Y. Times, March 28, 2000, at A12.

8. *The Federal Government Steps In.* In 1999, the federal government ceased its criminal investigation of the tobacco industry and filed a civil class action lawsuit, alleging that the largest manufacturers of cigarettes conspired to defraud and mislead the public about the dangers of smoking. Filed in the United States District Court for the District of Columbia, the suit is the first time the government has sued an entire industry using RICO, the federal Racketeering Influenced and Corrupt Organizations Act.

Although the government's case is based on some of the information that was disclosed in the state tobacco litigation and individual lawsuits, it seeks recovery under different statutes: the Medical Care Recovery Act ("Medicare"), which provides medical payments for the elderly; the Medicare Secondary Payer Act, used by the government to recover medical costs in individual cases; and statutes regulating military and veterans' health insurance payments made directly by the federal government. Marc Lacey, Tobacco Industry Accused of Fraud in Lawsuit by U.S., N.Y. Times, Sept. 23, 1999, at A1; Associated Press, U.S. Sues Cigarette Makers for Billions, Arizona Daily Star, Sept. 23, 1999, at A7.

Initially, the government attempted to persuade Congress to grant $20 million to finance the costs of the lawsuit. When that effort failed, the Department of Justice turned to a provision that allows other agencies to help defray litigation costs if that agency would be affected by the litigation in question. Specifically, DOJ targeted the departments of Veterans' Affairs, Health and Human Services, and Defense. The House of Representatives voted to block the transfer of that portion of the funds requested from the Department of Veterans' Affairs, claiming that to do so would deprive veterans of funds for care.

On June 22, 2000, the House reversed itself and allowed the Department of Veterans' Affairs to send $4 million to DOJ. After subsequent wrangling, on June 24, 2000, the House approved an amendment to a bill that allowed Veterans' Affairs and the Department of Health and Human Services to provide $12 million to DOJ to help subsidize litigation costs. Steven A. Holmes, Financing Approved for Tobacco Suit; Justice Department Prevails Despite Opposition of GOP Leadership, S.F. Chronicle, June 24, 2000, at A7.

9. *Gun Manufacturers.* A suit in California against gun manufacturers suggests that they may be subject to the same kinds of class action lawsuits

as is the tobacco industry. In reinstating a criminal lawsuit against the manufacturer of a semiautomatic pistol used to kill eight people in a San Francisco law office in 1993, the California First District Court of Appeals was the first appellate court to rule that a gun manufacturer might be held responsible for a criminal's use of its weapon.

While acknowledging that every other state and federal appellate court has determined that manufacturers of legal and properly functioning weapons would not be sued for misuse of the weapons by criminals, the Court of Appeals made significant distinctions. First, although the gun (the Tec-DC-9) is legal in Florida, where it is produced, and Nevada, where the weapon in question was purchased, it has been banned in California. Second, there is evidence that the Tec-DC-9 has "no legitimate civilian use." And last, the manufacturer's advertisement for the gun as fingerprint-resistant suggests that criminals were an intended market for the weapon. Merrill v. Navegar, Inc., 75 Cal. App. 4th 500 (1999), *cert. granted and opinion superseded by* 991 P.2d 755 (Cal. 2000). See also Associated Press, Kin of 8 Massacred by Gunman Can Sue Gun Maker, Court Rules, Ariz. Daily Star, Sept. 30, 1999, at A7.

Note: The Class Suit in Equity

The class suit was known to seventeenth-century equity. Stephen C. Yeazell, in Group Litigation and Social Context: Toward a History of the Class Action, 77 Colum. L. Rev. 866 (1977), points out that the ancestor of the class action, the Bill of Peace, was an outgrowth of waning feudalism and typically involved a manor or parish in conflict with its lord or clergyman. Although villagers formed a cohesive "class," the status did not confer power or cement a group of strangers as it does in the modern class action. A few of the tenants or parishioners represented the group. The controversy to be settled was not a conflict over a sum of money that was owed according to settled substantive law. Rather, the parties came before the chancellor to decide what had been the historical custom of the manor.

For instance, in Brown v. Vermuden, 22 Eng. Rep. 196 (1676), the parishioners of the village of Wem sued their vicar. The chancellor was to determine whether the custom of the village required them to pay tithes on the coal they mined. Professor Yeazell describes the judgment in this case and others as follows:

> It is not difficult to understand why the Chancellor in these cases did not award damages in the first instance. . . . [I]n these cases, he was engaged in a process that to a modern observer looks more like legislation than adjudication. A rule, generally applicable to a group of persons in particular social circumstances, was promulgated for the first time—a rule that, unlike a common law judgment, did not purport to result from simply applying a pre-existing legal standard to particular facts. The particularity of the

> custom, Chancery's power to alter in accordance with a vaguely defined standard of "reasonableness," and the Chancellor's willingness to range far from the original issues posed by the parties in seeking a resolution of the dispute distinguished these cases from run-of-the-mill common law adjudication. Moreover, the decree governed future behavior of the parties, not merely in the sense that they could (as with any decided case) guide themselves by reference to its ratio decidendi, but because in its own terms it established the mode of their future conduct to one another; its command was explicit rather than implicit. . . .
>
> Understanding the relief sought and given in the early cases clarifies the apparent abandon with which courts bound absent group members. Once one realizes that the relief sought was a declaration of custom, the problem seems far less urgent. Having one's day in court loses some of its significance if what the court does at the end of that day is simply to declare what shall be the law tomorrow, without retrospectively applying that law to a specific dispute.

Yeazell, supra, 77 Colum. L. Rev. at 890-891.

In a later article, From Group Litigation to Class Action, Part I: The Industrialization of Group Litigation, 27 UCLA L. Rev. 514 (1980), Yeazell traces the mutations that occurred in group litigation as equity gradually bent the old feudal procedure to fit the litigation of industrial society. In place of the manorial or parochial community, there arose artificially created communities — the joint-stock companies and friendly societies (social organizations that served as primitive insurance companies). "Both were voluntary associations replacing an older, traditional, and smaller way of accomplishing the same thing — communal mutual assistance in the case of friendly societies and partnership in the case of jointstock companies." Id. at 533.

> Since the beginning of the nineteenth century, we have moved from a rural, customary, agricultural world to one that is urban, individualistic, entrepreneurial-capitalist. . . .
>
> No longer are the "multitude" who seek litigative recognition a social group. . . . The group is on its way to becoming a class — not a social organism but a number of individuals sharing some interest, here a straightforwardly economic one. Moreover, the nature of the law applied to the dispute has changed, as has the remedy sought and administered. No longer do the plaintiffs seek a prospective declaration of reciprocal rights and duties that are to govern a continuing relation. Instead one sees the assimilation of group litigation to a more familiar legal model: acts in the past are measured against a previously existing legal standard and parties are amerced money damages for failure to comply. We are in a world recognizably "legal" and recognizably modern: group litigation has become one among many means of applying universally applicable rules of liability; it is no longer the peculiar procedure of a particularistic and moribund substantive law.

Id. at 521.

The Supreme Court sanctioned the class suit in America in Smith v. Swormstedt, 57 U.S. 288 (1853). That suit involved the Methodist church in schism over the issue of slavery. The ministers of the southern wing sued those of the northern wing to establish their right to share the proceeds of a pension fund provided by the church for "raveling and worn-out preachers." Although only nine individuals were joined as parties, the Court found that if the "persons brought on the record fairly represented the interest or right involved," the suit would be binding on the classes of 1,500 and 3,800 members. Id. at 302-303.

Note: The Right to Jury Trial

Given the class action's roots in equity, one may assume that no jury trial right attaches when an action is filed as a class action. This, however, is not necessarily so.

In Ross v. Bernhard, 396 U.S. 531 (1970), the United States Supreme Court concluded that the right to trial by jury attaches to the issues in a class action — in *Ross* it was a shareholder's derivative suit — as to which the right to trial by jury would have attached if the parties had litigated the matter in individual actions, rather than through the collective action device of a class action. Thus a court must analyze the issues in a class action and determine whether they are "legal" or "equitable" in the manner described more fully in Chapter 5.

2. Appeal of Class Certification

Blair v. Equifax Check Services, Inc.
181 F.3d 832 (7th Cir. 1999)

EASTERBROOK, Circuit Judge.

Last year the Supreme Court promulgated Fed. R. Civ. P. 23(f), which reads: "A court of appeals may in its discretion permit an appeal from an order of a district court granting or denying class action certification under this rule if application is made to it within ten days after entry of the order. An appeal does not stay proceedings in the district court unless the district judge or the court of appeals so orders."

We have for consideration the first application filed in this circuit (and, so far as we can tell, the nation) under the new rule. A motions panel directed the parties to file briefs discussing the standard the court should employ to decide whether to accept appeals under this rule.

The Committee Note accompanying Rule 23(f) remarks: "The court of appeals is given unfettered discretion whether to permit the appeal, akin to the discretion exercised by the Supreme Court in acting on a petition for certiorari. . . . Permission to appeal may be granted or denied on the basis of any consideration that the court of appeals finds persuasive." . . . Although

Rule 10 of the Supreme Court's Rules identifies some of the considerations that inform the grant of certiorari, they are "neither controlling nor fully measuring the Court's discretion." Likewise it would be a mistake for us to draw up a list that determines how the power under Rule 23(f) will be exercised. Neither a bright-line approach nor a catalog of factors would serve well — especially at the outset, when courts necessarily must experiment with the new class of appeals.

Instead of inventing standards, we keep in mind the reasons Rule 23(f) came into being. These are three. For some cases the denial of class status sounds the death knell of the litigation, because the representative plaintiff's claim is too small to justify the expense of litigation. Coopers & Lybrand v. Livesay, 437 U.S. 463 (1978), held that an order declining to certify a class is not appealable, even if that decision dooms the suit as a practical matter. Rule 23(f) gives appellate courts discretion to entertain appeals in "death knell" cases — though we must be wary lest the mind hear a bell that is not tolling. Many class suits are prosecuted by law firms with portfolios of litigation, and these attorneys act as champions for the class even if the representative plaintiff would find it uneconomical to carry on with the case. E.g., Rand v. Monsanto Co., 926 F.2d 596 (7th Cir. 1991). These law firms may carry on in the hope of prevailing for a single plaintiff and then winning class certification (and the reward of larger fees) on appeal, extending the victory to the whole class. A companion appeal, briefed in tandem with this one, presented just such a case. After class certification was denied, the plaintiff sought permission to appeal under Rule 23(f); although the remaining plaintiff has only a small stake, counsel pursued the case in the district court while we decided whether to entertain the appeal, and before the subject could be argued here the district judge granted summary judgment for the defendant. That plaintiff now has appealed on the merits and will seek to revive the class to boot. Many other cases proceed similarly; *Coopers & Lybrand* did not wipe out the small-stakes class action. But when denial of class status seems likely to be fatal, and when the plaintiff has a solid argument in opposition to the district court's decision, then a favorable exercise of appellate discretion is indicated.

Second, just as a denial of class status can doom the plaintiff, so a grant of class status can put considerable pressure on the defendant to settle, even when the plaintiff's probability of success on the merits is slight. Many corporate executives are unwilling to bet their company that they are in the right in big-stakes litigation, and a grant of class status can propel the stakes of a case into the stratosphere. In re Rhone-Poulenc Rorer Inc., 51 F.3d 1293 (7th Cir. 1995), observes not only that class actions can have this effect on risk-averse corporate executives (and corporate counsel) but also that some plaintiffs or even some district judges may be tempted to use the class device to wring settlements from defendants whose legal positions are justified but unpopular. Empirical studies of securities class actions imply that this is common. Janet Cooper Alexander, Do the Merits Matter? A Study of Settlements in Securities Class Actions, 43 Stan. L. Rev. 497 (1991);

Reinier Kraakman, Hyun Park & Steven Shavell, When Are Shareholder Suits in Shareholder Interests?, 82 Geo. L.J. 1733 (1994); Roberta Romano, The Shareholder Suit: Litigation Without Foundation?, 7 J.L. Econ. & Org. 55 (1991). Class certifications also have induced judges to remake some substantive doctrine in order to render the litigation manageable. See Hal S. Scott, The Impact of Class Actions on Rule 10b-5, 38 U. Chi. L. Rev. 337 (1971). This interaction of procedure with the merits justifies an earlier appellate look. By the end of the case it will be too late—if indeed the case has an ending that is subject to appellate review.

So, in a mirror image of the death-knell situation, when the stakes are large and the risk of a settlement or other disposition that does not reflect the merits of the claim is substantial, an appeal under Rule 23(f) is in order. Again the appellant must demonstrate that the district court's ruling on class certification is questionable—and must do this taking into account the discretion the district judge possesses in implementing Rule 23, and the correspondingly deferential standard of appellate review. However dramatic the effect of the grant or denial of class status in undercutting the plaintiff's claim or inducing the defendant to capitulate, if the ruling is impervious to revision there's no point to an interlocutory appeal.

Third, an appeal may facilitate the development of the law. Because a large proportion of class actions settles or is resolved in a way that overtakes procedural matters, some fundamental issues about class actions are poorly developed. Recent proposals to amend Rule 23 were designed in part to clear up some of these questions. Instead, the Advisory Committee and the Standing Committee elected to wait, anticipating that appeals under Rule 23(f) would resolve some questions and illuminate others. When an appellant can establish that such an issue is presented, Rule 23(f) permits the court of appeals to intervene. When the justification for interlocutory review is contributing to development of the law, it is less important to show that the district judge's decision is shaky. Law may develop through affirmances as well as through reversals. Some questions have not received appellate treatment because they are trivial; these are poor candidates for the use of Rule 23(f). But the more fundamental the question and the greater the likelihood that it will escape effective disposition at the end of the case, the more appropriate is an appeal under Rule 23(f). More than this it is impossible to say.

Judges have been stingy in accepting interlocutory appeals by certification under 28 U.S.C. § 1292(b), because that procedure interrupts the progress of a case and prolongs its disposition. That bogey is a principal reason why interlocutory appeals are so disfavored in the federal system. Disputes about class certification cannot be divorced from the merits—indeed, one of the fundamental unanswered questions is whether judges should be influenced by their tentative view of the merits when deciding whether to certify a class—and so this argument against interlocutory appeals carries some weight under Rule 23(f). But it has less weight than under § 1292(b), because Rule 23(f) is drafted to avoid delay. Filing a request for permission to appeal does not stop the litigation unless the district court or the court of appeals issues a stay—and a stay would depend on a demonstration that the probability of error in the class certification decision is high enough that the costs of pressing ahead in the district court exceed the costs of waiting. (This is the same kind of question that a court asks when deciding whether to issue a preliminary injunction or a stay of an administrative decision. See Illinois Bell Telephone Co. v. WorldCom Technologies, Inc., 157 F.3d 500 (7th Cir. 1998); American Hospital Supply Corp. v. Hospital Products Ltd., 780 F.2d 589, 593-594 (7th Cir. 1986).) We did not stay either of the two cases in which permission to appeal was sought; both continued in the district court and, as we related above, one already has been decided on the merits. Because stays will be infrequent, interlocutory appeals under Rule 23(f) should not unduly retard the pace of litigation.

So much for abstractions; what of this case? Equifax Check Services, which supplies a check-verification service to merchants, also attempts to collect fees imposed on dishonored checks. After we held that checks create "debts" within the meaning of the Fair Debt Collection Practices Act, 15 U.S.C. §§ 1692-1692o, see Bass v. Stolper, Koritzinsky, Brewster & Neider, S.C., 111 F.3d 1322 (7th Cir. 1997), many of Equifax's practices came under challenge. Until recently Equifax used a letter implying that it would refuse to verify checks written by anyone who had not paid all outstanding checks. Beverly Blair and Letressa Wilbon filed suits contending that this letter violated § 1692g of the Act because it did not adequately inform the recipients that they had 30 days within which to demand that Equifax obtain a verification of the debt from the merchant. Blair sought to represent a class of shoppers at Champs, and Wilbon a class of persons who had shopped at T.J. Maxx. The suits were consolidated and, after it became apparent that Equifax had sent the same letter to every person situated similarly to the plaintiffs, the district judge certified the case as a class action under Fed. R. Civ. P. 23(b)(3), defining the class as: "all Illinois residents (i) who were sent a demand letter by [Equifax] on or after a date one year prior to the filing of this action, (ii) in the form represented by Exhibit A . . . , (iii) in connection with an attempt to collect a check written to Champs or TJ Maxx for personal, family, or household purposes, where (iv) the letter was not returned by the Postal Service." 1999 U.S. Dist. LEXIS 2536, 3-4 (N.D. Ill. 1999). The court also certified a subclass of persons who received a particular follow-up letter less than 30 days after Equifax sent the first. Because plaintiffs sought only statutory penalties, the difficulties of proving individual loss did not block class treatment. Cf. Keele v. Wexler, 149 F.3d 589 (7th Cir. 1998). Equifax all but concedes that class certification was proper if the case is viewed in isolation, but it insists that what happened in another case requires a different outcome.

Several class actions against Equifax are pending in the Northern District of Illinois. On the same day Judge Plunkett certified the class in *Blair*, the plaintiffs in Crawford v. Equifax Check Services, Inc., No. 97 C 4240, which is pending before Magistrate Judge Schenkier, reached a settlement with Equifax. The class certified in *Crawford* is a superset of the class certified in *Blair,* and Equifax contends that as a result the terms of the *Crawford* settlement control here. A peculiar settlement it is. Equifax agreed to change the letters it sends in the future. Crawford personally receives $2,000. Members of the *Crawford* class get no relief for the letters sent to them, though Equifax agreed to donate $5,500 to Northwestern Law School's Legal Aid Clinic and (natch) [*sic*] the lawyers for the class receive fees for their work. According to the settlement, none of the class members will receive individual notice, and none will be offered the opportunity to opt out. The theory behind this is that the class was certified under Fed. R. Civ. P. 23(b)(2), even though it began as an action seeking damages. Finally, the settlement provides that all class members' claims for compensatory or statutory damages pass through the litigation unaffected and may be asserted elsewhere—but only in individual suits. The settlement forbids prosecution of any other case as a class action. It is this final feature of the *Crawford* settlement that Equifax contends should have led Judge Plunkett to decertify the *Blair-Wilbon* class. Maintaining *Blair* as a class action creates at least a possibility of inconsistent outcomes.

Judge Plunkett was not amused. He was piqued at Equifax's failure to ask the district court to consolidate *Crawford* with *Blair,* if indeed one comprises the other. He also concluded that the settlement in *Crawford* could not affect another pending suit. Because he deemed the *Crawford* settlement irrelevant, Judge Plunkett denied Equifax's motion for reconsideration of the class certification. This is the order Equifax wants to appeal under Rule 23(f). Before turning to that appeal, however, we need to describe additional proceedings before Magistrate Judge Schenkier.

Attorneys representing Blair and Wilbon were invited to a settlement conference in *Crawford* and there learned—for the first time, they say—that the *Crawford* class includes the *Blair* class. Counsel opposed the *Crawford* settlement as inadequate but did not persuade either Magistrate Judge Schenkier or Crawford's lawyers. Blair and Wilbon then sought to intervene in *Crawford* so that they would be able to appeal from final approval of the settlement, if their objections at the hearing under Rule 23(e) should be rejected. Magistrate Judge Schenkier denied the motion to intervene, concluding that counsel should have found out about the overlap and acted earlier. That decision is the subject of a separate appeal. . . .

[T]he appeal is within our jurisdiction—if we choose to accept it. We do accept it. This situation fits our third category of appropriate interlocutory appeals. Equifax contends that it is entitled to be rid of multiple overlapping class actions. Questions concerning the relation among multiple suits may evade review at the end of the case, for by then the issue will be the relation among (potentially inconsistent) *judgments,* and not the management of pending litigation. That neither side can point to any precedent in support of its position implies that this is one of the issues that has evaded appellate resolution, and the issue is important enough to justify review now.

Because both sides favored us with their view of the merits of the appeal, as well as the question whether we should entertain it, we can bring matters to a swift conclusion. That the issue has evaded appellate resolution does not imply that it is difficult. Far from it. Judge Plunkett is plainly right — though not altogether for the reason he gave. We do not see any reason in principle why the disposition of the *Crawford* litigation cannot be conclusive on the plaintiffs in *Blair.* All members of the class certified in *Blair* also are members of the class certified in *Crawford;* a judgment binding on members of the *Crawford* class therefore will bind all members of the *Blair* class. See Tice v. American Airlines, Inc., 162 F.3d 966 (7th Cir. 1998). If the judgment binds them not to pursue class actions, then the class in *Blair* must be decertified. But it does not *yet* have this effect, and the district judge was not required to jump the gun just to avoid all possibility of inconsistent outcomes.

Parallel cases often seek the same relief. There's nothing peculiar about class actions. Sometimes the same plaintiff will file in two courts; sometimes different plaintiffs will seek equivalent relief in the same court. Our situation has a little of each, since Blair, Wilbon, and Crawford are not the same person, but they are in the same class. No mechanical rule governs the handling of overlapping cases. Judges sometimes stay proceedings in the more recently filed case to allow the first to proceed; sometimes a stay permits the more comprehensive of the actions to go forward. Cf. Colorado River Water Conservation District v. United States, 424 U.S. 800 (1976). But the judge hearing the second-filed case may conclude that it is a superior vehicle and may press forward. When the cases proceed in parallel, the first to reach judgment controls the other, through claim preclusion (res judicata). Davis v. Chicago, 53 F.3d 801 (7th Cir. 1995); Rogers v. Desiderio, 58 F.3d 299 (7th Cir. 1995). *Crawford* has yet to produce a final and binding decision, however, so Judge Plunkett was entitled to proceed with *Blair* in the interim.

On occasion it will be so clear that the first-filed suit is the superior vehicle that it would be an abuse of discretion for the court in the second-filed suit to press forward. This is not such a case, however. *Crawford* is far from decision on the merits; it has seen negotiation, not combat. It is not clear that *Crawford*'s settlement will beat *Blair* to finality even if *Blair* is fully litigated. As we have recounted, Blair and Wilbon have tried to intervene in *Crawford,* and they have appealed from the order denying that motion. We anticipate that they will appeal again from any order giving final approval to the *Crawford* settlement after the Rule 23(e) hearing. The latter appeal will of course be contingent on success in the intervention appeal, because only parties may appeal from an order settling a class action. See Felzen v. Andreas, 134 F.3d 873 (7th Cir. 1998), *affirmed by an equally divided Court under the name* California Public Employees' Retirement System v. Felzen, 525 U.S. 315 (1999). But if Blair and Wilbon persuade us that Magistrate Judge Schenkier erred in excluding them from *Crawford,* or if some other class member intervenes and appeals from approval of the settlement, then this court will have to address the propriety of that deposition.

Approval cannot be called a foregone conclusion. *Crawford* was settled for a pittance, plus attorneys' fees. Some cases settle for tiny sums because they have little chance of success; maybe *Crawford* is such a case. (We have resisted all temptation to peek at its merits.) But if the class in *Crawford* has such a weak position, why were the debtors' rights to compensatory and statutory damages preserved? If damages are at issue, how can Rule 23(b)(2) be used to avoid opt-outs and notice? If damages claims survive, what's wrong with pursuing them in a separate class action? We have never heard of a class action being settled on terms that amount to: "For $7,500 plus attorneys fees, the class is disestablished." When the individual claims are small, class actions are most useful. Perhaps Equifax found a plaintiff (or lawyer) willing to sell out the class—a possibility that we discussed most recently in Greisz v. Household Bank, 176 F.3d 1012 (7th Cir. 1999)—and then tried to use *Crawford* as a way to thwart parallel actions where the class had more vigorous champions. Then again, perhaps the deal in *Crawford* was the best the class could obtain. We do not prejudge that issue. Enough questions have been raised, however, to show that Judge Plunkett was entitled to keep the *Blair* class in place until final decision in *Crawford*.

When overlapping suits are filed in separate courts, stays (or, rarely, transfers) are the best means of coordination. But both *Crawford* and *Blair* were filed in the Northern District of Illinois. By far the best means of avoiding wasteful overlap when related suits are pending in the same court is to consolidate all before a single judge. Rules of the Northern District permit just such a process. At oral argument we asked the parties why this had not been done. Plaintiffs' counsel replied that until shortly before they attended the settlement conference in *Crawford* they believed that the classes did not overlap. Counsel say that they were shocked to learn that *Crawford* is much the larger case and that the *Blair* class is its subset. Lawyers representing Equifax say that *Blair*'s lawyers knew this all along or should have deduced it, and Magistrate Judge Schenkier agreed. We can't tell who is right, but surely Equifax knew from the get-go the relative sizes of, and relations among, the different class actions pending against it. Equifax could not plausibly explain at oral argument why *it* had not asked the district court to transfer all related actions to a single judge for decision. It is still not too late for the district court to accomplish this—although Magistrate Judge Schenkier will drop out of the picture if either case is transferred. Unanimous consent of the parties is required for a magistrate judge to enter final decision in a civil case, see 28 U.S.C. § 636(c), and it is obvious that Blair and Wilbon won't consent to that procedure. But both *Crawford* and *Blair* easily could be handled by the same district judge—whether Judge Plunkett, to whom *Blair* is assigned, or Judge Andersen, to whom *Crawford* was initially assigned, does not matter for this purpose.

No matter what the district court does, we will do our own part to consolidate and expedite decision. *Crawford* is a related case for purposes of our Operating Procedure 6(b), so that any appeal in *Crawford*, and any further appeal in *Blair,* will come to this panel. For today, it is enough to hold that, until *Crawford* reaches final judgment, Judge Plunkett does not abuse his discretion by handling *Blair* as a class action

Affirmed.

Notes and Questions

1. *Appeals and Efficiency.* One of the reasons always given against allowing interlocutory appeals is the delay that ensues. Thus, though Rule 23(f) does not set any standards for when appeals should be taken, it does explicitly direct that the case should continue while the appeal is being decided, unless the trial or appellate court explicitly orders a stay. Isn't it likely, however, that trial judges will stay their orders pending appeal in most cases? Why spend time and effort on a case that may take an entirely different shape after the appeal is heard?

The court in *Blair* acted very expeditiously itself — hearing argument on the appeal in May and issuing a thoughtful and well-crafted opinion in June. The class certification occurred at the end of February. Another step promoting efficiency was the court's order that future appeals in these matters come back to the same panel (Judges Easterbrook, Posner and Rovner). Briefing the certification issue on the merits, at the same time appellate consideration was sought, also promoted efficiency and is a practice that will probably be followed in most cases.

Yet for all its concern for expedition, the panel also held that the ten-day period for seeking an appeal specified in the rule could be extended by filing a motion to reconsider an adverse certification in the district court. Blair argued that an order denying reconsideration is not the kind of "order" to which Rule 23(f) refers; only the order granting or denying class action certification qualifies as a basis for appeal. But Judge Easterbrook held that the opportunity for the trial judge to correct her own errors would in the long run save time and effort. See Asher v. Baxter Int'l Inc., 505 F.3d 736 (7th Cir. 2007) (affirming and extending *Blair* to renewed motions for certification; concluding that the Rule 23(f) ten-day limit begins running after the first denial of certification, even if plaintiffs bring new motions for certification after changes in the lead plaintiff designation were made to satisfy concerns that drove the judge to deny the first certification). For a case that may accord excessive weight to efficiency concerns, see In the Matter of Bridgestone/Firestone, Inc., Tires Products Liability Litigation, 333 F.3d 763 (7th Cir. 2003). A year earlier the Seventh Circuit had held that the district court abused its discretion by certifying nationwide classes covering plaintiffs alleging injuries suffered while driving Ford cars and trucks on Firestone tires. The court held that the need to apply multiple states' laws made nationwide classes (including owners of over 60 million tires and 3 million vehicles) improper. In response to this decision, plaintiffs refiled in numerous other courts, again seeking class certification of the same nationwide classes. Ford and Firestone then moved the district court "to enforce [the earlier Seventh Circuit] decision by enjoining other class actions." Id. at 765. The district court refused, but on appeal, the Seventh Circuit reversed, remanding the case with instructions that the lower court issue "an injunction that prevents all members of the putative national classes, and their lawyers, from again attempting to have nationwide classes certified over defendants' opposition with respect to the same claims." Id. at 769.

Although the preclusive effect of a judgment is usually left to the second court to determine, Judge Easterbrook invoked the Anti-Injunction Act, arguing that "when federal litigation is followed by many duplicative state suits, it is sensible to handle the preclusive effect once and for all in the original case, rather than put the parties and state judges through an unproductive exercise." Id. at 766. Judge Easterbrook was particularly concerned that lawyers for the plaintiff classes would simply shop around the country until they found a judge willing to certify nationwide classes. Id. at 766-767 ("A single positive trumps all the negatives. Even if just one judge in ten believes that a nationwide class is lawful, then if the plaintiffs file in ten different states the probability that at least one will certify a nationwide class is 65%. . . . This happens whenever plaintiffs can roll the dice as many times as they please. . . .").

Finally, consider the approach of the Ninth Circuit to interlocutory review:

> Bearing in mind that many class certification decisions "present familiar and almost routine issues that are no more worthy of immediate appeal than many other interlocutory rulings," Fed. R. Civ. P. 23(f), Advisory Committee Notes to 1998 Amendments, we adopt the following guidelines for consideration of Rule 23(f) petitions. Review of class certification decisions will be most appropriate when: (1) there is a death-knell situation for either the plaintiff or defendant that is independent of the merits of the underlying claims, coupled with a class certification decision by the district court that is questionable; (2) the certification decision presents an unsettled and fundamental issue of law relating to class actions, important both to the specific litigation and generally, that is likely to evade end-of-the-case review; or (3) the district court's class certification decision is manifestly erroneous.

Compare Chamberlan v. Ford Motor Co., 402 F.3d 952, 959 (9th Cir. 2005) (holding that manifest error is sufficient, by itself, to warrant interlocutory review; observing that the three factors are "merely guidelines, not a rigid test"); id. at 960 (rejecting Ford's claim that this case falls within the "death knell" category because well over one hundred thousand class members were seeking an award of nearly one hundred million dollars; Ford failed to show that it lacks resources to defend or that defending "runs the risk of ruinous liability").

2. *Appeals and Reform.* The interlocutory type appeal under Rule 23 may result in a lot more appellate law on important class action issues. The fact that most class action cases settle (as do most cases in general) has meant

that the definitive precedent has not developed at the same rate as the burgeoning use of the device. Because class actions can bind and affect so many people at once, the relatively stunted appellate case law in the area has, in the view of some, prevented needed improvement and reform in the administration of Rule 23. That is the import of *Blair*'s concern about issues that evade review as a main ingredient in allowing an appeal.

Coopers & Lybrand v. Livesay, discussed in *Blair,* held that a class certification order was not final, and also held that an appeal might be taken under 28 U.S.C. § 1292(b). That section requires that a "controlling question of law as to which there is a substantial ground for difference of opinion" be present and that an "immediate appeal from the order may materially advance the ultimate termination of the litigation." Are these reasons automatically sufficient under the new Rule 23(f)?

Another way in which appeals were gained before the passage of Rule 23(f) was through seeking an extraordinary writ of mandamus. In the Matter of Rhone-Poulenc Rorer Inc., 51 F.3d 1293 (7th Cir. 1995), was the best-known example of this tactic. Judge Posner decertified a class in that case, partly on the ground that there was an "undue and unnecessary risk of a monumental industry-busting error in entrusting the determination of potential multi-billion dollar liabilities to a single jury." Presumably, a case like *Rhone-Poulenc* would fit nicely into the requirements of Rule 23(f) for appeal.

Another case in which mandamus was employed to change the shape of a class action instead of to challenge the certification was In re Chevron U.S.A., Inc., 109 F.3d 1016 (5th Cir. 1997). This was a mass tort case in which the trial court had designated a "bellwether" group of plaintiffs whose individual claims would be tried to determine damages after common issues of causation were tried for the whole class. The circuit court held that the sample cases must be randomly selected and statistically significant. An appeal from this type of ruling would still require either certification under 28 U.S.C. § 1292(b) or mandamus.

3. *Appealing Certification of Defendant Classes.* Is the need for interlocutory appeal of certification orders any different for defendant classes? As the First Circuit observed in Tilley v. TJX Companies, Inc., 345 F.3d 34, 37 (1st Cir. 2003), "[d]efendant classes are a relatively rare breed, and no court of appeals has had the opportunity to consider whether the same set of standards should apply to petitions for leave to appeal orders certifying (or refusing to certify) defendant classes." Noting the "special solicitude" owed to the "due process interests of absent members of defendant classes," the court accepted interlocutory appeal and reversed certification of a defendant class on the grounds that (1) Rule 23(b)(2) is an improper vehicle for defendant classes, and (2) the stare decisis effect of separate actions against individual defendants on subsequent cases would not "be dispositive of the interests of the other members" within the meaning of Rule 23(b)(1)(B). Id. at 39-41 (plaintiff named defendant class consisting of wholesaler and individual retailers who allegedly infringed her copyright in a wallpaper design).

3. Who Is Bound? — Of Civil Rights and Class Actions

Hansberry v. Lee
311 U.S. 32 (1940)

JUSTICE STONE delivered the opinion of the Court.

The question is whether the Supreme Court of Illinois, by its adjudication that petitioners in this case are bound by a judgment rendered in an earlier litigation to which they were not parties, has deprived them of the due process of law guaranteed by the Fourteenth Amendment.

Respondents brought this suit in the Circuit Court of Cook County, Illinois, to enjoin the breach by petitioners of an agreement restricting the use of land within a described area of the City of Chicago, which was alleged to have been entered into by some five hundred of the landowners. The agreement stipulated that for a specified period no part of the land should be "sold, leased to or permitted to be occupied by any person of the colored race," and provided that it should not be effective unless signed by the "owners of 95 per centum of the frontage" within the described area. The bill of complaint set up that the owners of 95 per cent of the frontage had signed; that respondents are owners of land within the restricted area who have either signed the agreement or acquired their land from others who did sign; and that petitioners Hansberry, who are Negroes, have, with the alleged aid of the other petitioners and with knowledge of the agreement, acquired and are occupying land in the restricted area formerly belonging to an owner who had signed the agreement.

To the defense that the agreement had never become effective because owners of 95 per cent of the frontage had not signed it, respondents pleaded that that issue was *res judicata* by the decree in an earlier suit. Burke v. Kleiman, 277 Ill. App. 519 [1934]. To this petitioners pleaded, by way of rejoinder, that they were not parties to that suit or bound by its decree, and that denial of their right to litigate, in the present suit, the issue of performance of the condition precedent to the validity of the agreement would be a denial of due process of law guaranteed by the Fourteenth Amendment. It does not appear, nor is it contended that any of petitioners is the successor in interest to or in privity with any of the parties in the earlier suit.

The circuit court, after a trial on the merits, found that owners of only about 54 per cent of the frontage had signed the agreement, and that the only support of the judgment in the *Burke* case was a false and fraudulent stipulation of the parties that owners of 95 per cent had signed. But it ruled that the issue of performance of the condition precedent to the validity of the agreement was *res judicata* as alleged and entered a decree for respondents. The Supreme Court of Illinois affirmed. 372 Ill. 369. We granted certiorari to resolve the constitutional question. 309 U.S. 652.

The Supreme Court of Illinois, upon an examination of the record in Burke v. Kleiman, supra, found that that suit, in the Superior Court of Cook County, was brought by a landowner in the restricted area to enforce the agreement, which had been signed by her predecessor in title, on behalf of herself and other property owners in like situation, against four named individuals, who had acquired or asserted an interest in a plot of land formerly owned by another signer of the agreement; that, upon stipulation of the parties in that suit that the agreement had been signed by owners of 95 per cent of all the frontage, the court had adjudged that the agreement was in force, that it was a covenant running with the land and binding all the land within the described area in the hands of the parties to the agreement and those claiming under them, including defendants, and had entered its decree restraining the breach of the agreement by the defendants and those claiming under them, and that the appellate court had affirmed the decree. It found that the stipulation was untrue but held, contrary to the trial court, that it was not fraudulent or collusive. It also appears from the record in Burke v. Kleiman that the case was tried on an agreed statement of facts which raised only a single issue, whether by reason of changes in the restricted area, the agreement had ceased to be enforceable in equity.

From this the Supreme Court of Illinois concluded in the present case that Burke v. Kleiman was a "class" or "representative" suit, and that in such a suit, "where the remedy is pursued by a plaintiff who has the right to represent the class to which he belongs, other members of the class are bound by the results in the case unless it is reversed or set aside on direct proceedings"; that petitioners in the present suit were members of the class represented by the plaintiffs in the earlier suit and consequently were bound by its decree, which had rendered the issue of performance of the condition precedent to the restrictive agreement *res judicata,* so far as petitioners are concerned. The court thought that the circumstance that the stipulation in the earlier suit that owners of 95 per cent of the footage had signed the agreement was contrary to the fact, as found in the present suit, did not militate against his conclusion, since the court in the earlier suit had jurisdiction to determine the fact as between the parties before it, and that its determination, because of the representative character of the suit, even though erroneous, was binding on petitioners until set aside by a direct attack on the first judgment.

State courts are free to attach such descriptive labels to litigations before them as they may choose and to attribute to them such consequences as they think appropriate under state constitutions and laws, subject only to the requirements of the Constitution of the United States. But when the judgment of a state court, ascribing to the judgment of another court the binding force and effect of *res judicata,* is challenged for want of due process it becomes the duty of this Court to examine the course of procedure in both litigations to ascertain whether the litigant whose rights have thus been adjudicated has been afforded such notice and opportunity to be heard as are requisite to the due process which the Constitution prescribes.

It is a principle of general application in Anglo-American jurisprudence that one is not bound by a judgment *in personam* in a litigation in which he is not designated as a party or to which he has not been made a party by service of process. Pennoyer v. Neff, 95 U.S. 714 [1877]; 1 Freeman on Judgments (5th ed.), § 407. A judgment rendered in such circumstances is not entitled to the full faith and credit which the Constitution and statute of the United States, prescribe, . . . and judicial action enforcing it against the person or property of the absent party is not that due process which the Fifth and Fourteenth Amendments require. . . .

To these general rules there is a recognized exception that, to an extent not precisely defined by judicial opinion, the judgment in a "class" or "representative" suit, to which some members of the class are parties, may bind members of the class or those represented who were not made parties to it. Smith v. Swormstedt, [57 U.S. 288,] 16 How. 288 [1854]; cf. Christopher v. Brusselback, 302 U.S. 500 [1938].

The class suit was an invention of equity to enable it to proceed to a decree in suits where the number of those interested in the subject of the litigation is so great that their joinder as parties in conformity to the usual rules of procedure is impracticable. . . .

It is evident that the considerations which may induce a court thus to proceed, despite a technical defect of parties, may differ from those which must be taken into account in determining whether the absent parties are bound by the decree or, if it is adjudged that they are, in ascertaining whether such an adjudication satisfies the requirements of due process and of full faith and credit. Nevertheless, there is scope within the framework of the Constitution for holding in appropriate cases that a judgment rendered in a class suit is *res judicata* as to members of the class who are not formal parties to the suit. Here, as elsewhere, the Fourteenth Amendment does not compel state courts or legislatures to adopt any particular rule for establishing the conclusiveness of judgments in class suits . . . nor does it compel the adoption of the particular rules thought by this Court to be appropriate for the federal courts. With a proper regard for divergent local institutions and interests, this Court is justified in saying that there has been a failure of due process only in those cases where it cannot be said that the procedure adopted, fairly insures the protection of the interests of absent parties who are to be bound by it.

It is familiar doctrine of the federal courts that members of a class not present as parties to the litigation may be bound by the judgment where they are in fact adequately represented by parties who are present, or where they actually participate in the conduct of the litigation in which members of the class are present as parties . . . or where the interest of the members of the class, some of whom are present as parties, is joint, or where for any other reason the relationship between the parties present and those who are absent is such as legally to entitle the former to stand in judgment for the latter. Smith v. Swormstedt, supra; cf. Christopher v. Brusselback, supra, 503, 504 and cases cited.

In all such cases, so far as it can be said that the members of the class who are present are, by generally recognized rules of law, entitled to stand in judgment for those who are not, we may assume for present purposes that such procedure affords a protection to the parties who are represented, though absent, which would satisfy the requirements of due process and full faith and credit. . . .

Nor do we find it necessary for the decision of this case to say that, when the only circumstance defining the class is that the determination of the rights of its members turns upon a single issue of fact or law, a state could not constitutionally adopt a procedure whereby some of the members of the class could stand in judgment for all, provided that the procedures were so devised and applied as to insure that those present are of the same class as those absent and that the litigation is so conducted as to insure the full and fair consideration of the common issue. We decide only that the procedure and the course of litigation sustained here by the plea of *res judicata* do not satisfy these requirements.

The restrictive agreement did not purport to create a joint obligation or liability. If valid and effective its promises were the several obligations of the signers and those claiming under them. The promises ran severally to every other signer. It is plain that in such circumstances all those alleged to be bound by the agreement would not constitute a single class in any litigation brought to enforce it. Those who sought to secure its benefits by enforcing it could not be said to be in the same class with or represent those whose interest was in resisting performance, for the agreement by its terms imposes obligations and confers rights on the owner of each plot of land who signs it. . . .

Because of the dual and potentially conflicting interests of those who are putative parties to the agreement in compelling or resisting its performance, it is impossible to say, solely because they are parties to it, that any two of them are of the same class. Nor without more, and with the due regard for the protection of the rights of absent parties which due process exacts, can some be permitted to stand in judgment for all.

It is one thing to say that some members of a class may represent other members in a litigation where the sole and common interest of the class in the litigation, is either to assert a common right or to challenge an asserted obligation. . . . It is quite another to hold that all those who are free alternatively either to assert rights or to challenge them are of a single class, so that any group, merely because it is of the class so constituted, may be deemed adequately to represent any others of the class in litigating their interests in either alternative. Such a selection of representatives for purposes of litigation, whose substantial interests are not necessarily or even probably the same as those whom they are deemed to represent, does not afford that protection to absent parties which due process requires. The doctrine of representation of absent parties in a class suit has not hitherto been thought to go so far. . . . Apart from the opportunities it would afford for the fraudulent and collusive sacrifice of the rights of absent parties, we think that the representation in this case no more satisfies the requirements of due process than a trial by a judicial officer who is in such situation that he may have an interest in the outcome of the litigation in conflict with that of the litigants.

The plaintiffs in the *Burke* case sought to compel performance of the agreement in behalf of themselves and all others similarly situated. They did not designate the defendants in the suit as a class or seek any injunction or other relief against others than the named defendants, and the decree which was entered did not purport to bind others. In seeking to enforce the agreement the plaintiffs in that suit were not representing the petitioners here whose substantial interest is in resisting performance. The defendants in the first suit were not treated by the pleadings or decree as representing others or as foreclosing by their defense the rights of others; and, even though nominal defendants, it does not appear that their interest in defeating the contract outweighed their interest in establishing its validity. For a court in this situation to ascribe to either the plaintiffs or defendants the performance of such functions on behalf of petitioners here, is to attribute to them a power that it cannot be said that they had assumed to exercise, and a responsibility which, in view of their dual interests it does not appear that they could rightly discharge.

Reversed.

JUSTICE MCREYNOLDS, JUSTICE ROBERTS, and JUSTICE REED concur in the result.

Note: Hansberry *and the Concept of Persons Whose Interests Are Affected by Litigation*

An important aspect of *Hansberry*, of course, is that the covenant in the case was a racially restrictive one. The family in the case was that of Lorraine Hansberry, who drew on the event in creating her well-known play *A Raisin in the Sun.* In her autobiography, *To Be Young, Gifted and Black* (1969), she described the psychic costs of the litigation to her father, the named plaintiff, and the whole family. More on the background of the case, especially on the prior litigation, Burke v. Kleiman, is explored in Allen R. Kamp, The History Behind *Hansberry v. Lee*, 20 U.C. Davis L. Rev. 481 (1987).

Eight years after *Hansberry*, the United States Supreme Court finally ruled that all racially restrictive covenants are unenforceable. Shelley v. Kraemer, 334 U.S. 1 (1948). It later ruled that all governmentally sanctioned racial discrimination violated the Constitution. But in 1940, the Court was writing in a period of transition from a society that tolerated race-conscious laws to one that deemed them presumptively intolerable and unlawful. *Hansberry* gave the Court in 1940 a means by which it could strike down the results of a racially restrictive covenant without confronting head-on the legal and social problem it later could not, or chose not, to avoid. Consider the following passage from Stephen Yeazell's influential work From Medieval Group Litigation to the Modern Class Action 231 (1987), in which he characterizes the impact of

Hansberry on subsequent class action cases and the concept of "interest" within them:

> It may be that in situations of social flux the very concept of abstractly defined social interest dissolves, leaving only the individual as the definer of his good. It is less a question of whether or not the individual desires to assert his right, as the Court in *Hansberry* framed the question, than it is of figuring out the possible (and actual) combinations of economic and non-economic, long-run and short-run interests. *Hansberry*'s power flows from the elevation to constitutional status of its struggle to define interests. It equates due process with representation of interest but then defines interest in terms of individually expressed desire to enforce rights. Commentators have been trying to read the entrails ever since.

To what extent do *Hansberry*, and class actions generally, compel courts to rethink the meaning of individual interests and to consider the social and systemic impact of what may at first blush appear to be a "private" dispute? Doesn't a neighborhood's decision to enforce a race-restrictive covenant have community-wide reverberations? What about an individual's or single corporation's decision to deposit toxic substances in a river or into the atmosphere?

Note: Defendant Classes

Christopher v. Brusselback, 302 U.S. 500 (1938), held that a shareholder could not be subjected to personal liability by a judgment rendered against him in an action in which he was represented by a fellow shareholder but in which he was not personally joined as a party. Was that decision overruled by Hansberry v. Lee? It has been suggested that there is a difference between plaintiffs who may benefit from being represented in class actions and defendants who gain nothing from the representation. See, e.g., A. Peter Parsons and Kenneth W. Starr, Environmental Litigation and Defendant Class Actions: The Unrealized Viability of Rule 23, 4 Ecology L.Q. 881 (1975). The authors there suggest that the availability of the representative should be accepted as satisfying the requirements of due process, but only if the absent defendants are provided with notice and an opportunity to intervene. See In re Gap Sec. Litig., 70 F.R.D. 283 (N.D. Cal. 1978) (holding that notice is required).

Martin v. Wilks

490 U.S. 755 (1989)

CHIEF JUSTICE REHNQUIST delivered the opinion of the Court.

A group of white firefighters sued the city of Birmingham, Alabama (City), and the Jefferson County Personnel Board (Board) alleging that they were being denied promotions in favor of less qualified black firefighters.

They claimed that the City and the Board were making promotion decisions on the basis of race in reliance on certain consent decrees, and that these decisions constituted impermissible racial discrimination in violation of the Constitution and federal statutes. The District Court held that the white firefighters were precluded from challenging employment decisions taken pursuant to the decrees, even though these firefighters had not been parties to the proceedings in which the decrees were entered. We think this holding contravenes the general rule that a person cannot be deprived of his legal rights in a proceeding to which he is not a party.

The litigation in which the consent decrees were entered began in 1974, when the Ensley Branch of the National Association for the Advancement of Colored People and seven black individuals filed separate class-action complaints against the City and the Board. They alleged that both had engaged in racially discriminatory hiring and promotion practices in various public service jobs in violation of Title VII of the Civil Rights Act of 1964, 42 U.S.C. §§ 2000e et seq., and other federal laws. After a bench trial on some issues, but before judgment, the parties entered into two consent decrees, one between the black individuals and the City and the other between them and the Board. These proposed decrees set forth an extensive remedial scheme, including long-term and interim annual goals for the hiring of blacks as firefighters. The decrees also provided for goals for promotion of blacks within the fire department.

The District Court entered an order provisionally approving the decrees and directing publication of notice of the upcoming fairness hearings. Notice of the hearings, with a reference to the general nature of the decrees, was published in two local newspapers. At that hearing, the Birmingham Firefighters Association (BFA) appeared and filed objections as *amicus curiae.* After the hearing, but before final approval of the decrees, the BFA and two of its members also moved to intervene on the ground that the decrees would adversely affect their rights. The District Court denied the motions as untimely and approved the decrees. United States v. Jefferson County, 28 FEP Cases 1834 (N.D. Ala. 1981). Seven white firefighters, all members of the BFA, then filed a complaint against the City and the Board seeking injunctive relief against enforcement of the decrees. The seven argued that the decrees would operate to illegally discriminate against them; the District Court denied relief.

Both the denial of intervention and the denial of injunctive relief were affirmed on appeal. United States v. Jefferson County, 720 F.2d 1511 (11th Cir. 1983). The District Court had not abused its discretion in refusing to let the BFA intervene, thought the Eleventh Circuit, in part because the firefighters could "institut[e] an independent Title VII suit, asserting specific violations of their rights." And, for the same reason, petitioners had not adequately shown the potential for irreparable harm from the operation of the decrees necessary to obtain injunctive relief.

A new group of white firefighters, the *Wilks* respondents, then brought suit against the City and the Board in District Court. They too alleged that, because of their race, they were being denied promotions in favor of less qualified blacks in violation of federal law. The Board and the City admitted to making race-conscious employment decisions, but argued that the decisions were unassailable because they were made pursuant to the consent decrees. A group of black individuals, the *Martin* petitioners, were allowed to intervene in their individual capacities to defend the decrees.

The defendants moved to dismiss the reverse discrimination cases as impermissible collateral attacks on the consent decrees. The District Court denied the motions, ruling that the decrees would provide a defense to claims of discrimination for employment decisions "mandated" by the decrees, leaving the principal issue for trial whether the challenged promotions were indeed required by the decrees. After trial the District Court granted the motion to dismiss. The court concluded that "if in fact the City was required to [make promotions of blacks] by the consent decree, then they would not be guilty of [illegal] racial discrimination" and that the defendants had "establish[ed] that the promotions of the black individuals . . . were in fact required by the terms of the consent decree."

On appeal, the Eleventh Circuit reversed. It held that, "[b]ecause . . . [the *Wilks* respondents] were neither parties nor privies to the consent decrees, . . . their independent claims of unlawful discrimination are not precluded." In re Birmingham Reverse Discrimination Employment Litigation, 833 F.2d 1492, 1498 (1987). The court explicitly rejected the doctrine of "impermissible collateral attack" espoused by other Courts of Appeals to immunize parties to a consent decree from charges of discrimination by nonparties for actions taken pursuant to the decree. Although it recognized a "strong public policy in favor of voluntary affirmative action plans," the panel acknowledged that this interest "must yield to the policy against requiring third parties to submit to bargains in which their interests were either ignored or sacrificed." The court remanded the case for trial of the discrimination claims, suggesting that the operative law for judging the consent decrees was that governing voluntary affirmative-action plans.

We granted certiorari, and now affirm the Eleventh Circuit's judgment. All agree that "[i]t is a principle of general application in Anglo-American jurisprudence that one is not bound by a judgment *in personam* in a litigation in which he is not designated as a party or to which he has not been made a party by service of process." Hansberry v. Lee, 311 U.S. 32, 40 (1940). This rule is part of our "deep-rooted historic tradition that everyone should have his own day in court." A judgment or decree among parties to a lawsuit resolves issues as among them, but it does not conclude the rights of strangers to those proceedings.[2]

2. We have recognized an exception to the general rule when, in certain limited circumstances, a person, although not a party, has his interests adequately represented by someone with the same interests who is a party. See Hansberry v. Lee, 311 U.S. 32, 41-42 (1940) ("class" or "representative" suits); Fed. Rule Civ. Proc. 23 (same); Montana v. United States, 440 U.S. 147, 154-155 (1979) (control of litigation on behalf of one of the parties in the litigation). Additionally, where a special remedial scheme exists expressly foreclosing

Petitioners argue that, because respondents failed to timely intervene in the initial proceedings, their current challenge to actions taken under the consent decree constitutes an impermissible "collateral attack." They argue that respondents were aware that the underlying suit might affect them, and if they chose to pass up an opportunity to intervene, they should not be permitted to later litigate the issues in a new action. The position has sufficient appeal to have commanded the approval of the great majority of the Federal Courts of Appeals, but we agree with the contrary view expressed by the Court of Appeals for the Eleventh Circuit in these cases.

We begin with the words of Justice Brandeis in Chase National Bank v. Norwalk, 291 U.S. 431 (1934):

> The law does not impose upon any person absolutely entitled to a hearing the burden of voluntary intervention in a suit to which he is a stranger. . . . Unless duly summoned to appear in a legal proceeding, a person not a privy may rest assured that a judgment recovered therein will not affect his legal rights.

While these words were written before the adoption of the Federal Rules of Civil Procedure, we think the Rules incorporate the same principle; a party seeking a judgment binding on another cannot obligate that person to intervene; he must be joined. See [Zenith Radio Corp. v.] Hazeltine, [395 U.S. 100,] 110 [1969] (judgment against Hazeltine vacated because it was not named as a party or served, even though as the parent corporation of one of the parties it clearly knew of the claim against it and had made a special appearance to contest jurisdiction). Against the background of permissive intervention set forth in *Chase National Bank,* the drafters cast Rule 24, governing intervention, in permissive terms. See Fed. Rule Civ. Proc. 24(a) (intervention as of right) ("Upon timely application anyone shall be permitted to intervene"); Fed. Rule Civ. Proc. 24(b) (permissive intervention) ("Upon timely application anyone may be permitted to intervene"). They determined that the concern for finality and completeness of judgments would be "better [served] by mandatory joinder procedures." 18 Wright § 4452, p. 453. Accordingly, Rule 19(a) provides for mandatory joinder in circumstances where a judgment rendered in the absence of a person may "leave . . . persons already parties subject to a substantial risk of incurring . . . inconsistent obligations. . . ." Rule 19(b) sets forth the factors to be considered by a court in deciding whether to allow an action to proceed in the absence of an interested party.

---

successive litigation by nonlitigants, as for example in bankruptcy or probate, legal proceedings may terminate preexisting rights if the scheme is otherwise consistent with due process. See NLRB v. Bildisco & Bildisco, 465 U.S. 513, 529-530, n.10 (1984) ("[P]roof of claim must be presented to the Bankruptcy Court . . . or be lost"); Tulsa Professional Collection Services, Inc. v. Pope, 485 U.S. 478 (1988) (nonclaim statute terminating unsubmitted claims against the estate). Neither of these exceptions, however, applies in these cases.

Joinder as a party, rather than knowledge of a lawsuit and an opportunity to intervene, is the method by which potential parties are subjected to the jurisdiction of the court and bound by a judgment or decree.[6] The parties to a lawsuit presumably know better than anyone else the nature and scope of relief sought in the action, and at whose expense such relief might be granted. It makes sense, therefore, to place on them a burden of bringing in additional parties where such a step is indicated, rather than placing on potential additional parties a duty to intervene when they acquire knowledge of the lawsuit. The linchpin of the "impermissible collateral attack" doctrine — the attribution of preclusive effect to a failure to intervene — is therefore quite inconsistent with Rule 19 and Rule 24. . . .

Petitioners contend that a different result should be reached because the need to join affected parties will be burdensome and ultimately discouraging to civil rights litigation. Potential adverse claimants may be numerous and difficult to identify; if they are not joined, the possibility for inconsistent judgments exists. Judicial resources will be needlessly consumed in relitigation of the same question.

Even if we were wholly persuaded by these arguments as a matter of policy, acceptance of them would require a rewriting rather than an interpretation of the relevant Rules. But we are not persuaded that their acceptance would lead to a more satisfactory method of handling cases like these. It must be remembered that the alternatives are a duty to intervene based on knowledge, on the one hand, and some form of joinder, as the Rules presently provide, on the other. No one can seriously contend that an employer might successfully defend against a Title VII claim by one group of employees on the ground that its actions were required by an earlier decree entered in a suit brought against it by another, if the later group did not have adequate notice or knowledge of the earlier suit.

The difficulties petitioners foresee in identifying those who could be adversely affected by a decree granting broad remedial relief are undoubtedly present, but they arise from the nature of the relief sought and not because of any choice between mandatory intervention and joinder. Rule 19's provisions for joining interested parties are designed to accommodate the sort of complexities that may arise from a decree affecting numerous people in various ways. We doubt that a mandatory intervention rule would be any less awkward. . . .

6. The dissent argues, on the one hand, that respondents have not been "bound" by the decree but, rather, that they are only suffering practical adverse effects from the consent decree. On the other hand, the dissent characterizes respondents' suit not as an assertion of their own independent rights, but as a collateral attack on the consent decrees which, it is said, can only proceed on very limited grounds. Respondents in their suit have alleged that they are being racially discriminated against by their employer in violation of Title VII: either the fact that the disputed employment decisions are being made pursuant to a consent decree is a defense to respondents' Title VII claims or it is not. If it is a defense to challenges to employment practices which would otherwise violate Title VII, it is very difficult to see why respondents are not being "bound" by the decree.

Nor do we think that the system of joinder called for by the Rules is likely to produce more relitigation of issues than the converse rule. The breadth of a lawsuit and concomitant relief may be at least partially shaped in advance through Rule 19 to avoid needless clashes with future litigation. And even under a regime of mandatory intervention, parties who did not have adequate knowledge of the suit would relitigate issues. Additional questions about the adequacy and timeliness of knowledge would inevitably crop up. We think that the system of joinder presently contemplated by the Rules best serves the many interests involved in the run of litigated cases, including cases like the present ones.

Petitioners also urge that the congressional policy favoring voluntary settlement of employment discrimination claims, referred to in cases such as Carson v. American Brands, Inc., 450 U.S. 79 (1981), also supports the "impermissible collateral attack" doctrine. But once again it is essential to note just what is meant by "voluntary settlement." A voluntary settlement in the form of a consent decree between one group of employees and their employer cannot possibly "settle," voluntarily or otherwise, the conflicting claims of another group of employees who do not join in the agreement. This is true even if the second group of employees is a party to the litigation:

> [P]arties who choose to resolve litigation through settlement may not dispose of the claims of a third party . . . without that party's agreement. A court's approval of a consent decree between some of the parties therefore cannot dispose of the valid claims of nonconsenting intervenors.

Firefighters v. Cleveland, 478 U.S. 501, 529 (1986).

Insofar as the argument is bottomed on the idea that it may be easier to settle claims among a disparate group of affected persons if they are all before the court, joinder bids fair to accomplish that result as well as a regime of mandatory intervention.

For the foregoing reasons we affirm the decision of the Court of Appeals for the Eleventh Circuit. That court remanded the case for trial of the reverse discrimination claims. Birmingham Reverse Discrimination, 833 F.2d, at 1500-1502. Petitioners point to language in the District Court's findings of fact and conclusions of law which suggests that respondents will not prevail on the merits. We agree with the view of the Court of Appeals, however, that the proceedings in the District Court may have been affected by the mistaken view that respondents' claims on the merits were barred to the extent they were inconsistent with the consent decree.

Affirmed.

[The dissent of JUSTICE STEVENS, with whom JUSTICE BRENNAN, JUSTICE MARSHALL, and JUSTICE BLACKMUN join, is omitted.]

Notes and Questions

1. *The Significance of Martin v. Wilks.* Shortly after the case was decided Congress enacted a statute designed to reverse the decision.

Civil Rights Act of 1991

Pub. L. No. 102. 166, § 402(a), 105 Stat. 1071, 1099,
reprinted at 42 U.S.C. § 2000e-2(n)(1) (Supp. V. 1993)

§ 108. [A]n employment practice that implements and is within the scope of a litigated or consent judgment or order that resolves a claim of employment discrimination under the Constitution or Federal civil rights laws may not be challenged . . . in a claim under the Constitution or federal civil rights laws:

(i) by a person who, prior to the entry of the judgment or order . . . had —

(1) actual notice of the proposed judgment or order sufficient to apprise such person that such judgment or order might adversely affect the interests and legal rights of such person and that an opportunity was available to present objections to such judgment or order by a future data certain; and

(2) a reasonable opportunity to present objections to such judgment or order; or

(ii) by a person whose interests were adequately represented by another person who had previously challenged the judgment or order on the same legal grounds and with a similar factual situation, unless there has been an intervening change in law or fact.

The statute does reverse *Wilks* on its facts, doesn't it? But what about a discrimination claim outside of the employment discrimination area? If, for instance, you were representing the plaintiffs in a claim charging housing discrimination, how would you proceed to frame your class action in light of *Wilks*? The effect of the case is to place the burden of joining all affected parties on the plaintiffs (and secondarily on the court). Think about using Rule 19 or 24, or about creating subclasses under Rule 23(c)(4). Think also about the management problems involved in having involuntary and opposing parties on the same side of the "versus."

2. *Class Certification in Discrimination Cases.* The courts have struggled with the criteria for class certification as applied to employment discrimination cases; on the one hand, they have recognized "that racial discrimination is by definition class discrimination." General Tel. Co. of the Sw. v. Falcon, 457 U.S. 147, 148 (1982). On the other hand,

> there is a wide gap between (a) an individual's claim that he has been denied a promotion on discriminatory grounds, and his otherwise unsupported allegation that the company has a policy of discrimination, and (b) the existence of a class of persons who have suffered the same injury as

> that individual, such that the individual's claim and the class claims will . . . be typical of the class claims. . . . [T]o bridge that gap, [a plaintiff] must prove much more than the validity of his own claim.

Id. at 157-158. See also East Tex. Motor Freight Syst., Inc. v. Rodriguez, 431 U.S. 395, 405-406 (1977) ("The mere fact that a complaint alleges racial or ethnic discrimination does not in itself ensure that the party who has brought the lawsuit will be an adequate representative of those who may have been the real victims of that discrimination.").

3. *The Advantages of the Class Action.* Here are the first paragraphs of the introduction and the class action allegations in Rodriguez v. California Highway Patrol, 89 F. Supp. 2d 1131 (N.D. Cal. 2000). Do you think this is an appropriate kind of case for class action treatment? What are the advantages of a class action in this situation?

> 1. This is a class action lawsuit seeking declaratory, injunctive, and monetary relief against the California Highway Patrol ("CHP") and the Bureau of Narcotics Enforcement ("BNE") for engaging in and condoning a continuing pattern and practice of race-based stops, detentions and searches of motorists of color traveling on the public streets and highways of the State of California. The specific abuses giving rise to this action occurred on or in the area of Highway 152 in California, including, but not limited to, the area where Highway 152 intersects with Interstate Highway 5.
>
> 2. Plaintiffs in this case, Curtis Rodriguez ("Rodriguez"), Jose Lopez ("Lopez"), MacArthur Washington ("Washington"), California Branches of the NAACP ("NAACP"), and California League of United Latin American Citizens ("LULAC"), represent a class of people of color who have been or will be subjected to the humiliation of being targeted, interrogated, detained and searched by defendants in the area of Highway 152 due to the defendants' policy and practice of what is commonly known as "racial profiling." The moment Mr. Rodriguez, Mr. Lopez and Mr. Washington were stopped by the defendants they became victims of what the United States Court of Appeals for the Ninth Circuit called "an all too familiar set of circumstances—an intrusive law enforcement stop and seizure of innocent persons on the basis of suspicions rooted principally in the race of the 'suspects.'" Washington v. Lambert, 98 F.3d 1181, 1182 (1996).
>
> 3. To any person of color, regardless of ethnic background, level of education, or economic station in life, the insidious problem of racial profiling by law enforcement officers is all too familiar. It is a continuing reminder that, despite popular notions of progress in race relations, racial discrimination remains a day-to-day reality in our society.
>
> 4. By the complaint in this case, plaintiffs seek judicial redress for violations of their civil rights due to racial profiling. But they also seek to confirm what everyone has a right to expect in the United States: that people of color may use the public streets and highways, just like anybody else, without having to suffer the indignities of racial discrimination at the hands of government officials.
>
> 5. Plaintiffs' claims are brought pursuant to the Fourth, Fifth and Fourteenth Amendments to the United States Constitution; Title VI of the Civil

Rights Act of 1964 and its implementing regulations, 42 U.S.C. §§ 1982, 1983, 1985 and 1986; Article 1, Section 7(a) of the California Constitution; California Civil Code § 52. 1; California Government Code §§ 11135. . . .

Class Action Allegations

64. For the purposes of all relief sought in this case, plaintiffs Rodriguez, Lopez and Washington bring this action pursuant to Federal Rule of Civil Procedure 23 on behalf of themselves and all other persons similarly situated. Each of these individual class representatives is a person of color who has been stopped, detained, interrogated and searched by CHP and/or BNE officers while travelling on or in the area of Highway 152. The class which plaintiffs seek to represent consists of all people of color who, since June 1998, have been or will be stopped, detained, interrogated and/or searched on Highway 152 or on any road or highway near 152 including, but not limited to, Interstate Highway 5, by the CHP or the BNE. These class members are victims of the racially motivated and illegal pattern and practice of discrimination in the enforcement of traffic laws by the CHP and BNE.

65. The class of persons defined in paragraph 64 is so numerous that joinder of all members in one action is impracticable.

66. There are questions of law and fact common to all members of the class, because all class members have been, or will be, adversely affected by the challenged actions of the defendants. Common questions of fact and law include, but are not limited to: whether CHP and BNE officers target, stop, detain and/or search individual drivers in a racially discriminatory manner; and whether CHP and BNE officers are knowingly trained to employ methods that result in racial profiling and have an unjustified disparate impact on putative class members in violation of federal and state civil rights laws.

67. The claims of the representative plaintiffs are typical of the class as a whole who travel on or around Highway 152 and have been stopped, detained and/or searched by the defendants. The experiences of the plaintiffs at the hands of the defendants resulted from the defendants' policy and practice of discriminating on the basis of race and ethnicity, making their claims typical of those held by the class they seek to represent.

68. Plaintiffs can and will fairly and adequately protect the interests of the members of the class. Plaintiffs will be adequate representatives of the class in that all of the relevant questions of fact and law applicable to the class also apply to them.

69. Plaintiffs have retained counsel who are familiar with the applicable law and experienced in class action litigation, as well as litigation involving criminal law and civil rights. Counsel for plaintiffs have the resources necessary to pursue this litigation.

70. This action is properly maintained as a class action. The questions of law and fact common to the members of the class predominate over any questions affecting only individual members, and a class action is superior to other available methods for the fair and efficient adjudication of this controversy. Plaintiffs know of no difficulty to be encountered in the management of this action that would preclude its maintenance as a class action.

71. The prosecution of separate actions by individual class members would create a risk of inconsistent and varying adjudication concerning the subject of this action, and such adjudication could establish incompatible standards of conduct for defendants under the laws alleged herein.

4. Notice and the Opportunity to Be Heard

Eisen v. Carlisle & Jacquelin

417 U.S. 156 (1974)

JUSTICE POWELL delivered the opinion of the Court.

On May 2, 1966, petitioner filed a class action on behalf of himself and all other odd-lot[1] traders on the New York Stock Exchange (the Exchange). The complaint charged respondents with violations of the antitrust and securities laws and demanded damages for petitioner and his class. Eight years have elapsed, but there has been no trial on the merits of these claims. Both the parties and the courts are still wrestling with the complex questions surrounding petitioner's attempt to maintain his suit as a class action under Fed. Rule Civ. Proc. 23. We granted certiorari to resolve some of these difficulties. 414 U.S. 908 (1973).

Petitioner brought this class action in the United States District Court for the Southern District of New York. Originally, he sued on behalf of all buyers and sellers of odd lots on the Exchange, but subsequently the class was limited to those who traded in odd lots during the period from May 1, 1962, through June 30, 1966. 52 F.R.D. 253, 261 (1971). Throughout this period odd-lot trading was not part of the Exchange's regular auction market but was handled exclusively by special odd-lot dealers, who bought and sold for their own accounts as principals. Respondent brokerage firms Carlisle & Jacquelin and DeCoppet & Doremus together handled 99% of the Exchange's odd-lot business. S.E.C., Report of Special Study of Securities Markets, H.R. Doc. No. 95, pt. 21, 88th Cong., 1st Sess., 172 (1963). They were compensated by the odd-lot differential, a surcharge imposed on the odd-lot investor in addition to the standard brokerage commission applicable to round-lot transactions. For the period in question the differential was 1/8 of a point (12 1/2¢) per share on stocks trading below $40 per share and 1/4 of a point (25¢) per share on stocks trading at or above $40 per share.

Petitioner charged that respondent brokerage firms had monopolized odd-lot trading and set the differential at an excessive level in violation of §§ 1 and 2 of the Sherman Act, 15 U.S.C. §§ 1 and 2, and he demanded treble damages for the amount of the overcharge. Petitioner also demanded unspecified money damages from the Exchange for its alleged failure to regulate the differential for the protection of investors in

1. Odd lots are shares traded in lots of fewer than a hundred. Shares traded in units of a hundred or multiples thereof are round-lots.

violation of §§ 6 and 19 of the Securities Exchange Act of 1934; 15 U.S.C. §§ 78f and 78s. Finally, he requested attorneys' fees and injunctive prohibition of future excessive charges.

A critical fact in this litigation is that petitioner's individual stake in the damages award he seeks is only $70. No competent attorney would undertake this complex antitrust action to recover so inconsequential an amount. Economic reality dictates that petitioner's suit proceed as a class action or not at all. Opposing counsel have therefore engaged in prolonged combat over the various requirements of Rule 23. The result has been an exceedingly complicated series of decisions by both the District Court and the Court of Appeals for the Second Circuit. To understand the labyrinthian history of this litigation, a preliminary overview of the decisions may prove useful.

In the beginning, the District Court determined that petitioner's suit was not maintainable as a class action. On appeal, the Court of Appeals issued two decisions known popularly as *Eisen I* and *Eisen II*. The first held that the District Court's decision was a final order and thus appealable. In the second the Court of Appeals intimated that petitioner's suit could satisfy the requirements of Rule 23, but it remanded the case to permit the District Court to consider the matter further. After conducting several evidentiary hearings on remand, the District Court decided that the suit could be maintained as a class action and entered orders intended to fulfill the notice requirements of Rule 23. Once again, the case was appealed. The Court of Appeals then issued its decision in *Eisen III* and ended the trilogy by denying class action status to petitioner's suit. . . .

Thus, after six and one-half years and three published decisions, the Court of Appeals endorsed the conclusion reached by the District Court in its original order in 1966—that petitioner's suit could not proceed as a class action. In its procedural history, at least, this litigation has lived up to Judge Lumbard's characterization of it as a "Frankenstein monster posing as a class action." *Eisen II*, 391 F.2d, 555, 572 (1968). . . .

Turning to the merits of the case, we find that the District Court's resolution of the notice problems was erroneous in two respects. First, it failed to comply with the notice requirements of Rule 23(c)(2), and second, it imposed part of the cost of notice on respondents.

Rule 23(c)(2) provides that, in any class action maintained under subdivision (b)(3), each class member shall be advised that he has the right to exclude himself from the action on request or to enter an appearance through counsel, and further that the judgment, whether favorable or not, will bind all class members not requesting exclusion. To this end, the court is required to direct to class members "the best notice practicable under the circumstances, *including individual notice to all members who can be identified through reasonable effort*." We think the import of this language is unmistakable. Individual notice must be sent to all class members whose names and addresses may be ascertained through reasonable effort.

The Advisory Committee's Note to Rule 23 reinforces this conclusion. See 28 U.S.C. App., p. 7765. The Advisory Committee described subdivision (c)(2) as "not merely discretionary" and added that the "mandatory notice pursuant to subdivision (c)(2) . . . is designed to fulfill requirements of due process to which the class action procedure is of course subject." Id., at 7768. The Committee explicated its incorporation of due process standards by citation to Mullane v. Central Hanover Bank & Trust Co., 339 U.S. 306 (1950), and like cases.

In *Mullane* the Court addressed the constitutional sufficiency of publication notice rather than mailed individual notice to known beneficiaries of a common trust fund as part of a judicial settlement of accounts. The Court observed that notice and an opportunity to be heard were fundamental requisites of the constitutional guarantee of procedural due process. It further stated that notice must be "reasonably calculated, under all the circumstances, to apprise interested parties of the pendency of action and afford them an opportunity to present their objections." Id., at 314. The Court continued:

> But when notice is a person's due, process which is a mere gesture is not due process. The means employed must be such as one desirous of actually informing the absentee might reasonably adopt to accomplish it. The reasonableness and hence the constitutional validity of any chosen method may be defended on the ground that it is in itself reasonably certain to inform those affected.

Id. at 315. The Court then held that publication notice could not satisfy due process where the names and addresses of the beneficiaries were known. In such cases, "the reasons disappear for resort to means less likely than the mails to apprise them of [an action's] pendency." Id. at 318.

In Schroeder v. City of New York, 371 U.S. 208 (1962), decided prior to the promulgation of amended Rule 23, the Court explained that *Mullane* required rejection of notice by publication where the name and address of the affected person were available. The Court stated that the "general rule" is that "notice by publication is not enough with respect to a person whose name and address are known or very easily ascertainable. . . ." Id. at 212-213. The Court also noted that notice by publication had long been recognized as a poor substitute for actual notice and that its justification was "'difficult at best.'" Id. at 213.

Viewed in this context, the express language and intent of Rule 23(c)(2) leave no doubt that individual notice must be provided to those class members who are identifiable through reasonable effort. In the present case, the names and addresses of 2,250,000 class members are easily ascertainable, and there is nothing to show that individual notice cannot be mailed to each. For these class members, individual notice is clearly the "best notice practicable" within the meaning of Rule 23(c)(2) and our prior decisions.

Petitioner contends, however, that we should dispense with the requirement of individual notice in this case, and he advances two reasons for our doing so. First, the prohibitively high cost of providing individual notice to 2,250,000 class members would end this suit as a class action and effectively frustrate petitioner's attempt to vindicate the policies underlying the antitrust and securities laws. Second, petitioner contends that individual notice is unnecessary in this case, because no prospective class member has a large enough stake in the matter to justify separate litigation of his individual claim. Hence, class members lack any incentive to opt out of the class action even if notified.

The short answer to these arguments is that individual notice to identifiable class members is not a discretionary consideration to be waived in a particular case. It is, rather, an unambiguous requirement of Rule 23. As the Advisory Committee's Note explained, the Rule was intended to insure that the judgment, whether favorable or not, would bind all class members who did not request exclusion from the suit. 28 U.S.C. App., pp. 7765, 7768. Accordingly, each class member who can be identified through reasonable effort must be notified that he may request exclusion from the action and thereby preserve his opportunity to press his claim separately or that he may remain in the class and perhaps participate in the management of the action. There is nothing in Rule 23 to suggest that the notice requirements can be tailored to fit the pocketbooks of particular plaintiffs.

Petitioner further contends that adequate representation, rather than notice, is the touchstone of due process in a class action and therefore satisfies Rule 23. We think this view has little to commend it. To begin with, Rule 23 speaks to notice as well as to adequacy of representation and requires that both be provided. Moreover, petitioner's argument proves too much, for it quickly leads to the conclusion that no notice at all, published or otherwise, would be required in the present case. This cannot be so, for quite apart from what due process may require, the command of Rule 23 is clearly to the contrary. We therefore conclude that Rule 23(c)(2) requires that individual notice be sent to all class members who can be identified with reasonable effort.

We also agree with the Court of Appeals that petitioner must bear the cost of notice to the members of his class. The District Court reached the contrary conclusion and imposed 90% of the notice cost on respondents. This decision was predicated on the court's finding, made after a preliminary hearing on the merits of the case, that petitioner was "more than likely" to prevail on his claims. Apparently, that court interpreted Rule 23 to authorize such a hearing as part of the determination whether a suit may be maintained as a class action. We disagree.

We find nothing in either the language or history of Rule 23 that gives a court any authority to conduct a preliminary inquiry into the merits of a suit in order to determine whether it may be maintained as a class action. Indeed, such a procedure contravenes the Rule by allowing a representative plaintiff to secure the benefits of a class action without first satisfying the requirements for it. He is thereby allowed to obtain a determination on the merits of the claims advanced on behalf of the class without any assurance that a class action may be maintained. This procedure is directly contrary to the command of subdivision (c)(1) that the court determine whether a suit denominated a class action may be maintained as such "[a]s soon as practicable after the commencement of [the] action. . . ." In short, we agree with Judge Wisdom's conclusion in Miller v. Mackey International, 452 F.2d 424 (5th Cir. 1971), where the court rejected a preliminary inquiry into the merits of a proposed class action:

> In determining the propriety of a class action, the question is not whether the plaintiff or plaintiffs have stated a cause of action or will prevail on the merits, but rather whether the requirements of Rule 23 are met.

Id. at 427. Additionally, we might note that a preliminary determination of the merits may result in substantial prejudice to a defendant, since of necessity it is not accompanied by the traditional rules and procedures applicable to civil trials. The court's tentative findings, made in the absence of established safeguards, may color the subsequent proceedings and place an unfair burden on the defendant.

In the absence of any support under Rule 23, petitioner's effort to impose the cost of notice on respondents must fail. The usual rule is that a plaintiff must initially bear the cost of notice to the class. The exceptions cited by the District Court related to situations where a fiduciary duty preexisted between the plaintiff and defendant, as in a shareholder derivative suit. Where, as here, the relationship between the parties is truly adversary, the plaintiff must pay for the cost of notice as part of the ordinary burden of financing his own suit.

Petitioner has consistently maintained, however, that he will not bear the cost of notice under subdivision (c)(2) to members of the class as defined in his original complaint. See 479 F.2d at 1008; 52 F.R.D. at 269. We therefore remand the cause with instructions to dismiss the class action as so defined.

The judgment of the Court of Appeals is *vacated* and the cause *remanded*. . . .

JUSTICE DOUGLAS, with whom JUSTICE BRENNAN and JUSTICE MARSHALL concur, dissenting in part.

While I am in general agreement with the phases of this case touched on by the Court, I add a few words because its opinion does not fully explore the issues which will be dispositive of this case on remand to the District Court.

Federal Rule Civ. Proc. 23(c)(4) provides: "When appropriate (A) an action may be brought or maintained as a class action with respect to particular issues, or (B) a class may be divided into subclasses and each subclass treated as a class, and the provisions of this rule shall then be construed and applied accordingly."

As Judge Oakes, speaking for himself and Judge Timbers, said below:

> The plaintiff class might, for example, be divided into much smaller subclasses . . . of odd-lot buyers for particular periods, and one subclass treated as a test case, with the other subclasses held in abeyance. Individual notice

> at what would probably be a reasonable cost could then be given to all members of the particular small subclass who can be easily identified.

479 F.2d 1005, 1023 (dissenting from denial of rehearing en banc).

Or a subclass might include those on monthly investment plans, or payroll deduction plans run by brokerage houses.[1] The possibilities, though not infinite, are numerous.

The power to create a subclass is clear and unambiguous. Who should be included and how large it should be are questions that only the District Court should resolve. Notice to each member of the subclass would be essential under Rule 23(c)(2); and under Rule 23(c)(2)(A) any notified member may opt out. There would remain the question whether the subclass suit is manageable. But since the subclass could be chosen in light of the non-manageability of the size of the class whose claims are presently before us, there is no apparent difficulty in that sense. . . .

The class action is one of the few legal remedies the small claimant has against those who command the status quo. I would strengthen his hand with the view of creating a system of law that dispenses justice to the lowly as well as to those liberally endowed with power and wealth.

Notes and Questions

1. *The Centrality of Notice. Eisen* was the first big Supreme Court case after the revision of Rule 23 in 1966, and its weary path through the courts was not an inspiring example of the greater simplicity the new rule sought

1. The parties and courts below concentrated on whether a class action could be sustained on behalf of all six million odd-lot investors, so that the record is limited in information bearing on what manageable subclasses could be created.

There is, nonetheless, indication that certain subclasses might be economically manageable. Counsel for respondent Carlisle & Jacquelin stated in oral argument before the Court of Appeals that 100,000 shareholders participate in his client's Monthly Investment Plan, and that Carlisle & Jacquelin corresponds with those investors. Merrill Lynch corresponds with 150,000 people participating in a pay-roll deduction investment plan. Whether Eisen or any other plaintiff who may come forward to intervene fits in such a subclass, we do not know. But if brokerage houses correspond regularly in the course of business with such odd-lot investors, the marginal cost of providing the individual notice required by Rule 23(c)(2) might be nothing more than printing and stuffing an additional sheet of paper in correspondence already being sent to the investor, or perhaps only programming a computer to type an additional paragraph at the bottom of monthly or quarterly statements regularly mailed by the brokers.

A subclass of those who had engaged in numerous transactions might also be defined, so that the recovery per class member might be large enough to justify the cost of notice and management of the action. A survey of only four of 14 wire firms revealed 2,000 customers with 10 or more transactions between 1962 and 1966. 52 F.R.D. 253, 259, 267, and n.10.

By defining more definite subclasses such as those discussed, moreover, the problems inherent in distributing an eventual judgment would be reduced. Class members would be more readily identifiable, with more readily accessible transaction records and individually provable damages.

to promote. The case established the principle that new procedural tools must still adhere to due process fundamentals. A few years after *Eisen*, the court decided Oppenheimer Fund, Inc. v. Sanders, 437 U.S. 340 (1978), in which it held that the costs of providing notice to class members must be borne by the party seeking class treatment. Thus if a plaintiff requests in discovery defendants' records in an effort to define and locate potential class members, the plaintiff may be required to bear the cost of producing such lists. Ordinarily, the party responding to a discovery request pays for the cost of responding; *Oppenheimer* suggests an exception to that general rule.

If, however, the plaintiff succeeds in the lawsuit, then the costs of notice can be deducted from the class recovery. Of course, when the notice costs are exceptionally high, this up-front expense can be an insurmountable obstacle for some litigants, despite the potential for reimbursement at litigation's close.

2. *Making Sense of Notice*. Professor Deborah Rhode cites the following responses to a notice advising potential class members of their right to opt out of a suit seeking damages from several drug companies. Do they suggest that notice may not be of much use in some situations?

> Dear Sir:
>
> I received your pamphlet on drugs, which I think will be of great value to me in the future.
>
> Due to circumstances beyond my control I will not be able to attend this class at the time prescribed on your letter due to the fact that my working hours are from 7:00 until 4:30.
>
> Dear Sir:
>
> Our son is in the Navy, stationed in the Caribbean some place. Please let us know exactly what kind of drugs he is accused of taking.
>
> From a mother who will help if properly informed.
>
> Dear Attorney General:
>
> . . . I received a card from you and I don't understand it, and my husband can't read his. Most of the time all I buy is olive oil for healing oil after praying over it, it is anointed with God's power and ain't nothing like dope.

Deborah L. Rhode, Class Conflicts in Class Actions, 34 Stan. L. Rev. 1183, 1235, 1235 n.212 (1983).

Consider also the following remarks by Professor Arthur R. Miller, the Reporter of the Judicial Conference's Advisory Committee on the Federal Civil Rules, in Problems of Giving Notice in Class Actions, 58 F.R.D. 313, 321-322 (1972), in connection with the intelligibility of notice:

> Obviously, the federal courts should not involve themselves in Madison Avenue activities. I am not advocating the use of gayly colored judicial mail

embossed: "Important! Open this envelope! You may be entitled to a cash reward!!" The courts cannot act as if they were hawking the *Reader's Digest*. Nevertheless, the notice-giving process under Rule 23 must be reasonably pragmatic. The sad truth is that notices issued by courts or attorneys typically are much too larded with legal jargon to be understood by the average citizen.

A good illustration of this also is offered by the tetracycline cases. The Attorney General of North Carolina sent notice of the action to citizens of his state who had paid income taxes during a particular period. The theory underlying this procedure was sound enough. Given the wide use of the medication it was important to send notice to a broadly based list of citizens. Some of the responses are worth reading because they are symptomatic of the difficulty with the wording of most notices and reflect the problem of communicating to lay people about legal matters.

Dear Mr. Clerk:

I have your notice that I owe you $300 for selling drugs. I have never sold any drugs, especially those you have listed; but I have sold a little whiskey once in a while.

Dear Sir:

I received this paper from you. I guess I really don't understand it, but if I have been given one of those drugs, nobody told me why. If it means what I think it does, I have not been with a man in nine years. . . .

Dear Mr. Attorney General:

I am sorry to say this, but you have the wrong John Doe, because in 1954, I wasn't but three years old and didn't even have a name. Mother named me when I got my driver's license. Up to then, they just called me Baby Doe.

3. *Sample Notice of Settlement in Securities Fraud Action*. Recall In re Time Warner, Inc. Sec. Litig., 9 F.3d 259 (2d Cir. 1993), which you encountered in connection with pleading specificity (Chapter 2, section B(1)(b) supra). Shortly after the major pleading issues were resolved, the parties settled. Below is a summary of the notice of that settlement. A longer, more detailed version was mailed to known interested parties. This shorter version was published in the newspaper.

UNITED STATES DISTRICT COURT
SOUTHERN DISTRICT OF NEW YORK

IN RE TIME WARNER INC.	)	MASTER FILE NO.
SECURITIES LITIGATION	)	91 CIV. 4081(MEL)

SUMMARY NOTICE OF PROPOSED SETTLEMENT OF CLASS ACTION AND SETTLEMENT HEARING

TO: ALL PERSONS WHO PURCHASED, OR OTHERWISE ACQUIRED FOR CONSIDERATION, COMMON STOCK (CUSIP NO. 887315109) OF TIME WARNER INC. ("TIME WARNER") AT ANY TIME FROM APRIL 25, 1991 THROUGH THE CLOSE OF TRADING ON JUNE 5,

> 1991 (THE "CLASS PERIOD"), AND WHO SUFFERED A LOSS THEREBY, EXCLUDING DEFENDANTS AND ANY MEMBERS OF THEIR IMMEDIATE FAMILIES, ANY ENTITY IN WHICH THEY HAVE A CONTROLLING INTEREST, AND THE LEGAL REPRESENTATIVES, HEIRS, SUCCESSORS OR ASSIGNS OF ANY SUCH EXCLUDED PERSON OR ENTITY (THE "CLASS").

YOU ARE HEREBY NOTIFIED, pursuant to Rule 23 of the Federal Rules of Civil Procedure and an order of the United States District Court for the Southern District of New York (the "Court") dated October 11, 1994, that a hearing will be held on November 10, 1994 at 9:30 a.m., before the Court at the United States Courthouse, Southern District of New York, 40 Centre Street, New York, New York (the "Settlement Hearing"). The purpose of the Settlement Hearing is to determine whether the proposed $5,500,000 settlement of the above-captioned action against defendants should be approved by the Court as fair, reasonable and adequate, whether the application for an award of attorneys' fees and reimbursement of costs and expenses should be approved, and whether the action should be dismissed on the merits and with prejudice.

IF YOU PURCHASED SHARES OF COMMON STOCK OF TIME WARNER (CUSIP NO. 887315109) DURING THE CLASS PERIOD YOUR RIGHTS MAY BE AFFECTED BY THE ACTION AND YOU MAY BE ENTITLED TO MONEY. If you purchased common stock during the Class Period and have not yet received the "Notice of Pendency of Class Action and Proposed Settlement And Settlement Hearing" (the "Settlement Notice") and accompanying "Proof of Claim," which describe the Settlement and your rights and obligations thereunder in detail, you may obtain copies thereof by calling (415) 461-0410 or by writing to Time Warner Securities Litigation, c/o Gilardi & Co., P. O. Box 990, Corte Madera, CA 94976-0990. To participate in the settlement, you must file a Proof of Claim no later than January 16, 1995. IF YOU DO NOT FILE A PROPER PROOF OF CLAIM FORM OR DO NOT EXCLUDE YOURSELF FROM THE CLASS IN ACCORDANCE WITH THE SETTLEMENT NOTICE'S INSTRUCTIONS, YOU WILL NOT SHARE IN THE SETTLEMENT BUT YOU WILL BE BOUND BY THE FINAL JUDGMENT OF THE COURT.

Bankers and/or brokers requesting materials should contact Time Warner Securities Litigation, c/o Gilardi & Co., P.O. Box 990, Corte Madera, CA 94976-0990.

Bankers, brokers and/or other nominees will be entitled to reimbursement of the reasonable out-of-pocket expenses, service and research charges, handling fees, postage and similar charges that they incur in connection herewith.

PLEASE DO NOT CONTACT THE COURT OR THE CLERK'S OFFICE FOR INFORMATION.

Dated: New York, New York	By Order of the United States
October 11, 1994	District Court for the Southern District of New York

4. *Notice and Statutes of Limitation.* In a standard civil action, a plaintiff is barred from filing after the applicable statute of limitation has run. Statutes of limitation exist to protect defendants from stale claims, to prevent plaintiffs from sleeping on their rights, and to protect the integrity of the judicial process by ensuring that litigation occurs when memories are fresh and relevant evidence is more likely to be available. Normally, however, statutes of limitation are tolled while litigation is pending. How should statutes of limitation and tolling rules apply to class actions?

The Supreme Court has held that the filing of a class action automatically tolls the statute of limitations for putative class members, at least until class certification is denied. See Crown Cork & Seal Co., Inc. v. Parker, 462 U.S. 345 (1983); Am. Pipe & Constr. Co. v. Utah, 414 U.S. 538 (1974). A contrary rule, the Court observed in *Crown Cork & Seal*, would defeat the purposes of Rule 23—class members would have to file their own suits or intervene in the class suit to protect their rights, thereby inviting the very inefficiencies Rule 23 was designed to avoid. And as the Court emphasized in *American Pipe*, once a class action is filed, the defendants are on notice "not only of the substantive claims being brought against them, but also of the number and generic identities of the potential plaintiffs who may participate in the judgment." 414 U.S. at 554-555. Thus there is no harm to defendants in tolling the statute of limitations for class members.

The plaintiff in *Crown, Cork & Seal* was an African-American male fired by the defendant. He filed a charge of racial discrimination under Title VII with the EEOC which then issued him a "Notice of Right to Sue within 90 days." In the meantime, two other black employees filed a class action alleging discrimination under Title VII. Plaintiff, a putative member of the class suit, filed his individual claim nearly two years after the Notice of Right to Sue was issued, but within 90 days of the district court's decision denying class certification. The Supreme Court held that the 90-day statute of limitations was tolled while the unsuccessful class action was pending.

The courts of appeals have split, however, on whether tolling applies where class certification is denied in the first action and, rather than proceed individually, putative class members file a second class action suit. Can you see why it would be controversial to give plaintiffs the benefit of tolling to relitigate a denial of class certification? Justice Blackmun warned in *American Pipe* that the Court's decision to permit tolling in some circumstances "must not be regarded as encouragement to lawyers in a case of this kind to frame their pleadings as a class action, intentionally, to attract and save members of the purported class who have slept on their rights." 414 U.S. at 561 (Blackmun, J., concurring). The concern is that class members or their lawyers will "piggyback one class action onto another . . . and thereby engage in endless rounds of litigation" in an attempt to win certification. Griffin v. Singletary, 17 F.3d 356, 359 (11th Cir. 1994) (categorically disallowing tolling for successive class actions) (internal quotations omitted).

Are the grounds for the initial denial of class certification relevant to deciding whether tolling should apply? See Catholic Soc. Servs., Inc. v. I.N.S., 232 F.3d 1139 (9th Cir. 2000) (en banc). What if class certification is first denied on adequacy grounds because there is a problem with the class representative, but in the second suit the class members have cured the defect? See Yang v. Odom, 392 F.3d 97, 111 (3d Cir. 2004) (canvassing circuit split and holding that tolling is allowed).

What if class certification is first denied because of some deficiency in the class itself? See Basch v. Ground Round, Inc., 139 F.3d 6 (1st Cir. 1998) (no tolling for sequential class action where initial certification denied because the class members were not "similarly situated"); Korwek v. Hunt, 827 F.2d 874 (2d Cir. 1987) (no tolling where first class action failed because of manageability problems and intraclass conflicts); Salazar-Calderon v. Presidio Valley Farmers Ass'n, 765 F.2d 1334 (5th Cir. 1985) (tolling does not permit putative class members to file a subsequent class action where certification of first class denied because common questions did not predominate and class action was not a superior method for handling the controversy). If class members can take advantage of tolling to sue individually, why give them the option of filing another class action? Why allow two (or more) bites at the class certification apple?

5. Choice of Forum and Mode of Trial Issues: Personal Jurisdiction

Phillips Petroleum Co. v. Shutts

472 U.S. 797 (1985)

JUSTICE REHNQUIST delivered the opinion of the Court.

Petitioner is a Delaware corporation which has its principal place of business in Oklahoma. During the 1970's it produced or purchased natural gas from leased land located in 11 different States, and sold most of the gas in interstate commerce. Respondents are some 28,000 of the royalty owners possessing rights to the leases from which petitioner produced the gas; they reside in all 50 States, the District of Columbia, and several foreign countries. Respondents brought a class action against petitioner in the Kansas state court, seeking to recover interest on royalty payments which had been delayed by petitioner. They recovered judgment in the trial court, and the Supreme Court of Kansas affirmed the judgment over petitioner's contentions that the Due Process Clause of the Fourteenth Amendment prevented Kansas from adjudicating the claims of all the respondents, and that the Due Process Clause and the Full Faith and Credit Clause of Article IV of the Constitution prohibited the application of Kansas law to all of the transactions between petitioner and respondents. 679 P.2d 1159 (1984). We granted certiorari to consider these claims. 469 U.S. 879 (1984). We reject petitioner's jurisdictional claim, but sustain its claim regarding the choice of law.

Because petitioner sold the gas to its customers in interstate commerce, it was required to secure approval for price increases from what was then the Federal Power Commission, and is now the Federal Energy Regulatory Commission. Under its regulations the Federal Power Commission permitted petitioner to propose and collect tentative higher gas prices, subject to final approval by the Commission. If the Commission eventually denied petitioner's proposed price increase or reduced the proposed increase, petitioner would have to refund to its customers the difference between the approved price and the higher price charged, plus interest at a rate set by statute. See 18 C.F.R. § 154. 102 (1984).

Although petitioner received higher gas prices pending review by the Commission, petitioner suspended any increase in royalties paid to the royalty owners because the higher price could be subject to recoupment by petitioner's customers. Petitioner agreed to pay the higher royalty only if the royalty owners would provide petitioner with a bond or indemnity for the increase, plus interest, in case the price increase was not ultimately approved and a refund was due to the customers. Petitioner set the interest rate on the indemnity agreements at the same interest rate the Commission would have required petitioner to refund to its customers. A small percentage of the royalty owners provided this indemnity and received royalties immediately from the interim price increases; these royalty owners are unimportant to this case.

The remaining royalty owners received no royalty on the unapproved portion of the prices until the Federal Power Commission approval of those prices became final. Royalties on the unapproved portion of the gas price were suspended three times by petitioner, corresponding to its three proposed price increases in the mid-1970's. In three written opinions the Commission approved all of petitioner's tentative price increases, so petitioner paid to its royalty owners the suspended royalties of \$3.7 million in 1976, \$4.7 million in 1977, and \$2.9 million in 1978. Petitioner paid no interest to the royalty owners although it had the use of the suspended royalty money for a number of years.

Respondents Irl Shutts, Robert Anderson, and Betty Anderson filed suit against petitioner in Kansas state court, seeking interest payments on their suspended royalties which petitioner had possessed pending the Commission's approval of the price increases. Shutts is a resident of Kansas, and the Andersons live in Oklahoma. Shutts and the Andersons own gas leases in Oklahoma and Texas. Over petitioner's objection the Kansas trial court granted respondents' motion to certify the suit as a class action under Kansas law. Kan. Stat. Ann. §§ 60-223 et seq. (1983). The class as certified was comprised of 33,000 royalty owners who had royalties suspended by petitioner. The average claim of each royalty owner for interest on the suspended royalties was \$100.

After the class was certified respondents provided each class member with notice through first-class mail. The notice described the action and informed each class member that he could appear in person or by counsel; otherwise each member would be represented by Shutts and the Andersons, the named plaintiffs. The notices also stated that class members would be included in the class and bound by the judgment unless they "opted out" of the lawsuit by executing and returning a "request for exclusion" that was included with the notice. The final class as certified contained 28,100 members; 3,400 had "opted out" of the class by returning the request for exclusion, and notice could not be delivered to another 1,500 members, who were also excluded. Less than 1,000 of the class members resided in Kansas. Only a minuscule amount, approximately one quarter of one percent, of the gas leases involved in the lawsuit were on Kansas land.

After petitioner's mandamus petition to decertify the class was denied, Phillips Petroleum v. Duckworth, No. 82-54608 (Kan., June 28, 1982), *cert. denied,* 459 U.S. 1103 (1983), the case was tried to the court. The court found petitioner liable under Kansas law for interest on the suspended royalties to all class members. . . . The trial court did not determine whether any difference existed between the laws of Kansas and other States, or whether another State's laws should be applied to non-Kansas plaintiffs or to royalties from leases in States other than Kansas. 235 Kan., at 221.

Petitioner raised two principal claims in its appeal to the Supreme Court of Kansas. It first asserted that the Kansas trial court did not possess personal jurisdiction over absent plaintiff class members as required by International Shoe Co. v. Washington, 326 U.S. 310 (1945), and similar cases. Related to this first claim was petitioner's contention that the "opt-out" notice to absent class members, which forced them to return the request for exclusion in order to avoid the suit, was insufficient to bind class members who were not residents of Kansas or who did not possess "minimum contacts" with Kansas. Second, petitioner claimed that Kansas courts could not apply Kansas law to every claim in the dispute. The trial court should have looked to the laws of each State where the leases were located to determine, on the basis of conflict of laws principles, whether interest on the suspended royalties was recoverable, and at what rate.

The Supreme Court of Kansas held that the entire cause of action was maintainable under the Kansas class-action statute, and the court rejected both of petitioner's claims. 235 Kan. 195 (1984). First, it held that the absent class members were plaintiffs, not defendants, and thus the traditional minimum contacts test of *International Shoe* did not apply. The court held that nonresident class-action plaintiffs were only entitled to adequate notice, an opportunity to be heard, an opportunity to opt out of the case, and adequate representation by the named plaintiffs. If these procedural due process minima were met, according to the court, Kansas could assert jurisdiction over the plaintiff class and bind each class member with a judgment on his claim. The court surveyed the course of the litigation and concluded that all of these minima had been met.

The court also rejected petitioner's contention that Kansas law could not be applied to plaintiffs and royalty arrangements having no connection with Kansas. The court stated that generally the law of the forum controlled all claims unless "compelling reasons" existed to apply a different law. The court found no compelling reasons, and noted that "[t]he plaintiff class members have indicated their desire to have this action determined under the laws of Kansas." 235 Kan. at 222. The court affirmed as a matter of Kansas equity law the award of interest on the suspended royalties, at the rates imposed by the trial court. . . .

II

Reduced to its essentials, petitioner's argument is that unless out-of-state plaintiffs affirmatively consent, the Kansas courts may not exert jurisdiction over their claims. Petitioner claims that failure to execute and return the "request for exclusion" provided with the class notice cannot constitute consent of the out-of-state plaintiffs; thus Kansas courts may exercise jurisdiction over these plaintiffs only if the plaintiffs possess the sufficient "minimum contacts" with Kansas as that term is used in cases involving personal jurisdiction over out-of-state defendants. E.g., International Shoe Co. v. Washington, 326 U.S. 310 (1945); Shaffer v. Heitner, 433 U.S. 186 (1977); World-Wide Volkswagen Corp. v. Woodson, 444 U.S. 286 (1980). Since Kansas had no prelitigation contact with many of the plaintiffs and leases involved, petitioner claims that Kansas has exceeded its jurisdictional reach and thereby violated the due process rights of the absent plaintiffs.

In *International Shoe* we were faced with an out-of-state corporation which sought to avoid the exercise of personal jurisdiction over it as a defendant by a Washington state court. We held that the extent of the dependant's due process protection would depend "upon the quality and nature of the activity in relation to the fair and orderly administration of the laws. . . ." 326 U.S. at 319. We noted that the Due Process Clause did not permit a State to make a binding judgment against a person with whom the State had no contacts, ties, or relations. Id. If the defendant possessed certain minimum contacts with the State, so that it was "reasonable and just, according to our traditional conception of fair play and substantial justice" for a State to exercise personal jurisdiction, the State could force the defendant to defend himself in the forum, upon pain of default, and could bind him to a judgment. Id. at 320.

The purpose of this test, of course, is to protect a defendant from the travail of defending in a distant forum, unless the defendant's contacts with the forum make it just to force him to defend there. As we explained in *Woodson*, supra, the defendant's contacts should be such that "he should reasonably anticipate being haled" into the forum. 444 U.S. at 297. In Insurance Corp. of Ireland v. Compagnie des Bauxites de Guinee, 456 U.S. 694, 702-703, and n.10 (1982), we explained that the requirement that a court have personal jurisdiction comes from the Due Process Clause's protection of the defendant's personal liberty interest, and said that the requirement "represents a restriction on judicial power not as a matter of sovereignty, but as a matter of individual liberty." (Footnote omitted.)

Although the cases like *Shaffer* and *Woodson* which petitioner relies on for a minimum contacts requirement all dealt with out-of-state defendants or parties in the procedural posture of a defendant, cf. New York Life Ins. Co. v. Dunlevy, 241 U.S. 518 (1916); Estin v. Estin, 334 U.S. 541 (1948), petitioner claims that the same analysis must apply to absent class-action plaintiffs. In this regard petitioner correctly points out that a chose in action is a constitutionally recognized property interest possessed by each of the plaintiffs. Mullane v. Central Hanover Bank & Trust Co., 339 U.S. 306 (1950). An adverse judgment by Kansas courts in this case may extinguish the chose in action forever through res judicata. Such an adverse judgment, petitioner claims, would be every bit as onerous to an absent plaintiff as an adverse judgment on the merits would be to a defendant. Thus, the same due process protections should apply to absent plaintiffs: Kansas should not be able to exert jurisdiction over the plaintiffs' claims unless the plaintiffs have sufficient minimum contacts with Kansas.

We think petitioner's premise is in error. The burdens placed by a State upon an absent class-action plaintiff are not of the same order or magnitude as those it places upon an absent defendant. An out-of-state defendant summoned by a plaintiff is faced with the full powers of the forum State to render judgment *against* it. The defendant must generally hire counsel and travel to the forum to defend itself from the plaintiff's claim, or suffer a default judgment. The defendant may be forced to participate in extended and often costly discovery, and will be forced to respond in damages or to comply with some other form of remedy imposed by the court should it lose the suit. The defendant may also face liability for court costs and attorney's fees. These burdens are substantial, and the minimum contacts requirement of the Due Process Clause prevents the forum State from unfairly imposing them upon the defendant.

A class-action plaintiff, however, is in quite a different posture. The Court noted this difference in Hansberry v. Lee, 311 U.S. 32, 40-41 (1940), which explained that a "class" or "representative" suit was an exception to the rule that one could not be bound by judgment *in personam* unless one was made fully a party in the traditional sense. Id., citing Pennoyer v. Neff, 95 U.S. 714 (1878). As the Court pointed out in *Hansberry,* the class action was an invention of equity to enable it to proceed to a decree in suits where the number of those interested in the litigation was too great to permit joinder. The absent parties would be bound by the decree so long as the named parties adequately represented the absent class and the prosecution of the litigation was within the common interest. 311 U.S. at 41.

Modern plaintiff class actions follow the same goals, permitting litigation of a suit involving common questions when there are too many plaintiffs for proper joinder. Class actions also may permit the plaintiffs to pool claims which would be uneconomical to litigate individually. For example, this lawsuit involves claims averaging about $100 per plaintiff;

most of the plaintiffs would have no realistic day in court if a class action were not available.

In sharp contrast to the predicament of a defendant haled into an out-of-state forum, the plaintiffs in this suit were not haled any-where to defend themselves upon pain of a default judgment. As commentators have noted, from the plaintiffs' point of view a class action resembles a "quasi-administrative proceeding, conducted by the judge." 3B J. Moore & J. Kennedy, Moore's Federal Practice ¶23.45 [4-5] (1984); Kaplan, Continuing Work of the Civil Committee: 1966 Amendments to the Federal Rules of Civil Procedure (I), 81 Harv. L. Rev. 356, 398 (1967).

A plaintiff class in Kansas and numerous other jurisdictions cannot first be certified unless the judge, with the aid of the named plaintiffs and defendant, conducts an inquiry into the common nature of the named plaintiffs' and the absent plaintiffs' claims, the adequacy of representation, the jurisdiction possessed over the class, and any other matters that will bear upon proper representation of the absent plaintiffs' interest. See, e.g., Kan. Stat. Ann. § 60-223 (1983); Fed. Rule Civ. Proc. 23. Unlike a defendant in a civil suit, a class-action plaintiff is not required to fend for himself. See Kan. Stat. Ann. § 60-223(d) (1983). The court and named plaintiffs protect his interests. Indeed, the class-action defendant itself has a great interest in ensuring that the absent plaintiffs' claims are properly before the forum. In this case, for example, the defendant sought to avoid class certification by alleging that the absent plaintiffs would not be adequately represented and were not amenable to jurisdiction.

The concern of the typical class-action rules for the absent plaintiffs is manifested in other ways. Most jurisdictions, including Kansas, require that a class action, once certified, may not be dismissed or compromised without the approval of the court. In many jurisdictions such as Kansas the court may amend the pleadings to ensure that all sections of the class are represented adequately. Kan. Stat. Ann. § 60-223(d) (1983); see also, e.g., Fed. Rule Civ. Proc. 23(d).

Besides this continuing solicitude for their rights, absent plaintiff class members are not subject to other burdens imposed upon defendants. They need not hire counsel or appear. They are almost never subject to counterclaims or cross-claims, or liability for fees or costs. Absent plaintiff class members are not subject to coercive or punitive remedies. Nor will an adverse judgment typically bind an absent plaintiff for any damages, although a valid adverse judgment may extinguish any of the plaintiff's claims which were litigated.

Unlike a defendant in a normal civil suit, an absent class-action plaintiff is not required to do anything. He may sit back and allow the litigation to run its course, content in knowing that there are safeguards provided for his protection. In most class actions an absent plaintiff is provided at least with an opportunity to "opt out" of the class, and if he takes advantage of that opportunity he is removed from the litigation entirely. This was true of the Kansas proceedings in this case. The Kansas procedure provided for the mailing of a notice to each class member by first-class mail. The notice, as we have previously indicated, described the action and informed the class member that he could appear in person or by counsel, in default of which he would be represented by the named plaintiffs and their attorneys. The notice further stated that class members would be included in the class and bound by the judgment unless they "opted out" by executing and returning a "request for exclusion" that was included in the notice.

Petitioner contends, however, that the "opt out" procedure provided by Kansas is not good enough, and that an "opt in" procedure is required to satisfy the Due Process Clause of the Fourteenth Amendment. Insofar as plaintiffs who have no minimum contacts with the forum State are concerned, an "opt in" provision would require that each class member affirmatively consent to his inclusion within the class.

Because States place fewer burdens upon absent class plaintiffs than they do upon absent defendants in nonclass suits, the Due Process Clause need not and does not afford the former as much protection from state-court jurisdiction as it does the latter. The Fourteenth Amendment does protect "persons," not "defendants," however, so absent plaintiffs as well as absent defendants are entitled to some protection from the jurisdiction of a forum State which seeks to adjudicate their claims. In this case we hold that a forum State may exercise jurisdiction over the claim of an absent class-action plaintiff, even though that plaintiff may not possess the minimum contacts with the forum which would support personal jurisdiction over a defendant. If the forum State wishes to bind an absent plaintiff concerning a claim for money damages or similar relief at law, it must provide minimal procedural due process protection. The plaintiff must receive notice plus an opportunity to be heard and participate in the litigation, whether in person or through counsel. The notice must be the best practicable, "reasonably calculated, under all the circumstances, to apprise interested parties of the pendency of the action and afford them an opportunity to present their objections." *Mullane,* 339 U.S. at 314-315; cf. Eisen v. Carlisle & Jacquelin, 417 U.S. 156, 174-175 (1974). The notice should describe the action and the plaintiffs' rights in it. Additionally, we hold that due process requires at a minimum that an absent plaintiff be provided with an opportunity to remove himself from the class by executing and returning an "opt out" or "request for exclusion" form to the court. Finally, the Due Process Clause of course requires that the named plaintiff at all times adequately represent the interests of the absent class members. *Hansberry,* 311 U.S. at 42-43, 45.

We reject petitioner's contention that the Due Process Clause of the Fourteenth Amendment requires that absent plaintiffs affirmatively "opt in" to the class, rather than be deemed members of the class if they do not "opt out." We think that such a contention is supported by little, if any precedent, and that it ignores the differences between class-action plaintiffs, on the one hand, and defendants in nonclass civil suits on the other. Any plaintiff may consent to jurisdiction. Keeton v. Hustler Magazine, Inc., 465 U.S. 770 (1984). The essential question, then, is how stringent the requirement for a showing of consent will be.

We think that the procedure followed by Kansas, where a fully descriptive notice is sent first-class mail to each class member, with an explanation of the right to "opt out," satisfies due process. Requiring a plaintiff to affirmatively request inclusion would probably impede the prosecution of those class actions involving an aggregation of small individual claims, where a large number of claims are required to make it economical to bring suit. See, e.g., *Eisen*, supra, at 161. The plaintiff's claim may be so small, or the plaintiff so unfamiliar with the law, that he would not file suit individually, nor would he affirmatively request inclusion in the class if such a request were required by the Constitution. If, on the other hand, the plaintiff's claim is sufficiently large or important that he wishes to litigate it on his own, he will likely have retained an attorney or have thought about filing suit, and should be fully capable of exercising his right to "opt out."

In this case over 3,400 members of the potential class did "opt out," which belies the contention that "opt out" procedures result in guaranteed jurisdiction by inertia. Another 1,500 were excluded because the notice and "opt out" form was undeliverable. We think that such results show that the "opt out" procedure provided by Kansas is by no means *pro forma*, and that the Constitution does not require more to protect what must be the somewhat rare species of class member who is unwilling to execute an "opt out" form, but whose claim is nonetheless so important that he cannot be presumed to consent to being a member of the class by his failure to do so. Petitioner's "opt in" requirement would require the invalidation of scores of state statutes and of the class-action provision of the Federal Rules of Civil Procedure, and for the reasons stated we do not think that the Constitution requires the State to sacrifice the obvious advantages in judicial efficiency resulting from the "opt out" approach for the protection of the *rara avis* portrayed by petitioner.

We therefore hold that the protection afforded the plaintiff class members by the Kansas statute satisfies the Due Process Clause. The interests of the absent plaintiffs are sufficiently protected by the forum State when those plaintiffs are provided with a request for exclusion that can be returned within a reasonable time to the court. See Insurance Corp. of Ireland, 456 U.S., at 702-703 and n.10. Both the Kansas trial court and the Supreme Court of Kansas held that the class received adequate representation, and no party disputes that conclusion here. We conclude that the Kansas court properly asserted personal jurisdiction over the absent plaintiffs and their claims against petitioner.

Note: Venue in Class Actions

Should the venue requirement be fully satisfied if venue would be proper for an action against the class representative? For plaintiff classes, correct venue for the representative suffices for the absent parties, e.g., Research Corp. v. Pfister Assoc. Growers, 301 F. Supp. 497 (N.D. Ill. 1969).

For an isolated case holding that the defendant class judgment is not binding on members for whom the venue was improper, see Sperberg v. Firestone Tire & Rubber Co., 61 F.R.D. 70 (N.D. Ohio 1973).

Note: Federal Jurisdiction in Class Actions

The United States Supreme Court held in Supreme Tribe of Ben-Hur v. Cauble, 255 U.S. 356 (1921), that only the citizenship of the named representatives of a class action suit based on diversity need be considered for jurisdictional purposes. Thus a class member whose citizenship was not diverse from all of the defendants nevertheless was bound by a prior decree, even though it would have destroyed diversity had he been a named class representative.

Ben-Hur may suggest that only the claims of the named representatives likewise should be considered in determining the amount-in-controversy requirement. Yet Snyder v. Harris, 394 U.S. 332 (1969), and Zahn v. International Paper Co., 414 U.S. 291 (1973), hold otherwise. The Court explained this result in *Zahn* as follows:

> None of the plaintiffs in Snyder v. Harris alleged a claim exceeding $10,000, but there is no doubt that the rationale of that case controls this one. As previously indicated, *Snyder* invoked the well-established rule that each of several plaintiffs asserting separate and distinct claims must satisfy the jurisdictional amount requirement if his claim was to survive a motion to dismiss: This rule plainly mandates not only that there may be no aggregation and that the entire case must be dismissed where none of the plaintiffs claims more than $10,000 but also requires that any plaintiff without the jurisdictional amount must be dismissed from the case, even though others allege jurisdictionally sufficient claims. . . .
>
> It also seems to us that the application of the jurisdictional amount requirement to class actions was so plainly etched in the federal courts prior to 1966 that had there been any thought of departing from these decisions and, in so doing, of calling into question the accepted approach to cases involving ordinary joinder of plaintiffs with separate and distinct claims, some express statement of that intention would surely have appeared, either in the amendments themselves or in the official commentaries. But we find not a trace to this effect. As the Court thought in Snyder v. Harris, the matter must rest there absent further congressional action.

Id. at 300, 302. Justices Brennan, Marshall, and Douglas dissented, arguing that to assert ancillary jurisdiction over the claims that failed to satisfy the amount-in-controversy requirement would promote efficiency. In Justice Brennan's words,

> Class actions were born of necessity. The alternatives were joinder of the entire class, or redundant litigation of the common issues. The cost to the litigants and the drain on the resources of the judiciary resulting from either alternative would have been intolerable. And this case presents precisely

> those difficulties: approximately 240 claimants are involved, and the issues will doubtless call for extensive use of expert testimony on difficult scientific issues.
>
> It is, of course, true that an exercise of ancillary jurisdiction in such cases would result in some increase in the federal courts' workload, for unless the class action is permitted many of the claimants will be unable to obtain any federal determination of their rights. But that objection is applicable to every other exercise of ancillary jurisdiction. It should be sufficient answer that denial of ancillary jurisdiction will impose a much larger burden on the state and federal judiciary as a whole, and will substantially impair the ability of the prospective class members to assert their claims. . . .
>
> Not only does the practical desirability of sustaining jurisdiction bring Rule 23(b)(3) class actions within the logic of our decisions, but the Court has long since recognized the fact, and has sustained ancillary jurisdiction over the nonappearing members in a class action who do not meet the requirements of [the] traditional rule of complete diversity laid down in Strawbridge v. Curtis, 3 Cranch 267 (1806). In Supreme Tribe of Ben-Hur v. Cauble, 255 U.S. 356 (1921), the Court not only held that only the original named plaintiffs and defendants had to satisfy the diversity requirements, but it also stated that intervention by nondiverse members of the class would not destroy the District Court's jurisdiction. Id., at 366. Particularly in view of the constitutional background on which the statutory diversity requirements are written, see Zahn v. International Paper Co., 469 F.2d 1033, 1038 ([2d Cir.] 1972) (Timbers, J., dissenting), it is difficult to understand why the practical approach the Court took in *Supreme Tribe of Ben-Hur* must be abandoned where the purely statutory "matter in controversy" requirement is concerned.

Id. at 307-309 (Brennan, J., dissenting). Does the adoption of the supplemental jurisdiction statute (28 U.S.C. § 1367) alter this result? The Supreme Court has said "yes." See section A of this chapter, supra, for discussion of Exxon Mobile Corp. v. Allapattah Servs., Inc., 545 U.S. 546 (2005) (holding that § 1367 overrules *Zahn*; as long as the claims of one plaintiff satisfy the amount-in-controversy requirement, the court has supplemental jurisdiction over the claims of other class members.).

Congress has also intervened, passing a major expansion of the original and removal jurisdiction of federal courts over "interstate" plaintiff class actions where the aggregate amount in controversy exceeds $5,000,000 and the parties are minimally diverse. See The Class Action Fairness Act of 2005, PL 109-2; see especially 28 U.S.C. §§ 1332(d) and 1453. The Act's findings state that while class actions

> are an important and valuable part of the legal system when they permit the fair and efficient resolution of legitimate claims of numerous parties . . . there have been abuses of the class action device that have . . . harmed class members with legitimate claims and defendants that have acted responsibly . . . [and] undermined public respect for our judicial system.
>
> Class members often receive little or no benefit from class actions, and are sometimes harmed, such as where (A) counsel are awarded large fees, while leaving class members with coupons or other awards of little or no value; (B) unjustified awards are made to certain plaintiffs at the expense of other

class members; and (C) confusing notices are published that prevent class members from being able to fully understand and effectively exercise their rights. . . .

Abuses in class actions undermine the national judicial system . . . and the concept of diversity jurisdiction as intended by the framers of the United States Constitution, in that State and local courts are (A) keeping cases of national importance out of Federal court; (B) sometimes acting in ways that demonstrate bias against out-of-State defendants; and (C) making judgments that impose their view of the law on other States and bind the rights of the residents of those States.

PL 109-2, § 2; 28 U.S.C. § 1711, Note. In addition to expanding federal court jurisdiction over class actions, the Act sets standards for "coupon settlements," see 28 U.S.C. §§ 1711-1712, requires evenhandedness in the distribution of awards, see 28 U.S.C. §§ 1713-1714, and mandates that defendants notify appropriate state and federal officials of proposed settlements. See 28 U.S.C. § 1715.

If state courts are in fact doing what Congress accuses them of doing in the third paragraph quoted above, expanding federal subject matter jurisdiction arguably is a legitimate response. But are federal courts in any better position to deal with the other alleged abuses?

6. Settlement

Amchem Products, Inc. v. Windsor
521 U.S. 591 (1997)

Justice Ginsburg delivered the opinion of the Court.

This case concerns the legitimacy under Rule 23 of the Federal Rules of Civil Procedure of a class action certification sought to achieve global settlement of current and future asbestos-related claims. The class proposed for certification potentially encompasses hundreds of thousands, perhaps millions, of individuals tied together by this commonality: each was, or some day may be, adversely affected by past exposure to asbestos products manufactured by one or more of 20 companies. Those companies, defendants in the lower courts, are petitioners here.

The United States District Court for the Eastern District of Pennsylvania certified the class for settlement only, finding that the proposed settlement was fair and that representation and notice had been adequate. That court enjoined class members from separately pursuing asbestos-related personal-injury suits in any court, federal or state, pending the issuance of a final order. The Court of Appeals for the Third Circuit vacated the District Court's orders, holding that the class certification failed to satisfy Rule 23's requirements in several critical respects. We affirm the Court of Appeals' judgment.

I

A

The settlement-class certification we confront evolved in response to an asbestos-litigation crisis. A United States Judicial Conference Ad Hoc Committee on Asbestos Litigation, appointed by THE CHIEF JUSTICE in September 1990, described facets of the problem in a 1991 report:

> [This] is a tale of danger known in the 1930s, exposure inflicted upon millions of Americans in the 1940s and 1950s, injuries that began to take their toll in the 1960s, and a flood of lawsuits beginning in the 1970s. On the basis of past and current filing data, and because of a latency period that may last as long as 40 years for some asbestos-related diseases, a continuing stream of claims can be expected. The final toll of asbestos-related injuries is unknown. Predictions have been made of 200,000 asbestos disease deaths before the year 2000 and as many as 265,000 by the year 2015.
>
> The most objectionable aspects of asbestos litigation can be briefly summarized: dockets in both federal and state courts continue to grow; long delays are routine; trials are too long; the same issues are litigated over and over; transaction costs exceed the victims' recovery by nearly two to one; exhaustion of assets threatens and distorts the process; and future claimants may lose altogether. Report of The Judicial Conference Ad Hoc Committee on Asbestos Litigation 2-3 (Mar. 1991).

Real reform, the report concluded, required federal legislation creating a national asbestos dispute-resolution scheme. . . . To this date, no congressional response has emerged. . . .

[T]he federal courts—lacking authority to replace state tort systems with a national toxic tort compensation regime—endeavored to work with the procedural tools available to improve management of federal asbestos litigation. . . . [T]he MDL [Multidistrict Litigation] Panel transferred all asbestos cases then filed, but not yet on trial in federal courts to a single district, the United States District Court for the Eastern District of Pennsylvania; pursuant to the transfer order, the collected cases were consolidated for pretrial proceedings before Judge Weiner. The order aggregated pending cases only; no authority resides in the MDL Panel to license for consolidated proceedings claims not yet filed.

B

After the consolidation, attorneys for plaintiffs and defendants formed separate steering committees and began settlement negotiations. . . . [S]ettlement negotiations included efforts to find a "means of resolving . . . future cases."

Settlement talks thus concentrated on devising an administrative scheme for disposition of asbestos claims not yet in litigation. In these negotiations, counsel for masses of inventory plaintiffs endeavored to represent the interests of the anticipated future claimants, although those lawyers then had no attorney-client relationship with such claimants.

Once negotiations seemed likely to produce an agreement purporting to bind potential plaintiffs, CCR [the group defendants — a consortium of 20 former asbestos manufacturers] agreed to settle, through separate agreements, the claims of plaintiffs who had already filed asbestos-related lawsuits....

C

The class action thus instituted was not intended to be litigated. Rather, within the space of a single day, ... the settling parties ... presented to the District Court a complaint, an answer, a proposed settlement agreement, and a joint motion for conditional class certification.

The complaint identified nine lead plaintiffs, designating them and members of their families as representatives of a class comprising all persons who had not filed an asbestos-related lawsuit against a CCR defendant as of the date the class action commenced, but who (1) had been exposed — occupationally or through the occupational exposure of a spouse or household member — to asbestos or products containing asbestos attributable to a CCR defendant, or (2) whose spouse or family member had been so exposed. Untold numbers of individuals may fall within this description. All named plaintiffs alleged that they or a member of their family had been exposed to asbestos-containing products of CCR defendants. More than half of the named plaintiffs alleged that they or their family members had already suffered various physical injuries as a result of the exposure. The others alleged that they had not yet manifested any asbestos-related condition. The complaint delineated no subclasses; all named plaintiffs were designated as representatives of the class as a whole.

The complaint invoked the District Court's diversity jurisdiction and asserted various state-law claims for relief....

A stipulation of settlement accompanied the pleadings; it proposed to settle, and to preclude nearly all class members from litigating against CCR companies, all claims not filed before January 15, 1993, involving compensation for present and future asbestos-related personal injury or death.... The stipulation describes four categories of compensable disease: mesothelioma; lung cancer; certain "other cancers" (colon-rectal, laryngeal, esophageal, and stomach cancer); and "non-malignant conditions" (asbestosis and bilateral pleural thickening). Persons with "exceptional" medical claims — claims that do not fall within the four described diagnostic categories — may in some instances qualify for compensation, but the settlement caps the number of "exceptional" claims CCR must cover....

Class members are to receive no compensation for certain kinds of claims, even if otherwise applicable state law recognizes such claims. Claims that garner no compensation under the settlement include claims by family members of asbestos-exposed individuals for loss of consortium, and claims by so-called "exposure-only" plaintiffs for increased risk of cancer, fear of future asbestos-related injury, and medical monitoring. "Pleural" claims, which might be asserted by persons with asbestos-related plaques on their lungs but no accompanying physical impairment, are also excluded. Although not entitled to present compensation, exposure-only claimants and pleural claimants may qualify for benefits when and if they develop a compensable disease and meet the relevant exposure and medical criteria. Defendants forgo defense to liability, including statute of limitations pleas.

Class members, in the main, are bound by the settlement in perpetuity, while CCR defendants may choose to withdraw from the settlement after ten years. A small number of class members—only a few per year—may reject the settlement and pursue their claims in court. Those permitted to exercise this option, however, may not assert any punitive damages claim or any claim for increased risk of cancer. Aspects of the administration of the settlement are to be monitored by the AFL-CIO and class counsel. Class counsel are to receive attorneys' fees in an amount to be approved by the District Court.

D

[A]s requested by the settling parties, the District Court conditionally certified, under Federal Rule of Civil Procedure 23(b)(3), an encompassing opt-out class.... In a separate order, Judge Weiner assigned to Judge Reed, also of the Eastern District of Pennsylvania, "the task of conducting fairness proceedings and of determining whether the proposed settlement is fair to the class." Various class members raised objections to the settlement stipulation, and Judge Weiner granted the objectors full rights to participate in the subsequent proceedings.

In preliminary rulings, Judge Reed held that the District Court had subject-matter jurisdiction, and he approved the settling parties' elaborate plan for giving notice to the class. The court-approved notice informed recipients that they could exclude themselves from the class, if they so chose, within a three-month opt-out period.

Objectors raised numerous challenges to the settlement. They urged that the settlement unfairly disadvantaged those without currently compensable conditions in that it failed to adjust for inflation or to account for changes, over time, in medical understanding. They maintained that compensation levels were intolerably low in comparison to awards available in tort litigation or payments received by the inventory plaintiffs. And they objected to the absence of any compensation for certain claims, for example, medical monitoring, compensable under the tort law of several States. Rejecting these and all other objections, Judge Reed concluded that the settlement terms were fair and had been negotiated without collusion. He also found that adequate notice had been given to class members, and that final class certification under Rule 23(b)(3) was appropriate.

As to the specific prerequisites to certification, the District Court observed that the class satisfied Rule 23(a)(1)'s numerosity requirement, a matter no one debates. The Rule 23(a)(2) and (b)(3) requirements of commonality and preponderance were also satisfied, the District Court held. . . .

The District Court held next that the claims of the class representatives were "typical" of the class as a whole, a requirement of Rule 23(a)(3), and that, as Rule 23(b)(3) demands, the class settlement was "superior" to other methods of adjudication.

Strenuous objections had been asserted regarding the adequacy of representation, a Rule 23(a)(4) requirement. Objectors maintained that class counsel and class representatives had disqualifying conflicts of interests. In particular, objectors urged, claimants whose injuries had become manifest and claimants without manifest injuries should not have common counsel and should not be aggregated in a single class. Furthermore, objectors argued, lawyers representing inventory plaintiffs should not represent the newly-formed class.

Satisfied that class counsel had ably negotiated the settlement in the best interests of all concerned, and that the named parties served as adequate representatives, the District Court rejected these objections. Subclasses were unnecessary, the District Court held, bearing in mind the added cost and confusion they would entail and the ability of class members to exclude themselves from the class during the three-month opt-out period. Reasoning that the representative plaintiffs have a strong interest that recovery for *all* of the medical categories be maximized because they may have claims in *any*, or several categories, the District Court found "no antagonism of interest between class members with various medical conditions, or between persons with and without currently manifest asbestos impairment." Declaring class certification appropriate and the settlement fair, the District Court preliminarily enjoined all class members from commencing any asbestos-related suit against the CCR defendants in any state or federal court.

The objectors appealed. The United States Court of Appeals for the Third Circuit vacated the certification, holding that the requirements of Rule 23 had not been satisfied.

E

While stating that the requirements of Rule 23(a) and (b)(3) must be met "without taking into account the settlement," the Court of Appeals . . . closely considered the terms of the settlement as it examined aspects of the case under Rule 23 criteria. . . .

The Third Circuit, after intensive review, ultimately ordered decertification of the class and vacation of the District Court's anti-suit injunction. . . .

We granted certiorari, and now affirm.

II

Objectors . . . maintain that the settlement proceeding instituted by class counsel and CCR is not a justiciable case or controversy within the confines of Article III of the Federal Constitution. In the main, they say, the proceeding is a nonadversarial endeavor to impose on countless individuals without currently ripe claims an administrative compensation regime binding on those individuals if and when they manifest injuries. . . .

We agree that "[t]he class certification issues are dispositive, 'because their resolution here is logically antecedent to the existence of any Article III issues, it is appropriate to reach them first.'" . . . We therefore follow the path taken by the Court of Appeals, mindful that Rule 23's requirements must be interpreted in keeping with Article III constraints, and with the Rules Enabling Act, which instructs that rules of procedure "shall not abridge, enlarge or modify any substantive right," 28 U.S.C. § 2072(b). See also Fed. Rule Civ. Proc. 82 ("rules shall not be construed to extend . . . the [subject matter] jurisdiction of the United States district courts").

III

In addition to satisfying Rule 23(a)'s prerequisites, parties seeking class certification must show that the action is maintainable under Rule 23(b)(1), (2), or (3). . . .

In the 1966 class-action amendments, Rule 23(b)(3), the category at issue here was "the most adventuresome" innovation. See Kaplan, A Prefatory Note, 10 B.C. Indus. & Com. L. Rev. 497, 497 (1969) (hereinafter Kaplan, *Prefatory Note*). Rule 23(b)(3) added to the complex-litigation arsenal class actions for damages designed to secure judgments binding all class members save those who affirmatively elected to be excluded. . . .

Framed for situations in which "class-action treatment is not as clearly called for" as it is in Rule 23(b)(1) and (b)(2) situations, Rule 23(b)(3) permits certification where class suit "may nevertheless be convenient and desirable." Adv. Comm. Notes, 28 U.S.C.A. p. 697. To qualify for certification under Rule 23(b)(3), a class must meet two requirements beyond the Rule 23(a) prerequisites: Common questions must "predominate over any questions affecting only individual members"; and class resolution must be "superior to other available methods for the fair and efficient adjudication of the controversy." . . .

In the decades since the 1966 revision of Rule 23, class action practice has become ever more "adventuresome" as a means of coping with claims too numerous to secure their "just, speedy, and inexpensive determination" one by one. See Fed. Rule Civ. Proc. 1. The development reflects concerns about the efficient use of court resources and the conservation of funds to compensate claimants who do not line up early in a litigation queue.

Among current applications of Rule 23(b)(3), the "settlement only" class has become a stock device. Although all Federal Circuits recognize the utility of Rule 23(b)(3) settlement classes, courts have divided on the extent to which a proffered settlement affects court surveillance under Rule 23's certification criteria. . . .

A proposed amendment to Rule 23 would expressly authorize settlement class certification, in conjunction with a motion by the settling parties for Rule 23(b)(3) certification, "even though the requirements of subdivision (b)(3) might not be met for purposes of trial." Proposed Amendment to Fed. Rule Civ. Proc. 23(b), 117 S. Ct. No. 1 CXIX, CLIV to CLV (Aug. 1996) (Request for Comment). In response to the publication of this proposal, voluminous public comments—many of them opposed to, or skeptical of, the amendment—were received by the Judicial Conference Standing Committee on Rules of Practice and Procedure. The Committee has not yet acted on the matter. We consider the certification at issue under the rule as it is currently framed.

IV

We granted review to decide the role settlement may play, under existing Rule 23, in determining the propriety of class certification. The Third Circuit's opinion stated that each of the requirements of Rule 23(a) and (b)(3) "must be satisfied without taking into account the settlement." That statement, petitioners urge, is incorrect.

We agree with petitioners to this limited extent: Settlement is relevant to a class certification. The Third Circuit's opinion bears modification in that respect. But, as we earlier observed, the Court of Appeals in fact did not ignore the settlement; instead, that court homed in on settlement terms in explaining why it found the absentees' interests inadequately represented. The Third Circuit's close inspection of the settlement in that regard was altogether proper.

Confronted with a request for settlement-only class certification, a district court need not inquire whether the case, if tried, would present intractable management problems, see Fed. Rule Civ. Proc. 23(b)(3)(D), for the proposal is that there be no trial. But other specifications of the rule—those designed to protect absentees by blocking unwarranted or overbroad class definitions—demand undiluted, even heightened, attention in the settlement context. Such attention is of vital importance, for a court asked to certify a settlement class will lack the opportunity, present when a case is litigated, to adjust the class, informed by the proceedings as they unfold. See Fed. Rule Civ. Proc. 23(c), (d).[1] . . .

1. Portions of the opinion dissenting in part appear to assume that settlement counts only one way—in favor of certification. To the extent that is the dissent's meaning, we disagree. Settlement, though a relevant factor, does not inevitably signal that class action certification should be granted more readily than it would be were the case to be litigated.

And, of overriding importance, courts must be mindful that the rule as now composed sets the requirements they are bound to enforce. Federal Rules take effect after an extensive deliberative process involving many reviewers: a Rules Advisory Committee, public commenters, the Judicial Conference, this Court, the Congress. See 28 U.S.C. §§ 2073, 2074. The text of a rule thus proposed and reviewed limits judicial inventiveness. Courts are not free to amend a rule outside the process Congress ordered, a process properly tuned to the instruction that rules of procedure "shall not abridge . . . any substantive right." § 2072(b).

Rule 23(e), on settlement of class actions, reads in its entirety: "A class action shall not be dismissed or compromised without the approval of the court, and notice of the proposed dismissal or compromise shall be given to all members of the class in such manner as the court directs." This prescription was designed to function as an additional requirement, not a superseding direction, for the "class action" to which Rule 23(e) refers is one qualified for certification under Rule 23(a) and (b). . . .

The safeguards provided by the Rule 23(a) and (b) class-qualifying criteria, we emphasize, are not impractical impediments—checks shorn of utility—in the settlement class context. . . .

Federal courts, in any case, lack authority to substitute for Rule 23's certification criteria a standard never adopted—that if a settlement is "fair," then certification is proper. Applying to this case criteria the rulemakers set, we conclude that the Third Circuit's appraisal is essentially correct. Although that court should have acknowledged that settlement is a factor in the calculus, a remand is not warranted on that account. The Court of Appeals' opinion amply demonstrates why—with or without a settlement on the table—the sprawling class the District Court certified does not satisfy Rule 23's requirements.

A

The District Court concluded that predominance was satisfied based on two factors: class members' shared experience of asbestos exposure and their common "interest in receiving prompt and fair compensation for their claims, while minimizing the risks and transaction costs inherent in the asbestos litigation process as it occurs presently in the tort system." . . .

The predominance requirement stated in Rule 23(b)(3), we hold, is not met by the factors on which the District Court relied. The benefits asbestos-exposed persons might gain from the establishment of a grand-scale compensation scheme is a matter fit for legislative consideration, but it is not pertinent to the predominance inquiry. That inquiry trains on the legal or factual questions that qualify each class member's case as a genuine controversy, questions that preexist any settlement. . . .

For reasons the Third Circuit aired, proposed settlement classes sometimes warrant more, not less caution on the question of certification.

Predominance is a test readily met in certain cases alleging consumer or securities fraud or violations of the antitrust laws. Even mass tort cases arising from a common cause or disaster may, depending upon the circumstances, satisfy the predominance requirement. . . . The Advisory Committee for the 1966 revision of Rule 23, it is true, noted that "mass accident" cases are likely to present "significant questions, not only of damages but of liability and defenses of liability, . . . affecting the individuals in different ways." And the Committee advised that such cases are "ordinarily not appropriate" for class treatment. But the text of the rule does not categorically exclude mass tort cases from class certification, and district courts, since the late 1970s, have been certifying such cases in increasing number. The Committee's warning, however, continues to call for caution when individual stakes are high and disparities among class members great. . . . [T]he certification in this case . . . rests on a conception of Rule 23(b)(3)'s predominance requirement irreconcilable with the rule's design.

B

Nor can the class approved by the District Court satisfy Rule 23(a)(4)'s requirement that the named parties "will fairly and adequately protect the interests of the class." The adequacy inquiry under Rule 23(a)(4) serves to uncover conflicts of interest between named parties and the class they seek to represent.

As the Third Circuit pointed out, named parties with diverse medical conditions sought to act on behalf of a single giant class rather than on behalf of discrete subclasses. In significant respects, the interests of those within the single class are not aligned. Most saliently, for the currently injured, the critical goal is generous immediate payments. That goal tugs against the interest of exposure-only plaintiffs in ensuring an ample, inflation-protected fund for the future.

The disparity between the currently injured and exposure-only categories of plaintiffs, and the diversity within each category are not made insignificant by the District Court's finding that petitioners' assets suffice to pay claims under the settlement. Although this is not a "limited fund" case certified under Rule 23(b)(1)(B), the terms of the settlement reflect essential allocation decisions designed to confine compensation and to limit defendants' liability. For example, the settlement includes no adjustment for inflation; only a few claimants per year can opt out at the back end; and loss-of-consortium claims are extinguished with no compensation.

The settling parties, in sum, achieved a global compromise with no structural assurance of fair and adequate representation for the diverse groups and individuals affected. Although the named parties alleged a range of complaints, each served generally as representative for the whole, not for a separate constituency. . . .

C

Many persons in the exposure-only category, the Court of Appeals stressed, may not even know of their exposure, or realize the extent of the harm they may incur. Even if they fully appreciate the significance of class notice, those without current afflictions may not have the information or foresight needed to decide, intelligently, whether to stay in or opt out.

Family members of asbestos-exposed individuals may themselves fall prey to disease or may ultimately have ripe claims for loss of consortium. Yet large numbers of people in this category — future spouses and children of asbestos victims — could not be alerted to their class membership. And current spouses and children of the occupationally exposed may know nothing of that exposure.

Because we have concluded that the class in this case cannot satisfy the requirements of common issue predominance and adequacy of representation, we need not rule, definitively, on the notice given here. . . . [H]owever, we recognize the gravity of the question whether class action notice sufficient under the Constitution and Rule 23 could ever be given to legions so unselfconscious and amorphous.

V

The argument is sensibly made that a nationwide administrative claims processing regime would provide the most secure, fair, and efficient means of compensating victims of asbestos exposure. Congress, however, has not adopted such a solution. And Rule 23, which must be interpreted with fidelity to the Rules Enabling Act and applied with the interests of absent class members in close view, cannot carry the large load CCR, class counsel, and the District Court heaped upon it. As this case exemplifies, the rulemakers' prescriptions for class actions may be endangered by "those who embrace [Rule 23] too enthusiastically just as [they are by] those who approach [the rule] with distaste." C. Wright, Law of Federal Courts 508 (5th ed. 1994).

For the reasons stated, the judgment of the Court of Appeals for the Third Circuit is

Affirmed.

JUSTICE O'CONNOR took no part in the consideration or decision of this case.

JUSTICE BREYER, with whom JUSTICE STEVENS joins, concurring in part and dissenting in part.

Although I agree with the Court's basic holding that "settlement is relevant to a class certification," I find several problems in its approach that lead me to a different conclusion. First, I believe that the need for settlement in this mass tort case, with hundreds of thousands of lawsuits, is greater than the Court's opinion suggests. Second, I would give more weight than would the majority to settlement-related issues for purposes of determining whether common issues predominate. Third, I am uncertain about the Court's determination of adequacy of representation, and do not believe it appropriate for this Court to second-guess the District Court on the matter without first having the Court of Appeals consider it. Fourth, I am uncertain about the tenor of an opinion that seems to suggest the settlement is unfair. And fifth, in the absence of further review by the Court of Appeals, I cannot accept the majority's suggestions that "notice" is inadequate. . . .

I

First, I believe the majority understates the importance of settlement in this case. Between 13 and 21 million workers have been exposed to asbestos in the workplace—over the past 40 or 50 years—but the most severe instances of such exposure probably occurred three or four decades ago. This exposure has led to several hundred thousand lawsuits, about 15% of which involved claims for cancer and about 30% for asbestos. About half of the suits have involved claims for pleural thickening and plaques—the harmfulness of which is apparently controversial. Some of those who suffer from the most serious injuries, however, have received little or no compensation. . . . These lawsuits have taken up more than 6% of all federal civil filings in one recent year, and are subject to a delay that is twice that of other civil suits. Judicial Conference Report 7, 10-11. . . .

[T]he majority, in reviewing the District Court's determination that common "issues of fact and law predominate," says that the predominance "inquiry trains on the legal or factual questions that qualify each class member's case as a genuine controversy, questions that preexist any settlement." . . . If the majority means that these presettlement questions are what matters, then how does it reconcile its statement with its basic conclusion that "settlement is relevant" to class certification, or with the numerous lower court authority [sic] that says that settlement is not only relevant, but important?

Nor do I understand how one could decide whether common questions "predominate" in the abstract—without looking at what is likely to be an issue in the proceedings that will ensue, namely, the settlement. . . . How can a court make a contextual judgment of the sort that Rule 23 requires without looking to what proceedings will follow? Such guideposts help it decide whether, in light of common concerns and differences, certification will achieve Rule 23's basic objective—"economies of time, effort, and expense." Advisory Committee's Notes on Fed. Rule Civ. Proc. 23(b)(3), 28 U.S.C.A., p. 697. . . .

The majority may mean that the District Court gave too much weight to the settlement. But I am not certain how it can reach that conclusion. It cannot rely upon the Court of Appeals, for that court gave no positive weight at all to the settlement. Nor can it say that the District Court relied solely on "a common interest in a fair compromise," for the District Court did not do so. Rather, it found the settlement relevant because it explained the importance of the class plaintiffs' common features and common interests....

The settlement is relevant because it means that these common features and interests are likely to be important in the proceeding that would ensue—a proceeding that would focus primarily upon whether or not the proposed settlement fairly and properly satisfied the interests class members had in common. That is to say, the settlement underscored the importance of (a) the common fact of exposure, (b) the common interests in receiving *some* compensation for certain rather than running a strong risk of *no* compensation, and (c) the common interest in avoiding large legal fees, other transaction costs, and delays.

Of course, as the majority points out, there are also important differences among class members. Different plaintiffs were exposed to different products for different durations of time; each has a distinct medical history and a different history of smoking; and many cases arise under the laws of different States. The relevant question, however, is *how much* these differences matter in respect to the legal proceedings that lie ahead. Many, if not all, toxic tort class actions involve plaintiffs with such differences. And the differences in state law are of diminished importance in respect to a proposed settlement in which the defendants have waived all defenses and agreed to compensate all those who were injured....

Third, the majority concludes that the "representative parties" will not "fairly and adequately protect the interests of the class." Rule 23(a)(4).... I agree that there is a serious problem, but it is a problem that often exists in toxic tort cases.... And it is a problem that potentially exists whenever a single defendant injures several plaintiffs, for a settling plaintiff leaves fewer assets available for the others. With class actions, at least, plaintiffs have the consolation that a district court, thoroughly familiar with the facts, is charged with the responsibility of ensuring that the interests of no class members are sacrificed....

Further, certain details of the settlement that are not discussed in the majority opinion suggest that the settlement may be of greater benefit to future plaintiffs than the majority suggests....

I do not know whether or not the benefits are more or less valuable than an inflation adjustment. But I can certainly recognize an argument that they are....

Fourth, I am more agnostic than is the majority about the basic fairness of the settlement. The District Court's conclusions rested upon complicated factual findings that are not easily cast aside.... I do not intend to pass judgment upon the settlement's fairness, but I do believe that these matters would have to be explored in far greater depth before I could reach a conclusion about fairness. And that task, as I have said, is one for the Court of Appeals.

Finally, I believe it is up to the District Court, rather than this Court, to review the legal sufficiency of notice to members of the class. . . .

II

The issues in this case are complicated and difficult. The District Court might have been correct. Or not. Subclasses might be appropriate. Or not. I cannot tell. And I do not believe that this Court should be in the business of trying to make these fact-based determinations. That is a job suited to the district courts in the first instance, and the courts of appeal on review. But there is no reason in this case to believe that the Court of Appeals conducted its prior review with an understanding that the settlement could have constituted a reasonably strong factor in favor of class certification. For this reason, I would provide the courts below with an opportunity to analyze the factual questions involved in certification by vacating the judgment, and remanding the case for further proceedings.

Notes and Questions

1. *Implications of* Amchem: *Ortiz v. Fibreboard Corp., 527 U.S. 815 (1999).* Post-*Amchem,* courts have shown far less appetite for settlement classes, and for broad-gauged mass tort class actions in general. See, e.g., Thomas v. Albright, 139 F.3d 227 (D.C. Cir. 1998) (ruling that *Amchem* did not invalidate an earlier holding that opt-outs are allowable, but concluding that the district court abused its discretion in allowing dissident class members to opt out in this Title VII race discrimination suit); Barnes v. American Tobacco Co., Inc., 984 F. Supp. 842 (E.D. Pa. 1997) (decertifying class); O'Connor v. Boeing North Am., Inc., 180 F.R.D. 359 (C.D. Cal. 1997) (denying class certification); Wilks v. Ford Motor Co., 174 F.R.D. 332 (D.N.J. 1997) (denying certification); Ford v. Murphy Oil USA, Inc., 703 So. 2d 542 (La. 1997) (decertifying an environmental toxic tort suit based on *Amchem*).

An important post-*Amchem* case suggests that the Court means business in demanding that settlement classes satisfy Rule 23 criteria. The background was the effort of a number of courts to find some path outside of Rule 23(b)(3) by which to establish a settlement class. In Flanagan v. Ahearn (In re Asbestos Litigation), 134 F.3d 668 (5th Cir. 1998), the Fifth Circuit held that a settlement class action was properly certified as a limited fund under 23(b)(1)(B), which does not require the "predominance" showing of 23(b)(3), and thus avoids some of the problems of *Amchem.* In Ortiz v. Fibreboard Corp., 527 U.S. 815 (1999), the Supreme Court reversed the Fifth Circuit's rationale and held that before a court can certify a mandatory settlement class on a limited fund rationale, it must assure the inadequacy of the fund to pay all claims. There was insufficient evidence in this case, the Court concluded, on which to base a finding that the fund was indeed inadequate.

Justice Souter, writing for the majority, laid out the history of class actions in general, and of the limited fund doctrine in particular. He concluded that "the limited fund cases . . . ensur[e] that the class as a whole [is] given the best deal; they [do] not give a defendant a better deal than seriatim litigation would have produced." Rule 23(b)(1)(B) should be construed, according to the Court, in a way that "stay[s] close to the historical model." The Court ultimately concluded that the applicability of Rule 23(b)(1)(B) to a fund and plan purporting to liquidate actual and potential tort claims was questionable in any case and improper in the case before it, where the fund was not shown to be limited "independently of the agreement of the parties to the action." The Court thus intimated that bankruptcy may be a necessary precursor to invoking 23(b)(1)(B) on a limited fund rationale.

Amchem's insistence on close adherence to Rule 23(a) and (b) criteria has not been interpreted to preclude the lower court practice of invoking 23(d)(5) as authority to allow dissident members to opt out of 23(b)(1) or (2) classes in "appropriate" cases, despite the absence of express opt-out authority under either section. See Thomas v. Albright, supra; see also Alex Raskolnikov, Note, Is There a Future for Future Claimants After Amchem Products, Inc. v. Windsor?, 107 Yale L.J. 2545 (1998) (arguing that a principal source of concern in *Amchem* was future claimants and that satisfaction of class action standards in mass tort cases thus will depend primarily on whether courts can devise a regime that would guarantee adequate protection for these claimants).

The United States Supreme Court added another layer of protection against unfair class action settlements in Devlin v. Scardelletti, 536 U.S. 1 (2002). The Court held that non-named class members who object in a timely manner to approval of a settlement at a fairness hearing may bring an appeal without first intervening in the suit. The right to appeal in a class action is not restricted to named parties. The key is whether they are parties in the sense of being bound by the settlement, which non-named class members are.

2. *Legislation and Rulemaking*. In *Ortiz*, Justice Souter said of the asbestos litigation that it "defies customary judicial administration and calls for national legislation." Though the Justice was probably thinking of legislation directed toward resolving such claims through an administrative process, as mentioned also by Justice Ginsburg, legislative exasperation was expended on the class action device itself. One bipartisan bill, for instance, the Class Action Fairness Act of 1999 (S. 353), would have altered class actions in several respects. (See also H.R. 1875.) For instance, notice of both the class action and of settlements was required to be given in easily understood terms. Settlement notices were to include the amount and source of attorneys' fees, among other information. The Act would also limit class action attorneys' fees to a reasonable percentage of actual damages paid to class members, the actual costs of complying with the

terms of a settlement agreement, and any future financial benefits. In the alternative, the bill provided that, to the extent the law allows, fees would be based on a reasonable hourly rate.

Finally, it allowed removal from state court to federal court, either by a defendant, or an unnamed class member, and altered diversity of citizenship requirements to permit removal whenever the parties include citizens of different states. Cases would remain in state court, however, if the substantial majority of class and primary defendants were from the same state and that state's law would govern, or if the primary defendants were states and a federal court could not order the relief requested. See Stephen Labaton, Asbestos Cases in for Overhaul by Lawmakers, N.Y. Times, June 18, 1999, at A1.

Critics of the bill argued that it would unduly limit access to state court class actions and that there was inadequate evidence that state court class actions suffer from systematic problems that warrant the federalizing effect on class actions that would result from this last provision. Although the bill failed, possibly under the threat of a presidential veto, it was another indication of deep dissatisfaction with the efficacy of the class action device in mass tort situations.

Amchem came down just as the Advisory Committee was gearing up to add a new section to Rule 23, providing specifically for "settlement class actions." Specifically, the provision endorsed the much disputed practice of certifying a class under (b)(3) for settlement, even though it did not meet the requirements for trial. There were three main arguments against the new rule, which were basically the same as those made against the *Amchem* certification. First, the trial judge's discretion was unbounded as to when a settlement class was appropriate. Second, the legislation had potential constitutional flaws (violating due process, violating the case or controversy requirement for courts to act). There was also the argument, suggested in *Amchem*, too, that such a provision would encroach on the Rules Enabling Act by affecting substantive rights.

Needless to say, although *Amchem* did not hold settlement classes unconstitutional, it put a real crimp in an already-embattled rulemaking process. The new Rule 23(b)(4) was withdrawn. According to the Reporter of the Advisory Committee, Professor Edward Cooper, the committee thought that class action law would better develop through the ad hoc reforms enabled by the new provision, "allowing immediate appeals of certification rulings" [see note on new 23(f) below]. 68 U.S.L.W. 2259, 2259-2260 (Nov. 9, 1999).

But the Advisory Committee did not leave the matters entirely to "ad hoc reforms" for long. In 2003, it returned to the general problem of managing class action settlements, promulgating new amendments to Rule 23 setting specific rules for court approval (including a requirement that the court provide a hearing on the settlement and specifically find it to be "fair, reasonable, and adequate"), notice to class members, and the right to object. See Rule 23(e).

The Advisory Committee also added two new subsections: Rule 23(g), which distinguishes scrutiny of the class representative (under Rule 23(a)(4)) from the process and standards for evaluation and appointment of class counsel, and Rule 23(h) which governs attorney fee awards. Significantly, Rule 23(g) requires that the court, not named plaintiffs, appoint counsel to represent the class in all federal class actions, and it lists factors that should bear on the court's decision, including the work the lawyer has done in identifying potential claims; the experience of the lawyer, particularly in handling class actions; and the resources the lawyer can commit to representing the class. Under Rule 23(h), any class member is entitled to object to a motion for an award of attorneys' fees.

An even more comprehensive set of reforms was enacted by Congress in 2005. For materials on the Class Action Fairness Act, see section A.d.2, supra.

3. *Lawyer's Ethics and Class Actions.* In *Amchem,* the Court did not examine the issues of the potential conflicts of interest between class counsel and the class itself, though these conflicts were of great concern in *Ortiz.* There Justice Souter warned that in drafting global settlement agreements especially, "Class counsel . . . had great incentive to reach any agreement . . . that they thought might survive a Rule 23(e) fairness hearing, rather than the best possible arrangement for the substantially unidentified global settlement class." *Ortiz,* 527 U.S. at 815. Another ethical issue, one that often arises and is present but not mentioned in the Court's opinion in *Amchem,* is the possible collusion between the class counsel and the defendants, who (ironically, perhaps) sometimes turn out to desire class certification. Can you see why, especially if the settlement is "global" and binds future claimants as well as past ones? In *Amchem* in the lower court, the trial judge found specifically that neither of these potential ethical difficulties existed. Georgine v. Amchem Prods. Inc. 157 F.R.D. 246, 294-311 (E.D. Pa. 1994).

Professor Susan P. Koniak, who was an expert witness for the objectors, lays out the reasons she found such conflicts to exist. Without pulling punches, she charges that class counsel traded the interests of future claimants in order to obtain a better settlement for their "inventory clients" and higher fees for themselves. Feasting While the Widow Weeps: Georgine v. Amchem Products, Inc., 80 Com. L. Rev. 1045 (1995). See also Professor Carrie J. Menkel-Meadow, Ethics and the Settlement of Mass Torts: Where the Rules Meet the Road, 80 Cornell L. Rev. 1159 (1995).

Most of the ethical dilemmas faced by class counsel arise because our professional norms and rules are based on a traditional bipolar lawsuit, where all lawyers know exactly whom they represent, and where the fee potential is related to the amount of work actually performed. Class actions in general, and especially settlement class actions, do not fit the traditional model at all. Perhaps most notably, and raising the greatest temptation, the class action lawyer is often less a representative of clients' interests than an entrepreneur, putting together a suit for himself.

Professor Judith Resnik describes the usual relationship of attorney-client as an unregulated, contractually bound unit. "Agent-principal relations are presumed sufficient [for regulation], in that the lawyer is imagined to be monitored by the client, and the charter for representation is assumed to be adequately controlled by the client." She argues that in *Amchem* and *Ortiz*, the Supreme Court refused to transpose this ethic into the mass tort context, and effectively calls for judicial intervention to make certain that not only individuals within the group litigation but also the group itself are fairly represented. Money Matters: Judicial Market Interventions Creating Subsidies and Awarding Fees and Costs in Individual and Aggregate Litigation, 148 U. Pa. L. Rev. 2119, 2169 (2000).

Also in the background of the class action lawyer's special ethical dilemmas is the fact that his interests and those of the clients may diverge very early in the case.

In particular, the lawyer may stand to profit from a large, early settlement in the dispute far more than the class members. The issue may be most visible in the arena of securities fraud litigation, where it has received extended treatment in the media, before Congress, and in academic journals. See, e.g., David Marcus, Some Realism About Mass Torts, 75 U. Chi. L. Rev. 1949 (2008); Jonathan R. Macey and Geoffrey P. Miller, The Plaintiffs' Attorney's Role in Class Action and Derivative Litigation: Economic Analysis and Recommendations for Reform, 58 U. Chi. L. Rev. 1 (1991); Janet Cooper Alexander, Do the Merits Matter? A Study of Settlements in Securities Class Actions, 43 Stan. L. Rev. 497 (1991); Elliott J. Weiss and John S. Beckerman, Let the Money Do the Monitoring: How Institutional Investors Can Reduce Agency Costs in Securities Class Actions, 104 Yale L.J. 2053 (1995). See also Private Securities Litigation Reform Act of 1995, Pub. L. No. 104-67, § 102, 109 Stat. 737.

Consider the following materials addressing the ethical features of this problem, which appear in Deborah Rhode's Professional Responsibility: Ethics by the Pervasive Method 594-599 (1994):

> You work for Ford Motor Company's in-house general counsel. Assume that the following facts described in the American Lawyer are true. Would you recommend accepting the settlement? If the settlement is approved, what if any action would you recommend concerning Cohn's conduct?
>
> Event 1: A lawyer [Cohn], using his partner's children as the aggrieved "shareholders," decides to bring a shareholders' derivative suit against a company, charging the chairman with stealing. The charges are so scandalous, and the company and its chairman so well known, that the suit makes big headlines.
>
> Event 2: After he files the suit he tells a reporter, as he waves various papers in the air, that he has "an open and shut" case on all the charges.
>
> Event 3: The suit has not been filed in the right jurisdiction. It is thrown out.
>
> Event 4: The lawyer vows to file the suit in the right jurisdiction.

Event 5: Telling the other side that he plans to file again, and that this will mean a rehash of the charges in the press, the lawyer inquires if a "settlement" might be possible.

Event 6: The company, which has denied all the charges but is beset by bad publicity on other fronts, including a criminal trial for allegedly having made dangerous products, gives the lawyer $100,000 in "legal fees" on the condition that he not bring the suit in the right jurisdiction.

Event 7: The lawyer declares that "it now appears" that the company chairman was not guilty of any wrongdoing.

The lawyer's supposed clients — the shareholders — get nothing. Nor do they give up anything: the shareholders can sue again on the same charges. It's just that the headline-making lawyer can't represent them. Contrary to what would be required in any other shareholders' suit, a judge does not have to approve this settlement. With the first suit thrown out and the second one only threatened, there is no suit pending and, therefore, no judge with jurisdiction.

In short, the lawyer, having filed a claim in the wrong jurisdiction, having produced no proof, and having now admitted that the charges were unsupportable, gets $100,000 in return for dropping his client and not generating any more bad headlines.

In many circles this would be called extortion. At Hughes Hubbard & Reed, it is called a "settlement." And Cohn's $100,000 is called "legal fees," although Hughes Hubbard lawyers say that his time and work were not documented in any way.

How can it be a "settlement" if no suit was pending and if the shareholders can sue again on the same charges?

"Because we weren't buying off the lawsuit," says Hughes Hubbard senior partner Jerome Shapiro, who negotiated the deal with Cohn. "We were buying off Roy Cohn. It's Cohn we were interested in, and what he said he could do to us in the press if he started the suit again in Michigan [the correct jurisdiction]. Cohn has a special relationship with the press," Shapiro continues. "He can get a headline in The Wall Street Journal or The New York Times by picking up a phone. . . . These papers printed uncritical, big-headline accounts of Cohn's charges." . . .

"No, he doesn't deserve this as a fee, and it doesn't make me happy that he's received anything," Shapiro concludes. Then won't this just encourage him to go after other big-business targets? "Of course it will," Shapiro says, "but I represent the Ford Motor Company, not the next guy." . . .[20]

Jonathan R. Macey and Geoffrey Miller, The Plaintiffs' Attorney's Role in Class Action and Derivative Litigation: Economic Analysis and Recommendations for Reform

58 U. Chi. L. Rev. 1, 22-26 (1991)

[C]onsider incentive effects in class and derivative litigation. The lack of monitoring [by nominal plaintiffs] . . . in these settings would not be

20. Steven Brill, Roy Cohn Rides Again, Am. Law., March 1980, at 5.

especially problematic if the interests of plaintiffs' counsel were closely aligned with those of their clients. Unfortunately, there is a substantial deviation of interests between attorney and client. The nature of the conflict varies depending on the type of litigation involved and the procedure used in the jurisdiction for determining the attorney's fee. But at least under the existing regulatory system, the conflict remains significant in all cases.

In "common fund" cases, where the plaintiffs' attorney generates a fund for the benefit of the class, the majority of American courts award fees out of the fund based on the lodestar calculation. Under this approach, the hours reasonably expended by the lawyer are multiplied by the lawyer's reasonable hourly fee to calculate a lodestar. The lodestar is then adjusted by a multiplier to account for a variety of factors including [any unusual degree of skill, superior or inferior, and,] most significantly, the risk of the litigation. Attorneys in these cases thus have an incentive to run up excessive hours, delay the litigation unnecessarily, or even to exaggerate the number of hours expended in order to obtain a larger fee. Plaintiffs' attorneys may also wish to settle for a relatively low sum on the eve of trial, knowing that in so doing they obtain most of the benefits they can expect from the litigation while eliminating their downside risk. These abuses are checked, to a degree, by the required judicial scrutiny of fee awards and settlements in class and derivative litigation. Nevertheless, agency costs in cases where fees are calculated using the lodestar method are no doubt substantial.

Further, plaintiffs' attorneys may sometimes substantially reduce their risk by reaching an understanding with defense counsel early on about the contours of the eventual settlement. Then they can expend a mutually acceptable number of additional hours on the case, charging them against the settlement fund under the lodestar calculation. The social disutility of this procedure is obvious; it represents an essentially meaningless exercise that ties up the resources of plaintiffs' counsel, defense counsel, and others such as witnesses who must submit to depositions that all parties understand will never be used in court. The principal losers are members of the plaintiff class who must pay over part of their recovery to counsel for work that serves no purpose other than to justify an enhanced attorney's fee.

The other method of calculating attorneys' fees in common fund cases, which has become more popular recently is the "percentage" method, in which fees are awarded based on some fixed percentage of the fund. There are obvious incentive problems with this arrangement as well. First, plaintiffs' attorneys will earn windfall profits, at the expense of the class members, in cases presenting large damages and low proof costs. . . .

The second incentive problem in percentage-of-the-recovery cases is settlement. Attorneys compensated on a percentage method have an incentive to settle early for an amount lower than what might be obtained by further efforts. The attorney who puts in relatively few hours to obtain an early settlement is likely to earn a much greater compensation per hour of effort than an attorney who expends greater efforts and litigates a case to the point where the plaintiffs' recovery is maximized. Again the plaintiff class loses.

Consider now common benefit . . . cases. Common benefit cases are typically shareholders' derivative suits in which the plaintiffs' attorney does not generate a fund, but rather causes the defendant to do something that confers a nonpecuniary benefit on the corporation. . . . In common benefit . . . cases the attorneys' fee comes from the defendant rather than from the class recovery. Unlike common fund cases, therefore, there is a counter-party in common benefit and fee-shifting cases with an incentive to bargain over the fee in order to keep it within reasonable limits.

This feature, however, does not effectively obviate the attorney-client conflict. Defendants in common benefit and fee-shifting cases typically wish to minimize the sum of three costs: the costs of the relief on the merits, the costs of their own attorney's fees, and the costs of the plaintiffs' attorney's fees. Defendants are typically indifferent about how the total cost of litigation is distributed among these elements. Plaintiffs' attorneys, on the other hand, have an interest in increasing their own fees, even at the expense of a reduction in the relief afforded to the putative client. Thus the conditions are present for a bargain under which the plaintiffs' attorneys agree to a lower overall settlement on the merits of the litigation in exchange for a higher fee.

A related problem occurs when the defendant offers a relatively generous settlement on the merits on condition that the plaintiffs' attorney agrees to waive any fee request (or to accept a low fee). This conflict has led some courts and commentators to call for a mandatory rule separating the fee negotiation from the settlement on the merits in fee-shifting cases. Whether such a rule could be effectively enforced is open to question, however. Moreover, separating the fee negotiation from the merits determination raises the possibility that plaintiffs' attorneys who believe that a favorable settlement will eventually be reached will string out litigation well past the point where settlement first becomes possible in order to justify a higher fee request. Splitting the fee and merits negotiations is no panacea for the agency problems in the common benefit and fee-shifting contexts.

Example: A Lawyer's Fairy Tale

A, *B*, and *C* are three makers of widgets. Together, they have made and sold 100 million units a year for the last few decades.

Twelve years ago, the widget price went up from $1.00 to $1.20. There had been some rises in preceding years, and there have been some since, but this was the biggest single jump.

Two years ago, disgruntled former officers of *A* gave evidence that the 20¢ price increase was conspiratorial. This was hotly disputed. The Justice Department prosecuted and won. A fine in the amount of $50,000 was imposed on each of the companies.

Class Action I was brought on behalf of wholesalers against the three companies. The defendants conceded (as they could not dispute) that the government's judgment foreclosed litigation on the issue of liability. As to damages, however, they sought to prove that the price increase was largely, if perhaps not entirely, passed on to the retailers in higher wholesale prices. The jury found otherwise, ruling that the wholesalers had suffered a 20¢ loss on every widget for ten years. With the appropriate trebling, this resulted in a verdict of $600 million.

Class Action II was brought on behalf of retailers against the three companies. Again there was no issue as to liability. The plaintiffs offered substantially the same evidence on damages that the defendants had offered in Class Action I. This time the evidence was persuasive; the jury found that the retailers had, indeed, been caused to pay an extra 20¢ for each widget for ten years. The defendants' efforts to prove that the retailers had passed the price increase on to the consumers were unsuccessful. A second verdict and judgment in the amount of $600 million resulted.

Class Action III was brought on behalf of the consumers. Again there was no room for dispute as to liability; as to damages, the jury evaluated the conflicting testimony and concluded that consumers had, indeed, paid an extra 20¢ for each widget for ten years. Every consumer able to prove a purchase was held to be entitled to a 60¢ compensation.

Is there any question about the wisdom of this outcome? Is it required by the statute or by Rule 23? Is it unlikely that all three judgments can in fact be executed? If not, is there any priority among the payments from the assets of the three companies? If it were possible to satisfy all three judgments, is it not probable that the net worth of the lawyer representing the claimants would be greater than the net worth of the widget industry? Is this fairy tale a "miracle" of overstatement?

Note: Rule 68 and Class Actions

You have just read about the ethical dilemmas and temptations that plaintiff's-side lawyers face in the class action context. Defense lawyers are not without temptations in this setting. Consider the conduct of defense counsel in Weiss v. Regal Collections, 385 F.3d 337 (3d Cir. 2004), a nationwide consumer class action challenging certain unfair debt collection practices by the defendant collection agency. Before filing an answer, and before the named plaintiff moved to certify the class, defendants made a Rule 68 offer of judgment to the named plaintiff for $1,000 plus attorneys' fees and expenses. The named plaintiff turned down the offer because he also wanted declaratory and injunctive relief, and the offer included no remedy for the class. Defendants then promptly filed a motion to dismiss under Rule 12(b)(1), arguing that the named plaintiff's claim was moot, and that the court therefore lacked subject matter jurisdiction, because the settlement amount was the maximum recoverable for a violation of the Fair Debt Collections Practices Act.

Conceding that "[a]n offer of complete relief will generally moot the plaintiff's claim, as at that point the plaintiff retains no personal interest in the outcome of the litigation," the Third Circuit held that defendants had not offered complete relief here. 385 F.3d at 340. Although the Fair Debt Collections Practices Act does not authorize declaratory or injunctive remedies in private enforcement actions, it does authorize "additional recovery" for unnamed class members "'not to exceed the lesser of $500,000 or 1 per centum of the net worth of the debt collector.'" Id. at 342. Defendants argued that the case was still moot because they made their Rule 68 offer *before* a class was certified. The Third, Fifth, and Seventh Circuits all prohibit dismissal on mootness grounds if a class certification motion is pending, but in *Weiss*, the plaintiff had not even moved to certify. Id. at 346 (discussing precedent from other circuits).

Extending the reasoning of United States Parole Commission v. Geraghty, 445 U.S. 388 (1980) (holding that a named plaintiff whose individual claims have been mooted may still appeal a denial of class certification because, as the representative of the class, plaintiff retains a "personal stake" in the certification decision), and Deposit Guaranty National Bank v. Roper, 445 U.S. 326 (1980) (same result where bank tendered maximum individual damages to named plaintiffs after district court denied certification), the court refused to apply the mootness doctrine. As the court reasoned:

> allowing the defendants here to "pick off" a representative plaintiff with an offer of judgment less than two months after the complaint is filed may undercut the viability of the class action procedure, and frustrate the objectives of this procedural mechanism for aggregating small claims, like those brought under the FDCPA. . . . Allowing defendants to "pick off" putative lead plaintiffs contravenes one of the primary purposes of class actions — the aggregation of numerous similar (especially small) claims in a single action. Moreover, a rule allowing plaintiffs to be "picked off" at an early stage . . . may waste judicial resources by "stimulating successive suits brought by others claiming aggrievement." *Roper*, 445 U.S. at 339.

Id. at 344-345. The court remanded the case to permit the plaintiff to move for class certification and held that the motion would relate back to the filing of the complaint in order to prevent the Rule 68 offer from mooting class relief.

What exactly is wrong with "picking off" named plaintiffs? After all, they are the class members most motivated to vindicate their rights and we know that many unnamed class members would not bother to sue. The court counters that an endless succession of suits will follow if Rule 68 offers to named plaintiffs can moot class relief, or that the "private attorney general" function of class actions will be undermined if defendants can avoid paying the full cost of their wrongdoing by buying off named plaintiffs. But if these are the driving concerns, why should the named plaintiff have to decline the Rule 68 offer to prevent dismissal for mootness?

Is there anything ethically suspect about defeating an otherwise meritorious class action through a Rule 68 offer to the named plaintiff? Or is the real problem reconciling mootness doctrine with the complexities of interest representation — the fact that a named plaintiff sues not only to obtain individual relief but also to vindicate interests of the class?

Note: The Aggregation Alternative

Note that *Amchem* involved the transfer of cases from many forums to one court, effected under 28 U.S.C. § 1407. This aggregating of multiple claims has been used both as an alternative and accessory to class actions, and has aroused considerable commentary. For a sample see Edward F. Sherman, Aggregate Disposition of Related Cases: The Policy Issues, 10 Rev. Litig. 231 (1991). See also Richard Epstein, Commentary, The Consolidation of Complex Litigation: A Critical Evaluation of the ALI Proposal, 10 J.L. & Com. 1 (1990); Judith Resnik, From "Cases" to Litigation, 54 Law & Contemp. Probs. 5 (1991); Charles Silver, Comparing Class Actions and Consolidations, 10 Rev. Litig. 495 (1991); Roger H. Transgrud, Joinder Alternatives in Mass Tort Litigation, 70 Cornell L. Rev. 779 (1985).

After considering the policy issues, take any class action case or problem considered in this chapter and contemplate the possible application of § 1407. Imagine that several individual members of the classes have brought their own claims in different districts around the country. Perhaps some of these are class actions, and possibly multiple class actions with overlapping classes. Perhaps in some of these cases the plaintiffs are asserting multiple claims against the same defendants; in others, perhaps the defendants have asserted counterclaims.

It is possible in all of these situations that § 1407 might be applied. If none of the consolidated actions were previously class actions, the litigation would nevertheless begin to partake of some aspects of class litigation. There are, however, some important differences between multiple actions consolidated for pretrial under § 1407 and a class action proceeding under Fed. R. Civ. P. 23. The statute was enacted in 1968 for the purpose of enhancing efficiency in administration, inspired by an enormous saving achieved by voluntary consolidation of hundreds of duplicate antitrust suits in the electrical equipment industry.

In examining the text of the statute, consider the following questions:

1) Who decides whether an action should be transferred for consolidation?
2) Must the transfer be on motion of a party?
3) Can the panel select the transferee judge ad hominem?
4) Is there appellate review of panel decisions?
5) Does the transferee judge have authority under the statute to entertain a motion for summary judgment?

One of the practices that grew up under § 1407 was for the transferee court, which had become familiar with the case through all the pretrial proceedings, to then assign the trial to itself under § 1404. But in Lexecon, Inc. v. Milberg, Weiss, Bershad, Hynes & Lerach, 523 U.S. 26 (1998), the United States Supreme Court unanimously disapproved the practice. According to the Court, the "plain meaning" of § 1407(a) requires that "[e]ach action so transferred shall be remanded by the [JPML] at or before the conclusion of such pretrial proceedings to the district court from which it was transferred unless it shall have been previously terminated." In reversing the Ninth Circuit, the Court repudiated a practice followed by the appellate courts for over 30 years. Federal legislation subsequently was adopted that reinstates the practice of self-transfer and effectively undoes *Lexecon*. It also created a new 28 U.S.C. § 1369, which allows for original jurisdiction over single-event accidents in which there is minimal diversity between adverse parties, and at least 75 persons have died.

7 *Repose: Ending Disputes*

In this chapter we address direct and collateral post-trial avenues by which a party may seek to overturn a judgment or to give it preclusive effect in another, collateral lawsuit, and the procedural rules and decisional law that apply to these strategies. Before turning to the technical aspects of these maneuvers, however, consider the policy reasons why even an incorrect judgment nevertheless might be hard to overturn. The most obvious one is that disputes should end, and that even an incorrect outcome has in its favor that it concludes the dispute. Just as obvious, however, is that incorrect judgments are a strain on a judicial process that prides itself on arriving at just—which must mean reasonably accurate—outcomes. Yet, given the impressive array of procedural devices already available to litigants to question outcomes—such as the motions for judgment as a matter of law and for a new trial, and especially the opportunity to appeal—are any *other* means of challenging or avoiding these judgments necessary?

We first take up the subject of direct attacks on judgments. Read Fed. R. Civ. P. 60, which lists conditions under which a party may attack a judgment rendered by a federal judge. Then consider the following cases that construe the Rule and its limits.

A. DIRECT ATTACKS ON JUDGMENTS

Problem Case: A Time to Reconsider

For some years, the school board encouraged teachers and others employed at Senior High School to attend home football and basketball games, to sit in assigned areas among the students, and thus to assist in crowd control. Free tickets and free refreshments were provided, and those who regularly attended were warmly praised by school administrators for their loyalty and professionalism.

As counsel for 15 teachers led by Aldrich, Olvida filed an action in the county court against the school district, alleging that the plaintiffs were coerced to attend games and thus performed overtime work without overtime pay, in violation of the Federal Fair Labor Standards Act. The plaintiffs sought double damages, as provided by § 16(b) of the Act, and also an injunction against further violations of federal law by the school board.

The school board, through its counsel, Elder, answered and denied that any of the plaintiffs had been coerced.

At pretrial, the county judge questioned whether he had the power to issue an injunction against a local school board to enforce a federal law in a suit brought by a private plaintiff. Responding to this concern, Olvida contended that the applicability of this federal law to local school districts was controlled by Maryland v. Wirtz, 392 U.S. 183 (1968), and that injunctions to enforce the Act are authorized by § 17 of the Act. Elder contested neither of these statements.

At trial, the plaintiffs each testified to some form of coercion brought to bear upon them to assure their attendance at games. The defense witnesses denied each of the threats to which the plaintiffs testified.

The county judge found that there was at least implicit coercion, entitling the plaintiffs to double damages and an injunction. The school board did not appeal, and satisfied the money judgments.

Two years later, Elder retired. In reviewing the files, his successor, Newman, encountered the case. Newman is aware that Maryland v. Wirtz was overruled in National League of Cities v. Usery, 426 U.S. 833 (1976), which held that the Fair Labor Standards Act cannot constitutionally be applied to local governments. He is also aware that the Act authorizes injunctive relief only in suits brought by the Department of Labor, e.g., Roberg v. Henry Phipps Estate, 156 F.2d 958 (2d Cir. 1946). And Newman is now informed by Bailey, one of the claimants in the action, that Bailey is prepared to recant his testimony, which was given only on the assurance of Aldrich that all of the plaintiffs would give similar false testimony. Bailey has, indeed, refunded to the school district the money received in satisfaction of the judgment, and has voluntarily paid interest on that amount.

What action should Newman recommend on behalf of the school board?

1. Judgments of Courts Lacking Jurisdiction

Durfee v. Duke

375 U.S. 106 (1963)

JUSTICE STEWART delivered the opinion of the Court.

The United States Constitution requires that "Full Faith and Credit shall be given in each State to the . . . judicial Proceedings of every other State." The case before us presents questions arising under this constitutional provision and under the federal statute enacted to implement it.[2]

2. The Acts of the legislature of any State, Territory or Possession of the United States, or copies thereof, shall be authenticated by affixing the seal of such State, Territory or Possession thereto.

In 1956 the petitioners brought an action against the respondent in a Nebraska court to quiet title to certain bottom land situated on the Missouri River. The main channel of that river forms the boundary between the States of Nebraska and Missouri. The Nebraska court had jurisdiction over the subject matter of the controversy only if the land in question was in Nebraska. Whether the land was Nebraska land depended entirely upon a factual question—whether a shift in the river's course had been caused by avulsion or accretion. The respondent appeared in the Nebraska court and through counsel fully litigated the issues, explicitly contesting the court's jurisdiction over the subject matter of the controversy. After a hearing the court found the issues in favor of the petitioners and ordered that title to the land be quieted in them. The respondent appealed, and the Supreme Court of Nebraska affirmed the judgment after a trial de novo on the record made in the lower court. The State Supreme Court specifically found that the rule of avulsion was applicable, that the land in question was in Nebraska, that the Nebraska courts therefore had jurisdiction of the subject matter of the litigation, and that title to the land was in the petitioners. Durfee v. Keiffer, 95 N.W.2d 618. The respondent did not petition this Court for a writ of certiorari to review that judgment.

Two months later the respondent filed a suit against the petitioners in a Missouri court to quiet title to the same land. Her complaint alleged that the land was in Missouri. The suit was removed to a Federal District Court by reason of diversity of citizenship. The District Court after hearing evidence expressed the view that the land was in Missouri, but held that all the issues had been adjudicated and determined in the Nebraska litigation, and that the judgment of the Nebraska Supreme Court was res judicata and "is now binding upon this court." The Court of Appeals reversed. . . . 308 F.2d 209. We granted certiorari. . . . 371 U.S. 946. For the reasons that follow, we reverse. . . .

It is not questioned that the Nebraska courts would give full res judicata effect to the Nebraska judgment quieting title in the petitioners. It is the respondent's position, however, that whatever effect the Nebraska courts might give to the Nebraska judgment, the federal court in Missouri was free independently to determine whether the Nebraska court in fact had

---

The records and judicial proceedings of any court of any such State, Territory or Possession, or copies thereof, shall be proved or admitted in other courts within the United States and its Territories and Possessions by the attestation of the clerk and seal of the court annexed, if a seal exists, together with a certificate of a judge of the court that the said attestation is in proper form.

Such Acts, records and judicial proceedings or copies thereof, so authenticated, shall have the same full faith and credit in every court within the United States and its Territories and Possessions as they have by law or usage in the courts of such State, Territory or Possession from which they are taken.

Act of June 25, 1948, c. 646, 62 Stat. 947, 28 U.S.C. § 1738.

The progenitor of the present statute was enacted by the First Congress in 1790. 1. Stat. 122. "The Act extended the rule of the Constitution to all courts, federal as well as state, Mills v. Duryee, [11 U.S.] 7 Cr. 481, 485 [1813]." Davis v. Davis, 305 U.S. 32, 40 [1938].

jurisdiction over the subject matter, i.e., whether the land in question was actually in Nebraska.

In support of this position the respondent relies upon the many decisions of this Court which have held that a judgment of a court in one State is conclusive upon the merits in a court in another State only if the court in the first State had power to pass on the merits — had jurisdiction, that is, to render the judgment. As Mr. Justice Bradley stated the doctrine in the leading case of Thompson v. Whitman, [85 U.S.] 18 Wall. 457 (1874),

> we think it clear that the jurisdiction of the court by which a judgment is rendered in any State may be questioned in a collateral proceeding in another State, notwithstanding the provision of the fourth article of the Constitution and the law of 1790, and notwithstanding the averments contained in the record of the judgment itself. [18 Wall. at 469.]

The principle has been restated and applied in a variety of contexts.

However, while it is established that a court in one State, when asked to give effect to the judgment of a court in another State, may constitutionally inquire into the foreign court's jurisdiction to render that judgment, the modern decisions of this Court have carefully delineated the permissible scope of such an inquiry. From these decisions there emerges the general rule that a judgment is entitled to full faith and credit — even as to questions of jurisdiction — when the second court's inquiry discloses that those questions have been fully and fairly litigated and finally decided in the court which rendered the original judgment.

With respect to questions of jurisdiction over the person,[8] this principle was unambiguously established in Baldwin v. Iowa State Traveling Men's Assn., 283 U.S. 522 [1931]. There it was held that a federal court in Iowa must give binding effect to the judgment of a federal court in Missouri despite the claim that the original court did not have jurisdiction over the defendant's person, once it was shown to the court in Iowa that the question had been fully litigated in the Missouri forum. "Public policy," said the Court,

> dictates that there be an end of litigation; that those who have contested an issue shall be bound by the result of the contest, and that matters once tried shall be considered forever settled as between the parties. We see no reason why this doctrine should not apply in every case where one voluntarily appears, presents his case and is fully heard, and why he should not, in the absence of fraud, be thereafter concluded by the judgment of the tribunal to which he has submitted his cause. [283 U.S. at 525-526.]

Following the *Baldwin* case, this Court soon made clear in a series of decisions that the general rule is no different when the claim is made that

8. It is not disputed in the present case that the Nebraska courts had jurisdiction over the respondent's person. She entered a general appearance in the trial court, and initiated the appeal to the Nebraska Supreme Court.

the original forum did not have jurisdiction over the subject matter. Davis v. Davis, 305 U.S. 32 [1938]; Stoll v. Gottlieb, 305 U.S. 165 [1938]; Treinies v. Sunshine Mining Co., 308 U.S. 66 [1939]; Sherrer v. Sherrer, 334 U.S. 343 [1948]. In each of these cases the claim was made that a court, when asked to enforce the judgment of another forum, was free to retry the question of that forum's jurisdiction over the subject matter. In each case this Court held that since the question of subject-matter jurisdiction had been fully litigated in the original forum, the issue could not be retried in a subsequent action between the parties. . . .

The reasons for such a rule are apparent. In the words of the Court's opinion in Stoll v. Gottlieb, supra,

> We see no reason why a court, in the absence of an allegation of fraud in obtaining the judgment, should examine again the question whether the court making the earlier determination on an actual contest over jurisdiction between the parties, did have jurisdiction of the subject matter of the litigation. . . . Courts to determine the rights of parties are an integral part of our system of government. It is just as important that there should be a place to end as that there should be a place to begin litigation. After a party has his day in court, with opportunity to present his evidence and his view of the law, a collateral attack upon the decision as to jurisdiction there rendered merely retries the issue previously determined. There is no reason to expect that the second decision will be more satisfactory than the first. [305 U.S. at 172.]

It is argued that an exception to this rule of jurisdictional finality should be made with respect to cases involving real property because of this Court's emphatic expressions of the doctrine that courts of one State are completely without jurisdiction directly to affect title to land in other States. This argument is wide of the mark. Courts of one State are equally without jurisdiction to dissolve the marriages of those domiciled in other States. But the location of land, like the domicile of a party to a divorce action, is a matter "to be resolved by judicial determination." Sherrer v. Sherrer, 334 U.S. at 349. The question remains whether, once the matter has been fully litigated and judicially determined, it can be retried in another State in litigation between the same parties. Upon the reason and authority of the cases we have discussed, it is clear that the answer must be in the negative.

It is to be emphasized that all that was ultimately determined in the Nebraska litigation was title to the land in question as between the parties to the litigation there. Nothing there decided, and nothing that could be decided in litigation between the same parties or their privies in Missouri, could bind either Missouri or Nebraska with respect to any controversy they might have, now or in the future, as to the location of the boundary between them, or as to their respective sovereignty over the land in question. Fowler v. Lindsey, 3 Dall. 411 [1799]; New York v. Connecticut, 4 Dall. 1 [1799]; Land v. Dollar, 330 U.S. 731, 736-737 [1947]. Either State may at any time protect its interest by initiating independent judicial proceedings here. Cf. Missouri v. Nebraska, 196 U.S. 23 [1904].

For the reasons stated, we hold in this case that the federal court in Missouri had the power and, upon proper averments, the duty to inquire into the jurisdiction of the Nebraska courts to render the decree quieting title to the land in the petitioners. We further hold that when that inquiry disclosed, as it did, that the jurisdictional issues had been fully and fairly litigated by the parties and finally determined in the Nebraska courts, the federal court in Missouri was correct in ruling that further inquiry was precluded. Accordingly the judgment of the Court of Appeals is *reversed*, and that of the District Court is *affirmed*.

It is so ordered.

---

2. Judgments Obtained by Fraud or Mistake

Kupferman v. Consolidated Research & Mfg. Co.

459 F.2d 1072 (2d Cir. 1972)

[Kupferman was the receiver of an insolvent underwriter, Vickers, Christy & Co. Among the assets of Vickers, Christy were 12,500 shares of stock in Consolidated acquired pursuant to a 1960 underwriting agreement. By 1962, these shares were diminished in value. Kupferman brought this action against Consolidated, alleging that it had violated the underwriting agreement by its inadequate compliance with SEC filing requirements. Ross, Kupferman's attorney, had in his possession a copy of a release executed in 1961 by Vickers, Christy which purported to absolve Consolidated for any breach of the underwriting agreement. Purcell, the lawyer for Consolidated, did not discover the release, although he had a copy of a letter of February 3, 1961, referring to it. The release was not pleaded as a defense. The trial resulted in a judgment for the plaintiff receiver in 1962.

When the judgment against Consolidated proved unenforceable because of the absence of corporate assets, Kupferman brought an action in state court against its monied directors, asserting that their mismanagement of Consolidated gave rise to the loss resulting in the adverse judgment. In this litigation, Jacobsen, one of the defendant directors, discovered the release in 1971, and thereupon filed a motion in the court that had rendered the 1962 judgment, seeking a vacation of that judgment.]

FRIENDLY, Chief Judge. . . .

Fed. R. Civ. P. 60(b) authorizes a court on motion to "relieve a party or his legal representative from a final judgment" for "(1) mistake, inadvertence, surprise, or excusable neglect" or "(3) fraud (whether heretofore denominated intrinsic or extrinsic), misrepresentation, or other misconduct of an adverse party." However, motions seeking relief under these broad provisions may not be made "more than one year after judgment was entered." Any rights of appellant to have the 1962 judgment vacated must therefore stem from the saving clause in Rule 60(b): "This rule does not limit the power of a court to entertain an independent action to relieve a party from a judgment . . . or to set aside a judgment for fraud upon the court." [See Rule 60(d). EDS]

Since appellant has not initiated an independent action for fraud *inter partes*, he can prevail only upon a showing that Ross practiced "fraud upon the court" by not disclosing the release.

The meaning of the quoted phrase has not been much elucidated by decisions. Obviously it cannot be read to embrace any conduct of an adverse party of which the court disapproves; to do so would render meaningless the one-year limitation on motions under Fed. R. Civ. P. 60(b)(3). See 7 Moore, *Federal Practice* 60.33 at 511 (1971 ed.). Professor Moore submits that the concept should "embrace only that species of fraud which does or attempts to, defile the court itself, or is a fraud perpetrated by officers of the court so that the judicial machinery cannot perform in the usual manner its impartial task of adjudging cases that are presented for adjudication." Id. at 515. . . . We accepted that formulation in Martina Theatre Corp. v. Schine Chain Theatres, Inc., 278 F.2d 798, 801 (2d Cir. 1960). Professor Moore explains Hazel-Atlas Glass Co. v. Hartford-Empire Co., 322 U.S. 238 (1944), setting aside a judgment on motion because of conduct which, shocking as it was, was a shade less flagrant than that held insufficient to sustain a plenary action in United States v. Throckmorton, 98 U.S. 61 (1878), largely on the basis, claimed by appellant to be presented here, that an attorney was implicated in perpetrating the fraud. While an attorney

> should represent his client with singular loyalty that loyalty obviously does not demand that he act dishonestly or fraudulently; on the contrary his loyalty to the court, as an officer thereof, demands integrity and honest dealing with the court. And when he departs from that standard in the conduct of a case he perpetrates a fraud upon the court. [7 Moore, supra, at 513.]

If there were no facts other than those stated up to this point, it would be hard to resist the conclusion that the case came within the boundaries of the concept of fraud upon the court which this court recognized in *Martina Theatre*, supra, 278 F.2d at 801, strict as these are. Contrary to views intimated by the district court, Purcell's negligent failure to discover the release would not of itself operate against such a conclusion if Ross had instituted, or allowed a judgment to be recovered in, an action to which he knew there was a complete defense. Hazel-Atlas Glass Co. v. Hartford-Empire Co., supra, 322 U.S. at 246. However, the full story has not yet been told; when it has been, Ross' conduct appears in a different light. . . . In his affidavit opposing the instant motion he averred that, pursuant to court order, he had been examining Vickers under oath from time to time in an endeavor to obtain evidence that would assist the receiver in carrying out his duties.

On May 10, 1962, Ross interrogated Vickers about the release. Vickers answered that the release, prepared by Friedman & Friedman, had been signed at the closing in Consolidated's office in Connecticut; that its purpose was simply to show "that Vickers, Christy & Co., Inc., had actually received the 12,500 shares"; and that Mr. Friedman "had given that as the reason for asking him to sign it." While it is hard to square this explanation with the [general language] of the release, particularly when that is read in light of the letter of February 3, Ross was not aware of the latter, and Vickers' construction gained credence from Consolidated's failure promptly to reject his demands. . . . Ross cannot therefore be criticized for *continuing* to prosecute the litigation after learning of the release; he could have expected that his adversary would also be armed with such knowledge and that the court would have to determine whether the release meant what it said or only what Vickers alleged he had been told.

The crucial question thus becomes whether it was fraud upon the court for Ross to fail to disclose the release when, as the trial came to an end, Purcell had said nothing about it. . . .

If this had been a criminal case, such nondisclosure by a prosecutor of a piece of evidence that might have been so material to the defense would almost certainly have afforded ground for collateral attack. See United States v. Keogh, 391 F.2d 138, 147-148 (2d Cir. 1968). But it was not. Neither was this a case where Ross and his client stood in a fiduciary relation to Consolidated or were under any order to produce all relevant documents. Cf. Alleghany Corp. v. Kirby, 333 F.2d 327, 341-343 (2d Cir. 1964) (dissenting opinion), aff'd by an equally divided court, 340 F.2d 311 (2d Cir. 1965). . . . Although Judge Frank said in Phelan v. Middle States Oil Corp., 154 F.2d 978, 991-992 (2d Cir. 1946), that a receiver "is a trustee with the highest kind of fiduciary obligations," the next sentence of the opinion makes clear that these obligations are those that run "to all persons interested in the receivership estate," and the many illustrations given relate to failure to discharge such duties, the issue there before the court, not to proceedings against adversaries. The duty of a receiver's attorney, when seeking to recover monies for the estate, like that of all other attorneys, is the high one of "integrity and honest dealing with the court," 7 Moore, supra, at 513, not something vaguely higher.

Whether Ross' failure to apprise the court of the release before the trial ended was such a breach of that duty as to constitute a fraud upon the court is not altogether easy to decide. Doubtless the highest standards of professional conduct would have suggested that he should have sought counsel from the judge . . . concerning where his duty lay. However, it is all too easy to fall into the error of condemning conduct with the aid afforded by the bright glare of hindsight — specifically our knowledge of Purcell's ignorance of the release and of the contents of the February letter. Ross had to make his decision without benefit of such knowledge. He could hardly have supposed that so experienced a lawyer as Purcell would have failed to contact the attorneys who had represented Consolidated when the sale of the 12,500 shares was consummated and obtain the papers Ross had secured for the asking. He could have thought not unreasonably, particularly in light of Friedman's letter of August 8, that such inquiry had been made but had resulted in Friedman's confirming the construction of the release to which Vickers had testified, and that therefore Purcell had made a tactical decision to defend on another ground.

Broad statements that a trial is a search for the truth must be read in the context that, under our legal system, the method for reaching this goal is a properly conducted adversary proceeding. The vague requirement of "candor and fairness" in the Canons of Professional Ethics in force in 1962 could hardly be read as requiring Ross to make certain that his opponent was fully aware of every possible defense that could be advanced. The present Code of Professional Responsibility does not advance matters greatly when it tells us that a lawyer shall not "conceal or knowingly fail to disclose that which he is required by law to reveal," D.R. [Disciplinary Rule] 7-102(A)(3) (1970). So far as we can see, Ross made no misrepresentations: it would be going too far to characterize as "fraud upon the court" his failure to disclose an instrument which he could have supposed reasonably — although, as it now appears, erroneously — to have been known to his adversary. . . .

The order denying the motion to vacate the judgment is *affirmed*.

Note: Rozier v. Ford Motor Co., 573 F.2d 1332 (5th Cir. 1978)

Return to Chapter 3 and review *Rozier*, at page 569, now with the Rule 60(b)(3) aspect of the case in mind. The appellate court in *Rozier* held that the trial court had abused its discretion in denying plaintiff's 60(b)(3) motion, and that a new trial was necessary. Was this a sound result? See also Summers v. Howard Univ., 374 F.3d 1188 (D.C. Cir. 2004) (attempting to conceal filing of related action qualifies as misconduct but does not warrant setting aside consent decree); Cummings v. General Motors Corp., 365 F.3d 944 (10th Cir. 2004) (failure to produce videos not misconduct when not specifically requested; distinguishing *Rozier*); Ty Inc. v. Softbelly's Inc., 353 F.3d 528 (7th Cir. 2003) (discussing witness tampering as misconduct under Rule 60(b)(3)).

Note: Extrinsic Fraud

In Dowdy v. Hawfield, 189 F.2d 637 (D.C. Cir. 1951), it was held that an independent action requires proof of "extrinsic fraud." An early description of the term appears in United States v. Throckmorton, 98 U.S. 61 (1878):

> Where the unsuccessful party has been prevented from exhibiting fully his case by fraud or deception practiced on him by his opponent, as by keeping

> him away from court, a false promise or compromise; or where the defendant never had knowledge of the suit, being kept in ignorance by the acts of the plaintiff or where an attorney fraudulently or without authority assumes to represent a party or connives at his defeat; or where the attorney regularly employed corruptly sells out his client's interest to the other side—these and similar cases which show that there never has been a real contest in the trial or hearing of the case, are reasons for which a new suit may be sustained to set aside and annul the former judgment or decree, and open the case for a new and fair hearing.

Id. at 65-66.

The distinction was repudiated in Publicker v. Shallcross, 106 F.2d 949 (3d Cir. 1939). But it was applied in Salvation Army v. Morris, 421 F.2d 805, 808 (10th Cir. 1970). Note that it is explicitly inapplicable to motions under Fed. R. Civ. P. 60(b)(3). One reason for doubt about the value of the distinction is the curious results it may produce. New York Life Ins. Co. v. Nashville Trust Co., 292 S.W.2d 749 (1956), is a case in which the insurer recovers the proceeds of a life insurance policy when the insured reappears. The fraud was extrinsic because the "widow" was also deceived by the disappearance. The implication is that she would have been able to keep the money if she had proved her own complicity, because the fraud would then be intrinsic.

Despite these sorts of unwelcome consequences, many states still observe the elusive distinction between extrinsic and intrinsic fraud, and deem only extrinsic fraud to be a valid basis for overturning a judgment.

3. Judgments Contrary to Law

Pierce v. Cook & Co.

518 F.2d 720 (10th Cir. 1975)

BREITENSTEIN, Circuit Judge.

Plaintiffs-appellants have moved for relief under Rule 60(b), Fed. R. Civ. P., from a judgment of this court. The problem is that the same vehicular accident has produced divergent results in federal and state courts. We grant the motion and remand the case to the district court with directions.

Edwards, the owner and driver of a tractor-trailer combination, was hauling wheat for defendant-appellee Cook. On January 11, 1968, Edwards' rig collided on an Oklahoma highway with a car driven by Ted Pierce. Pierce was killed and passengers in his car were injured. Claudiatte Pierce brought suit in an Oklahoma state court for herself as surviving widow of Ted and for their minor daughter Letitia. Similar state suits were brought against Cook by Stephen Ellenwood and Mike Davis, passengers in the Pierce car.

On the motion of defendant Cook each case was removed to federal court on diversity grounds. The *Mike Davis* case was dismissed by the federal court on the motion of the plaintiff. It was later refiled in state court by coguardians of Mike, a minor. The guardianship maneuver apparently destroyed diversity and prevented removal.

The federal district court granted defendant Cook summary judgment on the ground that under the Oklahoma decision in Marion Machine, Foundry & Supply Co. v. Duncan, 101 P.2d 813 [1940], the shipper, Cook, was not liable for the torts of the independent contractor, Edwards.

Claudiatte Pierce and Ellenwood appealed. They conceded the effect of the *Marion Machine* decision and argued that, because of the Motor Carrier Act, 49 U.S.C. §§ 301 et seq., federal common law controlled. We held that the Motor Carrier Act did not indicate a congressional intent to supersede state tort law with respect to liability of a shipper, and concluded that Oklahoma law controlled. Pierce v. Cook & Co., 10th Cir., 437 F.2d 1119 [1970].

In the *Mike Davis* case the Oklahoma state court gave summary judgment for Cook on the basis of the *Marion Machine* decision. The case then went to the Oklahoma Supreme Court which specifically overruled *Marion Machine* and said, Hudgens v. Cook Industries, Inc., 521 P.2d 813, 816 [1974]:

> Where there is foreseeable risk of harm to others unless precautions are taken, it is the duty of one who is regularly engaged in a commercial enterprise which involves selection of motor carriers as an integral part of the business, to exercise reasonable care to select a competent carrier. Failure to exercise such care may create liability on the part of the employer for the negligence of the carrier.

The court remanded the case for jury trial. The case was then settled favorably to the plaintiff.

The Tenth Circuit decision became final in January, 1971. The Oklahoma Supreme Court decision became final in May, 1974. In November, 1974, Claudiatte Pierce and Ellenwood filed the pending Rule 60(b) motion for relief from judgment.

The first question is the propriety of consideration of the motion by the court of appeals. Movants seek relief as a matter of law from a judgment of this court. This is not a case like Wilkin v. Sunbeam Corporation, 10th Cir., 405 F.2d 165 [1968], where a motion was filed in the court of appeals for leave to file in the district court a Rule 60(b) motion on the grounds of newly discovered evidence and fraud. Saying that the district court was in a better position to decide the issues presented, we held that the motion was unnecessary. The procedural problems involved have been the subject of much discussion.... Because our judgment is final and mandate issued, the trial court could well believe that it is without power to determine a legal question contrary to the decision of the court of appeals. Accordingly, we shall consider the motion.

Rule 60(b) provides that a court may grant relief from a judgment on five stated grounds and then says: "(6) any other reason justifying relief from the operation of the judgment." The one-year limitation provided in the rule does not apply to (6).

An adjudication must at some time become final. We recognized this principle in the *Collins* litigation. There, the plaintiffs attacked the constitutionality of a Kansas statute and lost. Collins v. City of Wichita, Kansas, 10th Cir., 225 F.2d 132 [1955]. A year later in an unrelated case the Supreme Court held the Kansas statute unconstitutional. Plaintiffs then sought Rule 60(b)(6) relief which we denied, Collins v. City of Wichita, Kansas, 10th Cir., 254 F.2d 837, 839 [1958], saying (1) "in extraordinary situations, relief from final judgments may be had under Rule 60(b)(6), when such action is appropriate to accomplish justice," and (2) "[a] change in the law or in the judicial view of an established rule of law is not such an extraordinary circumstance which justifies such relief." *Collins* differs from the instant case in that there the decisional change came in an unrelated case. Here it came in a case arising out of the same accident as that in which the plaintiffs now before us were injured. The question is whether we have here an extraordinary situation justifying Rule 60(b)(6) relief.

Our attention is called to no case considering the situation before us. Plaintiffs were forced into federal court by Cook's removal of their state court actions on diversity grounds. They lost because state law controls and the *Marion Machine* decision defeated their claims as a matter of law. Another party, exercising a stratagem not shown to be available to these plaintiffs, obtained the reversal of the *Marion Machine* decision and a settlement thereafter.

Research has disclosed only one case considering divergent results from a common vehicular accident and it afforded relief to the previously unsuccessful party. Gondeck v. Pan American World Airways, Inc., 382 U.S. 25 [1965], was concerned with a claim for death benefits under the Longshoremen's and Harbor Workers' Compensation Act. Two men were killed in the same accident. An award made by the Department of Labor to the survivors of one of the men was set aside in the United States District Court for the Southern District of Florida. The Fifth Circuit affirmed. United States v. Pan American World Airways, Incorporated, 5th Cir., 299 F.2d 74 [1962]. The Supreme Court denied certiorari, 370 U.S. 918, and on October 8, 1962, denied rehearing, 371 U. S. 856.

The survivors of a second man killed in the same accident litigated in the Eastern District of Virginia and lost but the Fourth Circuit reversed and upheld the right to recover. Pan American World Airways, Incorporated v. O'Hearne, 4th Cir., 335 F.2d 70 [1964].

The survivors of the first then went back to the Supreme Court in 1965 with a petition for rehearing. The Supreme Court granted the rehearing, granted certiorari, and reversed the Fifth Circuit court of appeals. In so doing, it said, 382 U.S. 25, 27, . . . "since, of those eligible for compensation from the accident, this petitioner stands alone in not receiving it, 'the interests of justice would make unfair the strict application of our rules.'"

The reasons for relief in the instant case are more compelling than those in *Gondeck*. There two federal courts differed as to the construction and application of a federal statute. We are concerned with an action in which federal jurisdiction depends on diversity. In diversity jurisdiction cases the results in federal court should be substantially the same as those in state court litigation arising out of the same transaction or occurrence. Erie Railroad Co. v. Tompkins, 304 U.S. 64, 74-75 [1938]; Guaranty Trust Co. v. York, 327 U.S. 99, 109 [1945]; Hanna v. Plumer, 380 U.S. 460, 468 [1965]; and Merchants Transfer & Warehouse Co. v. Ragan, 10th Cir., 170 F.2d 987, 991 [1948], *aff'd* 337 U.S. 530 [1949]. Here they were not.

The unusual combination of events which have occurred make the situation extraordinary. The federal courts in which plaintiffs were forced to litigate have given them substantially different treatment than that received in state court by another injured in the same accident. The outcome determination principle mandated by Erie v. Tompkins has been violated.

Relief under Rule 60(b)(6) "is appropriate to accomplish justice" in an extraordinary situation. *Collins,* 254 F.2d 837, 839. Accordingly, our judgment heretofore entered in this case is vacated and the case is remanded. We do not set aside the judgment of the trial court. If plaintiffs file a Rule 60(b)(6) motion for relief from the trial court's judgment, that court shall consider the motion, and any response thereto, in the light of the *Hudgens* opinion, and of this opinion and shall make such determination as it deems proper.

Motion granted and case remanded with directions.

BARRETT, Circuit Judge (concurring in the result).

I concur in the result reached by the majority. Notwithstanding my strong disinclination to disturb a final judgment, I conclude that under the circumstances of this case that such is necessary in order to effect fundamental justice, thus justifying application of Rule 60(b)(6), Fed. R. Civ. P. on behalf of plaintiffs-appellants (hereinafter referred to as Pierce-Ellenwood). . . .

In my view, Rule 60(b)(6) should always be applied in order to relieve a party who did not invoke the jurisdiction of the federal court in a diversity suit from a judgment adverse to that which would otherwise have been favorable in the state court forums. One who invokes the jurisdiction of the federal court when the diversity requirements are present should pay the consequences of that election. A change in state law should not be cause for relief to one who has voluntarily selected that forum. Such a litigant is not entitled to the proverbial "two bites at the apple." Furthermore, such application should do much to promote and strengthen proper Federal-State court relations.

LEWIS, Chief Judge, with whom SETH, Circuit Judge, joins, dissenting.

I am completely uncertain as to what impact the ruling of the majority has, or is intended to have, on established procedural and substantive law or in the administration of justice generally. The opinion would appear to recognize that relief under Rule 60(b) is directed to the sound discretion of the trial court (except in this case) and remands the case to the trial court for consideration under Rule 60(b)(6) but in accord with the views expressed in the opinion. There is, of course, no existent motion under Rule 60(b)(6), or any motion under Rule 60(b)(6), or any motion at all, before the trial court but the majority suggests to plaintiffs that one be filed. This unusual judicial direction is surprising especially since the case was presented to this court in reliance upon Rule 60(b)(5) and counsel for plaintiffs expressly disavowed reliance on Rule 60(b)(6) during oral argument. The impact, if any, of Rule 60(b)(6) was neither argued nor briefed for this court and the authorities cited in the majority opinion appear in the case for the first time. . . .

The factual background of this case is based on a common disaster and, although the majority opinion does not specifically so state, I assume that the majority ruling is intended to be limited by this "extraordinary circumstance." But the driving force of the ruling, the desire to obtain consistent results in state and federal cases involving state law, to me, seems equally applicable to identical accidents and even to such instances as this court considered in Collins v. City of Wichita, 254 F.2d 837 [10th Cir. 1958].

Perhaps such a breakthrough would be desirable; perhaps not, for consistency, even in criminal cases, is not an invariable exaction of the law. United States v. Cudd, 10th Cir., 499 F.2d 1239, 1242 [1974]. In any event, I do not agree that the court has properly exercised its appellate function in this case and accordingly I dissent and join with Judge Seth in his expressed views. . . .

In Ackerman v. United States, 340 U.S. 193, 198 (1950), the petitioner's citizenship had been revoked in a case joined with that of his brother-in-law, Keilbar. Keilbar appealed, but Ackerman did not, on the advice of an officer of the Immigration and Naturalization Service and because his attorney told him that he would have to sell his house to pay the cost of an appeal. When Keilbar's case was reversed, Ackerman sought relief under 60(b)(6) and was denied. The Supreme Court wrote:

> Petitioner made a considered choice not to appeal. . . . [H]is choice was a risk, but calculated and deliberate and such as follows a free choice. Petitioner cannot be relieved of such a choice because hindsight seems to indicate to him that his decision not to appeal was probably wrong. . . . There must be an end to litigation some day, and free calculated choices are not to be relieved from.

Notes and Questions

1. *Finality and "the Law."* The federal courts have been reluctant to find changes in law to be a reason to set aside a judgment as void. As the First Circuit explained in Lubben v. Selective Service System Local Bd. No. 27, 453

F.2d 645, 649 (1st Cir. 1972), "[a] void judgment is one which, from its inception, was a complete nullity and without legal effect. In the interest of finality, the concept of void judgments is narrowly construed. . . . Only in the rare instance of a clear usurpation of power will a judgment be rendered void."

Nevertheless, the presumption in favor of finality can be overcome by a subsequent change in the law when especially compelling public policy reasons so dictate. See, e.g., Moch v. East Baton Rouge Parish School Bd., 548 F.2d 594, 598 (5th Cir. 1977) (holding that a judgment could be set aside where it had the effect of allowing to continue "ad infinitum a constitutionally infirm [school] system outlawed everywhere else"); but see Celestine v. Petroleos De Venezuela, 108 Fed. Appx. 180 (5th Cir. 2004) (change in decisional law is not an extraordinary circumstance in itself; distinguishing *Pierce* on ground that the divergent judgments did not arise out of the same transaction).

Moreover, the United States Supreme Court took the 60(b) route to revising Aguilar v. Felton, 473 U.S. 402 (1985), in Agostini v. Felton, 521 U.S. 203 (1997). In *Aguilar,* New York City taxpayers complained of a program that sent public school teachers to various schools to provide remedial education for disadvantaged children. Since some of the qualifying disadvantaged children attended parochial schools, this meant that city funds were paying for classes in parochial schools, a practice that the Supreme Court held entangled church and state. On remand, the district court issued a permanent injunction preventing the city from sending public school teachers to teach remedial classes in parochial schools. Twelve years later, the Court in *Agostini* held that *Aguilar* was inconsistent with subsequent Supreme Court Establishment Clause decisions and that petitioners thus were entitled to 60(b)(5) relief from the prospective injunction issued earlier by the district court judge in *Aguilar.* Although the majority expressly rejected the dissent's argument that its approach could inspire a flurry of 60(b)(5) motions arguing that the applicable law has changed, *Agostini* does seem to invite such a response. As the dissent emphasizes, the factual conditions of *Aguilar* had not changed, and *Aguilar* itself had not been formally overruled when the district court acted.

Implicated by these results is an interesting and quite basic question about what the law is, or should be. At a superficial level, law is simply whatever rules are in force at the time of a decision. To disrupt a result simply because that law later changes in no way undermines the correctness of the result, provided it was consistent with the law of its time. By permitting such results to be disrupted — even if rarely — aren't courts suggesting that "law" is sometimes found outside the controlling cases and statutes, such that this superficial definition of law is misleading?

2. *Default Judgments.* One important caveat to the general principle that Rule 60(b) motions tend not to succeed is that the motion applies to default judgments as well as to judgments after appearance by a defendant. As you might imagine, motions to set aside a default judgment are far

more likely to prevail than ones filed after a trial. Indeed, the motion's likely success may be a reason not to take a default judgment, lest the judgment simply be set aside later, and the expenses of this process be added to other expenses of pursuing the case.

3. *Appeal Versus Rule 60(b).* The courts' interpretation of Rule 60(b) must be evaluated in light of the alternatives available to a litigant who is unhappy with a judgment. The most important of these, of course, is the right to appeal. As the courts have repeatedly observed, "Rule 60(b) was not intended to provide relief for error on the part of the court or to substitute for appeal." Title v. United States, 263 F.2d 28, 31 (9th Cir.), *cert. denied*, 359 U.S. 989 (1959).

4. *Independent Actions.* Note that Rule 60 also anticipates the possibility of an independent action to challenge a judgment. When might such an action be filed? Isn't allowing such challenges a waste of judicial resources that runs counter to the efficiency concerns that tend to govern rulings on Rule 60(b) motions?

Another question raised by Rule 60 challenges is whether this independent action requires an independent source of jurisdiction. The United States Supreme Court held in United States v. Beggerly, 524 U.S. 38 (1998), that an independent action to set aside a judgment under 60(b) does not require this independent jurisdiction. *Beggerly* also discussed the history of the rule preserving such independent actions and stressed their rarity:

> [A]n independent action should be available only to prevent a grave miscarriage of justice. In this case, it should be obvious that respondents' allegations do not nearly approach this demanding standard. Respondents allege only that the United States failed to "thoroughly search its records and make full disclosure to the Court" regarding the Boudreau grant. Whether such a claim might succeed under Rule 60(b)(3) we need not now decide; it surely would work no "grave miscarriage of justice," and perhaps no miscarriage of justice at all, to allow the judgment to stand.

524 U.S. at 47.

An example of the rare case justifying an independent action is Marshall v. Holmes, 141 U.S. 589 (1891), in which the underlying judgment was based on forged evidence.

B. COLLATERAL EFFECTS OF JUDGMENTS — CLAIM AND ISSUE PRECLUSION

Res judicata (or "thing(s) decided") is the doctrine determining when and how a judgment in one action will be dispositive in a second, later action. Essentially, it is a doctrine of repose, reflecting the belief that part of due process is closure—that is, that a litigation system should be able to bring a matter to an end.

Because of the increased burden on courts and litigants, and the increased chance for varying results, our system has always resisted relitigation of claims. The legal vessels for this resistance are the ancient, much respected, though little loved, doctrines of res judicata and collateral estoppel. In modern parlance, "res judicata" means claim preclusion and "collateral estoppel" means issue preclusion.

The trend in the federal cases and in general is to impose strict requirements on litigants that force them to raise as many issues and facts as they can in the first litigation forum. In fact, courts seem to be moving toward a rule that would require a plaintiff not only to raise as many transactionally related claims as she can in the first forum, but also to choose the forum that allows her to raise the greatest number of claims—lest she be deemed to have waived those claims that cannot be heard in her chosen forum.

In the following sections, we explore claim and issue preclusion and the growing significance of both doctrines. Before turning to these materials, however, you should distinguish the preclusion doctrines from stare decisis, double jeopardy, and the law of the case. Professors Friedenthal, Kane, and Miller explain the distinctions as follows:

> Stare decisis describes the effect of previous judicial decisions on present litigation. Stare decisis principles, also referred to as the doctrine of precedent, dictate that like cases should be decided alike by courts in a single jurisdiction. To adhere to precedent is a fundamental doctrine of Anglo-American law. Like former adjudication, stare decisis has the task of ensuring stability and consistency in judicial decisions, allowing people to plan their conduct. The law must appear to be rationally consistent if it is to be accepted as an impersonal arbiter of disputes. . . .
>
> Res judicata effect is given to any valid judgment, civil or criminal, that is final and on the merits. Double jeopardy depends on the concept of "jeopardy," which is unique to criminal cases. Jeopardy attaches to a criminal proceeding when the accused is in imminent danger of conviction. Once this has occurred, double jeopardy forbids the prosecution from renewing the same charges in a second proceeding no matter how the case was dealt with in the original court. Ordinarily, jeopardy is deemed to have attached when the jury is sworn, or a witness examined. Because res judicata and double jeopardy rely on different standards, one can imagine criminal cases in which one doctrine would apply but not the other. For example, if a criminal prosecution is dismissed before a jury is empaneled on a finding that the relevant statute of limitations has expired, the defendant has not yet been placed in jeopardy. Nevertheless, he might avoid later prosecution for the same offense by invoking res judicata.
>
> The last doctrine to be distinguished from former adjudication is "law of the case." Law of the case refers to the principle that issues once decided in a case that recur in later stages of the same case are not to be redetermined. Thus, just as notions of collateral estoppel prevent the relitigation of the same issues in successive suits, this doctrine limits relitigation in successive stages of a single suit. For example, law of the case will apply when an issue

> in the case is decided by the trial court and appealed. If the appellate court reverses and rules on the law to be applied and how it affects certain issues of the case, those findings will be binding on the trial court when the action is remanded for a new trial. In practice, the doctrine is not enforced with the rigor that attends the rules of res judicata and collateral estoppel. As noted by the Supreme Court, it "merely expresses the practice of courts generally to refuse to reopen what has been decided, not a limit on their power." [Messinger v. Anderson, 225 U.S. 436, 444 (1912).]

Jack Friedenthal, Mary Kay Kane, and Arthur R. Miller, Civil Procedure 629-631 (3d ed. 1993).

Note: Planned Parenthood v. Casey

The United States Supreme Court relied heavily on stare decisis in reaching its controversial decision not to overrule Roe v. Wade, 410 U.S. 113 (1973). Consider the following excerpts of Planned Parenthood v. Casey, 505 U.S. 833, 854-855 (1992), in which the Court expands on the force and limits of precedent:

> The obligation to follow precedent begins with necessity, and a contrary necessity marks its outer limit. With Cardozo, we recognize that no judicial system could do society's work if it eyed each issue afresh in every case that raised it. See B. Cardozo, The Nature of the Judicial Process 149 (1921). Indeed, the very concept of the rule of law underlying our own Constitution requires such continuity over time that a respect for precedent is, by definition, indispensable. See Powell, Stare Decisis and Judicial Restraint, 1991 Journal of Supreme Court History 13, 16. At the other extreme, a different necessity would make itself felt if a prior judicial ruling should come to be seen so clearly as error that its enforcement was for that very reason doomed.
>
> Even when the decision to overrule a prior case is not, as in the rare, latter instance, virtually foreordained, it is common wisdom that the rule of stare decisis is not an "inexorable command," and certainly it is not such in every constitutional case, see Burnet v. Coronado Oil Gas Co., 285 U.S. 393, 405-411 (1932) (Brandeis, J., dissenting). . . . Rather, when this court reexamines a prior holding, its judgment is customarily informed by a series of prudential and pragmatic considerations designed to test the consistency of overruling a prior decision with the ideal of the rule of law, and to gauge the respective costs of reaffirming and overruling a prior case. Thus, for example, we may ask whether the rule has proved to be intolerable simply in defying practical workability, Swift & Co. v. Wickham, 382 U.S. 111, 116 (1965); whether the rule is subject to a kind of reliance that would lend a special hardship to the consequences of overruling and add inequity to the cost of repudiation, e.g., United States v. Title Ins. & Trust Co., 265 U.S. 472 (1924); whether related principles of law have so far developed as to have left the old rule no more than a remnant of abandoned doctrine, see Patterson v. McLean Credit Union, 491 U.S. 164, 173-174 (1989); or whether facts have so changed or come to be seen so differently, as to have robbed the old rule of significant application or justification, e.g., Burnet, supra, 285 U.S. at 412 (Brandeis, J., dissenting).

Applying these factors, the Court concluded that the central holding of *Roe* — that viability of the fetus marks the earliest point at which the State's interest in fetal life is sufficient to justify a legislative ban on nontherapeutic abortions — was still valid and should be given stare decisis effect. The Court further justified its conclusion by underlining the importance of preserving the Court's authority. To overrule precedent on such a divisive issue, it argued, might create the appearance of a Court that acts not for legally principled reasons, but in response to political pressure. When the arguments for the debatable precedent on a hotly contested issue are at least as strong as those against it, the Court should not risk its authority by overruling precedent. Rather, "the justification claimed must be beyond dispute. The Court must take care to speak and act in ways that allow people to accept its decisions on the terms the Court claims for them, as grounded truly in principle, not as compromises with social and political pressures having, as such, no bearing on the principled choices that the Court is obliged to make." Id. at 865.

1. Claim Preclusion

a. In General

"Claim preclusion" means that a party may not relitigate all or part of a previously litigated claim. It prevents plaintiffs from splitting a cause of action into two separate claims, in effect precluding them from raising in a second action not only what they *actually* raised in the first, but *issues they could have raised* as well.

There are policy exceptions to what can operate as a harsh rule, but courts are becoming less and less forgiving as they feel the pressure for efficiency. As we shall see in Federated Department Stores v. Moitie, infra, the Court even has refused to excuse the only plaintiff in a multiparty case who failed to appeal a judgment against them all. Moitie simply wanted to join in the retrial that his coplaintiffs had won, but the Court invoked res judicata to bar him from further action.

The terms "merger" and "bar" have been much fussed over by courts and commentators. Simply put: If plaintiff wins in the first suit, claim preclusion acts as a merger, such that all causes are merged in the judgment and cannot be split. If plaintiff loses in the first suit, then the judgment acts as a bar to bringing a second action on the same claim.

An example of "merger" is the following verbatim account of a case from King's Bench in 1697, 91 Eng. Rep. 1122, a res judicata classic:

Fetter v. Beale

Plaintiff had brought an action for battery against defendant and recovered. *Subsequently* "part of his skull by reason of the said battery came out of his head," and plaintiff brought another action. Plaintiff's counsel argued that "this action differed from the nature of the former . . . because the recovery in the former action was only for the bruise and battery, but here there is a mayhem by the loss of the skull."

[T]he jury in the former action considered the nature of the wound, and gave damages for all the damages that it had done to the plaintiff; and therefore a recovery in the said action is good here. And *it is the plaintiff's fault, for if he had not been so hasty, he might have been satisfied for this loss of the skull also.* Judgment for the defendant. . . .

In general, then, a plaintiff cannot sue again on the same matter, alleging a new theory, new type of relief, or extension of damages. In Fetter v. Beale, the plaintiff sought an extension of the damages.

b. Conditions of Claim Preclusion

The conditions of claim preclusion are sometimes summarized as follows:

1. Valid final judgment in forum 1:
   - Notice
   - Subject matter jurisdiction
   - Personal jurisdiction
2. Same parties
3. Same claim

As a matter of due process, a person cannot be bound by a judgment unless made a party thereto (or represented, as in a class action). See, e.g., South Central Bell Telephone Co. v. Alabama, 526 U.S. 160 (1999), in which the Court held that where a prior case involving different plaintiffs and tax years was not a class action and had entailed no privity or special relationship between the plaintiffs in the prior case and the one at hand, no claim or issue preclusion from the first case could bar the second action, as the plaintiffs in the section action were "strangers" to the earlier suit. A corollary is that a judgment has preclusive effect only for the parties to the judgment. The major exception to this rule occurs when a person is a successor in interest to a party in a previous lawsuit, for example, when he inherits the land from a party. He then may be bound by any previous judgment that touched on the land.

Much trickier is the requirement that for res judicata to apply, the *same claim* must be involved. Many jurisdictions, though not all, define a claim from the standpoint of transactional relatedness.

As modern procedural rules have become more flexible in defining the outer contours of a "claim" and in allowing a joinder of claims and parties, there has been a corresponding expansion of the preclusive effects of a judgment. When you add to this joinder flexibility the expanded federal subject matter jurisdiction (through supplemental jurisdiction), you find a much broader definition of what "claim" is precluded.

Gone are the days when, in Yogi Berra's immortal words, "It ain't over 'til it's over." It may be over a lot sooner than that.

Problem Case: A Woman Partner (Yet Again)

Return now to the problem case, Shayes v. McKenzie, Brachman, et al. (page 360, supra). In summary, Rosalind Shayes sued her former law partners in federal court for sex discrimination. In the course of discovery, she learns that defendants are saying vicious things about her. She moves to amend her complaint to add a claim for defamation.

a) Would the court allow her to amend the complaint? This would be influenced partly by its assessment of the res judicata effect of failure to raise the claim in this case. This in turn depends on how closely it is related to the sex discrimination claim in the original complaint. If it is found to be very closely related, then if this sex discrimination claim goes to judgment first, Shayes will be barred by res judicata from suing for libel.

b) Does the possible res judicata effect of the amendment mean that the trial judge *must* grant the motion to add the libel claim? Practically speaking, this factor is a strong motivator for the judge unless he thought that Shayes had deliberately sat on the claim until late in the proceedings for some strategic reason, such as delay or limiting discovery time for the defendants.

c) Assume that McKenzie argued against the libel amendment on the ground that it would delay the proceedings and the court refused to allow the libel claim. Shayes then filed a libel suit in state court. The federal case went to trial and lost and the defendants move to dismiss the state case on grounds of res judicata. (Note that they would argue that she was barred from the claim.)

In ruling on the motion, the state court would probably apply its own preclusion law, though this approach is questionable. Can you see why a judgment's reach should be governed by the law of the rendering forum? For a cogent discussion of claim and issue preclusion effects of a judgment on subsequent judicial proceedings in another jurisdiction, see Howard M. Erichson, Interjurisdictional Preclusion, 96 Mich. L. Rev. 945 (1998), concluding, based on a study of several hundred cases, that state courts typically, but improperly, apply their own preclusion law.

Whatever law it applied, however, the state court would be making some of the same determinations that the federal court considered in ruling on the motion to amend. How closely related is it to the original sex discrimination claim? Under one view the libel claim is transactionally related because it arose out of the partnership dissolution. But a state court might find that Shayes was nevertheless not barred because here the defendants specifically denied the relationship of the claims in opposing the motion to amend, and because that motion was argued without any discussion or warning of a possible res judicata effect. As with everything that is judge-made and controlled, there is a great expanse for the play of discretion. And more and more, appellate courts are deferring to the discretion of trial judges on these matters.

McConnell v. Travelers Indemnity Co.

346 F.2d 219 (5th Cir. 1965)

WISDOM, Circuit Judge.

This hard case involving, for the plaintiff, disastrous effects from splitting his cause of action, is an invitation to make bad law. We decline the invitation.

Mr. and Mrs. Archie McConnell, Louisiana residents, were both injured in an automobile accident. Under Louisiana community property law, the wife's claim for personal injuries is her separate property; the husband's claim for personal injuries belongs to the community. Claims for medical expenses for either spouse also belong to the community. LSA-Civil Code, Article 2334 and 2402. As head and master of the community, only the husband may sue on claims belonging to the community. LSA-Code of Civil Procedure, Article 686. . . .

In August 1960 Mrs. McConnell brought suit against the Travelers Indemnity Company and Employers Casualty Company in the 24th Judicial District Court for the Parish of Jefferson, State of Louisiana, to recover damages of $8500 for personal injuries.[2] Her husband joined in the suit seeking recovery of $362.50 he had paid for medical expenses for treatment of Mrs. McConnell's injuries. A week later, Mr. McConnell filed the present suit in the district court to recover $85,000 for his personal injuries and $352.75 for his medical expenses. The state court suit was submitted in May 1963. In June 1963 the defendants filed a motion in the district court for a summary judgment of dismissal based upon the contention that the plaintiff had split his cause of action by filing suit in the state court for medical expenses; that under Article 425 of the LSA-Code of Civil Procedure the plaintiff is precluded from splitting a cause of action. While this motion was under submission, the plaintiff moved in the state court to dismiss his suit "with prejudice." That court therefore dismissed his claim for $362.50, with prejudice and at his cost. The district court then denied the motion for summary judgment in the instant case. The defendants then filed in the district court a renewed motion for summary judgment, contending that the plaintiff could have pursued his claim for personal injuries only by amending his petition in the state court; but that since that court had dismissed the action with prejudice, the dismissal was a final judgment of his entire claim, and was res judicata as to his action in the United States district court. The trial judge granted the motion and dismissed the complaint.

2. The suits were brought under the Louisiana Direct Action Statute, LSA-R.S. 22:655.

"Under Louisiana law, the splitting of tort claims is forbidden and the effect of such a split is to waive the right to recover the excess." Comment, 30 Tul. L. Rev. 462, 469 (1956). . . .

[Art. 425 provides:]

> An obligee cannot divide an obligation due him for the purpose of bringing separate actions on different portions thereof. If he brings an action to enforce only a portion of the obligation, and does not amend his pleading to demand the enforcement of the full obligation, he shall lose his right to enforce the remaining portion. . . .

Although there is no Louisiana case dealing specifically with the type of action-splitting this case presents, there is little doubt that a Louisiana court would hold that Mr. McConnell did indeed split his action. Louisiana courts hold that a plaintiff cannot split his claims for personal injuries and property damage arising from the same accident. Fortenberry v. Clay, 68 So. 2d 133; Thompson v. Kivett & Reel, Inc., 25 So. 2d 124. In addition, in wrongful death cases courts forbid the survivor to split his damages and the decedent's damages. . . .

We are aware that the result we reach produces an anomaly. The husband and wife may split their tort claims, but the husband's lawsuit must include any claim for the wife's medical expenses. In effect, therefore, the parties may twice litigate the issue of the wife's injuries. On the other hand, the plaintiff's theory of the case would also produce an anomaly. The purpose of the tort claims is compensation. Under Louisiana law the community of acquets [i.e., property that has been acquired by purchase, gift, or otherwise rather than by succession] and gains suffers the injury. The plaintiff's theory would divide community damages among several potential lawsuits. It is the Louisiana community property system that causes the anomaly, not the rules of res judicata. This Court must apply the Louisiana law as the Court finds it.

The judgment is *affirmed.*

Consumers Union of United States v. Consumer Product Safety Commission

590 F.2d 1209 (D.C. Cir. 1978)

SPOTTSWOOD W. ROBINSON, III, Circuit Judge.

At the core of this litigation is appellants' challenge under the Freedom of Information Act (FOIA) to the Consumer Product Safety Commission's failure to disclose data concerning accidents attributable to the operation of television sets. When their cause was first before us, we reversed the District Court's ruling that no case or controversy was presented. That determination had been premised on the Commission's acknowledged willingness to release the data save for a ban imposed thereon by a preliminary injunction awarded television manufacturers by the District Court for the District of Delaware in a reverse-FOIA suit involving the same information. We held that the Delaware action, to which appellants were not parties, was no obstacle to their effort in the District Court here. We reasoned that a preliminary injunction is designed merely to preserve the status quo ante pending final decision, and "is not an adjudication of rights in any proper sense of the term. . . ." Because the Delaware court had entered an order "closing out" the case before any final stage had been reached, we concluded that the Delaware proceeding was not "an insuperable barrier to the suit at bar." . . .

Our prior opinions spurred the manufacturers to renew vigorously their pursuit of a judgment on the merits in Delaware, and appellants made no effort to have the District Court here enjoin them from that course. And the Commission, at long last, moved in the Delaware court for a change of venue to the District of Columbia, but added no alternative motion to join the FOIA requesters in the Delaware case — in which, we are now told, their rights have been fully and finally adjudicated. The Delaware court denied transfer primarily on the ground that, though the Commission faced the possibility of inconsistent outcomes on the merits, "[t]he time for the Commission to have moved for a transfer of these cases was in the early stages of this litigation in 1975 before all the effort and work had been expended here."

While a petition to the Supreme Court for a writ of certiorari in this case was pending, the Delaware court issued a permanent injunction. The Supreme Court subsequently granted certiorari and remanded the case to us "for further consideration in light of the permanent injunction." Thus we are now brought face-to-face with the issue we had earlier reserved: Does a judgment in favor of information-suppliers in a reverse-FOIA suit bar requesters not parties thereto from litigating their contention that the Freedom of Information Act mandates disclosure? The answer, we think, becomes clear once one investigates the interrelationship of the Act and reverse-FOIA suits in light of traditional principles governing preclusion of subsequent litigation.

Before the Freedom of Information Act was adopted, official dissemination of information was frequently marked by caprice, and suits to obtain information or to forestall its release met with "far from uniform" judicial treatment. The Act was intended to rationalize agency disclosure policies by providing a mechanism for balancing the public's "right to know" against the agency's interest in preserving confidentiality. If a court finds that the Act applies to material for which a request has been properly made, that is the end of the matter; the material *must* be disclosed, for the Act effectuates a congressional judgment that in those circumstances no public or private interest in secrecy outweighs the benefits attending public access. Moreover, in determining whether the Act is operative, the legislative command that disclosure be the rule and exemptions be narrowly construed must be sedulously observed. But

Congress in the same breath specified classes of information to which the Act — and its policy of openness — "do[] not apply." When a court finds that requested material falls into one of these categories, and resultantly that its divulgence is not compelled by the Act, the propriety of voluntary disclosure by the agency must hinge on reconciliation with such other law as is pertinent — whether statute, regulation, the administrative "common law" or general principles of equity.

Some of these residual legal rules may endow private parties with legally cognizable interests in the confidentiality of exempted information; others may bestow on some a greater entitlement to information than the Act itself gives the general public. Since the agency's purposes will only coincidentally correspond with those of nongovernmental parties, it would be folly to entrust these often-critical private interests to unreviewable bureaucratic discretion. This court has accordingly held that when an agency asserts its intention to comply with a demand for information, parties who would be aggrieved by compliance may sue for a declaration whether that release would be lawful. But such litigants must first pass through the needle's eye of the Freedom of Information Act, for if the Act calls for disclosure they have, of course, no right whatsoever to confidentiality. Only if the Act does not govern need the court examine other sources of law — which may prohibit dissemination, give the agency judicially reviewable or unreviewable discretion to release or retain, or even mandate disclosure, depending on the circumstances. . . .

Federal courts in different jurisdictions may sometimes reach conflicting conclusions on the duties of an administrative agency, but normally without placing it in an impossible dilemma or bringing on a direct clash of judicial power. A serious conundrum, however, arises when, as here, the subject matter is information and the dispute is over whether it should be disclosed to the public. Once released pursuant to judicial decree, the data cannot be bottled up within the court's geographical area; with modern communications, information made public at any one point may soon be available throughout the country, often within moments. By the same token, when a court orders an agency to retain information, its edict is absolutely useless unless it stops agency action everywhere. Consequently, the first court to decide — in either a FOIA or a reverse-FOIA suit — will have pronounced a judgment that might reach across the Nation, or, on the other hand, might not have any practical effect even in its own jurisdictional domain.

That is exactly the situation here. The Delaware proceeding began, and the Commission was temporarily enjoined, before the appellant-requesters filed their own action in the District of Columbia seeking disclosure. By the time appellants sued, the District Court here knew that should the litigation before it continue, a decision contrary to that of the Delaware court might be reached, and that the Commission could not possibly comply with each of the conflicting orders.

Thus focused, the issue is the proper response of the court chronologically second. We earlier rejected one solution — dismissal for absence of a case or controversy—and we adhere to that position for the reasons then stated. That still leaves other alternatives—dismissal on a theory of stare decisis, collateral estoppel or comity, or continuation of the suit in some manner. For more than ample reason, we have chosen the latter course.

A. Stare Decisis

We surely do not gainsay that "the doctrine of stare decisis is still a powerful force in our jurisprudence." So, a court resolving a FOIA claim may choose to defer to a previous judicial decision that the Act does or does not apply to particular documents, whether the prior action sought disclosure or restraint. It has not, however, been our experience that federal judges are either careless or timorous. The notion that any would defer on stare decisis grounds to a decision by a co-ordinate court with which he disagreed is unworthy of comment.

B. Collateral Estoppel

Furthermore, the doctrine of collateral estoppel, which does bind parties to a previous suit to such determinations of material issues as are encompassed in the judgment, only rarely precludes nonparties from litigating the same issues afresh. If the FOIA applicant has neither been a party nor otherwise represented in a prior successful reverse-FOIA suit, he will not be blocked from taking his controversy to the courts.

The only parties here who were litigants in Delaware are the Consumer Product Safety Commission and the manufacturers who sought to prevent disclosure of materials that the Commission was prepared to turn over to appellants. An agency's interests in FOIA suits of either stripe diverge markedly from private interests, and raise serious doubt whether the agency could ever be deemed to represent members of the public. Indeed, congressional appreciation of that divergence underlies the Act. The institutional predilections that distinguish the agency's position from the citizens argue against permitting the Commission to do via litigation what it may not do by agreement—to bar applicants from information to which the Act mandates access. Far less do they justify departure from the rule, articulated in the milieu of antitrust enforcement, that "just as the Government is not bound by . . . litigation to which it is a stranger, so private parties, similarly situated, are not bound by government litigation."

Nor can the agency's role in reverse-FOIA litigation be likened to that of the named representative of a class in a defendant class action, and thus raise the spectre that a judgment against the agency would extend to bind all putative members of the hypothetical class it supposedly represents. At the outset, the clash of purposes would render the bureaucracy suspect as a representative of any class composed of FOIA requesters. Even passing that, when—as in the present circumstances—no class has been convened, no preclusive effect can possibly follow, and the public's right to know remains secure.

C. Comity

That brings us lastly to comity, here reflected in the principle that "[o]rdinarily, the court first acquiring jurisdiction of a controversy should be allowed to proceed with it without interference from other courts under suits subsequently instituted." . . . Created to assure judicial efficiency and to reflect abiding respect for other courts, the doctrine surely does not contemplate that fundamental rights of citizens will be adjudicated in forums from which they are absent. . . .

The decisions invoking the principle involve circumstances in which the plaintiff in the later federal suit was a party to the earlier action involving the same issues and subject matter. When everyone with an interest could have had his claim resolved in one court, it would be senseless to allow some of the parties to initiate concurrent litigation over the same dispute. But that is not this case. Some — at least appellants — with a stake in the controversy were not before the Delaware court, and accordingly the principle of comity is inapplicable. Even if comity might be thought at all relevant, it would not outweigh the nonparties' right, guaranteed by the Act and the Constitution, to have their claims adjudicated.

The sum of the foregoing is that none of the familiar anti-relitigation doctrines operates to deprive nonparty requesters of their right to sue for enforcement of the Freedom of Information Act; rather, they remain unaffected by prior litigation solely between the submitters and the involved agency. One obvious consequence is that federal agencies that are prey to reverse-FOIA suits may by that token find themselves subject to the possibility of inconsistent judgments. Threats of that nature are not unprecedented, however, and there are procedural devices aplenty designed to avoid the hazard of conflicting obligations. Resort to them in the present context, moreover, would have brought about representation of all interests before the court that first addressed the merits, and thereby would have eliminated the problem completely.

Another consequence is that reverse-FOIA plaintiffs may find that, to prevent judgments in their favor from becoming nugatory, they must join in their lawsuits anyone whose request for information quickened the submitter's controversy with the agency — or perhaps even, by way of a defendant class action, all those who likely may subsequently make such requests. That, too, can only be salutary, for it will assure that the public's interest will be represented by at least one of its own. It will also relieve courts of the temptation — to which we earlier succumbed — to undertake a critique of the agency's litigative strategy.

The manufacturer-plaintiffs could have named appellant-requesters as defendants in the Delaware lawsuit, or they could have maintained it as a defendant class action against the Commission and all possible requesters.

They did not. The Commission, with some creativity, could have filed an interpleader counterclaim and joined the requesters on the theory that otherwise the Commission might be exposed to multiple accountability and that, in a dispute over disclosure, information is an indivisible res over which the parties contest. It did not. At the very least, the Commission could have urged that the requesters were parties whose joinder was required under Civil Rule 19. But no consideration was given to the mandates of that rule, though, as we now elucidate, its applicability could hardly have been questioned.

If, as the manufacturers and the Commission assert, the Delaware reverse-FOIA suit so affected appellants' interest in disclosure of the information sought that they are now barred from litigating it in the District Court here, the Delaware action certainly could have been said, in the words of Rule 19, "as a practical matter [to] impede [their] ability to protect that interest or . . . [to] leave [the agency] subject to a substantial risk of incurring double, multiple, or otherwise inconsistent obligations by reason of [appellants'] claimed interest." Indeed, the concept of joinder was created to resolve the problem of conflicting exercise of equity jurisdiction. . . . In our view, those factors, had anyone in the Delaware action paused to look at them, surely demanded dismissal of the manufacturers' Delaware suit, or at least an injunction shaped to impact to the smallest possible extent upon the absent requesters' interest.

Joinder of the requesters would have been the better course, for it would have avoided the duplicative litigation in which we now are unfortunately entangled, but it was not the only solution. A well-crafted judgment in Delaware could have steered clear of any embarrassment to appellants' claim. Indeed, the inherent tension between reverse-FOIA and FOIA suits could often be mitigated by a rule that, unless the party resisting disclosure joins in his reverse-FOIA suit those seeking release, any injunction therein must be drafted to halt only voluntary disclosure by the agency, and to leave unaffected the requesters' right to seek a subsequent judicial determination that the Act mandates disclosure.

Appellant requesters were not made parties to the Delaware action, and the effect of that omission on this litigation is, to us, indisputable. A judgment cannot bind those who were not before the court either in person or through some sort of representative. . . . This basic tenet of due process can hardly be circumvented through the ritualistic invocation of "comity." The manufacturers have no valid objection to relitigation of disclosure of this information "for clearly the plaintiff [in the earlier suit], who himself chose both the forum and the parties defendant, will not be heard to complain about the sufficiency of the relief obtain[ed] against them." Nor can the Commission legitimately bemoan the threat of inconsistent obligations since it never attempted to foreclose that possibility by seeking the joinder of appellants in Delaware.

The only factor even remotely capable of preventing appellants from prosecuting their FOIA suit toward a result contrary to the broad Delaware reverse-FOIA injunction is their failure to intervene in the proceeding there. We believe, however, that appellants, and perhaps information-requesters generally, should not suffer from bypasses of this sort. To decide otherwise would force them to accept the choice of a forum possibly sympathetic to the submitter and surely inconvenient or impossible for the requester. Congress specified the sites proper for judicial consideration of FOIA claims; to allow submitters to force FOIA litigation to occur in other arenas would free the tail to wag the dog.

This, in our opinion, is the type of "undue hardship" expressly discountenanced by the Advisory Committee when it discussed amended Rule 19 in 1966. The rule puts the burden on existing parties and the court to bring in those whose presence is necessary or desirable, and to work out a fair solution when joinder is jurisdictionally impossible. A generally applicable theory of waiver by one who declines to voluntarily step into the proceeding would abrogate the rule and its purpose completely. It is the party's — not the nonparty's — responsibility to make certain that the court has before it all those needed to enable it to serve the ends of justice. And if the essential nonparty cannot, for reasons of personal jurisdiction, be joined in the suit, then the litigation must proceed elsewhere, if at all.

This case, therefore, must finally continue toward a decision on the merits in the District Court for the District of Columbia. Its first task is to analyze closely the Delaware court's reasoning, for it may turn out that the court here will agree with the Delaware court. Should, however, the court decide that the failure to release the information was indeed improper, it will have to ascertain the relief appropriate in the circumstances. Since the manufacturers are party-defendants, it might consider enjoining them from enforcing their Delaware judgment against the Commission. In short, our decision is a narrow one — that this litigation is not prohibited by the earlier action — and we have not attempted to decide whether or not actual disclosure should be the final result.

Remanded.

Note: GTE Sylvania, Inc. v. Consumers Union

Notwithstanding the D.C. Circuit's assurance that its decision was both "narrow" and "indisputable," the Supreme Court reversed. GTE Sylvania, Inc. v. Consumers Union, 445 U.S. 375 (1979). Without any discussion of necessary parties, mandatory intervention, or due process, the Court held that disclosure could not be ordered under the FOIA:

> The issue squarely presented is whether the Court of Appeals erred in holding that the requesters may obtain the accident reports under the Freedom of Information Act when the agency with possession of the documents has been enjoined from disclosing them by a Federal District Court. The terms of the Act and its legislative history demonstrate that the court below was in error.

> The Freedom of Information Act gives federal district courts the jurisdiction "to enjoin the agency from withholding agency records and to order the production of any agency records improperly withheld." 5 U.S.C. § 552(a)(4)(B). This section requires a showing of three components: the agency must have (1) improperly (2) withheld (3) agency records. Kissinger v. Reporters Committee for Freedom of the Press, [445 U.S. 136, 150 (1980)]. In this case the sole question is whether the first requirement, that the information has been "improperly" withheld, has been satisfied. . . .
>
> The CPSC has not released the documents sought here solely because of the orders issued by the Federal District Court in Delaware. At all times since the filing of the complaint in the instant action the agency has been subject to a temporary restraining order or a preliminary or permanent injunction barring disclosure. . . .
>
> To construe the lawful obedience of an injunction issued by a federal district court with jurisdiction to enter such a decree as "improperly" withholding documents under the Freedom of Information Act would do violence to the common understanding of the term "improperly" and would extend the Act well beyond the intent of Congress.
>
> We conclude that the CPSC has not "improperly" withheld the accident reports from the requesters under the Freedom of Information Act.

What happened? Who should have done what to whom to prevent it from happening? Why didn't they?

Federated Department Stores v. Moitie

452 U.S. 394 (1981)

JUSTICE REHNQUIST delivered the opinion of the Court.

The only question presented in this case is whether the Court of Appeals for the Ninth Circuit validly created an exception to the doctrine of res judicata. The court held that res judicata does not bar relitigation of an unappealed adverse judgment where, as here, other plaintiffs in similar actions against common defendants successfully appealed the judgments against them. We disagree with the view taken by the Court of Appeals for the Ninth Circuit and reverse. . . .

In 1976 the United States brought an antitrust action against petitioners, owners of various department stores, alleging that they had violated § 1 of the Sherman Act, 15 U.S.C. § 1, by agreeing to fix the retail price of women's clothing sold in Northern California. Seven parallel civil actions were subsequently filed by private plaintiffs seeking treble damages on behalf of proposed classes of retail purchasers, including that of respondent Moitie in state court (*Moitie I*) and respondent Brown (*Brown I*) in the United States District Court for the Northern District of California. Each of these complaints tracked almost verbatim the allegations of the Government's complaint, though the *Moitie I* complaint referred solely to state law. All of the actions originally filed in the District Court were assigned to a single federal judge, and the *Moitie I* case was removed there on the basis of diversity of citizenship and federal question jurisdiction. The District Court dismissed all of the actions "in their entirety" on the grounds that plaintiffs had not alleged an "injury" to their "business or property" within the meaning of § 4 of the Clayton Act, 15 U.S.C. § 15. Weinberg v. Federated Department Stores, 426 F. Supp. 880 (N.D. Cal. 1977).

Plaintiffs in five of the suits appealed that judgment to the Court of Appeals for the Ninth Circuit. The single counsel representing Moitie and Brown, however, chose not to appeal and instead refiled the two actions in state court, *Moitie II* and *Brown II.* Although the complaints purported to raise only state-law claims, they made allegations similar to those made in the prior complaints, including that of the Government. Petitioners removed these new actions to the District Court for the Northern District of California and moved to have them dismissed on the ground of res judicata. In a decision rendered July 8, 1977, the District Court first denied respondents' motion to remand. It held that the complaints, though artfully couched in terms of state law, were "in many respects identical" with the prior complaints, and were thus properly removed to federal court because they raised "essentially federal law" claims. The court then concluded that because *Moitie II* and *Brown II* involved the "same parties, the same alleged offenses, and the same time periods" as *Moitie I* and *Brown I,* the doctrine of res judicata required that they be dismissed this time. Moitie and Brown appealed.

Pending that appeal, this Court on June 11, 1979, decided Reiter v. Sonotone Corp., 442 U.S. 330, . . . holding that retail purchasers can suffer an "injury" to their "business or property" as those terms are used in § 4 of the Clayton Act. On June 25, 1979, the Court of Appeals for the Ninth Circuit reversed and remanded the five cases which had been decided with *Moitie I* and *Brown I,* the cases that had been appealed, for further proceedings in light of *Reiter.*

When *Moitie II* and *Brown II* finally came before the Court of Appeals for the Ninth Circuit, the court reversed the decision of the District Court dismissing the cases. 611 F.2d 1267.[2] Though the court recognized that a "strict application of the doctrine of res judicata would preclude our review of the instant decision," it refused to apply the doctrine to the facts of this case. It observed that the other five litigants in *Weinberg* cases had

2. The Court of Appeals also affirmed the District Court's conclusion that *Brown II* was properly removed to federal court, reasoning that the claims presented were "federal in nature." We agree that at least some of the claims had a sufficient federal character to support removal. As one treatise puts it, courts "will not permit plaintiff to use artful pleading to close off defendant's right to a federal forum . . . [and] occasionally the removal court will seek to determine whether the real nature of the claim is federal, regardless of plaintiff's characterization." 14 C. Wright, A. Miller, & E. Cooper, Federal Practice and Procedure § 3722, pp. 564-566 (1976) (citing cases) (footnote omitted). The District Court applied that settled principle to the facts of this case. After "an extensive review and analysis of the origins and substance of" the two Brown complaints, it found, and the Court of Appeals expressly agreed, that respondents had attempted to avoid removal jurisdiction by "[artfully] casting their 'essentially federal law claims'" as state-law claims. We will not question here that factual finding.

successfully appealed the decision against them. It then asserted that "non-appealing parties may benefit from a reversal when their position is closely interwoven with that of appealing parties," and concluded that "because the instant dismissal rested on a case that has been effectively overruled," the doctrine of res judicata must give way to "public policy" and "simple justice." Id. at 1270. We granted certiorari . . . to consider the validity of the Court of Appeals' novel exception to the doctrine of res judicata. . . .

. . . As this Court explained in Baltimore Steamship Co. v. Phillips, 274 U.S. 316, 325 (1927) an "erroneous conclusion" reached by the court in the first suit does not deprive the defendants in the second action

> of their right to rely upon the plea of res judicata. . . . A judgment merely voidable because based upon an erroneous view of the law is not open to collateral attack, but can be corrected only by a direct review and not by bringing another action upon the same cause of action.

We have observed that "the indulgence of a contrary view would result in creating elements of uncertainty and confusion and in undermining the conclusive character of judgments, consequences which it was the very purpose of the doctrine of res judicata to avert." Reed v. Allen, 286 U.S. 191, 201 (1932). . . . [T]his Court recognizes no general equitable doctrine, such as that suggested by the Court of Appeals, which countenances an exception to the finality of a party's failure to appeal merely because his rights are "closely interwoven" with those of another party. . . . Respondents here seek to be the windfall beneficiaries of an appellate reversal procured by other independent parties, who have no interest in respondents' case. . . .

Moreover . . . it is apparent that respondents here made a calculated choice to forego their appeals. . . .

The Court of Appeals also rested its opinion in part on what it viewed as "simple justice." But we do not see the grave injustice which would be done by the application of accepted principles of res judicata. "Simple justice" is achieved when a complex body of law developed over a period of years is evenhandedly applied. The doctrine of res judicata serves vital public interests beyond any individual judge's ad hoc determination of the equities in a particular case. There is simply "no principle of law or equity which sanctions the rejection by a federal court of the salutary principle of res judicata." Heiser v. Woodruff, 327 U.S. 726, 733 (1946). The Court of Appeals' reliance on "public policy" is similarly misplaced. This Court has long recognized that "[p]ublic policy dictates that there be an end of litigation; that those who have contested an issue shall be bound by the result of the contest, and that matters once tried shall be considered forever settled as between the parties." Baldwin v. [Iowa] Traveling Men's Association, 283 U.S. 522, 525 (1931). We have stressed that "the doctrine of res judicata is not a mere matter of practice or procedure inherited from a more technical time than ours. It is a rule of fundamental and substantial justice, 'of public policy and of private peace,' which should be cordially regarded and enforced by the court." Hart Steel Co. v. Railroad Supply Co., 244 U.S. 294, 299 (1917). The language used by this Court half a century ago is even more compelling in view of today's crowded dockets:

> The predicament in which respondent finds himself is of his own making. . . . [W]e cannot be expected, for his sole relief, to upset the general and well-established doctrine of res judicata, conceived in the light of the maxim that the interest of the state requires that there be an end to litigation — a maxim which comports with common sense as well as public policy. And the mischief which would follow the establishment of precedent for so disregarding the salutary doctrine against prolonging strife would be greater than the benefit which would result from relieving some case of individual hardship. [Reed v. Allen, supra, 283 U.S. at 198-199.]

Respondents . . . argue that "the District Court's dismissal on grounds of res judicata should be reversed, and the District Court directed to grant respondents' motion to remand to the California State Court." In their view, *Brown I* cannot be considered res judicata as to their *state* law claims, since *Brown I* raised only federal law claims and *Brown II* raised additional state law claims not decided in *Brown I,* such as unfair competition, fraud and restitution. It is unnecessary for this Court to reach that issue. It is enough for our decision here that *Brown I* is res judicata as to respondents' federal law claims. Accordingly, the judgment of the Court of Appeals is reversed, and the cause remanded for proceedings consistent with this opinion.

It is so ordered.

JUSTICE BLACKMUN, with whom JUSTICE MARSHALL joins, concurring in the judgment. . . .

. . . I would flatly hold that *Brown I* is res judicata as to respondents' state law claims. Like the District Court, the Court of Appeals found that those state law claims were simply disguised federal claims; since respondents have not cross-petitioned from that judgment, their argument that this case should be remanded to state court should be itself barred by res judicata. More important, even if the state and federal claims are distinct, respondents' failure to allege the state claims in *Brown I* manifestly bars their allegation in *Brown II.* The dismissal of *Brown I* is res judicata not only as to all claims respondents actually raised, but also as to all claims that could have been raised. . . . See Commissioner v. Sunnen, 333 U.S. 591, 597 (1948). . . . Since there is no reason to believe that it was clear at the outset of this litigation that the District Court would have declined to exercise pendent jurisdiction over state claims, respondents were obligated to plead those claims if they wished to preserve them. . . . Because they did not do so, I would hold the claims barred.

JUSTICE BRENNAN, dissenting. . . .

Respondent Floyd R. Brown filed this class action lawsuit (*Brown II*) against petitioners in California state court. The complaint stated four state law causes of action: (1) fraud and deceit, (2) unfair business practices, (3) civil conspiracy, and (4) restitution. . . . *All four* of the causes of action rested wholly on California statutory or common law; *none* rested in any fashion on federal law. Removability depends solely upon the nature of the plaintiff's complaint: an action may be removed to federal court only if a "right or immunity created by the Constitution or laws of the United States [constitutes] an element, and an essential one, of the plaintiff's cause of action." Gully v. First National Bank in Meridian, 299 U.S. 109, 112 (1936).

An important corollary is that "the party who brings a suit is master to decide what laws he will rely upon and therefore does determine whether he will bring a 'suit arising under' the . . . law[s] of the United States" by the allegations in his complaint. The Fair v. Kohler Die & Specialty Co., 228 U.S. 22, 25 (1913). Where the plaintiff's claim might be brought under either federal or state law, the plaintiff is normally free to ignore the federal question and rest his claim solely on the state ground. If he does so, the defendant has no general right of removal. La Chemise Lacoste v. Alligator Co., 506 F.2d 339, 346 (3d Cir. 1974). . . .

This corollary is well grounded in principles of federalism. So long as States retain authority to legislate in subject areas in which Congress has legislated without preempting the field, and so long as state courts remain the preferred forum for interpretation and enforcement of state law, plaintiff must be permitted to proceed in state court under state law. It would do violence to state autonomy were defendants able to remove state claims to federal court merely because the plaintiff *could have* asserted a federal claim based on the same set of facts underlying his state claim. . . .

The Court relies on what it calls a "factual finding" by the District Court, with which the Court of Appeals agreed, that "respondents had attempted to avoid removal jurisdiction by 'artfully' casting their 'essentially federal law claims' as state-law claims." . . . But this amounts to no more than a pejorative characterization of respondents' decision to proceed under state, rather than federal, law. "Artful" or not, respondents' complaint was not based on any claim of a federal right or immunity, and was not, therefore, removable. . . .

Even assuming that this Court and the lower federal courts have jurisdiction to decide this case, however, I dissent from the Court's disposition of the res judicata issue. . . .

Like Justice Blackmun, I would hold that the dismissal of *Brown I* is res judicata not only as to every matter that was actually litigated, but also as to every ground or theory of recovery that might also have been presented. . . .

I therefore respectfully dissent. . . .

Note: Pleading and Preclusion

Post-*Moitie*, courts and commentators had struggled over the meaning of footnote 2, in which the Court discussed "artful pleading" used by plaintiffs to close off defendant's right to a federal forum. Some very influential observers concluded that the Court in *Moitie* had "departed from the traditional scope of the artful-pleading doctrine." See Arthur R. Miller, Artful Pleading: A Doctrine in Search of a Definition, 76 Tex. L. Rev. 1781, 1802 (1998). In Rivet v. Regions Bank, 522 U.S. 470, 478 (1998), however, a unanimous Supreme Court stated that "*Moitie* did not create a preclusion exception to the rule, fundamental under currently governing legislation, that a defendant cannot remove on the basis of a federal defense. In sum, claim preclusion by reason of a prior federal judgment is a defensive plea that provides no basis for removal under § 144(b). Such a defense is properly made in the state proceedings, and the state courts' disposition of it is subject to this Court's ultimate review."

Note: Are Defects in Subject Matter Jurisdiction Ever Res Judicata?

Recall that subject matter jurisdiction defects can be raised at any time, as we saw in *Belleville Catering*. See Chapter 2, supra page 220. How should an appellate court treat lack of diversity when a case settles, the settlement agreement is incorporated into the trial court's judgment disposing of the case, and one side then raises a defect in subject matter jurisdiction for the first time as part of an appeal of the trial court's enforcement of terms of the settlement? Normally, a settlement is just a private contract and enforcing it requires an entirely new lawsuit for breach of contract. However, when the court that entertained the original suit incorporates the agreement into its judgment, the agreement becomes enforceable by that court. Rather than file a new action, parties can just go back to the original court with proof of breach and request a remedy.

In Baella-Silva v. Hulsey, 454 F.3d 5 (1st Cir. 2006), an attorney sued his co-counsel when co-counsel refused to pay his fees under a fee-sharing agreement. The parties settled and the district court agreed to incorporate the agreement into its judgment. No objection was raised to the agreement and no appeal was taken from the judgment.

When the attorney later breached the terms of the settlement, defendants moved the district court to award the liquidated damages provided in the contract. The court imposed the sanctions and the attorney appealed. In the First Circuit, for the first time, the attorney argued that there was incomplete diversity in the original action for attorneys' fees. The First Circuit rejected the argument. To be sure, the court conceded, "a lack of complete diversity between the parties deprives the federal courts of jurisdiction over the lawsuit," but "[w]eighing against this seemingly 'inflexible' jurisdictional requirement . . . is a strong interest in the finality of judgments. A district court's express or implicit determination that it has jurisdiction is open to direct review, but it is res judicata when collaterally attacked." Id. at 9 (internal quotation marks omitted). Thus as long as "the record supports an 'arguable basis' for concluding that subject-matter jurisdiction existed, a final judgment cannot be collaterally attacked." Id. at 9-10.

Here, the court concluded, there was evidence that the nondiverse parties may have been fraudulently joined. Id. at 10. The court viewed Baella-Silva's attempt to raise the subject matter jurisdiction issue for the first time on appeal of the enforcement of the settlement agreement as "collateral" because neither he nor defendants "[brought] a direct appeal challenging the district court's jurisdiction or any other aspect of the settlement judgment within the time period provided for appeal." Id. at 9. Thus Baella-Silva's collateral attack on the trial court's jurisdiction was analogous to "an appeal from the denial of a motion for relief from a void judgment pursuant to Federal Rule of Civil Procedure 60(b)(4)." Id. at 10.

Isn't a settlement agreement over which the trial court retains enforcement jurisdiction quite different from a final judgment as to which no appeal is taken? Surely the interest in finality is not identical in the two cases. The First Circuit noted the traditional doctrine that "[a] court without subject-matter jurisdiction may not acquire it by consent of the parties," id. at 9 (internal quotation marks omitted), but isn't that precisely the result the court sanctions in this case?

Note: Subject Matter Jurisdiction and Remedies

What happens if a plaintiff fails to request an available remedy in her first suit, say, damages for emotional distress, and wants to file a new suit to recover these damages? The answer is the same as it would be if the plaintiff omitted an available cause of action arising from the same transaction or occurrence — res judicata bars relitigation.

Matters are different, however, if the subject matter jurisdiction of the court in which the plaintiff first sued is limited in such a way that damages for emotional distress are not available.

Gale Nestor worked as a machinist for Pratt & Whitney for 20 years until she was fired in 1992 following an altercation with a male employee. She filed a complaint with the Connecticut Commission on Human Rights and Opportunities alleging that she had been terminated because of sex discrimination in violation of Title VII and parallel state law. Nestor v. Pratt & Whitney, 466 F.3d 65 (2d Cir. 2006). The Commission informed Nestor that it could not award compensatory damages, just back pay, and that proceedings before the Commission include representation by staff counsel at a reduced fee, "flexible evidentiary rules, and speedy proceedings." Id. at 68. The proceedings were not, in fact, speedy; they took six years. But the Commission eventually returned a finding for Nestor and awarded her back pay. Pratt appealed to the Connecticut courts, the state courts upheld the award, and Pratt eventually paid the judgment with interest.

In 2003 the federal Equal Employment Opportunity Commission issued Nestor a right-to-sue letter, and she promptly filed suit against Pratt seeking remedies available under Title VII, including compensatory damages, punitive damages, attorneys' fees, and prejudgment interest. Pratt moved for summary judgment on the theory that res judicata barred Nestor's federal suit. Recognizing a division of authority in the circuit courts, compare Jones v. Am. State Bank, 857 F.2d 494 (8th Cir. 1988) (state administrative litigation does not preclude Title VII suit for attorneys' fees); Patzer v. Bd. of Regents of the Univ. of Wis. Sys., 763 F.2d 851, (7th Cir. 1985) (state administrative litigation upheld by state courts does not bar Title VII action for additional relief), with Chris v. Tenet, 221 F.3d 648 (4th Cir. 2000) (federal court cannot entertain Title VII action to recover attorneys' fees incurred in prior state administrative proceeding), the Second Circuit held that a plaintiff who prevails in state administrative proceedings can "subsequently file suit in federal court seeking relief that was *unavailable* in the state proceedings." Nestor, 466 F.3d at 69 (emphasis added).

Reasoning that the result would be the same under either federal or Connecticut preclusion law, the court rejected Pratt's argument that it was "unfair to allow plaintiff to (in effect) re-litigate damages while binding the defendant to liability findings, particularly when (as here) liability was decided in an administrative forum that did not afford such basic procedures as discovery." Id. at 73. According to New York Gaslight Club, Inc. v. Carey, 447 U.S. 54 (1980), a prevailing plaintiff in state administrative proceedings is entitled to pursue supplemental relief afforded by Title VII — the federal statute operates as "a 'supplement' to state remedies 'when the State does not provide prompt or complete relief.'" Nestor, 466 F.3d at 71. And Connecticut preclusion doctrine, the court explained, follows the Restatement (Second) of Judgments § 26(1)(c), see infra, page 1161, in recognizing an exception to res judicata "for later actions that assert claims or seek relief that could not have been pressed or recovered in the prior proceeding." Id. at 74.

c. Counterclaims and Cross-Claims

Remember that res judicata (claim preclusion) applies not only to issues that were raised but also to issues that could or should have been raised in the prior lawsuit. Thus we bring in the compulsory counterclaim rules — Fed. R. Civ. P. 13(a) and many similar state provisions.

If a counterclaim was compulsory, then by definition it could and should have been raised in the first suit and is precluded. In fact, courts may even bar a party from later raising a transactionally related counterclaim when the defendant defaulted on the claim. See Todd David Peterson, The Misguided Law of Compulsory Counterclaims in Default Cases, 50 Ariz. L. Rev. 1107 (2008). But what if a jurisdiction does *not* have a compulsory counterclaim rule, or if an action is dismissed before the counterclaim rule kicks in? The answer is that the action may still be barred based on an unasserted counterclaim if it would completely contradict the result in the first action. This is sometimes called the "logical inconsistency" exception.

Here is an example of how this works.

A sues *B* in state court for damages resulting from an automobile accident. The jury returns a verdict for *B*. *B* then sues *A* in federal court (diversity) for damages *B* incurred in the same accident. What result:

(a) if state court has a procedural rule identical to Rule 13(a)? (precluded)
(b) if state has no compulsory counterclaim rule? (This depends on whether it fits the logical inconsistency exception. For example, might this happen if the result for *B* occurred in the first action because *A* and *B* were equally negligent?)

Problem Case: A Woman Partner (One More Time)

Return again to Shayes v. McKenzie, Brachman. Assume that Shayes brings a civil rights suit in federal court and amends her complaint to include a claim of libel. If McKenzie, Brachman wants to assert a libel claim—that she said equally horrible things about the firm—*must it do so in the original suit?* In other words, is McKenzie, Brachman's libel action a compulsory counterclaim?

It is a compulsory counterclaim under Rule 13(a) if it arose out of the same transaction or occurrence. "Compulsory" means that if McKenzie does not raise libel as a counterclaim, it will be precluded from bringing a separate libel suit later; that is, a final judgment in Shayes v. McKenzie, Brachman will preclude the libel claim, *even if it was never asserted;* Rule 13(a) refers, by definition, to claims that *should have been asserted.*

The interests of efficiency are likely to override those that deal with McKenzie's right to choose his own forum for his claims. If his libel claim sheds any light on the plaintiff's sex discrimination claim (for example, "This is not sex discrimination—I disliked her because of the outrageous things she said about the firm"), a court ruling on whether he must assert it now would be strongly inclined to say it grows out of the same transaction or occurrence. Once more: If it is a compulsory counterclaim, McKenzie will be barred from bringing any later state claim regardless of the outcome in federal court.

Could McKenzie choose to bring a separate libel claim in state court while the Shayes case is pending in federal courts? Technically yes, since only valid final judgments have res judicata effect. Thus even if the counterclaim is "compulsory," there is nothing to prevent McKenzie from entering this inefficient and potentially nasty situation. The solution is for either court to "stay" or "abate" its proceedings pending resolution of the other suit. Most likely the court in the later-filed action will do so, which means that when two feuding parties have competing claims against one another, either of which might be a compulsory counterclaim to the other, there may be an unseemly race to the courthouse to attain choice of forum.

Martino v. McDonald's System, Inc.

598 F.2d 1079 (7th Cir. 1979)

PELL, Circuit Judge.

The plaintiffs, Louis J. Martino and McDonald's Drive-In of Ottumwa, Iowa, Inc. (McDonald's Ottumwa), appeal from the district court's entry of summary judgment against them on one count of their two count antitrust complaint against the defendants, McDonald's System, Inc. (McDonald's System) and Franchise Realty Interstate Corporation (FRIC). The only issue before this court is whether a 1973 consent judgment against Martino precludes the cause of action set forth in Count I of the present complaint. The district court held that both res judicata and the compulsory counterclaim rule of Fed. R. Civ. P. 13(a) barred the plaintiffs from suing on their first cause of action. Martino v. McDonald's System, Inc., 432 F. Supp. 499 (N.D. Ill. 1977).

In 1962 the plaintiff Louis Martino and three brothers not involved in this action entered into a franchise and lease agreement with the defendants. Martino and his brothers then organized McDonald's Ottumwa, the corporate plaintiff here, to operate the business. The contract to which Martino and the defendants were parties provided that neither Martino nor a member of his immediate family would acquire a financial interest in a competing self-service food business without the written consent of McDonald's System and FRIC. In 1968 Martino's son purchased a Burger Chef franchise in Pittsburg, Kansas. Martino financed this transaction.

On the basis of this transaction FRIC and McDonald's System brought a federal diversity action in Iowa against Martino and his three brothers, charging that Martino had violated the contract provision restricting acquisitions described above. This lawsuit, commenced in 1972, ended in 1973 with a consent judgment to which the district court appended findings of fact and conclusions of law. The court order also provided that the parties had entered an agreement for the sale of McDonald's Ottumwa franchise to FRIC for $140,000. The sale was completed according to the terms of the agreement. Martino's brothers later cancelled their stock in McDonald's Ottumwa, leaving Martino as the sole shareholder.

Martino and McDonald's Ottumwa brought this action in 1975. Count I of their complaint alleges that the enforcement of the restriction on acquisition in the franchise and lease agreements violated Section 1 of the Sherman Act, 15 U.S.C. § 1. As a basis for damages, Martino claims profits he would have earned as owner of the McDonald's franchise. Both plaintiffs claim damages for having had to sell the franchise, allegedly below its market value.

The defendants have presented two theories for barring Count I of the plaintiffs' antitrust complaint. The first theory is based on the preclusive effect of Fed. R. Civ. P. 13(a), applying to compulsory counterclaims. The second theory is based on the principle of res judicata. We shall now consider the merits of each theory.

The defendants argue that the district court correctly held that Count I is precluded by Fed. R. Civ. P. 13(a). Claims coming within the definition of "compulsory counterclaim" are lost if not raised at the proper time. Baker v. Gold Seal Liquors, Inc., 417 U.S. 467, 469 n.1 (1974); Fagnan v. Great Central Insurance Co., 577 F.2d 418 (7th Cir. [1978]), *cert. denied*, [439] U.S. [1004] (1978). According to the defendants, Rule 13(a) required Martino to raise this antitrust challenge to the contract provision in the earlier suit based on the same provision. If Rule 13(a) were applicable to these facts, the defendants' argument might have merit. Rule 13(a), however, by its own terms does not apply unless there has been some form of pleading.

The rule expressly says that "a *pleading* shall state as a counterclaim any claim which at the time of serving the *pleading* the *pleader* has against any opposing party. . . ." (Emphasis added.) In the prior Iowa action at issue here, Martino filed no pleading as the word is defined in Fed. R. Civ. P. 7(a). For this reason, Martino argues that we must not apply Rule 13(a) to the claim stated in Count I of his complaint. We agree.

Rule 13(a) is in some ways a harsh rule. It forces parties to raise certain claims at the time and place chosen by their opponents, or to lose them. The rule, however, is the result of a balancing between competing interests. The convenience of the party with a compulsory counterclaim is sacrificed in the interest of judicial economy. See Southern Construction Co. v. Pickard, 371 U.S. 57 (1962); Dindo v. Whitney, 451 F.2d 1, 3 (1st Cir. 1971). We do not believe that the drafters of Rule 13 chose the term "pleading" unadvisedly. It no doubt marks, although somewhat arbitrarily, a point at which the judicial burden of the earlier lawsuit outweighs the opposing party's interest in bringing an action when and where it is most convenient. The earlier action between these parties was terminated by a consent judgment before the answer was filed. We see little sense in applying the broad bar established in Rule 13(a) to an action that ended with virtually no burden on the judicial calendar.

McDonald's System and FRIC emphasize, however, that the deadline for filing the answer in the earlier action had passed[5] and that Rule 13(a) should therefore apply regardless of the absence of a responsive pleading. Citing as support several cases construing rules similar to Rule 13(a), McDonald's System and FRIC argue that to hold otherwise is to reward noncompliance with the Federal Rules. We believe that this argument exaggerates the effect of not applying Rule 13(a). The Rules themselves provide for default judgments against a party for failure to plead, Fed. R. Civ. P. 55, and the effect of such a judgment as res judicata . . .

5. Almost immediately after the complaint was filed, the parties entered into settlement negotiations. The resulting consent judgment was entered before Martino filed an answer.

prevents the nonpleading party from profiting as the result of his noncompliance. . . .

Although Rule 13(a) does not dispose of Martino's antitrust claim, longstanding principles of res judicata establish a narrowly defined class of "common law compulsory counterclaims." . . . We hold that the antitrust claim set forth in Count I of Martino's complaint falls within this narrow class of claims and that the res judicata effect of the earlier consent judgment is a bar to raising it now.

The principle of res judicata at issue here treats a judgment on the merits as an absolute bar to relitigation between the parties and those in privity with them of every matter offered and received to sustain or defeat the claim or demand and to every matter which might have been received for that purpose. Commissioner v. Sunnen, 333 U.S. 591, 597 (1948); Chicot County Drainage District v. Baxter State Bank, 308 U.S. 371, 375 (1940); Cromwell v. County of Sac, 94 U.S. 351, 352 (1876).

The conclusion of the earlier contract lawsuit with a consent judgment does not prevent the earlier judgment from having a res judicata effect. The plaintiffs argue that the former judgment has no res judicata effect because the parties did not sign mutual releases. We recognize that if a consent decree is expressly entered without prejudice or reserving rights the decree will not have a preclusive effect. . . . The mere absence of releases, however, is insufficient to indicate the unambiguous intent of the parties to counteract what would otherwise be the preclusive effect of the judgment. Although the earlier judgment at issue here was entered pursuant to the agreement of the parties, it was accompanied by judicial findings of fact and conclusions of law that go to the merits of the controversy. The court described Martino's actions as "a material breach of the agreements sufficient to justify termination."[8] The trial "court is not properly a recorder of contracts, but is an organ of government constituted to make judicial decisions and when it has rendered a consent judgment it has made an adjudication." 1B Moore's Federal Practice ¶0.409[5] at 1030 (2d ed. 1974).

Having determined that the prior consent judgment is an adjudication on the merits, we conclude that this judgment precludes Count I of this antitrust action. As a predicate for our discussion of the res judicata effect of the prior judgment we turn to the basis of Martino's present antitrust claim.

The gravamen of Count I of Martino's antitrust complaint is the 1973 lawsuit. In paragraph 12 of Count I, the complaint describes the 1973 lawsuit seeking termination of the franchise. Paragraph 13 continues,

8. The court held that "the defendant, Louis J. Martino, or a member of his immediate family, has violated the terms of the sublease and the franchise agreement by engaging in a business in which food and beverages are dispensed other than [at] the location covered by the agreements without the prior consent of Franchise Realty or McDonald's System, and that such action constitutes a material breach of agreement sufficient to justify termination."

describing the personal pressures on Martino to settle the suit.[9] Paragraph 15 alleges that

> By enforcing the provisions of the franchise agreement and the sublease that prohibited the acquisition of any financial interest in a non-McDonald's self-service food and beverage establishment against plaintiffs, defendants discouraged competition and unreasonably restrained trade and commerce in violation of Section 1 of the Sherman Act (15 U.S.C. § 1).

Paragraph 16 concludes Count I, alleging that Martino lost profits he would have earned as owner of the McDonald's franchise and that Martino was forced to sell the franchise at below its market value.

It is impossible to interpret this count as anything but a direct challenge to the outcome of the 1973 lawsuit. The 1973 lawsuit concluded that termination was justified. The plaintiff now contends that termination was not justified, because the federal antitrust laws forbade it. If Martino's antitrust theory had merit, it would have been a defense in 1973, changing the outcome of the litigation. Milsen Company v. Southland Corporation, 454 F.2d 363 (7th Cir. 1971).

The well-settled rule for the purpose of determining the res judicata effect of a judgment is that a "cause of action" comprises defenses, such as the alleged antitrust violation here, that were or might have been raised. As the Supreme Court said long ago:

> [A judgment on the merits] is a finality as to the claim or demand in controversy, concluding parties, and those in privity with them, not only as to every matter which was offered and received to sustain or defeat the claim or demand, but as to any other admissible matter which might have been offered for that purpose. Thus, for example, a judgment rendered on a promissory note is conclusive as to the validity of the instrument and the amount due upon it, although it be subsequently alleged that perfect defenses actually existed, of which no proof was offered, such as forgery, want of consideration, or payment. If such defenses were not presented in the action, and established by competent evidence, *the subsequent allegation of their existence is of no consequence.* [Cromwell v. County of Sac, 94 U.S. 351, 352 (1876) (emphasis added). See Chicot County Drainage District v. Baxter State Bank, 308 U.S. 371, 375 (1940); Lambert v. Conrad, 536 F.2d 1183, 1185 (7th Cir. 1976).]

Because the alleged antitrust violation constitutes a separate ground for recovery as well as a defense to the suit to terminate the franchise, however, Martino argues that Count I of this action constitutes a different "cause of action" for the purpose of res judicata and that the prior judgment does not preclude relitigation of the defendants' termination rights under the antitrust laws. For cases like this one, to which Rule 13(a) is inapplicable, Martino's argument correctly states the general rule. When

9. The personal pressures were not attributable to the defendants but were in part from his brothers who owned other McDonald's franchises which they feared might be jeopardized by fighting the lawsuit and in part from the recent death of his wife.

facts form the basis of both a defense and a counterclaim, the defendant's failure to allege these facts as a defense or a counterclaim "does not preclude him from relying on those facts in an action subsequently brought by him against the plaintiff." . . . Virginia-Carolina Chemical Co. v. Kirven, 215 U.S. 252 (1909); Scott, Collateral Estoppel by Judgment, 56 Harv. L. Rev. 1, 27 (1942). The logic of this rule in circumstances not subject to Rule 13(a) is manifest. Should the earlier litigation end in its very first stage, no great burden on the courts results from permitting a counterclaim to be raised at a more convenient time and place. Notions of judicial economy give way to fairness. The defendant in the earlier action has his day in court when and where he sees fit.

The rule is not absolute, however. Both precedent and policy require that res judicata bar a counterclaim when its prosecution would nullify rights established by the prior action. Judicial economy is not the only basis for the doctrine of res judicata. Res judicata also preserves the integrity of judgments and protects those who rely on them. McDonald's System and FRIC have terminated and repurchased Martino's franchise in reliance on the trial court's 1973 judgment telling them they were justified in doing so. Now Martino seeks to impose significant financial liability on the defendants for these actions. We cannot hold that the counterclaim exception to the res judicata rule, based merely on notions of convenience, permits the plaintiff here to wage this direct attack on the rights established by the prior judgment.

A comparison between two Supreme Court decisions illustrates the rule and the exception to the rule we have discussed. In Chicot County Drainage District v. Baxter State Bank, 308 U.S. 371 (1940), a case similar in relevant respects to the one before us, the Supreme Court applied res judicata to preclude a claim. In *Chicot County* the Court held that a judgment effecting a plan of readjustment of indebtedness, resulting in a cancellation of certain bonds, precluded a subsequent suit on the same bonds. The subsequent suit on the bonds alleged the unconstitutionality of the 1934 Readjustment Act which was the basis of the prior action. Although the question of constitutionality in *Chicot County,* like the antitrust issue here, was not actually litigated in the earlier action, and although the suit to recover on the bonds, like the antitrust claim here, was a different cause of action, the Supreme Court applied the principle of res judicata to bar the second action. . . .

. . . In contrast, in Virginia-Carolina Chemical Co. v. Kirven, 215 U.S. 252 (1909), a purchaser sued for damages to his crops caused by the defendant's fertilizer. The defendant chemical company argued that its earlier successful suit against the purchaser for the price was a bar to the present suit. The Supreme Court held that the purchaser was entitled to bring the action for damages, drawing a distinction between claims which is crucial to the result in this case. A claim for crop damage in the earlier action for the purchase price would merely have effected a set-off to the Chemical Company's recovery of the purchase price. The claim for crop damage "[did not] go to the validity of the [Chemical Company's] demand [for the price] in its inception . . . such as . . . forgery, want of consideration, or payment." 215 U.S. 252, 257. . . . Concluding that Martino's claim set forth in Count I of his complaint is a direct attack on the termination rights established in the earlier judgment, we hold that Martino is barred from raising that claim. . . .

Accordingly, the judgment of the district court is *affirmed*. . . .

d. Sources of Preclusion Law

Claim and issue preclusion law is judge-made. Rules and cases vary from jurisdiction to jurisdiction. Since it is considered substantive on the whole, rather than procedural, federal courts follow state law on this matter in diversity actions.

But procedural rules about whether claims are compulsory or not may enter the picture, and federal courts follow their own rules about what is a compulsory counterclaim while taking into account the possible claim-preclusive effects of their decisions on joinder.

Though there are lots of cases on both issue and claim preclusion, and both doctrines arise often in practice, the major source of the law is the Restatement of Judgments, major excerpts of which appear below. Produced by the American Law Institute, a group of distinguished lawyers and judges, this is a very influential document, often followed by both courts and legislators.

Restatement (Second) of Judgments

§§ 17-29, 86-87

§ 17. Effects of Former Adjudication—General Rules

A valid and final personal judgment is conclusive between the parties, except on appeal or other direct review, to the following extent:

(1) If the judgment is in favor of the plaintiff, the claim is extinguished and merged in the judgment and a new claim may arise on the judgment (see § 18);

(2) If the judgment is in favor of the defendant, the claim is extinguished and the judgment bars a subsequent action on that claim (see § 19);

(3) A judgment in favor of either the plaintiff or the defendant is conclusive, in a subsequent action between them on the same or a different claim, with respect to any issue actually litigated and determined if its determination was essential to that judgment (see § 27).

§ 18. Judgment for Plaintiff—The General Rule of Merger

When a valid and final personal judgment is rendered in favor of the plaintiff:

(1) The plaintiff cannot thereafter maintain an action on the original claim or any part thereof, although he may be able to maintain an action upon the judgment; and

(2) In an action upon the judgment, the defendant cannot avail himself of defenses he might have interposed, or did interpose, in the first action.

§ 19. Judgment for Defendant—The General Rule of Bar

A valid and final personal judgment rendered in favor of the defendant bars another action by the plaintiff on the same claim.

§ 20. Judgment for Defendant—Exceptions to the General Rule of Bar

(1) A personal judgment for the defendant, although valid and final, does not bar another action by the plaintiff on the same claim:

(a) When the judgment is one of dismissal for lack of jurisdiction, for improper venue, or for nonjoinder or misjoinder of parties; or

(b) When the plaintiff agrees to or elects a nonsuit (or voluntary dismissal) without prejudice or the court directs that the plaintiff be nonsuited (or that the action be otherwise dismissed) without prejudice; or

(c) When by statute or rule of court the judgment does not operate as a bar to another action on the same claim, or does not so operate unless the court specifies, and no such specification is made.

(2) A valid and final personal judgment for the defendant, which rests on the prematurity of the action or on the plaintiff's failure to satisfy a precondition to suit, does not bar another action by the plaintiff instituted after the claim has matured, or the precondition has been satisfied, unless a second action is precluded by operation of the substantive law.

§ 21. Judgment for Defendant on His Counterclaim

(1) Where the defendant interposes a counterclaim on which judgment is rendered in his favor, the rules of merger are applicable to the claim stated in the counterclaim, except as stated in Subsection (2).

(2) Where judgment on a counterclaim is rendered in favor of the defendant, but he is unable to obtain full recovery in the action because of the inability of the court to render such a judgment and the unavailability of such devices as removal to another court or consolidation with another action in the same court, the defendant is not precluded from

subsequently maintaining an action for the balance due on the claim stated in the counterclaim.

§ 22. Effect of Failure to Interpose Counterclaim

(1) Where the defendant may interpose a claim as a counterclaim but he fails to do so, he is not thereby precluded from subsequently maintaining an action on that claim, except as stated in Subsection (2).

(2) A defendant who may interpose a claim as a counterclaim in an action but fails to do so is precluded, after the rendition of judgment in that action, from maintaining an action on the claim if:

(a) The counterclaim is required to be interposed by a compulsory counterclaim statute or rule of court, or

(b) The relationship between the counterclaim and the plaintiff's claim is such that successful prosecution of the second action would nullify the initial judgment or would impair rights established in the initial action.

§ 23. Judgment for Plaintiff on Defendant's Counterclaim

Where the defendant interposes a claim as a counterclaim and a valid and final judgment is rendered against him on the counterclaim, the rules of bar are applicable to the judgment.

§ 24. Dimensions of "Claim" for Purposes of Merger or Bar—General Rule Concerning "Splitting"

(1) When a valid and final judgment rendered in an action extinguishes the plaintiff's claim pursuant to the rules of merger or bar (see §§ 18, 19), the claim extinguished includes all rights of the plaintiff to remedies against the defendant with respect to all or any part of the transaction, or series of connected transactions, out of which the action arose.

(2) What factual grouping constitutes a "transaction," and what groupings constitute a "series," are to be determined pragmatically, giving weight to such considerations as whether the facts are related in time, space, origin, or motivation, whether they form a convenient trial unit, and whether their treatment as a unit conforms to the parties' expectations or business understanding or usage.

§ 25. Exemplifications of General Rule Concerning Splitting

The rule of § 24 applies to extinguish a claim by the plaintiff against the defendant even though the plaintiff is prepared in the second action

(1) To present evidence or grounds or theories of the case not presented in the first action, or

(2) To seek remedies or forms of relief not demanded in the first action.

§ 26. Exceptions to the General Rule Concerning Splitting

(1) When any of the following circumstances exists, the general rule of § 24 does not apply to extinguish the claim, and part or all of the claim subsists as a possible basis for a second action by the plaintiff against the defendant:

(a) The parties have agreed in terms or in effect that the plaintiff may split his claim, or the defendant has acquiesced therein; or

(b) The court in the first action has expressly reserved the plaintiff's right to maintain the second action; or

(c) The plaintiff was unable to rely on a certain theory of the case or to seek a certain remedy or form of relief in the first action because of the limitations on the subject matter jurisdiction of the courts or restrictions on their authority to entertain multiple theories or demands for multiple remedies or forms of relief in a single action, and the plaintiff desires in the second action to rely on that theory or to seek that remedy or form of relief; or

(d) The judgment in the first action was plainly inconsistent with the fair and equitable implementation of a statutory or constitutional scheme, or it is the sense of the scheme that the plaintiff should be permitted to split his claim; or

(e) For reasons of substantive policy in a case involving a continuing or recurrent wrong, the plaintiff is given an option to sue once for the total harm, both past and prospective, or to sue from time to time for the damages incurred to the date of suit, and chooses the latter course; or

(f) It is clearly and convincingly shown that the policies favoring preclusion of a second action are overcome for an extraordinary reason, such as the apparent invalidity of a continuing restraint or condition having a vital relation to personal liberty or the failure of the prior litigation to yield a coherent disposition of the controversy.

§ 27. Issue Preclusion—General Rule

When an issue of fact or law is actually litigated and determined by a valid and final judgment, and the determination is essential to the judgment, the determination is conclusive in a subsequent action between the parties, whether on the same or a different claim.

§ 28. Exceptions to the General Rule of Issue Preclusion

Although an issue is actually litigated and determined by a valid and final judgment, and the determination is essential to the judgment, relitigation of the issue in a subsequent action between the parties is not precluded in the following circumstances:

(1) The party against whom preclusion is sought could not, as a matter of law, have obtained review of the judgment in the initial action; or

(2) The issue is one of law and (a) the two actions involve claims that are substantially unrelated, or (b) a new determination is warranted in order to take account of an intervening change in the applicable legal context or otherwise to avoid inequitable administration of the laws; or

(3) A new determination of the issue is warranted by differences in the quality or extensiveness of the procedures followed in the two courts or by factors relating to the allocation of jurisdiction between them; or

(4) The party against whom preclusion is sought had a significantly heavier burden of persuasion with respect to the issue in the initial action than in the subsequent action; the burden has shifted to his adversary; or the adversary has a significantly heavier burden than he had in the first action; or

(5) There is a clear and convincing need for a new determination of the issue (a) because of the potential adverse impact of the determination on the public interest or the interests of persons not themselves parties in the initial action, (b) because it was not sufficiently foreseeable at the time of the initial action that the issue would arise in the context of a subsequent action, or (c) because the party sought to be precluded, as a result of the conduct of his adversary or other special circumstances, did not have an adequate opportunity or incentive to obtain a full and fair adjudication in the initial action.

§ 29. Issue Preclusion in Subsequent Litigation with Others

A party precluded from litigating an issue with an opposing party, in accordance with §§ 27 and 28, is also precluded from doing so with another person unless the fact that he lacked full and fair opportunity to litigate the issue in the first action or other circumstances justify [sic] affording him an opportunity to relitigate the issue. The circumstances to which considerations should be given include those enumerated in § 28 and also whether:

(1) Treating the issue as conclusively determined would be incompatible with an applicable scheme of administering the remedies in the actions involved;

(2) The forum in the second action affords the party against whom preclusion is asserted procedural opportunities in the presentation and determination of the issue that were not available in the first action and could likely result in the issue being differently determined;

(3) The person seeking to invoke favorable preclusion, or to avoid unfavorable preclusion, could have effected joinder in the first action between himself and his present adversary;

(4) The determination relied on as preclusive was itself inconsistent with another determination of the same issue;

(5) The prior determination may have been affected by relationships among the parties to the first action that are not present in the subsequent action, or apparently was based on a compromise verdict or finding;

(6) Treating the issue as conclusively determined may complicate determination of issues in the subsequent action or prejudice the interests of another party thereto;

(7) The issue is one of law and treating it as conclusively determined would inappropriately foreclose opportunity for obtaining reconsideration of the legal rule upon which it was based;

(8) Other compelling circumstances make it appropriate that the party be permitted to relitigate the issue.

§ 86. Effect of State Court Judgment in a Subsequent Action in Federal Court

A valid and final judgment of a state court has the same effects under the rules of res judicata in a subsequent action in a federal court that the judgment has by the law of the state in which the judgment was rendered, except that:

(1) An adjudication of a claim in a state court does not preclude litigation in a federal court of a related federal claim based on the same transaction if the federal claim arises under a scheme of federal remedies which contemplates that the federal claim may be asserted notwithstanding the adjudication in state court; and

(2) A determination of an issue by a state court does not preclude relitigation of that issue in federal court if according preclusive effect to the determination would be incompatible with a scheme of federal remedies which contemplates that the federal court may make an independent determination of the issue in question.

§ 87. Effect of Federal Court Judgment in a Subsequent Action

Federal law determines the effects under the rules of res judicata of a judgment of a federal court.

Notes and Questions

1. *Raise It or Waive It.* Given the principles of claim preclusion, the merger of law and equity, the expansion of federal courts' supplemental jurisdiction, and the liberal joinder of parties and claims now permitted by the Federal Rules of Civil Procedure and most states' rules of

procedure, the most prudent step for trial lawyers is to raise anything in the first litigation that arguably may be deemed res judicata in a second litigation, or risk being precluded from asserting the matter. As was true with counterclaims that are arguably compulsory, the safest course is to raise it, lest you waive it. The trial judge then may exercise discretion to sever some matters and try them separately, if warranted. See Fed. R. Civ. P. 42(b).

2. *Mechanics of Preclusion.* By what procedural move does a party raise the issues of claim or issue preclusion? See Fed. R. Civ. P. 8(c). Can it be waived? If it can, how does the doctrine promote judicial efficiency, versus the parties' interest in repose?

3. *Defining "Same Claim."* Determining what constitutes one "claim" for purposes of claim preclusion can be quite difficult. Different tests have been proposed—such as the same cause of action test, the same evidence test, and the same transaction or occurrence test—yet none is entirely satisfactory or workable in all cases. As was true with joinder and subject matter jurisdiction, the key seems to be transactional relatedness such that matters that logically belong together should be tried together. The test inevitably must consider context, and thus cannot avoid the fuzziness and flexibility aspects that seem to undermine the parties' interest in predictability.

4. *Defining "On the Merits."* Reread Restatement (Second) of Judgments § 20. This section summarizes courts' general approach to determinations of whether a prior judgment was "on the merits" or addressed only a threshold issue that should not bar relitigation. Reconsider the various procedural objections that a defendant can assert under Fed. R. Civ. P. 12 in a pre-answer motion to dismiss. Which of these would bar a plaintiff from relitigating the same claim in a different forum? Which would not? What about a default judgment? Voluntary dismissal after an out-of-court settlement? A consent judgment? See Jack H. Friedenthal, Mary Kay Kane, and Arthur R. Miller, Civil Procedure 667-673 (4th ed. 2005). See also Semtek Int'l Inc. v. Lockheed Martin Corp., 531 U.S. 497 (2001) (adjudication "on the merits" in Rule 41(b) does not necessarily mean that the judgment has claim preclusive effect; dismissal "with prejudice" on statute of limitations grounds bars refiling in federal court, but it may or may not preclude relitigation in another forum); Styskal v. Weld County Bd. Of County Comm'rs, 365 F.3d 855, 859 (10th Cir. 2004) (dismissal with prejudice for want of supplemental jurisdiction over state law claims under 28 U.S.C. § 1367 bars refiling in federal court: "The state court's decision regarding whether claim preclusion prevents a state lawsuit will depend upon the basis of the federal court's dismissal, not the nomenclature employed by the federal court to describe the dismissal."); Legnani v. Alitalia Linee Aeree Italiane S.P.A., 400 F.3d 139 (2d Cir. 2005).

5. *Contract Issues and Claim Preclusion.* Claim preclusion in contract matters operates under the general principle that one contract will support only one cause of action. See, e.g., Pakas v. Hollingshead, 77 N.E. 40 (1906). When the contract is an installment contract, however, then the contract is

considered severally, such that breach of one installment does not necessarily breach the whole contract. See Uniform Commercial Code § 2-612(3). Courts nevertheless have developed the rule that a party who sues for breach of an installment contract must raise (or waive) all claims that arose before the time that the suit is brought. Thus, if a party to an installment contract brings suit after unsatisfactory performance of the first installment, she is still free to sue for any subsequent installments that are unsatisfactory. But if she sues on the fifth installment but fails to raise any complaints about the first four installments, she waives these claims.

2. Issue Preclusion

Problem Case: Using a Friendly Decision

Bob Hesse recently was fired from his management job at ABC Photos, Inc., a corporation that provides driver's license image machines to state agencies. The reason for his termination was that Hesse, along with other corporate officials, was responsible for alleged questionable financial dealings by the corporation.

Hesse filed an arbitration proceeding against the company, claiming that his termination violated the employment agreement with ABC. ABC filed a complaint in the state district court to stay the arbitration proceedings on the ground that there was no employment agreement. In response to the state court action, Hesse filed a motion for partial summary judgment, alleging that ABC was estopped from relitigating the existence of an employment agreement, given a recent decision against ABC in the federal district court. The federal court action was filed by a fellow management employee, Adrian Spears. In that suit, one of the issues litigated was the existence of an employment agreement that entitled Spears to executive retirement plan benefits, unreimbursed expenses, and stock funds. The federal court concluded there was such an agreement. Hesse testified in the action, but was not a party in it. The federal case is now on appeal.

Can Hesse invoke this prior federal court judgment against ABC to bar relitigation of the employment agreement issue in the state court action? Should the federal court judgment have any stare decisis effect in the state court action? For a case based on similar facts, see Tofany v. NBS Imaging Systems, Inc., 616 N.E.2d 1034 (Ind. 1993).

a. In General

Issue preclusion, also called "collateral estoppel," prevents a party who has had a full and fair opportunity to litigate a question from relitigating the same matter. This branch of preclusion law applies *only* to issues that were actually litigated and determined in the first lawsuit, *not* matters that could have been raised but were not.

Thus, if a defendant chooses to assert a cross-claim against a codefendant (which she is not required to do under any pleading or procedural rules), then the defendant is bound by the outcome on the issue and cannot raise it in a subsequent suit.

Unlike claim preclusion, issue preclusion does not require that the claim in the first suit be the same as that asserted in the second suit.

Rather, the conditions of issue preclusion, generally stated, are as follows: 1) An issue of fact that 2) was actually litigated, and that was afforded 3) a full and fair opportunity to be litigated, received 4) a final and valid judgment, and 5) the issue to be precluded was essential to that judgment.

Issue preclusion can be asserted defensively or offensively. Defensive collateral estoppel occurs when a defendant asserts estoppel to prevent a plaintiff from relitigating issues. Offensive collateral estoppel occurs when a plaintiff uses it against a defendant to prevent relitigation of issues.

Examples

a) Assume that *P* sues *D* claiming that *D*'s product infringes her patent. The court decides that *P*'s patent is invalid. If *P* later sues *D*(2) claiming that *D*(2)'s product infringes the same patent, then *D*(2) would invoke *defensive collateral estoppel (issue preclusion).*

b) Assume that *P* sues *D*, claiming *D*'s mass-produced product is defective and that *D* knew of the defect. *P* wins. If *P*(2) now sues *D*, making the same claims and invoking the prior determination of the issue of knowledge against *D*, *this is offensive collateral estoppel (issue preclusion).*

Commissioner of Internal Revenue v. Sunnen

333 U.S. 591 (1948)

[Respondent taxpayer made gifts to his wife of various patent license contracts during the years 1937-1941. The Tax Court held that, with one exception, all the royalties paid to the wife during those years were part of the taxpayer's taxable income. The one exception involved royalties paid in 1937 under a 1928 contract. In an earlier proceeding, the Board of Tax Appeals had concluded Sunnen could not be taxed on the royalties he had received during the years 1929-1931 on the 1928 contract. This determination led the Tax Court to apply res judicata to bar a different result for the royalties received in 1937 on the same contract.]

Opinion of the Court by JUSTICE MURPHY. . . .

Relying upon its own prior decision in Estate of Dodson v. Commissioner, 1 T.C. 416 [1943], the Tax Court held that, with one exception, all the royalties paid to the wife from 1937 to 1941 were part of the taxable income of the taxpayer. 6 T.C. 431. The one exception concerned the royalties of $4,881.35 paid in 1937 under the 1928 agreement. In an earlier proceeding in 1935, the Board of Tax Appeals dealt with the taxpayer's income tax liability for the years 1929-1931; it concluded that he was not taxable on the royalties paid to his wife during those years under the 1928 license agreement. This prior determination by the Board caused the Tax Court to apply the principle of res judicata to bar a different result as to the royalties paid pursuant to the same agreement during 1937.

The Tax Court's decision was affirmed in part and reversed in part by the Eighth Circuit Court of Appeals, 161 F.2d 171 [8th Cir. 1947]. . . .

We then brought the case here on certiorari. . . .

If the doctrine of res judicata is properly applicable so that all the royalty payments made during 1937-1941 are governed by the prior decision of the Board of Tax Appeals, the case may be disposed of without reaching the merits of the controversy. We accordingly cast our attention initially on that possibility, one that has been explored by the Tax Court and that has been fully argued by the parties before us.

It is first necessary to understand something of the recognized meaning and scope of res judicata, a doctrine judicial in origin. The general rule of res judicata applies to repetitious suits involving the same cause of action. It rests upon considerations of economy of judicial time and public policy favoring the establishment of certainty in legal relations. The rule provides that when a court of competent jurisdiction has entered a final judgment on the merits of a cause of action, the parties to the suit and their privies are thereafter bound "not only as to every matter which was offered and received to sustain or defeat the claim or demand, but as to any other admissible matter which might have been offered for that purpose." Cromwell v. County of Sac, 94 U.S. 351, 352 [1877]. The judgment puts an end to the cause of action, which cannot again be brought into litigation between the parties upon any ground whatever, absent fraud or some other factor invalidating the judgment. . . .

But where the second action between the same parties is upon a different cause or demand, the principle of res judicata is applied much more narrowly. In this situation, the judgment in the prior action operates as an estoppel, not as to matters which might have been litigated and determined, but "only as to those matters in issue or points controverted, upon the determination of which the finding or verdict was rendered." Cromwell v. County of Sac, supra, 353. Since the cause of action involved in the second proceeding is not swallowed by the judgment in the prior suit, the parties are free to litigate points which were not at issue in the first proceeding, even though such points might have been tendered and decided at that time. But matters which were actually litigated and determined in the first proceeding cannot later be relitigated. Once a party has fought out a matter in litigation with the other party, he cannot later renew that duel. In this sense, res judicata is usually and more accurately referred to as estoppel by judgment, or collateral estoppel. . . .

These same concepts are applicable in the federal income tax field. Income taxes are levied on an annual basis. Each year is the origin of a new liability and of a separate cause of action. Thus if a claim of liability or nonliability relating to a particular tax year is litigated, a judgment on the merits is res judicata as to any subsequent proceeding involving the same claim and the same tax year. But if the later proceeding is concerned with a similar or unlike claim relating to a different tax year, the prior judgment acts as a collateral estoppel only as to those matters in the second proceeding which were actually presented and determined in the first suit. Collateral estoppel operates, in other words, to relieve the government and the taxpayer of "redundant litigation of the identical question of the statute's application of the taxpayer's status." Tait v. Western Md. R. Co., 289 U.S. 620, 624 [1933]. . . .

It is readily apparent in this case that the royalty payments growing out of the license contracts which were not involved in the earlier action before the Board of Tax Appeals and which concerned different tax years are free from the effects of the collateral estoppel doctrine. That is true even though those contracts are identical in all important respects with the 1928 contract, the only one that was before the Board, and even though the issue as to those contracts is the same as that raised by the 1928 contract. For income tax purposes, what is decided as to one contract is not conclusive as to any other contract which is not then in issue, however similar or identical it may be. In this respect, the instant case thus differs vitally from Tait v. Western Md. R. Co., supra, where the two proceedings involved the same instruments and the same surroundings facts.

A more difficult problem is posed as to the $4,881.35 in royalties paid to the taxpayer's wife in 1937 under the 1928 contract. Here there is complete identity of facts, issues and parties as between the earlier Board proceeding and the instant one. The Commissioner claims, however, that legal principles developed in various intervening decisions of this Court have made plain the error of the Board's conclusion in the earlier proceeding, thus creating a situation like that involved in Blair v. Commissioner, [300 U.S. 5 (1937)]. This change in the legal picture is said to have been brought about by such cases as Helvering v. Clifford, 309 U.S. 331 [1940]; Helvering v. Horst, 311 U.S. 112 [1940]; Helvering v. Eubank, 311 U.S. 122 [1940]; Harrison v. Schaffner, 312 U.S. 579 [1941]; Commissioner v. Tower, 327 U.S. 280 [1946]; and Lusthaus v. Commissioner, 327 U.S. 293 [1946]. These cases all imposed income tax liability on transferors who had assigned or transferred various forms of income to others within their family groups, although none specifically related to the assignment of patent license contracts between members of the same family. It must therefore be determined whether this *Clifford-Horst* line of cases represents an intervening legal development which is pertinent to the problem raised by the assignment of the 1928 agreement and which makes manifest the error of the result reached in 1935 by the Board. If that is the situation, the doctrine of collateral estoppel becomes inapplicable. A different result is then permissible as to the royalties paid in 1937 under the agreement in question. . . .

. . . True, [the *Clifford-Horst*] cases did not originate the concept that an assignor is taxable if he retains control over the assigned property or power to defeat the receipt of income by the assignee. But they gave much added emphasis and substance to that concept, making it more suited to meet the "attenuated subtleties" created by taxpayers. So substantial was the amplification of this concept as to justify a reconsideration of earlier Tax Court decisions reached without the benefit of the expanded notions, decisions which are now sought to be perpetuated regardless of their present correctness. Thus in the earlier litigation in 1935, the Board of Tax Appeals was unable to bring to bear on the assignment of the 1928 contract the full breadth of the ideas enunciated in the *Clifford-Horst* series of cases. And . . . a proper application of the principles as there developed might well have produced a different result, such as was reached by the Tax Court in this case in regard to the assignments of the other contracts. Under those circumstances collateral estoppel should not have been used by the Tax Court in the instant proceeding to perpetuate the 1935 viewpoint of the assignment. . . .

. . . The transactions were simply a reallocation of income within the family group, a reallocation which did not shift the incidence of income tax liability.

The judgment below must therefore be reversed and the case remanded for such further proceedings as may be necessary in light of this opinion.

Reversed.

JUSTICE FRANKFURTER and JUSTICE JACKSON believe the judgment of the Tax Court is based on substantial evidence and is consistent with the law, and would affirm that judgment. . . .

Allen v. McCurry

449 U.S. 90 (1980)

JUSTICE STEWART delivered the opinion of the Court. . . .

In April 1977, several undercover police officers, following an informant's tip that McCurry was dealing in heroin, went to his house in St. Louis, Mo., to attempt a purchase. Two officers, petitioners Allen and Jacobsmeyer, knocked on the front door, while the other officers hid nearby. When McCurry opened the door, the two officers asked to buy some heroin "caps." McCurry went back into the house and returned soon thereafter, firing a pistol at and seriously wounding Allen and Jacobsmeyer. After a gun battle with the other officers and their reinforcements, McCurry retreated into the house; he emerged again when the police demanded that he surrender. Several officers then entered the house without a warrant, purportedly to search for other persons inside. One of the officers seized drugs and other contraband that lay in plain view, as well as additional contraband he found in dresser drawers and in auto tires on the porch.

McCurry was charged with possession of heroin and assault with intent to kill. At the pretrial suppression hearing, the trial judge excluded the evidence seized from the dresser drawers and tires, but denied suppression of the evidence found in plain view. McCurry was convicted of both the heroin and assault offenses.

McCurry subsequently filed the present § 1983 action for $1 million in damages against petitioners Allen and Jacobsmeyer, other unnamed individual police officers, and the city of St. Louis and its police department. The complaint alleged a conspiracy to violate McCurry's Fourth Amendment rights, an unconstitutional search and seizure of his house, and an assault on him by unknown police officers after he had been arrested and handcuffed. The petitioners moved for summary judgment. The District Court apparently understood the gist of the complaint to be the allegedly unconstitutional search and seizure and granted summary judgment, holding that collateral estoppel prevented McCurry from relitigating the search and seizure question already decided against him in the state courts. McCurry v. Allen, 466 F. Supp. 514 (E.D. Mo. 1978).

The Court of Appeals reversed the judgment and remanded the case for trial. McCurry v. Allen, 606 F.2d 795 (8th Cir.). . . .

This Court has never directly decided whether the rules of res judicata and collateral estoppel are generally applicable to § 1983 actions. But in Preiser v. Rodriguez, 411 U.S. 475, 497 [1973], the Court noted with implicit approval the view of other federal courts that res judicata principles fully apply to civil rights suits brought under that statute. . . . And the virtually unanimous view of the Court of Appeals since *Preiser* has been that § 1983 presents no categorical bar to the application of res judicata and collateral estoppel concepts. These federal appellate court decisions have spoken with little explanation or citation in assuming the compatibility of § 1983 and rules of preclusion, but the statute and its legislative history clearly support the courts' decisions.

Because the requirement of mutuality of estoppel was still alive in the federal courts until well into this century, see Blonder-Tongue Laboratories, Inc. v. University of Illinois Foundation . . . , 402 U.S. [313], at 322-323 [1971],* the drafters of the 1871 Civil Rights Act, of which § 1983 is a part, may have had less reason to concern themselves with rules of preclusion than a modern Congress would. Nevertheless, in 1871 res judicata and collateral estoppel could certainly have applied in federal suits following state-court litigation between the same parties or their privies, and nothing in the language of § 1983 remotely expresses any congressional intent to contravene the common law rules of preclusion or to repeal the

* [Mutuality of estoppel required that for a prior judgment to be determinative of an issue in current litigation, both parties must have been involved in the earlier suit. *Blonder-Tongue* severely undercut the doctrine of mutuality by holding that a defendant could raise collateral estoppel to a charge of patent infringement that was based on an earlier determination that the patent was invalid in a suit to which he was not a party. For a further discussion of the doctrine of mutuality, see Parklane Hosiery Co. v. Shore, infra. EDS.]

express statutory requirements of the predecessor of 28 U.S.C. § 1738. . . . Section 1983 creates a new federal cause of action. It says nothing about the preclusive effect of state-court judgments.

Moreover, the legislative history of § 1983 does not in any clear way suggest that Congress intended to repeal or restrict the traditional doctrines of preclusion. . . . To the extent that it did intend to change the balance of power over federal questions between the state and federal courts, the 42d Congress was acting in a way thoroughly consistent with the doctrines of preclusion. . . . The . . . basis of the Court of Appeals' holding appears to be a generally framed principle that every person asserting a federal right is entitled to one unencumbered opportunity to litigate that right in a federal district court, regardless of the legal posture in which the federal claim arises. But the authority for this principle is difficult to discern. It cannot lie in the Constitution, which makes no such guarantee, but leaves the scope of the jurisdiction of the federal district courts to the wisdom of Congress. And no such authority is to be found in § 1983 itself. For reasons already discussed at length, nothing in the language or legislative history of § 1983 proves any congressional intent to deny binding effect to a state court judgment or decision when the state court, acting within its proper jurisdiction, has given the parties a full and fair opportunity to litigate federal claims, and thereby has shown itself willing and able to protect federal rights. And nothing in the legislative history of § 1983 reveals any purpose to afford less deference to judgments in state criminal proceedings than to those in state civil proceedings. There is, in short, no reason to believe that Congress intended to provide a person claiming a federal right an unrestricted opportunity to relitigate an issue already decided in state court simply because the issue arose in a state proceeding in which he would rather not have been engaged at all.

Through § 1983, the 42d Congress intended to afford an opportunity for legal and equitable relief in a federal court for certain types of injuries. It is difficult to believe that the drafters of that Act considered it a substitute for a federal writ of habeas corpus, the purpose of which is not to redress civil injury, but to release the applicant from unlawful physical confinement. . . .

The only other conceivable basis for finding a universal right to litigate a federal claim in a federal district court is hardly a legal basis at all, but rather a general distrust of the capacity of the state courts to render correct decisions on constitutional issues. . . .

. . . Accordingly, the judgment is reversed, and the case is remanded to the Court of Appeals for proceedings consistent with this opinion.

It is so ordered.

JUSTICE BLACKMUN, with whom JUSTICE BRENNAN and JUSTICE MARSHALL join, dissenting. . . .

. . . The Court repeatedly has recognized that § 1983 embodies a strong congressional policy in favor of federal courts' acting as the primary and final arbiters of constitutional rights. In Monroe v. Pape, 365 U.S.

167 (1961), the Court held that Congress passed the legislation in order to substitute a federal forum for the ineffective, although plainly available, state remedies:

> It is abundantly clear that one reason the legislation was passed was to afford a federal right in federal courts because, by reason of prejudice, passion, neglect, intolerance or otherwise, state laws might not be enforced and the claims of citizens to the enjoyment of rights, privileges, and immunities guaranteed by the Fourteenth Amendment might be denied by the state agencies. [Id. at 180.]

. . . The Court's conclusion was that this remedy was to be available no matter what the circumstances of state law:

> It is no answer that the State has a law which if enforced would give relief. The federal remedy is supplementary to the state remedy, and the latter need not be first sought and refused before the federal one is invoked. Hence the fact that Illinois by its constitution and laws outlaws unreasonable searches and seizures is no barrier to the present suit in the federal court. [Id. at 183.]

One should note also that in England v. Medical Examiners, 375 U.S. 411 (1964), the Court had affirmed the federal courts' special role in protecting constitutional rights under § 1983. In that case it held that a plaintiff required by the abstention doctrine to submit his constitutional claim first to a state court could not be precluded entirely from having the federal court, in which he initially had sought relief, pass on his constitutional claim. The Court relied on "the unqualified terms in which Congress, pursuant to constitutional authorization, has conferred specific categories of jurisdiction upon the federal courts," and on its "fundamental objections to any conclusion that a litigant who has properly invoked the jurisdiction of a federal district court to consider federal constitutional claims can be compelled, without his consent and through no fault of his own, to accept instead a state court's determination of those claims." Id. at 415. . . . The Court set out its understanding as to when a litigant in a § 1983 case might be precluded by prior litigation, holding that

> if a party freely and without reservation submits his federal claims for decision by the state courts, litigates them there, and has them decided there, then— whether or not he seeks direct review of the state decision in this Court—he has elected to forgo his right to return to the District Court. [Id. at 419.]

I do not understand why the Court today should abandon this approach. . . .

In this case, the police officers seek to prevent a criminal defendant from relitigating the constitutionality of their conduct in searching his house, after the state trial court had found that conduct in part violative of the defendant's Fourth Amendment rights and in part justified by the circumstances. I doubt that the police officers, now defendants in the

§ 1983 action, can be considered to have been in privity with the State in its role as prosecutor. Therefore, only "issue preclusion" is at stake.

The following factors persuade me to conclude that this respondent should not be precluded from asserting his claim in federal court. First, at the time § 1983 was passed, a nonparty's ability, as a practical matter, to invoke collateral estoppel was nonexistent. One could not preclude an opponent from relitigating an issue in a new cause of action, though that issue had been determined conclusively in a prior proceeding, unless there was "mutuality." Additionally, the definitions of "cause of action" and "issue" were narrow. As a result, and obviously, no preclusive effect could arise out of a criminal proceeding that would affect subsequent *civil* litigation. Thus, the 42d Congress could not have anticipated or approved that a criminal defendant, tried and convicted in state court, would be precluded from raising against police officers a constitutional claim arising out of his arrest.

Also, the process of deciding in a state criminal trial whether to exclude or admit evidence is not at all the equivalent of a § 1983 proceeding. The remedy sought in the latter is utterly different. In bringing the civil suit the criminal defendant does not seek to challenge his conviction collaterally. At most, he wins damages. In contrast, the exclusion of evidence may prevent a criminal conviction. A trial court, faced with the decision whether to exclude relevant evidence, confronts institutional pressures that may cause it to give a different shape to the Fourth Amendment right from what would result in civil litigation of a damages claim. Also, the issue whether to exclude evidence is subsidiary to the purpose of a criminal trial, which is to determine the guilt or innocence of the defendant, and a trial court, at least subconsciously, must weigh the potential damage to the truth-seeking process caused by excluding relevant evidence. See Stone v. Powell, 428 U.S. 465, 489-495 (1976).

A state criminal defendant cannot be held to have chosen "voluntarily" to litigate his Fourth Amendment claim in the state court. The risk of conviction puts pressure upon him to raise all possible defenses. He also faces uncertainty about the wisdom of forgoing litigation on *any* issue, for there is the possibility that he will be held to have waived his right to appeal on that issue. The "deliberate by-pass" of state procedures, which the imposition of collateral estoppel under these circumstances encourages, surely is not a preferred goal. To hold that a criminal defendant who raises a Fourth Amendment claim at his criminal trial "freely and without reservation submits his federal claims for decision by the state courts," see England v. Medical Examiners, 375 U.S. at 419, . . . is to deny reality. The criminal defendant is an involuntary litigant in the state tribunal, and against him all the forces of the State are arrayed. To force him to a choice between forgoing either a potential defense or a federal forum for hearing his constitutional civil claim is fundamentally unfair.

I would affirm the judgment of the Court of Appeals.

---

b. Mutuality of Estoppel

Mutuality is an old rule on its way out, though a few jurisdictions still follow it. Essentially, it says that no party can benefit from a judgment in which she was not also at risk. If she stood to lose nothing, she should likewise be unable to gain. Thus where *P*(2) sues a defendant who previously was found in a different lawsuit to have been liable, she would be invoking nonmutual offensive collateral estoppel. She was not a party to the original lawsuit, so could not be hurt by it. Likewise, a second defendant on the patent would be invoking nonmutual defensive estoppel.

Most courts would allow issue preclusion in both of these nonmutual examples. Mutuality requirements have been much relaxed over the years, especially in defensive estoppel cases.

Parklane Hosiery Co. v. Shore, 439 U.S. 322 (1979), is the leading federal case on offensive collateral estoppel. In brief, it holds that courts should weigh numerous factors in deciding whether issue preclusion is fair, and should not simply apply the old doctrines of mutuality.

Parklane Hosiery Co. v. Shore

439 U.S. 322 (1979)

JUSTICE STEWART delivered the opinion of the Court.

This case presents the question whether a party who has had issues of fact adjudicated adversely to it in an equitable action may be collaterally estopped from relitigating the same issues before a jury in a subsequent legal action brought against it by a new party.

The respondent brought this stockholder's class action against the petitioners in a Federal District Court. The complaint alleged that the petitioners, Parklane Hosiery Co., Inc. (Parklane), and 13 of its officers, directors, and stockholders, had issued a materially false and misleading proxy statement in connection with a merger. The proxy statement, according to the complaint, had violated §§ 14(a), 10(b), and 20(a) of the Securities Exchange Act of 1934, 48 Stat. 895, 891, 899, as amended, 15 U.S.C. §§ 78n(a), 78j(b), and 78t(a), as well as various rules and regulations promulgated by the Securities and Exchange Commission (SEC). The complaint sought damages, rescission of the merger, and recovery of costs.

Before this action came to trial, the SEC filed suit against the same defendants in the Federal District Court, alleging that the proxy statement that had been issued by Parklane was materially false and misleading in essentially the same respects as those that had been alleged in the respondent's complaint. Injunctive relief was requested. After a four-day trial, the District Court found that the proxy statement was materially false and misleading in the respects alleged, and entered a declaratory judgment to that effect. SEC v. Parklane Hosiery Co., 422 F. Supp. 477 [1976]. The Court of Appeals for the Second Circuit affirmed this judgment. 558 F.2d 1083 [1977].

The respondent in the present case then moved for partial summary judgment against the petitioners, asserting that the petitioners were collaterally estopped from relitigating the issues that had been resolved against them in the action brought by the SEC. The District Court denied the motion on the ground that such an application of collateral estoppel would deny the petitioners their Seventh Amendment right to a jury trial. The Court of Appeals for the Second Circuit reversed. . . . [W]e granted certiorari, 435 U.S. 1006.

The threshold question to be considered is whether, quite apart from the right to a jury trial under the Seventh Amendment, the petitioners can be precluded from relitigating facts resolved adversely to them in a prior equitable proceeding with another party under the general law of collateral estoppel. Specifically, we must determine whether a litigant who was not a party to a prior judgment may nevertheless use that judgment "offensively" to prevent a defendant from relitigating issues resolved in the earlier proceeding.

Collateral estoppel, like the related doctrine of res judicata, has the dual purpose of protecting litigants from the burden of relitigating an identical issue with the same party or his privy and of promoting judicial economy by preventing needless litigation. Blonder-Tongue Laboratories, Inc. v. University of Illinois Foundation, 402 U.S. 313, 328-329 (1971). Until relatively recently, however, the scope of collateral estoppel was limited by the doctrine of mutuality of parties. Under this mutuality doctrine, neither party could use a prior judgment as an estoppel against the other unless both parties were bound by the judgment. Based on the premise that it is somehow unfair to allow a party to use a prior judgment when he himself would not be so bound, the mutuality requirement provided a party who had litigated and lost in a previous action an opportunity to relitigate identical issues with new parties.

By failing to recognize the obvious difference in position between a party who has never litigated an issue and one who has fully litigated and lost, the mutuality requirement was criticized almost from its inception. Recognizing the validity of this criticism, the Court in Blonder-Tongue Laboratories, Inc. v. University of Illinois Foundation, supra, abandoned the mutuality requirement, at least in cases where a patentee seeks to relitigate the validity of a patent after a federal court in a previous lawsuit has already declared it invalid. The "broader question" before the Court, however, was "whether it is any longer tenable to afford a litigant more than one full and fair opportunity for judicial resolution of the same issue." 402 U.S. at 328. The Court strongly suggested a negative answer to that question:

> In any lawsuit where a defendant, because of the mutuality principle, is forced to present a complete defense on the merits to a claim which the plaintiff has fully litigated and lost in a prior action, there is an arguable misallocation of resources. To the extent the defendant in the second suit may not win by asserting, without contradiction, that the plaintiff had fully

> and fairly, but unsuccessfully, litigated the same claim in the prior suit, the defendant's time and money are diverted from alternative uses—productive or otherwise—to relitigation of a decided issue. And, still assuming that the issue was resolved correctly in the first suit, there is reason to be concerned about the plaintiff's allocation of resources. Permitting repeated litigation of the same issue as long as the supply of unrelated defendants holds out reflects either the aura of the gaming table or "a lack of discipline and of disinterestedness on the part of the lower courts, hardly a worthy or wise basis for fashioning rules of procedure." Kerotest Mfg. Co. v. C-O-Two Co., 342 U.S. 180, 185 (1952). Although neither judges, the parties, nor the adversary system performs perfectly in all cases, the requirement of determining whether the party against whom an estoppel is asserted had a full and fair opportunity to litigate is a most significant safeguard. [Id. at 329.]

The *Blonder-Tongue* case involved defensive use of collateral estoppel—a plaintiff was estopped from asserting a claim that the plaintiff had previously litigated and lost against another defendant. The present case, by contrast, involves offensive use of collateral estoppel—a plaintiff is seeking to estop a defendant from relitigating the issues which the defendant previously litigated and lost against another plaintiff. In both the offensive and defensive use situations, the party against whom estoppel is asserted has litigated and lost in an earlier action. Nevertheless, several reasons have been advanced why the two situations should be treated differently.

First, offensive use of collateral estoppel does not promote judicial economy in the same manner as defensive use does. Defensive use of collateral estoppel precludes a plaintiff from relitigating identical issues by merely "switching adversaries." Bernhard v. Bank of America Nat. Trust & Savings Assn., 122 P.2d at 895 (1942). Thus defensive collateral estoppel gives a plaintiff a strong incentive to join all potential defendants in the first action if possible. Offensive use of collateral estoppel, on the other hand, creates precisely the opposite incentive. Since a plaintiff will be able to rely on a previous judgment against a defendant but will not be bound by that judgment if the defendant wins, the plaintiff has every incentive to adopt a "wait and see" attitude, in the hope that the first action by another plaintiff will result in a favorable judgment. . . . Thus offensive use of collateral estoppel will likely increase rather than decrease the total amount of litigation, since potential plaintiffs will have everything to gain and nothing to lose by not intervening in the first action.

A second argument against offensive use of collateral estoppel is that it may be unfair to a defendant. If a defendant in the first action is sued for small or nominal damages, he may have little incentive to defend vigorously, particularly if future suits are not foreseeable. The Evergreens v. Nunan, 141 F.2d 927, 929 (2d Cir. 1944); cf. Berner v. British Commonwealth Pac. Airlines, 346 F.2d 532 (2d Cir. 1965) (application of offensive collateral estoppel denied where defendant did not appeal an adverse judgment awarding damages of $35,000 and defendant was later sued for over $7 million). Allowing offensive collateral estoppel may also be unfair to a defendant if the judgment relied upon as a basis for the estoppel is itself inconsistent with one or more previous judgments in favor of the defendant. Still another situation where it might be unfair to apply offensive estoppel is where the second action affords the defendant procedural opportunities unavailable in the first action that could readily cause a different result.

We have concluded that the preferable approach for dealing with these problems in the federal courts is not to preclude the use of offensive collateral estoppel, but to grant trial courts broad discretion to determine when it should be applied. The general rule should be that in cases where a plaintiff could easily have joined in the earlier action or where, either for the reasons discussed above or for other reasons, the application of offensive estoppel would be unfair to a defendant, a trial judge should not allow the use of offensive collateral estoppel.

In the present case, however, none of the circumstances that might justify reluctance to allow the offensive use of collateral estoppel is present. The application of offensive collateral estoppel will not here reward a private plaintiff who could have joined in the previous action, since the respondent probably could not have joined in the injunctive action brought by the SEC even had he so desired. Similarly, there is no unfairness to the petitioners in applying offensive collateral estoppel in this case. First, in light of the serious allegations made in the SEC's complaint against the petitioners, as well as the foreseeability of subsequent private suits that typically follow a successful Government judgment, the petitioners had every incentive to litigate the SEC lawsuit fully and vigorously. Second, the judgment in the SEC action was not inconsistent with any previous decision. Finally, there will in the respondent's action be no procedural opportunities available to the petitioners that were unavailable in the first action of a kind that might be likely to cause a different result.[19]

We conclude, therefore, that none of the considerations that would justify a refusal to allow the use of offensive collateral estoppel is present in this case. Since the petitioners received a "full and fair" opportunity to litigate their claims in the SEC action, the contemporary law of collateral estoppel leads inescapably to the conclusion that the petitioners are collaterally estopped from relitigating the question of whether the proxy statement was materially false and misleading.

The question that remains is whether, notwithstanding the law of collateral estoppel, the use of offensive collateral estoppel in this case would violate the petitioners' Seventh Amendment right to a jury trial....

Recognition that an equitable determination could have collateral-estoppel effect in a subsequent legal action was the major premise of this Court's decision in Beacon Theatres, Inc. v. Westover, 359 U.S. 500 (1959).

19. It is true, of course, that the petitioners in the present action would be entitled to a jury trial.... But the presence or absence of a jury as fact finder is basically neutral, quite unlike, for example, the necessity of defending the first lawsuit in an inconvenient forum.

In that case the plaintiff sought a declaratory judgment that certain arrangements between it and the defendant were not in violation of the antitrust laws, and asked for an injunction to prevent the defendant from instituting an antitrust action to challenge the arrangements. The defendant denied the allegations and counterclaimed for treble damages under the antitrust laws, requesting a trial by jury of the issues common to both the legal and equitable claims. The Court of Appeals upheld denial of the request, but this Court reversed, stating:

> [T]he effect of the action of the District Court could be, as the Court of Appeals believed, "to limit the petitioner's opportunity fully to try to a jury every issue which has a bearing upon its treble damage suit," for determination of the issue of clearances by the judge might "operate either by way of res judicata or collateral estoppel so as to conclude both parties with respect thereto at the subsequent trial of the treble damage claim." [Id. at 504.]

It is thus clear that the Court in the *Beacon Theatres* case thought that if an issue common to both legal and equitable claims was first determined by a judge, relitigation of the issue before a jury might be foreclosed by res judicata or collateral estoppel. To avoid this result, the Court held that when legal and equitable claims are joined in the same action, the trial judge has only limited discretion in determining the sequence of trial and "that discretion . . . must, wherever possible, be exercised to preserve jury trial." Id. at 510.

Both the premise of *Beacon Theatres,* and the fact that it enunciated no more than a general prudential rule were confirmed by this Court's decision in Katchen v. Landy, 382 U.S. 323 (1966). In that case the Court held that a bankruptcy court, sitting as a statutory court of equity, is empowered to adjudicate equitable claims prior to legal claims, even though the factual issues decided in the equity action would have been triable by a jury under the Seventh Amendment if the legal claims had been adjudicated first. The Court stated: Both *Beacon Theatres* and *Dairy Queen* recognize that there might be situations in which the Court could proceed to resolve the equitable claim first even though the results might be dispositive of the issues involved in the legal claim. Id. at 339. Thus the Court in Katchen v. Landy recognized that an equitable determination can have collateral-estoppel effect in a subsequent legal action and that this estoppel does not violate the Seventh Amendment. . . .

The petitioners have advanced no persuasive reason . . . why the meaning of the Seventh Amendment should depend on whether or not mutuality of parties is present. A litigant who has lost because of adverse factual findings in an equity action is equally deprived of a jury trial whether he is estopped from relitigating the factual issues against the same party or a new party. In either case, the party against whom estoppel is asserted has litigated questions of fact, and has had the facts determined against him in an earlier proceeding. In either case there is no further factfinding function for the jury to perform, since the common factual issues have been resolved in the previous action. . . .

The Seventh Amendment has never been interpreted in the rigid manner advocated by the petitioners. On the contrary, many procedural devices developed since 1791 that have diminished the civil jury's historic domain have been found not to be inconsistent with the Seventh Amendment. See Galloway v. United States, 319 U.S. 372, 388-393 (1943). . . .

The *Galloway* case is particularly instructive. There the party against whom a directed verdict had been entered argued that the procedure was unconstitutional under the Seventh Amendment. In rejecting this claim, the Court said:

> The Amendment did not bind the federal courts to the exact procedural incidents or details of jury trial according to the common law in 1791, any more than it tied them to the common-law system of pleading or the specific rules of evidence then prevailing. Nor were "the rules of the common law" then prevalent, including those relating to the procedure by which the judge regulated the jury's role on questions of fact, crystallized in a fixed and immutable system. . . .
>
> The more logical conclusion, we think, and the one which both history and the previous decisions here support, is that the Amendment was designed to preserve the basic institution of jury trial in only its most fundamental elements, not the great mass of procedural forms and details, varying even then so widely among common-law jurisdictions. [319 U.S. at 390, 392 (footnote omitted).]

The law of collateral estoppel, like the law in other procedural areas defining the scope of the jury's function, has evolved since 1791. Under the rationale of the *Galloway* case, these developments are not repugnant to the Seventh Amendment simply for the reason that they did not exist in 1791. Thus if, as we have held, the law of collateral estoppel forecloses the petitioners from relitigating the factual issues determined against them in the SEC action, nothing in the Seventh Amendment dictates a different result, even though because of lack of mutuality there would have been no collateral estoppel in 1791.

The judgment of the Court of Appeals is *affirmed*.

JUSTICE REHNQUIST, dissenting. . . .

. . . Neither respondent nor the Court doubts that at common law as it existed in 1791, petitioners would have been entitled in the private action to have a jury determine whether the proxy statement was false and misleading in the respects alleged. The reason is that at common law in 1791, collateral estoppel was permitted only where the parties in the first action were identical to, or in privity with, the parties to the subsequent action. It was not until 1971 that the doctrine of mutuality was abrogated by this Court in certain limited circumstances. Blonder-Tongue Laboratories, Inc. v. University of Illinois Foundation, 402 U.S. 313 (1971). But developments in the judge-made doctrine of collateral estoppel, however salutary, cannot, consistent with the Seventh Amendment, contract in any material fashion the right to a jury trial that a defendant would have enjoyed in 1791. In the instant case, resort to the doctrine of collateral estoppel does more than merely contract the right to a jury trial: It eliminates the right entirely and therefore contravenes the Seventh Amendment.

The Court responds, however, that at common law "a litigant was not entitled to have a jury [in a subsequent action at law between the same parties] determine issues that had been previously adjudicated by a chancellor in equity," and that "petitioners have advanced no persuasive reason . . . why the meaning of the Seventh Amendment should depend on whether or not mutuality of parties is present." . . .

But that is tantamount to saying that since a party would not be entitled to a jury trial if he brought an equitable action, there is no persuasive reason why he should receive a jury trial on virtually the same issues if instead he chooses to bring his lawsuit in the nature of a legal action. The persuasive reason is that the Seventh Amendment requires that a party's right to jury trial which existed at common law be "preserved" from incursions by the government or the judiciary. Whether this Court believes that use of a jury trial in a particular instance is necessary, or fair or repetitive is simply irrelevant. If that view is "rigid," it is the Constitution which commands that rigidity. To hold otherwise is to rewrite the Seventh Amendment so that a party is guaranteed a jury trial in civil cases unless this Court thinks that a jury trial would be inappropriate.

Even accepting, arguendo, the majority's position that there is no violation of the Seventh Amendment here, I nonetheless would not sanction the use of collateral estoppel in this case. The Court today holds:

> The general rule should be that in cases where a plaintiff could easily have joined in the earlier action or where, either for the reasons discussed above or for other reasons, the application of offensive estoppel would be unfair to a defendant, a trial judge should not allow the use of offensive collateral estoppel.

In my view, it is "unfair" to apply offensive collateral estoppel where the party who is sought to be estopped has not had an opportunity to have the facts of his case determined by a jury. Since in this case petitioners were not entitled to a jury trial in the Securities and Exchange Commission (SEC) lawsuit[,] I would not estop them from relitigating the issues determined in the SEC suit before a jury in the private action. I believe that several factors militate in favor of this result.

First, the use of offensive collateral estoppel in this case runs counter to the strong federal policy favoring jury trials, even if it does not, as the majority holds; violate the Seventh Amendment. The Court's decision in Beacon Theatres, Inc. v. Westover, 359 U.S. 500 (1959), exemplifies that policy. . . . Today's decision will mean that in a large number of private cases defendants will no longer enjoy the right to jury trial. Neither the Court nor respondent has adverted or cited to any unmanageable problems that have resulted from according defendants jury trials in such cases. I simply see no "imperative circumstances" requiring this wholesale abrogation of jury trials.

Second, I believe that the opportunity for a jury trial in the second action could easily lead to a different result from that obtained in the first action before the Court and therefore that it is unfair to estop petitioners from relitigating the issues before a jury. This is the position adopted in the Restatement (Second) of Judgments, which disapproves of the application of offensive collateral estoppel where the defendant has an opportunity for a jury trial in the second lawsuit that was not available in the first action. The Court accepts the proposition that it is unfair to apply offensive collateral estoppel "where the second action affords the defendant procedural opportunities unavailable in the first action that could readily cause a different result." . . . Differences in discovery opportunities between the two actions are cited as examples of situations where it would be unfair to permit offensive collateral estoppel. . . . But in the Court's view, the fact that petitioners would have been entitled to a jury trial in the present action is not such a "procedural opportunit[y]" because "the presence or absence of a jury as factfinder is basically *neutral*, quite unlike, for example, the necessity of defending the first lawsuit in an inconvenient forum." . . . (emphasis added).

As is evident from the prior brief discussion of the development of the civil jury trial guarantee in this country, those who drafted the Declaration of Independence and debated so passionately the proposed Constitution during the ratification period, would indeed be astounded to learn that the presence or absence of a jury is merely "neutral," whereas the availability of discovery, a device unmentioned in the Constitution, may be controlling. It is precisely because the Framers believed that they might receive a different result at the hands of a jury of their peers than at the mercy of the sovereign's judges, that the Seventh Amendment was adopted. And I suspect that anyone who litigates cases before juries in the 1970's would be equally amazed to hear of the supposed lack of distinction between trial by court and trial by jury. The Court can cite no authority in support of this curious proposition. The merits of civil juries have been long debated, but I suspect that juries have never been accused of being merely "neutral" factors.

The ultimate irony of today's decision is that its potential for significantly conserving the resources of either the litigants or the judiciary is doubtful at best. That being the case, I see absolutely no reason to frustrate so cavalierly the important federal policy favoring jury decisions of disputed fact questions. The instant case is an apt example of the minimal savings that will be accomplished by the Court's decision. As the Court admits, even if petitioners are collaterally estopped from relitigating whether the proxy was materially false and misleading, they are still entitled to have a jury determine whether respondent was injured by the alleged misstatements and the amount of damages, if any, sustained by respondent. . . . Thus, a jury must be impaneled in this case in any event. The time saved by not trying the issue of whether the proxy was materially false and misleading before the jury is likely to be insubstantial. It is just as probable that today's decision will have the result of coercing defendants to agree to consent orders or settlements in agency enforcement action in order to preserve their right to jury trial in the private actions. In that event, the Court, for no compelling reason, will have simply added a powerful club to the administrative agencies' arsenals that even Congress was unwilling to provide them.

Notes and Questions

1. *Implications of* Parklane. The factors to consider in whether there was a full and fair opportunity for litigation in the first suit and whether the claim may be asserted in the second suit now are:

(a) Size of claim. If the first lawsuit was for $1,000 and the second for $100,000, there may be a real difference in how the parties litigate. In *Parklane*, the parties knew the importance of the SEC suit, so they litigated the suit flat out.
(b) Forum of first suit. Is there any indication that the first forum had odd procedures, discovery, or other limitations that make preclusion unfair? In Parklane, the first forum was the federal court.
(c) Extent of litigation. Was the matter given full adversarial attention?
(d) Competence and experience of counsel in first action.
(e) New evidence or changed circumstances that have developed since the first trial.
(f) Differences in applicable law.
(g) Foreseeability of future litigation.
(h) Whether the party who now seeks to use the previously adjudicated case is a "wait and see" plaintiff. Could she have joined the first case? In Parklane, definitely not.
(i) Public interest. Is there a public interest in allowing relitigation of the claims?

2. *Prediction and Issue Preclusion.* After you review the list of factors in note, supra, the following question should seem inevitable: How workable is a doctrine of repose that depends on such a flexible, multifactored test for determining when an issue can be relitigated? Indeed, both claim and issue preclusion are highly context-dependent. Does the uncertainty that goes with such fact-bound inquiries cut against the policy interest that underlies a doctrine of repose? See In re Microsoft Corp. Antitrust Litigation, 355 F.3d 322 (4th Cir. 2004) (limiting nonmutual offensive collateral estoppel to previously litigated facts that are "critical and necessary" to, not just "supportive" of, the result).

3. *Policy Factors Revisited*. What is wrong with being a "wait and see" plaintiff anyway? Isn't this prudent behavior that promotes judicial economy? Are the policy factors invoked by the Court as reasons not to permit nonmutual estoppel persuasive?

4. *Inscrutable Verdicts and Issue Preclusion.* Another way in which jury trials play into the application of collateral estoppel is that the verdicts of juries are often "inscrutable." A general verdict may mean many things, none of them clearly. Consider the following examples:

a) *P* sues *D* for negligence. Jury enters a general verdict for *D*. What issue-preclusive effect does this judgment have if *P* then wants to sue *D*(2) for negligence in the same accident? None, because the general verdict could mean that 1) the jury found *P* contributorily negligent, 2) *P* has assumed the risk, or 3) *P* suffered no damages, and thus the verdict is inscrutable.

(b) *P*, the owner of a building, sues *D*, a gas utility, and *D*(2), a contractor doing repair work on the building, contending that through the negligence of both, a gas line in the building was ruptured, resulting in an explosion that demolished the building. *D* and *D*(2) each contend that he was not negligent and that the other was. If they have a full and fair opportunity to litigate these contentions, a judgment in favor of *P* against *D*(2) but in favor of *D* is preclusive of the issue that *D* was not negligent in a subsequent action between *D*(2) and *D*.

5. *Preclusion in Litigation with Nonparties.* Can a person or entity who was *not* a party (or represented as in a class action) in an earlier action ever be precluded from relitigating matters there decided? Due process would seem to require that a nonparty should be allowed to relitigate the issue, because the nonparty had no opportunity to be heard in the first place. But see Robert G. Bone, Rethinking the "Day in Court" Ideal and Nonparty Preclusion, 67 N.Y.U. L. Rev. 193 (1992) (arguing against the general rule that a nonparty may relitigate a matter). Review this question after you have read Montana v. United States.

6. *Preclusion in Alternative Dispute Resolution.* As arbitration and other forms of alternative dispute resolution grow increasingly common, courts have extended the doctrine of collateral estoppel to these new contexts, holding that where the prerequisites for collateral estoppel are satisfied, arbitrators must give preclusive effect to prior federal judgments. See, e.g., Collins v. D.R. Horton, Inc., 505 F.3d 874, 882 (9th Cir. 2007); Aircraft Braking Sys. Corp. v. Local 856, 97 F.3d 155, 159 (6th Cir. 1996); Miller v. Runyon, 77 F.3d 189, 193 (7th Cir. 1996); see also Miller Brewing Co. v. Fort Worth Distrib. Co., 781 F.2d 494, 499 (5th Cir. 1986) ("Since an arbitration award involves the entry of judgment by a court, parties should be barred from seeking relief from arbitration panels when, under the doctrine of res judicata, they would be barred from seeking relief in the courts.").

Should arbitrators have the same broad discretion as district courts in determining when to apply offensive nonmutual collateral estoppel? Will they have the same expertise as trial judges in making such determinations? See *Collins*, 505 F.3d at 882 (holding that arbitrators should have the same discretion possessed by district courts in applying the *Parklane* factors to determine whether offensive nonmutual collateral estoppel is appropriate). In *Collins*, the Ninth Circuit affirmed the arbitrators' refusal to give collateral estoppel effect to a district court decision that was pending on appeal. Unlike an Article III court's judgment, the arbitrators reasoned, an arbitration award cannot normally be corrected on appeal if the decision to which it gives collateral estoppel effect is later reversed. Interestingly, this suggests that collateral estoppel will be less binding before arbitrators, at least in part because their own awards are so binding. Finality cuts both ways.

Montana v. United States

440 U.S. 147 (1979)

JUSTICE MARSHALL delivered the opinion of the Court.

The State of Montana imposes a one percent gross receipts tax upon contractors of public, but not private, construction projects. Montana Rev. Codes Ann. § 84-3505 (Supp. 1975). A public contractor may credit against the gross receipts tax its payments of personal property, corporate income, and individual income taxes. Any remaining gross receipts liability is customarily passed on in the form of increased construction costs to the governmental unit financing the project. At issue in this appeal is whether a prior judgment by the Montana Supreme Court upholding the tax precludes the United States from contesting its constitutionality and if not, whether the tax discriminates against the Federal Government in violation of the Supremacy Clause. . . .

In 1971, Peter Kiewit Sons' Co., the contractor on a federal dam project in Montana, brought suit in state court contending that the Montana gross receipts tax unconstitutionally discriminated against the United States and the companies with which it dealt. The litigation was directed and financed by the United States. Less than a month after the state suit was filed, the Government initiated this challenge to the constitutionality of the tax in the United States District Court for the District of Montana. On stipulation by the parties, the instant case was continued pending resolution of the state-court litigation.

That litigation concluded in a unanimous decision by the Montana Supreme Court sustaining the tax. Peter Kiewit Sons' Co. v. State Board of Equalization, 505 P.2d 102 (1973) (*Kiewit I*). The court found the distinction between public and private contractors consistent with the mandates of the Supremacy and Equal Protection Clauses. Id. at 149-154, 505 P.2d, at 108-110. The contractor subsequently filed a Notice of Appeal to this Court, but abandoned its request for review at the direction of the Solicitor General. . . . It then instituted a second action in state court seeking a refund for certain tax payments different from those involved in *Kiewit I*. On determining that the contractor's second legal claim was, in all material respects, identical to its first, the Montana Supreme Court invoked the doctrines of collateral estoppel and res judicata to affirm the dismissal of the complaint. Peter Kiewit Sons' Co. v. Department of Revenue, 531 P.2d 1327 (1975) (*Kiewit II*).

After the decision in *Kiewit II*, a three-judge District Court heard the instant case on the merits. In a divided opinion, the court concluded that the United States was not bound by the *Kiewit I* decision, and struck down the tax as violative of the Supremacy Clause. 437 F. Supp. 354 (Mont. 1977).

We noted probable jurisdiction. 436 U.S. 916 (1978). Because we find that the constitutional question presented by this appeal was determined adversely to the United States in a prior state proceeding, we reverse on grounds of collateral estoppel without reaching the merits. . . .

A fundamental precept of common-law adjudication, embodied in the related doctrines of collateral estoppel and res judicata, is that a "right, question or fact distinctly put in issue and directly determined by a court of competent jurisdiction . . . cannot be disputed in a subsequent suit between the same parties or their privies. . . ." Southern Pacific R. Co. v. United States, 168 U.S. 1, 48-49 (1897). . . .

. . . To preclude parties from contesting matters that they have had a full and fair opportunity to litigate protects their adversaries from the expense and vexation attending multiple lawsuits, conserves judicial resources, and fosters reliance on judicial action by minimizing the possibility of inconsistent decisions.

These interests are similarly implicated when nonparties assume control over litigation in which they have a direct financial or proprietary interest and then seek to redetermine issues previously resolved. As this Court observed in Souffront v. Compagnie des Sucreries, 217 U.S. 475, 486-487 (1910), the persons for whose benefit and at whose direction a cause of action is litigated cannot be said to be

> strangers to the cause. . . . [O]ne who prosecutes or defends a suit in the name of another to establish and protect his own right, or who assists in the prosecution or defense of an action in aid of some interest of his own . . . is as much bound . . . as he would be if he had been a party to the record.

See Schnell v. Peter Eckrich & Sons, Inc., 365 U.S. 260, 262 n.4 (1961); cf. Zenith Radio Corp. v. Hazeltine Research, Inc., 395 U.S. 100, 111 (1969). Preclusion of such nonparties falls under the rubric of collateral estoppel rather than res judicata because the latter doctrine presupposes identity between causes of action. And the cause of action which a nonparty has vicariously asserted differs by definition from that which he subsequently seeks to litigate in his own right. . . .

That the United States exercised control over the *Kiewit I* litigation is not in dispute. The Government has stipulated that it:

(1) required the *Kiewit I* lawsuit to be filed;
(2) reviewed and approved the complaint;
(3) paid the attorneys' fees and costs;
(4) directed the appeal from state district court to the Montana Supreme Court;

(5) appeared and submitted a brief as amicus in the Montana Supreme Court;
(6) directed the filing of a Notice of Appeal to this Court; and
(7) effectuated Kiewit's abandonment of that appeal on advice of the Solicitor General . . .

Thus, although not a party, the United States plainly had a sufficient "laboring oar" in the conduct of the state-court litigation to actuate principles of estoppel.

To determine the appropriate application of collateral estoppel in the instant case necessitates three further inquiries: first, whether the issues presented by this litigation are in substance the same as those resolved against the United States in *Kiewit I;* second, whether controlling facts or legal principles have changed significantly since the state-court judgment; and finally, whether other special circumstances warrant an exception to the normal rules of preclusion.

A review of the record in *Kiewit I* dispels any doubt that the plaintiff there raised and the Montana Supreme Court there decided the precise constitutional claim that the United States advances here. . . .

Relying on Commissioner v. Sunnen, 333 U.S. 591 (1948), the United States argues that collateral estoppel extends only to contexts in which "the controlling facts and applicable legal rules remain unchanged." Id., at 600. In the Government's view, factual stasis is missing here because the contract at issue in *Kiewet I* contained a critical provision which the contracts involved in the instant litigation do not.

Under its contract with the Army Corps of Engineers, Kiewit was unable to take advantage of the credit provisions of the gross receipts tax. In 1971, however, the United States altered its policy and has since required Montana contractors to seek all available refunds and credits. . . . But we do not construe the opinion in *Kiewit I* as predicated on the factual assumption that the gross receipts tax would cancel out if public contractors took all available refunds and credits.

Thus, unless there have been major changes in the law governing intergovernmental tax immunity since *Kiewit I,* the Government's reliance on Commissioner v. Sunnen, 333 U.S. 591, is misplaced. . . No such considerations obtain here. The Government does not contend and the District Court did not find that a change in controlling legal principles had occurred between *Kiewit I* and the instant suit. That the Government's amended complaint in this action replicates in substance the legal argument advanced by the contractor's complaint in *Kiewit I* further suggests the absence of any major doctrinal shifts since the Montana Supreme Court's decision.

Because the factual and legal context in which the issues of this case arise has not materially altered since *Kiewit I,* normal rules of preclusion should operate to relieve the parties of "redundant litigation [over] the identical question of the statute's application to the taxpayer's status." Tait v. Western Maryland R. Co., 289 U.S. 620, 624 (1933). . . .

The sole remaining question is whether the particular circumstances of this case justify an exception to general principles of estoppel. Of possible relevance is the exception which obtains for "unmixed questions of law" in successive actions involving substantially unrelated claims. United States v. Moser, 266 U.S. 236, 242 (1924). As we recognized in *Moser*:

> Where, for example, a court in deciding a case has enunciated a rule of law, the parties in a subsequent action *upon a different demand* are not estopped from insisting that the law is otherwise, merely because the parties are the same in both cases. But a *fact, question* or *right* distinctly adjudged in the original action cannot be disputed in a subsequent action, even though the determination was reached upon an erroneous view or by an erroneous application of the law. [Id. (emphasis added.)]

Thus, when issues of law arise in successive actions involving unrelated subject matter, preclusion may be inappropriate. This exception is of particular importance in constitutional adjudication. Unreflective invocation of collateral estoppel against parties with an ongoing interest in constitutional issues could freeze doctrine in areas of the law where responsiveness to changing patterns of conduct or social mores is critical. To be sure, the scope of the *Moser* exception may be difficult to delineate, particularly where there is partial congruence in the subject matter of successive disputes. But the instant case poses no such conceptual difficulties. Rather, as the preceding discussion indicates, the legal "demands" of this litigation are closely aligned in time and subject matter to those in *Kiewit I.*

Nor does this case implicate the right of a litigant who has "properly invoked the jurisdiction of a Federal District Court to consider federal constitutional claims," and who is then "compelled, without his consent . . . , to accept a state court's determination of those claims." England v. Medical Examiners, 375 U.S. 411, 415 (1964) (footnote omitted). As we held in *England*, abstention doctrine may not serve as a vehicle for depriving individuals of an otherwise cognizable right to have federal courts make factual determinations essential to the resolution of federal questions. Id. at 417. See NAACP v. Button, 371 U.S. 415, 427 (1963). However here, as in *England*, a party has "freely and without reservation submitt[ed] his federal claims for decision by the state courts . . . and ha[d] them decided there. . . ." England v. Medical Examiners, supra, at 419. Considerations of comity as well as repose militate against redeterminations of issues in a federal forum at the behest of a plaintiff who has chosen to litigate them in state court.

Finally, the Government has not alleged unfairness or inadequacy in the state procedures to which it voluntarily submitted. We must conclude therefore that it had a full and fair opportunity to press its constitutional challenges in *Kiewit I.* Accordingly, the Government is estopped from seeking a contrary resolution of those issues here.

The judgment of the District Court is *reversed*.

Notes and Questions

1. *Binding Strangers to the Cause.* The Court thought the government had "a sufficient 'laboring oar,' to actuate principles of estoppel." What other facts besides having a controlling hand might establish privity? What if the nonparty's interests align with those of a party to the original suit such that one could say its interests were effectively represented in the original suit? Would that suffice? What if a "horse-switching" attorney refiles the same legal claims against the same defendant on behalf of a different plaintiff?

The Ninth Circuit has summarized privity doctrine in the following terms:

> Even when the parties are not identical, privity may exist if there is substantial identity between parties, that is, a sufficient commonality of interest. . . . First, a nonparty who has succeeded to a party's interest in property is bound by any prior judgment against the party. Second, a nonparty who controlled the original suit will be bound by the resulting judgment. Third, federal courts will bind a nonparty whose interests were represented adequately by a party in the original suit. In addition, "privity" has been found where there is a "substantial identity" between the party and nonparty, where the nonparty had a significant interest and participated in the prior action, and where the interests of the nonparty and party are so closely aligned as to be virtually representative. Finally, a relationship of privity can be said to exist when there is an express or implied legal relationship by which parties to the first suit are accountable to parties who file a subsequent suit with identical issues.

Tahoe-Sierra Pres. Council, Inc. v. Tahoe Regional Planning Agency, 322 F.3d 1064, 1081-1082 (9th Cir. 2003) (internal quotations omitted). Do any of these rules apply where the same attorney files a suit raising federal environmental challenges to timber sales by the United States Forest Service on behalf of a consortium of environmental groups, stipulates to dismissal with prejudice according to a settlement agreement, and then refiles on behalf of a new environmental group challenging the same timber sales under the same federal environmental statutes? See Headwaters, Inc. v. U.S. Forest Service, 399 F.3d 1047, 1053-5104 (9th Cir. 2005) (reversing district court's application of privity doctrine to two environmental organizations who had not before litigated the validity of certain timber sales where counsel for the organizations, a year earlier, signed a dismissal with prejudice of a similar suit); see id. at 1050, 1054-1056 (privity doctrine only applies if "the present plaintiffs were adequately represented in the prior suit" but "parallel legal interests alone, identical or otherwise, are not sufficient to establish privity, or to bind a plaintiff to a decision reached in another case involving another plaintiff"; remanding for reconsideration and a fact hearing on the ties between plaintiffs in the two suits and whether the first suit was "structured to protect 'strangers' to that case"). On the one hand, there is a danger of endless litigation if privity is too narrowly defined. On the other hand, if privity is too broadly defined—if future litigants stand in privity with prior litigants whose purely legal interests align—a great deal of public law litigation would be precluded. Indeed, privity would function as a kind of class action rule for preclusion purposes, binding strangers to the litigation who were "virtually" represented in only the most trivial sense. See Irwin v. Mascott, 370 F.3d 924, 930 (9th Cir. 2004) ("a close relationship, substantial participation, and tactical maneuvering all support a finding of virtual representation: identity of interests and adequate representation are necessary to such a finding").

Does this square with the reasoning in Martin v. Wilks about an individual's right to be heard?

2. *Stare Decisis Versus Collateral Estoppel.* Even a judgment that does not qualify for issue-preclusive effect may nevertheless be pesky for a party seeking to avoid its adverse consequences. After all, if the issue is very similar, and a prior court ruled against another litigant on very similar facts, then stare decisis may make it difficult to avoid a similar fate in the subsequent action. For a case that addresses the differences between issue preclusion and stare decisis, see Meredith v. Beech Aircraft Corp., 18 F.3d 890 (10th Cir. 1994).

3. *Preclusion and Criminal Actions.* Should issues resolved against a party in a civil action be used against her in a criminal action? How about the reverse scenario? The standard of proof differences obviously play a role here, such that—stated generally—the answer to the first question is "no," whereas the answer to the second is "yes." Similarly, acquittal in a criminal trial will not insulate the defendant from a civil suit based on the same facts. Do you see why? See Restatement (Second) of Judgments § 28(4), supra.

4. *Alternative Grounds and Preclusion.* If a judge provides alternative grounds for a holding in an action, should both receive preclusive effect? Neither? The Restatement (Second) of Judgments § 27 holds that alternative grounds should not be given preclusive effect unless an appeal is taken and the appellate court affirms the judgment on both grounds. The rationale is that neither alternative ground can be said to be "essential to the judgment." Moreover, a party may lack an incentive to appeal when she disagrees with only one of the alternative grounds, and there is also the risk that each ground was not weighed as carefully in conjunction with the other as it might have been in isolation. For a contrary view, see Winters v. Lavine, 574 F.2d 46 (2d Cir. 1978), in which the court concluded that it should be presumed that the judge considered fully all issues raised by the parties, and that the parties would have appealed if they disagreed with the holding.

3. Preclusion in a Federal System

Among the most complicated issues within the complex field of claim and issue preclusion are the effects of judgments by state courts in federal court and vice versa. Below we introduce these problems of inter-sovereign relations, though an appreciation of their fuller dimension will come through your future work in courses on constitutional law, federal courts, conflicts, and complex litigation. The decisions demonstrate how powerful, conflicting ideals for full hearings and forum choice on the one hand, and for efficiency and repose on the other, can make for hard cases. This is an area of the law to which you will often return.

a. State Court Judgments in Federal Courts

Kremer v. Chemical Corp.

456 U.S. 461 (1982)

JUSTICE WHITE delivered the opinion of the Court.

As one of its first acts, Congress directed that all United States courts afford the same full-faith-and-credit to state court judgments that would apply in the state's own courts. Act of May 26, 1790, ch. 11, 1 Stat. 122, 28 U.S.C. § 1738 (1976). More recently, Congress implemented the national policy against employment discrimination by creating an array of substantive protections and remedies which generally allows federal courts to determine the merits of a discrimination claim. Title VII of the Civil Rights Act of 1964, 78 Stat. 253, as amended, 42 U.S.C. §§ 2000e et seq. (1976). The principal question presented by this case is whether Congress intended Title VII to supersede the principles of comity and repose embodied in § 1738. Specifically, we decide whether a federal court in a Title VII case should give preclusive effect to a decision of a state court upholding a state administrative agency's rejection of an employment discrimination claim as meritless when the state court's decision would be res judicata in the state's own courts. . . .

Petitioner Rubin Kremer emigrated from Poland in 1970 and was hired in 1973 by respondent Chemical Corporation ("Chemico") as an engineer. Two years later he was laid off, along with a number of other employees. Some of these employees were later rehired, but Kremer was not although he made several applications. In May 1976, Kremer filed a discrimination charge with the Equal Employment Opportunity Commission (EEOC), asserting that his discharge and failure to be rehired was due to his national origin and Jewish faith. Because the EEOC may not consider a claim until a state agency having jurisdiction over employment discrimination complaints has had at least 60 days to resolve the matter, § 706(c), 42 U.S.C. § 2000e-5(c), the Commission referred Kremer's charge to the New York State Division of Human Rights ("NYHRD"), the agency charged with enforcing the New York law prohibiting employment discrimination. N.Y. Exec. Law §§ 295(6), 296(1)(a) (McKinney Supp. 1980).

After investigating Kremer's complaint, the Department concluded that there was no probable cause to believe that Chemico had engaged in the discriminatory practices complained of. The Department explicitly based its determination on the finding that Kremer was not rehired because one employee who was rehired had greater seniority, that another employee who was rehired filled a lesser position than that previously held by Kremer, and that neither Kremer's creed nor age was a factor considered in Chemico's failure to rehire him. The NYHRD's determination was upheld by its Appeal Board as "not arbitrary, capricious, or an abuse of discretion." Kremer again brought his complaint to the attention of the EEOC and also filed, on December 6, 1977, a petition with the Appellate Division of the New York Supreme Court to set aside the adverse administrative determination. On February 21, 1978, five justices of the Appellate Division unanimously affirmed the Appeal Board's order. Kremer could have, but did not seek review by the New York Court of Appeals.

Subsequently, a District Director of the EEOC ruled that there was no reasonable cause to believe that the charge of discrimination was true and issued a right-to-sue notice. The District Director refused a request for reconsideration, noting that he had reviewed the case files and considered the EEOC's disposition as "appropriate and correct in all respects."

Kremer then brought this Title VII action in District Court, claiming discrimination on the basis of national origin and religion. . . .

. . . The District Court . . . dismissed the complaint on grounds of res judicata. 477 F. Supp. 587 (S.D.N.Y. 1979). The Court of Appeals [affirmed.] 623 F.2d 786 (2d Cir. 1980).

. . . [P]etitioner filed for a writ of certiorari. We issued the writ . . . to resolve [an] important issue of federal employment discrimination law over which the Courts of Appeals are divided. We now *affirm*. . . .

Section 1738 requires federal courts to give the same preclusive effect to state court judgments that those judgments would be given in the courts of the state from which the judgments emerged. Here the Appellate Division of the New York Supreme Court has issued a judgment affirming the decision of the NYHRD Appeals Board that the discharge and failure to rehire Kremer were not the product of the discrimination that he had alleged. There is no question that this judicial determination precludes Kremer from bringing "any other action, civil or criminal, based upon the same grievance" in the New York courts. N.Y. Exec. Law § 300 (McKinney 1972). By its terms, therefore, § 1738 would appear to preclude Kremer from relitigating the same question in federal court.

Kremer offers two principal reasons why § 1738 does not bar this action. First, he suggests that in Title VII cases Congress intended that federal courts be relieved of their usual obligation to grant finality to state court decisions.

Allen v. McCurry , 449 U.S. 90, 99 (1980), made clear that an exception to § 1738 will not be recognized unless a later statute contains an express or implied partial repeal. There is no claim here that Title VII expressly repealed § 1738; if there has been a partial repeal, it must be implied. "It is, of course, a cardinal principle of statutory construction that repeals by implication are not favored." Radzanower v. Touche Ross & Co., 426

U.S. 148, 154 (1976); United States v. United Continental Tuna Corp., 425 U.S. 164, 168 (1976), and whenever possible, statutes should be read consistently.

. . . Congress enacted Title VII to assure equality of employment opportunities without distinction with respect to race, color, religion, sex or national origin. Alexander v. Gardner-Denver Co., 415 U.S. 36, 44 (1974); McDonnell Douglas Corp. v. Green, 411 U.S. 792, 800 (1973). To this end the EEOC was created and the federal courts were entrusted with ultimate enforcement responsibility. State anti-discrimination laws, however, play an integral role in the Congressional scheme. Whenever an incident of alleged employment discrimination occurs in a state or locality which by law prohibits such discrimination and which has established an "authority to grant or seek relief from such [discrimination] or to institute criminal proceedings with respect thereto," no charge of discrimination may be actively processed by the EEOC until the state remedy has been invoked and at least 60 days have passed, or the state proceedings have terminated. § 706(c), 42 U.S.C. § 2000e-5(c). Only after providing the appropriate state agency an opportunity to resolve the complaint may an aggrieved individual press his complaint before the EEOC. In its investigation to determine whether there is reasonable cause to believe that the charge of employment discrimination is true, the Commission is required to "accord substantial weight to final findings and orders made by State and local authorities in proceedings commenced under State or local law" pursuant to the limited deferral provisions of § 706, but is not bound by such findings. Alexander v. Gardner-Denver Co., supra, at 48, n.8. If the EEOC finds reasonable cause to believe that discrimination has occurred, it undertakes conciliation efforts to eliminate the unlawful practice; if these efforts fail, the Commission may elect to bring a civil action to enforce the Act. If the Commission declines to do so, or if the Commission finds no reasonable cause to believe that a violation has occurred, "a civil action" may be brought by an aggrieved individual. § 706(f)(1); 42 U.S.C. § 2000e-5(f)(1).

No provision of Title VII requires claimants to pursue in state court an unfavorable state administrative action, nor does the Act specify the weight a federal court should afford a final judgment by a state court if such a remedy is sought. While we have interpreted the "civil action" authorized to follow consideration by federal and state administrative *agencies* to be a "trial de novo," Chandler v. Roudebush, 425 U.S. 840, 844-845 (1976); Alexander v. Gardner-Denver Co., supra, 415 U.S., at 38; McDonnell Douglas Corp. v. Green, 411 U.S. at 798-799 (1973), neither the statute nor our decisions indicate that the final judgment of a state *court* is subject to redetermination at such a trial. Similarly, the Congressional directive that the EEOC should give "substantial weight" to findings made in state proceedings, § 706(b), 42 U.S.C. § 2000e-5(b), indicates only the minimum level of deference the EEOC must afford all state determinations; it does not bar affording the greater preclusive effect which may be required by § 1738 if judicial action is involved. To suggest otherwise, to say that either the opportunity to bring a "civil action" or the "substantial weight" requirement implicitly repeals § 1738, is to prove far too much. For if that is so, even a full trial on the merits in state court would not bar a trial de novo in federal court and would not be entitled to more than "substantial weight," before the EEOC. The state courts would be placed on a one-way street; the finality of their decisions would depend on which side prevailed in a given case. . . .

At the time Title VII was written, over half of the states had enacted some form of equal employment legislation. . . . Senator Humphrey, an advocate of strong enforcement, emphasized the state role under the legislation:

> We recognized that many States already have functioning antidiscrimination programs to insure equal access to places of public accommodation and equal employment opportunity. We sought merely to guarantee that these States — and other States which may establish such programs — will be given every opportunity to employ their expertise and experience without premature interference by the Federal Government. [110 Cong. Rec. 12725 (1964).]

Indeed, New York's fair employment laws were referred to in the Congressional debates by proponents of the legislation as an example of existing state legislation effectively combatting employment discrimination.

Because Congress must "clearly manifest" its intent to depart from § 1738, our prior decisions construing Title VII in situations where § 1738 is inapplicable are not dispositive. They establish only that *initial resort* to state administrative remedies does not deprive an individual of a right to a federal trial de novo on a Title VII claim. In McDonnell Douglas Corp v. Green, 411 U.S. 792 (1973) and Chandler v. Roudebush, 415 U.S. 820 (1976), we held that the "civil action" in federal court following an EEOC decision was intended to be a trial de novo. This holding, clearly supported by the legislative history, is not a holding that a prior state court judgment can be disregarded.

The petitioners and the Courts of Appeals which have denied res judicata effect to such judgments rely heavily on our statement in Alexander v. Gardner-Denver, supra, that "final responsibility for enforcement of Title VII is vested with federal courts." 415 U.S. at 44. We did not say, and our language should not be read to imply, that by vesting "final responsibility" in one forum, Congress intended to deny finality to decisions in another. The context of the statement makes this clear. In describing the operation of Title VII, we noted that the EEOC cannot adjudicate claims or impose sanctions; that responsibility, the "final responsibility of enforcement," must rest in federal court.

The holding in *Gardner-Denver* was that a private arbitration decision concerning an employment discrimination claim did not bind the federal courts. Arbitration decisions, of course, are not subject to the mandate of § 1738. Furthermore, unlike arbitration hearings under collective bargaining agreements, state fair employment practice laws are explicitly made part of the Title VII enforcement scheme. Our decision in *Gardner-Denver* explicitly recognized the "distinctly separate nature of these contractual and statutory rights." Id. at 50. Here we are dealing with a state statutory right, subject to state enforcement in a manner expressly provided for by the federal Act.

Finally, the comity and federalism interests embodied in § 1738 are not compromised by the application of res judicata and collateral estoppel in Title VII cases. Petitioner maintains that the decision of the Court of Appeals will deter claimants from seeking state court review of their claims ultimately leading to a deterioration in the quality of the state administrative process. On the contrary, stripping state court judgments of finality would be far more destructive to the quality of adjudication by lessening the incentive for full participation by the parties and for searching review by state officials. Depriving state judgments of finality not only would violate basic tenets of comity and federalism, Board of Regents v. Tomanio, 446 U.S. 478, 488, 491-492 (1980), but also would reduce the incentive for states to work towards effective and meaningful anti-discrimination systems. . . .

The petitioner nevertheless contends that the judgment should not bar his Title VII action because the New York courts did not resolve the issue that the District Court must hear under Title VII — whether Kremer had suffered discriminatory treatment — and because the procedures provided were inadequate. Neither contention is persuasive. Although the claims presented to the NYHRD and subsequently reviewed by the Appellate Division were necessarily based on New York law, the alleged discriminatory acts are prohibited by both federal and state laws. The elements of a successful employment discrimination claim are virtually identical; petitioner could not succeed on a Title VII claim consistently with the judgment of the NYHRD that there is no reason to believe he was terminated or not rehired because of national origin or religion. The Appellate Division's affirmance of the NYHRD's dismissal necessarily decided that petitioner's claim under New York law was meritless, and thus it also decided that a Title VII claim arising from the same events would be equally meritless.

The more serious contention is that even though administrative proceedings and judicial review are legally sufficient to be given preclusive effect in New York, they should be deemed so fundamentally flawed as to be denied recognition under § 1738. We have previously recognized that the judicially created doctrine of collateral estoppel does not apply when the party against whom the earlier decision is asserted did not have a "full and fair opportunity" to litigate the claim or issue, Allen v. McCurry, 449 U.S. at 95; Montana v. United States, 440 U.S. 147, 153 (1979); Blonder-Tongue Laboratories, Inc. v. University of Illinois Foundation, 402 U.S. 313, 328-329 (1971). "Redetermination of issues is warranted if there is reason to doubt the quality, extensiveness, or fairness of the procedures followed in the prior litigation." Montana v. United States, 440 U.S. at 164 n.11. Cf. Gibson v. Berryhill, 411 U.S. 564 (1973).

We have little doubt that Kremer received all the process that was constitutionally required in rejecting his claim that he had been discriminatorily discharged contrary to the statute. We must bear in mind that no single model of procedural fairness, let alone a particular form of procedure, is dictated by the Due Process Clause. Mitchell v. W. T. Grant Co., 416 U.S. 600, 610 (1974); Inland Empire Council v. Millis, 325 U.S. 697, 710 (1945). "The very nature of due process negates any concept of inflexible procedures universally applicable to every imaginable situation." Mitchell v. W.T. Grant Co., 416 U.S. at 610 (internal quotations omitted). Under New York law, a claim of employment discrimination requires the NYHRD to investigate whether there is "probable cause" to believe that the complaint is true. Before this determination of probable cause is made, the claimant is entitled to a "full opportunity to present on the record, though informally, his charges against his employer or other respondent, including the right to submit all exhibits which he wishes to present and testimony of witnesses in addition to his own testimony." State Div. of Human Rights v. New York State Drug Abuse Commn., 59 A.D. 332, 336 (1977). The complainant also is entitled to an opportunity "to rebut evidence submitted by or obtained from the respondent." 9 N.Y.C.R.R. § 465.6. He may have an attorney assist him and may ask the division to issue subpoenas. 9 N.Y.C.R.R. § 465.12(c).

If the investigation disclosed probable cause and efforts at conciliation fail, the NYHRD must conduct a public hearing to determine the merits of the complaint. N.Y. Exec. Law § 297(4)(a) (McKinney 1972). A public hearing must also be held if the Human Rights Appeal Board finds "there has not been a full investigation and opportunity for the complainant to present his contentions and evidence, with a full record." State Div. of Human Rights v. New York State Drug Abuse Commn., 59 A.D.2d at 337. Finally, judicial review in the Appellate Division is available to assure that a claimant is not denied any of the procedural rights to which he was entitled and that the NYHRD's determination was not arbitrary and capricious. N.Y. Civ. Prac. Law § 7803 (McKinney 1972). . . .

We have no hesitation in concluding that this panoply of procedures, complemented by administrative as well as judicial review, is sufficient under the Due Process Clause. Only where the evidence submitted by the claimant fails, as a matter of law, to reveal any merit to the complaint may the Department make a determination of no probable cause without holding a hearing. Flah's, Inc. v. Schneider, 71 A.D.2d 993 (1979). . . . And before that determination may be reached, New York requires the Commission to make a full investigation, wherein the complainant has full opportunity to present his evidence, under oath if he so requests. State Div. of Human Rights v. New York State Drug Abuse Control Commission, 59 A.D. at 336. The fact that Mr. Kremer failed to avail himself of the full procedures provided by state law does not constitute a sign of their inadequacy. Cf. Judice v. Vail, 430 U.S. 327, 337 (1977). . . .

In our system of jurisprudence the usual rule is that merits of a legal claim once decided in a court of competent jurisdiction are not subject to redetermination in another forum. Such a fundamental departure from traditional rules of preclusion, enacted into federal law, can be justified only if plainly stated by Congress. Because there is no "affirmative showing" of a "clear and manifest" legislative purpose in Title VII to deny res judicata or collateral estoppel effect to a state court judgment affirming that a claim of employment discrimination is unproven, and because the procedures provided in New York for the determination of such claims offer a full and fair opportunity to litigate the merits, the judgment of the Court of Appeals is

Affirmed.

JUSTICE BLACKMUN, with whom JUSTICE BRENNAN and JUSTICE MARSHALL join, dissenting.

Title VII provides that no charge may be filed until 60 days "after proceedings have been commenced under the State or local law, unless such proceedings have been earlier terminated." § 706(c), 42 U.S.C. § 2000e-5(c). After a charge is filed, the Equal Employment Opportunity Commission (EEOC) may take action and, eventually, the complainant may file suit, §§ 706(b) and (f)(1). By permitting a charge to be filed after termination of state proceedings, the statute expressly contemplates that a plaintiff may bring suit despite a state finding of no discrimination.

This fact is also made clear by § 706(b). In 1972, by Pub. L. 92-261, § 4, 86 Stat. 104, Congress amended that section by directing that the EEOC "accord substantial weight to final findings and orders made by State or local authorities in proceedings commenced under State or local law." If the original version of Title VII had given the outcomes of state "proceedings" preclusive effect, Congress would not have found it necessary to amend the statute in 1972 to direct that they be given "substantial weight." And if in 1972 Congress had intended final decisions in state "proceedings" to have preclusive effect, it certainly would not have instructed that they be given "substantial weight."

Thus, Congress expressly recognized in both § 706(b) and § 706(c) that a complainant could bring a Title VII suit in federal court despite the conclusion of state "proceedings."

Yet the Court nevertheless finds that petitioner's Title VII suit is precluded by the termination of state "proceedings." In this case, the New York State Division of Human Rights (NYHRD) found no probable cause to believe that petitioner had been a victim of discrimination. Under the Court's own rule, that determination in itself does not bar petitioner from filing a Title VII suit in federal district court. According to the Court, however, petitioner lost his opportunity to bring a federal suit when he unsuccessfully sought review of the state agency's decision in the New York courts. As the Court applies preclusion principles to Title VII, the state court affirmance of the state agency decision—*not* the state agency decision itself—blocks any subsequent Title VII suit.

State court review is merely the last step in the administrative process, the final means of review of the state *agency's* decision. For instance, in New York, the NYHRD "is primarily responsible for administering the law and to that end has been granted broad powers to eliminate discriminatory practices." Imperial Diner, Inc. v. State Human Rights Appeal Bd., 52

N.Y.2d 72, 77 (1980). When, as in this case, the NYHRD finds no probable cause, a reviewing court must affirm the division's decision unless it is "arbitrary, capricious or characterized by abuse of discretion or clearly unwarranted exercise of discretion," see N.Y. Exec. Law § 297-a(7)(e) (McKinney 1972), that is, unless the decision is "devoid of a rational basis." . . . If the agency decides to hold a hearing, its decision must be affirmed if it is "supported by substantial evidence on the whole record." N.Y. Exec. Law § 297-a(7)(d) (McKinney Supp. 1981). . . .

This review therefore, is not de novo in the state courts. When it affirms the agency's decision, the reviewing court does not determine that the division was correct. In fact, the court may not "substitute its judgment for that of the [NYHRD]," State Division of Human Rights v. Mecca Kendall Corp., 53 App. Div. 2d 201, 203-204 (1976); the court is "not empowered to find new facts or take a different view of the weight of the evidence if the [NYHRD's] determination is supported by substantial evidence," State Division of Human Rights v. Columbia University, 39 N.Y.2d 612, 616 (1976). . . . In affirming, the reviewing court finds only that the agency's conclusion "was a reasonable one and thus may not be set aside by the courts although a contrary decision may 'have been reasonable and also sustainable.'" Imperial Diner, Inc. v. State Human Rights Appeal Bd., 52 N.Y.2d at 79 (internal quotations omitted).

The Court purports to give preclusive effect to the New York court's decision. But the Appellate Division made no finding one way or the other concerning the *merits* of petitioner's discrimination claim. The NYHRD, not the New York court, dismissed petitioner's complaint for lack of probable cause. In affirming, the court merely found that the *agency's* decision was not arbitrary or capricious. Thus, although it claims to grant a state *court* decision preclusive effect, in fact the Court bars petitioner's suit based on the state *agency's* decision of no probable cause. The Court thereby disregards the express provisions of Title VII, for, as the Court acknowledges, Congress has decided that an adverse state agency decision will not prevent a complainant's subsequent Title VII suit.

Finally, if the Court is in fact giving preclusive effect only to the state *court* decision, the Court misapplies 28 U.S.C. § 1738 by barring petitioner's suit. The state reviewing court never considered the merits of petitioner's discrimination claim, the subject matter of a Title VII suit in federal court. It is a basic principle of preclusion doctrine . . . that a decision in one judicial proceeding cannot bar a subsequent suit raising issues that were not relevant to the first decision. . . . Here, the state court decided only whether the state agency decision was arbitrary or capricious. Since the discrimination claim, not the validity of the state agency's decision, is the issue before the federal court, under § 1738 the state court's decision by itself cannot preclude a federal Title VII suit.

Thus, the Court is doing one of two things: either it is granting preclusive effect to the state agency's decision, a course that it concedes would violate Title VII, or it is misapplying § 1738 by giving preclusive effect to a state court decision that did not address the issue before the federal court. . . .

The Court's decision is directly contrary to . . . congressional intent. The lesson of the Court's ruling is: *An unsuccessful state discrimination complainant should not seek state judicial review.* If a discrimination complainant pursues state judicial review and loses—a likely result given the deferential standard of review in state court—he forfeits his right to seek redress in a federal court. If, however, he simply bypasses the state courts, he can proceed to the EEOC and ultimately to federal court. Instead of a deferential review of an agency record, he will receive in federal court a de novo hearing accompanied by procedural aids such as broad discovery rules and the ability to subpoena witnesses. Thus, paradoxically, the Court effectively has eliminated state reviewing courts from the fight against discrimination in an entire class of cases. Consequently, the state courts will not have a chance to correct state agency errors when the agencies rule against discrimination victims, and the quality of state agency decisionmaking can only deteriorate. It is a perverse sort of comity that eliminates the reviewing function of state courts in the name of giving their decision due respect.

. . . Invariably, there will be some complainants who will not be aware of today's decision. The Court has thus constructed a rule that will serve as a trap for the unwary pro se or poorly represented complainant. For these complainants, their sole remedy lies in the state administrative processes. Yet, inevitably those agencies do not give all discrimination complaints careful attention. Often hampered by "inadequate procedures" or "an inadequate budget," see 110 Cong. Rec. 7205 (1964), the state antidiscrimination agency may give a discrimination charge less than the close examination it would receive in federal court. When, as in this case, the state agency dismisses for lack of probable cause, the discrimination complainant is particularly at risk, because inadequate staffing of state agencies can lead to "a tendency to dismiss too many complaints for alleged lack of probable cause." Though state courts may be diligent in reviewing agency dismissals for no probable cause, the nature of the agency's deliberations combined with deferential judicial review can lead only to discrimination charges receiving less careful consideration than Congress intended when it passed Title VII. The Court's decision thus cannot be squared with the congressional intent that the fight against discrimination be a policy "of the highest priority." Newman v. Piggie Park Enterprises, 390 U.S. 400, 402 (1968). . . .

I dissent.

Note: England v. Louisiana State Bd. of Medical Examiners, 375 U.S. 411 (1964)

Chiropractors brought an action challenging the Louisiana Medical Practice Act as applied to them by the Louisiana State Board of Medical Examiners, who had decided that the practice of chiropractic is the practice of medicine and requires full compliance with the educational requirements of the act. The plaintiffs sought an injunction, claiming that the interpretation violated the Fourteenth Amendment. The district court abstained from deciding the federal constitutional issue, pending state court review of the board's action to determine its legality under the act and the Louisiana Constitution.

Plaintiffs proceeded then to present their challenge in state court, arguing that the board's action was a violation of the act, the Louisiana Constitution, and the Fourteenth Amendment. The Louisiana courts upheld the board. Plaintiffs then returned to the district court and sought federal court consideration of the federal constitutional challenge. The district court held that the Louisiana state court judgment was a bar to further litigation inasmuch as the plaintiffs had submitted the federal challenge to the state court. The proper remedy, if any, for possible error by the Louisiana courts should be sought in the Supreme Court of the United States.

Plaintiffs then appealed to the Supreme Court from this federal judgment. The Court indicated that the district court was correct in the view that an unreserved submission of the federal constitutional challenge to the state court should serve as a bar to further litigation. But, the Court cautioned, it was also correct that the Louisiana court was entitled to hear argument on the federal constitutional issue as a means of interpreting the state law, which it would, of course, normally prefer to interpret in a way that would avoid serious constitutional challenge. Inasmuch as these chiropractors may have been confused by Supreme Court cases making this distinction, and may have unreservedly submitted the issue to state court in the mistaken belief that this was required, they should be given another chance to present their federal constitutional argument. But now that the Supreme Court has clarified the law in this regard, other litigants will not be permitted to avail themselves of two opportunities to make unreserved presentations of constitutional arguments to both state and federal courts.

For discussion and application of *England*, see DLX Inc. v. Kentucky, 381 F.3d 51 (6th Cir. 2004).

Note: Matsushita Electrical Indus. Co. v. Epstein, 516 U.S. 367 (1996)

The Court held that where a claim would have been barred by Delaware law, the statutory version of the Full Faith and Credit Clause (28 U.S.C. § 1738) required federal courts to give the same preclusive effect to the claims as Delaware law would give it. The case involved a shareholders' derivative suit filed in Delaware state court based on state law, and a class action suit filed in federal court based on federal law, over which federal courts had exclusive jurisdiction. The parties in the Delaware suit reached a global settlement, which stated that the parties gave up all state and federal claims. The court approved and entered judgment on the settlement. The defendant in the federal action then invoked the settlement as preclusive of the then-pending federal claims. Even though these federal claims could *not* have been filed in Delaware court, the Supreme Court held that they were barred in federal court, because under Delaware law the unasserted claims would have been barred.

On remand from the Supreme Court, a panel of the appellate court held that the plaintiffs' lawyers' decision to settle the Delaware state court action and thus to forgo the federal claims was inadequate representation that served the plaintiffs' counsels' interests at the expense of the shareholders' interests. 126 F.3d 1235 (9th Cir. 1997).

Note: Effect of Res Judicata on Amount in Controversy

Generally, "waivable affirmative defenses" may not be used "to whittle down the amount in controversy." Scherer v. The Equitable Life Assurance Soc. of U.S., 347 F.3d 394, 398 (2d Cir. 2003). This means that the res judicata effect of a prior state court judgment against a plaintiff cannot be used in a subsequent federal suit to establish that the amount in controversy is below the jurisdictional limit. Id. at 399 (reversing 12(b)(1) dismissal of federal suit for insurance benefits covering the period after plaintiff's earlier suit for benefits in state court).

Brown v. Felsen

442 U.S. 127 (1979)

JUSTICE BLACKMUN delivered the opinion of the Court.

Petitioner G. Garvin Brown III was a guarantor for respondent Mark Paul Felsen and Felsen's car dealership, Le Mans Motors, Inc. Petitioner's guaranty secured a bank loan that financed the dealership's trading in Lotus, Ferrari, and Lamborghini automobiles. In 1975, the lender brought a collection suit against petitioner, respondent, and Le Mans in Colorado state court. Petitioner filed an answer to the bank's complaint, and a cross-claim against respondent and Le Mans. The answer and the cross-claim, by incorporating the answer, alleged that respondent and Le Mans induced petitioner to sign the guaranty "by misrepresentations and nondisclosures of material facts." . . . The suit was settled by a stipulation. It provided that the bank should recover jointly and severally against all three defendants, and that petitioner should have judgment against respondent and Le Mans. Neither the stipulation nor the resulting judgment indicated the cause of action on which respondent's liability to petitioner was based. Because the case was settled, respondent's sworn deposition was never made part of the court record.

A short time later, respondent filed a petition for voluntary bankruptcy and sought to have his debt to petitioner discharged. Through discharge the Bankruptcy Act provides "a new opportunity in life and a clear field for future effort, unhampered by the pressure and discouragement of preexisting debt," Local Loan Co. v. Hunt, 292 U.S. 234, 244 (1934). By seeking discharge, however, respondent placed the rectitude of his prior dealings squarely in issue, for, as the Court has noted, the Act limits that opportunity to the "honest but unfortunate debtor." Ibid. Section 14 of the Act, 11 U.S.C. § 32, specifies that a *debtor* may not obtain a discharge if he has committed certain crimes or offenses. Section 17a, the focus of this case, provides that certain *types* of debts are not affected by a discharge. These include, under § 17a(2), "liabilities for obtaining money or property by false pretenses or false representations . . . or for willful and malicious conversion of the property of another" and, under § 17a(4), debts that "were created by his fraud, embezzlement, misappropriation, or defalcation while acting as an officer or in any fiduciary capacity."

In the bankruptcy court petitioner sought to establish that respondent's debt to petitioner was not dischargeable. Petitioner alleged that the guaranty debt was the product of respondent's fraud, deceit, and malicious conversion and so came within §§ 17a(2) and 17a(4). Petitioner contended that respondent had prepared false title certificates, sold automobiles out of trust, and applied the proceeds to private purposes. Respondent answered and moved for summary judgment. Respondent said that the prior state-court proceeding did not result in a finding of fraud, and contended that res judicata barred relitigation of the nature of respondent's debt to petitioner, even though the application of § 17 had not been in issue in the prior proceeding.

Before 1970, such res judicata claims were seldom heard in federal court. Traditionally, the bankruptcy court determined whether the debtor merited a discharge under § 14, but left the dischargeability under § 17 of a particular debt to the court in which the creditor sued, after bankruptcy, to enforce his prior judgment. Typically, that court was a state court. In 1970, however, Congress altered § 17 to require creditors to apply to the bankruptcy court for adjudication of certain dischargeability questions, including those arising under §§ 17a(2) and 17a(4). . . .

The bankruptcy court here . . . confined its consideration to the judgment, pleadings, exhibits, and stipulation which were in the state-court record. It declined to hear other evidence, and it refused to consider respondent's deposition that had never been made part of that record. The court concluded that, because neither the judgment nor the record showed that petitioner's allegation of misrepresentation was the basis for the judgment on the cross-claim against respondent, the liability had not been shown to be within §§ 17a(2) and 17a(4). The court granted summary judgment for respondent and held that the debt was dischargeable.

Both the United States District Court for the District of Colorado and the United States Court of Appeals for the Tenth Circuit affirmed. . . . We granted certiorari. . . .

Bankruptcy often breeds litigation, and respondent contends that the policy of repose which underlies res judicata has particular force here. Respondent argues that petitioner chose not to press the question of fraud in the state-court proceeding even though an adjudication of fraud would have entitled petitioner to extraordinary remedies such as exemplary damages and body execution.[5] Respondent says that because petitioner did not obtain a stipulation concerning fraud in the prior state-court proceeding, he is now barred from litigating matters that could have been concluded in the consent judgment. See United States v. Armour & Co., 402 U.S. 673, 681-682 (1971). Applying res judicata in bankruptcy court, it is argued, prevents a creditor from raising as an afterthought claims so insubstantial that they had previously been overlooked. In respondent's view, res judicata stops harassment and promotes the orderly processes of justice by encouraging the consolidation of the entire dispute between debtor and creditor into one prior proceeding.

Because res judicata may govern grounds and defenses not previously litigated, however, it blockades unexplored paths that may lead to truth. For the sake of repose, res judicata shields the fraud and the cheat as well as the honest person. It therefore is to be invoked only after careful inquiry. Petitioner contends, and we agree, that here careful inquiry reveals that neither the interests served by res judicata, the process of orderly adjudication in state courts, nor the policies of the Bankruptcy Act would be well served by foreclosing petitioner from submitting additional evidence to prove his case.

. . . [P]etitioner readily concedes the prior decree is binding. That is the cornerstone of his claim. He does not assert a new ground for recovery, nor does he attack the validity of the prior judgment. Rather, what he is attempting to meet here is the new defense of bankruptcy which respondent has interposed between petitioner and the sum determined to be due him. A substantial minority of state-court decisions, particularly those following Fidelity & Casualty Co. v. Golombosky, 50 A.2d 817, 819-820 (1946) (Maltbie, C.J.), have recognized this distinction and have refused to apply res judicata in determining the dischargeability of debts previously reduced to judgment. Respondent has upset the repose that would justify treating the prior state-court proceeding as final, and it would hardly promote confidence in judgments to prevent petitioner from meeting respondent's new initiative. . . .

Respondent contends that the § 17 questions raised here, or similar issues of state law, could have been considered in the prior state-court proceeding and therefore are not "new." Respondent argues that the state-court collection suit is the appropriate forum for resolving all debtor-creditor disputes, including those concerning dischargeability. While in some circumstances the consolidation of proceedings may be desirable, here consolidation would undercut a statutory policy in favor of resolving § 17 questions in bankruptcy court, and would force state courts to decide these questions at a stage when they are not directly in issue and neither

5. In Colorado, body execution is a statutory remedy which, under certain circumstances, permits a creditor to have a tortious judgment debtor imprisoned at the creditor's expense. See Hershey v. People, 12 P.2d 345 (1932); Colo. Rev. Stat. § 13-59-103 (1973).

party has a full incentive to litigate them. See In re Pigge, 539 F.2d 369, 371-372 (4th Cir. 1976).

Considerations material to discharge are irrelevant to the ordinary collection proceeding. The creditor sues on the instrument which created the debt. Even if an issue similar to those created by § 17 should arise, the state-law concept is likely to differ from that adopted in the federal statute.... For example, in Davis v. Aetna Acceptance Co., 293 U.S. 328 (1934), the Court held that a mere technical conversion by a bankrupt dealer in automobiles was not "willful and malicious" within the meaning of § 17 by virtue of being actionable under state law, nor was a misappropriation of funds, held pursuant to a "trust receipt," a breach of an express trust sufficient to constitute an act done "as an officer or in any fiduciary capacity."

When § 17 issues are not identical to those arising under state law, the parties have little incentive to litigate them. In the collection suit, the debtor's bankruptcy is still hypothetical. The rule proposed by respondent would force an otherwise unwilling party to try § 17 questions to the hilt in order to protect himself against the mere possibility that a debtor might take bankruptcy in the future. In many cases such litigation would prove, in the end, to have been entirely unnecessary, and it is not surprising that at least one state court has expressly refused to embroil itself in an advisory adjudication of this kind. See Pioneer Finance & Thrift Co. v. Powell, 443 P.2d 389 (1968). And absent trial on the merits, there is no particular reason to favor extraneous facts thrown into a record for § 17 purposes over facts adduced before the bankruptcy court.

... If a state court should expressly rule on § 17 questions, then giving finality to those rulings would undercut Congress' intention to commit § 17 issues to the jurisdiction of the bankruptcy court. The 1970 amendments eliminated postbankruptcy state-court collection suits as a means of resolving certain § 17 dischargeability questions. In those suits, creditors had taken advantage of debtors who were unable to retain counsel because bankruptcy had stripped them of their assets. Congress' primary purpose was to stop that abuse. A secondary purpose, however, was to take these § 17 claims away from state courts that seldom dealt with the federal bankruptcy laws and to give those claims to the bankruptcy court so that it could develop expertise in handling them. By the express terms of the Constitution, bankruptcy law is federal law, U.S. Const., Art. I, § 8, cl. 4, and the Senate Report accompanying the amendment described the bankruptcy court's jurisdiction over these § 17 claims as "exclusive," S. Rep. No. 91-1173, p.2 (1970). While Congress did not expressly confront the problem created by prebankruptcy state-court adjudications, it would be inconsistent with the philosophy of the 1970 amendments to adopt a policy of res judicata which takes these § 17 questions away from bankruptcy courts and forces them back into state courts....

Respondent ... contends that petitioner had an adequate incentive to prove state-law fraud, which might have entailed proof identical to that required by § 17. Petitioner, however, rejected whatever lure exemplary damages and body execution may have provided. That rejection does not conclusively show that petitioner thought respondent was innocent of fraud. Petitioner may have thought those remedies would not be advantageous to him.[8] While respondent is certainly entitled to claim that res judicata would bar further pursuit of those extraordinary remedies in state court, their hypothetical desirability provides no basis for preventing petitioner from recovering on the debt, the remedy he elected from the beginning. . . .

Refusing to apply res judicata here would permit the bankruptcy court to make an accurate determination whether respondent in fact committed the deceit, fraud, and malicious conversion which petitioner alleges. These questions are now, for the first time, squarely in issue. They are the type of question Congress intended that the bankruptcy court would resolve. That court can weigh all the evidence, and it can also take into account whether or not petitioner's failure to press these allegations at an earlier time betrays a weakness in his case on the merits.

The judgment of the Court of Appeals is *reversed*.

Baker v. General Motors Corporation

522 U.S. 222 (1998)

JUSTICE GINSBURG delivered the opinion of the Court.

This case concerns the authority of one State's court to order that a witness' testimony shall not be heard in any court of the United States. In settlement of claims and counterclaims precipitated by the discharge of Ronald Elwell, a former General Motors Corporation (GM) engineering analyst, GM paid Elwell an undisclosed sum of money, and the parties agreed to a permanent injunction. As stipulated by GM and Elwell and entered by a Michigan County Court, the injunction prohibited Elwell from "testifying, without the prior written consent of [GM], . . . as . . . a witness of any kind . . . in any litigation already filed, or to be filed in the future, involving [GM] as an owner, seller, manufacturer and/or designer. . . ." GM separately agreed, however, that if Elwell were ordered to testify by a court or other tribunal, such testimony would not be actionable as a violation of the Michigan court's injunction or the GM-Elwell agreement.

8. So long as a debtor is solvent, the debtor and creditor alike may prefer a simple contract suit to complex tort litigation. Default and consent judgment are common in collection proceedings. For the creditor, the prospect of increased attorneys' fees and the likelihood of driving the debtor into bankruptcy may offset the advantages of exemplary damages or other extraordinary remedies. Bankruptcy deprives the debtor of his creditworthiness and so impairs his ability to repay. In the words of a Shakespearean creditor, fearing the worst: "When every feather sticks in his own wing, Lord Timon will be left a naked Gull, Which flashes now a Phoenix." Timon of Athens, Act 2, Scene 1, in VII The Works of Shakespeare 294 (Henley ed. 1903). Nor does body execution aid in the collection of a debt if the creditor needs to be out of jail in order to earn the money to repay the debt.

After entry of the stipulated injunction in Michigan, Elwell was subpoenaed to testify in a product liability action commenced in Missouri by plaintiffs who were not involved in the Michigan case. The question presented is whether the national full faith and credit command bars Elwell's testimony in the Missouri case. We hold that Elwell may testify in the Missouri action without offense to the full faith and credit requirement.

I

Two lawsuits, initiated by different parties in different states, gave rise to the full faith and credit issue before us. One suit involved a severed employment relationship, the other, a wrongful-death complaint. We describe each controversy in turn.

A

The Suit Between Elwell and General Motors

Ronald Elwell was a GM employee from 1959 until 1989. For fifteen of those years, beginning in 1971, Elwell was assigned to the Engineering Analysis Group, which studied the performance of GM vehicles, most particularly vehicles involved in product liability litigation. Elwell's studies and research concentrated on vehicular fires. He assisted in improving the performance of GM products by suggesting changes in fuel line designs. During the course of his employment, Elwell frequently aided GM lawyers engaged in defending GM against product liability actions. Beginning in 1987, the Elwell-GM employment relationship soured. GM and Elwell first negotiated an agreement under which Elwell would retire after serving as a GM consultant for two years. When the time came for Elwell to retire, however, disagreement again surfaced and continued into 1991.

In May 1991, plaintiffs in a product liability action pending in Georgia deposed Elwell. The Georgia case involved a GM pickup truck fuel tank that burst into flames just after a collision. During the deposition, and over the objection of counsel for GM, Elwell gave testimony that differed markedly from testimony he had given when serving as an in-house expert witness for GM. Specifically, Elwell had several times defended the safety and crashworthiness of the pickup's fuel system. On deposition in the Georgia action, however, Elwell testified that the GM pickup truck fuel system was inferior in comparison to competing products.

A month later, Elwell sued GM in a Michigan County Court, alleging wrongful discharge and other tort and contract claims. GM counterclaimed, contending that Elwell had breached his fiduciary duty to GM by disclosing privileged and confidential information and misappropriating documents. In response to GM's motion for a preliminary injunction, and after a hearing, the Michigan trial court, on November 22, 1991, enjoined Elwell from "consulting or discussing with or disclosing to any person any of General Motors Corporation's trade secrets[,] confidential information or matters of attorney-client work product relating in any manner to the subject matter of any products liability litigation whether already filed or [to be] filed in the future which Ronald Elwell received, had knowledge of, or was entrusted with during his employment with General Motors Corporation." Elwell v. General Motors Corp., No. 91-115946NZ (Wayne Cty.) (Order Granting in Part, Denying in Part Injunctive Relief, pp. 1-2), App. 9-10.

In August 1992, GM and Elwell entered into a settlement under which Elwell received an undisclosed sum of money. The parties also stipulated to the entry of a permanent injunction and jointly filed with the Michigan court both the stipulation and the agreed-upon injunction. . . .

Elwell and GM included in their separate settlement agreement a more general limitation. If a court or other tribunal ordered Elwell to testify, his testimony would "in no way" support a GM action for violation of the injunction or the settlement agreement:

> It is agreed that [Elwell's] appearance and testimony, if any, at hearings on Motions to quash subpoena or at deposition or trial or other official proceeding, if the Court or other tribunal so orders, will in no way form a basis for an action in violation of the Permanent Injunction or this Agreement. [Settlement Agreement, at 10, as quoted in 86 F.3d 811, 820, n.11 (8th Cir. 1996).]

In the six years since the Elwell-GM settlement, Elwell has testified against GM both in Georgia (pursuant to [an agreed-upon] exception contained in the injunction) and in several other jurisdictions in which Elwell has been subpoenaed to testify.

B

The Suit Between the Bakers and General Motors

Having described the Elwell-GM employment termination litigation, we next summarize the wrongful-death complaint underlying this case. The decedent, Beverly Garner, was a front-seat passenger in a 1985 Chevrolet S-10 Blazer involved in a February 1990 Missouri highway accident. The Blazer's engine caught fire, and both driver and passenger died. In September 1991, Garner's sons, Kenneth and Steven Baker, commenced a wrongful death product liability action against GM in a Missouri state court. The Bakers alleged that a faulty fuel pump in the 1985 Blazer caused the engine fire that killed their mother. GM removed the case to federal court on the basis of the parties' diverse citizenship. On the merits, GM asserted that the fuel pump was neither faulty nor the cause of the fire, and that collision impact injuries alone caused Garner's death.

The Bakers sought both to depose Elwell and to call him as a witness at trial. GM objected to Elwell's appearance as a deponent or trial witness on the ground that the Michigan injunction barred his testimony. In response, the Bakers urged that the Michigan injunction did not override a Missouri subpoena for Elwell's testimony. The Bakers further noted that, under the Elwell-GM settlement agreement, Elwell could testify if a court so ordered, and such testimony would not be actionable as a violation of the Michigan injunction.

After *in camera* review of the Michigan injunction and the settlement agreement, the Federal District Court in Missouri allowed the Bakers to depose Elwell and to call him as a witness at trial. Responding to GM's objection, the District Court stated alternative grounds for its ruling: (1) Michigan's injunction need not be enforced because blocking Elwell's testimony would violate Missouri's "public policy," which shielded from disclosure only privileged or otherwise confidential information; (2) just as the injunction could be modified in Michigan, so a court elsewhere could modify the decree.

At trial, Elwell testified in support of the Bakers' claim that the alleged defect in the fuel pump system contributed to the post-collision fire. In addition, he identified and described a 1973 internal GM memorandum bearing on the risk of fuel-fed engine fires. Following trial, the jury awarded the Bakers, $11.3 million in damages, and the District Court entered judgment on the jury's verdict.

The United States Court of Appeals for the Eighth Circuit reversed the District Court's judgment, ruling, *inter alia,* that Elwell's testimony should not have been admitted. 86 F.3d 811 (8th Cir. 1996). Assuming, *arguendo,* the existence of a public policy exception to the full faith and credit command, the Court of Appeals concluded that the District Court erroneously relied on Missouri's policy favoring disclosure of relevant, nonprivileged information, see id. at 818-19, for Missouri has an "equally strong public policy in favor of full faith and credit," id. at 819.

The Eighth Circuit also determined that the evidence was insufficient to show that the Michigan court would modify the injunction barring Elwell's testimony. See id. at 819-20. The Court of Appeals observed that the Michigan court "has been asked on several occasions to modify the injunction, [but] has yet to do so," and noted that, if the Michigan court did not intend to block Elwell's testimony in cases like the Bakers', "the injunction would . . . have been unnecessary." Id. at 820.

We granted certiorari to decide whether the full faith and credit requirement stops the Bakers, who were not parties to the Michigan proceeding, from obtaining Elwell's testimony in their Missouri wrongful death action. 520 U.S. 1142 (1997).

II

A

The Constitution's Full Faith and Credit Clause provides:

> Full Faith and Credit shall be given in each State to the public Acts, Records, and judicial Proceedings of every other State. And the Congress may by

general Laws prescribe the Manner in which such Acts, Records and Proceedings shall be proved, and the Effect thereof. [U.S. Const., Art. IV, § 1.]

Pursuant to that Clause, Congress has prescribed:

Such Acts, records and judicial proceedings or copies thereof, so authenticated, shall have the same full faith and credit in every court within the United States and its Territories and Possessions as they have by law or usage in the courts of such State, Territory or Possession from which they are taken. [28 U.S.C. § 1738.]

The animating purpose of the full faith and credit command, as this Court explained in Milwaukee County v. M.E. White Co., 296 U.S. 268 (1935),

was to alter the status of the several states as independent foreign sovereignties, each free to ignore obligations created under the laws or by the judicial proceedings of the others, and to make them integral parts of a single nation throughout which a remedy upon a just obligation might be demanded as of right, irrespective of the state of its origin. [Id. at 277.]

Our precedent differentiates the credit owed to laws (legislative measures and common law) and to judgments. "In numerous cases this Court has held that credit must be given to the judgment of another state although the forum would not be required to entertain the suit on which the judgment was founded." *Milwaukee County,* 296 U.S. at 277. The Full Faith and Credit Clause does not compel "a state to substitute the statutes of other states for its own statutes dealing with a subject matter concerning which it is competent to legislate." Pacific Employers Ins. Co. v. Industrial Accident Comm'n, 306 U.S. 493, 501 (1939); see Phillips Petroleum Co. v. Shutts, 472 U.S. 797, 818-819 (1985). Regarding judgments, however, the full faith and credit obligation is exacting. A final judgment in one State, if rendered by a court with adjudicatory authority over the subject matter and persons governed by the judgment, qualifies for recognition throughout the land. For claim and issue preclusion (res judicata) purposes, in other words, the judgment of the rendering State gains nationwide force.

A court may be guided by the forum State's "public policy" in determining the law applicable to a controversy. See Nevada v. Hall, 440 U.S. 410, 421-424 (1979). But our decisions support no roving "public policy exception" to the full faith and credit due judgments. See Estin v. Estin, 334 U.S. 541, 546 (1948) (Full Faith and Credit Clause "ordered submission . . . even to hostile policies reflected in the judgment of another State, because the practical operation of the federal system, which the Constitution designed, demanded it."); Fauntleroy v. Lum, 210 U.S. 230, 237 (1908) (judgment of Missouri court entitled to full faith and credit in Mississippi even if Missouri judgment rested on a misapprehension of Mississippi law). In assuming the existence of a ubiquitous "public policy exception" permitting one State to resist recognition of another State's judgment, the District Court in the Bakers' wrongful-death action, see supra, at 662, misread our precedent. "The full faith and credit clause is one of the provisions incorporated into the Constitution by its framers for the purpose of transforming an aggregation of independent, sovereign States into a nation." Sherrer v. Sherrer, 334 U.S. 343, 355 (1948). We are "aware of [no] considerations of local policy or law which could rightly be deemed to impair the force and effect which the full faith and credit clause and the Act of Congress require to be given to [a money] judgment outside the state of its rendition." Magnolia Petroleum Co. v. Hunt, 320 U.S. 430, 438 (1943).

The Court has never placed equity decrees outside the full faith and credit domain. Equity decrees for the payment of money have long been considered equivalent to judgments at law entitled to nationwide recognition. We see no reason why the preclusive effects of an adjudication on parties and those "in privity" with them, *i.e.*, claim preclusion and issue preclusion (res judicata and collateral estoppel), should differ depending solely upon the type of relief sought in a civil action. . . .

Full faith and credit, however, does not mean that States must adopt the practices of other States regarding the time, manner, and mechanisms for enforcing judgments. Enforcement measures do not travel with the sister State judgment as preclusive effects do; such measures remain subject to the even-handed control of forum law. . . .

Orders commanding action or inaction have been denied enforcement in a sister State when they purported to accomplish an official act within the exclusive province of that other State or interfered with litigation over which the ordering State had no authority. Thus, a sister State's decree concerning land ownership in another State has been held ineffective *to transfer title*, see Fall v. Eastin, 215 U.S. 1 (1909), although such a decree may indeed preclusively adjudicate the rights and obligations running between the *parties* to the foreign litigation, see e.g., Robertson v. Howard, 229 U.S. 254, 261 (1913) ("[I]t may not be doubted that a court of equity in one State in a proper case could compel a defendant before it to convey property situated in another State."). And antisuit injunctions regarding litigation elsewhere, even if compatible with due process as a direction constraining parties to the decree, . . . in fact have not controlled the second court's actions regarding litigation in that court. . . . Sanctions for violations of an injunction, in any event, are generally administered by the court that issued the injunction. . . .

B

What matters did the Michigan injunction legitimately conclude?

As earlier recounted, . . . the parties before the Michigan County Court, Elwell and GM, submitted an agreed-upon injunction, which the presiding judge signed. While no issue was joined, expressly litigated, and determined in the Michigan proceeding, that order is *claim* preclusive between Elwell and GM. Elwell's claim for wrongful discharge and his related contract and tort claims have "merged in the judgment," and he cannot sue again to recover more. See Parklane Hosiery Co. v. Shore, 439 U.S. 322, 326, n.5 (1979) ("Under the doctrine of res judicata, a judgment on the merits in a prior suit bars a second suit involving the same parties or their privies based on the same cause of action."); see also Restatement (Second) of Judgments § 17 (1980). Similarly, GM cannot sue Elwell elsewhere on the counterclaim GM asserted in Michigan. See id., § 23, Comment *a*, p. 194 ("A defendant who interposes a counterclaim is, in substance, a plaintiff, as far as the counterclaim is concerned, and the plaintiff is, in substance, a defendant.").

Michigan's judgment, however, cannot reach beyond the Elwell-GM controversy to control proceedings against GM brought in other States, by other parties, asserting claims the merits of which Michigan has not considered. Michigan has no power over those parties, and no basis for commanding them to become intervenors in the Elwell-GM dispute. See Martin v. Wilks, 490 U.S. 755, 761-63 (1989). Most essentially, Michigan lacks authority to control courts elsewhere by precluding them, in actions brought by strangers to the Michigan litigation, from determining for themselves what witnesses are competent to testify and what evidence is relevant and admissible in their search for the truth. . . .

As the District Court recognized, Michigan's decree could operate against Elwell to preclude him from *volunteering* his testimony. But a Michigan court cannot, by entering the injunction to which Elwell and GM stipulated, dictate to a court in another jurisdiction that evidence relevant in the Bakers' case—a controversy to which Michigan is foreign—shall be inadmissible. This conclusion creates no general exception to the full faith and credit command, and surely does not permit a State to refuse to honor a sister state judgment based on the forum's choice of law or policy preferences. Rather, we simply recognize that, just as the mechanisms for enforcing a judgment do not travel with the judgment itself for purposes of Full Faith and Credit, . . . and just as one State's judgment cannot automatically transfer title to land in another State, . . . similarly the Michigan decree cannot determine evidentiary issues in a lawsuit brought by parties who were not subject to the jurisdiction of the Michigan court. . . .

In sum, Michigan has no authority to shield a witness from another jurisdiction's subpoena power in a case involving persons and causes outside Michigan's governance. Recognition, under full faith and credit, is owed to dispositions Michigan has authority to order. But a Michigan decree cannot command obedience elsewhere on a matter the Michigan court lacks authority to resolve.

For the reasons stated, the judgment of the Court of Appeals for the Eighth Circuit is reversed, and the case is remanded for further proceedings consistent with this opinion.

It is so ordered.

JUSTICE KENNEDY, with whom JUSTICES O'CONNOR and THOMAS join, concurring in the judgment.

In my view the case is controlled by well-settled full faith and credit principles which render the majority's extended analysis unnecessary and, with all due respect, problematic in some degree. This separate opinion explains my approach.

I

The majority, of course, is correct to hold that when a judgment is presented to the courts of a second State it may not be denied enforcement based upon some disagreement with the laws of the State of rendition. Full faith and credit forbids the second State from questioning a judgment on these grounds. . . . We have often recognized the second State's obligation to give effect to another State's judgments even when the law underlying those judgments contravenes the public policy of the second State. . . .

My concern is that the majority, having stated the principle, proceeds to disregard it by announcing two broad exceptions. First, the majority would allow courts outside the issuing State to decline to enforce those judgments "purport[ing] to accomplish an official act within the exclusive province of [a sister] State." . . . Second, the basic rule of full faith and credit is said not to cover injunctions "interfer[ing] with litigation over which the ordering State had no authority." . . . The exceptions the majority recognizes are neither consistent with its rejection of a public policy exception to full faith and credit nor in accord with established rules implementing the Full Faith and Credit Clause. As employed to resolve this case, furthermore, the exceptions to full faith and credit have a potential for disrupting judgments, and this ought to give us considerable pause.

Our decisions have been careful not to foreclose all effect for the types of injunctions the majority would place outside the ambit of full faith and credit. These authorities seem to be disregarded by today's holding. For example, the majority chooses to discuss the extent to which courts may compel the conveyance of property in other jurisdictions. That subject has proven to be quite difficult. Some of our cases uphold actions by state courts affecting land outside their territorial reach. . . . Nor have we undertaken before today to announce an exception which denies full faith and credit based on the principle that the prior judgment interferes with litigation pending in another jurisdiction. . . . As a general matter, there is disagreement among the state courts as to their duty to recognize decrees enjoining proceedings in other courts.

Subjects which are at once so fundamental and so delicate as these ought to be addressed only in a case necessarily requiring their discussion, and even then with caution lest we announce rules which will not be sound in later application. We might be required to hold, if some future case raises the issue, that an otherwise valid judgment cannot intrude upon essential processes of courts outside the issuing State in certain narrow circumstances, but we need not announce or define that principle here. Even if some qualification of full faith and credit were required where the judicial processes of a second State are sought to be controlled in their procedural and institutional aspects, the Court's discussion does not provide sufficient guidance on how this exception should be construed in light of our precedents. . . . The Court's reliance upon unidentified principles to justify omitting certain types of injunctions from the doctrine's application leaves its decision in uneasy tension with its own rejection of a broad public policy exception to full faith and credit.

In any event, the rule would be an exception. Full faith and credit requires courts to do more than provide for direct enforcement of the judgments issued by other States. It also "requires federal courts to give the same preclusive effect to state court judgments that those judgments would be given in the courts of the State from which the judgments emerged." Kremer v. Chemical Constr. Corp., 456 U.S. 461, 466 (1982). Through full faith and credit, "the local doctrines of res judicata, speaking generally, become a part of national jurisprudence. . . ." Riley v. New York Trust Co., 315 U.S. 343, 349 (1942). And whether or not an injunction is enforceable in another State on its own terms, the courts of a second State are required to honor its issue preclusive effects.

II

The Bakers were neither parties to the earlier litigation nor subject to the jurisdiction of the Michigan courts. The majority pays scant attention to this circumstance, which becomes critical. . . . In our most recent full faith and credit cases, we have said that determining the force and effect of a judgment should be the first step in our analysis. A conclusion that the issuing State would not give the prior judgment preclusive effect ends the inquiry, making it unnecessary to determine the existence of any exceptions to full faith and credit. We cannot decline to inquire into these state-law questions when the inquiry will obviate new extensions or exceptions to full faith and credit.

If we honor the undoubted principle that courts need give a prior judgment no more force or effect than the issuing State gives it, the case before us is resolved. Here the Court of Appeals and both parties in their arguments before our Court seemed to embrace the assumption that Michigan would apply the full force of its judgment to the Bakers. Michigan law does not appear to support the assumption.

The simple fact is that the Bakers were not parties to the Michigan proceedings, and nothing indicates Michigan would make the novel assertion that its earlier injunction binds the Bakers or any other party not then before it or subject to its jurisdiction. For collateral estoppel to apply under Michigan law, "the same parties must have had a full opportunity to litigate the issue, and there must be mutuality of estoppel." Nummer v. Treasury Dept., 533 N.W.2d 250, 253 (internal quotations omitted), *cert. denied*, 516 U.S. 964 (1995). Since the Bakers were not parties to the Michigan proceedings and had no opportunity to litigate any of the issues presented, it appears that Michigan law would not treat them as bound by the judgment.

It makes no difference that the judgment in question is an injunction. The Michigan Supreme Court has twice rejected arguments that injunctions have preclusive effect in later litigation, relying in no small part on the fact that the persons against whom preclusion is asserted were not parties to the earlier litigation. Bacon v. Walden, 152 N.W. 1061, 1063 (1915) ("Defendant was not a party to [the prior injunctive] suit and was not as a matter of law affected or bound by the decree rendered in it."); Detroit v. Detroit Ry., 95 N.W. 992, 993 (1903) ("[T]he fact that defendant was in no way a party to the record is sufficient answer to the contention that the holding of the circuit judge in that [prior injunctive] case is a controlling determination of the present."). . . .

Although inconsistent on this point, GM disavows its desire to issue preclude the Bakers. . . . This is difficult to accept because in assessing the preclusive reach of a judgment we look to its practical effect. Despite its disclaimer, GM seeks to alter the course of the suit between it and the Bakers by preventing the Bakers from litigating the admissibility of Elwell's testimony. Furthermore, even were we to accept GM's argument that the Bakers are essentially irrelevant to this dispute, GM's argument is flawed on its own terms. Elwell, in the present litigation, does not seek to relitigate anything; he is a witness, not a party.

In all events, determining as a threshold matter the extent to which Michigan law gives preclusive effect to the injunction eliminates the need to decide whether full faith and credit applies to equitable decrees as a general matter or the extent to which the general rules of full faith and credit are subject to exceptions. Michigan law would not seek to bind the Bakers to the injunction and that suffices to resolve the case.

What about parties who lose in state court but believe the state court's decision violates federal constitutional law? Do the federal district courts have authority to entertain such claims or is an appeal to the United States Supreme Court the only option? Take a look at 28 U.S.C. § 1257. It provides a clear answer, doesn't it?

But what if the state court decision is quasi-legislative? And what is the effect of a state judgment on a related and still pending federal case? These issues converged in the following case interpreting the so-called *Rooker-Feldman* doctrine.

Exxon Mobil Corp. v. Saudi Basic Indus. Corp.

544 U.S. 280 (2005)

JUSTICE GINSBURG delivered the opinion of the Court.

This case concerns what has come to be known as the *Rooker-Feldman* doctrine, applied by this Court only twice, first in Rooker v. Fidelity Trust Co., 263 U.S. 413 (1923), then, 60 years later, in District of Columbia Court of Appeals v. Feldman, 460 U.S. 462 (1983). Variously interpreted in the lower courts, the doctrine has sometimes been construed to extend far beyond the contours of the *Rooker* and *Feldman* cases, overriding Congress' conferral of federal-court jurisdiction concurrent with jurisdiction exercised by state courts, and superseding the ordinary application of preclusion law pursuant to 28 U.S.C. § 1738. See, e.g., Moccio v. New York State Office of Court Admin., 95 F.3d 195, 199-200 (2d Cir. 1996).

Rooker was a suit commenced in Federal District Court to have a judgment of a state court, adverse to the federal court plaintiffs, "declared null and void." 263 U.S. at 414. In *Feldman*, parties unsuccessful in the District of Columbia Court of Appeals (the District's highest court) commenced a federal-court action against the very court that had rejected their applications. Holding the federal suits impermissible, we emphasized that appellate jurisdiction to reverse or modify a state-court judgment is lodged, initially by § 25 of the Judiciary Act of 1789, 1 Stat. 85, and now by 28 U.S.C. § 1257, exclusively in this Court. Federal district courts, we noted, are empowered to exercise original, not appellate, jurisdiction. Plaintiffs in *Rooker* and *Feldman* had litigated and lost in state court. Their federal complaints, we observed, essentially invited federal courts of first instance to review and reverse unfavorable state-court judgments. We declared such suits out of bounds, i.e., properly dismissed for want of subject-matter jurisdiction.

The *Rooker-Feldman* doctrine, we hold today, is confined to cases of the kind from which the doctrine acquired its name: cases brought by state-court losers complaining of injuries caused by state-court judgments rendered before the district court proceedings commenced and inviting district court review and rejection of those judgments. *Rooker-Feldman* does not otherwise override or supplant preclusion doctrine or augment the circumscribed doctrines that allow federal courts to stay or dismiss proceedings in deference to state-court actions.

In the case before us, the Court of Appeals for the Third Circuit misperceived the narrow ground occupied by *Rooker-Feldman*, and consequently erred in ordering the federal action dismissed for lack of subject-matter jurisdiction. We therefore reverse the Third Circuit's judgment.

I

In Rooker v. Fidelity Trust Co., 263 U.S. 413, the parties defeated in state court turned to a Federal District Court for relief. Alleging that the adverse state-court judgment was rendered in contravention of the Constitution, they asked the federal court to declare it "null and void." Id. at 414-415. This Court noted preliminarily that the state court had acted within its jurisdiction. Id. at 415. If the state-court decision was wrong, the Court explained, "that did not make the judgment void, but merely left it open to reversal or modification in an appropriate and timely appellate proceeding." Id. Federal district courts, the *Rooker* Court recognized, lacked the requisite appellate authority, for their jurisdiction was "strictly original." Id. at 416. Among federal courts, the *Rooker* Court clarified, Congress had empowered only this Court to exercise appellate authority "to reverse or modify" a state-court judgment. Id. Accordingly, the Court affirmed a decree dismissing the suit for lack of jurisdiction. Id. at 415, 417.

Sixty years later, the Court decided District of Columbia Court of Appeals v. Feldman, 460 U.S. 462. The two plaintiffs in that case, Hickey and Feldman, neither of whom had graduated from an accredited law school, petitioned the District of Columbia Court of Appeals to waive a court Rule that required D.C. bar applicants to have graduated from a law school approved by the American Bar Association. After the D.C. court denied their waiver requests, Hickey and Feldman filed suits in the United States District Court for the District of Columbia. Id. at 465-473. The District Court and the Court of Appeals for the District of Columbia Circuit disagreed on the question whether the federal suit could be maintained, and we granted certiorari. Id. at 474-475.

Recalling *Rooker*, this Court's opinion in *Feldman* observed first that the District Court lacked authority to review a final judicial determination of the D.C. high court. "Review of such determinations," the *Feldman* opinion reiterated, "can be obtained only in this Court." 460 U.S. at 476. The "crucial question," the Court next stated, was whether the proceedings in the D.C. court were "judicial in nature." Ibid. Addressing that question, the Court concluded that the D.C. court had acted both judicially and legislatively.

In applying the accreditation Rule to the Hickey and Feldman waiver petitions, this Court determined, the D.C. court had acted judicially. Id. at 479-482. As to that adjudication, *Feldman* held, this Court alone among federal courts had review authority. Hence, "to the extent that Hickey and Feldman sought review in the District Court of the District of Columbia Court of Appeals' denial of their petitions for waiver, the District Court lacked subject-matter jurisdiction over their complaints." Id. at 482. But that determination did not dispose of the entire case, for in promulgating the bar admission rule, this Court said, the D.C. court had acted legislatively, not judicially. Id. at 485-486. "Challenges to the constitutionality of state bar rules," the Court elaborated, "do not necessarily require a United States district court to review a final state-court judgment in a judicial proceeding." Id. at 486. Thus, the Court reasoned, 28 U.S.C. § 1257 did not bar District Court proceedings addressed to the validity of the accreditation Rule itself. *Feldman,* 460 U.S. at 486. The Rule could be contested in federal court, this Court held, so long as plaintiffs did not seek review of the Rule's application in a particular case. Ibid.

The Court endeavored to separate elements of the Hickey and Feldman complaints that failed the jurisdictional threshold from those that survived jurisdictional inspection. Plaintiffs had urged that the District of Columbia Court of Appeals acted arbitrarily in denying the waiver petitions of Hickey and Feldman, given that court's "former policy of granting waivers to graduates of unaccredited law schools." Id. That charge, the

Court held, could not be pursued, for it was "inextricably intertwined with the District of Columbia Court of Appeals' decisions, in judicial proceedings, to deny [plaintiffs'] petitions." Id. at 486-487.

On the other hand, the Court said, plaintiffs could maintain "claims that the [bar admission] rule is unconstitutional because it creates an irrebuttable presumption that only graduates of accredited law schools are fit to practice law, discriminates against those who have obtained equivalent legal training by other means, and impermissibly delegates the District of Columbia Court of Appeals' power to regulate the bar to the American Bar Association," for those claims "do not require review of a judicial decision in a particular case." Id. at 487. The Court left open the question whether the doctrine of res judicata foreclosed litigation of the elements of the complaints spared from dismissal for want of subject-matter jurisdiction. Id. at 487-488.

Since *Feldman*, this Court has never applied *Rooker-Feldman* to dismiss an action for want of jurisdiction. The few decisions that have mentioned *Rooker* and *Feldman* have done so only in passing or to explain why those cases did not dictate dismissal. See Verizon Md. Inc. v. Public Serv. Comm'n of Md., 535 U.S. 635, 644, n.3 (2002) (*Rooker-Feldman* does not apply to a suit seeking review of state agency action); Johnson v. De Grandy, 512 U.S. 997, 1005-1006 (1994) (*Rooker-Feldman* bars a losing party in state court "from seeking what in substance would be appellate review of the state judgment in a United States district court, based on the losing party's claim that the state judgment itself violates the loser's federal rights," but the doctrine has no application to a federal suit brought by a nonparty to the state suit.); Howlett v. Rose, 496 U.S. 356, 370, n.16 (1990) (internal citations omitted); ASARCO Inc. v. Kadish, 490 U.S. 605, 622-623 (1989) (If, instead of seeking review of an adverse state supreme court decision in the Supreme Court, petitioners sued in federal district court, the federal action would be an attempt to obtain direct review of the state supreme court decision and would "represent a partial inroad on *Rooker-Feldman*'s construction of 28 U.S.C. § 1257."); Pennzoil Co. v. Texaco Inc., 481 U.S. 1, 6-10 (1987) (abstaining under Younger v. Harris, 401 U.S. 37 (1971), rather than dismissing under *Rooker-Feldman*, in a suit that challenged Texas procedures for enforcing judgments); 481 U.S. at 18 (Scalia, J., concurring) (The so-called *Rooker-Feldman* doctrine does not deprive the Court of jurisdiction to decide Texaco's challenge to the Texas procedures.); id. at 21 (Brennan, J., concurring in judgment) (*Rooker* and *Feldman* do not apply; Texaco filed its federal action to protect its "right to a meaningful opportunity for appellate review, not to challenge the merits of the Texas suit."). But cf. 481 U.S. at 25-26 (Marshall, J., concurring in judgment) (*Rooker-Feldman* would apply because Texaco's claims necessarily called for review of the merits of its state appeal). See also Martin v. Wilks , 490 U.S. 755, 784, n.21 (1989) (Stevens, J., dissenting) (it would be anomalous to allow courts to sit in review of judgments entered by courts of equal, or greater, authority (internal citations omitted)).

II

In 1980, two subsidiaries of petitioner ExxonMobil Corporation (then the separate companies Exxon Corp. and Mobil Corp.) formed joint ventures with respondent Saudi Basic Industries Corp. (SABIC) to produce polyethylene in Saudi Arabia. 194 F. Supp. 2d 378, 384 (D.N.J. 2002). Two decades later, the parties began to dispute royalties that SABIC had charged the joint ventures for sublicenses to a polyethylene manufacturing method. 364 F.3d 102, 103 (3d Cir. 2004).

SABIC preemptively sued the two ExxonMobil subsidiaries in Delaware Superior Court in July 2000 seeking a declaratory judgment that the royalty charges were proper under the joint venture agreements. 194 F. Supp. 2d at 385-386. About two weeks later, ExxonMobil and its subsidiaries countersued SABIC in the United States District Court for the District of New Jersey, alleging that SABIC overcharged the joint ventures for the sublicenses. Id. at 385; App. 3. ExxonMobil invoked subject-matter jurisdiction in the New Jersey action under 28 U.S.C. § 1330 which authorizes district courts to adjudicate actions against foreign states. 194 F. Supp. 2d at 401.

In January 2002, the ExxonMobil subsidiaries answered SABIC's state-court complaint, asserting as counterclaims the same claims ExxonMobil had made in the federal suit in New Jersey. 364 F.3d, at 103. The state suit went to trial in March 2003, and the jury returned a verdict of over $400 million in favor of the ExxonMobil subsidiaries. Id.; Saudi Basic Industries Corp. v. Mobil Yanbu Petrochemical Co., 866 A.2d 1, 11 (Del. 2005). SABIC appealed the judgment entered on the verdict to the Delaware Supreme Court.

Before the state-court trial, SABIC moved to dismiss the federal suit, alleging, *inter alia*, immunity under the Foreign Sovereign Immunities Act of 1976, 28 U.S.C. §§ 1602 *et seq.* (2000 ed. and Supp. II). The Federal District Court denied SABIC's motion to dismiss. 194 F. Supp. 2d, at 401-407, 416-417. SABIC took an interlocutory appeal, and the Court of Appeals heard argument in December 2003, over eight months after the state-court jury verdict. 364 F.3d at 103-104.

The Court of Appeals, on its own motion, raised the question whether "subject matter jurisdiction over this case fails under the *Rooker-Feldman* doctrine because ExxonMobil's claims have already been litigated in state court." Id. at 104. The court did not question the District Court's possession of subject-matter jurisdiction at the outset of the suit, but held that federal jurisdiction terminated when the Delaware Superior Court entered judgment on the jury verdict. Id. at 104-105. The court rejected ExxonMobil's argument that *Rooker-Feldman* could not apply because ExxonMobil filed its federal complaint well before the state-court judgment. The only relevant consideration, the court stated, "is whether the state judgment precedes a federal judgment on the same claims." 364 F.3d at 105. If *Rooker-Feldman* did not apply to federal actions filed prior to a state-court judgment, the Court of Appeals worried, "we would be encouraging parties to maintain federal actions as 'insurance policies' while their state court claims were pending." 364 F.3d at 105. Once ExxonMobil's claims had been litigated to a judgment in state court, the Court of Appeals held, *Rooker-Feldman* "preclude[d] [the] federal district court from proceeding." 364 F.3d at 104 (internal quotation marks omitted).

ExxonMobil, at that point prevailing in Delaware, was not seeking to overturn the state-court judgment. Nevertheless, the Court of Appeals hypothesized that, if SABIC won on appeal in Delaware, ExxonMobil would be endeavoring in the federal action to "invalidate" the state-court judgment, "the very situation," the court concluded, "contemplated by *Rooker-Feldman*'s 'inextricably intertwined' bar." Id. at 106.

We granted certiorari to resolve conflict among the Courts of Appeals over the scope of the *Rooker-Feldman* doctrine. We now reverse the judgment of the Court of Appeals for the Third Circuit.

III

Rooker and *Feldman* exhibit the limited circumstances in which this Court's appellate jurisdiction over state-court judgments, 28 U.S.C. § 1257, precludes a United States district court from exercising subject-matter jurisdiction in an action it would otherwise be empowered to adjudicate under a congressional grant of authority, *e.g.*, § 1330 (suits against foreign states), § 1331 (federal question), and § 1332 (diversity). In both cases, the losing party in state court filed suit in federal court after the state proceedings ended, complaining of an injury caused by the state-court judgment and seeking review and rejection of that judgment. Plaintiffs in both cases, alleging federal-question jurisdiction, called upon the District Court to overturn an injurious state-court judgment. Because § 1257, as long interpreted, vests authority to review a state court's judgment solely in this Court, e.g., *Feldman*, 460 U.S. at 476; Atlantic Coast Line R. Co. v. Locomotive Engineers, 398 U.S. 281, 286 (1970); *Rooker*, 263 U.S. at 416, the District Courts in *Rooker* and *Feldman* lacked subject-matter jurisdiction. See *Verizon Md. Inc.*, 535 U.S. at 644, n.3 ("The *Rooker-Feldman* doctrine merely recognizes that 28 U.S.C. § 1331 is a grant of original jurisdiction, and does not authorize district courts to exercise appellate jurisdiction over state-court judgments, which Congress has reserved to this Court, see § 1257(a).").[8]

When there is parallel state and federal litigation, *Rooker-Feldman* is not triggered simply by the entry of judgment in state court. This Court has repeatedly held that "the pendency of an action in the state court is no bar to proceedings concerning the same matter in the Federal court having jurisdiction." McClellan v. Carland, 217 U.S. 268, 282 (1910); accord Doran v.

8. Congress, if so minded, may explicitly empower district courts to oversee certain state-court judgments and has done so, most notably, in authorizing federal habeas review of state prisoners' petitions. 28 U.S.C. § 2254(a).

Salem Inn, Inc., 422 U.S. 922, 928 (1975); *Atlantic Coast Line R. Co.*, 398 U.S. at 295. Comity or abstention doctrines may, in various circumstances, permit or require the federal court to stay or dismiss the federal action in favor of the state-court litigation. See, e.g., Colorado River Water Conservation Dist. v. United States, 424 U.S. 800 (1976); Younger v. Harris, 401 U.S. 37 (1971); Burford v. Sun Oil Co., 319 U.S. 315 (1943); Railroad Comm'n of Tex. v. Pullman Co., 312 U.S. 496 (1941). But neither *Rooker* nor *Feldman* supports the notion that properly invoked concurrent jurisdiction vanishes if a state court reaches judgment on the same or related question while the case remains *sub judice* in a federal court.

Disposition of the federal action, once the state-court adjudication is complete, would be governed by preclusion law. The Full Faith and Credit Act, 28 U.S.C. § 1738 originally enacted in 1790, ch. 11, 1 Stat. 122, requires the federal court to "give the same preclusive effect to a state-court judgment as another court of that State would give." Parsons Steel, Inc. v. First Alabama Bank, 474 U.S. 518, 523 (1986). Preclusion, of course, is not a jurisdictional matter. See Fed. Rule Civ. Proc. 8(c) (listing res judicata as an affirmative defense). In parallel litigation, a federal court may be bound to recognize the claim- and issue-preclusive effects of a state-court judgment, but federal jurisdiction over an action does not terminate automatically on the entry of judgment in the state court.

Nor does § 1257 stop a district court from exercising subject-matter jurisdiction simply because a party attempts to litigate in federal court a matter previously litigated in state court. If a federal plaintiff "present[s] some independent claim, albeit one that denies a legal conclusion that a state court has reached in a case to which he was a party, then there is jurisdiction and state law determines whether the defendant prevails under principles of preclusion." GASH Assocs. v. Village of Rosemont, 995 F.2d 726, 728 (7th Cir. 1993).

This case surely is not the "paradigm situation in which *Rooker-Feldman* precludes a federal district court from proceeding." 364 F.3d at 104. ExxonMobil plainly has not repaired to federal court to undo the Delaware judgment in its favor. Rather, it appears ExxonMobil filed suit in Federal District Court (only two weeks after SABIC filed in Delaware and well before any judgment in state court) to protect itself in the event it lost in state court on grounds (such as the state statute of limitations) that might not preclude relief in the federal venue. Tr. of Oral Arg. 46; App. 35-36.[9] *Rooker-Feldman* did not prevent the District Court from exercising

9. The Court of Appeals criticized ExxonMobil for pursuing its federal suit as an "insurance policy" against an adverse result in state court. 364 F.3d 102, 105-106 (3d Cir. 2004). There is nothing necessarily inappropriate, however, about filing a protective action. See, e.g., Rhines v. Weber, ante, at 7-8 (permitting a federal district court to stay a federal habeas action and hold the petition in abeyance while a petitioner exhausts claims in state court); Union Pacific R. Co. v. Dept. of Revenue of Ore., 920 F.2d 581, 584, and n.9 (9th Cir. 1990) (noting that the railroad company had filed protective actions in state court to prevent expiration of the state statute of limitations); Government of Virgin Islands v. Neadle, 861 F. Supp. 1054, 1055 (M.D. Fla. 1994) (staying an action brought by plaintiffs "to protect themselves" in the event that personal jurisdiction over the defendants failed in the

jurisdiction when ExxonMobil filed the federal action, and it did not emerge to vanquish jurisdiction after ExxonMobil prevailed in the Delaware courts.

For the reasons stated, the judgment of the Court of Appeals for the Third Circuit is reversed, and the case is remanded for further proceedings consistent with this opinion.

It is so ordered.

---

b. Federal Court Judgments in State Courts

The following case involves the reverse scenario from that of Kremer v. Chemical Corp. Here the court is a state court, and it must determine the preclusive effects of a prior federal court judgment. But the case also raises several procedure issues from earlier chapters: adequacy of service of process, the scope of Article III, the contours of a claim, and the reach of federal subject matter jurisdiction under the supplemental jurisdiction statute. The decision therefore offers an excellent opportunity to review these concepts and to admire your progress. Many once-familiar and elusive aspects of procedure are now well within your grasp. These pieces now should fit together in a sturdy procedure framework that you will spend a career filling in, remodeling, and critiquing.

Watkins v. Resorts International Hotel and Casino, Inc.

591 A.2d 592 (1991)

POLLOCK, J.

This appeal concerns the preclusive effect of a federal judgment in a state court. Specifically, it requires us to decide whether state law claims brought in a state court are precluded by a prior federal court judgment dismissing federal law claims based on the same facts, if the federal claims were dismissed for insufficient service of process and for lack of standing.

Plaintiffs, Murrell Watkins and Abraham McDaniel and their wholly-owned company, sued Resorts International (Resorts), Bally's Park Place Casino (Bally's), and other defendants in federal district court, claiming that as minority bus-line owners they had been the targets of discriminatory practices. The claims, which sought relief pursuant to 42 U.S.C. sections 1981, 1983, 1985(3), and 1988, were dismissed on motion for various reasons, including insufficient service of process and lack of standing.

United States District Court for the Virgin Islands); see also England v. Louisiana Bd. of Medical Examiners, 375 U.S. 411, 421 (1964) (permitting a party to reserve litigation of federal constitutional claims for federal court while a state court resolves questions of state law).

Relying on state law, Watkins and McDaniel then filed this action in the Superior Court based on the same allegations of discrimination that underlay their federal claims. The Law Division granted defendants' motion to dismiss, on the ground that plaintiffs were barred by the entire controversy doctrine from relitigating the same cause of action that had already been decided in federal court. In an unreported decision, the Appellate Division affirmed on grounds of res judicata, collateral estoppel, and the entire controversy doctrine. We granted certification, 584 A.2d 253 (1990), and now reverse the judgment of the Appellate Division and remand the matter to the Law Division. Although state courts must honor judgments of federal courts, dismissals for insufficient service of process or lack of standing do not preclude relitigation. Consequently, the federal judgments against Watkins and McDaniel do not bar their state claims.

I

For purposes of this appeal, we accept the facts as alleged in the complaint. Plaintiff Watkins and his wife were the sole shareholders in Ocean Breeze Transit Company (Ocean Breeze), a bus company that operated service to Atlantic City casinos. Plaintiff McDaniel owned Cobra Coach Lines, Inc. (Cobra), which also operated bus service to Atlantic City. Plaintiffs, who are black, allege that Resorts and Bally's discriminated against them by interfering with their efforts to operate bus lines to the casinos. . . .

On August 27, 1984, Watkins, McDaniel, Ocean Breeze, and Cobra filed suit in the United States District Court for the District of New Jersey, claiming civil rights violations under 42 U.S.C. sections 1981, 1983, 1985(3), and 1988. The complaint named the same defendants as in the instant matter: Resorts, Bally's, McClain, McDermott, the DOT, and Fitzsimmons. Plaintiffs did not assert any pendent state claims. Eventually, the federal court dismissed all of the claims. First, on June 12, 1985, the court dismissed plaintiffs' section 1983 claim. Plaintiffs stipulated to a dismissal with prejudice of their section 1983 claim, leaving only the section 1985 claim and the derivative section 1981 claim for attorneys' fees. Then, on November 27, 1985, the court dismissed the complaint against Bally's for insufficient service of process under Federal Rule of Civil Procedure 4(j).* Specifically, the court dismissed the complaint without prejudice because plaintiffs had failed to serve the summons and complaint on Bally's within 120 days of filing the complaint, contrary to Federal Rule of Civil Procedure 4(j). Plaintiffs voluntarily dismissed their complaint against DOT. . . .

Shortly thereafter, Watkins and McDaniel brought suit in the Law Division. As in the federal action, they claimed that as minority bus-line owners they were the targets of discrimination by the two casinos, their employees, and DOT. Plaintiffs alleged the same facts as those in their federal complaint.

* [The provision of Rule 4 to which the court refers now appears as 4(m), not 4(j). Eds.]

Instead of alleging violations of federal anti-discrimination laws, however, plaintiffs founded their claims entirely on state law.

Resorts moved to dismiss the complaint, arguing that the entire controversy doctrine, res judicata, or collateral estoppel precluded plaintiffs' action. It argued that no private cause of action existed under the Casino Control Act. The court agreed that the state cause of action was essentially the same as the federal action, and that the entire controversy doctrine barred plaintiffs from relitigating the matter. The trial court therefore granted the motion to dismiss. As to DOT, the court dismissed plaintiffs' complaint for failure to state a claim.

Before the Appellate Division, plaintiffs argued that the federal court had not determined the matter on its merits and that therefore neither res judicata, collateral estoppel, nor the entire controversy doctrine should bar the state court action. The Appellate Division disagreed, and affirmed the dismissal. As to Resorts, the court viewed the dismissal for lack of standing as a resolution on the merits, stating that the district court's "holding was that the claims which the individual plaintiffs were asserting belonged solely to their corporations and, therefore, the individuals were not entitled to redress." The court held that plaintiffs' claims against Resorts were barred by res judicata or collateral estoppel. As to Bally's, the court affirmed the dismissal on the ground of the entire controversy doctrine. The court determined that although the federal dismissal for insufficient service of process was not on the merits and therefore did not itself preclude the state suit, Bally's was a necessary party and the dismissal of the federal suit against Resorts barred a later action against Bally's.

II

A fundamental feature of the relationship between state and federal courts is that the courts of each system must respect the judgments of courts of the other system. That respect is essential to the fair and efficient functioning of our federalist system of justice. The rule that state courts must accord preclusive effect to prior federal court judgments is . . . settled. . . . This case requires that we search for the reasons beneath the rule.

Our inquiry begins with the full faith and credit clause of the United States Constitution, which provides that "[f]ull Faith and Credit shall be given in each State to the public Acts, Records, and judicial Proceedings of every other State." U.S. Const. art. IV, § 1. That clause directs the courts of each state to give preclusive effect to the judgments of a sister state. The clause, however, does not expressly require state courts to accept the judgments of a federal court.

Nor does the federal full faith and credit statute, 28 U.S.C.A. § 1738, impose that requirement. The statute provides that

> judicial proceedings [of any State, Territory or Possession of the United States] . . . shall have the same full faith and credit in every court within the

> United States and its Territories and Possessions as they have by law or usage in the courts of such State, Territory or Possession from which they are taken.

Because they are included in "every court within the United States," federal courts are required to give full faith and credit to the judgments defined in the statute. The judgments so defined, however, are those "of any State, Territory, or Possession of the United States," not those of the federal courts. Thus, the statute does not compel state courts to give preclusive effect to judgments of the federal courts. In sum, neither the constitutional full faith and credit clause nor the corresponding federal statute solves the problem.

Some older cases purported to find the answer in the full faith and credit clause of the federal constitution. See Bigelow v. Old Dominion Copper Mining & Smelting Co., 225 U.S. 111, 129 (1912) (addressing federal-state preclusion issue as one governed by the full faith and credit clause and its implementing statute, and holding that a federal court judgment "is entitled to the same sanction which would attach to a like judgment of a court of the state"); National Foundry & Pipe Works v. Oconto City Water Supply Co., 183 U.S. 216, 237 (1902) (holding that state court's failure to give due effect to federal court decree raises federal question (internal citations omitted)). Courts also looked to the federal full faith and credit statute or its predecessor. . . .

As previously noted, however, neither the full faith and credit clause of the Constitution nor the corresponding federal statute applies. In brief, positive law does not expressly mandate that state courts give preclusive effect to the judgments of federal courts.

Generally without analysis, state courts have accepted federal court judgments as binding. [Ronan E.] Degnan, 85 Yale L.J. 744, at 744 n.17 [1976]. In the absence of any such analysis, respected scholars have theorized about the basis for the preclusive effect in state courts of federal court judgments. For example, Professor Charles Alan Wright, drawing on an explanation of Professor Ronan Degnan, states

> Article III limits the federal judicial power to cases and controversies. To decide a case or controversy implies some binding effect. Proceedings that do not have at least the potential effect of precluding later relitigation of the same claims and issues would constitute something other than the exercise of the judicial power. Once it is accepted that Article III and its implementing legislation have created courts with the power to issue judgments that will have preclusive effects in other litigation, the Supremacy Clause of Article VI mandates that those preclusive effects are binding on state courts. [C. Wright, The Law of Federal Courts 694-695 (4th ed. 1983) (internal citations omitted).]

See also Degnan, supra, 85 Yale L.J. at 772-773 (federal-state preclusion "will have to be placed forthrightly on the ground that the integrity of the federal judicial power is at stake"); cf. Burbank, Interjurisdictional

Preclusion, Full Faith and Credit and Federal Common Law: A General Approach, 71 Cornell L. Rev. 733, 753-755 & n.92 (1986) (questioning how far Professor Degnan's article III analysis can go, but acknowledging article III's significance in imposing basic obligation to respect federal judgments). Professor Wright's analysis echoes the earlier analysis in Dupasseur v. Rochereau, 88 U.S. (21 Wall.) 130 (1875), in which the United States Supreme Court held that a state court's failure to honor a federal court judgment constituted a federal question triggering the jurisdiction of the Supreme Court.

By insulating courts from the relitigation of claims, res judicata prevents the judicial inefficiency inherent in multiplicitous litigation. At some point litigation over a particular controversy should end. By preventing harassment of parties, preclusion serves the interest of fairness. Preclusion further protects the integrity of the judgments of state and federal courts. The strength of a judgment derives from the expectation that it will be binding. Essential to the proper functioning of state and federal courts is the principle that a disappointed litigant may not circumvent a judgment entered in one system by relitigating the claim or the decided issues in the other system. Generally speaking, whether started in state or federal courts, the determination of a case in one system should conclude the matter.

Beyond the general policy favoring finality, interjurisdictional preclusion serves the vital function of unifying the nation. The United States Supreme Court, this Court, and scholars have recognized that the full faith and credit clause, by obliging each state to enforce the judgments of another state, fulfills this function. As the United States Supreme Court has written,

> [t]he full faith and credit clause like the commerce clause thus became a nationally unifying force. It altered the status of the several states as independent foreign sovereignties, each free to ignore rights and obligations created under the laws or established by the judicial proceedings of the others, by making each an integral part of a single nation, in which rights judicially established in any part are given nation-wide application. [Magnolia Petroleum Co. v. Hunt, 320 U.S. 430, 439 (1943).]

Just as cohesion between state courts is necessary for national unity, cohesion between state and federal courts is necessary for the continuing vitality of the federalist system. Maintaining a cohesive federal system requires not only that federal courts honor state court judgments, as mandated by 28 U.S.C. § 1738, but also that state courts honor federal court judgments. . . .

Plaintiffs ordinarily have one chance to prove their case. Overlapping jurisdiction frequently gives plaintiffs the option of suing in either the state or the federal system. The availability of alternative forums should not give plaintiffs the additional luxury of suing first in one system and then in the other.

When a state court considers the binding effect of a federal court judgment, nothing less is at stake than the integrity of federal judicial power and the coherence of the federalist judicial system. See Degnan, supra, 85 Yale L.J. at 773. So viewed, state courts are bound by federal court judgments, just as they are bound by the judgments of sister states. Consequently, a cause of action finally determined on the merits by a competent federal court cannot be relitigated by the same parties or their privies in a state court.

We now consider the question of what law governs the preclusive effect of a federal judgment in state court. In general, the binding effect of a judgment is determined by the law of the jurisdiction that rendered it. Restatement (Second) of Conflict of Laws § 95 comment e (1971). This rule applies not only when considering the preclusive effect of a judgment of one state court on the courts of another state, but also when determining the preclusive effect in a state court of a federal court judgment. The Restatement (Second) of Judgments . . . § 87, states the rule plainly: "Federal law determines the effects under the rules of res judicata of a judgment of a federal court."

In principle, the preclusive effect of a judgment is the logical consequence of the procedures of the issuing court. See id. Introduction at 6-13. "Within the constitutional limits, the contours of res judicata are determined by the particulars of the opportunity to litigate afforded by the system of procedure in question." Id. at 7. The underlying consideration is whether the contending party in the second forum was accorded a "full and fair" opportunity to litigate in the first forum. Id. at 9.

It follows that ordinarily a federal court judgment would be neither more nor less binding in the courts of this State than it would be in the federal courts. The reason is that the preclusive effect of the judgment is a function of the procedures of the federal court that rendered it. Id. at 5. These considerations affect the applicability of the entire controversy doctrine, on which the Appellate Division relied. That doctrine, like res judicata, advances the goals of fairness, efficiency, and finality. In limited circumstances, the entire controversy doctrine may preclude an action that is not otherwise precluded by the federal law of res judicata. We note in this context the decision of the Appellate Division in Blazer Corp. v. New Jersey Sports & Exposition Authority, 488 A.2d 1025 (1985). There, the court relied on the entire controversy doctrine to bar a Superior Court action that "formed the foundation," id. at 1026, of a previously dismissed federal action. Our reading of that opinion leads us to conclude that the Appellate Division may not have sufficiently considered the federal law of claim preclusion in resorting to the entire controversy doctrine.

We turn therefore to the federal law of claim preclusion. Federal law requires the same three basic elements as New Jersey law: (1) the judgment in the prior action must be valid, final, and on the merits; (2) the parties in the later action must be identical to or in privity with those in the prior action; and (3) the claim in the later action must grow out of the same transaction or occurrence as the claim in the earlier one. Federated

Dept. Stores v. Moitie, 452 U.S. 394, 398 (1981). Claim preclusion applies not only to matters actually determined in an earlier action, but to all relevant matters that could have been so determined. For the purposes of res judicata, causes of action are deemed part of a single "claim" if they arise out of the same transaction or occurrence. Restatement (Second) of Judgments, supra, § 24. If, under various theories, a litigant seeks to remedy a single wrong, then that litigant should present all theories in the first action. Otherwise, theories not raised will be precluded in a later action. Thus, if a federal court in a prior action would have exercised pendent jurisdiction over related state claims that were not asserted, a final judgment on the merits by the federal court precludes raising those claims in a subsequent action in state court. Federated Dept. Stores, supra, 452 U.S. at 404 (Blackmun, J., concurring). If, on the other hand, a claim could not have been presented in the first action, then it will not be precluded in a later action. The Restatement (Second) of Judgments explains:

> When the plaintiff brings an action on the claim in a court, either state or federal, in which there is no jurisdictional obstacle to his advancing both theories or grounds, but he presents only one of them, and judgment is entered with respect to it, he may not maintain a second action in which he tenders the other theory or ground. If, however, the court in the first action would clearly not have had jurisdiction to entertain the omitted theory or ground (or, having jurisdiction, would clearly have declined to exercise it as a matter of discretion), then a second action in a competent court presenting the omitted theory or ground should be held not precluded. [§ 25 comment e.]

See also id. § 26(1)(c) (subject matter jurisdiction exception to rule against claim splitting). If the plaintiffs could not have asserted both state and federal claims in a single forum, it would be unfair to force them to sacrifice the claims that could not be so asserted in order to bring a single action in one forum.

In the present case, therefore, we must determine whether the federal district court had jurisdiction to entertain plaintiffs' omitted state law claims. A federal court can hear pendent state claims when the state and federal claims "derive from a common nucleus of operative fact." United Mine Workers of Am. v. Gibbs, 383 U.S. 715, 725 (1966). In cases asserting violations of civil rights, federal courts routinely exercise pendent jurisdiction over state claims. E.g., Hayden v. Chrysler Corp., 486 F. Supp. 557, 558 (E.D. Mich. 1980). Some scholars believed that the Supreme Court's decision in Finley v. United States, 490 U.S. 545 (1989), spelled the demise of pendent and ancillary jurisdiction. See Mengler, The Demise of Pendent and Ancillary Jurisdiction, 1990 BYU L. Rev. 247; Perdue, Finley v. United States: Unstringing Pendent Jurisdiction, 76 Va. L. Rev. 539 (1990). Congress, however, rescued the doctrines by passing the Judicial Improvements Act of 1990. None of this affects our resolution of the present case, however, because the federal action at issue here occurred before *Finley* and the Act.

Here, defendants argue that because plaintiffs could have appended their state claims to the federal action, the federal dismissal precludes presentation of those claims. In reply, plaintiffs argue that the federal court dismissal of their federal claims does not preclude the present action because the federal court would have declined to exercise pendent jurisdiction over their state claims. A federal court may choose not to exercise jurisdiction over pendent state claims when the federal claims have been dismissed before trial. *Gibbs*, supra, 383 U.S. at 726. In such a case, perhaps plaintiffs should not be precluded from later asserting their state claims in a state court. Restatement (Second) of Judgments, supra, § 25 comment e, illustration 10 (state action barred "unless it is clear that the federal court would have declined as a matter of discretion to exercise that jurisdiction (for example, because the federal claim, though substantial, was dismissed in advance of trial)"); Note, The Res Judicata Implications of Pendent Jurisdiction, 66 Cornell L. Rev. 608, 621-24 (1981) (generally, if federal claims dismissed before trial, then later court should presume federal court would not have invoked pendent jurisdiction despite common nucleus of operative fact, and therefore should hold omitted state claims not precluded). We need not decide that issue, however, because we conclude that even if plaintiffs could have asserted all their claims in federal court, the federal court's determination of the federal claims was not of such a nature as to preclude plaintiffs' subsequent assertion of their state claims in the state courts.

Only a judgment "on the merits" will preclude a later action on the same claim. Respected authorities reject the phrase "on the merits" as "question-begging," C. Wright, supra, at 679 (internal quotations omitted), and "possibly misleading," Restatement (Second) of Judgments, supra, § 19 comment a. Because "on the merits" may connote too limited a view of judgments that are entitled to preclusive effect, the Restatement (Second) of Judgments avoids the phrase. Compare Restatement (First) of Judgments § 48 (1942) ("Where a valid and final personal judgment is rendered on the merits in favor of the defendant, the plaintiff cannot thereafter maintain an action on the original cause of action.") with Restatement (Second) of Judgments, supra, § 19 ("A valid and final personal judgment rendered in favor of the defendant bars another action by the plaintiff on the same claim."). Semantics aside, the rule remains that a dismissal based on a court's procedural inability to consider a case will not preclude a subsequent action on the same claim, Restatement (Second) of Judgments, supra, § 19 comment a, § 20, but a judgment can be preclusive even if it does not result from a plenary hearing on the substantive claims. For example, in Velasquez [v. Franz,] 589 A.2d [143,] 151-52 [1991], we recently recognized the preclusive effect of a federal court dismissal based on a dissolved corporation's lack of capacity to be sued, although the federal court did not reach the facts underlying plaintiff's tort claim. In the present case, the issue is whether federal court dismissals for insufficient service of process and lack of standing preclude subsequent actions.

Concerning the dismissal for insufficient service of process, Federal Rule of Civil Procedure 4(j) provides that if service is not made on a defendant within 120 days after the filing of the complaint, and no good reason is given for the delay, "the action shall be dismissed as to that defendant without prejudice." Cf. Degnan, supra, 85 Yale L.J. at 763 ("To the extent, then, that the Federal Rules of Civil Procedure do speak about the preclusive effect of federal adjudications, they speak authoritatively, and determinations based upon them are entitled to res judicata effect or full faith and credit. They have been given that effect by state and federal courts alike." (footnote omitted)). Consequently, the November 27, 1985, federal court order dismissing Watkins' and McDaniel's individual claims against Bally's was necessarily "without prejudice." . . .

III

Plaintiff's state court and federal court actions arose from the same factual occurrences. Hence, they constitute the same claim for res judicata purposes. Although the corporations, which were plaintiffs in the federal action, do not join as plaintiffs in the state action, the individual plaintiffs and all defendants are identical. Thus, two of the requirements for claim preclusion, identity of parties and of claim, are satisfied.

In the federal courts, however, the complaint against Bally's was dismissed for insufficient service of process under Federal Rule of Civil Procedure 4(j). A dismissal on that ground is not a judgment on the merits for res judicata purposes. Rule 4(j) specifically provides for dismissal "without prejudice." Moreover, the opinion on which the order is based states that "plaintiffs will not be barred from refiling the action," and that the claim against Bally's "shall be dismissed, without prejudice, in accord with Fed. R. Civ. P. 4(j)." Consequently, we conclude that the federal dismissal of the complaint against Bally's is not entitled to claim preclusive effect. . . .

Initially, the federal courts dismissed the claims of the individual plaintiffs against Bally's and Resorts for improper service and lack of standing. The subsequent dismissal "with prejudice" on May 27, 1987, applied only to those claims remaining at that time, the claims of the corporate plaintiffs. Thus, the provision in the May 27, 1987, order that the dismissal is "with prejudice" could not affect the previously dismissed claims of the individual plaintiffs.

To conclude, the only issue precluded by the federal court judgment is the standing of the individual plaintiffs to maintain an action under federal law. The federal courts did not resolve the question whether Watkins and McDaniel have standing under the New Jersey Constitution, the Casino Control Act, and the Law Against Discrimination. Plaintiffs deserve the opportunity to be heard on that issue. We state no view concerning plaintiffs' standing or concerning the merits of their claims. Our opinion goes no further than holding that because the federal court judgment was not on the merits, it does not preclude plaintiffs from raising their state claims in state court.

The judgment of the Appellate Division is *reversed,* and the matter is remanded to the Law Division.

Notes and Questions

1. *Federal Judgments in State Court.* The foregoing cases construe Article IV, § 1 of the United States Constitution and § 1738 of the United States Code. Review both provisions carefully. Notice that neither provides any obligation for state courts to respect federal judgments. Nevertheless, as *Watkins* demonstrates, the obligation is well recognized. What arguments support this practice? What exceptions might there be to this general obligation to respect the judgments of another sovereign?

2. *Policy Bars to Respect for Other States' Judgments.* In Baehr v. Lewin, 71 Haw. 530, 852 P.2d 44 (1993), the Hawaii Supreme Court held that the Hawaii constitution required that the state justify its proscription of same-sex marriage with compelling reasons, a standard that is difficult to meet. If a state court were to hold that denial of a marriage license on the basis of gender or sexual orientation was unconstitutional, would all states be obliged to respect that holding? What if the courts in the state of Utah were to hold that the state could not deny multiple marriage licenses to consenting adults who wish to engage in bigamy? For a thorough discussion of these potential enforcement implications of *Baehr,* see Note, Aloha, Marriage? Constitutional and Choice of Law Arguments for Recognition of Same-Sex Marriages, 47 Stan. L. Rev. 499 (1995).

What does Baker v. General Motors Corp. suggest about the obligation of sister courts to respect another state's decision to recognize same-sex marriage? What, if anything, does the federal Defense of Marriage Act ("DOMA"), 1 U.S.C. § 7 (1997), 28 U.S.C. § 738C, which provides that a state "shall not be required to recognize same-sex marriages performed in other states," add to this full faith and credit analysis? Is a marriage a judicial act within the meaning of the Full Faith and Credit Clause?

These questions are now more pressing than ever. In a landmark decision concluding that the state of Massachusetts "failed to identify any constitutionally adequate reason for denying civil marriage to same-sex couples," the Massachusetts Supreme Court held that civil marriage under state law could no longer be construed to exclude same-sex couples. Goodridge v. Dep't of Public Health, 798 N.E.2d 941, 948 (Mass. 2003). The California Supreme Court followed suit several years later, holding that "the state interest in limiting the designation of marriage exclusively to opposite-sex couples . . . cannot properly be considered a compelling state interest for equal protection purposes" and that provisions in the Family Code limiting marriage to a union between a woman and a man violated the state constitution. In re Marriage Cases, 43 Cal. 4th 757, 854 (Cal. 2008). Marriage licenses between same-sex couples have been issued to Massachusetts and California residents, as well as residents of other states. In the November 4, 2008, election, however, California voters adopted a ballot measure altering the state constitution to provide that "[o]nly marriage between a man and a woman is valid or recognized in California." Cal. Const. art. I, § 7.5. As of this writing, there are three cases challenging the constitutionality of the ballot measure consolidated for review in the California Supreme Court. The questions presented include (1) whether the ballot measure was a procedurally valid method of amending the declaration of rights in the California constitution, (2) whether the measure violates separation of powers, and (3) whether the measure affects marriages between same-sex couples that took place before the measure passed.

For an excellent analysis of the conflict-of-laws questions presented by same-sex marriage as well as the issues likely to arise in the event of divorce, see Herma Hill Kay, Same Sex Divorce in the Conflict of Laws, 15 King's C. L.J. 63 (2004). See also 2005 Symposium, Current Debates in the Conflict of Laws: Recognition and Enforcement of Same-Sex Marriage, 153 U. Pa. L. Rev. (2005).

What weight should the courts give to congressional input in deciding whether a judicial act should receive full faith and credit? Recall that in the text immediately following the Full Faith and Credit Clause, U.S. Const. art. IV, § 1 gives Congress the power to "prescribe the manner in which such Acts, Records and Proceedings shall be proved, and the Effect thereof." Does this Effects Clause provide the constitutional basis for the passage of DOMA? For the argument that DOMA is unconstitutional and that Congress does not have the power to authorize states to refuse to recognize same-sex marriages, see Larry Kramer, Same-Sex Marriage, Conflict of Laws, and the Unconstitutional Public Policy Exception, 106 Yale L.J. 1965, 2008 (1997) ("[I]f states cannot selectively discriminate against each other's laws, Congress cannot authorize them to do so."). But see Mark D. Rosen, Why the Defense of Marriage Act Is Not (Yet?) Unconstitutional: Lawrence, Full Faith and Credit, and the Many Societal Actors that Determine What the Constitution Requires, 90 Minn. L. Rev. 915 (2006).

A unanimous United States Supreme Court held that Nevada courts could refuse to accord full faith and credit to California, when California immunized its tax collection agency from suit. In Franchise Tax Board v. Hyatt, 538 U.S. 488, 495 (2003), the Court rejected California's argument that Nevada must give effect to the "legislatively immunized acts" of California when refusing to do so "would interfere with [California's] capacity to fulfill its own core sovereign responsibilities." Applying Nevada v. Hall, 440 U.S. 410 (1979), the Court concluded that extending full faith and credit to California law was not required because the law would violate the home court state's "legitimate public policy." Id. at 497. The exception to this rule — that full faith and credit should be given when failure to do so would pose a substantial threat to cooperative federalism — did not apply.

What is required in order for a state to demonstrate a "legitimate public policy" against same-sex marriage? Is it sufficient that the state does not itself grant marriage licenses to same-sex couples, or must the state pass its own defense of marriage act, as some 40 states have now done? If there is already a recognized public policy exception to a state's full faith and credit obligations with respect to foreign laws, perhaps DOMA is superfluous. But see Andrew Koppelman, The Difference the Mini-DOMAs Make, 38 Loy. U. Chi. L.J. 265 (2007).

3. *The "One Bite" Test in a Federal System.* If a party files an action in state court when she could have filed in federal court, should she subsequently be precluded from litigating a claim related to the original action that is within the exclusive jurisdiction of the federal courts? She clearly could not have raised that issue in state court; should she nevertheless be precluded from litigating it later on the theory that she chose the forum with narrower jurisdiction and should get only one bite at the apple? The United States Supreme Court confronted the issue in Marrese v. American Academy of Orthopaedic Surgeons, 470 U.S. 373 (1985), and concluded that the answer depends on the state's law of preclusion. If it precludes subsequent litigation of issues that the party could not have raised in an earlier suit for jurisdictional reasons, then the federal claim is precluded. What arguments might support preclusion in such a case? What reasons can you offer in support of no preclusion?

What is required in order for a state to demonstrate a "legitimate public policy" against same-sex marriage? Is it sufficient that the state does not itself grant marriage licenses to same-sex couples, or must the state pass its own defense of marriage act, as some 40 states have now done? If there is already a recognized public policy exception to a state's full faith and credit obligations with respect to foreign laws, perhaps DOMA is superfluous. Why not? But see Andrew Koppelman, The Difference the Mini-DOMAs Make, 38 Loy. L.A. L. Rev. 265 (2005).

3. The One Bite Test in a Federal System. If a party files an action in state court when she could have filed in federal court, should she subsequently be precluded from litigating a claim related to the original action that is within the exclusive jurisdiction of the federal courts? She clearly could not have raised that issue in state court. Should she nevertheless be precluded from litigating it later on the theory that she chose the forum with narrower jurisdiction and should get only one bite at the apple? The United States Supreme Court confronted this issue in Marrese v. American Academy of Orthopaedic Surgeons, 470 U.S. 373 (1985), and concluded that the answer depends on the state's law of preclusion. If it precludes subsequent litigation of issues that the party could not have raised in an earlier suit for jurisdictional reasons, then the federal claim is precluded. What arguments might support preclusion in such a case? What reasons can you offer in support of no preclusion?

Appendix: Style Changes to the Federal Rules of Civil Procedure

Beginning in 2003, the Civil Rules Advisory Committee undertook the process of restyling the Federal Rules of Civil Procedure. In the most comprehensive overhaul since the rules were first adopted in 1937, the Committee restyled every rule, from Rule 1 to Rule 86, and redesigned every associated form. The proposed amendments to the rules were approved by the Supreme Court in April 2007, and the project culminated on December 1, 2007 with the promulgation of the new, restyled Civil Rules.

The amendments to the Rules took two basic forms. The first was a set of "style only" amendments to Rules 1-86, intended to simplify the rules and improve readability and comprehension. These "stylistic" changes included minor alterations to the language of the Rules, along with the addition of new labels and internal subparts. The second was a set of "style-substance" changes to Rules 4(a), 9(h), 11(a), 14(b), 16(c), 26(g), 30(b), 31(c), 40, 71.1(d), and 78(a); these changes were also intended to improve the Rules but arguably involved changes to their substantive meaning. The "style-substance" alterations were approved separately from the stylistic changes but also took effect on December 1, 2007. For an overview of all of the 2007 revisions, see Memorandum from the Comm. on Rules of Practice and Procedure of the Judicial Conference of the U.S. to C.J. John Roberts, Summary of Proposed Amendments to the Federal Rules (Nov. 1, 2006), available at http://www.uscourts.gov/rules/supct1106/summary_proposed_amend.pdf.

The following chart provides a side-by-side comparison of the pre-restyling text and the newly restyled text of every Rule that appears in the casebook. It is intended to highlight the respects in which the restyled Rules track, and the areas in which they depart from, the pre-2007 versions.

Rule	Pre-Restyling Text	Restyled Text	Casebook References
1	**Rule 1. Scope and Purpose of Rules** These rules govern the procedure in the United States district courts in all suits of a civil nature whether cognizable as cases at law or in equity or in admiralty, with the exceptions stated in Rule 81. They shall be construed and administered to secure the just, speedy, and inexpensive determination of every action.	**Rule 1: Scope and Purpose** These rules govern the procedure in all civil actions and proceedings in the United States district courts, except as stated in Rule 81. They should be construed and administered to secure the just, speedy, and inexpensive determination of every action and proceeding.	286, 288, 390, 394, 630, 644, 737, 1095
3	**Rule 3. Commencement of Action** A civil action is commenced by filing a complaint with the court.	**Rule 3: Commencing an Action** A civil action is commenced by filing a complaint with the court.	878, 888
4(a)	**Rule 4. Summons** **(a) FORM.** The summons shall be signed by the clerk, bear the seal of the court, identify the court and the parties, be directed to the defendant, and state the name and address of the plaintiff's attorney or, if unrepresented, of the plaintiff. It shall also state the time within which the defendant must appear and defend, and notify the defendant that failure to do so will result in a judgment by default against the defendant for the relief demanded in the complaint. The court may allow a summons to be amended.	**Rule 4: Summons** **(a) Contents; Amendments.** **(1)** ***Contents.*** A summons must: **(A)** name the court and the parties; **(B)** be directed to the defendant; **(C)** state the name and address of the plaintiff's attorney or—if unrepresented—of the plaintiff; **(D)** state the time within which the defendant must appear and defend; **(E)** notify the defendant that a failure to appear and defend will result in a default judgment against the defendant for the relief demanded in the complaint; **(F)** be signed by the clerk; and **(G)** bear the court's seal. **(2)** ***Amendments.*** The court may permit a summons to be amended.	Rule 4 generally: 26, 35, 36, 38, 42, 43, 45, 46, 48, 49, 50, 51, 52, 154, 981, 1221
4(b)	**(b) ISSUANCE.** Upon or after filing the complaint, the plaintiff may present a summons to the clerk for signature and seal. If the summons is in proper form, the clerk shall sign, seal, and issue it to the plaintiff for service on the defendant. A summons, or a copy of the summons if addressed to multiple defendants, shall be issued for each defendant to be served.	**(b) Issuance.** On or after filing the complaint, the plaintiff may present a summons to the clerk for signature and seal. If the summons is properly completed, the clerk must sign, seal, and issue it to the plaintiff for service on the defendant. A summons—or a copy of a summons that is addressed to multiple defendants—must be issued for each defendant to be served.	

Rule	Pre-Restyling Text	Restyled Text	Casebook References
4(c)	**(c) SERVICE WITH COMPLAINT; BY WHOM MADE.** (1) A summons shall be served together with a copy of the complaint. The plaintiff is responsible for service of a summons and complaint within the time allowed under subdivision (m) and shall furnish the person effecting service with the necessary copies of the summons and complaint. (2) Service may be effected by any person who is not a party and who is at least 18 years of age. At the request of the plaintiff, however, the court may direct that service be effected by a United States marshal, deputy United States marshal, or other person or officer specially appointed by the court for that purpose. Such an appointment must be made when the plaintiff is authorized to proceed in forma pauperis pursuant to 28 U.S.C. §1915 or is authorized to proceed as a seaman under 28 U.S.C. §1916.	**(c) Service.** **(1)** ***In General.*** A summons must be served with a copy of the complaint. The plaintiff is responsible for having the summons and complaint served within the time allowed by Rule 4(m) and must furnish the necessary copies to the person who makes service. **(2)** ***By Whom.*** Any person who is at least 18 years old and not a party may serve a summons and complaint. **(3)** ***By a Marshal or Someone Specially Appointed.*** At the plaintiff's request, the court may order that service be made by a United States marshal or deputy marshal or by a person specially appointed by the court. The court must so order if the plaintiff is authorized to proceed in forma pauperis under 28 U.S.C. §1915 or as a seaman under 28 U.S.C. §1916.	36, 42, 51
4(d)	**(d) WAIVER OF SERVICE; DUTY TO SAVE COSTS OF SERVICE; REQUEST TO WAIVE.** (1) A defendant who waives service of a summons does not thereby waive any objection to the venue or to the jurisdiction of the court over the person of the defendant. (2) An individual, corporation, or association that is subject to service under subdivision (e), (f), or (h) and that receives notice of an action in the manner provided in this paragraph has a duty to avoid unnecessary costs of serving the summons. To avoid costs, the plaintiff may notify such a defendant of the commencement of the action and request that the defendant waive service of a summons. The notice and request (A) shall be in writing and shall be addressed directly to the defendant, if an individual, or else to an officer or managing or general agent (or other agent authorized by appointment or law to receive service of process)	**(d) Waiving Service.** **(1)** ***Requesting a Waiver.*** An individual, corporation, or association that is subject to service under Rule 4(e), (f), or (h) has a duty to avoid unnecessary expenses of serving the summons. The plaintiff may notify such a defendant that an action has been commenced and request that the defendant waive service of a summons. The notice and request must: **(A)** be in writing and be addressed: **(i)** to the individual defendant; or **(ii)** for a defendant subject to service under Rule 4(h), to an officer, a managing or general agent, or any other agent authorized by appointment or by law to receive service of process; **(B)** name the court where the complaint was filed; **(C)** be accompanied by a copy of the complaint, two copies of a	39, 40, 41, 42, 47, 51, 52, 203, 204, 881, 882, 883, 884, 885

Rule	Pre-Restyling Text	Restyled Text	Casebook References
	of a defendant subject to service under subdivision (h); (B) shall be dispatched through first-class mail or other reliable means; (C) shall be accompanied by a copy of the complaint and shall identify the court in which it has been filed; (D) shall inform the defendant, by means of a text prescribed in an official form promulgated pursuant to Rule 84, of the consequences of compliance and of a failure to comply with the request; (E) shall set forth the date on which the request is sent; (F) shall allow the defendant a reasonable time to return thewaiver, which shall be at least 30 days from the date on which the request is sent, or 60 days from that date if the defendant is addressed outside any judicial district of the United States; and (G) shall provide the defendant with an extra copy of the notice and request, as well as a prepaid means of compliance in writing. If a defendant located within the United States fails to comply with a request for waiver made by a plaintiff located within the United States, the court shall impose the costs subsequently incurred in effecting service on the defendant unless good cause for the failure be shown. (3) A defendant that, before being served with process, timely returns a waiver so requested is not required to serve an answer to the complaint until 60 days after the date on which the request for waiver of service was sent, or 90 days after that date if the defendant was addressed outside any judicial district of the United States. (4) When the plaintiff files a waiver of service with the court, the action shall proceed, except as provided in paragraph (3), as if a summons and complaint had been served at the	waiver form, and a prepaid means for returning the form; **(D)** inform the defendant, using text prescribed in Form 5, of the consequences of waiving and not waiving service; **(E)** state the date when the request is sent; **(F)** give the defendant a reasonable time of at least 30 days after the request was sent—or at least 60 days if sent to the defendant outside any judicial district of the United States—to return the waiver; and **(G)** be sent by first-class mail or other reliable means. **(2)** ***Failure to Waive.*** If a defendant located within the United States fails, without good cause, to sign and return a waiver requested by a plaintiff located within the United States, the court must impose on the defendant: **(A)** the expenses later incurred in making service; and **(B)** the reasonable expenses, including attorney's fees, of any motion required to collect those service expenses. **(3)** ***Time to Answer After a Waiver.*** A defendant who, before being served with process, timely returns a waiver need not serve an answer to the complaint until 60 days after the request was sent—or until 90 days after it was sent to the defendant outside any judicial district of the United States. **(4)** ***Results of Filing a Waiver.*** When the plaintiff files a waiver, proof of service is not required and these rules apply as if a summons and complaint had been served at the time of filing the waiver. **(5)** ***Jurisdiction and Venue Not Waived.*** Waiving service of a summons does not waive any objection to personal jurisdiction or to venue.	

Rule	Pre-Restyling Text	Restyled Text	Casebook References
	time of filing the waiver, and no proof of service shall be required. (5) The costs to be imposed on a defendant under paragraph (2) for failure to comply with a request to waive service of a summons shall include the costs subsequently incurred in effecting service under subdivision (e), (f), or (h), together with the costs, including a reasonable attorney's fee, of any motion required to collect the costs of service.		
4(e)	**(e) SERVICE UPON INDIVIDUALS WITHIN A JUDICIAL DISTRICT OF THE UNITED STATES.** Unless otherwise provided by federal law, service upon an individual from whom a waiver has not been obtained and filed, other than an infant or an incompetent person, may be effected in any judicial district of the United States: (1) pursuant to the law of the state in which the district court is located, or in which service is effected, for the service of a summons upon the defendant in an action brought in the courts of general jurisdiction of the State; or (2) by delivering a copy of the summons and of the complaint to the individual personally or by leaving copies thereof at the individual's dwelling house or usual place of abode with some person of suitable age and discretion then residing therein or by delivering a copy of the summons and of the complaint to an agent authorized by appointment or by law to receive service of process.	**(e) Serving an Individual Within a Judicial District of the United States.** Unless federal law provides otherwise, an individual — other than a minor, an incompetent person, or a person whose waiver has been filed — may be served in a judicial district of the United States by: **(1)** following state law for serving a summons in an action brought in courts of general jurisdiction in the state where the district court is located or where service is made; or **(2)** doing any of the following: **(A)** delivering a copy of the summons and of the complaint to the individual personally; **(B)** leaving a copy of each at the individual's dwelling or usual place of abode with someone of suitable age and discretion who resides there; or **(C)** delivering a copy of each to an agent authorized by appointment or by law to receive service of process.	42, 52, 180, 203
4(f)	**(f) SERVICE UPON INDIVIDUALS IN A FOREIGN COUNTRY.** Unless otherwise provided by federal law, service upon an individual from whom a waiver has not been obtained and filed, other than an infant or an incompetent person, may be effected in a place not within any judicial district of the United States: (1) by any internationally agreed means reasonably calculated to give	**(f) Serving an Individual in a Foreign Country.** Unless federal law provides otherwise, an individual — other than a minor, an incompetent person, or a person whose waiver has been filed — may be served at a place not within any judicial district of the United States: **(1)** by any internationally agreed means of service that is reasonably calculated to give notice, such as those authorized by the Hague	36, 42, 43, 44

Rule	Pre-Restyling Text	Restyled Text	Casebook References
	notice, such as those means authorized by the Hague Convention on the Service Abroad of Judicial and Extrajudicial Documents; or (2) if there is no internationally agreed means of service or the applicable international agreement allows other means of service, provided that service is reasonably calculated to give notice: (A) in the manner prescribed by the law of the foreign country for service in that country in an action in any of its courts of general jurisdiction; or (B) directed by the foreign authority in response to a letter rogatory or letter of request; or (C) unless prohibited by the law of the foreign country, by **(i)** delivery to the individual personally of a copy of the summons and the complaint; or **(ii)** any form of mail requiring a signed receipt, to be addressed and dispatched by the clerk of the court to the party to be served; or (3) by other means not prohibited by international agreement as may be directed by the court.	Convention on the Service Abroad of Judicial and Extrajudicial Documents; **(2)** if there is no internationally agreed means, or if an international agreement allows but does not specify other means, by a method that is reasonably calculated to give notice: **(A)** as prescribed by the foreign country's law for service in that country in an action in its courts of general jurisdiction; **(B)** as the foreign authority directs in response to a letter rogatory or letter of request; or **(C)** unless prohibited by the foreign country's law, by: **(i)** delivering a copy of the summons and of the complaint to the individual personally; or **(ii)** using any form of mail that the clerk addresses and sends to the individual and that requires a signed receipt; or **(3)** by other means not prohibited by international agreement, as the court orders.	
4(g)	**(g) SERVICE UPON INFANTS AND INCOMPETENT PERSONS.** Service upon an infant or an incompetent person in a judicial district of the United States shall be effected in the manner prescribed by the law of the state in which the service is made for the service of summons or other like process upon any such defendant in an action brought in the courts of general jurisdiction of that state. Service upon an infant or an incompetent person in a place not within any judicial district of the United States shall be effected in the manner prescribed by paragraph (2)(A) or (2)(B) of subdivision (f) or by such means as the court may direct.	**(g) Serving a Minor or an Incompetent Person.** A minor or an incompetent person in a judicial district of the United States must be served by following state law for serving a summons or like process on such a defendant in an action brought in the courts of general jurisdiction of the state where service is made. A minor or an incompetent person who is not within any judicial district of the United States must be served in the manner prescribed by Rule 4(f)(2)(A), (f)(2)(B), or (f)(3).	

Rule	Pre-Restyling Text	Restyled Text	Casebook References
4(h)	**(h) SERVICE UPON CORPORATIONS AND ASSOCIATIONS.** Unless otherwise provided by federal law, service upon a domestic or foreign corporation or upon a partnership or other unincorporated association that is subject to suit under a common name, and from which a waiver of service has not been obtained and filed, shall be effected: (1) in a judicial district of the United States in the manner prescribed for individuals by subdivision (e)(1), or by delivering a copy of the summons and of the complaint to an officer, a managing or general agent, or to any other agent authorized by appointment or by law to receive service of process and, if the agent is one authorized by statute to receive service and the statute so requires, by also mailing a copy to the defendant, or (2) in a place not within any judicial district of the United States in any manner prescribed for individuals by subdivision (f) except personal delivery as provided in paragraph (2)(C)(i) thereof.	**(h) Serving a Corporation, Partnership, or Association.** Unless federal law provides otherwise or the defendant's waiver has been filed, a domestic or foreign corporation, or a partnership or other unincorporated association that is subject to suit under a common name, must be served: **(1)** in a judicial district of the United States: **(A)** in the manner prescribed by Rule 4(e)(1) for serving an individual; or **(B)** by delivering a copy of the summons and of the complaint to an officer, a managing or general agent, or any other agent authorized by appointment or by law to receive service of process and—if the agent is one authorized by statute and the statute so requires—by also mailing a copy of each to the defendant; or **(2)** at a place not within any judicial district of the United States, in any manner prescribed by Rule 4(f) for serving an individual, except personal delivery under (f)(2)(C)(i).	43, 44
4(i)	**(i) SERVING THE UNITED STATES, ITS AGENCIES, CORPORATIONS, OFFICERS, OR EMPLOYEES.** (1) Service upon the United States shall be effected (A) by delivering a copy of the summons and of the complaint to the United States attorney for the district in which the action is brought or to an assistant United States attorney or clerical employee designated by the United States attorney in a writing filed with the clerk of the court or by sending a copy of the summons and of the complaint by registered or certified mail addressed to the civil process clerk at the office of the United States attorney and (B) by also sending a copy of the summons and of the complaint by	**(i) Serving the United States and Its Agencies, Corporations, Officers, or Employees.** **(1)** ***United States.*** To serve the United States, a party must: **(A)** **(i)** deliver a copy of the summons and of the complaint to the United States attorney for the district where the action is brought—or to an assistant United States attorney or clerical employee whom the United States attorney designates in a writing filed with the court clerk—or **(ii)** send a copy of each by registered or certified mail to the civil-process clerk at the United States attorney's office; **(B)** send a copy of each by registered or certified mail to the	

Rule	Pre-Restyling Text	Restyled Text	Casebook References
	registered or certified mail to the Attorney General of the United States at Washington, District of Columbia, and (C) in any action attacking the validity of an order of an officer or agency of the United States not made a party, by also sending a copy of the summons and of the complaint by registered or certified mail to the officer or agency. (2) (A) Service on an agency or corporation of the United States, or an officer or employee of the United States sued only in an official capacity, is effected by serving the United States in the manner prescribed by Rule 4(i)(1) and by also sending a copy of the summons and complaint by registered or certified mail to the officer, employee, agency, or corporation. (B) Service on an officer or employee of the United States sued in an individual capacity for acts or omissions occurring in connection with the performance of duties on behalf of the United States — whether or not the officer or employee is sued also in an official capacity — is effected by serving the United States in the manner prescribed by Rule 4(i)(1) and by serving the officer or employee in the manner prescribed by Rule 4(e), (f), or (g). (3) The court shall allow a reasonable time to serve process under Rule 4(i) for the purpose of curing the failure to serve: (A) all persons required to be served in an action governed by Rule 4(i)(2)(A), if the plaintiff has served either the United States attorney or the Attorney General of the United States, or (B) the United States in an action governed by Rule 4(i)(2)(B), if the plaintiff has served an officer or employee of the United States sued in an individual capacity.	Attorney General of the United States at Washington, D.C.; and **(C)** if the action challenges an order of a nonparty agency or officer of the United States, send a copy of each by registered or certified mail to the agency or officer. **(2)** ***Agency; Corporation; Officer or Employee Sued in an Official Capacity.*** To serve a United States agency or corporation, or a United States officer or employee sued only in an official capacity, a party must serve the United States and also send a copy of the summons and of the complaint by registered or certified mail to the agency, corporation, officer, or employee. **(3)** ***Officer or Employee Sued Individually.*** To serve a United States officer or employee sued in an individual capacity for an act or omission occurring in connection with duties performed on the United States' behalf (whether or not the officer or employee is also sued in an official capacity), a party must serve the United States and also serve the officer or employee under Rule 4(e), (f), or (g). **(4)** ***Extending Time.*** The court must allow a party a reasonable time to cure its failure to: **(A)** serve a person required to be served under Rule 4(i)(2), if the party has served either the United States attorney or the Attorney General of the United States; or **(B)** serve the United States under Rule 4(i)(3), if the party has served the United States officer or employee.	

Rule	Pre-Restyling Text	Restyled Text	Casebook References
4(j)	**(j) SERVICE UPON FOREIGN, STATE, OR LOCAL GOVERNMENTS.** (1) Service upon a foreign state or a political subdivision, agency, or instrumentality thereof shall be effected pursuant to 28 U.S.C. §1608. (2) Service upon a state, municipal corporation, or other governmental organization subject to suit shall be effected by delivering a copy of the summons and of the complaint to its chief executive officer or by serving the summons and complaint in the manner prescribed by the law of that state for the service of summons or other like process upon any such defendant.	**(j) Serving a Foreign, State, or Local Government.** **(1) *Foreign State.*** A foreign state or its political subdivision, agency, or instrumentality must be served in accordance with 28 U.S.C. §1608. **(2) *State or Local Government.*** A state, a municipal corporation, or any other state-created governmental organization that is subject to suit must be served by: **(A)** delivering a copy of the summons and of the complaint to its chief executive officer; or **(B)** serving a copy of each in the manner prescribed by that state's law for serving a summons or like process on such a defendant.	42, 1221, 1228
4(k)	**(k) TERRITORIAL LIMITS OF EFFECTIVE SERVICE.** (1) Service of a summons or filing a waiver of service is effective to establish jurisdiction over the person of a defendant (A) who could be subjected to the jurisdiction of a court of general jurisdiction in the state in which the district court is located, or (B) who is a party joined under Rule 14 or Rule 19 and is served at a place within a judicial district of the United States and not more than 100 miles from the place from which the summons issues, or (C) who is subject to the federal interpleader jurisdiction under 28 U.S.C. §1335, or (D) when authorized by a statute of the United States. (2) If the exercise of jurisdiction is consistent with the Constitution and laws of the United States, serving a summons or filing a waiver of service is also effective, with respect to claims arising under federal law, to establish personal jurisdiction over the person of any defendant who is not subject to the jurisdiction of the courts of general jurisdiction of any state.	**(k) Territorial Limits of Effective Service.** **(1) *In General.*** Serving a summons or filing a waiver of service establishes personal jurisdiction over a defendant: **(A)** who is subject to the jurisdiction of a court of general jurisdiction in the state where the district court is located; **(B)** who is a party joined under Rule 14 or 19 and is served within a judicial district of the United States and not more than 100 miles from where the summons was issued; or **(C)** when authorized by a federal statute. **(2) *Federal Claim Outside State-Court Jurisdiction.*** For a claim that arises under federal law, serving a summons or filing a waiver of service establishes personal jurisdiction over a defendant if: **(A)** the defendant is not subject to jurisdiction in any state's courts of general jurisdiction; and **(B)** exercising jurisdiction is consistent with the United States Constitution and laws.	42, 154

Rule	Pre-Restyling Text	Restyled Text	Casebook References
4(l)	***(l)* PROOF OF SERVICE.** If service is not waived, the person effecting service shall make proof thereof to the court. If service is made by a person other than a United States marshal or deputy United States marshal, the person shall make affidavit thereof. Proof of service in a place not within any judicial district of the United States shall, if effected under paragraph (1) of subdivision (f), be made pursuant to the applicable treaty or convention, and shall, if effected under paragraph (2) or (3) thereof, include a receipt signed by the addressee or other evidence of delivery to the addressee satisfactory to the court. Failure to make proof of service does not affect the validity of the service. The court may allow proof of service to be amended.	**(l) Proving Service.** **(1) *Affidavit Required.*** Unless service is waived, proof of service must be made to the court. Except for service by a United States marshal or deputy marshal, proof must be by the server's affidavit. **(2) *Service Outside the United States.*** Service not within any judicial district of the United States must be proved as follows: **(A)** if made under Rule 4(f)(1), as provided in the applicable treaty or convention; or **(B)** if made under Rule 4(f)(2) or (f)(3), by a receipt signed by the addressee, or by other evidence satisfying the court that the summons and complaint were delivered to the addressee. **(3) *Validity of Service; Amending Proof.*** Failure to prove service does not affect the validity of service. The court may permit proof of service to be amended.	42
4(m)	**(m) TIME LIMIT FOR SERVICE.** If service of the summons and complaint is not made upon a defendant within 120 days after the filing of the complaint, the court, upon motion or on its own initiative after notice to the plaintiff, shall dismiss the action without prejudice as to that defendant or direct that service be effected within a specified time; provided that if the plaintiff shows good cause for the failure, the court shall extend the time for service for an appropriate period. This subdivision does not apply to service in a foreign country pursuant to subdivision (f) or (j)(1).	**(m) Time Limit for Service.** If a defendant is not served within 120 days after the complaint is filed, the court—on motion or on its own after notice to the plaintiff—must dismiss the action without prejudice against that defendant or order that service be made within a specified time. But if the plaintiff shows good cause for the failure, the court must extend the time for service for an appropriate period. This subdivision (m) does not apply to service in a foreign country under Rule 4(f) or 4(j)(1).	51, 52, 53
4(n)	**(n) SEIZURE OF PROPERTY; SERVICE OF SUMMONS NOT FEASIBLE.** (1) If a statute of the United States so provides, the court may assert jurisdiction over property. Notice to claimants of the property shall then be sent in the manner provided by the statute or by service of a summons under this rule. (2) Upon a showing that personal jurisdiction over a defendant	**(n) Asserting Jurisdiction over Property or Assets.** **(1) *Federal Law.*** The court may assert jurisdiction over property if authorized by a federal statute. Notice to claimants of the property must be given as provided in the statute or by serving a summons under this rule. **(2) *State Law.*** On a showing that personal jurisdiction over a defendant cannot be obtained in the	42

Rule	Pre-Restyling Text	Restyled Text	Casebook References
	cannot, in the district where the action is brought, be obtained with reasonable efforts by service of summons in any manner authorized by this rule, the court may assert jurisdiction over any of the defendant's assets found within the district by seizing the assets under the circumstances and in the manner provided by the law of the state in which the district court is located.	district where the action is brought by reasonable efforts to serve a summons under this rule, the court may assert jurisdiction over the defendant's assets found in the district. Jurisdiction is acquired by seizing the assets under the circumstances and in the manner provided by state law in that district.	
5(a)	**Rule 5. Service and Filing of Pleadings and Other Papers** (a) SERVICE: WHEN REQUIRED. Except as otherwise provided in these rules, every order required by its terms to be served, every pleading subsequent to the original complaint unless the court otherwise orders because of numerous defendants, every paper relating to discovery required to be served upon a party unless the court otherwise orders, every written motion other than one which may be heard ex parte, and every written notice, appearance, demand, offer of judgment, designation of record on appeal, and similar paper shall be served upon each of the parties. No service need be made on parties in default for failure to appear except that pleadings asserting new or additional claims for relief against them shall be served upon them in the manner provided for service of summons in Rule 4. In an action begun by seizure of property, in which no person need be or is named as defendant, any service required to be made prior to the filing of an answer, claim, or appearance shall be made upon the person having custody or possession of the property at the time of its seizure.	**Rule 5. Serving and Filing Pleadings and Other Papers** **(a) Service: When Required.** **(1)** *In General.* Unless these rules provide otherwise, each of the following papers must be served on every party: **(A)** an order stating that service is required; **(B)** a pleading filed after the original complaint, unless the court orders otherwise under Rule 5(c) because there are numerous defendants; **(C)** a discovery paper required to be served on a party, unless the court orders otherwise; **(D)** a written motion, except one that may be heard ex parte; and **(E)** a written notice, appearance, demand, or offer of judgment, or any similar paper. **(2)** ***If a Party Fails to Appear.*** No service is required on a party who is in default for failing to appear. But a pleading that asserts a new claim for relief against such a party must be served on that party under Rule 4. **(3)** ***Seizing Property.*** If an action is begun by seizing property and no person is or need be named as a defendant, any service required before the filing of an appearance, answer, or claim must be made on the person who had custody or possession of the property when it was seized.	

Rule	Pre-Restyling Text	Restyled Text	Casebook References
5(b)	**(b) MAKING SERVICE.** (1) Service under Rules 5(a) and 77(d) on a party represented by an attorney is made on the attorney unless the court orders service on the party. (2) Service under Rule 5(a) is made by: (A) Delivering a copy to the person served by: **(i)** handing it to the person; **(ii)** leaving it at the person's office with a clerk or other person in charge, or if no one is in charge leaving it in a conspicuous place in the office; or **(iii)** if the person has no office or the office is closed, leaving it at the person's dwelling house or usual place of abode with someone of suitable age and discretion residing there. (B) Mailing a copy to the last known address of the person served. Service by mail is complete on mailing. (C) If the person served has no known address, leaving a copy with the clerk of the court. (D) Delivering a copy by any other means, including electronic means, consented to in writing by the person served. Service by electronic means is complete on transmission; service by other consented means is complete when the person making service delivers the copy to the agency designated to make delivery. If authorized by local rule, a party may make service under this subparagraph (D) through the court's transmission facilities. (3) Service by electronic means under Rule 5(b)(2)(D) is not effective if the party making service learns that the attempted service did not reach the person to be served.	**(b) Service: How Made.** **(1)** ***Serving an Attorney.*** If a party is represented by an attorney, service under this rule must be made on the attorney unless the court orders service on the party. **(2)** ***Service in General.*** A paper is served under this rule by: **(A)** handing it to the person; **(B)** leaving it: **(i)** at the person's office with a clerk or other person in charge or, if no one is in charge, in a conspicuous place in the office; or **(ii)** if the person has no office or the office is closed, at the person's dwelling or usual place of abode with someone of suitable age and discretion who resides there; **(C)** mailing it to the person's last known address—in which event service is complete upon mailing; **(D)** leaving it with the court clerk if the person has no known address; **(E)** sending it by electronic means if the person consented in writing—in which event service is complete upon transmission, but is not effective if the serving party learns that it did not reach the person to be served; or **(F)** delivering it by any other means that the person consented to in writing—in which event service is complete when the person making service delivers it to the agency designated to make delivery. **(3)** ***Using Court Facilities.*** If a local rule so authorizes, a party may use the court's transmission facilities to make service under Rule 5(b)(2)(E).	36
5(c)	**(c) SAME: NUMEROUS DEFENDANTS.** In any action in which there are unusually large numbers of defendants, the court, upon motion or of its own initiative,	**(c) Serving Numerous Defendants.** **(1)** ***In General.*** If an action involves an unusually large number of defendants, the court	

Rule	Pre-Restyling Text	Restyled Text	Casebook References
	may order that service of the pleadings of the defendants and replies thereto need not be made as between the defendants and that any cross-claim, counterclaim, or matter constituting an avoidance or affirmative defense contained therein shall be deemed to be denied or avoided by all other parties and that the filing of any such pleading and service thereof upon the plaintiff constitutes due notice of it to the parties. A copy of every such order shall be served upon the parties in such manner and form as the court directs.	may, on motion or on its own, order that: **(A)** defendants' pleadings and replies to them need not be served on other defendants; **(B)** any crossclaim, counterclaim, avoidance, or affirmative defense in those pleadings and replies to them will be treated as denied or avoided by all other parties; and **(C)** filing any such pleading and serving it on the plaintiff constitutes notice of the pleading to all parties. **(2)** ***Notifying Parties.*** A copy of every such order must be served on the parties as the court directs.	
5(d)-(e)	**(d) FILING; CERTIFICATE OF SERVICE.** All papers after the complaint required to be served upon a party, together with a certificate of service, must be filed with the court within a reasonable time after service, but disclosures under Rule 26(a)(1) or (2) and the following discovery requests and responses must not be filed until they are used in the proceeding or the court orders filing: (i) depositions, (ii) interrogatories, (iii) requests for documents or to permit entry upon land, and (iv) requests for admission. **(e) FILING WITH THE COURT DEFINED.** The filing of papers with the court as required by these rules shall be made by filing them with the clerk of court, except that the judge may permit the papers to be filed with the judge, in which event the judge shall note thereon the filing date and forthwith transmit them to the office of the clerk. A court may by local rule permit or require papers to be filed, signed, or verified by electronic means that are consistent with technical standards, if any, that the Judicial Conference of the United States establishes. A local rule may require filing by electronic means only if reasonable exceptions are allowed. A paper filed by electronic means in compliance with a local rule constitutes a written paper for the purpose of applying these rules.	**(d) Filing.** **(1)** ***Required Filings; Certificate of Service.*** Any paper after the complaint that is required to be served—together with a certificate of service—must be filed within a reasonable time after service. But disclosures under Rule 26(a)(1) or (2) and the following discovery requests and responses must not be filed until they are used in the proceeding or the court orders filing: depositions, interrogatories, requests for documents or tangible things or to permit entry onto land, and requests for admission. **(2)** ***How Filing Is Made—In General.*** A paper is filed by delivering it: **(A)** to the clerk; or **(B)** to a judge who agrees to accept it for filing, and who must then note the filing date on the paper and promptly send it to the clerk. **(3)** ***Electronic Filing, Signing, or Verification.*** A court may, by local rule, allow papers to be filed, signed, or verified by electronic means that are consistent with any technical standards established by the Judicial Conference of the United States. A local rule may require electronic filing only if reasonable exceptions are allowed. A paper filed electronically in compliance with a local rule is a	37

Rule	Pre-Restyling Text	Restyled Text	Casebook References
	The clerk shall not refuse to accept for filing any paper presented for that purpose solely because it is not presented in proper form as required by these rules or any local rules or practices.	written paper for purposes of these rules. **(4) *Acceptance by the Clerk.*** The clerk must not refuse to file a paper solely because it is not in the form prescribed by these rules or by a local rule or practice.	
6(e) [now 6(d)]	**Rule 6. Time** **(e) ADDITIONAL TIME AFTER CERTAIN KINDS OF SERVICE.** Whenever a party must or may act within a prescribed period after service and service is made under Rule 5(b)(2)(B), (C), or (D), 3 days are added after the prescribed period would otherwise expire under subdivision (a).	**Rule 6. Computing and Extending Time, Time for Motion Papers** **(d) Additional Time After Certain Kinds of Service.** When a party may or must act within a specified time after service and service is made under Rule 5(b)(2)(C), (D), (E), or (F), 3 days are added after the period would otherwise expire under Rule 6(a).	36
7(a)	**Rule 7. Pleadings Allowed; Form of Motions** **(a) PLEADINGS.** There shall be a complaint and an answer; a reply to a counterclaim denominated as such; an answer to a cross-claim, if the answer contains a cross-claim; a third-party complaint, if a person who was not an original party is summoned under the provisions of Rule 14; and a third-party answer, if a third-party complaint is served. No other pleading shall be allowed, except that the court may order a reply to an answer or a third-party answer.	**Rule 7. Pleadings Allowed; Form of Motions and Other Papers** **(a) Pleadings.** Only these pleadings are allowed: **(1)** a complaint; **(2)** an answer to a complaint; **(3)** an answer to a counterclaim designated as a counterclaim; **(4)** an answer to a crossclaim; **(5)** a third-party complaint; **(6)** an answer to a third-party complaint; and **(7)** if the court orders one, a reply to an answer.	Rule 7 generally: 344, 345, 362 7(a): 328, 343, 344, 346, 347, 1154
7(b)	**(b) MOTIONS AND OTHER PAPERS.** (1) An application to the court for an order shall be by motion which, unless made during a hearing or trial, shall be made in writing, shall state with particularity the grounds therefor, and shall set forth the relief or order sought. The requirement of writing is fulfilled if the motion is stated in a written notice of the hearing of the motion. (2) The rules applicable to captions and other matters of form of pleadings apply to all motions and other papers provided for by these rules. (3) All motions shall be signed in accordance with Rule 11.	**(b) Motions and Other Papers.** **(1) *In General.*** A request for a court order must be made by motion. The motion must: **(A)** be in writing unless made during a hearing or trial; **(B)** state with particularity the grounds for seeking the order; and **(C)** state the relief sought. **(2) *Form.*** The rules governing captions and other matters of form in pleadings apply to motions and other papers.	

Rule	Pre-Restyling Text	Restyled Text	Casebook References
8(a)	**Rule 8. General Rules of Pleading** **(a) CLAIMS FOR RELIEF.** A pleading which sets forth a claim for relief, whether an original claim, counterclaim, cross-claim, or third-party claim, shall contain (1) a short and plain statement of the grounds upon which the court's jurisdiction depends, unless the court already has jurisdiction and the claim needs no new grounds of jurisdiction to support it, (2) a short and plain statement of the claim showing that the pleader is entitled to relief, and (3) a demand for judgment for the relief the pleader seeks. Relief in the alternative or of several different types may be demanded.	**Rule 8. General Rules of Pleading** **(a) Claim for Relief.** A pleading that states a claim for relief must contain: **(1)** a short and plain statement of the grounds for the court's jurisdiction, unless the court already has jurisdiction and the claim needs no new jurisdictional support; **(2)** a short and plain statement of the claim showing that the pleader is entitled to relief; and **(3)** a demand for the relief sought, which may include relief in the alternative or different types of relief.	Rule 8 generally: 286, 287, 290, 291, 293, 305, 306, 311, 313, 314, 315, 320, 324, 326, 327, 330, **335**, 340, 345, 363, 437, 439, 973 8(a): 218, 292, 293, 310, 311, 319, 320, 323, 325, 330, 331, 335, 336, 338, 345, 355, 437, 439, 440
8(b)	**(b) DEFENSES; FORM OF DENIALS.** A party shall state in short and plain terms the party's defenses to each claim asserted and shall admit or deny the averments upon which the adverse party relies. If a party is without knowledge or information sufficient to form a belief as to the truth of an averment, the party shall so state and this has the effect of a denial. Denials shall fairly meet the substance of the averments denied. When a pleader intends in good faith to deny only a part or a qualification of an averment, the pleader shall specify so much of it as is true and material and shall deny only the remainder. Unless the pleader intends in good faith to controvert all the averments of the preceding pleading, the pleader may make denials as specific denials of designated averments or paragraphs or may generally deny all the averments except such designated averments or paragraphs as the pleader expressly admits; but, when the pleader does so intend to controvert all its averments, including averments of the grounds upon which the court's jurisdiction depends, the pleader may do so by general denial subject	**(b) Defenses; Admissions and Denials.** **(1)** ***In General.*** In responding to a pleading, a party must: **(A)** state in short and plain terms its defenses to each claim asserted against it; and **(B)** admit or deny the allegations asserted against it by an opposing party. **(2)** ***Denials — Responding to the Substance.*** A denial must fairly respond to the substance of the allegation. **(3)** ***General and Specific Denials.*** A party that intends in good faith to deny all the allegations of a pleading — including the jurisdictional grounds — may do so by a general denial. A party that does not intend to deny all the allegations must either specifically deny designated allegations or generally deny all except those specifically admitted. **(4)** ***Denying Part of an Allegation.*** A party that intends in good faith to deny only part of an allegation must admit the part that is true and deny the rest.	361, 368, 370

Rule	Pre-Restyling Text	Restyled Text	Casebook References
	to the obligations set forth in Rule 11.	**(5)** ***Lacking Knowledge or Information.*** A party that lacks knowledge or information sufficient to form a belief about the truth of an allegation must so state, and the statement has the effect of a denial. **(6)** ***Effect of Failing to Deny.*** An allegation — other than one relating to the amount of damages — is admitted if a responsive pleading is required and the allegation is not denied. If a responsive pleading is not required, an allegation is considered denied or avoided.	
8(c)	**(c) AFFIRMATIVE DEFENSES.** In pleading to a preceding pleading, a party shall set forth affirmatively accord and satisfaction, arbitration and award, assumption of risk, contributory negligence, discharge in bankruptcy, duress, estoppel, failure of consideration, fraud, illegality, injury by fellow servant, laches, license, payment, release, res judicata, statute of frauds, statute of limitations, waiver, and any other matter constituting an avoidance or affirmative defense. When a party has mistakenly designated a defense as a counterclaim or a counterclaim as a defense, the court on terms, if justice so requires, shall treat the pleading as if there had been a proper designation.	**(c) Affirmative Defenses.** **(1)** ***In General.*** In responding to a pleading, a party must affirmatively state any avoidance or affirmative defense, including: • accord and satisfaction; • arbitration and award; • assumption of risk; • contributory negligence; • discharge in bankruptcy; • duress; • estoppel; • failure of consideration; • fraud; • illegality; • injury by fellow servant; • laches; • license; • payment; • release; • res judicata; • statute of frauds; • statute of limitations; and • waiver. **(2)** ***Mistaken Designation.*** If a party mistakenly designates a defense as a counterclaim, or a counterclaim as a defense, the court must, if justice requires, treat the pleading as though it were correctly designated, and may impose terms for doing so.	361, 362, 370, 373, 375, 376, 377, 378, 1164, 1219
8(d)-(f)	**(d) EFFECT OF FAILURE TO DENY.** Averments in a pleading to which a responsive pleading is required, other than those as to the amount of damage, are admitted when not denied in the responsive pleading. Averments in a pleading to which no responsive pleading is	[Former Rule 8(d) has become restyled Rule 8(b)(6).] **(d) Pleading to Be Concise and Direct; Alternative Statements; Inconsistency.** **(1)** ***In General.*** Each allegation must be simple, concise, and	292, 344, 345, 355, 358

Rule	Pre-Restyling Text	Restyled Text	Casebook References
	required or permitted shall be taken as denied or avoided. **(e) PLEADING TO BE CONCISE AND DIRECT; CONSISTENCY.** (1) Each averment of a pleading shall be simple, concise, and direct. No technical forms of pleading or motions are required. (2) A party may set forth two or more statements of a claim or defense alternately or hypothetically, either in one count or defense or in separate counts or defenses. When two or more statements are made in the alternative and one of them if made independently would be sufficient, the pleading is not made insufficient by the insufficiency of one or more of the alternative statements. A party may also state as many separate claims or defenses as the party has regardless of consistency and whether based on legal, equitable, or maritime grounds. All statements shall be made subject to the obligations set forth in Rule 11. **(f) CONSTRUCTION OF PLEADINGS.** All pleadings shall be so construed as to do substantial justice.	direct. No technical form is required. **(2)** ***Alternative Statements of a Claim or Defense.*** A party may set out 2 or more statements of a claim or defense alternatively or hypothetically, either in a single count or defense or in separate ones. If a party makes alternative statements, the pleading is sufficient if any one of them is sufficient. **(3)** ***Inconsistent Claims or Defenses.*** A party may state as many separate claims or defenses as it has, regardless of consistency. **(e) Construing Pleadings.** Pleadings must be construed so as to do justice.	
9(a)	**(a) CAPACITY.** It is not necessary to aver the capacity of a party to sue or be sued or the authority of a party to sue or be sued in a representative capacity or the legal existence of an organized association of persons that is made a party, except to the extent required to show the jurisdiction of the court. When a party desires to raise an issue as to the legal existence of any party or the capacity of any party to sue or be sued or the authority of a party to sue or be sued in a representative capacity, the party desiring to raise the issue shall do so by specific negative averment, which shall include such supporting particulars as are peculiarly within the pleader's knowledge.	**Rule 9. Pleading Special Matters** **(a) Capacity or Authority to Sue; Legal Existence.** **(1)** ***In General.*** Except when required to show that the court has jurisdiction, a pleading need not allege: **(A)** a party's capacity to sue or be sued; **(B)** a party's authority to sue or be sued in a representative capacity; or **(C)** the legal existence of an organized association of persons that is made a party. **(2)** ***Raising Those Issues.*** To raise any of those issues, a party must do so by a specific denial, which must state any supporting facts that are peculiarly within the party's knowledge.	Rule 9 generally: 317, 338, 340, 344, 437

Rule	Pre-Restyling Text	Restyled Text	Casebook References
9(b)	**(b) FRAUD, MISTAKE, CONDITION OF THE MIND.** In all averments of fraud or mistake, the circumstances constituting fraud or mistake shall be stated with particularity. Malice, intent, knowledge, and other condition of mind of a person may be averred generally.	**(b) Fraud or Mistake; Conditions of Mind.** In alleging fraud or mistake, a party must state with particularity the circumstances constituting fraud or mistake. Malice, intent, knowledge, and other conditions of a person's mind may be alleged generally.	317, 325, 333, 334, 336, 338, 343, 344, 345, 346, 347, 348, 349, 350, 351, 353, 354, 394
9(c)	**(c) CONDITIONS PRECEDENT.** In pleading the performance or occurrence of conditions precedent, it is sufficient to aver generally that all conditions precedent have been performed or have occurred. A denial of performance or occurrence shall be made specifically and with particularity.	**(c) Conditions Precedent.** In pleading conditions precedent, it suffices to allege generally that all conditions precedent have occurred or been performed. But when denying that a condition precedent has occurred or been performed, a party must do so with particularity.	317, 370
11(a)	**Rule 11. Signing of Pleadings, Motions, and Other Papers; Representations to Court; Sanctions** **(a) SIGNATURE.** Every pleading, written motion, and other paper shall be signed by at least one attorney of record in the attorney's individual name, or, if the party is not represented by an attorney, shall be signed by the party. Each paper shall state the signer's address and telephone number, if any. Except when otherwise specifically provided by rule or statute, pleadings need not be verified or accompanied by affidavit. An unsigned paper shall be stricken unless omission of the signature is corrected promptly after being called to the attention of the attorney or party.	**Rule 11. Signing Pleadings, Motions, and Other Papers; Representations to the Court; Sanctions** **(a) Signature.** Every pleading, written motion, and other paper must be signed by at least one attorney of record in the attorney's name—or by a party personally if the party is unrepresented. The paper must state the signer's address, e-mail address, and telephone number. Unless a rule or statute specifically states otherwise, a pleading need not be verified or accompanied by an affidavit. The court must strike an unsigned paper unless the omission is promptly corrected after being called to the attorney's or party's attention.	Rule 11 generally: 329, 337, 353, 400, 401, 402, 403, 404, 406, 407, 409, 411, 412, 413, 415, 416, 417, 419, 420, 421, 422, 423, 424, 425, 427, 428, 429, 430, 432, 433, 434, 435, 436, 437, 438, 443, 444, 445, 447, 448, 451, 452, 453, 454, 455, 456, 457, 461, 462, 464, 465, 466, 467, 468
11(b)	(b) REPRESENTATIONS TO COURT. By presenting to the court (whether by signing, filing, submitting, or later advocating) a pleading, written motion, or other paper, an attorney or unrepresented party is certifying that to the best of the person's knowledge,	**(b) Representations to the Court.** By presenting to the court a pleading, written motion, or other paper—whether by signing, filing, submitting, or later advocating it—an attorney or unrepresented party certifies that to the best of the person's knowledge, information,	329, 424, 433, 438, 444, 445, 446, 447, 451, 452, 455

Rule	Pre-Restyling Text	Restyled Text	Casebook References
	information, and belief, formed after an inquiry reasonable under the circumstances, (1) it is not being presented for any improper purpose, such as to harass or to cause unnecessary delay or needless increase in the cost of litigation; (2) the claims, defenses, and other legal contentions therein are warranted by existing law or by a nonfrivolous argument for the extension, modification, or reversal of existing law or the establishment of new law; (3) the allegations and other factual contentions have evidentiary support or, if specifically so identified, are likely to have evidentiary support after a reasonable opportunity for further investigation or discovery; and (4) the denials of factual contentions are warranted on the evidence or, if specifically so identified, are reasonably based on a lack of information or belief.	and belief, formed after an inquiry reasonable under the circumstances: **(1)** it is not being presented for any improper purpose, such as to harass, cause unnecessary delay, or needlessly increase the cost of litigation; **(2)** the claims, defenses, and other legal contentions are warranted by existing law or by a nonfrivolous argument for extending, modifying, or reversing existing law or for establishing new law; **(3)** the factual contentions have evidentiary support or, if specifically so identified, will likely have evidentiary support after a reasonable opportunity for further investigation or discovery; and **(4)** the denials of factual contentions are warranted on the evidence or, if specifically so identified, are reasonably based on belief or a lack of information.	
11(c)	**(c) SANCTIONS.** If, after notice and a reasonable opportunity to respond, the court determines that subdivision (b) has been violated, the court may, subject to the conditions stated below, impose an appropriate sanction upon the attorneys, law firms, or parties that have violated subdivision (b) or are responsible for the violation. (1) How Initiated. (A) By Motion. A motion for sanctions under this rule shall be made separately from other motions or requests and shall describe the specific conduct alleged to violate subdivision (b). It shall be served as provided in Rule 5, but shall not be filed with or presented to the court unless, within 21 days after service of the motion (or such other period as the court may prescribe), the challenged paper, claim, defense, contention, allegation, or denial is not withdrawn or appropriately corrected. If warranted, the court	**(c) Sanctions.** **(1)** ***In General.*** If, after notice and a reasonable opportunity to respond, the court determines that Rule 11(b) has been violated, the court may impose an appropriate sanction on any attorney, law firm, or party that violated the rule or is responsible for the violation. Absent exceptional circumstances, a law firm must be held jointly responsible for a violation committed by its partner, associate, or employee. **(2)** ***Motion for Sanctions.*** A motion for sanctions must be made separately from any other motion and must describe the specific conduct that allegedly violates Rule 11(b). The motion must be served under Rule 5, but it must not be filed or be presented to the court if the challenged paper, claim, defense, contention, or denial is withdrawn or appropriately corrected within 21 days after service or within another time the court sets. If warranted, the court	329, 396, 412, 456

Rule	Pre-Restyling Text	Restyled Text	Casebook References
	may award to the party prevailing on the motion the reasonable expenses and attorney's fees incurred in presenting or opposing the motion. Absent exceptional circumstances, a law firm shall be held jointly responsible for violations committed by its partners, associates, and employees. (B) On Court's Initiative. On its own initiative, the court may enter an order describing the specific conduct that appears to violate subdivision (b) and directing an attorney, law firm, or party to show cause why it has not violated subdivision (b) with respect thereto. (2) Nature of Sanction; Limitations. A sanction imposed for violation of this rule shall be limited to what is sufficient to deter repetition of such conduct or comparable conduct by others similarly situated. Subject to the limitations in sub paragraphs (A) and (B), the sanction may consist of, or include, directives of a nonmonetary nature, an order to pay a penalty into court, or, if imposed on motion and warranted for effective deterrence, an order directing payment to the movant of some or all of the reasonable attorneys' fees and other expenses incurred as a direct result of the violation. (A) Monetary sanctions may not be awarded against a represented party for a violation of subdivision (b)(2). (B) Monetary sanctions may not be awarded on the court's initiative unless the court issues its order to show cause before a voluntary dismissal or settlement of the claims made by or against the party which is, or whose attorneys are, to be sanctioned. (3) Order. When imposing sanctions, the court shall describe the conduct determined to constitute a violation of this rule and explain the basis for the sanction imposed.	may award to the prevailing party the reasonable expenses, including attorney's fees, incurred for the motion. **(3)** ***On the Court's Initiative.*** On its own, the court may order an attorney, law firm, or party to show cause why conduct specifically described in the order has not violated Rule 11(b). **(4)** ***Nature of a Sanction.*** A sanction imposed under this rule must be limited to what suffices to deter repetition of the conduct or comparable conduct by others similarly situated. The sanction may include nonmonetary directives; an order to pay a penalty into court; or, if imposed on motion and warranted for effective deterrence, an order directing payment to the movant of part or all of the reasonable attorney's fees and other expenses directly resulting from the violation. **(5)** ***Limitations on Monetary Sanctions.*** The court must not impose a monetary sanction: **(A)** against a represented party for violating Rule 11(b)(2); or **(B)** on its own, unless it issued the show-cause order under Rule 11(c)(3) before voluntary dismissal or settlement of the claims made by or against the party that is, or whose attorneys are, to be sanctioned. **(6)** ***Requirements for an Order.*** An order imposing a sanction must describe the sanctioned conduct and explain the basis for the sanction.	

Rule	Pre-Restyling Text	Restyled Text	Casebook References
11(d)	**(d) IN APPLICABILITY TO DISCOVERY.** Subdivisions (a) through (c) of this rule do not apply to disclosures and discovery requests, responses, objections, and motions that are subject to the provisions of Rules 26 through 37.	**(d) Inapplicability to Discovery.** This rule does not apply to disclosures and discovery requests, responses, objections, and motions under Rules 26 through 37.	
12(a)	**Rule 12. Defenses and Objections — When and How Presented — By Pleading or Motion — Motion for Judgment on the Pleadings** **(a) WHEN PRESENTED.** (1) Unless a different time is prescribed in a statute of the United States, a defendant shall serve an answer (A) within 20 days after being served with the summons and complaint, or (B) if service of the summons has been timely waived on request under Rule 4(d), within 60 days after the date when the request for waiver was sent, or within 90 days after that date if the defendant was addressed outside any judicial district of the United States. (2) A party served with a pleading stating a cross-claim against that party shall serve an answer thereto within 20 days after being served. The plaintiff shall serve a reply to a counterclaim in the answer within 20 days after service of the answer, or, if a reply is ordered by the court, within 20 days after service of the order, unless the order otherwise directs. (3)(A) The United States, an agency of the United States, or an officer or employee of the United States sued in an official capacity, shall serve an answer to the complaint or cross-claim — or a reply to a counterclaim — within 60 days after the United States attorney is served with the pleading asserting the claim. (B) An officer or employee of the United States sued in an individual capacity for acts or omissions occurring in connection with the performance	**Rule 12. Defenses and Objections: When and How Presented; Motion for Judgment on the Pleadings; Consolidating Motions; Waiving Defenses; Pretrial Hearing** **(a) Time to Serve a Responsive Pleading.** **(1) *In General.*** Unless another time is specified by this rule or a federal statute, the time for serving a responsive pleading is as follows: **(A)** A defendant must serve an answer: **(i)** within 20 days after being served with the summons and complaint; or **(ii)** if it has timely waived service under Rule 4(d), within 60 days after the request for a waiver was sent, or within 90 days after it was sent to the defendant outside any judicial district of the United States. **(B)** A party must serve an answer to a counterclaim or crossclaim within 20 days after being served with the pleading that states the counterclaim or crossclaim. **(C)** A party must serve a reply to an answer within 20 days after being served with an order to reply, unless the order specifies a different time. **(2) *United States and Its Agencies, Officers, or Employees Sued in an Official Capacity.*** The United States, a United States agency, or a United States officer or employee sued only in an official capacity must serve an answer to a complaint, counterclaim, or crossclaim within 60 days after service on the United States attorney. **(3) *United States Officers or Employees Sued in an Individual Capacity.*** A United States officer or employee sued in an individual capacity for an act or omission	Rule 12 generally: 144, 342, 389, 390, 1164 Rule 12(a): 390, 391

<table>
<tr><th>Rule</th><th>Pre-Restyling Text</th><th>Restyled Text</th><th>Casebook References</th></tr>
<tr><td></td><td>of duties on behalf of the United States shall serve an answer to the complaint or cross-claim — or a reply to a counterclaim — within 60 days after service on the officer or employee, or service on the United States attorney, whichever is later.

(4) Unless a different time is fixed by court order, the service of a motion permitted under this rule alters these periods of time as follows:

(A) if the court denies the motion or postpones its disposition until the trial on the merits, the responsive pleading shall be served within 10 days after notice of the court's action; or

(B) if the court grants a motion for a more definite statement, the responsive pleading shall be served within 10 days after the service of the more definite statement.</td><td>occurring in connection with duties performed on the United States' behalf must serve an answer to a complaint, counterclaim, or crossclaim within 60 days after service on the officer or employee or service on the United States attorney, whichever is later.

(4) Effect of a Motion. Unless the court sets a different time, serving a motion under this rule alters these periods as follows:

(A) if the court denies the motion or postpones its disposition until trial, the responsive pleading must be served within 10 days after notice of the court's action; or

(B) if the court grants a motion for a more definite statement, the responsive pleading must be served within 10 days after the more definite statement is served.</td><td></td></tr>
<tr><td>12(b)</td><td>(b) HOW PRESENTED. Every defense, in law or fact, to a claim for relief in any pleading, whether a claim, counterclaim, cross-claim, or third-party claim, shall be asserted in the responsive pleading thereto if one is required, except that the following defenses may at the option of the pleader be made by motion: (1) lack of jurisdiction over the subject matter, (2) lack of jurisdiction over the person, (3) improper venue, (4) insufficiency of process, (5) insufficiency of service of process, (6) failure to state a claim upon which relief can be granted, (7) failure to join a party under Rule 19. A motion making any of these defenses shall be made before pleading if a further pleading is permitted. No defense or objection is waived by being joined with one or more other defenses or objections in a responsive pleading or motion. If a pleading sets forth a claim for relief to which the adverse party is not required to serve a responsive pleading, the adverse party may assert at the trial any defense in law or fact to that claim for relief. If, on a motion asserting the defense numbered (6) to dismiss for failure of the pleading to state a claim upon</td><td>(b) How to Present Defenses. Every defense to a claim for relief in any pleading must be asserted in the responsive pleading if one is required. But a party may assert the following defenses by motion:

(1) lack of subject-matter jurisdiction;

(2) lack of personal jurisdiction;

(3) improper venue;

(4) insufficient process;

(5) insufficient service of process;

(6) failure to state a claim upon which relief can be granted; and

(7) failure to join a party under Rule 19.

A motion asserting any of these defenses must be made before pleading if a responsive pleading is allowed. If a pleading sets out a claim for relief that does not require a responsive pleading, an opposing party may assert at trial any defense to that claim. No defense or objection is waived by joining it with one or more other defenses or objections in a responsive pleading or in a motion.</td><td>51, 174, 229, 266, 290, 294, 302, 306, 310, 317, 319, 330, 332, 333, 334, 347, 362, 363, 364, 372, 387, 388, 409, 410, 434, 439, 440, 441, 947, 973, 1110, 1200</td></tr>
</table>

Rule	Pre-Restyling Text	Restyled Text	Casebook References
	which relief can be granted, matters outside the pleading are presented to and not excluded by the court, the motion shall be treated as one for summary judgment and disposed of as provided in Rule 56, and all parties shall be given reasonable opportunity to present all material made pertinent to such a motion by Rule 56.		
12(c)	**(c) MOTION FOR JUDGMENT ON THE PLEADINGS.** After the pleadings are closed but within such time as not to delay the trial, any party may move for judgment on the pleadings. If, on a motion for judgment on the pleadings, matters outside the pleadings are presented to and not excluded by the court, the motion shall be treated as one for summary judgment and disposed of as provided in Rule 56, and all parties shall be given reasonable opportunity to present all material made pertinent to such a motion by Rule 56.	**(c) Motion for Judgment on the Pleadings.** After the pleadings are closed—but early enough not to delay trial—a party may move for judgment on the pleadings.	292, 363
12(d)	**(d) PRELIMINARY HEARINGS.** The defenses specifically enumerated (1)–(7) in subdivision (b) of this rule, whether made in a pleading or by motion, and the motion for judgment mentioned in subdivision (c) of this rule shall be heard and determined before trial on application of any party, unless the court orders that the hearing and determination thereof be deferred until the trial.	**(d) Result of Presenting Matters Outside the Pleadings.** If, on a motion under Rule 12(b)(6) or 12(c), matters outside the pleadings are presented to and not excluded by the court, the motion must be treated as one for summary judgment under Rule 56. All parties must be given a reasonable opportunity to present all the material that is pertinent to the motion.	425
12(e)	**(e) MOTION FOR MORE DEFINITE STATEMENT.** If a pleading to which a responsive pleading is permitted is so vague or ambiguous that a party cannot reasonably be required to frame a responsive pleading, the party may move for a more definite statement before interposing a responsive pleading. The motion shall point out the defects complained of and the details desired. If the motion is granted and the order of the court is not obeyed within 10 days after notice of the order or within such other time as the court may fix, the court may strike the pleading to which the motion was directed or make such order as it deems just.	**(e) Motion for a More Definite Statement.** A party may move for a more definite statement of a pleading to which a responsive pleading is allowed but which is so vague or ambiguous that the party cannot reasonably prepare a response. The motion must be made before filing a responsive pleading and must point out the defects complained of and the details desired. If the court orders a more definite statement and the order is not obeyed within 10 days after notice of the order or within the time the court sets, the court may strike the pleading or issue any other appropriate order.	292, 298, 304, 323, 327, 328, 346, 363

Rule	Pre-Restyling Text	Restyled Text	Casebook References
12(f)	**(f) MOTION TO STRIKE.** Upon motion made by a party before responding to a pleading or, if no responsive pleading is permitted by these rules, upon motion made by a party within 20 days after the service of the pleading upon the party or upon the court's own initiative at any time, the court may order stricken from any pleading any insufficient defense or any redundant, immaterial, impertinent, or scandalous matter.	**(f) Motion to Strike.** The court may strike from a pleading an insufficient defense or any redundant, immaterial, impertinent, or scandalous matter. The court may act: **(1)** on its own; or **(2)** on motion made by a party either before responding to the pleading or, if a response is not allowed, within 20 days after being served with the pleading.	292
12(g)	**(g) CONSOLIDATION OF DEFENSES IN MOTION.** A party who makes a motion under this rule may join with it any other motions herein provided for and then available to the party. If a party makes a motion under this rule but omits therefrom any defense or objection then available to the party which this rule permits to be raised by motion, the party shall not thereafter make a motion based on the defense or objection so omitted, except a motion as provided in subdivision (h)(2) hereof on any of the grounds there stated.	**(g) Joining Motions.** **(1)** ***Right to Join.*** A motion under this rule may be joined with any other motion allowed by this rule. **(2)** ***Limitation on Further Motions.*** Except as provided in Rule 12(h)(2) or (3), a party that makes a motion under this rule must not make another motion under this rule raising a defense or objection that was available to the party but omitted from its earlier motion.	362
12(h)	**(h) WAIVER OR PRESERVATION OF CERTAIN DEFENSES.** (1) A defense of lack of jurisdiction over the person, improper venue, insufficiency of process, or insufficiency of service of process is waived (A) if omitted from a motion in the circumstances described in subdivision (g), or (B) if it is neither made by motion under this rule nor included in a responsive pleading or an amendment thereof permitted by Rule 15(a) to be made as a matter of course. (2) A defense of failure to state a claim upon which relief can be granted, a defense of failure to join a party indispensable under Rule 19, and an objection of failure to state a legal defense to a claim may be made in any pleading permitted or ordered under Rule 7(a), or by motion for judgment on the pleadings, or at the trial on the merits. (3) Whenever it appears by suggestion of the parties or otherwise that the court lacks jurisdiction of the subject	**(h) Waiving and Preserving Certain Defenses.** **(1)** ***When Some Are Waived.*** A party waives any defense listed in Rule 12(b)(2)-(5) by: **(A)** omitting it from a motion in the circumstances described in Rule 12(g)(2); or **(B)** failing to either: **(i)** make it by motion under this rule; or **(ii)** include it in a responsive pleading or in an amendment allowed by Rule 15(a)(1) as a matter of course. **(2)** ***When to Raise Others.*** Failure to state a claim upon which relief can be granted, to join a person required by Rule 19(b), or to state a legal defense to a claim may be raised: **(A)** in any pleading allowed or ordered under Rule 7(a); **(B)** by a motion under Rule 12(c); or	216, 302, 378, 937, 938

Rule	Pre-Restyling Text	Restyled Text	Casebook References
	matter, the court shall dismiss the action.	**(C)** at trial. **(3) *Lack of Subject-Matter Jurisdiction.*** If the court determines at any time that it lacks subject-matter jurisdiction, the court must dismiss the action.	
12(i)		**(i) Hearing Before Trial.** If a party so moves, any defense listed in Rule 12(b)(1)-(7)—whether made in a pleading or by motion—and a motion under Rule 12(c) must be heard and decided before trial unless the court orders a deferral until trial.	
13(a)	**Rule 13. Counterclaim and Cross-Claim** **(a) COMPULSORY COUNTERCLAIMS.** A pleading shall state as a counterclaim any claim which at the time of serving the pleading the pleader has against any opposing party, if it arises out of the transaction or occurrence that is the subject matter of the opposing party's claim and does not require for its adjudication the presence of third parties of whom the court cannot acquire jurisdiction. But the pleader need not state the claim if (1) at the time the action was commenced the claim was the subject of another pending action, or (2) the opposing party brought suit upon the claim by attachment or other process by which the court did not acquire jurisdiction to render a personal judgment on that claim, and the pleader is not stating any counterclaim under this Rule 13.	**Rule 13. Counterclaim and Crossclaim** **(a) Compulsory Counterclaim.** **(1) *In General.*** A pleading must state as a counterclaim any claim that—at the time of its service—the pleader has against an opposing party if the claim: **(A)** arises out of the transaction or occurrence that is the subject matter of the opposing party's claim; and **(B)** does not require adding another party over whom the court cannot acquire jurisdiction. **(2) *Exceptions.*** The pleader need not state the claim if: **(A)** when the action was commenced, the claim was the subject of another pending action; or **(B)** the opposing party sued on its claim by attachment or other process that did not establish personal jurisdiction over the pleader on that claim, and the pleader does not assert any counterclaim under this rule.	Rule 13 generally: 362, 904, 1154 13(a): 229, 386, 739, 964, 1151, 1152, 1153, 1154, 1155, 1156, 1157
14(a)	Rule 14. Third-Party Practice (a) WHEN DEFENDANT MAY BRING IN THIRD PARTY. At any time after commencement of the action a defending party, as a third party plaintiff, may cause a summons and complaint to be served upon a person not a party to the action who is or may be liable to the third-party plaintiff for all or part of the plaintiff's claim against	**Rule 14. Third-Party Practice** **(a) When a Defending Party May Bring in a Third Party.** **(1) *Timing of the Summons and Complaint.*** A defending party may, as third-party plaintiff, serve a summons and complaint on a nonparty who is or may be liable to it for all or part of the claim against it. But the third-party plaintiff must,	Rule 14 generally: 901, 902, 904, 905, 906, 913, 921, **972**, 973, 974, 975, 976, 977, 989 14(a): 967, 973, 976

Rule	Pre-Restyling Text	Restyled Text	Casebook References
	the third-party plaintiff. The third-party plaintiff need not obtain leave to make the service if the third-party plaintiff files the third-party complaint not later than 10 days after serving the original answer. Otherwise the third-party plaintiff must obtain leave on motion upon notice to all parties to the action. The person served with the summons and third-party complaint, hereinafter called the third-party defendant, shall make any defenses to the third-party plaintiff's claim as provided in Rule 12 and any counterclaims against the third-party plaintiff and cross-claims against other third-party defendants as provided in Rule 13. The third-party defendant may assert against the plaintiff any defenses which the third-party plaintiff has to the plaintiff's claim. The third-party defendant may also assert any claim against the plaintiff arising out of the transaction or occurrence that is the subject matter of the plaintiff's claim against the third-party plaintiff. The plaintiff may assert any claim against the third-party defendant arising out of the transaction or occurrence that is the subject matter of the plaintiff's claim against the third-party plaintiff, and the third-party defendant thereupon shall assert any defenses as provided in Rule 12 and any counterclaims and cross-claims as provided in Rule 13. Any party may move to strike the third-party claim, or for its severance or separate trial. A third-party defendant may proceed under this rule against any person not a party to the action who is or may be liable to the third-party defendant for all or part of the claim made in the action against the third-party defendant. The third-party complaint, if within the admiralty and maritime jurisdiction, may be in rem against a vessel, cargo, or other property subject to admiralty or maritime process in rem, in which case references in this rule to the summons include the warrant of arrest, and references to the	by motion, obtain the court's leave if it files the third-party complaint more than 10 days after serving its original answer. **(2)** ***Third-Party Defendant's Claims and Defenses.*** The person served with the summons and third-party complaint — the "third-party defendant": **(A)** must assert any defense against the third-party plaintiff's claim under Rule 12; **(B)** must assert any counterclaim against the third-party plaintiff under Rule 13(a), and may assert any counterclaim against the third-party plaintiff under Rule 13(b) or any crossclaim against another third-party defendant under Rule 13(g); **(C)** may assert against the plaintiff any defense that the third-party plaintiff has to the plaintiff's claim; and **(D)** may also assert against the plaintiff any claim arising out of the transaction or occurrence that is the subject matter of the plaintiff's claim against the third-party plaintiff. **(3)** ***Plaintiff's Claims Against a Third-Party Defendant.*** The plaintiff may assert against the third-party defendant any claim arising out of the transaction or occurrence that is the subject matter of the plaintiff's claim against the third-party plaintiff. The third-party defendant must then assert any defense under Rule 12 and any counterclaim under Rule 13(a), and may assert any counterclaim under Rule 13(b) or any crossclaim under Rule 13(g). **(4)** ***Motion to Strike, Sever, or Try Separately.*** Any party may move to strike the third-party claim, to sever it, or to try it separately. **(5)** ***Third-Party Defendant's Claim Against a Nonparty.*** A third-party defendant may proceed under this rule against a nonparty who is or may be liable to the third-party	

Rule	Pre-Restyling Text	Restyled Text	Casebook References
	third-party plaintiff or defendant include, where appropriate, a person who asserts a right under Supplemental Rule C(6)(a)(1) in the property arrested.	defendant for all or part of any claim against it. **(6)** ***Third-Party Complaint In Rem.*** If it is within the admiralty or maritime jurisdiction, a third-party complaint may be in rem. In that event, a reference in this rule to the "summons" includes the warrant of arrest, and a reference to the defendant or third-party plaintiff includes, when appropriate, a person who asserts a right under Supplemental Rule C(6)(a)(i) in the property arrested.	
15(a)	**Rule 15. Amended and Supplemental Pleadings** **(a) AMENDMENTS.** A party may amend the party's pleading once as a matter of course at any time before a responsive pleading is served or, if the pleading is one to which no responsive pleading is permitted and the action has not been placed upon the trial calendar, the party may so amend it at any time within 20 days after it is served. Otherwise a party may amend the party's pleading only by leave of court or by written consent of the adverse party; and leave shall be freely given when justice so requires. A party shall plead in response to an amended pleading within the time remaining for response to the original pleading or within 10 days after service of the amended pleading, whichever period may be the longer, unless the court otherwise orders.	**Rule 15. Amended and Supplemental Pleadings** **(a) Amendments Before Trial.** **(1)** ***Amending as a Matter of Course.*** A party may amend its pleading once as a matter of course: **(A)** before being served with a responsive pleading; or **(B)** within 20 days after serving the pleading if a responsive pleading is not allowed and the action is not yet on the trial calendar. **(2)** ***Other Amendments.*** In all other cases, a party may amend its pleading only with the opposing party's written consent or the court's leave. The court should freely give leave when justice so requires. **(3)** ***Time to Respond.*** Unless the court orders otherwise, any required response to an amended pleading must be made within the time remaining to respond to the original pleading or within 10 days after service of the amended pleading, whichever is later.	Rule 15 generally: 292, 379, 389, 390, 391, 393, 394, 447, 481, 482 15(a): 378, 379, 387, 388, 390, 391, 394, 395
15(b)	**(b) AMENDMENTS TO CONFORM TO THE EVIDENCE.** When issues not raised by the pleadings are tried by express or implied consent of the parties, they shall be treated in all respects as if they had been raised in the pleadings. Such amendment of the pleadings as may be necessary to cause them to conform to the evidence and to raise these issues may be made upon motion of any	**(b) Amendments During and After Trial.** **(1)** ***Based on an Objection at Trial.*** If, at trial, a party objects that evidence is not within the issues raised in the pleadings, the court may permit the pleadings to be amended. The court should freely permit an amendment when doing so will aid in presenting the merits and the objecting party fails to	379

Rule	Pre-Restyling Text	Restyled Text	Casebook References
	party at any time, even after judgment; but failure so to amend does not affect the result of the trial of these issues. If evidence is objected to at the trial on the ground that it is not within the issues made by the pleadings, the court may allow the pleadings to be amended and shall do so freely when the presentation of the merits of the action will be subserved thereby and the objecting party fails to satisfy the court that the admission of such evidence would prejudice the party in maintaining the party's action or defense upon the merits. The court may grant a continuance to enable the objecting party to meet such evidence.	satisfy the court that the evidence would prejudice that party's action or defense on the merits. The court may grant a continuance to enable the objecting party to meet the evidence. **(2)** ***For Issues Tried by Consent.*** When an issue not raised by the pleadings is tried by the parties' express or implied consent, it must be treated in all respects as if raised in the pleadings. A party may move—at any time, even after judgment—to amend the pleadings to conform them to the evidence and to raise an unpleaded issue. But failure to amend does not affect the result of the trial of that issue.	
15(c)	**(c) RELATION BACK OF AMENDMENTS.** An amendment of a pleading relates back to the date of the original pleading when (1) relation back is permitted by the law that provides the statute of limitations applicable to the action, or (2) the claim or defense asserted in the amended pleading arose out of the conduct, transaction, or occurrence set forth or attempted to be set forth in the original pleading, or (3) the amendment changes the party or the naming of the party against whom a claim is asserted if the foregoing provision (2) is satisfied and, within the period provided by Rule 4(m) for service of the summons and complaint, the party to be brought in by amendment (A) has received such notice of the institution of the action that the party will not be prejudiced in maintaining a defense on the merits, and (B) knew or should have known that, but for a mistake concerning the identity of the proper party, the action would have been brought against the party. The delivery or mailing of process to the United States Attorney, or United States Attorney's designee, or the Attorney General of the United States, or an agency or officer who would have been a proper defendant if named, satisfies	**(c) Relation Back of Amendments.** **(1)** ***When an Amendment Relates Back.*** An amendment to a pleading relates back to the date of the original pleading when: **(A)** the law that provides the applicable statute of limitations allows relation back; **(B)** the amendment asserts a claim or defense that arose out of the conduct, transaction, or occurrence set out—or attempted to be set out—in the original pleading; or **(C)** the amendment changes the party or the naming of the party against whom a claim is asserted, if Rule 15(c)(1)(B) is satisfied and if, within the period provided by Rule 4(m) for serving the summons and complaint, the party to be brought in by amendment: **(i)** received such notice of the action that it will not be prejudiced in defending on the merits; and **(ii)** knew or should have known that the action would have been brought against it, but for a mistake concerning the proper party's identity. **(2)** ***Notice to the United States.*** When the United States or a United States officer or agency is added as a defendant by amendment, the	380, 383, 388, 389, 479, 481, 482, 484

Rule	Pre-Restyling Text	Restyled Text	Casebook References
	the requirement of subparagraphs (A) and (B) of this paragraph (3) with respect to the United States or any agency or officer thereof to be brought into the action as a defendant.	notice requirements of Rule 15(c)(1)(C)(i) and (ii) are satisfied if, during the stated period, process was delivered or mailed to the United States attorney or the United States attorney's designee, to the Attorney General of the United States, or to the officer or agency.	
15(d)	**(d) SUPPLEMENTAL PLEADINGS.** Upon motion of a party the court may, upon reasonable notice and upon such terms as are just, permit the party to serve a supplemental pleading setting forth transactions or occurrences or events which have happened since the date of the pleading sought to be supplemented. Permission may be granted even though the original pleading is defective in its statement of a claim for relief or defense. If the court deems it advisable that the adverse party plead to the supplemental pleading, it shall so order, specifying the time therefor.	**(d) Supplemental Pleadings.** On motion and reasonable notice, the court may, on just terms, permit a party to serve a supplemental pleading setting out any transaction, occurrence, or event that happened after the date of the pleading to be supplemented. The court may permit supplementation even though the original pleading is defective in stating a claim or defense. The court may order that the opposing party plead to the supplemental pleading within a specified time.	
16(a)	**Rule 16. Pretrial Conferences; Scheduling; Management** **(a) PRETRIAL CONFERENCES; OBJECTIVES.** In any action, the court may in its discretion direct the attorneys for the parties and any unrepresented parties to appear before it for a conference or conferences before trial for such purposes as (1) expediting the disposition of the action; (2) establishing early and continuing control so that the case will not be protracted because of lack of management; (3) discouraging wasteful pretrial activities; (4) improving the quality of the trial through more thorough preparation, and; (5) facilitating the settlement of the case.	**Rule 16. Pretrial Conferences; Scheduling; Management** **(a) Purposes of a Pretrial Conference.** In any action, the court may order the attorneys and any unrepresented parties to appear for one or more pretrial conferences for such purposes as: **(1)** expediting disposition of the action; **(2)** establishing early and continuing control so that the case will not be protracted because of lack of management; **(3)** discouraging wasteful pretrial activities; **(4)** improving the quality of the trial through more thorough preparation; and **(5)** facilitating settlement.	Rule 16, generally: 287, 292, 296, 328, 379, 394, 395, 484, 500, 602, 603, 622, 626, 628, 629, 630, 853

Rule	Pre-Restyling Text	Restyled Text	Casebook References
16(b)	**(b) SCHEDULING AND PLANNING.** Except in categories of actions exempted by district court rule as inappropriate, the district judge, or a magistrate judge when authorized by district court rule, shall, after receiving the report from the parties under Rule 26(f) or after consulting with the attorneys for the parties and any unrepresented parties by a scheduling conference, telephone, mail, or other suitable means, enter a scheduling order that limits the time (1) to join other parties and to amend the pleadings; (2) to file motions; and (3) to complete discovery. The scheduling order also may include (4) modifications of the times for disclosures under Rules 26(a) and 26(e)(1) and of the extent of discovery to be permitted; (5) provisions for disclosure or discovery of electronically stored information; (6) any agreements the parties reach for asserting claims of privilege or of protection as trial-preparation material after production; (7) the date or dates for conferences before trial, a final pretrial conference, and trial; and (8) any other matters appropriate in the circumstances of the case. The order shall issue as soon as practicable but in any event within 90 days after the appearance of a defendant and within 120 days after the complaint has been served on a defendant. A schedule shall not be modified except upon a showing of good cause and by leave of the district judge or, when authorized by local rule, by a magistrate judge.	**(b) Scheduling.** **(1)** ***Scheduling Order.*** Except in categories of actions exempted by local rule, the district judge—or a magistrate judge when authorized by local rule—must issue a scheduling order: **(A)** after receiving the parties' report under Rule 26(f); or **(B)** after consulting with the parties' attorneys and any unrepresented parties at a scheduling conference or by telephone, mail, or other means. **(2)** ***Time to Issue.*** The judge must issue the scheduling order as soon as practicable, but in any event within the earlier of 120 days after any defendant has been served with the complaint or 90 days after any defendant has appeared. **(3)** ***Contents of the Order.*** **(A)** *Required Contents.* The scheduling order must limit the time to join other parties, amend the pleadings, complete discovery, and file motions. **(B)** *Permitted Contents.* The scheduling order may: **(i)** modify the timing of disclosures under Rules 26(a) and 26(e)(1); **(ii)** modify the extent of discovery; **(iii)** provide for disclosure or discovery of electronically stored information; **(iv)** include any agreements the parties reach for asserting claims of privilege or of protection as trial-preparation material after information is produced; **(v)** set dates for pretrial conferences and for trial; and **(vi)** include other appropriate matters.	
		(4) ***Modifying a Schedule.*** A schedule may be modified only for good cause and with the judge's consent.	

Rule	Pre-Restyling Text	Restyled Text	Casebook References
16(c)	**(c) SUBJECTS FOR CONSIDERATION AT PRETRIAL CONFERENCES.** At any conference under this rule consideration may be given, and the court may take appropriate action, with respect to (1) the formulation and simplification of the issues, including the elimination of frivolous claims or defenses; (2) the necessity or desirability of amendments to the pleadings; (3) the possibility of obtaining admissions of fact and of documents which will avoid unnecessary proof, stipulations regarding the authenticity of documents, and advance rulings from the court on the admissibility of evidence; (4) the avoidance of unnecessary proof and of cumulative evidence, and limitations or restrictions on the use of testimony under Rule 702 of the Federal Rules of Evidence; (5) the appropriateness and timing of summary adjudication under Rule 56; (6) the control and scheduling of discovery, including orders affecting disclosures and discovery pursuant to Rule 26 and Rules 29 through 37; (7) the identification of witnesses and documents, the need and schedule for filing and exchanging pretrial briefs, and the date or dates for further conferences and for trial; (8) the advisability of referring matters to a magistrate judge or master; (9) settlement and the use of special procedures to assist in resolving the dispute when authorized by statute or local rule; (10) the form and substance of the pretrial order; (11) the disposition of pending motions; (12) the need for adopting special procedures for managing	**(c) Attendance and Matters for Consideration at a Pretrial Conference.** **(1)** ***Attendance.*** A represented party must authorize at least one of its attorneys to make stipulations and admissions about all matters that can reasonably be anticipated for discussion at a pretrial conference. If appropriate, the court may require that a party or its representative be present or reasonably available by other means to consider possible settlement. **(2)** ***Matters for Consideration.*** At any pretrial conference, the court may consider and take appropriate action on the following matters: **(A)** formulating and simplifying the issues, and eliminating frivolous claims or defenses; **(B)** amending the pleadings if necessary or desirable; **(C)** obtaining admissions and stipulations about facts and documents to avoid unnecessary proof, and ruling in advance on the admissibility of evidence; **(D)** avoiding unnecessary proof and cumulative evidence, and limiting the use of testimony under Federal Rule of Evidence 702; **(E)** determining the appropriateness and timing of summary adjudication under Rule 56; **(F)** controlling and scheduling discovery, including orders affecting disclosures and discovery under Rule 26 and Rules 29 through 37; **(G)** identifying witnesses and documents, scheduling the filing and exchange of any pretrial briefs, and setting dates for further conferences and for trial; **(H)** referring matters to a magistrate judge or a master; **(I)** settling the case and using special procedures to assist in resolving the dispute when	289, 328, 329, 622, 626, 628, 633

Rule	Pre-Restyling Text	Restyled Text	Casebook References
	potentially difficult or protracted actions that may involve complex issues, multiple parties, difficult legal questions, or unusual proof problems; (13) an order for a separate trial pursuant to Rule 42(b) with respect to a claim, counterclaim, cross-claim, or third-party claim, or with respect to any particular issue in the case; (14) an order directing a party or parties to present evidence early in the trial with respect to a manageable issue that could, on the evidence, be the basis for a judgment as a matter of law under Rule 50(a) or a judgment on partial findings under Rule 52(c); (15) an order establishing a reasonable limit on the time allowed for presenting evidence; and (16) such other matters as may facilitate the just, speedy, and inexpensive disposition of the action. At least one of the attorneys for each party participating in any conference before trial shall have authority to enter into stipulations and to make admissions regarding all matters that the participants may reasonably anticipate may be discussed. If appropriate, the court may require that a party or its representative be present or reasonably available by telephone in order to consider possible settlement of the dispute.	authorized by statute or local rule; **(J)** determining the form and content of the pretrial order; **(K)** disposing of pending motions; **(L)** adopting special procedures for managing potentially difficult or protracted actions that may involve complex issues, multiple parties, difficult legal questions, or unusual proof problems; **(M)** ordering a separate trial under Rule 42(b) of a claim, counterclaim, crossclaim, third-party claim, or particular issue; **(N)** ordering the presentation of evidence early in the trial on a manageable issue that might, on the evidence, be the basis for a judgment as a matter of law under Rule 50(a) or a judgment on partial findings under Rule 52(c); **(O)** establishing a reasonable limit on the time allowed to present evidence; and **(P)** facilitating in other ways the just, speedy, and inexpensive disposition of the action.	
16(d)	**(d) FINAL PRETRIAL CONFERENCE.** Any final pretrial conference shall be held as close to the time of trial as reasonable under the circumstances. The participants at any such conference shall formulate a plan for trial, including a program for facilitating the admission of evidence. The conference shall be attended by at least one of the attorneys who will conduct the trial for each of the parties and by any unrepresented parties.	**(d) Pretrial Orders.** After any conference under this rule, the court should issue an order reciting the action taken. This order controls the course of the action unless the court modifies it.	

Rule	Pre-Restyling Text	Restyled Text	Casebook References
16(e)	**(e) PRETRIAL ORDERS.** After any conference held pursuant to this rule, an order shall be entered reciting the action taken. This order shall control the subsequent course of the action unless modified by a subsequent order. The order following a final pretrial conference shall be modified only to prevent manifest injustice.	**(e) Final Pretrial Conference and Orders.** The court may hold a final pretrial conference to formulate a trial plan, including a plan to facilitate the admission of evidence. The conference must be held as close to the start of trial as is reasonable, and must be attended by at least one attorney who will conduct the trial for each party and by any unrepresented party. The court may modify the order issued after a final pretrial conference only to prevent manifest injustice.	
16(f)	**(f) SANCTIONS.** If a party or party's attorney fails to obey a scheduling or pretrial order, or if no appearance is made on behalf of a party at a scheduling or pretrial conference, or if a party or party's attorney is substantially unprepared to participate in the conference, or if a party or party's attorney fails to participate in good faith, the judge, upon motion or the judge's own initiative, may make such orders with regard thereto as are just, and among others any of the orders provided in Rule 37(b)(2)(B), (C), (D). In lieu of or in addition to any other sanction, the judge shall require the party or the attorney representing the party or both to pay the reasonable expenses incurred because of any noncompliance with this rule, including attorney's fees, unless the judge finds that the noncompliance was substantially justified or that other circumstances make an award of expenses unjust.	**(f) Sanctions.** **(1)** ***In General.*** On motion or on its own, the court may issue any just orders, including those authorized by Rule 37(b)(2)(A)(ii)-(vii), if a party or its attorney: **(A)** fails to appear at a scheduling or other pretrial conference; **(B)** is substantially unprepared to participate—or does not participate in good faith—in the conference; or **(C)** fails to obey a scheduling or other pretrial order. **(2)** ***Imposing Fees and Costs.*** Instead of or in addition to any other sanction, the court must order the party, its attorney, or both to pay the reasonable expenses—including attorney's fees—incurred because of any noncompliance with this rule, unless the noncompliance was substantially justified or other circumstances make an award of expenses unjust.	461, 462
17(a)	**Rule 17. Parties Plaintiff and Defendant; Capacity** **(a) REAL PARTY IN INTEREST.** Every action shall be prosecuted in the name of the real party in interest. An executor, administrator, guardian, bailee, trustee of an express trust, a party with whom or in whose name a contract has been made for the benefit of another, or a party authorized by statute may sue in that person's own name without joining the party for whose benefit	**Rule 17. Plaintiff and Defendant; Capacity; Public Officers** **(a) Real Party in Interest.** **(1)** ***Designation in General.*** An action must be prosecuted in the name of the real party in interest. The following may sue in their own names without joining the person for whose benefit the action is brought: **(A)** an executor;	960

Rule	Pre-Restyling Text	Restyled Text	Casebook References
	the action is brought; and when a statute of the United States so provides, an action for the use or benefit of another shall be brought in the name of the United States. No action shall be dismissed on the ground that it is not prosecuted in the name of the real party in interest until a reasonable time has been allowed after objection for ratification of commencement of the action by, or joinder or substitution of, the real party in interest; and such ratification, joinder, or substitution shall have the same effect as if the action had been commenced in the name of the real party in interest.	**(B)** an administrator; **(C)** a guardian; **(D)** a bailee; **(E)** a trustee of an express trust; **(F)** a party with whom or in whose name a contract has been made for another's benefit; and **(G)** a party authorized by statute. **(2)** ***Action in the Name of the United States for Another's Use or Benefit.*** When a federal statute so provides, an action for another's use or benefit must be brought in the name of the United States. **(3)** ***Joinder of the Real Party in Interest.*** The court may not dismiss an action for failure to prosecute in the name of the real party in interest until, after an objection, a reasonable time has been allowed for the real party in interest to ratify, join, or be substituted into the action. After ratification, joinder, or substitution, the action proceeds as if it had been originally commenced by the real party in interest.	
17(b)	**(b) CAPACITY TO SUE OR BE SUED.** The capacity of an individual, other than one acting in a representative capacity, to sue or be sued shall be determined by the law of the individual's domicile. The capacity of a corporation to sue or be sued shall be determined by the law under which it was organized. In all other cases capacity to sue or be sued shall be determined by the law of the state in which the district court is held, except (1) that a partnership or other unincorporated association, which has no such capacity by the law of such state, may sue or be sued in its common name for the purpose of enforcing for or against it a substantive right existing under the Constitution or laws of the United States, and (2) that the capacity of a receiver appointed by a court of the United States to sue or be sued in a court of the United States is governed by Title 28, U.S.C., Sections 754 and 959(a).	**(b) Capacity to Sue or Be Sued.** Capacity to sue or be sued is determined as follows: **(1)** for an individual who is not acting in a representative capacity, by the law of the individual's domicile; **(2)** for a corporation, by the law under which it was organized; and **(3)** for all other parties, by the law of the state where the court is located, except that: **(A)** a partnership or other unincorporated association with no such capacity under that state's law may sue or be sued in its common name to enforce a substantive right existing under the United States Constitution or laws; and **(B)** *28 U.S.C.* §§754 and 959(a) govern the capacity of a receiver appointed by a United States court to sue or be sued in a United States court.	960

Rule	Pre-Restyling Text	Restyled Text	Casebook References
18(a)	**Rule 18. Joinder of Claims and Remedies** **(a) JOINDER OF CLAIMS.** A party asserting a claim to relief as an original claim, counterclaim, cross-claim, or third-party claim, may join, either as independent or as alternate claims, as many claims, legal, equitable, or maritime, as the party has against an opposing party.	**Rule 18. Joinder of Claims** **(a) In General.** A party asserting a claim, counterclaim, crossclaim, or third-party claim may join, as independent or alternative claims, as many claims as it has against an opposing party.	Rule 18 generally: 737 18(a): 437
18(b)	**(b) JOINDER OF REMEDIES; FRAUDULENT CONVEYANCES.** Whenever a claim is one heretofore cognizable only after another claim has been prosecuted to a conclusion, the two claims may be joined in a single action; but the court shall grant relief in that action only in accordance with the relative substantive rights of the parties. In particular, a plaintiff may state a claim for money and a claim to have set aside a conveyance fraudulent as to that plaintiff, without first having obtained a judgment establishing the claim for money.	**(b) Joinder of Contingent Claims.** A party may join two claims even though one of them is contingent on the disposition of the other; but the court may grant relief only in accordance with the parties' relative substantive rights. In particular, a plaintiff may state a claim for money and a claim to set aside a conveyance that is fraudulent as to that plaintiff, without first obtaining a judgment for the money.	
19(a)	**Rule 19. Joinder of Persons Needed for Just Adjudication** **(a) PERSONS TO BE JOINED IF FEASIBLE.** A person who is subject to service of process and whose joinder will not deprive the court of jurisdiction over the subject matter of the action shall be joined as a party in the action if (1) in the person's absence complete relief cannot be accorded among those already parties, or (2) the person claims an interest relating to the subject of the action and is so situated that the disposition of the action in the person's absence may (i) as a practical matter impair or impede the person's ability to protect that interest or (ii) leave any of the persons already parties subject to a substantial risk of incurring double, multiple, or otherwise inconsistent obligations by reason of the claimed interest. If the person has not been so joined, the court shall order that the person be made a party. If the person should join as a plaintiff but refuses to do so, the person may be made a	**Rule 19. Required Joinder of Parties** **(a) Persons Required to Be Joined if Feasible.** **(1)** ***Required Party.*** A person who is subject to service of process and whose joinder will not deprive the court of subject-matter jurisdiction must be joined as a party if: **(A)** in that person's absence, the court cannot accord complete relief among existing parties; or **(B)** that person claims an interest relating to the subject of the action and is so situated that disposing of the action in the person's absence may: **(i)** as a practical matter impair or impede the person's ability to protect the interest; or **(ii)** leave an existing party subject to a substantial risk of incurring double, multiple, or otherwise inconsistent obligations because of the interest.	Rule 19 generally: 773, 905, 913, 916, 917, 966, 967, 969, 972, 989, 1065, 1066, 1067, 1142, 1143 19(a): 967, 968, 969, 1064

Rule	Pre-Restyling Text	Restyled Text	Casebook References
	defendant, or, in a proper case, an involuntary plaintiff. If the joined party objects to venue and joinder of that party would render the venue of the action improper, that party shall be dismissed from the action.	**(2)** ***Joinder by Court Order.*** If a person has not been joined as required, the court must order that the person be made a party. A person who refuses to join as a plaintiff may be made either a defendant or, in a proper case, an involuntary plaintiff. **(3)** ***Venue.*** If a joined party objects to venue and the joinder would make venue improper, the court must dismiss that party.	
19(b)	**(b) DETERMINATION BY COURT WHENEVER JOINDER NOT FEASIBLE.** If a person as described in subdivision (a)(1)–(2) hereof cannot be made a party, the court shall determine whether in equity and good conscience the action should proceed among the parties before it, or should be dismissed, the absent person being thus regarded as indispensable. The factors to be considered by the court include: first, to what extent a judgment rendered in the person's absence might be prejudicial to the person or those already parties; second, the extent to which, by protective provisions in the judgment, by the shaping of relief, or other measures, the prejudice can be lessened or avoided; third, whether a judgment rendered in the person's absence will be adequate; fourth, whether the plaintiff will have an adequate remedy if the action is dismissed for nonjoinder.	**(b) When Joinder Is Not Feasible.** If a person who is required to be joined if feasible cannot be joined, the court must determine whether, in equity and good conscience, the action should proceed among the existing parties or should be dismissed. The factors for the court to consider include: **(1)** the extent to which a judgment rendered in the person's absence might prejudice that person or the existing parties; **(2)** the extent to which any prejudice could be lessened or avoided by: **(A)** protective provisions in the judgment; **(B)** shaping the relief; or **(C)** other measures; **(3)** whether a judgment rendered in the person's absence would be adequate; and **(4)** whether the plaintiff would have an adequate remedy if the action were dismissed for nonjoinder.	967, 968, 969, 970, 971, 1064
20(a)	**Rule 20. Permissive Joinder of Parties** **(a) PERMISSIVE JOINDER.** All persons may join in one action as plaintiffs if they assert any right to relief jointly, severally, or in the alternative in respect of or arising out of the same transaction, occurrence, or series of transactions or occurrences and if any question of law or fact common to all these persons will arise in the action. All	**Rule 20. Permissive Joinder of Parties** **(a) Persons Who May Join or Be Joined.** **(1)** ***Plaintiffs.*** Persons may join in one action as plaintiffs if: **(A)** they assert any right to relief jointly, severally, or in the alternative with respect to or arising out of the same transaction, occurrence, or series	Rule 20, generally: 229, 905, 913, 914, 917, 921, 962, 963, 964, 965 20(a): 963, 964, 965

Rule	Pre-Restyling Text	Restyled Text	Casebook References
	persons (and any vessel, cargo or other property subject to admiralty process in rem) may be joined in one action as defendants if there is asserted against them jointly, severally, or in the alternative, any right to relief in respect of or arising out of the same transaction, occurrence, or series of transactions or occurrences and if any question of law or fact common to all defendants will arise in the action. A plaintiff or defendant need not be interested in obtaining or defending against all the relief demanded. Judgment may be given for one or more of the plaintiffs according to their respective rights to relief, and against one or more defendants according to their respective liabilities.	of transactions or occurrences; and **(B)** any question of law or fact common to all plaintiffs will arise in the action. **(2)** ***Defendants.*** Persons — as well as a vessel, cargo, or other property subject to admiralty process in rem — may be joined in one action as defendants if: **(A)** any right to relief is asserted against them jointly, severally, or in the alternative with respect to or arising out of the same transaction, occurrence, or series of transactions or occurrences; and **(B)** any question of law or fact common to all defendants will arise in the action. **(3)** ***Extent of Relief.*** Neither a plaintiff nor a defendant need be interested in obtaining or defending against all the relief demanded. The court may grant judgment to one or more plaintiffs according to their rights, and against one or more defendants according to their liabilities.	
20(b)	**(b) SEPARATE TRIALS.** The court may make such orders as will prevent a party from being embarrassed, delayed, or put to expense by the inclusion of a party against whom the party asserts no claim and who asserts no claim against the party, and may order separate trials or make other orders to prevent delay or prejudice.	**(b) Protective Measures.** The court may issue orders — including an order for separate trials — to protect a party against embarrassment, delay, expense, or other prejudice that arises from including a person against whom the party asserts no claim and who asserts no claim against the party.	963
22	**Rule 22. Interpleader** (1) Persons having claims against the plaintiff may be joined as defendants and required to interplead when their claims are such that the plaintiff is or may be exposed to double or multiple liability. It is not ground for objection to the joinder that the claims of the several claimants or the titles on which their claims depend do not have a common origin or are not identical but are adverse to and independent of one another, or that the plaintiff avers that the plaintiff is not liable in whole or in part to any or all of the	**Rule 22. Interpleader** **(a) Grounds.** **(1)** ***By a Plaintiff.*** Persons with claims that may expose a plaintiff to double or multiple liability may be joined as defendants and required to interplead. Joinder for interpleader is proper even though: **(A)** the claims of the several claimants, or the titles on which their claims depend, lack a common origin or are adverse and independent rather than identical; or	Rule 22, generally: 978, 980, 981

Rule	Pre-Restyling Text	Restyled Text	Casebook References
	claimants. A defendant exposed to similar liability may obtain such interpleader by way of cross-claim or counterclaim. The provisions of this rule supplement and do not in any way limit the joinder of parties permitted in Rule 20. (2) The remedy herein provided is in addition to and in no way supersedes or limits the remedy provided by Title 28, U.S.C., §§1335, 1397, and 2361. Actions under those provisions shall be conducted in accordance with these rules.	**(B)** the plaintiff denies liability in whole or in part to any or all of the claimants. **(2)** ***By a Defendant.*** A defendant exposed to similar liability may seek interpleader through a crossclaim or counterclaim. **(b) Relation to Other Rules and Statutes.** This rule supplements—and does not limit—the joinder of parties allowed by Rule 20. The remedy this rule provides is in addition to—and does not supersede or limit—the remedy provided by 28 U.S.C. §§1335, 1397, and 2361. An action under those statutes must be conducted under these rules.	
23(a)	**Rule 23. Class Actions** **(a) PREREQUISITES TO A CLASS ACTION.** One or more members of a class may sue or be sued as representative parties on behalf of all only if (1) the class is so numerous that joinder of all members is impracticable, (2) there are questions of law or fact common to the class, (3) the claims or defenses of the representative parties are typical of the claims or defenses of the class, and (4) the representative parties will fairly and adequately protect the interests of the class.	**Rule 23. Class Actions** **(a) Prerequisites.** One or more members of a class may sue or be sued as representative parties on behalf of all members only if: **(1)** the class is so numerous that joinder of all members is impracticable; **(2)** there are questions of law or fact common to the class; **(3)** the claims or defenses of the representative parties are typical of the claims or defenses of the class; and **(4)** the representative parties will fairly and adequately protect the interests of the class.	Rule 23 generally: 907, 914, 921, 962, 1019, 1020, 1023, 1024, 1030, 1032, 1033, 1036, 1037, 1041, 1048, 1054, 1055, 1061, 1063, 1069, 1070, 1071, 1072, 1073, 1074, 1075, 1077, 1078, 1079, 1090, 1094, 1095, 1096, 1097, 1098, 1099, 1100, 1102, 1104, 1110, 1112 23(a): 965, 1023, 1024, 1025, 1026, 1035, 1093, 1094, 1095, 1096, 1097, 1098, 1101, 1103, 1105
23(b)	**(b) CLASS ACTIONS MAINTAINABLE.** An action may be maintained as a class action if the prerequisites of subdivision (a) are satisfied, and in addition: (1) the prosecution of separate actions by or against individual	**(b) Types of Class Actions.** A class action may be maintained if Rule 23(a) is satisfied and if: **(1)** prosecuting separate actions by or against individual class members would create a risk of:	1023, 1026, 1029, 1030, 1031, 1033, 1035, 1036, 1049, 1050, 1052, 1055, 1071, 1089,

Rule	Pre-Restyling Text	Restyled Text	Casebook References
	members of the class would create a risk of (A) inconsistent or varying adjudications with respect to individual members of the class which would establish in-compatible standards of conduct for the party opposing the class, or (B) adjudications with respect to individual members of the class which would as a practical matter be dispositive of the interests of the other members not parties to the adjudications or substantially impair or impede their ability to protect their interests; or (2) the party opposing the class has acted or refused to act on grounds generally applicable to the class, thereby making appropriate final injunctive relief or corresponding declaratory relief with respect to the class as a whole; or (3) the court finds that the questions of law or fact common to the members of the class predominate over any questions affecting only individual members, and that a class action is superior to other available methods for the fair and efficient adjudication of the controversy. The matters pertinent to the findings include: (A) the interest of members of the class in individually controlling the prosecution or defense of separate actions; (B) the extent and nature of any litigation concerning the controversy already commenced by or against members of the class; (C) the desirability or undesirability of concentrating the litigation of the claims in the particular forum; (D) the difficulties likely to be encountered in the management of a class action.	**(A)** inconsistent or varying adjudications with respect to individual class members that would establish incompatible standards of conduct for the party opposing the class; or **(B)** adjudications with respect to individual class members that, as a practical matter, would be dispositive of the interests of the other members not parties to the individual adjudications or would substantially impair or impede their ability to protect their interests; **(2)** the party opposing the class has acted or refused to act on grounds that apply generally to the class, so that final injunctive relief or corresponding declaratory relief is appropriate respecting the class as a whole; or **(3)** the court finds that the questions of law or fact common to class members predominate over any questions affecting only individual members, and that a class action is superior to other available methods for fairly and efficiently adjudicating the controversy. The matters pertinent to these findings include: **(A)** the class members' interests in individually controlling the prosecution or defense of separate actions; **(B)** the extent and nature of any litigation concerning the controversy already begun by or against class members; **(C)** the desirability or undesirability of concentrating the litigation of the claims in the particular forum; and **(D)** the likely difficulties in managing a class action.	1093, 1094, 1095, 1096, 1097, 1098, 1100, 1102, 1103, 1104
23(c)	**(c) DETERMINING BY ORDER WHETHER TO CERTIFY A CLASS ACTION; APPOINTING CLASS COUNSEL; NOTICE AND MEMBERSHIP IN CLASS; JUDGMENT; MULTIPLE CLASSES AND SUBCLASSES.** (1)(A) When a person sues or is sued as a representative of a class,	**(c) Certification Order; Notice to Class Members; Judgment; Issues Classes; Subclasses.** **(1)** *Certification Order.* **(A)** *Time to Issue.* At an early practicable time after a person sues or issued as a class representative, the court must	1030, 1031, 1067, 1071, 1072, 1073, 1074, 1075, 1096

Rule	Pre-Restyling Text	Restyled Text	Casebook References
	the court must—at an early practicable time—determine by order whether to certify the action as a class action. (B) An order certifying a class action must define the class and the class claims, issues, or defenses, and must appoint class counsel under Rule 23(g). (C) An order under Rule 23(c)(1) may be altered or amended before final judgment. (2)(A) For any class certified under Rule 23(b)(1) or (2), the court may direct appropriate notice to the class. (B) For any class certified under Rule 23(b)(3), the court must direct to class members the best notice practicable under the circumstances, including individual notice to all members who can be identified through reasonable effort. The notice must concisely and clearly state in plain, easily understood language: • the nature of the action, • the definition of the class certified, • the class claims, issues, or defenses, • that a class member may enter an appearance through counsel if the member so desires, • that the court will exclude from the class any member who requests exclusion, stating when and how members may elect to be excluded, and • the binding effect of a class judgment on class members under Rule 23(c)(3). (3) The judgment in an action maintained as a class action under subdivision (b)(1) or (b)(2), whether or not favorable to the class, shall include and describe those whom the court finds to be members of the class. The judgment in an action maintained as a class action under subdivision (b)(3), whether or not	determine by order whether to certify the action as a class action. **(B)** *Defining the Class; Appointing Class Counsel.* An order that certifies a class action must define the class and the class claims, issues, or defenses, and must appoint class counsel under Rule 23(g). **(C)** *Altering or Amending the Order.* An order that grants or denies class certification may be altered or amended before final judgment. **(2)** ***Notice.*** **(A)** *For (b)(1) or (b)(2) Classes.* For any class certified under Rule 23(b)(1) or (b)(2), the court may direct appropriate notice to the class. **(B)** *For (b)(3) Classes.* For any class certified under Rule 23(b)(3), the court must direct to class members the best notice that is practicable under the circumstances, including individual notice to all members who can be identified through reasonable effort. The notice must clearly and concisely state in plain, easily understood language: **(i)** the nature of the action; **(ii)** the definition of the class certified; **(iii)** the class claims, issues, or defenses; **(iv)** that a class member may enter an appearance through an attorney if the member so desires; **(v)** that the court will exclude from the class any member who requests exclusion; **(vi)** the time and manner for requesting exclusion; and **(vii)** the binding effect of a class judgment on members under Rule 23(c)(3). **(3)** ***Judgment.*** Whether or not favorable to the class, the judgment in a class action must:	

Rule	Pre-Restyling Text	Restyled Text	Casebook References
	favorable to the class, shall include and specify or describe those to whom the notice provided in subdivision (c)(2) was directed, and who have not requested exclusion, and whom the court finds to be members of the class. (4) When appropriate (A) an action may be brought or maintained as a class action with respect to particular issues, or (B) a class may be divided into subclasses and each subclass treated as a class, and the provisions of this rule shall then be construed and applied accordingly.	**(A)** for any class certified under Rule 23(b)(1) or (b)(2), include and describe those whom the court finds to be class members; and **(B)** for any class certified under Rule 23(b)(3), include and specify or describe those to whom the Rule 23(c)(2) notice was directed, who have not requested exclusion, and whom the court finds to be class members. **(4)** ***Particular Issues.*** When appropriate, an action may be brought or maintained as a class action with respect to particular issues. **(5)** ***Subclasses.*** When appropriate, a class may be divided into subclasses that are each treated as a class under this rule.	
23(d)	**(d) ORDERS IN CONDUCT OF ACTIONS.** In the conduct of actions to which this rule applies, the court may make appropriate orders: (1) determining the course of proceedings or prescribing measures to prevent undue repetition or complication in the presentation of evidence or argument; (2) requiring, for the protection of the members of the class or otherwise for the fair conduct of the action, that notice be given in such manner as the court may direct to some or all of the members of any step in the action, or of the proposed extent of the judgment, or of the opportunity of members to signify whether they consider the representation fair and adequate, to intervene and present claims or defenses, or otherwise to come into the action; (3) imposing conditions on the representative parties or on intervenors; (4) requiring that the pleadings be amended to eliminate therefrom allegations as to representation of absent persons, and that the action proceed accordingly; (5) dealing with similar procedural matters. The orders may be combined with an order under Rule 16, and may be altered	**(d) Conducting the Action.** **(1)** ***In General.*** In conducting an action under this rule, the court may issue orders that: **(A)** determine the course of proceedings or prescribe measures to prevent undue repetition or complication in presenting evidence or argument; **(B)** require—to protect class members and fairly conduct the action—giving appropriate notice to some or all class members of: **(i)** any step in the action; **(ii)** the proposed extent of the judgment; or **(iii)** the members' opportunity to signify whether they consider the representation fair and adequate, to intervene and present claims or defenses, or to otherwise come into the action; **(C)** impose conditions on the representative parties or on intervenors; **(D)** require that the pleadings be amended to eliminate allegations about representation of absent	1085, 1096, 1103

Rule	Pre-Restyling Text	Restyled Text	Casebook References
	or amended as may be desirable from time to time.	persons and that the action proceed accordingly; or **(E)** deal with similar procedural matters. **(2)** ***Combining and Amending Orders.*** An order under Rule 23(d)(1) may be altered or amended from time to time and may be combined with an order under Rule 16.	
23(e)	**(e) SETTLEMENT, VOLUNTARY DISMISSAL, OR COMPROMISE.** (1)(A) The court must approve any settlement, voluntary dismissal, or compromise of the claims, issues, or defenses of a certified class. **(B)** The court must direct notice in a reasonable manner to all class members who would be bound by a proposed settlement, voluntary dismissal, or compromise. **(C)** The court may approve a settlement, voluntary dismissal, or compromise that would bind class members only after a hearing and on finding that the settlement, voluntary dismissal, or compromise is fair, reasonable, and adequate. (2) The parties seeking approval of a settlement, voluntary dismissal, or compromise under Rule 23(e)(1) must file a statement identifying any agreement made in connection with the proposed settlement, voluntary dismissal, or compromise. (3) In an action previously certified as a class action under Rule 23(b)(3), the court may refuse to approve a settlement unless it affords a new opportunity to request exclusion to individual class members who had an earlier opportunity to request exclusion but did not do so. (4)(A) Any class member may object to a proposed settlement, voluntary dismissal, or compromise that requires court approval under Rule 23(e)(1)(A). (B) An objection made under Rule 23(e)(4)(A) may be withdrawn only with the court's approval.	**(e) Settlement, Voluntary Dismissal, or Compromise.** The claims, issues, or defenses of a certified class may be settled, voluntarily dismissed, or compromised only with the court's approval. The following procedures apply to a proposed settlement, voluntary dismissal, or compromise: **(1)** The court must direct notice in a reasonable manner to all class members who would be bound by the proposal. **(2)** If the proposal would bind class members, the court may approve it only after a hearing and on finding that it is fair, reasonable, and adequate. **(3)** The parties seeking approval must file a statement identifying any agreement made in connection with the proposal. **(4)** If the class action was previously certified under Rule 23(b)(3), the court may refuse to approve a settlement unless it affords a new opportunity to request exclusion to individual class members who had an earlier opportunity to request exclusion but did not do so. **(5)** Any class member may object to the proposal if it requires court approval under this subdivision (e); the objection may be withdrawn only with the court's approval.	1050, 1051, 1097, 1104, 1105

Rule	Pre-Restyling Text	Restyled Text	Casebook References
23(f)	**(f) APPEALS.** A court of appeals may in its discretion permit an appeal from an order of a district court granting or denying class action certification under this rule if application is made to it within ten days after entry of the order. An appeal does not stay proceedings in the district court unless the district judge or the court of appeals so orders.	**(f) Appeals.** A court of appeals may permit an appeal from an order granting or denying class-action certification under this rule if a petition for permission to appeal is filed with the circuit clerk within 10 days after the order is entered. An appeal does not stay proceedings in the district court unless the district judge or the court of appeals so orders.	1046, 1047, 1048, 1049, 1050, 1053, 1054, 1055, 1104
23(g)	**(g) CLASS COUNSEL.** (1) Appointing Class Counsel. (A) Unless a statute provides otherwise, a court that certifies a class must appoint class counsel. (B) An attorney appointed to serve as class counsel must fairly and adequately represent the interests of the class. (C) In appointing class counsel, the court **(i)** must consider: • the work counsel has done in identifying or investigating potential claims in the action, • counsel's experience in handling class actions, other complex litigation, and claims of the type asserted in the action, • counsel's knowledge of the applicable law, and • the resources counsel will commit to representing the class; **(ii)** may consider any other matter pertinent to counsel's ability to fairly and adequately represent the interests of the class; **(iii)** may direct potential class counsel to provide information on any subject pertinent to the appointment and to propose terms for attorney fees and nontaxable costs; and **(iv)** may make further orders in connection with the appointment.	**(g) Class Counsel.** **(1)** ***Appointing Class Counsel.*** Unless a statute provides otherwise, a court that certifies a class must appoint class counsel. In appointing class counsel, the court: **(A)** must consider: **(i)** the work counsel has done in identifying or investigating potential claims in the action; **(ii)** counsel's experience in handling class actions, other complex litigation, and the types of claims asserted in the action; **(iii)** counsel's knowledge of the applicable law; and **(iv)** the resources that counsel will commit to representing the class; **(B)** may consider any other matter pertinent to counsel's ability to fairly and adequately represent the interests of the class; **(C)** may order potential class counsel to provide information on any subject pertinent to the appointment and to propose terms for attorney's fees and nontaxable costs; **(D)** may include in the appointing order provisions about the award of attorney's fees or nontaxable costs under Rule 23(h); and **(E)** may make further orders in connection with the appointment. **(2)** ***Standard for Appointing Class Counsel.*** When one applicant seeks appointment as class counsel, the court may appoint that applicant only if the applicant is adequate	1105

Rule	Pre-Restyling Text	Restyled Text	Casebook References
	(2) Appointment Procedure. (A) The court may designate interim counsel to act on behalf of the putative class before determining whether to certify the action as a class action. (B) When there is one applicant for appointment as class counsel, the court may appoint that applicant only if the applicant is adequate under Rule 23(g)(1)(B) and (C). If more than one adequate applicant seeks appointment as class counsel, the court must appoint the applicant best able to represent the interests of the class. (C) The order appointing class counsel may include provisions about the award of attorney fees or nontaxable costs under Rule 23(h).	under Rule 23(g)(1) and (4). If more than one adequate applicant seeks appointment, the court must appoint the applicant best able to represent the interests of the class. **(3)** ***Interim Counsel.*** The court may designate interim counsel to act on behalf of a putative class before determining whether to certify the action as a class action. **(4)** ***Duty of Class Counsel.*** Class counsel must fairly and adequately represent the interests of the class.	
23(h)	**(h) ATTORNEY FEES AWARD.** In an action certified as a class action, the court may award reasonable attorney fees and non-taxable costs authorized by law or by agreement of the parties as follows: (1) Motion for Award of Attorney Fees. A claim for an award of attorney fees and nontaxable costs must be made by motion under Rule 54(d)(2), subject to the provisions of this subdivision, at a time set by the court. Notice of the motion must be served on all parties and, for motions by class counsel, directed to class members in a reasonable manner. (2) Objections to Motion. A class member, or a party from whom payment is sought, may object to the motion. (3) Hearing and Findings. The court may hold a hearing and must find the facts and state its conclusions of law on the motion under Rule 52(a). (4) Reference to Special Master or Magistrate Judge. The court may refer issues related to the amount of the award to a special master or to a magistrate judge as provided in Rule 54(d)(2)(D).	**(h) Attorney's Fees and Nontaxable Costs.** In a certified class action, the court may award reasonable attorney's fees and nontaxable costs that are authorized by law or by the parties' agreement. The following procedures apply: **(1)** A claim for an award must be made by motion under Rule 54(d)(2), subject to the provisions of this subdivision (h), at a time the court sets. Notice of the motion must be served on all parties and, for motions by class counsel, directed to class members in a reasonable manner. **(2)** A class member, or a party from whom payment is sought, may object to the motion. **(3)** The court may hold a hearing and must find the facts and state its legal conclusions under Rule 52(a). **(4)** The court may refer issues related to the amount of the award to a special master or a magistrate judge, as provided in Rule 54(d)(2)(D).	1105

Rule	Pre-Restyling Text	Restyled Text	Casebook References
24(a)	**Rule 24. Intervention** **(a) INTERVENTION OF RIGHT.** Upon timely application anyone shall be permitted to intervene in an action: (1) when a statute of the United States confers an unconditional right to intervene; or (2) when the applicant claims an interest relating to the property or transaction which is the subject of the action and the applicant is so situated that the disposition of the action may as a practical matter impair or impede the applicant's ability to protect that interest, unless the applicant's interest is adequately represented by existing parties.	**Rule 24. Intervention** **(a) Intervention of Right.** On timely motion, the court must permit anyone to intervene who: **(1)** is given an unconditional right to intervene by a federal statute; or **(2)** claims an interest relating to the property or transaction that is the subject of the action, and is so situated that disposing of the action may as a practical matter impair or impede the movant's ability to protect its interest, unless existing parties adequately represent that interest.	Rule 24 generally: 905, 913, 914, 985, 1064, 1065, 1067 24(a): 986, 1064
24(b)	**(b) PERMISSIVE INTERVENTION.** Upon timely application anyone may be permitted to intervene in an action: (1) when a statute of the United States confers a conditional right to intervene; or (2) when an applicant's claim or defense and the main action have a question of law or fact in common. When a party to an action relies for ground of claim or defense upon any statute or executive order administered by a federal or state governmental officer or agency or upon any regulation, order, requirement, or agreement issued or made pursuant to the statute or executive order, the officer or agency upon timely application may be permitted to intervene in the action. In exercising its discretion the court shall consider whether the intervention will unduly delay or prejudice the adjudication of the rights of the original parties.	**(b) Permissive Intervention.** **(1)** ***In General.*** On timely motion, the court may permit anyone to intervene who: **(A)** is given a conditional right to intervene by a federal statute; or **(B)** has a claim or defense that shares with the main action a common question of law or fact. **(2)** ***By a Government Officer or Agency.*** On timely motion, the court may permit a federal or state governmental officer or agency to intervene if a party's claim or defense is based on: **(A)** a statute or executive order administered by the officer or agency; or **(B)** any regulation, order, requirement, or agreement issued or made under the statute or executive order. **(3)** ***Delay or Prejudice.*** In exercising its discretion, the court must consider whether the intervention will unduly delay or prejudice the adjudication of the original parties' rights.	1064

Rule	Pre-Restyling Text	Restyled Text	Casebook References
26(a)	**Rule 26. General Provisions Governing Discovery; Duty of Disclosure** **(a) REQUIRED DISCLOSURES; METHODS TO DISCOVER ADDITIONAL MATTER.** (1) *Initial Disclosures.* Except in categories of proceedings specified in Rule 26(a)(1)(E), or to the extent otherwise stipulated or directed by order, a party must, without awaiting a discovery request, provide to other parties: **(A)** the name and, if known, the address and telephone number of each individual likely to have discoverable information that the disclosing party may use to support its claims or defenses, unless solely for impeachment, identifying the subjects of the information; **(B)** a copy of, or a description by category and location of, all documents, electronically stored information, and tangible things that are in the possession, custody, or control of the party and that the disclosing party may use to support its claims or defenses, unless solely for impeachment; **(C)** a computation of any category of damages claimed by the disclosing party, making available for inspection and copying as under Rule 34 the documents or other evidentiary material, not privileged or protected from disclosure, on which such computation is based, including materials bearing on the nature and extent of injuries suffered; and **(D)** for inspection and copying as under Rule 34 any insurance agreement under which any person carrying on an insurance business may be liable to satisfy part or all of a judgment which may be entered in the action or to indemnify or reimburse for payments made to satisfy the judgment. **(E)** The following categories of proceedings are exempt from	**Rule 26. Duty to Disclose; General Provisions Governing Discovery** **(a) Required Disclosures.** **(1)** ***Initial Disclosure.*** **(A)** *In General.* Except as exempted by Rule 26(a)(1)(B) or as otherwise stipulated or ordered by the court, a party must, without awaiting a discovery request, provide to the other parties: **(i)** the name and, if known, the address and telephone number of each individual likely to have discoverable information—along with the subjects of that information—that the disclosing party may use to support its claims or defenses, unless the use would be solely for impeachment; **(ii)** a copy—or a description by category and location—of all documents, electronically stored information, and tangible things that the disclosing party has in its possession, custody, or control and may use to support its claims or defenses, unless the use would be solely for impeachment; **(iii)** a computation of each category of damages claimed by the disclosing party—who must also make available for inspection and copying as under Rule 34 the documents or other evidentiary material, unless privileged or protected from disclosure, on which each computation is based, including materials bearing on the nature and extent of injuries suffered; and **(iv)** for inspection and copying as under Rule 34, any insurance agreement under which an insurance business may be liable to satisfy all or part of a possible judgment in the	Rule 26 generally: 329, 340, 475, 476, 477, 482, 483, 490, 491, 492, 493, 499, 500, 502, 504, 514, 537, 549, 560, 565, 568, 584, 586, 593, 597, 629 26(a): 469, 477, 479, 480, 482, 483, 484, 485, 486, 487, 491, 496, 506, 564, 1017

Rule	Pre-Restyling Text	Restyled Text	Casebook References
	initial disclosure under Rule 26(a)(1): **(i)** an action for review on an administrative record; **(ii)** a forfeiture action in rem arising from a federal statute; **(iii)** a petition for habeas corpus or other proceeding to challenge a criminal conviction or sentence; **(iv)** an action brought without counsel by a person in custody of the United States, a state, or a state subdivision; **(v)** an action to enforce or quash an administrative summons or subpoena; **(vi)** an action by the United States to recover benefit payments; **(vii)** an action by the United States to collect on a student loan guaranteed by the United States; **(viii)** a proceeding ancillary to proceedings in other courts; and **(ix)** an action to enforce an arbitration award. These disclosures must be made at or within 14 days after the Rule 26(f) conference unless a different time is set by stipulation or court order, or unless a party objects during the conference that initial disclosures are not appropriate in the circumstances of the action and states the objection in the Rule 26(f) discovery plan. In ruling on the objection, the court must determine what disclosures—if any—are to be made, and set the time for disclosure. Any party first served or otherwise joined after the Rule 26(f) conference must make these disclosures within 30 days after being served or joined unless a different time is set by stipulation or court order. A party must make its initial disclosures based on the information then reasonably available to it and is not excused from making its disclosures because	action or to indemnify or reimburse for payments made to satisfy the judgment. **(B)** *Proceedings Exempt from Initial Disclosure.* The following proceedings are exempt from initial disclosure: **(i)** an action for review on an administrative record; **(ii)** a forfeiture action in rem arising from a federal statute; **(iii)** a petition for habeas corpus or any other proceeding to challenge a criminal conviction or sentence; **(iv)** an action brought without an attorney by a person in the custody of the United States, a state, or a state subdivision; **(v)** an action to enforce or quash an administrative summons or subpoena; **(vi)** an action by the United States to recover benefit payments; **(vii)** an action by the United States to collect on a student loan guaranteed by the United States; **(viii)** a proceeding ancillary to a proceeding in another court; and **(ix)** an action to enforce an arbitration award. **(C)** *Time for Initial Disclosures—In General.* A party must make the initial disclosures at or within 14 days after the parties' Rule 26(f) conference unless a different time is set by stipulation or court order, or unless a party objects during the conference that initial disclosures are not appropriate in this action and states the objection in the proposed discovery plan. In ruling on the objection, the court must determine what disclosures, if	

Rule	Pre-Restyling Text	Restyled Text	Casebook References
	it has not fully completed its investigation of the case or because it challenges the sufficiency of another party's disclosures or because another party has not made its disclosures. (2) *Disclosure of Expert Testimony.* (A) In addition to the disclosures required by paragraph (1), a party shall disclose to other parties the identity of any person who may be used at trial to present evidence under Rules 702, 703, or 705 of the Federal Rules of Evidence. (B) Except as otherwise stipulated or directed by the court, this disclosure shall, with respect to a witness who is retained or specially employed to provide expert testimony in the case or whose duties as an employee of the party regularly involve giving expert testimony, be accompanied by a written report prepared and signed by the witness. The report shall contain a complete statement of all opinions to be expressed and the basis and reasons therefor; the data or other information considered by the witness in forming the opinions; any exhibits to be used as a summary of or support for the opinions; the qualifications of the witness, including a list of all publications authored by the witness within the preceding ten years; the compensation to be paid for the study and testimony; and a listing of any other cases in which the witness has testified as an expert at trial or by deposition within the preceding four years. (C) These disclosures shall be made at the times and in the sequence directed by the court. In the absence of other directions from the court or stipulation by the parties, the disclosures shall be made at least 90 days before the trial date or the date the case is to be ready for trial or, if the evidence is intended solely to contradict or rebut evidence on	any, are to be made and must set the time for disclosure. **(D)** *Time for Initial Disclosures—For Parties Served or Joined Later.* A party that is first served or otherwise joined after the Rule 26(f) conference must make the initial disclosures within 30 days after being served or joined, unless a different time is set by stipulation or court order. **(E)** *Basis for Initial Disclosure; Unacceptable Excuses.* A party must make its initial disclosures based on the information then reasonably available to it. A party is not excused from making its disclosures because it has not fully investigated the case or because it challenges the sufficiency of another party's disclosures or because another party has not made its disclosures. **(2)** ***Disclosure of Expert Testimony.*** **(A)** *In General.* In addition to the disclosures required by Rule 26(a)(1), a party must disclose to the other parties the identity of any witness it may use at trial to present evidence under Federal Rule of Evidence 702, 703, or 705. **(B)** *Written Report.* Unless otherwise stipulated or ordered by the court, this disclosure must be accompanied by a written report—prepared and signed by the witness—if the witness is one retained or specially employed to provide expert testimony in the case or one whose duties as the party's employee regularly involve giving expert testimony. The report must contain: **(i)** a complete statement of all opinions the witness will express and the basis and reasons for them;	

Rule	Pre-Restyling Text	Restyled Text	Casebook References
	the same subject matter identified by another party under paragraph (2)(B), within 30 days after the disclosure made by the other party. The parties shall supplement these disclosures when required under subdivision (e)(1). (3) *Pretrial Disclosures.* In addition to the disclosures required by Rule 26(a)(1) and (2), a party must provide to other parties and promptly file with the court the following information regarding the evidence that it may present at trial other than solely for impeachment: (A) the name and, if not previously provided, the address and telephone number of each witness, separately identifying those whom the party expects to present and those whom the party may call if the need arises; (B) the designation of those witnesses whose testimony is expected to be presented by means of a deposition and, if not taken stenographically, a transcript of the pertinent portions of the deposition testimony; and (C) an appropriate identification of each document or other exhibit, including summaries of other evidence, separately identifying those which the party expects to offer and those which the party may offer if the need arises. Unless otherwise directed by the court, these disclosures must be made at least 30 days before trial. Within 14 days thereafter, unless a different time is specified by the court, a party may serve and promptly file a list disclosing (i) any objections to the use under Rule 32(a) of a deposition designated by another party under Rule 26(a)(3)(B), and (ii) any objection, together with the grounds therefor, that may be made to the admissibility of materials identified under Rule 26(a)(3)(C). Objections not so disclosed, other than objections under	**(ii)** the data or other information considered by the witness in forming them; **(iii)** any exhibits that will be used to summarize or support them; **(iv)** the witness's qualifications, including a list of all publications authored in the previous 10 years; **(v)** a list of all other cases in which, during the previous four years, the witness testified as an expert at trial or by deposition; and **(vi)** a statement of the compensation to be paid for the study and testimony in the case. **(C)** *Time to Disclose Expert Testimony.* A party must make these disclosures at the times and in the sequence that the court orders. Absent a stipulation or a court order, the disclosures must be made: **(i)** at least 90 days before the date set for trial or for the case to be ready for trial; or **(ii)** if the evidence is intended solely to contradict or rebut evidence on the same subject matter identified by another party under Rule 26(a)(2)(B), within 30 days after the other party's disclosure. **(D)** *Supplementing the Disclosure.* The parties must supplement these disclosures when required under Rule 26(e). **(3)** ***Pretrial Disclosures.*** **(A)** *In General.* In addition to the disclosures required by Rule 26(a)(1) and (2), a party must provide to the other parties and promptly file the following information about the evidence that it may present at trial other than solely for impeachment:	

Rule	Pre-Restyling Text	Restyled Text	Casebook References
	Rules 402 and 403 of the Federal Rules of Evidence, are waived unless excused by the court for good cause. (4) *Form of Disclosures.* Unless the court orders otherwise, all disclosures under Rules 26(a)(1) through (3) must be made in writing, signed, and served. (5) *Methods to Discover Additional Matter.* Parties may obtain discovery by one or more of the following methods: depositions upon oral examination or written questions; written interrogatories; production of documents or things or permission to enter upon land or other property under Rule 34 or 45(a)(1)(C), for inspection and other purposes; physical and mental examinations; and requests for admission.	**(i)** the name and, if not previously provided, the address and telephone number of each witness — separately identifying those the party expects to present and those it may call if the need arises; **(ii)** the designation of those witnesses whose testimony the party expects to present by deposition and, if not taken stenographically, a transcript of the pertinent parts of the deposition; and **(iii)** an identification of each document or other exhibit, including summaries of other evidence — separately identifying those items the party expects to offer and those it may offer if the need arises. **(B)** *Time for Pretrial Disclosures; Objections.* Unless the court orders otherwise, these disclosures must be made at least 30 days before trial. Within 14 days after they are made, unless the court sets a different time, a party may serve and promptly file a list of the following objections: any objections to the use under Rule 32(a) of a deposition designated by another party under Rule 26(a)(3)(A)(ii); and any objection, together with the grounds for it, that may be made to the admissibility of materials identified under Rule 26(a)(3)(A)(iii). An objection not so made — except for one under Federal Rule of Evidence 402 or 403 — is waived unless excused by the court for good cause. **(4)** ***Form of Disclosures.*** Unless the court orders otherwise, all disclosures under Rule 26(a) must be in writing, signed, and served.	

Rule	Pre-Restyling Text	Restyled Text	Casebook References
26(b)	**(b) DISCOVERY SCOPE AND LIMITS.** Unless otherwise limited by order of the court in accordance with these rules, the scope of discovery is as follows: (1) *In General.* Parties may obtain discovery regarding any matter, not privileged, that is relevant to the claim or defense of any party, including the existence, description, nature, custody, condition, and location of any books, documents, or other tangible things and the identity and location of persons having knowledge of any discoverable matter. For good cause, the court may order discovery of any matter relevant to the subject matter involved in the action. Relevant information need not be admissible at the trial if the discovery appears reasonably calculated to lead to the discovery of admissible evidence. All discovery is subject to the limitations imposed by Rule 26(b)(2)(i), (ii), and (iii). (2) *Limitations.* (A) By order, the court may alter the limits in these rules on the number of depositions and interrogatories or the length of depositions under Rule 30. By order or local rule, the court may also limit the number of requests under Rule 36. (B) A party need not provide discovery of electronically stored information from sources that the party identifies as not reasonably accessible because of undue burden or cost. On motion to compel discovery or for a protective order, the party from whom discovery is sought must show that the information is not reasonably accessible because of undue burden or cost. If that showing is made, the court may nonetheless order discovery from such sources if the requesting party shows good cause, considering the limitations of	**(b) Discovery Scope and Limits.** **(1)** ***Scope in General.*** Unless otherwise limited by court order, the scope of discovery is as follows: Parties may obtain discovery regarding any nonprivileged matter that is relevant to any party's claim or defense—including the existence, description, nature, custody, condition, and location of any documents or other tangible things and the identity and location of persons who know of any discoverable matter. For good cause, the court may order discovery of any matter relevant to the subject matter involved in the action. Relevant information need not be admissible at the trial if the discovery appears reasonably calculated to lead to the discovery of admissible evidence. All discovery is subject to the limitations imposed by Rule 26(b)(2)(C). **(2)** ***Limitations on Frequency and Extent.*** **(A)** *When Permitted.* By order, the court may alter the limits in these rules on the number of depositions and interrogatories or on the length of depositions under Rule 30. By order or local rule, the court may also limit the number of requests under Rule 36. **(B)** *Specific Limitations on Electronically Stored Information.* A party need not provide discovery of electronically stored information from sources that the party identifies as not reasonably accessible because of undue burden or cost. On motion to compel discovery or for a protective order, the party from whom discovery is sought must show that the information is not reasonably	477, 478, 479, 491, 492, 493, 494, 501, 505, 506, 507, 509, 514, 518, 520, 521, 522, 549, 550, 551, 552, 553, 562, 563, 565, 566, 567, 574, 627, 629, 101

Rule	Pre-Restyling Text	Restyled Text	Casebook References
	Rule 26(b)(2)(C). The court may specify conditions for the discovery. (C) The frequency or extent of use of the discovery methods otherwise permitted under these rules and by any local rule shall be limited by the court if it determines that: (i) the discovery sought is unreasonably cumulative or duplicative, or is obtainable from some other source that is more convenient, less burdensome, or less expensive; (ii) the party seeking discovery has had ample opportunity by discovery in the action to obtain the information sought; or (iii) the burden or expense of the proposed discovery outweighs its likely benefit, taking into account the needs of the case, the amount in controversy, the parties' resources, the importance of the issues at stake in the litigation, and the importance of the proposed discovery in resolving the issues. The court may act upon its own initiative after reasonable notice or pursuant to a motion under Rule 26(c). (3) *Trial Preparation: Materials.* Subject to the provisions of subdivision (b)(4) of this rule, a party may obtain discovery of documents and tangible things otherwise discoverable under subdivision (b)(1) of this rule and prepared in anticipation of litigation or for trial by or for another party or by or for that other party's representative (including the other party's attorney, consultant, surety, indemnitor, insurer, or agent) only upon a showing that the party seeking discovery has substantial need of the materials in the preparation of the party's case and that the party is unable without undue hardship to obtain the substantial equivalent of the materials by other means. In ordering discovery of such materials when the required showing has been made, the court shall protect against disclosure of	accessible because of undue burden or cost. If that showing is made, the court may nonetheless order discovery from such sources if the requesting party shows good cause, considering the limitations of Rule 26(b)(2)(C). The court may specify conditions for the discovery. **(C)** *When Required.* On motion or on its own, the court must limit the frequency or extent of discovery otherwise allowed by these rules or by local rule if it determines that: **(i)** the discovery sought is unreasonably cumulative or duplicative, or can be obtained from some other source that is more convenient, less burdensome, or less expensive; **(ii)** the party seeking discovery has had ample opportunity to obtain the information by discovery in the action; or **(iii)** the burden or expense of the proposed discovery outweighs its likely benefit, considering the needs of the case, the amount in controversy, the parties' resources, the importance of the issues at stake in the action, and the importance of the discovery in resolving the issues. **(3)** ***Trial Preparation: Materials.*** **(A)** *Documents and Tangible Things.* Ordinarily, a party may not discover documents and tangible things that are prepared in anticipation of litigation or for trial by or for another party or its representative (including the other party's attorney, consultant, surety, indemnitor, insurer, or agent). But, subject to Rule 26(b)(4),	

Rule	Pre-Restyling Text	Restyled Text	Casebook References
	the mental impressions, conclusions, opinions, or legal theories of an attorney or other representative of a party concerning the litigation. A party may obtain without the required showing a statement concerning the action or its subject matter previously made by that party. Upon request, a person not a party may obtain without the required showing a statement concerning the action or its subject matter previously made by that person. If the request is refused, the person may move for a court order. The provisions of Rule 37(a)(4) apply to the award of expenses incurred in relation to the motion. For purposes of this paragraph, a statement previously made is (A) a written statement signed or otherwise adopted or approved by the person making it, or (B) a stenographic, mechanical, electrical, or other recording, or a transcription thereof, which is a substantially verbatim recital of an oral statement by the person making it and contemporaneously recorded. (4) *Trial Preparation: Experts.* (A) A party may depose any person who has been identified as an expert whose opinions may be presented at trial. If a report from the expert is required under subdivision (a)(2)(B), the deposition shall not be conducted until after the report is provided. (B) A party may, through interrogatories or by deposition, discover facts known or opinions held by an expert who has been retained or specially employed by another party in anticipation of litigation or preparation for trial and who is not expected to be called as a witness at trial only as provided in Rule 35(b) or upon a showing of exceptional circumstances under which it is impracticable for the party seeking discovery to obtain facts	those materials may be discovered if: **(i)** they are otherwise discoverable under Rule 26(b)(1); and **(ii)** the party shows that it has substantial need for the materials to prepare its case and cannot, without undue hardship, obtain their substantial equivalent by other means. **(B)** *Protection Against Disclosure.* If the court orders discovery of those materials, it must protect against disclosure of the mental impressions, conclusions, opinions, or legal theories of a party's attorney or other representative concerning the litigation. **(C)** *Previous Statement.* Any party or other person may, on request and without the required showing, obtain the person's own previous statement about the action or its subject matter. If the request is refused, the person may move for a court order, and Rule 37(a)(5) applies to the award of expenses. A previous statement is either: **(i)** a written statement that the person has signed or otherwise adopted or approved; or **(ii)** a contemporaneous stenographic, mechanical, electrical, or other recording—or a transcription of it—that recites substantially verbatim the person's oral statement. **(4)** ***Trial Preparation: Experts.*** **(A)** *Expert Who May Testify.* A party may depose any person who has been identified as an expert whose opinions may be presented at trial. If Rule 26(a)(2)(B) requires a report from the expert, the deposition	

Rule	Pre-Restyling Text	Restyled Text	Casebook References
	or opinions on the same subject by other means. (C) Unless manifest injustice would result, (i) the court shall require that the party seeking discovery pay the expert a reasonable fee for time spent in responding to discovery under this subdivision; and (ii) with respect to discovery obtained under subdivision (b)(4)(B) of this rule the court shall require the party seeking discovery to pay the other party a fair portion of the fees and expenses reasonably incurred by the latter party in obtaining facts and opinions from the expert. (5) *Claims of Privilege or Protection of Trial-Preparation Materials.* (A) Information Withheld. When a party withholds information otherwise discoverable under these rules by claiming that it is privileged or subject to protection as trial preparation material, the party shall make the claim expressly and shall describe the nature of the documents, communications, or things not produced or disclosed in a manner that, without revealing information itself privileged or protected, will enable other parties to assess the applicability of the privilege or protection. (B) Information Produced. If information is produced in discovery that is subject to a claim of privilege or of protection as trial-preparation material, the party making the claim may notify any party that received the information of the claim and the basis for it. After being notified, a party must promptly return, sequester, or destroy the specified information and any copies it has and may not use or disclose the information until the claim is resolved. A receiving party may promptly present the information to the court under seal for a determination of the claim. If the receiving party disclosed the information before being notified,	may be conducted only after the report is provided. **(B)** *Expert Employed Only for Trial Preparation.* Ordinarily, a party may not, by interrogatories or deposition, discover facts known or opinions held by an expert who has been retained or specially employed by another party in anticipation of litigation or to prepare for trial and who is not expected to be called as a witness at trial. But a party may do so only: **(i)** as provided in Rule 35(b); or **(ii)** on showing exceptional circumstances under which it is impracticable for the party to obtain facts or opinions on the same subject by other means. **(C)** *Payment.* Unless manifest injustice would result, the court must require that the party seeking discovery: **(i)** pay the expert a reasonable fee for time spent in responding to discovery under Rule 26(b)(4)(A) or (B); and **(ii)** for discovery under (B), also pay the other party a fair portion of the fees and expenses it reasonably incurred in obtaining the expert's facts and opinions. **(5)** ***Claiming Privilege or Protecting Trial-Preparation Materials.*** **(A)** *Information Withheld.* When a party withholds information otherwise discoverable by claiming that the information is privileged or subject to protection as trial-preparation material, the party must: **(i)** expressly make the claim; and **(ii)** describe the nature of the documents, communications, or tangible things not	

Rule	Pre-Restyling Text	Restyled Text	Casebook References
	it must take reasonable steps to retrieve it. The producing party must preserve the information until the claim is resolved.	produced or disclosed — and do so in a manner that, without revealing information itself privileged or protected, will enable other parties to assess the claim. **(B)** *Information Produced.* If information produced in discovery is subject to a claim of privilege or of protection as trial-preparation material, the party making the claim may notify any party that received the information of the claim and the basis for it. After being notified, a party must promptly return, sequester, or destroy the specified information and any copies it has; must not use or disclose the information until the claim is resolved; must take reasonable steps to retrieve the information if the party disclosed it before being notified; and may promptly present the information to the court under seal for a determination of the claim. The producing party must preserve the information until the claim is resolved.	
26(c)	**(c) PROTECTIVE ORDERS.** Upon motion by a party or by the person from whom discovery is sought, accompanied by a certification that the movant has in good faith conferred or attempted to confer with other affected parties in an effort to resolve the dispute without court action, and for good cause shown, the court in which the action is pending or alternatively, on matters relating to a deposition, the court in the district where the deposition is to be taken may make any order which justice requires to protect a party or person from annoyance, embarrassment, oppression, or undue burden or expense,	**(c) Protective Orders.** **(1)** ***In General.*** A party or any person from whom discovery is sought may move for a protective order in the court where the action is pending — or as an alternative on matters relating to a deposition, in the court for the district where the deposition will be taken. The motion must include a certification that the movant has in good faith conferred or attempted to confer with other affected parties in an effort to resolve the dispute without court action. The court may, for good cause, issue an order to protect a party or person from annoyance, embarrassment,	174, 329, 494, 496, 501, 503, 551, 593, 992, 997

Rule	Pre-Restyling Text	Restyled Text	Casebook References
	including one or more of the following: (1) that the disclosure or discovery not be had; (2) that the disclosure or discovery may be had only on specified terms and conditions, including a designation of the time or place; (3) that the discovery may be had only by a method of discovery other than that selected by the party seeking discovery; (4) that certain matters not be inquired into, or that the scope of the disclosure or discovery be limited to certain matters; (5) that discovery be conducted with no one present except persons designated by the court; (6) that a deposition, after being sealed, be opened only by order of the court; (7) that a trade secret or other confidential research, development, or commercial information not be revealed or be revealed only in a designated way; and (8) that the parties simultaneously file specified documents or information enclosed in sealed envelopes to be opened as directed by the court. If the motion for a protective order is denied in whole or in part, the court may, on such terms and conditions as are just, order that any party or other person provide or permit discovery. The provisions of Rule 37(a)(4) apply to the award of expenses incurred in relation to the motion.	oppression, or undue burden or expense, including one or more of the following: **(A)** forbidding the disclosure or discovery; **(B)** specifying terms, including time and place, for the disclosure or discovery; **(C)** prescribing a discovery method other than the one selected by the party seeking discovery; **(D)** forbidding inquiry into certain matters, or limiting the scope of disclosure or discovery to certain matters; **(E)** designating the persons who may be present while the discovery is conducted; **(F)** requiring that a deposition be sealed and opened only on court order; **(G)** requiring that a trade secret or other confidential research, development, or commercial information not be revealed or be revealed only in a specified way; and **(H)** requiring that the parties simultaneously file specified documents or information in sealed envelopes, to be opened as the court directs. **(2)** ***Ordering Discovery.*** If a motion for a protective order is wholly or partly denied, the court may, on just terms, order that any party or person provide or permit discovery. **(3)** ***Awarding Expenses.*** Rule 37(a)(5) applies to the award of expenses.	
26(d)	**(d) TIMING AND SEQUENCE OF DISCOVERY.** Except in categories of proceedings exempted from initial disclosure under Rule 26(a)(1)(E), or when authorized under these rules or by order or agreement of the parties, a party may not seek discovery from any source before the parties have	**(d) Timing and Sequence of Discovery.** **(1)** ***Timing.*** A party may not seek discovery from any source before the parties have conferred as required by Rule 26(f), except in a proceeding exempted from initial disclosure under Rule 26(a)(1)(B),	

Rule	Pre-Restyling Text	Restyled Text	Casebook References
	conferred as required by Rule 26(f). Unless the court upon motion, for the convenience of parties and witnesses and in the interests of justice, orders otherwise, methods of discovery may be used in any sequence, and the fact that a party is conducting discovery, whether by deposition or otherwise, does not operate to delay any other party's discovery.	or when authorized by these rules, by stipulation, or by court order. **(2)** ***Sequence.*** Unless, on motion, the court orders otherwise for the parties' and witnesses' convenience and in the interests of justice: **(A)** methods of discovery may be used in any sequence; and **(B)** discovery by one party does not require any other party to delay its discovery.	
26(e)	**(e) SUPPLEMENTATION OF DISCLOSURES AND RESPONSES.** A party who has made a disclosure under subdivision (a) or responded to a request for discovery with a disclosure or response is under a duty to supplement or correct the disclosure or response to include information thereafter acquired if ordered by the court or in the following circumstances: (1) A party is under a duty to supplement at appropriate intervals its disclosures under subdivision (a) if the party learns that in some material respect the information disclosed is incomplete or incorrect and if the additional or corrective information has not otherwise been made known to the other parties during the discovery process or in writing. With respect to testimony of an expert from whom a report is required under subdivision (a)(2)(B) the duty extends both to information contained in the report and to information provided through a deposition of the expert, and any additions or other changes to this information shall be disclosed by the time the party's disclosures under Rule 26(a)(3) are due. (2) A party is under a duty seasonably to amend a prior response to an interrogatory, request for production, or request for admission if the party learns that the response is in some material respect incomplete or incorrect and	**(e) Supplementing Disclosures and Responses.** **(1)** ***In General.*** A party who has made a disclosure under Rule 26(a)—or who has responded to an interrogatory, request for production, or request for admission—must supplement or correct its disclosure or response: **(A)** in a timely manner if the party learns that in some material respect the disclosure or response is incomplete or incorrect, and if the additional or corrective information has not otherwise been made known to the other parties during the discovery process or in writing; or **(B)** as ordered by the court. **(2)** ***Expert Witness.*** For an expert whose report must be disclosed under Rule 26(a)(2)(B), the party's duty to supplement extends both to information included in the report and to information given during the expert's deposition. Any additions or changes to this information must be disclosed by the time the party's pretrial disclosures under Rule 26(a)(3) are due.	530, 573, 639

Rule	Pre-Restyling Text	Restyled Text	Casebook References
	if the additional or corrective information has not otherwise been made known to the other parties during the discovery process or in writing.		
26(f)	**(f) CONFERENCE OF PARTIES; PLANNING FOR DISCOVERY.** Except in categories of proceedings exempted from initial disclosure under Rule 26(a)(1)(E) or when otherwise ordered, the parties must, as soon as practicable and in any event at least 21 days before a scheduling conference is held or a scheduling order is due under Rule 16(b), confer to consider the nature and basis of their claims and defenses and the possibilities for a prompt settlement or resolution of the case, to make or arrange for the disclosures required by Rule 26(a)(1), to discuss any issues relating to preserving discoverable information, and to develop a proposed discovery plan that indicates the parties' views and proposals concerning: (1) what changes should be made in the timing, form, or requirement for disclosures under Rule 26(a), including a statement as to when disclosures under Rule 26(a)(1) were made or will be made; (2) the subjects on which discovery may be needed, when discovery should be completed, and whether discovery should be conducted in phases or be limited to or focused upon particular issues; (3) any issues relating to disclosure or discovery of electronically stored information, including the form or forms in which it should be produced; (4) any issues relating to claims of privilege or of protection as trial-preparation material, including—if the parties agree on a procedure to assert such claims after production—whether to ask the court to include their agreement in an order; (5) what changes should be made in the limitations on discovery	**(f) Conference of the Parties; Planning for Discovery.** **(1)** ***Conference Timing.*** Except in a proceeding exempted from initial disclosure under Rule 26(a)(1)(B) or when the court orders otherwise, the parties must confer as soon as practicable—and in any event at least 21 days before a scheduling conference is to be held or a scheduling order is due under Rule 16(b). **(2)** ***Conference Content; Parties' Responsibilities.*** In conferring, the parties must consider the nature and basis of their claims and defenses and the possibilities for promptly settling or resolving the case; make or arrange for the disclosures required by Rule 26(a)(1); discuss any issues about preserving discoverable information; and develop a proposed discovery plan. The attorneys of record and all unrepresented parties that have appeared in the case are jointly responsible for arranging the conference, for attempting in good faith to agree on the proposed discovery plan, and for submitting to the court within 14 days after the conference a written report outlining the plan. The court may order the parties or attorneys to attend the conference in person. **(3)** ***Discovery Plan.*** A discovery plan must state the parties' views and proposals on: **(A)** what changes should be made in the timing, form, or requirement for disclosures under Rule 26(a), including a statement of when initial disclosures were made or will be made; **(B)** the subjects on which discovery may be needed,	469, 549, 553

Rule	Pre-Restyling Text	Restyled Text	Casebook References
	imposed under these rules or by local rule, and what other limitations should be imposed; and (6) any other orders that should be entered by the court under Rule 26(c) or under Rule 16(b) and (c). The attorneys of record and all unrepresented parties that have appeared in the case are jointly responsible for arranging the conference, for attempting in good faith to agree on the proposed discovery plan, and for submitting to the court within 14 days after the conference a written report outlining the plan. A court may order that the parties or attorneys attend the conference in person. If necessary to comply with its expedited schedule for Rule 16(b) conferences, a court may by local rule (i) require that the conference between the parties occur fewer than 21 days before the scheduling conference is held or a scheduling order is due under Rule 16(b), and (ii) require that the written report outlining the discovery plan be filed fewer than 14 days after the conference between the parties, or excuse the parties from submitting a written report and permit them to report orally on their discovery plan at the Rule 16(b) conference.	when discovery should be completed, and whether discovery should be conducted in phases or be limited to or focused on particular issues; **(C)** any issues about disclosure or discovery of electronically stored information, including the form or forms in which it should be produced; **(D)** any issues about claims of privilege or of protection as trial-preparation materials, including—if the parties agree on a procedure to assert these claims after production—whether to ask the court to include their agreement in an order; **(E)** what changes should be made in the limitations on discovery imposed under these rules or by local rule, and what other limitations should be imposed; and **(F)** any other orders that the court should issue under Rule 26(c) or under Rule 16(b) and (c). **(4)** ***Expedited Schedule.*** If necessary to comply with its expedited schedule for Rule 16(b) conferences, a court may by local rule: **(A)** require the parties' conference to occur less than 21 days before the scheduling conference is held or a scheduling order is due under Rule 16(b); and **(B)** require the written report outlining the discovery plan to be filed less than 14 days after the parties' conference, or excuse the parties from submitting a written report and permit them to report orally on their discovery plan at the Rule 16(b) conference.	

Rule	Pre-Restyling Text	Restyled Text	Casebook References
26(g)	**(g) SIGNING OF DISCLOSURES, DISCOVERY REQUESTS, RESPONSES, AND OBJECTIONS.** (1) Every disclosure made pursuant to subdivision (a)(1) or subdivision (a)(3) shall be signed by at least one attorney of record in the attorney's individual name, whose address shall be stated. An unrepresented party shall sign the disclosure and state the party's address. The signature of the attorney or party constitutes a certification that to the best of the signer's knowledge, information, and belief, formed after a reasonable inquiry, the disclosure is complete and correct as of the time it is made. (2) Every discovery request, response, or objection made by a party represented by an attorney shall be signed by at least one attorney of record in the attorney's individual name, whose address shall be stated. An unrepresented party shall sign the request, response, or objection and state the party's address. The signature of the attorney or party constitutes a certification that to the best of the signer's knowledge, information, and belief, formed after a reasonable inquiry, the request, response, or objection is: (A) consistent with these rules and warranted by existing law or a good faith argument for the extension, modification, or reversal of existing law; (B) not interposed for any improper purpose, such as to harass or to cause unnecessary delay or needless increase in the cost of litigation; and (C) not unreasonable or unduly burdensome or expensive, given the needs of the case, the discovery already had in the case, the amount in controversy, and the importance of the issues at stake in the litigation. If a request, response, or objection is not signed, it shall be stricken unless it is signed promptly after the omission is called to the	**(g) Signing Disclosures and Discovery Requests, Responses, and Objections.** **(1)** ***Signature Required; Effect of Signature.*** Every disclosure under Rule 26(a)(1) or (a)(3) and every discovery request, response, or objection must be signed by at least one attorney of record in the attorney's own name—or by the party personally, if unrepresented—and must state the signer's address, e-mail address, and telephone number. By signing, an attorney or party certifies that to the best of the person's knowledge, information, and belief formed after a reasonable inquiry: **(A)** with respect to a disclosure, it is complete and correct as of the time it is made; and **(B)** with respect to a discovery request, response, or objection, it is: **(i)** consistent with these rules and warranted by existing law or by a nonfrivolous argument for extending, modifying, or reversing existing law, or for establishing new law; **(ii)** not interposed for any improper purpose, such as to harass, cause unnecessary delay, or needlessly increase the cost of litigation; and **(iii)** neither unreasonable nor unduly burdensome or expensive, considering the needs of the case, prior discovery in the case, the amount in controversy, and the importance of the issues at stake in the action. **(2)** ***Failure to Sign.*** Other parties have no duty to act on an unsigned disclosure, request, response, or objection until it is signed, and the court must strike it unless a signature is promptly supplied after the omission is	289, 459, 461, 537, 538, 547

Rule	Pre-Restyling Text	Restyled Text	Casebook References
	attention of the party making the request, response, or objection, and a party shall not be obligated to take any action with respect to it until it is signed. (3) If without substantial justification a certification is made in violation of the rule, the court, upon motion or upon its own initiative, shall impose upon the person who made the certification, the party on whose behalf the disclosure, request, response, or objection is made, or both, an appropriate sanction, which may include an order to pay the amount of the reasonable expenses incurred because of the violation, including a reasonable attorney's fee.	called to the attorney's or party's attention. **(3)** ***Sanction for Improper Certification.*** If a certification violates this rule without substantial justification, the court, on motion or on its own, must impose an appropriate sanction on the signer, the party on whose behalf the signer was acting, or both. The sanction may include an order to pay the reasonable expenses, including attorney's fees, caused by the violation.	
30(a)	**Rule 30. Depositions Upon Oral Examination** **(a) WHEN DEPOSITIONS MAY BE TAKEN; WHEN LEAVE REQUIRED.** (1) A party may take the testimony of any person, including a party, by deposition upon oral examination without leave of court except as provided in paragraph (2). The attendance of witnesses may be compelled by subpoena as provided in Rule 45. (2) A party must obtain leave of court, which shall be granted to the extent consistent with the principles stated in Rule 26(b)(2), if the person to be examined is confined in prison or if, without the written stipulation of the parties, **(A)** a proposed deposition would result in more than ten depositions being taken under this rule or Rule 31 by the plaintiffs, or by the defendants, or by third-party defendants; **(B)** the person to be examined already has been deposed in the case; or **(C)** a party seeks to take a deposition before the time specified in Rule 26(d) unless the notice contains a certification, with supporting facts, that the	**Rule 30. Depositions by Oral Examination** **(a) When a Deposition May Be Taken.** **(1)** ***Without Leave.*** A party may, by oral questions, depose any person, including a party, without leave of court except as provided in Rule 30(a)(2). The deponent's attendance may be compelled by subpoena under Rule 45. **(2)** ***With Leave.*** A party must obtain leave of court, and the court must grant leave to the extent consistent with Rule 26(b)(2): **(A)** if the parties have not stipulated to the deposition and: **(i)** the deposition would result in more than 10 depositions being taken under this rule or Rule 31 by the plaintiffs, or by the defendants, or by the third-party defendants; **(ii)** the deponent has already been deposed in the case; or **(iii)** the party seeks to take the deposition before the time specified in Rule 26(d), unless the party certifies in	Rule 30 generally: 586 30(a): 593

Rule	Pre-Restyling Text	Restyled Text	Casebook References
	person to be examined is expected to leave the United States and be unavailable for examination in this country unless deposed before that time.	the notice, with supporting facts, that the deponent is expected to leave the United States and be unavailable for examination in this country after that time; or **(B)** if the deponent is confined in prison.	
30(b)	**(b) NOTICE OF EXAMINATION: GENERAL REQUIREMENTS; METHOD OF RECORDING; PRODUCTION OF DOCUMENTS AND THINGS; DEPOSITION OF ORGANIZATION; DEPOSITION BY TELEPHONE.** (1) A party desiring to take the deposition of any person upon oral examination shall give reasonable notice in writing to every other party to the action. The notice shall state the time and place for taking the deposition and the name and address of each person to be examined, if known, and, if the name is not known, a general description sufficient to identify the person or the particular class or group to which the person belongs. If a subpoena duces tecum is to be served on the person to be examined, the designation of the materials to be produced as set forth in the subpoena shall be attached to, or included in, the notice. (2) The party taking the deposition shall state in the notice the method by which the testimony shall be recorded. Unless the court orders otherwise, it may be recorded by sound, sound-and-visual, or stenographic means, and the party taking the deposition shall bear the cost of the recording. Any party may arrange for a transcription to be made from the recording of a deposition taken by nonstenographic means. (3) With prior notice to the deponent and other parties, any party may designate another method to record the deponent's testimony in addition to the method specified by the person taking the deposition. The additional record or transcript shall be made at that	**(b) Notice of the Deposition; Other Formal Requirements.** **(1)** ***Notice in General.*** A party who wants to depose a person by oral questions must give reasonable written notice to every other party. The notice must state the time and place of the deposition and, if known, the deponent's name and address. If the name is unknown, the notice must provide a general description sufficient to identify the person or the particular class or group to which the person belongs. **(2)** ***Producing Documents.*** If a subpoena duces tecum is to be served on the deponent, the materials designated for production, as set out in the subpoena, must be listed in the notice or in an attachment. The notice to a party deponent may be accompanied by a request under Rule 34 to produce documents and tangible things at the deposition. **(3)** ***Method of Recording.*** **(A)** *Method Stated in the Notice.* The party who notices the deposition must state in the notice the method for recording the testimony. Unless the court orders otherwise, testimony may be recorded by audio, audiovisual, or stenographic means. The noticing party bears the recording costs. Any party may arrange to transcribe a deposition. **(B)** *Additional Method.* With prior notice to the deponent and other parties, any party may designate another method	174, 289, 521, 532, 533, 539, 540, 542, 593

Rule	Pre-Restyling Text	Restyled Text	Casebook References
	party's expense unless the court otherwise orders. (4) Unless otherwise agreed by the parties, a deposition shall be conducted before an officer appointed or designated under Rule 28 and shall begin with a statement on the record by the officer that includes (A) the officer's name and business address; (B) the date, time, and place of the deposition; (C) the name of the deponent; (D) the administration of the oath or affirmation to the deponent; and (E) an identification of all persons present. If the deposition is recorded other than stenographically, the officer shall repeat items (A) through (C) at the beginning of each unit of recorded tape or other recording medium. The appearance or demeanor of deponents or attorneys shall not be distorted through camera or sound-recording techniques. At the end of the deposition, the officer shall state on the record that the deposition is complete and shall set forth any stipulations made by counsel concerning the custody of the transcript or recording and the exhibits, or concerning other pertinent matters. (5) The notice to a party deponent may be accompanied by a request made in compliance with Rule 34 for the production of documents and tangible things at the taking of the deposition. The procedure of Rule 34 shall apply to the request. (6) A party may in the party's notice and in a subpoena name as the deponent a public or private corporation or a partnership or association or governmental agency and describe with reasonable particularity the matters on which examination is requested. In that event, the organization so named shall designate one or more officers, directors, or managing agents, or other persons who consent to testify on its behalf, and may set forth, for each person designated, the matters on which the person will testify. A subpoena shall advise a non-party	for recording the testimony in addition to that specified in the original notice. That party bears the expense of the additional record or transcript unless the court orders otherwise. **(4)** ***By Remote Means.*** The parties may stipulate — or the court may on motion order — that a deposition be taken by telephone or other remote means. For the purpose of this rule and Rules 28(a), 37(a)(2), and 37(b)(1), the deposition takes place where the deponent answers the questions. **(5)** ***Officer's Duties.*** **(A)** *Before the Deposition.* Unless the parties stipulate otherwise, a deposition must be conducted before an officer appointed or designated under Rule 28. The officer must begin the deposition with an on-the-record statement that includes: **(i)** the officer's name and business address; **(ii)** the date, time, and place of the deposition; **(iii)** the deponent's name; **(iv)** the officer's administration of the oath or affirmation to the deponent; and **(v)** the identity of all persons present. **(B)** *Conducting the Deposition; Avoiding Distortion.* If the deposition is recorded non-stenographically, the officer must repeat the items in Rule 30(b)(5)(A)(i)-(iii) at the beginning of each unit of the recording medium. The deponent's and attorneys' appearance or demeanor must not be distorted through recording techniques. **(C)** *After the Deposition.* At the end of a deposition, the officer must state on the record that the deposition is complete and must set out any stipulations	

Rule	Pre-Restyling Text	Restyled Text	Casebook References
	organization of its duty to make such a designation. The persons so designated shall testify as to matters known or reasonably available to the organization. This subdivision (b)(6) does not preclude taking a deposition by any other procedure authorized in these rules. (7) The parties may stipulate in writing or the court may upon motion order that a deposition be taken by telephone or other remote electronic means. For the purposes of this rule and Rules 28(a), 37(a)(1), and 37(b)(1), a deposition taken by such means is taken in the district and at the place where the deponent is to answer questions.	made by the attorneys about custody of the transcript or recording and of the exhibits, or about any other pertinent matters. **(6)** ***Notice or Subpoena Directed to an Organization.*** In its notice or subpoena, a party may name as the deponent a public or private corporation, a partnership, an association, a governmental agency, or other entity and must describe with reasonable particularity the matters for examination. The named organization must then designate one or more officers, directors, or managing agents, or designate other persons who consent to testify on its behalf; and it may set out the matters on which each person designated will testify. A subpoena must advise a nonparty organization of its duty to make this designation. The persons designated must testify about information known or reasonably available to the organization. This paragraph (6) does not preclude a deposition by any other procedure allowed by these rules.	
30(c)	**(c) EXAMINATION AND CROSS-EXAMINATION; RECORD OF EXAMINATION; OATH; OBJECTIONS.** Examination and cross-examination of witnesses may proceed as permitted at the trial under the provisions of the Federal Rules of Evidence except Rules 103 and 615. The officer before whom the deposition is to be taken shall put the witness on oath or affirmation and shall personally, or by someone acting under the officer's direction and in the officer's presence, record the testimony of the witness. The testimony shall be taken stenographically or recorded by any other method authorized by subdivision (b)(2) of this rule. All objections made at the time of the examination to the qualifications of the officer taking the deposition, to the manner of taking it, to the evidence presented, to the conduct	**(c) Examination and Cross-Examination; Record of the Examination; Objections; Written Questions.** **(1)** ***Examination and Cross-Examination.*** The examination and cross-examination of a deponent proceed as they would at trial under the Federal Rules of Evidence, except Rules 103 and 615. After putting the deponent under oath or affirmation, the officer must record the testimony by the method designated under Rule 30(b)(3)(A). The testimony must be recorded by the officer personally or by a person acting in the presence and under the direction of the officer. **(2)** ***Objections.*** An objection at the time of the examination—whether to evidence, to a party's conduct, to the officer's qualifications, to the	

Rule	Pre-Restyling Text	Restyled Text	Casebook References
	of any party, or to any other aspect of the proceedings shall be noted by the officer upon the record of the deposition; but the examination shall proceed, with the testimony being taken subject to the objections. In lieu of participating in the oral examination, parties may serve written questions in a sealed envelope on the party taking the deposition and the party taking the deposition shall transmit them to the officer, who shall propound them to the witness and record the answers verbatim.	manner of taking the deposition, or to any other aspect of the deposition — must be noted on the record, but the examination still proceeds; the testimony is taken subject to any objection. An objection must be stated concisely in a nonargumentative and nonsuggestive manner. A person may instruct a deponent not to answer only when necessary to preserve a privilege, to enforce a limitation ordered by the court, or to present a motion under Rule 30(d)(3). **(3)** ***Participating Through Written Questions.*** Instead of participating in the oral examination, a party may serve written questions in a sealed envelope on the party noticing the deposition, who must deliver them to the officer. The officer must ask the deponent those questions and record the answers verbatim.	
30(d)	**(d) SCHEDULE AND DURATION; MOTION TO TERMINATE OR LIMIT EXAMINATION.** (1) Any objection during a deposition must be stated concisely and in a non-argumentative and non-suggestive manner. A person may instruct a deponent not to answer only when necessary to preserve a privilege, to enforce a limitation directed by the court, or to present a motion under Rule 30(d)(4). (2) Unless otherwise authorized by the court or stipulated by the parties, a deposition is limited to one day of seven hours. The court must allow additional time consistent with Rule 26(b)(2) if needed for a fair examination of the deponent or if the deponent or another person, or other circumstance, impedes or delays the examination. (3) If the court finds that any impediment, delay, or other conduct has frustrated the fair examination of the deponent, it may	**(d) Duration; Sanction; Motion to Terminate or Limit.** **(1)** ***Duration.*** Unless otherwise stipulated or ordered by the court, a deposition is limited to 1 day of 7 hours. The court must allow additional time consistent with Rule 26(b)(2) if needed to fairly examine the deponent or if the deponent, another person, or any other circumstance impedes or delays the examination. **(2)** ***Sanction.*** The court may impose an appropriate sanction — including the reasonable expenses and attorney's fees incurred by any party — on a person who impedes, delays, or frustrates the fair examination of the deponent. **(3)** ***Motion to Terminate or Limit.*** **(A)** *Grounds.* At any time during a deposition, the deponent or a party may move to terminate or limit it on the ground that it is being conducted in bad faith or in a manner that unreasonably	591, 593

Rule	Pre-Restyling Text	Restyled Text	Casebook References
	impose upon the persons responsible an appropriate sanction, including the reasonable costs and attorney's fees incurred by any parties as a result thereof. (4) At any time during a deposition, on motion of a party or of the deponent and upon a showing that the examination is being conducted in bad faith or in such manner as unreasonably to annoy, embarrass, or oppress the deponent or party, the court in which the action is pending or the court in the district where the deposition is being taken may order the officer conducting the examination to cease forthwith from taking the deposition, or may limit the scope and manner of the taking of the deposition as provided in Rule 26(c). If the order made terminates the examination, it may be resumed thereafter only upon the order of the court in which the action is pending. Upon demand of the objecting party or deponent, the taking of the deposition must be suspended for the time necessary to make a motion for an order. The provisions of Rule 37(a)(4) apply to the award of expenses incurred in relation to the motion.	annoys, embarrasses, or oppresses the deponent or party. The motion may be filed in the court where the action is pending or the deposition is being taken. If the objecting deponent or party so demands, the deposition must be suspended for the time necessary to obtain an order. **(B)** *Order.* The court may order that the deposition be terminated or may limit its scope and manner as provided in Rule 26(c). If terminated, the deposition may be resumed only by order of the court where the action is pending. **(C)** *Award of Expenses.* Rule 37(a)(5) applies to the award of expenses.	
30(e)	**(e) REVIEW BY WITNESS; CHANGES; SIGNING.** If requested by the deponent or a party before completion of the deposition, the deponent shall have 30 days after being notified by the officer that the transcript or recording is available in which to review the transcript or recording and, if there are changes in form or substance, to sign a statement reciting such changes and the reasons given by the deponent for making them. The officer shall indicate in the certificate prescribed by subdivision (f)(1) whether any review was requested and, if so, shall append any changes made by the deponent during the period allowed.	**(e) Review by the Witness; Changes.** **(1)** ***Review; Statement of Changes.*** On request by the deponent or a party before the deposition is completed, the deponent must be allowed 30 days after being notified by the officer that the transcript or recording is available in which: **(A)** to review the transcript or recording; and **(B)** if there are changes in form or substance, to sign a statement listing the changes and the reasons for making them. **(2)** ***Changes Indicated in the Officer's Certificate.*** The officer must note in the certificate prescribed by Rule 30(f)(1) whether a review was requested	

Rule	Pre-Restyling Text	Restyled Text	Casebook References
		and, if so, must attach any changes the deponent makes during the 30-day period.	
30(f)	**(f) CERTIFICATION AND DELIVERY BY OFFICER; EXHIBITS; COPIES.** (1) The officer must certify that the witness was duly sworn by the officer and that the deposition is a true record of the testimony given by the witness. This certificate must be in writing and accompany the record of the deposition. Unless otherwise ordered by the court, the officer must securely seal the deposition in an envelope or package indorsed with the title of the action and marked "Deposition of [here insert name of witness]" and must promptly send it to the attorney who arranged for the transcript or recording, who must store it under conditions that will protect it against loss, destruction, tampering, or deterioration. Documents and things produced for inspection during the examination of the witness, must, upon the request of a party, be marked for identification and annexed to the deposition and may be inspected and copied by any party, except that if the person producing the materials desires to retain them the person may (A) offer copies to be marked for identification and annexed to the deposition and to serve thereafter as originals if the person affords to all parties fair opportunity to verify the copies by comparison with the originals, or (B) offer the originals to be marked for identification, after giving to each party an opportunity to inspect and copy them, in which event the materials may then be used in the same manner as if annexed to the deposition. Any party may move for an order that the original be annexed to and returned with the deposition to the court, pending final disposition of the case. (2) Unless otherwise ordered by the court or agreed by the parties, the officer shall retain stenographic notes of any deposition taken	**(f) Certification and Delivery; Exhibits; Copies of the Transcript or Recording; Filing.** **(1)** ***Certification and Delivery.*** The officer must certify in writing that the witness was duly sworn and that the deposition accurately records the witness's testimony. The certificate must accompany the record of the deposition. Unless the court orders otherwise, the officer must seal the deposition in an envelope or package bearing the title of the action and marked "Deposition of [witness's name]" and must promptly send it to the attorney who arranged for the transcript or recording. The attorney must store it under conditions that will protect it against loss, destruction, tampering, or deterioration. **(2)** ***Documents and Tangible Things.*** **(A)** *Originals and Copies.* Documents and tangible things produced for inspection during a deposition must, on a party's request, be marked for identification and attached to the deposition. Any party may inspect and copy them. But if the person who produced them wants to keep the originals, the person may: **(i)** offer copies to be marked, attached to the deposition, and then used as originals—after giving all parties a fair opportunity to verify the copies by comparing them with the originals; or **(ii)** give all parties a fair opportunity to inspect and copy the originals after they are marked—in which event the originals may be used as if attached to the deposition. **(B)** *Order Regarding the Originals.* Any party may move	

Rule	Pre-Restyling Text	Restyled Text	Casebook References
	stenographically or a copy of the recording of any deposition taken by another method. Upon payment of reasonable charges therefor, the officer shall furnish a copy of the transcript or other recording of the deposition to any party or to the deponent. (3) The party taking the deposition shall give prompt notice of its filing to all other parties.	for an order that the originals be attached to the deposition pending final disposition of the case. **(3)** ***Copies of the Transcript or Recording.*** Unless otherwise stipulated or ordered by the court, the officer must retain the stenographic notes of a deposition taken stenographically or a copy of the recording of a deposition taken by another method. When paid reasonable charges, the officer must furnish a copy of the transcript or recording to any party or the deponent. **(4)** ***Notice of Filing.*** A party who files the deposition must promptly notify all other parties of the filing.	
30(g)	**(g) FAILURE TO ATTEND OR TO SERVE SUBPOENA; EXPENSES.** (1) If the party giving the notice of the taking of a deposition fails to attend and proceed therewith and another party attends in person or by attorney pursuant to the notice, the court may order the party giving the notice to pay to such other party the reasonable expenses incurred by that party and that party's attorney in attending, including reasonable attorney's fees. (2) If the party giving the notice of the taking of a deposition of a witness fails to serve a subpoena upon the witness and the witness because of such failure does not attend, and if another party attends in person or by attorney because that party expects the deposition of that witness to be taken, the court may order the party giving the notice to pay to such other party the reasonable expenses incurred by that party and that party's attorney in attending, including reasonable attorney's fees.	**(g) Failure to Attend a Deposition or Serve a Subpoena; Expenses.** A party who, expecting a deposition to be taken, attends in person or by an attorney may recover reasonable expenses for attending, including attorney's fees, if the noticing party failed to: **(1)** attend and proceed with the deposition; or **(2)** serve a subpoena on a nonparty deponent, who consequently did not attend.	461
31	**Rule 31. Depositions Upon Written Questions** **(a) SERVING QUESTIONS; NOTICE.** (1) A party may take the testimony of any person,	**Rule 31. Depositions by Written Questions** **(a) When a Deposition May Be Taken.** **(1)** ***Without Leave.*** A party may, by written questions, depose any	174, 586

Rule	Pre-Restyling Text	Restyled Text	Casebook References
	including a party, by deposition upon written questions without leave of court except as provided in paragraph (2). The attendance of witnesses may be compelled by the use of subpoena as provided in Rule 45. (2) A party must obtain leave of court, which shall be granted to the extent consistent with the principles stated in Rule 26(b)(2), if the person to be examined is confined in prison or if, without the written stipulation of the parties, (A) a proposed deposition would result in more than ten depositions being taken under this rule or Rule 30 by the plaintiffs, or by the defendants, or by third-party defendants; (B) the person to be examined has already been deposed in the case; or (C) a party seeks to take a deposition before the time specified in Rule 26(d). (3) A party desiring to take a deposition upon written questions shall serve them upon every other party with a notice stating (1) the name and address of the person who is to answer them, if known, and if the name is not known, a general description sufficient to identify the person or the particular class or group to which the person belongs, and (2) the name or descriptive title and address of the officer before whom the deposition is to be taken. A deposition upon written questions may be taken of a public or private corporation or a partnership or association or governmental agency in accordance with the provisions of Rule 30(b)(6). (4) Within 14 days after the notice and written questions are served, a party may serve cross questions upon all other parties. Within 7 days after being served with cross questions, a party may serve redirect questions upon all other parties. Within 7 days after being	person, including a party, without leave of court except as provided in Rule 31(a)(2). The deponent's attendance may be compelled by subpoena under Rule 45. **(2)** ***With Leave.*** A party must obtain leave of court, and the court must grant leave to the extent consistent with Rule 26(b)(2): **(A)** if the parties have not stipulated to the deposition and: **(i)** the deposition would result in more than 10 depositions being taken under this rule or Rule 30 by the plaintiffs, or by the defendants, or by the third-party defendants; **(ii)** the deponent has already been deposed in the case; or **(iii)** the party seeks to take a deposition before the time specified in Rule 26(d); or **(B)** if the deponent is confined in prison. **(3)** ***Service; Required Notice.*** A party who wants to depose a person by written questions must serve them on every other party, with a notice stating, if known, the deponent's name and address. If the name is unknown, the notice must provide a general description sufficient to identify the person or the particular class or group to which the person belongs. The notice must also state the name or descriptive title and the address of the officer before whom the deposition will be taken. **(4)** ***Questions Directed to an Organization.*** A public or private corporation, a partnership, an association, or a governmental agency may be deposed by written questions in accordance with Rule 30(b)(6). **(5)** ***Questions from Other Parties.*** Any questions to the deponent from other parties must be served	

Rule	Pre-Restyling Text	Restyled Text	Casebook References
	served with redirect questions, a party may serve recross questions upon all other parties. The court may for cause shown enlarge or shorten the time. **(b) OFFICER TO TAKE RESPONSES AND PREPARE RECORD.** A copy of the notice and copies of all questions served shall be delivered by the party taking the deposition to the officer designated in the notice, who shall proceed promptly, in the manner provided by Rule 30(c), (e), and (f), to take the testimony of the witness in response to the questions and to prepare, certify, and file or mail the deposition, attaching thereto the copy of the notice and the questions received by the officer. **(c) NOTICE OF FILING.** When the deposition is filed the party taking it shall promptly give notice thereof to all other parties.	on all parties as follows: cross-questions, within 14 days after being served with the notice and direct questions; redirect questions, within 7 days after being served with cross-questions; and recross-questions, within 7 days after being served with redirect questions. The court may, for good cause, extend or shorten these times. **(b) (b) Delivery to the Officer; Officer's Duties.** The party who noticed the deposition must deliver to the officer a copy of all the questions served and of the notice. The officer must promptly proceed in the manner provided in Rule 30(c), (e), and (f) to: **(1)** take the deponent's testimony in response to the questions; **(2)** prepare and certify the deposition; and **(3)** send it to the party, attaching a copy of the questions and of the notice. **(c) (c) Notice of Completion or Filing.** **(1) *Completion.*** The party who noticed the deposition must notify all other parties when it is completed. **(2) *Filing.*** A party who files the deposition must promptly notify all other parties of the filing.	
32(a)	**Rule 32. Use of Depositions in Court Proceedings** **(a) USE OF DEPOSITIONS.** At the trial or upon the hearing of a motion or an interlocutory proceeding, any part or all of a deposition, so far as admissible under the rules of evidence applied as though the witness were then present and testifying, may be used against any party who was present or represented at the taking of the deposition or who had reasonable notice thereof, in accordance with any of the following provisions: (1) Any deposition may be used by any party for the purpose of	**Rule 32. Using Depositions in Court Proceedings** **(a) Using Depositions.** **(1) *In General.*** At a hearing or trial, all or part of a deposition may be used against a party on these conditions: **(A)** the party was present or represented at the taking of the deposition or had reasonable notice of it; **(B)** it is used to the extent it would be admissible under the Federal Rules of Evidence if the deponent were present and testifying; and	Rule 32 generally: 593

Rule	Pre-Restyling Text	Restyled Text	Casebook References
	contradicting or impeaching the testimony of deponent as a witness, or for any other purpose permitted by the Federal Rules of Evidence. (2) The deposition of a party or of anyone who at the time of taking the deposition was an officer, director, or managing agent, or a person designated under Rule 30(b)(6) or 31(a) to testify on behalf of a public or private corporation, partnership or association or governmental agency which is a party may be used by an adverse party for any purpose. (3) The deposition of a witness, whether or not a party, may be used by any party for any purpose if the court finds: (A) that the witness is dead; or (B) that the witness is at a greater distance than 100 miles from the place of trial or hearing, or is out of the United States, unless it appears that the absence of the witness was procured by the party offering the deposition; or (C) that the witness is unable to attend or testify because of age, illness, infirmity, or imprisonment; or (D) that the party offering the deposition has been unable to procure the attendance of the witness by subpoena; or (E) upon application and notice, that such exceptional circumstances exist as to make it desirable, in the interest of justice and with due regard to the importance of presenting the testimony of witnesses orally in open court, to allow the deposition to be used.	**(C)** the use is allowed by Rule 32(a)(2) through (8). **(2) *Impeachment and Other Uses.*** Any party may use a deposition to contradict or impeach the testimony given by the deponent as a witness, or for any other purpose allowed by the Federal Rules of Evidence. **(3) *Deposition of Party, Agent, or Designee.*** An adverse party may use for any purpose the deposition of a party or anyone who, when deposed, was the party's officer, director, managing agent, or designee under Rule 30(b)(6) or 31(a)(4). **(4) *Unavailable Witness.*** A party may use for any purpose the deposition of a witness, whether or not a party, if the court finds: **(A)** that the witness is dead; **(B)** that the witness is more than 100 miles from the place of hearing or trial or is outside the United States, unless it appears that the witness's absence was procured by the party offering the deposition; **(C)** that the witness cannot attend or testify because of age, illness, infirmity, or imprisonment; **(D)** that the party offering the deposition could not procure the witness's attendance by subpoena; or **(E)** on motion and notice, that exceptional circumstances make it desirable—in the interest of justice and with due regard to the importance of live testimony in open court—to permit the deposition to be used.	
	A deposition taken without leave of court pursuant to a notice under Rule 30(a)(2)(C) shall not be used against a party who demonstrates that, when served with the notice, it was unable through the exercise of diligence to obtain counsel to represent it at the taking of the deposition; nor shall a deposition be used against a party who, having	**(5) *Limitations on Use.*** **(A)** *Deposition Taken on Short Notice.* A deposition must not be used against a party who, having received less than 11 days' notice of the deposition, promptly moved for a	

Rule	Pre-Restyling Text	Restyled Text	Casebook References
	received less than 11 days notice of a deposition, has promptly upon receiving such notice filed a motion for a protective order under Rule 26 (c)(2) requesting that the deposition not be held or be held at a different time or place and such motion is pending at the time the deposition is held. (4) If only part of a deposition is offered in evidence by a party, an adverse party may require the offeror to introduce any other part which ought in fairness to be considered with the part introduced, and any party may introduce any other parts. Substitution of parties pursuant to Rule 25 does not affect the right to use depositions previously taken; and, when an action has been brought in any court of the United States or of any State and another action involving the same subject matter is afterward brought between the same parties or their representatives or successors in interest, all depositions lawfully taken and duly filed in the former action may be used in the latter as if originally taken therefor. A deposition previously taken may also be used as permitted by the Federal Rules of Evidence.	protective order under Rule 26 (c)(1)(B) requesting that it not be taken or be taken at a different time or place—and this motion was still pending when the deposition was taken. **(B)** *Unavailable Deponent; Party Could Not Obtain an Attorney.* A deposition taken without leave of court under the unavailability provision of Rule 30(a)(2)(A)(iii) must not be used against a party who shows that, when served with the notice, it could not, despite diligent efforts, obtain an attorney to represent it at the deposition. **(6)** ***Using Part of a Deposition.*** If a party offers in evidence only part of a deposition, an adverse party may require the offeror to introduce other parts that in fairness should be considered with the part introduced, and any party may itself introduce any other parts. **(7)** ***Substituting a Party.*** Substituting a party under Rule 25 does not affect the right to use a deposition previously taken. **(8)** ***Deposition Taken in an Earlier Action.*** A deposition lawfully taken and, if required, filed in any federal- or state-court action may be used in a later action involving the same subject matter between the same parties, or their representatives or successors in interest, to the same extent as if taken in the later action. A deposition previously taken may also be used as allowed by the Federal Rules of Evidence.	
32(b)	**(b) OBJECTIONS TO ADMISSIBILITY.** Subject to the provisions of Rule 28(b) and subdivision (d)(3) of this rule, objection may be made at the trial or hearing to receiving in evidence any deposition or part thereof for any reason which would require the exclusion of the evidence if the witness were then present and testifying.	**(b) Objections to Admissibility.** Subject to Rules 28(b) and 32(d)(3), an objection may be made at a hearing or trial to the admission of any deposition testimony that would be inadmissible if the witness were present and testifying.	593

Rule	Pre-Restyling Text	Restyled Text	Casebook References
33(a)	**Rule 33. Interrogatories to Parties** **(a) AVAILABILITY.** Without leave of court or written stipulation, any party may serve upon any other party written interrogatories, not exceeding 25 in number including all discrete subparts, to be answered by the party served or, if the party served is a public or private corporation or a partnership or association or governmental agency, by any officer or agent, who shall furnish such information as is available to the party. Leave to serve additional interrogatories shall be granted to the extent consistent with the principles of Rule 26(b)(2). Without leave of court or written stipulation, interrogatories may not be served before the time specified in Rule 26(d).	**Rule 33. Interrogatories to Parties** **(a) In General.** **(1)** ***Number.*** Unless otherwise stipulated or ordered by the court, a party may serve on any other party no more than 25 written interrogatories, including all discrete subparts. Leave to serve additional interrogatories may be granted to the extent consistent with Rule 26(b)(2). **(2)** ***Scope.*** An interrogatory may relate to any matter that may be inquired into under Rule 26(b). An interrogatory is not objectionable merely because it asks for an opinion or contention that relates to fact or the application of law to fact, but the court may order that the interrogatory need not be answered until designated discovery is complete, or until a pretrial conference or some other time.	Rule 33 generally: 174, 549
33(b)	**(b) ANSWERS AND OBJECTIONS.** (1) Each interrogatory shall be answered separately and fully in writing under oath, unless it is objected to, in which event the objecting party shall state the reasons for objection and shall answer to the extent the interrogatory is not objectionable. (2) The answers are to be signed by the person making them, and the objections signed by the attorney making them. (3) The party upon whom the interrogatories have been served shall serve a copy of the answers, and objections if any, within 30 days after the service of the interrogatories. A shorter or longer time may be directed by the court or, in the absence of such an order, agreed to in writing by the parties subject to Rule 29. (4) All grounds for an objection to an interrogatory shall be stated with	**(b) Answers and Objections.** **(1)** ***Responding Party.*** **The interrogatories must be answered:** **(A)** by the party to whom they are directed; or **(B)** if that party is a public or private corporation, a partnership, an association, or a governmental agency, by any officer or agent, who must furnish the information available to the party. **(2)** ***Time to Respond.*** The responding party must serve its answers and any objections within 30 days after being served with the interrogatories. A shorter or longer time may be stipulated to under Rule 29 or be ordered by the court. **(3)** ***Answering Each Interrogatory.*** Each interrogatory must, to the extent it is not objected to, be answered	296

Rule	Pre-Restyling Text	Restyled Text	Casebook References
	specificity. Any ground not stated in a timely objection is waived unless the party's failure to object is excused by the court for good cause shown. (5) The party submitting the interrogatories may move for an order under Rule 37(a) with respect to any objection to or other failure to answer an interrogatory.	separately and fully in writing under oath. **(4) *Objections*.** The grounds for objecting to an interrogatory must be stated with specificity. Any ground not stated in a timely objection is waived unless the court, for good cause, excuses the failure. **(5) *Signature*.** The person who makes the answers must sign them, and the attorney who objects must sign any objections.	
34(a)	**Rule 34. Production of Documents, Electronically Stored Information, and Things and Entry Upon Land for Inspection and Other Purposes** **(a) SCOPE.** Any party may serve on any other party a request (1) to produce and permit the party making the request, or someone acting on the requestor's behalf, to inspect, copy, test, or sample any designated documents or electronically stored information — including writings, drawings, graphs, charts, photographs, sound recordings, images, and other data or data compilations stored in any medium from which information can be obtained — translated, if necessary, by the respondent into reasonably usable form, or to inspect, copy, test, or sample any designated tangible things which constitute or contain matters within the scope of Rule 26(b) and which are in the possession, custody or control of the party upon whom the request is served; or (2) to permit entry upon designated land or other property in the possession or control of the party upon whom the request is served for the purpose of inspection and measuring, surveying, photographing, testing, or sampling the property or any designated object or operation thereon, within the scope of Rule 26(b).	**Rule 34. Producing Documents, Electronically Stored Information, and Tangible Things, or Entering onto Land, for Inspection and Other Purposes** **(a) In General.** A party may serve on any other party a request within the scope of Rule 26(b): **(1)** to produce and permit the requesting party or its representative to inspect, copy, test, or sample the following items in the responding party's possession, custody, or control: **(A)** any designated documents or electronically stored information — including writings, drawings, graphs, charts, photographs, sound recordings, images, and other data or data compilations — stored in any medium from which information can be obtained either directly or, if necessary, after translation by the responding party into a reasonably usable form; or **(B)** any designated tangible things; or **(2)** to permit entry onto designated land or other property possessed or controlled by the responding party, so that the requesting party may inspect, measure, survey, photograph, test, or sample the property or any designated object or operation on it.	Rule 34 generally: 549, 550

Rule	Pre-Restyling Text	Restyled Text	Casebook References
35(a)	**Rule 35. Physical and Mental Examinations of Persons** **(a) ORDER FOR EXAMINATION.** When the mental or physical condition (including the blood group) of a party or of a person in the custody or under the legal control of a party, is in controversy, the court in which the action is pending may order the party to submit to a physical or mental examination by a suitably licensed or certified examiner or to produce for examination the person in the party's custody or legal control. The order may be made only on motion for good cause shown and upon notice to the person to be examined and to all parties and shall specify the time, place, manner, conditions, and scope of the examination and the person or persons by whom it is to be made.	**Rule 35. Physical and Mental Examinations** **(a) Order for an Examination.** **(1)** ***In General.*** The court where the action is pending may order a party whose mental or physical condition — including blood group — is in controversy to submit to a physical or mental examination by a suitably licensed or certified examiner. The court has the same authority to order a party to produce for examination a person who is in its custody or under its legal control. **(2)** ***Motion and Notice; Contents of the Order.*** The order: **(A)** may be made only on motion for good cause and on notice to all parties and the person to be examined; and **(B)** must specify the time, place, manner, conditions, and scope of the examination, as well as the person or persons who will perform it.	563, 564
35(b)	**(b) REPORT OF EXAMINER.** (1) If requested by the party against whom an order is made under Rule 35(a) or the person examined, the party causing the examination to be made shall deliver to the requesting party a copy of the detailed written report of the examiner setting out the examiner's findings, including results of all tests made, diagnoses and conclusions, together with like reports of all earlier examinations of the same condition. After delivery the party causing the examination shall be entitled upon request to receive from the party against whom the order is made a like report of any examination, previously or thereafter made, of the same condition, unless, in the case of a report of examination of a person not a party, the party shows that the party is unable to obtain it. The court on motion may make an order against a party requiring delivery of a report on such terms as are just, and if an examiner fails or refuses to make a report the court	**(b) Examiner's Report.** **(1)** ***Request by the Party or Person Examined.*** The party who moved for the examination must, on request, deliver to the requester a copy of the examiner's report, together with like reports of all earlier examinations of the same condition. The request may be made by the party against whom the examination order was issued or by the person examined. **(2)** ***Contents.*** The examiner's report must be in writing and must set out in detail the examiner's findings, including diagnoses, conclusions, and the results of any tests. **(3)** ***Request by the Moving Party.*** After delivering the reports, the party who moved for the examination may request — and is entitled to receive — from the party against whom the examination order was issued like reports of all earlier or later examinations of the same	562, 563, 564

Rule	Pre-Restyling Text	Restyled Text	Casebook References
	may exclude the examiner's testimony if offered at trial. (2) By requesting and obtaining a report of the examination so ordered or by taking the deposition of the examiner, the party examined waives any privilege the party may have in that action or any other involving the same controversy, regarding the testimony of every other person who has examined or may thereafter examine the party in respect of the same mental or physical condition. (3) This subdivision applies to examinations made by agreement of the parties, unless the agreement expressly provides otherwise. This subdivision does not preclude discovery of a report of an examiner or the taking of a deposition of the examiner in accordance with the provisions of any other rule.	condition. But those reports need not be delivered by the party with custody or control of the person examined if the party shows that it could not obtain them. **(4)** ***Waiver of Privilege.*** By requesting and obtaining the examiner's report, or by deposing the examiner, the party examined waives any privilege it may have—in that action or any other action involving the same controversy—concerning testimony about all examinations of the same condition. **(5)** ***Failure to Deliver a Report.*** The court on motion may order—on just terms—that a party deliver the report of an examination. If the report is not provided, the court may exclude the examiner's testimony at trial. **(6)** ***Scope.*** This subdivision (b) applies also to an examination made by the parties' agreement, unless the agreement states otherwise. This subdivision does not preclude obtaining an examiner's report or deposing an examiner under other rules.	
36	**Rule 36. Requests for Admission** **(a) REQUEST FOR ADMISSION.** A party may serve upon any other party a written request for the admission, for purposes of the pending action only, of the truth of any matters within the scope of Rule 26(b)(1) set forth in the request that relate to statements or opinions of fact or of the application of law to fact, including the genuineness of any documents described in the request. Copies of documents shall be served with the request unless they have been or are otherwise furnished or made available for inspection and copying. Without leave of court or written stipulation, requests for admission may not be served before the time specified in Rule 26(d). Each matter of which an admission is requested shall be separately set forth. The matter is admitted unless,	**Rule 36. Requests for Admission** **(a) Scope and Procedure.** **(1)** ***Scope.*** A party may serve on any other party a written request to admit, for purposes of the pending action only, the truth of any matters within the scope of Rule 26(b)(1) relating to: **(A)** facts, the application of law to fact, or opinions about either; and **(B)** the genuineness of any described documents. **(2)** ***Form; Copy of a Document.*** Each matter must be separately stated. A request to admit the genuineness of a document must be accompanied by a copy of the document unless it is, or has been, otherwise furnished or made available for inspection and copying.	174

Rule	Pre-Restyling Text	Restyled Text	Casebook References
	within 30 days after service of the request, or within such shorter or longer time as the court may allow or as the parties may agree to in writing, subject to Rule 29, the party to whom the request is directed serves upon the party requesting the admission a written answer or objection addressed to the matter, signed by the party or by the party's attorney. If objection is made, the reasons therefor shall be stated. The answer shall specifically deny the matter or set forth in detail the reasons why the answering party cannot truthfully admit or deny the matter. A denial shall fairly meet the substance of the requested admission, and when good faith requires that a party qualify an answer or deny only a part of the matter of which an admission is requested, the party shall specify so much of it as is true and qualify or deny the remainder. An answering party may not give lack of information or knowledge as a reason for failure to admit or deny unless the party states that the party has made reasonable inquiry and that the information known or readily obtainable by the party is insufficient to enable the party to admit or deny. A party who considers that a matter of which an admission has been requested presents a genuine issue for trial may not, on that ground alone, object to the request; the party may, subject to the provisions of Rule 37(c), deny the matter or set forth reasons why the party cannot admit or deny it. The party who has requested the admissions may move to determine the sufficiency of the answers or objections. Unless the court determines that an objection is justified, it shall order that an answer be served. If the court determines that an answer does not comply with the requirements of this rule, it may order either that the matter is admitted or that an amended answer be served. The court may, in lieu of these orders,	**(3)** ***Time to Respond; Effect of Not Responding.*** A matter is admitted unless, within 30 days after being served, the party to whom the request is directed serves on the requesting party a written answer or objection addressed to the matter and signed by the party or its attorney. A shorter or longer time for responding may be stipulated to under Rule 29 or be ordered by the court. **(4)** ***Answer.*** If a matter is not admitted, the answer must specifically deny it or state in detail why the answering party cannot truthfully admit or deny it. A denial must fairly respond to the substance of the matter; and when good faith requires that a party qualify an answer or deny only a part of a matter, the answer must specify the part admitted and qualify or deny the rest. The answering party may assert lack of knowledge or information as a reason for failing to admit or deny only if the party states that it has made reasonable inquiry and that the information it knows or can readily obtain is insufficient to enable it to admit or deny. **(5)** ***Objections.*** The grounds for objecting to a request must be stated. A party must not object solely on the ground that the request presents a genuine issue for trial. **(6)** ***Motion Regarding the Sufficiency of an Answer or Objection.*** The requesting party may move to determine the sufficiency of an answer or objection. Unless the court finds an objection justified, it must order that an answer be served. On finding that an answer does not comply with this rule, the court may order either that the matter is admitted or that an amended answer be served. The court may defer its final decision until a pretrial conference or a specified time	

<table>
<tr><th>Rule</th><th>Pre-Restyling Text</th><th>Restyled Text</th><th>Casebook References</th></tr>
<tr><td></td><td>determine that final disposition of the request be made at a pre-trial conference or at a designated time prior to trial. The provisions of Rule 37(a)(4) apply to the award of expenses incurred in relation to the motion.

(b) EFFECT OF ADMISSION. Any matter admitted under this rule is conclusively established unless the court on motion permits withdrawal or amendment of the admission. Subject to the provision of Rule 16 governing amendment of a pre-trial order, the court may permit withdrawal or amendment when the presentation of the merits of the action will be subserved thereby and the party who obtained the admission fails to satisfy the court that withdrawal or amendment will prejudice that party in maintaining the action or defense on the merits. Any admission made by a party under this rule is for the purpose of the pending action only and is not an admission for any other purpose nor may it be used against the party in any other proceeding.</td><td>before trial. Rule 37(a)(5) applies to an award of expenses.

(b) Effect of an Admission; Withdrawing or Amending It. A matter admitted under this rule is conclusively established unless the court, on motion, permits the admission to be withdrawn or amended. Subject to Rule 16(e), the court may permit withdrawal or amendment if it would promote the presentation of the merits of the action and if the court is not persuaded that it would prejudice the requesting party in maintaining or defending the action on the merits. An admission under this rule is not an admission for any other purpose and cannot be used against the party in any other proceeding.</td><td></td></tr>
<tr><td>37(a)</td><td>Rule 37. Failure to Make Disclosures or Cooperate in Discovery; Sanctions

(a) MOTION FOR ORDER COMPELLING DISCLOSURE OR DISCOVERY. A party, upon reasonable notice to other parties and all persons affected thereby, may apply for an order compelling disclosure or discovery as follows:

(1) Appropriate Court. An application for an order to a party shall be made to the court in which the action is pending. An application for an order to a person who is not a party shall be made to the court in the district where the discovery is being, or is to be, taken.

(2) Motion.

(A) If a party fails to make a disclosure required by Rule 26(a), any other party may move to compel disclosure and for appropriate sanctions. The motion must include a</td><td>Rule 37. Failure to Make Disclosures or to Cooperate in Discovery; Sanctions

(a) Motion for an Order Compelling Disclosure or Discovery.

(1) In General. On notice to other parties and all affected persons, a party may move for an order compelling disclosure or discovery. The motion must include a certification that the movant has in good faith conferred or attempted to confer with the person or party failing to make disclosure or discovery in an effort to obtain it without court action.

(2) Appropriate Court. A motion for an order to a party must be made in the court where the action is pending. A motion for an order to a nonparty must be made in the court where the discovery is or will be taken.</td><td>Rule 37 generally: 461, 483, 489, 499, 537, 584

37(a): 174, 537</td></tr>
</table>

Rule	Pre-Restyling Text	Restyled Text	Casebook References
	certification that the movant has in good faith conferred or attempted to confer with the party not making the disclosure in an effort to secure the disclosure without court action. (B) If a deponent fails to answer a question propounded or submitted under Rules 30 or 31, or a corporation or other entity fails to make a designation under Rule 30(b)(6) or 31(a), or a party fails to answer an interrogatory submitted under Rule 33, or if a party, in response to a request for inspection submitted under Rule 34, fails to respond that inspection will be permitted as requested or fails to permit inspection as requested, the discovering party may move for an order compelling an answer, or a designation, or an order compelling inspection in accordance with the request. The motion must include a certification that the movant has in good faith conferred or attempted to confer with the person or party failing to make the discovery in an effort to secure the information or material without court action. When taking a deposition on oral examination, the proponent of the question may complete or adjourn the examination before applying for an order.	**(3)** ***Specific Motions.*** **(A)** *To Compel Disclosure.* If a party fails to make a disclosure required by Rule 26(a), any other party may move to compel disclosure and for appropriate sanctions. **(B)** *To Compel a Discovery Response.* A party seeking discovery may move for an order compelling an answer, designation, production, or inspection. This motion may be made if: **(i)** a deponent fails to answer a question asked under Rule 30 or 31; **(ii)** a corporation or other entity fails to make a designation under Rule 30(b)(6) or 31(a)(4); **(iii)** a party fails to answer an interrogatory submitted under Rule 33; or **(iv)** a party fails to respond that inspection will be permitted — or fails to permit inspection — as requested under Rule 34. **(C)** *Related to a Deposition.* When taking an oral deposition, the party asking a question may complete or adjourn the examination before moving for an order.	
	(3) *Evasive or Incomplete Disclosure, Answer, or Response.* For purposes of this subdivision an evasive or incomplete disclosure, answer, or response is to be treated as a failure to disclose, answer, or respond.	**(4)** ***Evasive or Incomplete Disclosure, Answer, or Response.*** For purposes of this subdivision (a), an evasive or incomplete disclosure, answer, or response must be treated as a failure to disclose, answer, or respond.	
	(4) *Expenses and Sanctions.* (A) If the motion is granted or if the disclosure or requested discovery is provided after the motion was filed, the court shall, after affording an opportunity to be heard, require the party or deponent whose conduct necessitated the motion or the party or attorney advising such conduct or both of them to pay to the moving party the reasonable	**(5)** ***Payment of Expenses; Protective Orders.*** **(A)** *If the Motion Is Granted (or Disclosure or Discovery Is Provided After Filing).* If the motion is granted — or if the disclosure or requested discovery is provided after the motion was filed — the court must, after giving an opportunity to be heard,	

Rule	Pre-Restyling Text	Restyled Text	Casebook References
	expenses incurred in making the motion, including attorney's fees, unless the court finds that the motion was filed without the movant's first making a good faith effort to obtain the disclosure or discovery without court action, or that the opposing party's nondisclosure, response, or objection was substantially justified, or that other circumstances make an award of expenses unjust. (B) If the motion is denied, the court may enter any protective order authorized under Rule 26(c) and shall, after affording an opportunity to be heard, require the moving party or the attorney filing the motion or both of them to pay to the party or deponent who opposed the motion the reasonable expenses incurred in opposing the motion, including attorney's fees, unless the court finds that the making of the motion was substantially justified or that other circumstances make an award of expenses unjust. (C) If the motion is granted in part and denied in part, the court may enter any protective order authorized under Rule 26(c) and may, after affording an opportunity to be heard, apportion the reasonable expenses incurred in relation to the motion among the parties and persons in a just manner.	require the party or deponent whose conduct necessitated the motion, the party or attorney advising that conduct, or both to pay the movant's reasonable expenses incurred in making the motion, including attorney's fees. But the court must not order this payment if: **(i)** the movant filed the motion before attempting in good faith to obtain the disclosure or discovery without court action; **(ii)** the opposing party's nondisclosure, response, or objection was substantially justified; or **(iii)** other circumstances make an award of expenses unjust. **(B)** *If the Motion Is Denied.* If the motion is denied, the court may issue any protective order authorized under Rule 26(c) and must, after giving an opportunity to be heard, require the movant, the attorney filing the motion, or both to pay the party or deponent who opposed the motion its reasonable expenses incurred in opposing the motion, including attorney's fees. But the court must not order this payment if the motion was substantially justified or other circumstances make an award of expenses unjust. **(C)** *If the Motion Is Granted in Part and Denied in Part.* If the motion is granted in part and denied in part, the court may issue any protective order authorized under Rule 26(c) and may, after giving an opportunity to be heard, apportion the reasonable expenses for the motion.	

Rule	Pre-Restyling Text	Restyled Text	Casebook References
37(b)	**(b) FAILURE TO COMPLY WITH ORDER.** (1) *Sanctions by Court in District Where Deposition Is Taken.* If a deponent fails to be sworn or to answer a question after being directed to do so by the court in the district in which the deposition is being taken, the failure may be considered a contempt of that court. (2) *Sanctions by Court in Which Action Is Pending.* If a party or an officer, director, or managing agent of a party or a person designated under Rule 30(b)(6) or 31(a) to testify on behalf of a party fails to obey an order to provide or permit discovery, including an order made under subdivision (a) of this rule or Rule 35, or if a party fails to obey an order entered under Rule 26(f), the court in which the action is pending may make such orders in regard to the failure as are just, and among others the following: (A) An order that the matters regarding which the order was made or any other designated facts shall be taken to be established for the purposes of the action in accordance with the claim of the party obtaining the order; (B) An order refusing to allow the disobedient party to support or oppose designated claims or defenses, or prohibiting that party from introducing designated matters in evidence; (C) An order striking out pleadings or parts thereof, or staying further proceedings until the order is obeyed, or dismissing the action or proceeding or any part thereof, or rendering a judgment by default against the disobedient party; (D) In lieu of any of the foregoing orders or in addition thereto, an order treating as a contempt of court the failure to obey any orders except an order to submit to a physical or mental examination; (E) Where a party has failed to comply with an order under Rule	**(b) Failure to Comply with a Court Order.** **(1) *Sanctions in the District Where the Deposition Is Taken.*** If the court where the discovery is taken orders a deponent to be sworn or to answer a question and the deponent fails to obey, the failure may be treated as contempt of court. **(2) *Sanctions in the District Where the Action Is Pending.*** **(A)** *For Not Obeying a Discovery Order.* If a party or a party's officer, director, or managing agent—or a witness designated under Rule 30(b)(6) or 31(a)(4)—fails to obey an order to provide or permit discovery, including an order under Rule 26(f), 35, or 37(a), the court where the action is pending may issue further just orders. They may include the following: **(i)** directing that the matters embraced in the order or other designated facts be taken as established for purposes of the action, as the prevailing party claims; **(ii)** prohibiting the disobedient party from supporting or opposing designated claims or defenses, or from introducing designated matters in evidence; **(iii)** striking pleadings in whole or in part; **(iv)** staying further proceedings until the order is obeyed; **(v)** dismissing the action or proceeding in whole or in part; **(vi)** rendering a default judgment against the disobedient party; or **(vii)** treating as contempt of court the failure to obey any order except an order to submit to a physical or mental examination.	174, 484, 584

Rule	Pre-Restyling Text	Restyled Text	Casebook References
	35(a) requiring that party to produce another for examination, such orders as are listed in paragraphs (A), (B), and (C) of this subdivision, unless the party failing to comply shows that that party is unable to produce such person for examination. In lieu of any of the foregoing orders or in addition thereto, the court shall require the party failing to obey the order or the attorney advising that party or both to pay the reasonable expenses, including attorney's fees, caused by the failure, unless the court finds that the failure was substantially justified or that other circumstances make an award of expenses unjust.	**(B)** *For Not Producing a Person for Examination.* If a party fails to comply with an order under Rule 35(a) requiring it to produce another person for examination, the court may issue any of the orders listed in Rule 37(b)(2)(A)(i)-(vi), unless the disobedient party shows that it cannot produce the other person. **(C)** *Payment of Expenses.* Instead of or in addition to the orders above, the court must order the disobedient party, the attorney advising that party, or both to pay the reasonable expenses, including attorney's fees, caused by the failure, unless the failure was substantially justified or other circumstances make an award of expenses unjust.	
37(c)	**(c) FAILURE TO DISCLOSE; FALSE OR MISLEADING DISCLOSURE; REFUSALTO ADMIT.** (1) A party that without substantial justification fails to disclose information required by Rule 26(a) or 26(e)(1), or to amend a prior response to discovery as required by Rule 26(e)(2), is not, unless such failure is harmless, permitted to use as evidence at a trial, at a hearing, or on a motion any witness or information not so disclosed. In addition to or in lieu of this sanction, the court, on motion and after affording an opportunity to be heard, may impose other appropriate sanctions. In addition to requiring payment of reasonable expenses, including attorney's fees, caused by the failure, these sanctions may include any of the actions authorized under Rule 37(b)(2)(A), (B), and (C) and may include informing the jury of the failure to make the disclosure. (2) If a party fails to admit the genuineness of any document or the truth of any matter as requested under Rule 36, and if the party requesting the admissions	**(c) Failure to Disclose, to Supplement an Earlier Response, or to Admit.** **(1)** ***Failure to Disclose or Supplement.*** If a party fails to provide information or identify a witness as required by Rule 26(a) or (e), the party is not allowed to use that information or witness to supply evidence on a motion, at a hearing, or at a trial, unless the failure was substantially justified or is harmless. In addition to or instead of this sanction, the court, on motion and after giving an opportunity to be heard: **(A)** may order payment of the reasonable expenses, including attorney's fees, caused by the failure; **(B)** may inform the jury of the party's failure; and **(C)** may impose other appropriate sanctions, including any of the orders listed in Rule 37(b)(2)(A)(i)-(vi). **(2)** ***Failure to Admit.*** If a party fails to admit what is requested under Rule 36 and if the	174, 483, 485, 584

Rule	Pre-Restyling Text	Restyled Text	Casebook References
	thereafter proves the genuineness of the document or the truth of the matter, the requesting party may apply to the court for an order requiring the other party to pay the reasonable expenses incurred in making that proof, including reasonable attorney's fees. The court shall make the order unless it finds that (A) the request was held objectionable pursuant to Rule 36(a), or (B) the admission sought was of no substantial importance, or (C) the party failing to admit had reasonable ground to believe that the party might prevail on the matter, or (D) there was other good reason for the failure to admit.	requesting party later proves a document to be genuine or the matter true, the requesting party may move that the party who failed to admit pay the reasonable expenses, including attorney's fees, incurred in making that proof. The court must so order unless: **(A)** the request was held objectionable under Rule 36(a); **(B)** the admission sought was of no substantial importance; **(C)** the party failing to admit had a reasonable ground to believe that it might prevail on the matter; or **(D)** there was other good reason for the failure to admit.	
37(d)	**(d) FAILURE OF PARTY TO ATTEND AT OWN DEPOSITION OR SERVE ANSWERS TO INTERROGATORIES OR RESPOND TO REQUEST FOR INSPECTION.** If a party or an officer, director, or managing agent of a party or a person designated under Rule 30(b)(6) or 31(a) to testify on behalf of a party fails (1) to appear before the officer who is to take the deposition, after being served with a proper notice, or (2) to serve answers or objections to interrogatories submitted under Rule 33, after proper service of the interrogatories, or (3) to serve a written response to a request for inspection submitted under Rule 34, after proper service of the request, the court in which the action is pending on motion may make such orders in regard to the failure as are just, and among others it may take any action authorized under subparagraphs (A), (B), and (C) of subdivision (b)(2) of this rule. Any motion specifying a failure under clause (2) or (3) of this subdivision shall include a certification that the movant has in good faith conferred or attempted to confer with the party failing to answer or respond	**(d) Party's Failure to Attend Its Own Deposition, Serve Answers to Interrogatories, or Respond to a Request for Inspection.** **(1)** ***In General.*** **(A)** *Motion; Grounds for Sanctions.* The court where the action is pending may, on motion, order sanctions if: **(i)** a party or a party's officer, director, or managing agent—or a person designated under Rule 30(b)(6) or 31(a)(4)—fails, after being served with proper notice, to appear for that person's deposition; or **(ii)** a party, after being properly served with interrogatories under Rule 33 or a request for inspection under Rule 34, fails to serve its answers, objections, or written response. **(B)** *Certification.* A motion for sanctions for failing to answer or respond must include a certification that the movant has in good faith conferred or attempted to confer with the party failing to act in an effort	174, 584, 593

Rule	Pre-Restyling Text	Restyled Text	Casebook References
	in an effort to obtain such answer or response without court action. In lieu of any order or in addition thereto, the court shall require the party failing to act or the attorney advising that party or both to pay the reasonable expenses, including attorney's fees, caused by the failure unless the court finds that the failure was substantially justified or that other circumstances make an award of expenses unjust. The failure to act described in this subdivision may not be excused on the ground that the discovery sought is objectionable unless the party failing to act has a pending motion for a protective order as provided by Rule 26(c).	to obtain the answer or response without court action. **(2)** ***Unacceptable Excuse for Failing to Act.*** A failure described in Rule 37(d)(1)(A) is not excused on the ground that the discovery sought was objectionable, unless the party failing to act has a pending motion for a protective order under Rule 26(c). **(3)** ***Types of Sanctions.*** Sanctions may include any of the orders listed in Rule 37(b)(2)(A)(i)-(vi). Instead of or in addition to these sanctions, the court must require the party failing to act, the attorney advising that party, or both to pay the reasonable expenses, including attorney's fees, caused by the failure, unless the failure was substantially justified or other circumstances make an award of expenses unjust.	
37(e) [formerly 37(f)]	**(f) ELECTRONICALLY STORED INFORMATION.** Absent exceptional circumstances, a court may not impose sanctions under these rules on a party for failing to provide electronically stored information lost as a result of the routine, good-faith operation of an electronic information system.	**(e) Failure to Provide Electronically Stored Information.** Absent exceptional circumstances, a court may not impose sanctions under these rules on a party for failing to provide electronically stored information lost as a result of the routine, good-faith operation of an electronic information system.	
37(f) [formerly 37(g)]	**(g) FAILURE TO PARTICIPATE IN THE FRAMING OF A DISCOVERY PLAN.** If a party or a party's attorney fails to participate in good faith in the development and submission of a proposed discovery plan as required by Rule 26(f), the court may, after opportunity for hearing, require such party or attorney to pay to any other party the reasonable expenses, including attorney's fees, caused by the failure.	**(f) Failure to Participate in Framing a Discovery Plan.** If a party or its attorney fails to participate in good faith in developing and submitting a proposed discovery plan as required by Rule 26(f), the court may, after giving an opportunity to be heard, require that party or attorney to pay to any other party the reasonable expenses, including attorney's fees, caused by the failure.	549
38(a)	**Rule 38. Jury Trial of Right** **(a) RIGHT PRESERVED.** The right of trial by jury as declared by the Seventh Amendment to the Constitution or as given by a statute of the United States shall be preserved to the parties inviolate.	**Rule 38. Right to a Jury Trial; Demand** **(a) Right Preserved.** The right of trial by jury as declared by the Seventh Amendment to the Constitution—or as provided by a federal statute—is preserved to the parties inviolate.	Rule 38 generally: 723

Rule	Pre-Restyling Text	Restyled Text	Casebook References
38(b)	**(b) DEMAND.** Any party may demand a trial by jury of any issue triable of right by a jury by (1) serving upon the other parties a demand therefor in writing at any time after the commencement of the action and not later than 10 days after the service of the last pleading directed to such issue, and (2) filing the demand as required by Rule 5 (d). Such demand may be indorsed upon a pleading of the party.	**(b) Demand.** On any issue triable of right by a jury, a party may demand a jury trial by: **(1)** serving the other parties with a written demand—which may be included in a pleading—no later than 10 days after the last pleading directed to the issue is served; and **(2)** filing the demand in accordance with Rule 5(d).	735
39(a)	**Rule 39. Trial by Jury or by the Court** **(a) BY JURY.** When trial by jury has been demanded as provided in Rule 38, the action shall be designated upon the docket as a jury action. The trial of all issues so demanded shall be by jury, unless (1) the parties or their attorneys of record, by written stipulation filed with the court or by an oral stipulation made in open court and entered in the record, consent to trial by the court sitting without a jury or (2) the court upon motion or of its own initiative finds that a right of trial by jury of some or all of those issues does not exist under the Constitution or statutes of the United States.	**Rule 39. Trial by Jury or by the Court** **(a) When a Demand Is Made.** When a jury trial has been demanded under Rule 38, the action must be designated on the docket as a jury action. The trial on all issues so demanded must be by jury unless: **(1)** the parties or their attorneys file a stipulation to a nonjury trial or so stipulate on the record; or **(2)** the court, on motion or on its own, finds that on some or all of those issues there is no federal right to a jury trial.	739
41(a)	**Rule 41. Dismissal of Actions** **(a) VOLUNTARY DISMISSAL: EFFECT THEREOF.** (1) *By Plaintiff; by Stipulation.* Subject to the provisions of Rule 23(e), of Rule 66, and of any statute of the United States, an action may be dismissed by the plaintiff without order of court (i) by filing a notice of dismissal at any time before service by the adverse party of an answer or of a motion for summary judgment, whichever first occurs, or (ii) by filing a stipulation of dismissal signed by all parties who have appeared in the action. Unless otherwise stated in the notice of dismissal or stipulation, the dismissal is without prejudice, except that a notice of dismissal operates as an adjudication upon the merits when filed by a plaintiff who has once dismissed in any court of the United States or of any	**Rule 41. Dismissal of Actions** **(a) Voluntary Dismissal.** **(1)** ***By the Plaintiff.*** **(A)** *Without a Court Order.* Subject to Rules 23(e), 23.1(c), 23.2, and 66 and any applicable federal statute, the plaintiff may dismiss an action without a court order by filing: **(i)** a notice of dismissal before the opposing party serves either an answer or a motion for summary judgment; or **(ii)** a stipulation of dismissal signed by all parties who have appeared. **(B)** *Effect.* Unless the notice or stipulation states otherwise, the dismissal is without prejudice. But if the plaintiff previously dismissed any	Rule 41 generally: 801 41(a): 402, 620

Rule	Pre-Restyling Text	Restyled Text	Casebook References
	state an action based on or including the same claim. (2) *By Order of Court.* Except as provided in paragraph (1) of this subdivision of this rule, an action shall not be dismissed at the plaintiff's instance save upon order of the court and upon such terms and conditions as the court deems proper. If a counterclaim has been pleaded by a defendant prior to the service upon the defendant of the plaintiff's motion to dismiss, the action shall not be dismissed against the defendant's objection unless the counterclaim can remain pending for independent adjudication by the court. Unless otherwise specified in the order, a dismissal under this paragraph is without prejudice.	federal-or state-court action based on or including the same claim, a notice of dismissal operates as an adjudication on the merits. **(2) *By Court Order; Effect.*** Except as provided in Rule 41(a)(1), an action may be dismissed at the plaintiff's request only by court order, on terms that the court considers proper. If a defendant has pleaded a counterclaim before being served with the plaintiff's motion to dismiss, the action may be dismissed over the defendant's objection only if the counterclaim can remain pending for independent adjudication. Unless the order states otherwise, a dismissal under this paragraph (2) is without prejudice.	
41(b)	**(b) INVOLUNTARY DISMISSAL: EFFECT THEREOF.** For failure of the plaintiff to prosecute or to comply with these rules or any order of court, a defendant may move for dismissal of an action or of any claim against the defendant. Unless the court in its order for dismissal otherwise specifies, a dismissal under this subdivision and any dismissal not provided for in this rule, other than a dismissal for lack of jurisdiction, for improper venue, or for failure to join a party under Rule 19, operates as an adjudication upon the merits.	**(b) Involuntary Dismissal; Effect.** If the plaintiff fails to prosecute or to comply with these rules or a court order, a defendant may move to dismiss the action or any claim against it. Unless the dismissal order states otherwise, a dismissal under this subdivision (b) and any dismissal not under this rule—except one for lack of jurisdiction, improper venue, or failure to join a party under Rule 19—operates as an adjudication on the merits.	465, 901, 1164
42(a)	**Rule 42. Consolidation; Separate Trials** **(a) CONSOLIDATION.** When actions involving a common question of law or fact are pending before the court, it may order a joint hearing or trial of any or all the matters in issue in the actions; it may order all the actions consolidated; and it may make such orders concerning proceedings therein as may tend to avoid unnecessary costs or delay.	**Rule 42. Consolidation; Separate Trials** **(a) Consolidation.** If actions before the court involve a common question of law or fact, the court may: **(1)** join for hearing or trial any or all matters at issue in the actions; **(2)** consolidate the actions; or **(3)** issue any other orders to avoid unnecessary cost or delay.	
42(b)	**(b) SEPARATE TRIALS.** The court, in furtherance of convenience or to avoid prejudice, or when separate trials will be conducive to expedition and economy, may order a separate trial of any claim,	**(b) Separate Trials.** For convenience, to avoid prejudice, or to expedite and economize, the court may order a separate trial of one or more separate issues, claims, crossclaims, counterclaims, or	736, 737, 740, 963, 1164

Rule	Pre-Restyling Text	Restyled Text	Casebook References
	cross-claim, counterclaim, or third-party claim, or of any separate issue or of any number of claims, cross-claims, counterclaims, third-party claims, or issues, always preserving inviolate the right of trial by jury as declared by the Seventh Amendment to the Constitution or as given by a statute of the United States.	third-party claims. When ordering a separate trial, the court must preserve any federal right to a jury trial.	
45(a)	**Rule 45. Subpoena** **(a) FORM; ISSUANCE.** (1) Every subpoena shall (A) state the name of the court from which it is issued; and (B) state the title of the action, the name of the court in which it is pending, and its civil action number; and (C) command each person to whom it is directed to attend and give testimony or to produce and permit inspection, copying, testing, or sampling of designated books, documents, electronically stored information, or tangible things in the possession, custody or control of that person, or to permit inspection of premises, at a time and place therein specified; and (D) set forth the text of subdivisions (c) and (d) of this rule. A command to produce evidence or to permit inspection, copying, testing, or sampling may be joined with a command to appear at trial or hearing or at deposition, or may be issued separately. A subpoena may specify the form or forms in which electronically stored information is to be produced. (2) A subpoena must issue as follows: (A) for attendance at a trial or hearing, from the court for the district where the trial or hearing is to be held; (B) for attendance at a deposition, from the court for the district where the deposition is to be	**Rule 45. Subpoena** **(a) In General.** **(1)** ***Form and Contents.*** **(A)** *Requirements—In General.* Every subpoena must: **(i)** state the court from which it issued; **(ii)** state the title of the action, the court in which it is pending, and its civil-action number; **(iii)** command each person to whom it is directed to do the following at a specified time and place: attend and testify; produce designated documents, electronically stored information, or tangible things in that person's possession, custody, or control; or permit the inspection of premises; and **(iv)** set out the text of Rule 45(c) and (d). **(B)** *Command to Attend a Deposition—Notice of the Recording Method.* A subpoena commanding attendance at a deposition must state the method for recording the testimony. **(C)** *Combining or Separating a Command to Produce or to Permit Inspection; Specifying the Form for Electronically Stored Information.* A command to produce documents, electronically stored information, or tangible things or to permit the inspection of premises may be included in a subpoena commanding	

Rule	Pre-Restyling Text	Restyled Text	Casebook References
	taken, stating the method for recording the testimony; and (C) for production, inspection, copying, testing, or sampling, if separate from a subpoena commanding a person's attendance, from the court for the district where the production or inspection is to be made. (3) The clerk shall issue a subpoena, signed but otherwise in blank, to a party requesting it, who shall complete it before service. An attorney as officer of the court may also issue and sign a subpoena on behalf of (A) a court in which the attorney is authorized to practice; or (B) a court for a district in which a deposition or production is compelled by the subpoena, if the deposition or production pertains to an action pending in a court in which the attorney is authorized to practice.	attendance at a deposition, hearing, or trial, or may be set out in a separate subpoena. A subpoena may specify the form or forms in which electronically stored information is to be produced. **(D)** *Command to Produce; Included Obligations.* A command in a subpoena to produce documents, electronically stored information, or tangible things requires the responding party to permit inspection, copying, testing, or sampling of the materials. **(2)** ***Issued from Which Court.*** **A subpoena must issue as follows:** **(A)** for attendance at a hearing or trial, from the court for the district where the hearing or trial is to be held; **(B)** for attendance at a deposition, from the court for the district where the deposition is to be taken; and **(C)** for production or inspection, if separate from a subpoena commanding a person's attendance, from the court for the district where the production or inspection is to be made. **(3)** ***Issued by Whom.*** The clerk must issue a subpoena, signed but otherwise in blank, to a party who requests it. That party must complete it before service. An attorney also may issue and sign a subpoena as an officer of: **(A)** a court in which the attorney is authorized to practice; or **(B)** a court for a district where a deposition is to be taken or production is to be made, if the attorney is authorized to practice in the court where the action is pending.	

Rule	Pre-Restyling Text	Restyled Text	Casebook References
45(b)	**(b) SERVICE.** (1) A subpoena may be served by any person who is not a party and is not less than 18 years of age. Service of a subpoena upon a person named therein shall be made by delivering a copy thereof to such person and, if the person's attendance is commanded, by tendering to that person the fees for one day's attendance and the mileage allowed by law. When the subpoena is issued on behalf of the United States or an officer or agency thereof, fees and mileage need not be tendered. Prior notice of any commanded production of documents and things or inspection of premises before trial shall be served on each party in the manner prescribed by Rule 5(b). (2) Subject to the provisions of clause (ii) of subparagraph (c)(3)(A) of this rule, a subpoena may be served at any place within the district of the court by which it is issued, or at any place without the district that is within 100 miles of the place of the deposition, hearing, trial, production, inspection, copying, testing, or sampling specified in the subpoena or at any place within the state where a state statute or rule of court permits service of a subpoena issued by a state court of general jurisdiction sitting in the place of the deposition, hearing, trial, production, inspection, copying, testing, or sampling specified in the subpoena. When a statute of the United States provides therefor, the court upon proper application and cause shown may authorize the service of a subpoena at any other place. A subpoena directed to a witness in a foreign country who is a national or resident of the United States shall issue under the circumstances and in the manner and be served as provided in Title 28, U.S.C. §1783. (3) Proof of service when necessary shall be made by filing with the clerk of the court by which the subpoena is issued a statement of the date and manner of service and	**(b) Service.** **(1)** ***By Whom; Tendering Fees; Serving a Copy of Certain Subpoenas.*** Any person who is at least 18 years old and not a party may serve a subpoena. Serving a subpoena requires delivering a copy to the named person and, if the subpoena requires that person's attendance, tendering the fees for 1 day's attendance and the mileage allowed by law. Fees and mileage need not be tendered when the subpoena issues on behalf of the United States or any of its officers or agencies. If the subpoena commands the production of documents, electronically stored information, or tangible things or the inspection of premises before trial, then before it is served, a notice must be served on each party. **(2)** ***Service in the United States.*** Subject to Rule 45(c)(3)(A)(ii), a subpoena may be served at any place: **(A)** within the district of the issuing court; **(B)** outside that district but within 100 miles of the place specified for the deposition, hearing, trial, production, or inspection; **(C)** within the state of the issuing court if a state statute or court rule allows service at that place of a subpoena issued by a state court of general jurisdiction sitting in the place specified for the deposition, hearing, trial, production, or inspection; or **(D)** that the court authorizes on motion and for good cause, if a federal statute so provides. **(3)** ***Service in a Foreign Country.*** 28 U.S.C. §1783 governs issuing and serving a subpoena directed to a United States national or resident who is in a foreign country. **(4)** ***Proof of Service.*** Proving service, when necessary, requires	593

Rule	Pre-Restyling Text	Restyled Text	Casebook References
	of the names of the persons served, certified by the person who made the service.	filing with the issuing court a statement showing the date and manner of service and the names of the persons served. The statement must be certified by the server.	
45(c)	**(c) PROTECTION OF PERSONS SUBJECT TO SUBPOENAS.** (1) A party or an attorney responsible for the issuance and service of a subpoena shall take reasonable steps to avoid imposing undue burden or expense on a person subject to that subpoena. The court on behalf of which the subpoena was issued shall enforce this duty and impose upon the party or attorney in breach of this duty an appropriate sanction, which may include, but is not limited to, lost earnings and a reasonable attorney's fee. (2)(A) A person commanded to produce and permit inspection, copying, testing, or sampling of designated electronically stored information, books, papers, documents or tangible things, or inspection of premises need not appear in person at the place of production or inspection unless commanded to appear for deposition, hearing or trial. **(B)** Subject to paragraph (d)(2) of this rule, a person commanded to produce and permit inspection, copying, testing, or sampling may, within 14 days after service of the subpoena or before the time specified for compliance if such time is less than 14 days after service, serve upon the party or attorney designated in the subpoena written objection to producing any or all of the designated materials or inspection of the premises—or to producing electronically stored information in the form or forms requested. If objection is made, the party serving the subpoena shall not be entitled to inspect, copy, test, or sample the materials or inspect the premises except pursuant to an order of the court	**(c) Protecting a Person Subject to a Subpoena.** **(1)** ***Avoiding Undue Burden or Expense; Sanctions.*** A party or attorney responsible for issuing and serving a subpoena must take reasonable steps to avoid imposing undue burden or expense on a person subject to the subpoena. The issuing court must enforce this duty and impose an appropriate sanction—which may include lost earnings and reasonable attorney's fees—on a party or attorney who fails to comply. **(2)** ***Command to Produce Materials or Permit Inspection.*** **(A)** *Appearance Not Required.* A person commanded to produce documents, electronically stored information, or tangible things, or to permit the inspection of premises, need not appear in person at the place of production or inspection unless also commanded to appear for a deposition, hearing, or trial. **(B)** *Objections.* A person commanded to produce documents or tangible things or to permit inspection may serve on the party or attorney designated in the subpoena a written objection to inspecting, copying, testing or sampling any or all of the materials or to inspecting the premises—or to producing electronically stored information in the form or forms requested. The objection must be served before the earlier of the time specified for compliance or 14 days after the subpoena is served. If an objection is	593, 1014, 1017, 1019

Rule	Pre-Restyling Text	Restyled Text	Casebook References
	by which the subpoena was issued. If objection has been made, the party serving the subpoena may, upon notice to the person commanded to produce, move at any time for an order to compel the production, inspection, copying, testing, or sampling. Such an order to compel shall protect any person who is not a party or an officer of a party from significant expense resulting from the inspection, copying, testing, or sampling commanded. (3)(A) On timely motion, the court by which a subpoena was issued shall quash or modify the subpoena if it (i) fails to allow reasonable time for compliance; (ii) requires a person who is not a party or an officer of a party to travel to a place more than 100 miles from the place where that person resides, is employed or regularly transacts business in person, except that, subject to the provisions of clause (c)(3)(B)(iii) of this rule, such a person may in order to attend trial be commanded to travel from any such place within the state in which the trial is held; (iii) requires disclosure of privileged or other protected matter and no exception or waiver applies; or (iv) subjects a person to undue burden. If a subpoena (i) requires disclosure of a trade secret or other confidential research, development, or commercial information, or (ii) requires disclosure of an unretained expert's opinion or information not describing specific events or occurrences in dispute and resulting from the expert's study made not at the request of any party, or (iii) requires a person who is not a party or an officer of a	made, the following rules apply: **(i)** At any time, on notice to the commanded person, the serving party may move the issuing court for an order compelling production or inspection. **(ii)** These acts may be required only as directed in the order, and the order must protect a person who is neither a party nor a party's officer from significant expense resulting from compliance. **(3)** ***Quashing or Modifying a Subpoena.*** **(A)** *When Required.* On timely motion, the issuing court must quash or modify a subpoena that: **(i)** fails to allow a reasonable time to comply; **(ii)** requires a person who is neither a party nor a party's officer to travel more than 100 miles from where that person resides, is employed, or regularly transacts business in person — except that, subject to Rule 45(c)(3)(B)(iii), the person may be commanded to attend a trial by traveling from any such place within the state where the trial is held; **(iii)** requires disclosure of privileged or other protected matter, if no exception or waiver applies; or **(iv)** subjects a person to undue burden. **(B)** *When Permitted.* To protect a person subject to or affected by a subpoena, the issuing court may, on motion, quash or modify the subpoena if it requires: **(i)** disclosing a trade secret or other confidential research,	

Rule	Pre-Restyling Text	Restyled Text	Casebook References
	party to incur substantial expense to travel more than 100 miles to attend trial, the court may, to protect a person subject to or affected by the subpoena, quash or modify the subpoena or, if the party in whose behalf the subpoena is issued shows a substantial need for the testimony or material that cannot be otherwise met without undue hardship and assures that the person to whom the subpoena is addressed will be reasonably compensated, the court may order appearance or production only upon specified conditions.	development, or commercial information; **(ii)** disclosing an unretained expert's opinion or information that does not describe specific occurrences in dispute and results from the expert's study that was not requested by a party; or **(iii)** a person who is neither a party nor a party's officer to incur substantial expense to travel more than 100 miles to attend trial. **(C)** *Specifying Conditions as an Alternative.* In the circumstances described in Rule 45(c)(3)(B), the court may, instead of quashing or modifying a subpoena, order appearance or production under specified conditions if the serving party: **(i)** shows a substantial need for the testimony or material that cannot be otherwise met without undue hardship; and **(ii)** ensures that the subpoenaed person will be reasonably compensated.	
45(d)	**(d) DUTIES IN RESPONDING TO SUBPOENA.** (1)(A) A person responding to a subpoena to produce documents shall produce them as they are kept in the usual course of business or shall organize and label them to correspond with the categories in the demand. (B) If a subpoena does not specify the form or forms for producing electronically stored information, a person responding to a subpoena must produce the information in a form or forms in which the person ordinarily maintains it or in a form or forms that are reasonably usable. (C) A person responding to a subpoena need not produce the same electronically stored	**(d) Duties in Responding to a Subpoena.** **(1)** ***Producing Documents or Electronically Stored Information.*** These procedures apply to producing documents or electronically stored information: **(A)** *Documents.* A person responding to a subpoena to produce documents must produce them as they are kept in the ordinary course of business or must organize and label them to correspond to the categories in the demand. **(B)** *Form for Producing Electronically Stored Information Not Specified.* If a subpoena does not specify a form for producing electronically stored information, the person	549

Rule	Pre-Restyling Text	Restyled Text	Casebook References
	information in more than one form. (D) A person responding to a subpoena need not provide discovery of electronically stored information from sources that the person identifies as not reasonably accessible because of undue burden or cost. On motion to compel discovery or to quash, the person from whom discovery is sought must show that the information sought is not reasonably accessible because of undue burden or cost. If that showing is made, the court may nonetheless order discovery from such sources if the requesting party shows good cause, considering the limitations of Rule 26(b)(2)(C). The court may specify conditions for the discovery. (2)(A) When information subject to a subpoena is withheld on a claim that it is privileged or subject to protection as trial-preparation materials, the claim shall be made expressly and shall be supported by a description of the nature of the documents, communications, or things not produced that is sufficient to enable the demanding party to contest the claim. (B) If information is produced in response to a subpoena that is subject to a claim of privilege or of protection as trial-preparation material, the person making the claim may notify any party that received the information of the claim and the basis for it. After being notified, a party must promptly return, sequester, or destroy the specified information and any copies it has and may not use or disclose the information until the claim is resolved. A receiving party may promptly present the information to the court under seal for a determination of the claim. If the receiving party disclosed the information before being notified, it must take reasonable steps to retrieve it. The person who produced the information must	responding must produce it in a form or forms in which it is ordinarily maintained or in a reasonably usable form or forms. **(C)** *Electronically Stored Information Produced in Only One Form.* The person responding need not produce the same electronically stored information in more than one form. **(D)** *Inaccessible Electronically Stored Information.* The person responding need not provide discovery of electronically stored information from sources that the person identifies as not reasonably accessible because of undue burden or cost. On motion to compel discovery or for a protective order, the person responding must show that the information is not reasonably accessible because of undue burden or cost. If that showing is made, the court may nonetheless order discovery from such sources if the requesting party shows good cause, considering the limitations of Rule 26(b)(2)(C). The court may specify conditions for the discovery. **(2)** ***Claiming Privilege or Protection.*** **(A)** *Information Withheld.* A person withholding subpoenaed information under a claim that it is privileged or subject to protection as trial-preparation material must: **(i)** expressly make the claim; and **(ii)** describe the nature of the withheld documents, communications, or tangible things in a manner that, without revealing information itself privileged or protected, will enable the parties to assess the claim. **(B)** *Information Produced.* If information produced in response to a subpoena is	

Rule	Pre-Restyling Text	Restyled Text	Casebook References
	preserve the information until the claim is resolved.	subject to a claim of privilege or of protection as trial-preparation material, the person making the claim may notify any party that received the information of the claim and the basis for it. After being notified, a party must promptly return, sequester, or destroy the specified information and any copies it has; must not use or disclose the information until the claim is resolved; must take reasonable steps to retrieve the information if the party disclosed it before being notified; and may promptly present the information to the court under seal for a determination of the claim. The person who produced the information must preserve the information until the claim is resolved.	
45(e)	**(e) CONTEMPT.** Failure of any person without adequate excuse to obey a subpoena served upon that person may be deemed a contempt of the court from which the subpoena issued. An adequate cause for failure to obey exists when a subpoena purports to require a nonparty to attend or produce at a place not within the limits provided by clause (ii) of subparagraph (c)(3)(A).	**(e) Contempt.** The issuing court may hold in contempt a person who, having been served, fails without adequate excuse to obey the subpoena. A nonparty's failure to obey must be excused if the subpoena purports to require the nonparty to attend or produce at a place outside the limits of Rule 45(c)(3)(A)(ii).	593
47	**Rule 47. Selection of Jurors** **(a) EXAMINATION OF JURORS.** The court may permit the parties or their attorneys to conduct the examination of prospective jurors or may itself conduct the examination. In the latter event, the court shall permit the parties or their attorneys to supplement the examination by such further inquiry as it deems proper or shall itself submit to the prospective jurors such additional questions of the parties or their attorneys as it deems proper. **(b) PEREMPTORY CHALLENGES.** The court shall allow the number of peremptory	**Rule 47. Selecting Jurors** **(a) Examining Jurors.** The court may permit the parties or their attorneys to examine prospective jurors or may itself do so. If the court examines the jurors, it must permit the parties or their attorneys to make any further inquiry it considers proper, or must itself ask any of their additional questions it considers proper. **(b) Peremptory Challenges.** The court must allow the number of peremptory challenges provided by 28 U.S.C. §1870. **(c) Excusing a Juror.** During trial or deliberation, the court	725, 755

Rule	Pre-Restyling Text	Restyled Text	Casebook References
	challenges provided by 28 U.S.C. §1870. **(c) EXCUSE.** The court may for good cause excuse a juror from service during trial or deliberation.	may excuse a juror for good cause.	
48	**Rule 48. Number of Jurors—Participation in Verdict** The court shall seat a jury of not fewer than six and not more than twelve members and all jurors shall participate in the verdict unless excused from service by the court pursuant to Rule 47(c). Unless the parties otherwise stipulate, (1) the verdict shall be unanimous and (2) no verdict shall be taken from a jury reduced in size to fewer than six members.	**Rule 48. Number of Jurors; Verdict** A jury must initially have at least 6 and no more than 12 members, and each juror must participate in the verdict unless excused under Rule 47(c). Unless the parties stipulate otherwise, the verdict must be unanimous and be returned by a jury of at least 6 members.	725
49(a)	**Rule 49. Special Verdicts and Interrogatories** **(a) SPECIAL VERDICTS.** The court may require a jury to return only a special verdict in the form of a special written finding upon each issue of fact. In that event the court may submit to the jury written questions susceptible of categorical or other brief answer or may submit written forms of the several special findings which might properly be made under the pleadings and evidence; or it may use such other method of submitting the issues and requiring the written findings thereon as it deems most appropriate. The court shall give to the jury such explanation and instruction concerning the matter thus submitted as may be necessary to enable the jury to make its findings upon each issue. If in so doing the court omits any issue of fact raised by the pleadings or by the evidence, each party waives the right to a trial by jury of the issue so omitted unless before the jury retires the party demands its submission to the jury. As to an issue omitted without such demand the court may make a finding; or, if it fails to do so, it shall be deemed to have made a finding in accord with the judgment on the special verdict.	**Rule 49. Special Verdict; General Verdict and Questions** **(a) Special Verdict.** **(1) *In General.*** The court may require a jury to return only a special verdict in the form of a special written finding on each issue of fact. The court may do so by: **(A)** submitting written questions susceptible of a categorical or other brief answer; **(B)** submitting written forms of the special findings that might properly be made under the pleadings and evidence; or **(C)** using any other method that the court considers appropriate. **(2) *Instructions.*** The court must give the instructions and explanations necessary to enable the jury to make its findings on each submitted issue. **(3) *Issues Not Submitted.*** A party waives the right to a jury trial on any issue of fact raised by the pleadings or evidence but not submitted to the jury unless, before the jury retires, the party demands its submission to the jury. If the party does not demand	Rule 49 generally: 374, 776, 778

<table>
<tr><th>Rule</th><th>Pre-Restyling Text</th><th>Restyled Text</th><th>Casebook References</th></tr>
<tr><td></td><td></td><td>submission, the court may make a finding on the issue. If the court makes no finding, it is considered to have made a finding consistent with its judgment on the special verdict.</td><td></td></tr>
<tr><td>49(b)</td><td>(b) GENERAL VERDICT ACCOMPANIED BY ANSWER TO INTERROGATORIES.

The court may submit to the jury, together with appropriate forms for a general verdict, written interrogatories upon one or more issues of fact the decision of which is necessary to a verdict. The court shall give such explanation or instruction as may be necessary to enable the jury both to make answers to the interrogatories and to render a general verdict, and the court shall direct the jury both to make written answers and to render a general verdict. When the general verdict and the answers are harmonious, the appropriate judgment upon the verdict and answers shall be entered pursuant to Rule 58. When the answers are consistent with each other but one or more is inconsistent with the general verdict, judgment may be entered pursuant to Rule 58 in accordance with the answers, notwithstanding the general verdict, or the court may return the jury for further consideration of its answers and verdict or may order a new trial. When the answers are inconsistent with each other and one or more is likewise inconsistent with the general verdict, judgment shall not be entered, but the court shall return the jury for further consideration of its answers and verdict or shall order a new trial.</td><td>(b) General Verdict with Answers to Written Questions.

(1) In General. The court may submit to the jury forms for a general verdict, together with written questions on one or more issues of fact that the jury must decide. The court must give the instructions and explanations necessary to enable the jury to render a general verdict and answer the questions in writing, and must direct the jury to do both.

(2) Verdict and Answers Consistent. When the general verdict and the answers are consistent, the court must approve, for entry under Rule 58, an appropriate judgment on the verdict and answers.

(3) Answers Inconsistent with the Verdict. When the answers are consistent with each other but one or more is inconsistent with the general verdict, the court may:

(A) approve, for entry under Rule 58, an appropriate judgment according to the answers, notwithstanding the general verdict;

(B) direct the jury to further consider its answers and verdict; or

(C) order a new trial.

(4) Answers Inconsistent with Each Other and the Verdict. When the answers are inconsistent with each other and one or more is also inconsistent with the general verdict, judgment must not be entered; instead, the court must direct the jury to further consider its answers and verdict, or must order a new trial.</td><td>774</td></tr>
</table>

Rule	Pre-Restyling Text	Restyled Text	Casebook References
50(a)	**Rule 50. Judgment as a Matter of Law in Jury Trials; Alternative Motion for New Trial; Conditional Rulings** **(a) JUDGMENT AS A MATTER OF LAW.** (1) *In General.* If a party has been fully heard on an issue during a jury trial and the court finds that a reasonable jury would not have a legally sufficient evidentiary basis to find for the party on that issue, the court may: (A) resolve the issue against the party; and (B) grant a motion for judgment as a matter of law against the party on a claim or defense that, under the controlling law, can be maintained or defeated only with a favorable finding on that issue. (2) *Motion.* A motion for judgment as a matter of law may be made at any time before the case is submitted to the jury. The motion must specify the judgment sought and the law and facts that entitle the movant to the judgment.	**Rule 50. Judgment as a Matter of Law in a Jury Trial; Related Motion for a New Trial; Conditional Ruling** **(a) Judgment as a Matter of Law.** **(1) *In General.*** If a party has been fully heard on an issue during a jury trial and the court finds that a reasonable jury would not have a legally sufficient evidentiary basis to find for the party on that issue, the court may: **(A)** resolve the issue against the party; and **(B)** grant a motion for judgment as a matter of law against the party on a claim or defense that, under the controlling law, can be maintained or defeated only with a favorable finding on that issue. **(2) *Motion.*** A motion for judgment as a matter of law may be made at any time before the case is submitted to the jury. The motion must specify the judgment sought and the law and facts that entitle the movant to the judgment.	Rule 50 generally: 667, 786, 791, 796, 798, 807, 808, 809, 810, 811, 816, 821 50(a): 641, 664, 796, 808, 812, 813
50(b)	**(b) RENEWING THE MOTION AFTER TRIAL; ALTERNATIVE MOTION FOR A NEW TRIAL.** If the court does not grant a motion for judgment as a matter of law made under subdivision (a), the court is considered to have submitted the action to the jury subject to the court's later deciding the legal questions raised by the motion. The movant may renew its request for judgment as a matter of law by filing a motion no later than 10 days after the entry of judgment or—if the motion addresses a jury issue not decided by a verdict—no later than 10 days after the jury was discharged. The movant may alternatively request a new trial or join a motion for a new trial under Rule 59.	**(b) Renewing the Motion After Trial; Alternative Motion for a New Trial.** If the court does not grant a motion for judgment as a matter of law made under Rule 50(a), the court is considered to have submitted the action to the jury subject to the court's later deciding the legal questions raised by the motion. No later than 10 days after the entry of judgment—or if the motion addresses a jury issue not decided by a verdict, no later than 10 days after the jury was discharged—the movant may file a renewed motion for judgment as a matter of law and may include an alternative or joint request for a new trial	787, 800, 810, 811

Rule	Pre-Restyling Text	Restyled Text	Casebook References
	In ruling on a renewed motion, the court may: (1) if a verdict was returned: (A) allow the judgment to stand, (B) order a new trial, or (C) direct entry of judgment as a matter of law; or (2) if no verdict was returned: (A) order a new trial, or (B) direct entry of judgment as a matter of law.	under Rule 59. In ruling on the renewed motion, the court may: **(1)** allow judgment on the verdict, if the jury returned a verdict; **(2)** order a new trial; or **(3)** direct the entry of judgment as a matter of law.	
50(c)-(d) [formerly 50 (c)]	**(c) GRANTING RENEWED MOTION FOR JUDGMENT AS A MATTER OF LAW; CONDITIONAL RULINGS; NEW TRIAL MOTION.** (1) If the renewed motion for judgment as a matter of law is granted, the court shall also rule on the motion for a new trial, if any, by determining whether it should be granted if the judgment is thereafter vacated or reversed, and shall specify the grounds for granting or denying the motion for the new trial. If the motion for a new trial is thus conditionally granted, the order thereon does not affect the finality of the judgment. In case the motion for a new trial has been conditionally granted and the judgment is reversed on appeal, the new trial shall proceed unless the appellate court has otherwise ordered. In case the motion for a new trial has been conditionally denied, the appellee on appeal may assert error in that denial; and if the judgment is reversed on appeal, subsequent proceedings shall be in accordance with the order of the appellate court. (2) Any motion for a new trial under Rule 59 by a party against whom judgment as a matter of law is rendered shall be filed no later than 10 days after entry of the judgment.	**(c) Granting the Renewed Motion; Conditional Ruling on a Motion for a New Trial.** **(1)** ***In General.*** If the court grants a renewed motion for judgment as a matter of law, it must also conditionally rule on any motion for a new trial by determining whether a new trial should be granted if the judgment is later vacated or reversed. The court must state the grounds for conditionally granting or denying the motion for a new trial. **(2)** ***Effect of a Conditional Ruling.*** Conditionally granting the motion for a new trial does not affect the judgment's finality; if the judgment is reversed, the new trial must proceed unless the appellate court orders otherwise. If the motion for a new trial is conditionally denied, the appellee may assert error in that denial; if the judgment is reversed, the case must proceed as the appellate court orders. **(d) Time for a Losing Party's New-Trial Motion.** Any motion for a new trial under Rule 59 by a party against whom judgment as a matter of law is rendered must be filed no later than 10 days after the entry of the judgment.	806, 808, 810, 811

Rule	Pre-Restyling Text	Restyled Text	Casebook References
50(e) [formerly 50(d)]	**(d) SAME: DENIAL OF MOTION FOR JUDGMENT AS A MATTER OF LAW.** If the motion for judgment as a matter of law is denied, the party who prevailed on that motion may, as appellee, assert grounds entitling the party to a new trial in the event the appellate court concludes that the trial court erred in denying the motion for judgment. If the appellate court reverses the judgment, nothing in this rule precludes it from determining that the appellee is entitled to a new trial, or from directing the trial court to determine whether a new trial shall be granted.	**(e) Denying the Motion for Judgment as a Matter of Law; Reversal on Appeal.** If the court denies the motion for judgment as a matter of law, the prevailing party may, as appellee, assert grounds entitling it to a new trial should the appellate court conclude that the trial court erred in denying the motion. If the appellate court reverses the judgment, it may order a new trial, direct the trial court to determine whether a new trial should be granted, or direct the entry of judgment.	
51	**Rule 51. Instructions to Jury; Objections; Preserving a Claim of Error** **(a) REQUESTS.** (1) A party may, at the close of the evidence or at an earlier reasonable time that the court directs, file and furnish to every other party written requests that the court instruct the jury on the law as set forth in the requests. (2) After the close of the evidence, a party may: (A) file requests for instructions on issues that could not reasonably have been anticipated at an earlier time for requests set under Rule 51(a)(1), and (B) with the court's permission file untimely requests for instructions on any issue. **(b) INSTRUCTIONS.** The court: (1) must inform the parties of its proposed instructions and proposed action on the requests before instructing the jury and before final jury arguments; (2) must give the parties an opportunity to object on the record and out of the jury's hearing to the proposed instructions and actions on requests before the	**Rule 51. Instructions to the Jury; Objections; Preserving a Claim of Error** **(a) Requests.** **(1)** ***Before or at the Close of the Evidence.*** At the close of the evidence or at any earlier reasonable time that the court orders, a party may file and furnish to every other party written requests for the jury instructions it wants the court to give. **(2)** ***After the Close of the Evidence.*** After the close of the evidence, a party may: **(A)** file requests for instructions on issues that could not reasonably have been anticipated by an earlier time that the court set for requests; and **(B)** with the court's permission, file untimely requests for instructions on any issue. **(b) Instructions.** The court: **(1)** must inform the parties of its proposed instructions and proposed action on the requests before instructing the jury and before final jury arguments; **(2)** must give the parties an opportunity to object on the record and out of the jury's	768, 775

Rule	Pre-Restyling Text	Restyled Text	Casebook References
	instructions and arguments are delivered; and (3) may instruct the jury at any time after trial begins and before the jury is discharged. **(c) OBJECTIONS.** (1) A party who objects to an instruction or the failure to give an instruction must do so on the record, stating distinctly the matter objected to and the grounds of the objection. (2) An objection is timely if: (A) a party that has been informed of an instruction or action on a request before the jury is instructed and before final jury arguments, as provided by Rule 51(b)(1), objects at the opportunity for objection required by Rule 51 (b)(2); or (B) a party that has not been informed of an instruction or action on a request before the time for objection provided under Rule 51(b)(2) objects promptly after learning that the instruction or request will be, or has been, given or refused. **(d) ASSIGNING ERROR; PLAIN ERROR.** (1) A party may assign as error: (A) an error in an instruction actually given if that party made a proper objection under Rule 51(c), or (B) a failure to give an instruction if that party made a proper request under Rule 51(a), and — unless the court made a definitive ruling on the record rejecting the request — also made a proper objection under Rule 51(c). (2) A court may consider a plain error in the instructions affecting substantial rights that has not been preserved as required by Rule 51(d)(1)(A) or (B).	hearing before the instructions and arguments are delivered; and **(3)** may instruct the jury at any time before the jury is discharged. **(c) Objections.** **(1)** ***How to Make.*** A party who objects to an instruction or the failure to give an instruction must do so on the record, stating distinctly the matter objected to and the grounds for the objection. **(2)** ***When to Make.*** An objection is timely if: **(A)** a party objects at the opportunity provided under Rule 51(b)(2); or **(B)** a party was not informed of an instruction or action on a request before that opportunity to object, and the party objects promptly after learning that the instruction or request will be, or has been, given or refused. **(d) Assigning Error; Plain Error.** **(1)** ***Assigning Error.*** A party may assign as error: **(A)** an error in an instruction actually given, if that party properly objected; or **(B)** a failure to give an instruction, if that party properly requested it and — unless the court rejected the request in a definitive ruling on the record — also properly objected. **(2)** ***Plain Error.*** A court may consider a plain error in the instructions that has not been preserved as required by Rule 51 (d)(1) if the error affects substantial rights.	

Rule	Pre-Restyling Text	Restyled Text	Casebook References
52(a)	**Rule 52. Findings by the Court; Judgment on Partial Findings** **(a) EFFECT.** In all actions tried upon the facts without a jury or with an advisory jury, the court shall find the facts specially and state separately its conclusions of law thereon, and judgment shall be entered pursuant to Rule 58; and in granting or refusing interlocutory injunctions the court shall similarly set forth the findings of fact and conclusions of law which constitute the grounds of its action. Requests for findings are not necessary for purposes of review. Findings of fact, whether based on oral or documentary evidence, shall not be set aside unless clearly erroneous, and due regard shall be given to the opportunity of the trial court to judge of the credibility of the witnesses. The findings of a master, to the extent that the court adopts them, shall be considered as the findings of the court. It will be sufficient if the findings of fact and conclusions of law are stated orally and recorded in open court following the close of the evidence or appear in an opinion or memorandum of decision filed by the court. Findings of fact and conclusions of law are unnecessary on decisions of motions under Rules 12 or 56 or any other motion except as provided in subdivision (c) of this rule.	**Rule 52. Findings and Conclusions by the Court; Judgment on Partial Findings** **(a) Findings and Conclusions.** **(1)** ***In General.*** In an action tried on the facts without a jury or with an advisory jury, the court must find the facts specially and state its conclusions of law separately. The findings and conclusions may be stated on the record after the close of the evidence or may appear in an opinion or a memorandum of decision filed by the court. Judgment must be entered under Rule 58. **(2)** ***For an Interlocutory Injunction.*** In granting or refusing an interlocutory injunction, the court must similarly state the findings and conclusions that support its action. **(3)** ***For a Motion.*** The court is not required to state findings or conclusions when ruling on a motion under Rule 12 or 56 or, unless these rules provide otherwise, on any other motion. **(4)** ***Effect of a Master's Findings.*** A master's findings, to the extent adopted by the court, must be considered the court's findings. **(5)** ***Questioning the Evidentiary Support.*** A party may later question the sufficiency of the evidence supporting the findings, whether or not the party requested findings, objected to them, moved to amend them, or moved for partial findings. **(6)** ***Setting Aside the Findings.*** Findings of fact, whether based on oral or other evidence, must not be set aside unless clearly erroneous, and the reviewing court must give due regard to the trial court's opportunity to judge the witnesses' credibility.	152
52(b)	**(b) AMENDMENT.** On a party's motion filed no later than 10 days after entry of judgment, the court may amend its findings—or make	**(b) Amended or Additional Findings.** On a party's motion filed no later than 10 days after the entry of judgment, the court may amend	409

Rule	Pre-Restyling Text	Restyled Text	Casebook References
	additional findings—and may amend the judgment accordingly. The motion may accompany a motion for a new trial under Rule 59. When findings of fact are made in actions tried without a jury, the sufficiency of the evidence supporting the findings may be later questioned whether or not in the district court the party raising the question objected to the findings, moved to amend them, or moved for partial findings.	its findings—or make additional findings—and may amend the judgment accordingly. The motion may accompany a motion for a new trial under Rule 59.	
53(a)	**Rule 53. Masters** **(a) APPOINTMENT.** (1) Unless a statute provides otherwise, a court may appoint a master only to: (A) perform duties consented to by the parties; (B) hold trial proceedings and make or recommend findings of fact on issues to be decided by the court without a jury if appointment is warranted by (i) some exceptional condition, or (ii) the need to perform an accounting or resolve a difficult computation of damages; or (C) address pretrial and post-trial matters that cannot be addressed effectively and timely by an available district judge or magistrate judge of the district. (2) A master must not have a relationship to the parties, counsel, action, or court that would require disqualification of a judge under 28 U.S.C. §455 unless the parties consent with the court's approval to appointment of a particular person after disclosure of any potential grounds for disqualification. (3) In appointing a master, the court must consider the fairness of imposing the likely expenses on the parties and must protect against unreasonable expense or delay.	**Rule 53. Masters** **(a) Appointment.** **(1)** ***Scope.*** Unless a statute provides otherwise, a court may appoint a master only to: **(A)** perform duties consented to by the parties; **(B)** hold trial proceedings and make or recommend findings of fact on issues to be decided without a jury if appointment is warranted by: **(i)** some exceptional condition; or **(ii)** the need to perform an accounting or resolve a difficult computation of damages; or **(C)** address pretrial and posttrial matters that cannot be effectively and timely addressed by an available district judge or magistrate judge of the district. **(2)** ***Disqualification.*** A master must not have a relationship to the parties, attorneys, action, or court that would require disqualification of a judge under 28 U.S.C. §455, unless the parties, with the court's approval, consent to the appointment after the master discloses any potential grounds for disqualification. **(3)** ***Possible Expense or Delay.*** In appointing a master, the court must consider the fairness of imposing the likely expenses on the parties and must protect against unreasonable expense or delay.	Rule 53 generally: 683, 853 53(a): 683

Rule	Pre-Restyling Text	Restyled Text	Casebook References
53(b)	**(b) ORDER APPOINTING MASTER.** (1) *Notice*. The court must give the parties notice and an opportunity to be heard before appointing a master. A party may suggest candidates for appointment. (2) *Contents*. The order appointing a master must direct the master to proceed with all reasonable diligence and must state: (A) the master's duties, including any investigation or enforcement duties, and any limits on the master's authority under Rule 53(c); (B) the circumstances—if any—in which the master may communicate ex parte with the court or a party; (C) the nature of the materials to be preserved and filed as the record of the master's activities; (D) the time limits, method of filing the record, other procedures, and standards for reviewing the master's orders, findings, and recommendations; and (E) the basis, terms, and procedure for fixing the master's compensation under Rule 53(h). (3) *Entry of Order*. The court may enter the order appointing a master only after the master has filed an affidavit disclosing whether there is any ground for disqualification under 28 U.S.C. §455 and, if a ground for disqualification is disclosed, after the parties have consented with the court's approval to waive the disqualification. (4) *Amendment*. The order appointing a master may be amended at any time after notice to the parties, and an opportunity to be heard.	**(b) Order Appointing a Master.** **(1)** ***Notice.*** Before appointing a master, the court must give the parties notice and an opportunity to be heard. Any party may suggest candidates for appointment. **(2)** ***Contents.*** The appointing order must direct the master to proceed with all reasonable diligence and must state: **(A)** the master's duties, including any investigation or enforcement duties, and any limits on the master's authority under Rule 53(c); **(B)** the circumstances, if any, in which the master may communicate ex parte with the court or a party; **(C)** the nature of the materials to be preserved and filed as the record of the master's activities; **(D)** the time limits, method of filing the record, other procedures, and standards for reviewing the master's orders, findings, and recommendations; and **(E)** the basis, terms, and procedure for fixing the master's compensation under Rule 53(g). **(3)** ***Issuing.*** The court may issue the order only after: **(A)** the master files an affidavit disclosing whether there is any ground for disqualification under 28 U.S.C. §455; and **(B)** if a ground is disclosed, the parties, with the court's approval, waive the disqualification. **(4)** ***Amending.*** The order may be amended at any time after notice to the parties and an opportunity to be heard.	683

Rule	Pre-Restyling Text	Restyled Text	Casebook References
53(c) [formerly 53 (c)-(d)]	**(c) MASTER'S AUTHORITY.** Unless the appointing order expressly directs otherwise, a master has authority to regulate all proceedings and take all appropriate measures to perform fairly and efficiently the assigned duties. The master may by order impose upon a party any noncontempt sanction provided by Rule 37 or 45, and may recommend a contempt sanction against a party and sanctions against a nonparty. **(d) EVIDENTIARY HEARINGS.** Unless the appointing order expressly directs otherwise, a master conducting an evidentiary hearing may exercise the power of the appointing court to compel, take, and record evidence.	**(c) Master's Authority.** **(1)** ***In General.*** Unless the appointing order directs otherwise, a master may: **(A)** regulate all proceedings; **(B)** take all appropriate measures to perform the assigned duties fairly and efficiently; and **(C)** if conducting an evidentiary hearing, exercise the appointing court's power to compel, take, and record evidence. **(2)** ***Sanctions.*** The master may by order impose on a party any noncontempt sanction provided by Rule 37 or 45, and may recommend a contempt sanction against a party and sanctions against a nonparty.	
53(d) [formerly 53(e)]	**(e) MASTER'S ORDERS.** A master who makes an order must file the order and promptly serve a copy on each party. The clerk must enter the order on the docket.	**(d) Master's Orders.** A master who issues an order must file it and promptly serve a copy on each party. The clerk must enter the order on the docket.	
53(e) [formerly 53(f)]	**(f) MASTER'S REPORTS.** A master must report to the court as required by the order of appointment. The master must file the report and promptly serve a copy of the report on each party unless the court directs otherwise.	**(e) Master's Reports.** A master must report to the court as required by the appointing order. The master must file the report and promptly serve a copy on each party, unless the court orders otherwise.	683
54(a)	**Rule 54. Judgments; Costs** **(a) DEFINITION; FORM.** "Judgment" as used in these rules includes a decree and any order from which an appeal lies. A judgment shall not contain a recital of pleadings, the report of a master, or the record of prior proceedings.	**Rule 54. Judgment; Costs** **(a) Definition; Form.** "Judgment" as used in these rules includes a decree and any order from which an appeal lies. A judgment should not include recitals of pleadings, a master's report, or a record of prior proceedings.	
54(b)	**(b) JUDGMENT UPON MULTIPLE CLAIMS OR INVOLVING MULTIPLE PARTIES.** When more than one claim for relief is presented in an action, whether as a claim, counterclaim, cross-claim, or third-party claim, or when multiple parties are involved, the court may direct the entry of a final judgment as to one or more but fewer than all	**(b) Judgment on Multiple Claims or Involving Multiple Parties.** When an action presents more than one claim for relief—whether as a claim, counterclaim, crossclaim, or third-party claim—or when multiple parties are involved, the court may direct entry of a final judgment as to one or more, but fewer than all, claims or parties only if the court expressly determines	667

Rule	Pre-Restyling Text	Restyled Text	Casebook References
	of the claims or parties only upon an express determination that there is no just reason for delay and upon an express direction for the entry of judgment. In the absence of such determination and direction, any order or other form of decision, however designated, which adjudicates fewer than all the claims or the rights and liabilities of fewer than all the parties shall not terminate the action as to any of the claims or parties, and the order or other form of decision is subject to revision at any time before the entry of judgment adjudicating all the claims and the rights and liabilities of all the parties.	that there is no just reason for delay. Otherwise, any order or other decision, however designated, that adjudicates fewer than all the claims or the rights and liabilities of fewer than all the parties does not end the action as to any of the claims or parties and may be revised at any time before the entry of a judgment adjudicating all the claims and all the parties' rights and liabilities.	
54(c)	**(c) DEMAND FOR JUDGMENT.** A judgment by default shall not be different in kind from or exceed in amount that prayed for in the demand for judgment. Except as to a party against whom a judgment is entered by default, every final judgment shall grant the relief to which the party in whose favor it is rendered is entitled, even if the party has not demanded such relief in the party's pleadings.	**(c) Demand for Judgment; Relief to Be Granted.** A default judgment must not differ in kind from, or exceed in amount, what is demanded in the pleadings. Every other final judgment should grant the relief to which each party is entitled, even if the party has not demanded that relief in its pleadings.	
54(d)	**(d) COSTS; ATTORNEYS' FEES.** (1) *Costs Other than Attorneys' Fees.* Except when express provision therefor is made either in a statute of the United States or in these rules, costs other than attorneys' fees shall be allowed as of course to the prevailing party unless the court otherwise directs; but costs against the United States, its officers, and agencies shall be imposed only to the extent permitted by law. Such costs may be taxed by the clerk on one day's notice. On motion served within 5 days thereafter, the action of the clerk may be reviewed by the court. (2) *Attorneys' Fees.* (A) Claims for attorneys' fees and related nontaxable expenses shall be made by motion unless the substantive law governing the action provides for the recovery	**(d) Costs; Attorney's Fees.** **(1)** ***Costs Other Than Attorney's Fees.*** Unless a federal statute, these rules, or a court order provides otherwise, costs — other than attorney's fees — should be allowed to the prevailing party. But costs against the United States, its officers, and its agencies may be imposed only to the extent allowed by law. The clerk may tax costs on 1 day's notice. On motion served within the next 5 days, the court may review the clerk's action. **(2)** ***Attorney's Fees.*** **(A)** *Claim to Be by Motion.* A claim for attorney's fees and related nontaxable expenses must be made by motion unless the substantive law requires those fees to be	606, 609

Rule	Pre-Restyling Text	Restyled Text	Casebook References
	of such fees as an element of damages to be proved at trial. (B) Unless otherwise provided by statute or order of the court, the motion must be filed no later than 14 days after entry of judgment; must specify the judgment and the statute, rule, or other grounds entitling the moving party to the award; and must state the amount or provide a fair estimate of the amount sought. If directed by the court, the motion shall also disclose the terms of any agreement with respect to fees to be paid for the services for which claim is made. (C) On request of a party or class member, the court shall afford an opportunity for adversary submissions with respect to the motion in accordance with Rule 43(e) or Rule 78. The court may determine issues of liability for fees before receiving submissions bearing on issues of evaluation of services for which liability is imposed by the court. The court shall find the facts and state its conclusions of law as provided in Rule 52(a). (D) By local rule the court may establish special procedures by which issues relating to such fees may be resolved without extensive evidentiary hearings. In addition, the court may refer issues relating to the value of services to a special master under Rule 53 without regard to the provisions of Rule 53(a)(1) and may refer a motion for attorneys' fees to a magistrate judge under Rule 72(b) as if it were a dispositive pretrial matter. (E) The provisions of subparagraphs (A) through (D) do not apply to claims for fees and expenses as sanctions for violations of these rules or under 28 U.S.C. §1927.	proved at trial as an element of damages. **(B)** *Timing and Contents of the Motion.* Unless a statute or a court order provides otherwise, the motion must: **(i)** be filed no later than 14 days after the entry of judgment; **(ii)** specify the judgment and the statute, rule, or other grounds entitling the movant to the award; **(iii)** state the amount sought or provide a fair estimate of it; and **(iv)** disclose, if the court so orders, the terms of any agreement about fees for the services for which the claim is made. **(C)** *Proceedings.* Subject to Rule 23(h), the court must, on a party's request, give an opportunity for adversary submissions on the motion in accordance with Rule 43(c) or 78. The court may decide issues of liability for fees before receiving submissions on the value of services. The court must find the facts and state its conclusions of law as provided in Rule 52(a). **(D)** *Special Procedures by Local Rule; Reference to a Master or a Magistrate Judge.* By local rule, the court may establish special procedures to resolve fee-related issues without extensive evidentiary hearings. Also, the court may refer issues concerning the value of services to a special master under Rule 53 without regard to the limitations of Rule 53(a)(1), and may refer a motion for attorney's fees to a magistrate judge under Rule 72(b) as if it were a dispositive pretrial matter. **(E)** *Exceptions.* Subparagraphs (A)-(D) do not apply to claims for fees and expenses as	

Rule	Pre-Restyling Text	Restyled Text	Casebook References
		sanctions for violating these rules or as sanctions under 28 U.S.C. §1927.	
55	**Rule 55. Default** **(a) ENTRY.** When a party against whom a judgment for affirmative relief is sought has failed to plead or otherwise defend as provided by these rules and that fact is made to appear by affidavit or otherwise, the clerk shall enter the party's default. **(b) JUDGMENT.** Judgment by default may be entered as follows: (1) *By the Clerk.* When the plaintiff's claim against a defendant is for a sum certain or for a sum which can by computation be made certain, the clerk upon request of the plaintiff and upon affidavit of the amount due shall enter judgment for that amount and costs against the defendant, if the defendant has been defaulted for failure to appear and is not an infant or incompetent person. (2) *By the Court.* In all other cases the party entitled to a judgment by default shall apply to the court therefor; but no judgment by default shall be entered against an infant or incompetent person unless represented in the action by a general guardian, committee, conservator, or other such representative who has appeared therein. If the party against whom judgment by default is sought has appeared in the action, the party (or, if appearing by representative, the party's representative) shall be served with written notice of the application for judgment at least 3 days prior to the hearing on such application. If, in order to enable the court to enter judgment or to carry it into effect, it is necessary to take an account or to determine the amount of damages or to establish the truth of any averment by evidence or to make an investigation of any other matter, the court may conduct such hearings or order such	**Rule 55. Default; Default Judgment** **(a) Entering a Default.** When a party against whom a judgment for affirmative relief is sought has failed to plead or otherwise defend, and that failure is shown by affidavit or otherwise, the clerk must enter the party's default. **(b) Entering a Default Judgment.** **(1) *By the Clerk.*** If the plaintiff's claim is for a sum certain or a sum that can be made certain by computation, the clerk — on the plaintiff's request, with an affidavit showing the amount due — must enter judgment for that amount and costs against a defendant who has been defaulted for not appearing and who is neither a minor nor an incompetent person. **(2) *By the Court.*** In all other cases, the party must apply to the court for a default judgment. A default judgment may be entered against a minor or incompetent person only if represented by a general guardian, conservator, or other like fiduciary who has appeared. If the party against whom a default judgment is sought has appeared personally or by a representative, that party or its representative must be served with written notice of the application at least 3 days before the hearing. The court may conduct hearings or make referrals — preserving any federal statutory right to a jury trial — when, to enter or effectuate judgment, it needs to: (A) conduct an accounting; (B) determine the amount of damages; (C) establish the truth of any allegation by evidence; or (D) investigate any other matter.	Rule 55, generally: 370, 1154

Rule	Pre-Restyling Text	Restyled Text	Casebook References
	references as it deems necessary and proper and shall accord a right of trial by jury to the parties when and as required by any statute of the United States. **(c) SETTING ASIDE DEFAULT.** For good cause shown the court may set aside an entry of default and, if a judgment by default has been entered, may likewise set it aside in accordance with Rule 60(b). **(d) PLAINTIFFS, COUNTERCLAIMANTS, CROSS-CLAIMANTS.** The provisions of this rule apply whether the party entitled to the judgment by default is a plaintiff, a third-party plaintiff, or a party who has pleaded a cross-claim or counterclaim. In all cases a judgment by default is subject to the limitations of Rule 54(c). **(e) JUDGMENT AGAINST THE UNITED STATES.** No judgment by default shall be entered against the United States or an officer or agency thereof unless the claimant establishes a claim or right to relief by evidence satisfactory to the court.	**(c) Setting Aside a Default or a Default Judgment.** The court may set aside an entry of default for good cause, and it may set aside a default judgment under Rule 60(b). **(d) Judgment Against the United States.** A default judgment may be entered against the United States, its officers, or its agencies only if the claimant establishes a claim or right to relief by evidence that satisfies the court.	
56(a)	**Rule 56. Summary Judgment** **(a) FOR CLAIMANT.** A party seeking to recover upon a claim, counterclaim, or cross-claim or to obtain a declaratory judgment may, at any time after the expiration of 20 days from the commencement of the action or after service of a motion for summary judgment by the adverse party, move with or without supporting affidavits for a summary judgment in the party's favor upon all or any part thereof.	**Rule 56. Summary Judgment** **(a) By a Claiming Party.** A party claiming relief may move, with or without supporting affidavits, for summary judgment on all or part of the claim. The motion may be filed at any time after: (1) 20 days have passed from commencement of the action; or (2) the opposing party serves a motion for summary judgment.	Rule 56 generally: 174, 216, 292, 323, 325, 326, 346, 363, 633, 634, 640, 642, 644, 645, 646, 648, 654, 664, 668, 670, 673, 797 56(a): 642
56(b)	**(b) FOR DEFENDING PARTY.** A party against whom a claim, counterclaim, or cross-claim is asserted or a declaratory judgment is sought may, at any time, move with or without supporting affidavits for a summary judgment in the party's favor as to all or any part thereof.	**(b) By a Defending Party.** A party against whom relief is sought may move at any time, with or without supporting affidavits, for summary judgment on all or part of the claim.	642, 667

Rule	Pre-Restyling Text	Restyled Text	Casebook References
56(c)	**(c) MOTION AND PROCEEDINGS THEREON.** The motion shall be served at least 10 days before the time fixed for the hearing. The adverse party prior to the day of hearing may serve opposing affidavits. The judgment sought shall be rendered forthwith if the pleadings, depositions, answers to interrogatories, and admissions on file, together with the affidavits, if any, show that there is no genuine issue as to any material fact and that the moving party is entitled to a judgment as a matter of law. A summary judgment, interlocutory in character, may be rendered on the issue of liability alone although there is a genuine issue as to the amount of damages.	**(c) Serving the Motion; Proceedings.** The motion must be served at least 10 days before the day set for the hearing. An opposing party may serve opposing affidavits before the hearing day. The judgment sought should be rendered if the pleadings, the discovery and disclosure materials on file, and any affidavits show that there is no genuine issue as to any material fact and that the movant is entitled to judgment as a matter of law.	217, 639, 641, 642, 643, 645, 649, 658
56(d)	**(d) CASE NOT FULLY ADJUDICATED ON MOTION.** If on motion under this rule judgment is not rendered upon the whole case or for all the relief asked and a trial is necessary, the court at the hearing of the motion, by examining the pleadings and the evidence before it and by interrogating counsel, shall if practicable ascertain what material facts exist without substantial controversy and what material facts are actually and in good faith controverted. It shall thereupon make an order specifying the facts that appear without substantial controversy, including the extent to which the amount of damages or other relief is not in controversy, and directing such further proceedings in the action as are just. Upon the trial of the action the facts so specified shall be deemed established, and the trial shall be conducted accordingly.	**(d) Case Not Fully Adjudicated on the Motion.** **(1) *Establishing Facts.*** If summary judgment is not rendered on the whole action, the court should, to the extent practicable, determine what material facts are not genuinely at issue. The court should so determine by examining the pleadings and evidence before it and by interrogating the attorneys. It should then issue an order specifying what facts — including items of damages or other relief — are not genuinely at issue. The facts so specified must be treated as established in the action. **(2) *Establishing Liability.*** An interlocutory summary judgment may be rendered on liability alone, even if there is a genuine issue on the amount of damages.	
56(e)	**(e) FORM OF AFFIDAVITS; FURTHER TESTIMONY; DEFENSE REQUIRED.** Supporting and opposing affidavits shall be made on personal knowledge, shall set forth such facts as would be admissible in evidence, and shall show affirmatively that the affiant is competent to testify to the matters stated therein. Sworn or certified copies of all papers or parts thereof	**(e) Affidavits; Further Testimony.** **(1) *In General.*** A supporting or opposing affidavit must be made on personal knowledge, set out facts that would be admissible in evidence, and show that the affiant is competent to testify on the matters stated. If a paper or part of a paper is referred to in an affidavit, a sworn or certified copy must be attached to or	639, 641, 642, 643, 645, 646, 649, 657, 658, 662

Rule	Pre-Restyling Text	Restyled Text	Casebook References
	referred to in an affidavit shall be attached thereto or served therewith. The court may permit affidavits to be supplemented or opposed by depositions, answers to interrogatories, or further affidavits. When a motion for summary judgment is made and supported as provided in this rule, an adverse party may not rest upon the mere allegations or denials of the adverse party's pleading, but the adverse party's response, by affidavits or as otherwise provided in this rule, must set forth specific facts showing that there is a genuine issue for trial. If the adverse party does not so respond, summary judgment, if appropriate, shall be entered against the adverse party.	served with the affidavit. The court may permit an affidavit to be supplemented or opposed by depositions, answers to interrogatories, or additional affidavits. **(2) *Opposing Party's Obligation to Respond.*** When a motion for summary judgment is properly made and supported, an opposing party may not rely merely on allegations or denials in its own pleading; rather, its response must—by affidavits or as otherwise provided in this rule—set out specific facts showing a genuine issue for trial. If the opposing party does not so respond, summary judgment should, if appropriate, be entered against that party.	
56(f)	**(f) WHEN AFFIDAVITS ARE UNAVAILABLE.** Should it appear from the affidavits of a party opposing the motion that the party cannot for reasons stated present by affidavit facts essential to justify the party's opposition, the court may refuse the application for judgment or may order a continuance to permit affidavits to be obtained or depositions to be taken or discovery to be had or may make such other order as is just.	**(f) When Affidavits Are Unavailable.** If a party opposing the motion shows by affidavit that, for specified reasons, it cannot present facts essential to justify its opposition, the court may: (1) deny the motion; (2) order a continuance to enable affidavits to be obtained, depositions to be taken, or other discovery to be undertaken; or (3) issue any other just order.	639, 643, 646
56(g)	**(g) AFFIDAVITS MADE IN BAD FAITH.** Should it appear to the satisfaction of the court at any time that any of the affidavits presented pursuant to this rule are presented in bad faith or solely for the purpose of delay, the court shall forthwith order the party employing them to pay to the other party the amount of the reasonable expenses which the filing of the affidavits caused the other party to incur, including reasonable attorney's fees, and any offending party or attorney may be adjudged guilty of contempt.	**(g) Affidavit Submitted in Bad Faith.** If satisfied that an affidavit under this rule is submitted in bad faith or solely for delay, the court must order the submitting party to pay the other party the reasonable expenses, including attorney's fees, it incurred as a result. An offending party or attorney may also be held in contempt.	
57	**Rule 57. Declaratory Judgments** The procedure for obtaining a declaratory judgment pursuant to Title 28, U.S.C., §2201, shall be in accordance with these rules, and the	**Rule 57. Declaratory Judgment** These rules govern the procedure for obtaining a declaratory judgment under 28 U.S.C. §2201. Rules 38 and 39 govern a demand	736

Rule	Pre-Restyling Text	Restyled Text	Casebook References
	right to trial by jury may be demanded under the circumstances and in the manner provided in Rules 38 and 39. The existence of another adequate remedy does not preclude a judgment for declaratory relief in cases where it is appropriate. The court may order a speedy hearing of an action for a declaratory judgment and may advance it on the calendar.	for a jury trial. The existence of another adequate remedy does not preclude a declaratory judgment that is otherwise appropriate. The court may order a speedy hearing of a declaratory-judgment action.	
59(a)	**Rule 59. New Trials; Amendment of Judgments** **(a) GROUNDS.** A new trial may be granted to all or any of the parties and on all or part of the issues (1) in an action in which there has been a trial by jury, for any of the reasons for which new trials have heretofore been granted in actions at law in the courts of the United States; and (2) in an action tried without a jury, for any of the reasons for which rehearings have heretofore been granted in suits in equity in the courts of the United States. On a motion for a new trial in an action tried without a jury, the court may open the judgment if one has been entered, take additional testimony, amend findings of fact and conclusions of law or make new findings and conclusions, and direct the entry of a new judgment.	**Rule 59. New Trial; Altering or Amending a Judgment** **(a) In General.** **(1)** ***Grounds for New Trial.*** The court may, on motion, grant a new trial on all or some of the issues — and to any party — as follows: **(A)** after a jury trial, for any reason for which a new trial has heretofore been granted in an action at law in federal court; or **(B)** after a nonjury trial, for any reason for which a rehearing has heretofore been granted in a suit in equity in federal court. **(2)** ***Further Action After a Nonjury Trial.*** After a nonjury trial, the court may, on motion for a new trial, open the judgment if one has been entered, take additional testimony, amend findings of fact and conclusions of law or make new ones, and direct the entry of a new judgment.	Rule 59 generally: 375, 808, 821, 891, 894, 897, 898, 899 59(a): 894
59(b)	**(b) TIME FOR MOTION.** Any motion for a new trial shall be filed no later than 10 days after entry of the judgment.	**(b) Time to File a Motion for a New Trial.** A motion for a new trial must be filed no later than 10 days after the entry of judgment.	
59(c)	**(c) TIME FOR SERVING AFFIDAVITS.** When a motion for new trial is based on affidavits, they shall be filed with the motion. The opposing party has 10 days after service to file opposing affidavits, but that period may be extended for up to 20 days, either by the court for good cause or by the parties' written stipulation. The court may permit reply affidavits.	**(c) Time to Serve Affidavits.** When a motion for a new trial is based on affidavits, they must be filed with the motion. The opposing party has 10 days after being served to file opposing affidavits; but that period may be extended for up to 20 days, either by the court for good cause or by the parties' stipulation. The court may permit reply affidavits.	

Rule	Pre-Restyling Text	Restyled Text	Casebook References
59(d)	**(d) ON COURT'S INITIATIVE; NOTICE; SPECIFYING GROUNDS.** No later than 10 days after entry of judgment the court, on its own, may order a new trial for any reason that would justify granting one on a party's motion. After giving the parties notice and an opportunity to be heard, the court may grant a timely motion for a new trial for a reason not stated in the motion. When granting a new trial on its own initiative or for a reason not stated in a motion, the court shall specify the grounds in its order.	**(d) New Trial on the Court's Initiative or for Reasons Not in the Motion.** No later than 10 days after the entry of judgment, the court, on its own, may order a new trial for any reason that would justify granting one on a party's motion. After giving the parties notice and an opportunity to be heard, the court may grant a timely motion for a new trial for a reason not stated in the motion. In either event, the court must specify the reasons in its order.	
59(e)	**(e) MOTION TO ALTER OR AMEND JUDGMENT.** Any motion to alter or amend a judgment shall be filed no later than 10 days after entry of the judgment.	**(e) Motion to Alter or Amend a Judgment.** A motion to alter or amend a judgment must be filed no later than 10 days after the entry of the judgment.	389
60(a)	**Rule 60. Relief From Judgment or Order** **(a) CLERICAL MISTAKES.** Clerical mistakes in judgments, orders or other parts of the record and errors therein arising from oversight or omission may be corrected by the court at any time of its own initiative or on the motion of any party and after such notice, if any, as the court orders. During the pendency of an appeal, such mistakes may be so corrected before the appeal is docketed in the appellate court, and thereafter while the appeal is pending may be so corrected with leave of the appellate court.	**Rule 60. Relief from a Judgment or Order** **(a) Corrections Based on Clerical Mistakes; Oversights and Omissions.** The court may correct a clerical mistake or a mistake arising from oversight or omission whenever one is found in a judgment, order, or other part of the record. The court may do so on motion or on its own, with or without notice. But after an appeal has been docketed in the appellate court and while it is pending, such a mistake may be corrected only with the appellate court's leave.	Rule 60 generally: 1115, 1130
60(b)	**(b) MISTAKES; INADVERTENCE; EXCUSABLE NEGLECT; NEWLY DISCOVERED EVIDENCE; FRAUD, ETC.** On motion and upon such terms as are just, the court may relieve a party or a party's legal representative from a final judgment, order, or proceeding for the following reasons: (1) mistake, inadvertence, surprise, or excusable neglect; (2) newly discovered evidence which by due diligence could not have been discovered in time to move for a new trial under Rule 59(b); (3) fraud (whether heretofore denominated intrinsic or extrinsic), misrepresentation, or	**(b) Grounds for Relief from a Final Judgment, Order, or Proceeding.** On motion and just terms, the court may relieve a party or its legal representative from a final judgment, order, or proceeding for the following reasons: **(1)** mistake, inadvertence, surprise, or excusable neglect; **(2)** newly discovered evidence that, with reasonable diligence, could not have been discovered in time to move for a new trial under Rule 59(b); **(3)** fraud (whether previously called intrinsic or extrinsic),	39, 44, 45, 50, 375, 571, 572, 577, 619, 817, 1120, 1121, 1123, 1124, 1125, 1126, 1127, 1128, 1129, 1130, 1150

Rule	Pre-Restyling Text	Restyled Text	Casebook References
	other misconduct of an adverse party; (4) the judgment is void; (5) the judgment has been satisfied, released, or discharged, or a prior judgment upon which it is based has been reversed or otherwise vacated, or it is no longer equitable that the judgment should have prospective application; or (6) any other reason justifying relief from the operation of the judgment. The motion shall be made within a reasonable time, and for reasons (1), (2), and (3) not more than one year after the judgment, order, or proceeding was entered or taken. A motion under this subdivision (b) does not affect the finality of a judgment or suspend its operation. This rule does not limit the power of a court to entertain an independent action to relieve a party from a judgment, order, or proceeding, or to grant relief to a defendant not actually personally notified as provided in Title 28, U.S.C., §1655, or to set aside a judgment for fraud upon the court. Writs of coram nobis, coram vobis, audita querela, and bills of review and bills in the nature of a bill of review, are abolished, and the procedure for obtaining any relief from a judgment shall be by motion as prescribed in these rules or by an independent action.	misrepresentation, or misconduct by an opposing party; **(4)** the judgment is void; **(5)** the judgment has been satisfied, released or discharged; it is based on an earlier judgment that has been reversed or vacated; or applying it prospectively is no longer equitable; or **(6)** any other reason that justifies relief.	
65(a)	**Rule 65. Injunctions** **(a) PRELIMINARY INJUNCTION.** (1) *Notice.* No preliminary injunction shall be issued without notice to the adverse party. (2) *Consolidation of Hearing With Trial on Merits.* Before or after the commencement of the hearing of an application for a preliminary injunction, the court may order the trial of the action on the merits to be advanced and consolidated with the hearing of the application. Even when this consolidation is not ordered, any evidence received upon an application for a preliminary injunction which would be admissible upon the trial on the merits becomes part of the	**Rule 65. Injunctions and Restraining Orders** **(a) Preliminary Injunction.** **(1) *Notice.*** The court may issue a preliminary injunction only on notice to the adverse party. **(2) *Consolidating the Hearing with the Trial on the Merits.*** Before or after beginning the hearing on a motion for a preliminary injunction, the court may advance the trial on the merits and consolidate it with the hearing. Even when consolidation is not ordered, evidence that is received on the motion and that would be admissible at trial becomes part of the trial record and need not be repeated at trial.	Rule 65 generally: 458, 721 65(a): 217

Rule	Pre-Restyling Text	Restyled Text	Casebook References
	record on the trial and need not be repeated upon the trial. This subdivision (a)(2) shall be so construed and applied as to save to the parties any rights they may have to trial by jury.	But the court must preserve any party's right to a jury trial.	
65(b)	**(b) TEMPORARY RESTRAINING ORDER; NOTICE; HEARING; DURATION.** A temporary restraining order may be granted without written or oral notice to the adverse party or that party's attorney only if (1) it clearly appears from specific facts shown by affidavit or by the verified complaint that immediate and irreparable injury, loss, or damage will result to the applicant before the adverse party or that party's attorney can be heard in opposition, and (2) the applicant's attorney certifies to the court in writing the efforts, if any, which have been made to give the notice and the reasons supporting the claim that notice should not be required. Every temporary restraining order granted without notice shall be indorsed with the date and hour of issuance; shall be filed forthwith in the clerk's office and entered of record; shall define the injury and state why it is irreparable and why the order was granted without notice; and shall expire by its terms within such time after entry, not to exceed 10 days, as the court fixes, unless within the time so fixed the order, for good cause shown, is extended for a like period or unless the party against whom the order is directed consents that it may be extended for a longer period. The reasons for the extension shall be entered of record. In case a temporary restraining order is granted without notice, the motion for a preliminary injunction shall be set down for hearing at the earliest possible time and takes precedence of all matters except older matters of the same character; and when the motion comes on for hearing the party who obtained the temporary restraining order shall proceed with the application for a preliminary injunction and, if the party does not do so, the court shall dissolve the	**(b) Temporary Restraining Order.** **(1)** ***Issuing Without Notice.*** The court may issue a temporary restraining order without written or oral notice to the adverse party or its attorney only if: **(A)** specific facts in an affidavit or a verified complaint clearly show that immediate and irreparable injury, loss, or damage will result to the movant before the adverse party can be heard in opposition; and **(B)** the movant's attorney certifies in writing any efforts made to give notice and the reasons why it should not be required. **(2)** ***Contents; Expiration.*** Every temporary restraining order issued without notice must state the date and hour it was issued; describe the injury and state why it is irreparable; state why the order was issued without notice; and be promptly filed in the clerk's office and entered in the record. The order expires at the time after entry—not to exceed 10 days—that the court sets, unless before that time the court, for good cause, extends it for a like period or the adverse party consents to a longer extension. The reasons for an extension must be entered in the record. **(3)** ***Expediting the Preliminary-Injunction Hearing.*** If the order is issued without notice, the motion for a preliminary injunction must be set for hearing at the earliest possible time, taking precedence over all other matters except hearings on older matters of the same character. At the hearing, the party who obtained the order must proceed with the motion; if	

Rule	Pre-Restyling Text	Restyled Text	Casebook References
	temporary restraining order. On 2 days' notice to the party who obtained the temporary restraining order without notice or on such shorter notice to that party as the court may prescribe, the adverse party may appear and move its dissolution or modification and in that event the court shall proceed to hear and determine such motion as expeditiously as the ends of justice require.	the party does not, the court must dissolve the order. **(4) *Motion to Dissolve.*** On 2 days' notice to the party who obtained the order without notice—or on shorter notice set by the court—the adverse party may appear and move to dissolve or modify the order. The court must then hear and decide the motion as promptly as justice requires.	
65(c)	**(c) SECURITY.** No restraining order or preliminary injunction shall issue except upon the giving of security by the applicant, in such sum as the court deems proper, for the payment of such costs and damages as may be incurred or suffered by any party who is found to have been wrongfully enjoined or restrained. No such security shall be required of the United States or of an officer or agency thereof. The provisions of Rule 65.1 apply to a surety upon a bond or undertaking under this rule.	**(c) Security.** The court may issue a preliminary injunction or a temporary restraining order only if the movant gives security in an amount that the court considers proper to pay the costs and damages sustained by any party found to have been wrongfully enjoined or restrained. The United States, its officers, and its agencies are not required to give security.	
65(d)	**(d) FORM AND SCOPE OF INJUNCTION OR RESTRAINING ORDER.** Every order granting an injunction and every restraining order shall set forth the reasons for its issuance; shall be specific in terms; shall describe in reasonable detail, and not by reference to the complaint or other document, the act or acts sought to be restrained; and is binding only upon the parties to the action, their officers, agents, servants, employees, and attorneys, and upon those persons in active concert or participation with them who receive actual notice of the order by personal service or otherwise.	**(d) Contents and Scope of Every Injunction and Restraining Order.** **(1) *Contents.*** Every order granting an injunction and every restraining order must: (A) state the reasons why it issued; (B) state its terms specifically; and (C) describe in reasonable detail—and not by referring to the complaint or other document—the act or acts restrained or required. **(2) *Persons Bound.*** The order binds only the following who receive actual notice of it by personal service or otherwise: (A) the parties; (B) the parties' officers, agents, servants, employees, and attorneys; and (C) other persons who are in active concert or participation with anyone described in Rule 65(d)(2)(A) or (B).	715

Rule	Pre-Restyling Text	Restyled Text	Casebook References
68	**Rule 68. Offer of Judgment** At any time more than 10 days before the trial begins, a party defending against a claim may serve upon the adverse party an offer to allow judgment to be taken against the defending party for the money or property or to the effect specified in the offer, with costs then accrued. If within 10 days after the service of the offer the adverse party serves written notice that the offer is accepted, either party may then file the offer and notice of acceptance together with proof of service thereof and thereupon the clerk shall enter judgment. An offer not accepted shall be deemed withdrawn and evidence thereof is not admissible except in a proceeding to determine costs. If the judgment finally obtained by the offeree is not more favorable than the offer, the offeree must pay the costs incurred after the making of the offer. The fact that an offer is made but not accepted does not preclude a subsequent offer. When the liability of one party to another has been determined by verdict or order or judgment, but the amount or extent of the liability remains to be determined by further proceedings, the party adjudged liable may make an offer of judgment, which shall have the same effect as an offer made before trial if it is served within a reasonable time not less than 10 days prior to the commencement of hearings to determine the amount or extent of liability.	**Rule 68. Offer of Judgment** **(a) Making an Offer; Judgment on an Accepted Offer.** More than 10 days before the trial begins, a party defending against a claim may serve on an opposing party an offer to allow judgment on specified terms, with the costs then accrued. If, within 10 days after being served, the opposing party serves written notice accepting the offer, either party may then file the offer and notice of acceptance, plus proof of service. The clerk must then enter judgment. **(b) Unaccepted Offer.** An unaccepted offer is considered withdrawn, but it does not preclude a later offer. Evidence of an unaccepted offer is not admissible except in a proceeding to determine costs. **(c) Offer After Liability Is Determined.** When one party's liability to another has been determined but the extent of liability remains to be determined by further proceedings, the party held liable may make an offer of judgment. It must be served within a reasonable time — but at least 10 days — before a hearing to determine the extent of liability. **(d) Paying Costs After an Unaccepted Offer.** If the judgment that the offeree finally obtains is not more favorable than the unaccepted offer, the offeree must pay the costs incurred after the offer was made.	602, 603, 604, 606, 607, 608, 609, 610, 611, 612, 613, 617, 618, 619, 1110, 1111, 1112
69	**Rule 69. Execution** **(a) IN GENERAL.** Process to enforce a judgment for the payment of money shall be a writ of execution, unless the court directs otherwise. The procedure on execution, in proceedings supplementary to and in aid of a judgment, and in proceedings on and in aid of execution shall be in accordance with the practice and procedure of the state in which the district court is held, existing at the time the remedy is sought, except	**Rule 69. Execution** **(a) In General.** (1) ***Money Judgment; Applicable Procedure.*** A money judgment is enforced by a writ of execution, unless the court directs otherwise. The procedure on execution — and in proceedings supplementary to and in aid of judgment or execution — must accord with the procedure of the state where the court is located,	433

Rule	Pre-Restyling Text	Restyled Text	Casebook References
	that any statute of the United States governs to the extent that it is applicable. In aid of the judgment or execution, the judgment creditor or a successor in interest when that interest appears of record, may obtain discovery from any person, including the judgment debtor, in the manner provided in these rules or in the manner provided by the practice of the state in which the district court is held. **(b) AGAINST CERTAIN PUBLIC OFFICERS.** When a judgment has been entered against a collector or other officer of revenue under the circumstances stated in Title 28, U.S.C., §2006, or against an officer of Congress in an action mentioned in the Act of March 3, 1875, ch. 130, §8 (18 Stat. 401), U.S.C., Title 2, §118, and when the court has given the certificate of probable cause for the officer's act as provided in those statutes, execution shall not issue against the officer or the officer's property but the final judgment shall be satisfied as provided in such statutes.	but a federal statute governs to the extent it applies. **(2) *Obtaining Discovery.*** In aid of the judgment or execution, the judgment creditor or a successor in interest whose interest appears of record may obtain discovery from any person—including the judgment debtor—as provided in these rules or by the procedure of the state where the court is located. **(b) Against Certain Public Officers.** When a judgment has been entered against a revenue officer in the circumstances stated in 28 U.S.C. §2006, or against an officer of Congress in the circumstances stated in 2 U.S.C. §118, the judgment must be satisfied as those statutes provide.	
82	**Rule 82. Jurisdiction and Venue Unaffected** These rules shall not be construed to extend or limit the jurisdiction of the United States district courts or the venue of actions therein. An admiralty or maritime claim within the meaning of Rule 9(h) shall not be treated as a civil action for the purposes of Title 28, U.S.C., §§1391–1392.	**Rule 82. Jurisdiction and Venue Unaffected** These rules do not extend or limit the jurisdiction of the district courts or the venue of actions in those courts. An admiralty or maritime claim under Rule 9(h) is not a civil action for purposes of 28 U.S.C. §§1391-1392.	1095
84	**Rule 84. Forms** The forms contained in the Appendix of Forms are sufficient under the rules and are intended to indicate the simplicity and brevity of statement which the rules contemplate.	**Rule 84. Forms** The forms in the Appendix suffice under these rules and illustrate the simplicity and brevity that these rules contemplate.	296

Table of Cases

Principal cases are in italics.

A & M Records Inc., et al. v. Napster, 722
Abbott Labs, In re, 908
Abdullah v. Acands, Inc., 446
Able v. Upjohn Co., 936
Abrahams, United States v., 526
Abrego Abrego v. Dow Chem. Co., 924
ACA Fin. Guar. Corp. v. Advest, Inc., 330, 440
Ackerman v. United States, 1128
Addington v. Texas, 7
Adickes v. S. H. Kress & Co., 635-640, 641, 642, 643, 645, 646, 647, 648
Adler v. Berg Harmon Assocs., 233
Adlman, United States v., 507, 508, 526
Admiral Insurance Co. v. United States District Court, 521
Ager v. Jane C. Stormont Hospital & Training School for Nurses, 566-567
Agostini v. Felton, 1129
Aguilar v. Felton, 1129
Airborne Beepers & Video, Inc. v. AT&T Mobility, L.L.C., 331
Aircraft Braking Sys. Corp. v. Local 856, 1183
Air Crash Disaster Near Dayton, Ohio, In re, 984
Air Line Pilots Assn. v. Miller, 842
Airlines Reporting Corp. v. S&N Travel, Inc., 223
Aktieselskabet AF 21 November 2001 v. Fame Jeans, Inc., 331, 440
Alabama v. Blue Bird Body Co., 1034
Albemarle Paper Co. v. Moody, 841
Albright v. R.J. Reynolds Tobacco Co., 1013
Aldinger v. Howard, 904, 911, 912
Alexander v. Anthony Intl. L.P., 844
Alexander v. Chicago Park District, 299-300
Alexander v. Gardner-Denver Co., 835, 843, 1192, 1193
Alexander v. Sandoval, 257
Alexander Proudfoot Co. World Headquarters v. Thayer, 890
Allapattah Services, Inc. v. Exxon Corp., 908, 914, 922
Alleghany Corp. v. Kirby, 1122
Allen v. Hardy, 756
Allen v. McCurry, 1169-1174, 1191, 1194
Allen v. United States, 806
Allen v. Wright, 961
Allendale Mut. Ins. Co. v. Bull Data Sys., Inc., 527
Allied-Bruce Terminix Companies, Inc. v., Dobson, 844
Allied Chemical Corp. v. Daiflon, Inc., 806
Allied Chemical Corp. v. Mackay, 377
Allison v. Citgo Petroleum Corp., 734, 1035
Allstate Ins. Co. v. Hague, 176
Al-Marri v. Pucciarelli, 18
Al-Marri v. Wright, 18
Aloe Coal Co. v. Clark Equipment Co., 809
Alvarez v. Uniroyal Tire Co., 942
Alyeska Pipeline Service Co. v. Wilderness Society, 462, 606, 609, 613
Amalgamated Transit Union Local 1309 v. Laidlaw Transit Servs., Inc., 939
Ambrosia Coal & Constr. Co. v. Pages Morales, 223
Amchem Prods., Inc. v. Windsor, 1090-1102, 1103, 1104, 1105, 1112
American Fiber & Finishing, Inc. v. Tyco Healthcare Group, LP, 388
American Fid. & Cas. Co. v. Greyhound Co., 977
American Fire & Casualty Co. v. Finn, 933, 934, 937
American Hospital Supply Corp. v. Hospital Products Ltd., 1049
American Lung Association v. Reilly, 985-987
American Mills Co. v. American Surety Co., 739
American Nurses' Assn. v. Illinois, 294-300, 301, 305, 306, 333, 334, 363, 437
American Pipe & Const. Co. v. Utah, 1079
American Protection Insurance Co. v. MGM Grand Hotel-Las Vegas, Inc., 562

American Surety Co. v. Baldwin, 390
American Tel. & Tel. Co. v. Grady, 994
American Tobacco Co., In re, 1006
American Well Works Co. v. Layne & Bowler Co., 232, 242
Anderson v. Dunn, 462
Anderson v. Liberty Lobby, Inc., 641, 664-666, 797
Anderson v. Sara Lee Corp., 440
Ankenbrandt v. Richards, 218
Apodaca v. Oregon, 726
Arabian Am. Oil Co. v. Scarfone, 630
Arbaugh v. Y&H Corp., 302
Arenson v. Southern University Law Center, 806
Argentine Republic v. Amerada Hess Corp., 428
Argersinger v. Hamlin, 74
Ariel Land Owners, Inc. v. Dring, 945
Arista Records LLC v. Does 1-27, 438-447
Armco, Inc. v. Penrod-Stauffer Building Systems, Inc., 47
Armendariz v. Foundation Health Psychcare Services, 845
Armour & Co., United States v., 1202
Armstrong v. Manzo, 75
Armstrong v. Pomerance, 165
Armstrong v. Rushing, 387
Arnold v. Panhandle & S.F.R. Co., 772, 774
Arnold v. United Artists Theatre Circuit, Inc., 1031
Asahi Metal Industry Co. v. Superior Court, 132-139, 141, 173, 174
ASARCO Inc. v. Kadish, 1216
Asbestos and Asbestos Insulation Material Products Liability Litigation, In re, 1010
Ascon Properties, Inc. v. Mobil Oil Co., 314
Asahi Glass Co. v. Pentech Pharmaceuticals, Inc., 311
Ashcroft v. Iqbal, 333
Asher v. Baxter Int'l Inc., 1053
Associated Builders, Inc. v. Alabama Power Co., 296
Associated Gen. Contractors of Cal., Inc. v. Carpenters, 312
Association of Haystack Property Owners v. Sprague, 322
AT&T Corp. v. Iowa Utilities Bd., 307
Atari Corp. v. Sega of America, 566
Atkins v. Fischer, 329
Atkinson Trading Co. v. Shirley, 265
Atlantic & Gulf Stevedores, Inc. v. Ellerman Lines, Ltd., 772
Atlantic Coast Line R. Co. v. Locomotive Engineers, 1218, 1219
Atlantic Pipe Corp., In re, 630
Atlantic Recording Corp. v. Howell, 443
Austin v. Owens-Brockway Glass Container, Inc., 843

Bacon v. Walden, 1213
Baehr v. Lewin, 1229
Baella-Silva v. Hulsey, 468, 1149
Baggs v. Martin, 934
Baker v. F & F Investment, 496
Baker v. General Motors Corporation, 1204-1213, 1229
Baker v. Gold Seal Liquors, Inc., 1154
Baldwin v. Iowa State Traveling Men's Assn., 1118, 1146
Baldwin v. New York, 725
Ballew v. Georgia, 726
Bally Exp. Corp. v. Balicar, Ltd., 50
Baltimore & Carolina Line v. Redman, 740, 800, 810
Baltimore Steamship Co. v. Phillips, 1146
Bancroft & Masters, Inc. v. Augusta National, Inc., 191
Barber v. Miller, 456
Barcume v. City of Flint, 381-386
Barkema v. Williams Pipeline Co., 322
Barnes v. American Tobacco Co., Inc., 1102
Barnett v. Wash. Mut. Bank, FA, 1028
Barr v. City of Columbia, 702
Barrentine v. Arkansas-Best Freight System, Inc., 841
Barry Wright Corp. v. ITT Grinnell Corp., 661
Baruan v. Young, 385
Basch v. Ground Round, Inc., 1080
Basha v. Mitsubishi Motor Credit of America, Inc., 620
Bass v. Stolper, 1049
Batson v. Kentucky, 753, 754, 759, 766, 767
Baxter Healthcare Corp. v. U.S. Dist. Court for Cent. Dist. of Cal., 1037
Beacon Theaters, Inc. v. Westover, 735-740, 1177, 1178, 1180
Bechtel v. Robinson, 482, 484
Beck v. Alabama, 762
Becker v. Montgomery, 389
Beech Aircraft Corp. v. Rainey, 392
Beggerly, United States v., 1130
Bell Atlantic Corp. v. Twombly, 306-330, 331, 332, 333, 334, 335, 336, 338, 347, 353, 355, 387, 439, 440, 441, 442, 443, 447, 448
Belleville Catering Co. v. Champaign Marketplace, L.L.C., 220-221, 301, 1149
Bender v. City of St. Ann, 233
Bendix Aviation Corp. v. Glass, 739

Bennett v. Circus U.S.A., 48
Benny v. Pipes, 42
Benusan Restaurant Corp. v. King, 182, 184
Bercovitch v. Baldwin School, Inc., 843
Berger v. United States, 694
Berkey Photo, Inc. v. Eastman Kodak Co., 554-559
Berner v. British Commonwealth Pac. Airlines, 1176
Bernhard v. Bank of America Nat. Trust & Savings Assn., 1176
Bernhardt v. Polygraphic Co. of America, 887, 888
Best Ban Lines, Inc., v. Walker, 188
Betts v. Brady, 74
Bevevino v. Saydjari, 898
Bigelow v. Old Dominion Copper Mining & Smelting Co., 967, 1223
Bill Johnson's Restaurants, Inc. v. NLRB, 664
Bilzerian, United States v., 518
Birmingham Reverse Discrimination Employment Litigation, In re, 1063, 1066
B.K.B. v. Maui Police Department, 421
Black & White Taxicab & Transfer Co. v. Brown & Yellow Taxicab & Transfer Co., 869, 873
Blackhawk Heating & Plumbing Co. v. Turner, 41
Blackie v. Barrack, 1023
Blackjack Bonding v. Las Vegas Munic. Ct., 321
Blair v. Equifax Check Services, Inc., 1046-1053, 1055
Blank v. Sullivan & Cromwell, 489-491, 693
Blazer v. Black, 387
Blazer Corp. v. New Jersey Sports & Exposition Authority, 1225
Blessing v. Freestone, 257
Blockbuster, Inc. v. Galeno, 924
Blonder-Tongue Labs, Inc. v. University Foundation, 984, 1170, 1175, 1176, 1179, 1194
Blue Chip Stamps v. Manor Drug Stores, 311, 312, 313, 349, 355
BMW of North America, Inc. v. Gore, 825, 827
Board of Regents v. Roth, 373
Boddy v. Dean, 383, 384
Boeing Co. v. Shipman, 787
Boelens v. Redman Homes, Inc., 906
Boit v. Gar-Tec Products, Inc. 140
Boles v. Federal Electric Co., 368
Bolivia, Republic of, v. Philip Morris Companies, Inc., 948-949, 1011
Bolling v. Sharpe, 753
Bond v. United Railroads, 355
Boston Maritime Corp. v. Hampton, 349
Boumediene v. Bush, 19, 20
Boyd v. Illinois State Police, 776
Bradford v. Rockwell Semiconductor Systems, Inc., 845, 846
Brady v. Maryland, 488
Branch v. Tunnell, 340
Brand Name Prescription Drugs Antitrust Litigation, In re, 908, 985
Brandt v. Schal Assocs., Inc., 416
Branzburg v. Hayes, 1003
Bray v. Alexandria Women's Health Clinic (498 U.S. 1119), 716
Bray v. Alexandria Women's Health Clinic (506 U.S. 263), 716
Breier v. Northern Cal. Bowling Proprietors' Assn., 387
The Bremen v. Zapata Off-Shore Co., 194, 195, 196, 197, 199
Breon v. Coca-Cola Bottling Co. of New England, 494
Breuer v. Jim's Concrete of Brevard, Inc., 945
Brickwood Contractors, Inc. v. Datanet Engineering, 456, 457
Bridgestone/Firestone, Inc., Tires Products Liability Litigation, In the Matter of, 1053
Brill v. Countrywide Home Loans, Inc., 924
Brockmeyer v. May, 43
Broin v. Philip Morris Cos., 1042
Brooke Group Ltd. v. Brown & Williamson Tobacco Corp., 309, 812
Brown v. Federation of State Medical Bds., 410
Brown v. Felsen, 1200-1204
Brown v. Vermuden, 1044
Browning v. Pendleton, 382
Browning-Ferris Ind. of Utah, Inc. v. Kelco Disposal, Inc., 894, 897
Bryan, United States v., 1008
Brzozowski v. Correctional Physician Services, Inc., 394
Buckeye Boiler Co. v. Superior Court of Los Angeles County, 115
Buckhannon Bd. & Care Home, Inc. v. W. Va. Dept. of Health and Human Res., 616, 617
Bull's Corner Restaurant v. Director, Federal Emergency Management Agency, 377
Bunker Ramo Corp. v. United Business Forms, Inc., 300
Burda Media, Inc. v. Viertel, 50

Burger King Corp. v. MacShara, 148
Burger King Corp. v. Rudzewicz, 89, 136, 138, 145-153, 173, 181, 182, 183, 187, 192, 201, 865
Burke v. Kleiman, 1056-1057
Burlington Northern R.R. Co. v. Woods, 888, 898
Burnet v. Coronado Oil and Gas Co., 1132
Burnett, United States v., 789
Burnham v. Superior Court of Cal., 32, 110, 117, 157, 165-176
Burns v. Joseph Flaherty Co., 368
Burns v. Windsor Ins. Co., 945
Business Guides, Inc. v. Chromatic Communications Enterprises, Inc., 329, 402, 406, 407, 412, 419
Buster v. Greisen, 417
Butler, Del. Supr., In re, 591
Butterfield Patent Infringement, In re, 984, 985
Butz v. Economou, 373
Byrd v. Blue Ridge Rural Electric Cooperative, Inc., 822, 879-880, 883, 893, 900

Calder v. Jones, 132, 191
Califano v. Yamasaki, 608
California Public Employees' Retirement System v. Felzen, 1051
Campbell v. General Dynamics Govt. Sys. Corp., 844
Canel v. Topinka, 322
Cannon v. University of Chicago, 253
Canton v. Harris, 336
Cape Shore Fish Co., Inc. v. United States, 978
Capital Traction Co. v. Hof, 725, 859
Capitol Life Ins. Co. v. Rosen, 41
Car Carriers, Inc. v. Ford Motor Co., 312
Carden v. Arkoma Assoc., 223, 933
Carefirst of Maryland, Inc. v. Carefirst Pregnancy Ctrs., Inc., 188
Carey v. Bayerische Hypo-Und Vereinsbank AG, 957
Carey v. Piphus, 8
Carnegie-Mellon University v. Cohill, 927, 930
Carnival Cruise Lines v. Shute, 143, 193-202, 889
Carota v. Johns Manville Corp., 889
Carpa, Inc. v. Ward Foods, Inc., 429
Carson v. American Brands, Inc., 1066
Carter v. Delta Air Lines, Inc., 384
Carter v. Jury Commission of Greene County, 754
Carter v. Sparkman, 857, 858, 859
Cary v. Allegheny Technologies, Inc., 806
Cascade Corp. v. Hiab-Foco AB, 191
Castano v. American Tobacco Corp., 1041
Caterpillar Inc. v. Lewis, 916, 920, 930-938
Caterpillar Inc. v. Williams, 942
Catholic Social Services v. I.N.S., 1080
Catrett, Administratrix of the Estate of Louis H. Catrett, Deceased v. Johns-Manville Sales Corporation, et al., 648-651, 668
Cedant Corp. Securities Litigation, In re, 568
Cedars-Sinai Med. Ctr. v. Sup. Ct., 530
Celestine v. Petroleos de Venezuela, 1129
Celotex Corp. v. Catrett, 640-648, 651, 653, 654, 671, 797
Certain Asbestos Cases, In re, 563
Cesar v. Rubie's Costume Co., 619
Chad S., Matter of, 77
Chalick v. Cooper Hosp., et al., 479-485
Chamberlan v. Ford Motor Co., 1054
Chambers v. NASCO, 457-466, 467, 537, 889
Champion Produce, Inc. v. Ruby Robinson Co., Inc., 618
Chandler v. Roudebush, 1192, 1193
Chaney v. City of Orlando, 787
Chase National Bank v. Norwalk, 1064
Chauffers Local No. 391 v. Terry, 733
Chemetall GMBH v. ZR Energy, Inc., 667
Cheney v. United States District Court for the District of Columbia, 695
Chesapeake Paper Products Co. v. Stone & Webster Eng'g Corp., 667
Chevron U.S.A., Inc., In re, 1055
Chicago & Southern Air Lines, Inc. v. Waterman S.S. Corp., 15
Chicago, City of, v. International College of Surgeons, 249, 904-905, 915-916, 921, 927
Chicago Council of Lawyers v. Bauer, 996
Chicago, R.I. & P.R. Co. v. Stude, 905, 935
Chicago, R.I. & P.R.R. v. Williams, 963
Chicot County Drainage District v. Baxter State Bank, 1155, 1156, 1157
Chris v. Tenet, 1151
Christian v. Mattel, Inc., 413-421, 423
Christianburg Garment Co. v. EEOC, 409
Christianson v. Colt Industries Operating Corp., 249
Christopher v. Brusselback, 1058, 1061
Church v. Adler, 359
Circuit City Stores, Inc. v. Adams (279 F.3d 889), 844
Circuit City Stores, Inc. v. Adams (532 U.S. 105), 844
Cities Service Oil v. Dunlap, 887
Clady v. County of Los Angeles, 518

Clapp v. Stearns & Co., 217-218
Clark v. Paul Gray, Inc., 911, 912, 915, 917, 919, 921
Clark v. United Parcel Serv., Inc., 456, 457
Clark v. United States, 517
Clarke v. American Commerce National Bank, 518
Clausman v. Nortel Networks, Inc., 1028
Clawson v. St. Louis Post-Dispatch, LLC, 321
Clement v. American Honda Finance Corp., 1032
Cleveland v. Policy Management System Corp., 671
Cleveland Board of Education v. Loudermill, 9, 21, 23, 24
Clinton v. Jones, 340
Cloud v. Superior Court [Little Industries, Inc.], 497
Coates v. AC & S, Inc., 562-564
Cobbledick v. United States, 595, 596
Cocksedge v. Fanshaw, 781
Coday, In re, 322
Cohen v. Beneficial Indus. Loan Corp., 877-878, 885
Cole v. Burns Intl. Sec. Servs., 845
Coleman (Parent) Holdings, Inc. v. Morgan, Stanley & Co., Inc., 529
Colgrove v. Battin, 725, 726, 741
Collins v. City of Wichita, 1126, 1127, 1128
Collins v. D.R. Horton, Inc., 1183
Colman v. Utah State Land Bd., 322
Colonial Penn Ins. Co. v. Coil, 619
Colorado River Water Conservation District v. United States, 1051, 1219
Colosi v. Electric-Flex Co., 672
Commissioner v. Estate of Bosch, 888
Commissioner v. Tower, 1168
Commissioner of Internal Revenue v. Duberstein, 743
Commissioner of Internal Revenue v. Sunnen, 1147, 1155, 1166-1169, 1186
Compton v. Luckenbach Overseas Corp., 806
CompuServe, Inc. v. Patterson, 182, 183, 186, 188
Comshare, Inc. Sec. Litig., In re, 351
Concrete Pipe & Products of Cal., Inc. v. Construction Laborers Pension Trust for Southern Cal., 9
Cone v. West Virginia Pulp & Paper, 801, 810
Conley v. Gibson, 291-294, 300, 305, 306, 310, 313, 314, 321, 322, 323, 324, 326, 330, 331, 332, 335, 338, 355
Conlin v. Blanchard, 382
Connecticut v. Doehr, 22, 23
Consorti v. Armstrong World Industries, Inc., 893, 894, 895
Construction Products Research, Inc., United States v., 518, 525, 595
Consumers Union of United States v. Consumer Product Safety Commission, 1137-1143
Continental Collieries, Inc. v. Shober, 323, 324
Continental Illinois Securities Litigation, In re, 996, 997
Cook v. McPherson, 670
Cook v. Wikler, 939
Cooper v. R.J. Reynolds Tobacco Co., 1013
Cooper Industries, Inc. v. Leatherman Tool Group, Inc., 827
Coopers & Lybrand v. Livesay, 936, 1047
Cooter and Gell v. Hartmax, 402, 406, 407, 415, 425, 429, 464
Copeland v. Marshall, 614
Copperweld Corp. v. Independence Tube Corp., 309, 435
Corbitt, United States v., 995
Cordy v. The Sherwin-Williams Co., 559-562, 596
Corley v. Detroit Bd. of Ed., 322
Cort v. Ash, 237, 253, 254
Cottman Transmission Systems Inc. v. Martino, 186
County of Washington v. Gunther, 295, 299
Covey v. Town of Somers, 34
Cox v. State of Louisiana, 701
Cox v. State of New Hampshire, 701
CP Kelco U.S. Inc. v. Pharmacia Corp., 567
Craig v. Craig, 213
Crane v. Int'l Paper Co., 582
Crawford v. Board of Education, 299
Crawford v. Equifax Check Services, Inc., 1049, 1050, 1051, 1052
Crawford v. Honig, 1025
Crawford v. Zeitler, 378
Crawford-El v. Britton, 346
Crawford Packing Co., United States v., 978
Crist v. Division of Youth and Family Services, 77
Cromwell v. County of Sac., 1155, 1156, 1167
Crossman v. Marcoccio, 618
Crown Cork & Seal Co., Inc. v. Parker, 1079
CSC Holdings, Inc. v. Redisi, 1017
CSX Transp., Inc. v. Miller, 815
Cudd, United States v., 1128
Cummings v. General Motors Corp., 1123

CUNA Mut. Ins. Soc. v. Office & Prof'l Employees Int'l Union, Local 39, 851
Cunningham v. City of McKeesport, 614
Curtis v. Loether, 728-731, 733
Curtis Publishing Co. v. Butts, 816-821
Cybersell, Inc. v. Cybersell, Inc., 188

Daggett v. Comm'n on Gov't Ethics & Election Practices, 991
Dairy Queen, Inc. v. Wood, 729, 731, 1178
Danforth v. Maine Dept. of Health and Welfare, 77
Daubert v. Merrell Dow Pharmaceuticals, Inc., 807, 808, 809, 813, 814, 815
Davenport v. International Brothers of Teamsters, AFL-CIO, 972
Daves v. Hawaiian Dredging Co., 311
Davis v. Aetna Acceptance Co., 1203
Davis v. Chicago, 1051
Davis v. Coca-Cola Bottling Co., 303, 304
Davis v. Davis, 1117, 1119
Davis v. Farmer's Coo. Equity Co., 876
Davis v. Gaona, 852
Davis v. Minnesota, 766
Davis, United States v., 508
Day v. NLO, Inc., 630
Dean Witter Reynolds Inc. v. Byrd, 836
Dehmlow v. Austin Fireworks, 141
Deitchman v. R.R. Squibb & Sons, Inc., 1008 1009, 1014
Delta Air Lines, Inc. v. August, 604, 605, 608, 609, 610
Demsey & Assocs. v. S.S. Seat Star, 378
Dennis v. Sparks, 410
Denny v. Barbar, 350
Department of Health & Social Servs. v. Native Village of Curyung, 321
Department of Navy v. Egan, 8
Department of Public Welfare v. J.K.B., 77
Deposit Guaranty National Bank v. Roper, 1111
Dery v. Wyer, 976
Detroit v. Detroit Ry, 1213
Devlin v. Scardelletti, 1103
D.H. Overmyer Co. v. Frick Co., 201
Diamond v. Charles, 991
Diebold, Inc., United States v., 639, 658
Dillon, United States v., 91
Dimick v. Schiedt, 821
Dindo v. Whitney, 1154
Dioguardi v. Durning, 323, 324
District of Columbia Court of Appeals v. Feldman, 1213-1214, 1215, 1216
Dixon v. 80 Pine Street Corp., 1007
DL Res., Inc. v. FirstEnergy Solutions Corp., 667
DLX Inc. v. Kentucky, 1199
Doe v. Blue Cross & Blue Shield of Rhode Island, 961
Doe v. Norwalk Cmty. Coll., 548
Doe v. Smith, 334
Doe v. United States, 388
Dollar v. Long Mfg., N.C., Inc., 577
Donaldson v. United States Steel Corp., 975
Donovan v. Penn Shipping Co., 821-829, 896
Doran v. Salem Inn, Inc., 1218-1219
Dow Chemical Co. v. Allen, 1004, 1008
Dowdy v. Hawfield, 1123
Dowling v. American Hawaii Cruises, Inc., 497
Dreis & Krump Mfg. Co. v. Int'l Assn of Machinists, Dist. No. 8, 851
Dupasseur v. Rochereau, 900-901, 1224
Duplan Corp. v. Moulinage et Retorderie de Chavonoz, 521, 522
Dura Pharmaceuticals, Inc. v. Broudo, 311, 312, 313, 354, 355
Durfee v. Duke, 1116-1120
Dusenbery v. United States, 33, 34
Dyer v. MacDougall, 672

East Texas Motor Freight Sys., Inc. v. Rodriguez, 1068
Eastern Associated Coal Co. v. United Mine Workers of Am., District 17, 850
Eastern Medical Billing, Inc., United States v., 806
Eastway Constr. Corp. v. City of New York, 402
Eberhart v. United States, 303
EB Invs., LLC v. Atlantis Development, Inc., 321
Edleman v. Lynchburg College, 389
Edmonson v. Leesville Concrete Co., 753-757, 761, 765
Edwards v. Bates County, 919
Edwards v. Logan, 832
Edwards v. South Carolina, 711
Edwards, United States v., 997
EEOC v. ____. *See* Equal Employment Opportunity Comm'n v.
E. I. DuPont De Nemours & Company-Benlate Litgation, In re, 720-721
Eisen v. Carlisle & Jacquelin, 1023, 1070-1075, 1086
Elliott v. Perez, 337, 342, 343, 344, 346
El Paso Co., United States v., 508
Elvig v. Calvin Presbyterian Church, 492
Elwell v. General Motors Corp., 1206

Emerald Investors Trust v. Gaunt Parsippany Partners, 223
Empire Healthchoice Assurance, Inc. v. McVeight, 255
Employing Plasterers Assn., United States v., 298
England v. Louisiana State Bd. of Medical Examiners, 1198-1199, 1220
England v. Medical Examiner, 1172, 1173, 1187
English Lot, Inc. v. Norden Lab, 561
Entertainment Research Group, Inc. v. Genesis Creative Group, Inc., 418
Epstein v. MCA, Inc., 1032
Equal Employment Opportunity Comm'n v. Caesars Entertainment, Inc., 494
Equal Employment Opportunity Comm'n v. Concentra Health Servs., Inc., 334
Equal Employment Opportunity Comm'n v. Luce, 843
Equal Employment Opportunity Comm'n v. Lutheran Soc. Servs., 508
Equal Employment Opportunity Comm'n v. Peabody Western Coal Co., 972
Equal Employment Opportunity Comm'n v. University of Notre Dame du Lac, 1009
Equal Employment Opportunity Comm'n v. Waffle House, Inc., 844
Equal Employment Opportunity Comm'n v. Wyoming, 837
Erie R.R. v. Tompkins, 858, 865, 866, 870, 871-877, 879, 880, 882, 883, 884, 887, 888, 889, 890, 892, 897, 900, 923, 936, 946, 1127
Erikson v. Pardus, 331
Erlanger Mills, Inc. v. Cohoes Fibre Mills, Inc., 123
ESAB Group, Inc. v. Centricut, Inc., 929
Estate of Dodson v. Commissioner, 1166
Estin v. Estin, 1084, 1208
Evans v. Jeff D., 613
Evans v. Walter Industries, Inc., 924
The Evergreens v. Nunan, 1176
Ex parte Bollman, 13
Ex parte Merryman, 13
Ex parte Milligan, 8
Ex parte Robinson, 462, 464
Exxon Corp. v. Burglin, 345
Exxon Mobil Corp. v. Allapattah Services, Inc., 1089
Exxon Mobil Corp. v. Saudi Basic Indus. Corp., 1213-1220
Exxon Shipping Co. v. Baker, 827, 828
Fioravanti, United States v., 806
First National City Bank, United States v., 136
Fort Sill Apache Tribe, United States v., 969
Factor v. Pennington Press, Inc., 218
Fagnan v. Great Central Insurance Co., 1154
The Fair v. Kohler Die & Specialty Co., 1148
Falkirk Mining Co. v. Japan Steel Words, Ltd., 140
Fall v. Eastin, 1209
Falls Indus., Inc. v. Consolidated Chem. Indus., Inc., 977
Faranza K. v. Indiana Dep't of Educ., 303
Fauntleroy v. Lum, 1208
Favale v. Roman Catholic Diocese of Bridgeport, 493
Fay v. New York, 759
F.D.I.C. v. Maxxam, Inc., 432
F. D. Rich Co. v. United States ex rel. Industrial Clumber Co., 463
Federal Reserve Bd. of Minneapolis v. Carrey-Canada, Inc., 630
Federated Department Stores v. Moitie, 1133, 1144-1148, 1225-1226
Feist Publ'n, Inc. v. Rural Tel. Serv. Co., Inc., 417
Feldberg, In re, 528
Feltner v. Columbia Pictures Television, Inc., 733
Felzen v. Andreas, 1051
Ferguson v. Moore-McCormack Lines, Inc., 775
Fetter v. Beale, 1133-1134
Fidelity & Casualty Co. v. Golombosky, 1202
Fields v. City of Fairfield, 703
Fields v. Ramada Inn Inc., 185
Fink v. Bryant, 320
Fink v. Gomez, 421
Finley v. United States, 904, 910, 911, 912, 913, 917, 919, 920, 921, 1226
Firefighters v. Cleveland, 1066
Firelock, Inc. v. District Court of the 20th Judicial District, 852
First Federal Savings Bank v. United States, 524
First National Bank & Trust Co. v. Ingerton, 41
First National Bank of Arizona v. Cities Service Co., 646, 657, 658
Fisher v. Stolaruk Corp., 620
Fisher v. United States, 526
Fisons, Ltd. v. United States, 936
Fjelstad v. Am. Honda Motor Co., Inc., 537

Flagg Bros., Inc. v. Brooks, 24
Flah's, Inc. v. Schneider, 1195
Flanagan v. Ahearn, 1102
Fleischman Distilling Co. v. Maier Brewing Co., 84, 462
Fleitman v. Welsbach Street Lighting Co., 729, 736
Fleshner v. Copeland, 359
Flournoy v. Wiener, 232
Fode v. Farmers Ins. Exch., 522
Folding Carton Antitrust Litig., In re, 1034
Foltz v. State Farm Mut. Auto. Ins. Co., 998
Foman v. Davis, 395
Ford v. Murphy Oil USA, Inc., 1102
Fortenberry v. Clay, 1137
Fortunato v. Ford Motor Co., 803
Foucha v. Louisiana, 7, 8
Fowle v. Alexandria, 783
Fowler v. Lindsey, 1119
Fox v. City of West Palm Beach, 675
Fragante v. City and County of Honolulu, 399, 400
Franchise Tax Board v. Construction Laborers Vacation Trust, 232-233, 241, 246, 249, 943
Franchise Tax Board v. Hyatt, 1230
Franklin v. Gwinnett Public Schools, 723
Frantz v. United States Powerlifting Federation, 411, 434-438, 447
Frazier v. Pioneer Americas, 924
Freeport-McMoRan, Inc. v. K.N. Energy, Inc., 388
Freisz, In re, 77
Friend v. General Motors Corp., 575
Friends of the Earth v. Laidlaw Envtl. Servs. (TOC), Inc., 617
Fritzinger v. Weist, 217
Fuentes v. Shevin, 9, 22, 86
Fuentes v. Tucker, 364-366

Gagliardi v. Sullivan, 442
Gagne v. Clanbro Corp., 321
Gagnon v. Scarpelli, 75, 77
Gagnon v. State, 322
Galbraith v. County of Santa Clara, 347
Galella v. Onassis, 1011
Gallick v. Baltimore & Ohio R.R. Co., 769-775
Galloway v. United States, 778-786, 799, 1179
Gannis v. Ordean, 28
Gannon v. Circuit City Stores, Inc., 844
Gant v. Union Bank, 745
Gap Securities Ltig., In re, 1061
Garofalo v. Praiss, 185
Garr v. U.S. Healthcare Inc., 423
GASH Assocs. v. Village of Rosemont, 1219
Gasior v. Massachusetts Gen. Hospital, 321
Gasperini v. Center for Humanities, Inc., 890-899, 900
Gator.com Corp. v. L.L. Bean, Inc., 188
Gault, In re, 75, 80
Gavoni v. Dobbs House, Inc., 619
Gehling v. St. George's School of Medicine, Ltd., 185
General Electric Co. v. Joiner, 813, 814
General Electric Co. v. Wabash Appliance Corp., 743
General Motors Corp., In re, 528
General Tel. Co. of the Southwest v. Falcon, 328, 1024, 1067
Georgine v. Amchem Prods. Inc., 1105
G. Heileman Brewing Co. v. Joseph Oat Corp., 626
Gibbs v. Buck, 214, 216, 217
Gibson v. Berryhill, 1194
Gibson v. Chrysler Corp., 908
Gibson v. Hunter, 781
Gibson v. Mayor & Council of Wilmington, 667
Gideon v. Wainwright, 74, 79
Gilbert v. Homar, 23
Gillette Foods Inc. v. Bayerwald-Fruchteverwertung, 467
Gilly v. City of New York, 1008
Gilmer v. Interstate/Johnson Lane Corp., 834-842, 843, 844, 846
Gilmour v. Gates, McDonald & Co., 394
Glasser v. United States, 750
Glassman v. Computervision Corp., 441
Glenfed, Inc., In re, 349
Globe Liquor Co. v. San Roman, 810
Globe Newspaper Co. v. Superior Court, 995
Goad v. Mitchell, 347
Gober v. City of Birmingham, 706
Gold v. Deutsche AG, 844
Goldberg v. Kelly, 24, 744
Golden Eagle Distrib. Corp. v. Burroughs Corp., 417
Goldlawr, Inc. v. Heiman, 957
Gomes v. Avco Corp., 387
Gomez v. Toledo, 370-374, 377
Gompers v. Bucks Stove & Range Co., 718
Gondeck v. Pan American World Airways, Inc., 1126, 1127
Gonzaga University v. Doe, 257
Goodridge v. Dep't Public Health, 1229
Gorman v. Ameritrade Holding Corp., 177

Government of Virgin Islands v. Neadle, 1219
Grable & Sons Metal Products, Inc. v. Darue Engineering & Mfg., 232, 247-253, 255, 256, 257
Graduate Admission Council v. Raju, 42
Grand Jury Proceedings, In re (87 F.3d 377, 381), 517
Grand Jury Investigation, In re (399 F.3d 527), 519
Grand Jury Proceedings, In re (473 F.2d 840, 848), 514
Grand Jury Investigation, In re (974 F.2d 1068, 1071), 526
Grand Jury Subpoena Duces Tecum, In re, 519
Grand Jury Subpoena (Mark Torf), In re, 507
Granfinanciers, S.A. v. Nordberg, 741
Gray v. American Radiator and Standard Sanitary Corp., 115, 119, 124
Gray v. Board of Higher Education, 1008
Green v. Wolf, 1033
Green, In re, 700, 710, 712
Green Tree Financial Corp. v. Randolph, 845, 846, 851
Greene v. Lindsey, 26-31, 32, 34, 36
Greenleaf v. Birth, 784
Greenwood v. City of Yoakum, 347
Greisz v. Household Bank, 1052
Grendal's Den v. Larking, 615
Griffin v. Singletary, 1079
Grinnell Corp., United States v., 694
Groh v. Brooks, 217
Gross v. British Broadcasting Corp., 957
Grove Fresh Distributors, Inc. v. Everfresh Juice Co., 992-998
Grubb v. KMS Patriots, L.P., 417
Grubbs v. General Elec. Credit Corp., 933, 934, 935
Grupo Dataflux v. Atlas Global Group, LP, 221
GTE Sylvania, Inc. v. Consumers Union, 1143
Guaranty Trust Co. v. York, 870, 877, 878, 879, 881, 882, 883, 885, 886, 887, 889, 892, 893, 1127
Guidry v. Clare, 423
Guidry v. Continental Oil Co., 584
Gulf Coast Shrimpers & Oysterman's Assn. v. United States, 977
Gulf Oil Corporation v. Gilbert, 463, 951, 953, 955
Gully v. First National Bank in Meridian, 233, 240, 246, 249, 943, 1148
Gupta v. Florida Board of Regents, 734
Guthrie National Bank v. Guthrie, 730
Hageman v. Signal L.P. Gas, Inc., 383
Hague v. C.I.O., 708, 711
Haig v. Agee, 15
Haines v. Hampshire Cty. Comm'n, 322
Haines v. Liggett Group Inc., 528, 691
Haley v. Pan American World Airways, 564
Hall v. Clifton Precision, E.D. Pa., 591
Hall v. Werthan Bag Corp., 965
Halprin v. Mora, 773
Hamdan v. Rumsfeld, 18
Hamdi v. Rumsfeld, 2-16, 17, 18, 19, 20, 21, 24
Handgards, Inc. v. Johnson & Johnson, 522
Hanlon v. Chrysler Corp., 1024, 1025, 1026
Hanna v. Plumer, 628, 822, 858, 880, 881-887, 890, 892, 893, 894, 897, 898, 899, 900, 1126
Hanon v. Dataproducts Corp., 1023
Hansberry v. Lee, 1025, 1056-1060, 1061, 1063, 1084, 1086
Hanson v. Denckla, 116, 123, 124, 125, 126, 149, 164, 181
Harbor Motor Co., Inc. v. Arnell Chevrolet-Geo, Inc., 618
Harris v. Balk, 160, 162
Harris v. Palm Springs Alpine Estates, Inc., 1024
Harris v. Secretary, Department of Veterans Affairs, 378
Harris v. Zurich Ins. Co., 802
Hart Steel Co. v. Railroad Supply Co., 1147
Hatahley, United States v., 691
Havenfied Corp. v. H & R Block, Inc., 573
Hayden v. Chrysler Corp., 1226
Hazel-Atlas Glass Co. v. Hartford-Empire Co., 462, 1121
Hazen Paper Co. v. Biggins, 792
Headwaters, Inc. v. U.S. Forest Service, 1188
Heaton v. Monogram Credit Card Bank, 988
Heiser v. Woodruff, 1146
Helicopteros Nacionales de Columbia v. Hall, 117, 149, 171, 180
Heller v. Doe, 7
Heller v. Miller, 77
Helvering v. Clifford, 1168
Helvering v. Eubank, 1168
Helvering v. Horst, 1168
Helzberg's Diamonds Shops, Inc. v. Valley West Des Moines Shopping Center, 968-971, 972
Henry v. Metro. Sewer Dist., 944
Hensley v. Eckerhart, 607, 612
Hepner v. United States, 729
Herbert v. Lando, 493

Hermsdorfer v. American Motors Corp., 567
Herron v. Southern Pacific Co., 880, 885
Hershey v. People, 1202
Herzfeld & Rubin v. Robinson, 130
Herzog Contracting Corp. v. McGowen Corp., 223
Hess v. Pawloski, 110, 113, 124
Hicklin Eng'g., L.C. v. Bartell, 222
Hickman v. Taylor, 321, 475, 498-505, 506, 511, 513, 514, 521, 522, 523, 576, 629
Hicks v. Ass'n of Am. Med. Colls., 332
Hicks v. Feiock, 718
HIF Bio, Inc. v. Yung Shin Pharm. Ind., 942
Hillman Constr. Corp. v. Wainer, 321
Hishon v. King & Spaulding, 300, 361
Holland v. Illinois, 761
Holmes Group, Inc. v. Vornado Air Circulation Systems, Inc., 236
Holmgren v. State Farm Mutual Automobile Ins. Co., 520, 522
Home Building & Loan Assn. v. Blaisell, 10
Honda Power Equipment Mfr., Inc. v. Woodhouse, 370
Hooker Chemicals & Plastics Corp., United States v., 566, 986
Hooters of Am., Inc. v. Phillips, 847
Hope Clinic v. Ryan, 1018
Hopkins v. Walker, 232
Hospital Building Co. v. Trustees of Rex Hospital, 326
Hotaling v. Church of Jesus Christ of Latter-Day Saints, 443
Household Bank v. JFS Group, 236
Howard v. Mo. Bone & Joint Ctr., Inc., 188
Howat v. State of Kansas, 699, 700, 703, 709, 710, 712
Howlett v. Rose, 1216
Howsam v. Dean Witter Reynolds, Inc., 842
H.P. Hood & Sons, Inc. v. Du Mond, 123
Hudgens v. Cook Industries, Inc., 1125
Hudson v. National Academy of Sciences Inst. of Medicine, 233
Hudson, United States v., 462
Huff, United States v., 804
Hunter v. Earthgrains Co. Bakery, 452
Hurtado v. California, 169, 172
Hutchinson v. Chase & Gilbert, 112
Hutto v. Finney, 463, 464
Hy Cite Corp. v. Badbusinessbureau.com L.L.C., 188

Iacurci v. Lummus Co., 811
IBM Peripheral EDP Devices Antitrust Litigation, In re, 583
Ideal Instruments, Inc. v. Rivard Instruments, Inc., 423
IFC Credit Corp. v. Aliano Bros. General Contractors, 890
Illinois v. Allen, 463
Illinois Bell Telephone Co. v. WorldCom Technologies, Inc., 1049
Imbler v. Pachtman, 372
IMO Indus. v. Kiekert AG, 141
Imperial Diner, Inc. v. State Human Rights Appeal Bd., 1196, 1197
Improvement Co. v. Monsanto, 665
Inamed Corp. v. Kuzmak, 191
Indianapolis Colts v. Metro Baltimore Football, 186, 187
Ingle v. Circuit City Stores, Inc., 847
Ingraham v. Carroll, 206
Ingraham v. United States, 373-376
Inland Empire Council v. Millis, 1195
Inman v. Baltimore & O.R. Co., 771
INS v. St. Cyr, 6
Inset Systems, Inc. v. Instruction Set, 183, 184
Insituform Technologies, Inc. v. Cat Contracting, Inc., 393
Insurance Corp. of Ireland v. Compagne des Bauxites de Guinee, 128, 148, 1083, 1087
Intamin Ltd. v. Magnetar Tech. Corp., 422
Intel Corp. v. Advanced Micro Devices, Inc., 597, 598
International Brotherhood of Teamsters v. United States, 972
International Business Machines Corp. v. Edelstein, 998-1000
International Harvester Co. v. Kentucky, 112, 113
International Shoe Co. v. Washington, 110-118, 122, 124, 125, 126, 128, 145, 148, 149, 150, 157, 159, 161, 162, 163, 164, 165, 167, 168, 170, 173, 181, 186, 205, 1082, 1083
International Telemedia Assocs., Inc., In re, 36
Intervet, Inc. v. Merial Ltd., 566
Iowa Mutual Ins. Co. v. LaPlante, 264
Iqbal v. Hasty, 331, 332, 333, 440
Irving v. Owens-Corning Fiberglass Corp., 141
Irwin v. Dep't of Veterans Affairs, 945
Irwin v. Mascott, 1189
Italia Societa per Azioni di Navigazione v. Oregon Stevedoring Co., 379

IUE AFL-CIO Pension Fund v. Herrmann, 929

Jackson v. Pleasant Grove Health Care Center, 812
Jacob v. New York, 880
James Julian, Inc. v. Raytheon Corp., 509
Japanese Electronic Products Antitrust Litig., In re, 744
JDS Uniphase Corp. Sec. Litig., In re, 540
J.E.B. v. Alabama ex rel. T.B., 758-763, 766, 767
Jeff D. v. Evans, 615
Jefferson County, United States v., 1062
Jimenez v. Domino's Pizza, Inc., 1031
Jinks v. Richland County, 928
Joe Grasso & Son, Inc., United States v., 975-978
Johns v. Harborage I, Ltd., 392
Johnson v. Campbell, 767
Johnson v. Columbia Props. Anchorage, LP, 222
Johnson v. De Grandy, 1216
Johnson v. Mammoth Recreations, Inc., 394
Johnson v. McRee, 365
Johnson v. New York, 810
Johnson v. Wadell & Reed, Inc., 456
Johnston v. Nebraska Dept. of Correctional Servs., 321
Joiner v. Hercules, Inc., 497
Jones v. American State Bank, 1151
Jones v. Flowers, 33-35
Jones v. Montana Univ. System, 321
Jones v. United States, 8
Jordan v. Time, Inc., 618
Judice v. Vail, 1195
Judin v. United States, 422

Kaepa, Inc. v. Achilles Corp., 599
Kaiser Aluminum & Chemical Sales, Inc. v. Avondale Shipyards, Inc., 296
Kamsler v. H.A. Seinscheimer Co., 387
Kansas-Nebraska Natural Gas Co. v. Marathon Oil Co., 567
Kaplan v. DaimlerChrysler, A.G., 452
Kaplan v. Kaplan, 321
Karim-Panahi v. Los Angeles Police Dept., 337
Karnes v. Skrutski, 789
Karvelas v. Melrose Wakefield Hosp., 349
Kasper v. Brittain, 703
Katchen v. Landy, 730, 1178
Kathrein v. Monar, 438
Keele v. Wexler, 1049
Keeper of the Records, In re, 518
Keeshan v. Elgin A. & S. Traction Co., 358
Keeton v. Hustler Magazine, Inc., 131-132, 149, 181, 1086
Kemp v. Gay, 595
Keogh, United States v., 1122
Kerotest Mfg. Co. v. C-O-Two Co., 1176
Kimberlin v. Quinlan, 340
Kimbrough v. Holiday Inn, 852
Kincheloe v. Farmer, 378
Kinser v. Gehl Co., 809, 812
Kircher v. Putnam Funds Trust, 303, 939, 940, 942
Kirk, United States v., 803
Kissinger v. Reporters Committee for Freedom of the Press, 1144
KL Group v. Case, Kay & Lynch, 518
Klaudt v. Flink, 522
Klaxon v. Stentor-Electric Manufacturing Co., 870, 876, 887
Klein v. Board of Supervisors, 112
Klonoski v. Mahlab, 483
Knop v. McMahan, 937
Koenig, United States v., 410
Koerner v. Club Mediterranee, S.A., 898
Kohn v. Royall, Koegel & Wells, 490
Kokkonen v. Guardian Life Ins. Co. of America, 620, 909
Kolupa v. Roselle Park Dist., 334
Koon v. Lakeshore Contractors, 384
Korwek v. Hunt, 1080
Koster v. Lumbermen's Mut. Cas. Co., 951
Kothe v. Smith, 629
Kraemer v. Grant County, 407-412, 425
Kramer v. Kansas City Power and Light Co., 285
Krause v. Rhodes, 324
Kremer v. Chemical Corp., 1190-1198, 1212, 1220
Krueger v. Pelican Prod. Corp., 582
Krumwiede v. Brighton Assocs., 548
Kruse v. Hawaii, 944
Kulko v. Superior Court, 116, 122, 123, 124, 125, 126, 153, 175, 180, 187
Kumho Tire Co. v. Carmichael, 813, 815
Kupferman v. Consolidated Research & Mfg. Co., 1120-1123
KVOS, Inc. v. Associated Press, 216, 218

La Chemise Lacoste v. Alligator Co., 1148
Laffey v. Northwest Airlines, Inc., 429
Lakin v. Prudential Securities, Inc., 188
Lamb v. Schmitt, 55
Lambert v. Conrad, 1156
Land v. Dollar, 216, 1119
Langley v. Coughlin, 1018
Lanzetta v. New Jersey, 466

LaPrade v. Kidder, Peabody & Co. Inc., 846
Larkin v. Grendel's Den, 615
Larsen v. General Motors Corp., 575
Larter & Sons, Inc. v. Dinkler Hotels Co., 378
Lassiter v. Department of Social Services, 72-81, 84, 92
Lassiter, William L., In the Matter of, 74
Lawlor v. National Screen Service Corp., 967
Le v. University of Pennsylvania, 619
Leary v. Daeschner, 394
Leatherman v. Tarrant County Narcotics Intelligence and Coordination Unit, 317, 324-325, 332, 333, 336-339, 340, 342, 344, 345, 346, 347, 350, 378
Legal Services Corp. v. Velasquez, 87
Legnani v. Alitalia Linee Aeree Italiane, S.P. A., 1164
Leimer v. State Mut. Life Assur. Co. of Worcester, Mass., 323, 324
LeJeune v. Armstrong World Indus., 1004
Lemon v. Int'l Union of Operating Eng'rs, 1035
Leonhardt v. Western Sugar Co., 909
Lesnick v. Hollingsworth & Vose Co., 139, 140
Lexecon, Inc. v. Milberg, Weiss, Bershad, Hynes & Lerach, 1113
Lightning Lube, Inc. v. Witco Corp., 812
Limestone Dev. Corp. v. Village of Lemont, 332, 440
Lincoln Property Co. v. Roche, 930
Lindsey, In re, 519
Lindsey v. Normet, 31
Ling, United States v., 803
Link v. Wasbash R.R. Co., 462, 463, 464, 622, 628
Liteky v. United States, 693-695
Local Joint Executive Bd. of Culinary/Bartender Trust Fund v. Las Vegas Sands, Inc., 1026
Local Loan Co. v. Hunt, 1201
Local 36, International Fishermen & Allied Workers of America v. United States, 978
Logan v. Commercial Union Ins. Co., 507
Logerquist v. McVey, 815
Lopez v. Smith, 386
Louisville & Nashville R. Co., United States v., 511
Louisville & Nashville R.R. Co. v. Mottley, 232, 234-235, 236, 238, 943
Lovell v. City of Griffin, 712
Lubben v. Selective Serv. Sys. Local Bd. No. 27, 1128-1129
Lucas v. United States, 377
Lujan v. Defenders of Wildlife, 961
Lujan v. National Wildlife Federation, 813
Lumbermen's Mut. Cas. Co. v. Wright, 885
Lumbermen's Mutual Insurance Co. v. Bowman, 370
Lundy v. Adamar of New Jersey, Inc., 484
Lussier v. Dollar Tree Stores, Inc., 924
Lusthaus v. Commissioner, 1168
Lutz v. Glendale Union High School, 723
Mackey v. Montrym, 96
Mackler Productions, Inc. v. Cohen, 718
Magnolia Petroleum Co. v. Hunt, 1209, 1224
Mallard v. United States Dist. Court, 91
Malpiede v. Townson, 322
ManaSota-88, Inc. v. Tidwell, 987
Mandanici, United States v., 518
Mangold v. Neuman, 41
Marano Enters. of Kan. v. Z-Tecca Rests., L.P., 200
Marbury v. Madison, 208
Marbury-Patillo Construction Co., Inc. v. Bayside Warehouse Co., 956
Marek v. Chesny, 603-613, 614, 617, 618
Marion Machine, Foundry & Supply Co. v. Duncan, 1125, 1126
Maritz, Inc. v. Cybergold, Inc., 182, 183, 184
Markham v. Allen, 219, 220
Markman v. Westview Instruments, Inc., 740-744, 746
Marrero Hernandez v. Esso Standard Oil, 553
Marrese v. American Academy of Orthopedic Surgeons, 1006, 1231
Marriage Cases, In re, 1229
Marriage of Gong and Kwong, In re, 542
Marron v. Stromstad, 815
Marshall v. Holmes, 1130
Marshall v. Marshall, 219
Mars Steel Corp. v. Continental Bank N.A., 409, 411
Martin v. Hunter's Lessee, 243
Martin v. Miqueu, 365
Martin v. Refrigeration School, Inc., 1028
Martin v. Wilks, 972, 1061-1070, 1210, 1216
Martina Theatre Corp. v. Schine Chain Theatres, Inc., 1121
Martino v. McDonald's System, Inc., 1153-1158
Maryland v. Wirtz, 1116
Mas v. Perry, 211-213, 224
Mason v. United States, 873
Master Key Antitrust Litigation, In re, 1034

Mathews v. Eldridge, 7, 8, 9, 10, 14, 15, 20, 24-25, 75, 77, 95, 101
Matsushita Electrical Indus. Co. v. Epstein, 1199-1200
Matsushita Electrical Indus. Co. v. Zenith Radio Corp., 310, 313, 325, 332, 654-664, 797
Maty v. Grasselli Co., 384
Mausolf v. Babbitt, 991
May v. Anderson, 75
Mayle v. Felix, 387
McBratney, United States v., 262
McConnell v. Travelers Indemnity Co., 1136-1137
McConney, United States v., 743
McCormick v. Kopmann, 355-360
McCulloch v. State of Maryland, 884
McCurry v. Allen, 1170
McDonald v. Mabee, 28, 30
McDonnell Douglas Corp. v. Green, 317, 325, 490, 791, 792, 799, 1192, 1193
McDonnell Douglas Corp. v. Polin, 956
McFaul v. Ramsey, 285
McGee v. International Life Ins. Co., 115, 122, 136, 150, 181, 186
McGuire v. Turnbo, 52
McHenry County v. Shadur, 1018
McKay v. Boyd Constr. Co., 944
McLaughlin, United States v., 52
McNabb v. United States, 752
McNutt v. General Motors Acceptance Corp., 216, 218
McSparran v. Weist, 217
McVey v. Phillips Co., 772, 773
McZeal v. Sprint Nextel Corp., 331
Medtronic, Inc. v. Endologix, Inc., 200
Mellon Bank (East) FSFS, N.A. v. Farino, 180, 181
Melong v. Micronesian Claims Commn., 429
Merchants Transfer & Warehouse Co. v. Ragan, 1127
Meredith v. Beech Aircraft Corp., 1189
Meritcare, Inc. v. St. Paul Mercury Ins. Co., 909, 917
Merrell Dow Pharmaceutical v. Thompson, 232, 237-246, 247, 249, 250, 251, 253, 257
Merrill v. Navegar, Inc., 1044
Merrill v. Waffle House, Inc., 493
Merrill v. Yeomans, 743
Merrill Lynch, Pierce, Fenner & Smith, Inc. v. Curran, 240
Mesirow v. Duggan, 370
Messinger v. Anderson, 1132
Metro-Goldwyn-Mayer Studios Inc. v. Grokster, Ltd., 442
Metropolitan Life Ins. Co. v. Robertson Ceco Corp., 205
Metropolitan Life Ins. Co. v. Taylor, 943
Microsoft Corp. Antitrust Litigation, In re, 1182
Microsoft, United States v., 188
Microsystems Software, Inc. v. Scandinavia Online AB, 190
Mid-Continent Broadcasting Co. v. North Central Airlines, Inc., 809
Mid-Continent Wood Products v. Harris, 44-50, 51, 52
Miles v. Illinois Central R.R. Co., 868
Miller v. Fenton, 742
Miller v. Holzmann, 509
Miller v. Mackey International, 1074
Miller v. Public Storage Management, 843
Miller v. Runyon, 1183
Miller Brewing Co. v. Fort Worth Distrib. Co., 1183
Milliken v. Meyer, 112, 122, 165, 167
Mills v. Duryee, 1117
Milsen Company v. Southland Corporation, 1156
Milwaukee County v. M.E. White Co., 1208
Mink v. AAA Dev., LLC, 188
Minnesota Commercial Assn. v. Benn, 113
Miserandino v. Resort Properties, Inc., 32
Mississippi, United States v., 964
Missouri v. Nebraska, 1119
Mitchell v. W.T. Grant, 22, 1195
Mitsubishi Motors Corp. v. Soler Chrysler-Plymouth, Inc., 836, 837, 838, 840, 944
M.L.B. v. S.L.J., 82
Moccio v. New York State Office of Court Admin., 1214
Moch v. East Baton Rouge Parish School Bd., 1129
Mollenhauer Laboratories, Inc., United States v., 47
Molski v. Gleich, 1035
Moncharsh v. Heily & Blasé, 850
Monell v. New York City Dept. of Social Services, 336, 337, 338
Moneypenny v. Dawson, 322
Monroe v. Pape, 373, 1171
Monsanto Co. v. Spray-Rite Service Corp., 325, 658, 660
Montana v. United States, 264, 265, 1063, 1183, 1184-1189, 1194

Monterey, City of, v. Del Monte Dunes at Monterey, Ltd., 733
Montgomery County v. MicroVote Corp., 507
Montgomery Ward & Co. v. Duncan, 810
Moore v. Baker, 387
Moore v. New York Cotton Exchange, 964
Moore v. Hughes Helicopters, Inc., 1023
Moose Lodge No. 107 v. Irvis, 755
Moran, United States v., 453
Morris v. Pennsylvania R. Co., 772
Morrison v. Circuit City Stores, Inc., 846
Morrissey v. Brewer, 75
Moser, United States v., 1187
Moses H. Cone Memorial Hospital v. Mercury Construction Corp., 836
Mosley v. General Motors Corp., 962-966
Mount Sinai School of Medicine v. American Tobacco Co., 1001-1011, 1019
Mullane v. Central Hanover Bank & Trust Co., 9, 21, 27, 28, 29, 30, 32-33, 34, 41, 203, 1072, 1084, 1086
Mullin v. Skains, 967
Murdock v. Commonwealth of Pennsylvania, 711
Murray v. Auslander, 1035
Muza, United States v., 802
Myricks, In re, 77

NAACP v. Button, 89, 1187
Nadherny v. Roseland Property Co., 453
Napster, Inc., In re, 518, 528
Narensky et al. v. HMO, 902
NASCO v. Calcasieu Television & Radio, Inc., 458, 459, 460, 461
Natale v. Pfizer, Inc., 924
National Assn. of Radiation Survivors v. Brown, 101
National Assn. of Radiation Survivors v. Derwinski, 101, 102
National Assn. of Radiation Survivors v. Turnage, 579
National Assn. of Radiation Survivors v. Walters, 101
National City Bank v. Aronson, 225
National Collegiate Athletic Assn. v. Tarkanian, 755
National Development Co. v. Triad Holding Corp. and Adnan Khashoggi, 38-42, 52
National Equipment Rental, Ltd. v. Szukhent, 202-206
National Farmers Union Inc. Cos. v. Crow Tribe, 264
National Foundry & Pipe Works v. Oconto City Water Supply Co., 1223
National Hockey League v. Metropolitan Hockey Club, 595
National League of Cities v. Usery, 1116
National Org. for Women v. Operation Rescue, 720
National Presto Indus., Inc., In re, 946
National Rental v. Szukhent, 882
Navarro Savings Assoc. v. Lee, 222
Nebraska Press Assn v. Stuart, 996
Neely v. Eby Construction Co., 807, 810, 811, 812, 813, 814
Neff v. Pennoyer, 107
Neitzke v. Williams, 310
Nelson v. Adams, USA, Inc., et al., 389-393
Nelson v. Cyprus Bagdad Copper Corp., 843
Nelson v. Keefer, 218
Nemmers v. United States, 410
Nestor v. Pratt & Whitney, 1150
Network Computing Systems v. Cisco Systems, Inc., 581
Nevada v. Hall, 1208, 1230
Nevada v. Hicks, 265
Newman v. GHS Osteopathic, Inc., 483
Newman v. Maricopa Cty, 321
Newman v. Piggie Park Enterprises, 1198
Newman-Green, Inc. v. Alfonzo-Larrain, 225, 910, 936, 937
New York v. Connecticut, 1119
New York Central R.R. Co. v. Johnson, 820
New York Gaslight Club, Inc. v. Carey, 11151
New York Life Ins. Co. v. Nashville Trust Co., 1124
New York State Natl. Organization for Women v. Terry, 713-721
Nguyen v. Excel Corp., 506
Nicholas W. v. Northwest Indep. Sch. Dist., 347
Nicholson v. CPC Intl. Inc., 839
Nike, Inc. v. Comercial Iberica de Exclusivas Deportivas, S.A., 223
Nixon v. Warner Communications, 995
Nixon, United States v., 517
NLRB v. Bildisco & Bildisco, 1064
NLRB v. Jones & Laughlin Steel Corp., 730
Nobles, United States v., 506
Nokomis, City of v. Sullivan, 358
Noonan v. Winston Co., 206
Northern District of Cal., Dalkon Shield IUD Prods. Liability Litigation, In re, 1037
North Georgia Finishing, Inc. v. Di-Chem, Inc., 22

Northwestern Memorial Hosp. v. Ashcroft, 1014
Nottingham v. General American Communications Corp., 967
Nowak v. Tak How Investment Ltd., 206
NRC Management Servs. Corp. v. First Va. Bank-Southwest, 322
Nummer v. Treasury Dept., 1212
Nuwesra v. Merrill Lynch, Fenner & Smith, Inc., 455

Oberkramer v. Ellisville, 322
O'Brien v. Alexander, 423, 424
O'Brien v. City of Greers Ferry, 618
O'Brien v. City of Syracuse, 1007
O'Brien v. DiGrazia, 314
O'Brien v. Okemo Mountain, Inc., 200
O'Brien v. R.J. O'Brien & Assocs., Inc., 50
O'Connor v. Boeing North Am., Inc., 1102
O'Connor v. Donaldson, 8
Ohio Cellular Prods., Inc. v. Adams USA, Inc., 390
Okla. Tax Comm'n v. Graham, 920
Olden v. LaFarge Corp., 908
Omni Capital International v. Rudolf Wolff & Company, Ltd., 47
Omokehinede v. Detroit Board of Education, 496
One Parcel of Property Located at 31-33 York Street, United States v., 1018
Oppenheimer Fund, Inc. v. Sanders, 551, 1017, 1076
Ormel Corp. v. Ohio Power Co., 248
Ortega v. Star-Kist Foods, Inc., 901, 908, 914, 919, 920
Orthman v. Apple River Campground, Inc., 296
Ortiz v. County of Westchester, 51
Ortiz v. Fibreboard Corp., 1102, 1103, 1105
Osborn v. Bank of United States, 209, 238
Osborn v. Haley, 940, 941, 942
Osloond v. Farrier, 322
Owen v. City of Independence, 372
Owen Equipment & Erection Co. v. Kroger, 904, 910, 912, 914

PacifiCare Health Systems, Inc. v. Book, 844
Pacific Employers Ins. Co. v. Industrial Accident Comm'n, 1208
Pacific Mutual Life Insurance Co. v. Haslip, 822, 826
Padilla v. Hanft, 17
Padilla-Mangual v. Pavia Hosp., 224
Padovani v. Liggett & Myers Tobacco Co., 1013
Page v. Lincoln Electric Co., 1002
Pakas v. Hollingshead, 1164
Paladino v. Avnet Computer Tech, Inc., 845
Palmer v. Hoffman, 887
Palmer v. San Antonio, 338
Pan American World Airways, Inc. v. O'Hearne, 1126
Pan American World Airways, Inc., United States v., 1126
Panavision Intern., L.P. v. Toeppen, 182
Pannill v. Roanoke Times Co., 217
Paramount Communications v. Viacom Inc., 587-592
Parham v. J.R., 7
Parker v. Columbia Pictures Indus., 395
Parker v. Hulme, 742
Parklane Hosiery Co. v. Shore, 1170, 1174-1182, 1210
Parkson v. Central DuPage Hospital, 1015, 1016
Parsons v. Bedford, 729, 783
Parsons Steel, Inc. v. First Alabama Bank, 1219
Passa v. Derderian, 925
Patterson v. McLean Credit Union, 1132
Patzer v. Bd. of Regents of the Univ. of Wis. Sys., 1151
Paul v. WinCo Foods, Inc., 1024
Pavelic & LeFlore v. Marvel Entertainment Group, 401
P.C. v. Nadjari, 1007
Pearson v. Planned Parenthood Margaret Sanger Clinic, Manhattan (507 U.S. 901), 716
Pearson v. Planned Parenthood Margaret Sanger Clinic, Manhattan (512 U.S. 1249), 716
Penfield Co. v. Securities & Exchange Comm'n, 718
Pennie & Edmonds LLP, In re, 452, 457
Pennix, United States v., 803
Pennoyer v. Neff, 104, 105-110, 112, 113, 115, 159, 160, 161, 167, 168, 173, 1058, 1084
Pennsylvania v. Local Union 542, Intl. Union of Operating Engineers, 691-693
Pennsylvania Fire Ins. Co. v. Gold Issue Mining Co., 110
Pennzoil Co. v. Texaco Inc., 1216
Pennzoil Prods. Co. v. Colelli Associates, Inc., 141
People v. Garcia, 766
People v. Operation Rescue National, 719
People v. Skaggs, 360
PepsiCo Inc. v. Baird, Kurtz & Dobson LLP, 507

Perkins v. Benguet Consolidated Mining Co., 149
Perkins v. U.S. West Commc'ns, 619
Pernell v. Southall Realty, 732
Perry v. U.S. Bank, 1027
Peter Kiewit Sons' Co. v. Department of Revenue, 1184-1185, 1186, 1187
Peter Kiewit Sons' Co. v. State Board of Equalization, 1184
Peters v. Public Service Corporation, 369
Peterson v. Chesapeake & Ohio Rv., 497
Phelan v. Middle States Oil Corp., 1122
Philadelphia, City of, v. Westinghouse Electric Corp., 511
Philip Morris, Inc. v. Angletti, 1041
Philip Morris USA v. Williams, 827
Philip Morris USA, Inc., United States v., 529, 530
Philips Med. Sys. Int'l B.V v. Bruetman, 599
Phillips v. County of Allegheny, 440
Phillips Petroleum Co. v. Duckworth, 1082
Phillips Petroleum Co. v. Shutts, 178, 1080-1087, 1208
Pierce v. Cook & Co., 1124-1128
Pierson v. Ray, 372
Pigge, In re, 1203
Pinsky v. Duncan, 23
Pintando v. Miami-Dade Hous. Agency, 906
Pioneer Finance & Thrift Co. v. Powell, 1203
Pioneer Village v. Bullitt Cty., 322
Piper Aircraft Co. v. Reyno, 950-955
Pizza Time Theatre Securities Litig., In re, 565
Planned Parenthood v. Casey, 1132-1133
Plummer v. R.H. Macy & Co., 1008
Plymovent Corp. v. Air Tech Solutions, Inc., 565
Polin v. Conductron Corp., 956
Poller v. Columbia Broadcasting System, Inc., 326, 654
Pollux Holding Ltd. v. The Chase Manhattan Bank, 956
Postal Service Bd. of Governors v. Aikens, 792
Poulos v. State of New Hampshire, 701
Powell v. Alabama, 80
Powerex Corp. v. Reliant Energy Servs., 941, 942
Powers v. Allstate Insurance Co., 821
Powers v. Graff, 387
Powers v. Ohio, 754, 756, 760
Preferred Capital, Inc. v. Sarasota Kennel Club, Inc., 889
Presider v. Rodriguez, 1170
Pres-Kanp, Inc. v. System One, Direct Access, Inc., 184
Press-Enterprise Co. v. Superior Court, 995, 996, 997
Prewitt Enterprises, Inc. v. Organization of Petroleum Exporting Countries, 43
Prime Care, LLC v. Humana Ins. Co., 939
Primerica Life Ins. Co. v. Brown, 842
Primus Auto. Fin. Serv., Inc. v. Batarse, 420
Pritchard v. Liggett & Myers Tobacco Co., 1013
Probe v. State Teachers' Ret. Sys., 1031
Procter & Gamble Co., United States v., 577
Procunier v. Navarette, 373
Provident Tradesmen's Bank & Trust Co. v. Patterson, 967
Prudential Oil Corp. v. Phillips Petroleum Co., 223
Pryner v. Tractor Supply Co., 843
PSEG Power N.Y., Inc. v. Alberici Constructors, Inc., 552
Publicker v. Shallcross, 1124
Public Service Co. of Colorado v. Van Wyk, 321
Puertorriquenos en Accion v. Hernandez, 347
Purcell v. Gonzalez, 722

Quaak v. KPMG-Belgium, 597, 598-599
Quackenbush v. Allstate Ins. Co., 928, 930
Qualcomm Inc. v. Broadcom Corp., 531-546, 547, 548
Quill v. North Dakota, 155
Quinby v. WestLB AG, 551

Rabiolo v. Weinstein, 47
Raddatz, United States v., 682
Radio Corp. of Am. (RCA) v. Radio Station KYFM, Inc., 378
Radzanower v. Touche Ross & Co., 1191
Ragan v. Merchants Transfer & Warehouse Co., 612, 878, 881, 882, 888
Railroad Comm'n of Tex. v. Pullman Co., 1219
Railroad Trainmen v. Virginia Bar, 89
Rambus, Inc. v. Infineon Technologies AG, 518
Ramunno, In re, 590
Rand v. Monsanto Corp., 1047
Rannard v. Lockheed Aircraft Corp., 285
R.A.R., Inc. v. Turner Diesel, Ltd., 206
Rasul v. Bush, 18

Raygor v. Regents of the University of Minnesota, 928
Reavis v. Metropolitan Property & Liability Ins. Co., 521, 522
Redman v. John D. Brush & Co., 809
Reeb v. Ohio Dep't of Rehab. & Corr., 1035
Reed v. Allen, 1146, 1147
Reeves v. Sanderson Plumbing Prods., Inc., 789-799, 815, 816
Reich v. National En'g & Contracting Co., 595
Reid v. San Pedro, Los Angeles & Salt Lake R.R., 788
Reilly v. Phil Tolkan Pontiac, Inc., 124
Reiter v. Sonotone Corp., 1145
Reno v. ACLU, 832
Research Corp. v. Pfister Assoc. Growers, 1087
Rhimes v. Weber, 1219
Rhone-Poulenc Rorer, Inc., In re, 1047, 1055
Rice, United States v., 940
Richardson v. Nat'l R.R. Passenger Corp., 619
Richardson v. Philip Morris, Inc., 1041
Richmond Newspapers, Inc. v. Virginia, 995
Ridder v. City of Springfield, 455
Ridge at Red Hawk, L.L.C. v. Schneider, 330
Riley v. Merrill Lynch, 222
Riley v. New York Trust Co., 1212
Ring v. Spina, 737
Rio Properties, Inc. v. Rio International Interlink, 36
Rivera v. Riverside, 614
Rivet v. Regions Bank of Louisiana, 236, 943, 1149
R.J. Reynolds Tobacco Co., In re, 1002, 1005, 1006, 1007, 1008, 1009
R.J. Reynolds Tobacco Co. v. Engle, 1040, 1041
Roadway Express, Inc. v. Piper, 462, 463
Robbins v. Okla. ex rel. Dep't of Human Servs., 440
Roberg v. Henry Phipps Estate, 1116
Roberson v. Giuliani, 616
Roberts v. Shawnee Mission Ford, Inc., 1014
Robertson v. Howard, 1209
Robinson v. Audi NSU Auto Union Aktiengesellschaft, 129
Robinson v. Metro North Commuter R.R. Co., 734, 1035
Robinson v. Volkswagen of Am., 129
Robinson v. Volkswagenwerk, 129-130
Rock Island Bank & Trust Co. v. Ford Motor Co., 574
Rockwell Int'l Corp. v. United States, 906
Rocky Mountain Tool & Machine Co. v. Tecon Corp., 821
Rodgers, United States v., 250
Rodriguez v. California Highway Patrol, 1068
Rodriguez de Quijas v. Shearson/American Express, Inc., 836, 839
Rodriguez-Ortiz v. Margo Caribe, Inc., 440, 442, 443
Roe v. Wade, 1132
Roell v. Winthrow, 683
Rogers v. Desiderio, 1051
Rogers v. Loether, 728
Rogers v. Missouri Pacific R. Co., 772, 773
Romero v. International Terminal Operating Co., 239
Ronco, Inc., In re, 409
Rooker v. Fidelity Trust Co., 905, 1213-1215, 1216
Rose v. Giamatti, 222
Rose v. Mitchell, 756
Rose v. United Equitable Ins. Co., 322
Rosenberg v. Merrill Lynch, Pierce, Fenner & Smith, Inc., 845
Rosmer v. Pfizer, Inc., 908
Ross v. A.H. Robins Co., 348
Ross v. Bernhard, 729, 744, 1046
Rozier v. Ford Motor Co., 569-586, 1123
Ruhrgas AG v. Marathon Oil Co., 230
Ruiz v. Estelle, 991
Rumely, United States v., 205
Russell v. Chicago Trust & Savings Bank, 360
Russell v. Richardson, .58
Ryan v. New York Telephone Co., 1007
Ryan, United States v., 595
S.A. Auto Lube, Inc. v. Jiffy Lube Intl., Inc., 410
St. Mary's Honor Center v. Hicks, 792, 795, 796, 799
St. Paul Mercury Indem. Co. v. Red Cab Co., 920
Salazar-Calderon v. Presidio Valley Farmers Ass'n, 1080
Salerno, United States v., 7, 8
Salgado v. General Motors Corp., 483
Saltany v. Bush, 428-430
Saltany v. Reagan (702 F. Supp. 319), 426, 427, 429
Saltany v. Reagan (886 F.2d 438), 426-428, 429

Salvation Army v. Morris, 1124
Samuel v. University of Pittsburgh, 213
Sanden v. Mayo Clinic, 378
Sanders-El v. Wencewicz, 801-804
Sanyo Laser Prods., Inc. v. Arista Records, Inc., 492
Saudi Basic Industries Corp. v. Mobile Yanbu Petrochemical Co., 1217
Sawyer v. LaFlamme, 55
Scarborough v. Principi, 388
Schacht v. Wisconsin Dep't of Corrections, 944
Schall v. Martin, 7
Scherer v. The Equitable Life Assurance Soc. of U.S., 1200
Scherk v. Alberto-Culver Co., 836
Scheuer v. Rhodes, 310, 314, 324, 335, 373
Schnell v. Peter Eckrich & Sons, Inc., 1185
Schroeder v. City of New York, 203, 1072
Schudel v. General Electric Co., 812
Schultea v. Wood, 340-346, 347, 378
Schuylkill and Dauphin Improvement Co. v. Munson, 784
Schuykill Fuel Corp. v. B & C Nieberg Realty Corp., 1007
Scott v. American Tobacco Co., 1041
Seaboldt v. Pennsylvania R.R. Co., 574
Sealed Case, In re (146 F.3d 881), 507
Sealed Case, In re (877 F.2d 976), 518
Sealed Case (Medical Records), In re (381 F.3d 1205, 1215), 492
Seattle Times Co. v. Rhinehart, 996
Seattle Totems Hockey Club, Inc. v. National Hockey League, 599
SEC v. Internet Solutions for Bus. Inc., 50
SEC v. Parklane Hosiery Co., 1174
Seinfeld v. Austen, 248
Semtek Int'l, Inc. v. Lockheed Martin Corp., 900, 901, 1164
Shaffer v. Heitner, 104, 122, 124, 125, 126, 148, 149, 157, 158-165, 169, 170, 172, 173, 174, 1083, 1084
Shamsuddin v. Vitamin Research Prods., 188
Shanaghan v. Cahill, 905
Shankle v. B-G Maint, Mgmt. of Col., Inc., 845
Shaumyan v. O'Neill, 23
Shayes v. McKenzie, Brachman, et al., 1135, 1152
Shearson American Express v. McMahon, 836, 839
Shearson American Express, Inc. v. McNulty, 844
Shelley v. Kraemer, 713, 1060
Shell Oil Refinery, In re, 566, 567
Shelton v. American Motors Corp., 506
Shepard v. Ocwen Fed. Bank, 322
Sherrer v. Sherrer, 1119, 1209
Shillitani v. United States, 718
Shires v. The Celotex Corp., 1004
Shore v. Cornell-Dubilier Elec. Corp., 41
Shulthis v. McDougal, 249, 250
Shute v. Carnival Cruise Lines, 192, 193, 194
Shuttlesworth, In re, 706
Shuttlesworth v. Birmingham (43 Ala. App 68), 702
Shuttlesworth v. Birmingham (373 U.S. 262), 706
Shuttlesworth v. Birmingham (376 U.S. 339), 706
Shuttlesworth v. Birmingham (382 U.S. 87, 91), 701, 706
Sibbach v. Wilson & Co., 613, 882, 885, 887
Silicon Graphics, Inc. Sec. Litig., In re, 351
Simpson v. Nickel, 334
Sinochem Intern. Co., Ltd. v. Malaysia Intern. Shipping Corp., 956
Skaff v. Meridien N. Amer. Beverly Hills, L. L.C., 334
Skelly Oil Co. v. Phillips Petroleum Co., 236
Skidmore v. Baltimore & Ohio R.R. Co., 776
Skoda v. Fontani, 614
Slocum v. New York Life Insurance Co., 800
Smelser v. Norfolk Southern R. Co., 809
Smith v. Kansas City Title & Trust Co., 232, 238, 239, 242, 248
Smith v. Lincoln Brass Works, Inc., 322
Smith v. North American Rockwell Corp., 963
Smith v. Swormstedt, 1046, 1058
Smith v. Texas, 750, 756
Smith v. United States Dist. Court, 995
Smolik v. Philadelphia & Reading Co., 110
Sniadach v. Family Finance Corp., 21, 22
Snyder v. Alternate Energy, Inc., 36
Snyder v. Harris, 919, 1088
Solem v. Bartlett, 261
Soma Medical Int'l v. Standard Chartered Bank, 188
Souffront v. Compagnie des Sucreries, 1185
South Central Bell Telephone Co. v. Alabama, 1134
Southern Construction Co. v. Pickard, 1154
Southern Methodist University Assn. v. Wynne & Jaffe, 961

Southern Pacific R. Co. v. United States, 1185
Southland Corp. v. Keating, 844
Southland Securities Corp. v. INSpire Ins. Solutions, Inc., 351, 394
Spahr v. Secco, 842
Spaulding v. University of Washington, 295
Sperberg v. Firestone Tire & Rubber Co., 1088
Sporck v. Peil, 509
Sprague v. Ticonic National Bank, 463
Sreter v. Hynes, 1007
SRI Intl. v. Matsushita Electric Corp. of Am., 745
Stanley v. Illinois, 75
Starling v. Gulf Life Ins. Co., 800
State Division of Human Rights v. Columbia University, 1197
State Division of Human Rights v. Mecca Kendall Corp., 1197
State Division of Human Rights v. New York State Drug Abuse Control Commission, 1195
State Farm Fire & Casualty Co. v. Tashire, 910, 979-984
State Farm Mutual Automobile Insurance Co. v. Campbell, 827
State of Maine v. U.S. Dept. of Interior, 507
State-Record Co., In re, 997
Steele v. Louisville & Nashville R. Co., 292
Steffel v. Thompson, 255
Steinbuch v. Cutler, 549
Stenberg v. Carhart, 1015, 1017-1018
Stewart Organization, Inc. v. Ricoh Corp., 887, 889
Stine v. Moore, 212
Stoll v. Gottlieb, 1119
Stomp Inc. v. NeatO LLC, 187
Stone v. Powell, 1173
Stoneridge Inv. Partners v. Scientific Atlanta, 257
Strandell v. Jackson County, Illinois, 626-629
Strate v. A-1 Contractors, 263, 264, 265
Strauder v. West Virginia, 759
Strawbridge v. Curtiss, 210, 211, 912, 932
Stromberg Metal Works, Inc., v. Press Mechanical, Inc., 908, 917
Styskal v. Weld County Bd. of County Comm'rs, 901, 1164
Subpoena Issued to Dennis Friedman, In re, 506
Sugar Antitrust Litigation, In re, 1034
Summers v. Howard Univ., 1123
Sun Printing & Pub. Assn. v. Edwards, 218
Supreme Tribe of Ben-Hur v. Cauble, 918, 1088, 1089
Surles v. Air France, 492
Sussman v. Bank of Israel, 432
Swain v. Alabama, 761
Sweeney v. Sherman Williams Co., 966
Swidler & Berlin v. United States, 515-517
Swierkiewicz v. Sorema N.A., 310, 314, 317, 318, 320, 325, 327, 334, 335, 347, 355
Swift v. Tyson, 866, 867, 869, 872, 873, 874, 875, 883
Swift & Co. v. Wickham, 1132
Swiss American Bank, Ltd., United States v., 42
Syngenta Crop Protection, Inc. v. Henson, 920, 944
Szabo Food Serv., Inc. v. Canteen Corp., 432, 437

Tabrizi v. Village of Glen Ellyn, 409
Tahoe-Sierra Pres. Council, Inc. v. Tahoe Regional Planning Agency, 1188
Tait v. Western Maryland R. Co., 1186
Talamini v. Allstate Insurance Co., 427
Tango Music, LLC v. DeadQuick Music, Inc., 222
Tanzymore v. Bethlehem Steel Corp., 213-218
Taylor v. Maile, 321
Taylor v. Washington Terminal Co., 894
T.B. Harms Co. v. Eliscu, 232
Tedford v. Warner-Lambert Co., 944
Tefal, S.A. v. Products Int'l Co., 186, 187
Temple v. Synthes Corp., 966-968, 971, 972
Temple Community Hosp. v. Sup. Ct., 530
Tenaska Washington Partners II L.P. v. United States, 844
Tennessee v. Lane, 102-103
Tennessee Coal, Iron & R.R. Co. v. George, 220
Textainer P'ship Sec. Litig., In re, 924
Textron Lycoming Reciprocating Engine Division Arvo Corp. v. United Automobile Aerospace and Agricultural Implement Workers of Am. Intl. Union and Its Local 787, 236
Theatre Enterprises, Inc. v. Paramount Film Distributing Corp., 308, 309, 313, 318
Thermtron, Products, Inc. v. Hermansdorfer, 629, 930, 939, 940
Thiel v. Southern Pacific Co., 749-752, 754, 756
Thomas v. Albright, 1102, 1103
Thompson v. Deloitte & Touche LLP, 225

Thompson v. Dept. of Housing and Urban Development, 492
Thompson v. Kivett & Reel, Inc., 1137
Thompson v. Whitman, 1118
Thomson v. Washington, 321
Throckmorton, United States v., 1121, 1123
Tice v. American Airlines, Inc., 1051
Ticke v. Barton, 55
Ticor Title Ins. Co. v. Brown, 1033
Tiller v. Atlantic Coast Line R.R. Co., 383
Tilley v. TJX Companies, Inc., 1055
Time Warner, Inc. Sec. Litig., In re, 348, 1077
Title v. United States, 1130
Title Ins. & Trust Co., United States v., 1132
Toberman v. Copas, 972-975
Tofany v. NBS Imaging Systems, Inc., 1165
Toledo Scale Co. v. Computing Scale Co., 463
Torres v. Walker, 616
Townsend v. Holman Consulting Corp., 432
Toys "R" Us, Inc. v. Step Two, S.A., 188
Traina v. United States, 456
Trammel v. United States, 1007
Trans-Spec Truck Serv., Inc. v. Caterpillar, Inc., 440
Travelers Health Assn. v. Virginia, 181
Travelers Ins. Co. v. Byers, 365
Travis v. Irby, 966
Treinies v. Sunshine Mining Co., 1119
Trezza v. Dame, 776
Trimble v. Asarco, Inc., 909
Tull v. United States, 731, 732, 741
Tulsa Professional Collection Services, Inc. v. Pope, 1064
Turner v. City of Taylor, 52
Turner v. Houk, 322
Twin City Fire Ins. Co. v. Ben Arnold-Sunbelt Beverages Co., 583
TXO Production Corp. v. Alliance Resources Corp., 823, 826
Ty Inc. v. Softbelly's Inc., 1123

Unauthorized Practice of Law Committee v. Parsons Technology, Inc., 92
Union Pacific R. Co. v. Dept. of Revenue of Ore, 1219
United Carbon Co. v. Binney & Smith Co., 743
United Food and Commercial Workers Union v. Alpha Beta Company, 48
United Mine Workers of America v. Bagwell, 468, 716, 717, 718, 719, 720
United Mine Workers of America v. Gibbs, 902-903, 909, 910, 911, 912, 927, 928, 964, 1226, 1227
United Mine Workers, United States v., 710, 711, 712, 718, 719
United National Ins. Co. v. R & D Latex Corp., 452
United Stars Ind. v. Plastech Engineered Prods., Inc., 423
United States v. *See* opposing party name
United States ex rel. Bradford Hunt v. Merck-Medco Managed Care, LLC, 486
United States ex rel. Karvelas v. Melrose-Wakefield Hospital, 349
United States ex rel Snapp, Inc. v. Ford Motor Co., 440
United States ex rel Tex. Portland Cement Co. v. McCord, 988
United States Gypsum Co., United States v., 152
United States Parole Commission v. Geraghty, 1111
Universal Oil Products Co. v. Root Refining Co., 462, 453
Upjohn Co. v. United States, 509-515, 519, 521, 523, 525
Uppgren v. Executive Aviation Services, Inc., 124
Urrutia v. Harrisburg County Police Dept., 484
U.S. Financial Securities Litigation, In re, 745
U2 Home Entm't, Inc. v. Kylin Tv., Inc., 332

Valley Forge Christian College v. Americans United for Separation of Church and State, Inc., 961
Vance v. United States of America, 483
Van Dusen v. Barrack, 954
Velasquez v. Franz, 1227
Velazquez v. Thompson, 28
Verizon Communications, Inc. v. Law Offices of Curtis v. Trinko, LLP
Verizon Md. Inc. v. Public Serv. Comm'n of Md., 1216
Vieux Carre Prop. Owners, Residents & Assoc., Inc. v. Brown, 972
Village of Oakwood v. State Bank & Trust Co., 988
Virginia-Carolina Chemical Co. v. Kirven, 1157
Vitek v. Jones, 75
von Bulow by Auersperg v. von Bulow, 526
Vons Companies, Inc. v. Seabest Foods, Inc., 206

Wachovia Bank v. Schmidt, 222
Wade v. Lynn, 378
Wagner v. Fawcett Publication, 378
Waitt v. Merck & Co., 924
Walker v. Armco Steel Corp., 888, 894
Walker v. Carnival Cruise Lines, 200
Walker v. City of Birmingham, 697-713, 721, 722
Walker v. Hutchinson, 203
Walker v. Sauvinet, 727
Wallace v. La. Citizens Prop. Ins. Co., 942, 943
Walpole v. Hill, 6
Walters v. National Assn. of Radiation Survivors, 93-100, 101, 102, 579
Wang v. Chinese Daily News, 1027
Wang Laboratories, Inc. v. Toshiba Corporation, 561
Ware v. Howard University, 233
Warner Communications Sec. Litig., In re, 603
Warren v. Hart, 322
Warth v. Seldin, 961
Washington v. Confederated Tribes of the Colville Indian Reservation, 263
Washington v. Lambert, 1068
Washington Elec. Coop., Inc. v. Mass. Mun. Wholesale Elec. Co., 986
Watkins v. Resorts International Hotel and Casino, Inc., 1220-1231
Watson v. INCO Alloys Int'l, Inc., 815
Watson v. Philip Morris Cos., Inc., 940
Webb v. James, 619
Weber v. Grand Lodge of Kentucky, F. & A. M., 28
Weber v. Mobil Oil Corp., 939
Weil v. Markowitz, 427
Weinberg v. Federated Department Stores, 1145
Weinberger v. Romero-Barcelo, 463
Weisgram v. Marley Co., 796, 807-814, 815
Weiss v. Regal Collections, 1110
Wellness Cmty. Nat'l v. Wellness House, 906
Wells Fargo Home Mortgage Overtime Pay Litigation, In re, 1020-1032, 1035
Westchester Fire Ins. Co. v. Hanley, 803
Westmoreland v. CBS, Inc., 427, 497
West Virginia Div. of Highways v. Butler, 815
Westwood Chemical Co. v. Kulick, 1007
Wetmore v. Rymer, 214, 216
White v. Pence, 805
Whitehead v. Food Max of Mississippi, Inc., 433, 434
Wildlands CPR v. U.S. Forest Serv., 617
Wilk v. American Medical Assn., 994, 998
Wilkerson v. McCarthy, 796
Wilkes v. Ford Motor Co., 1102
Wilkin v. Sunbeam Corporation, 1125
Will-Drill Resources, Inc. v. Samson Resources Co., 843
Williams v. Florida, 725, 726
Williams v. Green Bay & Western R., 952
Williams v. Lee, 258-260, 263
Williams v. Mensey, 802
Williams v. Sprint/United Management Co., 550
Williams v. Walker-Thomas Furniture Co., 198
Williams Packing & Nav. Co. v. Enoch, 978
Willy v. Coastal Corp., 402
Windham v. American Brands, Inc., 1034
Winget v. Rockwood, 323
Winters v. Levine, 1189
Wisconsin Dept. of Corrections v. Schacht, 910, 944
A Witness Before the Special Grand Jury 2000-2, In re, 519
Wolters Kluwer Fin. Servs., Inc. v. Scivantage, 465
Wonson, United States v., 740
Wood v. Strickland, 372, 373
Woods v. Holy Cross Hospital, 855-860
Woods v. Interstate Realty Co., 878-879
Worcester v. Georgia, 262
World-Wide Volkswagen Corp. v. Woodson (444 U.S. 286), 121-128, 130, 135, 136, 137, 139, 149, 150, 173, 181, 185, 186, 1083, 1084
World-Wide Volkswagen Corp. v. Woodson (585 P.2d 351), 118-120
World Wrestling Fed'n Entm't, Inc. v. William Morris Agency, Inc., 494
Wright v. Home Depot U.S.A., 321
Wright v. State of Georgia, 703
Wright v. Universal Maritime Service Corp., 843
Wright v. Willamette Industries, Inc., 809
Wuchter v. Pizzutti, 203
Wyman v. Newhouse, 53-55

Yagman, In re, 415, 418
Yahoo!, Inc. v. La Ligue Contre la Racisme et L'Antisemitisme, 190-191
Yang v. Odom, 1080
Young, In re, 322
Young v. City of Providence ex rel. Napolitano, 448-454

Young v. United States ex rel. Vuitton el Fils S.A., 462
Younger v. Harris, 1216, 1219
Youngstown Sheet & Tube Co. v. Sawyer, 10, 13

Zachair Ltd. v. Driggs, 388
Zadvydas v. Davis, 7
Zahn v. International Paper Co., 907, 911, 912, 915, 917, 918, 919, 921, 1088, 1089
Zenith Radio Corp. v. Hazeltine Research, Inc., 1064, 1185
Zielinski v. Philadelphia Piers, Inc., 366-369
Zinermon v. Burch, 7
Zinser v. Accufix Research Inst., Inc., 1023, 1026, 1029
Zippo Mfg. Co. v. Zippo Dot Com, Inc., 178-187, 188, 189
Zolin, United States v., 527
Zubulake v. UBS Warburg LLC, 528, 529, 530, 551, 552
Zuni Public School District No. 89 v. Department of Education, 329
Zyprexa Prods. Liab. Litig., In re, 670

Table of Federal Rules of Civil Procedure

Rule 1 286, 288, 390, 394, 630, 644, 737, 1095
3 878, 888
4 26, 35, 36, 38, 42, 43, 45, 46, 48, 49, 50, 51, 52, 154, 1221
4(c) 36, 42, 51
4(d) 39, 40, 41, 42, 47, 51, 52, 203, 204, 881, 882, 883, 884, 885
4(e) 42, 52, 180, 203
4(f) 36, 42, 43, 44
4(h) 43, 44
4(j) 42, 1221, 1228
4(k) 42, 154
4(l) 42
4(m) 51, 52, 53
4(n) 42
5(b) 36
5(d) 37
6(b) 52
6(d) 36
7 344, 345, 362
7(a) 328, 343, 344, 346, 347, 1154
8 286, 287, 290, 291, 293, 305, 306, 311, 313, 314, 315, 317, 320, 324, 326, 327, 330, 335, 340, 345, 363, 437, 439, 973
8(a) 218, 292, 293, 310, 311, 319, 320, 323, 325, 330, 331, 335, 336, 338, 345, 355, 437, 439, 440
8(b) 361, 368, 370
8(c) 361, 362, 370, 373, 375, 376, 377, 378, 1164, 1219
8(d) 344
8(e) 345, 355, 358
8(f) 292
9 317, 338, 340, 344, 437
9(b) 317, 325, 333, 334, 336, 338, 343, 344, 345, 346, 347, 348, 349, 350, 351, 353, 354, 394
9(c) 317, 370
11 329, 337, 353, 400, 401, 402, 403, 404, 406, 407, 409, 411, 412, 413, 415, 416, 417, 419, 420, 421, 422, 423, 424, 425, 427, 428, 429, 430, 432, 433, 434, 435, 436, 437, 438, 443, 444, 445, 447, 448, 451, 452, 453, 454, 455, 456, 457, 461, 462, 464, 465, 466, 467, 468
11(b) 329, 424, 433, 438, 444, 445, 446, 447, 451, 452, 455
11(c) 329, 396, 412, 456
12 144, 342, 389, 390, 1164
12(a) 390, 391
12(b) 51, 174, 229, 266, 290, 294, 302, 306, 310, 317, 319, 330, 332, 333, 334, 347, 362, 363, 364, 372, 387, 388, 409, 410, 434, 439, 440, 441, 947, 973, 1110, 1200
12(c) 292, 363
12(d) 425
12(e) 292, 298, 304, 323, 327, 328, 346, 363
12(f) 292
12(g) 362
12(h) 216, 302, 378, 937, 938
13 362, 904, 1154
13(a) 229, 386, 739, 964, 1151, 1152, 1153, 1154, 1155, 1156, 1157
14 901, 902, 905, 906, 913, 921, 972, 973, 974, 975, 976, 977, 989
14(a) 967, 973, 976
15 292, 379, 389, 390, 391, 393, 394, 447, 481, 482
15(a) 378, 379, 387, 388, 390, 391, 394, 395
15(b) 379
15(c) 380, 383, 388, 389, 479, 481, 482, 484

16 287, 292, 296, 328, 379, 394, 395, 484, 500, 602, 603, 622, 626, 628, 629, 630, 853
16(c) 289, 328, 329, 622, 626, 628, 633
16(f) 461, 462
17(a) 960
17(b) 960
18 737
18(a) 437
19 773, 905, 913, 914, 916, 917, 966, 967, 969, 972, 989, 1065, 1066, 1067, 1142, 1143
19(a) 967, 968, 969, 1064
19(b) 967, 968, 969, 970, 971, 1064
20 229, 905, 913, 914, 917, 921, 962, 963, 964, 965
20(a) 963, 964, 965
20(b) 963
22 978, 980, 981
23 907, 914, 921, 962, 1019, 1020, 1023, 1024, 1030, 1032, 1033, 1036, 1037, 1041, 1048, 1054, 1055, 1061, 1063, 1069, 1070, 1071, 1072, 1073, 1074, 1075, 1077, 1078, 1079, 1090, 1094, 1095, 1096, 1097, 1099, 1100, 1102, 1104, 1110, 1112
23(a) 965, 1023, 1024, 1025, 1026, 1035, 1093, 1094, 1095, 1096, 1097, 1098, 1101, 1103, 1105
23(b) 1023, 1026, 1029, 1030, 1031, 1033, 1035, 1036, 1049, 1050, 1052, 1055, 1071, 1089, 1093, 1094, 1095, 1096, 1097, 1098, 1100, 1102, 1103, 1104
23(c) 1030, 1031, 1067, 1071, 1072, 1073, 1074, 1075, 1096
23(d) 1085, 1096, 1103
23(e) 1050, 1051, 1097, 1104, 1105
23(f) 1046, 1047, 1048, 1049, 1050, 1053, 1054, 1055, 1104
23(g) 1105
23(h) 1105
24 905, 913, 914, 985, 1064, 1065, 1067
24(a) 986, 1064
24(b) 1064
26 329, 340, 475, 476, 477, 482, 483, 490, 491, 492, 493, 499, 500, 502, 504, 514, 537, 549, 560, 565, 568, 584, 586, 593, 597, 629
26(a) 469, 477, 479, 480, 482, 483, 484, 485, 486, 487, 491, 496, 506, 564, 1017
26(b) 477, 478, 479, 491, 492, 493, 494, 501, 505, 506, 507, 509, 514, 518, 520, 521, 522, 549, 550, 551, 552, 553, 562, 563, 565, 566, 567, 574, 627, 629, 1017
26(c) 174, 329, 494, 496, 501, 503, 551, 593, 992, 997
26(e) 530, 573, 639
26(f) 469, 549, 553
26(g) 289, 459, 461, 537, 538, 547
30 586
30(a) 593
30(b) 174, 289, 521, 532, 533, 539, 540, 542, 593
30(d) 591, 593
30(g) 461
31 174, 586
31(c) 289
32 593
32(b) 593
33 174, 549
33(b) 296
34 549, 550
35(a) 563, 564
35(b) 562, 563, 564
36 174
37 461, 483, 489, 499, 537, 584
37(a) 174, 537
37(b) 174, 484, 584
37(c) 174, 483, 485, 584
37(d) 174, 584, 593
37(f) 549
38 723
38(b) 735
39(a) 739
41 801
41(a) 402, 620
41(b) 465, 901, 1164
42(b) 736, 737, 740, 963, 1164
45(b) 593
45(c) 593, 1014, 1017, 1019
45(d) 549
45(e) 593
47 725, 755
48 725
49 374, 776, 778
49(b) 774
50 667, 786, 791, 796, 798, 807, 808, 809, 810, 811, 816, 821
50(a) 641, 664, 796, 808, 812, 813
50(b) 787, 800, 810, 811
50(c) 806, 811
50(d) 808, 810, 811
51 768, 775

52(a) 152
52(b) 409
53 683, 853
53(a) 683
53(b) 683
53(e) 683
54(b) 667
54(d) 606, 609
55 370, 1154
56 174, 216, 292, 323, 325, 326, 346, 363, 633, 634, 640, 642, 644, 645, 648, 654, 664, 668, 670, 673, 797
56(a) 642
56(b) 642, 667
56(c) 217, 639, 641, 642, 643, 645, 649, 658
56(e) 639, 641, 642, 643, 645, 646, 649, 657, 658, 662
56(f) 639, 643, 646
57 736
59 375, 808, 821, 891, 894, 897, 898, 899
59(a) 894
59(e) 389
60 1115, 1130
60(b) 39, 44, 45, 50, 375, 571, 572, 577, 619, 817, 1120, 1121, 1123, 1124, 1125, 1126, 1127, 1128, 1129, 1130, 1150
65 458, 721
65(a) 217
65(d) 715
68 602, 603, 604, 606, 607, 608, 609, 610, 611, 612, 613, 617, 618, 619, 1110, 1111, 1112
69 433
82 1095
84 296

Table of Judicial Code Citations — U.C.C.

Code	Section	Pages
28 U.S.C.	144	690, 693, 695
	144(b)	1149
	455	690, 695
	455(a)	694, 696
	473(a)	853
	636	680
	636(c)	682, 1052
	652	852
	725	872
	738C	1229
	1257	1213, 1214, 1215, 1216, 1218, 1219
	1291	595, 938
	1292	595, 938
	1292(b)	936, 963, 976, 1048, 1055
	1331	209, 230, 231, 232, 237, 239, 240, 241, 242, 243, 244, 245, 247, 248, 249, 251, 252, 290, 303, 903, 904, 905, 906, 909, 915, 919, 943, 948, 1218
	1332	209, 212, 217, 228, 479, 856, 890, 901, 902, 903, 904, 905, 906, 907, 909, 910, 913, 915, 918, 919, 920, 921, 931, 944, 948, 1218
	1332(a)	221, 222, 908, 909, 910, 911, 912, 933
	1332(d)	922, 923, 1089
	1335	978, 979, 980, 981, 983
	1367	209, 210, 228, 386, 902, 904, 905, 906, 907, 908, 909, 911, 912, 913, 914, 915, 916, 917, 918, 919, 920, 921, 922, 944, 1089, 1164
	1367(a)	905, 906, 907, 908, 913, 914, 915, 916, 917, 919, 920, 921, 927, 988
	1367(b)	905, 906, 907, 912, 913, 914, 916, 917, 918, 920, 921
	1367(c)	906, 912, 913, 927, 928, 930, 939, 942
	1367(d)	928
	1369	925, 942, 1113
	1369(a)	925
	1369(b)	925, 926, 942
	1391	266
	1391(a)	980
	1392	266
	1397	978, 980
	1401	266
	1404	174, 266, 945, 946, 947, 956, 1113
	1404(a)	946, 948, 949, 951, 954
	1406	266, 945, 946, 947, 957
	1406(a)	957
	1407	984, 985, 1010, 1112, 1113
	1407(a)	1113
	1441	209, 246, 920, 929, 945
	1441(a)	222, 248, 915, 916, 920, 933, 935, 943, 944
	1441(b)	238, 933, 943
	1441(c)	929
	1441(e)	942
	1446	210
	1446(b)	931, 933, 936, 944
	1447	209
	1447(c)	933, 937, 938, 940, 941, 944
	1447(d)	937, 938, 939, 940, 941, 942

Section	Pages
1453	922, 1089
1453(c)	939
1651	738, 944, 998
1652	866, 876
1711	1090
1712	1090
1713	1090
1714	1090
1715	1090
1738	1117, 1171, 1190, 1191, 1192, 1193, 1194, 1197, 1199, 1208, 1214, 1219, 1222, 1224, 1229
1781	597
1782	597, 598
1861	756
1862	749, 756
1915	91
1915(e)	387
1927	403, 420, 421, 427, 428, 456, 460, 461, 466
2071	286
2072	286, 322, 609, 612, 628, 876, 881
2072(a)	894
2072(b)	286, 894, 901, 1095, 1097
2073	286, 322, 876, 1097
2074	286, 322, 876, 1097
2075	286, 876
2076	286, 876
2077	286, 876
2201	236, 736
2202	736
2361	154, 978, 980, 982, 983
2412(d)	425

Index

Access to justice as a fundamental right, 92-103
Additur, 820-821
ADR. *See* Alternative dispute resolution (ADR)
Adversarial legalism, 63-68
Adversary system
  defined, 57, 58-68
  due process, 83-84
  expectations of lay people and, 69-71
  necessities of, 505-506
Advocacy
  creative, 395-466
  "later" written submission, 423-425
  no-holds-barred, 421-423
Affidavits, summary judgment, 636-642, 672
Affirmative defenses, 370-379
  apparent from complaint, 378
  denial, distinguished, 377-378
  waiver of, 378-379
Agents for service of process, 110, 202-203
Aggregation, 922-925, 985, 1112-1113
Alternative dispute resolution (ADR), 833-864. *See also* Arbitration; Mediation
  arbitration, 834-858
  "court-annexed" arbitration, 851-853
  critical perspectives on, 862-864
  early neutral evaluation (ENE), 862
  forms of, 861-862
  mediation-arbitration, 861
  mini-trials, 861
  multidisciplinary practice, 862
  negotiation, 861
  preclusion in, 1183-1184
  summary jury trial, 862
Amendment
  adding non-diverse parties, 388
  adding party after judgment, 393
  motion to dismiss, after, 387-388
  pleadings, 379-395
  pretrial orders and, 379
  statute of limitations, 380-381
American approach to adjudication, 58-68
American Indian law. *See* Tribal courts
American Rule, 84
Ancillary jurisdiction. *See* Supplemental jurisdiction
Anonymous parties, 961
Answer, 364-370. *See also* Counterclaims
  admissions in, 370
  affirmative defenses, 370-379
  amendment of, 379-395
  counter-claims, 362
  defined as pleading, 362
  denial, 370, 377-378, 451-454
  moving for a stay, 379
  objections, 362
  pre-answer motion, relation to, 362-364. *See also* Motions
  responding to complaint, 361-395
  rules and forms, 361-362
  unpleased defenses, 378
Appellate review
  arbitration, 850-851
  class certification, 1046-1055
  discovery orders, 594-596
  jury verdicts, 807-816
  new trial motion, 806
  procedure 38, 348
  remand, 938-943
  remittitur, 821-822
  removal, 938-943
  Rule 60(b) motions compared, 1129-1130
  Seventh Amendment, 900
  unfavorable verdict by trial judge, 678
Arbitration, 834-854. *See also* Alternative dispute resolution (ADR)
  appealability of awards, 850-851
  "court-annexed," 851-853
  international, rise of, 853-854
  justification of, 848-850
  mediation distinguished, 854
  paying for, 845-847
  post-*Gilmer* developments, 842-844
  procedure, 842
  settlement-promotion strategies, 624-626
  state law application, 887
"Artful pleading" doctrine, 1149
Article III courts, 208-209

Attachment. *See also* Personal jurisdiction
property, 157
requirement, 104-110

Attorneys
access to, 84-103
access to justice as fundamental right, 92-103
American Rule, 84
appointment of, 84-85, 90-91
assistance of, 81-85
for causes, 430-433
civil vs. criminal cases, 92
competence, negotiation vs. litigation, 618
constitutional rights to counsel, 92-93
contingent fees, 85-86
due process and representation by, 57-103
ethics, 395-457, 556-559, 804-805, 1105-1107
fees, 84-103, 427-428, 603-618, 1107-1110
frivolous pleadings, 395-466
government-provided legal services, 86-88
group legal services, 88
indigent defendants, representing, 86-88
in forma pauperis proceedings, 91
insurance fee plans, 82
lay competition, 91-92
legal service providers, 86-92
mediation, role in, 64, 860
misconduct by, 540-542, 804-805
multidisciplinary practice, 862
necessity of having, 93-100
new trial for misconduct, 804-805
nonfrivolous arguments, 438
prepayment movement, 89
price of advice, 84-100
private fee agreements, 89
privilege, 497-530, 541
pro bono legal services, 84, 89-91
problems that warrant retrial, 804-805
reasonable fees, 94-85
representation by and due process, 57-103
Rule 11, effects of, 412-413
tendency to be protective of clients' interests, 1011-1014
termination of parental rights, representation by, 72-83
work-product privilege, 497-530

Bracton's Note Book, 271

Burden of pleading
federal law application, 887
summary judgment, 651-664

Burden of production, summary judgment, 651-654. *See also* Judgment as a matter of law (JMOL)

Burden of proof
state law application, 887
summary judgment, 651-664

Bureaucratic legalism, 64-65

Capacity to sue or be sued, 960-961

Catalogue sales, personal jurisdiction and, 155

Cause of action, right of private action requirement, 237-257. *See also* Claim and issue preclusion; Complaint

Certiorari, granting, 775

Chancery, Court of, 282-283

Choice of law, 151, 176
diversity jurisdiction, 869, 886

Civil Justice Reform Act of 1990
overview, 287-288
voluntary disclosure, 482

Civil lawsuit, constructing, 270-468

Civil procedure
global rules, 71-81
history of, 270-289

Civil rights
cases, special pleading in, 346-347
class actions, 1056-1070
jury trial and, 733-735
order of trial, 735-740

Claim and issue preclusion, 1130-1132
claim preclusion, 1134-1165
collateral estoppel, 1131, 1140-1141, 1165-1166
comity, 1141-1143
contract issues and, 1164-1165
counterclaims and cross-claims, 1151-1158, 1159-1160
criminal actions, 1189
double jeopardy, 1131
federal court judgments in state courts, 1220-1231
federal system, preclusion in, 1189-1231
inscrutable verdicts, 1183
issue preclusion, 1165-1189
law of the case, 1131-1132
merger and bar, 1133, 1159
mutuality of estoppel, 1170, 1174-1182
"one bite" test, 1231
"on the merits" defined, 1164
other states' judgments, 1229-1231
raising the issues of, 1163-1164
repose, doctrine, of, 1130-1131
res judicata, 1130-1165

same claim, defining, 1164
sources of preclusion law, 1158-1163
splitting claims, 1160-1161
stare decisis distinguished, 1131-1132, 1140, 1189
state court judgments in federal courts, 1190-1220
waiver, 1163-1164
Claim preclusion, 1134-1165
conditions of, 1134-1135
generally, 1133-1134
sources of preclusion law, 1158-1165
Class Action Fairness Act of 2005, 922-925
Class actions, 1019-1113. *See also* Joinder of claims
adequacy of representation, 1032-1033
advantages of, 1068-1070
aggregation alternative, 1112-1113
appeal of class certification, 1046-1055
argument for, 1019-1020
asbestos claims, 1090-1107
attorneys and, 1105-1110
choice of forum and mode of trial issues, 1080-1090
civil rights and, 1056-1070
Class Action Fairness Act of 2005, 922-925
class certification, 1046-1055, 1067-1068
class suit in equity of, 1044-1046
consumer-type, 1033-1037
defendant classes, 1055, 1061
discrimination cases, 1056-1070
diversity jurisdiction, 1088-1090. *See also* Diversity
efficiency, 1053-1054
federal jurisdiction, 1088-1090
gun manufacturers, 1043-1044
history of, 1019-1020
introduction, 1019-1046
jury trial, right to, 1046
legislative attempts to manage, 1037-1041
notice and opportunity to be heard, 1070-1080
opting out, 1033-1035
personal jurisdiction, 1080-1090
predominance of class questions, 1033-1035
reforming, 1054-1055
Rule 68 and, 1110-1112
sample notice of, 1077-1078
settlement, 1090-1113
supplemental jurisdiction and, 907-926, 1089
tobacco-related actions and their progeny, 1037, 1041-1043
venue, 1087-1088
Class certification
appeal of, 1046-1055
discrimination cases, 1067-1068
Clickwrap agreement, 187
Closing arguments, 677
Code pleading, 282-285
Cognovit notes, 201
Collateral attack on judgment, 1130-1132. *See also* Claim and issue preclusion
Collateral estoppel
defined, 1131, 1140-1141, 1165-1166
issue preclusion, 1165-1166
Common-law procedure, 271-282
equity, 280-282
methods of proof, 277-280
pleading process, 271-272
writ system, 273-277
Common law vs. civil law systems of law, 71-72
Complaint, 289-360. *See also* Pleading
allegations and details required, 289-360
amendment of, 379-395
basic standard, 291-305
civil rights cases, 346-347
code pleading, historical development, 282-285
common law pleading and procedure, 271-282
creative advocacy, 395-466
defined as pleading, 362
discovery and, 340. *See also* Discovery
ethical constraints, 395-466
factual contentions, 438-457
factual vs. substantive sufficiency, 293-294
Field Code, 283
fraud, securities litigation, 347-355
frivolous pleadings, 395-466
heightened pleading requirements, 336-355
inadequate investigation, 406, 421
modern federal court procedure, 285-289
nonfrivolous arguments, 438
notice pleading, 293
pleading and substantive law, 305-336
pleading in the alternative, 356-360
post-pleading improper purposes, 433-434
responding to, 361-395. *See also* Answer; Motions
Rule 8, 291-305

Complaint, (*cont.*)
  rule-imposed and judge-made burdens, 336-355
  same transaction or occurrence, 380, 447
  securities fraud litigation, 347-355
  special pleading requirements, 336-355
  well-pleaded requirement, 234-236
Complex litigation, 620, 865-1113
Compurgator, 278
Conflict of interest, settlements, 620-621
Conflict of laws, 176
  litigation strategies, 946-947
  multistate litigation, 946
  state law application, 887
Consolidation, transfer for, 984-985
Contempt power, 467-468, 697
Corporations, diversity jurisdiction and, 210, 220
Costs. *See* Fees and costs
Counterclaims
  answer in, 362
  collateral attack on judgment, 1151-1158
  compulsory, 1151-1158
  general rules, 1159-1160
  multiple claims and parties, 989-991
Court records, sealing, 992-998
Cross-claims
  ancillary jurisdiction, 902-903
  collateral attack on judgment, 1151-1158
  issue preclusion, 1151-1158, 1159-1160
Cyberspace, personal jurisdiction in, 177-192

Decisionmakers, neutral and passive, 58-59
Default judgment, Rule 60(b) motions and, 1129-1130
Demurrer, 634
Denial
  affirmative defenses distinguished, 377-378
  general, 370
  reasonably based on a lack of information or belief, 451-454
Deposition, 472-474, 675
  and the adversarial advocate, 586-596
  compel attendance, 593
  deciding whether to depose witness, 473-474
  enforcement, 483
  guide to, 470-474
  misconduct at, 593
  preparing clients for, 594
  sequence of, 474
  strategies, 470-474
  use and advantages of, 472
  video, 593-594
Direct attacks on judgment. *See* Relief from judgment
Directed verdict, 678, 686. *See also* Judgment as a matter of law (JOML)
Discovery, 469-600
  advanced issues in, 992, 998
  adversary litigation, necessities of, 505-506
  any matter not privileged, 495-530
  appealing discovery orders, 594-596
  attorney-client privilege, 496-530, 541
  complex organizations, 577-586
  criticism of, 475-489
  defined, 469
  deposition, 470-474, 483, 586-596, 675
  digital data and, 530-548
  disclosure requirements, 482-485
  documents, under protective order, 992-998
  dual purpose documents, 508
  electronic, 530-548
  enforcement, 483, 546
  ethics of nondisclosure, 487-489
  expert testimony, 554-569
  formal discovery tools, guide to, 471-472
  impeachment, solely for, 473, 477
  inadvertent disclosure, 552-554
  international litigation and, 596-600
  interrogatories, 457, 470-474, 480-481, 483, 569-586
  joinder strategies, 992-998
  mandatory disclosure, 476, 477-478, 485-487
  opinion work product, 520-523
  orders, appealing, 594-596
  overview, 469-474
  physical or mental examination of party, federal law application, 887
  pleading and, 340
  primary tools for, 471-472
  private investigation and third party's duty to give evidence, 998-1000
  privileges, 495-530, 541
  progression, 485
  protective orders, 992-998
  public access, 992-998
  reform of, solution as problem, 475-489
  relevance, Rule 26, 480, 491-494
  relevant to claim or defense, 477, 491
  relevant to subject matter, 477, 489-495
  sanctions, 537, 538-546

scope of, 489-569
strategies, 470-474
subpoena power, 1001-1019
Rule 26, e-discover amendments, 549-550
timing and sequence of, 472-473
unduly burdensome or expensive, 494-495
voluntary disclosure, 482, 518
work-product privilege, 506-515
Dismissal, 51-53, 601
amendment of pleadings after, 387-388
for failure to state a claim, 361-362
motion for, service of process defects, 51-53
placing conditions on, 955-956
Diversity jurisdiction, 209-230. *See also* Personal jurisdiction; Subject matter jurisdiction
amount in controversy, 209, 210, 228-230
Article III, 208-209
choice of law, 866, 869
class actions, 1088-1090
corporations and businesses, 210, 220
counterclaims, 220, 229
determining, 209-225
domestic relations, 213-214, 218-219
Erie doctrine and development, 866-877
exceptions, 213, 218-219
Federal Employers' Liability Act, 868
fictitious parties, 222
forum selection clauses, 889-890
Hanna presumption, 880-890
history and current controversies, 225-228
illustrative cases, 877-890
injunctions, 210
law governing, 865-901
litigation strategies, 946-947
nominal parties, 222
probate claims, 218, 219-220
removal, 210, 222, 929-945
sanctions, 889
statutory authority, 207-208
substantive and procedural rules, 877-880
supplemental jurisdiction, 901-929
Swift doctrine, 866, 867, 869
time-of-filing rule, 210, 221
Domestic relations claims, diversity jurisdiction exception, 213, 218-219
Domicile. *See also* Diversity jurisdiction; Personal jurisdiction
corporations, 210
libel actions, 131-132
married women, 213
venue compared, 266-268
Double jeopardy, 1131
Due process. *See also* Personal jurisdiction; Service of process
adversary system, 57-70, 83-84
attorney representation and, 57-103. *See also* Attorneys
choice of law, 151, 176
citizens vs. non-citizens, 16-20
class action, 1070-1080
common law vs. civil law systems of law, 71-72
common understanding of, 68-69
conflict of law, 176
constitutional notice, 25-35
of context and subcontext, 2-25, 246
contracts and, 144-155
excessive verdicts and, 822-829
hearing requirement, 24-25, 56-103
jurisdiction. *See* Personal jurisdiction; Subject matter jurisdiction
lawyers and, 83-84
limits of state power over persons and property, 103-106
Mathews test, 24-25
notice and opportunity to be heard, 1-55
private vs. public official conduct, 23-24
procedural, 53-103
service of process, 25-55. *See also* Service of process
state action, 23-24
Transnational Rules of Civil Procedure, 71-72

Early neutral evaluation (ENE), 862
Ejectment, writ of, 274
Enforcement of out-of-state judgment. *See* Collateral attack on judgment; Full faith and credit
Equity
class suit in equity, 1044-1046
"clean up" doctrine, 902
historical development, 280-282
Erie doctrine, history and development, 866-877. *See also* Federal common law; Rules Enabling Act; Rules of Decision Act
Ethics
attorneys' trial behavior, 804-805
class actions, attorneys' and, 1105-1107
complaint, 395-466
discovery, nondisclosure during, 487-489

Evidence
  documentary, 675
  expert testimony, 675
  hearsay, 676
  historical methods of proof, 277-280
  judicial notice, 675
  motions testing sufficiency of, 677
  nonparties' duty to give, 1001-1019
  party responsibility to present, 59-60
  presentation of, 676-677
  proof at trial, 677
  subpoena power, 1001-1019
  third parties, duty to give, 998-1000
  willful destruction of, 528-530
Execution. *See* Appellate review; Collateral attack on judgment; Default judgment; Relief from judgment; Summary judgment
Expert testimony, 554-569
  and attorney-client privilege, 567
  court-appointed, 568-569
  as litigation consultants, 568
  nontestifying, 565-566
  scientific, 814-815
  temptation to rely on, 559-564
  trial testimony, 564, 675

Fair procedure, 25
Federal common law, 869-870
Federal Employers' Liability Act, 775, 868
Federal Jury Selection Act of 1968, 749
Federal question jurisdiction
  private right of action and, 237-257
  removal, 943-945
  statutory requirements, 230-237
  well-pleaded complaint rule, 234-236
Federal Rules of Civil Procedure, 288-289
Fees and costs
  arbitration, 845-847
  attorneys' fees, 84-103
  class actions, 1107-1110
  discovery sanctions, 537, 538-546
  fee-cap statutes, 93-102
  offer of settlement, 603-618
  recovery of, by reason of frivolous appeal, 427-428
  settlements, 603-618
  waiver, 613-615
Field Code, 283
Finality. *See* Appellate review
Forensic procedure, highly structured, 60-61
Former adjudication. *See* Claim and issue preclusion
Forms of action. *See* Common-law pleading and procedure; Complaint; Equity
Forum non conveniens. See Venue
Forum shopping, 867, 869-870, 883, 944-945, 956
Forum state, personal jurisdiction
  direction "product" toward, 130-144
  importance of, 141-143
  selection clauses, 192-201, 889-890
Fraud. *See also* Common-law pleading and procedures; Complaint
  extrinsic motions, 1123-1124
  obtaining service of process and, 53-55
  relief from judgment based on, 1120-1124
Frivolous pleading, 395-466
  inquiry reasonable under the circumstances, 406-426
  presented for any improper purpose, 426-434
  warranted by existing law, 434-438
Full faith and credit, personal jurisdiction and, 109

Garnishment. *See* Personal jurisdiction
Global rules of civil procedure, 71-81
Government-provided legal services, 86-88
Group legal services, 88
Gun manufacturers, 1043-1044

Habeas corpus, writ of, 12, 13, 16
Hearing requirement, due process, 24-25, 56-103

Impeachment materials, discovery of, 473, 477
Impleader, 972-978
Indigent defendants, representing, 86-88
Indispensable parties. *See* Necessary and indispensable parties
In forma pauperis proceedings, 91
Injunctions, 697-722. *See also* Appellate review
  diversity jurisdiction, 210
  temporary restraining order, 721-722
Inscrutable verdicts, 776, 1183
Instructions. *See* Jury trial, instructions
Insurance for attorneys' fees, 82
Interlocutory appeal. *See* Appellate review
International litigation, discovery in, 596-600

Internet, personal jurisdiction and, 171-192
Interpleader, 978-984
Interrogatories, 480-481, 569-586
  enforcement, 457, 483
  guide to, 471
  strategies, 470-474
Intervention, 985-988
Issue preclusion, 1165-1189
  alternative dispute resolution and, 1183-1187
  alternative grounds and, 1189
  criminal actions, 1189
  generally, 1165-1173
  general rule, 1161-1162
  mutuality of estoppel, 1170, 1174-1182
  nonparties, 1183
  prediction and, 1182
  stare decisis distinguished, 1189

JMOL. *See* Judgment as a matter of law (JMOL)
Joinder of claims. *See also* Claim and issue preclusion; Class actions
  aggregation alternative, 1112-1113
  cross-claims, 902-903, 1151-1160
  counterclaims, 361, 989-991, 1151-1160
  impleader, 972-978
Joinder of parties. *See also* Class actions
  anonymous, 961
  capacity to sue or be sued, 960-961
  compulsory joinder, 966-972
  constitutional limitations, 961
  examples of, 989-991
  fictitious names, 961
  fraudulent joinder, 966
  impleader, 972-978
  interpleader and statutory interpleader, 978-984
  intervention, 985-988
  "limited trough," 991-992
  making decisions about, 988
  multiple, 958-961
  permissive joinder, 962-966
  persons affected, 991
  protective orders, 992-998
  real party in interest, 960
  restraints on, 988-989
  rules of, 962-992
  standing, 961, 991
  strategies, 971-972, 992-998
  transfer for consolidation, 984-985
Judges, 679-722
  appointment and election, 680-686
  disqualification of, 689-696
  diversity and, 681, 691-693
  federal, 680, 725
  injunction and contempt, 697-722
  judicial notice, 675
  magistrates, 682-683, 689
  mediators, as, 861
  philosophy of candidate, 686, 687
  powers of, 697-722
  presidential appointments, diversity and, 681
  qualifications, 686-689
  recusal, grounds for, 695-696
  selection, 680, 683, 684-686
  special masters, 680, 682-683
  state, 683
  trial by, advantages of, 724
Judgment. *See also* Appellate review; Collateral attack on judgment; Default judgment; Judgment as a matter of law (JMOL); Summary judgment
  contrary to law, 1124-1128
  courts lacking jurisdiction and, 1116-1120
  default, 1129-1130
  finality of, 1119-1120, 1128-1129
  obtained by fraud or mistake, 1120-1123
Judgment as a matter of law (JMOL), 778-786
  attorney misconduct, 804-805
  credibility, 788-789, 799
  order at trial, 677
  post-verdict motions, 678
  procedure for motion, 800-801
  renewed, 678
  standard for, 786-788
Judgment notwithstanding the verdict (JNOV), 678. *See also* Judgment as a matter of law (JMOL)
Judicial notice, 675
Jurisdiction. *See* Diversity jurisdiction; Personal jurisdiction; Subject matter jurisdiction; Supplemental jurisdiction
Jury trial. *See also* Judgment as a matter of law (JMOL); New trial
  advantage of, 723-725
  appellate review, 806-816
  challenges, 749-767
  choosing a jury, 747-767
  civil rights cases and, 733-735
  competence of jury, 740-747
  complexity exception, 744-745
  control of juries, 814
  courtroom of the future, 831-833

Jury trial (*cont.*)
deadlocked jury, 806
deliberation, 678
equal protection, 763-764
experts, 814-815
Federal Jury Selection Act of 1968, 749
functional analysis of jury's competence, 747-767
gender exclusion, 759-763
guiding, 769-778
instructions, 678, 755-776
judge trial compared, 724
legal and equitable claims, 727-735
managing the jury, 767-833
misconduct by juror, 678, 804-805
number of jurors, 725-727
order of trial, 735-740
peremptory challenges, 749-767, 863-864
post-verdict motions, 678
racial exclusion, 753-754
reforms, 746-747
reversal as remedy for improper selection, 752-753
right of individual potential juror, 757-758
right to, 723-724, 727-735, 744-745, 1046
selection and challenges, 749-767
Seventh Amendment, 723-747
size and unanimity of jury, 725-727
summary jury trial (SJT), 862
technology and, 831-833
venire, 747-749
verdicts, 678, 725-727, 769-778, 786, 807-831, 899
virtual juries, 831-832
voir dire, 749, 755
women's rights and, 764-765

Law of the case, 1131-1132
Lawyers. *See* Attorneys
Libel actions, personal jurisdiction, 131-132
"Limited trough," 991-992
Long-arm statutes, 115-116, 118-121, 133, 140, 145, 153, 156, 180, 192, 193

Magistrates, 680, 682-683
Masters, special, 680, 682-683
Mediation, 854-861. *See also* Alternative dispute resolution (ADR)
arbitration distinguished, 854
attorney's role in, 64, 860
as a "business," 861
cultural preference, 854-855
mediator's obligation, 860
settlement-promotion strategies, 624-626
Merger and bar. *See also* Claim and issue preclusion
defined, 1133
general rule, 1159
Metadata, discovery of, 550-552
Mistake, relief from judgments based on, 1120-1124
Motions
answer vs., 362-364
to compel discovery, 537-538
defined, 362
to dismiss, 51-53, 361-362, 387-388, 601
in limine, 633
new trial, 801-807
parts of, 362-363
post-verdict, 678
pre-answer, 362-364
pre-trial motions, affirmative defenses, 370-377
relief from judgment, 1116-1139
responding to complaint, 361-395
Rule 12(c) and Rule 12(b)(6), compared, 363-364
Rule 60, 1115-1139
summary judgment, 363-364. *See also* Summary judgment
testing sufficiency of evidence, 677
Multiparty, Multiform Trial Jurisdiction Act of 2002, 925-927

Napster, 517
Necessary and indispensable parties, 967-971
Negotiation. *See* Alternative dispute resolution (ADR); Mediation
New trial. *See also* Jury trial
appellate review of motion, 806
attorney or juror misconduct, 804-805
judges vs. juries, 805-806
motion for, 678, 801-807
problems warranting, 804-805
Nonparties
duty to give evidence, 1001-1019
issue preclusion and, 1183
subpoena power, 1001-1019
Nonsuit. *See* Dismissal
Notice. *See* Due process; Injunctions; Personal jurisdiction; Service of process

Offer of settlement, 604-613
  attorneys' fees, 603-618
OPEN Government Act, 617
Opening argument, 676
Opportunity to be heard. *See* Due process

Parties. *See also* Class actions; Joinder of parties
  adding after judgment, 393
  amendment of pleadings, 379-381
  anonymous, 961
  capacity to sue or be sued, 960-961
  fictitious, 961
  impleader, 972-978
  interpleader, 978-984
  intervention, 985-988
  necessary and indispensable, 967-971
  nominal, 222
  real party in interest, 960
  standing, 961, 991
Pendent jurisdiction. *See* Subject matter jurisdiction; Supplemental jurisdiction
Personal jurisdiction, 103-206. *See also* Service of process
  agents for service of process, 110
  attachment of property, 104-110, 157
  capias ad repondendum, 104, 112
  case law, applying, 205-206
  catalogue sales, 155
  choice of law, 151, 176, 869, 886
  class actions, 1080-1090
  cognovit notes, 201
  conflict of laws, 176, 887, 946-947
  consent to, 110
  contracts, 144-155
  corporate officers and directors, 165-174
  cyberspace in, 177-192
  dangerous instrumentality concept, 124
  dot-com litigation overseas, 190-192
  direct attack on, 144
  directing "product" toward forum state, 130-144
  domicile, 131-132, 210, 213, 265-267
  due process basis, 105-110
  enforceability, 189-190
  extraterritorial conduct and, 130-144
  fair play in the modern age and, 130-144
  federal courts, 154
  foreseeability and, 118-130
  forum state, 130-144, 192-201, 889-890
  full faith and credit, 109
  general jurisdiction, 117-118
  generally, 103-104
  geography as litigation weapon, 141-143
  implied consent, 110
  Internet and, 177-192
  judgments lacking, 1116-1120
  libel actions, 131-132
  limited appearance, 144
  limited jurisdiction, 117-118
  limits of state power over persons and property, 103-206
  litigating, 143-144
  long-arm statutes, 115-116, 118-121, 133, 140, 145, 153, 156, 180, 192, 193
  magazine circulation and, 131-132
  minimum contacts, 110-150, 154, 927-928
  nonresidents, 154-155
  pendant, 928-929
  Pennoyer v. Neff, 104, 105-110
  in personam judgment, 104, 157
  persons or property within the state, 155-176
  presence in state, 110-118, 156
  purposeful availment, 190-192
  quasi in rem, 104, 144, 157
  in rem, 104, 157
  special appearance, 144
  specific jurisdiction, 117-118
  state boundaries and jurisdiction, 104
  state-sovereignty, 104, 110, 128
  stream-of-commerce analysis, 118-121, 126, 137-141
  substance and procedure, 189
  substantial justice and, 110-118
  supplemental jurisdiction and, 927-928
  territorial conceptions of, 110
  traditional framework, 180-181
  two-step process, 144-150, 154
  waiving due process objections by agreement, 192-206
Physical examination. *See* Discovery
Pleading. *See also* Answer; Complaint; Motions
  amendment of, 379-395
  cause of action, right of private action requirement, 237-257
  common-law procedure, 271-282
  creative advocacy, 395-466
  defined, 271, 362
  discovery and, 340
  ethical constraints, 395-466
  excessive, 294
  frivolous, 395-466
  historical overview, 271-272
  nonfrivolous, 438
  subject matter jurisdiction and, 293
  writ system, history of, 273-277

Pretrial conference and procedure, 603, 622-633
motion in limine, 633
settlements, 602, 624-626, 632-633
Pretrial disposition with judgment, 633-674
Pretrial evidentiary motions, 627
Pretrial orders, amendment and, 379
Private investigations, 998-1000
Private right of action, 237-257
Private Securities Litigation Reform Act of 1995, 351, 352
Privileges, 495-530. *See also* Discovery
accurate outcome implications, 524-525
administering claim of, 525-530
attorney-client, 497-530, 541
civil litigation and, 496-505
corporate context, 523-524
logs, 552-554
opinion work product, 520-523
self-critical analysis, 496-497
work-product, 408-530
Probate claims, diversity jurisdiction exception, 218, 219-220
Pro bono legal services, 84, 89-91
Procedural rules. *See* Substantive and procedural rules
Proof. *See* Evidence
Protective orders, 992-998
Public access issues, 992-998
Punitive damages, 816-821

Quasi-in-rem jurisdiction, 104, 144, 157. *See also* Personal jurisdiction

Real party in interest, 960
Recusal, grounds for, 695-696
Relevance and discovery. *See* Discovery
Relief from judgment
appeal compared, 1130
default judgment and, 1129-1139
finality of judgments, 1128-1129
fraud or mistake, 1120-1124
judgments contrary to law, 1124-1130
jurisdiction, lacking, 1116-1120
Remand, 930-943
Remedies. *See* Injunctions
Remittitur, 820-821
appellate court's role in remittitur, 821-822
Removal, 210, 222, 929-945
appellate review, 938-943
exceptions, 945
federal question jurisdiction, 943-945
fictitious parties, 222
forum shopping, 944-945
generally, 929-930
nominal parties, 222
remand, 930-938
statutory requirements, 929-930
Replevin, 22
Reply
amendment of, 379-395
defined as pleading, 362
Repose, 1115-1231
Res judicata, 1130-1165
claim preclusion, 1132-1165
defined, 1130-1132
Right to jury trial, 723-724
class actions, 1046
complexity exception, 744-745
legal and equitable claims, 727-735
"Rubber-stamping," 68
Rule 4, 35-53, 203
Rule 8, 291-305
Rule 11, 400-406, 409, 412-413, 427-428, 466-467
Rule 12(c) and Rule 12(b)(6), compared, 363-364
Rule 26, 480, 491-494
e-discovery amendments to, 549-550
Rule 59, 899-900
Rule 60, 1115-1130
Rule 60(b), 1129-1130
Rules Enabling Act of 1934, 286-287, 868, 881, 882
Rules of Decision Act, 866, 876

Sanctions
contracting for, 468
discovery, 537, 538-546
diversity jurisdiction, 889
inherent power to sanction, 457-468
monetary, de-emphasizing, 455-457
nonmonetary for frivolous pleadings, 401-406, 412-413
Rule 11, 400-406, 409, 417-419, 466-467
Sealing court records, 992-998
Securities fraud litigation, 347-355
settlement notice, 1077-1078
Securities Litigation Uniform Standards Act of 1998, 353
Self-critical analysis privilege, 496-497
Service of process. *See also* Due process; Personal jurisdiction
agents for, 110, 202-203
attempted service, 45-50

constitutional notice, 27-35
due process, 25-55
dwelling house or usual place of abode, 38-41
electronic, 36-37
fax, service by, 36
foreign defendants, 42-44
foreign entity, 42
fraud, 53-55
immunity from, 55
improper conduct to effect, 53-55
impropriety and immunity from, 55
incompetents, 42
mail and waiver provisions, 42
motion to dismiss, 51-53
personal service, 28, 30, 35, 37-38
posting, 27-29, 31-32
process servers, 35-36, 42
publication, 32-33
Rule 4, 35-53
seizure of assets, 42
United States government, 42
waiver of, 51

Settlements, 601, 602-622
advantages, 603, 632
attorneys' fees, 603-618
catalyst theory of prevailing parties, 616-617
class actions, 1090-1113
complex litigation, 620
conflicts of interest in, 620-621
costs and fees, 603-618
criticism, 602, 632-633
enforcement, 618-620
offer of, 604-613
Rule 68, 617, 618-620
sample notice, 1077-1078
sentiment and, 621-622
special procedures to encourage, 629-631
strategies for judges, 624-626
waiver of fees and costs, 613-615

Seventh Amendment, 724-747, 900
appellate review and, 900
historical test, 725-735

Shareware, 183
Sliding scale test, 188
Special masters, 680, 682-683
Spoliation, 528-530
Standard of care, state law application, 887
Standing, 961, 991
Stare decisis, 1131-1132, 1140, 1189
State law. See *Erie* doctrine, history and development; Federal common law; Supplemental jurisdiction

Statute of limitations
state law applications, 887
tolling provision, 928

Statutory interpleader, 978-984
Stay, moving for, 379
Stipulations, 675
Sua sponte transfer. *See* Venue
Subject matter jurisdiction, 207-267. *See also* Diversity jurisdiction; Supplemental jurisdiction
ancillary jurisdiction. *See* Supplemental jurisdiction
appellate review, 938-943
Article III courts, 208-209
attacks on judgments based on, 1115-1130
class actions, 1088-1090
complaint requirements, 293
defects, 1149-1150
diversity jurisdiction. *See* Diversity jurisdiction
dual court system, 207-209, 865-958
federal courts, 208-209
federal judicial authority, 208-209
federal question jurisdiction, 208, 230-257, 943-945
federal vs. state, 207-208
forum selection, clauses, 889-890
general jurisdictions, 117-118, 207
intervention and, 987-988
judgments lacking, 1116-1120
legislative authority, federal vs. state, 207-208
limited jurisdiction, 117-118, 207
litigating, 229-230
Multiparty, Multiform Trial Jurisdiction Act of 2002, 925-927
pleading and, 293
private right of action requirement, 237-257
remand, 930-938
and remedies, 1150-1151
removal, 210, 222, 929-945
state claims in federal courts, 209
substantive and procedural rules, 871, 887-889
supplemental jurisdiction, 901-929
Supremacy Clause, 208
Tenth Amendment, 207
tribal courts, 257-265

Subpoena
power, 1001-1019

Subpoena (*cont.*)
unduly burdensome, 1014-1019
Substantive and procedural rules, 877-880
arguments, 887
compared, 871
conflicting procedural rules, 887, 900-901
sanctions, 889
separating, 890-901
state vs. federal law, 887-889
Summary judgment, 601, 633-634
affidavits, 636-642, 672
appeal, 666-668
certificate of service, 673-674
demurrer, 634
genuine issue for trial, 643-648, 657-658
historical perspectives, 633-640
new standard for, 668-671
partial, 667
parts of, 673-674
"piercing the pleading," 634-640
pleading, burden of, 651-664
problems with, 671-672
production, burden of, 651-664
proof, burden of, 651-664
sua sponte, 667
Supreme Court trilogy, 640-651
Summary jury trial (SJT), 802
Summons. *See* Service of process
Supplemental jurisdiction, 209, 901-929
class actions, 907-927, 1089
cross-claims, 902-903
declining to exercise, 927-928
efficiency and institutional competence, 922
Gibbs test, 902-903
modern approach, 904-905
pendent personal jurisdiction, 928-929
post-*Gibbs* developments, 904
statutory background, 902
tolling provision, statute of limitation, 928
Supremacy Clause, 208
Suspension Clause, 12, 13
Swift doctrine, 866, 867, 869

Technology, impact on litigation, 831-833
Temporary restraining order, 721-722. *See also* Injunctions
Tenth Amendment, 207
Termination of parental rights, attorney representation and, 72-83
Third-party practice. *See* Impleader
Tobacco-related class actions and their progeny, 1037, 1041-1043
Trademark infringement, 188
Transfer of actions. *See also* Venue
aggregation, 1112-1113
consolidation, for, 984-985
within federal court systems, 945-948
litigation strategies, 946-947
for reasons other than inconvenience, 957-958
sua sponte transfer, 948-949
Transient jurisdiction, 156, 172
Transnational Rules of Civil Procedure, 71-72
Trespass, writ of, 271, 274
Trial. *See also* Judgment as a matter of law; Jury trial; New trial
appeal, 678
courtroom of the future, 831-833
closing arguments, 677
evidence, presentation of, 676-677
by judge, advantage of, 724
judgment as a matter of law (JMOL), 677
judicial notice, 675
jury instructions, 677
jury trial compared, 724
mini-trials, 861
motions testing sufficiency of evidence, 677
opening argument, 676
overview, 674-676
post-verdict motions, 678
practice, 674-676
proof, 278-280, 675-676
stages of, 676-678
stipulations, 675
technology and, 831-833
witnesses, 675, 677
Tribal courts, 257-265
civil jurisdiction, 263-265
jurisdiction, 257-263

United States government, service of process on, 42

Venue, 265-267
aggregation, 1112-1113
arbitration, 842
change of, for reasons other than inconvenience, 957-958
class actions, 1087-1088
consolidation, for, 984-985

domicile compared, 265-267
federal court system, transfers within, 945-948
federal law application, 868, 887
federal statutes, applying, 265-267
forum non conveniens, 867
litigation strategies, 946-947
plaintiff's choice, deference to, 956-957
sua sponte transfer, 948-949
Verdict, 678
additur and remittitur, 820-822
anticipating, 829-831
appellate review, 807-816
directed, 678, 786. *See also* Judgment as a matter of law (JMOL)
due process when excessive, 822-829
excessive, 899, 816-829
form of, 769-778
gauging the chance of winning, 830-831
general, 678, 776-778
general with interrogatories, 678
prejudice, passion and punitive damages, 816-820
special, 678, 776-778
unanimity requirement, 725-727, 821
Voluntary disclosure, 482, 518

Waivers
affirmative defenses, of, 378-379
claim preclusion, 1163-1164
fees, 613-615
Witnesses, 677
credibility, 815
deposition of, 473-474
expert, 554-569, 675, 814-815
Work-product privilege, 408-530
World Wide Web, personal jurisdiction and, 177-192
Writs, history of, 273-277